A Guide to Irish Fiction, 1650-1900

'Serena' showing Honora Sneyd, second wife of Richard Lovell Edgeworth
(they married in 1773), reading a novel until daybreak (mezzotint engraving
by J.R. Smith after G. Romney, published London, 28 Sept. 1782).
The book she is reading is [Frances Burney's] *Evelina, or a young lady's entrance
into the world* (London, 1778, 3 vols; reprinted Dublin, 1779, 2 vols).

A Guide to Irish Fiction
1650–1900

Rolf Loeber and Magda Loeber

with Anne Mullin Burnham

FOUR COURTS PRESS

Set in 9 on 11 point Ehrhardt for
FOUR COURTS PRESS LTD
7 Malpas Street, Dublin 8, Ireland
e-mail: info@four-courts-press.ie
http://www.four-courts-press.ie
and in North America by
FOUR COURTS PRESS
c/o ISBS, 920 N.E. 58th Avenue, Suite 300, Portland, OR 97213.

A catalogue record for this title
is available from the British Library.

ISBN (10 digit) 1–85182–940–7 hbk
ISBN (13 digit) 978–1–85182–940–8 hbk

Printed in England
by MPG Books, Bodmin, Cornwall.

SPECIAL ACKNOWLEDGMENT

This publication has been generously supported by
The National Library of Ireland.

'Literary fiction, whether directed to the purpose of transient amusement, or adopted as an indirect medium of instruction, has always in its more genuine form exhibited a mirror of the times in which it was composed; reflecting morals, customs, manners, peculiarity of character, and prevalence of opinion. Thus, perhaps, after all, it forms the best history of nations ...'

Lady Morgan, O'Donnel. A national tale (London, 1815), 3rd edn, p. [vii]

'The novel, at first view, seems the most insignificant of all writings, and scarcely deserving the sober thoughts of the philosopher; but when we consider the influence it bears upon the morals and taste of a vast part of the population, the insignificance fades away, and its importance stands forth, and appears in its true proportions.'

Revd John Keefe Robinson, Leisure hours to a country parsonage;
or, strictures on men, manners, and books (Dublin, 1850), p. 28.

'I fear I have such a confused account of my publications – ... I have not many of my works and do not remember [publication] dates exactly.'

Selina Bunbury to Mr Blewitt, Letter to the Royal Literary Fund
requesting financial assistance [n.d., written in old age]
(British Library, Royal Literary Fund, Loan 96, No. 1089/93).

*To the late Mary 'Paul' Pollard in gratitude to her friendship,
encouragement and inspiration*

Contents

Plates, Figures, and Tables

Plates, Figures and Tables

FIGURES

TABLES

Foreword by Joep Leerssen

How do we write literary history? The origins of the genre lie in the biographical celebration of great artists (going back to Dr Johnson's *Lives of the Poets* and, before him, to Vasari), and in the academic institutionalization of literary criticism (going back to the Schlegel brothers and to Hugh Blair). Those origins between them determine the established mode of writing literary history: chronologically tracing the activities of authors over time, and discussing how their poetical agendas shifted, and their artistic achievements developed, from one generation to the next. This generative paradigm also means that literary history is in fact traced on the basis of a relatively fixed set of texts preselected by their critical acclaim and canonicity. In literary history, 'merit' and 'importance' are almost interchangeable terms.

The two underlying assumptions on which literary history rests have lost credit: the self-justified importance and separate status of something like a *canon* based on artistic merit/importance, as well as the *author* as the premier organizing focus of literary praxis and of the analysis of literary praxis. This shift has affected literary criticism more than literary history, however. True, countercanonical revisionism has made its voice heard: for example, in the rise of feminist-inspired historiography or postcolonial studies (preceded by the earlier attention for 'Commonwealth Literature'); and there has been an increasing awareness that 'literature' is not easily cordoned off from other media or genres, or from orality and manuscript cultures. Still, when it comes to the writing of literary history, all these critical innovations present themselves as revisions rather than revolutions, as additions and correctives to the established historiography rather than as fundamental overhauls. But there is also a truly revolutionary, fundamental change in perspective emerging, one which will present the most thorough overhaul of how we deal with the diachronicity of literature. That challenge comes from the field of book history; and although Rolf and Magda Loeber are not card-carrying book historians, their *magnum opus* presents one of the most impressive examples to date of what literary history must reckon with in the future.

What is presented here is not a narrative, but an alphabetical list; and if the central concern is Irish literature, then the Irishness lies, not in the background of surveyed authors, but in the content of the surveyed texts. What is more, the aim is total inclusiveness. Any distinction (so fundamental for traditional literary history) between an included canon (noteworthy material of merit/importance) and all the excluded rest, has been abandoned. The texts that take, alphabetically at least, pride of place are not the Great Works of famous authors, but a great body of Anonyma.

The organizing principle of the *Guide to Irish Fiction* is thematic. Any fictional text dealing with Irish matters, regardless of size, sub-genre, provenance or fame, has been included. The commentaries are descriptive, almost as in a library's or in a bookseller's catalogue, but they do point out (again) thematic as well as bibliographical features: religious, historical, domestic or regional setting. Information on authors is given, by way of background, and also a printing history. In this factualist avoidance of all the presuppositions of literary history, the *Guide* at once clears the deck of all the ingrained pieties, nostrums and received wisdoms that critics and historians have been mulling over for decades, and in their place sets up the data that allow us to review, reassess and recalibrate what Irish literature for the period 1650 to 1900 was all about. Data, I should add, that are much more voluminous, much more diverse, much more challenging than the received apostolic succession from Swift to Edgeworth to Joyce had accustomed us to seeing.

Like any revolution, this one comes from unexpected quarters. The compilers are Dutch-born North Americans, albeit with a long-standing interest in Ireland; their academic background lies, not in literary studies but in the epidemiology of delinquency and mental health problems in juveniles. They are used to conducting long-term, large-scale surveys involving great quantities of data. That empirical approach they have, for many years and with exemplary dedication, applied to their bibliophile study of Ireland-related fiction. Their work had already acquired a great reputation and authority among Irish scholars even when it was still in the preliminary database stage. That reputation was due to two things; one was the unfailing courtesy and generosity with which the Loebers shared their insights and information with inquisitive colleagues; the other, more important perhaps, lay in the fact that what they presented was not based on any received wisdom or academic debate in Irish studies, but on a wholly unbiased inventory of what they had encountered in their long, meticulous inventory. Rolf and Magda Loeber, in their collaboration with Anne Mullin Burnham, approach and present the material in an almost perfect descriptive and inclusive innocence.

In its finished form, the *Guide to Irish Fiction* will make all this available in its totality to the wider field, and to whatever line of inquiry one wishes to trace across the data collected and assembled here. Questions of domesticity, age-group cohorts, crime, religious morality, social class, politics or popular culture can be put to this *Guide*, and answers will be returned that are not based on anyone's critical parti-pris or perspective, nor on any canonical or counter-canonical view of the corpus, but on *what is actually there*. The patterns of Irish literature emerge from the actual raw material of Irish literature, not from the things a given historian or critic chooses to highlight.

In its own, understated way, the *Guide to Irish Fiction* marks a revolution; it subverts the ascendancy of doxa over data. So many treatments of the nineteenth century (my own not excluded) scanned and surveyed ad-hoc samples of literary materials for things we were looking for; now those things, the trends and patterns of literary history, are allowed to emerge from the large, generous totality of the actual stuff of literature, so assiduously and scrupulously assembled here. Like all real revolutions, this one will not be a sudden flash in the pan. The *Guide* will, it is safe to predict, emit its influence quietly and steadily for decades to come, and will probably generate and open up research perspectives beyond the uses we can discern at present. Its impact will be far greater than its citation frequency will indicate – that is the fate of all true works of reference; but in future years, the study of literature (and cultural history) for the period 1650 to 1900 will be marked by the great caesura of this book's appearance.

Foreword by Seamus Deane

Ever since the novel became an established literary form there have been endless debates about the influence it exerts over its readers. It was always suspect because it always conceded that it was not history, or a sermon, a political pamphlet or a philosophical treatise; yet, it still made a claim to truth. This worried a lot of people. Did fiction 'influence' how people behaved or what they believed? This anxiety remains to the present day, although it is now more focussed on film, video, internet sites and the like. But fiction, however transmitted, remains a problem. How can something 'made up' have the power it does? In a country like Ireland, where the official versions of history were sustained exercises in concealment and propaganda, what people, especially young people, read was a matter of great concern to the authorities. In the early nineteenth century, for instance, as literacy expanded and technological advances began to open up what we call the mass market, the government began to shoulder out the missionary and proselytising societies, many of them deeply corrupt, which had hitherto taken charge of educating Irish children. They began to look at what these children, especially papist children, read when they were left in the care of the local schoolmaster. The books available to pupils in Irish hedge schools were uniformly castigated as 'a selection alike pernicious and ridiculous'.[1] In the view of the commentators and commissioners involved in the period between the first Commission for Education in 1811 and the establishment of National Schools in 1830, the chapbooks, fables and novels commonly read by children glorified highwaymen, rebels, or women of dubious morals. The reading diet was wholly different from that of the Protestant charity schools, so-called, because their selections were dominated by catechisms, bibles and the standard propaganda of the state and established Church – *Foxe's Martyrs*, for instance, being a favourite It was recognised then that the control of what people read was of fundamental importance for the preservation of the state and the state religion and that fiction – quite as much as history, propaganda, or religious works – was a form of knowledge or, at the very least, a mode of writing that moulds attitudes towards knowledge. In the more coercive kind kinds of reading associated with school, or with, public issues around which a whole pamphlet and book literature would form like a coral reef, it is easy to see the polemical intent of the authors and to envisage the target audiences. (For instance, we can still hear echoes of the uproar occasioned by Bishop Woodward's pamphlet on tithes and loyalty in 1787, or the Burke Paine controversy over the Revolution and the Rights of Man, or the Rebellion of 1798, the Union of 1800.)[2] In such instances, the relationship between the text and the context is dramatically important and obvious. But there is another kind of reading, associated with leisure and, in the case of fiction, more specifically, although by no means exclu-

---

For explanation of abbreviated references see Abbreviations.

1 Leslie Foster in an Appendix to *Reports from the Commissioners of the Board of Education in Ireland, 1809–1812* (London, 1813), 346. This is an opinion widely repeated in histories and reports of the period 1809–35.   2 See, for example, J. Kelly, 'Inter-denominational relations and religious toleration in late eighteenth-century Ireland', *Eighteenth-Century Ireland* 3 (1988), 39–67; W.J. McCormack, *The Pamphlet debate on the Union between Great Britain and Ireland, 1797 to 1800* (Dublin, 1996)

sively, with women and juveniles or young people. The pleasure of reading and of writing has for long been associated with the leisure that allows one to read and write; and leisure has also been itself gendered, that is to say, regarded as a condition enjoyed or endured by women more than by men. Removed from the press of the busy world and thus fatally prone to concede an important role to fantasy, romance and fable, fiction was often infantilised, along with its audience, as a refuge from the real world. In almost equal measure, the senior role of women in the novel has confirmed the view that the domestic realm, with its hard work and social demands, and most of all with its sexual-commercial marital relationships, is the central zone of all fiction, because all its historical and philosophical pretensions are sourced in that private and interior realm. Since this realm was assigned to women, according to convention, they were especially equipped to provide its most vivid narratives. In Ireland, where so much fiction was produced by Protestant women who had a Catholic servant class in their employ, there was a always an element of sectarian as well as class tension or assumption quite visibly governing aspects of their novels. One important feature of this *Guide* is that it identifies Catholic writers where possible, thereby revealing the political and social visibility they began to achieve in the nineteenth century.

Such faint outlines have had to do in place of a detailed map up until now. This magnificent *Guide*, the work of Rolf and Magda Loeber in collaboration with Anne Mullin Burnham, changes that situation entirely. For it is laden with all kinds of information that we did not have before and, further, that we did not know we didn't have. With this publication, we now learn of the international appeal of and audience for Irish fiction in the Anglophone empire in the Antipodes, South Africa, India and North America, as well as in Great Britain and notably, via translation, in Europe. We can now see in some detail the intricate publishing network that linked cities such as Philadelphia (created as a centre for publications of Irish interest by the United Irishman, publisher, printer and author, Matthew Carey),[3] Sydney, Melbourne, New York, to Dublin or London. We see too the fertilising effects of piracy. Many works pirated editions of what had initially been published in London, attracted audiences they would otherwise not have reached; this was no fun for the author, but it did actually increase an author's readership, although with no corresponding rise in income. The fact that no copyright had to be paid, because English copyright laws did not apply in Ireland, was unfair; but it might actually have helped to create the mass-market conditions that later evolved, in part because piracy allowed for lower prices in Ireland than in England. It thereby enhanced the appeal of low-price mass-market international circulation in general.

So too, whether pirated or reprinted legally, do the books change – in illustrations, typeface, paper and binding and price. All of these are part of a book's cultural meaning, a fact that is perhaps underestimated in relation to novels when compared with, say, the acknowledgment paid to these features of political, philosophical, scientific or religious works. It is especially important that this be recognised, since so much emphasis has been (understandably) given to the flourishing nature of the book trade in eighteenth century Ireland, the elegance and excellence

---

3 Matthew Carey (1760–1839), born in Dublin, left for Philadelphia in 1784, became a successful journalist, publisher and author on political and economic affairs.

of book production and of bindings, and the steep decline in that followed upon the Union. The publication of novels, and the phenomenon of the best seller, linked obviously to technological advances as well as to the expansion of audiences and literacy rates, makes the book (and the newspaper and the periodical publication in which fiction would find more opportunities for growth) after 1800 a new and different kind of object. Still a commodity, it is now produced to a much more thunderous rhythm of consumption; old hierarchies begin to falter and disintegrate. Thus, when we speak of the popularity of chapbooks and romances in the early nineteenth century in the hedge schools of Ireland, this is not the popularity enjoyed by Byron, Walter Scott, Thomas Moore, or Mrs. Sadleir in the nineteenth century. With them comes a more complicated apparatus of publicity – reviews, advertisements, gossip. An author can now achieve in his or her lifetime both canonical status and popularity. The commercial drive does not always bring this about; but there are not many examples in which it did not play a part. It is not just by looking at a first or a late edition of a novel that we can get a sense of its status; by seeing the number of editions, and where they were published, and what quality of production was involved, we can see how the writer's work moved in a market that had a sturdy and identifiable structure, although its organisational advances were never sufficient to clear out all capricious elements. Status can certainly be bought in a market, but then it would be useful to know why people bought it in one case rather than another. The answer obviously demands some consideration of taste, but then that too can be dictated and obscurely stimulated by clever marketing

Besides, with so many thousands of books printed, and so relatively few surviving, or surviving only in small numbers, it is invaluable to be given information, as here, on where they have been found. That helps us understand something of the role played by institutional and private collecting, especially in the retention of much material that – as we can see from the quality of its production – was from the outset regarded as ephemeral, by both producer and consumer. This *Guide* retrieves a vast amount of information – biographical, bibliographical, social – that helps us to rebuild some of the features of a world that had largely disappeared in its detail because it had not been built to survive anyway. In saying so, I am not simply referring to the use of acid paper, which was in itself not designed to abbreviate the life of the books printed on it but seems now symbolic of the regard in which many of them were held by their publishers. The cost of retrieval for such books for libraries is today many times any production cost that could have been initially laid out; but such is the price now of cultural rescue.

For many readers, especially those acclimatised to the idea that the number of novels in the 'Irish tradition' is fairly limited and readily identifiable as such, the appearance of a work of this magnitude presents an alarming prospect. Yet its effect is to enrich rather than demolish our sense of what a particular genre or sub-genre might be. The 'national marriage' novel, and 'the 'improvement' novel, are not genres in quite the sense that the gothic novel is, nor have they been defined with the political suavity that has been brought to the proposition that there is an Irish gothic. But all of these, even the gothic itself, can be understood as subordinate examples of the historical novel, whether Scott or Edgeworth, is taken to be the originator, or Mazzini or Lukacs the theorist. Thomas Leland, with his curious 'first' historical novel *Longsword*, which many regarded then as no less fictional than his *History of Ireland*, certainly has a claim to priority in chronological terms, although that is not at all the same as being 'first' in the production of a genre. For instance, the 'philosophical history' of Ireland which many hoped Leland would write, would have been the first of its kind in Ireland, already pioneered elsewhere by Voltaire and Hume. The disappointment that followed on the publication of Leland's work was marked, because the writing of history in Ireland, especially by those who wrote to defend policies of extermination and dispossession, was so clearly an exercise in propaganda, that some more impartial and serene survey was much hoped for. History and, even more particularly, antiquarianism remained a battleground; but the most common accusation among historians was that their predecessors or colleagues in the profession had produced fiction. The line of division between history and fiction is often invisible; novels often call themselves 'histories' and many histories should be read as novels. Thus, because the case is so contested, the historical novel, as a genre, claims special attention, although that sometimes is given it on the grounds of prestige (it's about serious matters), sometimes on the grounds of derision (it's merely an amateurish exercise in drum-banging prejudice). Exactly how many versions of the war of 1689–90, or of 1798 can be invented? Yet, when we look at the swarms of novels centred on these events, there is actually little variation in the range of polemical intent or of historical interpretation that they display. All have their creaky plots borne along by hefty and durable stereotypes. The durability of these stereotypes is at times disturbing. The Irish historical novel (if the epithet 'Irish' has here any clarifying force in identifying a genre), leans heavily upon them. Perhaps what we need to do is recognize that their political function alters from decade to decade, but their sedimented contents remain intact. For instance, one could select a letter – say 'P'– and find Peter Paradox's *The Land of the Kelt* (1860) as a close neighbour to William Parnell's *The Irish heiress. A Novel* (1797) and be surprised at the family resemblance that links them across the intervening six decades or so, one that even survives the very different historical circumstances of their production. The shadow of the French Revolution and of the Irish rebellion of 1798, their menace and aftermath, falls across both. Yet, such is the range of material offered here that even the stereotypes begin to alter their appearance after a sojourn in another part of the world. Thus, when we discover a novel of 1858, published in Melbourne, Richard Henry Horne's *Rebel Convicts. An Australian novel*, which is concerned with the transportation of 1798 rebels to New South Wales and Van Diemen's Land, the notion of what constitutes an Irish or Australian novel, or an historical novel, or what was recognisably an audience for such fiction, begins to be sorely tested.

Since there is an enormous range of novels on religious topics – conversion, bigotry, oppression, propaganda, the social and intellectual subjection of women – is it possible to categorise these by redistributing them among the accepted sub-genres? Are religious novels, to call them that, always a species of historical novel? Or are they often parables of some other, confessional, kind? And what is their role in the promotion of anti-Popery, for instance, so monotonously a popular and toxic theme in Protestant Ireland, in other forms of discourse? Perhaps too we would see William Carleton's fiction and his *Autobiography* (if that can be characterised as non-fiction) differently in the light of Thomas Aveling's *The Irish Scholar; or, Popery and Protestant Christianity: a Narrative* (1851), published in New York for the Sunday-School Union of the Methodist Episcopal School. It is also surprising to find just how much American Irish fiction contributed to or else simply absorbed the idea of the Celt and the Celtic race from as early as the mid-nineteenth century. This was possibly more required in New York and Boston, as a marker of specific communal and racial identity, than at home. Another sidelight on this is provided by Captain Mayne Reid's *The Quadroon; or, a Lover's Adventures in Louisiana* (London and New York, 1856, with a German translation in Leipzig in 1857), in which a young Englishman falls in love with and eventually marries a beautiful quadroon slave. Dion Boucicault made this into a play that was performed in New York in 1859. The whole question of racial identity among emigrants is so often posed in so many different ways in these novels (not just in the USA; also in Australia, South Africa, the West Indies) that the existing commentary on it seems impoverished indeed. Might this be understood as a development of the kind of early nineteenth-century novel that has come to be known as the national tale?

A strange feature of the novel as a form is that it so readily lends itself to and so readily exploits national stereotypes, yet remains steadfastly transnational in its appeal. This is no doubt because it absorbs into its plots so many epic, biblical, romance and folk tale elements that it has widespread recognition. But this *Guide* demonstrates more than any before it, just how many admixtures of the generic and the national can be achieved, while also asking if there is any way to make sense or pattern of these correlations. In that regard, the Irish novel, partly because of its diasporic writers and audiences, poses the question of the national in such a manner that it can neither be affirmed nor denied in any of the orthodox ways. This question has been raised, especially in recent years, by various writers – Terry Eagleton, Joe Cleary, Emer Nolan, David Lloyd, Siobhan Kilfeather, Jacqueline Belanger – in relation to the issues surrounding 'realism' and especially concerning the question of Irish nineteenth-century realism as a defective form of its French or English models.[4] Tucked within the idea of realism is always the question, 'How real is realism?', more especially acute when novels are so often given to homiletic or didactic purposes – don't drink too much, wash more often, don't fall into evil sexual ways, remember the love of Jesus, don't join a rebel gang, etc., etc. Can you trust realism? That is maybe not the best question to ask. It's not so much a question of trust, as of appeal; and the appeal of a work can lie in its exotic or fabulous elements or in its domestic and recognisable features. Novels with strong picaresque elements, about love, adventure, or serial escapades, including tales of murder, espionage and kidnap, can easily exercise both forms of appeal. In many of the items listed here we can see how powerful is the influence of or even just the idea of the folk tale with its miraculous or satiric elements, but always

---

4 See, for example, T. Eagleton, *Heathcliff and the Great Hunger* (London, 1995); E. Nolan, *Catholic emancipations* (Syracuse, 2007); J. Belanger (ed.), *The Irish novel in the nineteenth century: facts and fictions* (Dublin, 2005). For general reference, see Raymond Gillespie and Andrew Hadfield (eds), *The Oxford history of the Irish book: Volume III, The Irish book in English, 1550–1800* (Oxford, 2006).

with its erosion of the idea of chronological time or sequenced historical events. It is obvious that the Roman Catholic Church laid claim, in one phase of its history, especially during the long night of the Penal Laws, to its peculiar access to or possession of the manners and customs of the native Irish; staying faithful to these was of a piece with staying faithful to the Church; and the antiquity and the universality of the idea of the human conserved in these belonged also to the Church, as well as to the people. Once the folk tale begins to migrate, via collections and early anthropological studies of the Irish, into fiction, the association between customs and oppression begins to be modified; very often, novels of an improving intent wanted to consolidate a linkage between freedom (emancipation) and the preservation of traditional mores. This was sustained into the Irish Revival and beyond as a particular cultural/political blend peculiar to the Irish (although it was not); but the point here, borne out by the listings before us, is that the novel was the literary form in which this mutation and ambition was first tested

Even to use the term 'the novel' is in itself misleading, because, although all novels are fiction, it is equally obvious that not all fictions are novels. This *Guide* reveals many stories that have appeared, for instance, in booklet form. They are single stories, not married to the novel as a form, nor to its more precious cousins (like the Short Story as a literary form, despite its great reputation in Ireland). This is fiction that never disentangled itself from the thickets of cautionary tale, parable, sermon, tract in which it first appeared. There is so much of it that it needs to be distinguished from other forms of narration. These are not folk tales, nor novels. It is not just a matter of naming this kind of fiction. Finding a description and name for it, involves understanding more about novels.

There cannot be any reader who will not make discoveries here, about authors such as Mrs Sadlier (and her daughter) to, say, Father Thomas Joseph Potter. However, in the spirit of the nineteenth-century commissioners for education, we should perhaps give more attention to the kinds of fiction provided for children, of which a many examples are given. This might illuminate both the difficulty and the importance of the 'coercive' and the 'leisure' elements in that literature, reproduced as it is in novels for adults. The ratio between these is often measurable as a stable, even fixed, energy in the work itself; but it often alters, especially in retrospect and, at a hazard, one might say that the most 'literary' works show greater instability and variation in that ratio over time. Works are discovered in many ways; in a catalogue, in an advertisement or through being mentioned in a letter; they are also often discovered by being read again in the light of a time that alters the shape they once had for their contemporaries.

This *Guide* then, is more than a literary resource, although it is clearly that. Its value lies not just in its range and variety, not just in its exposure of our ignorance (although it helps greatly to alleviate that), but also in its power to persuade us to look again at the categories we use to describe fiction. For their frailty is exposed here, in the most severe test of received opinion that meticulous scholarship and miraculous dedication have provided in a very long time. It is proper to salute this magnificent achievement in the best way – by trying to absorb it. That will take some time.

Acknowledgments

This book would have never been completed without the advice, stimulation and encouragement of many people. Foremost, we wanted to thank our informal advisory group, which included the following individuals: Charles Benson (Trinity College, Dublin), Seamus Deane (University of Notre Dame), Pat Donlan (former director of the National Library of Ireland, Dublin), Desmond Fitzgerald, Knight of Glin (Glin Castle, Co. Limerick), Christopher Fox (University of Notre Dame), Dónall Ó Luanaigh (National Library of Ireland, Dublin), the late Miss Paul (Mary) Pollard (Dublin), and Kevin Whelan (University of Notre Dame, Dublin and Notre Dame, IN). They were always ready to help and inspired us to overcome the many barriers we faced. Many of the strengths of this volume are due to their most helpful advice. However, the weaknesses of this work are our responsibility.

We are also very grateful to the University of Notre Dame for financial support for this project over several years, and to Christopher Fox, Seamus Deane, and Kevin Whelan for facilitating this support. In addition, we received a grant from the Trinity College Dublin Print Culture project to defray some of the costs of employing researchers. Most importantly, we are much indebted to Aongus Ó hAonghusa and Brendan O Donoghue, acting and past directors of the National Library of Ireland, respectively, for a subvention in support of the publication of this *Guide*. The first author also acknowledges his gratitude for the Fellowship of the Centre of the Book at the British Library, awarded to him for the period 2000–3.

We received much help from James McGuire, director of the Dictionary of Irish Biography. The DIB staff checked their database against ours, which led to the identification of several authors not known to us. Also, we were able to consult the large database of the Dictionary of Irish Biography.

We employed scholars to assist us in our research. We are highly indebted to them: Johanna Archbold (Trinity College, Dublin), Malcolm Ballin (University of Cardiff), Fionnuala Dillane (Trinity College, Dublin), Carmel Doyle (Dictionary of Irish Biography), Neil Hitchin (University of Cambridge), Tara Keenan (Trinity College, Dublin), Matthew Lamberti (Harvard University), Jessica Marsh (Dictionary of Irish Biography), Turlough O'Riordan (Dictionary of Irish Biography), and Catherine Morris (Sheffield). Further, we are grateful for several scholars who looked up materials for us, including Jacqueline Belanger (University of Cardiff who also read and commented on the manuscript), Irene Danks (Edinburgh, National Library of Scotland), Clare Hutton (University of Oxford) and Eileen Reilly (New York University). In addition, Debra Anthony (University of Pittsburgh) and Tamia Hayes (University of Pittsburgh) most effectively provided secretarial assistance. Cheon Graham expertly created the access data base to quantify the information in the *Guide*.

The research could not have been accomplished without the assistance of librarians and staff of many of the major libraries with holdings of Irish fiction. Foremost, we are greatly indebted to Kevin Brown and the staff of the National Library of Ireland who were most helpful and greatly facilitated our research in that library. Special mention should be made of many other librarians, including Robin C. Alston (British Library), Charlotte Ames (University of Notre Dame), Tricia Boyd (University of Edinburgh), Gavin Bridson (Institute for Botanical Documentation, Carnegie-Mellon University), Michel Brisebois (National Library, Ottawa), Mary Clarke (City of Dublin Archives), Conny Crossey (University of Pittsburgh), Stephen Enniss (Emory University), Laura Fuderer (University of Notre Dame), Nora Geurtsen (Koninklijke Bibliotheek, The Hague), Brian Jenkins (Cambridge University Library), Marion

Acknowledgments

Keyes (The Children's Book Collection, London), Máire Kennedy (Public Library, Pearse Street, Dublin), Muriel MacCarthy (Marsh's Library, Dublin), Leslie McGrath (Osborne Collection, Toronto), David McKitterick (Trinity College, University of Cambridge), the late Carolyn T. Nee (The Catholic University of America), Robert O'Neill (Boston College), Benjamin Panciera (University of Notre Dame), Raymond Refaussé (Representative Church Body Library, Dublin), Candida Ridler (British Library), and Sara Weber (University of Notre Dame).

In addition, we received assistance from staff of the following libraries: the main library of the University of Cambridge (Cambridge), Ryland Library (Manchester), the Bodleian Library (Oxford), the Robarts Library (Toronto), the Hillman Library (University of Pittsburgh), the library of the University of Cardiff (Cardiff), the Henry E. Huntington Library (San Marino, CA), the Newberry Library (Chicago, IL), the University of Chicago Library (Chicago, IL), Special Collections at the University of Texas (Austin, TX), Special Collections at the University of Georgia (Atlanta, GA), Special Collections, University College, Dublin, Special Collections, University College, Cork, Athlone Regional Library, and the Central Catholic Library (Dublin).

We received a great deal of advice and assistance from many antiquarian book dealers. Special mention should be made of: Eamonn de Búrca (de Búrca Rare Books, Blackrock, Co. Dublin, and Dublin), John Hart (John Hart, Antiquarian Bookseller, Salthouse, Norfolk, England), Tom Joyce (Joyce & Co., Chicago, IL), David Mason and Debra Deerlove (Mason Books, Toronto), John Schulman (Caliban Books, Pittsburgh, PA) and Steve Weissman (Ximenes, New York, London, Kempsford). In addition, we are greatly indebted to numerous other book dealers for their assistance: Angela Carter (Irish Books, New York City), Marsha Carter (Booked Up, Washington, DC), Aisling, David, and Enda Cunningham (Cathach Books, Dublin), James Fenning (Dun Laoghaire, Co. Dublin), Neville Figgis (The House of Figgis, Dublin, now Moyard, Co. Galway, Ireland), Jack A. Gamble (Emerald Isle Books, Belfast, Northern Ireland), Denise Byrne Gogarty (Quixote Books, Potomac, MD), Sylvia Harlow (Tiger Books, Westbere, Canterbury, Kent), Theodore Hoffman and Mary James (Quaritch, London), the late Noel Jameson (Carrigtohill, Co. Cork), Chris R. Johnson and his colleague Chris A. Forster (London), the Kenny brothers (Kenny's Bookshops, Galway), Brian Lake, Janet Nassau and Helen Smith (Jarndyce, London), Patrick McGahern (Patrick McGahern Books, Ottawa, Canada), Peter Rowan (P. & B. Rowan Antiquarian Books, Belfast), Stephen Stokes (Passage Books, Dublin), and Neal and Beverly Townsend (Townsend Books, Pittsburgh).

We greatly benefited from the generosity of several private collectors who opened their libraries for us to view: Andrew and the late Dolores Carpenter (Dalkey, Co. Dublin), Desmond Fitzgerald, The Knight of Glin (Glin Castle, Co. Limerick), Liam O'Leary (Clonegal, Co. Wexford), Valerie Pakenham (Tullynally, Co. Westmeath), Moira Robertson (Huntington Castle, Co. Wexford), Aidan Heavey (Dublin), the late Mary Pollard (Dublin), Piers O'Conor (Clonalis, Co. Roscommon) and Tony Sweeney (Dalkey, Co. Dublin).

Throughout the project we received much help from friends and colleagues. Special mention should be made of Don Acheson (Queen's University, Kingston, ON), David Alexander (York, England), Toby Barnard (University of Oxford), the late Sir Charles Brett (Belfast), Jack Burtchaell (Waterford), Michael Byrne (Tullamore, Co. Offaly), Marc Caball (University College, Dublin), Nicholas Canny (University College, Galway), Andrew Carpenter (University College, Dublin), George Casey (Memorial University of Newfoundland), Marion Casey (New York University), Lady Christina Colvin (Oxford), Claire Connolly (University of Cardiff), Tom Connors (University of Iowa, Cedar Falls, IA), Brian Cosgrove (National University of Ireland, Maynooth), Cecil Courtney (University of Cambridge), Anne Crookshank (Trinity College, Dublin), Peter Costello (Dublin), Bernadette Cunningham (Royal Irish Academy, Dublin), Andrew Davies (University of Cardiff), Marysa Demoor (University of Gent, Gent,

Acknowledgments

Belgium), Jane Desmarais (University of London), David Dickson (Trinity College, Dublin), Arch Elias (Philadelphia, PA), Elizabeth FitzPatrick (University College, Galway), Antonia Forster (University of Akron, OH), Peter Garside (formerly at the University of Cardiff), Raymond Gillespie (National University of Ireland, Maynooth), Charles Ginnane (Cork), Luke Gibbons (University of Notre Dame), George and Suzie Gossip (Birr, Co. Offaly; Ballinderry, Co. Galway), Jennifer Harrison (University of Queensland, Australia), Ronald Hoffman (Omohundro Institute of Early American History and Culture, Williamsburg, VA), Margaret Kelleher (National University of Ireland, Maynooth), Joep Leerssen (University of Amsterdam, Amsterdam, Netherlands), Pat Lysaght (University College, Dublin), William J. McCormack (University of London), Robert B. MacDowell (emeritus Trinity College, Dublin), Edward McParland (Trinity College, Dublin), Anthony Mandal (University of Cardiff), Con Manning (Duchas, Dublin), Patrick Maume (Dictionary of Irish Biography), Mrs M. Maume (Cork), Kathy Mezei (Simon Fraser University, Vancouver, BC), David W. Miller (Carnegie Mellon University), Angus Mitchell (Huntington Castle, Co. Wexford), James Murphy (De Paul University, Chicago, IL), Sidney Neff (Sewickley, PA), Breandán Ó Buachalla (University of Notre Dame), Niall Ó Ciosáin (University College, Galway), Jane Ohlmeyer (Trinity College, Dublin), James Quinn (Dictionary of Irish Biography, Royal Irish Academy, Dublin), the late William O'Sullivan (Trinity College, Dublin), James Raven (University of Essex), Ann Rigney (University of Utrecht), Ian Campbell Ross (Trinity College, Dublin), Ann Martha Rowan (Irish Architectural Archive, Dublin), Gavin Selerie (England), Anngret Simms (University College, Dublin), Keith D.M. Snell (University of Leicester), Janet Todd (University of Glasgow), Nathan Wallace (Notre Dame University) and Christopher Woods (Royal Irish Academy, Dublin). We are very grateful to Matthew Stout for drawing the maps for this *Guide*, and to Sharon Corcoran for making several of the indexes. We hope to be forgiven if we have not mentioned any one else who has assisted us in this work. In this category belong all our close friends and relatives, who, despite having heard us talk about Irish fiction for more than a decade, and are still associating with us.

Permission to Quote Sources

Every honest effort has been made to obtain copyright permission. In the event of a lack of permission, please notify the publisher so that it can be rectified in a later edition. For permission to reproduce material from the following copyright works and booksellers catalogues, the authors and publisher gratefully acknowledge the following. Jacqueline Belanger, for her 'Some preliminary remarks on the production and reception of fiction relating to Ireland, 1800–1829', version 6/1/00; Stuart Bennett, Mill Valley, CA, USA, for his catalogues; V. Blain, for V. Blain, I. Grundy & P. Clements, *The feminist companion to literature in English* (New Haven: Yale University Press, 1990); John Crichton of the Brick Row Book Shop, San Francisco, CA, USA, for his catalogues; the Provincial of the Jesuits in Ireland, for S.J. Brown, SJ, *Ireland in fiction* (Dublin, 1919; first published in 1916); Bernard Browne, for his 'Bio-bibliography of the 1798 Rebellion' (unpublished computer database 1982–2005), Old Ross, Co. Wexford, unpublished manuscript [1992]; Seamus Deane (general editor), for the five volumes of the *The Field Day anthology of Irish writing* (Derry, 1992, 3 vols and Cork, 2002, 2 vols); Eamonn de Búrca of de Búrca Rare Books, Blackrock (Co. Dublin), Ireland, for his catalogues; James Burmester, Upton Cheyney, Bristol, England, for his catalogues; Charles Cox, Treglasta, Launceton, Cornwall, England, for his catalogues; James Cummins, New York, NY, USA, for his catalogues; Arthur Davidson, Ballynahinch (Co. Down), Northern Ireland, for his catalogues; Christopher Edwards, Hurst, Berks., England, for his catalogues; John A. Gamble of Emerald Isle Books, Belfast, Northern Ireland, for his catalogues; the University of Notre Dame Press, Notre Dame, IN, USA, for C. Fanning (ed.), *The exiles of Erin: nineteenth-century Irish-American fiction* (copyright 1987); the University Press of Kentucky, Lexington (KY), USA, for C. Fanning, *The Irish voice in America: Irish-American fiction from the 1760s to the 1980s.* (1990); James Fenning, Dun Laoghaire (Co. Dublin), Ireland, for his catalogues; Neville Figgis of The House of Figgis, Moyard, Co. Galway, Ireland, for his catalogues; Alex Fotheringham, West Woodburn, Hexham, Northants., England, for his catalogues; F.S. Frank, for *The first Gothics. A critical guide to the English Gothic novel* (1987), Garland Publishing Inc., New York, USA; Oxford University Press for P. Garside & R. Schöwerling, *The English novel 1770–1829: A bibliographic survey of prose fiction published in the British Isles. Volume II: 1800–1829* (2000); John Hart Antiquarian Bookseller, Salthouse, Norfolk, England, for his catalogues; Epoch Books Inc., Kenmore, NY, USA, for D.K. Hartman, *Historical figures in nineteenth century fiction* (1999); Norman Healy, Galway, Ireland, for his catalogues; C.P. Hyland, Rosscarbery (Co. Cork), Ireland, for his catalogues; Brian Lake of Jarndyce, London, England, for his catalogues; C. Forster of C.R. Johnson Rare Book Collections, London, England, for his catalogues; Colin Smythe, Gerrards Cross Publishing, Gerrards Cross, Bucks., England, for M. Keane, *Mrs S.C. Hall. A literary biography* (1997); Oxford University Press for S. Kemp, C. Mitchell & D. Trotter, *Edwardian fiction. An Oxford companion* (1997); Siobhan Kilfeather, for her "Strangers at home': Political fictions by women in eighteenth-century Ireland', unpublished dissertation (1989); Regina de Búrca of Lullaby Children's Books, Blackrock (Co. Dublin), Ireland, for her catalogue; W.J. McCormack, for his *Sheridan Le Fanu and Victorian Ireland* (Oxford University Press, 1980); Patrick Maume, for his *The margins of subsistence: The novels of Shan Bullock* (Enniskillen, n.d.); Howard S. Mott, Sheffield, MA, USA, for his catalogues; Greenwood Publishing Group, Inc., Westport CT, USA:, for J.H. Murphy, *Catholic fiction and social reality in Ireland, 1873–1922* (copyright 1997 by James H. Murphy); John Price, London, England, for his catalogues; Oxford

University Press for J. Raven, A. Forster & S. Bending (eds), *English novel 1770–1829. A bibliographical survey of prose fiction published in the British isles. Vol. I: 1770–1799* (2000); Eileen Reilly, for her 'Fictional histories: An examination of Irish historical and political novels 1880–1914', unpublished dissertation (1997); P. & B. Rowan Antiquarian Booksellers, Belfast, Northern Ireland, for their catalogues; Garrett H. Scott II, Ann Arbor, MI, USA, for his catalogues; Robert B. Slocum, for his *New England in fiction, 1787–1990. An annotated bibliography* (West Cornwall, CT, 1994, 2 vols); Richard Loomis Jnr. of Sumner & Stillman, Yarmouth, ME, USA, for his catalogues; Pearson Educational Limited; the Longman Group UK Limited, for J. Sutherland, *The Longman companion to Victorian literature* (London, 1988; paperback edn, 1990); The Continuum Publishing Company, Routledge, for J. Todd (ed.), *Dictionary of British women writers* (London, 1989); the University Press of Kentucky, for A.B. Tracy, *The Gothic novel, 1790–1830* (Lexington, KY, 1981); Oxford University Press, for R. Welch (ed.), *The Oxford companion to Irish literature* (1996); British Library, for N. Wilson, *Shadows in the attic. A guide to British supernatural fiction, 1820–1950* (London, 2000); Routledge/Taylor & Francis Group, LLC, Garland Publishing, Inc., for R.L. Wolff, *Introduction to the Nineteenth century fiction. Series two. Ireland from the Act of the Union ... to the death of Parnell. 1891* ([New York], n.d.); Steve Weissman of Ximenes Rare Books Kempsford, Glos., England, for his catalogues.

In addition, we are indebted to the staff of the Hesburgh Library, University of Notre Dame, for photographs of the books from the Loeber collection used as illustrations in this volume.

Abbreviations

§	After a name in the text, indicates an author whose work is listed in the present work
?	doubtful or unknown
[ ]	editorial comment
'...'	for a name or initials, this indicates a pseudonym
+	book has been examined by one of the authors or researchers
A. Hall cat.	Amanda Hall Rare Books, London, and later Upper Bucklebury, Berks., England
ABE books	ABE books (website of book dealers)
AD	Andrew Davies (researcher)
Adamnet	On line: Internet: <http://picarta.pica.nl> (access date: Aug. 2005).
Adams	J.R.R. Adams, *The printed word and the common man. Popular culture in Ulster, 1700–1900* (Belfast, 1987).
Addenda, Waterford	[anon.], Addenda to W.H. Rennison, Bishops, cathedral and parochial clergy of the diocese of Waterford & Lismore (1920). Unpublished manuscript. Representative Church Body Library, Dublin.
adv. (advs)	advertisement(s)/advertised
AIHS	American-Irish Historical Society, New York, NY, USA
Allen cat.	William H. Allen, Philadelphia, PA, USA
Allibone	S.A. Allibone, *A critical dictionary of English literature and British and American authors*, 3 vols. (Philadelphia, 1858; republished Detroit, MI, 1895).
Allibone Suppl.	J.F. Kirk (ed.), *A supplement to Allibone's critical dictionary of English literature and British and American* authors, 2 vols. (Philadelphia, 1891; republished Detroit, MI, 1895).
Alphabetische naamlijst 1790–1832	[anon.], *Alphabetische naamlijst van boeken,welke sedert her jaar 1790 tot en met her jaar 1832 in Noord-Nederland zijn uitgekomen* ('s Gravenhage, 1835).
Alphabetische naamlijst 1833–49	[anon.], *Alphabetische naamlijst van boeken, plaat- en kaartwerken die gedurende de jaren 1833 tot en met 1849 in Nederland uitgegeven of herdrukt zijn* (Amsterdam, 1858).
Alston & Evans	S. Alston & K. Evans (eds), *A bibliography of Canadiana*, 5 vols. (Toronto, 1986).
Alston	R.C. Alston, *A checklist of women writers, 1801–1900* (London, 1990).
AMB	Anne Mullin Burnham (researcher)
ANB	J.A. Garraty & M.C. Carnes (eds), *American national biography*, 24 vols. (New York, 1999).
Anderson 1	J. Anderson, *Catalogue of early Belfast printed books, 1694 to 1830* (Belfast, 1890, new and enlarged edn).
Anderson 2	J. Anderson, *Catalogue of early Belfast printed books, 1694 to 1830* (Belfast, 1894, suppl. to the 3rd, 1890 edn).
Anderson 3	J. Anderson, *Catalogue of early Belfast printed books, 1694 to 1830* (Belfast, 1902, another suppl. to the 3rd, 1890 edn).

anon.	anonymous
Ave	Avenue
B & S	G.D. Burtchaell & T.U. Sadleir (eds), *Alumni Dublinenses* (Dublin, 1935, new edn).
B. Browne	Bernard Browne, Bio-bibliography of the 1798 Rebellion. Old Ross, Co. Wexford: Unpublished MS computer print out [1992].
b.	born
BA	Bachelor of Arts
Baker	E.A. Baker, *A guide to historical fiction* (London, 1914).
Baldwin	*Index to the Baldwin library of books in English before 1900 primarily for children. University of Florida Libraries, Gainesville*, 2 vols. (Boston, MA, 1981).
Bary	V. Bary, *Historical, genealogical, architectural notes of some houses of Kerry* (Whitegate, Co. Clare, 1994).
BD	*Biographical dictionary of the living authors of Great Britain and Ireland* (London, 1816).
BD	Bachelor of Divinity (when associated with an individual)
Beasley	J.C. Beasley, *A check list of prose fiction published in England 1740–1749* (Charlottesville, VA, 1972).
Beds.	Bedfordshire
Belanger	J. Belanger, 'Some preliminary remarks on the production and reception of fiction relating to Ireland, 1800–1829'. On line: Internet: <http://www.cardiff.ac.uk/encap/corvey/articles/cc04_ no2.html> (access date: May 2003)
Bennett cat.	Stuart Bennett, Mill Valley and San Rafael, CA, USA
Berks.	Berkshire
BFl	Linen Hall Library, Belfast, Northern Ireland
BGL	Bethnal Green Museum of Childhood, London, England
Bickersteth cat.	David Bickersteth, Bassingbourne, Royston, Herts., England
Bigger	*Catalogue of the Francis Joseph Bigger collection in the Belfast Public Library* (Belfast, 1930).
BL	British Library, London
Black	F.G. Black, *The epistolary novel in the late eighteenth century. A descriptive and bibliographical study* (Eugene, OR, 1940).
Blackwell cat.	Blackwell's Rare Books, Oxford, England
Blain	V. Blain, I. Grundy & P. Clements, *The feminist companion to literature in English* (New Haven, 1990).
Blakey	D. Blakey, *The Minerva Press, 1780–1820* (Oxford, 1939).
BLC	*Catalogue of Printed Books in the British Museum*, 263 vols. (London, 1960–66).
Blessing	P.J. Blessing, *The Irish in America. A guide to the literature and the manuscript collections* (Washington, DC, 1992).
Block	A. Block, *The English novel, 1740–1850. A catalogue including prose romances, short stories, and translations of foreign fiction* (London, 1961, new and revsd edn).
BNF	Bibliothèque Nationale de France, Paris, France
Bn-Opale plus	On line: Internet: <http://catalogue.bnf.fr/framesWEB.jsp; jsessionid=0000cQskFoonSVp-IZYe7A8Nqui:-1?host=catalogue> (access date: May 2005)

Boase	F. Boase, *Modern English biography*, 6 vols. (Truro, 1887, 1908; repr. London, 1965).
Bologna cat.	Peter A. Bologna Rare Books, Kilbrittain, Bandon, Co. Cork, Ireland
Bolton	H.P. Bolton, *Women writers dramatized. A calendar of performances from narrative works published in English to 1900* (London, 2000).
Boylan	H. Boylan, *A dictionary of Irish biography* (New York, 1988, 2nd edn).
Bradshaw	*A catalogue of the Bradshaw collection of Irish books in the University Library, Cambridge*, 3 vols. (Cambridge, 1916).
Brady	A.M. Brady & B. Cleeve, *A biographical dictionary of Irish writers* (New York, 1985).
Brick Row cat.	The Brick Row Book Shop, San Francisco, CA, USA
Brig.	Brigadier
British Fiction	P.D. Garside, J.E. Belanger, & S.A. Ragaz, *British fiction, 1800–1829: A database of production, circulation and reception*. On line: Internet <http://www.british.fiction.cf.ac.uk> (access date: Feb. 2005).
Brooke	R.S. Brooke, *Recollections of the Irish church* (London, 1877).
Bros	Brothers
Brown 2	S.J. Brown & D. Clarke, *Ireland in fiction. A guide to Irish novels, tales, romances and folklore. Volume 2* (Cork, 1985).
Brown	S.J. Brown, *Ireland in fiction* (Dublin, 1919; first published in 1916).
Browne	B. Browne, *Living by the pen. The authors, poets, and writers of Co. Wexford* (n.l., n.p., 1997).
Bt	Baronet
Bucks.	Buckinghamshire
Burke	W.J. Burke & W.D. Howe, *American authors and books, 1640 to the present day* (New York, 1962, revsd edn).
Burke, 1878	Sir B. Burke, *A genealogical and heraldic dictionary of the peerage and baronetage, together with memoirs of the Privy Councillors and knights* (London, 1878, 40th edn).
Burke's	*Burke's Irish family records* (London, 1976).
Burmester cat.	James Burmester, Upton Cheyney, Bristol, England
Burmester list	Lists of Irish novels provided by James Burmester, Upton Cheyney, Bristol, England, July 2005
Butler	M. Butler, *Maria Edgeworth: a literary biography* (Oxford, 1972).
C	Cambridge Univ., Cambridge, England
c.	circa
c.	century
CA	California
CaACU	Univ. of Alberta, Edmonton, Alberta, Canada
CaBVAU	Univ. of British Columbia, Vancouver, BC, Canada
Cahalan	J.M. Cahalan, *Great hatred, little room. The Irish historical novel* ([Syracuse, NY], 1983).
Cambs.	Cambridgeshire
CaOKQ	Queen's Univ., Kingston, ON, Canada
CaOONL	National Library, Ottawa, ON, Canada

CaOTP	Toronto Public Library, Toronto, ON, Canada
Capt.	Captain
Carpenter	A. Carpenter (ed.), *Verse in English from eighteenth-century Ireland* (Cork, 1998).
Carraig cat.	Carraig Books, Blackrock, Co. Dublin, Ireland
Carter	J. Carter, *Binding variants in English publishing, 1820-1900* (London, 1932).
Casey & Rowan	C. Casey & A. Rowan, *North Leinster. The buildings of Ireland* (London, 1993).
Cat. Dcc	S.J. Brown, SJ, *Catalogue of novels and tales by Catholic writers* (Dublin, 1932, 5th edn, revsd).
cat.	catalogue
Cathair cat.	Cathair Books, Dublin (later Rathdrum, Co. Wicklow), Ireland
CCF	Catalogue Collectif de France. On line: Internet: <http://www.ccfr.bnf.fr/accdis/accdis.htm> (access date: June 2004).
CD	Carmel Doyle (researcher)
CEWW	*Canada's Early Women Writers: An online directory.* On line: Internet: <http://www.lib.sfu.ca/researchtools/databases/dbofdb. htm?DatabaseID=424> (access date: 15 Nov. 2004).
Ches.	Cheshire
Chronology	J.M. Cahalan, *Modern Irish literature and culture. A chronology* (New York, 1993).
CIHM	Canadian Institute for Historical Microreproductions
CKu	Univ. College, Cork, Ireland
Clements cat.	R.W. Clements, Hampton, Middx, England
CLU	Univ. of California at Los Angeles, CA, USA
Clyde	T. Clyde, *Irish literary magazines. An outline history and descriptive bibliography* (Dublin, 2003).
CM	Catherine Morris (researcher)
CO	Colorado
Co.	Company
Co.	County (when followed by the name of the county)
Col.	Colonel
Cole	R.C. Cole, *Irish booksellers and English writers, 1740-1800* (London, 1986).
Collinson Black	R.D. Collinson Black, *A catalogue of pamphlets on economic subjects published between 1750 and 1900 and now housed in Irish libraries* (Belfast, 1969).
Colman	A.U. Colman, *Dictionary of nineteenth-century Irish women poets* (Galway, 1996).
Colvin	C. Colvin, *Maria Edgeworth. Letters from England, 1813-1884* (Oxford, 1971).
Comerford	R.V. Comerford, *Charles J. Kickham, a biography* (Portmarnock [Co. Dublin], 1979).
Commoners	J. Burke, *A genealogical and heraldic history of the commoners of Great Britain and Ireland, enjoying territorial possessions or high official rank; but invested with heritable honours,* 4 vols. (London, 1838).
COPAC	Consortium of University Research Libraries in the United Kingdom and Ireland (on line)

Corbett	E. Corbett, *Dublin in fiction* (Dublin, 1992).
Cork	W.M. Brady, *Clerical and parochial records of Cork, Cloyne, and Ross*, 3 vols. (Dublin, 1863–64).
Corn.	Cornwall
Corvey	Corvey Microfiche Collection of English language novels based on the collection in Schloss Corvey, near Höxter, Germany
Cox cat.	Charles Cox, Chagford, Devon; later Treglasta, Launceton, Corn., England.
CP	F.E. Cocayne (ed.), *The complete peerage of England, Scotland and Ireland*, 13 vols. (Gloucester, 1982, [new, revsd edn]).
Crookshank	A. Crookshank & The Knight of Glin, *The watercolours of Ireland. Works on paper in pencil, pastel and paint, c.1600–1914* (London, 1994).
Crowley	D.O. Crowley, *Irish poets and novelists* (San Francisco, CA, 1893, 3rd edn).
CSmH	Henry E. Huntington Library, San Marino, CA, USA
CSt	Stanford Univ., Palo Alto, CA, USA.
CT	Connecticut
CtY	Yale Univ., New Haven, CT, USA
Cummins cat.	James Cummins Bookseller, New York, NY, USA
Curran index	E.M. Curran (ed.), The Curran index. Additions to and corrections of the Wellesley index to Victorian periodicals. On line: Internet: <http://victorianresearch.org/curranindex.html> (access date: 10 Feb. 2005).
D & P	Dime novels and Penny Dreadfuls. Stanford Univ.'s dime novel and story paper collection. On line: Internet: <http://www-sul.stanford.edu/depts/dp/pennies/home.html> (access date: Oct. 2005).
D	National Library of Ireland, Dublin, Ireland
d.	died
D. & D.	M. Daly & D. Dickson (eds), *The origins of popular literacy in Ireland. Language change and educational development, 1700–1920* (Dublin, 1990).
d.	pence or penny
DAB	A. Johnson & D. Malone (eds), *Dictionary of American biography*, 20 vols. (New York, 1937).
Daims	D. Daims & J. Grimes, *Toward a feminist tradition. An annotated bibliography of novels in English by women, 1891–1920* (New York, 1982).
Dalby	R. Dalby, *Bram Stoker. A bibliography of first editions* (London, 1983).
Davidson cat.	Davidson Books, Ballynahinch, Co. Down, Northern Ireland
DC	District of Columbia
DCB	*Dictionary of Canadian biography*, 16 vols. (Toronto, 1966–ongoing).
Dcc	Central Catholic Library, Dublin, Ireland
DCL	Library of Congress, Washington, DC, USA
DCU	Catholic Univ. of America, Washington, DC, USA
DD	Doctor of Divinity
de Búrca cat.	de Búrca Rare Books, Blackrock, Co. Dublin, Ireland

DE	Delaware
Derbys.	Derbyshire
Devonshire	M.G. Devonshire, *The English novel in France, 1830–1870* ([London], 1929; repr. New York, 1967).
Dime novels	A. Johannson, The house of Beadle and Adams and its dime and nickel novels. The story of a vanished literature. On line. A project of the Northern Illinois Univ. Libraries, DeKalb, IL 60115. Internet: <http://www.niulib.niu.edu/badndp/bibindex.html> (access date: 28 Apr. 2005).
Dixson	Z.A. Dixson, *The comprehensive subject index to universal prose fiction* (New York, 1897).
DL	Deputy Lieutenant
DLB	*Dictionary of literary biography*, 307 vols. (Farmington Hills, MI, 1999–2005).
DLitt.	Doctor of Letters
Dm	Marsh's Library, Dublin, Ireland
Dnce	National College of Education, Dublin, Ireland
Donegal	B. O'Hanrahan, *Donegal authors: a bibliography* (Blackrock, [Co. Dublin, *c.*1982]).
Doolin Dinghy cat.	Doolin Dinghy, Doolin, Co. Clare, Ireland
DPL	Dublin Public Library, Pearse Street, Dublin, Ireland
Dr	Doctor
Drury cat.	John Drury, Manningtree, Essex, England
DSAB	W.J. De Kock (ed.), *Dictionary of South African Biography*, 5 vols. ([Pretoria], 1968).
Dt	Trinity College, Dublin, Ireland
E	National Library of Scotland, Edinburgh, Scotland
E. Reilly	E. Reilly, Fictional histories: An examination of Irish historical and political novels, 1880–1914. Unpublished dissertation, Oxford Univ., Oxford, 1997.
E. Sussex	East Sussex
ed.	edited/editor
edn/edns	edition/s
eds	editors
Edwards cat.	Christopher Edwards, Hurst, Berks., England
EF	S. Kemp, C. Mitchell & D. Trotter, *Edwardian fiction. An Oxford companion* (Oxford, 1997).
Ellis	S.M. Ellis, *Wilkie Collins, Le Fanu and others* (London, 1931; repr. 1951).
Elmes	R.M. Elmes, *Catalogue of engraved Irish portraits mainly in the Joly collection and of original drawings* (Dublin, [n.d.]).
Emerald Isle cat.	Emerald Isle Books, Belfast, Northern Ireland
ER	Eileen Reilly (researcher)
Esdaile	A. Esdaile, *A list of English tales and prose romances printed before 1740* (London, 1912; repr. 1970).
ESTC	*The English eighteenth century short title catalogue.* On line (available by subscription only).
exhib.	Exhibition

Exiles	C. Fanning (ed.), *The exiles of Erin: nineteenth-century Irish-American fiction* (Notre Dame, IN, 1987).
F.A. van S.	F.A. van S., *Nederlandsche letterkunde. Populaire prozaschrijvers der xvii^e en xviii^e eeuw* (Amsterdam, 1893).
Falkner Greirson cat.	Falkner Greirson, Dublin, Ireland
Fanning	C. Fanning, *The Irish voice in America: Irish-American fiction from the 1760s to the 1980s* (Lexington, KY, 1990).
Fegan	M. Fegan, *Literature and the Irish famine, 1845–1919* (Oxford, 2002).
Fenning cat.	James Fenning, Dun Laoghaire, Co. Dublin, Ireland
Ferguson	K. Ferguson (ed.), *King's Inns barristers 1868–2004* (Dublin, 2005).
ff.	and following
FFF	*Fiction, folklore, fantasy & poetry for children, 1876–1985* (New York, 1986).
Field Day	S. Deane (general ed.), *The Field Day anthology of Irish writing*, 3 vols. (Derry, 1992).
Field Day 2	A. Bourke, S. Kilfeather, M. Luddy, M. MacCurtain, G. Meany, M. Ní Dhonnchadha, M. O'Dowd, & C. Wills (eds), *The Field Day anthology of Irish writing*, 2 vols. (Cork, 2002 [vols. 4 and 5]).
Figgis cat.	The House of Figgis, Dublin, and later Moyard, Co. Galway, Ireland
fl.	flourished
FL	Florida
Fleming, *Armagh*	Fleming, W.E.C., *Armagh clergy, 1800–2000* (n.l., 2001).
FD	Fionnuala Dillane (researcher)
FitzPatrick	W.J. FitzPatrick, *The life of Charles Lever* (London, n.d., new edn).
Forster	A. Forster, *Index to book reviews in England 1749–1774* (Carbondale, IL, 1990).
Forster 2	A. Forster, *Index to book reviews in England, 1775–1800* (London, 1997).
Fotheringham cat.	Alex Fotheringham, West Woodburn, Hexham, Northumb., England
Fr	Father
Frank	F.S. Frank, *The first Gothics. A critical guide to the English Gothic novel* (New York, 1987).
GA	Georgia
Gains and losses	R.L. Wolff, *Gains and losses. Novels of faith and doubt in Victorian England* (New York, 1977).
Galway	H. Maher, *Galway authors* (Galway, 1976).
Garside (2003)	P.D. Garside, 'Subscribing fiction in Britain, 1780–1829', *Cardiff Corvey* (Dec. 2003). On line: Internet: <http://www.cf.ac.uk/encap/corvey/articles/cc11_n03. html> (access date: 18 Feb. 2005).
Garside	P. Garside & R. Schöwerling, *The English novel, 1770–1829: A bibliographic survey of prose fiction published in the British Isles. Volume II: 1800–1829* (Oxford, 2000).
Garside 2	P. Garside, A. Mandal, V. Ebbes, A. Koch, & R. Schöwerling (eds), *The English novel, 1830–1836. A bibliographical survey of fiction published in the British Isles.* On line: Internet:

<http://www.cf. ac.uk/encap/corvey/1830s/1836.html> (access date: 15 Feb. 2005).

Gecker — S. Gecker (ed.), *English fiction to 1820 in the University of Pennsylvania Library based on the collections of Godfrey F. Singer and John C. Mendenhall* (Philadelphia, 1954).

Gen. — General

GEU — Emory Univ., Atlanta, GA, USA

Gilbert — D. Hyde & D.J. O'Donoghue (eds), *Catalogue of the books & manuscripts comprising the library of the late Sir John T. Gilbert* (Dublin, 1918).

Gilcher — E. Gilcher, *A bibliography of George Moore* (DeKalb, IL, [c.1970]).

Glam. — Glamorganshire

GLOL — German Libraries on Line. On line: Internet: <http://www.hbz-nrw.de/produkte_dienstl/germlst/index-engl.html> (access date: May 2005).

Glos. — Gloucestershire

Gov. — governor

Grail — The Galway Resource for Anglo-Irish Literature. Microfiche of Anglo-Irish fiction and other works from the NLI, completed 1987. Copies in the microfiches are in the National Library of Ireland and the James Hardiman Library, Univ. College Galway, Galway, Ireland

Griffin — S.M. Griffin, *Anti-Catholicism and nineteenth-century fiction* (Cambridge, 2004).

Hajba — A.M. Hajba, *Houses of Cork. Volume I: North Cork* (Whitegate, Co. Clare, 2002).

Halkett & Laing — *A dictionary of anonymous and pseudonymous publications in the English language*, 9 vols. (Edinburgh, Oliver & Boyd, 1926–34; Edinburgh, 1926–62, enlarged edn).

Hall — N.J. Hall, *Trollope. A biography* (Oxford, 1991).

Hall, S.C. — See S.C. Hall.

Hall, W.E. — See W.E. Hall.

Hants. — Hampshire

Hardy — J.C. Hardy, *A catalogue of English prose fiction mainly of the eighteenth century from a private library* (Foss, OK, 1982).

Harris — W.V. Harris, *British short fiction in the nineteenth century* (Detroit, 1979).

Harrison — R.S. Harrison, *A biographical dictionary of Irish Quakers* (Dublin, 1997).

Hart cat. — John Hart Antiquarian Bookseller, London, later Holt, and more recently, Salthouse, Norfolk, England

Hart — J.D. Hart (ed.), *The Oxford companion to American literature* (New York, Oxford, 1983, 5th edn).

Hartman — D.K. Hartman, *Historical figures in nineteenth century fiction* (Kenmore, NY, 1999).

Hayley — B. Hayley, *A bibliography of the writing of William Carleton* (Gerrards Cross, 1985).

Hayley 2 — B. Hayley, *Carleton's Traits and stories and the 19th century Anglo-Irish tradition* (Gerrards Cross, 1983).

Healy cat.	Healy Rare Books, Galway, Ireland
Heath cat.	A.R. Heath, Clifton, Bristol, England
Herbert	R. Herbert, *Limerick printers & printing* (Limerick, 1941).
Herefs.	Herefordshire
Herlihy	J. Herlihy, *Royal Irish Constabulary officers. A biographical dictionary and genealogical guide, 1816–1922* (Dublin, 2005).
Herts.	Hertfordshire
HIP	E.M. Johnston-Liik, *History of the Irish parliament, 1692–1800*, 6 vols. (Belfast, 2002).
Hislop	H. Hislop, The Kildare Place Society. Unpublished PhD dissertation, TCD, 1990.
Hodges Figgis cat.	Hodges, Figgis & Co., Dublin, Ireland
Hodgson	T. Hodgson, *The London catalogue of books published in Great Britain with their sizes, prices, and publisher's names, 1816–1851* (London, 1851).
Hogan	R. Hogan (ed.), *Dictionary of Irish literature* (Westport, CT, 1979).
Hogan 2	R. Hogan (ed.), *Dictionary of Irish literature, revised and expanded version*, 2 vols. (London, 1996).
Holmes cat.	David J. Holmes, Philadelphia, PA, and later Collingswood, NJ, USA
Hon.	Honourable
Howard	R.A. Howard, 'Domesticating the novel: Moral-domestic fiction, 1820–1834'. In *Cardiff Corvey* (Winter 2004). On line: Internet: http://www.cf.ac.uk/encap/corvey/articles/cc13_no3.html> (access date: 24 Mar. 2005).
Howes cat.	Howes Bookshop, Hastings, E. Sussex, England
HS	High Sheriff
Hudson	E. Hudson (ed.), *A bibliography of the first editions of the works of E.Œ. Somerville and Martin Ross* (New York, 1942).
Hyland cat.	C.P. Hyland, Wales, and later Rosscarbery, Co. Cork, Ireland
IA	Iowa
IBL	*Irish Book Lover* (London, 1909–57).
ICN	Newberry Library, Chicago, IL, USA
ICU	Univ. of Chicago, Chicago, IL, USA
ID	Irene Danks (researcher)
Igoe	V. Igoe, *A literary guide to Dublin. Writers in Dublin: Literary associations and anecdotes* (London, 1994).
IL	Illinois
ill.	illustrated (when no name follows, the artist is unknown)
impr.	impression
IN	Indiana
InND	Univ. of Notre Dame, South Bend, IN, USA
InND Loeber coll.	Loeber collection of Irish fiction, Univ. of Notre Dame, South Bend, IN, USA
introd.	introduction/introduced
IRA	Irish Republican Army
IRB	Irish Republican Brotherhood
Ireland related fiction	J. Belanger & C. Connolly (eds), *Ireland related fiction, 1793–1837*, 120 cd-roms (Boyle, Roscommon; Belser Wissenschaftlicher Dienst, 2001).

Irish Book Shop cat.	The Irish Book Shop, New York, NY, USA
Irish pseudonyms	R. Loeber & M. Loeber (eds), *Irish poets and their pseudonyms in early periodicals* (Dublin, 2006).
IU	Univ. of Illinois, Urbana, IL, USA
J & S	James & H.R. Smith (eds), *Penny dreadfuls and boys' adventures* (London, 1998).
JA	Johanna Archbold (researcher)
JAPMDI	*Journal of the Association for the Preservation of the Memorials of the Dead, Ireland* (Dublin, 1888–1934).
Jarndyce cat.	Jarndyce, London, England
JB	Jacqueline Belanger (researcher)
Jnr	Junior
Johnson cat.	C.R. Johnson Rare Book Collections, London, England
JP	Justice of the Peace
Jrnl	Journal
Kaser	D. Kaser, *The cost book of Carey & Lea, 1825–1838* (Philadelphia, PA, 1963).
Keane	E. Keane, P.B. Phair & T.U. Sadleir (eds), *King's Inns admission papers, 1607–1867* (Dublin, 1982).
Kelley	M.E. Kelley, *The Irishman in the English novel of the nineteenth century* (Washington, DC, 1939).
Kenny's cat.	Kenny's Bookshops, Galway, Ireland
Kersnowski	F.L. Kersnowski, C.W. Spinks & L. Loomis, *A bibliography of modern Irish and Anglo-Irish literature* (San Antonio, TX, 1976).
Kilfeather	S. Kilfeather, 'Strangers at home': Political fictions by women in eighteenth-century Ireland. Unpublished Ph.D. dissertation. Princeton Univ., 1989.
King cat.	Patrick King, Stony Stratford, Bucks., England
Knt	Knight
Krishnamurti	G. Krishnamurti, *Women writers of the 1890s* (London, 1991).
KS	Kansas
Kunitz & Haycraft	S.J. Kunitz & H.H. Haycraft (eds), *British authors of the nineteenth century* (New York, 1936).
KU-S	Univ. of Kansas, Spencer Research Library, Lawrence, KS, USA
KY	Kentucky
L	British Library, London, England
LA	Louisiana
Lancs.	Lancashire
Landed gentry	Sir B. Burke, *A genealogical and heraldic history of the landed gentry of Ireland* (London, 1904, 10th edn; 1912 new edn).
Law	G. Law, *Serializing fiction in the Victorian press* (Houndmills, 2000).
Leaves of Grass cat.	Leaves of Grass, Ann Arbor, MI, USA
Leclaire	L. Leclaire, *A general analytic bibliography of the regional novelists of the British Isles, 1800–1950* (Paris, 1954).
Leics.	Leicestershire
Leslie, *Ardfert*	J.B. Leslie, *Ardfert & Aghadoe clergy and parishes* (Dublin, 1940).
Leslie, *Clogher*	J.B. Leslie, *Clogher clergy and parishes* (Enniskillen [Co. Fermanagh], 1929).

Leslie, *Connor*	J.B. Leslie, *Clergy of Connor from patrician times to present day* Belfast, 1993).
Leslie, *Derry*	J.B. Leslie, *Derry clergy and parishes* (Enniskillen [Co. Fermanagh], 1937); (in Belfast: Ulster Historical Foundation, *Clergy of Derry and Raphoe*, 1999).
Leslie, *Down*	J.B. Leslie & H.B. Swanzy, *Biographical succession lists of the clergy of diocese of Down* (Enniskillen [Co. Fermanagh], 1936); (in Belfast: Ulster Historical Foundation, *Clergy of Down and Dromore*, 1996).
Leslie, *Ferns*	J.B. Leslie, *Ferns clergy and parishes* (Dublin, 1936).
Leslie, *Ossory*	J.B. Leslie, *Ossory clergy and parishes* (Enniskillen [Co. Fermanagh], 1933).
Leslie, *Raphoe*	J.B. Leslie, *Raphoe clergy and parishes* (Enniskillen [Co. Fermanagh], 1940); (in Belfast: Ulster Historical Foundation, *Clergy of Derry and Raphoe*, 1999).
Leslie & Wallace	J.B. Leslie & W.J.R. Wallace, *Clergy in Dublin and Glendalough* (Belfast, 2001).
Lewis	G. Lewis, *Somerville and Ross. The world of the Irish R.M.* (London, 1987).
Lincs.	Lincolnshire
Linen Hall cat.	Belfast Library and Society for Promoting Knowledge (Linen Hall Library), *Catalogue of the books in the Irish section* (Belfast, 1917).
List of catalogues	[anon.], *List of catalogues of English book sales 1676–1900 in the British Museum* (London, 1915).
LLB	Bachelor of Law
LLD	Doctor of Law
Lohrli	A. Lohrli, *Household Words: A Weekly Journal, 1850–1859, conducted by Charles Dickens* (Toronto, 1973).
Longford	S. Ó Suilleabháin, *Longford authors. A biographical and bibliographical dictionary* (Mullingar [Co. Westmeath], 1978).
Lough Fea cat.	*Catalogue of the library at Lough Fea, in illustrations of the history and antiquities of Ireland* (London, 1872).
Lowndes	W.T. Lowndes, *The bibliographer's manual of English literature containing an account of rare, curious and useful books, published in or relating to Great Britain and Ireland*, 4 vols. (London, 1871, new edn, revsd).
Lt.	Lieutenant
Lullaby cat.	Lullaby Children's Books, Blackrock, Co. Dublin, Ireland
LVP	C.W. Reilly, *Late Victorian poetry, 1880–1899* (London, 1994).
MA	Massachusetts
MA	Master of Arts (when associated with an individual)
Macartney	F.T. Macartney (ed.), *Australian literature. A bibliography by E. Morris Miller ... extended to 1950* (Sydney, 1956).
MacDonald	M.L. MacDonald, *Literature and society in the Canadas, 1817–1850* (Lewiston, NY, 1992).
MacLeod	A.S. MacLeod, *A moral tale. Children's fiction and American culture, 1820–1860* (Hamden, CT, 1975).
Macmillan	*A bibliographical catalogue of Macmillan and Co.'s publications from 1843 to 1889* (London, 1891).

Maggs cat.	Maggs Bros, London, England
Maj.	Major
Marlborough cat.	Marlborough Rare Books, London, England
Mateboer	J. Mateboer, *Bibliographie van het Nederlandstalig narratief fictioneel proza 1701–1800* (Nieuwkoop, 1996).
Mayo	R.D. Mayo, *The English novel in the magazines, 1740–1815* (Evanston, IL, 1962).
MB	Boston Public Library, Boston, MA, USA
MB	Bachelor of Medicine (when associated with an individual)
MB	Manitoba
McBurney	W.H. McBurney, *A check list of English prose fiction, 1700–1739* (Cambridge, 1960).
McBurney & Taylor	W.H. McBurney & C.M. Taylor (eds), *English prose fiction, 1700–1900 in the University of Illinois Library* (Urbana, IL, 1965).
McCarthy	J. McCarthy (ed.), *Irish literature*, 10 vols. (New York, 1904).
McCormack	W.J. McCormack, *Sheridan Le Fanu and Victorian Ireland* (Oxford, 1980).
McGahern cat.	Patrick McGahern Books, Ottawa, Canada
MChB	Boston College, Boston, MA, USA
McHenry	Cameron & Ferguson (publishers). Catalogue in James McHenry, *McHenry's Irish tales* (Glasgow, [190–?]).
McKenna	B. McKenna, *Irish Literature, 1800–1875, a guide to information sources* (Detroit, MI, 1978).
McVeagh	J. McVeagh, *Irish travel writing. A bibliography* (Dublin, 1996).
MD	Maryland
MD	Doctor of Medicine (when associated with an individual)
MDCB	W.S. Wallace, & W.A. McKay (eds), *The Macmillan dictionary of Canadian biography* (Toronto, 1978).
ME	Maine
Mealy's cat.	Mealy's Auctioneers, Castlecomer, Co. Kilkenny, Ireland
Mercantile Library	[anon.], *Finding list for novels in the Mercantile Library of Philadelphia.* (Philadelphia, 1878).
Mes	G. Mes, *The Katholieke pers van Nederland. 1853–1887* (Maastricht, 1887–88).
MH	Harvard Univ., Boston, MA, USA
MI	Michigan
Middx.	Middlesex
Miller	E.M. Miller, *Australian literature from its beginning to 1935*, 2 vols. (Melbourne, 1940).
M. Keane	M. Keane, *Mrs. S.C. Hall. A literary biography* (Gerrards Cross, 1997).
ML	Magda Loeber (researcher)
MLa	Matthew Lamberti (researcher)
Mme	Madame
Moon	M. Moon, *Benjamin Tabart's juvenile library* (Winchester [Hants.], 1990).
Mott cat.	Howard S. Mott, Sheffield, MA, USA
MP	Member of Parliament
MS/MSS	manuscript(s)
Msgr	Monsignor

Munter	R. Munter, *A dictionary of the print trade in Ireland, 1550–1775* (New York, 1988).
Murphy	J.H. Murphy, *Catholic fiction and social reality in Ireland, 1873–1922* (Westport, CT, 1997).
MVP	C.W. Reilly, *Mid-Victorian poetry, 1860–1879* (London, 2000).
n.	note
NB	*Nederlandse bibliographie, 1801–1832* (Houten, 1993), 3 vols.
NC	North Carolina
n.l.	no location for place of publication
n.p.	no publisher
n.s.	new series
NCBEL 2	G. Watson (ed.), *The new Cambridge bibliography of English literature, vol. 2, 1660–1800* (Cambridge, 1971).
NCBEL 3	G. Watson (ed.), *The new Cambridge bibliography of English literature, vol. 3, 1800–1900* (Cambridge, 1969).
NCBEL 4	G. Watson (ed.), *The new Cambridge bibliography of English literature, vol. 4, 1900–1950* (Cambridge, 1977).
Newmann	K. Newmann, *Dictionary of Ulster biography* (Belfast, 1993).
NGI	National Gallery of Ireland, Dublin, Ireland
NH	New Hampshire
NIC	Cornell Univ., Ithaca, NY, USA
Nield	J. Nield, *A guide to the best historical novels and tales* (n.l., 1911).
Nineteenth Century Books cat.	Nineteenth Century Books, Warborough, Wallingford, Oxon., England
NJ	New Jersey
NjP	Princeton Univ., Princeton, NJ, USA
NLI	National Library of Ireland, Dublin, Ireland
NLS	National Library of Scotland, Edinburgh, Scotland
NM	New Mexico
NN	New York Public Library, New York, NY, USA
NNC	Columbia Univ., New York, NY, USA
No./Nos.	number(s)
Northants.	Northamptonshire
Northumb.	Northumberland
Notts.	Nottinghamshire
NRU	Univ. of Rochester, Rochester, NY, USA
NS	Nova Scotia
NSTC	*Nineteenth Century Short Title Catalogue*, series 1, 6 vols; series 2, 33 vols. (Newcastle-upon-Tyne, 1984–86, [c.1993]).
NSW	New South Wales
NUC	National Union Catalogue; for location(s) see this source
NUI	National Univ. of Ireland
NY	New York
NYPL	New York Public Library. *Dictionary catalogue of research libraries through 1971.* Vols. in the NYPL, New York, NY, USA
NYU	New York Univ., New York, NY, USA
O	Bodleian Library, Oxford, England
O'Brien	[J. O'Brien], A member of the Michigan Bar, *Irish Celts. A cyclopedia of race history, containing biographical sketches of more*

	than *fifteen hundred distinguished Irish Celts, with a chronological index* (Detroit [MI], 1884).
OCCL	W. Toye (ed.), *The Oxford companion to Canadian literature* (Toronto, 1983).
OCIL	R. Welch (ed.), *The Oxford companion to Irish literature* (Oxford, 1996).
OCLC	OCLC First Search Service. Worldcat. (on line; available for subscribers only).
ODNB	H.G.C. Matthew and B. Harrison (eds), *Oxford Dictionary of National Biography*, 60 vols. (Oxford, 2004).
O'Donoghue	D.J. O'Donoghue, *The poets of Ireland. A biographical and bibliographical dictionary of Irish writers of English verse* (Dublin, 1912).
O'Donoghue 2	D.J. O'Donoghue, *The humour of Ireland* (London, 1894).
OH	Ohio
OK	Oklahoma
ON	Ontario
opp.	opposite
OR	Oregon
Osborne	J. St John (ed.), *The Osborne collection of children's books, 1566–1910*, 2 vols. (Toronto, revsd edn, 1975).
O'Toole	T. O'Toole (ed.), *Dictionary of Munster women writers, 1800–2000* (Cork, 2005).
OU	Ohio State Univ., Columbus, OH, USA
Oxon.	Oxfordshire
p./pp	page/s
PA	Pennsylvania
PC	Private collection
PEI	Prince Edward Island
PhD	Doctor of Philosophy
Pickering & Chatto cat.	Pickering & Chatto, London, England
Pollard	M. Pollard, *Dublin's trade in books, 1550–1800* (Oxford, 1989).
Pollard 2	M. Pollard, *A dictionary of members of the Dublin book trade, 1550–1800* (London, 2000).
PP	Athenaeum, Philadelphia, PA, USA
PP	parish priest (when abbreviation after a personal name)
PpiU	Univ. of Pittsburgh, Pittsburgh, PA, USA
PPL-R	Library Company of Philadelphia, Philadelphia, PA, USA
Price cat.	John Price Antiquarian Books, London, England
PRONI	Public Record Office of Northern Ireland, Belfast, Northern Ireland
pseud.	pseudonym
pseuds	pseudonyms
pt.	part
PU	Van Pelt Library, Univ. of Pennsylvania, Philadelphia, PA, USA
PVU	Villanova Univ., Villanova, PA, USA
Quaritch cat.	Bernard Quaritch, London, England
Quinn	*Complete catalogue of the library of John Quinn sold by auction in five parts*, 2 vols. (New York, 1924; repr. 1969).
RA	Royal Artillery

Rafroidi	P. Rafroidi, *Irish literature in English: The romantic period*, 2 vols. (Atlantic Highlands, NJ, 1980).
Rauchbauer	O. Rauchbauer (ed.), *Ancestral voices. The big house in Anglo-Irish literature* (Dublin, 1992).
Raven	J. Raven (ed.), *British fiction 1750–1770. A chronological check-list of prose fiction printed in Britain and Ireland* (Newark, NJ, 1987).
Raven 2	J. Raven, A. Forster & S. Bending (eds), *The English novel 1770–1829. A bibliographical survey of prose fiction published in the British isles. Vol. I: 1770–1799* (Oxford, 2000).
RB	Books seen at P. & D. Rowan, Belfast, Northern Ireland, Mar. 1995
RCB	Representative Church Body Library, Dublin, Ireland
Rd	Road
Reese cat.	William Reese, New Haven, CT, USA
Reeve cat.	M. & D. Reeve, Wheatley, Oxon., England
Reilly	J.M. Reilly, *Twentieth-century crime and mystery writers* (New York, 1985, 2nd edn).
Rennison	W.H. Rennison, *Succession list of the bishops, cathedral and parochial clergy of the diocese of Waterford and Lismore, from the earliest times* (n.l., n.d.).
repr.	reprinted
rev.	reviewed
Revd	Reverend
revsd	revised
RHA	Royal Hibernian Academy
Rhodenizer	V.B. Rhodenizer, *Canadian literature in English* (Montreal, [1965]).
RIA	Royal Irish Academy
RIA/DIB	*Data base of the Dictionary of Irish biography*, Dublin, Royal Irish Academy, in progress.
RIC	Royal Irish Constabulary
Right	Rt
RL	Rolf Loeber (researcher)
RLIN	RLG Union Catalogue (on line; available to subscribers only)
RM	Resident Magistrate
RN	Royal Navy
Robertshaw cat.	John Robertshaw, Ramsey, Huntingdon, Cambs., England
Rochedieu	C.A. Rochedieu, *Bibliography of French translations of English works, 1700–1800* (Chicago, IL, 1948).
Rogal	S.J. Rogal, *The education of the British literati: A guide to their schools, colleges, and universities* (Lewiston, NY, [c.1982]).
Roscommon	H. Maher, *Roscommon authors. A contribution towards a biographical and bibliographical index of Roscommon authors* (Roscommon, 1978).
Rose cat.	Paulette Rose, Fine & Rare Books, New York, NY, USA
Rosenbach	A.S.W. Rosenbach, *Early American children's books* (Portland, ME, 1933; repr. New York, 1971).
Roth	W.H. Roth, *A catalogue of English and American first editions of William Butler Yeats*. Exhibition cat. (New Haven, CT, 1939).
Rowan cat. P. & . B. Rowan cat	Antiquarian Booksellers, Belfast, Northern Ireland

Rowe & Scallan	D. Rowe & E. Scallan, *Historical genealogical architectural notes on some houses of Wexford* (Whitegate, Co. Clare, 2004).
Ryan	W.P. Ryan, *The Irish literary revival: Its history, pioneers and possibilities* (London, 1894).
s.	shilling, or twelve pence
S.C. Hall	S.C. Hall, *A book of memoirs of great men and women of the age from personal acquaintance* (London, n.d., new edn).
Sadleir	M. Sadleir, *XIXth century fiction*, 2 vols. (London, 1957).
SC	South Carolina
Schulz	H.C. Schulz, 'English literary manuscripts in the Huntington Library' in *The Huntington Library Quarterly*, 31 (1968), pp 251–302.
Scott cat.	Garrett Scott, Ann Arbor, MI, USA
Scott	Millgate Union Catalogue of Sir Walter Scott's correspondence. On line: Internet: <http://www.nls.uk/catalogues/resources/scott/bio.cfm?id=25> (access date: 2 Apr. 2005).
Shrops.	Shropshire
SJ	Society of Jesus
Slade	B.C. Slade, *Maria Edgeworth, 1767–1849, a bibliographical tribute* (London, 1937).
Slocum	R.B. Slocum, *New England in fiction, 1787–1990. An annotated bibliography*, 2 vols. (West Cornwall, CT, 1994).
Snell	K.D.M. Snell, *The bibliography of regional fiction in Britain and Ireland, 1800–2000* (Aldershot, 2002).
Snr	Senior
Soc.	Society
Som.	Somerset
Sotheby's cat.	Sotheby's, London, England
Spelman cat.	Ken Spelman Rare Books, York, England
St	Saint
Staffs.	Staffordshire
Streeter	H.W. Streeter, *The eighteenth century English novel in French translation* (New York, 1970).
Strickland	W.G. Strickland, *A dictionary of Irish artists*, 2 vols. (Dublin, 1913; repr. Dublin, 1968).
Summers	M. Summers, *The gothic quest. A history of the Gothic novel* (London, n.d).
Summers 2	M. Summers, *A gothic bibliography* (London, [1941]; repr. New York, 1964).
Sumner & Stillman cat.	Sumner & Stillman, Yarmouth, ME, USA
Suppl.	Supplement
Survey C A	[various authors] *A survey of Catholic Americana and Catholic books in the United States* (Series of dissertations submitted to the Catholic Univ. of America, Washington, DC, 1950-onward (microfilm Z7837. C3 at the Catholic Univ. of America)
Sutherland	J. Sutherland, *The Longman companion to Victorian literature* (London, 1988).
Sutton	D.C. Sutton, *Location register of English literary manuscripts and letters. Eighteenth and nineteenth centuries*, 2 vols. (London, 1995).

Swanzy	H.B. Swanzy, *Succession Lists of the Diocese of Dromore* (Belfast, 1933); in Belfast, Ulster Historical Foundation, *Clergy of Down and Dromore*, 1996).
Sweeney	T. Sweeney, *Ireland and the printed word* (Dublin, 1997).
T & B	W.B. Todd & A. Bowden, *Tauchnitz international editions in English, 1841–1955. A bibliographical history* (New York, 1988).
TCD	Trinity College, Dublin, Ireland
Teerink/Scouten	A.H. Scouten, *A bibliography of the writings of Jonathan Swift, second edition, revised by Dr. H. Teerink* (Philadelphia, PA, 1963).
Thuente 1	M.H. Thuente, *W.B. Yeats and Irish folklore* (Towota, NJ, 1980).
Thuente 2	M.H. Thuente, *The harp restrung. The United Irishmen and the rise of literary nationalism* (Syracuse, NY, 1994).
Tiger cat.	Tiger Books, Westbere, Canterbury, Kent, England
TK	Tara Keenan (researcher)
TN	Tennessee
Todd	J. Todd (ed.), *Dictionary of British women writers* (London, 1989).
Topp 1	C.W. Topp, *Victorian yellowbacks & paperbacks, 1849–1905. Vol. 1: George Routledge* (Denver, CO, 1993).
Topp 2	C.W. Topp, *Victorian yellowbacks & paperbacks, 1849–1905. Vol. II: Ward & Lock* (Denver, CO, 1995).
Topp 3	C.W. Topp, *Victorian yellowbacks & paperbacks, 1849–1905. Vol. III: John Camden Hotten; Chatto & Windus; Chapman & Hall* (Denver, CO, 1997).
Topp 4	C.W. Topp, *Victorian yellowbacks & paperbacks, 1849–1905. Vol. IV: Frederick Warne & Co.; Sampson Low & Co* (Denver, CO, 1999).
Topp 5	C.W. Topp, *Victorian yellowbacks & paperbacks. 1849–1905. Vol. V: Macmillan & Co.; Smith, Elder & Co.* (Denver, CO, 2001).
Topp 6	C.W. Topp, *Victorian yellowbacks & paperbacks, 1849–1905. Vol. VI: Longmans, Green & Co.; C.H. Clarke; John Maxwell & Co.; Tinsley Bros.* (Denver, CO, 2003).
Topp 7	C.W. Topp, *Victorian yellowbacks & paperbacks, 1849–1905. Vol. VII: F.V. White & Co.; Cassell & Co.; William Blackwood & Sons; Vizetelly & Co.* (Denver, CO, 2003).
Tracy	A.B. Tracy, *The Gothic novel, 1790–1830* (Lexington, KY, 1981).
trans.	translated
Trebizond cat.	Trebizond Rare Books, New Preston, CT, USA
TX	Texas
TxU	Univ. of Texas, Austin, TX, USA
UBP	Brigham Young Univ., Salt Lake City, UT, USA
UCC	Univ. College, Cork, Ireland
UCD	Univ. College, Dublin, Ireland
UK	United Kingdom
Univ.	University
US	United States of America
UT	Utah
UVA	Universiteit van Amsterdam, Amsterdam, Netherlands
VA	Virginia
Vanishing country houses	The Knight of Glin, D.J. Griffin & N.K. Robinson, *Vanishing country houses in Ireland* (Dublin, 1989, 2nd edn).

Ven.	Venerable
Venn	J.A. Venn (ed.), *Alumni Cantabrigienses*, 10 vols. (Cambridge, 1947).
ViU	Univ. of Virginia, Charlottesville, VA, USA
vol./vols.	volume/s
VT	Vermont
W.E. Hall	W.E. Hall, *Dialogues in the margin. A study of the Dublin University Magazine* (Washington, DC, 1999).
Wade	A. Wade, *A bibliography of the writings of W.B. Yeats* ([London], 1968, 3rd edn, revised and ed. by R.K. Alspach).
Walford	E. Walford, *The county families of the United Kingdom or Royal manual of the titled and untitled aristocracy of Great Britain and Ireland* (London, 1873).
War.	Warwickshire
Watters	R.E. Watters, *A checklist of Canadian literature and background materials, 1628–1960* (Toronto, 1972, 2nd edn).
Weekes	A.O. Weekes, *Unveiling treasures. The Attic guide for the published works of Irish women literary writers* (Dublin, 1993).
Welch	d'A.A. Welch, *A bibliography of American children's books printed prior to 1821* (n.l., 1972).
Westmeath	M. Keaney, *Westmeath authors* (Mullingar, Co. Westmeath, 1969).
WI	Wisconsin.
Williams	J. Williams, *A companion guide to architecture in Ireland, 1837–1921* (Dublin, 1994).
Wilson	N. Wilson, *Shadows in the attic. A guide to British supernatural fiction, 1820–1950* (London, 2000).
Wilts.	Wiltshire
Wing	Wing's *Short Title Catalogue of Books Printed in England, Scotland, Ireland, Wales, and North America from the late sixteenth century to the present day* (on line).
Wintermans	C. Wintermans, 'Dutch translations of English novels, 1770–1829' *Cardiff Corvey* (Dec. 2001); On line: Internet: <http://www. cf. ac. uk/encap/corvey/articles/cc07_n05. html> (access date: Feb. 2002).
Wolff	R.L. Wolff, *Nineteenth century fiction: a bibliographical catalogue based on the collection formed by Robert Lee Wolff*, 5 vols. (New York, 1981–86).
Wolff introd.	R.L. Wolff, *Introduction to the Nineteenth century fiction. Series two. Ireland from the Act of the Union ... to the death of Parnell. 1891* ([New York], n.d.).
Worcs.	Worcestershire
Wright	L.H. Wright, *American fiction*, 3 vols. (San Marino, CA, 1957, 1969, 1978).
Wright web	Wright American fiction, 1851–1875. Indiana Univ. On line: Internet: <http://www.letrs.indiana.edu/web/w/wright2> (digitized texts of novels; access date: Jan. 2005).
Ximenes cat.	Ximenes Rare Books, New York, USA, later London, later Kempsford, Glos., England
Yorks.	Yorkshire
Zimmermann	G.D. Zimmermann, *The Irish storyteller* (Dublin, 2001).

Organization of the *Guide*

The *Guide* is organized as follows. The first part consists of: (I) General introduction; (II) The scope of the *Guide*; (III) How we worked and editorial procedures; (IV) Arrangement of the entries; (V) Summary of selected key issues based on the findings from the *Guide*; and (VI) This *Guide and beyond*, which illustrates examples of research projects that could flow from the *Guide*.

The second part consists of: the *Guide* itself, which starts with anonymous authors of single works, then anonymous authors of multiple works (a total of 286 works of fiction), 1455 identified authors alphabetically arranged, each with his or her work(s), covering a total of 5,889 works of fiction; and five indexes (Persons; Book titles; Historic periods, themes, and settings; Publishers; and Places relating to authors).

Introduction

I. GENERAL INTRODUCTION

If there is a national art of a country, then literary fiction must surely qualify as the prime national art of Ireland. Four Irish authors, William Butler Yeats, George Bernard Shaw, Samuel Beckett and Seamus Heaney were awarded the Nobel Prize in literature in the twentieth century. In the nineteenth century, this national art is represented by well-known authors such as Maria Edgeworth, Lady Morgan, William Carleton, Gerald Griffin, and Charles Maturin, Bram Stoker, and Oscar Wilde, to mention only a few. Several Irish authors have become national icons, with their pictures on bank notes, plaques on the houses they lived in, dedicated memorial day (Bloomsday for James Joyce), summer seminars (Yeats, Joyce, Charles Kickham, etc.), and numerous statues in various Irish cities. The portraits of Irish literary heroes inducted by acclaim into the pantheon of world-famous writers now adorn even the walls of Irish pubs around the world. In the scholarly literature, a large body of criticism has sprung up based on the studies of Irish literary figures and their works.[1] Yet, beyond well-known names the majority of Irish authors are little known nowadays despite making sometimes substantial contributions to Irish literature in the English language and to literature in general. A host of other authors, some with Irish ancestors, also contributed through their writings to the story of the Irish in Ireland and the Irish abroad. We agree with Leerssen (see his preface to the *Guide*), who wrote that 'The two underlying assumptions on which literary history rests have lost credit: the self-justified importance and separate status of something like a *canon* based on artistic merit/importance, as well as the *author* as the premier organizing focus of literary praxis and of the analysis of literary praxis'.

In the spirit of Leerssen's words, this *Guide to Irish Fiction* is different from earlier publications on Irish literature in that it attempts to reset the parameters of what is generally considered Irish fiction between 1650 and 1900 to expand dramatically the known number of Irish authors and their Irish and non-Irish works, and to extend the number of known books about the Irish and Ireland written by non-Irish writers.

When we began our exploration of Irish fiction, we did not know in advance that eventually we would end up with just under 6,000 titles (5,889)[2] and 1,455 authors. The contents of these volumes have been our companions for more than a decade, and have provided immense joy and puzzlement at the same time.[3] Our search for forgotten authors and their books was partly aimed at improving the profile of fiction in Irish literary history, but a large part of our motivation was to document literature as social and cultural history – in Lady Morgan's words (see her statement above), to understand literary fiction as 'a mirror of the times in which it was composed'.[4] In a similar vein, William Butler Yeats in his compilation of *Representative Irish*

---

1 Belanger (ed.), *Irish novel*; S. Deane, *Strange country* (Oxford, 1997); S. Deane, *A short history of Irish literature* (Notre Dame, 1986); Murphy; Field Day; Field Day 2; T. Eagleton, *Scholars and rebels in nineteenth century Ireland* (London, 1999); I. Ferris, *The romantic national tale and the question of Ireland* (Cambridge, 2002); J. Leerssen, *Remembrance and imagination. Patterns in the historical and literary representation of Ireland in the nineteenth century* (Notre Dame, 1997); N. Vance, *Irish literature since 1800* (London, 2002). 2 This takes into account that one title *The mayor of Wind-gap and Canvassing* is twice in this *Guide* because it was written by two different authors, John Banim and Harriet Letitia Martin. 3 The puzzlement predates to the 1960s when Rolf Loeber published his *Moderne Ierse verhalen* [Modern Irish short stories] (Amsterdam, 1966), an anthology of twentieth-century Irish short stories translated into Dutch. Since that time, he published two other books (a biographical dictionary of Irish architects, and a book on the settlement of Ireland during the sixteenth century) and, often in collaboration with his wife Magda, a set of papers on architecture, colonial settlement, and Irish fiction. 4 The process of such search, as is also emphasized by Cleary, improves knowledge of 'the

tales (New York, [1891]), said that he was 'trying to make all the stories illustrations of some phase of Irish life, meaning the collection to be a kind of social history'.⁵ Fiction is the closest that we can ever come to understand, through the words of authors, how people in the past thought and acted in all types of contexts. Works of fiction provide evidence of places of the past, occupations and manners, and the condition of society.⁶ These books also give multiple details about material culture, popular entertainments,⁷ and the experience of religious issues.

W.J. McCormack has rightly stated that the 'Irish people have been acutely responsive to language over the centuries, [and] have extensively contributed to literature and song' in the Irish and English languages.⁸ When one of the characters in J.F. Molloy's *What has thou done?* (London, 1883) asked why there were so many Irishmen engaged in literature, he received as answer: 'because literature requires no special training, but wants vivid imagination and fluency – two gifts Irishmen almost always possess; they find it suits them, and serves as a refuge from physical labour or business, things they detest and despise'.⁹ Certainly, though, as our *Guide* reveals, many Irish authors did not avoid the labour involved in writing. The verbal agility of Irishmen has been known for centuries, and even nowadays the telling of stories, often of a gossipy nature, is common at the dinner tables of Irish families. The nineteenth-century Irish scholar J.P. Mahaffy observed that 'the average man [in Ireland] is able to talk well'.¹⁰ Vance has characterized the Irish as follows: 'Despite social and economic marginality the Irish writer often had special linguistic advantages, developed in youth by competitive talk and verbal duelling among witty compatriots in a tight-knit and intensely sociable society.'¹¹ The verbal skills were not confined to men; for example, William Butler Yeats's mother, who lived in Howth, outside of Dublin, read no books, 'but she and the fisherman's wife would tell each other stories that Homer would have told, pleased with any moment of sudden intensity and laughing together over any point of satire'.¹² This verbal agility also meant an unusual perception of and memory for what other people said or did, and an ability to record this.

Another aspect that applies to many Irishmen and authors (and nonwriters) is a retentive memory of the distant past. Flanagan went even as far as stating that 'the Irish mind had always been influenced, to the point of obsession, 'by the deeds and passions of the past'',¹³ which once introduced into the present provided ample fuel for literary stories and full-fledged novels, of which more below.

These verbally gifted Irish authors were able to create and reproduce stories in the form of novels and tales. They did so in their own inimitable way, which was often distinct from a great deal of English fiction. Foster emphasized that the Irish 'have an idiosyncratic approach to telling stories. A powerful oral culture, a half-lost language, the necessary stratagems of irony, collusion and misdirection …, the deliberate gap in the narrative, [and] story within story' all are elements that 'give a distinctive twist to the way the Irish account for themselves'.¹⁴ Similarly, Samuel Lover, one hundred and seventy years earlier than Foster, explained in the preface to his *Legends and stories of Ireland* (Dublin, 1831) that the stories

> are given in the manner of the Irish peasantry; and this has led to some peculiarities that
> might be objected to, were not the cause explained – namely, frequent digressions in the

material infrastructures of publication, circulation, reviewing and anthologizing' (J. Cleary, 'The nineteenth-century Irish novel: notes and speculations on literary historiography' in J. Belanger (ed.), *Irish novel*, p. 202. **5** Cited in M.H. Thuente (ed.), *Representative Irish tales. Compiled, with an introduction and notes by W.B. Yeats* (Atlantic Highlands, NJ, 1979), pp 8, 11. Other calls to examine the social-cultural aspects of Irish fiction can be found, for example, in Morash, 'Minor literature', passim. **6** M. Hill, 'Reading the past: literature and local history' in R. Gillespie & M. Hill (eds), *Doing Irish local history. Pursuit and practice* (Belfast, 1998), p. 63. **7** Zimmermann, pp 258–9. **8** W.J. McCormack (ed.), *The Blackwell companion to modern Irish culture* (Oxford, 1999), p. 1. **9** J.F. Molloy, *What has thou done?* (London, 1883), i, pp 156–7. **10** Eagleton, *Scholars & rebels*, p. 47. **11** Vance, *Irish literature*, p. 31; see also Zimmermann, p. 73. **12** Zimmermann, p. 326. **13** T. Flanagan, *The Irish novelists, 1800–1850* (New York, 1958), p. 188. **14** R.F. Foster, *The Irish story. Telling tales and making it up in Ireland* (London, 2001), p. 3.

course of the narrative, occasional adjurations, and certain words unusually spelt. As to the first, I beg to answer, that the stories would be deficient in national character without it; – the Irish are so imaginative, that they never tell a story straight forward, but constantly indulge in episode: for the second, it is only fair to say, that in most cases, the Irish peasant's adjurations are not meant to be in the remotest degree irreverent; but arise merely from the impassioned manner of speaking, which an excitable people are prone to.[15]

Now, it could be assumed that the above qualities of writing would be repellent to readers and doom the popularity of authors. This was not necessarily the case: the most popular Irish novel of the late-eighteenth century, Maria Regina Roche's *The children of the abbey* (London, 1796, 4 vols.), was full of digressions and the introduction of numerous characters and subplots. Also, the Fenian leader Charles Kickham's hugely popular *Knocknagow, or the homes of Tipperary* (Dublin, [1873]) was in Vance's words a 'preposterously melodramatic and episodic novel'.[16] Storytelling was almost equally shared by Irish authors from Gaelic stock and Irish authors from Ascendancy or English descent.

Other distinguishing characteristics of Irish fiction were the continuously perplexing aspects and conflicts of Irish life, which provided the inspiration and substance for the majority of Irish novels and stories. The Reverend Charles Robert Maturin in his dedication to *The Milesian chief* (London, 1812) explained that

> I have chosen my country for the scene because I believe it the only country on earth, where, from the strange existing opposition of religion, politics and manners, the extremes of refinement and barbarism are united, and the most wild and incredible situations of romantic story are hourly passing before modern eyes.[17]

Mrs S.C. Hall in her *Sketches of Irish character* (London, 1829) summarized the conflicting characteristics in another perceptive way: 'There are two nations on one soil; Celt and Saxon, Roman and Protestant, Irish and English Irish ...'[18]

Irish writers appear to draw directly from their own experiences, but also often based their novels and tales on what they heard from others. If necessary, urban writers were prepared to travel around the countryside and collect stories from the peasantry or from their friends living there. Thus, many Irish writers became the public voices of storytellers. A Major Darcy from the west of Ireland commented in 1839 on this 'raiding' of materials for books:

> The genius of the rest of Ireland uses Connaught as a species of literary store-farm. Ulster, Leinster, and Munster, breed men of genius who, so soon as they have exhausted their own provinces of lay and legend, incontinently cross the Shannon to carry on a predatory warfare against Fin Varra and Grana Uaile. These they rob and pillage without mercy; driving prays of ghost stories, and taking black mail of songs and tunes as unceremoniously as ever the Finns of old lifted sheep and black cattle. Meanwhile, the Connasians go on coshering, and story telling, and droning on their bagpipes; fighting, joking, ghost-seeing; acting comedies and romances every day; but never dreaming of taking pen in hand to turn themselves to account ...[19]

Peasant storytelling surely existed from times immemorial, but emerged 'from obscurity only in the second half of the eighteenth century'.[20] However, the raiding of peasant stories reached its

15 S. Lover, *Legends and stories of Ireland* (Dublin, 1831), preface. 16 Vance, *Irish literature*, p. 85; Murphy, p. 79. 17 Cited in Rafroidi, i, p. 265. 18 Cited in Zimmermann, p. 239; see also [anon.], *The periodical press of Great Britain and Ireland* (London, 1824), p. 189. 19 W.J. FitzPatrick, *The life of Charles Lever* (London, n.d., new edn), p. 175. 20 Zimmermann, p. 49.

height during the early – and much less the latter half of the nineteenth century. Although some English speakers collected these stories in the countryside, a few could do this from the comfort of their home. Dr William Wilde, father of the famous playwright and novelist Oscar Wilde, was consulted by poor patients from all over the island and, instead of a fee, collected folklore from some of them.[21] Wilde then recast these stories, most of which were eventually published by his wife, Lady Wilde. Yeats commented that storytellers would not necessarily 'think sufficiently about the shape of the poem or the story', and that for oral tradition to become a superior art, it needed writers who could mold the stories and give them 'a deliberate form'.[22]

Maturin's comments on the tensions in Irish history and politics applied to both the times in which he lived and to the past, and were to be reflected after his *The Milesian chief* (London, 1812) was published. In fact, for both Irish and non-Irish authors, the past contained a veritable storehouse of inspiration for Irish novels and tales. Ireland's history was full of lost causes, lost wars, disasters, agricultural agitation, secret societies, debilitating legal discrimination through penal laws, and famines (see summary in Table 1).

Irish literature was also permeated with the theme of 'lost' land, 'lost' heroes, 'lost' culture, and the 'loss' of a sense of original nationhood without British dominance. In the same vein, the literature is full of peasantry who have lost home and family and are displaced through eviction from their homesteads, transportation to penal exile, or through semi-voluntary exile through joining armies abroad (the 'Wild Geese'), and emigration due to famine and poverty. Not surprisingly, William Carleton, who came from a peasant background in Co. Tyrone, appointed himself as 'the historian' of the habits and manners of his people. In a flight of fancy, one storyteller, when questioned about the fairies of his times, lamented that they 'had gone to Scotland'.

The theme of loss in literature also applied to the gentry and Ascendancy, who towards the end of the time period covered by the *Guide* lost or were about to lose their estates and their formerly leisurely and sporting lifestyle. In either case, literature often functioned as a tool to recover the memory of important aspects of Irish society prior to its having been 'mislaid'.[23]

Thus, through such laments, Irish literature gave hope to peasant heirs of lost estates for the recovery of their fortunes, the regaining of the Gaelic and Catholic ownership of the land, the expulsion of the English and Scottish intruders and confiscators of Irish soil, and, less frequently, the restoration of the Irish kingship.

Mirroring the diversities of strife on the land and in daily life, all types of conflict were featured in fiction. Writers of English and Scottish stock promulgated in their works notions of the anti-Christ nature of the Catholic Church, the secret machinations of priests, monks, and nuns, and the reach of Rome into domestic matters.

Another aspect of literature sprang from the Protestant Ascendancy writers featuring the cruelties and violence committed by the Irish during the rebellions – the Desmond rebellion of the late sixteenth century, and the 1641 and the 1798 rebellions. As the title of Leerssen's important study expressed, *Remembrance and imagination*[24] are frequently recurring themes in Irish fiction.

The full cast of Irish authors and a great deal of Irish fiction in the English language published in Ireland, England and North America before 1900 is little known or, even worse, has fallen in virtual oblivion. A large proportion of Irish writers were single-book authors (perhaps those who only had a single, major story to tell, or who only published a more or less fixed set of favourite stories), and were never pressed into public memory because of the lack of their names on further title pages, the smallness of the editions of their book, barriers to the distribution of their books, or the public's lack of appreciation of their writing.[25]

---

21 B. Earls, 'Supernatural legends in nineteenth-century Irish writing' in *Béaloideas*, lx–lxi (1992–3), p. 127. 22 Cited in Zimmermann, p. 328. 23 Zimmermann, pp 209–10, 238, 242. 24 Leerssen, *Remembrance and imagination*. 25 It

	Rebellions, Military campaigns, Agrarian disturbances	Other events
5th and 6th centuries		Coming of Christianity to Ireland (St Patrick, d. 493)
8th century	Start of Viking raids	
1169	Norman invasion	
1541		English King Henry VIII made King of Ireland
1569–73	The earl of Desmond's rebellion	
1579–83		
1586 onwards		Munster plantation
1593–1603	Nine-Years' War	
1601–2	Spanish landing and defeat	
1607		Flight of the earls of Tyrconnell and Tyrone to the Continent
1612 onwards		Ulster confiscation and plantation
Late 1610, early 1620s		Confiscations and plantations in Co. Wexford and the midlands
1641	Irish rebellion	
1642–47		(Catholic) Confederation of Kilkenny
1649	Cromwell's campaign	
1650s		Confiscations all over Ireland
1660		Restoration of King Charles II
1685		Succession by Catholic James II
1689–91	Williamite War	
1690s		Confiscations
Early 18th c.		Anti-Catholic and anti-Dissenter penal laws
1769	Outbreak of 'Hearts of steel' disturbances in Ulster	
1798	Rebellion by United Irishmen	
1801		Union between England and Ireland
1803	Emmet's rebellion	
1829		Catholic Emancipation
1831	Terry Alt disturbances begin in Cos. Clare and Limerick	
1832	Whitefeet disturbances begin Cos. Laois, Kilkenny, and midland counties	
1845–9		Great Famine
1848	Young Ireland rebellion failed	
1867	Unsuccessful Fenian rising	
1869		Disestablishment of the Church of Ireland
1879	Land League founded	
1880s		Defeat of Home Rule bills in English Parliament
1893		Foundation of the Gaelic League to cultivate the use of the Irish language
1916	Easter rising	
1919–21	Anglo-Irish war	
1920		Partition between six Ulster counties and the Irish Free State
1922–23	Civil war	

Table 1 Summary of the main rebellions, military campaigns, agrarian disturbances, and other key political and religious events.

Introduction

We argue that the appreciation of Irish fiction should not just rest on well-known authors alone, nor can generalizations about Irish fiction be based on single case studies, or even studies of a handful of major authors. Morash, in his argument to examine the minor literature of Ireland, stated that no chemist or psychologist 'worthy of name would draw a conclusion on the basis of a single experiment' or a 'case study', and advanced that minor literature needs to be included in order to come to valid conclusions about the true nature of Irish literature.[26]

We also agree with Seamus Deane's comment that 'The near deification of a few [Irish authors] has been to the detriment of the majority'.[27] As Robert Lee Wolff, the expert on nineteenth-century Irish fiction, expressed it in the early 1980s, 'there are literally hundreds of other novelists of Ireland [than the most famous ones] and many hundreds of Irish novels waiting in obscurity'.[28] Our *Guide* to Irish fiction attempts to rectify some of the limitations of past surveys of Irish literature by expanding the known body of literature through a systematic search for 'hidden' authors and their books. Irish literary history has been plagued for a long time by what we did not know, and to use Seamus Deane's words from his preface to this *Guide* 'that we did not know we didn't have'. The challenge for us was to ferret out these authors and books, and encourage friends, booksellers and librarians to do the same. Thus, we were fortunate to kindle an enthusiasm in many individuals to identify Irish fiction, all of whom contributed greatly to the present *Guide*.

The true richness and variety of Irish fiction can only become apparent when the full spectrum of Irish fiction and its authors can be marshalled, irrespective of the current, perceived literary status of the books. The main purpose of the present work is to address the void faced by generations of scholars interested in addressing the development of Irish fiction between 1650 and 1900.[29]

Strangely enough, many Irish literary historians, at least starting with Flanagan, have mostly written about Irish novels,[30] while relatively few scholars have written about Irish tales and stories.[31] Although the focus on novels is understandable, it ignores the fact that most Irish fiction was characterized either as 'a tale' in its title, or in fact consisted of a short story of varied length, which in the course of the nineteenth century became a dominant force beside the Irish folktale (see Section V).

In yet another development, prose fiction in the English language started to replace poetry in the first part of the nineteenth century. Samuel Whyte anticipated this change in a poem published in Dublin in 1795: 'If thou must write, and would'st thy works disperse, Write novels, sermons, and any thing but verse.'[32] He was right about novels, which became a popular genre of writing attracting readers of every faith, but he was wrong about sermons which even among the Protestants became less-favoured reading.

Literary Changes

Based on information from this *Guide*, we can now document better when the number of Irish authors writing fiction in the English language started to change. In the early-eighteenth century, the number of new Irish fiction writers was small (see Figure 1) and their literary output was modest. Figure 2 displays the number of new titles per year of fiction books from 1650 to 1900 included in this *Guide*,[33] and shows that the yearly rate was very small for much of the late-seventeenth and

should be taken into account, however, that some of the single-book fiction writers were also authors of poetry, plays, or non-fictional works. 26 C. Morash, 'On the minor literature: nineteenth century Ireland' in J. McMinn (ed.), *The internationalism of Irish literature and drama* (Savage, MD, 1992), p. 211. 27 Quoted in the *Irish Times*, 4 Jan. 2002, p. 15. 28 Wolff, i, p. xvi. 29 The choice of excluding authors who published their first book of fiction after 1900 was governed by the fact that the works of many of the twentieth-century authors have been inventoried better than those of the preceding period. 30 Flanagan, *Irish novelists*, passim. 31 E.g., Foster, *Irish story*; P. Rafroidi & T. Brown (eds), *The Irish short story* (Lille, n.d.); Zimmermann. 32 S. Whyte, *Poems on various subjects* (Dublin, 1795), p. 161. 33 This excludes books in this *Guide* appearing after 1900.

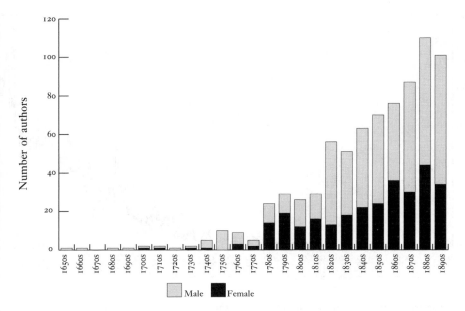

Figure 1 Number of new Irish authors writing fiction in the
English language between 1650 and 1899.

early-eighteenth centuries. Only in the 1750s was there a slight rise, but it wasn't until the 1780s that the rate of publishing original fiction started to increase. Some notable changes took place during this century. Print culture increased during the 1790s as a result of the United Irishmen promoting newspapers and songs, but they contributed little to fiction.[34] There was a modest increase of publishing of works of fiction during the 1820s and 1830s during the first Irish revival, which was dominated by male authors such as the Banim brothers, William Carleton, and Gerald Griffin. A second period of accelerated growth took place during the 1880s and 1890s.[35]

During much of the nineteenth century the majority of the population was Irish-speaking and illiterate. The production of *new* works of fiction (in contrast to poetry) in the Irish language was virtually nonexistent, and remained so through much of the nineteenth century. As Denvir states, 'Most of the prose written [in Irish] in the nineteenth century is a continuation of the scribal activity of *copying* [our emphasis] earlier texts.'[36] John Bernard Trotter complained in 1812 that 'Books in Irish are not to be had.'[37] Chronicling the history of earlier literature, Leerssen remarked that 'Until the end of the nineteenth century, literary dissemination [of Irish literature] had been either oral, or else in scribal manuscripts' only.[38] Thus, despite the majority status of

34 Thuente 2, passim; K. Whelan, 'The Republic in the village: The dissemination and reception of popular political literature in the 1790s' in G. Long (ed.), *Books beyond the Pale* (Dublin, 1996), pp 101–40. **35** There were peaks in publishing in 1886, 1889, 1895, and 1898. Our figures over the period 1700 to 1840 are somewhat comparable with the figures for British fiction published by Moretti for Britain for that period (F. Moretti, *Graphs, maps, tress. Abstract models for a literary history* (London, 2005, p. 7), and are comparable for the period 1770–1779 (Raven 2, p. 27), and for the period 1800–1829 (Garside, p. 38). Note however, that the inclusion criteria of fiction for this *Guide* are broader than those used by Moretti, Raven or Garside. **36** G. Denvir, 'Literature in Irish, 1800–1890: from the Act of the Union to the Gaelic League' in M. Kelleher & P. O'Leary (eds), *The Cambridge history of English literature* (Cambridge, 2006), i, pp 566–7. **37** J.B. Trotter, *Walks through Ireland in … 1812, 1814, and 1817* (London, 1819), p. 46. **38** J. Leerssen, 'A la recherche d'une littérature perdue. Literary history, Irish identity and Douglas Hyde' in M. Spiering, *Nation building and writing literary history* (Amsterdam, 1999), p. 96; D. Ó hOgáin, 'Folklore and literature: 1700–1850' in M. Daly & D. Dickson (eds), *The origins of popular literacy in Ireland* (Dublin, 1990), p.4.

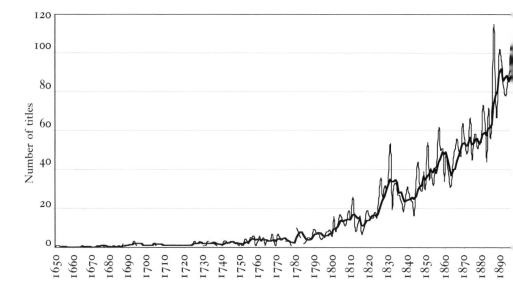

Figure 2 Number of fiction titles by Irish authors and by foreign authors writing about Ireland and the Irish between 1650 and 1899 (dark line is the five-year moving average).

Irish speakers, prose fiction in the Irish literary tradition remained frozen outside of print culture, its manuscripts were in private hands and not represented in publicly-accessible libraries.[39] Only in the public sphere of social gatherings of the peasantry were manuscripts read aloud. Their contents also remained disconnected from English literature because, as Cronin remarked, of the striking 'paucity of printed translations [from the English or other languages] into Irish'.[40]

Several other factors contributed to the decline of the Irish language and its literature and the massive adoption of the English language by formerly Irish-speakers. The decay of Irish literature coincided with the disappearance of the old patronage system that had fostered and preserved Irish poetry and narratives. As Cullen remarked, 'By the end of the eighteenth century, it was not so much a case of the continuing decline of the old-style patronage as a collapse of it'. The approximately 2,500 surviving eighteenth-century manuscripts in Irish showed that English content increased in these artefacts – as evident from notes by owners of the documents, and by inscriptions of the scribes as well. Cullen also noted major geographic differences in people's familiarity with written language in Irish, which was highest in Munster and east Ulster, and 'scarcely existed in Connaught, which had a much weaker scribal and a stronger song tradition than Munster'.[41] In addition, in the eighteenth century poets were concentrated in Munster. Dickson, in a recent summary of the evidence, suggests that 'as many as half of all Irish-language poets ... known to have been active [in Ireland] between 1690 and 1760 were principally resident in Kerry, Cork or west Waterford'.[42] We will return to this point in Section V, when we will review the concentration of English-language writers in Munster a century later.

39 J. Leerssen, *Hidden Ireland, public sphere* (Galway, 2002), p. 36. **40** M. Cronin, *Translating Ireland. Translation, languages, cultures* (Cork, 1996), p. 115. However, in some instances, English fiction was incorporated into narrative in the Irish language. **41** Cullen, 'Patrons', p. 33. **42** D. Dickson, *Old World colony. Cork and South Munster 1630–1830* (Cork, 2005), p. 260, and sources mentioned on p. 578*n*.57. See also T.F. O'Reilly, 'Irish poets, historians, and judges in English documents, 1538–1615' in *Proceedings of the RIA*, xxxvi (1921–4), pp 86–120.

Introduction

The gradual decline in the use of the Irish language took place especially after 1780. For instance, Maria Edgeworth, when living at Edgeworthstown, Co. Longford, wrote in 1782 that 'The Irish language is now almost gone into disuse, the class of people all speak English except in their quarrels with each other ...' During the nineteenth century, the decline of spoken Irish accelerated over large parts of the country, with Irish-speaking areas preserved in the south and west.[43]

The decline of the Irish language occurred at a time when the number of schools increased, and with them came an increased demand for reading materials.[44] In late-eighteenth- and early-nineteenth-century Ireland the Catholic country schools, usually known as hedge schools, did not have educational books specifically written for children and, instead, used reading materials of all kinds, including novels and chapbooks in the English language.[45] Probably, part of the death-knell of the Irish language spoken by the younger generations was the establishment of government-sponsored national schools in 1831. In these schools English was the only language of instruction and English textbooks and references to British works of fiction became the norm.

Irish education policy reflected British imperial approaches to extend British rule through educational institutions. In the case of India this was expressed in Baron MacAulay's notorious *Minutes on Indian Education* in 1835, which proposed 'the formation of a class of persons, Indian in blood and colour, but English in taste, in opinions, in morals, and in intellect'. Although we have not found such a bold statement regarding national Irish education, the impact was the same – with British literature introduced as instruction material for pupils in schools. However, Ireland differed much from India. Whereas in India, education in native languages was not abandoned by the English, in the Irish national schools education in Irish was prohibited. This had a major, divergent impact on the publishing industry in each country. In India the publishing of fiction flourished both in English *and* in native languages,[46] whereas in Ireland only publishing in English took place and no publishing of fiction in the Irish language emerged until the end of the nineteenth century.

The literary historian Norman Vance has noted that the Irish novel emerged with 'no established tradition of the novel' in the Irish language. Thus, for Ireland novel writing was an imported literary form,[47] tied to the English language and which appears to have been inspired by English and continental examples. Yet the infusion of English as spoken in Ireland, Irish matters, and Irish imagination and discourse, all contributed to a unique shape of novels which often differed from those written by British novelists.

A major change that inhibited creative forces in Ireland was the Great Famine of 1845–9 which through death and vastly accelerated emigration led to an unprecedented reduction in the Irish population. As Sir William Wilde stated: 'The great convulsions which society of all grades has lately experienced, the failure of the potato crop, and a most unparalleled extent of emigration, together with bankrupt landlords, pauperizing poor-laws, grinding officials, and decimating workhouses, have broken up the very foundations of social intercourse, have swept away the established theories of political economists, and uprooted many of our long-cherished opinions.' He lamented the many changes in society, including 'the Shannaghie and the

43 Butler, p. 91; G. FitzGerald, 'Estimates for baronies of minimum level of Irish-speaking among successive decennial cohorts: 1771–1781 to 1861–1871' in *Proceedings RIA*, Section C, lxxxiv (1984), 3–155; G. FitzGerald, 'The decline of the Irish language, 1771–1871' in Daly & Dickson (eds), *Origins of popular literacy in Ireland*, pp 59–72.   44 L. Cullen, 'Patrons, teachers, and literacy in Irish' in M. Daly & D. Dickson (eds), *The origins of popular literacy in Ireland* (Dublin, 1990), pp 22, 24, 27, 29–30, 32.   45 A. McManus, *The Irish hedge school and its books, 1695–1831* (Dublin, 2002), pp 182–4, 248–56; J. Glasscock, *Notes of three tours in Ireland in 1824 and 1826*. Bristol, 1832, passim; R. Loeber & M. Stouthamer-Loeber, 'Fiction available to and written for cottagers and their children' in B. Cunningham and M. Kennedy (eds), *The experience of reading: Irish historical perspectives* (Dublin, 1999), pp 124–72; J. Logan, 'Book learning: The experience of reading in the national schools 1831–1900' in B. Cunningham and M. Kennedy, *Experience of reading*, pp 173–95 46 P. Joshi, 'Fiction, the reading public, and the British novel in Colonial India' in E. Greenspan & J. Rose (eds), *Book history. Volume 1* (University Park, PA, 1998), pp 199–202.   47 Vance, *Irish Literature*, pp 20, 24.

Introduction

Callegh in the chimney corner, tell no more the tales and legends of the other days' and the 'rapid decay of the Irish vernacular, in which most of our legends, romantic tales, ballads, and bardic annals, the vestiges of Pagan rites, and the relics of fairy charms were preserved ...', which were '*the poetry of the people*, the bond that knit the peasant to the soil, and cheered and solaced many a cottier's fireside.' Emigration, according to Sir William Wilde, had an enormous cultural impact: 'Everyone who can muster three pounds ten ... are [*sic*] on the move to America, leaving us the idle and ill-conditioned ..., so that it may well be said, the heart of Ireland now beats in America'.[48] This was a bit of an exaggeration. As this *Guide* shows, Irish fiction continued to be produced in Ireland and England and accelerated in the second half of the nineteenth century.

It is not sufficiently recognized that emigration was only part of the outflow of people from Ireland. Irishmen, like the Scots and the Welsh, became instrumental in the expansion and government of the British Empire and found employment as government officials, officers, soldiers, and planters in British dominions on both sides of the Atlantic from Africa to the Caribbean and Canada, and around the Indian Ocean in South Africa, India, Hong Kong, Australia, and New Zealand.

In addition, emigration from Ireland to North America which had started in the early-eighteenth century and which was then mostly Presbyterian from the north of Ireland, was followed by a massive influx of Irish Catholics to the United States from the 1820s onward. Eventually, about five million Irish emigrated to the United States between 1820 and 1920, and another one million to Canada, Australia and New Zealand. In addition, at least one-and-a-half million Irish moved to England. At the end of the nineteenth century, 'Two out of every five Irish-born people were living overseas ...'[49]

The Irish diaspora is in some ways comparable to the emigration of the Italians, Poles, and Portuguese from their home countries to the United States. However, the Irish, partly because of their connection to the expanding British Empire, and partly because of their use of the English language, could take advantage of opportunities more quickly than emigrants from other European countries. As R.M. Martin expressed in 1843, 'What enabled these distinguished [Irishmen and women] to inscribe their names to the Scroll of Fame, and to add to the honor and to the welfare of their country? The wide and noble field of British enterprise.'[50] In contrast to emigrants from most other countries in Europe, Irish emigrants were enormously facilitated in their move to Anglophone colonies by their knowledge of a common language.[51]

This facility with the English language created opportunities for the Irish to contribute to the national literatures of the United States and several countries within the British Empire (e.g., Canada and Australia). The shared English language greatly facilitated Irish participation in commerce, trade and the professions, including journalism, which as this *Guide* shows, gave employment to large numbers of Irish men and women. For those Irish emigrants who became authors abroad, the Anglophone environments provided a wide readership outside of Ireland. Thus, Irish fiction, unlike the fiction of Italy, Poland, or Portugal, was the only European fiction that became truly transnational without the need for translation.

The transnational movement of Irish fiction was strongest in the United States. By 1850, the Catholic Irish population had grown into the single largest Catholic population in the country, fed in good measure by the one-and-a-half million Irish who entered America in the decade

48 W. Wilde, *Irish popular superstitions* (Dublin, [1852]), pp 9–11, 21; for other accounts of the impact of the Famine on storytelling and singing, see Zimmermann, pp 273–4. 49 K. Kenny, 'The Irish and the Empire' in K. Kenny (ed.), *Ireland and the British Empire* (Oxford, 2004), p. 100. According to R.M. Martin, *Ireland before and after the Union with Great Britain* (London, 1843), p. 167, under half a million of Irish had already emigrated to Britain by 1841. 50 Martin, *Ireland before and after the Union*, p. 188. 51 Kenny, 'The Irish and the Empire', pp 93, 96, 98–9. One should not forget, however, that Irish was the only language of a proportion of Irishmen and women who emigrated.

between 1845 and 1854.[52] As this *Guide* shows, some of the immigrants turned to writing fiction, while many non-Irish American authors introduced Irish characters and themes in their novels. Only some of the Irish-American fiction made its way back into Ireland: Mrs J. Sadlier's works, for example, which were first published in Montreal and Boston, were republished by Duffy in Dublin. Otherwise, most of Irish-American fiction appears to have had no direct impact on Irish readers.

One of the distinct developments of Irish authorship was the link between the collapse of social orders and changes in authorship.[53] An early example of such social collapse occurred in the eighteenth century with the disappearance of patronage for poets in the Irish language. At that time, one could hardly speak of individual authorship as we know it nowadays. Leerssen stressed that the concept of authorship in bardic poetry was 'largely meaningless' with the same text being attributed to different poets often living 'hundreds of years apart'.[54] Sometime between the late-seventeenth and early-eighteenth century, the notion of authorship in the English language as an occupation emerged in Ireland and Britain. Jonathan Swift is an example of this emerging class of authors, but few of the Irish authors in the eighteenth century were able to earn a living from their writing alone.

Ireland saw another type of collapse of the social order in the nineteenth century when the role of the Ascendancy in Irish society diminished and shifted towards literary engagement. The rise of Ascendancy writers took place under worsening economic and social conditions for their classes, especially during the second half of the nineteenth century when their minority position in Irish society started to lose its economic hegemony.[55] Seamus Deane has remarked that 'Irish culture became the new property of those who were losing their grip on Irish land', which constituted 'a strategic retreat from political to cultural supremacy'.[56] We will show in Section V that an increase of authorship by the Irish gentry, both Protestant and Catholic, and by ministers of the Church of Ireland and their children took place during the nineteenth century.[57] For instance, George Moore, a scion of the Moores of Moor Hall in Co. Mayo, realized in 1879 that as a result of estate mismanagement and poor harvests and rent failures, he would have to leave Ireland to earn a living as an author. Most of these Irish authors had not been trained for any profession and traditionally saw trade and physical work as beneath their status, and therefore turned to writing instead, this new occupation being acceptable to their station in life. A few of the gentry, notably women authors such as Maria Edgeworth, Edith Somerville, and Dorothea Conyers were able to keep up their country house establishments only by their literary earnings, and incorporated many local aspects and characters of their country house world in their writings.[58] In fact, the gentry who stayed in Ireland, in contrast to those who left, contributed more to literature with an Irish content.[59] However, their numbers appear to have decreased at the beginning of the twentieth century. In their place came a solid foundation of middle-class authors, often from a Catholic background, a movement that began during the second half of the nineteenth century.

Eventually, emigrant Irish writers, because of writing in the English language, became participants and leaders in other national literatures that emerged in countries such as Canada and Australia.

---

52 S.M. Griffin, *Anti-Catholicism and nineteenth-century fiction* (Cambridge, 2004), p. 3. 53 D. Kiberd, 'Literature and politics' in M. Kelleher & P. O'Leary (eds), *Cambridge history of Irish literature*, ii, p. 12. 54 J. Leerssen, 'A la recherche', p. 104. 55 T. Dooley, *The decline of the Big House in Ireland. A study of Irish landed families 1860–1960* (Dublin, 2001), passim. 56 S. Deane, 'Heroic styles: the tradition of an idea' cited in T.E. Hachey & L.J. McCaffrey (eds), *Perspective on Irish nationalism* (Lexington, KY, 1989), p. 77; Deane, *Short history*, p. 74. 57 R. Loeber & M. Stouthamer-Loeber, 'Literary absentees: Irish women authors in nineteenth-century England' in J. Belanger (ed.), *The Irish novel in the nineteenth century* (Dublin, 2005), pp 167–186. 58 Vance, *Irish literature*, p. 125. 59 Loeber & Stouthamer-Loeber, 'Literary absentees', pp 167–86; for daughters of Church of Ireland ministers in the early twentieth century, see O. Walsh, *Anglican women in Dublin* (Dublin, 2005).

Literature and Nation Building

Perhaps more strikingly, new generations of Irish authors living and working in Ireland and Britain contributed to a new form of nationalism in Ireland. The Irish patriot John O'Leary once stated that 'there is no great literature without nationality, no great nationality without literature'.[60] Even before the Union, the Dublin publishing industry, in contrast to publishing houses in London, did little to support native authors writing in the English language, and this indirectly stimulated an exodus of Irish writers to England. After the Union, and even more strongly during the second half of the nineteenth century, the publishing industry in Dublin declined, which further encouraged Irish authors to become literary 'absentees'[61] and leave Ireland for journalism, translation, and other literary work in England.[62] There were various motivations for moving, but one articulated by George Bernard Shaw stands out: 'Every Irishman [*sic*] who felt that his business in life was on the higher planes of the cultural professions felt that he must have a metropolitan domicile and an international culture: that is, he felt that his first business was to get out of Ireland.'[63] Speaking much earlier, Thomas Moore told John Banim (who had returned to Ireland) that 'if he had confined his labours to Ireland, he would be a beggar'.[64] The exodus was no small matter: between 1650 and 1900, six out of ten Irish authors died abroad (see Section V), largely because of the fact that their professional lives as writers were situated outside of Ireland.

One of the paradoxes of Irish literary history is that the majority of authors who developed an interest in Ireland, Irish problems, and the Irish language did not spring out of the Catholic Irish peasantry or middle classes. Instead, as Leerssen explained, 'a massive cultural transfer' took place in Ireland 'between the Gaelic tradition and the urban, English-speaking, educated classes'. This constituted an as yet poorly-understood cross-cultural exchange, which was more complex than cultural changes found in 'monocultural or monolingual societies'. This change in the expression of the culture in fiction was all the more remarkable because of the growth of 'an educated English-speaking, city-dwelling middle class' which began to identify itself with Gaelic culture.[65] The reorientation within certain members of this class from British to Irish interests fostered a new cadre of Irish authors in the English language with strong interests in Irish history. This did not mean that the initial advocates insisted on expressing themselves in Irish rather than in English. Yeats firmly believed that English could be the language for an Irish national literature.[66] Many of the English-speaking literati interested in Irish Ireland appear to have agreed. However, dissent emerged slowly during the second half of the nineteenth century. As pointed out by Foster, in 1858 the weekly periodical *The Celt* published a leader which stated that 'To be Anglicised is to lose our national and characteristic identity, to merge everything Irish and Celtic in, not a British union, but a British supremacy.'[67] Thirty-four years later, Douglas Hyde famously advocated the de-Anglicization of Irish literature. Foster speaks of the emergence in the 1890s of an Anglophobia, which was to persist for decades.[68] The second Irish literary revival which started in the 1890s, however, produced mostly English-language poetry and plays (the latter not known in old Gaelic Ireland) and few works of fiction.

60 Cited in P.L. Marcus, *Yeats and the beginning of the Irish renaissance* (Ithaca, 1970), pp 1, 3, 14.   61 William Carleton, preface to his *Traits and stories* (Dublin: William Curry Jnr & Co.; London: William S. Orr & Co., 1843), I, pp v–vi; [anon.], *Periodical press*, p. 195.   62 See Loeber & Stouthamer-Loeber, 'Literary absentees', pp 171–82; *Bolster's Magazine* (Cork, 1826), i, no. 1, cited in D. & M. Coakley, *Wit and wine* (Peterhead, 1975), p. ix.   63 Cited in S. Haddelsey, *Charles Lever: The last Victorian* (Gerrards Cross, 2000), p. 23.   64 P.J. Murray, *The life of John Banim* (New York, 1869), p. 288.   65 Leerssen, *Hidden Ireland*, pp 13–5, 23–4. The complexity of cultural transfer was increased by the fact that (a) many Irish legends were in ancient Irish, which was no longer current in the countryside, and was initially studied and made available through German, French and English scholars; (b) in certain parts of the countryside and even as late as the nineteenth century, the Irish peasantry (not to mention the clergy) knew Latin and had read classical authors (Vance, *Irish literature*, p. 113).   66 Cited in Marcus, *Yeats*, pp 1, 3, 14.   67 Foster, *Irish story*, p. 68.   68 Foster, *Irish story*, p. 77; on Hyde and the introduction of Irish literature, see also Leerssen 'A la recherche', pp 95–108.

Starting in the eighteenth century, several Irish authors in the English language turned their attention to history writing and rewrote Irish history in the form of historical fiction.[69] In the nineteenth century, the availability of Irish historical novels compensated for the prohibition of Irish history books for young people in national schools which were thought to be too controversial. It is the retelling of past historical calamities experienced by the Irish (failed rebellions, the loss of the language and culture, the irretrievable Celtic past, the loss of the peasant population through famine and emigration, the oppressive rule of the conquerors) that provided the grist of much literary production by Irish authors.

This orientation to the past was common in many emerging nations searching for a national and native identity, including Greece, Italy, Catalonia, Poland and Estonia, and in that respect Ireland was no exception. These and other emerging nations in Europe all produced national movements with cultural expressions and accoutrements – including a national literature (fiction, poems, and plays), histories of the nation, national symbols, national anthems, monuments commemorative of crucial events in the history of the nation, museums and libraries to preserve the national heritage, national organizations for youth, inventories of ancient archaeological sites and the preservation of the built heritage of the modern period, and national sports. As Leerssen points out, these different forms of cultural nationalism are essential elements in the study of cultural history as it evolved over time.[70]

Lady Morgan turned to fiction to express political arguments: 'A novel is especially adapted to enable the advocate of any cause to steal upon the public, through the by-ways of the imagination, and win from it sympathies what its reason so often refuses to yield to undeniable demonstration.'[71] Both Terry Eagleton and Joep Leerssen have noted that, since readership often was English rather than Irish, a national tale in a perplexing manner was developed for a 'readership of foreigners'.[72] John Banim's biographer remarked that an objective of the work by the brothers John and Michael Banim was 'To raise the national character in the estimation of other lands, by a portrayal of the people as they really were, but at the same time to vindicate them of the charges of violence and bloodthirstiness, by showing in the course of fiction, the various causes which he supposedly concurred to draw forth and foster these evil qualities'.[73]

Much has been written about the definition of Irish fiction as part of the emergence of a national literature of Ireland.[74] Although its study has begun, the growing knowledge of this literature as evident from this *Guide*, is likely to boost future investigations of the cultural significance of Irish literature. Leerssen stresses that the study of cultural nationalism in literature should examine the development of Irish fiction in the context of the spread of ideas in Europe about cultural aspects of nationhood. Citing the work of Miroslav Hroch, Leerssen points out that cultural preoccupations (such as 'The national tale'), rather than being a reflection of past political events, tend to precede political events. Hroch formulated a hierarchical model of influences, during which in phase A: 'a small circle of intellectuals rediscovers the national culture and past and formulates the idea of a nation'. This can be followed by phase B, which consists of 'the crucial process of dissemination of the idea of the national by agita-

69 See e.g., *Cahalan*, p. 22, which discusses a modest number of Irish historical novels; E. Reilly, Fictional histories: An examination of Irish historical and political novels 1880–1914. Ph.D. dissertation, Univ. of Oxford, 1997. **70** J. Leerssen, 'The cultivation of culture. Towards a definition of romantic nationalism in Europe'. Working Papers, European Studies, Amsterdam, No. 2. Opleiding Europese Studies, University of Amsterdam, Amsterdam, Netherlands, 2005, p. 10. **71** Cited in Ferris, *Romantic national tale*, p. 13. **72** Ferris, pp 46–7, citing Eagleton, *Heathcliff*, p. 201, and J. Leerssen, 'On the treatment of Irishness in romantic Anglo-Irish fiction', *Irish University Review*, xx (1990), p. 257. **73** Cited in Zimmermann, p. 244. **74** For example, R.V. Comerford, *Inventing the nation – Ireland* (London, 2003); Deane, *Strange country*, p. 49ff; Ferris, *Romantic national tale*, passim; L. Gibbons, 'Constructing the canon: versions of national identity' in Field Day, ii, pp 950–5; Leerssen, *Remembrance and imagination*, passim; D. Lloyd, *Nationalism and minor literature* (Berkeley, CA, 1987); P. Rafroidi, 'Defining the Irish literary tradition in English', in Princess Grace Library (ed.), *Irishness in a changing society* (Towata, NJ, 1988), pp 32–47; Thuente 2, passim; K. Trumpener, *Bardic nationalism. The romantic novel and the British isles* (Princeton NJ, 1997).

tor-professionals who politicise cultural nationalism in the growing towns' In the final phase C 'the state of popular involvement in nationalism creates a mass movement'.[75]

In Ireland, the development of the national tale with its emphasis on injustices inflicted upon the Catholic population, the adoption of the idea of Catholic Emancipation by Daniel O'Connell, and his translation of this idea into a mass movement, all somewhat fit this dissemination model. However, in the thicket of conflict, Irish revolutionaries had different ideas about the relationship between literature and social and political change. Some of them believed that that the real battle for nationhood was to be fought not on the cultural front, but was to be waged with land reform and Home Rule as the key pawns. For instance, James Stephens stated that a free Ireland would not be achieved by 'amiable and enlightened young men ... pushing about in drawing room society ... creating an Irish national literature, schools of Irish art, and things of the sort'. He likened these idealists in 1863 to 'dilettante patriots, perhaps the greatest fools of all'.[76] Michael Davitt's Land League movement which operated from 1879 onward, also had little room for the literary ideals articulated by Thomas Davis in the 1840s and, instead, advanced the idea that control of land was essential for the Irish nation.[77]

In the middle of controversies and conflicts, however, readers decided for themselves. In the words of William Carleton in 1843, 'Ireland was not then what is she is now fast become, a reading, and consequently a thinking, country'.[78] This thinking stimulated by literature, included thinking of these wrongs inflicted on Ireland and its people, and ways to redress these through land reform and, eventually, through political independence from England.

Although certain aspects of cultural nationalism are common to many European nations, the expression of this nationalism varied widely from country to country. Consequently, specific reactions to historical events and perceived wrongs and calamities varied much among different nations. In the case of Ireland, there were salient events (such as various famines, mass emigration, and the second Reformation with its attempts by Protestant ministers and Bible readers to evangelize and convert Irish Catholics), which helped to shape a specifically Irish tradition of literary fiction.

At the same time, Ireland shared with other European nations the emergence of the 'national tale'. The earliest known Irish instance was Sydney Owenson's (later Lady Morgan] *The wild Irish girl. A national tale* which appeared in 1806. Within the next four decades, the epithet *national* was attached to the title of an Irish work only six times. Other books advertising themselves as Irish novels and tales (without the adjective 'national') emerged subsequently. In fact, one of the most surprising facts is that novels referring to Ireland or the Irish as advertised by their title increased significantly during the nineteenth century (see Section V). Deane, in discussing Irish national fiction, emphasizes that the emergence of Irish national tales rested on three claims, that 'a) Ireland was a culturally distinct nation; b) it had been mutilated beyond recognition by British colonialism; and c) it could nevertheless rediscover its lost features and thereby recognize once more its true identity'.[79]

Thus, a century prior to Irish independence from Britain, various notions of Irishness developed through the medium of fiction. Curiously, however, Lady Morgan's national tales appear to have addressed an English readership,[80] were never reprinted in Ireland and, therefore, may have reached only a small Irish readership, who would have had to rely on her English-published works. Remarkably, it was an English and not an Irish publisher – Henry Colburn – who issued in 1834 a fiction series with the title *Irish National Tales*, which consisted of books produced from the remainder sheets of earlier editions of Irish novels. Most

75 Leerssen, 'Cultivation of culture', p. 10n.8.   76 Cited in D.G. Boyce, *Nationalism in Ireland* (London, 1982), p. 177. 77 Deane, *Short history*, p. 76.   78 William Carleton's preface to his *Traits and stories of the Irish peasantry* (1843 ed.), i, p. vi.   79 Deane, *Strange country*, p. 53; see also Deane, *Short history*, p. 62ff.   80 K. Trumpener, *Bardic nationalism*, p. 17.

Irish literature with nationalistic themes was not published in Ireland but was produced by London printing presses and financed by English publishing houses (more about this in Section V). This coincided with a shift by Irish authors wishing to address English rather than Irish readerships about matters Irish. The first known Irish novel clearly aimed at English readership was Stephen Cullen's Gothic tale, *The castle of Inchvally: A tale-alas! too true* (London, 1796, 3 vols.), which has footnotes to explain Irish customs. Better known are Maria Edgeworth's *Castle Rackrent. An Hibernian tale* (London, 1800), and Mary Leadbeater's *Cottage dialogues among the Irish peasantry* (London, 1811), each of which contained an extensive glossary of Irish phrases and notes for the use of English readers.

The elucidation by Irish authors of Irish matters sprang from different impulses. There were many social and political reasons to counteract English negative perceptions of Irish people and Irish conflicts with the English. Irish topics also could have their charm for English readers, but these readers needed some information to make Irish fiction palatable. The Irish differed from the English in their customs and their use of the English language. Thus, several Irish writers highlighted the 'peculiar Irish ways' in which the Irish used the English language,[81] and might try to render an Irish brogue in their writings (e.g., T.S. Arthur's *Before and after the election; or, The political experiences of Mr. Patrick Murphy*, Philadelphia, 1853; or W.P. French, *The first Lord Liftinant, and other tales*, Dublin, 1890). One of the Irish characters in the Irish novel *Blue-stocking Hall* (London, 1827) set in Co. Kerry states 'You speak English amongst your poor, as we speak Irish, by ear, and so we speak it badly enough, and differently in different places; but *our English* we learn out of books, because it is *not* our natural language, and so perhaps we may speak it nearer to the manner in which it is written than you do at your side of the water'.[82] The result often was, as Lady Augusta Gregory explained, that the Irish from the countryside spoke English while apparently thinking in Irish.[83] This mixture of English and Irish languages became part of Irish literary history.

Critics and Irish Writers

A key link connecting books to the reading public were the critics who reviewed works of fiction. Reviews in eighteenth- and nineteenth-century periodicals were important as they helped to set standards by commenting on structure, narrative and plot.[84] Richard Lovell Edgeworth and Maria Edgeworth noted that 'General principles of taste and criticism have been spread in society by reviews and magazines'.[85] The worst that could happen to any writer was that his or her book was not reviewed at all. This was a particular problem for Irish writers publishing in Ireland, because these books were often not reviewed in England or Scotland.[86] Much Irish fiction was published by subscription[87] or because the author paid for its publication, it probably did not reach the usual distribution networks and was, therefore, less likely to come to the notice of the major review periodicals in England or Scotland. This meant that such volumes encountered an extra barrier in reaching an English reading audience. In contrast, novels by Irish authors published in Britain were more likely to be reviewed by British-based

81 Zimmermann, p. 260.   82 ii, p. 70.   83 Cited in Zimmermann, p. 331.   84 R. Loeber, M. Stouthamer-Loeber and J. Leerssen, 'Early calls for an Irish national literature, 1820–1877' in N. McCaw (ed.), *Writing Irishness in nineteenth century British culture* (London, 2004), pp 12–33; W. Hall, passim; J. Belanger, Educating the reading public: Critical reception of the Irish fiction of Maria Edgeworth and Lady Morgan, 1800–1830. Ph.D. dissertation, Univ. of Kent, Canterbury, 1999; Belanger (see index of short titles, this volume); K. Lubbers, 'Author and audience in the early nineteenth century' in P. Connolly (ed.), *Literature and the changing Ireland* (Gerrards Cross, 1982), pp 25–36.   85 R.L. Edgeworth & M. Edgeworth, *Readings on poetry* (London, 1816), 2nd edn (corrected), pp xix–xx.   86 For evidence in the eighteenth century, see Raven 1788:18, 1791:54. This is also evident from titles that were first published in Ireland and subsequently in England, where the English review was based on the English but not on the Irish edition (see e.g., Raven 1780:11, 1781:4, 1786:21). For additional information about reviews, see Foster and Foster 2. The situation was basically similar for much of the nineteenth century.   87 See the person index of the *Guide*, and also M. Kennedy, 'Women and reading in eighteenth-century Ireland' in Cunningham and Kennedy, *Experience of reading*, p. 89.

periodicals and occasionally by Irish-based periodicals as well. Several periodicals published in London, were edited by Irishmen (e.g., the *Dublin and London Magazine*; the *Dublin University Magazine*; *The Nation*; the *Irish Harp*), and periodicals such as the *Dublin and London Magazine* and the *Dublin Review*, although published in London, carried much Irish writing as well as reviews directed at Irish readers.

Although Irish critics also wrote about their strong literary preferences, many of them took upon themselves the task of delineating who they considered Irish authors, and of distinguishing between Irish and non-Irish fiction. Their critiques often reflected the tensions of Irish society – Protestants against Catholics, nationalists versus Unionists, Ascendancy against the tenantry. Many critical comments also reflected battles over suitable reading materials for young readers. For example, critics representing the Hibernian Bible Society called the books available in hedge schools 'foolish legends which poisoned the minds of youth'. The Report of the Commissioners of Irish Education of 1825 lamented the absence of appropriate books, and argued that children's minds were being 'corrupted by Books calculated to incite to lawless and profligate Adventure, to cherish Superstition, or to lead to Dissension or Disloyalty'.[88] The pioneering educational booklets issued by the Kildare Place Society for use in Irish schools, often couched in a semi-fictional format and aimed at self-improvement through knowledge of biology, nature, and the world outside of Ireland (but not Irish history),[89] were not approved of by the Catholic hierarchy. The Roman Catholic Education Society 'denounced the Kildare Place Society as anti-Catholic and un-Christian'.[90]

Several of the major Irish fiction writers – the Banim brothers, William Carleton, and Maria Edgeworth – were regularly and generally positively reviewed by Irish and English critics.[91] However, as the idea of a national literature emerged, authors and critics restricted the criteria of what constituted 'good' Irish fiction and what it meant to be an Irish writer. It was very easy for an Irish author to be attacked on any one of several fronts such as being of the Ascendancy class rather than from a farmer background,[92] or being a Protestant rather than a Catholic.

A major problem faced by Irish writers was not being recognized by reviewers as 'truly' Irish. For example, the Roscommon-born Mrs Bithia Croker published 52 works of fiction, of which at least ten were set in Ireland. In 1919 she wrote to the publisher Edmund Downey: 'It is strange to me that I never receive any acknowledgement from my native land as an Irish novelist ... Irish papers rarely notice me, save *The Freeman's Journal,* whose abuse is most amusing'.[93]

Irish reviewers did pay attention to the content of Irish novels, but tended often to criticize authors for the authenticity of their depictions of Ireland, or for choosing not to write about Ireland at all. Irish authors writing about Ireland and the Irish were not exempt from criticism, often because they might be accused of depicting less than authentic or positive views of the Irish. When William Carleton was told that his pictures of the Irish were 'really more reliable than those of Mrs S.C. Hall', he boisterously answered 'Why, of course, they are! Did she ever live with the people as I did? Did she ever dance and fight with them as I did? Did she ever get drunk with them as I did?'[94] Carleton, in turn, was reproached by one reviewer for 'his libels on the Irish priesthood' and 'beastly slanders'.[95] Another critic complained that Lady Morgan let her Irish peasantry speak 'in a jargon meant for the Irish dialect',[96] as if there was a prescribed manner to record dialects and intonations. Several Irish

88 P.J. Dowling, *The hedge schools of Ireland* (Cork, [1968]); Loeber & Stouthamer-Loeber, 'Fiction for cottagers', passim. 89 For example, McManus, *Irish hedge schools*, pp 218–36. 90 M. Casteleyn, *A history of literacy and libraries in Ireland* (Aldershot, 1984), p. 30. The society succumbed after 1831 during the period that Daniel O'Connell's Catholic Emancipation program succeeded. 91 For examples, see sources in British Fiction. 92 C.G. Duffy, *Young Ireland. A fragment of Irish history, 1840–1845* (Dublin, 1884), i, p. 25. 93 Loeber & Stouthamer-Loeber, 'Literary absentees', p. 185. 94 Cited in P. Rafroidi, 'The Irish short story in English. The birth of a new tradition,' in P. Rafroidi & T. Brown (eds), *The Irish short story* (Lille, n.d.), p. 34. 95 B. Hayley, 'The Eerishers are marchin' in leeterature' in W. Zach & H. Kosok (eds), *Literary interrelations. Ireland, England, and the world* (Tübingen, 1987), p. 41. 96 Hayley, 'Eerishers',

authors, especially those who depicted Irishmen in a comic way (e.g., Charles Lever, Samuel Lover, Edith Somerville and Violet Martin), were rebuked for presenting caricatures of Irish life and personalities.[97] Yeats criticized authors for representing an Ireland which was not 'the real Ireland' and presenting a 'false Ireland of sentiment'.[98] Other critics could not stand Mrs S.C. Hall's pointing out defects in the Irish character and her attempts to reform the Irish by making them more English.[99] Political orientation sometimes overrode religious beliefs: even if an author was a Catholic, he or she could still be attacked for being a Unionist rather than an Irish nationalist.[100]

Those Irish writers who did not write about Ireland or the Irish also came in for criticism from their compatriots. One critic categorically stated that the Munster author and politician Justin McCarthy could have been 'a much greater novelist than he if he had lived all his life in Ireland'.[101] The fact that Irish literature became incorporated into British literature led one critic to remark that Irish authors were selling out to the English and asked why should 'the Celtic genius of Ireland ... go to perfect and glorify English literature when it might have a literature of its own?[102] Another critic, under the headline *'We do not work in our own material'*, complained that Irish authors were not writing about the Irish.[103]

The diverse criticisms of Irish fiction often had in common the absence of a desire to arrive at a common ground over what constituted Irish fiction. Very little or no effort was put forward by reviewers to create an encompassing range of criteria for Irish authorship.[104] Even nowadays, this problem occasionally emerges from its grave. We agree with the Irish literary scholar Norman Vance's view that 'A more relaxed and pragmatic understanding of the sub-category 'Irish Literature (in English)' is clearly needed.[105]

The critics who held up some of the standards represented by these criticisms were a very diverse group of individuals: reviewers, priests, authors (William Carleton, Douglas Hyde, George Augustus Moore, William Butler Yeats, etc.), and proponents of a distinct Irish culture (Thomas Davis, Daniel Corkery).[106] In all, some of the criticisms could be devastating, but could also attract public attention to a particular volume or author. Among the most celebrated literary fights is the Irish author John Wilson Croker's critique of Miss Owenson's (later Lady Morgan) *The wild Irish girl* (London, 1806, 3 vols.). He wrote, 'I accuse her of attempting to vitiate mankind – of attempting to undermine morality by sophistry – and that under the insidious mask of virtue, sensibility and truth.'[107] The Munster author Canon Patrick Sheehan counter-attacked the critics by writing that 'we have no Catholic reading public because *constructive* criticism [our emphasis] is unknown'. Instead, he stated, 'we have a good deal of negative criticism ...'[108] O'Donoghue believed that 'an Irish writer publishing in London does not cater solely for his countrymen at home, who are necessarily more exacting in the manner of the right sort of national sentiment'.[109] In a frank appraisal, William Butler Yeats concluded in 1908 that it proved impossible to make a distinction between essential Irish elements in Irish fiction from 'foreign' [read British] qualities.[110]

Other more amorphous groups of individuals, whose direct opinions have not been well-documented exercised major influences on what Irish readers could access. Among these 'selectors' were compilers of anthologies, librarians and library committees of convents, parish and

p. 46.   97 Murphy, *Catholic fiction*, p. 18.   98 Critique in *United Ireland* (Feb. 1891), cited in J.S. Kelly, 'The fall of Parnell and the rise of Irish literature: an investigation' in *Anglo-Irish Studies*, ii (1976), p. 11.   99 Cited in Thuente 2, pp 10, 17.   100 Murphy, *Catholic fiction*, p. 16.   101 Cited in Kelly, 'Fall of Parnell', p. 13.   102 Ibid., pp 13–14.   103 Ibid., p. 11.   104 Foster, *The Irish story*, p. 110; P. Ward, *Exile, emigration and Irish writing* (Dublin, 2002), p. 180.   105 Vance, *Irish Literature*, p. 25.   106 Hall, *Dialogues*, p. 131; see also M. Kelleher, '"Wanted an Irish novelist": the critical decline of the nineteenth-century novel' in J. Belanger (ed.), *The Irish novel in the nineteenth century*, p. 193ff.   107 C. Connolly, '"*I accuse Miss Owenson*": The wild Irish girl *as media event*' in *Colby Quarterly*, xxxvi (2000), p. 98.   108 P.C. Canon Sheehan, *Literary life essays: poems* (Dublin, n.d), p. 76.   109 Cited in Loeber et al., 'Literary absentees', p. 183.   110 Thuente 1, p. 18.

public libraries, owners of circulating libraries, and booksellers who were importers of fiction, including Irish fiction published in England. For instance, Father S.J. Brown in selecting books for Dublin's Central Catholic Library in the 1930s admitted that 'a certain number of novels by Catholic authors have been deliberately omitted as objectionable from the moral standpoint'.[111] School and university teachers' choices of literary materials for their pupils were a major force in moulding and restricting what pupils and students were exposed to in terms of Irish fiction. In addition, according to Irish readers, parish priests exercised control over what their flocks were reading and some Irish readers hid their reading materials from priests' eyes.[112] In a book of conduct for juveniles published in Dublin 1870, a priest addressed the question, 'Which are Bad Books?'

> There are six sorts of bad books. 1. Books which are plainly about very bad things. 2. Many novels and romances, which do not seem to be so bad, but often are bad. 3. Idle books, which do no good, but take people's minds off what is good. 4. Bad newspapers, and journals, and miscellanies. 5. Superstitious books, fate books, &c. 6. Protestant books and tracts.[113]

Father John O'Rourke in the preface to his *Holly & ivy for the Christmas holidays* (Dublin, [1852]) alludes to the Synod of Thurles (1850) when the Irish hierarchy, led by Archbishop Paul Cullen, warned the faithful of the dangers of modern literature and suggests that his own story could both amuse and edify the reader. An Ursuline nun of Waterford writing in 1850 addressed her pupils:

> We do not ask you never to read novels; but remember that the mere novel-reader is a useless, insipid, tasteless being. Imagination becomes her conscience, her guide, her counsellor, her God. By such reading the understanding is blinded, the heart becomes selfish, and barren of noble and affectionate feelings. Egotism, not duty, not religion, not sacred domestic love, rules the mere novel-reader.[114]

When the novelist Katharine Tynan finished her education at the Siena Dominican Convent in Drogheda, she had to sign the convent pledge that she would not dance 'fast dances', go the theatre, or read novels. In her autobiography, she wryly remarks that the pledge did not say anything about the writing of novels.[115] Owners of circulating libraries had their own, unique manner of screening literary texts. A Mrs Lord who kept a circulating library in Dublin had several copies of the English Gothic novel the *Monk*, which was in universal request. As Summers relates it, the story goes that

> a highly correct *paterfamilias* having reproved her for imperilling the morality of the metropolis by admitting such a book in her catalogue, she naively replied: 'A shocking bad book to be sure, sir; but I have carefully looked through every copy, and *underscored* all the naughty passages, and cautioned my young ladies what they are to skip without reading it'.[116]

---

111 S.J. Brown, *Catalogue of novels and tales by Catholic writers* (Dublin, 1832, 5th edn), p. v; see also Casteleyn, *History of literacy*, p. 104.   112 See e.g., P. Ward, *Exile, emigration and Irish writing* (Dublin, 2002), pp 179–80; the theme is also mentioned in novels, such as J.F. Molloy, *What hast thou done?* (London, 1883), ii, pp 68–69; M. Coleman, '"Eyes big as bowls with fear and wonder": Children's responses to the Irish national schools, 1850–1922' in *Proceedings of the RIA*, iic (No. 5), 1998, p. 194.   113 J. Furniss, *The book of young persons* (Dublin, 1860), p. 25.   114 A member of the Ursuline Community, *The Catholic Lady's keepsake; or the gleanings offered to increase the store of our young friends educated at St. Mary's* (Dublin, 1850), p, 65.   115 K. Tynan, *Twenty-five years: reminiscences* (New York, 1913), pp 54–5, 69. See also, M. Cullen, *Girls don't do honours* (Dublin, 1987), pp 37–41.   116 Summers, p. 219.

Much remains to be learned about what literature by Irish authors was actually available to readers to Ireland, and what was available to authors themselves.

Where Have All the Books Gone?

When Yeats was preparing his book on William Carleton's stories in 1889 – only twenty years after Carleton's death – he borrowed some of Carleton's books from friends, but found himself 'seeking vainly for others which even then had disappeared from bookshops and library shelves'.[117] Carleton was famous during his lifetime and many of his books were reprinted in the nineteenth century, but still it proved difficult for Yeats to locate all of Carleton's work. Yeats's dilemma would have been even greater if he had searched for the works of lesser-known Irish writers. Now, more than one hundred years later, locating thousands of books written by Irish authors has proven a very arduous task. Even after enormous efforts using on-line bibliographies, accessing the stock of dozens of antiquarian dealers, personally searching innumerable old and rare bookstores through Europe and the North America, and searching extensive library collections, we have not been able to locate hundreds of titles.

The relative lack of knowledge about Irish fiction is aggravated by the fact that there is no single comprehensive repository of Irish fiction either in Ireland or abroad. The National Library of Ireland, Trinity College Dublin, University College Dublin, Queen's University Belfast, and the Linen Hall Library, the latter two both in Belfast, have large but by no means comprehensive collections. The Bradshaw collection of Irish books at the university library of Cambridge has only small holdings of fiction, but the university's general collection is very rich indeed. Remarkably, the Royal Irish Academy de-accessioned many of its novels in 1993.[118]

The history of some of the major holdings of Irish books is sometimes bizarre. In the past, novels at the copyright library of Trinity College, Dublin, received low priority for indexing by librarians. Also novels were lent out to staff and faculty without record, and large numbers of novels were sent to the front during the First World War.[119] Although in recent decades the college has been active in acquiring novels, its old and intricate cataloguing system makes it nearly impossible to access easily all novels published during the eighteenth and nineteenth.

Fires and neglect have seriously limited the availability of Irish fiction. Father Brown complained in the 1930s about the books that had 'disappeared from the [Central Catholic] library' in Dublin, a situation which had been aggravated by the library burning down in 1932.[120] The section of religious fiction in the British Library, which contained much Irish fiction, was largely demolished when the library was hit by a German bomb in the Second World War. The library of the Belfast Reading Society, now better known as the Linen Hall Library, suffered when an adjoining house was bombed during the 'troubles' in recent times and about 8,000 works of Victorian and Edwardian fiction were lost.[121]

Much of late-nineteenth-century Irish fiction at one time was housed in public libraries. The Irish Joint Fiction Reserve, which is a depository of older fiction withdrawn from Ireland's public libraries, is scattered all over the country. For instance, fiction by authors whose names starts with the letter 'A' can now be found at the Western Education & Library Board in Omagh (Co. Tyrone), the letter 'K' at the Kildare County Library, while short stories are housed at the Donegal County Library, and the undemanding letter 'Z' is housed at the Laois County Library. Unfortunately, the letters 'L' and 'M', once situated in the Dublin City & County Libraries, were destroyed by a fire in June 1987, but the collection is being rebuilt.[122]

117 The words are by Wolff, introd. p. 8. 118 Typescript of de-accession list of Irish fiction, formerly in the Royal Irish Academy, 1993. 119 Personal communications by William O'Sullivan, Oct. 1993 and May 1994; anonymous staff member of Trinity College Library, Jan. 2001; Peter Costello, May 1994. 120 S.J. Brown, *Catalogue of novels and tales by Catholic writers* (Dublin, 1932, 5th edn), pp 49–51, 56. 121 M. Casteleyn, *A history of literacy and libraries in Ireland* (Aldershot, 1984), p. 106.

It is nearly impossible to access this large body of fiction spread over thirty-two counties, and much of the national heritage of Irish fiction situated in Ireland remains scattered, inaccessible and underestimated.

In former times, major repositories of fiction could be found in thousands of Irish country houses. However, the large-scale departure of the Ascendancy, and the deserting, demolition and burning of country houses during the Anglo-Irish War has seriously diminished these holdings. Key collections once housed in country houses such as Castle Bellew (Co. Galway), Edgeworthstown House (Co. Longford), Doneraile Court (Co. Cork), the Gage/McCausland collection at Bellanrena (Co. Derry), and the Granard collection at Castle Granard (Co. Longford) have been dispersed in recent years. Also, the libraries of Church of Ireland clergymen and their offspring, many of whom became fiction writers, had the same fate.[123] For example, the library of the Le Fanu family, which produced several authors, was dispersed not too long ago.

The upshot of all of this is that thousands of Irish works of fiction published between 1650 and 1900 are very rare and hundreds are known to have survived only as single copies. This *Guide*, partly based on our own collection (now the Loeber Collection of Irish fiction at the Hesburgh Library of the University of Notre Dame, South Bend, IN, consisting of 2,444 books)[124] provides the location of almost all surviving titles.

It is likely that the future will reveal titles that we have missed. The holdings of some libraries are vast and their catalogues are not set up to identify Irish fiction (the exceptions are for major modern Irish authors such as Joyce and Beckett). In fact, Irish fiction in major libraries remains buried among English language fiction. In that sense, it is not different from the literatures of former British colonies such as Jamaica, Canada or other former British dominions. These literatures, including Irish fiction, all need special efforts to identify native authors, discover and document their works, and appreciate their contributions to their national heritages.

II. THE SCOPE OF THIS 'GUIDE'

This is an annotated bibliography of all known books of fiction by Irish authors and foreign authors writing about Ireland and the Irish. For authors to be included an author had to publish his/her first work after 1650 and prior to 1901. In the case of anonymous works and manuscripts, the work had to be published between 1650 and 1900. The lower year was set because we have not come across works of fiction from earlier decades. The top date was set at 1900, partly for convenience, partly because Irish fiction of the twentieth century has been much better documented than fiction of earlier centuries. Several other aspects of this bibliography make it distinct from earlier bibliographies: it includes, for example, updated biographical sketches of hundreds of authors and thousands of summaries of works of fiction. In addition, the key information in the *Guide* was entered into a spread-sheet database. This step proved most important because, unlike prior bibliographies, we could then quantify many of the basic features of the authors, their works, their publishers, and other characteristics of the publication process. The results of some of the analyses based on these data are presented in Section V.

We were particularly interested in Irish fiction as a historical rather than literary phenomenon. Not being trained in literary studies, this approach suited us best. Whatever was

122 *Guide to the Joint Fiction Reserves* (n.p., n.l.), p. 8. **123** For the contents of such libraries in the eighteenth century see T. Barnard, *A new anatomy of Ireland: the Irish Protestants, 1649–1770* (New Haven, 2003), chapter 4; Cole, pp 24–25 and passim. **124** Dr Michael W.J. Smurfit facilitated the purchase of the Loeber Collection of Irish Fiction by the University of Notre Dame.

published and read at the time was part of the culture and from that point of view is worth preserving. To apply standards of high literary merit, transient as these standards are, would be to exclude a large part of a country's national and cultural heritage. Even the so-called badly written books convey information about the times and conditions in which they were written. As stated previously, many novels that would not attract wide attention nowadays were heavily reprinted and read in their time (see Table 2).

This *Guide* serves several other purposes. It contributes to literary history and to the history of book publishing by documenting the first edition of each work, followed by, where applicable, reprint(s) in cities other than where the first edition appeared. The bibliography also documents other editions with alternative titles and translations that appeared in France, Germany and the Netherlands. Because of restricted search capabilities for translations, our listings cannot claim to be comprehensive.[125] To further show the spread of Irish fiction abroad, we included English-language editions of Irish fiction published in North America, Australia, and to a lesser extent in India and the West Indies, but we also list English-language Irish fiction that was published in France and Germany.

The *Guide* records the publication location and the publisher(s) of each title and the number of volumes in which it was published. We provide source material for this information (which provides detailed imprint information and often the catalogue number in major libraries), and also provide the location in key libraries in Ireland, England and North America. In the commentary that follows the bibliographical information we have often provided information about where the work may have been previously published as a serial or as an article in a periodical (however, we cannot claim that this is an exhaustive survey). Further, we provide a sampling of reviews of the works, indicated in either the source materials (e.g., British Fiction, Forster, Forster 2, and Garside) or mention this in the commentary section (again, it was beyond our capacities to present a comprehensive survey of reviews).

III. HOW WE WORKED AND EDITORIAL PROCEDURES

We started with the work of documenting authors and their works in October 1989, and it has occupied and enriched our lives since then. Our initial list of Irish fiction covered four pages. Increasingly confident that there must have been more fiction, we decided to expand the search. This led to the discovery of hundreds of unknown novels and the identification of scores of previously undocumented novelists. In addition, we started to build a more comprehensive catalogue of the works of known authors.

In the distribution of the work between the authors of this *Guide*, Magda Loeber (and to a much lesser extent, Rolf Loeber) read over 900 Irish novels, which she summarized and dictated. Rolf Loeber systematically read autobiographies, biographies, volumes of letters, booksellers' catalogues, and other source material to document biographical aspects of authors' lives and to expand the bibliographical history of works of Irish fiction. Anne Mullin Burnham made invaluable contributions in complementing the biographical sketches, checking source materials, making the glossary, and entering data in the database.

Jointly, Rolf and Magda Loeber spend vacations over seven years working in the National Library of Ireland making an inventory of the largest collection of Irish fiction in Ireland. We found many undocumented books both there and at other locations. Rolf Loeber visited dozens of libraries searching for books of Irish fiction.

---

125 Thus, we excluded the relatively small number of translations of Irish fiction that appeared in such countries as Italy, Sweden and Hungary.

Author	Title, and original place and date of printing	Place and date of reprint	Edition	Source
Period 1745 to 1799				
McCarthy, Charlotte	*The fair moralist* (London, 1745)	Dublin, 1747 onwards	Remained in print in Ireland until 1783	Addenda to this *Guide*, p. 1401
Johnstone, Charles	*Chrysal* (London, 1760)		Reprinted over a period of 50 years	*Guide*, J44.
Sheridan, Frances	*Memoirs of Miss Sidney Bidulph* (London, 1761)	London, 1796	5th edn	Burmester cat. 38/315. RL; V.E. Neuburg, *Popular literature* (Harmondsworth, 1977), pp 184.
Roche, Maria Regina	*The children of the abbey* (London, 1796)		About 80 reprints. Milner edn alone sold over 75,000 copies	
[Potter, James]	*Billy bluff* (Belfast, 1796)	Belfast, 1840	13th edn	Thuente 2, p. 235.
Period 1800 to 1849				
[Bunbury, Selina]	*A visit to my birthplace* (Dublin, 1826)		11 edns	*Guide*, B435
[Roberts, Abigail]	*The cottage fire-side* (Dublin, 1821)	Dublin, 1821	20,000 copies printed of which 15,000 had been sold in 1821	*Guide*, R203
[Moore, Thomas]	*Memoirs of Captain Rock* (London, 1824)		Highly popular	*Guide*, M530
'Elizabeth Charlotte' [Elizabeth Tonna]	*Derry. A tale of the revolution* (London, 1833)	London, 1890	30th thousand	Copy at D
Edgeworth, Maria	*Helen* (London, 1834)	London, 1834	8,000 copies for 1st edn; 1,500 copies for 2nd edn; 1,500 copies subsequently	Butler, p. 492
'Doyle, Martin' [William Hickey]	*Common sense for common people* (Dublin, 1835)	Dublin, 1837	14th edn	*Guide*, H272
[Sargent, Lucius]	*An Irish heart* (Boston, 1836)	Boston, 1843	9th thousand	Wright, i, 2290
'A., E.C.' [E.C. Agnew]	*Geraldine. A tale of conscience* (London, 1837–9)	London, n.d.	12th edn	Copy at D

Author	Title, and original place and date of printing	Place and date of reprint	Edition	Source
Period 1850 to 1905				
Sadlier, Mrs. J.	The Blakes and Flanagans (New York, 1855)	New York, 1859	16th thousand	Guide, S9
Power, Philip Bennett	The eye doctor (London, [1866?])		23,000 sold	Guide, P137
C., W.A.	Mick Tracy, the Irish scripture reader (London, [1863])	London, 1869	19th thousand	Guide, C187
Caddell, Cecilia	Never forgotten; or, the home of the lost child (London, 1871)	–	12th edn	Guide, C12
Wright, Julia	Priest and nun (Philadelphia, [1869])	Cincinnati, 1871	16th thousand	Guide, W162
Kickham, Charles	Knocknagow (Dublin, [1873]).	[after 1879]	26th edn	Clements cat. Winter 1997/196
'Allen, T.M.' [Edmund Downey]	A house of tears (London, 1886)	London, 1893	21st thousand	Guide, D159
	Through green glasses (London, 1887)	London, c.1890	23rd thousand	Guide, 382
	Voyage of the ark (London, 1888)	London, 1888	20th thousand	Guide, 382
	From the green bag (London, 1889)	London, c.1890	14th thousand	Guide, 382
'Meade, L.T.' [Elizabeth Smith]	A world of girls (London, 1886)	London, 1894	21st thousand	Guide, S192
	Polly (London, 1889)	London, 1908	32nd thousand	Guide, S204
	A madcap (London, 1904)	London, n.d.	15th thousand	Guide, S330
'Grand, Sarah' [Frances McFall]	The heavenly twins	(London, 1893)	Sold about 100,000 copies in 1893	Guide, M104.
Caffyn, Kathleen	A yellow aster (London, 1894)	London, 1894	13th edn, completing 22nd thousand	Jarndyce cat. 126/56
[Moore, Frank Frankfort]	The diary of an Irish cabinet minister (Belfast, 1893)		30th edn appeared in 1893	Guide, M432
Croker, B.M.	Beyond the Pale (New York, 1896)	London, 1905	Republished with a print run of 25,000 copies; 2nd edn of 10,000 copies, 3rd edn of 11,000 copies	E. Reilly, 'Beyond gilt shamrock' in L.W. McBride (ed.), Images (Dublin, 1999), p. 97.

Table 2 Examples of popular novels by Irish authors first published between 1745 and 1905.

Because many of the volumes were rare and generally could not be obtained through the University of Pittsburgh's Interlibrary Loan, Rolf Loeber during his travels in North America and Western Europe, acquired a large collection of Irish fiction. The presence of this collection in the main authors' Pittsburgh apartment over many years allowed them to systematically read hundreds of volumes and prepare the brief summaries included in this volume.

The Guide was compiled by consulting prior bibliographies and listings of works of Irish fiction in current and past catalogues of antiquarian booksellers; by retrieving 'new' titles from the collections of major libraries in Ireland, England, and North America, and from the holdings of scores of antiquarian booksellers. In the process of this work, we issued 22 newsletters to friends and colleagues (entitled *18th and 19th Century Irish Fiction Newsletter*) from 1998 to 1999, which raised several of the key issues pertaining to the development of Irish fiction or individual works within that framework.[126]

Our work was greatly helped by prior bibliographies of Irish fiction, but as the reader will see, we have gone beyond earlier works. Ninety years ago, Father Stephen Brown published his seminal *Ireland in fiction* (1916, reprinted 1919), which was followed by a second volume, published in 1985 and co-authored by Desmond Clarke. Although pioneering in many respects, as reference sources the volumes are inadequate (incomplete titles abound, first editions are not consistently identified, and many inaccuracies are apparent). Moreover, because of their focus on fiction dealing with the Irish and with Ireland only, the volumes excluded fiction by Irish authors on non-Irish themes, and narrowly evaluated the suitability of fiction for a Roman Catholic readership. Also, Brown's volumes do not reveal how widely republished Irish fiction was in other cities and countries.[127] As a result, it is difficult to grasp from them the extent to which the Irish abroad remained in touch with literature from the mother country.

Perhaps most frustratingly, Brown's bibliographies do not reveal the location of volumes in public repositories. This is an acute problem aggravated by the fact that many of the volumes are very rare. In recent years several other guides to Irish fiction have been published, each advancing knowledge in the field. These volumes have been very helpful to us, but overall they were either more concerned with authors' biographical sketches rather than detailed bibliographies or with an in-depth appraisal of well-known authors to the exclusivity of lesser-known writers (see bibliographies by, for example, Brady & Cleeve, Hogan, McKenna, Newmann, Rafroidi, Weekes, Welch, and more recently, O'Toole). Problems with other compilers such as Brady and Boylan included incomplete listings of works (often excluding major

---

126 Copies of the newsletters are lodged at the NLI and the library of the Univ. of Notre Dame, South Bend, IN. The following is a full list of the titles of the newsletters: An early Irish novel on women's education (Jan. 1998 – No. 1); An example of an unreliable narrator (Feb. 1998 – No. 2); An unusual novel about the Union (March 1998 – No. 3); 'Lost' Irish novels of the eighteenth century (April 1998 – No. 4); John Connor: A maverick Cork publisher of literature (May 1998 – No. 5); The early Development of a national literature of fiction published in Dublin after the Union (June 1998 – No. 6); Puzzles in Irish literary biography and bibliography (July 1998 – No. 7); The early and later development of fiction relating to Ireland, 1680 – 1900 (August 1998 – No. 8); Rooms, books and reading in Irish country houses, Part 1 (September 1998 – No. 9); Rooms, books and reading in Irish country houses, Part 2 (October 1998 – No. 10); An epoch of publishing history: James Duffy and the lowering of prices and the diversification of bindings (December 1998/January 1999 – Nos. 12–13); Fiction for charity: Literature as a link between benefactors and beneficiaries. With an addendum to Newsletters 9 and 10 by Toby C. Barnard (February 1999 – No. 13 [14]); Libertine fiction of the eighteenth century: Irishmen as 'Petticoat-Pensioners' (March 1999 – No. 15); Informal prohibitions of works of fiction in 18th and 19th Century Ireland (April 1999 – No. 16); John Banim's letters written from England and France concerning his stories for English annuals (May 1999 – No. 17); Early calls for an Irish national literature, 1822–1877, Part 1 (June 1999 – No. 18); Early calls for an Irish national literature, 1822–1877, Part 2 (July 1999 – No. 19); The prodigious Mrs. L.T. Meade (August 1999 – No. 20); The Beaufort sisters and educational fiction (Sept. 1999 – No. 21); A House of Tears: A little known horror novel (Dec. 1999 – No. 22). Note that some of the information from the newsletters, thanks to feedback from colleagues and friends, has been amended and corrected since the instalments appeared. Some of the information from the newsletters has been incorporated in the current Guide.   127 An additional problem was that the dating of books by Brown often deviated from that of more certain sources, such as the catalogue of the British Library.

categories of fiction such as religious stories, and fiction for children and juveniles); minimal bibliographic references; and a far-from-exhaustive listing of authors.

Thanks to the support of directors and staff of libraries, we were able to work in the National Library of Ireland and the British Library. Although we covered most of the fiction contents in the various sections of the National Library, the task in the British Library, with its miles of stacks of novels, was far more daunting and we limited ourselves mostly to the stacks of small fiction, which contained much material that was generally unknown. The lack of available time away from our regular work always put frustrating restraints on our investigation of Irish fiction. We occasionally investigated publishers' archives and the records of the Royal Literary Fund in the British Library, but we cannot say that we have exhausted all unpublished sources. Since a great deal of Irish fiction was published in Britain, there is still much work to be done in publishers' archives to uncover the dealings between Irish authors and British publishers. Access to sources is greatly facilitated nowadays through the portal http://www.sharpweb.org/.

Another mode by which we increased the corpus of known Irish fiction was by scouring thousands of older and current catalogues of book dealers (see the reference section of this volume). They proved an important source because of the rarity of many of the volumes. In addition, a large collection of eighteenth- and nineteenth-century library catalogues was used to add to our list of books to be investigated. We routinely read contemporary advertisements and reviews of books, many of which proved very useful in identifying early and sometimes extremely rare editions (for bibliographic references to reviews of works of fiction published between 1749 and 1800, see Forster, and Forster 2; and for the period 1800 to 1830, see Belanger). We also used standard and unusual bibliographies of collections of eighteenth- and nineteenth-century fiction (see our bibliography), including a set of bibliographies on specific authors (e.g., Hayley on William Carleton, Slade on Maria Edgeworth, Teerink and Scouten on Jonathan Swift, Dalby on Stoker). The publication of key reference works in the period of writing this *Guide* helped us immensely.

One of the principal difficulties in documenting original Irish fiction was the extensive reprint industry of fiction in Dublin during the eighteenth century. James Raven's works were particularly helpful in distinguishing between original works and Irish reprints,[128] although some uncertainty remained when books were published in London and Dublin in the same year.[129] If a book of fiction was published in Dublin, but not in England, then we have included this title here. We addressed in the following way the problem of determining whether an Irish edition had precedence over a London edition: if the title appeared in same year in Dublin and London, we did not include it unless: (a) we knew it was by an Irish author, or if (b) it had Irish content. In a rare instance, it is possible that what appeared as a unique Irish edition was in fact not so because of the non-survival of an English edition.

Matters were further complicated by the late-eighteenth-century practice of Irish booksellers purchasing from an English printer the copyright of his/her works. After an English printer had typeset the English edition, the author forwarded the novel's manuscript to the Irish publisher for it to be typeset in Ireland. This allowed the Irish publisher to produce the book very soon after its publication in England but prior to likely piracy by other Dublin publishers. This practice was in evidence in the case of Charlotte Smith's *The banished man*, which appeared almost simultaneously in London and Dublin in 1794. She complained that 'I do

---

128 Raven; Raven 2; Garside; Garside 2.   129 We erred on the side of caution and generally excluded the volumes with the same publication date published in London and Dublin, and only included them when there was clear evidence through an inscription or other evidence that the work was by an Irish author or concerned Ireland and the Irish. For the exact date at which Irish novels were published in London during the period 1800–29, see J. Belanger, P. Garside, A. Mandal & S. Ragaz, 'British fiction 1800–1829' in http://www.cf.ac.uk/encap/corvey/articles/database/star.html.

think it hard that The Irish Booksellers should derive so much profit from a very successful English work, injure the sale to the English proprietor, and be at no expence whatever but the printing & paper'.[130]

During the fifteen years that we worked on this project, electronic databases became available. Access to databases such as ESTC, OCLC, COPAC, RLIN (now RLG Union Catalogue) were particularly useful because they allowed us to search for Irish and English publishers, verify titles, and identify libraries in which the volumes could be found.

Inclusions and Exclusions

It was inevitable that we had to make difficult decisions about the nature and scope of this *Guide*, such as whether to give details of material written in Irish as well as English, the types of fiction we wished to cover, and the criteria for including authors. In discussions with our advisors, we decided to prepare a guide to rather than a bibliography of Irish fiction, an essential distinction that warrants explanation. We knew from the outset, while working part-time on this project, that we could not possibly examine all the volumes during our lifetime. This led to the rather painful conclusion that we could include only essential bibliographical information. Table 3 shows how our entries are organized.

Authors For this *Guide*, we included three categories of authors and their works. First, we focused on authors of Irish birth, and those authors of British parentage who had lived in Ireland for most of their lives, whose first published work of fiction appeared prior to 1901. Of these authors *all* works of fiction are included irrespective of whether the works dealt with Ireland or the Irish. The criterion of Irish birth or residence in Ireland was not always easy to establish and we were generally cautious to attribute either of these without documentary evidence. Second, we included authors of Irish descent who were born elsewhere (for example, North America, India or Australia), but only those who wrote works of fiction dealing with Ireland or with the Irish people. The terminal cut-off for these publications was 1901. Finally we included a third and smaller group of authors who were not Irish by birth or descent, but who published fiction about the Irish abroad or in Ireland (their non-Irish works are excluded). The cut-off date for this category of works was 1901 as well.

We often encountered problems in identifying Irish authors. For us to go beyond known Irish authors, we needed do extensive research to determine Irish birth or extended residence in Ireland. We defined Irish by birth as any person born in Ireland; this approach works well as a rule. However, its limitation is that authors born in Ireland who left Ireland at a young age (e.g., Elizabeth Hamilton), in contrast to those who left in late adolescence or adulthood, rarely wrote about Ireland. These individuals, representing a relatively small group, were still counted by us (and by most other editors of Irish fiction) as Irish authors. We also included authors born in England of Irish parents if they came to live in Ireland for extended periods of time (this applied to, for example, to the Edgeworths, Maria and her father Richard Lovell).

Sometimes there was insufficient information about residence in Ireland. We then employed the following criteria to establish whether the individual was a probable Irish author: (a) the person only published in Ireland or published earliest known books in Ireland; and (b) the person published fiction on Ireland or Irish topics and other nonfiction about Irish matters.

In few rare instances, the name of an author given on a title page is incorrect. This occurred where a relative took responsibility for the authorship of a work. For example, Thomas Crofton Croker's name appears on volumes written by his wife, Marianne Croker;

---

130 J.P. Stanton, *The collected letters of Charlotte Smith* (Bloomington, IN, 2003), pp 53, 57, 94, 103.

and Charles Lever's name is on a novel by his daughter Sydney Lever). Sometimes someone is listed as an 'editor' of a work written by someone else (e.g., Viscount Wolseley). There are likely to be other examples of this practice which have not come to our attention.

It was common to find a list of authors' other works on the title pages of one of their books. However, in a number of instances it proved impossible to locate these works. It is possible that these literary productions may have appeared in periodicals and remain to be identified. It is also possible that some authors included fictitious titles in order to appear more important in the eyes of the critics and the reading public.

One of the problems we faced was the large number of anonymous books published in the period covered by this *Guide*, including titles by anonymous 'ladies', later called 'Aggravating Ladies' by Ralph Thomas because of the immense difficulties in discovering their true identities (some were actually male authors seeking to disguise their identity or who masqueraded as women in order to disarm any potential critical hostility to male authors of novels).[131] This meant that a proportion of known fiction could not be included simply because the identity, and – hence the nationality – of its author could not be ascertained. However, in a good number of cases we were able to identify a previously anonymous author. We included in all cases those anonymous works which clearly referred to Ireland in their title or content.

Books The scope of this *Guide* is on Irish fiction in the English language, which means that we excluded fiction published in the Irish language (in fact very few works of fiction in Irish were published prior to the 1890s). We included English language fiction in the form of novels, tales, short stories, short fiction, manuscripts and anthologies (but not short stories published only in periodicals). The title index shows, whenever possible, which books were Anthologies (a), and manuscripts (MS). Poetry and plays are excluded, but mainly to set a limit to our endeavours, partly because of our central focus on fiction.[132]

Fiction is defined here broadly as literary narratives in prose, but it is not often easy to make distinctions between fiction and autobiographical works, imaginary voyages, tales of criminals' lives and trials, and educational works. We faced many perplexing questions: for example should fictionalized autobiographical accounts be included? What about satires referring to contemporary events? Which educational books could be classified as educational fiction? In general, we decided to include rather than exclude, often using as a criterion whether or not a volume included dialogues. This meant that we included, for example, a modest number of Irish travel books, but only if these contained folk tales or legends (e.g., the works of the Revd Caesar Otway and Lady Chatterton). Further, we decided that inclusion of novels *only* would be too restrictive for a country where storytelling was an inherent part of the national heritage. For that reason, we included books of stories and tales by specific authors, and anthologies of stories by different authors. However, to make our task more manageable, we excluded the following material: chapbooks and religious tracts with 24 or fewer pages, serialized and magazine fiction that was never published in book form, jest books, and primers and grammar books that contain illustrative stories. If we knew of novels or short stories that had first been published in a magazine, we mention this. However, given the vast number of Irish, British, and North American periodicals that published Irish fiction, a complete coverage of this aspect of Irish literary history was beyond the scope of this *Guide*, and clearly remains a challenge for future literary researchers.

---

131 *Aggravating ladies, being a list of works published under the pseudonym of 'A Lady'* (London, 1880), referred to in Brick Row cat. 140/147; Raven, p. 18.   132 D.J. O'Donoghue, *The poets of Ireland, a biographical and bibliographical dictionary of Irish writers of English verse* (London, 1912).

Many of the authors listed in this *Guide* wrote for juveniles as well as adults. We decided not to exclude their works of fiction written for juveniles, because this would distort authors' contributions to Irish fiction. Another reason was that in practice it proved very difficult to separate fiction written for adolescents from that aimed at young adults. Perhaps most importantly was the fact that fiction for young people constituted the core reading material for generations of Irish (and non-Irish) readers, and where that fiction dealt with Ireland and the Irish, it helped to mould concepts of the Irish nation, and the history of Ireland under British rule.

There is no golden standard as to what makes a book Irish in content. Should the principal character be Irish? What if secondary characters were Irish? In general, we developed a standard that at least one of the characters had to be Irish and had to be present for a significant portion of the work. This character, however, did not have to be the principal hero or heroine. In North American fiction especially this often meant a focus on menial workers and domestic servants, because the Irish were highly represented in these social strata during the nineteenth century. Anthologies raised another sticky problem. Under a given author, we decided not to include anthologies in which that author had published a single story and where the other authors were non-Irish. However, anthologies of Irish stories are included in the *Guide*.

In summary, in contrast to prior guides to Irish fiction, we attempted to achieve a fuller description of the national Irish literature that included all large varieties of fiction, published and unpublished, surviving and lost.

IV. ARRANGEMENT OF THE ENTRIES

A typical entry consists of information in the following order:

Author's name,
Biographical sketch,
Sources for the biographical sketch,

For each title we included the following information:

Book identification number,
Book title,
Whether we or our collaborators have seen the volume(s),
Publication details,
Sources for the publication details.

If possible, we added:

A commentary about the contents or features of the volume(s),
Sources for this information.

Each of these aspects can be identified using as an example the author William Allingham and his single work of fiction (Table 3).

1. **Author's Name** Author's name is given in its most complete form as noted in bibliographical sources. Because of variant names, we also list those where they are either used in publications or under which the author was commonly known. We also separately list co-authors, with a cross-reference to the author entry where more information can be found. The 'anonymous section' begins with anonymous authors known because of a single volume, followed by those known because of multiple works of fiction. Attributions usually rest on the mention on the title page of other titles written by an author. However, the attributions are

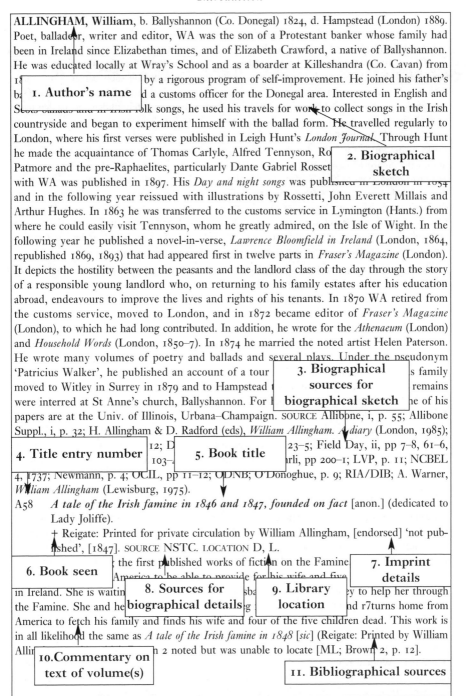

Table 3 Lay-out of entries in the *Guide*.

not always sound, because another author could steal such a list and add it to his or her own works. The identification of inconsistencies in publishing houses of strings of associated titles can then provide clues of multiple authorships.

The naming convention for known authors used is to first mention the author's birth name in full, and then if applicable, the most common name used during their career. For women authors, we used the name they most often used as an author, and if married, followed by their maiden name. In all cases we indexed a woman author separately under her maiden name to credit her as an individual and to facilitate research on female authors' writing careers prior to marriage. If applicable, we also listed the author's pseudonym(s), but only those used for works of fiction that are listed here (in other words, other pseudonyms used in periodicals or in non-fiction works have not been given; for these, see R. Loeber and M. Loeber, *Irish poets and their pseudonyms in early periodicals* [Dublin, 2006]). The authors and the pseudonyms are listed alphabetically, but the 'an' and 'the' of a pseudonym are ignored. Surnames with the prefix 'Mc' or 'M'' are filed under 'Mac', while surnames starting with 'O' (as O'Brien) are filed under 'O'. Surnames that start with 'De' are listed under that prefix, but the name is cross referenced under its main name (thus, Madame de Genlis is found under 'de Genlis'). Names that start with 'Le' are listed under that prefix (e.g., 'Le Fanu').

2. **Biographical Sketch** Where possible, we included a brief biographical sketch of the author. The biographical sketches included in this volume are often based on summaries of other biographical works, but many of the entries have been expanded by new findings on the lives and works of the authors. Length of the sketches is not uniform, partly to accommodate new information, and because our emphasis is on the lesser-known rather than the better-known writers (for whom complete biographical and reference material is readily available elsewhere). Readers are referred to standard works cited at the end of the biographical sketches for further information on individual authors. Wherever possible we referred to unpublished manuscripts of novels. We set a limit, however, to novels that were planned but not written. Thus, Daniel O'Connell's projected novel (possibly begun as early as Feb. 1796), which is only known from a sketched plot, is not included in this *Guide*, neither is the antiquarian John O'Donovan's romantic tale, for which he wrote a plot only, or the poet Jeremiah Joseph Callanan's lost manuscript novel based on a legendary tale concerning Lough Ine (near Skibbereen, Co. Cork).[133] However, we noted manuscripts of works of fiction (but not single short stories) and listed them as separate items under the books by an author.

In many instances, an author's name on the title page is accompanied by the phrase 'author of', followed by a listing of some of his/her earlier works. For reasons of space, this listing is not repeated in the *Guide*. Exceptions are little-known authors, whose identification hinges on the mention of his/her earlier works. Also, authors' names as listed on title pages varied (sometimes only initials of first names were used); except where confusion might arise, these variations are not specifically mentioned here. Whenever other authors are mentioned in the biographical sketch that are included in this *Guide*, then the symbol § indicates that more information can be found under that person's last name.

Pseudonymous authors are listed under their real name, when this could be established, but the pseudonym is listed after the work's title (if applicable); the pseudonym is also listed in the alphabetical name list. For titled persons, the principal entry can be found under that title (e.g., Blessington, earl of), with a cross-reference to the individual's family name (Gardiner). Women who married into the nobility are listed under the title of their husband (e.g., Blessington, Lady). Within the biographical sketches, titles of other works are in italics, but works that are not known to have been published are in single quotes.

133 O. MacDonagh, *The hereditary bondsman Daniel O'Connell, 1775–1829* (London, 1988), p. 39; P. Boyne, *John O'Donovan (1806–1861), A biography* (Kilkenny, 1987), p. 140; Connolly, 'Irish romanticism', p. 438.

The biographical sketch also contains information about other works published or unpublished by a particular author. Our mention of such works emphasizes authors' contribution to culture in different genres other than prose literature (e.g., poetry, plays, travel books, and scientific books), and contributions to the periodical literature (many of which never appeared in book form). In all cases, we avoided flooding the biographical text with this information, and chose to give examples of such publications rather than a complete listing. We provided, however, the place of publication of other works and periodicals. We thought that this information was important because it clarifies the contribution of authors to book culture both inside and outside of Ireland.

An author's religious affiliation is mentioned where known. Every effort was made to identify Catholic authors because, on the whole, their lives and work have been less-documented than those of Protestant authors.

3. **Bibliographical Sources for Biographical Sketch** This section lists the source material(s) which we consulted for the biographical sketch. Abbreviations for the source material can be found in the Index of Abbreviations.

4. **Title Entry Number** Each title of an author's prose work is preceded by a letter and a number. The letter denotes the first letter of the author's last name, followed by a number in sequence across all authors under that letter. For example, the only novel by William Allingham (see Table 3) carries the title number of 'A58'. Note that all anonymous works are numbered under the prefix 'anon.' and then given a sequential number.

5. **Book Title** All titles in bold are of the first edition. Only in a minority of instances, when the first edition was not located, does the title reflect the next known edition. The book title is a literal transcription of its title, but is kept in lower case (on the original title page, lower and upper case was often used, but since we were not able to examine all books, we imposed some uniformity on the form used for the title). Whenever applicable, we give the full title including, where appropriate, a subtitle. The transcription, in most cases, is done from a copy of the first edition we have examined (and then often confirmed through the spelling in a major reference work). However, when we were not able to inspect a volume, we relied on a bibliographical source. Spelling in the title was kept as found (e.g., a subtitle often was preceded by '; or, the…'). In the case of subtitles on a new line without punctuation, a semicolon was inserted. In all instances, we included the full title, rather than abbreviating the title. If in later editions the title of the volume was changed, then we inserted another line with that information, including when and where this alternative title was published (indicated in italics). If there is no reference to a title following the publication of the work in another city, this means that the title was identical to that given in the main entry of the book. If the work was published anonymously but the author's identity is known, then the abbreviation [anon.] follows the title.

Book titles are listed chronologically wherever possible, starting with the earliest known work of fiction. If a title is undated, then that title precedes other dated titles. For reasons of space and legibility, we did not include all published editions of a given work. Instead, we only listed other editions if: (a) there was a variant title under which the work appeared (b) if the volume of fiction was republished in a different or new condition (such as illustrations or stories added, or a revision of the text).[134] In some instances, a bundle of short stories changed in its composition and title over time with some stories included but other stories not in subsequent reprints. Often this became so complex that we decided to list all variants of a bundle of short stories

---

134 We included reprints principally when they were published in the author's lifetime. However, this standard proved not always workable.

under its main, original title (e.g. all the stories in Maria Edgeworth's *Manoeuvring, Madame de Fleury, & The Dun* (London, 1856) derived from her *Tales of fashionable life* (London, 1809) and for that reason, can be found on the latter title). To make this mass of information even more interpretable, we arranged later publications under each location where they appeared (e.g., London, Dublin, etc.) and we listed the alternative titles in the title index.

Collected works, if applicable, are listed at the end of the individual titles. For reasons of space, individual titles published as part of collected works could not be listed. Also, titles belonging to collected works are not listed under each main title, largely because they were almost always reprints. We noted that some collected works were not issued with a title, but are often recognizable as a separate series because of their unique binding and decoration. Such untitled collected works are included: the work is mentioned in brackets and is accompanied by a commentary explaining binding details. An example in the *Guide* is G174 [*Gerald Griffin's works*] (Dublin: James Duffy, 1857), 8 vols, without a title signifying that this constituted a collected works.

6. **Book Seen** A plus sign (+) indicates which, if any, of the editions of the title we or our collaborators have examined. For reasons of space, we do not indicate which copy we have seen, other than that they were most likely in our own collection (as evident from the location InNDLoeber coll., now in the Hesburgh Library of the University of Notre Dame), the National Library of Ireland, or the British Library. Although both libraries are copyright libraries, they are far from complete as to Irish imprints.

7. **Imprint Details** For each work, we note its place of publication, name of publisher(s), date, number of volumes if more than one, the author's pseudonym or alternative name, and, where applicable, we mention the presence of subscribers' lists, the illustration(s) and the name of the illustrators. The place of publication generally is that of the first edition, with other locations only included for other editions. If an English edition is not listed but an Irish edition is, this means that we have not identified and located an English edition.

In general, we attempted to list republications in major parts of the English speaking world, including Ireland, England, Europe, and North America (in that order), but only when they were contemporaneous with a first edition, usually published in London or Dublin. This serves to illustrate the spread of Irish fiction to other countries. At the end of this listing of publications, we mention whether the book was reprinted in recent times.

The names of publishers are transcribed literally, but this often led to inconsistencies because of lack of uniformity across different publications. If two or more publishing houses have collaborated in the publication of the book, all publishers are listed, and the order of names was standardized. If the publisher's name is not known this is indicated in brackets [publisher?], but we made every attempt to minimize such missing information. In cases where no publisher is known, we included the name of the printer (other than that, printer's names could not be included here). For the sake of brevity, we used some abbreviations such as '&' replacing 'and', and 'Co.' replacing 'Company'. Some volumes were privately published, printed for the author, or remained 'unpublished' and this is noted in the bibliographical details. We also note if a work was printed in a limited edition and the size of that edition. However, we do not generally note the format of books (e.g., folio, octavo, duodecimo), partly because of widespread rebinding of volumes and cutting of margins.

The date of publication is based on information on the title page, allusions in the text, and/or the date of preface. Where it was not possible for us to inspect the book in person, the date was gleaned from bibliographical sources. In the case of undated publications, the conjectured date of publication is given in brackets. This information is generally obtained from the British Library Catalogue, or from the dates that a publisher was established at a certain address (e.g., the Dublin publisher James Duffy changed addresses repeatedly and the dates of his moves provide an indication of a title's publication date). The year of publication as given on the title page in some instances may be different than the actual publication date. The actual publication date may be known from newspaper advertisements (sometimes publishers post-dated the date on the title page, a practice often used for books published late in the year. For example, a novel actually published in December 1814 may carry the date of 1815 on its title page). When there is doubt about the publication date, this is indicated by a question mark (e.g., [1877?]). In the case of books published in the United States, the year of publication often is the year that copyright was registered. If the date of publication could not be ascertained, this is indicated by '[date?]'. Occasionally an author would publish more than one volume of prose fiction in a given year. Because of the poor documentation of actual publication dates, it proved impossible to rank the publication of titles within a given year.

If there was a dedication in the volume, this information is listed in parentheses after the date of publication. We thought that the inclusion of the information was important because the dedicatee(s) often represent members of an author's social circle (although sometimes an author selected a dedicatee because of that person's social standing in society). Because of space limitations, we provide information about the background of dedicatee(s) if such information clarified aspects of an author's life. We do not repeat in entries for later editions of a work the mention of dedicatee(s) with the exception of those cases where the dedication changed subsequent to the first publication.

Following the date of publication, we mention the number of volumes in which the title was published (if more than one). We indicate whenever different volumes were published in a single volume, which often applied to later editions (e.g., '3 volumes in 1').

We also note whether a volume is illustrated (indicated by 'ill.'). Since the study of illustrations in works of Irish works of fiction is much neglected, mention is made, where possible, of artists' names.[135] However, information about illustrations is not as comprehensive as we would have liked, because we have not been able to inspect all titles first-hand. Occasionally, the name of an artist on the illustration was not legible. Since most works of Irish fiction were published in London, the illustrators used were mostly non-Irish.

As much as possible, we included the first 'new' edition of a work, which could be a revision of the text, but this was not necessarily so in all instances. Clearly, the term 'new edition' was used inconsistently by publishers, and, for some, was a ploy to imply that the book had been in demand by readers.

We noted when the book was republished under a different title than the first edition (including a shortened version of the original title, often caused by the deletion of the subtitle), or if the contents changed (e.g., republication of a subset of stories in a volume, or the introduction of one or more stories). In such instances, we provided all relevant bibliographic details for that volume.

Whenever possible, translations of the work in French, German and Dutch are provided, but such listings are not meant to be exhaustive. For translated works, we note where known the name of the translator.

We also included information about a series in which a given title might have appeared (e.g., 'Mrs L.T. Meade Series'). Pagination of volumes is not given, because of our inability to examine all copies and because of insurmountable variations among copies due to rebinding (however, when we encountered a slim volume, we included the number of pages, so that the reader would be alerted to look for a smaller-sized book).

---

135 Studies on individual Irish illustrators of the period are rare, but see, for example, R. Engen, *Richard Doyle* (Stroud, Glos., 1983).

The books covered in this *Guide* were issued in a variety of bound forms, including soft-bound books, paperbacks, or yellow-backs; and some were issued in wrappers. However, details of such binding types have not been included, but can be found in several reference sources (e.g., Topp, Dime Novels, etc.). For bound books, we mention variant bindings, but we cannot say that we have exhausted this topic.

8. **Sources for Bibliographic Details** The information *Source* at the end of each title entry serves to inform the reader about reference source(s) in which the volume is mentioned or discussed in more in detail. Often these sources include more detailed bibliographical information, such as the pagination of volumes, blank pages, advertisements, etc. (for example, the collections of Sadleir and Wolff, the bibliographies of Rafroidi, Raven, Garside and their colleagues), or reviews (e.g., Belanger; British Fiction; Forster; Forster 2). For books published between 1800 and 1829, reviews, newspaper advertisements, publishing papers, subscription lists, and library catalogue information are given in *British fiction, 1800–1829. A database of production, circulation, and reception* (<http://www.british-fiction.cf.ac.uk>). Note that the accuracy of many of the source materials was mostly high, but we noted occasional errors in our bibliographical information (e.g., Brown 'mistakenly states…'). Although Father Brown's *Ireland in fiction* (Dublin, 1916, repr. 1919) is a pioneering work, it often referred to earlier editions than we could document in a large variety of other sources (we noted this in the **Source** section).

9. **Location** consists of a brief listing of libraries that hold a copy of the volume(s), but this information is not exhaustive. The main aim was to show the availability of copies in three main locations: Ireland, Britain and North America but this was not always possible, largely because of the rarity of some of the books. For the NUC locations, readers are referred to the NUC volumes (or to the more recent OCLC database). We also checked whether the British Library had a copy of books in our list (initially using the British Library catalogue up to 1965, later complemented by the British Library electronic integrated catalogue and the electronic union catalogue, COPAC). In addition, we inspected the sections on Irish fiction in the National Library of Ireland, but it is possible that we may have missed some books lodged outside the main Irish fiction section, as some fiction is scattered in many other sections of that library. We also note whether a volume was reproduced in microfiche (see references to the Grail and to Corvey), and whether a volume was reprinted in the twentieth or twenty-first century. Despite extensive searches, we have not been able to locate copies of many of the volumes: this is indicated by the phrase 'No copy located'.

Occasionally, we found that a volume was published in North America but, apparently, not in Ireland or Britain. We can speculate that this was because the author had contact with a North American publisher only, or because the publisher reprinted a novel from an earlier publication in a periodical. It should be noted, however, that prior to 1891, many North American publishers pirated Irish and English authors' works.[136] The competition for issuing the pirated works often was high, and this is documented in our list of publication by rival publishing houses in cities such as New York or Chicago.

10. **Commentary** Where possible, we included a brief summary of the content of the books. Our method in providing such summaries was to give a précis of the story, main characters, but to exclude evaluative remarks (either our own or those of scholars). When we used other compilers' summaries of novels, we deleted their appraisals (but readers interested in these can follow this as we have provided the source) and, instead, concentrated on the content. The length of the summaries varies. Sometimes all that is known is whether the book does or does

---

136 The U.S.A.'s Chace Act was passed in that year and offered protection to qualified foreign, non-resident authors.

not have Irish content (e.g., descriptions of Irish historical events, significant Irish characters, etc.). Where appropriate, we note whether the volume contains poetry or plays, which we do not list in detail, and whether the book had been issued earlier in parts. Given the thrust of this *Guide*, books with Irish content are described in greater detail than books with non-Irish content. For anthologies, we attributed individual stories to authors wherever possible, including their names in square brackets following the story title.

The Commentary section also lists the titles of stories for those volumes that appear in anthologies of multiple authors or in a collection of short stories by a particular author. Unless a book consisted of a few relatively long stories, it proved impossible to provide summaries of each short story. Occasionally, the *Commentary* section contains additional bibliographical information, such as whether the work or stories had been published earlier in book form or in a periodical.

11. **Sources for Commentary** Many of the summaries have been provided by the second author (indicated by ML), but because of the volume of titles and because of their limited accessibility, we also relied on summaries from other sources, such as those by Brown, Nield, Sutherland, Field Day and from catalogues of antiquarian book dealers. We are much indebted to these sources for this information. Other sources for commentary often reflect the more extensive information mentioned in the sources listed at the end of the biographical sketch. For books that we did not see ourselves, we had to rely on the best available reference sources with their inherent limitations.

V. SELECTED KEY ISSUES BASED ON FINDINGS FROM THIS 'GUIDE'

To address several key issues about Irish literary history, particularly its authors, publishers, and books for the period 1650 to 1900, we coded and entered many aspects of the information of this guide into a data system. The following text illustrates examples of analyses based on the access data system.

AUTHORS

Irish and Non-Irish Authors
This *Guide* contains information about 1455 named authors, but the actual number is higher because it does not include the 286 titles written by an unknown number of anonymous authors. Among the named authors, we identified 760 authors who either were certainly Irish or probably Irish. It should be noted that because of inadequate biographical information, the nationality of a fairly large number of authors (188) who wrote about Ireland and the Irish could not be established. Although it is probable that a proportion of these authors were Irish, they have been excluded from summaries on Irish authors.

The *Guide* also includes non-Irish authors (thus excluding Irish emigrants) who wrote fiction about Ireland or the Irish (Figure 3). Out of a total of 241 foreign authors, just over half were English (145, or 60.2%), and one quarter (59, or 24.5%) were from the United States. A few of the foreign authors came from Canada (10), and fewer hailed from Australia (3) or India (4). Among Europeans authors, France produced the highest number of authors writing about Ireland (14), with smaller numbers from Belgium, the Netherlands, and Germany.

Emergence of Foreign Authors Writing about Ireland
Figure 4 shows that, not surprisingly, British authors emerged first and that their numbers increased from the 1800s onward. Writers from the United States began writing about Ireland during the 1790s, but only steadily increased from the 1830s onward. Thus, the efflorescence

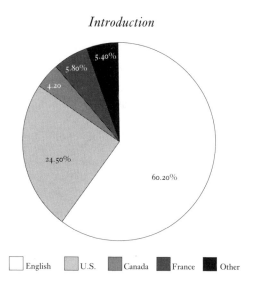

Figure 3 Nationality of foreign authors writing about Ireland and the Irish.

of Irish literature during the 1820s and 1830s was strengthened by the rise of authors from the United States (and to a lesser extent Canada) writing about Irish matters, particularly conflicts in Ireland.

Gender

The results show that only four out of ten Irish authors (38.2%) were women. However, in the period 1780 to 1819, the number of new female authors exceeded the number of new male authors by a ratio of almost six to four (61 vs. 47). This is also found in data on British authors.[137] It should be noted, however, that this female dominance reversed itself in the 1820s when the female to male ratio became about three to seven (a mere 13 new female authors compared to 43 new male authors), and never became equitable afterwards. The shift in the gender balance in Irish authorship coincided with the increased output of Irish fiction during the first Irish literary revival of the 1820s and 1830s.

The proportional decrease in women writers after the 1810s coincided with the decline in at least two genres of fiction which Irish women writers had favoured: Gothic tales and epistolary novels, both of which, as the *Guide* shows, went out of fashion in the late 1820s. While these two genres declined in the period 1790–1820, there was a growth in the popularity of other types of fiction, most notably in educational fiction for young people (e.g., Maria Edgeworth and Abigail Roberts), and the national tale (Sydney Owenson, later Lady Morgan). What also changed in the same period was a decrease in the use of pseudonyms by women authors and an increase in publishing of fiction under their own names.

Religious Background

Of the documented Irish authors, just over one quarter (136; 28.5%) came from a Catholic background and/or professed the Catholic faith, and the remainder were overwhelmingly Protestant.[138] These figures are rough estimates, because the religion of many Irish authors is

---

137 This includes Irish authors. Sources: Garside, p. 74; R. Schöwerling, H. Steinecke & G. Tiggesbäumker, 'Literatur und Ergfahrungswandel 1789–1830', printed paper presented at the Internationalen Corvey-Symposions, 8–12 June 1993, Paderborn, Germany. 138 This includes individuals who we thought were in all probability Protestant.

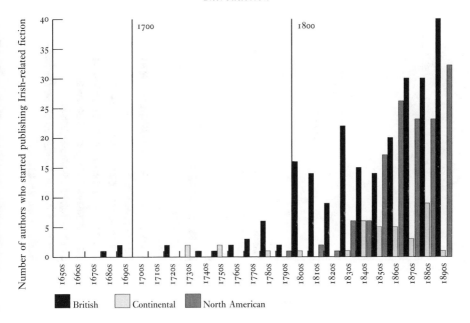

Figure 4 Number of foreign authors writing about Ireland
and the Irish between 1650 and 1899.

not documented. Moreover, some Catholics converted to protestantism (e.g., William Carleton, Mortimer and Richard O'Sullivan), while some Protestants converted to catholicism (e.g., Miss Eleanor Agnew, Trevor Lloyd Ashe, Nathaniel Burton, and Margaret Anne Cusack, later known as the Nun of Kenmare).

Figure 5 shows that the number of new Protestant authors (i.e., those producing their first volume of fiction) was modest until the 1780s and only increased to 10 for the decade of the 1790s, after which the numbers dropped slightly during the next two decades. Only in the 1830s did the number of new Protestant authors increase to about 20 per decade, a level which, with the exception of the 1840s was maintained through the 1880s to drop back to 12 in the 1890s.

The majority of the Protestant authors were members of a congregation of the Church of Ireland, and only a handful of dissenters are known to have been authors of fiction (9 were Quakers, 9 Presbyterians and one Methodist). Relative to their population, Church of Ireland authors appear to have contributed more to authorship of fiction than dissenters.

Figure 5 also shows those decades in which Catholic authors became active. Compared to their Protestant counterparts, the number of new Catholic authors during the first half of the nineteenth century was low and only accelerated in the 1820s. The number remained about constant at 5 to 6 new Catholic authors per decade over the 1830s through the 1850s but, starting in the 1860s, the rate almost tripled to about 13–18 per decade, and this remained somewhat stable over the 1870s and 1880s. Only in the 1890s did the number of new Catholic authors exceed the number of new Protestant authors (18 versus 12).

Many contemporary sources commented on the exodus of Irish authors to England, particularly London (see Introduction, Section I). Out of the total number of Irish authors, in the case of 431 the place of death is not known. Of those whose place of death is known, six out of ten died outside of Ireland (Figure 6): 40.5% died in England, 11.6 percent died in

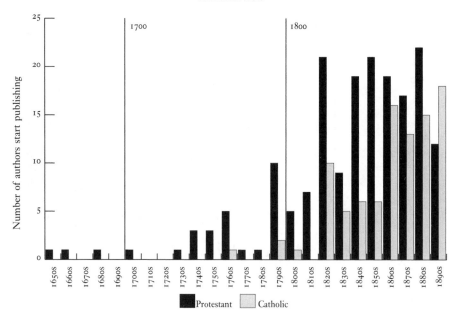

Figure 5 Changes in religious affiliation of new Irish authors
of fiction between 1650 and 1899.

North America, 5.6% died on the European Continent, while the remaining died in Australia,
New Zealand, India and South Africa, and a few other places.[139]

Geographic Concentration of Authors' Birthplaces in Ireland
When David J. O'Donoghue published his *The geographical distribution of Irish ability* (Dublin,
1906), he included all types of persons of talent (including authors of any type of writing) and
concluded that the six highest concentrations were in Cos. Dublin, Waterford, Limerick, Cork,
Meath and Kilkenny, and the lowest six concentrations were in Cos. Longford, Monaghan,
Leitrim, Mayo, Cavan, and Armagh.

Since O'Donoghue's tally one hundred years ago, numerous other Irish authors of fiction
have been identified. Based on our count of Irish birthplaces of authors, Figure 7 shows that
the highest concentration of writers of fiction were in Co. Dublin, and second, in Co. Cork.
Whereas in Co. Dublin more authors were born in the city rather than in the county, the
reverse was true for Co. Cork. The county producing the third-highest number of authors
was Co. Tipperary, followed by Co. Down and Co. Antrim. Thus, there were two clusters of
high author-producing counties: one in Munster (Cos. Cork, Tipperary, Limerick and
Waterford), constituting one quarter of authors (25.4%), and one in East Ulster (Cos. Down
and Antrim). It is remarkable that a string of counties on the border of South Ulster and
Leinster and Connaught (Cos. Armagh, Fermanagh, Tyrone, Monaghan, and Sligo) produced
few authors. A similarly low-producing cluster of counties was situated in central Leinster
(Cos. Kildare, Offaly, Wicklow and Carlow). In slight contrast, several counties in the mid-

---

139 The figures include certain and probable Irish status. It should be noted that these figures are tentative because of
the fact that for a large number of Irish authors whose place of death was not known (N = 431).

Introduction

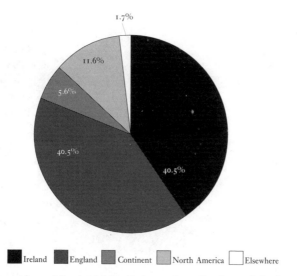

Ireland ■ England ■ Continent ■ North America □ Elsewhere

Figure 6 Known place of death of Irish fiction authors for the period 1650 to 1899.

dle of the country – Cavan, Leitrim, Longford, Louth, Mayo, Meath, Offaly, Roscommon, and Westmeath – were in the mid-range of producing literary authors. Thus, in large parts of Ireland, authorship emerged in relative isolation. However, authorship *and* readership among the gentry and Protestant clergy often took place in small networks as was the case between members of the Edgeworth family, the Forbes family (earl of Granard) of Castle Forbes (Co. Longford), the Pakenhams of Tullynally (Co. Westmeath), the Ruxtons of Black Castle (Co. Meath), and the Beauforts of Collon (Co. Louth).[140] Subscribers' list of works to fiction also show networks that must have linked the novelist Charlotte McCarthy to mostly Catholic readers in Cos. Kilkenny, Waterford and Tipperary during the 1750s.[141]

The reasons why authorship was concentrated in some and not in other counties needs further study. We surmise that regional differences in authorship had much to do with the presence or absence of factors that stimulated the reading of fiction, such as the availability of bookshops, reading societies, and educational institutions. Usually these facilities were concentrated in towns, meaning that counties with few towns were at a disadvantage in producing authors. However, the mere presence of towns in a county was no guarantee that writers would emerge. For example, several towns in Co. Tipperary, which was one of the counties with a strong presence of authors, produced few authors (this applied to, for example, Cashel, Roscrea, Thurles, and Nenagh). The exception was Clonmel, which generated 8 authors of prose works and 5 poets, more than some entire Irish counties. Readership and probably authorship in Clonmel, compared to other towns in Co. Tipperary, was stimulated by the confluence of a higher-than-average number of educational institutions, bookshops, reading rooms, circulating libraries, and locally produced newspapers and books.[142]

Our conclusions on the geographic spread of birthplaces of Irish authors should be viewed with some caution. First, the time frame considered – 1650 to 1900 – is long and may hide con-

140 A.J.C. Hare (ed.), *The life and letters of Maria Edgeworth* (London, 1894), i, pp 160, 162, 315. 141 C. MacCarthy, *The fair moralist* (n.l., 1752). 142 R. Loeber, 'The geography of Irish literary talent at home and abroad, 1650–1900: a historical cartographic approach to authors' lives and the fictional content of their novels in the English language'. Lecture presented at the National University of Ireland, Maynooth, Feb. 2006. The fact that Clonmel had slightly more residents than other towns in Tipperary does not fully explain why it produced more authors.

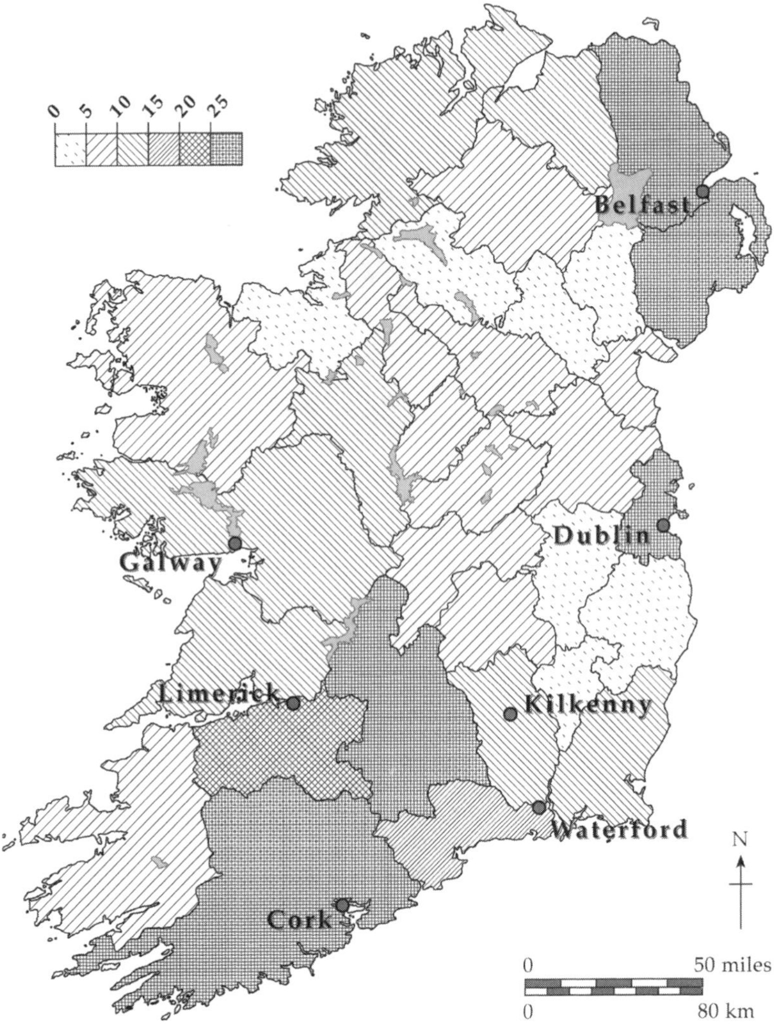

Antrim	25	Down	25	Laois	8	Roscommon	10
(Belfast 14)		Dublin	109	Leitrim	7	Sligo	4
Armagh	2	(Dublin city 99)		Limerick	21	Tipperary	32
Carlow	1	Fermanagh	3	(Limerick city 9)		Tyrone	5
Cavan	7	Galway	14	Longford	8	Waterford	17
Clare	12	(Galway city 6)		Louth	7	(Waterford city 9)	
Cork	47	Kerry	6	Mayo	8	Westmeath	6
(Cork city 20)		Kildare	3	Meath	9	Wexford	12
Derry	12	Kilkenny	12	Monaghan	3	Wicklow	3
Donegal	14	(Kilkenny city 6)		Offaly	8		

Figure 7 Map of Ireland showing the birth county of Irish authors born between 1650 and 1899.

siderable variations per county over the two-and-a-half centuries. Second, the numbers of authors per county in many instances are modest. Third, these statistics reflect the county of birth only, which can be misleading: it is very possible that an author was born in one county, but did not actually live there or even have close ties to that place (this applies, for example to Laurence Sterne and his association with Clonmel). Lastly, the results are tentative; once better biographical information becomes available, it is likely that the above conclusions will need to be modified.

Although we may celebrate those counties with heavy concentrations of authors, there is also a need to highlight those authors who were exceptions to the trends and came from low-producing counties. For example, among the few Monaghan authors is the Revd John Wright, who was the author of *The last of the corbes, or, The MacMahon country: a legend connected with Irish history in 1641* (London, 1835), a historical novel set in that county.

Historical Continuity of Literary Output in Specific Regions in Ireland

A tentative case can be made that there is historical continuity of literary output in certain regions of Ireland. We mentioned in Section I the concentration of Irish poets in Munster and east Ulster during the eighteenth century, and in this Section we observed that the same areas produced more fiction writers in the English language than in other areas in Ireland in the next century. Thus, it is possible that a shift took place from Irish poetry to English prose over a period of hundred years and that this can be best studied in Munster and east Ulster. As an example, Welch noted that the prolific author Justin McCarthy (1830–1912), was a descendant of the McCarthys of Blarney Castle (Co. Cork), who had been patrons and protectors of Dámhscoil na Blárnan (The Bardic School of Blarney).[143] We would add that Justin McCarthy was one of a line of writers: his father was the founder of and a contributor to the *Cork Magazine*, while his son, John Huntly McCarthy (1860–1936), also became an author. Of course, such a single instance of a literary lineage in different media is a mere illustration rather than proof of geographic continuity and transmission of literary skills over time. The question of why such continuity might have taken place should include a study of patrons, readers and teachers and the spread of printed books in these areas.

The possible persistence of literary traditions flourishing in the same area should also take into account that sometime prior to the nineteenth century there was a shift away from the professional poet to peasantry reciting legends in a non-poetic, more narrative form, which did not require training, since almost anyone could recite legends. Several Catholic authors – John Banim, William Carleton (he became oriented towards protestantism later), Gerald Griffin, John Keegan, and Michael James Whitty – were among the first to publish legends in book form during the 1820–1840s. Other writers who in the 1850s and 1860s became standard-bearers of the folk legends from their neighbourhoods were Patrick Kennedy, Canon John O'Hanlon, and somewhat later, Séumas MacManus. In probably all cases, the writer was a necessary intermediary in translating and editing orally-transmitted stories and legends into the written word. As Gerald Griffin said, 'Avowing the sources from which the materials were taken the collector thinks himself entitled to tell the stories after his own liking'.[144]

Family Background of Irish Authors

The social status of writers of Irish fiction changed much over time and several major trends can be identified. Earlier we mentioned Seamus Deane's proposition that Irish literary activity in the nineteenth century sprang in part from economic retrenchments experienced by the Ascendancy. Figure 8 lends some support to this, in that it shows that the number of gentry (including nobil-

---

143 R. Welch, *A history of verse translation from the Irish, 1789–1897* (Gerrards Cross, 1988), p. 58.   144 Earls, 'Supernatural legends', pp 95–7, 102–3, 109.

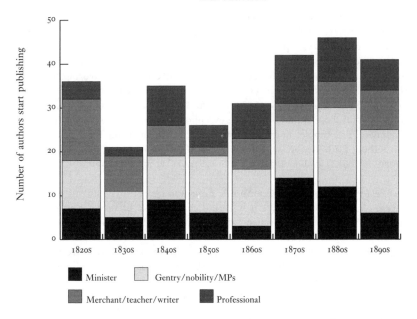

Figure 8 Changes in family background of Irish fiction authors between 1650 and 1899.

ity and MPs) publishing fiction increased, especially from the 1840s onwards, and by the 1890s the mostly Protestant gentry constituted one third (33.9%) of the Irish authors writing fiction.

The number of writers whose father were ministers, although smaller than those whose fathers were of the gentry, gradually grew and peaked in the 1870s and 1880s, decreasing afterwards. This group included many ministers themselves and their daughters and sons. Although several of them contributed to religious fiction, a large proportion also produced other forms of fiction, such as Gothic fiction, love and courtship stories, and fiction centred around women's issues. The waxing and waning of literary contributions of this group needs to be studied in the context of the second Reformation with its emphasis on converting Irish Catholics to protestantism, and as a function of changing economic conditions such as the tithe wars and the disestablishment of the Church of Ireland. The offspring of ministers, once these ministers retired or died, often lost their homes and as a consequence were more pressed into alternative modes of earning money, including journalism and writing fiction, than were the off-spring of the Irish gentry.

Figure 8 shows that the number of Irish authors from the middle class (merchants, teachers, and writers) peaked in the 1820s and did not reach a higher level throughout the remainder of the century (it is not clear why this was the case). The number of writers who came from a farming background (such as William Carleton) remained small throughout the century (not shown in Figure 8). In contrast, the number of Irish authors who came from a professional background (such as doctors and lawyers) increased particularly after the 1850s. Most of the male authors had a concurrent or previous occupation other than writing. However, for the majority of the female authors writing was their mainstay in life.

In summary, the *Guide* provides a glimpse of the changing social backgrounds of Irish authors, but much more detailed study is needed to clarify which forces differentially affected various social strata in Irish society in nurturing authorship. This is all the more important since authors from different social strata in Ireland wrote in different ways about the country and its problems, and thus influenced the shape of Irish literature.

Introduction

PUBLISHERS

Dublin publishers produced in the eighteenth century record numbers of reprints of English, and translations of French and to a lesser extent German novels at about half the price of the London originals.[145] The situation was similar in the Netherlands where English, French, and German fiction was pirated very widely.[146] In both countries, this meant that a larger segment of the reading population could purchase novels (compared to those countries where cheap reprints were not available), and that more of these novels found homes in lending libraries, and thus could foment literary taste and ambitions, especially in towns where such libraries were established. In the 1790s, however, the Dublin publishing industry, partly because of difficulties in the paper supply, had gone into a decline. However, Cork and Belfast became modestly-sized centres for publishing of novels at this time.

A decisive plunge in the Dublin publishing and printing industry took place as a result of the Union between Ireland and England in 1801, and with the introduction of the Copyright Act. The act made the publishing of pirated books illegal, and thus seriously diminished Irish publishing enterprises. It also led to an increase in the price of books for Irish readers, which must have restricted their access to literature. Reduced financial strength of Dublin publishing houses undermined their patronage of new Irish fiction writers.[147] Figure 9 shows that the number of original Irish fiction titles (that is, not reprints) published in Dublin decreased between the 1780s and 1820s, but accelerated in the 1830s, after which the rate remained somewhat stable, but decreased after the 1860s, perhaps as a result of increased competition by London publishers (see below). James Duffy, who published Catholic fiction, figures prominently among the nineteenth century Dublin publishers. Other regular publishers of Irish fiction prior to 1900 were William Curry, Richard Moore Tims, M'Glashan (also spelled McGlashan), Sealy, Bryers and Walker, and M.H. Gill. Compared to Dublin, the publication of fiction in Cork and Belfast remained much smaller (see Figure 9), peaking around 1790s to 1830s for Cork, and around the 1830s and again around the 1870s to 1890s for Belfast. No other provincial towns in Ireland consistently contributed to the publication of Irish fiction before 1900. Belanger rightly speaks of a shift in publishing from the provincial Irish towns to Dublin during the eighteenth and nineteenth centuries.[148]

A study by Garside has made it possible to compare the output of original fiction between Dublin and Edinburgh, which shows that Dublin publishers produced more original fiction in the period 1770 to 1799, and continued to do so in the period 1808 to 1829 (publishers in other Scottish towns published far less original fiction than those in Edinburgh).[149] Thus, in the British Isles, Dublin was the second city after London in terms of the publication of original fiction, albeit on a much smaller scale.

Dublin publishing houses, however, in turn succumbed to the dominance of the London publishing house in the production of fiction and this became more manifest during the course of the nineteenth century (see Figures 9 and 10). The number of original Irish fiction titles and works by Irish authors published in London increased slowly from the 1750s onwards, accelerated during much of the nineteenth century, particularly in the 1880s and 1890s. In the latter decade, 656 works of Irish fiction were published in London, compared to 28 in Dublin (a mere 2.8%). In London, among the major publishers who sponsored Irish authors were William Lane (the Minerva Press), Richard Bentley, and Henry Colburn (for the many other publishers who issued Irish fiction, see publishers' index at the end of this *Guide*).

---

145 Raven, p. 29.   146 See Mateboer, passim.   147 J. Benson, The Dublin book trade 1801–1850. Unpublished Ph.D. dissertation, Trinity College, Dublin, 2000, pp 15–17, 136; Munter, passim; Pollard, passim; Pollard 2, passim.   148 Belanger, *Irish novel*, p. 24.   149 P. Garside, 'National fictions of Scotland, 1789–1834'. Paper presented at Centre for Editorial and Intertextual Research, Cardiff University, Cardiff, Wales, England, Sept. 2001.

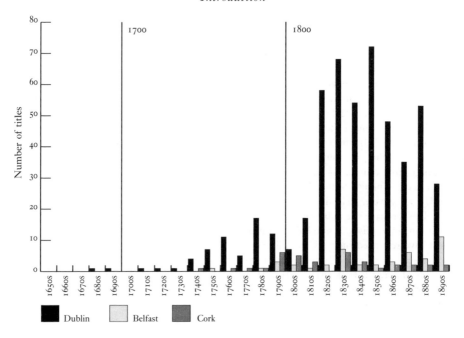

Figure 9 Changes in the number of original Irish fiction titles published in
Dublin, Belfast and Cork between 1650 and 1899.

In North America, original Irish fiction became more prominent, especially during the
second half of the nineteenth century. Some of the titles were produced by Irish men and
women who had emigrated from Ireland. Other titles were produced by North American
authors often with no obvious link to Ireland. Within the North American continent, most
works of Irish fiction were published in the United States. Figure 11 shows the publication
of Irish fiction in the largest US cities (leaving aside a scattering of publications from smaller
towns for which see index of publishers). The number of Irish fiction titles published in New
York increased from the 1830s and overtook those published in Philadelphia and Boston in
the 1840s. By the 1890s, more Irish works of fiction were published in New York than in
Dublin (Figure 9 shows 88 in New York versus 28 in Dublin). Among the New York publishing houses, D. & J. Sadlier and P.J. Kenedy published Irish-Catholic fiction, but dime-
novel publishers such as Beadle & Adams and many other publishers also contributed to the
spread of Irish-related fiction in North America (see publishers' index at the end of this *Guide*).

BOOKS

Bindings and Prices
Irish bindings of the eighteenth century have been studied, but those of the nineteenth century
have received scant attention.[150] The colour illustrations in this volume supply examples of the
many different types of bindings. Cloth and paper covers were simultaneously used throughout

150 E. Reilly, 'Beyond gilt shamrock' in L.W. McBride (ed.), *Images, icons and the Irish national imagination* (Dublin,
1999), pp 98–112; M. Craig, *Irish book bindings, 1600–1800* (London, 1954); S. Bennett, *Trade bookbinding in the British
Isles* (London, 2004).

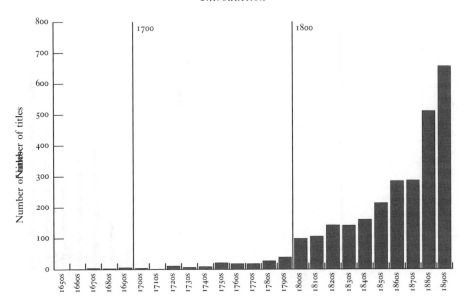

Figure 10 Changes in the number of original Irish-related fiction titles published in London between 1650 and 1899.

the century, with paper covers being the norm for dime novels and short fiction in general. In the course of the nineteenth century, the same titles were issued in different binding types, with less expensive bindings being at least half the cost of the most expensive bindings. Another major way that publishers improved the affordability of fiction was to issue volumes in parts. The earliest-known publication of fiction in parts was undertaken by the Dublin publisher William Curry Jnr in 1839 (three years after Chapman and Hall in London pioneered the publication in parts of Charles Dickens's *Pickwick papers*). The first printing in parts by the Dublin publisher James Duffy that we have come across is an advertisement in 1857 for the publication of Brother James's *Tales and stories for the amusement and instruction of youth* with the announcement that the 'The twelve takes [i.e., parts] may be had in Neatly printed Covers, price 4d. each'.[151] The publication of fiction in parts, however, became uncommon after the 1850s, possibly as a result of the proliferation of magazines and newspapers, which made fiction available at much lower prices.

Illustrations and Problems of Representation
The depiction of Irish settings and interpretation of Irishness became a major issue in the illustration of Irish fiction. During the eighteenth and nineteenth centuries, many Irish illustrators (draughts-men and engravers) had migrated to England, leaving few behind to work on Irish-produced books. Among the earliest illustrators of Irish fiction were members of the Edgeworth family, including Maria's sister Charlotte, and her step-mother Frances, who made drawings, later engraved for *The parent's assistant* (London, 1800 edn).[152]

As a program of national literature developed in the early 1840s, Thomas Osborn Davis observed 'how suited for countless illustrations are our Irish novels'.[153] Around this time the

---

151 Advertised in Gerald Griffin, *The half Sir* (Dublin, 1857). 152 [Book of drawings by members of the Edgeworth family], endorsed 'This book belonged to Aunt Harriet Beaufort ...', [n.d., but late 1790s through 1820s?] (Private collection). 153 A. Griffith (ed.), *Thomas Davis: the thinker & teacher* (Dublin, 1916), p. 138; see also S. Burdy, *Ardglass, or the*

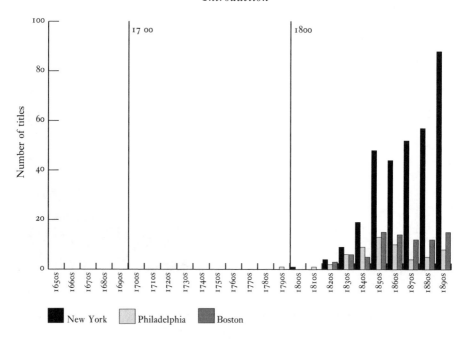

Figure 11 Changes in the number of original Irish-related fiction titles published in New York, Philadelphia and Boston between 1650 and 1899.

Dublin publisher Duffy advertised Irish fiction illustrated by Irish authors, using this as a selling point in his advertisement in *The New Irish Journal of Information for the People* (Dublin, 1842). Among the Irish artists illustrating Irish works were John Kirkwood and George Measom.

Since most Irish fiction was published in England, the majority of its illustrators were English. Thus, stereotypes of Irish matters were common.[154] Charles Lever, to counteract ignorance about matters Irish, advised his friend, the English illustrator Hablot Browne, better known as Phiz, to study the features of the Irish delegates in the British House of Commons as a source of inspiration for the illustration of Lever's novels.[155] Since illustrations and book covers influenced book purchasing and communicated to readers many aspects of Irish life, they remain a fertile field for further study.

Popular Books and Popular Authors
Most Irish authors wrote a single book of fiction, and that book was usually published in a single edition only. The reasons for this are not clear, but may have to do with the age at which such an author came to write, because many of the single-volume authors first published when they were in their forties or later and usually published recollections of their life couched in fiction. This combination of late publishing of a single volume in a single edition made it rare for a particular book or author to become popular. Table 2 provides examples of much reprinted Irish works of fiction, many of which are not well-known nowadays.

During the period 1750 to 1770, three famous Irish authors, Laurence Sterne, Charles Johnson, and Oliver Goldsmith, were among the twenty most republished authors from Ireland

ruined castles (Dublin, 1802), pp iii–iv.   **154** L.P. Curtis, *Apes and angels. the Irishman in Victorian caricature* (Washington DC, 1971).   **155** V.B. Lester, *Phiz. The man who drew Dickens* (London, 2004), p. 112.

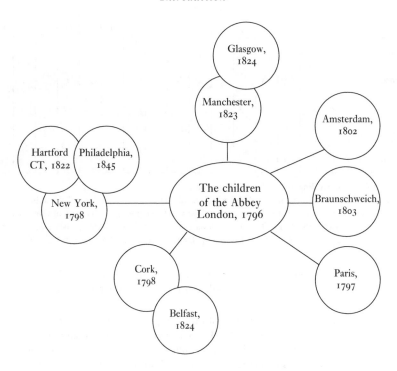

Figure 12 Geographic spread of the reprints of Regina Maria Roche's *The children of the abbey* between 1797 and 1845.

and Britain. Their most reprinted works were *Tristam Shandy, gentleman* (Sterne; York, 1760), *Chrysal; or the adventures of a guinea* (Johnson; London, 1760), and *The vicar of Wakefield* (Goldsmith; London, 1766).[156] In addition, Henry Brooke's *The fool of quality*, published in stages between 1766 and 1770 was in high demand by readers.[157]

Among the most popular books of Irish fiction published in the 1790s was Regina Maria Roche's *The children of the abbey* (London, 1796, 4 vols.) which was reprinted about eighty times throughout the nineteenth century. Figure 12 shows the early history of its reprinting and the high speed with which this novel spread throughout Europe and North America. Remarkably, it was republished over the longest period of time in the United States – almost one hundred years – after it first appeared in London in 1796.

Aside from *The children of the abbey*, Roche wrote fourteen other novels. Figure 13 shows the extent that her novels (all first published in London) were republished in Ireland, France, Holland, Germany, and the United States. Republication of her works was more concentrated in France and the United States than in other countries (this also applied to the republication of the works of the Banim brothers). Despite the fact that during the course of her writing career Mrs Roche moved back from England to Ireland and set more of her fiction in Ireland, she continued to rely on English rather than Irish publishers to publish her books, and her later works of fiction were never republished in Ireland.

156 See also Cole, p. 29 for a list of the most popular works by Sterne and Goldsmith in Irish private libraries in the eighteenth century. Sterne and Goldsmith lived for most of their life in England and are often seen as English rather than Irish novelists. 157 Raven, pp 14–15, 17, 19.

Novel (total)	1	2	3	4	5	6	7	8	9	10	11	12	13	14	15
Ireland (4)		x	x	x	x										
France (11)	x	x	x	x	x	x		x		x	x	x	x		
Holland (2)			x			x									
Germany (4)	x		x					x					x		
United States (10)	x	x	x	x	x		x	x	x	x				x	

x = republication; Shading = novels with Irish content;
1 = Vicar of Lansdowne (1789); 2 = Maid of the hamlet (1793); 3 = Children of the abbey (1796); 4 = Clermont (1798); 5 = Nocturnal visit (1800); 6 = Discarded son (1807); 7 = Houses of Osma and Almeria (1810); 8 = Monastery (1813); 9 = Trecothiek bower (1814); 10 = Munster cottage boy (1820); 11 = Bridal (1823); 12 = Tradition (1824); 13 = Castle chapel (1825); 14 = Contrast (1828); 15 = Nun's picture (1836).

Figure 13 The republication of Regina Maria Roche's novels (first published in London) in Ireland, France, Holland, Germany, and the United States.

Turning to the nineteenth century, with the exception of several novels published by Sir Walter Scott, Maria Edgeworth's *Helen* (London, 1834, 3 vols.) had 'almost the largest circulation of any novel of its time in three volumes'.[158] The majority of editions of Maria Edgeworth's collected works appeared in London. However, the majority of collected works of several other Irish authors, especially those writing about Ireland, appeared in the United States. For instance, the collected works of the Banim brothers and Gerald Griffin were mostly published in New York, where they remained in print for decades.

By far the most productive Irish-born novelist for the entire period covered by this *Guide* was Elizabeth Smith, better known under her pseudonym of 'L.T. Meade'. She produced about 300 titles as well as innumerable stories for periodicals. The exact number of her books of fiction is elusive because some of her volumes may have been reprinted in the United States under different titles. Her readership extended throughout the British dominions. Constance A. Barnicoat's survey of British vs. Colonial and Indian girls' reading, published in 1906, showed that Colonial and Indian girls ranked Elizabeth Smith's works fifth among the first ten most popular 'British' authors.[159] However, often overlooked is the fact that aside from fiction for girls, Elizabeth Smith wrote crime fiction, social protest fiction, science fiction, medical fiction, and fiction expressly written for young women entering the work force.

The Market for Irish Fiction
As mentioned previously, much Irish fiction was written for the British reading market. However, authors, critics and publishers varied in their perception of how much the British book market could tolerate in terms of Irish works. The information in this *Guide* makes it possible to test statements by these individuals against the production numbers of works with Irish titles.

An early instance of a reviewer commenting on the feasibility of publishing Irish fiction is a review of Samuel Lover's *Legends and stories of Ireland* in the *London Literary Gazette* of 1832,

158 Wolff, 1991a, citing from the Bentley Private Catalogue; Butler, p. 492; M. Sadleir, *The evolution of publishers' binding styles, 1770–1900* (London, 1930), p. 34*n*; D. Kaser, *The cost book of Carey & Lea, 1825–1838* (Philadelphia, 1963), passim. 159 Table in K. Flint, *The woman reader* (Oxford, 1993), pp 160–1).

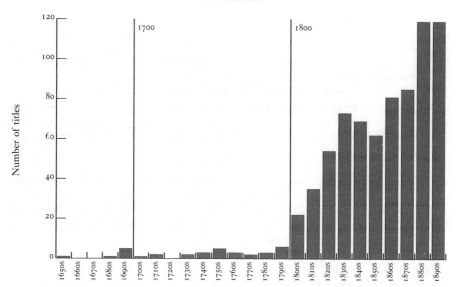

Figure 14 Changes in the number of books with Irish titles published between 1650 and 1899.

which mentioned that 'Irish tales and legends have been both so very good and so very plentiful that, to use a Dublin bay simile, 'there's a glut of herrings in the market".[160] After the poor sale of Anthony Trollope's *The Kellys and the OKellys* (London, 1848), the publisher Henry Colburn wrote 'it is evident that readers do not like novels on Irish subjects so well as on others'.[161] Trollope, however, continued to write Irish novels. In the introduction to his London-published *Castle Richmond* (*c*.1860) he observed: 'I wonder whether the novel-reading world ... will be offended if I lay the plot of my story in Ireland ... Irish stories are not popular with the booksellers ... Irish novels were once popular enough. But there is a fashion in novels, as there is in colours and petticoats, and now I fear they are a drug on the market'.[162] In contrast, the author M. Doyle writing in 1885 claimed that Irish fiction had made a comeback in popularity during the previous decades. 'Of late, *Irish novels* have been rather the fashion; and it is said that one of our most successful authors has expressed his desire to 'be able' to write an Irish novel.'[163]

It is instructive to compare comments with a tabulation of the terms 'Irish', 'Ireland', 'Emerald Isle', and 'Erin' in titles published in Ireland and England between 1650 and 1899. Figure 14 shows that the number of books with Irish titles was modest during the eighteenth century; increased sharply from about 1800 onward; leveled off in the 1840s to 1860s and increased especially during the 1880s and 1890s. Thus, the popularity of Irish fiction varied significantly over the period and confirmed the comments by contemporary authors, critics, and publishers cited above.

Novels, Romances, Tales and Stories
The present-day classification of works of fiction in categories such as novels, romances, and stories is not a precise science (illustrated by Seamus Deane in his preface to this *Guide*). In

---

160 Cited in Hayley, 'Eerishers', p. 46. 161 N. John Hall (ed.), *The letters of Anthony Trollope* (Stanford, 1983), i, p. 17. 162 Cited in Kelley, *The Irishman in the English novel*, p. 29, from undated ed. of *Castle Richmond*, pp 1–2 (this novel first appeared in 1860). 163 Preface by M. E. T. [i.e., M. Doyle] to *Exiled from Erin: A story of Irish peasant life* (Dublin: James Duffy & Sons [1885 or later]).

the eighteenth and nineteenth centuries, authors' or publishers' use of subtitles of, for example, a 'novel' or a 'romance', on title pages[164] formed a kind of guide to readers about different categories of fiction. Some novelists, including Maria Edgeworth, never used the subtitle 'a novel' to any of her works of fiction. This reflected the negative impact she believed that novels had on readers.[165]

The *Guide* shows that of all subtitles (including novel, romance, sketch, story or tales), the designation a 'tale' or 'tales' was the most often used (697), followed by 'story' (or its plural form) which occurred on 544 title pages. In comparison, 'novel' was less used (468 instances) and 'romance' was less common (201 instances), while 'sketch' or 'sketches' was used least (63 instances).

As mentioned in previous sections, most attention in Irish literary studies has been devoted to novels and much less to stories. This was certainly not because stories were less common than novels: according to our count, two thirds (66.1%) of books on Irish fiction were characterised as story (or stories), tale(s) or sketch(es), with the remainder being novels and romances. Thus, a very strong tradition of publishing Irish stories, tales, and sketches existed, especially during the nineteenth century.

Facts and Realities in Fiction
Thuente emphasized that 'numerous introductions and prefaces to Irish novels had declared [their intention] ... to represent Ireland 'as it really is''.[166] In fact a large proportion of Irish works of fiction present a blend of facts and fiction (also stressed by Seamus Deane in his preface to the *Guide* and by other literary historians).[167] Some nineteenth-century Irish authors commented on the need to describe facts about Ireland and the Irish. For example, Lady Morgan's preface to her *Florence Macarthy* (London, 1819), states that "the national tale', with which the reader is here presented, is no pathetic appeal to public compassion. It is, indeed, impossible to speak of Ireland, still less to take it as the scene of a narrative, without frequent allusion to its starving, squalid, and diseased population ...'[168] Also in the preface to her *O'Donnel, a national tale* (London, 1814) she claimed to present a novel revealing the 'flat realities of life'.[169] Numerous other examples of factual representations of Irish individuals, life circumstances and Irish settings can be found in a multitude of Irish works of fiction published in the nineteenth century. It should be understood, however, that an author's claim of factuality may not have been accurate, and that other authors not claiming factuality may actually have written their fiction on a partly factual basis.

Book titles are one method of clarifying changes over time in the mix of fact and fiction. Figure 15 shows that the number of works of Irish fiction referring in their titles or prefaces to facts and comparable terms[170] was very uncommon during first half of the eighteenth century, and remained small during most of the second part of that century, and increased during the early-nineteenth century. The rate peaked during the decade after the Famine, and although fluctuating subsequently, remained high. Changes in the presentation of 'factual' or 'real' stories in fiction reflect the choice of different genres of fiction, and the move away from fantasy fiction, epistolary and Gothic novels.

---

164 P. Garside, J. Raven & R. Schöwerling, 'General introduction' in Raven 2, p. 3; see also Raven 2, pp 21–25. **165** W. H. Häusermann (ed.), *The Genevese background* (London, 1952), p. 68; J. Newcomer, *Maria Edgeworth the novelist* (Fort Worth, 1967), p. 60; Butler, pp 307–8. **166** Thuente, *Representative Irish tales*, p. 10. **167** For example, J. Leerssen, '"Interesting to all the world": fiction, interest, and the public sphere' in Belanger, *Irish novel*, pp 52–62. **168** i, pp iv–v. **169** i, p. ix. **170** Defined as fiction containing one of the following key terms: 'fact', 'true', 'truthful', 'real', 'actual', or 'genuine', in either the title of a volume, title of a story within a volume, or a book's introduction or preface.

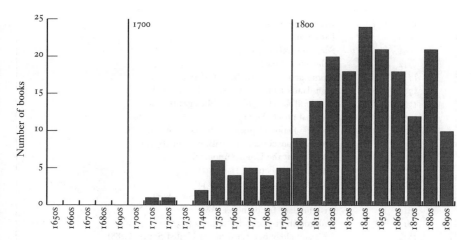

Figure 15 Changes in the number of Irish novels and books of stories based on facts published between 1650 and 1899.

Changes in the Themes of Fiction and the Emergence of New Forms of Fiction
Table 4 provides some examples of the earliest forms of specific types of fiction that we have documented. Irish fiction was much embedded primarily in British and, secondarily, in continental, particular French fiction.[171] Therefore, themes and new forms of fiction in Irish fiction waxed and waned largely in concert with that of other literatures. However, against this backdrop, Irish fiction had its unique features, as in its preoccupations with Irish matters and Irish settings. In addition, stories, often based on oral tradition and inspired by ancient Irish legends, perhaps with the exception of Ossianic legends, did not have direct counterparts in Britain.

Historical Fiction
As mentioned previously, Irish fiction was often preoccupied with the Irish past, and works of historical fiction describing many aspects of Irish historical events proliferated throughout the nineteenth century, especially during the 1880s and 1890s (see Figure 16). Our search revealed 20 novels set in Ireland prior to the middle ages, 26 set during the middle ages, 29 set during the sixteenth century, 68 during the seventeenth century, and largest number, 117, set during the eighteenth century.

Many novels dealt with particular periods of conflict in Ireland. Novels on the 1641 rebellion and its immediate aftermath were less common than novels about the 1798 rebellion. The subjects of historical fiction had their own peaks of popularity. For example, Figure 17 shows that the number of novels published on the 1798 rebellion and the United Irishmen peaked in the 1820s and accelerated in the late nineteenth century, especially around the centennial of the 1798 rebellion.[172]

Ireland as a Setting for Irish Fiction
By definition, the setting of Irish historical fiction was Ireland. However, many examples of other types of fiction – such as country house novels and novels on agrarian unrest and the

171 See several essays in G. Gargett & G. Sheridan (eds), *Ireland and the French enlightenment, 1700–1800* (Houndmills, 1999). 172 Our graph varies slightly from that published by K. Whelan, in his *Fellowships of freedom. The United Irishmen and 1798* (Cork, 1998), p. 130, probably because of a larger range of novels being included in Figure 18.

1689, 1693	Irish erotic fiction (Anon.258; Anon.69)
1690	Irish rogue (S2)
1694	Satire on Ireland (S84)
1742	Religious fiction (S670)
1747	Stories about Irish robbers (C382)
1749	Irish dandies and women seducers in London (F2)
1762	Historical novel on Irish middle ages (L140)
1770	Regional novel (M281)
1780	Didactic fiction of practical stories for children (E83)
1792–7	American novel featuring Irish servant (B312)
[1799?]	Novel about the Union (Anon.57)
1806	Anti-Catholic fiction (Anon.193)
1807	Fiction about absenteeism (R234)
1809	Fiction about Catholic Emancipation (T97)
1810	Irish military fiction novel (A85)
1811	Didactic short stories for farmers (L51)
1812	Irish anthology published in the United States (C288)
1817	Juvenile didactic fiction published by Kildare Place Society (B134)
1819	Juvenile didactic fiction on biology (B127; B131)
[1825 or earlier]	Irish stories (Anon.220; W69)
1829	History of Ireland written as stories for children (Anon.209)
1831	Fiction on plight of working children (C74)
1832	Fiction about emigration ship to Australia (B290)
1835	Fiction on the plights of women (H14)
1837	Fiction on religious conversion to Catholicism (A10)
1838	Fiction written by a maid servant (O41)
1839	Fiction about 1641 rebellion (M362)
1839	Catholic fiction (C180)
1845	Temperance tale (C84)
1846–7	Fiction about the Great Famine (A58; C88; H336)
1847	Fiction on working conditions for women (P49)
1850	Novel about a girls' school (K6)
1850	Novel about Irish orphan in America (R253)
1853	Novel on the Irish poor in London (M303)
1885	Novel on Irish dynamiters in London (Anon.53)
1886	Horror fiction featuring man-created monster (D159)
1889	Internal monologue novel (W4)
1890	Interplanetary novel (C484)
1896	Horror fiction featuring vampire (S622)

Table 4: Examples of earliest known works of fiction with Irish content.

Land League movement – were set in specific locations in Ireland (e.g., William Carleton writing about south Co. Tyrone, where he grew up). This aspect of Irish fiction is important because of the large regional differences in the make-up of the population, in Irish legends and folk tales, and in economic and social conditions.

The geography of Irish fiction shows an approximation of the extent that certain regions or counties of Ireland featured more often than others.[173] Figure 18 shows that on the east coast, fiction settings were concentrated in Dublin, but beyond Dublin, fiction settings were

173 Other helpful cartographic sources are: Welch (pp 616–17), who published a map of places of literary interest in Ireland; and Leclaire, who published a map of regional novelists in Ireland and Britain.

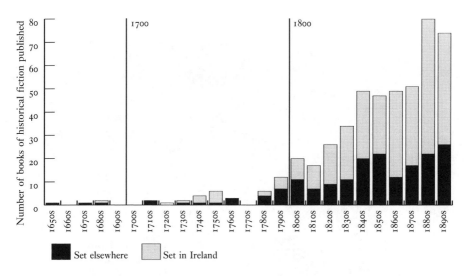

Figure 16 Changes in the number of historical fiction novels
published between 1650 and 1899.

most commonly found in the west, especially in south-west Munster (Cos. Cork and Kerry), and in Co. Donegal. In contrast, books of fiction set in a broad swath of the Irish midlands (Cos. Armagh, Carlow, Cavan, Laois, Leitrim, Longford, Monaghan, Offaly, Roscommon, Tyrone) were uncommon for the period between 1650 and 1900.[174]

Regional differences in the setting of Irish fiction partly reflect where Irish authors grew up, the location of Irish historical events, and partly the places that took writers' fancies. In

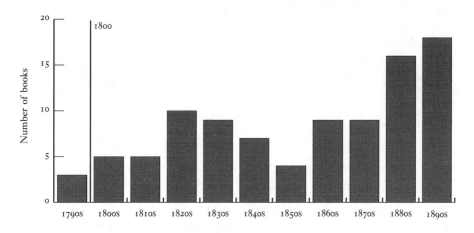

Figure 17 Changes in the number of historical novels or stories about the
1798 rebellion and the United Irishmen published between 1650 and 1899.

174 See also distribution of regional novels between 1800 and 1990 in England, Wales, Scotland, and Ireland (K.D.M. Snell, *The regional novel in Britain and Ireland, 1800–1990* (Cambridge, 1998), pp 24–5.

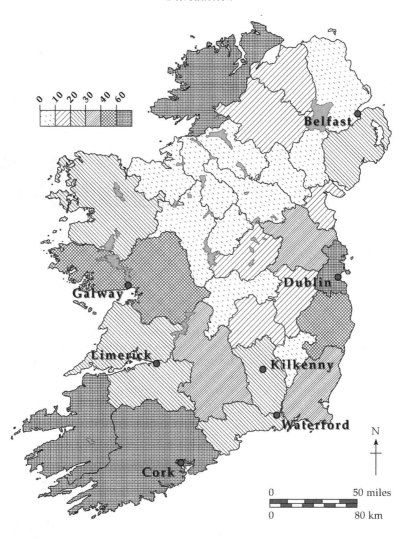

Antrim	5	Down	25	Leitrim	6	Roscommon	4
Armagh	6	Dublin	217	Limerick	26	Sligo	9
Carlow	2	Fermanagh	14	Longford	3	Tipperary	33
Cavan	3	Galway	52	Louth	16	Tyrone	8
Clare	24	Kerry	70	Mayo	25	Waterford	22
Cork	101	Kildare	14	Meath	33	Westmeath	14
Derry	15	Kilkenny	23	Monaghan	4	Wexford	38
Donegal	70	Laois	10	Offaly	7	Wicklow	53

Figure 18 Map of Ireland showing the approximate number of titles of
Irish fiction set in each county.

part, the place where a writer spent his/her first two decades of life helped to determine which region he/she highlights in subsequent fiction. This means that there is a correlation[175] between the number of authors born in a given county (Figure 7) and the likelihood that eventually the county becomes the setting of works of fiction (this applies, for example, to Cos. Cork and Tipperary). Conversely, some counties such as Monaghan, Laois, and Louth had few native authors, while the geographic distribution of regional novels also shows that these counties are underrepresented (Figure 18).

It is important, however, to consider those counties that are much represented in Irish fiction but which have produced few authors. Three counties qualify in this respect. First, Co. Wicklow is the setting of much Irish fiction, partly due to the fact that it formed the backdrop to much historical fiction relating to the 1798 rebellion. The case of Co. Kerry being prominent in fiction is different, however. The lure of Killarney, its lakes, and scenery formed the backdrop to many novels, probably fuelled by it being a centre of tourism and attracting the imagination of Irish and non-Irish writers alike. Figure 18 also shows that Co. Donegal was a favoured setting, partly due to the large number of the works of fiction written by Séumus MacManus (see Figure 19 for the geographic distribution of regional novelists). Thus, there are various reasons why counties with relatively few native authors still may still feature frequently in Irish fiction. It should also be noted that Co. Antrim which had a high number of authors did not commonly features as a setting in Irish fiction. In summary, even though there is a correlation between the number of authors born in a county and the number of works of fiction set in that county, future studies are likely to qualify our conclusions and explain why exceptions occur.

Disguised Settings

A tension sometimes existed for Irish authors writing for an English readership whether to set their stories in Ireland or to disguise the setting by transforming it to an English environment. There are several instances in which Irish authors concealed the setting of their fiction by moving it to England. For example, Sheridan Le Fanu's 'The haunted baronet' in his *Chronicles of Golden Friars* (London, 1871) is populated with English characters and set either in Northumberland or the Lake District, but the real setting was Ireland. In the same manner, Le Fanu's *Uncle Silas* (London, 1864), ostensibly set in Derbyshire, derived from a short story 'A passage in the secret history of an Irish countess' set in Ireland, but its title – on the urging of the publisher Richard Bentley – was changed because he had insisted on the 'story of an English subjects and in modern times'.[176] Likewise, Charlotte Riddell set her *Miss Gascoigne* (London, 1887) in an English seaside resort. However, she told Edmund Downey that she had in mind a particular spot in her native Ulster.[177] The reverse, replacing English setting by introducing Irish settings was also known, particularly in fiction written for juveniles.[178]

VI. THIS 'GUIDE' AND BEYOND

The preceding text merely constitutes a limited number of examples of issues and questions raised by the *Guide*. However, many questions remain about the authors, their books, the illustrations and publishers that may inspire future research. There are many other ways to bet-

---

175 The Spearman rank correlation = .571, p = .002 (two-tailed).   176 M. Cogan, 'Exotics or provincials Anglo-Irish writers and the English problem' in W. Zach & H. Kosok (eds), *Literary interrelations. Ireland, England and the world* (Tübingen, 1987), iii, pp 35–6. See also McCormack, pp 140–1.   177 M. Kelleher, 'Charlotte Riddell's *A Struggle for fame*: the field of women's literary production', *Colby Quarterly*, xxxvi (2000), p. 121.   178 Loeber & Stouthamer-Loeber, 'Fiction for cottagers', p. 166n.115.

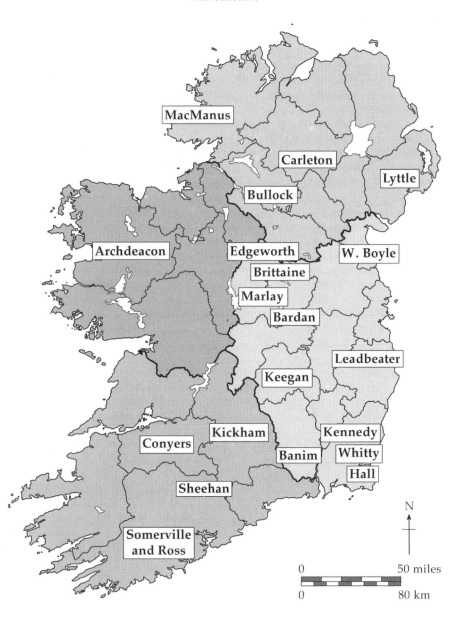

Figure 19 Map of Ireland showing the locations of regional novelists.

ter document the lives of those authors about whom very little is currently known. There are more public and private Irish archives of authors and their relatives and friends than we have been able to access, and the chances are high that much new material will be found in the archives of families and publishing houses in Britain and North America.

Much knowledge about the growth of Irish fiction is still hidden because it was often published in the periodical literature that appeared in Ireland, Britain, and the United States. Making an inventory of this large literature will greatly help to better understand the intellectual and artistic growth of writers in this *Guide*, the timing and context of their literary activities, and undoubtedly will reveal hundreds of additional authors, some of whom may have written books also.

The different databases that we consulted for this *Guide* offer great inspiration for future work. Some excel because they have made available on line the texts of the actual books in a searchable format (see for example, Wright American fiction, 1851–1875. Indiana Univ. On line: <http://www.letrs.indiana.edu/web/w/wright2>). The availability of such primary and searchable source material is likely to enhance scholarship and more permanently make available books that are now kept in rare book departments. Other data systems that currently exist, such as the one developed by P.D. Garside, J.E. Belanger and S.A. Ragaz, *British fiction, 1800–1829: A database of production, circulation and reception* (On line: http://www.british.fiction.cf.ac.uk) offer a wealth of easily searchable information about Romantic-era fiction, including publishing papers, newspaper advertisements, reviews in British periodical literature, subscribers' lists and records of the books in contemporary libraries. The study of the critical reception of most of Irish literature is still in its infancy and is likely to reveal much about how changing tastes and changing criteria influenced contemporary understanding of this literature and the market for fiction.

Much of Irish fiction published in the eighteenth and early-nineteenth centuries was supported by subscribers guaranteeing the purchase of copies of the works. The subscribers constitute a largely unexplored entry into patronage and readership. Since many of the subscribers were resident in Ireland, the subscription lists also shed light on local and regional networks of writers and readers, which often are not apparent from other contemporary sources.

Since a large portion of Irish fiction was published in North America, further work on the primary sources of that literature and on the lives of its North American authors is likely to deepen our understanding about Irish fiction.

A largely unexplored area is the relationship between Irish prose fiction and Irish poetry and songs. In the *Guide*, we recorded whether works of fiction contained poetry or songs, but space did not allow us to examine them in any great detail.

It is our hope that this *Guide* will fuel enthusiasm and energy for all or some of the tasks that we outlined. We hope that scholars and students will experience the intensity of pleasures that sustained our work, and will marvel at the richness of what constitutes Irish fiction.

Glossary

*A brief background guide to topics or persons appearing in the fiction
or part of the historical background of the period.*

§ Indicates a writer included in the *Guide*.   + Indicates another topic in the Glossary.

Abbey Theatre
The name given to the Irish National Theatre founded in 1903 by William Butler Yeats§, Augusta Lady Gregory§ and John Millington Synge from its performing space in Old Abbey Street in Dublin. The Abbey Theatre opened on 27 December 1904. It was the successor to the Irish Literary Theatre begun in 1899 by Lady Gregory, Edward Martyn§ and Yeats, whose aim was to present a national and poetic – rather than popular and commercial – theatre.

Absenteeism/Absentee Landlords
The common practice of English or Irish owners of estates in Ireland residing elsewhere for the greater part of their time and delegating the running of their estates to land agents. This led to a large segment of the landlord class unfamiliar at first hand with – and often unsympathetic to – issues concerning their tenants.

Act of Union
Legislation passed by both British and Irish parliaments creating in 1801 the United Kingdom of Great Britain and Ireland. It was prompted by British reactions to efforts towards greater Irish legislative independence from the 1780s on and by the United Irishmen+ rebellion of 1798 against British rule in Ireland. After passage of the Act of Union, the Irish parliament was disbanded and Irish members took their seats in Westminster, from where Ireland was governed directly.

Ascendancy
The Anglican Protestant, Anglo-Irish elite of the eighteenth and early-nineteenth century who constituted the ruling class and dominated the law and the professions. Ascendancy life centered on the Irish Parliament in Dublin before the Act of Union+ and depended in great measure on the exclusion or marginalization of Catholics.

Association for Discountenancing Vice and Promoting the Practice of Virtue and Religion
A Protestant organization founded in 1792 to fight immorality and sedition and support efforts to reform prostitutes and the criminal poor through the distribution of bibles and religious tracts. Women were admitted only as honorary members.

Boycott/Boycotting
A form of ostracism named after a Capt. Charles Cunningham Boycott (1823–97), a British land agent for Lord Erne, who fought the campaign of the Land League+ and, as a result of resistance tactics suggested by Charles Stewart Parnell+, was shunned by the local community, which refused to deal with or speak to him. Boycotting thus became a term for tactics of ostracism used subsequently for non-violent civil and political disobedience and in civil rights campaigns.

Catholic Emancipation
A campaign, waged primarily under the leadership of Daniel O'Connell+, to remove the last of the penal laws+ that prohibited Catholics from sitting in parliament without taking the Oath of Supremacy to the king of England as head of the church, or from holding senior gov-

ernment office, judgeships, membership in the Privy Council, king's counsel or county sheriff. This was accomplished by the enactment in April 1829 of the last of a series of Catholic Relief Acts, begun in 1778.

Chartism/Chartists
A working-class movement for social and political reform in the United Kingdom created in response to economic depression during the mid-nineteenth century. It got its name from the *People's Charter* of 1838, which set out the main aims of the movement including suffrage, abolition of property qualifications for MPs, equal constituencies, annual elections and payment of MPs. Rejection of the charter by the government led to strikes and riots but by 1858 the movement had mostly died out.

Celtic Revival
A movement begun in Wales and Scotland and taken up in Ireland by William Butler Yeats§, Augusta Lady Gregory§, John Millington Synge and others, that stimulated new appreciation of traditional Celtic literature. The movement, part of the greater Irish Literary Revival+, encouraged the creation of works written in the spirit of Irish culture, as distinct from English or Continental culture

Civil War in England
A series of wars between 1642 and 1648 pitting the forces loyal to the English crown and King Charles I, against the forces of Parliament, resulting in the execution of Charles in 1649 and a period of republican or parliamentary government in England that lasted until the restoration of Charles II to the throne in 1660.

Clearances
The process of clearing the land of impoverished or starving tenants, most especially during and after the Great Famine (1845–9) when the 1847 the Poor Law Extension Act put the responsibility for destitute tenants on the landlords and increased the Poor Rate, which was based on the number of poor tenants on their land. This was an incentive to the landlords to evict tenants. Many offered 'assisted passages', whereby tenants were given assistance to emigrate, and the cleared land was converted from tillage to pasture.

Coercion Acts
A number of legislative acts passed by the British parliament in response to increasing agrarian violence and civil unrest in Ireland triggered by land issues and the efforts of the Land League+ towards land reform. Under one such act, the Land League+ was suppressed and Charles Stewart Parnell+ imprisoned.

Confederation of Kilkenny
An association of Catholics formed in Kilkenny in 1642 in the wake of the 1641 rising to administer the Catholic-controlled parts of the country. It set up provincial councils, raised armies and levied taxes. Members asserted their rights while swearing allegiance to Charles I. The Confederate army was decisively beaten by Parliamentary army in 1647 and the Confederation broke up soon after.

Congested Districts Board
Established in 1891 to assist the heavily-populated areas of the west of Ireland to overcome persistent poverty and hunger by building roads, railroads, piers and harbours, encourage fishing, land improvement and cottage industries. The CDB purchased large land holdings, broke them into small parcels and made loans available for their purchase. In 1923 it was succeeded by the Land Commission.

Cromwell, Oliver (1599–1658)

Parliamentary military and republican leader in the civil wars in England who was a signatory to the death warrant of King Charles I and later lord lieutenant and commander-in-chief of Parliamentary forces in Ireland. He led an army of 20,000 soldiers on a campaign to Ireland (Aug. 1649 to May 1650) to enforce Parliament's control and ensure Protestant land settlement in Ireland, resulting in defeat of the royalists and their Catholic and Old English allies at Drogheda, Wexford and Limerick, many of whom were dispossessed of their lands and resettled in less-fertile land in the west of Ireland and some of whom were sent to slavery or indentured servitude in the West Indies. Cromwell, who became Lord Protector of England in 1653, believed in religious toleration (except for Catholics and dissenters+) and in representative government (but limited to men of property).

Curran, John Philpot

A noted barrister and MP famous for his wit and oratorical skills, he resigned from the Irish parliament in 1797 in despair of reforming its corrupt practices. He defended many of the United Irishmen+, including the brothers John and Henry Sheares. His daughter Sarah was the fiancée of patriot and insurrectionist Robert Emmet+.

Disestablishment

The removal of the Anglican Church, or Church of Ireland, as the established church in Ireland. In 1869 British prime minister William Gladstone+ pushed a bill through parliament effecting the disestablishment, almost 50 years before similar legislation for Wales (introduced first in 1870) achieved the same result.

Dissenters/Non-Conformists

Protestants who did not conform to the established church, the Church of England (or Ireland). These included initially Congregationalists, Baptists and Presbyterians, and later Unitarians and Methodists.

Duffy, Sir Charles Gavan (1816–1903)

A politician and author and member of the Young Ireland+ movement who with Thomas Davis founded in 1842 the influential nationalist newspaper the *Nation*. His advocacy of revolutionary measures resulted in imprisonment and the shutting-down of the paper. He was defended by Isaac Butt§. He later founded the Tenant League but, disillusioned with prospects for land reform, left for Australia where he served in parliament and was briefly prime minister of Victoria, for which he was knighted. He later wrote about the Young Ireland movement and his experiences as a politician on two continents.

Emmet, Robert (1778–1803)

A member of the United Irishmen+ movement, orator and revolutionary, born in Dublin and educated at TCD, he went to France after the rebellion of 1798 where he endeavored to obtain French support for another insurrection. He led an abortive rebellion in 1803, for which he was hanged. He is remembered chiefly for his eloquent speech from the dock, which became a rallying cry for future generations of Irish nationalists.

Famine, The Great (1845–1849)

Although periods of famine occurred frequently over centuries in Ireland, the scale of death from hunger or illness during the Great Famine was unprecedented. Caused by fungal infection of the potato crop (the staple diet of one-third of the population) for several years running, it resulted in a one-fifth decline in the population by 1851 and an altered social structure due to death, widespread emigration, the decimation of the cottier class and the reversion of large acreage from tillage to pasture.

Fenians/Fenian Brotherhood
A revolutionary secret society and movement to free Ireland of British rule founded in the
US by John O'Mahony in 1855 and named after the Fianna, a legendary group of Irish war-
riors led by Fionn MacCumhail. Members were required to take an oath of allegiance to the
Irish republic. The movement, which quickly aligned with the Irish Republican Brotherhood
founded by James Stephens, was active in the US, in Ireland, in England, Canada and
Australia. It was proscribed by the Catholic church for its advocacy of force. The Fenian ris-
ing of 1867 in Ireland was unsuccessful, as were a series of attempts by a Fenian army in the
US to invade Canada and hold it hostage to Britain in exchange for Irish independence.

Gaelic League
A non-political organization founded in 1893 by Douglas Hyde§ and Eoin MacNeill for the
purpose of revitalizing the use of the Irish language as a spoken tongue in Ireland. Known in
Irish as Conradh na Gaeilge, it published a newspaper, *An Claidheamh Soluis* (the sword of
light), the most noted editor of which was the later revolutionary leader Patrick Pearse. When
the constitution of the organization was changed in 1915 to include the idea of a free Ireland,
Hyde resigned in protest.

Giraldus Cambrensis or Gerald of Wales (*c*.1146–*c*.1223)
A medieval clergyman and chronicler of Norman and Welsh blood who became chaplain to
King Henry II of England in 1184 and accompanied the king's son, John, on an expedition to
Ireland, an account of which he published as *Topographia Hibernica* (1188). Later he wrote an
account of Henry's conquest of Ireland, the *Expugnatio Hibernica*.

Gladstone, William Ewart (1809–1898)
British Liberal politician and prime minister (1868–74, 1880–5, 1886, and 1892–4) and a political reformer known for his populist speeches during whose tenures as prime minister major
legislation regarding Ireland was introduced, including the disestablishment+ of the Church
of Ireland and various land reform acts that began to redress longstanding issues regarding
land tenure and ownership in Ireland. Gladstone's Home Rule+ bills of 1886 and 1892,
although defeated, set the precedent of a British political party backing some form of legislative autonomy for Ireland.

Grattan, Henry (1746–1820)
A member of the Irish Ascendancy, a graduate of TCD and a parliamentary reformer and orator who led a campaign in the 1770s and 1780s for legislative freedom for the Irish parliament, specifically for the overthrow of Poynings's Law, a statute by which all proposed Irish
legislation had to be submitted to the privy council in England for approval before it could
be passed by the Irish Parliament, as well as other constraints on Irish legislative independence. The reforms were approved by the Irish parliament in 1782 and conceded to by Britain
soon after. Grattan's Parliament was the popular name given to the Irish parliament from then
until 1801 when the Act of Union+ destroyed it.

Hearts of Steel/Steelboys
A group of agrarian agitators active principally in Cos. Antrim and Down between 1769 and
1772 that protested rent increases, evictions and local taxes. The Steelboys sent threatening
letters to landlords and made nocturnal raids on their properties. The movement also spread
to Cos. Armagh, Tyrone and Derry. See also Whiteboys+.

Hedge Schools
A feature of education for mostly peasant children in the countryside in Ireland in the eighteenth and early nineteenth centuries when education for Catholics was restricted by the penal

laws+. These informal schools were held in barns or outhouses – or under hedges – with pupils paying small fees to the master, who conducted lessons in Irish and often taught Latin and Greek as well as literature and mathematics. The introduction of a national, English, system of education in 1831 caused their gradual decline.

Hell Fire Club

A club similar to ones of the same name in England, where Dublin 'bucks', or young men of means and fashion in the 18th century, met to engage in drinking and alleged satanic rites and sexual orgies. It was based on Cork Hill, next to Dublin Castle, but is associated also with a summer residence owned by William Conolly on the slopes of the Dublin mountains, the ruins of which can still be seen.

Home Rule

A movement to secure legislative autonomy for Ireland (lost by the Act of Union+ of 1801) that dominated Irish politics from the 1870s until 1914. It grew out of the Home Government Association founded by Isaac Butt§, became the Home Rule League, and from the 1880s on was the chief legislative objective of the Irish Parliamentary Party under the leadership of Charles Stewart Parnell+. With funds from Irish-Americans in the US, the party built its electoral strength until with 80 members after the 1884 election it held the balance of power in Westminster. In response to IPP pressure, prime minister William Gladstone+ introduced a Home Rule bill in 1886 that gave separate legislative powers to Ireland, with Britain retaining control of the army, navy, trade and navigation. The bill was opposed by the Liberal Unionist members and when it failed to carry, Gladstone resigned. A second Home Rule bill introduced by Gladstone in 1892 also failed, and a third – opposed by the Ulster Unionists and the Irish nationalist Sinn Féin party – received royal assent in Sept. 1914 but because of the outbreak of the First World War was accompanied by an act of suspension and never came into force. The constitutional efforts of the Home Rule movement were overtaken by the uprising of 1916 and the subsequent war of independence.

Huguenots

French Calvinists who were aided by England in the Wars of Religion in France (1562–98). After the St Bartholomew Day massacre of Huguenots in Paris in 1572, many left for England and Ireland, and after the 1685 revocation of the Treaty of Nantes, which had guaranteed them religious freedom, many more emigrated, including to the American colonies. In Ireland they contributed greatly to the growth of the linen and textile industries.

Irish Brigade

A military brigade in the French army composed initially of Irish soldiers who, according to the terms of the Treaty of Limerick+ that ended the Williamite Wars+ in Ireland, were allowed to leave Ireland for France. In 1692 the Irish Brigade consisted of the Mountcashel, Butler, Fielding, O'Brien and Dillon regiments, with a total strength of over 6,000 men. Until the French Revolution (1789), the Irish Brigade was part of the French army and distinguished itself at such battles as that at Fontenoy (1745).

Irish 'Bulls' Deliberately illogical but amusing utterances made by 'stage-Irishmen' or stereotypical Irish characters, usually on the English stage or in Anglo-Irish literature.

Irish Literary Revival See also **Celtic Revival**

A renaissance of Irish literary activity, written in English, but inspired by Irish poetry, myth and legend and spurred by an effort to create a distinct Irish literary identity. Its leading exponents included William Butler Yeats§, Katharine Tynan§, Douglas Hyde§, Augusta Lady

Gregory, and John Millington Synge. It helped foster an increased sense of Irish nationalism in the late-nineteenth and early-twentieth centuries.

Irish National League
The new name for the Land League+ after it was suppressed by a Coercion Act of 1881 and reformed in 1883 under the leadership of Charles Stewart Parnell+ who ensured that home rule+, as well as land reform, was its objective.

Irish Volunteers See Volunteers

Jacobins/Jacobites
Supporters of the cause of the Stuart (also Stewart) monarchy, mainly Catholics in England and Ireland and the Scots, united in restoring the Stuart king James II to the monarchy after he was deposed by the Glorious Revolution in England (1688) in favour of William of Orange. The Jacobites fought and were defeated in the Williamite Wars+ in Ireland and the Jacobite cause died out with the defeat of the grandson of James II, 'Bonnie Prince Charlie', at the battle of Culloden in Scotland in 1746.

Kildare Place Society
Society for the Education of the Poor of Ireland, known as the Kildare Place Society, active 1816 to 1827, it published popular, non-sectarian works covering, among other subjects, religion, natural history, the arts and travel. The books were written or rewritten under strict superintendence of the Society's publication committee. A report in 1824 to the commissioners inspecting the state of education in Ireland stated that almost one million copies were in circulation.

Land Acts
A series of parliamentary acts passed between 1870 and 1903 to settle the contentious and politically powerful issues of land tenure and ownership in Ireland.

Land League, National
Founded as the Land League of Mayo by Michael Davitt, it became the National Land League in 1879 with Charles Stewart Parnell+ as its president and Davitt one of its secretaries. The Land League fought for 'fair rents, fixity of tenure, free sale' for Irish tenants initially, with the long-term objective of land ownership for peasants.

Land War
The period roughly between 1879 and 1882 and beyond during which the Land League+ fought politically and through intimidation, coercion and boycotting for its objectives. Through an agreement made between British prime minister William Gladstone+ and Charles Stewart Parnell+ while the latter was imprisoned in Kilmainham gaol for encouraging agrarian agitation, it was agreed that in exchange for Gladstone introducing a bill by which tenants could have arrears in rent paid and thus take advantage of the Land Act of 1880, Parnell would discourage violence.

Molly Maguires
Agrarian agitators in the tradition of the Whiteboys+ active in the early-nineteenth century. Later this organization re-formed in the US in the coal mining regions of eastern Pennsylvania where it used similar tactics to agitate for miners' rights.

Moonlighters/Captain Moonlight Agrarian agitators in the tradition of the Whiteboys+ active in the early nineteenth century who used force and intimidation against landlords and their agents, as well as against prospective tenants of properties from which previous tenants had been evicted for non-payment of rent.

Glossary

Non-Conformists See **Dissenters**

O'Connell, Daniel (1775–1847)
Lawyer, politician, orator and advocate of non-violent protest, he led the movement for Catholic emancipation+ or the abolishment by 'legal and constitutional means' of the last of the penal laws+ that prevented Catholics from serving in Parliament, in the inner Bar or in high civil or military office. He founded the Catholic Association in 1823 which raised money for Catholic candidates and he was returned to parliament himself with a huge electoral victory in Co. Clare in 1828. His refusal to take the Oath of Supremacy to the king as the head of the church led to the Catholic Relief Act of 1829. He later founded the Repeal Association to repeal the Act of Union+ and instituted the non-violent political tactic of 'monster meetings', some attended by hundreds of thousands of people, the last of which, at Clontarf (Dublin) was proclaimed by the government. He was imprisoned for sedition, and on his release the Famine+, conflicts with the Young Ireland+ movement and his broken health reduced his political effectiveness. He was known popularly as the 'Liberator'.

OGAM (or OGHAM)
The earliest form of script writing in Ireland, preserved on over 300 stones or pillars in Ireland and in Irish colonies in Wales. It consists of an alphabet of 20 (later 25) letters differentiated by varying numbers of slashes and by the side of the pillar on which they are incised. The language is a primitive form of Old Irish.

Orange Order/Orangemen
A Protestant sectarian organization, successor to the vigilante Peep O'Day boys, founded in 1795 in Ulster and named after the Protestant king William III of Orange, who replaced the Catholic James II of England in 1688. It spread throughout Ulster and the east and south of Ireland which resulted in an increase in anti-Catholic activity. The first parade of the Orange Order was held on 12 July 1796 in commemoration of the day of the battle of the Boyne (1690) at which the Williamite forces decisively beat James and his Jacobite+ army. The Orange Order remains a significant organization and the tradition of Orange marches on July 12 continues in contemporary Northern Ireland.

Parnell, Charles Stewart (1846–1891)
An Anglo-Irish Protestant member of parliament from a land-owning family in Co. Wicklow and the leading Irish parliamentarian and Irish nationalist of his day, Parnell joined the Home Rule League of Isaac Butt§ and was founding president of the Land League+ in 1879. He became leader of the Irish Parliamentary Party, uniting its members by tying land reform to home rule+ and imposing strict party discipline. He helped to raise funds from Irish Americans in the US to aid in electing new members committed to home rule and by 1884 the party held the balance of power in Westminster when the Liberals under William Gladstone+ were returned to office. Gladstone introduced a Home Rule+ bill in 1886 which was defeated, but it set the precedent of a British party supporting some measure of Irish autonomy. Parnell was named as co-respondent in a divorce case brought by Capt. William O'Shea in 1889. The Irish Parliamentary Party split over whether Parnell could continue to be an effective leader in light of the ensuing scandal. Some members remained loyal to Parnell and others believed his continuance as leader would ruin the party's effectiveness and the chances for home rule. He lost the leadership to Justin McCarthy§, but refused to resign. He carried his case to Ireland in 1891 where in three by-elections he was defeated. He married Mrs O'Shea that year, but died soon after. The Parnell divorce split Ireland, with the Catholic hierarchy and many Catholics opposing him on moral grounds, and many nationalists and supporters of home rule remaining loyal. He was known popularly as 'the uncrowned king of Ireland'.

Glossary

Penal Laws
A series of laws begun in 1560 in the reign of Queen Elizabeth I with a Penal Code against Catholics and dissenters+ but usually a reference to the laws enacted after the defeat of the Jacobites+ in 1691 at the end of the Williamite Wars+ and in violation of the Treaty of Limerick+. Passed over the course of a number of years, the penal laws were intended primarily to consolidate Protestant power in Ireland and secondly to encourage conversion to protestantism. By these laws, Catholics were excluded from parliament, disarmed, forbidden to keep schools, take degrees, and excluded from the Bar. Catholic bishops were banished, seminaries banned, and education of new priests forbidden. Catholics were excluded from the professions and deprived of the franchise. The laws restricted inter-marriage between Catholics and Protestants, inheritance, land ownership and trade. Catholics could avoid some of the laws by conversion. Many of them applied also to dissenters+. In practice, not all of the laws were strictly enforced and they affected the Catholic aristocracy and landowners more than peasants. The penal laws were gradually repealed starting in 1778 with a series of Catholic Relief Acts, the final one enacted in 1829 (see Catholic Emancipation+).

Peninsular Wars (1808–1814)
A long drawn-out and hard-fought part of the Napoleonic Wars, fought on the Iberian Peninsula. Britain, with Spanish and Portuguese allies, gradually forced the French army out of the Peninsula and defeated it at Toulouse in 1814. Napoleon's abdication put an end to further hostilities.

Pitt, William (1759–1806)
Son of an eponymous prime minister of England, William Pitt (the younger) was one of the youngest and longest-serving prime ministers in England, in office from 1783 to 1801 and from 1804 until his death. His time in office was dominated by major events in Europe, and in Ireland by dissatisfaction with English rule and the example of the American and French Revolution leading to the rebellion of 1798. His government introduced the Act of Union+ between England and Ireland but he deplored the outright bribery of members needed to get it passed. He supported Catholic emancipation+ and resigned when he failed to effect it.

Rack Rents
Inordinately high rents charged tenants by landlords – often absentee+ – wishing to maximize income from their estates. Rack rents were one of the principal causes of agrarian arrest in Ireland. When rents could not be met because of bad harvests, famines, or other calamities, tenants were often evicted peremptorily, causing visible hardship and resulting in resentment against the landlord class.

Repeal Association/Movement
A non-violent movement founded by Daniel O'Connell+ in 1840 to agitate for repeal the Act of Union+.

Rebellion of 1798 See **United Irishmen**

Ribbonmen/Ribbonism
A secret sectarian society of agrarian agitators formed in the north of Ireland in response to land issues in early-nineteenth-century Ireland. It attacked landlords and their agents seen to be unfair in their dealings with tenants.

Rockites
A group that took its name from the initials of Capt. Roger O'Connor and was involved in various agrarian and anti-tithe activities in the early 1820s, especially in Cos. Cork, Kerry, Limerick and Tipperary.

Glossary

Smock Alley Theatre
The first theatre built in Dublin after the Restoration of Charles II to the throne of England in 1660 (theatre had been in disfavour under the Parliamentary government). Smock Alley flourished from 1662 until 1786 under a variety of managers (including Thomas Sheridan, father of playwright Richard Brinsley Sheridan) and through various mergers of rival theatrical companies. Irish playwrights George Farquhar§, Arthur Murphy§ and John O'Keefe all produced works at Smock Alley.

'Souper', 'Souperism'
The practice by some proselytizing evangelical Protestant organizations during the Great Famine+ of 1845–49 and other times of hunger of offering food – often soup – and sometimes clothing and shelter to starving peasants on condition they convert to Protestantism.

'Squireen'
A derisory name given in the Irish countryside to men who assumed airs above their station or emulated the manners and dictatorial ways of a squire.

Terry Alts
Agrarian agitators in Munster in the early-nineteenth century. See also Whiteboys+, Ribbonmen+, Hearts of Steel+, Molly Maguires+.

Tithes/Tithe War
A compulsory tax in support of the established Anglican church, the Church of Ireland, that was greatly resented by Catholics, Quakers and Presbyterians and gave rise to acts of terrorism from the 1760s on. This agitation culminated in the Tithe War of the 1830s and the Tithe Commutation Act of 1838 that substituted a rent charge fixed at 75% of the original tithe.

Transportation
The practice of sending political prisoners, convicted criminals, agitators, priests and others deemed by English governing forces to be dangerous or undesirable, to penal or indentured servitude in British possessions outside Ireland. Begun in large numbers by Cromwell with the dispatch of thousands to the West Indies in the 1650s, later groups were sent to North America and after the American Revolution to penal colonies in Tasmania and Australia, which received over 40,000 persons before the practice was abandoned in 1868.

Treaty of Limerick
The treaty concluding the Siege of Limerick and the end of the Williamite Wars+ in Ireland (1689–91). Under the treaty, Jacobite+ soldiers had the option of leaving Ireland for France (where they formed the Irish Brigade+) or joining the Williamite Army. The civil articles of the treaty protected the rights, with certain conditions, of defeated Jacobites who remained in Ireland. The civil articles were honoured only briefly and were followed by the imposition of the penal laws+, making in Irish folk memory the Treaty synonymous with betrayal.

Trinity College
The single college of Dublin University, founded in 1592 by Queen Elizabeth I. Dedicated to educating a Protestant elite in Ireland, Catholics were excluded until 1793 and only in 1873 were all religious tests abolished. In 1904 Trinity became the first of the old universities of Great Britain and Ireland to admit women.

United Irishmen, Society of
A revolutionary republican organization founded in Belfast (Co. Antrim) and in Dublin by Protestants Theobald Wolfe Tone§ and Thomas Russell to seek democracy, religious freedom and complete independence for Ireland from England. United with Catholics and inspired

both by American independence and the French Revolution, the organization sought help from the French to overthrow English rule. The United Irishmen rebellion of 1798, the first significant rebellion since 1641, was quickly and brutally suppressed and many of its leaders executed. It became the inspiration for future Irish revolutionary nationalist movements.

Volunteers, Irish
A corps of predominantly Protestant, middle-class volunteers formed in 1779 to protect Ireland from invasion while England was engaged in war with the American colonies, France and Spain. By 1782 it consisted of over 80,000 men. The Volunteers became a powerful element in political life and a threat to English rule in Ireland and were instrumental in England conceding some legislative freedom to the Irish Parliament, fought for by Henry Grattan+ and other reformers. By 1785 the force had subsided. It was abolished by the Arms Act of 1793.

Whiteboys
An illegal secret society and agrarian agitation movement named for the white shirts worn by its members, it began in Munster in 1761 to protest tithes+, the enclosure of common land, evictions, and the encroachment of pasture on tillage. It stimulated in reaction the passage of various Whiteboy Acts that provided for severe penalties, including capital punishment.

Whitefeet
An early-eighteenth century rural protest movement committed to the abolition of tithes+ to support the established, or Anglican, church in Ireland.

Wild Geese
A poetic term given to the surviving remnants of the Catholic Jacobite+ resistance that, under the terms of the Treaty of Limerick+, left Ireland after the Williamite Wars+ to fight in Continental armies, particularly those of Spain and France where Irish soldiers formed the famed Irish Brigade+.

Williamite Wars (1689–91)
The continuation on Irish soil of the conflict between the deposed English king, James II, and his Jacobite+ supporters in Ireland and William III and his Ulster Protestant allies. Williamite victories at the battles of the Boyne (1690), Aughrim (1691) and the collapse of the Jacobite resistance after the siege of the city of Limerick were followed by the Treaty of Limerick+. The war, followed by the imposition of a series of draconian measures against Catholics known collectively as the penal laws+, resulted in the consolidation of Protestant power in Ireland.

Young Ireland/Young Irelanders
A nationalist, non-denominational movement begun by young intellectuals in the 1840s that grew out of the weekly newspaper the *Nation*, begun in 1842 by Charles Gavan Duffy+ and Thomas Davis. It was in conflict with Daniel O'Connell's+ efforts for repeal of the Act of Union+ through legal agitation, and was distrusted by the Catholic church, which accused it of spreading an anti-Catholic secular philosophy. In 1847 the Young Irelanders founded the Irish Confederation as an alternative to O'Connell's Repeal Association+. Inspired by the French revolution of 1848, Confederate Clubs began drilling for rebellion. Pre-emptive arrests and the repeal of the habeas corpus act removed many of the leaders from active involvement. An abortive uprising led by William Smith O'Brien in Co. Tipperary was quickly quashed. Leaders of Young Ireland, including O'Brien, John Mitchel and Thomas Meagher were transported+ to Van Diemen's Land (Tasmania). Some Young Irelanders later joined the Fenian+ movement.

THE GUIDE

Anonymous Works

ANONYMOUS AUTHORS OF ONLY ONE WORK

Anon.1 *The abduction; or, the adventures of Major Sarney. A story of the times of Charles the Second.*

+ London: Charles Knight, 1825, 3 vols. SOURCE British Fiction; Garside, 1825:1. LOCATION Corvey CME 3–628–47011–0, Ireland related fiction, Dt, L, MH.
COMMENTARY Historical fiction set in Ireland from the reign of King Charles II (1660–85) up to the coming of James II to Ireland (1689). The story starts at the coast near Dublin. A mysterious boat drops a stranger ashore. A fisherman, called Brennan, helps him to go to Dublin and protects him from robbers. The scene changes. The family of MacDonnell of Baldunaven are staunch Catholics. A son, Louis, is short of money since a great deal of the family's fortune has been given to the Catholic church. Louis falls in love with Cicely Tyrconnel, whose father is rich. However, she is a Protestant and the MacDonnell family refuse Louis permission to marry her. He becomes a Protestant, marries Cicely and obtains his brother's estate and title. His mother and sister continue to live on the estate. They are summoned to Dublin Castle to testify about what they know concerning the abduction of Louis' two children. On their way to Dublin Castle, the carriage carrying his mother and sister breaks down. The sister is rescued by an officer, Ludowic Kennedy. Kennedy is warned by a mysterious midnight visitor not to fall in love with the daughter. Louis hears that Brennan was involved in the abduction and arranges the arrest of him and his companions. However, the abduction had been set in motion by the deposed brother, who has become a monk. After a while, one daughter is returned to her parents; the other daughter returns much later and subsequently reconverts and becomes a nun. Louis dies in the bosom of the Catholic church [ML].

Anon.2 *Adelaide. An original East Indian story.*

London: A. Neil, [1807?]. SOURCE BLC. LOCATION L (not found).
COMMENTARY No copy located. 'Written for' and first published as a serial in the *Sentimental and Masonic Magazine*, Dublin (Mar. 1794–June 1795), 16 parts. The London edn probably was a novelette, similar to other novelettes published by Neil [Mayo, 10; RL].

Anon.3 *The adventures of a black coat. Containing a series of remarkable occurrences and entertaining incidents, that it was a witness to in its peregrinations through the cities of London and Westminster, in company with a variety of characters. As related by itself.*

London: J. Williams & J. Burd, 1760. SOURCE Raven, 524; ESTC t128642. LOCATION L.
+ Dublin: Robert Bell, 1762. SOURCE ESTC t070296. LOCATION D (incomplete), L.
Edinburgh: Printed [for the author?] by Alex M'Caslan, [*c.*1770?]. SOURCE ESTC t86017; LOCATION E, L, MH.
Paris: Lagrange, 1790 (trans. by R. Girard-Raigné as *Aventures d'un habit noir: où l'on trouvera les vènements les plus remarquables dont il a été témoin dans les circonstances présentes*). SOURCE Rochedieu, p. 363; COPAC. LOCATION Univ. of Leeds.

[Boston]: London: printed, Boston: repr. Edes & Evans, 1767. LOCATION InND.
COMMENTARY 166pp for the London edn, 188pp for the Dublin edn and 62pp for the Boston edn. The plot centres on a sable coat and the experiences of its owners, beginning with an Irish footman ambitious to get onto the stage [Edwards cat. 16/11; RL].

Anon.4 *The adventures of Patrick O'Donnell, in his travels through England and Ireland, written by himself* (dedicated to Thomas Newburgh).
    London: J. Williams, 1763. SOURCE Raven, 756; Forster, 31; Brown 2, 1; ESTC n029833. LOCATION D (1763, 2nd edn).
    Dublin: James Potts, [1764?]. SOURCE Adv. in W. Mason, *Elfrida: a dramatic poem* (Dublin, 1764).
COMMENTARY No copy of the Dublin edn located. Patrick O'Donnell is a native of Cork, where his father has ruined himself by gambling. The family moves to its small property in Banbridge (Co. Down). After the father dies, Patrick studies law in Dublin. He travels through England as a strolling player. When he returns to Ireland, he is robbed by highwaymen. He brings them to justice by pretending to join them. In the end, he recovers his property and marries his first love [Brown 2].

Anon.5 *The adventures of Shelim O'Blunder, Esq; the Irish beau, who within a very few years has passed through many surprizing vicissitudes, and remarkable scenes of life. The whole founded on real facts, and interspersed with several diverting and amusing incidents. With a few cursory reflections on the common ingredients of a Teague-land beau, or fortune hunter, by way of salutary advice, or friendly caution to the fair sex of Great Britain* (dedicated to the Ladies of Great Britain).
    + London: H. Carpenter, [c.1750]. SOURCE Forster, 32; ESTC t16632. LOCATION Di, L.
COMMENTARY Set in the eighteenth century, a short story of an Irish fortune-hunter leading a dissipated life and trying by means of deception to marry a rich bride. He ends up in prison. A related farce by Thomas Sheridan, *Captain O'Blunder; or, the brave Irishman,* was published in about 1746 and was an adaptation of Molière's *Monsieur de Pourceaugnac* (Paris, 1673) [ESTC t212766; ML; COPAC; Hart cat. 64/20].

Anon.6 *Amusing stories: A collection of histories, adventures and anecdotes.*
    + Dublin: Graisberry & Campbell [for the Kildare Place Society], 1819 (ill.). SOURCE Hislop, p. 1035; NSTC (1820 edn); Gilbert, p. 20 (1820 edn); Osborne, p. 798. LOCATION D, DPL Gilbert Coll. (1820 edn), C (1824 edn), CaOTP (1824 edn), InND Loeber coll. (1824 edn).
    + London: C.J.G. & F. Rivington [for the Society for Promoting Christian Knowledge], 1831. SOURCE Hislop, p. 1035; Osborne, p. 798. LOCATION L, CaOTP.
COMMENTARY Stories from different countries; their origins remain unclear. Contents: 'Adventures of Madame Godin in the country of Amazons', 'Description of a tiger hunt in India', 'The cataract of Niagara, in Canada', 'Perseverance, – A story', 'Account of the salt mines of Wielitska', 'Short account of the plague in London in 1665', 'Wonderful escapes of a hunter from the Blackfeet [*sic*] Indians', 'Account of the earthquake in Calabria, in 1638', 'Muly Moluc' [ML].

Anon.7 *The ancient Irish tales. Being a collection of the stories told by the peasantry, in the winter evenings.*
    + Drogheda: For the booksellers, 1829. SOURCE *Béaloideas,* 40–41 (1992–3), p. 135. LOCATION D.

COMMENTARY Chapbook of 96pp consisting of stories mostly taken from other books. Contents: 'The wonderful adventures of Daniel O'Rourke and the eagle' (O'Rourke lived at the bottom of Hungary Hill [*sic*] 'just as you go to Bantry'), 'Lusmore and the fairies' (about a man who lived at the foot of the Galtee mountains; after [William Maginn†] 'The legend of Knockgrafton'), 'Mick Purcell and the fairy' (after [William Maginn§] 'Legend of Bottle Hill'), 'The soldier and the blue light', 'The soldier and the three crows', 'Paddy M' Dermid and the fairies', 'Mick M' Connell and the fairies', 'Sir Walter Whitty and his cat', 'Robert Barry and the soldier' [ML; CD; Thuente 1, p. 61 (who misattributes some of the stories); Zimmermann, p. 172].

Anon.8 *Annie; or, memorials of a sister.*
+ Dublin: Hodges & Smith, 1852. SOURCE NSTC. LOCATION L.
COMMENTARY Religious fiction. Described in the preface as a picture of domestic suffering, and commemorates the love of God. Annie is an Irish girl who wants to love Jesus and go to heaven, but finds many temptations in her way. She is consumptive, and as such is given a warning to become religious and saintly before she dies [ML].

Anon.9 *Arthur Russel, the deaf and dumb boy; and The Gordon family.*
+ Dublin: R.M. Tims, 1830 (ill.). LOCATION DPL Dix coll.
COMMENTARY The author of the first story, 'Arthur Russell', might be Charlotte Elizabeth Tonna§, who was in Ireland in this time and who was interested in the education of deaf and dumb children. The author of the second story, 'The Gordon family', according to its separate preface, was 'a young lady' aged 15. This story starts out in Killarney (Co. Kerry) [RL].

Anon.10 *Autobiography of an Irish traveller* (dedicated to Tsar Nicholas I).
+ London: Longman, Rees, Orme, Brown, Green & Longman, 1835, 3 vols. SOURCE Hodgson, p. 29; Sadleir, 75; Garside 2, D:9. LOCATION L, MH.
London: Longman, Rees, Orme, Brown, Green & Longman, 1837, 3 vols. (as *Autobiography of an Irish traveller: Or travels in various parts of the world*). SOURCE Garside 2, D:9; OCLC. LOCATION PVU.
COMMENTARY Account and anecdotes written in the form of a novel of an Irishman who travelled in Ireland, America, Africa, China and Russia [ML].

Anon.11 *Ballyblunder. An Irish story.*
+ London: John W. Parker & Son, 1860. SOURCE Brown, 5; Wolff, 7414; NSTC. LOCATION Dt, D, L.
COMMENTARY A novel of agrarian agitation, set on the north-east coast of Ireland. A priest instigates people to kill sheep on the Ballyblunder estate of the Kindly family. Mr Kindly's son tries to track the sheep-killers, and a friend of his is murdered. Brady, the murderer, falls off a cliff and is killed. The Kindly family eventually sells the estate [Brown].

Anon.12 *The Barrow pilot; or, a tale of the Irish sea.*
+ Barrow: [addendum to the *Barrow Times*], [1870]. SOURCE NSTC. LOCATION L.
COMMENTARY The *Barrow Times* was published by Joseph Richardson in Cumbria (England). The story, consisting of two chapters, is set on the coast of Co. Wexford and concerns a pilot by the name of Kruvvus, an ill-natured person, who lives with his daughter. A stranger comes to visit and the father wants his daughter to use a different name so that the stranger will not know who she is [ML; JB; On line: Internet <http://www.cumbria.gov.uk/elibrary/view.asp?ID=1075> (access date: Nov. 2005)].

Anon.13 *The battle of the Moy; or, how Ireland gained her independence 1892–94.*
Boston: Lee & Shepard; New York: C.T. Dillingham, 1883. SOURCE OCLC. LOCATION L, CtY.
COMMENTARY 74pp, sold for 25¢. Intended as a satire rather than a prophecy of changes brought about by Irish independence [R.L. Kilgour, *Lee and Shepard. Publishers for the people* (n.l., 1965), p. 209].

Anon.14 *The battle of Ventry Harbour, which took place in the fourth century; and which continued without intermission for 366 days!!! Being a literal translation from an old Irish manuscript.*
+ Limerick: Printed [for the author?] by George M. Goggin, 1835 (ill.). LOCATION D, L.
+ Cork: Charles Dillon & Son, [1840s?]. SOURCE RL; COPAC. LOCATION D.
Worcester (MA): J. Grout, Jnr, 1847. LOCATION DCL.
New York: P.J. Kenedy, [1856 or earlier] (as *Battle of Ventry Harbor*). SOURCE Adv. in A.D Dorsey, *Conscience* (New York, 1856).
COMMENTARY No copy of the New York edn located. The frontispiece of the Limerick edn shows a woodcut of 'Fergus carrying Beaul M'Gromstain to the Ship'. Based on an early Irish story known as Cath Fionntragha – the battle of Ventry, part of the Fenian cycle or Fiannaiocht. The earliest manuscript copies date from the sixteenth century. Edited edns of the original can be found in K. Meyer, *Anecdota Oxoniensia* (Oxford, 1884), i, part iv, and C. O'Rahilly, *Cath Finnträga* (Dublin, 1962) [RL; Personal communication, Kevin Whelan, May 2004; Personal communication, Breandán Ó Buachalla, Oct. 2004].

Anon.15 *Benevola. A tale: in two parts. Part the first – England, Part the second – Ireland.*
+ London: Charles Knight & Co., 1840. SOURCE Block, p. 19; COPAC. LOCATION L.
COMMENTARY A story about a fairy who wants to do good. When she finds in England a labourer threatened with destitution because he is struck blind, she goes to the prime minister and induces him to establish the poor laws. However, when she visits England again she finds that the effect of the poor laws is exactly the opposite from what she had in mind. The village is unkempt and the people are not happier. Later she flies to Ireland and finds that there often is fighting and great animosity between the Protestant landowners and the Catholic tenants. She finds that the tenants have all the burden and she wants to distribute this more equally. Poor laws are established here too. However, great good is being effected by landlords taking a personal interest in their tenants [ML].

Anon.16 *The biblicals; or, Glenmoyle Castle. A tale of modern times* (dedicated to Power Le Poer Trench, archbishop of Tuam).
Dublin: T. O'Flanagan, 1830. SOURCE Wolff, 7418; COPAC. LOCATION Dt, L.
London: Keating & Brown, 1831. SOURCE Sadleir, 76. LOCATION L.
COMMENTARY Religious fiction. Purports to describe conditions in 1827, and was written in answer to a novel entitled *Father Clement* (Edinburgh, 1823) by Grace Kennedy§. The dedicatee, Power Le Poer Trench, archbishop of Tuam, was a fervent Evangelical clergyman. One of his daughters, a Miss Trench§, wrote fiction, but is only known from a volume published twenty-two years later than *The biblicals; or, Glenmoyle Castle* [RL; Wolff].

Anon.17 *A biographical sketch of the adventures of Jeremiah Grant, commonly called Captain Grant; who was tried, found guilty, and executed, at the summer assizes,*

1816, held at Maryborough, in the Queen's County. With a faithful report of his trial, and conduct at the place of execution. The narrative taken from his own detail, after his conviction.
+ Dublin: Printed [for the author?] by A. O'Neil, [1816]. SOURCE NSTC. LOCATION L, O.
Athy: Thomas French, 1836. SOURCE OCLC. LOCATION L.
COMMENTARY 137pp. Reprinted soon afterwards by the Dublin publisher C.M. Warren in a 144 pp edn. Written in a narrative, fictional style, but apparently based on notes taken over three days of interviews before Grant's execution. He was hanged for burglary. Not repentant, he explained his behaviour as a consequence of his seeking revenge against a man who had seduced his sister [RL; BLC].

Anon.18 *The birth day of Rosina.*
Dublin, London, Edinburgh, Glasgow: R.M. Timms, 1829. LOCATION PC.
COMMENTARY Religious fiction set in the mountainous part of Co. Down [Personal communication, Mary Pollard, Sept. 2003].

Anon.19 *Blacklegs and Whitefeet. A tale of the extra super-improved era of Irish tranquillity.*
+ Dublin: Martin Keene & Son, [1838] (Nos. 1, 2 and 3; ill. B. Clayton). SOURCE Block, p. 22 (gives [1840]); Bradshaw, 2892; IBL, 13 (1922), p. 177 (mistakenly lists the title as 'Blackfeet and Whiteboys'). LOCATION L (No. 3 missing), C.
COMMENTARY Humorous story about a court case involving some Whitefeet (part of the Whiteboy agrarian protest movement) who set fire to the house of a parson. Probably reprinted in the *Irish Union Magazine* (Dublin, Mar. 1845), as a serial under the title 'Mary Mansfield; or, Ireland ten years since' [ML; IBL, 13 (1922), p. 178].

Anon.20 *Blind George, the Irish schoolmaster. A true narrative.*
+ London: William Macintosh, 1864. LOCATION O.
+ Bristol: J. Wright and Co., 1864. LOCATION L (destroyed), O.
COMMENTARY Religious fiction set in Cork [BLC; CM].

Anon.21 *Blind Tom: or the lost found.*
+ Philadelphia: William S. & Alfred Martien, 1857 (ill. Van Ingen Snydert). SOURCE OCLC. LOCATION DCL, InND Loeber coll. (1861 edn).
COMMENTARY Religious fiction for juveniles set in a North American city, it is the story of blind Tom, the son of Mr Ryan, an Irishman, and Mrs Ryan, a drunk. Tom is taken in by a Christian family. He is taught religion and given a chance to learn an occupation in a school for the blind. Tom is able to teach his mother to mend her ways. He dies of consumption, but he dies happily [ML].

Anon.22 *Bridget Clancy, or the Lord's working-woman.*
London: [n.p.], [1859]. LOCATION L (destroyed).
COMMENTARY No other copy located [RL].

Anon.23 *Bridget Sullivan; or, the cup without a handle. A tale.*
+ London: Wertheim & MacIntosh, 1854. SOURCE Brown, 11. LOCATION O.
Philadelphia: Presbyterian Board of Publication, 1858. SOURCE OCLC. LOCATION Presbyterian Historical Society, Philadelphia (PA).

COMMENTARY Anti-Catholic religious fiction. The volume starts with a quote from a poem by Charlotte Elizabeth§. The introductory chapter compares Protestant and Catholic parts of Ireland and concludes that in the Protestant as compared to the Catholic parts the inhabitants are better off, happier and better educated. Protestant clergymen often do not bother with the Catholics in the parish. One excuse is that the Catholics speak Gaelic. The story is set between 1824 and 1834 in Co. Galway. When a new clergyman arrives and rebuilds the Protestant church, Michael Sullivan refuses to send his children to the school – particularly his daughter Bridget. She converts of her own accord and is violently assaulted by her father and the priest and cast from the house. After she is rescued from starvation and death by the Protestant clergyman, her father renounces the Catholic church and converts to protestantism: 'And then Mr. O'Neil would come and read to them the sweet story of peace in their own loved Irish tongue'. The volume ends with: 'And now, dear reader, farewell! And while you feel thankful to God for having made you a "happy English child", do not look with pride and contempt on "Irish children". Think rather of Bridget Sullivan, and instead of despising, learn to love and help and pray for them' [CM].

Anon.24 *Busy Peter.*
      Dublin: James Duffy & Co., [1892 or earlier] (Duffy's Juvenile Library). SOURCE Adv. in J.J. O'Dea, *The beauties of nature* (Dublin, 1892).
      COMMENTARY No copy located [RL].

Anon.25 *Caroline Tracy, the Spring Street milliner's apprentice; or, life in New York in 1847–8. Being the narrative of actual occurrences which came to the knowledge of a young physician of New York City.* [Also contains] *The sister-in-law: a tale of real life.*
      New York: Stearns & Co., 1849 (ill.). SOURCE Fanning, p. 377; Wright, i, 483. LOCATION CtY.
      New York: W.F. Burgess; Cincinnati (OH): Burgess & Wood, 1849. SOURCE Wright, i, 483a.
COMMENTARY 91pp. No copy of the New York/Cincinnati edn located. Consists of the story of an Irish prostitute in New York. Also advertised by Dick & Fitzgerald in New York at 25¢ in the 1850s [Fanning, p. 78; Adv. in O. Bradbury, *Ellen Grant* (New York, [185?])].

Anon.26 *Castle Martyr. A tale of old Ireland.*
      London: Hugh Cunningham & Mortimer, 1839, 2 vols. SOURCE Hodgson p. 97; Block, p. 36; Wolff, 7426; Sadleir, 78; Brown 2, 5 (London, Thomas Curson Hansard, 1839 edn.). LOCATION C.
COMMENTARY Describes the 1798 movement towards rebellion in east Co. Cork and west Co. Waterford and gives an account of an alleged visit by Lord Edward Fitzgerald to the Youghal area [Brown 2].

Anon.27 *A castle of Christmas eve; or, the tales the portraits told.*
      + Dublin: United Ireland Offices, 1885. SOURCE Brown, 14. LOCATION D.
COMMENTARY Contributions by T.M. Healy, MP, John Augustus O'Shea§, J.H. M'Carthy [Justin Huntley McCarthy§], M.T. Pender§, Edmund Leamy, MP§, Katharine Tynan§, William Redmond, MP, E. O'Shea Dillon, James O'Connor, Hannah Lynch§, J.J. O'Shea [Mrs. J.J. O'Shea Dillon§], William O'Brien, MP§. Originally appeared as the Christmas number of *United Ireland* (Dublin, 20 Dec. 1884). The story is about a reporter, Michael Kelly, who goes to Dublin Castle with a deputation on the subject of the deterioration of the Irish oyster. He

is inadvertently locked in one of the rooms where he has fallen asleep. He dreams of a banquet in which the vice-regal portraits come to life and each of them tells a story [Brown; OCLC].

Anon.28 *The Castle of Savina; or, the Irishman in Italy. A tale.*
> + London: Ann Lemoine & J. Roe, [*c*.1807] (ill. W. Grainger, S. Sharp). LOCATION InND Loeber coll. (incomplete).

COMMENTARY Novelette of 6opp ending with a poem by Sir John Moore. Engraving dated 1807. Set in Italy. Terence is an Irish servant who has lost his master in Italy. He has attached himself as a servant to a young profligate, but when he sees that the young man has designs on a young girl, he switches sides and helps the girl and her lover to survive. The story was also published as a serial in *Weekly Selector, or Sligo Miscellaneous Magazine* (Sligo, May–July 1812), 8 parts, and as part of a collection of stories, *Wild roses; or, cottage tales* (London, 1808) [ML; Mayo, 191; ViU cat.].

Anon.29 *Cathleen.*
> Dublin: James Duffy & Co., [1892 or earlier] (Duffy's Juvenile Library). SOURCE Adv. in J.J. O'Dea, *The beauties of nature* (Dublin, 1892).
> COMMENTARY No copy located [RL].

Anon.30 *Catholic tales.*
> + Dublin: James Duffy, [1882–5]. LOCATION PC.

COMMENTARY Consists of three stories bound together, but with separate title pages, separately paginated, and each published by James Duffy in Dublin. Contents: 'The white hen: An Irish fairy tale', 'The favourite child; or, Mary Ann O'Halloran. An Irish tale' (by an Irish priest [Fr William Crolly§]), 'The Queen of Italy. Canova's cake, and the prudent choice' (1880 [anon., but by William Bernard MacCabe§]). 'The white hen' had been first anonymously published by James Duffy in 1852, while 'The favourite child' was first published separately in 1851 [PC; RL].

Anon.31 *Charley Chalk; or, the career of an artist; being sketches from real life; comprising a narrative of his extraordinary adventures in Great Britain and Ireland, France and Greece.*
> + London: C. Berger, [*c*.1839] (ill. 'Jacob Parallel'). SOURCE Sadleir, 79; Ximenes cat. 103/190. LOCATION L, InND Loeber coll.

COMMENTARY First published in the *Romancist and Novelist's Library* (London). An amusing comic novel about the hapless career of an artist [Fotheringham cat. 56/34; Ximenes; Sadleir 3757a].

Anon.32 *The chimney sweep.*
> + Dublin: Printed [for the author?] by M. Goodwin, 1825. SOURCE NSTC. LOCATION O.

COMMENTARY Revd Lambert and his son visit a chimneysweep's home in an unnamed city and are amazed by its cleanliness and spirituality. They ask for the story of his life. The moral is told by Revd Lambert: James [the chimneysweep] had been brought up by a pious man. He ought to have profited by the instruction offered to him – he was brought to religious meetings – but all without effect. He persisted in evil. Then the Lord addressed him in another language. James understood this language and obeyed the voice that called him [CM].

Anon.33 *Clarissa Leland; an interesting narrative detailing in the history of Charles M'Kenzie and Clarissa Leland, a faithful picture of the oppressions endured by the Irish peasantry.*
> London: Dean & Munday, [1830] (ill.). SOURCE RLIN. LOCATION MH.
> COMMENTARY 28pp [RLIN].

Anon.34 *Coast Castle, its environs, its inhabitants and its visitors. A sketch.*
> Belfast: Marcus Ward & Co., 1864. SOURCE Emerald Isle cat. 88/33, 91/39. LOCATION L.
COMMENTARY Printed for private circulation and published posthumously. Written by a female author (whose presumed portrait is shown on the frontispiece), who carefully concealed the identity of her castle (called Sea Castle) and its inhabitants. Set in the north of Ireland, it mentions Earlsdale, two miles from Coast Castle and Gracehill, the Moravian Village [Emerald Isle].

Anon.35 *Confessions of an homoeopathist.*
> + Dublin: Samuel B. Oldham; London: Whittaker & Co.; Edinburgh: J. Johnstone, 1846. SOURCE COPAC. LOCATION L.
COMMENTARY The preface states that the tale is intended to show the dangers of homoeopathy. The story is set on the Continent and in England and tells the tale of a poor German boy of humble background who found out that he was able to manipulate people to his own benefit. He makes a fortune practicing in homoeopathy in England. Because of some failures in his craft, he also makes a deadly enemy of one of his former patients. He returns to the Continent, where he buys a title and marries. However, he is pursued by his enemy and accidentally falls into a well, from which an Irish doctor and his English friend rescue him. While recovering he tells the story of his life. The Englishman introduces him to religion. Eventually he dies, having gained faith and the forgiveness of his enemy. When the scene is set in England, there is a description of a group of Connacht men who have come to England to work in the harvest [ML].

Anon.36 *Cooper's Irish dialect. Readings and recitations.*
> + New York: Henry J. Wehman, 1891. SOURCE RLIN. LOCATION Syracuse Univ. (NY), DCL.
COMMENTARY 109pp. A mixture of stories and poems. Contents of the prose: 'Jimmy Butler and the owl' [earlier published by J.A. Smith in *Humorous sketches and poems* (Toronto, 1875)], 'The Irish philosopher' ([William?] MacCabe§), 'Mrs. Magoogin's daughter' (John J. Jennings), 'Paudeen O'Rafferty's say [*sic*] voyage', 'Nora Murphy and the spirits' (Henry Hatton), 'Her cake was dough', 'Paddy's dream' [by 'G.C.', first published in the *Irish Penny Magazine* (Dublin, 1833), pp 11–13], 'Pat O'Flaherty on women's rights', 'The illigant affair at Muldoon's. Terry O'Dodd's version', 'Miss Maloney goes to the dentist', 'Pat at the post-office' (Mrs S.C. Hall§), 'The Chinaman and Mickey Finn's goat' (Ernest Jerrold), 'That recommend' (S.D. Richardson), 'Father Phil's subscription list' (abridged from Samuel Lover§), 'Biddy's trials among the Yankees', 'Con Lafferty's coon' (Wade Whipple), 'Winning a widow', 'Patrick O'Rourke and the frogs' (George W. Bungay), 'That fire at the Nolans', 'The Kildare grip' (Henry Llewellyn Williams§) [ML].

Anon.37 *The cottagers of the glen.*
> Dublin: [sold at 22 Upper Sackville St.], [1827 or earlier]. SOURCE Adv. in Charlotte Elizabeth§, *The moth* (Dublin), 1827.
> COMMENTARY No copy located. Priced at 4*d*. [RL].

Anon.38 *The danger of ignorance.*
    Dublin: James Duffy & Co. [1886 or earlier]. SOURCE: Adv. in W. Carleton, *Redmond, Count O'Hanlon* (Dublin: Duffy, 1886).
COMMENTARY No copy located. Priced at 6*d*. Possibly a reprint of *The danger of ignorance, The cardinal's dinner, William and his monkey, and The way to be happy* (Baltimore: Kelly, Piet & Co., 1868) a work written for juveniles, in which the full title of the first story is 'Aline de Coulanges, or the danger of ignorance' (perhaps a take-off of 'Emilie de Coulanges', one of the *Tales of fashionable life* (London, 1809) by Maria Edgeworth§) [OCLC; RL].

Anon.39 *Darby Fagan's journey from Armagh, and his visits to the first and second exhibition of paintings at Belfast in 1836 and 1837.*
    Belfast: Greer, [1837?]. SOURCE de Búrca cat. 65/112; NSTC. LOCATION MH.
COMMENTARY Satire on the progress of the fine arts in Belfast in a series of humorous letters submitted to the *Belfast Commercial Chronicle*, which describe the author's reactions to the two exhibitions. At the end are two poems and a page of music [de Búrca cat. 65/112].

Anon.40 *The Davenels; or, a campaign of fashion in Dublin* (dedicated to Arthur Wellesley, duke of Wellington).
    + London: Henry Colburn, 1829, 2 vols. SOURCE Brown, 21; British Fiction; Garside, 1829:1. LOCATION Corvey CME 3–628–47413–2, Ireland related fiction, Dt, E, MH.
COMMENTARY The *La Belle Assemblée* (London, 10 [1829], p. 304) notes that the novel has been '[a]scribed, ... we think erroneously to Lady Morgan'§. Set in Dublin and in Ireland around the time of Catholic emancipation (1829), and describes fashionable life. The parents of the Davenel girls attempt to marry off their daughters. However, Irish girls do not have a chance of finding a husband in England, and they have to be content with setting their sights on Irishmen [ML; British Fiction].

Anon.41 *The delightful history of the life and death of that renowned & famous St Patrick, champion of Ireland, containing his heroick actions and valorous atchievements in Europe, Asia, and Africk. With other remarkable passages, from his cradle to his grave.*
    + London: D. Newman, 1685 (ill.). SOURCE Esdaile, p. 282; Wing D903; Gilbert, p. 201; Sweeney 1369. LOCATION DPL Gilbert coll., L.
COMMENTARY Describes the adventures of St Patrick who, like a medieval knight, performs great acts of bravery and chivalry in fighting monsters and rescuing ladies, subsequent to his stay in Ireland. His travels bring him to the countries around the Mediterranean [ML].

Anon.42 *Denis O'Grady's Irish stories.*
    [London: publisher?, *c*.1820 or earlier]. SOURCE Adv. in [anon.], *Irish bulls, selected by that tight lad, Teddy O'Flannigan* (London, [1820?]) as being just published, and priced at 6*d*.
COMMENTARY No copy located [RL].

Anon.43 *Dennis McArthy; or, a home in New Brunswick.*
    + London: William Macintosh, 1867. LOCATION L.
COMMENTARY Religious fiction. After their conversion to protestantism, an Irish couple decides to emigrate to New Brunswick in Canada where they will be free to be openly Protestant. They prosper and convert an Indian tribe to protestantism [ML].

Anon.44 *Dermot, the fisher-boy of Inniskerry.*
+ London: Society for Promotion of Christian Knowledge, n.d. (ill.). LOCATION
CaOTP.
COMMENTARY Religious fiction. The narrator, although born in Ireland, mostly lived abroad
but returns to one of the western sea ports, where he stays in a rectory. There is much Bible
reading, followed by the conversion of Dermot and others [RL].

Anon.45 *The devil's stroll through Dublin, a satiric sketch from the comic periodical literature of old Dublin.*
+ Dublin: Edward Smith, 1880 (ill.). SOURCE OCLC; COPAC. LOCATION L, NUC
(1880, 2nd edn, revsd), InND Loeber coll.
COMMENTARY 60pp. The preface refers to claims of the English poets Samuel Taylor Coleridge
and Robert Southey to the authorship of the *Devil's walk* (London, 1830). The Dublin work
was inspired by this and is written in a satirical form. Preface is written from the same address
as that of the publisher, Edward Smith, who may have been the author [RL].

Anon.46 *Duffy's tales for the young.*
Dublin: J. Duffy & Co., [1886 or earlier]. SOURCE Adv. in W. Carleton, *Redmond,
Count O'Hanlon* (Dublin, 1886).
COMMENTARY No copy located [RL].

Anon.47 *Dunsany. An Irish story.*
London: Sherwood, Neely & Jones, 1818, 2 vols. (subscribers' list). SOURCE Brown,
23; Belanger, 49; Block, p. 64; British Fiction; Garside, 1818:8. LOCATION Corvey
CME 3-628-47714-X, Ireland related fiction, MH.
COMMENTARY The scene is set in England and the characters are English in sympathy and
education, although some happen to have been born in Ireland. The story deals with the marrying of impecunious sons and daughters and gives a picture of Irish society from the English
viewpoint. There are a few Irish subscribers to this novel (e.g., Viscount Kilmorey and his
wife), but most of the subscribers are from Wales and the west of England [Brown; RL; British
Fiction].

Anon.48 *The dying woodcutter.*
Dublin: James Duffy & Co., [1886 or earlier]. SOURCE Adv. in W. Carleton, *Redmond,
Count O'Hanlon* (Dublin, 1886).
COMMENTARY No copy located. Priced at 6*d*. [RL].

Anon.49 *Edith; or, life's changes.*
+ Dublin: William Robertson; London: Simpkin, Marshall & Co., 1858 (Railway
Edition). SOURCE COPAC; Topp 8, 81. LOCATION L, InND Loeber coll.
COMMENTARY Set in England. A young man, Mr Wycherly, dallies with the affections of
Edith Waldron. He leaves suddenly without a word to her, making her very unhappy. Her
father dies and she becomes a governess in a household where the mother is mad and eventually kills one of the daughters. She meets Sir Mark Meredith, a rich man who falls in love
with her, but she still has warm feelings for Mr Wycherly. However, Mr Wycherly comes
back on the scene and cures her of her lingering love for him. She marries Sir Mark and
with him visits his estates in Ireland. Wycherly falls in love and marries Edith's former pupil
[ML].

Anon.50 *Emerald gems: A chaplet of Irish fireside tales, historic, domestic, and legendary. Compiled from approved sources.*
+ Boston: Marlier, Callanan & Co., 1878. SOURCE Brown, 28 (Boston: Noonan, 1879 edn). LOCATION InND Loeber coll.

COMMENTARY Contents: 'Deirdri, or the sorrowful fate of the children of Usna', 'The moat of Cromogue', 'Jack, the cunning thief', 'The Donagh; or, the horse-stealers' [William Carleton§], 'The fairy finder', 'Clontarf, or the death of King Brian Boru', 'Hairy Rouchy' [Patrick Kennedy§], The Whiteboy tragedy of "seventy five"' [Patrick Kennedy§], 'Roney Maher', 'A legend of clever women', 'Kate Connor' [Mrs S.C. Hall§], 'The gridiron; or Paddy Mullowney's travels in France' [Samuel Lover§], 'The bier that conquered', 'The earl of Stairs' son', 'Shan an Omadhan and his master', 'The wise thought', 'The fight of Shroughmore', 'The twelve wild geese', 'The usurer's ghost', 'Jack, the shrimp', 'The three gifts', 'The burial of the tithe' [Samuel Lover§], 'The battle of Ballinvegga' [Patrick Kennedy§], 'The giant and his royal servants', 'The dance-school', 'Coursing and fowling extraordinary', 'The Gilla na Gruaga Donna', 'The battle of Beal-an-atha-buie', 'The grateful beasts', 'The three geese' [RL; Personal communication, Kevin Whelan, July 2004].

Anon.51 *Emma; or, the child of sorrow.*
+ London: T. Lowndes, 1776, 2 vols. SOURCE Gecker, 295; Raven 2, 1776:2; ESTC t108372. LOCATION L, PU.
Dublin: S. Price, D. Chamberlaine, W. Watson, J. Potts, W. Sleater [and 21 others], 1776, vol. 1. SOURCE ESTC n050813. LOCATION Dt (Dublin, Watson et al. edn, 1777, 2 vols.), L (not located).
Dublin: S. Price, D. Chamberlaine, W. Watson, J. Potts, W. Sleater [and 21 others], J. Beatty, 1776, vol. 2. SOURCE McBurney & Taylor, 253; Raven 2, 1776:2; ESTC n050813. LOCATION PC, IU.
Paris [London]: Buisson, 1788, 2 vols. (trans. by Mlle Haudry as *Emily, ou l'enfant du malheur*). SOURCE Streeter, 18; ESTC t229577. LOCATION L.
Londres [Paris]: Crapart; Volland; Briand & la veuve Lesclapart, 1788, 2 vols. SOURCE ESTC t229576; Bn Opale-Plus. LOCATION Biblioteka Publiczna, Warsaw, Poland.
+ Paris: Marchand, [1798], 2 vols. in 1 (trans. as *Emma ou l'enfant du malheur*; ill.). SOURCE InND Loeber coll.
Leipzig: J.F. Junius, 1776 (trans. as *Emma oder das Kind des Kummers*). SOURCE Raven 2, 1776:2. LOCATION Staatsbibliothek, Berlin.
COMMENTARY Widely reprinted Irish epistolary novel of sentiment set mostly in London among the upper-classes, making a case for single women. Slim Irish content [RL; *Irish University Review*, 10(2), 1980, p. 235, citing 1777 edn].

Anon.52 *English hearths and Irish homes. Life scenes from an editor's note book, and social sketches for sunny nooks and winter firesides. Profusely illustrated* (new edn of 'Leaves from an editor's note-book').
+ London: W. Kent & Co., 1868. SOURCE NSTC. LOCATION L (missing), O.
+ Leamington: J. Arthur, the Library, 1868. LOCATION O.
COMMENTARY The text mentions that 'The flattering reception which was accorded to this volume when it first appeared has encouraged its reissue,' but no earlier edn is known [CM].

Anon.53 *An episode in the dynamite war.*
+ Salisbury: Brown & Co.; Leeds: J.W. Petty & Sons; London: Simpkin & Marshall, 1885. SOURCE Topp 8, 761. LOCATION L.

COMMENTARY 31pp. Priced at 6*d*. Set in Dublin and England. An English commercial traveller becomes suspicious about people in his hotel in Dublin. They are plotting to blow something up (the story does not state whether they are Fenians or not). The traveller is found spying and the conspirators threaten to kill his daughter. Eventually, one of the conspirators reunites the traveller with his daughter and the conspirator commits suicide [ML].

Anon.54 *Errors and their consequences; or, memoirs of an English family.*
> London: Longman, Hurst, Rees, Orme & Brown, 1819, 2 vols. SOURCE Ximenes List
> M15/67; COPAC; Garside, 1819:7. LOCATION Corvey CME 3–628–47620–8, L, C.
COMMENTARY A contemporary tale of match-making, social ambition and greed, involving members of a provincial family of considerable means. Several of the characters are Irish. A preface discusses the problems of novelty in modern novel-writing [Ximenes List M15/67].

Anon.55 *Eva Desmond; or, mutation.*
> London: Smith, Elder & Co., 1858, 2 vols. SOURCE Brown 2, 7; OCLC. LOCATION
> L, C.
COMMENTARY Eva Desmond's father, of Glenmore House (Co. Cavan), became a Protestant in order to marry into the Clifton family of Wiltshire. The novel describes a number of family members' amorous intrigues and gives a picture of the impoverished Irish gentry [Brown 2].

Anon.56 *Eva Fitzgerald; or, scenes in Erin and the sister isle* (dedicated 'To the long suffering and noble-hearted Catholics of Ireland').
> + London: Burns & Lambert, 1861 (subscribers' list: including several convents and
> Christian Brothers' schools). SOURCE Brown 2, 8; COPAC. LOCATION L, InND
> Loeber coll.
COMMENTARY A Catholic tale. Eva Fitzgerald's father is Irish and her mother English. They live in England. When her father dies, her mother remarries but her new husband deserts her. The story describes the struggles of Eva and her sisters to survive. Eva goes to St Petersburg (Russia) as a governess. Two sisters go to the workhouse, after which a rich Protestant family takes one of them in. Eva returns in time to rescue the other sister. It describes proselytism and evictions in Ireland [Brown 2].

Anon.57 *Extracts from a narrative of the conversion of an Asiatic prince to the Christian faith, and from letters on religious subjects.*
> + [London]: W. Flexney, [1799 or earlier] (subscribers' list, many of whom are Irish
> nobility). SOURCE Figgis cat. 47/99; ESTC t122073. LOCATION L, CKu, InND
> Loeber coll.
COMMENTARY Rare example of a novel about the proposed Act of Union between Ireland and England. For eighteenth-century books published in Ireland the proportion of women subscribers to the novel was very high, and for a book with a political message, the proportion was exceptional. A man educated in England goes into the world to make his fortune as a merchant. However, he ends up as a slave of an Asian monarch of two domains. This king treats his slaves in a benevolent fashion by insisting on them being clean and provided for. He also instructs the supervisor of the slaves to look out for people with special skills or knowledge so that his nation might benefit from them. The narrator plays the flute and the king wishes to learn to play that instrument. He learns the English language in the process of reading the Old and the New Testaments. The king spontaneously remarks that he likes the prophet Jesus

much better than Mahomet, which gives the narrator the courage to instruct the king in the Christian religion. He sends the narrator back to Europe to recruit missionaries to convert his people to Christianity. While in England, he learns that the relaxation in the adherence to religious rules leads to revolutions. Fraternal love as a political principle (alluding to the revolution in France) is mentioned as one of the negative outcomes. An appendix to the volume deals with the need to have a common language. A second appendix deals with the way that public punishment and rewards are dealt out in the Asian kingdom and stresses private and public conformity to laws. In a third appendix, the story is linked to two kingdoms, a greater and a lesser, divided by a narrow channel of the sea (representing England and Ireland), and a brief history of their relations is provided. The question is raised about what should be done about the troublesome smaller island. The final appendix contains some religious notes, showing the way to religious consolation experienced by righteous believers. We have seen a reference to *Extracts from a narrative of the conversion of an African prince to the Christian faith, and from letters on religious subjects* (London, 1798), but this must be a mistaken title for the above work, because no work with that title is known [ML; W.J. McCormack, *The pamphlet debate on the Union* (Blackrock, 1996), p. 42].

Anon.58 *Extraordinary adventures of a watch.*
> Dublin: James Duffy & Co., [1886 or earlier]. SOURCE Adv. in W. Carleton, *Redmond, Count O'Hanlon* (Dublin: Duffy, 1886).
> COMMENTARY No copy located [RL].

Anon.59 *The fair Hibernian.*
> + London: G.G.J. & J. Robinson, 1789, 2 vols. SOURCE Hardy, 47; Black, 98; Forster 2, 1358; Raven 2, 1789:6; ESTC t119711. LOCATION L.
> + Dublin: P. Byrne, P. Wogan, B. Dornin, J. Halpin, J. Jones, J. Moore & W. Jones, 1790. SOURCE Gecker, 301; Raven 2, 1789:6; ESTC n008161. LOCATION D, PU.
> Dublin printed: Re-printed at Newburyport [MA]: by George Jerry Osborne, 1794. SOURCE Black, 98; McBurney & Taylor, 256; ESTC w012185. LOCATION IU.

COMMENTARY Rev. in the *European Magazine* (Feb. 1790) and reproduced in Byrne's *Universal Magazine* in Dublin. An epistolary novel, written by persons of quality in England, Ireland and France, which features as main character an Irish girl, Valeria O'Bryen. It contains very little on Ireland. Mary Wollstonecraft critiqued this novel by writing: 'Without a knowledge of life, or the human heart, why will young misses presume to write?' The same title is included in Joseph Moser's *Turkish tales* (London: William Lane, 1794) [ML; Blakey, p. 168; S.M. Conger (ed.), *Sensibility in transformation* (Cranbury, NJ, 1990), p. 128; M. Deane (ed.), *Belmont Castle or suffering sensibility* (Dublin, 1998), p. 23].

Anon.60 *Fair Rosamond to the fair Hibernian. An epistle.*
> London: T. Howard, [1752]. SOURCE Forster, 826; ESTC n1444. LOCATION Univ. of Cincinnati (OH).

COMMENTARY A novelette priced at 6*d*. Rev. in the *Monthly Review* (London, 1752, vol. vi, p. 79), which states that 'this little piece contains some general hints to the fair Hibernian, to caution against the fatal effects, which the ladies so often experience from the flattery and adulation of men … the whole deduced from the melancholy example of the famous *Unfortunate concubines: or, the history of Fair Rosamond, mistress to Henry II, and Jane Shore, concubine to Edward IV* (a chapbook that continued to be published well into the nineteenth century) [RL].

Anon.61 *False appearances; or, memoirs of Henry Auberville interspersed with legendary*
romances (dedicated to Sir Fenton Aylmer, Bt).
Dublin: William Porter, 1803. SOURCE British Fiction; Garside, 1807:7. LOCATION IU.
COMMENTARY 179pp. Preface dated Dublin, May 1803. Summers mentions 'an English edn
of the same year, but some months earlier'. No such edn has been located. The dedicatee, Sir
Fenton Aylmer, was of Donadea (Co. Kildare) [Garside, 1803:7; RL].

Anon.62 *Faversham Grange; or, the daughter of the Piscatori.*
Dublin: James Duffy & Co., [1886 or earlier]. SOURCE Adv. in W. Carleton, *Redmond,*
Count O'Hanlon (Dublin, 1886).
COMMENTARY No copy located [RL].

Anon.63 *La fée de la famille O'Toole, ou le signal de départ* (imitated from the English,
followed by *La fée irlandaise* (a play in three acts), translated by Mme Daring).
Paris: Lance, 1833. SOURCE Devonshire, p. 459; CCF. LOCATION BNF.

Anon.64 *The female barbers. An Irish tale, after the manner of Prior.*
London: Williams, 1765. SOURCE Forster, 881; Raven, 949; ESTC t189992. LOCATION
Dt, O.
COMMENTARY Various edns from 1750 are in verse and refer to the Irish poet Thomas Prior.
This title is known from a review in 1765, indicating that this edn was not in verse, but no
copy has been located. The same title appeared in London in about 1770 and consisted of
12pp but it is unclear whether this was an abridgement. A slip-song in a single sheet, *The*
female barbers. A tale, was published in Dublin in or about 1765 [ESTC t189992; ESTC
t007726; Raven, 949].

Anon.65 *Forlorn, but not forsaken: a story of the "bad times" in Ireland.*
Dublin: [publisher?], 1871. LOCATION L (destroyed).
COMMENTARY No copy located. Religious fiction that deals with the Famine in 1848–9
[RL; BLC].

Anon.66 *The fortune hunter; or, history of Jack FitzPatrick: With four other novels. Being,*
the modern novelist.
+ Dublin: Printed [for the author?] by James Hoey Jnr, 1762 (ill.). SOURCE ESTC
t203460. LOCATION D.
COMMENTARY This must be the same as *The adventures of Jack FitzPatrick, embellished with a*
copper-plate frontispiece of a night-scene, known from an advertisement in Sarah Fielding's *The*
history of Ophelia (Dublin: James Hoey, 1763). Contents: 'The fortune hunter' (set in London
and concerns various Irish characters in pursuit of heiresses and widows), 'The story of Bianca
Capello' (set in Italy). The NLI copy does not have 'four other novels' as announced in its
title. The fortune hunter may be based on a story published under the title 'The fortune-
hunter, a modern tale', which appeared in the *Royal Female* (London, 1760, in six parts) [RL;
Raven, 754; Mayo, 449].

Anon.67 *Frailities of fashion; or, the adventures of an Irish smock, interspersed with whim-*
sical anecdotes of a nankeen pair of breeches; containing among a great variety
of curious connexions between the most celebrated demi reps and beaux garçons
upon the ton. The secret memoirs of Madame D'Eon, as related to herself. Amours

de Count D'Artois. Private intrigues of Lady W—Y and Mrs N—N; never before published. The frolics of boarding school misses. The gambols of maids of honour, &c. &c.
London: Lister, 1782. SOURCE Raven 2, 1782:6.
COMMENTARY No copy located. Rev. in the *Critical Review* (London) states: 'One of those pernicious incentives to vice that are a scandal to decency', while the *Monthly Review* (London) found it 'equally remarkable for its stupidity and obscenity'. The story features the famous transvestite D'Eon (1728–1810) and possibly the Count d'Artois, later king of France (1757–1836) [Raven 2; RL].

Anon.68 *The fugitives. A narrative of the adventures, sufferings, and escape of Messrs. Doheny and Stephens, until their arrival in the United States of America, taken from the Cork Examiner.*
+ Cork: Printed [for the author?] by Wm. Hurley, [c.1860]. LOCATION UCC.
COMMENTARY Fictional adventure story with some poems appended, based on the escape of the Fenians Michael Doheny and James Stephens [RL; Personal communication, Kevin Whelan, Jan. 2006].

Anon.69 *Galanteries d'une religieuse mariée à Dublin.*
Cologne: Marteau, 1693. SOURCE *Ulster J. of Archaeology*, 1949, xii, p. 89; Sweeney, 2079.
COMMENTARY No copy located. Probably a sexually titillating story. The imprint 'Cologne: Marteau' is known from at least one other volume, *La source des malheurs d'Angleterre* (Cologne, 1689) and may have originated in Amsterdam. The NUC lists *Galanteries d'une religieuse*, published in Cologne, chez les héritiers de P. Martineau, 1758, which may be a late reprint [Fotheringham cat. 56/170; NUC; RL].

Anon.70 *Genuine letters between a married couple 1767–68.*
Dublin: proposal by Elizabeth Lynch for the publication of this book, and subscriptions taken, 1770.
COMMENTARY Broadside of announced novel. Not in ESTC; no copy of this novel has been located, and possibly it was never published. Probably the title alludes to an imitation or a continuation of Elizabeth§ and Richard Griffith's§ *A series of genuine letters between Henry and Frances* (London, 1757, 1766, 4 vols.). Elizabeth Lynch (née Watson) was a Dublin bookseller, stationer and circulating library keeper [RL; Pollard 2, p. 597]

Anon.71 *Gerard Carlton. A novel* (by the author of 'Twice married').
+ New York: American News Co., [1860s–80s]. LOCATION Wright web.
COMMENTARY Calvin Wheeler Philleo (1787–1874) was the author of *Twice married. A story of Connecticut life* (New York, 1855), but as he is not listed by Wright as the author of *Gerald Carlton*, it is unlikely that he is connected with this work. Story is mainly set in Ireland where a woman came to live in Athy (Co. Kildare) after she had given birth to a son in England and her lover had left her. Her son does not know his real name and his mother refuses to tell him. He has to give up the girl he loves. In the meantime his real father is trying to find out where the mother of his child and the child have gone. Eventually all are united and the riddle is solved [ML; Wright web].

Anon.72 *Gloriously happy. The story of an Irish convert.*
+ London: Wertheim, MacIntosh & Hunt for the Office of Irish Church Mission, [1862]. LOCATION L.

COMMENTARY 32pp. Religious fiction, reprinted from the 'Banner of the Truth in Ireland' (not identified). George Connor is a Roman Catholic, but his wife is a Protestant. 'So far, George Connor's was a very common case – an earnest enquirer sorely persecuted. Alas! It is an everyday tale. None know this better than we who are engaged on the instruction of poor Roman Catholics' (p. 10) [BLC; CM].

Anon.73 *Grace Lindsay; or, one day's experience.*
+ Dublin: Printed [for the author?] by T.I. White for the Book and Tract Society for Ireland, 1829, 3rd edn (ill.). SOURCE Adv. in 'P.D.H.', *The Northern cottage* (Dublin, 1842); OCLC. LOCATION Duke Univ., Chapel Hill, NC.
COMMENTARY 36pp. For sale at 4*d*. No 1st edn located. Religious fiction. Discussion between eleven-year-old Grace Lindsay and her mother about religious matters and dedication to use time better. The story chronicles what Grace does during the day. The booklet ends with a hymn [OCLC; RL].

Anon.74 void

Anon.75 *The green bushes; or, a hundred years ago. A romance.*
London: E. Lloyd, 1847. SOURCE Cox cat. 45/9. LOCATION L.
COMMENTARY 62pp. An early penny dreadful in eight parts set in Ireland and America, by one of the publisher Edward Lloyd's 'Salisbury Square School' of authors. Presumably based on John Baldwin Buckstone's 1845 drama of the same name [Cox cat. 45/9].

Anon.76 *Half hours with Irish authors. Selections from Griffin, Lover, Carleton, and Lever.*
New York: J.A. McGee, 1873 (ill.). LOCATION NUC.
COMMENTARY The selections are from the works of Gerald Griffin§, Samuel Lover§, William Carleton§, and Charles Lever§ [RL].

Anon.77 *Harcourt; a sentimental novel. In a series of letters* (by the authoress of *Evelina* [*sic*]).
+ Dublin: C. Jackson, 1780, 2 vols. in 1. SOURCE Bradshaw, 1684; Black, 140 (variant title); Gecker, 421; Raven 2, 1780:3; Pollard 2, p. 72; ESTC t140056. LOCATION Dt, L, CU, PU.
COMMENTARY Not by Frances Burney, the author of *Evelina* (London, 1778) and not to be confused with [Mrs Mary Meeke's] *Harcourt. A novel* (London, 1799, 4 vols.). An epistolary novel set in London concerning matters of love [Raven 2; ML].

Anon.78 *The Hibernian keepsake, for 1832* (dedicated to the marchioness of Westmeath).
+ London: C. Fleming, [1832] (ill. A. Colin, W. Greatbatch). SOURCE NSTC. LOCATION E, InND Loeber coll.
COMMENTARY A collection of prose and poetry, none of it dealing with Ireland. The stories are by various authors, of whom only one, Sir Aubrey de Vere, is an Irish poet. Internal evidence indicates that this volume may have been a revamped version of a story in the periodical the *Gem* (London) [RL].

Anon.79 *Hibernian tales, being a choice collection of popular stories descriptive of Irish life, from several eminent authors.*
+ Dublin: James M'Cormick, 1844 [cover has 1845]. LOCATION D.
COMMENTARY 90pp. Contents: 'An account of a remarkable trial for murder', 'The robber. A tale of the North of Ireland' (from [Dr. John] Gamble§, 'Sketches of the society and manners' [i.e., *Sketches of history, politics, and manners, taken in Dublin and the North of Ireland, in the autumn of 1810* (London, 1811, suppressed; 1826, new edn)], 'Brien O'Dempsey, A tale of Eyemali' (P. Mooney), 'The Whiteboy's revenge' [Denis O'Donoho] [ML].

Anon.80 *History of the Burnett family, or the life and adventures of Albert de Clerville. An interesting tale.*
+ Dublin: Printed [for the author?] by John Martin, n.d. [18th c.]. LOCATION D.
COMMENTARY Not in ESTC. Set in Spain [RL].

Anon.81 *A history of the customs, manners, and religion, of the moon. To which are annexed, several specimens of lunar poetry; and the characters of the most distinguished personages* (dedicated to 'My dearly beloved self').
+ Dublin: Printed [for the author?] by John Hillary, 1782. SOURCE Pollard 2, p. 289; ESTC t212453. LOCATION Dt, Di.
COMMENTARY A satirical work describing a society of 'beings' living among the heavenly constellations, where time is measured by the revolutions of Saturn. Women play a subordinate role and are banished as soon as their fertile years are over. Contains some poetry and instructions for a newly married lady [ML].

Anon.82 *The history of the honest widow Riley. With an account of Mrs. Buckley, the huxter's wife.*
+ Dublin: Printed by John Jones [for the Kildare Place Society], 1820 (ill.). SOURCE Hodges Figgis cat. 10 n.s./1580; Adams, pp 103, 191. LOCATION D, L.
+ Dublin: Printed by P. Dixon Hardy [for the Kildare Place Society], [1821 or later] (as *James Talbot; or, the importance of recollecting "God sees me at all times." Also, The history of the honest widow Riley. With an account of Mrs. Buckley, the huxter's wife*; ill.). SOURCE RL.
COMMENTARY 72pp. Set in Dublin and concerns the widow Riley, who has a street stall selling vegetables. The story mentions the custom of waking the dead, and features her son Paddy. The Hardy edn consists of two separately paginated booklets, each of 72pp. Of these, the story of James Talbot is by the American storywriter for children, Sarah Savage (1785–1837), and was first published in Cambridge (MA), in 1821. It does not have Irish content [Adams, p. 191; BLC; RL].

Anon.83 *The history of Jacob Newman, the shipwrecked Irish boy: A tale for youth.*
Boston: Crocker & Brewster, 1825. SOURCE RLIN. LOCATION Free Library of Philadelphia (PA).
COMMENTARY 36pp. Fiction for juveniles [RLIN].

Anon.84 *The history of James Reilly and his family; to which is added, John Sands the shoe-boy.*
Dublin: Bentham, 1822. SOURCE Rev. in the *Family Gazette* (Dublin, 4 May 1822).
COMMENTARY 127pp. No copy located. Rev. in the *Family Gazette* and intended for the instruction of 'the lower classes' and relates how a landlord prefers to live among his tenantry rather

than abroad, and wishes to improve the condition of the poor, particularly by promoting education. The second tale is of a poor boy who raises himself and his family to comfort and independence by probity and industry [RL].

Anon.85 *The history of Kitty and Molly Ross; or, the progress of vanity and virtue; a most entertaining novel.*
 Dublin: James Hoey, [1767 or earlier]. SOURCE Adv. in *Memoirs of the remarkable life of Mr. Charles Brachy* (Dublin, [1767]).
 COMMENTARY Not in ESTC and no copy located [RL; Quaritch cat. 1208, p. 49].

Anon.86 *The history of a nobleman and his family.*
 + Dublin: Printed for Benjamin Gunne, 1756. SOURCE ESTC t204531; Raven, 534 ([1760] edn). LOCATION D.
 COMMENTARY 93pp. Included because it is known only from a Dublin edn. No Irish content. Set mainly in France and Turkey [ML].

Anon.87 *The history of Peggy Black and Wilmot Bond. Some truths, some fiction, some things trite, the author now intends to write* (dedicated to Revd Laurence Sterne§).
 + Dublin: Printed [for the author?] by Michael Mills, 1784, 5 vols. SOURCE ESTC n7880. LOCATION D, PU (vols. 1–4), ViU (vols. 2–3).
COMMENTARY Written in a style reminiscent of Laurence Sterne's§ *The life and opinions of Tristram Shandy* (York, 1760–7, 9 vols.), the novel contains bawdy passages, and extensive irreverent conversations about religion, philosophy, and literature. Several Irish authors, including Leonard McNally§ (1752–1820), have been inspired by Sterne's works, but no author of *The history of Peggy Black* has been identified. The text is interspersed with poems and verses. Peggy Black had a rough start in life, helping her mother as a beggar in Ireland until a lady took fancy to her and gave her some education. This was interrupted by the jealousy of a servant causing Peggy to be accused of theft. She leaves her benefactress and has a number of adventures making a living. She meets an Irishman, Wilmot Bond with whom she falls in love. Wilmot and his servant Tom are eloquent characters, who create pun after pun, and bull after bull. Wilmot leaves Peggy and travels to England, where he has new amorous connections. He qualifies to be a ship's surgeon and enters the navy. In his journeys, he visits America and France. Upon his return to England, he visits Peggy now reunited with her father Sir William. She is still in love with Wilmot and, having been long distraught by his absences, dies in his arms. Wilmot marries the pregnant Olivia, a previous love [ML; RL].

Anon.88 *The history of Susan Blake. A true story.*
 + Dublin: P. Dixon Hardy & Sons [for the Religious Book and Tract Depository for Ireland], 1846. LOCATION D.
 COMMENTARY 48pp. Religious fiction set in Co. Wexford near the river Slaney. Susan Blake is a Protestant, has a serious illness and, eventually, dies a happy death [ML].

Anon.89 *The history of Sophronia. A novel founded on truth.*
 Dublin: James Williams, [1764?]. SOURCE Raven, 815.
 COMMENTARY No copy located, and known only from an advertisement Possibly a piracy of *Sophronia, or letters to the ladies* (London, 1761; Dublin, 1763) [Raven].

Anon.90 *Holy and blessed children. Legends for children.*
Dublin: James Duffy & Co., [1892 or earlier]. SOURCE Adv. in J.J. O'Dea, *The beauties of nature* (Dublin, 1892).
COMMENTARY No copy located. Religious fiction for juveniles [RL].

Anon.91 *The holy well. An Irish story to which is added An Irish convert's letter.*
+ London: Religious Tract Society, [1874] (ill.). LOCATION L (destroyed), InND Loeber coll.
COMMENTARY Religious fiction. A conversion story in which an old soldier returns from the Continent to spend his last days in his birthplace in Co. Cork. His parents' cottage has disappeared, but the well is still there. It is now called a holy well after a priest had consecrated it when the original holy well had become too crowded and a place for fighting. The soldier teaches his relatives who live nearby that believing that the well is holy is superstitious. With the help of the Bible in Irish he helps them to convert to protestantism. Attached to the narrative is a letter from a man who had emigrated to North America telling how his wife had died happily as a Protestant. The story was earlier published in another Religious Tract Society publication, [anon.], *The new casket. A gift book for all seasons* (London, [1851]) [ML; RL].

Anon.92 *Honor O'More's three homes.*
New York: Catholic Publication Society, 1871. SOURCE Brown, 39; OCLC. LOCATION Saint John's Univ. Library, New York.
COMMENTARY A story for girls, Catholic in its outlook [Brown; IBL, 8 (Feb.–Mar. 1916–17), p. 88].

Anon.93 *The house of refuge; or, the history of Sally Smith and Kitty Hacket.*
+ Dublin: B. Dugdale, M. Keene, J. Charrurier & T. Johnson, 1810. SOURCE NSTC. LOCATION O.
COMMENTARY 71pp. Story of two children, Sally Smith and Kitty Hacket, 'deposited' in a basket at the Foundling Hospital of Dublin [RL].

Anon.94 *Hyde Nugent. A tale of fashionable life.*
+ London: Henry Colburn, 1827, 3 vols. SOURCE Wolff, 7491; British Fiction; Garside, 1827:7. LOCATION Corvey CME 3–628– 47868–5, L, InND Loeber coll.
COMMENTARY A silver-fork novel, mainly set in a southern county in England at a house called Nugent Hall. The Irish interest is in a side plot. An Irish visitor, Narcissus Moyle, from Castle Moyle in Co. Kilkenny, is a suitor to Louisa Nugent. However, Moyle is presented as the butt of jokes. He then makes advances to Mrs Markham, a rich widow. She consents to marry him, and he goes off to Ireland to prepare Castle Moyle for her arrival. The residence is described as a very old castle. As a part of the preparations, Moyle creates a new avenue to the castle. His bride does not like the castle and the marriage is not a success. Horace St Quentin, an Englishman, comes to visit. He describes Ireland and the Irish in somewhat unflattering terms. St Quentin and Mrs Moyle fall in love. However, a letter summons him back to England, which stops the affair [ML].

Anon.95 *Into the sunlight.*
Dublin: James Duffy & Co., [1892 or earlier]. SOURCE Adv. in J.J. O'Dea, *The beauties of nature* (Dublin, 1892).
COMMENTARY No copy located [RL].

Anon.96 *Ireland's authors.*
+ Dublin: M.H. Gill & Son, 1886 (The O'Connell Press Popular Library; see Plate 1). LOCATION InND Loeber coll.
COMMENTARY Originally issued separately, at 3*d.* (advertised in this volume). Contents: 'The vicar of Wakefield' (Oliver Goldsmith§), 'The bit o' writing' (Michael Banim§), 'On Irish affairs' (Edmund Burke) [RL].

Anon.97 *The Irish brothers and other interesting stories.*
New York: Carleton & Porter, [1856?]. SOURCE OCLC. LOCATION Drew Univ., Madison (NJ).
COMMENTARY Written for Sunday Schools [OCLC].

Anon.98 *Irish bubble and squeak; a selection of the most popular Irish tales, anecdotes, wit, & humour illustrative of the manners and customs of the Irish peasantry.*
+ London: Clarke, Beeton & Co., 1854. SOURCE Brown, 41; NSTC; Topp 6, 79.
LOCATION L (n.d. edn), InND Loeber coll. (n.d. edn).
COMMENTARY Contents: 'Peter Mulrooney in America. – How he was deceived into marrying Mrs Connolly', 'O'Connell's tact in cross-examination', 'Darby and the ram', 'The stolen sheep' [John Banim§], 'Barney M'Connell, the Irish giant', 'Rare discovery', 'Serving a writ in Ireland', 'Peter Mulrooney bothering the lawyers in America', 'Thady and the bear', 'Darby Doyle's voyage to Quebec' [Thomas Ettingsall], 'Anecdotes of [John Philpot] Curran', 'How to save fuel', 'How Peter Mulrooney became a widdy', 'Reward of merit', 'Irish bulls', 'The eagle's nest', 'Paddy Doyle's first trip to Cork' [Edward Walsh], 'The biter bitten', 'Colonel Maribus', 'Kedagh and the counsellor', 'Petit sessions sketch', 'Paddy and the oysters', 'Condy Cullen and the gauger' [William Carleton§], 'Lending a congregation', 'Shane Fadgh's wedding' [William Carleton§], 'Morgan Prussia', 'The beggerman and the blacksmith', 'Paddy Corcoran', 'Tim Rooney', 'Hamilton Rowan and the watch', 'Pether Brierly's inn adventure', ' Tullerdoon', 'The resurrections of Barney Bradley' [William Carleton§], 'The ghost and the two blacksmiths', 'The deserter' [ML].

Anon.99 *The Irish coquette. A novel.*
+ London: Saunders & Otley, 1844, vol. 1 [no other vols. published]. SOURCE Hodgson, p. 289; Brown, 42; NSTC (all mention vol. 1, no further vols. published); Block, p. 119 (mentions 3 vols., which appears a mistake). LOCATION L (vol. 1 only).
COMMENTARY Historical fiction, which starts out in an Elizabethan house, Shamrock Hall, in the south of Ireland. Its owner, Col. O'Grady, has just lost his wife. He is left with a young daughter, Minna. Before her death Minna's mother tried to contact a rich relative of hers so that her daughter would not be wholly unprotected in this world. She was unsuccessful and charged her husband to try again [ML].

Anon.100 *The Irish cottage.*
London: [publisher?], [1835 or earlier]. LOCATION L (destroyed).
Augsburg: M. Rieger, 1835 (trans. as *Die irländische Hütte. Eine Erzählung für die reifere Jungend*; ill.). SOURCE OCLC. LOCATION Univ. of Oregon.
Amsterdam: J.H. Laarman, 1837 (trans. as *De Iersche hut. Een verhaal voor de volwassen jeugd*; new edn). SOURCE Alphabetische naamlijst 1833–49, p. 316.
+ Amsterdam: G.J.A. Beijerinck, 1844 (new edn; trans. from the German as *De Iersche hut. Een verhaal voor de jeugd*). LOCATION InND Loeber coll.

's Hertogenbosch: P. Verhoeven, 1864 (trans. into Dutch by J. Gouverneur as *De Iersche hut*; Mes mentions that this is by the author of *Beatus-kluis*, which has not been identified). SOURCE Brown 2, 559; Mes, pp 20, 116.

Paris: J. Langlumé & Peletier, [1837?] (trans. by F.C. Gérard from the German as *La chaumière irlandaise*; ill.). LOCATION D.

Paris: Langlois & Laclerq, [1845] (trans. by Jacob Glantz [Glatz?] as *La chaumière Irlandaise*; ill.). SOURCE Brown 2, 555.

Regensburg: G.J. Manz, 1874 (trans. as *Die irländische Hütte: eine Erzählung für die gesammte edlere Lesewelt, besonders für die reifere Jungend*; ill.). SOURCE OCLC. LOCATION Mount Angel Abbey Library, Mount Angel (OR).

COMMENTARY No copies of the London, 's Hertogenbosch, and Paris [1845] edns located. Fiction for juveniles set in Co. Wicklow in an idyllic valley. The story is about two brothers and their parents, who live a happy life despite their poverty. Various misadventures befall them: the father drowns while trying to save someone in Dublin Bay, and the sons are pressed into military service. At the end of the story they return to the valley, where they live happily again [RL].

Anon.101 *Irish diamonds.*
+ Philadelphia: J.B. Lippincott, 1891. LOCATION D.
COMMENTARY Contents: 'On the road', 'Young Ireland', 'Irish wit', 'Irish life', 'Irish traits', 'The latter end'. Not to be confused with Emily Bowles's§ *Irish diamonds* (London, 1864) [ML; RL].

Anon.102 *Irish female jockey club.*
[location?]: [publisher?], [date?].
COMMENTARY Mentioned in *The autobiography of William Carleton* (London, 1968), p. 177. No copy located. According to Carleton§, it consists of 'a repertory of the antique scandal of the fashionable demireps ... Only the initials of the names of the characters were given, but so well had they been known to several of the readers, that the names were found pencilled in full in the margins. How so much private scandal was got together, and whether by one or many contributors, it is impossible to say. All I can add is, that the minuteness of the details, and the acquaintance with the localities exhibited by the author or authors, proved those sketches to contain a vast deal of truth – a fact which probably accounted for their escape from prosecution'. Probably the volume was inspired by [Charles Pigott's] *The female jockey club* (London, 1794) [RL; *The autobiography of William Carleton* (London, 1968), p. 177].

Anon.103 *Irish fireside stories, tales and legends.*
New York: P.J. Kenedy, 1879 (ill.). LOCATION D (1904 edn), Boston College (MA).
COMMENTARY Partly the same contents as *Irish bubble and squeak* (London, 1854). This US volume was published by subscription of $1. Contents of 1904 edn: 'Phil Purcel, the pig-driver' [William Carleton§], 'Paul Doherty's visit to Squire Beamton's', 'The wake', 'The wreckers', 'Paddy Doyle's first visit to Cork' [Edward Walsh], 'The boccaugh's curse', 'The pooka', 'The gamblers', 'Kedagh and the counsellor', 'The Duhallow cow-boy', 'Caoine, or Irish death-song', 'The Whiteboy', 'The proctor's daughter', 'Nick Nowlan, the noggin-weaver', 'The hedge schoolmaster' [William Carleton§], 'Condy Cullen and the gauger' [William Carleton§], 'Ellen Duncan' [Denis O'Donoho], 'Legend of Ossheen', 'The biter bitten', 'Legend of Jack-o'-the-lantern', 'Tale of the old wars', 'Darby Dooley and his white horse', 'The dead hand', 'Murder will out', 'Fox and cat hunting', 'Case of assault and battery', 'The ghost and the two blacksmiths', 'The poteen still', 'The mowin' match', 'Fairies, or no fairies', 'Paddy

Corcoran', 'Mickey the sportheen', 'An ocular demonstration', 'A troublesome customer', 'The widow's curse', 'A secret well kept', 'The excursion of Malachi O'Neil', 'The miser outwitted', 'Barney O'Shea, and the Justice of Kilmacshockery', 'First visit to the post-office' [ML; RL].

Anon.104 *The Irish girl, a story of today* .
New York: P.M. Haverty, [1871 or earlier]. SOURCE Adv. by P.M. Haverty in *Haverty's Irish-American Illustrated Almanac* (New York, 1871), p. 104.
COMMENTARY No copy located [RL].

Anon.105 *The Irish girl; or, the true love and the false.*
Glasgow: Cameron & Ferguson, [date?]. SOURCE Brown, 47.
COMMENTARY No copy located. Priced at 6*d*. An Irish girl, Alice, goes to England to stay with an aunt. An Englishman falls in love with her, but he contracts an unhappy marriage with someone else. He is tried for poisoning his wife, but is saved by Alice, whom he marries in the end [Brown; RL].

Anon.106 *Irish highway-men. The lives and actions of the most notorious stories and rapparees comprising interesting narratives of Captain Jeremiah Grant, James Freney, Redmond O'Hanlon, Cahir Na Cuppul, Manus M'Coniel &c.*
Dublin: James Duffy, 1840. SOURCE ABE books (access date: 20 Jan. 2004).
COMMENTARY No other copy located. Largely supplementary to Cosgrave's *A genuine history of the lives and actions of the most notorious Irish highwaymen* (Dublin, 1747). The first story is based on *A biographical sketch of the adventures of Jeremiah Grant* [Dublin, 1816]), while the second story derives from *The life and adventures of James Freney*§ (Dublin, 1754) [RL].

Anon.107 *Irish lives.*
London: [publisher?], 1840, 2 vols. SOURCE *Catalogue of the library of the late Roger Chambers Walker, Q.C.* (Dublin, 1854), p. 10, where it is indicated as a novel (cat. seen at de Búrca, Blackrock, May 1994); RL.
COMMENTARY No copy located [RL].

Anon.108 *The Irish mail calamity.*
London: [publisher?], [1868]. SOURCE NSTC. LOCATION L (destroyed).
COMMENTARY No other copy located. Religious fiction [RL; BLC].

Anon.109 *The Irish outlaws. A romance.*
London: A.K. Newman, 1832, 3 vols. SOURCE Summers, p. 368.
COMMENTARY No copy located. According to Summers this was 'Advertisement among A.K. Newman's New Publications' [Personal communication, Peter Garside, Nov. 2001].

Anon.110 *The Irish pearl. A tale of the time of Queen Anne.*
+ Dublin: Samuel B. Oldham; London: Seeley; Edinburgh: Johnstone, 1850 (ill. Forster). SOURCE Brown, 53; NSTC. LOCATION D, PC, L.
COMMENTARY Repr. from the *Christian Ladies' Magazine* (1847). Advertisement in 1850 states that the profits of this volume were to 'aid in providing home-occupation for the female peasantry, in a poor and comparatively unfriendly district in the South of Ireland'. A religious, strongly anti-Catholic historical tale in which a hermit, Fr Eustace of Gougane Barra (Co.

Cork), tells Lady Glengeary about his conversion to protestantism. Lady Glengeary tells about her conversion to Lady Ormond, who in turn, tells the story to Queen Anne [Brown].

Anon.111 *Irish pleasantry and fun. A selection of the best humorous tales by Carleton, Lover, Lever, and other popular writers.*
Dublin: M.H. Gill & Son, 1881 (ill. J.F. O'Hea). SOURCE OCLC; Brown, 54 (mistakenly states that the 1892 edn is the 1st edn); Hayley, p. 179 (1882 edn); Topp 8, 1224 (1892 edn). LOCATION D (part 2 only), InND Loeber coll. (1892 edn).
+ Dublin: M.H. Gill & Son, 1885 (new edn). SOURCE COPAC. LOCATION E.
COMMENTARY Possibly first issued in parts, because the copy in the NLI (not examined, but listed in OCLC) consists of part 2 and is dated Dec. 1881. Contents of 1892 edn (excluding poetry): 'Barny Bradley's resurrection' (William Carleton§), 'Barny O'Reirdon, the navigator' (Samuel Lover§), 'The bewitched pudding' (William Carleton§), 'Billy Malowney's taste of love and glory' [Joseph Sheridan Le Fanu§], 'Bob Burke's duel with ensign Brady' (William Maginn§), 'The captain's story' (William Hamilton Maxwell§), 'The captured leprauchaun', 'Condy Cullen and the gauger' (William Carleton§), 'Corny Keho's birth and Christening' (William Carleton§), 'Darby Doyle's voyage to Quebec' [Thomas Ettingsall], 'Denis O'Shaughnessy's story of Luther' (William Carleton§), 'The devil and Tom Connolly ([W.F.?] Barry§), 'The devil's mill' (Samuel Lover§), 'An extraordinary phenomenon' ([Thomas Caulfield] Irwin§), 'The fairy finder' (Samuel Lover§), 'Father Malachi's supper' (Charles Lever§), 'Father Phil Blake's collection' (Samuel Lover§), 'The gauger outwitted' (William Carleton§), 'The ghost and the bone-setter', 'The gridiron; or Paddy Mullowney in France' (Samuel Lover§), 'The hare-hound and the witch' ([Michael] Banim§), 'Handsome Kate Kavanagh', 'How I escaped matrimony' (William Hamilton Maxwell§), 'How Father Tom taught the pope to mix punch' (William Maginn§), 'How Peter Connell took the pledge' (William Carleton§), 'An Irish election' (Samuel Lover§), 'An Irish wake' (William Carleton§), 'Jack Mullany's fish story', The keg of poteen', 'King O'Toole and Saint Kevin' (Samuel Lover§), 'Laying a ghost' (William Carleton§), 'Legend of Garry Castle', 'Legend of Fin-mac-Cool', 'The little weaver of Duleek Gate' (Samuel Lover§), 'Little fairy' (Samuel Lover§), 'Mail-coach adventure' (Charles Lever§), 'Mat Kavanagh, the hedge schoolmaster' (William Carleton§), 'Mickey Free and the editor' (Charles Lever§), 'Mickey Free's father and the ghost' (Charles Lever§), 'M'Garry's wake' (Samuel Lover§), 'Miss Judy Macan' (Charles Lever§), 'The monks of the screw' (Charles Lever§), 'Mr. O'Leary's two loves' (Charles Lever§), 'Mr. Dempsey's grandfather' (Charles Lever§), '"My new Pittayatees"' (Samuel Lover§), 'Othello at drill' (Charles Lever§), '"Paddy the piper"' (Samuel Lover§), 'Paddy Flynn', 'Paddy the sport' (Samuel Lover§), 'Paddy Corbett's first smuggling trip', 'Peggy the pishoge', 'The peregrinations of Mac-Brady', 'Phil Purcel, the pig driver' (William Carleton§), 'The pugnacious tailor' (William Carleton§), 'Puss in brogues: A legend', 'Riches in spite of ill-luck' (William Carleton§), 'Saint Bridget's shawl: A legend' [Thomas Ettingsall], 'Saint Sinan's warning', 'Shamus O'Brien' ([Sheridan] Le Fanu§), 'Shane Fadgh's wedding' (William Carleton§), 'Shawn Gow and the cluricaun', 'The shebeen house, and the curse of Kishoge' (Samuel Lover§), 'Spree at Donnybrook Fair', 'Terrible Tim' (W.F. Lynam§), 'The three tasks' (William Carleton§), 'The three wishes' (William Carleton§), 'Tim Hogan's ghost' (J.S. Coyne), 'Trinity College in old times' (Charles Lever§), 'Two queer ladies' (Charles Lever§), 'The white trout' (Samuel Lover§), 'The witch of Kilkenny' (W.F. Barry§) [RL].

Anon.112 *The Irish priest; or, what for Ireland?* (dedicated to Mary).
+ London: Longman, Brown, Green & Longmans, 1847. SOURCE Hodgson, p. 289; Brown, 55; NSTC. LOCATION D, L.

COMMENTARY Supposed to be a manuscript given by a dying priest to a doctor in the west of Ireland. It contains a series of incidents in the priest's life and offers suggestions on how to make Ireland better [Brown].

Anon.113 *The Irish register: or a list of the duchess dowagers, countesses, widow ladies, maiden ladies, widows, and misses of large fortunes in England, as register'd by the Dublin Society, for the use of their members. Together with the places of their several abodes. Also, the charge given by their president, at their last general assembly.*
+ Dublin printed: London re-printed for T. Cooper, 1742. SOURCE ESTC t116018. LOCATION D, L, InND Loeber coll.

COMMENTARY A satire on the pursuits of London heiresses by Irish males. The first thirteen pages consist of 'The President's speech to the Hibernian Society, advising a speedy Draught of their Members to be Imported into England for the Service of the English Ladies'. The president mentions 'with a bleeding Heart ... the miserable State of our dear Nation is reduced to, by the great Numbers of Absentees, now residing in *England*, who spend their Fortune there ... that as we are reduced to this extreme Poverty by our own dear selves, we ought, by the indefatigable Tenderness and Care of the *English* Ladies of large Fortunes, to redress our present Calamities, by cultivating those valuable Talents which Nature has kindly provided us with'. Then follows a list of the ladies, most of them with addresses, listed by rank. This list includes several ladies of Irish nobility, such as the ladies Castlecomer, Kildare and Dillon. The last few pages contain 'Orders and Resolutions of the Brave and Heroic Society of Adventurers at Dublin, for Incorporating and Manufacturing of *British* Commodities,' which refers to the registers kept by Patrick Macguire [*sic*] on Cork Hill, near Pall-Mall, and Owen O'Bourne at his 'Ale-Cabin' at Covent Garden. This document is signed by M. Fitz-Patrick, secretary. The book led to the publication of *The English register: or the Irish register match'd ... to prevent the English ladies from going astray* (London, 1742). An earlier account of Irish fortune-hunters in London was written by E. Jones, entitled *A trip through London: Containing observations on men and things* (London, 1728), while the anonymous *The adventures of Shelim O'Blunder, Esq; the Irish beau* (London, *c.*1750) is of a similar genre [RL; Edward cat. 29/29].

Anon.114 *The Irish rogue: or, the comical history of the life and actions of Darby Ó Brolaghan, from his birth to this present time. To which is added, The gold-merchant; ... Also, Letters of courtship, and love-letter. By the late Earl of Rochester.*
Dublin: James Dalton, 1740. SOURCE Pollard, p. 171; Pollard 2, p. 141; ESTC n001432. LOCATION CSmH.

COMMENTARY Apparently a different book than J.S.'s§, *The Irish rogue; or, the comical history of Teague O'Divelley, from his birth to the present year, 1690* (London, [1690]).

Anon.115 *The Irish scholar: or, the shipwrecked boy.*
Philadelphia: American Baptist Publication, 1853. SOURCE OCLC. LOCATION D.

Anon.116 *Irish stories.*
+ London: Religious Tract Society, [*c.*1854 or 1855] (ill. John Gilbert; see Plate 3. SOURCE Brown 2, 16; NSTC. LOCATION L (destroyed), C, InND Loeber coll.

COMMENTARY Religious fiction. Four stories about how poor Irish children are weaned from the Catholic faith and are taught that salvation lies in the study of the Bible. Contents: 'The good and bad names; or, the workhouse children' (a possible later edn has the title 'The good and bad names'), 'The little Irish girl's holiday', 'Terence Moran; or, the life of an Irish boy', 'Margaret Conolly; or, the snares of business' (a possible later edn has the title 'The snares of business') [RL; Brown 2].

Anon.117 *Irish stories for thoughtful readers.*
New York: Carlton & Phillips, 1855. SOURCE OCLC. LOCATION Drew Univ., Madison (NJ).
Richmond (VA): Presbyterian Committee of Publication, 1867. SOURCE OCLC. LOCATION Virginia Historical Society Library, Richmond (VA).
COMMENTARY Religious (Methodist) fiction for juveniles [OCLC].

Anon.118 *The Irish widow. Founded on facts.*
+ Dublin: R.M. Tims, 1821. SOURCE Block, p. 119; Bradshaw, 3280. LOCATION L (1828 edn), C.
Paris: Delay, 1847 (trans. as *La veuve Irlandaise et son fils; histoire véritable*). SOURCE Brown, 106. LOCATION L.
COMMENTARY 72pp. Proselytizing religious fiction. A young Englishman accompanies his Irish friend Charles to Ireland for a vacation. Charles lives in the remote part of a southern county. His sisters lead busy lives with reading, music, drawing, their schools and other charitable institutions. The Englishman tells the story of a widow, the daughter of a Catholic farmer, who converted to the Protestant religion. At age 16 Elinor had married a young Protestant man, but at that time in her life she would rather dance than listen to the Bible. One Sunday she went to a dance and came back with a cold. Her husband caught the cold from her and died. Elinor married a second time but things did not prosper and her second husband died also. Her son by her first husband had inherited his father's Bible and hymnbook and had learned how to read. When his teacher gives him an Irish Bible, he reads this to his mother and converts her to protestantism. Her son drowns in the river, but her faith supports her [ML; COPAC].

Anon.119 *The Irishman at home: Characteristic sketches of the Irish peasantry.*
+ Dublin: James McGlashan; London: W.S. Orr, 1849 (ill. Geo. Measom). SOURCE Brown, 50; Sadleir, 505; Harris, p. 170; COPAC; Hayley, pp 174–5; NSTC. LOCATION L, C.
COMMENTARY Sadleir, Harris, and COPAC mistakenly attribute all of the following stories to William Carleton§ (but only one is his). The stories were partly reprinted from the *Dublin Penny Journal*. Contents: 'The Whiteboys', 'The Rockite' [Charlotte Elizabeth Tonna§?], 'The wrestlers', 'The mowin' match', 'The false step', 'The fatal meeting', 'The gauger captured and The gauger outwitted' [William Carleton§] [RL].

Anon.120 *Jack Cade; or, the bondsman's struggle. A tale of feudal oppression.*
+ New York: De Witt & Davenport, 1853. LOCATION Wright web.
COMMENTARY Historical fiction set in the fourteenth and fifteenth centuries. The Cade family living in Ireland want to ensure that their property stays in their hands. Therefore, the son, Jack, fights with the Yorkist forces and the father moves to Kent in England. His landlord is a terrible man and almost the whole family is extirpated. In the end Jack organizes an uprising and kills the landlord. Jack is also killed, however [ML].

Anon.121 *Jesuit executorship; or, passages in the life of a seceder from Romanism. An autobiography.*
+ London: John W. Parker & Son, 1853, 2 vols. LOCATION Dt, L.
+ New York: DeWitt & Davenport, [185?] (as *Helen Mulgrave; or, Jesuit executorship: being passages in the life of a seceder from Romanism. An autobiography*).
SOURCE Wright, ii, 115; Griffin, p. 169; RL. LOCATION D, Wright web.
COMMENTARY Anti-Catholic religious fiction. The New York edn is probably the American version of the London edn. The editor's preface to the London edn states that 'the following autobiography is that of a young and highly gifted woman, struggling in the midst of Roman Catholic society, with her own almost spontaneous perception of the errors of the religion in which she has been born and educated'. Set in Ireland (Cork) and France, it concerns Catholic girls' struggles with their perception of errors in Catholic religion. It mentions the governess Miss White, 'who as a rigid catholic was very much confined in her acquaintance with literature'. Extensive notes are appended to the end of each volume [ML; CM].

Anon.122 *Jim Eagan.*
New York: Pratt, [date?]. SOURCE Brown, 57.
COMMENTARY No copy located. Brown was also unable to locate a copy of this volume in 1916–17 [RL; IBL, 8 (Feb.–Mar. 1916–17), p. 88].

Anon.123 *The jolly harper man and his good fortune, and other amusing tales.*
+ Dublin: M.H. Gill & Son, 1890. LOCATION L.
COMMENTARY Stories set in Ireland. Contents: 'Fergus O'Mara and the air demons', 'Mun Carbery and the phooka', 'The leprechaun and the blacksmith' [CM].

Anon.124 *Julia Stanley: A novel. In a series of letters* (published by the author of *The man of feeling, The man of the world, Roubigne* [sic], &c.).
Dublin: C. Jackson, 1780, 2 vols. SOURCE Black, 192; Raven 2, 1780:7; Pollard 2, p. 310; ESTC t127869. LOCATION D, L, MH.
COMMENTARY Epistolary novel. A blatant attempt to profit from the success of Henry Mackenzie's *Man of the world* (London, 1773, 2 vols.) and *Julia de Roubigné* (London, 1777, 2 vols.). The advertisement, signed by C. Jackson, states that the book was to promote 'the cause of virtue' [Johnson cat. 38/41].

Anon.125 *The juvenile annual; or, 100 tales for youth.*
Dublin: James Duffy, [1857 or earlier]. SOURCE Adv. in [anon.], *The young crusader* (Dublin, [1857]).
COMMENTARY No copy located [RL].

Anon.126 *Kate and Rosalind; or, early experiences.*
+ London: Grant & Griffith, 1853 (ill. John Gilbert). LOCATION L.
COMMENTARY Story about two cousins, Kate O'More from Ireland and Rosalind Vernon from England. Initially, Kate lives with her aunt, Mrs Vernon, in Sussex. After her aunt dies, she returns to Ireland, where she marries an Irishman. Eventually, Rosalind also marries an Irishman [ML].

Anon.127 *The kind Irishman, and other tales.*
London: [publisher?], [1877], 6 pts. LOCATION L (destroyed).
COMMENTARY No copy located. Religious fiction [BLC].

Anon.128   *Laura's impulses; or, principle a safer guide than feeling.*
Philadelphia: American Sunday School Union, 1854. SOURCE MacLeod, p. 181; OCLC. LOCATION L (1881 edn), Florida Univ.
COMMENTARY A story for children set in America. Laura offers to teach some poor Irish children to read and is soon bored with the task and chafes at their lack of gratitude [MacLeod].

Anon.129   *The legend of Moilena; or, the priest of Ashinroe.*
London: Geo. Corvie & Co.; Dublin: John Cumming, 1823. SOURCE IBL, 12 (Aug.–Sept. 1920), p. 21.
+ London: A.K. Newman, 1828. LOCATION D.
COMMENTARY Summers notes *The legend of Moleiria* (London: Minerva Press, [1812]), which may relate to the above title, but no copy of this or of the London 1823 edn (perhaps a misprint for 1828?) has been located. The story starts at Moilena, a mansion on the north-west coast of Ireland. It includes information on the Irish bards. It also contains a poem on wild Irish scenery and the painter Salvator Rosa [RL; British Fiction (Update 4)].

Anon.130   *Legends and fairy tales of Ireland.*
New York: P.M. Haverty, 1872 (ill.). SOURCE Fanning, p. 382. LOCATION NUC.
COMMENTARY Announced to be 'ready Nov. 1st, 1871' and advertised as 'being a complete collection of all the fairy tales published by Thomas Crofton Croker§, Thomas Keightley, and embodying the entire volume of [Patrick] Kennedy's§ fictions of the Irish Celts'. 408pp and 50 illustrations [Adv. in *Haverty's Irish-American Illustrated Almanac* (New York, 1872), p. 104; RL].

Anon.131   *Legends and stories of Ireland: containing the dead boxer, and other tales.*
Philadelphia: J.B. Perry, 1848. SOURCE OCLC. LOCATION NUC (mistakenly gives [1820?] edn).
COMMENTARY Contents: 'The dead boxer' [William Carleton§], 'Halloran the peddler', 'Kate Connor' [Mrs S.C. Hall§], 'Mabel O'Neill's curse' [RL].

Anon.132   *Legends and tales of Ireland.*
London: Simpkin, Marshall, Hamilton, Kent & Co., [*c*.1900] (ill.). SOURCE Brown, 964. LOCATION L, InND.
COMMENTARY Contents: Stories from Samuel Lover's§ *Legends and stories of Ireland* (London, 1834), and Thomas Crofton Croker's§ *Fairy legends of the South of Ireland* (London, 1825) [Brown].

Anon.133   *Leonora Hervey. Morad and Abima. Obidah and the hermit. An Irish schoolmaster.*
+ London: J. Arliss, [*c*.1810] (Fireside Amusement from the Juvenile Library; ill. Edwards, Henry Brooke). SOURCE Osborne, p. 275. LOCATION CaOTP.
COMMENTARY Pagination starts at p. 99. The last story concerns a schoolmaster, Mr Thady O'Conolan, teacher at a classical 'seminary' in Connacht. The story has been copied from Sydney Owenson's (later Lady Morgan§), *Patriotic sketches of Ireland, written in Connaught* (London, 1807) ii, pp 138–42. Describes his school in a two-room cabin and the limited availability of reading books [RL].

Anon.134 *Letters from an Irish student in England to his father in Ireland.*
+ London: C. Cradock & Joy, 1809, 2 vols. (ill.). SOURCE COPAC; Falkner
Greirson cat. 17/289 (where W. Lewis is noted as publisher, but he was the
printer). LOCATION L, InND (1812 edn).
London: [n.p.], 1809, 2 vols. SOURCE COPAC. LOCATION Dt.
COMMENTARY A second edn appeared in 1812 at the Minerva Press. Erroneously mentioned
as an 'extraordinary picaresque novel' (Falkner Greirson cat. 17/289), but instead contains a
description by a future student at the London inns of court of a trip from northern Ireland
via Dublin to London, with a side trip to Oxford, interspersed with 'anecdotes' in the form
of observations and stories [ML; RL].

Anon.135 *The life, actions and exploits of the most notorious and famous Mary Field,*
otherwise Thompson, otherwise Webb, otherwise Davis, the blind harper's wife,
otherwise Milliner the rope-maker's wife, otherwise Wild, otherwise Johnston,
the captain of the trading billender to Holland, otherwise Smokes, otherwise,
Mary Clarke, who was lately convicted for defacing his Majesty's coin, and
received sentence to be burnt, but obtained his Majesty's most gracious pardon
for transportation for life in six months after the date hereof, March the 1st,
1747–48. Her several intercourses with her ceremonial husbands, mostly deliv-
ered by herself. Illustrated with curious and moral observations: Her character
under Jonathan Wild, delivered by his nephew to the author. Her transactions
in Ireland for nineteen years, coming little short of her exploits in England.
Collected by the author on good authority.
+ Dublin: Printed for the author by Bartholomew Corcoran, 1748 (ill.). SOURCE
Pollard 2, p. 119; COPAC; ESTC t168943. LOCATION Dt.
COMMENTARY 47pp. The story of a female criminal. The main character was born in Hereford
(England). The subject's life in Ireland, even though mentioned in the title, is not discussed.
For Wild, referred to in the above title, see below, Anon.138 *The life and glorious actions of*
the most heroic and magnanimous Jonathan Wilde, generalissimo of the prig-forces of Great-Britain
and Ireland ... With an explanation of the most usual terms of the art in the canting dialect
(London, 1725) [ML; COPAC].

Anon.136 *The life and death of the indefatigable Tory, Redmond Ó Hanlyn, commonly*
called Count Hanlyn.
[Dublin]: John Foster, 1682. SOURCE Pollard 2, p. 223; Wing L2017. LOCATION
L. COMMENTARY Dublin edn consists of 23pp [COPAC].
+ London: Dean & Munday, 1819 (as *The Irish freebooter; or, surprising adventures*
of Captain Redmond O'Hanlan, a celebrated robber who, for many years, commanded
a banditti and laid a considerable part of the country under annual contributions, together
with The life and adventures of Humphrey Kynaston; Plate 2). SOURCE OCLC.
LOCATION L, NUC.
+ New York: W. Borradaile, 1823 (as *The Irish freebooter; or, surprising adventures*
of Captain Redmond O'Hanlan, a celebrated robber ... together with The life and
adventures of Humphrey Kynaston...). SOURCE OCLC. LOCATION D.
COMMENTARY Story of the famous Irish outlaw, Redmond O'Hanlon, who died in 1681. Related
publications are *Count O'Hanlon's downfall. A true and exact account of the killing of the arch-*
tory and traitor Redmond O'Hanlon, 25 April 1681 (Dublin, 1681), and a poem, *An elegy on the*
modern heroe, Redmond O'Hanlan, surnamed the Tory (Dublin, [?1681]). These publications

were followed by the story in prose in Dublin the next year. O'Hanlon's history was later published in John Cosgrave's§ *A genuine history* (Dublin, 1747). Possibly another version *The life of Redmond O'Hanlon, the robber* is mentioned in the *First report of the Commission of Education Inquiry* (London, 1825), Appendix No. 221, p. 557. The London edn consists of 25pp [Hartman, 741; ML; N. Ó Ciosáin, 'The Irish rogues' in J.D. Donnelly & K.A. Miller (eds.), *Irish popular culture* (Dublin, 1998), pp 84–93. RL; Sweeney 1647].

Anon.137   *The life and extraordinary adventures of C. Netterville with the various hardships and vicissitudes that he encountered both by sea and land, until his safe return to Ireland; his native country* (written by himself).
+ Dublin: John Martin, [*c.*1806] (ill.). LOCATION Dt.
COMMENTARY 42pp, priced at 6½*d*. Charles Netterville was born near Carlow, the son of very poor parents. On the day of his birth, a wounded man, Mr Westbury, who had been thrown off his horse during a storm, is carried into the cottage. He takes a fancy to the newborn baby. When Charles reaches his seventh year, he joins Mr Westbury in England and then joins the navy. After he marries, he accepts a lucrative post in the East Indies. On the way, the ship stops at Madagascar for repairs. There he and his wife meet with 'savages'. Returning to England, their ship is captured by a French privateer who takes them to Trinidad. In one of his adventures, he loses his wife and remarries. However, in a later adventure, his first wife is rescued. His second wife conveniently expires and Charles and his wife settle in England. The story was reprinted in the *Marvellous Magazine* (Dublin, [1822], Nos. 25–6) [ML; RL; Dt cat.].

Anon.138   *The life and glorious actions of the most heroic and magnanimous Jonathan Wilde, generalissimo of the prig-forces of Great-Britain and Ireland ... With an explanation of the most usual terms of the art in the canting dialect.*
+ London: H. Whitridge, 1725 (ill.). LOCATION InND Loeber coll.
COMMENTARY Not in ESTC. One of the many accounts, including one by Henry Fielding, of the celebrated receiver of stolen goods, thief-taker and informer Jonathan Wild (as it is usually spelled). However, this edn is almost entirely devoted to a wholly imaginary account of Wild's Irish ancestry and youth. The historic character, Wild, was in fact born in Wolverhampton and is not known to have had anything to do with Ireland. But this version traces his lineage back to his great-grandfather's father, named Patrick Mac Judas Wild, who lived in a cave on the mountains of Newry (Co. Down) in the year 1524. It includes the activities of relations such as O Neal Wild and Patrick Fitz Wild of Armagh. All generations were leaders of robbers and thieves and most ended their lives on the gallows. When Ireland became too dangerous for him, Patrick Fitz Wild moved to England, where new generations continued similar nefarious activities. Some of them became bailiffs and enriched themselves in this profitable profession. Included also is a description of terms for various illegal activities. The real Jonathan Wilde's final words were published in Dublin in 1725 (as *The last speech, confession and dying words of Jonathan Wilde, the notorious thief taker and keeper of Newgate in London, who was executed at Tyburn on Monday the twenty fourth of May 1725*) [ML; RL; G. Howson, *The thief-taker general. The rise and fall of Jonathan Wild* (New York, 1970); J. Kelly, *Gallows speeches from eighteenth-century Ireland* (Dublin, 2001), pp 29–30; Personal communication, Steve Weissman, Ximenes, Nov. 1999].

Anon.139   *The life and travels of James Tudor Owen: who, amidst a variety of other interesting particulars, gives an account of his being in an East Indian campaign; and his singular adventures among the Hindoos; as also his voyage, shipwreck, and journey with a troop of wild roving Arabs over immense burning sands, and trackless dessarts, he embarks from the Egyptian shore for Ireland, and there, during the late war with America, gains an ensigncy to with the British forces against that country: is wounded in battle, and taken by the Agiguans, a war-like nation inhabiting the wilds of America.*

London: S. Fisher & T. Hurst, 1802. SOURCE OCLC. LOCATION D, DCL.

New York: Garland, 1977 (Garland Library of Narratives of North American Captivities, vol. 25). SOURCE RLIN. LOCATION DCL.

COMMENTARY 42pp [NUC].

Anon.140 *Life displayed: Fugitive novels.*
Dublin: John Mitchell, 1771. SOURCE Pollard 2, p. 412.
COMMENTARY Not in ESTC and no copy located [RL].

Anon.141 *The life of a collegian. A novel.*
+ London: Charles J. Skeet, 1853, 2 vols. SOURCE Wolff, 7506. LOCATION D (2 vols. in 1), Dt.
COMMENTARY Setting is Trinity College, Dublin and Galway City [ML].

Anon.142 *The life of Dick En—l—d, alias Captain En—l—d; of turf memory. With notes and illustrations* (dedicated to 'the public, and more particularly to the two universities of Cambridge and Oxford; schools of Winchester, Eton, Westminster and Harrow …').
+ London: T. Boosey, 1792 (ill.). SOURCE Scott cat. 42/21. ESTC t40946.
LOCATION L.

COMMENTARY 53pp. Both a life of Dick Enfield, a native of Dublin, and his biographer, who share dissolute careers. Enfield, an Irishman, broke out of a Dublin goal, fled to England, where he graduated from porter to bully at a Charing Cross brothel. He becomes a pimp, and with the proceeds buys an army commission, plays tennis every morning, and concentrates on all forms of gambling, including horse-racing. The story tells of his fleecing other fellow officers, engaging in frauds, and his final disgrace [Scott cat.].

Anon.143 *The life of Nicholas Mooney, alias Jackson, born at Regar near Rathfarnham in the County of Dublin.*
Dublin: Elizabeth Golding & James Esdall, 1752. SOURCE ESTC t110617.
LOCATION Dt, O.

London, Philadelphia repr. by William Bradford, 1752 (as *The life of Nicholas Mooney. Wherein is contained his parentage and education, an account of his joining the rebel army at Carlisle, and his part he acted therein, 'till the defeat thereof at Culloden Moor: The adventuers [sic] he met with both before and after this, 'till he took to the highway, with a brief account of his vicious life, 'till he committed the robbery at Bristol, for which he was executed on Friday April 24, 1752. Together with his moral religious and reflections upon the most remarkable passages of his whole life; and an account of his conversation [i.e., conversion] the Sunday before the trial. Taken from his own mouth by a friend, and published at his request*). SOURCE ESTC w24072.
LOCATION Haverford College (PA).

COMMENTARY 48pp for the Dublin edn. A moral tale. Regar refers to the modern Rathgar [J. Kelly, *Gallows speeches from eighteenth-century Ireland* (Dublin, 2001), p. 38; Personal communication, Kevin Whelan, Jan. 2006].

Anon.144 *The life of Paddy O'Flarrity, who, from a shoe black, has, by perseverance and good conduct, arrived to a member of Congress, interspersed with many curious anecdotes, calculated to improve as well as divert the youths of America.*
[Washington?, DC]: [n.p.], 1834. SOURCE Fanning, p. 384; partly repr. in Exiles, pp 35–48. LOCATION NUC.
COMMENTARY Set in St Louis (MO) and Washington (DC). Title on cover: *A spur to youth, or Davy Crockett beaten.* The story of Paddy O'Flarrity, a wily, amoral immigrant boy, and his rise in the world of American politics, subsequent to his landing in Baltimore (MD). Paddy marries the daughter of the governor; is elected to the Missouri legislature; becomes speaker of the house; rises from a public speaker who has been hissed to a famous orator; fights the Indians to save his beloved, and is elected to the US Congress. The anon. author concludes with a puzzle. He tells the reader to remember Paddy when undertaking a project 'as a spur to the accomplishment of it. I leave you now to guess who I am' [Exiles, p. 34; Mott cat. 231/134].

Anon.145 *Life in the home.*
+ Dublin: [n.p.], 1883 (Stories of the Ragged Boys' Home, No. 17). LOCATION D.
COMMENTARY 32pp. Set in Ireland and describes the Ragged Boys' Home (probably in Dublin) and relates the story of a student who caused trouble [RL].

Anon.146 *Lilie Dunbar; or, the Irish wedding.*
Dublin: Samuel B. Oldham, [c.1850]. SOURCE Brown 2, 17. LOCATION L ([1858?]).
COMMENTARY Religious fiction. A tale showing, from the Protestant point of view, the danger of intermarriage [Brown 2].

Anon.147 *The little adventurer.*
Dublin: James Duffy & Co., [1892 or earlier] (Duffy's Juvenile Library). SOURCE Adv. in J.J. O'Dea, *The beauties of nature* (Dublin, 1892).
COMMENTARY Possibly a reprint. A book with the title *The little adventurer founded on fact*, appeared in London in 1820 [OCLC].

Anon.148 *Little Andy's legacy; or, for the master's sake. An Irish story.*
London: Religious Tract Society, [1882]. LOCATION L (destroyed), E.

Anon.149 *Little Frank; or, the painter's progress.*
Dublin: James Duffy, [1857 or earlier] (Duffy's Cottage Library). SOURCE Adv. in Anon., *The young crusader* (Dublin, [1857]).
COMMENTARY No copy located [RL].

Anon.150 *Little Maggie's trials and triumphs.*
+ Philadelphia, New York, Boston, Louisville: American Sunday-School Union, 1852 (ill.). LOCATION NUC, InND Loeber coll.
COMMENTARY Some Irish content [RL].

Anon.151 *Little Nelly; and, The dying Irish girl.*
Philadelphia: Presbyterian Board of Publication, [c.1865]. SOURCE RLIN. LOCATION Rutgers Univ. Libraries, New Brunswick, (NJ).
COMMENTARY 144pp. Religious fiction. Includes 'Hope for Ireland' [RLIN].

Anon.152 *The London Mathews; containing an account of Master Charles Mathews's youthful days, and six original and humorous songs, viz. Trade chusing. Stratford on a market-day. An Irish rubber at whist. Volunteer field day, and sham fight. Croskeen lawn. London green rooms. And, the Jew and the pig. Embellished with eight copper-plate engravings, representing him in several characters he assumes in his last entertainment.*
+ London: Hodgson & Co., [1827] (ill.). SOURCE COPAC. LOCATION Univ. of Bristol, PC.

COMMENTARY 36pp. One of several comical, unnumbered series of partly fictionalized lives of the celebrated actor Charles Mathews (1776–1835). This one relates his visit to Dublin where he had been engaged by Charles Daly for the Dublin Theatre. There he played the roles of George Augustus Fipley, Mr. Trombone, one Flannagan (also known as O'Finnigan), Old Hurst and others. Also contains several songs, two of which are Irish [RL].

Anon.153 *The loss of the Kent, East Indiaman.*
+ Dublin: Printed by John Jones [for the Kildare Place Society], [1827] (title on cover: *The loss of the Kent*; Printed by Bentham & Hardy, Dublin, 1827). SOURCE Hislop, p. 1041 (n.d. edn [1827]). LOCATION InND Loeber coll.
London: C.J.G. & F. Rivington [for the Society for the Promotion of Christian Knowledge], 1831. SOURCE Hislop, p. 1041. LOCATION L (1837 edn).

COMMENTARY Although not stated, the story is based on Lt Gen. Sir Duncan MacGregor's *A narrative of the loss of the Kent East Indiaman* (Edinburgh, 1825, which was co-published by R.M. Tims in Dublin), who later served in Ireland. The Kildare Place Society version is written in the form of a letter by 'Servatus', dated London, April 1825, and addressed to 'Dear Miss E—'. The *Kent*, bound for Bengal and China, caught fire in a storm. The exemplary and Christian behaviour of the officers and crew in the face of the disaster is described. They evacuated the ship in an orderly fashion with little loss of life. An appendix contains several letters commending the bravery of the men. Earlier, much shorter edns are known from London imprints. According to the London (1837) edn, the book had been originally prepared for the Society for Promoting the Education of the Poor in Ireland, Kildare Place, Dublin, and was reprinted by permission. However, the Irish edn must be based on another work, since the quarterly report of the publication subcommittee of the Kildare Place Society in 1826 mentions that permission has been requested from Lt Col. [*sic*] MacGregor for the publication of *The loss of the Kent* [ML; RL; BLC; The Church of Ireland College of Education, Dublin, MS BS 40; Herlihy, pp 215–16].

Anon.154 *Love betray'd; or, the unexpected wife. A novel.*
Dublin: Z. Martineau, [1743 or earlier]. SOURCE Adv. in [anon.], *Memoirs of an unfortunate young nobleman* (Dublin, 1743).
COMMENTARY No copy located, and not in ESTC. A comedy *Love betray'd; or, the agreeable disappointment* was published and acted in London in 1703, but may be an unrelated work. Zachariah Martineau was a Dublin printer and bookseller, fl.1743, d. 1793 [RL; Pollard 2, p. 401].

Anon.155 *Love in the Brazils, or, the honest criminal: exemplified in the interesting history of Henry Monkville and Zara D'Almaida.*
Dublin: A. O'Neil, [18—]. SOURCE OCLC. LOCATION Univ. of Delaware, Newark (DE).
COMMENTARY A novelette of 40pp [OCLC].

Anon.156 *Love tales Irish.*
+ London: William Paterson, 1890. LOCATION C, InND Loeber coll.
+ Philadelphia: George W. Jacobs & Co., n.d. (as *Irish love tales, selected from standard authors*). LOCATION InND Loeber coll.
COMMENTARY Contents of the London edn: 'The mistletoe bough' (Thomas Crofton Croker §[*sic*]), 'The dispensation' (Mrs S.C. Hall§), 'Ensign O'Donoghue's "first love"', 'The love draught. A tale of the Barrow-side' [*sic*][1] [Thomas Colley Grattan§], 'Shane Fadh's wedding' (William Carleton§), 'A legend of Killarney' (Thomas Haynes Bayly§), 'Paddy Kelleher and his pig. A tale' (Thomas Crofton Croker [*sic*]), 'Mary M'Donnell' (Mrs James Gray), 'Annie Leslie' (Mrs S.C. Hall§) [RL].

Anon.157 *Love without artifice; or, the disappointed peer. A history of the amour between Lord Mauritio and Emilia. Being the case of Elizabeth Fitz-Maurice, alias Leeson, and the Lord William Fitz-Maurice, relating to a marriage-contract between them; which was confirmed by a Court of Delegates, in the Lady's behalf, on Wednesday, March 14th 1732–3, at Serjeant's-Inn, in Chancery-Lane (dedicated to the duchess of M******).*
+ London: E. Curll, 1733. SOURCE McBurney, 279; ESTC t070439. LOCATION L (imperfect), ICN, InND Loeber coll.
London: E. Curll, 1734, 2nd edn (as *Love and artifice; or, a complete history of the amour between Lord Mauritio and Emilia, etc.* [as above]). SOURCE McBurney, 279a; Gecker, 561; ESTC t038612. LOCATION Dt, L (imperfect), O, PU.
COMMENTARY Epistolary novel, probably partly based on [anon.], *The secret history of Medilla* (London, 1731), and historical facts, in which the identities of Lord Mauritio and Emilia are not hidden. Lord Mauritio is William FitzMaurice, commonly called Lord FitzMaurice, son of the 1st earl of Kerry, of Lixnaw (Co. Kerry), and later 2nd earl of Kerry (b. 1694/5?, d. Lixnaw 1747), while Emilia is Elizabeth Leeson. With one exception, the letters are all written by Emilia and are dated between 1724 and 1726. The letters are interspersed with commentary from the narrator of the story. Lodge states that William married Elizabeth, daughter of one Moss, and widow of Mr Leeson of Dublin, in 1730. Once the court had pronounced judgement as to the validity of the marriage between the former lovers, the narrator concludes that his Lordship escaped the law by entrenching himself in the 'Fastnesses of Glanflest [Glenflesk] or Mangerty' [Mangerton mountain, Co. Kerry]. Archdall states that the marriage contract was confirmed, 14 Mar. 1732, and relates that Elizabeth died in 1736, upon which William remarried [RL; Gecker, p. 59; M. Archdall, *The peerage of Ireland by John Lodge* (Dublin, 1799), ii, p. 206].

Anon.158 *Love's pilgrimage; a story founded on facts. Compiled from the journal of a deceased friend.*
+ London: T.N. Longman, 1796, 3 vols. SOURCE ESTC t078888. LOCATION L, O, InND Loeber coll. (vol. 2 only).
Dublin: P. Wogan, P. Byrne, W. Jones, J. Rice & H. FitzPatrick, 1796. SOURCE ESTC n0339909. LOCATION PU.
Philadelphia: John Bioren & Robert Campbell, 1799. SOURCE ESTC w023287. LOCATION American Antiquarian Society, Worcester (MA).
COMMENTARY The story starts in Somerset and covers parts of southern Europe. Irish content because of the presence of a Mr Maurice Fitzgerald [Personal communication, Neville Figgis; ML].

1 'A tale of the Barrow-side' in the Philadelphia edn.

Anon.159 *Lucy O-Neil, ou la jeune irlandaise.*
Paris: And.-Aug. Lottin, [1799]. SOURCE Hart cat. 73/88. LOCATION InND.
COMMENTARY In the preamble, the author claims that the story is based on a translation from the English, and that the manuscript was discovered in a Devonshire garden. However, Hart is of the opinion that this concerns an original work. Consists of a tale of a juvenile nature set among the old Gaelic aristocracy [Hart cat. 73/88].

Anon.160 *The maid of Erin: or, the lily of Tyrconnel.*
+ London: Star Publishing Office, 1885. LOCATION D, Dt, InND Loeber coll.
COMMENTARY Contents: 'The maid of Erin; or, the chief of the red hand', 'The knight-errant and the snow storm' [ML].

Anon.161 *Mary Irvine; or, a tale by a convert.*
Dublin: John Mullany, [1888 or earlier]. SOURCE Adv. in *The Irish Catholic Directory* (Dublin, 1888).
COMMENTARY No copy located. Published in cloth limp at 6*d*. and cloth gild at 1*s*. [Adv. in *The Irish Catholic Directory* (Dublin, 1888)].

Anon.162 *May eve; or, the lost sheep restored in the fold.*
Dublin: J. Duffy, 1853 (Duffy's Popular Library). LOCATION L (destroyed).
COMMENTARY 46pp [BLC]. No other copy located [RL].

Anon.163 *May waters; or, the experiences of an artist.*
+ Dublin: John Mullany, n.d. LOCATION D.
COMMENTARY A love story [ML].

Anon.164 *Memoir of Mrs. Manon, or self-delusion discovered.*
+ Dublin: Religious Tract and Book Society for Ireland, 1836. LOCATION PC.
COMMENTARY 36pp. Religious fiction [RL].

Anon.165 *Memoirs of Francis Dillon, Esq; In a series of letters written by himself* (dedicated to the duchess of Cumberland).
+ London: T. Hookham, 1772, 2 vols. SOURCE Forster, 1801; Raven 2, 1772:17. LOCATION ICU.
COMMENTARY Epistolary adventure novel set in London, Gibraltar and France. Gilbert Stuart in his review in the London *Monthly Review* stated that 'The details of this performance are most insufferably tedious, and are mixed with vulgarity which is disgusting in the highest degree'. Part of the story concerns Irishmen who are fortune-hunters living in London. Aside from Francis Dillon, allegedly born in England, one of the principal Irish characters is Patrick Callaghan [RL; Raven 2].

Anon.166 *The memoirs of George Barrington, containing every remarkable circumstance, from his birth to his present time, including the following trials – 1. For robbing Mrs. Dudman; 2. Elizabeth Ironmonger; 3. Returning from transportation; 4. Robbing Sir G. Webster; 5. Mr. Bagshaw; 6. Mr. Le Mesurier; 7. For outlawry; 8. For robbing Mr. Townsend. With the whole of his celebrated speeches, taking from the records from the King's Bench, Old Bailey, &c.*
+ London: J. Bird; Simmonds, [1790]. SOURCE Burmester cat. 56/19; ESTC t73567. LOCATION L.

+ London: John Wilson, [*c*.1820] (as *The life, times, and adventures of George Barrington, the celebrated thief and pickpocket, embracing the whole of his history, and a full account of all his extraordinary feats, which procured him the name of 'The Prince of Thiefs!' His attempted murder of O'Neill, robbery of the Duke of Leinster, the Duke's attack on Barrington's wife, &c.; also full details of the many desperate robberies committed by Barrington, in England, Ireland, etc.*). SOURCE Heath cat. April 2003/2. LOCATION L (n.d., 2nd edn).

+ [London]: J. Sadler, J. Eves & M. Clements, n.d. (as *The genuine life and trial of G. Barrington, from his birth in June 1755, to the time of his conviction in September, 1790, to the Old Bayley, for robbing Henry Hare Townsend, Esq. of his gold watch, seals, &c.*; ill. W. Green). LOCATION O.

COMMENTARY 73pp for the London, [*c*.1820], 2nd edn, and 48pp for the [London], n.d. edn. Based on [anon.], *The genuine life and trial of George Barrington* (London, 1791). George Barrington's real name was Waldron. He was born in Maynooth (Co. Kildare) in 1755, where his father was a silversmith. Barrington's life of crime started at an early age. He attempted to murder his school friend, O'Neill, when he was age 16. This was followed by years of robberies committed in Ireland and subsequently in England, to where he fled to avoid trial. He was arrested numerous times and served several sentences of hard labour. In 1790 he was sentenced to transportation for seven years. Having played a considerable part in suppressing a mutiny on the voyage, he was introduced favourably to the governor at Port Jackson (New South Wales), who appointed him superintendent of the convicts. Barrington amassed a very considerable fortune, lived to an old age and died at Botany Bay, much respected by all who knew him. Barrington did not write any of the works associated with his name, neither did he write any of the subsequent publications, including *Barrington's annals of suicide* (London, 1803), *Barrington's new London spy* (London, 1804, 1805, etc.). Wilde et al. (1985) list several other works that were inspired by Barrington's life [W.H. Wilde, J. Hooton, & B. Andrews (eds), *The Oxford companion to Australian literature* (Melbourne, 1985), pp 72–3; Heath cat. April 2003/2].

Anon.167 *Memoirs of Madam de Granson; or, virtue invincible. An historical novel. Interspersed with anecdotes of persons of the first quality. English and French; and a lively and interesting account of the siege of Calais, by Edward of England ... Translated from the French of the celebrated Crebillon, the elder.*

+ Dublin: Printed [for the author?] by D. Chamberlaine, 1761, 2 vols. in 1. SOURCE *A catalogue of the library of the late Rev. Dr. John Barrett* (Dublin, 1822), item 128; seen at C.R. Johnson, London, Jan. 1994; ESTC t226122. LOCATION L.

COMMENTARY No copy of a London edn located and the original French title not found. Crebillon the Elder, the supposed author on the title page, is presumably to be distinguished from Claude Prosper Crebillon, or Crebillon Fils, author of *The Sopha* and various other novels (Crebillon's *The wanderings of the heart and mind, or memoirs of M. de Meilcour* was advertised by Ewing in Dublin in 1747 (*Female Spectator*, i, of that date and location; but see Raven, 81, which only notes a 1751 edn)). It is at least possible that, with its partially English subject, the novel is an original, masquerading as a translation and attempting to benefit from the vogue for foreign romances of this kind. It consists of an historical romance set in the time of Edward II of England. An 'Advertisement to the London edn' which follows the title page, states that this novel 'is esteemed for its politeness equal to the *Princess of Cleves*, and according to the report of a certain great lady (not long since arrived from Paris ...) is at present the most in vogue of any book of the kind, not only at the French court, but among all the Beau

Monde at Paris and elsewhere in that kingdom' [RL; ESTC t226122; Personal communication, Chris R. Johnson; Personal communication, Máire Kennedy, July 1996].

Anon.168 *Memoirs of the life, travels and transactions, of the Reverend Mr. Kelly, from his birth, to escape, from his imprisonment, out of the Tower of London, October 26, 1736.*
+ London: E. Curll, 1736. SOURCE McBurney 310; ESTC t1221653. LOCATION DPL, L.
COMMENTARY 32pp. Probably based on historical facts. Kelly was born in Co. Roscommon, studied at TCD and became a minister. He went to Paris and participated in the Mississippi scheme. Afterwards he went to England and married a widow. He was suspected to be in contact with the Pretender to the English throne living in Paris and was jailed [ML].

Anon.169 *Memoirs of the Nutrebian court: discovering the distresses of the Queen, happy birth, and surprizing deliverance of her children* (dedicated to William Benn, Mayor of London).
+ London: M. Laughan, J. Robinson & W. Reeves, 1747, 2 vols. SOURCE Beasley, 220; ESTC t057810. LOCATION L, IU.
COMMENTARY Jacobite pseudo-orientalized, sentimental story of love, scandal and political intrigue in a kingdom overrun by a usurper (Ireland?), but saved through the magical intervention of a sprite named Papaglia and his care of the rightful heirs, who finally regain the throne [Beasley].

Anon.170 *The minor; or, history of George O'Nial, Esq.* (dedicated to A****** D**** Esq.).
+ Dublin: Watson, White, Colbert, Moore & Halpen, 1787, 2 vols. SOURCE Block, p. 162. LOCATION L.
London: W. Lane, 1788, 2 vols. SOURCE Hardy, 132; Blakey, p. 141; Forster 2, 2883; ESTC t070098. LOCATION L.
COMMENTARY Probably issued in Dec. 1786. The page header is labelled 'The adventures of a minor'. The book is presumably an autobiography and concerns the story of George O'Nial, born in Co. Tyrone. It describes the ups and downs of the family fortune, a long stay in London, and the return of the family to the north of Ireland. The story ends with his marriage. Mentions the Volunteers in 1782 [ML; Pollard 2, p. 109].

Anon.171 *The miscellany; or, evening's occupation for the youthful peasantry in Ireland.* Dublin: printed by R. Conolly [for the Kildare Place Society], 1818. SOURCE Hislop, p. 1042; Dm exhib. cat., 1981, p. 31; OCLC; COPAC. LOCATION O.
+ Dublin: Printed by C. Betham [for the Kildare Place Society], 1821 (as *The miscellany, or evening's occupation for youth*; ill.). SOURCE Gilbert, p. 553. LOCATION D (1830 edn), DPL, L, IU (*c.*1821 edn), InND Loeber coll. (1823 edn).
+ London: Printed by the executrix of the late W. Wotton, n.d. (as *The miscellany; or, evening's occupation for youthful peasantry*; ill.). LOCATION InND Loeber coll.
COMMENTARY A collection of articles, stories and moral reflections. Contents of 1830 edn: 'The two bees', 'Appearances often deceive', 'The four seasons', 'Ingenuity and industry rewarded', 'Tenderness to mothers', 'The pious son', 'Cruelty to insects condemned', 'The fatal effects of cruelty', 'The eagle', 'The humming-bird', 'Mortality', 'The horse', 'The ass',

'Natural appearances of the year as displayed in the different months' [following by an account for each month], 'Description of the Laplanders', 'The Salisbury shepherd', 'Rural felicity', 'The advantage of a constant adherence to truth', 'Temptation resisted', 'Truth recommended', 'Gratitude', 'The ungrateful guest', 'Heaven', 'The father redeemed from slavery by his son', 'Religion the foundation of content – an allegory', 'Noble behaviour of Scipio', 'Virtue rewarded', 'Love between brothers and sisters', 'With a good conscience we sleep soundly', 'The banyan tree, or Indian fig', 'The discovery of America, by Columbus', 'The coffee tree', 'The tea plant', 'The sugar cane', 'The lion', 'Leonidas, the king of Sparta', 'Filial piety', 'The covering of different animals', 'The Ouran-Outang', 'The grotto of Antiparos', 'The hospitable negro woman', 'The manufacture of paper', 'Health', 'Respect due to old age', 'The good example', 'The camel', 'The old man and his ass', 'Valentine and Unnion', 'Integrity and modesty rewarded', 'Damon and Pythias', 'The secret of being always satisfied', 'The generous negro', 'Dangers of sloth and luxury', 'Properties and uses of cork', 'Franklin's lessons', 'Night', 'Selfish sorrow reproved', 'Benevolence its own reward' [RL].

Anon.172 *Modern Irish tales and stories, anecdotes, &c &c.*
Belfast: Joseph Smyth, 1837. SOURCE Adams, pp 146–7, 196.
+ Dublin: Printed [for the author?] by C.M. Warren, n.d. (ill.). SOURCE Adams, p. 196. LOCATION InND Loeber coll.
COMMENTARY No copy of the Belfast edn located. Several of the stories are in Anglo-Hibernian dialect. Contents: 'One night's adventures of Denis Delaney', 'The Irish priest', 'The Dublin shoeblack', 'The love marriage – authorship', 'Paddy and the bear' [Samuel Lover§], 'The Hibernian mendicant', 'The rival dreamers' [John and Michael Banim§], 'Irish wit and eloquence', 'Evelyn L – Gambling', 'Denis Delaney's misfortunes. Founded on fact', 'Patty Conway – A story of Irish life' [Mrs S.C. Hall§; reprinted in the *Irish Penny Magazine* (Dublin, 1833), pp 148–52 from the *Amulet*], 'The sportheen', 'The sleeping warriors; or, Dhaarah Dheerlig and his men. A legend of Mulahether' [first published in the *Irish Penny Magazine* (Dublin, 1833), pp 309–10], 'Kate Connor' [Mrs S.C. Hall§], 'Shane Fadh's wedding' [abbreviated version of tale by William Carleton§], 'The wake', 'Paddy's dream – The scalp' [by 'G.C.', first published in the *Irish Penny Magazine* (Dublin, 1833), pp 11–13], 'An Irish cross-examination' [RL; Adams, p. 147].

Anon.173 *The Molly Maguires : a thrilling narrative of the rise, progress and fall of the most noted band of cut-throats in modern times …: supplemented by the statement of Detective McParlan … and the confession of that prince of villains, Jimmy Kerrigan, which corroborates the statement of McParlan.*
Tamaqua (PA): Eveland & Harris, c.1876. SOURCE RLIN. LOCATION DCL.
St Clair (PA): Kelly Printing, 1969. SOURCE RLIN. LOCATION Pennsylvania State Univ.
COMMENTARY 30pp [RLIN].

Anon.174 *My own story. A tale of old times.*
+ Dublin: William Curry Jnr & Co., 1829 (ill. George Petrie, Kirkwood). SOURCE Brown, 69. LOCATION D, L (destroyed).
COMMENTARY The story of James O'Donnell, who joins the United Irishmen. Later he becomes a 'Bible Christian', and turns traitor, and in the end is hanged [Brown].

Anon.175 *The mysterious pilgrim; or, fatal duplicity. An Italian romance … To which is added, The Hibernian mendicant. A tale.*

London: Langley & Bruce, 1810. LOCATION ViU.

COMMENTARY 32pp. The *Hibernian mendicant* was also published in [anon.], *Modern Irish tales and stories, anecdotes* (Belfast, 1837) [RL; ViU cat.].

Anon.176 *Narmo and Aimata; a tale of the Jesuits in Tahiti.*
+ Dublin: Samuel H. Oldham; London: P. Seeley, Jackson & Halliday; Edinburgh: R. Grant & Sons, 1855 (ill.). LOCATION D, Dt.
COMMENTARY Religious fiction [RL].

Anon.177 *Narratives and stories for the instruction of young persons.*
+ Dublin: J. & M. Porteous, 1825 [for the Religious Tract and Book Society for Ireland], 2 vols. in 1 (ill.). SOURCE Burmester cat. 39/205; OCLC. LOCATION Indiana Univ
COMMENTARY Consists of mostly earlier published stories between 8 and 30pp in length, published for the Religious Tract and Book Society for Ireland. Each story carries its own title page and pagination with various Dublin imprints. Contents: 'The history of Peter Lacy and his wife Susan', 'Blind Mary', 'The history of John Buller', 'The cottage in Connaught', ' The good minister', 'The orphan', 'The reduced tradesman', 'The murder of the Christian Indians in North America', 'Mary Jones, or the soldier's daughter', 'The hospital patient', 'The history of David Thompson and Mrs S—', 'A cottage conversation', 'The friendless boy', 'The Jew and his daughter', 'The happy poor man', 'The king's visit', 'The chimney sweep', 'The poor widow', 'Light in darkness', 'Remarks on New Zealanders', 'The gardener of Glammis', 'The village of the mountains', 'The laundry maid' [Elizabeth Tonna§], 'The wake house', 'Robert Shaw', 'John Pascal, or the temptations of the poor' [Elizabeth Tonna§], 'Sarah Hopkins', 'The peasant's daughter', 'The life of Cyprian', 'The Bible revered', 'Ararat', 'Tschoop and Shabasch, Christian Indians in North America', 'The dying Sunday school girl', 'The life of St. Augustine', 'The two friends' [Elizabeth Tonna§], 'John Papunhank', 'The pensioner'. The copy of this volume in the Burmester cat. has annotations showing that three of the stories were heavily corrected, revsd and abridged in a contemporary hand, possibly for a reprint by the publisher James Gall of Edinburgh [RL; Burmester cat. 39/205; OCLC].

Anon.178 *The new casket. A gift book for all seasons.*
+ London: Religious Tract Society [1851] (ill. J.M. Kronheim & Co.). SOURCE COPAC. LOCATION L, C.
COMMENTARY Religious fiction set in Ireland. Contents (excluding poetry): 'The three flowers', 'The party of pleasure' (set in Ireland), 'A tale of Constantius; or, the trial and reward of Christian integrity', 'The holy well' (set in Ireland), 'Old Humphrey on seed sowing', 'Romanist friendship', 'The threepenny omnibus' [ML].

Anon.179 *New Irish legendary tales; or, entertaining stories, illustrative of the Irish character.*
+ Belfast: Simms & M'Intyre, [c.1835]. SOURCE Adams, pp 146, 201 (where title is mistakenly given as *Irish legendary tales*); *Béaloideas*, 60–1 (1992–3), p. 136; OCLC; COPAC. LOCATION D, Dt, O.
Dublin: C.M. Warren, n.d. SOURCE Adams, pp 146, 201.
COMMENTARY No copy of the Dublin edn located. Belfast edn consists of 120pp. Contents: 'The rival dreamers', 'Paddy the piper', 'The station; an Irish sketch', 'Kate Connor' [Mrs S.C. Hall§], 'Paul Doherty', ' 'The gridiron; or, Paddy Mullowney's travel in France' [Samuel

Lover§], 'The three advices' [from *Royal Hibernian tales*, [Dublin?, 1825 or earlier], 'A tough yarn', 'Flory Cantillon's funeral', 'Dreaming Tim Jarvis' [from Thomas Crofton Croker's§ *Fairy legends*], 'Rent-day', 'The little shoe' [ML].

Anon.180 *Newminster Abbey; or, the daughter of O'More. A novel, founded on facts and interspersed with original poetry and picturesque and faithful sketches of various countries.*
+ London: J.F. Hughes, 1808, 2 vols. SOURCE British Fiction; Garside, 1808:10. LOCATION Corvey CME 3–628–48266–6, Ireland related fiction, L.
COMMENTARY Preface implies male authorship. An Irish Capt. O'More and his daughter Geraldine are travelling through England when Capt. O'More is suddenly taken ill and dies. As O'More's Irish estates are entailed, the property passes to Geraldine's uncle, who refuses to give any of his inheritance to Geraldine. The orphaned and penniless Geraldine is taken in by the family of Lord Newminster. Geraldine and Newminster's son Theodore fall in love and are married, against the wishes of Lord Newminster, who is largely characterized by his violent anti-Irish prejudice (repeatedly calling Geraldine 'an Irish adventurer, a papist, a rebel'). Disinherited by Lord Newminster, Theodore and Geraldine travel to Portugal, North Africa and, finally, Ireland. They are eventually forgiven by Lord Newminster, after which they settle in England [JB].

Anon.181 *Newry bridge; or, Ireland in 1887.*
+ Edinburgh, London: William Blackwood & Sons, 1886. LOCATION L.
COMMENTARY 72pp. Reprinted from the London *St. James's Gazette*. A father tells a story to his children, predicting civil war in Ireland if the Home Rule bill of 1886 is passed [BLC; OCLC].

Anon.182 *Nouvelles irlandaises.*
Paris: A. Eymery, 1819, 2 vols. (trans. by Mme Elisabeth de Bon). LOCATION BNF.

Anon.183 *Nouvelles irlandaises.*
Paris: Casterman, 1877 (trans. by M. de Jorel). SOURCE Brown 2, 689; ABE Books (accessed 22 Jan. 2003, 1884 edn).
COMMENTARY Translated from English with authorship not indicated. Contents: 'Nelly', 'Histoire d'une âme', 'Les heros du Fossoyeur', 'La fontaine de Pen-Morsa', 'Les trois fêtes d'Elizabeth', 'La coeur et la main' [Brown 2].

Anon.184 *The novelist's magazine.*
Philadelphia: C. Alexander, 1833, 2 vols. SOURCE OCLC. LOCATION MH.
COMMENTARY Contents: 'The ghost hunter and his family' [Michael Banim§], 'The Nowlans' [John Banim§], 'The collegians' [Gerald Griffin§] and other stories [OCLC].

Anon.185 *Obadiah's address from Ireland to the worshipful and all-potent people of Almack's.*
+ London: J. Hatchard, 1827. SOURCE Sadleir, 3137. LOCATION L.
COMMENTARY The author addresses all the chief characters in Marianne Spencer Hudson's *Almacks* (London, 1826, 3 vols.), a 'silver-fork school' novel about Almack's Assembly Rooms in London. The identity of the personages in the novel is assumed (or known) by the author as stated in the key of the *Literary Gazette*, and include 'Lady Hauton' [Lady Jersey], 'Lady Stavordale' [duchess of Bedford] and 'Lady Bellamont' [countess of Sefton]. The author con-

demns the unseemliness of the despotic manner of the Almack's committee, 'this is very strange, and quite unnatural that women should act in such a manner' [Sadleir, 3136–7; Quaritch Nov. 1999].

Anon.186 *O'Brien's lusorium: being a collection of convivial songs, lectures, &c. entirely original, in various styles. With characteristic cuts of the author, music to the songs, suggestions for promoting convivial enjoyment, &c. &c.*
+ London: Durham, Lewis, Steel, Peat, 1782 (with improvements; ill.). SOURCE ESTC t128544. LOCATION L, O, InND Loeber coll.
COMMENTARY Consists of prose and songs. Contents of the prose: 'Suggestions in view of promoting genuine jocundity at the convivial board', 'A lecture on eating and drinking: Spoken in the character of a drunken parson', 'A Methodist love-feast, or class-meeting', 'A Methodist sermon, by a cobbler', 'An anti-dramatic Methodist sermon', 'Foreign empiric and Irish Andrew', 'An anti-theatric Quaker's oration, or holding forth', 'Female Quaker', 'A Roman Catholic mass-house lecture, addressed to the vulgar Irish, and delivered by an Irish priest', 'A lecture on punch, wine, pipes and tobacco, and a merry song: Spoken in the character of a half-tipsy parson', 'The St. Giles Tatterdemallion ballad-singer' [RL].

Anon.187 *O'Connor's child; or, the harp of Innisfail.*
+ London: James Henderson, 1873 (The People's Pocket Story Book). SOURCE L.
COMMENTARY Historical fiction in a Gothic mode set in fourteenth-century Ireland [RL].

Anon.188 *The old country. A Christmas annual.*
+ Dublin: Sealy, Bryers & Walker, 1893 (ill. Edith Œnone Somerville§, Jack Yeats, J. Wilson Leitch, Walter F. Osborne). SOURCE Brown, 72. LOCATION L.
COMMENTARY Irish stories and poems: 'The Rorytight militia' (Terence Hourigan), 'The serpent's string' (Mary H. Tennyson), 'Winter months' (Hon. Mrs Arthur Henniker), 'The legend of Vanderdecken' (W.G. Wills§), 'November eve' (Katharine Tynan§), 'The five enormous gooseberries' (F. Langbridge§), 'Mrs. Wynniatt's skeleton' (Dick Donovan§), 'An immoderate man' (Edwin Hamilton§), 'Michael Clancy, the great dhoul, and death' (William Butler Yeats§), 'The strong man' (Lewis Morris), 'A ghost to order (Walter Parke), 'An Italian from Cork' (Edmund Downey§), 'Locksley Hall Hotel' (Samuel K. Cowan), 'The grace of Queen Clare' (Nora Vynne), 'Nocturne' (Edward Dowden) [CM].

Anon.189 *The Olio: Collected by a literary traveler.*
+ Boston: n.p., 1833. LOCATION NUC.
COMMENTARY Some Irish content: 'A journey to Dublin', 'Knipe and the Irishman', and 'Dublin Theatre – A Free Night' [RL].

Anon.190 *On the snow clad heights.*
Dublin: James Duffy & Co., [1886 or earlier]. SOURCE Adv. in J.J. O'Dea, *The beauties of nature* (Dublin, 1892).
COMMENTARY No copy located [RL].

Anon.191 *The Orientalist. A volume of tales after the Eastern taste* (by the author of *Roderick Random* [*sic*], *Sir Launcelot Greaves*, &c. and others).
+ Dublin: Printed [for the author?] by James Hoey Jnr, 1764. SOURCE Raven, 822; ESTC t043418. LOCATION L, PC, C.

COMMENTARY Not by the English writer Tobias Smollett, author of *The adventures of Roderick Random* (London, 1748, 2 vols.). The present volume may be a re-telling of existing stories, most of which are set in the Arab world. Contents: 'The history of Omrah, the son of Abulfaid', 'The history of Hindbad, the merchant', 'The history of Jaher and Massaoud', 'The history of Banou Rassid', 'The history of Hazikin, king of Gazna', 'The history of the peasant Yaarab', 'The history of Aouge, the peasant', 'The history of Malicknazir, king of Carizme and the Princess Farzana', 'The history of Ibrahim Hassan, the hermit', 'The history of Abraoulf', 'The history of Musidorus and Abdulla', 'The history of Zadick', 'The history of Hussendgiar, the hermit', 'The history of Almoraddin, Dogandar, and Hanif', 'The history of Firnaz and Mirvan', 'The history of Abdallah', 'The history of Atelmoule', 'The history of Zemin and Galhinda', 'The history of Ardostan', 'The history of Abah Rabieh', 'Zara: or royal justice', 'Mahmut and Idris', 'The history of Almira', 'The history of Princess Padmani', 'Mirza; or, the moralist', 'Alladin: A tale. Translated from the Arabic of Ebn Sadoc', 'Zulima; or the coquette', 'The history of Abdallah, the son of Aboan', 'The magic combat: or, power of beauty', 'The history of Assan', 'The history of Selim', 'The history of Ibrahim and Almira', 'Soliman II. A tale', 'Igluka and Sibbersik, a Greenland tale', 'The concluding tale' [RL; Raven].

Anon.192 *Original legends & stories of Ireland.*
+ Dublin: G.P. Warren, [1880s?]. LOCATION D, UCD Folklore Dept.
COMMENTARY 120pp. Contents: 'Cup tossing', 'Paddy's dream – The scalp' [by 'G.C.', first published in the *Irish Penny Magazine* (Dublin, 1833), pp 11–13], 'Morrogh Delany', 'Legend of Killarney', 'The water witch', 'A visit from the grave, or, the carpenter's promise', 'The sportheen', 'FitzStephen's tower', 'The herb doctor and the fairies' [by 'Tim Telltale', first published in the *Irish Penny Magazine* (Dublin, 1833), pp 261–2], 'The wake', 'The breaking heart', 'The wish', 'The widow's curse', 'The miser outwitted', 'The dead watcher' [by 'G.C.', first published in the *Irish Penny Magazine* (Dublin, 1833), pp 29–30] [ML].

Anon.193 *The orphan heiress of Sir Gregory. An historical fragment, of the last century.*
+ Cork: J. Connor, 1806. LOCATION D.
COMMENTARY Historical anti-Catholic fiction set in England at the time of Cromwell. A rich widow adopts a shipwrecked orphan, whom she calls Margaret, and brings her up in the Protestant religion. This inflames her Catholic relatives, who had expected to inherit from her. Margaret falls in love with a Catholic nephew who has been sent by her mother and a priest to infiltrate the household. Margaret narrowly avoids being married to a good, young Protestant man. The nephew is sent abroad and to be sure that Margaret does not get in contact with him, the priest kidnaps her and sends her to America, where she meets her real relatives. The Catholic nephew turns Protestant, and eventually they marry, thwarting the priest's plans. She becomes an heiress of her adoptive family and of her real relatives [ML].

Anon.194 *O'Ruarc, an Irish tale* (dedicated to Lady Morgan§).
+ Dublin: Richard Milliken & Son, 1832. SOURCE Brown, 75; Garside 2, 1832:6.
LOCATION D.
COMMENTARY In the dedication, the author, a student or fellow at TCD, from where he signed the preface in June 1832, expresses his admiration for Lady Morgan's§ talent, especially her 'recording of Irish grievances and observations on events resulting from absentee landlords'. The present novel originated from Lady Morgan's mentioning in her work the death of O'Ruarc, prince of Breffini [*sic*]. The author explains that by means of his novel he wants to

draw young people's attention to the 'history of their own country' and the evil consequences of absentee landlords in Ireland. This historical novel is set during Elizabethan times [ML; Brown].

Anon.195 *Our Katie.*
+ New York: American Tract Society, n.d. (ill.; on cover: Life Ill.). SOURCE OCLC. LOCATION NN, InND Loeber coll.
COMMENTARY 32pp. Protestant religious fiction for juveniles. Katie was born in Ireland but at an early age emigrated with her parents and settled in Brooklyn (NY). She becomes absorbed in the Protestant Sabbath school and develops strong religious feelings. She brings with her as many children as she can collect. She often washes and combs them before they enter the school. At an early age she goes into service to help her parents financially. Everybody loves her. One evening her dress catches fire and she is badly burnt. She dies peacefully [ML].

Anon.196 *The outcast: A story of the modern Reformation.*
Dublin: William Curry Jnr & Co.; London: Hurst, Chance & Co., 1830, 2 vols. SOURCE COPAC (1831 edn); Brown, 76; Garside 2, 1830:11. LOCATION L (2nd edn, revsd and corrected, 2 vols. in 1), C (2nd edn).
COMMENTARY No copy of the first edn located. Reviewed in the *Christian Examiner* (Dublin, Mar. 1831). A Catholic studying for the priesthood reads widely and by reading Lady Morgan's§ *Italy*, (London, 1821, 2 vols.) he becomes aware of the errors of the Roman Catholic church. His father turns him out, and his mother dies of a broken heart. It contains a description of the river Slaney in the south-east of Ireland [Brown; RL].

Anon.197 *Paddy's leisure hours in the poor house; or, priests, parsons, potatoes, and poor rates.*
+ London: John W. Parker; Dublin: Hodges & Smith, 1849. SOURCE NSTC. LOCATION Dt, L, C, O.
COMMENTARY Religious fiction dealing with effects of poverty and famine. Paddy eventually emigrates to America to rescue his family from the Irish poor house. An appendix contains political answers to the fictional narrative [CM].

Anon.198 *Passaw; or, the German prince. Being a genuine relation of the late transactions of Sir William Newsted alias Passaw, wherein that potable piece of knight errantry is trac'd from its first original to its final exit.*
Dublin: John Crawford, 1719. SOURCE Pollard 2, p. 127; ESTC t180497. LOCATION D, Di.
Printed at Dublin: and [London] for T. Bickerton, 1720. SOURCE COPAC; ESTC N23647. LOCATION O, CSmH.
COMMENTARY 45pp in London edn. Sometimes attributed to Daniel Defoe [ESTC].

Anon.199 *Passion and pedantry. A novel illustrative of Dublin life.*
London: T.C. Newby, 1853, 3 vols. SOURCE Brown, 77. LOCATION L.
COMMENTARY A tale of the fortunes of Charles Desmond, an officer. He inherits his uncle's money and marries. Gives a portrayal of Dublin life [Brown].

Anon.200 *The pearl of great price; or, the autobiography of an Irish convert* (dedicated to 'My Christian friends and benefactors').

+ Dublin: W. Curry & Co., P.D. Hardy & Co., J. Robertson; G. Herbert; London: J. Nisbet & Co., [1851]. SOURCE Bradshaw, 3543. LOCATION C.

COMMENTARY 48pp. Account of a man's conversion from catholicism to protestantism [RL].

Anon.201 *Phelim O'Neil; or, man's extremity is God's opportunity. An Irish story founded on fact* (dedicated to Lady Isabella King,[2] the text being 'illustrative of the priestly tyranny & spiritual bondage of unhappy Ireland').

+ Liverpool: W. Grapel, 1844. SOURCE COPAC. LOCATION L.

COMMENTARY Protestant religious fiction that describes the labours of a Protestant clergyman in Ireland and the problems of having Catholics read the Bible. At the end of the story the question of emigration for the converted Protestants is brought up [ML].

Anon.202 *Philip O'Hara's adventures.*

+ Edinburgh: W. & R. Chambers, 1885. SOURCE Brown, 79; COPAC. LOCATION L.

COMMENTARY The adventures of Philip O'Hara in the American Civil War. Also contains other stories, 'A boy's first fight', 'The Christmas tree', 'The little shepherd', but they do not have a connection with Ireland [Brown; ML].

Anon.203 *The pleasures of a new life; or, the miseries of matrimony.*

Newry: Dan Carpenter, n.d. [18th c.]. SOURCE Emerald Isle cat. 68/788.

COMMENTARY Not in ESTC, and no copy located other than the one referred in the Emerald Isle cat. [RL].

Anon.204 *The polite companion; or, stories for the ladies.*

+ Dublin: Will Sleater, 1767. SOURCE Raven, 1158; ESTC n011866. LOCATION MH.

COMMENTARY A miscellany that includes a collection of tales or short novels with no Irish content. Contents: 'Fortitude and patience triumphant over barbarity and deceit', 'The reward of avarice', 'Love repaid by gratitude', 'The precipitate marriage', 'The fatal amusement', 'The wicked revenge', 'Reciprocal generosity', 'The twice-united pair', 'The extraordinary oeconomist [*sic*]', 'The fair indiscreet', 'Virtue rewarded', 'The thoughtless beauty', 'The unfortunate prejudice', 'The disappointed lady', 'The power of beauty', 'The dreaming projector', 'The lady's punishment', 'The happy stratagem', 'The perjur'd mistress', 'The avaritious [*sic*] lover requited', 'The virtuous wife', 'Female humility and benevolence' [Raven; ML].

Anon.205 *The polite tutoress, or, young lady's instructor; being a series of dialogues between Mrs. Affable, a sensible governess, and several of her pupils of the first rank; in which they are made to think, speak, and act, in a manner suitable to their respective tempers, dispositions, and capacities. No less care being taken to form their hearts to virtue than to cultivate their understandings with useful knowledge. In this work are included lessons in geography, and a clear abridgement of sacred and prophane history, interspersed with useful reflections, fables, moral tales, songs, etc. for their amusement: a very proper study for chil-*

2 This is probably Isabella, daughter of Sir Edward King, Bt (later created first earl of Kingston). She died unmarried (R.D. King-Harman, *The Kings, Earls of Kingston* (Cambridge, 1959), p. 125).

dren of fashion, especially those at boarding schools. By Madame Le Princesse de Beaumont; translated from the French. To which is added Margaretta, the profidious orphan; and Sophia, or the double escape; two new novels, never before printed. With an address to the masters and governesses of boarding-schools (dedicated by the 'editor' to Lady Emilia Fitzgerald, eldest daughter of the Rt Hon. James, earl of Kildare).

Dublin: James Hoey Jnr , [1760 or earlier], 2 vols. SOURCE Adv. in the *Angler's Magazine; or, complete fisherman* (Dublin, 1760).

London: J. Coote, 1761. SOURCE ESTC n12395. LOCATION Rice Univ., Houston (TX).

COMMENTARY No copy of the Dublin edn located. Madame Marie Le Princesse de Beaumont (1711–80) was a French author, specializing in juvenile fiction [RL].

Anon.206 *The poor Irish woman: or, the labourers and the penny.*
[London]: Religious Tract Society, [*c*.1840] (Narrative Series, No. 892). SOURCE COPAC. LOCATION Methodist Archives, John Rylands Univ. Library, Manchester Deansgate.

Anon.207 *Popular tales and legends of the Irish peasantry* (ed. by Samuel Lover§ [*sic*, see below]).
+ Dublin: William Frederick Wakeman; London: R. Groombridge; Edinburgh: Oliver & Boyd, 1834 (ill. Samuel Lover§). SOURCE Hayley, 9a; Rafroidi, ii, p. 219; Sadleir, 508; OCLC; Garside 2, 1834:17. LOCATION Grail, D, L, InND Loeber coll.

COMMENTARY Samuel Lover§ in the preface to his *Legends and stories of Ireland* (London, 1834, 4th edn, first series) stated that 'A book, entitled, *Popular stories and legends of the peasantry of Ireland, with illustrations, by Samuel Lover, &c. &c.* has lately been published in Dublin, with the authorship of which book I am totally unconnected. Six illustrations for the volume were supplied by me, and those who are answerable for the work should have let the public distinctly understand that *so far only* was I concerned, and not have imputed to me, by a questionable use of my name, an authorship which I feel it necessary to disavow. From the duplicity of this title many have been induced to imagine that the work, to which it is prefixed, is *my* Second Series of Legends and Stories; and this very name, too, has been assumed, with a mere transposition, the book being entitled "Stories and Legends," although *there is not a single legend in its pages*. I leave the Public to call such conduct by its right name' (pp vii–viii). Binding title is *Sketches of Ireland and the Irish [sic]*. Contents: 'Alley Sheridan; or, the runaway marriage' (William Carleton§), 'Kate Connor' (Mrs S.C. Hall§), 'Charley Fraser; or, the victim of jealousy' (Selina Bunbury§), 'The Whiteboy's revenge' (Denis O'Donoho), 'Laying a ghost' (William Carleton§), 'The wife of two husbands' (J.L.L.), 'Reminiscences of an Irish landlord – the rebel chief – 1799' (P.D.H. [Philip Dixon Hardy?§]), 'Mick Delany' (Denis O'Donoho), 'The lost one' (J.L.L.), 'The abduction and rescue' (Denis O'Donoho), 'The dance' (J.L.L.), 'The shooting excursion' (Denis O'Donoho), 'The unwedded mother' (Denis O'Donoho), 'The Fetch. A tale of superstition' (J.L.L.), 'The three devils' (B.A.P.) [ML].

Anon.208 *Power of religion, moral and entertaining tales.*
Dublin: John Gough, [1795?]. SOURCE Pollard 2, p. 245.
COMMENTARY Not in ESTC, and no copy located [RL].

Anon.209 *The principal events in the history of Ireland, in the form of stories* (dedicated to the Honourable Augusta and Frederic Ponsonby).[3]
+ London: E. Lloyd & Co., 1829. SOURCE Fenning cat. 133/188. LOCATION L, InND Loeber coll.
COMMENTARY Written by a 'friend', possibly a relative of the Ponsonbys. One of the earliest historical books on Ireland for children. Includes a list of sources used. Written from the Ascendancy point of view, but gives a very balanced view of Irish history, and apportions blame and praise in a non-partisan manner. The form is more first-person narrative about history than fiction [RL].

Anon.210 *Publications of the Religious Tract and Book Society for Ireland.*
+ Dublin: Sold at 22 Upper Sackville St.; London: James Nesbit & Houlston & Son, 1828, vol. 2 (ill.). LOCATION PC.
COMMENTARY Volume 1 not located. Volume 2 consists of a bound volume of tracts, individually paginated and dated (ranging from 1824 to 1828). Some of the tracts first appeared in book form in [anonymous], *Narratives and stories for the instruction of young persons* (Dublin, 1825). Contents of volume 2 (only fiction listed, leaving aside religious and practical agricultural advice): 'The Jew and his daughter, converted to Christianity' (from an American publication), 'John Elliot, the friend of the American Indians', 'The murder of the Christian Indians in North America in the year 1782. A narrative of facts', 'A happy poor woman. A true story' (English in content), 'The wake house' (Irish content), 'The evils of illicit distillation' (temperance tale; Irish content), 'The cottage in Connaught', 'The reduced tradesman' [RL].

Anon.211 void

Anon.212 *Reasons against coition. A discourse (on I Cor.vii.I.27) deliver'd to a private congregation. By the reverend Stephen M*****, D.D., chaplain to the ... earl of ***** ... To which is added A proposal for making religion and the clergy useful; with the author's observations on the cause and cure of the piles ...*
London: H. Hook, 1732. LOCATION MH.
COMMENTARY 64pp. A plea for the extinction of the human race in Ireland [C. Welsh & W.H. Tillinghast (eds.), *Catalogue of English and American Chapbooks and broadside ballads in Harvard College Library* (repr. Detroit, 1968), p.138].

Anon.213 *The rebel chief. An historical tale.*
+ London: John Duncombe, n.d. (ill.;). LOCATION D.
COMMENTARY Chapbook. Pagination is from p. [123]–152. Dramatic tales of the rebellion of 1798. The bibliographical origin of the larger publication of which this is part remains unclear [RL].

---

3 Children of the 4th earl of Bessborough, who were age 15 and 14 in 1829; Augusta became countess of Kerry; Frederic became the 6th earl of Bessborough.

Anon.214 *The rebels of Glenfawn. A romance of the last century.*
+ London: Shoberl, 1852, 3 vols. SOURCE Brown 2, 22. LOCATION L.
COMMENTARY Historical fiction set in 1797 in the village of Glenfawn (Co. Cork), it gives a vivid description of the events at that time and shows the conflicting loyalties of those who espoused the cause of the United Irishmen. Interwoven is a love story. This book was advertised in 1853 as *The rebels of Glenfawn. A tale of Ireland's troubles in 1798* and is possibly based on a manuscript *A tale of the last century, or a visit to Ireland in 1798* listed in the *Catalogue of the library of Dr. R.R. Madden* (Dublin, 1846), p. 20 (current location not known). Madden purchased the manuscript at the sale of the library of Sir F. Shaw, recorder of Dublin. A serial 'The rebel – a tale of '98''' by one Melior, published in the *Dublin Saturday Magazine c.*1865, may refer to one or more of the above sources [RL; Brown 2; Personal communication, Kevin Whelan, Dec. 2001].

Anon.215 *The robber chieftain: A tale of Dublin Castle.*
+ Dublin: James Duffy, 1857 (ill. J. Lonecht?, Geo. Measom). SOURCE Brown, 89 (1858 edn); Brown 2, 198 (1858 edn). LOCATION L, InND Loeber coll.
+ Dublin, London: James Duffy, 1863 (as *The robber chieftain. A historical tale of Dublin Castle*; ill. George Measom). LOCATION DPL, L.
COMMENTARY Ascribed by Brown 2 to William Carleton§, but not so by Hayley. Set in the seventeenth century, mainly in Dublin Castle. The story describes the cruelties of the Cromwellians under Ludlow and the early years of the Restoration. The robber chieftain is Robert O'Hanlon, the rapparee. O'Hanlon's escapades were first published in the anonymous *The life and death of the indefatigable Tory, Redmond Ô Hanlyn* ([Dublin], 1682), see Anon.136 [Brown; Brown 2; Hayley; RL].

Anon.216 *Robert and Adela; or, the rights of women, best maintained by the sentiments of nature.*
London: G.G. & J. Robinson, 1795, 3 vols. SOURCE Black, p. 124; ESTC n013038. LOCATION CtY.
+ Dublin: P. Byrne, P. Wogan, W. Jones & G. Folingsby, 1795, 2 vols. SOURCE ESTC n013039. LOCATION Dm.
COMMENTARY An epistolary novel, with some of the letters addressed by Mr Harrowby from 'Black Rock, near Dublin' and featuring nobility from various countries. Harrowby is descended from a Gaelic family originally named 'O'Hara-bagh' [ML; RL].

Anon.217 *The Roman Catholic priest.*
+ Dublin: W. Curry Jnr & Co.; London: Hamilton, Adams & Co.; Edinburgh: W. Oliphant, 1827 (ill. Kirkwood). SOURCE Brown, 90; British Fiction; Garside, 1827:8; LOCATION L.
COMMENTARY Anti-Catholic fiction in which Doyle, a Catholic boy, heroically saves a Protestant boy from drowning. The boy's father offers to send Doyle to TCD, guaranteeing that he can continue to be a Catholic. However, the local priest refuses to let Doyle go to Trinity. In the end, Doyle converts to protestantism [Brown].

Anon.218 *Rosalind; or, an apology for the history of a theatrical lady.*
Dublin: Printed and sold by the booksellers, 1759. SOURCE Raven, 518; ESTC t072051. LOCATION L (mislaid), MH.
COMMENTARY A fictional, biographical account of the actress Ann Crawford, formerly Mrs Dancer and Mrs Barry. No Irish content [CM; ML].

Anon.219   *A round table of the representative Irish and English Catholic novelists, at which is served a feast of excellent stories ... with portraits, biographical sketches, and bibliography.*
+ New York, Cincinnati, Chicago: Benziger Bros, 1897 (2nd edn; ill.). LOCATION InND, NUC.
COMMENTARY Contents: 'A dress ring' (Louisa Emily Dobrée), 'In St. Patrick's ward' (M.E. Francis§), 'A soldier's wife' (Theo. Gift), 'Fairy Dorothy Wilmot' (baroness Pauline von Hügel), 'Just what was wanted' (Lady Anabel Kerr), 'Hyancinth's regrets' (R.B. Sheridan Knowles§), 'Miss Packe' (Frances M. Maitland), 'A paste buckle' (Sophie Maude), 'Ma[e]ve's repentance' (Clara Mulholland§), 'Granny Grogan' (Rosa Mulholland Gilbert§), 'Her last stake' (Mrs Bartle Teeling), 'The wardrobe' (Katharine Tynan Hinkson§) [RL].

Anon.220   *The Royal Hibernian tales; being a collection of the most entertaining stories now extant.*
[Dublin?], [publisher?], [1825 or earlier]. SOURCE First report of the Commission of Education Inquiry (London: House of Commons, 1825), p. 555, as 'Hibernian tales'. COMMENTARY *1825 or earlier edn* No copy of this edn located [RL].
+ Dublin: Printed [for the author?] by C.M. Warren, [1835?] (ill.; cover: 'Hibernian tales'; see Plate 4). SOURCE Adams, p. 197; NSTC (1844 edn); Garside 2, 1832:8. LOCATION D, L [c.1880 edn], O (1844 edn), InND Loeber coll.
Belfast: Joseph Smyth, [1832]. SOURCE Adams, p. 197; Garside 2, 1832:8. LOCATION D, Dt.
COMMENTARY This is said to be the earliest known collection of Irish popular tales, some of which are clearly from Ulster. Note that the Dublin, Warren edn (Plate 4) has a harp without the crown. The compiler of this volume was either a native of Co. Antrim, or at least very familiar with its topography. The compiler states in the preface that the stories are meant to be instructive moral tales. Contents of the NLI copy: 'The black thief and the Knight of the Glen' (set in the south of Ireland), 'Will o' the wisp' (set in Loughhile, Ballymoney, Co. Antrim), 'The apprentice thief', 'Manus O'Mallaghan and the fairies' (set in Ahoghill, Co. Antrim), 'Fool Tom and his brother Jack', 'The hermit turn pilgrim' (set in Killarney, Co. Kerry), 'The farmer and his servant', 'The three advices', 'The spaeman' (set in Derry), 'Donald and his neighbours' (set at Balinconlig), 'The priest and the robber' (set in Ulster), 'Teague Sloan' (set in Kiltonrella, containing 'The story of Oldemar'), 'Peter Megrab & his brother John', 'The jackdaw' (set in Dublin), 'The blacksmith' (set in the north of Ireland), 'Jack Withers' (set in Athlone, Co. Westmeath). The collection closes with a page of anecdotes. The Belfast edn contains the following, additional stories: 'The young priest and Brien Braar', 'Mac Turkill', 'The fisherman's son', 'The generous Irishman', 'Annie Bonney, the female pirate', 'James Butler'. The volume is mentioned by William Makepeace Thackeray§ in his *The Paris sketch book, the Irish sketch book* (Boston, 1883, pp 162–9). With the exception of one story, it was reprinted in *Béaloideas*, 10 (1940), pp 148–203. Many of the stories survived in oral tradition in Irish and English and were recorded by the Irish Folklore Commission. Several of the stories were recycled in other anthologies [ML; Adams, pp 147, 197; S. Delargy, 'Royal Hibernian tales' in *Béaloideas*, 10 (1940), pp 148–203; RL; Garside].

Anon.221   *The school for majesty: An oriental tale* (dedicated to Lady Louisa Conolly [of Castletown House, Co. Kildare]).
+ Dublin: Printed for the author by S. Colbert, 1780. SOURCE Raven 2, 1780:11; ESTC t107629. LOCATION Dt, L.

+ Dublin: Printed for the author by S. Colbert, 1781, 2nd edn (as *The sufferings of Zomelli; or, school for majesty: An oriental history*). SOURCE ESTC t212585. LOCATION Dt.

London: William Lane, 1783 (as *School for majesty; or, the sufferings of Zomelli*). SOURCE Summers, p. 496; Raven 2, 1793: ESTC n021579.

COMMENTARY A mighty eastern monarch is dethroned through the machinations of his crafty chief minister [ML].

Anon.222 *The schoolboys and other tales.*
+ London: Burns & Lambert, [1860]. SOURCE COPAC. LOCATION L.
COMMENTARY Contents: 'The schoolboys', 'The story of Giovanni', 'Gudbrand on the hill-side', 'The French orphan' (set in Dublin). Ascribed in the BL entry in COPAC to Maria Edgeworth§, but this appears to be an error [RL].

Anon.223 *The secret history of Medilla: containing a faithful account of her birth and parentage; her amour with a gentleman of Ireland ... Together with the whole series of her amour with Count Onslorio, and their extraordinary nuptials ... With the proceedings, as they are going on in the Ecclesiastical Court, on behalf of Medilla, for conjugal rights. The whole concluded, with a parallel between the cases of Count Onslorio and Medilla, the Ld. FitzMaurice and Mrs Eliz. Leeson.*
London: T. Reynolds, 1731. SOURCE Falkner Greirson cat. Maude/674.
London: T. Reynolds, 1733 (as *The secret history of M—d—lla. Containing a faithful account of her birth and parentage; her amour with a gentleman of Ireland, etc.*). SOURCE Esdaile, p. 270; ESTC t047391. LOCATION L.
COMMENTARY No copy of the London 1731 edn located (other than one mentioned by Falkner Greirson). Rev. in the *Gentleman's Magazine* (London, May 1733). Another version of the same events appeared as the anonymous *Love without artifice* (London, 1731). The title here is not to be confused with *The secret history of Mama Oella, Princess Royal of Peru* (London, 1733?), which is based on the marriage of Anne, daughter of King George II [RL; NCBEL 2, p. 933].

Anon.224 *The secret memoirs of Miss Sally Dawson: otherwise Mrs. Sally M'Clane: otherwise Mrs. Sarah Mayne, – widow. To which is annexed, a genuine will.*
+ Dublin: Printed [for the author?] by Holmes & Charles, 1805, 2nd ed. (ill.). LOCATION L.
COMMENTARY No copy of the first edn located. 50pp (second edn). The narrative of Sally Dawson who was born near Armagh. Her father was a cooper and farmer, her mother descended from a respectable family named D—n—s. Sally in her adolescence befriended the third son of the Earl Vere P—l—t [3rd Earl Poulett], and Viscount H—n—t—n [?Huntingdon] and fled with him to England. The story relates her adventures there and, following her return, further adventures in Ireland [RL].

Anon.225 *The select story teller; a collection of shipwrecks, anecdotes, and adventures.*
+ Dublin: Printed by Graisberry & Campbell [for the Kildare Place Society], 1819 (ill.). SOURCE Hislop, p. 1047. LOCATION D (1822 edn), L (1820 edn).
London: C.J.G. & F. Rivington [for the Society for the Promotion of Christian Knowledge], 1831. SOURCE Hislop, pp 1047–8.

COMMENTARY No copies of the Dublin 1819 edn and the London 1831 edn located. Retelling of stories of disasters and hardships set in different countries (no Irish content). Contents of the 1822 edn: 'Account of the great earthquake in Lisbon in the year 1755', 'Miraculous escape of a boy cast away on a rock', 'Singular account of the death of Thomas Clark, a miser', 'Hardships endured by four Russian sailors on the island of Spitsbergen', 'Description of a lion hunt in India', 'Shipwreck of Emanuel de Sosa, on the coast of Africa', 'The two brothers', 'Extraordinary adventures of William Bontekoe' [RL].

Anon.226 *The serpent's sting, and other stories.*
> Dublin: Sealy, Bryers & Walker, [1898 or earlier] (ill.). SOURCE RL; Adv. by Sealy, Bryers & Walker, 1898.
COMMENTARY No copy located. Priced at 6*d*. Perhaps associated with R.R. Engle's *The serpent's sting, or worse than death: a tale of drink and woe* (Hamilton, OH, 1874) [RL; Adv. of Sealy, Bryers & Walker; OCLC].

Anon.227 *Shamrock leaves; gleaned in the fertile field of Irish literature: being tales and stories of Ireland selected from the most popular authors.*
> + Boston: Thomas Sweeney, 1854 (ill.). LOCATION NUC, InND Loeber coll.
> + Boston: Patrick Donahoe, 1854. SOURCE Hayley, p. 175. LOCATION D, NUC.
COMMENTARY Rev. in the *Catholic Herald* (29 Aug. 1857), p. 284. Mostly, but not fully, a subset of the stories published from *Tales & stories of Ireland* (Halifax, 1846), for which see below. Contents of the Sweeney edn (that of the Donahoe edn is practically the same, but does not identify the authors): 'Light hearts and light heels', 'Ned M'Keown' (William Carleton§), 'The stolen sheep; an Irish sketch' ([John & Michael] Banim§), 'Darby Doyle's voyage to Quebec' [Thomas Ettingsall], 'The three tasks; or the little house under the hill' (William Carleton§), 'Confessions of a reformed Ribbonman (An owre true tale)' (William Carleton§), 'Barny O'Reirdon, the navigator' (Samuel Lover§), 'The dead watcher' [by 'G.C.', first published in the *Irish Penny Magazine* (Dublin, 1833), pp 29–30], 'Neal Malone. A tale of a tailor' (William Carleton§), 'Tubber Derg' (William Carleton§), 'Cup tossing', 'The wish', 'It's my luck' (Mrs D.C. Hall [*sic*, Mrs S.C. Hall§]), 'The Irish magistrate', 'The poor scholar' (William Carleton§), 'Duke Dorgan' (Gerald Griffin§), 'Story of Hogan' (Gerald Griffin§), 'The three advices. An Irish moral tale' (Thomas Crofton Croker§ [*sic*; actually from *Royal Hibernian tales*, [Dublin?, 1825 or earlier]), 'The two brothers. An Irish tale' (William Carleton§), 'Owen and Ellen. A legend of Clare', 'The pass of Cooleagh', 'The Whiteboys' [RL].

Anon.228 *The siege of Belgrade: An historical novel. Translated from a German manuscript* (dedicated to Lord Rawdon).
> London: H.D. Symonds, 1741 [*sic*, 1791], 4 vols. in 2. SOURCE ESTC t71920; Raven 2, 1791:24. LOCATION L.
COMMENTARY The alluded origin of a German manuscript is likely to be a fictive device. Set in 1789, the novel concerns the French Revolution and mixes reprehension of the *ancien régime* with disdain for the revolution. Features Viscount Leinster, a likely personification of Lord Edward Fitzgerald (whose father was the duke of Leinster; Lord Edward did not visit France until 1792). Although Viscount Leinster censored the violence committed, he described the 'abstract virtue and necessity of reformation: alleging, that the spirit of the constitution, and the indispensable rights of men, had been totally absorbed in a blind and slavish obedience to despotism'. The story is set in a vague Serbian context, in which Viscount Leinster stresses the evils of insurrection. When the inevitable revolt erupts with its attendant violence, Leinster's attitude to it is that the grievances of the people do not warrant an insurrection and blood-

shed. However, in the face of the mob, Leinster reluctantly contributes to the violence by commanding his troops to fire on the rebels who then disperse into the country. James Cobbe's comic opera *The siege of Belgrade* (London, 1791) appears to be associated with this novel [G.O. Grenby, *The anti-Jacobin novel* (Cambridge, 2001), pp 46, 48; RL].

Anon.229 *The siege of Drogheda; or, reminiscences of the families of Ireland, Celtic and Anglo – founded on incidents of Irish history.*
> Dublin, London: John Mullany, Catholic Publishing and Bookselling Company, [1870?]. SOURCE COPAC. LOCATION D, L.
> COMMENTARY Historical fiction set in the seventeenth century [RL].

Anon.230 *The siege of Maynooth; or, romance in Ireland.*
> + London: James Ridgway, 1832, 2 vols (spine title: Romance in Ireland. SOURCE Brown, 94; COPAC; Garside 2, 1832:10. LOCATION Corvey, 3–628–48698–X, D, L, C.

COMMENTARY Historical fiction set in sixteenth-century Ireland that tells of incidents during the Desmond wars and of the rebellion of Silken Thomas, and features the old countess of Desmond. The story includes the attack on Desmond Castle by the Butlers, the defeat and capture of the lord deputy Grey in Glendalough (Co. Wicklow), the escape of Lord Thomas Fitzgerald from the Black Castle of Wicklow, and the siege and betrayal of the Castle of Maynooth (Co. Kildare). The story starts with the young Lord Grey who, in search of shelter from a storm, stumbles upon a hut in southern England inhabited by 'something not belonging to this world'. This 'Irish witch' is the countess of Desmond who asks: 'Who reigns in England now? I have seen many reigns, but all are away like unto a dream. – Oh! Young man, I have passed from a throne to a prison, I have been steeped in the blood of those nearest and dearest; I have sojourned on this earth one hundred and forty years; I have been a Queen; I am a Beggar'. She passes an ancient manuscript to Lord Gray containing the story of her life in Ireland. His reading of this narrative provides the central part of the novel. Block relates that the anonymous *Romance of Irish history* is mentioned in the *Literary Gazette* as also published in London by the same publisher in the same year (Ridgway, 1832, 2 vols.). The latter title has not been traced or located, and plausibly is a mix-up with the above title. A serial, *Romance of Irish history*, was published in the *Dublin Journal* (Dublin, 1842), and is also set in late-sixteenth-century Ireland [Brown; CM; RL; Block, p. 200].

Anon.231 *Simple Sarah.*
> Dublin: James Duffy & Co., [1892 or earlier] (Duffy's Juvenile Library). SOURCE Adv. in J.J. O'Dea, *The beauties of nature* (Dublin, 1892).
> COMMENTARY No copy located [RL].

Anon.232 *The singular life, amatory adventures, and intrigues of John Wilmot, Earl of Rochester: The constant companion of that merry monarch, King Charles the second, in most of his famous freaks and intrigues. Interspersed with curious anecdotes of the Duke of Buckingham – Lord Chancellor Hyde – Nell Gwynn – Jane Stanley – The Duchess of Cleveland – Lady Holbert – Dir E. Hilton – Sophia Waller – Countess of Shrewsbury, &c. With an interesting account of his various mistresses, &c. &c. To which is added, his amorous poems. Founded on a manuscript in the hand-writing of his Lordship, by a living descendant of the family.*
> New York: Printed for the publisher, 1831 (ill.). SOURCE Scott cat. 42/93.

COMMENTARY No other copy located. Historical fiction featuring John Wilmot, earl of Rochester (1647–1680). The book starts with a 'key', describing Nell Gwynn and Jane Stanley as the mistresses of both King Charles and Rochester; Janet, the maid, as Rochester's mistress; the French ambassador, duc de Vignon, 'cuckolded by Rochester'; various Dutch and German officers killed by Rochester; 'A certain Dutch officer, eunuchised by Rochester'; and Teresa Tonkins, 'released from the Inquisition and —— by Rochester'. It is possible that the imprint is false and that this is an English production. Contains some of Rochester's poems and other, unidentified poems [Scott cat.].

Anon.233   *Six months in a House of Correction, or, the narrative of Dorah Mahony, who was under the influence of the Protestants about a year, and an inmate of the House of Correction, in Leverett St., Boston, Massachusetts, nearly six months, in the years 18–. With some preliminary suggestions by the committee of publication.*
        + Boston: Benjamin B. Mussey, 1835. SOURCE Partly printed in Exiles, pp 49–60; Griffin, pp 34–5. LOCATION L, InND Loeber coll.
COMMENTARY A counterattack against anti-Catholic feelings and a rejoinder to Rebecca T. Reed's *Six months in a convent* (Boston, 1835; also Glasgow, 1835). It starts with the emigration of Dorah Mahony from Ireland to Lowell (MA). She lives under the protection of Thaddeus Murrough, but then falls in love with a Mr McS. from Boston, who is a Protestant and from the north of Ireland. She leaves for Boston, but is soon arrested for drunkenness. False evidence by the police about her recidivism leads to her being sentenced to six months' hard work in the house of correction. Much of the text is filled with details of life in prison, its inmates and the guards, and ways that her religious beliefs are undermined. Eventually, she escapes from the prison and finds a safe haven in the house of one Costello in Boston [RL; Exiles, pp 49–50].

Anon.234   *Souvenirs du Sacré-Coeur de Paris.*
        Tours: Alfred Mame & Sons, 1852. LOCATION BNF.
        + Tours: Alfred Mame & Sons, 1878 (new edn; ill.). LOCATION BNF.
COMMENTARY Catholic religious fiction based on the life of Monique-Françoise-Malvina O'Connor, who was born in Martinique in 1823. Her father was a Catholic of a 'noble famille irlandaise'. She received her education from her niece, Elmire de Courcy, a daughter of the baroness de Courcy (perhaps Sarah, the wife of John Stapleton de Courcy, 23rd Lord Kingsale; see CP, vii, p. 291). Both parents died when Malvina and her sister were still young, after which their aunt, the baroness de Courcy took them in her house. She and the children went to France for their education. Here the story starts with Malvina eventually joining the order of the Sacré-Coeur. An appendix relates the biographies of other girls, who, after joining the order, had died [RL].

Anon.235   *Spectacles for young ladies; exhibiting the various arts made use of for seducing young women, and the dreadful consequences of straying from the paths of innocence and virtue, in a stile that cannot offend the chastest ear; and, at the same time that it amuses with its surprising variety, conveys instruction by the most effectual method, example. Containing the most remarkable histories of the lives and actions of those young women, who, conscious of their past guilt, have dedicated the remainder of their time in the service of God, and making atonement, by repentance, for their past crimes, by retiring from the world to the Magdalen-Hospital, London, erected for the reception of penitent prostitutes. As related by themselves.*

+ Cork: Printed for the proprietor, 1767, 2 vols. SOURCE COPAC; Mott cat. 249/12. LOCATION L.

COMMENTARY Series of autobiographical tales set in England supposedly related by the former prostitutes themselves. A number of young women, teenagers to age 30, innocent or naive to a fault, come to the big city and experience the school of hard knocks with eyes wide open or shut, often going from poverty to elegant living and back again. Describes dens of iniquity; grinding poverty; kept women who believe they will be wed; children born out of wedlock, and men as cads. The publication of this novel coincided with the opening of the first Magdalen Asylum in Dublin under the patronage of Lady Arabella Denny, modelled after the recently opened refuge in London [Mott cat.; RL; T. Barnard, *A new anatomy of Ireland* (New Haven, 2003), p. 277; RL].

Anon.236 *The spirit of Irish wit; or, post-chaise companion; being an eccentric miscellany of Hibernian wit, fun, and humour, much the greater part never before in print, with a selection of such as may have appeared; calculated for the meridian of the United Kingdoms, and consisting of bon mots, repartees, smart puns, high jokes, queer hoakes, humorous anecdotes, laughable bulls, devilish good things, and various other articles of intellectual confectionary, adapted to the risible muscles, and designed to dispel care, purge melancholy, cure the spleen, and raise the drooping spirits in these gloomy times.*

+ London: [publisher?], 1809, 4th edn. SOURCE Emerald Isle cat. 50/14; Gilbert, p. 773 ([1811?] edn). LOCATION DPL Gilbert coll. ([1811?] edn), L (1812 edn), O (1812 edn), InND Loeber coll. (n.d. edn).

Glasgow: R. Griffin, 1812. LOCATION O.

COMMENTARY No copy of 1809, 4th edn located other than in Emerald Isle cat. Earlier edns not located either. Short pieces of wit, bulls etc., but no sustained stories [ML].

Anon.237 *The stage coach: Containing the character of Mr. Manly, and the history of his fellow travellers.*

Dublin: H. Saunders, [1766 or earlier]. SOURCE Adv. in *Chrysal: or, the adventures of a guinea* (Dublin, 1766).

COMMENTARY Not in ESTC, and no copy located. Declared as having been lately published by H. Saunders, as advertised in *Chrysal: or, the adventures of a guinea* (Dublin, 1766), vol. 1 [RL].

Anon.238 *Stories by English authors. Ireland.*

+ New York: Charles Scribner's Sons, 1896 (ill.). SOURCE Hayley, p. 185. LOCATION D (1900 edn), NUC, InND Loeber coll.

COMMENTARY Volume 5 out of a series of ten volumes. Contents of volume 5: 'The gridiron' (Samuel Lover§), 'Emergency men' (George [Henry] Jessop§), 'A lost recruit' (Jane Barlow§, first published in the London *Pall Mall Magazine*), 'The rival dreamers' (John [or Michael] Banim§), ' Neal Malone' (William Carleton§), 'The banshee' (anon.) [RL; NUC].

Anon.239 *Taciturna and Jocunda; or, Genius Alaciel's journey through these two islands. A satirical work* (trans. from French [*sic*]).

+ London: R. Withy & J. Cook, 1760. SOURCE Hardy, 172; Raven, 553; ESTC t088560. LOCATION L, MH.

COMMENTARY A tale of a visit by a spirit to two islands where the people hate each other. In one island [which must be England] everyone is prosperous but gloomy; in the other island

[Ireland] people are happy but poor and improvident. The spirit formulates twenty laws to bring both islands closer together and to regulate the defects of both [ML].

Anon.240 *Tales and legends of Ireland, illustrative of society, history, antiquities, manners, and literature; to which are added translations from the Irish, biographical essays, &c.*
+ Cork: Bolster, 1831, 2 vols. SOURCE Brown, 99. LOCATION D.
London: Thomas Hurst, 1834. LOCATION D.
COMMENTARY This is a reissue in book form of *Bolster's Magazine* (Cork, 1827). Contents: 'Origin of the O's and Macs', 'Gerevra; the lament of O'Gnive, a translation from the Irish Tasso and Byron', 'Night thoughts by the author of Zedechias', 'Reading made easy', 'Woman can love but once', 'Stanzas; Irish art and artists-fine arts in Cork, Barry, Butts, Grogan, Corbet, &c', 'To the Memory of ——', 'Sir Walter Raleigh; a tale of the South ballad', 'Recollections of an absentee', 'Stanzas', 'Shea's Rudekki', 'Stanzas', 'An epistle from Mac Rinco', 'Why should we love the laurel tree' [CD; TCD cat.].

Anon.241 *Tales & stories of Ireland.*
+ Halifax: William Milner, 1846 (ill.). SOURCE Hayley, 13f. LOCATION NUC (1852 edn), InND Loeber coll.
London: Milner & Co., n.d. LOCATION UCD Folklore Dept.
COMMENTARY The Halifax edn was issued in two different bindings: the earliest with spine impressed in four compartments, three of which showing Irish scenes, and with woodcut frontispiece. The later binding in plain cloth blind embossed, with engraved frontispiece. This volume is not to be confused with *Tales and stories of Ireland. Carleton, Lover and Mrs. Hall* [ed. by P. Dixon Hardy] (Dublin, 1834). Contents: 'Light hearts and light heels', 'Ned M'Keown', 'The stolen sheep' (John Banim§), 'Ensign O'Donoghue's first love', 'The furlough', 'Paddy the piper' (Samuel Lover§), 'The sportheen' (Samuel Lover§), 'The good woman', 'The first and last run', 'Darby Doyle's voyage to Quebec' [Thomas Ettingsall], 'The horse stealers' (William Carleton§), 'Philip Garraty; or, "We'll see about it"' (Mrs S.C. Hall§), 'Confessions of a reformed Ribbonman' [William Carleton§], 'Barny O'Reirdon the navigator' (Samuel Lover§), 'Sir Darby Monaghan', 'The dead watcher' [by 'G.C.', first published in the *Irish Penny Magazine* (Dublin, 1833), pp 29–30], 'Squire Warnock' (William Carleton§), 'Owen Macarthy' (William Carleton§), 'Cup tossing', 'The wish', 'It's my luck', 'Kate Connor' [Mrs S.C. Hall§], 'A legend of Clonmacnoise' (Samuel Lover§), 'Sir Turlough; or, the churchyard bride' [William Carleton§], 'The Irish magistrate', 'The gridiron' (Samuel Lover§), 'Duke Dorgan' (Samuel Lover§), 'The night attack', 'The illicit distiller', 'Story of Hogan', 'The three advices' (Thomas Crofton Croker§ [*sic*], actually from *Royal Hibernian tales*, [Dublin?, 1825 or earlier]), 'The two brothers', 'Owen and Ellen', 'The billet', 'The pass of Cooleagh'. Contents of 1846 edn slightly different and include 'The three tasks', 'Neal Malone' (William Carleton§), 'The poor Irish scholar' (William Carleton§) [ML; AMB].

Anon.242 *Those Irish eyes.*
+ London: William Stevens, [1890] (The Family Story Teller series). LOCATION L.
COMMENTARY Love story set in England. The main female character is Irish [ML].

Anon.243 *The tower of Clanmalloch. A romance.*
+ Dublin: Saunders & Kempston, 1828. SOURCE British Fiction; Garside, 1828:14. LOCATION Corvey CME 3–628–48756–X, L.

COMMENTARY Although the setting is Scotland, the fact that the author published in Dublin suggests a possible Irish link [ML].

Anon.244 *The transplanted shamrock; or, the way to win an Irish heart.*
+ Boston: American Tract Society, [1860] (ill. Nathaniel Rudd). LOCATION NUC, InND Loeber coll.

Anon.245 *The treacherous confident [sic]: or, fortune's change, a novel.*
Dublin: Printed [for the author?] by Sylvanus Pepyat, 1733. SOURCE ESTC n63311; ESTC t17633; ESTC t2736. LOCATION D, Dt, L, CSmH.
COMMENTARY 28pp in most copies but 32pp in the NLI copy. First appeared in a 22pp edn in Dublin. Syphon, a confidant of a prince, leaves the prince's service to spend his remaining years with his daughter at his country seat. The prince goes to war, but dies in it. His advisor, Thetes, flees to Syphon and falls in love with Syphon's daughter, Almiana. However, her father and the king wish her to marry Scomes. Thetes is apparently killed by Scomes, but in the end he reappears and the two lovers are united [ML].

Anon.246 *The two boys.*
Dublin: James Duffy & Co., [1892 or earlier] (Duffy's Juvenile Library). SOURCE Adv. in J.J. O'Dea, *The beauties of nature* (Dublin, 1892).
COMMENTARY No copy located [RL].

Anon.247 *The two cottagers, showing how many more families may be comfortable and happy than are so.*
+ New York: P.J. Kenedy, 1872 (ill.).
COMMENTARY No copy located. Concerns the Irish in America [RL (source unclear)].

Anon.248 *The Ulster miscellany, containing, I. A voyage to O'Brazeel, the sub-marine island, lying West off the coast of Ireland. II. Advice to a son, in the exemplary way of stories, fables, etc. III. The brute philosophers; in six dialogues. IV. The Ladies' monitor; or, the way of the army. A farce. V. Poems on humorous subjects. VI. Thoughts on various subjects. VII. Poems on humorous subjects; consisting of tales, epistles, songs, epigrams, &c., &c.* (dedicated to The very worthy gentlemen of the north of Ireland).
+ Belfast: Hamilton & Bird, 1753. SOURCE Falkner Greirson cat. Maud/589; Gilbert, p. 856. LOCATION DPL Gilbert coll.
+ [Dublin?]: Printed in the year, 1753. SOURCE ESTC t128828. LOCATION L, MH.
COMMENTARY The volume is a compilation of prose pieces; it was not a periodical, because its pagination is continuous. Story no. I is presented as a translation from the original sixteenth-century Irish manuscript, and gives details of a trip by Manus O'Donnell of Cloughaneely (Co. Donegal) to the legendary island of O'Brazeel, where there is a perfectly governed society. The volume also contains a farce, poems, and other material. The island of O'Brazeel first appeared in print in Richard Head's§ *Western wonder: or O-Brazile, an inchanted island discovered* (London, 1694) [ML; RL].

Anon.249 *The United Irishman; or, the fatal effects of credulity. A tale founded on facts.*
Dublin: Printed for the author, 1819, 2 vols. SOURCE Brown, 103; British Fiction; Field Day, iv, pp 841–2; Garside, 1819:20; NYPL. LOCATION Dt, NN.

Dublin: Printed for the author by James Charles, 1821, 2 vols. (as *The cavern in the Wicklow mountains; or, fate of the O'Brien family. A tale founded on facts*). SOURCE Brown, 15; Black, 46; British Fiction; Garside, E:8. LOCATION L.

COMMENTARY An epistolary novel told in a series of letters between Augustus Tranton and Sir Edward Elbe. It concerns O'Brien, a United Irishman who with the help of his sister escapes from Dublin Castle. Having lost everything, he hides in a cave near the Dargle river. He tells his tale of woe to an Englishman he meets accidentally. The Englishman in turn tells his equally woeful story [Brown; B. Browne].

Anon.250 *The upper circles of New York; burial before death! Or, the marble bride.*
+ Dublin: John Mullany, [1867]. LOCATION PC.
COMMENTARY Published as a supplement to the *Dublin Saturday Magazine* (1867). Set in New York and France. A number of medical students are working in the dissecting room when they are visited by the famous doctor Mannikin, a specialist in poisons. The dead body of a woman is brought in and Mannikin says that he would like to purchase it, but the students do not agree. It transpires that the woman is not dead, and the students take her home to recuperate. She is the granddaughter of a very wealthy man but had been raised by her French grandfather. Her appearance in New York made a number of jealous relatives very unhappy. One of these had a relationship with Mannikin, hence the attempt on her life by poison [ML].

Anon.251 *The velvet coffee-woman: or, the life, gallantries and amours of the famous Mrs. Anne Rochford. Particularly, I. The history of her going by that name. II. The adventure of her noted Irish-lover MacDermot. III. An account of that unparalleled impostor Count Brandenburgh. IV. A funeral oration to her memory, and all ladies of industry, as well among the Grecians and Romans, as those of our own nation.*
+ Westminster [London]: Simon Green, 1728. SOURCE ESTC t100189. LOCATION L, CSmH.
COMMENTARY 46pp. The picaresque story of Anne Woase, later Mrs Rochford, whose father was waterman to the late earl of Torrington. It mentions that she had in her library several libertine books, including *MacDermot; or, the Irish-fortune hunter, a mock-heroic poem in six cantos*, printed for a bookseller at the Strand in London. MacDermot also features in her life [RL].

Anon.252 *Veritas vincit; or, incidents of real life.*
Dublin: Printed [for the author?] by James Stuart, 1827. SOURCE Anderson 1, p. 76. LOCATION L.
+ Dublin: Carson & Knox, William Curry Jnr & Co.; London: Hamilton. Adams & Co; Belfast: M. Jellett, 1827. SOURCE British Fiction; Garside, 1827:11; Emerald Isle cat. 83/27. LOCATION D, L.
COMMENTARY Written by a female author, who in the preface thanks the ladies and gentlemen of Larne (Co. Antrim) for their kind support. The book has Irish content. The opening paragraph eulogizes a Col. Percival of Irish birth who served in the East India Company's service [ML].

Anon.253 *Verschoyle, a Roman Catholic tale of the nineteenth century.*
+ London: J. Hatchard & Son, 1837. LOCATION L, InND Loeber coll.
COMMENTARY An anti-Catholic novel relating how the Catholic church tries to convert rich Protestants in order to lay claim to their money. The novel warns of the danger of being tol-

erant to catholicism. An English Protestant girl, Millicent, is brought to Italy and placed in a convent by her liberal-minded guardians. The nuns work on her to effect a conversion and an Irish girl, Teresa Fitzgerald, warns her not to give in. An Irish priest, Kenelm Verschoyle, himself a convert, succeeds in converting her. When she returns to England, she marries an Irishman, Mr Fitzgerald, who is after her money. She leads a miserable life. The Protestant minister in her neighbourhood leads Verschoyle back to protestantism and to a reconciliation with his father before Verschoyle dies from an injury he had received in Italy at the hand of Millicent's husband [ML].

Anon.254 *Vertue rewarded; or, the Irish princess. A new novel.*
> London: R. Bentley, 1693. SOURCE NCBEL 2, p. 983; Esdaile, p. 324; Sweeney, 5399. LOCATION Dm, L, O.
> + Gerrards Cross: Colin Smythe, 1992. SOURCE Dt, O, InND Loeber coll.

COMMENTARY Set in 1690 in Clonmel (Co. Tipperary). A foreign officer who served in the army of King William III is billeted in Clonmel where he immediately falls in love with an Irish girl. He is set on seducing this girl and makes numerous unsuccessful attempts. Finally, he gives way before the girl's virtue and makes her his wife. The novel is apparently a *roman-à-clef*, with Gen. Schomberg, first commander of William's forces in Ireland who was killed at the Battle of the Boyne, as the likeliest model for the foreign officer [ML; Welch, p. 588].

Anon.255 *The vicar of Bray: A tale.*
> London: R. Baldwin, 1771, 2 vols. SOURCE Raven 2, 1771:35; Forster, 2852; Hardy, 188; ESTC t117343. LOCATION L, CtY.
> + Dublin: J. Williams, W. Wilson & T. Walker, 1771, 2 vols. in 1. SOURCE Raven 2, 1771:35; ESTC t177069. LOCATION L.
> Belfast: Printed by James Magee, 1771. SOURCE Anderson 3, p. 9 (known from Pinkerton MSS).

COMMENTARY No copy of the Belfast edn located. Mostly set in England with some of the action taking place in Ireland. Charts the infamous career and downfall of a fictional clergyman who is loosely based on the vicar of the ballad, 'The vicar of Bray', with which the book ends. This ballad, which was first printed in 1734, is set in the parish of Bray in Berkshire rather than in the parish of the same name in Co. Dublin. The vicar becomes an adviser to the powerful Windham family. He seduces a cottager's beautiful daughter. One of the characters, Louisa, whose face is disfigured by smallpox, is the first to discern the vicar's hypocrisy. Thomas Leland§ was appointed in 1768 vicar of Bray (Co. Dublin), which is close to Powerscourt, the seat of the Wingfield family, but these names remain unconnected to this novel [RL; Raven 2; Quaritch cat. Autumn 2003/103; Personal communication, Andrew Carpenter, Nov. 2003].

Anon.256 *The vision of Tara: Containing a view of the oppression inflicted upon Irishmen, by that infernal demon, bigotry, the mother of injustice, oppression, murder, ignorance, famine, tyranny, & hypocrisy: With an account of the monster's final defeat by the liberator of his country.*
> New York: Printed [for the author?] by P. O'Halloran, 1836. SOURCE OCLC. LOCATION Univ. of Delaware, Madison (DE).

COMMENTARY 48pp. Historical fiction written in the form of an allegory, which features Daniel O'Connell. Perhaps a reprint of [M.L. Grimstone's§] *The vision of Tara* (London, 1831) [Hartman, 738; OCLC; RL].

Anon.257 *Walter O'Niel; or, the pleasure of doing good.*
+ London: Darton & Harvey, 1838 (ill.). SOURCE Brown, 107. LOCATION L.
COMMENTARY 83pp. A story for juveniles featuring Walter O'Niel, who becomes an orphan at a young age. He is sent from the south of Ireland to live with his aunt and uncle, Mr and Mrs Lovett, in England. He is a good boy, and when he meets a wayward boy he decides to try and rescue him. The story has strong religious overtones [ML; RL].

Anon.258 *The wanton friar; or, the Irish amour. A new novel.*
London: Sold by R. Baldwin, 1689. SOURCE Esdaile, p. 325 (citing Term Cat., ii, pp 251, 286).
COMMENTARY Not in Wing and no copy located [RL].

Anon.259 *Weird tales. Irish.*
+ London, Edinburgh: W. Paterson, [1886] (Nuggets for Travellers Series, No. 7). SOURCE Brown, 108. LOCATION L, NN, InND Loeber coll.
+ London: J.M. Dent & Co., n.d. (as *Weird tales by Irish writers*; ill., portrait of Samuel Lover§). LOCATION InND Loeber coll.
New York: White & Allen, 1888 (as *Weird tit-bits; Irish*). SOURCE NYPL. LOCATION NN.
COMMENTARY Contents: 'The lots upon the raft', 'A night in the haunted house. Being a passage in the life of Mr. Midas Oldwiche', 'The burial of O'Grady' (Samuel Lover§), 'The lianhan shee' (William Carleton§), 'The mountain pass' (Charles Lever§), 'The banshee', 'Legends of the banshee' (Thomas Crofton Croker§ [*sic*])', 'The faction fights' (Mr & Mrs S.C. Hall§), 'The drunkard's dream' [Joseph Sheridan Le Fanu§], 'A terrible night', 'A realized dream' (J.B. O'Meara). The New York edn contains fewer stories [ML; NYPL].

Anon.260 *The West-Indian, or the brothers. A novel.*
Dublin: John Cumming; London: A.K. Newman & Co., 1820, 3 vols. SOURCE British Fiction; Garside, 1820:11. LOCATION Corvey CME 3–628–48896–6.
COMMENTARY Note that Richard Cumberland wrote a comedy *The West Indian*, which was published in Dublin in 1795 [RL].

Anon.261 *What news to-day? or, blind Charlie, the Irish beggar.*
Birmingham: J. Groom, [1855?] (ill.). SOURCE Emerald Isle cat. 86/908. LOCATION L (missing), E.
COMMENTARY 32pp. Classified as conduct of life/literature for juveniles [COPAC].

Anon.262 *"What shall I render?" or, social touches in Ireland* (dedicated to the archdeacon of Meath).
+ Dublin: George Herbert; London: Hamilton & Co., Jas. Nisbet & Co., 1873. LOCATION D, DPL.
COMMENTARY Religious fiction. The NLI copy has an inscription showing that the author was from Bandon (Co. Cork). Religious fiction. Two young women authors, Margaret Wolfe Hungerford§ and Elizabeth Thomasina Toulmin Smith§ (later known under her pseudonym 'L.T. Meade') had connections with Bandon around this time, and both came from Church of Ireland families, but authorship of this volume remains unclear [ML; RL].

Anon.263 *The white hen. An Irish fairy tale.*
Dublin, London: James Duffy & Sons, 1852 (Duffy's Popular Library). LOCATION D (n.d. edn), L (destroyed), PC (n.d. edn).

COMMENTARY 43pp for the n.d. edn, priced at 6*d*. Catholic tale. Repr. in a 32pp format in the anonymous *Catholic tales* (Dublin, [1882–5]) [RL].

Anon.264 *The wild-Irish captain; or, villainy display'd: being the exploits, and memoirs, of that famous boglander, the pretended Marshall of the King's Bench, David Fitzgerald, truly and faithfully related.*
+ London: Sold by the Booksellers, 1692. SOURCE Bradshaw, 7211; Wing W2156. LOCATION L, C.
COMMENTARY 32pp. Descriptive account of the exploits of David Fitzgerald, who was the son of an outlaw, one of the 'cut-throats of the Irish massacres'. Starts out in Ireland. The son becomes foot boy to one Capt. Buttler [*sic*] and afterwards to one Col. Piggott. He then takes a cottage from Sir Thomas Southwell, who sues him for non-payment. Fitzgerald counter-sues and is freed. He leaves for England where he continues in a life of extortion and fraud, with the duke of Ormond and the earl of Shaftsbury as victims. He appoints himself a captain and engages in many adventures [RL].

Anon.265 *The witty and extravagant exploits of George Buchanan: To which is added, The comical sayings of Paddy from Cork. Being a conference between English Tom and Irish Teague.*
Philadelphia: J.B. Perry, 1840. SOURCE OCLC. LOCATION Balch Inst. for Ethnic Studies, Historical Society of Pennsylvania, Philadelphia (PA).
COMMENTARY 45pp, plus 26pp. The first story was independently published at an earlier date (e.g., New York, 1789, 36pp). *The comical sayings of Paddy from Cork* was also published as a chapbook of 24pp (Glasgow, n.d.) [RL; OCLC].

Anon.266 *Wonderful escapes! Containing The interesting narrative of the shipwreck of the Antelope packet, upon the coast of an unknown island: with an account of the dangers and sufferings of the crew. The distressing account of the loss of the Lady Hobart packet, on an island of ice. The narrative of the shipwreck of the Hercules, on the coast of Africa. And an account of the extraordinary escape from the effects of a storm in a journey over the frozen sea in North America.*
+ Dublin: Printed by Brett Smith [for the Kildare Place Society], 1818 (ill.). SOURCE Hislop, p. 1051. LOCATION L (1819 edn), InND Loeber coll. (also 1830 edn).
COMMENTARY The *Shipwreck of the Antelope East-India packet* was first published in London in 1788. Contains several stories as mentioned in the title, all dealing with dire escapes on the sea or on the ice. The stories include some details concerning natural history and geography [ML; Pollard 2, p. 612].

Anon.267 *The wreath of friendship. A series of popular and amusing tales.*
Dublin: James Duffy, [1857 or earlier]. SOURCE Adv. in [anon.], *The young crusader* (Dublin, [1857]).
COMMENTARY No copy located [RL].

Anon.268 *Young ladies' book of romantic tales* [anon. compiler] (by Thomas Moore§, Mrs S.C. Hall§, The author of *The king's own*, [Capt. Marryat§], the author of *Stories of Waterloo* [William Hamilton Maxwell§], Charles Lamb, J.M. Wilson, Miss Mitford and others).

+ Boston: E. Littlefield, 1839. SOURCE Copy seen at Mason Books, Toronto, Aug. 2001; RL.

COMMENTARY No other copy located. Anthology of several Irish and English authors. Contents: 'Ali's bride. A tale from the Persian' (Thomas Moore§), 'The last of the line' (Mrs S.C. Hall§), 'The wine merchant's story' (by the author of *The king's own* [Capt. Marryat§]), 'The procrastinator' (Thomas Crofton Croker [*sic*]§), 'The legend of Rose Roche' (by the author of *Stories of Waterloo* [William Hamilton Maxwell§]) [RL].

Anon.269 *The young musicians.*
　　　　 Dublin: James Duffy & Co., [1892 or earlier] (Duffy's Juvenile Library). SOURCE Adv. in J.J. O'Dea, *The beauties of nature* (Dublin, 1892).
　　　　 COMMENTARY No copy located [RL].

ANONYMOUS AUTHORS OF MORE THAN ONE WORK OF FICTION

ANONYMOUS AUTHOR, fl. 1810s.
Anon.270 *Prodigious!!! Or, Childe Paddie in London.*
　　　　 + London: For the author, 1818, 3 vols. SOURCE Belanger, 50; British Fiction; Garside, 1818:12. LOCATION Corvey CME 3–28–47481–7, Ireland related fiction, L, MH.
COMMENTARY Innocent Anglo-Irish aristocrat 'Childe Paddie' visits London and is exposed to the various temptations and vices of fashionable life there. While the novel offers some commentary on Irish affairs and argues strongly against English prejudice towards Ireland and the Irish, it is primarily a series of loosely organized satirical sketches of the English *haut ton* using 'Paddie' as an outside observer of this society [JB].
Anon.271 *Gogmagog-Hall; or, the philosophical lord and the governess* (by the author of *Prodigious!! or Childe Paddie in London*).
　　　　 + London: G. & W.B. Whittaker, 1819, 3 vols. SOURCE British Fiction; Garside, 1819:9. LOCATION Corvey CME 3–628–47911–8, L.
COMMENTARY Set in England. The author makes the case that if in Ireland Protestants and Catholics can live together, then Christians and Muslims can also live together [ML].

ANONYMOUS AUTHOR, fl. 1810s. In all likelihood the author of the following books was a clergyman of the Church of England or the Church of Ireland. SOURCE RL.
Anon.272 *Coelebs married, being intended as a continuation of Coelebs in search of a wife.*
　　　　 + London: G. Walker, 1814. SOURCE British Fiction; Garside, 1814:3. LOCATION L, InND Loeber coll.
COMMENTARY In the preface the author states that he is a different author than the person who wrote *Coelebs in search of a wife* (London, 1809, written by Hannah More). There were several other spin-offs of Hannah More's book. For example, Maria Edgeworth§ considered writing a sequel, to be called *Caelia in search of a husband*, but rejected the idea. A book of a similar title *Celia in search of a husband* (London, 1809) has been ascribed to Medora Gordon Byron (but also to Miss Byron, and Medora Gordon). In addition, Robert Torrens§, published *Coelibia*

choosing a husband; A modern novel (London, 1809, 2 vols.). *Coelebs married* is set in England, mainly Westmoreland. The story describes the bliss of virtuous and Christian married life and is interspersed with discussions on religion and politics in which Ireland, the Irish and the Catholic church are frequently criticized. The main character has an estate both in Westmoreland and in Co. Cork, but does not want to live on his Irish estate due to the unsettled times [ML; Christina Colvin, letter, 4 Oct. 1993; RL; Ximenes List M5/40].

Anon.273　*The Irish girl. A religious tale* (by the author of *Coelebs married*).

> London: George Walker, 1814 (ill.). SOURCE Brown, 46; British Fiction; Garside, 1814:5. LOCATION L.

COMMENTARY A poor Irish girl, born in a mud hut, is found in a barn and taken in by English people. She is converted to protestantism at age 14. A visit to some Roman Catholic churches, in one of which the dust of a saint is sold, seals her conversion. The book represents the Irish as driven by their priests [Brown].

ANONYMOUS AUTHOR, fl. 1820s. The author was probably a Church of Ireland clergyman. SOURCE RL.

Anon.274　*Ellmer Castle; A Roman Catholic story of the nineteenth century* (by the author of *Edmund O'Hara: an Irish tale*).

> + Dublin: William Curry Jnr & Co.; London: Hamilton, Adams & Co., J. Nisbet, J. Hatchard & Son; Edinburgh: William Oliphant, Waugh & Innes; William Whyte & Co., 1827. SOURCE Brown, 27; British Fiction; Garside, 1827:3. LOCATION Corvey (1828, 3rd edn) CME 3–628–47488–4, Ireland related fiction, Dt, L, InND Loeber coll. (1828, 3rd edn).
>
> Dublin: William Curry Jnr & Co., [1829 or earlier] (new edn). SOURCE Adv. in [S. Bunbury], *The abbey of Innismoyle* (Dublin, 1829).
>
> + London: Houlston & Stoneman, 1848, 6th edn. SOURCE Nineteenth Century Books cat. 19/73. LOCATION InND Loeber coll.
>
> + Boston: James Loring, 1833 (revsd American edn). SOURCE British Fiction; Garside, 1827:3. LOCATION D, NUC.
>
> Philadelphia: Wilson & Stokes, 1845. LOCATION NUC.

COMMENTARY No copy of the Dublin (new edn) located. Religious fiction set on the west coast of Ireland. Henry Ellmer, a Roman Catholic of the landed gentry, sets out on a tour and comes back converted to protestantism. He tries to read his Bible and discusses with his sisters why reading the Bible is important. The priest finds out that he is doing this and reports it to Henry's father. The father gives Henry an ultimatum to give up Bible reading. Henry wants to discuss this with his father, but is not given a chance. He is turned out of his home. However, he and his father are reconciled at his father's deathbed [ML].

Anon.275　*Edmund O'Hara, an Irish tale* (by the author of *Ellmer Castle*).

> + Dublin: William Curry Jnr & Co., 1828 (ill. Kirkwood & Son). SOURCE Brown, 26; Wolff, 7452; British Fiction; Garside, 1828:3. LOCATION Corvey CME 3–628–47487–6, Ireland related fiction, Dt, DPL, L.

COMMENTARY Anti-Catholic religious fiction. Edmund O'Hara, a Catholic Irishman, goes to Spain to be educated for the priesthood. He meets a Protestant, Hamilton, who teaches him about the Protestant faith. On their return voyage home, their ship is wrecked off the Irish coast, and when they get to shore they are helped by Protestants to get to the north of Ireland, whereas a priest refuses them his aid. Edmund falls in love with the Protestant Miss Williams, who gives him a year's probation to make sure that he is steadfast in his protestantism before she will marry him. Edmund dies, however, and Miss Williams marries Hamilton [Brown].

ANONYMOUS AUTHOR, fl. 1820s.

Anon.276 *The ball-room window: A tale founded on facts.*
Dublin: Richard Moore Tims [for the Dublin Tract Society], 1824. SOURCE Adv.
in J. Anderson, *Extracts from Roman Breviary, literally translated into English*
(Dublin, 1829); RLIN; COPAC. LOCATION L, PP (incomplete).
COMMENTARY 62pp according to RLIN, but 42pp according to COPAC. Religious
fiction [RLIN].

Anon.277 *The stay-maker; a true story* (by the author of *The ball-room window*).
+ Dublin: Richard Moore Tims; London: Hatchard & Son, J. Nesbit; Edinburgh:
William Oliphant, 1826. LOCATION D.
COMMENTARY 42pp. Religious fiction [RL].

ANONYMOUS AUTHOR, fl. 1830s. Probably a Church of Ireland clergyman. The preface
to *The curate's grave* (Dublin, 1838) states that the author had engaged in Gospel ministry. He
also wrote an anonymous pamphlet, *The Jew and his daughter converted to Christianity. From an
American publication*, which was published by the Religious Tract and Book Society for Ireland
(Dublin, 1826, 3rd edn). SOURCE COPAC.

Anon.278 *The curate's grave* (by the author of 'The Jew and his daughter converted to
Christianity').
+ Dublin: Richard Moore Tims; London: Robert H.C. Tims; Longman & Co;
Hamilton, Adams & Co; Simpkin, Marshall & Co.; Whittaker & Co.; Edinburgh:
Frazer & Co.; V. Innes, 1838. LOCATION L.
COMMENTARY Religious fiction contrasting Roman Catholics with Protestants [RL].

Anon.279 *The Home mission. An Irish story, founded on fact* (by the author of *The curate's
grave*).
Dublin: Robertson; R. Groombridge; Edinburgh: J. Johnstone, 1840. SOURCE
Brown, 38 ([*c.*1849] edn); Hodgson, p. 270; Block, p. 112. LOCATION L.
COMMENTARY Describes the trials in the life of a Protestant clergyman engaged
for the Home Mission in the south of Ireland [Brown].

ANONYMOUS AUTHOR, fl. 1830s. This female writer of travel stories for children also
wrote *Portugal, or the young travellers* (London, 1830) SOURCE RLIN.

Anon.280 *The new estate; or, the young travellers in Wales and Ireland* (by the author of
Portugal).
+ London: Harvey & Darton, 1831 (ill.). SOURCE OCLC ([1843] edn). LOCATION L.
COMMENTARY Fiction for juveniles consisting of a travel account partly in Ireland, a sequel to
The young travellers in Portugal (London, 1830). Contains a description of the elections in
Clonmel (Co. Tipperary) and, in addition, relates the history of Ireland [RL].

ANONYMOUS AUTHOR, fl. 1830s.

Anon.281 *Real scenes in Irish life.*
Dublin: [publisher?], 1838. SOURCE OCLC. LOCATION NNC (not located).
COMMENTARY 53pp [OCLC].

Anon.282 *Mary Leslie's visit to Ireland* (by the author of *Real scenes in Irish life*).
Dublin: Tims; London: J. Nisbet & Co., [1840 or earlier]. SOURCE Rev. in the
Christian Lady's Magazine (Mar. 1840, p. 277).
COMMENTARY No copy located. Priced at 9*d*. Religious fiction concerned with scriptural
education. The main character is an English visitor to Ireland [RL; *Christian Lady's Magazine*].

ANONYMOUS AUTHOR, fl. 1830s. The author probably was a resident of Connacht, and had knowledge of the Irish language. SOURCE RL.

Anon.283 *The captain of the horse; or, the triumph of good nature: An Irish tale of 1798.*
COMMENTARY Unpublished manuscript [*c*.1830], 3 volumes [anon.]. Gives an insight into country life in small Irish villages during the time of the 1798 rebellion, while also describing various battles fought between the English troops and the rebel Irish army [CD; NLI, MS 4,697–99].

Anon.284 *Tales told in Connaught – viz. 'Cathal Criobdearg,' 'The Calliagh Buey'.*
COMMENTARY Unpublished manuscript [*c*.1830], 3 volumes [anon.]. Contents: 'Cathal Croibdearg or the old nurses tale or tales told in Connacht', 'The Calliagh buey or Irish occurrences in the time of James I' [CD; NLI, MS 4,696].

ANONYMOUS AUTHOR, fl. 1830s to 1850s.

Anon.285 *The valley of the Clusone, a tale of the Vaudois in the seventeenth century, as related by Carloman D'Andilli.*
+ Dublin: Richard Moore Tims; London: Hamilton & Adams; Wellington: Houlston & Son; Edinburgh: Waugh & Innes, 1830. SOURCE NSTC; Garside 2, 1830:15. LOCATION C.
COMMENTARY Religious fiction in a Gothic setting. The phrase *Carloman D'Andilli* is similar in sound to 'Carlow man Dan Dilli(n)' [RL; AMB].

Anon.286 *Villeroi; or, religion founded on principle, not on excitement* (by the author of *The valley of the Clusone*).
+ Dublin: William Curry Jnr & Co.; London: Simpkin & Marshall; Edinburgh: Fraser & Co., 1835. SOURCE NSTC; Garside 2, 1835:15. LOCATION D, L, O.
COMMENTARY Religious fiction reviewed in the *Christian Lady's Magazine* (London, Mar. 1835), where it is called a 'wholesome' work [RL].

Anon.287 *Home Sunday library. A series of stories* (by the author of *The valley of Clusone*).
+ Dublin: Samuel B. Oldham, 1854, 1st ser. LOCATION L, C.
COMMENTARY 88p. Religious fiction originally issued in six chapbooks, but here continuously paginated. Contents: 'The widow of Nain, and The gleaners', 'Nannie's first Sabbath in the country', 'Self-confidence', 'Harriet Compton; or, bear another's burden', 'Edward; or, the wild strawberries', 'Grand-papa and the sandhills' [RL].

ANONYMOUS AUTHOR, fl. 1840s. The author probably was a resident of Cork or its vicinity. He or she also published anonymously in Cork in 1847 *The widow O'Leary. A story of the present famine*, which is a chapbook (24pp), written in the form of a letter. SOURCE Block, p. 252; RL.

Anon.288 *Charles Mowbray; or, duelling. A tale founded on fact* (by the author of *The widow O'Leary*).
+ Cork: J. O'Brien, 1847. SOURCE Brown, 17. LOCATION D, DPL Dix coll., L.
COMMENTARY 82pp. A young Irish physician goes to live in England, where he is much liked by the people in his neighbourhood. A dissipated baronet is planning to marry a young lady who deserves a better husband. The doctor acquaints her with her intended's true character and she breaks her engagement. The baronet wants to find out who has told her and under duress she divulges the name of the doctor. A duel ensues in which the doctor is wounded. The baronet flees to the colonies and the doctor dies, but not before he is converted to the Protestant religion. His parents both die from shock [ML].

ANONYMOUS AUTHOR, fl. 1840s. According to *The orphans of Glenbirkie* (Dublin, 1841), this was a female author, probably connected with the Deaf and Dumb Society, founded by Revd Edward Herbert Orpen. This society promoted the founding of Claremont, a residence and school for deaf and dumb children at Glasnevin, near Dublin. SOURCE RL; E.L.L. [Emma Le Fanu], *Life of the Reverend Charles Edward Herbert Orpen* (London, 1840).

Anon.289 *Norman Lyndesay, the orphan mute. A narrative of facts.*
> + Dublin: Will. Curry Jnr & Co., P.D. Hardy; London: R. Groombridge, 1841 (ill. J. Kirkwood). LOCATION L.
> + Dublin: Will Curry Jnr & Co., P.D. Hardy; London: R. Groombridge, 1841, 3rd thousand (revsd, corrected, and considerably enlarged; preface to the first, and a preface to the 2nd edn, introd. by Revd Charles Stanford, superintendent of the Claremont Institution; ill. J. Kirkwood). SOURCE OCLC. LOCATION UCD, L, InND Loeber coll.

COMMENTARY Published for the benefit of the Juvenile Deaf and Dumb Society, founded by Revd Charles Edward Herbert Orpen. The London title page is evident from the BL copy of the Dublin edn, where it was inserted after the Dublin title page. The title page of the Dublin imprint carries an engraving of the Claremont institution. The story is set in England and concerns the widow of a soldier who lives with her mute boy. After her death, a Scottish lord becomes his guardian. The boy leads a Christian life and it transpires that he is of noble birth. After his death he is buried with his ancestors [ML; Fenning cat. 212/186].

Anon.290 *The orphans of Glenbirkie. A story founded on facts* (by the authoress of *Norman Lyndesay*).
> + Dublin: The Protestant Orphan Society, 1841. LOCATION D.
> + Dublin: Philip Dixon Hardy & Co.; London: B. Groombridge; Edinburgh: Oliver & Boyd, 1841. LOCATION D (1841, 4th thousand impression), L (3rd thousand impression).

COMMENTARY In the preface the author claims that the facts came from the *Protestant Orphan Report* of 1837. The profits of *The orphans of Glenbirkie* were to be given to the Protestant Orphan Society. The story is about James and Jannette Forrest. Their mother had been mistreated by their father and as a result had lost her mind. The father and the children go to Ireland where the father dies by a fall from his horse. The children stay with a Mrs Murphy, a Catholic, and are in danger of being converted to catholicism. However, a scripture reader realizes what is happening and places the children under the protection of the Orphan Society in Wicklow. In the end the children are reunited with their mother in Scotland [ML].

Anon.291 *Inshivogue. A tale of the Irish peasantry* (by the authoress of *Norman Lyndesay*).
> Dublin: P. Dixon Hardy & Sons, [1846 or earlier].
> SOURCE Adv. in [anon.], *The history of Susan Blake. A true story* (Dublin, 1846).
> COMMENTARY No copy located [RL].

ANONYMOUS AUTHOR, fl. 1850s. The author was most likely a military officer. SOURCE RL.

Anon.292 *Tales of military life.*
> [London?]: [publisher?], [1853 or earlier]. SOURCE Mentioned on title page of *The militia; or, army of reserve* (London, [1853]).
> + London: Society for Promoting Christian Knowledge, 1855–6, 6 parts (ill.). LOCATION D, InND Loeber coll. (incomplete).

COMMENTARY No copy of the first edn located. This title is not to be confused with *Tales of military life* (London, 1829, 3 vols.) by 'An officer of the line'. The present tales start in the 1840s in Ireland, where new recruits from England are conveyed to the Beggar's Bush barracks in Dublin. Two recruits from the same village are contrasted; one is hardworking and pious, the other gets into serious trouble. Only parts 1 and 2 deal with Ireland. However, some of the other soldiers featured in the stories are Irish. Contents Part 1: 'The two recruits', 'The lance-corporal'; Part 2: 'Promotion', 'The depôt'; Part 3: 'Foreign service', 'The rock'; Part 4: 'West Indies', 'Nova Scotia'; Part 5: 'Detachment', 'Old friends'; Part 6: 'Old England', 'The commission' [ML].

Anon.293   *The militia; or, army of reserve* (by the author of *Tales of military life*)
    London: Christian Knowledge Society, [1853]. LOCATION L (destroyed), E.

ANONYMOUS AUTHOR, fl. 1860s.

Anon.294   *Lyntonville; or, the Irish boy in Canada* (by the author of *Nellie Newton*).
    + London: Religious Tract Society, [1865] (ill.). SOURCE Alston & Evans, iii, 9355.
    LOCATION L, NUC, InND Loeber coll.
    + New York: American Tract Society, [1867] (ill.; Life Illustrated Series).
    LOCATION D, L, InND Loeber coll.
    New York: Hunt & Eaton; Cincinnati: Cranton & Curts, [*c.*1880] (as *Life in Lyntonville; or, the Irish boy in Canada*). SOURCE McGahern cat. 42/4; OCLC.
    LOCATION D, CtY.
COMMENTARY Fiction for juveniles featuring Phillip Quin, a young Irish boy, as hero; set most likely in Ontario. The main plot stems from the jealousy of Phillip's schoolmate, who cannot stand that Phillip wins prizes and who sets fire to the house where Phillip and his mother live. This requires Phillip to abandon school and to work in a store, which undermines his health. The boy who started the fire is consumed by guilt and finally confesses [ML].

Anon.295   *Nellie Newton; or, patience and perseverance.*
    + London: Religious Tract Society, [1866]. SOURCE Mentioned on title page of *Lyntonville* (London, [1865]). SOURCE COPAC. LOCATION L, O.
COMMENTARY Religious fiction. An earlier, not located edn, is suggested by the fact that this title is referred to on the title page of *Lyntonville; or, the Irish boy in Canada* (London, [1865]) [CM].

ANONYMOUS AUTHOR, fl. 1870s. American writer. According to the title page of *Nora Mavourneen*, the author also wrote 'Miles O'Lynn', and 'O'Huala', which have not been located. SOURCE RL.

Anon.296   *Nora Mavourneen; or, the romantic and thrilling story of "Shawn Dhuv"* (by the author of 'Miles O'Lynn', 'O'Huala' &c.).
    New York: R.M. De Witt, [1872]. LOCATION NUC.

ANONYMOUS AUTHOR, fl. 1870s. American writer and lawyer, who was probably the author of *Mysteries of crime, as shown in remarkable capital trials, by a member of the Massachusetts Bar* (Boston, 1870). SOURCE RL; OCLC.

Anon.297   *Roger O'Donnell, or the Irish Claude Duval, being a tale of woman's vengeance* (by the author of *Mysteries of crime*).
    New York: R.M. De Witt, [18—] (De Witt's Handsome Jack Series, No. 3).
    SOURCE RLIN. LOCATION NRU.
    COMMENTARY 112pp [RLIN].

ANONYMOUS AUTHOR, fl. 1877. Neither Lehmann's biography or ODNB's entry on the Irish general Sir Garnet Wolseley ascribe the following two vols to him (he is mentioned only as the editor the first novel). The two novels probably were written by an unidentified author, who may have been a friend of Sir Garnet Wolseley. SOURCE J.H. Lehmann, *All Sir Garnet: A life of Field-Marshal Lord Wolseley* (London, 1964); ODNB; RL.

Anon.298 *Marley Castle: A novel* (ed. by Sir Garnet Wolseley).
+ London: Remington & Co. 1877, 2 vols. SOURCE McCarthy, ix, p. 3636.
LOCATION L.
COMMENTARY The book tells about a love story set in England. An army major loves a woman who is unhappily married. Eventually the husband dies and the couple can be united. No Irish content [ML]

Anon.299 *Corrafin* (by the author of *Marley Castle*).
+ London: Tinsley Bros, 1878, 2 vols. LOCATION L, InND Loeber coll.
COMMENTARY The life stories of a number of officers quartered in Limerick. The main character, Sir Herbert Corry of Corrafin, is destined to marry Laurie, a relative who was brought up in India. When they meet it is not love at first sight, but the feeling of appreciation grows. However, an old flame of Sir Herbert's thwarts their love, and they part. After many vicissitudes, they meet again when Sir Herbert returns wounded from a foreign military campaign. They discover they love each other and, even though Sir Herbert is dying, they marry [ML].

ANONYMOUS AUTHOR, fl. 1880s. According to the title page of the *Fox and the goose* (London, 1887) the author also wrote 'Spavin Hall', but this has not been located. SOURCE RL.

Anon.300 *The fox and the goose. A tale of The Curragh of Kildare* (title on cover: *A sporting novel*).
+ London: Ward & Downey, 1887. SOURCE NUC. LOCATION D (1888 edn), L, InND Loeber coll. (1888 edn).
COMMENTARY Describes life in and around The Curragh (Co. Kildare) in the second half of the nineteenth century, including the buying and selling of horses, racing and betting, with a love story interwoven [ML].

ANONYMOUS AUTHOR, fl. 1880s. Since this writer published in Dublin, it is likely that he or she was Irish. SOURCE RL.

Anon.301 *Geoffrey of Killingworth; or, the grey friar's legacy.*
Dublin: James Duffy & Co., [1886 or earlier]. SOURCE Adv. in W. Carleton, *Redmond, Count O'Hanlon* (Dublin, 1886).
COMMENTARY No copy located [RL].

Anon.302 *Dalkey; or, Christmas in the olden time* (by the author of *Geoffrey of Killingworth*).
+ Dublin: James Duffy, [1886 or earlier]. LOCATION D.

Anon.303 *From sunrise to sunrise; or, Christmas in the olden time* (by the author of *Geoffrey of Killingworth*).
+ Dublin: James Duffy & Co., [1886 or earlier]. SOURCE Adv. in J.J. O'Dea, *The beauties of nature* (Dublin, 1886). LOCATION D.
COMMENTARY Set in medieval England. No Irish content [ML].

Anon.304 *Penalty of a crime. A tale of the middle ages* (by the author of *Geoffrey of Killingworth*).
+ Dublin: James Duffy & Co., [1886 or earlier]. SOURCE Adv. in J.J. O'Dea, *The beauties of nature* (Dublin, 1892). LOCATION D.
COMMENTARY Set in 1325 in the castle of Bruavent, stronghold of the Count de Ramorintin in the Palatinate. The count wishes for the hand of Adele de Bruavent in marriage. Sir Raol,

a cousin of Adele, wants to forbid the marriage as he wants to marry her himself. Sir Raol and Adele are married at Christmas, but it is an unholy contract. One day Sir Raol argues with the Abbot of Moulin-Frou. The latter falls to the ground leaving the holy particles of the blessed host exposed. Raol is summoned to the court of Lord Palatine and is excommunicated. Following the trial, he is banished from France and must relinquish his knighthood. He is not allowed to re-enter Bruavent until an eagle flies over his head and a bear licks his hand. When the miracle finally occurs twenty years later, he returns to Bruavent [CD].

ANONYMOUS AUTHOR, fl. late-nineteenth century. Religious fiction writer who, according to the title page of *Sarah & Harriet*, also authored 'Sympathies of Jesus', which has not been located. SOURCE RL.

Anon.305   *Sarah & Harriet; or, the Sunday scholars* (by the author of *Sympathies of Jesus*).
    + [?Bristol]: Wright & Albright, [late nineteenth century]. LOCATION InND Loeber coll.
    COMMENTARY 28pp. No other copy located. Religious fiction set in Ireland. Contains 'Hymn for a little child' [RL].

A

'A., A.', pseud. See ANDERSON, Adam, and ARMSTRONG, A.

'A., C.W.', pseud. See ASHBY, Caroline W.

'A., E.', fl. 1880. Pseudonym of an historical novelist. Probably Irish since this person published in Belfast. SOURCE RL.

A1   *Kathleen. A tale of the fifth century* (by 'E.A.').
        Belfast: W. Mullan & Son, 1880. SOURCE Brown 58. LOCATION L.
COMMENTARY Set in the fifth century, an Irish slave girl is carried off by Norse sea robbers and she converts some of them to Christianity. She sings and plays native songs on her Irish harp, taken with her into captivity [Brown].

'A., E.C.' See AGNEW, Miss Eleanor C. Note that BLC (Alston, p. 1) equates 'E.C.A.' with Miss M.G.T. Crumpe, but this is probably an error.

'A., F.C.' pseud. See ARMSTRONG, Florence C.

'A., S.E.', fl. 1832. Historical fiction writer, possibly English. The preface to *Father John* is signed from Mere Lodge, Springfield, Everton (England). According to the title page, the author also wrote 'The Luddite's sister', which has not been located. *Richard of York; or, the white rose of England* (London, 1832, 3 vols.) by the same author does not have Irish content. SOURCE ML; RL.

A2   *Father John; or, Cromwell in Ireland* (by 'S.E.A.', author of *Richard of York*, and *The Luddite's sister*).
        + London: Whittaker & Co.; Dublin: Curry & Co.; Liverpool: H. Perris, 1842. SOURCE Brown 31; Block, p. 72; Hodgson, p. 190; NSTC. LOCATION D, L, NUC, InND Loeber coll.
COMMENTARY Historical fiction set during the Cromwellian period in Ireland. The plot turns largely on the sufferings brought about by a priest's fidelity to the secrecy of the confessional. The hero is a young Irish Protestant who converts all the non-villains in the story. His parentage is shrouded in mystery, but eventually it appears he is of noble birth. The villain in the story is one O'Neill, who murders his kinsman Owen Roe O'Neill. The massacres of Drogheda and Wexford are described, but also the murder of the Protestants in the north of Ireland. The text is heavily footnoted and has an historical appendix [ML; Brown].

ABBOT, —, pseud. 'An Irish bachelor', fl. 1845. Novelist.

A3   *The freaks of cupid. A novel* (by 'An Irish bachelor'; dedicated to Charles Lever§).
        + London: T.C. Newby, 1845, 3 vols. SOURCE NSTC. LOCATION O.
        COMMENTARY Has Irish content [CM].

ACHESON, Harriet (née Glasgow), fl. 1890s. Poet and temperance writer, HA was the daughter of Revd Professor James Glasgow, DD, a missionary in Gujarat, India. She received her initial education at Walthamstow, London, and later at Victoria College, Belfast. Her first poem appeared in 1867 and her poetry was printed in several Armagh papers. She published *Ulster ballads of today* (not located). A staunch advocate of temperance, she married John

Acheson, JP, of Portadown (Co. Down) in 1879. SOURCE Colman, p. 97 [under Glasgow]; O'Donoghue, p. 6.

A4 *Willie's quest* (by Harriet Acheson).
London: Religious Tract Society, [*c.*1894]. SOURCE Colman, p. 97.
COMMENTARY No copy located [RL].

ADAMS, Alexander Maxwell, pseud. 'A physician', d. 1867. Scottish physician and medical tract writer who published *The Crawfurd peerage* (Edinburgh, 1829). AAM studied at the universities of Edinburgh, Glasgow and Aberdeen, where he received his MD. The dedication of the following book is signed from 26, St Patrick's Square, Edinburgh, May 1835. SOURCE BLC; Boase, i, pp. 14–15; Ximenes, list 97–4/1; Garside 1835:18.

A5 *Sketches from life* (by 'a physician'; dedicated to Sir George Ballingall, MD).
+ Glasgow: W.R. M'Phun; London: Simpkin, Marshall & Co., 1835. SOURCE Davidson cat. 19/15; COPAC; Ximenes, list 97–4/1; Garside 2, 1835:18. LOCATION Univ. of Glasgow; InND Loeber coll.
COMMENTARY Themes involve medicine and psychology, often rather Gothic in flavour: 'The curate's daughter; or, the victim of Irish anarchy and English despotism' (set in 'one of the northern Provinces of Ireland' and the Isle of Man at the time of the 1798 rebellion; the heroine is seduced by an English officer and the atrocities of the yeomen are vividly described), 'The casuist; or, delineations and observations of a sentimentalist', 'Mrs Mackintosh; and public charities', 'Elizabeth; or, the fatal bereavement', 'The death-bed; or, child of two fathers', 'Fanaticism and Miss P***; or, the unique Christians analyzed', 'MDCCXXII; or, the reign of terror; with cases and observations' [RL].

ADAMS, Bertha Jane Leith (née Grundy, also known as Mrs Leith Adams, later Mrs Robert de Courcy Laffan), b. Moss-side (Lancs.) 1837, d. London 1912. BJLA was an English novelist, dramatist, poet and editor who published stories and serialized novels in Charles Dickens's *All the Year Round* (London) where she also worked on the staff in 1880. Her first husband was Andrew Leith Adams, a surgeon in the army, with whom she lived in New Brunswick, Canada, and who became professor of zoology in the College of Science, Dublin, and professor of natural history in Queen's College, Cork. One of her sons died of tuberculosis in Queensland, the other was the novelist and poet Francis Adams. Her second husband was a Church of Ireland clergyman, Revd Robert Stuart de Courcy Laffan, but she retained her former married name as her pen name. Many of her novels reflect her travels and experiences with the military. In London she lived at 119 St George's Road. SOURCE Allibone Suppl., ii, p. 966 [under Laffan]; Alston, pp 1–2; Blain, p. 6; DLB, ccxl; EF, p. 2; LVP, p. 265; NCBEL 2, pp 1623–4; ODNB; Sutherland, p. 7; Wolff, i, pp 5–6.

A6 *Colour sergeant, No.1 Company. A novel* (by Bertha Jane Leith Adams; dedicated 'to the dear and precious memory of one who died in a far-off land').
+ London: Jarrold & Sons, 1894, 2 vols. LOCATION D, L, InND Loeber coll. (1897 edn).
COMMENTARY Set in Cork, a romance between a major's niece and a disguised nobleman during the time of the Fenians [RL; ODNB].

ADAMS, Mrs Leith. See ADAMS, Bertha Jane.

ADAMS, William Taylor, pseud. 'Oliver Optic', b. probably Boston (MA) 1822, d. United States? 1897. American author who specialized in fiction for juveniles, son of Capt. Laban Adams of Boston and Catherine Johnson. WTA was a teacher in the Boston public schools; a member of the school board of Dorchester (MA), and a state legislator for one term. He was a prolific writer, with 126 titles and over one million copies sold. He always published under a pseudonym He made about twenty visits to all parts of Europe (presumably including Ireland), Asia and Africa. SOURCE ANB; Allibone Suppl., i, p. 14; DAB; Wright, ii, p. 6.

A7   *Shamrock and thistle; or, young America in Ireland and Scotland. A story of travel and adventure* (by 'Oliver Optic'; dedicated to Robinson Locke).

+ Boston: Lee & Shepard, 1868 (ill. Kilburn). LOCATION UC, MH, InND Loeber coll.

COMMENTARY Fiction for juveniles. The story of an American school ship that crosses the Atlantic with a number of boys aboard. The boys form the crew of the ship and are also taught on board. Many of the lessons are about the countries to be visited. In Ireland, they visit Cork City; Blarney Castle; the Lakes of Killarney; Dublin and Belfast. Some of the boys find the discipline on board too strict and desert the ship, but after some adventures they return [ML].

ADDISON, Lt.-Col. Henry Robert, b. Calcutta (India) 1805, d. London 1876. Born of Irish parents in India, HRA was a writer of dramas and farces, a journalist and a novelist. He was commissioned in the 2nd Dragoon Guards in 1827 and was stationed in Co. Clare during Daniel O'Connell's election campaign of 1828. That same year he married Mary Vokes, daughter of a Limerick magistrate. He served with the army in India but after going on half-pay in 1833 he became a police magistrate and began a writing career that produced over sixty dramas and farces. The family moved to Bruges in Belgium in 1837 where they could live more cheaply and there HRA met Charles Lever§, who later fictionalized him as Captain Bubbleton in his *Tom Burke of 'Ours'* (London, 1844). Through Lever, HRA contributed to the *Dublin University Magazine*, which also published his portrait (Dublin, 1841). SOURCE Allibone Suppl., i, p. 14; Irish pseudonyms; NCBEL 4, p. 1991; ODNB; O'Donoghue, p. 6; Sutherland, p. 10; Wolff, i, p. 6.

A8   *Recollections of an Irish police magistrate, and other reminiscences of the South of Ireland* (by Henry Roberts Addison; dedicated to John Henry Law, of Urmstone House).

+ London: Ward & Lock, 1862. SOURCE Sadleir, 3518; Topp 2, 339; NSTC. LOCATION Dt ([1862] edn), L.

+ London: John & Robert Maxwell, [1883] (as *Recollections of an Irish police magistrate*). SOURCE Topp 6, 146. LOCATION UCD Folklore Dept.

COMMENTARY Semi-fictional account of a policeman's career and an early depiction of Victorian criminal detective work. Author states in the introduction that he has not written an essay but he has narrated some scenes with names suppressed and some circumstances changed. The story deals with the secret society of the Terry Alts; sheriffs' seizures; an elopement; O'Connell's election; an abduction, etc. [ML; Sutherland, p. 10].

'AN ADEPT', pseud. See **JOHNSTONE, Charles.**

AGG, John, fl. 1810. JA was a printer and bookseller at Evesham in England and published mainly novels of an historical nature in London between 1808 and 1819. SOURCE Allibone, i, p. 40; BD, pp 3, 409; Brown 2, p. 10; NCBEL 4, pp 869–70; Wolff, i, p. 7.

A9   *Mac Dermot; or, the Irish chieftain. A romance, intended as a companion to the Scottish chiefs* (by John Agg).

London: George Shade, 1810, 3 vols. SOURCE Brown 2, 29; Block, p. 4; British Fiction; Garside 1810:20; NCBEL 4, p. 869. LOCATION Corvey CME 3–628–47024–2, Ireland related fiction.

COMMENTARY Historical fiction with Gothic touches intended as a companion piece to Jane Porter's§ *The Scottish chiefs* (London, 1810, 5 vols.). Set during the Norman invasion of Ireland, the hero is Dermot MacMurrough. Strongbow and Eva (Aoife) also appear. The story centres on the illicit love of Dermot for Devorgilla, wife of O'Rourke of Breffny [Brown 2].

AGNEW, Miss Eleanor C., pseud. 'E.C.A.', fl. 1837. ECA was a writer of moral and religious tales and verse who often published under 'Mrs Agnew'. According to Maria Edgeworth§, she was a niece of Sir Andrew Agnew, 7th Bt of Lochnaw (born at Kinsale, Co. Cork). ECA probably was the daughter of Sir Andrew's brother, and a grandchild of Andrew Agnew (d. 1792) and Martha, the eldest daughter of John De Courcy, 26th Lord Kingsale, premier baron of Ireland. This explains Maria Edgeworth's statement that ECA was 'of good family and used to live in the higher ranks of society' (Maria Edgeworth, letter to unnamed correspondent). Maria admired ECA's *Geraldine. A tale of conscience*, but lamented her conversion to catholicism, which took place before Nov. 1838 and probably inspired her to write *Geraldine*. It is unclear whether ECA was Irish, but she published her subsequent works in Dublin first. There is a gap in her known publications between 1851 and 1863. In total, she wrote twelve works of historical, Catholic fiction, and two volumes of religious verse (London, 1851, 1868), and *The young communicants* (London, 1840). The BLC mistakenly equates ECA with Miss M.G.T. Crumpe§. SOURCE Allibone Suppl., i, p. 17; BLC; G.E.C. [G.E. Cocayne], *Complete baronetage* (Exeter, 1902), ii, p. 369; NCBEL 4, p. 1736; Pickering & Chatto cat. 729/33, 1 Nov. 1838, Maria Edgeworth, letter to unnamed correspondent (courtesy of Amanda Hall, Pickering & Chatto, Summer 1995); Wolff, i, p. 7.

A10   *Geraldine. A tale of conscience* (by 'E.C.A.').
+ London: Booker & Dolman, 1837, vols. 1 and 2. SOURCE NSTC. LOCATION L, O, NUC, InND Loeber coll. (also 1875, 12th edn).
+ London: Charles Dolman, 1839, vol. 3. SOURCE NSTC. LOCATION L, O, NUC, InND Loeber coll. + Philadelphia: Eugene Cummiskey, 1839, 2 vols. (recommended by Francis Patrick Kenrick, B[isho]p. &c. [of Philadelphia]. SOURCE NSTC. LOCATION D (vol. 2 only), DCU, NUC, InND Loeber coll.

COMMENTARY Extensively reviewed in the *Dublin Review* (Oct. 1838 and May 1839), and may have been inspired by Mary Jane MacKenzie's *Geraldine; or, modes of faith and practice. A tale* (London, 1821, 3 vols.). The story is set in England and describes the process by which a rich heiress, Geraldine Carrington, changes from a high-church Protestant to a Catholic, and eventually becomes a nun. The seeds of her doubt were planted by the fact that there were so many versions of protestantism, all of which purported to be the true version. Geraldine is surrounded by people of different religious persuasions, which provides ample opportunity for discussions of the pros and cons of various church doctrines and the history of the Christian faith. Charlotte Elizabeth's [Mrs Tonna's§] novel *Derry. A tale of the revolution* (London, 1833) is mentioned. The publications of the Tract Society are discussed but are disapproved of because they are written in a 'wrangling spirit'. At an evangelical meeting, which was meant to be an attack on catholicism, only two people speak out to defend the old religion: Sir Eustace De Grey, a nobleman, and an Irish Catholic priest, whose words make a deep impression. Geraldine's Catholic friends do not try to persuade her to become a Catholic because they want her to reach this conclusion of her own accord. After her conversion, Geraldine marries Sir Eustace. Even though the marriage is a happy one, Geraldine feels that it detracts from her religious duties. Her husband dies, and she decides to join the Sisters of Mercy in Ireland so that she can devote herself entirely to religion and good works. As a nun, she learns to serve the poor and the sick. Eventually, she returns to England with six other nuns of the order and sets up a convent in the abbey buildings on her estate. G. Lowther's§ *Gerald; a tale of conscience* (London, 1840) was written in response to this volume [ML].

A11   *Tales explanatory of the sacraments* [anon.].

London: C. Dolman, 1846, 2 vols. SOURCE Wolff, 27. LOCATION L.

Dublin, London: James Duffy, 1846 (as *The Catholic souvenir or tales explanatory of the sacraments*). SOURCE OCLC. LOCATION PC (n.d. edn).

Philadelphia: McGrath, [1856?] (as *Tales of the sacraments*). SOURCE Rev. in the Boston *Pilot*, 1 Nov. 1856, p. 4.

COMMENTARY Religious fiction. Contents: 'The vigil of St. Laurence or an infant's baptism', 'Blanche's confirmation', 'The sister penitents', 'The altar of Woodbank, or the midnight banquet and the daybreak feast', 'Clyff Abbey, or the last anointing', 'Priest of Northumbria, an Anglo-Saxon tale', 'The spousal cross' [Wolff, 27].

A12   *Rome and the abbey. The sequel to, and by the author of Geraldine: a tale of conscience* [anon.] (dedicated to Princess Doria Pamphili).

+ London: James Burns, 1849. LOCATION L.

+ New York, Boston, Montreal: D. & J. Sadlier & Co., 1852 (as *Rome and the abbey: A tale of conscience*). LOCATION NUC, InND Loeber coll. (1857 edn).

COMMENTARY A sequel to *Geraldine* (London, 1837–39, 3 vols.). A party of English people, mainly Catholics, makes its way from England to Rome. The purpose of the visit is for the nun, Geraldine, to ask permission from the pope to found an Order of the Religious Solitaries of Jesus and Mary. While in Rome, the party observes and participates in a great variety of Roman Catholic rites and occasions. The permission is granted. One of the party is converted to catholicism. They all return to England, and the order opens a house in London [ML].

A13   *Clyff Abbey; or, the last anointed* [anon.].

+ Philadelphia: H. McGrath, 1863 (St Mary's Library, No. 5). LOCATION OCLC; InND.

Dublin: James Duffy & Co., [1886 or earlier] (as *Knight of Clyff Abbey; a tale of extreme unction*). SOURCE Advertised in W. Carleton, *Redmond O'Hanlon* (Dublin, 1886).

COMMENTARY Philadelphia edn is 78pp. Religious story reprinted from *Tales explanatory of the sacraments* (London, 1846, 2 vols.) and tells about an anointing in an abbey [RL].

A14   *The merchant prince and his heir; or, the triumphs of duty. A tale for the world* [anon.].

+ Dublin, London: James Duffy, 1863. LOCATION Dcc, L.

Boston: Donahoe, 1863 (as *The triumphs of duty; or, the merchant prince and his heir*). LOCATION NUC.

A15   *The vigil of St. Laurence and other tales* [anon.].

+ Dublin, London: James Duffy, 1865. LOCATION Dcc.

+ Philadelphia: Henry McGrath, n.d. (as *The vigil of St. Laurence; or, an infant's baptism*; Sister Mary's Library, No. 1; see Plate 5. LOCATION InND Loeber coll.

COMMENTARY Story first published in *Tales explanatory of the sacraments* (London, 1846). The Philadelphia edition has a single story, set in England, explaining the importance of Catholic baptism [ML].

A16   *Captive mother; a tale of confirmation* (by Eleanor C. Agnew).

Dublin: James Duffy & Co., [1886 or earlier]. SOURCE Advertised in W. Carleton, *Redmond O'Hanlon* (Dublin, 1886).

COMMENTARY Probably a reprint of an unidentified original. This may also apply to the following volumes. Priced at 6*d*. No copy located [RL].

A17   *Eve of St. Michael; a tale of penance* (by Eleanor C. Agnew).

Dublin: James Duffy & Co., [1886 or earlier]. SOURCE Advertised in W. Carleton, *Redmond O'Hanlon* (Dublin, 1886).

COMMENTARY Priced at 6*d*. No copy located [RL].

A18   *Heir of Rochdale; a tale of baptism* (by Eleanor C. Agnew).

Dublin: James Duffy & Co., [1886 or earlier]. SOURCE Advertised in W. Carleton, *Redmond O'Hanlon* (Dublin, 1886).
COMMENTARY No copy located [RL].

A19   *Priest of Northumbria; a tale of holy orders* (by Eleanor C. Agnew).
Dublin: James Duffy & Co., [1886 or earlier]. SOURCE Advertised in W. Carleton, *Redmond O'Hanlon* (Dublin, 1886).
COMMENTARY No copy located. First published in *Tales explanatory of the sacraments* (London, 1846) [RL].

A20   *Emily Sunderland; a tale explanatory of the holy sacrament of matrimony* (by Eleanor C. Agnew).
+ Dublin: James Duffy, [1886 or earlier]. SOURCE Advertised in W. Carleton, *Redmond O'Hanlon* (Dublin, 1886). LOCATION DPL.

A21   *The altar at Woodbank; a tale of holy eucharist* (by Eleanor C. Agnew).
Dublin: James Duffy, [1886 or later]. SOURCE Advertised in W. Carleton, *Redmond O'Hanlon* (Dublin, 1886); NSTC. LOCATION O.
COMMENTARY First published in *Tales explanatory of the sacraments* (London, 1846) [RL].

AIKEN, Albert W., pseud. 'Col. Delle Sara', b. Boston *c*.1846, d. Keyport (NJ) 1894. American actor, vocalist, playwright and writer, AWA was the younger brother of the author George L. Aiken. He was a prolific novelist and dramatist, writing under many pseuds, and he often acted in his own plays. He wrote the first detective story in the Beadle dime series. He and his brother lived in Brooklyn, New York in 1872–3. He retired temporarily from the stage in 1881 but returned to it four years later. He married Mary A.T. Crawford in 1873. SOURCE Dime novels.

A22   *The Molly Maguires* (by Albert W. Aiken).
New York: Beadle, 1876 (The Fireside Companion). SOURCE Biographical sketch in Dime novels.
COMMENTARY Later rewritten as play, produced in 1876. The Molly Maguires was an agrarian agitation secret society that began in Ireland in the early-nineteenth century and later was active in the coal mining regions of Pennsylvania [Dime novels].

A23   *Shamus O'Brien, the bould boy of Glingal; or, Irish hearts and homes* (by 'Col. Delle Sara').
New York: Beadle, 1880 (Saturday Journal, No. 527). SOURCE Dime novels.
COMMENTARY No copy located. It is not clear whether this dime novel was the inspiration for Charles Villars Stanford's comic opera, *Shamus O'Brien* (London, *c*.1896), for which George Henry Jessop§ wrote the libretto [RL].

AINSWORTH, William Harrison, b. Manchester (England) 1805, d. Reigate (Surrey) 1882. English novelist, magazine editor and publisher who, after Sir Walter Scott, became the leading historical novelist in Great Britain and published some forty popular titles. His early works specialized in crime, but responding to criticism for glorifying crime, he switched to historical fiction. He succeeded Charles Dickens as editor of *Bentley's Miscellany* (London), later establishing *Ainsworth's Magazine* (London) and also owning and editing the *New Monthly Magazine* (London). He also wrote for *Fraser's Magazine* (London) in its early years. Many of his works were illustrated by George Cruikshank. He attended the salon of Lady Blessington§. SOURCE Allibone, i, p. 42; Allibone Suppl., i, p. 18; Brown 2, p. 11; DLB, xxi; NCBEL 4, p. 1091; ODNB; J.A. Sutherland, 'Lever and Ainsworth: missing the first rank', in *Victorian novelists and publishers* (Chicago, 1976), pp 152–65; Sutherland, pp 13–15; T & B, p. 962; Wolff, i, pp 8–22.

A24   *Old Court. A novel* (by William Harrison Ainsworth).
London: Chapman & Hall, 1867, 3 vols. SOURCE Brown 2, 31 (mistakenly mentions 1830 as date); DNB; NSTC; Sadleir, 23; Wolff, 63. LOCATION L, MH.
Leipzig: Bernard Tauchnitz, 1867, 2 vols. SOURCE NSTC; T & B, 899–900. LOCATION L, NUC.
COMMENTARY Set in Sussex and Kent. Concerns the love and sorrows of an Irish beauty, whose heart has been disturbed by the showy qualities of an Irish soldier and rake, Sir Walter Darcy, the last relic of a long line of Irish foxhunters, who has inherited their habits of carelessness, luxury and gallantry [Brown 2; Leclaire, p. 87].

ALCOCK, D. See ALCOCK, Deborah.

ALCOCK, Deborah (also known as D. Alcock), b. Waterford 1835, d. St Leonards (E. Sussex) 1913. DA was a writer of adventure and morally-uplifting stories for juveniles, historical novels about religious conflicts in Europe, and a memoir of her father, the Ven. John Alcock, archdeacon of Waterford (1867–86). Her mother, Jane Innes, died when she was an infant. Initially the family lived at Tralee (Co. Kerry), and later at Frankfield, near Cork, where DA spent most of her childhood and where she received a strong Protestant, evangelical upbringing. She recounted later that during this period she and her girl friends 'wove endless stories beginning with the wildest and most impossible figments, and going on, through the practice of years, to long historical romances', and she developed an intense interest in poetry and history. A letter of that time, cited by Bayly, mentions her 'want of observation, or absence of mind. She lives in an imaginary world of her own, while totally unacquainted with the realities of life around her'. Her father disapproved of her reading fiction. In 1848 the family moved to the Isle of Man where her father had become minister of Douglas. Here DA developed her interest in history and writing. She never married, and lived with her father until his death in 1886, after which she wrote a memoir of him, *Walking with God* (London, 1887). In 1891, at age 56, she moved to England. She wrote a total of twenty-four historical and religious novels, set in various countries in Europe, all dealing with Protestant issues. Several of these volumes were published under the auspices of the Religious Tract Society. She also wrote a biographical sketch of Hannah More, *The great and good* (London, 1855); a volume on protestantism (*The romance of protestantism*, London [1908]), and *Lessons on early church history* (London, 1879). Her portrait was published by her biographer, E.B. Bayly, an annotated copy of which in a private collection reveals that DA, under the pseudonym of 'A' is likely to be the author of an article in *Sunday at Home* (London, 1893–4), on 'Children's books of fifty years ago', which gives an account of the favourite books she read as a child. SOURCE Allibone Suppl., i., p. 20; EF, p. 4; E.B. Bayly, *The author of The Spanish brothers; Deborah Alcock, her life and works* (London, 1914) [available at: http://www.telusplanet.net/public/inhpubl/webip/Alcockoo.htm]; Leslie, *Ardfert*, p. 154; NCBEL 4, p. 1737; RIA/DIB; Sutherland, p. 15.

A25   *Sunset in Provence, and other tales of martyr times* [anon.].
+ London, Edinburgh, New York: T. Nelson & Sons, 1864. SOURCE NSTC. LOCATION L.
COMMENTARY Contents: 'The martyr's widow' (Set in the Netherlands under Spanish reign), 'Sunset in Provence', 'The stranger in the valleys' (set in the valleys of the Dauphinese Alps), 'The carpenter of Nimes' (concerns a Huguenot from Nimes), 'A child's victory' (set mainly in Cologne) [ML].

A26   *The dark year of Dundee. A tale of the Scottish reformation* [anon.].
London, New York: T. Nelson, 1867. SOURCE NSTC. LOCATION L, NUC.

London: T. Nelson, 1873 (as *No cross no crown.*). LOCATION PC; L (destroyed [1910] edn).

COMMENTARY Fiction based on religious history. As *No cross no crown A tale of the Scottish reformation.*, this volume was advertised in *Under the Southern Cross* (London, 1884), where it is described as a tale of the plague in Dundee, 1544, and the life and times of George Wishart [RL].

A27   *The days of Knox. A tale of the sixteenth century* [anon.].
      London: Nelson, 1869. SOURCE NSTC. LOCATION L, NUC.
      + London, New York: T. Nelson & Son, 1884 (as *Arthur Erskine's story. A tale of the days of Knox*). SOURCE Alston, p. 4 (1886 edn). LOCATION L (1886 edn, destroyed), NUC, InND Loeber coll. (1893 edn).
      Amsterdam: Hoveker, [188?] (trans. into Dutch as *Arthur Erskine. Een verhaal uit de dagen van John Knox*). SOURCE OCLC. LOCATION Calvin College and Theological Seminary.
      COMMENTARY Fiction based on religious history, set in Scotland after the Reformation. Features the Scottish religious reformer John Knox [ML].

A28   *The Spanish brothers. A tale of the sixteenth century* [anon.].
      London: T. Nelson & Sons, 1871. SOURCE Sutherland, p. 15; Nield, p. 51; NSTC. LOCATION DPL (1893 edn), L (1927 edn), NUC.
      + London, Edinburgh, New York: T. Nelson & Sons, 1891 (ill.). LOCATION InND Loeber coll.
      + Rotterdam: B. Bolle, n.d., 4th edn (trans. into Dutch as *De Spaanse broeders. Een verhaal uit den tijd der reformatie in Spanje in de zestiende eeuw;* ill. L.W.R. Wenckebach). LOCATION InND Loeber coll.
      Leipzig: Bernard Tauchnitz, 1891, 2 vols. SOURCE T & B, 2766–7.
COMMENTARY Fiction based on religious history, set in Seville in Spain in 1599 and deals with the Inquisition and Protestant martyrdom. Describes the *autos-da-fé* of the heretics [ML; Nield; Sutherland].

A29   *Under the Southern Cross. A tale of the New World* [anon.].
      London, New York: T. Nelson & Sons, 1874. SOURCE Nield, p. 54. LOCATION NUC.
      + London, Edinburgh, New York: T. Nelson & Sons, 1884 (ill.). LOCATION InND Loeber coll.
COMMENTARY Historical novel set in sixteenth-century Peru after the Spanish conquest; describes the cruelty of the Spaniards toward the Incas. A priest takes a young Indian boy under his protection. The story describes the clashes between the beliefs of the Indian boy and of the Catholic faith. The English are depicted as the deliverers of the Indians from Spanish oppression [ML; Nield].

A30   *In the shadow of God: Sketches of life in France during the eighteenth century* [anon.].
      London: Dalby, Isbister & Co., 1877. SOURCE OCLC; COPAC. LOCATION C, Boston Public Library.
      COMMENTARY Historical fiction set in France [COPAC; RL].

A31   *In the shadow of God. In the desert. A story of the church under the cross* [anon.].
      London: J.F. Shaw & Co., 1880. LOCATION L.
      + London: Women's Protestant Union & W. Stanley Martin, n.d. (new edn; as *In the desert. A story of the church under the cross* (ill.). LOCATION InND Loeber coll.
COMMENTARY Fiction based on religious history set in France in the mountainous region of the Cévennes around the middle of the eighteenth century and tells of government persecution of the Protestants. Church services have to be held in secret places, and ministers, if caught, might lose their lives [ML].

A32   *In the shadow of God. In the city. A story of old Paris* [anon.].
London: J.F. Shaw & Co., 1880. LOCATION L (destroyed).
COMMENTARY No copy located [RL].

A33   *The czar. A tale of the time of the first Napoleon* [anon.].
+ London: Nelson & Sons, 1882. SOURCE Alston, p. 4. LOCATION L, NUC (1888 edn),
InND Loeber coll. (1885 edn).
COMMENTARY Historical fiction. Story for juveniles about Napoleon's invasion of
Russia. Features Alexander I, czar of Russia [Sutherland].

A34   *The Roman students; or, on the wings of the morning. A tale of the Renaissance* [anon.].
+ London; T. Fisher Unwin, [1883] (ill. P.J.H.). SOURCE Alston, p. 4. LOCATION L,
NUC (n.d. edn).
COMMENTARY Historical fiction for juveniles set in Italy [RL].

A35   *The King's service. A story of the thirty-years' war* [anon.].
London: [publisher?], [1885] (ill.). SOURCE COPAC. LOCATION E.
COMMENTARY Fiction based on religious history, set in seventeenth-century Europe [BLC].

A36   *The cross and the crown. A tale of the revocation of the Edict of Nantes, two hundred years ago* [anon.] (dedicated to the children of the Huguenot refugees).
+ London: Religious Tract Society, [1886] (ill.). SOURCE Alston, p. 4. LOCATION L,
InND Loeber coll.

COMMENTARY Fiction based on religious history set in the seventeenth century. The hero Gabriel
De Vaur is born at his father's castle near Caudebec, Normandy. He has a twin, Desirée, two
younger sisters and a younger brother. The family are Protestants. They live near the castle of
the marquis of Vigny, whose only daughter, Aimée, is Gabriel's playfellow. Gabriel's two
younger sisters die of smallpox, and when threats of religious persecution increase, his mother
dies also. Gabriel escapes capture but his sister and infant brother are put into religious institutions to be brought up as Catholics. His father is also imprisoned. Gabriel saves his sister
from a burning nunnery. She, however, has lost her reason because of the abuse she has undergone. They wander through northern France and eventually escape to England. Aimée and her
family also escape; they would gladly look after Gabriel and his sister, but Gabriel insists on
living in Southwark and becomes a glovemaker to provide for himself and his sister. One day
he discovers that Aimée is poor and he comes to her rescue. Desirée dies and Gabriel meets
an old French acquaintance who, while they were both fleeing persecution in France, had carried Gabriel's little store of money to safety and with it had started a business in Waterford in
Ireland. He persuades Gabriel to become his business partner and to live in that city, which
Gabriel does, after first marrying Aimée. Features King Louis XIV [ML].

A37   *Archie's chances and The child's victory* [anon.].
London: Nelson & Sons, 1886. LOCATION PC, L (destroyed).
COMMENTARY Religious fiction [BLC].

A38   *Geneviève; or, the children of Port Royal. A story of old France* [anon.].
London: Religious Tract Society, [1889]. SOURCE Alston, p. 4. LOCATION L (destroyed).
+ London: Religious Tract Society, [1902] (as *The friends of Pascal; or, the children of
Port Royal. A story of old France*). SOURCE COPAC. LOCATION E.
+ Philadelphia: J.B. Lippincott, 1889 (ill.). LOCATION NUC, InND Loeber coll.
New York: G. Munro, [1889]. LOCATION NUC.
COMMENTARY Fiction based on religious history, set in France. The volume was issued
in two similar binding types: one in brown, the other in blue cloth [BLC; RL].

A39   *Crushed yet conquering. A story of Constance and Bohemia* [anon.].
+ London: Religious Tract Society, [1891] (ill. W.S.S.). SOURCE Alston, p. 4. LOCATION
L (destroyed), NUC, InND Loeber coll.

London: Religious Tract Society, 1940 (as *A torch to Bohemia; or, crushed yet conquering*). LOCATION L.

New York: P.H. Revell, [1894]. LOCATION NUC.

Neerlandia [Alberta]: Inheritance Publications, *c*.2002. SOURCE RLIN. LOCATION DCL.

COMMENTARY Fiction based on religious history, set in France, Switzerland and Bohemia at the beginning of the fifteenth century. The story deals with the death of the religious reformer Johannes Huss in Constance, and the persecution of the Hussites in Bohemia [ML].

A 40   *Prisoners of hope. A story of the faith* [anon.].

London: Religious Tract Society, [1894]. SOURCE Alston, p. 4. LOCATION L (destroyed).

COMMENTARY Religious fiction. Advertised in 1914 as *Prisoners of hope. A Bohemian story* [BLC; Advertised in E.B. Bayly, *The author of The Spanish brothers; Deborah Alcock, her life and works* (London, 1914)].

A41   *The well in the orchard* (by D. Alcock).

+ London: Religious Tract Society, [1895] (ill. W.J. Morgan). SOURCE Alston, p. 4; COPAC. LOCATION L (destroyed), InND Loeber coll.

COMMENTARY Fiction based on religious history, set in France at the time of the French Revolution, just after King Louis XVI has been beheaded. The story deals with the resistance against the revolutionaries in some rural areas. The main character is a young Protestant man who learns to extend Christian forgiveness, even to his enemies [ML].

A42   *Doctor Adrian. A story of old Holland* [anon.].

+ London: Religious Tract Society, [1897] (ill.). SOURCE Alston, p. 4. LOCATION L (destroyed), InND Loeber coll.

COMMENTARY Fiction based on religious history, set in the Netherlands in the sixteenth century when Spain is in power and protestantism is suppressed. It describes the liberation of the Netherlands by the Dutch resistance fighters called the 'geuzen'. The life of a doctor who becomes a Protestant is interwoven with the political events [ML].

A43   *By far Euphrates. A tale* (by D. Alcock).

+ London: Hodder & Stoughton, 1897. SOURCE Alston, p. 4. LOCATION L (destroyed), InND Loeber coll. (1901, 2nd edn).

Neerlandia [Alberta]: Inheritance Publications, 2001 (as *By far Euphrates, a tale of Armenia in the 19th century*). SOURCE RLIN. LOCATION DCL.

COMMENTARY Fiction based on religious history. Concerns the Armenian massacres, 1894–6 [BLC; RLIN].

A44   *The little captives, and other stories* (by Deborah Alcock).

+ London: Religious Tract Society, [1898]. SOURCE Alston, p. 4; NSTC. LOCATION L, C.

COMMENTARY Religious fiction. Contents: 'The little captives', 'The cloak in pledge', 'The story of a poor scholar' [BLC].

A45   *Not for crown or sceptre* (by Deborah Alcock).

London: Hodder & Stoughton, 1902. SOURCE Nield, p. 46. LOCATION L.

New York: American Tract Society, [1903?]. SOURCE NUC.

COMMENTARY Fiction based on religious history. Concerns the Reformation in Sweden at the time of Gustavus Vasa (1496–1560) [Nield].

A46   *Under Calvin's spell; a tale of the heroic times in old Geneva* (by Deborah Alcock).

London: Religious Tract Society, 1902. SOURCE Nield, p. 52; COPAC. LOCATION Dt ([1929?] edn), L (destroyed).

New York: F.H. Revell, [1910–19?]. SOURCE OCLC. LOCATION DCL.

London: Protestant Truth Society, 1950 (as *Under Calvin's spell*; ill.). SOURCE COPAC. LOCATION L.

COMMENTARY Fiction based on religious history, set in Geneva during John Calvin's time (1509–64) [Nield].

A47 *Done and dared in old France* (by Deborah Alcock).
London: S.W. Partridge & Co., [1907]. SOURCE BLC. LOCATION L (destroyed), NUC (1931 edn).
Neerlandia [Alberta]: Inheritance Publications, 2002. SOURCE RLIN. LOCATION DCL.
COMMENTARY Fiction based on religious history [BLC].

A48 *Robert Musgrave's adventure. A story of old Geneva* (by Deborah Alcock).
London: S.W. Partridge & Co., [1909] (ill.). LOCATION L.

ALDRICH, Thomas Bailey, b. Portsmouth (NH) 1836, d. Boston (MA) 1907. American poet, novelist, short story writer and editor. TBA's early poetry was influenced by Henry Wadsworth Longfellow. As a scion of two of America's colonial families, he enjoyed the friendship of Boston's literary circle that included Nathaniel Hawthorne and Oliver Wendell Holmes. He was editor of a number of publications, including the Boston *Atlantic Monthly* which under his leadership became very successful. SOURCE Allibone Suppl., i, p. 47; ANB; DAB; DLB, xlii, lxxii, lxxiv, lxxix; T & B, p. 963; Wright, iii, pp 8–9.

A49 *Marjorie Daw, and other people* (by Thomas Bailey Aldrich).
+ Boston: James R. Osgood & Co., 1873. SOURCE Wright, ii, 36; Wright, iii, 49. LOCATION NUC, InND Loeber coll., Wright web.
London, New York: George Routledge & Sons, [1873]. LOCATION L.
Leipzig: Bernard Tauchnitz, 1879. SOURCE T & B 1838; OCLC. LOCATION MH.
+ Boston: James R. Osgood & Co., 1877 (as *A rivermouth romance*; ill.). LOCATION InND Loeber coll.
COMMENTARY Stories of the Irish in America. Contents: 'Marjorie Daw', 'A rivermouth romance', 'Quite so', 'A young desperado', 'Miss Mehetabel's son', 'A struggle for life', 'The friend of my youth', 'Mademoiselle Olympe Sabrieski', 'Père Antoine's date-palm' [NUC].

'ALEXANDER, Mrs', pseud. See **HECTOR, Annie**.

ALEXANDER, Cecil (not Cecilia) **Frances** (Fanny; née Humphreys), pseud. **'C.F.H.'**, b. Dublin, 1818, d. Derry (Co. Derry) 1895. Hymnist, poet and writer of religious stories for children, CFA was the second daughter of Maj. John Humphreys, who had served in the Royal Marines, and Elizabeth Frances Reed. The family lived at Ballykean (also known as Ballykeane; Co. Wicklow) while her father was land agent for the earl of Wicklow, moving to Milltown House, Strabane (Co. Tyrone) when he was appointed agent to the marquess of Abercorn. CFA began to write poetry by age 9. In her collaboration with Lady Harriet Howard§, daughter of the 4th earl of Wicklow, on a number of religious tracts she provided the poetry and Lady Howard provided the prose. A collected volume of their work was published in 1848, the same year her *Hymns for little children* (London, 1848) appeared. This became immensely popular (the 69th edn was published in 1896). She was deeply influenced by the Tractarian movement at Oxford and John Keble, one of its leading proponents, wrote the introd. to her *Hymns*. Many of these, including 'All things bright and beautiful', and 'Once in royal David's city', remain in almost universal use. CFA contributed to the *Dublin University Magazine*. She married in 1850 Revd William Alexander, later the Church of Ireland bishop of Derry and Raphoe, archbishop of Armagh and, after her death, primate of all Ireland, with whom she had four children. She ceased publishing fiction after her marriage. She helped to found the Derry and Raphoe Diocesan Institution of the Education of the Deaf and Dumb in Strabane. CFA was known for other charitable works and for her delight in congenial gatherings, for which she often wrote musical verse.

Alfred Lord Tennyson greatly admired her ballad 'Legend of Stumpie's brae', written in an Ulster-Scots dialect. SOURCE Allibone Suppl., i, pp 22–3; Blain, pp 15–16; Burke's, p. 13; DLB, cic; Field Day, iv, pp 462, 562–6, 568–9, 1151–3; Hogan 2, pp 101–2; Irish pseudonyms; S. McMahon, 'All things bright and beautiful' in *Eire–Ireland*, Winter 1975; NCBEL 4, pp. 621–2; OCIL, p. 10; ODNB; O'Donoghue, p. 7; Osborne, pp 857–8; RIA/DIB; V. Wallace, *Mrs. Alexander: a life of the hymn-writer Cecil Frances Alexander, 1818–1895* (Dublin, 1995).

A50   *The lord of the forest and his vassals, an allegory* (by 'C.F.H.'; dedicated to the author's little cousins).
     + London; Joseph Masters, 1848. LOCATION L.
     COMMENTARY Religious fiction [ML].

A51   *The baron's little daughter, and other tales in prose and verse* [anon.] (ed. by Revd William Gresley; dedicated to Ladies Katherine and Maria Howard, daughters of the 4th earl of Wicklow).[1]
     + London: Joseph Masters, 1848. SOURCE Osborne, p. 857. LOCATION L (6th edn), CaOTP.

COMMENTARY Fiction for juveniles. Stories told by a young man of the Isle of Wight. The stories are moral lessons, which are accompanied by ballads written by the young man's deceased sister. Contents: 'A tale of the first Christians', 'The baron's little daughter', 'New Year's eve', 'The guardian angel', 'Lilian', 'The rising at Aix' [ML].

ALEXANDER, Rupert, fl. 1897. Novelist.

A52   *The vicar of St. Nicholas'* (by Rupert Alexander).
     + London: Digby, Long & Co., [1897]. SOURCE Brown, p. 18. LOCATION L.
     COMMENTARY Has some Irish characters [ML].

A53   *Ballyronan* (by Rupert Alexander).
     + London: Digby, Long & Co., [1897]. SOURCE Brown, 122. LOCATION L, NUC.
     COMMENTARY Set mainly in Ireland [ML].

A54   *Maureen Moore. A romance of '98* (by Rupert Alexander).
     London: T. Burleigh, 1899. SOURCE Brown, 123. LOCATION L.

COMMENTARY Historical fiction set during the 1798 rebellion. John Moore is driven into rebellion by the persecution of the yeomanry, and is joined by his two sons, one of whom is a captain in the army and the other a priest. The battle of New Ross and the atrocities of Wexford are vividly described. The book sides with the rebels. A love story involving Maureen Moore, an American niece of John Moore, is interwoven with the events of the day [Brown].

ALEXANDER, Mrs Thomas, fl. 1895. Romance novelist, Mrs TA was probably Irish since she is known only from a single Irish work, published in Dublin. According to the title page she was also the author of 'A cloak of hodden grey', which as not been located [RL].

A55   *Ierne: a romance of St. Patrick's well, Trinity College* (by Mrs Thomas Alexander).
     + Dublin: Edward Ponsonby; London: Simpkin, Marshall, Hamilton, Kent & Co., 1895. SOURCE Topp 8, 1362; COPAC. LOCATION Dt, L.

COMMENTARY 61pp. Set in Dublin. Esther Lanigan is an elderly widow who has one son, Corny, 'a poor crazed man of twenty-five' (p. 5). Esther looks after the orphaned Penelope, who has an illegitimate child, the Ierne of the title. Ierne is cared for by Mrs Doyle, her cruel grandmother, but is kidnapped by Corny. Eventually, Corny dies, Ierne is reunited with her mother, and Penelope and the father of her child (a student at TCD) are married. Illustration on cover is of a young woman by a well, with the information 'price one shilling' [JB; COPAC].

---

1 See Lady Harriet Howard§.

ALGER, Horatio Jnr, b. Massachusetts 1832, d. New York, 1899. American author of over 130 stories for boys. He was raised by strictly Puritan parents and graduated from Harvard's Divinity School in 1852. As a Unitarian minister, he moved to New York where the lives of the street boys drew his interest. Leaving the pulpit in 1866 to devote himself to writing, his tales in which the hero overcomes great odds to escape poverty and achieve success became immensely popular, so much so that HA's name has become synonymous with 'pull oneself up by the bootstraps' transformations. SOURCE Allibone Suppl., i., pp 25–6; ANB; Brown, p. 18; DAB; DLB, xlii; Hart, p. 18.

A56   *Only an Irish boy; or, Andy Burke's fortunes and misfortunes* (by Horatio Alger).
Chicago: J.C. Winston, [*c.*1894]. LOCATION NUC.
Philadelphia: J.C. Winston, [1910?]. LOCATION NUC.
+ New York: Hurst & Co., [189?] (as *Only an Irish boy; or, Andy Burke's fortunes*).
LOCATION NUC; InND Loeber coll. ([1904] edn).
COMMENTARY Set in the US, a story for boys about the adventures of a young Irish boy [ML].

ALLEN, Charlotte Gibson. See **BOGER, Charlotte Gibson**.

'ALLEN, F.M.', pseud. See **DOWNEY, Edmund**.

ALLEN, Dr —, fl. 1753. Attributed author, according to a note in the BL copy of the following work. SOURCE ESTC t1588.
A57   *A fragment of the history of Patrick* [anon.].
London [Dublin?], [n.p.], 1753. SOURCE Scott cat. 15/8; ESTC t1588. LOCATION D, Dt, L.
COMMENTARY 47pp. One of two edns published, the other a 16pp edn with an identical publication date, priority undetermined. A satire on Irish politics and relations with England and Scotland, cast as a domestic drama that follows the fortunes of Patrick and his brothers George and Andrew [Scott cat. 15/8].

ALLINGHAM, William, b. Ballyshannon (Co. Donegal) 1824, d. Hampstead (London) 1889. Poet, balladeer, writer and editor, WA was the son of a Protestant banker whose family had been in Ireland since Elizabethan times, and of Elizabeth Crawford, a native of Ballyshannon. He was educated locally at Wray's School and as a boarder at Killeshandra (Co. Cavan) from 1837, and advanced himself by a rigorous program of self-improvement. He joined his father's bank and was later appointed a customs officer for the Donegal area. Interested in English and Scots ballads and in Irish folk songs, he used his travels for work to collect songs in the Irish countryside and began to experiment himself with the ballad form. He travelled regularly to London, where his first verses were published in Leigh Hunt's *London Journal*. Through Hunt he made the acquaintance of Thomas Carlyle, Alfred Tennyson, Robert Browning, Coventry Patmore and the pre-Raphaelites, particularly Dante Gabriel Rossetti, whose correspondence with WA was published in 1897. His *Day and night songs* was published in London in 1854 and in the following year reissued with illustrations by Rossetti, John Everett Millais and Arthur Hughes. In 1863 he was transferred to the customs service in Lymington (Hants.) from where he could easily visit Tennyson, whom he greatly admired, on the Isle of Wight. In the following year he published a novel-in-verse, *Lawrence Bloomfield in Ireland* (London, 1864, republished 1869, 1893) that had appeared first in twelve parts in *Fraser's Magazine* (London). It depicts the hostility between the peasants and the landlord class of the day through the story of a responsible young landlord who, on returning to his family estates after his education abroad, endeavours to improve the lives and rights of his tenants. In 1870 WA retired from the customs service, moved to London, and in 1872 became editor of *Fraser's Magazine* (London), to which he had long contributed. In addition, he wrote for the *Athenaeum* (London) and *Household Words* (London, 1850–7). In 1874 he married the noted artist Helen Paterson. He wrote many volumes of poetry and ballads and several plays. Under the pseudonym 'Patricius Walker', he published an account of a tour through England. He and his family moved to Witley in Surrey in 1879 and to Hampstead two years later. His cremated remains were interred at St Anne's church, Ballyshannon. In his diary he left vivid recollections of his many literary friends. A collection, *Varieties in prose*, was published posthumously (London, 1893). For his portraits, see ODNB. Some of his papers are at the Univ. of Illinois, Urbana–Champaign. SOURCE Allibone, i, p. 55; Allibone Suppl., i, p. 32; H. Allingham & D. Radford (eds), *William Allingham. A diary* (London, 1985); Brady, pp 3–4; Brown 2, p. 12; DLB, xxxv; Donegal, pp 23–5; Field Day, ii, pp 7–8, 61–6, 113, iv, p. 1169; Hogan 2, pp 103–4; Irish pseudonyms; Lohrli, pp 200–1; LVP, p. 11; NCBEL 4, 1737; Newmann, p. 4; OCIL, pp 11–12; ODNB; O'Donoghue, p. 9; RIA/DIB; A. Warner, *William Allingham* (Lewisburg, 1975).

A58   *A tale of the Irish famine in 1846 and 1847, founded on fact* [anon.] (dedicated to Lady Joliffe).

+ Reigate: Printed for private circulation by William Allingham, [endorsed] 'not published', [1847]. SOURCE NSTC. LOCATION D, L.

COMMENTARY Among the first published works of fiction on the Famine. Honour McCarthy's husband has gone to America to be able to provide for his wife and five children, who are left in Ireland. She is waiting for a letter from her husband with some money to help her through the Famine. She and her children are forced to beg for food. Her husband returns home from America to fetch his family and finds his wife and four of the five children dead. This work is in all likelihood the same as *A tale of the Irish famine in 1848* [*sic*] (Reigate: Printed by William Allingham, n.d.), which Brown 2 noted but was unable to locate [ML; Brown 2, p. 12].

'AN AMATEUR', pseud. See **EGAN, Pierce**.

'AMÉRO, J.' pseud. See **TRENCH, William Steuart**.

AMORY, Thomas, b. Bunratty? (Co. Clare) 1691 (this is uncertain; the ODNB states that, like his semi-fictional, semi-autobiographical hero, John Buncle, he probably was born in London, but grew up from infancy in Ireland), d. Westminster, London, 1788. A writer who combined fiction, biography and prose, TA was apparently the son of a Councillor Amory who accompanied William III to Ireland and who became secretary for the forfeited estates after the Williamite War. His father acquired property close to Ardfert in the barony of Iraghticonnor in Co. Kerry (but some sources say that the estate was in Co. Clare). TA attended TCD and lived for some time in Dublin, where he claimed to have been a friend of Jonathan Swift§. After 1755 he left Ireland, toured the north of England, and settled in London. His wife, whom he married in 1757, was related to the earl of Orrery. TA lived a very secluded life, rarely venturing out except in the evening, and died at a great age. He claims to have learned Irish and seems to have been familiar with Irish antiquities. His two novels are part fiction, part biography, part autobiography, part religious speculation and part near-pornography, prompting a description of Amory in *Hazlitt's Round Table* as 'the English Rabelais'. He also wrote works on religion and on antiquities. TA's portrait was published in *The life of John Buncle* (London, 1756, vol. 1). SOURCE Allibone, i, p. 58; Boylan, p. 4; Brady, p. 4; A. Clarke, *Prelude to Restoration in Ireland* (Cambridge, 1999), p. 222; DLB, xxxix; Field Day, i, p. 758, iv, p. 765; Hogan 2, p. 105; OCIL, p. 12; ODNB; RIA/DIB; I.C. Ross, 'Thomas Amory, John Buncle, and the origins of Irish fiction', *Éire-Ireland*, 18(3) (Fall, 1983), pp 71–85.

A59   *Memoirs containing the lives of several ladies of Great Britain. Interspersed with*
       literary reflexions, and accounts of antiquities and curious things. In several let-
       ters [anon.].
       London: John Noon, 1755 (vol. 1 all published). SOURCE ESTC t205966; Raven, 336;
       Forster, 70. LOCATION L, MH, NUC.
       London: Johnson & Payne, 1769 [1766?] (as *Memoirs: Containing the lives of several ladies*
       of Great Britain. A history of antiquities, productions of nature, and monuments of art. In
       several letters). SOURCE ESTC t074615; Gecker, 28 (1769 edn). LOCATION L, O, DCL.
COMMENTARY Characterized by A. Hall as a novel with 'a Utopian, ornithological, bodice-rip-
ping, Gothic, Scottish, anti-papist imaginary voyage with learned footnotes'. A miscellany of
biography, literary criticism and observations on religious matters. The title and text were
inspired by George Ballard's rather more conventional *Memoirs of several ladies of Great Britain*
(London, 1752). TA evidently intended to write twenty such 'memoirs', to be contained in
eight volumes, but in fact only this first volume appeared. Contents: 'The history of Mrs
Mardina Benlow. With notes. And some occasional remarks by the way. In two letters to
Hugolin Jewks, Esq.' Consists of a fantastic voyage in which a company of exemplary women
visit various imaginary islands west of Scotland, and then goes on to Cape Verde and the
Canary Islands before returning north for a stay in a kind of utopian community on Green
Island (location unclear). Included are elaborate descriptions of natural history, and extraordinary digressive discussions of philosophy and theology, with extensive comments on the
ideas of the philosophers Isaac Newton, John Locke, George Berkeley, the bishop of Cloyne,
and many others [Boylan; Ximenes cat. 99–1/3; A. Hall cat. 3/1].

A60   *The life of John Buncle, Esq.; containing various observations and reflections, made*
       in several parts of the world, and many extraordinary relations [anon.] (dedicated
       to the 'criticks').
       + London: J. Noon, 1756, vol. 1. SOURCE Field Day, i, pp 694–704; Raven, 362;
       Forster, 68; Gecker, 26; ESTC t108506. LOCATION D, L, PU, IU, NUC.
       + London: J. Johnson & B. Davenport, 1766, vol. 2. SOURCE Raven, 990; Forster, 69;
       ESTC t128392. LOCATION D, L, MH, IU.
       + London: T. Becket, P.A. Dehondt & T. Cadell, 1770, 4 vols. (new edn). SOURCE
       ESTC t071403; Gecker, 27; Gilbert, p. 20. LOCATION Dt, DPL Gilbert coll., PU,
       InND Loeber coll., NUC.
       London: C. Stocking, 1823 (as *The spirit of John Buncle; or, the surprising adventures*
       of that original and extraordinary character John Buncle). SOURCE NSTC. LOCATION L,
       NUC. COMMENTARY London 1823 edn An abridged version [BLC].
       London: Septimus Prowett, 1825, 3 vols. (new edn; ed. by Jacob Henry Burn as *The*
       life of John Buncle Esq.). SOURCE Tiger cat. 06/04/8. LOCATION Dt, L.
       + Berlin: Friedrich Nicholai, 1778, 4 vols. (trans. as *Leben, Bemerkungen, und Meinungen*
       Johan Bunkels, nebst den Leben verschiedener merkwundiger Frauenzimmer; ill.). LOCATION
       D, L.
       's Gravenhage: J.H. Munnikhuisen & C. Plaat, 1778–9, 4 vols. (trans. into Dutch (from
       the German edn) by J.H. Munnikhuisen as *Het leven, de aanmerkingen en gevoelens van*
       Johan Bonkel; ill. Chodowiecki, Bakker). SOURCE F.A. van S. LOCATION Koninklijke
       Bibliotheek, The Hague.
       + London: George Routledge & Sons; New York: E.P. Dutton, 1904 (as *The life and*
       opinions of John Buncle, Esq.; introd. by Ernest A. Baker). LOCATION InND Loeber coll.
COMMENTARY Story of a seventeenth-century gentleman, narrated in the first person. Buncle
recounts his life from youth to middle age. Born in London, he arrives in Ireland as an infant.
He enters TCD at age 17, where he studies for five years before departing for his father's estate

in the west of Ireland. Frustrated by a wicked stepmother, he is forced to return to Dublin and takes the boat to England. He lives principally in the Lake District and in Yorkshire. He soon marries, but his wife dies shortly afterwards. Over the years, Buncle enjoys eight happy marriages and sees eight happy wives to their graves. After the death of his last wife, he travels to China and the Far East. In between the description of his travels, he discourses on topics such as philosophy and morality; Spanish fly; integrity; poverty, and the history of metals. A review in the *Christian Register* (1 Jan. 1920), calls the book the first novel devoted to Unitarianism. T. Cogan's *John Buncle, Junior, gentleman* (London, 1776-8, 2 vols.) extends the story but is not set in Ireland. German and Dutch translations of the *Life of John Buncle* were prohibited in Germany and in Holland in 1779. A German sequel (A. Stein, *Geschichte einiger Esel, oder Fortsetzung des Lebens und der Meynungen des Weltberümten John Bunkels*) was published in Hamburg in 1782 [Corbett, p. 8; Field Day, i, pp 683-4, 694-704, iv, p. 765; *Catalogus van zeldzame boeken der J.F.M. Scheepers* (Utrecht, [1953]), p. 30; ODNB; RL].

'AMOS READE', pseud. See **ROWAN, Anne Margaret.**

'AMY', fl. 1868. Pseudonym of an author who, given that she or he published in Dublin, is likely to be Irish. Other works by someone using this pseudo. are *Sketches of Wales and the Welch* (London, 1847) and a religious work for young people (London, 1875). SOURCE BLC.
A61   *The breaking up of the ice. A Christmas tale* (by 'Amy').
        + Dublin: Moffat & Co., 1868. SOURCE NSTC. LOCATION L (destroyed).
        COMMENTARY Religious fiction. No copy located [BLC; RL].

'AN ANTIQUARY', pseud. See **RENNIE, James.**

ANCKETILL, William Robert, b. Co. Monaghan? 1820, d. 1889. Novelist and political writer, WRA was the second son of William Ancketill, of Ancketill's (also Anketell's) Grove, Emyvale (Co. Monaghan) and Sarah, daughter of Lt.-Col. John C.F. Waring-Maxwell of Finnebrogue (Co. Down). WRA resided at Quintin Castle, near Portaferry (Co. Down), served as captain in the Monaghan militia and became a JP for Co. Down. He married in 1844, Madelina Selina, second daughter of David Ker of Portavo (Co. Down). His works on Irish political matters were written under the pseudonym 'Scrutator'. SOURCE Allibone Suppl., i, p. 35; Brown, p. 19; Landed gentry, 1912, p. 8; BLC; NUC.
A62   *The adventures of Mick Callighin, M.P., a story of Home Rule; and The De Burgos. A romance* (by William Robert Ancketill).
        + London: Samuel Tinsley, 1874 (ill.). SOURCE Allibone Suppl., i, p. 35; Brown, 125. LOCATION D, Dt, L.
        + Belfast: James Reed, 1875, 2nd edn (as *The adventures of Mick Callighin, M.P., a story of Home Rule*). LOCATION InND Loeber coll.
        + Chicago, Detroit: Railroad News Co., 1875. LOCATION InND Loeber coll., NUC.
        + Toronto, Detroit: Belford & Co., 1875. SOURCE McGahern cat. 42/1. LOCATION InND Loeber coll.
        COMMENTARY The first story concerns Mick Callighin leaving Ballypooreen (Co. Tipperary) near the Galtee mountains for Dublin and London, where he meets his future wife in Kensington Gardens. The second story is set in the west of Ireland. Arthur Mervyn meets Col. De Burgo and his daughter, Nora, who has returned home from Italy. An Italian count comes after Nora and carries her off. She is rescued, however, and marries Mervyn [Brown].
A63   *Dowdenham. A tale of high life in the present period* (by William Robert Ancketill).
        London, Belfast: Marcus Ward & Co., 1879. SOURCE Allibone Suppl., i, p. 35; Brown, 126. LOCATION L.

COMMENTARY Set largely in aristocratic circles in England. One of the Irish characters is Revd Hercules Mulligan, who settled in England after the disestablishment of the Church of Ireland. Another Irishman, George Fitzwalter, a young absentee landlord visiting his estates, realizes the evils of landlordism [Brown].

ANDERDON, Blanche (formerly Blanche Partridge), pseud. 'Whyte Avis', b. England? 1880. Novelist and religious writer, BA was probably English. She was the daughter of Revd W.E. Partridge, an Anglican clergyman, and cousin of the poet and author William Henry Anderdon who became dean of the Catholic University, Dublin (1858–63) and who joined the Jesuit order in 1874. She assumed the name of Anderdon on her conversion to catholicism. SOURCE Brown 2, p. 14 [under Avis]; LVP, p. 13.

A64   *A noble revenge* (by 'Whyte Avis').
    London: Burns & Oates, 1898. SOURCE Brown 2, 48. LOCATION L (destroyed), C, E.
COMMENTARY Religious fiction. A story of French life. One of the noteworthy characters is Bridget O'Callaghan, outwardly grim and forbidding, but underneath shrewd and humorous [BLC; Brown 2].

ANDERSON, Adam, pseud. 'A.A.', fl. 1867, d. 1867. The following book has been variously ascribed to either Adam Anderson (annotation in copy in PC) or to A. Armstrong (Linen Hall cat. p. 11), as both used the pseudonym 'A.A.' Either one was probably a friend of the painter Erskine Nicol (1825–1904), who lived and painted in Ireland from 1846 to 1850 and worked for the Department of Science and Art in Dublin. Nichol, who subsequently lived mostly in England, returned to Ireland on regular visits. He often depicted peasant life in Ireland, and considering the following work must have spent time in Co. Westmeath. SOURCE Crookshank, pp 178, 181, 308; RIA/DIB.

A65   *Jim Blake's tour from Clonave to London* (preface and notes by 'A.A.').
    + Dublin: Printed for private distribution by M.H. Gill, 1867 (ill. Erskine Nichol). SOURCE Allibone Suppl., i., p. 35; Linen Hall cat. p. 11. LOCATION BFl, InND Loeber coll.
COMMENTARY An autobiographical account of a trip by James Blake, a servant to the painter Erskine Nichol, from Clonave Island (Co. Westmeath) to London. It shows Blake's unsophisticated views of the wonders of travel and of London [ML].

ANDERSON, Alexander. Co-author. See **EDGEWORTH, Maria**.

ANDERSON, L., fl. 1896. Given the details of this novel, LA was probably an Irish author. SOURCE RL.

A66   *Lockwood Godwin. A tale of Irish life* (by L. Anderson).
    + London: Gay & Bird, 1896. LOCATION L, InND Loeber coll.
COMMENTARY The love stories of two young Irishmen who had been friends from childhood. Some of the action takes place in Ireland. The evils of absenteeism are portrayed [ML].

ANDERSON, Paris, b. 1819, d. Cincinnati (OH) 1857. Novelist, poet, editor and antiquary, PA was the son of Louis Anderson and Eliza Carpenter and cousin of the antiquary and Church of Ireland minister James Graves. At age 16, PA contributed a story to the *Dublin Penny Journal* and later wrote verse, published in the *Kilkenny Moderator*. From 1835 to 1838 he resided at Belvedere Place, Dublin, and in 1839 went to England as a schoolteacher. A year later he became editor of a paper in Macclesfield (Ches.). He returned to Ireland to become secretary of the Barony of Kilkenny Relief Committee for the Famine. In 1853 he left for America, partly in protest against the dealings of the Church of Ireland. *Nooks and corners of the County Kilkenny*, formerly ascribed to him, is actually by his relative John G.A. Prim (republished Dundalk, 2003). His single novel *The warden of the marches* (Kilkenny, 1884) was published after his death. SOURCE Brady, p. 4; Brown, p. 19; C. Manning, preface to *Nooks and corners of the County Kilkenny* (reprint Dundalk, 2003), pp xiii–xviii; W.J. Phelan, 'Paris Anderson' in *Old Kilkenny Review* 11 (1959), p. 31; Hogan 2, p. 106; IBL, 10 (1919), p. 92; O'Donoghue, p. 10; Personal communication, Con Manning, July 2003; Personal communication, George Gossip, July 2003; RIA/DIB.

A67   *The warden of the marches. A Kilkenny story of the Pale* (by Paris Anderson).

+ Kilkenny: Printed at the 'Moderator' Office, 1884. SOURCE Brown, 127. LOCATION D, NUC, InND Loeber coll.

COMMENTARY Historical fiction first published in the *Kilkenny Moderator* (1884). Advertised as being published by P.M. Egan in Kilkenny, but appeared at the Moderator Office in that city. Said to be an old legend still current in the nineteenth century; the story is partly based on historical documents. Set in Co. Kilkenny in and around the marches of Ballygowran. The period is the middle of the fourteenth century. Cantwell, while on a pilgrimage to the Holy Land, falls in love in Florence, marries, and brings his Italian wife to Ireland. His marriage is not happy, because he is jealous, and because of his wife's connection with the alleged witch, Alice Kyteler, which meant that she is in disfavour with the church. Oliver De La Fraine, on hearing that the church would take action against Cantwell's wife, convinces her to flee with him from her home. On their way, however, they are embroiled in a skirmish with Le Poer and Cantwell's men and are taken to be imprisoned in Kilkenny. They escape and flee to De La Fraine's territory. Eventually, Cantwell kills De La Fraine and takes his wife home with him. She, however, poisons him that same day. She is taken prisoner, but dies before a sentence can be pronounced [ML; Brown; C. Manning, preface to *Nooks and corners of the County Kilkenny* (reprint Dundalk, 2003), p. xviii].

ANDERSON, Revd Samuel, b. Co. Armagh *c.*1835, d. Upper Falls, Belfast (Co. Antrim) 1886. Church of Ireland cleric and novelist, SA was the son of Robert Anderson, a merchant. He was educated at the Armagh Royal School; entered TCD in 1852 at age 17; graduated BA in 1857, sat his Divinity Test the same year; was ordained deacon in 1858 and priest in 1859. He was appointed curate of Glenavy (Co. Antrim, 1859), later at Belfast (1859–60) and perpetual curate Upper Falls (Belfast, 1860–86). In 1861 he married Eliza daughter of Nelson Trafalgar Foley and Katherine Frances of Ballygally (Co. Waterford), and with her had one daughter. SA was buried at the Upper Falls church, where there is a tablet commemorating him. The following novel has been ascribed to him, but this novel is set in Co. Waterford (home to his wife's family) rather than in his native Ulster. SOURCE Brown, p. 6; B & S, Appendix B, p. 2; IBL, 10 (1919), pp 67–8; Leslie, *Connor*, p. 199.

A68   *Hugh Bryan. The autobiography of an Irish rebel* [anon.].

+ London: Trübner & Co., 1866. LOCATION L (destroyed), InND Loeber coll.

Belfast: Archer & Son, 1866. SOURCE Brown, 40. LOCATION D.

Dublin: Hodges, Smith & Co., [1866]. SOURCE Falkner Greirson cat. 'Jane'/4; OCLC. LOCATION Rice Univ., Houston (TX).

COMMENTARY Historical fiction set in the Blackwater valley near Lismore (Co. Waterford) in the eighteenth and nineteenth centuries. Describes the last struggles of the Irish against the English planters. The main character converts to protestantism and marries an escaped nun he meets while engaged in slum-work in an English town [Brown].

ANDREWS, Marion, fl. 1890s. Writer of juvenile fiction between 1891 and 1900, who possibly was English. SOURCE Alston, p. 7; NCBEL 4, p. 1739.

A69   *Cousin Isabel. A tale of the siege of Londonderry* (by Marion Andrews).
    + London: Wells Gardner, Darton & Co., [1892] (ill.). SOURCE Dixson, p. 221;
    NCBEL 4, p. 1739. LOCATION D, L, InND Loeber coll.
COMMENTARY Historical fiction for juveniles set in 1689 recounting the events inside of the
city of Derry while it is under siege. Written from a Protestant point of view [Baker].

ANDREWS, Mary. See **DENISON, Mary Andrews.**

ANGOU, Germaine D'. See **D'ANGOU, Germaine.**

'ANN JANE', pseud. See **MORGAN, Ann Jane.**

'ANN OF SWANSEA' (also **'ANNE of SWANSEA'**), pseud. See **HATTON, Anne Julia
    Kemble.**

ANNESLEY, Lady Dorothea. See **DU BOIS, Lady Dorothea.**

ANNESLEY, James, b. Dunmain (near New Ross, Co. Wexford) 1715, d. Blackheath (Kent)
1760. Peerage claimant, indentured servant and writer, JA was the son of the 4th Baron Altham
of Dunmain. The identity of his mother is uncertain and may have been Lord Altham's second
wife, Mary Sheffield, the natural daughter of the duke of Buckingham, or a maid, Joan (Juggy)
Landy. JA's fame rests on his claim to be the disinherited son of the Lord Altham. He alleged
that he had been kidnapped and transported to America by his uncle Richard Annesley, 5th
Lord Altham and 6th earl of Anglesey, to make room for his uncle's accession to the honours
and estates of the family after his father's death. In America, he was sold as an indentured servant and when in 1740 his term of servitude was over, he secured employment on a ship and
was able to return to England. In 1742 JA was tried for the murder of a poacher in Staines
(Middx.) but was acquitted. JA went to court against his uncle to be recognized as the rightful
heir of the Altham estate. A trial to this effect took place in Dublin in 1743 in the court of
exchequer. JA obtained a positive verdict, but eighteen years later his uncle was still claiming
to be earl of Anglesey. JA married in 1742 or 1743, and in 1751 married, Margaret, daughter
of Thomas l'Anson, Bt. JA died without assuming the family title; with the death of his two
sons within a few years, the Annesley claim came to an end. JA's story captured the imagination of several authors, including Tobias Smollett, who used it in a long chapter in *The adventures of Peregrine Pickle* (London, 1751, 4 vols.); Sir Walter Scott in his *Guy Mannering*
(Edinburgh, 1815), and the English author, Charles Reade, in his *The wandering heir* (London,
1872). JA's portrait was published by Lang. SOURCE J.C. Beasley, *Novels of the 1740s* (Athens,
GA, 1982), pp 66–7; Sir Bernard Burke, *A genealogical history of the dormant peerages* (London,
1866), p. 7; CP, i, pp 115–16; Elmes, p. 4; Johnson cat. 44/305; A. Lang, *The Annesley case*
(Edinburgh, 1912); Rowe & Scallan, 450; *The trial at large between James Annesley Esqr., plain-
tiff, and the Rt Hon. Richard Earl of Anglesea, defendant, before the Hon. the Barons of the Exchequer
in Ireland, Nov. 11, 1743, etc.* (London, 1744); *The trial of James Annesley and Joseph Redding*
(London, 1742); *Minutes of the proceedings before the Lords Committees for Privileges, upon the several claims to the titles of Viscount Valentia, &c.* (Dublin, 1773); ODNB; RIA/DIB.

A70   *Memoirs of an unfortunate young nobleman, return'd from a thirteen years slav-
    ery in America, where he had been sent by the wicked contrivances of his cruel uncle.
    A story founded on truth, and address'd equally to the head and heart* [anon.].
    + London: J. Freeman, 1743, vols. 1 and 2. SOURCE ESTC t081623; Hardy, 204;
    McBurney & Taylor, 25. LOCATION L (1743 edn), IU, InND Loeber coll. (vol. 1 only).

+ London: J. Freeman, 1747, vol. 3. SOURCE ESTC t081624; Hardy, 204; Beasley, 113. LOCATION PC, IU, CtY.

+ Dublin: Z. Martineau, 1743 [part 1]. SOURCE Pollard 2, p. 401; ESTC t081625. LOCATION L.

Dublin: Z. Martineau & J. Kenier, 1744 [part 2.]. SOURCE Pollard 2, p. 401; ESTC t171555. LOCATION UCD.

Belfast: Samuel Wilson & James Magee, 1743. SOURCE ESTC t175311. LOCATION O. COMMENTARY The account of JA's adventures in exile, 'done in the manner of a novel', advertised in *The trial at Bar* (London, 1744). Written in the third-person, this is a fictionalized account of his unsuccessful attempt to gain a title which he claimed his uncle Richard, the earl of Angelsea, had usurped after selling him as an indentured servant in America. The third volume drops the pretence of fiction which the first two vols. attempt. It was issued as an incomplete serial in the *Gentleman's Magazine* (London, Feb.–June 1743) under the title 'Memoirs of an unfortunate young nobleman'. It also appeared, abbreviated as a serial, as 'The beggar boy, or history and adventures of James Altamont', in *Tell-Tale* (London?, 1805) [Beasley; Lang, p. 9; Mayo, 149, 876; Scott cat. 41/3].

A71   *The case of the Honourable James Annesley Esqr., being a sequel to the Memoirs of an unfortunate young nobleman* [anon.].

London: repr. for W. Bickerton, 1745. SOURCE ESTC n043758. LOCATION NYPL.

A72   *The case of the Honourable James Annesley, humbly offered to all lovers of truth and justice* [anon.].

+ [London?]: [n.p.], 1756. SOURCE ESTC t001498; Bradshaw, 7410. LOCATION L, C. COMMENTARY The volume in the BL contains correspondence concerning subscriptions to the book and subscription volumes to be left at booksellers in London and Bath [RL].

'AN ANTIQUARY', pseud. See **RENNIE, James**.

APJOHN, Isabella Lloyd. See **FITZGERALD, Isabella Lloyd**.

APPERSON, John, d. 1849. Novelist. JA probably was a resident of Drogheda or its vicinity. SOURCE RL.

A73   *Life and adventures of Michael Collier, the celebrated Leinster highwayman* (compiled with care by John Apperson).

+ Drogheda: Printed for the author, 1850. LOCATION UCD Folklore Dept., D (n.d. edn). COMMENTARY 72pp, priced at 6*d*. A moral tale describing the life of Michael Collier, the convicted highwayman, who was born in Bellewstown (Co. Meath) in 1750. While he was working as a car man between Drogheda and Dublin, he began a life of crime. His life as a highwayman stopped abruptly when he was arrested and brought to Trim jail. He was sentenced to seven years' transportation, which was commuted to allow him enlist in one of Britain's African or West Indian corps. Upon his return to Ireland he opened a public house in Ashbourne (Co. Meath). He died from Asiatic cholera on 13 Aug. 1849 [CD; RL].

'ARAMI', fl. 1852. Pseudonym of a novelist, possibly with the first name Maria. SOURCE RL.

A74   *Cathal More; or, self-love and self-control* (by 'Arami'; dedicated to Ramia).

+ London: W. Shoberl, 1852, 2 vols. LOCATION D. COMMENTARY Set around 1800 and opening at Cappagh House, the seat of the Mores. Cathal More, a member of the Church of Ireland, gets entangled with a German visitor from whom he borrows money. The German then insists on building a Unitarian chapel. In the end the German commits suicide and Cathal pulls down the chapel and places a cross in its place as repentance for his sins [ML].

ARCHDEACON, Matthew, b. Castlebar (Co. Mayo), *c.*1800, d. Castlebar 1863 (1862 according to O'Donoghue). A novelist, poet and short story writer, MA taught at his own private academy in Castlebar from 1825 until the year of his death. From a young age he was interested in the history of Connacht under the penal laws, which provided themes for his novels, in which he also included poems. He married the daughter of an officer in the English army named Maguire, and with her had three sons and three daughters. He applied to the Royal Literary Fund for support but died in destitute circumstances. MA wrote four works of fiction, all set in Ireland. He should not be confused with Matthew Archdeacon (b. 1843), a verse writer from Kanturk (Co. Cork). SOURCE Brady, p. 4; Brown, p. 20; *Dublin Journal*, 1 (June 1887); W.H.G.F., 'Matthew Archdeacon', IBL, 3 (11) (June 1912); Hogan 2, p. 109; Irish pseudonyms; McKenna, p. 92; OCIL, p. 20; O'Donoghue, p. 12; RIA/DIB; I. Sleater, *National commercial directory of Ireland* (London, 1846), p. 113; Sutherland, p. 26.

A75   *Connaught, a tale of 1798* [anon.].

    + Dublin: Printed for M. Archdeacon, 1830 (subscribers' list). SOURCE Brown, 131; Rafroidi, ii, p. 44; Garside 2, 1830:18. LOCATION Grail, D, L (imperfect), NUC.

    Dublin: Printed for the author, 1830 (as *Connaught in 1798. An historical tale*). SOURCE NSTC; Falkner Greirson cat. 'Jane'/6. LOCATION Dt.

COMMENTARY Preface dated 'Castlebar, June 12, 1830'. The subscribers' list is one of the earliest of Connacht sponsors of a novel. Consists of historical fiction, describing French Gen. Jean Joseph Humbert's campaign during the 1798 rebellion [Brown].

A76   *Everard: An Irish tale of the nineteenth century* [anon.].

    + Dublin: Printed for M. Archdeacon by J. Taaffe, 1835, 2 vols. (subscribers' list). SOURCE Brown, 132; NSTC; Garside 2, 1835:20. LOCATION Grail, Dt (2 vols. in 1), D, L, InND Loeber coll. (first volume only).

COMMENTARY Describes the activities of the Ribbonmen in Connacht during the tithe war of the 1830s. Everard is a young man of good education, but down in the world. The leader of the Ribbonmen enlists him in the conspiracy to make use of his superior talents. NSTC mistakenly lists an 1830 edn [Brown; Garside].

A77   *Legends of Connaught, Irish stories, &c. &c.* [anon.].

    + Dublin: John Cumming, 1839 (subscribers' list). SOURCE Brown, 130; Rafroidi, ii, p. 44. LOCATION Grail, D, Dt, L, MH, NUC, InND Loeber coll.

    London: Longman, Orme, Brown, Green & Longmans, 1839. SOURCE Hodgson, p. 329; NSTC. LOCATION L (not found).

COMMENTARY The author states in his preface that each of the stories is based on fact. Contents: 'Fitzgerald' (based on the life of the notorious George Robert Fitzgerald, executed in 1786; the appendix extensively quotes from his *An appeal to the public by George Robert Fitzgerald*, Dublin, 1782), 'The banshee', 'The election', 'Alice Thomson', 'M'Mahon', 'The rebel's grave', 'The Ribbonman' [Brown; RL].

A78   *Shawn na soggarth; or, the priest-hunter. An Irish tale of the penal times* (by Matthew Archdeacon).

    + Dublin: James Duffy, 1844. SOURCE Brown, 133; Sadleir, 60; Rafroidi, ii, p. 45; Hogan 2, p. 109. LOCATION Grail, D, Dt, NUC.

    Dublin: James Duffy, 1844 (as *The priest hunter*). SOURCE Hogan 2, p. 109. LOCATION Dt.

    Dublin: James Duffy, 1862 (as *The priest hunter. An Irish tale of the penal times*). SOURCE NSTC. LOCATION L.

COMMENTARY Historical fiction set in west Connacht during the penal days of the early-eighteenth century. The plot turns around the efforts of a priest-hunter to capture a priest and a friar but his schemes are foiled by a peddler. Only one person, a Protestant rector, exhibits forbearance and charity [Brown; Murphy, p. 40].

'ARDEN, Humphrey', fl. 1829. Pseudonym of a female author of tales for juveniles who, according to the title page of the following volume, was also the author of 'The juvenile Sunday library' and 'Very little tales' (both not located). The preface to the undated Dublin, 6th edn of the latter title indicates the author was female. She also published *Progressive tales* (Edinburgh, 1835). SOURCE BLC; Personal communication, Mary Pollard, July 2003; RL.

A79　*The trial of skill; or, which is the best story?* (preface by 'Humphrey Arden').
　　　London: N. Hailes, 1829, 2 vols. LOCATION L.
　　　+ Edinburgh: Fraser & Co.; London: Smith, Elder & Co., H. Washbourne; Dublin: W. Curry Jnr & Co., 1837 (ill.). LOCATION InND Loeber coll.

COMMENTARY Fiction for juveniles. According to the preface to the 1837 edn the stories are based on fact. Contents: 'The little gambler', 'The black oak necklace' (set in Ireland), 'The midshipman and his sisters', 'The soldier's return' [RL].

ARGENS, Marquis Jean Baptiste de Boyer D'. See D'ARGENS, Marquis Jean Baptiste de Boyer.

'ARGYLE, Anna', fl. 1862. Probable pseudonym of an American novelist who published several other works of fiction in New York during these years. SOURCE Allibone Suppl., i, p. 45; NUC; Wright, i, pp 12–13.

A80　*Money and marriage: A modern story* (by 'Anna Argyle').
　　　New York: S. & A. Hoyt, 1862. LOCATION Wright web.

COMMENTARY Author states in the introd. that her goal is to draw attention to the complete pecuniary dependence of women during married life. She feels that a diffusion of wealth would benefit the world. The main character, Miss Digby, is of the opinion that women need a chance to be educated. Some women in the story take up writing, or think of opening a school, to earn enough to look after themselves and their dependents. Part of the story is set in Ireland. A visit is made to Carrickfergus Castle (Co. Antrim). Miss Digby has inherited a secluded cottage in the south of the country, where she retires [ML].

A81　*Olive Lacey. A tale of the Irish rebellion of 1798* (by 'Anna Argyle').
　　　Philadelphia: J.B. Lippincott & Co., 1874. SOURCE Brown, 135 (mentions earlier edns, which have not been located); Wright, ii, 73; OCLC. LOCATION NUC, DCL, Wright web.

COMMENTARY Historical fiction set in Co. Wicklow during the 1798 rebellion. Olive Lacey is a Protestant peasant girl, whose father was a Catholic. She is adopted into a country gentleman's family. Her father becomes a United Irishman, and among his adventures is a betrayal by a foreign monk, which leads to his being shot. The story contains historical figures, such as Lord Castlereagh and John Philpot Curran. The Union between England and Ireland is seen as having been accomplished by a complete paralysis of the weaker country. The book finishes with the wish for Ireland's thraldom to come to an end [Brown; ML].

ARMSTRONG, A. See ANDERSON, Adam.

ARMSTRONG, F.C. See ARMSTRONG, Capt. Francis Claudius.

ARMSTRONG, Miss Florence C., b. Ireland? 1843, d. 1875. Hymnist and novelist, FCA was the daughter of William Armstrong, a medical officer in the district of Collooney (Co. Sligo). She left Sligo at an early age and almost nothing is known of her later life. Her *The King in his beauty, and other hymns* was published in London in 1875. O'Donoghue describes her as a 'clever novelist', and Coleman and Allibone list *The Sunny South* (London, 1880) as one of her novels, but Allibone also lists the novel, *The Sunny South or the battle of the*

Bosphorus (London, 1866) as one of Capt. F. Claudius Armstrong's§ twenty-one novels. A novel under the title *Sisters of Pheaton* (London, 1890) appeared under her name, but she had died fifteen years earlier. FCA is not to be confused with the author Frances Charlotte Armstrong who used the same pseudonym of 'F.C.A.' SOURCE Allibone Suppl., i, p. 46; Coleman, pp 33–4; O'Donoghue, p. 13.

A82   *Lilian: A tale of three hundred years ago* [anon.].
        London: Religious Tract Society, [1864]. SOURCE Allibone Suppl., i., p. 46; COPAC. LOCATION: L (destroyed).
COMMENTARY Historical fiction set in the sixteenth century. This novel is not to be confused with the novel *Lilian*, published in Boston in 1863 and ascribed to Mrs Richard S. Greenough [RL].

ARMSTRONG, Capt. Francis Claudius (also known as **F.C. Armstrong**), fl. 1855. Novelist, FCA's ancestry has not been found in Irish sources, so he probably was not Irish. SOURCE Allibone, i, p. 68 (list of novels); Allibone Suppl., i., p. 46; Brown 2, p. 13; BLC; IBL, 23 (1935), p. 17; NCBEL 4, pp 1740–1; Wolff, i, pp 37–8.

A83   *The Warhawk. A tale of the sea* (by F.C. Armstrong).
        London: T.C. Newby, 1855, 3 vols. SOURCE COPAC. LOCATION L, NUC.
        London: Charles H. Clarke, [1861?] (as *The Warhawk*). SOURCE Topp 6, 238.
COMMENTARY No copy of the London [1861?] edn located. Set mostly in Ireland in Banagher (Co. Offaly), on the river Suir near Waterford, and various places between the Kenmare River and the Old Head of Kinsale (Co. Cork), but later shifts to London and Turin (Italy). It deals mainly with the fortunes of the children and nephews of Sir Vance Granville of Castle Granville, Glandore (Co. Cork) and is anti-Irish and anti-Catholic in tone. Three of the most admirable characters convert to protestantism and the villains are mostly Catholics. The Warhawk is a smuggling lugger, cruising off the Cork coast [Brown 2, 42].

ARNOLD, Lt. —, pseuds. '**A naval officer**', and '**A native officer**', fl. 1810. Given that this author signed his *The Irishmen* (London, 1810, 2 vols.), with the pseudonym, 'A native officer', it is likely that he was an Irishman, and given the large number of titled subscribers to his *The British admiral* (London, 1808, 3 vols.) and *The Irishmen* (London, 1810, 2 vols.), he was probably well-connected. According to the preface to the former, he was imprisoned for a relatively small debt in 1808. He appears to have published only from 1808 to 1810. SOURCE Blakey, p. 327; Garside, 1808:22, 1809:13.

A84   *The British admiral* (by 'A naval officer'; dedicated to Sir Home Popham).
        London: Lane, Newman & Co., 1808, 3 vols. SOURCE Garside, 1808:22. LOCATION Corvey CME 3–628–47160–5.

A85   *The Irishmen; a military-political novel, wherein the idiom of each character is carefully preserved, and the utmost precaution constantly taken to render the ebullitionary phrases, peculiar to the sons of Erin, inoffensive as well as entertaining* (by 'a native officer'; dedicated to Mrs Edwin).
        + London: A.K. Newman & Co., 1810, 2 vols. (subscribers' list). SOURCE Blakey, p. 232; Brown, 52; Block, p. 10; British Fiction; Garside, 1810:22. LOCATION D, L.
COMMENTARY Epistolary novel in which all the main characters with Irish names live in England. The content of the letters is generally gossip of fashionable or domestic life [Brown].

ARNOLD, Charlotte, fl. 1878. Short story writer and poet, CA lived in Lismore (Co. Waterford) and along with her sister Henrietta published a volume of poetry, *Village lyrics* (London, 1878). She collected and edited the following volume, but it is unclear what her sources were. SOURCE Allibone Suppl., i, p. 48; Colman, p. 34; MVP, p. 16; O'Donoghue, p. 13; RL.

A86   *Tales of my father's fireside* (collected and edited by Charlotte Arnold; dedicated to the duchess of Abercorn).
+ London: Provost & Co., 1879. LOCATION L.
COMMENTARY Each of the following short stories starts with a poem. Contents: 'Moira Rhu, an Irish story, as related by a descendant of the heroine to the writer', 'The blue-room catastrophe', 'The inconvenience of good nature', 'Autobiography of a transmigrated soul', 'The widow bird', 'C'est l'amour', 'A true story', and several sketches, including 'Irish stew; or, café à la mode irlandaise' [RL].

ARTHUR, T.S. See ARTHUR, Timothy Shay.

ARTHUR, Timothy Shay (also known as T.S. Arthur), b. Newburgh (NY) 1809, d. Philadelphia (PA) 1885, pseudonym 'Mrs John Smith'. Irish-American novelist, temperance writer and editor, TSA was the grandson of a Revolutionary War soldier. He grew up in Baltimore and joined the first temperance society of Maryland. He edited a number of Baltimore literary journals before moving to Philadelphia where he became fully involved with the temperance movement. He wrote didactic, moralizing tales with domestic settings. His novel, *Ten nights in a barroom and what I saw there* (Philadelphia, 1897), achieved great success and its sales in the 1850s were second only to the American classic, Harriet B. Stowe's *Uncle Tom's Cabin* (Boston, 1852, 2 vols.). SOURCE Allibone, i, p. 71; ANB; DAB; DLB, iii, xlii, lxxix, ccl; Hart, p. 38; [J. O'Brien], *Irish Celts* (Detroit, 1884), n.p.; NUC; see Wright, i, pp 11–29, ii, pp 14–24 and iii, p. 17 for lists of novels.

A87   *Stories for young housekeepers* (by T.S. Arthur).
+ Philadelphia: J.B. Lippincott, Grambo & Co., 1851. SOURCE Wright, ii, 128; RLIN. LOCATION NUC, InND Loeber coll. (1864 edn), Wright web.
COMMENTARY Contains a story 'Hiring a servant', which concerns the hiring of an Irish cook, Margaret Coyle, in a middle-class American family, and how the initial hurdles in her employment are overcome [RL].

A88   *Confessions of a housekeeper* (by 'Mrs John Smith').
+ Philadelphia: Lippincott, Grambo & Co., 1851 (ill.). SOURCE Wright, ii, 89. LOCATION DCL, Wright web.
Philadelphia: Lippincott, Grambo & Co., 1854 (as *Trials and confessions of an American housekeeper*). SOURCE Wright, i, 135.
London: James Blackwood, [c.1875] (as *Trials and confessions of a housekeeper. Being practical, instructive, humorous and exciting experiences taken from life*). SOURCE Jarndyce cat. 143/238.
COMMENTARY No copy of the London edn located other than that noted in the Jarndyce cat. A series of tales of domestic life: speculations on china ware; tales of cooks; cheap furniture; the picked-up dinner; shirt buttons; boiling a lobster; experiences in taking in boarders, etc. Some of the domestics are Irish [ML; Jarndyce cat. 143/238].

A89   *Before and after the election; or, the political experiences of Mr. Patrick Murphy* (by T.S. Arthur).
+ Philadelphia: J.W. Bradley; Boston: L.P. Crown, 1853 (ill.; Tales for the People). SOURCE Wright, ii, 87; RLIN. LOCATION L, NUC, Wright web.
COMMENTARY 46pp. Set in the US. Features the adventures of a naturalized Irishman, Patrick Murphy, who becomes a voter in the election, joins a political party, but then leaves it in disgust. Written in an Irish brogue [OCLC; RL].

ASHBY, Caroline W., pseud. 'C.W.A.', fl. 1880s. Religious fiction writer.
A90   *Lillies and shamrocks* (by 'C.W.A.'; in memory of F[rances] R[idley] H[avergal]).

+ London: John Nisbet & Co., [1883] ([ed. by M.V.H. Havergal]; ill. Frances Ridley Havergal). SOURCE Alston, p. 10. LOCATION L.

COMMENTARY Religious fiction, consisting of letters and memorials related to the good work of the Irish Society, an evangelical group devoted to Bible reading. Also contains a prayer for Ireland [ML].

ASHE, Capt. —. See ASHE, Capt. Thomas.

ASHE, Capt. Thomas (also known as **Capt. Ashe**), b. Glasnevin (Dublin) 1770, d. Bath 1835. Novelist, travel writer, editor and adventurer, TA was the son of a half-pay officer living near Limerick, whose ancestor had served with William of Orange in Ireland and had been awarded a forfeited Irish estate, and Margaret Hickman of Co. Clare. TA was educated at Cheators school at Clonmel (Co. Tipperary) and was sent to Bordeaux to enter the wine trade, but became involved in a duel with the brother of a young woman he had seduced. He returned to Dublin, where he became secretary to the Diocesan and Endowed School Commission. However, he ran into trouble and debt, robbed money from his father, and left Ireland. He met Lord Edward Fitzgerald in Switzerland and accompanied him on a walking tour. He returned to London and after more debt and more travel, he went to Ireland and was sent on government work to Co. Wexford during the 1798 rebellion. Fleeing debt yet again, he travelled to Boston and settled in Maryland on the Patuxent River where he left his family with a backwoodsman while he went to Washington (DC) to edit the *National Intelligencer*. He was soon sacked, and after a lecture tour he went back to England, joined a regiment and went to Canada. There he became a trader, learned Indian dialects, and started to hunt for mammoth bones. Aside from several novels, he wrote a book on his travels in America (London, 1808) as well as *Memoirs of mammoth and other ... bones found in the vicinity of the Ohio* (Liverpool, 1806?) and *A commercial and geographical sketch of Brazil and Madeira* (London, 1812). He published his memoirs in London in 1815 (3 vols.). SOURCE Allibone, i, p. 74; Brady, p. 5; Falkner Greirson cat. 17/14; Hogan 2, p. 113; NSTC; E.E.T. Martin (ed.), *The Ash MSS, written in the year 1735, by Lieut. Col. Thomas Ash [sic], and other family records* ([Belfast], 1890); Personal communication, Kevin Whelan, Feb. 2003; I. McCalman, *Radical underworld* (Cambridge, 1988), pp 41, 163–5; OCIL, p. 23; ODNB; RIA/DIB.

A91   *The spirit of "The book;" or, memoirs of Caroline, Princess of Hasburgh, a political and amatory romance* (ed. by Thomas Ashe).

+ London: Allen & Co., 1811, 3 vols. SOURCE Hardy, 211; Wolff, 187; Black, 350; Block, p. 11; British Fiction; Garside, 1811:15. LOCATION Dt, MH ([1812?] edn), L, NUC, InND Loeber coll.

London: W. Mason, 1812 (as *The spirit of the spirit, being a concise abridgement of that popular and interesting work, The spirit of the book, or memoirs of Caroline, Princess of Hasburgh, comprising the particulars of the delicate enquiry, and a memoir of the life of that most virtuous and illustrious princess, respecting whom it concerns.*). LOCATION L (4th edn).
COMMENTARY *London 1812 edn* Abridged edn of 36pp [BLC].

London: W. Mason, 1820 (as *Algernon & Caroline; or, the spirit of the spirit, being a concise abridgement of that popular and interesting work. The spirit of the book, comprising political and amatory memoirs of Queen Caroline, late Princess of Hasburgh*). SOURCE NSTC. LOCATION L.

+ Leipzig: Paul Gotthelf Rumer, 1813, 2 vols. (trans. as *Denkwürdigkeiten der Prinzessin Caroline. In Briefen an ihre Tochter, die Prinzessin Charlotte*). LOCATION L.

Philadelphia: Moses Thomas, 1812. SOURCE Gecker, 53. LOCATION PU.

Philadelphia: Bradford & Inskeep; New York: Inskeep & Bradford, 1812. LOCATION NUC.

COMMENTARY Written in the Newgate prison, London. Epistolary novel consisting of letters purporting to be from Queen Caroline to Princess Charlotte. Published as a reply to a suppressed book, *The delicate investigation* [Newcastle-upon-Tyne, 1820?] [Black; COPAC; NUC; I. McCalman, *Radical underworld* (Cambridge, 1988), pp 41, 163–5].

A92 *The liberal critic; or, memoirs of Henry Percy. Conveying a correct estimate of the manners and principals of the present times* (by Thomas Ashe).

London: B. & R. Crosby & Co., 1812, 3 vols. SOURCE Block, p. 11 (mistakenly mentions 1811 edn); Gecker, 51; British Fiction; Garside, 1812:19. LOCATION Corvey CME 3–628–47074–9, L, PU.

A93 *The soldier of fortune: An historical and political romance* (by Thomas Ashe; dedicated to Viscount Castlereagh).

+ London: Sherwood, Neely & Jones, 1816, 2 vols. SOURCE Block, p. 11; British Fiction; Garside, 1816:15. LOCATION Corvey CME 3–28–470725, L.

COMMENTARY According to the preface, the story is based on 'real incidents in the Annals of Ancient Spain, but the characters are all drawn from existing personages, such as Lord Wellington, Bonaparte, &c.' [RL].

A94 *The charms of dandyism; or living in style ... by Olivia Moreland, chief of the female dandies* (ed. by Captain Ashe).

+ London: A.K. Newman & Co., 1819, 3 vols. SOURCE Blakey, p. 265; British Fiction; Garside, 1819:22. LOCATION Corvey CME 3–628–48290–9, L.

ASHE, Trevor Lloyd, fl. 1844. Irish temperance writer, TLA was a resident of Castle Mary, near Bansha (Co. Tipperary). He attended St Alban's Hall, Oxford, and described himself as a 'Deacon of the Roman Catholic Church'. Apparently he was a convert to catholicism. He probably was related to Capt. Thomas Ashe§, whose father lived at Ashegrove, close to Castle Mary in the late-eighteenth century. SOURCE B & S, p. 23; Brown, p. 21; J. Foster (ed.), *Alumni Oxonienses 1715–1886* (London, 1887), vol. 1, p. 34; RL.

A95 *The attorney; or, the contrast. A descriptive tale illustrative of the advantages of teetotalism, both in its physiological and moral bearings* (by Trevor Lloyd Ashe; frontispiece of Castle Mary; dedicated to the Very Revd Theobald Mathew).

+ London: Ackerman, 1844 (ill.). SOURCE Brown, 137. LOCATION D.

COMMENTARY Temperance tale set in Co. Tipperary; the story describes the author's views on teetotalism and the evils of litigation [Brown].

ASHWORTH, Revd John Hervey, b. Elland (Yorks.) 1795, d. 1882. Anglican clergyman, novelist, travel writer and antiquarian, JHA was the son of John Ashworth of Halifax (Yorks.). He was educated at Manchester Grammar School and University College, Oxford, where he obtained his BA in 1819 and MA in 1825. In 1820 he took holy orders. A keen antiquarian, he not only wrote on history but acquired a castle, Craggaunowen (also Graggane) Tower, near Kilkishen (Co. Clare) which he restored. His travels in Ireland were published anonymously as *The Saxon in Ireland; or, the rambles of an Englishman in search of a settlement in the West of Ireland* (London, 1851). According to COPAC, he is alleged to have written *Hurstwood: A tale of year 1715*, (London, 1823, 3 vols.), but recent research has assigned this to Augustus French. SOURCE Allibone Suppl., i, p. 57; British Fiction (Update 3 under 1823); J.F. O'Flanagan, *The Munster circuit* (London, 1880), pp 220–1; H. Weir, *Historical genealogical architectural notes on some houses of Clare* (Whitegate, Co. Clare, 1986), p. 89; J. Foster (ed.), *Alumni Oxonienses 1715–1886* (Oxford, 1888), i, p. 36; Sutherland, p. 31.

A96 *Rathlynn* [anon.].

+ London: Hurst & Blackett, 1864, 3 vols. SOURCE Brown, 138; Wolff, 189; NSTC. LOCATION D, L, InND Loeber coll.

COMMENTARY When this book was reviewed in the *Emerald* (Liverpool, 1 June 1864, p. 31), it was criticized as 'a book of but moderate merit as a delineation of Irish character, and of no Irish interest whatever'. The story centres on a young Englishman, Wyville, son of an admiral, who takes up a property in a remote district in the west of Ireland. The family on the neighbouring estate, the FitzPatricks, befriend him. Their daughter wishes to marry Mr Wyville. This is encouraged by her father and her brother, particularly because their estate is in debt. FitzPatrick's son, who is ruthless, wants to marry a girl, Marian, who lives a secluded life with her father in a remote spot. She refuses, and he tries to abduct her. Mr Wyville resists the charms of Miss FitzPatrick and becomes the protector of Marian. He knows that he can not marry her because his family would disapprove. In the end, all turns out well because Marian is revealed to be a relative of Mr Wyville's uncle, who has a large estate in Wales [ML].

ASHWORTH, Robert, b. Dublin 1777. Presumed but unconfirmed author and a barrister, the son of Robert Ashworth, Esq., of Dublin, and Eliza Woodward. Entered TCD at age 15 in 1792, graduated BA in 1796 and was called to the Irish Bar in 1798. Brown and Clarke suggest that he was the author of the anonymously published, *O'Hara; or 1798*, which traditionally (and by R.L. Wolff) has been attributed to Revd William Hamilton Maxwell§. Brown and Clarke do not reveal the source of their attribution (but see Garside 2, 1825:59). SOURCE Brown 2, p. 14; B & S, p. 24; Keane, p. 12; Wolff, 4669.

'ARVOR, Gabrielle D'', pseud. See DE BELBE, Bagriella Isnard.

'ATHÈNE', pseud. See HARRIS, Miss S.M.

ATKINS, Miss Harriet Westrop, fl. 1788. Epistolary novelist, probably from Cork given that her only novel was privately printed there. A Harriette Atkins, possibly this author, was the daughter of William Atkins (b. 1757) of Fountainsville (near Buttevant, Co. Cork) and Mary Roberts of Ardmore House (Co. Cork). Her father dismantled Fountainsville 'completely, and for many years resided at several places, but chiefly in Mallow' (Burke, iv, p. 571). One of her ancestors was Charles Atkins of Currakerry West (later Fountainsville), who married as his first wife the daughter of John Westropp (b. 1688) of Killard (Co. Clare) and Cahirduggan (Co. Cork), which would explain HWA's middle name, which possibly was also spelled Westropp. SOURCE Hajba, pp 171–2; J. Burke, *A history of the commoners* (London, 1838), iv, pp 570–1; Landed gentry, 1912, p. 757; RL.
A97　*The vale of Irvine: or, memoirs of the Countess of Douglass. In a series of letters to Miss Charlotte Aldersey, Aldersey Castle, Wales* (by Miss Harriet Westrop Atkins).
　　　+ Cork: Printed for the authoress by James P. Trant, 1788, 2 vols. in 1. SOURCE ESTC t193197; Raven 2, 1788:41. LOCATION D.
　　　COMMENTARY Epistolary novel in two slim volumes: vol. 1, 74pp, vol. 2, 68pp. Set in Scotland and France. The tale of an unhappy love affair [ML].

ATTERIDGE, H. See ATTERIDGE, Helen.

ATTERIDGE, Helen (also known as H. Atteridge), fl. 1886. Poet and writer of religious fiction mainly for young people, HA was an Irishwoman who contributed to Catholic periodicals. Apparently none of her fiction has Irish content. SOURCE Allibone Suppl., i, p. 60; Colman, pp 34–5; NCBEL 4, p. 1741; O'Donoghue, p. 15; RIA/DIB; RL.
A98　*"Foremost if I can," etc* (by Helen Atteridge).
　　　London, Paris, New York, Melbourne: Cassell & Co., 1886 (Golden Mottoes Series). SOURCE COPAC. LOCATION L (destroyed), E.

COMMENTARY Religious fiction [BLC].

A99   *Bunty and the boys* (by Helen Atteridge).
+ London, Paris, New York, Melbourne: Cassell & Co., 1888 (ill. Gordon Brown).
SOURCE COPAC. LOCATION L.
COMMENTARY Fiction for juveniles. [ML].

A100   *The bravest of the brave, and The story of a soldier, a donkey, and a doll* (by Helen Atteridge).
+ London, Paris, New York, Melbourne: Cassell & Co., 1900 (ill.). LOCATION L.
COMMENTARY Fiction for juveniles. [ML].

A101   *Fluffy and Jack* (by H. Atteridge).
+ London, Paris, New York, Melbourne: Cassell & Co., 1900 (ill.). SOURCE COPAC.
LOCATION L.
COMMENTARY Fiction for juveniles. [ML].

A102   *The mystery of Master Max, and the Shrimps of Shrimpton* (by Helen Atteridge).
+ London, Paris, New York, Melbourne: Cassell & Co., 1900 (ill.). LOCATION L.
COMMENTARY Fiction for juveniles. [ML].

A103   *To school and away* (by Helen Atteridge).
+ London, Paris, New York, Melbourne: Cassell & Co., 1900 (ill.). SOURCE COPAC.
LOCATION L.
COMMENTARY Fiction for juveniles. [ML].

A104   *Uncle Silvio's secret* (by Helen Atteridge).
+ London, Paris, New York, Melbourne: Cassell & Co., 1900 (ill.). SOURCE COPAC.
LOCATION L.
COMMENTARY Fiction for juveniles [ML].

A105   *Dolly's golden slippers, and The queer house next door* (by Emilie Searchfield and H. Atteridge).
+ London, Paris, New York, Melbourne: Cassell & Co., 1900 (ill.). LOCATION L.
COMMENTARY Fiction for juveniles. Contents: 'Dolly's golden slippers' (by Emilie Searchfield), 'The queer house next door' (by H. Atteridge) [ML; BLC].

A106   *At the sign of the silver cup* (by Helen Atteridge).
London: B. Herder, [1927]. SOURCE COPAC. LOCATION L.
New York: P.J. Kenedy & Sons, [1926]. LOCATION NUC.

A107   *The old-world house* (by Helen Atteridge).
London: Catholic Truth Society, 1929. SOURCE COPAC. LOCATION L.

AUBIN, Mrs Penelope, b. London, 1679? (*c.*1685 according to Blain), d. London, 1731? Novelist, translator, poet and dramatist, PA was the daughter of a French émigré officer. Her family may have been Huguenots, but judging from positive portraits of Catholics in her work, it is possible she was brought up a Catholic. A businesswoman and orator on moral and religious topics, she preached from her own oratory in London. She may have married the French merchant Abraham Aubin in 1698, with whom she had two children. They lived in London until at least 1709. One of her novels is about Ireland, but there is no evidence that she ever visited the country. Her *The noble slaves* (London, 1722) was republished in Dublin (1736) and Belfast (1775). SOURCE Allibone, i, p. 81; Adams, p. 78; Blain, p. 39; DLB, xxxix; Esdaile, p. 136; ODNB; Todd, pp 20–1.

A108   *The life and adventures of Lady Lucy, the daughter of an Irish lord, who marry'd a German officer and was by him carry'd into Flanders, where he became jealous of her and a young nobleman, his kinsman, whom he kill'd, and afterwards left her wounded and big with child in a forest. Of the strange adventures that befell both him and her afterwards and the wonderful manner in which they met again, after living eighteen years asunder* (by Mrs Penelope Aubin; dedicated to Lord Colerain [probably Henry Hare, 3rd Baron Coleraine]).

+ London: J. Darby, A. Bettesworth, F. Fayram, J. Pemberton, C. Rivington, J. Hooke, F. Clay, J. Batley & E. Symon, 1726. SOURCE ESTC to98943; Esdaile, p. 155; McBurney, 189. LOCATION L, MB.

London: D. Midwinter, A. Bettesworth & C. Hitch, 1739 (published in *A collection of entertaining histories and novels, designed to promote the cause of virtue and honour. Principally founded on facts, and interspersed with a variety of beautiful incidents*, London, 3 vols.). SOURCE NCBEL 2, p. 991; McBurney, 334; Gecker, 54. LOCATION PU.

Dublin: George Golding, 1741. SOURCE ESTC t168215. LOCATION Dt (incomplete).

+ Clonmel [Co. Tipperary]: Printed by T. Gorman for P. Wogan, Dublin, 1808 (as above, with the additional title: *To which is added The adventures of Yarico. Also, Lindor and Eugenia. A tale.* LOCATION D, UCC.

Belfast: Joseph Smyth, [1826]. SOURCE Adams, p. 195.

New York: Garland, 1973 (introd. by J. Grieder). SOURCE COPAC. LOCATION O, InND.

COMMENTARY No copy of the Belfast Smyth edn located. Historical fiction initially set in Ulster during the Williamite War. The father of the heroine supported King James and was killed. When his castle was plundered, his wife and daughter begged the protection of a German captain to prevent attacks on their virtue. The captain falls in love with the daughter and marries her and takes mother and daughter with him to Heidelberg where they live happily until, in a fit of unjust jealousy, he attacks his wife and leaves her in a wood, thinking she is dead. After a number of years living the life of a libertine, he repents and becomes a hermit. His wife is rescued by a monk and lives a retired life in a monastery. At the end of their lives they are brought together again and the husband realizes that his wife's virtue always was unblemished. There are a number of side stories, all with the theme of attacks on virtue and the fate of those who repent and those who do not repent [ML].

'AN AUSTRALIAN ', pseud. See BUNN, Anna Maria.

'AN AUSTRALIAN COLONIST ', fl. 1893. A fiction writer who was resident in New South Wales (Australia). SOURCE Miller, ii, p. 653.

A109 *A victim of circumstantial evidence. A sensational story* (by 'An Australian colonist').
Sidney [*sic*]: Published by the author, 1893. SOURCE Miller, ii, p. 653; COPAC. LOCATION E.

COMMENTARY Account of a murder trial and miscarriage of justice. Contains references to Killarney in Ireland, Liverpool and Sydney; set in the early-nineteenth century [Miller].

'AUNT PENN'. Possible pseud. See SMITH, Elizabeth (Lillie) Thomasina Toulmin.

'AUTOMATHES', pseud. See GRIFFITH, Richard.

AVELING, Thomas William Baxter, b. Castletown, Isle of Man 1815, d. Reedham, near Caterham (Surrey), 1884. Congregationalist minister, biographer and religious fiction and travel writer, TWBA was the son of a soldier and an Irish mother. He was a non-conformist minister at the Kingsland Congregational Church, Hackney (London), who was known for his eloquence, learning and philanthropy. He became chairman of the Congregational Union in 1874. Many of his sermons were published. SOURCE Allibone Suppl., i, p. 63; Brown 2, p. 14; ODNB.

A110   *The Irish scholar; or, Popery and Protestant Christianity: A narrative* (by Thomas William Baxter Aveling).
New York: Lane & Scott for the Sunday-School Union of the Methodist Episcopal Schools, 1851. SOURCE OCLC. LOCATION Drew Univ., Madison (NJ).
London: Sabbath School Union, 1870. SOURCE Brown 2, 47. LOCATION D, InND.
COMMENTARY Religious fiction inspired, according to the author, by the writings of William Carleton§. The story relates the rescue of a baby from a shipwreck on the coast of Co. Clare who is adopted by a fisherman and grows up to become a 'poor scholar'. Having made the pilgrimage to Lough Derg, he meets a scripture reader who converts him to protestantism. He turns out to be an heir to an estate in Connemara. The author advocates the reading of the scriptures in the Irish language [Brown 2].

AVERY, Samuel Putnam, b. New York City, 1822, d. New York City, 1904. An engraver, art dealer, and rare book and print collector, SPA trained as a wood-engraver in New York and worked for periodicals such as *Appleton's, Harper's* and the *New York Herald* (all New York). He illustrated several anthologies, including *Laughing gas: an encyclopedia of wit, wisdom and wind* by 'Sam Slick, Jnr', and the volume below. SPA expanded his work of engraving artists' illustrations into an art dealership. After organizing American artists' paintings at the Universal Exhibition in Paris in 1867, he became an agent for both American and European art for such clients as William Walters (whose collection is now in the Walters Art Gallery in Baltimore (MD)), William Henry Vanderbilt, Edward Morgan, William Corcoran and James Hill. He had a special interest in old Dutch paintings and in romantic French landscapes. He was involved in the founding of the Metropolitan Museum of Art in New York and, as an influential collector of prints, worked to establish a separate print room at the NYPL, to which he gave his priceless collection of engravings and etchings. He also collected rare books and exceptional bindings. He was active in social reform and in support of the arts in New York. SOURCE Allibone Suppl., i, p. 63; ANB, DAB.
A111   *Mrs. Partington's carpet bag of fun* (by Samuel Putnam Avery).
New York: Garrett, 1854 (ill. S.P. Avery). SOURCE Allibone Suppl., i, p. 63. LOCATION Wright web.
COMMENTARY Consists of very short, illustrated sketches, some with Irish content: 'Pat too much for the Yankee', 'Irish coolness', 'Irish innocence', 'An Irish mistake', 'A strange creature or Pat's discovery', 'Irish moderation', 'The Irish have to suffer', 'One of the bhoys', 'Milesian advice', 'Pathrick too much for the bishop', 'Irish natural history', 'Irish flavor', 'An Irishman's answer' [ML].
A112   *The harp of a thousand notes; or laughter for a lifetime. Konceived, kompiled, and komically konkoted by Spavery, &c.* (by Samuel Putnam Avery).
New York: Dick & Fitzgerald, 1858 (ill. S.P. Avery). SOURCE Allibone Suppl., i, p. 63 [gives 1868 edn]. LOCATION Wright web.
COMMENTARY Consists of short pieces and poems, the following of which have Irish content: 'MacDermot on the widow Green', 'An Irish highwayman', 'The Irish priest's frolic', 'The fairy oak' [ML].

'AVIS, Whyte', pseud. See **ANDERDON, Blanche**.

'AYRTON, J.C[alder].', pseud. See **CHAPMAN, Mary Francis**.

'AZA'. Pseud of introd. writer. See **CARTAN, Joseph**.

B

'B******, Lord', pseud. See **CHICHESTER, Frederick Richard, earl of Belfast**.

'B., C.F.' See **BLAKE-FORSTER, Charles Ffrench**.

'B., F.F.', alternative pseud. of 'A Lady of New York', fl. 1860.
B1   *The romance of an Irish girl; or, life in two worlds. An autobiography* (with an introd. by a 'Lady of New York' [who signed F.F.B.]).
New York: Derby & Jackson, 1860. SOURCE Wright, i, 2122. LOCATION C, Brown Univ. Library.

'B., J.', pseud. See **BORTHWICK, James**.

'B., M.'. Possible editor. See **FINNY, Revd Thomas Henry Cotter**.

'B., S.', pseud. of **Samuel Bentley**, editor. See **ST. LEGER, Francis Barry Boyle**.

'B., S.D.' Pseudonym of a novelist who, according to the title page of the following book, also wrote 'Dulcie de Sandoval', and 'Through darkest night' (both not located), *Aquaviva: a tale* (London, n.d.) and *The curse recalled: a tale* (London, n.d.). SOURCE Personal communication, Mary Pollard, Sept. 2003; RL.
B2   *Kathleen's motto; or, the sea king* (by 'S.D.B.').
+ Barnet [London]: St Andrew's Press, 1898. SOURCE Brown, 59; OCLC. LOCATION D, MChB.
COMMENTARY The scene is laid in Ireland, England and India. The story relates the devotedness of an Irish girl to her invalid father and unfortunate brother. A kind relative, the sea king, helps to set some wrongs right. Note that Rosa Mulholland§ also wrote a novel entitled *Kathleen's motto* (New York, [1890?]) [Brown; ML].

'B., S.W.', pseud. See **BRISCOE, C.W.**

'B., W.H.', fl. 1850. Pseudonym of a story writer, it may be identified as the possible pseud. of the portrait painter and draughtsman, William Henry Brooke (1772–1860), who illustrated the books of William Carleton§ and Thomas Crofton Croker§ from the 1820s to the 1840s. WHB was the son of the artist Henry Brooke and related to the author Henry Brooke§. He died at Chichester after a long illness. He would have been age 78 when publishing the following work. SOURCE Crookshank, pp 95–6; RL; W.G. Strickland, *A dictionary of Irish artists* (Shannon, 1969), i, pp 97–9.
B3   *Pictures of life from the cottage and the camp* (by 'W.H.B.'; dedicated to James Hartley).
+ London: George Flintoff; Dublin: M'Glashan, 1850 (ill.). LOCATION D.
COMMENTARY 'My uncle Tom', 'The rock of Bannow', 'Rivalry of Murat and Davoust', 'Pat Leary's eventful trip to Dublin, by steam', 'The lost child', 'Jacques Barn', 'Prelude to Dick Vernon's first campaign', 'Pat Leary's return trip to London', 'The lucky escape', 'The consul of Montauban', 'The sentinel of five years' standing', 'The diligence', 'The snuff-box', 'The sun-dial of Malines', 'Romieu and the porter', 'The wig', 'The general', 'Dick Vernon again' [RL].

BAGE, Robert, b. Darley (Derbys) 1728, d. Tamworth (Staffs.) 1801. Popular English novelist and industrialist, RB was the son of a paper maker and was a precocious child. He married Elizabeth Woolley in 1751 and moved to Staffordshire where he bought and operated a paper mill. RB taught himself music, French and Italian and studied mathematics with a tutor. In 1766 he sold his mills to the Irish nobleman Arthur Chichester, 5th earl of Donegall (later earl of Belfast and 1st marquess of Donegall) who soon rebuilt the nearby Fisherwick Hall into a Palladian mansion. RB turned to writing after suffering financial setbacks in his ironwork business in 1779. In his novels he creates fictional settings in which contemporary scientific, philosophical and political ideas are discussed and in which satire highlights the rigidity of the established order. Although Ireland features in two of his novels, the lack of detail suggests that RB never came to Ireland, but issues involved in political unrest in Ireland in the 1780s were of interest to him, as were those of the American War of Independence and the French Revolution. Aside from these novels, several of his other works were reprinted in Dublin, including *Mount Henneth* (London, 1782; Dublin, 1782), *Man as he is* (London, 1792; Dublin, 1793), and *Hermsprong; or, man as he is not* (London, 1796; Dublin, 1796). SOURCE Allibone, i, p. 98; DLB, xxxix; P. Faulkner, *Robert Bage* (Boston, 1979), passim; ODNB.

B4　　*Barham Downs. A novel* [anon.].

London: G. Wilkie, 1784, 2 vols. SOURCE Gecker, 65; Raven 2, 1784:11; ESTC t1033005. LOCATION L, PU, NUC.

Dublin: S. Colbert, 1786, 2 vols. (as *Barham Downs: or, memoirs of the Whitaker family. With anecdotes of Lord Winterbottom. A novel*). SOURCE Raven 2, 1784:11. LOCATION ESTC n043386.

New York: Garland, 1979, 2 vols. LOCATION L, CtY.

COMMENTARY Epistolary novel set in England with a large number of correspondents among the landed gentry and deals with their various romantic intrigues and betrayals. There are a number of subplots, one of which involves Kitty Ross, a girl who is seduced by Mr Corrane, an Irishman. He leaves for Ireland with promises of eternal love. When Kitty finds that she is pregnant, she sets out for Ireland but falls ill on the way. An honest Quaker, Dr Isaac Arnold of Dublin, takes a fatherly interest in Kitty and she lives happily with him there. Another Irish character is O'Donnell, a soldier on the Continent, who is described as an ardent duellist. All bad characters eventually die, or flee, or are converted to more sensible lives. The good characters marry and live happily [ML].

B5　　*The fair Syrian. A novel* [anon.].

London: J. Walter, J. Bew & P. Sandford, 1787, 2 vols. SOURCE Gecker, 66; Raven 2, 1787:28; ESTC n009659. LOCATION PU, NUC.

Dublin: Gilbert, Byrne, H. Whitestone, Heery, Lewis, Moore, Jones & Halpen, 1787, 2 vols. SOURCE Raven 2, 1787:28; ESTC t126825. LOCATION NUC.

Londres [Paris]: Briand, 1788, 3 vols (trans. as *La belle Syrienne*). LOCATION L.

+ New York, London: Garland, 1979, 2 vols. LOCATION C.

COMMENTARY Epistolary novel. Part of the action is set in Turkey and Ireland (Killarney, Kilkenny, the north of Ireland, and Dublin), but this is not crucial to the plot. The story concerns the triumph of virtue over evil and over fashionable life. A French and an English nobleman fall in love with two young women in distress. Honoria, presumed an orphan and brought up in the Middle East where she was sold several times to harems, is saved by a woman who adopts her and brings her to Ireland. Honoria has been falsely accused of murdering her benefactress. The other woman, Aurelia, who is Irish, is being forced by her father into a marriage with her wastrel cousin. The two noblemen prove Honoria's innocence and succeed in securing Aurelia's inheritance. The novel abounds with comparisons between high life and virtuous living. In the end, Honoria is reunited with her father, who had been languishing in jail in Constantinople. In the end, all villains die, and the two couples are married and decide to live withdrawn from society on the Continent [ML].

BAGOT, Harriet Frances. See **THYNNE, Lady Charles.**

BAILEY, Margaret. See **MAGUIRE, Mrs John Francis.**

BAKER, Dorothea. See **TOWNSHEND, Dorothea Baker.**

BAKER, Harriet. See **NUNN, Mrs Lorenzo N.**

BAKER, Henry Barton, fl. 1878. English author of historical works who also wrote about the London stage, much of which appeared as essays in the London *Temple Bar* magazine. SOURCE Allibone Suppl., i, p. 76; BLC; *Saturday Review* (London), 46, p. 664.
B6   *Strafford. A romance* (by Henry Barton Baker).
         + London: Tinsley Bros, 1878, 3 vols. SOURCE COPAC. LOCATION L, NUC, InND
         Loeber coll. (1878 edn, 3 vols. in 1).
COMMENTARY Historical fiction relating the life of Thomas Wentworth, earl of Strafford. The story begins soon after the death of the duke of Buckingham when King Charles I is in need of a new strongman. Wentworth deserts his Parliamentarian friends and casts his lot with the king. He first becomes lieutenant of the north, afterwards lord deputy of Ireland. He is depicted as a stern but honest man who in the service of the king makes many enemies. His stay in Ireland is described as a period of great improvements, at least for the king's revenues. Finally, the growing power of the Parliament leads to Strafford's attainder. The weak King Charles signs the document that leads to his execution. A side story is about Strafford's love for his wife Ethel, who in the book dies from distress at his execution [ML].

BALDREY, Walter Burton. Co-author. See **OUSELEY, John Mulvey.**

BALFOUR, Mrs Clara Lucas (née Liddell), b. New Forest (Hants.) 1808, d. Croydon (London) 1878. Writer of fiction for juveniles and on moral and social reform and a poet, CLB was an English temperance activist and orator. As a child she lived in poverty with her mother in London. At age 16 she married James Balfour, with whom she had eight children. Their poverty was exacerbated by his heavy drinking and this first-hand experience of the effects of alcoholism informed her later writings. In 1837, influenced by the nascent temperance movement, the Balfours forswore alcohol. It was around this time that CLB began to write. She came to the notice of the essayist and historian Thomas Carlyle, who became a patron and friend. In 1840 she met the temperance campaigner John Dunlop, author of *Artificial and compulsory drinking usages in Great Britain and Ireland* (Glasgow, 1837). Her writings on temperance were popular and successful and she contributed regularly to temperance periodicals. For thirty years she lectured widely on teetotalism and on women in society. She also wrote a work about the author Elizabeth Tonna§ (*A sketch of Charlotte Elizabeth*, London, 1854). For CLB's portrait, see ODNB. SOURCE Allibone Suppl., i, pp 80–1; Blain, p. 53; Boase, i, p. 143; BLC; NCBEL 4, p. 1744; ODNB; Sutherland, pp 38–9.
B7   *Confessions of a decanter* (by Mrs Clara Lucas Balfour).
         Philadelphia: American Baptist Publication Society, [1862]. SOURCE RLIN; NCBEL.
         LOCATION Free Library of Philadelphia.
         London: S.W. Partridge, [1862] (ill.). LOCATION L.
         COMMENTARY 144pp for the Philadelphia edn, which has as other title: *Lame Irish girl* [RLIN].

BALFOUR, Frederic Henry, pseuds 'Ross Dering' and 'Ross George Dering', fl. 1889. A novelist and writer on China, FHB was a resident of Dering House (Co. Wicklow) in 1889, and therefore possibly an Irish author. At least one of his works has Irish content. SOURCE Allibone Suppl., i, p. 81; BLC; Wolff, i, pp 43–4; *Saturday Review* 43, p. 300.

B8   *Giraldi; or, the curse of love* (by 'Ross George Dering'; dedicated to Thomas Lowestoft of Braybrooke Hall, Lincs.).
        London: Trübner & Co., 1889. SOURCE Wolff, 217. LOCATION NUC.
        New York: D. Appleton & Co., 1889. LOCATION NUC.

B9   *The virgin's vengeance; or, how the Irish got Home Rule* (by 'Ross Dering').
        + Oxford: J. Oliver, 1889. LOCATION L, NUC.

B10   *The undergraduate. A sketch* (by 'Ross George Dering').
        London: Richard Bentley & Son, 1891, 2 vols. SOURCE Wolff, 218. LOCATION NUC.
        COMMENTARY An Oxford story [Wolff].

B11   *Dr. Mirabel's theory. A psychological study* (by 'Ross George Dering').
        London: Richard Bentley & Son, 1893, 3 vols. SOURCE Wolff, 216. LOCATION NUC.
        New York: Harper & Bros, 1893. LOCATION NUC.
        COMMENTARY The prefatory note by the author counters accusations of plagiarism [Jarndyce cat. 158/24].

B12   *Cherryfield Hall. An episode in the life of an adventuress* (by 'Ross George Dering').
        + London: Richard Bentley & Son, 1895. SOURCE Wolff, 215. LOCATION L.
        New York: G.P. Putnam's Sons, 1895 (The Hudson Library, No. 11). LOCATION NUC.
        COMMENTARY The setting is imaginary [RL].

B13   *The expiation of Eugene. A novel* (by Frederic Henry Balfour).
        London: Greening & Co., 1905. SOURCE COPAC. LOCATION L.

B14   *Austin and his friends* (by Frederic Henry Balfour).
        London: Greening & Co., 1906. LOCATION L.

'BALLINASLOE', pseud. See **TAYLOR, Frederick**.

BALME, E., fl. 1898. A novelist, possibly related to Edward Balme Wheatley Balme (b. 1819), sheriff of Westmoreland (England) in 1876, who with others was the author of *Observations on the treatment of convicts in Ireland* (London, 1862). SOURCE Allibone Suppl., i, p. 85.

B15   *The luck of the four-leaved shamrock* (by E. Balme).
        London: George Routledge & Sons, 1898. SOURCE Brown 2, 54. LOCATION L.
COMMENTARY Concerns the growing love of Leslie Desmond, a professed woman-hater, for a little Irish girl and the process by which, having set her affections on the wrong man, Kitty is gradually brought to appreciate the right one [Brown 2].

BAMPFYLDE, the Hon. Marcia Warwick (known as the **Hon. Marcia Bampfylde**), fl. 1892. English novelist and writer of juvenile fiction, MWB was the daughter of Augustus Frederick George Warwick (Bampfylde), 7th Bt and 2nd Baron Poltimore (seated at Poltimore Park, Devon) and Flora Sara Wilhelmine, descendant of Irish playwright Richard Brinsley Sheridan and Maria Marcia Grant. She probably wrote only a single work with Irish content. SOURCE CP, x, p. 568; but not mentioned as daughter of the 2nd Baron Poltimore in Burke's *Peerage and baronetage* (London, 1970), p. 2143.

B16   *In the hush of the evening hour* (by the Hon. Marcia Bampfylde).
        + London: Wells Gardner, Darton & Co.; Exeter: Henry S. Eland, 1892 (ill. Dellagana). LOCATION D.
        COMMENTARY Set on the west coast of Ireland [ML].

'BANIM'. See **MARTIN, Harriet Letitia**. Pseud. used by French publisher for translation of HLM's novel *Canvassing* (*Le candidat – moeurs irlandaises* [Paris, 1836, 2 vols.]) originally included with *The mayor of Wind-gap* (London, 1835) by 'the O'Hara Family', pseud. of the brothers John§ and Michael§ Banim.

'BANIM, Dan', pseud. See **DOWNEY, Edmund**.

BANIM, John, pseud. 'the O'Hara family', b. Kilkenny 1798, d. Kilkenny 1842. Novelist, playwright, poet and artist, JB was the son of Michael Banim, a Catholic shopkeeper, and Joannah or Judith Carroll, and brother of Michael Banim§. Educated at Kilkenny College, JB later studied drawing at the academy of the Royal Dublin Society and after graduating returned to Kilkenny in 1816 to teach drawing at a girls' boarding school. Disappointed in love, he went to Dublin in 1820 where he contributed to various publications, including the *Leinster Journal* (Kilkenny) and the *Limerick Evening Post*. He moved to London shortly afterwards, where he tried to make a living by writing, being helped by the Irish playwright and poet Richard Lawlor Sheil. His long poem *The Celt's paradise* (London, 1821) was admired by Sir Walter Scott. JB was successful in having his second play 'the celebrated tragedy of *Damon and Pythias*' ([London], 1821) produced at Covent Garden and the proceeds enabled him to return to Ireland, pay off his debts, marry Ellen Ruth [or Rothe] of Inistioge (Co. Kilkenny) and return to set up house in Brompton, London, where he joined the staff of the *Literary Register*. In 1822 he suggested to his brother Michael that they write a series of stories, corresponding to Sir Walter Scott's Scottish stories, that would present Irish characters, history and society free of literary stereotypes and condescending caricatures, while advancing the cause of Catholic emancipation and explaining to an English audience the underlying grievances behind outbreaks of agrarian aggression. From then on the two collaborated closely on some (but not all) of their novels and in the process helped to develop Irish realist and historical fiction with regional authenticity, the tone of which was always conciliatory between England and Ireland. In London JB met Gerald Griffin§ and lived in the same 'cottage' as S.C. Hall, who later married the Irish author Anna Maria Fielding (Mrs S.C. Hall§). JB also probably met Michael James Whitty§, with whom he and his brother competed to be the first in England to publish Irish stories, Whitty's collection appearing in 1824, and the first collection by the Banim brothers in 1825. JB and/or his brother contributed short stories to the *Dublin and London Magazine* (London, 1826), the *Keepsake* (London, 1830–31), *Friendship's Offering* (London, 1830–31), and the *New Monthly Magazine* (London, Sept. 1833). To recuperate from illness (he suffered from a progressive spinal disease that eventually crippled him), JB lived in France from 1829 to 1835 (he was visited by Thomas Haynes Bayly§ in Boulogne, who wrote a poem about Banim's suffering). His health failing, he retired to Kilkenny in 1836, living an invalid's life at Windgap Cottage on a Civil List pension. Later in life he occasionally lectured on geology and literature at a school in Kilkenny that his brother helped to found. S.C. Hall described JB 'in his prime' as 'a good specimen of the Irish Celt. His face was full, somewhat too much so … [and] somewhat pitted with the small-pox, but his face was handsome …' (S.C. Hall, pp 227–8). An advertisement on the back cover of a book of songs, *Chaunt of the cholera* (London, 1831) by the Banim brothers, announced a three-volume novel *The dwarf bride* by 'the O'Hara family', but this is not known to have been published. A French book of fiction, *Le candidat – moeurs irlandaises* (Paris, 1836, 2 vols.), by 'Banim' is a translation of *Canvassing* by Harriet Letitia Martin§. Since there is not full agreement among scholars about what role each brother played in the various publications, the following listing follows the division applied by Rafroidi. Their works became very popular, were much reprinted in the US, and were translated into French and German. For JB's portraits, see Elmes, Strickland, and Laffan & Rooney. For unpublished letters, see ODNB. SOURCE Allibone, i, p.

112; Boyle, p. 11; Brady, p. 6; J.T. Campion, Manuscript memoir of John Banim (NLI, MS 18,489); Clyde, pp 86,188; DLB, cxvi, clviii, clix; Elmes, p. 9; Field Day, i, pp 1139–49, 1171–2; T. Flanagan, *The Irish novelists 1800–1850* (New York, 1958), pp 167–202; S.C. Hall, pp 227–8; Hogan 2, pp 115–17; *The Harp* (Cork), 1855, i, pp 117–24; R. Horne (ed.), *The new spirit of the age* (London, 1844), ii, pp 143–52; Irish pseudonyms; *Irish Quarterly Review* (Dublin, 1851–60), issues 14–21 (200pp biographical study of the Banims; not examined); W. Laffan & B. Rooney, '"One of our brilliant ornaments": the death and life of Thomas Foster' in *Irish Architectural and Decorative Studies*, 7 (2004), pp 197, 201–2, 213, 217, 200, 220; McKenna, pp 95–8; J.O'K. Murray, *Prose and poetry of Ireland* (New York, 1877, p. 436; contains letters); P.J. Murray, *The life of John Banim* (London, 1857); NCBEL 4, pp 883–5; OCIL, pp 29–30; ODNB; O'Donoghue, p. 18; Rafroidi, ii, pp 49–53; RIA/DIB; RL; Sadleir, i, pp 23–6; Scott (correspondence with Sir Walter Scott); Strickland, i, p. 380; Wolff, i, pp 44–8; Sutherland, p. 40.

B17   *Revelations of the dead-alive* [anon.].

  London: W. Simpkin & R. Marshall, 1824. SOURCE COPAC. LOCATION L.

  London: Simpkin, Marshall & Co. (as *London and its eccentricities in the year 2023; or, revelations of the dead-alive*). SOURCE COPAC; Rafroidi, ii, p. 50; British Fiction; Garside, 1824:15; Sadleir, 148; Wolff, 231. LOCATION D, Dt, L, NUC, L.

COMMENTARY Futuristic novel set in the time of Napoleon I and the duke of Wellington, mainly in England, but going up to the year 2023. The main character goes into a semi-death and for every day he is 'dead', he can see a year into the future. Mentions the year 1829 in Ireland and the political changes that took place at that time. There are other references to Ireland as well [Hartman, 723, 1022; ML].

B18   *Tales by the O'Hara family: Containing Crohoore of the bill-hook. The fetches, and John Doe* [first series] [anon.].

  Editorial note Because of the large number of versions of this collection of short stories, reprints and publications in parts, the following is organized by city of first publication. Unless stated otherwise, the title of the publication is as above. Commentary showing the contents of the first publication follows the first issue so that is clearer to readers what the significance is of titles comprising one or more of the stories. The same lay-out is repeated below for JB's other books of stories [RL].

  — LONDON

  + London: W. Simpkin & R. Marshall, 1825, 3 vols. SOURCE Rafroidi, p. 52; British Fiction; Garside, 1825:13; Sadleir, 150; Wolff, 233. LOCATION Grail, Corvey CME 3–628–47950–9, Ireland related fiction, D, L, DCL, NUC, InND Loeber coll.

  COMMENTARY *London 1825 edn* Reviewed in the *Dublin and London Magazine* (London, 1825, pp 141–4), the stories both support Catholic emancipation and try to explain the causes of agrarian unrest. Contents: 'Crohoore of the bill-hook' (by Michael Banim; concerns the Whiteboys, who make savage attacks on tithe proctors), 'The fetches' (by John Banim; a story set in Kilkenny in the eighteenth century in which an Irish superstition comes true), 'John Doe' (by John and Michael Banim; later reissued under title *The peep o' day*, is set in Co. Tipperary, near Clonmel. John Doe is a Whiteboy leader. The story was later turned into a play under the title of 'The last of the guerrillas', when its location was changed from Ireland to Spain [B. Bernard, *The life of Samuel Lover, R.H.A.* (New York 1874), p. 193; ODNB; Wolff introd., p. 16].

  London: Simms & McIntyre, 1848 (as *Crohoore of the bill-hook*). LOCATION Dt, NUC.

  + London, Belfast: Simms & M'Intyre, 1853 (as *John Doe*; Parlour Library, No. 88). SOURCE Sadleir, ii, p. 155; NSTC. LOCATION L, C, NUC, InND Loeber coll.

  London: Charles H. Clarke, 1861 (as *The peep o'day; or, savourneen deelish*; Parlour Library, No. 255). SOURCE Topp 1, p. 219; NSTC. LOCATION E.

+ London: George Newnes, [ca.1896?] (as *The peep of day or, John Doe*; preface by C.S.C.; Penny Library of Famous Books, No. 8). SOURCE COPAC. LOCATION O.

London: George Newnes, [ca.1896–1899], 2 vols. (as *Crohoore of the bill hook*; Penny Library of Famous Books, Nos. 31, 32). SOURCE Sadleir, 3643.

COMMENTARY *London Newnes edn* No copy located [RL].

— BELFAST

+ Belfast: Simms & M'Intyre; London: W.S. Orr & Co., 1846 (as *Tales by the O'Hara family. Part I. Containing Crohoore of the bill-hook and The fetches*; The Parlour Novelist, vol. 1; ill. F.P. Becker). SOURCE Sadleir, ii, p. 148. LOCATION D, Dt (1848 edn), NUC.

— PARIS

Paris: Gosselin, 1828, 2 vols. (trans. by A.J.B. Defauconpret as *John Doe, ou le chef des rebelles*). SOURCE Rafroidi, ii, p. 360.

Paris: Gosselin, 1828, 3 vols. (trans. by A.J.B. Lefauconpret as *Crohoore na Bilhoge, ou les Whiteboys*). SOURCE Rafroidi, ii, p. 359. LOCATION L.

— STUTTGART

Stuttgart: Carl Hoffman, 1828 (trans. as *Hauptmann Reh*; Pantheon Series). SOURCE Garside, 1825:13, OCLC. LOCATION NjP.

— HAMBURG

+ Hamburg: August Campe, 1828 (trans. by E.L. Domeier as *Der Zwerg, ein irländisches Sittengemälde*). SOURCE Garside, 1825:13. LOCATION L.

— AMSTERDAM

Amsterdam: M.H. Binger, 1847 (trans. into Dutch by G.H. Nagel as *Crohoorne met de bijl*). SOURCE Alphabetische naamlijst 1833–49, p. 39.

— NEW YORK

New York: Peterson Publishing Co., n.d. LOCATION NUC.

+ New York, Montreal: D. & J. Sadlier & Co., 1881 (*The fetches, evidence of academic decadence*, by 'the O'Hara family'; Sadlier's Household Library). LOCATION D. COMMENTARY *New York 1881 edn* This volume appears to be have been published separately from the series of collected works listed below [RL].

— MODERN EDN

+ New York: Garland, 1978, 3 vols. (introd. by R.L. Wolff). LOCATION D, CtY.

B19   *Tales by the O'Hara family. Second series. Comprising The Nowlans, and Peter of the castle* [anon.].

— LONDON

+ London: Henry Colburn, 1826, 3 vols. SOURCE British Fiction; Garside, 1826:14; Sadleir, 151; Wolff, 234. LOCATION Grail, Corvey CME 3–628–47940, Ireland related fiction, D, Dt (1834 edn), DPL (incomplete), L, NUC, InND Loeber coll.

COMMENTARY *London 1826 edn* Reviewed in the *Literary Chronicle* (London, 18 Nov., 1826). Contents: 'The Nowlans' (by John Banim. A story of a 'spoiled priest', it concerns the son of a prosperous farming family intended for the priesthood who finds his education interrupted when he is sent to live with his profligate uncle where he is exposed to sexual temptation. He elopes with the niece of a liberal Protestant Ascendancy landowner. The ex-priest is allegedly based on Revd Mortimer O'Sullivan§), 'Peter of the castle' (by John and Michael Banim. The plot revolves around a series of uncertain identities, and was set in the Priory church at Kells, Co. Kilkenny). William Butler Yeats§ included 'The Nowlans' in his list of the thirty best Irish novels. It was later turned into a play, the 'Sergeant's wife', with the location changed from Ireland to France. Note that the subject matter of 'The Nowlans' was also the inspiration for Anna Brownell Jameson's§ 'Halloran the peddler', which although written in 1826 appears not to have been printed until the publication of her *Visits and sketches at home and abroad* (London, 1834, 4 vols.) [B. Bernard, *The life of Samuel Lover, R.H.A.* (New York 1874), p. 193; ODNB; [J.G.A. Prim], *Nooks and corners of the County Kilkenny* (Kilkenny, 2003), p. 54; RL; Wolff introd., pp 16–17; Wolff, introd. to *The Boyne Water*, p. xviii].

London: Henry Colburn, 1827, 2nd edn, 3 vols. (new edn; dedicated to Thomas Moore§). SOURCE Davidson cat. 24/67. LOCATION NUC.

London: Henry Colburn & R. Bentley; Edinburgh: Bell & Bradfute; Dublin: John Cumming, 1834, 3 vols. (as *The Nowlans and Peter of the Castle*, by 'the O'Hara family'); Colburn's Irish National Tales Nos. 1–3). SOURCE Sadleir 3736c(ii); Rowan cat. 45/330. LOCATION MH.

London, Belfast: Simms & M'Intyre, 1847 (as *The Nowlans and Peter of the Castle*, by 'the O'Hara family'); Parlour Library, No. 93). SOURCE Sadleir, ii, p. 155; NSTC. LOCATION DPL (1853 edn), L, E.

— BELFAST

+ Belfast: Simms & M'Intyre; London: W.S. Orr & Co., 1846 (as *Tales by the O'Hara family. Part II. Containing The Nowlans*; dedicated to Thomas Moore§; The Parlour Novelist, vol. 7). SOURCE Sadleir, ii, p. 149. LOCATION D, NUC, InND Loeber coll.

— DEVENTER

Deventer: De Lange, 1838 (freely trans. by H. van der Sprong into Dutch as *Peter uit den ouden burg: Een familiegeschiedenis*). SOURCE Adamnet. LOCATION UVA.

PARIS

Paris: Gosselin, 1829, 4 vols. (trans. by A.J.B. Defauconpret as *L'Apostat, ou la famille Nowlan*). SOURCE Rafroidi, ii, p. 359; NSTC. LOCATION O.

— LEIPZIG

Leipzig: Brockhaus, 1835, 2 vols. (trans. by Gottlob Heinrich Adolf Wagner as *Das Haus Nowlan, oder Hang und Geschick. Ein irländisches Familiengemählde*). SOURCE Garside, 1826:14. LOCATION Bibliotheks Verbund Bayern.

— MODERN EDNS

+ Belfast: Appletree Press, 1992 (*The Nowlans*, introd. by Kevin Casey). LOCATION D.

Philadelphia: H.C. Carey & I. Lea, 1827, 2 vols. (as *The Nowlans and Peter of the Castle*, by 'the O'Hara family'). SOURCE Kaser, 59; OCLC. LOCATION MH, NUC.

+ New York: Garland, 1978, 3 vols. (introd. by R.L. Wolff). LOCATION D, DCL.

+ Belfast: The Appletree Press, 1992 (as *The Nowlans*, introd. by Kevin Casey). LOCATION D.

B20　*The Boyne water. A tale* (by 'the O'Hara family').

+ London: W. Simpkin & R. Marshall, 1826, 3 vols. SOURCE Block, p. 14 (probably mistakenly refers to a Dublin, 1826 edn); British Fiction; Garside, 1826:13; Sadleir, 137; Wolff, 225; Rafroidi, ii, p. 50. LOCATION Grail, Corvey CME 3-628-47272-5, Ireland related fiction, D, Dt (1836, 2nd edn), DPL (1836, 2nd edn), L, NUC, InND Loeber coll.

Paris: Gosselin, 1829, 5 vols. (trans. by A.J.B. Defauconpret as *La bataille de la Boyne, ou Jacques II en Irlande; roman historique irlandais*). SOURCE Rafroidi, ii, p. 359; NSTC. LOCATION L.

+ Lille: University of Lille, 1976 (introd. by P. Rafroidi). LOCATION InND Loeber coll.

+ New York, London: Garland, 1979, 3 vols. (introd. by R.L. Wolff). LOCATION Dt, InND Loeber coll.

COMMENTARY Historical fiction describing the Williamite War and the treaty of Limerick. Features Patrick Sarsfield and George Walker, hero of the siege of Derry. The offspring of a Protestant family and a Catholic family in Ulster who before the war were friends, find themselves torn between their friendship and loyalty to their respective causes. The novel presents an appeal for Catholic emancipation based on the idea that the English had reneged on the conciliatory attitude to Catholics expressed in the treaty of Limerick [ML; Hartman, 880, 1008; ODNB].

B21   *The Anglo-Irish of the nineteenth century. A novel* [anon.].

+ London: Henry Colburn, 1828, 3 vols. SOURCE Rafroidi, ii, p. 51; British Fiction; Garside, 1828:16; Wolff 223. LOCATION Grail, Corvey CME 3–628–47060–9, Ireland related fiction, D, Dt, L, MH, NUC.

+ London: Henry Colburn & R. Bentley; Edinburgh: Bell & Bradfute; Dublin: John Cumming, 1834, 3 vols. (as *The Anglo-Irish*; Irish National Tales, Nos. 10–12). SOURCE Sadleir, 3736c(ii); Rowan cat. 45/330. LOCATION O, NUC, InND Loeber coll. (3 vols. in 1).

+ Glasgow: Cameron & Ferguson [1877 or later]. (as *Gerald and Augusta; or, the Irish aristocracy*). SOURCE Brown, 35; RL. LOCATION D.

+ Paris: Charles Gosselin, 1829, 4 vols. in 2 (trans. by A.J.B. Defauconpret as *L'Anglo-irlandais du XIXe siècle. Roman historique irlandais*, par M. Banim; Collection de Romans Historiques sur l'Irlande). SOURCE Rafroidi, ii, p. 359. LOCATION Dt (1829 edn), InND Loeber coll.

+ New York: Garland, 1978, 3 vols. (introd. by R.L. Wolff). LOCATION Dt, D.

Washington (DC): Woodstock, 1997. LOCATION InND.

COMMENTARY A satire on divisions between Irish social classes, the opening scenes are set in London among the Anglo-Irish who have been living there, almost permanently, since the Act of Union (1801). They discuss the perilous state of Ireland with its unruly peasants, secret societies and agrarian unrest. The hero, Gerald (not George as in ODNB) Blount, son of the Irish peer Lord Glangore, shares the belief of his class that all things English are automatically superior to all things Irish. Some time later he is obliged to go to Ireland and begins to contrast what he has heard about the country all his life with what he sees with his own eyes. He visits Dublin where he meets an old London friend, Captain Flood, now of the Dragoons, who reveals the authorities' preparations for revolt by the Irish. Gerald is won over to the Irish cause and falls in love with an Irishwoman. The character of 'The Secretary' is based on John Wilson Croker§ [Corbett, pp 13–15; ODNB; Wolff introd. to *The Boyne water*, p. xxxii].

B22   *The denounced* [anon.] (dedicated to Arthur, duke of Wellington).

+ London: Henry Colburn & Richard Bentley, 1830, 3 vols. SOURCE Brown, 149 (mistakenly mentions Duffy, [1826] edn); Sadleir, 142; Wolff, 227; NSTC; Garside 2, 1830:21. LOCATION Grail, Corvey CME 3–628–47934–7, Ireland related fiction, D, L, NUC.

+ New York: Printed by J. & J. Harper, 1830, 2 vols. SOURCE Wolff, 227a; NSTC. LOCATION Dt, DCL, NUC, InND Loeber coll.

+ New York: Garland, 1979, 3 vols. (introd. by R.L. Wolff). LOCATION Dt, D, MH.

COMMENTARY By John Banim (but John and Michael Banim according to Garside 2). Contents: 'The last baron of Crana', 'The conformists'. Both stories are set in the period after the Treaty of Limerick and describe the struggles of two Catholic families to practice their religion while being intimidated by hostile Protestants [Brown; Garside 2].

B23   *The smuggler; a tale* [anon.].

+ London: Henry Colburn & Richard Bentley, 1831, 3 vols. SOURCE Rafroidi, ii, p. 51; Sadleir, 149; Wolff, 232; Garside 2, 1831:33. LOCATION Corvey 3–628–47933–9, L, DCL, NUC, InND Loeber coll.

+ London: Richard Bentley; Dublin: Cumming; Edinburgh: Bell & Bradfute; Paris: Galignani, 1833 (ill. Pickering, Greatbatch; Standard Novels, vol. 29). SOURCE NSTC. LOCATION Grail, D, MH, InND Loeber coll.

London: Ward & Lock, 1856 (as *The smuggler*; Standard Novels). SOURCE Topp 2, p. 62.

New York: J.J. Harper, 1832, 2 vols. (Library of Select Novels). SOURCE Topp 2, p. 11; NSTC. LOCATION NUC, MH.

COMMENTARY By John Banim. Only novel by JB which was set in England. Michael Mutford, a Yorkshire man who lost his estate through legal wrangling, is driven to crime and exile in order to support his family [OCIL, p. 529].

B24   *The bit o' writin' and other tales* (by 'the O'Hara family').
+ London: Saunders & Otley, 1838, 3 vols. (with introductory notes by M. Banim). SOURCE Rafroidi, ii, p. 53; Wolff, 224; NSTC. LOCATION Grail (1865 edn), D (1865 edn), Dt, L, InND Loeber coll.

COMMENTARY *London 1838 edn* By John and Michael Banim. Contents 'The bit o' writin'', 'The Irish Lord Lieutenant and his double', 'The family of the cold feet', 'The harehound and the witch', 'The soldier's billet', 'A peasant girl's love', 'The hall of the castle' (first published in the *Keepsake*, London, 1830), 'The half-brothers' (first published in the *Keepsake*, London, 1829), 'Twice lost, but saved' (first published in the *Keepsake*, London, 1831), 'The faithful servant' (first published in the *Keepsake*, London, 1830), 'The Roman merchant' (first published in the *Amulet*, London, 1831), 'Ill got, ill gone', 'The church-yard watch' (first published in *Friendship's Offering*, London, 1832), 'The last of the storm' (first published in the *Literary Souvenir*, London, 1830), 'The rival dreamers' (first published in *The Gem*, London, 1829), 'The substitute' (first published in *Friendship's Offering*, London, 1832), 'The "White Bristol"' (first published in *Friendship's Offering*, London, 1830), 'The stolen sheep' (first published in *Friendship's Offering*, London, 1831; also published in the *Imperial*, London, 1839), 'The publican's dream' (first published in *Friendship's Offering*, London, 1829) 'The ace of clubs' [Rafroidi, ii, p. 53; RL; Wolff, Introduction to *The Boyne water*, p. lii].
    + Philadelphia: E.L. Carey & A. Hart, 1838, 2 vols. SOURCE Sadleir, 224b; NSTC. LOCATION NUC, DCL, InND Loeber coll. COMMENTARY *Philadelphia edn* Two binding types, one plain boards, the other marble paper boards [RL].
    + Dublin: M.H. Gill & Son, 1886 (*The bit o' writin' and The ace of clubs*, by Michael Banim [*sic*]; The O'Connell Press Popular Library). LOCATION D, InND Loeber coll.
    New York: Garland, 1979, 3 vols. (introd. by R.L. Wolff). SOURCE COPAC. LOCATION Dt, L.

B25   *Father Connell* (by 'the O'Hara family').
+ London: T.C. Newby & T. & W. Boone, 1842, 3 vols. SOURCE Rafroidi, ii, p. 53; Sadleir, 143; Wolff, 228; DNB. LOCATION Grail, D, Dt, L, NUC.
+ Dublin: O'Byrne & Co., 1858 (as *Father Connell. A tale*; new edn, introd. and notes by the author; ill. Swain). SOURCE DPL, InND Loeber coll.
New York: Wilson & Co., [1842], 3 vols. (as *Father Connell. A romance of Ireland*). SOURCE NSTC. LOCATION DCL.

COMMENTARY By John and Michael Banim (but appeared in the year of JB's death, when he had been very ill for some time). Set in Kilkenny, it features Fr Connell, an Irish country priest who tries to guide and protect his people, particularly Neddy Fennell, an orphan he has taken under his protection. To save his protégé from an unjust sentence, Fr Connell goes to the viceroy but dies at his feet. The character of Fr Connell is based on the person of Fr Richard O'Donnell, Catholic dean of Ossory, and the novel paints a realistic and grim picture of cabin life and poverty in pre-Famine Ireland [Brown; P.J. Murray, *The life of John Banim* (New York, 1869), p. 297; ODNB].

B26   *Tales by the O'Hara family. Part III. Containing John Doe, and Peter of the Castle.*

+ Belfast: Simms & M'Intyre; London: W.S. Orr & Co., 1846 (The Parlour Novelist, vol. 11). SOURCE Sadleir, ii, p. 149. LOCATION DPL, NUC.

Paris: Gosselin, 1829, 2 vols. (trans. by A.J.B. Defauconpret as *Padhré na-moulh, ou le mendiant des ruines. Roman irlandais*). SOURCE Rafroidi, ii, p. 360; NSTC. LOCATION Dt, L.

COMMENTARY Posthumous republication from the *Tales by the O'Hara family*, first and second series. Contents: 'John Doe' and 'Peter of the Castle' [RL].

B27 *The Peep o' Day; or, John Doe, and The last baron of Crana* (by 'the O'Hara family').

Boston: Patrick Donahoe, [1866]. LOCATION NUC.

COMMENTARY Contents: 'The Peep o' Day; or, John Doe' (originally published in the first series of *Tales by the O'Hara family*, London, 1825, 3 vols.), 'The last baron of Crana' (first appeared in *The denounced*, London, 1830, 3 vols.) [RL].

COLLECTED WORKS

B28 [*Works by the Banim brothers*].

+ Dublin, London: James Duffy, 1865–66, 12 vols. (new edn, each with introd. and notes by Michael Banim§). LOCATION InND Loeber coll. (selection of the various binding types).

COMMENTARY Unnumbered and untitled series advertised as *Duffy's National edition of the works of the Brothers Banim* ('by the O'Hara family'). Issued in at least four binding types: (a) printed boards in red, black and green, with shamrocks. The 1865 edn carries the name Mellish on the board; the later undated edns do not (seen at C; see Plate 6); (b) plain cloth with text on spine; (c) cloth with decorative gold stamped spine, gold stamped cover with shamrock, central harp surrounded by shamrocks, and gold leafed, see Plate 7; (d) leather spine and corners; spine impressed with BANIM [RL].

B29 *Banim's works.*

+ New York, Montreal, Boston (later New York, Montreal): D. & J. Sadlier & Co., 1866, 1869, 1872, 1881, [c.1888], [10 vols] (Sadleir Household Library; new edn, with introd. and notes by Michael Banim). LOCATION DCU, NUC, InND Loeber coll. (incomplete).

COMMENTARY These collected works stayed in print for about twenty years. Series title on spine, volumes not numbered; numbering as advertised by D. & J. Sadlier in T.N. Burke, *Ireland's case stated* (New York, 1873); three binding variants: (a) blind stamped cloth with shamrock on cover, and spine stamped in gold with shamrock, earliest edn seen is 1866, but also 1869; (b) leather spines with marbled boards, earliest edn seen is 1869 and n.d.; (c) blind stamped cloth with harp on cover, and spine stamped in gold with shamrock and harp, n.d. The series in cloth and half morocco were sold in 1875 at $20, and in half calf at $25. Note that *The Anglo-Irish* appeared in this series as *Lord Glangore; or, the Anglo-Irish* [DCU, Catholic Americana files; RL; Advertised in M.J. Hoffman, *The orphan sisters* (New York, 1875)].

B30 [*Works of the Banim brothers*].

New York: P.J. Kenedy, [1895], 10 vols. (new edn). SOURCE Brown, p. 22. LOCATION InND (one vol.).

COMMENTARY Unnumbered and untitled series. Two binding types: (a) crushed leather at $7 for the series; (b) half calf, gilt edges at $20 for the series. This probably is a reissue of the collected works first published by D. & J. Sadlier. The Kenedy series of the brothers Banim's works was advertised as part of 'Kenedy's Gilt-top Series of Irish Novelists', and included the works of William Carleton§, Gerald Griffin§, and Samuel Lover§, in total 35 uniformly bound volumes, which was priced at $22 [Broadsheet advertised P.J. Kenedy, New York, [1895]; RL].

BANIM, Michael, pseud. 'the O'Hara family', b. Kilkenny 1796, d. Booterstown (Co. Dublin) 1874. Novelist and merchant, he was the son of Michael Banim, a Catholic shop-keeper and farmer, and Joannah or Judith Carroll, and brother of John Banim§. MB was edu-cated first in Kilkenny and then studied for the Bar, but business difficulties suffered by his father obliged him to give up his studies and take over the family business, which he restored to its former prosperity. With his brother, John Banim§, he collaborated in researching and writing the novels and stories published under their joint pseud. Consequently, some of MB's works are listed under John Banim§. He also produced works of fiction on his own. MB seems to have gathered much material for his stories first-hand, especially in 1825 when he travelled in the south of Ireland and corresponded with the folklorist Patrick Kennedy§. He later inter-viewed leaders of the Whitefeet, a rural protest movement committed to abolishing church tithes. *The bit o' writing*, which appeared in 1838 and contained sketches by both brothers and a selection of John's periodical writing, made money for both brothers. In 1840 he married Catherine O'Dwyer of Tipperary. Shortly after this, he lost his fortune through the failure of a merchant. He became postmaster in Kilkenny in 1852, which position he resigned in 1873 because of failing health. He was elected member of the Kilkenny Archaeological Society in 1850. In 1865 and 1866 when the Dublin publisher Duffy reissued many of the volumes of the Banim brothers, MB wrote additional comments for each volume. He survived his brother John by over thirty years and he assisted Patrick Murray in writing John Banim's§ biography, which was published in 1857 and which went into ten edns in both London and Dublin. He may have contributed the story 'The furze-cutters' to the *Dublin Journal* (1842). He became ill in 1873 and retired to Booterstown (Co. Dublin), where he died in the next year. A por-trait of MB is mentioned by Laffan & Rooney. SOURCE Allibone Suppl., i, p. 87; Boyle, pp 11–12; Brady, p. 6; DLB, clviii, clix; British Fiction (Update 4); Hogan, pp 91–3; Hogan 2, pp 115–17; W. Laffan & B. Rooney, '"One of our brilliant ornaments": the death and life of Thomas Foster' in *Irish Architectural and Decorative Studies*, 7 (2004), p. 221; McKenna, pp 95–8; NCBEL 4, pp 883–5; OCIL, p. 30; ODNB; RIA/DIB; RL; Sutherland, p. 40 [under John Banim]; Wolff, i, pp 44–8.

B31 *The hellfire club* (by Michael Banim).

  COMMENTARY Manuscript fragment of a novel; edited and published by B. Escarbelt in *Études Irlandaises*, new series 1, 1976, pp 51–61 [Rafroidi, ii, p. 52].

B32 *The croppy. A tale of the Irish rebellion of 1798* [anon.] (dedicated to Sheffield Grace).

  + London: Henry Colburn, 1828, 3 vols. SOURCE Rafroidi, ii, p. 52; British Fiction; Garside, 1828:17; Sadleir, 140; Wolff, 226. LOCATION Grail, Corvey CME 3–628–47353, Ireland related fiction, D, Dt, L, MchB, NUC.

  London: Henry Colburn & R. Bentley; Edinburgh: Bell & Bradfute; Dublin: John Cumming, 1834, 3 vols. (as *The croppy*; Colburn's Irish National Tales Nos. 7–9). SOURCE Sadleir 3736c(ii); Rowan cat. 45/330; COPAC. LOCATION Univ. of Sheffield.

  Paris: Gosselin, 1832, 4 vols. (trans. by A.J.B. Lefauconpret as *Les croppys, épisode de l'histoire de la rébellion d'Irlande en 1798*). SOURCE Rafroidi, ii, p. 360; NSTC. LOCATION L.

  Philadelphia: E.L. Carey & A. Hart, 1839. SOURCE Wolff, 226a. LOCATION NUC.

  + New York: Garland, 1978, 3 vols. (introd. by R.L. Wolff). SOURCE COPAC. LOCATION Dt, D.

COMMENTARY Set in Co. Wexford during the 1798 rebellion. Deals with some of the outrages by which people were driven to revolt. Events at Enniscorthy, Wexford, and New Ross form the main part of the novel. Describes cruelties on both sides [Brown; Wolff introd., p. 17; British Fiction (Update 4)].

B33 *The ghost hunter and his family* (by 'the O'Hara family').
+ London: Smith, Elder & Co., 1833 (The Library of Romance, No. 1; preface by Leitch Ritchie). SOURCE Sadleir, 144; ii, p. 171; Wolff, 229; Rafroidi, ii, p. 52 (mistakenly mentions London, 1835 as first edn); Garside 2, 1833:9. LOCATION Grail, D, L, DLC, InND Loeber coll.
+ London, Belfast: Simms & M'Intyre, 1852 (by John Banim [*sic*, he had died in 1842]; The Parlour Library, No. 70). SOURCE Sadleir, ii, p. 154; NSTC. LOCATION Dt, L, InND Loeber coll.
+ London, New York: George Routledge & Sons, [1870] (as *Joe Wilson's ghost*; Railway Library, No. 541). SOURCE Topp 1, p. 204; NSTC. LOCATION Dt, L, InND Loeber coll. (Warne edn, 1888; see Plate 8).
Paris: Levasseur, 1833, 2 vols. (trans. by A. Pichard as *Le chasseur de spectres et sa famille*). SOURCE Rafroidi, ii, p. 360; NSTC. LOCATION L, BNF.
+ Philadelphia: Carey, Lea & Blanchard, 1833 (The Library of Romance; preface by Leitch Ritchie). SOURCE Kaser, 339; NSTC. LOCATION DCL, NUC, InND Loeber coll.
New York: D. & J. Sadlier, 1833. SOURCE Garside 2, 1833:9; OCLC. LOCATION D.
+ New York: Garland, 1979 (introd. by R.L. Wolff). LOCATION D.
COMMENTARY Serialized in the *Novelist's Magazine* (Philadelphia, 1833). Describes Irish family life near Kilkenny in the eighteenth century. It apparently portrays the authors' own grandparents, uncle and aunt [Wolff introd., p. 18; Topp 4, p. 197].

B34 *The mayor of Wind-gap and Canvassing* (by 'the O'Hara family' [see commentary below]).
+ London: Saunders & Otley, 1835, 3 vols. SOURCE Sadleir, 147; Wolff, 230; Garside 2, 1835:22. LOCATION DPL, L, NUC.
+ Brussels: Ad Wahlen; Frankfort O/M: Fred. Wilmans, 1835, 2 vols. in 1 (Wahlen's Modern British Authors). LOCATION DPL, InND Loeber coll.
Paris: A. & W. Galignani & Co., 1835. SOURCE de Búrca cat. 28/30; COPAC. LOCATION L.
Paris: Baudry, 1835 (Baudry's European Library). SOURCE Maggs cat. 1162/26; NSTC. LOCATION L, NUC.
+ New York: Harper & Bros, 1835 (as *The Mayor of Wind-Gap*). SOURCE NSTC. LOCATION NUC, MH, InND Loeber coll.
+ Philadelphia: Carey, Lea & Blanchard, 1835, 2 vols. in 1 (as *The Mayor of Wind-Gap*). SOURCE Kaser, 473. LOCATION PPAt, NUC, InND Loeber coll.
+ New York: Garland, 1979, 3 vols. (introd. by R.L. Wolff). LOCATION Dt, D.
COMMENTARY 'Mayor of Windgap' (Set in Kilkenny in 1779, where John Banim§ lived at Windgap Cottage. A story of jealousy, revenge and murder involving a stolen inheritance. An ex-pirate is the mysterious villain. The unofficial mayor of Windgap brings about a reconciliation among the feuding members of the family); 'Canvassing' (by Harriet Letitia Martin§; describes details of electioneering and match-making) [Brown; Wolff introd., p. 18; OCIL, p. 361].

B35 *The town of the cascades* (by Michael Banim, survivor of 'the O'Hara family').
+ London: Chapman & Hall, 1864, 2 vols. SOURCE Rafroidi, ii, p. 52; Sadleir, 152; Wolff, 235; NSTC. LOCATION Grail, D, Dt, L, NUC.
+ London: Chapman & Hall, 1866 (as *Irish tales*). SOURCE NSTC. LOCATION O.
COMMENTARY Set in a coastal town in Co. Clare. The story revolves around a tragedy brought on by drink. Written in support of Fr Mathew's temperance movement [Brown; OCIL, p. 566].

B36 *Clough Fionn; or, the stone of destiny* (by 'the O'Hara family').
New York, Boston, Montreal: D. & J. Sadlier & Co., 1869. SOURCE DCU, Catholic Americana files. LOCATION Grail (n.d. edn), D (n.d. edn), NUC.

'Banna-Borka'

COMMENTARY First appeared in the *Dublin University Magazine* (Aug. to Dec., 1852). Apparently not published in an English or Irish edn [Rafroidi, ii, p. 52; RL].

'BANNA-BORKA', pseud. See **FITZPATRICK, Thomas**.

BANNAC, Adolphus, fl. 1756. ESTC states that this novel is sometimes attributed to Adolphus Bannac, who also wrote *The apparition; or, female cavalier* (London, [1756], 3 vols.) and, possibly *The life and surprizing adventures of Crusoe Richard Davis* (London, [1756], 2 vols.). SOURCE ESTC n3936.

B37　*The history of my own life. Being an account of the severest trials imposed by an implacable father, upon the most affectionate pair that ever entered the marriage-state* [anon.].

　　London: F. Noble & J. Noble, 1756, 2 vols. SOURCE Raven, 293. LOCATION L.

　　+ Dublin: Benjamin Gunne, 1757. LOCATION D.

　　Dublin: Printed for Richard Watts, 1760 (*As The history of Biddy Farmer, or, memoirs of my own life. Interspersed with a variety of characters, both in high and low life*). SOURCE ESTC n3936. LOCATION CtY.

COMMENTARY The marital adventures and misadventures of Biddy Farmer, set mostly in England but a significant part in Dublin, where, eventually, Biddy is accused of bigamy and is imprisoned. Her first husband, Lord G—r—d, had purchased an Irish earldom to advance his family. He disappears, but re-emerges at the end of the story [RL].

BARBOUR, Margaret Fraser, fl. 1850s. Scottish writer of works for juveniles and religious tracts. SOURCE Allibone Suppl., i, p. 90; BLC; NCBEL 4, p. 1745; NSTC.

B38　*The Irish orphan in a Scottish home* [anon.] (dedicated to 'The young of the Scottish churches').

　　+ London, Edinburgh, New York: T. Nelson & Sons, 1866. SOURCE Brown, 158; NCBEL 4, p. 1745; NSTC. LOCATION L.

　　London: James Nisbet & Co., 1872 (enlarged edn). LOCATION L.

COMMENTARY This is a sequel to *The way home* (Edinburgh, 1856). Set in Edinburgh, it is a Protestant religious tract in story form with chapters on 'The orphan's funeral', 'The Irish nurse', 'The orphan's home' [Brown; CM; RL].

BARDAN, Patrick, b. Co. Westmeath 1855?, d. Co. Westmeath? 1936. Poet, folklorist and antiquarian, PB was a native of Kneadsbridge, Killucan (Co. Westmeath), where he attended the local National School. Known locally as 'the poet', he published widely in magazines (e.g., the *Dublin Journal*, 1887) and in newspapers, but many of his writings have been destroyed. He spent some time in New York towards the end of the nineteenth century. He was buried at Coralstown cemetery, near Mullingar. SOURCE Irish pseudonyms; RIA/DIB; RL; Westmeath, pp 4–5.

B39　*The dead-watchers, and other folk-lore tales of Westmeath* (by Patrick Bardan).

　　+ Mullingar: Printed at the Westmeath Guardian Office, 1891. SOURCE Brown, 159. LOCATION D, NUC.

COMMENTARY Tales set in Co. Westmeath. Contents: 'The dead-watchers; a weird tale of Westmeath', 'The ghost's warning', 'The haunted miller, a tale of St. Martin's night', 'Oscar and Maura. A tradition of St. John's eve', 'Legend of the black pig', 'The weird woman of Dernaveagh', 'The hag of the ivy tree', 'The white lady', 'The churchyard bride', followed by an appendix [ML].

BARDIN, Revd Charles Peter, b. Dublin 1788, d. 1842. Church of Ireland clergyman, writer and editor, CPB was the son of Peter Bardin, a revenue officer. He was admitted to TCD in 1807 where he obtained his BA in 1817, his MA a year later, and a DD in 1828. He was canon of St Mark's (Dublin,1818–20), St Mary's (Dublin, 1824), Dundalk (Co. Louth, 1827–29), and rector of Derryloran (Co. Tyrone, 1820–41). He was an active member of the Association for Discountenancing Vice. While working in Dublin he became literary assistant to the Society for the Education of the Poor of Ireland, known as the Kildare Place Society, a position he held from 1818 to 1827, during which time most of its books were produced (our attributed books were published from 1822 to 1834). These popular books, intended to be non-sectarian, covering natural history, the arts and travel, were mainly written, rewritten, abridged or edited by CPB under strict superintendence of the Society's publication committee. In 1824 he testified to the commissioners inspecting the state of education in Ireland that almost 1,000,000 copies were in circulation. When he was appointed a curate in Dundalk in 1827, he gave up his position with the Society but continued to supply copy, his work appearing anonymously. He is especially known for having produced a series of travel books on different parts of the world, but it cannot be excluded that other authors were involved as well. As a rule, the Society's travel books appear based on original works (but usually unattributed), and are included here because they were re-formatted as stories about travellers. CPB married Julia Helen Hodgkinson in 1820 and they had six children. The following volumes are attributed to CPB as he is the most likely candidate and names of other, possible authors have not yet emerged. He also published several sermons and an essay, *The importance of religious education* (Dublin, 1840). Strickland notes CPB's bust by Thomas Kirk. SOURCE Adams, pp 101–2; B & S, p. 39; W.E.C. Fleming, *Armagh clergy 1800–2000* (n.l., 2001), pp 340–1 (information in this source is somewhat in variance with Leslie & Wallace, see below); Hislop, pp 207–13; Leslie & Wallace, pp 372–3; H.K. Moore, *An un-written chapter in the history of education* (London, 1904), p. 256–8; NUC; RIA/DIB; Strickland, i, p. 588.

B40　*Travels in Southern Asia: compiled from the most authentic and recent sources* [anon.].
　　　Dublin: Printed by C. Bentham [for the Kildare Place Society], 1822 (ill.). SOURCE Hislop, p. 1049; COPAC. LOCATION PC, C.

B41　*Travels in South America* [anon.].
　　　+ Dublin: Printed by C. Bentham [for the Kildare Place Society], 1822 (ill.). LOCATION D.
　　　COMMENTARY Narrative account, written for juveniles [RL].

B42　*Travels in South-Eastern Asia: compiled from the most authentic and recent sources* [anon.].
　　　+ Dublin: Printed by J. Jones [for the Kildare Place Society], 1823 (ill.). SOURCE Bradshaw, 2472; Hislop, p. 1049. LOCATION D (1832 edn), C.
　　　COMMENTARY Narrative account, written for juveniles [RL].

B43　*Travels in South-Western Asia* [anon.].
　　　+ Dublin: Printed by J. Jones [for the Kildare Place Society], 1823 (ill.). SOURCE Bradshaw, 2473; Hislop, p. 1049. LOCATION D (1832 edn), PC, C.
　　　COMMENTARY Narrative account, written for juveniles [RL].

B44　*Travels in Northern Asia, compiled from authentic sources* [anon.].
　　　Dublin: Printed by C. Bentham [for the Kildare Place Society], 1823 (ill.). SOURCE Bradshaw, 3324; Hislop, p. 1048. LOCATION D (1832 edn), C.
　　　COMMENTARY Narrative account, written for juveniles. Features the travellers William Walsh, an Irishman, and Capt. Blisset, RN [RL].

B45　*Travels in North America* [anon.].

+ Dublin: Printed by Brett Smith [for the Kildare Place Society], 1824 (ill.). LOCATION D.

COMMENTARY Narrative account, written for juveniles [RL].

B46   *Travels in Africa* [anon.].
Dublin: Printed by A. O'Neil [for the Kildare Place Society], 1824 (ill.). SOURCE COPAC. LOCATION PC, L, C.
London: Rivington & Society for Propagating Christian Knowledge, 1831. LOCATION PC.
COMMENTARY Note that O'Neil also published Mungo Park's *Travels in the Interior of Africa* in 1820 [RL].

B47   *A voyage through the islands of the Pacific Ocean: compiled from the most authentic and recent authorities* [anon.].
Dublin: Printed by Bentham & Gardiner [for the Kildare Place Society], 1824 (ill.). LOCATION D (1831 edn).

B48   *Voyages through the Northern Pacific Ocean, Indian Ocean, and Chinese Sea* [anon.].
+ Dublin: Printed by Bentham & Hardy [for the Kildare Place Society], 1825. SOURCE Hislop, p. 1049. LOCATION D.

B49   *Arctic voyages: being an account of discoveries in the North Polar Seas, in the years 1818, 1819, & 1820. With an account of the Esquimaux people. Compiled from the most authentic sources* [anon.].
Dublin: P.D. Hardy [for the Kildare Place Society], [1825]. SOURCE Osborne, p. 798 ([1825] edn. LOCATION D (1831 edn), L, CaOTP.
London: C.J.G. & F. Rivington, 1831. LOCATION L.

COMMENTARY Fiction for juveniles. William and Patrick Jones of Waterford learn of Parry's three voyages to the polar regions from Captain Mackay, who supposedly accompanied him. The author of *Arctic voyages* explains in the introd. that, to make the text more attractive for the young, 'the events which it relates are faithfully extracted from the works of those celebrated men, who have recently so much extended our knowledge of the geography and inhabitants of North America, and the North Polar Regions'. The main character allegedly accompanied Edward Parry on his Arctic explorations in 1818, 1819 and 1820. However, the identity of this Capt. Mackay has not been established since his name is not evident from known works of the period [Osborne; A. Parry, *Parry of the Arctica. The life story of Admiral Sir Edward Parry* (London, 1963)].

B50   *Travels in England and Wales, compiled from the most authentic and recent authorities* [anon.].
+ Dublin: Printed by R. Napper [for the Kildare Place Society], 1825 (ill. Clayton). SOURCE Hislop, p. 1049. LOCATION D (1832 ed), InND Loeber coll.
COMMENTARY Narrative account, written for juveniles [RL].

B51   *Travels in Sweden, Denmark, and Norway* [anon.].
+ Dublin: Printed by Bentham & Hardy [for the Kildare Place Society], 1826 (ill.). SOURCE Bradshaw, 3340; Hislop, p. 1050. LOCATION D, C.
COMMENTARY Narrative account, written for juveniles [RL].

B52   *Travels in European Russia* [anon.].
Dublin: Bentham & Hardy, 1826. SOURCE Bradshaw, 3339; Hislop, p. 1049. LOCATION PC, L (destroyed), C.
COMMENTARY Narrative account, written for juveniles [RL].

B53   *Travels in Spain and Portugal* [anon.].
+ Dublin: Printed by Thomas I. White [for the Kildare Place Society], 1828 (ill.). SOURCE Bradshaw, 3587; Hislop, p. 1049. LOCATION D, C.
COMMENTARY Narrative account, written for juveniles [RL].

B54   *Travels in Southern Italy. Compiled from the most recent authorities* [anon.].
+ Dublin: Printed by Thomas I. White [for the Kildare Place Society], 1830 (ill.).
SOURCE Bradshaw, 3599; OCLC; Hislop, p. 1049. LOCATION D, C.
COMMENTARY Narrative account, written for juveniles [RL].

B55   *Travels in Switzerland. Compiled from the most recent authorities* [anon.].
+ Dublin: Printed by P.D. Hardy [for the Kildare Place Society], 1830 (ill.). SOURCE
Bradshaw, 3371; Hislop, p. 1050. LOCATION D, C.
COMMENTARY Narrative account, written for juveniles [RL].

B56   *Arctic travels; or, an account of the several land expeditions to determine the geog-*
raphy of the Northern part of the American Continent [anon.].
+ Dublin: Printed by T.I. White [for the Kildare Place Society], 1830 (ill.). SOURCE
Emerald Isle cat. 55/100; Bradshaw, 3592; Hislop, p. 1048; OCLC. LOCATION D, DLC
([1830] edn).
COMMENTARY Written for juveniles, a sequel to *Arctic voyages* (Dublin, [1825]) consisting of
the narrative of Sir John Franklin's search for the north-west passage. The preface suggests
that the author was a Captain Mackay, who narrated the account for the children of a Mr
Jones of Waterford [Emerald Isle cat. 55/100; Osborne, p. 798; OCLC].

B57   *The Dublin reading book* [anon.].
+ Dublin: P.D. Hardy [for the Kildare Place Society], 1830 (ill.). SOURCE Emerald
Isle cat. 79/380. LOCATION L (1839 edn, 1840 edn).
COMMENTARY Contains a selection of short narrative pieces, poetry, and natural his-
tory [RL].

B58   *Voyages in the Arctic Seas, from 1821 to 1825, for the discovery of a North-West*
Passage to the Pacific Ocean [anon.].
+ Dublin: Printed by R. Napper, 1830 [for the Kildare Place Society] (ill.). LOCATION D.

B59   *Travels in Northern Italy; compiled from the most recent authorities* [anon.].
+ Dublin: Printed by Thomas I. White [for the Kildare Place Society], 1831 (ill.).
SOURCE Hislop, p. 1049. LOCATION D.
COMMENTARY Narrative account, written for juveniles [RL].

B60   *Travels in Northern France* [anon.].
+ Dublin: Printed by R. Webb [for the Kildare Place Society], 1832. SOURCE Bradshaw,
3637. LOCATION D (incomplete), PC, C.
COMMENTARY Narrative account, written for juveniles [RL].

B61   *Travels in Southern France; compiled from the most authentic sources* [anon.].
+ Dublin: Printed by W. Folds [for the Kildare Place Society], 1832 (ill.). SOURCE
Bradshaw, 1832; Hislop, p. 1049. LOCATION D, C.
COMMENTARY Narrative account, written for juveniles [RL].

B62   *Travels in European Turkey. Compiled from the best authorities* [anon.].
+ Dublin: P. Dixon Hardy [for the Kildare Place Society], 1833 (ill.). SOURCES Hislop,
p. 1049. LOCATION D.
COMMENTARY Narrative account, written for juveniles. The title page does not mention that Hardy printed this volume, as was customary in these publications [RL].

B63   *Travels in Greece. Compiled from the most authentic accounts* [anon.].
+ Dublin: Printed by P.D. Hardy [for the Kildare Place Society], 1834 (ill.). SOURCE
Bradshaw, 3376; Hislop, p. 1049. LOCATION D, C.
COMMENTARY Narrative account, written for juveniles [RL].

BARKER, Mary, fl. 1798. Novelist. Given that there were many Irish subscribers to the following volume, it is likely that MB was Irish with connections in Dublin and Newry. SOURCE
COPAC; RL.

B64   *A Welsh story* [anon.] (dedicated to the duchess of York).
        + London: Hookham & Carpenter, 1798, 3 vols. (subscribers' list). SOURCE Raven 2,
        1798:15; Garside (2003); COPAC. LOCATION L.
COMMENTARY A sentimental domestic novel in a country setting, of which 750 copies were
printed at a cost of about £120 and a loss to the author of some £80. Subscribers' list shows
residents of London, Bath, the Midlands, Wales, Dublin, several in Newry, a Mrs Leslie of
Donagh[a]dee (Co. Down), a Lady Morgan (now deceased), Miss [Maria] Edgeworth§, and
the author Mrs Hannah More [Raven 2; Garside (2003); ML].

BARKER, M.H. See **BARKER, Matthew Henry.**

BARKER, Matthew Henry (also known as **M.H. Barker**), pseuds '**The old sailor**' and '**An
old sailor**', b. Deptford (London) 1790, d. 1846. English sailor, editor and author of popular nautical novels, MHB joined a ship of the East India Company while still a boy, later serving in the Royal Navy and in the merchant marine. He saw action during the Napoleonic Wars
and spent some time as a prisoner. After retiring in 1825 he wrote to satisfy popular demand
for nautical novels. He was naval editor of the *United Service Gazette* (London) and contributed
to various periodicals, including *Bentley's Miscellany* (London), and the *Dublin and London
Magazine* (London, 1825). Several of his novels, some of which feature Irish characters, were
illustrated by his friend George Cruikshank. SOURCE BLC; ODNB; Sutherland, p. 44.
B65   *Greenwich Hospital, a series of naval sketches descriptive of the life a man-of-war's
       man* (by 'An old sailor').
        + London: James Robins & Co.; Dublin: Joseph Robins Jnr & Co., 1826 (ill. George
        Cruikshank). LOCATION D.
        COMMENTARY Contains some Irish characters [RL].
B66   *Hamilton King, or, the smuggler and the dwarf* (by 'The old sailor'; dedicated to G.
       Cruikshank).
        + London: Richard Bentley, 1839, 3 vols. LOCATION L.
        + Calcutta: William Rushton & Co., 1840. LOCATION InND Loeber coll.
COMMENTARY Maritime story set in the eighteenth century containing adventures of smug-
glers and pirates, many of whom are Irish. The action ranges from Bantry in Ireland, to France,
England and the West Indies and is woven around the fate of two presumed orphans, who
are in actuality the son and daughter of the heir of The O'Connor. They are persecuted by
their uncle, a dwarf, who wishes them dead so that he can claim the title of The O'Connor.
Eventually his plot unravels and the young man, known in the story as Arthur King, is installed
as The O'Connor heir [ML].
B67   *Jem Bunt* (by 'The old sailor').
        London: How & Parsons, [1841] (ill. R. Cruikshank and others). LOCATION L.
        + London: Henry Lea, n.d. (as *Jem Bunt: A tale of the land and the ocean*). LOCATION
        InND Loeber coll.
COMMENTARY Set mainly in London. Story of an abandoned child, Jem Bunt, who is
befriended by an Irish labourer. For a while Jem is employed as a chimney-sweep. Several sea
adventures are related. Eventually it turns out that Jem is of noble birth [ML].
B68   *The old sailor's jolly boat: laden with tales, yarns, scraps, fragments, etc., etc. to
       please all hands; pulled by wit, fun, humour, and pathos* (by M.H. Barker).
        London: W. Strange, 1844. LOCATION L (1855 edn), InND.
        COMMENTARY Contains short stories, one of which, 'Anne of Munster', has Irish con-
        tent and is 100pp. [ML].

BARLOW, Jane, b. Clontarf (Dublin) 1857, d. Bray (Co. Wicklow) 1917. Short story writer, novelist and poet, JB was the elder daughter of Revd James Barlow, history professor and later vice-provost of TCD (for whom see RIA/DIB), and his wife and niece Mary Louisa Barlow of Clontarf. JB was very shy and was educated at home. She lived most of her life at Raheny (Co. Dublin), never marrying. Her early poetry was published by the *Dublin University Magazine* and is collected in *Bogland studies* (London, 1892), and *The end of Elfintown* (London, 1894). She had great sympathy for the nationalist cause, contributed to *Hibernia* (Dublin), and in many of her novels was critical of Irish landowners. She was a friend of Katharine Tynan§ and of William Butler Yeats§, who included her *Irish idylls* (London, 1892) in his list of 'Best Irish Books'. A member of the National Literary Society, she was the first woman to be awarded an honorary DLitt from Dublin University. JB published 19 titles of fiction, consisting mainly of collected stories, mostly set in Ireland and many of Irish peasant life, on which her fame mainly rests. Collections of her letters can be found in the LOCATION *register of twentieth-century English literary manuscripts* (Boston, 1988, p. 47), the NLI (MSS 8,186–8, 10,751), and ODNB. Her portrait was painted by the Irish artist Sarah Purser (Hugh Lane Municipal Gallery of Art, Dublin), who also illustrated some of her stories. SOURCE Blain, p. 62; Boyle, p. 12; Brady, p. 7; Brown, pp 25–6; Colman, pp 35–7; EF, p. 18; Hogan 2, pp 124–5; IBL, 8 (June–July 1917), pp 141–2; Irish pseudonyms; NCBEL 4, pp 701–2; OCIL, p. 34; ODNB; O'Donoghue, p. 18; RIA/DIB; Ryan, p. 146; Sutherland, p. 44; K. Tynan, *The middle years* (London, 1916), p. 74.

B69   *Irish idylls* (by Jane Barlow).
+ London: Hodder & Stoughton, 1892. SOURCE Hogan, p. 95; Wolff, 301 (1893 edn). LOCATION D, DPL (1895 edn), L, NUC.
+ Leipzig: Heinemann & Balestier, 1893. SOURCE Maggs cat. 1162/30. LOCATION D, NUC.
+ New York: Dodd, Mead & Co., 1893. SOURCE NYPL. LOCATION D, NUC, InND Loeber coll. (1897 and 1898 edns).
+ London: Sphere Books, 1984. LOCATION D.
COMMENTARY Sketches of peasant life in the poor, fictional village of Lisconnell in Connemara, which is surrounded by bogland. The sketches attracted the notice and approval of Lady Augusta Gregory, folklorist and co-founder of the Abbey Theatre [Brown; ODNB].

B70   *Kerrigan's quality* (by Jane Barlow).
+ London: Hodder & Stoughton, 1894 (ill. St.C.S.). SOURCE Brown, 161 ([1893] edn, probably in error); Wolff, 302. LOCATION D, DPL, L, NUC, InND Loeber coll. (1895, 2nd edn).
+ New York: Dodd, Mead & Co., 1894 (ill.). SOURCE NYPL. LOCATION NN, NUC, InND Loeber coll.
COMMENTARY After twenty years in Australia, the hero Martin Kerrigan returns to Ireland with a large inheritance from an Australian relative. He is disappointed by the coldness of his reception by his relatives at Drumclogher, and leaves his native village. He lives in seclusion in a small farmhouse where he had spent his early years. He buys the 'big house' at Glenore, but continues to live in the farmhouse. One day the young Sir Benjamin O'Connor, who has met with an accident, is brought to his house. Kerrigan nurses him back to health. He lets the big house to Sir Ben and his relatives. Kerrigan becomes quite fond of Sir Ben and wants to make him his heir. However, one of the house party drowns and Sir Ben and his party depart. After a while, he returns and Kerrigan proposes that he come back for good to live in the big house and help to develop the area for the good of the people around Glenore. Sir Ben agrees. Through Kerrigan's eyes, the novel shows the effects of the Famine and evictions on rural Ireland [ML; ODNB].

B71   *Strangers at Lisconnel. A second series of Irish idylls* (by Jane Barlow; dedicated to M.L.B. [Mary Louisa Barlow, author's mother]).

+ London: Hodder & Stoughton, 1895. SOURCE Wolff, 305; Brown, 162. LOCATION D, L, NUC (1896 edn), InND Loeber coll. (1896 edn).

+ New York: Dodd, Mead & Co., 1895. SOURCE Hogan, p. 95. LOCATION D, NUC.

+ London: Sphere Books, 1984. LOCATION D.

COMMENTARY Set of interconnected stories, a sequel to *Irish idylls* (London, 1892), telling about the everyday lives of people in a small isolated village and the effects of occasional visits from strangers [Brown; ML].

B72   *Maureen's fairing and other stories* (by Jane Barlow).

+ London: J.M. Dent & Co., 1895 (ill. Bertha Newcombe). LOCATION D, DPL, L, InND Loeber coll.

+ London, New York: Macmillan, 1895. SOURCE Brown, 163; Hogan, p. 95. LOCATION DPL, L, NUC.

New York: Books for Libraries Press, 1972. SOURCE Weekes, p. 27; OCLC. LOCATION D.

COMMENTARY Some of these stories about small incidents in the lives of country people in the west of Ireland first appeared in the *Cornhill Magazine* (London) and in the *Whitehall Review* (London). Contents: 'Maureen's fairing', 'A cream-coloured cactus', 'The formidable rival', 'A year and a day', 'Mac's luncheon', 'Stopped by a signal', 'An escape', 'The Murphs' supper' [RL; Krishnamurti, p. 7].

B73   *Mrs. Martin's company and other stories* (by Jane Barlow).

+ London: J.M. Dent & Co., 1896 (ill. Bertha Newcombe; Iris Series). SOURCE Brown, 164; Wolff, 304. LOCATION DPL, L, NUC, InND Loeber coll.

+ New York: Macmillan & Co., 1896 (ill. Bertha Newcombe; Iris Series). LOCATION DPL

COMMENTARY A selection of these stories set in rural Ireland originally appeared in the *National Review* (London) and in the *Pall Mall Magazine* (London). Contents: 'Mrs. Martin's company', 'A lost recruit', 'After seven years', 'A case of conscience', 'A provident person', 'A very light railway', 'Rosanne' [ML].

B74   *A creel of Irish stories* (by Jane Barlow; dedicated to J.W.B. [probably James Barlow, author's father]).

+ London: Methuen & Co., 1897. SOURCE Brown, 174 (n.d. edn); Hogan, p. 95. LOCATION D, L, NUC.

+ New York: Dodd, Mead & Co., 1898. SOURCE Hogan, p. 95; NYPL. LOCATION NUC, NN, InND Loeber coll.

COMMENTARY Contents: 'The keys of the chest', 'A deserted child', 'An account settled', 'M'Neills' tiger-sheep', 'The snakes and Norah', 'Three pint measures', 'The surree at Mahon's', 'The shortest way', 'The stay-at-homes', 'A proud woman' [ML].

B75   *From the East unto the West* (by Jane Barlow; dedicated to Katharine).

+ London: Methuen & Co., 1898. SOURCE Wolff, 298; Brown, 165. LOCATION D (1901 edn), DPL, L, NUC, InND Loeber coll.

COMMENTARY The first six stories are set in the Middle East and around the Mediterranean; the remainder are set in the west of Ireland. All are about ordinary people. Contents: 'The evil Abenooyahs', 'The puzzle of Jarbek', 'The mockers of the shallow waters', 'At Krinori', 'A caprice of Queen Pippa', 'An advance sheet', 'The field of the frightful beasts', 'A long furrow', 'Moggy Goggin', 'Cocky', 'As luck would have it', 'Her bit of money', 'Some jokes of Timothy', 'Notice to quit', 'Pilgrims from Lisconnel' [Brown; RL].

B76   *From the land of the shamrock* (by Jane Barlow).

+ New York: Dodd, Mead & Co., 1900. SOURCE RLIN; NYPL. LOCATION NUC, NN, InND Loeber coll.

+ New York: Dodd, Mead, 1902 (as *At the back of beyond*; cover: L.H.). SOURCE Hogan, p. 96. LOCATION NUC, InND Loeber coll.

+ London: Methuen & Co., 1901. SOURCE Brown, 166; Wolff, 229. LOCATION DPL (1907 edn), L, NUC, InND Loeber coll.

COMMENTARY Contents of the London edn: 'A white kerchief', 'Danny and the Dans', 'A Christmas dole', ' A wedding gown', ' The aunt of the Savages', 'A magpie's nest', 'The counsel of Widdy Coyle', 'An ould torment', 'Two sacks of potatoes', 'A story on sticks', 'Perry's show', ' The vengeance of Joe Mahoney', 'At an opening door', 'Cocky's conscience'; the New York 1900 end has the following additional stories culled from *From the East unto the West* (London, 1898): 'In the winding walk', 'Pilgrims from Lisconnel', 'The field of the frightful beasts', 'The aunt of the savages', 'Some jokes of Timothy', 'Cocky', 'As luck would have it', 'Moggy Goggin'. The New York 1902 edn has only the first set of stories [Wolff; RL].

B77   *The founding of fortunes* (by Jane Barlow).
+ London: Methuen & Co., 1902. SOURCE Brown, 167. LOCATION DPL, L, NUC (1906 edn).

+ New York: Dodd, Mead & Co., 1902. SOURCE NYPL. LOCATION D, NUC, NN.

COMMENTARY Story about a young, poor boy, Timothy Galvin, who is given a start in life and rises to wealth by his own dishonesty and his mother's wit [Brown].

B78   *By beach and bog-land. Some Irish stories* (by Jane Barlow).
+ London: T. Fisher Unwin, 1905 (ill. Paul Henry). SOURCE Brown, 168. LOCATION D, L, NUC, InND Loeber coll.

COMMENTARY Contents: 'In the winding walk', 'A money-crop at Lisconnel', 'The high tide and the man-trappers', 'The foot-sticks and slughnatraigh', 'Old Isaac's biggest haul', 'The wrong turning', 'Crazy Mick', 'Widow Farrell's wonderful age', 'The Hins' housekeeper', 'Two pair of truants', 'Their new umbrellas', 'A small practice', 'A lingering guest', 'Loughnaglee', 'Moriarty's meadow', 'Delayed in transmission', 'For company' [ML].

B79   *Irish neighbours* (by Jane Barlow; dedicated to J.W.B. [James William Barlow]).
+ London: Hutchinson & Co., 1907. SOURCE Brown, 169. LOCATION D, L, NUC, InND Loeber coll.

COMMENTARY Contents: 'The migration of Murtagh Gilligan', 'A rebel's breakfast', 'An invincible ignoramus', 'The Morrogh's dreams', 'The Libby-Anns', 'For luck', 'A cold reception', 'A long holiday', 'On his own confession', 'A dinner of salt leaves', 'A false start', 'A false alarm', 'Cured dead', 'A Christmas quarrel', 'The clock and the cock', 'The little house', 'A test of truth' [RL].

B80   *A strange land* (by 'Felix Ryark').
London: Hutchinson & Co., 1908 SOURCE RIA/DIB. LOCATION L.
COMMENTARY A fantasy [RIA/DIB].

B81   *Irish ways* (by Jane Barlow; dedicated to James William Barlow).
+ London: George Allen & Sons, 1909 (ill. Warwick Goble). SOURCE Brown, 170 LOCATION D, DPL (1911 edn), BFl, L, NUC, InND Loeber coll. (1911, 2nd edn).

COMMENTARY All stories set in Ireland. Contents: 'Ourselves and our island', 'Under the hill', 'Joanna's two fortunes', 'An unfinished romance', 'Mr. William's collection', 'John the ghost', 'A woman ever vext', 'The loan of a pencil', 'The first drive', 'A transfer', 'Julia's borrowing', 'A storm of terror', 'And no thanks to them', 'Michael the meditator', 'A corner of a county' [RL].

B82   *Flaws. A novel* (by Jane Barlow).
+ London: Hutchinson & Co., 1911. SOURCE Brown, 171. LOCATION D, L, NUC.

COMMENTARY Unlike in her other books, the characters here are from the Protestant middle- and upper-classes. Their petty jealousies and snobbery are satirized in the story, set in the south of Ireland. The story tells of a downtrodden daughter (a son was wanted) who unexpectedly takes the advice of a meek old spinster to assert herself and defies her family to marry [ML; Blain, p. 62; ODNB].

B83   *Mac's adventures* (by Jane Barlow; dedicated to Algernon Charles Swinburne).
       + London: Hutchinson & Co., 1911. SOURCE Wolff, 303; Brown, 172. LOCATION D, L, NUC.

COMMENTARY Eight stories featuring a little boy, Macartney Valentine O'Neill Barry, are about how he affects the lives of the adults around him. Contents: 'A luncheon party', 'A formidable rival', 'Mac's ways and means', 'Some jokes of Timothy', 'A wedding gown', 'The field of the frightful beast', 'The aunt of the Savages', 'An invincible ignoramus' [Brown; RL].

B84   *Loughnaglee* (by Jane Barlow).
       Dublin: James Duffy, [1912 or earlier] (Duffy's Penny Library). SOURCE Advertised in *Catalogue of books* (Dublin: James Duffy & Co., 1912). LOCATION C (not found).
       COMMENTARY No copy located. First appeared in *By beach and bog-land* (London, 1905) [RL].

B85   *Doings and dealings* (by Jane Barlow).
       + London: Hutchinson & Co., 1913. SOURCE Brown, 173. LOCATION D, L, NUC.

COMMENTARY Contents: 'Nemesis in a garden', 'Quin's rick', 'A white roof', 'At a safe distance', 'A bad sixpence', 'Judy's bribe', 'By the whitethorn bush', 'Wishers at the well', ' A blank page', 'Among the honey-blobs', 'A stroke of business', 'A short loan', 'Namesakes' [ML].

B86   *In Mio's youth. A novel* (by Jane Barlow).
       + London: Hutchinson & Co., 1917. SOURCE Brown, 176; Blain, p. 62 (mistakenly mentions at title: *In Mio's path*); OCIL, ODNB (both mistakenly give title as *In Mio's country*). LOCATION D, L, NUC.

COMMENTARY Published posthumously. Set in Ireland, the story features the Delaneys, a country family that has come down in the world. The sons are described as happy-go-lucky, and the mother and daughters as aiming at respectability and good matches. Mio is an adopted child [Brown].

'BARON NA CARRIAG', pseud. See **CONVILLE, Thomas M.**

BARR, Robert. Co-author. See **CRANE, Stephen.**

BARRETT, C.F., fl. 1800. Gothic and sensational novelette writer, CFB was probably English, but with a possible Irish background. Among his other publications are: *Laugh when you can* (London, [1800–9?]), which includes Irish bulls, and the chapbooks *Brazen mask: or, singular memoirs of Sigismund, a Polish baron* (Dublin, 1803), and *Fair Rosamund; or, Woodstock bower* (Dublin, 1803). SOURCE BLC; COPAC; OCLC.

B87   *The round tower; or, the mysterious witness: An Irish legendary tale of the sixth century* (by C.F. Barrett).
       London: Tegg & Castleman, 1803 (ill.). SOURCE Frank, 25; COPAC. LOCATION Dt.
       London: Ann Lemoine & J. Roe, [1803] (as [anon.] *The round tower; or, the mystery: A romantic tale. To which is added, The noble Genoese. A tale*). SOURCE COPAC. LOCATION O.

COMMENTARY 35pp. Gothic novelette, set in sixth-century Ireland. Features the monstrous Cobthach, who is 'sensible of the unjustness of his title to the throne of Munster', and his fellow usurper, the Danish chief Sitric, and a blood-smeared infant who is draped with chains when first seen in the dungeon of Cobthatch's castle. Sitric and Gobthatch had joined forces to take over the kingdom of Moriat, after which Sitric plots the murder of Cobthatch. Sitric uses the round tower of his castle in the Wicklow mountains as a retreat. At the execution of Moriat's son, Maon, O'Brian accompanied by Kildare rush in with their peasants. Sitric is incinerated by lightning coming out of a blue cloud and Maon is saved [COPAC; Frank, 25].

BARRETT, Eaton Stannard, pseuds '**Cervantes Hogg, F.S.M.**', and '**A late resident**', b. Cork 1786, d. Glamorgan (Wales) 1820. Burlesque novelist, playwright, poet, and a newspaper owner known for his satire, ESB was the son of Richard Barrett, a gentleman of Mallow (Co. Cork), and Eleanor Stannard, and probably through his mother he was descended from Eaton Stannard (*c.*1685–1755), recorder of Dublin. ESB was educated at Wandsworth Common (Surrey) and at TCD where he was admitted in 1801 and graduated BA in 1805. He was admitted to the King's Inns in 1803 and entered the Middle Temple (London) the same year but was never called to the Bar. He was the author of a number of political satires, including *All the talents* (London, 1807), in three dialogues, published under a pseud., which became the most well-known of his poems and went into at least nineteen edns. He founded a satirical newspaper in London, the *Comet*, not to be confused with a volume of miscellaneous topics with the same title (London, 1808). His comedy *My wife, what wife?* appeared in 1816 and was well-received. Despite his successes, ESB was poor. He died suddenly in Wales and was buried there. SOURCE Allibone, i, p. 128; Brady, p. 7; B & S, p. 42; DLB, cxvi; Hogan 2, pp 125–6; Keane, p. 21; NCBEL 4, pp 885–6; NSTC; OCIL, p. 34; ODNB; O'Donoghue, p. 19; O'Donoghue 2, p. 423; RIA/DIB; RL.

B88   *The rising sun, a serio-comic satiric romance* (by 'Cervantes Hogg, F.S.M.').
       London: Appleyards, 1807, 2 vols. (ill.). SOURCE Wolff, 318; British Fiction; Garside: 1807:8; Gecker, 80. LOCATION L, NUC.
       + London: Appleyards, 1807, 3 vols. 4th edn (revsd, corrected, and enlarged; ill. J. Brown, O'Keefe). LOCATION D, InND Loeber coll. (5th edn, revsd, corrected, and enlarged).

B89   *The mis-led general; a serio-comic, satiric, mock-heroic romance* [anon.].
       + London: H. Oddy, 1808 (ill.). SOURCE British Fiction; Garside, 1808:25; Hardy, 225; Wolff, 317. LOCATION Corvey CME 3–628–48215–1, D, L, NUC, InND Loeber coll.
       COMMENTARY Satire on Frederick, duke of York, who is depicted as a very inept and cowardly general involved in campaigns against France [NSTC; ML].

B90   *The tarantula; or, the dance of fools. A satirical work* [anon.].
       + London: Holmes & Witterton, 1809, 2 vols. LOCATION D, L.
       London: J.F. Hughes, 1809, 2 vols. SOURCE Wolff, 320. LOCATION NUC.

B91   *The setting sun; or, devil among the placemen. To which is added a new musical drama being a parody on the Beggar's Opera, as lately acted, with universal eclat, at the Theatre Royal, Glyster Place; with hints for a masquerade jubilee on a grand scale* (by 'Cervantes Hogg').
       + London: T. Hughes, Gray & Son, Kirby & Co., Blacklock, & Wilson, 1809, 3 vols. (ill.). LOCATION D.

B92   *The metropolis; or, a cure for gaming. Interspersed with anecdotes of living characters in high life* (by 'Cervantes Hogg').
       London: A.K. Newman & Co., 1811, 3 vols. SOURCE Blakey, p. 235; British Fiction; Garside, 1811:18. LOCATION Corvey CME 3–28–48106–6, O, NUC.
       COMMENTARY Not to be confused with *The metropolis. A novel* (London, 1819) [Garside].

B93   *The heroine; or, adventures of a fair romance reader* (by Eaton Stannard Barrett; dedicated to George Canning).
       + London: Henry Colburn, 1813, 3 vols. SOURCE British Fiction; Garside, 1813:9; Wolff, 316. LOCATION D, L, O, NUC.

+ London: Henry Colburn, 1814, 2nd edn, 3 vols. (as *The heroine; or, adventures of Cherubina*, with considerable additions and alterations). SOURCE Rafroidi, ii, p. 55; Gecker, 79 (3rd edn). LOCATION Dt, D, L, NUC, InND Loeber coll. (1815, 3rd edn).

Philadelphia: M. Carey, 1815, 2 vols. (as *The heroine; or, adventures of Cherubina*). SOURCE NCBEL 3, p. 709. LOCATION NUC.

+ Boston: West & Richardson, 1816, 2 vols. (as *The heroine; or, adventures of Cherubina*). SOURCE InND Loeber coll.

Baltimore: J. Robinson, 1832 (as *The heroine; or, adventures of Cherubina*). SOURCE NSTC. LOCATION NUC.

Richmond (VA): Peter D. Bernard, 1835 (as *The heroine; or, adventures of Cherubina*). SOURCE OCLC; NSTC (1835, 2nd edn). LOCATION MH (1835, 2nd edn).

London: E. Mathews & Marrot, 1927 (introd. by Michael Sadleir; The Rescue Series). LOCATION NUC.

COMMENTARY A popular satire of Gothic and sentimental novels, reprinted in London and the US. Set in England, it is an epistolary novel featuring a girl who wishes to be a heroine and starts out with imagining that her father is not her real father. She flees from her home to discover her 'real' background. The book is full of adventures and high-flown language suitable to heroines, sources for some of which are given as Regina Maria Roche's§ *The children of the abbey* (London, 1796, 4 vols.), Wolfgang Goethe's *Die Leiden des jungen Werther* (Leipzig, 1774), and Ann Radcliffe's *Mysteries of Udolpho* (London, 1794). Features a Jerry Sullivan, who persuaded by others that 'old Ireland was going to ruin; I forget how now', becomes an United Irishman [ML; Frank, 26; ODNB; M.O. Grenby, *The anti-Jacobin novel* (Cambridge, 2001), p. 60; Allibone, i, p. 128].

B94 *Six weeks at Long's* (by 'A late resident').

+ London: Printed for the author, 1817, 3 vols. SOURCE Rafroidi, ii, p. 55; Gecker, 82 (2nd edn); British Fiction; Garside, 1817:11; Wolff, 319 (1817, 3rd edn). LOCATION Dt (1817, 2nd edn), L (1817, 3rd edn), O, NUC, InND Loeber coll. (1817, 3rd edn, 3 vols. in 1).

COMMENTARY A humorous novel set in a famous Bond Street hotel in London. The plot involves the gulling of a wealthy provincial by a band of high-life swindlers. Provides an elaborate portrait of Lord Byron as Lord Leander, and includes caricatures of many prominent figures of the day such as Thomas Moore§, Robert Southey, and William Wordsworth. There are also many references to Lady Caroline Lamb's§ *Glenarvon* (London, 1816). The anonymously published *London: or, a month at Steven's* (1819, 3 vols.) was influenced by this volume [Ximenes cat. 102/110].

BARRETT, J.G., pseud. 'Erigena', fl. 1870s. Novelist. The preface to the following volume is dated from Birmingham Jan. 1870. SOURCE Brown, p. 28; RL.

B95 *Evelyn Clare; or, the wrecked homesteads. An Irish story of love and landordism* (by 'Erigena').

+ London, Derby: Thomas Richardson & Sons, [1870]. SOURCE Brown, 180. LOCATION D, L, InND Loeber coll.

COMMENTARY Set in the west of Ireland around 1850. Contains all the elements of agrarian unrest such as a bad landlord and land agent, evictions, murders, a poteen still and abhorrence of catholicism. However, in the end several Protestants have been converted to catholicism [Brown].

'BARRINGTON, F. Clinton', pseud. See **PIPER, A.G.**

BARRINGTON, Laurel, fl. 1888. Novelist, LB lived in New South Wales (Australia). SOURCE Miller, ii, p. 635.

B96   *The tragedy of Druids' Glen, or, the shadows of the cross: A story of Irish and Australian life* (by Laurel Barrington).
Sidney [*sic*]: Sidney Newspaper Co., 1888. SOURCE Miller, ii, p. 635. LOCATION State Library of New South Wales (Australia).
COMMENTARY Concerns the fate of an heir presumptive to an Irish estate. The action is mainly in Ireland during the 1860s, but also deals with squatters in Queensland (Australia) [Miller].

'A BARRISTER', pseud. See **SAMPSON, William**.

BARRY, Mrs —, fl. 1790. A novelist, possibly Irish, who dedicated the following book to Lady St George, Elizabeth Baroness St George, daughter of Christopher Dominick of Dublin and wife of St George St George, 1st Baron St George (d. Naples 1774), eldest son of John Usher of Headford (Co. Galway). Mrs B was probably in Italy before 1790 because most of the subscribers to her novel were members of the British merchant communities in Leghorn, Genoa and Naples at the time, but the list also includes George Foster Dalton of Dublin. She certainly was in Leghorn in 1794. SOURCE J. Ingamells, *A dictionary of British and Irish travellers in Italy* (New Haven, 1997), pp 57, 227, 835.

B97   *Memoirs of Maria, a Persian slave* [anon.] (dedicated to Lady [Elizabeth] St George).
London: G.G.J. & J. Robinson, 1790, 2 vols. (subscribers' list). SOURCE Raven 2, 1790:21 (where not identified as by Mrs Barry); ESTC t067639. LOCATION L, IU.

BARRY, Msgr William Francis, b. London 1849, d. 1930. English-born cleric, novelist, theological historian and biographer of Irish and Catholic descent, according to the preface to *Memoirs and opinions* (London, 1926), WFB's parents, William Barry (b. 1819) and Ellen Downey (b. 1818) came from Liscarroll (Co. Cork). He was educated at Oscott College (Birmingham) and Rome, and became a Roman Catholic theologian and man of letters. He contributed to the *Catholic Times* (Liverpool); the *Pilot* (London or Boston?); the *Tablet*, *Westminster Libraries*, the *Dublin Review* (all London), and the *Contemporary* (London?). In the 1890s he joined the Irish Literary Society in London, where he lectured on Edmund Burke in 1897. At the end of his life, he made a final visit to Ireland. He must have been familiar with the Irish language because the Irish words in the second story are 'printed nearly according to sound'. Only his books with Irish content are listed here. SOURCE BLC; Brown, p. 29; W.F. Barry, *Memoirs and opinions* (London, 1926), p. 3, passim; E. Reilly, p. 241; O'Donoghue, p. 20; RL; Sutherland, pp 49–50.

B98   *The place of dreams: Four stories* (by William Francis Barry; dedicated to Ella, Harry, and May).
+ London: Catholic Truth Society, 1893. SOURCE COPAC. LOCATION L, InND.
COMMENTARY Contents: 'The house of shadows', 'Lost Artie: A legend of Candlemas' (set in Ireland), 'The mystery of Drerewater', 'St. Anthony's flask' [RL].

B99   *The wizard's knot* (by William Francis Barry; dedicated to Douglas Hyde§ and Standish Hayes O'Grady).
London: T. Fisher Unwin, 1900. SOURCE Brown, 183. LOCATION Queen's Univ., Belfast, L (1901 edn), NUC (1901 edn).
New York: The Century Co., 1901. SOURCE Brown, 183. LOCATION NUC.
Toronto: The Publishers' Syndicate, 1901. LOCATION NUC.
COMMENTARY The author in his *Memoirs and opinions* (London, 1926) wrote that 'I have always regarded "The Wizard's Knot" with peculiar affection, as my mother's own fairy-tale. My hope was to reproduce the atmosphere of that ancient folk-lore which lives under all outward

changes ...' (pp 234–5). Set on the coast of south-west Cork during famine times. Contains a slight embroidery of an Irish legend and superstitions [Brown].

BARTER, Laura A. See **BARTER, Laura Anna**.

BARTER, Laura Anna, later Snow, fl. 1890s. A writer of religious fiction for juveniles under the name **Laura A. Barter-Snow** and **Laura A. Barter**. Considering the following works with Irish content, she probably was Irish. SOURCE BLC; RL.

B100 *Harold; or, who died for me* (by Laura A. Barter; dedicated to Lucy, Temple, Ronald, Godfray, Evelyn, and Donald Cargill with Auntie Laura's love).
+ London: S.W. Partridge & Co., [1891] (ill. [illegible] W. Burton). LOCATION L.
COMMENTARY Fiction for juveniles, set in Ireland and featuring the Ellestone family [RL].

B101 *Marjory; or, what would Jesus do?* (by Laura A. Barter).
+ London: S.W. Partridge & Co., 1893 (ill. H.J. Rhodes). LOCATION L.
COMMENTARY Further stories of the Elleston family [RL].

B102 *Aileen; or, 'the love of Christ constraineth us.'* (by Laura A. Barter).
+ London: S.W. Partridge & Co., [1895] (ill.). LOCATION L.
COMMENTARY Features Aileen Ellestone and has some slight Irish content [RL].

B103 *Barney boy* (by Laura A. Barter-Snow).
+ London: S.W. Partridge & Co., [1912] (ill. Victor Prout). LOCATION L.
COMMENTARY Fiction for juveniles. The main character's home, which is near the Derrynasaggart mountains (Co. Kerry), is to be sold. He moves to England but returns by the end of book [Personal communication, Mary Pollard, Sept. 2003].

BARTER-SNOW, Laura A. See **BARTER, Laura Anna**.

BARTON, Eustace Robert, pseud. 'Robert Eustace'. Co-author. See **SMITH, Elizabeth Thomasina Toulmin**.

BARTON, Revd Richard, b. Painstown (Co. Meath) 1706, d. Lurgan (Co. Antrim) 1759. Church of Ireland evangelizing clergyman, natural and topographical historian, poet and prose writer, RB was the son of John Barton, dean of Ardagh (Co. Longford) and Elinor Jenney, daughter of the Revd Henry Jenney, Church of Ireland archdeacon of the Dromore diocese. Admitted to TCD in 1722, RB graduated BA in 1726 and MA in 1731. He became a deacon in 1728 and was ordained the following year. He never married. He had a successful clerical career, first as curate of Donaghcloney (Co. Down, 1728–42), and then as rector of Shankill, near Lurgan (Co. Armagh, 1742–59). John Wesley met him on his tour through Armagh in 1756 and records that the somewhat eccentric RB lived in a house with no doors and few windows on Lough Neagh. RB's *The analogy of divine wisdom* (London 1737–8; Dublin, 1750) attempted to enlist all human knowledge in the Christian cause. *Farrago; or, miscellanies in verse and prose* (London, 1739) mostly deals with education, and he also published *Dialogue respecting Ireland* (Dublin, [1751]). As a member of the Physico-Historical Society, he and others collected material for a history of Co. Armagh, illustrating the importance of Lough Neagh and the surrounding counties, which they advertised in *Faulkner's Journal* in Mar. 1745 and 1746, but which does not appear to have been published. Some of RB's letters to this society refer to the fact that he was working on a dictionary of place names for the county, but this material appears to have been lost (but see also ODNB). He also published a pamphlet, *Remarks respecting Lough Lene* (Dublin, 1751), which deals with one of the lakes of Killarney. His preoccupation with Lough Neagh resulted eight years later in the publication of a poem in English and Latin: *A physico-poetical essay on the wonders of Lough Neah [sic] in Ireland, in imitation of Lucretius* (Dublin, 1759). He also published a few religious works. SOURCE Allibone, i, p. 137; B.F. Barton, 'Some account of the family of Barton' in *Ulster Folklore*, 10 (1964), p. 64; B & S, p. 46; BLC; E. Magennis, 'A land of milk and honey' in *RIA Proc.*, 102C, No. 6 (2002), pp 202, 210n.56; ODNB; O'Donoghue, p. 21; RIA/DIB; RL.

B104 *Dialogue, concerning some things of importance to Ireland; particularly to the County of Ardmagh [sic]. Being part of a design to write the natural, civil and ecclesiastical history of that county* (by Richard Barton; dedicated to George Lord Archbishop of Ardmagh [sic]).

+ Dublin: For the author, 1751 (ill. Domina Bush, T. Chambars). SOURCE ESTC t88509. LOCATION D, Dm, Dt, BFl, L, InND Loeber coll.

COMMENTARY Dialogues between Gorgias, a farmer, Odontes, a traveller, Othonius, a linen-draper, Philedones, a man of pleasure, and Hierophantes and Cenophotus, two clergymen of different persuasions. They converse about the merits of the landscape around Lough Neagh, its salmon, the market for linen at Lurgan (Co. Armagh), the canal connecting Lough Neagh with the sea, and the commerce of coal and other wares which served to relieve the famine of 1745. They mention farmers' infatuation with emigration to America in the late 1720s, give accounts of Irish history based on Spenser, Morrison and Davies, and extol the virtues of the Scots-Irish. The discussion closes with a poorly disguised advertisement for RB's book on Lough Neagh and its environs. On the verso of this booklet is an advertisement to *Lectures in natural philosophy ... upon the petrifications, gems, crystals, and sanative quality of Lough Neagh in Ireland* (Dublin, 1751), as an introd. to his larger historical work on Co. Armagh [RL].

BARTRAM, George, fl. 1897. A novelist, poet and prose writer who was probably English. His six volumes of fiction published between 1897 and 1914 are mostly historical romances set in the English provinces. SOURCE BLC; EF, p. 21.

B105 *The white-headed boy* (by George Bartram).

London: T. Fisher Unwin, 1898. SOURCE Brown, 184; COPAC. LOCATION L.

COMMENTARY Set in Kerry in Fenian times and describes the inadequacy of the Fenians as rebels but also their heroic spirit [Brown].

'BASIL', pseud. See **KING, Richard Ashe**.

BATTERSBY, Mrs —, fl. 1880s. Poet and writer of juvenile religious fiction, she may be identified with either the religious tract writer and poet C. Maud Battersby§ or the lyric writer Hannah S. Battersby. A Mary Battersby (fl. 1804–41), a possible relative, was a flower and bird painter in Ireland. A branch of the Battersby family resided at Loughbawn (Co. Westmeath), but there is no reference to Mrs B. in M. Keaney's *Westmeath authors* (Mullingar, 1869). SOURCE Allibone Suppl., i, p. 108; Crookshank, pp 116–17, 298; Landed gentry, pp 33–4; NCBEL 4, p. 1747; O'Donoghue, p. 21.

B106 *The riband oath. An Irish story. And The lighthouse keepers of Anticosti* (by Mrs Battersby).

+ London: Sunday School Union, [1886] (ill. C. Hewitt). SOURCE NCBEL 4, p. 1747. LOCATION L (destroyed); D, InND.

COMMENTARY 95pp. Religious fiction for juveniles. Contents: 'The riband oath' (set in Ireland and involving a romantic triangle between Nelly Cregan, who refuses to marry Corny Marten unless he takes an oath to join the secret Riband Society, of which her brothers are members, and Moira Clare, a young woman who has lived with the Martens since she was orphaned who loves Corny and tries to dissuade him. The activities of the Riband society are featured when a young member, Andy Doolan, is nominated to shoot Mr Lambert, a prominent businessman, as he returns from Knockdera fair. Since Lambert has helped Andy in the past, Andy issues a secret warning to him, but he goes to the fair anyway. Andy attempts to shoot but misfires and is injured by Lambert's gamekeeper. Lambert realizes that Andy has been an unfortunate victim of the society. Meanwhile, Corny learns the truth about the scheming Nelly. He discovers the depth of Moira's love and they marry two years later), 'The lighthouse keepers of Anticosti' (set on the gulf of St Lawrence in North America. Two lighthouses exist on the island of Anticosti. The western lighthouse is inhabited by a Scottish family named McLeod, while the eastern one is inhabited by an Irishman named O'Bryan, who has four children. They are the sole inhabitants of the island, but they have never met. Donald McLeod gets caught in a storm and is rescued by the O'Bryans and the families meet) [CD].

B107   *John Elton; or, the results of anger. And Johnnie the 'Bocher'* (by Mrs Battersby).
London: Sunday School Union, [1888]. SOURCE Alston, p. 20. LOCATION L (destroyed), CtY.
COMMENTARY Religious fiction [BLC].

BATTERSBY, C. Maud, fl. 1890s. Religious fiction and tract writer and poet, CMB was a Protestant, probably from the north of Ireland, whose *Twilight and dawn: hymns, fragments and poems* was published in London in 1899. Perhaps the same person as Mrs Battersby§.
SOURCE Colman, pp 38–9; O'Donoghue, p. 21; RL.

B108   *Gaspar; or, the story of a street Arab* (by C. Maude [*sic*] Battersby).
London: George Cauldwell, [1891]. SOURCE COPAC. LOCATION L.
COMMENTARY Religious fiction about a poor boy [BLC].

B109   *Seven times in the fire. A story of France in revolution times* (by C. Maud Battersby).
London: Religious Tract Society, [1892]. SOURCE COPAC. LOCATION L (destroyed), E.
COMMENTARY Historical fiction set during the French Revolution [RL].

BATTERSBY, H.F. Prevost. See **BATTERSBY, Henry Francis Prevost.**

BATTERSBY, Henry Francis Prevost (also known as **H.F. Prevost Battersby**), pseud. **'Francis Prevost'** and **'H.F. Prevost'**, b. 1862, d. 1949. Short story writer, war correspondent, novelist, poet, and man of letters, HFPV was the son of Maj.-Gen. John Prevost Battersby, originally from Listoke House, Drogheda (Co. Louth) and Louisa Dillon, second daughter of Sir William [O'Donoghue has John] Dillon, Bt. He was educated at Westminster School and at the military academies at Woolwich and Sandhurst, where he graduated with honours and special mention. He was a lieutenant in the 1st Battalion of Royal Irish Rifles and, after leaving the service, a war correspondent for the London *Morning Post* in South Africa, Somaliland, France and Flanders, where he was wounded. He married Frances Muriel (Pearl) Saunders in 1909. HPVB was a prolific writer: he published collections of poetry; translations of Tolstoy; plays; reviews, and a number of books on sport. Some of his papers are at Cambridge University Library, NRA 44066; Ref. Add 9530. SOURCE Landed gentry, 1912, p. 34; O'Donoghue, p. 21; RIA/DIB; Sutherland, p. 510 [under Prevost].

B110   *Rust of gold* (by 'Francis Prevost').
+ London, New York, Melbourne: Ward, Lock & Bowden, 1895. SOURCE RLIN.
LOCATION L, NIC.
COMMENTARY Contents: 'False equivalents', 'Someone's sister', 'Grass upon the house-tops', 'Pity's prisoner', 'A ghost of the sea', 'The crown of pride', 'An exotic virtue', 'The balance',

'The skirts of chance'. Note that the following are not short stories, but very short (no longer than ten pages) dramatic interludes: 'Someone's sister', 'Pity's prisoner', 'The crown of pride', 'The balance'. All but 'The crown of pride' consist of dialogues between two characters; 'The crown of pride' has four characters [JB].

B111　*On the verge* (by 'Francis Prevost'; dedication: 'For a summer, to M.C.B.').
+ London, New York, Melbourne: Ward, Lock & Bowden, 1896. SOURCE RLIN. LOCATION L, NYU.
COMMENTARY Contents: 'A great forsaking', 'Qui Regis Israel', 'Head winds' (first published in *Pall Mall Magazine*, London), 'A modern instance', 'Derelict', 'Honour's Pawn' [JB].

B112　*False dawn* (by 'Francis Prevost').
London, New York, Melbourne: Ward & Lock, 1897. SOURCE RLIN. LOCATION L, NIC.
COMMENTARY A psychological study of forbidden love with an ambitious politician as hero [Sutherland].

B113　*Entanglements: The woman's weaving* (by 'Francis Prevost').
+ London: Service & Paton, 1898. SOURCE RLIN. LOCATION L, NIC.
COMMENTARY Short stories [RLIN].

B114　*The plague of the heart* (by 'Francis Prevost'; dedicated to 'April').
London, New York, Melbourne: Ward, Lock & Co., 1902. SOURCE COPAC. LOCATION L.
COMMENTARY Contents: 'The siege of Sar', 'Her reputation', 'The measure of a man' [JB].

B115　*The avenging hour* (by 'H.F. Prevost').
London: Hurst & Blackett, 1906. SOURCE COPAC. LOCATION L.
New York: D. Appleton, 1906. SOURCE RLIN. LOCATION NN.

B116　*The last resort* (by H.F. Prevost Battersby).
London, New York: John Lane, 1912. SOURCE COPAC. LOCATION L.

B117　*The silence of men* (by H.F. Prevost Battersby).
London: John Lane, 1913. SOURCE COPAC; OCLC. LOCATION L, E.

B118　*The lure of romance* (by H.F. Prevost Battersby).
London: John Lane, 1914. SOURCE COPAC. LOCATION L.

B119　*The edge of doom* (by H.F. Prevost Battersby).
London, New York: John Lane, 1919. SOURCE COPAC; OCLC. LOCATION L.

BATTERSBY, John. See **ELRINGTON, John Battersby.**

BAYLY, Ada Ellen, pseud. **'Edna Lyall',** b. Brighton (E. Sussex) 1857, d. Eastbourne (E. Sussex) 1903. English novelist of religious and political fiction and supporter of suffrage for women, AEB was the daughter of Robert Bayly, a barrister of the Inner Temple, and Mary Winter. She used her novels to express, for example, her support for the Armenians and her opposition to the second South African war. As an ardent advocate of Home Rule for Ireland, her novel *Doreen* (London, 1894) drew a response from prime minister William Gladstone who commended her for the 'singular courage with which you stake your wide public reputation upon the Irish cause' (ODNB). In the preparation of *Doreen*, she visited Ireland in 1892. A previous novel, *Donovan* (London, 1882), does not have Irish content. AEB had a strong faith but was also a loyal supporter of liberal causes and was secretary of the Eastbourne branch of the Women's Liberal Association. William O'Brien§ eulogized that she 'was one of those English women who might have done more than laws or armies to gain the good-will of the Irish nation' (Reilly). SOURCE Allibone Suppl., i, p. 112; Blain, p. 677 [under Lyall]; EF, p. 252; NCBEL 4, p. 1627 [under Lyall]; ODNB; E. Reilly, pp 226–7; Sutherland, p. 52; T & B, p. 996; Todd, pp 428–9.

B120   *Doreen. The story of a singer* (by 'Edna Lyall'; dedicated to W.E. Gladstone).
+ London: Longman, Green & Co., 1894. SOURCE Daims, 222; Sadleir, 1457; Wolff, 4209. LOCATION L, InND Loeber coll. (1902 edn).
Leipzig: Bernard Tauchnitz, 1899, 2 vols. SOURCE T & B, 3345. LOCATION NUC.
+ New York: Longmans, Green & Co., 1894 (ill.). SOURCE Daims, 222. LOCATION D (1895 edn), NUC.
COMMENTARY Doreen is a great popular singer and an Irish patriot who helps the cause of Irish Home Rule by her singing. She is engaged to an Englishman, whom she converts to the Irish cause. She cannot marry him immediately because she has the care of her younger siblings, for whom she feels entirely responsible. At different times both she and her lover are imprisoned in Dublin. Their love is severely tried by a secret that needs to be kept. After Doreen comes out of prison and has lost her voice, she marries the Englishman and they live part of the time in Ireland. Her hero, Donal Moore, stands for the Fenian leader Michael Davitt, founder of the Land League [ML].

BAYLY, Nathaniel Thomas Haynes (known as **Thomas Haynes Bayly**), b. Bath (Avon) 1797, d. Cheltenham (Glos.) 1839. English song writer, novelist and dramatist, THB was the son Nathaniel Bayly, a solicitor. His father entered him at St Mary's Hall, Oxford, but THB left after three years without taking a degree. He went to Dublin, where he performed in private theatricals, and visited Killarney. From this period is his *Erin, and other poems* (Dublin, 1822), and his *The Lover's Mistake: together with Paddy Blaney, Billy Taylor, etc.* (Dublin, [1830?]). In 1826 he married Helena Beecher Hayes, the daughter of Benjamin Hayes of Marble Hill (Co. Cork). In England, the couple stayed at Lord Ashtown's villa, Chessel, on the Southampton River, where THB wrote some of his most famous songs (the Ashtowns, Irish nobility, were later subscribers to his book published in Boulogne, see below). THB published a novel *The Aylmers* (London, 1827, 3 vols.), which despite its Irish-sounding title, mostly consists of sketches of Oxford college life. Among his plays is 'Perfection, or the Lady of Munster' (performed at Drury London, 1830), which featured an Irish heiress, Kate O'Brien. In 1831 his financial situation deteriorated, partly because of the loss of his wife's fortune in unproductive Irish coal mines. He became depressed, and seeking to recover, moved his family to Boulogne in France, where two years later he published the following volume. He fell ill, recovered temporarily but died young and was buried at Cheltenham. His portrait is in the National Portrait Gallery, London; a portrait engraving was made after a miniature by Samuel Lover§. SOURCE Allibone, i, p. 145; DNB; NCBEL, 4, p. 231[under Nathaniel Thomas]; O'Donoghue, p. 23; ODNB; RL.
B121   *Musings and prosings* (by Thomas Haynes Bayly).
+ Boulogne: Printed [for the author] by F. Birlé, 1833 (subscribers' list). LOCATION L, PC.
COMMENTARY Although this work contains only a single Irish story, it is included because of the fact that many of its subscribers are Irish. Also, one of poems in this volume is about John Banim§, who like THB was living at Boulogne (France) at the time of publication. Contents: 'Lines written after Mr. John Banim, the author of the O'Hara tales' (which chronicles Banim's suffering). Contents of the prose pieces, excluding a play, poetry and songs: 'Sigmon Dumps', 'My great-grandmother's harpsichord', 'Kings, queens', and knaves', 'Lunatic lays', 'Faults on both sides', 'Autobiography of a landaulet', 'A legend of Killarney', 'The Arabian steed', 'Retrenchment' [RL].

BAYLY, Thomas Haynes. See **BAYLY, Nathaniel Thomas Haynes.**

BAYNE, Marie. Co-author. See **FINLEY, Fr Thomas A**.

'BEACH, Charles', pseud. See **REID, Capt. Thomas Mayne**.

'BEACH, Charles A.', pseud. See **REID, Capt. Thomas Mayne**.

'BEACON, Evelyn', pseud. See **SMITH, Elizabeth Thomasina Toulmin**.

BEAMISH, North Ludlow, b. Beaumont House (Co. Cork) 1796 (1797 in ODNB and RIA/DIB), d. Annemount (Co. Cork), 1872. Military historian, translator and novelist, NLB was the fifth son of William Beamish of Beaumont House (Co. Cork) and Anne Jane Margaret Delacour of Short Castle (Co. Cork). At an early age he was one of the subscribers to M. Despourrin's§ *The Neville family* (Cork, 1814, 3 vols.). He was educated at Sandhurst and received his commission in the 4th Royal Irish Dragoon Guards in Nov. 1816, and held the rank of captain, and then lieutenant-colonel, *à la suite*, in the Hanoverian service. In 1837, as president of the Cork Scientific and Literary Society, he gave an address in which he showed that he favoured a British rather than an Irish national literature for the Irish. In the same year, after the separation of England and Hanover, he was given the honour, unusual for a British citizen, of being decorated by King Ernst of Hanover. At that time he was a Fellow of the Royal Society. He translated into English several German books on cavalry and on military history. He wrote the preface to the following book from Regent's Park, London, April 1829. NLB became very interested in Norse antiquities and he published *The discovery of America by the Northmen* [*sic*] (London, 1841), that included notices on the early settlements of the Irish in the western hemisphere. That same year he married Aline Marie, daughter and co-heiress of Revd John Eric Forsström, dean of Munktorp in Sweden, with whom he had one son and two daughters. After he became seated at Annemount (Co. Cork; not Ann Mount in as ODNB) he served as JP and was HS in 1855. SOURCE Allibone, i, p. 146; N.L. Beamish, *Address to the Cork Scientific and Literary Society* (Cork, 1837); BLC; T. Eagleton, *Crazy John and the bishop* (Cork, 1998), p. 162n.24; Landed gentry, 1912, p. 39; ODNB; RIA/DIB.
B122 *Peace campaigns of a cornet* [anon.].
+ London: John Ebers & Co., 1829, 3 vols. SOURCE British Fiction; Garside, 1829:16.
LOCATION Corvey CME 3–628–48406–5, L, DCL.
COMMENTARY The preface states that the author furnished the story from 'a few loose and ill-connected memoranda, found among the papers of a deceased and valued friend ...' The main character is Pierse Butler, a younger scion of a family living at Bally-butler, who gives up a boring, administrative job to join the army. A picaresque novel, which features the Apollo Society in Cork, it was later suppressed by the publisher [Personal communication, Terry Eagleton, Feb. 2000; RL].

BEAUCLERC, Amelia, fl. 1810. Novelist, probably English, AB wrote eight Gothic and moralistic novels published in London, of which three have Irish content. According to Blain several of her works are attributed in error to Emma Parker. SOURCE Blain, p. 74; Garside, 1811:19–20, 1812:22, 1814:13, 1817:12, and 1820:16 (list of her works); NCBEL 4, p. 886.
B123 *Alinda; or, the child of mystery. A novel* [anon.].
+ London: B. & R. Crosby & Co, 1812, 4 vols. SOURCE British Fiction; Garside, 1812:21. LOCATION Corvey CME 3–628–47042–0, Ireland related fiction, L.
COMMENTARY According to the *Monthly Review* (London, 1813), this novel contained 'a tolerable representation of a poor Irish domestic, which character is now much in vogue with novel-writers; perhaps from the ample material for its delineation, which have been furnished

by Miss Edgeworth'. The story centres on Alinda, abandoned in childhood to the care of an impoverished curate and his wife in Yorkshire. When she comes of age she meets an Irishman, Mr Fitzgerald, who wants to marry her and carries her off to Scotland against her will. When he finds out she is pregnant he orders her to Ireland, where she is conveyed to a distant farmhouse inside a ruin of an old castle. The farmer's daughter becomes her maid. Her husband visits her rarely and when she delivers a baby boy he wants her to give it to a peasant, but she refuses. His father wants him to marry an heiress and he consents, writing to his wife that once his father dies she can put in a prior claim. Alinda leaves Ireland for Devon with her servant Judy, but not before writing to the heiress to warn her. A stranger who comes to Alinda in her new home and asks her how she is related to the Fitzgeralds turns out to be Isabella Montgommerie, the heiress Fitzgerald is to marry. She has fled to escape the marriage. Isabella stays with Alinda and the story ends happily when Isabella falls in love and Alinda inherits vast estates [ML; *Éire-Ireland*, 19(2) (1984), p. 118].

B124   *Husband hunters!!! A novel* [anon.].
+ London: A.K. Newman & Co., 1816, 4 vols. SOURCE Blakey, p. 255; British Fiction; Garside, 1816:17. LOCATION Corvey CME 3–28–47919–3, L.
COMMENTARY Slight Irish content [ML].

B125   *The deserter. A novel* (by Amelia Beauclerc).
+ London: A.K. Newman & Co., 1817, 4 vols. SOURCE Blakey, p. 258; British Fiction; Garside, 1817:12. LOCATION L, C.
COMMENTARY Set in France and refers to some Irish characters [RL].

BEAUFORT, Frances Anne. See EDGEWORTH, Mrs Frances Anne.

BEAUFORT, Henrietta (Harriet), b. Allenstown (Co. Meath) 1778, d. 1865. Botanist, novelist and juvenile fiction writer, HB was the second daughter of Revd Dr Daniel Augustus Beaufort, rector of Navan (Co. Meath) and vicar of Collon (Co. Louth), and Mary Waller of Allenstown. Henrietta was brought up by the Wallers and later kept house for them at Allenstown, a country house situated in an estate of about 700 acres. She had a great interest in botany and wrote several didactic books for children in a fictional style, while her sister, Louisa Catherine Beaufort§, in the same manner wrote on entomology for children. In these works the two sisters were probably inspired by the recommendation of their brother-in-law, Richard Lovell Edgeworth§ (father of Maria Edgeworth§) to teach science to children. Their eldest sister, Frances Anne, became Richard Lovell Edgeworth's fourth wife. HB stayed with the Edgeworths for several months in 1800, when Maria Edgeworth wrote about her approvingly. HB and her sister Louisa gave Maria Edgeworth the idea for the story 'The orphans', published in Maria's *The parent's assistant* (London, 1800). Given HB's educational interests, it is likely that she taught school while staying at the Wallers, since Mrs Waller sponsored a small school for females near the demesne. At one point HB was slated to become the wife of Lovell, Maria Edgeworth's§ brother, but she remained a spinster all her life. HB's works, *Dialogues on botany* (London, 1819), *Bertha's visit* (London, 1830), and *The heiress in her minority* (London, 1850), formerly have been ascribed in error to Jane Marcet. Her writing career spans 1819 to 1854, but so far only four books have been identified. Letters by Frances Edgeworth to HB are in the Bodleian Library, Oxford (MS Eng. Lett. C. 738). A volume of her letters (1835–45) can be found in TCD (MS 8,782). SOURCE Alston, p. 279 (wrongly identified the author, copying information from the BLC); Butler, p. 237n.3; Colvin, pp 307–12, 449n.2; E.E. MacDonald, *The education of the heart: The correspondence of Rachel Mordecai Lazarus and Maria Edgeworth* (Chapel Hill, NC, 1977), pp 36, 52; C.C. Ellison, 'Remembering Dr. Beaufort' in *Quarterly Bulletin of the Irish Georgian Society*, 18 (Jan.–Mar. 1975), p. 2;

C.C. Ellison, *The hopeful traveller. The life and times of Daniel Augustus Beaufort LL.D. 1739–1821* (Kilkenny, 1987), pp 6, 78–9, 117; Field Day, iv, p. 1187; *A topographical dictionary of Ireland* (1837, republ. Baltimore, 1984), ii, p. 345; Wolff, i, p. 69 (who cites various sources dismissing Jane Marcet's authorship and stressing HB's); Mrs [Frances] Edgeworth, *A memoir of Maria Edgeworth* (London, 1867), i, p. 104; iii, p. 66.

B126   **The little white hen** (by Henrietta Beaufort).

COMMENTARY Mentioned in the Edgeworth manuscripts, but no copy located. Different from *The white hen. An Irish fairy tale*. Dublin: James Duffy, 1852 (Duffy's Popular Library), which was a Catholic tale [RL; Personal communication, Lady Christina Colvin, in a letter, 13 Sept. 1993].

B127   *Dialogues on botany, for the use of young persons; explaining the structure of plants, and the progress of vegetation* [anon.].

+ London: R. Hunter, 1819. LOCATION L, InND Loeber coll.

COMMENTARY Highly praised by Maria Edgeworth§. Written for young children in response to books on the Linnaean classification of botany, 'by which the young memory is loaded with systematic arrangements and technical terms, while the really instructive parts of the science – the physiology of plants, and the progress of vegetation – are deferred till the ardour of the learner has subsided' (p. v). Instead, it deals with such topics as bulbs, roots, bark, leaves, etc., in brief, daily lessons in botany written in the form of dialogues between three 'very happy' children, Fanny, Emma, and Cecil and their aunt, Miss Mary Percival. The book has an extensive index but no illustrations because the author felt that 'children should be induced to study nature, rather than engraved representations' (p. viii). The volume provides a fairly extensive overview of the structure of plants, enhanced by the use of a microscope. The volume may have been written in response also to *Conversations on botany* (London, 1817) by Jane Marcet which was very technical, but this work is not mentioned in HB's volume [ML; RL; [F. Edgeworth], *A memoir of Maria Edgeworth* (London, 1867), ii, p. 41].

B128   *Bertha's visit to her uncle in England* [anon.].

London: John Murray, 1830, 3 vols. SOURCE Garside 2, A:4. LOCATION L, Corvey 3–628–47118–4, CaOTP, NUC.

+ London: John Murray, 1831, 3 vols. (new edn). LOCATION InND Loeber coll.

COMMENTARY *London 1831 edn* Reset and some textual revsd [Personal communication, Mary Pollard, Oct. 2004].

London: John Murray, 1836, 3rd ed (as *Bertha's journal while on a visit to her uncle in England*). SOURCE Alston, p. 279; Ellison, 1975 (p. 2 probably mistakenly mentions a 1829 edn, also mentioned by Colvin). LOCATION L, NUC (1843 edn)]

London: John Murray, 1851, 7th edn (as *Bertha's journal during a visit to her uncle in England. Containing a variety of interesting and instructive information*). LOCATION NUC

+ Boston: Lilly & Wait, Carter, Hendee & Babcock; New York: G. & C. & H. Carvill & E. Bliss; Philadelphia: Carey & Hart; Baltimore: W. & J. Neal; Albany: Little & Cummings; New-Orleans: M. Carroll; Portland: S. Colman, 1831, 2 vols. (ill.; 'improved from the London edn'). LOCATION NUC, InND Loeber coll.

COMMENTARY This book became very popular and is known from a 7th edn. It is wrongly ascribed to Jane Marcet in BLC, NUC, and Osborne (p. 722). The story for juveniles concerns Bertha Montague who is sent from Rio de Janeiro to live with her uncle in a country house in England. She promises her mother to keep a journal and send the pages to her. The journal is a mixture of brief sketches and pieces of information on a diverse range of topics, such as biology, botany, geology, physics, agriculture, etc. The text also contains reminders on how to behave, and lessons of life as well as religious discussions. The encyclopaedic range of topics covered is summarized in an index in the last volume. In North America the book was recommended in *The young lady's own book* (Philadelphia, 1832) as suitable for young women [ML; RL].

B129   *The heiress in her minority; or, the progress of character* [anon.].

+ London: John Murray, 1850, 2 vols. SOURCE Wolff, 371. LOCATION D, L, NUC.

COMMENTARY Wrongly ascribed to Jane Marcet in BLC and NUC. Written prior to the Famine of 1845–47. The advertisement states that 'the author had endeavoured, in the following pages, to trace the steps by which the power of self control may be practically developed in a young and ardent mind when brought under the influence of high and noble motives; and further, to show how materially the happiness of the individual may be enlarged by turning it from selfish indolence of pride to the active and habitual exercise of the faculties in the acquisition of useful and varied knowledge. The scene is laid in the west of Ireland, and a few slight sketches are given of its many interesting objects; but they were all written before that country had become a prey to the late dreadful evils of rebellion and famine; and the reader is assured that all the characters are purely imaginary'. The main character is Evelyn Desmond, a young girl of Irish descent whose grandfather is Sir Connor O'Brien, with whom she has lived in England until his death. Afterwards she travels through Ireland with her father and his second wife. Many places are described including the Isles of Aran, Lough Derg, Dingle, Kenmare and Killarney. The book consists mainly of a succession of discussions on a great variety of topics, ranging from the utility of insects, the management of horses in South America, moon-worship, and Irish land agents. Most unusually for a novel, a topical index is provided. Evelyn is greatly improved by the experience of the tour and the interesting conversations she has with various people. Her view of the Irish is completely altered [ML].

B130   *Lessons and trials of life* [anon.].

+ London: James Nisbet & Co., 1854 (ill. E. Evans). SOURCE Alston, p. 279. LOCATION L.

COMMENTARY Mistakenly identified as by Jane Marcet. Society fiction set in England [Alston, p. 279; RL].

BEAUFORT, Louisa Catherine, b. Penylan, Carmarthenshire, Wales 1781 (1791 according to Colvin), d. Dublin? 1867. Botanist, entomologist, writer of juvenile fiction, artist and antiquarian, LCB was the second daughter of Revd Dr Daniel Augustus Beaufort, rector of Navan (Co. Meath) and vicar of Collon (Co. Louth), and Mary Waller of Allenstown (Co. Meath). Her parents were on a visit to Wales at the time of her birth. She had a special interest in botany and gardening which developed early in life. She became very interested in insects and wrote *Dialogues on entomology* (London, 1819) to accompany her sister Henrietta Beaufort's§ *Dialogues on botany* (London, 1819). Whether she was also responsible for *The natural history of remarkable insects, with their habits and instincts* (Dublin, 1819), published under the aegis of the Kildare Place Society, is not clear. LCB also published on botany in *RIA Trans.* ((15)1828, pp 101–243). Another of her interests was architecture. In 1820 her father wrote to his son Francis in England, inquiring for Louisa whether 'small books on architecture or bees be likely to sell in London … [because] her fingers are itching to write and her full mind seeking for vent' (Ellison, p. 78). We have not been able to confirm that she ever published such 'small books'. LCB became the first woman in Ireland known to have written about monuments in the Irish countryside. She delivered *An essay upon the state of architecture and antiquities of Ireland, previous to the landing of the Anglo-Normans* at the RIA in 1827 and published it later, illustrated with her own drawings (*RIA Trans.*, 1828). This earned her the unusual distinction of honorary membership of the RIA (her father had taken a prominent part in founding the RIA). She was also elected member of the Kilkenny Archaeological Society in 1851. LCB and her sister Henrietta Beaufort§ gave Maria Edgeworth§ the idea for the story 'The orphans', published in Maria's *The parent's assistant* (London, 1800). Occasionally LCB joined her parents on their travels, for example in 1794 to England and later on several occasions in Ireland (in 1810 they travelled together to Killarney and Limerick and her mother kept a diary of that trip (TCD, MS 4,035)). LCB helped her father with the making of maps and also designed the elaborately patterned glass in some of the windows of his church at Collon. In 1853 she was living in Dublin at 9 Hatch Street. LCB's Irish journal for 1842 to 1843, containing archaeological sketches, is in the Henry E. Huntington Library, San Marino (CA, MS FB 58), which also has several of her letters (MS FB 152). Other of her papers are in the NLI (MS 8,783), and in TCD (MSS 4,034, 9,217). Letters by Frances Edgeworth§ to LCB are in the Bodleian Library, Oxford (MS Eng. Lett. C. 738). SOURCE Butler, p. 237n.3; Colvin, pp xxxvii, 376–7, 560; C.C. Ellison, *The hopeful traveller. The life and times of Daniel Augustus Beaufort LL.D. 1739–1821* (Kilkenny, 1987), pp 6–7, 78, 83, 87, 97, 104, 117; J. Leerssen, *Remembrance and imagination.* (Notre Dame [IN], 1997), passim; J.B. Leslie, *Armagh clergy and parishes* (Dundalk, 1911), p. 201; RL.

B131 *Dialogues on entomology, in which the forms and habits of insects are familiarly explained* [anon.] (dedicated to Miss [Maria] Edgeworth§).
+ London; R. Hunter, 1819 (ill.). LOCATION L, InND Loeber coll.
COMMENTARY According to the introduction, the text was written for children between the ages of eight and ten. The work consists of dialogues between a mother and her daughter, Lucy, about many aspects of entomology. In the process Lucy learns about the classification of insects and many of the Latin and Greek terms that are used to describe them. The daily discussions are brief, so as not to make the topic burdensome for children. The discussions are aided by specimen found in the garden and aim to train children to observe nature. The volume has an index [ML].

B132 *Animal sagacity, exemplified by facts: shewing the force of instinct in beasts, birds, &c.* [anon.].
+ Dublin: Printed by W.H. Tyrrell [for the Kildare Place Society], 1819 (ill.). SOURCE Osborne, p. 819; Bradshaw, 3239. LOCATION D (1824 edn), C, CaOTP, InND Loeber coll. (1824 edn).
COMMENTARY Fiction for juveniles. A series of thirty letters between Emily and Caroline concerning the behaviour of animals. Many of the letters concern animals, mostly in the east and north of Ireland, and some of the stories related in the letters are by Irishmen, including Capt. Beaufort (p. 113), LCB's brother. Several of the stories concern insects, which were LCB's special interest. Revd Palmer in the stories is probably modelled on Dr. Daniel Augustus Beaufort, LCB's father [RL: Osborne].

'BEAUMONT, Edgar', pseud. of Clifford Halifax, MD. Co-author. See SMITH, Elizabeth Thomasina Toulmin.

BEAVAN, Emily Elizabeth (née Shaw; also known as Mrs F. Beavan), b. Belfast c.1820. Story and sketch writer, EEB was the daughter of Samuel Shaw, a sea captain. Around 1836 she emigrated to New Brunswick in Canada (settling at Long Creek), where she studied, taught school, and in 1838 married Frederick Cadwallader Beavan, a medical doctor. She frequently contributed stories to the *Amaranth*, a periodical published in St John in the early 1840s. She returned to Ireland in 1843 and two years later published her only volume. SOURCE CEWW.

B133 *Sketches and tales illustrative of life in the backwoods of New Brunswick, North America : gleaned from actual observation and experience during a residence of seven years in that interesting colony* (by Mrs F. Beavan).
London: G. Routledge, 1845. SOURCE CEWW; COPAC. LOCATION L.

COMMENTARY Mingles sketches of daily life, scenery and customs of early-nineteenth-century New Brunswick (Canada) with tales of gothic adventure and romance. Describes a community bound together by isolation and hardship that takes pleasures from literature and sociability [CEWW].

BEAVAN, Mrs. F. See **BEAVAN, Emily Elizabeth.**

BEDDOES, Thomas, b. 1760 Shifnal (Shrops.), d. Clifton, near Bristol (Avon) 1808. English physician, chemist, and writer on medicine and politics, TB graduated BA from Oxford in 1779, then studied medicine in Edinburgh in 1784, returning to Oxford in 1786 to take his MB and MD in 1788. He believed in the advancement of medicine through new research in chemistry and in public health through a reformed social order at all levels. A liberal and anti-imperialist, his anti-government views were shared by writers such as Robert Southey and Samuel Taylor Coleridge. In 1794 he married Anna, a sister of Maria Edgeworth§, and daughter of Richard Lovell Edgeworth§, but the marriage was not a happy one. He lived with his wife at Clifton where in 1798 he opened a 'pneumatic hospital' at which research into the uses of gases in medicine was carried out. This later became the Preventive Medical Institution for the Sick and Drooping Poor. Here TB aimed at the early treatment of disease while despairing of the lifestyles of the poor that brought illness upon them. Among his writings are *Hygeia* (Bristol, 1802–3), and *The manual of health* (London, 1806). At his death, Southey wrote: 'From Beddoes I hoped for more good to the human race than any other individual'. Few of his papers survived him. The following highly-popular moral tale appeared in an English and Irish version, but it is not clear whether TB was responsible for the Irish version as well, and whether that version was published with the encouragement of his father-in-law, whom he first met in 1793. SOURCE Allibone, i, p. 156; BLC; Butler, pp 109–11, 142, 170–1, 442ff; DLB, clviii; NCBEL 4, pp 535–7; ODNB; Osborne, p. 860; RL; D.A. Stansfield, *Thomas Beddoes M.D., 1760–1808* (Dordrecht, 1984), pp 87–9, 120–2.

B134   *The history of Isaac Jenkins, and of the sickness of Sarah, his wife, and their three children* [anon.].
Madeley: Printed [for the author?] by J. Edmunds, 1792. SOURCE Mayo, 581; ESTC t18476. LOCATION L (destroyed), C, O.
Bristol: Bulgin & Rosser, [1793], 5th edn (as *The history of Isaac Jenkins, and Sarah his wife, and their three children*). SOURCE ESTC t018479. LOCATION L, NUC (1796 edn).
London: J. Murray & J. Johnson, 1793 (as *The history of Isaac Jenkins, and Sarah his wife, and their three children*). SOURCE ESTC t018477; Forster 2, 262. LOCATION Univ. of Glasgow.
Cork: A. Edwards, 1793, 3rd edn. SOURCE ESTC t226290. LOCATION CKu.
Edinburgh: [n.p.], 1793 (as *The history of Isaac Jenkins, and Sarah his wife, and their three children*). SOURCE ESTC t200512. LOCATION E.
Birmingham: J. Belcher & Son, 1816. LOCATION L.
+ Dublin: Printed by R. Napper [for Kildare Place Society], 1817 (as *The history of Isaac Jenkins, and Sarah his wife, and their three children; to which is added, A friendly gift for servants and apprentices*). SOURCE Adams, pp 103–4, 193. LOCATION L.
+ Dublin: J.J. Nolan [for the Kildare Place Society], 1818 (as *The story of Isaac Jenkins, to which are added, A friendly gift to servants and apprentices, and The brazier, or mutual gratitude*; ill. T. Kelly). SOURCE Gilbert, p. 430. LOCATION DPL Gilbert coll.
+ Dublin: Printed by Wm. Espy [for the Kildare Place Society], 1820 (as *The history of Isaac Jenkins, to which are added, A friendly gift to servants and apprentices, and The*

brazier, or, mutual gratitude; ill.; see Plate 9). SOURCE Bradshaw, 2999; Osborne, p. 860. LOCATION D (1830 edn), L (destroyed), NUC, CaOTP, InND Loeber coll.

Belfast: Simms & M'Intyre, 1818. SOURCE Anderson 1, p. 61. LOCATION BFl.

COMMENTARY Twenty-thousand copies had been sold at the end of 1816 and the beginning of 1817. Contents of Dublin 1820 edn: 'The history of Isaac Jenkins', 'A friendly gift for servants and apprentices', 'The brazier; or, mutual gratitude. Translated from the French'. The story of 'Isaac Jenkins' exemplifies TB's medical and public health approach to alcoholism and illnesses, and consists of a moral tale concerning the poor family of the drunken Isaac Jenkins. The earliest version of the story, printed at Madeley (Shrops.) in 1792 is set at Titterstene, some twenty miles southwest of Madeley. Through the services of a kindly doctor, Isaac's dying children recover from their fever and the father is reformed. The story concludes with the doctor's rules for good health and sobriety and his advice concerning the opening of savings bank accounts. An Irish version appeared in 1831, which was set during the Irish famine of 1783 (but this is not mentioned in the 1817 or 1820 Dublin edns) and has the drunken Isaac Jenkins also as principal character. The 1820 Dublin edn refers to a famine in 1783, but the location is not indicated. Later in the story it mentions a savings bank in Dublin. 'A friendly gift for servants and apprentices' refers to various gravestones erected by grateful employers, one of which celebrates the faithful servant of Dean Swift§ in St Patrick's Cathedral, Dublin. The story may have been extracted from Mrs Taylor's *Present of a mistress to a young servant* (London, 1816). The last story 'The brazier' was by Mme de Genlis§. The main character, Mme de Varonne, was descended from 'one of the best families' in Ireland, but she and her husband had retired to France [ML; Adams, pp 103–4; Mayo, 581; Osborne; Stansfield, *Beddoes*, pp 87–9; Hislop, p. 202].

BELBE, Bagriella Isnard de. See **DE BELBE, Bagriella Isnard.**

BELFAST, earl of. See **CHICHESTER, Frederick Richard.**

BELL, Miss Catherine Douglas (also **Miss C.D. Bell**), d. Edinburgh 1861 (other sources give 1866). CDB was a writer of religious and moral fiction for children. SOURCE Allibone Suppl., i, p. 123; Boase, i, p. 227; NCBEL 4, p. 1748; NUC; Personal communication, Mary Pollard, Sept. 2003.

B135 *Mike, the shop-boy* (by Catherine Douglas Bell).
London: T. Nelson & Sons, 1859. LOCATION L (destroyed).
London, New York, Edinburgh: T. Nelson & Sons, 1871 (as *Love thy neighbour as thyself; or, the story of Mike, the Irish boy*, by 'Cousin Kate' (the late Miss C.D. Bell); ill.). LOCATION L (destroyed), O, NUC (1872 edn).
COMMENTARY 62pp. No copy of London, 1859 edn located. Religious fiction for children [COPAC; BLC].

BELL, Revd Charles Dent, pseud. '**An old hand**', b. Ballymaguigan, near Castledawson (Co. Derry) 1819, d. London 1898. Anglican clergyman, poet and miscellaneous writer, CDB was the son of Henry Humphrey Bell of Ballymaguigan (Co. Derry). CDB attended the Royal School, Dungannon (Co. Tyrone), graduated BA, MA, and DD from TCD and was ordained in 1843. He moved to England and became curate of St Mary's (Reading, 1845–47); St Mary-in-the-Castle (Hastings, 1847–54); St John's Chapel (Hampstead,1854–61); vicar of Ambleside (Westmoreland, 1861–72); Rydal (Cumbria, 1872); rector of Cheltenham (Glos., 1872–95), and was honorary canon of Carlisle for many years. Some of his poetry was published in *The four seasons at the lake* (London, n.d.) and with H.E. Fox he published the Church of England hymnal ([London], 1894). He wrote several books on travel in the Middle East. SOURCE

Allibone Suppl., i, p. 123; B & S, p. 56 (for some conflicting information); Boase, iv, p. 345; Irish pseudonyms; LVP, p. 38; MVP, pp 35–6; NCBEL 4, p. 537; NSTC; O'Donoghue, p. 24; RIA/DIB; Rogal, p. 264.

B136 *Blanche Neville; or, a record of married life* [anon.].
London: [publisher?], 1853. SOURCE Allibone Suppl., i, p. 123; NCBEL 4, p. 537. LOCATION L (destroyed).
COMMENTARY No copy located. Perhaps written in response to A.M. Stewart's *Humility, or, Blanche Neville and the fancy fair* (London, 1848).

B137 *Reminiscences of a boyhood in the early part of the century. A fragment of a life. A new story* (by 'An old hand').
+ London: Sampson Low, Marston, Searle & Rivington, 1889. SOURCE NCBEL 4, p. 537. LOCATION L, C, InND Loeber coll.
COMMENTARY Fictionalized biographical account set in Lough Neagh House, which may be identified with the author's boyhood home at Ballymaguigan (Co. Derry). Contains much on childhood in the country and what individuals read in this small country house [RL].

B138 *Tales told from the fireside* (by Charles Dent Bell).
+ London: Elliot Stock, 1896. SOURCE NCBEL 4, p. 536; COPAC. LOCATION L, C.
COMMENTARY The stories are said to be based on fact. The volume carries the motto: 'Fiction may be used as one of the Gateways to the Temple of Truth'. Contents: 'My father's story', 'Rose Oge: A vignette of Irish peasant life', 'My mother's story', 'My uncle's story' (set near Lough Neagh), 'My aunt's story' (set in Co. Wicklow), 'My grandmother's story', 'My cousin's story', 'The vicar's story' [CM; RL].

B139 *Home sunshine, etc.* (by Charles Dent Bell).
+ London, Glasgow: Collins, [1904] (ill.). SOURCE COPAC. LOCATION L.
COMMENTARY Fiction for juveniles published posthumously. Set in Scotland and features the fate of the family of the Gordons of Eagle's Crag [NSTC; RL].

BELL, Henry Nugent. See **BELL, Nugent.**

BELL, Mrs Martin. See **MARTIN, Mary Letitia.**

BELL, Nugent (possibly Henry Nugent), fl. 1817, d. prior to 1826. Novelist and attorney, NB was probably the first son of George and Catherine Nugent of Bellview (Co. Fermanagh). He was educated by Dr. Burrowes at Portora Royal School in Enniskillen (Co. Fermanagh) and admitted to the King's Inns in 1808. He was not called to the Irish Bar, but is likely to have practiced as an attorney. He may be the same person or be related to the genealogist Henry Nugent Bell (1792–1822), also from Belleview [*sic*], who successfully solved and wrote about the long-dormant earldom of Huntington (London, 1820). For his portraits, see ODNB. SOURCE Keane, p. 31; W. Laffan & B. Rooney, '"One of our brilliant ornaments": the death and life of Thomas Foster' in *Irish Architectural and Decorative Studies*, 7 (2004), p. 220; ODNB; RL.

B140 *Alexena; or, the Castle of Santa Marco, a romance* [anon.].
+ London: A.K. Newman & Co., 1817, vol. 1. SOURCE British Fiction (see also Update 1); Garside, 1817:13, LOCATION D, ViU.
+ Dublin: Printed by Brett Smith, 1817, vols. 2 and 3 (ill.). SOURCE British Fiction (see also Update 1); Garside 1817:13. LOCATION D, ViU.
COMMENTARY Anon. in volume 1, but author's name, Nugent Bell, is annotated in volume 2 (NLI copy). Gothic fiction set in the sixteenth century beginning with Lord Mortimer and his Irish servant Tom Rourke. The action takes place in Spain [RL; British Fiction (Update 1)].

BELL, Priscilla. See **WAKEFIELD, Priscilla.**

BELL, Robert, b. Cork 1800, d. London 1867. Journalist, editor, dramatist, novelist and biographer, RB was the son of an Irish magistrate and was educated at TCD, where he began his career in journalism. At TCD he founded the Dublin Historical Society in the wake of the College Historical Society having been suppressed by the college authorities. After graduation in 1818 he was editor of the *Patriot* (Dublin), founded the *Dublin Inquisitor*, and wrote two dramas, 'Double disguises' and 'Comic lectures'. He moved to London in 1828, wrote a pamphlet supporting Catholic emancipation, and became editor of the London weekly journal *Atlas*. With Edward Bulwer Lytton§ he helped establish and then edit the *Monthly Chronicle* (London), and became a major book reviewer of and contributor to *Bentley's Miscellany* (London, at least from 1848 onward) and to *Household Words* (London, 1851). He edited several volumes of stories, poems, and ballads; wrote five more dramas; contributed to many histories and compendiums of biographies and published the *Life of Canning* (London, 1846). He was an active member of the committee of the Literary Fund and in his later years edited the *Home News* (London), a monthly journal for English residents in India and the east. RB was a close friend of the authors Charles Dickens, Anthony Trollope§ and William Makepeace Thackeray§, next to whose grave in Kensal Green cemetery he requested he be buried. Trollope said of him, 'I have known no man better read in English literature' (Sadleir, p. 138). RB left incomplete at his death his annotated edn of *English poets* (London, 1854–7). For correspondence, see ODNB. SOURCE Allibone, i, p. 160; Allibone Suppl., i, p. 125; Brady, p. 10; Curran index, BentM 1579ff; Irish pseudonyms; Lohrli, p. 205; ODNB; O'Donoghue, p. 24; RIA/DIB; M. Sadleir (ed.), *An autobiography by Anthony Trollope* (London, 1923), p. 138; Sutherland, p. 56.

B141   *The ladder of gold. An English story* (by Robert Bell).
    London: Richard Bentley, 1850, 3 vols. SOURCE Rafroidi, ii, p. 60; NSTC. LOCATION L, NUC.
    New York: W.F. Purgess, 1851. LOCATION NUC.
COMMENTARY Follows the rise and fall of a clerk, Richard Rawlings, who marries his employer's widow, and finds himself rich. He turns to railway speculation, makes himself even richer and aspires to a seat in parliament. Finally, his wealth evaporates, and he is left with the love of his family [Sutherland].

B142   *Hearts and altars. A narrative* (by Robert Bell).
    London: Henry Colburn & Co., 1852. SOURCE Rafroidi, ii, p. 60; NSTC. LOCATION L, NUC.

BELLEW, Capt. Francis John, fl. 1843. Novelist and army member, FJB is identified by Block, who also indicates that the same person (listed by him as Capt. F.H.T. Bellew [*sic*]) wrote *The cockney in Scotland*. According to an advertisement seen by Block, the latter work was published by H.J. Gibbs in London in 1850 and was illustrated by the author. We have been unable to locate a copy under this title. FJB also wrote a small illustrated book, *View in India* (London, 1833), where he must have served in the army. SOURCE Block, p. 18; OCLC; RL.

B143   *Memoirs of a griffin; or, a cadet's first year in India* (by Capt. Bellew).
    + London: Wm. H. Allen & Co., 1843, 2 vols. (ill. the author; Plate 10). LOCATION L.
    London: Wm. H. Allen & Co., 1880 (new edn; ill. the author). LOCATION L.
    New York: H. Long & Brother, 1848 (as *Frank Gernon, or, a cadet's first year in India*). SOURCE OCLC. LOCATION OU. COMMENTARY *New York edn.* A book entitled *The young cadet. A novel* (by Capt. Ballew [*sic*]) appeared in New York in the 1880s and may be a late reprint [RL].

COMMENTARY Partially autobiographical. The main character, Frank Gernon, was born in England of an Irish father. He sets out to join the army in India, where newly arrived people are called griffins, and the story is about his first year there. He arrives by ship in Calcutta and then traverses the continent by boat and horse to New Delhi where he joins his regiment. On the way, he meets a number of soldiers of Irish extraction and he gives vivid descriptions of the countryside, the native population and their habits [ML].

BELSON, Mary. See ELLIOTT, Mary Belson.

BENNETT, Susanna. See LE FANU, Susanna.

BENTLEY, Samuel. Editor. See ST. LEGER, Francis Barry Boyle.

BERENS, Mrs E.M. See STEWART, Miss Elizabeth M.

BERESFORD, G. de la Poer. See BERESFORD, Maj.-Gen. George de la Poer.

BERESFORD, Maj.-Gen. George de la Poer (also known as G. de la Poer Beresford), b. 1826 (1830 according to Allibone), d. 1865. Novelist and travel writer, GPB was the seventh and youngest son of John-Barré Beresford, of Learmont (Co. Derry), and Sophia Montgomery. He probably served or travelled in the Balkans since he published *Twelve sketches ... in Southern Albania* (London, 1855). He married in 1849 Anne, daughter of Lt.-Gen. Charles-Edward Conyers. In all likelihood GPB was related to George de la Poer Beresford, 2nd earl of Tyrone and 1st marquess of Waterford (1735–1800) and John George de la Poer Beresford (1773–1862), vice-chancellor of Dublin University and archbishop of Armagh. For his portraits, see ODNB. SOURCE Allibone Suppl., i, p. 136; E. Lodge, *The peerage and baronetage* (London, 1897, 66th edn), p. 679; ODNB.
B144　*Clara Leicester. A novel* (by G. de la Poer Beresford).
　　London: Hurst & Blackett, 1858, 3 vols. SOURCE NSTC; COPAC. LOCATION L.
B145　*Hoods and masks* (by George de la Poer Beresford).
　　London: C.J. Skeet, 1865, 3 vols. SOURCE NSTC ; COPAC. LOCATION L, DCL.

BERLIN, Eliza Annie (also known as E.A. Berlin), fl. 1868. American novelist, EAB states in the introduction to the following volume that she received little education, and that the story is based on 'truth'. She thanks Mr and Mrs C— of Ashland County (OH), who provided her with a home while writing this work. SOURCE RL.
B146　*Earth angels and hidden oppression: or the life of little Annie* (by E.A. Berlin).
　　+ Columbus: Printed [for the author?] by Nevins & Myers, 1868. LOCATION Wright web.
COMMENTARY Possibly an autobiographical story about an Irish emigrant family by the name of Milony. They leave Ireland with two children but one dies at sea. They settle in a rural area and have more children. Annie is a Presbyterian but her husband Robert does not practice his religion. The hardships of life in the colonies are discussed and the problems of rearing children are exemplified [ML; RL].

BERTHET, Élie-Bertrand (also known as Élie Berthet), b. 1815 (not 1818 as indicated by Wolff), d. 1891. French or Belgian novelist and dramatist, E-BB was the son of a lawyer. His *The draper's daughter. A tale of Paris in the olden time* appeared in a translation by Frank Thorpe Porter§ in Dublin in 1852. SOURCE Personal communication, Andrew Carpenter, July 1996; CCF; NUC; RL; Wolff, 410.

B147 *Le dernier Irlandais* (by Élie Berthet).
Brussels: Meline, Cans & Co., 1851, 3 vols. SOURCE Brown, 191; COPAC (Brussels, du Panthéon, 1851, 4 vols in 2 edn). LOCATION NUC.
+ Deventer : P. Hovenaar Ruterine, 1853, 2 vols. (trans. into Dutch as *De laatste Ier: Een romantisch verhaal uit de tijd der laatsten Iersche oproer*; ill.). SOURCE Adamnet. LOCATION UVA.
+ Paris: J.-J. Ledoyen & Paul Giret, 1852, 3 vols. LOCATION L, NUC (1865 edn), InND Loeber coll. (Bourdilliat & Co., 1860 edn; see Plate 11).
COMMENTARY Reviewed in the *Irish Quarterly Review* (Dublin, June 1852). Describes an abortive rising under one of the O'Byrnes of Wicklow in the 1840s as a result of an insult to O'Byrne's sister by a scoundrel named Clinton. O'Byrne flees to Connemara with Nelly Avondale, daughter of the landlord of Glendalough. Nelly returns to marry the scoundrel and O'Byrne flees again [Brown].

'BERWICK, E.L.A.', pseud. See REYNOLDS, James.

BESANT, Sir Walter, b. Portsea (Hants.) 1836, d. Hampstead (London) 1901. A popular English novelist, historian and juvenile fiction writer who campaigned for authors' rights, women's employment, and on behalf of workers and the poor. WB was educated at Cambridge and taught at the Royal College in Mauritius for over six years, where he studied French literature and wrote his first novel. In 1868 he became secretary to the Palestine Exploration Fund and collaborated on writing *Jerusalem: the city of Herod and Saladin* (London, 1871). In 1869 he began a collaboration with James Rice, editor of *Once A Week* (London), that produced a number of successful novels, some of which became immensely popular and sold hundreds of thousands of copies. After Rice's death, WB continued to write novels as well as works on social, historical and religious themes. He was a central figure in setting up the Society for Authors in 1883. SOURCE Allibone Suppl., i, pp 139–40; Brown 2, p. 19; DLB, cxxxv, cxc; EF, p. 30; NCBEL 4, pp 1455–61; ODNB; Sutherland, pp 59–61; T & B, pp 966–7.
B148 *This son of Vulcan. A novel* (by Sir Walter Besant and James Rice).
London: Sampson Low, Marston, Searle & Rivington, 1876, 3 vols. SOURCE Brown 2, 76; Wolff, i, p. 79. LOCATION NUC.
New York: New York Tribune, [1878?]. LOCATION NUC.
COMMENTARY Life story of a boy orphaned in tragic circumstances and adopted by Myles Cuolahan, a hard-drinking Irishman, who falls deeper and deeper into drunken ways but is saved from a dreadful crime while in delirium tremens. He takes a pledge of temperance from Fr [Theobald] Mathew and goes off on his travels, leaving the boy to the care of a spiritualist named Bastable. The remaining story turns on the discovery of a hidden treasure in the shape of rich vein of ironstone, leading to the rise of 'this son of Vulcan' to prosperity [Brown 2].

BEST, Henry Digby. See BESTE, Henry Digby.

BESTE, Revd Henry Digby (known also as Henry Best), b. Lincoln (Lincs.) 1768, d. Brighton (E. Sussex) 1836. English novelist, poet and travel writer, HDB was the son of the prebendary of Lincoln. He was educated at Magdalen College, Oxford, and graduated BA in 1788 and MA in 1791 when he entered the Church of England, serving as curate of St Martin's, Lincoln. His studies and friendships with Roman Catholic clerics led him to convert to catholicism in 1798. In 1801 HDB married Sarah Sealy and the couple lived in Bath. They had six children in all and moved to France in 1818, returning to England in 1827. Aside from one novel that deals with Ireland, he wrote accounts of his Continental travels, while his

Personal and literary memoirs was published in 1829. SOURCE Allibone i, p. 182; Brown, p. 31; NSTC; ODNB [under Best].

B149 **Poverty and the baronet's family.** *An Irish Catholic novel* (by Henry Digby Beste, MA, Fellow of St Mary Magdalen College, Oxford; 'Originator of the religious opinions of modern Oxford').

London: T. Jones, 1845. SOURCE Brown, 192; Sadleir, 210; Wolff, 471. LOCATION L.

COMMENTARY Published posthumously. Concerns the early stages of Catholic Irish immigration to England. The story opens in 1805 with Bryan O'Meara, the son of a poor Irish migratory labourer, being educated in England by Sir Cecil Foxglove in gratitude for Bryan's father's rescue of his daughter. When Bryan is grown up he returns to his father's people in Athlone, after having been refused by the baronet's daughter. Although Bryan is poor, he is a descendant of Irish gentry, who following the battle of the Boyne in 1690 were dispossessed as part of the Williamite confiscations. After his return to Ireland as a tenant farmer, he gets involved in rebellious activities. By chance he becomes wealthy and returns to England to marry the baronet's daughter, Arabella. Her decision to convert to catholicism did not spring from strong religious feelings. An appendix has a sketch of Beste's decision to convert to catholicism [Brown; Gains and losses, pp 28–31].

BIANCONI, Mary Anne. See O'CONNELL, Mrs Mary Anne.

'BICKERDYKE, John', pseud. See COOKE, Charles Henry.

BIDDLE, Anthony J. Drexel. See BIDDLE, Anthony Joseph Drexel.

BIDDLE, Anthony Joseph Drexel (known as Anthony J. Drexel Biddle), b. 1874, d. 1948. American sketch writer who also wrote a manual on individual combat and may have self-published some of his works. SOURCE NUC; RL; Wright, iii, p. 53.

B150 **Shantytown sketches** (by Anthony J. Drexel Biddle).

Philadelphia: Drexel Biddle, 1897 (ill. Clarence Snyder). SOURCEs Fanning, pp 177, 375; Wright, iii, 516; COPAC. LOCATION NUC

COMMENTARY Contents: 'Mrs. Mulhooney's receiving day', 'O'Blather's lecture on "Arnithololgy"', 'A petition from dwellers in Shantytown', 'Remember and take varning', 'Advice to a newspaper reporter', 'An heiress', 'An interrupted debate on the woman's rights question', 'Brother Winslow's discourse on "De modern people am exactly like de ancients"', 'At the theatre – from the gallery standpoint' [NUC].

'BIOGRAPHER TRIGLYPH', pseud. See GRIFFITH, Richard.

BISHOP, Revd R.F., fl. 1893. Novelist, RFB was a clergyman of the Ohio Conference. SOURCE RL.

B151 **Camerton Slope: A story of mining life** (by Revd R.F. Bishop).

+ Cincinnati: Cranston & Curtis; New York: Hunt & Eaton, 1893 (ill.). SOURCE Scott cat. 4/7; Wright, iii, 532; COPAC. LOCATION D, NUC, InND Loeber coll.

COMMENTARY A novel of life in a small mining community in Pennsylvania, largely consisting of individuals of Irish descent. Boys are employed in the mines at a very young age, the work is hard and dangerous and their education is curtailed. The Molly Maguires, an organization with roots in Ireland, tries to exploit the miners' hardships by proposing a strike, planning to kill those who are against it. However, the miners' good sense prevails and the Molly Maguires are banished from the area [ML].

BISSET, Robert, b. 1759, d. 1805. Novelist and essayist, RB was the author of *Douglas; or, the Highlander* (London, 1800, 4 vols.), which was printed at the Anti-Jacobin Press and also published in Dublin in that year. The dedication to it and to the following volume were dated Sloane Terrace [London], 1 Feb. 1800, and 8 May 1804, respectively. RB's degree is given as LLD on the title pages of vols. 2 and 3 of *Modern Literature* (London, 1804). He also wrote *A defence of the slave trade on the grounds of humanity, policy, and justice* (London, 1804). SOURCE Garside, 1800:18, 1804:13; NSTC; COPAC.

B152   *Modern literature. A novel* (by Robert Bisset).
+ London: T.N. Longman & O. Rees, 1804, 3 vols. SOURCE Garside, 1804:13.
LOCATION Corvey CME 3–628–47137, L.
COMMENTARY Tells of the adventures of the villain Roger O'Rourke. Fleeing from law, O'Rourke, a former Jacobin and Methodist, ends up in Ireland in the early 1790s, and declares himself a Catholic and United Irishman. He pretends to be a Catholic priests, but reverts at times to the role of Methodist minister. He travels through the country 'confessing the women; and exhorting the men to what he called the emancipation of Ireland', while defrauding widows and committing highway robberies. In the end, he is captured, sentenced and executed [M.O. Grenby, *The anti-Jacobin novel* (Cambridge, 2001), p. 61].

BLACHFORD, Mary. See **TIGHE, Mary.**

BLACK, William, b. Glasgow (Scotland) 1841, d. Brighton (E. Sussex) 1898. WB was a journalist, editor and of one the foremost nineteenth-century novelists, with a formidable output. He was educated at the Glasgow School of Art but soon turned to journalism. He moved to London and was a correspondent for the *Morning Star* in the Franco-Prussian war. His novels, of which Queen Victoria was a fan, combine fictional adventures with closely observed scenes of travel and sport. Many are set in Celtic Scotland and include lush descriptions of the scenery there. Only one is known to deal with Ireland. SOURCE Allibone Suppl., i, pp 156–7; Brown, p. 34; NCBEL 4, pp 1466–7; ODNB; Sutherland, pp 64–5; T & B, p. 967.

B153   *Shandon bells. A novel* (by William Black).
London: Macmillan & Co., 1883, 3 vols. SOURCE Brown, 212 (1893 edn); Wolff, 508; Macmillan, p. 428. LOCATION Dt (1885 edn), NUC.
Leipzig: Bernard Tauchnitz, 1883, 2 vols. SOURCE T & B, 2155. LOCATION NUC.
New York: G. Munro, [1883] (Seaside Library, No. 1556). LOCATION NUC.
New York: Harper & Bros, 1883 (Harper's Franklin Square Library, No. 297). LOCATION D (1893 revsd edn), NUC.
New York: J.W. Lovell Co., [1883] (Lovell's Library, vol. 2, No. 85). LOCATION NUC.
COMMENTARY Serialized in Harper's *New Monthly Magazine* (May 1882 to Apr. 1883). Set partly in Co. Cork and partly in London and tells the story of a young man, Willie Fitzgerald, who goes to London to make his fortune. He is disappointed in love and turns to love of nature. The character of Willie Fitzgerald is based on the journalist William Barry [Brown; IBL, 10 (1919), pp 51–3; Topp 4, p. 399].

'BLACKBURNE, E. Owens', pseud. See **CASEY, Elizabeth Owens Blackburne.**

BLACKWOOD, Lady Helen Selina. See **DUFFERIN, Lady Helen Selina, baroness of Dufferin and Clandeboye.**

BLAKE, Sir Henry Arthur, pseud. '**Terence McGrath**', b. Corbally (Co. Limerick) 1840, d. Youghal? (Co. Cork) 1918. Short story writer and chronicler of his service as an RM, HAB was the son of Peter Blake, county inspector of the RIC, and Jane, daughter of John Lane, of Lanes Park. He joined the constabulary also and was appointed special RM of the Irish midland counties before becoming governor of the Bahamas in 1884; Newfoundland (1887); Hong Kong (1897); Jamaica (1889), and Ceylon (1903). He retired in 1907. He was the author of 'The Irish police' in the nineteenth century (1881, not located), a book on China (London, 1909), and a volume on Ceylon (Colombo, 1907). He remained interested in Newfoundland and in 1910 was chairman of Newfoundland Oilfields Ltd. At the end of his life he lived in Myrtle Grove, near Youghal (Co. Cork), where he was buried. The community of Blaketown in Newfoundland was named in his honour. He was married first to Jeannie Irwin of Boyle (Co. Roscommon), and then to Edith, daughter of Bernal Osborne and Catherine Isabella Osborne§ of Newtown Anner (Co. Tipperary), who became a botanical artist. SOURCE Allibone Suppl., i, p. 162; BLC; R.H. Cuff (ed.), *Dictionary of Newfoundland and Labrador biography* (St John's, 1990), pp 23–4; Herlihy, pp 63–4; IBL, 6 (1914), p. 24, and 9 (1918), pp 110–11; O'Toole, pp 14–15; RIA/DIB; W.A. Shaw, *The knights of England* (London, 1906), i, pp 345, 373.

B154 *Pictures from Ireland* (by 'Terence McGrath').
+ London: Kegan Paul & Co., 1880. LOCATION L, NUC.
+ New York: Henry Holt & Co., 1881 (Holt's Leisure Hour Series, No. 120). LOCATION NUC, InND Loeber coll.
COMMENTARY Reviewed in the *Saturday Review* (London). Stories about social tensions in the countryside. Contents: 'An Irish landlord of the old school', 'A land jobber', 'An absentee's agent', 'The tenant's friend', 'A gentleman farmer', 'A parish priest', 'An agitator', 'A Home Ruler', 'An Orangeman', 'A successful shopkeeper', 'A western tenant', 'The country's difficulty', 'A distressed landlord', 'A dispensary doctor', 'The voter of the future', 'The national schoolmaster', '"A gombeen" man', 'The true story of the Irish famine' [ML].

BLAKE, Nicholas, fl. 1846. Farmer, poet and unpublished novelist, NB was a native of Marley (Co. Meath) whose farming was ruined by the Famine of 1846 and 1847. He left for London, taking with him the manuscript of a novel, which he was unable to get published. He died there in his fifties. SOURCE O'Donoghue, p. 29.

B155 *The absentee* (by Nicholas Blake).
COMMENTARY Unpublished novel. Present location not known. Note that Maria Edgeworth's§ 'The absentee' was published about forty years earlier in her *Tales of fashionable life* (London, 1809) [O'Donoghue, p. 29; RL].

BLAKE-FORSTER, Charles Ffrench, b. Galway 1851, d. 1874. Historical novelist, genealogist and periodical writer, CFB-F was the eldest son of Capt. Francis Blake-Forster of the Connaught Rangers, and was privately educated. He became town councillor of Galway and HS of the county in 1874. His estate was located at Kinvara (Co. Galway). CFB-F was expelled from the county clubs of Galway and Clare for his nationalist opinions, and especially for publishing *The Irish chieftains* (Dublin, 1872) with a crownless harp on the cover, denoting the absence of royal dominion over Ireland. On the title page of this work he listed several historical tracts and pieces of fiction. Some of the former had been published in local newspapers and among the latter are: 'General Forster's rebellion; or, the rising of 1715'; 'The Lady Adeliza Dillon: A story of the penal laws', and 'A collection of the oldest and most popular legends of the peasantry of Clare and Galway'. It is not clear if and where these were published. He died unmarried in 1874 at age 23 and was buried in the family vault at Busheyfield, outside Galway. SOURCE Brown, p. 36; Galway, pp 4–5; IBL, 13 (1921), pp 74–6; 13 (1922), pp 165–6; RIA/DIB [under Forster].

B156 *The Irish chieftains; or, a struggle for the crown: with numerous notes and a copious appendix* (by Charles Ffrench Blake-Forster; dedicated to 'the descendants of

those ... who fought at the Boyne, Aughrim, Athlone, Galway, Limerick and on the Continent').
+ Dublin: M'Glashan & Gill; London: Whitaker & Co.; Simpkin, Marshall & Co.; Edinburgh: John Menzies & Co., 1872. SOURCE Brown, 220; Linen Hall cat. p. 95. LOCATION D, BFl, L, NUC, InND Loeber coll.
COMMENTARY First part is an historical novel of the Williamite War from the landing of James II at Kinsale to the surrender of Galway. Interwoven are large sections of the history of the O'Shaughnessy and Blake-Forster clans of Co. Galway. The family histories are carried down to the final dispossession of the O'Shaughnessys in 1770. The second part has 300pp of notes and appendices on pedigrees, reports, documents, etc. on west of Ireland families [Brown; RL].

BLAKENEY, Hope, fl. late-nineteenth century. Story writer who published in Belfast and hence probably was a resident of the north of Ireland. Source RL.
B157 *Shillelaghs; or, the Irish at home* (by Hope Blakeney).
+ Belfast: L. M'Kay, n.d. (ill. Barney O'Hea). LOCATION D.
COMMENTARY Publication date unclear, but clearly late-nineteenth century. Contents: 'Dandy (from life)', 'The fair thorn (a sketch from life)', 'Mickey; or, how they court in Ireland', 'Little Irish Jim (a sketch from life)', 'Ireland's private stills' [RL].

BLAND, E.A., pseud. **'E.A.B.D.'** Novelist and writer of religious fiction and fiction for juve-niles, EAB may be identified with Emma Alice Bland, eldest daughter of Francis Christopher Bland, of Derriquin (also known as Derryquin; Co. Kerry; since demolished), and Jane, daugh-ter of a Church of Ireland clergyman, Archibald Robert Hamilton. Her father converted to the Plymouth Brethren congregation in the 1860s, forsook his estate and travelled around Ireland and England as a missionary. His son, James Franklin, sold the Derriquin estate. EAB, who remained single, published 17 works of fiction, which were mostly issued by the Religious Tract Society. She is not to be confused with Edith Bland (née Nesbit). SOURCE Bary, p. 97; Landed gentry, pp 53–4.
B158 *Us three* (by 'E.A.B.D.').
London: J.F. Shaw & Co., [1885]. LOCATION L (destroyed), O.
B159 *'Gran'* (by 'E.A.B.D.').
London: James Nisbet & Co., 1886. LOCATION L (destroyed), O.
B160 *Barney. A soldier's story* (by 'E.A.B.D.'; dedicated to Thompson O'Gow and Thompson Mac).
+ London: John F. Shaw, 1887 (ill. by M. Irwin). LOCATION L, O.
COMMENTARY Set mostly in Ireland and contrasts people from the cabin and the castle. Barney and his sister beg for a living. Barney enlists and is shipped to India, where he meets Mr Cheniston, the son of the castle owner, and they become friends. Mr Cheniston is killed and when Barney returns Mr Cheniston's father gives Barney the watch that had belonged to his son [ML].
B161 *Young Ishmael Conway* (by 'E.A.B.D.').
London: J.F. Shaw & Co., [1887]. LOCATION L (destroyed), O.
B162 *Constable 42 Z* (by 'E.A.B.D.').
London: Religious Tract Society, [1888]. LOCATION L (destroyed).
COMMENTARY No copy located [RL].
B163 *Pincherton Farm. The story of Maurice Hamilton* (by 'E.A.B.D.').
+ London, Edinburgh, New York: Thomas Nelson & Sons, 1889 (ill.). LOCATION L, O.
COMMENTARY No Irish content [ML].

B164 *Adopted; or, the old soldier's embarrassments* (by 'E.A.B.D.').
London: Religious Tract Society, [1890]. LOCATION L (destroyed), O.

B165 *The tenants of paradise row* [anon.].
+ London: Religious Tract Society, [1890] (ill.). LOCATION L, O.
COMMENTARY No Irish content [ML].

B166 *A marked man.*(by 'E.A.B.D.').
+ London: Religious Tract society, [1890] (ill. C.W.). LOCATION L, O.
COMMENTARY An English farrier comes to work in an Irish town and is viewed with suspicion. He gets into trouble in Ireland, and in the end he goes to London to work for the poor [ML].

B167 *Foxy Fielding's friend* (by 'E.A.B.D.').
London: Religious Tract Society, [1891]. LOCATION L (destroyed), O.
COMMENTARY Religious fiction [BLC].

B168 *The outlaw of Huntstown* [anon.].
London: Religious Tract Society, [1892]. LOCATION L (destroyed), O.
COMMENTARY Religious fiction [BLC].

B169 *Annie Deloraine's aunt* (by E.A. Bland).
+ London: Religious Tract Society, 1895 (ill. W.J.M.; see Plate 12). SOURCE COPAC.
LOCATION L, InND Loeber coll. (n.d. edn).
COMMENTARY Set in England, Miss Ann Harrison, a fairly sour, upright spinster, receives a request from a niece, Annie Deloraine, who is coming from India to England having lost her parents and her husband, to take her and her small twin daughters in. Miss Harrison reluctantly agrees. A friend of Annie and her husband in India, Gerard Leigh, becomes a regular visitor and is somehow able to befriend Miss Harrison. Eventually Annie, who is consumptive, dies and leaves her daughters in her aunt's care. When Miss Harrison is about to die, a sister whom she had not seen for many years, shows up just in time to take over the care of the little orphans [ML].

B170 *Old chickweed* (by E.A. Bland).
+ London: John F. Shaw & Co., [1895] (ill.). SOURCE COPAC. LOCATION L, O.
COMMENTARY Set in England [ML].

B171 *The next thing* (by E.A. Bland).
+ London: John F. Shaw, [1896] (ill.). SOURCE COPAC. LOCATION L, O.
COMMENTARY No Irish content [ML].

B172 *Alice Courtenay's legacy. An Irish tale* (by E.A. Bland).
London: J. Snow & Co., 1898 (ill.). SOURCE COPAC. LOCATION L.
COMMENTARY Religious fiction set in Ireland [BLC].

B173 *'A hind let loose'* (by E.A. Bland).
+ London: S.W. Partridge & Co, [1910] (ill.). LOCATION L, O.
Sterling: Drummond's Tract Depot, [1910]. SOURCE COPAC. LOCATION L.
COMMENTARY Set in England, concerns giving to charity [ML].

B174 *'O carry me back!' or the friend of my youth* (by E.A. Bland).
+ London, Glasgow, Edinburgh: Pickering & Inglis, [1934] (ill.). SOURCE COPAC.
LOCATION L, O.
COMMENTARY No Irish content [ML].

BLATHWAYT, Mrs Sarah Margaret, pseud. **'Maggie Symington'**, b. Hinckley (Leics.) 1841. English fiction writer, MSB wrote also for children. The dedication of the following novel was from Hunstanton (Norfolk), 1894. SOURCE Allibone Suppl., ii, p. 165 [under Blathwayt]; Alston, p. 425; NCBEL 4, p. 1875.

B175   *Hollyberry Janet; or, the girls of Ballyowen* (by 'Maggie Symington'; dedicated to
Lucinda Bowser).
+ London: A.D. Innes & Co., 1894. SOURCE Alston, p. 425. LOCATION L.
COMMENTARY Fiction for juveniles. Set in Ireland. Janet and her family live in a country house.
She is the odd-child-out; she likes to read books, but her parents burn them [ML].

'BLAYNEY, Owen', pseud. See WHITE, Robert.

'BLENKINSOP, Adam', pseud. See WALROND, Robert Francis.

BLESSINGTON, Charles John Gardiner, earl of Blessington, b. 1782, d. Paris 1829.
Bon vivant, landowner and occasional writer, he was the son of the Rt Hon. Luke Gardiner
who became Baron and Viscount Mountjoy in 1789 and 1795 respectively, and Elizabeth,
daughter of Sir William Montgomery. In 1798, at age 17, CJG succeeded to the title Viscount
Mountjoy and to a 32,000 acre estate in Co. Tyrone and considerable property in the city of
Dublin, which his father had developed. In 1816 he was created earl of Blessington. He married first Mary Campbell (by whom he fathered the author Harriet Anne d'Orsay§), and secondly in 1818, Marguerite Power Farmer (later known as the countess of Blessington§). Aside
from a single novel, he also wrote *Observations addressed to … Marquis Wellesley … on the state
of Ireland* (London, 1822), and anonymously, *Critic on the Roman portraits, a poem in heroic
verse* (*Gentleman's Magazine*, London, Dec. 1794), in response to the poem of that name by
Robert Jephson§. In the course of CJG's life, he spent extravagantly and at his death left little money for his widow. Madden considered him 'a man of an unsound judgement', but noted
that the tenants on his Mountjoy estate praised him as a landlord. Lady Morgan§ satirized
him as Lord Rosbrin in her *Florence Macarthy* (London, 1818). SOURCE Bradshaw, 5473;
Gardiner's Dublin (Dublin, 1991), pp 22–9; R.R. Madden, *The literary life and correspondence
of the Countess of Blessington* (London, 1855), i, p. 63; RIA/DIB [under Gardiner]; M. Sadleir,
The strange life of Lady Blessington (Boston, 1933), p. 31.
B176   *De Vavasour: A tale of the fourteenth century* [anon.].
London: Henry Colburn, 1826, 3 vols. SOURCE Block, p. 22; British Fiction; Garside,
1826:16; Wolff, 548. LOCATION Corvey CME 3–628–48861–3, L, NUC.
COMMENTARY Historical fiction set in the fourteenth century. Reviewed in the *New Monthly
Magazine* (London, June 1826), and the *Literary Gazette* (London, May 1826), where it is
ascribed to Lord Blessington [RL].

BLESSINGTON, countess of. See BLESSINGTON, Marguerite countess of.

BLESSINGTON, Marguerite countess of (née Power; known as the countess of
Blessington), b. Knockbrit, near Clonmel (Co. Tipperary) 1789 (1790 according to E. Rennie),
d. Paris 1849. A novelist, short story writer, editor, poet, periodical contributor and society
hostess, MB was the daughter of Edmund Power of Curragheen (Co. Waterford), a former
Catholic, who was a magistrate, a minor landowner, a dandy and a drunken bully. Her mother,
Ellen Sheehy, belonged to 'an ancient catholic stock in co. Tipperary' (DNB). Because of her
father's strong partisanship of Lord Donoughmore, he got into a major conflict and was forced
to move to Co. Tipperary where the young Margaret (as she was baptized) became familiar
with the poet Edward Lysaght. As a child, she entertained her siblings with numerous tales
she invented. Her father forced her into a marriage with Capt. Maurice St Leger Farmer when
she was less than age 15. After three months she left her husband, who had an ungovernable
temper, and returned home. In 1809 she moved to Dublin and took refuge with another army

officer, Capt. Thomas Jenkins, with whom she lived for some years. During this period she read widely and grew into a great beauty. She met Charles John Gardiner, first earl of Blessington§ and after Farmer's death, she married him in London in 1818, Gardiner compensating Jenkins, her former protector, with £10,000. The earl, supported by his large income, took his wife on a honeymoon to Ireland. They set up house in London in St James's Square and their home became a magnet for London society and literary notables. In 1821 MB met Count Alfred D'Orsay, a handsome young Frenchman who became the earl's son-in-law in 1827 by marrying the Hon. Harriet Anne Gardiner (see Harriet Anne D'Orsay§), a daughter by the earl's first wife. The Blessingtons travelled to Europe in 1822, meeting up with D'Orsay and spending time in Genoa where MB formed a close friendship with Lord Byron. After five years in Italy, they moved to Paris in 1828. The earl died suddenly in 1829 and MB returned to London the following year and set up house first near Park Lane and later at Gore House, Kensington. She resumed her role as society hostess, praised for her wit, beauty and intelligence. Since the earl had not left her much money, she increasingly turned to writing to supplement her income and to support numerous dependent members of her family. D'Orsay and Harriet became estranged and his liaison with MB and the ensuing scandal created a rift between her and London society from which she never fully recovered. Her income was cut by the Famine in Ireland, leading to her bankruptcy in 1849, whereupon she fled to Paris with D'Orsay to escape her debts. She died there in the same year. Aside from novels, she wrote short stories, as well as *Flowers of loveliness* (London, 1836; with E.T. Parris). She was editor of *Gems of Beauty* (London, 1835–40); *The Keepsake* (London, 1841–50 – she had already contributed a short story to this annual in 1831, and continued to write regularly for it); *The Book of beauty or regal gallery* (London, 1848–49), and *Heath's Book of Beauty* (London, 1834–49, for which she regularly wrote, including biographical sketches on women). In addition, she contributed to annuals such as the *Amulet* (London, 1835), and *The Gift for All Seasons* (London, 1840). She also became the first columnist on record to furnish the *Daily News* with society intelligence. In addition, she wrote travel books, including *Journal of a tour through the Netherlands to Paris in 1821* (London, 1822) and *Rambles in Waltham Forest* (London, 1827). The novel *Lionel Deerhurst* (London, 1846, 3 vols.) was 'edited' by MB, but was written by Barbara Hemphill§. MB is most well-known for her *Conversations of Lord Byron* (London, 1833–34), based on their Genoa friendship. Her *One hundred valuable receipts for the young lady of the period* was published in 1878. She mostly wrote high society novels, and only two deal directly with Ireland. Her *Desultory thoughts and reflections* (London, 1839) constitutes a miscellany, and her *The idler in Italy* (London, 1839) and *The idler in France* (London, 1848) are rich in anecdotes of both native society and English society abroad. An anonymous novel written by John Mills, *D'Horsay; or, the follies of the day, by a man of fashion* (London, 1844), satirizes MB and Count D'Orsay. *The honey-moon by the Countess of Blessington, and other tales* (Philadelphia, 1837, 2 vols.) contains only one of her short stories. It is likely that MB was also an artist: an alpine scene by 'Lady Blessington' was published in *Passage du Mont Saint-Gothard* by Georgiana, duchess of Devonshire, and Elizabeth Foster ([Paris], c.1817). Her portrait by Thomas Lawrence is in the Wallace Collection in London; for engraved portraits, see Elmes. Her letters were auctioned on 14 March, 1866 (for other correspondence, see ODNB). SOURCE Allibone i, pp 205–6; Blain, p. 105; Boylan, pp 24–5; Brady, p. 207; DLB, clxvi; Elmes, pp 19–20; Field Day, v, pp 843–6, 870–5, 893–4; S.C. Hall, pp 399–407; Hogan 2, pp 1032–4 [under Power]; *The collection of autograph letters and historical documents formed by Alfred Morrison (second series, 1882–1893). The Blessington papers* [n.l.], 1895, pp 81, 166–76; Holmes cat. 59/13; Jarndyce cat. 162/460, 515, 517–27; List of catalogues; p. 314; E.J. Lovell (ed.), *Lady Blessington's conversations of Lord Byron* (1969); R.R. Madden, *The literary life and correspondence of the Countess of Blessington* (London, 1855, 3 vols.); [E. Rennie], *Traits of char-*

acter (London, 1860), ii, pp 31, 34; NCBEL 4, pp 887–8; OCIL, p. 480 [under Power]; ODNB [under Gardiner]; O'Donoghue, p. 388; O'Toole, pp 256–7; RIA/DIB [under Power]; M. Sadleir, *The strange life of Lady Blessington* (Boston, 1933); M. Sadleir, *Blessington-D'Orsay a masquerade* (London, 1933); M.A. Shee, *My contemporaries, 1830–1870* (London, 1893), pp 73–5, 97–9, 167–9; Sutherland, pp 72–3; T & B, p. 968; H. Wyndham, *Serena. A biography of Lady Wilde* (London, 1951), p. 140.

B177 **The magic lantern; or, sketches of scenes in the metropolis** [anon.].
   London: Longman, Hurst, Rees, Orme & Brown, 1822. SOURCE Rafroidi, ii, p. 63; Sadleir, 24. COMMENTARY 72pp. Shows the fashions and follies of society life in London. Contents: 'The auction', 'The park', 'The tomb', 'The Italian opera' [Burmester list 20/22].

B178 **Sketches and fragments** [anon.].
   London: Longman, Hurst, Rees, Orme & Brown, 1822. SOURCES Rafroidi, ii, p. 63. LOCATION L, MH.
COMMENTARY Authorship is in doubt; the book would have been written prior to or during Lady B's journey in Italy. Contents: 'Blighted hopes', 'Marriage', 'The ring', 'Journal of a week of a lady of fashion', 'An allegory', 'Fastidiousness of taste', 'Coquetry', 'Egotism', 'Reflections', 'Sensibility', 'Friendship', 'Wentworth fragments' [Sadleir].

B179 **The Repealers. A novel** (by the countess of Blessington).
   London: Richard Bentley, 1833, 3 vols. SOURCE Brown, 223; Rafroidi, ii, p. 63; Block, p. 23; Sadleir, 247; Garside 2, 1833:26. LOCATION Corvey 3–628–47229–6, Ireland related fiction, Dt, L.
   London: Richard Bentley, 1833, 3 vols. (as *Grace Cassidy; or, the Repealers*). SOURCE Rafroidi, ii, p. 64; Sadleir, 247a (1834, 2nd edn); COPAC. LOCATION Dt.
   + Philadelphia: Carey, Lea & Blanchard, 1833, 2 vols. in 1. SOURCE Kaser, 408. LOCATION NUC, DCL, InND Loeber coll.
COMMENTARY Written rapidly when Lady B. was badly in need of money, and for which she received £400 for the copyright from Richard Bentley. The story is a *roman à clef* that satirizes the affectations and fashionable jealousies of English society, while also highlighting the distress of the Irish peasantry of the time, many of whom were tenants of fashionable London landlords. M. Sadleir published a complete key to the characters. Some examples are: duchess of Heaviland = duchess of Northumberland; Lady Elsinore = Lady Tullamore; Mrs Grantly = Mrs Norton; marchioness of Stuartville = marchioness of Londonderry; marchioness of Burton = marchioness of Conyngham; marchioness of Glanricarde = marchioness of Clanricarde; Mr Thiel = Mr Shiel; Lady Castlemount = Lady Charlemont; Lord Leath = Lord Meath; duke and duchess of Cartoun = duke and duchess of Leinster. The Abbervilles probably were the earl and countess of Charleville [Sadleir, *The strange life*, p. 329].

B180 **The two friends. A novel** (by the countess of Blessington).
   + London: Saunders & Otley, 1835, 3 vols. SOURCE Rafroidi, ii, p. 64; Block, p. 23; Wolff, 553; Garside 2, 1835:45. LOCATION D, L, DLC.
   Dordrecht: Van Houtrijve & Bredius, 1839 (trans. into Dutch as *De twee vrienden: Een verhaal*; ill.). SOURCE Adamnet. LOCATION UVA.
   Paris: A. & W. Galignani & Co., 1835. SOURCE OCLC. LOCATION O, NN.
   Seitz: Johann Christian Senckenberg, [1837] (trans. by Hermann Franz as *Die beiden Freunde*). SOURCE Garside 2, 1835:45; GLOL.
   + Philadelphia: Carey, Lea & Blanchard, 1835, 2 vols. SOURCE Kaser, 491. LOCATION NUC, MH, InND Loeber coll.
COMMENTARY Set in England, France, and Italy. Relates the amorous adventures of two friends who are both rich but who have contrasting characters. One is stable and serious and the other

gambles and has a liaison with a married woman. They both fall in love with girls whom they wish to marry. However, the path of love does not run smooth for either of them and it is only after many obstacles are overcome that the lovers can marry [ML].

B181 *The confessions of an elderly gentleman* (by the countess of Blessington).
London: Longman, Rees, Orme, Brown, Green & Longman, 1836 (ill. E.T. Parris). SOURCE Wolff, 549; Sadleir, 236; Rafroidi, ii, p. 64 (1838 edn); Garside 2, 1836:36. *Location* D (1837 edn), Dt, L, DLC.
+ London, Belfast: Simms & M'Intyre, 1848 (Parlour Library, No. 22; also contains 'Confessions of an elderly lady' by Lady B., and 'Modern flirtations' by C. Sinclair). SOURCE Sadleir, ii, p. 152. LOCATION InND Loeber coll.
+ Paris: Baudry, 1836 (Baudry's European Library). SOURCE Wolff, 549a. LOCATION InND Loeber coll.
+ Philadelphia: Carey, Lea & Blanchard, 1836 (ill. E.T. Parris, W. Holl, H. Cook). LOCATION NUC, InND Loeber coll.
Berlin: [publisher?], 1837 (trans. by R.Z. Ende as *Lady Blessingtons Bekenntnisse eines alten Junggesellen*). SOURCE British Fiction; GLOL. LOCATION Niedersächsische Staats – und Universitätsbibliothek.
COMMENTARY Follows sequentially through headings from 'My first love' to 'My sixth love' [Garside 2, 1836:26].

B182 *The victims of society* (by the countess of Blessington).
London: Saunders & Otley, 1837, 3 vols. SOURCE Rafroidi, ii, p. 64; Wolff, 554; Sadleir. LOCATION L.
Paris: Baudry's European Library, 1837. SOURCE Sadleir, 249a.
+ Paris: A. & W. Galignani & Co., 1837. LOCATION D.
Philadelphia: Carey, Lea & Blanchard, 1837, 2 vols. SOURCE Kaser, 650. LOCATION DCL, InND Loeber coll. (1838 edn).
COMMENTARY Written at least in part by Lady Blessington's friend Edward Bulwer Lytton§. Tells the story of a young wife driven to death by the malicious slanders of heartless fashionables. It is likely to have been founded on fact [Cox cat. 48/29].

B183 *The confessions of an elderly lady* (by the countess of Blessington).
London: Longman, Orme, Brown, Green & Longmans, 1838 (ill. E.T. Parris). SOURCE Rafroidi, ii, p. 64; Sadleir, 237. LOCATION L.
+ London, Belfast: Simms & M'Intyre, 1848 (Parlour Library, No. 22, also includes 'Confessions of an elderly gentleman', first published in London in 1836). SOURCE Sadleir, ii, p. 153. LOCATION D, InND Loeber coll.
Paris: A. & W. Galignani & Co., 1838. SOURCE OCLC. LOCATION CLU.
+ Paris: Baudry's European Library, 1838. LOCATION InND Loeber coll.
Cincinnati: U.P. James, 1838. LOCATION NUC.
Philadelphia: Carey & Lea, 1838, 2 vols. (as *Confessions of an elderly lady and gentlemen* [*sic*]). SOURCE Kaser, 667, 909.
COMMENTARY No copy of the Philadelphia edn located [RL].

B184 *The governess* (by the countess of Blessington).
+ London: Longman, Orme, Brown, Green & Longmans, 1839, 2 vols. (ill. E.T. Parris, W.H. Mote). SOURCE Rafroidi, ii, p. 64; Sadleir, 241. LOCATION L.
Amsterdam: J.D. Sijbrandi, 1842 (trans. into Dutch as *De gouvernante*; ill.). SOURCE Adamnet. LOCATION UVA.
Paris: Baudry's European Library, 1840 (as *The governess and The belle of a season*). SOURCE NCBEL 3, p. 711; OCLC. LOCATION CLU.
Philadelphia: Lea & Blanchard, 1839. LOCATION NUC.

COMMENTARY The Paris edn also contains *The belle of the season,* which is a poem about fashionable society. Madden gives a key to its characters, e.g., marchioness of Stewartville = marchioness of Londonderry; marchioness of Glanricarde = marchioness of Clanricarde; Mr Thiel = Mr R.L. Shiel; Lady Castlemont = Lady Charlemont; duke and duchess of Cartoun = duke and duchess of Leinster, etc. [RL; Madden, i, p. 259].

B185   *The lottery of life* (by the countess of Blessington).
   London: Henry Colburn, 1842, 3 vols. SOURCE Rafroidi, ii, p. 64; Sadleir, 251g. LOCATION L.
   + Amsterdam: P.N. van Kampen, 1844 (trans. into Dutch as *'s Levens loterij: Een verhaal*; ill. H.J. Backer). SOURCE Adamnet. LOCATION UVA.
   + Paris: A. & W. Galignani & Co., 1842. SOURCE NCBEL 3, p. 711. LOCATION InND Loeber coll.
   New York: J. Winchester, 1842. LOCATION NUC.

B186   *Meredith* (by the countess of Blessington).
   London: Longman, Brown, Green & Longmans, 1843, 3 vols. SOURCE Rafroidi, ii, p. 65; Wolff, 551; Sadleir, 251. LOCATION L.
   Arnhem: J.A. Nijhoff, 1845 (trans. into Dutch as *Meredith*). SOURCE Alphabetische naamlijst 1833–49, p. 76.
   + Leipzig: Bernh. Tauchnitz Jun., 1843. SOURCE T & B, 52. LOCATION InND Loeber coll.
   Paris: Baudry's European Library, 1843. SOURCE Jarndyce cat. 137/147.
   COMMENTARY *Paris Baudry edn* No copy located other than that in Jarndyce cat. [RL].
   Paris: A. & W. Galignani & Co., 1843. SOURCE Tiger cat. 12–04/53.
   Philadelphia: Printed by J. Crissy, 1837. SOURCE OCLC. LOCATION ViU.
COMMENTARY According to the publisher Longman, this novel did not sell well in the year it was first published. The story is set in England and the Continent. A young man, Meredith, sets out for a tour of the Continent accompanied by his tutor after his parents' deaths. He gets embroiled in the rescue of a young woman in distress and falls in love with her. A horrible woman claims to be her mother, but in the end she turns out to be the long-estranged daughter of a French duke. Meredith and the girl marry and they live happily with the girl's new-found parents [ML; *The collection of autograph letters and historical documents … The Blessington papers* [n.l.], 1895, p. 161].

B187   *Strathern; or, life at home and abroad. A story of the present day* (by the countess of Blessington).
   Leipzig: Bernard Tauchnitz, 1844. SOURCE T & B, 69. COMMENTARY *Leipzig edn* Probably predated by the publisher [RL].
   London: Henry Colburn, 1845, 4 vols. (ill. Landseer). SOURCE Rafroidi, ii, p. 65; Wolff, 552; Sadleir, 248. LOCATION L.
   + Paris: Baudry's European Library, 1845, 2 vols. (Baudry's Collection of Ancient and Modern British Authors). LOCATION InND Loeber coll.
   Paris: A. & W. Galignani & Co., 1845, 2 vols. SOURCE Wolff, 552a. LOCATION Univ. of California, Berkeley.
COMMENTARY First serialized in the *Sunday Times.* A novel of high fashion and social life set in contemporary Rome with some characters based on individuals living at that time (for example, the author Edward Bulwer Lytton§ is maliciously portrayed as the simpering Webworth, a word play on his estate at Knebworth) [Ximenes List M5/26; Madden, i, p. 260].

B188   *The memoirs of a femme de chambre. A novel* (by the countess of Blessington).
   + London: Richard Bentley, 1846, 3 vols. SOURCE Rafroidi, ii, p. 66; Sadleir, 246. LOCATION L.

Amsterdam: P.N. van Kampen, 1847, 3 vols. (trans. into Dutch as *Gedenkschriften van eene kamenier*). SOURCE Adamnet. LOCATION UVA.

Leipzig: Bernard Tauchnitz, 1846. SOURCE T & B, 104. LOCATION D.

Philadelphia: T.B. Peterson, [1850] (as *Ella Stratford; or, the orphan child: A thrilling novel, founded on facts*). SOURCE NCBEL 3, p. 711; OCLC. LOCATION NN.

New York: D. & J. Sadlier, [Rev. 1850] (as *Ella Stratford; or, the orphan child*). SOURCE Survey Catholic Americana, 1841–1850, No. 484.

COMMENTARY Copy of the New York edn not located. Set in England. Relates the life of an impoverished girl of good background who is obliged to earn her living as a governess and a ladies' maid. She finds that her beauty brings out the worst in her mistresses' husbands, which makes them jealous. When she is obliged to leave positions, people of lower classes take pity on her and provide shelter. Eventually a kind mistress leaves her a small inheritance which allows her to live in peace [ML].

B189 *Marmaduke Herbert; or, the fatal error. A novel, founded on fact* (by the countess of Blessington).

London: Richard Bentley, 1847, 3 vols. SOURCE Rafroidi, ii, p. 66; Sadleir, 251h. LOCATION L.

+ Amsterdam: P. Kraaij Jnr, 1848, 3 vols. (trans. into Dutch as *De vloek der zelfzucht*; ill.). SOURCE Adamnet. LOCATION UVA.

Paris: A.W. Galignani & Co., 1847. SOURCE Devonshire, p. 456; CCF. LOCATION BNF.

Paris: Baudry's European Library, 1847. SOURCE CCF. LOCATION BNF.

Leipzig: Bernard Tauchnitz, 1847, 2 vols. SOURCE T & B, 123. LOCATION D.

+ New York: Burgess, Stringer, 1847. LOCATION NUC, InND Loeber coll.

COMMENTARY Marmaduke Herbert, whose father has died, grows up under the guidance of his tutor, Mr Trevyllan, a cold-hearted, selfish man devoid of sentiment from whom Marmaduke learns to be suspicious of other people. As a result, he is unhappy at school and college. He comes across the sleeping daughter of his mother's friend. She awakes when he kisses her brow and in great fright runs away from him and falls to her death over a precipice. Although strictly speaking he is not to blame for her death, he feels extremely guilty and hides her body in a cavern. He tells nobody, and goes on to marry the sister of the dead girl. However, his whole life is influenced by this event and at the end of his life he writes the tale so that his daughter, after his death, may understand why he was such a moody person [ML].

B190 *Country quarters. A novel ... with a memoir by her niece, Miss Power* (by the countess of Blessington).

London: W. Shoberl, 1850, 3 vols. SOURCE Rafroidi, ii, p. 64; Wolff, 550; Sadleir, 238. LOCATION L.

Leipzig: Bernard Tauchnitz Jnr, 1850, 2 vols. SOURCE D & B, 183. LOCATION D, Dt.

+ Philadelphia: T.B. Peterson & Bros, [1877] (as *Country quarters. A love story*). LOCATION D, NUC, InND Loeber coll.

COMMENTARY Published posthumously by Margarite Power§. First published in an unidentified newspaper. Set in the south of Ireland among the landed gentry and garrison communities. Grace is loved by two officers, Mordaunt and Vernon, who are friendly rivals. Mordaunt makes Vernon propose. Vernon is refused but Mordaunt is too poor to marry. In the end, however, Grace and Mordaunt marry [Brown; Lady Wilde§, *Notes on men, women, and books* (London, 1891), p. 147].

COLLECTED WORKS

B191 *The works of Lady Blessington.*

Philadelphia: Carey & Hart, 1838, 2 vols. SOURCE Sadleir, 250. LOCATION NUC.

New York: AMS Press, 1975, 2 vols. in 1. LOCATION InND.

BLOOD, Gertrude Elizabeth. See CAMPBELL, Lady Colin.

BLOOD-SMYTH, Dorothea Spaight. See CONYERS, Dorothea (Minnie) Spaight.

BLUNDELL, Agnes Mary Frances, also Agnes Blundell. Co-author. See BLUNDELL, Mary E.

BLUNDELL, Mrs Francis. See BLUNDELL, Mary E.

BLUNDELL, Margaret Elizabeth Clementina Mary, also Margaret Blundell. Co-author. See BLUNDELL, Mary E.

BLUNDELL, Mary E. (née Sweetman; also known as Mrs Francis Blundell), pseud. 'M.E. Francis', b. Killiney (Co. Dublin) 1859, d. Mold (Wales) 1930. A novelist and Catholic writer, MEB was the second daughter of John Michael Sweetman of Lamberton Park (since demolished), near Stradbally (Co. Laois) and Margaret, heiress of Michael Powell of Fitzwilliam Square, Dublin, and Richview (Co. Dublin). Her sister Agnes wrote under her married name, Mrs L.A. Egerton Castle§. MEB was educated at home by governesses and in Brussels, where the family lived for some years, and began to write – with her sisters – at an early age. Her first printed tale was written when she was age 14, and her first long story, *Molly's fortunes*, appeared in the *Irish Monthly* (Dublin, 1889–90) whose editor, Fr Matthew Russell, encouraged her to write. After her marriage to Francis Blundell in 1879, they settled near Crosby (Lancs.), the residence of her father-in-law and the setting for many of her subsequent stories. She was widowed in 1884, started to publish about eight years later, and moved to Dorset. She wrote 60 works of fiction, some of which were published by the Catholic Truth Society. A few of her books were co-authored by Agnes Mary Frances Blundell and Margaret Elizabeth Clementina Mary Blundell, who probably were close relatives. MEB published her semi-fictional autobiography, *The things of a child* (London, 1918), which focused on her childhood in Ireland. At the end of her life she wrote *Memoirs and opinions* (London, 1926). MEB died at her home in Wales but was buried at Little Crosby Church (Lancs.). The author Walter Sweetman§ was a relative. SOURCE Blain, p. 393 [under 'M.E. Francis']; Brady, p. 84; Brown, p. 110; M. Blundell, *M.E. Francis, an Irish novelist's own story* (Dublin, 1935); Colman, pp 211–12 [under Sweetman]; EF, pp 139–40; Hogan 2, pp 458–60 [under Francis]; Irish pseudonyms; Landed gentry, 1912, p. 677; Murphy, p. 59; *A round table of the representative Irish and English Catholic novelists* (New York, 1897), pp 27–8; OCIL, p. 203; RIA/DIB; Ryan, p. 117; Sutherland, p. 73; T & B, p. 981; Vanishing country houses, p. 97.

B192   void

B193   *Whither? A novel* (by 'M.E. Francis'; dedicated to the memory of author's husband [Francis Blundell]).
London: Griffith Farran & Co., 1892, 3 vols. SOURCE McCarthy, i, p. 215. LOCATION L, InND.
+ London: Griffith Farran & Co., 1893 (new and cheaper edn; ill. Hal Ludlow). LOCATION InND Loeber coll.

B194   *In a North country village* (by 'M.E. Francis'; dedicated to The squire).
+ London: Osgood, McIlvaine & Co., 1893 (ill. F. Felloes; Short Stories by British Authors).
SOURCE Colman, p. 213. LOCATION NUC (1894 edn), InND Loeber coll.
+ London: Osgood, McIlvaine & Co., 1896 (ill. Frank Fellows). LOCATION Dcc.

Boston: Little, Brown & Co., 1893. SOURCE McCarthy, i, p. 215. LOCATION D (1894 edn), Dt (1896 edn), NUC.

COMMENTARY. Stories about Lancashire village life. Contents 'Thornleigh', 'Gaffer's child', 'Celebrities', 'Nancy', 'Politics', 'The gilly-f'ers', 'Aunt Ginny', 'On the other side of the wall', 'Little paupers', 'Here and there', '"Our Joe"', 'Mates' [ML].

B195 *The story of Dan* (by 'M.E. Francis').

+ London: Osgood, McIlvaine & Co., 1894. SOURCE Brown, 611. LOCATION D, Dt, L, NUC, InND Loeber coll.

Boston, New York: Houghton, Mifflin & Co., 1894. LOCATION NUC.

COMMENTARY Set in Wales. The tragic story of a generous peasant who adores a worthless girl and sacrifices himself for her by not revealing that her retarded brother had committed the murder for which he stands accused [Brown; ML].

B196 *Town mice in the country: A story of holiday adventure* (by 'M.E. Francis').

London, Glasgow, Edinburgh, Dublin: Blackie & Son, 1894. SOURCE McCarthy, i, p. 215. LOCATION D (n.d. edn), L.

B197 *A daughter of the soil* (by 'M.E. Francis'; dedicated to author's sister Gertrude [Sweetman]).

+ London: Osgood, McIlvaine & Co., 1895. LOCATION D, Dt, L.

New York: Harper & Bros, 1895 (as *A daughter of the soil. A novel*). LOCATION NUC.

COMMENTARY The first novel to be published as a serial in the weekly edn of the London *Times*. A story of bigamy set in Lancashire, of which the *Times'* reviewer said, it 'leaves one better for the reading of it and more disposed to regard human nature as fundamentally good' [Sutherland; M. Blundell, *M.E. Francis, An Irish novelist's own story* (Dublin, 1935), p. 29].

B198 *Frieze and fustian* (by 'M.E. Francis' (Mrs Francis Blundell); dedicated to the author's mother [Margaret Sweetman]).

+ London: J.R. Osgood, McIvaine & Co., 1896. SOURCE Brown, 612. LOCATION D, L, NUC., InND Loeber coll.

COMMENTARY Sketches and stories arranged in two parts so as to contrast Irish ('frieze') and northern English ('fustian') manners of peasants. Contents of the frieze section: 'Father Pat', 'Queen O'Toole', 'Long Jack', 'Honnie'. Contents of the fustian section: 'Daddy Jack and Daddy Jim', 'The third time of asking', 'Owd lads', 'Squire's Mon', 'Old folks' tales' [ML; Sutherland; Brown].

B199 *Among the untrodden ways* (by 'M.E. Francis'; dedicated to Lady Butler (Elizabeth Thompson)).

+ Edinburgh, London: William Blackwood & Son, 1896. SOURCE McCarthy, i, p. 215. LOCATION D, L, InND Loeber coll.

COMMENTARY Stories set in the North Country in England. Contents: 'Th' ploughin' o' th' sunnyfields', 'Tom's second Missus', 'Tea-time in the village', 'The wooing of William', 'Jack O' th' warren', 'The lady of the lock', 'Merrymaking', 'A village prodigal' [RL].

B200 *Maime o' the corner* (by 'M.E. Francis'; dedicated to author's sister Elinor Sweetman).

New York: Burr, 1897. SOURCE Daims, 308. LOCATION NUC.

+ London, New York: Harper & Bros, 1898. SOURCE Jarndyce cat. 94/459; Daims, 308. LOCATION D, L.

B201 *The duenna of a genius* (by 'M.E. Francis').

+ London, New York: Harper & Bros, 1898. SOURCE Daims, 306. LOCATION Dt, D, L, NUC.

Boston: Little, Brown & Co., 1898. SOURCE Daims, 306. LOCATION NUC.

Leipzig: Bernard Tauchnitz, 1899. SOURCE T & B, 3368, NUC.

COMMENTARY Love story of two Hungarian musicians in London [Sutherland].

B202 *Miss Erin* (by 'M.E. Francis' (Mrs Francis Blundell); dedicated to K.M.S. [?Sweetman]).
+ London: Methuen & Co., 1898. SOURCE Brown, 613. LOCATION D, L, InND Loeber coll.
+ New York, Cincinnati, Chicago: Benziger Bros, 1898 (as *Miss Erin. A novel*). LOCATION D, NUC.

COMMENTARY A Gerald Fitzgerald, who had participated in the 1848 uprising, has died in California and leaves behind a baby girl who he entrusts to his friend to take to his brother in Ireland. The brother rejects the child and the parish priest places her with a peasant family where she is treated with great affection. Over time all the people she loves die and she decides to dedicate herself to Ireland's cause. On her way to Brussels to finish her education she meets an Englishman, Mr Wimbourne, who takes pity on the sad bedraggled girl. They meet again a few years later after she has inherited her uncle's wealth. Mr Wimbourne, a member of parliament, is very much against Home Rule. Although they fall in love, their differences on Ireland seem to make a union impossible. She returns to Ireland to do the best she can for her tenants and for Ireland, and finds out how difficult that is. She is willing to marry Mr Wimbourne if he will give up his parliamentary career, but he has promised to stand for election. Their difficulties are solved when he is defeated [ML].

B203 *Yeoman Fleetwood* (by 'M.E. Francis', Mrs Francis Blundell; dedicated to the Hon. Mrs Carrington Smythe, 'Aunt Laura').
+ London, New York, Bombay: Longman, Green & Co., 1900. SOURCE Alston, p. 33; Wolff, 559 (1902 edn). LOCATION L, NUC.

COMMENTARY Historical fiction chronicling country life in southern Lancashire during the eighteenth century. A yeoman of faultless character loves a girl who is above him in social rank and who has captivated George prince of Wales at Brighton. The plot features Mrs Maria Anne Fitzherbert, Beau Brummell, etc. [Baker].

B204 *Pastorals of Dorset* (by 'M.E. Francis').
London, New York: Longman, Green & Co., 1901 (ill. Claude C. Du Pré Cooper). LOCATION D (1915 edn), L, NUC.

COMMENTARY Set in Dorset. Contents: 'Shepherd Robbins', 'Private Griggs', 'Up at the 'lotments', 'The only soldier', 'A rustic Argus', 'The rosy plate', 'Becky and Bithey', 'The lover's wraith', 'Johnny at Shroton fair', 'The rout of the conqueror', 'How Granfer volunteered' [ML].

B205 *Fiander's widow* (by 'M.E. Francis'; dedicated to 'my kind hostess of Tenantees').
+ London: Longman, Green & Co., 1901. SOURCE Jarndyce cat. 137/719. LOCATION Dt, D (n.d. edn), L.
New York, London: Longmans, Green, 1901. SOURCE Daims, 307. LOCATION L. NUC.
COMMENTARY Set in Dorset [ML].

B206 *The manor farm. A novel* (by 'M.E. Francis'; dedicated to Agnes [Castle§] and Egerton Castle).
New York: Longman, Green & Co., 1902 (ill. Claude C. Du Pré Cooper). LOCATION L, NUC.
+ London, New York, Bombay, Calcutta, Madras: Longman, Green & Co., 1915 (ill. Claud C. du Pré Cooper). LOCATION DPL.

COMMENTARY Set in Dorset. Two cousins in a farming family rebel against the family order that they should marry. However, they fall in love after all [EF, p. 139; Leclaire, p. 187].

B207 *North, South, and over the sea* (by 'M.E. Francis' (Mrs Francis Blundell)).
+ London: 'Country Life' & George Newnes, 1902 (ill. H.M. Brock; cover: G.J.; Country Life Library of Fiction). SOURCE Brown, 614. LOCATION L, NUC, InND Loeber coll.

COMMENTARY Deals with life in Lancashire, Dorset, and in Ireland, each described in five stories, all dealing with humble life. Contents: 'Golden Sally', '"Th' owdes member,"' 'The conquest of radical Ted', 'Heather in Holborn', 'Sentiment and "feelin"', 'The romance of Brother John', 'Giles in luck', '"The wold love and the noo"', 'Blackbird's inspiration', 'The girl he left behind him', 'Elleney', 'In St. Patrick's ward', 'The flitting of the old folks', '"The spider and the gout"', 'Roseen' [Brown; ML].

B208   *Christian Thal. A novel* (by 'M.E. Francis' (Mrs Francis Blundell); dedicated to 'those makers of music who have brought joy into my life').
+ London, New York, Bombay: Longman, Green & Co., 1903. SOURCE Jarndyce cat. 94/456. LOCATION D (1915 edn), L, NUC, InND Loeber coll.

COMMENTARY Set mainly on the Continent and describes the relationship between artists and the rest of society. Juliet, an impressionable daughter of a professor, falls in love with a young musician [EF, p. 139].

B209   *Lychgate Hall. A romance* (by 'M.E. Francis').
London: Longman, Green & Co., 1904. LOCATION L, NUC.

COMMENTARY An historical romance set in the early years of the eighteenth century at Lychgate Hall, a haunted, old mansion at Great Crosby, near Liverpool [Baker; EF, p. 139].

B210   *Wild wheat, a Dorset romance* (by 'M.E. Francis').
+ London, Bombay: Longman, Green & Co., 1905. LOCATION D, L, NUC.
COMMENTARY A well-to-do yeoman takes a job as an under-keeper out of love for the young lady of the house in Dorset [EF, p. 139].

B211   *The Lord's ambassador, and other tales* (by 'M.E. Francis').
London: Catholic Truth Society, 1905. LOCATION L, NUC.

COMMENTARY 'The Lord's ambassador', 'Father Anselm', 'About poor Judy', 'Mick's badge', 'In St. Patrick's ward', 'The little cross-bearer', 'Anne's husband', 'Bridget's holy habit', 'Number 6 Parade'. The story of 'Anne's husband' was also published as a separate booklet by the Catholic Truth Society of Ireland [NUC; RL].

B212   *Dorset dear. Idylls of country life* (by 'M.E. Francis'; dedicated to Lady Smith-Marriott).
+ London, New York, Bombay: Longman, Green & Co., 1905. LOCATION D, L.
New York, Bombay: Longmans, Green & Co., 1905. LOCATION NUC.

COMMENTARY Stories set in Dorset. Contents: 'Witch Ann', 'A runaway couple', 'Postman Chris', 'Keeper Guppy', 'The worm that turned', 'Olf and the little maid', 'In the heart of the green', 'The wold stockin'', 'A woodland idyll', 'The carrier's tale', 'Mrs Sibley and the sexton', 'The call of the woods', 'The home-coming of dada', 'The majesty of the law', 'The spur of the moment', 'A terr'ble voolish little maid', 'Sweetbriar lane' [NYPL].

B213   *Simple annals* (by 'M.E. Francis'; dedicated to Mrs Ritchie (Anne Thackeray)).
+ London, New York, Bombay: Longman, Green & Co., 1906. LOCATIONs D, L, NUC.

COMMENTARY Lancashire stories. Contents: 'Madame Félicie', 'The breadwinner', 'Mrs. Angel', 'Patchwork', 'The widow indeed', 'Mr. Brown and Tilly', 'Cwortin' corner', 'The woodpecker', 'The "Tallygraft"', '"Forty-bags"', 'The philanthropist and the unit', 'Mademoiselle and Fräulein', 'Mrs. Gradwell's piano', 'The transplanting of a daisy' [RL].

B214   *Matthew Strong, the story of a man with a purpose* (by 'M.E. Francis').
Philadelphia: J.B. Lippincott; London: Sampson Low, Marston & Co., 1906. LOCATION NUC.

B215   *Margery o' the mill* (by 'M.E. Francis').
+ London: Methuen & Co., [1907]. LOCATION D (1907, 3rd edn), L, NUC.

B216   *Stepping Westward* (by 'M.E. Francis'; dedicated to Elina, Lady d'Oyly).
+ London: Methuen & Co., 1907. LOCATION D, L.

COMMENTARY Dorset stories. Contents: 'Tranter Sally', '"Lwonesome [*sic*] Lizzie"', 'Jess Domeny on strike', '"Jarge's little "ooman"', 'Ann-Car'line', 'One another's burden', 'How Ned Blanchard emigrated', 'Farmer Barne's dilemma', 'The missus's chair', 'The rules o' the house', 'Lady Lucy', 'A prisoner of war', 'Through the cottage window', 'April fools' [NYPL].

B217   *Children of light, and other stories* (by 'M.E. Francis').
     London: Catholic Truth Society, 1908. SOURCE Brown, 615. LOCATION L, NUC.

COMMENTARY Some of the stories are set in Ireland. Contents: 'Children of light', 'Dinny and St. Anthony', 'Dublin Bay herrin', 'Toppy', 'Little Jack and the Christmas pudding', 'The home coming of Godfrey Davis' [NUC].

B218   *Hardy-on-the-hill* (by 'M.E. Francis').
     + London: Methuen & Co., 1908. LOCATION D, L, NUC.
     COMMENTARY Set in Dorset [Leclaire, p. 188].

B219   *Madge make-the-best-of-it* (by 'M.E. Francis' (Mrs Francis Blundell)).
     + London: MacDonald & Evans, 1908 (ill. J.B.G.; The St Nicholas Series). LOCATION D, InND Loeber coll.

COMMENTARY Set in England, A Protestant minister's family has been impoverished by their conversion to catholicism and a rich relative has broken off with them as a result. One of the daughters becomes a companion to a rich but spoiled French girl. Her stay in the girl's family is far from easy, but eventually she teaches the girl to be less egocentric and to care for others. In the end the rich aunt comes to the rescue and releases her niece from having to work for a living [ML].

B220   *Noblesse oblige* (by 'M.E. Francis').
     London: John Long, 1909. LOCATION L.

COMMENTARY Historical fiction set in the eighteenth and nineteenth centuries. Story of a goddaughter of Marie Antoinette and playmate of the royal family of France and her marriage to an English admiral. Features Admiral Horatio Nelson, Lady Hamilton, Joshua Romney, and Charles-Maurice de Talleyrand-Périgord [Baker].

B221   *Galatea of the wheatfield* (by 'M.E. Francis').
     London: Methuen & Co., [1909]. LOCATION L, NUC (1909, 2dn edn).
     COMMENTARY Set in Dorset. A young undergraduate courts a milkmaid [EF, p. 139; Leclaire, p. 188].

B222   *The tender passion* (by 'M.E. Francis').
     + London: John Long, 1910. SOURCE Brady, p. 84. LOCATION D, L, NUC.

B223   *The wild heart* (by 'M.E. Francis').
     + London: Smith, Elder & Co., 1910. LOCATION D, L, NUC.
     COMMENTARY Set in Dorset. Story about a poacher, unpremeditated crime, and disastrous love [Leclaire, p. 188].

B224   *Gentleman Roger* (by 'M.E. Francis').
     + London, Edinburgh: Sands & Co., 1911. LOCATION D, L, NUC.
     COMMENTARY A man becomes a labourer in order to marry a farmer's daughter [Leclaire, p. 188].

B225   *Our Alty* (by 'M.E. Francis').
     + London: John Long, 1912. LOCATION D (n.d. edn), L.

B226   *Honesty* (by 'M.E. Francis').
     + London, New York, Toronto: Hodder & Stoughton, [1912]. LOCATION D, L, NUC.

B227   *Molly's fortunes* (by 'M.E. Francis'; dedicated to Fr Matthew Russell, SJ).
     + London, Edinburgh, Glasgow: Sands & Co., [1913]. SOURCE Brown 2, 520.
     LOCATION D, L.

COMMENTARY First serialized in the *Irish Monthly* (Dublin, 1889–90). The plot turns mainly around the will of Miss O'Neill, an eccentric old lady, who leaves her fortune to Molly, an orphan working as a governess, provided the real heir does not turn up. But he does, proves his claim and offers marriage to Molly. She refuses and goes as a governess to a family in France. It turns out that baron de Sauvigny is the real heir. He comes to Ireland and marries Molly [Brown 2; Murphy, p. 156].

B228   *The story of Mary Dunne* (by 'M.E. Francis').
        London: John Murray, 1913. SOURCE Brown, 616; OCIL (where it is mistakenly called *Molly Dunne*). LOCATION L, NUC.
        New York: Longman, Green & Co., 1913. SOURCE OCLC. LOCATION NUC.
        COMMENTARY Set in Glenmalure in Wales [*sic*], the story describes the love of Mat for Mary and ends in a law-court where Mat is on trial for murder and Mary has to publicly tell the story of her wrongs – that she has been a victim of the white slave trade [Brown; Leclaire, p. 188].

B229   *Dark Rosaleen* (by 'M.E. Francis').
        London, Paris, Melbourne: Cassell & Co., 1915. SOURCE Brown, 617. LOCATION L, NUC.
        New York: P.J. Kenedy & Sons, 1917 (as *Dark Rosaleen. A story of Ireland today*). LOCATION NUC.
        COMMENTARY The story of a mixed marriage gone wrong. Norah, a Connemara peasant girl, marries Hector, a young engineer from Belfast. They go to live in Derry but their love turns to misery [Brown].

B230   *Penton's captain* (by 'M.E. Francis').
        London: Chapman & Hall, 1916. LOCATION L.

B231   *Little pilgrims to Our Lady of Lourdes* (by 'M.E. Francis').
        London: Burns & Oates, 1917. LOCATION L.
        New York: P.J. Kenedy & Sons, [1916]. LOCATION NUC.
        COMMENTARY Catholic religious fiction [BLC].

B232   *A maid o' Dorset* (by 'M.E. Francis').
        London, Paris, Melbourne: Cassell & Co., 1917. LOCATION L, NUC.
        COMMENTARY Set in Dorset [ML].

B233   *The things of a child* (by 'M.E. Francis'; dedicated to author's three children).
        + London, Glasgow, Melbourne, Auckland: W. Collins Sons & Co., 1918. SOURCE Brown, p. 110. LOCATION D, L, NUC, InND Loeber coll.
        COMMENTARY Semi fictional autobiographical story of the author's childhood in Ireland, describing a child's anxieties in life [Brown; RL].

B234   *Beck of Beckford* (by 'M.E. Francis').
        London: G. Allen & Unwin, 1920. SOURCE Brady, p. 84. LOCATION L, NUC.

B235   *Rosanna Dew* (by 'M.E. Francis').
        London: Odhams, [1920]. LOCATION L.

B236   *Renewal* (by 'M.E. Francis').
        London: George Allen & Unwin, [1921]. LOCATION L, NUC.

B237   *Many waters* (by 'M.E. Francis').
        London: Hutchinson & Co., [1922]. LOCATION L.
        COMMENTARY A tale of Welsh country life [Leclaire, p. 188].

B238   *The runaway* (by 'M.E. Francis').
        London: Hutchinson & Co., [1923]. LOCATION L.

B239   *Lady Jane and the smallholders* (by 'M.E. Francis' and Margaret Elizabeth Clementine Mary Blundell).

London: Hutchinson & Co., [1924]. LOCATION D, NUC.

B240 *Young Dave's wife. A novel* (by 'M.E. Francis' and M. Blundell [M. Blundell, only on cover]).

+ London: Hutchinson & Co., [1924]. LOCATION D (n.d., 2nd edn), L, NUC (1925 edn). COMMENTARY Set in Wales [Leclaire, p. 188].

B241 *Golden Sally* (by 'M.E. Francis' and Agnes Mary Frances Blundell).

+ London, Edinburgh: Sands & Co., 1925. LOCATION D.

B242 *Napoleon of the looms* (by 'M.E. Francis').

+ London: Hutchinson & Co., [1925]. LOCATION D, L.

B243 *Cousin Christopher* (by 'M.E. Francis').

London: T. Fisher Unwin, 1925. LOCATION L.

+ Dublin: Phoenix Publishing Co., n.d. (ill. K. Maidment; The Library of Modern Irish Fiction). LOCATION D, DPL, InND Loeber coll.

COMMENTARY Concerns the romantic adventures of Christopher and his sister Oonagh, poor Irish relations of Mr Prescott, when they come to England where Christopher is to be agent at Mr Prescott's estate. Mr Prescott has a son, Cuthbert, and two daughters, Joan and Susan. The latter is engaged to a Mr Travers, about whom Christopher knows some very disagreeable facts. Mr Travers in turn insinuates that Christopher is a disreputable character. Eventually, the truth comes out and Christopher is reinstated as agent. Oonagh is going to marry Cuthbert, and Christopher will marry Joan [ML].

B244 *Tyrer's lass* (by 'M.E. Francis' and Agnes Blundell).

London: Sands & Co., 1926. LOCATION L.

B245 *Idylls of old Hungary* (by 'M.E. Francis' (Mrs Francis Blundell)).

+ London: Sheed & Ward, 1926. LOCATION D, L, NUC, InND Loeber coll.

COMMENTARY Stories set in Hungary. Contents: 'The forest hut', 'A Slavonian Shylock', 'Berthe's dream-melody', 'Pista's short-sleeves', 'Mariska and the garden-boy', 'The little Jew girl', 'The countess and the frying-pan' [NUC].

B246 *Mossoo: A comedy of a Lancashire village* (by 'M.E. Francis').

London: Hutchinson, 1927. SOURCE Blain, p. 393; Colman, p. 215; Hogan 2, p. 460; COPAC. LOCATION Dt.

COMMENTARY Stories set in Lancashire [RL].

B247 *The evolution of Oenone* (by M.E. Blundell).

London: Hutchinson & Co., [1928]. LOCATION L.

B248 *Wood sanctuary* (by 'M.E. Francis' and Margaret Blundell).

+ London: George Allen & Unwin, 1930. LOCATION D, L.

COMMENTARY Set in a Welsh village [Leclaire, p. 188].

B249 *Hannie and her father Pat* (by M.E. Blundell).

Dublin: Catholic Truth Society of Ireland, 1935. SOURCE Murphy, p. 156.

COMMENTARY No copy located. Possibly first published in 1895? [Murphy, p. 156; RL].

BOATE, Mrs Edward Wellington (née Henrietta Bruce O'Neill; also known as Mrs Wellington Boate and Henrietta Bruce Boate), fl. 1847. Catholic poet, songwriter and novelist, Mrs EWB's volume of poetry *Nugæ canoræ, or melodious trifles* (Dublin, 1847) was, according to an advertisement in *The maid of Avoca*, 'to be had from the author' only. *Carlo Marillo, and other poems* (London, 1857) includes 'Recollections of Ireland'. She married Edward Wellington Boate, who was from Waterford, and became a journalist. They emigrated to the US and lived in New York. According to the title page of the following book, she published 'Tales of the Sacred Heart' and 'Lays of the Irish peasantry', but these have not been located. She is said to have published *Tales of the Sacred Heart*, but this has not been located. She is not to be confused with the poet and actress the Hon. Henrietta O'Neill (b. 1758). SOURCE Allibone, ii, p. 1458 [under O'Neill]; Boase, i, p. 322; Colman, p. 180 [under O'Neill]; O'Donoghue, p. 36 [under Boate] and p. 365 [under O'Neill]; RIA/DIB; RL.

B250   *The maid of Avoca: or, the maniac's prophesy* (by Mrs Edward Wellington Boate; dedicated to Sir Edward Blakeney, Commander of the Forces in Ireland).
    + Dublin: William Curry & Co., 1851 (Tales of the Indian Wars, No. 1). LOCATION D.
COMMENTARY First part (22pp) of a projected series of *Tales of the Indian Wars* to be 'published in distinct parts, price 1s. 6d. each'. No. 1 also contains 'Songs of the camp' by the same author. No other issues are known [RL].

BOATE, Henrietta Bruce. See **BOATE, Mrs Edward Wellington.**

BOATE, Mrs Wellington. See **BOATE, Mrs Edward Wellington.**

BODDINGTON, Mary (née Comerford), b. Cork 1776, d. 1839 or 1840. Poet, travel, short story and song writer, MB was the daughter of Patrick Comerford. She frequently wrote verse for Cork papers. She left Cork in 1803 to marry a Mr (probably Samuel) Boddington of London, a wealthy merchant in the West Indian trade. Her travel writing includes *Sketches in the Pyrenees* (London, 1837, 2 vols.) and *Slight reminiscences of the Rhine, Switzerland, and a corner of Italy* (London, 1834, 2 vols.). SOURCE Allibone, i, p. 212; O'Donoghue, p. 30; O'Toole, p. 15.

B251   *The gossip's week* [anon.] (dedicated to Samuel Boddington).
    + London: Longman, Rees, Orme, Brown, Green & Longman & John Rodwell, 1836, 2 vols. (ill.). SOURCE O'Donoghue, p. 30. LOCATION L, DLC.
COMMENTARY Most of the stories are set on the Continent. Contents: 'The glove', 'The king's daughter', 'The roc's egg', 'Count Dalberg and his son', 'Janet Hamilton', 'The story of Flammetta', 'The veiled woman', 'Antonia' [ML].

BODKIN, Matthias McDonnell George (also known as **M. M'D. Bodkin, M McD. Bodkin, M. Bodkin, Matthias McDonnell Bodkin,** and **M. McDonnell Bodkin**), pseud. 'Crom a Boo', b. Tuam (Co. Galway) 1850 (not 1849 as in several other sources), d. 1933 (not in 1928 as in OCIL). A novelist, journalist, MP and judge, MMGB was the second son of Dr Bodkin of Eastland House, Tuam (Co. Galway) and Maria McDonnell. MMGB was educated at Tullabeg Jesuit College and at the Catholic University, Dublin, after which he studied law, was admitted to the Irish Bar in 1877, and practiced on the Connaught circuit. He was a nationalist MP for North Roscommon and an anti-Parnellite. He was the chief leader writer for *United Ireland* and later for the *Freeman's Journal* (both in Dublin). From 1907 to 1924 he was county court judge of Co. Clare. During the Anglo-Irish war, he criticized government forces from the bench and in *The Bodkin report* (Dublin, 1921) listed many atrocities. Former British prime minister Herbert Asquith described this in the house of commons as 'one of the gravest indictments ever presented by a judicial officer against the Executive Government in a free country' (Hogan 2, p. 160). MMGB became best known for his crime and historical fiction (we have identified 30 volumes). In addition, he published several plays, some poetry and *Grattan's Parliament, before and after* (London, 1912), *Recollections of an Irish judge* (London, 1914), and *Famous Irish trials* (Dublin, 1918). He also wrote about his travels in the US in *A trip through the States and a talk with the President* (Dublin, 1907). In 1889 he married Arabella Norman of Dublin. He resided mostly in Dublin. SOURCE Brady, p. 15; Brown, p. 37; EF, p. 37; DLB, lxx; Ferguson, p. 141; Galway, pp 6–7; Hogan, ii, pp 160–1; OCIL, p. 52; O'Donoghue, p. 30; Sutherland, p. 73; OCIL, p. 52; RIA/DIB; Wolff, i, p. 105.

B252   *Peggy Dillon and the brave Mr. Balfour* (by 'Crom a Boo').

Dublin: W.P. Swan, 1889 (cover title: *Peggy Dillon, the midwife, and "the brave Mr. Balfour"*). SOURCE Galway, p. 6; COPAC. LOCATION D.

B253 *Poteen punch, strong, hot and sweet, made and mixed ... being a succession of Irish after-dinner stories of love-making, fun, and fighting, some of which have already appeared in various Christmas numbers of 'United Ireland'* (by 'Crom a Boo').

+ Dublin: M.H. Gill & Son, 1890. SOURCE Brown, 225. LOCATION D, NUC.

COMMENTARY Stories with a strong nationalist flavour supposed to have been told in the presence of the viceroy, Lord Carlisle, in a house at Cong (Co. Mayo). Contents: 'The Lord Lieutenant's misadventure', 'Why Lord Leitrim slammed the door', 'A fox hunt by moonlight', 'Bought and sold', 'Under police protection', 'The bailiff in possession', 'The right man hanged', 'A dance at a bonfire', 'By wire', 'Upside down', ' Love's stratagem', 'Cupid at pistol practice', 'Next morning'. An appendix contains a poem, 'The earl's revenge' [RL].

B254 *Pat o' nine tales and one over* (by M. M'D. Bodkin).

+ Dublin: M.H. Gill & Son, 1894. SOURCE Brown, 226. LOCATION D, L, NUC, InND Loeber coll.

COMMENTARY Stories set in Ireland. Contents: 'Of the same flesh and blood', 'The leprechaun', 'Hanging by a thread', 'Nobbled', 'Showing the white feather', 'Death, the deliverer; or, the fight at Fontenoy', 'Hoist with his own petard', 'The prodigal daughter' [ML].

B255 *Lord Edward Fitzgerald. A historical romance* (by M.McD. Bodkin).

London: Chapman & Hall, 1896 (ill. Leonard Linsdell). SOURCE Brown, 227; Nield 1647. LOCATION D (1921 edn), Dt, L, NUC.

+ Dublin: Phoenix, n.d. (as *Lord Edward Fitzgerald*; ill. W.C. Mills; The Library of Modern Irish Fiction). LOCATION DPL, InND Loeber coll.

COMMENTARY Historical fiction chronicling Lord Edward Fitzgerald's career, mostly within the period 1780 to 1795. It begins with when he served in the English army during the American War of Independence (battle of Eutaw Springs, 1781), then rapidly sketches his experiences in Dublin, in America among the Indians, in Canada, and in London. The later portions of the novel deal with Lord Edward's domestic affairs (marriage etc.) as well as with politics and the Irish parliament. Many other historic figures, including William Pitt, Lord Castlereagh, Henry Grattan and John Philpot Curran appear [Nield, 1647].

B256 *White magic. A novel* (by M.McD. Bodkin).

+ London: Chapman & Hall, 1897 (ill.). SOURCE Wolff, 565. LOCATION D, Dt, L, NUC, InND Loeber coll.

COMMENTARY Set in England and Ireland. A very rich London gentleman, Mr Merlyn, tries to increase his fortune by chemically treating his gold. He is found dead in his laboratory, the gold gone and only a pile of black dust left. His daughter, Dorothy, is left nearly destitute and rents out rooms. Two of her boarders, Gerald and Grace Daly, have also been left penniless by their father. Gerald had become a newspaper man in Dublin and then an MP in London. Grace is deaf but has learned to lip read. Gerald and Dorothy fall in love, but after a while a coldness springs up between them because of Dorothy's unexplained closeness to a man who claims to be her long-estranged brother. In reality he is after the pile of black dust, which can be reconverted into gold. Gerald exposes the impostor and happiness returns to Dorothy and Gerald [ML].

B257 *Paul Beck: the rule of thumb detective* (by M.McD. Bodkin).

London: C. Arthur Pearson, 1898. LOCATION Dt, L, NUC.

+ Dublin: Talbot Press, 1929 (as *Paul Beck, detective*). LOCATION D.

COMMENTARY Crime fiction [RL].

B258 *A stolen life* (by Matthias McDonnell Bodkin).

+ London, New York, Melbourne: Ward, Lock & Co., [1899] (ill. Frances Ewan). SOURCE Topp 2, p. 371. LOCATION Dt, D, L.

B259 *The rebels* (by Matthias McDonnell Bodkin).
London, New York, Melbourne: Ward, Lock & Co., 1899 (ill.). SOURCE Brown, 228 (Dublin: Duffy, 1899 edn, not located); Wolff, 564; Topp 2, p. 377. LOCATION D (n.d. edn), L, NUC.
+ Dublin: Talbot Press; London: T. Fisher Unwin, 1921 (as *The rebels. A romance of Ireland in 1798*). LOCATION DPL, NUC, InND Loeber coll.
COMMENTARY Historical fiction. A sequel to *Lord Edward Fitzgerald* (London, 1896), set mainly in Dublin and Wexford at the time of the 1798 rebellion. A considerable portion deals with the tracking, capture, and death of Lord Edward. Covers the period of the Wexford fighting and gives glimpses of Fr John Murphy. Describes the French invasion under Gen. Humbert at Killala and the races of Castlebar. Besides Fitzgerald and his wife, Lord Clare, Sir Ralph Abercombie, Lord Camden, Henry Grattan, and Lord Castlereagh appear. The book has a decided rebel bias [Nield, 1656; B. Browne].

B260 *The quests of Paul Beck* (by M. McDonnell Bodkin).
+ London: T. Fisher Unwin, 1900 (ill. Ernest Prater). LOCATION D, L (1908 edn), NUC (1908 edn)
Boston: Little, Brown & Co., 1910. LOCATION NUC.
COMMENTARY Crime fiction, sequel to *Paul Beck* (London, 1898) [RL].

B261 *Dora Myrl, the lady detective* (by M.McD. Bodkin).
+ London: Chatto & Windus, 1900. SOURCE Wolff, 562. LOCATION D, L, NUC.
COMMENTARY Crime fiction. Story of an independent female detective, who carries a small revolver and can pick a lock [EF, p. 37].

B262 *A bear squeeze; or, her second self* (by M. McDonnell Bodkin).
+ London, New York, Melbourne: Ward, Lock & Co., 1901 (Copyright Novels, No. 34; ill. Harold Copping). SOURCE Topp 2, 2482; Wolff, 561. LOCATION D, L.

B263 *A modern miracle* (by M.McD. Bodkin).
London, New York, Melbourne: Ward, Lock & Co., 1902. LOCATION L.

B264 *Shillelagh and shamrock* (by M.McD. Bodkin).
+ London: Chatto & Windus, 1902. SOURCE Brown, 229. LOCATION D, L, InND Loeber coll.
COMMENTARY Some of the following stories had been first published in *Poteen punch* (Dublin, 1890) and in *Pat o' nine tales* (Dublin, 1894). Contents: 'The holy well', 'A fox-hunt by moonlight', 'Hoist with his petard', 'Vote early – vote often', 'The leprechaun', 'A well-decked jury', 'Down the red lane', 'Rival distillers', 'The banshee', 'A friend of the fairies', 'The four-leaved shamrock', 'Hen Castle', 'An Irish Christmas', 'Cupid at pistol practice', 'Bought and sold', 'Showing the white feather' [ML].

B265 *In the days of Goldsmith* (by M.McD. Bodkin).
+ London: John Long, 1903. SOURCE Brown, 230; Wolff, 563. LOCATION D, L, NUC.
COMMENTARY Historical fiction set in the eighteenth century. Deals with Oliver Goldsmith's§ life while he lived in England. Introduces Joshua Reynolds, Dr. Samuel Johnson, etc. [Brown].

B266 *A modern Robyn Hood* (by M. McDonnell Bodkin).
London, New York, Melbourne: Ward, Lock & Co., 1903. LOCATION L.

B267 *Patsey the omadaun* (by M.McD. Bodkin).
+ London: Chatto & Windus, 1904. SOURCE Brown, 231; OCIL (where mistakenly called *Patsy*). LOCATION D, L, NUC, InND Loeber coll.
+ Dublin: James Duffy & Co., n.d. LOCATION DPL.
COMMENTARY Twelve stories set in Ireland in which the village tailor, Patsey, recounts his exploits. He is less of a fool than he seems. Contents: 'How Patsey raffled the milch cow',

'How Patsey lost his memory', 'How Patsey forgot the pishogue', 'How Patsey played with dynamite', 'How Patsey employed the iron man', 'How Patsey cheated the devil', 'How Patsey found a sweetheart', 'How Patsey made true love run smooth', 'How Patsey made the big bear commit suicide', 'How Patsey met the grand lady', 'How Patsey met the fine gentleman', 'How Patsey caught the leprechaun' [ML; Brown].

B268   *A madcap marriage* (by M. MacDonnell [*sic*] Bodkin).
+ London: John Long, 1906. LOCATION D, L.

B269   *The capture of Paul Beck* ((by M. McDonnell Bodkin).
London: T. Fisher Unwin, 1909. LOCATION L.
+ Boston: Little, Brown & Co., 1911 (ill. Grunwald). LOCATION D, NUC.
COMMENTARY Crime fiction. Detective Paul Beck is pitted against Dora Myrl, a female detective. Eventually Dora gives up her independent life and marries Paul. Their child is young Beck, who features later in *Young Beck* (London, 1911) [EF, p. 37].

B270   *True man and traitor; or, the rising of Emmet* (by M. McDonnell Bodkin).
Dublin: James Duffy, 1910. SOURCE Brown, 232. LOCATION L.
London: T. Fisher Unwin, 1910. LOCATION NUC.
COMMENTARY Historical fiction. Recounts the career of Robert Emmet from his days in TCD to his tragic end. Emmet is represented as an able organizer and the story of his love for Sarah Curran is interwoven [Brown].

B271   *Young Beck, a chip of the old block* (by M. McDonnell Bodkin).
London: T. Fisher Unwin, 1911. LOCATION L, NUC.
Boston: Little, Brown & Co., 1912 (ill. Ernest Prater). LOCATION NUC.
COMMENTARY Sequel to *The capture of Paul Beck* (London, 1909). Crime fiction featuring the son of the detectives Paul Beck and Dora Myrl [RL].

B272   *His brother's keeper* (by M.McD. Bodkin).
London: Hurst & Blackett, 1913. LOCATION L.

B273   *Behind the picture* (by M.McD. Bodkin).
London, Melbourne, Toronto: Ward, Lock & Co., 1914 (ill.). SOURCE COPAC.
LOCATION L.

B274   *The test* (by M. McDonnell Bodkin).
London: Everett & Co., [1914]. LOCATION L.

B275   *Pigeon blood rubies* (by M. McDonnell Bodkin).
London: Eveleigh Nash, 1915. LOCATION L.

B276   *Old Rowley* (by M. McDonnell Bodkin).
+ London: Holden & Hardingham, [1916]. SOURCE Brown, 233. LOCATION D, L
([1917] edn).
COMMENTARY Historical fiction set in the seventeenth century. Begins with Cromwell's siege of Drogheda where a Hugh O'Donnell escapes. His son, also named Hugh, refuses under torture to betray his father. Young Hugh goes to France and becomes a courtier at Versailles. After the Restoration he goes to the court of Charles II in London, under the nickname of Old Rowley. His early love has become one of the ladies of the court but she does not recognize him. Despite the shameless amours and intrigues of Charles's court, the lovers remain true to each other's memory and are united in the end [Brown].

B277   *When youth meets youth* (by M.McD. Bodkin).
+ Dublin: Talbot Press; London: T. Fisher Unwin, 1920. SOURCE Brown 2, 119.
LOCATION D, L.

B278   *Kitty the madcap. A romance of to-day* (by M. McDonnell Bodkin).
+ Dublin, Cork: Talbot Press, [1927]. SOURCE Brown 2, 120. LOCATION D, L, InND
Loeber coll.

COMMENTARY Concerns young people and their lives and contains a description of holiday-making at Achill (Co. Mayo) [Brown 2].

B279 *Guilty or not guilty?* (by M. McDonnell Bodkin).

+ Dublin: Talbot Press, 1928. SOURCE Brown 2, 121. LOCATION D, L (1929 edn), NUC (1929 edn), InND Loeber coll. (n.d. edn).

COMMENTARY Set in Dublin and in the west of Ireland. The heir of the wealthy marquis of Clanrogan is accused of having killed him. The plot against the heir is unravelled by his friend who is a barrister who writes mystery novels. His so-called fiancée and his cousin had set him up to clear the way for their own union and to inherit the marquis' wealth [ML].

B280 *Borrowed days* (by M. Bodkin; dedicated to the son of Maurice's three homes, Belvedere College, St Mary's, Emo, and Clongowes Wood College).

Dublin: Browne & Nolan, 1942. SOURCE Galway, p. 7. LOCATION D.

COMMENTARY A posthumously published historical novel about Catholic landlords at the end of the eighteenth century. About half of the characters are based on historical figures such as Robert Emmet, Lord Edward Fitzgerald, and Daniel O'Connell [ML; Cathair cat. Spring 1999/47].

BOGAERTS, Félix. See BOGAERTS, Félix Guillaume Marie.

BOGAERTS, Félix Guillaume Marie (also known as Felix Bogaerts), b. Antwerp (Belgium) 1805, d. Antwerp 1851. Belgian novelist, playwright and art historian, FGMB was secretary of the Archaeologische Academie van Belgium. He mainly wrote historical novels, including *La bataille de Nieuport* (Antwerp, 1844). SOURCE NUC; Koninklijke Bibliotheek, The Hague, Netherlands; W.J.A. Huberts, W.A. Elberts, & F.Joz.P. van den Branden, *Biographisch woordenboek der Noord- en Zuid-Nederlandsche letterkunde* (Deventer, 1878), p. 45 [under Bogaerts].

B281 *Dympne d'Irlande, légende du septième siècle* (by Félix Bogaerts; dedicated to Mlle Théodora van den Nest).

+ Antwerp: L.J. de Cort, 1840 (ill. N. de Keyser). LOCATION L.

COMMENTARY Historical fiction set in seventh-century Ireland [ML].

B282 *Lord Strafford* (by Félix Bogaerts).

Brussels: Alex. Jamar & Ch. Hen, [1843] (ill. Nicaise de Keyser). LOCATION NUC.

Antwerp: J.E. Buschmann, 1846 (trans. into Dutch by Jozef Colveniers; ill. N. de Keyser). LOCATION Univ. of Ghent.

Rotterdam: G.W. van Belle, 1858 (trans. into Dutch as *Lord Strafford, eene episode uit de laatste jaren der regeering van Karel I, koning van Engeland*). Source Mes, p. 30.

BOGER, Charlotte Gibson (née Allen), b. Ilminster (Som.) 1826. English historical novelist and writer, CGB published under the name **Mrs Edmund Boger**, including works on Southwark and Somerset. SOURCE Allibone Suppl., i, p. 172; BLC; RL.

B283 *Elfrica. A historical romance of the twelfth century* (by Mrs Edmund Boger).

+ London: W. Swan Sonnenschein, 1885, 3 vols. LOCATION D, L.

COMMENTARY Historical novel, partly set in Ireland in the twelfth century, and relates the conquest of Ulster [ML].

BOGER, Mrs Edmund. See BOGER, Charlotte Gibson.

BONESTEEL, Mary G. fl. 1900. American writer of fiction for juveniles.

B284 *Recruit Tommy Collins* (by Mary G. Bonesteel).

+ New York, Cincinnati, Chicago: Benziger Bros, 1900. SOURCE OCLC. LOCATION InND.

COMMENTARY Fiction for juveniles. Main character is Tommy Collins, a boy whose parents are from Ireland. His father is a soldier and the book describes life in a military fort, where Tommy has many adventures. He leaves with a troop for war in Cuba. Most of the characters are Irish and the book is written for Catholic children as they discuss mass and Lent [ebay. Access date: 26 July 2001].

BOOLE, Ethel Lilian. See **VOYNICH, Ethel Lilian.**

BOREL, Joseph Pierre Borel d'Hautterive (also known as **Pétrus Borel**), b. Lyons (France) 1809, d. 1859 (not 1880 as in Brown 2). French poet, novelist and colonial administrator, he was the son of André Borel and Madeline-Victoire Garnaud. He moved to Paris where he trained as an architect but he did not succeed in this profession. He spent some time in Algeria and held various posts as inspector of colonization. His well-received book of poems, *Rhapsodies*, was published in 1832. SOURCE Brown 2, p. 26; DBF, xvi; DLB, cxix; NUC.

B285 *Madame Putiphar* (by Pétrus Borel; dedicated to L.P.).
+ Paris: Ollivier, 1839, 2 vols. (ill.). LOCATION L, NUC.
Paris: Léon Willem, 1877, 2 vols. (new edn, with preface by Jules Claretie). SOURCE Brown 2, 124. LOCATION NUC.
Paris: Phébus, [*c*.1999] (introd. and notes by Jean-Luc Steinmetz). LOCATION InND.
COMMENTARY Historical fiction. MacPahadrig, or Patrick MacWhyte, is in love with Deborah, daughter of Lord Cockermouth, who has an estate near Killarney where Patrick lives. He elopes with her to France where he joins the king's musketeers, among whom he finds his boyhood friend Kildare Fitzharris. He and Fitzharris are both thrown into prison because of some real or fancied slight to Mme Putiphar (Madame de Pompadour). Deborah joins the crowd that storms the Bastille in the revolution. Fitzharris has died in prison and her husband has lost his reason. The story tells much about the Irish language and about conditions in Ireland [Brown 2].

BOREL, Pétrus. See **BOREL, Joseph Pierre Borel d'Hautterive.**

BORLASE, James Skipp, pseud. '**J.J.G. Bradley**', b. Truro (Corn.) fl. 1870s. An English writer of stories for boys who had been a soldier in Australia but after his retirement about 1870 lived in England, where he continued to write for the next thirty years. SOURCE Allibone Suppl., i, p. 179 [under Borlase]; BLC; Brown 2, p. 28.

B286 *Ned Kelly: The ironclad Australian bushranger* [anon.].
London: A.J. Isaacs & Sons, 1881. SOURCE COPAC. LOCATION L.
COMMENTARY Historical fiction featuring Ned Kelly, an Australian horse-thief and bushranger, who had come from Ireland [Hartman, 574].

B287 *A sword for a fortune; or, Sir Redmond the rover* (by 'J.J.G. Bradley).
+ London: C. Fox, [1891]. SOURCE Brown 2, 131. LOCATION L.
COMMENTARY 68pp. Crime fiction written for juveniles, originally published in the *Boys' Standard* (London, 1875). Set in England. Describes the adventures of young Redmond O'Neill, the unknown heir to the earldom of Inchmore. His dying father hands him a sword and a sealed package, not to be opened until his twenty-first birthday. He is captured by pirates at the instigation of the usurper of the family estate. After many adventures at sea and in India, Redmond becomes earl of Inchmore [Brown 2; ML].

BORTHWICK, James, pseud. '**J.B.**', fl. mid-eighteenth century. Unpublished historical fiction writer, JB was a resident of Kilkenny. According to the preface to the following manuscript, the author composed the story 'while watching the sick bed of a dying parent … The

Night – the midnight lamp – was often witness to the close of a chapter, and probably was not unfavourable to many terrific ideas which the very silence of that hour, are wont to suggest'. The manuscript was intended for publication because it includes at the end a table for the insertion of a list of subscribers, at five shillings a copy, but the list has only two names. JB may be related to the Irish author, Norma Borthwick, whose writings promoted the Gaelic language, and to Catherine Borthwick, a watercolorist who drew Kilkenny Castle. Allibone Suppl. i, p. 180 has an entry for J.D. Borthwick with the title *Three years in California* (Edinburgh, 1857), but gives no biographical information. SOURCE BLC; Personal communication, Chris R. Johnson, London, Oct. 1996; Crookshank, p. 199.

B288   *The wanderer of Carrickfergus; A legend* (by 'J.B.').

COMMENTARY Manuscript [*c*.1835–40?] (current location not known) with preface initialled 'J.B.' Historical fiction set during the troubles of 1641 when the hero, Connor O'Brien, joined in 'the confederation for the stability of the reigning monarch [Charles I], against the usurpation of Oliver Cromwell'. O'Brien had been a respectable farmer living near Carrickfergus but had been ruined as the result of the war [Personal communication, Chris R. Johnson, Oct. 1996].

BOSWELL, George, fl. 1832. A writer of novelettes, GB was, according to the title page of *Eleanor of the village* (London, 1832), the author of the 'Orphan'; 'Village cottage'; 'Aged musician'; 'St. John's knights', and 'Juvenile poems'. None of these has been located. He probably can be identified with the George Boswell who published a bundle of poems, *Forlorn Anna, a tale* (London, 1826, 10th edn), which like the following works was privately published. Given that the two novelettes below are largely set in Ireland, GB may have been Irish. SOURCE COPAC; RL.

B289   *Maria of the mountain; or, The castle of Balahana. (Founded on facts)* [anon.].
    + London: Printed for the author by R. Brown, 1832. SOURCE OCLC; Summers 2, pp 402, 571. LOCATION MH.

COMMENTARY 60pp. Historical fiction set at the end of the seventeenth century. Lord and Lady Balahana, named for the estate they own (possibly Balahana refers to Ballyhana, Co. Kerry), are kind to all their tenants and generous to all supplicants. Their 8-year-old son is likewise charitably-disposed. Their happiness is interrupted by the outbreak of war. Lord Balahana, being a pacifist at heart, allows members of King William's army to camp on his estate on their way to the river Boyne. One of the generals insults him, however, so a few days later Lord Balahana sets out with his followers to aid King James's army. He is wounded defending the river crossing from Williams's attack, and dies. News of his death puts Castle Balahana in despair. A rumour spreads that all its inhabitants and tenants will be wiped out. Lady Balahana, along with her son and faithful domestics Henry and Harriet, sets out for Dublin. They arrive at a safe house there, but the stable boy's vociferous denunciation of the English army alerts several English veterans to Lady Balahana's presence. The four flee to the country for safety, hiding out in a cornfield for days. Henry, however, visits the cottage of the stable boy's father, and the family invites all four to stay with them. Lady Balahana and her companions try again to get to Dublin but are delayed by weather. Holed up in a townhouse, Lady Balahana meets the landlady, also formerly a noblewoman. This woman tells Lady Balahana her sad tale of loss and betrayal, and then the four set out again, led by the landlady's generous peasant friend, McDowal. On their way the five of them are forced to shelter in a cave, where they meet a hermit who was – *mirabile dictum* – also once a noble. He lectures Lady Balahana and her son on all the vices of his former life. After his house has burned down, he gave all his land to his tenants and villagers, claiming that he had learned that 'prosperity was the only barrier between mortals and knowledge'. Shortly thereafter, McDowal returns with Henry, who had been reconnoitring their route. Henry had been shot by English soldiers and dies. Lady Balahana never makes it to Dublin and she, McDowal, and Harriet also die. A 'mechanic' adopts the orphaned boy and teaches him the trade. The boy grows up, settles there, marries, and has many children, the descendants of whom still sigh for the original lord's folly. Summers 2 mentions a 1827 edn of this book, but that edn has not been located [ML; OCLC; RL; Summers 2, pp 402, 571].

B290 *Eleanor of the village; or, the persecuted servant* (by George Boswell).
+ London: Printed for the author by R. Brown, 1832. LOCATION PC.
COMMENTARY 63pp. Only late in the story is it is evident that it is set in Ireland, but the time is inconstant and switches between the late-seventeenth and the early-nineteenth centuries. Eleanor Finglass, the daughter of a prosperous farmer, becomes governess to the children of a landowner. She falls in love with Edwin, a shepherd. They marry and she announces her intention to leave her position. She commits a minor transgression and her employer, dissatisfied with her planned departure, takes revenge by seeing that she is prosecuted, convicted, and sentenced to be transported to New South Wales in Australia. After a terrifying journey in the hold of a ship, she arrives and manages to become a governess to the children of a friendly lady. The distressed Edwin decides to make the voyage to New South Wales to seek his wife. Through the friendly assistance of several sea captains, including one Will Donovan, he embarks as a sailor. His ship, however, goes down in a storm and he is the only survivor to land on the Isle of France (Mauritius). There he is taken in by an Irish family, originally from Co. Down, who had fled Ireland after the battle of the Boyne and settled there. Eventually, Edwin reaches New South Wales, finds Eleanor, after which they return to Ireland to live there happily [RL].

BOSWELL, John Whittley, pseud. '**Doctor Hastler, M.R.S.P.Q.L.M.N.A.S.T. and L.L.Z.**', b. Dublin *c*.1767. Humorous writer, the son of John Boswell, a merchant, JWB was admitted to TCD at age 17 in 1784, and graduated BA in 1788. SOURCE B & S, p. 83; ESTC.

B291 S YL LETOMENA *of the antiquities of Killmackumpshaugh, in the county of Roscommon, and Kingdom of Ireland, in which it is clearly proven that Ireland was originally peopled by Ægyptians* (by 'Doctor Hastler, M.R.S.P.Q.L.M.N.A.S.T. and L.L.Z.'; dedicated to the Members of the Royal Irish Academy).
+ Dublin: Printed for the Author, 1790. SOURCE ESTC t105278; Lough Fea cat. p. 22. LOCATION D, Dt, L, MH, InND Loeber coll.
COMMENTARY This is a quip on Charles Vallancey's thesis that the Irish descended from the Phaeno-Scythians [RL].

BOUCICAULT also **BOURCICAULT, BOURSIQUOT, Dionysius Lardner**, b. Dublin 1820, d. New York 1890. DLB was a playwright, actor, theatre manager and writer whose dates and parentage are not fully clear, but he is said to be the youngest child of Dionysius Lardner Boursiquot, a wine merchant in Dublin, and Anne Maria Darley (OCIL says that he was the illegitimate son of Dionysius Lardner Boucicault, a scientist). However, the ODNB states that he was the fifth and final son of Samuel Boursiquot, but the natural son of Dionysius Lardner who was lodging with the Boursiquots at the time and who had a relationship with Anne Boursiquot, who later followed Lardner to London with four of her children. Lardner took care of DLB's education. DLB became first an actor under the stage name Lee Moreton and then a highly-productive and successful playwright. His first major success was his play *London assurance*, which was staged to acclaim at the Theatre Royal, Covent Garden, in 1841. Quickly squandering his considerable earnings, he wrote for *Bentley's Miscellany* (London) and the *Musical Examiner*

(London), attempted a three-volume novel, and wrote several unsuccessful plays. Bankruptcy followed and he married a wealthy French widow and lived in Paris until her death in 1846. Back in London, he adapted French plays, campaigned to reform the royalty system for plays, and fell in love with his leading lady, Agnes Kelly Robertson, with whom he moved to New York, where they were married in 1853. DLB wrote plays in which Agnes could star, mining contemporary events in melodramas that captured the public's imagination. The Boucicaults made several forays into theatre ownership and management and DLB acted as well (he played the title role in the stage adaptation of Samuel Lover's§ *Rory O'More*). His adaptation of Gerald Griffin's§ *The collegians* into a play, *The Colleen Bawn; or, the brides of Garryowen* (New York, [1860]), was a huge success, with DLB playing the role of Myles-na-Coppaleen. The Boucicaults brought the production to London and stayed there for twelve years. DLB wrote several other Irish plays: *Andy Blake; or, the Irish diamond* (Boston, 1854), *Arrah-na-Pogue* (Dublin, 1864), *The lily of Killarney* (Philadelphia, 1867), and his greatest success, *The shaughraun* (New York, 1874). Praised for their melodrama, sentiment and vivid characterization, these plays turned the negative English stereotype of the 'stage-Irishman' on its head by creating charming, witty characters who in turn made light fun of the English and the upper-classes. George Bernard Shaw§ and Sean O'Casey both acknowledged DLB's influence on their writing. After years of acting and touring in America and abroad, DLB died in 1890 and was buried in the Mount Hope cemetery in New York. At the end of his life he published a highly nationalistic, historical work of 24pp, *A fireside story of Ireland* (London, 1881). For his portraits and papers, see ODNB. For complete biography and discussions of DLB's career as a playwright and his over 150 plays, see the following sources. SOURCE R. Fawkes, *Dion Boucicault: a biography* (London, Melbourne, New York, 1979); Field Day, i, p. 505; ii, pp 108–9, 234–8, 366–7; Hogan 2, pp 169–73; R. Hogan, *Dion Boucicault* (New York, 1969), pp 59–60, passim; NCBEL 4, pp 1994–6; OCIL, pp 57–8; ODNB; O'Donoghue, p. 31; Rafroidi, ii, p. 70.

B292   *Adventures and works of Hugh Darley* (by Dion Boucicault).

London: Andrews, [1842 or 1843], 3vols.

COMMENTARY No copy located. Mentioned as in press in DLB's play *The Irish heiress* published by Andrews in London in 1842, but may never have been published. DLB's mother was a Darley and a son was named Darley George [R. Hogan, *Dion Boucicault* (New York, 1969), p. 134; ODNB].

B293   *Foul play. A novel* (by Charles Reade and Dion Boucicault).

+ London: Bradbury, Evans, & Co., 1868, 3 vols. LOCATION L.

+ London: Bradbury, Evans & Co., 1869 (new edn; ill. D.M.). LOCATION L.

Paris: Hachette & Co., 1880 (trans. by D. Bochet as *L'Isle proventielle*). LOCATION L.

+ Boston: Ticknor & Fields, 1868 (ill. George de Maurier). LOCATION InND Loeber coll.

New York: A.L. Burt, [1903]. LOCATION NUC.

COMMENTARY Complicated plot, part of which had been borrowed from *Le portefeuille rouge* by Narcisse Fournier and Henri-Horace Meyer. There is an announcement at the start of the London 1869 new edn, stating: 'Notice to Managers. A Drama entitled "Foul Play" has been written by the Authors of the Story, and produced at the Theatre Royal, Leeds. So that no other person can legally dramatise the Story'. The authors, however, fell out about the dramatization of the novel [NUC; R. Hogan, *Dion Boucicault* (New York, 1969), pp 59–60; JB].

BOURCICAULT, Dion. See **BOUCICAULT, Dion.**

BOURSIQUOT, Dion. See **BOUCICAULT, Dion.**

BOURKE, Dermot Robert Wyndham. See **MAYO, Dermot Robert Wyndham, 7th earl of**.

BOURKE, Mrs Hubert, fl. 1891. Novelist, the wife of Hubert E.M. Bourke, author of a broadsheet, *The labourers who abused the parson and demanded disestablishment* ([London, 1890?]). SOURCE COPAC.

B294 *A political wife* (by Mrs Hubert Bourke; dedicated to H.E.M.B. [Hubert E.M. Bourke] in the recollection of many a political contest).
+ London: Eden, Remington & Co., 1891. SOURCE Alston, p. 35. LOCATION L.
COMMENTARY Mostly set in England and partly in Ireland. Deals with the Land League and Home Rule [RL].

BOURKE, Fr U.J. Editor. See **ROONEY, Miss Teresa J.**

'BOURREAU, Jacques', possible pseud. See **JEPHSON, Robert**.

BOWLES, Emily (afterwards Southey), fl. 1861. Novelist, poet, translator and author of religious fiction, EB was the daughter of Thomas Bowles, JP, of Milton Hall (Berks.) and lord of the manor of Streatley. She converted to catholicism. She may have had some connection to Ireland considering that she published in Dublin. Only her known Irish works are included here. Many of the books appearing under her name between 1861 and 1888 were translations from French Catholic literature, such as Mme Augustus [Pauline de la Ferronays] Craven's *A sister's story* (London, 1868). She also wrote a biography of Madame de Maintenon (London, 1888). SOURCE Allibone Suppl., i, p. 188; Alston, p. 38; Brown, p. 39; MVP, p. 51; Wolff, i, p. 113.

B295 *Irish diamonds; or, a chronicle of Peterstown* (by Emily Bowles).
+ London, Dublin, Derby: Thomas Richardson & Son, 1864. SOURCE Brown, 235.
LOCATION DPL, L, NUC, InND (1866 edn), InND Loeber coll. (1867 edn).
+ Leamington, London: Art and Book Co., n.d. LOCATION D.
COMMENTARY A satire on the anti-popery evangelizing efforts of the London branch of the Protestant Association, based at Exeter Hall in the Strand. In Ireland, Powerscourt House (Co. Wicklow) was a centre of its militant missionary zeal. The novel features Lord Powderhouse as Lord Powerscourt. Eudora, Lord Powderhouse's sister, refers to the pious Theodosia, Lady Powerscourt. Lefroy, a character in the book who is a justice in Dublin, may refer to Thomas Lefroy, the Irish chief justice, who appears to have been one of the people in the Powerscourt circle [D. Bowen, *The Protestant crusade in Ireland*, 1800–70 (Dublin, 1978), pp. 65, 74–5, 115–5, 195–266 passim; ML]

B296 *St. Martha's home; or, work for women* (by Emily Bowles).
+ Dublin: London: James Duffy, 1864. LOCATION D.
COMMENTARY Contents: 'The good neighbour', 'St. Joseph's night', 'The new servant', 'The wife's victory', 'How Dora went into business', 'What became of the cock and pin' [ML].

BOWMAN, Anne, fl. 1830s. American author of adventure stories for children, poetry and works on domestic economy. SOURCE NCBEL 4, pp 1754–5.

B297 *The bear hunters of the Rocky Mountains* (by Anne Bowman).
Philadelphia: Porter & Coates, [not before 1868?]. SOURCE NCBEL 4, p. 1754; RLIN.
LOCATION CSt.
COMMENTARY Classified as Irish juvenile fiction [RLIN].

BOYCE, Fr John, pseud. **'Paul Peppergrass'**, b. Co. Donegal 1810, d. Worcester (MA) 1864. Catholic cleric, novelist, religious writer and journalist, JB was the son of a hotel owner and county magistrate. He was educated for the priesthood in Navan and Maynooth and was ordained in 1837. He served in Fanad and Glenties, Irish-speaking parishes in the Raphoe diocese, for eight years, during which time he became involved with the Young Ireland movement, contributing to its newspaper, the *Nation* (Dublin). In 1845 he went to the US and assumed an isolated pastorate at Eastport (ME). Two years later he moved to the increasingly-Irish parish of St John's in Worcester (MA), then a destination of massive immigration due to the Famine. He soon became a contributing member of the intellectual circle of Boston-area priests, many of them Irish. He edited *The lady of the beacon of Araheera* (Quebec, 1859), but it has been attributed to Margaret McDougall§. He corresponded with leading figures of the day, including Charles Dickens, William Makepeace Thackeray§, Charles Lever§, Thomas D'Arcy Magee and William Smith O'Brien. SOURCE Allibone, ii, p. 1556 [under Peppergrass]; Allibone Suppl., i, p. 190; Brady, p. 16; Brown, p. 39; Donegal, pp 35–6; Fanning, pp 75, 97; Hogan 2, p. 177; McKenna, p. 105; Newmann, p. 20; OCIL, p. 59; RIA/DIB.

B298   *Shandy McGuire; or, tricks upon travellers. Being a story of the North of Ireland* (by 'Paul Peppergrass, Esq.').
         + New York: Edward Dunigan & Brother, 1848. SOURCE Fanning, p. 375; Wright, i, 347; LOCATION Grail, D, DCL, NUC, InND Loeber coll. (1853 edn).
         + Boston: Patrick Donahoe, 1853. LOCATION D, DCU, NUC, InND Loeber coll. (Noonan, 1879 edn).
         + Dublin: P.C.D. Warren, [ca.1895]. LOCATION D, Dt.

COMMENTARY First appeared in a Boston periodical and reviewed in *Brownson's Quarterly Review* (Boston, 1849), which alleged that the Irish-American author's insistence on making 'the tyrant ... a Saxon, and the victim a Celt ...' turned 'a war against oppression for common justice into a war of races'. Set in Co. Donegal after a period of famine, it concerns the conflict between the local Ribbonmen and the Orange Lodge. The main characters are Shandy McGuire, a popular Ribbon society leader, and Revd Baxter Cantwell and his son Archy, organizer of the Orange Lodge and estate agent for Colonel Templeton, the local landlord. Intermixed is the story of the aristocrat Ellen O'Donnell who marries Capt. O'Brien, a convert to catholicism who encourages the revolutionary zeal of the Ribbonmen. When the local priest's chapel, house and library are set on fire by the Orangemen, the priest warns of the eventual revolt of the Irish against English rule. A dramatized version of this novel was staged in 1851 [RIA/DIB; C.M. Eagon, '"White", if "not quite": Irish whiteness in the nineteenth century' in *Éire/Ireland*, 36, 2001, p. 74; Fanning, pp 98–103, 108].

B299   *The spaewife; or, the Queen's secret. A story of the reign of Elizabeth* (by 'Paul Peppergrass, Esq.'; dedicated to R.R., J.B.F., DD).
         Baltimore: Kelly, Hedian & Piet, 1852, 2 vols. SOURCE OCLC; Wright, ii, 330 (1853 edn). LOCATION Grail, Boston College, Wright web (1853 edn).
         Boston: Patrick Donahoe, 1860. LOCATION NUC.
         Boston: Pilot Publishing Co., 1876 (revsd edn). SOURCE DCU, Catholic Americana files.

COMMENTARY Historical romance set in the days of Elizabeth I and based on a note in the work of John Lingard (the historian, 1771–1851?) concerning the illegitimate child born to the queen and the duke of Leicester. This child is saved from execution and brought up by a Scots 'spaewife' or fortune-teller. The ostensible subject is the queen's defection from youthful sympathy for catholicism in order to gain power. One of the characters is Roger O'Brien, an Irishman attached to the court of Mary, queen of Scots [Brown; Donegal, p. 35; Fanning, p. 104].

B300   *Mary Lee; or, the Yankee in Ireland* (by 'Paul Peppergrass, Esq.').
         Boston: Noonan & Co., [1859]. LOCATION Donegal County Library, MB, NUC.
         + Baltimore: Patrick Donahoe, 1859. LOCATION InND Loeber coll.

+ Baltimore: Kelly, Hedian & Piet; Boston: P. Donahoe, 1860 (ill. Harley, Keating). SOURCE Wright, ii, 329. LOCATION D, L, NUC, InND Loeber coll. (1864 edn).

+ Dublin: G.P. Warren, [1880]. LOCATION D, NUC.

COMMENTARY Set in Co. Donegal in the 1850s. Ephraim C.B. Weeks, an American from Ducksville (CT), arrives in Ireland to seek a bride and woos Mary Lee, the daughter of the lighthouse keeper at Inishowen Head. Weeks knows that she is really the orphaned child of the Talbots, wealthy Irish aristocrats, whose fortune he hopes to gain by marrying her. He is aided in his scheme by Robert Hardwrinkle of Crohan, a grim Presbyterian landlord. Weeks turns out to be only a cousin of the man that he pretends to be. The novel contrasts the American scramble for social mobility with the old Irish order, and Weeks' values with those of his Irish hosts [Fanning, pp 105–8].

BOYD, Arabella, fl. 1818. Novelist, AB may be identified with the daughter of a Church of Ireland clergyman, William Boyd (b. *c*.1762 at Wexford, still alive in 1862, said to be age 90 at that time [*sic*]) and Frances Arabella Waring. AB's father was curate at Castletowndelvin (Co. Westmeath, 1788), vicar of Ballywalter (Co. Down, 1799–1828), and vicar of Donaghadee (Co. Down, 1824–30). SOURCE Landed gentry, 1912, p. 747; Leslie, *Down*, pp 137–8.

B301   *The foundling orphan and heiress; a novel* (by Arabella Boyd).
        Belfast: Printed [for the author?] by F.D. Finlay, 1818, 2 vols. SOURCE C.N. Greenough card coll. LOCATION BFl, MH (not found).

BOYD, Elizabeth, fl. 1727. Novelist and poet, possibly Irish (she is included in O'Donoghue), whose verses appeared in London in 1730, 1733, 1743 and 1745 and who also published a ballad opera, *Don Sancho, or, the students' whim ... with Minerva's triumph, a masque* (London, 1739). EB's background is unknown but in the only issue of her proposed periodical, *The Snail*, she mentions 'her deceased father having long and zealously serv'd the *Stuart* family in a creditable Employ'. The following volume is identified in the ODNB as by EB, who seems to have lived in London while writing it (she had an address in Georges Court, Princes Street). She was married, but the identity of her husband is not known. SOURCE Brady, p. 16; NUC; ODNB; O'Donoghue, p. 33; RL.

B302   *The happy unfortunate; or, the female page. A novel in three parts* (by Elizabeth Boyd).
        + London: Thomas Edlin, 1732. SOURCE ESTC n012313; Brady, p. 17; McBurney, 275. LOCATION L, ICN.
        London: Olive Payne, 1737 (as *The female page: A genuine and interesting history, relating to some persons of distinction. Intermix'd with a great variety of affecting intrigues in love and gallantry. Also the remarkable letters that passed between the several person's concerned*; by 'the ingenious Mrs. Elizabeth Boyd'; subscribers' list, which includes some Irish names). SOURCE McBurney, 275a. LOCATION L.
        New York: Garland, 1972 (ed. by W. Graves). LOCATION L, InND.

COMMENTARY A highly romantic novel of disguise and adventure. Set in Cyprus, it deals with the evil effects of arranged or loveless marriages. No Irish content [ML; ODNB].

BOYLE, Robert, b. Lismore (Co Waterford) 1627, d. London 1691, pseud. 'A person of honour'. Scientist, Christian philosopher and theologian, philanthropist and writer, he was the seventh son and fourteenth child of Richard Boyle, 1st earl of Cork, and Catherine Fenton. After the death of his mother when he was age 8, he was sent to Eton with his brother Francis, where he was particularly studious. He was privately tutored after he left Eton and, like his brother Roger Boyle§, spent time travelling on the Continent and studying in Geneva where he experienced a religious conversion that was the foundation of his life-long devotion to Christianity. Returning to London in 1644, he associated with members of the Philosophical College (later the Royal Society), and developed a passion for chemistry and physics. In 1645 he moved to Stallbridge (Dorset), which his father had bequeathed to him, where he stayed for the next decade, writing, and setting up his scientific laboratory in 1649. After dispiriting visits in 1652 and 1653 to his estates in Ireland, which he described as 'a barbarous country', he settled in Oxford and continued his experiments. Among his many scientific achievements, RB is credited with originating the definition of an element, inventing a compressed air pump, directing the manufacture of the first hermetically sealed thermometers in England, and confirming the body's high blood temperature, earning him the sobriquet of 'the father of modern chemistry'. Equally important to him were his theological studies. He learned Hebrew, Greek, Chaldee and Syriac in order to study the Scriptures in the originals. RB underwrote the printing of the Bible in Indian, Irish and Welsh; the New Testament in Turkish, and the Gospel and Acts of the Apostles in Malay. In his will he endowed the Boyle lectures for the defence of Christianity against unbelievers. He was instrumental in procuring a charter for the East India Company and became a director, strenuously working to spread Christianity where it operated. In 1668 he moved to London where he lived with his sister Catherine, Lady Ranelagh, and until his death wrote voluminously on scientific and religious matters. He refused many offers of a peerage and was the only one of his family to die untitled. For RB's portraits, see Elmes and ODNB. SOURCE Allibone, i, p. 232; Elmes, pp 22–3; ODNB; RIA/DIB.

B303   *The martyrdom of Theodora, and of Didymus* (by 'A person of honour').

London: J. Taylor & C. Skegnes, 1687. SOURCE ESTC r002732; Hardy, 255; Esdaile, p. 166; Sweeney, 548. LOCATION Dt, L, C, CtY.

London: John Taylor, 1703 (as *Love and religion demonstrated in the martyrdom of Theodora and of Didymus* by the late Honourable Robert Boyle Esq., 2nd edn, corrected). SOURCE ESTC t064724; Esdaile, p. 167; McBurney & Taylor, 98. LOCATION L, IU, NUC.

Los Angeles: Augustan Reprint Society, 1953. SOURCE NCBEL 2, p. 981; COPAC. LOCATION O.

COMMENTARY Written by RB at a young age, but published forty years later. Historical fiction about St Theodora of Alexandria, who died in 304, and is set in Rome during the early Christian era. The novel is said to incorporate autobiographical aspects of RB's life [NCBEL 2, p. 981; Ximenes cat. 100/68; Sweeney, 548].

BOYLE, R. Whelan. See **BOYLE, Robert Whelan.**

BOYLE, Robert Whelan (known as **R. Whelan Boyle**), b. north of Ireland 1822, d. London? 1889. Journalist, novelist and poet, RWB, was the son of Thomas Boyle. He was editor of the London *Daily Chronicle* from 1877. His published poetry includes *Quietude* (London, 1879). He was buried at Woking (Surrey). SOURCE Allibone Suppl., i, p. 193; Brown, p. 40; MVP, p. 52; O'Donoghue, p. 35.

B304   *Love until death. An Irish story* (by R. Whelan Boyle).

London: Spencer Blackett, [1888]. SOURCE Brown, 239. LOCATION D.

COMMENTARY The scene is set in Heathborough (i.e., Maryborough, Co. Laois) about 1820. The love story of the young Protestant Dr Parnell and Miss Desmond who, in the end, rejects the doctor and enters a convent. The novel includes descriptions of the location and discusses religious issues [Brown].

BOYLE, Roger, pseud. '**A person of honour**', 1st earl of Orrery (earlier known as **Lord Broghill**), b. Lismore (Co. Waterford) 1621, d. Castlemartyr? (Co. Cork) 1679. Soldier, politician, statesman, novelist, playwright, poet and amateur architect, he was the third son of Richard Boyle, lst earl of Cork, and Catherine Fenton. He shared the same pseud. with his brother Robert Boyle§. He was created Baron Broghill in childhood. He entered TCD in 1630, moved to London in 1634, and was admitted to Gray's Inn in 1636. He travelled to France and Italy and in Geneva stayed at the house of the Calvinist theologian Diodati. In 1639 he was sent by his father to attend the king at Berwick as he prepared to fight the Scots. After RB's marriage to Lady Margaret Howard in 1641 he set out for Ireland and arrived on the outbreak of the rebellion. He was actively involved in the subsequent fighting. He had a chequered military career during the Civil War, joining the Parliamentarians after the king's execution, in contrast to his brothers, and becoming a confidant of Henry Cromwell. In 1655 he was appointed lord president of the Scottish council in Edinburgh and in 1654 and 1656 he was elected to the Westminster parliament for Co. Cork. After the restoration of Charles II in 1660 he declared for the king, who created him earl of Orrery. He was appointed lord president of Munster and subsequently named one of the three lord justices to rule Ireland, but with little decision-making power. He lobbied hard for the retention of the Cromwellian land settlements, from which he had greatly benefited. An eloquent and insistent voice for Protestants as the best hope for English rule in Ireland, RB embodied this idea in his writings and in his dramas, but his shrill anti-catholicism eventually alienated Charles and he was removed from the privy council in 1679. An adroit soldier, politician and statesman, he is credited with writing the first heroic verse play in English, *Altemera, or the general*, performed in the 1660s and printed 1702, but the DNB questions RB's authorship. RB's papers are in the NLI, the BL, Chatsworth House and Petworth House. For his portraits, see ODNB. SOURCE Allibone i, p. 233; Brady, p. 18; B & S, p. 89; R. Loeber, *A biographical dictionary of architects in Ireland, 1600–1720* (London, 1981), pp 25–9; K. Lynch, *Roger Boyle, first Earl of Orrery* (Knoxville [TN], 1965); OCIL, p. 61; ODNB; O'Donoghue, pp 35–6; RIA/DIB.

B305   *Parthenissa. A romance in six tomes* (by Lord Broghill; dedicated to Lady Northumberland and Lady Sunderland).

    Waterford: Peter de Pienne, 1651, 4 vols. SOURCE Bradshaw, ii, p. 900; Summers, p. 107 (mistakenly states 5 parts); Sweeney, 615.

    London: Richard Lownes, 1654 (as *Parthenissa, that most fam'd romance, etc.* [part 1 only]). LOCATION L.

    London: Humphrey Moseley, 1655–69 (as *Parthenissa. A romance. In four parts*). SOURCE Esdaile, p. 167; Bradshaw, 5315. LOCATION L, C, NUC.

    London: Henry Herringman, 1656, part 5. LOCATION L, NUC.

    London: Henry Herringman, 1669, part 6. SOURCE Esdaile, p. 167. LOCATION L, NUC.

    + London: Henry Herringman, 1676, 6 vols. (as *Parthenissa. That most fam'd romance*, by the earl of Orerry). SOURCE Hardy, 256; Esdaile, p. 167; Gecker, 783. LOCATION D, L, PU, NUC.

    Los Angeles: Augustan Reprint Society, 1953. SOURCE NCBEL 2, p. 977.

COMMENTARY Waterford edn not located. Heroic novel in the French tradition. The sixth part was written 'by particular command' of Henrietta Maria, duchess of Orleans (daughter of King Charles I); other parts were to follow, but the novel remained unfinished [*The whole works of Sir James Ware* (Dublin, 1769), i, p. 178; RL].

B306   *English adventures* (by 'A person of honour').

    + London: H. Herringman, 1676, vol. 1 [all published]. SOURCE DNB; Esdaile, p. 167; ESTC r20367. LOCATION L, NUC.

COMMENTARY Historical novel set in the sixteenth century, in which Henry VIII is supposed to be travelling incognito among his subjects with Charles Brandon, duke of Suffolk, as his companion. Inevitably they meet with many striking experiences, which give rise to the relating of various narratives. One of these told by the duke is 'The history of Brandon' (which formed the plot for Otway's tragedy *The Orphan*, first staged in 1680). Further tomes of this novel were promised, but never written [Summers, pp 157–8].

BOYLE, William, b. Dromiskin (Co. Louth) 1853, d. London 1923. Playwright, songwriter and short story writer, WB was educated at St Mary's College, Dundalk (Co. Louth). He entered the civil service in 1874 and was employed as an excise officer at Glasgow, and probably other locations, until his retirement in 1914. A nationalist, he was a friend of Charles Stewart Parnell and of John Redmond. Many of his plays are realistic and humorous looks at rural and small-town Ireland. *The building fund* (Dublin, 1905) staged by the Abbey Theatre (25 Apr. 1905), was well-received in Dublin and went on to successful runs in London and America, causing Boyle to be compared to Molière and Ibsen but alienating him from William Butler Yeats§ and his idea of a loftier, more poetic Irish drama. He also had productions of 'The eloquent Dempsey' (20 Jan. 1906) and *The Mineral Workers* (20 Oct. 1906, published Dublin, 1910) at the Abbey and, after an absence protesting the staging of J.M. Synge's *Playboy of the Western world* at the Abbey in Jan. 1907, he returned with *Family failing* on 28 Mar. 1912 (Dublin, 1912). He contributed to Dublin periodicals, including the *Nation, United Ireland, Irish Fireside* and *Young Ireland*. Settling back in Dromiskin after retirement, he became a magistrate but returned to England after the Easter Rising of 1916. For his correspondence, see ODNB. SOURCE Boylan, p. 30; Brady, p. 18; Brown, p. 40; Field Day, ii, pp 563–4; Hogan 2, p. 183; Irish pseudonyms; OCIL, p. 61; ODNB; O'Donoghue, p. 36; RIA/DIB.

B307   *A kish of brogues* (by William Boyle).

+ London: Simpkin, Marshall, Hamilton, Kent & Co.; Dublin, M.H. Gill & Son; O'Donoghue & Co., 1899. SOURCE Brown, 240. LOCATION D, L, NUC, InND Loeber coll.

COMMENTARY Describes country life in Co. Louth in several stories and poems. Contents: 'The livery servant', 'In the interest of science. A tale of sixty years ago', 'The downfall of Donovan, as described by his conqueror', 'The fairy pipes', 'Oiny Oge', 'Only an omadhawn', 'Micksey', 'The incorrigible of Slievemore', 'A country courtship', 'Larry Maloney's charm', 'The bocca's revenge', 'The cow charmer', 'The end of the faction fight', 'Mrs. Good's ducklings', 'Wooing by theft', 'An exile of Erin', 'An inquisitive mortal' [ML].

BOYSE, E.C., fl. 1886. This person also published '*Murdered or —?*' (Bristol, [1890]), which has no Irish content. SOURCE Allibone Suppl., i, p. 193; NCBEL 4, p. 1755; RL.

B308   *That most distressful country. A novel* (by E.C. Boyse).

London: F.V. White & Co., 1886, 3 vols. SOURCE Brown, 241; Wolff, 622; COPAC. LOCATION L, NUC.

COMMENTARY Historical novel consisting of a love story interwoven with incidents of the 1798 rebellion. The standpoint is loyalist. The scene is set in Wexford, London, Dublin and Tuam (Co. Galway), where word is brought of Gen. Humbert's campaign in the west [Brown].

BRABAZON, Elizabeth Jane (née Levinge), probable pseud. '**Adelaide Vernon**', fl. 1834. Novelist, travel, history and religious fiction writer and poet, EJB also published *Outlines of the history of Ireland for schools and families … to the Union in 1800 with questions for examination* (Dublin, 1844), and *Statistical account of Ireland* (announced on title page of her volume of verse *Jessy Grey; or biblical instruction*, Dublin, 1841, but not located). She married in

1828 a Church of Ireland clergyman, James Brabazon, rector of Portnashangan (Co. Westmeath, 1826), who became rector of Almoritia (Co. Westmeath, 1841–84). They had one son, who died at age 21. EJB was also the author of *Russia and the czars* (London, 1855); *A month at Gravesend* (London, 1863); *Exmouth and its environs* (Exmouth, 1866), and *Historical tales from the history of the Muslims in Spain* (London, [1853]). SOURCE Allibone Suppl., i, p. 193; BLC; J.B. Leslie, *Biographical succession list of the clergy of Meath Diocese*, i, p. 71 (unpublished MS, Representative Church Body Library, Dublin); NCBEL 4, p. 1755.

B309   *Home happiness, or, three weeks in snow* (by 'Adelaide Vernon').
        Dublin: R. Moore Tims; London: Hatchard & Son, J. Nisbet, Hamilton & Adams, Seeley & Son, Simpkin & Marshall, W. Darton & Son; Edinburgh: Waugh & Innes, 1834. SOURCE OCLC; COPAC; Garside 2, A:30. LOCATION Univ. of Glasgow.
        London: John Hughes, 1855 (by Elizabeth Jane Brabazon). SOURCE Alston, p. 39. LOCATION L (destroyed).
COMMENTARY Classified as religious fiction in the BLC. Preface declares the moral educational purpose of the work. Stories incorporated, within the framework context of a family group isolated by snow, include: 'Fanny Beauchamp', 'The jasmine wreath', 'Hope deferred' (set in Ceylon) [BLC; Garside 2, A:30].

B310   *Stories from the rectory: containing Henry Wilford, and The exile of Upama* [anon.].
        + Dublin: R.M. Tims, 1840. LOCATION D.
COMMENTARY 'Henry Wilford' is a tale of deceit and murder in which Augustus Ilderton, proprietor of Westham, adopts his two nephews, Henry Wilford and Edmund Maitland, as prospective heirs to his dynasty. An evil character, Robert Harris, lures the indecisive and unassuming Wilford into a web of deceit, which eventually ends in the murder of Ilderton, who has already disowned Wilford. Wrongly accused of the murder, Wilford flees and travels to faraway lands. When he returns twenty years later, he amends his broken friendship with Edmund, who is now proprietor of Westham. 'The exile of Upama', set in China, is a tale of the efforts of an English clergyman, Robert Edwards, to convert the island of Upama to Christianity and of the romantic relationship between his son, Alfred, and Lia-Kin, daughter of his host Tse-Ming. Forced to flee from the island or conform to a Chinese religious sect, Alfred goes to Canton, where he studies theology for two years. Upon his return to Upama as a missionary, he discovers that Tse-Ming and his beloved Lia-King have been captured by the mandarin of China. Following their release, Alfred vows to marry Lia-Kin [CD].

BRACKEN, Thomas, pseud. **'Paddy Murphy'**, b. Ireland 1843, d. probably New Zealand 1898. Journalist, political commentator, politician and poet, TB had emigrated to Australia as a child where he successively worked as a farm boy, chemist's assistant, station-hand and shearer. He crossed over to Otago in New Zealand in the late 1860s and became a journalist, an occupation varied by excursions into politics. As 'Paddy Murphy' he acquired fame for his comments on parliamentary affairs written in doggerel Irish. His poems, *Musings on Maoriland*, were published in 1890. He became a newspaper proprietor in Dunedin and a member of the legislature in New Zealand. SOURCE Allibone Suppl., i, p. 194; E.H. McCormick, *New Zealand literature. A survey* (London, 1959), pp 67–8; O'Donoghue, p. 36.

B311   *Paddy Murphy's budget; a collection of humorous 'pomes, tiligrams, an' ipistols.'*
        Dundedin [New Zealand]: Mackay, Bracken, 1880. SOURCE McCormick, p. 166. LOCATION National Library of Canada.
        COMMENTARY 94pp [National Library of Canada].

BRACKENRIDGE, Hugh Henry (also known as Hugh Montgomery Brackenridge), b. near Campbeltown (Scotland) 1748, d. Carlisle (PA) 1816. A writer, newspaper man, propagan-

Braddon

dist for the American Revolution, judge, legislator and satirist, HHB had emigrated with his family to York County (PA) in 1753. He graduated in 1771 from the College of New Jersey at Princeton, where he was a classmate of James Madison, and received his MA in 1774. ODNB says that while at Princeton he and poet Philip Freneau, a classmate, collaborated on *Father Bombo's pilgrimage* (1770; reprinted Princeton, NJ, 1975), 'often considered the first novel in America' (ODNB). He served as a chaplain in the American War of Independence and wrote propaganda in the form of pamphlets and dramas. Having left the church, he studied law and was admitted to the Bar in Philadelphia in 1781. He settled in western Pennsylvania where he helped found the *Pittsburgh Gazette*, the city's first academy (later the University of Pittsburgh), and its first bookstore. He mediated in the Whiskey Rebellion (1793–94), served briefly as a state legislator, and was appointed a judge of the supreme court of Pennsylvania in 1799. His writings often satirized the abuses of the new American democracy. His portrait was painted by Gilbert Stuart. SOURCE Allibone, i, p. 234; ANB; DAB; DLB, xi, xxxvii; R.A. Harrison, *Princetonians, 1769–1775: a biographical dictionary* (Princeton, 1980); C.M. Newlin, 'The writings of Hugh Henry Brackenridge' in *Western Pennsylvania History Magazine*, Oct. 1927; ODNB; Wright, i, pp 51–2.

B312 *Modern chivalry: containing the adventures of Captain John Farrago, and Teague O'Regan, his servant* (by Hugh Henry Brackenridge).
Philadelphia: Printed [for the author?] by John M'Culloch, 1792–97, 4 vols. SOURCE Wright, i, 354; ESTC w26247. LOCATION L (1846 edn), NUC.
Carlisle [PA], Printed by Archibald Loudon, 1804–5, 2 vols. (as *Modern chivalry: containing the adventures of a captain, &c.*). SOURCE Wright, i, 355. LOCATION NUC.
Philadelphia: J. Conrad & Co., 1804, vols. 1 and 2 (as *Modern chivalry: containing the adventures of a captain and Teague O'Regan, his servant*). SOURCE Wright, i, 356. LOCATION NUC.
Philadelphia: Jacob Johnson, 1807–8, 4 vols in 2. SOURCE Wright, i, 357; OCLC. LOCATION CtY.
+ Philadelphia: Carey & Hart, 1846, 2nd edn, 2 vols. in 1 (as *Modern chivalry: containing the adventures of Captain John Farrago, and Teague O'Regan*; ill. Darley). LOCATION InND Loeber coll.
Wilmington (DE): Printed by George Metz, 1815. SOURCE Wright, i, 361. LOCATION CtY.
+ Pittsburgh (PA): R. Patterson & Lambdin, 1819, 2 vols. (with the last corrections and additions of the author). SOURCE Wright, i, 362. LOCATION CtY.
New York, Cincinnati: American Book Co., [1937] (as *Modern chivalry*; ed. by Claude M. Newlin). LOCATION L, NUC.

COMMENTARY A humorous social and political satire contrasting a patrician, intellectual master and an assertive Irish servant, it is one of the earliest portrayals in American fiction of a drinking, whistling, blarneying Irishman. It was a bestseller for over fifty years. The novel also features an array of other Irishmen: Oconama (a 'Scotch-Irishman'), Phelim Clonmel (a ballad singer), and O'Fin. HB worked on it and published it in instalments over a period of 23 years (1792–1815). Consequently, it is one of the most bibliographically complex of early American novels [RL; Brick Row cat. 35/31; Fanning; ODNB].

BRADDON, M.E. See BRADDON, Mary Elizabeth.

BRADDON, Mary Elizabeth (later Maxwell; known as M.E. Braddon), b. London 1835, d. 1915. An immensely popular novelist and an editor, MEB was the daughter of Henry Braddon of Cornwall and Fanny White, an Irish journalist from Co. Cavan. Her parents separated in 1839 and MEB received her education first at school but then largely from her mother, who wrote occasionally for *Ainsworth's Magazine* (London). MEB started with an acting career and wrote several plays, which remained mostly unpublished. She was the editor of a number of periodicals, including *Temple Bar* and *Belgravia* (London), and of the *Mistletoe Bough* (a Christmas fiction annual). She wrote over 70 novels, becoming notorious for her 'bigamy' stories: *Lady Audley's secret* (London, 1862) and *Aurora Floyd* (London, 1863), which became bestsellers and helped make her 'the queen of the circulating libraries'. From 1861 onward she lived in London with the Irish publisher John Maxwell, whose wife was in a Dublin asylum, and supported his five children and the six she bore him. They married in 1874 after his wife died. In 1874, she published 'Ireland for tourists. A reminiscence of a recent excursion' in *Belgravia* (London). In 1883 she wrote that she was working on an 'Irish novel', but the work has not been identified. Only her work with Irish content is listed below. SOURCE Allibone Suppl., ii, pp 1094–5 [under Maxwell]; Blain, p. 129; DLB, xviii, lxx, clvi; NCBEL 4, pp 1467–71; ODNB; Sutherland, pp 80–1; T & B, pp 968–9; Wolff, i, pp 115–54.

B313   *Like and unlike. A novel* [anon.].

    + London: Spencer Blackett, [1887], 3 vols. SOURCE Wolff, 663. LOCATION L, InND Loeber coll.

    Leipzig: Bernard Tauchnitz, 1887, 2 vols. LOCATION NUC.

    New York: G. Munro, [1887]. LOCATION NUC.

COMMENTARY A story of romance, betrayal and murder, it was first published by Tillotson in his newspapers. Set in England and featuring Sir Adrian Belfield and his twin brother, Valentine, who are alike in many ways but Adrian is ponderous and interested in books, while Valentine is impetuous and a sportsman. A neighbouring house is rented by an Irishman, Colonel Deverill, who has two daughters. Adrian falls in love with Helen Deverill, but when his brother Valentine shows up, Helen falls in love with him and they marry, Valentine neglects her and Helen starts a dangerous relationship with another man. She is on the point of eloping when her husband finds out and kills her. It takes the arrest of his brother for Valentine to own up to what he has done. He is sentenced to two years in prison and dies of tuberculosis when he is released. The novel formed the basis for MEB's play, 'For better for worse' [ML; Wolff, i, p. 135].

B314   *The rose of life* (by M.E. Braddon).

    London: Hutchinson, [1905]. SOURCE COPAC. LOCATION L.

    Leipzig: Bernard Tauchnitz, 1905. SOURCE COPAC; Wolff, 682. LOCATION L.

    COMMENTARY The main character, Daniel, is a portrait of Oscar Wilde§ [Wolff].

'BRADEY, Barney', pseud. See PARKES, William Theodore.

BRADFORD-WHITING, Mary. See WHITING, Mary Bradford.

'BRADLEY, J.J.G.', pseud. See BORLASE, James Skipp.

BRADLEY, Margaret Louisa. See WOODS, Margaret Louisa.

BRADSHAW, Mrs John (née Wilmot), fl. 1885. According to O'Donoghue, Mrs Bradshaw, was a Cork author. The poet Edward Wilmot was her nephew. SOURCE O'Donoghue, p. 485.

B315   *Roger North* (by Mrs John Bradshaw).

    London: W. Swan Sonnenschein & Co., 1885, 3 vols. SOURCE Allibone Suppl., ii, p. 197; COPAC. LOCATION L.

B316   *Merevale* (by Mrs John Bradshaw).

    London: Swan Sonnenschein & Co., 1886. SOURCE Allibone Suppl., ii, p. 197; COPAC. LOCATION L.

B317 *Gabrielle; or, worth the winning* (by Mrs John Bradshaw).
London: W.H. Allen & Co., 1887. SOURCE Allibone Suppl., ii, p. 197; COPAC.
LOCATION L.

B318 *Rivets of gold* (by Mrs John Bradshaw).
London: Jarrold & Sons, [1890]. SOURCE Allibone Suppl., ii, p. 197 (1888 edn);
COPAC. LOCATION L.

BRADSTREET, Capt. Dudley, b. Co. Tipperary 1711, d. Multifarnham (Co. Westmeath) 1763. A merchant, secret agent and adventurer, DB was the son of John Bradstreet, whose family had obtained land in Tipperary under the Cromwellian settlement. He was raised by a foster-family and educated in a boarding school near Templemore (Co. Tipperary) and at Granard (Co. Longford). DB spent time in the army, was apprenticed to an attorney, married several times, and dabbled in business as a linen merchant and a brewer. In 1739 he went to England and joined the army there. Making money on liquor, gambling and prostitution, he eventually was encouraged to become a government spy. Infiltrating various Irish groups to assess Jacobite disaffection, he was present at the Council of Derby where the Stuart prince Charles Edward and his army decided not to engage and to return to Scotland. DB took credit for this development and for it he received a gift of £120 from George II. After various other schemes to get rich, he returned to Ireland, where he tried unsuccessfully to trade as a brewer in Dublin. He built a house in Westmeath and raised subscriptions for his first book (*The life and uncommon adventures*, Dublin, 1755), the success of which prompted him to write *Bradstreets lives* (Dublin, 1757). DB also wrote a play *The magician, or the bottle conjurer* (included in the Dublin, 1755 edn of *The life and uncommon adventures* ...), which was suppressed by the authorities after only four performances. SOURCE Allibone, i, p. 236; ODNB; J. O'Donoghue, 'Dudley Bradstreet-a Tipperary spy and adventurer', *Tipperary Historical Jrnl* (1992), pp 174–85; RIA/DIB.

B319 *The life and uncommon adventures of Capt. Dudley Bradstreet. Being the most genuine and extraordinary, perhaps, ever published. Containing a full account of his and others amours. His being employ'd in secret service by the M[ini]stry of G[rea]t B[ritai]n, in the late rebellion. His M[ajest]y's present to him, receiv'd by the hands of Mr. S—ne. His letters to his M[ajest]y, and the answers received from the K[in]g. The reward he got for his services, occasioning his scheme of the bottle conjurer. His passing as a magician in Covent-garden, where many of high-Birth and fortune of both sexes, and even famed for wisdom, resorted to him, upon his promising to renew their age, making them thirty or forty years younger than they were, informing others when their husbands or wives would die. His being made governor and judge in the finest seraglio in England, and his promised feast to the city of London; facts well known to all the courts of Europe. With the lives of Mrs. Winnett, Mrs. Collison, Mrs. Churchill, &c. &c.*
+ Dublin: Printed for the author by S. Powell, 1755 (subscribers' list). SOURCE Cole, p. 230; Raven, 296; Gilbert, p. 83; ESTC t074215. LOCATION D, DPL Gilbert coll., L, O, NUC.
+ London: John Hamilton, [1929] (ed. by G.S. Taylor, with a foreword by E.H.W. Meyerstein as *The life and uncommon adventures of Captain Dudley Bradstreet*). LOCATION L, NUC, InND Loeber coll.
COMMENTARY Presumably an autobiographical story of a gambler and spy whose romantic involvements are fairly sordid. He is not faithful to any party or principle but is governed by what may give him profit or pleasure [ML].

B320 *Bradstreet's lives: being the genuine history of several gentlemen and ladies living within these ten years past, remarkable for their virtues or their vices, to which is*

added *The author's system of government. His speech to the Grand Jury, remarks upon the last dying agonies of the Roman empire. His opinions on the fighting bucks of his age. His observations on the miseries of this kingdom for want of tillage, and how it may be remedied. With a letter from the river Seine to the river Shannon, &c. &c.*
+ Dublin: S. Powell, 1757 (subscribers' list). SOURCE ESTC t65520; Gilbert, p. 83. LOCATION D, DPL Gilbert coll., O, ICN.
COMMENTARY A sequel to the author's first book, but in this one, as he states, he 'has no recourse to Invention, but gives my Reader real and well known Examples of virtuous and vicious Lives, and their Consequences ...' Includes a miscellany. Raven mentions that Bradstreet's' play 'The magician' is appended to this work, but it is not present in the NLI copy [Raven; RL].

BREEN, Henry H. See BREEN, Henry Hegart.

BREEN, Henry Hegart (known as Henry H. Breen), b. Co. Kerry 1805, d. 1882. Novelist, poet, critic and colonial administrator, HHB was educated in Paris before settling in St Lucia in the West Indies. In 1838 he received an official appointment and was 'administrator of the government' on the island (1857–61). Among his work is a book on *Modern English literature* (London, 1857), and a history of St Lucia (London, 1844). SOURCE Allibone, i, p. 240; Allibone Suppl., i, p. 203; BLC; Boase, iv, p. 489; O'Donoghue, p. 38; Wolff, i, p. 162.
B321   *Warrawarra, the Carib chief. A tale of 1770* (by Henry H. Breen).
London: Tinsley Bros, 1876, 2 vols. SOURCE Wolff, 800. LOCATION L.
COMMENTARY Story is set on the island of 'Sidonie' in the French Antilles [Wolff].

BRENNAN, John. See BRENNAN, John Frederick.

BRENNAN, John Frederick (known as John Brennan), fl. 1892. An American historical novelist, perhaps Irish-born, whose dedication of the following book is dated from San Francisco, 1 May 1892. SOURCE ER.
B322   *Erin Mor: the story of Irish republicanism* (by John Brennan; dedicated to President Benjamin Harrison).
+ San Francisco: P.M. Diers & Co., 1892. SOURCE Wright, iii, 662; COPAC. LOCATION C, NN.
COMMENTARY In the dedication JFB expressed his intention 'neither to excite nor perpetuate any form of foreignism, but the earnest desire of creating in the minds of his Celtic brethren a deep, intense and fervid American national spirit'. The story concerns an Irishman who emigrates to San Diego (CA). Beginning with the Famine era, the author details Irish history until 1892, focusing in particular on Fenianism and the Irish in America through the story of the Dillon family. John Devoy, exiled Fenian and chief organizer of American support for Irish nationalism, is a central character. The tale ends in the year of publication, 1892, when the author perceives that America and the Irish are growing in mutual tolerance, respect and admiration [Wright; ER].

BRERETON, William H., fl. 1877. Short story writer and solicitor, WB was resident in Hong Kong in the late 1870s. He may the same person who published *The truth about opium* (London, 1882), but he should not be confused with Lt.-Gen. Sir William Brereton (1789–1864), a descendant of the Breretons of Carrigslaney (Co. Carlow) who was inspector-general of the Irish Constabulary from 1839 to 1842, commanded troops in Hong Kong in

1846, at the Canton River, China, in 1847 and in the Crimea. SOURCE BLC; Burke's, p. 168; ODNB; RIA/DIB.

B323 *Tales of Irish life* (by William H. Brereton).
+ Hong Kong: Noronha & Sons, Printed for private circulation, 1877. SOURCE Brown 2, 140. LOCATION D, Dt, NUC, InND Loeber coll.
COMMENTARY Contents: 'The sale of Cloonmore, a romance of the Incumbered Estates Court' [Cloonmore, Co. Limerick], 'Engaging a governess', 'The managing mamma. A comedy of errors', 'The story of an Orange Lodge. A chronicle of Dublin' [RL].

BRESLIN, J. William, fl. 1899. Historical novelist, JWB was perhaps related to William Breslin of Co. Fermanagh, who studied at TCD in 1822. SOURCE B & S, p. 96; NUC.

B324 *Thady Halloran of the Irish Brigade* (by J. William Breslin).
London: T. Fisher Unwin, 1899. SOURCE Brown, 245. SOURCE COPAC. LOCATION L, NUC.
COMMENTARY The story of a young Irishman in the Irish Brigade in France. Opens with a description of the conditions in Ireland towards the end of the reign of Queen Anne, and depicts the recruiting for the Wild Geese, Irish soldiers who served in foreign armies in the eighteenth century. Describes a number of dashing adventures, such as the escape of Chevalier Wogan and other Jacobites from Newgate prison, and the rescue of the Princess Clementina. In the end, the hero is disgusted with his treatment by the French king and quits the French service [Brown].

BRETT, Edwin John, b. Canterbury (Kent) 1828, d. London 1895. English illustrator, editor, publisher and perhaps writer, EJB was the son of an army officer. He began his professional life as an illustrator, but then became a bookseller and publisher. He edited stories for boys and published penny dreadfuls for boys, notably the 'Wild Boys' series, and the weekly *Boys of England* (London, 1866–99). He grew wealthy and became a collector of ancient armour, about which topic he wrote. SOURCE Boase, iv, p. 491; Brown 2, p. 257 (probably mistakenly mentions him under W.T. Townsend); Sutherland, p. 83.

B325 *Fred Frolic, his life and adventures* [anon.].
London: Edwin J. Brett, 1872 (ill. Hebblewaite). SOURCE Brown 2, 1536 (n.d. edn). LOCATION L.
COMMENTARY A rollicking story of the stage Irishman type crammed with incidents – hunting, racing, faction-fights, illicit stills, etc. Young Fred overcomes his enemies in the end [Brown 2].

B326 *Wildfoot the wanderer of Wicklow* [anon.].
London: Edwin J. Brett, 1875 (ill.). SOURCE Brown 2, 1535 ([1900] edn); J & S, 689. LOCATION L.
COMMENTARY Reprinted from the *Boys of England* (London). Historical fiction of the 1798 rebellion. Redmond O'Hanlon, perhaps named after the legendary seventeenth-century Ulster outlaw, is the hero and a Major Sirr one the characters. Before the insurrection takes place, O'Hanlon escapes to France. Among places mentioned are the Devil's Glen and the Dargle River (both Co. Wicklow) [Brown 2; J & S, 689–90; ML; RL].

B327 *Pat O'Connor's schooldays or the boys of Shannon* [anon.].
+ London: Edwin J. Brett, [*c*.1905]. SOURCE COPAC; RL. LOCATION L.
COMMENTARY Originally issued as a penny dreadful in nine separate issues at ½*d.* each [RL].

BREW, Miss M.W. See BREW, Miss Margaret W.

BREW, Miss Margaret W. (also known as **M.W. Brew**), b. Co. Clare 1850, died 1905? Novelist, poet and short story writer. Members of the Brew family belonged to the landed gentry in Co. Clare (who resided at Applevale, Clonkerry, Mullineen, Leadmore House, and at Springmount), but it is unclear to which of these families MWB belonged. MWB may be identified with a person of her name who owned a small estate at Lisduff, near Corrofin in 1876. She contributed poetry and stories to the *Irish Monthly* (Dublin, 1886–91). The novels are described as works that seek 'social accommodation between religions and classes' (OCIL, p. 63). In addition, she contributed to *Duffy's Hibernian Magazine* (Dublin, 1860). Given the Catholic themes in the fiction, she probably was a Catholic. SOURCE Allibone Suppl., i, p. 205; Brown, p. 41; Ferguson, p. 145; Hogan, ii, p. 187; Irish pseudonyms; JAPMDI, 5(3) (1903), pp 316–17; A. Leet, *Directory* (Dublin, 1814), pp 8, 117, 303, 335, 360; OCIL, p. 63; O'Donoghue, p. 39; O'Toole, pp 26–27; E. Reilly, p. 242; *Return of owners of land* (Dublin, 1876), p. 107; RIA/DIB; RL.

B328   *The Burtons of Dunroe* (by M.W. Brew).
+ London: Samuel Tinsley & Co., 1880, 3 vols. SOURCE Brown, 246; Wolff, 809. LOCATION D, L.
New York: Garland, 1979, 3 vols. (introd. by R.L. Wolff). SOURCE COPAC. LOCATION Dt.
COMMENTARY Set in the early years of the nineteenth century, it tells of the love of William Burton of the Burton estate, the son of a strict Protestant landowner of Cromwellian origins, for Rosha Dhuv (Rose O'Brien). Her family have ulterior motives in the romance: they wish to gain control of the Burton estate by the river Shannon in Co. Limerick. Despite his father's protests, William marries Rose. His father disowns him and orders him to the Peninsular War. When he returns he lives in poverty with his wife, who dies in childbirth. He then marries his cousin, Isabella Burton, to whom he was pledged in marriage from the beginning [CD; Wolff, preface, p. v].

B329   *Chronicles of Castle Cloyne; or, pictures of the Munster people* (by M.W. Brew; dedicated to Lady Florence Dixie).[1]
+ London: Chapman & Hall, 1884, 3 vols. SOURCE Brown, 247 (1886 edn); Wolff, 810 (1885 edn). LOCATION D, Dt, L (1885 edn), NUC (1885 edn).
New York: Garland, 1979, 3 vols. (introd. by R.L. Wolff). SOURCE COPAC. LOCATION D, Dt.
COMMENTARY An English reviewer in the *Athenaeum* wrote that 'one could hardly wish for a better Irish story, more touching, more amusing, more redolent of the soil – the hand of the native is manifest throughout in these pictures of Munster folk'. Deals with the 1845–47 Famine years and gives a detailed description of the local scene in Munster [*Athenaeum* (1884), p. 821; Wolff introd., pp 36–7; Fegan, p. 208].

BRISCOE, C.W., pseud. **'S.W.B.'**, fl. 1786, b. Manchester? (England). According to the preface to the following book of memoirs, the author's father was born on an estate in Cheshire but due to declining family finances he became a teacher in a school in Manchester, where the author grew up. An Irish branch of the Briscoe family had settled in Co. Offaly in the late-sixteenth century and later resided in Co. Westmeath. SOURCE Landed gentry, 1912, p. 72; RL.

B330   *Clerimont, or, memoirs of the life and adventures of Mr. B****** (written by himself) interspersed with original anecdotes of living characters* [anon.] (dedicated to 'his Highness, the Lord of Oblivion').
+ Liverpool: Printed [for the author?] by Charles Wosencroft, 1786. SOURCE Raven 2, 1786:19; ESTC t068953. LOCATION L, CtY.
COMMENTARY Preface signed S.W.B.; the name Briscoe is written in the BL copy. Memoirs containing dialogues, partly set in Ireland, particularly Dublin and the adjoining countryside.

---

1 Lady Florence Dixie assisted the poor in Co. Mayo in 1882 ('Veritas', *Lady Florence Dixie vindicated*, Dublin, 1883).

The main character meets an Irishman returning to Dublin after seven years of service in India. He also encounters the Rt Hon. E.S. Pery§, speaker of the Irish house of commons. Contains some poems, one of which was written after a visit to Lord Charlemont's seat at Marino (Co. Dublin) [CM; RL].

BRISTOW, Amelia, fl. 1824. Novelist, translator and poet, AB was from Ulster, according to O'Donoghue. Aside from Protestant religious fiction about Jewish life, she also wrote poetry. Note that the mother of author Robert Torrens§, born in Derry in 1780, was Elizabeth Bristow and thus he may have been related to AB. Sometime prior to 1830, AB moved to London; according to the title page of *The twin sisters* (London, 1835), she lived at 3 Catherine Place, Blackheath Road, whereas the preface to the following work is dated from Greenwich, Sept. 1835. SOURCE Garside 2, 1835:30; O'Donoghue, p. 40; RL.

B331   *The faithful servant; or, the history of Elizabeth Allen* [anon.] (dedicated to her subscribers).

    London: Francis Westley, 1824 (subscribers' list). SOURCE British Fiction; Garside 1824:18. LOCATION L (1824, 2nd edn), O.

    London: R.B. Seeley & W. Burnside, 1832 (as *Elizabeth Allen; or, the faithful servant*). SOURCE Garside 1824:18); COPAC. LOCATION L.

    COMMENTARY Reached a 5th edn in 1835. The subscribers' list contains some Irish individuals. Evangelical and didactic story for servants [British Fiction; RL; Garside (2003)]

B332   *Sophia de Lissau; or, a portraiture of the Jews of the nineteenth century: being an outline of their religious and domestic habits of this most interesting nation with explanatory notes* [anon.].

    London: Published for the author by T. Gardiner & Son, Simpkin & Marshall, 1826. SOURCE Garside 1826:20. LOCATION L (1828, 2nd edn).

    Amsterdam: C.J.A. Beyerinck, 1829 (trans. into Dutch by J. Cortius as *Sophia van Lissau; eene bijdrage tot de geschiedenis van het tegenwoordige Jodendom*). SOURCE Alphabetische naamlijst 1790–1832, p. 561.

    Leipzig: [publisher?], 1829 (trans. by P.H.W. Schnaase as *Die Familie de Lissa, oder sonderbare Begebenheiten einer aus Polen nach London gezogenen jüdischen Familie; mit Schilderung der jüdischen Gebräuche und Sitten*). SOURCE Garside 1826:20; GLOL. LOCATION Niedersächsische Staats- und Universitätsbibliothek, Göttingen.

    COMMENTARY The first of the Lissau trilogy (see below for the other two volumes) [RL].

B333   *Emma de Lissau; a narrative of striking vicissitudes, and peculiar trials; with explanatory notes illustrative of the manners and customs of the Jews* [anon.].

    London: T. Gardiner & Son, 1828, 2 vols. (subscribers' list). SOURCE Rowan cat. 58/37; Garside (2003); Topp 8, p. 28. LOCATION Corvey CME 3-628-47171-0, L.

    Toulouse: Société de Livres Religieux, 1855 (trans. as *Emma de Lissau ou la conversion d'une jeune juive*). SOURCE OCLC; Bn-Opale plus. LOCATION NN.

    COMMENTARY Reached a 6th edn in 1847. The subscribers' list contains some Irish names, and includes the writers Hannah More, Jane Porter§ and Anna Maria Porter§. Didactic novel describing contemporary Jewish life with the underlying purpose of advancing the claims of Christianity over Judaism [Rowan cat. 58/37: RL; Topp 8, p. 23].

B334   *The orphans of Lissau, and other interesting narratives, immediately connected with Jewish customs, domestic and religious, with explanatory notes* [anon.].

    London: T. Gardiner & Son, 1830, 2 vols. SOURCE Garside 2, 1830:27. LOCATION L.

    London : Simpkin, Marshall & Co., 1859 (revsd and abridged edn; The Run and Read Library, No. 51). SOURCE Garside 2, 1830:27; OCLC. LOCATION CtY.

COMMENTARY Final volume of the Lissau trilogy. Preface is dated from 'Blackheath, May 5, 1830', and states that 'The following narratives are authentic. The Explanatory notes illustrating, in the simplest form, Judaism, as it is in the present day, are drawn from eminent Jewish authorities ...' Contents: essays and stories (latter listed only): 'The orphans of Lissau', 'The widow and her son, or brief annals of the Jewish poor', 'Brief annals of the Jewish poor. The widow and her son, continued', 'Margaret Warburton, or, the double apostasy'. Contains explanatory footnotes [Garside 2; RL].

B335 *The scrap book: containing a variety of articles in prose and verse. Chiefly original* [anon.].
  London: R.B. Seeley, 1833. SOURCE OCLC. LOCATION TxU.

B336 *The twin sisters; a Jewish narrative of the eighteenth century* [anon.].
  Deptford Bridge: Printed for the author, 1835. SOURCE Garside 2, 1835:30. LOCATION CLU.
  London: C. Tilt, 1837 (as *Miriam and Rosette; a Jewish narrative of the eighteenth century*). SOURCE L (1847, 3rd edn). LOCATION GEU.
  London: C. Tilt, 1837, 3rd edn (as *Miriam and Rosette; or, the twin sisters; a Jewish narrative of the eighteenth century*). SOURCE Garside 2: 1835:30; OCLC. LOCATION GEU.

B337 *Village walks: A series of sketches from life* [anon.].
  London: Thomas Ward & Co., 1834. SOURCE Garside 2: Appendix C:10. LOCATION O (1834, n.d. edn).
  COMMENTARY No copy of first edn located. Consists of 12 religious and didactic sketches [Garside 2].

'A BRITON', pseud. See JOHNSTONE, Charles (1719–1802).

BRITTAINE, Revd George, b. 1788 d. Dublin 1848. Church of Ireland clergyman and novelist, GB wrote about Irish situations with wit and sometimes in an anti-Catholic tone. He was the son of Revd Patrick Brittain [*sic*], curate at St James's (Dublin 1789–1804). GB was admitted to TCD in 1804 and graduated BA in 1809. Initially vicar of Castleblaney (Co. Monaghan), he became rector of Kilmactranny (Co. Sligo) where he was warned that the location was very isolated. However, he saw to the building of the church and glebe house there. In 1823 GB was appointed rector of Kilcommock, near Ballymahon (Co. Longford) at £500 per annum, where he lived for over twenty years. His parish was very close to Edgeworthstown where Maria Edgeworth§, who admired his works, lived. It remains to be established to what extent his stories are based on the border area between Cos. Longford and Westmeath. Isaac Butt§ introd. him to the *Dublin University Magazine* and GB became one of its stalwart contributors, whose published pieces included a serial novel 'The orphans of Dunasker' (1837–8), and 'Tales of Irish life'. His contemporary, Revd Richard S. Brooke§, characterized GB as 'a striking and interesting preacher [who] had a noble and intellectual countenance and presence' (Brooke, p. 144). GB married Anna Maria Monck Mason in 1816. GB's novels were often reprinted in Dublin. SOURCE B & S, p. 98; Brady, p. 7; Brooke, pp 144–5, 171; Butler, p. 455; Colvin, pp 542–3, 558; J.C. Erck, *The ecclesiastical register* (Dublin, 1820), pp 121–2; B. Hayley & E. McKay (eds), *Three hundred years of Irish periodicals* (Mullingar, 1987), p. 47n.18; Hogan, ii, pp 187–8; Leslie & Wallace, p. 424; McKenna, p. 107; OCIL, p. 64; Rafroidi, ii, pp 74–5; RIA/DIB; J. D'A. Sirr, *A memoir of ... Power Le Poer Trench* (Dublin, 1845), pp 251–4; Wolff, i, p. 166.

B338 *Recollections of Hyacinth O'Gara* [anon.].
  + Dublin: Richard Moore Tims; London: Hamilton & Adams, J. Nesbitt, Hatchard & Son; Edinburgh: Wm. Oliphant, Waugh and Innes; Glasgow: Chalmers & Collins, 1828. SOURCE Block, p. 28; Bradshaw, 3279. LOCATION L, C.

+ Dublin: Richard Moore Tims; London: Hamilton & Adams, J. Nesbitt, Hatchard & Son; Edinburgh: Wm. Oliphant; Waugh & Innes; Glasgow: Chalmers & Collins, 1829, 3rd edn (enlarged). SOURCE Rafroidi, ii, p. 74; McKenna, p. 107. LOCATION L (1829, 3rd edn, destroyed; 1831, 4th edn), O, NUC, InND Loeber coll.

Dublin: Richard Moore Tims, 1837 (new edn). SOURCE Davidson cat. 33/34.

COMMENTARY No copy of the Dublin 1837 edn located. Set in Lisnamennigan, Ardrossil (Co. Clare) and describes the Methodists there. At the end of the novel, Hyacinth hopes to die without the benefits of a priest [ML; CM].

B339　*The confessions of Honour Delany* [anon.].

+ Dublin: Richard Moore Tims; London: Hamilton & Adams, J. Nesbitt, Hatchard & Son; Edinburgh: William Oliphant, Waugh & Innes; Glasgow: Chalmers & Collins, 1829.

SOURCE Rafroidi, ii, p. 74; Brown, 248 (3rd edn, 1839). LOCATION Grail, D, Dt (2nd edn, imperfect), L, O (1830 edn).

+ Dublin: Richard Moore Tims; London: Hamilton & Adams; James Nesbitt; Hatchard & Son; Edinburgh: W.M. Oliphant; Waugh & Innes; Glasgow: Chalmers & Collins, 1829, 2nd edn. LOCATION InND Loeber coll.

Dublin: Richard Moore Tims, 1830, 3rd edn (new edn). LOCATION L.

London: R.B. Seeley, 1852. LOCATION L.

COMMENTARY Religious fiction. A proselytizing story about Honour Delany, foster mother to Miss Clara of the 'big house', who suffers the death of several children and her husband. Her brother Richard comes to live with her to tend the farm. Richard becomes a Protestant and is banished by his older brother, after which the one servant leaves also. Through reading the Bible, Honour also becomes a Protestant. Her landlord, the earl of Innisfallan, stops her pension because he does not want any unrest on his land caused by conversions. However, the earl's two daughters make it up out of their own pockets. Honour lives a contented life in old age [ML].

B340　*Irish priests and English landlords* [anon.].

+ Dublin: Richard Moore Tims, 1830. SOURCE Rafroidi, ii, p. 74; Brown, 249; Wolff, 823 (1830, 2nd edn); NSTC; Garside 2, 1830:28. LOCATION Grail, D, BFl (1871 edn), L, O (1830, 2nd edn), NUC (1830, 2nd edn), InND Loeber coll.

+ London: William Hunt & Co., 1871 (new edn, revsd and corrected by Revd Henry Seddall; ill.). LOCATION L (destroyed), O, InND Loeber coll.

COMMENTARY Religious fiction. A priest, with authority from his bishop, tries to marry a girl who had become a Protestant to a Catholic man against her will. The girl refuses and dies a martyr to her faith. Most of the book revolves around the animosity between Protestants and Catholics. Maria Edgeworth§ found this book 'the most powerful' of GB's works [Brown; Colvin, pp 542–3; ML].

B341　*Irishmen and Irishwomen* [anon.].

+ Dublin: Richard Moore Tims; London: Hamilton & Adams; Edinburgh: Waugh & Innes, 1830.

SOURCE Rafroidi, ii, p. 74 (1831, 2nd edn); McKenna, p. 107 (mistakenly states first edn, Dublin, 1831); Brown, 250 (1831, 3rd edn); Bradshaw, 8690 (1831, 3rd edn); Garside 2, 1830:29. LOCATION Grail (1831 edn), D (1831, 3rd edn), Dt, DPL (1831, 3rd edn), L (1831, 2nd edn, destroyed), C (1831, 3rd edn), O (1831, 3rd edn), NUC (1831 edn), InND Loeber coll.

COMMENTARY Set in the north-west of Ireland and deals with agrarian outrages in which the peasantry are depicted as cold-blooded murderers. Also describes the conversion of Mrs Costigan to protestantism. Contains long discussions on religion [Brown].

B342 *Mothers and sons* [anon.].

+ Dublin: Richard Moore Tims; London: Hatchard & Son, Longman & Co., Simpkin & Marshall; Edinburgh: Waugh & Innes, White & Co., 1833. SOURCE Rafroidi, ii, p. 74; Brown, 253; Wolff, 824 (2nd edn); Garside 2, 1833:10. LOCATION Grail, Dt, D, L (destroyed), O, NUC, InND Loeber coll. (1833, 2nd edn).

COMMENTARY A group of Irish peasants, headed by the local schoolmaster, plot to do something to improve their lot. They meet at the cottage of the schoolmaster's mother, who is very much against their insurrectionist talk. The local curate has been brought up by a Mrs Tudor, who has become a Methodist. His own mother had eloped with an earl, married him, and they have lived abroad for many years. They return to his estate but the curate does not have any contact with his mother. The curate has a fiancée whose mother has high hopes that the earl will give the curate a rich living. When this does not happen, the engagement is broken. Subsequently the curate is shot by one of the disgruntled peasants and on his deathbed is reunited with his mother [RL].

B343 *Johnny Derrivan's travels* [anon.].

+ Dublin: Richard Moore Tims, 1833. SOURCE Rafroidi, ii, p. 74; Brown, 252; Bradshaw, 3290. LOCATION Grail, Dt (2nd edn), D (2nd edn), L (destroyed), C.

COMMENTARY 36pp and originally published in yellow wrapper. Set in Tubbercully, near Lough Gara (Co. Sligo). Johnny Derrivan returns to his family home in Ireland to tell of his adventurous journey to Wales as 'Master George's' servant (his main job was to look after the dogs on top of the carriage.) He describes to his family and a cabin packed with neighbours the strange customs he witnessed in Dublin, the ship's stormy departure from Howth, Holyhead and Wales. The wit of the narrative derives from Derrivan's literal understanding of events and his misunderstanding of Irish stereotypes: The Welsh are described as 'them wild people'. Johnny's father comments: 'the respect they must have shewed to one of your cultivation and breeding!' His mother asks of England: 'in that country, is there houses fit for the family to live in?' Johnny replies, 'Them people wouldn't know how to run up a grand house, if they went about it' [CM; Bradshaw, 3290].

B344 *Nurse McVourneen's story* [anon.].

+ Dublin: R.M. Tims; London: Simpkin & Marshall, Hatchard & Son; Edinburgh: Waugh & Innes, 1833. SOURCE Rafroidi, ii, p. 74 (1833, 2nd edn); Brown, 254; Bradshaw, 3287. LOCATION Grail, Dt, D, C.

Dublin: W. Curry & Co., 1862. SOURCE Bradshaw, 3561. LOCATION C.

COMMENTARY Religious fiction. Reviewed in the *New Monthly Magazine* (London); concerns 'the history of a child whose father contracts a second marriage, and is supposed to be told by her nurse' [RL; *New Monthly Magazine* (Nov. 1833, p. 367)].

B345 *Hyacinth O'Gara, Honor Delany, Irish priests and English landlords* [anon.].

+ Dublin: Richard Moore Tims; London: Simpkin, Marshall & Co., 1839 (new edn, corrected by the author). LOCATION DPL, L.

+ Dublin: Richard Moore Tims; London: Simpkin, Marshall & Co., 1839, 5th edn [on outside label] (new edn, corrected). LOCATION NUC (1839 edn), InND Loeber coll.

COMMENTARY An anthology of the first three published works by GB [RL].

B346 *The election* [anon.].

+ Dublin: Richard Moore Tims; London: Simpkin, Marshall & Co., 1840. SOURCE Rafroidi, ii, p. 74; Brown, 255; Hodgson p. 174; Block, p. 27. LOCATION Grail, L (destroyed), O, NUC, InND Loeber coll.

COMMENTARY Set in Ireland and describes election manoeuvres, particularly how people are torn between family ties, loyalty to their landlord, and fear of the priest [ML].

BROGHILL, Lord. See BOYLE, Roger.

BRONTE, Revd P. See BRONTË, Revd Patrick.

BRONTË, Revd Patrick (also known as the Revd P. Bronte), b. Drumballyroney (Co. Down) 1777, d. Haworth (Yorks.) 1861. Anglican Protestant clergyman, writer and poet, PB was the son of Hugh Prunty, a peasant farmer of Ahaderg (Co. Down) and Eleanor, called Alice, McClory. His original family name was O'Prunty or Brunty. PB worked as a blacksmith's labourer before opening his own school in Drumgooland (Co. Down) at age 16. He subsequently became private tutor to the children of Revd Thomas Tighe, the local evangelical minister, who arranged for him to go to St John's College, Cambridge, Tighe's alma mater. PB matriculated in 1802, received his BA in 1806, was ordained deacon in 1806 and priest in 1807. On arriving in Cambridge, PB's name changed from Brunty to Bronte in 1802 and to Brontë in 1811, but whether it was volitional or not is disputed The diaeresis first appeared on the 'e' in the first edn of *The cottage in the woods* (Bradford, 1815), apparently a printer's error. PB was ordained in the Church of England and held various curacies in England (Wethersfield, Essex; Wellington, Shrops.; Dewsbury, West Yorks.; Hartshead, West Yorks.), settling at Haworth in 1820. In 1812 he married Maria Branwell and their children included the authors Charlotte, Emily and Anne, many of whose writings are said to be influenced by the 'wild Irish tales' told them by their father. The four eldest daughters were sent to Cowan Bridge School where Maria and Elizabeth fell ill, and were subsequently brought home to die on 6 May and 15 June 1825. The remaining children were educated at home from this date. PB outlived his children, sharing his parsonage in his old age with Charlotte's husband, his curate Arthur Nicholls. He assisted Elizabeth Gaskell with her biography of Charlotte, which appeared in 1857. PB's published poetry includes *Cottage poems* (Halifax, 1811), *The rural minstrel* (Halifax, 1813) and *The phenomemon* (Bradford, 1824).For his portraits and papers, see ODNB. SOURCE Allibone, i, p. 250; J. Barker, *The Brontës* (London, 1994); Boylan, p. 35; Brady, p. 20; E. Chitham, *The Brontës' Irish background* (New York, 1986); NCBEL 4, pp 1118–20; NSTC; Newmann, p. 23; ODNB; O'Donoghue, p. 40; OCIL, p. 65; RIA/DIB.

B347   *The cottage in the wood; or, the art of becoming rich and happy* (by the Revd P. Brontë).
+ Bradford: T. Inkersley, 1815. SOURCE NSTC. LOCATION L, NUC (1818, 2nd edn).
COMMENTARY Reprinted in *Brontëana* (see below). Contains long diatribe against bad novels. The main character is Mary, daughter of one of the cottagers, who has more resources to overcome troubles and temptations than some 'gay and fashionable ladies'. William Bower, gentleman and drunk, arrives at the cottage and refutes the Bible. Mary rejects William's offer of marriage because she will not be 'yoked together with unbelievers'. He repents, finds God and temperance. The volume ends with four poems [CM].

B348   *The maid of Killarney; or, Albion and Flora: A modern tale; in which are interwoven some cursory remarks on religion and politics* [anon.].
London: Baldwin, Cradock & Joy, 1818. SOURCE Brown, 256; Rafroidi, ii, p. 77; British Fiction; Garside, 1818:21; Sadleir, 345. LOCATION Corvey CME 3–628–48148–1, Ireland related fiction, L, NUC.
COMMENTARY Reprinted in *Brontëana* (see below). Albion, an Englishman, falls in love with Flora Loughlen, while on a visit to Killarney. The tale is anti-Catholic in tone. Some of the discussion between Albion and Doctor O'Leary revolves around the ill effects of Catholic emancipation. Contains lyrical descriptions of the beauties of the Lakes of Killarney and the pitiable poverty of the Irish peasants that suggest firsthand knowledge, as well as a diatribe against certain types of novels [Brown; RL].

— COLLECTED WORKS

B349 *Brontëana. The Rev. Patrick Brontë, A.B., his collected works and life. The works; and the Brontës of Ireland.*
+ Bingley [West Yorks.]: T. Harrison, 1898 (ed. by J. Horsfall Turner. Printed for the ed.; ill. with photographs). LOCATION L, NUC, InND Loeber coll.
COMMENTARY Contents: *The cottage in the wood* (first published in Bradford, 1815), and *The maid of Killarney* (first published in London, 1818). Also contains poetry, including 'The Irish cabin' [RL].

BROOKE, Mr. See **BROOKE, Henry.**

BROOKE, Miss —. See **BROOKE, Charlotte.**

BROOKE, Miss —, pseud. **'E. Fairfax Byrrne'**, fl. 1881 to 1887. Poet and novelist, Miss B was a daughter of the Irish Revd Stopford Augustus Brooke, author of *English literature* (London, 1876) and *The need and use of getting Irish literature into the English tongue* (London, 1893). Miss B was the granddaughter of Revd Richard Sinclair Brooke§. She first published a poem, 'Millicent', which appeared in London in 1881. SOURCE Allibone Suppl., ii, p. 270 [under Byrrne]; COPAC; O'Donoghue, p. 52.
B350 *A fair country maid* (by 'E. Fairfax Byrrne').
London: R. Bentley & Son, 1883, 3 vols. SOURCE Allibone Suppl., ii, p. 270; COPAC. LOCATION L.
New York: Harper & Bros., 1884. SOURCE OCLC. LOCATION DCL.
B351 *Entangled* (by 'E. Fairfax Byrrne').
London: Hurst & Blackett, 1885, 3 vols. SOURCE Allibone Suppl., ii, p. 270; COPAC. LOCATION L.
B352 *The heir without a heritage* (by 'E. Fairfax Byrrne').
London: R. Bentley & Son, 1887, 3 vols. SOURCE Allibone Suppl., ii, p. 270 [where listed as *An heir without a heritage*]; COPAC. LOCATION L.

BROOKE, Charlotte (also known as **Miss Brooke**), b. Rantavan (Co. Cavan) 1740, d. Cottage, near Longford (Co. Longford) 1793. Translator, anthologist and miscellaneous writer, CB was the daughter of the writer Henry Brooke§, a descendant of Henry Brooke of Brookeborough (Co. Fermanagh), and Catherine Meares of Meares Court (Co. Westmeath). Educated by her father, she developed an interest in the Irish language and in Gaelic literature (her nurse, Mary Kelly, spoke mainly Irish to her) and later taught herself Old Irish. CB also encountered the Irish language among the labourers in the estates in Cavan and in Kildare, where the family moved in 1758. Her father's success as a Dublin dramatist brought her theatrical and literary friends, including Maria Edgeworth§. After her mother and last surviving sister died in 1773 she devoted herself to her stricken father. She was left in poverty after his death in 1783 due to an ambitious scheme involving a model industrial village in Kildare going bankrupt. In 1787, CB applied unsuccessfully for the post of housekeeper of the newly-founded RIA, which disappointment forced her to rely on her writing for support. While much of her own poetry was written early and destroyed, she is mostly known for her pioneering work *Reliques of Irish poetry* (Dublin, 1789, facsimile 1970) in which she published original Irish texts with her own translations and in which she argues that Irish poetry is the 'elder sister' to English poetry. The collection, which exemplified a growing Anglo-Irish cultural identification with Ireland, contains a single Irish tale, 'A Oisín, is binn linn do sgéala' ('Oisín, sweet is your story to us'). CB also wrote an unpublished tragedy, 'Belisarious', and edited her father's works. In 1795 she published in the first and only issue of *Bolg an tSolair; or Gaelic Magagine*. Rafroidi refers to *A dialogue between a lady and her pupils* (London, [1800?]), but this does not appear to be by CB. Some of her correspondence is in the RIA. SOURCE Allibone, i, p. 251; Blain, pp 141–2; Boylan, p. 35; Brady, p. 21; BD, pp 39–40; Field Day, i, pp 980–1,1008, iv, pp 508–9, 516, 1143–4; v, pp 811–12, 831; Hogan 2, pp 192 [under Henry Brooke]; *The Irish Shield* ([New York], 1829), i, pp 407–13 (biographical entry); Newmann, p. 23; OCIL, p. 66; ODNB; O'Donoghue, pp 40, 496; S. Ó Mórdha, 'Charlotte Brooke. Her background and achievements' in *Breifne*, vi (1986), pp 320–40; Rafroidi, ii, pp 77–8; RIA, MS 12/R/21 vol. 13/13, 114; RIA/DIB; Zimmerman, p. 93.

B353   *The school for Christians: in dialogues, for the use of children* (by Miss Brooke).
    Dublin: Bernard Dornin, 1791 (subscribers' list). SOURCE Blain, p. 142; Pollard 2, p. 161; ESTC t104982. LOCATION D, L.
    + Dublin: B. Dugdale, 1809. SOURCE NSTC. LOCATION L, InND Loeber coll.
COMMENTARY Dialogues between a father and his son about religious matters. According to the preface, the author was inspired by her father's childrearing skills. The book was among the volumes recommended by the Kildare Place Society for lending libraries in Ireland in 1824 [ML; *Hints on the formation of lending libraries in Ireland* (Dublin, 1824), pp 13–19].

B354   *Emma; or, the foundling of the wood. A novel* (by Miss Brooke).
    + London: J.F. Hughes, 1803. SOURCE British Fiction; Garside, 1803:17; BD, p. 40; Corvey CME 3–62847163. LOCATION NUC.
COMMENTARY Published posthumously. The preface states that the volume is most likely from an unfinished manuscript. Not set in Ireland or with Irish characters. A child is put out in the wood by her mother and is taken up by the family living in Hammond Castle [ML].

BROOKE, Henry (also known as **Mr Brooke**), b. Rantavan (Co. Cavan) *c*.1703, d. Dublin 1783. Dramatist, poet and miscellaneous writer, HB was the eldest son of a Church of Ireland minister, Revd William Brooke, and Lettice Digby. He was schooled initially at Rantavan, later at Dr Sheridan's School in Dublin, and subsequently at TCD where he was admitted in 1720. He studied law in London and was befriended by Jonathan Swift§ and the poet Alexander Pope. HB and his father were among the subscribers to the reprint of Robert L'Estrange's *Godfrey of Bulloigne: or the recovery of Jerusalem* (Dublin, 1726), and to Samuel Boyse's *Translations of poems* (Edinburgh, 1731). His six-book philosophical classical poem, *Universal beauty*, was published in London in 1735. He became well-known for his politically sensitive plays. 'Gustavus Vasa: the deliverer of his country' was prohibited after four performances in London in 1739 but sold to over 1,000 subscribers in a printed version. It was later produced in Dublin as 'The patriot' and viewed in the context of Irish-English relations. The play, along with his satirical opera *Jack the giant-queller* (Dublin, 1751), made it prudent for HB to move back to Ireland where he is said to have taken a minor post as a barracks master in Co. Kildare and to have been the author of *The secret history and memoirs of the barracks of Ireland* (London, 1747). His political pamphlets included the anti-Catholic, anti-Jacobite *The farmer's letter to the Protestants* (Dublin, 1745 onward), *The spirit of party* ([Dublin?], 1753) and *Interests of Ireland* (Dublin, 1759). However later, at the behest of the Catholic Committee, he wrote *The case of the Roman-Catholics of Ireland* (Dublin, 1760) in which he argued for a relaxation of the penal laws. He is the attributed author of *An essay on the antient and modern state of Ireland* (Dublin, 1759). His project for the publication of a history of Ireland was advertised by Faulkner in Dublin, but was not realized. Similarly, his plans for the 'Ogygian tales: or a curious collection of Irish fables, allegories, and histories from the relations of Fintane the aged', advertised in 1743 and intended to be based on the work of the antiquarian Charles O'Conor§, does not appear to have been printed. In 1763 he became the first editor of the *Public Register, or Freeman's Journal* (Dublin), but his editorship was short. HB translated and anonymously published, without acknowledging its French authors, *A new system of fairery; or, a collection of fairy tales* (Dublin, 1750, 2 vols.). He was best known for his novels, which were much reprinted. He was inclined towards the mystical beliefs of Jakob Boehme and his exponent William Law, and probably for that reason sponsored the translation into English of the German original of the life of the mystic Charles Hector de St George, marquis de Marsay (not published but known from manuscript). HB is said to have survived all but one of his twenty-two children, but this is probably not correct as the families of Henry and his brother Robert were often put together since they had a joint household. His daughter, the poet Charlotte Brooke§, cared for him in his last years when he was in a state of mental depression. She re-edited his poetic and dramatic works in 1792, and corrected imperfect edns that had appeared in 1778 and 1779. These included a poem *Conrade*, which is an Ossianic evocation of ancient Ulster. For his portraits, see ODNB. SOURCE Allibone, i, p. 251; Brady, p. 21; B & S, p. 99; [C.H. Wilson] *Brookiana* (London, 1804, 2 vols.); Carpenter, pp 235–40; DLB, xxxix; I. D'Olier, *Memoirs of the life of ... Henry Brooke* (Dublin, 1816); Elmes, p. 25; Fenning cat. 225/28; Field Day, i, pp 427–9, 502, 685–6, 759, 900–2, 909–12; Hogan 2, pp 191–2; King cat. 41/66 (translation of ms); R.R. Madden, *The history of Irish periodical literature* (London, 1867), ii, pp 374, 391–2, 407; Newmann, p. 23; OCIL, p. 66; ODNB; O'Donoghue, p. 41; RIA/DIB; RL; R. Ward, *Letters of Charles O'Conor of Belanagare* (Washington, DC, 1988), i, p. xxiii; R.E. Ward, *Prince of Dublin printers. The letters of George Faulkner* (Lexington, KY, 1972), p. 31.

B355 *The fool of quality; or, the history of Henry, Earl of Moreland* (by Mr Brooke).

+ Dublin: Printed for the author by Dillon Chamberlaine, 1765–1770, 5 vols. SOURCE Raven 2, 1770:24; Pollard 2, p. 98; ESTC t059854. LOCATION Dt, InND Loeber coll. (vol. 3 only).

Dublin: P. Wogan, 1796, 3 vols. (new edn, greatly altered and improved). SOURCE ESTC t057315. LOCATION NUC.

Dublin: T. Jackson, 1799 (abridged as *The story of David Doubtful; or, the reprobate reformed*). SOURCE ESTC n036430. LOCATION McMaster Univ., Hamilton (ON).

London: W. Johnston, 1766, vols. 1 and 2. SOURCE Raven, 993; Forster, 263; ESTC t057311; Gecker, 131 (1766–70, 2nd edn); Gilbert, p. 92; McBurney & Taylor, 104. LOCATION DPL Gilbert coll. (partly 2nd edn), D (1767 edn), L (imperfect), IU, PU, NUC.

London: W. Johnston, 1768–70, vols. 3, 4, and 5. SOURCE Raven, 1202; Raven 2, 1770:24; Forster, 264–66; ESTC t147806; ESTC t147805. LOCATION L, PU, NUC.

+ London: Edward Johnston, 1776, 4 vols. (new edn, greatly altered and improved; ill. H. Brooke, Isaac Taylor). SOURCE ESTC t144077. LOCATION L.

+ London: Edward Johnston, 1777, 5 vols. (new edn, greatly altered and improved; ill.). SOURCE ESTC t144135; Gecker, 132; McBurney & Taylor,108. LOCATION Dt, PU, IU, NUC, InND Loeber coll.

London: J. Paramore, 1781, 2 vols. (as *The history of Henry, Earl of Moreland*). SOURCE ESTC t068577. LOCATION NUC.

London: For the booksellers, 1784 (as *The history of a reprobate; being the life of David Doubtful*). SOURCE ESTC t073511. LOCATION NUC.

COMMENTARY *London 1784 edn* Abridged and revsd by Revd John Wesley [CM].

London: Vernor & Hood, 1798 (abridged as *The story of David Doubtful; or, the reprobate reformed*). SOURCE ESTC t118188. LOCATION L (imperfect), C, Toronto Public Libraries.

+ Chiswick: Printed by C. Whittingham, 1829 (ed. by the Revd John Wesley). LOCATION D, InND Loeber coll.

+ London: George Routledge & Sons; New York: E.P. Dutton, 1906 (with author's portrait, and biographical preface by Charles Kingsley§, and new life by E.A. Baker). SOURCE NCBEL 2, p. 1001. LOCATION InND Loeber coll.

Plymouth: John Bennett, 1815 (ed. by Revd John Wesley, as *The history of Henry Earl of Moreland*). SOURCE Gilbert, p. 92. LOCATION DPL Gilbert coll.

+ Liverpool: Nuttell, Fisher & Dickson, [1811 or later] (introd. signed by J.W. [?John Wesley], dated 1780; under title: *The history of Henry, Earl of Moreland*). LOCATION InND Loeber coll.

Paris: Royez, 1789, 2 vols. (trans. by Griffet de la Baume as *Le fou de qualité, ou histoire de Henri, Comte de Moreland*).

Frankfurt am Main: Kessler, 1776, 3 vols. (trans. as *Der vornehme Thor, oder Heinrichs Grafen von Moreland Geschichte*). SOURCE Raven 2, 1770:24. LOCATION Bayerische Staatsbibliothek.

Philadelphia: Robert Campbell, 1794, 3 vols. SOURCE ESTC w012240. LOCATION NUC.

Philadelphia: Rev. M.L. Weems, 1795 (abridged as *The very interesting and surprising adventures of David Doubtful*). LOCATION NUC.

Philadelphia: H. & P. Rice, 1796 (as *The history of a reprobate; being the life of David Doubtful*). SOURCE ESTC w0392230. LOCATION McMaster Univ., Hamilton (ON).

Alexandria [VA]: Printed by John Westcott, 1803 (abridged edn consisting of chapters 7 and 8 only). SOURCE RL. LOCATION CSmH.

+ Baltimore: J. Kingston, 1810, 2 vols. SOURCE Allen cat. 316/2272. LOCATION NUC. COMMENTARY Abridged edn with some of the dialogues appended in the rear [RL].

New York: E. Duyckinck, 1818, 2 vols. (new edn, greatly altered and improved [unclear by whom, because HB died in 1783]). LOCATION NUC.

New York: Garland, 1979, 5 vols. LOCATION L.

COMMENTARY A highly popular sentimental novel that was reprinted many times and also extracted in several contemporary periodicals including, in Ireland, the *New Magazine* (Dublin, 1800) and the *Strabane Magazine* (1800). Inspired by the life and teachings of the philosopher Jean-Jacques Rousseau, the story is set in England and describes the education of a boy by his uncle, stressing the learning of Christian virtues of humility, forgiveness, and charity through real experiences rather than book learning. The story contains many sub-plots since many of the characters that are introduced tell their life histories. The feminist author Mary Hays adapted this book for her *Harry Clinton* (London, 1804). The book was admired by the founder of methodism, John Wesley, who edited an abbreviated version [ML; Burmester cat. 49/209; Field Day, i, pp 738–45; Mayo, 537, 655; ODNB].

B356 *Juliet Grenville; or, the history of the human heart* (by Mr Brooke).

+ London: G. Robinson, 1774, 3 vols. SOURCE Hardy, 272; Block, p. 28; McBurney & Taylor, 110; Forster, 267; Raven 2, 1774:24; ESTC t130243. LOCATION D, L, IU, NUC, InND Loeber coll.

Dublin: James Williams, 1774, 3 vols. SOURCE Raven 2, 1774:24; ESTC t107653. LOCATION Dt (vols. 1 and 2 only), L.

Leipzig: Schwickert, 1774 (trans. as *Julie Grenville oder Die Geschichte des menschlichen Herzens*). SOURCE Raven 2, 1774:24. LOCATION BibliotheksVerbund Bayern.

Paris: Lavillette, 1801, 2 vols. (trans. by G. Garnier as *Juliette Granville; ou, histoire du coeur humain*). SOURCE Streeter, 91. LOCATION NUC.

Philadelphia: John Sparhawk & John Dunlap, 1774, 2 vols. SOURCE Gecker, 135. LOCATION PU, NUC.

COMMENTARY A tale of romance, adventure and extravagant sentiment set in England and on the Continent. Juliet Grenville and Thomas, the son of the earl of Cranfield, fall in love as children. Their parents intend them to marry. However, the parents have a disagreement and Thomas is sent to the Continent. Juliet pines and is sick for a long time. When she recovers, her father interests her in works of benevolence. Part of the book consists of stories about the recipients of their benevolence. Another part consists of Thomas's adventures on the Continent, where he wanders among people who need his help and sympathy. When Thomas and Juliet finally meet again and are about to married, letters from their former nurses say that they cannot marry because they are brother and sister. After severe heartaches, the mystery is solved and Juliet and Thomas are happily united and live together with their four parents [ML].

BROOKE, Revd Richard Sinclair, b. *c.*1798, d. England? 1882. Church of Ireland clergyman, writer of historical fiction and religious prose and poetry, RSB was the son of Dr William Brooke and descended from the author Henry Brooke§. He was admitted at TCD in 1817 where he graduated BA in 1827, MA in 1858 and DD in 1860. He became curate of Kinnitty (Co. Offaly) in 1828, subsequently held the living of Glendoan (Co. Donegal) and later was the incumbent of Mariners' Church, Kingstown (now Dun Laoghaire, Co. Dublin). After the disestablishment of the Church of Ireland (1869) he left for England and became rector of Wyton (Cambs.; Eyton according to Brown). His serial, 'The Darragh' appeared in the *Dublin University Magazine* (1856). He published privately and anonymously an historical fiction of the Irish rebellion in 1641, *A True romance* (n.l., printed Huntington, [*c.*1870], 13pp). He was also the author of *Recollections of the Irish church* (London, 1877), which contains sketches of many of his contemporaries. RSB was the father of the author and clergyman Stopford Augustus Brooke (1832–1916) and grandfather of the novelist Miss Brooke§. SOURCE Allibone Suppl., i, p. 216; Brooke, passim. Brown, p. 42; B & S, p. 99; Fenning cat. 158/43; IBL, 13 (1921), p. 65; O'Donoghue, p. 41; RIA/DIB.

B357 *The story of parson Annaly* (by Richard Sinclair Brooke).
    + Dublin: Printed [for the author?] by George Drought, 1870. SOURCE Brown, 257; COPAC. LOCATION D, Dt, BFl, NUC.
COMMENTARY In part reprinted from the *Dublin University Magazine*. Tells of a parson who has been sent on a tour in Ireland to regain his health. Contains many philosophical ruminations and descriptions of the people he meets and the adventures he has. The story contains descriptions of Donegal, including Glenveagh and Barnesmore [Brown; IBL; ML; Burmester list].

BROOKE, William Henry. See possible pseud. 'W.H.B.'.

BROPHY, Michael, fl. 1886. According to the title page of *Tales of the Royal Irish Constabulary* (Dublin, [1888]) MB also wrote *Carlow, past and present* (Carlow, 1888), *Forgotten chapters of Carlow history* (Carlow, 1888), and 'Historical reminiscences of Kildare' (no copy located). The preface to his *Sketches* (London, 1886) is from Emily Cottage, Carlow. MB is not to be confused with a namesake who was a member of the RIC from 1913 to 1922, and who received the Constabulary medal in 1920. SOURCE Brown, p. 42; IBL, 10 (1919), p. 69; J. Herlihy, *The Royal Irish Constabulary* (Dublin, 1997), p. 159; RIA/DIB; RL.

B358 *Sketches of the Royal Irish Constabulary* (by Michael Brophy; dedicated to Sergeant Sir Thomas Echlin, Bt, RIC. Depot, Phoenix Park).
    + London: Burns & Oates; New York: The Catholic Publication Society Co., 1886. SOURCE DCU, Catholic Americana files. LOCATION L, NUC.
COMMENTARY Preceded by the history of the RIC, the stories are fictionalized and probably autobiographical accounts of the activities of members of the RIC under two headings, 'Eccentric units' ('H.B.', 'Tiger Townshend', 'Billy', 'Sartor resartus', 'The shaughraun of the constabulary', 'Vi et armis',) and 'A hunt for a skeleton' ('"Pyramid" of Heapstown', 'An extraordinary wager') [RL].

B359 *Tales of the Royal Irish Constabulary* (by Michael Brophy).
+ Dublin: Bernard Doyle, [1888], 1896, vol. 1 [no more published]. SOURCE Brown, 258. LOCATION D, L, NUC.
Edinburgh: William Blackwood, 1921 (as *Tales of the R.I.C.*). LOCATION D, O, NYPL.
COMMENTARY The Edinburgh edn carries the advertisement, 'Hazardous adventures worthy of the pen of Dumas'. Consists of short stories, among which are 'The Lord of Kilrush', 'Fate of Marion', 'Last vicissitudes of Lord Edward Fitzgerald's estate', 'Episodes of '48', 'The story of a sword'. The IBL mentions that no other volume appeared as MB was not able to find a sufficient number of subscribers and for that reason was compelled to issue the work 'by a number of series' [Brown; IBL, 7 (1915–16), p. 176; RL].

'BROTHER JAMES', pseud. See REYNOLDS, James.

'BROTHER WAGTALE', fl. 1864. Pseudonym of chronicler of an Orange Order lodge.
B360 *The story of an Orange lodge; a chronicle of Dublin* (by 'Brother Wagtale').
+ Dublin: McGlashan & Gill; London: Simpkin, Marshall & Co., 1864. SOURCE Topp, 183. LOCATION D.

BROUGH, Robert Barnabas, b. London 1828, d. 1860. English journalist, novelist, poet, burlesque and short story writer, RBB was a portrait painter in Manchester before moving to Liverpool, where he started a weekly satirical journal, the *Liverpool Lion*. After moving to London he contributed to a number of periodicals and was for a time Brussels correspondent of the London *Sunday Times*. SOURCE Allibone Suppl., i, p. 219; Boase, i, p. 425; Brown 2, p. 31; ODNB; NCBEL 4, pp 1997–8; Wolff, i, p. 169 (lists other novels).
B361 *Which is which? or, Miles Cassidy's contract. A picture story* (by Robert Barnabas Brough).
+ London: W. Kent & Co., 1860, 2 vols. in 1 (ill. the author, Swain). SOURCE Brown 2, 151; Wolff, 847; NCBEL 4, p. 1998; COPAC. LOCATION D, L, NUC, InND Loeber coll.
COMMENTARY The story of an Irishman who in 1813 emigrates with two little boys to England. He settles in Oxford because he wants the boys to have the best education. He takes on all kinds of jobs and becomes a builder. Only one of the boys is his son, the other comes from gentry stock. However, it is not clear who is who. After the mystery has been resolved, both young men continue to consider the old man their father [ML].

BROUGHAM, John, b. Dublin 1810 (according to ODNB, DLB, Allibone and OCIL, and not 1814 as elsewhere), d. New York 1880. Playwright, actor, story and verse writer and theatre manager, JB was of Irish and French ancestry. He graduated at TCD and after his medical studies were cut short by family adversity, he went to London where he became an actor of note and a manager of theatres. He is thought to be the model for Charles Lever's§ character of Harry Lorrequer in *The confessions of Harry Lorrequer* (Dublin, 1839). In 1842 JB went to New York where he acted, managed theatres, including the short-lived Brougham's Lyceum, and wrote more than 75 plays (including *The Irish Yankee*, New York, 1856), libretti and burlesques, the most famous of which was 'Po-ca-hon-tas'. He collaborated with and acted in several plays by Dion Boucicault§. Popular, handsome and charming, he was most successful as an actor in impersonating comic characters, especially Irish ones, and in particular the role of Sir Lucius O'Trigger in Richard Brinsley Sheridan's *The Rivals* (1775). He was married twice. For his portraits, see *The Bunsby papers* (New York, 1856) and ODNB. SOURCE Allibone Suppl., i, p. 220; ANB; Brady, p. 21; DAB; DLB, xi; Hogan 2, p. 193; *Illustrated Celtic*

Monthly (New York, 1879), pp 300–2; OCIL, p. 67; ODNB; O'Donoghue, p. 42; RIA/DIB; W. Winter (ed.), *Life, stories and poems of John Brougham* (Boston, 1881).

B362 *The incendiary! A tale of love and revenge* (by John Brougham).
   Boston: H.L. Williams, 1845 (ill.). SOURCE Wright, i, 417a; COPAC. LOCATION L.
   COMMENTARY 40pp [Wright].

B363 *A basket of chips* (by John Brougham; dedicated to Dr William B. Egan of Illinois).
   + New York: Bunce & Brother, 1855 (ill. J. McLuan). SOURCE Rafroidi, ii, p. 80;
   Wright, ii, 374. LOCATION L, NUC, InND Loeber coll., Wright web.
COMMENTARY Contents (excluding poetry and drama): 'Some passages in the life of a dog',
'Love and loyalty, an episode in English history', 'O'Dearmid's ride' (set in Ireland), 'The
fairies' warning' (set in Ireland), 'Kitt Cobb, the cabman. A story of London life', 'Fatality.
A condensed novel', 'Ned Geraghty's luck' (set in Ireland), 'The eagle and her talons. An
Eastern apologue', 'Evenings at our club', 'Romance and reality', 'Jasper Leech. The man who
never had enough', 'Nightmares', 'The Bunsby papers' [RL].

B364 *The Bunsby papers (second series)* [on title page:] *Irish echoes* (by John Brougham;
   dedicated to Samuel Lover§).
   + New York: Derby & Jackson; Cincinnati: W.H. Derby & Co., 1856 (ill. McLenan).
   SOURCE Rafroidi, ii, p. 74 (1857 edn); Wright, ii, 375. LOCATION D, L (1857 edn),
   NUC, InND Loeber coll., Wright web.
   New York: Derby & Jackson, 1857, 8 vols. (as *Humorous stories*). SOURCE Allibone
   Suppl. i, p. 220; RLIN; Wright, ii, p. 53. LOCATION D, DCL, NUC (1859 edn), Univ.
   of Minnesota Libraries.
COMMENTARY Sketches of Irish life. Contents: 'Dan Duff's wish, and what came of it', 'The Blarney
stone', 'The gospel charm', 'The test of blood', 'The morning dream', 'The fortune-teller', 'The
fairy circle', 'O'Bryan's luck. A tale of New York', 'The Tipperary Venus' [RL].

B365 *The light of home: A Christmas story* (by John Brougham).
   + New York: American News Company, 1868 (ill.). SOURCE Wright, ii, 376; RLIN.
   LOCATION Univ. of California, Berkeley, Wright web.
   COMMENTARY 96 pp [RL].
   — COLLECTED WORKS

B366 *Life, stories and poems of John Brougham* (ed. by W. Winter).
   Boston: J.R. Osgood & Co., 1881. SOURCE COPAC. LOCATION L.

BROWN, Charles Brockden, b. Philadelphia (PA) 1771, d. 1810. American novelist, editor
and miscellaneous writer, CBB is considered to be the first person in the US to make writing his profession. He was the son of Elijah Brown and Mary Armitt and was trained as a
lawyer. He wrote *Alcuin: a dialogue* (New York, 1798), a treatise on the rights of women, and
edited various magazines. His *Ormond* (New York, 1799) does not appear to have Irish content. According to the DLB, the novel deals with the horrors of the plague and is a sensational novel with an attempted rape of the heroine, who kills Ormond. SOURCE Allibone i, p.
256; ANB; DAB; DLB, xxxvii, lix, lxxiii; Hart, pp 102–3; RL.

B367 *Carwin, the biloquist, and other American tales and pieces* (by Charles Brockden
   Brown).
   + London: Henry Colburn & Co., 1822, 3 vols. SOURCE British Fiction; Garside,
   1822:21. LOCATION Corvey CME 3–628–47135–4, L, NUC.
COMMENTARY Originally published in the US in instalments (1803–05). Contents: 'Carwin,
the biloquist' (partially set in Ireland), 'Stephen Calvert' (some thin links to Ireland), 'Jessica',
'The scribbler' [ML; Garside].

BROWN, David, pseud. 'A Northern man', b. 1786, d. 1875. American writer. SOURCE Wright web.

B368   *The planter: or, thirteen years in the South* (by 'A Northern man').
+ Philadelphia: H. Hooker, 1853. LOCATION Wright web.
COMMENTARY An anti-abolitionist story where the situation in the American states is compared favourably with the condition of the people in Ireland. Posits that the laws in Ireland protect property but not life [ML].

BROWN, Frances. See **BROWNE, Frances.**

BROWN, James Moray. Co-author. See **CROMMELIN, Maria Henrietta.**

'BROWN, Mahan A.', pseud. See **ELLIS, Edward Sylvester.**

BROWNE, Charles Farrar, pseud. 'Artemus Ward', b. Waterford (ME) 1834, d. Southampton (Hants.) 1867. American journalist and comic sketch writer, CFB was the son of Levi Browne and Caroline Farrar. He began his working life apprenticed to a printer in New Hampshire, where he started to write for a newspaper. Moving to Cleveland (OH) he worked on the *Plain Dealer* contributing comic sketches, and later to New York where he became a staff member of *Vanity Fair*. His comic sketches, based on the incongruities of life, were collected into a series of books published under his pseud. and he toured widely and very successfully, including to London, giving lectures based on them. He contributed also to the Boston weekly the *Carpet Bag*, and to *Punch* (London). SOURCE Allibone, iii, p. 2573 [under Artemus Ward]; ANB; DAB; DLB, xi; Wright ii, pp 55–6.

B369   *Artemus Ward among the Fenians. With the showman's observations upon life in Washington, and military ardour in Baldinsville* (by 'Artemus Ward').
+ London: John Camden Hotten, [1866] (title on cover: *Among the Fenians*). SOURCE Topp 3, p. 9. LOCATION L, InND Loeber coll.
+ London, New York: Ward, Locke & Co., [n.d.] (as *Babies and ladders by Emanuel Kink. And Among the Fenians*, by 'Artemus Ward', *With the showman's observations upon life in Washington, and military ardour in Baldinsville*). LOCATION InND Loeber coll.
New York: Carleton, 1862 (as *Artemus Ward, his book*; ill.). SOURCE Wright, ii, 392; OCLC. LOCATION CtY.

BROWNE, Charlotte Elizabeth. See **TONNA, Mrs Charlotte Elizabeth.**

BROWNE, Frances (also known as **Frances Brown**), b. Stranorlar (Co. Donegal) 1816, d. London 1879. Poet, novelist and writer of stories for children, FB was the seventh child in a Presbyterian village postmaster's family of twelve. As a small child she contracted smallpox, which left her blind. She educated herself by listening to lessons read aloud. She contributed poems to the *Irish Penny Journal* (Dublin, 1840–44), the *Athenaeum* (London), the *Ulster Monthly Magazine* (Belfast, 1845), the *Belfast Penny Journal* (1845–46), and the *Northern Whig* (Belfast). She published a short story, 'The fairy and the flirt. An Irish legend', in the *Forget Me Not* (London, 1838), and made a contribution to the *Keepsake* (London, 1843). In 1847, accompanied by her sister who acted as her amanuensis, she went to Edinburgh to further her literary career and while living there published her 'Legends of Ulster' in *Fraser's Magazine* (London) and *Tait's Edinburgh Magazine*. In 1848 she published *Lyrics and miscellaneous poems* (Edinburgh). A gift of £100 from the marquess of Lansdowne made it possible for her to move to London in 1852. There she was known as 'the blind poetess of

Donegal' and earned her living by writing, contributing to a variety of magazines such as *Leisure Hour* (London) and *Chambers's Journal* (Edinburgh). Later in life she wrote much for the Religious Tract Society, but she also published short stories in the *Lady's Annual* (New York, n.d.), and in the *Magnet Stories* (London, [1862]). Her autobiography, *My share in the world,* appeared in 1862 in a fictional format. She was awarded a Civil List pension in 1863. SOURCE Allibone, i, p. 257; Allibone Suppl., i, p. 229; Alston, p. 52; Blain, p. 149; Brady, p. 21; DLB, cic; Clyde, pp 110–11; Donegal, pp 49–51; Field Day, iv, p. 893; v, 776–7, 728; Hogan 2, pp 195–6; IBL, 8 (Dec. 1916–17), pp 49–51; Irish pseudonyms; Jarndyce cat. 162/154; NCBEL 4, p. 1114; Newmann, pp 24–5; OCIL, p. 67; ODNB; O'Donoghue, p. 42; RIA/DIB; RL; Sutherland, pp 90–1.

B370   *The Ericksons. The clever boy; or, consider another (Two stories for my young friends)* (by Frances Brown[e]).
+ Edinburgh: Paton & Ritchie, 1852. SOURCE Hogan, p. 128; COPAC. LOCATION L.
COMMENTARY Contents: 'The Ericksons' (set in Norway), 'The clever boy' (set in England). Another version of the first story was published as a short story in Gustav Nieritz's *Tales for the young* (London, 1855) [Colman, p. 46; ML].

B371   *Granny's wonderful chair and the stories it told* (by Frances Browne).
London: Griffith, Farran, Okedan & Welsh, 1856 (ill. Kenny Meadows). SOURCE Weekes, p. 61; Alston, p. 52. LOCATION L (1857 edn), NUC.
+ London: Griffith & Farran, 1857 (as *Granny's wonderful chair, and its tales of fairy times*; ill. Kenny Meadows; cover: J.L.). SOURCE Hogan, p. 128; Donegal, p. 51; Osborne, p. 972. LOCATION CaOTP, InND Loeber coll.
London: A. & C. Black, 1909 (as *Lords of the castles, and other stories from Granny's wonderful chair ... with composition exercises*). LOCATION L.
London, New York: McClure, Phillips & Co., 1904 (as *The story of the lost fairy book*). LOCATION L.
+ New York: Macmillan, 1924 (as *Granny's wonderful chair*; ill. Emma L. Brock). LOCATION InND Loeber coll.
+ New York: McLoughlin Bros, n.d. (as *Granny's wonderful chair and its tales of fairy times*; ill.). LOCATION InND Loeber coll.
Harmondsworth: Puffin, 1985 (Puffin Classics). SOURCE OCLC. LOCATION Dt, L, Rochester Public Library.
COMMENTARY For many other edns, see BLC. Collection of fairy stories for children, illustrating Christian values, but having no links with Ireland. Contents: 'The Christmas cuckoo', 'The Lords of the White and the Grey Castles', 'The greedy shepherd', 'The story of Fairyfoot', 'The story of Childe Charity', 'Sour and civil', 'The story of Merrymind', 'Prince Wisewhit's return' [RL].

B372   *Our uncle the traveller's stories* (by Miss Frances Browne).
London: Kent, 1859. SOURCE RIA/DIB; Donegal, p. 51; COPAC. LOCATION L.

B373   *My share of the world. An autobiography* (by Frances Browne).
London: Hurst & Blackett, 1861, 3 vols. in 2. SOURCE Hogan, p. 128. LOCATION L, MH, NUC.
COMMENTARY Despite its sub-title, this is fictionalized autobiography [Wolff, i, p. 175].

B374   *The Castleford case* (by Frances Browne).
London: Hurst & Blackett, 1862, 3 vols. SOURCE Hogan, p. 128; COPAC. LOCATION L.

B375   *The orphans of Elfholm* (by Frances Browne).
+ London: Groombridge, [1862] (Magnet Stories, No. 30). SOURCE Hogan, p. 128; Donegal, p. 51; COPAC. LOCATION L, InND Loeber coll.

B376 *The poor cousin* (by Frances Browne).
+ London: Groombridge & Sons, [1863] (Magnet Stories for Summer Days and Winter Nights). SOURCE NCBEL 4, p. 1144; RLIN. LOCATION C.
COMMENTARY Story set in England, where a poor cousin comes to help look after an afflicted girl in a rich family. However, she is unhappy there and returns home [ML].

B377 *The young foresters* (by Frances Browne).
London: Groombridge & Son, [1864] (Magnet Stories for Summer Days and Winter Nights, No. 45; ill.). SOURCE Hogan, p. 128; Donegal, p. 51; RLIN. LOCATION L, C.

B378 *The hidden sin. A novel* [anon.].
London: Richard Bentley, 1866, 3 vols. SOURCE Hogan, p. 128; Wolff, 884. LOCATION L.
+ New York: Harper & Bros, 1866 (ill.). SOURCE NYPL; OCLC. LOCATION NN, InND Loeber coll.
COMMENTARY Contents different from most of FB's work. Also attributed to Sara Eliza Baughman Hubbard. Set in banking circles in Armagh, Dublin, and London and revolves around the mysterious disappearance of the son of one of the Latouches, just after he had collected a large sum of money. A very prosperous Scottish banker who comes across as religious and charitable eventually appears to have been the murderer. Members of a Greek banking firm lend a mysterious and exotic flavour to the story [ML; OCLC].

B379 *The exile's trust. A tale of the French Revolution, and other stories* (by Frances Browne).
London: Leisure Hour, [1869]. SOURCE Hogan, p. 128. LOCATION L.

B380 *The nearest neighbour, and other stories* (by Frances Browne).
+ London, Manchester, Brighton: Religious Tract Society, [1875] (ill.). SOURCE Hogan, p. 128. LOCATION L (destroyed), InND Loeber coll.
COMMENTARY Contents: 'The nearest neighbour', 'Found in the far North', 'The city of debtors' [ML].

B381 *The dangerous guest. A story of 1745* (by Frances Browne).
London: Religious Tract Society, [1886]. SOURCE Hogan, p. 128. LOCATION L (destroyed), E.
COMMENTARY Religious fiction [BLC].

B382 *The foundling of the Fens. A story of a flood* (by Frances Browne).
London: Religious Tract Society, [1886]. SOURCE Hogan, p. 128; Donegal, p. 51. LOCATION L (destroyed), C.
COMMENTARY Religious fiction [BLC].

B383 *The first of the African diamonds* (by Frances Browne).
London: Religious Tract Society, [1887] (ill.). SOURCE Hogan, p. 128; OCLC. LOCATION L (destroyed), CtY.
COMMENTARY 80pp. Religious fiction [BLC].

BROWNE, Jemmett J. (also known as J. Jemmett-Browne), b. 1832, d. 1897. Novelist, balladeer and songwriter, JJB was the eldest son of a Church of Ireland clergyman, John Browne of Riverstown (Co. Cork). JJB matriculated at Worcester College, Oxford, in Mar. 1852 and graduated BA from Corpus Christi College in 1855. He entered Lincoln's Inn in 1859 and was called to the Bar in 1867. He married Frances Mary Custance in 1864 and following her death, he married in 1877 his cousin Frances Caroline Cecil, eldest daughter of Major William Walter Stephenson of the Rifle Brigade. JJB was private secretary to the permanent secretary of the Board of Trade (1868–84). His *Songs of Many Seasons* was published in London in 1879. SOURCE Burke's, 1904, p. 67; J. Foster (ed.), *Alumni Oxonienses* (1715–1866), i, p. 174; Leslie, *Down*, p. 14; O'Donoghue, p. 44; RIA/DIB.

B384   *A lone lassie. An autobiography* (by J. Jemmett-Browne).
London: Sampson Low & Co., 1886, 3 vols. SOURCE COPAC. LOCATION L.
B385   *So the world wags. A tale of town and travel* [anon.].
London: Sampson Low & Co., 1886, 3 vols. SOURCE COPAC. LOCATION L.

BROWNE, J. Ross. See **BROWNE, John Ross**.

BROWNE, John Ross (also known as J. Ross Browne), b. Dublin 1821 (1817 according to Allibone and Boase), d. Oakland (CA) 1875. Reporter, travel writer, novelist and illustrator, JRB and his parents, Thomas Egerton Browne and Elana Buck, emigrated from Ireland to Louisville (KY) around 1832. He was largely self-taught and in order to travel he studied shorthand and moved to Washington (DC), where he became a reporter in the US Senate. In 1842 he shipped out on a whaler and largely spent the next twenty-five years travelling and writing about his experiences. His articles for *Harper's Magazine* (New York) were accompanied by his own sketches. A California pioneer, he was the official reporter of the convention that drew up the state's first constitution in 1849. He left for Europe as a newspaper correspondent in 1851. In 1868 he was appointed US minister to China but was recalled the following year after expressing views contrary to those of the government. He settled in Oakland (CA) and went into the real estate business. SOURCE Allibone, i, p. 262 [under J. Ross Browne]; Allibone Suppl., i, pp 230–1; ANB; Boase, i, p. 445; Burke, p. 99; DAB; DLB, ccii; Wright, ii, p. 56 (list of novels).
B386   *Confessions of a quack; or, the autobiography of a modern Aesculapian* (by J. Ross Browne).
Louisville (KY): Printed [for the author?] by James B. Marshall, 1841. SOURCE Wright, i, 434. LOCATION NUC .
COMMENTARY All copies incomplete, ending at p. 32 [NUC].
B387   *Etchings of a whaling cruise, with notes on Zanzibar; and a brief history of the whale fishery* (by J. Ross Browne).
London: John Murray, 1846. SOURCE Burke, p. 99; Hodgson, p. 76. LOCATION NUC.
+ New York: Harper & Bros, 1846 (as *Etchings of a whaling cruise, with notes of a sojourn on the island of Zanzibar. To which is appended a brief history of the whale fishery*). LOCATION L, NUC.
Cambridge (MA): Belknap Press, 1968. LOCATION InND.
COMMENTARY Autobiographical novel, narrated by an American [ML].
B388   *Yusef; or, the journey of the Frangi. A crusade in the East* (by J. Ross Browne).
+ New York: Harper & Bros, 1853 (ill.). SOURCE Wright, ii, 401. LOCATION L, NUC, Wright web.
London: Sampson Low & Co., 1853. LOCATION NUC, L.
B389   *Crusoe's island: A ramble in the footsteps of Alexander Selkirk. With sketches of adventure in California and Washoe* (by John Ross Browne).
New York: Harper & Bros, 1864. SOURCE Wright, ii, 399. LOCATION L, NUC.
London: Sampson Low, Son & Marston, 1864. SOURCE OCLC. LOCATION NUC
B390   *An American family in Germany* (by J. Ross Browne).
+ New York: Harper & Bros, 1866 (ill. the author). SOURCE Wright, ii, 398. LOCATION L, NUC, Wright web.
B391   *The land of Thor* (by J. Ross Browne).
New York: Harper & Bros, 1867 (ill. the author). SOURCE Wright, ii, 400; COPAC. LOCATION L, NUC, Wright web.

BROWNSON, O.A. Editor. See **CLARKE, D.W.C.**

'BRUNEFILLE, G.E.', pseud. See **CAMPBELL, Lady Colin.**

BRYCE, William. Co-author. See **STACPOOLE, Henry de Vere.**

BRYSON, Revd James, b. Holywood (Co. Down) 1730, d. Belfast (Co. Antrim) 1796. A Presbyterian clergyman and prolific sermonizer, JB was the son of John Bryson, Presbyterian minister of Holywood, and his wife, Ann. Ordained at Lisburn (Co. Antrim) in 1764, he moved to Belfast in 1773 where he was minister of the Second Congregation until 1792, when after some internal dissension he left and formed the Fourth Congregation. He was chaplain to the First Belfast Volunteer Company when it was formed in 1778. JB became a Freemason in 1782, one of the founders of the Orange Society, and a member of Lodge 257. He married twice and fathered twenty-one sons and three daughters. His youngest son, Samuel Maziere, was a doctor in Belfast and a collector of Irish manuscripts. Twelve volumes of JB's sermons survive in manuscript at Queen's University, Belfast, and one at the Antrim Presbytery Library. For JB's portraits, see ODNB. SOURCE Allibone, i, p. 273; Brown 2, p. 32; ODNB; RIA/DIB.
B392 *Primus aut Imus. A tale of primogeniture. With sketches of contemporary and current history* (by James Bryson).
+ Belfast: New Letter Office, 1877. SOURCE Brown 2, 154. LOCATION D.
COMMENTARY Published posthumously. Set mostly in Dublin at the end of the eighteenth century, it opens with a conversation between the knight of Glenturk and Phelon Shrigley Tarley, QC, on the rights and wrongs of primogeniture. It introduces the earl of Dermon of Castle Col and his son, Lord Walter Newton, a model young man who decides to enter the ministry of the Church of Ireland. The story presents a picture of social and other conditions as seen from the Protestant standpoint. Lord Newton carries out social and moral reforms and preaches to Catholics against catholicism. He marries and becomes the father of twins who are named jointly Primus and Imus. There is much mystery as to which was born first. The story follows the twins' fortunes, first at Eton and then at Cambridge. There is a long polemic against the Roman Catholic Church, Jesuits, priest craft, Irish marriage and sacerdotal celibacy [Brown 2].

BUCHANAN, Robert Williams, b. Caverswell (Staffs.) 1841, d. London 1901. English poet, playwright and novelist of Irish ancestry, RWB was the son of Robert Buchanan, a Scottish tailor who became a noted socialist and disciple of Robert Owen. He was educated in Glasgow and moved to London to make a living as a writer. There he had some success with his plays and worked with the *Athenaeum* (London) and other periodicals. He lived in Scotland again from 1866 to 1874, when he moved to Rosspoint (Co. Mayo) in an effort to reduce his living expenses, leaving Ireland in 1877. RWB is known for an acrimonious literary dispute concerning his criticism of the poetry of Algernon Swinburne that went on for years, with friends of both parties weighing in, and about which RWB brought a suit for libel. He subsequently produced numerous plays and novels in an effort to improve his circumstances, which had taken a downturn due to an unwise speculation. For his portraits and papers, see ODNB. Only those novels with known Irish content are listed below. SOURCE Allibone Suppl., i, pp 240–1; Brown, p. 43; DLB, xviii, xxxv; IBL, 14 (1924), p. 73; H. Jay, *Robert Buchanan* (London, 1903), passim; LVP, p. 73; MVP, pp 65–6; NCBEL 4, p. 722; OCIL, p. 68; ODNB; Sutherland, pp 91–2.
B393 *The Queen of Connaught. A story* [anon.].
+ London: Richard Bentley & Son, 1875, 3 vols. SOURCE Wolff, 3606. LOCATION L.
+ London: Chatto & Windus, 1878 (new edn; Piccadilly Library). SOURCE Brown, 808; Topp 3, p. 60. *Location* InND Loeber coll.

New York: Harper & Bros, 1875 (Library of Select Novels, No. 452). SOURCE Topp 3, p. 60; OCLC. LOCATION NN.

COMMENTARY Harriet Jay§, RWB's adopted daughter, identified RWB as the author of this novel. Previously, the volume has been attributed to Charles Reade and Harriet Jay. Introductory poem relates that Shana O'Mara, the queen of Connaught, meets Queen Elizabeth I in the company of the earl of Ormond. The novel concerns an Englishman, John Bermingham, who becomes involved with a west of Ireland community when he marries Kathleen O'Mara. He tries but fails to reform the Connaught peasantry with English ideas [Sutherland; Brown; CM].

B394 **The dark Colleen. *A love story*** [anon.].
 London: Richard Bentley & Son, 1876, 3 vols. LOCATION L.
 + New York: Lovell, Adam, Wesson & Co., 1877. LOCATION InND Loeber coll.

COMMENTARY Set on a remote island off the west coast of Ireland and in France. The captain of a shipwrecked French boat is rescued by a girl, Morna, who against the islanders' wishes nurses him back to health. He flirts with her, eventually marries her and takes her to France. She is unhappy in France and the captain secretly starts an affair with another woman. To get rid of Morna, he asks the mate of his ship to take her to sea and drown her. Morna, however, jumps overboard and swims to shore. After many wanderings she finds her way back to her island. There, however, she still pines for her husband. Another shipwreck takes place and none of the islanders is willing to rescue the man who is clinging to the mast. Morna recognizes her husband just before the ship keels over and he drowns [ML].

B395 **Madge Dunraven. *A tale*** [anon.].
 + London: Richard Bentley & Son, 1879, 3 vols. SOURCE Wolff, 3605. LOCATION L.

COMMENTARY Part one is entitled 'Old Ireland' and is set in Co. Sligo. There is a description of a wake and a dilapidated big house (Shranamonragh Castle), which is visited by an Englishman, Mr Aldyn, brother of the deceased. Mr Dunraven's wife has died and his lands in Ireland are all mortgaged off. The family moves to England. Part two is set in England. Madge Dunraven, who is a niece of Mr. Dunraven and an orphan, refuses to attend a Protestant school, performs Irish dances and would not wear shoes. Finally, she returns to Nallymoy [CM].

B396 **A child of nature. *A romance*** (by Robert Williams Buchanan).
 + London: Richard Bentley & Son, 1881, 3 vols. *Locatio*n L.
 COMMENTARY Set in Scotland, but 'coloured by his Irish experience' [DNB; RL].

B397 **Matt. *A story of a caravan*** (by Robert Williams Buchanan).
 London: Chatto & Windus, 1885 (Piccadilly Library). LOCATION L.
 + London: Chatto & Windus, 1886 (new edn). SOURCE Topp 3, p. 151. LOCATION InND Loeber coll.
 New York: D. Appleton & Co., 1885 (as *Matt: A tale of a caravan*; Seaside Library Pocket Edition, No. 398). LOCATION Topp 3, p. 151; OCLC. LOCATION NN.

COMMENTARY An amateur painter, Mr Charles Brinkley, and his servant, Tim-na-Chaling, travel by caravan through Wales. Tim-na-Chaling comes from Co. Mayo where Mr Brinkley had lived for a while and to which he makes several references. They settle in a quiet place near the coast where they meet Matt, an unsophisticated girl, who proclaims herself an orphan. She is being brought up by a sinister 'wrecker', who is paid for his troubles by a Mr Monk, the local landlord. Mr Brinkley solves the mystery of Matt's background. She appears to be an heiress. Mr Monk is shown to have come into her estate under false pretences. When Matt is grown she marries Mr Brinkley [ML].

B398 **A marriage by capture. *A romance of to-day*** (by Robert Williams Buchanan).
 + London: T. Fisher Unwin, 1896 (Autonym Library). SOURCE Brown 2, 158.
 LOCATION L, NUC, InND Loeber coll.

COMMENTARY A tale of Co. Mayo in the 1890s, allegedly based on fact. The hand of a heiress is sought by two suitors, one her cousin, a rogue who tried to abduct her but failed. She disappears and he is arrested on suspicion but discharged. She suddenly returns, having been carried off by the other suitor, to whom she is eventually married by the parish priest who plays a prominent part in the tale [Brown 2].

B399   *Father Anthony. A romance of to-day* (by Robert Williams Buchanan; dedicated to the Revd John Melvin, formerly parish priest of Rossport, Co. Mayo).
+ London: John Long, 1898. SOURCE Brown, 262 (1903 edn). LOCATION L, NUC (1899 edn), InND Loeber coll. (1899, 2nd edn).

COMMENTARY Set in a village in the west of Ireland. Fr Anthony has, for his brother's sake, sacrificed a career in the world. He is called upon to keep the secret of the confessional when by a word he could save his brother from the hangman's hand [Brown].

B400   *The 'Peep-o'-Day Boy'. A story of the 'ninety-eight'* (by Robert Williams Buchanan).
+ London: John Dicks, [1902] (ill. cover: Harry Evans; see Plate 13). SOURCE Brown, 263; RLIN. LOCATION C, InND Loeber coll.

COMMENTARY Historical fiction about the 1798 rebellion. The daughter of the absentee landlord loves O'Connormore, the expelled owner of an estate. The plot contains meetings of secret societies in underground caves, abductions and informers. The three chapters on the insurrection are based on *Cassell's History of Ireland* (London, 1852) [Brown].

BUGG, Lelia Hardin, fl. 1892. American novelist and short story writer, LHB also wrote *The correct thing for Catholics* (New York, 1892). SOURCE BLC.

B401   *The prodigal daughter, and other tales* (by Lelia Hardin Bugg).
New York, Cincinnati etc.: Benziger Bros, 1898. SOURCE Fanning, p. 376; Wright, iii, 767. LOCATION NUC.
COMMENTARY Contents: 'The prodigal's daughter, 'Westgate's past' (Irish content), 'At the pension Roget', 'The major' [NUC; Fanning].

'BUISSON, Ada', pseud. See **BRADDON, Mary Elizabeth**.

BULLOCK, Mrs —. For attribution, see British Fiction (Update 1). She was also the author of *Susanna; or, traits of a modern Miss* (London, 1795, 4 vols.). SOURCE Raven 2, 1795:15.

B402   *Dorothea; or, a ray of the new light* [anon.].
London: G.G. & J. Robinson, 1801, 3 vols. SOURCE Garside, 1801:4; British Fiction (Update 1); M.O. Grenby, *The anti-Jacobin novel* (Cambridge, 2001), pp 58–9. LOCATION O.
+ Dublin: P. Wogan, H. Colbert, W. Porter, B. Dornin, J. Rice, T. Burnside & J. Parry, 1801. SOURCE Garside, 1801:4. LOCATION L.

COMMENTARY Anti-Jacobin novel, which recounts the beginning of the French Revolution and the fall of the Bastille in the context of the 1798 rebellion in Ireland. Starts out in England, but partially set in Ireland. Dorothea is a girl who has been brought up to think for herself. However, in the end she abdicates the right to equality and finds happiness as a wife and mother. She exploits her active spirit not in awakening discontent and rebellion, but in ameliorating the needs of the poor. Tells of a crowd preventing the execution of several rebels by seizing them from the scaffold, and once emboldened they forcibly attack the prison in Kilkenny to set free its inmates. Under the motto that 'the good things of the world are common stock', the crowd invades a house in the country, steal its contents, and murder the owners and their children [M.O. Grenby, *The anti-Jacobin novel*, pp 58–9; ML].

BULLOCK, John William (later called himself Shan Fadh; also known as **Shan Bullock** and **Shan F. Bullock**), b. Crom (RIA/DIB has 'Inisherk'; Co. Fermanagh) 1865, d. Cheam (Surrey) 1935. JWB was a novelist, story writer and poet whose father was a steward on the earl of Erne's estate and later became a full-time tenant farmer at Killynick, on the southern shore of Lough Erne. JWB received a strict, evangelical Protestant upbringing. He attended Farra School (Co. Westmeath) and went to London in 1883, where in rebellion against his father's harshness, he adopted the Gaelic version of John and added 'Fadh' (long, or tall) to his name and rejected presbyterianism in favour of anglicanism. In 1889 he married Emma Mitchell and they had a son and a daughter. He worked as a civil servant most of his life, supplementing his income with journalism. In all, we have identified 19 works of fiction, principally collections of short stories. Most of his novels are set in south-eastern Co. Fermanagh, in an area bounded by Belturbet, Clones, and Lisnaskea, with occasional excursions to Bundoran (Co. Donegal), and draw from his childhood memories. The stories explore the lives and hardships of small farmers and their families. He also wrote a play, completed Emily Lawless'§ *The race of Castlebar* (London, 1913), and published his autobiography, *After sixty years*, in 1931, which is described by author Benedict Kiely as the last description of a great estate produced by someone who had seen it before the Land War. JWB was a member of the Irish Academy of Letters, supported social reform in Ireland but was opposed to Home Rule, and while rejecting Orange sectarianism was equally against Irish nationalism. He wrote an account of his son in the First World War, *The making of a soldier* (London, 1916). For his portraits, see ODNB. Many of his papers are in the special collections of Queen's University, Belfast, including the unpublished novels 'Little Victorians' and 'Sheila passes' (see further in the ODNB). His portrait is in the Great Hall there. SOURCE Brady, p. 22; Brown, p. 44; EF, p. 49; Field Day, ii, pp 1023, 1217–18; J.W. Foster, *Forces and themes in Ulster fiction* (Dublin, 1974); Hogan 2, pp 197–8; P. Maume, 'The Papist minister: Shan Bullock, John Haughton Steele, and the literary portrayal of the nineteenth century clergyman' in L. Litvack & G. Hooper (eds.), *Ireland in the nineteenth century* (Dublin, 2000), pp 108–22; P. Maume (ed.), *The foundling by Shan Bullock and The margins of subsistence: The novels of Shan Bullock* (Enniskillen, n.d.), passim; Newmann, p. 27; OCIL, pp 69–70; ODNB; RIA/DIB; Sutherland, p. 92.

B403   *The awkward squads, and other stories* (by Shan F. Bullock).
    London, Paris, Melbourne: Cassell & Co., 1893. SOURCE Brown, 267. LOCATION L, NUC.
COMMENTARY Set at the borders of Cos. Cavan and Fermanagh, consists of four stories: 'The awkward squads', 'The white terror', 'A State official', 'One of the unfortunates' [Brown].

B404   *By Thrasna river. The story of a townland* (given by one John Farmer and edited by his friend Shan F. Bullock).
    + London, New York, Melbourne: Ward, Lock & Bowden, 1895 (ill. St Clair Simmons). SOURCE Brown, 268. LOCATION D, Dt, L, NUC.
COMMENTARY Semi-autobiographical novel. Story of fatally powerful forces in Co. Fermanagh: poverty, land-hunger, and an adverse climate. The Englishman Harry Thomson is driven off by the narrow-minded tenants of an estate for courting one of their daughters [Hogan; Brown; Leclaire, p. 191; Maume, *Margins*, pp 12–13].

B405   *Ring o' rushes* (by Shan F. Bullock; dedicated to Clement King Shorter [husband of Dora Mary Sigerson§]).
    + London, New York, Melbourne: Ward, Lock & Co., 1896 (ill.). SOURCE Topp 2, p. 361. LOCATION D, L, NUC, InND Loeber coll.
    New York: Stone & Kimball, 1896. LOCATION NUC.
    Chicago: Stone & Kimball, 1896 (as *Rogue Bartley*). SOURCE Kersnowski, p. 9. LOCATION NUC.

Chicago: Stone & Kimball, 1896 (as *The splendid shilling*). SOURCE Kersnowski, p. 9. LOCATION NUC.

COMMENTARY Many of these stories first appeared in various English magazines and are concerned with aspects of Ulster life in the neighbourhood of Lough Erne. Contents: 'His magnificence', 'They that mourn', 'The rival swains', 'They twain', 'Shan's diversion', 'Th' ould boy', 'Her soger boy', 'Rogue Bartley', 'The splendid shilling', 'The emigrant', 'The beggar's benefit' [RL; Brown].

B406   *The charmer. A seaside comedy* (by Shan F. Bullock).
       London: James Bowden, 1897 (ill. Bertha Newcombe). SOURCE Hogan, p. 130. LOCATION L, NUC.
       + London, New York: Harper & Bros, 1900 (ill. Bertha Newcombe). LOCATION DPL.

COMMENTARY A work of fiction, set in Kyle (Bundoran, Co. Donegal), and describing the awkwardness of holidaying farmers meeting English tourists [NUC; Maume, 'Papist minister', p. 108].

B407   *The Barrys* (by Shan F. Bullock; dedicated to A.T. Quiller-Couch).
       London: Methuen, 1899. SOURCE Brown, 270. LOCATION D (n.d. edn).
       + London, New York: Harper & Bros, 1899. LOCATION Dt, DPL, L.
       + New York: Doubleday & McClure, 1899. SOURCE Brown, 270. LOCATION NUC; InND Loeber coll.

COMMENTARY Frank Barry is on a visit from London to his uncle at Innishrath, an island in Lough Erne. While there he has a liaison with a peasant girl named Nan Butler. Frank returns to London. Nan follows him and finds out that he is already married. Frank's wife becomes aware of the affair. Nan returns to Ireland, where her faithful lover, Ted, is still waiting for her [Brown].

B408   *Irish pastorals* (by Shan F. Bullock; dedicated to Coulson Kernahan§).
       + London: Grant Richards, 1901 (ill.). SOURCE Brown, 271. LOCATION D, L.
       + New York: McClure, Phillips & Co., 1901 (ill.). SOURCE Brown, 271. LOCATION D, NUC, InND Loeber coll.

COMMENTARY Short stories set among the rural classes in Co. Cavan in which various rural activities are described. Contents: 'The planters', 'The turf-cutters', 'The mowers', 'The haymakers', 'The reapers', 'The diggers', 'The herd', 'Spotty', 'The brothers' [ML; Brown; Leclaire, p. 191].

B409   *The squireen* (by Shan F. Bullock).
       + London: Methuen & Co., 1903 (ill. with map). SOURCE Brown, 272 (1904 edn); Kersnowski, p. 9. LOCATION D (1904 edn), L, NUC.
       + New York: McClure, Phillips & Co., 1903. LOCATION D, NUC.

COMMENTARY Set among Ulster Protestants. Jane Fallon, who comes from a family of Orangemen, is pressed by them into marriage with a squireen, who is a spendthrift and a roué. After a long resistance she marries him, and he reforms. However, when their child dies, he descends into madness [Brown; EF, p. 49].

B410   *The red-leaguers* (by Shan F. Bullock).
       London: Methuen & Co., 1904 (ill.). SOURCE Brown, 273. LOCATION L, NUC.
       + New York: McClure, Phillips, 1904. SOURCE Brown, 273; Kersnowski, p. 9. LOCATION D.

COMMENTARY Set in Co. Fermanagh. A story of an imaginary rebellion against the English in which the Irish win and declare an Irish republic. Subsequently, in a very short time-span, the country is going to wreck and ruin. At the end of the story, English troops land in Ireland again, showing that the Irish could not manage by themselves [Brown].

B411 *Dan the Dollar* (by Shan F. Bullock).
  + Dublin: Maunsel & Co., [1905]. SOURCE Brown, 275 (1906 edn); Kersnowski, p. 9.
  LOCATION D, L ([1907] edn), NUC.
COMMENTARY Set on a farm in Co. Fermanagh. Describes five persons, one is the easy-going
Felix on his neglected farm, his wife, Mary Troy, a Catholic girl living with them, and a char-
acter called Felim. Dan the Dollar comes among them, after years of having worked in the
US [Brown; Leclaire, p. 192].

B412 *The cubs. The story of a friendship* (by Shan F. Bullock).
  + London: T. Werner Laurie, [1906]. SOURCE Brown, 274. LOCATION DPL, L, NUC.
COMMENTARY The story of life in an Irish school, possibly the author's old school at Thalma
(i.e., Farra, near Mullingar, Co. Westmeath). The story describes the development of a great
friendship between two boys [Brown; RIA/DIB].

B413 *Robert Thorne. The story of a London clerk* (by Shan F. Bullock).
  London: T. Werner Laurie, 1907. SOURCE Hogan, p. 129. LOCATION L, NUC.
COMMENTARY Semi-autobiographical novel, which contains an editorial introd. and numerous
footnotes. Sortie in Edwardian realism replete with documentary details of the lives, at desk
and hearth, of 'pen-drivers', emasculated drudges beset by poverty, duty, and routine. London
is displayed in all its misery. Thorne's deliverance at novel's end is by emigration to New
Zealand [Hogan; Maume, *Margins*, pp 12–13].

B414 *A laughing matter* (by Shan F. Bullock).
  + London: T. Werner Laurie, [1908]. SOURCE Brown, 276 (Murray edn); Kersnowski,
  p. 9. LOCATION D, L, NUC.
COMMENTARY The story is set in London but told by an Irish gardener who has come
to London to find his daughter [Brown].

B415 *Master John* (by Shan F. Bullock).
  London: T. Werner Laurie, [1909]. SOURCE Brown, 277. LOCATION L, NUC.
COMMENTARY Master John has worked his way up in the world and, when wealthy, settles in
Fermanagh. However, his new place has a curse on it and strange things happen [Brown].

B416 *Hetty. The story of an Ulster family* (by Shan F. Bullock).
  + London: T. Werner Laurie, [1911]. SOURCE Brown, 278. LOCATION D, L, NUC.
COMMENTARY Set in Co. Westmeath. A domestic story contrasting Hetty, a quiet and retiring girl, with her wilful, wayward younger sister. Hetty fancies herself as a New Woman and
flirts with the fiancé of her sister, but is eventually reabsorbed in the countryside through
marriage [Brown; Leclaire, p. 192; Maume, *Margins*, p. 12].

B417 *Mr. Ruby jumps the traces* (by Shan F. Bullock).
  London: Chapman & Hall, 1917. SOURCE Kersnowski, p. 9. LOCATION L.

B418 *The loughsiders* (by Shan F. Bullock; dedicated to author's brother Willie [Bullock]).
  + London, Calcutta, Sydney: George G. Harrap & Co., 1924. SOURCE Brown 2, 162;
  Kersnowski, p. 9. LOCATION D, L, NUC, InND Loeber coll.
  New York: L. Macveagh, 1924. LOCATION NUC.
COMMENTARY Set in Ulster and presents a picture of the countryside and reproduces the local
dialect. Richard Jebb is a small farmer, a returned American emigrant, age 40. He thinks it is
time to settle down and he bestows his attentions on Rachel Nixon. A misunderstanding sep-
arates them. Misfortune befalls the Nixon family and gives Richard a chance of proving him-
self a friend in need. The Nixon children emigrate and he secures the farm by marrying not
Rachel, but her mother, who is a compulsive shoplifter [Brown 2; Maume, *Margins*, p. 18;
OCIL, p. 317].

BULLOCK, Shan Fadh. See **BULLOCK, John William.**

BULWER LYTTON, Sir Edward George (created Baron Lytton of Knebworth in 1866) , b. 1803 or 1805, d. 1873. English writer and politician, EGBL married Rosina Anne Doyle Wheeler of Co. Limerick (see under Rosina Bulwer Lytton§) in 1827. At this time, possibly under the influence of his wife, he wrote an anonymous poem, *O'Neill; or, the rebel* (London, 1827), which he dedicated to her, and in the same year started writing chapters for a novel *Glenallan*, set in Ireland, which was never finished but which featured his wife as Ellen St Aubyn and himself as her hero. He visited Ireland in 1834 when he travelled to Limerick. His marriage was a disaster and the couple soon separated. He was a friend of Lady Blessington§, who stayed loyal to him in the face of his marital problems and he collaborated with her on her *The victims of society* (London, 1837, 3 vols.). SOURCE Allibone, i, p. 1151 [under Lytton]; Allibone Suppl., ii, p. 1031 [under Lytton]; Brown 2, 854; *The collection of autograph letters ... historical documents formed by Alfred Morrison* ([London], second series, 1882–93); *The Blessington papers* (n.l., 1895), p. 15; Cox cat. 48/29; DLB, xxi; ODNB [under Lytton]; IBL, 6 (1914), p. 80; NCBEL 4, pp 1144–60; M. Sadleir, *Bulwer: A panorama* (London 1931), passim; Sutherland, p. 388 [under Lytton]; T & B, p. 970.

BULWER LYTTON, Lady Rosina Doyle (née Wheeler; also known as **Lady Bulwer Lytton, Lady Lytton Bulwer**, and **Lady Lytton**), pseud. 'George Gordon Scott', b. Ballywire House (Co. Limerick) 1802 (and not 1794 as in Allibone), d. Kent 1882. Novelist and essayist, RDBL was the youngest daughter of Francis Massey-Wheeler, a landowner, and Anna Doyle, a feminist, who collaborated with William Thompson on *Appeal of one-half the human race, women against the pretensions of the other half* (London, 1825) and whose father was Revd Nicholas Milley Doyle. RDBL's father was an alcoholic and violent and her parents separated in 1812. Mrs Wheeler and her two daughters moved in with their relative, Sir John Doyle, the retired governor of Guernsey. Eventually they left to live in Caen in France, but RDBL, unable to endure conflicts with her mother, returned first to her uncle Doyle in London, and then moved in with her mother's brother, a clergyman living at Kilsallaghan (Co. Dublin). There she met Mary Greene, who would become her life-long friend and support, and whose diary chronicles the major upheavals of RDBL's life. She eventually settled in London where she mixed with a bohemian literary group that centred around Lord Byron's former lover, Lady Caroline Lamb§. In 1826 she claimed to have contributed text to Elizabeth Spence's§ *Dame Rebecca Berry; or, court scenes in the reign of Charles the Second* (London, 1827, 3 vols.). In the next year she married Edward George Bulwer Lytton§, whose mother cut off his allowance in disapproval of the alliance. Financial pressures and her husband's infidelities made it an unhappy marriage and a separation was signed in 1838. Her two children were forcibly taken from her. She fought back with bitter lawsuits and public defamation of her husband, who retaliated by having her briefly and illegally confined to an asylum. She started writing only after the separation, when her allowance proved inadequate to cover her expenses. Many of her novels fictionalize her marital distress and its aftermath and highlight the plight of unhappily-married and separated women. Early in life, RDBL had rejected her mother's feminist convictions, but in this phase of her life, she 'hardened into a permanent replica of her mother' (Sadleir, p. 76). She contributed to *Fraser's Magazine* (London) and she wrote a set of essays, *Shells from the sands of time* (London, 1876). Her library was auctioned in Aug., 1882. For her portraits, see ODNB. SOURCE Allibone, i, p. 1154 [under Lytton]; Allibone Suppl., ii, p. 1032 [under Lytton]; Blain, p. 680 [under Lytton]; Brady, p. 139; D. Dooley, *Equality in community. Sexual equality in the writings of William Thompson and Anna Doyle Wheeler* (Cork, 1996), pp 60–1; List of catalogues, p. 381; NCBEL 4, pp 1160–1; ODNB [under Lytton]; M. Sadleir, *Bulwer: a panorama* (London 1931); O'Toole, pp 128–9 [under Rosina Lytton], 309–11 [under Anna Weeler]; Sutherland, p. 93 [under Bulwer]; Todd, pp 109–11.

B419   *Cheveley; or, the man of honour* (by Lady Lytton Bulwer).
London: Edward Bull, 1839, 3 vols. SOURCE Hodgson, p. 349; NCBEL 3, p. 921 (states 3 edns); Wolff, 970. LOCATION L, NUC.
Paris: Baudry, 1839 (Baudry's European Library). LOCATION NUC.
+ New York: Harper & Bros, 1839, 2 vols. SOURCE Wolff, 970a. LOCATION NUC, InND Loeber coll. (vol. 2 only).
Calcutta: William Rushton & Co., 1839, 3 vols. in 1. LOCATION NUC.
COMMENTARY Partly autobiographical, the novel focuses on the unhappy marriage of the Cliffords. Lord De Clifford is portrayed as a brute, a fool and the ill-bred son of a vulgar harridan. His wife is pure, long-suffering and quite innocent in the passionate love which springs up between herself and Mowbray (later to be marquis of Cheveley). De Clifford has a 'predilection for governesses' and spawns a bastard by a village girl on the estate. He frames her father on a charge of stealing to keep him quiet during his election campaign. There is a complicated unravelling of the plot in which the husband-villain is killed falling from his horse [Sutherland, pp 119–20].

B420   *The budget of the Bubble family* (by Lady Bulwer Lytton; dedicated to Frances Trollope).
London: Edward Bull, 1840, 3 vols. SOURCE Hodgson, p. 349; Sadleir, 455; Wolff, 969. LOCATION L, NUC.
Paris: Baudry, 1840 (Baudry's European Library). LOCATION L, NUC.
New York: Harper & Bros, 1843, 2 vols. LOCATION NUC.

B421   *Bianca Cappello. An historical romance* (by Lady Bulwer Lytton).
London: Edward Bull, 1843, 3 vols. SOURCE Hodgson, p. 349; Sadleir, 454; Wolff, 968. LOCATION L, NUC.
+ New York: William H. Colyer, 1843. SOURCE Wolff, 968a. LOCATION InND Loeber coll.
New York: J. Winchester, 1843. LOCATION NUC.

B422   *Memoirs of a Muscovite* (ed. by Lady Bulwer Lytton).
London: T.C. Newby, 1844, 3 vols. SOURCE Hodgson, p. 349; Sadleir, 464. LOCATION L, NUC.
COMMENTARY A fantasy romance that ends in a happy marriage. It is unclear for whom Lady BL edited this novel [Todd, p. 110; RL].

B423   *The peer's daughters. A novel* (by Lady Bulwer Lytton).
London: T.C. Newby, 1849, 3 vols. SOURCE Hodgson, p. 349; Sadleir, 549. LOCATION L, NUC.
+ New York: Stringer & Townsend, 1850. SOURCE NUC. LOCATION InND Loeber coll.
COMMENTARY Historical fiction set among the aristocracy in France and England at the time of Madame de Pompadour [ML].

B424   *Miriam Sedley; or, the tares and the wheat. A tale of real life* (by Lady Bulwer Lytton).
London: W. Shoberl, 1851, 3 vols. SOURCE Hodgson, p. 349; NCBEL 3, p. 922; Sadleir, 458. LOCATION L, NUC.
COMMENTARY Largely autobiographical [Blain].

B425   *The school for husbands; or, Molière's life and times* (by Lady Bulwer Lytton).
London: Charles J. Skeet, 1852, 3 vols. SOURCE Sadleir, 460. LOCATION L, NUC.
+ London: Charles J. Skeet, 1854, 3 vols. (as *The school for husbands*). LOCATION InND Loeber coll.
Philadelphia: A. Hart, 1852. LOCATION NUC.

COMMENTARY Historical fiction consisting of a fictionalized life of the playwright Molière in which the author makes the 'tragedy' of his life heroic. Includes preface detailing Lady Bulwer Lytton's literary persecution by various publishers [ML; Todd, p. 110].

B426 *Behind the scenes. A novel* (by Lady Bulwer Lytton; dedicated to 'the great - and will be greater – American nation').
London: C.J. Skeet, 1854, 3 vols. SOURCE Sadleir, 453; Wolff, 967. LOCATION L, NUC.
+ New York: Riker, Thorne & Co., 1854, 3 vols. in 1. SOURCEs Wolff, 967a. LOCATION NUC, InND.
COMMENTARY The story is set in Scotland and London. A young heir to a Scottish estate dies just before coming of age. The estate is sold by the next heir, and the mother and Edith, sister of the deceased, are left without a home. They move to London to live with a relative, a pompous archdeacon. Edith leads a virtuous and withdrawn life but is continuously besieged with attention from a Mr Ponsonby Ferrars. He was her brother's friend at Cambridge and later became a celebrated author and politician. A large part of the book is devoted to showing what a base person Mr Ferrars is, having seduced and deserted several women. Edith escapes from his clutches, marries a duke, but contracts a fatal illness [ML].

B427 *Very successful!* (by Lady Bulwer Lytton).
London: Whittaker & Co.; F.R. Clarke; Taunton, Frederick B. Clarke, 1856. SOURCE Sadleir, 462; Wolff, 971; Topp 6, 132. LOCATION L.
COMMENTARY Due to the threat of legal action no second edn was issued as planned [Topp 6, 132].

B428 *The world and his wife; or, a person of consequence. A photographic novel* (by Lady Bulwer Lytton).
London: C.J. Skeet, 1858, 3 vols. SOURCE Sadleir, 463; Wolff, 972. LOCATION L.

B429 *The household fairy* (by the Lady Lytton; dedicated to 'every householder in Great Britain').
+ London: Hall & Co., 1870. SOURCE NCBEL 3, p. 922; Sadleir, 457. LOCATION L, NUC.
COMMENTARY A story praising the virtues of a well-run household [ML].

B430 *Clumber chase, or, love's riddle solved by a royal sphinx: a tale of the Restoration* (by 'George Gordon Scott').
London: T. Cautley Newby, 1871, 3 vols. SOURCE ODNB; COPAC. LOCATION L.
COMMENTARY An historical novel set in the late-seventeenth century [ODNB].
— UNCERTAIN WORKS

B431 *The prince-duke and the page. A historical novel* (ed. by Lady Bulwer Lytton).
London: T. & W. Boone, 1841, 3 vols. SOURCE Sadleir, 465. LOCATION L, NUC.
COMMENTARY Wolff is uncertain about RDBL's authorship, and it is unclear for whom Lady BL edited this novel [Wolff, i, p. 190; RL].

B432 *The man of the people* (by the author of *The prince-duke and the page*).
London: T.C. Newby, 1845, 3 vols. SOURCE Wolff, 973; OCLC. LOCATION TxU.
COMMENTARY For its authorship, see commentary under *The prince-duke and the page* [RL].

BUNBURY, Selina, b. Kilsaran Rectory, near Castlebellingham (Co. Louth) 1802, d. Cheltenham (Glos.) 1882. SB was one of fifteen children of Revd Henry Bunbury, a Church of Ireland clergyman (and not a Methodist as sometimes stated), and Henrietta Eleanor Shirley. Her mother was the daughter of Revd Walter Shirley, a brother of Earl Ferrers, and rector of Loughrea (Co. Galway). SB was named after her relative, Lady Selina Shirley, who later became the countess of Huntingdon. Through her father she descended from a landed gentry family in Co. Carlow. He was rector of Mansfieldstown (Co. Louth) from 1793 to 1815, after which he became treasurer of Ossory and the family moved to Beaulieu on the river Boyne. However, he went bankrupt in 1819 and as a consequence her mother and the children were forced to move to Dublin. There SB taught in a primary school and started writing in secret, against her mother's wishes. Eventually, she published at least 34 works of fiction and numerous tracts. Her first published work, *A visit to my birthplace* (Dublin, 1826), went through twelve edns during her lifetime. Her early works, published anonymously, were generally tales about Protestant society in Ireland. Unlike most Irish authors at that time, she published her books in Dublin. In the introd. to her *Coombe abbey* (Dublin, 1843), she took pride in seeing the book, illustrated by Irish artists, published in Dublin. (She may have undertaken this earlier than William Carleton§, who claimed this distinction.) From 1828 to 1830 SB edited the *Dublin Magazine*, to which she contributed 'Constance De Ceselli' and a serialized story 'Guy de Valence, an Albigensic tale' (1829). She also contributed stories to *Fraser's Magazine* (London), *Sharpe's London Magazine*, and the *Christian Lady's Magazine* (London). She often used Ireland as a backdrop for her religious fiction, which was strongly anti-Roman Catholic. Around 1830 the family moved to Liverpool where SB kept house for her twin brother, but she continued to publish in Dublin. She returned to Ireland (1842–3) to attend to her dying mother. After her brother's marriage in 1845, she began to travel in Europe recording her experiences in many volumes, including *Rides in the Pyrenees* (London, 1844); *A Visit to the catacombs* (London, 1849); *A summer in Northern Europe* (London, 1856); *Russia after the war* (London, 1857), and *My first travels* (London, 1859). Some of her travel stories are fictionalized, such as *Evelyn; or, a journey from Stockholm to Rome in 1847–48* (London, 1849), which also shows a strong awareness of female oppression. She also wrote juvenile fiction and biographies, including *Sketches in the life of Alfred the Great* (London, 1847). Many of her works are slim volumes, some of which were published by the Religious Tract Society and the Society for Promoting Christian Knowledge. Despite her industry, it is evident from her applications for financial support to the Royal Literary Fund that she was very poor in later life. In 1844 she stated that from age 17 onward she had supported her family (father, mother, brother and sister) by writing and had lost the use of her right arm due to the physical stress of writing, compelling her to use her left hand. The author Francis Edward Smedley organized a subscription volume to raise money for her. Entitled *Seven tales by seven authors* (London, 1849), it included a story 'The trust' by SB under the pseud. 'E.J.B.' Shortly before her death she contributed to *Leisure Hour* (London) and *Sunday at home* (London), and her last work *Lady Flora* (London, 1870, 2 vols.), was written when she was living in Kent in 1869. She died at Percy House, her nephew's home at Cheltenham and was buried in Cheltenham cemetery where a memorial was erected to commemorate her. Her portrait was published in the IBL (7 (1916), p. 104). Collections of her letters (some to William Carleton§) can be found among D.J. O'Donoghue's papers at UCD (LA15), among the publisher Gill's papers in TCD (MS 10,308), in the BL. She is not to be confused with Selina Bunbury, author of *Florence Sackville; or, self-dependence.* SOURCE Allibone, i, p. 282; Allibone Suppl., i, p. 247; Blain, pp 156–7; Brady, p. 23; BL, M 1077, reel 37, No. 1089; Brown, pp 46–7; Casey & Rowan, p. 186; Curran index, FM 2210; Field Day, v, pp 836, 838, 894; Hogan 2, p. 199; IBL, 7 (1916), pp 105–7; McKenna, pp 108–9; J.B. Leslie, *History of Kilsaran* (Dundalk, 1908), pp 236, 285, opp. p. 56; NCBEL 4, pp 1161–2; Personal communication, Jacqueline Belanger, Aug. 2000; OCIL, p. 70; ODNB; Rafroidi, ii, pp 82–4; RIA/DIB; Sutherland, p. 93.

B433   ***The burning bush*** [anon?].

> Edinburgh: [publisher?], 1825. SOURCE BL, Royal Literary Fund, Loan 96, 1089 (37); also advertised in *Tales of my country* (London, 1833) as mentioned in Wolff, i, p. 191.

COMMENTARY No copy located [RL].

B434   *Early recollections. A tale* [anon.] (dedicated to Christian parents).
    Edinburgh: William Oliphant, 1825. SOURCE Blain, p. 156. LOCATION L.
    COMMENTARY Religious fiction: tale about the importance of Eustace's early moral training [Blain].

B435   *A visit to my birth place* [anon.].
    Dublin: William Curry Jnr, 1826. SOURCE Brown, p. 46 (mistakenly mentions 1821 edn); IBL, 7 (1916), pp 105–6 (ditto). LOCATION D (1829, 3rd edn), O.
    London: George Routledge & Sons, 1863 (new edn). SOURCE COPAC. LOCATION C, InND Loeber coll. (n.d., 7th edn).
    Boston: J. Loring, [1828]. LOCATION MH, NUC.
COMMENTARY SB variously gave as date of publication of this work: 1820, 1821, 1824, 1825, and most often 1826. The IBL states that *A visit to my birthplace* was published in 1821 (No copy located). It passed through 11 edns during her lifetime. The story of a young English officer and his wife who move abroad where the officer's duties lie. A son is born to them. Over the course of their stay abroad, the wife finds consolation from all anxieties in religion, which she imparts to her son. The husband is not very interested in religion. After the husband is severely wounded and his wife has died, he returns to England. His son grows up with the wish to become a missionary, but dies just after his ordination. His father, touched by his son's faith, turns to the Lord and finds peace. The story is told by a friend and fellow missionary of the son, who visits his own birthplace and spends time at the grave of his friend [ML; Brown; BL, Royal Literary Fund, Loan 96, 1089 (37); IBL, 7 (1916)].

B436   *The pastor's tales* [anon.].
    + Edinburgh: William Oliphant, 1826. SOURCE British Fiction; Garside, 1826:22.
    LOCATION L, O.
    COMMENTARY 116pp. Religious fiction not set in Ireland [CM].

B437   *Cabin conversations and castle scenes. An Irish story* [anon.].
    + London: James Nisbet, 1827 (ill.). SOURCE Brown, 279; Rafroidi, ii, p. 82; British Fiction; Garside, 1827:19. LOCATION L.
COMMENTARY Religious fiction. Set in 1815 in the west of Ireland, and tells of the evils of popery and of efforts to convert Catholics to protestantism. Frontispiece shows a man returning from Dublin to the country bringing with him a parcel of books for the family to read [Brown; RL].

B438   *Annot and her pupil* [anon.].
    Edinburgh: William Oliphant, 1827. LOCATION L, O, NUC.
    + Edinburgh: W. Oliphant, 1830 (as *Annot and her pupil. A simple story*). SOURCE Falkner Greirson cat. 'Jane'/36; Rafroidi, ii, p. 82 (1830, 2nd edn). LOCATION L (1830, 2nd edn).
    Salem: Whipple & Lawrence, 1829. LOCATION NUC.
COMMENTARY Religious story set in Castle Harwood in Ireland where the orphan Annot Clive lives in the household of Mr Harwood and his Spanish wife. Annot, after a shipwreck, had grown up in the house of a Spanish family and had befriended the daughter Rosalba, who married Mr Harwood. Annot reads her Bible and loves the plain Irish parish church, but Mrs Harwood prefers the Roman Catholic faith. Alonzo, the Harwoods' son, attended by Annot, dies in the Protestant faith [BLC; RL].

B439   *Stories from church history; from the introduction of Christianity, to the sixteenth century* [anon.].
    + London: R.B. Seeley & W. Burnside, 1828 (ill.). LOCATION L, O.

COMMENTARY Religious fiction for juveniles written in response to earlier Christian histories [RL].

B440 *The abbey of Innismoyle: A story of another century* [anon.].

+ Dublin: W. Curry Jnr, 1828. SOURCE McKenna, p. 108; British Fiction; Garside, 1828:25. LOCATION Grail, Corvey CME 3–628–47001–3, Ireland related fiction, D, C, NUC, InND Loeber coll. (1829, 2nd edn).

Philadelphia: J.M. Campbell; New York: Sarton & Miles, 1845. LOCATION NUC.

COMMENTARY Religious fiction set in Ireland in the eighteenth century. The Raymonds, of Norman descent, have clung to their Catholic faith, despite punitive financial consequences. The daughter, Edith, is brought up along strict religious principles by a resident Jesuit priest. As she grows older, she begins to question the tenets of the Catholic church after she has been given a Bible by a consumptive Protestant curate. She keeps the Bible a secret. Her disobedience in religious matters escalates and her Catholic husband-to-be is called in by her parents and the priest. She rejects him and is locked in her rooms and threatened with transportation to a French convent. She falls ill and on her deathbed exhorts her mother to give up praying to the Virgin and the saints and to pray directly to Jesus Christ. At the end of the story the abbey of Innismoyle is in Protestant hands [ML; Burmester list].

B441 *My foster brother* [anon.].

+ Dublin: R.M. Tims; London: Houlston & Son; J. Nesbitt, Hatchard & Son; Edinburgh: Waugh & Innes; Glasgow: Chalmers & Collins, 1829. SOURCE Brown, 280; Rafroidi, ii, p. 82 (1833, 2nd edn); British Fiction; Garside, 1829:23. LOCATION Dt, L (1833, 2nd edn), InND Loeber coll.

COMMENTARY Religious fiction, set in Ireland. A boy converts his foster brother to protestantism. The foster brother then dies a pious death [Brown].

B442 *Retrospections; A soldier's story* [anon.].

+ Dublin: William Curry Jnr & Co., 1829 (ill. Kirkwood & Son). SOURCE Rafroidi, ii, p. 83; British Fiction; Garside, 1829:24. LOCATION Grail (1839 ed), L.

COMMENTARY Religious fiction, set in Spain [BLC; RL].

B443 *Gertrude and her family* [anon.].

+ Dublin: Richard Moore Tims, 1830. SOURCE Garside 2, 1830:32. LOCATION L.

COMMENTARY Religious fiction set in England [RL].

B444 *Laura Conyngham* [or Cunningham] [anon?].

Edinburgh: [publisher?], 1830.

COMMENTARY Note that this is based on SB's often faulty recollections (BL, Royal Literary Fund, Loan 96, 1089 (37)). No copy located [RL].

B445 *Eleanor* [anon.].

+ Dublin: W. Curry Jnr & Co., W. Carson, 1830. SOURCE Rafroidi, ii, p. 83; Garside 2, 1830:31. LOCATION Dt, L.

COMMENTARY Religious story of a Roman Catholic girl, who lives with her Protestant grandmother, and who is eventually converted. Title page states that the profits of this work are in part appropriated to the promotion of the Greek mission [BLC; RL; Garside 2, 1830:31].

B446 *Tales of my country* [anon.].

+ Dublin: William Curry Jnr & Co.; London: Simpkin & Marshall, 1833. SOURCE Brown, 282; Rafroidi, ii, p. 83; Wolff, 980; Garside 2, 1833:14. LOCATION Grail, D, Dt, DPL, L, O, InND.

COMMENTARY Contents: 'A visit at Clairville Park, including the story of Rose Mulroon' (set in Ireland in 1798), 'Eveleen O'Connor (entitled in index: 'An arrival at Moneyhaigue and the Doctor's story of Eveleen O'Connor'), 'A tale of Monan-a-Glena', 'Six weeks at the rectory' (entitled in index: 'Six weeks at the rectory, including the account of a parish history') [RL].

B447   *Recollections of Ireland* [anon.].
        + Dublin: William Curry Jnr & Co., 1839 (ill. L.A. Wheeler; see Plate 14). LOCATION
        D, InND Loeber coll.
COMMENTARY Religious short stories set in Ireland and written from the Protestant point of
view. Many of the stories first appeared in the *Christian Lady's Magazine* (London, 1835, ed.
by Elizabeth Tonna§), which also contains other stories not included in the book version (see
1840 volume of the magazine). Contents: 'The fatal funeral', 'The dying Romanist', 'The
contrast', 'The curate's wife', 'An invalid's excursion', 'The outcast', 'My early friends' [ML].

B448   *Stories of Alfred the Great* [anon.].
        Dublin: Browne, 1840. SOURCE Reviewed in *The Catholic Luminary* (Dublin, 1840), p.
        139.
COMMENTARY No copy located. Children's story about the Catholic king Alfred the Great.
Probably by SB, who published *Sketches in the life of Alfred the Great* in 1847 [RL].

B449   *Eily O'Connor: or, the foster brother* [anon.].
        London: J. Duncombe, [c.1840] (Dramatic Tales). SOURCE See COMMENTARY.
COMMENTARY Attributed. The correspondence with the Royal Literature Fund mentions
Eveleen O'Connor (London, 1849, 2 vols.), which had been first published in the *Cornhill
Magazine* (London). Also mentioned as *Eva O'Connor* and *Evaleen*. 'Eveleen O'Connor'
appeared as a short story in SB's *Tales of my country* (London, 1833) [BL, Royal Literary
Fund, Loan 96, 1089 (37); RL].

B450   *Coombe abbey. An historical tale of the reign of James the First* (by Selina Bunbury;
        dedicated to the Earl Craven, the owner of Coombe Abbey).
        + Dublin: William Curry Jnr & Co.; London: William S. Orr & Co.; Edinburgh:
        Fraser & Co., 1843 (ill. G.F. Sargent, Henning, J.C. Robinson, E. Evans, Hanlon).
        SOURCE Rafroidi, ii, p. 83; McKenna, p. 108; Sutherland, p. 93 (mistakenly mentions
        1844 as first edn). LOCATION Grail, L, InND Loeber coll. (1843 and 1844 edns).
        + Dublin: William Curry Jnr & Co., 1844 (ill. G.T. Sargent, Henning, Robinson,
        Fraser & Co., E. Evans). SOURCE Jarndyce cat. 151/51. LOCATION InND Loeber coll.
        COMMENTARY *Dublin 1844 edn* A reissue of the 1843 edn, but published in 15 parts
        [Jarndyce cat. 151/50].
        + London: Willoughby & Co., [1843] (on spine: Illustrated Standard Edition; title on
        spine: *Coombe abbey. A tale of Guy Fawkes*). LOCATION NUC; InND Loeber coll.
        London: Willoughby & Co.; Glasgow: R. Griffin & Co., [c.1850] (ill.). SOURCE Jarndyce
        cat. 151/51.
COMMENTARY Advertised as to be published shortly in parts by William Curry, Dublin, in
Mar. 1842 (Advertised in Part 3 of Lever's *Jack Hinton*), and again issued in 76 parts in
London (c.1850). The stereotype plates were purchased by Willoughby (Warwick Lane,
London), and were issued by him in penny weekly numbers. Written many years before its
publication date during a prolonged stay in Warwickshire. The story, set in England in the
early-seventeenth century, shows SB's predilection for historical religious fiction. SB states in
the introd. that 'I am in between two parties, one of which will think the book is not enough
of a novel, the other that it is too much so; – one, that I have appeared too friendly to Popery
– the other, that I have denounced either the system or its adherents, but suffered history to
tell its own tale, and carry its own moral'. Historical fiction set in England in the seventeenth
century at the time of the Gunpowder Plot and features the conspirator Guy Fawkes [RL;
Jarndyce cat. 151/51].

B451   *Interesting narratives* [anon.].
        Dublin: John Robertson, [1844 or earlier]. SOURCE OCLC; Advertised in [S. Martin],
        Sketches of Irish history (Dublin, 1844).

COMMENTARY No copy located. Contents as advertised: 'Story of Betsey', 'Broken pledge', 'Happy family', 'Captain and his crew' [RL].

B452 *Stories for children* (by the authors [*sic*] of *The invalid's hymn book*, *Pastoral annals*, *Visit to my birthplace*).
   Dublin: John Robertson, [1844 or earlier] (ill.). SOURCE Advertised in [S. Martin], *Sketches of Irish history* (Dublin, 1844).

COMMENTARY No copy located. Contents as advertised: 'Early roses', 'Lost day', 'Sunday school girl', 'Resignation', 'I never knew you', 'Say your prayers in fair weather', 'Way of the transgressor', 'Mary Calvert' [Advertised in [S. Martin], *Sketches of Irish history* (Dublin, 1844); RL].

B453 *The star of the court; or, the maid of honour and Queen of England, Anne Boleyn* (by Selina Bunbury).
   + London: Grant & Griffith, 1844 (ill.). SOURCE Rafroidi, ii, p. 83; McKenna, p. 108; Block, p. 29; Wolff, 978. LOCATION Grail, D, L, O, NUC.
   COMMENTARY Religious historical fiction about Anne Boleyn. The author's introd. is dated Nov. 1843 from the Hautes Pyrenées [RL].

B454 *The castle and the hovel; or, the two sceptics* (by Selina Bunbury).
   + London: B. Wertheim, Aldine Chambers, J. Masters, 1844. SOURCE Rafroidi, ii, p. 83. LOCATION L (1864 edn).

COMMENTARY Short story of religious fiction in which two sceptics, a Mr Parnell, living in a castle, and Judith, living in a hovel, are converted to protestantism [BLC; RL].

B455 *'I am so happy'* (by Selina Bunbury).
   + London: B. Wertheim & J. Masters, 1844. LOCATION O.
   COMMENTARY Religious fiction for children set in London [CM].

B456 *The blind girl of the moor, a shepherd's child* (by Selina Bunbury).
   + London: B. Wertheim, 1845. LOCATION O.
   COMMENTARY Set in Scotland [CM].

B457 *The Indian babes in the wood. Tales from fact* (by Selina Bunbury).
   + London: B. Wertheim, Aldine Chambers, [1845?]. SOURCE Alston, p. 56. LOCATION L.
   COMMENTARY Religious short story written for juveniles and based on a report in a missionary newspaper [BLC; RL].

B458 *Evenings in the Pyrenées; comprising the stories of wanderers from many lands* (ed. and arranged by Selina Bunbury).
   + London: J. Masters, 1845 (ill. McGahey, T.H. Jones, Oliver, J.N. Hulme, Anelay). SOURCE Rafroidi, ii, p. 83. LOCATION L, O, NUC, InND Loeber coll.

COMMENTARY Contents: 'La Donzelle; or the hunter of the Pyrenées and the fair Bearnaise', 'Hedwig. A simple Swedish story. By the count de B–', 'The courier's story of Mademoiselle Geraldine', 'The wolf-fight. A tale of Brittany', 'Souvenirs of the veteran of the Empire. A French story', 'The heiress of Morelands. An Irish history' (set in the north-east of Ireland) [RL].

B459 *The triumph of truth; or, Henry and his sister* (by Selina Bunbury).
   London: Religious Tract Society, [1846]. SOURCE Alston, p. 56; Rafroidi, ii, p. 84. LOCATION L ([1847], destroyed), O.
   COMMENTARY Religious fiction for children [BLC].

B460 *A happy new-year!* (by Selina Bunbury).
   + London: B. Wertheim, Aldine Chambers, [1847]. SOURCE NCBEL 4, p. 1161; NSTC. LOCATION O.
   COMMENTARY 28pp. Religious story centred around the new year. Includes a poem by one H.B. [RL].

B461 *Evelyn; or, a journey from Stockholm to Rome in 1847–48* (by Selina Bunbury).
London: Richard Bentley, 1849, 2 vols. SOURCE Rafroidi, ii, p. 84. LOCATION L, O, NUC.
COMMENTARY A novel-cum-travel book, describing a trip from Stockholm to Rome. Features Albert O'Donnell and his new wife Geraldine, who are Irish, and who plan to settle in Ireland [Sutherland; CM].

B462 *Fanny the flower girl; or, honesty rewarded* (by Selina Bunbury).
London: Wertheim & MacIntosh, [1850 or earlier]. SOURCE: Advertised in S. Bunbury, *The blind clergyman* (London, 1850).
Philadelphia: Presbyterian Board of Publication, n.d. LOCATION NUC.
+ New York: Hurst & Co., n.d. (as *Fanny the flower girl; or, honesty rewarded ... to which are added other tales*). LOCATION InND Loeber coll.
COMMENTARY No copy of the London edn located, which was priced at 6*d.* or in cloth at 1*s.* Contents of New York edn: 'Fanny, the flower-girl', 'Convenient food', 'The little pavior' [*sic*], 'The silver knife', 'The modern Dorcas', 'The tract found by the way-side' [RL; Advertised in S. Bunbury, *The blind clergyman* (London, 1850)].

B463 *The blind clergyman, and his little guide* (by Selina Bunbury).
+ London: Wertheim & Macintosh, 1850 (ill.). SOURCE Rafroidi, ii, p. 84 (mistakenly lists this as 'The blind man'). LOCATION L, O.
COMMENTARY 34pp. Religious fiction for children [BLC].

B464 *The little dumb boy. An Irish story* (by Selina Bunbury).
London: Wertheim & MacIntosh, [1850 or earlier]. SOURCE Advertised in S. Bunbury, *The blind clergyman* (London, 1850).
COMMENTARY No copy located. Priced at 2*d.* [RL; Advertised in S. Bunbury, *The blind clergyman* (London, 1850)].

B465 *The image-worshipper converted* (by Selina Bunbury).
London: Wertheim & MacIntosh, [1850 or earlier]. SOURCE Advertised in S. Bunbury, *The blind clergyman* (London, 1850).
COMMENTARY No copy located. Priced at 2*d.* [RL; Advertised in S. Bunbury, *The blind clergyman* (London, 1850)].

B466 *It is enough; or, trust in providence* (by Selina Bunbury).
London: Wertheim & MacIntosh, [1850 or earlier]. SOURCE Advertised in S. Bunbury, *The blind clergyman* (London, 1850).
COMMENTARY No copy located. Priced at 2*d.* [RL; Advertised in S. Bunbury, *The blind clergyman* (London, 1850)].

B467 *Victory to Jesus Christ; a missionary story* (by Selina Bunbury).
London: Wertheim & MacIntosh, [1850 or earlier]. SOURCE Advertised in S. Bunbury, *The blind clergyman* (London, 1850).
COMMENTARY No copy located. Priced at 2*d.* Also published as a chapbook (24pp) in Philadelphia in 1840 and 1850s [RL; Advertised in S. Bunbury, *The blind clergyman* (London, 1850); OCLC].

B468 *The brother's sacrifice. A French story* (by Selina Bunbury).
London: Wertheim & MacIntosh, [1850 or earlier]. SOURCE Advertised in S. Bunbury, *The blind clergyman* (London, 1850).
+ London: J. Masters, [*c.*1851] (new edn; ill.). SOURCE Alston, p. 55. LOCATION L.
COMMENTARY No copy of the earliest edn located. Religious fiction consisting of a short story. Priced at 2*d.* [RL; Advertised in S. Bunbury, *The blind clergyman* (London, 1850)].

B469 *Little Dora Playfair; or, 'I won't go to school'* (by Selina Bunbury).

London: Society for Promoting Christian Knowledge, 1851. LOCATION L.

B470 *Stories for schools* (by Selina Bunbury).
London: Society for Promoting Christian Knowledge, 1851–53, 4 parts. LOCATION L.

B471 *Glory, glory, glory. A story for children* (by Selina Bunbury).
London: Houlston & Stoneman: [1855?]. SOURCE RLIN. LOCATION L (destroyed), Rutgers Univ. (1856 edn).
COMMENTARY 47pp [RL].

B472 *Our own story; or, the history of Magdelene and Basil St. Pierre* (by Selina Bunbury; dedicated to Colonel and Lady Louisa Tighe).
+ London: Hurst & Blackett, 1856, 3 vols. SOURCE Rafroidi, ii, p. 84; Wolff, 977. LOCATION L, NUC.
COMMENTARY Set on an estate in Ireland, a first-person narrative by a girl who, given the same education as her twin brother, moves to London and grows up to be a writer. When her fiancée forbids writing after marriage, she says 'Then I must have my book edited, if I can have no name'. Part of the story deals with religious controversy in the Church of England [Blain; ML].

B473 *The lost one found* (by Selina Bunbury).
London: J. Masters, 1856. SOURCE Alston, p. 56. LOCATION L (destroyed), O.
COMMENTARY Religious fiction [O cat.].

B474 *Silent John; or, the picture of the good shepherd expounded* (by Selina Bunbury).
London: Joseph Masters, 1856. LOCATION L.
COMMENTARY Silent John, under the guidance of a minister, dies a Christian [ML].

B475 *Little Mary, or the captain's gold ring* (by Selina Bunbury).
London: Joseph Masters, 1857. SOURCE NCBEL 4, p. 1162. LOCATION L, O.

B476 *Sir Guy d'Esterre* (by Selina Bunbury).
+ London, New York: George Routledge & Co., 1858, 2 vols. SOURCE Brown, 283; Rafroidi, ii, p. 74. LOCATION L, O, NUC.
Dublin: McGlashan & Gill, 1874, 2 vols. in 1. LOCATION NUC.
COMMENTARY Historical fiction. Sir Guy is a young soldier in the service of Sir Philip Sidney, and later of Essex. In Ireland Sir Guy is captured and taken to the castle of the O'Connors. Here he falls in love. His enemies cause him to be thrown in to the Tower. He is released by Essex and goes with him to Ireland on Essex's fatal campaign [Brown].

B477 *Edward, the infant-school boy* (by Selina Bunbury).
London: J.F. Shaw, [1860]. LOCATION L.

B478 *The good name and the bad name* (by Selina Bunbury).
+ London: Society for Promoting Christian Knowledge, [1860?] (ill.). LOCATION InND Loeber coll.
COMMENTARY 36pp. Set in England. Orphan Kate Thorndike herds cattle on the Downs, where she frequently reads her Bible. She befriends Walter Tyrell who comes from a bad family. Kate convinces Walter to work to earn a good name. When Walter leaves, Kate gives him her Bible and some money. After several years he returns from sea, a respected man. They marry, and Walter is offered a position on a demesne where they live happily [ML].

B479 *Madame Constance, the autobiography of a French-woman in England* (ed. by Selina Bunbury).
London: Thomas Cautley Newby, 1861, 2 vols. SOURCE Rafroidi, ii, p. 84. LOCATION Grail, D, L, O.
COMMENTARY Biography in the form of a novel, 're-written' by Selina Bunbury from Madame Constance's autobiography [RL].

B480 *Tales. The recovered estate. The blind curate's child. Christmas eve in the forests of Sweden* (by Selina Bunbury).
+ London: Rivington; Oxford: W.R. Bowden, [1862], 2 issues. SOURCE McKenna, p. 109; Alston, p. 56. LOCATION L, O, C, NUC.
COMMENTARY Religious fiction. Contents: 'The recovered estate', 'The blind curate's child', 'Christmas eve in the fir forests of Sweden'. The first story first appeared separately as a reward book in London in 1863 [BLC; RL].

B481 *Florence Manvers* (by Selina Bunbury).
London: T.C. Newby, 1865, 3 vols. SOURCE Rafroidi, ii, p. 84; Wolff, 975. LOCATION L, O.

B482 *Lady Flora; or, the events of a winter in Sweden, and a summer in Rome, in the years 1846 and 1847* (by Selina Bunbury).
+ London: T. Cautley Newby, 1870, 2 vols. SOURCE Alston, p. 56. LOCATION L, O, NUC. COMMENTARY According to the preface, this work consists of a 'compilation of memories ...' [RL].

B483 *The smuggler's cave* (by Selina Bunbury).
+ London: Religious Tract Society, [1897] (ill.). SOURCE Alston, p. 56. LOCATION L (destroyed), O.
COMMENTARY Published posthumously. Religious fiction set in Ireland based on a narrow escape SB and her brother had from drowning while boating at the mouth of the river Boyne [RL; IBL, 7 (1916), p. 105].

SPURIOUS WORK

B484 *My early adventures during the Peninsular campaign of Napoleon* ('by the author of *A visit to my birth place*, and *Abbey of Innismoyle*').
Boston: J. Loring, 1834. SOURCE RLIN. LOCATION NN.
COMMENTARY This is almost certainly not by SB [RL].

BUNN, Anna Maria (née Murray), pseud. **'An Australian'**, b. Balliston, Co. Limerick 1808, d. St Omer, near Braidwood, New South Wales (Australia) 1889. Author of a single novel, AMB was the only daughter of Terence Murray, an army officer, and Ellen Fitzgerald. Following her mother's death in 1814, she was sent to the Ursuline Convent, Cork, and later attended a private school in Limerick. She and her father and brother emigrated to Australia and arrived at Sydney in 1827. In the following year she married George Bunn, a ship-owner and whaler. According to the ODNB , she was 'the first woman to publish a novel in Australia', and her *The guardian* (Sidney [sic], 1838) was the second novel to appear in Australia. For her portraits, see ODNB. Many of her letters, along with her paintings of plants and insects, are in the National Library of Australia. SOURCE ADB, ii [included in entry for her brother, politician Terence Aubrey Murray]; Blain, p. 157; Personal communication, Sr Ursula (Clarke), Ursuline Convent, Blackrock (Co. Dublin), Jan. 1998; ODNB; G. Wilson, *Murray of Yarralumla* (Melbourne, 1968).

B485 *The guardian. A tale* (by 'An Australian').
Sidney [sic]: J. Spillsbury, 1838. SOURCE C.H. Hadgraft, *Australian literature* (London, 1960), p. 12; Miller, i, p. 398; RLIN. LOCATION National Library of Australia.
Canberra: Mulini Press, 1994 (introd. by Elizabeth Webby). SOURCE ODNB. LOCATION National Library of Australia.
COMMENTARY Set in the west of Ireland during the first three decades of the nineteenth century, a story of the misfortunes that beset the heroine, Jessie Errol, born out of wedlock, who believes she has unknowingly married her half-brother, Francis Gambier. To ensure that a murder she has inadvertently mentioned will not be revealed, an old woman tells Jessie that

she and her husband had the same father. This drives Jessie distracted, and she drops her infant son down a cliff and then follows him into the sea [Hadgraft, pp 12–13; Miller, i, p. 398].

BURGESS, Joseph Tom, b. Cheshunt (Herts.) 1828, d. Leamington (War.) 1866. English author and journalist, JBB wrote a lot about Warwickshire. The details in the following volume attest that the author visited Ireland. SOURCE Allibone Suppl., i, p. 250; BLC; DNB; Davidson cat. 29/115.

B486 *Harry Hope's holidays: What he saw, what he did, and what he learnt during a year's rambles in country places* (by Joseph Tom Burgess).

London, New York: George Routledge & Sons, [1871] (ill.). SOURCE Davidson cat. 29/115 ; COPAC. LOCATION L.

COMMENTARY Children's book containing two chapters regarding Ireland. Includes a landing at Waterford, a visit to the copper mine at Knockmahon, and a description of the wreck of 'The Selim of Beyrout' off the coast of Wexford [Davidson cat. 29/115].

BURKE, John, fl. 1881. A fiction writer who may be the same person who translated *The fable of Phoedrus* (Dublin, 1881). This JB is probably a different person than Sir John Bernard Burke, son the genealogist John Burke, who was his father's assistant and co-author and who became Ulster king-of-arms in Ireland. SOURCE Allibone Suppl., i, p. 252; DNB [for the Burke genealogists]; O'Donoghue, p. 47.

B487 *Carrigaholt. A tale of eighty years ago* (by John Burke).

+ Dublin: Hodges Figgis; London: Simpkin, Marshall & Co., 1885. SOURCE Allibone Suppl., i, p. 252; Brown, 285; Topp 8, 723. LOCATION D, L, NUC.

COMMENTARY Set in the south-west of Ireland in the beginning of the nineteenth century and describes a good-natured but spendthrift landlord, young ladies who have been 'finished' in Belgium, and young men of leisure whose lives revolve around sport and girls. A scapegrace youth narrowly escapes being hanged for forgery [Brown].

BURKE, Oliver Joseph, b. Galway 1825 or 1826, d. Dublin 1889. Catholic barrister, historian, biographer and juvenile fiction writer, OJB was the second son of Joseph Burke of Ower, Headford (Co. Galway) and Margaret Martyn. He was admitted to Gray's Inn (London) in 1843, to the King's Inns (Dublin) in 1854, was called to the Irish Bar that year, when he also graduated BA at TCD, and became a land commissioner. He kept a residence at Ower during the 1880s. Aside from the following work of fiction, he was the author of two topographical works: *The abbey of Ross, its history and details* (Dublin, 1869), and *The south isles of Aran, Co. Galway* (London, 1887); two works relating to the law: *The history of the Lord Chancellors of Ireland* (Dublin, 1879), and the *Anecdotes of the Connaught circuit* (Dublin, 1885). In addition, he wrote among other works, *The history of the Catholic archbishops of Tuam* (Dublin, 1882). At the end of his life he lived at Lower Baggot Street, Dublin. After his death, his library was sold in Dublin. SOURCE Allibone Suppl., i, p. 252; B & S, p. 115; Boase, iv, p. 546; *Catalogue of the libraries of the late Oliver J. Burke, etc.* (Dublin, 1889); COPAC; OCLC; Galway, pp 10–11; Keane, p. 63; RL.

B488 *The bridegroom of Barna* [anon.].

New York, Boston, Montreal: D. & J. Sadlier & Co., 1870. SOURCE Brown, 10 (1884 edn); OCLC (1884 edn). LOCATION NUC.

COMMENTARY 80pp. Author identified from the 1884 edn as Oliver J. Burke. Reprinted from *Tales from "Blackwood"* (Edinburgh, xii [1861]). Fiction for juveniles set in Co. Tipperary near Ballymore. Lawlor, a bridegroom, ill-treats a tramp who then tells the authorities about a murder committed by Lawlor years earlier. The bride dies of a broken heart, and in the end Lawlor is arrested at his wife's grave, but shoots the informer [Brown; NUC; OCLC].

BURKE, Ulick Ralph. b. Milltown (Co. Dublin), 1845, d. en route to Lima (Peru) 1895. Lawyer, novelist, historian and Spanish scholar, URB was the eldest son of Charles Granby Burke, who was master of the court of common pleas, and Emma Jane Crayke of Yorkshire. He was educated at TCD, where he graduated BA in 1873. He was admitted to the King's Inns in the next year and he was called to the Bar at the Middle Temple (London) in 1870. His lifelong interest in Spanish language, literature and history began after a tour to Spain and he published after his return a collection of the proverbs of Don Quixote and in 1872 a collection of Sancho Panza's proverbs, translated and annotated (reprinted in 1877 as *Spanish salt*). URB practiced as a barrister in the Northwest Provinces high court, India (1873–8), and in Cyprus (1885–9). He published works on Spanish and Mexican history and on Brazil. His *History of Spain from the earliest times to the death of Ferdinand the Catholic* appeared in 1895. He was clerk of the peace in Co. Dublin (1886–95). He was appointed agent-general to the Peruvian Corporation in 1895 and was on his way to Peru when he became ill and died on board ship. Brown wrongly ascribed *Couleur de rose. A novel* (London, 1884, 2 vols.) to URB, which in fact was written by Ulick John Burke, possibly a relative. SOURCE Allibone Suppl., i, p. 252; B & S, p. 32; Boase, iv, p. 546; Keane, p. 63; ODNB; E. Reilly, p. 242; RIA/DIB; Wolff, i, p. 192.

B489   *Beating the air* (by Ulick Ralph Burke).
    London: Chapman & Hall, 1879, 3 vols. SOURCE Wolff, 988. LOCATION L, NUC.
B490   *Loyal and lawless* (by Ulick Ralph Burke).
    + London: Chapman & Hall, 1880, 2 vols. SOURCE Brown, 286. LOCATION D, L.
COMMENTARY Describes the matrimonial affairs of a number of titled persons. The novel is anti-Catholic and anti-Irish in viewpoint and denounces Fenianism and priests [Brown].

BURNABY, Frederick Gustavus, b. Bedford (Beds.) 1842, d. Khartoum (Sudan) 1885. English military man, novelist, journalist and travel writer, FGB was educated at Harrow and at age 16 became the youngest cornet in the army. John Churchill found him a 'gentle-voiced, amiable man, notwithstanding an enormous frame and gigantic strength' (Waller, p. 433n.4). He was known for his feats of strength and by 1881 was colonel of his regiment. His family's wealth enabled him to travel, and his natural abilities as a linguist enhanced his work as a *Times* correspondent in Spain, Russia, and throughout Europe while on leave from the army. His *A ride to Khiva, or On horseback through Asia Minor*, (London, 1876) warned of Russian expansion through central Asia towards India and made him a minor celebrity. He joined the Irish-born Gen. Garnet Wolseley in the Sudan in the effort to relieve Gen. Gordon at Khartoum and died in battle there. SOURCE Allibone Suppl., i, p. 253; ODNB; J.H. Waller, *Gordon of Khartoum* (New York, 1988), pp 177–8, 389, 424–5; Wolff, i, p. 193.

B491   *Our radicals. A tale of love and politics* (by Frederick Gustavus Burnaby; published posthumously, with a preface, by his private secretary, J. Percival Hughes).
    + London: Richard Bentley & Son, 1886, 2 vols. SOURCE Wolff, 991 (1886, 1 vol. edn).
    LOCATION D, L, NUC; InND Loeber coll. (vol. 2 only).
    New York: Harper & Bros, 1886. LOCATION NUC.
COMMENTARY Concerns world-wide politics and the Fenians, who are planning to destroy a tunnel connecting Ireland and England. The sentiment is expressed that Ireland as a country should be taken over by the US [ML].

BURN, Jacob Henry. Editor. See AMORY, Thomas.

BURTCHAELL, Emily, b. Kilkenny 1817, d. 1890. A short story writer, she may be identified with Elizabeth Emily, third daughter of Peter Burtchaell, county surveyor of Kilkenny and Carlow, and Maria Isabella Foot, and granddaughter of David Burtchaell of Brandondale, Graignamanagh (Co. Kilkenny). SOURCE Brown 2, p. 34; Landed gentry, 1912, p. 89.

B492   *Sacrificed and other tales* (by Emily Burtchaell).
        + Kilkenny: Coyle Bros, 1873. SOURCE Brown 2, 165. LOCATION D.
COMMENTARY Contents: 'Sacrifice' (story told at a picnic party at Howth, Co. Dublin), 'The haunted forge' (set in the Mount Leinster district of Co. Carlow), 'A London story' [Brown 2].

BURTON, Revd Nathaniel Judson (also known as Nathaniel Burton), b. Co. Clare *c*.1794. Church of Ireland minister, convert, and fiction writer, NJB was the son of Edward Burton, gentleman. He was educated at TCD where graduated BA in 1814, and LLB and LLD in 1829. According to *Battersby's Registry for the Catholic World, or the complete Catholic Directory, Almanac, and Registry for 1847* (Dublin, 1847), 'On Friday 5th May (1846) the Rev. N. Burton D.D. the Protestant Chaplain of the Royal Hospital, near Kilmainham, and formerly of St Paul's Church, Dublin, made his abjuration of the Protestant form of worship, and his formal profession of the Catholic Faith, in the Church of Jesus, St Francis Xavier, Upper Gardiner St.' (p. 306). Aside from the following work of fiction, he was also the author of *History of the Royal Hospital, Kilmainham* (Dublin, 1843). Eventually, he retired to Mount Argus (Co. Dublin), where he died. Brown 2 mistakenly identifies NJB as an American cleric and writer who was a Congregational minister of Hartfield [*sic*] (CT) and lectured on preaching at Yale. SOURCE Allibone Suppl., i, p. 260; B & S, p. 119; Brown 2, p. 34; DAB; Hodgson, p. 86; de Búrca cat. 75/58.

B493   *Oxmantown and its environs; or, some suburban sketches of the eighteenth century* [anon.].
        + Dublin: T. O'Gorman, 1845 (ill.). SOURCE Brown 2, 166. LOCATION D, DPL (Dix coll., Gilbert coll.).
COMMENTARY Despite the title, this is a story that centres on the family of Mr and Mrs Crofts and their daughter Henrietta. A wastrel named Knockeade (alias Cuffe) tries to force his attention on the daughter. On one occasion she is rescued by Sir Marcus Somers, who afterwards marries her. Meanwhile Knockeade goes from bad to worse and ends by committing a horrible murder [Brown 2].

BURY, Lady Charlotte Susan Maria (née Campbell), b. London 1775, d. London 1861. English novelist, poet and diarist, CSMB was the youngest daughter of John Campbell, 5th duke of Argyll, and Elizabeth Gunning of Castle Coote (Co. Roscommon). She was married first to her cousin, Col. John Campbell, and later to Revd Edward John Bury, an Anglican clergyman and her children's tutor. Her first poems were published anonymously in 1797. She was appointed lady-in-waiting to the princess of Wales, later Queen Caroline, in 1810 and began to keep a diary of her time at court. An intimate account of the royal family and the literary and political figures of the day, she published it anonymously as a *Diary Illustrative of the Times of George IV* in 1838. Financial constraints throughout her life led her to write and she published over a dozen novels, some of which became very popular. *Self-indulgence* (Edinburgh, 1812, 2 vols.) is her only novel with Irish content. SOURCE Allibone, i, p. 308; Blain, pp 162–3; DLB, cxvi; NCBEL 4, p, 891; ODNB; Wolff, pp 195–6.

B494   *Self-indulgence; a tale of the nineteenth century* [anon.].
+ Edinburgh: G.R. Clarke; London: Longman, Hurst, Rees, Orme & Brown, 1812, 2 vols. SOURCE British Fiction; Garside, 1812:25; Wolff, 101bb4. LOCATION InND Loeber coll. (vol. 1 only).

COMMENTARY Lord Donneraile [*sic*] and his wife and son live in London, but have to sell their house and possibly return to their Irish estate. When the son turns twenty-one he goes to Paris and witnesses the political unrest there [ML].

BUSTEED, N. William, b. Ireland 1814, d. New York 1872. Novelist, NWB was buried in Greenwood cemetery, Brooklyn (NY). Possibly he was a member of the Busteed family of Co. Cork, who in the eighteenth century had an estate at Kilvocry. SOURCE B & S, p. 121; Dime novels; HIP, iii, p. 338; E. MacLysaght, *The surnames of Ireland* (Dublin, 1973), p. 31.

B495   *King Barnaby: or, The maidens of the forest. A romance of the Mickmacks* (by N. William Busteed).
New York: Beadle, 1861 (Beadle's Dime Novels, No. 28). SOURCE OCLC; Dime novels. LOCATION NNC.
New York: Beadle, 1884 (as *The Indian king: or, The maidens of the forest*; Beadle's Pocket Novels, No. 263). SOURCE OCLC; Dime novels. LOCATION NNC.

BUTLER, Lt.–Col. —. See BUTLER, Gen. Sir William Francis.

BUTLER, A., fl. 1886. Story writer AB perhaps can be identified with the Irish-American author Revd Thomas Ambrose Butler (b. Dublin 1837, d. St Louis [MO] 1897) who lived in Kansas, contributed to a wide variety of periodicals and published a collection of poetry, *The Irish on the prairies, and other poems* (New York, 1874). SOURCE Irish pseudonyms; O'Donoghue, p. 51.

B496   *Shamrock leaves: Cead mile failte* (by A. Butler).
Dublin: Sealy, Bryers & Walker, 1886. SOURCE Brown, 289; COPAC. LOCATION Univ. of Manchester.

COMMENTARY Stories presumably founded on fact. Contents (excluding poem): 'Abbey-Brien', 'A noble sacrifice', 'A night adventure', 'The pieon's [*sic*] castle', 'A memorable night' [Brown; COPAC].

BUTLER, Josephine Elizabeth (née Grey), pseud. 'M.T.C.', b. Glendale (Northd.) 1828, d. Wooler (Northd.) 1906. English political activist, social reformer and religious writer, JEB was the daughter of a radical agricultural reformer. In 1852 she married George Butler, an educationalist and ecclesiastic. She established the Ladies' National Association for the Repeal of the Contagious Diseases Acts, branches of which were formed in Ireland in 1871, and worked for women's issues such as health and education. An annotation in the NLI copy of the following book identified JEB as its author. Among her other books is *Our Christianity tested by the Irish question* (London, [1887]). SOURCE Allibone Suppl., i, pp 264–5; Blain, pp 163–4; BLC; DLB, cxc; Field Day, iv, pp 876–7, 894; NCBEL 4, pp 2216–18; ODNB; RL.

B497   *The hour before dawn. An appeal to men* [anon.].
London: Trübner & Co., 1876 (Published for the Social Purity Alliance). SOURCE NCBEL 4, p. 2217. LOCATION L.
+ Dublin: John Mullany, 1878 (by 'M.T.C.'; as *The hour before day. A tale*). LOCATION D.

COMMENTARY Set in Ireland. The main female character plans to enter a convent to free her fiancée to make a more advantageous marriage. Eventually, the lovers are united [ML].

BUTLER, Mary. See BUTLER, Mary E.L.

BUTLER, Mary E.L. (later Mrs Thomas O'Nowlan; also known as **Mary Butler**), b. Co. Clare 1874, d. Rome (Italy) 1919 (1920 according to O'Toole). Novelist and short story writer, MELB was the daughter of Peter Lambert Butler, granddaughter of William Butler of Bunnahow (Co. Clare) and cousin of Sir Edward Carson, the barrister who defended Oscar Wilde§ and who later became the leader of the Irish Unionist Parliamentary Party. She was educated privately and at Alexandra College (Dublin) and learned Irish on the Aran Islands. She edited a women's page in the *Irish Weekly Independent* (Dublin, 1889–1903). She married in 1907 Thomas O'Nowlan, professor of classics and Irish at UCD and at Maynooth. They lived in Dublin. She was an enthusiastic member of the Gaelic League and was active in the women's movement. She established a conference of writers in 1913 to consider publication practices, such as minimum payment for the publication of serials in newspapers. An unpublished account of her life is in the NLI. It includes Arthur Griffith's acknowledgment of MELB's naming of the political party Sinn Féin (Butler Papers, MS 7,321). SOURCE Brown, p. 48; O'Toole, p. 28; E. Reilly, pp 222–4, 242; RIA/DIB.

B498   *A bundle of rushes* (by Mary E.L. Butler; dedicated to author's mother).
+ Dublin: Sealy, Bryers & Walker, 1900. SOURCE Brown, 290 (mistakenly identified a 1899 edn, but preface is dated 1900). LOCATION D, NUC, InND Loeber coll.
COMMENTARY Stories mainly set in Ireland. Contents: 'The three caskets', 'The two gardeners', 'The perfect gift', 'Tír na n-óg', 'Maelcho's quest', 'The song of the bard', 'At the Galway races', 'Noreen', 'A judgment in the Court of Appeal', 'A priceless possession', 'The man from the North', 'A courtship in Clare', 'The letter from the States', 'A good rest', 'Cécile' [ML].

B499   *The ring of day* (by Mary Butler).
London: Hutchinson & Co., 1906. SOURCE Brown, 291; COPAC. LOCATION L.
COMMENTARY This novel, a romantic story centred around the aspirations of the 'Irish Ireland' movement, received very mixed reviews in the *World*, the *Times*, the *Dublin Evening Mail* and *Sinn Féin*. The manuscript is in the NLI (Butler Papers, MS 8,323) [Brown; E. Reilly, pp 222–3].

BUTLER, Lady Rachel Evelyn (née Russell; known as **Lady Rachel Butler**), b. 1826, d. 1898. An English historical novelist, REB was the daughter of the 6th duke of Bedford. In 1856 she married Capt. Lord James Wandesford Butler, son of the 19th earl and 1st marquess of Ormonde, with whom she had four children. Her husband was state steward to the lord lieutenant of Ireland from 1867 to 1868. REB and her husband must have lived in Ireland before that since her introd. to the following book is dated Oct. 1862 from Drumcondra Castle (Dublin), where her husband had a small estate. SOURCE Allibone Suppl., i, p. 265; Burke, 1878, p. 926; Wolff, i, p. 197.

B500   *The prophecy* (by Lady Rachel Butler; dedicated to Lord Clermont, author's brother-in-law).
+ London: Richard Bentley, 1862, 2 vols. SOURCE Wolff, 1018; Brown 2, 167 (1863 edn); COPAC. LOCATION D, L, NUC, InND Loeber coll.
COMMENTARY Historical fiction consisting of family story of the Butlers of Kilkenny said to be founded on a manuscript discovered in Brussels in the year 1822 by the earl of Clancarty and subsequently transferred to Kilkenny Castle. The story tells how the black earl of Ormonde foretold the reverse of the family fortunes and their restoration by one Jimmy Butler of Kilcash, and how things turned out as prophesied when in the early-seventeenth century King James I gave away the family estates to Sir Richard Preston. Lord Walter Butler and his grandson, Lord Thurles (the Jimmy Butler of the prophesy) experience the ups-and-downs of fortune

until the latter elopes with his cousin, Lady Elizabeth Preston. The scene for the most part is set in England, but there are many allusions to Kilkenny, Callan, Carrick, etc. A retainer of King James I and a follower of the house of Ormonde play important roles [Brown 2; ML].

BUTLER, Mrs Sarah, fl.1716, d.1735? Historical fiction writer, SB can perhaps be identified with the Sarah Butler whose husband, Capt. James Butler, was killed at the battle of Aughrim (1691) during the Williamite War, and whose three sons died in subsequent wars. However, historical research on officers of King William III's army has failed to identify this Capt. James Butler. William III granted her an allowance of £30 per annum, which ceased when the king died in 1702. Two years later she petitioned Queen Anne for relief, particularly since she was incarcerated in Marshalsea prison because of a debt. Two years after that she still was in prison and she petitioned again so that she could return to 'her country' [i.e., Ireland], repeating the above, but also stating that her daughter had been murdered before her eyes; that she escaped with wounds; that her house was burned and that she was left with two grandchildren and no income. The Sarah Butler who wrote *Irish tales* ... is said to have been dead when the shady Edmund Curll published the book as hers, which would nullify the date of death suggested in OCIL. SOURCE Blain, pp 164–5; Field Day, v, pp 773, 775*n*, 830; Historical Manuscript Commission, *Portland*, VIII, pp 323, 345 (we are indebted to Joep Leerssen for drawing attention to this reference); OCIL, p. 74; Personal communication, Harman Murtagh, Oct. 2004; RIA/DIB; RL; I.C. Ross, '"One of the principal nations in Europe": The representation of Ireland in Sarah Butler's *Irish tales*', *Eighteenth-century fiction*, vol. 7, no. 1 (Oct. 1994), pp 1–16.

B501   *Irish tales; or, instructive histories for the happy conduct of life. Containing the following events. Viz. I. The captivated monarch. II. The banish'd prince. III. The power of beauty. IV. The distrest lovers. V. The perfidious gallant. IV. The constant fair-one. VII. The generous rival. VIII. The inhuman father. IX. The depos'd usurper. X. The punishment of ungenerous love* (by Mrs Sarah Butler; dedicated to the earl of Lincoln).
    + London: E. Curll & J. Hooke, 1716 (dedicatory epistle by Charles Gildon). SOURCE Hardy, 285; Blain, p. 165; ESTC t119241. LOCATION Dt, L, NUC.
    London: E. Curll & J. Roberts, 1719 (as *Milesian tales; or, instructive novels for the happy conduct of life. Containing the following events. Viz. I. The captivated monarch ... X. The punishment of ungenerous love* (by Mrs Butler). SOURCE McBurney, 96; Bradshaw, 5542. LOCATION C, ICN, NUC.
    + London: printed, and Dublin, reprinted, and sold by Ebenezer Rider, 1735 (with subtitle: *and An historical preface, of the learning and politeness of the ancient Irish*). SOURCE Brown 2, 168; McBurney, p. 36; ESTC t167049. LOCATION UCD Folklore Dept., D, Di, NUC.
COMMENTARY The 1716 edn has 116pp, while 1735 edn is 67pp. Another London edn of 1727 is 130pp. The author used historical sources such as Geoffrey Keating's *Foras feasa ar Éirinn* (in 1716 not yet published), Bede's *History of the English church and people* (Antwerp, 1565), and Camden's *Britannia* (London, 1607). She asserts that in former times Ireland had been a centre of culture. The London, 1716 edn contains a learned preface claiming historical accuracy about the kings of Ireland before its subjection to English rule. It celebrates 'Heroic Love, and all the Patriot Virtues', but lets its 'Lovers die unmarried: since I could find no Authority to the contrary'. The book is unusually well-versed in Gaelic culture for its date. The Dublin reprinted copy, according to the preface, contains 'The love and amorous discourses of Muchoe and Dooneflaith', and does not list the stories in the main title [Blain; B. Cunningham, *The world of Geoffrey Keating. History, myth and religion in seventeenth-century Ireland* (Dublin, 2000), pp 215–16; RL].

BUTLER, Revd Thomas Ambrose. See BUTLER, A.

BUTLER, W.F. See BUTLER, Gen. Sir William Francis.

BUTLER, Gen. Sir William Francis (known as W.F. Butler and Lt.-Col. Butler), pseud.
'An old soldier', b. Suirville (Co. Tipperary) 1838, d. Bansha Castle (Co. Tipperary) 1910
(not in 1911 as elsewhere). Soldier, biographer and author, WFB was a Catholic descendant
of the Butlers of Ormond and his mother was Ellen Dillon of Donnybrook (Co. Dublin). As
a child he experienced the hardships of the Famine and witnessed evictions near his home.
He was educated by the Jesuits at Tullabeg (Co. Offaly) and later in Dublin and was commissioned ensign in the 69th Foot in 1858. He served in the British army in Burma and India,
where he gained a dislike of imperialism. In 1867 his regiment was sent to Canada to forestall
a threatened Fenian invasion. Later he was appointed special commissioner to the Indian tribes
of Saskatchewan (Canada) and embarked on a 2700-mile exploratory reconnaissance mission
to the Red River settlements, which took him over the western prairies and the Rockies (narrated in his *The wild north land: being the story of a winter journey with dogs across northern
North America*, London, 1872). He served in West Africa, South Africa and in Egypt and was
deeply involved in the effort to relieve Gen. Charles Gordon at Khartoum. He was commander
of the British forces in South Africa prior to the outbreak of the Boer War. His criticism of
British aims in South Africa and his sympathy with the Boers led him in 1899 to resign his
position. He related his experiences in his *Autobiography* (London, 1911). After his retirement
in 1905 his efforts were directed towards Irish issues. He was appointed a member of the Irish
privy council, the senate of the newly-constituted National University of Ireland, and a commissioner of the board of national education in Ireland. He took a keen interest in the Gaelic
League. Many of his Irish ideas can be found in his *The light of the west* (Dublin, 1909). Among
his many works are several biographies, including *Charles George Gordon* (London, 1889), and
Sir Charles Napier§ (London, 1890). For his portraits and papers, see ODNB. SOURCE Allibone
Suppl., i, p. 266; Brady, p. 25; Brown, p. 48; DLB, clxvi; Field Day, ii, p. 1012; OCIL, p.
74; ODNB; RIA/DIB.

B502   *Akim-Foo: the history of a failure* (by Major W.F. Butler).
        + London: Sampson Low, Marston, Low & Searle, 1875 (ill.). SOURCE COPAC.
        LOCATION L.
        COMMENTARY Semi-fictionalized account of events connected with Sir Garnet
        Wolseley's§ march from Cape Coast Castle to Coomassie in 1873–74 [AMB; RL].
B503   *Far out: Rovings retold* (by Lt.-Col. W.F. Butler).
        + London: Wm. Isbister, 1880. LOCATION InND Loeber coll.
COMMENTARY Consists of travel stories covering various parts of the globe, including South
Africa, northern Canada and Afghanistan. Borders on straight travel accounts of a nonfictional
nature [ML].
B504   *The invasion of England: Told twenty years after by an old soldier* (by 'An old sol-
        dier').
        London: Sampson Low, Marston, Searle & Rivington, 1882. SOURCE COPAC.
        LOCATION L.
B505   *Red cloud, the solitary Sioux. A story of the great prairies* (by Lt.-Col. Butler).
        London: Sampson, Low & Co., 1882. SOURCE Brown, 292; COPAC. LOCATION L.
        + London: Sampson Low, Marston & Co., 1896 (new edn; ill. H. Petherick). LOCATION
        D, NUC.
        Dublin: Browne & Nolan, n.d. SOURCE de Búrca cat. 44/55; OCLC. LOCATION D.
        New York: G. Munro, [1882] (Seaside Library). LOCATION NUC.

Boston: Roberts Bros, 1884 (also published as *The hero of Pine Ridge*). LOCATION NUC. COMMENTARY Fiction for juveniles. The story starts at Glencar in Co. Kerry and relates the hero's childhood there. The remainder of the story is set in the wilds of north-west Canada where the hero and his friend Donogh have many adventures. An Indian is one of the chief heroes of the book [Brown].

B506   *The light of the west. With some other wayside thoughts, 1865–1908* (by Sir William Francis Butler).

Dublin, Waterford: M.H. Gill & Son, 1909. SOURCE COPAC. LOCATION L.

BUTT, Isaac, b. Glenfin, Stranorlar (Co. Donegal) 1813, d. Roebuck, Dundrum (Co. Dublin) 1879. Barrister, professor, politician, a writer of fiction and on history and politics, editor and orator, IB was the son of Revd Robert Butt, Church of Ireland rector of Stranorlar, and his second wife, Berkeley Cox. IB was a prodigy who was initially educated locally and later at TCD, where he was admitted at age 15, graduated BA in 1835, LLB in 1836, and MA and LLD in 1840. At age 20 he published a translation of *Ovid's Fasti* (Dublin, 1833) and in the same year was one of the founders of the *Dublin University Magazine*, to which he contributed fiction and which he edited from 1834 to 1838 when the magazine published writers such as William Carleton§, Charles Lever§, William H. Maxwell§, Sheridan Le Fanu§, Samuel Lover§ and James Clarence Mangan§. He married Elizabeth Swanzy of Co. Monaghan in 1837. He had been appointed professor of political economy at TCD at age 23 and was called to the Bar in 1838, becoming QC in 1844. He was called to the English Bar at the Inner Temple in 1859. Originally a vigorous supporter of the Union who argued against its repeal and was a staunch opponent of the inclusion of Catholics in civic office, he debated Daniel O'Connell and grew to respect his views, beginning the transition from conservative to liberal to nationalist. He was one of the vice-presidents elected at the founding of the Celtic Society in 1845. After what he considered England's inadequate response to the Famine, he opposed the Union and defended many Young Irelanders, including William Smith O'Brien and T.F. Meagher, and later in the 1860s Fenians such as Charles Kickham§. While raising his standing with and incurring the gratitude of the nationalists, the trials meant financial hardship for him (he was earlier imprisoned in Kilmainham gaol for debt). He was an elected MP, representing Harwich, then Youghal (Co. Cork, 1852–65), and later Limerick. He founded the Home Government Association in 1870 (later called the Home Rule League) based on the idea of Ireland in a federal union with Britain without destruction of 'the unity of the empire'. He led the Irish Party in Westminster, putting the idea of Home Rule on the political agenda, but lack of progress in reforms and disagreements over tactics lost him the leadership of the party to Charles Stewart Parnell. His influence dwindled and he withdrew from public life. He died in Dublin but was buried at Stranorlar. The historian Thomas Carlyle described him in 1849 as 'a terribly black burly son of earth: talent visible in him, but still more animalism: big bison-head, black, not *quite* unbrutal ...' (Carlyle, p. 54). IB's writings include *The famine in the land* (Dublin, 1847), *Land tenure in Ireland: A plea for the Celtic race* (Dublin, 1866), and *Home government for Ireland* (Dublin, 1874). *What does she do with it?* (London, 1871) is attributed by Donegal to IB under the pseud. 'Solomon Temple'; in COPAC this is also under the pseud., but it is not confirmed to be by IB. Likewise, Donegal attributes 'The heiress', a novel, to IB, but this has not been confirmed and no copy has been located. For his portraits and papers, see ODNB. SOURCE Allibone, i, p. 316; Allibone Suppl., pp 266–7; Brady, p. 26; Brooke, pp 72–3; Brown, p. 49; T. Carlyle, *Reminiscences of my Irish journey in 1849* (London, 1882), p. 54; Donegal, pp 51–7; Elmes, p. 32; Field Day, i, pp 1200–10, 1297–8, ii, pp 116, 161–5, 223–33; W.E. Hall, p. 145; Hogan 2, pp 207–8; Keane, p. 68; McKenna, pp 110–11; NCBEL 4, p. 2473; Newmann, p. 29; J. O'Donovan (ed.), *The book* *of rights* (Dublin, 1847), n.p. list of officers [in 1845]; OCIL, p. 75; ODNB; RIA/DIB; D. Thornley, *Isaac Butt and Home Rule* (London, 1964); T. de Vere White, *The road to excess* (Dublin, n.d.); Wolff, i, p. 197.

B507 *Irish life in the castle, the courts, and the country* [anon.].
+ London: How & Parsons, 1840, 3 vols. SOURCE Hodgson, p. 289; Brown, 293; Rafroidi, ii, p. 92; NSTC. LOCATION Grail, D, L.
COMMENTARY A young barrister, Tarleton, while studying in London forms a friendship with Gerald MacCullagh, an alias for O'Donnell. O'Donnell becomes a national leader in Ireland, but sees the national movement drift away from high ideals to mere criminal acts. Tarleton is disowned by his father for refusing to give up his friend. He moves to Dublin and lives in a boarding-house. The novel presents extensive pictures of Dublin life [Brown].

B508 *The gap of Barnesmore. A tale of the Irish highlands and the revolution of 1688* [anon.].
London: Smith, Elder & Co., 1848, 3 vols. SOURCE Hodgson, p. 210; McKenna, p. 111; Brown, 294; Rafroidi, ii, p. 92; Wolff, 1023. LOCATION Grail, City of Belfast Public Libraries, L, DCL, NUC.
COMMENTARY Historical fiction set in Co. Donegal. Deals with a feud arising out of the revolution in 1688. Relates the issues between the colonists and the native Irish in a conversation between Captain Spencer, representing the former, and Fr Meehan, representing the latter [Donegal, p. 52; Brooke, p. 173; Brown].

B509 *Chapters of college romance* (by Isaac Butt).
+ London: Charles J. Skeet, 1863 (first series) [all published]. SOURCE Brown, 295; Hogan, 2, p. 208; Rafroidi, ii, p. 74. LOCATION Grail, D, L, C, NUC.
COMMENTARY First serialized in the *Dublin University Magazine* (1834–37) under the pseud. of 'Edward J. O'Brien'. Contents: 'The billiard table', 'Reading for honours', 'The mariner's son', 'The murdered fellow; an incident of 1734', 'The sizar – Arthur Johns', 'The bribed scholar', 'The duel' [Brown; W.E. Hall, p. 81; ML; Hogan].

B510 *Children of sorrow* (by Isaac Butt).
[location?]: [publisher?], [date?].
COMMENTARY No copy located. Brown has only seen mention of it. The volume should not be confused with *The children of sorrow. A tale* (Dublin, 1830), written by a member of the Committee of the Juvenile Deaf and Dumb Association. A note in the IBL, 5 (1913), 54–6, states that this book is only heard of [RL; Brown, p. 50].

BUTTS, Eleanor L. de. See **DE BUTTS, Eleanor L.**

BYRNE, May (also known as Mrs Mary Catherine Lawrie, née Wheland), pseud. '**Cape Colonist**', b. Kilkenny 1855, d. South Africa 1920. Novelist, generally listed as South African, MB was brought to South Africa by her mother. She became a teacher and began writing at an early age. SOURCE Allibone Suppl., i, p. 269; RIA/DIB.
B511 *Ingram Place. A novel* (by 'Cape Colonist').
+ London: Longman, Green & Co., 1874, 2 vols. LOCATION L.
B512 *Power's partner* (by May Byrne).
London: Hurst & Blackett, 1876, 3 vols. LOCATION L.

'**BYRRNE, E. FAIRFAX**', pseud. See **Brooke, Miss —**.

C

'C—D, Mr', pseud. See **CHETWOOD, William Rufus**.

'C., M.L.', fl. 1874. Pseudonym of a fictionalizing memoirist. Judging from the content of the following work and its preface, the author was a Protestant, female member of an Anglo-Irish family who opposed the Union and absenteeism of landlords. She lived in the Kilkenny/Waterford area and later married and lived in England. SOURCE RL.

C1　　*Some time in Ireland. A recollection* (preface signed 'M.L.C.').
　　　　+ London: Henry S. King & Co., 1874. SOURCE NSTC. LOCATION D, L, NUC, InND
　　　　Loeber coll.

COMMENTARY According to the preface, the author's 'aim [was] to depict, from vivid recollections of my earlier years and from my later experience, views, feeling, habits, and principles, more really and truly characteristic of the gentry of Ireland'. Fictitious setting includes a seat called Kilkreen near the river Dour, with a view of the city of Landford. The identity of this setting remains unclear. (There was a Kilcreene House in Co. Kilkenny but it is uncertain whether this is what is referred to.) Describes the childhood of Kathleen, the youngest of eight children living in a country house. There is great concern for marrying off the daughters in the proper order. Daniel O'Connell's politics are discussed and a contested election and the murder of a tithe process-server are described. Eventually Kathleen moves to Waterford to stay with her aunt and uncle, a canon in the Church of Ireland. Due to the uncertainty of tithes for the clergy, the aunt and uncle and Kathleen move to England, where Kathleen marries an Englishman [ML].

'C., M.T.', pseud. See **BUTLER, Josephine**.

'C., W.', pseud. See **CHAIGNEAU, William**.

'C., W.A.', pseud. See **CAWTHORNE, William Anderson**.

CADDELL, Cecilia Mary (also known as **Maria Caddell**), b. Harbourstown, Fournocks (Co. Meath) 1814, d. Kingstown (now Dun Laoghaire, Co. Dublin) 1877. A Catholic short story and historical fiction writer; CMC wrote some works with an anti-Protestant tone. She came from an old Catholic family. Her father, Richard O'Ferrall Caddell, built Harbourstown House which has been demolished since but a model of which survives at Castletown House (Co. Kildare). Her mother was the Hon. Paulina (not Pauline as in Brady, Brown and the *Irish Monthly*, March 1916, pp 202–3), daughter of Thomas Arthur, Viscount Southwell. CMC was an invalid for much of her life and remained unmarried. She had a prolific output, contributing to the Dublin *Irish Monthly* and to Catholic periodicals; writing stories for collections of fiction; hymns, and pieces on Irish history and on the Catholic faith. She wrote *A history of the missions in Japan and Paraguay* (London, 1856) and a biography, *Hidden saints: life of Soeur Marie* (London, 1869). In 1872 she visited Lourdes and may have travelled to Italy, which is the background of her most famous novel *Blind Agnese* (Dublin, 1856). CMC wrote 16 works of historical fiction about the plight of Catholics, some set in Ireland. She should not be confused with Cecilia Mary Cadell, author of *Massenburg* (London, 1825, 3 vols.) and *The reformer* (London, 1832, 3 vols.). A volume entitled *Father De Lisle; or, Tyborne and its victims* (New

York, 1861) has been ascribed to CMC, but in fact is by Fanny Margaret Taylor§. SOURCE Allibone Suppl., i, p. 270; Blain, p. 168; Brady, p. 27; Brown, p. 50; Colman, pp 48–9; Hogan 2, pp 213–14; *Irish Monthly*, 1874, pp 332–5; Irish pseudonyms; Landed gentry, 1912, p. 94; NCBEL 4, p. 1763; OCIL, p. 76; ODNB; O'Donoghue, p. 53; RIA/DIB; Vanishing country houses, p. 113; Wolff, i, pp 198–9.

C2   *Tales for the young* (by Cecilia Mary Caddell).
London: Burns, Oates & Washbourne, n.d. SOURCE Colman, p. 49.
COMMENTARY No copy located. Advertised in [anon.], *Tales of faith and loyalty* (London, n.d.), which states that there was a first and second series, each priced at 1s. [RL].

C3   *Blanche Leslie; or, the living rosary* [anon.].
London: Burns & Oates [1849]. SOURCE Cat. Dcc, p. 19. LOCATION L.

C4   *Lost Geneviève; or, the child of an especial providence* (by Cecilia Mary Caddell).
Dublin: James Duffy, [1857 or earlier] (Duffy's Cottage Library). SOURCE Adv. in [anon.], *The young crusader* (Dublin, 1857). LOCATION D ([1880] edn).
London: Burns & Oates, [?date]. SOURCE Brown, p. 50; Cat. Dcc, p. 19.
Paris: H. Casterman, 1862 (trans. as *Geneviève, ou l'enfant de la providence*). SOURCE Devonshire, p. 457; CCF. LOCATION BNF.
New York, Boston, Montreal: D. & J. Sadlier & Co. [1856] (as *Lost Genoveffa; or the spouse of the Madonna. A tale of Brittany*). LOCATION NUC.
COMMENTARY No copy of the London and the earliest Dublin edns located. It is plausible that the New York edn is a reprint, but this needs confirmation [RL].

C5   *The miner's daughter. A Catholic tale* (by Cecilia Mary Caddell).
New York, Boston, Montreal: D. & J. Sadlier & Co., 1859 (Young People's Library). SOURCE OCLC; Colman, p. 49 (where mistakenly called *Minister's daughter*). LOCATION NUC, Villanova Univ.
+ Dublin: James Duffy & Co., n.d. (new edn). LOCATION DPL.

C6   *Chateau Lescure; or, the last marquis. A tale of Brittany and the Vendée. New and charming tale of the French Revolution* [anon.].
New York: Edward Dunigan & Brother, 1856. SOURCE OCLC. LOCATION UBP.
COMMENTARY Reviewed in the *Catholic Mirror* (17 Mar. 1855, p. 6) [RL].

C7   *Blind Agnese; or, little spouse of the blessed sacrament* (by Cecilia Mary Caddell; dedicated to the sacred heart of Jesus, dated 1853).
+ Dublin: James Duffy, 1856 (pictorial title dated 1855). SOURCE Brown, 300 (1856, 2nd edn); Alston, p. 65. LOCATION PC, L, InND Loeber coll. (n.d. edn).
Amsterdam: J.M. Vincent, 1884 (trans. into Dutch as *Agnes, het bruidje van her Allerh. Sacrament*). SOURCE Mes, p. 47.
's Hertogenbosch: G. Mosmans Snr, 1885 (trans. into Dutch as *Agnes, the kleine bruid van het H. Sacrament*). SOURCE Mes, p. 4.
Paris: A. Vaton, 1861 (trans. as *Agnès l'aveugle, ou la petite épouse du très-saint sacrement*). SOURCE Devonshire, p. 457; CCF. LOCATION BNF.
Paris: Tolra & Haton, 1868 (trans. as *Agnès l'aveugle; épisode des persecutions d'Irlande*). SOURCE Hyland cat. 205/111. LOCATION D, NUC.
New York: E. Dunigan & Bros, 1855. SOURCE MacLeod, p. 179.
COMMENTARY *New York, Dunigan 1855 edn* No copy located [RL].
+ New York: P.J. Kenedy, [c.1855] (ill.). SOURCE RLIN. LOCATION State Univ. at Albany (NY).
COMMENTARY Reprinted many times. Religious, historical fiction set in the seventeenth century. The story opens in a church in Naples where Lady Oranmore, an Irish Protestant, finds that the blind beggar girl she discovers deep in prayer is her granddaughter, Agnese. She takes

her to Ireland where Agnese meets her uncle, Squire Netterville, while he is priest-hunting. Netterville, the youngest of three brothers, by becoming a Protestant has obtained the estate of Agnese's father. The second brother, Fr Netterville, is surprised by the priest-hunters. He saves his younger brother from the fury of the Catholics but is murdered by the Cromwellians. The squire converts back to catholicism. Agnese dies young, but not before she has been the instrument of the conversion of Lady Oranmore [Brown; ML].

C8   *Flower and fruit; or, the use of tears* (by Cecilia Mary Caddell).
      Dublin: James Duffy, 1856 (with additional title page as *Flowers and fruits*, etc., 1855).
      SOURCE Alston, p. 65; Brown, p. 50. LOCATION L (destroyed), PC.
      COMMENTARY Religious fiction [BLC].

C9   *Home and the homeless. A novel* (by Cecilia Mary Caddell).
      + London: T.C. Newby, 1858, 3 vols. LOCATION L, NUC.
      COMMENTARY The enemy in this story, set partly in France, is agnosticism [Blain; *Saturday Review*, 7, p. 158; ML].

C10   *Snowdrop, ou les trois baptêmes* (by Maria Caddell).
      Paris: H. Casterman, 1859. SOURCE Devonshire, p. 457; CCF. LOCATION BNF.
      's Hertogenbosch: G. Mosmans, 1881 (trans. into Dutch from the French as *Sneeuwklokje, of de drie doopsels*). SOURCE Mes, p. 47.
      Philadelphia: H. McGrath, 1860 (as *Little snowdrop, the unbaptized one; or, the story of the three baptisms*; Parochial and Sunday School Library, No. 10). SOURCE Rev. in the *Catholic Mirror* (31 Dec. 1859), p. 5; DCU, Catholic Americana files (1872 edn); OCLC. LOCATION NYU.
      London, New York: T. Nelson, 1875 (as *Little snowdrop and her golden casket*). LOCATION L, NUC.
      COMMENTARY Probably an English edn preceded the Paris edn, but none has been located [RL].

C11   *Nellie Netterville; or, one of the transplanted. A tale of the times of Cromwell in Ireland* [anon.].
      London: Burns, Oates & Co., [1867]. SOURCE Alston, p. 65; Brown, 299; Dixson, p. 221. LOCATION L.
      's Hertogenbosch: Maatschappij Katholieke Illustratie, 1883 (trans. into Dutch as *De laatste der Nettervilles. Een Iersch verhaal uit de dagen van Cromwell*). SOURCE Mes, p. 237.
      COMMENTARY 's Hertogenbosch edn Also was published in the periodical *Leesbibliotheek voor Christelijke Huisgezinnen* ('s Hertogenbosch, 1883) [Mes, p. 287].
      New York: Catholic Publication Society, 1868. SOURCE DCU, Catholic Americana files. LOCATION InND, NUC.

COMMENTARY Historical fiction set in the middle of the seventeenth century. The story is about the trials and travails of an Anglo-Irish family who lose their land in the Cromwellian confiscations and are ordered to move to Connacht. Nellie leaves with her grandfather, while her English mother will follow. A strange woman tells Nellie that she has put a curse on her mother for once sending her away. Mrs Netterville and her household are left in a desolate condition, but find strength in prayer. Mrs Netterville is falsely accused by the woman who cursed her of shooting a Cromwellian soldier. Meanwhile, Nellie and her grandfather arrive in Clew Bay (Co. Mayo), to find that their allotted land has been occupied by a party of Puritans led by a Major Hewitson. He denies their claim on the grounds they did not exercise it right away. Hewitson's daughter Henrietta is appalled at her father's rudeness and points to a hut where they can shelter for the night. The hut is inhabited by another fugitive, Roger O'More, who had known Nellie's father on the battlefield of Benburb. Roger has a home on

Clare island where he takes the Nettervilles. When the Cromwellians find out where the fugitives worship they set the chapel on fire. O'More saves Nellie and with Henrietta's help they escape. Hamish, Nellie's foster brother, comes with news of Mrs Neterville's incarceration in a Dublin jail. He has been wounded and cannot accompany Nellie to Dublin, so Roger offers to help. They secretly visit the Netterville home and find that the woman who had cursed her mother is dying. She confesses that Nellie's mother is innocent. Nellie goes to Dublin to obtain her mother's release but finds her dying. She marries O'More in the prison and her mother dies happy in her belief in Christian mercy [ML].

C12 *Never forgotten; or, the home of the lost child* (by Cecilia Mary Caddell).
London: Burns, Oates & Co., 1871. SOURCE Alston, p. 65; COPAC. LOCATION L.
+ New York: P.J. Kenedy, 1893 (ill. P.J. Kenedy). LOCATION InND Loeber coll.
COMMENTARY Also known from a 12th edn. Religious fiction. According to the author's introduction, the outline of the story had been handed to her by the Mother Provincial of the order of the 'Bon Pasteur' in England, 'with the full permission of the lady by whom they had been originally collected' who had long been resident in the convent. The proceeds of the books were to benefit the order [BLC; RL; Personal communication, Mary Pollard, June 2004].

C13 *Wild times. A tale of the days of Queen Elizabeth* (by Cecilia Mary Caddell).
London: Burns, Oates & Co., 1872 (new edn). SOURCE Alston, p. 65. LOCATION L.
+ New York: The Catholic Publication Society, [1873] (new edn). SOURCE DCU, Catholic Americana files, NUC, InND Loeber coll.
COMMENTARY Historical fiction about the persecution of a noble English Catholic family during the reign of Queen Elizabeth I. No Irish content [ML].

C14 *Summer talks about Lourdes* (by Cecilia Mary Caddell).
London: Burns & Oates, 1874. SOURCE *Irish Monthly* (1874), p. 619. LOCATION L, NUC.
Mainz: F. Kirchheim, 1875 (trans. as *Somergespräche über Lourdes*). LOCATION NUC.
COMMENTARY Religious fiction. The talks, between Mrs de Grey and her little daughter, feature the Lady of Lourdes and all kinds of miracles. At the end, a Mr de Sommerie is introduced, who gives an account of the Feast of the Banners in 1872 [*Irish Monthly* (1874), p. 619].

C15 *Tales of the festivals* (by Cecilia Mary Caddell).
New York: P.J. Kenedy, 1896. LOCATION NUC.
COMMENTARY Published posthumously. Contents: 'Ash Wednesday', 'The annunciation', 'Holy week', 'Easter', 'Mimi's grave; or, Rogation Day', 'Our Lady the Deliverer', 'Pentecost' [RL].

CADDELL, Maria. See **CADDELL, Cecilia Mary.**

CAFFYN, Kathleen (**Katharine**, according to ODNB; née Hunt also known as **Kathleen Mannington Caffyn** and **Mrs Mannington Caffyn**), pseud. '**Iota**', b. Co. Tipperary 1853 (1855? in OCIL and Sutherland), d. Turin (Italy) 1926. Novelist, sometimes described as 'a new-woman writer', KMC was the daughter of William de Vere Hunt and Louisa Going. She was educated by English and German governesses and later trained as a nurse in London hospitals. In 1879 she married a surgeon, Stephen Mannington Caffyn. They went to Australia and lived in Sydney and then Melbourne where he held a number of medical posts, made some useful inventions, and wrote some fiction. Both husband and wife were involved in improving public health. In Melbourne KMC was one of the founders of the District Nursing Society of Victoria and was instrumental in professionalizing nursing in the province. She contributed to local magazines. She returned to England in 1892 where her first novel, *A yellow aster* (London, 1894), was very successful. This and subsequent works – she wrote 18 novels in all – had a strong appeal to women as they often dealt with women's changing relationships with men, but a review in the *Times* lamented KMC's 'terrible gift of familiarity in speaking of things sacred'. She liked to ride, hunt and watch polo, and horses feature prominently in her work. She died after an operation in Turin. For her portrait and correspondence, see ODNB. She should not be confused with the author John Francis Waller§, who also wrote under the pseudonym 'Iota'. SOURCE ADB, vol. 3; Blain, p. 170; G. Cunningham, *The new woman and the Victorian novel* (London, 1978); EF, p. 208; Miller, i, p. 446; NCBEL 4, p. 1478; OCIL, p. 262 [under 'Iota']; ODNB; O'Toole, p. 101; Sutherland, pp 319–20 [under 'Iota']; T & B, p. 990 [under 'Iota']; Wolff, i, p. 198.

C16   *A yellow aster* (by 'Iota').

+ London: Hutchinson & Co., 1894, 3 vols. SOURCE Macartney, p. 94; Wolff, 1029; Topp 8, 230. LOCATION D (1894 edn 1 vol.), L (1894, 6th edn), NUC, InND Loeber coll. (1894, 3 vols., 7th edn).

Leipzig: Bernard Tauchnitz, 1894. SOURCE T & B, 2988. LOCATION NUC.

New York: D. Appleton & Co., 1894 (Town & Country Library, No. 139). LOCATION NUC.

Chicago: E.A. Weeks, [1894]. SOURCE Topp 8, 230. LOCATION NUC (1896 edn).

Chicago: C.H. Spergel, [1894]. SOURCE Topp 8, 230.

COMMENTARY No copy of the Chicago, Spergel edn located. A highly popular and much reprinted novel, set in England. Centres on Gwen Waring, a girl brought up by scientific parents who are unable to display warmth or affection to their children. The atmosphere in the home is non-religious. Gwen grows up without being able to form ties or display affection. She marries as an experiment. When she finds herself pregnant, she requests a separation from her husband, who leaves on an expedition to Africa. Gwen learns what love is after her baby is born and she is reunited with her husband. The final volume includes a chapter from another novel, *Hooks of steel*, by Helen Prothero-Lewis printed as an advertisement [ML; Burmester list].

C17   *Children of circumstance. A novel* (by 'Iota'; dedicated to M.A. Townsend).

+ London: Hutchinson & Co., 1894, 3 vols. SOURCE Macartney, p. 94. LOCATION D (n.d. edn), L, NUC (n.d. edn).

Leipzig: Bernard Tauchnitz, 1894, 2 vols. SOURCE T & B, 3019–20. LOCATION NUC.

New York: D. Appleton & Co., 1894. LOCATION NUC.

COMMENTARY The hero marries his cousin but subsequently falls in love with a social worker in London's East End. The three meet and discuss this triangular 'mistake' in adult fashion. The wife nobly arranges for her rival to take over after her death [Sutherland].

C18   *A comedy in spasms* (by 'Iota').

+ London: Hutchinson & Co., [1895] (ill. G.H.E. Edwards; Zeit-Geist Library, No. 4). SOURCE Macartney, p. 94; Daims, 465. LOCATION D, L, InND Loeber coll.

New York: F.A. Stokes, [1895]. SOURCE Daims, 465. LOCATION NUC.

COMMENTARY Paper and cloth edns were published simultaneously. Set Initially in Australia, a station-owner's death during a drought forces his family to move to England rather than face genteel poverty in Melbourne. In England, the daughter marries a physically weak but intellectual man in order to solve the family's financial problems. After her marriage she meets her ideal lover and is about to leave her husband when her lover stops her. She remains in her unhappy marriage [Miller, i, p. 446; Krishnamurti, p. 67].

C19   *A Quaker grandmother* (by 'Iota').

+ London: Hutchinson & Co., 1896. SOURCE Macartney, p. 94. LOCATION L, InND Loeber coll.

COMMENTARY A Canadian heroine brings the energy and freshness of life lived on a Canadian ranch into English provincial society. She has more wisdom that is expected of her and eventually brings happiness to her aunt and cousin who had been estranged from each other [ML; Miller, i, p. 447].

C20   *Poor Max. A novel* (by 'Iota').

+ London: Hutchinson & Co., 1898. SOURCE Macartney, p. 94; Daims, 472. LOCATION L, InND Loeber coll.

Philadelphia: Lippincott, 1898 (Lippincott's Select Novels). SOURCE Daims, 472. LOCATION NUC.

COMMENTARY Judith, an Irish woman, marries Max Morland, a Jew, after a whirlwind courtship in Ballybruff. Max's impulsive generosity leads to desperate financial straits. Judith becomes involved with another man but faithfully nurses a sick Max. After his death she leaves her lover to marry a rich debauchee in order to look out for her own financial interests [Sutherland, p. 508].

C21   *Anne Mauleverer* (by 'Iota').

London: Methuen & Co., 1899. SOURCE Macartney, p. 94; Wolff, 1027. LOCATION L.

Leipzig: Bernard Tauchnitz, 1899, 2 vols. SOURCE T & B, 3373–74. LOCATION NUC.

Philadelphia: J.B. Lippincott, 1899. LOCATION NUC.

COMMENTARY The half-Irish heroine, a sculptress, nurses the man she loves. After he dies she adopts his child and remains defiantly celibate for the rest of her life. Her knowledge of horses wins her the favour of the king of Italy [Sutherland; Miller, ii, p. 660].

C22   *The minx. A novel* (by 'Iota').

New York: F.A. Stokes, 1899. LOCATION NUC.

+ London: Hutchinson & Co., 1900. SOURCE Macartney, p. 94. LOCATION D, L, InND Loeber coll.

COMMENTARY A young woman of scientific training and radical views contends with the conservative prejudices of English provincial society. There are discussions on factory legislation, housing and other social reforms. Of her two suitors, she eventually chooses the one who is less rich and less obviously socially involved [Miller, ii, p. 660; ML].

C23   *The happenings of Jill* (by 'Iota').

London: Hutchinson & Co., 1901. SOURCE Daims, 467. LOCATION L.

C24   *He for God only* (by Kathleen Mannington Caffyn).

London: Hurst & Blackett, 1903. SOURCE Daims, 468; Macartney, p. 94 (London, Hutchinson, 1903 edn). LOCATION L.

C25   *At a rest house of the foot-hills* [anon.].

London: Daily Mail, [1904]. LOCATION L.

C26   *Patricia: a mother* (by 'Iota').

London: Hutchinson & Co., 1905. SOURCE Daims, 471. LOCATION L.

New York: D. Appleton, 1905. SOURCE Daims, 471. LOCATION NUC.

C27   *Smoke in the flame* (by 'Iota').

+ London: Hutchinson & Co., 1906. SOURCE Macartney, p. 94. LOCATION D, L.

C28   *The magic of May* (by 'Iota').

+ London: Eveleigh Nash, 1908. SOURCE Macartney, p. 94. LOCATION D, L.

COMMENTARY Concerns the religious training of a young girl who responds to the stories of the lives of prophets and apostles as if they are living presences [Miller, ii, p. 660].

C29   *'Whoso breaketh an hedge'* (by 'Iota').

London: Hurst & Blackett, 1909. SOURCE Daims, 473. LOCATION L, NUC.

C30   *Dorinda and her daughter* (by Mrs Mannington Caffyn).

+ London: Hurst & Blackett, 1910. SOURCE Macartney, p. 94; Wolff, 1028; OCLC. LOCATION D, L.

COMMENTARY Set in England, and features an Irish nurse [ML; Miller, i, p. 446].

C31   *The fire-seeker* (by 'Iota').

+ London: Eveleigh Nash, 1911. SOURCE Macartney, p. 94. LOCATION D, L, NUC.

COMMENTARY Analyzes the emotional development of an adolescent girl [Miller, ii, p. 660; RL].

C32   *Two ways of love* (by Mrs Mannington Caffyn).
London: Hurst & Blackett, 1913. SOURCE Macartney, p. 94; COPAC. LOCATION L, NUC.

C33   *Mary Mirrilies* (by 'Iota').
London: Hurst & Blackett, 1916. SOURCE Daims, 470; OCLC. LOCATION L.

CAFFYN, Kathleen Mannington. See CAFFYN, Kathleen.

CAHILL, Charles, pseud. 'An old commercial traveller', fl. 1892. Story and sketch writer.
C34   *Anecdotes and reminiscences of the road in coach days* (by 'An old commercial traveller').
+ London: Stead & Lashmar, [1892] (ill. Paul Gilardoni). LOCATION L.
COMMENTARY Sketches of Killarney, Waterford elections, and many other topics [RL].

CALLAN, Mrs Margaret (née Hughes), pseud. 'Thornton MacMahon', b. Newry (Co. Down) 1817, d. Melbourne (Australia) c.1883. Nationalist and writer, MC was the daughter of Philip Hughes, merchant, of Newry and Susanna Gavan of Co. Monaghan, whose mother was a MacMahon and the aunt of the nationalist leader Charles Gavan Duffy. After her father's death, MC and her mother opened a boarding-school for young women in Blackrock (Co. Dublin) where she taught until she married a doctor, John B. Callan. Through Charles Gavan Duffy she, her sister Susan and her brother became involved in the Young Ireland movement. Susan later married her cousin Charles Gavan Duffy. MC contributed anonymously to the *Nation* (Dublin) and two reports on a trip to France, identified as by her, are considered to be the first lengthy pieces by a woman published in that periodical. In these she urged the Irish to show the kind of national pride exhibited by the French and reported on the high regard in which Daniel O'Connell was held in France. After the arrest of the leaders of the Young Ireland movement, she and Jane Francesca Elgee (late Lady Wilde§) continued to publish in the *Nation* until it was suppressed. In 1856 MC and her husband and the Gavan Duffys emigrated to Australia. She kept in correspondence with Irish writers and politicians. Any later writings have not been identified. For her portrait, see ODNB. SOURCE B. Anton, 'Northern voices: Ulsterwomen in the Young Ireland movement', in J. Holmes and D. Urquhard (eds), *Coming into the light: the work, politics and religion of women in Ulster* (Belfast, 1994), pp 60–92; T. Bradshaw, *General directory of Newry, Armagh ...* (Newry, 1819; republ. [Ballynahinch], n.d.), p. 12; 'More about "Mary" of the *Nation*', *Irish Monthly*, 36 (1908), pp 69–83; ODNB; RL.
C35   *The casket of Irish pearls. A selection of prose and verse from the best Irish writers* (compiled by 'Thornton MacMahon'; dedicated to 'the young men of Ireland').
+ Dublin, London: James Duffy; London: Simpkin, Marshall & Co., 1846. SOURCE Linen Hall cat. p. 162; OCLC. LOCATION BFl, L, MChB, InND Loeber coll.
COMMENTARY In the introd. MC urges the Irish people to gain knowledge and self-respect through education, attacks the English policy of 'divide and conquer' and urges all Irish factions to unite and obtain self-government through peaceful means. Contents: short historical and biographical pieces, poetry, and a few short stories and extracts: 'An Irish Wake' (William Carleton§), 'Catholic gentlemen in the penal times' (Lady Morgan§), 'Mental and personal charms' (Maria Edgeworth§) [RL; ODNB].

CALLENDER, Caroline Henrietta. See SHERIDAN, Caroline Henrietta.

CALLWELL, J.M. See **CALLWELL, Josephine M.**

CALLWELL, Josephine M. (née Martin; also known as **J.M. Callwell**), d. Ballycastle (Co. Antrim) 1935. Historical fiction and children's writer and a translator with an interest in German literature. According to Brown, JMC was born into the Martin family of Ross (Co. Galway), (see Violet Florence Martin§). She may have been related to Sir Charles Edward Callwell (1859–1928), an army officer and writer, who was the son of Henry Callwell of Ballycastle, and who had married Maud Martin of Ross. JMC became a frequent contributor to *Blackwood's Magazine* (Edinburgh). Aside from fiction, she published *Old Irish life* (Edinburgh, 1912), which deals with Galway city and county. JMC published 10 works of fiction, including historical fiction, Irish fiction, and fiction for juveniles. SOURCE Allibone Suppl., i, p. 274; Brown, p. 51; Brown 2, p. 38; NCBEL 4, p. 1764; ODNB [under Charles Edward Callwell].

C36   *Legends of olden times, adapted from the Old German* (by J.M. Callwell). London: Newman & Co., [1880]. SOURCE Alston, p. 66. LOCATION L.

C37   *Little curiosity: The story of a German Christmas* (by J.M. Callwell). + London, Glasgow, Edinburgh, Dublin: Blackie & Son, [1887] (ill.). SOURCE Alston, p. 66. LOCATION L, InND Loeber coll.

COMMENTARY Small volume of fiction for juveniles originally published in a six-penny series, presumably in wrappers, and in a cloth edn. Contents: 'A sleighing party', 'The new aunt', 'Lost!', 'The pastor's home' [RL].

C38   *The squire's grandson. A Devonshire story* (by J.M. Callwell). + London, Glasgow, Edinburgh, Dublin: Blackie & Son, 1888 (ill. H.P.). SOURCE Alston, p. 66. LOCATION D (n.d. edn), L.

C39   *Timothy Tatters. A story for the young* (by J.M. Callwell; on cover: T.M. Calwell [*sic*]). + London: T. Nelson & Sons, 1890 (ill. A.J.R., on cover, *Eileen*; title on spine: *Timothy Tatters, an Irish story*). SOURCE Alston, p. 66; Brown 2, 188 (who mistakenly mentions Dublin: Thomas Nelson & Sons, n.d. edn), D (1896 edn), L, InND Loeber coll. (also 1892, 2nd edn).

COMMENTARY Two binding variants, grey and blue cloth. Fiction for juveniles. Timothy Tatters is the nickname of Rose Moore, elder daughter and one of four children of a Co. Galway family. The children are up in arms at the idea of their mother's approaching marriage with an English captain. They form a 'Land League' and one night fire at him with blank cartridges to frighten him out of the country. He catches Patsey, one of Rose's protégées whom she had taken in when he had returned from Liverpool after his mother's death and found his relatives dead. Patsey is brought to court and to save him from being sentenced, Rose has to own up to the escapade. The children reconcile themselves to the idea of having a new father [Brown 2; ML; Personal communication, Mary Pollard, June 2004].

C40   *Dorothy Arden. A story of England and France two hundred years ago* (by J.M. Callwell). + London: T. Nelson & Sons, 1890 (ill. H. Rhind). SOURCE Alston, p. 66; Personal communication, Mary Pollard, June 2004. LOCATION L [1897 edn], NUC, InND Loeber coll. (n.d. edn).

COMMENTARY Historical fiction set in France and England at the end of the seventeenth century. Dorothy, a young girl, and Maurice her brother, born in France to an English father and brought up as Huguenots, flee France when their relative who was to bring them up dies and the Huguenots are actively persecuted. They go to England to ask their uncle for protection. They expect England to be a country where people can practise their religion freely but they find out that this is not the case. The short campaign of the earl of Monmouth is described. Eventually Dorothy marries her cousin, who has been involved in the political upheavals [ML].

C41   *Town and country mice* (by J.M. Callwell).
London: T. Nelson & Sons, 1891. SOURCE Alston, p. 66. LOCATION L.
COMMENTARY Fiction for juveniles [RL].

C42   *The rival princess. A story of the fourteenth century (his sacred majesty of France)* (by J.M. Callwell).
London: T. Nelson & Sons, 1893. SOURCE Alston, p. 66. LOCATION L (not located), E.

C43   *A champion of the faith. A tale of Prince Hal and the Lollards* (by J.M. Callwell).
London, Glasgow, Edinburgh, Dublin: Blackie & Son, 1894. SOURCE Alston, p. 66. LOCATION D (n.d. edn), L, NUC (1893 edn).
COMMENTARY Religious, historical fiction [BLC].

C44   *One summer by the sea* (by J.M. Callwell).
+ London, Edinburgh, New York: Thomas Nelson & Sons, [1899] (ill. John H. Bacon). SOURCE Alston, p. 66. LOCATION D, L, InND Loeber coll.

COMMENTARY Fiction for juveniles. Three orphans are treated badly by their English relatives with whom they live. They decide to run away and live with their half-brother, Rolf, a doctor in Ireland. Even though Rolf is very poor, he accepts the charge of the three children. Eventually it turns out that the eldest boy is in direct succession for an earldom and their poverty is ended [ML].

C45   *A little Irish girl* (by J.M. Callwell).
+ London, Glasgow, Dublin: Blackie & Son, 1902 (ill. Harold Copping; cover R.H.). LOCATION D, L, InND Loeber coll.

COMMENTARY Fiction for juveniles set in the west of Ireland. A story about how two poor orphans make peace with their rich uncle who had been estranged from the orphans' parents and inherit a small property on the coast of Clare [ML].

CAMERON, John, b. near Edinburgh (Scotland) 1725, d. Derry (Co. Derry) 1799. Scottish-born religious writer and missionary Presbyterian preacher, JC worked as an apprentice bookseller before receiving an MA at Edinburgh University He belonged to the 'reformed Presbyterians' and travelled to the north of Ireland as a missionary preacher in 1750, remaining there for the rest of his life. In 1754 he was called by the breakaway parish of Dunluce (Co. Antrim) to be their minister on condition he leave the Covenanters and join the regular Presbyterian church. He consented and was ordained for Dunluce in 1755. He was moderator of the Presbyterian synod in Ulster (1768–69). JC gained wide recognition for his sermons, which were often borrowed. His published works include *The policy of Satan to destroy the Christian religion* (Dublin, 1766), *The Catholic Christian* (Belfast, 1769), and the posthumously-published *The doctrine of the Holy Scriptures* (London, 1828), in which he laid out his anti-Trinitarian views. The volume below is his only prose work. He was buried in the parish churchyard at Dunluce. SOURCE Allibone, i, p. 321; ODNB; RIA/DIB; T. Witherow, *Historical and literary memorials of Presbyterianism in Ireland, 1725–1799* (London, 1880).

C46   *The Messiah; in nine books* (by John Cameron).
+ Belfast: J. & W. Magee, 1789. LOCATION Dt, L (destroyed).
Dublin: Simms & McIntyre, Archer & Worling, 1811. SOURCE ODNB; COPAC (1811 2nd edn); OCLC. LOCATION D (1811, 2nd edn), C (1811, 2nd edn), DCL (1811, 2nd edn).

COMMENTARY No copy of the Dublin 1811 edn located. Described in the preface as a work designed 'to amuse and to instruct', the text combines details of Christ's life from the Bible (which Cameron takes as facts) with 'fictitious' sections 'invented from short hints'. Each book begins with a section called 'Argument', which offers a summary of historical incidents from the life of Christ. Each 'argument' is followed by a fictitious rendering of the 'factual' summary. The various 'characters' who speak in the text are 'intelligent beings of which we have any knowledge, namely God, Angels, men and devils'. The book remained popular throughout the nineteenth century [FD; ODNB].

CAMPBELL, Dr —, d. 1811. Novelist, and author of *The female minor* (London, 1808, 2 vols.), Dr C should not be confused with the Irish minister Dr Thomas Campbell who wrote on Irish travels and history. SOURCE RL.

C47 *The heroine of Almeida, A novel: founded on facts, relating to the campaigns in Spain and Portugal, under Lord Wellington and General Beresford* (by Dr Campbell).
+ Dublin: Printed [for the author?] by J. Charles, 1811. SOURCE British Fiction; Garside, 1811:26. LOCATION Dt, C, NUC (imperfect).
COMMENTARY Novelette of 145pp relating military campaigns on the Continent and containing references to several Irishmen during the Peninsular campaigns [RL].

CAMPBELL, Lady Charlotte Susan Maria. See **BURY, Lady C.S.M.**

CAMPBELL, Lady Colin (Gertrude Elizabeth, née Blood; also known as **Gertrude Elizabeth Blood**), pseud. **'G.E. Brunefille'**, b. Cratloe (Co. Clare; but possibly born in London, according to RIA/DIB) 1861 (1857 according to ODNB), d. London 1911. Writer, painter, poet, journalist, translator and art critic, GEC was the youngest daughter of Edmond Maghlin Blood, of Brickhill (Co. Clare), sheriff of Co. Clare, and Mary Amy Fergusson of Leixlip (Co. Kildare). She was educated in England, Italy and France, studied art in Florence, and later exhibited her work in England at the Society of Women Artists and at the Society of British Artists. Her marriage in 1881 to Lord Colin Campbell, a younger son of the duke of Argyll, was ended by legal separation in 1883 on the grounds of his cruelty. The subsequent sensational divorce proceedings ruined her reputation and left her socially disgraced. She supported herself by her writing. She was a staff writer for London *Saturday Review*, her subjects including science, literature and political economy, as well as reviews of Italian, German, French and Spanish books. She contributed to *Pall Mall Gazette* and *National Review* (both London), among other publications, and later became art editor for the *World*, the first woman editor on a London paper not exclusively aimed at women. She founded a short-lived weekly review, the *Realm* (London, 1894–95) and became the editor of *Ladies Field* (London) in 1901. Her published works include *The book of the running brook and still waters* (London, 1886), a compilation of her *Saturday Review* essays on natural history and the possibilities of inland commercial fisheries; she edited and revised a popular book on etiquette *Etiquette and good society* (London, 1893), and *A woman's walks: studies in colour abroad and at home* appeared in London in 1903. With Clo Graves§, an Irish artist and playwright, she wrote a full-length melodrama 'St. Martin's summer', which, as well as a one-act drama of hers, played in the West End. McCarthy reported that she wrote 'A miracle in rabbits', but this has not been located. She lived at 67 Carlisle Mansions, Victoria, London. A portrait painted by James McNeill Whistler has been lost. For other portraits, see ODNB. SOURCE Allibone Suppl., i, p. 279; Brady, p. 27; *Burke's genealogical and heraldic history of the peerage, baronetage and knightage* (London, 1949, 99th edn), p. 74; G.H. Fleming, *Victorian 'sex goddess': Lady Colin Campbell* (1990); LVP, p. 83; McCarthy, ii, p. 448; NCBEL 4, p. 1765; ODNB; O'Toole, pp 29–30; RIA/DIB; Sutherland, p. 102.

C48 *Topo. A tale about English children in Italy* (by 'G.E. Brunefille').
London, Belfast: Marcus Ward & Co., 1878 (ill. Kate Greenaway). SOURCE Sutherland, p. 102. LOCATION L, NUC.

COMMENTARY Fiction for juveniles, which became very popular. The heroine, a young 'pickle of a girl', is forever getting into scrapes with her siblings. The story draws on the author's childhood experiences in Italy [ODNB; Sutherland].

C49 *Darell Blake. A study* (by Gertrude Elizabeth Blood; dedicated to my inexorable critic).

   + London: Trischler & Co., [1889]. SOURCE Alston, p. 33. LOCATION L.

   New York: The National Publication Co., 1889 (The Red Letter Series of Select Fiction, No. 4). LOCATION NUC.

COMMENTARY A 'society novel' set in England that draws on the publicity of the author's recent court case against her husband and her first-hand knowledge of journalism. The plot revolves around the destruction of a newspaper editor's happiness through his seduction by the scheming aristocrat Lady Alma Vereker. The main character, Blake, is distantly related to the Blakes of Co. Galway [ML; ODNB; Sutherland].

CAMPBELL, John Francis (known as **J.F. Campbell**), b. Islay (Scotland) 1821?, d. Cannes (France) 1885. Scottish folklorist, scientist and inventor, JFC was heir to the island of Islay but his father, William Frederick Campbell, MP, the second laird, was forced to sell Islay to pay the debts he had incurred improving it. JFC was educated at Eton and at the University of Edinburgh, and subsequently worked with the lighthouse and coal commissions. He was a native speaker of Gaelic and spent a great deal of time collecting folklore in the Western Isles, which resulted in his *Leabhair na Feinne* (London, 1872). SOURCE Allibone Suppl., i, pp 280–1; Brown, p. 51; ODNB; R.M. Dorson, *The British folklorists: a history* (London, 1968), pp 392–418.

C50 *Popular tales of the West highlands orally collected* (by J.F. Campbell and others).

   + Edinburgh: Edmonston & Douglas, 1860–62, 4 vols. SOURCE Brown, 304; *Saturday Review* (London), 11, p. 197. LOCATION L.

   Paisley, London: Alexander Gardner, 1890–93, 4 vols. (new edn). LOCATION L.

COMMENTARY A collection of folklore; the stories are mostly Irish in origin. The Gaelic text is given along with the translation. Contents: 'The young king of Easaidh Ruadh', 'The battle of the birds', 'The tale of the hoodie', 'The sea-maiden', 'Conall cra bhuidhe', 'Conal Crovi', 'The tale of Connal', 'Murchag a's mionachag', 'The brown bear of the green glen', 'The three soldiers', 'The white pet', 'The daughter of the skies', 'The girl and the dead man', 'The king who wished to marry his daughter', 'The poor brother and the rich', 'The king of Lochlann's three daughters', 'Maol a chilobain', 'Fables', 'Baillie lunnain', 'The slim swarthy champion', 'The shifty lad', 'The chest', 'The inheritance', 'The three wise men', 'A puzzle', 'The knight of riddles', 'The burgh', 'The tulman', 'The isle of Pabhaidh', 'Sanntraigh', 'Cailliagh mhor chlibhrich', 'The smith and the three fairies', 'The fine', 'The two shepherds', 'Osean after the feen', 'Barra Widow's son', 'The queen who sought a drink from a certain well', 'The origin of Loch Ness', 'Conall', 'Maghach Colgar', 'Brollaghan', 'Murachadh Mac Brian' [ML].

CAMPBELL, J.G. See **CAMPBELL, John Gregorson**.

CAMPBELL, John Gregorson (also known as **J.G. Campbell**), fl. 1891. A folklorist of Tiree (Scotland). SOURCE Brown, p. 52.

C51 *The fians; or, stories, poems, & traditions of Fionn and his warrior band, collected entirely from oral sources* (collected by J.G. Campbell; introd. by Alfred Nutt).

   + London: David Nutt, 1891 (ill.; Waifs and Strays of Celtic Tradition. Argyleshire Series, No. 4). SOURCE Brown, 306. LOCATION L.

COMMENTARY Contents: 'The Fians', 'The cattle of the Fians', 'End of the Féinne', 'Ossian after the Fians', 'Lay of the red cataract', 'Stormy night', 'Manus', 'Alvin', 'Conn, son of the red', 'The muileartach', 'The lay of the smithy', 'Brugh farala', 'The day of the battle of sheaves, in the true hollow of Tiree', 'Fin Mac Coul in the kingdom of the big men', 'How Fionn found his missing men', 'Fionn and his men', 'How Fionn found Bran', 'Fionn and Bran', 'Ceudach, son of the king of the Colla men', 'How Fionn was in the house of the yellow field', 'Fionn's ransom', 'Numbering of Duvan's men', 'The lad with the skin coverings' [RL].

CAMPBELL, Lady Pamela, fl. 1854. A novelist and children's writer. Only one of her books is set in Ireland. SOURCE NCBEL 4, p. 1765; RL.
C52   *The cabin by the wayside: A tale for the young* (by Lady Pamela Campbell).
        + London, New York: George Routledge & Co., 1854 (ill. Dalziel Bros). SOURCE OCLC. LOCATION DPL, Univ. of Florida.
        COMMENTARY Fiction for juveniles, set north of Dublin and depicts the struggles of poor cottagers who have taken in an orphan [ML].

CAMPBELL, Ross, fl. 1880s. According to the title page of the following book, RC was a teacher of elocution at Dundee (Scotland). SOURCE RL.
C53   *Humorous Irish sketches* (by Ross Campbell; dedicated to Thomas Harrower of Glasgow).
        + Edinburgh, Glasgow: John Menzies & Co.; Dundee: Wm. Kidd, [1888]. LOCATION D.
        COMMENTARY Two of the sketches first appeared in the *People's Friend* (Dundee) and *Scottish Nights* (Glasgow). Contents: 'Hints on gesture, and how to prepare a piece', 'Key to letters in directions', 'Professor Augustus D'Alberta', 'The wiles and the guiles most women work', 'Selling a mountain roe', 'Pleasures of angling', 'Kissed in the dark', 'Why Phil Carson stopped the whiskey bottle' [RL].

CAMPION, Dr —. See **CAMPION, John Thomas.**

CAMPION, John T. See **CAMPION, John Thomas.**

CAMPION, John Thomas (known as **John T. Campion** and **Dr Campion**), b. Kilkenny 1814 (1812 according to Maher), d. Dublin 1898. Physician, writer of historical fiction and poet, JTC contributed to nationalist journals such as the *Nation* (1842), *United Irishman* and the *Irish Felon* (all Dublin). His 'Sketches' appeared in the *Celt* (Dublin, 1857–58), of which he becameeditor in 1859. He was also the author of *Traces of the crusaders in Ireland, with notes, and some poems* (Dublin, 1856). He practiced medicine in Kilkenny and later in Rathgar (Dublin). He wrote for the *Kilkenny Journal* and the *Leinster Independent* (Athy, Carlow, etc.) and he was the secretary of the [John] Banim§ Testimonial Committee in 1883 and wrote a manuscript memoir of the author. JTC died in Simpson's Hospital, Dublin, and was buried in an unmarked grave in Glasnevin cemetery. SOURCE Allibone Suppl., i, p. 283; Brady, p. 28; Brown, pp 52, 336; Hogan 2, pp 222–3; Irish pseudonyms; McKenna, p. 114; J. Maher (ed.), *Chief of the Comeraghs* (Mullinahone, 1957), p. 140; NLI, MS 18,489; O'Donoghue, p. 56; OCIL, p. 79.
C54   *Alice. A historical romance of the crusaders in Ireland (embracing many remarkable traditions)* (by John T. Campion).
        + Kilkenny: Coyle Bros, 1862. SOURCE Brown, 307; McKenna, p. 114; NLI cat.
        LOCATION D, Dcc.
COMMENTARY Historical fiction set in Kilkenny city in the early-fourteenth century. Describes a horse race by the Knights of St John and the preaching of the Crusaders at the market cross as well as the manners and dress of the period. One of the characters is Friar Clynn, the annalist who died in 1328 [Brown].

C55   *Adventures of Michael Dwyer* (by John Thomas Campion).

New York: P.J. Kenedy, [1856 or earlier]. SOURCE Adv. in A.D Dorsey, *Conscience* (New York, 1856).

New York: P.J. Kenedy, [1856 or earlier] (as *Michael Dwyer. An Irish story of 1798*). SOURCE Adv. in A.D Dorsey, *Conscience* (New York, 1856).

COMMENTARY *New York Kenedy [1856 or earlier edn]* Both variant titles are advertised in the same catalogue, each at $1.00 [RL].

New York: P.J. Kenedy, 1875 (as *Michael Dwyer: or, the insurgent captain of the Wicklow mountains: and, reminiscences of '98*). SOURCE OCLC. LOCATION Boston College.

+ New York: P.J. Kenedy, 1897 (as *Adventures of Michael Dwyer; or, the insurgent captain of the Wicklow mountains. And reminiscences of '98*; ill.; Irish Fireside Library). LOCATION InND Loeber coll.

New York: P.M. Haverty, [1871 or earlier] (as *Michael Dwyer; or, the insurgent captain of the Wicklow mountains: a tale of the rising in '98*). SOURCE Adv. in *Haverty's Irish-American Illustrated Almanac* (New York, 1871), p. 104.

+ Glasgow, London: Cameron & Ferguson [1877 or later]. SOURCE McKenna, p. 114; OCLC; RL. LOCATION D (n.d. edn), NUC (n.d. edn).

+ Dublin: M.H. Gill & Son, 1890. SOURCE Brown, 309 (n.d. edn); OCLC. LOCATION UCD, DPL (n.d. edn), Dcc (n.d. edn), NUC (n.d. edn). InND Loeber coll. (n.d. edn).

COMMENTARY No copy of the earliest New York edn located. The book stayed in print until at least 1893 (when advertised in C. Caddell's§ *Never forgotten*, New York,1893, where it was listed as *Adventures and daring deeds of Michael Dwyer*). Historical fiction of an account of the life of a Wicklow outlaw from 1798 to 1805. It describes how Michael Dwyer evades his pursuers for a long time before making terms with the government for his surrender. However, the terms are not kept and along with his wife and companions he is transported for life to Australia. The New York edn has an appendix with reminiscences of the rebellion of 1798 [ML; RL].

C56   *The last struggles of the Irish sea smugglers. A historical romance of the Wicklow coast* (by Dr. Campion).

Glasgow, London: Cameron & Ferguson, 1869 (cover: *The Irish sea smuggler*). SOURCE Brown, 308; McKenna, p. 114; OCLC; COPAC. LOCATION NUC (n.d. edn).

New York: P.M. Haverty, [1871 or earlier] (as *The Irish sea-smugglers*). SOURCE Adv. in Haverty's *Irish-American Illustrated Almanac* (New York, 1871), p. 104.

COMMENTARY No copy of the New York edn located. Historical fiction set on the Wicklow coast around Bray Head around the time of the Union, the book describes the clashes between smugglers and government officials. A love story is interwoven [Brown; RL].

— COLLECTED WORKS

C57   *Dr. Campion's Irish tales.*

Glasgow: Cameron & Ferguson, [following 1869]. SOURCE Adv. in *McHenry Irish tales* (Glasgow, n.d.).

COMMENTARY No copy located. Contents according to the advertisement: 'Michael Dwyer', 'The last struggles of the Irish sea smugglers' and 'Minor tales' [Advertised in *McHenry Irish tales* (Glasgow, n.d.); RL].

'CANDIDA' pseud. See **PECK, Mrs Frances.**

'CANDIDA', fl. 1847. Pseudonym of writer of moral and satiric tales probably Irish.

C58   *Life in the Irish militia; or, tales of the barrack room* (by 'Candida'; dedicated to Daniel O'Connell).

+ London: James Ridgway & Sons, 1847. SOURCE Brown, 65. LOCATION D.

COMMENTARY Tales of satire and moral instruction. Contents: 'The sojourner in Dublin – The modern Pharisees of the city of Shim-shan in Ireland', 'Life in the Irish militia', 'A visit to the lakes of Killarney', 'An allegorical tale', '"A new earth, a new heaven – a fragment."' [RL; CD].

CANNING, the Hon. Albert S.G. See **CANNING, the Hon. Albert Stratford George**.

CANNING, the Hon. Albert Stratford George (known as **Albert S.G. Canning**), b. Ireland 1832, d. Rostrevor (Co. Down) 1916. Novelist and prolific miscellaneous writer, ASGC was the second son of George, 1st Baron Garvagh and his second wife, Rosabelle Charlotte Isabella Bonham. He was landlord of a 4,500 acre estate and spent most of his life in Rostrevor (Co. Down) where he was a DL and a JP. He wrote mostly historical fiction about conflicts in Ireland, from a moderate Unionist and Protestant standpoint. He also published *History in fact and fiction. A literary sketch* (London, 1897), and *The divided Irish* (London, 1888). SOURCE Allibone Suppl., i, pp 283–4; Brown, p. 52; Landed gentry, 1912, p. 95; E. Lodge, *The peerage and baronetage* (London, 1897), p. 294; OCIL, p. 79; E. Reilly, pp 242–3; RIA/DIB; Sutherland, pp 103–4; Topp 8, 880; Wolff, i, pp 205–6.

C59 *Kilsorrel Castle. An Irish story* (by the Hon. Albert Stratford George Canning).
London: Chapman & Hall, 1863, 2 vols. SOURCE Brown, 310 (where misspelled as 'Kilsorrell'); *Saturday Review* (London), 16, p. 368; Sutherland, p. 104. LOCATION L.
COMMENTARY Set in the neighbourhood of Carlingford Lough, a rambling story about two men who have been murdered, one of whom is the illegitimate son of Lord Kilsorrel. The murderer is a villain but the people show him some sympathy [Brown].

C60 *Kinkora. An Irish story* (by Albert Stratford George Canning).
+ London: Chapman & Hall, 1864, 2 vols. SOURCE Brown, 311. LOCATION D, L.
COMMENTARY Historical fiction set at the end of the 1798 rebellion and written from a Unionist point of view. The author describes a number of true incidents, including a public attack on Vincent Lorton, illegitimate son of Lord Delamont. Several rebels are executed at Mullahone, and some people appear after their deaths as ghosts [Brown].

C61 *Baldearg O'Donnell. A tale of 1690–91* (by Albert S.G. Canning).
+ London: T. Cautley Newby, 1867, 2 vols. SOURCE Brown, 312 (1881 edn); Wolff, 1071 (1881 edn); COPAC. LOCATION D, L.
COMMENTARY Historical fiction set in Ireland in 1690–91. Baldearg O'Donnell is the colonel of a regiment in Spain. When returning to Ireland poses as a representative of the Gaelic Irish. For a brief time he becomes an independent, half-guerilla leader on the Irish side. On the promise of a pension, however, he deserts to the English. According to the introd., the story is based on accounts by Leland and Lord Macaulay [Brown; RL].

C62 *Sir Marmaduke Lorton, bart. A tale* (by Albert Stratford George Canning).
+ London: Samuel Tinsley, 1875, 3 vols. SOURCE Wolff, 1072; COPAC. LOCATION D, L.
COMMENTARY The story is set at the seat of the Lorton family in the English midlands. Features several Irish characters, such as Mike Gaffney, and Mr and Mrs Dornan. Some of the discussions concern the fact that in Ireland English authors are not much read. The land agent on the Lorton estate is an Irishman by the name of O'Gorman, whose role in the 1798 rising is revealed. The story contains discussions about religion [ML].

C63 *Heir and no heir. A tale* (by Albert Stratford George Canning).
London: Eden Remington & Co., 1890. SOURCE Brown, 313. LOCATION L.
COMMENTARY Historical fiction set in Co. Derry and London on the eve of the outbreak of the 1798 rebellion. The plot is based on the well-known story of the disinheritance of George

Canning, father of the prime minister, who in the book is called Randolph Stratford. The sharply divided religious and political opinions of the time are described [Brown].

CANNON, Charles James, b. New York (NY) 1800, d. New York (NY) 1860. An Irish-American poet, novelist and dramatist, CJC earned his living as a clerk. His drama *Oath of office*, set in Ireland in the fifteenth century and produced at the Bowery Theatre (New York) in 1850, was described as 'a tragedy of unrelieved intensity'. Only his work of known Irish content is listed below. SOURCE Allibone Suppl., i, p. 284; ANB; DAB; Irish pseudonyms; O'Donoghue, p. 57; Wright, i, p. 67; Wright, ii, p. 64.

C64   *Bickerton; or, the immigrant's daughter. A tale* [anon.].
        + New York: P. O'Shea, 1855. SOURCE Fanning, p. 376; Wright, ii, 456. LOCATION DCU, InND Loeber coll., Wright web.
        New York: O'Shea, 1885 (as *Bickerton; or, the immigrant's daughter. A tale by a distinguished writer*). SOURCE DCU, Catholic Americana files.
        + London: Burns & Lambert, n.d. (as *Bickerton; or, the emigrant's daughter. A tale of Irish-American life*; ill. L. Wing). LOCATION D.
        COMMENTARY Manus O'Hanlon and his wife and daughter emigrate from Ireland to America. They speak Gaelic, but the text is in English and contains songs [RL].

'CAPE COLONIST', pseud. See **BYRNE, May**.

CAREW, Miss —, pseuds **'Mrs Frank Petrill'**, married name Mrs William A. Rafferty, fl. 1885. A poet, essayist, prose and travel writer who lived in the Dublin area and set her work in France. SOURCE Colman, p. 50.

C65   *Lina's tales* (by 'Mrs Frank Petrill').
        + Dublin: M.H. Gill & Son, 1885. LOCATION L.
        COMMENTARY Contents: 'Minette and Fife', 'Two little donkeys'. Both stories are set in France [ML].
C66   *Odile, a tale of the commune* (by 'Mrs Frank Petrill').
        + Dublin: M.H. Gill & Sons, 1886. LOCATION L.
        COMMENTARY Set in France [ML].

CAREY, Mrs Albert, fl. 1863. Religious fiction writer who, since she published in Dublin, may have been Irish. SOURCE Allibone Suppl., i, p. 286; RL.

C67   *'There is but a step between me and death'. A true story* (by Mrs Albert Carey).
        Dublin: W. Curry & Co., 1863. SOURCE Alston, p. 72; COPAC. LOCATION L (destroyed), C.
        COMMENTARY 33pp. Religious fiction [BLC].

CAREY, Margaret Dixon. See **MC DOUGALL, Margaret Dixon**.

CAREY, Mrs Stanley, fl. 1864. Historical fiction writer. Since Mrs SC published only in Dublin, she was probably Irish and most likely a Catholic. SOURCE RL.

C68   *The out-quarters of St. Andrew's priory: A tale of penal times* (by Mrs Stanley Carey).
        Dublin: James Duffy, 1864. SOURCE Falkner Greirson cat. 'Jane'/51. LOCATION Dt.
        + Dublin: James Duffy, [1886 or earlier] (as *Gerald Marsdale; or, the out-quarters of St. Andrew's priory*). SOURCE Adv. in W. Carleton, *Redmond Count O'Hanlon* (Dublin, 1886); Personal communication, Mary Pollard, June 2004. LOCATION InND Loeber coll. ([c.1875–81] edn).

COMMENTARY First serialized in *Duffy's Hibernian Sixpenny Magazine* (Dublin, 1862). Historical fiction set in Cornwall at the beginning of the seventeenth century. It tells of the persecution of a family who had lived on the Continent for some time, who had not given up the Catholic faith. A disgruntled nephew informs on them, and a neighbour who has lost a law suit with them, seizes the opportunity to get rid of them. The family escapes from prison and returns to the Continent [ML].

'CARLETON, Cousin May', pseud. See FLEMING, May Agnes.

CARLETON, Gerald, pseud. 'Bernard Wayde'. Novelist. It is unclear whether this GC can be identified with the Irish-American poet GC, born in Galway in 1844, who later wrote for English papers before emigrating to the US in 1866, and who does not seem to have lived in Ireland for an extended period of time. SOURCE Brown 2, p. 267; O'Donoghue, p. 58.
C69   *Arthur O'Donnell; or, the outcast's revenge* (by 'Bernard Wayde').
+ London: James Henderson, [1867] (The People's Pocket Story Books). SOURCE Brown 2, 1599 (1873 edn). LOCATION L.
COMMENTARY Set in Kilmurry (Co. Waterford) around 1845. The characters include landlords, agents, spies, informers and smugglers. The author does not seem to have had first-hand knowledge of conditions in Ireland [Brown 2; ML].

CARLETON, John William, pseud. 'Craven', b. Hermitage (according to Boase, but Mohill, Co. Leitrim, according to Keane) 1813, d. Dublin 1878. A barrister, novelist and legal writer, JWC was the eldest son of Andrew Carleton, 'pragmaticus', of Hermitage, Mohill (Co. Leitrim), and Elizabeth O'Brien. Educated at Elphin, JWC was admitted to TCD in 1829, graduated BA in 1834 and MA in 1856. He was admitted to the King's Inns in 1834, Gray's Inn (London) the next year, and was called to the Irish Bar in 1839. From 1844 onward he published several tracts on Irish legal and election matters. He must have been an ardent sportsman as he was editor of the *Sporting Review* (London). SOURCE Allibone Suppl., i, p. 287; BLC; B & S, p. 134; Boase, i, p. 549; Keane, p. 75.
C70   *Hyde Marston; or, a sportsman's life* (by 'Craven').
+ London: Henry Colburn, 1844, 3 vols. LOCATION D, L.
COMMENTARY Set in the 1810s and 1820s in England, Ireland and France, it is a story of Hyde Marston, an Englishman born on the banks of the Severn. The Irish section has much on jovial entertainments, the turf and hunting [RL].

CARLETON, Maria Georgina. See FETHERSTONHAUGH, the Hon. Mrs Maria Georgina.

CARLETON, William, pseud. 'Wilton', b. Prillisk (Co. Tyrone) 1794, d. Dublin 1869. A novelist and short story writer, WC was the youngest son in a family of fourteen children of Catholic and Gaelic-speaking farmers. He was educated by hedge-school masters and studied for the priesthood, later abandoning his vocation and his affiliation with catholicism. He joined the Ribbonmen society in 1813, but repudiated its radicalism and remained a supporter of the Union throughout his life. Arriving in Dublin in 1818, he converted to protestantism, found temporary work as a teacher and married Jane Anderson, a Protestant, in 1822. He worked briefly as a teacher in Mullingar and Carlow before returning to Dublin in 1826, where he wrote the home secretary, Sir Robert Peel, and offered to prove that Daniel O'Connell's Catholic Association was involved in agrarian aggression. In Dublin he met Caesar Otway§, the editor of the anti-Catholic *Christian Examiner* (Dublin) and one of the founders of *Dublin*

University Magazine, for whom he started to write (1833–34) anti-Catholic pieces based on his intimate knowledge of peasant life. He also contributed short stories to the *Dublin and London Magazine* (London, 1825–28), the *Dublin Penny Journal* (1840–41), the *Irish Penny Journal* (Dublin, 1840–41), the *Nation* (Dublin, 1842 onward), the *Citizen* (Dublin, 1839, 1841), *Duffy's Hibernian Sixpenny Magazine* (Dublin, 1860–62), and the *Illustrated Dublin Journal* (Dublin, 1861–62). He resided at various addresses in Dublin, and eventually at Dollymount, on the coast road past Clontarf. During his career he wrote for anyone who would pay him, taking on different points of view. But his stories, built on the oral tradition, incorporate realistic descriptions of the hardships of rural life, typically drawn from the south Tyrone locality, as well as politics and social commentary. He met the poet and folklorist Samuel Ferguson§ with whom he went on walking tours, and members of the Young Ireland movement, which may have caused him to soften the harsh anti-Catholic tone of many of his early stories when they were reprinted in the early 1850s. In later novels he highlighted the evils of drink, the land tenure system, Orange bigotry, agrarian violence and famine. He made some efforts to move his base to London and toyed with the idea of emigrating to Canada, where three of his daughters had settled, but stayed in Ireland. WC was awarded an annual government grant of £200 in 1848 but when he died, he had been dogged by poverty and his talents had been eroded by drink. S.C. Hall described him as '[more] above than below the middle size, thick-set ...' (S.C. Hall, p. 237). In 1896 *The Life of William Carleton,* composed of an autobiographic fragment together with biographical commentary by Frances Hoey§ and D.J. O'Donoghue§ was published. A copy of WC's will is among the O'Donoghue papers at UCD (MS LA15/1794), where there are also many of his letters. Additional manuscript materials by WC are in the NLI (MSS 5,756–57, 10,862, 13,993), the NLS (MSS 4,024, 4,083, 4,137 passim). Other manuscripts are mentioned in the ODNB. His portrait by J.J. Slattery is in the NGI, while Elmes lists engraved portraits. SOURCE Allibone, i, p. 342; Allibone Suppl., i, pp 287–8; Brady, p. 29–30; Clyde, pp 103, 105, 107, 128, 130; DLB, clix; Elmes, p. 35; Field Day, ii, pp 205–6, 837–40, iii, pp 391–9, iv, pp 369–72; T. Flanagan, *The Irish novelists 1800–1850* (New York, 1958), pp 255–330; S.C. Hall, p. 237; W.E. Hall, pp 44–5, 75–9, passim; Hogan 2, pp 224–6; Igoe, pp 40–1; Irish pseudonyms; B. Kiely, *Poor scholar* (London, 1847); McKenna, pp 115–20; NCBEL 4, pp 893–5; NUC; OCIL, pp 81–3, 311; ODNB; O'Donoghue, pp 58–9; RIA/DIB; E.A. Sullivan, *William Carleton* (Boston, 1983); Sutherland, pp 106–7; Wolff, i, pp 210–16; R.L. Wolff, *William Carleton. Irish peasant novelist* (New York, 1980).

C71 *Ann Cosgrave; or, the chronicles of Silver Burn* (by William Carleton).
COMMENTARY Manuscript novel in 3 vols. left unpublished at Carleton's death in 1869. Deals with the manners and customs and religious feelings of the Ulster people. Partly published in *Blackwood's Magazine* (Edinburgh, 179 (1906), pp 273–7). SOURCE NCBEL 3, p. 715; Brown; Hayley, p. 166; UCD, MS LA15/313.

C72 *Father Butler. The Lough Dearg pilgrim. Being sketches of Irish manners* [anon.].
+ Dublin: William Curry Jnr & Co., 1829 (ill. [George] Petrie, Kirkwood). SOURCE Hayley, 1a; British Fiction; Garside, 1829:25; Wolff, 1109. LOCATION Grail, D, Dt, BFl, L, InND Loeber coll.

+ Dublin: W. Curry Jnr & Co., 1839, 2nd edn (as *Father Butler. The Lough Dearg pilgrim*). SOURCE Hayley, 1b. LOCATION DPL, NUC.

Philadelphia: Thomas Latimer, 1834 (as *Father Butler; or, sketches of Irish manners*). SOURCE Brown, 30; Hayley, 7a. LOCATION Dt, L (1835 edn), NUC.

Philadelphia: T.K. & P.G. Collins, 1839, 2 vols. (as *Father Butler and the Lough Dearg pilgrim ... to which is added National tales* [by Thomas Hood]). SOURCE NYPL. LOCATION NN.

+ New York: Garland, 1979. LOCATION D, Dt.

COMMENTARY Anti-Catholic stories first published in the *Christian Examiner* (Dublin, 1828). Contents: 'Father Butler' (about a Catholic young man who was committed to the priesthood by his mother's vows, but against his own inclination. The plan had been masterminded by a sinister Jesuit. Eventually, the young man converts to protestantism) and 'The Lough Dearg pilgrim' (a reminiscence of the author's own pilgrimage) [Wolff introd., p. 22; Brown].

C73   *Traits and stories of the Irish peasantry* [anon.; first series] (dedicated to Isaac Butt§, Alderman of the City of Dublin).

Editorial note Because of the large number of versions of this collection of short stories, reprints and publications in parts, the following is organized by city of first publication. Unless stated otherwise, the title of the publication is as above. Commentary showing the contents of the first publication follows the first issue so that it is clearer to readers what the significance is of titles comprising one or more of the stories. The same layout is repeated below for WC's other books of stories [RL].

— DUBLIN

+ Dublin: William Curry Jnr & Co., 1830, 2 vols. (ill. W.H. Brooke). SOURCE Hayley, 2a; Sadleir, 518; Wolff, 1121; Garside 2, 1830:37. LOCATION Corvey 3–28–51141–0, Grail, Ireland related fiction, D, L, NUC, InND Loeber coll. COMMENTARY *Dublin 1830 edn*. Reviewed in Selina Bunbury's§ *Dublin Monthly Magazine* (May 1830). The preface addresses a reading public in England. Contents: 'Ned M'Keown', 'The three tasks, or the little house under the hill; a legend', 'An Irish wedding' (listed in index as 'Shane Fadh's wedding'), 'Larry M'Farland's wake', 'The battle of the factions. By a hedge schoolmaster', 'Funeral and party fight', 'The hedge school' (listed in index as 'The hedge school and the abduction of Mat Kavanagh'), 'The station' (first published in the *Christian Examiner* (London) Jan.–Mar. 1829, signed 'Wilton') [ML; Hayley 2, p. 24].

Dublin: William Curry Jnr & Co.; London: Simpkin & Marshall; Edinburgh: Oliver & Boyd, 1832 (2nd edn, corrected). SOURCE Hayley 2, p. xiii. LOCATION ViU. COMMENTARY *Dublin 1832 edn* In this edn 'The funeral and party fight' is now retitled as 'The party fight and funeral' [Hayley 2, p. 24].

+ Dublin: William Frederick Wakeman; London: Simpkin & Marshall, & Rich. Groombridge, 1834, 2 vols., 3rd edn (corrected; ill. W.H. Brooke). SOURCE Hayley, 2d. LOCATION InND Loeber coll.

— LONDON

+ London: George Routledge & Co., 1853 (as *Traits and stories of the Irish peasantry. Comprising Ned M'Keown, The three tasks, Shane Fadh's wedding, Larry M'Farland's wake, Battle of the factions*; ill. Phiz). SOURCE Hayley, 37a. LOCATION NUC, L (vol. 1 only out of a series of 5). COMMENTARY *London edn* Contains some of the stories [Hayley].

London: George Routledge & Co., 1853 (*Traits and stories of the Irish peasantry. Comprising Shane Fadh's wedding*; Cheap Series, No. 26; ill. Phiz). SOURCE Hayley, 37a; Topp 1, p. 32. COMMENTARY *London 1853 Traits and stories ... Shane Fadh's wedding*. No copy located [RL].

London: George Routledge & Co., 1853 (*Traits and stories of the Irish peasantry. Comprising The station. The party fight and funeral. The hedge school*. Vol. 2; Cheap Series, No. 27; cover embossed Routledge's New Series; ill. Phiz). SOURCE Hayley, 38a; Topp 1, p. 36; COPAC. LOCATION C, NUC.

— MODERN EDN.

+ New York: Garland, 1979, 2 vols. LOCATION D, Dt.

Gerrards Cross: Colin Smythe, 1990, 2 vols. SOURCE COPAC. LOCATION O.

C74 *The little chimney-sweep. An affecting narrative; with authentic facts illustrative of the sufferings of climbing-boys* [anon.].
Dublin: W. Curry Jnr & Co.; R.M. Tims, 1831. SOURCE Hayley, 3a, pp 153–6; Ximenes cat. 108/66. LOCATION InND.
COMMENTARY 58pp. Reviewed in the *Christian Examiner* (Dublin), which stated that 'it is not unworthy of the pen of WILTON', which was Carleton's pseudonym in periodicals. Story of the plight of Irish child chimney-sweeps in the early-nineteenth century, and describes one climbing-boy who is suffocated in a fall of soot as his master curses him for delaying. At the end of the booklet is a section of 'Authentic facts', with such headings as 'Child sold by a father', 'Child stolen', 'Manner of learning the business', 'Losing their way in chimneys and burnt to death', 'Suffocation and burning', etc. This book appeared two years after Samuel Roberts' *Tales of the poor* (London, 1829) which was to benefit the Society for Abolishing the Employment of Climbing Boys in Sweeping Chimneys [Burmester cat. 31/216; Ximenes cat. 108/66; Hayley, 3a, pp 153–6].

C75 *Traits and stories of the Irish peasantry* (second series) [anon.].
— DUBLIN
+ Dublin: William Frederick Wakeman, 1833, 3 vols. (ill. W.H. Brooke). SOURCE Hayley, 4a; Sadleir, 519; Wolff, 1122; Garside 2, 1833:15. LOCATION Grail, Corvey CME 3–628–51141–0, Ireland related fiction, D, Dt, L, NUC. COMMENTARY *Dublin 1833 edn* The first printing was destroyed by a fire which consumed the Dublin printing premises that also published the *Dublin Penny Journal*. First of the three volumes was reviewed in the Dec. 1832 issue of the *New Monthly Magazine* (London, Feb. 1833, pp 147–8) before the other volumes had come out. Contents: 'The midnight mass', 'The Donagh, or the horse-stealers', 'Phil Purcell, the pig-driver. An outline', 'An essay on Irish swearing', 'The geography of the an Irish oath', 'The lianhan shee, an Irish superstition', 'The poor scholar', 'Wildgoose Lodge' (based on the death of eight people resulting from the burning of this huntsman's lodge in Co. Louth in 1816; first published in the *Dublin Monthly Magazine*, 1833, as 'Confessions of a reformed Ribbonman'), 'Tubber Derg, or the red well', 'Denis O'Shaughnessy going to Maynooth' (first serialized in the *Christian Examiner*, Dublin, as 'Dennis [*sic*] O'Shaughnessy going to Maynooth', from which it was adapted), 'Phelim O'Toole's courtship'. The third volume contains an appendix with notes on the text [ML; Hayley 2, pp 88, 124].
Dublin: W.F. Wakeman, 1834, 3rd edn, 2 vols. (corrected; ill. W.H. Brooke). SOURCE Hayley, 4b (1834, 2nd edn, 3 vols.); Hayley, 4c (1835, 3rd edn, 3 vols.). LOCATION NUC.
+ Dublin: William Curry Jnr & Co., 1854 (new edn; ill. Harvey, Phiz, Franklin, Macmanus, Gilbert etc.). LOCATION DPL.
— LONDON
+ London: George Routledge, 1845 (as *Denis O'Shaugnessy going to Maynooth*; ill. W.H. Brooke). SOURCE Hayley, 17a; Brown, 325; Sadleir, 497; Wolff, 1104. LOCATION D, DPL, L, NUC, InND Loeber coll. COMMENTARY *London 1845 edn* Single story concerning Denis O'Shaughnessy who, from an early age, was destined for the priesthood [Brown].
+ London: George Routledge & Co., 1853 (as *Traits and stories of the Irish peasantry. Comprising The midnight mass. The Donagh. Phil Purcel, the pig-driver. The geography of an Irish oath. An essay on Irish swearing.* Vol. 3; Cheap Series, No. 28; ill. Phiz). SOURCE Hayley, 39a; Topp 1, p. 36. LOCATION PC, NUC.
London, New York: George Routledge & Co., 1854 (as *Traits and stories of the Irish peasantry. Comprising The lianhan shee. The poor scholar. Wildgoose lodge. Tubber Derg,*

or the red well. Vol. 4; Cheap Series, No. 29; ill. Phiz). SOURCE Hayley, 40a; Topp 1, p. 39. LOCATION NUC.

London, New York: George Routledge & Co., 1854 (as *Traits and stories of the Irish peasantry. Comprising Phelim O'Toole's courtship. Denis O'Shaughnessy going to Maynooth.* Vol. 5; Cheap Series, No. 30; ill. Phiz). SOURCE Hayley, 41a; Topp 1, p. 40. LOCATION NUC. COMMENTARY *London 1853–54 edns* These edns contain a selection of the stories [Hayley].

— PHILADELPHIA

+ Philadelphia: E.L. Carey & A. Hart; Baltimore: Carey, Hart & Co., 1833, 2 vols. SOURCE Hayley, 5a. LOCATION NUC (1834 edn), InND Loeber coll. COMMENTARY *Philadelphia 1833 edn* Contents: 'The Donagh, or the horse-stealers' (first published in the *Dublin Literary Gazette and National Magazine*, Dec. 1830), 'Phil Purcell, the pig-driver', 'The poor scholar', 'Phelim O'Toole's courtship', 'The geography of an Irish oath' [Hayley; RL].

Philadelphia: E.L. Carey & A. Hart; Boston: Allen & Ticknor, 1833, 2 vols. SOURCE Hayley, 5a. LOCATION NUC.

+ Philadelphia: E.L. Carey & A. Hart; Baltimore: Carey, Hart & Co., 1834, 2 vols. in 1. SOURCE Hayley, 6a. LOCATION NUC, InND Loeber coll. COMMENTARY *Philadelphia 1834 edn* Contents: 'The midnight mass', 'The Lianhan shee', 'Tubber Derg, or the red well', 'An essay on Irish swearing', 'Wildgoose Lodge', 'Denis O'Shaughnessy going to Maynooth' [Hayley].

Philadelphia: Carey & Hart, 1845 (as *Phelim O'Toole's courtship and The poor scholar*). LOCATION D, NUC. COMMENTARY *Philadelphia 1845 edn* Consists of only a few of the stories [RL].

— TORONTO

Toronto: Adam, Stevenson & Co., 1871. SOURCE Hayley, 55a; OCLC. LOCATION Univ. of Ottawa. COMMENTARY *Toronto edn* Contents: 'Geography of an Irish oath', 'Going to Maynooth', 'The midnight mass' [Hayley].

— MODERN EDN

+ New York: Garland Press, 1979, 3 vols. SOURCE COPAC. LOCATION Dt, L, InND Loeber coll.

C76   *Tales of Ireland* [anon.].

+ Dublin: William Curry Jnr & Co.; London: Simpkin & Marshall, 1834 (ill. W.H. Brooke). SOURCE Hayley, 8a; Brown, 319; Sadleir, 516; Wolff, 1119; Bradshaw, 3498; Garside 2, 1834:18. LOCATION Corvey CME 3–28–51152–6, Grail, Ireland related fiction, D, Dt, L, C, DCL, MH, InND Loeber coll.

Philadelphia: E.L. Carey & A. Hart, 1839, 2 vols. (as *Neal Malone, and other tales of Ireland*). SOURCE Hayley, 12a; NYPL. LOCATION NUC.

+ New York: Garland, 1979. LOCATION D, Dt.

COMMENTARY According to the preface, some of the tales were written to demonstrate 'the deplorable effects which too frequently proceed from marriages between Roman Catholics and Protestants'. Most of these anti-Catholic stories first appeared in the *Christian Examiner* (Dublin, 1829–30). Contents: 'The death of a devotee', 'The priest's funeral', 'Neal Malone', 'The brothers. A narrative', 'The illicit distiller', 'The brothers', 'The dream of a broken heart', 'Lachlin Murray and the blessed candle' [ML].

C77   *Traits and stories of the Irish peasantry* [first and second series combined] (by William Carleton; dedicated to John Birney).

— LONDON

+ London: Baldwin & Cradock; Dublin: William F. Wakeman, 1836, 5 vols. (4th edn, ill. W.H. Brooke). SOURCE Hayley, 10a. LOCATION DPL, L, InND Loeber coll.

COMMENTARY This combined series was issued in parts by James Curry, Dublin, advertised in June 1842, with the first of 23 parts, appearing Aug. 1842–June 1844. It has some new illustrations. For contents, see contents of the first and second series. This edn also includes 'The Lough Dearg pilgrim', and 'Neal Malone' [RL; Haley, 15a; Hayley 2, p. xiv; Advertised in pt. 6 of C. Lever, *Jack Hinton* (Dublin, 1843–44)].

+ London: George Routledge & Co., 1852, 2 vols. (new edn; dedicated to Isaac Butt§; with an autobiographical introd. by WC, and explanatory notes; ill. Harvey, Phiz, Macmanus, Gilbert, S. Holden, E. Evans). LOCATION D. COMMENTARY *London 1852 edn* Probably a reissue of unsold sheets of the first printing. The BL copy contains an extra title page with the imprint, Dublin: Wm. Curry Jnr; London: W.S. Orr, n.d. [Rowan cat. 60/80; RL].

+ London: William Tegg, 1865, 2 vols., 6th edn (new edn; with author's latest corrections and introd., and explanatory notes; ill.). LOCATION D (n.d. edn), DPL (n.d., 11th edn), InND Loeber coll.

London: William Tegg & Co.; New York: Scriber, Welford & Armstrong, 1875 (new edn). SOURCE Hayley, 58a.

+ London, Manchester, New York: George Routledge & Sons, 1895 (as *Phil Purcell the pig-driver and other stories*; The Caxton Novels). SOURCE Hayley, 81a; Brown 2, 197. LOCATION D. COMMENTARY *London 1895 edn* A subset of the stories. Contents: 'The hedge school', 'The station', 'The midnight mass', 'The Donagh; or, the horse stealers', 'Phil Purcell, the pig-driver', 'The lianhan shee' [Hayley].

— DUBLIN

+ Dublin: William Curry Jnr & Co.; London: William S. Orr & Co., 1843, 2 vols. (new edn; new introd.; ill.). SOURCE Hayley, 15a (issued in 25 parts). LOCATION D, InND Loeber coll.

— LEIPZIG

Leipzig: Weber, 1837, 3 vols. (trans. by H. Roberts as *Skizzen und Erzählungen aus dem Leben des Irishen Landvolks*; preface by K. Jürgens). SOURCE Hayley, p. 190; GLOL. LOCATION Gemeinsamer Bibliotheksverbund.

— PARIS

Paris: E. Dentu, 1861 (trans. by Léon de Wailly as *Romans irlandais, scènes de la vie champêtre*). SOURCE P.S. O'Hegarty, 'Notes and comment ...' *The Bibliographical Society of Ireland*, 6(4), (1954), p. 60; Rafroidi, ii, p. 361; Brown, 1647; OCLC; CCF. LOCATION BNF. COMMENTARY *Paris edn* Contents 'Denis O'Shaughnessy', 'The three tasks', 'Wildgoose lodge' [P.S. O'Hegarty, 'Notes and comment ...' *The Bibliographical Society of Ireland*, 6(4), 1954, p. 60].

— PHILADELPHIA

Philadelphia: Carey & Hart, 1845 (as *Phil Purcel, and other tales of Ireland*). LOCATION NUC. COMMENTARY *Philadelphia edn* Contents: 'Phil Purcel', 'Ned M'Keown', 'The three tasks', 'Shane Fadh's wedding', 'Larry M'Farlane's wake' [NUC].

— NEW YORK

+ New York: Wilson & Hawkins, 1862, 2 vols. (new edn with autobiographical introd., explanatory notes; ill. Harvey, Phiz, Franklin, Macmanus, Gilbert etc.). SOURCE Hayley, 15e. LOCATION D.

— MODERN EDNS

+ Gerrards Cross: Colin Smythe, 1990, 2 vols. (ed. by B. Hayley). LOCATION D.

+ Cork, Dublin: Mercier Press, 1973 (as *The party fight and funeral*; introd. by Maurice Harmon). LOCATION DPL. COMMENTARY *Cork edn The party fight* A subset of the stories. Contents: 'The party fight and funeral', 'The midnight mass' [RL].

+ Cork, Dublin: Mercier Press, 1973 (as *Phelim O'Toole's courtship and other stories*; introd. by Maurice Harmon). LOCATION DPL. COMMENTARY *Cork edn Phelim O'Toole's courtship* A subset of the stories. Contents: 'Phelim O'Toole's courtship', 'The three tasks', 'An essay on Irish swearing' [RL].

C78   *The chronicles of Ballymacruiskeen. With the lives, deaths, marriages, and other misfortunes of its inhabitants* (by William Carleton).

COMMENTARY Announced for publication in 1839 and 1840, to be published monthly in parts with illustrations; not known to have been published. An agreement between Carleton and James McGlashan to write this book is among the O'Donoghue papers at UCD (MS LA/15/1791). The prospective of 'Mr. Carleton's New Work', attached to his *The miser; or, the convicts of Lisnamona* (Philadelphia: Carey & Hart, 1840), i, n.p., contains 'a peep at the larder' for the prospective readers, of its 'rough bill of fare': 'Roe and progress of the village', 'Decline and fall of another', 'Opposing principles', 'Good landlord and bad', 'The Pelts of Castle Pelt – as landlords – their system', 'Silky Sisk the factotum', 'The old forties', 'Kate Karney', 'Glimpses at '98', 'The humours of an Irish election', 'Convert hunting – an Irish pastime', 'The two converts', 'Mat Kavanagh *redivius*', 'Priests and parsons', 'Controversy', 'The month's mind', 'Old Irish dances – the *Horo Liege*', 'The blessings of conacre', 'Poor Laws', 'The cow saddled', 'Vagrants', 'Workhouses', 'Combination among beggars', 'The Crutch conspiracy', 'Battle of the guardians', 'Father O'Flaherty', 'An excommunication', 'Coroner's inquest', 'Election sermon', 'Kate Karney's wooers', 'Abduction', 'Orange Lodge', 'Grand Jury in the old style', 'Willy Reilly and Cooleen Bawn – their loves and sorrows', 'Swearing an alibi', 'Presbyterian singing meetings', 'The Rev. Sergeant M'Swig', 'Method of keeping lent', 'Location of salvation', 'Education', 'New schools and old masters', 'Mat Kavanagh under training', 'Story of Alice Dun', 'The holy cruiskeen', 'Barny Green, the polygamist – his own chaplain', 'The struggles of Malachy O'More – his ruin and emigration', 'Legend of Peggy Slevin – origin of the air and song', 'The rakes of Ballyfaddy', 'The murdered landlord', 'Judicial death of Silky Sisk', 'Ribbonism', 'Orange and Green', 'Progress of the spirit of Irish society', 'Kate Karney – her character – story wound up by her marriage and happiness' [RL; Hayley, p. 32].

C79   *Fardorougha, the miser; or, the convicts of Lisnamona* (by William Carleton; dedicated to James McCullagh, Fellow of TCD).
       + Dublin: William Curry Jnr & Co., 1839. SOURCE Hayley, 11a; Sadleir, 502; Wolff, 1108. LOCATION Grail, D, Dt (1841 edn), L, NUC.
       + Dublin: William Curry Jnr & Co.; London: Longman, Orme & Co., 1841, 2nd edn. LOCATION InND Loeber coll.
       Dublin: J. Duffy, 1846, 4th edn (carefully revised and corrected; ill.). SOURCE Hayley, 11e. LOCATION D, L, NUC.
       + Dublin: James Duffy & Co., n.d. (as *Fardorougha the miser*). LOCATION DPL.
       + London, Belfast: Simms & M'Intyre, 1848 (Parlour Library, No. 21; with a new introd.). SOURCE Sadleir, ii, p. 153; Sadleir, 502a. LOCATION D, Dt, NUC, InND Loeber coll.
       London: Newnes, [*c.*1896–99], 2 vols. (Newnes' Penny Library of Famous Books, Nos. 99, 100). SOURCE Sadleir, 3643.
       + Philadelphia: Carey & Hart, 1840, 2 vols. (as *The miser; or, the convicts of Lisnamona*; contains prospectus of Mr Carleton's new work). SOURCE Hayley, 11b; Wolff, 1108a. LOCATION NUC.
       New York: P.M. Haverty, 1868. SOURCE Hayley, 11i.
       Boston, New York: Little, n.d. (as *Fardorougha: the miser, a tale*). SOURCE Hayley, 11m. LOCATION NUC.

+ New York: Garland, 1979. LOCATION D, Dt.

+ Dublin: Appletree Press, 1992 (introd. by Benedict Kiely). LOCATION D.

COMMENTARY First serialized in the *Dublin University Magazine* (1837). The story starts with the birth of a child, Connor, after thirteen years of marriage between Fardorougha O'Donovan, a peasant farmer, and his wife Honor. The father's temperamental miserliness is complicated and exacerbated by his love for his son. He takes on as a servant in his household Bartle Flanagan, the son of a man he previously ruined. Bartle, a secret Ribbonman, plots O'Donovans' downfall. He burns the barn of Bodagh Buie, whose daughter Una has refused Connor in marriage because of Fardorougha's meanness. Connor is brought to trial and condemned to hang, but the sentence is commuted on account of his gentle nature. Suffering tempers Fardorougha, who sells his farm and with his wife follows Connor to transportation in New South Wales. Bartle is eventually caught and confesses. The O'Donovans are brought back to their home by public subscription. The novel is a grim study of avarice and Catholic family life. The story was adapted into a play by Anna Jane Magrath, which ran for some time in Dublin, but Carleton did not like it [Sutherland, p. 222; W.E. Hall, pp 78–9; Colman, p. 154; O'Donoghue, p. 297].

C80   *The fawn of Spring-Vale, The clarionet, and other tales* (by William Carleton; dedicated to William Wordsworth).[1]

+ Dublin: William Curry Jnr & Co.; London: Longman, Orme & Co., 1841, 3 vols. SOURCE Hayley, 14a; Topp 1, p. 2; Wolff, 1110. LOCATION Grail, D, L, NUC. COMMENTARY *Dublin 1841 edn* Contents: 'Jane Sinclair; or, the fawn of Spring Vale', 'Lha Dhu; or, the dark day', 'The clarionet', 'The dead boxer', 'The misfortunes of Barney Branagan', 'The resurrections of Barney Bradley' [Hayley].

+ Dublin: William Curry Jnr; London: George Routledge, 1843, 3 vols. (as *Jane Sinclair; or, the fawn of Spring Vale, The clarionet, and other tales*). SOURCE Hayley, 14b; Sadleir, 504. LOCATION D, NUC, InND Loeber coll.

London: G. Routledge, 1847, 3 vols. in 1 (as *Barney Branagan, Fawn of Spring Vale, Barney Bradley, and other tales*). SOURCE Hayley, 26a; OCLC. LOCATION NUC.

+ London: George Routledge & Co., 1850 (as *The clarionet, The dead boxer, and Barney Branagan*; Railway Library, No. 14). SOURCE Hayley, 34a. LOCATION D, DPL, Dt, L, NUC. COMMENTARY *London 1850 edn* A subset of the stories. Contents: 'The clarionet', 'The dead boxer', 'Barney Branagan' [Hayley].

+ New York: Garland, 1979, 3 vols. LOCATION D, Dt.

C81   *Valentine M'Clutchy, the Irish agent; or, chronicles of the Castle Cumber property, with the pious aspirations of Solomon M'Slime* (by William Carleton).

+ Dublin: James Duffy; London: Chapman & Hall; Edinburgh: Oliver & Boyd, 1845, 3 vols. (ill. H.K. Browne [Phiz]). SOURCE Hayley, 16a; Brown, 323; Block, p. 35; Sadleir, 521; Wolff, 1126. LOCATION Grail, D, L, NUC, InND Loeber coll.

+ Dublin: James Duffy, 1847 (as *Valentine M'Clutchy, the Irish agent; or, the chronicles of Castle Cumber, together with the pious aspirations, permissions, vouchsafements and other sanctified privileges of Solomon M'Slime, a religious attorney* (ill. Phiz;Valentine McClutcy [*sic*] on spine). SOURCE Hayley, 16c. LOCATION D, DPL (1848 edn), Dt (1848 edn), NUC, InND Loeber coll. (1848 edn).

Dublin: James Duffy & Co., 1859 (as *Valentine McClutchy, the Irish agent, and Solomon M'Slime, his religious attorney*; ill. Geo. Measom). SOURCE Hayley, 16h; Sadleir, ii, p. 25 (n.d.). LOCATION D (n.d., 8th edn), L.

+ London: Henry Lea, [1846] (as *Valentine McClutchy, the Irish agent*; ill. Phiz).

---

1 Probably the English poet.

SOURCE Hayley, 16n. LOCATION D, Dt (imperfect), NUC.

Paris: L'Univers, 1845 (trans. by L. de Wailly as *Les chroniques de Chateau Cumber*). SOURCE Rafroidi, ii, p. 367.

+ New York, Montreal: D. & J. Sadlier, 1846 (as *Valentine M'Clutchy, the Irish agent; or, chronicles of the Castle Cumber property*). SOURCE Hayley, 16b. LOCATION D, InND Loeber coll.

New York, Montreal: D. & J. Sadlier, 1854 (as *Valentine M'Clutchy, the Irish agent; or, the chronicles of Castle Cumber, together with the pious aspirations, permissions, vouchsafements and other sanctified privileges of Solomon M'Slime, a religious attorney*). SOURCE Haley, 16f. COMMENTARY *New York 1854 edn* No copy located [RL].

+ New York: Garland, 1979. LOCATION D, Dt.

COMMENTARY Evoked very contradictory reactions from reviewers. Remained popular, with an 8th Dublin edn in about 1889. A social problem novel written against absentee Protestant landlords. A landlord comes back to Ireland and publicly humiliates and dismisses his agent. Before the landlord's return, the wicked agent and his son, the Methodist lawyer, and the bailiff had committed some atrocious crimes [Wolff introd., pp 24–5; Brown; T. Flanagan, *The Irish novelists 1800–1850* (New York, 1958), pp 312–13].

C82   *Rody the rover; or, the Ribbonman* (by William Carleton).

+ Dublin: James Duffy, 1845 (Duffy's Library of Ireland, No. 3; Plate 15). SOURCE Brown, 324; Sadleir, 512; ii, p. 37; Wolff, 1116. LOCATION Grail, D, Dt, L, NUC, InND Loeber coll. COMMENTARY *Dublin 1845 edn* Originally published in soft cover, printed in two colours green with shamrocks and primitive decoration, priced at 1*s*. as part of Duffy's Library of Ireland for Sept. 1845 [BLC; RL.; Advertised in W. Carleton, *Tales and sketches* (Dublin, 1845)].

+ New York: Stringer & Townsend, 1850. LOCATION InND Loeber coll.

+ Philadelphia: T.B. Peterson & Bros, [186–] (as *The life and adventures of Rody the rover; the Ribbonman of Ireland*; complete and unabridged edn; see Plate 16). LOCATION NUC, InND Loeber coll.

COMMENTARY According to the introd., the volume initially had been planned as the second volume to WC's *Tales for the Irish people*. This volume is addressed to Irishmen to show them the terrible consequences of joining the Ribbonmen. Consists of a story about Ribbonism, which is represented as an organization whose leaders are self-interested rascals who make use of the peasantry and were often double-dealing by being in the pay of Dublin Castle [Brown; RL].

C83   *Parra Sastha; or, the history of Paddy-go-easy and his wife Nancy* (by William Carleton; dedicated 'to the people of Ireland … to improve their condition').

+ Dublin: James Duffy, 1845 (Duffy's Library of Ireland, No. 5). SOURCE Brown, 322; Sadleir, 506; ii, p. 38; Wolff, 1113. LOCATION Grail, D, L, InND Loeber coll. COMMENTARY *Dublin 1845 edn* The NLI copy has original soft cover, printed in green and red, in primitive, nationalistic design [RL].

Dublin: James Duffy, 1846, 2nd edn (carefully revised … new matter amounting to more than one-third off the book added; Duffy's Library of Ireland). LOCATION Dt, NUC.

+ Boston: Patrick Donahoe, 1865. LOCATION D, NUC.

COMMENTARY Supposedly written for farmers. Contains a sketch of a good-natured but good-for-nothing Irishman called Paddy, who has not improved his land holding and is critical of his improving neighbour. However, when Paddy marries he is turned into an industrious farmer under the gentle direction of his wife who has many ideas about the improvement of the house, the farmyard and the fields. The appendix contains instructions on agricultural and other farm matters, copied from Martin Doyle's [William Hickey's§] *Hints to the small farm-*

ers of the County of Wexford (Dublin, 1833). The Irish revolutionary Jeremiah O'Donovan Rossa read the book when he was young and found 'The whole book ... a dirty caricature of the Irish character' [Brown; OCIL, p. 466; *Rossa's recollections, 1838 to 1898, memoirs of an Irish revolutionary* (Guilford, CT, 2004), p. 128].

C84   *Art Maguire; or, the broken pledge. A narrative* (by William Carleton; dedicated to Fr Theobald Mathew).
+ Dublin: James Duffy, 1845 (ill.; Duffy's Library of Ireland, No. 19). SOURCE Hayley, 19a; Block, p. 34 (who mistakenly mentions 1841 as first edn); Brown, 326; Sadleir, 482; ii, p. 38; Wolff, 1101. LOCATION D, Dt (1847 edn), DPL (n.d. edn), L, NUC, InND Loeber coll. COMMENTARY *Dublin 1845 edn* Back cover of the InND copy has embossed: Traveller's Library, but no evidence of other books in this series [RL].
+ Dublin: James Duffy, 1847. LOCATION D, L. COMMENTARY *Dublin 1847 edn* 214pp, instead of earlier 263pp. Deluxe edn, in gold stamped boards with a harp on cover; 'Duffy's Library of Ireland' plus title on spine; gold edge [RL].
+ Dublin: James Duffy; London: Simpkin, Marshall & Co., 1847. LOCATION D. COMMENTARY *Dublin and London 1847 edn* The NLI copy has a soft cover, ill. in black, with primitive nationalistic drawings [RL].
New York, Montreal: D. & J. Sadlier, 1846. SOURCE Hayley, 19c. LOCATION NUC ([1846?] edn).
COMMENTARY In the preface WC stated that 'In proposing to write a series of 'Tales for the Irish people', it is his intention 'to improve their physical and social condition'. This is a temperance tale, a cautionary story of a man who is ruined by drink. Art Maguire is an intelligent man with a good profession of carpenter, well-regarded and married to a loving wife. Despite all these advantages, he falls time and again under the influence of alcohol. Even Fr Mathew cannot keep him on the straight and narrow. Art is compared to his cautious brother, Frank, who follows a steady course through life and who is able to support his sister-in-law when Art is not contributing any money to the household. Art dies in the poor house [ML; RL].

C85   *O'Sullivan's love: A legend of Edenmore; and the history of Paddy Go-Easy and his wife Nancy* (by William Carleton).
Philadelphia: Carey, 1847. SOURCE OCLC. LOCATION D, NUC.
COMMENTARY Contents: 'O'Sullivan's love: A legend of Edenmore', 'Parra Sastha; or, the history of Paddy Go-Easy' (first published in Dublin, 1845) [NUC].

C86   *Tales and sketches illustrating the character, usages, traditions, sports and pastimes of the Irish peasantry* (by William Carleton; dedicated to Charles Gavan Duffy).
Dublin: James Duffy, 1845 (ill. Phiz). SOURCE Hayley, 18a; Sadleir, 514; Wolff, 1118. LOCATION Grail, NUC.
+ Dublin: James Duffy, 1846 (ill. Phiz; contains extra title page *Tales and stories of the Irish peasantry*, 1846, followed by a title page, which is dated 1845). LOCATION D, InND Loeber coll. (also 1849 edn). COMMENTARY *Dublin 1846 edn* Two binding types: (a) green cloth, gold stamped with Irish dancing, music playing, and fighting figures on spine, title: 'Tales & Stories' [*sic*]; (b) the same in red cloth [RL].
London: Henry Lea, [*c.*1855] as *Irish life and character; or, tales and stories of the Irish peasantry*). SOURCE Hayley, 79a; OCLC (1855 edn); Sadleir, ii, p. 24. LOCATION L ([1860] edn). COMMENTARY *London edn* First issued in 35 parts, then bound as a book; omits last story in *Tales and sketches* [Hayley].
+ New York: Garland, 1979. LOCATION D, Dt, InND Loeber coll.
COMMENTARY Contents: 'Micky M'Rorey, the Irish fiddler', 'Buckramback, the country dancing master', 'Mary Murray, the Irish match-maker', 'Bob Pentland; or, the gauger outwitted',

'The fate of Frank M'Kenna', 'The rival kempers', 'Frank Martin and the fairies', 'A legend of Knockmany', 'Rose Moan, the Irish midwife', 'Talbot and Gaynor, the Irish pipers', 'Frank Finnegan, the foster-brother', 'Tom Cressiey, the Irish senachie', 'The castle of Aughentain; or, a legend of the brown goat. Narrated by Tom Cressiey, the Irish senachie', 'Barney M'Haigney, the Irish prophesy man', 'Moll Roe's marriage; or, the pudding bewitched', 'Barney Brady's goose; or, dark doings at Slathbeg' (first published in the *Dublin University Magazine*, Dublin, 1838), 'Condy Cullen; or, the exciseman defeated', 'A record of the heart; or, the parents' trial', 'The three wishes; an Irish legend', 'The Irish rake', 'Stories of the second-sight and apparition' [Hayley].

C87   *The battle of the factions, and other tales of Ireland* (by William Carleton).
+ Philadelphia: Carey & Hart, 1845 (ill.). SOURCE Sadleir, 493. LOCATION NUC, InND Loeber coll.

COMMENTARY Collection of stories from *Traits and stories* (1st and 2nd series, London, 1836, 5 vols.), and *Tales of Ireland* (Dublin, 1834). Contents: 'The battle of the factions', 'The geography of an Irish oath', 'Neal Malone', 'The Donagh; or, the horse-stealers', 'The station' [ML].

C88   *The black prophet. A tale of Irish famine* (by William Carleton; dedicated to Lord John Russell, prime minister of Great Britain and Ireland).
+ Belfast: Simms & M'Intyre, 1847 (Parlour Library, No. 1). SOURCE Topp 6, 256; LOCATION D, NUC.
+ London, Belfast: Simms & M'Intyre, 1847 (Parlour Library, No. 1; ill. W. Harvey, Dickes: cover: Owen Jones). SOURCE NCBEL 3, p. 714; Brown, 327; Sadleir, 495; Wolff, 1102. LOCATION D, Dt, BFl, L, InND Loeber coll.

COMMENTARY *London and Belfast 1847 edn* Issued as the first volume of the famous Parlour Library. Two binding variants, one blind embossed cloth, the other in pale yellow glazed boards printed in gold and red in arabesque design by Owen Jones [Sadleir, 495; RL].
Niewe Diep: C. Bakker, 1847, 2 vols. (trans. into Dutch as *De zwarte profeet: Een verhaal uit den tijd van de Ierschen hongersnood*). SOURCE Adamnet; Alphabetische naamlijst 1833–49, p. 131. LOCATION UVA.
New York: Burgess, Stringer, 1847. LOCATION NUC.
+ Shannon: Irish Univ. Press, 1972. LOCATION D.
+ New York: Garland, 1979. LOCATION D, Dt, L.

COMMENTARY First serialized in the *Dublin University Magazine* (1846–47). According to the author's preface, some of the scenes are in part based on the lesser famines of 1817 and 1822. The plot centres round a murder mystery and chronicles several families and their suffering. The novel attacks various groups such as landlords, moneylenders, middlemen and the government for their role in the dire state of the country prior to the Great Famine of the 1840s [Brown; Field Day, ii, pp 124–9; Wolff introd., p. 25].

C89   *The emigrants of Ahadarra: A tale of Irish life* (by William Carleton).
+ London, Belfast: Simms & M'Intyre, 1848 (Parlour Library, No. 11). SOURCE Hayley, 30a; Brown, 328 (mistakenly mentions a [1847] edn); Sadleir, 499; Wolff, 1106. LOCATION Grail, D, Dt, L, NUC, InND Loeber coll.
London, New York: George Routledge & Co., 1857 (as *The emigrants: A tale of Irish life*; Railroad Library, No. 141). SOURCE Hayley, 30c; Topp 1, p. 83. LOCATION L, NUC.
+ New York: Garland, 1979. LOCATION D, Dt.

COMMENTARY Describes the ravages of Irish depopulation in the wake of the Famine and the necessity of emigration in order to stay alive. The story is about a worthy young farmer who narrowly escapes ruin at the hands of a neglectful landlord, a corrupt would-be squireen allied with illegal distillers. However, another absentee landlord is reformed and the planned emigration to America never takes place [Brown; Field Day, v, pp 518–20; Wolff introd., p. 25].

C90 *The tithe proctor: A novel. Being a tale of the tithe rebellion in Ireland* (by William Carleton).

+ London, Belfast: Simms & M'Intyre, 1849 (Parlour Library, No. 24). SOURCE Hayley, 31a; Brown, 329; Sadleir, 517; Wolff, 1120. LOCATION Grail, D, DLP, Dt, L, InND Loeber coll.

London, New York: George Routledge & Co., 1857 (as *The tithe-proctor. A novel*; Railway Library, No. 142; ill. Phiz). SOURCE Hayley, 31b; Topp 1, p. 82. LOCATION NUC.

+ New York: Garland, 1979. LOCATION D, Dt.

COMMENTARY Concerns the tithe war and is based on a real event, the murder of the Bolands by the Whiteboys in 1808. The 1849 edn has an additional story: 'The hand and word' [Brown; RL; Wolff introd., p. 25].

C91 *Jane Sinclair; or, the fawn of Spring Vale; and The dark day* (by William Carleton). London: George Routledge & Co., 1849 (Railway Library, No. 2). SOURCE Hayley, 32a; Topp 1, p. 2. LOCATION NUC. COMMENTARY *London 1849 edn* Contents: 'Jane Sinclair; or, the fawn of Spring Vale', 'The dark day'. Both stories were first published in *The fawn of Springvale*, Dublin, 1841, 3 vols. [NUC; RL].

+ London: George Routledge & Co., 1850 (as *Jane Sinclair. Neal Malone, &c. &c.*). SOURCE Hayley, 33a; OCLC. LOCATION D, Dt, L (1852 edn), NUC. COMMENTARY *London 1850 edn* Contents: 'Jane Sinclair; or, the fawn of spring-vale', 'Lha Dhu; or the dark day', 'Barney Bradley' (first published in *The fawn of Springvale*, Dublin, 1841, 3 vols.), 'Neal Malone' (first published in *Tales of Ireland*, Dublin, 1834), 'Wildgoose lodge' (first published in *Tales and stories*, Dublin, 1834) [RL].

+ London, New York: George Routledge & Sons, [1875] (as *Jane Sinclair, Neal Malone and other tales*). SOURCE Hayley, 33c. LOCATION D. COMMENTARY *London and New York [1875] edn* Contents: 'Jane Sinclair; or the fawn of Spring-vale', 'Lha Dhu; or, the dark day', 'Barney Bradley', 'Neal Malone', 'Wildgoose lodge' [Hayley, 33a; CD].

New York, Montreal: D. & J. Sadlier & Co., 1872, probably three parts (as *Jane Sinclair; or, the fawn of Spring Vale*). SOURCE Hayley, 56a; OCLC. LOCATION NN. COMMENTARY *Montreal 1872 edn* Contents: 'Jane Sinclair; or, the fawn of Spring Vale', 'Lha Dhu; or, the dark day', 'The dead boxer' [Hayley].

C92 *The dead boxer, an Irish legend* (by William Carleton).

+ Philadelphia: A. Winch, 1850. LOCATION InND Loeber coll. COMMENTARY *Philadelphia edn* Stories from *The fawn of Spring Vale* (Dublin, 1841, 3 vols.), and *Tales of Ireland* (Dublin, 1834). Contents: 'The dead boxer', and 'Neal Malone' [RL].

Boston: J. Jones, [18–?] (as *The dead boxer; or, the secret blow and the counter secret*). SOURCE Hayley, 82a. LOCATION NUC.

New York: N.L. Munro, 1877 (New York Boys' Library, vol. 2 as *The dead boxer*). LOCATION NUC.

C93 *Dominick, the poor scholar* (by William Carleton). London: Ward, Lock & Co., [185?]. SOURCE OCLC. LOCATION NUC.

C94 *Red Hall or the baronet's daughter* (by William Carleton). London: Saunders & Otley, 1852, 3 vols. SOURCE Hayley, 36a. LOCATION Grail (1854 edn), Dt (1854 edn), L.

+ Dublin: James Duffy, 1858 (as *The black baronet; or, the chronicles of Ballytrain*; ill. Geo. Measom). SOURCE Hayley, 36c; Sadleir, 494. LOCATION D, L, NUC (1875 edn).

+ New York: P.M. Haverty, 1858 (as *The black baronet; or, the chronicles of Ballytrain*; ill. S.C. Keating). LOCATION InND Loeber coll.

Boston: Patrick Donahoe, 1869 (as *The black baronet; or, the chronicles of Ballytrain*). SOURCE Hayley, 36d. LOCATION NUC.

C95   *The Squanders of Castle Squander* (by William Carleton).
+ London: Illustrated London Library, 1852, 2 vols. (ill. Topham, [George] Measom, T. Williams; The Illustrated Family Novelist). SOURCE Hayley, 35a; Brown, 333; Sadleir, 514, 3747; Topp 2, p. 159. LOCATION Grail, Dt (2 vols. in 1), DPL, L, NUC, InND Loeber coll.

COMMENTARY Issued in two binding types (a) carmine red cloth, embossed in silver; (b) olive green or bright blue morocco cloth. Depicts the life of the gentry. However, the book turns from a novel into a political essay [ML; Carter, pp 101–2].

C96   *Jane Sinclair; or, the fawn of Spring Vale; The clarionet, and other tales* (by William Carleton).
London: George Routledge & Co., 1852. LOCATION BL, NUC.

COMMENTARY *London 1852 edn* Mostly stories from *The fawn of Spring Vale* (Dublin, 1831, 3 vols.), but also from *Tales of Ireland* (Dublin, 1834). Contents: 'Jane Sinclair; or, the fawn of Spring Vale', 'Lha dhu; or, the dark day', 'Barney Bradley', 'Neal Malone', 'Wildgoose lodge', 'The clarionet', 'The dead boxer', 'Barney Branagan' [NUC; RL].

C97   *The poor scholar* (by William Carleton).
New York, Montreal: D. & J. Sadlier, 1854 (Sadlier's Fireside Library, No. 6; ill.). SOURCE Hayley, 42a; NUC.
+ New York, Montreal: D. & J. Sadlier, 1877 (as *The poor scholar, and other tales of Irish life*; Sadlier's Fireside Library, No. 6; ill.; has extra title page, 1873, just for 'The poor scholar'). LOCATION InND Loeber coll.

COMMENTARY Stories from *Traits and stories* (Dublin, 1833, 3 vols., 2nd series), and *Tales and sketches* (Dublin, 1845). Contents: 'The poor scholar', 'A peasant girl's love' [by John Banim'], 'Talbot and Gaynor, the Irish pipers', 'Frank Finnegan, the foster brother' [Hayley].

C98   *Tubber Derg; or, the red well, and other tales of Irish life* (by William Carleton).
+ New York, Boston, Montreal: D. & J. Sadlier, 1854 (Sadlier's Fireside Library, No. 8). SOURCE Hayley, 43a; DCU, Catholic Americana files; NUC (1866 edn), InND Loeber coll. (1860 edn).

COMMENTARY Mostly stories from *Tales and sketches* (Dublin, 1845), but also from *Traits and stories* (Dublin, 1833, 3 vols., 2nd series). Contents: 'Tubber Derg; or, the red well', 'Barney Brady's goose; or, dark doings at Slathbeg', 'Tom Gressiey, the Irish senachie', 'The castle of Aughentain; or, the legend of the brown goat', 'The white horse of the Peppers' [by Samuel Lover§], 'Mick M'Rorey, the Irish fiddler' [Hayley].

C99   *Willy Reilly and his dear Coleen Bawn: A tale, founded upon fact* (by William Carleton).
+ London: Hope & Co., 1855, 3 vols. SOURCE Hayley, 44a; Brown, 334; Sadleir, 522; Wolff, 1127. LOCATION Grail, D, L, NUC, InND Loeber coll.
+ Dublin: James Duffy, 1857, 2nd edn (ill. George Measom; additional preface). SOURCE Hayley, 44c; Topp 1, p. 461. LOCATION Dt ([c.1890] edn), L, InND Loeber coll.
Boston: Thomas P. Noonan, 1855. SOURCE OCLC. LOCATION InND.
New York: P.J. Kenedy, 1855 (as *Willy Reilly and his dear Colleen [sic] Bawn*). SOURCE OCLC. LOCATION InND (also Geo. Munro edn; see Plate 17).
Philadelphia: John E. Potter & Co., [1883] (Lovell's Library, No. 4). SOURCE Hayley, 44z; NCBEL 3, p. 715. LOCATION NUC.
+ Chicago: Belford, Clarke & Co., [1856]. SOURCE Hayley, 44y. LOCATION D (1881 edn), NUC, InND Loeber coll. (1885 edn).

COMMENTARY A highly popular novel, it is known from at least eight different New York imprints (represented in the InND Loeber coll.). Romantic story set in the penal days, and based on the famous ballad 'Now rise up, Willy Reilly'. Story of crossed Catholic and Protestant love. It ends happily after many harrowing events with Willy safely united with his Colleen Bawn on the Continent. Colleen Bawn is said to represent the daughter of squire ffolliott of Holybrook, Co. Sligo [Sutherland; Brown; RL; J.C. Ternan, *Historic Sligo* (Sligo, 1965), p. 28].

C100   *Alley Sheridan, and other stories* (by William Carleton).

+ Dublin: P. Dixon Hardy & Sons, [1857] (ill.). SOURCE Hayley, 45a; Brown, 335a; Sadleir, 491; Wolff, 1100. LOCATION D (n.d. edn), L, NUC, InND Loeber coll.

COMMENTARY Advertised in *Hardy's tourist guide through Ireland* (Dublin, 1858) as part of an unidentified series entitled *Hardy's Genuine Edition of Tales and Stories of the Irish Peasantry* (sold in 'fancy covers' at the price of 1s. 6d., both published by Philip Dixon Hardy), but no further volumes of this series have been identified. Contents: 'Alley Sheridan, or the Irish runaway marriage', 'Laying a ghost', 'Owen M'Carthy, or the landlord and tenant', 'Condy Cullen and the gauger' (first published in *Tales and sketches*), 'The Donagh, or the horse-stealers' (first published in *Traits and stories*, 2nd series), 'Sir Turlough, or the church-yard bride' [Hayley; RL].

C101   *The evil eye; or, the black spectre. A romance* (by William Carleton; dedicated to Edward and Anthony Fox).

+ Dublin, London: James Duffy, 1860 (portrait of Carleton, ill. Edmund FitzPatrick). SOURCE Hayley, 47a; Brown, 336; NCBEL 4, p. 894; Sadleir, 500; Wolff, 1107. LOCATION Grail (1880 edn), D (1880 edn), Dt (1864 edn), L, NUC, InND Loeber coll.

+ Dublin, London: James Duffy & Sons, 1880 (as *The evil eye; or, the black spectre*; ill.). SOURCE Hayley, 47f. LOCATION DPL.

Tournai: H. Casterman, 1865 (trans. as *Le mauvais oeil, ou le spectre noir, suivi de cela seulement*). SOURCE Hayley, p. 189; Rafroidi, ii, p. 361; Bn-Opale plus. LOCATION BNF.

+ Boston: Patrick Donahoe, 1860. LOCATION NUC (1875 edn), InND Loeber coll.

C102   *The double prophecy; or, trials of the heart* (by William Carleton; dedicated to the earl of Carlisle, lord lieutenant of Ireland).

+ Dublin, London: James Duffy, 1862, 2 vols. SOURCE Hayley, 48a; Brown, 337a; NCBEL 4, p. 894; Sadleir, 498; Wolff, 1105. LOCATION Grail, D, L, NUC.

COMMENTARY First serialized in *Duffy's Hibernian Magazine* (Dublin, 1861), and the *Irish American* (New York, 1861) [NCBEL; BLC; RL].

C103   *Redmond, Count O'Hanlon, the Irish rapparee. An historical tale* (by William Carleton).

+ Dublin, London: James Duffy, 1862. SOURCE Hayley, 49a; Brown, 337; NCBEL 3, p. 715; Wolff, 1115. LOCATION Grail, D, L, C, NUC.

COMMENTARY *Dublin and London 1862 edn* Simple blind pressed binding with leave pattern – gold title on spine [RL].

+ Dublin: James Duffy & Sons, 1886 (new edn; with an appendix by Thomas Clarke Luby). LOCATION D, DPL, NUC (n.d. edn), InND Loeber coll.

COMMENTARY WC first published this in *Duffy's Hibernian Magazine* (Dublin, 1860) as 'The rapparee'. Set in Ireland in 1696, it tells of the exploits of a daring rapparee. The plot consists mainly of the rescue by O'Hanlon of a girl who has been abducted. A poem, *An elegie on … Redmond O'Hanlan* was published in 1681, followed by the Dublin story in prose the next year. The history of Redmond O'Hanlon was later published in John Cosgrave's§ *A genuine history* (Dublin, 1747) [Brown; RL].

C104   *The silver acre and other tales* (by William Carleton).

+ London: Ward & Lock, 1862 (Stirling Volume Library, No. 15; ill. Phiz). SOURCE Hayley, 50a; Brown, 338. LOCATION Grail, D, Dt, L, InND Loeber coll.

London: Ward, Lock & Tyler, 1869 (as *The fair of Emyvale, and The master and scholar*; The Parlour Library Sixpenny Series, No. 10; ill. Phiz]). SOURCE Hayley, 54a (1870 edn); NCBEL 3, p. 715; Topp 2, 602. LOCATION L ([1870] edn).

COMMENTARY Serialized in *Illustrated London Magazine* (1853). Contents: 'The silver acre', 'The fair of Emyvale', 'Master and scholar'. The London 1869 edn consists of two of the three stories [Brown; NCBEL 4, p. 894; RL].

C105   *The poor scholar, Frank Martin and the fairies, The country dancing master, and other Irish tales* (by William Carleton).

+ Dublin, London: James Duffy, 1869. SOURCE Hayley, 51a; Sadleir, 507; Wolff, 1114. LOCATION D (1869 edn), DPL, NUC, InND Loeber coll. COMMENTARY *Dublin 1869 edn* Two binding types: (a) green boards, blind stamped with gold harp and shamrock in the centre, gold on spine; (b) green paper cover with black type, with cover title: *The poor scholar, and other Irish tales*, at 6*d*. [RL].

+ Dublin: James Duffy & Sons, 1874 (as *The poor scholar and other tales*). LOCATION D.

COMMENTARY *Dublin 1874 edn* Green paper cover with black type, at 6*d*. Mostly stories from *Tales and sketches* (Dublin, 1845) and *Traits and stories* (Dublin, 1833, 3 vols., 2nd series). Contents: 'The poor scholar', 'Mickey M'Rorey, the Irish fiddler', 'Buckram Back, the country dancing master', 'Mary Murray, the Irish match maker', 'Bob Pentland, or the gauger outwitted', 'The fate of Frank M'Kenna', 'The rival kempers', 'Frank Martin and the fairies', 'The legend of Knockmany' [RL].

C106   *Barney Brady's goose, The hedge school, The three tasks, and other Irish tales* (by William Carleton).

+ Dublin, London: James Duffy, 1869. SOURCE Hayley, 52a. LOCATION D, DPL (n.d. edn), NUC.

COMMENTARY Published in green paper cover with black printed title, 6*d*., with cover title: *Traits and stories of the Irish peasantry*. Stories from *Tales and sketches* (Dublin, 1845), *Traits and stories* (Dublin, 1830, 2 vols., 1st series), and *Tales of Ireland* (Dublin, 1834). Contents: 'Barney Brady's goose; or, dark doings at Slathbeg', 'The three tasks', 'Second sight and apparition', 'Neal Malone', 'The hedge school', 'Condy Cullen; or, the exciseman defeated', 'Moll Roe's marriage; or, the pudding bewitched' [RL].

C107   *Tubberderg; or, the red well. Party fight and funeral, Dandy Kehoe's christening, and other Irish tales* (by William Carleton).

+ Dublin, London: James Duffy, 1869. SOURCE Hayley, 53a; Wolff, 1125. LOCATION D, DPF (n.d. edn), NUC.

COMMENTARY Two binding types: (a) blind stamped green cloth, with central harp surrounded by shamrock; gold title on spine; (b) green printed paper cover with black type, at the price of 6*d*. Mostly stories from *Tales and sketches* (Dublin, 1845), but also from *Traits and stories* (London, 1836, 5 vols., 1st and 2nd series). Contents: 'Tubber Derg; or, the red well', 'Party fight and funeral', 'Dandy Kehoe's christening', 'Talbot and Gaynor, the Irish pipers', 'Frank Finnegan, the foster brother', 'The three wishes' [Hayley].

C108   *Parra Sastha; or, the history of Paddy go-easy and his wife Nancy. To which is added Rose Moan, the Irish midwife* (by William Carleton; dedicated to the People of Ireland).

+ Dublin, London: James Duffy & Co., 1875, 12th edn. SOURCE Hayley 21d; LOCATION D (n.d. edn), NUC (n.d., 14th edn).

Dublin: James Duffy & Co., [1892 or earlier] (as *Paddy go easy and his wife Nancy*).
SOURCE Adv. in J.J. O'Dea, *The beauties of nature* (Dublin, 1892).
COMMENTARY No copy of the Dublin [1892 or earlier] edn located. Contents: 'Parra Sastha; or, the history of Paddy go-easy', 'Rose Moan, the Irish midwife'. Binding type: green boards, blind stamped with gold harp and shamrock in the centre, gold on spine [RL].

C109 *The Fardorougha miser, Tithe proctor, The poor scholar, and other tales* (by William Carleton).
New York: Sadlier, 1880, 3 vols. LOCATION NUC.
COMMENTARY The first story was published separately in Dublin in 1839; the second story separately in London in 1849; and the third story in *Traits and stories of the Irish peasantry* (second series) (Dublin, 1833) [RL].

C110 *The red-haired man's wife* (by William Carleton).
+ Dublin: Sealy, Bryers & Walker; London: Simpkin, Marshall & Co., 1889. SOURCE Brown, 340; Hayley, 78a; Sadleir, 509. LOCATION Grail, D, Dt, L.
COMMENTARY Serialized in *Carlow College Magazine* (Carlow, 1870). Carleton's last work, published posthumously as a volume. The story of a notorious lady-killer, set in Fenian times [Brown; RL; NCBEL 4, 894].

C111 *Stories from Carleton* (dedicated to the author of *Shamrocks* [Katharine Tynan§]).
+ London: Walter Scott; New York, Toronto: W. J. Gage & Co., [1889] (introd. by W.B. Yeats§; The Camelot Series). SOURCE Hayley, 80a. LOCATION D, DPL, NUC.
+ London, Felling-on-Tyne, New York: Walter Scott, [1889] (introd. by W.B. Yeats§; The Camelot Series). SOURCE Hayley, 80b. LOCATION L, NUC, InND Loeber coll.
New York: Lemma, 1973. SOURCE Hayley, 80c.
COMMENTARY Stories from *Traits and stories* (London, 1836, 5 vols., 1st and 2nd series). Contents: 'The poor scholar', 'Tubber Derg; or, the red well', 'Wildgoose Lodge', 'Shane Fadh's wedding', 'The hedge school' [RL].

C112 *Amusing Irish tales* (by William Carleton).
+ London: Hamilton, Adams & Co.; Glasgow: Thomas D. Morison, 1889. SOURCE Hayley, 77a. LOCATION D (n.d., 4th edn), L, NUC ([1889], 4th edn), InND Loeber coll.
+ London: Hamilton, Adams & Co.; Glasgow: Thomas D. Morison, 1892 (new edn). SOURCE Hayley, 77b. LOCATION D.
COMMENTARY Mostly stories from *Tales and sketches* (Dublin, 1846), but also *Traits and stories* (Dublin, 1833, 3 vols., 2nd series). Contents: 'Buckram-back, the country dancing master', 'Mary Murray, the Irish match-maker', 'Bob Pentland, the Irish smuggler; or, the gauger outwitted', 'Tom Gressiey, the Irish senachie; or, the origin of the name of Gordon', 'Barney M'Haigney, the Irish prophesy man', 'Fin M'Coul, the Knockmany giant', 'Around Ned's fireside; or, the story of the squire' (based on 'Ned M'Keown'), 'The Irish student; or, how the Protestant church was invented by Luther and the devil' (based on 'O'Shaughnessy going to Maynooth'), 'Mickey M'Rorey, the country fiddler', 'Rose Moan, the country mid-wife', 'Corney Keho's baby; or, the Irish Christening', 'Barney Brady's goose; or, mysterious doings at Slathbeg', 'Condy Cullen; and how he defeated the exciseman', 'Phil Purcel, the Connaught pig-driver', 'Father Phelimy; or, the holding of the station' [Hayley; RL].

C113 *Irish tales. Wildgoose lodge. Condy Cullen. The curse. Battle of the factions* (by William Carleton).
New York, London: G.P. Putnam's Sons, [1904] (ed. and introd. by W.B. Yeats§). SOURCE Hayley, 85a.
COMMENTARY Stories from *Traits and stories* (London, 1836, 5 vols., 1st and 2nd series), and *Tales and sketches* (Dublin, 1845). Contents: 'Wildgoose lodge', 'Condy Cullen', 'The curse',

'The battle of the factions'. These are all the Carleton stories which William Butler Yeats§ published in his *Representative Irish tales* (New York, [1891]) [Hayley; RL].

C114 *Stories by William Carleton.*
+ London, Glasgow, Edinburgh, Bombay: Blackie & Son, [1905] (ed. by Tighe Hopkins§). LOCATION D.
COMMENTARY Stories from *Traits and stories* (London, 1836, 5 vols., 1st and 2nd series), and *Tales of Ireland* (Dublin, 1834). Contents: 'The party fight and funeral', 'The hedge school', 'Phelim O'Toole's courtship', 'Neal Malone' [Hayley; RL].

C115 *Carleton's stories of Irish life.*
+ Dublin: Talbot Press; London: T. Fisher Unwin, [1918] (introd. by Darrell Figgis; ill.; Every Irishman's Library). LOCATION L, DCU, NUC, InND Loeber coll.
COMMENTARY Stories from *Tales of Ireland* (Dublin, 1834), *Traits and stories* (London, 1836, 5 vols., 1st and 2nd series), and *Tales and sketches* (Dublin, 1845). Contents: 'Neal Malone', 'Phelim O'Toole's courtship', 'The geography of an Irish oath', 'Bob Pentland, or the gauger outwitted', 'The party fight and funeral', 'The midnight mass', 'The hedge school', 'Denis O'Shaughnessy going to Maynooth' [RL].

C116 *Wildgoose lodge and other stories* (by William Carleton).
+ Cork, Dublin: Mercier Press, 1973 (introd. by Maurice Harmon). LOCATION DPL.
COMMENTARY Stories from *Traits and stories* (London, 1836, 5 vols., 1st and 2nd series), and *Father Butler*. Contents: 'Wildgoose lodge', 'Ned M'Keown', 'The lianhan shee', 'The Lough Dearg pilgrim' [RL; Field Day, ii, pp 873–83 (*Wildgoose Lodge*)].

C117 *King Richard McRoyal or the dream of an antiquarian* (by William Carleton).
+ Armagh: Southern Education and Library Board, 1983 (introd. by Liam Bradley). LOCATION Dt, L, O, InND Loeber coll.

— COLLECTED WORKS
C118 *Mr. Carleton's works.*
+ Dublin: William Curry Jnr & Co.; London: Longman & Orme & Co., 1841, 4 vols. SOURCE Adv. in C. Lever§, *Charles O'Malley* (Dublin, 1841). LOCATION InND Loeber coll. (one vol. only).

C119 *Carleton's traits and stories of the Irish peasantry.*
+ London: Ward, Lock & Co., [1881], 10 vols. (ill. E. Evans, C.H. Weigall; G.F. Sargent, S. Prout). SOURCE Topp 2, 1443. LOCATION InND Loeber coll. (vols. 3, 7 and 10 bound in 1).
COMMENTARY Priced at 6*d*. each [RL].

C120 *Tales and stories of the Irish peasantry.*
New York, Boston, Montreal: D. & J. Sadlier & Co., 1860, 9 vols. SOURCE Hayley, p. 93; RL.
COMMENTARY Also known from an 1875 edn. Possibly a publisher's binding, but without publisher's name on the binding [RL].

C121 *Carleton's work.*
+ New York: D. & J. Sadlier & Co., 1875–[76?], 10 vols. SOURCE DCU, Catholic Americana files; Hayley, pp 93–4 (who mentions 1875 as the earliest edn). LOCATION NUC, InND Loeber coll. (a few vols.).
COMMENTARY Possibly the series started in 1872. Remained in print in 1880 and 1886. Advertised in 1875 and mentions that the series in cloth was priced at $15, in half morocco at $20, and in half calf at $25 [RL; Advertised in M.J. Hoffman, *The orphan sisters* (New York, 1875)].

C122 *The works of William Carleton.*
+ New York: P.F. Collier, 1881, 2 vols. and 3 vols. edns (Collier's Unabridged Edition). LOCATION NUC, InND Loeber coll.

COMMENTARY For contents of three variant edns of the 1881 issue, see Hayley, pp 127–135. NUC mentions a [1856] edn, but this probably is an undated edn of one the Collier 1881 edns [see Hayley, pp 127–135; RL].

C123 *[William Carleton's works]*.

New York: P.J. Kenedy, [1895], 10 vols. [Broadsheet advertised P.J. Kenedy, [1895]; RL].

COMMENTARY Unnumbered and untitled series. Two binding types: (a) crushed leather at $7 for the series; (b) half calf, gilt edges at $20 for the series. The series probably is a reissue of the collected works first published by D. & J. Sadlier. The Kenedy series of Carleton's works was advertised as part of 'Kenedy's Gilt-top Series of Irish Novelists', and included the works of the Banim brothers§, Gerald Griffin§, and Samuel Lover§, in total 35 uniformly bound volumes and priced at $22 [Broadsheet advertisement P.J. Kenedy, [1895]; RL].

C124 *The works of William Carleton*.

+ Freeport (NY): Books for Libraries Press, 1970, 2 vols. (ill. M.L. Flanery). LOCATION D, InND Loeber coll.

COMMENTARY Reprint of Collier, 1881, 2 vols. edn [RL].

CARR, Ellis, fl. 1881. Novelist. Judging from the following volume, EC was probably Catholic and Irish. A person of this name ill. C. Wilson's *Mountaineering* (London, 1893) and W.P. Haskett Smith's *Climbing in the British Isles, Ireland* (London, 1894). SOURCE BLC.

C125 *An eviction in Ireland, and its sequel* (by Ellis Carr).

+ Dublin: M.H. Gill & Son, 1881. SOURCE Allibone Suppl., i, p. 294. LOCATION L.

COMMENTARY 51pp. A grandfather and his granddaughter are going to be evicted by a landlord. Many neighbours are ready to fight for them, but the priest exhorts them to stay calm. The grandfather dies at the doorstep. The granddaughter wishes to kill the landlord's agent, but does not. She ends up in England, where one day she is hit by the coach of the landlord's son, who has succeeded his father. The agent's wife and the young landlord visit her in the hospital and she recognizes the agent's wife. Before dying, she tells the young landlord the story of the eviction, and he promises to reverse the wrongs done in his father's time [ML].

CARROLL, Revd John, b. Bay of Fundy (Canada) 1809, d. 1884. Canadian Methodist minister, religious writer and biographer, JC moved with his parents to York (Toronto) in 1818. He became an itinerant Methodist preacher and wrote several religious works and biographies of Methodist figures. He published his sermons and documented the evangelization of Canadian society. His first book, *The stripling preacher; or a sketch of the life and character, with the theological remains of the Rev. Alexander S. Byrne* (Toronto, 1852), concerned a romantically charismatic Irish convert. JC also published *My boy life presented in a succession of true stories* (Toronto, 1882). SOURCE DCB; DLB, ic; Rhodenizer, pp 357, 707.

C126 *The school of prophets; or Father McRory's class, and Squire Firstman's kitchen fire* (by John Carroll).

Toronto: Burrage & Magurn, 1876. SOURCE Rhodenizer, p. 707. LOCATION L (not found), Robarts Library, Toronto.

COMMENTARY Announced as 'fiction founded on fact' [Rhodenizer, p. 707].

CARROLL, Mary Augustine, pseud. '**A member of the Order of Mercy**', b. probably Clonmel (Co. Tipperary) 1835, d. 1909. Biographer, children's writer and nun, it is not known when MAC emigrated to the US but it is clear that she was working in the Convent of Mercy in St Louis in 1866. She wrote the biography of Mother McAuley, foundress of the order, as well as 'Happy hours of childhood', and 'Angel dreams', which have not been located. SOURCE [anon.], 'The writings of an Irish-American nun', in *Donahoe's Magazine*, 9 (1883), pp 49–51, copied from the *Irish Monthly*; RIA/DIB; RL.

C127 *Glimpses of pleasant homes. A few tales for youth* (by 'A member of the Order of Mercy').
    + New York: Catholic Publication Society, 1869. LOCATION InND.

CARTAN, Joseph, b. Tullyallen (Co. Louth) 1811, d. 1891. Journalist, writer and entrepreneur, JC joined the staff of the *Drogheda Argus* in the 1830s. He temporarily abandoned journalism to found a car service between Newry and Dundalk but in 1849 established the *Dundalk Democrat and People's Journal*. Interested in politics from an early age, JC used his paper to endorse nationalism and tenant rights, and later the Tenant League. His often vitriolic editorials were widely criticized. Lord Clermont won a judgment against him which he could not pay in full. Consequently he was imprisoned in Dundalk jail. The paper ran until 1870, when he sold it. SOURCE O'Donoghue, p. 61; RIA/DIB.

C128 *An essay on patriotism, together with legends and stories of Louth, and a variety of songs to the most celebrated Irish airs* (by Joseph Cartin [*sic*]; introd. by 'AZA').
    + Drogheda: Thomas Kelly, 1839. SOURCE O'Donoghue, p. 61; RIA/DIB. LOCATION D.
    COMMENTARY The legends and stories are in prose; the rest of the volume consists of songs. Contents: 'Thubber na sullis (The well of light): A legend of Belgathern', 'Peter Callan; or the forty shilling freeholder of Louth. A story of the election of 1826' (Catholic emancipation movement and the events surrounding the election of Alexander Dawson in 1826), 'The friar's white horse. A legend of Mellifont Abbey', 'Jemmy Mooney and his man Dick Hanratty. A story of difficulties and disappointments' [O'Donoghue; RIA/DIB].

CARTIN [*sic*], Joseph. See CARTAN, Joseph.

CASEY, Elizabeth Owens Blackburne, pseud. 'E. Owens Blackburne', b. Slane (Co. Meath) 1848, d. Fairview (Dublin) 1894. Novelist, journalist and short story writer, EOBC was the daughter of Andrew Casey and his wife (née Mills) and granddaughter of Richard Blackburne of Mulladillon House (Co. Meath). At age 11 she lost her sight, recovering it after an operation by Sir William Wilde§ seven years later. EOBC went to London in 1873 or 1874, and became a prolific journalist, contributing to such Dublin publications as the *Irish Fireside* (1883–84), the *Nation*, and the *Shamrock*. Her stories are mostly descriptions of Irish peasant life. She wrote ten novels, two of which are autobiographical and mostly deal with Ireland. In 1877 she published *Illustrious Irishwomen* (London), a scholarly compilation of women from different political and religious backgrounds. She never married and although later in life she received assistance from the Royal Bounty Fund, she became almost destitute. Eventually she returned to Ireland where she died in a fire at her home in Fairview. McCarthy and Hogan 2 mention several works ('Aunt Delia's heir'; 'In the vale of honey'; 'Shadows in the sunlight'; and 'A chronicle of Barham') which have been not been located in book form and which may have been published in – as yet unidentified – periodicals. *Source* Allibone Suppl., i, pp 299–300; Blain, pp 97–8; Boylan, p. 54; Brady, p. 14; Brown, p. 35; Colman, p. 50; Field Day, v, pp 1103, 1108, 1120 [under Blackburne]; Hogan 2, pp 156–7 [under Blackburne]; Irish pseudonyms; OCIL, p. 49 [under Blackburne]; O'Donoghue, p. 62; RIA/DIB; Rowan cat. 53A/594; Sutherland, p. 67 [under Blackburne]; Wolff, i, p. 218.

C129 *A modern Parrhasius* (by 'E. Owens Blackburne' and A.A. Clemës).
    London: Tinsley Bros, 1875, 2 vols. SOURCE McCarthy, ii, p. 565; Hogan 2, p. 157. LOCATION NUC.

Casey

C130   *A woman scorned. A novel* (by 'E. Owens Blackburne').
London: Tinsley Bros, 1876, 3 vols. SOURCE Brown, 213; Alston, p. 74. LOCATION L, NUC.
COMMENTARY Probably autobiographical fiction. Set near the river Boyne. Describes life in an upper-class Irish household fallen on hard times. A Capt. Fitzgerald falls in love with Katherine, the second daughter. The jealous elder sister plots to marry Katherine to a rich elderly suitor. Her plot fails and the elder sister dies [Brown; RL].

C131   *The way women love. A novel* (by 'E. Owens Blackburne').
+ London: Tinsley Bros, 1877, 3 vols. SOURCE Brown, 214; Wolff, 1141. LOCATION D, L.
COMMENTARY Tells of the love life of the two daughters of a Donegal man who, after an unsuccessful career as an artist in London, settles near Weirford [Waterford]. Gives descriptions of local society [Brown].

C132   *A bunch of shamrocks. A collection of Irish tales and sketches* (by 'E. Owens Blackburne'; dedicated to author's god-daughter Norah Ivatts).
+ London: Newman & Co., 1879. LOCATION D, L, NUC.
New York: G. Munro, 1879 (Seaside Library). SOURCE Brown, 215. LOCATION NUC.
COMMENTARY Contents: 'Biddy Brady's banshee', 'The priest's boy', 'The stray sod of Tiernach bog', 'Ould Butler's wake', 'Philosopher Push', 'Lovely Katty Keogh', 'Norah Kinsellagh', 'Dean Swift's ghost', '"Denis Dhuv"', 'An unsolved mystery', 'Miss Honor's patients', 'Maureen', '"Till the sea gives up its dead"', 'Dick Wilkin's adventure', 'Story of a deaf mute' [RL].

C133   *Molly Carew. A novel* (by 'E. Owens Blackburne').
London: Tinsley Bros, [1879], 3 vols. SOURCE Brown, 216. LOCATION L.
COMMENTARY Partly autobiographical: a young Irish writer seeks work in London and is obsessed with a male writer who had befriended her as a child. The plot is sensational but unpredictable and is relentless in depicting the sacrifices the heroine make to protect her ideal and in its refusal of a 'happy ending' [Blain, p. 98].

C134   *The glen of silver birches. A novel* (by 'E. Owens Blackburne').
London: Remington & Co., 1880, 2 vols. SOURCE Brown, 217 (1881 edn); Alston, p. 74. LOCATION L.
's Hertogenbosch: Maatschappij Katholieke Illustratie, 1886 (trans. into Dutch as *De laatste der O'Donnell's. Een zedenschets uit Ierland*). SOURCE Mes, p. 28.
COMMENTARY *'s Hertogenbosch edn* Also was published in the periodical *Leesbibliotheek voor Christelijke Huisgezinnen* ('s Hertogenbosch, 1883) [Mes, p. 287].
New York: Harper & Bros, 1881. SOURCE Colman, p. 51. LOCATION NUC.
COMMENTARY Nuala O'Donnell lives with her extravagant father who has mortgaged his estate in the Donegal highlands. A scheming attorney tries to get possession of the estate and to marry Nuala. However, she marries an English landlord who has bought the neighbouring estate [Brown].

C135   *'My sweetheart when a boy'* (by 'E. Owens Blackburne').
+ London: Moxon, [1880] (Moxon's Select Novelettes, No. 1; ill. J. Moyr Smith).
SOURCE Alston, p. 74. LOCATION L.
COMMENTARY Has Irish content [CM].

C136   *As the crow flies* (by 'E. Owens Blackburne').
+ London: Moxon, Saunders & Co., [1880] (Moxon's Select Novelettes, No. 4).
SOURCE Alston, p. 74; COPAC. LOCATION L.
COMMENTARY Has Irish content. Set in Magheragh. This place name occurs in several counties in the west of Ireland [CM; RL].

C137   *The love that loves always. A novel* (by 'E. Owens Blackburne').
London: F.V. White & Co., 1881, 3 vols. SOURCE Alston, p. 74. LOCATION L.

New York: G. Munro, 1881 (Seaside Library). LOCATION NUC.

C138 *The heart of Erin. An Irish story of to-day* (by 'E. Owens Blackburne').
+ London: Sampson Low, Marston, Searle & Rivington, 1882, 3 vols. LOCATION D, NUC.
New York: G. Munro, 1882 (Seaside Library). SOURCE Brown, 218.
COMMENTARY No copy of the New York edn located. Set in Co. Meath at the time of the campaign of the Land League. Tells the story of an Irish MP who, when he moves up in society, breaks with his faithful girl at home. There is a mystery surrounding his birth, but in the end he appears to be the heir to an estate [Brown; RL].

CASSIDY, Patrick Sarsfield, b. Dunkineely (Co. Donegal) 1852. Journalist, poet and novelist, PSC emigrated to the US around 1869. He wrote a long story in verse, *The borrowed bride, a fairy love legend of Donegal* (New York, 1892), and contributed poetry to the *Harp* (Montreal, Mar., 1880). He worked for the Associated Press from 1875 to 1885, during which time he also edited the *Celtic Magazine* (New York). According to O'Donoghue, he became city editor of *New York Mercury*. SOURCE Allibone Suppl., i, p. 300; Brown, p. 60; Donegal, p. 60; Irish pseudonyms; O'Donoghue, p. 64; RL; Wright, ii, p. 66.

C139 *Glenveigh, or, the victims of vengeance. A tale of Irish peasant life in the present* (by Patrick Sarsfield Cassidy).
+ Boston: Patrick Donahoe, 1870. SOURCE Fanning, p. 377; Brown, 349; Wright, ii, 475. LOCATION L, NUC, InND Loeber coll., Wright web.
COMMENTARY First serialized in the Boston *Pilot*. Based on an actual set of evictions in Co. Donegal in 1863. A young girl is clubbed to death by a 'crowbar brigade' of ruffians imported from the Glasgow docks to enforce court eviction orders. The dissolute landlord rents out his reclaimed farms to Scottish shepherds and takes off for a life of sinful self-indulgence in Venice [Fanning, p. 81].

CASTLE, Agnes, also Mrs Egerton (née Sweetman), b. *c.*1860, d. 1922. Novelist, AC came from a Catholic family, the fourth daughter of Michael James Sweetman of Lamberton Park (near Stradbally, Co. Laois, since demolished) and his wife Adela Jane, daughter of the Hon. Arthur Petre. Her sister was Mrs Francis Blundell§, who wrote under the pseudonym 'M.E. Francis'. AC married an English critic, Capt. Anthony Egerton Castle, MA, FSA, in 1883, with whom she collaborated on most of her fiction as well as on a play, 'Desperate remedies', but the division of work is unclear. She wrote 41 works of fiction, of which only a few are set in Ireland and the remainder in England. Several of the novels have women as main characters. SOURCE Brown 2, p. 43; EF, pp 59–60; Landed gentry, 1912, p. 677; RIA/DIB; Sutherland, p. 109 [under Egerton Castle]; T & B, pp 971–2; Vanishing country houses, p. 97; Wolff, i, pp 218–19.

C140 *My little Lady Anne* (by Agnes Castle).
London: John Lane; Philadelphia: Henry Altemus, 1896 (Pierrot's Library, No. 2; ill. Aubrey Beardsley). LOCATION L, NUC.
+ New York: Frederick A. Stokes, 1905 (as *The heart of Lady Anne*; ill. Ethel Franklin Betts, Frederick Garrison Hall). LOCATION NUC, InND Loeber coll.
COMMENTARY The story told by an old woman servant of a retarded young girl who is forced into marriage and dies of fright [EF, p. 60].

C141 *The pride of Jennico, being a memoir of Captain Basil Jennico* (by Agnes and Egerton Castle).
New York: Macmillan, 1897. SOURCE McCarthy, ii, p. 576. LOCATION D (n.d. edn), NUC.

COMMENTARY *New York 1897 edn* This consists of part of the volume, but it is not mentioned by Topp [NUC; Topp 5, p. 164].

New York: Macmillan, 1898. LOCATION NUC. COMMENTARY *New York 1898 edn* This consists of the complete volume. [NUC].

London: Richard Bentley & Son, 1898. SOURCE Alston, p. 75. LOCATION L.

COMMENTARY First serialized in *Temple Bar* (London, July–Dec. 1897) and subsequently transformed into a play in 1899. An English aristocrat, Capt. Basil Jennico, inherits a princedom in 'Moravia' [Bolton, p. 115; Sutherland, p. 109; Topp 5, p. 163].

C142   *The Bath comedy* (by Agnes and Egerton Castle).

London: Macmillan & Co., 1900. SOURCE Alston, p. 75; McCarthy, ii, p. 576 (perhaps mistakenly mentions 1898 edn); COPAC. LOCATION D (n.d. edn), L.

New York: Frederic Stokes, [1900]. LOCATION NUC.

COMMENTARY Historical fiction, it reconstructs the watering place of Bath in its Beau Nash eighteenth-century era [Sutherland, p. 109].

C143   *The house of romance; certain stories, including La Bella and others* (by Agnes and Egerton Castle).

New York: F.A. Stokes, [1901]. SOURCE RLIN; NYPL. LOCATION NN.

C144   *The secret orchard* (by Agnes and Egerton Castle).

London: Macmillan & Co., 1901. SOURCE McCarthy, ii, p. 576; COPAC. LOCATION L, InND Loeber coll. (London, n.d. edn (with Egerton Castle); see Plate 18).

Toronto: McLeod & Allan, 1901 (ill. C.D. Williams). LOCATION L.

C145   *Incomparable Bellairs* (by Agnes and Egerton Castle; dedicated to Austin Dobson).

+ New York: Frederick A. Stokes, 1903 (ill.). LOCATION L, NUC, InND Loeber coll.

+ Westminster [London]: Archibald Constable & Co., 1904 (ill. Fred Pegram). LOCATION D, L, NUC.

Leipzig: Bernard Tauchnitz, 1904. SOURCE T & B, 3733. LOCATION NUC.

COMMENTARY Sequel to *The Bath comedy* (London, 1900), set mainly in Bath and London. The ups-and-downs in the love life of a beautiful, rich and young eighteenth-century widow and of her various suitors, the foremost of which is O'Hara, an Irishman [ML].

C146   *The star dreamer. A romance* (by Agnes and Egerton Castle; dedicated to Lady Stanley).

+ Westminster [London]: Archibald Constable, 1903. LOCATION D.

New York: Frederick A. Stokes, [1903]. SOURCE Sumner & Stillman cat. 46/18. LOCATION InND Loeber coll. ([1903] 3rd edn).

+ Leipzig: Bernhard Tauchnitz, 1903, 2 vols. in 1. SOURCE T & B, 3666. LOCATION InND Loeber coll.

COMMENTARY The story of an eccentric astronomer, Sir David Cheveral, and his equally eccentric relative, a chemist and herbalist named Simon Rickart who live in Sir David's castle near Bath. Sir David and his cold-blooded sister have been estranged since she married the man who had seduced Sir David's betrothed and had wounded him in a subsequent duel. The sister's son stands to inherit the property. At the opening of the story, Simon's daughter Ellinor returns after the death of her husband. She becomes her father's amanuensis and slowly thaws Sir David's heart. The housekeeper writes to Sir David's sister to warn her of the danger to her son's inheritance if Ellinor and Sir David should marry. The sister visits, bringing a number of unsavoury society characters, one of whom she sets to seduce Ellinor. As a last resort, she tries to poison her brother, but fails. Eventually, Ellinor and Sir David marry [ML].

C147   *French Nan* (by Agnes and Egerton Castle; dedicated to the Hon. Mrs Everard Pepys).

+ London: Smith, Elder & Co., 1905. LOCATION D (1905, 2nd edn), L, NUC.

Leipzig: Bernard Tauchnitz, 1905. SOURCE T & B, 3852. LOCATION NUC.

COMMENTARY Historical fiction. Another sequel to *The Bath comedy* (London, 1900). Set in London in the reign of George II, and consists of a comedy of character and manners [Baker].

C148 *Rose of the world* (by Agnes and Egerton Castle).

+ London: Smith, Elder & Co., 1905. LOCATION L, NUC, InND Loeber coll.

Leipzig: Bernard Tauchnitz, 1905. SOURCE T & B, 3822. LOCATION NUC.

New York: A.L. Burt, 1905. LOCATION NUC.

New York: F.A. Stokes, 1905 (ill. Harrison Fisher, Clarence F. Underwood). LOCATION NUC.

COMMENTARY A tale of disguise, deceit and love put to the test. Lady Gerardine, wife of the lieutenant governor of an Indian province had previously been married to Harry English, a soldier who had died in a battle in Kashmir. English's friend, Maj. Bethune, wishes to write a memoir of him and asks Lady Gerardine for her cooperation and for English's papers still in her possession. Lady Gerardine does not want to be confronted with her past but she is more or less forced to look over the papers before she gives them to Maj. Bethune. Meanwhile her husband, who is writing a history of the province, has hired a native to assist him. Lady Gerardine returns to England to the house which she has inherited from her first husband. There she goes through Harry English's diaries and falls in love with him again. Eventually it transpires that the native hired by the lieutenant governor is actually Harry English, who had survived the battle and had disguised himself in order to find out if his wife had really loved him. The lieutenant governor leaves and Lady Gerardine and Harry English are reunited [ML].

C149 *'If youth but knew!'* (by Agnes and Egerton Castle; dedicated to Marie Louise).

+ London: Smith, Elder & Co., 1906 (ill. Lancelot Speed). LOCATION D, L, InND Loeber coll.

Leipzig: Bernard Tauchnitz, 1906. SOURCE T & B, 3885. LOCATION NUC.

New York: Macmillan, 1906. LOCATION NUC.

C150 *My merry Rockhurst. Some episodes in the life of Viscount Rockhurst, a friend of King Charles the second, at one time constable of His Majesty's Tower* (by Agnes and Egerton Castle; dedicated to Randolph Henry Stewart, 11th earl of Galloway).

London: Smith, Elder & Co., 1907. LOCATION L, NUC.

Leipzig: Bernard Tauchnitz, 1908. SOURCE T & B, 4014. LOCATION NUC.

+ New York: Macmillan, 1907 (as *'My merry Rockhurst', being some episodes in the life of Viscount Rockhurst, a friend of King Charles the Second, and at one time constable of His Majesty's Tower of London*; ill.). LOCATION NUC, InND Loeber coll.

COMMENTARY Historical fiction set in seventeenth-century England [RL].

C151 *Flower o' the orange and other stories* (by Agnes and Egerton Castle; dedicated to Royal Cortissoz).

+ London: Methuen & Co., 1908 (ill. Arthur H. Buckland). SOURCE COPAC. LOCATION D (1908, 2nd edn), E.

Leipzig: Bernard Tauchnitz, 1908. SOURCE T & B, 4028.

New York: Macmillan, 1908 (as *Flower o' the orange and other tales of bygone days*). LOCATION NUC.

COMMENTARY Contents: 'Flower o' the orange', 'The young conspiracy', 'The great wide deeps', 'My rapier and my daughter', 'The great Todescan's secret thrust', 'Polmona', 'Hagar of the farm', 'The love-apple', 'The mirror of the faithful heart', 'The yellow slipper'. Three of the stories were omitted in the New York edn [ML; NUC].

C152 *Wroth* (by Agnes and Egerton Castle).

+ London: Smith, Elder & Co., 1908. LOCATION D.

Leipzig: Bernard Tauchnitz, 1908. SOURCE T & B, 4119.

COMMENTARY Romantic comedy of a theatrical kind set in Regency society at Tunbridge Wells, and at Compiègne and Florence. The main character is known as Mad Wroth [Baker].

C153 *A gift of the mist* (by Agnes Castle).
New York: R.H. Paget, 1909. LOCATION NUC.

C154 *Diamond cut paste* (by Agnes and Egerton Castle).
+ London: John Murray, 1909. LOCATION D, L.
Leipzig: Bernard Tauchnitz, 1911. SOURCE T & B, 4245. LOCATION NUC.
New York: Dodd, Mead & Co., 1909 (as *Diamonds cut paste*). LOCATION NUC.
+ New York: A.L. Burt, 1909 (as *Diamonds cut paste*; ill. John E. Sutcliffe). LOCATION InND Loeber coll.
COMMENTARY A family attempts to disentangle an elderly married general from a designing woman [EF, p. 59].

C155 *Panther's cub* (by Agnes and Egerton Castle).
+ London, Edinburgh, Dublin, Leeds, New York, Leipzig, Paris: Thomas Nelson & Sons, 1910 (ill. Dudley Tenant). LOCATION D, L, NUC.
+ Garden City (NY): Doubleday, Page & Co., 1911 (ill. Florence R.A. Wilde). LOCATION NUC, InND Loeber coll.

C156 *The ninth wave* (by Agnes and Egerton Castle).
New York: R.H. Paget, 1911. LOCATION NUC.

C157 *The lost Iphigenia* (by Agnes and Egerton Castle; dedicated to A.H.).
+ London: Smith, Elder & Co., 1911. LOCATION D, L, NUC.
Leipzig: Bernard Tauchnitz, 1911. SOURCE T & B, 4286. LOCATION NUC.
Garden City (NY): Doubleday, Page & Co., 1911 (as *The composer*). LOCATION NUC.

C158 *Love gilds the scene and woman guides the plot. No. 1. My lady's word is not to be doubted* (by Agnes and Egerton Castle).
New York: R.H. Paget, 1911. LOCATION NUC.
+ London: Smith, Elder & Co., 1912 (as *Love gilds the scene, and women guide the plot*). LOCATION D, L, NUC.
Leipzig: Bernard Tauchnitz, 1912 (as *Love gilds the scene, and women guide the plot*). SOURCE T & B, 4333. LOCATION NUC.
COMMENTARY Set in England but with a large number of Irish characters. The story concerns husbands and wives not trusting each other and having affairs [ML; Baker].

C159 *The grip of life* (by Agnes and Egerton Castle).
London: Smith, Elder & Co., 1912. LOCATION L.
Leipzig: Bernard Tauchnitz, 1913. SOURCE T & B, 4388. LOCATION NUC.
Garden City (NY): Doubleday, Page & Co., 1912 (as *The lure of life*). SOURCE NUC; RL. LOCATION NUC.
COMMENTARY Presumably, *The lure of life* is the American version of *The grip of Life* [RL].

C160 *The golden barrier* (by Agnes and Egerton Castle).
+ Garden City (NY): Doubleday, Page & Co., 1913. LOCATION NUC, InND Loeber coll.
+ London: Methuen & Co., 1914. LOCATION D (1918 edn), L, NUC (n.d. edn), InND Loeber coll.

COMMENTARY A rich, young heiress who supports her aunt is surrounded by a court of suitors who are attracted by her wealth. The girl marries her agent, who seems to be the only sensible man in her circle. The aunt and the rejected suitors create mischief by insinuating that the agent married her for her money and that she is not master over her own wealth anymore. For a while this plot succeeds. In the end, however, the girl returns to her husband to live with him on his terms [ML].

C161 *The haunted heart* (by Agnes and Egerton Castle).
New York: D. Appleton & Co., 1915 (ill. C.H. Taffs). LOCATION NUC.
London: Methuen & Co., 1915 (as *Forlorn adventurers*). LOCATION L, NUC (n.d. edn).
Paris: Nelson's Continental Library, [1915]. LOCATION L.

C162 *Chance the piper* (by Agnes and Egerton Castle; dedicated to Lord Parker of Waddington).
+ London: Smith, Elder & Co., 1915. LOCATION D, L, NUC.
Leipzig: Bernard Tauchnitz, 1913. SOURCE T & B, 4415. LOCATION NUC.
COMMENTARY Contents: 'The ninth wave', 'A gift of the mist', 'A house of care', 'Moon's gibbet', 'The death hussar', 'The unwritten chapter', '"Parson"', 'Soldier's red', 'Rosanna' [NUC].

C163 *The ways of Miss Barbara* (by Agnes and Egerton Castle).
+ London: Smith, Elder & Co., 1914. LOCATION D.

C164 *Our sentimental garden* (by Agnes Castle and Egerton Castle).
London: William Heinemann, 1914 (ill. Charles Robinson). LOCATION L.
Philadelphia: J.B. Lippincott, 1914. LOCATION NUC.

C165 *The hope of the house* (by Agnes and Egerton Castle; dedicated to Maj. M.J. Sweetman).
+ London, New York: Cassell & Co., 1915. LOCATION D, L, NUC (n.d. edn).
New York: D. Appleton & Co., 1915 (ill. C.A. Taffs). LOCATION NUC.

C166 *New wine* (by Agnes and Egerton Castle).
+ London: W. Collins Sons & Co., 1919. SOURCE Brown 2, 219. LOCATION D (1923, 5th edn), L, NUC.
New York: D. Appleton & Co., 1919. LOCATION NUC.
COMMENTARY Shane O'Connor is suddenly transferred from the village of Cleenane (Co. Clare) to a title and estate in England. London society fawns on him to his face and sneers behind his back at his countrified manners. Disillusionment follows. He joins the air force during the First World War. After an escape from an unscrupulous adventuress he is glad to return to Cleenane and sets about rebuilding the family fortunes [Brown 2].

C167 *A little house in war time* (by Agnes and Egerton Castle).
+ London: Constable & Co., 1916 (ill. Charles Robinson). LOCATION D, L, NUC.
New York: E.P. Dutton & Co., [1916]. LOCATION NUC.

C168 *Count Raven* (by Agnes and Egerton Castle).
London, New York: Cassell & Co., 1916. LOCATION L, NUC.

C169 *The black office, and other chapters of romance* (by Agnes and Egerton Castle).
London: John Murray, 1917. LOCATION NUC.
COMMENTARY Contents: 'The black office', 'The red kilns of Amblemont', 'The resurrectionist', 'The smile in the portrait', 'The belts of old', 'The arresting point' [NUC].

C170 *Minniglen* (by Agnes and Egerton Castle).
London: John Murray, 1918. LOCATION L, NUC.
New York: D. Appleton & Co., 1918. LOCATION NUC.

C171 *The chartered adventurer: being some episode in the life of Mr. Terence O'Flaherty and his friend Lord Marlowe* (by Agnes and Egerton Castle).
London: Skeffington & Son, [1919]. LOCATION NUC.

C172 *Little hours in great days* (by Agnes and Egerton Castle).
London: Constable & Co., [1919]. LOCATION L, NUC.
COMMENTARY Concerns life in England during the First World War [BLC].

C173 *John Seneschal's Margaret* (by Agnes and Egerton Castle; dedicated to Michael).
+ London: Hodder & Stoughton, [1920]. LOCATION D, L, NUC.
New York: D. Appleton & Co., 1920. LOCATION NUC.

C174   *Pamela Pounce. A tale of tempestuous petticoats* (by Agnes and Egerton Castle).
+ London: Hodder & Stoughton, [1921?]. LOCATION InND Loeber coll.
+ London, Toronto, New York: Hodder & Stoughton, [1921]. LOCATION D, L, NUC.
COMMENTARY Set in eighteenth-century London where a young milliner is involved in many intrigues and adventures. She manages to stay out of dangerous liaisons and in the end marries a gentleman, whom she had saved from scrapes several times [ML].

C175   *Romances in red* (by Agnes and Egerton Castle).
London: Hodder & Stoughton, [1921]. LOCATION L, NUC.
COMMENTARY Contents: 'The four invisibles', 'The vengeance of young glory', 'The accursed town', 'Amadine's day of glory', 'Auguste and the supreme being', 'The arch-tigress of Austria', 'Tallien and the bind-flower', 'The incredible macaroni', 'Flayer Hans', 'The red shepherdess' [NUC].

C176   *Kitty and others* (by Agnes and Egerton Castle).
+ London: Hutchinson & Co., [1922]. LOCATION D, L, NUC.

C177   *Minuet and foxtrot* (by Agnes and Egerton Castle).
London: Hutchinson & Co., [1922]. LOCATION L.

C178   *Enchanted casements* (by Agnes and Egerton Castle).
London: Hutchinson & Co., 1923. LOCATION L, NUC.

CASTLE, Egerton. Co-author. See CASTLE, Agnes.

'A CATHOLIC MISSIONARY', fl. 1880s. Pseudonym of a religious fiction writer.
C179   *Household story book* (by 'A Catholic missionary').
+ New York: P.J. Kenedy, 1880 (ill.; title on cover: *Life stories of dying penitents*).
SOURCE OCLC. LOCATION InND Loeber coll., Michigan State Univ.
COMMENTARY Religious Catholic stories set in London, many of them dealing with the Irish poor and all concerned with dying. The author is kindly inclined toward the Irish. Contents: 'The infidel', 'The dying banker', 'The drunkard's death', 'The miser's death', 'The hospital', 'The wanderer's death', 'The dying shirt-maker', 'The broken heart', 'The destitute poor', 'The cholera patient', 'The merchant's clerk', 'Death-beds of the poor', 'The missioner's Sunday work', 'The dying burglar', 'The Magdalen', 'The famished needlewoman' [RL].

'A CATHOLIC PRIEST', pseud. See CROLLY, Fr William.

'A CATHOLIC PRIEST', fl. 1830s. Pseudonym of a religious fiction writer, presumably a priest and Irish. This author may be identified with the poet of the same pseudonym who published *The vision of heresies, and other poems* (London, 1834), which he dedicated to his kinsman Daniel O'Connell. It is possible that the following volumes are by different authors. Note that Fr William Crolly§ also used the same pseudonym SOURCE O'Donoghue, p. 64.
C180   *The wooden cross. A religious tale* (by 'A Catholic priest', 'imitated from the German' of the Canons [*sic*] Schmid).
+ Dublin: T. O'Gorman, 1839 (see Plate 19). SOURCE de Búrca cat. 36/99. LOCATION InND Loeber coll.
COMMENTARY Early Irish Catholic religious fiction. Canon Johann Christoph von Schmid's fiction was quite popular in Ireland where it was published in several translations from 1835 onwards. This story concerns Sophy, a poor orphan, who is taken in by de Linden, a rich widow. She teaches Sophy to be charitable and to maintain her Catholic religion. When de Linden dies, Sophy is allowed to select one thing to take with her and chooses a simple wooden cross. Later, when she is married and she and her husband are in dire financial straits, she

finds that the wooden cross contains inside a cross covered with diamonds. By selling this she is able to avert disaster. She and her husband continue to lead virtuous lives and share their blessings with others [ML; BLC].

C181   *Thomas Martin, and how he turned out* (by 'a Catholic priest').
London: [publisher?], 1858. LOCATION L (destroyed).
COMMENTARY No copy located [RL].

C182   *Harry O'Brien. A tale for boys* (by the author of *Thomas Martin*).
+ London: Burns & Lambert, 1859. LOCATION L.
New York: Catholic Publication Soc., 1868 (as *Harry O'Brien and other tales*). SOURCE Brown, 36 (New York, Benziger 1859 edn, not located and may be a mistake); OCLC. LOCATION Univ. of Florida.
COMMENTARY 53pp for the London edn. A pious and moral Catholic story set among the Irish in London [Brown].

C183   *The lamentable story of Jim Fagan* (by the author of Harry O'Brien).
London: [publisher?], [1862]. SOURCE COPAC. LOCATION L (destroyed), E.
New York, Montreal: D. & J. Sadlier & Co., [1875 or earlier] (as *Jim Fagan*). SOURCE Adv. in M.J. Hoffman, *The orphan sisters* (New York, 1875); OCLC (1889 edn).
COMMENTARY No copy of the New York edn located [RL].

CAULFEILD (sometimes spelled Caulfield), **Edward Houston**, pseud. '**A country gentleman**', b. Dublin *c*.1807, d. 1878 or 1883? Didactic story writer, EHC was the son of James Caulfeild, a soldier, and was connected with the earl of Charlemont's family and lived at Drumcairn, Stewartstown (Co. Tyrone), and at Hockley (Co. Armagh). Author Sophia F.A. Caulfield§ (also Caulfeild) was the earl's niece. EHC was admitted to TCD in 1825 but does not appear to have obtained a degree. He also wrote instructive booklets on farming and education. SOURCE B & S, p. 143; Brown 2, pp 43–4; O'Donoghue, p. 64; RIA/DIB.

C184   *History of Paddy Blake and Kathleen O'More. A tale; into which are introduced observations on agriculture, chemistry, and various subjects, compiled and written for the instruction and amusement of the farmers of Tyrone* (by 'A country gentleman').
Dungannon: Printed [for the author?] by William Douglas, 1847. SOURCE Brown 2, 220; O'Donoghue, p. 64. LOCATION D.

COMMENTARY Attributed in the IBL 8 (Feb.–Mar. 1916–17, p. 76) to William Douglas, but by Brown 2 to EHC. It tells of the farming of Paddy and the housekeeping of his wife, Kitty, as models of their respective occupations. Presents practical details of farming as well as observations on agriculture, chemistry and various subjects. It includes songs and poems [Brown 2; O'Donoghue].

CAULFEILD, Sophia Frances Anne. See **CAULFIELD, Sophia Frances Anne.**

CAULFIELD, Edward Houston. See **CAULFEILD, Edward Houston.**

CAULFIELD, S.F.A. See **CAULFIELD** or **CAULFEILD, Sophia Frances Anne.**

CAULFIELD or **CAULFEILD, Sophia Frances Anne** (known as **S.F.A. Caulfield**), d. *c*.1900. Poet and miscellaneous writer, possibly Irish, SFAC was the daughter of an author of pamphlets and niece of the 2nd earl of Charlemont. She lived in Bath and wrote 13 books. Her first volume, *Desmond and other poems* (London, 1870), was followed by works in several genres: religious books; practical manuals; a book on needlework, and some fiction. She also wrote *House mottoes and inscriptions: old and new* (London, 1902) which contains a chapter on Scottish and Irish inscriptions. SOURCE Allibone Suppl., i, p. 302; Colman, pp 51–2; CM; MVP, p. 88; O'Donoghue, p. 65; RIA/DIB.

C185   *By land and sea; and, Ben, "a rough diamond"* (by S.F.A. Caulfield and [Jeanie Hering]).

> London: Cassell & Co.; New York: Petter & Galpin, [1880]. SOURCE OCLC; COPAC. LOCATION Wayne State Univ. (IN).

COMMENTARY Fiction for juveniles. The story 'By land and sea' is by S.F.A. Caulfield, while the second story is by the author of 'Honour and glory' [Jeanie Hering]. The stories initially appeared in volumes of *Little Folks* (London) [OCLC; COPAC].

C186   *A restful work for youthful hands* (by Sophia Frances Anne Caulfield).

> + London: Griffith, Farran & Co., 1888 (ill. E. Scannell). SOURCE COPAC. LOCATION L.

COMMENTARY Fiction for juveniles, but not set in Ireland [CM].

'CAVIARE', pseud. See **O'DONNELL, John Francis.**

CAWTHORNE, William Anderson, pseud. **'W.A.C.',** d. Canada? Writer of Protestant pros-elytizing fiction, and possibly a minister, but not of the Church of Ireland. In the preface to *Mick Tracy* (London, [1863]), WAC states that he had lived in Ireland and had witnessed the 'faithful labourers' who were Bible readers. Sometime prior to 1869, he emigrated to Canada, which is evident from his introd. to *Tim Doolan* (London, 1869). He probably is not the same W.A. Cawthorne who wrote about an Australian aboriginal legend. SOURCE Allibone Suppl., i, p. 304; Brown, 67; RLIN; TK.

C187   *Mick Tracy, the Irish scripture reader; or, the martyred convert and the priest. A tale of facts* (by 'W.A.C.').

> + London: The Book Society, Simpkin, Marshall & Co.; Clapham: S.M. Haughton; Edinburgh: Patton & Ritchie; Dublin: J. Robertson & Co.; Manchester: W. Bremner & Co.; Liverpool: A. Newling; Birmingham: H. Barclay, [1863] (ill. P.N. Row). LOCATION Dt, L, NUC, InND Loeber coll.
>
> + London: S.W. Partridge & Co., n.d (new edn; ill.; see Plate 20). LOCATION InND Loeber coll.
>
> Philadelphia: American Baptist Publication Society, [1867] (as *Mick Tracy, the Irish scripture reader. A tale of facts*). SOURCE Watters, p. 255. LOCATION L, NUC, Univ. of Montreal.

COMMENTARY Very popular work. The London edn reached the 19th thousand impression in 1869 or somewhat later. Religious fiction. A Catholic day labourer converts to protestantism. He is denounced by the priests and assaulted by the parishioners, who also kidnap converts. Despite this persecution, conversions multiply [Brown; InND Loeber coll.].

C188   *Tim Doolan, the Irish emigrant: being a full and particular account of his reasons for emigrating – his passage across the Atlantic – his arrival in New York – his brief sojourn in the United States, and his further emigration to Canada* [anon.].

> + London: S.W. Partridge & Co., 1869 (ill.). SOURCE Brown, 101 (1869, 3rd edn); Wolff, 7583. LOCATION D (n.d.), Dt, L, InND Loeber coll.

COMMENTARY Religious fiction. Tim is the son of a small farmer in Co. Cork who has con-verted to protestantism, after which his house is burned and his cattle are killed. He emigrates to the US and from there goes to Canada where he helps to repel the Fenian invasion [Brown].

'CELTIS, Emelobie de', pseud. See **O'BYRNE, M.L.**

CHABOT, Philippe Ferdinand Auguste de Rohan. See DE JARNAC, Philippe Ferdinand Auguste de Rohan, comte.

CHAIGNEAU, William, pseud. 'W.C.', b. Dublin 1709, d. Dublin 1781. Novelist, army agent and theatrical entrepreneur, WC was the son of John Chaigneau, a Huguenot vintner, and Margaret Martyr. He was probably related to Revd David Chaigneau (d. 1747), minister of the French church at Carlow, whose father, Isaac (Josias according to ODNB), was a merchant in Dublin. WC served in the British army in Flanders and became an army agent in Dublin. In 1730 he published a map of the post towns and barracks in Ireland. His literary interests must have emerged early in life because he subscribed to the Dublin edns of John Gay's poems in 1729 and to a volume of poems by John Winstanley and others in 1742. WC lived in Abbey Street, Dublin, but his dedication of *The history of Jack Connor* (London, 1752) is dated from Ashburton (Devon), 1 July 1751. WC later adapted and translated French farces. He must have become reasonably well-to-do because he and others furnished mortgages to the Music Hall property in Crow Street, Dublin, in 1757 and 1759, effectively becoming shareholders. A cabalistic manuscript of *c.*1746 owned by him, and possibly by him, was on the Dublin market in 1975 (current location unknown). SOURCE Brady, p. 34; Cork, iii, p. 163; Falkner Greirson cat. 25/13; Field Day, i, p. 758; Hogan 2, pp 239–40; JAPMDI, 5(1) (1901), p. 6; A.B. Law, *The printed maps of Ireland, 1812–1850* (Dublin, 1997), 71; T.P. Le Fanu, *Memoir of the Le Fanu family* (Privately printed, n.d.), p. 49; OCIL, p. 84; ODNB; RIA/DIB, RL; L.T. Stockwell, *Dublin theatres* (New York, 1968), pp 121, 125–6, 341, 383–4.

C189 *The history of Jack Connor* (title of vol. 2: *The history of Jack Connor, now Conyers*; introd. signed 'W.C.'; dedicated to the Rt Hon. Henry Fox, Secretary at War).
London: W. Johnston, 1752, 2 vols. SOURCE Raven, 124; McBurney & Taylor, 139; Forster, 362; ESTC t108074. LOCATION L, IU, NUC.
+ London: W. Johnston, 1753, 2nd edn, 2 vols. (corrected). SOURCE Raven, 179, ESTC t066943. LOCATION L, YU, NUC, InND Loeber coll. (vol. 2 only).
Dublin: Abraham Bradley, 1752, 2 vols. in 1. SOURCE Raven, 124; Brown, 352 (mistakenly mentions [1751] edn); ESTC t101674. LOCATION Dt, L, DCL.
Dublin: Abraham Bradley, 1753, 3rd edn, 2 vols. in 1 (corrected edn). SOURCE ESTC t066942. LOCATION Dt, L.
+ Dublin: Hulton Bradley, 1766, 2 vols., 4th edn (corrected and improved; ill.). SOURCE Raven, 997; Bradshaw, 1329a; ESTC n008043. LOCATION D, Dm, C, MH, NUC.

COMMENTARY A picaresque 'moral tale' of cultural identity whose hero, Jack Connor, resembles other mid-eighteenth-century heroes such as Gil Blas, Roderick Random and Tom Jones, but whose central theme is English prejudice against the Irish and includes commentary on Irish political, economic and social matters. Connor, born in Ireland in 1720, is the illegitimate and Protestant son of Sir Roger Thornton of Co. Limerick, a Williamite soldier blinded by an old wound. Jack has a difficult, impoverished childhood labouring and begging until his father dies and he is taken up by Lord and Lady Truegood of Bounty Hall and becomes a companion to their young son Harry. After an amorous adventure involving his schoolmaster's niece, the schoolmaster banishes him to England, advising him to change his Irish name and accent to prevent ridicule. He becomes John Conyers and one scandalous adventure follows another in London and Paris. He amasses some fortune and finds his mother (who has married a rich merchant) in Cadiz. Happily married, Jack settles on an Irish estate and is reunited with some of the people of his earlier life. The second edn contains in volume 2 an addendum of three letters discussing, among other topics, charter schools and the linen industry in Ireland. The novel includes the earliest example in English of mottoes, some forming chapter heads. A Conyers family was seated at least from the early-eighteenth century on at

Castletown Conyers (Co. Limerick; see Dorothy Conyers§) but it is unclear to what extent the story was inspired by them [ML; Burke's, pp 268–9; Field Day, i, pp 682–3, 688–94; ODNB; Quaritch cat. 1181/29; Rauchbauer, pp 18–19].

CHAMBERLAIN, Charles, Jnr, fl. 1873. American social satirist. SOURCE Allibone Suppl., i, p. 307; Wright, ii, p. 67.

C190 *The servant-girl of the period, the greatest plague of life. What Mr. and Mrs. Honeydew learned of housekeeping* (by Charles Chamberlain, Jnr).

+ New York: J.S. Redfield, 1873. SOURCE Wright, ii, 481. LOCATION InND Loeber coll., Wright web.

COMMENTARY Probably was inspired by Henry and Augustus Mayhew's§ *The greatest plague in life: or the adventures of a lady in search of a good servant* (London, [1847]), but set in New York instead of London. Mr and Mrs Honeydew, a newly married couple, wish to set up housekeeping. The main trial of their new life is the hiring of female servants, many of whom are Irish and none of whom gives satisfaction. Eventually they move back into a hotel so that they do not have to deal with the problem [ML].

CHAMBERLAINE, Frances. See **SHERIDAN, Frances.**

CHAPLIN, Mrs Jane D. (née Dunbar; also known as Mrs Jane Dunbar Chaplin), pseud. 'Hyla', b. 1819, d. 1884. American religious tract writer educated in New York, she married Revd Jeremiah Chaplin, a writer of religious and historical works. Aside from the following two works, she is also the author of *Out of the wilderness* (Boston, 1870). SOURCE Allibone, i, p. 368; Allibone Suppl., i, p. 313; NUC; RLIN; Wright, ii, pp 68–9.

C191 *The convent and the manse* (by 'Hyla').

+ Boston: John P. Hewett & Co; Cleveland (OH): Jewett, Proctor & Worthington; London: Low & Co., 1853. LOCATION Wright web.

COMMENTARY Contains some Irish characters [ML].

C192 *Gems of the bog: A tale of the Irish peasantry* (by Mrs Jane D. Chaplin).

Boston: American Tract Society; New York: Hurd & Haughton, [*c*.1869] (ill.). SOURCE RLIN. LOCATION NUC, NN.

CHAPMAN, M.F. See **CHAPMAN, Mary Francis.**

CHAPMAN, Mary Francis (known as **M.F. Chapman**), pseuds '**Francis Meredith**', and '**J.C. Ayrton**' (J. Calder Ayrton), b. Dublin 1838, d. Old Charlton (Kent) 1884. A novelist whose father worked in the port of Dublin when she was born and was transferred to London when MFC was still a child, she started writing very young and completed part of her *Mary Betrand* (London, 1860, 3 vols.) by age 15. She was educated at Staplehurst (Kent) and for the most part lived her life in Kent, never marrying. Under her pseudonym and in collaboration with her father, she wrote an historical tale, 'Bellasis; or, the fortunes of a cavalier', which appeared in the *Churchman's Family Magazine* (London, 1869) but may not have been published as a book. Her novels are mainly romantic tales of domestic life and she used literary epigrams from mostly English poets such as William Shakespeare, Alfred Lord Tennyson and the Romantics at the head of each chapter. Allibone mentions a Mary Chapman of the same era but she may not be this author. SOURCE Allibone Suppl., i, p. 315; Blain, p. 45 [under J. Calder Ayrton]; Boase, i, p. 591; ODNB; RIA/DIB; Sutherland, pp 114–15.

C193 *Mary Bertrand* (by 'Francis Meredith').

+ London: Hurst & Blackett, 1860, 3 vols. SOURCE Alston, p. 77. LOCATION L, NUC (1862 edn).

COMMENTARY A love story set in the village of Moorheath, near the town of Altham (15 miles from London); Mary's mother is English, her father French; no discernable Irish contents [Sutherland; JB; CM].

C194   *Lord Bridgenorth's niece* (by 'J.C. Ayrton').
+ London: Ward & Lock, 1862. SOURCE Alston, p. 77; ODNB (where misspelled 'Lord Bridgnorth'). LOCATION L.

C195   *A Scotch wooing* (by 'J.C. Ayrton').
London: H.S. King & Co., 1875. SOURCE Alston, p. 77. LOCATION L.
COMMENTARY A pretty young girl, 'English to the core', is forced to live with relatives north of the border [Sutherland].

C196   *Gerald Marlowe's wife* (by 'J.C. Ayrton').
London: Tinsley Bros, 1876, 3 vols. SOURCE Alston, p. 77; Blain, p. 45. LOCATION L.
COMMENTARY Melodrama, chronicling routine marital trials [Sutherland].

C197   *The gift of the gods* (by M.F. Chapman).
London: Chapman & Hall, 1879, 2 vols. SOURCE Alston, p. 77; COPAC. LOCATION L.

CHARLES, Mrs Elizabeth (née Rundle; known as **Mrs Rundle Charles**), b. Tavistock (Devon) 1828, d. Hampstead (London) 1896. English historical novelist, biographer, miscellaneous writer and social worker, EC was the daughter of John Rundle, MP for Tavistock. Many of her works are based on religious history. Only one of her novels has Irish content. SOURCE Allibone Suppl., i, pp 315–16; Boase, iv, p. 644; ODNB; Sutherland, pp 116–17; T & B, p. 972.

C198   *Attila and his conquerors. A story of the days of St. Patrick and St. Leo the Great* (by Mrs Rundle Charles).
London: Society for the Promotion of Christian Knowledge, [1894]. SOURCE Brown, 353. LOCATION L, NUC.
COMMENTARY Moral, didactic and historical novel set in the fifth century and deals with the Huns and their contact with Christianity, chiefly in the person of St Leo, from whose writings much of the matter is borrowed. Features Attila, king of the Huns. Two young Irish converts of St Patrick are carried off by British pirates. The story tells of their adventures in Rome and France [Brown].

CHARLES, Mrs Rundle. See **CHARLES, Mrs Elizabeth**.

CHASE, Lucien Bonaparte, b. 1817, d. 1864. American writer, who was also the author of *History of the Polk administration* (New York, 1850). SOURCE Allibone Suppl., i, p. 318; Wright web.

C199   *English serfdom and American slavery, or, ourselves as others see us* (by Lucien Bonaparte Chase; dedicated to the aristocratic ladies of Great Britain).
+ New York: H. Long & Brother, 1854. SOURCE Wright, ii, 493. LOCATION Wright web.
COMMENTARY Compares the condition of people in the British empire, i.e., the Irish, with the slaves in America. Describes the lot of the weavers in Ireland. The conclusion is that the slaves in America are not badly off. Quotes a report of the British parliament and a speech in Congress by the Hon. Charles Hudson, representative for Massachusetts [ML; RL].

CHATTERTON, Lady. See **CHATTERTON, Lady Henrietta Georgina Marcia Lascelles**.

Chatterton

CHATTERTON, Lady Henrietta Georgina Marcia Lascelles (née Iremonger; known as Lady Chatterton), b. London, 1806, d. Baddesley Clinton (War.) 1876. English poet, miscellaneous and travel writer, HGMLC was the daughter of Revd Lascelles Iremonger, Anglican prebendary of Winchester, and Harriet Gambier. She married in 1824 Sir William Abraham Chatterton, Bt, of Castle Mahon (Co. Cork). The couple lived at Castle Mahon but in her memoirs she states: 'The relaxing climate of that beautiful country disagreed with me very much, so we went to spend the next winter in Italy' (Dering, p. 25). At the time of the Famine, having been deprived of their Irish rents, the couple retired to Dorset. Sir William died in 1855, after which HGMLC married Edward Hineage Dering, a retired Coldstream Guards officer and author. Shortly after the marriage Dering converted to catholicism and Lady Chatterton followed ten years later. Thomas Crofton Croker§ dedicated his *Fairy legends and traditions of the South of Ireland* (London, 1825) to her. Two of her books, the popular *Rambles in the South of Ireland during the year 1838* (London, 1839, 2 vols.), and *Home sketches and foreign recollections* (London, 1841, 3 vols.) contain Irish legends and stories told by local individuals. She was a competent artist and illustrator of her own books. The originals of HGMLC's drawings for *Rambles* ... are now among the Heavey Collection, Public Library, Athlone (Co. Westmeath). A list of her more than 30 publications was published in her husband's memoir. SOURCE Allibone, i, p. 371; Blain, p. 199; Burke's, 1976, pp 225–6; de Búrca cat. 54/60; E.H. Dering, *Memoirs of Georgiana, Lady Chatterton* (London, 1878), pp 25, Appendix; NCBEL 4, pp 1162–3; MVP, p. 92; ODNB; O'Toole, p. 34; Sutherland, p. 118; Wolff, i, pp 223–4.

C200 *Rambles in the South of Ireland during the year 1838* (by Lady Chatterton).
London: Saunders, 1839, 2 vols. SOURCE NCBEL 4, p. 1162; OCLC. LOCATION D, O, CtY.
COMMENTARY Travel sketches including several Irish stories, such as 'A poor widower's tale', 'Legend of O'Donoghue', 'Legend of Oween-na-fahadee', 'A legend of Ferriter's Castle and Sybil Head', 'Legend of the golden bird', 'Legend of the green sheep', 'The widow Marney, or the effects of perseverance in prayer', 'The widowed bride', and 'The two wives' [RL].

C201 *Home sketches and foreign recollections* (by Lady Chatterton).
+ London: Saunders & Otley, 1841, 3 vols. (ill. Lady Chatterton, Day & Hague; see Plate 21). SOURCE NCBEL 4, p. 894; Wolff 1181. LOCATION D, C, InND Loeber coll.
COMMENTARY Contains several Irish stories in a travelogue and commonplace book: 'Clewen Castle', 'A tale from the ancient history of Ireland', 'A novel mode of proposing to a young lady', 'A peasant's story of Avelina and the Danes', 'Legend of the fairy Nil Rue' [RL].

CHESNEY, Mary. See DAMANT, Mary.

CHESSON, Mrs W.H. See HOPPER, Nora.

CHETWODE also CHETWOOD, Miss Anna Maria (probable first names), fl. 1827. Novelist daughter of Revd John Chetwode, a Church of Ireland clergyman of Glanmire (Co. Cork) and Elizabeth Hamilton, and granddaughter of Knightley Chetwode, friend of Jonathan Swift§. Her father, a literary-minded gentleman, wrote many small pieces of prose and verse but never published. Through his mother, he was related to Ralph Sneyd of Staffs. and may therefore have been distantly related to Honora Edgeworth§, Richard Lovell Edgeworth§ and Maria Edgeworth§. He was rector at Rathconey (i.e., Glanmire, Co. Cork) from 1790 until his death in 1814. His daughter belonged to a small coterie of Irish women who travelled in Russia in the first decades of the nineteenth century. AMC lived near Moscow with the Russian

Princess Daschkaw,[2] probably on the princess's estate at Troitskoe. The princess was a remarkably well-educated woman who became director of the Academy of Arts and Sciences in St Petersburg, first president of the Russian Academy, and as a patron of the arts invited in 1779 the Irish architect James Gandon to St Petersburg to work there. It is not clear whether AMC's support of learning for women predated or followed this sojourn. Her sister, Elizabeth Hester, married Robert Wilmot, deputy recorder of Cork.[3] Two of Robert's sisters, Martha and Catherine Wilmot also travelled in Russia, (1803–08 and 1805–07 respectively), mostly as guests of Princess Daschkaw. AMC was author of the following three and other – as yet unidentified – novels. Her *Blue-stocking Hall* and *Tales of my time* have been wrongly ascribed by Block, Wolff, NCBEL, BLC and other sources to William Pitt Scargill and a Mrs Wilmot. In addition, the second novel has been ascribed to Mrs J.C. Loudon. The Cork historian Windle in 1839 mentions AMC as the author of the first two books. Garside reports that the papers of the publisher Bentley ascribes authorship to 'Mrs Wilmot', but the Bentley account muddles this with an implausible attribution to the writer Barbarina Wilmot, Baroness Dacre (1768–1854). Instead, it is more plausible that AMC's sister, Elizabeth Wilmot as Mrs Wilmot mediated transactions for AMC with Bentley. AMC is said to have also written a work called 'Snugborough', that has not been located. She is one of the early Irish women fiction writers to deal with politics and improvements of the place of women in society. Among the books she owned was G. Belzoni's *Narrative of the operations and recent discoveries ... in Egypt and Nubia* (London, 1820), in which she inscribed her name as Anna Maria Chetwood, Glanmire, Mar. 1821.[4] An Alice Wilmot Chetwode, perhaps a member of the same family, translated the works of Mme Marie David§ and other French writers, which were published in Dublin and London between 1872 and 1888. SOURCE Allibone, iii, p. 2764; Block, p. 206; W.M. Brady (ed.), *Clerical and parochial records of Cork, Cloyne, and Ross* (London, 1864), i, pp 52–3; British Fiction (Update 2); J. Coleman (ed.), *Windele's Cork* (Cork, 1973, p. 87; based on the 1839 publication); H. Heany (ed.), *A Scottish Whig in Ireland 1835–38* (Dublin, 1999), pp 34, 118, 136; Landed gentry, p. 109; Leslie & Wallace, p. 478; marchioness of Londonderry & H.M. Hyde (eds), *The Russian journals of Martha and Catherine Wilmot* (New York, 1934, reprinted 1971), pp xvii, 30, 46*n*.2; E. McParland, *James Gandon* (London, 1985), p. 23; S. Tucker, *Pedigree of the family of Chetwode* (London, 1884), p. 31.

C202   *Blue-stocking Hall* [anon.].

> \+ London: Henry Colburn, 1827, 3 vols. SOURCE British Fiction; Garside, 1827:60; Wolff, 6202. LOCATION Corvey CME 3–628–47264–4, Ireland related fiction, L, InND Loeber coll.

> London: Henry Colburn & Richard Bentley, 1827, 3 vols. (as *Blue-stocking Hall; a work of fiction, designed to inculcate the various duties of domestic life*). SOURCE Block, p. 206.

> New York: Collins & Hannay, 1828, 3 vols. SOURCE OCLC; Allibone, iii, p. 2764 (where noted as by 'Mrs Wilmot', but is not mentioned by OCLC). SOURCE OCLC. LOCATION DCL.

COMMENTARY No copy of the joint Colburn and Bentley imprint located. An epistolary novel mostly set in Co. Kerry and partly in England and the Continent, devoted to comparing a simple lifestyle in which nature, reason, honesty and religion prevail, with an artificial lifestyle

---

2 The princess had befriended Catharine Hamilton (née Ryder), who married in 1751 the Revd Hutchinson Hamilton of Edgeworthtown (Co. Longford) (Londonderry & Hyde, *Russian journals*, p. 4*n*. 4). The princess visited Ireland in 1779-80 (W. Bradford (ed.), *Memoirs of the Princess of Daschaw* (London, 1840), pp 209-12). 3 Mary, another sister, married the Ven. William Thompson, archdeacon of Cork. A third sister, Henrietta, married Horatio Townsend of Firmount (Co. Cork) (Londonderry & Hyde, *Russian journals*, pp 46*n*.2, 179*n*.1). 4 In a private collection.

in which fashion, greed, and dishonesty reign. The novel strongly advocates women's education. Maria Edgeworth§ read it and wrote that 'notwithstanding its horrid title ... I thought that there was a great deal of good, and of good sense in it' (Mrs Edgeworth, iii, p. 31). The story starts with an Englishman, Arthur Howard, arriving at his relations' isolated house in Co. Kerry for a period of recuperation. On his first evening there he discovers – to his horror – that he is among several blue-stockings. However, he does stay, and is won over in a series of conversations with his cousins, their male tutor and his aunt to believe in the benefits of learning in women and of a simple, natural lifestyle. A distinction is made between knowledge that is useful and which gives enjoyment and knowledge that is used only to impress other people. Marriage is presented as a true intellectual partnership, and staying single is preferred over a marriage merely for money or title. The fashionable people in the novel are either won over or lead miserable lives. It also deals with education of the lower-classes in Ireland and is sympathetic to the Irish. Characters discuss contemporary literature (like Maria Edgeworth's§ *Absentee*), politics and religion. A visit to Killarney is described [Quaritch cat. Oct. 1996; Mrs Edgeworth, *A memoir of Maria Edgeworth* (London, 1867), iii, p. 31; ML; British Fiction (Update 2)].

C203   *Tales of my time* (by the author of *Blue-stocking Hall*).
         London: Henry Colburn & Richard Bentley, 1829, 3 vols. SOURCE British Fiction; Garside, 1829:74. LOCATION Corvey CME 3-628-48871-0, Ireland related fiction, D, Dt, L, DCL.

COMMENTARY Contents: 'Who is she?' (set in England and on the Continent. No Irish content), 'The young reformers' (set in Ireland, the Continent, and Canada. The main character, Albert Fitzmaurice, the son of a Church of Ireland minister, lives quietly with his sweet and accomplished wife in relative obscurity. Their neighbours, including one whose house is called 'Painesville', are deeply steeped in republican ideas, with bookcases filled with volumes by Thomas Paine, William Godwin§, Count Constantin François de Volney, and Mary Wollstonecraft, among others. They introduce Albert to members of the society of United Irishmen. Albert's parents send him to Quebec to avoid further contacts with the rebels. Over time he comes to appreciate religion and to see the dangers of rebelling against the established order. He visits France where he meets republicans such as Paine and Volney, who disappoint him. When he inherits some money he buys an estate in Ireland to further the cause of the country by peaceful means [ML; COPAC; British Fiction (Update 2)].

CHETWODE, William Rufus. See **CHETWOOD, William Rufus.**

CHETWOOD, Anna Maria. See **CHETWODE, Anna Maria.**

CHETWOOD, William Rufus (also Chetwode), pseud. 'Mr C—D', b. 1700?, d. Dublin 1766. WRC was a playwright, novelist, stage manager, bookseller and publisher whose real name was Chetwode. He might have been a sailor when young, because according to his *General history of the stage*, he had been in 'most Parts of the World in my Youth'. He was active in London by 1713 and published 'A poem on the memorable fall of Chloe's P—s Pot', attributed to Jonathan Swift§. The following year he spent in Dublin as assistant manager of Joseph Asbury's theatre company. His own first known publication, the *Life of Lady Jane Gray*, appeared in Dublin in 1715. Back in London he was an active bookseller and publisher, a theatre prompter, and a playwright and novelist. His first work of fiction, *The voyages and adventures of Captain Robert Boyle*, appeared in London in 1726. In about 1740 he came to Dublin, fleeing creditors, and was stage manager at Thomas Sheridan's Theatre Royal in Smock Alley for about a year. The Dublin bookseller and printer James Hoey took a subscription with the author for a reprint of WRC's *Five new novels* (London, 1741) in 1744 but they do not appear to have been published in Ireland. In Dublin WRC published a periodical, the *Meddler* and then *A tour through Ireland* (Dublin, 1746), and two years later a poem 'Kilkenny; or, the old man's wish' (Dublin, 1748). The work for which he is most remembered, a *General history of the stage*, appeared in London in 1749. He also published *The British Theatre: Containing the lives of the British dramatic poets and all their plays* in Dublin in 1750. WRC was chronically in debt, for which he was imprisoned in both London and Dublin several times. At the end of his life he was bedridden and appealed for charity. He is presumed to have died in Marshalsea prison, Dublin. Only works that have some relationship with Ireland or which were written in Ireland are listed here. The author Anna Maria Chetwode§ was his descendant. For his portrait, see ODNB. SOURCE Allibone, i, p. 377; O'Donoghue, p. 67; OCIL, p. 96; ODNB; Pollard 2, pp 104, 292; Quaritch list No. 2001/6/11.

C204   *The voyages, dangerous adventures and imminent escapes of Captain Richard Falconer: Containing the laws, customs, and manners of the Indians in America; his shipwrecks; his marrying an Indian wife; his narrow escape from the island of Dominico, &c. Intermix'd with the voyages and adventures of Thomas Randal, of Cork, pilot; with his shipwreck in the Baltick, being the only man who escap'd: His being taken by the Indians of Virginia &c. Written by himself, now alive* [anon.].
London: W. Chetwood, T. Jauncy, A. Betteswood, J. Brotherton, W. Meadows & J. Graves, 1720. SOURCE Hardy, 308; ESTC t720045. LOCATION L (1734 edn).
London: J. Marshal, W. Chetwood, N. Cox & T. Edlin, 1724, 2nd corrected edn. SOURCE ESTC t072046. LOCATION L.
COMMENTARY A popular imaginary voyage in the manner of Daniel Defoe. The narrative begins with a shipwreck not unlike the story of Robinson Crusoe [Ximenes cat. 99–1/32].

C205   *The twins; or, the female traveller. A novel* (written by 'Mr C—D').
+ London: [n.p.], 1742–43. SOURCE Block, p. 40; ESTC t107657; OCIL, p. 96. LOCATION L.
COMMENTARY 48pp. Set in Spain, and features some Irish characters [ESTC; RL].

CHICHESTER, Frederick Richard, earl of Belfast (also known as the **earl of Belfast**), pseud. '**Lord B********', b. Belfast 1827, d. Naples (Italy) 1853. Novelist, litterateur, composer and philanthropist, FRC was the son of the 2nd marquess of Donegall and his wife, Lady Harriet Anne Butler, daughter of the earl of Glengall. He was educated at Eton and displayed a precocious interest in art, literature, verse and music. On the death of his father in 1844 he succeeded to the heavily-encumbered family estate. In adult life he was actively philanthropic, contributing the proceeds from his musical compositions for famine relief and lecturing to working men's clubs. His *Poets and poetry of the xixth century* (London, 1852) was based on his lectures in the Music Hall, Belfast, for the benefit of the library fund of the local Working Classes Association. He contributed fiction and travel writing under the pseudonym 'Campana' to the *Northern Magazine* (London) and was active in plans to establish an Atheneum, as well as serving as president of the Belfast Classical Harmonists Society. Because of ill-health he moved to Naples where he managed to write *Naples; political, social and religious* (London, 1856) before he died at age 25. FRC's proclaimed radical tendencies were at odds with his background. After his death his family questioned his authorship of the anon. novels. The people of Belfast erected two statues in his memory. D. Florence MacCarthy wrote an ode on his death. SOURCE Allibone Suppl., i, p. 324; Boase, i, p. 609; Brady, p. 35; W.A. Maguire, *Living like a lord. The second Marquis of Donegall 1769–1844* (Belfast, 2002); D.F. MacCarthy, *Underglimpses and other poems* (London, 1857), pp 145–59; ODNB; O'Donoghue, pp 67, 497; RIA/DIB; Sutherland, p. 120; Wolff, i, pp 226–7.

C206 *Two generations; or, birth, parentage, and education. A novel* (by the earl of Belfast; dedicated to author's mother, the marchioness of Donegall).
+ London: Richard Bentley, 1851, 2 vols. SOURCE Wolff, 1202. LOCATION D.
COMMENTARY Mostly set in France [ML].

C207 *Masters and workmen. A tale illustrative of the social and moral conditions of the people* (by 'Lord B******').
London: T.C. Newby, 1851. SOURCE Sutherland, p. 120 (1852 edn). LOCATION L.

C208 *The farce of life* (by 'Lord B******').
London: T.C. Newby, 1852, 3 vols. SOURCE NSTC. LOCATION L.

C209 *Wealth and labour. A novel* (by 'Lord B******').
London: T.C. Newby, 1853. SOURCE Wolff, 1203; NSTC. LOCATION L.

C210 *The county magistrate. A novel* (by 'Lord B******').
London: T.C. Newby, [1855], 3 vols. SOURCE Sutherland, p. 120; NSTC. LOCATION L, O ([1854] edn).
COMMENTARY Not set in Ireland. Features a father who locks up evidence of his son's innocence of a murder charge in order to spare the feelings of the guilty man's family. The story is accompanied by interpolated essays on the virtues of sanitary improvement [Sutherland].

C211 *The fate of folly* (by 'Lord B******').
London: T.C. Newby, 1859, 3 vols. SOURCE NSTC. LOCATION L.

C212 *Uncle Armstrong. A narrative* (by 'Lord B******').
London: T.C. Newby, 1866, 3 vols. SOURCE Allibone Suppl., i, p. 324. LOCATION L.
COMMENTARY Published posthumously [AMB].

CHILD, Lydia Maria (née Francis), b. Medford (MA) 1802, d. United States? 1880. American novelist, children's and miscellaneous writer and abolitionist, LMC was the daughter of Susannah Rand and Convers Francis, an anti-slavery campaigner. She became an active abolitionist and published several works on the anti-slavery cause, which adversely affected the sales of her other books. She ran a school in Watertown (MA) and in 1826 began *Juvenile Miscellany*, a bi-monthly magazine. Besides her novels she wrote biographies of women; books for young girls; stories, and in 1829 *The frugal housewife*, the third edn of which appeared in Boston the following year. It was immensely popular in England and Germany. Her 'The power of love, a tale of '98' appeared in *Francis Davis, The Belfast Man's Journal* (Belfast, 1850). It is not clear how her connection with Ireland came about. SOURCE Allibone, i, p. 378; Allibone Suppl., i, p. 324; ANB; Blain, p. 202; BLC; Clyde, p. 116; DAB; DLB, I, lxxiv, ccxliii; Hart, p. 139; NCBEL 4, p. 1769.

C213 *Fact and fiction: A collection of stories* (by Lydia Maria Child).
New York: C.S. Francis; Boston: J.H. Francis, 1846. SOURCE OCLC. LOCATION NRU.
+ Dublin: James M'Glashan, 1849. LOCATION D, L.
COMMENTARY Contents: 'The children of Mount Ida', 'The youthful emigrant', 'The Quadroons', 'The Irish heart', 'The legend of the apostle John', 'The beloved tune', 'Elizabeth Wilson', 'The neighbour-in-law', 'The waits in the spirit-land', 'A poet's dream of the soul', 'The black Saxons', 'Hilda Silfverling', 'Rosenglory', 'The legend of the falls of St. Anthony', 'The brothers', 'The skeleton's cave' [ML].

CHISHOLM, A., b. Ballyclare (Co. Antrim), fl. 1870s. Author of a manuscript.
C214 *Mirth and amusement, or fireside talk* (by A. Chisholm).
COMMENTARY Unpublished manuscript (c.1870). Current location is unknown. SOURCE Emerald Isle cat. 87/845; RL.

CHURCH, Samuel Harden, b. 1858, d. 1943. American novelist and historian, SHC wrote *Oliver Cromwell, a history* (New York, 1894), *A short history of Pittsburgh* (New York, 1908), and various political works. SOURCE Brown, p. 62; NUC.

C215 *John Marmaduke: A romance of the English invasion in Ireland in 1649* (by Samuel Harden Church; dedicated to the author's mother).

New York, London: G.P. Putnam's Sons, 1897 (ill. Albert Grantley Reinhart). SOURCE Brown, 357 (mentions a probable date of 1889). LOCATION DPL (1899, 7th edn), L, NUC.

Toronto: Copp, Clark, [1898]. LOCATION L.

COMMENTARY Historical fiction. The main character is Marmaduke, an officer under General Ireton, who idolizes Oliver Cromwell. The story opens in 1649 at Arklow (Co. Wicklow) and ends shortly after the massacre at Drogheda (Co. Louth). The book reached a 7th edn in 1899 [Brown; RL].

'A CITIZEN OF THE UNITED STATES', fl. 1811. Pseudonym of a female epistolary novelist who in the preface to the following work uses the pseudonym **'Sinceritas'**, and who relates her great difficulties in getting the volumes published in Dublin with a fraudulent publisher and an incompetent printer. She states she also did a translation from French, but it is unclear whether that work was published. SOURCE RL.

C216 *Sketches of society in France and Ireland, in the years 1805–6–7* (by 'A citizen of the United States'; signed in preface 'Sinceritas').

+ Dublin: Printed for the author, 1811, 2 vols. (see Plate 22). LOCATION D, L, InND Loeber coll.

COMMENTARY An epistolary novel, possibly autobiographical, which includes a travel narrative. Narrator Edward Melville, an American of high-born and wealthy English stock from Philadelphia who, when he is defrauded of his money at the start of the War of Independence, goes to work for an Irish merchant, Mr Bagnel, and marries his daughter, Julia (later in the text called Miss Stanley). The story starts out in Meadville (PA) where Melville deplores the loss of Julia, who has recently drowned, leaving a young child. Melville sets out for Europe leaving his daughter in the care of a friend. He visits France and stays in Bordeaux where 'a vast number' of Irish are living. He observes differences between the French and the Irish émigrés, some of whom are United Irishmen (he mentions a number by name). Overall he favours the Irish. Later he visits Ireland where he continues to remark upon the Irish character. Topics which concern him are spending habits, entertainment, the subservient role and poor education of women, the over-reliance of women on their husbands' finances, women's occupation with embroidery, lack of education for the poor, how genius is undone by drinking, religious animosities, novel writers and the reading public. He visits the estate of his wife's family between Carlow and Dublin (possibly Cookstown close to Kiltiernan),[5] and tours other places around Dublin. The book stops abruptly when the narrator announces that he will return to the US [ML; RL].

CLARE, Sr Mary Francis. See **CUSACK, Margaret Anne**.

CLARKE, Charles Henry Montague, fl. 1868. Novelist, probably English and possibly a publisher. CHMC's wife was the author Mrs Charles Montague Clarke§. He may have been the physician who published *Corns and bunions: their causes and cures* (London, [1878]), and *The sea-side visitor's guide* (London, [1872]). A publisher in London, C.H. Clarke (possibly

---

5 A John Stanley had an estate at Cookstown, near Bray (Co. Wicklow) in 1814 (A. Leet, *A directory to the market towns, villages, gentlemen's seats, and other noted places in Ireland* (Dublin, 1814, 2nd ed.), p. 125).

CHMC), published CHMC's two novels and several works of fiction by Mrs CMC. Since his wife lived at her birthplace, Glenlogan, Dromara (Co. Down) in 1881, it is likely he also lived there. SOURCE Allibone Suppl., i, p. 337; RL.

C217   *The head-centre; or, the life of a Fenian informer* [anon.].
    + London: C.H. Clarke, 1868. LOCATION D, L, DCL, InND Loeber coll.

COMMENTARY A young man, Owen Dermot, born out of wedlock and the reputed son of the local priest, lives with the priest after his mother marries and has another child by her new husband. He becomes a bank clerk and is favoured by the bank manager's wife, who thinks he is turning towards protestantism. He marries Caroline Douglas without her father's approval, but has to flee because he is suspected of stealing £1,000 from the bank. After a number of years he returns from America under the name of Col. Masters and visits the Douglas family, where no one but his ailing wife recognizes him. Mr Douglas is an Orangeman, as is Mr Magennis, the fiancée of Caroline's sister, Kate. Mr Douglas asserts Orangemen's right to march through Catholic areas. Col. Masters slowly turns Magennis into a Fenian. Eventually, both are caught. Masters, at the behest of his wife, turns informer, while Magennis does not. Masters is disgraced and dies in prison, but not before he has made peace with God. His widow, her sister, and Magennis set out for New Zealand to start a new life [ML].

CLARKE, Mrs C. See **CLARKE, Mrs Charles Montague**.

CLARKE, Mrs Charles Montague (née Marion Doake; not Doak as in Brown and O'Donoghue; known as **Marion Clarke, Mrs C. Clarke**, and **Mrs Charles Clarke**), pseuds 'Miriam Drake' and 'Miriam D—', b. Dromara (Co. Down), fl. 1867. Novelist and writer of Protestant religious fiction for children, Mrs CMC wrote two books with her sister, Margaret Doake§, and another 15 works of works of fiction under her own name. An endorsement in the NLI copy of her sister's *May darling* [1881] states that Mrs CMC resided at Glenlogan, Dromara (Co. Down). Her husband was the author Charles Henry Montague Clarke§. SOURCE Allibone Suppl., i, p. 337; Blain, p. 213; Brown, p. 62; Colman, p. 68; NCBEL 4, p. 1770 [under Mrs C.M. Clark]; O'Donoghue, p. 69 [under Marion Clarke].

C218   *Farrago: A collection of stories and verses* (by Mabel and Miriam D—.).
    + Dublin: M'Glashan & Gill; London: Simpkin Marshall & Co., 1867. SOURCE MVP, p. 121; O'Donoghue, p. 69; Colman, p. 68. LOCATION L.

COMMENTARY Wrongly identified by O'Donoghue and Colman as *Figaro, a collection of prose and verse*. Consists of poetry and three long stories: 'Farrago: Unequally yoked' (story of an English girl going to Ireland to teach at a Mission school), 'Rather an unpopular hobby', 'Dick and I' [RL].

C219   *Oughts and crosses. A novel with a moral* (by Mrs Charles Clarke ('Miriam Drake')).
    + London: Charles H. Clarke, [1872] (Clarke's Standard Novel Library). SOURCE Alston, p. 84. LOCATION L, InND Loeber coll.

COMMENTARY A temperance novel probably set in Ireland in which all who persist in drinking die or cause harm to others. The message is that alcohol, even when consumed in small quantities or for medicinal purposes, might lead to habituation and drunkenness and therefore it is safest to abstain entirely [ML].

C220   *Munro of Fort Munro* (with Margaret Doake§, ed. by Mrs C. Clarke).
    London: C.H. Clarke, 1873. SOURCE Alston, p. 121; Topp 6, 356. LOCATION L.

C221   *No security; or, rights and wrongs* (by Mrs Charles Clarke).
    London: C.H. Clarke, 1873 (Standard Novel Library). SOURCE Alston, p. 83; Topp 6, 357. LOCATION L.

C222   *Strong as death* (by Marion Clarke).
London: Tinsley Bros, 1875, 3 vols. SOURCE Brown, 359; Wolff, 1245. LOCATION D, L.
COMMENTARY A novel of Ulster presbyterianism and set in the uprising of 1798. The author's sympathies are with the rebels, but she does justice to the men on the loyalist side. Dialect is used [Brown; Blain].

C223   *Not transferable; or, wooing, winning, and wearing* ([M. Clarke] and Margaret Doake§).
London: Charles Henry Clarke, 1875 (Standard Novel Library). SOURCE Alston, pp 84, 121; Topp 6, 397 (Standard Novel Library); OCLC. LOCATION L.

C224   *Anthony Ker; or, living it down. A story for the young. Together with Meg's race for life* (by Mrs C.M. Clarke).
London: Sunday School Union, [1881]. LOCATION L.

C225   *Cousin Dorry; or, three measures of meal* (by Mrs C. M. Clarke).
London: Sunday School Union, [1883]. SOURCE Alston, p. 83; COPAC. LOCATION L (destroyed), Univ. of London.

C226   *Con's acre. A tale of Gilcourt Farm* (by Marion Clarke).
London: Sunday School Union, [1884]. SOURCE Alston, p. 83; COPAC. LOCATION L (destroyed), E.

C227   *Johnny's search* (by Marion Clarke).
London: Sunday School Union, [1884]. SOURCE Alston, p. 83. LOCATION L (destroyed).
COMMENTARY No copy located [RL].

C228   *Polly's petition; or, bread for a stone* (by Marion Clarke).
London: Religious Tract Society, [1884] (ill. J.F. Weedon). SOURCE Alston, p. 84; Personal communication, Mary Pollard, June 2004; COPAC. LOCATION L (destroyed), E.
COMMENTARY Religious fiction [BLC].

C229   *The slippery ford; or, how Tom was taught* (by Marion Clarke).
London: Religious Tract Society, [1885]. SOURCE Alston, p. 84; OCLC. LOCATION L (destroyed), CSt.
COMMENTARY Religious fiction [BLC].

C230   *Out of step; or, the broken crystal* (by Marion Clarke).
London: S.W. Partridge & Co., [1886]. SOURCE Alston, p. 84; COPAC. LOCATION L (destroyed), E.

C231   *More true than truthful. A story and a study* (by Marion Clarke).
London: Hodder & Stoughton, 1887 (ill. H. Hebblethwaite). SOURCE Alston, p. 83. LOCATION L.
COMMENTARY Religious fiction [BLC].

C232   *Among thorns* (by Marion Clarke).
London: Religious Truth Society, [1887]. SOURCE Alston, p. 83; COPAC. LOCATION L (destroyed) E.

CLARKE, Mrs D.W.C., fl. 1857. American author of Catholic religious fiction. SOURCE Preface to *Lizzie Maitland*.

C233   *Lizzie Maitland* (by Mrs D.W.C. Clarke; ed. by O.A. Brownson).
New York: E. Dunigan & Brother, 1857. LOCATION Wright web.
COMMENTARY A Catholic story set in America but with several Irish characters. The story details the conversion to catholicism of several protestants. Religious discussions are detailed. Also presents several discussions about the state of Ireland [ML].

Clarke

CLARKE, Frances Elizabeth. See MC FALL, Mrs Frances Elizabeth.

CLARKE, Marion. See CLARKE, Mrs Charles Montague.

CLARKE, Rebecca Sophia, pseud. 'Sophia May', b. Norridgewock (ME) 1833, d. United States? 1906. American writer of fiction for juveniles, much of it published in series, such as the Dotty Dimple Stories (1868–70) and the Little Prudy's Flyaway Series (Boston, 1871–74). SOURCE Allibone Suppl., i, p. 340; R.L. Kilgour, *Lee and Shepard. Publishers for the people* (n.l., 1965), pp 138–9.
C234 *The doctor's daughter* (by 'Sophia May').
    Boston: Lee & Shepard, 1872. SOURCE Slocum, i, 860. SOURCE RLIN. LOCATION NYU.
    COMMENTARY Features Miss O'Neill, an odd but kind-hearted old Irish schoolmistress [Slocum].

CLARKE, Sara Jane. See LIPPINCOTT, Sara Jane.

CLARKE, Thomas, fl. 1874. American novelist and poet, TC was the author of several volumes of poetry published in London including *A day in May* (1838); *Love and duty, and other poems* (1843); *Erotophuseos* (1844), and *The silent village* (1844). His *Sir Copp, a poem for the times* was published in 1865 in Chicago, where his novel also appeared. He apparently was a professor. SOURCE Allibone Suppl., i, p. 341, no. l; ML.
C235 *Avondale. A story of English life* (by Thomas Clarke).
    + Chicago: Published by the author, 1874. LOCATION Wright web.
    COMMENTARY Story starts out in northern Ireland where a landowner loses his possessions because of a run on the bank. He moves with his son, Edward Montague, and daughter Ellen to England. On board the ship, an old man, Mr. Worthington, befriends the family and suggests they come and live with him at Avondale. To while away the time they tell each other stories. Mr. Worthington tells a love story, part of the which is set in Ireland, in which a mystery stands in the way of the union of two lovers [ML].

CLARKE, William, b. 1800, d. 1838. An English writer of humorous fiction and fiction for juveniles, WC was a solicitor and a naturalist. His *The boy's own book: a complete encyclopaedia of all the diversions, athletic, scientific, and recreative, of boyhood and youth* (London, 1828) became very popular. He also began a humorous publication, the *Cigar*, and for some time was editor of the *Monthly Magazine* (both London). SOURCE Allibone Suppl., i, p. 341; BLC; Brown 2, p. 46; ODNB.
C236 *Three courses and a dessert* [anon.].
    + London: Vizetelly, Branston & Co., 1830 (ill. Cruikshank). SOURCE Garside 2, 1830:38. LOCATION D, L, InND Loeber coll. (1830, 2nd edn).
    London: Vizetelly, Branston & Co., 1836 (as *Three courses and a dessert; comprising three sets of tales, West Country, Irish, and legal; and a melange*; ill. Cruikshank). LOCATION NUC.
    COMMENTARY Contents (excluding poetry): 'First course: – West Country chronicles', 'Second course: – Neighbours of an old Irish boy', 'Third course: – My cousin's clients'; only the second 'course' is Irish in content [RL].

CLAYTON, Ellen (also Eleanor) Creathorne, later Mrs Needham, also published under Ellen Creathorne Needham, and Ellen C. Clayton), b. Dublin 1834, d. London 1900. Novelist, biographer, children's' writer and artist, ECC was a daughter of Benjamin Clayton, a well-known Dublin engraver who also worked in London as an illustrator and miniature painter and who gained a reputation for his military drawings. Her mother was Mary Grahame. Both ECC's brothers became engravers and her aunt, Caroline Clayton Millard, was a wood engraver and a water colourist. The family moved to London in 1841 and by the time ECC was age 15 she was contributing to and partly editing her father's paper *Chat* (London?). Her stories and illustrations appeared in publications in Dublin and in London – in her father's *Punchinello*, in *Judy*, and Sala's *London*. She studied at the National Gallery and the British Museum and wrote to supplement her income. She designed and illustrated Christmas cards, comic calendars and Valentines for, among others, the perfumer Rimmel on the Strand. Her first publication, *The World's Fair*, appeared in 1851, the year of the exhibition (volume not located). She earned praise for her numerous biographies of women painters, vocalists, religious and historical figures, including *English Female Artists* (London, 1876), and *Female warriors* (London, 1879, 2 vols.). She mostly wrote fiction for juveniles, and according to the ODNB published another novel in an [unidentified] weekly journal. In Feb. 1879 she married James Henry Needham and after that wrote only a few works of fiction for juveniles. SOURCE Allibone Suppl., ii, pp 1166–7 [under Needham]; Boase, iv, p. 684; ODNB; RIA/DIB; Strickland, i, pp 182–4; Sutherland, p. 130.

C237 *Miss Milly Moss; or, sunlight and shade* (by Ellen Creathorne Clayton).
+ London: Dean & Son, 1862. SOURCE COPAC. LOCATION E.
Chicago: Belford & Clarke, 1895 (as *The record of a ministering angel*). SOURCE OCLC; ODNB. LOCATION NYU.
COMMENTARY A domestic romance for young girls, it was EC's most successful novel [RL; ODNB].

C238 *Cruel fortune* (by Ellen Creathorne Clayton).
London: John Maxwell & Co., 1876, 3 vols. SOURCE ODNB; COPAC. LOCATION L.
COMMENTARY A sensationalist novel, which according to the ODNB did not sell well as publishers found it 'painfully morbid' [ODNB].

C239 *Topsy turvy; or strange sights to see* (by Ellen Creathorne Needham, formerly Clayton).
London: Dean & Son, [1876] (ill.). SOURCE ODNB; COPAC. LOCATION L.
COMMENTARY Fiction for juveniles [ODNB].

C240 *Playing for love: A story* (by Ellen Creathorne Needham, formerly Clayton).
London: Tinsley Bros, 1876, 3 vols. SOURCE ODNB; COPAC. LOCATION L, E.
COMMENTARY The tale of a young widow vacillating between suitors [ODNB].

C241 *The world turned upside-down* (by Ellen Creathorne Needham, formerly Clayton).
London: Dean & Son, [1876] (ill.). SOURCE ODNB. LOCATION L.
COMMENTARY Fiction for juveniles [ODNB].

C242 *Crying for vengeance. A novel* (by Ellen C. Clayton).
London: Tinsley Bros, 1877, 3 vols. SOURCE COPAC. LOCATION L, C.

C243 *A girl's destiny. A love story* (by Ellen Creathorne Clayton).
London: Tinsley Bros, 1882, 3 vols. SOURCE Wolff, 5085; COPAC. LOCATION L.

C244 *Only a girl, and other tales: Regina's mistake. Mabel's brother's friend. Fruits of flattery* (by Ellen Creathorne Clayton).
London: Dean & Son, [1883] (ill.). SOURCE COPAC. LOCATION L.

CLAYTON, Revd F.H., pseud. **'An Irishman'**, d. Canada? Miscellaneous writer and clergyman, FHC probably grew up near Banagher (Co. Offaly) before emigrating to Canada, judging from the first part of *Scenes and incidents in Irish life* (Montreal, 1884). According to the title page of this work, he also published 'The adventures of a black-thorne', but no copy has been located. SOURCE Personal communication, Michel Brisebois, National Library, Ottawa, Aug. 1996; RL.; Watters, p. 262.

C245 *Scenes and incidents in Irish life* (by 'An Irishman'; dedicated to author's 'dearest mother, Erin ... and all thy children').

+ Montreal: Printed [for the author?] by John Lovell & Son, 1884 (ill.). SOURCE Watters. LOCATION CIMH (microfiche 00679), QUK, CaOONL.

COMMENTARY The volume starts with author's autobiographical reminiscences and some considerations about the plight of Ireland, and then moves to fiction, interspersed with some poetry. The story is set at Gurteen Lodge (Co. Galway) [RL].

'CLEMENTS, Albyn', fl. 1900. Possibly the pseud. of a Church of Ireland minister. According to the title page of the following novel, he also wrote 'Jephethaes' daughter'; 'Mrs. Haldane's jewels'; 'An artist's stratagem', and 'The green [illegible] of Ivyland'. SOURCE RL.

C246 *Carston's parisher* (by 'Albyn Clements').

COMMENTARY Unpublished manuscript novella (*c*.1900). Set in Ireland. The hero is a young Church of Ireland rector in 'Dunerin', and the plot turns on his successful struggle to bring spiritual and familial peace to the (wicked) absentee landlord. The story tells of a church restoration; a fatal fall from a horse; a protracted death-bed scene; a restored inheritance; a double wedding, and the departure of the hero and heroine to work in the mission service in India. The manuscript is now in the NLI [Fotheringham cat. 27/20].

CLEMENTS, Mary E., fl. 1884. Religious fiction writer, possibly English, MEC published several works between 1884 and 1889, including *Eagle and dove* (London, 1889). Only the following book has Irish content. SOURCE Allibone Suppl., i, pp 344–5.

C247 *'Sheltering arms;' or, the entrance of God's word gives light* (by Mary E. Clements).

+ London, Edinburgh, New York: T. Nelson & Sons, 1885. SOURCE OCLC. LOCATION L, CtY (1888 edn), InND Loeber coll.

COMMENTARY Set in the west of Ireland and describes the conversion of a boy, Pat, to the Protestant faith. One summer he works for a family who come to the seaside to restore the health of two little girls. Pat learns to read and is told Bible stories with the help of jig-saw puzzles. After the family leaves, he obtains a Bible in Gaelic from an itinerant salesman. He is made an assistant teacher, which is a great help to his mother as the crops have failed. However, when the priest finds out that Pat reads the Bible, he loses his job. His mother dies a Protestant. Pat joins the itinerant salesman and sets out with him to sail to America. The boat shipwrecks, however, and Pat washes ashore close to where some members of the family for whom he had worked live. Pat is educated further and becomes a Protestant minister [ML].

CLEMËS, A.A., co-author. See CASEY, Elizabeth O.B.

'CLEOPHIL', pseud. See CONGREVE, William.

'A CLERGYMAN', fl. 1824. Pseudonym of a religious fiction writer. According to the title page of the following volume, he was also the author of *Missionary geography* (London, 1825), for which he used the pseudonym 'An Irish clergyman'. He may be identified with 'An Irish clergyman,' who signed as 'H.B.' and who published his 'Reminiscences', that is, Irish religious tales, edited by Elizabeth Tonna§ in the *Christian Lady's Magazine* (London, 1837–38). SOURCE RLIN; RL.

C248   *Simple memorials of an Irish family. A narrative of facts* (by 'A clergyman').
+ London: L.B. Seeley & Son, 1824. LOCATION L.
Dublin: P. Dixon Hardy & Sons [for the Religious Book and Tract Depository for Ireland], [1846 or earlier]. SOURCE Adv. in [anon.], *The history of Susan Blake. A true story* (Dublin, 1846).
Boston: Perkins & Marvin, 1829. SOURCE RLIN. LOCATION American Antiquarian Society (Worcester, MA).
COMMENTARY No copy of Dublin edn located. Set in the Golden Vale of Iverk (a barony in south Co. Kilkenny) along the river Iver (Suir), which can be reached by boat from Carrick-on-Suir and Clonmel (Co. Tipperary). Scene is in a cottage, where an old mother lives with several daughters and grandchildren. They have been brought down in the world by the dissipated behaviour of the husband of the eldest daughter. The book is about the beneficial effects of scripture reading on behaviour and on peace of mind, even under difficult circumstances [ML].

'A CLERGYMAN', fl. 1850s. Pseudonym of a religious fiction writer.
C249   *The clergyman's orphans; an interesting story founded on facts* (by 'A clergyman').
Dublin: P.D. Hardy, [1850] (ill. W.G. Mason). LOCATION PC.
COMMENTARY Published in two binding types, dark green cloth and bright blue cloth. Advertised in Revd T.H.C. Finny's *The history of John Bergan* (Dublin, 1850) as just published. Probably different from [anon.], *The clergyman's orphan, and other tales* (New York, 1833, and London, 1834). Set in England or Wales. Only Irish reference is that the younger orphan's 'inseparable' Sunday-school friend was a Miss O'Brien, daughter of an Irish gentleman of 'immense fortune' [RL; Personal communication, Mary Pollard, June 2004].

'A CLERGYMAN', fl. 1863. Pseudonym of a religious fiction writer.
C250   *The Irish daisy; or, Elizabeth, the happy Sunday scholar* (by 'A clergyman').
London: John Snow, 1863. LOCATION L.
COMMENTARY Religious fiction set in Co. Meath [BLC; CM].

'A CLERGYMAN'S WIDOW', fl. 1849. Pseudonym of an anti-Catholic religious fiction writer. Although *Sister Agnes* appears to have been published only in New York in 1854, judging from the content the author may have been Irish or English. She was also the author of 'The widow's friend' (not located; mentioned on the title page of *Sister Agnes*) and *The orphan's friend* (London, 1849). SOURCE BLC.
C251   *Sister Agnes; or, the captive nun. A picture of convent life* (by 'A clergyman's widow').
+ New York: Riker, Thorne & Co., 1854 (ill. E. Evans Snr). SOURCE Wright, ii, 2233; Fanning, p. 390. LOCATION InND Loeber coll., NYU, Wright web.
COMMENTARY Anti-Catholic religious fiction. The story is set in England, Ireland and Italy, and details the vices and deceptions practised by the Roman Catholic church to ensnare rich heiresses. A rich, motherless girl is taught by a governess, who is a nun in disguise. She is lured into the Catholic religion and whisked away unbeknownst to her father to Ireland to enter a convent there. All communication between them is prevented and the girl's inheritance is signed over to the convent. The girl is extremely unhappy as a nun but realizes that she is not allowed to leave. Eventually, she is placed in a convent in northern Italy where an escape attempt fails and she is tortured to death and thrown into a lime pit. The book contains allusions to the political situation in Ireland and has many negative remarks about clergy educated at Maynooth [ML].

'CLINGTON, Allen H.', pseud. See **CONYNGHAM, David Power**.

CLOWES, Alice A. See **CLOWES, Alice Ada**.

CLOWES, Alice Ada (known as **Alicia A. Clowes**, fl. 1898. Novelist, AAC also wrote a biography of Charles Knight (London, 1892). Her work is located in the Irish literature section of the NLI, which suggests that she is Irish. SOURCE BLC; RL.

C252 *Senex. A novel* (by Alice A. Clowes).
      + London: W. Swan Sonnenschein & Co., 1898. LOCATION L.
      COMMENTARY Set in Wales and has no Irish content [ML].

C253 *Mona. A novel* (by Alice A. Clowes).
      + London: W. Swan Sonnenschein & Co., 1899. LOCATION L, NUC.
COMMENTARY Set in Ireland. The main character is Mona Keary, born in the west of Ireland in a place called Castle Toberoy. After her mother dies, aunt Bid takes over the mother's role. Mona becomes engaged to Richard Kennedy, an Englishman whom she marries. She lives in England. The marriage breaks up and Mona becomes a matron in a children's home. In the end her husband returns [ML].

C254 *Mrs. Frederick Graham. A novel* (by Alice A. Clowes).
      + London: W. Swan Sonnenschein & Co., 1900. LOCATION D, L.
      COMMENTARY Set near Chelsea and has no Irish content [ML].

C255 *Stranded. A tale* (by Alice A. Clowes).
      + London: W. Swan Sonnenschein & Co., 1902. LOCATION D, L.
      COMMENTARY Set in England and Switzerland and has no Irish content [ML].

C256 *Mabel Percival's marriage* (by Alice A. Clowes).
      + London: G. Routledge & Sons; New York: E.P. Dutton & Co., 1912. LOCATION L.
COMMENTARY Set in England. Mabel has a suitor, Capt. Payne, who is about fifteen years older than she. She rejects him and contracts a marriage in a private ceremony with Eugene Ferguson. The marriage does not work out; Eugene dies and Mabel is free to go on with her life [ML].

COATES, Mr —. See **COATES, H.J.**

COATES, H. See **COATES, H.J.**

COATES, H.J. (also known as **Mr Coates** and **H. Coates**), fl. 1830. Writer of historical fiction. SOURCE AMB.

C257 *The weird woman of the Wraagh; or, Burton and Le Moore. An historical tale* (by Mr Coates; dedicated to Arthur, duke of Wellington).
      London: A.K. Newman & Co., 1830, 4 vols. SOURCE Hodgson, p. 598; Brown, 361; Garside 2, 1830:39. LOCATION Corvey 3–628–47299–7, L.
COMMENTARY Historical fiction. Mentions in the dedication 'If the melancholy condition of Ireland and Irishmen is ever to be remedied by the British legislature, now is the time!' Chronicles adventures starting in 1783. The Wraagh is a cave near Baltinglass (Co. Wicklow), but the scene frequently shifts to other parts of Ireland such as Cork, Kilkenny and Cashel (Co. Tipperary). The story describes a kidnapping, escapes from robbers, a duel, and a love story [Brown; Garside 2].

C258 *Lucius Carey; or, the mysterious female of Mora's dell. An historical tale* [anon.] (dedicated to Daniel O'Connell).
      London: A.K. Newman & Co., 1831, 4 vols. SOURCE Brown, 362; Block, p. 42; Garside 2, 1832:18. LOCATION Corvey CME 3–628–48121–X, L.

COMMENTARY Historical fiction. Lucius Carey goes to England with his followers to fight in the royalist cause and finally returns to Ireland. The book has many allusions to astrology and Irish heroic legends [Brown].

C259 *The water Queen; or, the mermaid of Lough Lene, and other tales* (by H. Coates).
London: A.K. Newman & Co., 1832, 3 vols. SOURCE Brown, 363. LOCATION L.
COMMENTARY Set in Killarney at the time of Queen Elizabeth's wars with Hugh O'Neill. Sir Bertram Fitzroy, a young Englishman, comes over with Essex and is sent to Killarney where he befriends the Irish and falls in love with Eva, who teaches him to love Ireland. They are kept apart by the scheming of O'Fergus, a standard-bearer to O'Neill. After O'Fergus is slain, the lovers are united [Brown].

COBB, Sylvanus, Jnr, b. Waterville (ME) 1823, d. 1887. American writer of juvenile fiction, editor and temperance writer, SC was the son of Revd Sylvanus Cobb, a minister of the Universalist Church, and Eunice Hale Waite. He was one of the first prolific writers of stories for boys in which he 'allowed a maximum amount of excitement compatible with strict morality' (DAB). His early service and travels in the navy provided background for his fiction. He was on the staff of Gleason's *Flag of Our Union* (Boston) and *Pictorials* (location unclear) and contributed over 200 stories and 30 novelettes, many of them advocating temperance. He also contributed to the *New York Ledger* and was editor of the Boston *New England Washingtonian*. SOURCE Allibone, i, p. 398; Allibone Suppl., i, p. 351; Brown 2, p. 48; DAB; Dime novels.

C260 *Roderick of Kildare; or, the baron's compact* (by Sylvanus Cobb, Jnr).
London: Henderson, 1866. SOURCE Brown 2, 241.
New York: R. Bonner's Sons, 1891. LOCATION NUC.
COMMENTARY No copy of the London edn located. Historical novel set during the period of the Norman invasion of Ireland and the parcelling out of Irish lands among the invaders. Contrasts the power and the magnificence of the foreigner with the misery and state of 'barbarism' to which the Irish had been reduced. The chief characters are Roderick Fitzgerald, son of the earl of Kildare, Kate Mac Murrough, and the earl and countess of Catherlogh (Carlow), who join in a league against the barons. The story was dramatized by Julia McK. McBarron and Deborah McK. Walsh in 1903 [Brown 2; OCLC].

COBBE, Elizabeth Dorothea. See TUITE, Lady Elizabeth Dorothea.

COBBE, F.P. See COBBE, Frances Power.

COBBE, Frances Power (known as F.P. Cobbe), b. Dublin 1822 (not in 1828 as in Allibone), d. Hengwrt, near Dolgellau (Wales) 1904. Writer, poet, social activist, philosopher, and feminist, FPC was the daughter of Charles Cobbe of Newbridge House, Donabate, and Frances Conway. She was educated mainly at home, except for a brief time in Brighton, England. Raised in an evangelical Protestant family that had produced five archbishops, FPC rejected the Church of Ireland for a form of deism influenced by Theodore Parker, whose writings she later edited. Her first book, *The theory of intuitive morals* (London 1855, 1857, 2 vols.), was prompted by a reading of Kant's *Metaphysics of ethics*. After her father's death and her brother's inheritance of Newbridge House, she travelled in the Middle East and in Italy, to which she returned many times. She settled first in Bristol (Avon) and then in London and wrote and worked for the higher education and political enfranchisement of women. She contributed to most of the major periodicals of the day, composed hymns and poems, and wrote widely on faith and religion and on the many social movements in which she was involved, such as women's suffrage; prison reform; reform of the property laws, and anti-vivisectionism. She continued to travel, and was the Italian correspondent for the London *Daily News*. Her writings include *False beasts and true. Essays on natural and unnatural history* (London, [1876]), and *Re-echoes* (London, 1876), which consists of her contributions to the halfpenny periodical the *Echo* (location unclear). She contributed an article 'Wife-torture in England' to the *Contemporary Review* (1878) in which she sought to make aggravated assault on women grounds for judicial separation and which was influential in the passage of the Matrimonial Causes act of the same year. In 1884 she moved with Mary Lloyd, her companion of many years, to ML's home in Wales but continued her crusading writing. She published her autobiography, *Life of Frances Power Cobbe, by herself* (London, 1894, 2 vols.). For her portrait and papers, see ODNB. SOURCE Allibone Suppl., i, pp 351–2; Blain, p. 219; B. Caine, *Victorian feminists* (1992); DLB, cxc; LVP, p. 98; NCBEL 4, p. 2222; OCIL, p. 104; ODNB; O'Donoghue, p. 71; RIA/DIB; RL; T & B, p. 973; L. Williamson, *Power & protest: Frances Power Cobbe and Victorian society* (London, 2005).

C261   *Hours of work and play* (by Frances Power Cobbe).

+ London: N. Trübner & Co., 1867. LOCATION L, InND Loeber coll.

COMMENTARY Partly essays and short stories, published in various periodicals (1865–66). Contents of the short stories: 'A lady's adventure in the great pyramid', 'The state vault of Christ Church' (set in Dublin), 'The shadow of death' (on druids), 'Allured', 'The spectral rout: passages from the diary of a governess' (two Irish gentlewomen reduced to poverty), 'The Fenians of Ballybogmucky' [RL].

C262   *The confessions of a lost dog* (reported by her mistress F.P. Cobbe).

+ London: Griffith & Farran, 1867. LOCATION L.

COMMENTARY Fiction for children, which has as its frontispiece a photograph of the author's dog. The story, set in England, was written in support of the Lost Dog's Home. It tells the ups-and-downs in a dog's life, ending in the lost dog's home from where he is retrieved by his mistress [ML].

COBBE, Sarah, fl. 1800. Novelist, SC was the daughter of Richard Chaloner Cobbe, rector of Badenham (Bucks.) who descended from the Cobbe family of Newbridge House, Donabate (Co. Dublin). Her father was chaplain to the earl of Moira who had estates in Co. Down (at Moira and Altamont) and in England. SOURCE Falkner Grierson cat. 23/114; Landed gentry, 1912, p. 118; RL.

C263   *Julia St. Helen; or, the heiress of Ellisborough. A novel* (by Sarah Cobbe; dedicated to the earl of Moira).

+ London: Printed [for the author?] by J. Nichols, 1800, 2 vols. (subscribers' list). SOURCE Falkner Grierson cat. 23/114; British Fiction; Garside, 1800:23; ESTC t017266. LOCATION L.

COMMENTARY Among the Irish subscribers are Lady Moira, Lady Granard, Lady Kilkenny, the earl of Lanesborough, Lord Mountjoy, the countess of Oxmantown, and Lady Tuite§. Although Sarah Cobbe's name occurs on the title page of this novel, she claimed not to have been its author. It is unclear to what extent this is a ruse. The preface states 'that Julia St. Helen is not mine, but has been kindly obtained for me from the deceased author's relatives, through the interference of a friend, and upon the condition that I should publish it by subscription' (p. [vii]). High society novel, set in and around London [Garside; RL].

'**A COCKNEY**', pseud. See **GREEN, Mrs Sarah**.

COEN, P.J., fl. 1870s. American writer of religious fiction, PJC was possibly related to the Irish writer John Coen, contributor to the *Nation* (Dublin). SOURCE Irish pseudonyms.

C264 *Evaline; or, weighed and not wanting. A Catholic tale* (by P.J. Coen).
+ New York: P. O'Shea, [1872]. SOURCE Wright iii, 1127. LOCATION InND Loeber coll., AIHS.

COMMENTARY An English Protestant girl, Evaline, moves to New York to become a ward of her uncle. While there, she meets a Frenchman, Jean Baptiste. The two fall in love, but the uncle is very much against the match because of Jean Baptiste's nationality and religion. Eventually, they marry, and move to France. While on a visit to Rome, Evaline is converted to the Catholic faith, which increases the couple's happiness. Two Irish stories about fairies are introduced into the narrative by Paddy, an Irish servant of the uncle. One story is about Paddy's grandfather who was helped in a fight at a fair by a mysterious person in a red waistcoat. The person disappeared and all agreed that it must have been a fairy. The other is about a poor family whose cow dies and they seem to have run out of luck. After a while things go better, in a mysterious way, which is also attributed to the fairies [ML].

COLCHESTER, Reginald C.E. See COLCHESTER, Reginald Charles Edward Abbot, 3rd baron.

COLCHESTER, Reginald Charles Edward Abbot, 3rd Baron (also known as Reginald C.E. Colchester), b. 1842. Only son of Admiral Charles, 2nd Baron Colchester, and the Hon. Elizabeth-Susan Law, daughter of Edward, 1st Lord Ellenborough. RCEAC's grandfather had been appointed chief secretary to the lord lieutenant of Ireland, and keeper of the privy seal in Ireland. RCEAC produced several works pertaining to the political activities of his family members. He became a fellow of All Souls, Oxford, and was private secretary to the earl of Darby when first lord of the Treasury. RCEAC married the Hon. Isabella-Grace Maude, eldest daughter of the 4th Viscount Hawarden. Their seat was at Kidbrooke, Tunbridge Wells (Sussex). SOURCE B. Burke, *A genealogical and heraldic dictionary of the peerage and baronetage* (London, 1878, 40th edn), p. 265; OCLC.

C265 **Kathleen O'Dwyer: A tale of Tipperary under Cromwell** [anon.].
Tunbridge Wells [Sussex]: Printed [for the author?] by N.C. Colbran, 1872. SOURCE OCLC; Bow Windows cat. 172/42. LOCATION D.

COMMENTARY 94pp. The author's name, Reginald C.E. Colchester, is mentioned in OCLC. Copy in the Bow Windows cat. has small label tipped unto the title page bearing the signature [?] of Lord Colchester. Historical novel set in Ireland during the Commonwealth [OCLC; RL].

'COL. DELLE SARA', pseud. See AIKEN, Albert W.

COLLINS, Mabel (Mrs Keningale Cooke). Co-author. See DESPARD, Charlotte.

COLLINS, William, b. Co. Wicklow *c.*1740, d. London 1812. Fictionalizing autobiographer, WC was, according to the title page of his only work of semi-fiction, the author of a poem, *The slave trade* (London, [1788]), as well as *An ode to Sir Jeffrey Dunstan, an heroic effusion; with several detached pieces in prose and verse* published under various signatures from 1788 on. His son was the painter William Collins and his grandson the novelist William Wilkie Collins§. SOURCE Brady, p. 39; NSTC, ser. 1, i, p. 431; O'Donoghue, p. 74; RIA/DIB.

C266 *Memoirs of a picture. Containing the adventures of many conspicuous characters, and interspersed with a variety of amusing anecdotes of several very extraordinary personages connected with the arts; including a genuine biographical sketch of the celebrated original and eccentric genius, the late Mr. George Morland. Drawn from* the tolerably authentic source of more than twenty years' intimate acquaintance with him, his family, and connections. To which is added, a copious appendix, embracing every interesting subject relative to our justly admired English painter, and his most valuable works (by William Collins).

London: C. Stower & H.D. Symonds, 1805, 3 vols. (ill. Collins Jnr, W. Ward). SOURCE Hardy, 316; NSTC. LOCATION NUC.

COMMENTARY Fictionalized biography. Vol. 2 is entitled 'Memoirs of a painter'. A related work, *Authentic memoirs of the late George Morland* was published in London in 1805. WC's *Memoirs of a picture* was criticized by the *British Critic* (London, 1805, p. 684), where it was called 'the oddest farrago that was ever put together. The first volume outdoes Baron Munchhausen in its improbability, and has no more to do with Morland than with Bonaparte. The whole is very poor stuff indeed' [Hardy; RL].

COLLINS, William, b. Strabane (Co. Tyrone) 1838, d. United States? 1890. Novelist, poet and Fenian adventurer, WC's family originally came from Munster. At age 15 he ran away from home and emigrated to Canada, and thence to the US. He contributed poems to the Boston *Pilot*, worked for various newspapers, and published *Ballads, songs and poems* (New York, 1875), and 'Sybilla, a tale of the county of Tyrone' (no copy located). He took part in the Fenian raid on Canada in 1866. The title page of the following volume notes that he was the author of 'The wild geese', 'Desmond, or the two flags', and 'Songs, poems and ballads', but these have not been located. The 'L'envoi' of the latter volume was written from Brooklyn (NY) in 1879. SOURCE Brown, pp 64–5; A.A. Campbell, *Notes of the literary history of Strabane* (Omagh, 1902), pp 46–8; Irish pseudonyms; NUC; O'Donoghue, p. 74; Personal communication, Mary Pollard, June 2004.

C267 *Dalaradia; or, the days of King Milcho* (by William Collins).

+ New York: P.J. Kenedy, 1890 (ill. P.J. Kenedy). SOURCE Brown, 366. LOCATION Dc, D, InND Loeber coll. (1896 edn).

New York: D. & J. Sadlier & Co., 1890 (ill.). SOURCE OCLC. LOCATION Boston College.

COMMENTARY Historical novel set in Dalaradia (Co. Antrim) in the fifth century, it features the sons and daughters of Milcho, chief of Dalaradia, and tells about the conversion by St Patrick of many of the individuals in Milcho's household. Relates the arrival of St Patrick at Tara, and ends with the nuptials of Mahon and his love, Sybilla, who have both become converts [Brown; ML].

COLLINS, William Wilkie, b. London 1824, d. 1889. Prolific English novelist, playwright, editor and short story writer, WWC was the son of the painter William Collins and grandson of the Irish author William Collins§ (*c*.1740–1812). He wrote one Irish novel, his last, but he does not seem to have had any first-hand knowledge of Ireland. He was a friend of and collaborator with Charles Dickens and contributed to Dickens's London periodicals *All the Year Round* and *Household Words* as well as to *Bentley's Miscellany* and the *Leader* (both London). Among his many novels, *The woman in white* (London, 1860) and *The moonstone* (London, 1868) were particularly famous. SOURCE Allibone, i, p. 413; Allibone Suppl., i, pp 367–8; Brown, p. 65; DLB, xviii, lxxix, clix; NCBEL 4, pp 1166–80; ODNB; Sutherland, pp 141–2; T & B, p. 973.

C268 *Blind love* (by William Wilkie Collins; preface by Walter Besant§, who completed it after the author's death from notes left by the author).

London: Chatto & Windus, 1890, 3 vols. (ill. A. Forestier). SOURCE Brown, 365a; Topp 3, p. 198; Wolff, 1348. LOCATION L, NUC.

Leipzig: Bernard Tauchnitz, 1890, 2 vols. SOURCE T & B, 2629. LOCATION NUC.

New York: D. Appleton & Co., 1890 (Town & Country Library, No. 44). SOURCE Topp 3, p. 198. LOCATION NUC.

New York: Frank F. Lovell, 1890 (Household Library, No. 286). SOURCE Topp 3, p. 198.

New York: John W. Lovell, 1890 (Lovell's Library, No. 1482). SOURCE Topp 3, p. 198.

New York: George Munro, 1890 (Seaside Library Pocket Edition, No. 1260). SOURCE Topp 3, p. 198; OCLC. LOCATION DCL.

COMMENTARY No copies of the two New York Lovell edns located. First serialized in the *Illustrated London News* (Jul.–Dec. 1889), the central theme is the blind love of a London girl, Iris Hadley, for the worthless scapegrace Lord Harry Norland. Iris takes refuge from her father with her godfather, Sir C. Mordaunt, a banker, living at 'Ardoon' in Kerry. She will not marry his son, the devoted Hugh Mordaunt. Twice she saves Norland's life from murder by the Invincibles. A third time she saves him when he is on the point of suicide, and then marries him. He feigns death, and disappears, so as to get the insurance money with which to pay his debts. But soon he comes out of hiding and goes back to Ireland, to meet his death at the hands of the Invincibles [Brown; Topp 3, p. 198; RL].

COLOMB, Captain. See **COLOMB, Col. George Hatton**.

COLOMB, Colonel. See **COLOMB, Col. George Hatton**.

COLOMB, Col. George Hatton (also known as **Captain Colomb** and **Colonel Columb**), fl. 1862. Novelist, poet and playwright, GHC was Irish. He served in the Royal Artillery and was a member of the Society of Antiquaries. He also wrote poetry, verse plays, and *Blue stockings* (London, 1884), an adaptation of a comedy by Molière. Source Allibone Suppl., ii, p. 369; LVP, p. 102; MVP, p. 103.

C269   *Hearths & watch-fires* (by Captain Colomb; dedicated to the duchess of Beaufort).
+ London: T. Cautley Newby, 1862, 3 vols. SOURCE Allibone Suppl., ii, p. 369; COPAC. LOCATION L.
COMMENTARY Military novel, it starts out in England and discusses the Crimean War. No Irish content other than one Irish servant in Liverpool [ML].

C270   *For king and Kent, 1648. A true story of the great rebellion* (by Colonel Colomb).
London: Remington & Co., 1882, 3 vols. (with notes). SOURCE COPAC. LOCATION L.
London: W.H. Allen & Co., 1886 (new edn with notes). SOURCE COPAC. LOCATION L.
COMMENTARY No Irish content [ML].

C271   *The shadows of destiny. A romance* (by George Hatton Columb).
London: Chapman & Hall, 1866, 2 vols. SOURCE Allibone Suppl., ii, p. 369; COPAC. LOCATION L.

C272   *The Miss Crusoes: A curious story for big and little children. Compiled from original sources* (by Colonel Colomb).
+ London: W.H. Allen & Co., [1888] (ill. A. Hitchcock, some after designs by Miss Emily Lees). SOURCE COPAC. LOCATION L.
COMMENTARY In the preface, GHC names himself as 'editor, or compiler' of the volume. Fiction for juveniles, it chronicles the 'memoirs' of two orphans, Emma Jane and Mary Anne, who leave for New Zealand by sea to live there with an aunt. After rounding Cape Horn, they land on an island where they meet a 'Gentleman of the Country', who is an ape. GHC's pref-

ace states that he had 'the least design of ridiculing the legitimist party in a neighbouring country' [RL].

COLPOYS, Mrs A., fl. 1801. Fiction writer. Mrs AC's identity is not clear. A John Colpoys of the Middle Temple married a Miss Searle of Madeira Island in London in 1788, but it is not known if she is the same person as this author. The Colpoys family was from Co. Clare. A John Colpoys held the estate of Ballycarr near O'Brien's Bridge in 1780, and a John Colpoys (1742–1821) was a naval officer who saw action against the American revolutionaries and the French. SOURCE Farrar, i, p. 92; J. Lloyd, *A short tour; or, an impartial and accurate description of the County of Clare* (Ennis, 1780, reprinted 1986), p. 48; ODNB [under John Colpoys, 1742–1821].

C273   *The Irish excursion; or, I fear to tell you. A novel* [anon.].
    London: William Lane, 1801, 4 vols. SOURCE Blakey, p. 199; Brown, 367; Block, p. 43; British Fiction; Garside 1801:17. LOCATION Corvey CME 3-628-47462, Ireland related fiction, Dt, L.
    Dublin: H. Colbert, W. Porter, J. Moore, J. Rice, B. Dornin & J. Stockdale, 1801, 2 vols. SOURCE Brown, 367 (who mistakenly mentions Dublin: Lane). LOCATION Dt, L, NUC.
COMMENTARY Vignette on title page of three hands clasped together, joining sprays of shamrock, rose, and thistle, below the motto *Quis Separabit?* Set at the time of the Union and makes a plea for the Union. Tells of Mrs M'Gralahan and her family's trip to London and contains political discussions about Ireland [Brown; Blakey, p. 84].

COLQUHOUN, Lucy Bethia. See WALFORD, Lucy Bethia.

COLTHURST, Miss E., d. 1858? Short story writer and religious fiction writer, poet and novelist, EC was a resident of Cork and perhaps can be identified with Elizabeth Colthurst, third daughter of Charles Nicholas Colthurst, of Clonmoyle (Co. Cork) and Florence Campbell. When her book *Irrelagh* was published in London in 1849, she dedicated it from Danesfort, Killarney (Co. Kerry), now in ruins, which was the seat of Capt. Colthurst, probably a relative. She was associated with Revd Edward Nangle and his evangelical mission to Achill, but the specifics remain unclear. EC's published poetry includes *Emmanuel* (London, 1833); *Life: A Poem* (Cork, 1835); *Home* (Cork, 1836), and *The storm* (Liverpool, 1840). In addition, she published six works of fiction, some of which are set in Co. Kerry. She died unmarried. SOURCE Alston, pp 89–90; Bary, p. 95; BLC; Brown, pp 64–5; Burke's, p. 261; Colman, pp 55–6; NCBEL 4, p. 323; O'Donoghue, p. 75; O'Toole, p. 41; RIA/DIB.

C274   *Tales of Erin* [anon.].
    + London: J. Wright & Co.; Aldine Chambers, [1837 or earlier] (ill.). SOURCE Brown, 368; RL. LOCATION D.
COMMENTARY Proselytizing tales, poetry and songs. Contents of the stories: 'Dennis Dunleavy', 'The Kerry cows', 'The May feast', 'The contented Irishman', 'The friend departed', 'A peep into an Irish cabin', 'A reward of faith' [RL].

C275   *Futurity* [anon.] (dedicated to the Queen).
    + Cork: Osborne Savage & Son, 1837. SOURCE Brown 2, 244. LOCATION L, NUC, InND Loeber coll.
COMMENTARY The following tales are heavily religious in content and are aimed at pointing the reader to life after death. Contents (excluding poetry): 'A peep into an Irish cabin' (first published in *Tales of Erin*, London, n.d.), 'A dream', 'Rassellas', 'The infant school', 'Gerissimo Michaeletziano', 'Perseverance', 'The convert', 'Anticipation', 'The hurling match', 'Edward

Campbell', 'The cholera', 'The Jew', 'Night thoughts', 'The water-cut', 'The condemned soldier', 'The little old woman of Muckrus', 'The boatman of Lough-Lane', 'The fox's brush', 'Tomorrow' [ML].

C276 *Emmeline; or, trials sanctified* (by Miss E. Colthurst; dedicated to the author's father [Charles Nicholas Colthurst?]).
+ Cork: Printed for the author by F. Jackson, 1838. SOURCE OCLC. LOCATION D, UCC.
COMMENTARY Not to be confused with Mary Brunton's novel *Emmeline* (Edinburgh, 1819) [RL].

C277 *Futurity, continued* (by Miss E. Colthurst).
Cork: Osborne Savage, 1838. SOURCE Colman, p. 56. LOCATION D.

C278 *Innisfail; or, the Irish scripture reader. Narratives of facts* [anon.] (ed. by Joseph Wilson).
+ London: James Nisbet & Co., 1841. SOURCE Hodgson, p. 287. LOCATION L, NUC (1849 edn).
COMMENTARY Preface by Joseph Wilson, Clapham Common (London), Mar. 1841. Introd. calls for the Catholic Irish to pursue their national goals. Contents: short stories, sketches, and some poems (not listed here): 'The Irish inspector', 'The sand-pit', 'The school house', 'The Irish examination', 'The triumph of Kerry', 'The attack', 'The landscape', 'The arrest', 'The old Irish woman', 'The mountain fog', 'The priest's clerk', 'Knockanaro', 'Trust in the Lord', 'Blind George', 'The Kerryman's welcome to the first Irish testament', 'The mountain village', 'Paddy Conner', 'The pair of brogues', 'The robbery', 'The piper of Dunquin', 'Irish intellect (includes poem)', 'The Blasket Island (includes poem)', 'The Blasket Island (part II.)', 'The Carmelite', 'Gougane Barra', 'The Irish schoolmaster's journey from home', 'The convert rebuked by his horse', 'The sword of the spirit', 'The grateful Irishman', 'A visit to Inishfallan', 'The funeral', 'The Irish correspondent', 'Ventry'. It is possible that *The little ones of Innisfail*, mentioned by O'Donoghue, but not identified as such, refers to this volume. [RL; O'Donoghue, p. 75].

C279 *Irrelagh; or, the last of the chiefs. An Irish tale* [anon.] (dedicated to the Queen Dowager).
+ London: Houlston & Stoneman; Bristol: John Wright, 1849. SOURCE Hodgson, p. 289; Brown, 369. LOCATION D, L, InND Loeber coll.
COMMENTARY Religious fiction. Set in Killarney at the end of the seventeenth century but has no reference to historical events. A Waldensian pastor comes to live in the family of The O'Donoghue and converts that family and some of the neighbouring chieftains' families [Brown].

COMERFORD, Mary. See **BODDINGTON, Mary.**

CONGREVE, William, pseud. 'Cleophil', b. Bardsey Grange (Yorks.) 1670, d. London 1729. English dramatist and novelist, WC was the son of an army officer and his wife, Mary Browning of Doncaster. Shortly after his birth, his father was appointed commander of the garrison at Youghal (Co. Cork), serving later in Carrickfergus (Co. Antrim) and in Kilkenny, where WC attended Kilkenny School along with Jonathan Swift§. WC's father managed part of the estates of Richard Boyle, the earl of Cork, at Youghal and Lismore Castle (Co. Waterford) after he was discharged from the army. WC entered TCD in 1686 but left before graduation, probably in 1689 when TCD closed during the political upheavals of 1688 when many Protestants left Ireland as war between James II and William III appeared imminent. His first published work, *Incognita ...*, was written in Dublin but not published until after he had moved to England (London, 1692). He studied at the Middle Temple but soon gave up the law in favour of literature. His play *Old batchelor*, which he dedicated to Charles Boyle, eldest son of the earl of Cork, was performed in Drury Lane when he was age 21. He subsequently went on to become one of the most popular comic Restoration dramatists in England, famous for his wit, polished dialogue and social commentary. In 1696 he returned to Dublin where he received an MA from TCD. SOURCE Allibone, i, pp 413–14; DLB, xxxix, lxxxiv; Field Day, i. p. 502; Hogan 2, pp 278–9; ODNB (for full biography); RIA/DIB.

C280   *Incognita; or, love and duty reconcil'd. A novel* (dedicated to Katharine Leveson; dedication signed 'Cleophil').

+ London: P. Buck, 1692. SOURCE Esdaile, p. 190; McBurney & Taylor (1713, 2n edn); ESTC r2622; Hogan 2, p. 279; Sweeney, 1151. LOCATION L, IU (1713, 2nd edn), NUC (1770 edn).

Dublin: J. Rhames, 1743. SOURCE ESTC n054096. LOCATION NUC.

Columbia (SC): Univ. of South Carolina Press, [*c.*1966] (ed. by A.N. Jeffares). SOURCE NCBEL 2, p. 982. LOCATION DCL.

COMMENTARY A novel set in Italy that followed the conventions of romance in order to parody them. The main characters are Aurelian and the fair maiden Incognita. The novel was revived in the twentieth century by Egon Wellesz as a musical composition [RL; Hogan; Sweeney, 1151].

CONMEE, John S. See **CONMEE, Fr John Stephen.**

CONMEE, Fr John Stephen, SJ (known as **John S. Conmee**), b. Glanduff, near Athlone (Co. Westmeath) 1847, d. Dublin 1910. Catholic priest, poet and writer, JSC came from a well-to-do farming family that later moved to Kingsland, near Frenchpark (Co. Roscommon). He studied at Castleknock College (Co. Dublin) but moved to Clongowes Wood College (Co. Kildare) in 1863. After entering the Society of Jesus in 1869, he continued his studies at Roehampton and Stonyhurst in England. He returned to Ireland to teach at Tullybeg (Co. Offaly) in 1873, later studying theology in Innsbruck and travelling extensively in Europe. He was ordained at Thurles (Co. Tipperary) in 1881. Subsequently he was rector of Clongowes; prefect of studies and dean of UCD; superior of St Francis Xavier Church, Dublin; provincial of the Society (1905–09), and rector at Milltown Park. He published poetry in the Dublin *Irish Monthly*. JSC features in James Joyce's *A portrait of the artist* (New York, 1916) and in *Ulysses* (Paris, 1922). SOURCE Introd. to 1976 edn of *Old times in the barony* (Dublin, 1900); Irish pseudonyms; RIA/DIB.

C281   *Old times in the barony* (by John S. Conmee).

Dublin: Catholic Truth Society, 1900 (No. 16). SOURCE OCLC; COPAC; Blackrock, Carraig 1976 edn. LOCATION InND.

+ Blackrock: Carraig, 1976 (introd. by Dr Thomas Wall; ill.; Carraig Chapbooks 7). LOCATION InND Loeber coll.

COMMENTARY 36pp. First published in the *New Ireland Review* (Jan. 1895) [RL].

'CONNELL, F. Norryes', pseud. See **O'RIORDAN, Conal Holmes O'Connell.**

CONNER, Elizabeth Jane. See **LYSAGHT, Elizabeth Jane.**

CONNOR, Kate, fl. 1880s. Novelist, who possibly was the daughter of a Church of Ireland minister. SOURCE RL.

C282   *See-saw. An Irish story. A novel* (by Kate Connor).
+ London: London Literary Society, [1887]. SOURCE Allibone Suppl., i, p. 374; Brown 2, 265 ([1908] edn). LOCATION L.
COMMENTARY A family chronicle of Protestant life on the south coast of Ireland in the days of the Land League. It includes incidents of boycotting and violence against landlords, towards whom the narrative is sympathetic. The narrator is a daughter of Revd O'Brien, rector of Kilvar, who marries the marquis of Glenmore, heir to Glendufferin Castle [Brown 2].

CONNOR, Roger. See **O'CONNOR, Roger.**

CONOLLY, Revd L.A. See **CONOLLY, Revd Luke Aylmer.**

CONOLLY, Revd Luke Aylmer (known as the **Revd L.A. Conolly**), b. 1786, d. 1832. Church of Ireland clergyman, novelist and poet who in 1806 is noted by J. Carr as an Irish author. The preface to *The friar's tale* is dated from TCD, Mar. 1805, where LAC graduated in 1806. He was chaplain at Ballycastle (Co. Antrim, 1810–26) but resigned because of illness, which he endured until his death in 1832. Aside from two novels he published many well-known poems, *Legendary tales* (Belfast, 1813), and contributed a piece on the 'Parish of Ramoan' to W.S. Mason's *A statistical account or parochial survey of Ireland* (Dublin, 1816, ii, p. 511. SOURCE Allibone, i, p. 419; B & S, p. 171; J. Carr, *The stranger in Ireland* (Philadelphia, 1806), p. 153; J.C. Erck, *Ecclesiastical register* (Dublin, 1820), p. 25; Leslie, *Connor*, p. 272; NSTC, ser. 1, i, p. 444; *The Parliamentary Gazetteer* (Dublin, 1849), iii, p. 1100; O'Donoghue, p. 77.

C283   *The friar's tale; or, memoirs of the Chevalier Orsino, with other narratives* (by L.A. Conolly).
+ London: T. Caddell & W. Davies, 1805, 2 vols. SOURCE Hardy, 59; British Fiction; Garside, 1805:21. LOCATION Corvey CME 3–628–7318–7, L, ViU.
COMMENTARY Probably can be identified with the 'Friar's tale' which was published in the *Sentimental and Masonic Magazine* (Dublin, July–Oct. 1792). Gothic novel set in Italy, Vienna, Warsaw, the Black Forest and England, and featuring an ancient manuscript [Clyde, p. 70; Summers, p. 170; Quaritch cat. 1244/4].
C284   *The tournament: A legendary tale* (by the Revd L.A. Conolly).
Belfast: Printed [for the author?] by Drummond Anderson, 1827. SOURCE COPAC. LOCATION BFl, CtY.

CONTI, F. Carlo de', fl. 1652. Italian fiction writer.
C285   *La principessa d'Irlanda, historia sacra, descritta e moralizata dal cavalier F. Carlo de' Conti, della Lengveglia.*
Venice: Christoforo Tomasini, 1652. SOURCE Sweeney, 1171; Gilbert, p. 166. LOCATION DPL (Gilbert coll.).

'A CONVERT TO THE CATHOLIC FAITH', fl. 1852. Pseudonym of a religious fiction writer.
C286   *Annie and her aunt* (by 'A convert to the Catholic faith').
Dublin: James Duffy, 1852. LOCATION L (destroyed).
COMMENTARY 48pp. No copy located. Religious fiction [BLC].

CONVILLE, Thomas M., pseuds **'Baron na Carriag'** [*sic*] and **'T.M.',** fl. 1873. Comic romance novelist, TMC is identified in a handwritten note on the KU-S copy of the 1873 edn of the following volume. He was probably an Irish fortune-seeker in the Australian gold rush. SOURCE Miller, ii, 616; OCLC.

C287   *The artist of Collingwood* (by 'Baron na Carriag').

Dublin: McGlashan & Gill; London: Simpkin, Marshall, & Co.; Edinburgh: John Menzies & Co., 1873. SOURCE OCLC. LOCATION D, Dt, L, KU-S.

+ Dublin: McGlashan & Gill; London: Simpkin, Marshall, & Co., 1876 (as *Frank O'Meara; or, the artist of Collingwood*; by 'T.M.'). SOURCE Brown, 34; Topp 8, 502. LOCATION L.

Dublin: McGlashan & Gill; London: Simpkin, Marshall, & Co., 1882 (new edn). SOURCE Topp 8, 502.

COMMENTARY No copy of the Dublin 1882 new edn located. A comic romance set in Bray (Co. Wicklow) and in Collingwood, Australia. Frank falls in love with his landlord's daughter, whose father does not allow him to approach her, because of his low status. Frank deems it advisable to emigrate to Australia, where he and his comic sidekick Jerry Doolin have many adventures. Meanwhile in Ireland his father and friend contend for the favours of a widow, and Frank's girl Fanny opens a bookshop, awaiting his return. Frank returns a rich man from Australia and marries Fanny [Brown; ML].

CONWAY, Katherine Eleanor. Editor. See **O'REILLY, John Boyle**.

CONWAY, William D., fl. 1812. Publisher and writer in Philadelphia.

C288   *Beauties of the shamrock, containing biography, eloquence, essays and poetry* (introd. by William D. Conway).

+ Philadelphia: William D. Conway, 1812, vol. 1. [all published] (ill.). SOURCE Exiles, p. 23*n*.3; OCLC. LOCATION D, InND Loeber coll.

COMMENTARY One of the earliest Irish anthologies published in America. Contains history, biography, poetry and one story 'Nathos and Minona', translated from Irish [Exiles; RL].

CONYERS, Dorothea. See **CONYERS, Dorothea Spaight**.

CONYERS, Dorothea (Minnie) Spaight (née Blood-Smyth; known as **Dorothea Conyers**), b. Fedamore (Co. Limerick) 1869 (but some sources give 1871 and 1873), d. Co. Limerick? 1949. Novelist and story writer, DSC was the younger of twin daughters of John Blood-Smyth, JP, of Fedamore and Ardsollus (Co. Clare) and Amelia Spaight of Derry Castle (Co. Tipperary). She was educated at home and at Doncaster. She married in 1892 Lt.-Col. (or Col.) Charles Conyers of the Royal Irish Fusiliers, third son of Revd Charles Conyers of Castletown Conyers (Co. Limerick), who was stationed in various places in England and Ireland. He was killed in action in France in 1915. Two years later DSC married Capt. John Joseph White of Nantenan House, Ballinagrane (Co. Limerick) who died in 1940. She spent the rest of her life in Ballinagrane, where she wrote most of her 55 novels and collections of stories between 1900 and 1950. She had two children by her first marriage. She specialized in hunting novels depicting Anglo-Irish life, garrison officers, horse dealers, and peasants. She also wrote her autobiography, *Sporting reminiscences* (London, 1920). Some of her literary manuscripts were for sale at The Brick Row Bookshop, San Francisco, in Nov. 2000. SOURCE Brown, p. 66; Brown 2, p. 52; Burke's, pp 144, 268–9, 1205; EF, p. 76; Hogan 2, pp 284–5; OCIL, p. 114; O'Toole, pp 54–5; RIA/DIB; RL.

C289   *The thorn bit* (by Dorothea Conyers).

London: Hutchinson & Co., 1900. SOURCE Brown, 376. LOCATION L.

COMMENTARY Describes hunting days of society in a small country town in the west of Ireland (presumably Co. Limerick) [Brown; Leclaire, p. 231].

C290   *Bloom or blight* (by Dorothea Conyers).
London: Hurst & Blackett, 1901. LOCATION L.

C291   *The boy, some horse and a girl: A tale of an Irish trip* (by Dorothea Conyers).
London: Edward Arnold, 1903. SOURCE Brown, 379. LOCATION L, NUC (1905 edn).
COMMENTARY A competition between three men to win an heiress with a desirable house and stable yard in the west of Ireland. Story contains some comic Irish servants [EF, p. 76].

C292   *Peter's pedigree* (by Dorothea Conyers).
London: Edward Arnold, 1904 (ill. Nora K. Shelley). SOURCE Brown, 377. LOCATION L, NUC.
COMMENTARY Hunting, horse dealing and love making in Co. Cork [Brown].

C293   *Cloth versus silk* (by Dorothea Conyers).
London: Hutchinson & Co., 1905. LOCATION L, NUC.

C294   *The strayings of Sandy* (by Dorothea Conyers).
+ London: Hutchinson & Co., 1906. SOURCE Brown, 382. LOCATION L, NUC, InND
Loeber coll. (n.d. edn).
COMMENTARY Shows Irish country life as seen by a London businessman, Alexander Acland, on a holiday to restore his health. Set in a country house on the west coast where life revolves around horses. Acland, who initially does not know anything about horses, takes to them and to the life in Ireland. He decides not to return to England and marries a poor but warm-hearted woman [ML; Brown].

C295   *Aunt Jane and Uncle James* (by Dorothea Conyers).
London: Hutchinson & Co., 1908. SOURCE Brown, 378. LOCATION L.
COMMENTARY Sequel to *Peter's pedigree* (London, 1904). Set in Ireland and features hunting and a murder trial [Brown].

C296   *Three girls and a hermit* (by Dorothea Conyers).
London: Hutchinson & Co., 1908. SOURCE Brown, 380. LOCATION L.
New York: E.P. Dutton & Co., 1908. LOCATION NUC, InND.
COMMENTARY Life in a small garrison town in Ireland [Brown].

C297   *The conversion of Con Cregan, and other stories* (by Dorothea Conyers).
+ London: Hutchinson & Co., 1909. SOURCE Brown, 381. LOCATION L, NUC.
COMMENTARY Stories dealing mostly with horses and hunting in Ireland. Contents: 'The conversion of Con Cregan' (Con Gregan was the main character in Charles Lever's§ *The confessions of Con Cregan* (Dublin, 1848)), 'The vision of the dark woman', 'How the Roches found fortune', 'Is it worth it?', 'An Irish poultry fund', 'Mickey's training', 'Off the course', 'How the doctor took to horse-racing', 'Father Fitzroy Flanagan', 'What the red cow did', 'Burglary', 'A last practical joke', 'Paddy O'Rafferty's match' [ML; RL].

C298   *Lady Elverton's emeralds* (by Dorothea Conyers).
London: Hutchinson & Co., 1909. LOCATION L, NUC.
COMMENTARY Crime story with passages on hunting [EF, p. 76].

C299   *Two impostors, and tinker* (by Dorothea Conyers).
London: Hutchinson & Co., 1910. SOURCE Brown, 383. LOCATION L.
New York: E.P. Dutton & Co., 1911. LOCATION NUC.
COMMENTARY A hunting story set in the south-west of Ireland [Brown; Leclaire, p. 231].

C300   *For Henri and Navarre* (by Dorothea Conyers).
London: Hutchinson & Co., 1911. LOCATION L, NUC.
COMMENTARY Historical fiction [EF, p. 76].

C301   *Some happenings of Glendalyne* (by Dorothea Conyers).
London: Hutchinson & Co., 1911. SOURCE Brown, 384. LOCATION L, NUC.

COMMENTARY The O'Neill is a religious eccentric who keeps Hugh O'Neill, the heir who is supposed to be dead, in a deserted wing of the old mansion. Eve O'Neill, his ward, discovers Hugh and thrilling adventures ensue [Brown].

C302　*The arrival of Antony* (by Dorothea Conyers).

　　　London: Hutchinson & Co., 1912. SOURCE Brown, 385. LOCATION L, NUC.

　　　New York: E.P. Dutton & Co., [1912?]. LOCATION NUC.

COMMENTARY Antony Doyle, who was brought up as a gentleman in Germany, comes home to a remote part of the west of Ireland to help his old uncle, a horse-dealer. Describes Antony's inexperience in the ways of horse-sharpers, his devotion to his uncle, and the social barriers that for a long time keep him aloof from his own class and from his future wife [Brown].

C303　*Sally* (by Dorothea Conyers).

　　　London: Methuen & Co., 1912. SOURCE Brown, 386. LOCATION L, NUC.

　　　COMMENTARY Hunting story set in Connemara in which love has a more wholesome effect upon melancholia than the hunt [Brown; Leclaire, p. 231].

C304　*Sandy married* (by Dorothea Conyers).

　　　London: Methuen & Co., 1913. SOURCE Brown, 387. LOCATION L.

COMMENTARY Set in the south of Ireland among the sporting gentry and the horse-dealing middle classes. The will of a deceased relative requires an unamiable pair of cousins to maintain a stud of race horses to which they are very much opposed [Brown].

C305　*Old Andy* (by Dorothea Conyers).

　　　London: Methuen & Co., 1914. SOURCE Brown, 388. LOCATION L.

　　　COMMENTARY Describes peasant life in Co. Limerick [Brown].

C306　*Maeve* (by Dorothea Conyers).

　　　London: Hutchinson & Co., 1915. SOURCE Brown, 390. LOCATION L, NUC (1915, 3rd edn).

　　　COMMENTARY Set in England and full of hunting scenes, one of the main characters is a wild young Irish girl [Brown].

C307　*A mixed pack* (by Dorothea Conyers).

　　　+ London: Methuen & Co., 1915. SOURCE Brown, 389. LOCATION L.

　　　COMMENTARY Collection of varied stories including hunting sketches, the experiences of an engine driver, and the adventures of a traveller for a firm of jewellers [Brown].

C308　*The financing of Fiona* (by Dorothea Conyers).

　　　London: George Allen & Unwin, 1916. SOURCE Brown, 391. LOCATION L.

COMMENTARY Set in the south-west of Ireland. Fiona inherits a house but no money to keep it up. She takes in paying guests, among them a young English baronet. She tries to deal with the poverty and domestic troubles as best as she can. Contains many hunting scenes [Brown; Leclaire, p. 232].

C309　*The scratch pack* (by Dorothea Conyers).

　　　London: Hutchinson & Co., 1916. SOURCE Brown, 392. LOCATION L.

COMMENTARY Set on the Irish Atlantic coast in Castle Freyne. The Freynes live there with their stepdaughter Gheena. If Gheena marries, the estate will fall to her. Her stepfather plots to keep the estate by trying to marry her to someone under his control. Eventually, she marries a member of the English secret service, whom she had suspected of being a German spy. However, he proves his loyalty by rescuing her from a German submarine. Contains a number of hunting scenes [Brown].

C310　*The experiments of Ganymede Bunn* (by Dorothea Conyers).

　　　London: Hutchinson & Co., 1917. SOURCE Brown, 393. LOCATION L, NUC (n.d. edn).

COMMENTARY Ganymede, formerly a clerk in a London store, receives a bequest from an aunt after which he decides to live in the country, write, and speculate on horses. He goes to the west of Ireland, where he falls in love. His relatives try, unsuccessfully, to prove him mad [Brown; Leclaire, p. 232].

C311   *The blighting of Bartram* (by Dorothea Conyers).
London: Methuen & Co., 1918. SOURCE Brown, 394. LOCATION L.
COMMENTARY Set in Ireland. Concerns hunting and horse-dealing [Brown].

C312   *B.E.N.* (by Dorothea Conyers).
London: Methuen & Co., 1919. SOURCE Brown 2, 268. LOCATION L.
COMMENTARY Berenice Ermyntrude Nicosia Nevin lives in a tumbledown castle in a hunting district where her aunt survives by horse-dealing. She becomes a nurse in a Dublin hospital and later she is whip to the West Cara hounds [Brown].

C313   *Tiranogue* (by Dorothea Conyers).
London: Methuen & Co., 1919. SOURCE Brown 2, 267. LOCATION L.
COMMENTARY Irish life in a hunting district with rich English visitors who are taken advantage of [Brown 2].

C314   *Irish stew* (by Dorothea Conyers).
+ London: Skeffington & Son, [1920]. SOURCE Brown 2, 269. LOCATION L.
COMMENTARY Stories (not all Irish content). Contents: 'The story of Darby O'Toole: I. How he grew up and saw the daughter of the Geraldines', 'II. How he found the king's daughter', 'III. How he shot a seal', 'IV. How he went to Mayo', 'Mr. Jones helps Mosenthals', 'Mr. Jones is consulted by the firm', 'Mr. Jones has another adventure', 'Mr. Jones makes several matches and retires', 'A match for a match', 'Con Cassidy's stageen', 'When rogues fall out', 'Sir Hector Devereux's bet', 'Getting even', 'Lord Hillayton's settlement', 'A gamble for warmth', 'Maeve's ride', 'Phil Phelan's fantasy' [ML].

C315   *Uncle Pierce's legacy* (by Dorothea Conyers).
London: Methuen & Co., 1920. SOURCE Brown 2, 270. LOCATION L.
COMMENTARY Uncle Pierce left £5,000 a year to two elderly ladies, Honor and Evelyn Nutting, on condition that they keep the hounds and hunt with them in person, and that they spend all the money [Brown 2].

C316   *The waiting of Moya* (by Dorothea Conyers).
London: Hutchinson & Co., [1921]. SOURCE Brown 2, 271. LOCATION L, NUC.
COMMENTARY Moya will inherit some money from her old uncle. While waiting for this inheritance she enjoys herself with sport and horsemanship among the impoverished Irish gentry [Brown 2].

C317   *The toll of the Black Lake* (by Dorothea Conyers).
London: Hutchinson & Co., [1922]. LOCATION L.

C318   *Rooted out* (by Dorothea Conyers).
London: Hutchinson & Co., [1923]. SOURCE Brown 2, 272. LOCATION L.
COMMENTARY Set during the Irish Civil War, it pictures an Ireland impossible to live in so the characters must pursue their lives in the safety of Loamshire, England [Brown 2].

C319   *The adventures of Gerry* (by Dorothea Conyers).
London: Hutchinson & Co., [1924]. LOCATION L, NUC.

C320   *The two Maureens* (by Dorothea Conyers).
London: Hutchinson & Co., [1924]. SOURCE Brown 2, 273. LOCATION L, NUC.
COMMENTARY How Maureen Delmarten, faced with semi-starvation in London, determines to impersonate her absent aunt, Lady Maureen Delmarten, comes to Ireland and takes paying guests at Castle Creagh for the hunting season [Brown 2].

C321   *Hounds of the sea* (by Dorothea Conyers).
London: Hutchinson & Co., [1924]. SOURCE Brown 2, 276 (1927 edn). LOCATION L.

COMMENTARY Gerald Cantillon returns from London to Doonbeg, his dilapidated castle on the south coast of Cork. He returns despite a curse laid on the castle's inhabitants by a dying buccaneer, but succeeds in lifting the curse. It includes descriptions of rough hunting over wild country [Brown 2].

C322   *Sandy and others* (by Dorothea Conyers).

+ London: Mills & Boon, 1925. SOURCE Brown 2, 274. LOCATION L, NUC.

COMMENTARY Stories of hunting and the humorous side of Irish country life. The title story (in six parts) concerns Sandy Ackland, who comes to Ireland to buy horses for the British army at the start of the First World War, and Kit Hardress whose inheritance of the family estates depends on his breeding a winner of the Derby but who goes off to war while his wife successfully produces a winner in his absence. Contents: 'I. Sandy goes back to work', 'II. Sandy rescues a damsel in distress', 'III. Sandy backs a winner', 'IV. Sandy tries to be a comforter', 'V. Sandy listens to intimidation', 'VI. Sandy sees daylight', 'Ducal coronets', 'Cousins', 'The alibi', 'Too honest', 'A hundred and two', 'The river house', 'The light on the ford' [ML; Brown 2].

C323   *Treasury notes. A novel* (by Dorothea Conyers).

London: Hutchinson & Co., [1926]. SOURCE Brown 2, 275. LOCATION L, NUC.

COMMENTARY The story of Isobel who runs away from her straight-laced English home to be a paying guest in the happy-go-lucky household of the Floods and enjoys herself in an atmosphere of horses and hunting [Brown 2].

C324   *Grey brother, and others* (by Dorothea Conyers).

+ London: Mills & Boon, 1927. SOURCE Brown 2, 277. LOCATION L.

COMMENTARY Short stories: Seven are detective stories not set in Ireland, and two deal with horses and dogs and Irish country life. Contents: 'Grey brother', 'The fair-haired companion', 'Justice evaded', 'The Pitmaston duchess', 'Chase-me-Charlie', 'Creina's venture', 'Jock', 'The end of life', 'The murder on the Dover train', 'Diplomacy' [ML; Brown 2].

C325   *Bobbie* (by Dorothea Conyers).

London: Hutchinson & Co., [1927]. SOURCE Brown 2, 278. LOCATION L.

COMMENTARY Concerns the struggle between two strong personalities – Bobbie and his uncle, Robert Bryan of Knockbui – and features the meets and hunts of a country pack in post-war Ireland [Brown 2].

C326   *Follow Elizabeth* (by Dorothea Conyers).

London: Hutchinson & Co., [1929]. SOURCE Brown 2, 279. LOCATION L, NUC.

COMMENTARY Romantic story of Elizabeth Palliser who lets Dromin Abbey, her dilapidated house in the west of Ireland, to an Englishman, Sir James Hanniside, for the hunting season [Brown 2; Leclaire, p. 232].

C327   *Hunting and hunted* (by Dorothea Conyers).

London: Hutchinson & Co., [1930]. SOURCE Brown 2, 280. LOCATION L.

COMMENTARY Eighteen short stories, three of which deal with Ireland and feature an Irish RM, a friendly poacher, horse-dealing, and a county show [Brown 2].

C328   *Denton's Derby* (by Dorothea Conyers).

London: Hutchinson & Co., [1930]. LOCATION L, NUC.

C329   *Managing Ariadne* (by Dorothea Conyers).

London: Hutchinson & Co., [1931]. SOURCE Brown 2, 281. LOCATION L.

COMMENTARY Romantic thriller featuring Ariadne Hardress and her step niece Ann and describes life at Castle Hardress in Ireland during the hunting season [Brown 2].

C330   *Whoopee* (by Dorothea Conyers).

London: Hutchinson & Co., [1932]. SOURCE Brown 2, 282. LOCATION L, NUC.

COMMENTARY An involved story of impersonation, inheritance, hunting, and romantic intrigues set in contemporary Ireland and featuring an aged clergyman, his ward, and the ward's young American stepmother [Brown 2].

C331   *A Maeve must marry* (by Dorothea Conyers).

London: Hutchinson & Co., [1933]. SOURCE Brown 2, 283. LOCATION L, NUC.

COMMENTARY Humorous story set in an Irish country house about a 39-year-old spinster and her three suitors [Brown 2].

C332   *A good purpose* (by Dorothea Conyers).

London: Hutchinson & Co., [1934]. SOURCE Brown 2, 288. LOCATION L, NUC.

COMMENTARY A young man who has inherited a small legacy on condition that he puts it to a 'good purpose' and must convince the lawyers that his dream of starting a pack of hounds complies with these terms [Brown 2].

C333   *The fortunes of Evadne* (by Dorothea Conyers).

London: Hutchinson & Co., [1935]. SOURCE Brown 2, 284. LOCATION L, NUC.

COMMENTARY A hunting and love story set in the west of Ireland [Brown 2].

C334   *The elf* (by Dorothea Conyers).

London: Hutchinson & Co., [1936]. SOURCE Brown 2, 286. LOCATION L, NUC.

COMMENTARY Set in the west of Ireland, the story of Elfrida, 'the Elf', and the earl of Fitzgranly who marry, but whose high-spirited temperaments clash and lead to their separation. Later she returns from England disguised as a man and acts as second whip for her husband's pack. A fatal accident in the hunting field brings reconciliation before she dies [Brown 2; Leclaire, p. 233].

C335   *Phil's castle* (by Dorothea Conyers).

+ London: Hutchinson & Co., [1937]. SOURCE Brown 2, 287. LOCATION D, L, NUC.

COMMENTARY Set in Ireland, a tale of romance and adventure in which the heroine, Phil, comes to know the stranger who rents her castle. The story features wealthy Americans, gangsters and gun-play [Brown 2; RL].

C336   *A lady of discretion* (by Dorothea Conyers).

London: Hutchinson & Co., [1938]. SOURCE Brown 2, 288. LOCATION L.

COMMENTARY A romance set in west of Ireland among sporting, horse-loving people [Brown 2; Leclaire, p. 233].

C337   *Gulls at Rossnacorey* (by Dorothea Conyers).

London: Hutchinson & Co., [1939]. SOURCE Brown 2, 289. LOCATION L.

COMMENTARY Set in a lonely inlet on the coast of Cork, a governess to two young children discovers that their guardian is a notorious smuggler of drugs and other contrabands [Brown 2].

C338   *The best people* (by Dorothea Conyers).

London, Melbourne: Hutchinson & Co., [1941]. SOURCE Brown 2, 290. LOCATION L.

COMMENTARY Concerns hunting with the North Knockmurry hounds and marriage affairs [Brown 2].

C339   *Rosalie. A novel* (by Dorothea Conyers).

London: Hutchinson & Co., [1945]. LOCATION L.

C340   *Dark* (by Dorothea Conyers).

London: Hutchinson & Co., [1946]. SOURCE Brown 2, 291. LOCATION L.

COMMENTARY A 'Big House' novel featuring Anglo-Irish and English landed (formerly) gentry and military men. The story revolves around whether Dark O'Donnell of Ballymorare will be sacrificed to an unloving suitor for a debt to be paid [Brown 2].

C341   *Kicking foxes* (by Dorothea Conyers).

London: Hutchinson & Co., [1947]. SOURCE Brown 2, 292. LOCATION L.

COMMENTARY Set during the Second World War, a romantic adventure story of Felicia, who realizes her dream of coming to hunt in Ireland by helping Scotland Yard capture jewel thieves [Brown 2].

C342   *A kiss for a whip* (by Dorothea Conyers).
London: Hutchinson & Co., [1948]. SOURCE Brown 2, 293. LOCATION L.
COMMENTARY Set in the west of Ireland. Lord Dick Fitzgraly and his friends try to end what they view as an unsuitable alliance between Lord Dick's son, Rickie, and the glamorous but mercenary film star Viva de l'Enclos. The novel is set against a hunting background [Brown 2; Leclaire, p. 233].

C343   *The witch's samples* (by Dorothea Conyers).
London: Hutchinson & Co., [1950]. LOCATION L, NUC.

CONYNGHAM, D.P. See **CONYNGHAM, Major David Power.**

CONYNGHAM, Major David Power (also known as **D.P. Conyngham**), pseuds 'A **Tipperary boy**' and '**Allen H. Clington**', b. Killenaule (Crohane, according to RIA/DIB, both in Co. Tipperary) *c.*1825, d. New York 1883. Novelist, war correspondent and chronicler of the Irish Brigade in the American Civil War, DPC was the eldest son of John Cunningham and Catherine Power, a cousin of Charles Kickham§ with whom DPC participated in the 1848 rising, where he served as a local leader. He obtained a law degree, but appears not to have completed his studies at Queen's College, Cork. He contributed to the *Tipperary Free Press* (Clonmel) in the 1850s and he was a war correspondent for the Dublin *Irishman* during the early part of the American Civil War. Through introductions from William Smith O'Brien and P.J. Smyth he joined the Union army's Irish Brigade, where he served as staff officer to General Thomas Meagher. He was wounded and later received an honorary title of major from New York State. He accompanied General William Tecumseh Sherman through Georgia and the Carolinas and later published *Sherman's march through the South* (New York, 1865). After settling in New York he was involved in various newspaper ventures and made several return journeys to Ireland. He wrote many works on Irish and American subjects, including *Ireland past and present* (New York, 1887), and *The Irish brigade and its campaigns* (New York, 1867). He was awarded an honorary doctorate from the Univ. of Notre Dame (IN). DPC was buried in New York's Calvary cemetery. SOURCE Allibone Suppl., i, p. 377; Brady, p. 43; Brown, p. 69; OCIL, p. 114; RIA/DIB; Wright, iii, p. 119.

C344   *The old house at home; or, the surprising adventures of Frank O'Donnell* (by 'A Tipperary boy').
Dublin: James Duffy, [1850s]. SOURCE Brown, 395. COMMENTARY *Dublin [1850s] edn* No copy located [RL].
Dublin: James Duffy, 1861 (as *Frank O'Donnell: A tale of Irish life*, ed. by 'Allen H. Clington'). SOURCE Brown, 395. LOCATION L.
New York, Montreal: D. & J. Sadlier & Co., 1874 (as *The O'Donnells of Glen cottage. A tale of the famine years in Ireland*). SOURCE Brown, 397; DCU, Catholic Americana files. LOCATION NUC.
COMMENTARY Set during the Famine of 1846. A Tipperary family faces starvation, then eviction into a snow storm, after which the mother dies of exposure. Forced to emigrate, young Frank O'Donnell succeeds, makes money, returns to Ireland, and buys back his old home. The 'souper', Bob Sly, is condemned in the story. The local minister, Revd Smith, financially supports the parish priest through the Famine and takes in an evicted family [Brown 395; Fanning, p. 81; Fegan, p. 219].

C345   *Sarsfield; or, the last great struggle for Ireland* (by David Power Conyngham).
Boston: Patrick Donahoe, 1871. SOURCE Brown, 396; RIA/DIB. LOCATION L, NUC.

COMMENTARY Historical fiction set in the seventeenth century but begins with the past history of Ireland's national struggles. Patrick Sarsfield's career is described and is intertwined with the love story of Hugh O'Donnell and Eveleen, granddaughter of Florence McCarthy [Brown].

C346 *The O'Mahony, chief of the Comeraghs. A tale of the rebellion of '98* (by D.P. Conyngham).

+ New York, Montreal: D. & J. Sadlier & Co., 1879. SOURCE Brown, 398; RIA/DIB; Fanning, p. 378; Wright, iii, 1176. LOCATION D, NUC.

COMMENTARY Historical fiction. The last Gaelic chieftain of the Comeragh Mountains (Co. Waterford) struggles against the earl of Kingston,[6] known as 'the wolf of the Galtees', who terrorizes the peasantry from his Mitchelstown Castle (Co. Cork). The rising in Wexford in 1798 is the novel's climax [Fanning, p. 80].

C347 *Rose Parnell, the flower of Avondale. A tale of the rebellion of '98* (by D.P. Conyngham).

+ New York, Montreal: D. & J. Sadlier & Co., 1883 (Sadliers' [*sic*] Popular Library). SOURCE Brown, 399; RIA/DIB; Fanning, p. 378; Wright iii, 1177. LOCATION D (1892, 2nd edn, which states copyrighted 1882); NUC.

COMMENTARY Historical fiction. According to the author, the heroine represents all the patriotic qualities that have characterized the Parnell family 'down to the present day'. Set in Ireland, 1790–1800, with a full account of the United Irishmen and the 1798 rebellion [B. Browne].

COOKE, A.M.P. See **COOKE, Alice M. Peppard.**

COOKE, Alice M. Peppard (known as **A.M.P. Cooke**), fl. 1900. Novelist. SOURCE BLC.
C348 *His laurel crown. A player's romance* (by A.M.P. Cooke; dedicated to Col. C.G. Tottenham and F.I.C.).

London: Downey & Co., 1900. LOCATION L.

COMMENTARY Set partly in London and on the west coast of Ireland in the fictional town of Kilshane, famous for its horse fair. Tells about the performance there by a company of strollers, and about actors in London [RL].

COOKE, Charles Henry, pseud. '**John Bickerdyke**', b. London 1858. English angling and sporting novelist, CHC was educated at Cambridge and was called to the Bar. His published works include *Wild sports in Ireland* (London, 1897). SOURCE Allibone Suppl., i, p. 143 [under Bickerdyke]; Brown 2, p. 20.
C349 *An Irish midsummer-night's dream. A legend of the Shannon* (by 'John Bickerdyke').

+ London: W. Swan Sonnenschein & Co., 1884 (ill.). SOURCE Brown 2, 81. LOCATION D, L.

COMMENTARY Set at Lough Derg and the Shannon. One evening when Andy Allen is out pike-fishing on Lough Derg there is a fairy wedding on Cribby Island. The fairy queen of Carrigeen, who had not been invited, decides to spoil the fun by forcing Andy to land. He is changed into a fairy and as such has various adventures, but is changed back before dawn and goes home with a monster pike [Brown 2].

COOKE, Mrs John, fl. 1863. Historical novelist and poet, Mrs JC was probably Irish and a Protestant. She wrote *The temple of the Lord and minor poems* (Dublin, 1863). SOURCE Allibone Suppl., i, p. 380, NUC; RL.

6 Probably, Robert, 2nd earl of Kingston.

C350   *Phillipe. A tale, founded on historical facts* (by Mrs John Cooke).
        + Dublin: George Herbert, 1872. SOURCE Alston, p. 92; BL cat. LOCATION L.
COMMENTARY Historical fiction set in France at the time of Louis XIV featuring Patrick Delaney, an Irishman. It relates the escape of Huguenots from France who join with King William III of England to fight in Ireland to preserve the Irish from the cruelties that Huguenots had experienced [ML].

COOPER, E.H. See **COOPER, Edward Herbert.**

COOPER, Edward Herbert (known as **E.H. Cooper**), b. Trentham (Staffs.) 1867, d. England? 1910. English novelist and children's writer, EHC published many works not related to Ireland. He was Paris correspondent for the *New York World* and later a special reporter for the London *Daily Mail.* He was secretary of the Ulster Convention League in 1893 (not mentioned by the ODNB). EHC loved horses and gambling and died while watching a race at Newmarket. SOURCE BLC; EF, p. 76; ODNB; Sutherland, p. 146.
C351   *The enemies* (by E.H. Cooper).
        + Westminster [London]: Arch. Constable & Co., 1896. LOCATION L, InND Loeber coll.
COMMENTARY Set mainly in and around Belfast and in London in the last decade of the nineteenth century, the story deals with Irish politics, both in Belfast and in the English house of commons. A young landowning Unionist politician of Catholic origin marries a Protestant girl, to the disappointment of his family, who had hoped he would form a Catholic political party in England. The bride is very young and innocent and not prepared for the life of a politician's wife. Her husband neglects her somewhat, which allows a romance to develop between her and a friend of his who has always been jealous of him. The wife shrinks from fleeing with her lover and confesses all to her husband. They stay together. The friend lives a few more years, which he spends in misery [ML].

COOPER, Maria Susanna. See **HUNTER, Mrs Maria Susanna.**

'**COR**', fl. 1879. Pseudonym of an Irish author, presumably a Catholic. SOURCE RL.
C352   *The Sydenhams of Beechwood; or, the two espousals* (by 'Cor'; dedicated to Rt Revd Dom. Bruno, abbot of the Cistercians of Mount Melleray).
        + Dublin: M.H. Gill, 1879. LOCATION D, Dcc.

CORDNER, Catherine Adelaide, pseud. '**A.C.U. Marchmont**', b. Co. Longford 1836, d. 1931. Unpublished novelist and illustrator, CAC can likely to be identified with the fourth daughter of Revd Edward James Cordner (1795–1870), a Church of Ireland clergyman of Derramore (Co. Longford) who in 1824 married Maria, daughter of Henry Purdon, MD, of Belfast and of Rathwyre (Co. Westmeath). Through her mother, she was distantly related to the writer May [Maria Henrietta] Crommelin§. Her father was curate of Derryvaghy in the diocese of Connor (1818–33); there is no subsequent documented clerical appointment but he officiated occasionally at the Cathedral of Lisburn (Co. Antrim) and at Drumbo (Co. Down) between 1833 and 1844. His wife's mother's family, the de la Cherois, were from Lisburn. He died in 1870 in Dublin and was buried at Mount Jerome cemetery. It is likely that the family moved to Co. Longford, because according to an inscription of CAC's *The days that are past*, she resided at Derramore in 1864. The family is said to have also resided at Mullagh, close to the town of Longford. CAC's two unpublished novels, each under the pseudonym 'A.C.U. Marchmont', were donated by a member of the Cordner family to Revd Pollard, minister at Rathcline (Co. Longford), grandfather of Ms Mary Pollard, and by her donated to the

RIA. Both manuscripts are burnt on one side, suggesting a house fire. CAC probably remained unmarried. The pseudonym 'A.C.U. Marchmont' is perhaps inspired by Charlotte Smith's§ *Marchmont* (London, 1796, 4 vols.; Dublin, 1797, 2 vols.), or the heroine of Mrs Hamilton's§ *The monk's daughter; or, hypocrisy punished* (London, 1812, 3 vols.). SOURCE EF, p. 265; Leslie, *Connor*, pp 275–6; Personal communication, Mrs K. Green-Baxter, July, 1988; Personal communication, Mary Pollard, Oct. 2004; RL; Walford, p. 236.

C353   *The mysterious stranger* (by 'A.C.U. Marchmont', dedicated, July 23rd 1863, to the author's mother, 'by her fourth daughter').

COMMENTARY Unpublished manuscript, dated 1856 [*sic*], illustrated with pen drawings and calligraphy in colours, title page dated 1866; Belfast watermark. The novel starts with scenes on the Irish sea coast [RL. LOCATION RIA (SR/Bay29/1D)].

C354   *The days that are past* (dedicated, 27 July 1861 to Miss Lisette A. Cordner, 'for whom the story was expressly written'; front endpaper has endorsement, in different handwriting, 'Lisette A Cordner with her sister's best love Derramore April 18th 1864').

COMMENTARY Unpublished manuscript, dated 1863, illustrated with pen drawings (30) and calligraphy in colours, 1863, Belfast watermark. The story starts with childhood recollections of Adelaide, the daughter of Lord Altamont. Her grandmother had 'an unaccountable prejudice against Ireland'. Features Irish music [RL. LOCATION Di (SR/Bay29/1D)].

CORNE, Thomas, fl. 1820s. Religious fiction writer.

C355   *Plain friendly Irish whispers to watermen, rivermen, seamen, and others* (by Thomas Corne).

   London: Printed for the author, [1825?]. LOCATION L (destroyed).

COMMENTARY Religious fiction. No other copy located [BLC].

'CORNELIUS O'DOWD', pseud. See **LEVER, Charles James**.

'A CORONER', fl. 1869. Pseudonym of a temperance writer who was probably Irish, since he or she published in Dublin. SOURCE RL.

C356   *The bane and antidote. A tale founded chiefly on facts, illustrating the evils of intemperance, and the advantages of total abstinence from intoxicating liquors* (by 'A coroner').

   + Dublin: McGlashan & Gill, 1869. LOCATION D, L.

COMMENTARY A story about the effects of intemperance featuring Mr and Mrs Laurence, who live with their family at a country residence near the town of Anyborough [CD].

CORR, Revd Thomas J. See **CORR, Revd Thomas John**.

CORR, Revd Thomas John (known as **Thomas J. Corr**), b. Creggan (Co. Donegal) 1859, d. Crossmaglen (Co. Armagh) 1885 (1887, according to RIA/DIB). Church of Ireland clergyman, essayist, poet and miscellaneous writer, who was the son of William Corr of Urcher, Crossmaglen. He graduated BA at TCD in 1875, MA in 1878, and was ordained in 1876. He was curate of St Mary Magdalen (Belfast, 1877–83) and resigned due to ill health. He went to France and took light duty in Pau. At the time of his death he was assistant chaplain of Holy Trinity Church, Florence (Italy). According to an editorial note in *Favilla* (London, 1887), the author at his death left his manuscripts in the charge of his sister, Mrs Simpsons, desiring their publication, which was effected with the help of Charles J. Ward, MA. SOURCE Allibone Suppl., i, p. 391; Leslie, *Connor*, p. 276; O'Donoghue, p. 80; RIA/DIB; RL.

C357   *The dream of Melzar, and other allegories* (by Thomas J. Corr).

   + Belfast: Marcus Ward & Co., 1878 (ill.). SOURCE RB. LOCATION L (destroyed).

COMMENTARY Religious fiction. Contents: 'The dream of Melzar', 'The enchanted island', 'Soliloquy of Aletes; or, the wanderer', 'The old plantation', 'The slothful gardener, and the precious seedling' [RL].

C358   *Favilla: tales, essays, and poems* (by Thomas J. Corr; ed. by C.J. Ward).
        + London: Kegan Paul, Trench & Co., 1887. LOCATION L.
        COMMENTARY Published posthumously [RL].

CORRY, John, fl. 1782. A journalist, novelist and poet who lived near Newry (Co. Down), perhaps in Ravensdale (Co. Louth), JC was a self-taught man who went to Dublin and then settled in London in 1792. He wrote the histories of several English towns, the life of George Washington (Belfast, 1800), and the life of the poet William Cowper (London, 1803). He specialized in the writing of Gothic and adventure novelettes, some with Irish content. He may be identified with the John Corry who published *Odes and elegies ... with The patriot, a poem* (Newry, 1797). It is not clear whether the publisher J. Corry, who published much of JC's work from about 1805 onwards was the author or a relative. SOURCE Allibone, i, p. 431; BLC; ODNB; O'Donoghue, p. 80; RIA/DIB.

C359   *The adventures of Felix and Rosarito; or, the triumph of love and friendship, containing an account of several interesting events during the late war, between France and Spain in the Western Pyrenees* [anon.].
        London: Crosby & Co., 1782. LOCATION L, NUC (1802 edn).
        London: T. Tegg, [18—] (as *The adventures of Felix and Rosa; or, the triumph of love & friendship. A Spanish story*). SOURCE NSTC. LOCATION MH.
        COMMENTARY The hero is Felix Dillon. Although the story begins and ends in Dublin, it is set mainly in France and Spain [Brown].

C360   *Memoirs of Alfred Berkley; or, the danger of dissipation* (by John Corry; dedicated to The ladies of The United Kingdom).
        London: R. Dutton, Crosby & Co., J.F. Hughes, J. Henderson & C. Chapman, 1802. SOURCE British Fiction; Garside, 1802:19. LOCATION Corvey CME 3–628–47367.

C361   *Edwy and Bertha; or, the force of connubial love* (by John Corry).
        London: Crosby & Co., 1802. SOURCE NSTC. LOCATION L, ViU.

C362   *Tales for the amusement of young persons* (by John Corry).
        London: [publisher?], 1802. SOURCE DNB.
        COMMENTARY No copy located [RL].

C363   *The preservation of Charles and Isabella; or, the force of friendship* (by John Corry).
        London: B. Crosby & Co., [1803]. SOURCE RLIN. LOCATION NjP.
        COMMENTARY Republished later in *Corry's friend of youth* (London, 1803) [RL].

C364   *The Swiss revolution; or, the fall of Albert* (by John Corry).
        London: B. Crosby & Co., [1803] (ill.). LOCATION L, ViU.
COMMENTARY Features the wife and young son of the Swiss patriot Albert. The novel ends with the genuine 1802 proclamation of Napoleon Bonaparte to the Swiss, after which Bonaparte invaded Switzerland [Bennett cat. 41/38].

C365   *Memoirs of Edward Thornton; or, a sketch of modern dissipation in London* (by John Corry).
        + London: B. Crosby & Co., 1803 (ill. Cruikchank [*sic* Cruikshank]). SOURCE Brick Row cat. 137/46. LOCATION ViU, InND Loeber coll.

C366   *Arthur and Mary; or, the fortunate fugitives* (by John Corry).
        + London: B. Crosby & Co., Champante & Co., R. Ogle, T. Hughes & M. Jones, J. Stuart & J. Murray, A.H. Nairne, & C. Chapple, 1803 (ill. M. Betham, W. Wise). LOCATION ViU, InND Loeber coll.

COMMENTARY 36pp. Set in Ulster after the 1798 rebellion. Arthur, a farmer's son, had joined an insurrectionist party. A neighbour informs on him and he has to leave his parents' house. After a night of wandering, he is taken in by Owen Conolly, a farmer. Arthur helps him with his work and also tutors his daughter Mary, with whom he falls in love. Again, he is denounced to the authorities and is put in jail in Newry (Co. Down). Mary and her friend Anna visit him and Anna exchanges clothing with Arthur so that he can escape. Arthur takes a boat to Liverpool and as a Mr Desmond starts a school. When it succeeds, he writes to Mary to join him. Mary and Anne set out by boat but the boat founders off the Welsh coast. Mary reaches land but Anna drowns. Arthur hastens to Wales and marries Mary [ML].

C367   *The history of Henry Thomson, or the reward of filial affection* (by John Corry).
    + London: B. Crosby & Co., [1803] (ill. Cruikshank, Wise). LOCATION L, NUC.
    COMMENTARY Extracted from a larger work. The first gathering of pages is signed 'H', but complete in itself [Personal communication, John Price, Nov. 2003].

C368   *The unfortunate daughter; or, the danger of the modern system of female education* (by John Corry).
    London: B. Crosby & Co., [1803]. LOCATION ViU.

C369   *Memoirs of Francis Goodwin; or, the delusion of pride* (by John Corry).
    London: B. Crosby & Co., [1803 or earlier] (ill.). LOCATION L.

COMMENTARY A 36 pp novella satirizing the 'new philosophy' of William Godwin§ and Mary Wollstonecraft. The main character, Francis Goodwin, is the well-educated son of a rich merchant who becomes interested in the French Revolution and joins up with a group of like-minded young men who support the principles of liberty and equality. Francis meets Emma Vance, 'a young lady ... whose imagination has been inflamed by the perusal of novels, romances, and poems ...' She reads Wollstonecraft's *Rights of woman* and imbibes its principles 'with all ardour of a proselyte'. Francis seduces her, they live together without being married, and she becomes pregnant, whereupon Francis, feeling remorse, rejects her and attempts suicide. He is rescued by Mr Trueman who takes him to the 'Temple of Modern Philosophy', where he encounters Emanuel Kant, August Friedrich Ferdinand von Kotzebue, Thomas Paine and others. Eventually, Trueman effects reconciliation all round [Burmester cat. 33/237].

C370   *The vale of Clwyd; or, the pleasures of retirement. A Welch tale* (by John Corry).
    + London: B. Crosby & Co., Champante & Co., R. Ogle, T. Hughes & M. Jones, J. Stuart & J. Murray, A.H. Nairne, & C. Chapple, [1803 or earlier] (ill. Cruikshank; see Plate 23). LOCATION D ([*c*.1825] edn [*sic*]), InND Loeber coll.

COMMENTARY 36pp. The main character is Thomas Conolly, whose father was a farmer in the vicinity of Limerick. The story relates Thomas's military adventures against the French in Egypt [RL].

C371   *The adventures of Edmund and Emelia* (by John Corry).
    London: [publisher?], [1803 or earlier]. SOURCE Republished later in *Corry's friend of youth* (London, 1803).
    COMMENTARY No copy located [RL].

C372   *Corry's friend of youth* (by John Corry).
    London: B. Crosby & Co., 1803, 6 vols. in 1. LOCATION NUC.
    London: W. Nicholson, 1806, 5 vols. in 1 (as *Domestic distresses, exemplified in five pathetic original tales. Frances Goodwin, Vale of Clywd, Edmund and Amelia, Arthur and Mary, and Henry Thomson*). LOCATION NUC.

COMMENTARY Stories first published separately (see above). Contents: 'The adventures of Edmund and Emelia', 'Arthur and Mary', 'The history of Henry Thomson', 'The vale of Clwyd', 'The preservation of Charles and Isabella', 'Memoirs of Francis Goodwin'. The 1806 edn contains five of the stories [NUC; RL].

C373   *Sebastian and Zeila; or, the captive liberated by female generosity* (by John Corry).
London: B. Crosby & Co., [1804 or later]. LOCATION L; ViU ([1802] edn).

C374   *The gardener's daughter of Worcester; or, the miseries of seduction. A moral tale* (by John Corry).
London: Champante & Withrow, [1804] (ill.). SOURCE ESTC t144317. LOCATION L.

C375   *The suicide; or, the progress of error. A moral tale* (by John Corry).
London: J. Corry, [1805]. LOCATION L, NUC.

C376   *The mysterious gentleman farmer; or, the disguises of love. A novel* (by John Corry).
London: B. Crosby & Co., 1808, 3 vols. SOURCE British Fiction; Garside, 1808:38. LOCATION Corvey CME 3–628–47368–3, O, NUC.

C377   *The elopement; or, the imprudent connexion; containing the adventures of Edmund and Letitia* (by John Corry).
London: J. Corry, [1810?]. SOURCE NSTC. LOCATION L.

C378   *The pleasures of sympathy* (by John Corry).
London: [publisher?], [1803 or earlier]. SOURCE Republished later in *Narratives, illustrative of the passions and affections of the human mind* (Newcastle, 1815).
COMMENTARY No copy located [RL].

C379   *Narratives, illustrative of the passions and affections of the human mind* (by John Corry).
Newcastle: M. Smith, 1815. LOCATION NUC.
COMMENTARY Reprint of stories published earlier (see above). Contents: 'Edwy and Bertha; or, the force of connubial love', 'The pleasures of sympathy', 'The miseries of seduction' (originally published as *The gardener's daughter of Worcester; or, the miseries of seduction*), 'The elopement; or, the imprudent connection' [NUC; RL].

C380   *The English metropolis; or, London in the year 1820. Containing satirical strictures on public manners, morals, and amusements; a young gentleman's adventures; and characteristic anecdotes of several eminent individuals who now figure in this great theatre of temporary exhibition* (by John Corry).
London: Sherwood, Nealy & Jones, 1820. SOURCE Burmester cat. 35/45. LOCATION L, NUC.
COMMENTARY Describes the London literary and social scene as experienced by a young man newly arrived in town. Introduces authors such as Sir Walter Scott, Robert Southey, William Wordsworth, and Lord Byron. Much on reviewers, novelists (including William Godwin§ and Ann Radcliffe), 'the old book trade', the theatre, etc. An earlier, related but nonfictional edn, *A satirical view of London at the commencement of the nineteenth century*, appeared in London in 1801[Burmester cat. 35/45; Burmester cat. 61/21].

CORWIN, Jane H., d. OH, United States? Miscellaneous writer, JHC's family emigrated from Ireland to America in 1818. She lived at Rose Bank (OH). Her husband was the brother of the 'celebrated Thomas Corwin, the "wagoner boy", and the son of M. Corwin, for some years Speaker of the House [in Ohio] …' Her husband died by the 1870s, when she was in her 60s, leaving her in need of money. In an unpublished account, she mentions that her volume *The harp of home; or, the medley* (Cincinnati, 1858), sold well among the Irish in America, particularly in Chicago. Of her three sons who fought in the Civil War, only two returned. SOURCE *The harp of home; or, the medley* (Cincinnati, 1858), p. 283 (as cited in Leaves of Grass cat. 20/240. The latter source mentions unpublished details about her life).

C381   *The harp of home; or, the medley* (by Jane H. Corwin; dedicated to author's husband and eight children, 'five on earth, and three in heaven').

Cincinnati: Moore, Wilstach, Keys & Co., 1858. LOCATION NUC.
COMMENTARY Contains prose and poetry [NUC].

COSGRAVE, John, fl. 1740s. Story and sketch writer.

C382   *A genuine history of the lives and actions of the most notorious Irish highwaymen,*
tories and rapparees, from Redmond O'Brien [*sic*] *... to Cahier na Gappul ... To*
which is added, The gold-finder; or, the history of Manus Mac Oniel (by John
Cosgrave).

+ Dublin: Printed [for the author?] by C.W., sold by the booksellers, 1747, 3rd edn.
SOURCE ESTC t083416; N. Ó Ciosáin, 'The Irish rogues' in J.D. Donnelly & K.A.
Miller (eds.), *Irish popular culture* (Dublin, 1998), pp 83–4. LOCATION L.

Belfast: Printed by the booksellers, 1776, 9th edn. SOURCE ESTC t203880; Adams, p.
90. LOCATION D.

Belfast: Printed by J. Smyth, n.d. (as *The lives and actions of the most notorious high-*
waymen, tories and rapparees, from Redmond O'Hanlon to Cahier na Gappul, to which is
added The Goldfinder, or the history of Many Maconeil). SOURCE de Búrca cat. 75/78.

+ Dublin: R. Cross, 1801, 10th edn (as *A genuine history of the lives and actions of the*
most notorious Irish highwaymen, tories and rapparees, from Redmond O'Hanlon [*sic*] *the*
famous gentleman-robber, to Cahier na Gappul, the great horse-catcher, who was executed
at Maryborough, in August, 1735. To which are added, The gold-finder; or, the history of
Manus Maconiel, who, under the appearance of a stupid, ignorant country fellow (on the
bog of Allen, by his man Andrew) played the most notorious cheats, and remarkable tricks
on the people of Ireland, that were ever known. Also, the remarkable life of Gilderoy, a
murderer, ravisher, incendiary & highwayman: with several others, not in any former edi-
tion). SOURCE RLIN. LOCATION Univ. of California School of Law, InND Loeber coll.

Limerick: Printed by Stephen Goggin, 1827. LOCATION PC. COMMENTARY *Limerick*
edn 72pp. Title almost the same as that of the Dublin 1801 edn, except that it states
'August 1695' instead of 1735. SOURCE Personal communication, Mary Pollard, June
2004.

Wilmington (DE): Printed by Bonsal & Niles, 1799 (as *A genuine history of the lives*
and actions of the most notorious Irish highwaymen, tories and rapparees, from Redmond
O'Hanlon [*sic*]*, the famous gentleman-robber, to Cahier na Gappul, the great horse-catcher,*
who was executed at Maryborough, in August, 1735: To which is added, The gold-finder;
or, the history of Manus Mac Oniel, who under the appearance of a stupid, ignorant coun-
try fellow (on the bog of Allen, by the help of his man Andrew) played the most notori-
ous cheats, and remarkable tricks on the people of Ireland, that was ever known: Also, the
remarkable life of Gilder Roy, a murderer, ravisher, incendiary and highwayman, with
several others, not in any former edition). SOURCE RLIN. LOCATION Syracuse Univ.
Library.

COMMENTARY First Dublin edn not located. The Dublin 1747, 3rd edn consists of sketches
of the following highwaymen, tories and rapparees: Redmond O'Hanlon, Capt. Power, John
Mac-Farcin, Patrick Flemming, Irish Teague alias William Macquire, Richard Balf, James
Butler, John Mulhoni, James Carrick, Paul Lyddy, Will. Peters also Delany, Charles Dempsey
alias Cahier na Gappul, and Manus Mac Oniel. The Dublin (1801) edn features the following individuals: Redmond O'Hanlon, John Macpherson, Irish Teague alias William Macquire,
Richard Balf, James Butler, James Carrick, William Peters, alias Delany, Manus Mac Oneil
and his man Andrew, James MacFaul, Gilder Roy, and Capt. Martel and his crew (the last
three are not in the Dublin, 1747 edn). The Belfast n.d. edn has the following additional
biographies: Wee Harry Doraghan of Donaghadee; Anne Bonny the illegitimate daughter of

a Cork attorney; and John Fallstaff of Bedfordshire [RL; D. & D.; Pollard, p. 222; de Búrca cat 75/78].

COSTELLO, Mary, fl. 1884. Novelist and dramatist, MC was born in Kilkenny and contributed to periodicals such as the *Cornhill Magazine* (London). According to the title page of *Addie's husband* (London, [1884]) she was also the author of 'Kathleen; or, beauty and the beast', but this has not been located. SOURCE Brown, p. 70; McCarthy, ii, p. 640; RL.

C383 *Addie's husband* [anon.].
> London: William Stephens, [1884]. SOURCE McCarthy, ii, p.640; COPAC. LOCATION L.

C384 *Peggy the millionaire* (by Mary Costello).
> + Dublin: Christian Truth Society of Ireland, 1910 (Iona Series). SOURCE Brown, 402; COPAC. LOCATION L.

COMMENTARY Set in the west of Ireland, the story of a young girl whose mother is dissatisfied with her lack of luxury in life and unable to appreciate her husband's good heart. The daughter makes her fortune and scatters happiness and blessings around her [Brown; CM].

COTTON, Revd Henry. See pseud. **'CUI BONO'.**

COTTON, Revd Samuel George, b. Dublin 1824, d. 1900. Church of Ireland clergyman and religious tract writer, SGC was the son of Francis Cotton, a surgeon. He entered TCD in 1840, graduated in 1845 and was ordained in 1847. After various positions in the Church of Ireland, he was appointed vicar of Carogh (Co. Kildare, 1861–94) where he was also the manager of the Carogh orphanage. Some of his publications must have been inspired by his work at this orphanage. However, he was twice prosecuted and convicted of cruelty to orphans and was imprisoned 1893 to 1894. He contributed a short story to the *Dublin University Magazine* in 1850 and wrote *Tracts for Ireland* (Dublin, 1854) under the pseudonym 'Fidelis'. According to the title page of *Ellen Dalton* (Dublin, 1851) he was also the author of 'The orphan', but this has not been located. He married Elizabeth Gordon Johnson in 1855. SOURCE Allibone Suppl., i, p. 394; B & S, p. 183; BLC; Leslie & Wallace, p. 509; W.E. Hall, p. 141; RIA/DIB.

C385 *Ellen Dalton; or, the Sunday school* [anon.]
> Dublin: Samuel B. Oldham; London: Seeleys, 1851. LOCATION L.
> COMMENTARY 54pp. Religious fiction [BLC].

C386 *The three whispers, and other tales* (by Samuel George Cotton).
> Dublin: John Robertson & Co., 1870. SOURCE Brown, 403. LOCATION L.
> COMMENTARY Reprinted from the 'University' and the 'Sunday School' magazines [COPAC].

'A COUNTRY GENTLEMAN', pseud. See **CAULFEILD, Edward Houston.**

'COVERTSIDE', Naunton, pseud. See **DAVIES, Naunton.**

COWAN, Charlotte Eliza Lawson. See **RIDDELL, Mrs J.H.**

COX, Samuel Alfred, fl. 1856. A journalist and novelist, SAC lived at Eagle Cottage, Sandymount, Dublin. SAC is probably the same person who serialized a work of fiction in 1856, but there is an almost forty-year gap between his first and last known work of fiction . It is unlikely that he can be identified with Revd Samuel Alfred Cox (d. 1934), who was educated at TCD and served mostly in England. A Samuel Alfred Cox who wrote a play, *Shakespeare converted into Bacon* (Dublin, [1899]), published *Practical speech culture* (London, 1913), and was a co-author of *A copy book for teaching the art of writing with the left hand* (London, 1920). SOURCE Brown, p. 71; Leslie, *Down*, p. 88; NUC; RL.

C387 *Saints and sinners: A tale* (by Samuel Alfred Cox).

COMMENTARY Manuscript volume, dated Dublin 1856 (see Plate 24), composed of a serial which appeared in the *Dublin Commercial Journal* (1854). The manuscript shows signs of having been prepared for publication as a separate volume, but it does not appear to have been published in book form. LOCATION InND Loeber coll. [RL].

C388 *Jack Westropp: A autobiography* [anon.].

London: Downey & Co., 1895, 2 vols. SOURCE Brown, 404; COPAC. LOCATION L.

COMMENTARY Possibly autobiographical, the novel is set in Dublin and London. Recounts the life of Jack, who comes from a good family in Co. Clare, works as a freelance journalist in Dublin and develops into a clever, cynical, and unscrupulous person. When he marries the lady of his choice, Daniel O'Connell makes a speech at the wedding breakfast. Describes scenes in the law court [Brown; RL].

COX, Walter ('Watty'), b. Co. Westmeath 1770, d. Dublin 1837. Journalist, dramatist and editor, WC was the son of a Catholic master-blacksmith and a Miss Dease of Summer Hill (Co. Westmeath). At first a gunsmith, he moved to Dublin and in 1797 began a newspaper called the *Union Star* in support of the United Irishmen, in which he advocated a policy of assassination of selected loyalists. He acted as an informer in 1798. He travelled to Baltimore (MD) in 1801, working as a tallow chandler there in 1801 and 1802 (1804 according to ODNB), and subsequently visited New York and Nova Scotia, but returned to Ireland where he founded in 1807 the *Irish Magazine, or Monthly Asylum for Neglected Biography* (Dublin, 1807–15). He was frequently fined and imprisoned for sedition, scurrility and libel. In 1815 he was granted a government pension on condition that he leave Ireland. He published *The Exile* in New York City from 1817 to 1818. In the next year he went to Boston and in 1820 published a pamphlet *The snuff box*, that satirized American institutions. Tired of working in America, he left for Bordeaux in 1821 and probably returned to Ireland before the end of that year. His presence in Ireland was discovered by the authorities in 1835 and his pension forfeited. He died in poverty in Dublin in 1837 and was buried in Prospect cemetery, Glasnevin. He was twice married; he treated his first wife badly and was separated from his second wife, the Widow (probably Isabella) Powell, for upward of twenty-five years. In a letter to a friend written from New York on 20 Nov. 1819, he announced that he planned to return to Ireland, and added that upon arrival he would have ready a novel in Irish style for publication, which he esteemed would be superior to any of Lady Morgan's§. A bibliography of his works can be found in Ó Casaide, but his novel has not been located. SOURCE Brady, p. 46; S. Ó Casaide, 'Watty Cox and his publications' in *The Bibliographical Society of Ireland*, 5 (1935), pp 3–18; B. Clifford (ed.), *The origin of Irish Catholic nationalism: selections from Walter Cox's 'Irish Magazine' 1809–1815* (Belfast, 1992); Clyde, p. 77; M. Durey, *Transatlantic radicals and the early American republic* (Lawrence (KS), 1997), pp 119–20; Hogan 2, p. 292; McKenna, p. 124; OCIL, p. 118; ODNB; O'Donoghue, p. 84; Pollard 2, p. 124; RIA/DIB.

COX, 'Watty'. See **COX, Walter**.

COYNE, Joseph Stirling, b. Birr (Co. Offaly) 1803, d. London 1868 (not 1889 as in Brown 2). A playwright, journalist and humorist, JSC was the son of Denis Coyne, port surveyor of Waterford, and Bridget Cosgrave. He attended the Dungannon School (Co. Tyrone) and early success with submissions to periodicals gave him the confidence to pursue writing as a career. He wrote farces for the Theatre Royal in Dublin and his farce *The queer subject* was performed in London in 1837. That year, with an introd. to Thomas Crofton Croker§ from William Carleton§, he moved to London where he married Anne Comins, a widow, whose parents were from Galway. He wrote three short stories for *Bentley's Miscellany* (London, 1840–41), and wrote in all about 64 farces and theatrical pieces, some of which were translated into French and German. Plays with Irish subjects included 'Shandy Maguire' and 'The bashful Irishman', both produced in 1837. His *The scenery and antiquities of Ireland* (with Nathaniel P. Willis), illustrated by W.H. Bartlett was published in London in 1842. As secretary of the Dramatic Authors' Society for many years he worked to establish a fixed scale for performance fees and to make sure authors' copyrights were respected and fees paid. Although his farces are mostly forgotten, JSC's enduring fame is as a co-founder of *Punch* (London, 1842). For many years he was drama critic for the London *Sunday Times*. For his likenesses, see ODNB. SOURCE Allibone Suppl., i, p. 404; Boase, i, pp 744–5; Brady, p. 46; Brown 2, p. 59; Hogan 2, pp 293–4; Irish pseudonyms; NCBEL 4, pp 1999–2001; OCIL, p. 118; ODNB; O'Donoghue, pp 85–6; RIA/DIB; J.R. Stephens, *The profession of the British playwright: British theatre, 1800–1900* (Cambridge, 1992).

C389   ***Pippins and pies; or, sketches out of school. Being the adventures and misadventures of Master Frank Pickleberry during the month he was home for the holidays*** (by Joseph Stirling Coyne; dedicated to Young England).
     + London, New York: George Routledge & Sons, 1855 (ill. M'Connell, Dalziel).
     LOCATION InND Loeber coll. (also n.d. edn).

C390   ***Sam Spangles; or, the history of a harlequin*** (by Joseph Stirling Coyne).
     + London, New York: George Routledge & Sons, 1866 (ill.). SOURCE Brown 2, 313.
     LOCATION L, NUC.

CRAIG, J. Duncan. See **CRAIG, Revd John Duncan.**

CRAIG, Revd John Duncan (known as **J. Duncan Craig**), b. Dublin *c*.1830, d. San Remo (Italy) 1909. Church of Ireland clergyman, novelist, religious tract writer and poet, JDC was the son of John Craig, a silversmith of Horsehead (Co. Cork). He was raised in Sligo and Cork, and entered TCD as a fellow commoner in 1847, graduated BA in 1851, MA in 1857 and DD in 1869. He took holy orders and was a chaplain in the Irish Convict Service. He served in various parishes in the diocese of Cork; vicar of Kinsale (1866–72); chaplain of the Molyneux Asylum (Dublin, 1873–84) and then incumbent of Trinity Church, Lower Gardiner Street (Dublin). He was an authority on the language and literature of Provence. He contributed to periodicals including the *New Monthly Magazine*, *Ainsworth's Magazine*, the *Family Treasury of Sunday Reading* (all London), and *Chambers's Journal* (Edinburgh). He married Dorothea-Eliza, daughter of J. Sandys Bird of Kinsale in 1860 and they had a son. He was a voluntary chaplain in the Prussian army in the Franco-Prussian war (1870–71), and was wounded in the lung. Later in life he resided at Glenageary (Co. Dublin), but he died in Italy. SOURCE Allibone Suppl., i, p. 406; B & S, Appendix B, p. 27; Brown, p. 71; Cork, ii, p. 341; Leslie & Wallace, pp 514–15; LVP, p. 112; O'Donoghue, p. 86; E. Reilly, p. 243.

C391   ***The crew of the Florence Barton*** (by John Duncan Craig).
     [London?]: [publisher?], [date?].
     COMMENTARY No copy located; could refer to an expanded version of a sketch with this title published in *Real pictures of clerical life in Ireland* by the same author [mentioned in Cork, ii, p. 341; RL].

C392   ***The cross in Sardinia*** (by John Duncan Craig).
     [London?]: [publisher?], [date?].

COMMENTARY No copy located. Perhaps this title refers to the following book [mentioned in Cork, ii, p. 341; RL].

C393 *Lady Wilmerding of Maison Rouge: a startling tale of modern Sardinian life* (by J. Duncan Craig).

London: William MacIntosh, [1869]. LOCATION L.

London: Elliot Stock, 1901. LOCATION L.

COMMENTARY The 1901 edn is a much enlarged version [BLC].

C394 *Real pictures of clerical life in Ireland* (by J. Duncan Craig).

+ London: James Nisbet & Co., 1875. SOURCE Brown, 406. LOCATION L, InND Loeber coll. (Elliott Stock, n.d. edn).

COMMENTARY Sketches with autobiographical overtones that are mostly disguised as fiction. Most of the sketches are set in Ireland and a few in France. Contents: 'Retrospective', 'Very rambling', 'Angus Cameron', 'The scholar's deathbed', '48!', 'A night with the Mormons', 'The story of Sergeant Beatty', 'The squire of Ballyvourneen', 'The murder of the rector of Golden', 'The attack on Vaughan's Court', 'George Bond Lowe J.P.', 'The Reverend Florence MacCarthy M.A.', 'The monk', 'The Dean of Kiln-na-Martyr', 'The death of the scripture reader', 'The evangelist of La Place Dominique', 'Baus gaun Soggarth', 'The lone house of Sliev-na-Mon', 'The gathering of the thunder cloud', 'The burning of the Sheas', 'Retribution', 'Convict life', 'A convict hunt', 'The soldier convict', 'The Sunday school Bible', 'The attack on Heathfield Towers', 'Father Ulick's repentance', 'Father Ulick's confession', 'The two wills', 'The murder', 'The trial', 'The burning of Cloone glebe', 'The white ladye of Charles' Fort', 'The legend of the governor's house', 'The convert's deathbed', 'Priests and converts', 'The staff-surgeon's story', 'The meeting', 'The Royal Ulsters', 'The story of Mrs. Vannix', 'The Seine man's story', 'Left behind on Sliev-ruadh', 'The doctor's story', 'The Rev. Prebendary Middleton B.D.', 'Priests in Provence', 'The night mail', 'The silent lake', 'The home missionary', 'The dying French soldier', 'The crew of the "Florence Barton"', 'The cruise of the "Wild Duck"', 'The escape', 'The curate's wife', 'An exciting visit', 'The night of the fifth of March', 'Historical', 'Ireland in more recent days', 'Home Rule', 'The Whiteboys', 'Shaun Russell's vow', 'The execution of the vow', 'Kate Costello is wanted', 'The white wand', 'On the windlass', 'The death of surgeon-major', 'The disestablished Church of Ireland' [ML].

C395 *Bruce Reynell, M.A. (Locum tenens); or, the Oxford man in Ireland* (by J. Duncan Craig).

+ London: Elliot Stock, 1898. SOURCE Brown, 405. LOCATION Dt ([1903] edn), L, InND Loeber coll.

COMMENTARY Written in 1888, the story of an English curate who comes to Ireland as a temporary minister to fill in for a friend's absence at a time of great agrarian unrest and the rise of the Land League. Many families are boycotted, Roman Catholics are refusing to pay their rents to the landlords, there is fighting, in which the curate becomes involved. All Protestants are favourably depicted and the Catholic clergy come in for a great deal of criticism. After an aborted attempt at a general revolt, aided by American money and officers, the uprising seems to die down. The writer blames the state of affairs in Ireland on the establishment of National Schools, which prohibit Bible reading. Several characters from Provence (France), who also appear in other books by this author, play a role [ML].

C396 *John Maverell. A tale of the Riviera* (by J. Duncan Craig).

+ London: Elliot Stock, 1898. LOCATION L, InND Loeber coll.

CRAIG, R. Manifold. See CRAIG, Richard Manifold.

CRAIG, Richard Manifold (known as **R. Manifold Craig**), b. Dublin 1845?, d. 1913. Novelist and army surgeon, RMC was educated in Dublin. He retired with the rank of lieutenant-colonel. A copy of *The weird of 'The Silken Thomas'* (Aberdeen, 1900) was given to the BL when he was living at 69 York Mansions, Battersea Park, London. In the attached letter RMC explains that 'The written document [attached to the novel] is a re-production of the 'deceptfully prepared letter' referred to on p. 179, *et passim*, which by its 'devilish double meaning', as read from p. 1 to p. 4 made 'The Silken Thomas' come out as "Henry's rebel" '. SOURCE CM; E. Reilly, p. 243.

C397 *The sacrifice of fools* (by R. Manifold Craig).

+ London: Frederick A. Stokes; New York: John Lane, 1896. LOCATION L, InND Loeber coll. (1906, 2nd edn).

COMMENTARY No Irish content. A story of revenge by a widow of an Italian artist, who had deserted his wife to pursue an English heiress. The artist had been mentally unstable and his son, Ferdinand, was likewise afflicted. The widow plots to have her son marry the daughter, Salome, of the woman whom she blames for her misfortune. Ferdinand and Salome move to India, where they lead very unhappy lives. At one point Salome is rescued by a Capt. Savile. After Ferdinand dies, Salome returns to England, where eventually she marries Capt. Savile [ML].

C398 *The weird of 'The Silken Thomas.' An episode of Anglo-Irish history. Together with some romantic account of the humbler history (but greater happiness) of Martyn Baruk Fallon, scrivener, & cripple, sometime unofficially in the following of the Fitzgeralds, in their town of Maynooth, in Ireland AD 1532–1537* (by Richard Manifold Craig; dedicated to the duke of Leinster).

+ Aberdeen: Moran & Co., 1900. SOURCE Brown, 407. LOCATION L, InND Loeber coll.

COMMENTARY Cover has shield with motto 'Crom A Boo!', 'As yt is taky't. Thomas: FitzGera'. Historical fiction set in sixteenth-century Ireland and detailing how Thomas Fitzgerald, 10th earl of Kildare, was drawn into revolt by the treachery of a private enemy [Brown; CM].

CRANE, Stephen, b. Newark (NJ) 1871, d. Germany 1900. American journalist and novelist, SC was famous for his novel *The red badge of courage* (New York, 1895). He was the youngest of fourteen children of Revd Jonathan Tournley Crane, a Methodist minister, and Mary Helen Peck. After attending Syracuse Univ., he became a freelance journalist and moved to New York in 1892. His first novel, *Maggie* ([New York], 1893), failed to please the reading public but was well received by literary critics such as William Dean Howells. As a journalist SC reported from the American west, Mexico, Greece and Cuba. After he had appeared in court on behalf of a prostitute accused of solicitation while he was interviewing her, police officers harassed him to such an extent that he left for Florida and in 1899 settled with his wife, Cora, in England. His tuberculosis worsened due to his severe work schedule and he died in 1900 in a sanatorium in the Black Forest, Germany. SOURCE ANB; Burke, p. 165; S. Crane, *Maggie: a girl of the streets and other tales of New York*, ed. by Z. Ziff (New York, 2000); DAB; DLB, xii, liv, lxxviii; V. Starrett, *Stephen Crane: bibliography* (Philadelphia, 1923).

C399 *The O'Ruddy, a romance* (by Stephen Crane; finished by Robert Barr).

+ New York: Frederick A. Stokes Co., 1903 (ill. C.D. Williams). LOCATION NUC, InND Loeber coll. (incomplete).

London: Methuen & Co., 1904. LOCATION NUC.

COMMENTARY Published posthumously. A fairy story for grown-ups, with plenty of humorous incidents – love affairs, duels &c. The O'Ruddy is a reckless, rollicking, lovable character. There is little or no connection with real life. Set in south Co. Cork [RL; Brown].

'AN CRAOIBHINN AOIBHINN', pseud. See **HYDE, Douglas**.

'CRAVEN', pseud. See **CARLETON, John William**.

CRAWFORD, Mrs A. See **CRAWFORD, Sophia**.

CRAWFORD, Isabella Valancy, b. Dublin 1850 (1851 according to O'Donoghue), d. Toronto (Canada) 1887. Poet, novelist and short story writer, IVC was the sixth daughter of Dr Stephen Dennis Crawford, whose family had come from Scotland to Ireland in the early-seventeenth century, and Sydney Scott. When she was age five, the family emigrated to Wisconsin and then moved to Ontario (Canada) in 1857, where they lived in Paisley. Her father was an alcoholic and the family was poor; much of IVC's writing was done to support them. In 1862 the family attempted to move back to Ireland but instead were persuaded to relocate to North Douro (later known as Lakefield). In 1868, she moved with her family once again, this time to Peterborough, where her father died in July 1875 and her sister Emma six months later. In 1883 IVC and her mother settled in Toronto where she remained single and resided until her early death from a heart attack. IVC wrote for Canadian and American journals such as the *Favourite* (location unclear), *Fireside Weekly* (location unclear), the *Toronto Globe* and the *Toronto Evening Telegram*. She contributed several serialized novels and novellas to Frank Leslie's New York publications. While her poetry received early recognition and acclaim, it was not until the 1970s that her prose was published in book form. For her portrait, see ODNB. Manuscripts by her can be found in the Lorne Pierce collection at Queen's University, Kingston (ON). They were summarized by Frank Tierney and published in *The Halton boys* (Ottawa, 1979). SOURCE Blain, p. 247; CEWW; DCB, vol. 12, pp 212–14; DLB, xcii; IBL, 9 (1918), p. 76; OCCL, pp 145–6; ODNB; O'Donoghue, p. 497.

C400   *Selected stories* (by Isabella Valancy Crawford; ed. by Penny Petrone).
      Ottawa: University of Ottawa Press, 1975 (Canadian Short Story Library). SOURCE Blain, p. 247; ODNB; RLIN. LOCATION DCL.

C401   *Fairy tales* (by Isabella Valancy Crawford; ed. by Penny Petrone and Susan Ross).
      Ottawa: Burealis Press, 1977. SOURCE Blain, p. 247; ODNB. LOCATION CaOKQ.

C402   *The Halton boys* (by Isabella Valancy Crawford; ed. by Frank M. Tierney).
      Ottawa: Burealis Press, 1979. SOURCE Blain, p. 247. LOCATION CaOKQ.

COMMENTARY An adventure story for boys set in Canada. The volume includes other unpublished fiction such as 'The heir of Dremore', and 'Monsieur Phoebus or some of the adventures of an Irish gentleman' [RL; ODNB].

CRAWFORD, Louisa Julia MacCartney (née Montague; O'Donoghue and Irish pseudonyms mention 'Matilda Jane' as middle names) b. Co. Cavan 1790, d. 1858 (according to O'Donoghue; but 1800?–55 in OCIL; 1799–1860 in Newmann). Putative novelist, Irish-born poet and song writer LJC was the daughter of Col. Montague of Luckham Hall (Wilts.), a British soldier and a naturalist. Her mother was probably a MacCartney from Co. Cavan. She grew up in Wiltshire and wrote over a hundred songs, many of them Irish and some – such as 'Kathleen Mavourneen' and 'Dermot Astore' – very famous. Thomas Moore§ mentions writing lyrics for some 'Russian Airs' she composed. LJC published in the *Irish Metropolitan Magazine* (1830–5) and her *Irish songs* appeared in 1840. She is said to have written several novels, but to date we have not been able to identify them. SOURCE Irish pseudonyms; Newmann, p. 51; OCIL, p. 119; O'Donoghue, pp 86–7.

CRAWFORD, Mabel Sharman (Wolff mistakenly has Sherman), b. after 1818. Irish travel writer and author of a single novel, MSC was probably the third daughter of the radical Irish

MP William Sharman (who changed his name to Crawford) and Mabel Fridiswid. Her *Life in Tuscany* (London, 1859) was followed by *Through Algeria* (London, 1863), which contained a feminist preface, 'A plea for the lady tourists'. She was an advocate for the London Government Act, 1899, which made women eligible to become councillors and aldermen. SOURCE Allibone Suppl., i, p. 410; Blain, p. 248; Landed gentry, 1912, p. 141; PRONI, Dufferin & Ava papers, D/1071H/B/C/688/3; Wolff, i, p. 311.

C403   *The Wilmot family* (by Mabel Sharman Crawford).
            London: Richard Bentley, 1864, 3 vols. SOURCE Blain, p. 248; Wolff, 1595; COPAC.
            LOCATION L.
            COMMENTARY An old-fashioned didactic story of a family unexpectedly inheriting wealth, written from a high Tory standpoint [Blain].

CRAWFORD, Sophia (Mrs Abraham Crawford; known as **Mrs A. Crawford**), fl. 1850. Novelist and poet, SC also published a volume of poetry, *Stanzas* (n.l., *c*.1850). Since she is listed by O'Donoghue, we assume that she is Irish. SOURCE Allibone, i, p. 448 [under Mrs A. Crawford]; Allibone Suppl., i, p. 409 [under Mrs A. Crawford]; Alston, p. 102; Colman, p. 59; COPAC; O'Donoghue, p. 86 [under Mrs A. Crawford]; Wolff, i, p. 301 [under Mrs A. Crawford].

C404   *The lady of the bedchamber. A novel* (by Mrs A. Crawford).
            + London: T.C. Newby, 1850, 2 vols. SOURCE Hodges, p. 318; Alston, p. 102.
            LOCATION L.
            COMMENTARY Set in Seapoint, on the south coast of England, and in Wales. No Irish content [ML].

C405   *The double marriage. A novel* (by Mrs. A. Crawford).
            + London: T.C. Newby, 1852, 3 vols. SOURCE Wolff, 1547; COPAC. LOCATION L.
            COMMENTARY Set in the south of England [RL].

C406   *Lismore. A novel* (by Mrs A. Crawford).
            + London: Thomas Cautley Newby, 1853, 3 vols. SOURCE Allibone Suppl., i, p. 409; Brown, 409; COPAC. LOCATION Dt, L.
            COMMENTARY Set in Lismore (Co. Waterford) and in Italy. A sentimental tale set in the period 1659-60. The historical aspects are minimal [Brown].

C407   *The story of a nun* (by Mrs A. Crawford).
            + London: Thomas Cautley Newby, 1855, 3 vols. SOURCE Allibone Suppl., i, p. 409; COPAC. LOCATION L.
            COMMENTARY Historical fiction. Starts in Lisbon during the Peninsula War. No Irish content [ML].

C408   *Early struggles* (by Mrs A. Crawford).
            + London: T. Cautley Newby, 1857, 3 vols. SOURCE Allibone Suppl., i, p. 409.
            LOCATION L.
            COMMENTARY No Irish content [ML].

'CRAYON, Geoffrey Jr.', pseud. See **DARLEY, George**.

CREECH, Mrs ——, fl. 1796. Epistolary novelist, Mrs C probably was a resident of the Cork area, where she published her only known novel [RL].

C409   *Mary; or, the uses of adversity. A novel* (by Mrs Creech).
            + Cork: Printed [for the author?] by J. Connor, 1796, 2 vols. (subscribers' list). SOURCE Raven 2, 1796:33; ESTC t171970. LOCATION D, DCL.
COMMENTARY Epistolary novel containing letters between Mrs Elford and Miss Fitzmaurice dated from places in England, while other letters written by Miss Fitzmaurice are from Ashvale

in Ireland. Probably privately printed because among the subscribers is the Cork publisher John Connor, who took 100 copies [RL].

CROCKETT, S.R. See **CROCKETT, Revd Samuel Rutherford.**

CROCKETT, Revd Samuel Rutherford (known as **S.R. Crockett**), b. Kirkcudbrightshire (Scotland) 1860, d. Avignon (France) 1914. Scottish minister, novelist, poet and children's writer, SRC's early work as a journalist helped sustain him during his studies. He travelled widely on the Continent and his experiences there provided colourful background for many of his novels. His Scottish stories are typically set in Galloway. He produced 63 books of fiction. Only works with an Irish connection are listed below. SOURCE BLC; ODNB (for full biography); NCBEL 4, p. 1511; Sutherland, pp 160–1; T & B, p. 975.

C410　*Cleg Kelly, an Arab of the city* (by S.R. Crockett; dedicated to J.M. Barrie).
　　　+ London: Smith, Elder & Co., 1896. SOURCE Kelley, p. 32. LOCATION L, NUC, InND Loeber coll.
　　　Leipzig: Bernard Tauchnitz, 1896, 2 vols. LOCATION NUC.
　　　New York: D. Appleton, 1896. LOCATION NUC.
COMMENTARY Depicts Cleg, an Edinburgh street urchin of Irish parentage, who is a delight and a support to his friends but a terror to his enemies. He protects a girl who with her siblings had escaped her parents. Cleg inherits some money from an old general he had taken care of. He marries and shares some of his wealth with others [ML; Kelley].

C411　*Kit Kennedy: a country boy* (by S.R. Crockett).
　　　London: James Clarke & Co., 1899. SOURCE Kelley, p. 32. LOCATION L, NUC.
　　　New York, London: Harper & Bros, 1899. LOCATION NUC.
　　　COMMENTARY Concerns a street boy of Irish parentage and melodramatically evokes Crockett's own childhood in Galloway [Kelley; ODNB; Sutherland].

C412　*Joan of the sword hand* (by S.R. Crockett).
　　　London, New York, Melbourne: Ward, Lock & Co., 1900. SOURCE NCBEL 4, p. 1511; Sutherland, p. 161. LOCATION L.
　　　COMMENTARY Heroine is an Amazonian Irish princess [Sutherland].

CROFT, Sir Herbert, b. Dunster Park (Berks.) 1751, d. Paris, 1816. English miscellaneous writer and lexicographer, HC was educated at University College, Oxford, and studied law at Lincoln's Inn. He eschewed the law in favour of the church and was ordained in 1782. He succeeded to a baronetcy in 1797. In 1792 he proposed editing and expanding Johnson's dictionary by 20,000 words but the project was not completed due to lack of subscribers. Chronically short of funds, he withdrew to the Continent and his library was sold in 1797. He was a regular contributor to periodicals, including the London *Gentleman's Magazine*. He knew Latin, Greek, Hebrew and Anglo-Saxon and spoke German, French and Italian. He published several volumes in French. SOURCE Allibone, i, p. 451; ODNB; ESTC.

C413　*Love and madness. A story too true: in a series of letters between parties, whose names would perhaps be mentioned, were they less known, or less lamented* [anon.].
　　　London: G. Kearsly, 1780. SOURCE Raven 2, 1780:14; ESTC t113654. LOCATION L.
　　　+ London: G. Kearsly & R. Faulder, 1780 (new edn). SOURCE Raven 2, 1780:14; ESTC t143247 (1780, 3rd edn). LOCATION InND Loeber coll.
　　　Dublin: C. Jackson, [1781 or earlier]. SOURCE Adv. in *The new Eloisa* (Dublin, 1781); Raven 2, 1780:14 (1786 edn).
COMMENTARY Epistolary novel; no copy of the earliest Dublin edn located. For an account of the factual basis of this work, the 'most unprecedented murder ... committed on the person

of Miss Ray (or Reay) by the Revd Mr Hackman', see sources cited by Raven 2, p. 290 and ODNB. Some of the letters are addressed from Ireland, but that setting does not appear to have been essential. Inserted in the novel is a huge interpolation of the ill-fated boy poet Thomas Chatterton which, according to the ODNB, provides 'more graphic glimpses of the boy than all subsequent writers have supplied'. Letter XLIX prints three of Chatterton's poems and eight of his letters for the first time. HC was later accused by the poet Southey of falsely acquiring Chatterton's letters and publishing them without consent. The novel also includes material relating to Ossian [RL; Burmester cat. 49/190; ODNB].

CROFTON, Francis Blake, b. Crossboyne (Co. Mayo) 1842, d. Southsea (Hants.) 1911. Humorist and writer of fiction for juveniles, FBC was the son of Revd William Crofton. He graduated BA at TCD in 1862 and went to Nova Scotia the same year where he was appointed librarian to the Legislative Assembly, an appointment he held until 1909, when he retired to reside in England. He published poetry, a political work entitled *For closer union* (Halifax, NS, 1895), as well as a biography, *Haliburton§ (Sam Slick), the man and the writer* (Windsor, NS, 1889). SOURCE Allibone Suppl., i, p. 414; B & S, Appendix B, p. 27; BLC; IBL, 3 (1911–12), p. 101; O'Donoghue, pp 87–8.

C414   *The bewildered querist and other nonsense* (by Francis Blake Crofton).
    New York: G.P. Putnam's Sons, 1875. SOURCE IBL, 3 (1911–12), p. 101. LOCATION NUC.
    COMMENTARY American wit and humour [NUC].

C415   *The Major's big-talk stories* (by Francis Blake Crofton).
    + London: Frederick Warne & Co., 1881 (ill.). SOURCE IBL, 3 (1911–12), p. 101. LOCATION L.
    COMMENTARY Fiction for juveniles dealing mostly with adventures in Africa [RL].

C416   *Hairbreadth escapes of Major Mendax : his perilous encounters, startling adventures, and daring exploits with Indians, cannibals, wild beasts, serpents, balloons, geysers, etc., etc., all over the world, in the bowels of the earth, and above the clouds: a personal narrative* (by Francis Blake Crofton).
    Philadelphia: Hubbard Bros, 1889. SOURCE IBL, 3 (1911–12), p. 101; COPAC. LOCATION NUC.
    COMMENTARY Fiction for juveniles [NUC].

CROFTS, Charley, b. 1770. Fictionalizing autobiographer, CC was the eighth son of William Crofts of Velvetstown (Co. Cork) and Elizabeth Beare. He died unmarried. SOURCE Burke's, pp 293–4.

C417   *Memoirs of Charley Crofts, containing numerous highly entertaining anecdotes* ('written by himself').
    + Cork: Printed [for the author?] by Edwards & Savage, 1829. LOCATION D, CKu, NUC, InND Loeber coll.
    COMMENTARY Preface signed C. Crofts. A fictionalized autobiographical sketch of life in the eighteenth century. Opens in 1781 with the birth of CC on 1 Apr., the youngest son of a respectable country gentleman living in Velvetstown. CC gives an account of his schooldays in Cork and his adventures as a young man in both Cork and Dublin. He then manages a residence at Danesfort (Co. Kilkenny?) with his brother William. He writes about his experiences of the 1798 rebellion. The book includes a copy of his father's will, in which he gave CC the lease to an estate at Ballyhen [CD; RL].

CROKER, Mrs B.M. See **CROKER, Mrs Bithia Mary**.

CROKER, Mrs Bithia Mary (née Sheppard; also known as **Mrs B.M. Croker** and **Mrs John Croker**), b. Kilgefin (Co. Roscommon) *c*.1850, d. London 1920 (1921 according to Sutherland). Romantic novelist and short story writer of colonial and Anglo-Irish life, BMC was the daughter of a Church of Ireland clergyman, Revd William Sheppard (not Shepherd as in other sources) of Kilgefin whose family were Irish Puritans who had settled at Knockshegowna and Shinrone in Co. Offaly. Her mother was Bithia Watson of Warrenpoint (Co. Down). BMC was educated at Rockferry in Cheshire, England, and Tours, France. In 1871 she married an army officer, Lt.-Col. John Croker of the Royal Scots Fusiliers, whose Anglo-Irish family came from Drumkeen (Co. Limerick). They spent fourteen years in India and Burma. Up to 1880 she had no idea of adopting literature as a profession but started writing to distract herself from the heat and soon found a ready market for her work among British women in India. Some of her novels and short stories are set in Ireland but most centre on British colonial life in India and Burma, including *The road to Mandalay* (London, 1917), which became a famous motion picture. Other novels focus on the British upper class in varied settings on the Continent and in Australia. In the early 1880s BMC and her husband returned to England. He was on half-pay at this time and she often worked ten or twelve hours a day writing. After his retirement they lived at Bray (Co. Wicklow). In 1919 she wrote the publisher Edmund Downey§: 'It is strange to me that I never receive any acknowledgment from my native land as an Irish novelist ... Irish papers rarely notice me, save *The Freeman's Journal* [Dublin], whose abuse is most amusing'. Many of her short stories and novels were reprinted in the 1920s and 1930s when her work was most popular. We have identified 52 titles published between 1882 and 1921, of which at least 10 had Irish content. Some of her correspondence is in the NLI (MS 21,845). SOURCE Allibone Suppl., i, p. 415; H.C. Black, *Pen, pencil, baton and mask. Biographical sketches* (London, 1896), pp 83–92; Blain, pp 248–9; Brady, p. 47; Brown, p. 73; EF, pp 82–3; Hogan 2, pp 295–6; IBL, 12 (1920), pp 68–9; Landed gentry, 1912, p. 637; OCIL, p. 120; ODNB; RIA/DIB; Roscommon, pp 27–9; Sutherland, pp 161–2; T & B, p. 975; Wilson, pp 161–2; Wolff, i, pp 313–19; [J. Wright], *The King's County* (Parsonstown, [now Birr, Co. Offaly] 1890), pp 310–11.

C418   *Proper pride. A novel* [anon.].
> + London: Tinsley Bros, 1882, 3 vols. SOURCE Wolff, 1619; Roscommon, p. 27; Topp 8, 34. LOCATION D (1882, 3rd edn), NUC.
>
> London: Ward & Downey, 1885 (new edn). SOURCE Roscommon, p. 27. LOCATION L, InND Loeber coll. (Chatto & Windus, 1892, new edn).
>
> New York: George Munro, 1884 (Seaside Library, No. 1823). SOURCE Topp 3, p. 217–18. LOCATION NUC.

COMMENTARY First serialized in the London *Tinsley's Magazine*; a 6th edn appeared in 1887. A story of Anglo-Indian life with some lively military chapters set in Afghanistan. By the malicious invention of a false marriage certificate and some miscarried mail between them, a young couple is kept apart for years. Eventually, all is solved and happiness returns [Sutherland; ML].

C419   *Pretty Miss Neville* (by B.M. Croker).
> + London: Tinsley Bros, 1883, 3 vols. SOURCE Wolff, 1618; Topp 8, 33. LOCATION D (vol. 1 only), L.
>
> London: Chatto & Windus, [1893?] (new edn). SOURCE Topp 3, p. 225. LOCATION InND Loeber coll. (Collins n.d. edn).
>
> New York: Harper & Bros, 1884 (Franklin Square Library, No. 363). SOURCE Topp 3, p. 225. LOCATION NUC.
>
> New York: George Munro, 1884 (Seaside Library, No. 1822). SOURCE Topp 3, p. 225.

COMMENTARY No copy of the New York, Munro edn located. Has as heroine-narrator a faithless coquette (and huntswoman) in the Indian station of Mulkapore. The novel ends with Miss Neville marrying [Sutherland; Topp; RL].

C420   *Some one else* (by B.M. Croker; dedicated to my Anglo-Indian friends).
       + London: Sampson, Low, Marston, Searle & Rivington, 1885, 3 vols. SOURCE Wolff,
       1621; Sutherland, p. 161 (mistakenly mentions 1884 edn). LOCATION D, L, NUC.
       New York: Harper & Bros, [1885] (Franklin Square Library, No. 455). SOURCE Topp
       4, p. 359. LOCATION NUC.
       New York: George Munro, [1885] (Seaside Library, No. 1990). SOURCE Topp 4, p. 359.
       COMMENTARY Set in South Africa. Chronicles the mishaps that follow from a mis-
       taken kiss [Sutherland].
C421   *A bird of passage* (by B.M. Croker).
       + London: Sampson Low, Marston, Searle & Rivington, 1886, 3 vols. SOURCE Brown,
       415; Topp 8, 68. LOCATION D, L, NUC (1887, 2nd edn).
       + London: Chatto & Windus, 1903 (new edn). SOURCE Topp 3, 216. LOCATION InND
       Loeber coll.
COMMENTARY Study of a colonial flirtation in the Andaman Islands in the Indian Ocean. Two
lovers are separated by the scheming of an unsuccessful rival. The girl first lives with disagreeable
relations in London but finally goes to a relative in Ireland where life is better. In the end she
is reunited with her lover. Reviewed in the *Athenaeum* (London, July, 1888) [Brown].
C422   *Diana Barrington. A romance of central India* (by Mrs John Croker).
       + London: Ward & Downey, 1888, 3 vols. SOURCE Wolff, 1611; Topp 8, 103. LOCATION
       Dt (3 vols. in 1), D (1889, 4th edn), L, NUC, InND Loeber coll. (1890, 5th edn).
       New York: George Munro, 1888 (Seaside Library Pocket Edition, No. 1124). SOURCE
       Topp 3, p. 210. LOCATION NUC.
COMMENTARY The fifth London edn appeared in 1890. Set in India. Diana Barrington is
brought up by her father and an Irish nurse in seclusion in a deserted area of India. Her father
has told her that her mother died shortly after she was born. When Diana is aged about 18
she wants to see something of the world. Her father, very much against it, tells her the world
is a wicked place. He gives her a diamond necklace that once was her mother's. They meet
some Englishmen who are out hunting in the area, one a school-fellow of Mr Barrington. They
implore him to let his daughter visit. He finally agrees and Diana finds that many of her new
acquaintances are indeed very wicked. Her father dies, and she marries a Capt. Fitzroy. At
the settlement, a Mrs Vavasour becomes her particular friend. When Diana wears her diamond necklace, Mrs Vavasour realizes that Diana is her daughter. Rather than show moth-
erly feelings, she makes Diana pawn the necklace to pay for her mother's debts. Mrs Vavasour
swears Diana to secrecy. Eventually Diana's husband becomes aware that all is not in order
and takes her away to bring her to England. However, in Bombay Diana becomes ill and their
departure is delayed. Mrs Vavasour, on her deathbed, tells the whole story to Capt. Fitzroy.
This restores harmony, the Fitzroys are happy again and stay in India [ML].
C423   *Two masters. A novel* (by B.M. Croker).
       + London: F.V. White & Co., 1890, 3 vols. SOURCE Roscommon, p. 27; Topp 7, 188.
       LOCATION D (1890 edn, 1 vol.), L.
       Philadelphia: J.B. Lippincott & Co., 1890 (Series of Select Novels, No. 113). SOURCE
       Topp 3, pp 251–2. LOCATION NUC.
       New York: George Munro, 1890 (Seaside Library Pocket Edition, No. 1607). SOURCE
       Topp 3, pp 251–2.
       COMMENTARY No copy of the New York edn located. Set partly in Ireland [Brown; RL].
C424   *Interference. A novel* (by B.M. Croker).
       + London: F.V. White, 1891, 3 vols. SOURCE Daims, 713; Wolff, 1614; Topp 7, 214.
       LOCATION Dt (1905, new edn), L, NUC, InND Loeber coll. (also 1894, 3rd edn; see
       Plate 25).

+ Philadelphia: J.B. Lippincott, 1891. SOURCE Daims, 713. LOCATION D (1899 edn), NUC.

COMMENTARY A story of love and manipulation, it begins in Ireland with a fox-hunting scene. Mrs Redmond and her vain daughter Belle, on whom she dotes, have inherited a small property and take in a poor niece, Betty. An officer from India comes to visit and both Belle and Betty fall in love with him. He falls in love with Betty and after he has returned to India he writes Mrs Redmond asking for her hand. Instead of sending Betty to India, she sends her daughter Belle. The officer is taken aback but feels that he has no choice but to marry Belle. He is unhappy in his marriage and things get worse when Betty comes to India with her uncle. Belle finds out the truth of her mother's manipulations and is extremely jealous. In a fit of anger she rushes off into the night and falls to her death into a ravine [ML].

C425   *A family likeness. A sketch in the Himalayas* (by B.M. Croker).

+ London: Chatto & Windus, 1892, 3 vols. SOURCE Wolff, 1612. LOCATION D (1893, 2nd edn), L, NUC (1894 edn).

+ London: Chatto & Windus, 1894 (new edn). SOURCE Topp 3, pp 227–8. LOCATION InND Loeber coll.

Philadelphia: J.B. Lippincott, 1893 (Series of Select Novels, No. 140). SOURCE Topp 3, p. pp 227–8. LOCATION NUC.

COMMENTARY Set in England and India. Mr Carwithen, while in the army in India, makes a hasty marriage with a woman he considers to be inferior. She dies in childbirth and he leaves the baby in a school there. After his return to England he marries an heiress but omits telling her that he has a daughter in India as he is concerned to be seen only in the best of society. An acquaintance sees in his house a portrait of a beautiful woman and remarks that if he ever found anyone like that, he would fall in love. In India he meets the daughter, who is the image of the portrait in her father's house, and becomes engaged to her. The father is forced to admit the existence of his daughter [ML].

C426   *'To let' and other stories* (by B.M. Croker).

+ London: Chatto & Windus, 1893. SOURCE Topp 3, pp 222–3. LOCATION D (n.d. edn), L.

Philadelphia: J.B. Lippincott, 1893. LOCATION NUC.

COMMENTARY Stories of Anglo-Indian life, some with supernatural elements. Contents: "'To let'", 'Mrs. Raymond', 'The khitmatgar', 'The dâk bungalow at Dakor', "'The other Miss Browne'", "'If you see her face'", 'The former passengers', 'The secret of the amulet' [ML; Wilson, p. 161].

C427   *A third person. A novel* (by B.M. Croker).

+ London: F.V. White & Co., 1893, 2 vols. SOURCE Daims, 717; Wolff, 1624a (1895 edn); Topp 7, 246. LOCATION Dt (1895 edn), D (1894 edn), L, NUC.

London: Chatto & Window, 1899 (new edn). SOURCE Topp 3, p. 262; OCLC. LOCATION CSt.

Philadelphia: J.B. Lippincott & Co., 1893 (Series of Select Novels, No. 151). SOURCE Topp 3, p. 262. LOCATION NUC.

C428   *Mr. Jervis. A romance of the Indian hills* (by B.M. Croker).

London: Chatto & Windus, 1894, 3 vols. SOURCE Wolff, 1617. LOCATION Dt, D (n.d. edn), L, NUC.

London: Chatto & Windus, 1897 (new edn). SOURCE Topp 3, pp 247–8; OCLC. LOCATION GEU.

+ London, Edinburgh, Paris: Thomas Nelson & Sons, n.d. (as *Mr. Jervis*). LOCATION InND Loeber coll.

Philadelphia: J.B. Lippincott, 1895 (Select Novels, No. 163). SOURCE Topp 3, pp 247–8; Roscommon, p. 27. LOCATION NUC.

COMMENTARY First serialized in the *Social Review* (London?), and continued after the book was published. A tale of military life set in India. Jervis delays his marriage because he thinks insanity runs in his family [Burmester list].

C429 *Village tales and jungle tragedies* (by B.M. Croker).
> London: Chatto & Windus, 1895 (Piccadilly Novel). SOURCE Topp 3, p. 242; Roscommon, p. 27. LOCATION L, NUC.

COMMENTARY Contents: 'A free-offering' (first published in the *Graphic* (London), Christmas, No. 1894), '"The Missus"', 'The betrayal of Shere Bahadur', '"Proven or not proven"', 'An outcast of the people', 'An appeal to the Gods', 'Two little travellers' [NUC; Topp 3, p. 242].

C430 *Married or single?* (by B.M. Croker).
> + London: Chatto & Windus, 1895, 3 vols. SOURCE Daims, 715; Wolff, 1616. LOCATION D, L, NUC (1895 new edn).
> London: Chatto & Windus, 1896 (new edn). SOURCE Topp 3, p. 255 (1898 edn); COPAC. LOCATION Dt.
> New York: P.F. Collier, [c.1895], 2 vols. in 1 (The Fortnightly Library, Nos. 14–15). SOURCE Topp 3, p. 255; Daims, 715. LOCATION NUC.

C431 *The real Lady Hilda. A sketch* (by B.M. Croker).
> + London: Chatto & Windus, 1896 (Piccadilly Novel). SOURCE Topp 3, p. 258; Wolff, 1620 (1896, 2nd edn). LOCATION L, NUC.
> London: Chatto & Windus, 1898 (new edn). SOURCE Topp 3, p. 258; OCLC. LOCATION GEU.
> New York: F.M. Buckles & Co., 1899. LOCATION NUC.

C432 *In the kingdom of Kerry & other stories* (by B.M. Croker).
> + London: Chatto & Windus, 1896. SOURCE Brown, 416; Roscommon, p. 28. LOCATION D, L, NUC, InND Loeber coll.

COMMENTARY Stories mainly set in Ireland, others are set in India, and three are supernatural tales. Contents: 'In the kingdom of Kerry', 'Old Lady Ann', 'Tim Brady's boots', 'The first comer', 'Jack Straw's castle', 'The red woollen necktie', 'Her last wishes' [ML; Wilson, p. 161].

C433 *Beyond the Pale. A novel* (by B.M. Croker).
> New York: P.F. Collier, 1896. LOCATION NUC.
> + New York: R.F. Fenno & Co., 1896 (ill.). SOURCE Roscommon, p. 28. LOCATION D, NUC ([c.1897] edn).
> + London: Chatto & Windus, 1897. SOURCE Brown, 417. LOCATION Dt (1898, new edn). LOCATION Roscommon County Library, L, NUC, InND Loeber coll.

COMMENTARY First appeared in serial form in the weekly edition of the *Times* (Oct. 1896 to Feb. 1897). First English edn was published in a print run of 25,000 copies, and remained very popular until at least 1911. It features an Irish heroine, 'Galloping Jerry', and is set in Munster. Her family's estate is sold to an Englishman, Mr Money, who comes to reside there. His son falls in love with Jerry, who is very proud of her lineage but lives a miserable live as a horse trainer. The social gulf between them is gradually narrowed, particularly when it becomes clear that the Moneys are descended from the Mooneys, who used to live on a poor part of the estate. Eventually they marry [ML; E. Reilly, p. 230; Sutherland, pp 161–2].

C434 *Miss Balmaine's past* (by B.M. Croker).
> London: Chatto & Windus, 1898. SOURCE Roscommon, p. 28. LOCATION D (n.d. edn), L.
> Philadelphia: J.B. Lippincott, 1898. LOCATION NUC.

C435 *Peggy of the Bartons* (by B.M. Croker).
> London: Methuen & Co., 1898. SOURCE Roscommon, p. 28. LOCATION L.
> Leipzig: Bernard Tauchnitz, 1904. SOURCE T & B, 3738. LOCATION NUC.
> + New York: R.F. Fenno, 1898. SOURCE Roscommon, p. 28. LOCATION D, NUC.

C436   *Terence* (by B.M. Croker; dedicated to the Irish Tourist Development).
+ London: Chatto & Windus, 1899 (ill. Sidney Paget; see Plate 26). SOURCE Brown, 418; Wolff, 1623. LOCATION Dt, D, L, NUC, InND Loeber coll.
Toronto: W.J. Gage & Co., 1899. SOURCE Roscommon, p. 28; OCLC. LOCATION Simon Fraser Univ. (Burnaby, BC, Canada).
+ New York: F.M. Buckles & Co., [1899]. SOURCE Roscommon, p. 28. LOCATION D, NUC.
COMMENTARY A tale of love and jealousy set in Waterville (Co. Kerry) at an anglers' hotel. The characters belong to the Protestant upper classes. A dramatic version ran for two years in the US [Brown; ODNB].

C437   *Infatuation* (by B.M. Croker).
+ London: Chatto & Windus, 1899. LOCATION D, L, InND Loeber coll.
Philadelphia: J.B. Lippincott, 1899 (as *Infatuation; or, Maria's misfortunes*). LOCATION NUC.

C438   *Jason and other stories* (by B.M. Croker).
+ London: Chatto & Windus, 1899. SOURCE Roscommon, p. 28. LOCATION D (n.d. edn), L, NUC, InND Loeber coll. (1932 edn).
COMMENTARY This appeared in serial form in the weekly edition of the London *Times*, from July to Nov. 1898. Contents: 'Jason', 'The end of her tether', 'Tommy's nurse', 'The spider', 'Information', 'Mrs. Ponsonby's dream' (supernatural tale), 'My only adventure', 'The right man in the wrong place'. The 1932 edn has a revised title of the story 'Information', where it is called 'Trooper Thompson's information' (supernatural tale) [RL].

C439   *Angel. A sketch in Indian ink* (by B.M. Croker).
+ London: Methuen & Co., 1901. SOURCE Daims, 709. LOCATION D, L, NUC, InND Loeber coll.
New York: Dodd, Mead & Co., 1901. SOURCE Daims, 709. LOCATION NUC.
COMMENTARY A story of difficult family relations involving Angel, a girl born in India who, after her mother's death and when her step-father is not interested in her, becomes the ward of her cousin, Phil Gascoigne. Angel is sent to England to school and when she has finished she lives with her grandmother, with whom she does not get along. After an exchange of words about Angel's mother, Angel leaves her grandmother and takes passage to India to her guardian. This turns into an awkward situation because Angel is now grown up and he is still fairly young. Eventually, Phil and Angel marry, but it takes a long time for Angel to believe that Phil really loves her [ML].

C440   *A state secret, and other stories* (by B.M. Croker).
+ London: Methuen & Co., 1901. SOURCE Roscommon, p. 28. LOCATION D (1904, 3rd edn), L, InND Loeber coll. (1918 edn).
New York: F.M. Buckles & Co., 1901. LOCATION NUC.
COMMENTARY Stories on Irish and Indian themes: Contents: 'A state secret', 'Sullivan's bargain', 'The little blue jug', 'Lady Mark Slattery', 'The Glen Lammie shooting', '"An unexpected invitation"' (haunted house tale), 'Mrs. Van Byl', 'The clue', '"Incognito"', 'The proud girl' [RL; Wilson, p. 161].

C441   *The cat's paw* (by B.M. Croker; dedicated to the author's daughter, Eileen Whitaker).
+ London: Chatto & Windus, 1902 (ill. Fred. Pegram). LOCATION D, L.
Leipzig: Bernard Tauchnitz, 1908. SOURCE T & B, 4066. LOCATION NUC.
Philadelphia: J.B. Lippincott, 1902. SOURCE Daims, 710. LOCATION NUC.

C442   *Her own people* (by B.M. Croker); dedicated to Edith M. Vincent).
+ London: Hurst & Blackett, 1903. SOURCE Roscommon, p. 28. LOCATION D, L, NUC, InND Loeber coll. (n.d. edn).

COMMENTARY A story of mistaken identity and racial prejudice. Verona Chandos was adopted by the rich Mrs de Godez who has taken her from India to Europe. Before Mrs de Godez dies, she tells Verona that she has relatives in India. Verona set out to find them and discovers that her father had married a half-caste. Her father is an honourable, but beaten-down man, and her mother turns out to be a terrible money-lender. She is aghast at the sight of her mother and siblings and finds it hard to adjust to the fact that she has Indian blood. An officer, who in Europe had made love to her, drops her when he finds out about her relations. Another Englishman, Mr Salway, who is in the local police, professes his love for her, but she refuses him because of her Indian background. In a fit of anger her mother tells her that she is not her daughter at all but the daughter of a noble Englishwoman who died at her birth. Verona returns to England to meet her real relatives, but not before she tells Mr Salway that she will marry him [ML].

C443 *Johanna* (by B.M. Croker; dedicated to Mrs Rowan-Hamilton of Shanganagh Castle, Shankill, Co. Dublin).

+ London: Methuen & Co., 1903. SOURCE Brown, 419. LOCATION D (1917 edn), L.
Philadelphia: J.B. Lippincott, 1903. LOCATION NUC.

COMMENTARY The story of a beautiful but unsophisticated peasant girl who is forced by her stepmother to leave her home in Kerry. She sets off for Dublin but on the way she loses the address of the house to which she is going. The keeper of a lodging-house takes her in. She leads a terrible life there until her lover comes home from the wars and finds her [Brown].

C444 *The happy valley* (by B.M. Croker).

+ London: Methuen & Co., 1904. SOURCE Wolff, 1613. LOCATION D (n.d. edn), L, NUC, InND Loeber coll. (Collins, n.d. edn).
Leipzig: Bernard Tauchnitz, 1905. SOURCE T & B, 3792. LOCATION NUC.

COMMENTARY Possible autobiographical account of a summer spent in Norway among Englishmen who had come over for fishing. The Norwegians living in the valley are described as extremely poor. The river and the surrounding landscape are idyllic. The story includes some love affairs among the English [ML].

C445 *A nine days' wonder* (by B.M. Croker).

+ London: Methuen & Co., 1905. SOURCE Brown, 420. LOCATION D (1905, 2nd edn), L, NUC, InND Loeber coll. (1913, 5th ed).
Leipzig: Bernard Tauchnitz, 1906. SOURCE T & B, 3907. LOCATION NUC.

COMMENTARY A story of love between social classes set in Ireland and England. Mary Foley, a poor girl brought up in an Irish cabin, helps Ulick Doran, a member of the local gentry, when he falls off his horse. Over the years they become more friendly but this friendship is forbidden by Ulick's mother. Ulick joins the army and leaves the country, but not before he has pledged his love to Mary. An English peer suddenly claims Mary as his daughter. She is unsophisticated and initially has great difficulty fitting into her new environment. In the end she meets Ulick again and promises to marry him [ML; Brown].

C446 *The old Cantonment, with other stories of India and elsewhere* (by B.M. Croker).

London: Methuen & Co., 1905. SOURCE Roscommon, p. 28. LOCATION L.
Leipzig: Bernard Tauchnitz, 1905. SOURCE T & B, 3829. LOCATION NUC.

COMMENTARY Contains a few supernatural stories: 'La carcasonne', 'The door ajar', 'The helper', 'The little brass god', 'Who knew the truth?' [Wilson, p. 162].

C447 *The youngest Miss Mowbray* (by B.M. Croker).

London: Hurst & Blackett, 1906. SOURCE Roscommon, p. 28. LOCATION D (n.d. edn), L, NUC.
Leipzig: Bernard Tauchnitz, 1906. SOURCE T & B, 3930. LOCATION NUC.

COMMENTARY This novel became very popular: 119,000 copies had been printed by *c.*1920 [Tiger cat. 12/02/78].

C448 *The Company's servant. A romance of southern India* (by B.M. Croker).
+ London: Hurst & Blackett, 1907. SOURCE Roscommon, p. 28; Wolff, 1610 (1908 edn). LOCATION D, L, NUC, InND Loeber coll. (1907, 2nd edn).
Leipzig: Bernard Tauchnitz, 1906. SOURCE T & B, 3930. LOCATION NUC.

COMMENTARY This novel became very poplar, reaching a 62nd thousand printing. A disgraced gentleman has become a guard on an Indian railway. His best friend is an opium-smoking Englishman. Eventually, the gentleman is restored to respectability and prosperity [EF, p. 83; Davidson cat.34/879].

C449 *The Spanish necklace* (by B.M. Croker).
London: Chatto & Windus, 1907 (ill. F. Pegram). SOURCE Wolff, 1622. LOCATION L, NUC.
New York: Cupples & Leon, [1908]. LOCATION NUC.

COMMENTARY Hester Forde, a shy young heiress, tours the Continent with a chaperone because her home is made unpleasant by tyrannical servants. In Spain she is wooed by a Spanish nobleman [EF, p. 83].

C450 *Katherine, the arrogant* (by B.M. Croker); dedicated to the memory of author's friend, Nellie Bovill).
London: Methuen & Co., 1909. SOURCE Daims, 714. LOCATION D (1913, 7th edn), L.
Leipzig: Bernard Tauchnitz, 1909. SOURCE T & B, 4100. LOCATION NUC.

COMMENTARY A romance about the predicament of a penniless girl who takes a job as a maid and falls in love with a married man [EF, p. 83].

C451 *Babes in the wood. A romance of the jungles* (by B.M. Croker).
London: Methuen & Co., 1910. SOURCE Roscommon, p. 28. LOCATION D (1917, 9th edn), L, NUC.
Leipzig: Bernard Tauchnitz, 1910. SOURCE T & B, 4219. LOCATION NUC.
New York: Brentano, 1911. LOCATION NUC.

C452 *Fame* (by B.M. Croker).
+ London: Mills & Boon, 1910. SOURCE Daims, 712. LOCATION D (1910, 3rd edn), L, NUC.
Leipzig: Bernard Tauchnitz, 1910. SOURCE T & B, 4188. LOCATION NUC.

C453 *A rolling stone* (by B.M. Croker).
London: F.V. White & Co., 1911. SOURCE Roscommon, p. 28. LOCATION D (1927 edn), L.
Leipzig: Bernard Tauchnitz, 1911. SOURCE T & B, 4275. LOCATION NUC.
New York: Brentano's, 1912. LOCATION NUC.

C454 *The serpent's tooth* (by B.M. Croker).
+ London: Hutchinson & Co., 1912. SOURCE Daims, 716. LOCATION D, L, NUC.
Leipzig: Bernard Tauchnitz, 1912. SOURCE T & B, 4345; Daims, 716. LOCATION NUC.
New York: Brentano's, 1913. LOCATION NUC.

C455 *In old Madras* (by B.M. Croker).
+ London: Hutchinson & Co., 1913. SOURCE Roscommon, p. 29. LOCATION D (n.d. edn), L, NUC.
Leipzig: Bernard Tauchnitz, 1913. SOURCE T & B, 4414. LOCATION BL.

C456 *Lismoyle: an experiment in Ireland* (by B.M. Croker).
+ London: Hutchinson & Co., 1913. SOURCE Brown, 421; Roscommon, p. 29; Wolff, 1615. LOCATION D, L, NUC.
+ New York: Brentano's, 1914. SOURCE Roscommon, p. 29. LOCATION D, NUC.

Leipzig: Bernard Tauchnitz, 1914. SOURCE T & B, 4485. LOCATION NUC.
COMMENTARY The story of a six-month visit of a young English heiress to the stately but dilapidated mansion of Lismoyle in Co. Tipperary [Brown].

C457 *Quicksands* (by B.M. Croker).
+ London: Cassell & Co., 1915. SOURCE Roscommon, p. 29: D, L, NUC.

C458 *Given in marriage* (by B.M. Croker).
+ London: Hutchinson & Co., 1916. SOURCE Roscommon, p. 29. LOCATION D, L.

C459 *The road to Mandalay. A tale of Burma* (by B.M. Croker; dedicated to Lt.-Col. A.E. Congdon).
London, Toronto: Cassell & Co., 1917. SOURCE Roscommon, p. 29. LOCATION D (1919 edn), L.

C460 *What she overheard* (by B.M. Croker).
London: Hutchinson & Co., [1917]. LOCATION NUC.

C461 *A rash experiment* (by B.M. Croker).
London: Hutchinson & Co., 1917. SOURCE Roscommon, p. 29. LOCATION D (n.d. edn), L.

C462 *Bridget* (by B.M. Croker).
London: Hutchinson & Co., 1918. SOURCE Brown, 421a. LOCATION L.
COMMENTARY A story about Bridget, a beautiful but poor girl who lives in a far corner of Ireland. Her life is not easy, but in the end her circumstances improve [Brown].

C463 *Blue China* (by B.M. Croker).
London: Hutchinson & Co., [1919]. SOURCE Roscommon, p. 29. LOCATION D, L.
New York: Brentano's, [1919]. LOCATION NUC.
COMMENTARY Advertised as a tale woven around the great Oriental collection of a wealthy Shanghai merchant and the doings of his crafty niece [Adv. in De Vere Stacpoole's§ *Under blue skies* (London, 1927)].

C464 *Odds and ends* (by B.M. Croker).
London: Hutchinson & Co., [1919]. SOURCE Roscommon, p. 29. LOCATION L, NUC.
COMMENTARY Stories set in Ireland and India. Contents: 'The creaking board' (supernatural story), 'The north verandah', 'The red bungalow', 'The sword of Lanbryde' [Wilson, p. 162].

C465 *Jungle tales* (by B.M. Croker).
+ London: Holden & Hardingham, 1919. SOURCE Roscommon, p. 29. LOCATION L.
COMMENTARY The running header is 'Village Tales and Jungle Tragedies'. Contents: 'A free-will offering', '"The Missus." A dog tragedy', 'The betrayal of Shere Bahadur', '"Proven or not proven?" The true story of Naim Sing, Rajpoot', 'An outcast of the people', 'An appeal to the gods', 'Two little travellers' [JB].

C466 *The pagoda tree* (by B.M. Croker).
+ London, New York: Cassell & Co., 1919. SOURCE Roscommon, p. 29. LOCATION D, L, NUC.
+ Leipzig: Bernard Tauchnitz, 1921. SOURCE T & B, 4547. LOCATION InND Loeber coll.
COMMENTARY A story of love triumphing over greed and manipulation. John Crawford, a good-looking ne'er-do-well, travels to India with his daughter Helen to look for the riches that were hidden by his great-uncle. He is not successful and lives off other people. He wishes Helen to marry a rich man, but she refuses as she is in love with a man she met on the boat coming to India. While she and her fiancée are taking refuge from the rain in a cave, they find the treasure. But the incessant rain results in a huge landslide and it is buried forever [ML].

C467 *The chaperon* (by B.M. Croker).
London, New York: Cassell & Co., 1920. SOURCE Daims, 711. LOCATION D (1922 edn), L.

+ Leipzig: Bernard Tauchnitz, 1920. SOURCE T & B, 4583. LOCATION InND Loeber coll.

COMMENTARY Reminiscences of a divorcée who is neglected by her husband when they live in India. Her husband divorces her because he mistakenly thinks she had an affair. As a consequence, she is separated from her daughter and has to earn her own living as a chaperone to a spoiled English girl vacationing on the French Riviera. She meets her grown-up daughter but cannot tell her that she is her mother. Her ex-husband also appears on the scene, having long since regretted his hasty behaviour towards his wife. He proposes to remarry her and she accepts [ML].

C468   *The house of rest* (by B.M. Croker).

+ London, New York: Cassell & Co., 1921. SOURCE Roscommon, p. 29. LOCATION D (n.d. edn), L.

C469   *'Number ninety' and other ghost stories* (by B.M. Croker).

+ Mountain Ash [Kidwell, Wales]: Sarob Press, 2000 (ed. by Richard Dalby; ill. Paul Lowe). SOURCE Wilson, p. 161. LOCATION L.

COMMENTARY Collection of supernatural stories. Contents: '"Number ninety"', 'The former passengers', '"If you see her face"', 'The red bungalow', 'The Khitmatgar', 'Her last wishes', 'The Dâk bungalow at Dakor', '"To let"', 'The north verandah', 'The first comer', 'Trooper Thompson's information', 'Who knew the truth?', 'La Carcassonne', 'Mrs. Ponsonby's dream', 'The door ajar'. Contains: 'Appendix one: Mrs. Croker' by Helen C. Black; 'Appendix two: Hindi (and Urdu) glossary'; Sources; Acknowledgements [JB; Wilson, p. 161].

CROKER, Mrs John. See **CROKER, Mrs Bithia Mary.**

CROKER, John Wilson, b. Galway (Waterford according to B & S, p. 194) 1780, d. Hampton (Middx.) (West Molesey in ODNB) 1857. Politician, critic, historian, satirist, poet and miscellaneous writer, JWC was the son of John Croker, who was later surveyor-general of Customs and Excise, and of Hester Rathbone, a clergyman's daughter. He attended Hood's school in Portarlington (Co. Laois) where he commanded the school Volunteer regiment, which had been founded in about 1780. JWC was admitted to TCD in 1796, where he graduated BA in 1800, later LLB, and LLD in 1808. He entered the Lincoln's Inn (London) in 1800, but did not finish his studies there. He was admitted to the King's Inns in 1802, but there is no record that he was ever called to the Irish Bar. Among his early publications is the controversial *Familiar epistles ... on the present state of the Irish stage* (Dublin, 1804). He was elected MP for Downpatrick (Co. Down) in 1807. The poem *The Amazoniad; or, figure and fashion* (Dublin, 1806) is ascribed to him and he later published poems on the battles of Talavera and Trafalgar that were well-received. *A sketch of the state of Ireland past and present* (Dublin, 1808) ran to 20 edns and was reprinted in 1884. Moving to London, JWC founded there the *Athenæum*, and co-founded and contributed to the *Quarterly Review*. As a reviewer, he sometimes savagely treated other authors' works, for example, criticizing those of Lady Morgan§, Charles Robert Maturin§, and Thomas Macaulay, who loathed him 'more than cold boiled veal' (RIA/DIB) and said of JWC that he was 'the most inaccurate writer that ever lived ... a scandal to literature and to politics' (DNB). His main employment was as secretary of the Admiralty from 1809 to 1830. John Gamble§, who met him in 1818 at the election for TCD, described him as 'a good-looking young man ... One of the attributes he certainly has, which is irritability, and like the porcupine, he shoots his fretful quills on all who venture to assail him' (Gamble, pp 74, 81). JWC originated the scheme to build Nelson's Pillar in Dublin and helped to acquire the Elgin marbles for the British Museum. For his portraits and papers, see ODNB. He married Rosamond Pennell in 1806 and they had one son, who died when he was age 3.

JWC is buried at West Molesey (Surrey). The characters of 'The Secretary' in John Banim's§ *The Anglo-Irish* (London, 1828) and Counsellor Con Crawley in Lady Morgan's§ *Florence Macarthy* (London, 1818) are based on JWC. SOURCE Allibone, i, p. 452; Boase, i, p. 764; DLB, cx; DNB; Elmes, pp 50–1; *Dublin University Magazine*, 1842, pp 796–800; Field Day, i, pp 1170–1; Galway, pp 28–31; J. Gamble, *Views of society and manners in the North of Ireland in a series of letters written in the year 1818* (London, 1819), pp 74, 81; Hogan 2, pp 296–7; NCBEL 4, p. 2121; Newmann, p. 52; B & S, p. 194; OCIL, pp 120–1; ODNB; O'Donoghue, p. 88; J.S. Powell, *Huguenot planters Portarlington* ([Portarlington, Co. Laois], 1964, 2nd edn), p. 89; Rafroidi, i, pp 21–3; RIA/DIB; Wolff, introd. to *The Boyne Water* (New York, 1979), i, p. xxxii.

C470 *An intercepted letter from J— T—, Esq. Writer at Canton, to his friend in Dublin, Ireland* [anon.].

+ Dublin: M.N. Mahon, 1804. SOURCE Rafroidi, ii, p. 116; Field Day, i, pp 1103–5. LOCATION D, L (6th edn, 1805), NUC, InND Loeber coll.

COMMENTARY A 42pp satire in prose in the tradition of Montaigne's *Lettres Persanes* (1721). Reviewed in *Ireland's Mirror* (Dublin, Jan. 1805, pp 38–42), it contains discussions on public affairs, on the theatre, etc., in Dublin (after the Act of Union), which is called Quang-Tcheu. The satire gave rise to a response by one J.T., who wrote *A short letter from Quang-Tcheu* (Dublin, 1805), also reviewed in *Ireland's Mirror* (Feb. 1805, pp 95–6) [RL; Blackwell cat. B120/342; Field Day, i, pp 1103–5; Rafroidi].

C471 *Stories selected from the history of England, from the conquest to the revolution. For children* (by John Wilson Croker).

+ London: John Murray, 1817 (new edn). SOURCE OCLC. LOCATION CLU.

London: John Murray, 1828, 9th edn (corrected). SOURCE OCLC. LOCATION PpiU.

Hartford (CT): H. Huntington Jnr, 1825 (ill.). SOURCE OCLC. LOCATION CtY.

COMMENTARY No copy located of the 1st edn. The volume stayed in print until at least 1908. Contents: 'Robert of Normandy', 'Red William', 'The shipwreck', 'Stephen', 'Fair Rosamond', 'Coeur de Lion', 'Arthur', 'Edward's escape', 'The conquest of Wales', 'Edward of Carnarvon', 'The siege of Calais', 'Wat Tyler', 'Madcap Harry', 'The crown', 'The generous robber', 'The death of Clarence', 'Jane Shore', 'The murder in the Tower', 'Perkin Warbeck', 'King Henry and his six wives', 'Jane Grey', 'Bloody Mary', 'The ring', 'The gunpowder plot', 'King Charles's martyrdom', 'The royal oak', 'The escape' [RL].

CROKER, Marianne (Mrs Thomas Crofton Croker, née Nicholson), b. 1791 or 1792, d. England? 1854. Novelist and artist, MC was the daughter of the English water-colour artist Francis Nicholson. She married Thomas Crofton Croker§ in 1830 and was a substantial collaborator in his work, while much of her own writing has been mis-attributed to him. However, in a memoir of TCC written by his son, he assigned the following two books to his mother and states that they were published under her husband's name at her desire. MC is known to have exhibited two Scottish landscapes in 1815 and she illustrated a number of her husband's works. Some of her correspondence is in the NLI (MS 15,726). SOURCE Boase, i, p. 766; Brown, 425; D. & M. Coakley, *Wit and wine* (Peterhead, 1975), pp 23–31; T.F. Dillon Croker, *Fairy legends and traditions of the south of Ireland* (London, [c.1862]), p. xix; Crookshank, p. 95; ODNB [under Thomas Crofton Croker].

C472 *The adventures of Barney Mahoney* (by T. Crofton Croker§ [*sic*]).

London: Fisher, Son & Jackson, 1832. SOURCE Rafroidi, ii, p. 120 (n.d. edn); Brown, 425; Garside 2, 1832:21; NSTC; Sadleir, 659; Bradshaw, 5626. LOCATION Corvey CME 3–628–47356–X (1832, 2nd edn), Grail, Ireland related fiction, L (1832, 2nd edn), E (not located), NUC.

COMMENTARY Although published as by Thomas Crofton Croker, it was written by his wife. Republished in the *Novelist's Magazine* (London, 1833, vol. 1). Story about the escapades of a comic Irish servant who tries to make his way honestly or, if necessary, dishonestly [Brown; Garside; NUC].

C473 *My village, versus 'our village.'* (by the author of *Barney Mahoney*).
+ London: H. Fisher, R. Fisher & P. Jackson, 1833. SOURCE Rafroidi, ii, p. 120; Wolff, 1628; Bradshaw, 5627 (the last two sources wrongly attribute it to Thomas Crofton Croker§); Garside 2, 1833:19. LOCATION Corvey CME 3-628-48176-7, Dt, L, C, DCL, InND Loeber coll.

COMMENTARY Also reprinted as part of *Carey's Library of Choice Literature* (Philadelphia, 1836, vol. 2). It contrasts Mary Russell Mitford's§ series, *Our village* (London, 1824–32, 5 vols.), which contains an idyllic description of village life, with a village where neighbourly feelings are absent. The village is situated not far from London and contains several boarding-houses for the use of patients of a well-known quack. The inhabitants love to gossip and tell ill of each other. The arrival of a woman who opens yet another boarding-house leads to particularly ill feelings [ML; RL].

CROKER, T.C. See **CROKER, Thomas Crofton**.

CROKER, Thomas Crofton (also known as T.C. Croker), b. Cork 1798, d. Old Brompton (Middx.) 1854. An early Irish folklorist, TCC was the son of Maj. Thomas Croker of the 39th Infantry, who was descended from a family that came to Ireland in the seventeenth century. He received limited education and at age 15 was apprenticed to a local merchant. He spent his spare time travelling in the south of Ireland, where he collected songs, poetry and legends. Around 1818 he forwarded some of these to Thomas Moore§, who invited him to England. With the help of John Wilson Croker§ (no relation) he became a clerk in the Admiralty in London in 1818 and served there until his retirement in 1850. He visited Ireland in 1820, 1821 and 1825 to collect stories. In England he helped to found the Camden Society, the Percy Society, and the British Archaeological Association. TCC's contribution to the earliest printed popularization of Irish peasant stories (particularly superstitions and folk-beliefs) is beyond doubt. However, he is often wrongly credited with writing all the stories in *Fairy legends and traditions of the South of Ireland* (London, 1825), many of which were actually authored by his friends and acquaintances (see details below). S.C. Hall, who knew him well, said 'he was a small man – small in mind as well in body; doing many little things, but none of them well: his literary fame rests on his 'Irish Fairy Legends' – a book of which he was only the editor. Most of the stories – and those the best – were written ... [by others]' (S.C. Hall, p. 17). His unfounded authorship of this work was reinforced by later edns of the stories which were then attributed to him. In addition, TCC published under his own name the literary work of his wife, the artist Marianne Nicholson Croker§, although according to his son this was at her request. Gerald Griffin§ was reported horrified to learn that the *Literary Gazette* (London) compared his work with that of Croker. Sir Walter Scott's impression of him was more favourable and described him as 'little as a dwarf, keen-eyed as a hawk, and of easy, prepossessing manner' (DNB). TCC featured in Edward Kenealy's§ *Brallaghan, or the Deipnosophists* (London, 1845). TCC edited several historical works, wrote some poetry (e.g., *Daniel O'Rourk; or, rhymes of a pantomime founded on that story* [London, 1828]), and wrote several other works including *Researches in the South of Ireland* (London, 1824) based on a number of walking tours between 1812 and 1822. This is a compilation of descriptions of places, local and national history, fairy lore and folk customs, as well as discussions of national character and literature. He also edited the *Christmas box: An annual present for young persons* (London, 1829), and

Popular songs of Ireland (London, 1839). He contributed several pieces to the periodical *Captain Rock in London* (London, 1828). He published *Landscape illustrations of Moore's "Irish Melodies"* (London, 1835, part 1, all published), and had plans to publish 'The story of Moore's Irish Melodies' in 1854, but he died in that year. He liked to draw and etch and he contributed sketches to Mr and Mrs S.C. Hall's§ *Ireland, its scenery and character* (London, 1841–43, 3 vols.) and to some of his own books. TCC was befriended by Richard Alfred Millikin§, whose widow gave him Milliken's papers after her husband's death. A description of the contents of TCC's house, Rosamond's Bower, Fulham, was printed in 1843 and its library and contents were auctioned in London in 1854. He left a manuscript, 'Recollections of Cork', 2 vols., now in TCD (Ms 1206), and one on Henry Perronet Briggs and Thomas Foster (NGI). His letters are in the NLI; Cork City library (6 vols.); the Bodleian Library, Oxford; the Henry E. Huntington Library, San Marino (CA); Clements Library, University of Michigan (Ann Arbor, MI), and other repositories. For his portraits, see ODNB. SOURCE Allibone, i, p. 452; Bentley MS IU, microfilm in the University of Cambridge Library, Thomas Crofton Croker to Bentley, 3 Jan. 1854; Boase, i, p. 765; Boylan, p. 78; Brady, p. 48; *Catalogue ... books ... by ... Dr. J. Orr Kyle* (New York, 1924), i, pp 15, 18 (collection of TCC's letters), 35; D. & M. Coakley, *Wit and wine* (Peterhead, 1975), pp 135, 144; Elmes, p. 51; Field Day, iv, p. 1433; H. Giles, *Lectures and essays* (New York, 1869), p. 251; S.C. Hall, p. 17; Hogan 2, pp 297–8; N.C. Hultin & W.U. Ober, 'An O'Connellite in Whitehall: Thomas Crofton Croker, 1798–1854' in *Éire-Ireland*, 28(3) (1993), pp 61–86; Irish pseudonyms; W. Laffan & B. Rooney, '"One of our brilliant ornaments": the death and life of Thomas Foster' in *Irish Architectural and Decorative Studies*, 7 (2004), pp 184–231; J. Leerssen, *Remembrance and imagination* (Cork, 1996), pp 160–1; List of catalogues, p. 267; B.G. MacCarthy, 'Thomas Crofton Croker, 1798–1854', *Studies*, 32 (1943), pp 539–56; McKenna, pp 126–8; R. Ormond, *Daniel Maclise, 1806–1870* ([London], 1972), p. 23; J. Martineau (ed.), *Victorian fairy painting* (London, 1998), p. 27; OCIL, p. 121; ODNB; O'Donoghue, pp 88–9; RIA/DIB; Schulz, p. 264; Scott (correspondence with Sir Walter Scott); Thuente 1, pp 48–51, passim; Wolff, i, p. 319; Zimmermann, p. 174–5.

C474   **Fairy legends and traditions of the South of Ireland** [part 1] [anon.; but compiled by Thomas Crofton Croker] (dedicated to Lady Chatterton§, Castle Mahon [Co. Cork]).
+ London: John Murray, 1825 (ill. W.H. Brooke). LOCATION Grail, L, NUC, InND Loeber coll.
+ London: John Murray, 1826, 2nd edn, [part 1] (new introd., with letter by Sir Walter Scott; ill. W.H. Brooke, Daniel Maclise). LOCATION InND Loeber coll.
Leipzig: Friedrich Fleischur, 1826 (trans. by the brothers Grimm as *Irische Elfenmärchen*). SOURCE NSTC. LOCATION L. COMMENTARY *Leipzig edn* Also mentioned as *Mährchen und sagen aus Süd-Irland* in the preface to London, 1826 edn [RL].
Philadelphia: H.C. Carey & I. Lea, 1827. SOURCE Kaser, 62. LOCATION NUC, ViU.

COMMENTARY The first collection of oral legends ever assembled in the British Isles. The preface to the first London edn states that 'The following Tales are written in the style in which they are generally related by those who believe in them; and it is the object of the Compiler to illustrate, by their means, the Superstitions of the Irish Peasantry ...' However, not mentioned is that most of the stories were written by TCC's friends and acquaintances: William Maginn§, Joseph Humphreys (a Quaker), [John?] Pigot,[7] Thomas Keightley, Charles Dodd,

---

7 Possibly John Pigott, son of the chief baron, who was one of the writers for the *Nation* (J. Maher (ed.), *The valley near Slievenamon. A Kickham anthology* (Kilkenny, [1941], p. 185). 8 According to Sir William Wilde§, this story was first published in a periodical, *Dundee Repository* (*Irish popular superstitions* (Dublin, [1852]), p. 28n.

S.C. Hall, and two to four others. TCC functioned as 'only the editor' and may have written a few of the stories. Thomas Keightley also contributed 'a very large proportion of the Notes' (Keightley, p. 180). Contents arranged in sections: The shefro: 'The legend of Knockshegowna' [by William Maginn§], 'The legend of Knockfierna', 'The legend of Knockgrafton' [William Maginn§], 'The priest's supper', 'The young piper' [Thomas Keightley], 'The brewery of egg-shells', 'The changeling', 'Capture of Bridget Purcell', 'The two gossips', 'The legend of Bottle-Hill' [William Maginn§], 'The confessions of Tom Bourke', 'Fairies or no fairies'. The cluri-caune: 'The haunted cellar', 'Seeing is believing' [Thomas Keightley], 'Master and man', 'The field of boliauns' [Thomas Keightley], 'The little shoe'. The banshee: 'The Bunworth ban-shee', 'The MacCarthy banshee'. The phooka: 'The spirit horse', 'Daniel O'Rourke'[8] [William Maginn§], 'The crookened back', 'The haunted castle'. Thierna na oge: 'Fior Usga', 'The leg-end of Lough Gur', 'The enchanted lake', 'The legend of O'Donoghue' [RL; S.C. Hall, p. 17; Thuente 1, p. 49, 86–7; Zimmermann, pp 149, 180; T. Keightley, *Tales and popular fic-tions* (London, 1834), pp 179–80].

C475   *Fairy legends and traditions of the South of Ireland, Part II* [anon.] (compiled by Thomas Crofton Croker; dedicated to Sir Walter Scott).
+ London: John Murray, 1828 (ill. W.H. Brooke). LOCATION Grail, L, NUC, InND Loeber coll.
Philadelphia: Carey & Lea, 1829. SOURCE Kaser, 156.

COMMENTARY No copy of the Philadelphia edn located. TCC stated in the preface to the London edn that two of the stories came from the manuscript collection of legends of a Mr Lynch (probably R. Adolphus Lynch), who supplied stories for *Legends of the lakes* (London, 1829, 2 vols.), which TCC also edited and arranged in sections. In addition, the volume con-tains unacknowledged stories by Thomas Keightley, who also contributed 'a very large pro-portion of the Notes' (Keightley, p. 180). Contents: The merrow: 'The Lady of Gollerus', 'Flory Cantillon's funeral', 'The soul cages' [Thomas Keightley], 'The Lord of Dunkerron', 'The wonderful tune'. The dullahan: 'The good woman', 'Hanlon's mill', 'The harvest din-ner' [Thomas Keightley], 'The death coach', 'The headless horseman'. The fir-darrig: 'Diarmud Bawn, the piper' [Mr Lynch], 'Teigue of the Lee', 'Ned Sheehy's excuse', 'The lucky guest'. Treasure legends: 'Dreaming Tim Jarvis', 'Rent-day' [Mr Lynch], 'Scath-a-legaune' [Thomas Keightley], 'Linn-na-payshtha'. Rocks and stones: 'Legend of Cairn Thierna', 'The rock of the Candle', 'Clough-na-Cuddy' (first published in the *Literary Souvenir* (London), 1827), 'Barry of Cairn Thierna' [Thomas Keightley], 'The Giant's Stairs' [RL; Thuente 1, p. 86–7; T. Keightley, *Tales and popular fictions* (London, 1834), pp 179–80].

C476   *Fairy legends and traditions of the South of Ireland, Part III* (compiled by Thomas Crofton Croker).
+ London: John Murray, 1828, part 3 (dedicated to Dr Wilhelm Grimm; with addi-tional notes by the brothers Grimm on part 1; ill. W.H. Brooke, Sir R.C. Hoare, G.O. Delamotte). SOURCE Rafroidi, ii, p. 118; Brown, 424; Sadleir, 660; Bradshaw, 5623. LOCATION Grail, L, C, NUC, InND Loeber coll.

COMMENTARY Contents: Translation of the Brothers Grimm's essay, and Irish short stories pub-lished in sections. The elves in Ireland: 'The good people', 'The cluricaune', 'The banshee', 'The phooka', 'The land of youth'. The elves of Scotland: 'Descent', 'Form', 'Dwelling and mode of life', 'Intercourse with men', 'Skill', 'Good neighbours', 'Spiteful tricks', 'Changelings', 'Elf-bolt, weapons, and utensils', 'The elf-bull', 'Sea elves', 'The brownie'. On the nature of elves: 'Name', 'Degree and varieties', 'Extinction', 'Form', 'Dress', 'Habitation', 'Language', 'Food', 'Mode of life', 'Secret powers and ingenuity', 'Character', 'Connexion with mankind', 'Hostile disposition', 'Ancient testimonies', 'Elfin animals', 'Witches and sorceresses'. Additions to the authorities, from the manuscript communication of Dr Wilhelm Grimm, from Holland,

Finnland [*sic*], Livonia, Armenia, Africa, Lower Bretagne, Miscellaneous. The Mabinogion and fairy legends of Wales. The mabinogion: 'Pwyll, prince of Dyved', 'Sketch of the tale of Bran'. Mythological persons: 'Arianrod', 'Cawr', 'Don', 'Gwydion', 'Gwenidw', 'Gwidhan and Gwidhaes', 'Gwrach', 'Gwyn ap Nudd', 'Idris or Edris', 'Moll Walbee'. Fairy legends of Wales: 'The story of Gitto Bach', 'Llewellyn's dance', 'The egg-shell dinner', 'Stories of Morgan Rhys Harris', 'Fairy money', 'The knockers'. The Pwcca: 'Cwm Pwcca', 'Yanto's chase', 'The adventure of Elidurus', 'Stories of fairies'. Legends of Lakes: 'Llyn Cwm Llwch', 'Meddygon Myddvai', 'The island of the fair family', 'The headless lady', 'Owen Lawgoch's castle', 'Cwn Annwn; or the dogs of hell' 'The corpse-candle', 'Story of Polly Shone Rhys Shone', 'The kyhirraeth'. Additional notes on Irish legends in the first vol. [RL].

C477   *Legends of the lakes; or, sayings and doings at Killarney collected chiefly from the manuscripts of R. Adolphus Lynch, Esq. H.P. King's German Legion* (compiled by Thomas Crofton Croker; dedicated to Miss [Maria] Edgeworth§).

    + London: John Ebers & Co., 1829, 2 vols. (ill. W.H. Brooke). SOURCE Rafroidi, ii, p. 119; McKenna, p. 127; Brown, 411; Bradshaw, 5625; British Fiction; Garside: 1829:29. LOCATION Grail, Corvey CME 3–628–51008–2, Ireland related fiction, Dt, L, C, MH, InND Loeber coll.

    London: Fisher, Son & Jackson, 1831 (as *Killarney legends, arranged as a guide to the lakes*). SOURCE Brown, 423. LOCATION L. COMMENTARY The London, 1831 edn is an abbreviated edn [RL].

    + London: William Tegg & Co.; New York: Scribner, Welford & Armstrong, 1875 (new edn, as *Killarney legends*, revised by T. Wright, with introd. by T.F. Dillon Croker, dedicated to his aunt, Mrs Eyre Coote, Queenstown, Co. Cork; ill. L & E. Byrne, Alfred Nicholson, Mrs [Thomas] Crofton Croker§). LOCATION L ([1876] edn), NUC ([1875] edn), InND Loeber coll.

COMMENTARY Original title was *Legends of the lakes; or, sayings and doings at Killarney: being an apology for a guide-book*, which is a more accurate description of the work. Consists of a series of folk tales interwoven with a travel account about the lakes of Killarney. Contains a topographical index and pictorial and musical illustrations [Rafroidi; ML; *Killarney legends* (London. 1875), p. [xvi]].

C478   *Fairy legends and traditions of the South of Ireland* [parts 1 and 2] (compiled by Thomas Crofton Croker, dedicated to the Dowager Lady Chatterton§).

    + London: John Murray, 1834 (ill. Mr [William H.] Brooke, Mr M'Clise [Maclise], and Thomas Crofton Croker; Family Library, No. 47). SOURCE Osborne, pp 25–6; Gilbert, p. 178 (1838, 2nd edn). LOCATION DPL (1838, 2nd edn), CaOTP, InND Loeber coll.

    COMMENTARY *London 1834 edn* Condensed and revised edn of parts 1 and 2, containing 40 tales instead of 50; appended letter by Sir Walter Scott [RL; Osborne].

    + London: William Tegg, [*c.*1862] (new edn; ed. by Thomas Wright, with a memoir of the author by his son Thomas F. Dillon Croker). SOURCE McKenna, p. 126. LOCATION Grail, InND Loeber coll. COMMENTARY *London [c.1862] edn* This edn has additional stories: 'Capture of Brigid Purcell', 'The turf cutters', 'Cormac and Mary' [RL].

    + Philadelphia: Lea & Blanchard, 1844 (new edn; ill. William H. Brooke, Daniel M'Clise [Maclise], Thomas Crofton Croker). LOCATION InND Loeber coll.

    Doughcloyne, Wilton, Cork: Collins Press, 1998 (introd. by Francesca Diano). LOCATION InND.

    COMMENTARY A reissue of parts 1 and 2 of the *Fairy legends and traditions of the South of Ireland*, first published in London in 1825 and 1828, respectively.

CROLLY, Fr William, pseuds **'A retired priest'** and **'A Catholic priest'**, b. Ballykilbeg (Co. Down) 1780, d. Drogheda (Co. Louth) 1849. Catholic clergyman and writer, WC was the son of John Crolly, a tenant farmer, and Mary Maxwell. He was educated at St Patrick's College, Maynooth, where he was ordained and where he later held the professorship of logics, ethics and metaphysics for six years. In 1812 he was appointed parish priest of Belfast, where he was on close terms with local Presbyterians who contributed generously to the building of a second Catholic church in Belfast in 1815. In 1825 WC was consecrated bishop of Down and Connor, and in 1835 archbishop of Armagh. He differed from his episcopal colleagues in their support for the repeal of the Act of Union, their opposition to the new system of national education and the Charitable Bequests Act, and to the establishment of the Queen's Colleges. This exposed him to the charge of being a 'Castle Catholic' (i.e., a Catholic who aligned himself closely with British rule in Ireland). He was one of the few identifiable Irish Catholic tract writers, seeking, however modestly, to counter the heavy output of Protestant tract literature. He also wrote *The life and death of Oliver Plunkett, Primate of Ireland* (Dublin, 1850) and a serial, 'Reminiscences of the Irish mission', which appeared in *Duffy's Irish Catholic Magazine* (Dublin, 1847–48). He was elected as council member of the newly founded Celtic Society in 1845. He laid the foundation stone for St Patrick's Cathedral in Armagh. In the course of Famine relief, he died of cholera, and was buried in St Patrick's Cathedral, where there is a memorial statue. For his portraits and correspondence, see ODNB. SOURCE Brown, pp 75, 339 (who mistakenly mentions his first name as George); A. Macaulay, *William Crolly, archbishop of Armagh, 1835–1849* (Blackrock, Co. Dublin, 1994); Newmann, p. 52; ODNB; J. O'Donovan (ed.), *The book of rights* (Dublin, 1847), n.p. (list of officers); RIA/DIB.

C479   *The favourite child; or, Mary Anne O'Halloran* (by 'A retired priest').
    Dublin: James Duffy, 1851. SOURCE Brown, 426. LOCATION L.
    + Dublin, London: James Duffy & Sons, 1880, 4th edn (as *The favourite child; or, Mary Anne O'Halloran. An Irish tale* (by 'a Catholic priest'). LOCATION PC.
COMMENTARY 78pp for the Dublin 1880 edn. Catholic religious fiction. A spoiled child turns out badly but learns from her sufferings and becomes a Sister of Charity [Brown; RL].

CROLY, Revd George, b. Dublin 1780, d. London 1860. Church of Ireland clergyman, poet, journalist and man of letters, GC was the son of Robert Croly, a pharmacist, and came from a family he described as 'a living type of the Protestant and Orange party'. He was admitted to TCD in 1795 where he obtained his BA in 1800 and his MA in 1804, when he was ordained. He moved to London in 1810 and eventually was appointed rector of St Benet and St Stephen in Walbrook, where he was a celebrated preacher. In addition, he became a prolific writer, producing sermons, poetry, plays, novels (including one Gothic novel), and short stories. His play, *Pride shall have a fall* ([London], [1824]) had a successful run in 1824. For a time he was the *Times* theatre critic and a foreign correspondent. He wrote biography and fiction but he was always proudest of his poetry, which was inspired by Lord Byron and Thomas Moore§ and was praised by John Wilson Croker§ for blending what was 'splendid in imagination' with 'what is right in politics'. From 1839 to 1846 he wrote the leading articles for the weekly *Britannia* newspaper (location not clear), many stories for *Blackwood's Magazine* (Edinburgh) and the *Literary Gazette* (London), and contributed to *Forget-Me-Not* (London, 1826–7). He was thought to have contributed to *Bentley's Miscellany* (London), but this appears incorrect. In all his writings he energetically espoused Toryism and protestantism, but he published mostly anonymously so as not to jeopardize his ecclesiastical appointments. Henry Crabbe Robinson described him in 1813 as a 'fierce-looking Irishman, very lively in conversation … his eloquence, like his person, is rather energetic than elegant …' (Sadler, i, p. 264). He was awarded an honorary DD by TCD in 1831. He probably can be identified with Revd George Croly who wrote the historical descriptions to *The Holy Land ... from drawings made by Daniel Roberts* (London, 1842). For his portraits and correspondence, see ODNB. SOURCE Allibone, i, pp 452–3; B & S, p. 194; Boase, i, p. 766; Brady, p. 48; Curran index, BentM 1245ff; British Fiction (Update 4, under 1828); DLB, clix; Elmes, p. 51; S.C. Hall, pp 232–3; D.C. Hanson, 'George Croly' in J.R. Greenfield (ed.), *British short-fiction writers, 1800–1880* (Detroit, 1996), pp 69–83 (includes bibliography); Hogan 2, pp 298–9; NCBEL 4, pp 326–7; OCIL, p. 121; ODNB; O'Donoghue, p. 89; RIA/DIB; RL; T. Sadler, *Diary ... of Henry Crabbe Robinson* (Boston, 1870), i, p. 264; Sutherland, p. 162; Wolff, i, pp 319–20.

C480   *Tales of the great St. Bernard* [anon.].

> + London: Henry Colburn, 1828, 3 vols. SOURCE British Fiction; Garside, 1828:33; Sadleir, 662; Wolff, 1634. LOCATION Corvey CME 3–628–581149–6 (1829, 2nd edn), D, Dt, L (1829, 2nd edn), O, NUC, InND Loeber coll.

> + New York: J. & J. Harper, 1829, 2 vols. SOURCE NCBEL 4, p. 326. LOCATION NUC, InND Loeber coll.

COMMENTARY Serialized in *Waldie's Select Circulating Library* (Philadelphia, 1836). Contents: 'The squire's tale', 'The Wallachian's tale', 'The captain's tale', 'The Augustine's tale', 'The Englishman's tale', The Spaniard's tale', 'The Italian's tale' [ML].

C481   *Salathiel. A story of the past, the present and the future* [anon.] (dedicated to the duke of Newcastle).

> + London: Henry Colburn, 1828, 3 vols. SOURCE British Fiction; Garside, 1828:32; Sadleir, 661; Wolff, 1633. LOCATION Corvey CME 3–628–48505–3, Dt (1828, 2nd edn), NUC, InND Loeber coll.

> London: Henry Colburn, 1829, 3 vols. (new edn). SOURCE Rafroidi, ii, p. 122. LOCATION L.

> London: Hurst & Blackett, 1855 (new rev. edn). SOURCE NCBEL 4, p. 326; Topp 1, p. 99; COPAC. LOCATION L.

> Paris: Mame & Delaunay-Vallée, 1828, 3 vols. (trans. by J. Cohen as *Salathile ou le juif errant, histoire*). SOURCE Rafroidi, ii, p. 361; Bn-Opale plus. LOCATION BNF.

> New York: G. & C. Carvill; Philadelphia: Carey, Lea & Carey, 1828, 2 vols. SOURCE Topp 1, pp 99–100. LOCATION NUC.

> + Philadelphia: J. van Court, 1843 (ill. Spittall). LOCATION NUC, InND Loeber coll.

> Philadelphia: T.B. Peterson, 1848. SOURCE NYPL. LOCATION NN, NUC (1849 edn).

> + Cincinnati: J.A. & U.P. James, 1842, 2 vols. in 1. LOCATION NUC, InND Loeber coll. (1850 edn).

COMMENTARY Gothic tale on the theme of the medieval tale of Salathiel, the 'Wandering Jew', condemned by Jesus not to die until Jesus returns. The story starts on the morning after the crucifixion and traces the wanderings of Salathiel up to the Jewish rebellion and the destruction of the Temple by Titus in AD 70. Numerous narrow escapes and violent incidents follow as Salathiel becomes an avid patriot in the struggle to eliminate Roman rule. Contains dungeon episodes, shipwrecks, tortures, and a fantasy of premature burial. Taking part in the Jewish war of liberation, he hopes to redeem himself and to be able to die, but the curse remains. At the fall of the Temple walls he finds himself a man age 33 once more, condemning him again to wander [Frank, 77; Tracy, 19].

C482   *Marston; or, the memoirs of a statesman* (by George Croly).

> Philadelphia: Lea & Blanchard, 1845. LOCATION NUC.

> + London: Henry Colburn, 1846, 3 vols. (as *Marston: or, the soldier and statesman*). SOURCE Rafroidi, ii, p. 122; Wolff, 1631; Sadleir, 3494 (1860, 3rd edn). LOCATION Dt, D, L, NUC.

COMMENTARY First published in *Blackwood's Magazine* (Edinburgh). Set in the French Revolution, the narrative is autobiographical in form [Sutherland].

'CROM A BOO', pseud. See **BODKIN, Matthias McDonnell**.

CROMIE, Robert, b. Clough (Co. Down) 1856, d. 1907. A journalist, novelist and science fiction writer, RC was educated at the Royal Belfast Academical Institution and he worked in Belfast on the staff of the *Northern Whig*. SOURCE Brown, p. 76; EF, p. 84.

C483 *For England's sake* (by Robert Cromie).
London, New York: Frederick Warne & Co., 1889, 8th thousand. LOCATION L.
COMMENTARY Story on the struggle between Russia and England [RC's preface to *The next crusade* (London, 1896)].

C484 *A plunge into space* (by Robert Cromie).
London, New York: Frederick Warner & Co., 1890. LOCATION L, NUC.
London, New York: Frederick Warner & Co., 1891, 2nd edn (preface by Jules Verne§). LOCATION NUC.
Westport (CT): Hyperion, 1976 (Classics of Science Fiction). SOURCE COPAC. LOCATION Univ. of Liverpool.
COMMENTARY Interplanetary novel. A group of scientific adventurers journey to Mars in a steel globe which they have succeeded in insulating from earth's gravity. The Martian civilization that they discover is utopian but in decline. On the return trip a stowaway Martian girl overloads the spaceship's life support and each crew member must bring some essential skill to ensuring the ship's safe return to earth [Rowan cat. 62/101].

C485 *The crack of doom* (by Robert Cromie).
+ London: Digby, Long & Co., 1895. SOURCE Rowan cat. 37, part A/432. LOCATION D (1895, 3rd edn), DPL, L, NUC.
COMMENTARY Science fiction novel of a wicked scientist plotting to blow up the world [Rowan cat. 37].

C486 *The next crusade* (by Robert Cromie).
+ London: Hutchinson & Co., 1896. LOCATION D, L, NUC, InND Loeber coll. (1896, 2nd edn).
COMMENTARY In the preface the author stated, 'I make no apology for taking upon myself to write the history of the future. This method has already many students; and certainly some advantages over the writing of the history of the past. It can hardly be so full of error'. Set in England and the eastern Mediterranean. Describes war between Austria, Russia and Turkey. Two Englishmen join a cavalry regiment and are shipped out to the aid of Austria. The book describes terrible battles, culminating in the heroic behaviour of one of the Englishmen in saving the life of his friend [ML].

C487 *The King's oak and other stories* (by Robert Cromie).
+ London: Geo. Newnes; Belfast: R. Aickin & Co., [1897]. LOCATION D, L, InND Loeber coll.
COMMENTARY Contents: 'The King's oak', 'Mr. Markham's private secretary', 'Castle Slander', 'The Rev. Alexander M'Intosh', 'The moated grange' [ML].

C488 *The lost liner* (by Robert Cromie; dedicated to J.G.).
+ London: Geo. Newnes; Belfast: R. Aickin & Co., [1898]. LOCATION D, L ([1899] edn), InND Loeber coll.
COMMENTARY A liner leaving San Francisco bound for Australia founders. George Drury, a second cabin passenger, and Margery Bute, a saloon passenger, land on a deserted island. They survive on fish and the ship's stores. When they are finally rescued it seems that they will go

their own ways because of the difference in their social status. However, Margery does not want to lose George and so they marry [ML].

C489   *Kitty's Victoria Cross* (by Robert Cromie).
London, New York: Frederick Warne & Co., 1901. SOURCE Brown, 430. LOCATION L, NUC.

COMMENTARY Set at Woodbine Cottage, Innisboffin, Kitty O'Neill meets two English officers, Peterson and Linton. She falls in love with Peterson. At an eviction, Peterson orders his men to fire on the people. He goes away and leaves Kitty broken-hearted. When Kitty finds out from a newspaper that Peterson has died, she consoles herself with Linton, who has won a Victoria Cross [Brown].

C490   *The shadow of the cross* (by Robert Cromie).
London, New York, Melbourne: Ward, Lock & Co., 1902 (ill. Gordon Browne). SOURCE Brown, 431. LOCATION L.

COMMENTARY A romance set against a background of Ulster Presbyterian life that ends in the death of a young minister [Brown].

C491   *A new Messiah. A novel* (by Robert Cromie).
London: Digby, Long & Co., 1902. LOCATION L.

C492   *The romance of poisons, being weird episodes from life* (by Robert Cromie and S. Wilson).
+London: Jarrold & Sons, 1903. LOCATION D, L.

COMMENTARY Detective stories. The hero is Surgeon-Col. John Headford, late of the Indian medical service, who is good at detecting little-known poisons [EF, p. 84].

C493   *El Dorado* (by Robert Cromie).
+ London, New York, Melbourne: Ward, Lock & Co., 1904 (ill. Victor Prout). LOCATION D, L.

C494   *From the cliffs of Croghaun* (by Robert Cromie).
Akron (OH), New York: Saalfield, [1904] (ill. Victor Prout). LOCATION NUC.

CROMMELIN, Maria Henrietta de la Cherois (known as **May Crommelin**), b. Carrowdore Castle, Donaghadee (Co. Down) *c.*1850, d. England? 1930. Novelist, poet and travel writer, MHC was the daughter of Samuel de la Cherois-Crommelin, who descended from Louis Crommelin, the Huguenot founder of the Ulster linen industry, and Anna-Maria Thompson. She spent most of her early life in Ireland where she was largely educated at home by foreign governesses. The family moved to Devon during the Land War (started 1879) and her sister died there in 1881. After her father's death in 1885, she moved to London and earned her living by writing. As an adult she travelled widely in far-flung parts of the world and wrote travel books, such as *Over the Andes from the Argentine to Chili and Peru* (London, 1896). She was an early woman member of the Royal Geographical Society. In addition, she also wrote one volume of poems. Ireland is the main setting for her fiction, of which we have identified 46 titles. Financially her work was not very successful, however, and she applied twice for assistance from the Royal Literary Fund. Among the Bentley MSS there are several letters by her to the editor of the *Temple Bar* (London) concerning the publication of her second novel (not named) in that magazine. SOURCE Allibone Suppl., i, p. 416; Alston, p. 103; Bentley MS IU, microfilm in the University of Cambridge Library; Blain, pp 249–50; Brady, p. 48; Brown, p. 76; EF, p. 84; Hogan 2, pp 299–300; OCIL, p. 121–2; RIA/DIB; Sutherland, p. 162; Wolff, i, pp 320–1.

C495   *Queenie. A novel* [anon.].
London: Hurst & Blackett, 1874, 3 vols. SOURCE Wolff, 1641. LOCATION L, NUC.

C496   *My love, she's but a lassie* [anon.].

London: Hurst & Blackett, 1875, 3 vols. SOURCE Wolff, 1640. LOCATION L, InND Loeber coll. (Routledge, [1877 edn]).

COMMENTARY Set in England. A young girl, Mabel, is looked after by her cruel stepmother who has married her father only for his money. A soldier, Wat Huntley, falls in love with Mabel. The stepmother and her associates are initially able to prevent the romance from blossoming. However, in the end her evil schemes fail and after some adventures the lovers are reunited [ML].

C497　*A jewel of a girl* [anon.].
London: Hurst & Blackett, 1877, 3 vols. SOURCE Wolff, 1637. LOCATION L.
New York: Harper, 1878. LOCATION NUC.
COMMENTARY Set in Ireland and Holland [Brown, p. 76].

C498　*Orange Lily, and other stories* [anon.].
London: Hurst & Blackett, 1879, 2 vols. SOURCE Brown, 432. LOCATION L.
+ London, New York: George Routledge & Sons, 1880 (as *Orange Lily*; on half-title: *Orange lily and other tales*). SOURCE Topp 1, p. 314. LOCATION D, L, InND Loeber coll.
New York: Harper & Bros, 1879 (as *Orange Lily. A novel*; Franklin Square Library, No. 60). SOURCE Topp 1, p. 314. LOCATION NUC.
COMMENTARY Contents of the London edn: 'Orange Lily' (set in Co. Down), 'Lisa: the lily of Vaucourt', 'The witch of windy hill' (set in the north of Ireland), 'An old maid's marriage' (set in the north of Ireland), 'Notes on Nice' [ML].

C499　*Black abbey* (by May Crommelin).
London: Sampson Low, Marston, Searle & Rivington, 1880, 3 vols. SOURCE Topp 1, p. 325; Brown, 433. LOCATION L.
COMMENTARY Describes the life of three children of Black Abbey (Co. Down) and their German governess, an Irish nurse, and their playmate Bella, born in America but the granddaughter of the old Presbyterian minister. Life does not always run smoothly when they grow up, but circumstances seem to be righting themselves at the end of the story [Brown].

C500　*Miss Daisy Dimity* [anon.].
London: Hurst & Blackett, 1881, 3 vols. SOURCE Alston, p. 103. LOCATION L, NUC.

C501　*Brown-eyes* [anon.].
+ London: Arrowsmith, 1882 (Christmas Annual; ill. W.C.R. Browne). SOURCE Alston, p. 103. LOCATION L, InND Loeber coll.
's Hertogenbosch: G.W. van Belle, 1885 (trans. into Dutch as *Angela de vondeling*). SOURCE Mes, p. 157.
COMMENTARY The story of Angel, who is stolen from her home along the Thames in revenge against her father by a woman whose marriage he had thwarted. After a shipwreck, Angel ends up in the island of Marken in the Netherlands. While Angel is growing up there, her father never gives up his search for her. An English painter discovers her and falls in love with her. She is reunited with her father and marries the painter [ML].

C502　*My book of friends. Pen and ink portraits by themselves* (by May Crommelin).
London, New York: George Routledge & Sons, 1883. LOCATION L.

C503　*In the West countrie* (by May Crommelin).
London: Hurst & Blackett, 1883, 3 vols. SOURCE Topp 1, p. 358; Alston, p. 103. LOCATION L, NUC.
New York: Harper & Bros, 1884 (Franklin Square Library, No. 380). SOURCE Topp 1, p. 358. LOCATION NUC.

C504　*Joy or the light of cold-home ford* (by May Crommelin).
+ London: Hurst & Blackett, 1884, 3 vols. SOURCE Wolff, 1638. LOCATION L, InND Loeber coll.

New York: Harper & Bros, [1884] (Franklin Square Library, No. 406). SOURCE Topp 1, p. 366. LOCATION NUC.

COMMENTARY The story of two sisters, Magdalen and Rachel, who live as recluses on the Devonshire moors, to which they had fled after Magdalen is mistreated by her husband. Magdalen is at times mentally disturbed and the locals treat the sisters as witches. Magdalen's daughter, Joy, is being brought up by a servant, Hannah, and they live elsewhere. Eventually, Hannah and Joy move closer but Magdalen does not want much contact with her daughter. Joy marries her childhood friend, the son of an honest farmer, although her mother would have liked to see her be married into the gentry. Magdalen and Rachel die within a few days of each other [ML].

C505   *Goblin gold* (by May Crommelin).

+ London, New York: Frederick Warne & Co., [1885] (ill.; London Library, No. 8: on spine: Warne's Birthday Library). SOURCE Alston, p. 103; Topp 4, p. 177. LOCATION L, InND Loeber coll.

New York: Harper & Bros, 1885 (Handy Series, No. 36). SOURCE Topp 4, p. 177. LOCATION NUC.

New York: George Munro, [1885] (Seaside Library Pocket Edition, No. 647). SOURCE Topp 4, p. 177.

COMMENTARY Set in England. Two cousins live with their grandfather. By telling false stories, one of them ensures that the grandfather disinherits the other. However, in the end the true character of the deceiving cousin comes to light and he loses all he had inherited [ML].

C506   *Love, the pilgrim* (by May Crommelin).

London: Hurst & Blackett, 1886, 3 vols. SOURCE Alston, p. 103. LOCATION L.

C507   *Dead men's dollars* (by May Crommelin).

Bristol: J.W. Arrowsmith, [1887]. SOURCE Alston, p. 103; Topp 8, 53. LOCATION L.

C508   *The freaks of Lady Fortune* (by May Crommelin).

London: Hurst & Blackett, 1889, 2 vols. SOURCE Alston, p. 103. LOCATION L.

New York: J.W. Lovell, [1891]. LOCATION NUC.

C509   *Violet Vyvian, M.F.H.* (by May Crommelin and J[ames] Moray Brown).

+ London: Hurst & Blackett, 1889, 3 vols. SOURCE Topp 7, 169; BL cat. LOCATION L, NUC.

New York: J.W. Lovell, [1890] (International Series, No. 91). SOURCE Topp 7, 169. LOCATION NUC.

C510   *Midge* (by May Crommelin).

London: Trischler & Co., 1890, 3rd thousand. SOURCE Alston, p. 103. LOCATION L.

C511   *Cross-roads* (by May Crommelin).

London: Hurst & Blackett, 1890, 3 vols. SOURCE Weekes, p. 84. LOCATION L.

London, Sydney: Eden, Remington & Co., 1892 (as *Love knots; or, cross-roads*). SOURCE McCarthy, ii, p. 751. LOCATION L.

C512   *For the sake of the family* (by May Crommelin).

New York: J.D. Lovell, [c.1891]. SOURCE Daims, 720. LOCATION L, NUC.

London, Sydney: Eden, Remington, 1892. SOURCE Daims, 720. LOCATION L.

C513   *Mr. and Mrs. Herries* (by May Crommelin).

London: Hutchinson & Co., 1892. SOURCE Alston, p. 103. LOCATION L.

C514   *Bay Ronald* (by May Crommelin).

London: Hurst & Blackett, 1893, 3 vols. SOURCE Alston, p. 103. LOCATION D (1899 edn), L, NUC.

C515   *Dust before the wind. A novel* (by May Crommelin).

London: Bliss, Sands & Foster, 1894, 2 vols. SOURCE Daims, 719. LOCATION L, NUC.

C516 *Half round the world for a husband. A comedy of errors* (by May Crommelin; dedicated to the Hon. Francis and Mrs Pakenham).
+ London: T. Fisher Unwin, 1896. SOURCE Alston, p. 103. LOCATION D, L.
Chicago, New York: [publisher?], 1898. LOCATION NUC.

C517 void

C518 *'Divil-may-care'; alias Richard Burke, sometime adjutant of the Black Northerns* (by May Crommelin; dedicated to 'all Ulster friends').
+ London: F.V. White & Co., 1899. SOURCE Brown, 434. LOCATION D, L.
COMMENTARY The adventures of an officer home from India on sick leave. Most of these humorous episodes are located in Co. Antrim [Brown].

C519 *Kinsah, a daughter of Tangier* (by May Crommelin; dedicated to Lady Nicholson).
+ London: John Long, 1899 (ill. Tauber). SOURCE Daims, 723. LOCATION D (1899, 3rd edn), L.

C520 *Bettina* (by May Crommelin; dedicated to A.B.).
+ London: John Long, 1900. SOURCE Alston, p. 103. LOCATION D, L.

C521 *The luck of a lowland laddie* (by May Crommelin).
London: John Long, 1900. SOURCE Alston, p. 103. LOCATION L.
New York: F.M. Buckles & Co., [1900]. LOCATION NUC.

C522 *The Vereker family* (by May Crommelin).
London: Digby, Long & Co., 1900. SOURCE Alston, p. 103. LOCATION L, NUC.
COMMENTARY Set in Louisana [Burmester list].

C523 *A woman-derelict* (by May Crommelin).
+ London: John Long, [1901]. SOURCE McCarthy, ii, p. 751. LOCATION D, L.
COMMENTARY The heroine has amnesia. When she recovers she finds out that her husband has remarried. She nurses a madwoman, who eventually murders her [EF, p. 84].

C524 *A daughter of England* (by May Crommelin).
London: John Long, [1902]. LOCATION L.

C525 *Her faithful knight, a novel* (by May Crommelin).
New York: A.L. Burt, [1902] (The Manhattan Library of New Copyright Fiction).
LOCATION NUC, NN.

C526 *Partners three* (by May Crommelin).
London: John Long, 1903. LOCATION L.

C527 *Crimson lilies* (by May Crommelin).
London: John Long, 1903 (ill.). SOURCE Daims, 718. LOCATION D (n.d. edn), L.

C528 *One pretty maid, and others* (by May Crommelin).
London: John Long, 1904. LOCATION L.

C529 *The white lady* (by May Crommelin).
London: John Long, 1905. SOURCE Wolff, 1642. LOCATION L.

C530 *Phoebe of the white farm* (by May Crommelin).
London: John Long, 1906. LOCATION L.

C531 *The house of Howe* (by May Crommelin).
London: John Long, 1907. SOURCE Daims, 721. LOCATION L.

C532 *'I little knew—!'* (by May Crommelin).
London: John Milne [1908]. SOURCE Daims, 722. LOCATION L.

C533 *Madame Mystery. A romance in Touraine* (by May Crommelin).
+ London: Hutchinson & Co., 1910. LOCATION D, L.
Boston: D. Estes & Co., [1912]. LOCATION NUC.

C534   *Lovers on the green* (by May Crommelin).
        London: Hutchinson & Co., 1910. LOCATION L.

C535   *The isle of the dead* (by May Crommelin with A. Williams).
        + London: Hutchinson & Co., 1911. LOCATION D, L.

C536   *The golden bow* (by May Crommelin).
        London: Holden & Hardingham, 1912. SOURCE Brown, 435. LOCATION L.
        COMMENTARY Set in the north of Ireland. The story of how a poor, proud and pretty
        Irish girl grows up from an unhappy childhood to a happy engagement [Brown].

C537   *Pink lotus. A comedy in Kashmir* (by May Crommelin).
        London: Hurst & Blackett, 1914. LOCATION L.

C538   *Little soldiers* (by May Crommelin).
        London: Hutchinson & Co., [1916] (ill. Louis Wain). LOCATION L.

C539   *Sunshine on the Nile. A novel* (by May Crommelin).
        London: Jarrold, [1920]. LOCATION L.

C540   *Aunt Angel* (by May Crommelin).
        + London: Odhams Press, [1921]. LOCATION D, L.

C541   *Halfpenny house* (by May Crommelin).
        London: Hurst & Blackett, [1924]. LOCATION L.

CROMMELIN, May. See **CROMMELIN, Maria Henrietta de la Cherois.**

CROTTIE, Miss Julia M., b. Lismore (Co. Waterford) 1853, d. 1930. A novelist, short
story writer and chronicler of small town life, JMC was educated privately and at the
Presentation convent in Lismore. She moved from Ramsay (Isle of Man) to Chicago, in which
city she gained some newspaper experience and completed her novel *The lost land* (London,
1901). She returned to Ireland in 1890, but two years later she was looking for work in
London. She appears to have stayed in Waterford, contributing stories to the provincial press
and to Irish and American periodicals, including the *Catholic World* (New York). Financial
problems plagued her. Some of her letters are among the Downey Papers in the NLI (MS
10,005). She is buried in Lismore. SOURCE Brown, p. 77; E. Reilly, pp 218, 243; OCIL, p.
123; O'Toole, pp 49–50; RIA/DIB.

C542   *Neighbours: being annals of a dull town* (by Miss Julia M. Crotty).
        + London: T. Fisher Unwin, 1900. SOURCE Brown, 441. LOCATION D (1901, 2nd edn),
        DPL, L, NUC, InND Loeber coll.
        + Manchester (NH): The Magnificat Press, 1920 (as *Innisdoyle neighbours*). LOCATION
        D.
        COMMENTARY A series of stories about the fictional town of Innisdoyle (but actually, Lismore?).
        Contents: 'Gubinet', 'Rose Ellen's matchmaking', 'Miss Dunne's monument', 'Turned back',
        'A blast', 'Neighbourly talk', 'Miss Etty on the train', 'Moribound', 'The Sunday-boy', 'A
        sudden seizure', 'The town in danger', 'A burying', 'A little stratagem', 'A harvest evening',
        'The Terror's sheep', 'A Danish uprising', 'The delicate tinker', 'A tale of the "Big wind"',
        'A claim on France', 'Brothers of the soul' [ML].

C543   *The lost land. A tale of a Cromwellian-Irish town: being the autobiography of Miss
        Anita Lombard, 1780–1797* (by Miss Julia M. Crotty).
        + London: T. Fisher Unwin, 1901. SOURCE Brown, 442; Nield, p. 414. LOCATION RB,
        L, NUC.
        COMMENTARY Historical fiction. A gloomy fictional autobiography of Miss Anita Lombard,
        depicting an Irish town in Munster in the last part of the eighteenth century. It tells of the
        failure of the United Irishmen to inspire the people and satirizes various forms of Anglicized

catholicism. The noble Thad Lombard sacrifices all he has for Ireland, anticipating the ideals of the later Gaelic League [Brown; Nield; E. Reilly, pp 224–5].

CROW, Mrs L. See **CROW, Mrs Louisa A.**

CROW, Mrs Louisa A. (also known as **Mrs L. Crow**), fl. 1870s, d. 1895. Prolific English novelist, LC wrote many works for Dick's English Novels. Only one Irish work has been identified so far. SOURCE Allibone Suppl., i, p. 424; Boase, iv, p. 815.

C544 *The rose and shamrock. A domestic story* (by Mrs L. Crow).
London: Dick's English Novels, No. 11, [*c*.1876]. SOURCE Brown, 443 (1882 edn); Wolff, 1651.
COMMENTARY No copy located. Set in Co. Galway in the 1850s, with Ireland viewed by Anglicized upper-class people living on a small estate [Brown; RL].

CROWE, Eyre Evans, b. Redbridge, near Southampton (Hants.) 1798 (not in 1799 as in many sources), d. London, 1868. English novelist, journalist and historian, EEC was the son of David Crowe, captain of an East India regiment, and Miss Hayman of Walmer (Kent). OCIL, however, says he was born 'of Irish parents'. He descended from Revd William Crowe, Church of Ireland dean of Clonfert, who married Emilia, daughter of Eyre Evans of Portrane (Co. Dublin). EEC's parents died by the time he was age 10, after which he was reared by two aunts in Dublin. He was educated at a school in Carlow and was admitted at TCD in 1812, but at age 16 he left for London where he spent some years contributing prose and poetry to periodicals. In the early 1820s he went to Italy and contributed letters on his travels to *Blackwood's Magazine* (Edinburgh). He married Margaret Archer of Kiltimon (Newtownmountkennedy, according to Crowe, both in Co. Wicklow) at St Patrick's Cathedral, Dublin, in 1823. The couple settled in London but soon moved to Boulogne-sur-Mer in France and eventually settled in Paris, where he worked as a journalist. During the family's residence in France, they toured France, Switzerland and Germany. Among their occasional guests were Thomas Moore§ and Thomas Colley Grattan§. All of EEC's novels and short stories but one were written in the 1820s and 1830s and are set in Italy, France, England and Ireland. He wrote the first of the four-volume *Lives of the most eminent foreign statesmen* (London, 1832 onwards; later volumes by G.P.R. James). Between 1830 and 1844 he was the Paris correspondent of the London *Morning Chronicle* and returned to England to become a staff member on the paper. He moved to the new *Daily News* (founded by Charles Dickens) in 1843 and served as its editor from 1849 to 1851. In this period he also contributed to *Household Words* (London, 1852–3) and *Bentley's Miscellany* (London, 1852–4), and travelled to Belgium, Prussia, Austria and Italy. After a trip to the Levant he published *The Greek and the Turk* in 1853. He also contributed articles on foreign affairs to the *Examiner* (London?). He wrote a substantial five-volume history of France as well as a study of the reigns of Louis XVIII and Charles X (1858). In 1832, while living in Dublin, he was in needy circumstances, not finding a publisher for the novel he was then working on. With the help of Thomas Crofton Croker§, he applied to the Royal Literary Fund, from which he subsequently received £40. One of his sons was the artist Eyre Crowe, ARA, who was for a time secretary to William Makepeace Thackeray§, while another son, Joseph, became a journalist and diplomat. The following list of EEC's publications contains only those works with some Irish content. SOURCE Allibone, i, p. 455; BL, M1077, reel 23, No. 730; B & S, p. 198; Boase, i, p. 775; Brady, p. 49; J. Burke, *A ... history of the commoners* (London, 1835), i, pp 594–5; Sir J. Crowe, *Reminiscences of thirty-five years of my life* (London, 1895), passim; Curran index, BentM 2142ff; Garside, 1825:23; S.C. Hall, p. 240; Hogan 2, pp 304–5; Irish pseudonyms; W. Laffan & B. Rooney, '"One of our brilliant ornaments": the death and life of Thomas Foster' in *Irish*

Architectural and Decorative Studies, 7 (2004), pp 199–200, 228*n*.46; Lohrli, p. 244; NUC; OCIL, pp 124–5; ODNB; O'Donoghue, p. 90; Wolff, i, pp 323–4.

C545 **The English in Italy** [anon.].

> + London: Saunders & Otley, 1825, 3 vols. SOURCE British Fiction; Garside, 1825:23; Wolff 1655. LOCATION Corvey CME 3–628–47830–8, L, MH, InND Loeber coll.

COMMENTARY Authorship is variously ascribed to EEC or to Constantine Henry Phipps, marquess of Normanby, but Garside, ODNB and Wolff favour EEC. Contents: 'L'Amoroso', 'Il politico' (concerns an Irish peer, Lord Tara, travelling on the Continent; mentions Richard Lovell Edgeworth's§ educational experiments); a series of sketches, entitled 'I zingari', 'The boy connoisseur', 'Change of air', 'The forum', 'The British capuchin', 'The Vatican', 'The Gograms', 'Boyhood abroad', 'Cicisbeism', 'Extortion', 'The aristocracy of travel', 'Torlonia', 'The renegade converted', 'Roman sporting', 'The eruption', 'Mispatriotism', 'The yeomanry at congress', 'St. Mark's'; 'Sbarbuto', ' Il critico' (epistolary novella) [RL; Garside; OCIL, p. 125; ODNB; Wolff, i, p. 323; British Fiction (Update 2)].

C546 **To-day in Ireland** [anon.].

> + London: Charles Knight, 1825, 3 vols. SOURCE Brown, 444; Rafroidi, ii, p. 123; Wolff, 1658;
> Garside, 1825:24. LOCATION Corvey CME 3–628–48962–8, Ireland related fiction, Dt, DPL, L, NUC, InND Loeber coll.
> London: Henry Colburn & R. Bentley; Edinburgh: Bell & Bradfute; Dublin: John Cumming, 1834, 3 vols. (Colburn's Irish National Tales Nos. 17–19). SOURCE Sadleir 3736c(ii); Rowan cat. 45/330; OCLC. LOCATION ICU.
> Paris: Gosselin, 1830, 3 vols. ('The carders' trans. by A.J.B. Defauconpret as *Les cardeurs, ou patriotisme et vengeance*). SOURCE Rafroidi, ii, p. 362.
> Paris: Gosselin, 1830, 3 vols. ('Connemara' trans. by A.J.B. Defauconpret as *Le Connemara, ou une élection en Irlande*). SOURCE Rafroidi, ii, p. 362.

COMMENTARY Neither Paris edn located. Reviewed in the *Dublin and London Magazine* (London, 1825), pp 177–85. Stories set in Ireland. Contents: 'The carders' (set in the village of Rathfinnan, near Athlone, and concerns the dire consequences for a young man who accidentally joins a secret society), 'Connemara' (about an election in Co. Galway), 'Old and new light' (set at Ardenmore; concerns the tension between the established church and the evangelicals), 'The Toole's warning' (the fate of the Tooles of Co. Wicklow) [ML].

C547 **Yesterday in Ireland** [anon.] (dedicated to the marquis of Lansdowne).

> + London: Henry Colburn, 1829, 3 vols. SOURCE Rafroidi, ii, p. 123; Brown, 446; British Fiction; Garside, 1829:30; Wolff, 1660. LOCATION Corvey CME 3–628–48986–5, Ireland related fiction, D, Dt, DPL, L, NUC.
> London: Henry Colburn & R. Bentley; Edinburgh: Bell & Bradfute; Dublin: John Cumming, 1834, 3 vols. (Colburn's Irish National Tales Nos. 4–6). SOURCE Sadleir 3736c(ii); Rowan cat. 45/330; OCLC. LOCATION CtY.
> + New York: J. & J. Harper, 1829, 2 vols. LOCATION NUC.
> + New York, London: Garland, 1979, 3 vols. (introd. by R.L. Wolff). SOURCE COPAC. LOCATION Dt, InND Loeber coll.

COMMENTARY Contents: 'Corramahon' (set in Carlow in 1714 in the time of the penal laws, and features rapparees), 'The Northerns of 1798' (set in Co. Antrim and Ulster during the rebellion) [Wolff introd., p. 15; Hogan, p. 305].

CROWLEY, Mary Catherine, fl. 1889, b. Boston (MA). American poet and writer of children's books, MCC came from a well-known Catholic family. She wrote for the Boston *Pilot*, *Catholic World* and *Freeman's Journal* (both New York), *Irish Monthly* (Dublin) and other publications. She is best known for her stories for children. SOURCE Irish pseudonyms; O'Donoghue, p. 81; NUC.

C548   *Merry hearts and true. Stories from life* (by Mary Catherine Crowley).
+ New York, Montreal: D. & J. Sadlier & Co., 1889. SOURCE DCU, Catholic Americana files; OCLC. LOCATION DCL, NUC.
COMMENTARY Children's stories with some Irish characters in mostly American settings. Contents: 'Little beginnings', 'Potato', 'The blind apple-woman', 'Pollie's five dollars', 'Marie's triumph', 'A family frolic' [RL].

CRUMPE, Miss —. See CRUMPE, Miss Mary Grace Susan.

CRUMPE, Miss Mary Grace Susan (also known as **Miss Crumpe**; Garside gives her initials as M.G.T.), fl. 1823. Novelist, daughter of Dr Samuel Crumpe, RIA (1766–96), a noted Limerick physician who wrote on opium and on how to find employment for the people of Ireland, and his wife Susan Ingram. MGSC initially lived in Limerick (from where she dated the introd. to her *Isabel St. Albe* (Edinburgh, 1823) 24 Feb. 1823) and later in Dublin, where in 1826 she met Thomas Moore§, who became her friend. When she dedicated her *Geraldine of Desmond* (London, 1829) to him she was living in Welbeck Street, Cavendish Square, London. Maria Edgeworth§ reluctantly visited her and her mother in London in 1831 and found MGSC 'a very handsome too magnificently dressed lady! ... who talked and talked ... on admiration of me and of herself' (Colvin, p. 533). MGSC wrote mostly historical fiction set in Ireland. A few letters between her and Maria Edgeworth are in the NLI (MS 18,479), and some of her correspondence with Sir Walter Scott is in the NLS. She was among the subscribers to Catherine Luby's *The spirit of the lakes, or Muckross Abbey* (London, 1822). The BLC equates 'E.C.A.' (Eleanor C. Agnew§) with MGSC, but this is in error. SOURCE Alston, pp 1, 105; Colvin, pp 529, 533–4; Lord J. Russell (ed.), *Memoirs, journal, and correspondence of Thomas Moore* (London, 1854), v, pp 34, 36; ODNB (see Dr Samuel Crumpe); O'Toole, p. 50; Scott (correspondence with Sir Walter Scott); Wolff, i, p. 326.

C549   *Isabel St. Albe: or, vice or virtue. A novel* (by Miss Crumpe; dedicated to Sir Walter Scott).
+ Edinburgh: Archibald Constable & Co.; London: Hurst, Robinson & Co.; Dublin: John Cumming, 1823, 3 vols. SOURCE Block, p. 50; British Fiction; Garside, 1823:30. LOCATION Corvey CME 3–28–47354–3, L (3 vols. in 1), NUC.
COMMENTARY A society novel partly set in Ireland [RL].

C550   *Geraldine of Desmond; or, Ireland in the reign of Elizabeth. An historical romance* [anon.] (dedicated to Thomas Moore§).
+ London: Henry Colburn, 1829, 3 vols. SOURCE Rafroidi, ii, p. 124; Brown, 447; British Fiction; Garside, 1829:31; Wolff, 1670. LOCATION Corvey CME 3–628–47749–2, Ireland related fiction, D, Dt, L, NUC.
COMMENTARY Historical fiction. Misattributed in the *Irish Shield* ([New York], 1829), i, p. 269) to Lady Morgan§. Mentions Maria Edgeworth§ in its preface. Relates the story of the Desmond rebellion and describes the battle of Monasternenagh, Co. Limerick, and the massacre of Smerwick (Co. Kerry). The chief historical figures of the time are featured, such as the Desmonds and Ormonds, Fr Allen, SJ, Sanders, Sir Henry Sidney, Sir William Drury, Dr John Dee, the alchemist and astrologer, and Queen Elizabeth I. Historical notes are appended to each volume Maria Edgeworth§ thought the book 'of great pretensions' [Brown; Colvin, p. 529].

C551   *The death-flag; or, the Irish buccaneers* [anon.].
London: William Shoberl, 1851, 3 vols. SOURCE Brown, 448 (1852 edn); Wolff, 1669. LOCATION L (1852 edn), NUC (1852 edn).

COMMENTARY No copy of the first edn located. Historical fiction set between 1748 and 1788 in Ireland, France, England and Italy. The story deals with the O'Sullivans of Berehaven – the Irish buccaneers – and their ship, the *Death Flag*. Jacobite activities form the main plot. A love story between Lord Ogilvy, a Jacobite, and Eva O'Sullivan is interwoven [Brown].

'CUI BONO', fl. 1870s. Pseudonym of a Cork story writer, who signed the preface to the following work, Cork, 4 Feb. 1877. May possibly be identified with Revd Henry Cotton (1789–1879), Church of Ireland archdeacon of Cashel and treasurer of Christ Church cathedral, Dublin, who used this pseudonym in his *A letter to Right Hon. E.G. Stanley* (Dublin, 1833). SOURCE Leslie & Wallace, pp 508–9; RL.

C552   *St. Luke's; Montenotte; Tivoli; and Glanmire. A conversation* (by 'Cui Bono').
    + [Cork]: [privately published], [1877] (see Plate 27). LOCATION InND Loeber coll.
COMMENTARY 27pp. Consists of a short story about a man from Cork who takes an evening walk in the city's vicinity with an Italian visitor. While walking, they talk about art, libraries, Catholic education, and compare the landscape to some Italian places [ML].

CULLEN, Stephen, fl. 1794. Historical novelist, classified as an Irish author in the TCD catalogue. SC specialized in Gothic fiction. Among the Irish living in Bath in 1779 were a Mr and Mrs Cullen, but it is unclear whether this is the author. SOURCE Allibone, i, p. 458; M. Busteed, 'Identity and economy ...' in *Jrnl of Historical Geography*, xxvi (2000), p. 185.

C553   *The haunted priory: or, the fortunes of the house of Rayo. A romance, founded partly on historical facts* [anon.].
    + London: J. Bell, 1794. SOURCE Raven 2, 1794:20; Forster 2, 950; ESTC n017266. LOCATION L, PU.
    Dublin: William Jones, 1794. SOURCE Raven 2, 1794:20; Block, p. 50; ESTC t071311. LOCATION D, Dt, NUC.
    New York: Mathew Carey, 1794. SOURCE ESTC w012587. LOCATION NUC.
COMMENTARY Gothic tale set in fourteenth-century Spain. Contains supernatural horrors but also unusual poetic effects and descriptions. The central episode consists of Alfonso making a dangerous journey to avenge the death of his father. He leaves the Castilian court of Don Isidor de Haro to keep his appointment at the haunted priory of Rayo. Left behind by the young knight is the old Baron de Rayo who has come to Castile seeking his missing son. The two men are related but this is not revealed until the end of the story within the tomb of Alfonso's father, Gonsalvo [Frank, 86; ML; Tracy, 28].

C554   *The castle of Inchvally: A tale—alas! too true* (by Stephen Cullen).
    + London: J. Bell, 1796, 3 vols. (ill.). SOURCE Brown 2, 324; Forster 2, 949; Raven 2, 1796:34; ESTC t120483. LOCATION L, NUC.
COMMENTARY Gothic fiction set in the south-west of Ireland at a castle built in the time of Henry II. Explains the term 'discoverer' of titles for lands and refers to Protestants seeking to get possession of the castle, which is inhabited by Catholics. Cullen built this romance around a demonic laugh, which reverberates through the corridors of Inchvally Castle and freezes its victims. The book has footnotes to explain Irish customs to the English reader [ML; Frank, 87].

CUNINGHAME, Richard, b. Co. Donegal? *c.*1832? Novelist, RC was from Ulster and also wrote an historical work, *The broken sword of Ulster* (Dublin, 1904). He probably can be identified with Richard Cunninghame, of Portrush (Co. Antrim), who was the son of Dr Hugh Cunninghame (also spelled Cunningham), of Castlecooly, Burt (Co. Donegal), who in his early life was stationed at St Helena and was present at some interviews with Napoleon when he was imprisoned there. RC, was admitted to TCD at age 18 in 1851. RC's son was Revd Hugh Harvey Cunninghame. SOURCE B & S, Appendix B, p. 29; Brown, p. 79; Brown 2, p. 62; Fleming, *Armagh*, p. 131.

C555   *In bonds but fetterless* (by Richard Cuninghame).
> London: Samuel Tinsley, 1875, 2 vols. SOURCE Allibone Suppl., ii, p. 430; Brown 2, 330; COPAC. LOCATION L.

COMMENTARY Historical fiction set in Ulster in the time of Charles II. The novel's introd. mentions details of the plantation of the Scots in Ulster under King James I. The story opens in 1661 in a farmhouse of Scottish Presbyterians in Co. Down and deals mainly with relations between the Afton family of Ellerslie and survivors of the O'Neills, who still inhabit their ancient castle, some of whom have become Protestants. The book presents the reactions of the Ulster Presbyterians to the persecution started by the 'Prelatic Church' under Charles II. A conspiracy by the Covenant is begun by two dubious characters, Blood and Lecky, but Ulster Presbyterians hold aloof. Many personages of the day are introduced and the plot moves between Belfast ('Plekopolis') and Dublin [Brown 2].

CUNNINGHAME, Richard. See **CUNINGHAME, Richard.**

CURRAN, Henry Grattan, pseud. 'G.C.H.', b. Co. Tipperary 1800, d. Parsonstown (now Birr, Co. Offaly) 1876. Barrister, poet, translator and novelist, HGC was the natural son of John Philpot Curran of Rathfarnham Priory (Co. Dublin), master of the rolls in Ireland, and Marianne FitzGerald. He was educated at TCD in 1815, admitted to Gray's Inn (London) and the King's Inns in 1824. He was called to the Irish Bar in 1828. He translated poetry from Irish and is associated with the famous ballad, 'The wearing of the green', which he probably edited from a folk version. He was appointed RM for the Strokestown (Co. Roscommon) area in 1851 and in 1861 was transferred to Parsonstown. SOURCE B & S, p. 284; Boase, iv, p. 829; Brady, p. 50; B & S, p. 284 [under Fitzgerald]; Irish pseudonyms; Keane, p. 116; OCIL, p. 128; O'Donoghue, p. 93; RIA/DIB.

C556   *Confessions of a Whitefoot* (ed. by 'G.C.H.', Esq., barrister at law; dedicated to right hon. the earl of Devon, Sir Robert Alexander Hamilton, Bt, MP, George Alexander Hamilton, esq. MP, Thomas N. Redington, esq. MP, and John Wynne, esq., commissioners appointed to inquire into the state of the law, and practice respecting the occupation of land in Ireland).
> + London: Richard Bentley, 1844. SOURCE Rafroidi, ii, p. 125; Brown, 455, Block, p. 51; RIA/DIB. LOCATION L, NUC.

COMMENTARY A polemical novel designed to draw attention to aspects of the land system by showing how the narrator – who begins as a supporter of law and order – becomes entangled with the secret society of the Whitefeet, even though they often break the law, because of the injustices he endures on the part of self-interested landowners and corrupt magistrates [Brown; RIA/DIB].

CURTIN, Jeremiah, b. Detroit (MI) (Milwaukee [WI] according to Brown and DAB) 1838, d. Vermont 1906. American folklorist, ethnologist, linguist and diplomat, JC was the son of Irish parents David Curtin and Ellen Furlong who had emigrated from Thomond (in the west of Ireland) and who raised him on a farm in Milwaukee. A graduate of Harvard (1863), he was multilingual and went as a translator to Russia, later serving in the US government service in St Petersburg (Russia, 1864–70). He joined the staff of the Bureau of Ethnology of the Smithsonian Institution (1883–91) and became one of the best-known collectors of American Indian, Slavic, Mongol, British and Irish folk tales. He made frequent visits to Ireland where he collected stories in the Gaeltacht, the Irish-speaking areas of Ireland. SOURCE Boylan, p. 80; Brady, p. 50; Brown, p. 80; DAB; OCIL, p. 129; Zimmermann, pp 304–8.

C557 *Myths and folk-lore of Ireland* (by Jeremiah Curtin; dedicated to Maj. J.W. Powell, LLD of Harvard and Heidelberg).

+ Boston: Little, Brown & Co., 1890 (ill.). SOURCE Catholic Americana files; Quinn, 2263. LOCATION DCU, L, NUC, InND Loeber coll.

London: Sampson Low, Marston, Searle & Rivington, 1890. SOURCE Brown, 450; Fanning, p. 378. LOCATION L.

New York: Weathervane Books, [*c.*1975]. LOCATION InND.

COMMENTARY Tales of folklore collected from Gaelic speakers through an interpreter. Contents: 'The son of the king of Erin, and the giant of Loch Léin', 'The three daughters of King O'Hara', 'The weaver's son and the giant of the white hill', 'Fair, brown, and trembling', 'The king of Erin and the queen of the Lonesome Island', 'The Shee an Gannon and the Gruagach Gaire', 'The three daughters of the king of the East and the son of a king in Erin', 'The fisherman's son and the Gruagach of tricks', 'The thirteenth son of the king of Erin', 'Kil Arthur', 'Shaking-head', 'Birth of Fin MacCumhail and origin of the Fenians of Erin', 'Fin MacCumhail and the Fenians of Erin in the castle of Fear Dubh', 'Fin MacCumhail and the knight of the full axe', 'Gilla na Grakin and Fin MacCumhail', 'Fin MacCumhail, the seven brothers, and the king of France', 'Black, brown, and gray', 'Fin MacCumhail and the son of the king of Alba', 'Cucúlin', 'Oisin in Tir na n-Og' [RL; Brown].

C558 *Hero-tales of Ireland* (collected by Jeremiah Curtin; dedicated to the Rt Hon. John Morley, Secretary of State for Ireland).

Boston: Little, Brown & Co., 1894. LOCATION L, NUC.

+ London: Macmillan & Co., 1894. SOURCE Brown, 451. LOCATION L, NUC, InND Loeber coll.

COMMENTARY Contents: 'Elin Gow, the swordsmith from Erin, and the Cow Glas Gainach', 'Mor's sons and the herder from under the sea', 'Saudan Og and the daughter of the king of Spain', 'Young Conal and the Yellow king's daughter', 'The black thief and King Conal's three horses', 'The king's son from Erin, the Sprisawn, and the Dark king', 'The Amadan Mor and the Gruagach of the Castle of Gold', 'The king's son and the white-bearded Scolog', 'Dyeermud Ulta and the king in south Erin', 'Cud, Cad, and Micad, three sons of the king of Urhu', 'Cahal, son of King Conor, in Erin, and Bloom of Youth, daughter of the king of Hathony', 'Coldfeet and the queen of Lonesome Island', 'Lawn Dyarrig, son of the king of Erin, and the Knight of Terrible Valley', 'Balor on Tory Island', 'Balor of the Evil Eye and Lui Lavada, his grandson', 'Art, the king's son, and Balor Beimenach, two sons-in-law of king Under the Wave', 'Shawn MacBreogan and the king of the White Nation', 'The cotter's son and the half slim champion', 'Blaiman, son of Apple, in the kingdom of the White Strand', 'Fin MacCool and the daughter of the king of the white nation', 'Fin MacCool, the three giants, and the small men', 'Fin MacCool, Ceadach Og, and the fish-hag', 'Fin MacCool, Faolan, and the Mountain of Happiness', 'Fin MacCool, the hard Gilla, and the high king', 'The battle of Ventry' [RL].

C559 *Tales of the fairies and of the ghost world, collected from oral tradition in southwest Munster* (by Jeremiah Curtin; preface by Alfred Nutt).

Boston: Little, Brown & Co., 1895. LOCATION NUC.

+ London: David Nutt, 1895. SOURCE Brown, 452; Maggs cat. 1163/74. LOCATION L, NUC, InND Loeber coll.

COMMENTARY Contents: 'John Connors and the fairies', 'Fitzgerald and Daniel Donoghue', 'Fairies of Rahonain and Elizabeth Shea', 'The Knights of Kerry – Rahonain Castle', 'The cattle jobber of Awnascawil', 'The midwife of Listowel', 'Daniel Crowley and the ghosts',

'Tom Daly and the nut-eating ghost', 'Tom Connors and the dead girl', 'The farmer of Tralee and the fairy cows', 'The two gamblers and the fairies', 'The girl and the robber', 'Maurice Griffin and the fairy doctor', 'The three sisters and their husbands' three brothers', 'John Shea and the treasure', 'St. Martin's eve', 'James Murray and Saint Martin', 'Fairy cows', 'John Reardon and the sister ghosts', 'Maggie Doyle and the dead man', 'Pat Doyle and the ghost', 'The ghost of Sneem', 'The dead mother', 'Tim Sheehy sent back to this world to prove his innocence', 'Tom Moore and the seal woman', 'The four-leafed shamrock', 'John Cokeley and the fairy', 'Tom Foley's ghost', 'The blood-drawing ghost', 'Murderous ghosts' [RL].

C560   *Irish folk-tales* (by Jeremiah Curtin; edited and introd. by Seamus Ó Duilerga; ded-
        icated 'to the memory of the storytellers who told these tales').
        + Dublin: Educational Co. of Ireland, 1943. SOURCE de Búrca cat. 57/140; Brown 2,
        334 (1956 edn). LOCATION NUC, InND Loeber coll. (Talbot, 1944 edn; see Plate 28).
COMMENTARY Even though the 1944 edn states that it is the first edn, it was preceded by a
1943 edn. Contents: 'The son of the king of Erin and the queen of the moving wheel', 'The
bird of the golden land', 'The king's son in Erin and the king of the Green Island', 'The fisherman of Kinsale and the hag of the sea', 'The tinker of Ballingarry and his three wishes',
'Baranoir, son of a king of Erin, and the daughter of king Under the Wave', 'The share-smith
and the stranger', 'Gold Apple, son of the king of Erin', 'The widow's son, the devil, and the
fool', 'The three sons of the king of Antua', 'Sgiathán Dearg, and the daughter of the king of
the western world', 'Fáinne óir, daughter of the king of Erin, and the son of the king of Three
Seas', 'The high king of Lochlann, and the Fenians of Erin', 'Finn Mac Cumhaill and Conan
Maol in the house at the rock', 'Sál Fhada, the king's son and Finn Mac Cumhaill', 'Finn
Mac Cumhaill and Iolann Iolchrothach, son of the king of Spain' [RL].

CURTIS, Robert, b. Co. Offaly 1801, d. Dublin 1874. Novelist and detective story writer,
RC was the son of Robert Edward Curtis, sub-inspector of the RIC. RC was appointed 3rd
sub-inspector of the RIC in 1823 and county inspector in 1838. He was stationed in the north-
west of Ireland, probably including Co. Sligo. He contributed to the *Dublin University Magazine*
(1857), the *Dublin Lyceum*, and 'The reprieve: or the wild justice of revenge' and other stories (see below) to the *Dublin Saturday Magazine* (1865–7). He also published *The history of
the Royal Irish Constabulary* (Dublin, 1869). He married Eleanor, but the year of marriage is
not clear. He was buried in Deansgrange cemetery, Dublin. SOURCE Allibone Suppl., i, p. 435;
Brown, p. 80; R. Curtis, introd. to *Curiosities of detection* (London, 1862); W.E. Hall, p. 191;
J. Herlihy, p. 112; T.J. Morrissey, *Thomas A. Finlay SJ, 1848–1940* (Dublin, 2004), p. 43.

C561   *The Irish police officer. Comprising The identification, and other tales, founded
        upon remarkable trials in Ireland* (by Robert Curtis; dedicated to Sir Henry John
        Brownrigg).
        + London: Ward & Lock, 1861. SOURCE Topp 2, 277; Brown, 453; Sadleir, 3520.
        LOCATION DPL, L, NUC.
COMMENTARY Contents: 'The identification' (reprinted as a serial in the *Dublin Saturday
Magazine* in *c*.1865), 'The banker of Ballyfree', 'The reprieve', 'The two Mullanys' [*sic*,
Mulvanys], 'M'Cormack's grudge' (the last two reprints as serials in the *Dublin Saturday
Magazine*, *c*.1865) 'How the chief was robbed' [RL].

C562   *Curiosities of detection; or, the sea-coast station, and other tales* (by Robert Curtis;
        dedicated to E.J. Cooper of Markru Castle, Collooney [*sic*, Markree Castle, Co. Sligo]).
        + London: Ward & Lock, 1862. SOURCE Topp 2, 312; Brown 2, 337. LOCATION L,
        NUC, InND Loeber coll.
COMMENTARY Detective stories set on the north-west coast of Ireland narrated by an RIC officer.
Contents: 'The sea-coast station', 'James M'Grath; or, time's changes', 'The twin Joyces' [ML].

C563 *The trial of Captain Alcohol* (by Robert Curtis).
Dublin: Moffat & Co., 1868. SOURCE Brown, p. 80 (1871 edn). LOCATION L.
COMMENTARY 48pp. Temperance tale [RL].

C564 *Rory of the hills. An Irish tale* (by Robert Curtis).
+ Dublin, London: James Duffy, 1870. SOURCE Brown, 454. LOCATION D, L, InND
Loeber coll.
COMMENTARY Set in Co. Clare and purportedly based on fact. Two relatively well-to-do farm-
ers have farms adjoining each other. Kavana has a daughter, Winny, and Murdock has a son,
Thomas. The fathers plan to have their children marry so that the farms can be joined. Thomas,
although he does not care for Winny, likes the plan since he is short of money. Winny, however, does not trust Thomas and is in love with a poor labourer, Rory of the Hills. When
Thomas is refused by Winny, he vows revenge and has Winny abducted. When Rory comes to
the rescue, Thomas shoots him. Although there is no hope for Rory's recovery, he does not die
immediately and Winny insists on marrying him. After Rory's death, Winny and her father
move to a city in the north of Ireland where she spends her life working for the poor [ML].

CUSACK, Margaret Anne (Sr Mary Francis Clare, also 'The nun of Kenmare', also
known as Mary F. Cusack and M.F. Cusack), b. Dublin 1832, d. Leamington Spa (War.)
1899. Nun, prolific writer, poet and publisher, committed social worker and early feminist,
MAC was the daughter of Dr Samuel Cusack of Dublin and Sarah Stoney of Oakley Park
(Co. Offaly). Her parents separated in 1843 and MAC and her brother went to live with a
great-aunt in Exeter (Devon). MAC, raised a Protestant, joined the Plymouth Brethren, and
after the death of her fiancée entered an Anglican nunnery. But in 1858 she converted to
catholicism and in 1859 entered the religious order of the Poor Clares in Newry (Co. Down).
She moved to Kenmare (Co. Kerry) when her order established a convent there. There she
wrote and ran a publishing house, Kenmare Publications, in response to the need for educational texts on the history of catholicism in Ireland. She established a foundation to aid vulnerable young women and a famine relief fund to address food shortages in the 1870s. In her
A history of the kingdom of Kerry (London, 1871), she criticized absentee landlords, and particularly the Lansdowne family and its agents, who owned large holdings in Co. Kerry. Her
outside work caused disagreements with the convent community and she left Kenmare in 1881,
travelled to Rome, and returned to Ireland to open a convent and a vocational school for
women at Knock (Co. Mayo). Never on easy terms with the ecclesiastical hierarchy, her disagreements with the archbishop of Tuam increased to the point that her friend Cardinal
Manning advised her to go to England. She began the order of the St Joseph's of Peace Sisters
in 1884, but on the urging of the bishop of Nottingham she went to the US to open American
branches of the order and to organize guidance for emigrant Irish working girls. She opened
a home for working girls in Jersey City (NJ) in 1885. She did not receive the cooperation she
expected from the American clergy and, rejecting Rome and reverting to protestantism, she
returned to England where she lectured mainly to Protestant audiences about her experiences.
Her last conversion was to methodism. Her later writings are anti-Catholic and anti-clerical
in tone. She published over 50 books, including biographies of St Patrick, St Bridget, and St
Columba (London, [1877]), and of Daniel O'Connell. Her historical works included: *An illustrated history of Ireland* (Kenmare, 1868), in which she praised the Fenian movement as a
wholesome influence in Ireland's intellectual life; *A history of the city and county of Cork*
(Dublin, 1875), and *The present case of Ireland plainly stated* (New York, 1881). She wrote a
textbook: *The school history of Ireland* (London, 1871); a play; numerous pamphlets, and
Woman's work in modern society ([Kenmare], 1874). In 1889 she published her autobiography,
The nun of Kenmare ([London], 1889) and subsequently, *The story of my life* (London, 1891).

Several of her letters are in the Ardagh and Clonmacnoise Diocesan Archive (box marked Woodlock). For her portraits and correspondence, see ODNB. SOURCE Allibone Suppl., i, p. 436; Boase, iv, pp 833–4; Boylan, p. 80; Brady, p. 51; Brown, p. 31; Colman, pp 60–5; I.F. Eagar, *The nun of Kenmare* (Cork, 1970); Field Day, iv, pp 529–32, 536; Hogan 2, pp 312–14; IBL, 6 (1915), p. 134; J. Leerssen, *Remembrance and imagination* (Cork, Notre Dame [IN], 1997), pp 137, 144, 272n; LVP, p. 122; McKenna, pp 130–1; J.O'K. Murray, *The prose and poetry of Ireland* (New York), 1877), pp 709–16; Newmann, p. 55; OCIL, p. 130; ODNB; O'Donoghue, p. 94 [under Mary Frances Cusack (*sic*)]; O'Toole, pp 55–7; RIA/DIB.

C565 *Ned Rusheen; or, who fired the first shot?* [anon., but 'M.F. Cusack' on cover].

  + London: Burns & Oates; Dublin: Elwood; Boston: Patrick Donahoe; Melbourne, Australia: George Robertson, 1871. SOURCE Brown, 456. LOCATION Grail, D.

  Dublin: M.H. Gill & Son, [1880 or earlier] (as *Who fired the first shot? or, Ned Rusheen. An Irish story*). SOURCE Adv. in 'Eblana', *The last monarch of Tara* (Dublin, 1880). LOCATION L (1883 edn).

  Boston: P. Donahoe, 1871. SOURCE DCU, Catholic Americana files.

COMMENTARY No copy of the Dublin edn located. Religious fiction strongly Catholic in tone. A murder mystery in which the hero is wrongly accused but is acquitted when the real culprit confesses while dying [Brown].

C566 *Hornehurst rectory* (by Sr Mary Francis Clare).

  New York, Montreal: D. & J. Sadlier & Co., 1872, 2 vols. in 1. SOURCE DCU, Catholic Americana files. LOCATION NUC.

C567 *Tim O'Halloran's choice; or, from Killarney to New York* (by Mary F. Cusack; dedicated to the Committee of the Orphanage of Our Lady of Mount Carmel).

  + London: Burns & Co.; Dublin: M.H. Gill & Son; Melbourne, Australia: G. Robertson; New York: J.A. Magee; Paris: Fotheringham, 1877. SOURCE Brown, 457. LOCATION D, L.

  New York: D. O'Loughlin, [1877] (as *From Killarney to New York; or, how Thade became a banker*, by sister Mary Francis Clare). SOURCE Brown, 457; Catholic Americana files. LOCATION Grail, DCU, NUC.

COMMENTARY Anti-Protestant religious fiction, written specifically against the Protestant 'souper' proselytizers during the Famine in Co. Kerry. When Tim O'Halloran is dying, a priest and a souper are contending for the possession of his son. Tim stays faithful to the Catholic church, but after his death, the son is kidnapped by proselytizers. He escapes and finds shelter in a good Catholic family, after which a rich American takes him to New York [Brown].

C568 *His yarn, and another story (How Katie found Jesus)* (by M.F. Cusack).

  London: Marshall, Russell & Co.; Brighton: D.B. Friend & Co. [1897]. SOURCE Alston, p. 108. LOCATION L.

CUSACK, M.F. See **CUSACK, Margaret Anne**.

CUSACK, Mary F. See **CUSACK, Margaret Anne**.

CUTHBERTSON, Miss Catherine, fl. 1817. Gothic novelist, CC was English and is said to have been a sister of the poet and novelist Helen Craik. SOURCE Blain, p. 257; Frank, 97–100; NCBEL 4, p. 899 (list of novels).

C569 *Rosabella; or, a mother's marriage. A novel* [anon.].

  + London: Baldwin, Cradock & Joy 1817, 5 vols. SOURCE Summers, p. 40; British Fiction; Garside, 1817:20. LOCATION Corvey CME 3–628–48512, Ireland related fiction, L, NUC.

New York: James Eastburn & Co., 1818, 5 vols. in 3. LOCATION NUC.
COMMENTARY Irish content. The book starts with the plan to massacre the earl of Montalbert and all under his roof. This is prevented by McGuire, a faithful servant [ML].

CUTHELL, Edith E., fl. 1897. Children's book writer, EC contributed extensively to devotional periodicals for children. Her work deals a lot with India. SOURCE Allibone Suppl., i, p. 437; BLC; NCBEL 4, p. 1779 (list of works).
C570 *Sweet Irish eyes. A novel* (by Edith E. Cuthell).
    + London: Skeffington & Son, 1897. LOCATION D, L, NUC.
COMMENTARY Set in Scotland. Involves two girls who are of Irish extraction. One of them, Honor, is accused of stealing a diamond brooch. When the mystery is cleared up, she and her lover are united [ML].

D

'D., E.A.B.', pseud. See **BLAND, Emma Alice**.

'D., F.K.', fl. 1880s. Pseudonym of a religious fiction writer.

D1   *The dying Irish girl* (by 'F.K.D.').
+ London: [publisher?], [1881]. LOCATION L (destroyed), O (without cover).
Philadelphia: Presbyterian Board of Education, [19—?]. SOURCE RLIN; OCLC.
LOCATION MH.
COMMENTARY Religious fiction, set in Dublin. Mary Drinan dies of consumption, discontented
with her short and unfulfilled life. Story tells of the family's consolation in religion. The
Philadelphia edn is only eight pages [RL; CM].

'D., G.D.', fl. 1867. Pseudonym of a Catholic fiction and miscellaneous writer. A person with
the same initials published a serial, 'Recollection of country life from the diary of a
visitor', and 'Love and faith' in the *Dublin Saturday Magazine* (1867), ii. SOURCE RL.

D2   *The priest's prophesy. A tale of real life* (by 'D.G.D.').
Dublin: John Mullany, 1876. SOURCE Adv. in the *Irish Catholic Directory* (Dublin,
1888); RLIN. LOCATION CSmH.
COMMENTARY 96pp [RLIN].

D3   *The priest's sister; or, the silent sufferings of a blighted heart* (by 'D.G.D.').
Dublin: John Mullany [1888 or earlier]. SOURCE Adv. in the *Irish Catholic Directory*
(Dublin, 1888).
COMMENTARY No copy located [RL].

D4   *The unforgiven sister. A tale of every-day life* (by 'D.G.D.').
Dublin: John Mullany [1888 or earlier]. SOURCE Adv. in the *Irish Catholic Directory*
(Dublin, 1888).
COMMENTARY No copy located [RL].

'D., H.', pseud. See **DOHERTY, Hugh**.

'D., M.F.', pseud. See **DICKSON, Maria Frances**.

'D—., Mabel'. Pseud. of co-author. See **CLARKE, Mrs Charles Montague**.

'D—., Miriam', pseud. See **CLARKE, Mrs Charles Montague**.

'D., S.A.N.', fl. 1894. Pseudonym.

D5   *A vast experiment. An Irish tale of 1890* (by 'S.A.N.D.').
Edinburgh: Printed by Banks, 1894. SOURCE Emerald Isle cat. 89/1476; COPAC.
LOCATION E.
COMMENTARY 79pp [COPAC].

DALTON, Regina Maria. See **ROCHE, Mrs Regina Maria**.

DALY, Dominick. See **DALY, James Dominick**.

DALY, James Dominick (also known as **Dominick Daly**), fl. 1880s. Historical fiction writer and barrister, according to the title page of *Adventures* (London, 1896), JDD was at the Inner Temple, London, but does not appear to have been called to the Irish Bar. In addition to *The feudal theory of landlordism, a plea for its revival* (Birmingham, [1882]), *The O'Dalys of Muintiaravara. The story of a bardic family* (Dublin, 1905), and an abridged translation of *Don Quixote* (London, 1905), he published several legal works. It is likely that he was Irish and belonged to the O'Dalys of Muintiaravara (near Kilcohane, Co. Cork). SOURCE Ferguson, p. 169 [where not listed]; RL; BLC.

D6   *Adventures of Roger L'Estrange sometime Captain in the Florida army of His Excellency the Marquis Hernando de Soto governor of Cuba and Captain-General of all Florida. An autobiography, translated from the Spanish* (by Dominick Daly; preface by Henry M. Stanley, MP; with route map).
    + London: W. Swan Sonnenschein & Co., 1896. LOCATION D, L, NUC, InND Loeber coll.

COMMENTARY Historical fiction. Set in the sixteenth century, the story is based on a manuscript presumably written by Roger L'Estrange, a Catholic Englishman who briefly joined an English campaign in Ireland. His family lost their English estates, which forced him to remove to the Continent. He joined a Spanish expedition to the southern parts of America to explore for gold and silver. The hardships of the army and encounters with Indians are described. Roger falls in love with an Indian girl and settles in a village not far from the Mississippi where he teaches the Indians agricultural techniques and the making of iron. Eventually, his Spanish comrades catch up with him and Roger and his wife agree to leave with them and they settle in Mexico [ML].

DAMANT, Mary (née Chesney), b. probably Co. Down, fl. 1887. Historical fiction writer, MD was a daughter of Gen. Francis Rawdon Chesney, born in Annalong (Co. Down), a noted explorer who surveyed the Suez isthmus for the feasibility of a canal (on which Ferdinand de Lesseps based the project), and the navigability of the Euphrates for a possible overland route from the Mediterranean to India. As a young man he had assisted his own father defending against attacks of the United Irishmen in Co. Down during the rebellion of 1798. A biography of the general was written by his widow and his elder daughter, Jane. MD was a younger daughter by his third wife, Louisa Fletcher, whom he married in 1848. At some time prior to 1887, she married one Damant. She addressed the preface to the following work from Cowes (Isle of Wight) in Jan. of that year. SOURCE Brown, p. 82; ODNB [under Gen. Francis Rawdon Chesney]; RL.

D7   *Peggy: A tale of the Irish rebellion* (by Mary Damant).
    + London: W.H. Allen & Co., 1887. SOURCE Allibone Suppl., i, p. 444 (as *Peggy Thornhill: a tale*); Brown, 462; Dixson, p. 222; COPAC. LOCATION D, BFl, L, NUC, InND Loeber coll..

COMMENTARY Historical fiction, possibly inspired by the history of the Chesney family during the 1798 rebellion. Consists of a tale of domestic life in north Antrim previous to and during the rebellion that pictures the rebellious peasants as deluded. Peggy and her brother Aleck live with their father, a retired military man, near Dunluce Castle. Aleck appears to be involved with the rebellion. His father is so shocked that he leaves Antrim and goes to the Isle of Wight. For many years nothing is heard of Aleck. However, at the end of his father's life he reappears, having won laurels in the Austrian army, and in this manner redeems himself in his father's eyes [ML; Brown].

DAMMAST, Jeanie Selina (née Reeves; also known as **Jeanie Selina Reeves**), fl. 1864. Religious fiction writer. Given JSD's authorship of some Irish novels and the dedication of her first novel to the lord lieutenant of Ireland, it is possible she is Irish. SOURCE Allibone Suppl., i, p. 444; RL.

D8   *Shadow and sunshine; or, life notes* (by Jeanie Selina Reeves; dedicated to the earl of Carlisle, lord-lieutenant of Ireland).
+ London: William MacIntosh, 1864. LOCATION L, C.
COMMENTARY Protestant religious fiction written for juveniles [RL].

D9   *St. Mary's convent; or, chapters in the life of a nun* (by Jeanie Selina Dammast, formerly Reeves).
+ London: S.W. Partridge, 1866. SOURCE COPAC. LOCATION L (destroyed), O.
COMMENTARY Religious fiction set in Ireland condemning convent life. Mr Stewart is a Protestant convert to catholicism. In an attempt to convert his daughter Emily (and prevent her marriage to another Protestant), he sends her to spend time living in a convent. The rule in the convent is portrayed as tyrannical and the nuns with whom Emily converses articulate their deep unhappiness. After the nuns stage a rebellion, Emily escapes and recovers from the starvation punishment inflicted on her for reading the Bible. She is renounced by her father when she marries the Protestant she originally intended to marry [ML].

D10   *The cord of love* (by Jeanie Selina Dammast, formerly Reeves).
+ Edinburgh, London: Gall & Inglis, [1867] (ill.). LOCATION O, InND Loeber coll.
COMMENTARY Religious fiction. No Irish content. Tells the story of three boys who learn to care for each other [ML].

D11   *High and low; or, help each other. To which is added the story of our little drum-major* (by Jeanie Selina Dammast, formerly Reeves).
London: Sunday School Union, 1872. SOURCE COPAC. LOCATION L.

D12   *Bob the shoeblack* (by Jeanie Selina Reeves).
London: Sunday School Union, 1872. SOURCE COPAC. LOCATION L (destroyed).
COMMENTARY Religious fiction [BLC].

D13   *Thady D'Arcy; or, them that honour me, I will honour* (by Jeanie Selina Dammast).
+ London: Sunday School Union, [1887] (ill.). SOURCE COPAC. LOCATION L (destroyed), O.
COMMENTARY 96pp. Proselytizing religious fiction revolving around a narrative of conversion set in a small village in Ireland where animosity towards Protestants and the English is supposedly encouraged by the priests, while the Catholic peasants respect Protestants more than their own co-religionists. Thady, a Catholic educated in hedge-schools, is ordained at Maynooth and becomes Fr Mulcahy's curate in the village. A Protestant curate, Mr Grady, arrives and tries to befriend Thady and the other villagers. Thady and Lily, a Catholic, both convert to protestantism and marry. Thady becomes ill and in a fever expresses his new religious beliefs and renounces the Virgin Mary. He tells his family: 'I have seen the error of the Roman Catholic Church, and I have forever left her communion' [CM].

'DANBY, Frank', pseud. See FRANKAU, Julia.

D'ANGOU, Germaine, fl. 1888. French fiction writer.
D14   *La petite-nièce d'O'Connell* (by Germaine D'Angou).
Paris: Lecoffre, 1888. SOURCE Brown, 459; COPAC. LOCATION L.
COMMENTARY A story with religious and moral overtones set in Kenmare (Co. Kerry) and in Scotland. After the death of her mother, Ellen MacGaway is taken to Scotland by her uncle and guardian where she leads an adventurous life. She becomes the heiress of her uncle, who dies a Catholic. In the end, Ellen marries a young French officer [Brown].

D'ARGENS, Marquis Jean Baptiste de Boyer (known as the **Marquis D'Argens**), b. Aix en Provence (France) 1704, d. Provence 1771. Soldier and novelist, the Marquis D'Argens, spent some time in Constantinople (Istanbul). After he was disinherited by his father, he turned to writing as a profession. He received a position at the court of Potsdam (Germany), where he became the favourite of King Frederic II. SOURCE *Biographie universelle (Michaud)* (Paris, 1854), new edn, ii, pp 186–7; CCF.

D15   *Le mentor cavalier, ou les illustres infortunés de notre siècle* (by the Marquis D'Argens).

Londres [Paris?]: [n.p], 1736. SOURCE Raven, p. 109; CCF. LOCATION Bibliothèque Carré d'Art, Nîmes.

London: Aux Dépends de la Compagnie, 1736. SOURCE ESTC t203778. LOCATION L, NUC.

London: M. Cooper, 1754 (trans. by Samuel Derrick as *Memoirs of the Count du Beauval. Including some curious particulars relating to the Dukes of Wharton and Ormond, during their exile. With anecdotes of several other illustrious unfortunate noblemen of the present age*). SOURCE Raven, 270; Gilbert, p. 188; Hardy, 206 (perhaps mistakenly identified a 1764 edn); ESTC t106572; McBurney & Taylor, 38. LOCATION L, IU, NUC.

Dublin: W. Whiteston & B. Edmond, 1754. SOURCE ESTC n022042; McBurney & Taylor, 39. LOCATION IU.

COMMENTARY The London edn of 1736 probably has a false imprint and may have been published in the Netherlands. The story presumably is set in the early-eighteenth century. Raven classifies it as a miscellany, but it is a novel with historical characters describing French court life, political intrigue and amorous adventures. The duke of Ormond briefly features in chapter IV of book III, which carries the title 'The occasion of the duke of Ormond's leaving England. Ill us'd by the chevalier De George. Retires to Avignon, and has an affair with the marchioness de —'. [RL; Raven; Personal communication, Steve Weissman, Feb. 2001].

DARLEY, George, pseuds '**Guy Penseval**' and '**Geoffrey Crayon, Jr.**', b. Dublin 1795, d. London 1846. Poet, dramatist, critic and journalist, GD was the son of Arthur Darley, a Dublin grocer, and his second cousin Mary Darley of Co. Down, and the grandson of the builder George Darley. As a child he lived with his grandfather on the outskirts of Dublin at Ballybetagh, near Kiltiernan. He was admitted at TCD in 1815 where he studied classics and mathematics and received his BA in 1820. His family opposed his literary ambitions and he went to live in London where in 1822 he published his first book, *The errors of ecstasie: A dramatic poem. With other pieces*. He became a drama critic for the *London Magazine* (1823–25), and later a long-time contributor to several periodicals, including the *Athenaeum*, as well as contributing verse and short stories to *Bentley's Miscellany* and the *Illuminated Magazine*, all in London. Although he wrote dramas, these were not successful. To supplement his literary income, GD wrote a series of respected treatises on geometry, algebra, trigonometry and astronomy. Samuel Taylor Coleridge, Charles Lamb, Thomas Carlyle and Alfred Tennyson admired his poetry but, like his plays, it had little popular success. He suffered from a pronounced stutter and led a reclusive life, his writing being his easiest form of communication. He visited Ireland in 1839 and kept up correspondence with members of his family there. For his portrait, see ODNB. SOURCE Allibone, i, p. 476; Boylan, p. 84; Brady, p. 53; B & S, p. 211; DLB, xcvi; Field Day, ii, pp 6–7, 111; J. Heath-Stubbs, *The darkling plain: romanticism in English poetry from Darley to Yeats* (London, 1950); Hogan, p. 187; Hogan 2, pp 324–5; Igoe, p. 56; Irish pseudonyms; McKenna, pp 132–4; NCBEL 4, pp 328–9; OCIL, p. 134; ODNB; O'Donoghue, pp 97–8; Quinn, 2354–60; RIA/DIB.

D16   *The labours of idleness; or, seven nights' entertainments* (by 'Guy Penseval').
London: J. Taylor, 1826. SOURCE Rafroidi, ii, p. 129; McKenna, p. 134; Block, p. 53.
LOCATION L, NUC.
COMMENTARY Contents: 'The enchanted lyre', 'Love's devotion', 'Pedro Ladron', 'Aileen Astore',
'The dead man's dream', 'Ellinore', 'Lilian of the vale'. Also contains some poetry [Rafroidi].

D17   *The new sketch book* (by 'G. Crayon Jr.').
London: Printed for the author, 1829, 2 vols. SOURCE Rafroidi, ii, p. 129; McKenna,
p. 134. LOCATION L, NUC.
COMMENTARY The title and the pseudonym used must have been inspired by Washington
Irving's *My sketchbook* (New York, 1819–20), whose pseudonym was 'G. Crayon'. The sec-
ond volume of *The new sketch book* is a reprint of *The labours of idleness* (London, 1826)
[Personal communication, Jacqueline Belanger, Feb. 2005; Rafroidi].

'D'ARVOR, Gabrielle', pseud. See DE BELBE, Bagriella Isnard.

'THE DAUGHTER OF A CAPTAIN IN THE NAVY DECEASED', pseud. See WALSH,
Miss (or Mrs) —.

DAUNT, Alice Ismene (not Ismere as in ODNB) O'Neill, b. 1848, d. 1914. Catholic writer
of historical and religious fiction, AID was the only daughter of the politician and author William
Joseph O'Neill Daunt§, whose memoirs, *A life spent for Ireland* (London, 1896), she
. Her contributions to a number of periodicals such as the *Lamp* (New York?) and *Ireland's Own*
(Wexford, later Dublin), included several serials: 'Love's fruition'; 'Couma tower', and 'St.
Werburgh's abbey'. The IBL mentions two works, 'The white rose of Koncie', and 'In Norway
o'er the foam', which have not been located. SOURCE Brown, p. 82; IBL, 6 (1914), p. 63; RL.

D18   *Watch and hope: A tale of the wars of the roses* (by Alice Ismere [*sic*] Daunt).
+ Dublin: James Duffy, [1886 or earlier]. SOURCE Adv. in W. Carleton's, *Redmond
Count O'Hanlon* (Dublin, 1886); IBL, 6 (1914), p. 63; NLI cat. LOCATION D.
COMMENTARY Historical fiction set in the fifteenth century [ML].

D19   *Eva; or, as the child, so the woman* (by Alice Ismene Daunt).
London, Derby: Thomas Richardson & Son, 1882. SOURCE Brown, 463; Alston, p.
111; COPAC. LOCATION L (destroyed).
COMMENTARY Religious fiction for juveniles. One of a series of Catholic tales for the
young. This story is set in Ireland, but is not particularly Irish in any way [Brown].

DAUNT, William Joseph O'Neill (also known as William J. O'Neill Daunt), pseud.
'Denis Ignatius Moriarty', b. Tullamore (Co. Offaly) 1807, d. Kilcascan Castle, Ballyneen
(Co. Cork) 1894. Politician, historian and novelist, WJO'ND was the son of Joseph Daunt of
Kilcascan Castle and Jane Wilson of Ardstraw (Co. Tyrone). He was privately educated. After
his father's death in a duel, he converted to catholicism in 1827 and lived at Kilcascan. A supporter of Daniel O'Connell, he became MP for Mallow (Co. Cork) and later O'Connell's secretary when he became lord mayor of Dublin (1841). He was admitted to the King's Inns in
1845 but does not appear to have been called to the Irish Bar. He was a founding member of
the Loyal National Repeal Association, which published his *Letter from W.J. O'Neill Daunt,
Esq., of Kilcascan, County Cork, to the landlords of Ireland* [Dublin, 1846]. Along with Thomas
Davis, John Blake Dillon and Charles Gavan Duffy he helped to found the *Nation* (Dublin)
as the organ of the Young Ireland movement, to which he contributed. Later he agitated for
disestablishment and disendowment of the Established church in Ireland but also, urging complete separation of church and state, persuaded the Catholic hierarchy not to accept the gov-

ernment's grant to the Catholic college at Maynooth. A supporter of Isaac Butt's§ Home Government Association, he considered Home Rule the best compromise short of complete repeal of the Union. He was the author of *Catechism of the history of Ireland: ancient and modern* (Dublin, 1844), *Ireland and her agitators* (Dublin, 1845), and *Eighty-five years of Irish history 1800–1885* (London, 1886). He published four novels between 1838 and 1848 and may have published another novel, unnamed, which is mentioned in 1869 in a letter by John Mitchel, when Mitchel tried to get it published in New York. For his portrait and papers, see ODNB. His daughter, the author Alice O'Neill Daunt§, edited her father's journals, *A life spent for Ireland* (London, 1896). A collection of WJO'ND's letters is in the NLI (MSS 8,045–48). SOURCE Allibone Suppl., i, p. 451; Boase, v, pp 24–5; Brady, p. 53. Brown, pp 82–3; note that Block, p. 89 identifies 'Denis Ignatius Moriarty' as 'John O'Brien Grant', another of Daunt's pseuds; T.G. Connors, 'Letters of John Mitchel, 1848–1869', *Analecta Hibernica*, 37 (1998), p. 300; Hogan 2, p. 325; Keane, p. 122; McKenna, pp 135–6; OCIL, p. 134; ODNB; Rafroidi, ii, pp 130–1; RIA/DIB; Rowan cat. 54/202.

D20 *The wife hunter & Flora Douglas. Tales by the Moriarty family* (ed. by 'Denis Ignatius Moriarty, Esq.'; dedicated to Miss [Maria] Edgeworth§).
    + London: Richard Bentley, 1838, 3 vols. SOURCE Hodgson, p. 606; Rafroidi, ii, p. 131; Brown, 464. LOCATION Grail, D, L.
    + Dublin: John Mullany, 1867 (as *The wife-hunter: or, memoirs of 'MP'S.' A novel* (new revised edn, by W.J.O'N. Daunt). LOCATION D.
    Philadelphia: E.L. Carey & A. Hart, 1838 (as *The wife hunter, by the Moriarty family*). SOURCE McKenna, p. 135. LOCATION Dt, NUC.
COMMENTARY Prefatory notice is signed by the main character, John O'Brien Grant, from his seat Kilnaflesk (in Ireland, in a 'remote quarter of the kingdom'), Aug., 1834. The story concerns the matrimonial and political adventures of a hard-drinking Orange squireen. A late edn of this book was reviewed in the *Dublin Saturday Magazine*, 2 (1867), p. 363 [Brown; RL].

D21 *The husband hunter. A novel; or, 'Das Schiksal'* (by 'Denis Ignatius Moriarty').
    London: Richard Bentley, 1839, 3 vols. SOURCE Hodgson, p. 389; Block, p. 89; Brown, 465. LOCATION L.
    Philadelphia: Lea & Blanchard, 1839. SOURCE McKenna, p. 135. LOCATION NUC.
COMMENTARY A society novel set in Co. Kerry around 1830 describing the matrimonial complications of a lady and including such characters as a Russian prince and a German baron. The subtitle refers to fate in German [Brown].

D22 *Innisfoyle Abbey. A tale of modern times* (by 'Denis Ignatius Moriarty').
    + London: C. Dolman, 1840, 3 vols. SOURCE Hodgson, p. 389; McKenna, p. 136; Rafroidi, ii, p. 131; Brown, 465a. LOCATION Grail, D, L, InND.
    + Dublin: James Duffy, 1844, 2 vols. (revsd edn, condensed and altered, as *Saints and sinners. A tale of modern times*). SOURCE McKenna, p. 136; Brown, 466. LOCATION Dt (2 vols. in 1), D, NUC.
    + Glasgow: Cameron & Ferguson & Co., [1877 or later] (as *Saints and sinners: A romance illustrating the origin of Irish outrage*). SOURCE COPAC; RL. LOCATION E.
COMMENTARY Deals with the religious question in Ireland from the Catholic point of view. The hero's Protestant and anti-Irish prejudices are slowly made to give way as the real situation is forced on him. Represents the struggle between landlords and the peasants and includes actual incidents, such as the Rathcormack tithe massacres [Brown; RL].

D23 *Hugh Talbot. A tale of the Irish confiscations of the seventeenth century* (by William J. O'Neill Daunt).
    + Dublin: James Duffy, 1846. SOURCE Rafroidi, ii, p. 131; Brown, 467; Block, p. 54. LOCATION Grail, Dt, D, L, NUC, InND Loeber coll.

COMMENTARY Historical tale of the Irish confiscations in the reign of James I. The scene varies between England, Ireland and Scotland and describes the persecution, arrest, and adventures of Fr Hugh Talbot. Eveline Mac Orr, descendant of a noble Ulster family, decides to marry an ancient English earl because she feels that in that position she might give some protection to her Ulster friends. However, in the end she is not able to stem the tide of the Ulster confiscations [ML; Brown].

D24   *The gentleman in debt* (by William J. O'Neill Daunt; dedicated to Mrs Scott, of Parton, Kirkcudbrightshire).
Edinburgh: Cameron & Ferguson, 1848. SOURCE Brown, 468.
COMMENTARY *Edinburgh edn* No copy located [RL].
London: T.C. Newby, 1851. SOURCE McKenna, p. 136; OCLC. LOCATION L, NUC.
Dublin: John Mullany, [1867 or earlier]. SOURCE Adv. in W.J. O'Neill Daunt's *Ireland and her agitators* (Dublin, 1867) as *The gentleman in debt: A Connaught story of the 18th century*.
COMMENTARY *Dublin edn* No copy located [RL].
New York: R. Worthington, 1889 (as *The Irish gentleman. A novel*; Franklin Edition). SOURCE Hyland cat. 252/86. LOCATION InND Loeber coll. (n.d. edn).
COMMENTARY Set in the eighteenth century. The adventures of a penniless young gentleman trying to get a position. Depicts life in Galway among impecunious fox-hunting, hard-drinking squires, some of whom cannot leave their house for fear of the bailiff. Also describes the life of the Castle aristocracy in Dublin, the hard life of the Catholic landowners and the working of the penal laws [ML; Brown].

DAVID, Mme Marie (née de Saffron), pseud. 'Raoule de Navery', b. 1831, d. 1885. Novelist, probably French, MD also wrote *The treasure of the abbey* (Dublin, 1886; New York, [1886?]), translated by Alice Wilmot Chetwode (probably of Woodbrook, Co. Laois) who translated several of her other works, including *John Canada or New France* (Dublin, n.d.). MD's works were also translated by Anna Theresa Sadlier, daughter of Mrs J. (Mary Anne) Sadlier§.
SOURCE Allibone Suppl., ii, p. 1309; DCU cat.; Mes, p. 167.

D25   *Father Fitz-Roy; or, the martyr of a secret. A tale of the Irish famine* (by 'Raoule de Navery').
+ New York: P. O'Shea, 1872 (trans. from the *Tales from church history*). SOURCE DCU, Catholic Americana files. LOCATION NUC ([188?] edn), InND Loeber coll. (1890 edn).
COMMENTARY No French edn located. A story of murder and romance set in Ireland in the beginning of the nineteenth century. Fr Fitz-Roy is bound by his priestly oath not to divulge the confession of Hugh Peadcock, who has murdered Fr Fitz-Roy's brother. The brother was murdered because Peadcock coveted his fiancée, Maggy. Maggy is not interested in Peadcock's advances but he contrives that she and her aged mother lose their cottage and then promises he will look after her mother if Maggy marries him. Maggy, unable to see her mother suffer, gives in. The priest is extremely upset but cannot intervene. The night before the wedding, Peadcock has been drinking in a pub and on his way home he walks past the spot where he murdered his rival. The priest falls in with him, and even though Fr Fitz-Roy tells him that he is walking beside him not as a priest but just as a man, Peadcock spills his secret and points to where he committed the murder. Fr Fitz-Roy immediately overpowers him and brings him to the magistrate. He is now free to denounce his brother's murderer and to prevent Maggy's sacrifice [ML].

DAVIES, Miss —. See DAVIES, Sarah.

DAVIES, Naunton, pseud. 'Naunton Covertside', fl. 1898. Novelist and playwright. Some of ND's fiction is set in Wales. He probably was English by birth. SOURCE BLC.

D26   *Chester Creswell. A novel* (by 'Naunton Covertside').
+ London: Digby, Long & Co., 1898. LOCATION L.

COMMENTARY A story of friendship, romance and duty set in Galway, it tells of two friends who drift apart over a woman they both love. One marries her, the other engages in a relationship with a girl of humble background. When he finds that she is pregnant by him, he hypnotizes her so as to forget him and leaves for Rome to become a priest. He returns, however, finds his son and learns that the mother died in childbirth. His whole life becomes centred around the little boy. The mother, who in fact had taken refuge in a nunnery, returns and marries the boy's father. The two friends stay apart during most of the story, but eventually their misunderstandings are cleared up [ML].

DAVIES, Naunton Wingfield, fl. 1876. Novelist, NWD published more than twenty years earlier than Naunton Davies§, and therefore is likely to be a different individual but probably related. SOURCE RL.

D27   *Norvin of the tower. A novel* (by Naunton Wingfield Davies).
London: Charing Cross Publishing Co., 1876, 2 vols. SOURCE Allibone Suppl., i, p. 457. LOCATION L.

COMMENTARY Set in England, but features Mick Macket, an Irishman [RL].

DAVIES, Sarah (also known as **Miss Davies**), fl. 1853. A writer of religious fiction and an advocate for poor children (not to be confused with the English suffragist and feminist Sarah Emily Davies), SD appears to have worked alongside Revd Alexander Dallas for the 'Irish Church Missions' to the Catholics in Ireland. SD anonymously published *Wanderers brought home: The story of the Ragged Boys' Home* (London, 1871), and *St. Patrick's armour. The story of the Coombe Ragged School* (Dublin, 1880), which concerns a school for poor children founded in Dublin in 1852, as well as *Other cities also: The story of mission work in Dublin* (Dublin, 1881), which is a history of the Dublin schools for poor children. According to the preface to the third edn of her *Holly and ivy* (London, Dublin, 1864), she lived at 35 Upper Fitzwilliam Street, Dublin, in 1871, and was honorary secretary of the Children's Association. She probably can be identified with the Miss Davies who wrote a chapbook *Town sparrows. Stories of the Dublin ragged schools* (Dublin, 1880). On the title page of *Holly and ivy* she is mentioned as having written *Erin's hope*, which may refer to the Irish Church Mission's Juvenile Magazine, published in London (1853–5), which contains anonymous contributions. SOURCE Allibone Suppl., i, p. 458; Brooke, p. 168; CM; RIA/DIB; RL.

D28   *Holly and ivy. The story of a winter 'Bird's Nest'* (by Sarah Davies; dedicated to the members of the Children's Association).
London, Dublin: Marlborough, 1864. SOURCE Alston, p. 113; COPAC. LOCATION L.
+ Dublin: George Herbert; London: William Hunt, 1871, 3rd edn (by 'Miss Davies'; ill.). LOCATION D.

COMMENTARY Concerns destitute little children, who are gathered into a place called 'The Bird's Nest', where they learn Christian values. Written from a Protestant viewpoint. The 'Bird's Nest' was a children home, which opened in 1859 [ML; J. Prunty, *Dublin Slums 1800–1925: a study in urban geography* (Dublin, 1999), p. 248].

D29   *'Them also'. The story of the Dublin mission to Roman Catholics* [anon.].
+ London: James Nisbet & Co., 1866. SOURCE OCLC. LOCATION D.

COMMENTARY The preface states that 'It is our purpose in these pages to tell of all the efforts and successes of those who have sought those "other sheep" amongst the Roman Catholics of

Dublin'. Contains religious fiction in the form of short stories. OCLC mentions as its author John O'Rourke, but this is clearly mistaken because the title page states 'by the author of Holly and ivy' [CM; RL].

DAVIS, John, fl. 1805. Novelist, travel and miscellaneous writer, JD was a native of Bristol (Avon) who went to North America and wrote an account of the four-and-a-half years he spent travelling there, mostly on foot, from 1799 on. According to Allibone this contains 'some interesting facts relating to Pres. Jefferson, Col. Burr, &c.' He also wrote a novel about the first settlers of Virginia, a biography of Thomas Chatterton, and a volume on naval society and manners (Garside, 1806:26). SOURCE Allibone, i, p. 483; Ximenes cat. M13/54.

D30   *Walter Kennedy: An American tale* [anon.].
> London: Longman, Hurst, Reese & Orme, 1805. SOURCE COPAC; British Fiction; Garside, 1805:26. LOCATION L.
> London: J.F. Hughes, 1808 (as *Walter Kennedy: An interesting American tale*). SOURCE Ximenes cat. M13/54.
> COMMENTARY The 1808 edn is made up of the sheets of the 1805 edn. A story about the Indians of North America narrated by a young Irishman who comes to live among various tribes along the Mississippi. He marries an Indian princess. The book contains a vocabulary of the Kaskaskia language and many details of life among the Indians [Ximenes cat. M13/54].

DAVIS, Julia. See **FRANKAU, Julia.**

DAVYS, Mary, pseud. 'A Lady', b. Dublin 1674, d. Cambridge (Cambs.) 1732. Novelist, playwright and memoirist, MD married Revd Peter Davys, headmaster of the Free School of St Patrick's, Dublin. Allegedly she and her husband were part of Jonathan Swift's§ circle, but Swift referred to her as 'a rambling woman with very little taste in wit or humour'. After her husband's death at a young age in 1698, she moved to London in 1700, then in 1704 to York, where her play *The northern heiress, or, the humours of York* was performed in 1715 and in London the following year. With the proceeds she moved to Cambridge, where she kept a coffeehouse and continued to write. Her novels are notable for their humour, colloquial dialogue and for their portrayals of upper- and middle-class life and helped shape the course of novel-writing in English in the early-seventeenth century. Before she died she gave £5 to St Patrick's in Dublin for a large Oxford bible. SOURCE Adams, pp 66–7; Allibone, i, p. 485; Blain, pp, 271–2; Brady, p. 54; Carpenter, pp 135–7; DLB, xxxix; Field Day, v, pp 775, 830, 1092; Hogan 2, p. 327; Leslie & Wallace, p. 541; ODNB; O'Donoghue, p. 101; RIA/DIB; Todd, pp 179–81.

D31   *The amours of Alcippus and Lucippe: A novel* (by 'A Lady').
> London: James Round, 1704. SOURCE ESTC n30889; Blain, p. 271; McBurney, X5. LOCATION NUC.
> London: For the author, 1725 (in *Works of Mrs. Davys* as *The lady's tale*). SOURCE Blain, p. 271; McBurney, 171. LOCATION L, MH.
> COMMENTARY Dedication signed M. Davys. The manuscript sold at 3 guineas in 1700. The story is confided by one female friend to another [Blain; ESTC].

D32   *The fugitive. Containing several very pleasant passages and surprizing adventures, observ'd by a lady in her country ramble; being both useful and diverting for persons of all ranks. Now first published from her own manuscript* (by Mary Davys; dedicated to Esther Johnson [Swift's 'Stella']).
> London: G. Sawbridge, 1705. SOURCE ESTC t185069; McBurney, 16; ODNB. LOCATION O, NUC.

+ London: For the author, 1725 (in *The works of Mrs. Davys* as *The merry wanderer*). SOURCE McBurney, 16a. LOCATION L.

COMMENTARY Said to be autobiographical. The fugitive records her visit to various relatives and friends while she awaits the return of her brother on whose fortunes she depends. The main character is depicted as a man born in Ireland. Introduces Jonathan Swift§ [ML; Blain; Field Day, v. pp 777–8; Kilfeather, p. 96; ODNB].

D33 *The reform'd coquet; A novel* (by Mary Davys).

London: Printed by H. Woodfall, for the author, 1724 (subscribers' list). SOURCE ESTC t10261; Hardy, 356; Esdaile, p. 201; Field Day, v, p. 830. LOCATION L, ICN.

London: J. Stephens, 1736, 4th edn (corrected). SOURCE ESTC n22162; McBurney 154d. LOCATION O.

+ Dublin: R. Gunne, 1735 (as *The reform'd coquet; or, memoirs of Amoranda. A surprising novel*). SOURCE ESTC t8503; McBurney, 154c. LOCATION D, L, NUC.

Belfast: Printed by Daniel Blow, 1760. SOURCE Anderson 3, p. 6.

COMMENTARY *Belfast edn* No copy located [RL].

New York: Garland Publications, 1973 (introd. J. Grieder). LOCATION O, InND.

Lexington (KY): Univ. Press of Kentucky, [*c*.1999] (ed. by M.F. Bowden). SOURCE RLIN.

COMMENTARY Set in England. A popular, comic and satirical adventure, featuring Amoranda, a vain, independent young lady of great fortune who takes pleasure in encouraging suitors, but accepts none. She rejects a lover who wants to marry her. He leaves for the Continent but she cannot banish her memory of him. An elderly gentleman is injured in an accident in front of her castle and she cares for him in her house during his recovery. She admits to him her weakness with men and tells him about her only love, whom she rejected. The elderly man's disguise slips and her lover stands in front of her [Adams, p. 67; The novel is discussed in the preface to *Venetian tales* (London, 1737); ODNB; Ximenes List 97–1 (A to L)/69].

D34 *The cousins. A novel* (by Mary Davys).

London: For the author, 1725 (in *The works of Mrs. Davys*). SOURCE McBurney, 171. LOCATION L, MH.

London: T. Astley, 1732 (as *The false friend; or, the treacherous Portugueze. A novel. Interspersed with the adventures of Lorenzo and Elvira. Carlos and Leonora. Octavia and Clara*, by 'A Lady'). SOURCE McBurney, 171a; ESTC n009622.

London: Francis Noble & John Noble, 1767, 2 vols. (as *The country cousins; or, a journey to London. A novel*). SOURCE ESTC n4713. LOCATION CtY.

COMMENTARY Blain states that the London 1732 edn is pirated as *The false friend, or the treacherous Portugueze*, but the ODNB states that this was the original title she had given it when she wrote it in 1704 which was published, as above, in 1725 [ODNB].

D35 *The accomplish'd rake; or, the modern fine gentleman. Being the genuine memoirs, being an exact description of the conduct and behaviour of a person of distinction* (by Mary Davys).

London: Sold by the booksellers of London and Westminster, 1727 (subscribers' list). SOURCE ESTC n14929; McBurney, 207. LOCATION L (1756 edn), MH, NUC.

London: J. Millan, [1729] (possibly pirated as *The reform'd rake; or, the modern fine gentlemen. A novel*). SOURCE McBurney, X21.

Lexington (KY): Univ. Press of Kentucky, [*c*.1999] (ed. by M.F. Bowden). SOURCE RLIN.

COMMENTARY A frank satire on the fashionable pastimes of London's leisure class and on the plots of contemporary novels. It describes a seducer who, for revenge, is tricked into sleeping with a woman with venereal disease [ODNB; Todd, p. 180].

— COLLECTED WORKS

D36   *The works of Mrs. Davys: consisting of plays, novels, poems, and familiar letters.*
       Several of which never before published.
       + London: Printed for the author by H. Woodfall, 1725, 2 vols. SOURCE ESTC
       t202035; ESTC t119971; McBurney, 171. LOCATION L, MH.
COMMENTARY Contents: (excluding plays and poetry) vol. 1: 'The merry wanderer' (a series
of anecdotes based on visits to various great houses, a revision of *The fugitive*]); vol. 2: 'The
reform'd coquet; a novel', 'The Lady's tale', 'The cousins. A novel', 'Familiar letters betwixt
a gentleman and a lady' (political discussions between a lady with Whig leanings and a Jacobite
exile with Tory interests, ending in marriage. Two female friends devote much of their correspondence to critiques of English policy in Ireland, and discuss the relationship between
nationalism and feminism) [ML; Field Day, v. pp 778–81 (*Familiar letters*; Kilfeather, p. 338;
McBurney, 171; ODNB; Todd, pp 179–80].

DEACON, William Frederick, b. London 1799, d. Islington (London) 1845. English journalist, miscellaneous writer and editor, WFD was educated at Reading School and at
Cambridge, but did not graduate. He was a regular contributor of short stories, sketches and
reviews to a wide variety of publications, including *Blackwood's Magazine* (Edinburgh), and
Bentley's Miscellany (London, Mar.–Apr., 1844). In 1824 he published *Warreniana*, a series of
parodies of his contemporaries, including Samuel Taylor Coleridge, Lord Byron and Sir Walter
Scott, which proved very popular. He lived for a time in Wales and a collection of tales and
sketches, many with Welsh settings, appeared as *November Nights* (London, 1826). SOURCE
Allibone, i, p. 487; Brown, p. 84; Curran index, passim; ODNB; Venn, part ii, vol. ii, p. 262.

D37   *The exile of Erin; or, the sorrows of a bashful Irishman* [anon.].
       + London: Whittaker & Co., 1835, 2 vols. SOURCE Hodgson, p. 186; Brown, 469;
       Garside 2: 1835:41. LOCATION D, Dt, BFl, L, NUC.
       + London: David Bryce, [1854] (new edn; as *Adventures of a bashful Irishman*). SOURCE
       Brown, 470 (1862 ed.); Garside 2, 1835:41. LOCATION D, L, NUC (1862 edn).
       New York: Harper & Bros., 1835, 2 vols. SOURCE Topp 1, p. 134. LOCATION NUC.
COMMENTARY Not to be confused with Mrs Elizabeth Plunkett's§ *The exile of Erin. A novel*
(London, 1808, 3 vols.). Probably autobiographical fiction. The introd. states that 'The ground-
work of this tale is founded on fact, though the circumstances of the journey are in some degree
fictitious'. Contains satirical portraits of prominent Irish patriots, such as Daniel O'Connell (under
the unflattering name O'Cromwell). The main story, 'Adventures of a bashful Irishman' is divided
into four sections with the following headings: 'The adventurer', 'The politician', 'The village
doctor', and 'The patriot'. Mr O'Blarney, the hero of the main story, was born in Co. Galway.
The story of his life is set in Ireland, England and the Continent in the early-nineteenth century. O'Blarney turns out to be a cheerful villain who commits bigamy and embezzlement and
flees from place to place when he is about to be unmasked. He has a wide variety of professions:
actor, journalist, doctor and political organizer. Eventually, the law catches up with O'Blarney.
O'Cromwell is the lawyer for his defence, but he is transported for life. The second story, 'The
magic of love; or, the adventure of De Grey, of Gwynneavay', has no Irish content. The Chicago
edn has another story, 'Adventures of an old maid' [ML; RL; ODNB].

DE BELBE, Bagriella Isnard, pseud. 'Gabrielle d'Arvor'. French novelist BIDeB published strongly Catholic works mainly in the 1870s and 1880s. SOURCE Brown 2, p. 13.

D38   *Dent pour dent. Scènes irlandaises* (by 'Gabrielle d'Arvor').
       Paris: Blériot Bros., 1882. SOURCE IBL, 16 (1928), p. 60; Brown 2, 44 (n.d. edn); CCF.
       LOCATION BNF.

Montreal: La Lecture, 1906. SOURCE OCLC. LOCATION National Library of Canada, Ottawa.

COMMENTARY Set in Co. Cork. Includes evictions, risings, ambushes, bandits, and revenge. Interwoven is a love story between Tony and Colette, who are eventually married by a hermit [Brown 2].

DE BUTTS, Eleanor L., d. 1893. Children's and religious fiction writer, ELDeB published three books between 1883 and 1893. Although one of her works has Irish content, it is unclear whether she was Irish. However, members of the De Butts (also Debutts) family resided in Dublin, Co. Wicklow and Co. Sligo in the eighteenth and nineteenth centuries. SOURCE Allibone Suppl., i, p. 469; B & S, p. 220.

D39   *Great grandmother's days: A tale of the Irish rebellion* (by Eleanor L. De Butts; dedicated to the author's grandchildren).
+ London: Remington & Co., 1883. SOURCE COPAC. LOCATION Dt (cat. mentions a 1882 edn based on annotation in copy), L.
COMMENTARY Set in Ireland during the 1798 rebellion [RL].

DECCAN, Hilary, fl. 1892. Fiction writer.
D40   *Light in the offing* (by Hilary Deccan).
+ London: Hurst & Blackett, 1892, 3 vols. SOURCE COPAC. LOCATION L.
COMMENTARY The story starts at Kilcoran in the west of Ireland and is set in 1847 during the Famine [RL].
D41   *Where billows break* (by Hilary Deccan).
+ London: Digby, Long & Co., 1896. SOURCE COPAC. LOCATION D, L.
COMMENTARY Short stories. Contents: 'Where the billows break. One o' the Whijarls', 'Crookit Lanty', 'Marcus Aurelius O'Rourke', 'Mickie's quest' [ML].

'DE CELTIS, Emelobie', pseud. See **O'BYRNE, M. Louise**.

DE CHARRIÈRE, Mrs E. WARD. See **WARD DE CHARRIÈRE, Mrs E.**

DE GENLIS, Mme Stephanie-Félicité, marquise de Sillery, comtesse de Genlis (née du Crest de Mézières ; also known as **Madame Stephanie-Félicité de Genlis**), b. Champcry, near Autun (France) 1746, d. 1830. French fiction writer and educator, SFDeG's ideas on education had a great influence in England. She was a governess to the children of the duke of Orleans and left France from 1792 until the establishment of Napoleon Bonaparte, from whom she received a pension in 1805. SFDeG's daughter married the Irish revolutionary Lord Edward Fitzgerald and the translation of SFDeG's *A new method of instruction for children from five to ten years old* (Dublin, 1800) was dedicated to their children. Her work became quite popular in Ireland. Maria Edgeworth§ translated her *Adèle et Théodore* in 1783, but because of the appearance of a rival version, Edgeworth's translation was never published although one volume was printed. This novel and the translation of SFDeG's *The knights of the swan* both appeared in Dublin in 1797, followed by her *Lessons of a governess to her pupils* (Dublin, 1793, 2 vols.). A translation of her *Tales of the castle; or, stories of instruction and delight* was published in Dublin in 1789. One of her stories was reprinted in *The history of Isaac Jenkins* (Dublin, 1820; see Thomas Beddoes§). SOURCE Blain, p. 417; M. Butler, introd. to *Maria Edgeworth, Castle Rackrent and Ennui* (London, 1992), p. 6; BD, p. 433; Hodges Figgis cat. n.s. 15/230.

D42   *Le Comte de Corke, surnommé le grand, ou la séduction sans artifice, suivi de six nouvelles* (by Madame Stephanie-Félicité de Genlis).

+ Paris: Maradan, 1805, 2 vols. in 1. SOURCE Block, pp 55–6. LOCATION L, InND Loeber coll.

London: J.F. Hughes, 1808, 3 vols. (trans. as *The Earl of Cork; or, seduction without artifice. To which are added six interesting tales*). SOURCE Brown 2, 539; Mayo, p. 602; British Fiction; Garside, 1808:46; LOCATION NUC.

COMMENTARY The London edn was reviewed in the *Belfast Monthly Magazine* (Jan. 31, 1809, Feb. 28, 1809). Historical fiction of the courtship of Richard Boyle, afterwards known as the 'Great earl of Cork', and Lady Ranelagh, showing a poor understanding of the earl of Cork's life. Richard, an orphan, is brought up by old Mr Mulcroon at Blackrock (Co. Dublin). The earl of Essex visits and later Richard and his guardian go to London to see Queen Elizabeth and Essex. When he is age 18, Richard falls in love with Lady Ranelagh who, with her companion Mrs Brown, visits Mr Mulcroon. From that day on Richard is successful according to all the laws of eighteenth-century courtship. He becomes secretary to Sir Charles Manwood, who is a bounder. He lives near the Dargle and there, at the Lover's Leap, Richard again meets Lady Ranelagh. When Essex falls into disgrace, Sir Charles involves Richard in his fall. But Lady Ranelagh obtains for him the privilege of pleading his cause in person before the queen. He is successful and at last wins Lady Ranelagh. Other stories are 'The young penitent', 'Zumelinde; or, the young lady', 'The lovers without love', 'Introduction', 'The Tuli, an oriental tale, 'The Savinias; or the twins' [Brown 2; Belanger, 9].

'DEHAN, Richard', pseud. See GRAVES, Clo.

DE JARNAC, Philippe Ferdinand Auguste de Rohan Chabot, comte, pseud. 'Sir Charles Rockingham', b. France 1818, d. 1875. French nobleman and writer who was educated at Harrow. He was a nephew of the duke of Leinster and lived in Ireland from 1830 to 1870, after which he became secretary to the French embassy in London and French ambassador in London in 1874. SOURCE Allibone Suppl., i, p. 305, [under Chabot]; RIA/DIB.

D43 *Rockingham; or, the younger brother* [anon.].
London: Henry Colburn, 1849, 3 vols. LOCATION L.
COMMENTARY Set in England and presents the story of the son of Edward Plantagenet Rockingham, earl and marquis of Arlingford [RL].

D44 *Love and ambition* [anon.].
London: Henry Colburn, 1851, 3 vols. LOCATION L (1856 edn), MH.

D45 *Cécile; or, the pervert* (by 'Sir Charles Rockingham').
+ London: Colburn & Co., 1851. SOURCE COPAC. LOCATION L (destroyed), E.

D46 *Electra: a story of modern times* [anon.].
+ London: Hurst & Blackett, 1853 (ill. Lord Gerald Fitzgerald). SOURCE Wolff, 3603; Sadleir, 1300. LOCATION InND Loeber coll. (1853, 2nd edn), MH.

COMMENTARY A love story set in England and on the Continent. Young Lord Glenarlowe has fallen in love with his stepsister. His stepmother violently opposes the connection because she feels that Lord Glenarlowe stands in the way of her own son's advancement. The story moves to Italy and later on to the Iberian Peninsula where Lord Glenarlowe serves in the army. Helped by his stepmother's sisters, he is able to keep his love alive and eventually marries his sweetheart. No Irish content [ML].

D47 *Dark and fair* (by 'Sir Charles Rockingham').
London: Hurst & Blackett, 1857, 3 vols. SOURCE COPAC. LOCATION L.

DE LA CHEROIS CROMMELIN, Maria Henrietta. See CROMMELIN, May.

DE LAMOTHE, Alexandre Bessot, b. Périgueux (France) 1823, d. France ? 1897. French historical novelist. SOURCE Bn-Opale plus.

D48   *Le roi de la nuit* (by Alexandre Bessot De Lamothe).
    Paris: Bleriot, 1873. SOURCE Brown 2, 750.
COMMENTARY No copy located. The introd. to this work gives a description of contemporary Ireland, laying stress on the oppression suffered by the people. Set in Glengarriff (Co. Cork), the story's main character is Patrick Hadfield, son of Tom Joyce and Molly Hadfield, who retains his mother's surname. He is the 'king of the night', head of the 'children of the night', a secret society whose ambush of the leading landlords and others is a failure. Jealousy and treachery inside and outside the organization destroy the cause. Hadfield is taken prisoner but escapes. The story includes descriptions of the Famine and an eviction, and in the second volume of Keim-en-eigh and Gougane Barra (Co. Cork) [Brown 2].

DELANEY, Denis, fl. 1848. Story writer, DD is identified as the author of the following work from the cover of the copy in TCD, where he is called one of the Anchorites (hermits). *Bolster's Magazine* (Cork, Aug. 1828) contained 'Passages in the life of Denis Delaney, commonly called The rhymer'. He probably was a resident of Cork. SOURCE Brown 2, p. 67.

D49   *Sir Walter Raleigh. Brennan, the rapparee. Two Irish tales* [anon.].
    Cork: Bradford & Co., 1848. LOCATION Dt.
    Dublin: J. M'Glashan; Cork: Bradford & Co., 1848. SOURCE Brown 2, 354; COPAC.
    LOCATION Dt.
COMMENTARY The wrapper of the Dublin edn carries the imprint: 'Cork: Bradford and Co., Patrick Street. 1848'. Originally appeared in *Bolster's Magazine* (Cork, 1837). The rapparee referred to is Willie Brennan of the ballad 'Brennan on the Moor', the outlaw who roamed the Kilworth mountains in Co. Cork in the early-eighteenth century [Brown 2; Fenning cat. 183/70].

DELAP, James, pseud. **'Philantropos'**, fl. 1794. Editor and children's writer, JD's pseud. is mentioned in the *Waterloo directory of Irish newspapers*. He edited the *New Magazine; or, Moral and Entertaining Miscellany* ([Dublin?] 1799). Allibone mentions a Dr J. Delap, a playwright and poet with similar dates, but it is unclear whether this is the same person. Given that JD published in Dublin only, it is likely that he was Irish. SOURCE Allibone, i, p. 491; Personal communication, Mary Pollard, Dublin, May 1994.

D50   *The history of Harry Spencer; compiled for the amusement of good children; and the instruction of such as wish to become good* (by 'Philantropos').
    + Dublin: Printed by John Gough, 1794. SOURCE ESTC t167565; Dm exhib. cat., 1981, p. 21. LOCATION C.
    COMMENTARY Probably the earliest-known Dublin-printed children's book written by an Irishman [Dm exhib. cat., 1981, pp 21–2].

'DELLE SARA', pseud. See **AIKEN, Albert W.**

DE MILLE, James, b. St John, New Brunswick (Canada) 1837 (1833 according to DLB), d. 1880. Novelist, academic and miscellaneous writer, JDeM was the son of Elizabeth and Nathan DeMill, a school-teacher and founder of an academy. He added the last 'e' to his own name. He graduated from Brown Univ., Providence (RI) in 1854, was professor of classics in Acadia College (NS,1860–65), and held the chair of history and rhetoric at Dalhousie College (Halifax) until his death. He contributed to periodicals in the US and wrote 20 novels, some of which appeared first in serial form. He characterized them as 'pot–boilers'. He also authored *Elements of Rhetoric* (New York 1878). SOURCE Allibone Suppl., i, p. 474; DCB; DLB, ic, 251.

D51   *Andy O'Hara; or, the child of providence* [anon.].
New York: Carlton & Porter, 1861. SOURCE DLB, ic; OCLC. LOCATION Drew Univ.,
Madison (NJ).
COMMENTARY Religious fiction [OCLC].

D52   *The seven hills* (by James De Mille).
Boston: Lee & Shepard; New York: Lee, Shepard & Dillingham, 1873 (ill.). SOURCE
RLIN; OCLC. LOCATION NN.
COMMENTARY Classified as Irish juvenile fiction [RLIN].

DENANCÉ, L.V. Popular French novelist (Brown mistakenly has L.V. de Nance), fl. 1865.
SOURCE CCF.

D53   *O'Sullivan. Épisode de la dernière ensurrection d'Irlande* (by L.V. Denancé).
+ Limoges: Eugène Ardant & C. Thibaut, [1865]. SOURCE Brown, 482 ([1874?] edn).
LOCATION D, L, BNF ([1866] edn).
COMMENTARY Fiction for juveniles. Concerns the French invasion of Ireland in 1798,
as told by O'Sullivan himself [Brown].

D54   *Indomptable Irlande, épisode de l'ensurrection en 1640 d'Irlande* (by L.V. Denancé).
+ Paris: Hatier, n.d. (ill.; Bibliothèque Anecdotique et Littéraire). SOURCE Brown 2,
1091. LOCATION InND Loeber coll.
COMMENTARY Historical fiction. The scene is laid near Athlone (Co. Westmeath) at first, then
in the south, and finally between Killala Bay (Co. Mayo) and Sligo. Daniel O'Cousserys, an
Irish leader, gets into a Cromwellian fort near Athlone by means of a token. He hopes to seize
it but instead has difficulty in escaping from it to Connacht where he proceeds to organize
against the English. Cromwell resolves to do away with him and employs an Irishman,
O'Mearn. But O'Mearn goes over to the Irish side. He joins a leader, MacNeuill, in Tipperary
and together they go to warn O'Cousserys of his danger and to meet a French ship arriving
with aid. O'Cousserys is killed and his son Patrick and O'Mearn escape to France. The book
begins with an *aperçue historique* of Ireland before 1640 and concludes with a sketch of Irish
history from 1640. There is an account of Mme Maud Gonne (afterwards McBride) and the
frontispiece is a portrait of her [Brown 2].

D55   *Tradition de famille, ou l'Irlande en 1640 d'Irlande* (by L.V. Denancé).
Paris: Rigaud, [1877] (Bibliothèque Religieuse, Morale et Classique). SOURCE IBL, 16
(1928), p. 59; CCF. LOCATION BNF.
COMMENTARY Historical fiction surrounding the 1641 rebellion [RL].

'DE NAVERY, Raoule', pseud. See DAVID, Mme Marie.

DENISON, Mary Andrews (née Mary Andrews; also known as Mrs Charles Wheeler
Denison, Mary A. Denison, and Mrs M.A. Denison), b. Cambridge (MA) 1826, d. Baltimore
(MD) 1911. American novelist, short story writer and temperance supporter, MAD'S parents
were Thomas Franklin Andrews and Jerusha Robbins. The death of her father spurred her to
write to supplement the family's income. She became a prolific author of pulp fiction and
dime novels with over 60 titles to her name. Her husband, Revd Charles Wheeler Denison,
was the author of several nautical novels and editor of the *Emancipator*, the first anti-slavery
journal in New York, and of the *Olive Branch* (Boston), to which she contributed and also
edited. She lived for a time in British Guiana (where her husband was consul general), in
Philadelphia, Buffalo (NY) and in Washington (DC). She edited the *Lady's Enterprise* (location
not known) and published short stories and dialogues in *Gleeson's Literary Companion* (location
not known) in 1860. She appears to have maintained an interest in Irish matters. Aside from

the following short fiction, her 'The blue vein', published in the Dollar Newspaper (Philadelphia, [*c*.1855]) tells a love story set partly in Ireland and partly in the US at the time of the American Revolution. Her *Nobody's child, and other stories* (Philadelphia, 1857), includes a story, 'A genuine Pat'. Only her work with known Irish content is listed below. SOURCE Adv. in C.J. Peterson, *Kate Aylesford* (Philadelphia, [*c*.1855]); Allibone Suppl., i, p. 477; Brick Row cat. 35/11; Burke, p. 189; DAB; Dime novels; Wright, iii, pp 151–2 (list of her other novels); www.letrs.indiana.edu/web/w/wright2.

D56   *Zelda. A tale of the Massachusetts colony* (by Jane Howard and Mrs M.A. Denison).
+ Boston: Elliott, Thomes & Talbot, 1866 (Standard American Authors. Ten Cent Novelette Series, No. 32). SOURCE Brick Row cat. 127/6. LOCATION MH, InND Loeber coll.

COMMENTARY 100 pp, continuous pagination, consisting of three novellas: 'Zelda', 'On a lee-shore: A tale of the coast', and 'The Irish heiress' (by Mrs M.A. Denison). The last story is probably set in Ireland. Its main character is Nora McLester, who is caught stealing straw-berries from the garden of Miss Arminty. She stole the strawberries because her mother was sick and her father used all the money for drink. Miss Arminty goes with her to visit her mother and finds that Nora's father has just died. It turns out that Nora is an heiress and that Miss Arminty is poor. However, in this reversal of fortunes, Nora makes sure that Miss Arminty is provided for [ML].

D57   *Erin go bragh!* (by Mrs Mary A. Denison).
+ Washington (DC): Globe Printing & Publishing House, 1879 (Editor's edn, com-pliments of publishers). SOURCE Wright, iii, 1492. LOCATION D, NUC, InND Loeber coll.

COMMENTARY The plot revolves around a number of hidden identities and contains several villains, all English, and several heroes, almost all Irish. The scene is set in England, Ireland, the US and the Continent, and the action takes places toward the end of the eighteenth cen-tury and includes the 1798 rebellion. The book propounds the idea that Ireland will be saved in the future with the help of the US [ML].

DERENZY, Mrs Margaret Graves (née Graves; also known as **M.G. DeRenzy**), d. 1828 (1829 in NCBEL). Novelist, poet and children's author, MGD was a daughter of Anthony Graves of Thomastown (Co. Kilkenny) and a writer from a young age. Beginning with poetic tales of ghosts, fairies, and legendary heroes, she subsequently wrote poetry and became skilled in music, painting and French and Italian literature. Her *Parnassian geography; or, the little ideal wanderer* (Wellington, [1824]) is a geography book for children, partly in verse. She wrote *A whisper to a newly-married pair, from a widowed wife* (Wellington, 1824), which contains a brief biographical account of her by the editor of the *Irish Shield*. She married Maj. DeRenzy (first name not known), who had served in Spain and Portugal during the Peninsular War, and who presumably was of Irish descent. But the marriage was an unhappy one because of his 'illicit passion' for other women. He eventually eloped to Paris with a 'Miss L.'. MGD must have been widowed prior to 1824, and her writing career postdates this. She lived most of her life in Co. Kilkenny, but two years before her death she moved to the house of her brother in New Ross (Co. Wexford) where she wrote the following novel. She probably can be identified with the Mrs DeRenzy who lived at Ring-wood-lodge near Enniscorthy in 1814. She was the author of a chapbook of 15pp, *Nothing at all* (London, 1835, 5th edn). She died of consumption in 1828 or 1829, but several of her works for children remained in press after her death. SOURCE Alston, pp 13, 119; Colman, p. 66; A. Leet, *Directory* (Dublin, 1814), p. 336; NCBEL 4, p. 329; OCLC; O'Donoghue, p. 105; RIA/DIB.

D58   *The singular and extraordinary adventures of poor little bewildered Henry* [anon.]
+ Wellington: Houlston, 1825 (ill.; see Plate 53). Source Blackwell's cat. B148/187.
LOCATION PC.
COMMENTARY *Wellington edn* No other copy located [RL].
London: [publisher?], [1830 or earlier]. SOURCE Mentioned on the title page of M.G.
DeRenzy, *A gift from the mountains* (London, 1830, 3rd edn).
London: Houlston, 1835, 4th edn (as *The singular and extraordinary adventures of poor
little bewildered Henry: who was shut up in an old abbey for three weeks: A story founded
on fact*; ill.). SOURCE OCLC. LOCATION Univ. of North Carolina, Greensboro.
New York: Mahlon Day, 1832 (as *The singular and extraordinary adventures of poor lit-
tle bewildered Henry: who was shut up in an old abbey for three weeks: A story founded
on fact* by the author of 'Nothing at all'). SOURCE OCLC. LOCATION CtY.
COMMENTARY 31pp for the Wellington edn and 21pp for the New York edn. Fiction for juveniles. Remained in print in London until at least 1850. Wrongly ascribed to Mrs Mary
Margaret Sherwood in RLIN [RL; RLIN].

D59   *The old Irish knight: A Milesian tale of the fifth century* [anon.].
+ London: Poole & Edwards, 1828. SOURCE Brown, 485; Block, p. 58; British Fiction;
Garside, 1828:39. LOCATION Corvey CME 3-628-48291-7, Ireland related fiction, D, L.
COMMENTARY Contents: 'The old Irish knight' (set in ancient times in Ireland; has many
explanatory footnotes, and a poem 'The nun'); 'Story of Lorenzo. An allegory' (set in the val-
ley of 'Glenorbin') [RL].

D60   *A gift from the mountains; or, the happy Sabbath* (by M.G. DeRenzy).
+ London, Wellington: Houlston & Son, 1830, 3rd edn. SOURCE COPAC. LOCATION
PC, Univ. of Glasgow (n.d., 4th edn).
COMMENTARY No copy of the 1st edn located. Religious fiction for children. Advertisement
states: 'An excellent old lady, who lived among the mountains of Leinster, was in the habit
of bestowing on her young friends a number of Lilliputian productions. Her last gift was the
following little work' [RL].

DE RENZY, S.S. See DE RENZY, Capt. S. Sparow.

DE RENZY, Capt. S. Sparow (also know as S.S. De Renzy, and Sparow De Renzy), fl.
1813. Military man and novelist, possibly Irish, according to SSdeR's *Marian de Brittoon*
(London, 1822), he was formerly captain in the Royal South Gloucester Regiment and then
captain and adjutant of the duke of York's New Forest Rangers, both militia units in England.
SSdeR's descent is not clear but the De Renzy family resided in Ireland from the early-seventeenth century onward. He wrote two novels that feature women as main characters. The
poem *William Tell. A dramatic sketch* (London, 1824) has been ascribed to this author but is
by Mrs R. Trench (also known as Melesina Trench). SOURCE Fenning cat. 176/268; British
Fiction; Garside, 1813:18; 1822:28; RL.

D61   *The faithful Irishwoman, or the house of Dunder* (by S.S. De Renzy; dedicated to
the author's uncle, Sir Solomon Dunder, Bt).
London: Printed by J. Gillet, 1813, 2 vols. (subscribers' list). SOURCE Belanger, 34;
British Fiction; Garside, 1813:18; BD, p. 93. LOCATION CLU.
COMMENTARY Dedication signed 'Your affectionate Nephew, S.S. Dunder'. According to the
Monthly Review (1813), 'the character of a faithful Irish domestic is well drawn, her language
appears to have been copied from nature, and her uncouth expressions of attachment render
some scenes at once laughable and touching'. The subscribers' list contains only a few Irish
names [cited in *Éire-Ireland*, 19(2) (1984), p. 118; Garside; RL].

D62   *Marian de Brittoon; or, the rector's orphan granddaughter. A novel* (by S. Sparow De Renzy).

+ London: W. Wright, 1822, 3 vols. SOURCE Block, p. 58; British Fiction; Garside, 1822:28; COPAC. LOCATION Corvey CME 3–28–47432–9, L, NUC, InND Loeber coll.

COMMENTARY Set in Ireland and describing social life in the country, the story deals with the vulnerability of a woman left without financial support. Marian, the orphan granddaughter of a country minister, brings pleasure and love to his last years of life. When he dies, his son – a lawyer in Dublin – does not find a will. This leaves Marian penniless. Former acquaintances suddenly shun her. She has to live with her uncle in Dublin, whose family always hated her for being her grandfather's favourite. Life becomes unbearable and she goes to another uncle, the scapegrace of the family. An earl's son falls in love with her and pursues her, to the great annoyance of her Dublin relatives. Eventually, the grandfather's will is found and Marian inherits a goodly income. After various impediments in the way of true love, she marries the earl's son. He inherits his father's estate and title and Marian becomes a duchess. With the reversal of her fortune, her old friends return [ML].

D63   *Life, love, and politics; or the adventures of a novice. A tale* (by Sparow De Renzy).

+ London: Knight & Lacey, 1825, 2 vols. SOURCE British Fiction; Garside, 1825:26; COPAC. LOCATION Corvey CME 3–628–48566–5, L, NUC.

COMMENTARY No Irish content [RL].

DE RENZY, Sparow. See **DE RENZY, Capt. S. Sparow**.

'DERING, Ross', pseud. See **BALFOUR, Frederick Henry**.

'DERING, Ross George', pseud. See **BALFOUR, Frederick Henry**.

DE SAFFRON, Marie. See **DAVID, Mme Marie**.

DESART, William Ulick O'Connor Cuffe, 4th earl (styled Viscount Castlecuffe until 1865), b. Grosvenor Crescent (Middx.) 1845, d. Falmouth Harbour (Corn.) 1898 (not 1928 as in Brown 2). Novelist and sporting writer, WUO'CD was the eldest son of the 3rd earl of Desart and Elizabeth Lucy Campbell (daughter of the 1st Earl Cawdor) and was educated at Eton and Bonn. He served in the Grenadier Guards until assuming the earldom at age 20. His first marriage to Maria Emma Georgina Preston ended in divorce in 1878. He married secondly Ellen Odette Bischoffsheim in 1881. He wrote for the London papers, frequently on hunting, which was his passion. He often lived in London, away from the family seat, Desart Court (Co. Kilkenny), leading to its neglect. He was the nephew of the author Maria La Touche§. Only his novels with known Irish content are listed below. SOURCE Allibone Suppl, i, p. 427, [under 'Cuffe']; Brown, p. 87; Brown 2, p. 67; *CP*, iv, pp 229–30; M.F. Young (ed.), *Letters of a noble woman* (London, 1908), p. 65; O'Donoghue, p. 91 [under Cuffe]; Sutherland, p. 180; *Vanishing country houses*, p. 91.

D64   *Beyond these voices* (by William Ulick O'Connor Cuffe, earl of Desart).

London: Tinsley Bros, 1870, 3 vols. SOURCE Brown 2, 357; COPAC. LOCATION L.

COMMENTARY Set against a background of Fenianism, the story involves Tom Dillon, who lives with his sister Emily in Ballytoben House (Co. Tipperary). Tom seduces and then marries a peasant girl named Kathleen. Her brothers, in revenge for the eviction of their mother, shoot Tom's friend Verner. This and other incidents cause estrangement between Tom and his wife. He goes to London and forms a liaison with a married woman but comes back full of remorse to find that his wife has disappeared. Believing her dead, he is trapped into marriage with Lady Alice Rosemore, only to learn that his wife is alive. The denouement is tragic and yet happy. The villain is Fr Murphy, parish priest of Killblazer, while Church of Ireland clergy are mildly satirized [Brown 2].

D65   *Mervyn O'Connor and other tales* (by William Ulick O'Connor Cuffe, earl of Desart).
+ London: Hurst & Blackett, 1880, 3 vols. SOURCE Brown, 486; COPAC. LOCATION
D, L, NUC.

COMMENTARY Contents: 'Mervyn O'Connor', 'A capital match; and what came of it', 'Kilsheelah', 'A bear fight', 'The Arlmore mystery', 'Shocking! A fragment of the memoirs of an English lady', 'The pride of Kilclare', 'The mystery of Ellaby Castle', 'Our vigilance committee', 'John: A Cowes idyl', 'The lost lady: A very strange story', 'The ace of spades' [ML].

DESPARD, Mrs —. See **DESPARD, Charlotte.**

DESPARD, C. See **DESPARD, Charlotte.**

DESPARD, Charlotte (née French; also known as **C. Despard, Mrs Despard,** and **Mrs M.C. Despard**) b. Ripple Vale (Kent) 1844, d. Whitehead (Co. Antrim) 1939. An English-born romantic novelist, a suffragette, a social and political activist and a pacifist, CD was the daughter of William French, a descendant of the Frenches of Co. Roscommon, and an heiress, Margaret Eccles. Her brother John, Lord French, was the last lord lieutenant of Ireland. In 1870 she married Maximilian Despard of Queen's Co. (Co. Laois), a successful businessman in the opium and tea trade in China. Because of his ill-health they travelled each winter and with her husband's approval CD engaged herself in writing conventional romantic novels with exotic settings. To assuage her grief after his death in 1890 she turned to philanthropy and lived among the poor in south London, an area with many Irish immigrants, where she set up services such as a soup kitchen, health clinic and social clubs. She became increasingly militant politically, a Marxist, and president of the Women's Freedom League. She was imprisoned several times in Holloway prison for her work for women's suffrage and regularly engaged in passive resistance protests on the grounds of 'no taxation without representation'. She wrote articles and pamphlets on women's issues and on religion – she had earlier converted to catholicism. In defiance of her beloved brother's position, she became a supporter of the Irish Self-Determination League. After the Anglo-Irish peace, she moved to Ireland in 1921 where she agitated for better treatment of prisoners and worked closely with Maude Gonne McBride in relief efforts during the Irish civil war. Her commitment to world socialism grew and the new Irish Free State classified her as a dangerous subversive. After her house in Dublin was attacked by an anti-communist mob in 1933, she moved to Belfast where she interceded on behalf of the Catholics and supported anti-appeasement campaigns. She died in her ninety-fifth year, after a fall. CD published *Songs of the red dawn* ([Dublin], 1932), a small collection of political poems and works on the position of women in society. Many of her letters are in the NLI (MSS 24,102, 24,104), and TCD (MS 6,788), and other papers are listed in ODNB. SOURCE Allibone Suppl., i, p. 480 [under C. Despard and Mrs M.C.]; Blain, p. 283; Field Day, v. p. 93; M. Mulvihill, *Charlotte Despard* (London, 1989); C. Murphy, *The women's suffrage movement and Irish society in the early twentieth century* (Philadelphia, 1989), pp 63*ff*; NUC; ODNB; Rowan cat. 50, part A/284; Sutherland, pp 180–1.

D66   *Chaste as ice, pure as snow* (by Mrs M.C. Despard).
London: Samuel Tinsley, 1874, 3 vols. SOURCE Blain, p. 283; Sutherland, p.180;
COPAC. LOCATION L (2nd edn).

COMMENTARY Portrait of a wife wronged by her husband's suspicions [Sutherland].

D67   *Wandering fires* (by Mrs M.C. Despard).
      London: Samuel Tinsley, 1874, 3 vols. SOURCE Allibone Suppl., i, p. 480; Mulvihill,
      p. 203; COPAC. LOCATION C, E.
D68   *A modern Iago: a novel* (by C. Despard).
      London: Remington & Co., 1879, 2 vols. SOURCE Allibone Suppl., i, p. 480; Sutherland,
      p. 180; COPAC. LOCATION L.
      COMMENTARY A study of modern marriage [Sutherland].
D69   *A voice from the dim millions; being the true history of a working-woman* (ed. [*sic*]
      by C. Despard).
      + London: Griffith & Farran, [1884] (ill. F. Barnard). LOCATION L, InND Loeber
      coll. (n.d. edn).
COMMENTARY 128pp. Reached a 5th edn in 1899. Set in England. The story is narrated by a
woman who wants to tell about her family's suffering in the hope that such knowledge will
make people aware of the degrading circumstances under which many people live. Initially the
family lives comfortably on a small farm but the reversal of their fortunes starts when the eldest son develops fits, making him incapable of work, followed by the farm having some bad
years, and the death of the father. The mother and children move to London, thinking that
by fine needlework they can earn a living. Life is extremely hard and their circumstances go
from bad to worse. One daughter goes to work in Bristol but is seduced and disappears. The
two youngest children are sent to Canada for adoption through a charitable organization. Almost
all of the remaining members die in very needy circumstances. But just when the narrator
thinks that she is the only one left alive, she meets her wayward sister. The two set up a sewing
business which proves successful. They make sure that the people who work for them are better off than they themselves were in similar circumstances [ML].
D70   *Jonas Sylvester* (by C. Despard).
      London: W. Swan Sonnenschein, Lowrey & Co., 1886. SOURCE Allibone Suppl., i, p.
      480; Mulvihill, p. 203; COPAC. LOCATION L.
D71   *The rajah's heir* [anon.].
      London: Smith, Elder & Co., 1890, 3 vols. LOCATION L.
      London: Smith, Elder & Co., 1892 (new edn). SOURCE Topp 5, p. 274; COPAC.
      LOCATION Newcastle, Robinson Library
      Leipzig: Bernard Tauchnitz, 1890. SOURCE T & B, 2654.
      Philadelphia: J.B. Lippincott, 1890 (Series of Select Novels). SOURCE Topp 5, p. 274.
      COMMENTARY No copies of the Leipzig and Philadelphia edns located [RL].
D72   *Outlawed. A novel on the woman suffrage question* (by Mrs Despard and Mabel
      Collins (Mrs Keningale Cooke)).
      + London: Henry J. Drane, [1908]. LOCATION L.
      COMMENTARY No Irish content [ML].

DESPARD, Mathilda Pratt (née Pratt; known as **Mathilda Despard**), fl. 1878. American
novelist and children's writer, MD translated a children's book from German (Washington (DC),
1874) and published *Old New York* (New York, 1875). SOURCE Allibone Suppl., i, p. 480; NUC.
D73   *Kilrogan cottage: A novel* (by Mathilda Despard).
      New York: Harper & Bros, 1878 (Harper's Library of American Fiction). SOURCE
      Wright, iii, 1515; Emerald Isle cat. 25/260. LOCATION NUC.
      COMMENTARY Set in Co. Fermanagh [Emerald Isle cat.].

DESPOURRINS, M., pseud. 'A Lady', fl. 1814. Fiction writer, MD probably was from
Kinsale or another part of Co. Cork. The dedication of the following volume was signed M.

Despourrins; one of the subscribers is Mrs Despourrins of Biggar, Scotland, but most of the subscribers are from Kinsale and Co. Cork. According to the dedication, the writer's father was a friend of Lady Kingsale[1], resident in Kinsale, and the novel was written 'a few years back'. The Despourrins family name suggests a Huguenot or French origin, but this family has not been identified in Ireland. SOURCE Allibone i, p. 495 (probably mistakenly mentions the author's name as M. Despaurrius); RL.

D74   *The Neville family; an interesting tale, founded on facts* (by 'A Lady'; dedicated to Lady Kinsale [*sic*, Kingsale]).

+ Cork: Printed for the author by W. West & Co., 1814, 3 vols. (subscribers' list). LOCATION D.

London: Printed for T. Hughes, 1815, 3 vols. SOURCE British Fiction (also Update 3); Garside 1815:21; Garside (2003). LOCATION CME 3-628-48190-2.

COMMENTARY Set in England, the West Indies, France and Ireland, it tells the tale of a soldier, Charles Neville. According to the introd., 'some characters here represented, still exist' [ML; RL].

D'ESTERRE-KEELING, Elsa (also known as **Mrs Elsa Keeling**), b. Dublin 1860, d. 1935. Novelist, playwright, poet and translator, ED went to school in Dublin and finished her education in Germany. Evidently an able linguist, she worked for a while as a translator for the British Foreign Office and translated German songs. Afterwards she was a schoolmistress in Oxford and London (1884–90) and became principal of the Chelsea School of Elocution. In 1893 she lectured before the Irish Literary Society in London, of which she was a member. She contributed to the *Leisure Hour, Academy, Graphic, Belgravia, Temple Bar, Pall Mall Gazette*, and other London periodicals. Tauchnitz published her *A laughing philosopher* in their textbook series in 1916. Between 1884 and 1898 she published eight works of fiction. In later life, however, she suppressed reference to her novels and marriage. SOURCE Allibone Suppl., ii, p. 933 [under Keeling]; Alston, p. 138; Colman, p. 66; O'Donoghue, p. 224 [under Keeling]; RIA/DIB; Ryan, pp 74, 115–16; Sutherland, p. 346 [under Keeling].

D75   *Three sisters; or, sketches of a highly original family* [anon.] (dedicated to the mother of the dauntless three).

+ London: Sampson Low, Marston, Searle & Rivington, 1884, 2 vols. SOURCE Alston, p. 138. LOCATION L, InND Loeber coll.

Leipzig: Bernard Tauchnitz, 1884. SOURCE T & B, 2295. LOCATION NUC.

New York: G. Munro, 1885. LOCATION NUC.

COMMENTARY Possibly an autobiographical novel. A family story of travel and self-sufficiency involving Mrs O'Brien, her three daughters, and a nephew who move to a city in Germany to earn a living. They call themselves a jolly family and laugh a lot. The mother gives English lessons, one of the daughters teaches music and another does translations. The youngest daughter moves to Russia as governess to a family, and dies there. After many adventures in earning money and after many examples of how Germans pronounce English, one girl marries a relative and the mother and the remaining daughter move to London [ML].

D76   *Bib and Tucker: being the revelations of an infant in arms. An absurdity* (by Elsa D'Esterre-Keeling).

London: Sampson Low, Marston, Searle & Rivington, 1884. SOURCE Alston, p. 138; COPAC. LOCATION L.

---

1 This was Susan, daughter of Conway Blennerhassett of Castle Conway (Co. Kerry), who married John de Courcy, 21st Lord Kingsale in 1763, and who died in Kinsale in 1819 (CP, vii, p. 291).

D77 *The professor's wooing. Being the courtships of Monsieur La Mie* [anon.].
London: Sampson Low, Marston, Searle & Rivington, 1886, 2 vols. SOURCE Alston,
p. 138; COPAC. LOCATION L.
Leipzig: Bernard Tauchnitz, 1887. SOURCE T & B, 2471. LOCATION NUC.

D78 *In thoughtland and in dreamland* (by Elsa D'Esterre-Keeling).
London: T. Fisher Unwin, 1890. SOURCE Alston, p. 138; COPAC. LOCATION L.
Leipzig: Bernard Tauchnitz, 1890. SOURCE T & B 2653. LOCATION NUC.
COMMENTARY Short sketches [BLC].

D79 *Orchardscroft. The story of an artist* (by Elsa D'Esterre-Keeling).
London: T. Fisher Unwin, 1892. SOURCE Daims, 1616; COPAC. LOCATION L.
Leipzig: Bernard Tauchnitz, 1892. SOURCE T & B, 2866. LOCATION NUC.
New York: Cassell, 1892. SOURCE Daims, 1616. LOCATION NUC.

D80 *Appassionata. A musician's story* (by Elsa D'Esterre-Keeling; dedicated to Nelly).
London: William Heinemann, 1893. SOURCE Daims, 1614. LOCATION L.
+ Leipzig: Bernard Tauchnitz, 1894. SOURCE T & B, 3007. LOCATION InND Loeber
coll., NUC.
New York: R. Bonners' Sons, 1893. SOURCE Daims, 1614. LOCATION NUC.
COMMENTARY A novel of unhappy married life, it concerns a beautiful Finnish artist who loves
a female artist and is less in love with her husband, a Russian count. Against her husband's
will she gives a concert. Her husband deserts her and even after the birth of a baby boy is not
willing to take her back. He allows the baby and the nurse to live in one of his homes but
does not meet the baby until he is three years old. The nurse is actually his wife, but he does
not let on that he knows [ML].

D81 *Old maids and young* (by Elsa D'Esterre-Keeling).
London, Paris, New York, Melbourne: Cassell & Co., 1895.
Leipzig: Bernard Tauchnitz, 1896. SOURCE T & B, 3126; Daims, 1615; COPAC.
LOCATION L, NUC.

D82 *A return to nature. A Kentish idyll* (by Elsa D'Esterre-Keeling).
London: Jarrold & Son, 1896 (Daffodil Library). SOURCE Daims, 1617; COPAC.
LOCATION L (1897 edn). COMMENTARY No copy of the 1896 edn located [RL].

D83 *The Queen's serf. Being the adventures of Ambrose Gwinett in England and Spanish
America* (by Elsa D'Esterre-Keeling).
London: T. Fisher Unwin, 1898. SOURCE Alston, p. 138; COPAC. LOCATION L.
Leipzig: Bernard Tauchnitz, 1899. LOCATION NUC.

'DE SAIX, Tyler', pseud. See **STACPOOLE, Henry de Vere.**

DE WAILLY, Armand François Léon (known as Léon de Wailly), b. 1804, d. 1863. Popular
French writer and republican politician, AFLdeW can be identified with the L. de Wailly,
who translated into French several works by William Carleton§ and Laurence Sterne§. SOURCE
BLC; Brown, p. 304 [under Wailly]; RL; Topp 2, 211; Wolff, iv, p. 229.

D84 *Stella et Vanessa* (by Léon de Wailly).
Brussels: Meline, [1846], 2 vols. SOURCE Brown, 1646; Topp 2, p. 30; GLOL (n.d.
edn); OCLC. LOCATION NUC, CtY.
Paris: L. Hachette & Co., 1855. SOURCE OCLC. LOCATION Dt, NN, BNF.
London: Richard Bentley, 1850, 2 vols. (trans. by Lady Lucie Duff Gordon as *Stella
and Vanessa. A romance*). SOURCE Blain, p. 442 [under Gordon]; Brown, 528 [under
Duff, mistaking translator as Lady Gordon Duff]; Topp 2, p. 30; Topp 8, 24; Block,
p. 247; Wolff, 6968. LOCATION L, NUC.

London: Richard Bentley, 1853 (trans. by Lady Lucy [*sic*] Duff Gordon as *Stella and Vanessa; a romance of the days of Swift*). SOURCE COPAC. LOCATION E.

COMMENTARY Set in Ireland around 1730 with Jonathan Swift§ and the two important women in his life, Vanessa VanHomrigh and Esther Johnson (known as Stella) as the main characters [RL; Blain; Brown].

DE WIL, Ernest, fl. 1893. Novelist.

D85 *The Brookham mystery* (Ernest De Wil).

London, New York: The International Publishing Co., 1893. SOURCE Brown 2, 367 (not 1873); OCLC. LOCATION NUC.

COMMENTARY Begins with the abduction in Italy of the two-year-old son of the heir to an Irish baronetcy. The scene changes to Ireland. There is a trial of murder with remarks about jury-packing. Parts are anti-Catholic in tone [Brown 2].

DICKSON, Maria Frances, pseud. '**M.F.D.**' (later known as Mrs Maria Frances Smith), fl. 1838. Protestant religious fiction and travel writer, MFD was the niece of Stephen Creagh Sandes, bishop of Cashel (Co. Tipperary). She contributed to the *Christian Lady's Magazine* (London, 1836–37, edited by Elizabeth Tonna§), and probably to *Bentley's Miscellany* (London, April, 1838), but this is not confirmed. Other works of hers are, *Souvenirs of a summer in Germany in 1836* (London, 1838, 2 vols.) and a book on Norway (Dublin, 1870). The preface to her *Scenes on the shores of the Atlantic* was written from Vermont (Co. Limerick) in 1845 and recounts her journey in the west of Ireland in the company of Viscountess Guillamore. There is an unexplained gap in her writing between 1845 and 1870. MFD is not to be confused with a Mary Downing (1818?–1881?) who under the same pseud. contributed to periodicals around the same time. SOURCE BLC; Curran index; Irish pseudonyms; RL.

D86 *The happy family; or, talents well employed. A tale for youth* (by 'M.F.D.').

London: L. & G. Seeley, 1838, 2nd edn. LOCATION PC.

COMMENTARY No copy of the first edn located [RL].

D87 *Sabbath musings and every-day scenes* [anon.] (dedicated to Stephen Creagh Sandes, bishop of Cashel).

+ London: R.B. Seeley & W. Burnside, 1839 (ill. B? Smith). LOCATION L.

COMMENTARY Fiction for juveniles. 'Sabbath musings' was first published in the *Christian Lady's Magazine* (London, 1836–7), and the other stories first appeared in various periodicals. Contents: 'Reflections in a church-yard – an Irish cabin', 'Evil spirits – a sinner's death-bed', 'The Sabbath in the country – a pleasant rencontre at a German table d'hote', 'An interesting acquaintance', '"Glory to God!"', 'Remarks on conversion – sketch on a renewed character', 'Narrative of Ellen M—', 'An evening in autumn – a young girl who had "chosen the better part" – the three brothers', 'The uses of disappointments – a walk in the streets on an illumination night', 'The river Lee – death of Rev. Horace Townsend', 'The effects of religion on a woman's mind – young man at Rosstrevor', 'Power of the scriptures to give relief under mental distress illustrated', 'A domestic calamity', 'A morning ramble – narrative of a young officer and his Creole wife – visit to a cottage', 'Oriental expressions and customs met with among the Irish peasantry', 'Anecdotes illustrating the usefulness of giving away religious books – Mr. Venn and the inn-keeper – the traveller and the waiting maid – the "sinner's friend" – the soldier', 'Giving up all for Christ – David Margoschi – saying grace in an Irish cabin', 'Life without religion', 'The widow and her son', 'The evils of procrastination – visits to the widow' [RL].

D88 *The lost farm; or, the effects of a lie. An Irish story* (by 'M.F.D.').

+ London: L. & G. Seeley, 1838, 2nd edn. SOURCE Mentioned on title page of 'M.F.D', *The visit* (London, 1842). LOCATION PC.

COMMENTARY No copy of the first edn located. 70pp. Religious fiction reviewed in the *Christian Lady's Magazine* (London, 1842) as a sixpenny book [RL].

D89   *The visit to Clarina; or, the effects of revenge. An Irish story* (by 'M.F.D.').
+ London: L. & G. Seeley, 1842. LOCATION D, L.

COMMENTARY Religious and moral sketches written for young people set in the village of Clarina (Co. Limerick) near 'Carrig O'Gunniel [Carrigogunnel] Castle', where Quilan and his family live. Gleeson, a schoolmaster from Co. Kerry, and his nephew Lawrence come to visit. Gleeson values above all his Irish Bible. Lawrence extols to the Quilan children the virtues of the Bible. Gleeson advises about the removal of manure from in front of the Quilan house. In a later chapter, Quilan's desire for revenge on another person is curbed. Gleeson describes the characteristics of a true patriot [RL].

D90   *Scenes on the shores of the Atlantic* (by 'M.F.D.'; dedicated to the Viscountess Guillamore).
+ London: T.C. Newby, 1845, 2 vols. LOCATION L.
COMMENTARY Set in the west of Ireland and written in the form of a travelogue with dialogue [RL].

D91   *My first ring. A tale* (by 'M.F.D.').
Dublin: George Herbert, 1871. SOURCE Alston, p. 120. LOCATION L.
COMMENTARY 54 pp; also includes *In memoriam: Poems* by Francis Charles Hassard [BLC].

D92   *Childhood's happy and unhappy days* (by 'M.F.D.').
+ Dublin: George Herbert; London: Simpkin, Marshall & Co., 1873 (ill.). SOURCE Alston, p. 120. LOCATION L.
COMMENTARY Fiction for juveniles, consisting of a chapbook of 28pp. Contents (excluding poetry): 'Our dear governess', 'Our next governess', 'Fairy land'. The frontispiece consists of, incongruously, a series of oriental prints of acrobats [RL].

DILLON, Edwin, fl. 1807. Despite its autobiographical claim, the following work may have been written by another person. SOURCE RL.

D93   *A singular tale! or, the adventures of Edwin Dillon, a young Irishman. Interspersed with pathetic and comical stories ... written by himself.*
+ London: Printed for the author by E. Thomas, [1807] (ill. J. Oastler). SOURCE NSTC. LOCATION O, ViU, InND Loeber coll.
COMMENTARY Chapbook of 36pp. Edwin, the only son of Revd John Dillon finds himself almost penniless after his parents' deaths. He sets out from the west of Ireland to Dublin to meet his maternal grandfather, who had disinherited his mother because of her marriage. While walking to Dublin he meets various characters, such as a soldier and a Jewish peddler, who tell him their histories. In Dublin he has various adventures, one of which lands him in jail. When he finally meets up with his grandfather, he is received with open arms and eventually inherits the greater part of his grandfather's property [ML].

DILLON, Henry Augustus (Dillon-Lee), Viscount Dillon (also known as Viscount Dillon-Lee), b. Brussels 1777, d. London 1832. Novelist, pamphleteer and miscellaneous writer, HAD was the only son of Charles Dillon-Lee, 12th Viscount Dillon of Costello-Gallen, and Henrietta Maria Phipps. He was educated at Christ Church, Oxford, and became a colonel in the Irish Brigade in 1794, and colonel in the duke of York's Irish Regiment of foot in 1807. He succeeded his father in 1813, thereby becoming one of the largest landowners of his day in Ireland, with estates at Lough Glynn (Co. Roscommon). HAD was MP for Harwich (Essex) and then Co. Mayo from 1802 to 1813. He favoured the Union, but he advocated Catholic claims in Ireland in two pamphlets: *A short view of the Catholic question* (London, 1801) and *Letter to the noblemen and gentlemen who composed the deputation from the Catholics of Ireland* (Dublin, 1805). He married in 1807 at Castle McGarrett (Co. Mayo), Henrietta, sister of Dominick, 1st Baron Oranmore. Thomas Moore§ in his journal for 1829, referred to HAD 'reading aloud of an evening all the "good coarse novels"'. Aside from two novels, he wrote poetry and published *Eccelino da Romano, surnamed the tyrant of Padua* (London, 1828). SOURCE Allibone i, p. 503; Brady, p. 61; CP, iv, pp 361–2; Block, p. 60; Falkner Greirson cat. 'Jane'/91; J. Foster (ed.), *Alumni Oxonienses, 1715–1886* (Oxford, 1888), i, p. 371; NSTC, ser. 1, ii, p. 50; ODNB; O'Donoghue, p. 109; [E. Rennie], *Traits of character* (London, 1860), ii, pp 197–232; RIA/DIB; J. Russell (ed.), *Memoirs, journal, and correspondence of Thomas Moore* (London, 1854), v, p. 217.

D94   *The life and opinions of Sir Richard Maltravers, an English gentleman of the seventeenth century* [anon.].
    + London: G. & W.B. Whittaker, 1822, 2 vols. SOURCE Sadleir, 708; British Fiction; Garside, 1822:29. LOCATION Corvey CME 3–628–48097–3, D, L, NUC, InND Loeber coll.
COMMENTARY Contrasts the manners of the seventeenth century with those of the author's own day. No Irish content. Maria Edgeworth§ recounted in 1822 that Honora Edgeworth's§ experience of HD was 'as extraordinary [a] talker and egoist that ever existed. He treated her by reading her with great enthusiasm many passages from his strange book *The Life and Opinions of Sir Richard Maltravers* – Such a rhodomontade as I never saw except in a translation from a German novel' [ML; Sadleir; W.S. Scott (ed.), *Letters of Maria Edgeworth and Anna Letitia Barbauld* (London, 1953), p. 34].

D95   *Rosaline de Vere* [anon.].
    London: Treuttel & Würtz, Treuttel Jnr & Richter, 1824, 2 vols. SOURCE Black, 452; Block, p. 60; British Fiction; Garside, 1824:29. LOCATION Corvey CME 3–628–48547–9, L, NUC.
COMMENTARY Epistolary novel set in England and Italy [Black].

DILLON, Mrs J.J. O'Shea, b. Nenagh (Co. Tipperary), *c.*1839? Novelist and miscellaneous writer, Mrs JJO'SD was the daughter of journalist and poet John O'Shea§ and sister of John Augustus O'Shea§, a journalist and special correspondent well-known in his day. The year of her birth is not known, but her brother was born in 1839. Brown 2 mentions her brother's dates of birth and death and attributes *Roundabout recollections* to Mrs JJO'SD but they are in fact her brother's autobiographical writings. Perhaps she can be identified with E. O'Shea Dillon, who contributed to *A castle of Christmas eve; or, the tales the portraits told* (Dublin, 1885). SOURCE Brown 2, p. 72; E. Reilly, p. 243; RL; Sutherland, p. 482 [under John Augustus O'Shea].

D96   *Dark Rosaleen* (by Mrs J.J. O'Shea Dillon; dedicated to the author's brother, John Augustus O'Shea§).
    + London: Tinsley Bros, 1884, 3 vols. SOURCE Allibone Suppl., i, p. 490; Brown, 1359; Brown 2, 382. LOCATION D, L, InND Loeber coll.
COMMENTARY Set in the Vale of Lismore (Co. Waterford) *c.*1886–88. Relates the warm friendship between the Protestant rector, Adam Glover, and Fr John Kennedy, the parish priest. The priest, a fervent Young Irelander in his youth, is approached by two men from his past to enrol in the Fenian organization. He refuses, and forbids them to tamper with his parishioners. A love story between the priest's niece with the rector's nephew is interwoven, along with the murder of the rector. Pat Mahon, the schoolmaster and local villain, thief, spy and informer is suspected by everybody, but the murderer turns out to be the rector's mother, who confesses and dies [Brown 2].

DILLON, Sir John Talbot, Bt, b. Lismullen (Co. Meath) 1740, d. Dublin 1805. Literary historian, novelist and travel and history writer, JTD was the only son of Arthur Dillon and Elizabeth, daughter of Dr Ralph Lambert, bishop of Meath, and claimed descent from the Lords Roscommon and Dillon. He may be identified with the JD who entered TCD in 1757. He married in 1767, Millicent, daughter of George Drake of Fernhill (Berks.). He was MP for Co. Wicklow (1771–76) and for Blessington (Co. Wicklow, 1776–83). He travelled extensively in Italy and Spain and resided for some time at Vienna, where Emperor Joseph II created JTD and his heirs free barons of the Holy Roman Empire in 1782 in recognition of his 'exertions in Parliament to serve his country, by granting liberty to Roman Catholics to realize property in their native land'. JTD was a strong proponent of religious and political freedom and toleration and admired the Emperor's enlightened religious principles, publishing a *Political survey of the sacred Roman Empire* (London, 1782). He became an authority on Spain and Spanish literary history. His *Travels through Spain* (London, 1780) was widely translated and published. He published *The history of the reign of Peter the Cruel, King of Castile and Leon* (London, 1788, 2 vols.), and is probably best known for his *Historical and critical memoirs of the general revolution in France* (London, 1790), which contained original sources and eyewitness accounts of the French Revolution, with which Dillon was in sympathy. According to the title page of his *Alphonso and Eleonora* (London, 1800), he was late captain in the 2nd Surrey regiment of militia. At the time of the writing of this novel, he resided in Brompton, at that time just outside London. After the Act of Union he was created one of the first baronets of the United Kingdom of Great Britain and Ireland on 31 July 1801. SOURCE Allibone i, pp 503–4; BLC; Brady, p. 61; Burke's Peerage, 1963, i, p. 739; B & S, p. 230; HIP, iii, pp 59–61; ODNB; RIA/DIB.

D97 *Alphonso and Eleonora; or, the triumphs of valour and virtue. Illustrated by historical facts* (by John Talbot Dillon; dedicated to Patrick Dillon, earl of Roscommon, baron of Kilkenny-West).
+ London: J. Barker & W. Taylor, 1800, 2 vols. SOURCE Block, p. 60; British Fiction; Garside, D:1. LOCATION L, NUC.
COMMENTARY Story about Alphonso IX, king of Castile, and his wife, Eleonora of England. The author admires both for their virtues [ML].

DOAKE, Margaret, fl. 1880s, b. Co. Down. Novelist and poet, MD was the sister of Mrs Charles Montague Clarke§ (née Marion Doake), with whom she co-authored some works (see under Mrs Charles Montague Clarke§). An endorsement in the copy of *May darling* ([London], [1881]) in the NLI states that MD was 'late of Glen Logan, Dromara' (Co. Down). SOURCE Allibone Suppl., i, p. 494; Colman, pp 67–8; LVP, p. 139; O'Donoghue, p. 110; RL.
D98 *May darling* (by Margaret Doake).
+ [London]: The Literary Production Committee, [1881]. LOCATION D, L.
COMMENTARY No Irish content [ML].

DOAKE, Marion. See **CLARKE, Mrs Charles Montague**.

'DOCTOR HASTLER, M.R.S.P.Q.L.M.N.A.S.T. and L.L.Z.', pseud. See **BOSWELL, J.W.**

DOHERTY, Mrs Ann (née Hunter, also known as Ann Holmes Hunter Doherty,), b. 1789. English novelist, Block and Allibone spell AD's name as Dogherty, but this must be a mistake. In the second edn of *Ronaldsha* (London, 1815, 2 vols.) she is identified as Mrs Doherty, wife of Hugh Doherty§, Esq. (an Irish ex-Dragoon much older than she) and daughter of

Thomas Hunter of Beoley Hall (Worcs.), Gubbins (Herts.), and Mansfield Street, Portland Place (London). The couple lived together in Hertfordshire before she deserted him and their child, alleging cruelty. This evidently spurred her husband to respond by writing his own book, *The discovery* (London, 1807), which included her letters detailing how she had eloped with him from a private mad-house, where her parents had confined her. Hugh Doherty instituted a lawsuit in the court of king's bench, Westminster, against Philip William Wyatt (presumably the architect, son of James Wyatt) in 1811 for 'criminal conversation' with his wife, which was successful. AD's only Irish novel is listed below. SOURCE Allibone i, p. 511; Block, p. 61; Blain, p. 301; BLC; ViU cat.; NSTC, ser. 1, ii, p. 60; RL.

D99   *The Knight of the Glen. An Irish romance* [anon.].

      + London: G. Walker, 1815, 2 vols. SOURCE British Fiction; Garside, 1815:22; Block, p. 129; Belanger, 42. LOCATION Corvey CME 3–628–47982–7, Ireland related fiction, L.

COMMENTARY Gothic historical romance set largely in Connacht in the fourteenth century in the time of King Edward. The Prince O'Nial and his son 'the great Tyrone' have usurped lands and titles from Earl Ulick. Eventually they are restored to the earl's son who has been raised as a peasant, unaware of his true identity. The novel features the maiden Adelais, daughter of the exiled Uriel, Lord de Lacy, and ward of the calculating Prince O'Nial, a co-conspirator in Tyrone's schemes of power. The Knight of the Glen, Voltimorn, is Adelais's lover and Tyrone's nemesis. The plot resolves in the restitution of the heroine's father's title and estates, the exposure and defeat of the villain, and the revelation that the hero's heredity is much nobler than anticipated [RL; JB; Frank, 113].

DOHERTY, Hugh, pseud. 'H.D.', fl. 1807. HD was the son of John Doherty of Dublin, and M. Verner. His grandmother was the sister of George Canning of Garvagh (Co. Derry), who was the grandfather of the secretary of state and author George Canning. In 1807 HD was on half-pay from of the 23rd Light Dragoons and lived at 12 Temple Place, London, after his marriage to Ann Holmes Hunter Doherty§ had broken down. He wrote his novel about this in 1807 and in the next year he published a novel written by his wife (*Ronaldsha*, London, 1808, 2 vols.), for which he wrote the dedication and preface. In 1811 HD instituted a lawsuit in the court of king's bench, Westminster, against Philip William Wyatt (presumably, the architect, son of James Wyatt) for 'criminal conversation' with his wife, which was successful. SOURCE RL; Blain, p. 301.

D100   *The discovery; or, the mysterious separation of Hugh Doherty, Esq. and Ann his wife* (by 'H.D. Esq.').

      London: Printed by G. Sidney, 1807. SOURCE Block, p. 61; British Fiction; Garside, 1807:20. LOCATION D (1807, 3rd edn), L (1807, 3rd edn), ViU.

COMMENTARY The story, which is largely autobiographical, contains a 95pp introd. in which HD explains what happened to his wife. The author projected a second volume, which was never published [RL; NUC].

DOHERTY, J.M., fl. 1867. Irish-American writer.

D101   *Paddy Pungent; or, a rambling Irishman right from the ould sod* (by J.M. Doherty).

      + San Francisco: J. Winterburn & Co., 1867. SOURCE NSTC. LOCATION L, DCL.

COMMENTARY 110 pp. The travel account and comparative commentary of an Irishman living in America who visits Ireland and describes the sights and the people and their habits. He includes some history and eventually tries to place modern history in a larger frame by explaining archaeological and geological findings showing the age of the earth and the creatures that once lived on it. He praises America and its freedoms which, since they have led to people there being taller, smarter, and more enterprising, are an example to the rest of the world. He advocates free choice in marriage, which he believes will reduce the number of mentally impaired children resulting from forced marriages within classes [ML].

DOMENECH, L'Abbé. See **DOMENECH, L'Abbé Emmanuel Henri Dieudonné.**

DOMENECH, Emmanuel. See **DOMENECH, L'Abbé Emmanuel Henri Dieudonné.**

DOMENECH, L'Abbé Emmanuel Henri Dieudonné (known as **Emmanuel Domenech** and **L'Abbé Domenech**), b. Lyon (France) 1826, d. 1886. Priest, missionary, and travel writer, EHDD went to Mexico as a military chaplain and became a member of the cabinet of the Mexican emperor Maximilian. Upon his return to France, he was appointed book censor and minister of the department of the interior. As a writer, he is known mostly for his travel books, which include several volumes about Ireland, such as *La chaussée des géants* (Paris, 1868), about the Giants' Causeway (Co. Antrim). Many his books interweave local stories. He contributed to the *Paris Journal International*, 'Erin; A legendary tour', which was translated and published in Irish papers in 1863. SOURCE BLC; *Dictionnaire de biographie française* (Paris, 1967), xi; IBL, 8 (1917, June–July), p. 140; NUC.

D102   *Les gorges du diable; voyage et aventures en Irlande, souvenirs d'un touriste* (by Emmanuel Domenech; dedicated to Jacques Durant de Saint-Georges).
+ Paris: E. Maillet, 1864. SOURCE COPAC. LOCATION L, InND Loeber coll.
COMMENTARY Travel account of the south of Ireland, intermixed with accounts of legends: 'Légende du Saut-de-l'Amant', 'Légende de la belle Eva', 'Légende des alouettes', 'Légende du roi O'Toole et de son oie', 'Légende de Kathleen', 'Histoire d'O'Donnell', 'Brian Boroimhé', 'Histoire de sir Amory Tristam', 'Histoire de la vision de Conn-des-Batailles', 'Voyages d'Aithirné le barde', 'Histoire de Connor-Mac Nessa', 'Légende d'Anne More', 'Légende du *banshie* des O'Neil', 'Légende de l'étudiant Johnny Curtin', 'Légende de John Hackett, du Munster', 'Légende de deux bergers', 'Histoire des trois maris de la reine Gormlaith', 'Légende du roi Lavra Lyngsky', 'Légende du chavelier et du cheval sant têtes', 'Légende druidique', 'Histoire de Jean Fitz-James', 'Légende de lord Clancarty', 'Légende du roitelet', 'Histoire de Grâce du lac Mahon', 'Légende de l'Escalier du géant', 'Aventures nocturnes de Sheehy' [RL].

D103   *Légendes irlandaises; souvenirs d'un touriste* (by Emmanuel Domenech).
Paris: A. de Vresse, 1865. LOCATION NUC ([1862] edn).

D104   *Voyages & aventures en Irlande* (by Emmanuel Domenech).
+ Paris: J. Hetzel, 1866, vol. 1 [all published]. SOURCE COPAC. LOCATION L.
COMMENTARY Contains stories interwoven with travel account: 'Légende de Carrig-a-Droid', 'Légende de Maurice', 'Légende de l'ermite', 'Aventures de Billy Thompson et sa vache', 'Histoire des trois étudiants d'Innisfallen', ' Aventures de Tim Shea', 'Légende sur la fondation de l'abbaye', 'Légende de Dick et de la fille du roi des mers', 'Légende des quatre enfants de Lir', 'Légende de la reine Maev et du taureau Donn Chuailgné', 'Légende de Malachy', 'Légende des cloches', 'Légende de lac Inchiquin', 'Légende de la baie de Dunbeg', 'Histoire de Walter Lynch' [RL].

D105   *Voyages légendaires en Irlande* (by L'Abbé Domenech).
+ Lyon: Librarie Générale Catholique et Classique, 1894 (ill. P. Fauré, B. Delaye). SOURCE COPAC. LOCATION L, InND Loeber coll.
COMMENTARY Published posthumously. Diary of travels through Ireland intermixed with stories. Some legends are reprinted from the author's *Les gorges du diable* (Paris, 1864). Contents: 'Légende de la belle Eva', 'Légende du roi O'Toole et de son oie', 'Légende de Kathleen', 'Brian Boroimhé', 'Histoire de la vision de Conn-des-Batailles', 'Voyages d'Aithirné le barde',

'Histoire de Connor-Mac Nessa', 'Légende de John Hackett, du Munster', 'Légende du chavelier et du cheval sans têtes', 'Légende druidique', 'Histoire de Jean Fitz-James', 'Légende du roitelet', 'Histoire de Grâce du lac Mahon', 'Légende de l'Escalier du Géant', 'Aventures nocturnes de Sheehy', 'Légende de Maurice, le joueur de cornemuse', 'Légende de l'ermite', 'O'Sullivan et Fingal', 'L'Isle du Chêne', 'Aventures de Billy Thompson et de sa vache', 'O'Donoghue', 'Aventures de Tim Shea', 'La pierre de Clough-na-Cuddy', 'Légende de Dick et de la fille du roi de mers', 'Légende de la reine Maeve et du taureau Donn Chuailgné', Légende des cloches', Légende de lanie de Dunbeg', 'Histoire de Walter Lynch', 'Légende d'Enda et de Fanchea', 'Légende de la truite blanche', Légende de Knock-Mna', 'Légende de Cuchulainn', 'Légende de Saint Patrick' [RL].

DONBAVAND, Benjamin, fl. 1872. American author, BD also wrote *The Irish, who are they?* (Liverpool, 1856), which concerns the origins of the Irish language. SOURCE Allibone Suppl., i, p. 500; CM; RM.

D106 *Wild Ireland; or, recollections of some days and nights with Father Michael* (by Benjamin Donbavand).
+ Philadelphia: J.B. Lippincott & Co., 1872. SOURCE NYPL. LOCATION L, NN, NUC.
COMMENTARY Written in the form of a reminiscence about an experience in Ireland, the major theme is a lament for the decline of the Irish language. The narrator, Tim, describes his five days and nights living in a cabin with an Irish priest. They go fishing, discuss Irish superstitions, Irish books and history [ER; CM].

DONELAN, Miss A.M., d. 1873. Novelist, AMD is probably of Irish background. SOURCE Allibone Suppl. i, p. 501; Wolff, ii, p. 25.

D107 *Flora Adair; or, love works wonders* (by A.M. Donelan).
+ London: Chapman & Hall, 1867, 2 vols. SOURCE Wolff, 1856; COPAC. LOCATION L, NUC.
COMMENTARY Set in Italy and France [RL].

D108 *Sowing and reaping. A tale of Irish life* (by A.M. Donelan; dedicated to H.D. Langdon).
+ London: Chapman & Hall, 1868, 2 vols. SOURCE Wolff, 1857; COPAC. LOCATION D, Dt, NUC.
+ London: Chapman & Hall, 1871, 2 vols. (as *The value of Fosterstown. A tale of Irish life*). SOURCE Brown, 493; BLC (where mistakenly listed under Donclan, M.A.). LOCATION L.
COMMENTARY The original title, *Sowing and reaping*, was objected to on the grounds of its having been used previously, after which the title *The value of Fosterstown* was substituted. Set in Bray (Co. Wicklow), Dublin, Brussels, and Rome, the plot turns on two brothers, one of whom became a Protestant in penal times to save the family property. His descendants meet with all kind of misfortune. Margaret Foster wishes to make amends and restore the property to her cousin Reginald. In the end, Margaret and Reginald marry [Brown].

D109 *What 'tis to love* (by A.M. Donelan; dedicated to May).
+ London: Henry S. King & Co., 1873. SOURCE Brown, p. 88; Alston, p. 122; COPAC. LOCATION L, NUC, InND Loeber coll. (1872 [*sic*], 2nd edn, 3 vols. in 1).
COMMENTARY Set in England and France, this is a story of a husband and wife who grow further and further apart. The unselfishness of the woman with whom the husband has fallen in love brings them back together again [ML].

DONNELLY, Eleanor Cecilia, b. Philadelphia (PA) 1838 (not 1818 as in O'Donoghue), d. West Chester (PA) 1917. American Catholic writer of religious verse, hymns, biographies, stories for children and some fiction, ECD was the daughter of Irish parents: Dr Philip Carroll Donnelly and Catherine Gavin. Deeply religious and very supportive of the Catholic Church, she considered becoming a nun. Her brother Ignatius Loyola Donnelly, a lawyer, was also a novelist, in addition to writing extensively on the authorship of Shakespeare's plays. ECD's career spanned seventy years. SOURCE Allibone Suppl., i, pp 501–2; BLC; DAB; O'Donoghue, p. 113; Wright, iii, pp 159 (for other novels).

D110   *The lost Christmas tree and other little stories and verses for children* (by Eleanor Cecilia Donnelly).

+ Philadelphia: H.L. Kilner & Co., [1896]. SOURCE COPAC. LOCATION L.

COMMENTARY Stories and poems for juveniles, Catholic in nature, set in America. 'The true story of a half-sovereign', where a poor couple find in a second-hand coat a half-sovereign and decide it is not theirs and they cannot keep it, has Irish content. One poem in the volume is dedicated to the children of Maurice Francis Egan§; another concerns a French doll and an Irish doll [ML].

DOORNE, Hendrik van. See **VAN DOORNE, Fr Hendrik.**

DORAN, James, fl. 1891. American novelist.
D111   *Zanthon. A novel* (by James Doran).

+ San Francisco: Bancroft, 1891. SOURCE Fanning, p. 378; Wright, iii, 1584. LOCATION L, NUC.

COMMENTARY Set in Ireland in 1841. Mentions the Famine and ends in the US [ML].

'DORMOUSE, Dorothy', fl. 1806. Pseudonym of a novelist who, according to the preface to her only known work, was a resident of Dublin.
D112   *Edmond of Lateragh. A novel founded on facts* (by 'Dorothy Dormouse').

+ Dublin: Printed [for the author?] by J. Charles, 1806, 2 vols. SOURCE Brown, 25; Block, p. 66. LOCATION D, Dm, L.

COMMENTARY Based on the author's recollections of stories told by friends in her early youth, the novel is set in Ireland, England and the Continent. The main story concerns two lovers who are cruelly kept apart but finally meet and find happiness. The Irish in this book are practically all Protestant gentry [Brown].

D'ORSAY, Harriet Anne, Countess (née Gardiner; known as **Harriet Countess D'Orsay**), b. 1812, d. 1860. English-born daughter of Charles John Gardiner, 1st earl of Blessington, and Mary (Campbell) Browne, and stepdaughter of Margaret, countess of Blessington§, HAd'O is the author of a single novel based on unpublished writings from much earlier in her life. She is known principally through the relationship her husband, Count Alfred d'Orsay, had with her stepmother after their marriage had foundered. HAd'O remarried in 1852 the Hon Charles Spencer Cowper. She also published 'Mary O'Brien. A tale' in the London *Ainsworth's Magazine* (between 1842 and 1845). SOURCE Allibone Suppl., i, p. 503 [under Dorsay]; M. Sadleir, *Blessington-d'Orsay* (London, 1933), pp xi, 182–3; Tiger cat. 12/04/8.
D113   *L'Ombre du bonheur* (by Harriet Countess D'Orsay).

Paris: Comon, 1851, 3 vols. SOURCE Sadleir, pp 181–2. LOCATION L (1853 edn).

+ London: James Vizetelly, Henry Vizetelly, 1855 (trans. as *Clouded happiness. A novel*). SOURCE Allibone Suppl., i, p. 503 (1853 edn). LOCATION L.

COMMENTARY Probably autobiographical in origin, this is a complex, almost Gothic tale of concealed identities, lurid coincidences, agonized death-beds, pronounced vice and virtue set mainly in Naples in the early 1830s. Giuditta, the erring heroine, is the daughter of a courtesan and is supposed to have moral instability in her veins. But her only real lapse is to sell herself to a rich debauchee to save her mother's life – the sacrifice coming too late to achieve its purpose. Thereafter, although she lives with a man to whom she is not married, her moral standards are above criticism. Toward the end of the story, d'Arville, her lover, has grown tired of her; he observes that an English lord is inclined to make a bid for her favours and, for his own convenience, encourages the new liaison. Giuditta's brother is a bandit capable of blackmail, robbery and murder, but with the face of an angel and a manner of irresistible charm, while Beatrice, the brother's accomplice and mistress, has a beautiful face, but lacks feminine charm. Sadleir argues that the bandit brother and Beatrice represent the Count d'Orsay and Lady Blessington§ [Sadleir].

DORSEY, Anna Hanson (née McKenney; known as **Anna H. Dorsey**), b. Georgetown (Washington, DC) 1815, d. Washington (DC) 1896. Popular American novelist and religious writer, AHD was the daughter of Revd William McKenney and Chloe Ann Lanigan. Through her father she descended from Sarah Grubb, an Irish Quaker. She was educated in private schools in Georgetown and Norfolk (VA) where her father was a navy chaplain. In 1837 she married Lorenzo Dorsey and three years later converted to catholicism. Both were deeply influenced by the Catholic revival movement in England. She contributed to the magazine *Ave Maria* (Notre Dame, IN) and received two papal benedictions and the Lætare medal from the University of Notre Dame. The following are her known Irish books, but since she wrote many volumes, it is possible that further research will reveal others with Irish content. SOURCE Allibone Suppl., i, p. 503; Blain, p. 303; Brown, p. 88; Burke, p. 201; DAB; Obituary in the *Sunday Times*, Philadelphia, MS copy in the Archives of the Catholic University of America, Washington, DC; Wright, iii, pp 160–1.

D114 *Nora Brady's vow, and Mona the vestal* (by Anna H. Dorsey; dedicated to 'the Irish people, brave and unconquered').
+ Philadelphia: J.B. Lippincott & Co., 1869. SOURCE Fanning, p. 378; Wright, ii, 773; DCU, Catholic Americana files; COPAC. LOCATION NUC, InND Loeber coll. (1880 edn), Wright web.
Boston: P. Donahoe, 1869. SOURCE DCU, Catholic Americana files. LOCATION NUC.
+ New York: Christian Press Association Publishing Co., 1896. SOURCE Brown, 496 (n.d. edn). LOCATION D.
New York: Christian Press Association Publishing Co., n.d. SOURCE Brown, 495.
COMMENTARY New York, Donahoe, n.d. edn consists of only *Mona the vestal*. 'Nora Brady's vow' is set near Holy Cross Abbey (Co. Tipperary) and in Boston. Nora is a servant girl of the Halloran family. John Halloran flees to America after he had taken part in the rising of 1848, and Nora vows not to settle down in life until the fortunes of the Hallorans are restored. She emigrates to America and works to support the family. Eventually, she finds Halloran and reunites the family. 'Mona the Vestal' features a druidess who is converted to catholicism in the fifth century by St Patrick himself and contrasts the decaying druidic paganism against the heroic values of the new Christians [Fanning, p. 79; Brown; NUC].
D115 *The Flemmings; a true story* (by Anna H. Dorsey).
New York: P. O'Shea, 1869. SOURCE Slocum, i, 1327; COPAC. LOCATION NUC (n.d. edn).
New York: P. O'Shea, 1870 (as *The Flemmings; or, truth triumphant*; Notre Dame Series of Catholic Novels). SOURCE Wright, ii, 772. LOCATION NUC, Wright web.
COMMENTARY An Irish peddler and his family settle on a farm in New Hampshire. As the first Catholics in the area, they experience social ostracism and discrimination [Slocum].
D116 *The heiress of Carrigmona* (by Anna Hanson Dorsey).
+ Baltimore, New York: John Murphy & Co., 1887. SOURCE Wright, iii, 1594; Brown, 494 (Boston, 1910 edn); COPAC. LOCATION D, Dcc, C, DCU, NUC.

COMMENTARY Set in Co. Wicklow and the western US and concerns the fortunes of an Irish peasant family named Travers. Their son emigrates to America and gets into trouble. The story is a strong warning against emigration [RL; Brown].

D117　*The fate of the Dane, and other stories* (by Anna Hanson Dorsey).
　　　Baltimore: J. Murphy & Co., [1888]. SOURCE Wright, iii, 1593; COPAC. LOCATION NUC.
　　　COMMENTARY Contents: 'The druid's tower; or, the fate of the Dane', 'A brave girl', 'The story of Manuel', 'Mad penitent of Todi' [NUC].

D'ORSONNENS, Eraste, fl. 1860. French-Canadian writer who, according to the preface, started the following work as a school essay. It was first published in *Veillées canadiennes* (Montreal, 1854) and was interrupted by the premature closing of this magazine. This was followed by a republication in book form, after corrections. The author also planned to publish *Le parracide Huron*, but it is not clear if this happened. SOURCE RL.

D118　*Une apparition. Épisode de l'émigration irlandaise au Canada* (by Eraste D'Orsonnens; dedicated to the owners of La Guepe).
　　　+ Montreal: Printed by Cérat & Bourguignon, 1860 (Litterature Canadienne [series]).
　　　SOURCE R.J. Grace, *The Irish in Canada* (Quebec, 1993), p. 706. LOCATION CaOONL.
COMMENTARY This is a story about the emigration and reunion of an Irishman and his wife in a rural Quebec parish. Margaret O'Brien, an ambitious mother who is not concerned about her daughter's morals, encourages her to seduce a rich doctor [*Études Irlandaises*, 12 (1977), p. 117; Grace, 706].

DOUGLAS, Gertrude. See **DOUGLAS, Lady Gertrude Georgina**.

DOUGLAS, Lady Gertrude Georgina (known as **Gertrude Douglas**), fl. 1876. Religious fiction writer, GGD was probably a daughter of Archibald William Douglas, 7th marquess of Queensberry (1818–58) who married Caroline Margaret Clayton in 1840. SOURCE CP, x, p. 701.

D119　*Linked lives* (by Gertrude Douglas).
　　　London: Hurst & Blackett, 1876, 3 vols. SOURCE COPAC. LOCATION L, E.
COMMENTARY Katie, a beautiful Irish Catholic girl lives, at age 8, in the Glasgow slums among thieves. She has many misfortunes. Her story is connected to the fate of Mabel, a high-church Anglican girl, who has fallen in love with her cousin Hugh, who is an evangelical clergyman. Eventually, both Hugh and Mabel convert to catholicism [Gains and losses, p. 91; ML].

DOUGLAS, John, d. 1743. Scottish surgeon and writer on surgical matters, JD is the assumed author of the following work, although he had died before publication. This volume is not mentioned in the ODNB, but in other writings JD viciously criticized various contemporary physicians and surgeons. SOURCE ODNB.

D120　*The cornutor of seventy-five. Being a genuine narrative of the life, adventures, and amours, of Don Ricardo Honeywater, fellow of the Royal College of Physicians at Madrid, Salamanca, and Toledo; and president of the Academy of Sciences in Lapland. Containing (amongst many other diverting particulars) his intrigue with Dona Maria W—s, of Via Vinculosa in the city of Madrid. Written originally in Spanish by the author of Don Quixot [sic]; and translated into English, by a graduate of the College of Mecca in Arabia* (by John Douglas).
　　　London: J. Cobham, [1748?], 2nd edn (with many additions and improvements). SOURCE Johnson cat. 46/11; ESTC t34187. LOCATION L, Rutgers Univ. Library.

COMMENTARY 52pp. No copy of the first edn located. A satire on the Irish physician Dr Richard Meade, who worked in England. Meade is presented as an avid but not smart book collector. The story also refers to 'Dr Chimney', 'The Don's Rarity-Keeper' and hack writer of Irish extraction. Meade's medical knowledge is mocked, his writings treated with sarcasm or mock deference, and his gullibility as a book collector noted in various instances. On one occasion he purchases what he is told is a Chinese manuscript 'wrote by the famous Confucius'. On consulting an Irish Benedictine he learned that it was the legend of the giant 'Phan M'Coul', written in Irish and of no great antiquity. The satire elicited a response, *Don Ricardo Honeywater vindicated. In a letter to Doctor Salguod, ... the reputed author of a scurrilous pamphlet, entitled The cornutor of seventy-five* (London, 1748) [Johnson cat. 46/11].

DOUGLAS, Robert Kennaway. Co-author. See **SMITH, Elizabeth Thomasina Toulmin**.

DOUGLAS, William. Attributed author. See **CAULFEILD, Edward Houston**.

DOUGLASS, Adam, attributed pseud. 'An Hibernian', fl. 1817. American, or possibly Irish-American, novelist. The following work is attributed to AD on the grounds that his name appears on its copyright page. It is plausible that the story is autobiographical and that the author came from Co. Antrim and emigrated to the US. SOURCE Exiles, p. 24*n*.7; RL.

D121 *The Irish emigrant. An historical tale founded on fact* (by 'An Hibernian').
+ Winchester (VA): John T. Sharrocks, 1817, 2 vols. SOURCE Fanning, p. 382; Wright, i, 1367. LOCATION D, DCL.

COMMENTARY This is the first known Irish-American novel. It is a story of the loves and adventures of a Catholic Ulster patriot who flees from the 1798 rebellion in Co. Antrim. It includes a sorrowing farewell to Erin, the wondering arrival in the New World, leading to a comfortable life on a Potomac River estate [Exiles, p. 24, n.7]

DOUTRE, Joseph, b. Beauharnois, Lower Canada 1825, d. Montreal (Canada) 1880. Canadian lawyer and political and fiction writer, JD was the son of a shoemaker. He favoured the rebellion of 1837, attacked religious intolerance, and opposed the union between Upper and Lower Canada, which he expressed in his *Constitution of Canada* (Montreal, 1880). He played a prominent role in the Institute Canadien in Montreal, of which he was the first laureate. SOURCE Allibone i, p. 516; DCB, xi, pp 272–8; *Études Irlandaises*, 12 (1977), p. 119; NUC.

D122 *Les fiancés de 1812. Essaie de littérature Canadienne* (by Joseph Doutre).
Montreal: Louis Perrault, 1844, 3 vols. SOURCE *Études Irlandaises*, 12 (1977), p. 123. LOCATION CaOONL (vols. 1 and 2 only), NUC.
+ Montreal: Réédition-Quebec, 1973 (introd. by Léopold LeBlanc). LOCATION InND Loeber coll.

COMMENTARY Brandsome, an Irish soldier, leaves the British army to emigrate to the US and settle in Boston. He joins the American army but becomes a prisoner in French Canada during the war of 1812. He marries a Canadian, unlike the Anglo-Saxon officers who look down on the Francophone heroine [*Études Irlandaises*, 12 (1977), pp 117, 119].

DOWLING, Revd George Thomas, b. 1849, d. 1928. Novelist and minister in the Episcopal Church in America, GTD also published a volume of sermons (New York, [1904]). SOURCE Allibone Suppl., i, p. 509; NUC.

D123 *The wreckers. A social study* (by George Thomas Dowling).
Philadelphia: J.B. Lippincott Co., 1886. SOURCE Wright, iii, 1630. LOCATION NUC.
COMMENTARY Concerns the emigration of an Irishman to America [Wright].

DOWLING, James Herbert. See **HERBERT, James Dowling.**

DOWLING, Richard, pseuds '**Emmanuel Kink**' and '**Marcus Fall**' (not Marcus Fell as in Hogan), b. Clonmel (Co. Tipperary) 1846, d. London 1898. Novelist, journalist, short story writer and humorist, RD was son of a schoolmaster, David Jeremiah Dowling, and his wife Margaret. He was educated at Clonmel, Waterford, and St Munchin's College (Limerick). A cousin of the better-known Edmund Downey§, RD worked for some years in a shipping office in Waterford where he acquired a great love for things nautical. He moved to Dublin in 1870 and worked as a journalist on the *Nation*; edited the *Daily Summary* (a war-sheet for the Franco-German war) and a comic paper, *Zozimus*, and wrote for *Ireland's Eye*. As R.D. Dowling he published fiction and poetry in the *Irish Monthly* (Dublin) in 1874 and a short story 'The opening door' in the *Monitor* (Dublin, 1879). He moved to London in 1874 and later became a supporter of the Irish Literary Society there. He wrote popular Irish regional novels and contributed under his own name and a variety of pseudonyms to most of the leading London and Dublin magazines of the period, including the *Illustrated Sporting and Dramatic News* (London), the *Irish Fireside* (Dublin, 1883–84), *Tinsley's Magazine* (London), and detective fiction in the *Strand Magazine* (London, 1892), as well as editing the humorous paper *Yorick* (London). He wrote several volumes of essays and edited the poems of John Francis O'Donnell§. He died in London in 1898 and was buried at the Mortlake cemetery. SOURCE Allibone Suppl., i, p. 509; Boase, v, p. 145; Brady, p. 64; Brown, p. 90; Hogan, pp 210–11; Hogan 2, pp 372–3; Irish pseudonyms; McKenna, pp 152–3; OCIL, p. 153; O'Donoghue, p. 117; *Irish Monthly* (Dublin, 1899), pp 13–21, 347–54 (obituaries); J. Maher (ed.), *Chief of the Comeraghs* (Mullinahone, 1957), p. 176; RIA/DIB; RL; Rowan cat. 53A/594; Ryan, pp 91–4; Ximenes list M11/59; Sutherland, p. 196.

D124   *On babies and ladders. Essays on things in general* (by 'Emmanuel Kink').

    + London: John Camden Hotten, 1873. SOURCE Topp 3, p. 33. LOCATION L.

    + London: Ward, Lock & Tyler, [1877], 2 parts (as *Babies and ladders* (by 'E. Kirk' [*sic*]) *and Among the Fenians* (by 'Artemus Ward§') *with The showman's observations upon life in Washington, and military ardour in Baldinsville*). LOCATION L, InND Loeber coll.

D125   *The mystery of Killard. A novel* (by Richard Dowling; dedicated to the author's mother [Margaret Dowling]).

    + London: Tinsley Bros, 1879, 3 vols. SOURCE Brown, 500; McKenna, p. 153; Wolff, 1883. LOCATION Grail, L, NUC.

    + London: Tinsley Bros, 1884 (new edn; as *The mystery of Killard*). LOCATION D, Dt, DPL, InND Loeber coll.

    + New York: The Vatican Library Co., 1889 (ill. Richardson). LOCATION D.

COMMENTARY A story of Co. Clare fishermen in the 1820s, set on the Clare coast at a mysterious and romantic rock, which cannot be approached by the sea and is connected to the land by a single rope. The ownership of the rock is clouded in mystery and there is talk of gold. One of the central figures of the story is a deaf mute, who grows to hate his own child because the child can hear and speak [Brown; Sutherland].

D126   *The sport of fate* (by Richard Dowling; dedicated to Miss Fildes).

    + London: Tinsley Bros, 1880, 3 vols. SOURCE Hogan, p. 210. LOCATION L.

COMMENTARY A collection of short stories. Contents: 'Red hands', 'The astronomer royal', 'The toll of Charon', 'An anachronism from the tomb', 'The partners of leather lane', 'That night', 'The ghoul', 'Genius at the hammer', 'The going out of Alessandro Pozzone', 'The marine binocular', 'The Elba of the Thames' [ML; BLC].

D127   *Under St. Paul's. A romance* (by Richard Dowling).

London: Tinsley Bros, 1880, 3 vols. SOURCE Hogan, p. 210. LOCATION L.

London: Ward & Downey, 1885 (new edn). SOURCE Topp 8, 4.

New York: G. Munro, 1881 (Seaside Library Pocket Edition, No. 929). LOCATION NUC.

COMMENTARY No copy of the London 1885 edn located [RL].

D128 *High-water mark* (by Richard Dowling).

London: Tinsley Bros., 1880 (Christmas no. of *Tinsley's Magazine*; ill. Harry Furniss§).

SOURCE Top 6, 95. COMMENTARY *London edn* No copy located [RL].

New York: George Munro, [1880]. LOCATION NUC.

COMMENTARY 88pp for the London edn, and 28pp for New York edn [Topp 6, 95; NUC].

D129 *London town: Sketches of London life and character* (by 'Marcus Fall').

London: Tinsley Bros, 1880, 2 vols. SOURCE COPAC. LOCATION L, NUC.

D130 *The weird sisters. A romance* (by Richard Dowling).

London: Tinsley Bros, 1880, 3 vols. SOURCE Hogan, p. 211; Topp 6, 124. LOCATION L, NUC.

COMMENTARY First published in *Tinsley's Magazine* (1879). The plot involves murder and embezzlement and the story ends with a spectacular fire in which the villain perishes on the roof of a castle [Ximenes list M11/59; Topp]

D131 *My darling's ransom* (by Richard Dowling).

London: Tinsley Bros., 1881 (Christmas no. of *Tinsley's Magazine*). SOURCE Topp 6, 99; OCLC. LOCATION Univ. of North Carolina, Chapel Hill.

New York: George Munro, 1881 (Seaside Library, No. 1152). LOCATION NUC.

COMMENTARY 99pp for the London edn [Topp].

D132 *The Duke's sweetheart. A romance* (by Richard Dowling).

London: Tinsley Bros, 1881, 3 vols. SOURCE Hogan, p. 211. LOCATION L.

London: Ward & Downey, 1885 (new edn). SOURCE Topp 8, 1; OCLC. LOCATION CLU.

COMMENTARY First published as 'Strawberry leaves' in *Tinsley's Magazine* [Topp 8, 1].

D133 *The husband's secret* (by Richard Dowling).

London: Tinsley Bros, 1881, 3 vols. SOURCEs Hogan, p. 211. LOCATION L.

D134 *A sapphire ring, and other stories* (by Richard Dowling).

London: Tinsley Bros, 1882, 3 vols. SOURCE Hogan, p. 211. LOCATION L.

D135 *Last Christmas eve* (by Richard Dowling).

London: Tinsley Bros, 1882 (Christmas no. of *Tinsley's Magazine*). SOURCE Topp 6, 105. COMMENTARY *London edn* No copy located [RL].

New York: George Munro, 1882 (Seaside Library). LOCATION NUC.

COMMENTARY Topp relates the publishing history of this and other Christmas annuals published by Tinsley [Topp 6, 105].

D136 *Sweet Inisfail. A romance* (by Richard Dowling).

London: Tinsley Bros, 1882, 3 vols. SOURCE Brown, 501; McKenna, p. 153; Wolff, 1885. LOCATION Grail, L.

New York: G. Munro, 1883 (Seaside Library). LOCATION NUC.

COMMENTARY A romance set in the author's native Clonmel [Sutherland].

D137 *The last call. A romance* (by Richard Dowling).

London: Tinsley Bros, 1884, 3 vols. SOURCE Hogan, p. 211. LOCATION L.

D138 *On the Embankment* (by Richard Dowling).

+ London: Tinsley Bros, 1884. SOURCE Hogan, p. 211; Topp 6, 110. LOCATION L.

COMMENTARY Set in London [ML].

D139   *The hidden flame. A romance* (by Richard Dowling).
London: Tinsley Bros, 1885, 3 vols. SOURCE Hogan, p. 211; Wolff, 1877. LOCATION L.

D140   *Fatal bonds. A romance* (by Richard Dowling).
London: Ward & Downey, 1886, 3 vols. SOURCE Hogan 2, p. 373. LOCATION L, NUC.

D141   *School board essays* (by 'Emmanuel Kink').
London: Ward & Downey, 1888. LOCATION L.

D142   *The skeleton key. A story* (by Richard Dowling).
London: Ward & Downey, 1886. SOURCE Hogan, p. 211; Wolff, 1884; Topp 8, 17. LOCATION L.

D143   *Tempest-driven. A romance* (by Richard Dowling).
London: Tinsley Bros, 1886, 3 vols. SOURCE Hogan, p. 211; Topp 8, 328. LOCATION L, NUC.
New York: D. Appleton & Co., 1887. LOCATION NUC.

D144   *With the unhanged* (by Richard Dowling).
+ London: W. Swan Sonnenschein & Co., 1887. SOURCE Hogan, p. 211. LOCATION D (uncatalogued), L.

D145   *Miracle gold. A novel* (by Richard Dowling).
London: Ward & Downey, 1888, 3 vols. SOURCE Hogan, p. 211; Wolff, 1881; Topp 8, 104. LOCATION L, NUC.
London: Ward & Downey, 1890 (new edn). SOURCE Topp 8, 104.
New York: George Munro, [1891] (Seaside Library Pocket Edition, No. 1829. SOURCE Topp 8, 104.
COMMENTARY No copy of the London or New York edn located [RL].

D146   *An isle of Surrey. A novel* (by Richard Dowling).
+ London: Ward & Downey, 1889, 3 vols. SOURCE Hogan, p. 211; Wolff, 1879. LOCATION D, L, NUC, InND Loeber coll.
+ London: Ward & Downey, 1891 (new edn). SOURCE Topp 8, 122. LOCATION InND Loeber coll.

COMMENTARY Set in London along the Thames. A story of seduction, abduction, desertion, deception and romance involving the heroine, Kate Bramwell, her husband, brother and little boy, all of whose lives are affected by the villain Crawford, who in the end accidentally drowns, while Kate is reunited with her husband and child and her brother falls in love [ML].

D147   *A baffling quest. A novel* (by Richard Dowling).
+ London: Ward & Downey, 1891, 3 vols. SOURCE Hogan, p. 211 (n.d. edn); Topp 8, 144. LOCATION L.
New York: United States Book Co., [1891] (International Series, No. 150. SOURCE Topp 8, 144. LOCATION NUC.
COMMENTARY Detective story featuring George Tufnell, Private Inquiry Agent of the City of London and Dunkley, a private detective [RL].

D148   *The crimson chair, and other stories* (by Richard Dowling).
London: Ward & Downey, 1891. SOURCE Hogan, p. 211. LOCATION L.

D149   *Catmur's caves; or, the quality of mercy* (by Richard Dowling).
New York: National Book Co., [1891]. LOCATION NUC.
+ London: Adam & Charles Black, 1892. SOURCE Hogan, p. 211. LOCATION D (1893 edn), L.

D150   *A dark intruder* (by Richard Dowling).
London: Downey & Co., 1895, 2 vols. LOCATION L.

D151   *While London sleeps* (by Richard Dowling).

London: Ward & Downey, [1895]. SOURCE Hogan, p. 211; Topp 8, 150. LOCATION L.
COMMENTARY Contains sketches of London scenes [Topp].

D152 *Below bridge* (by Richard Dowling).

+ London: Ward & Downey, 1895, 3 vols. SOURCE Hogan, p. 211 (n.d. edn). LOCATION
L, InND Loeber coll.

COMMENTARY Set in London along the Thames. Frank Jeaters is tired of his wife and wants
to start a relationship with Miss Orr, who works in a watch shop. Knowing that his wife sleep-
walks, he opens a trap door to the Thames underneath the house. Although his wife falls
through, he does not realize that she is rescued. He rents rooms in Miss Orr's mother's house,
not realizing that Miss Orr has a lover, Mr Crane. While Mr Crane goes to South America
to claim an inheritance, Jeaters makes slow progress in his intimacy with Miss Orr and her
mother. When Mr Crane appears to be lost at sea and the watch shop is about to go bankrupt, Mr Jeaters offers financial security to Miss Orr and is about to be accepted when Crane
reappears, a very rich man. Mrs Jeaters is reintroduced to her husband, who flees the scene
[ML].

D153 *Old Corcoran's money* (by Richard Dowling).

+ London: Chatto & Windus, 1897. SOURCE Brown, 502 (mistakenly mentions 1892
edn); McKenna, p. 153 (mistakenly mentions 1892 edn); Hogan, p. 211. LOCATION
Grail, L, NUC, InND Loeber coll.

COMMENTARY A rather bleak tale of crime and punishment in the small town of Ballymore
(perhaps Waterford), where money has been stolen from an old miser. The plot centres on
the detection of the thief [Brown; Leclaire, p. 143; Sutherland].

D154 *The fate of Luke Ormerod* (by Richard Dowling).

London: Hurst & Blackett, 1905. LOCATION L.

DOWNE, Walmer, fl. 1898. Novelist, probably Scottish since according to an endorsement
on the NLI copy of *By shamrock and heather* (London, 1898) WD lived in Edinburgh.
Only his novel with an Irish connection is listed here. SOURCE RL.

D155 *Celeste. A story of the Southerners* (by Walmer Downe; dedicated to the Rt Hon.
W. Pirrie and Mrs Pirrie).

+ London: Digby, Long & Co., 1898. LOCATION L.

COMMENTARY Not set in Ireland, but features a character called Denis O'Flaherty,
'The Hibernian' [CM].

DOWNEY, Mrs Edmund (née **Frances Margaret Allen**). Co-author. See **DOWNEY,
Edmund**.

DOWNEY, Edmund, pseuds 'F.M. Allen' (not F.L. Allen as in Hogan) and 'Dan Banim', b.
Waterford, 1856, d. Waterford, 1937. Publisher, novelist, short story and miscellaneous writer,
ED was son of a ship owner and was educated at the Catholic University School and John's
College, Waterford. In 1878 he moved to London and worked with the publisher Tinsley Brothers,
and in 1880 became editor of the London periodical *Tinsley's Magazine*. In 1884 he formed his
own publishing house, Ward and Downey. He is recognized as one of the publishers who facilitated the publishing of works by living Irish authors, greatly contributing to the popularization of
the Irish novel. Under ED's guidance, the firm of Downey & Co. also issued reprints of nineteenth-century Irish fiction, including the works of William Carleton§, Gerald Griffin§, J. Sheridan
Le Fanu§, and Samuel Lover§. He retired to Waterford in 1890 where he founded in 1894 Downey
and Co., and where he was proprietor of the *Waterford News*. He contributed to the periodical the
Old Country (Dublin?, 1893); published his memoirs as *Twenty years ago* (London, 1905); wrote

Charles Lever, his life in his letters§ (Edinburgh & London, 1903); *The story of Waterford* (Waterford, 1914), and *Waterford, an illustrated guide* (Waterford, 1915). He also contributed to the literary magazine *Green and Gold* (Waterford, 1920–21), which was edited by Alan Downey, possibly ED's son. We have identified 25 works of fiction by ED, which cover a wide gamut of genres, including sea, Irish, and children's stories; a horror novel; humour, and crime fiction. ED lectured on J. Sheridan Le Fanu§ at the Ursuline school, Waterford, in 1911. W.P. Ryan§, who knew him well, told that ED 'once in a while ... will sketch for you in bold outline the sort of Irish novel which he would like to write', but then admitted that 'one cannot always select the best and favourite subjects' to write about. According to an unpublished letter addressed to the publisher Pearsons in 1902 he attempted to republish many of his novels, in addition to two unpublished works, 'Three fingers and a thumb' (a sensational story) and 'Rian-na-Shark' (a sensational and humorous novel). ED's wife, Frances Margaret Allen Downey, co-authored some of ED's books. The author Richard Dowling§ was his cousin. ED's papers and his correspondence with many authors are in the NLI (MSS 10,000–69) and in a private collection. SOURCE Allibone Suppl., i, p. 509; Brady, p. 3; Brown, p. 91; EF, p. 106; Hogan 2, pp 373–4; IBL, 8 (1916–17), p. 73, and 9 (1918), pp 69–71 (Edmund Downey's reminiscences), 123–4; Irish pseudonyms; OCIL, p. 153; O'Donoghue, p. 119; RIA/DIB; E. Reilly, p. 243; RL; Ryan, pp 66, 88–9; Sutherland, p. 196; *St. Ursula's Annual* (Waterford, 1911), p. 54; Wolff, ii, p. 29.

D156　*Cathair Conroy, and other tales* (by Edmund Downey?).
　　　Dublin: Sealy, Bryers [& Walker?], n.d. SOURCE Brown, 522.
　　　COMMENTARY No copy located [RL].

D157　*Anchor-watch yarns. Pictures of life in the coasting trade* (by 'F.M. Allen'; dedicated to William Tinsley).
　　　London: Tinsley Bros, 1883, 2 vols. SOURCE Brown, 506 (1884 edn); Topp 8, 136.
　　　LOCATION DPL (n.d. edn), Dcc (1884 edn), L, NUC.
　　　+ London: Ward & Downey, 1887 (new edn). LOCATION DPL.
　　　London: Ward & Downey, 1893 (cover: Dublin: J. Duffy & Co., n.d.). LOCATION InND.
　　　New York: Scribner & Welford, [1887?]. SOURCE Topp 8, 136.
COMMENTARY No copy of the New York edn located. Sea stories told by old sailors around the inn fire in Waterford, many of which have some Irish elements. Contents: 'Captain Jackson's yarns', 'The ship's cousin's yarn', 'A fog yarn', 'The yarn of the unlucky tar', 'The landlubber's yarn', 'The yarn of "Captain Tom"', 'The river pilot's yarn', 'The shipbroker's clerk's yarn', 'The ne'er-do-well's yarn', 'The yarn of the shipbuilder', ' The yarn of "Meeyogany Haughton"', 'The yarn of the phantom brigantine', '"Captain Gregory's" yarn', 'Captain Jackson's yarn (concluded)' [Leclaire, p. 147; RL].

D158　*In one town. A novel* [anon.].
　　　London: Ward & Downey, 1886, 2 vols. SOURCE Brown, 505 (mistakenly mentions 1884 edn); Wolff, 1892; Topp 8, 96. LOCATION D (2nd edn), L, NUC.
　　　+ London: Ward & Downey, 1887, 2nd edn (new introd.). LOCATION InND Loeber coll.
　　　New York: D. Appleton & Co., 1887. LOCATION NUC.
　　　New York: Norman Munro, [1887] (Munro's Library, No. 719). SOURCE Topp 8, 96.
COMMENTARY No copy of the New York, Munro edn located. Set in Waterford and describes the activities and life in this seafaring town as they take place in the shipbroker's office and in the inn where the sea captains congregate. Various love stories are interwoven [ML].

D159　*A house of tears. An original story* [anon.].
　　　London: Ward & Downey, 1886. SOURCE Wolff, 1891; Topp 8, 18. LOCATION L, NUC (1887 edn).

+ Toronto: William Bryce, 1887 (by Edmund Downey; as *A house of tears*; see Plate 29). LOCATION InND Loeber coll.

New York: John W. Lovell Co., [1888] (Lovell's Library, No. 1126). LOCATION NUC. COMMENTARY 21st thousand printing was issued in 1897. Set in England, a horror story of a man-created monster, told by a Dr Emanuel. Emanuel has bought a practice in the country from a Dr Stoker (the theme of a man-turned-snake was developed by Bram Stoker§ in his *The snake's pass*, London, 1891). A new patient, Mr Brabazon, who lives on an estate in the country isolated from other people, seeks Emanuel's help for a twisted ankle. Brabazon's father had been a morose and tyrannical man, who with a companion, Dr Bletsoe, performed experiments on living creatures. He collected snakes and forced his wife to enter the snake room, knowing that she was terrified of them. He once cursed her by saying, 'may the devil send you a serpent for a son, Madam'. Subsequently, a son was born with fangs and poisonous and deadly venom. As a grown-up, Brabazon lives with one servant who has been inoculated against his master's poison. They are in constant dread lest Brabazon's affliction become public knowledge. Brabazon only bites people when in pain or when upset. Dr Bletsoe's son, who knows of Brabazon's affliction, tries to blackmail him. He sends his wife with the demand and she dies when Brabazon bites her. Brabazon feels that public exposure is now inevitable. He realizes that in his agitated state, he might bite Dr Emanuel. Rather than hurt him, he bites his own arm and dies a horrible death [ML; Personal communication, Paul Murray, April 2005; Topp 8, 18].

D160   *Through green glasses* (by 'F.M. Allen').

+ London: Ward & Downey, 1887 (ill. M. Fitzgerald). SOURCE Brown, 507; Wolff, 1894; Topp 8, 60; Adv. in *Brayhard* (London, 1890). LOCATION D (1888 edn), Dcc (1888 edn), L, NUC (n.d. edn), InND Loeber coll. (1888, 6th edn).

+ Waterford: Waterford News, n.d. (by Edmund Downey; ill.). LOCATION D, InND Loeber coll.

New York: D. Appleton & Co., 1887 (as *Through green glasses. Andy Merrigan's great discovery and other Irish tales*). LOCATION NUC.

+ New York: F.M. Lupton, n.d. (with subtitle *Andy Merrigan's great discovery*, ill. M. Fitzgerald). LOCATION InND Loeber coll.

COMMENTARY An unidentified portion of this work was 'contributed' by the author's wife, Frances Margaret Allen Downey. Contents: 'Andy Merrigan's great discovery', 'From Portlaw to paradise', ' King John and the Mayor', ' The wonderful escape of James the Second', 'The last of the dragons', 'The siege of Don Isle', 'Raleigh in Munster' [RL; IBL, 9 (1918), p. 124].

D161   *The voyage of the ark. As related by Dan Banim* (by 'F.M. Allen').

+ London: Ward & Downey, 1888. SOURCE Brown, 508; Topp 8, 58. LOCATION L, NUC.

New York: J.S. Ogilvie & Co., 1890. SOURCE Topp 8, 58.

COMMENTARY No copy of the New York edn located. The 3rd edn, 20th thousand of the London edn was advertised in 1888. Fiction for juveniles. The story of Noah and the ark forms the basis of a series of farcical episodes [RL; Brown; Topp].

D162   *From the green bag* (by 'F.M. Allen').

+ London: Ward & Downey, 1889 (cover: A.C.; ill.). SOURCE Brown, 509; Wolff, 1890; Topp 8, 111. LOCATION DPL, Dcc, L, NUC, InND Loeber coll.

COMMENTARY The 14th thousand printing was advertised in 1890. Several of the stories are comic reinterpretations of history. Contents: 'Dan's pilgrimage', 'The discovery of the shamrock', 'How Horatius kept the bridge', 'Garry Baldwin and the pope', 'The siege of Troy', 'The conquest of Britain' [ML; Topp].

D163   *Brayhard: the strange adventures of one ass and seven champions* (by 'F.M. Allen').

+ London: Ward & Downey, 1890 (ill. Harry Furniss§, Swain). SOURCE Brown, 510 (n.d. edn); Wolff, 1887. LOCATION D, L, NUC, InND Loeber coll.

COMMENTARY A farcical story founded on the legends of the ancient chapbook *The seven champions of Christendom*. The binding of the copy of InND Loeber coll. is blue green instead of red as reported by Wolff [Brown; RL].

D164 *The round tower of Babel* (by 'F.M. Allen').

London: Ward & Downey, 1891. SOURCE Brown, 513 (1892 edn). LOCATION L, NUC.

COMMENTARY A sequel to *The voyage of the ark* (London, 1888) and describes the adventures in foreign parts of descendants of Co. Waterford voyagers in the ark [Brown].

D165 *Captain Lanagan's log: passages in the life of a merchant skipper* (by 'F.M. Allen').

+ London: Ward & Downey, 1891 (ill. Matt. Stretch). SOURCE Brown, 511; Wolff, 1888. LOCATION D, L, NUC, InND Loeber coll.

COMMENTARY The adventures of an Irish-Canadian boy who runs away to sea and ends up a captain. He meets with various rough crews. On one of his voyages his entire crew consists of Negroes because the owner of the vessel wants to guard against having an Irish crew, since he hates the Irish. However, it turns out that the Negroes all had Irish great-grandmothers, speak with an Irish brogue, have Irish names, and drink Irish whisky [Brown].

D166 *Green as grass* (by 'F.M. Allen').

+ London: Chatto & Windus, 1892 (ill. Joseph Smyth). SOURCE Brown, 512. LOCATION Dcc, D, L, NUC, InND Loeber coll.

New York: Lovell, Coryell & Co., [1899]. LOCATION NUC.

COMMENTARY The London edn came in two bindings: (a) red with 'The Times 1785' in medallion on spine; (b) green with cover ill. Contents: 'The last king of Leinster', 'The ordeal by griddle', 'The dark horse', 'The barber and the banshee' [RL].

D167 *The land smeller and other yarns* (by Edmund Downey).

+ London: Downey & Co., 1893. SOURCE Brown, 514 (1892 edn but not found); Wolff, 1893. LOCATION D, Dcc (n.d. edn), DPL (n.d. edn), L, NUC ([1890?] edn).

+ Dublin: James Duffy & Co., n.d. LOCATION InND Loeber coll.

COMMENTARY The Dublin edn is a remainder of the London, Ward & Downey, 1893 edn. Consists of yarns of sea captains: 'The land smeller', 'The skipper's secret', 'Mysterious disappearance of the "Emily" brig', 'Captain Walker's luggage', 'Greek joins Greek', 'The Captain's cornet', 'Billy Callaghan's conscience', 'A game of cards', 'The mate's pipe', 'Minus five', 'The champion skipper', 'A dishonoured Bill' [RL].

D168 *The merchant of Killogue. A Munster tale* (by 'F.M. Allen'; dedicated to the author's wife [Frances Margaret Allen Downey]).

+ London: William Heinemann, 1894, 3 vols. SOURCE Brown, 515. LOCATION D, Dt, Dcc, L, InND Loeber coll.

New York: P.F. Collier, 1894. LOCATION NUC.

COMMENTARY Set in Munster, possibly Clonmel (Co. Tipperary), the story relates shop-keeping life in a small town and takes place in the days preceding the introduction of the ballot system at elections [Brown].

D169 *Ballybeg junction: an episode* (by 'F.M. Allen').

+ London: Downey & Co., 1895 (ill. John F. O'Hea). SOURCE Brown, 516; McCarthy, iii, p. 891 (mistakenly mentions 1894 edn). LOCATION D, Dt, L, NUC, InND Loeber coll.

COMMENTARY Comic story of southern Irish life in Co. Waterford at the end of a junction railway line [Brown; Leclaire, p. 147].

D170 *The little green man* (by 'F.M. Allen'; dedicated to Mary).

+ London: Downey & Co., [1895] (ill. Brinsley LeFanu). SOURCE Brown, 519; McCarthy, iii, p. 891. LOCATION D, L, NUC, InND Loeber coll.

COMMENTARY The story of how a leprechaun helps his human friend, Denis, who is threatened with eviction. On his way home after he has pleaded in vain with his landlord, Denis meets the fairy-man who comes home with him, cures his sick daughter and leads him to the spot of a buried crock of gold. Later on he takes Denis's son, Patsy, with him to California, where he wishes to marry a fairy who can give him a soul. In California he is instrumental in discovering the gold fields. Patsy finds out that gold brings a lot of unhappiness to the gold-diggers and returns to Ireland, but with a chest of gold nuggets [ML].

D171 *Pinches of salt* (by 'F.M. Allen').
> + London: Downey & Co., 1896. SOURCE Brown, 517; Leclaire, p. 147 (notes an 1895 edn, but this has not been located). LOCATION Dcc, DPL, L, NUC, InND Loeber coll.

COMMENTARY Contents: 'The eviction at Ballyhack', 'An Italian from Cork', 'Silver sand', 'Father Crotty's hat', 'The boy and the bird', 'A theatrical performance', 'A man hunt', 'My friend's valise', 'Viceroy's visit' [ML].

D172 *The ugly man* [anon.].
> + London: Downey & Co., 1896. SOURCE McCarthy, iii, p. 891; Topp 8, 194. LOCATION L, InND Loeber coll. (n.d. edn).

COMMENTARY A mystery story set in the suburbs of London about the disappearance of a great emerald from Cawnpore, interwoven with a love story [ML].

D173 *Mr. Boyton* (by 'F.M. Allen')
> + London: Downey & Co., 1900. SOURCE Sutherland, p. 196 (1899 edn); OCLC. LOCATION D.

COMMENTARY 1899 edn not located [RL].

D174 *London's peril* (by 'F.M. Allen').
> + London: Downey & Co., [1900]. SOURCE Topp 8, 240. LOCATION D, L.

COMMENTARY Invasion scare story, in which the French (rather than the Germans) dig a tunnel from Cap Gris Nex to Hampstead, but they are foiled in time [EF].

D175 *Glimpses of English history* (by 'F.M. Allen').
> + London: Downey & Co., 1901 (ill. James F. Sullivan). SOURCE Brown, 518. LOCATION D, L.
>
> London: Simpkin, Marshall, Hamilton, Kent & Co., 1904 (new edn; ill. James F. Sullivan). LOCATION NUC.

COMMENTARY Fiction for juveniles [RL].

D176 *Clashmore. A novel* (by Edmund Downey; dedicated to Thomas Sexton).
> Waterford: Downey & Co., 1903. SOURCE Brown, 520; COPAC. LOCATION D (n.d. edn), L, NUC ([1909] edn)
>
> + Dublin: The Parkside Press, [1945]. LOCATION D, DPL, L.
>
> + London: Simpkin, Marshall, Hamilton, Kent & Co., 1903. LOCATIONs Dcc, L, InND Loeber coll.
>
> + Glasgow: P.J. O'Callaghan, 1920. LOCATION DPL, NUC.

COMMENTARY Set in the neighbourhood of Tramore and Dunmore (Co. Waterford) and concerns the mysterious disappearance of Lord Clashmore and his agent. The denouement is aided by Lord Clashmore's nephew who comes from England to investigate his uncle's disappearance. Not only does his uncle turn up, but he also admits to a certain young man being his son. In addition, the young Englishman falls in love with a distant Irish relative and is accepted [ML; Brown].

D177 *The brass ring. The extraordinary adventures of a city clerk* (by 'F.M. Allen').
> London: Simpkin, Marshall, Hamilton, Kent & Co., 1904. SOURCE Wolff, 1886; Topp 8, 1726. LOCATION L.

D178 *Dorothy Tuke: A story of the sea* (by Edmund Downey).
> London: Hurst & Blackett, 1905. LOCATION L.

COMMENTARY The main character is a captain's daughter. Of the two officers in charge of her ship, one is a villain and she marries the other [EF].

D179 *Dunleary. Humours of a Munster town* (by Edmund Downey).

+ London: Sampson Low, Marston & Co., [1911]. SOURCE Brown, 521; Wolff, 1889. LOCATION D, DPL, Dcc, L, NUC, InND Loeber coll.

COMMENTARY Interrelated stories set in a port in Munster (perhaps New Ross). Contents: 'Tit for tat', 'The retort discourteous', 'The rivals', 'The unneighbourly revenge', 'The conspirators', 'Daly of Deerpark', 'A little learning', 'Baiting a dragon', 'Mickey Maloney', 'Advice gratis', 'The melancholy merchant', 'Give and take', 'At a distance', 'Bought and sold' [Leclaire, p. 147; ML; RL].

D180 *Morrissey* (by Edmund Downey).

+ London: John Lane, 1924. SOURCE Brown 2, 402 (mistakenly mentions 'Land' as publisher); COPAC. LOCATION Dcc, D (n.d. edn), DPL, L, NUC, InND Loeber coll.

COMMENTARY Interrelated stories set in a seaport of Rockhaven in Munster (i.e., Waterford) where an old-timer tells about townspeople to someone who has been away for twenty years. Contents: 'The chance of the sea', 'Sherry – and bitters', 'The turning-table', 'Head or harp', 'Inspiration', 'Mrs. Flaherty's clock', 'The pier', 'The black ram', 'Virginia' [Leclaire, p. 147; ML; RL].

DOYLE, M. (Matthew?), pseud. 'M.E.T.', fl. 1880s. Novelist, the author is identified in copies of the volume below in the NLI and the DPL, with an inscription date of '85 in the NLI copy. In the introduction, MD explains that in few books has the Irish peasant 'been treated fairly', and presents the following story based on 'real life'. He can perhaps be identified with Matthew Doyle, author of *Visitors to Matthew Doyle* (Waterford, 1871), which consists of poetry and prose. SOURCE MVP, p. 140; RL.

D181 *Exiled from Erin: A story of Irish peasant life* (by 'M.E.T.').

+ Dublin, London: James Duffy & Sons, [1885]. SOURCE Brown, 525. LOCATION D, DPL, NUC, InND Loeber coll.

COMMENTARY Brown, 525, identified a New York edn, but this has not been located. A poignant tale of misery and heartache suffered by two brothers, Fergus and Art O'Toole, born to a peasant family in the vale of Shanganagh, near Shankhill (Co. Dublin). Fergus falls in love with his first cousin, Nora Rivis. They plan to marry but are forbidden by their families. When Nora moves to America with her family, Fergus and Art wander from home in search of employment. While they are working in England, they meet with a group of miners who have just returned from New York. They tell the two brothers that Nora has married Jim Bant. Fergus flees to America to make sure that his beloved is happy. His devoted brother follows him after a few months. While in Virginia, Fergus meets Nora. She does not recognize him, but he realizes that she is happier than he has ever seen her. While Fergus and Art work in the silver mines of Rock Creek, Art is blinded in an explosion. Fergus nurses him back to health. They make a heartbreaking decision to remain as exiles in America, never to return to Shankhill and their parents [CD].

'DOYLE, Martin', pseud. See **HICKEY, William**.

'DRAKE, Miriam', pseud. See **CLARKE, Mrs Charles Montague**.

DRAPES, Revd Vernon Russell, b. Co. Wexford *c.*1812, d. 1898. Church of Ireland clergyman and religious fiction writer, VRD was the son of Samuel Drapes and Mary Russell. He was admitted to TCD in 1828 at age 16 and graduated BA in 1836. He was curate of

Thomastown (Co. Kilkenny, 1838–42); St John's (Kilkenny, 1842–57); prebendary of Tascoffin (Co. Kilkenny, 1858–65); vicar of Durrow (Co. Laois, 1865–74), and rector of Kells (Co. Kilkenny, 1874–98). He married first Eliza Nowlan; secondly Helena Anne Griffith, and thirdly Frances Louisa, widow of Charles A. Bagot. Preaching after VRD's death, the bishop of Ossory spoke of him as 'gentle, unassuming, loving, stainless'. SOURCE B & S, p. 244; Leslie, *Ossory*, p. 135; RL.

D182   *Brief memorials of a Sunday scholar, intended principally for the higher classes in Sunday schools* (by Vernon Russell Drapes).

     + Dublin: William Curry & Co., 1845. LOCATION D.

     COMMENTARY Religious fiction for the 'higher' classes in society. Relates the story, partly in letters, of Annie A—, born in the city of Kilkenny, 18 Oct. 1829 [RL].

DREW, Catharine, b. Belfast 1825/26, d. London 1910. Pioneering journalist, novelist and women's rights activist, CD was the seventh daughter of the hymn writer, Revd Thomas Drew, a Church of Ireland clergyman of Limerick, and Isabella Dalton of Dublin. Her father was a militant Orange Order supporter and a clergyman in Belfast and Seaforde (Co. Down). Her brother, Sir Thomas Drew, was an ecclesiastical architect who became president of the Royal Society of Antiquaries in Ireland. CD was educated at home. She moved to Dublin, where she assisted her brother in editing the *Irish Builder*, before moving to London In 1871. There she began a career as a writer, contributing to a number of periodicals and writing fiction. She became the London correspondent for the *Belfast Newsletter*, for which she wrote a column for women, one of the first of a genre that was to become very popular by the end of the century. CD was active in philanthropic causes, particularly in promoting a fund for the education of orphan children of journalists. She was a founding member of the Institute of Journalists (IOJ) in 1885 and the first woman elected an honorary vice-president and councillor in 1895. In 1894 she represented the IOJ at the first International Conference on the Press in Antwerp. A powerful and eloquent advocate of equal pay for women journalists, she drew attention to the need for women to receive a living wage and to be able to provide for old age, especially since they were often responsible for children and older parents. From 1896 to 1906 she was on the London staff of the National Press Agency. She remained single and lived in Holland Street, Kensington, London. For her portrait and papers, see ODNB. SOURCE Allibone Suppl., i, p. 513; Leslie, *Connor*, p. 311; ODNB; O'Donoghue, p. 123; RIA/DIB.

D183   *Harry Chalgrave's legacy* (by Catherine Drew).

     + London: James Clarke & Co., 1876 (ill.). SOURCE RIA/DIB ; COPAC. LOCATION L.

     COMMENTARY Set in England. No Irish content [ML].

D184   *The Lutaniste of St. Jacobi's, a tale* (by Catherine Drew).

     + London: Marcus Ward & Co., 1881. SOURCE RIA/DIB. LOCATION L.

     New York: H. Holt & Co., 1881 (The Leisure Hour Series, No. 128). LOCATION L.

     COMMENTARY Set in Germany and concerns a musician and a lace maker. The making of lace is explained [ML].

DRISCOL, Denis, pseud. '**Baba Mongo**', b. Cork 1762, d. United States. Miscellaneous writer and novelist, DD was born into a Catholic family of means. He was sent to the seminary at Salamanca (Spain), where he was trained as a Catholic priest. However, he converted to protestantism and became a curate of the French Reformed Church in a Cork parish. But when he was influenced by French philosophy and radical theory, he lost his parish. He became editor of the *Cork Gazette* in 1791. Initially he was in support of the established order but in 1794, because of his writings, he was sentenced to prison for two years. The government suppressed the paper in 1797. It is unclear what role he played during the 1798 rising. The next year he was living in Dublin in abject poverty. He emigrated to the US, where he worked at various newspapers in New York, Philadelphia, Baltimore and Augusta (GA). He was an active member of the Theist Society and a bookseller in Augusta at the end of his life, stocking many political and anti-Christian books. Durey concluded that DD was 'Extremely well read in Enlightenment philosophy, [he] married continental thought with Painite radicalism to create a doctrine of Irish Jacobinism' (Durey, pp 75–6). SOURCE M. Durey, 'Irish deism and Jefferson's republic: Denis Driscol in Ireland and America, 1793–1810' in *Éire-Ireland*, 25 (1990), pp 56–76; Personal communication, Michael Durey, May 2003; P. Waters, The African traveller, unpublished MS.

D185   *The African traveller, or a tour through Fungeno; a province in the interior of Africa, during the years 1795, 1796, and 1797* (by 'Baba Mongo, a native of Mongala, on the coast of Zanguebar. Having for his guide and companion an Irish philosopher'). London: Printed for the author, 1798. SOURCE J.P. Waters, The African traveller, unpublished MS. LOCATION Library Company of Philadelphia, Northwestern Univ. Library, Evanston (IL).

COMMENTARY Attributed to DD by John Waters. Cast in an African setting, it concerns Ireland and the Irish. Anti-Catholic and anti-monarchy in tone [J.P. Waters, The African traveller, unpublished MS].

DRISCOLL, Miss —, fl. 1820. Novelist. A review of the following volume in the *Dublin Magazine* (May, 1820, p. 376) suggests that it was written by a Miss D—l, while the TCD copy has an annotation that it was written by Miss Driscoll. In all likelihood she was a Protestant. SOURCE COPAC; RL.

D186   *Nice distinctions. A tale* [anon.] (dedication, written Dublin, Sept. 30, 1819, to Jedediah Cleishbotham [Sir Walter Scott], schoolmaster and parish clerk of Gandercleugh).
+ Dublin: J. Cumming; London: Longman, Hurst, Rees, Orme, & Brown, 1820. SOURCE Brown, 71; British Fiction (also Update 3); Garside, 1820:7. LOCATION Corvey CME 3–628–8223, Ireland related fiction, Dt, D, L (not found), NN.

COMMENTARY The review in the *Dublin Magazine* (May, 1820, p. 376) states: 'The action of this tale is quite of a domestic nature, and displays a very intimate acquaintance with the passions, objects, and motives of female minds'. Set in Co. Wicklow and concerning Charles Delacour, a tutor at Glendalough Abbey, who befriends a clergyman's family. When Charles is eventually presented with a living, he marries the clergyman's daughter [Brown].

DROHOJOWSKA, Mme la Comtesse (née Symon Latreiche), fl. 1861. French author.
D187   *Légendes irlandaises, scènes de mœurs* (by Mme la Comtesse Drohojowska).
+ Paris: A. Josse, 1861. SOURCE Brown, 527. LOCATION L.
COMMENTARY Part of *Les récits du foyer, publiés par Madame la Comtesse Drohojowska*. A collection of legends about Ireland. The introduction dwells on religious faith and superstition in the country and does not appear to be based on first-hand information [BLC; Brown].

DRUMMOND, Hamilton, b. (probably Dublin) 1857, d. 1935. Historical romance writer and poet, HD was the son of a Dublin JP and later became a JP himself and a merchant in Dublin. He then moved to England and lived in Lincoln. In his 40s he began publishing novels, specializing in Spanish and French settings. We have counted 36 works of his prose fiction, mostly historical. His poetry includes *Sir Hildebrand, and other poems* (Dublin, 1882), and *Herod, and other poems* (London, 1893). SOURCE Allibone Suppl., i, p. 515; BLC; EF, p. 108; LVP, p. 146; O'Donoghue, p. 123; RIA/DIB; Sutherland, p. 199.

D188   *Gobelin Grange* (by Hamilton Drummond).
London: Adam & Charles Black, 1896. SOURCE Wolff, 1934. LOCATION L.

D189   *For the religion: Being the records of Blaise de Bernauld* (by Hamilton Drummond).
London: Smith, Elder & Co., 1898. SOURCE Sutherland, p. 199; COPAC. LOCATION
L, NUC.
New York: Brentano, 1901. LOCATION NUC.

D190   *A man of his age* (by Hamilton Drummond).
London, New York, Melbourne: Ward, Lock & Co., [1899]. SOURCE Sutherland, p.
199 (1900 edn). LOCATION L.
New York, London: Harper & Bros, 1899. LOCATION NUC.

D191   *A king's pawn* (by Hamilton Drummond).
Edinburgh, London: William Blackwood & Sons, 1900. SOURCE Sutherland, p. 199.
LOCATION L, NUC.
New York: Doubleday, Page & Co., 1901. LOCATION NUC.

D192   *The seven houses* (by Hamilton Drummond).
New York: F.A. Stokes & Co., 1901. LOCATION NUC.

D193   *The Beaufoy romances* (by Hamilton Drummond).
London, New York, Melbourne: Ward, Lock & Co., [1902]. LOCATION L.
Boston: L.C. Page & Co., 1902 (as *Le seigneur of Beaufoy*; ill. A. Van Anrooy).
LOCATION NUC.

D194   *A lord of the soil* (by Hamilton Drummond).
London, New York, Melbourne: Ward, Lock & Co., [1902]. LOCATION L.

D195   *On behalf of the firm* (by Hamilton Drummond).
London, New York, Melbourne: Ward, Lock & Co., 1903 (ill. Henry Austin).
LOCATION L, NUC.
COMMENTARY A Spanish-speaking clerk is sent to Haiti to deal with a bad debt after his pred-
ecessor has been shot there. He frustrates the firm's rival and returns victorious, having cleared
the name of his fiancée's father [EF].

D196   *A man's fear* (by Hamilton Drummond).
London, New York, Melbourne: Ward, Lock & Co., 1903. LOCATION L.

D197   *Room five* (by Hamilton Drummond).
London, New York, Melbourne: Ward, Lock & Co., 1904. LOCATION L.
COMMENTARY Two men are found dead in a hotel room. The reader is left to decide
which one has committed murder and which suicide [EF].

D198   *The King's scapegoat* (by Hamilton Drummond).
London, New York, Melbourne: Ward, Lock & Co., 1905. LOCATION L, NUC.

D199   *The cuckoo* (by Hamilton Drummond).
London: F.V. White & Co., 1906. LOCATION L.

D200   *The chain of seven lives* (by Hamilton Drummond).
London: F.V. White & Co., 1906. LOCATION L, NUC.
COMMENTARY Historical fiction. The story is initially set in Italy at the time of Albertus
Magnus (1206–80) and is based on the idea of a series of lives linked together through history
[EF].

D201   *Shoes of gold* (by Hamilton Drummond).
London: Stanley Paul & Co., 1909. LOCATION L.

D202   *The justice of the king* (by Hamilton Drummond).
London: Stanley Paul & Co., 1911. LOCATION L, NUC.
Cleveland (OH): International Fiction Library, [c. 1911]. LOCATION NUC.
New York: Macmillan, 1911. LOCATION NUC.

COMMENTARY Historical fiction set in the fifteenth century during the reign of French king Louis XI [NUC].

D203 *The three envelopes* (by Hamilton Drummond).
London: Stanley Paul & Co., [1912]. LOCATION L, NUC.

D204 *Sir Galahad of the army* (by Hamilton Drummond).
London: Stanley Paul & Co., [1913]. LOCATION L.

D205 *Winds of God* (by Hamilton Drummond).
London: Stanley Paul & Co., 1913. LOCATION L, NUC.

D206 *Little Madame Claude* (by Hamilton Drummond).
London: Stanley Paul & Co., 1914. LOCATION L.

D207 *Greater than the greatest* (by Hamilton Drummond).
London: Stanley Paul & Co., 1915. LOCATION L, NUC.
New York: E.P. Dutton & Co., [1917]. LOCATION L.

D208 *The half-priest* (by Hamilton Drummond).
London: Stanley Paul & Co., 1916. LOCATION L, NUC.

D209 *The grain of mustard* (by Hamilton Drummond).
London: Stanley Paul & Co., 1916. LOCATION L.

D210 *The great game* (by Hamilton Drummond).
London: Stanley Paul & Co., 1918. LOCATION L.

D211 *The betrayers* (by Hamilton Drummond).
New York: E.P. Dutton & Co., [1919]. LOCATION NUC.

D212 *A maker of saints* (by Hamilton Drummond).
London: Stanley Paul & Co., 1919. LOCATION L, NUC.
New York: E.P. Dutton & Co., [1920]. LOCATION NUC.

D213 *Her chosen past* (by Hamilton Drummond).
London: Stanley Paul & Co., 1920. LOCATION L.

D214 *Loyalty* (by Hamilton Drummond).
London: E. Nash & Grayson, 1921. LOCATION L.

D215 *Chattels* (by Hamilton Drummond).
London: Stanley Paul & Co., 1922. LOCATION L.

D216 *Babette of Montfort* (by Hamilton Drummond).
London: Stanley Paul & Co., 1928. LOCATION L ([1929] edn), NUC.

D217 *Montalain* (by Hamilton Drummond).
London: Stanley Paul & Co., [1930]. LOCATION L.

D218 *The custom of Brettinoro* (by Hamilton Drummond).
London: Stanley Paul & Co., [1931]. LOCATION L.

D219 *The keeper of the gate* (by Hamilton Drummond).
London: Stanley Paul & Co., [1931]. LOCATION L.

D220 *Quittance* (by Hamilton Drummond).
London: Stanley Paul & Co., [1932]. LOCATION L.

D221 *The Tournelles plot* (by Hamilton Drummond).
London: Stanley Paul & Co., [1933]. LOCATION L.

D222 *Devrigne of Chantal* (by Hamilton Drummond).
London: Stanley Paul & Co., [1933]. LOCATION L.

D223 *Young Navarre* (by Hamilton Drummond).
London: Stanley Paul & Co., [1934]. LOCATION L.

'DUBH, Scian', pseud. See **MC CARROLL, James**.

DU BOIS, Lady Dorothea (née Annesley), b. Dublin 1728, d. Dublin 1774. Poet, novelist and dramatist, DDuB was the eldest daughter of Richard Annesley, Lord Altham, 8th (not 6th as in ODNB) earl of Angelsea, who had his residence in Ireland at Camolin Park (Co. Wexford, demolished in 1974), and Ann Simpson, daughter of John Simpson, a wealthy clothier from Dublin. In 1740 her father began an affair, repudiated his marriage and his children, and turned his wife and three daughters out of his house. He refused to pay the alimony ordered by the ecclesiastical courts and his family had to subsist on a pension of £200 a year granted by George II. She married M. Du Bois, a French musician, in a private ceremony in 1752. He converted to protestantism, and together they had six children, born within eight years. Given her financial straits, DDuB wrote mostly to earn money. Her poetry includes *Poems on several occasions* (Dublin, 1764), which contains 'A true tale', a vivid account of her life story. In addition, she published *The case of Anne, Countess of Anglesea* (London, 1766); *The lady's polite secretary; or, new female letter writer* (London, 1771), and several musical theatre pieces. She died in poverty in Dublin. For her portrait, see ODNB. The NLI has copies of her correspondence with George Berkeley, bishop of Cloyne, on her proposed marriage to M. Du Bois and Berkeley's response (MS 987). SOURCE Blain, pp 310–11; BLC; Carpenter, pp 331–7; *CP*, i, pp 136–7; Field Day, iv, pp 762, 789–90, 796–8, 791–4, 823; ODNB; O'Donoghue, p. 124; RIA/DIB; Rowe & Scallan, 295; *Vanishing country houses*, p. 149.

D224 *Theodora, a novel* (by Lady Dorothea Du Bois; dedicated to the countess of Hertford).
+ London: Printed for the author by C. Kiernan, 1770, 2 vols. SOURCE Blain, pp 310–11; Raven 2, 1770:28; ESTC t106576. LOCATION L, NN.

COMMENTARY An autobiographical novel partly set in Ireland. The copy in the BL contains a key to the main characters and the following comment: 'This book contains the story of the author and of her mother, who asserted herself to be the wife of Richard Annesley Esq. of Anglesea though disowned by him. It is said that Richard Altham, the earl of Anglesea, the hero of this memoir never scrupled to marry any woman whom he pursued but who would not surrender on less honourable terms– and when these deluded ladies attempted to claim the benefit of their marriage he always set up some of his purony [*sic*] in barr of it' [RL; Blain; Field Day, iv, pp 794–6; CM].

DUBOIS, Edward, pseud. 'A knight errant', b. London 1774, d. London 1850. English barrister, novelist, translator and poet, ED stated that if other men enjoyed hunting or dancing, he did not see why he should not enjoy writing novels, particularly since he was paid for his pleasure and they had to pay dearly for theirs. He supplemented his work as a barrister with his literary output, regularly contributing art notices, drama criticism and verse to a number of periodicals, including the London *Morning Chronicle*. He also served as art critic on the staff of the *Observer* (London). Only ED's work relating to Ireland is listed below. SOURCE Allibone i, p. 525; Garside 1800:28 and 1801:22 (for other novels); ODNB; J.T. Taylor, *Early opposition to the English novel* (New York, 1943), p. 17; Wolff, ii, p. 35.

D225 *My pocket book; or, hints for 'A ryghte merrie and conceitede' tour, in quarto; to be called 'The stranger in Ireland' in 1805* (by 'A knight errant').
London: Vernor, Hood, & Sharpe; Poultry, J. & A. Arch, J. Murra, J. Hatcherd, & J. Booker, 1807 (ill.). SOURCE NSTC; Bradshaw, 7681. LOCATION BFl (1808 edn), L, O, C, NUC.
+ London: Vernor, Hood & Sharpe, Poultry; & J. Archer; R. Dugdale; M.N. Mahon; M. Keene; C. Legrange; Dublin: L. Tuggis, 1808 (new edn; dedicated to the paper manufacturers; as *My pocket book; or, hints for 'A ryghte merrie and conceitede' tour, in quarto; to be called 'The stranger in Ireland' in 1805 ... In which will be found, amongst other pleasant and satirical novelties, An introduction; A description of the plates; Illustrative*

anecdoctes from my 'Tour through Holland' in 1806; an Appendix, containing three MSS. Found in St. Patrick's Abbey; and An essay in defence of bad spelling; ill.). SOURCE Gilbert, p. 249 (1808, 3rd edn). LOCATION DPL Gilbert coll. (1808, 3rd edn), L (1808, 3rd edn), NUC (1808, 3rd edn), InND Loeber coll.

New York: Ezra Sargant, 1807. SOURCE Fanning, p. 378. LOCATION NUC.

COMMENTARY A parody on Sir John Carr's *Stranger in Ireland* (London, 1806), which gave rise to a libel suit brought by Sir John against the publishers. The court ruled that Dubois's burlesque constituted fair comment, and rejected the complainant's suit [Jarndyce cat. 132/90; *Sir John Carr against Hood and Sharpe ... 1808* (London, 1808)].

'THE DUCHESS', pseud. See HUNGERFORD, Mrs Margaret Wolfe.

DU CREST DE ST AUBIN, Stephanie-Félicité. See DE GENLIS, Stephanie-Félicité, Mme de.

DUDLEY, Mary Elizabeth Southwell. See LEATHLEY, Mary Elizabeth Southwell.

DUFFERIN, Lady Helen Selina Blackwood, baroness of (née Sheridan), later Helen Hay, countess of Gifford, b. England? 1807, d. London, 1867. English songwriter, poet and illustrator, HSB was the granddaughter of Irish playwright and politician Richard Brinsley Sheridan and the eldest sister of the author Caroline Norton. Early in her childhood she accompanied her parents to South Africa, returning to England on her father's death, when her mother was given lodgings at Hampton Court. At age 18 she married Capt. Price Blackwood, heir to the marquess of Dufferin and Ava. To escape the Dufferins' disapproval, the couple lived at first in Italy. In 1841 her husband died and she remained a widow for 21 years, marrying in 1862 George Hay, the dying earl of Gifford. She was widowed again after a few months. She published several volumes of songs and ballads, the best known of which are 'The lament of the Irish emigrant', and 'Terence's farewell'. A collection of her illustrations was published privately in 1894; in the same year as appeared *Songs, poems and verses by Helen, Lady Dufferin*, edited by her son, the marquess of Dufferin and Ava. For her portraits and papers, see ODNB. SOURCE Allibone i, pp 526–7; Alston, p. 31; Brady, p. 60; Colman, pp 201–3 [under Sheridan]; DLB, cic; Field Day, ii, pp 3, 67, 77, 103, 114; Hogan, pp 214–15; Hogan 2, pp 383–4; McKenna, pp 160–1; MVP, p. 142; Newmann, p. 18; NCBEL 4, pp 608–9; OCIL, p. 50 [under Blackwood]; ODNB [under Hay]; O'Donoghue, p. 124; RIA/DIB [under Blackwood].

D226   *Lispings from low latitudes; or, extracts from the journal of the Hon. Impulsia Gushington* [anon.].

+ London: John Murray, 1863 (ill. the author). SOURCE McKenna, p. 161. LOCATION NUC, InND Loeber coll.

COMMENTARY The title was inspired by Lady Dufferin's son's collection of poems *Letters from high latitudes* (London, 1857), and by Sarah Lushington's *Narrative of a journey from Calcutta to Europe, by way of Egypt* (London, 1829). The story is a satire on high life in the nineteenth century as expressed by Miss Gushington's diary of her travel to Egypt. The journey was undertaken to escape the ennui of society life. As an unprotected female she has many adventures. Her servants desert her and her gullibility makes her a victim of profiteers and thieves. The story is accompanied by comical illustrations, apparently done by the author [ML].

DUGANNE, A.J.H. See DUGANNE, Augustine Joseph Hickey.

DUGANNE, Augustine Joseph Hickey (known as **A.J.H. Duganne** and **Augustine J.H. Duganne**), b. Boston (MA) 1823, d. United States? 1884. American novelist, poet and dramatist, AJHD was also a prolific writer on philosophy, economics and government. His pre-Famine works include patriotic poems about Irish freedom. A sumptuous volume of his verse, complete with his portrait, was published in 1856. He was elected to the New York State Assembly in 1855; he helped raise the New York 176th Volunteers for the Civil War, and he was imprisoned by Confederate forces. After the war, he was associated with the *New York Tribune* and the *Sunday Dispatch*. SOURCE Allibone i, p. 527; ANB; Burke, p. 209; DAB; Fanning, p. 78; NUC; Wright, ii, p. 107 (list of novels).

D227 *The two clerks; or, the orphan's gratitude: Being the adventures of Henry Fowler and Richard Martin* (by Augustine J.H. Duganne).
Boston: Brainard & Co., 1843. SOURCE Fanning, p. 379; Wright, i, 874. LOCATION NUC.
COMMENTARY The story traces a poor boy from Boston's North End to valiant soldiering with the Irish Wild Geese under Simon Bolivar in South America [Fanning, p. 79].

D228 *The spirit of the ford; an Irish ghost story* (by A.J.H. Duganne).
Boston: F. Gleason, 1849. LOCATION NUC.

D229 *The tenant house; or, embers from poverty's hearthstone* (by A.J.H. Duganne).
+ New York: Robert M. De Witt, 1857 (ill.). SOURCE Fanning, p. 379; Wright, ii, 799. LOCATION NUC ([c. 1857] edn), Wright web.
COMMENTARY The story of a frightful New York tenement groaning with Irish Catholic depravity [Fanning, p. 78; Wright].

DUNBAR, Jane. See **CHAPLIN, Mrs Jane.**

DUNN, N.J., fl. 1884. Novelist, NJD may be identified with the American poet Nathaniel Dunn, who published a poem *Satan chained* (New York, 1876, 2nd edn). SOURCE Allibone Suppl., i, p. 524; O'Donoghue, p. 127.

D230 *The vultures of Erin. A tale of the penal laws* (by N.J. Dunn).
New York: P.J. Kenedy, 1884. SOURCE Brown, 534; Wright, iii, 1678 (1886 edn). LOCATION L, NUC.
COMMENTARY Set between the Slieve Bouchta and Lough Derg (Co. Donegal). Edward Fitzgerald is robbed of his property by his enemy Templeton, who falsely accuses him of a murder he instigated himself. Fitzgerald is condemned to death and his wife loses her reason. He escapes, however, and many years later returns with proof of Templeton's guilt. His wife recovers. The penal laws are denounced, and scripture-readers appear in an unfavourable light [Brown].

DUNNE, F.W. See **DUNNE, Frederick William.**

DUNNE, Frederick William (also known as **F.W. Dunne**), fl. 1832. Historical fiction writer, FWD probably worked in the customs office in London as he wrote *The case of F.W.D, late a clerk of the first class in Her Majesty's customs* (London, 1850). SOURCE BLC.

D231 *The pirate of Bofine. An historical romance* (by F.W. Dunne).
+ London: A.K. Newman & Co., 1832, 3 vols. SOURCE Hodgson, p. 440; Brown, 536; Block, p. 64; Garside 2, 1832:28; COPAC. LOCATION Corvey, CME 328–47510–4, L.
COMMENTARY The introd. tells how, in the ruins of a castle on an island off the north west coast of Ireland, a manuscript was discovered that forms the basis for this historical novel. Relates a series of melodramatic and disconnected episodes, set in the west of Ireland in the

reign of Henry VIII, but historical characters are not given any historical background. Extensive notes are added to each volume Bofine may refer to Inisbofin, 'island of the white cow', one of which is off the coast of Donegal and the other off Galway [Brown; Garside].

DUNNE, Mary Chavelita (married names Clairmonte and Bright), pseud **'George Egerton'**, b. Melbourne (Australia) 1859, d. Crawley (Sussex) 1945. Primarily a short story writer and translator, MCD was an independent and adventurous woman who was the eldest daughter of John Dunne, an Irish Catholic officer, and Isobel George, who was Welsh. Her actual career is at variance with her autobiographical accounts. Born in Australia, at age 11 she was brought to Ireland, where the family lived in relatively poor circumstances. Her father was relieved of prison governorships at Nenagh (Co. Tipperary) and Castlebar (Co. Mayo) due to debts. He had many talents but was said to be a born liar and gambler and had difficulties keeping a job. MCD is said to have spent part of her youth in Chile and in New Zealand, where she witnessed the war against the Maoris. She was trained as a nurse and in 1875 was sent to Germany for two years, where she taught and studied. Afterwards she worked in Dublin, New York and London and her experiences there of women struggling to support themselves informed many of her later stories. In 1887, when she was the travelling companion of a Mr and Mrs Higginson (Mrs Higginson was the widow of George Whyte-Melville§), she eloped with Mr Higginson to Norway, where she read Strindberg, Nietzsche and others and was imbued with Ibsenism, which is prominent in her later work. In Norway she fell in love with the writer Knut Pedersen, who used the pseudonym 'Knut Hamsun', and he encouraged her to write. MCD translated his novel *Hunger* (London, 1899). Higginson was, apparently, a drunken and abusive man. He died in 1889, although she may have left him earlier, and he left her a small annual income, most of which she used to support her family. She moved to England and in 1891 married what one commentator called 'an idle destitute Canadian', Egerton Tertius Clairmonte. They moved to Millstreet (Co. Cork) to live cheaply, and she supported her husband by writing. In 1895 the marriage broke up and the couple divorced in 1901. Meanwhile, she achieved a huge success with her collection of stories, *Keynotes* (London, 1893), and apparently became the mistress of its publisher, John Lane. She married in 1901 Golding Bright, a literary agent who was a leading drama critic and agent for writers such as G.B. Shaw§ and Somerset Maugham. Her attempts at drama, although encouraged by Shaw, were unsuccessful. She did several translations of French plays. MCD's stories were categorized as 'new woman' stories and their frankness and exploration of gender roles had a significant impact on contemporary notions of feminism and sexuality. She herself disliked this description, and was even opposed to the women's suffrage movement. MCD died in poverty in a nursing home in Sussex. For her portrait and papers, see ODNB. SOURCE Blain, p. 332 [under Egerton]; Brady, p. 71; DLB, cxxxv [under Egerton]; EF, pp 113–14; Field Day, iv, p. 895, v, p. 977 [under Egerton]; Hogan 2, pp 403–5 [under Egerton]; C. Murphy, *The women's suffrage movement and Irish society* (Philadelphia, 1989), p. 52; NCBEL 4, pp 1520–1 [under Egerton]; OCIL, p. 169 [under Egerton]; ODNB; O'Toole, pp 75–6; RIA/DIB [under Egerton]; E. Showalter, *A literature of their own* (Princeton, 1999), pp 210–14; M.D. Stetz, in *Turn-of-the-century women* (1984); Sutherland, pp 209–10 [under Egerton]; T. de V. White (ed.), *A leaf from the yellow book* (London, 1958), p. 12 (contains some of her correspondence and diaries).

D232 *Keynotes* (by 'George Egerton'; dedicated to Knut Hamsun).
+ London: Elkin Mathews & John Lane; Boston: Roberts Bros, 1893 (ill. Aubrey Beardsley). SOURCE Wolff, 2049; Weekes, p. 119; Field Day, iv, pp 1102–3. LOCATION L, InND Loeber coll.
Boston: Roberts Bros, 1893. LOCATION NUC.

COMMENTARY A sensationally successful collection of short stories about the 'new woman'. A copy inscribed by GE has the annotation 'A potent argument against matrimony = a good pal and a pretty home'. The volume was parodied by Owen Seaman (under the pseudonym 'Borgia Smudgiton') as 'She-notes' in *Punch* in 1894 [Krishnamurti, pp 38–9].

D233 *Discords* (by 'George Egerton'; dedicated to T.P. Gill).
+ London: John Lane; Boston: Roberts Bros, 1894. SOURCE Wolff, 2047. LOCATION L, NUC, InND Loeber coll. (1895 edn).
Boston: Roberts Bros, 1894, 5th edn. LOCATION NUC.

COMMENTARY A series of short stories exploring the effects of women's anger, disgust and rage in situations where their dependence on men makes it hard to express their emotions. Contents: 'A psychological moment at three periods', 'Her share', 'Gone under', 'Wedlock', 'Virgin soil', 'The regeneration of two' [Showalter, Literature, p. 213; RL].

D234 *Symphonies* (by 'George Egerton'; dedicated to J.A.M.).
+ London, New York: John Lane, 1897. SOURCE Wolff, 2050. LOCATION L, InND Loeber coll.
COMMENTARY Contents: 'A Chilian episode', 'The captain's book', 'Sea pinks', 'A nocturne', 'Oony', 'At the heart of the apple', 'Pan' [RL].

D235 *Fantasias* (by 'George Egerton').
+ London, New York: John Lane, 1898 (dedicated to Richard Le Gallienne). SOURCE Wolff, 2048. LOCATION Dt, L, NUC, InND Loeber coll.

COMMENTARY Stories set in a fantasy world. Contents: 'The star-worshipper', 'The elusive melody', 'The mandrake Venus', 'The futile quest', 'The kingdom of dreams', 'The well of truth' [ML].

D236 *The wheel of God* (by 'George Egerton'; dedicated to the author's father [John Dunne]).
+ London: Grant Richards, 1898. SOURCE Weekes, p. 119. LOCATION L.
New York: G.P. Putnam Sons, 1898. LOCATION NUC.

COMMENTARY A full-length autobiographical work showing the formation of a young Irish girl's character as she travels to New York, supporting herself as a journalist [Sutherland].

D237 *Rosa Amorosa. The love-letters of a woman* (by 'George Egerton').
London: Grant Richards, 1901. SOURCE Weekes, p. 119. LOCATION L, NUC.
New York: Brentano's, 1901. LOCATION NUC.

COMMENTARY Based on the author's letters to an anonymous Norwegian author [EF, p. 114].

D238 *Flies in amber* (by 'George Egerton'; dedicated to R.G.B.).
+ London: Hutchinson & Co., 1905. SOURCE Weekes, p. 119. LOCATION L.

COMMENTARY Contents: 'How the Christ-child came to the unregenerate', '"Mammy"', 'The third in the house', 'A conjugal episode', 'The chessboard of Guendolen', 'The Marriage of Mary Ascension' (a portrayal of middle-class Irish life), 'The interment of little Alice' [ML; Sutherland].

DUNNE, Peter Finley, b. Chicago (IL) 1867, d. United States 1936. American journalist, humorist and social critic, PFD was born to Irish immigrant parents Peter Dunne of Offaly and Ellen Finley of Kilkenny. He grew up in a large Irish Catholic family and was educated by the Jesuits. He began his writing career as a journalist in Chicago and created for newspapers the character of Mr Martin Dooley, a bar-room sage who, like PFD's father, was a Catholic, a Democrat, an active political worker and an Irish nationalist. Mr Dooley dispensed wit and wisdom on the affairs of greater Chicago and the world. The stories first appeared in the *Chicago Times* in 1893 and continued up to 1919. They helped portray the process of assimilation of Irish immigrants into American life. SOURCE ANB; E.J. Bander, *Mr. Dooley &*

Mr. Dunne. The literary life of a Chicago Catholic (Charlottesville, VA, 1981); Brown, p. 95; DAB; DLB, xi, xxiii; G. Eckley, *Peter Finley Dunne* (Boston, 1981); OCIL, p. 162.

D239   *Mr. Dooley in peace and in war* [anon.] (dedicated to W.H. Turner).

+ Boston: Small, Maynard & Co., 1898. SOURCE Wright, iii, 1679. LOCATION DPL, L, NUC.

Toronto: George N. Morang & Co., 1899. SOURCE Topp 1, p. 484. LOCATION L, NUC.

London: Grant Richards, 1899. SOURCE Topp 1, p. 483. LOCATION L, NUC.

London: George Newnes, [1899]. LOCATION L.

+ London: George Routledge & Sons, 1899. LOCATION L, InND Loeber coll. (1899, 3rd edn).

London: G.P. Putnam's Sons; Boston: Small, Maynard & Co., 1899. LOCATION L.

D240   *What Dooley says* [anon.].

Chicago: Kazmar & Co., [1899] (Pontiac Series, No. 1). SOURCE Blessing, p. 141. LOCATION L, NUC.

D241   *Mr. Dooley in the hearts of his countrymen* [anon.] (dedicated to Sir George Newnes, Messrs. George Rutledge & Sons).

+ Boston: Small, Maynard & Co., 1899. SOURCE Blessing, p. 141; Wright, iii, 1680. LOCATION L, NUC, InND Loeber coll.

Toronto: George N. Morang & Co., 1899. LOCATION L.

London: Grant Richards, 1899. LOCATION L, NUC.

D242   *Mr. Dooley's philosophy* [anon.].

New York: R.H. Russell, 1900 (ill. William Nicholson, E.W. Kemble, F. Opper). SOURCE Blessing, p. 141; Wright, iii, 1681. LOCATION NUC.

+ London: William Heinemann, 1900 (ill. William Nicholson, E.W. Kemble, F. Opper). LOCATION DPL (1903 edn), L, NUC, InND Loeber coll. (1901 edn).

D243   *Mr. Dooley's opinions* [anon.].

New York: R.H. Russell, 1901. SOURCE Blessing, p. 141. LOCATION NUC.

+ New York: Harper, 1901. LOCATION NUC, InND Loeber coll. (1906 edn).

Toronto: Copp, Clark, 1902. LOCATION NUC.

COMMENTARY Contents: 'Christian science', 'Life at Newport', 'The Supreme Court's decisions', 'Disqualifying the enemy', 'Amateur ambassadors', 'The city as a summer resort', 'An editor's duties', 'On the poet's fate', 'The yacht races', 'On athletics', 'On lying', 'Discusses party politics', 'The truth about Schley', 'Fame', 'Cross-examinations', 'Thanksgiving', 'On the Midway', 'Mrs. Carnegie's gift', 'The crusade against vice', 'The New York custom house', 'Some political observations', 'Youth and age', 'On Wall Street', 'Colleges and degrees', 'The Booker Washington incident' [ML].

D244   *Observations by Mr. Dooley* [anon.].

New York: R.H. Russell, 1902. SOURCE Blessing, p. 141. LOCATION NUC.

+ London: William Heinemann, 1903. LOCATION DPL, L, NUC.

New York: Greenwood Press, 1969. SOURCE Blessing, p. 141; OCLC. LOCATION NYU.

D245   *Mr. Dooley on timely topics of the day; on the life insurance investigation, on business & political honesty, on national housekeeping* [anon.].

[New York]: [n.p.], 1905. SOURCE Blessing, p. 141. LOCATION NUC.

D246   *Dissertations by Mr. Dooley* [anon.].

New York, London: Harper & Bros, 1906. SOURCE Blessing, p. 141. LOCATION L, NUC.

D247   *Mr. Dooley says* [anon.].

+ New York: Charles Scribner's Sons, 1910. SOURCE Blessing, p. 141. LOCATION NUC, InND Loeber coll.

IRELAND'S AUTHORS

GOLDSMITH
THE VICAR OF WAKEFIELD

BANIM
THE BIT O' WRITIN'

EDMUND BURKE
ON IRISH AFFAIRS

PRICE SIXPENCE

1 Cover of [anon.], *Ireland's authors* (Dublin, 1886). See **Anon.96**.

2 Frontispiece of [anon.], *The Irish freebooter; or, surprising adventures of Captain Redmond O'Hanlan* (London, 1819). See **Anon.136**.

THE WORKHOUSE CHILDREN.

Page 45.

THE R. T. S. LIBRARY—ILLUSTRATED

IRISH STORIES

*Miss Greeves
10 Myrtle Field Park
Balmoral
Belfast.*

*A M Greeves
Lismachan*

THE RELIGIOUS TRACT SOCIETY
56, PATERNOSTER ROW; 65, ST. PAUL'S CHURCHYARD;
AND 164, PICCADILLY

3 Title page of [anon.], *Irish stories* (London, [*c.*1854 or 1855]). See **Anon.116**.

4 Cover of [anon.], *The Royal Hibernian tales* (Dublin, [1835?]). **See Anon.220.**

SISTER MARY'S LIBRARY.—NO. 1.

THE

VIGIL OF ST. LAURENCE;

OR,

AN INFANT'S BAPTISM.

BY THE AUTHORESS OF

"GERALDINE, A TALE OF CONSCIENCE," AND
"THE YOUNG COMMUNICANTS."

Eleanor C. Agnew

PHILADELPHIA:

PUBLISHED BY HENRY McGRATH,

1019 Walnut Street.

5 Title page of Eleanor C. Agnew, *The vigil of St. Laurence and other tales* (Philadelphia, n.d.). See **A15**.

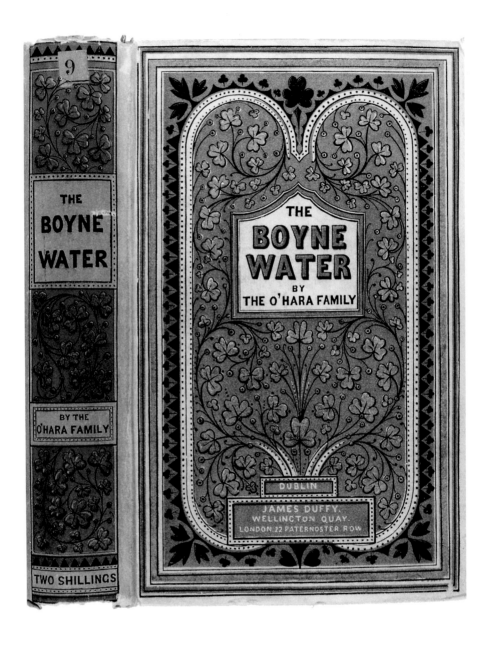

6 Cover of 'The O'Hara family' [John and Michael Banim],
The Boyne water (Dublin, 1865–66). See **B28**.

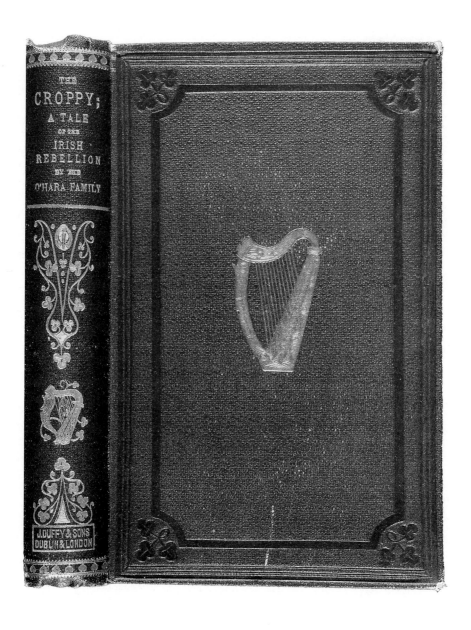

7 Cover of 'The O'Hara family' [Michael Banim], *The croppy.*
A tale of the Irish rebellion of 1798 (Dublin, 1865-66). See **B28**.

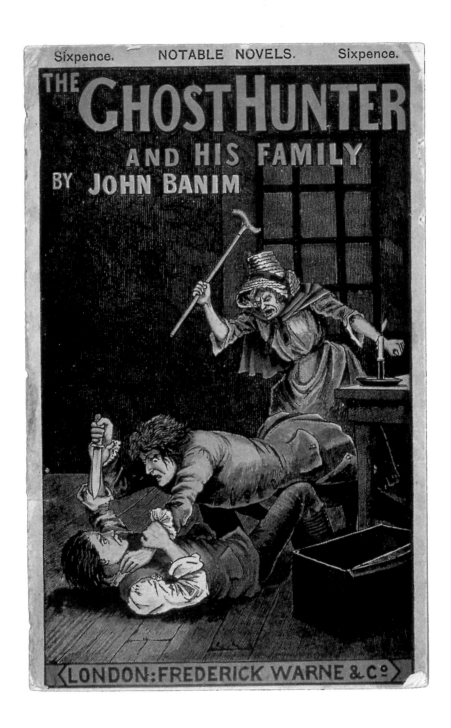

8 Cover of John Banim [*sic*, Michael Banim], *The ghost hunter and his family* (London, 1888). See **B33**.

THE

HISTORY

OF

ISAAC JENKINS,

To which are added,

A FRIENDLY GIFT

TO

𝕊𝖊𝖗𝖛𝖆𝖓𝖙𝖘 𝖆𝖓𝖉 𝕬𝖕𝖕𝖗𝖊𝖓𝖙𝖎𝖈𝖊𝖘,

AND

THE BRAZIER,

OR,

MUTUAL GRATITUDE.

DUBLIN:

PRINTED BY WM. ESPY, 6, LITTLE STRAND-ST.

1820.

[Price bound in Sheep, 8d. and in Grain, 6d.]

9 Title page of [Thomas Beddoes], *The history of Isaac Jenkins*
(Dublin, 1820). See **B134**.

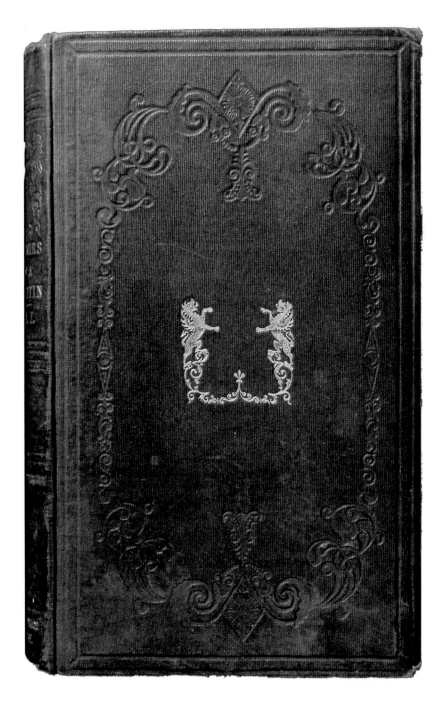

10 Cover of Capt. [Francis] Bellew *Memoirs of a griffin*
(London, 1843), 2 vols. See **B143**.

ÉLIE BERTHET

LE DERNIER

IRLANDAIS

PARIS

LIBRAIRIE NOUVELLE

BOULEVARD DES ITALIENS, 15

A. BOURDILLIAT ET Cᵉ, ÉDITEURS

La traduction et la reproduction sont réservées.

1860

11   Title page of Élie Berthet, *Le dernier Irlandais* (Paris, 1860). See **B147**.

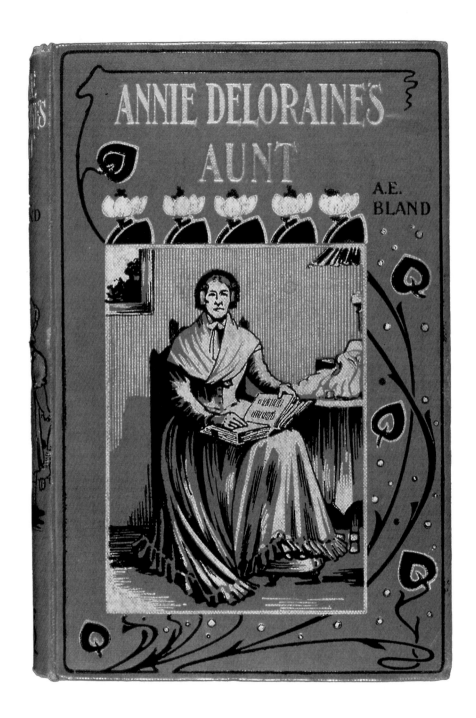

12   Cover of E.A. Bland, *Annie Deloraine's aunt* (London, 1895). See **B169**.

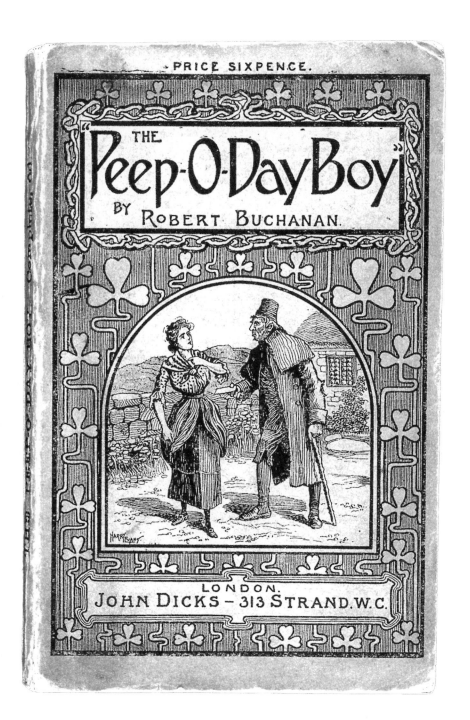

13 Cover of Robert Buchanan, *The 'Peep-o'-Day Boy*
(London, [1902]). See **B400**.

RECOLLECTIONS

OF

IRELAND.

BY THE AUTHOR OF

" A Visit to My Birth Place"—" Retrospections"—" Abbey
Innismoyle," &c.

DUBLIN

WILLIAM CURRY, JUN. AND COMPANY

9, UPPER SACKVILLE-STREET.

1839.

14 Title page of [Selina Bunbury], *Recollections of Ireland*
(Dublin, 1839). See **B447**.

15 Cover of William Carleton, *Rody the rover* (Dublin, 1845). See **C82**.

THE LIFE AND ADVENTURES

OF

RODY THE ROVER;

THE

RIBBONMAN OF IRELAND.

BY

WILLIAM CARLETON.

AUTHOR OF THE "TRAITS AND STORIES OF THE IRISH PEASANTRY,"
"VALENTINE McCLUTCHY," "ART MAGUIRE,"
"O'SULLIVAN'S LOVE," ETC.

COMPLETE AND UNABRIDGED EDITION.

Philadelphia:
T. B. PETERSON & BROTHERS,
306 CHESTNUT STREET.

16 Cover of William Carleton, *The life and adventures of Rody the rover*
(Philadelphia, [186-]). See **C82**.

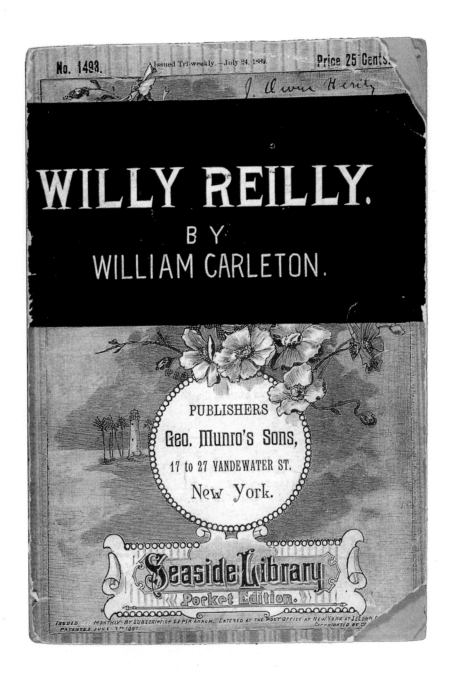

No. 1493. Issued Tri-weekly.—July 24, 1889. Price 25 Cents.

WILLY REILLY.

BY

WILLIAM CARLETON.

PUBLISHERS

Geo. Munro's Sons,

17 to 27 VANDEWATER ST.

New York.

Seaside Library

Pocket Edition.

ISSUED MONTHLY BY SUBSCRIPTION $3 PER ANNUM. ENTERED AT THE POST OFFICE AT NEW YORK AT SECOND
PATENTED JUNE 7TH 1887.

17 Cover of William Carleton, *Willy Reilly* (New York, n.d.). See **C99**.

18 Cover of Agnes and Egerton Castle, *The secret orchard*
(London, n.d.). See **C144**.

THE WOODEN CROSS:

𝕬 𝕽𝖊𝖑𝖎𝖌𝖎𝖔𝖚𝖘 𝕿𝖆𝖑𝖊.

IMITATED FROM THE GERMAN OF THE CANONS

SCHMID.

BY A CATHOLIC PRIEST.

" And the Lord is become a refuge for the poor :
a helper in due time in tribulation.

" And let them trust in thee who know thy name :
for thou hast not forsaken them that seek thee O Lord.

" To thee is the poor left : Thou wilt be a helper
to the Orphan."—Ps. ix. 10, 11, 14.

DUBLIN:

T. O'GORMAN, UPPER ORMOND QUAY.

MDCCCXXXIX.

19 Title page of 'A Catholic priest', *The wooden cross* (Dublin, 1839). See **C180**.

"HE PASSED THE DOOR BEFORE HE COULD PULL UP HIS HORSE."
[*Page* 53.

MICK TRACY

THE IRISH SCRIPTURE READER

OR

The Martyred Convert and the Priest

A TALE OF FACTS

BY THE AUTHOR OF "TIM DOOLAN, THE IRISH EMIGRANT"

"Hear the just law, the judgment of the skies,—
He that hates TRUTH, must be the dupe of lies;
And he that will be CHEATED to the last,
DELUSIONS strong as hell shall BIND him fast."
COWPER.

LONDON
S. W. PARTRIDGE & CO.
8 & 9, PATERNOSTER ROW.

20 Title page of [William Anderson Cawthorne], *Mick Tracy,
the Irish scripture reader* (London, n.d., new edn). See C187.

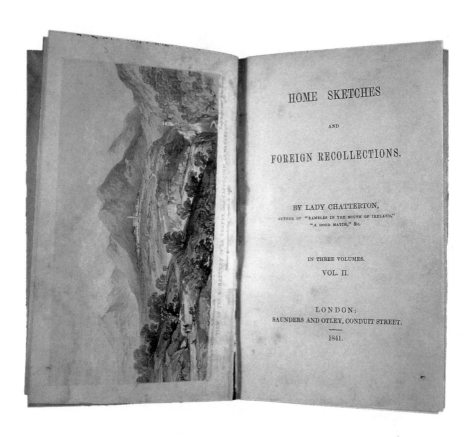

HOME SKETCHES

AND

FOREIGN RECOLLECTIONS.

BY LADY CHATTERTON,

AUTHOR OF "RAMBLES IN THE SOUTH OF IRELAND,"
"A GOOD MATCH," &c.

IN THREE VOLUMES.

VOL. II.

LONDON:
SAUNDERS AND OTLEY, CONDUIT STREET.

1841.

21 Title page of Lady Chatterton, *Home sketches and foreign recollections*
(London, 1841, 3 vols.). See **C201**.

SKETCHES

OF

SOCIETY

IN

FRANCE AND IRELAND,

IN THE

YEARS 1805—6—7.

By a CITIZEN of the UNITED STATES.

IN TWO VOLUMES.

VOL. I.

DUBLIN:

PRINTED FOR THE AUTHOR, AND SOLD BY THE
BOOKSELLERS.

1811.

22 Title page of 'A citizen of the United States', *Sketches of society in France and
Ireland, in the years 1805–6–7* (Dublin, 1811, 2 vols.). See **C216**.

Oruikshank del.   London sculp.

See Page 3.

Publish'd by J Corry, June 1.1803.

Rev⁰ Allan

THE

VALE OF CLWYD,

OR THE

PLEASURES OF RETIREMENT,

A WELCH TALE.

BY JOHN CORRY,

AUTHOR OF A SATIRICAL VIEW OF LONDON;
ORIGINAL TALES; &c.

Come see what pleasures in our plains abound,
The woods, the fountains, and the flow'ry ground;
As you are beauteous, were you half so true,
Here could I live, and love, and die with only you!
                                        DRYDEN'S VIRGIL.

LONDON:

Printed for B. CROSBY and Co. Stationers' Court; CHAMPANTE
and Co. Jewry Street, Aldgate; R. OGLE, Great Turnstile,
Holborn; T. HUGHES, and M. JONES, Paternoster-row;
J. STUART, and J. MURRAY, Prince's Street, Leicester Sq.
A. H. NAIRNE, Chandos Street,; and C. CHAPPLE, Pall
Mall.

Price Sixpence.

23   Title page of John Corry, *The vale of Clwyd; or, the pleasures of retirement* (London, [1803 or earlier]). See **C370**.

SAINTS AND SINNERS:

A TALE.

COMPLETE IN ONE VOLUME.

BY

SAMUEL ALFRED COX.

"My dear sir, clear your mind of CANT."—
Johnson.

DUBLIN.

1856.

---

24 Title page of Samuel Alfred Cox, *Saints and sinners: A tale*
(Unpublished manuscript vol., Dublin 1856). See **C387**.

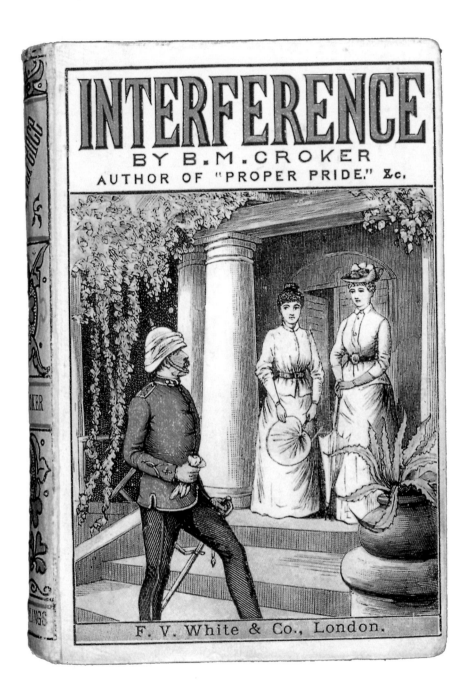

25 Cover of Bithia Mary Croker, *Interference* (London, 1894, 3rd edn). See **C424**.

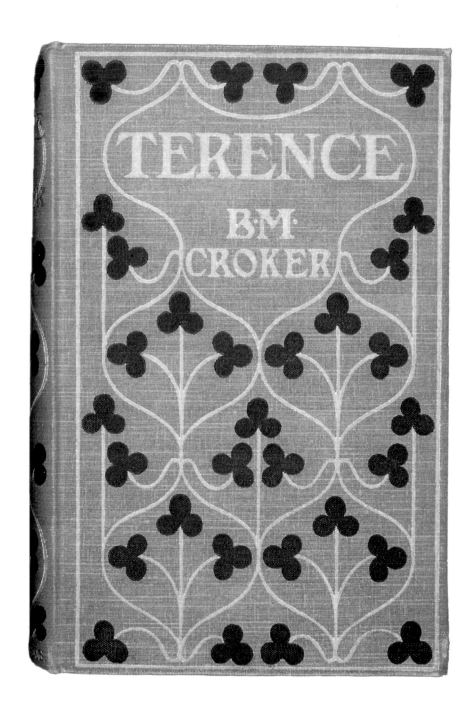

26 Cover of Bithia Mary Croker, *Terence* (London, 1899). See **C436**.

27   Cover of 'Cui Bono', *St. Luke's; Montenotte; Tivoli; and Glanmire. A conversation* ([Cork], [1877]). See **C552**.

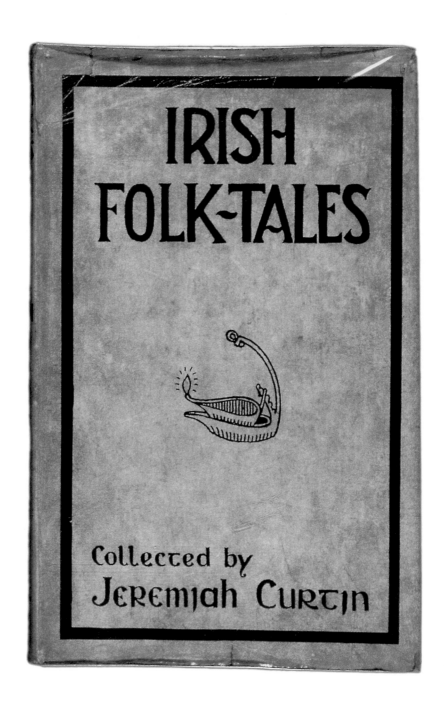

IRISH FOLK-TALES

Collected by
JEREMIAH CURTIN

28 Cover of Jeremiah Curtis, *Irish folk-tales* (Dublin, 1944). See **C560**.

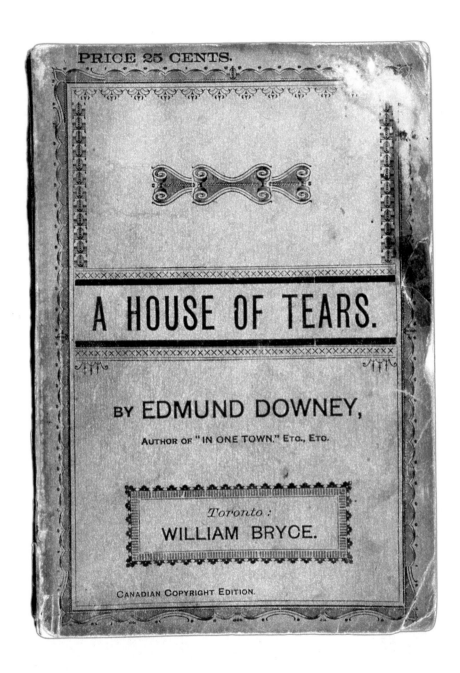

PRICE 25 CENTS.

A HOUSE OF TEARS.

BY EDMUND DOWNEY,

AUTHOR OF "IN ONE TOWN." ETC., ETC.

Toronto :
WILLIAM BRYCE.

CANADIAN COPYRIGHT EDITION.

29 Cover of Edmund Downey, *A house of tears* (Toronto, 1887). See **D159**.

THE

PARENT'S ASSISTANT,

OR

STORIES FOR CHILDREN.

IN ONE VOLUME.

BY

MARIA EDGEWORTH,

AUTHOR OF "PRACTICAL EDUCATION," "MORAL TALES," "EARLY LESSONS,"
&c. &c.

BOSTON:
MUNROE & FRANCIS, 128 WASHINGTON STREET.
CHARLES S. FRANCIS, NEW YORK.

30 Title page of Maria Edgeworth, *The parent's assistant,
or stories for children* (Boston, [1842 on cover]). See E19.

31 Cover of Maria Edgeworth, *Popular tales* (London, [1878?]). See **E24**.

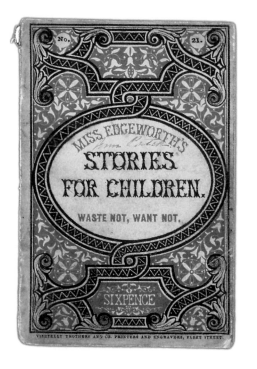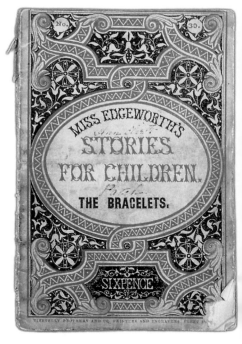

32 Covers of Maria Edgeworth, *Miss Edgeworth's stories for children* (London, 1846), showing two of its volumes. See **E59**.

London: William Heinemann, 1910. LOCATION L, NUC.

COMMENTARY A set of conversations between an Irish pub owner in Chicago and her Irish patrons. The conversations are commentaries on American political life and contemporary events [ML].

D248 *Mr. Dooley on the freedom of the seize* [anon.].

[New York?]: [n.p.], 1917. SOURCE Blessing, p. 141; OCLC. LOCATION NUC.

D249 *Mr. Dooley: on making a will and other necessary evils* [anon.].

+ New York: Charles Scribner's Sons, 1919. SOURCE Blessing, p. 141. LOCATION NUC, InND Loeber coll.

London: William Heinemann, 1920. LOCATION L, NUC.

D250 *Mr. Dooley at his best* (ed. by Elmer Ellis; dedicated to the Hennessys of the world 'who suffer and are silent').

+ New York: Charles Scribner's Sons, 1938 (ill., limited edn). LOCATION NUC, InND Loeber coll. (with page of original manuscript).

COMMENTARY Published posthumously [RL].

D251 *Mr. Dooley: now and forever, created by Finley Peter Dunne* (selected and introd. by Lewis Filler).

Stanford (CA): Academic Reprints, 1954. LOCATION NUC.

COMMENTARY Published posthumously [RL].

DUVAL, Kate Elizabeth. See **HUGHES, Mrs Kate Elizabeth.**

'DYCE, Gilbert', pseud. See **FITZGERALD, Percy Hetherington.**

E

'E., C.', fl. 1837. Pseudonym of a religious fiction writer. According to the preface to the following volume the author was a woman. SOURCE RL.

E1   *A few remarks on Ireland, with a true story of an aged man, and two little Irish mountaineers, who died happy in the faith of Jesus Christ* (by 'C.E.').
+ Plymouth: Jenkin Thomas, 1837. SOURCE COPAC. LOCATION C.
COMMENTARY 32pp. According to the title page this novelette was sold by Tims in Dublin. Religious fiction set in Ireland. The narrator deplores that relations between Protestants and Catholics have become worse over time. The story concerns a woman who keeps a school on her father's estate, which is regularly visited by priests to make sure that it is suitable for Catholic children to attend. One day some Jesuits visit. The only objections they have concern two books (one, a history of England because it is harsh on Mary Stuart; the other, a volume of Hannah More's tracts), but overall they approve of the school. After her father dies, the young woman travels around Ireland and eventually settles in one of the wildest, most mountainous parts where people speak only Irish and live in caves and hovels. She helps an old man die without the benefit of a priests and she starts a school for children. There is strife with priests but also with ministers. She teaches English and converts many of the children to the Protestant faith. Two of them die happy Protestants. Contains two poems 'On the death of my orphan Henry' and 'A few lines on little Mary' [ML].

'E., J.', fl. 1870. Pseudonym of a Canadian Protestant religious fiction writer.

E2   *The old and the new home. A Canadian tale* (by 'J.E.').
+ Edinburgh: W. Oliphant & Co., 1870 (ill. Paterson; Canadian Prize Sunday-School Books, Vol. 3). LOCATION L (destroyed), InND Loeber coll.
Toronto: Campbell, 1870. SOURCE Watters, p. 282; OCLC. LOCATION Univ. of Ottawa.
COMMENTARY Religious fiction extolling Protestant virtue and the power of the Bible. The O'Briens, an Irish Protestant family whose fortunes have declined, decide to emigrate to Canada. Their servants Biddy and Murty, who have converted to protestantism, do not want to be parted from them and secretly slip on board the ship. The captain, a rough man, is reformed by the O'Briens' youngest son, who dies on board in the full belief of his salvation. In Canada the family influence their neighbours by their Christian behaviour and by efforts to teach others from the Bible. Their eldest son, who had mysteriously disappeared before the emigration, returns to them with his name cleared. Biddy marries the ship's captain [ML].

'E., S.'. Editor. See **MOORE, Thomas**.

EARLY, May Agnes. See **FLEMING, Mrs May Agnes**.

'EBLANA', pseud. See **ROONEY, Miss Teresa J.**

EBRARD, Johannes Heinrich August, pseud. 'Gottfried Flammherz', b. 1818, d. Erlangen (Germany) 1888. A German theologian and writer on religion, JHAE was the son of Revd Franz Elias Ebrard and Wilhelmina Hohle. He was trained at Erlangen and Berlin and wrote many books on religious topics and on the early Irish and Scottish church (*Die* *iroschottische Missionskirche*, Gütersloh, 1873). SOURCE OCLC; *Neue Deutsche biographie* (Berlin, 1959), iv, pp 269–70; NUC.

E3   *Bilihild; eine Erzählung aus dem achten Jahrhundert* (by 'Gottfried Flammherz').
[location?]: Deutsche Jugend und Volksbibliothek, [before 1883]. LOCATION NUC.
+ London: Religious Tract Society, [1883] (trans. by J. Sutter as *Bilihild: a tale of the Irish missionaries in Germany, a.d. 703*; ill.). LOCATION L, MH.
COMMENTARY Historical religious fiction set in the eighth century [BLC].

ECCLES, C. See ECCLES, Charlotte O'Conor.

ECCLES, Charlotte O'Conor (also known as C. Eccles), pseud. 'Hal Godfrey', b. Ballinagard House (Co. Roscommon) 1863, d. London 1911. A novelist, pioneering journalist, translator and poet, CE was the oldest surviving daughter of Alexander O'Connor Eccles, JP, founder of the *Roscommon Messenger*. She was educated at Upton Hall, Birkenhead (Merseyside, England), and at convents in Paris and Germany. Her journalistic career began by writing for Irish periodicals. Later she and her sister settled with their mother in London in the 1880s and met considerable setbacks. Eventually she became a prominent journalist, working for the *New York Herald* and connected with a circle of leading women's papers. She published poetry and contributed under her name or her initials to the Dublin *Irish Monthly* from 1886 to 1905, and to the *Windsor Magazine* (London). Her didactic journalism was almost entirely directed toward social issues, such as the condition of the poor and the lack of education for women, and included a galvanizing article on the condition of hospitals in Vienna. With Sir Horace Plunkett, pioneer of the agricultural co-operative movement in Ireland, she lectured around Ireland for the Board of Agricultural and Technical Instruction. She was a fellow of the Institute of Journalists and she wrote an autobiographical article 'The experience of a woman journalist' (*Blackwood's Magazine*, Edinburgh, 1893). She published two comical books, one collection of short stories, and an instructional book on domestic economy cast in a fictionalized format. The RIA/DIB mentions that she wrote a work of fiction entitled '18, Blank Street' but this has not been located. After she was incapacitated by a stroke in 1908, she received assistance from the Royal Literary Fund. She remained unmarried and died at her home, 139A Alexander Road, St John's Wood, London. SOURCE Blain, pp 326–7; Colman, pp 75–6; EF, p. 112; H. Fraser et al., *Gender and the Victorian periodical* (Cambridge, 2003), p. 39; Irish pseudonyms; ODNB; O'Donoghue, p. 129; RIA/DIB; Roscommon, p. 38; Ryan, p. 116.

E4   *The rejuvenation of Miss Semaphore. A farcical novel* (by 'Hal Godfrey').
London: Jarrold & Sons, 1897. SOURCE Roscommon, p. 38. LOCATION L, InND Loeber coll. (1897, 4th edn).
Leipzig: Bernard Tauchnitz, 1899. SOURCE T & B, 3352. LOCATION NUC.
Boston: L.C. Page & Co., 1898. LOCATION NUC.
COMMENTARY The preface states that 'This story was partly suggested by "Dr Heidegger's Experiment" by Nathaniel Hawthorne'. Set in a London boarding-house where two spinster sisters read about an advertisement for the water of youth. They buy it and by chance one sister drinks the whole bottle and turns into a baby. The remainder of the book tells of the efforts of the other sister to conceal the event. In the end the effects wear off [ML].

E5   *Domestic economy reader for Irish schools: How Mary Fitzgerald learned house-keeping* (by C. Eccles).
Dublin, Belfast: Fallon & Co., 1903 (ill.). SOURCE RLIN. LOCATION D (1904 edn), DCL.
COMMENTARY Housekeeping instruction in the form of fiction, set in Ireland, and dealing with fire-lighting, tea-making, table-laying, preparation of meals etc. Each chapter has questions at the end for the students to answer [ML].

E6   *Aliens of the West* [anon.].
      + London, Paris, New York, Melbourne: Cassell & Co., 1904. SOURCE Brown, 537;
      Roscommon, p. 38. LOCATION RB, L.
COMMENTARY Six stories describing small town life set in Toomevara, an Irish country town
near the Shannon estuary. The characters are reputedly based on Roscommon originals.
Contents: 'Toomevara' (first published in the *American Ecclesiastical Review*, New York), 'A
voteen', 'Miss Kinahan's Kate', 'The wind bloweth where it listeth' (first published in the
American Ecclesiastical Review, New York), '"King William"' (first published in *Pall Mall
Magazine*, London), 'Tom Connolly's daughter' [ML; Brown; Roscommon, p. 38].
E7   *The matrimonial lottery* (by Charlotte O'Conor Eccles).
      London: Eveleigh Nash, 1906. SOURCE Roscommon, p. 38; COPAC. LOCATION L.
      + London: T. Fisher Unwin, 1906 (Colonial Edition). LOCATION InND Loeber coll.
      Leipzig: Bernard Tauchnitz, 1906. SOURCE T & B, 3934. LOCATION NUC.
COMMENTARY A light-hearted story set in London featuring Jack Darracott, the owner of an
ailing newspaper, the *Comet*. Jack's acquaintance, the impoverished Count MacCarthy de Burgo,
suggests a scheme to improve circulation: a matrimonial lottery in which women can subscribe
to a chance to marry the count, who will get the proceeds of the lottery. This scheme is a success from the point of view of increasing circulation, but it gives the count some anxious
moments when a very unattractive impostor tries to claim him. In the end he marries the real
prize-winner, a young American widow. With the prize money they repair to Ireland where
they pay off the mortgages on the count's estates [ML].

EDDY, Daniel C. See **EDDY, Daniel Clarke**.

EDDY, Daniel Clarke (known as **Daniel C. Eddy**), b. Salem (MA) 1823 (according to the
preface in *The Percy family*, the author was from Boston), d. Martha's Vineyard (MA) 1896.
An American travel, temperance and religious and ethical writer, he was the son of Daniel
and Martha Honeycomb Eddy. He graduated from New Hampshire Theological Institution
in 1845 and became a Baptist minister. To recover from illness, he travelled widely in Europe,
North Africa and Palestine. He was a supporter of the temperance movement and of the rights
of African-Americans, but intolerant of Catholics and Unitarians. He thought the novels of
Charles Dickens 'tended towards badness'. DCE became pastor of the Harvard Square Church
in Boston and speaker of the house in the Massachusetts legislature, elected on the Know
Nothing party ticket. SOURCE Allibone, i, p. 541; Allibone Suppl., i, p. 535; ANB; BLC; DAB;
RL.
E8   *The Percy family. A visit to Ireland* (by Daniel C. Eddy).
      + Boston: [Andrew F.] Graves & Young; New York: Sheldon & Co., 1859 (ill.
      Chadler-Duran, [Homer] Winslow). SOURCE OCLC. LOCATION D (1865 edn), L (1860
      edn), NUC, InND Loeber coll. (1861 edn).
COMMENTARY An additional title page reported in OCLC mentions *The Percy family:
sketches, travels, etc*. A story for juveniles [RL].
E9   *Our travelling party in Ireland* (by Daniel Clarke Eddy).
      + Boston: D. Lothrop & Co., [1882] (ill.). LOCATION NUC, InND Loeber coll.
      + Boston: Bradley & Woodruff, 1882. (ill.). LOCATION D.
COMMENTARY A story of travel in Ireland, interwoven with historical and topograph-
ical information, written for juveniles [ML].

'**EDGEWORTH, Mrs**', fl. 1806. Fictitious name for author(s) suggesting a spurious linkage
to Maria Edgeworth§ and her family. Novels listed below all appear in this category and were

troublesome to Maria Edgeworth and her relatives. In 1810 Bent's *Monthly Literary Advertiser* (location unknown) announced that 'What has appeared, or may hereafter be published, bearing her [ME's] name, which is not printed for her Bookseller, J. Johnson, in Paul's Churchyard, is spurious'. Two years later Maria Edgeworth's brother Lovell, while travelling in France, noted a spurious novel, 'Fanny' (i.e., *Fatherless Fanny*, probably the Paris, 1812 edn). In that year Maria Edgeworth published the following note in the fourth volume of her *Tales of fashionable life* (London, 1812 edn): 'It is painful to be obliged to address the public in a manner that has at first sight the appearance of a mean art to attract notice. But as certain books have been published under the name of Miss Edgeworth, Mrs Edgeworth, and Maria Edgeworth, some of which have not that moral tendency that alone can justify a female for appearing as an author; her father thinks it due for his daughter ... to request that the public will not consider any work under the name of Edgeworth that is not published by Messrs. Johnson & Co., Paul's Churchyard, London, as the production of any of his family'. (See also the 'correct' list of Mr and Miss Edgeworth's works in the rear of *Readings on poetry*, London, 1816.) In 1814, Maria Edgeworth mentioned in a letter that 'two books surreptitiously printed in our name, and are no better than they should be' (Mrs [Frances] Edgeworth, i, p. 296). This may refer to at least one book other than *The ballad singer: or, memoirs of the Bristol family*, which appeared later in that year under ME's name. SOURCE Personal communication, Lady Christina Colvin, Sept 1993; Mrs [Frances] Edgeworth, *A memoir of Maria Edgeworth* (London, 1867), i, p. 296; Moon, p. 205; Slade, pp. 224–6.

— SPURIOUS WORKS

E10   *Adelaide; or, the chateau de St. Pierre. A tale of the sixteenth century* (by 'Mrs Edgeworth').
+ London: J.F. Hughes, 1806, 4 vols. SOURCE Block, p. 65; British Fiction; Garside, 1806:28. LOCATION L.
COMMENTARY Spurious and not known to have been written by a member of the Edgeworth family. Gothic fiction set in France [RL].

E11   *The match girl. A novel* (by 'Mrs Edgeworth').
London: J.F. Hughes, 1808, 3 vols. SOURCE British Fiction; Garside, 1808:43. LOCATION L.
COMMENTARY Spurious and not known to have been written by a member of the Edgeworth family [RL].

E12   *The wife; or, a model for women. A tale* (by 'Mrs Edgeworth').
+ London: J.F. Hughes, 1810, 3 vols. SOURCE Block, p. 65; Blakey, p. 307; British Fiction; Garside, 1810:41. LOCATION Corvey CME 3-628-47556-2.
Paris: Galignani, 1813, 2 vols. (trans. by Mme Élizabeth de Bon as *Le modèle des femmes;* by 'Miss Edgeworth'). SOURCE Bn-Opale plus. LOCATION BNF.
COMMENTARY Spurious and not known to have been written by a member of the Edgeworth family. High society novel, which starts at a country house in Gloucestershire, the seat of Sir Henry Melmoth [RL].

E13   *Fatherless Fanny; or, the memoirs of a little mendicant, and her benefactors. A modern novel* (by 'Mrs Edgeworth', 'the authoress of 'The wife; or, a model of women').
London: James Taylor & Co.; Sherwood, Neeley & Jones, 1811, 4 vols. SOURCE British Fiction; Garside, 1811:31. LOCATION Corvey CME 3-628-47529-5, O.
London: J. Tallis, 1819 (by the author of *The old English Baron* [*sic*, Clara Reeve] as *Fatherless Fanny; or, a young lady's first entrance into life, being the memoirs of a little mendicant and her benefactors*). SOURCE Summers, p. 188; *Jrnl of English Literary History*, ix (1942), pp 224, 227. LOCATION L.

London: Fisher, Son & Co., 1833 (as *Fatherless Fanny; or, a lady's first entrance into life* by the late Miss Taylor [*sic*], edited and enlarged by Mrs Sarah Green§ [*sic*]). SOURCE British Fiction; Garside, 1811:31.

COMMENTARY *London 1833 edn* The ending of this version differs from earlier versions. No copy located [Garside; RL].

Sheffield: C. & W. Thompson; London: Lewis & Co., [1816]. LOCATION L.

Manchester: J. Gleave & Sons, 1819 (as *Fatherless Fanny; or, a young lady's first entrance into life: being the memoirs of a little mendicant and her benefactors*). SOURCE Falkner Greirson cat. 'Jane'/270. LOCATION L, NUC (1822 edn).

Derby: Thomas Richardson & Sons, 1841 (by the late Miss Taylor [*sic*], as *Fatherless Fanny; or, a young lady's first entrance into life*). SOURCE L. James, *English popular literature 1819–1851* (New York, 1976), p. 293. LOCATION L.

Paris: Galignani, 1812, 4 vols. (trans. by Josef Joly as *Fanni, ou mémoires d'une jeune orpheline et de ses bienfaiteurs*). SOURCE Devonshire, p. 271. LOCATION L, NUC.

[New York]: Thomas Kinnersley, 1836. LOCATION NUC.

COMMENTARY Spurious and not known to have been written by a member of the Edgeworth family. According to the BLC, this book is sometimes attributed to Thomas Peckett Prest, but it is also variously ascribed to Clara Reeve§, Sarah Green§ and Jane Taylor. It is improbable that the volume is by Reeve because she died in 1807 (however, there is a slight possibility that it was based on Reeve's *Castle Connor* in that its manuscript, which had been lost in transit, could have surfaced later). A London edn came out in 1833 by 'the late Miss Taylor, edited and enlarged by Mrs Sarah Green§', but is likely to have been derivative. James Malcolm Rymer, probably mischievously, claimed it as his own in about 1840. The story's heroine is Fanny, abandoned at the age 5, in rich clothing with money for her upkeep, outside the ladies' seminary of the termagant Mrs Bridewell. When payment for her education is not forthcoming, Mrs Bridewell advertises for her parents, threatening to farm her out to charity. A young man of fashion, Lord Ellencourt, in pursuit of his missing lapdog, Fanny, is hoaxed by his friends into answering the advertisement. There is a comic episode when he tells the headmistress that Fanny's father was hanged for sheep stealing and that he himself had 'kept' her mother. The misunderstanding resolved, and touched by the plight of the little fatherless girl, he becomes her first benefactor. He adopts Fanny, and falls in love with her. In society life she is looked down on as an illegitimate child of unknown origin. While keeping suitors at bay with her moral purity, Fanny falls into the hands of Lord Ballafyn, who imprisons her in his castle in Ireland. She learns that her mother died there. After experiencing rejection, adoption, abduction, and many other adventures, she marries a duke. Her early benefactor proves to be her uncle. The 'fascinating Duchess' is admired and fêted, and in a final scene at court as she leaves the queen's presence, her attention is sought by many strangers. The 1819 edn ends in a more domestic mode with Fanny as an older heroine with several children. This popular story was still being published in 1870 [H.J. Butler & H.E. Butler (eds), *The black book of Edgeworthstown and other Edgeworth memories* (London, 1927); J & S, pp 292–3; Jarndyce cat. 100/475, 477, title pages of Rymer's 'The Hebrew maiden' (1841), and 'Kathleen' [1840]; *Jrnl of English Literary History*, ix (1942), p. 224–26; Quaritch cat. 1193/121; Summers, pp 188–9].

E14   *The ballad singer; or, memoirs of the Bristol family. A most interesting novel* (by 'Mrs Edgeworth', author of *The chateau de St. Pierre*, and *Fatherless Fanny*).

+ London: A.K. Newman, 1814, 4 vols. SOURCE Block, p. 65; NSTC. LOCATION L.

London: Sherwood, Neely & Jones, 1814, 4 vols. SOURCE British Fiction; Garside, 1814:19. LOCATION Corvey CME 3–628–47528–7.

COMMENTARY Spurious and not known to have been written by a member of the Edgeworth family [RL].

E15   *Tales of real life, or, scenes in Ireland. Suited to the present condition of the Irish peasantry. With characteristic remarks of their national habits and manners* (by 'Mrs Edgeworth').
+ London: J. Bailey, 1817. SOURCE British Fiction; RLIN. LOCATION NjP, ICU.
COMMENTARY Spurious and not known to have been written by a member of the Edgeworth family. However, this title is among the earliest books written for and about Irish cottagers, following the example of Mary Leadbeater's§ *Cottage dialogues among the Irish peasantry*, with notes and preface by Maria Edgeworth§ (London, 1811), which was followed by another volume, published in 1813. *Tales of real life* has a subtitle (on the first text page): 'Tales for cottagers', and consists of stories, all of which are set in Ireland. Contents: 'Perseverance', 'Calculation', 'Economy', 'Early training', 'Temper', 'The Scotch plowman', 'High spirit', 'Honesty is the best policy' (in the form of a play). This volume differs in content from the anonymous *Tales of real life; forming a sequel to Miss Edgeworth's Tales of fashionable life* (London, 1810, 3 vols.) [RL].

EDGEWORTH, Charles Sneyd (also known as Sneyd Edgeworth), b. Edgeworthstown House? (Co. Longford) 1786, d. 1864. Barrister, poet, memoirist and reputed fiction writer, CSE was the fourth son of Richard Lovell Edgeworth§ and his third wife, Elizabeth Sneyd, and stepbrother of Maria Edgeworth§. He was partly reared by Maria but spent some time in England. He was admitted as a student at the King's Inns, Dublin, in 1802, and starting in 1804 he attended TCD. He became a barrister in 1810. He had some literary aspirations, intending to publish Maria's translation of Mme de Genlis's§ *Adèle and Théodore* in 1818. His father encouraged him to write poetry, which led to a long poem, *The transmigrations of Indur*, situated in India, which was based on a story by Mrs Barbauld and was published in *The New Year's Gift* (London, 1830). O'Brien in 1884 stated that CSE was 'the author of several popular works of fiction', but such works have not been identified. He published the *Memoirs of the Abbé Edgeworth* (London, 1815), with which he received help from his stepsister Maria. He furnished her some stories she incorporated in her *Patronage* (London, 1814). He helped her financially by purchasing part of the Edgeworthstown estate in 1826, while living in Kent, leaving Maria and other relatives to supervise the estate. He married Henrica Broadhurst in 1813. SOURCE Allibone i, p. 542; Butler, pp 148, 159, 214, 234, 246, 248, 285, 292n.4, 426; B & S, p. 258; Colvin, p. xxxiv; Keane, p. 150; O'Brien, n.p. [entry on Sneyd Edgeworth (*sic*)]; RIA/DIB.

EDGEWORTH, Mrs Frances (Fanny) Anne (née Beaufort), b. Navan (Co. Meath) 1769, d. Edgeworthstown? (Co. Longford) 1865. Artist, memoirist and possible novelist, FAE was a daughter of Dr Daniel Augustus Beaufort (clergyman and cartographer, who collaborated with Richard Lovell Edgeworth§), and Mary Waller. Her brother became Admiral Sir Francis Beaufort and her sisters Henrietta§ and Louisa§ were both writers. She attended Mrs Terson's School at Portarlington (Co. Laois), where she learned French and drawing. She studied art under Bowring of Gloucester, Francis Robert West of Dublin and Mons. Raymond Deshouilleres of London. She accompanied her father in 1788 on one of his many tours through Ireland to record sites and antiquities and later lived with her family in London (1789–90). According to her father's biographer, she was 'an exceptionally talented artist in oils and crayons' (Ellison, 1987, p. 5). She was also a water-colourist and was noted for her flower paintings. She illustrated her father's *A new map of Ireland* (1792), and later, her husband's engineering drawings. In 1796–77, she made drawings for Maria Edgeworth's§ *The parent's assistant*, which were included in its 3rd edn (London, 1800). Some of these drawings survive in an album from Edgeworthstown House (private collection). One year younger than

Maria, she became in 1798 the fourth wife of Maria's father, Richard Lovell Edgeworth. The Irish solicitor-general, Charles Kendal Bushe, characterized her as 'a perfect Scholar, and at the same time a good Mother and housewife ...' (Butler, p. 212). Her writing career was largely unknown to biographers of her stepchild, but is alluded to by James Hall, a visitor to Edgeworthstown in 1813, who mentioned that Mrs Edgeworth also was a 'successful' author and had published a novel, 'or what you choose to call it "The good wife"' (Hall, ii, p. 18). The same attribution is recorded by O'Brien in 1884, however no contemporary family account or papers mention it. It is possible that it is a mistake, based on a spurious volume, *The wife, or a model for women* that appeared under the name of 'Mrs Edgeworth' in London in 1810. More certain is that FAE wrote *A memoir of Maria Edgeworth, with a selection of her letters* which was edited by her children and privately published (London, 1867, 3 vols.). A volume of her botanical water-colours of plants around the house and on her travels through the country (1798–1807) is in the Henry E. Huntington Library, San Marino (CA, MS FB 59), while some of her letters are among the Edgeworth MSS in the NLI. SOURCE Allibone Suppl., i, p. 538; Butler, pp 130, 501; H.J. Butler & H.E. Butler (eds), *The black book of Edgeworthstown and other Edgeworth memories* (London, 1927); Butler, p. 212; D. Clarke, *The ingenious Mr. Edgeworth* (London, 1965), pp 152, 180; Colvin, p. xxxiii. Crookshank, pp 114, 302; Mrs [Frances] Edgeworth, *A memoir of Maria Edgeworth* (London, 1867), i, p. 105; C.C. Ellison, 'Remembering Dr. Beaufort' in *Quarterly Bulletin of the Irish Georgian Society*, 18 (1975, Jan.–Mar.), pp 2, 31; C.C. Ellison, *The hopeful traveller* (Kilkenny, 1987), pp 5, 48, 52, 54, 78–9; J. Hall, *Tour through Ireland* (London, 1813), ii, p. 18; S.C. Hall, pp 109–22; A.J.C. Hare (ed.), *The life and letters of Maria Edgeworth* (London, 1894), ii, p. 271; O'Brien, n.p., [entry under Sheyd [*sic*] Edgeworth]; RIA/DIB; Slade, pp 17–18, 29.

EDGEWORTH, Henrietta (Harriet), b. Edgeworthstown House? (Co. Longford) 1801, d. Kingstown? (Dún Laoghaire, Co. Dublin) 1889. Attributed fiction writer, HE was the daughter of Richard Lovell Edgeworth and his fourth wife, Frances Edgeworth§, and the half-sister of Maria Edgeworth§. In 1820 and again in 1821–2 she accompanied Maria to England, and in 1823 to Scotland. In 1825 she kept a diary of a tour with Sir Walter Scott in Ireland (NLS, MS 911, f. 50). According to Colvin, she was 'the most vigorous and practical of the Edgeworth sisters' (p. xxxv). In adulthood, she learned Greek, Spanish and several other languages, and was a handy carpenter. She married in 1826 Revd Richard Butler of Trim (Co. Meath), who later received the additional appointment of dean of Clonmacnoise. They paid yearly extended after-Christmas visits to Edgeworthstown House over a period of thirty-five years, went on a journey to England in 1829, and to Scotland in 1843. A drawing of her reading Samuel Lover's§ *Rory O'More* (London, 1837, 3 vols.) at Edgeworthstown House was published by Butler (opp. p. 429). She assisted her husband in his historical research and helped him to transcribe the 'Charter Book of Dublin'. She continued to advise Maria on her later writings, including her novel *Helen, a tale* (London, 1834, 3 vols.). She and her sister Honora also assisted Maria with the preparation of the collected edn of Maria's work, published in London in 1825. After her husband's death, she moved to Edgeworthstown House and privately published *A memoir of the very Rev. Richard Butler* (n.l., 1863), which chronicles their joint life at Trim, casting more light on her husband than on herself. She presented her husband's collection of Irish ancient coins and seals to the RIA. Many of her letters are at the NLI and the Bodleian Library, Oxford. Her portrait profile was published by Colvin. SOURCE Butler, pp 407, 424, 504, 499, 504, and passim; [H. Butler], *A memoir of the very Rev. Richard Butler* (n.l., 1863), pp 149; H.J. Butler & H.E. Butler (eds), *The black book of Edgeworthstown and other Edgeworth memories* (London, 1927), pp 244–6; E.A. Conwell, *A ramble round Trim* (Dublin, 1878), pp 55, 57; Colvin, opp. p. 214, and passim; RL.

E16   *The most unfortunate day of my life* (by Maria Edgeworth§ [*sic*]).
London: Cobden-Sanderson, 1931 (ill. Nora McGuinness). SOURCE COPAC. LOCATION
Dt, O.
COMMENTARY The 'The most unfortunate day of my life' is the late publication of a nine-
teenth-century manuscript in the collection of the late Hubert Butler (descendant of HE),
sometimes attributed to Maria Edgeworth§. However, the manuscript was formerly owned by
HE, and its authorship has been ascribed to her by Harold E. Butler (as cited by Slade).
Contents: 'The most unfortunate day of my life', and stories by Maria Edgeworth§: 'The purple jar', 'The two plums', 'The thorn', 'The rabbit', 'Waste not, want not', published in *Early
lessons* (London, 1801, 10 vols.), and *The Parent's assistant* (London, 1796, 3 parts) [Slade, p.
xxvii; Butler, p. 502].

EDGEWORTH, Honora (née Sneyd), b. England, d. Bighterton, near Shifnal (Shrops.) 1780.
Co-author. and attributed short story writer, HE was the daughter of Edward Sneyd, of Bishton
(Staffs.).[1] Honora's mother died when she was young and she was reared by a relative, Mrs
Thomas Seward. In 1773 Honora became the second wife of Richard Lovell Edgeworth§ in
Litchfield (also Lichfield), England. The couple moved soon afterwards to Edgeworthstown
(Co. Longford), but in 1776 they were back in England, living at Northchurch (Herts.). HE
and her husband wrote together a book for children, *Practical education: or, the history of Harry
and Lucy. Vol.2* (see under Richard Lovell Edgeworth§), begun in 1778 for their youngest
child Honora, which was privately published in Litchfield in 1780. She compiled a register of
children's reactions to new knowledge and experience in an effort to extend experimental science to the field of child education (2 vols., MSS, dated 1778–9; private collection; Butler, pp
65, 501), one of the premises leading her husband to write *Essays on professional education*
(London, 1809). The Bodleian Library has a small manuscript short story said to have been
composed by HSE in 1787 (Bodleian Library, Oxford, MS Eng poet.e.187–9). HE assisted
her husband in his mechanical experiments and became an 'excellent theoretick mechanic' herself (Uglow, p. 224). She succumbed to tuberculosis and was buried at King's Weston, near
Bristol (Avon). Her portrait, engraved after a painting by Romney, was published by Clarke
(see Elmes for other portraits), while the Wedgwood factory made a jasper medallion of her
after John Flaxman. SOURCE Butler, pp 64–5; H.J. Butler & H.E. Butler (eds.), *The black book
of Edgeworthstown and other Edgeworth memories* (London, 1927), pp 149, 151–4; D. Clarke,
The ingenious Mr Edgeworth (London, 1965), opp. p. 15; *Memoirs of Richard Lovell Edgeworth,
Esq. begun by himself and concluded by his daughter, Maria Edgeworth* (Boston, 1821) i, pp 106–7;
ii, pp 187–8; Elmes, p. 66; B. & H. Wedgwood, *The Wedgwood circle 1730–1897* (Don Mills,
ON, 1980), pp 55–6, 69–71, 75; J. Uglow, *The lunar men* (London, 2002), pl. 9, p. 317.

EDGEWORTH, Louisa. See **MAC NALLY, Mrs Louisa.**

EDGEWORTH, Maria, pseud. 'E.M.', b. Black Bourton (Oxon.) 1767, d. Edgeworthstown
(Co. Longford), 1849. Novelist, children's writer and educationalist, ME was the daughter of
Richard Lovell Edgeworth§, an inventor, author and landowner, and Anna Maria Elers. Initially
reared in England, she was educated in Derby and in London and was nearly blinded in 1781
by a friend of her father's trying to cure an eye disease. Her family returned to Edgeworthstown
the following year and eventually she became her father's chief assistant in dealing with their
tenants and running the estate, which gave her the background for some of her later novels.

---

1 She may have been related to Edward Sneyd, MP for Carrick 1777–81, who had married Hannah Honora, daughter
of James King of Gola (Co. Louth) (HIP, vi, pp 301–2).

She translated Mme de Genlis's§ *Adèle et Théodore* in 1783, but because of the appearance of a rival translation, only one volume was printed and it was recalled before publication (no known surviving copy). One of her duties in the Edgeworth household was to prepare moral tales for her many brothers and sisters in accordance with her father's theories of education. Her father is said to have had a great influence on her writing and wrote some of the story of 'Ormond', published in ME's *Harrington, a tale; and Ormond, a tale* (London, 1817), while ME contributed to *An essay on Irish bulls* (London, 1802), published under Richard Lovell Edgeworth's name. The novel for which she is most famous, *Castle Rackrent* (written between 1793 and 1796), was published in London in 1800. She travelled several times to England and Brussels, and to Paris in 1802 when a match between herself and the Swedish Count Abraham Clewberg-Edelcrantz foundered as she could not contemplate leaving Ireland, nor he Sweden. She never married. She was famous in her day: Byron, who met her in London in 1803, considered her simple and charming, and in Scotland Sir Walter Scott welcomed her warmly when she visited in 1823. Scott considered her descriptions of Irish characters inspiration for his Waverly novels. Jane Austen sent her a copy of *Emma* (London, 1816) when it was first published. As a writer, she was well-paid and commercially successful. She wrote little after her father's death in 1817 and was again troubled by eye problems, which prevented her from reading and writing for almost two years. Disillusioned with post-Union Ireland, she felt that it was impossible to write fiction about the Irish situation. However, she was able to finish her father's memoirs and to supervise an edn of her *Collected works* (London, 1832–33), which ran to 18 volumes. During the Famine she worked tirelessly to help the tenants and peasants of the area. Admirers in Boston sent 150 barrels of flour addressed to 'Miss Edgeworth for her poor', and to the porters who refused payment for carrying them ashore, she sent each a muffler she knitted herself. She died shortly after. She had relatively few contacts with other Irish novelists of the period, with the exception of Mary Leadbeater§ and Mary Letitia Martin§, but she admired the works of George Brittaine§, who lived close by in Co. Longford. The play *The row of Ballynavogue! or, the lily of Lismore*, partly based on ME's work (but is it not clear which of her works), was produced in London in 1819. She contributed to the *Scottish Annual* (Edinburgh, 1836). Collections of ME's works and letters can be found at the Bodleian Library, Oxford, the NLI, Dublin, and the Henry E. Huntington Library, San Marino (CA). For her portraits, see ODNB. A three-volume work edited by Frances Edgeworth, *A memoir of Maria Edgeworth, with a selection from her letters by the late Mrs. Edgeworth*, was printed but not published in 1867. For an overview of manuscripts by ME, see Butler (pp. 501–4) and ODNB. Spurious works associated with ME are listed at the end of this entry. SOURCE Allibone, i, p. 542; Blain, pp 328–9; JB; Bolton, pp 196–7; Boylan, p. 105; Brady, p. 68; Butler, pp 75, 280, 353, and passim; H.J. Butler & H.E. Butler (eds), *The black book of Edgeworthstown and other Edgeworth memories* (London, 1927); D. Clarke, *The ingenious Mr. Edgeworth* (London, 1965); Colvin, frontispiece, pp 542–3, 558, 594*n*.1; Elmes, p. 66; Field Day, i, pp 964, 1011, 1051–2, iv, 761, 1091, 1041, 1053, v, 622, 768, 847, 977*n*, 1072, 1118; T. Flanagan, *The Irish novelists 1800–1850* (New York, 1958), pp 53–106; S.C. Hall, pp 109–22; Hogan, pp 221–3; Hogan 2, pp 397–400; A.J.C. Hare (ed.), *The life and letters of Maria Edgeworth* (London, 1894), i, p. 272; Jarndyce cat. 162/603; W.J. McCormack, *Ascendancy and tradition in Anglo-Irish literature from 1789 to 1939* (Oxford, 1985); McKenna, pp 165–71; NCBEL 4, pp 901–07; OCIL, pp 167–8; ODNB; O'Donoghue, pp 129–30; RIA/DIB; Schulz, p. 269; Scott (correspondence with Sir Walter Scott); B.C. Slade, *Maria Edgeworth 1767–1849 a bibliographical tribute* (London, 1937); B. & H. Wedgwood, *The Wedgwood circle 1730–1897* (Don Mills, ON, 1980); H. Zimmern, *Maria Edgeworth* (London, 1, 883).

E17   *Letters of Julia and Caroline* [anon.].

+ London: J. Johnson, 1795. SOURCE ESTC t112216. LOCATION L, InND Loeber coll.

COMMENTARY Part of *Letters of literary ladies. To which is added, an essay on the noble science of self-justification* (London, 1795), see below, but *Letters of Julia and Caroline* has separate title page, pagination, and register. Epistolary novel that exemplifies the effects of a lifestyle based on feelings and emotions compared to one based on rational thought. Julia's lifestyle leads to great unhappiness and disastrous results, while Caroline's admonishes her to use more reason than feeling [ML; ESTC].

E18 *Letters for literary ladies. To which is added, an essay on the noble science of self justification* [anon.].

+ London: J. Johnson, 1795. SOURCE Slade, 1A; Rafroidi, 2, p. 149; Sadleir, 774; ESTC t064310. LOCATION Grail, L, O, DCL, NUC.

London: J. Johnson, 1799, 2nd edn (corrected and much enlarged). SOURCE Slade, 1B; Sadleir, 774a. LOCATION L, NUC.

+ George Town [Georgetown, Washington (DC)]: Joseph Milligan, 1810 (by Miss Edgeworth). LOCATION NUC, InND Loeber coll.

London: J.M. Dent, 1993 (ed. by C. Connolly). SOURCE COPAC. LOCATION Univ. of Liverpool.

COMMENTARY Contents: 'Letter from a gentleman to his friend upon the birth of a daughter', 'Answer to the preceding letter'; 'Letters of Julia and Caroline' (probably published earlier in the same year, see above). In the first letter, a gentleman advises his friend against turning his daughter into a literary lady [RL; Black, p. 73; Field Day, v, pp 641–4; ODNB].

E19 *The parent's assistant; or, stories for children* (by Maria Edgeworth).

Editorial note Because of the large number of versions of this collection of short stories, reprints and publications in parts, the following is organized by city of first publication. Unless stated otherwise, the title of the publication is as above. Commentary showing the contents of the first edition follows the first issue so that it is clearer to readers what the significance is of titles comprising one or more of the stories. The same layout is repeated below for ME's other books of stories for juveniles, such as *Early lessons* (London, 1801, 10 vols.) [RL].

— LONDON

+ London: J. Johnson, 1796, 3 parts (by 'E.M.' [*sic*]). SOURCE Rafroidi, ii, p. 149; Forster 2, 1211; Dm exhib. cat., 1981, p. 23; ESTC n023412; COPAC. LOCATION Grail, PC (vol. 1, part II), L, Univ. of Aberdeen.

London: J. Johnson, 1796, 2nd edn, 2 vols. SOURCE Osborne, p. 249; Slade, 2B; ESTC t133446. LOCATION CaOTP (Part I; Part II, 2nd edn).

London: J. Johnson, 1800, 3rd edn, 6 vols. (with additions; ill. C.P. [Charlotte Pakenham], F.A.B. [Frances Anne Beaufort], F.E. [ditto, Frances Edgeworth, after her marriage to Richard Lovell Edgeworth], C.E. [Charlotte Edgeworth], James Neagle, Angus). SOURCE Slade, 2C; Sadleir, 779; Osborne, p. 880 (1801 edn); ESTC t137066. LOCATION D, L, CaOTP, NUC, InND Loeber coll. (1804, 4th edn).

London: R. Hunter; Baldwin, Cradock & Joy; Simpkin & Marshall, 1822, 6 vols. (new edn). SOURCE Ximenes List 97–4/54; COPAC. LOCATION Univ. of Liverpool.

London: Whittaker, Treacher & Co., 1829 (trans. as *Laurent le paresseux, Tarlton, et le fause clef: trois contes*). SOURCE Slade, 2D. LOCATION L.

+ London, New York: George Routledge & Co., 1856 (as *The bracelets. A tale*). LOCATION D (1860 edn), L, NUC, InND Loeber coll. (also Willis & Hazard, 1853 edn).

+ London: Ward & Lock, [1861] (as *The orange man; or, the honest boy and the thief*; Frank Goodchild's Little Library; ill.). LOCATION L.

+ London: Longman & Co, Hamilton & Co., Simpkin, Marshall & Co., H. Washbourne, Houlston & Stoneman, E. Lumley; Darton & Co., Orr & Co., Routledge

& Co., Tegg & Co., Smith, Elder & Co., Whittaker & Co., 1848, 3 vols. (new edn; ill.). LOCATION InND Loeber coll.

+ London: Ward & Lock, [1861] (as *Little dog Trusty; or, the liar and the boy of truth*; Frank Goodchild's Little Library; ill.). LOCATION L.

London, New York: Routledge, Warne & Routledge, 1863 (as *The birth-day present, and The basket woman*). LOCATION L ([1871] edn). LOCATION NUC.

London, New York: George Routledge & Sons, 1866 (as *The orphans and Old Poz, stories for children*). LOCATION NUC.

+ London: G. Bell & Sons, 1875 (as *Select tales*). LOCATION L. COMMENTARY *London 1875 edn* Contents: 'Lazy Lawrence', 'Tarlton', 'Simple Susan', 'The white pigeon', 'Forgive and forget'. Stories are from different edns of *The parent's assistant* [ML].

+ London, New York, Glasgow, Manchester: George Routledge & Sons, [1890] (as *The birthday present, and other tales*). LOCATION L.
COMMENTARY Contents (except play): 'The birthday present', 'Forgive and forget' [RL].

— DUBLIN

+ Dublin: Printed by J. Chambers, 1798, 2 vols. SOURCE Dm exhib. cat., 1981, p. 23; Pollard 2, p. 100; ESTC n0234213. LOCATION PC.

+ Dublin: John Cumming, 1829, 3 vols. (new edn; ill. Kirkwood). LOCATION D.

— CORK

+ Cork: George Cherry, 1800 (as *The parent's assistant; or, stories for children. Containing Lazy Lawrence, Tarlton, and The false key*). SOURCE NCBEL; Slade, 2D; OCLC. LOCATION Grail, Boston College.

— DROGHEDA

+ Drogheda: Charles Evans, 1802 (as *Select stories from The parent's assistant*). SOURCE Slade, 2d; Bradshaw, ii, p. 860; G. Long (ed.), *Beyond the Pale* (Dublin, 1996), p. 50. LOCATION D, Dt. COMMENTARY *Drogheda edn* The advertised states that Mr Johnson, publisher of the English edn, 'permitted a Thousand Copies of this cheap Selection to be printed, for the Use of the Country Schools in Ireland'. Contents: 'The little dog Trusty: or the liar and the boy of truth', 'The orange man: or, the honest boy and the thief', 'Lazy Lawrence', 'The false key', 'The basket woman', 'The white pigeon', 'The orphans', 'Forgive and forget', 'Simple Susan' [RL].

— BELFAST

+ Belfast: Simms & M'Intyre, n.d. (as *The history of Susan Price, commonly called Simple Susan*). SOURCE Adams, p. 201. LOCATION PC. COMMENTARY *Belfast n.d. edn* 133p. Contents: 'The history of Susan Price', 'Travellers' wonders, from 'Evenings at home' [Welch].

Belfast: Simms & M'Intyre, n.d. (as *The little merchants*). SOURCE Adams, p. 201. COMMENTARY No copy of this edn located [RL].

— EDINBURGH

+ Edinburgh: Neill & Co., 1817 (trans. as *Contes choisis pour des enfants*). LOCATION L. COMMENTARY *Edinburgh edn* According to the title page, this edn was based on the Paris edn. Contents: 'Blaise le paresseux', 'Les bracelets', 'La femme aux paniers', 'Les orphelins' [RL].

+ Edinburgh: Alexander Hislop & Co., [1869] (as *The bracelets; or, habits of gentleness*; ill.). LOCATION L.

— PARIS

Paris: Théophile Grandin, 1820 (trans. and adapted by Mme Élizabeth De Bon as *L'Aimable enfant, ou, conversations d'Edouard; imité de l'Education practique*). SOURCE Slade, 2D; Bn-Opale plus. LOCATION BNF.

Paris: Baudry, 1827, 6 vols. LOCATION NUC.

+ Paris: Baudry, Galignani, 1827 (as *The basket-woman, the white pigeon, the orphans, waste not, want not, forgive and forget; stories for children*; on spine: *Miss Edgeworth's Parent's assistant*). LOCATION InND Loeber coll.

Paris: H. Fournier Jeune, 1832–33, 4 vols. (trans. by Mlle. A Sobry as *Le livre des familles*). LOCATION L. COMMENTARY *Paris 1827 end* Contents: 'The basket-woman', 'The white pigeon', 'The orphans', 'Waste not, want not', 'Forgive and forget' [ML].

Paris: Lavigne, 1837 (trans. by Ernest Garnier as *Contes des familles de Miss Edgeworth*; ill. M. de Sainson; Bibliothèque Familles). SOURCE Slade, 2D. LOCATION BNF.

Paris: Baudry, 1846 (new edn; as *The birthday present, and Simple Susan; stories for children*; Baudry's European Library). LOCATION L.

Paris: L. Hachette, 1859 (trans. by Armand le François as *Contes de l'enfance choisis de Miss Edgeworth*; ill. V. Foulquier). LOCATION NUC, InND Loeber coll. (1863 edn).

— GENEVA

Geneva: Manet & Paschoud, [1826?], 2 vols. (trans. by C. Pictet as *L'ami des parens*). SOURCE Slade, 2D; Sadleir, 779b. LOCATION L.

— GEORGETOWN

George Town [Georgetown, Washington (DC)]: Joseph Milligan, 1809, 3 vols. SOURCE Welch, 328.1; Slade, 2D. LOCATION NUC.

— BALTIMORE

Baltimore: F. Lucas Jnr, J. Vance & Co. & Anthony Miltenberger, 1811 (as *The little merchants*). SOURCE Slade 2D; Welch, 321.2. LOCATION DCL, NUC.

— BOSTON

+ Boston: W. Wells & T.B. Wait & Co.; New York: Eastburn, Kirk & Co.; Philadelphia: M. Carey, Moses Thomas & Edward Parker, [1814], 3 vols. (ill.). SOURCE Welch, 328.2, InND Loeber coll. (also 1842 edn; see Plate 30).

Boston: Munroe & Francis, [1820?] (as *Tarlton*). LOCATION NUC.

Boston, New York: Houghton, Mifflin & Co., [1889] (as *Waste not, want not, and The barring out; two tales*). LOCATION NUC.

— PHILADELPHIA

Philadelphia: J. Johnson, 1803 (as *Idleness and industry exemplified, in the history of James Preston and Lazy Lawrence* [anon.]; ill.). SOURCE Slade, 2D (1804 edn); Welch, 318.1; Rosenbach, 293 (1804 edn). LOCATION NUC.

Philadelphia: Jacob Johnson, 1804 (as *The bracelets*; ill. W.R.). SOURCE Slade, 2D; Welch, 310.1. LOCATION NUC.

Philadelphia: Jacob Johnson, 1805 (as *Three stories for young children* [anon.]. SOURCE Welch, 333; OCLC. LOCATION CtY.

Philadelphia: Johnson & Warner, 1809 (as *The barring out; or, party spirit*; ill.). SOURCE Slade, 2D; Rosenbach, 390; Welch, 307.1. LOCATION NUC (1809, 2nd edn).

+ Philadelphia: Geo. S. Appleton; New York: D. Appleton & Co., 1847 (as *Waste not, want not; or, two strings to your bow*; ill. W. Roberts, Herrick). LOCATION NUC, InND Loeber coll. (also 1850 edn). COMMENTARY *Philadelphia 1847 edn* Two binding types: (a) brown cloth impressed with gold lettering; (b) whitish cloth with multi-coloured printing [RL].

+ Philadelphia: Geo.S. Appleton; New York: D. Appleton & Co., 1847 (as *The bracelets; or, amiability and industry rewarded*; ill. N. Croome). LOCATION NUC, InND Loeber coll.

Philadelphia: Geo.S. Appleton, 1850 (as *Lazy Lawrence; or, industry and idleness contrasted*). LOCATION NUC.

Philadelphia: G.S. Appleton, 1850 (as *The fireside story book*; ill.). LOCATION NUC.
— NEW HAVEN (CT)
New Haven: Sidney's Press, 1808 (as *The little merchants, or honesty and knavery contrasted*). SOURCE Slade, 2D; Welch, 321.1. LOCATION NN, NUC.
New Haven: Sidney's Press, 1808 (as *Lazy Lawrence, an interesting story for children*). SOURCE Welch, 320.1. LOCATION NUC (1809 edn).
New Haven: John Babcock; Charleston (SC): S. & W.R. Babcock; Philadelphia: M'Carty & Davis, 1820 (as *The cherry-orchard: also, A description of a tiger*, [anon.]). SOURCE Welch, 311; OCLC. LOCATION CtY. COMMENTARY *New Haven 1820 edn* 'The cherry-orchard' was originally published in *The parent's assistant* (London, 1796, 3 parts) and later reprinted in *Early lessons* (London, 1801, 10 vols.). 'A description of a tiger' is not known to be by ME [RL].
— NEW YORK
New York: J. Miller, [187?] (as *Waste not, want not, and other stories*). LOCATION NUC.
New York: J. Miller, [187?] (as *Simple Susan, and other stories*). LOCATION NUC.
COMMENTARY Contents: Part 1, vol. 1: 'The little dog Trusty; or, the liar and boy of truth', 'The orange man; or, the honest boy and the thief', 'Tarlton', 'Lazy Lawrence', ' The false key', 'The barring out; or, party spirit'. Part 2, vol. 1: 'The purple jar', 'The bracelets', 'Mademoiselle Panache'. Part 2, vol. 2: 'The birth-day present', 'Old Poz' (a play), 'The mimic' (set in and around Bristol). The 1800, 3rd edn contains eight new stories, but omitted three. New: vol. 2: 'Simple Susan;' vol. 3: 'The little merchants' (set in Naples); vol. 5: 'The basket-woman', 'The white pigeon' (set in Ireland), 'The orphans' (set in Ireland, based on story by Harriet Beaufort§ and Louisa Beaufort§), 'Waste not, want not' (set in Bristol), 'Forgive and forget' (set in Bristol); vol. 6: 'Eton montem'. The story, 'Lazy Lawrence. A tale', was first published in two parts of the *Edinburgh Magazine* (1797) [Butler, pp 159, 161, 237*n*.3, 505; Mayo, 749; Slade; Osborne, p. 249].

E20   *Castle Rackrent. An Hibernian tale. Taken from facts, and from the manner of the Irish squires, before the year 1782* [anon.].
+ London: J. Johnson, 1800. SOURCE Slade, 5A; Rafroidi, 2, p. 150; Forster 2, 1209–10; Sadleir, 763; Wolff, 1984; Gilbert, p. 260; British Fiction; Garside, 1800:30. LOCATION Corvey CME 3–628–47575–9, Grail, Ireland related fiction, DPL Gilbert coll., D, Dt (1800, 2nd edn), L, NUC (1800, 2nd edn).
+ London: R. Hunter; Baldwin, Cradock & Joy, 1815 (new edn). LOCATION InND Loeber coll.
+ Dublin: P. Wogan, H. Colbert, P. Byrne, W. Porter, J. Halpen, J. Rice, H. Fitzpatrick, G. Folingsby, J. Stockdale, R.E. Mercier & Co., 1800. SOURCE Slade, 5D; Sadleir, 763a; ESTC t11109. LOCATION D, Dt, NUC.
Paris: Nicole, 1813–14 (trans. as *Le château de Rackrent*). SOURCE Rafroidi, ii, p. 363. COMMENTARY *Paris edn* No copy located [RL].
New York: X. Martin & J. Leclerc, [1802 or 1803]. SOURCE Leclaire, p. 16.
Newbern (NC): Martin & Ogden, [1802 or 1803]. SOURCE Slade, 5E.
COMMENTARY No copies of the New York and Newbern edns located [RL].
Boston: T.B. Wait & Sons, 1814. LOCATION NUC.
+ Oxford, London, New York: Oxford University Press, 1969. LOCATION InND Loeber coll.
+ New York: Garland, 1978 (introd. by R.L. Wolff). LOCATION D.
COMMENTARY Set in an eighteenth-century Irish country house with an oblique narration by Thady Quirk, an old retainer (based on John Langan, a steward on the Edgeworthstown estate),

who summarizes the lost opportunities and decline of his successive masters of Castle Rackrent. Thady's son, Jason Quirk, in the end acquires the estate. Part of the story is based on the household of Hugh Maguire of Castle Nugent (Co. Longford); other parts were derived from the history of earlier generations of the Edgeworth family. It contains a glossary [Butler, pp 16, 240–1; Field Day, i, pp 682–3, 687, 1013–25, 1071, 1081, 1084n, 1086n, ii, 832, 1009–10, v, 768, 847, 889n; Hogan 2, pp 397–8; W.A. Maguire, 'Castle Nugent and Castle Rackrent: Fact and fiction in Maria Edgeworth' in *Eighteenth-century Ireland*, 11 (1996), p. 153; ODNB; Wolff introd., p. 11].

E21   *Early lessons* (by Maria Edgeworth and Richard Lovell Edgeworth§; dedicated to the author's little brother William [Edgeworth]).

— LONDON

London: J. Johnson, 1801, 10 vols. SOURCE Slade, 6A; Rafroidi, ii, p. 149–50; Sadleir, 766; Wolf, 1986 (1820, 7th edn). LOCATION Grail, L (1809 edn), CLU.

COMMENTARY *London 1801 edn* Contents: 'Harry and Lucy', 'Rosamond' (containing 'The purple jar', 'The two plums', 'The day of misfortunes', 'Rivuletta', 'The thorn', 'The hyacinths', 'The story of the rabbit'), 'Frank' (dedicated to the author's 'little brother William'), 'The little dog Trusty', 'The orange man', 'The cherry orchard' ('The little dog Trusty', and 'The orange man' were originally published in *The parent's assistant*, London, 1796, 3 parts) [Field Day, iv, pp 1144, 1148–51; Slade].

   + London: J. Johnson, 1815, 2 vols. (new edn). LOCATION D.

   + London: Ward & Lock, [1861] (as *The cherry orchard*; Frank Goodchild's Little Library; ill.). LOCATION L.

— EDINBURGH

Edinburgh: Neill & Co.; London: A. Constable & Co., 1817 (trans. as *Contes choisis pour des enfants*). SOURCE Slade, 6C. COMMENTARY *Edinburgh edn* No copy located [RL].

— NORWICH

Norwich: Charles Muskett; London: Simpkin, Marshall & Co., 1846 (trans. by Frances K. Barnard as *Heinrich und Luzie*; dedicated to Miss Walker). SOURCE Slade, 6C. LOCATION L, O.

— DUBLIN

Dublin: Printed by J. Jones, 1817 (as *Entertaining stories for children: selected from Maria Edgeworth's Early lessons*). SOURCE OCLC. LOCATION NUC, CLU.

COMMENTARY *Dublin edn* 36pp. Contents: 'The orange man; or, the honest boy and the thief', 'The cherry orchard' [RL; OCLC].

— TRIM

   + Trim [Co. Meath]: Henry Griffith, 1835 (as *Dog Trusty, &c.*; Printed for the use of Trim School). SOURCE Bradshaw, 5303. LOCATION C.

COMMENTARY *Trim edn* 28pp. This probably was published for Revd Richard Butler (d. 1862), who took a great interest in the Trim School. He was dean of Clonmacnoise and vicar of Trim and married in 1829 Harriet Edgeworth (1801–89), second daughter of Richard Lovell Edgeworth by his fourth wife Frances Anne Beaufort§. Contents: 'Dog Trusty' (probably the same as 'The little dog Trusty'), 'The honest boy & the thief' (originally titled 'The orange man'), 'The cherry orchard' [RL; E.E. MacDonald, *The education of the heart: The correspondence of Rachel Mordecai Lazarus and Maria Edgeworth* (Chapel Hill, NC, 1977), p. 322].

— ROTTERDAM

Rotterdam: W. Locke, 1810 (trans. into Dutch as *Rosamunde, een leesboek voor de jeugd*). SOURCE Alphabetische naamlijst 1790–1832, p. 146; NB, i, p. 550. LOCATION UVA. COMMENTARY *Rotterdam edn* published in parallel English and Dutch texts [Adamnet].

— PARIS

Paris: Xhrouet & Defrelle, 1803, 5 vols. (trans. by M.L.C. Chéron). SOURCE Slade, 6C; OCLC. LOCATION CtY. COMMENTARY *Paris 1805 edn* Joint English and French version [Slade].

Paris: Alexandre Mesnier, 1829–34, 12 vols. (trans. as *Education familière ou séries de lectures pour les enfants depuis le premier age jusqu'à l'adolescence*). SOURCE Slade, 6C. LOCATION NUC.

Paris: Alexis Eymery, 1822, 4 vols. (trans. as *Les enfants, ou les caractères*). SOURCE Slade, 6C.

Paris: Fortric, 1826, 4 vols. (trans. by Mme Belloc as *Les jeunes industriels, ou découvertes, expériences, conversations et voyages de Henri et Lucie*). SOURCE Slade, 6C. LOCATION NUC.

Paris: Libraire d'Éducation de Didier, 1838 (imitated by Mme Viltardant as *Les jeunes savants, expériences, voyages, découvertes de Henri et Lucie, sous la direction de leur père*). SOURCE Slade, 6C; Bn-Opale plus. Location BNF.

— GENEVA

+ Geneva: Sèstié Fils, 1819 (trans. as *Rosamonde*). LOCATION D.

— NEW YORK

New York: William Burgess Jnr, [1826 or earlier] (ill.). SOURCE Adv. in [G. Kennedy], *Anna Ross*, 1826]. COMMENTARY *New York edn* No copy located [RL].

— PHILADELPHIA

Philadelphia: Jacob Johnson, 1808, 2 vols. (as *Rosamond*). SOURCE Slade, 6C; Welch, 330.1. LOCATION DCL, NUC.

Philadelphia: Jacob Johnson, 1808, 6 vols. (as *Frank* [anon.]). SOURCE Slade, 6C; Rosenbach, 364; Welch, 316.1. LOCATION NUC.

+ Philadelphia: Jacob Johnson, 1805, 2 vols. [anon.] (as *Harry and Lucy. Part I [II]*, being the first part of Early lessons). SOURCE Slade, 6C; Rosenbach, 304; Welch, 317.1. LOCATION NUC, InND Loeber coll.

Philadelphia: M. Fithian, 1840 (as *Extracts from Early lessons*; ill.). LOCATION NUC.

— BOSTON

+ Boston: Cummings & Hilliard, 1813 (as *Rosamond*; parts 1 & 2 together). SOURCE Welch, 330.2, InND Loeber coll. COMMENTARY *Boston 1813 edn* Contents: 'The purple jar', 'The two plums', 'The day of misfortunes', 'Rivuletta', 'The thorn', 'The hyacinth', 'The story of the rabbit' [RL].

Boston: Samuel T. Armstrong, Cummings & Hilliard, 1813, 2 volumes in 1 (as *Harry and Lucy, being the first part of Early lessons*). SOURCE OCLC. LOCATION C, NUC.

Boston: B. Mussey, [1845] (selected by Mrs Colman; as *The little dog Trusty, The cherry orchard, and The orange man*). LOCATION NUC.

— POUGHKEEPSIE (NY)

Poughkeepsie: Paraclete Potter, 1815 (as *Lucy, being the first part of Early lessons*). SOURCE Welch, 317.4; OCLC. LOCATION Univ. of Richmond.

— NEW HAVEN (CT)

New Haven: J. Babcock & Son; Charleston (SC): S. & W.R. Babcock, 1821 (as *Rosamond, or, the purple jar*). LOCATION NUC.

New Haven: J. Babcock & Son; Charleston (SC): S. & W.R. Babcock, 1821 (as *Harry and Lucy*). LOCATION NUC.

— WORCESTER (MA)

Worcester: Edward Livermore, 1847 (as *The little dog Trusty, The cherry orchard, and The orange man*). LOCATION NUC.

E22   *Belinda* (by Maria Edgeworth).
London: J. Johnson, 1801, 3 vols. SOURCE Slade, 8A; Rafroidi, ii, p. 149; Sadleir, 762; British Fiction; Garside, 1801:24. LOCATION Grail, D, L, NUC.
+ London: J. Johnson, 1802, 2nd edn, 3 vols. (corrected and improved). SOURCE Slade, 8B. LOCATION Corvey CME 3–628–47557, D, NUC.
+ London: F.C. & J. Rivington, 1810 (British Novelists series, vol. 49–50). SOURCE Butler, p. 505. LOCATION D, L, NUC.
COMMENTARY *London 1810 edn* Contains major alterations in the latter part of the story. Contents: 'Belinda', and 'The modern Griselda' [Slade; Butler, p. 505].
+ Dublin: H. Colbert & J. Stockdale, 1801, 2 vols. SOURCE Slade, 8C; NSTC. LOCATION D, Dt, O, NUC.
+ Paris: Maradan, 1802, 4 vols. (trans. by L.S. and F.S. [i.e., Octave Ségur] as *Bélinde, conte moral*). SOURCE Slade, 8C; NSTC; Sadleir, 762a; Pickering & Chatto cat. 729/28. LOCATION D, L.
+ Boston: Wells & Lilly; New York: Eastburn, Kirk & Co., 1814, 2 vols. SOURCE NCBEL 3, p. 667. LOCATION NUC, InND Loeber coll.
London: Dent, 1993 (ed. by E. ní Chuillenáin). SOURCE COPAC. LOCATION Dt, C.
COMMENTARY Set in high society in England and mainly concerned with the marrying off of young women in the most advantageous manner. The story contrasts dissipation and purity of mind. Dissipation leads to unhappiness whereas purity of mind allows for the possibility of positive marital and other relations. A side plot contains the experiment of training an innocent girl to be a perfect wife (in the manner of Jean-Jacques Rousseau and Thomas Day). See Butler for the evolution of the story [ML; Butler, pp 243, 494–9; Field Day, iv, pp 902*n*, 1095–9, v, 768, 836].

E23   *Moral tales for young people* (by Maria Edgeworth; preface by Richard Lovell Edgeworth§).
London: J. Johnson, 1801, 5 vols. (ill., C[harlotte] Edgeworth, F[rances] Edgeworth, Neagle). SOURCE Slade, 7A; Rafroidi, 2, p. 150; Garside, 1801:25; Osborne, p. 880; Sadleir, 777. LOCATION Grail, L, CaOTP, NUC.
COMMENTARY *London 1801 edn* Stories for juveniles. Contents: 'Forester', 'Angelina; or, l'amie inconnue' (initially written as a play, but then transformed into a short story), 'The knapsack', 'The Prussian vase', 'Mademoiselle Panache', 'The good aunt', 'The good French governess' [Slade; Butler, p. 165].
— LONDON
+ London: J. Johnson, 1809, 3 vols., 5th edn (as *Moral tales*). LOCATION D.
London: Schulze & Co., 1838 (trans. by Mlles M. and L. Shearburn as *Le vase Prussien, anecdote sur Frédéric Le Grand, roi de Prusse*). SOURCE Slade 7C. LOCATION L.
+ London: W. & R. Chambers, [1873] (as *The good aunt, and Forester*). LOCATION L, InND Loeber coll.
+ London: W. & R. Chambers, [1873] (as *The good French governess. Angelina and The Prussian vase*; ill. J. Corner). LOCATION L, InND Loeber coll.
— PARIS
+ Paris: A. Eymery & L. Colas, 1820, 2 vols. (liberally trans. by A.L.S as *Petites contes moraux a l'usage des enfans*; dedicated to Maria Edgeworth; ill.). SOURCE Slade, 7C (who stated that the translator was Mme Belloc). LOCATION InND Loeber coll.
Paris: Baudry, 1834, 3 vols. (as *Miss Edgeworth's moral tales*; Baudry's European Library). SOURCE Slade 7C. COMMENTARY No copy of the Paris, Baudry, 1834 edn located. Each story of this edn was also sold individually [Slade 7C; RL].

Paris: Fruger & Brunet, 1836 (liberally trans. As *Le petit trésor des enfant bien sage: ou choix de jolis contes moraux, propres à les faire persévérer, dans le bien*). LOCATION NUC. COMMENTARY *Paris 1836 edn* The settings of the stories have been transposed to France. Contents: 'Suzette, ou la reine de Mai', 'Laurent le paresseux', 'Les orphelins', 'Pardon et oubli' [RL].

Paris: Arthus Betrand, 1821, 2 vols. (trans. by Mme M. Tourte-Cherbuliez as *Forester, ou la manie de l'indépendance; suivi d'Angélina ou l'amie inconnue*). SOURCE Slade, 7C. LOCATION L.

Paris: Baudry, 1830, 2 vols. (trans. by M. Benj. Laroche as *Forester. A tale*). SOURCE Slade, 7C ([1834?] edn). LOCATION NUC.

Paris: Baudry's European Library, 1834 (as *The good aunt. A tale*). SOURCE Slade, 7C; Devonshire, p. 362 (mentions unidentified 1830 edn). LOCATION L, NUC.

Paris: Baudry, 1852 (as *The good French governess, a tale*). SOURCE CCF. LOCATION BNF.

— ROTTERDAM

Rotterdam: J. Hendriksen, [1818] (trans. from the German and English into Dutch as *Nieuwe verhalen voor de jeugd, ter vorming van het zedelijk gevoel*; ill). SOURCE Adamnet. LOCATION UVA.

Rotterdam: Mensing & Van Westreenen, 1823, 2 vols. (trans. into Dutch as *Zedelijke verhalen voor jonge lieden*). SOURCE Wintermans, 1801:25. SOURCE Adamnet; NB, i, p. 550. LOCATION UVA.

— PHILADELPHIA

Philadelphia: Johnson & Warner, 1810, 5 vols. (ill.). SOURCE Slade, 7C; Welch, 324.1. LOCATION NUC.

Philadelphia: Bennett & Walton, 1811 (as *Angelina, or, the unknown friend*). SOURCE Slade, 7C; Welch, 306. LOCATION NUC.

Philadelphia: Bennett & Walton, 1811 (as *The Prussian vase; or, the history of Sophia Mansfield*). SOURCE Welch, 329. LOCATION NUC.

— GEORGETOWN

George Town [Georgetown, Washington (DC)]: Joseph Milligan, 1811, 3 vols. SOURCE Welch, 324.2 (vol. 3 only). LOCATION NUC.

— NEW YORK

New York: W.B. Gilley, 1818, 3 vols. (ill. Anderson). SOURCE Slade, 7C (1819 edn), Rosenbach, 688 (1826 edn); Welch, 324.3–5. LOCATION NN, NUC (1818–19 edn).

New York: J.G. Shaw, 1838 (as *The good aunt: A moral tale*; ill.). LOCATION NUC, PpiU.

New York: Harper, 1842 (as *Forester; the Prussian vase and the good aunt*). LOCATION NUC.

— BOSTON

Boston: Munroe & Francis, 1832 (as *The knapsack: A tale*). LOCATION NUC.

E24   *Popular tales* (by Maria Edgeworth; preface by Richard Lovell Edgeworth§).

— LONDON

London: J. Johnson, 1804, 3 vols. SOURCE Slade, 10A; Rafroidi, ii, p. 151; Sadleir, 781; Wolff, 1994; British Fiction; Garside, 1804:17. LOCATION Grail, Corvey CME, 3–628–47576, L, NUC. COMMENTARY *London 1804 edn* The stories about trades people were written between 1799 and 1803, and were aimed at those of the 'lower' orders who could read. Contents: 'Lame Jervas', 'The will', 'The Limerick gloves', 'Out of debt out of danger', 'The lottery', 'Rosanna', 'Murad the unlucky', 'The manufacturers', 'The contrast', 'The grateful negro', 'To-morrow' [Slade; Butler, p. 287].

London: J. Johnson, 1805, 2nd edn, 3 vols. SOURCE Slade, 10B. LOCATION L, NUC. COMMENTARY *London 1805 edn* Considerably modified text [Slade, 10B].
+ London: Baldwin & Cradock, 1832, 2 vols. (new edn, ill. W. Harvey, F. Engelheart, C. Rolls). LOCATION InND Loeber coll. (also London, New York: Lock & Co., [1878?] edn; see Plate 31).
— EDINBURGH
+ Edinburgh: James Gordon; London: Simpkin, Marshall & Co., [1862] (as *To-mor-row*; ill., Gordon's School and Home Series). LOCATION L.
— HALIFAX (UK)
Halifax: Milner & Sowerby, 1863 (as *The will, and The Limerick gloves*). LOCATION NUC.
— PARIS
+ Paris: Dentu, 1813, 2 vols. (liberal trans. by T.P. Bertin as *Contes à mon fils*; ill.). SOURCE Slade, 10C. LOCATION InND Loeber coll.
Paris: J.A.S. Collin de Plancy, 1823, 2 vols. (trans. by Mmes. Elise Voyart and Read as *Contes populaires*). SOURCE Slade, 10C.
Paris: Baudry, 1837 (as *The Limerick gloves. Out of debt, out of danger*). SOURCE CCF. LOCATION BNF. COMMENTARY *Paris, Baudry edn.* Baudry also issued in the same year *Popular tales*, which consisted of the full range of the original stories [RL].
+ Paris: Hachette & Co., 1878, 2nd edn (trans. by H. Jousselin as *Demain, suivi de Morad le malheureux*; ill. Bertall; Bibliothèque Rose Illustrée). LOCATION L.
— AMSTERDAM
Amsterdam: H. Blad, 1845 (free trans. into Dutch as *De buren en het testament: Twee romantische verhalen*). SOURCE Adamnet. LOCATION UVA.
— BRUSSELS
+ Brussels: Meline, Cans & Co., 1837 (trans. by E. Garnier as *Contes populaires*; ill. M. de Saison, Boilly). LOCATION D.
— GÖRLITZ
Görlitz: Anton, 1807 (trans. by Wilhelm Adolf Lindau as *Einfache Erzählungen*). SOURCE Garside, 1804:17. LOCATION Staatsbibliothek, Berlin.
— HAMBURG
+ Hamburg: Perthes & Besser, 1832, 2nd edn (trans. as *Auswahl aus den Popular Tales*). SOURCE Adamnet. LOCATION UVA.
— PHILADELPHIA
Philadelphia: James Humphreys, 1804, 2 vols. SOURCE Slade, 10C; Topp 2, p. 131. LOCATION NUC.
— NEW BRUNSWICK (NJ)
New Brunswick: William Elliot, 1807 (as *To-morrow, or the dangers of delay*). LOCATION NUC.
New Brunswick: William Elliot, 1807 (as *The contrast*). SOURCE Slade, 10C. LOCATION NUC.
— CATSKILL (NY)
+ Catskill NY: Samuel Peck, 1811 (as *To-morrow, or the dangers of delay*; ill.). LOCATION D.
— POUGHKEEPSIE (NY)
Poughkeepsie NY: P. Potter, 1813, 2 vols. LOCATION NUC.
— NEW YORK
New York: Evert Duyckinck, 1813 (as *To-morrow, or the dangers of delay*). SOURCE Rosenbach, 472 (where misspelled Duyckigk). LOCATION NUC.

— NEW HAVEN (CT)

New Haven: J. Babcock & Son, 1819 (as *The basket-woman, and the orphans* [anon.]; ill.). SOURCE Welch, 308; OCLC. LOCATION CtY.

— PITTSBURGH (PA)

Pittsburgh: Cramer & Spear, 1818 (as *Lame Jervas; a tale*). SOURCE Welch, 319. LOCATION NUC. COMMENTARY *Pittsburgh 1818 edn* Includes 'The Lancashire collier girl', which is not by ME [RL; NUC].

Pittsburgh: Cramer & Spear, 1818 (as *Murad, the unlucky. A tale*). SOURCE Welch, 325. LOCATION NUC.

— BOSTON

Boston: Samuel H. Parker, 1823. LOCATION NUC.

— BALTIMORE

Baltimore: Kelly & Piet, 1870 (new edn). LOCATION NUC.

— CALCUTTA

Calcutta: R.C. LePage & Co., P.S. D'Rozario & Co., 1849. SOURCE Slade, 10C. COMMENTARY *Calcutta edn* No copy located [RL].

E25   *Choix de nouveau contes moraux offerts à la jeunesse* (by Maria Edgeworth).

+ Paris: Frechet & Co., 1804, 3 vols. (trans. by V.B.). SOURCE CCF. LOCATION L, BNF. COMMENTARY Contents: 'Mlle Panache', 'Les petits marchands', 'La bonne Susanne'. The first story is from *Moral tales* (London, 1801, 5 vols.), and last two are from *The parent's assistant* (London, 1796, 3 parts) [Slade; RL].

E26   *The modern Griselda. A tale* (by Maria Edgeworth).

London: J. Johnson, 1805. SOURCE Slade, 11A; Rafroidi, ii, p. 151; Sadleir, 776; Wolff, 1992; British Fiction; Garside, 1805:29. LOCATION Grail, Dt, L, NUC.

+ London: J. Johnson, 1805, 2nd edn (corrected). SOURCE Slade, 11B. LOCATION D, NUC, InND Loeber coll.

+ Paris: Galignani, 1813, 2 vols. (trans. as *Les deux Grisélidis, histoires ... l'une de Chaucher et l'autre de Mlle. Edgeworth*). SOURCE Slade 11C. LOCATION L. COMMENTARY *Paris edn* Only one of the stories is by ME [RL; ML].

+ George Town [Georgetown, Washington (DC)]: Joseph Milligan, 1810. SOURCE Slade, 11C. LOCATION NUC, InND Loeber coll.

COMMENTARY Set in England. A young woman tries various tactics to bring her husband into submission, with the result that she loses him [ML; Field Day, iv, pp 1156–7].

E27   *Leonora* (by Maria Edgeworth).

+ London: J. Johnson, 1806, 2 vols. SOURCE Slade, 12A; Rafroidi, ii, p. 151; Sadleir, 773; British Fiction; Garside, 1806:29. LOCATION Corvey CME 3–628–47571–6, Grail, Dt, L, NUC.

London: R. Hunter, 1815, 2 vols. (new edn). SOURCE Slade, 12B. LOCATION NUC.

Paris: Dentu, 1807, 3 vols. (trans. by C. Chenel as *Léonora*). SOURCE Slade 12C; Rafroidi, ii, p. 363. LOCATION L, NUC.

New York: I. Riley & Co., 1806, 2 vols. LOCATION Dt, NUC.

COMMENTARY Epistolary, moralistic novel in which virtue wins out over passion. A woman temporarily loses her husband to an affair in which he is engaged. However, she continues to be steadfast and when he falls ill on the Continent, she goes to nurse him. They reunite and live a happy life [ML].

E28   *Tales of fashionable life* (by Maria Edgeworth; preface by Richard Lovell Edgeworth§).

LONDON

+ London: J. Johnson, 1809, vols. 1–3. SOURCE Slade, 14A; Rafroidi, ii, p. 151–2; Sadleir, 786; Wolff, 1996; Block, p. 65; British Fiction; Garside, 1809:22. LOCATION

Corvey (1813, 4th edn), CME 3–628–47534–1, Grail, Ireland related fiction, D, Dt, L, InND Loeber coll.

+ London: J. Johnson, 1812, vols. 4–6. SOURCE Slade, 14A; Rafroidi, ii, p. 151–2; Sadleir, 786; Wolff, 1996; Block, p. 65; British Fiction; Garside, 1809:22. LOCATION Corvey (1813, 4th edn), CME 3–628–47534–1, Grail, D, Dt, L, InND Loeber coll.

COMMENTARY *London 1809 and 1812 edns* Contents: 'Ennui, or memoirs of the earl of Glenthorn' (the history a young dissipated Anglo-Irish nobleman, who makes his first visit to his Irish estates and is introduced to the problems of management on his own estate and elsewhere), 'Almeria', 'Madame de Fleury', 'The dun', 'Manoeuvring', 'Vivian', 'Emilie de Coulanges', 'The absentee' (first written as a play, the story relates how the young nobleman Colambre, an energetic man full of latent benevolence towards his tenants, sees his family's Irish estates for the first time. He encounters extraordinary cases both of good and of bad management, learns from the first, and deals drastically with the second. The story also describes the unsuccessful attempts by Colambre's Irish parents to dazzle London society) [Brown; Butler, p. 276; Field Day, i, pp 1029–51, ii, pp 768, 836–7, 1080, v, 812; RL; Wolff introd., p. 12; F.V. Barry (ed.), *Maria Edgeworth: Chosen letters* (Boston, [1931]), p. 161].

London, New York: George Routledge & Co., 1856 (as *Ennui, and Emilie de Coulanges: being Tales of fashionable life*; Cheap Series, No. 134). SOURCE Topp 1, p. 71. LOCATION L, NUC.

+ London: R. Hunter, Baldwin, Cradock & Joy, 1815, 6 vols. (new edn). LOCATION D, L.

London, New York: George Routledge & Co., 1856 (as *Manoeuvring, Madame de Fleury, & The Dun*; Cheap Series, No. 138). SOURCE Jarndyce cat. 116/351. LOCATION L, NUC.

London, New York: George Routledge & Co., 1856 (as *Vivian and Almeria.. Tales of fashionable life*; Cheap Series, No. 139). SOURCE Topp 1, p. 72. LOCATION L, NUC.

— PARIS

+ Paris: Galignani, 1812, 3 vols. (trans. by Mme E. de Bon as *L'Ennui, ou mémoires du Comte de Glenthorn*). SOURCE Slade 14C; Rafroidi, ii, p. 363. LOCATION L, NUC.

Paris: Henri Nicole & Renard, 1813–14, 7 vols. (trans. by P. L. Dubuc as *Scènes de la vie du grand monde*). SOURCE Slade 14C; Rafroidi, ii, p. 363. LOCATION NUC.

Paris: H. Nicolle, Renard, 1813, 3 vols. (trans. by [Pierre Louis Dubuc] as *Vivian*). LOCATION NUC.

Paris: Maradan, 1813, 3 vols. (trans. by M. Dubuc as *Vivian, ou l'homme sans caractère*). SOURCE Slade, 14C; Streeter, p. 222. LOCATION L.

Paris: H. Nicolle, Renard, 1813 (trans. by Dubuc as *Scènes de la vie du grand monde ... Emilie de Coulange*). LOCATION L, NUC.

+ Paris: Baudry's Foreign Library, 1831, 6 vols. in 3. SOURCE NCBEL 3, p. 667. LOCATION L, InND Loeber coll. COMMENTARY *Paris 1831 edn*. Also contains 'The modern Griselda', first published with *Belinda* (London, 1810, 3 vols.) [RL].

— LEIPZIG

Leipzig: in der Joachim'schen Buchhandling, [*c.*1812–15] (trans. as *Szenen aus dem Leben der grossen Welt*). SOURCE Burmester cat. 49/194. COMMENTARY *Leipzig edn* No other copy located than that mentioned in the Burmester cat.[RL].

— PESTH

Pesth: Hartleben, 1814, 2 vols. (as *Vivian, oder, Der Mann ohne Charakter; Szenen aus dem Leben der grossen Welt; 1. Gemälde*). SOURCE RLIN. LOCATION German Society of Pennsylvania.

— GRONINGEN

Groningen: W. Wouters, 1820 (trans. into Dutch as *Verhalen uit de groote wereld*). SOURCE Alphabetische naamlijst 1790–1832, p. 147.

— LEEUWARDEN

Leeuwarden: Steenbergen van Goor, 1817, 2 vols. (trans. into Dutch as *Vivian of the man zonder karakter*). SOURCE Wintermans,1809:22.

— GRONINGEN

Groningen: Wijbe Wouters, 1819 (trans. into Dutch as *Verveling; of de geschiedenis van de graaf van Glenthorne*). SOURCE Wintermans, 1809:22.

Groningen: Wijbe Wouters, 1819 (trans. into Dutch as *Verhalen uit de groote wereld*). SOURCE Wintermans, 1809:22.

— GEORGETOWN

George Town [Georgetown, Washington (DC)]: Joseph Milligan, 1809, 2 vols. (as *Ennui*). SOURCE Topp, p. 71. SOURCE Slade, 14C. LOCATION DCL. COMMENTARY *Georgetown edn* Reprint of London edn, vols. 1–3 [NUC].

— BOSTON

Boston: John Eliot Jnr, 1810–12, 3 vols. LOCATION NUC.

Boston: Bradford & Read, 1812, 3 vols. SOURCE Slade, 14C. COMMENTARY *Boston edns* Reprint of London edn, vols. 4–6. No copy of the Boston, 1812 edn located [Slade; RL].

— BRIDGEPORT

Bridgeport, CT: Lockwood & Backus, 1811 (as *Vivian*). SOURCE Topp 1, p. 72. COMMENTARY *Bridgeport edn* No copy located [RL].

Bridgeport, CT: Lockwood & Backus, 1811 (as *Almeria; a tale of fashionable life*). LOCATION NUC.

— NEW YORK

New York: Elliot & Crissy, 1810 (as *Ennui*). SOURCE Topp 1, p. 71. LOCATION NUC.

New York: Inskeep & Bradford, 1812, 2 vols. (as *Vivian*). SOURCE Topp 1, p. 72. LOCATION NUC.

+ New York: Inskeep & Bradford; Philadelphia: Bradford & Inskeep, 1812, 2 vols. (as *Vivian: and Emilie de Coulanges: tales*). LOCATION D, NUC.

New York: Inskeep & Bradford; Philadelphia: Bradford & Inskeep, 1812, 2 vols. (as *The absentee*). SOURCE OCLC. LOCATION NUC.

— WASHINGTON

Washington: W. Cooper, 1812, 2 vols. in 1 (as *The absentee*). SOURCE Slade, 14C; Topp 1, p. 71. LOCATION NUC.

— PHILADELPHIA

Philadelphia, Trenton: E. Littell, 1822–23, 6 vols. in 2. LOCATION NUC.

— MODERN REPRINTS

New York: Garland, 1979 (as *The absentee*; introd. by R.L. Wolff). SOURCE COPAC. LOCATION Univ. of Leeds.

+ New York: Garland, 1978 (as *Ennui*; introd. by R.L. Wolff). LOCATION D, L.

+ Oxford: Oxford University Press, 1988 (as *The absentee*; ed. by W.J. McCormack & Kim Walker). SOURCE OCLC. LOCATION L, MH.

London: Penguin, 1999 (as *The absentee*). LOCATION InND.

E29 *Conseils à mon fils ou les deux familles, la chaumière de Rosana et le nègre reconnaissant* (by Maria Edgeworth).

+ Paris: G.T. Dentu, 1814, 2 vols. (liberally trans. by T.P. Bertin). SOURCE Slade 10C. LOCATION L.

COMMENTARY French translations of 'Rosamond' and 'The grateful negro', originally published in *Early lessons* (London, 1801, 10 vols.) and *Popular tales* (London, 1804, 3 vols.), respectively [Slade, 10C].

E30   *Continuation of Early lessons:* [vol. 1] *Containing Frank, and the beginning of Rosamond,* [vol. 2] *The conclusion of Rosamond and Harry and Lucy* (by Maria Edgeworth; dedicated to the author's little brother Francis Beaufort Edgeworth).

— LONDON

London: J. Johnson & Co., 1814, 2 vols. SOURCE Slade, 15A; Rafroidi, ii, p. 152; Sadleir, 765; Wolff, 1986 (1816, 3rd edn). LOCATION Grail, NUC. COMMENTARY *London 1814 edn* Contents: 'Frank', 'Rosamond' (containing the following stories: 'The wager', 'The party of pleasure', 'The black bonnet', 'The India cabinet', 'The silver cup', 'The bee and the cow', 'The happy party', 'Wonders', 'The microscope'), 'Harry and Lucy' [Slade].

+ London: J. Johnson & Co., 1815, 2 vols. (new edn). SOURCE Slade, 15B. LOCATION D, L.

+ London: R. Hunter, Baldwin, Cradock & Joy, 1822, 3 vols. (as *Frank, a sequel to Frank in Early lessons*). SOURCE Slade, 22A; Rafroidi, ii, p. 153; Sadleir, 767. LOCATION Grail, D, L, NUC.

London: R. Hunter, Baldwin, Cradock & Joy, 1821, 2 vols. (as *Rosamond, a sequel to Early lessons*). SOURCE Rafroidi, ii, p. 153; Sadleir 783. LOCATION Grail, D, L, NUC.

London, New York: G. Routledge & Co., 1857 (as *Frank. A tale*). LOCATION NUC.

— PARIS

Paris: Truchy, 1835 (as *Frank, a sequel to Frank in Early lessons*). SOURCE NCBEL 3, p. 668; CCF. LOCATION BNF.

Paris: Baudry, 1836 (as *Rosamond, a sequel to Early lessons*). SOURCE NCBEL 3, p. 668, CCF. LOCATION BNF.

— BOSTON

Boston: Bradford & Read, 1815, 2 vols. SOURCE Slade, 15C; Welch, 312.1. LOCATION NUC.

Boston: Julius A. Noble, 1838 (as *Frank, a sequel to Frank in Early lessons*). COMMENTARY *Boston, Noble edn* No copy located [RL].

— PHILADELPHIA

Philadelphia: J. Maxwell, 1821, 2 vols. (as *Rosamond, a sequel to Early lessons*). SOURCE Slade, 21C. LOCATION NUC.

— CAMBRIDGE (MA)

+ Cambridge: Hilliard & Metcalf for the Trustees of the Publishing Fund, 1822, 2 vols. (as *Frank, a sequel to Frank in Early lessons*). SOURCE Slade, 22B. LOCATION NUC, InND Loeber coll.

— NEW YORK

New York: W.B. Gilley, 1822, 2 vols. (as *Frank, a sequel to Frank in Early lessons*). SOURCE Slade, 22B. LOCATION NUC.

New York: Allen, 1869, 2 vols. (new edn; *Frank: A book for boys*). LOCATION NUC.

— BALTIMORE

+ Baltimore: J. Smith Homans, 1836 (as *Frank, a sequel to Frank in Early lessons*). LOCATION NUC, InND Loeber coll.

Baltimore: Kelly & Piet, 1868, 2 vols. (new edn; as *Frank: A book for boys*). LOCATION NUC.

E31   *Patronage* (by Maria Edgeworth; preface by Richard Lovell Edgeworth§).

+ London: J. Johnson & Co., 1814, 4 vols. SOURCE Slade 16A; Rafroidi, ii, p. 152; British Fiction; Garside, 1814:20; Sadleir, 780; Wolff, 1993. LOCATION Grail, Corvey (1814, 2nd edn), CME 3–628–47574–0, D, Dt, L, NUC, InND Loeber coll.

London: R. Hunter, 1815, 3rd edn. SOURCE Slade 16C; Rafroidi, ii, p. 152. LOCATION CtY. COMMENTARY *London 1815 edn* Contains some changes to the plot [Slade, 14B; Mrs [Frances] Edgeworth, *A memoir of Maria Edgeworth* (London, 1867), i, p. 314].

Paris: Ledoux & Tenré, 1816, 5 vols. (freely trans. by J. Cohen as *Les protecteurs et les protégés*). SOURCE Slade 16D, Rafroidi, ii, p. 363. LOCATION L, NUC.

Frankfurt am Main: Sauerländer, 1828, 4 vols. (trans. by Louise Marezoll as *Die Gönnerschaft*). LOCATION IDS Bale/Bern.

Amsterdam: H. Moolenyser, 1816, 3 vols (trans. into Dutch as *Kruiwagens, of, hoe komt men het best door de wereld*). SOURCE Alphabetische naamlijst 1790–1832, p. 146. COMMENTARY *Amsterdam 1816 edn* Literal translation of the title is: 'Wheelbarrows, or, how can one go best through life'.

Philadelphia: Moses Thomas, 1814, 3 vols. SOURCE Slade, 16D. LOCATION NUC. COMMENTARY Epistolary novel, set almost entirely in England and based on a story Richard Lovell Edgeworth§ told his family. The first draft was completed as early as 1791 and revsd several times. The character of the lord chief justice was based on Charles Kendal Bushe, the Irish lord chief justice and ME's relative. In the 1825 collected edn there are substantial changes, including a rewritten last vol. (see Butler for a history of changes in this novel) [Butler, pp 257, 494–9, 505; Colvin, p. 318*n*.1; ODNB].

E32   *Harrington, a tale; and Ormond, a tale* (by Maria Edgeworth; preface by Richard Lovell Edgeworth§).

— LONDON

+ London: R. Hunter, Baldwin, Cradock & Joy, 1817, 3 vols. SOURCE Slade, 18A; Rafroidi, ii, p. 152; Sadleir, no number; Wolff, 1989; British Fiction; Garside, 1817:24. LOCATION Grail, Corvey (1817, 2nd edn), CME 3–628–47570–8, Ireland related fiction, Dt, L, NUC, InND Loeber coll. COMMENTARY *London 1817 edn* 'Harrington' (how education removed the protagonist's anti-Jewish prejudice), 'Ormond' (deals with the adventures and education of the youthful hero Harry Ormond. Ormond is first the ward of Sir Ulick O'Shane, who has abandoned the Catholic faith and has become a political 'jobber' dealing in patronage and various forms of corrupt practice, and then of Sir Ulick's cousin, King Corny, who rules over an isolated island estate in Lough Rea. The contrasting models of Irish life offered by Ulick and Corny are eventually rejected in favour of the paternalistic Anglo-Irish landlordism of the Annaly family). King Corny in 'Ormond' is based on John Corry of Shantonagh, Co. Monaghan, the husband of Mary (Maria?) Ruxton§. Sir Ulick in the same story is said to have been based on two men: Sir John de Blaquiere and Admiral Thomas Pakenham [Butler, pp 249–52; Field Day, v, p. 840 ('Ormond'); Wolff introd., p. 12].

+ London: R. Hunter, Baldwin, Cradock & Joy, 1817, 3 vols., 2nd edn (corrected). LOCATION D.

London: Baldwin & Cradock, 1833 (as *Harrington*). LOCATION NUC.

London: Baldwin & Cradock, 1833 (as *Ormond*). SOURCE Topp 8, 176; OCLC. LOCATION CtY.

+ London, New York: Macmillan & Co., 1895 (as *Ormond A Tale*, introd. Anne Thackeray Ritchie; ill. Carl Schloesser). LOCATION L, InND Loeber coll.

— PARIS

Paris: Gide fils et Nicolle, 1817, 2 vols. (trans. by C.A. Defauconpret as *Harrington*). SOURCE Slade, 18C; Rafroidi, ii, p. 363; Garside, 1817:24; CCF, DNB. LOCATION Dt, NUC.

Paris: Gide fils & Nicolle, 1817, 3 vols. (trans. by C.A. Defauconpret as *Ormond*).
SOURCE Slade, 18C; Rafroidi, ii, p. 363. LOCATION Dt, NUC.

— PHILADELPHIA
Philadelphia: Moses Thomas; New York: Van Winckle & Wiley, 1817, 3 vols. in 2.
SOURCE NCBEL 3, p. 668. LOCATION NUC.

— NEW YORK
New York: Van Winckle & Wiley, James Eastburn & Co., 1817. SOURCE Slade, 18C;
OCLC. LOCATION Univ. of Richmond.

New York: Kirk & Mercein, 1817, 3 vols. in 2. SOURCE OCLC. LOCATION Virginia
Historical Society Library.

New York: Harper, 1855 (as *Harrington*). LOCATION NUC.

— MODERN REPRINTS
+ New York: Garland, 1979, 2 vols. (introd. by R.L. Wolff). LOCATION D, L.
+ Dublin: Appletree Press, 1992 (as *Ormond*; introd. by John Banville). LOCATION D.
+ London: Penguin, 2000 (as *Ormond*; introd. by Claire Connolly). LOCATION Dt, L,
InND Loeber coll.

E33   *Harry and Lucy concluded; being the last part of Early lessons* (by Maria Edgeworth;
       dedicated to the children of Capt. [Francis] Beaufort [brother of Frances, the fourth
       wife of Richard Lovell Edgeworth, and of Henrietta Beaufort§ and Louisa Beaufort§]).
       + London: R. Hunter, Baldwin, Cradock & Joy, 1825, 4 vols. SOURCE Slade, 23A;
       Rafroidi, ii, p. 153; Sadleir, 769; Wolff, 1990. LOCATION Grail, D, Dt, L, NUC, InND
       Loeber coll.
       London: R. Hunter, Baldwin, Cradock & Joy, 1827, 2nd edn, 4 vols. (corrected).
       SOURCE Slade, 23B; Sadleir, 769a. LOCATION NUC.
       London: Baldwin & Cradock & George Routledge, 1837, 3rd edn (revsd and corrected).
       SOURCE Slade, 23C (1840, 3rd edn); Sadleir, 770 (1840, 3rd edn). LOCATION NUC.
       Boston: Munroe & Francis, 1825, 4 vols. SOURCE NCBEL 3, p. 668. LOCATION NUC.
       COMMENTARY A sequel to 'Harry and Lucy' from the *Continuation of Early lessons*
       (London, 1814, 2 vols.) [RL].

E34   *Garry-Owen; or, the snow-woman* (by Maria Edgeworth).
       Salem (MA): John M. & W. & S.B. Ives, 1829. LOCATION NUC.
COMMENTARY Originally published in *The Christmas Box* (London, 1828). Starts with a scene
of snipe-shooting, and the characters are Master Gerald and Patrick Carol. The scene then
moves to Mrs Crofton's cottage, where we find Molly and George. Part II is set at Castle
Gerald [Bolton, p. 195; Slade].

E35   *Garry Owen; or, the snow-woman; and Poor Bob, the chimney-sweeper* (by Maria
       Edgeworth).
       + London: John Murray, 1832 (ill.). SOURCE Slade, 25A. LOCATION Dt, L, NUC,
       InND Loeber coll. COMMENTARY London edn Priced at 2s. 6d. [Slade].
       Paris: Truchy, 1835 (as *The history of poor Bob the chimney sweep*). SOURCE Slade, 25B.
       Paris: Hachette, 1835 (trans. by Mme Belloc as *Contes aux jeunes garçons persévérance,
       Garry Owen ou la femme sous la neige*).
       COMMENTARY 'Garry Owen' was originally published in *The Christmas Box* (London,
       1828), while 'Poor Bob' appeared a year earlier, but it is not clear where [Slade].

E36   *Forgive and forget, a tale ... Rosanna* (by Maria Edgeworth; trans. into Irish for the
       Ulster Gaelic Society by Thomas Feenachty, teacher of Irish in Belfast; dedicated to
       the marquis of Downshire).
       + Belfast: Sold by Samuel Archer & William M'Comb; Dublin: Sold by William Curry
       Jnr & Richard Coyne, 1833 (the Irish text appeared as *Maith agus dearmad / sgéul beag*

d'ar b'ughdar Maria Edgeworth; Rosanna, ón ughdar chéadna. Air na d-tairuing go firineach ó Bhéurla go Gaoidheilg ... le Tómas Ó Fíanachtaigh, Oide Gaoidheilge a m-Béul fearsaide). SOURCE Slade, 2D; COPAC. LOCATION D, L, NUC, InND Loeber coll.

COMMENTARY This is one of the very few works of Irish fiction, initially written in English, that was contemporaneously translated into Irish and published with its English text. 'Forgive and forget' is from *The parent's assistant* (London, 1796, 3 parts), while 'Rosanna' was first published in *Popular tales* (London, 1804, 3 vols.) [Slade; RL].

E37　*Helen, a tale* (by Maria Edgeworth).

+ London: Richard Bentley, 1834, 3 vols. SOURCE Slade, 26A; Rafroidi, ii, p. 153; Sadleir, 771; Wolff, 1991; Garside 2, 1834:24. LOCATION Corvey CME 3–628–47569–4, Grail, D, Dt (1850, 1 vol. edn), L, NUC.

+ Paris: A. Guyot, 1834, 3 vols. (trans. by Mme L.Sw[anton] Belloc as *Hélène*). SOURCE Slade, 26C; Rafroidi, ii, p. 363; Sadleir, 771a. LOCATION L.

Paris: Baudry's European Library, 1834 (Modern British Novels and Romances Series, No. 55). SOURCE Slade, 26C. LOCATION D (1837 edn), NUC, InND Loeber coll. (1837 edn).

Amsterdam: M.H. Schonekat, 1835, 3 vols. (trans. into Dutch by J.J. Abbink as *Helena, of waarheid en logen: Eene schets der hedendaagsche groote wereld*). SOURCE Adamnet. LOCATION UVA.

Brussels: Meline [n.d.] (trans. by Louise Sw[anton]-Belloc as *Hélène*). SOURCE GLOG. LOCATION Universitätsbibliothek, Leipzig.

Aachen, Leipzig: Jacob Anton Mayer, 1834, 3 vols. (trans. by C. Richard as *Helene*). SOURCE Garside 2, 1834:24; COPAC. LOCATION L.

+ Philadelphia; Carey, Lea & Blanchard; Boston: Allen & Ticknor, 1834, 2 vols. SOURCE Kaser, 442; Sadleir, 771b; OCLC. LOCATION NUC, PU, InND Loeber coll.

New York: Carey, Lea & Blanchard; Boston: Allen & Ticknor, 1834, 2 vols. SOURCE Slade, 26C; Topp 1, p. 261. LOCATION NUC.

+ London, New York: Pandora, 1987 (as *Helen*). LOCATION Dt, L, InND Loeber coll.

COMMENTARY According to the Bentley Papers, 'This story had almost the largest circulation of any novel of its time in three-volume form, except Sir Walter Scott's [novels]'. A novel of domestic and fashionable life. A much corrected copy of *Helen* is in the BL (Add. MS 28,524–5) [Todd, p. 206; Garside 2, 1834:24; Slade, p. 199].

E38　*Le petit trésor des enfants bien sages, ou choix de jolis contes moraux, propres à les faire persévérer dans le bien* (by Maria Edgeworth).

Paris: Fruger & Brunet, 1836. SOURCE Slade, 4D. LOCATION NN.

E39　*Harry and Lucy* (by Maria Edgeworth).

+ London: Baldwin & Cradock & George Routledge, 1840, 3rd edn (as *Harry and Lucy*; revsd and corrected). LOCATION D.

London, New York: Routledge & Sons, [1856] (as *Harry and Lucy: to which are added The little dog Trusty, The cherry orchard, and The orange man*). LOCATION L (1860 edn), NUC.

Boston: Munroe & Francis, [185?] (as *Edgeworth's Harry and Lucy. With an address to mothers. The stories of Little dog Trusty, The orange man, and The cherry orchard*). LOCATION NUC.

New York: C.S. Francis & Co., 1859 (as *Harry and Lucy: with the stories of Little dog Trusty, the orange man & The cherry orchard & An address to mothers*). LOCATION NUC.

COMMENTARY 'Harry and Lucy' was originally published in *Early lessons* (London, 1801, 10 vols.); 'Little dog trusty was first published in *The parent's assistant* (London, 1796, 3 parts);

COMMENTARY 'The orange man', and 'The cherry orchard' were first published in *Early lessons* (London, 1801, 10 vols.) [RL].

E40   *Contes de Miss Edgeworth dédiée à la jeunesse comprenant les contes moraux, les contes des familles et les contes populaires* (by Maria Edgeworth).
Paris: Didier, 1842, 2 vols. (trans. by Ernest Garnier). LOCATION NUC.
COMMENTARY Stories from *Moral tales* (London, 1801, 5 vols.), *The parent's assistant* (London, 1796, 3 parts), and *Popular tales* (London, 1804, 3 vols.) [RL].

E41   *Illustrated tales for children* (by Maria Edgeworth).
Paris: J.H. Truchy, 1845 (ill.). SOURCE Devonshire, p. 462; COPAC (1850 edn). LOCATION D (1850 edn).
COMMENTARY No copy of the Paris, 1845 edn located. Contents of the 1850 edn: 'The bracelets', 'The orphans', 'Waste not, want not', 'Lazy Lawrence', 'Simple Susan', 'The good French governess', 'Orlandino'. The stories are from *The parent's assistant* (London, 1800, 3 parts) and *Moral tales* (London, 1801, 5 vols.), while 'Orlandino' was first published in Edinburgh in 1845 [COPAC; RL; but see, Slade, pp 202–4].

E42   *Frank; a tale, in two parts; to which are prefixed, The little dog Trusty; The cherry-orchard; and The orange-man* (by Maria Edgeworth).
+ Paris: Baudry's European Library, 1846. SOURCE Hart cat. 41/75. LOCATION InND Loeber coll.
COMMENTARY 'Frank' originally appeared in *Early lessons* (London, 1801, 10 vols.); the remaining stories were originally published in *The parent's assistant* (London, 1796, 3 parts) [RL].

E43   *Orlandino* (by Maria Edgeworth).
Edinburgh: William & Robert Chambers, 1848 (ill. G. Millar; Chambers's Library for Young People, [No. 1]). SOURCE Slade, 27A; Rafroidi, ii, p. 153; Osborne, p. 248; Sadleir, 778. LOCATION Grail, L, CaOTP, NUC.
+ London, Edinburgh: William & Robert Chambers, [185?] (ill.; Chambers's Library for Young People). LOCATION D (1871 edn), NUC, InND Loeber coll.
Paris: Baudry, 1849 (Juvenile Library Series, No. 46). SOURCE Slade 27C.
COMMENTARY *Paris edn* No copy located [RL].
Boston: Gould, Kendall & Lincoln, 1848 (Chambers's Library for Young People). SOURCE NCBEL 3, p. 668. LOCATION NUC.
COMMENTARY According to Osborne, this temperance story was written for the benefit of the Irish Poor Relief Fund, but the publisher's preface states that the volume is about self-denial and was expressly written for Chambers's Library for Young People. Orlandino, a young boy who ran away from home and joined a travelling entertainment group, returns to the area where his mother lives. He meets a boy called Walter who, with his family, tries to do good in the neighbourhood. Orlandino tells Walter his sorry story and the extent to which he is in debt. Walter's family is willing to assist Orlandino on condition that he will not drink for a year. Walter denies himself some pleasures in order to help Orlandino, who sticks to his promise and is asked by a learned doctor to become his secretary. In this way he is able to support his impoverished mother and sister [ML; Osborne].

E44   *Lazy Lawrence and other stories* (by Maria Edgeworth).
New York: D.J. Williams, [1850?]. LOCATION NUC.
COMMENTARY Stories originally published in *The parent's assistant* (London, 1796, 3 parts), *Moral tales* (London, 1801, 5 vols.), and *Popular tales* (London, 1804, 3 vols.): 'Lazy Lawrence', 'The basket-woman', 'The birthday present', 'Mademoiselle Panache', 'The barring out', 'The mimic' [RL].

E45   *Early lessons* (by Maria Edgeworth).
London, New York: George Routledge & Co., 1856 (ill. Birket Foster). LOCATION L.

+ London, New York: George Routledge & Sons, [1878 or earlier, judging from inscription] (new edn; ill. Birket Foster). SOURCE RL. LOCATION InND Loeber coll.

COMMENTARY Contents [combination of original series and continuation]: 'Little dog Trusty', 'The orange-man', 'The cherry orchard' [CM].

E46   *Rosamond: A series of tales* (by Maria Edgeworth).
London, New York: George Routledge & Sons, 1856. SOURCE COPAC. LOCATION E (not located), NUC.
Boston: Crosby, Nichols, Lee & Co., 1861, 2 vols. in 1. LOCATION NUC.
Baltimore: Kelly & Piet, 1868 (as *Rosamond: A series of tales for girls*). LOCATION NUC.

E47   *The purple jar, and other tales* (by Maria Edgeworth).
+ London, New York: Routledge, Warne & Routledge, 1860. LOCATION InND Loeber coll.

COMMENTARY Stories from *The parent's assistant* (London, 1796, 3 parts) and *Early lessons* (London, 1801, 10 vols.). Contents: 'The purple jar', 'The two plums', 'The injured ass', 'Rosamond's day of misfortunes', 'Rivuletta', 'The hyacinths', 'The party of pleasure', 'The black bonnet' [RL; Field Day, iv, pp 1148–51 ('The purple jar')].

E48   *Waste not, want not, and other tales* [anon.].
+ London: Ward & Lock, [1862] (ill.). LOCATION L.

COMMENTARY Contents: 'The golden touch', 'Waste not, want not; or, two strings to your bow' (originally published in *The parent's assistant*, London, 1796, 3 parts), 'The bracelets', 'The bank note', 'Unlucky Friday', 'The Sabbath: Sketches from a note-book of an elderly gentleman'. The last three stories are not by ME [RL].

E49   *Frank; The contrast, and other tales* (by Maria Edgeworth).
+ London: W. & R. Chambers, [1866] (ill. J.M. Corner). LOCATION L, InND Loeber coll.
Edinburgh: E. & S. Livingston, [1866]. LOCATION NUC.

COMMENTARY Contents: 'Frank' (originally published in *Early lessons*, London, 1801, 10 vols.), 'The contrast' (originally published in *Popular tales*, 3 vols.), 'The cherry orchard', 'The orange-man; or the honest boy and the thief' (the last two originally published in *The parent's assistant*, London, 1796, 3 parts) [RL].

E50   *The bracelets and The good French governess; two stories for girls* (by Maria Edgeworth).
+ London: Houlston & Wright, [1868] (new edn; ill.). LOCATION NUC, InND Loeber coll.

COMMENTARY Stories originally published in *The parent's assistant* (London, 1796, 3 parts) and *Moral tales* (London, 1801, 5 vols.), respectively [RL].

E51   *Harry and Lucy; Lame Jervas, and The grateful negro* (by Maria Edgeworth).
London, Edinburgh: W. & R. Chambers, 1873.

COMMENTARY First published in *Early lessons* (London, 1801, 10 vols.), and *Popular tales* (London, 1804, 3 vols.) [RL].

E52   *Miss Edgeworth's moral and popular tales* (by Maria Edgeworth; re-ed. and revsd by Laura Valentine).
+ London: Frederick Warne & Co.; New York: Scribner, Welford & Armstrong, 1874 (new edn; ill.). LOCATION L, NUC.
+ London, New York: George Routledge & Sons, [1881] (as *Moral and popular tales*). LOCATION L.

COMMENTARY Contents (except play): 'Forester', 'Angelina; or, L'amie inconnue', 'The Prussian vase', 'The good aunt', 'The good French governess', 'Mademoiselle Panache', 'Lame Jervas', 'The will', 'The Limerick gloves', 'Out of debt, out of danger', 'The lottery', 'Rosanna', 'Murad the unlucky', 'The manufacturers', 'The contrast', 'The grateful negro', 'To-morrow'. The stories were first published in *Moral tales for young people* (London, 1801, 5 vols.), and *Popular tales* (London, 1804, 3 vols.). The revsd stories were republished by Warne in 1889 in four separate vols. [ML; RL].

E53 **Classic tales** (by Maria Edgeworth).
Boston: Roberts Bros, 1883. LOCATION L, NUC.
New York: John W. Lovell, [1883]. LOCATION NUC.
COMMENTARY *Boston edn* Contents: 'Simple Susan', 'The mimic', 'Waste not, want; or, two strings to your bow', 'Mademoiselle Panache', 'Angelina; or, l'amie inconnue', 'The orphans'. The stories are from *The parent's assistant* (London, 1796, 3 parts), and *Moral tales* (London, 1801, 5 vols.) [NUC; RL].

E54 **Stories of Ireland** (by Maria Edgeworth).
+ London, New York: George Routledge & Sons, 1886 (Morley's Universal Library, No. 36; introd. by Henry Morley). LOCATION D.
COMMENTARY Contents: 'Castle Rackrent', 'The absentee' [RL].

E55 **Murad the unlucky, and other tales** (by Maria Edgeworth).
London: Cassell, 1889 (ed. by Henry Morley; Cassell's National Library). LOCATION L.
+ Dublin, Belfast: Blackie & Son, n.d. (includes notes). LOCATION InND Loeber coll.
COMMENTARY Contents: 'Murad the unlucky', 'The Limerick gloves', 'Madame de Fleury'. The first two stories were originally published in *Popular tales* (London, 1804, 3 vols.); the last story was originally published in *Tales of fashionable life* (London, 1809, 3 vols.) [RL].

E56 **The orphans, and other tales** (by Maria Edgeworth).
London, New York, Glasgow, Manchester: George Routledge & Sons, [1890]. LOCATION L.
COMMENTARY The first story originally was published in *The parent's assistant* (London, 1796, 3 parts) [RL].
COLLECTED WORKS

E57 **Tales and miscellaneous pieces** (by Maria Edgeworth).
+ London: R. Hunter; Baldwin, Cradock & Joy, Longman, Hurst, Rees, Orme & Co., J. Booker; Sherwood, Jones & Co., G.B. Whittaker, Harding, Triphook & Lepard, A.K. Newman & Co., R. Scholey, R. Saunders, T. Tegg, Hamilton, Adams & Co., Simpkin & Marshall, T. Mason, J. Duncan, Smith & Elder, 1825, 14 vols. SOURCE Slade, 29A; Rafroidi, ii, p. 153; Sadleir, 784; Wolff, 1995. LOCATION Grail, D, L, NUC.

E58 **Tales and novels** (by Maria Edgeworth).
+ London: Baldwin, Cradock, J. Murray, J. Booker, A.K. Newman & Co., Whittaker, Treacher & Arnot, T. Tegg, Simpkin & Marshall, E. Hodgson, Houlston & Son, J. Templeman, J. Bain, R. Mackie, Renshaw & Rush, G. & J. Robinson, 1832–33, 18 vols. (ill. W. Harvey, H. Robinson, C. Rolls, T.S. England, J.W. Cook). SOURCE Slade, 29B; Rafroidi, ii, p. 153; Sadleir, 785. LOCATION Grail, D, L, NUC.

E59 **Miss Edgeworth's stories for children.**
London: Longman & Co., T. Tegg, Hamilton & Co., Whittaker & Co., J. Murray, Smith, Elder & Co., Sherwood & Co., H. Washbourne, Houlston & Co., E. Lumley, Darton & Clark, Orr & Co., G. Routledge, Simpkin, Marshall & Co., 1846 [at least 32 vols] (see Plate 32). LOCATION InND Loeber coll. (Nos. 21–23, 30–32 only).
COMMENTARY Issued in paper cover, printed strap work in red and black; priced at 6*d*. [RL].

E60 **Tales and novels** (by Maria Edgeworth).
+ London: Whittaker & Co., Simpkin, Marshall & Co., H. Washbourne, H.G. Bohn, E. Hodgson, H. Renshaw, J. Bain, Houlston & Stoneman, J. Murray, R. Mackie,

Orr & Co., Smith, Elder & Co., Routledge & Co., Tegg & Co., R.S. Parry; Liverpool: G. & J. Robinson, 1848, 9 vols. (ill. W. Harvey, F. Engleheart, C. Rolls, E. Goodall, E. Smith, F. Bacon, H. Robinson, J.W. Cook). LOCATION D, Dt, InND Loeber coll.

E61   *Tales and novels* (by Maria Edgeworth).
+ London: Simpkin, Marshall & Co., Whittaker & Co., E. Hodgeson, Washbourne & Co., H.G. Bohn, Smith, Elder & Co., Halston & Stoneman, J. Bain, H. Renshaw, Tegg & Co., Routledge & Co., C. Templeman, Willis & Sotheran; Liverpool: G. & J. Robinson, 1857, 10 vols. LOCATION D, L.

E62   *Miss Edgeworth's tales.*
+ London: T.J. Allman, 1857, 16 vols. (new edn; New Juvenile Library; ill.). LOCATION NUC, InND Loeber coll. (vols. 1, 3, 9 only).

COMMENTARY Most of the known titles are from the advertised in *The birth-day present and Lazy Lawrence*. It is possible that the series already existed by 1857 because a volume. *The white pigeon – The mimic* was published by Allman in that year [RL; NUC].

E63   *Edgeworth's tales.*
+ London, New York: George Routledge & Co., 1858, [unknown number of vols]. LOCATION D (one vol. only).

E64   *Edgeworth's Juvenile Library.*
London: T.J. Allman, 1860 (new edn) [unknown number of vols]. LOCATION D (one vol. only).

E65   *Tales and novels* (by Maria Edgeworth).
+ London: Henry G. Bohn, Simpkin, Marshall & Co., 1874, 10 vols. (ill. J. Franklin, W. Greatbatch, W. Harvey, E. Finden, E. Goodall; H. Robinson, C. Rolls, E. Smith, J. Goodyear, F. Engleheart, J.W. Cook; F. Bacon). LOCATION D, DPL (1874 edn), InND Loeber coll.

E66   *Tales and novels* (by Maria Edgeworth).
+ London, New York: George Routledge & Sons, [before 1887], 10 vols. (ill. W. Harvey, C. Rolls). LOCATION D.

E67   *Miss Edgeworth's stories.*
+ London, Glasgow, Manchester, New York: George Routledge & Sons, 1893, 19 vols. LOCATION L, InND Loeber coll. (2 vols. only).

COMMENTARY A full list was advertised in M. Edgeworth, *The Limerick gloves*, which is part of this series [RL].

E68   *The novels of M. Edgeworth.*
London: J.M. Dent & Co.; New York: Dodd, Mead & Co., 1893, 12 vols. (ill.; edn of 250 copies). SOURCE Rafroidi, 2, p. 153. LOCATION L, NUC.

E69   *[Maria. Edgeworth's works].*
Boston: Wells & Lilly, [1815–19?], [at least 17 vols.] (ill. [Alexander] Anderson). SOURCE Welch, 309.1*ff.* SOURCE OCLC.

COMMENTARY Not listed as collected works, but obviously part of a series [RL].

E70   *Works of Maria Edgeworth.*
+ Boston: Samuel H. Parker; Munroe & Francis; Philadelphia, Trenton: E. Littell; New York: R. Norris Henry, [1822?–26], 13 vols. (vols. 1–6 issued as part of 12 vols. set). SOURCE Slade 29C (mentions slightly different set of publishers). LOCATION NUC, InND Loeber coll. (vols. 2, 7, 9–12 only).

E71   *Tales and novels* (by Maria Edgeworth).
New York: J. & P. Harper, 1832–33, 10 vols. COMMENTARY *New York 1832–33 edn*. Mentioned on extra title page of volume 2 in 1836 edn [RL].

+ New York: Harper & Bros, 1833–34, 18 vols. in 9 (ill. W. Harvey, Prudhomme, A. Dick, Pendleton; vol. no. on spine is indicated in square brackets). LOCATION NUC, InND Loeber coll. (vol. 4 only). COMMENTARY *New York 1833–34 edn* Green cloth binding embossed with flower design, vol. number on spine [RL].

+ New York: Harper & Bros, 1835–36, 18 vols. in 9 [and one added probably] (ill. W. Harvey, Prudhomme, A. Dick). LOCATION NUC, InND Loeber coll. (vols. 1, 2, 4–5, 7–9 only). COMMENTARY *New York 1835–36 edn* Two types of bindings: (a) plain green uniformly embossed, with gold printing and harp on spine; (b) brown cloth embossed with leave design, and gold on spine with harp [RL].

New York: Harper & Bros, 1839, 18 vols. in 9 (ill.). LOCATION InND (2 vols. only).

+ New York: Harper & Bros, 1845–46, 18 vols. in 9 (ill. W. Harvey, Prudhomme, Pendleton). LOCATION NUC (appeared in 10 vols.), InND Loeber coll. (3 vols. only).

+ New York: Harper & Bros, 1850, 20 vols. in 10 (ill. W. Harvey, Prudhomme, A. Dick, S.H. Gimber, Pendleton; J.L. Morton). LOCATION InND Loeber coll.

+ New York: Harper & Bros, 1856, 20 vols. in 10 (ill. W. Harvey, Prudhomme). LOCATION InND Loeber coll. (3 vols. only).

E72   *The juvenile works of Maria Edgeworth.*
+ New York: Harper & Bros, 1836, 5 vols. SOURCE Adv. in M. Edgeworth, *Rosamond: with other tales*, which is part of this series. LOCATION NUC, InND Loeber coll. (one vol. only). COMMENTARY Stayed in print until at least 1843, when the series was advertised in *Rosamond: with other tales*. In that year, *Rosamond: with other tales* appeared as part of the School District Library, No. 243 [RL].

E73   *The novels and selected works of Maria Edgeworth* (general eds. M. Butler & M. Myers).
Brookfield (VT): Pickering & Chatto, 1999–2003, 12 vols. SOURCE COPAC. LOCATION L.

SPURIOUS WORKS (wholly or partially). For review of and discussion of spurious works, see the biographical sketch on ME above and Slade (pp 132, 134, 136–7, 152–3, 178, 186).

E74   *Rosamond, parts I–IV and the sequel* (by 'Maria Edgeworth').
Boston: Munroe & Francis, [after 1801], 2 vols. SOURCE Slade, 21C; OCLC. LOCATION NUC.
COMMENTARY None of the stories is by ME. Contents: 'Rosamond' (containing the stories: 'Petty scandal', Airs and graces', 'The nine days' wonder', 'Egerton Abbey', 'The black lane', 'The palanquin', 'The forest drive', 'Morning visits', 'The bracelet of memory', 'Blind Kate', 'The print gallery', 'The departure') [Slade].

E75   *The watch-girl, a novel* (by 'Miss Edgeworth').
[London?], [publisher?], [1808], 3 vols. SOURCE C.N. Greenough card coll., MH.
COMMENTARY No copy located [RL].

E76   *Tales of real life; forming a sequel to Miss Edgeworth's Tales of fashionable life* [anon.].
London: Henry Colburn, 1810, 3 vols. SOURCE OCLC; British Fiction. LOCATION CLU.
Philadelphia: J. & A.Y. Humphreys, 1810. SOURCE OCLC. LOCATION Rutgers Univ.
COMMENTARY Seems to have taken advantage of ME's reputation, but does not appear to have an Irish connection. Announced in newspapers to be published in 1810. When Johnson, Maria Edgeworth's publisher complained, subsequent advs stated that it was merely a sequel to Maria

Edgeworth's§ *Tales of fashionable life* (London, 1809). Probably different from the spurious *Tales of real life* (London, 1817) by 'Mrs Edgeworth'§ [RL; Slade, p. 130].

E77　*La mère intrigante* (by 'Mlle Edgeworth').
+ Paris: Galignani, 1811, 2 vols. (trans. by J. Joly). SOURCE Slade, 14C; Rafroidi, ii, p. 363 (1812 edn). LOCATION D, L.
COMMENTARY A spurious work, not by ME. No Irish content [ML].

E78　void

E79　*Forget and forgive* (by 'Maria Edgeworth' and Alexander Anderson).
New Haven (CT): John Babcock & Son.; Charleston (SC): S. Babcock & Co., 1823. SOURCE OCLC. LOCATION NUC.
COMMENTARY Aside from 'Forget and forgive' (originally published in *The parent's assistant*, London, 1796, 3 parts), the volume contains Indian stories [NUC].

E80　*True charity: or, a tale of the year 1800* (by the author of *Moral tales* [*sic*]).
+ London: Poole & Edwards, 1827 (ill. Harvey, J. McGahey. LOCATION L.
COMMENTARY Spurious novel, not by ME [RL].

E81　*Real life; or, every day occurrences, a tale. Being a sequel to Tales of fashionable life* (by 'Maria Edgeworth').
London: Charles Knight, 1828, 2 vols. SOURCE OCLC. LOCATION MH.

E82　*Familien-Erziehung. In einer Reihe moralischer Erzählungen für Jugend von 5 bis 12 Jahren* (by 'Maria Edgeworth').
+ Duedlinburg, Leipzig: Gottfr. Basse, [1835 or earlier], 2nd edn (ill.; trans. by Fr. Uberobt). LOCATION InND Loeber coll.
COMMENTARY Probably abbreviated stories: 'Heinrich und Lucie' (first part), 'Franz', 'Rosamunde. Das blau Glas', 'Heinrich und Lucie' (second part), 'Rosamunde. Die Rosenknospe', 'Heinrich und Lucie. Der Elephant', 'Rosamunde. Die schwarze Hut' [RL].

EDGEWORTH, Richard Lovell, b. Bath (Avon) 1744, d. Edgeworthstown (Co. Longford) 1817. Inventor, writer, education theorist, reforming landlord and MP, RLE was the second son of Richard Edgeworth, an Irish landlord and MP, and Rachel Jane Lovell, daughter of a Welsh judge. His first tutor was Patrick Hughes of Edgeworthstown, who had been one of Oliver Goldsmith's§ teachers. RLE was admitted at TCD in 1760 but after only six months, his father removed him, because of his misbehaviour, to Corpus Christi College, Oxford, in 1761. In his free time he stayed at the estate of his father's friend, Paul Elers of Black Bourton, near Oxford, whose daughter Anna Maria (d. 1773), became his first wife. Subsequently he married Honora§ (1751–80), daughter of Maj. Edward Sneyd, of Byrkley Lodge (Staffs.); Elizabeth Sneyd (1753–97), Honora's sister, and Frances Anne Beaufort§ (1769–1865) of Navan (Co. Meath). RLE's many interests in engineering and mechanics included telegraphy, transport engineering, the design of roads and vehicles, and agricultural machinery. He received an honorary gold medal for mechanical inventions from the Royal Society of Arts in England and was a member of the Lunar Society of Birmingham, a group of inventors, scientists and industrialists that included James Watt and Josiah Wedgwood, to whom RLE suggested possible designs for dishes for meat pies. After settling in Ireland in 1782, he turned his attention to managing the neglected Edgeworth estate and to a study of children's education. His large family of, eventually, twenty-two children provided ample opportunities for practical application of his educational theories. These were based on intensive studies in child psychology and grounded in the treatment of children as rational beings who should be encouraged to think systemically rather than to repeat information, parrot-like. He and his second wife, Honora Sneyd Edgeworth§, had planned a three-volume work to be called *Practical education*, but only volume two was printed, anonymously, in 1780, the year of Honora's death.

In 1791 and 1792 Maria Edgeworth§ assisted her father in completing the work and it was published by Joseph Johnson in London in two volumes. in 1798. A second edn 'by Maria and R.L. Edgeworth' was published in 1801 and was widely translated, drawing much attention on the Continent. With Maria he wrote *Essays on professional education* (London, 1809). He contributed the story 'Ormond' to Maria Edgeworth's *Harrington, a tale; and Ormond, a tale* (London, 1817). Other educational works written by RLE included a reading book for children: *A rational primer* (London, 1799); *Poetry explained for young people* (London, 1802); *Readings on poetry* (London, 1816), and *School lessons* (Dublin, privately printed, 1817), the latter written for his son Lovell's school at Edgeworthstown. Confusingly, another volume, also entitled *School lessons*, was authored by RLE (Dublin, privately printed, 1817), which contains fables and myths written for boys. RLE wrote his first narrative storybooks for children with his second wife, Honora, and wrote another two children's stories later in life. With Maria he published *Essay on Irish bulls* (London, 1802). He wrote the first volume of his autobiography, but Maria completed the second volume (London, 1820, 2 vols.). There is little doubt that RLE exercised much influence on Maria Edgeworth's writings, but according to Butler, his role as co-author of her fiction is less than it was formerly thought to be. Politically he was a liberal, a supporter of the Irish parliament of 1782 and of Catholic emancipation. Although the family had to leave Edgeworthstown during the 1798 rebellion and narrowly escaped the rebels, he voted against the Union, disgusted with the corruption involved in bringing it about. He persuaded the government to construct a telegraph line from Dublin to Galway on the argument that the invasion of the French in 1798 made the experiment worthwhile, and he published *An essay on the construction of roads and carriages* (London, 1817). He was deeply concerned with optimizing education and became a member of the Irish Committee on Education. Josiah Wedgwood wrote of him, 'He is very sensible, acute and lively. He has many excellent notions of education and manners in general, with the nicer refinements and delicacies necessary to give the last finish and goût to the agreeables and pleasures of life' (Clarke, p. 90). For his portraits and papers, see ODNB. SOURCE Allibone i, p. 542; Butler, 271–304; H.J. Butler & H.E. Butler (eds), *The black book of Edgeworthstown and other Edgeworth memories* (London, 1927); D. Clarke, *The ingenious Mr Edgeworth* (London, 1965), passim; Colvin, pp xxii–xxiii; *Memoirs of Richard Lovell Edgeworth* (Boston, 1821), ii, pp 187–90; Elmes, p. 66; Field Day, iv, pp 837–40; W.H. Häusermann (ed.), *The Genevese background* (London, 1952), p. 91; HIP, iv, pp 105–6; OCIL, pp 168–9; ODNB; Scott (correspondence with Sir Walter Scott); D. Spender (ed.), *Living by the pen* (New York, 1992), pp 137–59; RIA/DIB; B. & H. Wedgwood, *The Wedgwood circle 1730–1897* (Don Mills, ON, 1980); J. Uglow, *The lunar men* (London, 2002).

E83   *Practical education: or, the history of Harry and Lucy. Vol. 2* [anon.] (by Richard Lovell Edgeworth and Honora Edgeworth§; dedicated to Dr [Joseph] Priestley). Lichfield: Printed [for the authors?] by J. Jackson, and sold by J. Johnson, 1780, 2 vols. (ill.). SOURCE Slade, p. 5; ESTC t211330. LOCATION C (vol. 2 only).

COMMENTARY Further publication of volumes 1 and 3 was interrupted by the death of Honora Edgeworth§ in 1780. Educational fiction for children, with Harry and Lucy asking questions and their parents giving answers, 'calculated to make brick making, or many other processes, intelligible to the very young'. The stories were intended to form the second volume in a set of three, but the first and third volumes were never written. A slightly amended version of volume 2 was later published under Maria Edgeworth's§ and Richard Lovell Edgeworth's§ authorship in *Early lessons* (London, 1801, 10 vols.) [Butler, p. 63; ODNB; Welch].

E84   *The history of the Freeman family* (by Richard Lovell Edgeworth).

COMMENTARY Unpublished manuscript, written in or shortly after 1787 (current location unknown), based on stories told by RLE to his third wife, Elizabeth Sneyd, and their children. Consists of the story of two families, one making its way in the world by independent efforts, the other by means of art and by courting the great. It formed the basis later for Maria Edgeworth's§ *Patronage* (London, 1814, 4 vols.) [Memoirs, ii, pp 192–3; ODNB (see also Maria Edgeworth)].

E85   *Essay on Irish bulls* (by Richard Lovell Edgeworth and Maria Edgeworth§).
    London: J. Johnson, 1802. SOURCE COPAC; Slade, 9A. LOCATION D, L, C.
    London: J. Johnson, 1803, 2nd edn (corrected). SOURCE Slade, 9B. LOCATION E, L (1808, 3rd edn), O (1808, 3rd edn), C (1808, 3rd edn), InND Loeber coll. (1808, 3rd edn).
    COMMENTARY *London 1803 and 1808 edns* The 1803 and the 1808 edn have been revsd and shortened [RL].
    + New York: Printed by J. Swaine, 1803 (ill.). SOURCE Slade 9C. LOCATION InND Loeber coll.
    + Philadelphia: Printed by William Duane, 1803 (ill. Akin). SOURCE Slade, 9C. LOCATION InND Loeber coll.

COMMENTARY Various examples of Irish bulls as well as several stories including 'Bath coach conversation', 'The Hibernian mendicant', 'Little Dominick' (born at Fort Reilly in Ireland), 'The Irish incognito'. However, the stories are not present in all edns [RL; Slade, 28(iii)].

EDGEWORTH, Sneyd. See **EDGEWORTH, Charles Sneyd**.

'EDGEWORTH, Theodore', possible pseud. fl. 1811. No such name is known among members of the Edgeworth family of Edgeworthstown (Co. Longford). It is plausible, as a reviewer in the *Monthly Review* (London, 2nd ser., 1811, p. 323) suggested, that the author might have used the Edgeworth name to advance his book. SOURCE Allibone i, p. 543; *Éire-Ireland*, 19 (1984), p. 118*n*.5; *The Parliamentary gazetteer of Ireland* (Dublin, 1846), i, p. 133; RIA/DIB; RL.

E86   *The shipwreck; or, memoirs of an Irish officer and his family* (by Theodore Edgeworth).
    + London: Thomas Tegg, 1811, 3 vols. SOURCE Brown, 548; British Fiction; Garside, 1811:32. LOCATION Corvey CME 3–628–7518–X, Ireland related fiction, D, Dt, L, NUC, InND Loeber coll.

COMMENTARY Capt. O'Neill, an Irish officer in the French service, is shipwrecked on the coast of Wicklow and befriended by a Maj. O'Hara. The story follows the fortunes of the two families and describes the life of squireens, the penal laws and life in TCD, all from an English perspective [Brown].

EDWARDS, Miss —. See **EDWARDS, Anna Maria**.

EDWARDS, Anna Maria, b. Ireland, fl. 1780 (known as **Miss Edwards?**). AME published her *Poems on various subjects* in Dublin in 1787, and in that volume she refers to a novel she had written. The most likely candidate is the one listed below by a Miss Edwards, but some uncertainty remains. SOURCE O'Donoghue, p. 130; Raven 2, 1780:15.

E87   *Otho and Rutha: A dramatic tale* (by Miss Edwards).
    Edinburgh: Printed by Murray & Cochran for the author, 1780. SOURCE Allibone, i, p. 544 [under Edwards, as *Otoa and Rutha*]; Raven 2, 1780:15; ESTC t145728. Location L.
    COMMENTARY A prose pastoral. The *Critical Review* stated that the tale was written in a style which resembles blank verse [Raven 2].

EDWARDS, C.L., fl. 1865. American novelist.

E88   *The Dacotah Queen, or, Pat Mulloney's pilgrimage: A romance of the Indian country* (by C.L. Edwards).

New York: Beadle & Co., 1865 (Beadle's Dime Fiction, No. 5). SOURCE Dime novels; OCLC. LOCATION Northern Illinois Univ.

New York: Beadle & Adams, 1892 (as An *Irish sport abroad; or, Pat Mulloney's adventures*; Beadle's Pocket Library, No. 435). SOURCE Dime novels; OCLC. LOCATION NNC.

COMMENTARY Dime novel. New York, 1865 edn consists of 44pp, while the New York, 1892 edn consists of 30pp [OCLC].

EDWARDS, R.W.K. See EDWARDS, Reginald Walter Kenrick.

EDWARDS, Reginald Walter Kenrick (known as R.W.K. Edwards), b. Isle of Wight 1862. English novelist and professor who was educated at Cambridge University. RWKE taught mathematics at the University of London and published mathematical textbooks. In 1884 he lived for a year in Ireland when he was a master at Foyle College (Co. Derry), and a frequent visitor to Donegal. SOURCE Brown, p. 98; Venn, part ii, vol. ii, p. 395.

E89   *Unchronicled heroes. A story of the siege of Londonderry, with an appendix of historical notes* (by R.W.K. Edwards).

Londonderry: William Gailey, 1888. SOURCE Brown, 550; Wolff, 2044; OCLC. LOCATION NUC.

COMMENTARY A chronicle of the siege of Derry in 1689. Revd George Walker, joint governor during the siege, and Presbyterian minister John Mackenzie, who questioned Walker's later glorification of his role, are introduced; the former highly lauded, the latter disparaged. The appendix, which comprises almost half of the book, gives extracts from rare documents relating to the siege [Brown].

E90   *The mermaid of Inish-uig* (by R.W.K. Edwards).

+ London: Edward Arnold, 1898. SOURCE Brown, 551. LOCATION D, L.

COMMENTARY A new lighthouse keeper settles in Inish-uig (Tory Island, Co. Donegal). He is a scoundrel, who leads 'Black Kate' astray. He tries to turn to account the illicit distilling by the people but is foiled [Brown].

E91   *Dick Vaughan's first turn* (by R.W.K. Edwards; dedicated to the Stevenagiangs of the Round Robin).

+ London: Wells Gardner, Darton & Co., [1901] (ill. Lancelot Speed). SOURCE COPAC. LOCATION L, InND Loeber coll.

COMMENTARY Contains reference to twins called Mulholland from Ulster. Otherwise no Irish content [CM].

EDWARDS, Rollin, fl. 1877. American novelist. According to the introd. to the volume below, RE resided for many years in the anthracite coal region of eastern Pennsylvania. SOURCE Allibone Suppl., i, p. 543.

E92   *Twice defeated, or the story of a dark society in two countries* (by Rollin Edwards; dedicated to the 'Judges of Schuylkill and Carbon Counties (PA), who, with great firmness and exact justice, presided at the Molly Maguire trials ...').

+ Philadelphia: J.B. Lippincott & Co., 1877. SOURCE Wright, iii, 1715. LOCATION L, NUC, InND Loeber coll.

COMMENTARY According to the author, the first half of the novel is indebted to William Steuart Trench's§ autobiographical *Realities of Irish life* (London, 1868). The second half is partly-based on the author's direct experiences in the coal regions of Pennsylvania. The story starts on the earl of Bath's estate in Co. Monaghan, where the tenants have learned not to pay the rent. A new agent, who is an extremely reasonable man, is finding it very difficult to collect any rent. The peasants, known as the Molly Maguires, organize into a Ribbon lodge and commit atrocities. One, when caught, turns informer, which gives the agent leverage to offer to a number of the tenants either emigration or the vengeance of the law. Many emigrate to the coal regions of Schuylkill and Carbon counties in Pennsylvania where they apply the same tactics of terrorism, in which again, in the end, they are defeated [ML].

EGAN, Maurice Francis, b. Philadelphia (PA) 1852, d. 1924. Irish-American novelist and short story writer whose father had emigrated to Philadelphia from Co. Tipperary. His mother, Margaret MacMullen, was of Scots-Irish descent. MFE was educated at LaSalle College, Philadelphia, and Georgetown College, Washington (DC), and became professor of English language and literature at the Catholic University of Washington (DC), and at the University of Notre Dame (IN). Later he was appointed American ambassador in Copenhagen (Denmark). He was a frequent contributor to American periodicals, became an associate editor of *Irish literature* (New York, 1904) and editor of the *Freeman's Journal* (presumably New York, 1881–8). He published a collection of sonnets, poems and legends, *Preludes* (Philadelphia: 1880). Further research may uncover Irish content in more of his many books. SOURCE Allibone Suppl., i, p. 544; Brown, p. 98; DAB; Fanning, pp 198, 379; Irish pseudonyms; McCarthy, iii, p. 1080; M.F. Egan, *Recollections of a happy life* (London, 1924); O'Donoghue, pp 130–1; RL.

E93　*A garden of roses. Stories and sketches* (by Maurice Francis Egan).
　　　+ Boston: Thomas B. Noonan & Co., 1887. SOURCE Blessing, p. 142; DCU, Catholic Americana files. LOCATION D.
COMMENTARY Consists of twenty-three stories of which four have Irish content: 'A sprig of shamrock'; 'A Christmas hymn'; 'Wilde by name and wilde by nature', and 'At school again' (which mentions Maria Edgeworth's§ *The parent's assistant*) [ML].

E94　*The disappearance of John Longworthy* (by Maurice Francis Egan).
　　　Notre Dame (IN): Office of the *Ave Maria*, 1890. SOURCE Fanning, p. 379; Wright, iii, 1717; OCLC. LOCATION CtY.
　　　New York: Arno Press, 1978. SOURCE OCLC. LOCATION NN.
COMMENTARY Deals with the Irish in New York [Wright].

E95　*The success of Patrick Desmond* (by Maurice Francis Egan; dedicated to Patrick O'Brien of South Bend, Indiana).
　　　+ Notre Dame (IN): Office of *Ave Maria*, 1893. SOURCE Brown, 552; Wright, iii, 1721; OCLC. LOCATION D, Dcc, NUC.

E96　*The vocation of Edward Conway* (by Maurice Francis Egan; dedicated to the author's mother [Margaret Egan]).
　　　+ New York, Cincinnati, Chicago: Benziger Bros, 1896. SOURCE Fanning, p. 379; Wright, iii, 1724; OCLC. LOCATION DCU.
COMMENTARY First published in *Ave Maria* (Notre Dame, IN). Set in New York State. Some of the characters are Irish [ML].

E97　*From the land of St. Lawrence. Sketches of French and American life* (by Maurice Francis Egan).
　　　St Louis: D. Herder, 1898. SOURCE Blessing, p. 142; RLIN. LOCATION NUC.
COMMENTARY Has Irish content [NUC].

E98　*The miles of sexton Maginnis* (by Maurice Francis Egan; dedicated to Theodore Roosevelt).

+ New York: The Century Co., [1902] (ill. Arthur I. Keller). SOURCE Brown, 553; Fanning, p. 379. LOCATION D (1909 edn).

+ Montreal: D. & J. Sadlier & Co., 1909 (ill. Arthur I. Keller; on spine: The Century Co.). LOCATION InND Loeber coll.

COMMENTARY A humorous social satire set in a Maryland town. The characters are almost all Catholic American-Irish of the lower classes, aspiring to respectability. Maginnis, the sexton, is full of guileless trickery and takes truth not too seriously [Brown].

EGAN, P.M. See **EGAN, Patrick M.**

EGAN, Patrick M. (known as **P.M. Egan**), fl. 1880s. Novelist, PME also wrote *History, guide, and directory of County and City of Waterford* (Kilkenny, [1895]) and several volumes. on geometry. SOURCE Brown, p. 99.

E99   *Scullydom: An Anglo-Irish story of to-day* (by P.M. Egan).
+ London: John & Robert Maxwell, [1886]. SOURCE Allibone Suppl., i, p. 544; Brown, 555. LOCATION D, L, InND Loeber coll.
+ London: R.E. King & Co., n.d. (as *Scullydom or husband no. 4. An Irish story of to-day*). LOCATION D.

COMMENTARY Scullydom is a term probably associated with William Scully of Co. Tipperary who was notorious for an armed affray with his tenants. The story is set in Kilkenny in the early–1880s. Lucifer Scully, a moneylender, accumulates much land and oppresses his tenants, who revolt. Scully spirits away Fred O'Brien's sweetheart. Many adventures ensue but in the end O'Brien and his sweetheart are united [Brown; Personal information, George Gossip, July 2003].

EGAN, Pierce, pseuds '**A real Paddy**' and '**An amateur**', b. probably in Dublin (but according to ODNB believed to be born in London) *c*.1774, d. London, 1849. Popular satirist, novelist and journalist, PE is credited with inventing modern sports journalism. He was the eldest son of James Egan, a labourer. His uncle was John Egan, a famous barrister and an Irish MP. The family moved to London early in his life. In 1786 he apprenticed to a printer, supplementing his income as a parliamentary reporter. Later he became a sports journalist and wrote *Sporting anecdotes* (London, 1807). He achieved fame with a history of pugilism, *Boxiana* (London, 1818–24), which appeared originally in monthly issues in 1812. In 1821 he began publication of the monthly *Life in London* (London) (ill. by George and Robert Isaac Cruikshank) which, with its scenes of high life and low life, became instantly popular and spawned several imitation publications and stage productions. Thackeray confessed to having been influenced by it. Soon PE was as popular a literary figure as Sir Walter Scott. In 1824 he began the periodical *Pierce Egan's life in London and sporting guide* (London), which merged with *Bell's Life* (London) and became the most-voluminous single record of nineteenth-century sport. Australian versions were published in Adelaide, Melbourne and Victoria. In 1827 he published his *Finish to life in London* and in 1834 he returned to Ireland to stage *Life in Dublin or Tom, Jerry and Logic on their travels* (never published). The Dublin newspapers commented on the novelty of depicting actual Dublin scenes on the stage. He also wrote verse, reported on criminal trials, and published a series of guides to Bath, Liverpool and Dublin. PE married Catherine Povey in 1806. Their son Pierce contributed to his father's works and became a writer of historical and romance novels. The elder PE's portrait was published by Reid. Some of his letters are in the BL. SOURCE Brady, p. 71; Brown, p. 99; Hogan 2, p. 403; NCBEL 2, pp 1279–80; NCBEL 4, pp 2141–2; OCIL, p. 169; ODNB;

O'Donoghue, p. 131; RIA/DIB; J.C. Reid, *Bucks and bruisers. Pierce Egan and Regency England* (London, 1971).

E100 *The mistress of royalty; or, the loves and Florizel and Perdita, portrayed in the amatory epistles, between an illustrious personage, and a distinguished female: with an interesting sketch of Florizel and Perdita, including other characters* [anon.].
London: P. Egan, 1814. SOURCE ODNB; British Fiction (Update 1). LOCATION L, NUC.
COMMENTARY A satire concerning the intrigue of George, prince of Wales, with Mrs Mary Robinson in the form of letters. Attribution in BL copy [NUC; OCIL; ODNB; British Fiction (Update 1)].

E101 *Real life in Ireland; or, the day and night scenes, rovings, rambles, and sprees, bulls, blunders, bodderation and blarney of Brian BORU, Esq. and his elegant friend Sir Shawn O'Dogherty; exhibiting a real picture of characters, manners, &c., in high and low life, in Dublin and various parts of Ireland. Embellished with humorous coloured engravings, from original designs by the most eminent artists* (by 'A real Paddy').
London: Jones & Co.; J.L. Marks, 1821 (ill. William Heath, Henry Alken). SOURCE Rafroidi, ii, p. 158; Brown, 554; Bradshaw, 7817; British Fiction; Garside, 1821:32. LOCATION D, BFl (n.d. edn), L, C.
+ London: Methuen & Co., 1904. LOCATION InND Loeber coll.
COMMENTARY Attributed to PE. Published in 18 parts, priced at 6*d*. Set in Ireland in the 1820s. Brian and his friend are what were then called bucks and bloods, who get into many adventures. George IV's visit to Ireland is described [Brown; Cumming cat. 92/16; Garside].

E102 *Life in London; or, the day and night scenes of Jerry Hawthorn, Esq., and his elegant friend Corinthian Tom, accompanied by Bob Logic, the Oxonian in their rambles and sprees through the metropolis* (by Pierce Egan; dedicated to King George IV).
London: Sherwood, Neely & Jones, 1821 (ill. I.R. & G. Cruikshank). SOURCE Block, p. 66; British Fiction; Garside, 1821:31. LOCATION Corvey CME 3–628–51309–X, L, NUC.
+ London: John Dicks, [1821] (as *Tom and Jerry; or, the day and night scenes of Jerry Hawthorn, Esq., and Corinthian Tom, accompanied by Bob Logic, the Oxonian, in their rambles and sprees through the metropolis*; ill. I. R. and G. Cruikshank). LOCATION NUC, InND Loeber coll.
New Orleans, LA: W. M'Kean, 1837, 2 vols. LOCATION NUC.
Philadelphia: E.L. Carey & A. Hart, 1837, 2 vols. LOCATION NUC.
COMMENTARY Adapted into a play, *Tom & Jerry, or, life in London* in 1821 [OCLC].

E103 *Real life in London; or, the rambles and adventures of Bob Tallyho, Esq. and his cousin, the Hon. Tom Dashall, through the metropolis; exhibiting a lively picture of fashionable characters, manners, and amusements in high and low life* (by 'An amateur').
London: Jones & Co., 1821–1822, 2 vols. (ill. Alken, Deighton, Brook, Rowlandson etc.). SOURCE Block, p. 66; British Fiction; Garside, 1821:33. LOCATION L, NUC.
COMMENTARY Title in second volume varies from that of the first volume [Garside].

E104 *The life and adventures of Samuel Denmore Hayward, the modern Macheath, giving an account of the extraordinary manner in which he raised himself from the mean situation of a tailor's apprentice, to an association with the most fashionable circles of society, his intrigues and villainies on the town, and final execution at the Old Bailey* (by Pierce Egan).
London: Sherwood & Co., 1822. LOCATION L, NUC.

E105   *The life of an actor* (by Pierce Egan; dedicated to Edmund Kean).
London: C.S. Arnold, 1825 (ill. Theodore Lane, Mr Thompson). SOURCE Block, p.
66; British Fiction; Garside, 1825:29. LOCATION Corvey CME 3–628–51310–3, L,
NUC.

E106   *Pierce Egan's anecdotes of the turf, the chase, the ring, and the stage.*
London: Knight & Lacey, 1827 (ill. T. Lane). LOCATION D, L.

E107   *Pierce Egan's finish to the adventures of Tom, Jerry and Logic in their pursuits
through life in and out of London* (dedicated to King George IV).
London: W. Strange, 1829. LOCATION L.
London, Manchester: G. Virtue, 1830 (ill. Robert Cruikshank). SOURCE Garside 2,
1830:44. LOCATION C.
+ London: John Dicks, n.d. (as *'Finish' or Tom and Jerry, being more life in and out of
London*; ill. Robert Cruikshank). LOCATION InND Loeber coll.

E108   *The pilgrims of the Thames, in search of the National!* (by Pierce Egan; dedicated,
by permission, to Queen Victoria).
London: W. Strange, 1838 (ill. Pierce Egan the Younger). SOURCE J & S, 156; Sadleir,
810 (1839 edn). LOCATION L, NUC.
COMMENTARY Penny dreadful [J & S, 156].

E109   *Captain MacHeath, or, the highwayman of a century since!: Interspersed with
numerous racy sketches of celebrated male and female characters* (by Pierce Egan).
London: F. Hextall, 1842 (ill. Pierce Egan the Younger). SOURCE NCBEL 4, p. 2142;
RLIN. LOCATION CtY.

'EGERTON, George', pseud. See DUNNE, Mary Chavelita.

'ELDON, Dr. Abraham', pseud. See WYSE, Thomas.

ELGEE, Jane Francesca. See WILDE, Lady Jane Francesca.

'ELIZABETH, Charlotte', pseud. See TONNA, Mrs Charlotte Elizabeth.

ELLIOTT, Mary Belson (also known as Mary Belson), b. 1794?, d. 1867? English author
and prolific writer of children's books, MBE was a Quaker and an anonymous author for the
Quaker publisher and engraver William Darton, who specialized in publishing children's books.
SOURCE Allibone, i, p. 552; NCBEL 4, pp 1786–7; ODNB [for William Darton]; Osgood, i,
pp 250–1; ii, pp 635, 881–2; Welch, 339–46.

E110   *The orphan boy; or, a journey to Bath. Founded on fact ... [part 2] The orphan
girl; or, sweets of benevolence. Being a sequel to The orphan boy* (by Mary Belson).
+ London: W. Darton, [1814] (ill. H. Corbould, C. Knight). SOURCE NCBEL 4, p.
1786. LOCATION L, NUC, InND Loeber coll.
New York: W.B. Gilley, 1816 (ill. Scoles). SOURCE Welch, 345.1–3. LOCATION NUC.
COMMENTARY The main story, which provides many occasions for moral lessons, is set in
England and unravels the mystery of a little orphan boy who lost his protector in an accident.
He meets several families willing to look after him who exert themselves to ascertain his origin. The mystery is solved by an Irish servant boy. The orphan turns out to be of Irish origin and is claimed by a rich uncle just returned from India. The second story is set in England
also and contrasts the life of a rich girl with that of a little orphan girl who sells matches. The
rich girl is touched by the misery of the orphan girl and asks her father to be allowed to set
up a school for six orphan girls to be trained in some useful fashion [ML].

ELLIOTT, Revd Robert, fl. 1796. Adventure and romance novelist, this author may possibly be the Revd Elliott of Waterford, who is identified as its author on the flyleaf of a copy in a private collection. However, the book has also been variously ascribed to Jane West and to Elizabeth Hervey. A note in the IBL states that the only Revd Elliott in the dioceses of Waterford and Lismore in the early-nineteenth century was the Revd Robert Elliott who in 1823 was appointed curate of Whitechurch and in 1828 became vicar of Ringagoonagh, where he remained until 1833. Both parishes are in the west of Co. Waterford, therefore the link between this author and the following volume, first published in 1796, remains elusive. SOURCE IBL (1947), p. 66.

E111   *The history of Ned Evans* [anon.].

+ London: G.G. & J. Robinson, 1796, 4 vols. SOURCE Raven 2, 1796:52; ESTC, t70090; Gecker, p. 113. LOCATION O, CtY.

+ Dublin: H. & T. Rice, Philadelphia, 1796, 2 vols. SOURCE Raven 2, 1796:52; Brown, 1660; Block, p. 250 (who mistakenly lists 4 vols.); Gecker, 1089; ESTC, t130957. LOCATION D (vol. 1 only), Dt (1797 edn), BFl (1805 edn), L, PU.

Dublin: John Milliken, 1796. SOURCE Pollard 2, p. 408.

+ Dublin: P. Wogan, 1797, 2 vols. (as *The history of Ned Evans. Interspersed with moral and critical remarks; anecdotes and characters of many persons well known in the polite world; and incidental strictures of the present state of Ireland*). SOURCE ESTC, t130957. LOCATION D, Dm (1805 edn).

Paris: Michel; Billois, 1800, 4 vols. (trans. as *Histoire de Ned Evans*). SOURCE Streeter, 42; Raven 2, 1796:52; COPAC. LOCATION Univ. of Leeds.

COMMENTARY Dublin 1796 edn published by Milliken has not been located. A story of romance and adventure. The hero, Ned Evans, is the son of a minister, born in Caernarvonshire (Wales). The story begins in 1799 when Ned brings home Lady Cecilia Rivers, daughter of the earl of Ravensdale in Ireland, and the body of her companion who had raised her after her mother's early death and who was killed when their coach is attacked by highwaymen. Lady Cecilia falls ill, but recovers slowly while living in the minister's home where she often speaks enthusiastically about Irish matters. She and Ned fall in love, although they both understand that their social positions are too different to contemplate marriage. While Ned's father is devising schemes to prevent his son from pining after Lady Cecilia, the earl of Ravensdale sends a letter which contains a commission for Ned. The regiment he is to join is in Ireland, and Ned travels there. A description of Dublin is given (with a note from the publisher of the 1805 edn to say that at the present time, Dublin has improved considerably). Ned is introduced to society and meets the family of Lord Ravensdale. Lord Squanderfield, an English nobleman, is a suitor to Lady Cecilia's hand. However, she still loves Ned. Ned's regiment sails for America, where he has many adventures during the American Revolutionary War. A stay with the Indians is recounted. Ned returns to Europe to find that he is the true earl of Ravensdale. He marries Lady Cecilia and they live in Ireland [ML; Falkner Greirson cat. 4/127; IBL, 30(2) (1947), pp 41, 66].

ELLIS, Edward S. See **ELLIS, Edward Sylvester**.

ELLIS, Edward Sylvester (known as **Edward S. Ellis**), pseud. '**Mahan A. Brown**', b. Geneva (OH) 1840, d. Cliff Island (ME) 1916. American teacher and prolific writer, ESE was the son of a famous rifle-shot and hunter, Sylvester Ellis, and his wife Mary Alberty. He grew up in New Jersey and received an MA from Princeton University in 1887. He was superintendent of the Trenton (NJ) public schools but at age 36 he resigned in order to devote himself to writing. He became a leading author of very successful dime novels; adventure stories for boys; inspirational biographies; histories, and textbooks in grammar, arithmetic, physiology and mythology. He wrote under a wide variety of pseuds, often favouring military titles. He edited *Golden Days* (Philadelphia), *Public Opinion* (a Trenton daily), and the *Boy's Holiday* (location not clear). ESE believed strongly in physical prowess and disapproved of cigarettes and alcohol. SOURCE Allibone Suppl., i, p. 551; ANB; Burke, p. 223; DAB; DLB, vol. 42; Dime novels; Hart, p. 227.

E112   *The Irish hunter; or, Pat Dogherty's adventures among the red skins* (by 'Mahan A. Brown').

New York: G. Munro, [1872]. LOCATION NUC.

New York: Beadle & Adams, 1880 (as *The Irish hunter; or, Pat Dogherty's adventures among the Indians*). SOURCE Brown 2, 153 (who mistakenly mentions his pseudynom as Mahlon A. Brown).

COMMENTARY Pat, with his Irish brogue, is a hunter in Missouri about 1840. He is always saving white people in the nick of time. Note that the DLB does not list this in Ellis's bibliography [Brown].

E113   *Adrift in the wilds; or, the adventures of two shipwrecked boys* (by Edward S. Ellis).

+ New York: A.L. Burt, 1887 (ill. Graves). SOURCE OCLC. LOCATION NUC, InND Loeber coll.

COMMENTARY Fiction for juveniles. Adventure story of two cousins, Howard and Elwood, who set out from New York by steamer to visit their parents in San Francisco. They are accompanied by a servant, Tim O'Rooney, and a Newfoundland dog called Terror. The ship catches fire and sinks near the California coast. They all make it to shore but the boys and Tim wander off inland, and miss the chance of being rescued by another boat, so they have to make their own way through the mountains. They meet with many adventures and are helped by a friendly Indian. Eventually, a search party finds them and takes them to their parents [ML].

E114   *The hunters of the Ozark* (by Edward S. Ellis).

Philadelphia: Porter & Coates, 1887. SOURCE OCLC. LOCATION NN.

+ London, Paris, New York, Melbourne: Cassell & Co., 1889 (ill.; The Deerfoot Series). LOCATION L.

COMMENTARY Fiction for juveniles set in the 1790s. Two boys, one American, one Irish, join Deerfoot, a heroic Shawanoe Indian warrior, in a trapping party in Missouri. They are captured by Winnebago Indians but delivered by the gallant Deerfoot [DLB, xlii].

ELMES, Revd John, fl. 1842. Cleric and short story writer, JE was resident in the province of Munster. Perhaps he can be identified with the JE (b. Cork *c.*1804), son of Thomas Elmes, who was admitted to TCD in 1824, and obtained his BA in 1830. JE was the author of *Quakerism exposed* (Limerick, 1842), and *Irish national education: The church and the Bible* (London, 1853). SOURCE B & S, p. 263; BLC; OCLC.

E115   *The last of the O'Mahoneys; and other historical tales of the English settlers in Munster* [anon.] (dedicated to the earl of Shannon).

+ London: Richard Bentley, 1843, 3 vols. SOURCE Brown, 62; BLC. LOCATION D, L.

COMMENTARY Author identified in the BLC. Historical fiction consisting of stories set in Co. Cork, chiefly around Bandon; all deal with the troubled times of the seventeenth century from the settlers' point of view. The Irish are described in negative terms. Contents: 'The last of the O'Mahoneys', 'The physician's daughter', 'The apprentice', 'Emma Cavendish', 'The puritan', Black Monday insurrection'. Appended to the stories are historical notes [Brown].

ELMORE, Wess, fl. 1884. American author.

E116   *The political biography of the Hon. Sylvester MacFinnigan, a man of high renown* (by Wess Elmore).

+ New York, Chicago, Washington: Brentano Bros, 1884 (ill. Frank Bellew, Chip).
LOCATION L.
COMMENTARY Set in the US. MacFinnigan's father was a member of the Orange Order [RL].

ELRINGTON, John. See **ELRINGTON, John Battersby.**

ELRINGTON, John Battersby (probably known also as John Battersby), pseud. 'Charles Sedley', fl. 1804. Novelist, translator and writer of licentious fiction. The probable identity of this novelist is clarified in *The Satirist* (London, *c*.1808–9), and reviewed in British Fiction. He wrote the preface to the following novel from Ramsgate (Kent). He is also the translator of *Confessions in Elysium; or the adventures of a platonic philosopher. From the German of C.M. Wieland* (London, 1804, 3 vols.), dedicated to Prince William Frederick of Gloucester. In the preface, the author states that it is a free translation to suit the English taste. SOURCE Allibone, i, p. 556; Personal communication, Jacqueline Belanger, Nov. 2001; British Fiction (Update 4, section B, and Addendum 1); for other possible works of fiction by JBE, see Block, NSTC, and British Fiction.

E117   *A winter in Dublin. A descriptive tale* (by 'Charles Sedley'; dedicated to Sheriff Phillips).
+ London: J.F. Hughes, 1808, 3 vols. SOURCE Brown 2, 1422; British Fiction; Garside, 1808:98, NSTC. LOCATION Corvey CME 3–628–48635–1 (1808, 3rd edn), Ireland related fiction, Dt, PC, L.
COMMENTARY Set in Ireland in the late 1790s. It describes Dublin and neighbourhood and Dublin high-society of the day. Mr Loftus leaves his fortune jointly to his nephew, Montague Burgoyne, and his niece, Ellen Perceval, if they marry within two years. Montague writes freeing Ellen and surrendering the fortune to her. She marries Col. Colville who shortly afterwards is put in command of the Dublin district. Ellen finds herself in fast society. Her husband is seduced by a Lady Butler; Ellen is pursued by a Mr Ponsonby. Husband and wife are reconciled, but then Montague appears on the scene. He and Ellen fall in love but keep apart (he on Rathlin Island, off the coast of Co. Antrim) until Col. Colville's death. Irish affairs are discussed in the preface, and throughout the novel there are footnotes to authenticate descriptions of Irish culture, politics, and history, perhaps showing the influence of Lady Morgan's§ *The Wild Irish Girl* (London, 1806, 3 vols.). There are fairly substantial descriptions of Irish landscape and customs. Often the long commentaries on subjects, such as the state of the Irish poor, seem to displace the fictional narrative [JB; Brown 2].

EMRA, Lucy (afterwards Groggon), fl. 1832. Poet, religious fiction and miscellaneous writer, LE was probably Irish. She published a volume of hymns (Dublin, 1850), and several volumes. of poetry in London (1832, 1836) and Sittingbourne [Kent] (1853). She wrote personal reminiscences and probably used her religious fiction in her work as a Sunday school teacher. Possibly she was related to Martha Pierce Rouch, née Emra, author of *Recollections of childhood; or, Sally, the faithful nurse* (London, 1840), and to the poet William Henry Atkinson Emra (1844–86). SOURCE Alston, p. 137; BLC; COPAC; MVP, p. 152; NCBEL 4, p. 336; RL.

E118   *Things new and old, or recollections by a district visitor, in prose and verse* (by Lucy Emra).
London: [publisher?], 1839. SOURCE L (destroyed).
COMMENTARY Religious fiction. No copy located [RL, BLC].

E119   *Things seen and known; or, a book of remembrance* [anon.].
London: [publisher?], 1844. SOURCE L (destroyed).
COMMENTARY Religious fiction. No copy located [RL, BLC].

E120   *Attempts at sketching* [anon.].
+ London: Hamilton, Adams & Co.; Bristol: J. Chilcott, 1846. SOURCE Pickering & Chatto cat. 739/57. LOCATION L.
COMMENTARY Partly literary pieces, mainly verse, the majority relating to Ireland. Contents: 'Glasnevin', 'Elliot, the missionary', 'Killarney, No. I', 'Killarney, No. II', 'Killarney, No. III', 'Killarney, No. IV', 'Olympia Morata (A tale of the reformation)', 'A New Zealand convert', 'A missionary meeting in the forest', 'Reminiscences', 'A school festival', 'The pool of Bethesda', 'Little kindness, or the sweet scented woodroofe', 'The isle of Portland', 'Recollections of pictures', 'St. Luke XXII. 35', 'Christmas time', '"Ireland and the Irish"' [ML].

E121   *Transcripts from my tablets by a lover of nature* [anon.] (dedicated to the author's fellow Sunday School teacher, Lady Jane Boyle).
+ Dublin: Printed [for the author?] by Goodwin, Son & Nethercott, 1849. SOURCE Pickering & Chatto cat. 739/58. LOCATION D, L (destroyed).
COMMENTARY Religious and nature stories, with some poems. Contents: 'Cool places', 'A dear old friend', 'Travelling – Somersetshire', 'Travelling – Worcestershire', 'Pictures', 'Sir Walter Raleigh's garden', 'The mines', 'Two walks', 'A little while together', 'Four-and forty hours', 'A disappointment', 'The first violets', 'The Moravian chapel', 'A scene in the Rotunda', 'The Belfast Botanic gardens', 'Kilrush and Kilkee', 'Ireland and the Irish, No. II', 'Ireland and the Irish, No. III', 'Ireland and the Irish, No. IV', 'A glimpse of Scotland', 'A glance at Edinburgh', 'Holyrood palace' [CD].

'ENGLISHMAN, A PLAIN', pseud. See SHEAHAN, Thomas.

ENNIS, Alice Margaret (Alicia), fl. 1817. Novelist. This writer may be identified with Miss Ennis, a friend of Dr Daniel Augustus Beaufort of Collon (Co. Louth), father of the authors Henrietta§ and Louisa Beaufort§. He asked his son Francis to arrange the printing of her 'Literary Folly' by the publisher Hunter in London. (Another letter to Francis Beaufort mentions the publisher Lloyd in London). Francis paid up to £124 for the publication of the volume, which probably refers to *Memoirs of the Montague family* (London, 1817) and had helped AME by reading the proofs, undoubtedly because he was in London while she was in Ireland. She signed the preface to her *The contested election* (London, 1820) at Grenville Street, Mountjoy Square, Dublin, in 1820, where she lived at least from 1817. She may be related to the F. Ennis who published *Complete system of modern geography* (Dublin, 1816). Branches of the Ennis family resided at Claremount, near Julianstown, and at Collierstown (both Co. Meath), not far from where Dr Beaufort lived, but it is unclear to which family AME belonged. SOURCE C.C. Ellison, *The hopeful traveller* (Kilkenny, 1987), p. 115; Henry E. Huntington Library, San Marino (CA), MS FB 1,246, letter by AME to Dr D.A. Beaufort; *Landowners in Ireland* (London, 1876), p. 67.

E122   *Memoirs of the Montague family* [anon.].
London: Edmund Lloyd, 1817, 3 vols. SOURCE British Fiction; Garside, 1817:25. LOCATION Corvey CME, 3–628–48065, Ireland related fiction, Dt, NUC.
+ London: E. Lloyd, 1820, 3 vols. (as *Ireland; or, memoirs of the Montague family*). SOURCE Brown, 560; Blakey, p. 271; British Fiction; Garside, E:7. LOCATION Corvey CME 3–628–47947–9.
COMMENTARY A story of family relationships and inheritance issues set in Ireland, but giving no description of the country. Sidney Montague, left an orphan by the death of her father, is involved in a lawsuit about her inheritance. While the outcome is still in doubt, she visits a paternal uncle. Her gentle manner makes her a favourite with her uncle and her male cousin.

Sidney marries and takes possession of the disputed property. Her cousin Fanny, who had been extremely haughty to her, elopes but eventually returns home with a child. Sidney helps to smooth out this embarrassing situation. She also helps to pay the debts of the claimant who had lost the lawsuit, enabling the young man to leave the prison and join a regiment. Sidney and her husband, Major Sedley, live a happy life blessed with several children [ML].

E123 *The contested election; or, a courtier's promises* (Alice Margaret Ennis; dedicated to the duke of Leinster).
+ London: A.K. Newman & Co., 1820, 3 vols. SOURCE Brown 2, 448; Blakey, p. 269; British Fiction; Garside, 1820:22. LOCATION Corvey CME 3-628-47461-2, Ireland related fiction, L.
COMMENTARY A story of thwarted love and family ambition set in Ireland about 1810. Frederick O'Moore loves Emily Vandeleur, but her father is resolved to uphold family pride by marrying her to her first cousin, Maj. Vandeleur. The major's father, Conynagham Vandeleur, schemes to bring about this alliance. Everything goes against the O'Moores until they are reduced almost to beggary, and then their fortunes turn [Brown 2].

ENSELL, Mrs E.J., fl. 1867. Novelist. Only Mrs EJE'S works associated with Ireland are listed below.
E124 *Meta's letters, A tale* (by Mrs E.J. Ensell).
+ London: Saunders, Otley & Co., 1867. SOURCE Allibone Suppl., i, p. 559; Alston, p. 138. LOCATION L.
COMMENTARY The story starts in England but ends in Ireland where a girl who has been in difficult circumstance is able to offer a curacy to her benefactor [ML].
E125 *The pearl of Lisnadoon; or, a glimpse of our Irish neighbours* (by Mrs E.J. Ensell).
London: Elliot Stock, 1886. SOURCE Allibone Suppl., i, p. 559; Brown, 561; Dixson, p. 306. LOCATION L, NUC.
COMMENTARY Set in Killarney following O'Connell's imprisonment [1844]. Describes the conditions in the country from a Protestant and landlord point of view [Brown].

ENSOR, Mathilda (or Matilda), b. 1807. Unpublished novelist and granddaughter of the architect George Ensor, ME was one of the ten children of George and Esther Weld Ensor who lived at the family seat, Ardress House (Co. Armagh), where she wrote the following manuscript. Her father was a lawyer and political and religious writer, educated at TCD, whose writings expressed progressive ideas on a wide range of issues, for example *A defence of the Irish* (Dublin, 1825). His papers are held in the Armagh County Museum. SOURCE Personal communication, F. Bailey, Curator, National Trust for Northern Ireland, May 2004; C.E.B. Brett, *Buildings of County Armagh* (Belfast, 1999), pp 82-4; ODNB (for George Ensor); RL.
E126 *Family annals* (by Mathilda Ensor).
COMMENTARY Unpublished 88pp manuscript dated 1818. If ME's birth date is correct, it means she was age 11 when she wrote this. The story features two families, the Elfords and the Lindleys, and is set at Castle Seldon, south of Limerick, with passing mention of social life in Dublin. It deals with love and marriage, the duties of parents and children, and the pitfalls of matrimony. The story does not seem to be finished, or perhaps the manuscript is incomplete. A book of the same title by Rachel Hunter was published in 1807 in London [Garside 1807: 30; Personal communication, Garrett Scott, Oct. 2003. LOCATION InND].

'ERIGENA', pseud. See **BARRETT, J.G.**

ESLER, E. Rentoul. See **ESLER, Mrs Erminda.**

ESLER, Mrs Erminda Rentoul (née Rentoul; also known as **Mrs E. Rentoul Esler**), b. Manorcunningham (Co. Donegal) *c.*1860 (1852 according to Blain), d. Bexley (Kent) 1924. Novelist and short story writer, EE was the daughter of Revd Alexander Rentoul, a Presbyterian clergyman of Manorcunningham. She was educated at Nîmes (France), at Berlin, and at Queen's University, Belfast. In 1879 she graduated at the Royal University of Ireland and in 1883 married Robert Esler, a doctor and scientific writer. The couple made their home in London. She contributed short stories to the *Cornhill Magazine* and *Sunday at Home* (both London), among other periodicals. Many of her novels are set in Co. Donegal and are imbued with the same Scots-Irish, Presbyterian values that informed her life. SOURCE Allibone Suppl., i, p. 561; Blain, p. 346; Brady, p. 74; Donegal, pp 92–3; EF, pp 118–19; Hogan 2, pp 414–15; W.T. Latimer, *A history of the Irish Presbyterians* (Belfast, [1893]), p. 190*n*; Newmann, p. 74; Sutherland, pp 215–16; McCarthy, iii, p. 1096; RIA/DIB; RL; TK.

E127   *Almost a pauper. A tale of trial and triumph* (by Mrs E. Rentoul Esler).
London: Christian Knowledge Society; New York: E. & J.B. Young & Co., [1888] (ill. F. Dadd). SOURCE Donegal, p. 92; COPAC. LOCATION L.
COMMENTARY Set in England [Sutherland].

E128   *The way of transgressors. A novel* (by Mrs E. Rentoul Esler).
London: Sampson Low, Marston, Searle & Rivington, 1890, 3 vols. SOURCE Wolff, 2098; Donegal, p. 92; COPAC. LOCATION L.
COMMENTARY Brief love stories set in England [Sutherland].

E129   *The way they loved at Grimpat: village idylls* (by Mrs E. Rentoul Esler).
London: Sampson Low, Marston & Co., 1893. SOURCE Brown, 565; Sutherland, p. 215 (1894 edn). Donegal, p. 93 (1894 edn); COPAC; OCLC. LOCATION City of Belfast Public Libraries, L, MB, NUC.
Leipzig: Bernard Tauchnitz, 1894. SOURCE T & B, 3004. LOCATION NUC.
New York: H. Holt, 1896. LOCATION NUC.
COMMENTARY Love stories touched with satire and set in England [Brown; Hogan; Sutherland].

E130   *A maid of the manse. A novel* (by Mrs E. Rentoul Esler; dedicated to 'the men of the press')
+ London: Sampson Low & Marston & Co., 1895. SOURCE Brown, 566; Donegal, p. 93. LOCATION D, L, MB, NUC.
COMMENTARY Describes Presbyterian clerical life in Co. Donegal in the 1850s [Brown; Hogan; Sutherland].

E131   *'Mid green pastures. Short stories* (by E. Rentoul Esler; dedicated to Frederick A. Atkins)
+ London: Sampson Low, Marston & Co., 1895. SOURCE Daims, 992. LOCATION D, L, NUC.
New York: J. Pott, 1895. SOURCE Daims, 992. LOCATION NUC.
COMMENTARY Contents: 'Miss Chrissie's protégé', 'Time, the alchemist', 'One lesson in life', 'Jamie Myles's vehicle', 'Jabez Gaunt's testament', 'An idealist', 'A tardy wooing', 'In the waning year' [ML].

E132   *The Wardlaws* (by E. Rentoul Esler).
+ London: Smith, Elder & Co., 1896. SOURCE Brown, 567; Donegal, p. 93. LOCATION City of Belfast Public Libraries, L, InND Loeber coll.
COMMENTARY Set in Ireland, the story covers a family's fifty years of genteel decay. The profligate Mr Wardlaw, who has lost practically all his possessions, is left a widower with a daughter, Margery. He marries again, and to earn money becomes the sub-agent on Lord Kilmoon's estate. His second wife dies in childbirth leaving a son. Mr Wardlaw gives up his sub-agency

as not worthy of a gentleman of his lineage. Margery is left to bring up her half-brother, John. At the death of her father, Lord Kilmoon promises to look after the little boy's schooling. Margery opens a grocery store, and although the Protestant minister is very fond of her, he can not contemplate marrying a businesswoman. She never marries. John becomes a stockbroker in England but rather than restoring the family's estate in Ireland, lives a comfortable life with his egocentric wife and children. At a certain point the brokerage firm is pretty much bankrupt and his family, except for his daughter Gladys, does not want to retrench. Not seeing a way out, John commits suicide. His partner, Tom Carstairs, is in love with Gladys, but does not ask her to marry him. Lord Kilmoon's son wishes to marry Gladys also, but she declines, realizing that she loves Tom. In the end, the Wardlaw's family fortunes are not restored, much to the chagrin of the old servants [ML].

E133   *Youth at the prow. A tale* (by E. Rentoul Esler).
           London: J. Long, 1898. SOURCE Donegal, p. 93; COPAC; OCLC. LOCATION L.
E134   *The awakening of Helena Thorpe* (by E. Rentoul Esler).
           London: Partridge, [1902]. SOURCE Donegal, p. 93; COPAC. LOCATION L.
E135   *The trackless way. A story of a man's quest for God* (by E. Rentoul Esler).
           + London: R. Brimley Johnson, 1903. SOURCE Brown, 568 (1904 edn); Daims, 993.
           LOCATION D, L.
           COMMENTARY Set mainly in Ulster, a study of the religious struggles of a Presbyterian minister and his difficulties in social relations [Brown].

'ESMOND, Henry', fl. 1878. Pseudonym, probably inspired by William Makepeace Thackeray's novel *Henry Esmond* (London, 1852). This pseudynom probably refers to the same person O'Donoghue identified as the author (living in Hampstead, London) of a poem *Hibernia Pacata* (London, 1886). The poem is most likely a version of, or response to, *Pacata Hibernia: Ireland appeased and reduced* (London, 1633), an English account of the campaign against Hugh O'Neill compiled by Thomas Stafford from the papers of Lord Carew, president of Munster. The BLC also suggests that HE is a pseudynom. SOURCE BLC; OCIL, p. 464; O'Donoghue p. 133.

E136   *A life's hazard; or, the outlaw of Wentworth Waste* (by 'Henry Esmond').
           London: Sampson Low, Marston, Searle & Rivington, 1878, 3 vols. SOURCE Brown, 569; Wolff, 2099. LOCATION L, NUC (1880 edn).
COMMENTARY A tale with many adventures such as supernatural events, abductions, attempted murders, perjury, imprisonment, rescues, etc., set in north Co. Dublin [Brown].

ESTERRE, Elsa D'. See D'ESTERRE, Elsa.

'ÉTOILE', pseud. See MITCHELL, Edward.

'EUSTACE, Robert', pseud. of Eustace Robert Barton. Co-author. See SMITH, Elizabeth Thomasina Toulmin.

'EVAN, May', fl. 1890. Pseudonym of a novelist who also published *Wanted – an heiress!* (Hull, 1891). SOURCE Topp 8, 1111.
E137   *The greatest of these. An Irish story* (by 'May Evan').
           + London: Simpkin, Marshall, Hamilton, Kent & Co., 1890. SOURCE Brown 2, 1015.
           LOCATION D, L, InND Loeber coll.
COMMENTARY The English Mr and Mrs Thornton are bequeathed an estate in Kerry. They come to Ireland determined to do their best by their tenants, although Mrs Thornton believes

there is danger in effecting any change, but they do what they can despite an attempt to murder them. The local parish priest is the Thorntons' ally throughout [Brown 2].

EVANS, Harriet. See **MARTIN, Harriet.**

'EVERGREEN, Anthony', pseud. See **O'ROURKE, Fr John.**

'AN EXILE OF ERIN', pseud. See **NEWMAN, M.W.**

'AN EX-OFFICER OF THE ROYAL IRISH CONSTABULARY', fl. 1879. Pseudonym of a writer and former policeman who appears to have been a native of Ballinakill (Co. Laois) and to have been educated at Kilkenny College. SOURCE Brown 2, p. 8.

E138   *Leaves from my note book; being a collection of tales, all positive facts portraying Irish life and character* (by 'An ex-officer of the Royal Irish Constabulary') London: Dean & Son, [1879] (ill.). SOURCE Brown, 63. LOCATION D, L, NUC ([1878] edn).

COMMENTARY The IBL mentions as its title: *Irish life and character: Being a collection of tales, all positive facts*, which may be in error. Consists of tales portraying Irish life, many of them concerned with crime and duels, and set in various parts of Ireland including Kilkenny, Athlone, and Dingle. Contents: 'A story of what happened on a Christmas day', 'Canal passenger boat', 'City of Kilkenny', 'Dingle', 'Cahirciveen', 'Murder of McDermott', 'Murder of Mr. Hall', 'Battle of the churchyard', 'Duel between Mr. Shaw, Sheriff of the Queen's County and Mr. Cooke', 'Duel between captain Smith and Mr. O'Grady at Harold's Cross, Dublin', 'Duel between captain Smith, 59th Regiment (uncle to Smith who shot O'Grady in Dublin) and Colonel MacDonald, 92nd Highlanders, at Fermoy', 'Torc Lake' [ML; Brown; IBL, 12 (1920 Aug.–Sept.), p. 8].

F

'F.', fl. 1773. Pseudonym of a moralizing novelist.

F1 *The dupe of love and friendship; or, the unfortunate Irishman. A moral founded on a fact; which happened at Liverpool* (by 'F.').
Plymouth: G. Walker, [18—?]. SOURCE RLIN. LOCATION NUC.
COMMENTARY Originally published in the *Westminster Magazine, or the Pantheon of Taste* (London, 1 (July, 1773), 1 part); and was subsequently published several other times in magazines, including the *Hibernian Magazine* [Mayo, 335].

'F., E.L.', pseud. See **FALLOON, Eliza Lee.**

'F., V.G.', pseud. See **FINNY, Violet Geraldine.**

'F., S., Philomath', fl. 1740s. Pseudonym of a writer of libertine fiction.

F2 *The petticoat-pensioners: being memoirs of the most remarkable of those gentlemen, in and about London and Westminster* (by 'S.F. Philomath').
+ London: J. Horner, [1749]. SOURCE ESTC t093802. LOCATION L, CtY, InND Loeber coll.
COMMENTARY A novel cast in the form of eleven letters from Thomas Harvey, Esq., to Sir Jacob Arnold, Bt, with each letter describing, often in vivid detail, the amorous adventures of a rogue but as often as not the women involved are just as corrupt as the men. The subtitle of the first episode is typical: 'The history and adventures of John C—y, Esq.; commonly called Count C—y [Courcey?], kept by Lady F—L*****'. The text has a somewhat xenophobic quality, as most of the villains come to London from distant parts in search of vice. Captain Alexander B—e is a native of Boston, in New England, Captain L—th is a 'Caledonian', and no fewer than five of the 'petticoat-pensioners' are Irish: from Dublin, Limerick, Connacht, etc. The Irish background is sometimes filled in at some length, as in 'The adventures of Captain C—ah' [Cavanagh?]. The volume is somewhat a spin-off of *The Irish register: or a list of the Duchess Dowagers, Countesses, Widow Ladies, Maiden Ladies, Widows, and misses of large fortunes in England, as register'd by the Dublin Society, for the use of their members* (Dublin printed; London repr., 1742) [RL; Personal communication, Steve Weissman, 15 Jan. 1999].

FABER, Mrs —, fl. 1869. Novelist and translator, Mrs F also translated Franz Hoffmann's *Sowing in tears and reaping in joy* (London, 1870). SOURCE Allibone Suppl., i, p. 570.

F3 *A legend of Dundrum Castle, within the County of Dublin: being a chronicle of the House of Bagod de la Rath* (done into English by Mrs. Faber).
+ London: Bell & Daldy, 1869. SOURCE Brown 2, 455. LOCATION D, Dt, L, NUC.
COMMENTARY Historical fiction. Purports to be edited by Geoffrey Bagod, an old man of eighty-five, from a manuscript entitled 'True Historie of the Tryals of Geraldine Bagod', written by her loving cousin and friend, Philippa Rochefort. The story opens in 1300 AD. Geraldine is engaged to Sir Walter de la Brett of Rathfarnham Castle (Co. Dublin). A Spaniard, Don Amador de Puerto-Garrero, woos Geraldine and on the eve of her marriage attempts to abduct her. He fights in single combat with Sir Walter. Both are wounded, but Don Amador dies. Philippa and an orphan named Kathleen, or Catalina, are mysteriously involved in the drama [Brown 2].

'FABER, Christine', pseud. See SMITH, Mary E.

'FAGG, Michael, Esq., K.C.', fl. 1836. Pseudonym of autobiographical fiction writer.

F4   *The life and adventures of a limb of the law; by Michael Fagg, K.C. and Bencher of the Hon. Society of Lincoln's Inn, interspersed with anecdotes of his contemporaries, members of the legal profession.*
+ London: A. Hancock, 1836. SOURCE Brown 2, 456; Wolff, 7636. LOCATION D, L, NUC.

COMMENTARY An autobiographical story set during the period 1793 to 1830. The narrator represents himself as born in Cork City but brought up mostly in Kenmare (Co. Cork). Describes O'Shaughnessy the schoolmaster and his school and relates the narrator's subsequent adventures in Cork and London [Brown 2].

'FALL, Michael', pseud. See DOWLING, Richard.

FALLOON, Eliza Lee (Mrs Garnett Falloon), pseud. 'E.L.L.' (probably referring to her maiden name), fl. 1840. The fourth edn of her *Wild flowers from the glens* (London, 1866 edn) mentions as her address Rosbercon, New Ross (Co. Wexford), at the end of which she signed herself as 'E.L.F.' SOURCE Alston, p. 140; Brown, p. 102; O'Donoghue, p. 240 [under L., E.L.]; RIA/DIB; RL.

F5   *Wild flowers from the glens* (by 'E.L.L.').
+ London: W.J. Cleaver; Dublin: William Curry. Jnr & Co.; Belfast: J. & R. Hodgson & G. Phillips, 1840. SOURCE Alston, p. 516; Brown, 572 (who identifies her real name from the 4th edn); Brown 2, 459 (who mentions a Belfast edn, 1866, but this is probably the joint London and Belfast edn). LOCATION D (1841, 4th edn), Dt, L (1866 edn, 3rd edn), NUC (1866, 4th edn).

COMMENTARY Contents: 'The glens', 'The dooming rose' (the love story of Maurice Fitzgerald and the daughter of Sir Raymond O'Neill), 'Old Moyna's story', 'The dooming rose (concluded)', 'The pic-nic', 'The fairy of Tivora' (a Cushendall, Co. Antrim love story with a *deus ex machina* in the shape of a friendly fairy), 'The wishing arch' (a tale of Portrush, Co. Antrim), 'The flower of Glenarriffe' (a love story with a sad ending) [ML].

FALY, Patrick C. Editor and grandson of John Hill. See HILL, John.

'FANE, Violet', pseud. See SINGLETON, Mary.

FAREWELL, James, possible pseud. 'Mac O Bonniclabbero', b. probably in England *c.*1666, d. 1689. A miscellaneous writer and satirist, JF was the son of Thomas Farewell of Horsington (Som.), and studied law at Lincoln's Inn, London. He is known mostly as the supposed editor of the poem *The Irish hudibras, or Fingallian prince* (London, 1689), which Field Day lists as anonymous but O'Donoghue attributes to 'J. Farewell', the pseudynom of Walter Jones (1693?–1765), but this is not confirmed in other sources. SOURCE Allibone i, p. 578; A. Bliss, *Spoken English in Ireland, 1600–1740* (Atlantic Highlands (NJ), 1979), pp 52–4, 56–8, 124–9; Field Day, i, pp 439–40, 492; O'Donoghue, p. 137.

F6   *Bogg-witticisms; or, dear joy's common-places. Being a compleat collection of the most pronounced punns, learned bulls, elabourate quibbles, and wise sayings of some of the natives of Teague-land. Shed fourd vor generaul nouddificaushion; and coullected bee de grete caare and panish-tauking of oour laurned countree-man Mac O Bonniclabbero of Drogheda Knight of the Mendicant Order.*

[n.l.]: Printed for Evidansh Swear-all [*sic*], [*c*.1687] (introd. signed 'Farewell'). SOURCE A. Bliss, *Spoken English in Ireland, 1600–1740* (Atlantic Highlands, NJ, 1979), pp 52–4, 124–5; IBL, 30 (1947), pp 59–62. LOCATION L (1700 edn).

London: [n.p.], 1690 (as *Teagueland jests, or bogg-witticisms. In two parts, the first being a complete collection of the most learned bulls, elabourate quibbles and wise sayings of some of the natives of Teagueland till the year 1688; the second contains many comical stories and famous blunders of those dear joys since the late King James's landing amongst them. Never before in print. Published for the entertainment of all those who are dispos'd to be merry.* SOURCE Bliss, p. 53; RLIN; Gilbert, p. 825. LOCATION DPL Gilbert coll., Syracuse Univ. Library, MH.

+ London: J. Pery, 1746 (as *The Irish miscellany, or Teagueland jests: being a compleat collection of the most profound puns, learned bulls, elabourate quibbles, amorous letters, sublime poetry, and wise sayings, of the natives of Teagueland. Being a sequel to Joe Miller's jests. Shet fourd vor Generaul Nouddificaushion: And coullected bee de grete caare and painsh-tauking of oour laurned countree-maun, Mac O Bonniclabbero of Drogheda, knight of the Mendicant Order;* ill.). SOURCE IBL, 30 (1947), pp 59/61; Bradshaw, 7369; ESTC t167442. LOCATION DPL Gilbert coll. (1747 edn), L (1749, 3rd edn), DPL (1747 edn), L (1749 edn), C.

COMMENTARY A miscellany of jests in brogue at the expense of the Irish [ML].

FARMER, John. Co-author. See **BULLOCK, John William.**

FARQUHAR, George, b. Derry (Co. Derry) 1677, d. London, 1707. A playwright, poet and epistolary writer who made the 'stage-Irishman' a staple of his late-period Restoration plays, GF was the son of a clergyman from an Ulster planter family which lost its fortunes in the siege of Derry in 1689. GF entered TCD in 1694 but soon abandoned his studies for the stage, appearing in 1696 as Othello in Dublin's Theatre Royal in Smock Alley. During a performance of Dryden's *Indian Emperor*, he accidentally stabbed a fellow actor. It was not a fatal wound but it caused him to give up acting and turn to writing. He left for London and soon his plays were being staged, several to great success, at the Drury Lane Theatre. In 1704 he received a commission in the army and worked as a recruiter in Shrewsbury and later in Dublin and Kildare. These experiences provided the background for *The recruiting officer* (London, 170?), one of his most highly-regarded plays which, along with *The constant couple* (London, 1700) , continue to be staples of the contemporary theatrical repertoire. In 1706 he sold his commission to meet debts. Some of his verse and letters appeared in *Love and business* (London, 1702), and his poem *Barcellona*, based on the Spanish expedition of the earl of Peterborough, appeared in London in 1707. His early death left the impression, according to Leigh Hunt, 'of a man called away who left the house ringing with his jest' (OCIL, p. 181). SOURCE Allibone, i, p. 580; Field Day, i, pp 502–6, 654–5; Hogan 2, pp 423–4; OCIL, pp 180–1; ODNB; O'Donoghue, p. 137; RIA/DIB.

F7 *The adventures of Covent-Garden, in imitation of Scarron's city romance* [anon.] (dedicated to 'all my ingenious acquaintances at Will's Coffee House').

+ London: R. Standfast, 1699. SOURCE Sweeney 1881. LOCATION L, NUC, CSmH.

COMMENTARY 58pp. This is actually an imitation of Antoine Furetière's *Le roman bourgeois* (Paris, 1666) translated as *Scarron's city romance* (London, 1671), and has no Irish content. The attribution to Farquhar has yet to be substantiated but since, as the ODNB points out, 'Farquhar was a man of rare creativity and great productivity, [who] seldom borrowed lines from others but often recycled his own plot ideas and lines of poetry; the romance is attributable to him because of materials he reused in the play *The constant couple*' [RL; BLC; ODNB; Sweeney 1881].

FARRIE, Hugh, pseud. 'Hugh Westbury', fl. 1887. Novelist.

F8   *Frederick Hazzleden. A novel* (by 'Hugh Westbury').

+ London, New York: Macmillan & Co., 1887, 3 vols. SOURCE Allibone Suppl., ii, p. 1505; Dixson, p. 218. LOCATION L, NUC.

COMMENTARY Describes a peasant-landlord conflict in Ireland over the peasant having used stones to build his cottage. The landlord tells him the stones are his and the peasant needs to pay for them. Also contains a description of an Irish election and of a Bible mission [ML].

'FATHER BAPTIST', pseud. See O'BRIEN, Fr (Mgr) Richard Baptist.

'FATHER CHARLES', pseud. See MEEHAN, Fr Charles Patrick.

FAUGHNAN, Thomas, b. Co. Leitrim, fl. 1835, d. Picton? (ON) 1891. Soldier, memoirist and writer, TF spent his childhood and youth in his native Co. Leitrim near the Shannon and went to a country school in Dromad. His autobiography recounts TF's home and school life and is a paean to his childhood village based on Oliver Goldsmith's§ *The deserted village* (London, 1770). He discusses the state of his area at the time: the poverty, the negative effects of absentee landlordism and exorbitant rents, and the Famine, before he decided to join the army and 'fight for the honour and glory of my Queen and country'. He joined the British army and saw service in many parts of Ireland as well as in the Crimea, Egypt, Gibraltar, Greece, Albania, the West Indies and Scotland. He rose to the rank of colour-sergeant in the 6th Royal Regiment before he finally emigrated to Canada, where he published his autobiography, *Stirring incidents in the life of a British soldier* (Picton, 1879). He settled at Picton (ON) where he had relatives and where he became a publisher. SOURCE T. Faughnan, *Stirring incidents in the life of a British soldier* (Toronto edn, 1882); RL; Rowan cat. 48 pt. I/236; Watters, p. 286.

F9   *The young hussar; or, Lady Iris's adventure. A story of love and war* (by Thomas Faughnan).

Picton (ON): Thomas Faughnan, 1890 (ill.). LOCATION L.

COMMENTARY According to the preface this is 'another narrative founded on fact' and uses disguised names. The story is that of a young Irish gentlewoman who, disguised as a man, follows her wronged lover, the heir to an Irish estate, into the army where both serve with distinction as hussars. Eventually she reveals her identity, they marry, and he is exonerated [Rowan cat. 48 pt. I/236].

FAY, M., fl. *c*.1900. Editor and possibly a short story writer. SOURCE AMB.

F10   *Fairy tales from Ireland. From Crofton Croker's 'Fairy legends of the South of Ireland'* (ed. by M. Fay).

+ London: Stead's, [*c*.1900] (ill. Brinsley Le Fanu; Books for the Bairns, No. 248). SOURCE RL. LOCATION InND Loeber coll.

COMMENTARY Contrary to the title, several of the stories are not from Thomas Crofton Croker's§ published stories. Contents: 'The princess Fior Usca and her golden pitcher', 'The fairy queen and Larry the Piper' [from Thomas Crofton Croker's *Fairy legends*], 'Two fairy gifts', 'The giant's stairs', 'The wonderful tune' [from Thomas Crofton Croker's *Fairy legends*], 'The enchanted lake, and what Paddeen found beneath its waters' [from Thomas Crofton Croker's *Fairy legends*], 'The legend of the O'Donaghue' [*sic*], 'The mermaid of Gollerus' [from Thomas Crofton Croker's *Fairy legends*], 'The enchanted bottle' [RL].

FENNELL, Charlotte, fl. 1897. Novelist, CF also published *The calico printer* (London, [1895]). She was the wife of Theodore Fennell. SOURCE RL; BLC.

F11   *A prince of Tyrone* (by Charlotte Fennell and J.P. O'Callaghan; dedicated to the author's husband, Theodore Fennell).
+ Edinburgh, London: William Blackwood & Sons, 1897 (ill.). SOURCE Brown, 575; Wolff, 2231. LOCATION D, DPL, L, NUC, InND Loeber coll.
New York: A.L. Burt, [1903]. LOCATION NUC.
COMMENTARY An historical romance set in mid-sixteenth-century Ireland that recounts the amorous adventures and military fortunes of Shane O'Neill, newly inaugurated as The O'Neill. In his castle he keeps as hostage the beautiful countess of Tyrconnell, with whom he is in love. However, on a visit to the court of Queen Elizabeth to argue his legitimacy as his father's heir, he falls in love with Anne Courtney, whom he forces to go back with him to Ireland. Eventually, O'Neill wants to get rid of Anne and she is placed in a convent run by his mother. O'Neill's military position worsens and in order to get help he gives the countess of Tyrconnell back to her relatives. He dies in battle, and the countess takes her own life [ML; Brown].

FERGUSON, Sir Samuel, pseuds 'A Fermanagh peasant', and 'Michael Heffernan', b. Belfast (Co. Antrim) 1810, d. Howth (Co. Dublin) 1886. Poet, antiquarian, folklorist, translator and archivist, SF came from an Ascendancy family, the son of John Ferguson of Collon House, Glenwhirry (Co. Antrim) and Agnes Knox. He was educated at the Royal Belfast Academical Institution and at TCD from which, by his own account, he never graduated. (The DNB credits SF with graduating BA in 1826 and MA in 1832). TCD conferred on him an honorary LLD in 1865 after the publication of *Lays of the western Gael* (London, 1865). Needing to support himself, SF studied law and was called to the Bar in Ireland in 1838. He contributed poems to the Belfast *Ulster Magazine* and to *Blackwood's Magazine* (Edinburgh) when he was age 21. Although not a founder of the *Dublin University Magazine* in 1833, he was involved from the beginning, contributing folk stories and poems. He also contributed to the *Irish Monthly* (Dublin), and the *Dublin Penny Journal*. In 1833 he published *A dialogue between the head and heart of an Irish Protestant* (not located). He was elected a council member of the newly founded Celtic Society in 1845. He married Mary Catherine Guinness in 1848, and eventually lived at 20 North Great George's Street, Dublin. He was a founder the same year of the Protestant branch of the *Repeal Association*. Despite his anti-nationalist and anti-Catholic views, he sought to provide strong Protestant leadership in cultural matters and to link Catholic and Protestant in a single, shared Irish identity. He made invaluable contributions to the collection, translation and dissemination of Irish folklore, especially the old Gaelic legends and sagas, and retells them in many of his most renowned poems, which made a major contribution to the development of Irish poetry in English. William Butler Yeats§, on whom Ferguson's work had a considerable influence, described these as 'truly bardic'. He was made queen's counsel in 1859 but in 1867 gave up the law when he was appointed deputy keeper of the public records of Ireland, the first to hold this position. His painstaking work in organizing and systemizing the Irish records garnered him a knighthood. Interest in native Irish culture dominated his life and he was elected president of the RIA in 1881. He wrote extensively on antiquarian subjects and is renowned for collecting and publishing the Ogham inscriptions of Ireland, Scotland and Wales. He was also interested in contemporary Irish fiction and wrote on 'Irish novelists' in the *Dublin University Magazine* (Dec., 1840). Some of the MSS of his poems can be found in the Belfast Library and Society for Promoting Knowledge. SOURCE Allibone Suppl., i, pp 583–4; Boylan, p. 112; Brady, p. 77; C.E.B. Brett, *Buildings of Co. Antrim* (Belfast, 1996), p. 184; Brown, p. 103; B & S, p. 277; A. Deering, *Sir Samuel Ferguson, poet and antiquarian* (Philadelphia, 1931); Lady Ferguson, *Sir Samuel Ferguson in the Ireland of his day* (Edinburgh, 1896, 2 vols., which lists Ferguson's publications in magazines); Field Day, i, pp 1053, 1174, 1297; ii, p. 7; W.E. Hall, p. 53*ff*; Hogan, pp 235–6; Hogan

2, pp 429–30; Igoe, p. 67; Irish pseudonyms; McKenna, pp 174–9; NCBEL 4, pp 611–12; ODNB; O'Donoghue, pp 139–40; J. O'Donovan (ed.), *The book of rights* (Dublin, 1847, n.p. list of officers); OCIL, pp 185–6; Rafroidi, ii, p. 160; RIA/DIB; RL.

F12   *Father Tom and the Pope; or, a night at the Vatican; as related by Mr. Michael Heffernan, Master of the National School at Tallymactaggart, in the County of Leitrim, to a friend, during his official visit to Dublin, for the purpose of studying political economy, in the Spring of 1838* [anon.].

+ Baltimore: Jos. Robinson, 1856 (published for subscribers only). SOURCE Hogan, p. 236 (1858 edn). LOCATION Grail (1858 edn), NUC (1858 edn), InND Loeber coll.

+ Philadelphia: Limited edn printed for Le Cercle Autour Du Poêle, 1861 (as *Father Tom and the Pope; or, a night at the Vatican*). LOCATION NUC, InND Loeber coll.

Philadelphia: T.B. Peterson, 1868 (as *Father Tom and the Pope; or, a night at the Vatican.* By the late John Fisher Murray§ [*sic*]). SOURCE Hodges Figgis cat. n.s. 12/152. LOCATION NUC (a note on the fly leaf signed by Ferguson admits authorship), InND Loeber coll. (1879 edn).

+ New York: A. Simpson & Co., 1867 (as *Father Tom and the Pope; or, a night at the Vatican*). LOCATION D, NUC, InND Loeber coll.

COMMENTARY Reprinted from *Blackwood's Magazine* (Edinburgh, May, 1838), and became very popular, a new edn appearing in New York as late as 1920. Authorship had been ascribed to SF, but ODNB states that it resulted from a collaboration between SF, William Maginn§ and John Fisher Murray§. The story is a take-off on Harriet Martineau's§ *Illustrations of political economy* (1832–34) which contains *Ireland: A tale*. A burlesque on Irish catholicism featuring Fr Tom, an Irish priest (based on Dr Thomas Maguire, a popular contemporary preacher) who spends an evening drinking poteen with the pope, while they discuss knotty religious issues [ML; Brady, p. 78; OCIL, p. 186; ODNB].

F13   *Hibernian nights' entertainments. A metrical romance* (by 'A Fermanagh peasant').

+ New York: P.M. Haverty, 1857. SOURCE McKenna, p. 178; Gilbert, p. 286. LOCATION D, DPL Gilbert coll.

+ New York: P.M. Haverty, 1872 (as *The Hibernian nights' entertainments*). LOCATION InND Loeber coll.

+ Dublin: Sealy, Bryers & Walker; London: George Bell & Sons, 1887, 3 vols. (first, second, and third series). SOURCE Rafroidi, ii, p. 167; Brown, 576; Rowan cat. 37, part A/365; Hogan, p. 236. LOCATION Grail, D, L, InND Loeber coll.

COMMENTARY Historical fiction first published in the *Dublin University Magazine* (1834–36) and reprinted many times since. Based on the famous *Arabian nights*, the narrator, Turlogh O'Hagan, who is O'Neill's shanachie, supposedly tells the stories to Hugh Roe O'Donnell and his companions, who are imprisoned in Dublin Castle in 1592. The stories are mainly fictitious and weave together history, myth and fiction, giving details of locality and contemporary customs. There is an historical introd. Contents: 'The death of the children of Usnach' (retelling of the saga of Deirdre), 'The return of Claneboy' (set in fourteenth-century Ulster and relating how Aodh Buidhe O'Neill regained his territory in Antrim on the death of William de Burgh, earl of Ulster), 'The captive of Killeshin' (fourteenth-century tale of the struggle of the Leinster clans, particularly the O'Nolans, against the English settlers), 'An adventure of Shane O'Neill's' (adventures in which O'Neill, and the old Irish in general, appear in an unfavourable light), 'Corby MacGillmore' (set in north Antrim at the beginning of the fifteenth century, it tells of the enmity of the MacGillmore clan and the Savage clan of north Down), 'The rebellion of Silken Thomas' (the main features of the rebellion are told in the form of a romance. A large part of the story is taken up by Sir John Talbot, who first joins Lord Thomas but afterwards leaves him). The story 'Corby

MacGillmore' was later serialized in the *Emerald* (New York, 1868) [Brown; Field Day, i, pp 1185–1200; RL].

FERGUSON, Walter, fl. 1826. Novelist, WF was the son of a Scottish minister and, according to the BLC, an astronomer. He was the author also of *An only son* (London, 1831). SOURCE OCLC; BLC.

F14   *My early days* (by Walter Ferguson; dedicated to the author's nephews Alan and Walter).
+ Edinburgh: Oliver & Boyd, 1826 (ill.). SOURCE Emerald Isle cat. 50/13 (1828 edn). LOCATION L, E (1828 edn).
Amsterdam: G. Portielje, 1837 trans. by G. Engelberts Gerrits as *Schetsen uit den jeugdige leeftijd van Walter Ferguson, den zoon van een Schotsch' predikant*; ill. P. Veldhuyzen, D. Sluyter). SOURCE Seen at Van der Steur, Haarlem, April 1999. LOCATION InND Loeber coll. (n.d. edn).
COMMENTARY Semi-fictional story based on autobiographical information. A Scottish minister moves to northern Ireland where he meets his future wife, a Maxwell. It describes his childhood follies and, eventually, having inherited from his grandfather, he buys the estate close to where he grew up to recreate the happiness of his youth [ML].

'A FERMANAGH PEASANT', pseud. See **FERGUSON, Sir Samuel**.

'FERNIA', fl. 1870s. Pseudonym of a religious fiction writer.
F15   *Lady Victorine; or, the triple cord. A story of Indian and home life* (by 'Fernia').
+ London: S.W. Partridge & Co., [1878]. LOCATION L, InND Loeber coll.
COMMENTARY Religious fiction set in Ireland and India. Three young women are about to leave the boarding school in Ireland where they have been brought up in Christian virtues and have learned to take the Bible as their example. Lady Victorine goes to India to join her brother, whose regiment is stationed there. The other two stay in Ireland, where one joins her family and the other goes to look after her aunt. Each of the three women, by her behaviour and the influence she has on those around her, brings others to true Christianity and form unions with men who share their beliefs [ML].

FETHERSTONHAUGH, the Hon. Mrs. See **FETHERSTONHAUGH, the Hon. Mrs Maria Georgina**.

FETHERSTONHAUGH, the Hon. Mrs Maria Georgina (née Carleton; known as the Hon. Mrs Fetherstonhaugh), b. 1847, d. 1918. English novelist, MGF was the daughter of Guy Carleton, 3rd Baron Dorchester and Anne Wauchope. She was a noted rider with the Quorn hunt. Perhaps she was related to the Fetherstonhaugh family of Bracklyn Castle (Co. Westmeath). According to the *Bentley List* she and her sister, Lady Dorchester, were readers for the firm of Bentley & Son. SOURCE Allibone Suppl., i, p. 586; Blain, p. 368; Brown 2, p. 89; CP, iv, p. 411; Personal communication, Ron Hoffman, Sept. 2001; RL; Wolff, ii, p. 81.
F16   *Kilcorran* (by the Hon. Mrs Fetherstonhaugh).
+ London: Richard Bentley & Son, 1877, 2 vols. SOURCE Brown 2, 485; COPAC. LOCATION D, L, NUC.
Hamburg: Karl Gradeuer, 1878. SOURCE Brown 2, 485. LOCATION L.
COMMENTARY A love story set in the north-west of Ireland and shifts to England and back again. Neal Trench, the owner of Kilcorran, falls in love with his neighbour, Lillis Fane, a fearless rider and a remarkable singer. As both are already engaged, complications ensue. But Lillis does the honourable thing and there is a happy ending [Brown 2].

F17   *Robin Adair* (by the Hon. Mrs Fetherstonhaugh).

+ London: Richard Bentley & Son, 1879, 2 vols. LOCATION L, InND Loeber coll.

COMMENTARY A story set in England and Ireland that contrasts two love affairs, one being broken off, and the other ending happily. Ellie Hamilton lives with her proverbially cold and unfeeling stepmother and stepsister at Thorncliffe Hall in England. Ellie, who has no money, falls in love with Col. Adair, who has large debts. He rejects Ellie in favour of her stepsister, who will inherit a large fortune. Ellie spends the rest of her short life continuing to love Adair and trying to forgive him for his treatment of her. The other love affair concerns Clare O'Neill, an Irish girl who lives in Gortnamore, a ramshackle castle on the west coast of Connemara. Her father has gone to the Continent to evade his debtors and Clare is left to her own devices. She meets and falls in love with the young Charles Anstruther. He accompanies her to England where she is going to stay at Thorncliffe Hall. The only problem on the way to marital bliss is to locate Clare's father, who has not left any forwarding address. Anstruther, who is rich, decides to buy the family castle and he and Clare marry and live at Gortnamore and make improvements to the castle [ML].

F18   *Dream faces* (by the Hon. Mrs Fetherstonhaugh).

+ London: Richard Bentley & Son, 1884, 2 vols. SOURCE Wolff, 2238; COPAC. LOCATION L, InND Loeber coll.

COMMENTARY The text of this edn is printed in an unusual violet, or mauve, ink. Set in aristocratic society, the novel charts the love of two women for Sir Horace, and ends with a suicide by poison of one of them. Injured in a sporting accident in the Cumbrian border country, Sir Horace falls in love with a local Carlisle girl. Their romance is jeopardized by his cousin, the beautiful widowed Lady Kirkpatrick, who hopes to save him from a *mésalliance*. Part of the story takes place at the Punchestown races in Co. Kildare and at a dramatic foxhunt at Sir Horace's Irish estate [Quaritch, Sept. 2001].

FÉVAL, Paul. FÉVAL, Paul-Henri-Corentin.

FÉVAL, Paul-Henri-Corentin (known as **Paul Féval**), b. Rennes (France) 1817, d. Paris 1887. French novelist, P-H-CF came from an old family of barristers. He set out to study law but eventually was employed at a newspaper, when he started to write fiction. Using the pseudonym 'Francis Trollopp' (an allusion to a member of the Trollope family of writers), he wrote *Les mystères de Londres* (Paris, 1848), which became a great success. A prolific novelist, he wrote two works about Ireland but it is not clear whether he ever visited the country. SOURCE Brown 2, p. 89; *The Catholic encyclopaedia* (London, 1909); NUC; RL; RLIN.

F19   *La quittance de minuit* (by Paul Féval).

Coulommiers: A. Moussin, 1846. SOURCE Bn-Opale plus; Brown 2, 486 (Paris, 1872–77 edn). LOCATION BNF.

London: George Peirce, 1846 (trans. as *The midnight reckoning, or, the Molly Maguires: A tale of real life in Ireland*). SOURCE RLIN. LOCATION NYU.

+ Zaltbommel: Jacob Pieter Crol, 1846, 4 vols. (trans. into Dutch as *De kwitanti te middernacht, of Iersche wraak*). SOURCE Adamnet. LOCATION UVA.

COMMENTARY Contents: 'L'Héritière', 'La galerie du géant'. One or both of the stories is set on the banks of the Corrib (Co. Galway) near the Maam Turk Mountains and concerns the agrarian and political troubles during the period of O'Connell's Repeal Movement [Brown 2; NUC].

FFORDE, A. Brownlow. See FFORDE, Arthur Brownlow.

FFORDE, Arthur Brownlow (known as **A. Brownlow Fforde**), fl. 1890. Mystery and detective novelist and illustrator, ABF may be Irish and a member of the Fforde family of Seaforde (Co. Down). Burke spells this family name as 'Forde', but the family listing includes many members with the middle-name Brownlow, suggesting a link to the Brownlow family of Ulster. Five of the following novels are set in India. SOURCE Burke's, pp 438–9; ML; RL; ODNB [under Arthur Frederic Brownlow].

F20   *The subaltern, the policeman, and the little girl. An Anglo-Indian sketch written in English* (by A. Brownlow Fforde).
    + London: Sampson Low, Marston, Searle & Rivington,1890. SOURCE COPAC. LOCATION L.

F21   *'The Trotter.' A Poona mystery* (by A. Brownlow Fforde).
    + London: Sampson Low, Marston, Searle & Rivington; Peter Lane, 1890. LOCATION L, InND Loeber coll.
COMMENTARY 94pp. Set in India among the British community. A man nicknamed 'the globetrotter' comes to stay. He poses as a scientist, studying ancient monuments. He is not loved by anyone and eventually it appears that he is responsible for a number of break-ins and thefts. He disappears and no one hears from him again [ML].

F22   *The maid and the idol: A tangled story of Poona* (by Arthur Brownlow Fforde).
    + Allahabad: A.H. Wheeler & Co., 1891 (ill. the author). SOURCE COPAC. LOCATION L.
COMMENTARY Set in India [ML].

F23   *The phantom of the dome. A telepathic tale* (by A. Brownlow Fforde).
    + Calcutta, Allahabad: A.H. Wheeler & Co., 1895. SOURCE COPAC. LOCATION L.
London: A.H. Wheeler & Co. & A.P. Marston, 1895. LOCATION L.

F24   *The sign of the snake. A study of the passion of revenge* (by A. Brownlow Fforde).
    + Calcutta, Allahabad: A.H. Wheeler & Co., 1895. SOURCE COPAC. LOCATION L.
COMMENTARY Set in London and India. No Irish content [ML].

F25   *An outraged society* (by A. Brownlow Fforde).
    + London: George Allen & Unwin, 1916. SOURCE COPAC. LOCATION L.
COMMENTARY Set on the south coast of England. No Irish content [ML].

FIELD, Mrs —. See **FIELD, Louise Frances**.

FIELD, Mrs E.M. See **FIELD, Louise Frances**.

FIELD, Mrs Louise Frances (née Story, also known as Frances (Fanny) Story, **Mrs Field** and **Mrs E.M. Field**), b. Cavan 1856. A novelist and children's writer, LF was the eldest daughter of Joseph Story, DL, of Bingfield (Co. Cavan), JP of Cos. Cavan and Leitrim, and Caroline Sophia Kenneth Reid. She married in 1882 Edward Maclane Field, an inspector of schools. She mostly wrote for children. Her book about children's literature, *The child and his book*, was published in London in 1891. She was a member of the Irish Literary Society in London. SOURCE Alston, p. 143; Brown, p. 104; Field Day, v, p. 924; Landed gentry, 1904, p. 571; NCBEL 4, p. 1792; E. Reilly, p. 244.

F26   *Mixed pickles: A story for boys and girls* (by Mrs Field).
    + London: Wells Gardner, Darton & Co.; New York: E. & J.B. Young & Co. [1886] (ill. T. Pym [Clara Creed]). SOURCE COPAC. LOCATION D, NUC.
COMMENTARY Fiction for juveniles [RL].

F27   *Bryda; a story of the Indian mutiny* (by Mrs E.M. Field).
    London: Wells Gardner, Darton, [1888] (ill. A. Forrestier). LOCATION NUC.

COMMENTARY Fiction for juveniles set in India describing the Sepoy rebellion in 1857–58 [NUC].

F28 *Ethne. Being a truthful historie of the great and final settlement of Ireland by Oliver Cromwell, and certain other noteworthy events, from the records of Ethne O'Connor and of Roger Standfast, Captain in the army of the Commons of England* (ed. by Mrs E.M. Field).
London: Wells Gardner & Co., 1889 (ill. G.W. Rhead). SOURCE Brown, 585 (1902 edn); Linen Hall cat. p. 92 (n.d. edn); Nield, pp 66, 190; COPAC. LOCATION D (n.d. edn), BFl (n.d. edn), L ([1889], 2nd edn), NUC ([1887] edn).

COMMENTARY A religious, historical novel dealing with Cromwell's transplantation of the Irish to Connacht. Purports to be taken partly from the diary of Ethne O'Connor, daughter of one of the transplanted, and partly from the 'record' of Roger Standfast-on-the-Rock. Ethne, a Catholic, is converted to Roger's protestantism by a single reading of the Bible [Brown].

F29 *Little Count Paul. A story of troublesome times* (by Mrs E.M. Field).
+ London: Wells Gardner, Darton & Co., [1893] (ill. A. Forrestier). SOURCE COPAC. LOCATION D, L.
COMMENTARY Fiction for juveniles [RL].

F30 *Master Magnus, or the prince, the princess and the dragon* (by Mrs Louise Frances Field).
+ London, New York: Edward Arnold, [1895] (ill.). SOURCE COPAC. LOCATION L, NUC.
COMMENTARY Fiction for juveniles [RL].

F31 *Denis. A study in black and white* (by Mrs. Louise Frances Field; dedicated to 'my kinsfolk and friends, among the landowners of Ireland').
London, New York: Macmillan & Co., 1896. SOURCE Brown, 584; COPAC. LOCATION D (1902 edn), L, InND Loeber coll. (1902 edn).

COMMENTARY A story of the Young Ireland movement and the Famine. Describes the trial of the Dublin periodical *The Nation*, which had been accused of seditious libel. A young English landlord tries to improve the lot of his Irish tenants by suggesting better agricultural methods and by building cottages. He has no success, and the seduction of a peasant girl costs him his life. Two Catholic clergymen are contrasted: the older one was educated at Douai, while the younger one received his training at Maynooth. The Famine is seen as an opportunity to convert Catholics [ML; Fegan, p. 220, 228].

F32 *At the King's right hand* (by Mrs Louise Frances Field).
London: Wells Gardner & Co., [1904]. SOURCE Brown, p. 104; COPAC. LOCATION L, NUC.
COMMENTARY An historical novel set in England around 870–910 [NUC].

F33 *Castle Dangerous of Canada* (by Mrs Louise Frances Field).
London: Wells Gardner & Co., [1913] (ill. Leonard S. Skeets). SOURCE COPAC. LOCATION L.

FIELDING, Anna Maria. See HALL, Mrs S.C.

FINGLASS, Miss Esther, fl. 1789. Epistolary novelist, EF was possibly of a Co. Dublin family, where this name appears. The following novel was dedicated to Lady Rutland, whose husband was lord lieutenant of Ireland (1784–87). SOURCE Allibone, i, p. 597; RL.

F34 *The recluse; or, history of Lady Gertrude Lesby* (by Miss Esther Flinglass; dedicated to the duchess of Rutland; recommendation by R. Lewes).
London: J. Barker, 1789, 2 vols. SOURCE Raven 2, 1789:39; Black, 475; Forster 2, 1444; ESTC n012840. LOCATION MH.

+ Dublin: P. Wogan, P. Byrne, J. Moore & J. Halper, 1789, 2 vols. in 1. SOURCE Raven 2, 1789:39; ESTC t1119662. LOCATION L, C.
COMMENTARY An epistolary novel set in England among the gentry concerning a clandestine marriage. No Irish content [Black; *Monthly Review* (Sept. 1790)].

FINLAY, Fr Thomas A., SJ, pseud. 'A. Whitelock' (not 'Thomas Whitelock' as in ODNB and RIA/DIB), b. on an island in the Shannon (Co. Roscommon), near Lanesborough 1848, d. Dublin 1940. Catholic academic, social reformer and writer, TAF was the son of William Finlay, an engineer and native of Fifeshire (Scotland), and Maria Mahgan from Co. Roscommon. With his brother Peter (who became a theologian), TAF was educated in Cavan before both entered the Society of Jesus novitiate at Miltown Park, Dublin, later studying at Amiens and at the Gregorian University in Rome. TAF also studied in Germany, taught German and French at the Jesuit college in Limerick, and was the co-founder of *Catholic Ireland* (which later became the influential Dublin-based *Irish Monthly*). He was ordained in 1880 and became rector of Belvedere College and a fellow of the Royal University of Ireland in classics. He and his brother were appointed joint professors of philosophy at UCD in 1883. With William Magennis, he edited the *Dublin Lyceum* (1887–91), and singly edited the *New Ireland Review* (Dublin, 1894–1911) which was succeeded by *Studies* (Dublin) in 1912. He was chairman of the *Irish Homestead* (Dublin), a journal edited by George Russell. In addition to his writings and translations on philosophy and other topics, around 1901 he edited a series of volumes, *The school and home library*. From 1900 to 1930 he held the chair of political economy at UCD. He was a commissioner of intermediate education, a vice-president of the Irish Agricultural Organization Society and was deeply involved in the Irish cooperative movement. George Moore§, and D.P. Moran were among his friends, and W.E.H. Lecky described him as one of the most universally respected men in Ireland. He was a founder member, with John O'Leary, William Butler Yeats§ and Maud Gonne of the National Literary Society, and was the chairman of the trustees of the NLI. After his retirement, a fund was subscribed that endowed an annual lecture in his name. The first of these was given by John Maynard Keynes. For his portraits and papers, see ODNB. SOURCE Allibone Suppl., i, p. 591; Brooke, p. 20; Brown, p. 105; Clyde, pp 123–4; Elmes, p. 72; Irish pseudonyms; T.J. Morrissey, *Thomas A. Finlay SJ, 1848–1940* (Dublin, 2004), passim; Murphy, p. 48; ODNB; RL; Ryan, p. 152; RIA/DIB [joint entry with Peter Finlay].

F35   *The chances of war. An Irish tale* (by 'A. Whitelock').
+ Dublin: M.H. Gill & Son, 1877. SOURCE Brown, 584. LOCATION D, Dt, InND Loeber coll.
+ Dublin, Belfast: Fallon & Co., 1901 (new edn; The School and Home Library, ed. by T.A. Finlay). LOCATION MChB.
Baile Áta Cliat [Dublin]: Oifig Díolta Foillseacáin Rialtais, 1935 (as *Saigdiúir de sluag Uí Néill* [*With the army of O'Neill*]). SOURCE Morrissey, *Finlay*, p. 16 (1930 edn not located); COPAC. LOCATION O.
COMMENTARY First published in the *Irish Monthly* (Dublin, 1875–77). The aim of this historical novel, set in the seventeenth century, is to indicate the causes that led to the failure of the Confederation of Kilkenny. The main character is an exile returned from a Continental army. The scene is chiefly set at an island in Lough Derg, although the relief of Derry, the battle of Benburb, and Ireton's siege of Limerick are also described. Owen Roe O'Neill, Cardinal Rinuccini, the duke of Ormond, Gen. Thomas, Preston, and Sir Charles Coote are among the characters [ML; Brown; Murphy, p. 155].

F36   *Tales of Ireland for Irish children* (series ed. by Rev. T.A. Finlay; Part 1 by Rev. T.A. Finlay).

+ Dublin: [n.p.], [1917], 4 parts (The Ideal Series; ill.; see Plate 33). SOURCE COPAC. LOCATION Dt.
COMMENTARY Part 1 consists of 85pp. Brief chapters, interspersed with poetry, telling hero stories of ancient Ireland. Part 2 is by Marie Bayne [COPAC; RL].

FINN, Edmund, b. Tipperary 1819, d. Melbourne (Australia) 1898. Teacher, journalist and writer, EF was the son of William and Catherine Mason Finn and was educated for the priesthood at Galbally Abbey (Co. Tipperary). He emigrated to Melbourne in 1841, first tutoring in the classics and then joining the staff of the *Port Phillip Herald* (Victoria). He became a regular contributor to the press, including the *Melbourne Punch*. He was a clerk to the Legislative Council from 1858 to 1886. Aside from fiction, he also published a collection of writings, *The Garryowen sketches*, by 'An old Colonist', in 1880, and at the suggestion of Charles Gavan Duffy, *The chronicles of early Melbourne, 1835–1852* (Melbourne, 1888, 2 vols.). SOURCE ADB, i; BLC; Miller, ii, p. 622; RIA/DIB.

F37   *Der Eggsberiences ov Hans Schwartz; with humorous interleaves* (by Edmund Finn). Melbourne: Alex. M'Kinley & Co., 1878 (ill.). SOURCE Miller, ii, p. 622. LOCATION National Library of Australia.
COMMENTARY 79pp [Libraries Australia (web site)].

F38   *A priest's secret; under seal of confession* (by Edmund Finn). Melbourne: Alex. M'Kinley & Co., 1888 (ill.). SOURCE Miller, ii, p. 622. LOCATION National Library of Australia.
COMMENTARY A murder mystery set in Australia [Miller].

F39   *The Hordern mystery* (by Edmund Finn). Melbourne: Alex. M'Kinley & Co., 1889. SOURCE Miller, ii, p. 622. LOCATION State Library of New South Wales.
COMMENTARY A murder mystery connected with mining speculations [Miller].

FINN, Fr Francis James, SJ, b. St Louis (MO) 1859, d. Cincinnati (OH) 1928. American writer of popular stories for Catholic schoolboys, JF was the son of John Finn and Mary Josephine White, who had emigrated from Ireland. He was educated by the Jesuits, entered the order, and became a teacher. Only his known Irish fiction is listed here. SOURCE ANB; DAB; D.A. Lord (ed.), *Father Finn, S.J.: The story of his life told by himself for his friends, young and old* (New York, 1929); ML.

F40   *Mostly boys: Short stories* (by Francis James Finn). New York: Benziger Bros, 1895. SOURCE OCLC. LOCATION D, Free Library of Philadelphia.
COMMENTARY Contents: 'The wager of Gerald O'Rourke', 'The pickerel prince', 'The last shall be first', 'A young hypocrite', 'Our western waits', 'The legend on the locket', 'Because he loved much', 'The butt of the school', 'Freddie's fishing adventure' [ML].

FINNY, Revd Thomas H.C. See FINNY, Revd Thomas Henry Cotter.

FINNY, Revd Thomas Henry Cotter (known as **Thomas H.C. Finny**), b. *c.*1799, d. prior to 1850. Church of Ireland clergyman, religious writer and memoirist, THCF in 1825 was curate of Tullyagnish in the diocese of Raphoe and in 1841 was licensed to the curacy of St Nicholas, Cork. He was chaplain of the Free (Episcopal) Church, Cork, for many years, and must have died prior to 1850. Given that his memoir accompanied *The history of John Bergan* and was published the same year, he probably was the author of the following volume. It is said he should not be confused with Thomas Henry Cotter Finny, curate of Dunleer, who died at Fermoy (Co. Cork) in 1872 at age 73, but that person was born approximately at that same time as this author. SOURCE AMB; Cork, ii, pp 127–8; Leslie, *Raphoe*; RL.

F41   *The history of John Bergan, a blind boy, a native of Ireland, who was converted from his errors of Romanism to true Christianity, as related by himself* (by the Revd T.C. Finny; with a memoir of the Revd Thomas H.C. Finny, chaplain of the Episcopal Church, Cork; preface signed M.B., and R.S., Exeter).

+ Dublin: P. Dixon Hardy & Sons, 1850, 2nd edn (ill. Millard). LOCATION D.

COMMENTARY No 1st edn located. The preface purports to be an authentication of the truth of the story, including that John Bergan, a native of Rathangan (Co. Kildare), 'was a wicked boy, addicted to almost every species of vice' [RL].

FINNY, Violet Geraldine, pseud. 'V.G.F.', fl. 1892. Writer of fiction for juveniles, VGF presumably was Irish, given the settings of her stories. SOURCE RL.

F42   *Ida's mistake; or, realities and trivialities. A tale* (by 'V.G.F.').

+ London: Digby & Long & Co., 1892. LOCATION L.

F43   *The revolt of the young MacCormacks* (by Violet Geraldine Finny).

London: Ward & Downey, 1896 (ill. Edith Scannell). SOURCE Brown, 592; COPAC. LOCATION L, NUC.

+ London, New York: Macmillan, 1898 (ill. Edith Scannell). LOCATION InND Loeber coll.

COMMENTARY Children's book set partly in Dublin and partly in the west of Ireland, about the pranks of the four MacCormack children [Brown].

F44   *A daughter of Erin* (by Violet Geraldine Finny).

London, Glasgow, Edinburgh, Dublin: Blackie & Son, 1898 (ill. G. Demain Hammond). SOURCE Brown, 592a; Pickering & Chatto cat. 160/16; COPAC. LOCATION D (n.d.), L, NUC ([1908?] edn).

COMMENTARY Set in the west of Ireland. The main character, Norah, initially dislikes her cousin John Herrick, but gradually learns to love him. Her old lover accepts the inevitable and loses his life in trying, for her sake, to do a service to the favoured suitor [Brown].

'A FIRST COUSIN OF ALLY SLOPER', fl. 1886. Pseudonym of a humour writer, who, given the Dublin publication of the following book, was probably Irish. 'Ally Sloper', invented by Charles Henry Ross§, was the first comic strip character in English.

F45   *Fun – humour – laughter. Sixpennyworth to while away an hour on a journey, whether by railroad, or on a steamboat, or up in a balloon* (by 'A first cousin of Ally Sloper').

+ Dublin, London: James Duffy & Co., 1886. LOCATION D, InND Loeber coll.

COMMENTARY Contents: 'On policemen', 'On eggs', 'On coals', 'On priests', 'On pokers', 'On pins', 'On fashions', 'On pens', 'On town councils', 'On matrimony', 'On balls' [ML].

FISHER, Fanny E. (née Lindsay), b. north of Ireland, d. England? Novelist and poet, FEF married a Dr Fisher of Limerick, and lived at Chelsea (London). She also published two volumes of poetry: *Lonely hours* (Dublin, 1864), and *Ainsworth's heir* (London, 1866). SOURCE Allibone Suppl., i, p. 592; COPAC; LVP, p. 166; MVP, p. 165; RL.

F46   *Love or hatred. A novel* (by Fanny E. Fisher; dedicated to the memory of Charles Dickens).

+ London: T. Cautley Newby, 1871, 3 vols. SOURCE COPAC. LOCATION L, C.

COMMENTARY Set in London among the upper classes and features a Lady De Burg, and members of the Werter family [RL].

F47   *The secret of two houses. A novel* (by Fanny E. Fisher; dedicated to the countess of Spencer ... in token of the high esteem in which she is held by the ladies of Ireland).
+ London: Samuel Tinsley, 1873, 2 vols. SOURCE COPAC. LOCATION L, C.
COMMENTARY Set in Co. Clare at the fictive Castlethomond, concerns a love story intertwined with the tensions between the current landowner, Sir Capel Sarsfield, and the dispossessed M'Dermotts [RL].

FISHER, Walter Mulrea, pseud. 'Andrew Quantock', b. Co. Down 1840, d. Glamorgan (Wales) 1919. Journalist and novelist, WMF was educated at Queen's College, Galway. He moved to California, where he worked as a journalist in San Francisco, and later to London, where he studied medicine and qualified in 1883. He practised in Australia, but returned toward the end of the century and settled at Glyncorrwg, Glam., Wales. His *The Californians* (London, 1876) is a demographic study. SOURCE Allibone Suppl., i, p. 594; IBL, 11 (1920), p. 67; RIA/DIB.
F48   *Tandra* (by 'Andrew Quantock').
+ London: C.A. Pearson, 1899 (ill.). SOURCE IBL, 11 (1920), p. 67. LOCATION L.
COMMENTARY Set in Australia [RL].

FITCH, Helen Eliza. See PARKER, Helen F.

FITZGERALD, G. Beresford. See FITZGERALD, Gerald Beresford.

FITZGERALD, Gerald Beresford (known as G. Beresford Fitzgerald), b. 1849. Novelist, GBF was the first son of Revd George Stephen Fitzgerald, Anglican rector of Wanstead, London, of the FitzGerald family of Coolanowle (Co. Laois), and Susan Anne Beresford, of the Lord Decies family. He matriculated at Balliol College, Oxford, in 1867 and married Lucy, daughter of Francis Wickham in 1881. GBF published 14 novels, of which we have identified one with Irish content, but there may be more. SOURCE Allibone Suppl., i, p. 596; BLC; Landed gentry, 1904, p. 190; RIA/DIB.
F49   *Clare Strong. A novel* (by G. Beresford Fitzgerald).
+ London: F.V. White, 1889, 2 vols. SOURCE Wolff, 2246. LOCATION L, NUC.
COMMENTARY Set in London among the upper classes, and features a young man, Clare Strong. The story is populated with characters with names common in Ireland, such as Penrose, Sherlock, Bandon, etc. Clare makes a trip to America, and visits New York and Baltimore, where he meets a Miss Dora M'Carthy, a daughter of a farmer from Co. Tyrone. Subsequently, he returns to London to claim an inheritance, but 'the laws of England' prohibited him from marrying her and two other women he knew. He goes to Rome, where Dora enters his life again [CM; RL].

FITZGERALD, Geraldine Penrose, pseud. 'Naseby', fl. 1870. Novelist. Given the Irish settings of GPF's stories, she was probably Irish or of Irish extraction. SOURCE BLC; RL.
F50   *Ereighda Castle. A novel* [anon.].
+ London: Chapman & Hall, 1870, 3 vols. SOURCE NSTC. LOCATION L, C.
COMMENTARY Set in Ireland. After he inherits the estate from his father, an absentee landlord, the son goes to Ireland and makes his life there [ML].
F51   *Only three weeks* (by 'Naseby').
+ London: Chapman & Hall, 1872, 2 vols. LOCATION L.
COMMENTARY Irish content [CM].
F52   *Oaks and birches. A novel* (by 'Naseby').

+ Edinburgh, London: William Blackwood & Sons, 1885, 3 vols. SOURCE Wolff, 7661. LOCATION L.

COMMENTARY Contains some Irish characters [ML].

F53   *The silver whistle. A novel* (by 'Naseby').

+ London: W.H. Allen & Co., 1890, 2 vols. LOCATION L, InND Loeber coll.

COMMENTARY A story of entangled romance set in Ireland, England and the Continent. Moyrah, a simple Irish girl, is expected to marry Cormack, but Cormack is enticed into seditious activities and has to flee to England. Sydney, an English visitor to Ireland, befriends Moyrah but is very aware of the social distance between them. Moyrah is enticed into marriage by a French agitator and follows him to the Continent, where he deserts her. Since he was already married, her marriage is void. At different times Moyrah and Sydney are instrumental in saving each other's lives, and even though it breaks Sydney's heart, he encourages her to marry Cormack [ML].

FITZGERALD, Isabella Lloyd (née Apjohn), pseud. '**Gerald Glyn**', d. 1907. A novelist and estate manager, ILF was the second daughter of Revd Michael Marshall Lloyd Apjohn of Linfield (Co. Limerick), a Church of Ireland clergyman, and Elizabeth Coote Barnes. She married Desmond John Edmund, 26th knight of Glin of Glin Castle (Co. Limerick), in 1861. In the 1860s the couple travelled on the Continent to retrench, and she is said to have written the novel *Sir Guy's ward* while abroad. In Ireland, she concerned herself with the management of the Glin estate in which her husband showed little interest. He died in 1895. Her portrait was published by Gaughan. SOURCE Burke's, pp 420, 727; J.A. Gaughan, *The knights of Glin* (Mount Merrion, 1978), pp 124–5, 137; Personal communication, knight of Glin, April 1993; RIA/DIB.

F54   *Sir Guy's ward. A novel* (by 'Gerald Glyn').

+ London: Tinsley Bros, 1876, 3 vols. SOURCE Allibone Suppl., ii, p. 680. LOCATION L.

COMMENTARY This is the story of a romance between a guardian and his ward. Maude, who is in a seminary for young ladies in Brussels and falls ill when she hears that her father has died in India. Guy, a friend of her deceased father, becomes her guardian. He is the owner of Treherne Abbey, (somewhere in England) where he and his mother reside. Maude goes to live there and despite obstacles in the way of their love, in the end they marry [ML].

FITZGERALD, John, called 'Bard of the Lee', b. 1825, d. 1910. A poet, painter, antiquary and woodcarver in Cork, JF was the son of John Fitzgerald and Martha Mary Deacy. He was educated at the North Monastery Christian Brothers school in Cork and at age 15 was apprenticed as a cabinetmaker to his brother in London. He returned to Cork in 1841 where he continued his work as a cabinetmaker and took up woodcarving. He supervised the woodcarving department at the Dublin exhibition of 1853 and won first prize in woodcarving at the Cork exhibition of 1883. Better known as a poet, some of his poems were including in *Gems of Cork poets*, published in 1883, and he published a volume of poems, *Echoes of '98*, in the centenary year of the rebellion. He contributed stories, prose and poems about Cork and its history and environs to local papers and he was a reader on the *Cork Examiner* for a number of years. Some of his paintings of Cork are in the Cork museum and some at the Crawford Municipal Gallery, Cork. He perhaps can be identified with a J.D. Fitzgerald who published *Glimpses of Irish life* (Dublin, 1860). SOURCE Allibone Suppl., i, p. 597; Irish pseudonyms; O'Donoghue, p. 143; RIA/DIB.

F55   *Legends, ballads, and songs of the Lee* (by John Fitzgerald).

+ Cork: Henry Coghlan, 1862. SOURCE de Búrca cat. 55/164; COPAC. LOCATION NN.

COMMENTARY Verse and prose fiction. The prose does not have Irish content [ML].

F56   *Echoes of 'Ninety-eight'* (by John Fitzgerald).
+ Cork: Guy & Co., 1898. SOURCE COPAC. LOCATION UCC.
COMMENTARY 45pp. Fictionalized account of the 1798 rebellion. Also contains poetry [RL].

FITZGERALD, Percy Hetherington, pseuds **'Gilbert Dyce'** and **'One of the boys'**, b. Fane Valley (Co. Louth) 1830, d. London 1925. A prolific writer, an artist, critic and barrister, PHF was the son of Thomas Fitzgerald, MP for Co. Louth from 1830 to 1834, who had made a fortune in business in the West Indies, and Maria Dillon. William Carleton§ when young applied in vain to Thomas Fitzgerald for a position as schoolmaster at the school he patronized. PHF was educated at the Catholic school, Stonyhurst (Lancs.) and at TCD, where he obtained his BA in 1855 and MA in 1863. He was admitted to the Lincoln's Inn (London) in 1851, to the King's Inn in 1853, and was called to the Irish Bar two years later. In time he rose to the rank of crown prosecutor on the north-eastern circuit. He was also a diligent sculptor and sometime painter. He published biographies (e.g. David Garrick, Richard Brinsley Sheridan, Laurence Sterne§, and William IV), books of history, plays, and writings on Catholic religious subjects: in all a reputed 200 volumes. He was befriended by Charles Dickens and the publisher Richard Bentley and contributed extensively to Dickens's *Household Words* (London, 1856–59) and to *All the Year Round* (London). He moved to London and wrote for a wide variety of periodicals including *Gentleman's Magazine*, *Cassell's Magazine* (London), the *Illustrated London News* (1876, 1879), the *Belgravia Annual* (London, 1870?), and the *London Society* (Christmas Number, 1873). After Dickens's death he helped to lay the foundation of early Dickens scholarship with his *Memoirs of an author* ([London], 1895). He wrote 30 works of fiction. In 1870 he married Dorcas Olivia Skeffington. He maintained contact with Ireland and his *Recollections of Dublin Castle and Dublin society* was published in London in 1902. His *Autobiography of a small boy* appeared in London in 1869. His *The story of the Incumbered Estates Court* (London, 1862) is not fiction. Some of his letters are among the Downey Papers (NLI, MS 10,013). SOURCE Allibone Suppl., i, pp 597–8; B & S, Appendix B, p. 40; *The autobiography of William Carleton* (London, 1968), pp 142, 144–5; Boylan, p. 117; Brady, p. 79; Hogan 2, pp 438–9; Keane, p. 166; Lohrli, pp 271–3; NCBEL 4, pp 1530–1; OCIL, p. 196; RIA/DIB; Sutherland, p. 227; Wolff, ii, p. 85.

F57   *Roman candles* [anon.] (dedicated to William Henry Wills).
+ London: Chapman & Hall, 1861. LOCATION D, L, E (1861 edn).

F58   *The night mail* (by Percy Hetherington Fitzgerald).
London: Ward & Lock, 1861 (Shilling Volume Library, No. 19). SOURCE Topp 2, p. 90; Sadleir, 3755b(i) ([1869] edn). LOCATION D (1885 edn), NUC (1883 edn).
+ London: Ward & Lock, 1862 (as *The night mail. Its passengers and how they fared at Christmas*). LOCATION D, L.

F59   *The woman with the yellow hair and other modern mysteries* [anon.] (dedicated to Edmund Waterton, F.S.A., of Walton).
+ London: Saunders, Otley & Co., [1862]. LOCATION D.
London: United Kingdom Press, [186—?] (as *The woman with the yellow hair: A romance of good and bad society*). LOCATION NUC.
COMMENTARY Contents: 'The woman with the yellow hair', 'The Balcombe street mystery', 'The blood of the Sundons', 'The old Yellow Tiger Inn', 'The canon's clock', 'The armourer's story', 'At the sign of the silver horn', 'A vision of a studious man', 'In a first-class carriage' [ML].

F60   *Mildrington the barrister. A romance* [anon.] (dedicated to Joseph Sheridan Le Fanu§).

+ London: Saunders, Otley & Co., 1863, 2 vols. SOURCE Sutherland, p. 227; Sadleir, 882 (1864, 2nd edn); Wolff, 2252 (1864, 2nd edn). LOCATION D, InND Loeber coll.
COMMENTARY First serialized in the *Dublin University Magazine*. Mildrington, a London barrister, has an extremely overbearing mother who holds the purse strings. She wishes him to marry well and has selected a girl for him. He, however, has secretly married a girl considered beneath him. In order to go along with his mother's ideas, he neglects his wife and is frequently seen at the home of the girl his mother has chosen for him. When he finally has to admit that he is already married, his mother disinherits him and his wife leaves him to go back to France. Mildrington's career is ruined. He goes to the colonies to start afresh [ML].

F61   *Rev. Alfred Hoblush and his curacies. A memoir* [anon.] (dedicated to the author's mother [Maria Fitzgerald]).
+ London: John Maxwell & Co., 1863. SOURCE Sadleir, 3755b(i) ([1869–70] edn); Topp 6, 3. LOCATION D, L ([1870] edn), NUC (1864 edn).
COMMENTARY First serialized in *Household Words* (London). Traces the life of Revd Hoblush through eight curacies. The sixth curacy is set in a fictitious seaport of Slopery with its 'Ebalana' square [*sic*], alluding to Dublin [Preface to the above book; RL].

F62   *Bella Donna; or, the cross before the name. A romance* (by 'Gilbert Dyce').
+ London: Richard Bentley, 1864, 2 vols. SOURCE Sadleir, 877; Wolff, 2248. LOCATION D, NUC.
London: Chapman & Hall, 1868 (new edn; Select Library of Fiction, No. 129). SOURCE Topp 3, p. 350; COPAC. LOCATION L.
COMMENTARY First serialized in the *Dublin University Magazine* (1863) [Topp].

F63   *Fairy Alice* (by Percy Hetherington Fitzgerald).
+ London: Richard Bentley, 1865, 2 vols. SOURCE Sadleir, 879. LOCATION D, L.

F64   *Never forgotten* (by Percy Hetherington Fitzgerald; dedicated to Charles Dickens).
+ London: Chapman & Hall, 1865, 3 vols. SOURCE Sadleir, 883; Wolff, 2253; COPAC. LOCATION D, L.
+ London: Chapman & Hall, 1867 (new edn, revsd; ill.; Select Library of Fiction, No. 137). SOURCE Topp 3, p. 352. LOCATION D, InND Loeber coll. (1881 edn).
COMMENTARY Serialized in *All the Year Round* (London, 1865). A story of romance, rejection and revenge that begins in an English coastal garrison town. An extremely egocentric officer, Fermor, who thinks that most people are beneath him, sets out to win a young girl, Violet. Fermor embarks on this exploit not so much because he loves Violet as to thwart her avowed lover, a Mr Hanbury. When it suits him, Fermor drops Violet and she wastes away and dies. Violet's sister and brother vow revenge for her death on anyone who had a hand in it. They take years to prepare the downfall of various people, and when everything is in place to accomplish this, they learn that Violet's last wish had been that no harm should come to those who had wronged her. However, the brother and sister are incapable of stopping what they have set in motion [ML; Topp].

F65   *The second Mrs. Tillotson. A story* (by Percy Hetherington Fitzgerald; dedicated to Viscountess Strangford).
+ London: Tinsley Bros, 1866, 3 vols. SOURCE Sadleir, 885. LOCATION D, L, NUC.
London: Chapman & Hall, 1868 (revsd edn; Select Library of Fiction, No. 136). SOURCE Topp 3, p. 352; OCLC. LOCATION GEU.
New York: Hilton & Co., 1866. LOCATION NUC.
COMMENTARY First serialized in *All the Year Round* (London) [Topp].

F66   *Jenny Bell. A story* (by Percy Hetherington Fitzgerald; dedicated to Walter Creyke, Esq.).
+ London: Richard Bentley, 1866, 3 vols. SOURCE Sadleir, 880. LOCATION D, Dcc, L.

F67   *Seventy-five Brooke Street. A story* (by Percy Hetherington Fitzgerald).
London: Tinsley Bros, 1867, 3 vols. SOURCE Sadleir, 886; Wolff, 2256. LOCATION L,
NUC.
London: Chapman & Hall, 1868 (new edn; Select Library of Fiction, No. 133). SOURCE
Topp 3, p. 350; OCLC. LOCATION GEU.

F68   *Polly. A village portrait* [anon.].
+ London: Tinsley Bros, 1867, 2 vols. SOURCE Wolff, 2255. LOCATION D.
London: Chapman & Hall, 1868 (new edn; Select Library of Fiction, No. 132). SOURCE
Topp 3, p. 351.
COMMENTARY *London Chapman edn* No copy located [RL].

F69   *School days at Saxonhurst* (by 'One of the boys').
Edinburgh: A. & C. Black, 1867 (ill., Phiz). SOURCE Osborne, p. 987 (1868, 2nd edn).
LOCATION L, CaOTP (1868, 2nd edn).
+ Deventer: W. Hulscher [1874] (trans. into Dutch by C. Stoffel as *Schetsen uit de
schoolwereld en het jongensleven*). LOCATION InND Loeber coll.

F70   *Diana Gay; or, the history of a young lady* (by Percy Hetherington Fitzgerald; ded-
icated to Mrs Charles Collins).
+ London: Tinsley Bros, 1868, 3 vols. SOURCE Wolff, 2246 (1881 edn). LOCATION D,
L, NUC.

F71   *The dear girl* (by Percy Hetherington Fitzgerald; dedicated to the countess of
Charlemont).
+ London: Tinsley Bros, 1868, 3 vols. SOURCE Sadleir, 878. LOCATION D, Dcc, L,
NUC.

F72   *Fatal zero, a diary kept at Homburg* [anon.].
+ London: Tinsley Bros, 1869, 2 vols. LOCATION D, L (1886 edn), NUC.
COMMENTARY Written in the form of a diary, it is a study of gambling mania
[Sutherland].

F73   *Beauty Talbot* (by Percy Hetherington Fitzgerald).
+ London: Richard Bentley, 1870, 3 vols. SOURCE Sadleir, 876; Wolff, 2247. LOCATION
D, L.

F74   *Two fair daughters* (by Percy Hetherington Fitzgerald; dedicated to Charles Dickens).
+ London: Hurst & Blackett, 1871, 3 vols. SOURCE Sadleir, 887. LOCATION D, L,
NUC.

F75   *The middle aged lover. A story* (by Percy Hetherington Fitzgerald).
London: Richard Bentley, 1873, 2 vols. SOURCE Sadleir, 881. LOCATION L, NUC.

F76   *The parvenu family; or, Phoebe: girl and wife* (by Percy Hetherington Fitzgerald).
+ London: Richard Bentley & Son, 1876, 3 vols. SOURCE Sadleir, 884; Wolff, 2254.
LOCATION D, L.
COMMENTARY Chronicles Phoebe Dawson as she progresses from finishing school to troubled
marriage into the parvenu Pringle family, followed by a resolution of all troubles [Sutherland].

F77   *Little Dorinda: who won and who lost her!* (by Percy Hetherington Fitzgerald).
+ London: Burns & Oates, 1878. LOCATION D (n.d. edn), L.
New York, Montreal: D. & J. Sadlier & Co., 1878. LOCATION NUC.

F78   *Young Coelebs* (by Percy Hetherington Fitzgerald; dedicated to Lady O'Hagan).
+ London: Tinsley Bros, 1881, 3 vols. SOURCE Wolff, 2258. LOCATION D, L.

F79   *Puppets. A romance* (by Percy Hetherington Fitzgerald).
+ London: Chapman & Hall, 1884, 3 vols. LOCATION D, L.

F80   *The lady of Brantome* (by Percy Hetherington Fitzgerald).
+ London: Chatto & Windus, 1884. SOURCE Topp 3, p. 123. LOCATION D.

COMMENTARY First appeared in the *Gentleman's Annual* (Christmas 1883) [Topp].

F81   *Topside & Turvey* (by Percy Hetherington Fitzgerald).
+ London, New York, Glasgow, Manchester: George Routledge & Sons, [1889] (Tillotson's Shilling Fiction). LOCATION D.

F82   *Three weeks at Mopetown; or, humours of a hydro* (by Percy Hetherington Fitzgerald).
+ London: Henry & Co., 1891 (Whitefriars Library of Wit and Humour, No. 4; photograph of the author). SOURCE Wolff, 2257. LOCATION D, L, NUC.

F83   *Pickwickian studies* (by Percy Hetherington Fitzgerald).
+ London: New Century Press, 1899. LOCATION L, InND Loeber coll.
COMMENTARY Humorous parody of Dickens's *Pickwick Papers* (London, 1837) [ML].

F84   *The bachelor's dilemma; and other stories, gay and grave* (by Percy Hetherington Fitzgerald).
London: Railway and General Automatic Library, [1892]. LOCATION L.

F85   *Lady Jean: the romance of the great Douglas cause* (by Percy Hetherington Fitzgerald).
London: T. Fisher Unwin, 1904. LOCATION L, NUC.

F86   *Josephine's troubles: a story of the great Franco-German war of 1870–1871* (by Percy Hetherington Fitzgerald).
London: Burns & Oates, [1907]. LOCATION L, NUC.

F87   *Worldlyman. A modern morality of our day setting forth how he passed from death to life, from sin to virtue; how he was lost and how he was found, by the agency of the good father S. Sepulchre, both going down in the 'Leviathan' liner* (by Percy Hetherington Fitzgerald).
+ London: Burns & Oates, [1913]. LOCATION D, L.

FITZMAURICE, John W., fl. 1889. American novelist.

F88   *'The shanty boy,' or, life in a lumber camp. Being pictures of the pine woods in descriptions, tales, songs and adventures in the lumbering shanties of Michigan and Wisconsin* (by John W. Fitzmaurice).
+ Cheboygan, MI: Democrat Steam Print, 1889. SOURCE Fanning, p. 381; OCLC. LOCATION L, NUC.
COMMENTARY A man of Irish extraction becomes a shanty boy (someone working in a lumber camp) on the advice of his doctor. He meets a number of other Irishmen among the woodsmen. The book contains several songs about Ireland, for example, 'The flower of Kildare'. The workings of the lumber industry are discussed [ML].

FITZPATRICK, Thomas, pseud. 'Banna-Borka', b. Gargory (Co. Down) 1845, d. Dublin 1912. Fiction and history writer, TF was a teacher at Blackrock College (Co. Dublin), St Malachy's College (Belfast), Athenry (Co. Galway), and headmaster of Birr School (Co. Offaly) in 1876. He was the author of two books on Ireland in the seventeenth century: *The bloody bridge* (Dublin, 1903) and *Waterford during the Civil War* (Waterford, 1912), as well as *A transatlantic holiday or notes of a visit to the Eastern states of America* (London, 1891), and *An autumn cruise in the Aegean in a sailing-yacht* (London, 1886). SOURCE Allibone Suppl., i, p. 599; BLC; Brady, p. 80; Newmann, p. 80; E. Reilly, p. 244; RIA/DIB; RL.

F89   *Jabez Murdock: Poetaster and 'adjint.' A romance of South Down* (by 'Banna-Borka').
Dublin: James Duffy & Sons, 1887, 2 vols. SOURCE Adv. in W. Carleton, *Redmond Count O'Hanlon* (Dublin, 1886); Brown, 601. LOCATION L (1888, 1 vol. edn), InND Loeber coll. (1888, 1 vol. edn).

COMMENTARY No copy of the Dublin 1887 (2 vols.) edn located. Set in south Co. Down in the first quarter of the nineteenth century where a rascally Scots settler attains wealth by unscrupulous means. The story gives many descriptions of peasant life and discusses the problem of landlords raising rents on the basis of improvements tenants have made to their holdings. Even after the defeat of Napoleon when produce is worth less, the rents stay high. It describes the processes of milling and weaving, the organization of a school and the distillation of whiskey [ML; Brown].

F90   *Newland; or, 'third class'. A Dublin sketch* (by 'Banna-Borka').
+ Dublin: Sealy, Bryers & Walker; London: Simpkin, Marshall & Co., 1889. SOURCE Topp 8, 957. LOCATION L.
COMMENTARY Set in Ireland, starting in Dublin, it traces the lives of two men of different social standing. Mr Doherty is poor, but he ends up well-to-do and happily married. Mr Newland turns out to be a crook and is sent to prison [ML].

F91   *The king of Claddagh. A story of the Cromwellian occupation of Galway* (by Thomas FitzPatrick).
+ London: Sands & Co., 1899 (ill.). SOURCE Brown, 602; COPAC. LOCATION D, DPL, L, NUC, InND Loeber coll.
Dublin: Mercier, [c.1979] (abridged by Uni Morrissy; Mercier Irish Classics). LOCATION L.
COMMENTARY Historical fiction set in Galway city and county during the Cromwellian period, it includes descriptions of the atrocities committed by the Cromwellians during the occupation of Galway city [ML; Brown].

FITZSIMON, E.A. See FITZSIMON, Elizabeth A.

FITZSIMON, Elizabeth A. (known as E.A. Fitzsimon), b. Lismore? (Co. Waterford) 1841, d. Boston (MA) 1921. A probably Catholic journalist, editor and writer, EAF was the daughter of Andrew FitzSimon, who had an academy in Lismore where she taught from 1864 to 1869. One of her pupils was Julia Crottie§. In 1869 EAF and her family moved to the US. She became a journalist in 1875 and in 1880 was editor of the *Providence Visitor*. In 1887 she married Dr M.A. Walsh of Providence (RI) who died in 1919. EAF also wrote educational works that were used in public schools in New England. SOURCE Brown, p. 109; IBL, 12 (1921), p. 144.

F92   *The joint venture. A tale in two lands* (by E.A. Fitzsimon; dedicated to 'the sons and daughters of Ireland, and their American cousins').
+ New York, Baltimore, Washington, Boston: James Sheehy, 1878 (ill.). SOURCE Brown, 603; Fanning, p. 381; Wright, iii, 1884. LOCATION DCU, NUC.
New York, Baltimore, Washington, Boston: James Sheehy, 1881 (as *Gerald Barry; or, the joint venture, tale of two lands*). SOURCE Brown, 603; Wright, iii, 1884. LOCATION D (1887 edn), NUC.
COMMENTARY Set in a valley of the Knockmealdown Mountains (Co. Tipperary) and in the US. Written from a Catholic point of view, it attacks Protestant divorce laws and includes the conversion of a person to catholicism [Brown].

'FLAMMHERZ, GOTTFRIED', pseud. See EBRARD, Johannes Heinrich August.

'A FLAT ENLIGHTENED "EXPERIENTA DOCET"', probable pseud. See LUTTRELL, Henry.

FLEMING, Mrs May Agnes (née Early; not Mary Agnes as in Brown), b. Portland, St John (New Brunswick, Canada) 1840, d. Brooklyn (NY) 1880. Canadian author of popular Catholic tales and Gothic and sentimental stories, May was the daughter of Irish immigrants, Bernard Early, a ship's carpenter and grocer, and Mary Doherty, who was a school teacher in the north of Ireland before moving to Canada. May married John William Fleming, a civil engineer of Brooklyn, in 1865. According to Mason, 'she was the best-selling Canadian author of her time … she wrote perhaps a hundred books or more. (The exact number is difficult to establish because the titles were changed regularly, not just between England and America, but also between publishers – a new publisher, often a pirate, would change a title to make his edn appear to be a new title)'. Many of her stories appeared in periodicals, notably in *Young Ireland* (Dublin), *Saturday Night* (Philadelphia), and the *New York Weekly* (1872 on). The volume *Hates and loves, or, the lesson of four lives* (New York, 1863), which appeared under the name of Arthur Townley, has been ascribed to her, but this and another work by Townley, *Clifton or modern fashions* (Philadelphia, 1852), are unlikely to be by her. Estranged from her husband, MAF was excluded from the upbringing of her children. She died of Bright's disease. Only her works currently known to have Irish content are listed below. SOURCE Allibone Suppl., i, p. 602; Blain, pp 379–80; Brown, p. 109; CEWW; DCB; Dime novels; DLB, ic; D. Mason, 'A tale of delusion, illusion and mystery: Booksellers and librarians', *Descant 91*, (4)26 (1995), p. 30; L. McMullen, 'A checklist of the works of May Agnes Fleming' in *Papers of the Bibliographical Society of Canada*, 28 (1990), pp 25–37; OCLC; NUC.

F93   *Lady Evelyn; or, the Lord of Royal Rest* (by Mrs May Agnes Fleming).
[n.l.]: National Publishing Co., 1869. SOURCE OCLC. LOCATION OU.
London: Henderson, 1882 (as *Lord Rory; or, the Lord of Royal Rest. A romance of old Ireland*). SOURCE Brown 2, 505.
COMMENTARY No copy of the London edn located. Scene opens on the Wicklow coast 'near the village of Clontarf' [*sic*]. Kathleen O'Neill, the village beauty, loves Lord Roderick Desmond, but his affections are given to another. Kathleen refuses Morgan, a villainous attorney. He murders her and suspicion falls on Lord Roderick, but the story ends happily [Brown 2; RL].

F94   *The star of De Vere; or, the mysteries of Bantry Hall* [anon.].
+ London: James Henderson, 1871–72 (The People's Pocket Story Books). SOURCE COPAC. LOCATION L.
+ London: James Henderson, n.d. (The People's Pocket Story Books) (as *Jacquetta; or, the star of De Vere*). LOCATION InND Loeber coll.
COMMENTARY Incongruously, whereas the date of the first volume in the London 1871–72 edn is 1872, the second volume carries the date 1871. Originally published as an American story in 1861, but ten years later the scene was changed to Ireland. The Irish version is a Gothic tale set in the neighbourhood of Bantry (Co. Cork) in which a large number of the characters are not aware of their true identity or live under the burden of a horrible, but a false secret. Other elements of the story involve secret happenings in a deserted wing of Bantry Hall; kidnappings by gypsies; pirates, and prophesies by an old hag. In the end all mysteries are revealed and the surviving characters live happily. The London 1871–2 edn also contains 'Prairie star', and 'The mysterie of Hazel Lodge' (by C.A. Read§) [Brown 2; ML; RL].

F95   *A wonderful woman. A novel* (by Mrs May Agnes Fleming; dedicated to Sara Hamilton Lemon).
+ New York: G.W. Carleton & Co.; London: S. Low, Son & Co., 1873. SOURCE Brown, 604 (1906 edn). LOCATION Wright web.
COMMENTARY Love story in which Redmond O'Donnell, an impoverished Irish gentleman, meets an English lady, who is visiting Ireland with her titled father. After many obstacles have been overcome they are married, but then it transpires that the lady is only the daughter of a servant who had exchanged babies with her mistress [Brown; ML].

F96   *A mad marriage. A novel* (by Mrs May Agnes Fleming).
New York: G.W. Carleton & Co.; London: Simpson Low & Co., 1875. SOURCE
Wright, ii, 913. LOCATION NUC, Wright web.
+ London: Tinsley Bros, 1875, 3 vols. LOCATION L.
+ Paris: Hachette, 1878, 2 vols. (trans. by C. Bernard-Derosne as *Un mariage extrav-
agant*). LOCATION L.
COMMENTARY Irish content [CM].

F97   *Maud Percy's secret: a novel* (by Mrs May Agnes Fleming).
New York: G.W. Carleton & Co., 1884. SOURCE Brown, 605; OCLC. LOCATION NUC.
COMMENTARY The story is set mainly in England, but some of the principal person-
ages are briefly shifted to Ireland [Brown].

'FLEMING, Zachary, writer', pseud. and editor. See JOHNSTON, Henry.

FLETCHER, Miss A., pseud. 'Sheelah', fl. 1857. American religious fiction writer, AF also
wrote *Within Fort Sumter* (New York, 1861). SOURCE Allibone Suppl., i, p. 602; Brown, p. 2;
NUC; Wright, ii, p. 923.

F98   *Ballyshan Castle. A tale founded on fact* (by 'Sheelah').
+ New York: N. Tibbals, 1857 (ill.). SOURCE Brown, 6; Wright, ii, 922. LOCATION D,
NUC.
New York: N. Tibbals, 1866 (as *The mother's request; or, Ballyshan Castle*). SOURCE
Wright, ii, p. 124. LOCATION NUC, Wright web.
COMMENTARY Religious fiction set in Athlone in the midlands of Ireland. Ellen Martin, a
Protestant, makes a love match with the O'Dougherty, Catholic owner of Ballyshan Castle.
The marriage is a failure, and Ellen declines and dies. Before her death she exacts a promise
from her sister to abduct her son and bring him up as a Protestant. The sister fulfils the prom-
ise and puts the child in the Foundling Hospital in Dublin. The child, grown into adulthood,
makes many converts to protestantism through Bible reading. He marries happily and emigrates to Canada [Brown].

'FLINT, Thaddeus', pseud. See GRIFFIN, Gerald.

FLOOD, William, fl. 1856. Regional fiction writer, WF was probably Irish because of the
settings of his work and because he published in Dublin only. SOURCE RL.

F99   *A peep into one of the corners of old Ireland* (by William Flood).
+ Dublin: Published for the author, 1856. LOCATION D.
COMMENTARY Concerns the inhabitants of the 'rustic' village of Castletown (Co. Laois), who
according to the author, 'will recognize the characters under their disguised names' [RL].

F100   *The Irishman's tour of ruin* (by William Flood).
+ Dublin: Published by the author, 1858. SOURCE Brown 2, 506. LOCATION D.
COMMENTARY 36pp. Set in a small village in the south of Ireland [Brown 2].

'FLOREDICE, W.H.', pseud. See HART, William.

FOGERTY, J., fl. 1873. Novelist, who in all likelihood was Irish or of Irish extraction (several of JF's novels deal with Ireland). A copy of *Countess Irene* formerly at Quaritch (cat.
1293/75), contains a manuscript family tree of the Fogerty family, but it has only first names
and no information regarding Irish nationality and does not clarify the author's descent. Only
JF's novels with Irish content are listed below. Brown 2 mistakenly identifies the author as J.

Fogarty. SOURCE Allibone Suppl., i, p. 605; BLC; Brown 2, 507; COPAC; Personal communication, T. Hoffman, Feb. 2000; RL; Wolff, ii, pp 86–7.

F101 *Lauterdale. A story of two generations* [anon.] (dedicated to the 'Masters and Men in England, in the Hope of Creating a Better Feeling Between Them').
+ London: Strahan & Co, 1873, 3 vols. SOURCE COPAC. LOCATION L.
COMMENTARY This does not appear to have any Irish content. Set in Lauterdale, a village in England, known for its iron and coal works [JB].

F102 *Caterina* [anon.].
+ London: Hurst & Blackett, 1887, 3 vols. SOURCE COPAC. LOCATION L.
COMMENTARY Novel opens: 'Colonel Harding had seen service in many lands, and plenty of it. He came of a fighting family – an old English family long settled in the west of Ireland ...' (p. 1). Col. Harding, whose estate is in Co. Clare, is the guardian of his niece Kate Harding. The action takes place in various locations across Europe [JB].

F103 *Countess Irene* [anon.].
+ Edinburgh, London: William Blackwood & Sons, 1888, 3 vols. SOURCE Brown 2, 507. LOCATION L, NUC.
COMMENTARY Depicts life and manners in Vienna and in an Austrian country seat; landscapes of the Salz Kammergut and the village of the Traun and the Inn, varied by pictures of Irish life and Shannon scenery [Brown 2].

F104 *Robert Leeman's daughters* (by J. Fogerty).
+ London: R. Bentley & Son, 1889, 3 vols. SOURCE COPAC. LOCATION L.
COMMENTARY Limited Irish contents: the story begins in Wexford, but shifts to other locations, primarily Holland and the United States [JB].

F105 *Mr. Jocko. A novel* (by J. Fogerty).
+ London: Ward & Downey, 1891, 3 vols. SOURCE COPAC. LOCATION L.
COMMENTARY No Irish contents. Mr Jocko is the name of a monkey in the novel [JB].

F106 *Juanita* (by J. Fogerty).
+ London: Ward & Downey, 1893, 3 vols. SOURCE COPAC. LOCATION L.
COMMENTARY Set mainly in Ireland (in 'Malbay', a bay on the west coast of Ireland) [JB].

F107 *A game at chess; or, when Jew meets Greek. And In and out of Zion* (by J. Fogerty).
+ London: Diprose & Bateman, [1894]. SOURCE COPAC. LOCATION L.
COMMENTARY No Irish content. Contents 'A game at chess; or, when Jew meets Greek'. 'In and out of Zion' [JB].

F108 *A hunted life. An episode* (by J. Fogerty).
London: Hutchinson & Co., 1894, 3 vols. SOURCE Burmester list; Wolff, 2275; COPAC. LOCATION L, NYU.
COMMENTARY Mystery novel of crime and adventure set on the west coast of Ireland. The hero starts out as an effeminate youth who receives serious injuries in an encounter with a bull [Burmester list].

FORDE, Arthur Brownlow. See FFORDE, Arthur Brownlow.

FORRESTER, Arthur M., b. Salford, Manchester (England) 1850, d. South Boston (MA) 1895. AMF's parents were Michael Forrester, a stonemason, and Ellen Magennis, a poet, who was born in Clones (Co. Monaghan). AMF was a printer by trade and wrote for the *Irish People* (Manchester). In 1865 he went to Dublin and became involved with the Fenian movement. He was arrested several times and served time in prison, after which he joined the French army (1870) and fought in the Franco-German war. According to O'Donoghue, he was implicated in the Phoenix Park murders in 1882 and went to America soon after. He was a frequent contributor to the *Irish World* (New York) and other American papers and was a proof-reader for the *Boston Herald*. With his mother, he published *Songs of the rising nation and other poems* (London, 1869). His sister was the author Mary Magdalen Forrester. SOURCE BLC; Irish pseudonyms; O'Donoghue, p. 151; OCLC; RL.

F109   *An Irish crazy-quilt. Smiles and tears, woven into song and story* (by Arthur M. Forrester; dedicated to the 'Felons' of Ireland).
+ Boston: Alfred Mudge & Son, 1891. SOURCE OCLC. LOCATION Brown Univ. Library, InND Loeber coll.
COMMENTARY Poems, stories and sketches. The stories are: 'Taming a tiger', 'Ryan's revenge', 'A seditious slide', 'Who shot Phlynn's hat?', 'A double surprise', 'Philipson's party', 'A picturesque penny-a-liner', 'A typical trial', 'Why Smithers resigned', 'Exploits of an Irish reporter', 'An Orange oration', 'Frederick's folly', 'A Sandy Row skirmish', 'Hobbies in our block', 'Not a John L. Sullivan', 'A windy day at Cabra', 'Apropos of the census', 'A mixed antiquarian', 'Jones's umbrella', 'Lessons in the French drama', 'A commercial crisis', 'A musical revenge', 'A lair laid out' [RL].

FORTESCUE, Walter, fl. 1898. Novelist.
F110   *An Irish patriot* (by Walter Fortescue).
+ London, New York: F. Tennyson Neely, 1898. SOURCE Brown 2, 509; OCLC. LOCATION D, NUC.
COMMENTARY Written from a Fenian point of view and set during a period of political chaos following the death of Parnell. The plot turns on four young men, Cornwell, Fenton, Lenwood, and the hero, James O'Nally, a student from Blackrock College, who meet in a train going from Dublin to Westport. Fenton becomes a Protestant for business purposes, and O'Nally's enemy No. 1; Lenwood, a somewhat insipid Englishman, goes to stay with his cousins, the Cornwells, and becomes O'Nally's rival for the hand of Helena Cornwell. O'Nally's father, Walter, is a devout Catholic but a lukewarm politician who drives his son out of the house when he learns that he is a Fenian. O'Nally is arrested, escapes, and is re-arrested, but gets away to the US. All comes right in the end and he marries Helena, a Protestant, with Fr Lavelle and a Protestant minister officiating [Brown 2].

FOSTER, Mrs J. Co-author. See HALL, Mrs S.C.

FOWLER, Eliza. See HAYWOOD, Eliza.

FOX, Mrs Emily, pseud. 'Toler King', fl. 1878. American novelist, EF was the author of *Gemini* (Boston, 1878) and *Off the rocks* (Chicago, 1882). SOURCE Allibone Suppl., i, p. 621; Brown, p. 159.
F111   *Rose O'Connor. A story of the day* (by 'Toler King').
Chicago: Legal News Co., 1880. SOURCE Brown, 871. LOCATION NUC.
COMMENTARY A romance set in Ireland during the 1845–49 Famine. Rose O'Connor and Tim Brady love each other. Tim has to go to America and while he is away, the Famine strikes Ireland. Rose's family is reduced to great poverty and she is compelled to promise marriage to Tim's rival. However, Tim returns in the nick of time [Brown; Fegan, p. 210].

FOX, Lady Mary. Editor. See WHATELY, Revd Richard.

'FRANCES', pseud. See GRIFFITH, Elizabeth.

467

FRANCES, Margaret Rose. American writer.

F112   *Carleton's reward* (by Margaret Rose Frances).
+ Cincinnati: Bosworth, Chase & Hall, 1871 (ill.). LOCATION Wright web.
COMMENTARY Story of an Irish family by the name of Carleton, who had lost all their belongings because the father had given surety for a friend. The father dies and the mother and five children emigrate to America. Life is very hard but by living as Christians and working hard they are successful [ML].

FRANCILLON, R.E. See **FRANCILLON, Robert Edward**.

FRANCILLON, Robert Edward (known as **R.E. Francillon**), b. Glos. 1841, d. 1919. An author of serial adventure novels, REF was the son of a county court judge of Huguenot origin and was educated at Cheltenham College and Trinity Hall, Cambridge. He was called to the Bar at Grey's Inn in 1864, but moved to journalism, joining the staff of the *Globe* (London), where he worked from 1872 to 1894. He published an autobiography, *Mid-Victorian memories* (n.l., 1914). SOURCE Allibone Suppl., i, p. 623; Sutherland, p. 232.

F113   *Under Slieve-Ban: a yarn in seven knots* [anon.].
New York: H. Holt & Co., 1881. SOURCE B. Browne. LOCATION NUC.
New York: G. Munro, [1881]. LOCATION NUC.
+ London: Grant & Co., [1882?] (Christmas Number). LOCATION InND Loeber coll.
COMMENTARY A love story set in the 1798 period [B. Browne].

F114   *Jack Doyle's daughter* (by R.E. Francillon).
+ London: Chatto & Windus, 1894, 3 vols. SOURCE Sutherland, p. 232. LOCATION L.
COMMENTARY Reviewers found the work about the misadventures of a heroine and heiress with six possible fathers pleasant but incoherent in the extreme. A group of bohemian friends includes two Irishmen, Ulick Ronaine, a Munster man, and Jack Doyle. Jack has a daughter, Phoebe, who turns out to be Alice Bassett of Cautleigh Hall. She marries, but keeps a place for Jack in her heart and home [ML; Sutherland].

FRANCIS, Lydia Maria. See **CHILD, Lydia Maria**.

'FRANCIS, M.E.', pseud. See **BLUNDELL, Mary E.**

FRANKAU, Julia (née Davis), pseud. **'Frank Danby'**, b. Dublin 1859, d. London 1916. Novelist, art historian and sportswoman, JF was the daughter of Hyman Davis, who came from an English Jewish family, and his wife Isabella. The family returned to London in 1863, where JF was educated by Karl Marx's daughter, Laura Lafargue. JF's brother James was a friend of Oscar Wilde§ and George Moore§ and Moore encouraged her in her writing. She was interested in art and she wrote on eighteenth-century colour prints and engravers. Four of her 15 novels attack Jewish materialism. She also contributed one of the 24 chapters of a novel edited by John Seymour Wood, *The fate of Fenella* (London, 1892), along with writers such as Justin McCarthy§, May Cromellin§, Bram Stoker§, Margaret Hungerford§, Clo Graves§, and others. JF was an inveterate card player, a bicyclist and a horsewoman, and described herself as 'half Celt and wholly impulsive'. She married Arthur Frankau, a wholesale cigar merchant, in 1883. Her sister Eliza Aria was also a writer as was her son Gilbert Frankau, a novelist and poet. She is buried in Hampstead cemetery (London). For her portrait, see ODNB. SOURCE Allibone Suppl., i, p. 445 [under Danby]; Blain, p. 262 [under Danby]; ODNB; RIA/DIB; Sutherland, p. 233; T & B, p. 976 [under Frankau]; Sutherland, p. 233; T & B, p. 976.

F115   *Dr. Phillips, a Maida Vale idyll* (by 'Frank Danby').
London: Vizetelly & Co., 1887. SOURCE RIA/DIB. LOCATION L.

COMMENTARY Supposedly based on a well-known doctor, it is the story of a Jewish doctor who, fearing to lose his gentile mistress, kills his wife with morphine. The book was offensive to Jews for its negative comparisons between Jewish and gentile life and it outraged conventional Victorian society for depicting a doctor with a mistress and baby. Nevertheless it was twice reprinted [RIA/DIB; ODNB; Sutherland, p. 233].

F116   *The copper crash: Founded on fact* (by 'Frank Danby').
London: Trischler & Co., 1889. LOCATION L.

F117   *A babe in Bohemia* (by 'Frank Danby').
London: Spencer Blackett, 1889. SOURCE RIA/DIB. LOCATION L.
COMMENTARY A tale of seduction. The main character is Lucilla Lewisham, a venereally-diseased epileptic girl who eventually cuts her own throat in a seizure [Sutherland].

F118   *Pigs in clover* (by 'Frank Danby').
London: William Heinemann, 1903. SOURCE RIA/DIB. LOCATION L.
COMMENTARY An anti-Semitic story caricaturing a well-known aesthete [RIA/DIB].

F119   *Baccarat. A novel* (by 'Frank Danby').
London: William Heinemann, 1904 (ill. Parys). LOCATION L.

F120   *The sphinx's lawyer* (by 'Frank Danby').
London: William Heinemann, 1906. SOURCE Sutherland, p. 233. LOCATION L.
COMMENTARY A satire on Judaism [Sutherland].

F121   *A coquette in crape. A tragedy of circumstance* (by 'Frank Danby').
London: Chatto & Windus, 1907. LOCATION L.

F122   *The heart of a child. Being passages from the early life of Sally Snape, Lady Kidderminster* (by 'Frank Danby').
London: Hutchinson & Co., 1908. LOCATION L.
Leipzig: Bernard Tauchnitz, 1908, 2 vols. SOURCE T & B, 4044. LOCATION L.

F123   *An incompleat Etonian* (by 'Frank Danby').
London: William Heinemann, 1909. SOURCE RIA/DIB. LOCATION L.
Leipzig: Bernard Tauchnitz, 1909, 2 vols. SOURCE T & B, 4109. LOCATION L.

F124   *Let the roof fall in* (by 'Frank Danby').
London: Hutchinson & Co., 1910. SOURCE BLC; ODNB (mistakenly has 'When the roof fell in'). LOCATION L.
Leipzig: Bernard Tauchnitz, 1910. SOURCE T & B, 4227. LOCATION L.

F125   *Joseph in jeopardy* (by 'Frank Danby').
London: Methuen & Co., 1912. SOURCE RIA/DIB. LOCATION L.

F126   *Concert pitch* (by 'Frank Danby').
London: Hutchinson & Co., 1913. LOCATION L.

F127   *Full swing* (by 'Frank Danby').
London: Cassell & Co., 1914. SOURCE RIA/DIB. LOCATION L.

F128   *Twilight* (by 'Frank Danby').
London: Hutchinson & Co., 1916. LOCATION L.

F129   *Mothers and children. Hitherto unpublished stories by the late 'Frank Danby'* (preface by author's son, Gilbert Frankau).
London: W. Collins Sons & Co., 1918. SOURCE RIA/DIB. LOCATION L.
COMMENTARY Published posthumously [RIA/DIB].

FRASER, Julia Agnes, fl. 1871. A novelist and playwright, JAF's works for the stage include *Pat of Mullingar* (Greenock, [1879]). According to the dedication to her *Shilrick, the drummer* (London, 1894, 3 vols.), she was the daughter of Maj.-Gen. Simon Fraser, JP, of the Royal

Marines. The title page of *Shilrick* mentions that JAF was the author of 'Skeletons in the cupboard; or, the captain's troubles'; 'Dermot O'Donoghue; or, the stranger of Belfast', and 'Patrick's vow; or, a rival's revenge', but these have not been located. Her portrait was published in *Shilrick the drummer*. SOURCE RL.

F130　*Universal equality; or, Jonathan Baxter's peep into the future* (by Julia Agnes Fraser).

　　+ Edinburgh, Glasgow: John Menzies & Co. 1871. SOURCE Alston, p. 151; COPAC. LOCATION L.

　　+ Strathaven: A. Morton, 1871. LOCATION L.

COMMENTARY 29pp. Partly written in an Irish brogue. A shopkeeper in England, concerned about the future, considers that universal equality would be the only great and lasting good that could befall a nation. He then dreams what the effect of universal equality would be on different countries, among which is Ireland. The scenario in Ireland would be that the landlords lose their land, which is divided among the people. Some people work very hard, while others do nothing and expect that they share the fruits of other people's labour. Things get so bad that people clamour to have the old landlords back [ML].

F131　*Shilrick the drummer; or, loyal and true. A romance of the Irish rebellion of 1798* (by Julia Agnes Fraser; dedicated to her father, Maj.-Gen. Simon Fraser, JP).

　　+ London: Remington & Co., 1894, 3 vols. (ill.). SOURCE Brown 2, 522; Sadleir, 907; Wolff, 2350. LOCATION D, L, NUC, InND Loeber coll.

COMMENTARY An historical novel set in the Wicklow Mountains that concerns divided loyalties during the rising of 1798. Rebels, led by Morwen O'Neill, are confronted by a regiment that has several Irish officers and an Irish drummer boy. Many of them are sympathetic to the Irish people but are loyal to their regiment. Certain actions of Shilrick O'Toole are misinterpreted as treason and he is sentenced to be shot. At the last moment he receives an amnesty [ML].

FRAZER, R.W. See **FRAZER, Robert Watson**.

FRAZER, Robert Watson, b. Dublin 1854, d. 1921. Sketch and story writer, RWF attended TCD and subsequently entered the Indian Civil Service. He became a noted scholar on the country, its history and languages. SOURCE Sutherland, p. 234; BLC.

F132　*Silent gods and sun-steeped lands* (by R.W. Frazer).

　　+ London: T. Fisher Unwin, 1895 (ill. A.D. McCormick). SOURCE Sutherland, p. 234; COPAC. LOCATION D, L, InND Loeber coll. (1896, 2nd edn).

COMMENTARY A collection of sketches and stories of ancient and modern India. Contents: 'The tailless tiger', 'The pearl of the temple; or the wantan vasantasena', 'The cry from the river', 'The wail of the woman', 'The last human sacrifice, and the Abbé Leroux', 'The dream of life', 'The cloud messenger (adapted from the Sanskrit)' [RL].

FREDERIC, Harold, b. near Utica (NY) 1856, d. Homefield, Kenley-on-Thames (Oxon.) 1898. American best-selling novelist, editor and foreign correspondent, HF's family name was Frederick, but he dropped the 'k' in order to create a new identity for himself as a writer. He was editor of the *Utica Daily Observer* and later the *Albany Evening Journal* and became London correspondent for the *New York Times* in 1884, where he was drawn into the ambit of the Irish Literary Society. He was known as a principled and individualistic journalist who wrote many sympathetic articles on Ireland. SOURCE Allibone Suppl., i, p. 627; ANB; Boase, v, p. 355; Brown, p. 112; DAB; NUC; Ryan, p. 122; Wright iii, pp 203–4 (list of other novels).

F133　*The return of the O'Mahoney. A romantic fantasy* (by Harold Frederic).

New York: Stone & Kimball, 1892. SOURCE Fanning, p. 381; OCLC. LOCATION DCL.
New York: Robert Bonner's Sons, 1892 (as *The return of the O'Mahoney. A novel*; ill.
Warren B. Davis). SOURCE Wright, iii, 2022; OCLC. LOCATION D (1899 edn), NUC.
+ London: William Heinemann, 1893 (ill.). SOURCE Brown, 618. LOCATION L, DPL,
DCU, NUC.

COMMENTARY No copy of the New York, Stone & Kimball edn located. Characterized by Ryan
as 'an experiment after [Charles] Lever'§. An adventure novel of impersonation and usurpation set in the south-west of Co. Cork in Fenian times. The person who comes to claim the
O'Mahoney title is actually a Mr Tisdale, who has managed to secure the papers of the real
O'Mahoney, who is not aware of his own origin and real name. Tisdale is a good landlord.
He tries his hand at Fenianism but abandons it and goes abroad to foreign wars. O'Daly, left
as manager, thrusts himself into his master's place. However, a young American engineer, 'the
real O'Mahoney', spoils his plans, but does not reveal his own identity until after Tisdale's
death [Brown; Ryan, p. 122].

F134 *The damnation of Theron Ware; or illumination* (by Harold Frederic).
New York: Stone & Kimball, 1896. SOURCE Fanning, p. 381; Wright, iii, 2013; OCLC.
LOCATION Concordia Univ.
New York: Hurst, [1896]. LOCATION NUC.
London: W. Heinemann, 1896 (as *The illumination*). LOCATION L, NUC.
Leipzig: Bernard Tauchnitz, 1896, 2 vols. in 1 (as *The illumination; or, the damnation
of Theron Ware*). LOCATION NUC.
COMMENTARY Favourably contrasts the Catholic Irish in America with the descendants
of the Puritans [Brown].

FRENCH, Annie. See HECTOR, Annie.

FRENCH, Arthur. See MURPHY, Arthur.

FRENCH, Charlotte. See DESPARD, Charlotte.

FRENCH, Henry Willard, b. West Hartford (CT) 1853. American author of fiction for juveniles and newspaper correspondent, HWF also published *Our boys in China* (Boston, 1883)
and *Our boys in India* (Boston, [*c*.1892]) and other works for juveniles. SOURCE Allibone Suppl.,
i, p. 630; O'Donoghue, p. 425; I.R. Weiss (ed.), *W.J. Burke & W.D. Howe, American authors
and books* (New York, 1962), p. 263; Wright, iii, p. 208 (list of novels).
F135 *Our boys in Ireland* (by Henry Willard French; dedicated to Gotty of Drumcormack
in Sligo).
+ New York: Worthington Co., 1891 (ill. W.H. Bartlett). LOCATION L, NUC, InND
Loeber coll.
COMMENTARY Fiction for juveniles. The story opens in Boston where a group of boys set sail
for Scotland, via Ireland. They land in Galway and travel around in Connemara and in the
south. Along the way they meet peasants, whose stories they relate. They visit Dublin, after
which they set sail for Scotland [CM].

FRENCH, James, fl. 1845. Historical novelist. An inscribed copy of the following volume
reveals that JF was the father of Margaret Josephine French of Frenchgrove, probably in Co.
Mayo (east of Ballinrobe). This address would make the author, together with Matthew
Archdeacon§, one of the earliest known fiction writers in English in Connacht. SOURCE Falkner
Greirson cat. L/74; RL.

F136   *Clongibbon; or, the White Knight of the forest. An Irish historical tale* (by James French).
+ Dublin: James Duffy, 1845. SOURCE Brown, 619. LOCATION D, Dt, InND Loeber coll.

COMMENTARY Historical fiction set mainly in Munster during the seventeenth century. A Gothic story that starts at Mitchelstown (Co. Cork) and abounds with abducted heroines locked up in dungeons, wicked villains of whom Clongibbon, The White Knight, is one, and gallant heroes. The background is formed by an account of the wars of the Confederation of Kilkenny from 1641 to about 1646, written from an Irish point of view. Much historical source material is referenced in footnotes. The White Knight falls in love with Olivia Hodder, daughter of a planter's family. She refuses to marry him and the White Knight arranges for the murder of her father and takes Olivia hostage. However, a servant of Clongibbon saves her and she is transported to France, where she enters a convent. Also features Owen Roe O'Neill [ML; Brown; Hartman, 748].

FRENCH, William Percy, b. Cloonyquin, near Elphin (Co. Roscommon) 1854, d. Formby (Lancs.) 1920. Songwriter, poet, librettist and writer, WPF was the third son of Christopher French of Cloonyquin (since demolished), and Susan Emma Percy of Carrick-on-Shannon (Co. Leitrim). Educated in England and at TCD, where he wrote his first and still famous song 'Abdula Bulbul Ameer', he received a BA in 1876, and a BE in 1881. He practiced for six years as a civil engineer in Co. Cavan, while continuing to write poems, comic operas, and the songs for which he became most famous. He also wrote a play 'The knights of the road'. In Dublin, he edited the comic periodical the *Jarvey*. He was a talented landscape painter and during concert tours of Ireland would hand out sketches he made en route. He reluctantly moved to London in 1896 to secure more remunerative work and played the London concert stage during winters, while touring Irish seaside resorts during summers. He also toured the US and Canada and performed for British troops in France during the First World War. He married first Ethel Kathleen Moore (of Arnmore, Co. Cavan) in 1890, and secondly Helen May Cunningham in 1894. In Dublin he lived at 3 St John's Road, Sandymount, and later at 35 Mespil Road. SOURCE Brady, p. 85; Crookshank, pp 217, 302; Hogan, pp 251–2; Hogan 2, p. 461; Igoe, pp 71–2; Landed gentry, 1904, p. 204; LVP, p. 174; OCIL, p. 204; O'Donoghue, p. 154; RIA/DIB; Vanishing country houses, p. 125.

F137   *The first Lord Liftinant, and other tales* (by William Percy French).
Dublin: Macredy & Kyle, 1890 (ill. R. Caulfeild Orpen; Rush-light Series, No. 1). SOURCE Brown 2, 485. LOCATION L, NYPL, NN.

COMMENTARY Three stories told in brogue and in a spirit of broad humour. Contents: 'The first liftinant' (burlesque account of Essex in Ireland during the reign of Elizabeth I), 'The rout of Rathmines' (similar account of the famous battle during the Parliamentary wars with Oliver Cromwell, John Milton, the earl of Ormond and others in the role of comedians), 'Strongbow' (set during the Norman invasion of Ireland) [Brown 2; NYPL].

FRENEY, James, b. Inistioge (Co. Kilkenny) *c*.1719, d. New Ross (Co. Wexford) 1788. A notorious robber and adventurer, JF was the son of John Freney, a servant of Joseph Robins, of Ballyduff (Co. Kilkenny), and Anne Phelan. JF is famous, or infamous, for the fictionalized account of his exploits as a robber and burglar. His gang terrified the countryside for almost five years (see e.g., *Extract from a letter from Waterfd* [*sic*]*, the following account of the bloody murther of J-M[oore] by Capt. Freany and his gang*, Dublin, [before Aug. 1749]). JF was described by his contemporary John Edward Walsh as 'a mean-looking fellow, pitted with the smallpox, and blind of an eye ... he was a coarse, vulgar, treacherous villain, much of the highway-man, and nothing of the hero'. From an account published in 1847, it is known that on the road between Clonmel and Kilkenny, the scene of many of his robberies, an elm known as 'Freney's tree' was pointed out to travellers. Popular tradition says that when the sunlight sparkles on the hill above Graiguenamanagh (Co. Kilkenny) it shows the location of 'Freney's gold', but when people search, the gold can never be found. The spot of his unmarked grave in the Inistioge (Co. Kilkenny) cemetery was still pointed out by locals in about 1900. The term 'Freney' became a soubriquet for all persons who had lost an eye. JF is also remembered in a ballad 'Bold Captain Freney'. SOURCE Adams, p. 91; JAPMDI, 5(1) (1901), p. 85; [anon.] *Sketches of Ireland sixty years ago* (Dublin, 1847), p. 106; J.J. Marshall, *Irish tories, rapparees, and robbers* (Dungannon, 1927), pp 67–8; C. Maxwell, *Country and town in Ireland under the Georges* (Dundalk, 1949, revsd edn), p. 289–91; ODNB; J. O'Keeffe, *Recollections* (London, 1826), i, pp 213–14; Pollard 2, p. 628; Personal communication, Con Manning, July 2003; [J.G.A. Prim], *Nooks and corners of the County Kilkenny* (Kilkenny, 2003), p. 93; J.G.A. Prim in *Jrnl of the Kilkenny and South-East of Ireland Archaeological Society*, 1 (1856–57), pp 52–61; RIA/DIB.

F138 *The life and adventures of James Freney, commonly called Captain Freney. From the time of his first entering on the highway, in Ireland, to the time of his surrender, being a series of five years remarkable adventures* (written 'by Himself'; dedicated to Somerset Hamilton Butler, earl of Garrick).
+ Dublin: Printed for the author by S. Powell, 1754 (subscribers' list). SOURCE Cole, p. 226; Raven, 223; ESTC t069293. LOCATION D, L.
Dublin: W. Jones, 1814 (title as above, and *To which is added The history of Sir John Falstaff*). SOURCE Gilbert, p. 307. LOCATION DPL Gilbert coll.
+ Dublin: Printed by C.M. Warren, [1830?] (as *The life and adventures of James Freney; together with an account of the actions of several noted highwaymen*). LOCATION D, NUC, InND Loeber coll.
Limerick: [publisher?], 1827 (as *James Freney. Life and adventures, written by himself. From the time of his first entering on the highway in Ireland, to the time of his surrender, being a series of five years' remarkable adventures* (ill.). SOURCE Quinn, 3143.
COMMENTARY *Limerick edn* No copy located [RL].
Kilkenny: Hebron Books, 1988 (ed. by Frank McEvoy; ill. David Holohan). SOURCE OCLC. LOCATION L.
COMMENTARY J.W. Phillips (*Printing & bookselling in Dublin* (Dublin, 1998), p. 284) states that there was a 1752 edn, but this has not been located. A fictionalized autobiographical story, characterized by James Glassford, one of the Education Commissioners, in 1826, as 'one of the worst of the popular books among the lowest Irish'. According to William Makepeace Thackeray§, writing in 1842, this was one of the most popular books ever known in Ireland and served as a 'class-book' in hedge-schools. Thackeray, who purchased his copy probably in Ennis (Co. Clare), extracted and incorporated more than twelve of its pages and published these in his *The Irish sketch book* (London, 1869). The story is set in the eighteenth century. The young James Freney becomes a pantry boy in the household of Joseph Robbins, Esq., of Ballyduff (Co. Kilkenny), where James Freney's father was a house-steward. However, James neglects his duty at an early age. He marries at age 20 and sets up in trade in Waterford, but soon runs into debt. He then becomes a highwayman who with many accomplices plies his trade mostly in Co. Kilkenny, where they also rob houses of money and plate. Freney is often induced by his victims to return their money or prized possessions. His greatest enemy is Counsellor Robbins, son of his former employer. Finally, he flees into Lord Dysart's [*sic*, Desart] deer park (at Desart Court, Co. Kilkenny), and escapes by foot to Waterford. He surrenders and receives a pardon on the condition he turn king's evidence. At the assizes, his fellow-robbers are executed and Freney is released. Lord Garrick tries to raise a subscription to help Freney and his family to leave Ireland

but as the local gentry refuse to assist him he is forced to raise money by writing his life story, but there are only twenty-six subscribers. Jack Butler Yeats celebrated this character in *Bold captain Freney*, which was published in Dublin, in 1913 [ML; Adams, pp 90–1; Cole, p. 226; J. Glasscock, *Notes of three tours in Ireland in 1824 and 1826* (Bristol, 1832); ODNB; W.M. Thackeray, *The Paris sketch book ..., the Irish sketch book* (Boston, 1883), pp 138–152].

FRICKER, Thomas, pseud. **'Humphrey Humbug'**, fl. 1835. Writer of satire. Attribution is tentative. Signature of 'Thos. Fricker' is noted on BL copy of the following work, but could be interpreted as owner's signature. However, another title (*Fireside lays and legends*, London, 1835) is authored by Fricker and bears a similar publisher imprint. TF was likely an Irish writer since, according to the dedication, he was indebted to Daniel O'Connell for support of his family. SOURCE Garside 2, Appendix 2, B:19; RL.

F139   *The life and confessions of Humphrey Humbug, M.D., M.P., F.R.S., F.A.S., F.Z.S., R.A., & A.S.S., with an account of his family, from 1 anno mundi to 1835 anno Christi. Related by himself* (by 'Humphrey Humbug'; dedicated to Dan. O'Connell, MP, with 'the sincerest feelings of gratitude for the many benefits of countenance he has bestowed upon the author's family').
+ London: Albert J. Attwood, 1835. SOURCE Garside 2, 1835:57. LOCATION InND Loeber coll.
COMMENTARY A satire on the lives of the author and his family (spread over England, Scotland, and Ireland), in which many adventures take place, with occasional reference to contemporary events [ML].

'A FRIEND', fl. 1767. Pseudonym of a probably Irish novelist, who only published in Dublin. SOURCE RL.
F140   *The history of Eliza* (by 'A friend').
+ Dublin: G. Faulkner, P. Wilson, J. Exshaw, H. Saunders, W. Sleater, J. Potts, D. Chamberlain, J. Hoey, Jnr, J. Williams, & J. Mitchell, 1767, 2 vols. SOURCE ESTC n033071. LOCATION D (vol. 1 only), L.
London: J. Dodsley, 1767, 2 vols. SOURCE ESTC t092326. LOCATION L.
COMMENTARY According to the preface, the story is based on facts. Irish content [RL].

'A FRIEND', fl. 1780s. Pseudonym of an adventure fiction writer.
F141   *The life and adventures of John Connor, commonly called Jack The Bachelor. The famous Irish buckler ... With alterations and additions. To which is added, the life of Mons. Thurot and the life of Captain Avery, two noted pirates* (by 'A friend').
+ Dublin: Printed [for the author?] by William Jones, [c.1785]. SOURCE RLIN; ESTC t118795. LOCATION L.
COMMENTARY The story of three men of the sea: John Connor, born in Wexford, recounts his travels and amours; Captain François Thurot, French but of Irish extraction, is involved in a ship battle at Carrickfergus (Co. Antrim), and Capt Avery, who is of English extraction, becomes a pirate and eventually settles in Ireland. The 2nd Dublin edn, published in 1821, contains a poem 'The pleasures of a single life' [ML; O'Donoghue, p. 77].

'A FRIEND TO THE PEACE AND PROSPERITY OF IRELAND', fl. 1753. Pseudonym of a fiction writer on topical subjects.
F142   *A dialogue between Dean Swift and Tho. Prior, Esq; in the isles [sic] of St. Patrick's Church, Dublin, on that memorable day, October 9th. 1753* (by 'A friend to the peace and prosperity of Ireland').

Dublin: G. & A. Ewing, 1753. SOURCE ESTC t65268. LOCATION D, L.

COMMENTARY Fictitious dialogue between Dean Swift§ and Thomas Prior, the founder of the Dublin Society, consisting of wide-ranging commentary on various aspects of Irish life in the 1750s, including agriculture; the arts; the clergy; drinking and gambling; manufactures and trade, etc. [Figgis cat. 50/73].

FROST, William Henry, fl. 1900. American miscellaneous writer, WHF signed the preface to the following book from New York, 1 Sept. 1900. He also published several books of medieval tales. SOURCE Brown, p. 112; NUC; RL.

F143   *Fairies and folk of Ireland* (by William Henry Frost; dedicated to Jane Grey Allen and Elizabeth Allen).

+ New York: Charles Scribner's Sons, 1900 (ill. Sydney Richmond Burleigh). SOURCE Brown, 620; Rowan cat. 52A/412. LOCATION NUC, InND Loeber coll.

COMMENTARY WHF states in the preface that 'The story which runs through and makes up the bulk of this is my own'. However, 'The shorter stories wherewith the main story is interspersed are all … genuine Irish folk-tales'. These stories are based on stories published by Patrick Kennedy§, Henry Charles Coote, Thomas Crofton Croker§, William Butler Yeats§, Samuel Lover§, Douglas Hyde§ and William Larminie§. Contents: 'O'Donoghue', 'The big poor people', 'The little good people', 'The cleverness of mortals', 'The time for Nageneen's plan', 'Little Kathleen and little Terence', 'A chapter that you can skip', 'The stars in the water', 'A year and a day', 'The iron crucifix', 'The old king comes back'. The main story concerns the O'Brien and Sullivan families who, finding life too difficult in Ireland, emigrate to New York, against old Mrs O'Brien's advice about the fairies. The fairies, however, have emigrated to Central Park and substitute a changeling for a Sullivan baby. All ends well and the O'Brien girl marries the re-found Sullivan boy [RL; Brown].

FROTHINGHAM, Charles W., fl. 1854. American anti-Catholic novelist, CWF also wrote a related work, *Six hours in a convent; or, the stolen nuns. A tale of Charlestown in 1834* (Boston, 1855).

F144   *The convent's doom. A tale of Charlestown in 1834. Also the haunted convent* (by Charles W. Frothingham).

Boston: Graves & Weston, 1854. SOURCE Fanning, p. 381; Wright, ii, 961. LOCATION NUC, InND, Wright web.

COMMENTARY An anti-Catholic novel featuring a wily Jesuit and a treacherous Irish servant. The story argues that the historical event of the destruction of the convent at Charlestown (MA) was justified since it was a prison for Protestants and a venue of pleasure for priests [Fanning, p. 79].

FROTHINGHAM, Washington, b. Fonda (NY) 1822. American religious fiction writer, WF was a businessman before becoming a Presbyterian minister. He established the West Side Presbyterian Church in Albany (NY) and also wrote *Zoe; or, the Martel papers* (New York, 1865). SOURCE Allibone Suppl., i, p. 634; RL; Wright, ii, 963.

F145   *Blind Peter. Written from his own statements* (by Washington Frothingham).

+ New York: C.A. Alvord, 1871. LOCATION InND Loeber coll.

COMMENTARY A temperance story involving a Mr Halloran, a Catholic born in the parish of Kilbacanty (Co. Galway), who leaves Ireland at the time of the Famine to go to New York, where he falls under the influence of alcohol. He goes steadily downhill until he enters the Protestant religion. During the rest of his life he attaches himself to various churches and spends most of his time discussing points of scripture. He becomes blind, but makes a living selling religious books [ML].

FROUDE, J.A. See FROUDE, James Anthony.

FROUDE, James Anthony (known as J.A. Froude), b. Dartington (Devon) 1818, d. Kingsbridge (Devon) 1894. English historian, biographer and man of letters, JAF was the son of the archdeacon of Totnes and his wife Margaret Spedding. After graduating from Oriel College, Oxford, where he was a friend of Matthew Arnold, he took deacon's orders in 1844, but later lost his faith and was considered an apostate. He spent some time in Ireland in 1840 when he tutored the son of the rector of Delgany (Co. Wicklow), returning in 1845 to do research. He collaborated with John Newman§ on a projected volume of the lives of Irish and English saints. JAF spent the summer of 1848 in Killarney, living in a lodge on Lord Kenmare's estate. He wrote an immensely popular *History of England* completed in twelve volumes in 1869. Between 1867 and 1870 he spent his summer holidays at the earl of Lansdowne's seat, Derreen, near Kenmare (Co. Kerry). There he began his book *The English in Ireland in the eighteenth century* (London, 1872–74), for the second edn of which in 1881 he wrote an additional chapter on recent events. His *A fortnight in Kerry* (published in *Short studies on great subjects*, London, 1871) was based on two articles published earlier in *Fraser's magazine* (London) which he edited from 1860 to 1874. Castletown Berehaven in nearby Co. Cork is the setting of his only Irish novel, *The two chiefs of Dunboy* (London, 1889). While JAF was critical of England's misgovernment of Ireland and was sympathetic to the plight of the peasants, he believed the Irish incapable of self-government and advocated that Ireland be ruled in the same imperial manner as India. His anti-Catholic and anti-nationalist writings spurred rebuttals by scholars such as W.E.H. Lecky and were used by Irish nationalists to illustrate English prejudices against Ireland. JAF, who had written a biography of Thomas Carlyle, edited Carlyle's *Reminiscences of my Irish journey in 1849* (London, 1882). He wrote prefaces for Mary Hickson's *Ireland in the seventeenth century* (London, 1884, 2 vols.) and J.A. Firth's *Our kin across the sea* (London, 1888). In 1892 he was appointed to the regius professorship of modern history at Oxford. He wrote several other novels. SOURCE Allibone i, p. 640; Brown, p. 112; W.H. Dunn, *James Anthony Froude. A biography* (Oxford, 1963), pp 558–60; Duke Univ., Durham (NC), Sir Arthur Helps papers; Field Day, ii, p. 366; NCBEL 4, p. 2425; OCIL, pp 205–6; ODNB; E. Reilly, 'J.A. Froude's use of history and his Irish prescription' in L.W. McBride (ed.), *Reading Irish histories* (Dublin, 2003), pp 140–55; RIA/DIB; Sutherland, pp 236–7; T & B, p. 981.

F146   *The two chiefs of Dunboy or an Irish romance of the last century* (by J.A. Froude).
+ London: Longmans, Green & Co., 1889. SOURCE Brown, 621. LOCATION D, DPL, BFl, L, NUC, InND Loeber coll.
+ London: Longmans, Green & Co., 1891 (new edn). LOCATION NUC, InND Loeber coll.
New York: G. Munro, [1889]. LOCATION NUC.
London: Chatto & Windus, 1969 (ed. and preface by A.L. Rowse). SOURCE Quaritch cat. 1290/14; COPAC. LOCATION Dt, O.
COMMENTARY A fictional reiteration of the key themes of JAF's *The English in Ireland* (London, 1872–74). Set in O'Sullivan country on the Beara Peninsula in west Cork in the second-half of the eighteenth century up to 1798, it is an expression of JAF's views on the relationship between England and Ireland, with England being a justifiable colonial power. It relates the story of Morty O'Sullivan, who after serving as an officer in the Austrian army, returns to Ireland to smuggle goods and to ferry away discontented Catholics for service in the Continental armies. John Puxley, the owner of the former O'Sullivan estate of Dunboy, attempts to thwart the smuggling operation. In a scathing review, Oscar Wilde§ said of this novel, 'Mr. Froude admits the martyrdom of Ireland but regrets [it] was not carried out' (Field

Day, ii, p. 375). The London 1969 edn is an abridged version [Brown; Field Day, ii, pp 375–6, 380–3; Reilly, pp 141, 153–4].

FULLER, Anne, pseud. '**A young Lady**', fl. 1786, d. Cork 1790, probably at a young age. An historical novelist, AF was a resident of Cork and came from a landed family. Her parents were William Fuller of West Kerries, near Tralee (Co. Kerry), and Jane Harnett. She is mentioned in the *Gentleman's Magazine* (London, July 1790) as the 'authoress of several interesting and ingenious novels', and in the *Dublin Chronicle* (25 Sept. 1790, p. 509) as 'the late Miss Anne Fuller of Cork'. The fact that she dedicated her novel *The son of Ethelwolf. An historical tale* (London, 1789) to the prince of Wales may indicate that she was connected to court circles. Thomas Townshend wrote an elegy on her after her death ('Ode to the memory of Miss Fuller, author of Alan FitzOsborne &c.' in *Poems*, Dublin, 1791). Her Gothic novels must have achieved some popularity and were reprinted in several locations on the Continent. AF did not marry and died of consumption. The novelist and architect James Franklin Fuller§ was of the same family. SOURCE Allibone i, p. 642; Blain, p. 401; Field Day, v, p. 831; J. Foster, *The royal lineage of our noble and gentle families* (London, 1887), ii, p. 744; Landed gentry, 1904, p. 206.

F147   *The convent; or, the history of Sophia Nelson* (by 'A young Lady').
London: Printed [for the author?] by T. Wilkins, 1786, 2 vols. SOURCE Blain, p. 401; Forster 2, 1542; Raven 2, 1786:22; ESTC t146879. LOCATION L, MH.
Dublin: P. Byrne, 1786. SOURCE Blain, p. 401. LOCATION NUC.
Londres [Paris?]: Brand, 1789–90, 3 parts (trans. by P.C. Briand as *Le couvent, ou histoire de Sophie Nelson*). SOURCE ESTC t14761; Streeter, 145. LOCATION L.
Leipzig: Weygand, 1789, 2 vols. (trans. as *Sophia Nelson, eine Geschichte nach dem Leben*). SOURCE Raven 2, 1786:22; Union Cat. Northern Germany. LOCATION Wolfenbütel, Herzog-August-Bibliothek.
+ Neuwied sur le Rhin: La Société Typographique; Paris: Garnery, 1792, 2 vols. (trans. by M.V.R.Y as *Histoire de Miss Nelson*). LOCATION NUC, InND Loeber coll.
COMMENTARY The book was advertised with the subtitle 'Letters to and from several Persons of England, France, and Ireland' [Raven 2, 1786:22].

F148   *Alan Fitz-Osborne. An historical tale* [anon.] (dedicated to Mrs Newenham of Maryborough [Portlaoise (Co. Laois)]).
+ Dublin: P. Byrne, 1786, 2 vols. (subscribers' list). SOURCE Raven 2, 1786:21; Forster 2, 1541; ESTC n29520. LOCATION PC, L.
London: Reprinted for the author, 1787, 2 vols. SOURCE Raven 2, 1786:21; ESTC t074659. LOCATION L.
Amsterdam, Paris: Briand, 1789, 2 vols. (trans. by Mlle** as *Alan Fitz-Osborne, roman historique*). SOURCE Streeter, 144; GLOL. LOCATION Bibliotheksverbund Bayern.
COMMENTARY A Gothic, historical tale set in the reign of Henry II. The hero, Alan, takes part in the Barons' Wars (1263–67). The *Critical Review* compares this work with Sophia Lee's§ *The Recess* (London, 1783) and finds 'great merit'. In the preface, the author states her intention of subordinating the historical to the horrific to achieve her ghostly effects. Mathilda, the 'posthumous heroine', makes her appearance at the bedside of her murdered brother-in-law, Walter Fitz-Osborne. A man attempts to rob his brother's wife by pretending that his brother has died in the crusades [Kilfeather, p. 283; Summer, p. 171; Raven 2; Frank, 135].

F149   *The son of Ethelwolf. An historical tale* [anon.] (dedicated to George, prince of Wales).
London: G.G.J. & J. Robinson, 1789, 2 vols. (subscribers' list). SOURCE Raven 2, 1789:40; Hardy, 404; Gecker, 347; McBurney & Taylor, 329; Forster 2, 1543; ESTC t120826. LOCATION L, PU, IU, NUC.

+ Dublin: L. White, P. Byrne, P. Wogan, H. Colbert, A. Grueber & M'Allister, C. Lewis, J. Jones & J. Moore, 1789. SOURCE Raven 2, 1789:40; Gecker, 348; ESTC t155651. LOCATION Dt, D, C, PU, NUC.

+ Paris: Ruedes Poitevins, 1789, 2 vols. (trans. by P.L. Le Bas as *Le fils d'Ethelwolf, conte historique* by Anne Faller [*sic*]). SOURCE Streeter, 146; Rochedieu, p. 117. LOCATION L.

Paris: Lavillette, 1792 (trans. by L. Lebas as *L'Adversité ou l'école des rois*). SOURCE Streeter, 143; Bn-Opale plus. LOCATION BNF.

Bremen: Wilmans, 1794 (trans. as *Alfred, König in England*). SOURCE Raven 2, 1789:40; Union Catalogue Bavaria. LOCATION Augsburg (Germany).

Prague, Vienna: Joseph Kottnauer, 1795 (trans. as *Alfred, König in England: Eine Geschichte aus dem neunten Jahrhundert*). SOURCE COPAC. LOCATION O.

COMMENTARY Subscribers' list includes many aristocrats (several with Irish titles); many of whom are located in London, Bath, Hotwells, and Ireland; one of the subscribers is the writer Miss Gunning§. A Gothic historical novel set in England during the time of Alfred and the threat of Danish invasion. A resourceful female character in disguise fights alongside Alfred in battle. The novel can be read as an allegory of contemporary conditions in Ireland [RL; Blain, p. 401; Burmester cat. 38/206; Field Day, v, pp 812–13; Garside (2003)].

FULLER, James Franklin, pseuds 'Ignotus' and 'An old boy', b. Nedanone, near Derriquin (Co. Kerry; not Denniquin as mentioned in Brady and Hogan) 1835, d. Dublin 1924. Architect, poet and writer, JFF was the eldest son of Thomas Harnett Fuller of Glashnacree (Co. Kerry) and Frances Diana Bland. Derriquin Castle was the seat of his mother's family, but he grew up at Reenaferrera also in Co. Kerry. JFF spent some time as an actor before qualifying as an architect. He became an architect to the Ecclesiastical Commissioners and to the Church Representative Body and in that function travelled extensively and lived in various parts of Ireland. He designed many churches, restored several cathedrals, built country mansions, wrote novels and published several historical papers in the *Cork Historical and Archaeological Society Jrnl* and the *Kerry Archaeological Magazine*. He married Helen Prospére Guivion in 1860, when he was living at Glashnacree (Co. Kerry) but from about 1871 lived at Great Brunswick Street, Dublin. Among Fuller's architectural works are St Anne's, Clontarf (Dublin, now destroyed), Ashford Castle (Co. Mayo), both for Sir Arthur Guinness (later Lord Ardilaun), and Kylemore Castle (Co. Galway). JFF, together with William Sheppard, laid out the gardens of Stephen's Green, Dublin, for Sir Arthur Guinness. He also rebuilt Derriquin Castle into a Victorian castle for his relatives, the Bland family. It was burnt during his lifetime in 1922 in the Anglo-Irish war. His portrait was published in his *Omniana ... the autobiography of an Irish octogenarian* (London, New York, 1916; not 1815 as in Brady). JFF is known for six novels, some of which have Irish connections. The author Anne Fuller§ was of the same family. SOURCE Allibone Suppl. i, p. 637; Bary, pp 97, 123–4; Brady, p. 86; Brown, p. 113; J. Foster, *The royal lineage of our noble and gentle families* (London, 1887), ii, pp 744–5; J.F. Fuller, *Omniana* (London, 1916), passim; Landed gentry, 1904, p. 206; Hogan 2, p. 464; E. Malins & P. Bowe, *Irish gardens and demesnes from 1830* (London, 1980), pp 48–51, 108, 115; LVP, p. 176; MVP, p. 174; RIA/DIB; D.S. Richardson, *Gothic revival architecture in Ireland* (New York, 1983), ii, pp 704–7; A.M. Rowan, James Franklin Fuller, database on Irish architects, 1720–1940, Irish Architectural Archive, Dublin; Vanishing country houses, p. 81; J. Williams, *A companion guide to architecture in Ireland, 1837–1921* (Blackrock, Co. Dublin, 1994), passim.

F150 *Culmshire folk* (by 'Ignotus').

London: Macmillan, 1873, 3 vols. SOURCE Brown, 622; Fuller, *Omniana*, p. 151. LOCATION D (1876 edn), L, NUC.

COMMENTARY Partly-based on the author's theatrical experiences, the plot centres on Sidney Bateman, heir of an impoverished family, his struggles against misfortune and his eventual attainment of fortune and happiness. Bateman owns an estate, Rathvarney, in the wilds of Co. Kerry [Fuller, pp 80, 151; Brown].

F151 *John Orlebar, clk* [anon.].
+ London: Smith, Elder & Co., 1878. SOURCE Fuller, *Omniana*, p. 157; Brown, 623 (London, Cassell 1878, 2nd edn); Topp 7, 828. LOCATION L, NUC.

COMMENTARY A villainous attorney and his clerk, a Fenian, try to cheat an heiress out of her estates. Her husband's friend suspects foul play, and he travels to Co. Kerry to make enquiries, which help to unravel the mystery. The novel contains descriptions of Ireland in the 1860s [Brown].

F152 *The young idea: A sketch for 'old boys' by one of them* [anon.].
London: Remington & Co., 1884. LOCATION L.
London: Field & Tuer, [?date], 2nd edn (enlarged). SOURCE Fuller, *Omniana*, pp 160, 295.

COMMENTARY First published as a Christmas book. No copy of the 2nd, enlarged edn located [Fuller, *Omniana*, pp 159, 160, 295].

F153 *Chronicles of Westerly: a provincial sketch* [anon.].
+ Edinburgh, London: William Blackwood & Sons, 1892, 3 vols. SOURCE Wolff, 2367. LOCATION L, NUC, InND Loeber coll.

COMMENTARY A romantic story set in a garrison town that contains a large number of clergy associated with the bishopric. In the course of the narrative several marriages are contracted and a number of mysteries as to people's descent are solved. One of the main characters is an Irish lieutenant, who is portrayed as jolly but also honest and loving. Some characters from *Culmshire folk* and *John Orlebar* re-appear [ML].

F154 *Dr. Quodlibet, a study in ethics* [anon.].
London: Field & Tuer, 1894. SOURCE Fuller, *Omniana*, pp 161, 299. LOCATION L.

F155 *Billy. A sketch for 'the new boy'* (by 'An old boy').
London: Leadenhall Press, [1900]. LOCATION L.

FURNISS, Harry, b. Wexford 1854, d. Hastings (E. Sussex) 1925. Artist, illustrator and writer, HF was the son of James Furniss, a civil engineer of Derbyshire, and Isabella Mackenzie, whose father Eneas was a writer, politician and publisher. His family moved to Dublin in 1864 where HF was educated at the Wesleyan School and the Hibernian Academy. He showed an early talent for drawing, contributing to *Zozimus* (the Dublin *Punch*), and worked for the engraver George Hanlon of Grafton Street. At age 19 he settled in London and became an illustrator and writer who sometimes worked under the signature of 'Lika Joko' (in 1894 he launched a humorous weekly of the same name, which lasted a year). He married Marian Rogers in 1877. He joined the staff of the *Illustrated London News* and also worked for London *Punch* and became one of the best-known cartoonists and caricaturists of his day. As a satirical illustrator he targeted politicians and chided the Royal Academy for its lack of recognition of the work of illustrators, publishing in 1890 *Royal Academy antics*. Although he resented the exploitation of a cartoon he drew of Pear's soap in 1884 showing a dirty tramp saying 'I used your soap two years ago; since then I have used no other', it became legendary in the world of advertising and contributed to his growing fame. HF illustrated Lewis Carroll's last book, *Sylvie and Bruno* (London, 1889), followed by a complete edn of the works of Charles Dickens (London, 1910) and of William Makepeace Thackeray§ (London, 1911). He also illustrated a parody of *Alice in wonderland* by Maggie Browne, *Wanted – a king* (London, 1890). In 1893 he caricatured in a simianized manner John G. Swift MacNeill, the Irish nationalist MP, which caused an uproar. He visited Belfast in 1891 with his show 'The "Humours of Parliament"' on tour. He was a pioneer of British cinematography, working first with Thomas Edison in New York as a writer, actor and producer before relocating back to London. Dorothy Furniss, probably a relative, made the vignettes to G.E. Farrow's *The missing prince* (London, 1897) for which HF prepared the illustrations. A self-portrait in pen and ink, dated 1921, is in the NLI. For his other portraits and papers, see ODNB. Some of his letters are among the Downey Papers (NLI, MS 10,016). An exhibition of his work was held at the National Portrait Gallery, London, in 1983. SOURCE M. Banim, *Here and there through Ireland* (Dublin, 1891), p. 80; Blackwell cat., Spring 2001/81; Cummins cat. 67/93; L.P. Curtis, *Apes and angels. The Irishman in Victorian caricature* (Washington, 1971), pp 54–5; EF, p. 142; Holmes cat. 77/129; P. Hunt, *Children's literature* (Oxford, 1995), p. 143; ODNB; RIA/DIB; Sutherland, p. 237.

F156   *Essence of Parliament: Parliamentary views. Extracted from the diary of Toby, M.P.* (by Harry Furniss).
+ London: Bradbury, Agnew & Co., [1885] (ill.). LOCATION L, InND Loeber coll.

F157   *'An artistic joke'* (by Harry Furniss).
London: For Harry Furniss, 1888 (ill. the author). SOURCE Marlborough cat. 175/64; COPAC. LOCATION L, E.

F158   *P & O sketches in pen and ink* (by Harry Furniss).
+ London: The Studio of Design, [1898] (ill. Harry Furniss; limited edn of 1000 copies). SOURCE COPAC. LOCATION E, InND Loeber coll.
London: G. Weidenfeld & Nicholson, 1987. SOURCE OCLC. LOCATION L, DCL.
COMMENTARY Consists of sketches of life on board a passenger steamer and life in the harbour cities it visits. The text is simply an elaboration of the drawings [ML].

F159   *Royal Academy antics* (by Harry Furniss).
+ London, Paris, Melbourne: Cassell & Co., 1890 (ill. by the author). SOURCE COPAC. LOCATION D (uncatalogued), L, E, InND Loeber coll.
COMMENTARY A humorous description of the history of the Royal Academy in London. HF also wrote a critical work on the Royal Academy, published by George Augustus Moore§ in 1895 [ML; Gilcher, A20].

F160   *Flying visits* (by Harry Furniss).
+ Bristol: J.W. Arrowsmith; London: Simpkin, Marshall, Hamilton, Kent & Co., [1892] (ill. Harry Furniss; Arrowsmith 3/6 Series, No. 12). SOURCE COPAC. LOCATION Dt, L, E, InND Loeber coll.
Leipzig: Heinemann & Balestier, 1893 (ill.). Source COPAC. Location L
COMMENTARY Describes in fictional form a visit to Dublin at the time of a horse show, various Irish characters, and different sports being played in the Phoenix Park [ML].

F161   *Poverty bay. A nondescript novel* (by Harry Furniss).
+ London: Chapman & Hall, 1905 (ill. the author). LOCATION L, InND Loeber coll.
COMMENTARY Set in England. A man who had grown up without experiencing much love from his parents and is living a solitary life, repairs to a seaside village and gets drawn into the lives of many of its residents, all of whom have stories to tell about their fortunes and misfortunes. He is enticed into buying a house because it supposedly has a ghost. In pursuit of the ghost, he tumbles down a set of stairs and requires some nursing care. He becomes very dependent on his nurse and eventually marries her [ML].

G

'G.', pseud. See NUGENT, George Nugent-Grenville, 3rd baron.

'G., C.', fl. 1852. Pseudonym of a French children's writer.
G1   *Daniel O'Connor* (by 'C.G.').
      + Tours: Ad. Mame, 1852 (Bibliothèque des Petits Enfants; ill.). SOURCE IBL, 16
      (1928), p. 43 (1861 edn). LOCATION L.
      COMMENTARY A tale of 1690 for Catholic children, reprinted in 1861, 1866, and 1867
      [IBL, 16 (1928), p. 43].

'G., J.P.', fl. 1870s. Pseudonym of a novelist.
G2   *Saved from the river and the fire. A simple story of Irish faith and Irish valour in
      the late American war* (by 'J.P.G.').
      + Glasgow, London: Cameron & Ferguson, [1876]. LOCATION L.
      COMMENTARY One of the characters is John Doyle, 'a fine manly Celt' [CM].

'G., L.E.', pseud. See GUERNSEY, Lucy Ellen.

'G., S.', pseud. See GREEN, Sarah.

GAFFNEY, H. Editor. See SHEEHAN, Canon Patrick Augustine.

GALE, Norman, fl. 1895. Fantasy novelist, NG can perhaps be identified with poet Norman
Rowland Gale (1862–1942). The author himself features in the following work. SOURCE BLC;
NCBEL 4, p. 736.
G3   *All expenses paid* [anon].
      Westminster [London]: A. Constable & Co., 1895. LOCATION L, NUC.
      + Chicago, New York: Stone & Kimball, 1896. SOURCE Hyland cat. 240/961. LOCATION
      NUC, InND Loeber coll.
COMMENTARY A fantasy novel of a green gnome who, having found a wealthy sponsor, instructs
William Butler Yeats§ to gather a group of 'Minor Poets' (including William Watson, Richard
Le Gallienne, Arthur C. Benson, Katharine Tynan§, Dolly Radford, Norman Gale, Arthur
Symons, Alfred Hayes, Francis Thompson, Jane Barlow§, Rudyard Kipling, and John
Davidson) and lead them to Mount Olympus, the fountain of poetic inspiration. There some
of them quarrel with the gods [ML; Hyland cat. 240/961].

GALLAHER, F.M. See GALLAHER, Frances M.

GALLAHER, Frances (Fannie or Fanny) M. (also known as F.M. Gallaher), pseud.
'Sydney Starr', fl. 1880. Novelist, poet and prose writer, FMG was the daughter of John
Blake Gallaher, long-time editor of the *Freeman's Journal* (which was published in Dublin and
New York). She was for many years secretary to the duchess of Bedford in London. Under
her pseudynom she published poems in the Dublin *Irish Monthly* and she also published *Lessons
in domestic science* (Dublin, 1885). SOURCE Allibone Suppl., i, p. 644; Alston, p. 154; BLC;
Brown, p. 113; Colman, pp 90–1; Field Day, v, pp 927, 973; RIA/DIB; K. Tynan, *Twenty-
five years: Reminiscences* (New York, 1913), p. 213.

G4 *Katty the flash; a mould of Dublin mud* (by 'Sydney Starr').
Dublin: M.H. Gill; London: Simpkin Marshall, 1880. SOURCE Brown, 626; Murphy, p. 156; Topp 8, 640. LOCATION L.
COMMENTARY 46pp. A story of the squalid lives of Katty and her mother, who were Dublin fisherwomen. Katty dies in Grangegorman prison, where she and her mother had often been before. This novel was altered by Mrs Mary (May) Laffan Hartley§ in 1883 and published in the *Temple Bar*, crediting 'Miss Gallaher'. In a letter to the *Morning and Evening Mail* (not located), FMG complained that her nom de plume had thus been violated for the first time [Brown; Field Day, v, pp 927, 939–44, 973].

G5 *A son of man. A story in three chapters* (by 'Sydney Starr').
+ Dublin: Gill & Son; London: Simpkin Marshall, 1880. SOURCE Alston, p. 154; Topp 8, 641. LOCATION L.
COMMENTARY Probably an autobiographical story of a young woman, educated at Alexandra (Pallas) College, Dublin, whose father is a journalist and who hopes to become a writer [Field Day, v. p. 973].

G6 *Thy name is truth. A social novel* [anon.].
London: John & Robert Maxwell, [1883], 3 vols. SOURCE Brown, 627 (mistakenly mentions [1884] edn); Topp 6, 173. LOCATION L, NUC.
COMMENTARY Probably autobiographical, the story is of a young woman, the daughter of a journalist, who has aspirations to become a writer. Set in Dublin in 1881, and describes the Hospice for the Dying at Harold's Cross, and the workings of a newspaper office. It discusses the politics of the time. The heroine is opposed to the Land League while sympathetic to land reform. A new landlord works to relieve the position of the peasantry [Brown; Field Day, v, pp 926, 973].

G7 *The dawn of day* [anon.].
+ London: John & Robert Maxwell, [1885], 3 vols. SOURCE Wolff, 2383. LOCATION L.
COMMENTARY Not clearly Irish in content, but features Sir Black Harman, successor to Sir Nugent Harman, and a grandfather who had established the family fortune on the Liverpool Exchange. A principal character is the occultist, Dr Harold Harman [RL].

G8 *Children's chimes: stories* (by F.M. Gallaher).
London: [publisher?], 1887 (ill.). SOURCE Allibone Suppl., i, p. 644.
COMMENTARY No copy located. Stories for juveniles [Allibone].

GAMBLE, John, b. Strabane (Co. Tyrone) 1770, d. 1831. Novelist and writer of travel and social commentary, JG was reared by his uncle, an apothecary. His family connections included the Lairds, Hendersons, and Sproules, and he was distantly related to the author Anna Maria Porter§. He obtained his MD in Edinburgh in 1793 and became an army surgeon in the Dutch campaigns. Returning to Ireland because of failing eyesight, he travelled the Ulster countryside on foot or by carriage, writing some travel sketches and stories based on his experiences. Among his non-fiction works are: [anon.], *Sketches of history, politics, and manners, taken in Dublin and the North of Ireland, in the autumn of 1810* (London, 1811, suppressed because it contained comments on the trial of Robert Emmet; 1826, new edn); '*A Protestant dissenter': Brief observations on the present state ... Ireland ... supplement ... Sketches of history, politics ... manners in Dublin* (London, 1811); *A view of society and manners in the North of Ireland in the summer and autumn of 1812* (London, 1813), and *Views of society and manners in the North of Ireland, in a series of letters written in the year 1818* (London, 1819). Cumulatively JG's books give a unique glimpse into the Ulster of his day. SOURCE Allibone i, p. 650; Brady, p. 88; Brown, p. 114; A.A. Campbell, *Notes of the literary history of Strabane* (Omagh, 1902), pp

28–31; Field Day, i, pp 1076, 1081, 1106–15, 1171; IBL, 1 (1909), pp 20–1; McKenna, p. 185; NCBEL 4, pp 915–16; Newmann, pp 84–5; OCIL, p. 211; Personal communication, John Gamble, June 1995; RIA/DIB.

G9   *Sarsfield; or, wanderings of youth. An Irish tale* (by John Gamble).
London: C. Cradock & W. Joy; Edinburgh: Doig & Stirling; Dublin: M. Keene; Belfast: S. Archer, 1814, 3 vols. SOURCE Brown, 628; McKenna, p. 185; British Fiction; Garside, 1814:22. LOCATION Corvey CME 3–628–47755–7, Ireland related fiction, Dt (lacks vol. 2), L, NUC.

COMMENTARY Historical fiction set around 1760. The hero is a young Irishman who, under the name of Glisson, is a French prisoner of war at Strabane (Co. Tyrone). Aided by the daughter of the postmaster, he escapes and wanders all over Ulster, where there are rumours of an expected French invasion. He goes to Scotland and England and then to the Continent. Later on he fights with François Thurot at the siege of Carrickfergus. Eventually, he returns to Strabane, where he meets with a tragic ending. The story embodies many local traditions and JG's own observations and experiences [Brown].

G10   *Howard. A novel* (by John Gamble).
London: Baldwin, Cradock & Joy, 1815, 2 vols. SOURCE Hardy, 408; McKenna, p. 185; Brown, 629; British Fiction; Garside, 1815:25. LOCATION Corvey CME 3–628–47908–8, Ireland related fiction, L, NUC.

COMMENTARY The hero is from a remote part of Ireland but the scene is set in London, where he seduces a young maiden who, after attempting suicide, dies of remorse [Brown].

G11   *Northern Irish tales* (by John Gamble).
+ London: Longman, Hurst, Rees, Orme & Brown, 1818, 2 vols. SOURCE Brown, 630; McKenna, p. 185; Block, p. 81; Bradshaw, 5753; British Fiction; Garside, 1818:31. LOCATION Corvey CME 3–28–51019–8, Ireland related fiction, L, C.

COMMENTARY This was issued in 500 copies. Reviewed in the *Literary and Political Examiner* (Cork, 1818, p. 203), which stated that 'We expected to have found some anecdotes illustrative of Irish manners, or some account of Irish scenery, interwoven with an imaginary story. But North American tales, or any other title, would have been just as applicable'. Contents: 'Stanley: A tale', 'Nelson: A tale', 'Lesley: A tale' (which concerns the American War of Independence) [RL; Belanger 52; British Fiction].

G12   *Charlton; or, scenes in the North of Ireland. A tale* (by John Gamble).
+ London: Baldwin, Cradock & Joy, 1823, 3 vols. SOURCE Brown, 631; McKenna, p. 185; British Fiction; Garside, 1823:36. LOCATION Corvey CME 3–628–47860–X, Ireland related fiction, L, NUC (1827 edn).
London: Baldwin, Cradock & Joy, 1827, 3 vols. (as *Charlton, or scenes in Ireland*). SOURCE Garside; NSTC; COPAC. LOCATION L.

COMMENTARY Issued in 1823 in an edn of 500 copies. In the preface, the author divides the Irish into three economic groups: The gentry consists of the English-Irish; the shopkeepers and manufacturers, the Scots-Irish, while the native Irish constitute all the labourers and servants. The author is mainly interested in the Presbyterians. The story deals with the United Irishmen in the years preceding the rebellion of 1798. The hero is a young doctor in an Ulster town who is tricked into becoming a United Irishman and leads the rebels at Ballynahinch (Co. Down). Revd James Porter§ is introduced in the story [Brown; CM].

'GANCONAGH', pseud. See YEATS, William Butler.

GANNON, Nicholas J. See GANNON, Nicholas John.

GANNON, Nicholas John (known as Nicholas J. Gannon), b. Ballyboy (Co. Meath; not Sligo or Co. Kildare as in other sources) 1829, d. Kingstown (now Dun Laoghaire, Co. Dublin) 1875. Novelist, barrister, critic and poet, NJG was the son of John Gannon of Ballyboy and was brought up at Benada Abbey (Co. Sligo), the residence of Daniel Jones, who was sheriff of Co. Sligo in 1837. He was educated at Clongowes Wood College (Co. Kildare), Stonyhurst, and TCD, and was a barrister of Gray's Inn. He became a JP, lived at Laragh, near Maynooth (Co. Kildare) and was sheriff of Kildare in 1864. He contributed to the *Irish Quarterly Review* (Dublin) and wrote *An essay on the characteristic errors of our most distinguished poets* (Dublin, 1853), and *The O'Donoghue of the lakes, and other poems* (London, 1858). He died at Crosthwaite Park, Kingstown and was buried at Trim (Co. Meath). SOURCE Allibone Suppl., i, p. 647; B & S, Appendix B, p. 44; Boase, v, p. 384; Brady, p. 88; Brown, p. 115; Hogan 2, p. 472; MVP, p. 177; O'Donoghue, p. 158; RIA/DIB; W.G. Wood-Martin, *Sligo and the Enniskilleners from 1688–1691* (Dublin, 1880), p. 177.

G13   *Rose Waldron; or, a drag on the wheel* (by Nicholas J. Gannon).
       Glasgow: Cameron & Ferguson, n.d. SOURCE Brown, 633.
COMMENTARY No copy located. Set partly in Ireland and partly in other parts of Europe around 1848. Rose and Robert McCloran are kept apart by the plotting of a wicked aunt and the inter-ference of a rival suitor, as well as by complications caused by mistaken identity. In the end they are united [Brown; RL].

G14   *Above and below. A novel* (by Nicholas J. Gannon).
       London: T.C. Newby, 1864, 2 vols. SOURCE Brown, 632. LOCATION L.
COMMENTARY A story of romance and class differences set in Co. Sligo. The offspring of two families of different station fall in love with each other and the vicissitudes of their love are described. Sir Redmond O'Leary's son loves Mary McCarthy, and his daughter loves John McCarthy. In the end, the McCarthys prove to be the better family. The novel contains many scenes of life in Co. Sligo [Brown].

GARD, Alison, fl. 1870. Religious fiction writer.
G15   *The O'Neiles; or, second sight* (by Alison Gard).
       + London: Provost & Co., 1870. SOURCE Allibone Suppl., i, p. 647; Alston, p. 154; OCLC; COPAC. LOCATION L (destroyed), E.
       London: Provost & Co., 1872 (as *The family priest or the O'Neiles*). SOURCE COPAC; OCLC. LOCATION L, E.
COMMENTARY Religious fiction [BLC].

GARDINER, the Hon. Harriet Anne. See D'ORSAY, countess Harriet Anne.

GARDNER, Mrs H.C., fl. 1859. American religious fiction writer, Mrs HCG published sev-eral novels other than the ones listed below. SOURCE Allibone Suppl., i, p. 649 (list of works), RL; Wright web.
G16   *Live to be useful; or, the story of Annie Lee and her Irish nurse* [anon.].
       + London, Edinburgh, New York: T. Nelson & Sons, 1859. LOCATION L, CaOTP (n.d. edn), InND Loeber coll. (1872 edn).
COMMENTARY Religious fiction set in North America. Annie Lee is a cripple in her early teens. She wants to do good and asks her mother to hire a nurse for her. She suggests an ill-tem-pered girl, Annorah, from an Irish family, to give this girl a chance to work. Although the road is not smooth, Annorah learns to read and is converted to protestantism. Annorah's brother, also a cripple, becomes a respectable shoemaker. Annie dies peacefully [ML].
G17   *Glimpses of our lake region in 1863 and other papers* (by Mrs H.C. Gardner).

+ New York: Nelson & Phillips; Cincinnati: Hitchcock & Walden, 1874 (Sunday School Department). LOCATION Wright web.

COMMENTARY Contents: 'Glimpses of our lake region' (concerns a region around a lake in New England, named New Ireland, settled by Irish immigrants. They are poor and not very cultivated but try to live Christian lives), 'Natural history', '"Provoking one another to love and good works"', '"A patch on the knee and gloves on"', 'Miss Phillisa's letters', 'Sympathy', 'The reverend Didymus Ego, M.D.' [ML].

GARLAND, Amelia. See **MEARS, Amelia Garland.**

GARSTIN, Norman, b. Cahirconlish (Co. Limerick) 1847, d. Penzance (Corn.) 1926. Architect, painter, illustrator and writer, NG was the son of an Anglo-Irish army officer, William Garstin, and Mary Hastings Moore, through whom he was related to George Augustus Moore§. According to the ODNB, he was raised by an aunt in Fetard (Co. Limerick; [*sic*, Fethard, Co. Tipperary?]), schooled at St Helier in Jersey, and briefly studied architecture at Queen's College, Cork. He studied art in Paris, where he met Edgar Degas and Edouard Manet. Losing interest in his studies, he went to South Africa where he worked in the diamond mines in Kimberly and shared a tent with Cecil Rhodes. Later he moved to Cape Town where he was sub-editor on the *Cape Times*. He returned to Ireland in 1877 but soon left to study painting in Antwerp and Paris. He travelled widely in Europe and Morocco before his marriage to Louisa Fanny Jones in 1886, after which the couple settled in Cornwall. NG became part of the influential school of artists gathered in Newlyn, Cornwall, which advocated individual expression in the face of Victorian conventionalism. Financial pressures forced him to combine painting with teaching and writing for the periodical press. He opened a school for artists, the Penzance and District Art Students School. His daughter Mary, known as Alethea Dochie Garstin, became a well-known Cornish painter and a joint exhibition of their work was held just before her death in 1978. SOURCE Personal communication, Teresa Johanson, April 2002; ODNB; R. Pryke, *Norman Garstin: Irishman and Newlyn artist* (Reading, 2005), mentioned in M. Hopkinson, 'Norman Garstin' in *Print Quarterly*, June (2005), p. 178; RIA/DIB.

G18 *The suitors of Aprille* (by Norman Garstin).
    London: J. Lane, [1899] (ill. Charles Robinson). LOCATION L, InND Loeber coll. (1900 edn).
    COMMENTARY Written in the manner of an Arthurian tale, with characters such as Prince Debonair, Lady Aprille, and the Red Duke [RL].

G19 *The shilling soldiers* (by Norman Garstin).
    London: Hodder & Stoughton, [1918] (preface by Hugh Walpole). SOURCE COPAC. LOCATION L.
    COMMENTARY War sketches [BLC].

G20 *Empty hands* (by Norman Garstin).
    London: Besant & Co., 1930. SOURCE COPAC. LOCATION L.
    COMMENTARY Published posthumously [RL].

G21 *The white Assegai* (by Norman Garstin).
    + London: G.G. Harrap & Co., 1937. SOURCE COPAC. LOCATION L.
COMMENTARY The story concerns Mark Shannon, who is a hunter in East Africa. He agrees to assist the young woman Consuelo Mansell in searching for a lost city, the details of which were passed down to her in a narrative by her Portuguese ancestors, who had died during a past expedition to Africa. Shannon's and Mansell's adventures in Africa to discover this lost city and its treasure are related [JB].

Gaspey

GASPEY, Thomas, b. Hoxton (London) 1788, d. Shooter's Hill (Kent) 1871. Political journalist, novelist, newspaper proprietor, biographer and poet, TG worked for sixteen years on the staff of the *Morning Post* (London). In 1828 he purchased part-ownership of the *Sunday Times* (London) and increased the paper's coverage of literature and drama. He published 'Shelah, the Fenian's daughter', which appeared in the *Dublin University Magazine* (Jan. 1871). Only the following novel is known to have Irish content. SOURCE Allibone, i, p. 654; Allibone Suppl., i, p. 654; Boase, i, p. 1130; W.E. Hall, p. 219; NCBEL 4, p. 916; OCLC; ODNB; Sutherland, pp 240–1.

G22   *The self-condemned. A romance* [anon.].
    + New York: Harper & Bros, 1836. LOCATION PC, NUC.
    COMMENTARY Historical fiction set in sixteenth-century Munster and features Lord President Carew [RL].

GEARY, Eleanor P., fl. 1876. Religious fiction writer.
G23   *Elsie's victory* (by Eleanor P. Geary).
    + London: Marcus Ward & Co., 1876 (ill.). SOURCE Allibone Suppl., i, p. 656; Alston, p. 157; COPAC. LOCATION L.
    COMMENTARY Religious fiction set in Carlington, Co. Louth, written for juveniles [CM].

'GEILLES HERRING', pseud. See **SOMERVILLE, Edith Anna Œnone**.

'GENEVIEVE', fl. 1830. Pseudonym of a regional fiction writer who, given that he or she published in Dublin, may have been Irish. SOURCE RL.
G24   *The five widows of Waterside: A story founded on facts* (by 'Genevieve').
    Dublin: Richard Moore Tims, 1830. SOURCE COPAC. LOCATION Dt.
    COMMENTARY 36pp. Based on marine accidents in Co. Wexford with an epigraph from the *Christian Year* (London?). The narrator is a Christian man, but not a Catholic [COPAC; FD].

GENLIS, Stephanie-Félicité, marquise de Sillery, comtesse de. See **DE GENLIS, Mme Stephanie-Félicité, marquise de Sillery**.

'A GENTLEMAN OF THE INNER-TEMPLE', fl. 1780s. Pseudonym of an adventure fiction writer.
G25   *Authentic memoirs of the life, numerous adventures, and remarkable escapes of the celebrated Patrick Madan; interspersed with a variety of genuine anecdotes of his contemporaries, and the character of his fair S—, the well-known c—rt—n, the influence of whose charms has so often saved the culprit. Likewise, in these memoirs is given a succinct account of the first introduction of the above lady to the beau monde, and the plan adopted by Lord S— effectually to accomplish so desireable an object* (by 'A gentleman of the Inner-Temple').
    + London: A. Milne, [1782]. SOURCE ESTC t025432. LOCATION D, L, CtY.
    London: Printed by Alexander Hogg, [1781?] (as *The life of Patrick Madan exhibiting the most extraordinary transactions, notorious villainies, and wonderful escapes, that ever happened to one man*). SOURCE ESTC t025429. LOCATION L, C.
    COMMENTARY 46pp for [1782] edn, and 35pp for [1781?] edn. Thomas Madan, Patrick's father, was head gardener and park-keeper of a 'nobleman' near Carrickfergus. The story treats of Patrick, who makes a life of crime. He acts as a burglar, swindler, pickpocket, highwayman

etc., but always manages to escape punishment. The narrative ends with his sentence to transportation to the coast of Africa [Personal communication, Steve Weissman, Dec. 1993].

'A GENTLEWOMAN', pseud. See MC CARTHY, Charlotte.

GEOFFROY, Auguste, b. Dizier, Haut Marne (France) 1850. French novelist. SOURCE Brown 2, p. 99.
G26   *Martyrs d'Irlande* (by Auguste Geoffroy).
       Paris: [publisher?], n.d. SOURCE Brown 2, 541.
       COMMENTARY No copy located [RL].
G27   *Fille d'Irlande, roman d'actualité* (by Auguste Geoffroy).
       Paris: Gautier, 1886. SOURCE Brown 2, 540 (1887 edn); CCF. LOCATION BNF.

GÉRIN-LAJOIE, Antoine, b. Yamachiche (Lower Canada) 1824, d. Ottawa (Canada) 1882. Canadian man of letters, AG-L was the son of Antoine Gérin, a farmer. He began to write poetry by age 15. He studied law, but only practiced intermittently and was mostly employed in government service. He lived for some time in Montreal, then Toronto and, finally, Ottawa. In 1844 he proposed the founding of the later famous Institut Canadien of Montreal. He published only two novels, one of which has Irish interest. He was intent on advancing Canadian literature and together with friends founded two literary periodicals (see below). He also wrote *Dix ans au Canada, de 1840 à 1850* (Quebec, 1888), which was published posthumously. SOURCE DCB, xi, pp 340–4; OCCL, pp 294–5; R. Dionne, *Antoine Gérin-Lajoie, homme de lettres* (Sherbrooke, [Quebec, 1978]).
G28   *Jean Rivard, économiste. Pour faire-suite à Jean Rivard le défricheur* (by Antoine Gérin-Lajoie).
       + Montreal: J.B. Rolland & Fils, 1876, 2nd edn (corrected). LOCATION CaOONL, NUC, InND Loeber coll.
       Montreal: Beau Chemin, 1953. LOCATION NUC.
COMMENTARY Sequel to *Jean Rivard le défricheur* (Montreal, 1874, 2nd edn), which first appeared in *Les Soirées Canadiennes* (Quebec, 1862). *Jean Rivard, économiste* first appeared in *Le Foyer Canadien* (Quebec, 1864, ii, pp 15–371). Set in the rural parish of Rivardville in French Canada, the priest notes the presence of several Irish families, who distinguish themselves by their industrious habits and their adherence to the Catholic faith. He favours intermarriage between the Irish and the French Canadians in order to cement the harmony between the two nationalities and in the hope that it will modify the habits of the French Canadians without affecting their national character [*Étude Irlandaises*, 12 (1977), p. 118].

GERMAINS, Mrs E.A., fl. 1878. Novelist, Mrs EAG probably was related to the American publisher A.Z. Germains, who published the following volume. SOURCE RL.
G29   *Left to starve, and no one wants the blame* (by E.A. Germains).
       New York: A.Z. Germains, 1878. SOURCE Allibone Suppl., i, p. 660; Emerald Isle cat. 88/562; COPAC. LOCATION NUC.
       London: Simpkin. Marshall & Co., [1880]. SOURCE Alston, p. 159. LOCATION L.
       COMMENTARY A story about Jewish life in Ireland [Emerald Isle cat.].

GETTY, Edmund, b. Belfast (Co. Antrim) 1799, d. 1857. Antiquarian and writer, EG was the son of a Belfast merchant, Robert Getty, and his wife Susanna Grimshaw, whose family was in the cotton industry in Belfast. He was educated at the Belfast Academical Institution, of which his father was a founder, and he became secretary of the Belfast Harbour Board. He was active in civic organizations such as the Belfast Natural History Society and the Belfast Literary Society and gave numerous papers on natural and antiquarian topics. He was involved in excavations at Drumbro (Co. Down) and on Tory Island (Co. Donegal); published *Notices of the round towers of Ulster* ([Belfast, *c.*1855–6]), and contributed to the *Ulster Jrnl of Archaeology*, including articles on his research on Tory and on his grandmother's family, the Sitlingtons of Dunagor (Co. Antrim). The Getty family papers are at the PRONI, Belfast. SOURCE *Belfast literary society* (Belfast, 1902), p. 82; Brown, p. 115; RIA/DIB; Rowan cat. 43/70.

G30   *The last king of Ulster* [anon.].

+ London: James Madden & Co., 1841, 3 vols. SOURCE Brown, 636; Wolff, 2480. LOCATION D, BFl, L.

COMMENTARY An historical miscellany of Elizabethan times containing memoirs, anecdotes and family history of the northern Irish chieftains [Brown].

GIBBON, Charles, b. Isle of Man 1843, d. Great Yarmouth (Suffolk) 1890. English novelist, CG was born of working-class parents and moved early in life to Glasgow where he first worked as an office clerk and later as a journalist. He migrated to London around 1861 or 1862, where he soon became well-known as a writer and club man. He published forty-seven novels, many of which are set in Scotland and were serialized in *All the Year Round* and *Once a Week* (both London). The last years of his life were spent in East Anglia in poor health and in poverty. SOURCE Allibone Suppl., i, p. 662; Boase, v, p. 399; NCBEL 4, pp 1533–4 (list of other novels); ODNB; Sutherland, p. 244; Wolff, i, pp 115–16.

G31   *In cupid's wars* (by Charles Gibbon).

London: F.V. White, 1884, 3 vols. SOURCE Brown, 637. LOCATION L, NUC.

COMMENTARY Historical fiction set in Kilkenny in 1798, but both the topographical and historical settings are vague. Most characters are Roman Catholics and secret societies abound [Brown].

GIBSON, Revd Charles Bernard, b. Ireland? 1808, d. London 1885. Clergyman, historical novelist and miscellaneous writer, CBG was a chaplain at Spike Island (Cork Harbour) and a minister of the Independent Congregation at Mallow (Co. Cork). He later joined the Church of England and was chaplain of the Shoreditch Workhouse and Infirmary from 1874 to his death. He wrote several historical works, including *The history of the County and City of Cork* (London, 1861, 2 vols.), and *Historical portraits of Irish chieftains and Anglo-Norman knights* (London, 1871), as well as *Irish convict reform* (Dublin, 1863) and other works. He was elected member of the RIA in 1854 and was granted a civil list pension in 1864. SOURCE Allibone Suppl., i, p. 664; Boase, v. p. 402; Brown, p. 116; NUC; RIA/DIB.

G32   *The last Earl of Desmond. A historical romance of 1599–1603* [anon.] (dedicated to Sir Denham Jephson Norreys).

+ Dublin: Hodges & Smith, 1854, 2 vols. SOURCE Brown, 638; Linen Hall cat. p. 31 (where misattributed to C.B. Bernard). LOCATION D, Dt, BFl, L, NUC, InND Loeber coll.

COMMENTARY Historical fiction set in sixteenth-century Munster. The author explains in the preface that his story does not accurately follow the historical events of the time. He frequently addresses the reader and inserts contemporary events to illustrate the historical narrative. The main character is James Fitz-Thomas, the last earl of Desmond. The story begins when Sir Thomas Norreys is lord president of Munster. He is succeeded by Sir George Carew, whose wily schemes to break up the resistance in Munster are matched by the plots and counterplots and shifts in allegiance among the Irish, such as John Nugent, Florence M'Carthy, Fitzgibbon and the White Knight. The earl of Desmond marries Ellen Spenser, an imaginary daughter of Edmund Spenser, who is unaware of her ancestry. She is a Protestant, however, and introduces the earl to the New Testament. She dies in childbirth, but the baby daughter lives, unbeknownst to the earl. The earl ends up in the Tower of London, where he meets Sir Walter Raleigh who proposes a scheme to break out of prison and seek gold in South America. The plan is frustrated by the sudden appearance of the earl's little daughter. She brightens his last months before he dies, and then returns to Munster. Raleigh becomes friendly with Florence M'Carthy, who is also in the Tower, and they plot to go for the gold in South America but M'Carthy at the last moment changes his mind. The book closes with a brief summary of the fate of some of the main characters, among them Raleigh, who dies on the scaffold [ML].

G33   *Dearforgil: the princess of Brefney. A historical romance of 1152–1172* [anon.] (dedicated to George Petrie).
London: J.F. Hope, 1857. SOURCE Brown, 639. LOCATION D (1884, 2nd edn), L, NUC.
COMMENTARY Historical fiction, which tells about the story of Diarmuid MacMorrough's abduction of the wife of O'Ruairc of Breffni and subsequent events, including the Norman invasion of Ireland [Brown].

G34   *Beyond the Orange River; or, scenes in Southern Africa* [anon.] (dedicated to Viscount Palmerston).
+ London: Thomas Cautley Newby, 1861. SOURCE NSTC. LOCATION Dt, C, L.

GILBERT, Lady. See **MULHOLLAND, Rosa.**

GLASCOCK, Capt. William Nugent, pseud. 'An officer of rank', b. 1787?, d. Baltinglass (Co. Wicklow) 1847. Naval officer, novelist and short story writer, WNG may have been a member of the Glascock family that had estates at Alderton and Killowen (Co. Wexford). He entered the Royal Navy in 1800 and served with distinction in the Napoleonic Wars. From 1818 until his death, he had various commands and distinguished himself in duty in Portugal, protecting British interests in the Duoro region. In 1847 he was one of the Poor Relief Act inspectors superintending aid to victims of the Famine, when he died suddenly at Baltinglass. He wrote five works of fiction, mostly dealing with naval adventures. SOURCE Allibone, i, p. 677; NCBEL 4, p. 917; ODNB; Rowe & Scallan, 9, 615; Sutherland, p. 249; Walford, p. 409.

G35   *Naval sketch-book; or, the service afloat and ashore; with characteristic reminiscences, fragments, and opinions on professional, colonial, and political subjects; interspersed with copious notes, biographical, historical, critical, and illustrative* (by 'An officer of rank').
London: Printed for the author, 1826, 2 vols. SOURCE British Fiction; Garside, 1826:29; Sadleir, 982. LOCATION L, NUC.
COMMENTARY Naval fiction [RL].

G36   *Sailors and saints; or, matrimonial manoeuvres* [anon.].
+ London: Henry Colburn, 1829, 3 vols. SOURCE British Fiction; Garside, 1829:34; Sadleir, 983; Wolff, 2566. LOCATION Corvey CME 3–628–51125–9, Dt, L, NUC.
COMMENTARY Fiction set in England, deals with naval matters but the story is largely set on shore [RL].

G37   *Tales of a tar, with characteristic anecdotes* [anon.].
+ London: Henry Colburn & Richard Bentley, 1830. SOURCE Sadleir, 984; Garside 2, 1830:52. LOCATION Corvey, CME 3–628–51159–3, L, NUC.
COMMENTARY Naval stories. Contents: 'The breeze at Spithead', 'Jack a biographer', 'Kind inquiries', 'Command o'mind', 'Obstetric consultation', 'Sailor Sal', 'Dreams at sea', 'A brush in the boats', 'A "call" for the cat' [ML].

G38   *Naval sketch book: or, the service afloat and ashore; with characteristic reminiscences, fragments, and opinion* (second series) (by 'An officer of rank').
+ London: Whittaker & Co., 1834, 2 vols. (ill.). SOURCE Wolff, 2564a; Garside 2, 1834:28; COPAC. LOCATION L, NUC.
COMMENTARY Naval stories. Contents: 'The chase – a tale founded on fact', 'Strictures on Smollett', 'Notes for naval maxims (found in the pocket-book of a post captain)', 'Jack's eccentricities', 'A new system of signals, by which the colours may be wholly dispensed with', 'Dialogue of the deck', 'Twenty-eight ships and ten gun-brigs', 'Recreation in rhyme', 'The boarders', 'Leaves of the private log of captain on half-pay', 'Jack in Parliament: Dialogue of the deck', 'Impressment of seaman', 'Jack the giant', 'Original of the shipwreck in Don Juan', 'Naval humorists – Sir T.P., Sir John P., Sir I.C., Sir J.D.', 'Jack at Oporto: A dialogue at the deck' [Personal communication, Debra Deerlove, Aug. 2003].

G39   *Land sharks and sea gulls* (by William Nugent Glascock).
London: Richard Bentley, 1838, 3 vols. (ill. G. Cruikshank). SOURCE Wolff, 2564; COPAC. LOCATION L, NUC.
COMMENTARY Naval fiction [RL].

GLASGOW, Harriet. See **ACHESON, Harriet.**

'GLYN, Gerald' pseud. See **FITZGERALD, Isabella Lloyd.**

'GODFREY, Hal', pseud. See **ECCLES, Charlotte O'Conor.**

GODWIN, William, the elder, pseud. **'Theophilus Marcliffe',** b. Wisbech (Cambs.) 1756, d. 1836. English novelist and philosopher, WG was the son of a dissenting minister in East Anglia and was reared in a strict Puritan tradition. For a short while he was a minister, after which he went to London to pursue a literary career. Although he objected to marriage on principle, in 1797 he wed Mary Wollstonecraft (former governess to Margaret Mount Cashell§), who died later that year after the birth of their daughter Mary (author of *Frankenstein* [London, 1818] and wife of the poet Percy Bysshe Shelley). One of his friends was John Philpot Curran, to whom he dedicated his *Mandeville* (London, 1817). Only his works with Irish content are listed here. SOURCE Allibone, i, pp 683–6; British Fiction; Brown 2, p. 103; Field Day, v, p. 55; NSTC, ser. 1, ii, pp 281–2; ODNB; Osborne, p. 164; G. Woodcock, *William Godwin. A biographical study* (London, 1944), pp 195–6; *London Gentlemen Magazine*, June 1836.

G40   *The looking-glass. A true history of the early years of an artist; calculated to awaken the emulation of young persons in the pursuit of every laudable attainment: particularly in the cultivation of the fine arts* (by 'Theophilus Marcliffe')
+ London: Thomas Hodgkins, 1805 (ill.). SOURCE Hodges Figgis cat. 10 n.s./1153. LOCATION L.
COMMENTARY This is a semi-fictionalized account of the Irish artist William Macready. The main character is a boy born in 'one of the principal towns in the county Clare' [Hodges Figgis cat. 10 n.s./1153; CM].

G41   *Mandeville. A tale of the seventeenth century in England* (by William Godwin; dedicated to John Philpot Curran).
+ Edinburgh: Archibald Constable & Co.; London: Longman, Hurst, Rees, Orme & Brown, 1817, 3 vols. SOURCE Brown 2, 558 (1818 edn); British Fiction; Garside, 1817:29; Wolff, 2588. LOCATION Corvey CME 3–628–47849–7, Ireland related fiction, Dt, D, L, NUC.
New York: W.B. Gilley; C. Wiley & Co., 1818, 2 vols. LOCATION NUC.

Philadelphia: M. Thomas, 1818, 2 vols. LOCATION NUC.

Paris: Béchet, 1818, 4 vols. SOURCE Garside, 1817:29; CCF. LOCATION BNF.

COMMENTARY The novel had been started eight years earlier as a rejoinder to the American novelist Charles Brockden Brown's§ *Wieland* (New York, 1798) and then laid aside. It was only completed at the insistence of Godwin's publisher, A. Constable. The narrator tells that he was born in Charlemont (Co. Armagh) in 1638 where his father was an officer under Lord Caulfield. The author discusses, on the whole fairly, the misgovernings and the grievances that led to the Rising of 1641 and Sir Phelim O'Neill's capture by Charlemont's stratagem. He admits that at first the rising succeeded almost without bloodshed, but developed later into excesses of various kinds, including massacres of prisoners, among them his father and mother. He himself escaped with a faithful nurse. At Kells they meet Revd Hilkish Bradford, who takes the child from the nurse. 'Was a woman of this accursed, savage, Irish, Popish breed to be supposed to have any feelings entitled to the sympathy and favour of a Protestant heart?' Revd Hilkish thought not and he leaves Ireland with the child. Here the Irish interest of the story ends [Brown 2; Falkner Grierson cat. 22/225].

G42   *Cloudesley. A tale* [anon.].

London: H. Colburn & Richard Bentley, 1830, 3 vols. SOURCE Wolff, 2586; Sadleir, 2586. LOCATION L, NUC.

New York: Collins & Hannay; Collins & Co., C. & H. Carwill etc., 1830, 2 vols. SOURCE OCLC. LOCATION MH, NUC.

COMMENTARY Reviewed in *Dublin Literary Gazette* (Mar. 27, 1830), this is a tale of two brothers, the sons of an Irish nobleman, who are brought up together but under very different circumstances. The elder, the heir, is the favourite; the younger is much neglected. Notwithstanding this differential treatment, they are much attached to each other. After their father's death, they join the Austrian army under Prince Eugene in the war against the Turks. Lord Alton, the eldest son, rescues a beautiful young Greek lady, whom he marries. He dies as a result of a duel instigated by his sensitivity to insults against the Greek nation. His wife also dies, leaving an infant son. The younger son, aiming to get the inheritance, leaves the infant with his servant Cloudesley. The new Lord Alton, by the death of a relative, now becomes Lord Danvers, and returns to his large estates in England. He marries and fathers four children. Sickness and death strike the children, and Lord Danvers is plagued by his bad conscience. Cloudesely also feels guilt as an accessory and decides to give the boy, Julian, the best education, but the boy becomes spoiled. Cloudesley attempts to travel to England to restore Julian to his rights, but is mortally wounded by banditti. In the meantime, Julian escapes but is pursued by an accomplice of Lord Danvers and eventually by Danvers himself. Danvers rescues his nephew from an ignominious death, makes a full confession, and dies [RL; *Dublin Literary Gazette*].

GOLDSMITH, Oliver, b. Pallas, Ballymahon (Co. Longford), probably in 1728, d. London, 1774. Poet, playwright, novelist, man of letters and an important contributor to English and Irish literature, OG was a son of Revd Charles Goldsmith, a Church of Ireland clergyman, and Ann Jones. Early in his childhood the family moved to Lissoy (Co. Westmeath), where he was educated locally and on which he probably based one of his most famous poems, *The deserted village* (London, 1770). He attended the parish schools at Athlone and Edgeworthstown and the Elphin Diocesan School in Roscommon. He was admitted to TCD in 1745 at age 15 and obtained his BA in 1750. When rejected by the church, and after squandering many opportunities to begin a career, he went to Edinburgh and afterwards to Leiden (Netherlands) to study medicine. He arrived in London poor, with a dubious medical degree, after having wandered through Europe on foot. In 1757 he became a contributor to the *Monthly Review* in London and published also in the *Bee* and the *Citizen of the World* (both London). He lived the rest of his life in England, mostly in poverty and hardship, but that Ireland remained close to his heart is evidenced in his letters to his friend Bob Bryanston. He alternated between journeywork and literature. His comedy *She stoops to conquer* remains in the contemporary dramatic repertoire. Elizabeth Griffith§ published a few of his stories in her *Novellettes* (London, 1780). Goldsmith counted among his friends some of the most eminent men of the day, including Edmund Burke and Dr Samuel Johnson, whose famous epitaph 'There was no kind of writing he did not touch on, and he enhanced everything he touched' is inscribed on Goldsmith's memorial in Westminster Abbey. For his portraits and papers, see ODNB. For an extensive discussion of Goldsmith as dramatist, poet and novelist, see the RIA/DIB, Field Day, and ODNB. His portraits are listed in ODNB and Elmes. SOURCE Allibone, i, pp 687–96; Boylan, p. 130; B & S, p. 331; Elmes, pp 80–1; Field Day, i, pp 656, 658–81, 686; Hogan 2, pp 486–7; OCIL, pp 219–20; ODNB; O'Donoghue, p. 164; RIA/DIB; Rogal, pp 144, 185, 187.

G43   *The citizen of the world: or, letters from a Chinese philosopher residing in London to his friends in the East* [anon.].

London: Printed for the author, 1762, 2 vols. SOURCE Raven, 716; Forster, 1085; ESTC t146033; McBurney & Taylor, 349. LOCATION Dt, L, MH, IU, NUC.

Dublin: George & Alex Ewing, 1762, 2 vols. SOURCE Cole, p. 245; Raven, 718; ESTC t146034. LOCATION Dt, L, H, NUC, InND Loeber coll. (1775 edn).

Amsterdam: J.F. Boitte, 1763, 3 vols. (trans. by M. P[oivre] as *Le citoyen du monde, ou lettres d'un philosophe chinois à ses amis dans L'Orient*). SOURCE Streeter, 153; Bn-Opale plus. LOCATION BNF.

Albany: Thomas Spencer, 1794. SOURCE Gecker, 369; ESTC t146041. LOCATION PU, NUC.

Philadelphia: D. Davies & J. Morgan, 1802. LOCATION NUC.

COMMENTARY Partly inspired by baron de Montesquieu's *Lettres Persanes* (Amsterdam, 1721) and Edmond Pery's§ *Letters from an Armenian in Ireland* (London, 1757), a series of fictional letters written by a Chinese traveller to Europe who is living in London and reporting back to his friends in China on a wide variety of contemporary topics such as religion, politics, the theatre, sports, morals, and society. In turn the letters from China add a note of exoticism [Field Day, i, pp 671–4, 686; *Modern Language Review*, 14(2) 1953 p. 209; ODNB].

G44   *The vicar of Wakefield. A tale. Supposed to be written by himself* [anon.].

London: F. Newbery, 1766, 2 vols. SOURCE Raven, 1007; Forster, 1094; ESTC t146175. LOCATION D (3rd edn), Dt, L, MH.

+ London [i.e., Cork]: [no publisher], 1766, vol. 1. SOURCE Pollard, p. 82; Raven, 1012; ESTC t146802. LOCATION Dt, L, MH, InND Loeber coll.

Corke [i.e., London]: Printed by Eugene Swiney, 1766, 2 vols. in 1. SOURCE Pollard, p. 82; Raven, 1011; ESTC t146179; Topp 8, p. 41. LOCATION Dt, L, MH, NUC.

Dublin: W. & W. Smith, A. Leathley, J. Hoey Snr, P. Wilson, J. Exshaw, E. Watts, H. Saunders, J. Hoey, Jnr, J. Potts & J. Williams, 1766, 2 vols. SOURCE Raven, 1010, 1010a; Cole, p. 245; Pollard 2, p. 114; ESTC t146177. LOCATION D (1767 edn), Dt, L, MH, NUC.

Dublin: Printed by G. Gilbert, 1797 (trans. by M.J.B. Bisset as *Le curé de Wakefield*). SOURCE Cole, p. 245; Pollard 2, p. 239; Emerald Isle cat. 76/334; Bn-Opale plus. LOCATION BNF.

Londres [Paris?]: Pissot, Dessaint, 1767, 2 vols. (trans. by Charlotte-Jeanne Béraud de la Haie de Riou, marquise de Montesson as *Le ministre de Wakefield. Histoire supposée écrite par lui-même*). SOURCE ESTC t098006; Streeter, 157; Bn-Opale plus. LOCATION Dt, L, BNF.

Paris: Barrois le Jeune, 1779 (revsd by Mr D**). LOCATION Dt.
Liège: J.J. Tutot, 1781, 2 vols. (trans. as *Le ministre de Wakefield*). SOURCE Rochedieu,
p. 127. SOURCE Bn-Opale plus. LOCATION BNF.
Deventer: Lucas Leemhorst, 1768, 2 vols. (trans. into Dutch as *De predikant van
Wakefield*). LOCATION Dt.
Leipzig: M.G. Weidmanns Erben & Reich, 1767 (trans. as *Der Landpriester von
Wakefield*). LOCATION Dt.
Berlin: Gottfried Carl Nauck, 1794. SOURCE ESTC t204878. LOCATION L.
Norwich (CT): Printed by Ebenezer Bushnell, 1791. LOCATION Dt, NUC.
Philadelphia: William Mentz, 1772, 2 vols. SOURCE Rosenbach, 74; ESTC w29876.
LOCATION Dt, L, NUC.
Dublin [i.e. Boston], printed [by Mein and Fleming], 1767, 4th edn. Source ESTC
w42510; w39851. Location CtY, MH. COMMENTARY *Dublin* [*i.e. Boston edn*] 'The
imprint is false' [it was not printed in Dublin, but] was printed by Mein and Fleming
in Boston' [ESTC w42510].
Providence [RI]: Printed by Bennett Wheeler, 1792. LOCATION Dt, NUC.
COMMENTARY Set in England. An Anglican minister goes bankrupt and moves with his family to a small farm. The landlord turns out to be a villain who seduces the minister's daughter and puts him and his son in jail. In the end, all turns out well. The story contains much social satire [Field Day, i, pp 746–51; OCIL, p. 586; ODNB].

— COLLECTED WORKS
G45 *The miscellaneous works of Oliver Goldsmith; now first uniformly collected.*
Perth: R. Morison & Son; Edinburgh: N.R. Cheyne, 1792, 7 vols. (ill.). SOURCE ESTC
t146786. LOCATION L.
Edinburgh: Geo. Mudie, 1792, 4 vols. SOURCE ESTC n006016. LOCATION C.
G46 *The miscellaneous works of Oliver Goldsmith, M.B. Consisting of his essays, poems,
plays, &c. &c.*
London: W. Griffin, 1775. SOURCE ESTCt146118. LOCATION D, Dt, L.
Edinburgh: R. Morison & Son, 1791, 2 vols. SOURCE ESTC t146120. LOCATION L,
CtY.
G47 *Collected works of Oliver Goldsmith* (ed. by A. Friedman).
Oxford: Clarendon, 1966, 5 vols. SOURCE COPAC. LOCATION O.
— SPURIOUS WORK
G48 void

GOLLAN, Eliza M. See HUMPHREYS, Mrs Desmond.

GOODRICH, Samuel Griswold, pseud. 'Peter Parley', b. Ridgefield (CT) 1793, d. New York City, 1860. American publisher, editor and novelist, SGG was self-educated and began his publishing business first in Hartford and then Boston, where he edited the *Token*, considered then to be the best of the American annuals. He travelled in England, France, Germany and Holland in 1823 and 1824, after which he began to write and publish the extensive Peter Parley series, for which he is best known. This series, numbering more than 100 books, was immensely popular and millions of books were sold. According to the DAB, SGG's claim to have written all of them has been disputed. The series' instructional aims are masked in the lightly-fictional conversations between a kindly, wise old gentleman and various curious children. SOURCE Allibone, i, pp 700–3; Brown, p. 117; DAB.

G49　*Peter Parley's tales about Great Britain: including England, Wales, Scotland, and Ireland* (by 'Peter Parley').
Baltimore: J. Jewett, 1832. LOCATION NUC.
London: William Tegg, 1839 (as *Tales about Great Britain and Ireland*; ill.). LOCATION NUC.
+ London: Thomas Tegg; Dublin: Tegg & Co.; Glasgow: Griffin & Co.; Sydney, Hobart Town: J. & S.A. Tegg, 1839, 3rd edn (as *Tales about Great Britain and Ireland*; ill.). LOCATION InND Loeber coll.
COMMENTARY Fiction for juveniles, which deals with Ireland. A fifth edn appeared in 1856 [RL].

G50　*Peter Parley's short stories for long nights* (by 'Peter Parley').
Boston: Allen & Ticknor, 1834. SOURCE MacLeod, p. 58. LOCATION NUC.
London: G. Limbird, 1837. LOCATION NUC.
COMMENTARY A tale for young children, recounting the story of an Irish boy who, after his mother's death in Ireland, emigrates to America with his father. His father works as a gardener, but then dies. The boy is destitute, but is found and adopted by a benevolent Christian [MacLeod].

G51　*Peter Parley's tales about Ireland and the Irish* (by 'Peter Parley'; dedicated to 'The young people of Ireland').
London: Darton & Clark, [1842] (ill.). LOCATION D ([1845] edn), UCD Folklore Dept., L ([1845] edn), NUC.
COMMENTARY Written for children in a non-fictional style. Alternative dedication of the same imprint: 'To the neglected people of Ireland' [RL].

G52　*The balloon travels of Robert Merry and his young friends over various countries in Europe* (by 'Peter Parley').
New York, Boston: J.C. Derby & Co.; Phillips, Sampson & Co., 1855. LOCATION CtY.
+ London: James Blackwood, 1857 (ill.). LOCATION MH, InND Loeber coll.
COMMENTARY Written in dialogue, the story starts with the arrival by balloon of the children and their adult friend to the Giant's Causeway and their trips to Belfast and Dublin, before setting off to England and the Continent. They discuss Irish national character and Irish patriotism [RL].

GORDON, Letitia, fl. 1803. Fiction writer, LG was a resident of Belfast or somewhere in the north of Ireland. SOURCE RL.

G53　*Anna; or, a picture of domestic happiness* (by Letitia Gordon; dedicated to the marchioness of Donegall).
+ Belfast: Smyth & Lyons, 1803, 2 vols. SOURCE Anderson 2, p. 10. LOCATION PC.
COMMENTARY Contains English names, but no indication of location [ML].

GORGES, Mary (née Kelly), d. Kingstown (now Dun Laoghaire, Co. Dublin) 1911. Poet and religious fiction writer, MG was the daughter of William Daniel Kelly of Castlepark, Turrock (Co. Roscommon). She married Maj. Gorges, an East India Company officer, and survived him by many years. Her poems appeared in *Chambers's Journal* (Edinburgh) and in the *Irish Monthly* (Dublin) and two volumes were published posthumously: *Killarney* (London, 1912), and *On life's journey: poems and ballads* (London, 1916). She is also the author of *Your heavenly father knoweth* (London, 1888). In an obituary she was described as 'a broad-minded, gentle-hearted, Christian woman' (Colman, p. 129, quoting IBL 3 (May 1912, p. 171)). SOURCE Allibone Suppl., i, p. 691; Colman, p. 129; Irish pseudonyms; O'Donoghue, p. 165.

G54   *A twelfth night king* (by Mary Gorges).
London, Edinburgh: W. & R. Chambers, 1897 (ill.). LOCATION L(destroyed), E.
COMMENTARY Religious fiction [BLC].

'THE GOVERNOR', pseud. See TEELING, Bartholomew J.

'GRACE, Saye', fl. 1889. Probable pseudonym, most likely of an Irish author, whose only work was published in Dublin. SOURCE RL; Topp 8, 963.
G55   *A snake in the grass* (by 'Grace Saye').
Dublin: Sealy, Bryers & Walker; London: Simpkin, Marshall & Co., 1889. SOURCE COPAC; Topp 8, 963. LOCATION L.

GRAHAM, Lady Beatrice Violet. See GREVILLE, Lady Beatrice Violet.

'GRAND, Sarah', pseud. See MC FALL, Frances Elizabeth.

'GRANNY', fl. 1885. Pseudonym of a children's writer who published in London several other books for children. SOURCE COPAC.
G56   *At Granny's; or, ten days without father and mother* (by 'Granny').
London: Masters & Co., 1885. LOCATION L.
COMMENTARY English children, age 5 and 6, stay with grandmother in Ireland [Personal communication, Mary Pollard, July 2003].

GRANT, Mrs Anne (née MacVicar), b. Glasgow (Scotland) 1755, d. 1838. Scottish translator, poet and miscellaneous writer, AG spent the years 1758 to 1768 in Albany (NY), where her father was posted with the army and where she became acquainted with the widow of Col. Philip Schuyler, whose friendship she memorialized in *Memoirs of an American lady* (London, 1808). After returning to Scotland, she married Revd James Grant of Laggan in the Scottish highlands in 1779. Here she farmed, translated from Gaelic and reared her children to speak Gaelic. She also wrote *Sketches of intellectual education* (Inverness, 1812), *Popular models ... for the sons and daughters of industry* (Edinburgh, 1815; repr. Philadelphia, 1816, 2 vols.), and several works on the Scots and Scotland. SOURCE Allibone, i, pp 718–20; Blain, pp 451–2; NCBEL 4, p. 344; NUC; ODNB; COPAC.
G57   *The history of an Irish family: in which, the unspeakable advantages of a virtuous education, in the formation of the human character, are strikingly exemplified, and its powerful effects in reclaiming and amending, even after vicious propensities have been formed, are amply demonstrated. To which is added, by way of sequel, the exemplary mother; or, dutiful parents and good children, by the same author* [anon.] (dedicated to the Prince Regent).
+ Haddington: George Miller, Dunbar, 1822 (ill.). LOCATION D, InND Loeber coll.
COMMENTARY Didactic religious fiction which first appeared in the *Cheap Magazine* (Haddington, 1814). A poor Irish family moves to Scotland to beg. The parents, weak from drinking whiskey, catch a fever and die. The children receive help from Lady L-, who divides them among several families, sending two back to Ireland. The children raised in Scotland all do very well. The two children raised in Ireland grow up under the influence of alcohol. One dies, while the other requires the help of all his siblings to improve his life and that of his children. The booklet is written to advise parents on how to raise children and in the story fathers as well as mothers are involved in childrearing. The book emphasizes self-improvement by reading, but note is made of the lack of appropriate material. Mention is made of

Maria Edgeworth's§ *Popular tales* (London, 1804) as filling a gap in reading materials for the education and entertainment of the lower classes [ML].

GRANT, James, b. Edinburgh (Scotland), 1822, d. London, 1887. A Scottish novelist and historical and military writer, JG was the son of an army captain and through his mother he was related to Sir Walter Scott. He was an ensign in the 62nd Regiment but resigned his commission in 1843, worked in an architect's office in Edinburgh, and began to devote himself to writing. Despite the fact that he was quite prolific: he produced 56 novels and wrote on Scotland (in particular Edinburgh) in addition to producing fiction for juveniles, he died penniless. Around 1855 he published short pieces in the *Dublin University Magazine*. His death in 1887 is mentioned in the *Irish Catholic Directory* (Dublin, 1888, p. 428) where it is noted that, prior to his conversion to catholicism, he had written in 'bigoted' terms about the religion. SOURCE Allibone Suppl., i, pp 701–02; BLC; W.E. Hall, p. 175; NCBEL 4, p. 1302; ODNB; Sutherland, pp 258–9.

G58   *Frank Hilton; or, "the Queen's own"* (by James Grant).
+ London, New York: George Routledge & Co., 1855. LOCATION L.
+ London, New York: Routledge, Warne & Routledge, 1861 (new edn). LOCATION InND Loeber coll.
COMMENTARY A military novel set mainly in the Arabian Peninsula where a regiment is stationed at Aden and officers make incursions into the desert. Features several Irish soldiers as side characters, including O'Hara and the Hon. Mr Morphew, the son of an Anglo-Irish peer, and O'Flannigan, 'a sterling Irishman of the right kind' [ML].

GRANT, Mary Ann, fl. 1810. Miscellaneous writer, MAG was the wife of a soldier and spent time at various military camps, as well as travelling with friends. She is not to be confused with the author Mrs Anne Grant§ (1755–1838). SOURCE Burmester cat. 47/61.

G59   *Sketches of life and manners, with delineation of scenery in England, Scotland, and Ireland: interspersed with moral tales and anecdotes in original letters* (by Mary Ann Grant; dedicated to the princess of Wales).
+ London: For the author, 1810, 2 vols. (subscribers' list, mostly Scottish and a few Irish names). LOCATION C, NUC, InND Loeber coll.
COMMENTARY A collection of letters, probably partly fictional, partly autobiographical, to various female correspondents written between 1795 and 1808. They describe a number of places where the main character stayed in various military camps. Includes some of the writer's own short stories and observations on a soldier's life. The description of her stay in Ireland covers various towns where her husband's regiment was stationed, such as Kildare, Tuam, Loughrea and the village of Eyrecourt (all Co. Galway). The author is fairly critical of the customs and traditions of the Irish. She remarks on the number of the balls that she and her husband have to attend, and the sudden moves that the regiment is required to make. She describes Irish markets and cabins, and discusses religion and superstitions. She relates a trip from Shannon Harbour to Dublin by canal boat [ML; Burmester cat. 47/61].

GRANT, Robert. Co-author. See **O'REILLY, John Boyle**.

GRATTAN, Thomas Colley, pseud. '**A walking gentleman**', b. Dublin 1791, d. London 1864. Short story and travel writer, historian, novelist and diplomat, TCG was the second son of Colley Grattan, coroner of Kildare, and Elizabeth Warren, and brother of the military author William Grattan. His family was related both to the Irish parliamentarian Henry Grattan and to Arthur Wellesley, duke of Wellington. TCG went to school in Athy (Co. Kildare), and after a false start in law in Dublin he joined the Louth militia and served in northern England. Failing to get a commission when war with France ended, he left Ireland, intending to fight in the South American wars of independence. On the voyage to Venezuela he met, fell in love with and married Eliza O'Donnel (Aliza Sarah, according to Burke's) in 1817. They settled in Bordeaux, and TCG took to writing as a living. Soon the family moved to Paris where he met Washington Irving, who advised him on the first edn of *High-ways and by-ways* (London, 1823) and where he began his own journal, the *Paris Monthly Review of British and Continental Literature*. He contributed extensively to London magazines (e.g., a ghost story in the *Keepsake*, 1833), especially to the *New Monthly Magazine* and to *Household Words* (London, 1856). He translated French poetry. His play *Ben Nazir, the Saracen* (London, 1827) was a financial and artistic failure, largely due to the inept performance of Edmund Kean, and under financial pressures TCG and his family left for Brussels. In 1828 he made a sojourn with the poets Samuel Taylor Coleridge and William Wordsworth on the Continent. Always suffering financially, he undertook a series of minor government commissions. Around this time, having moved to Antwerp after his house in Brussels was destroyed during the revolution of 1830, and then to The Hague, he wrote *The Netherlands* (London, 1830), and between 1838 and 1839 completed a manuscript on Belgium for the Society for the Diffusion of Useful Knowledge, but it remained unpublished (of which, perhaps, a segment was published in the Foreign Quarterly Review, Oct., 1839). TCG became interested in the boundary dispute between the US and Canada, which was being arbitrated by the Netherlands, and distinguished himself working on that issue. Returning to Brussels he became Brussels correspondent for the London *Times* and through the offices of King Leopold he was appointed British consul in Boston (MA) in 1839. In the US he wrote about the plight of Irish immigrants and helped found a society for their aid. In 1846 he returned to England and spent his last years in London, churning out volumes of commentary on Anglo-American affairs (for example, his *Civilized America*, London, 1859, 2 vols.), and a number of novels. His strengths were the writing of novellas, short stories and historical fiction novels, almost all of which he set on the Continent. In 1844 it was reported that he commanded £300 for a novel, which put him in the intermediate ranking of publishers' payment to authors. His partly-fictionalized reminiscences *Beaten paths; and those who trod them* (London, 1862, 2 vols.), written when he was age 70, show his friendship with the poets Thomas Campbell and Thomas Moore§, and the actors François Joseph Talma, John Kemble, and Edmund Kean. John Edward Jones's bust of 'Colley Grattan' is noted by Strickland. For his portraits and papers, see ODNB. SOURCE Allibone, i, p. 722; Allibone Suppl., i, pp 703–4; Brady, p. 92; Burke's, p. 489; Curran index, FQR 549; T.C. Grattan, *Beaten paths; and those who trod them* (London, 1862, 2 vols.); S.C. Hall, p. 235; Holmes cat. 59/163; Lohrli, p. 287; NCBEL 4, pp 922–3; ODNB; O'Donoghue, p. 168; RIA/DIB; Sutherland, pp 259–60; Personal communication, Steve Weissman, Dec. 2000; Strickland, i, p. 559; N.P. Willis, *Pencillings by the way* (New York, 1844), p. 191.

G60 *High-ways and by-ways; or tales of the roadside picked up in the French provinces* ([first series]; by 'A walking gentleman'; dedicated to Washington Irving).

+ London: G. & W.B. Whittaker, 1823. SOURCE Block, p. 90; British Fiction; Garside, 1823:39. LOCATION Corvey CME 3–628–51028–7, D (1824 edn), Dt, L, NUC, InND Loeber coll.

+ Paris: Haut-coeur & Gayet Jeune, 1825, 3 vols. (trans. by J.B. Defauconpret as *Contes sur les grandes et petites routes, par un voyageur a pied*). SOURCE NCBEL 3, p. 728. LOCATION L.

+ Paris: A-A. Renouard, 1825, 3 vols. (trans. by Mme Louise Belloc as *Contes recueillis dans les provinces françaises, par un irlandais voyageant a pied*). LOCATION InND Loeber coll.

Haarlem: de erven François Boon, 1827 (trans. into Dutch as *Groote wegen en binnen-wegen; of ontmoetingen van een voetreiziger in de Zuidelijke provincies van Frankrijk*). SOURCE Wintermans, 1823:39.

Boston: Wells & Lilly, 1824, 2 vols. LOCATION NUC.

COMMENTARY Contents: 'The father's curse', 'The exile of the Landes', 'The birth of Henry IV', 'La vilaine tête [*sic*]' [NUC].

G61 *High-ways and by-ways; or tales of the roadside picked up in the French provinces* (second series; by 'A walking gentleman'; dedicated to William Henry Coppinger, Esq., of the Inner Temple).

+ London: Henry Colburn, 1825, 3 vols. SOURCE Block, p. 90; British Fiction; Garside, 1825:35. LOCATION Corvey CME 3–628–51059–7, L, InND Loeber coll.

London, Belfast: Simms & M'Intyre, 1848 (Parlour Library, No. 17). SOURCE Sadleir, ii, p. 153.

Paris: A. & W. Galignani & Co., 1825, 3 vols. LOCATION NUC.

Paris: A-A. Renouard, [1825], 3 vols. (trans. by Mme Louise Belloc as *Grandes routes et chemins de traverse, ou contes recueillis dans les provinces françaises*). SOURCE Garside, 1825:35; Robertshaw cat. 78/145.

+ Philadelphia: H.C. Carey & I. Lea, 1825, 2 vols. SOURCE Kaser, 690. LOCATION DLC, NUC, InND Loeber coll.

COMMENTARY Contents: 'Caribert, the bear hunter', 'The priest, and the garde du-corps', 'The vouée au blanc' [ML].

G62 *High-ways and by-ways; or, tales of the roadside picked up in the French provinces* (third series; by 'A walking gentleman'; dedicated to Horace Smith).

+ London: Henry Colburn, 1827, 3 vols. SOURCE Block, p. 90; British Fiction; Garside, 1827:33. LOCATION Corvey CME 3–628–51042–2, Dt, L, NUC, InND Loeber coll.

+ London, Belfast: Simms & M'Intyre, 1847 (as *The Cagot's hut, and The conscript's bride*; Parlour Library, No. 82). SOURCE COPAC; Sadleir, 1059 (1852 edn). LOCATION L (not found). InND Loeber coll. (1852 edn).

COMMENTARY Contents: 'The Cagot's hut' (set in the Pyrenees around 1822 when Spain was in political upheaval), 'Seeing is not believing' (set in La Rochelle), 'The conscript's bride' (set in Picardy) [RL, ML].

G63 *Traits of travel; or, tales of men and cities* [anon.] (dedicated to Sir W.J. Hort)

+ London: Henry Colburn, 1829, 3 vols. SOURCE British Fiction; Garside, 1829:38; Wolff, 2721. LOCATION Corvey CME 3–628–51143–7, Dt, D, L, DCL, InND Loeber coll.

London: [publisher?], 1834 (new edn as *Tales of travel; or traits of men and cities*). SOURCE British Fiction (Update 3, section F).

Leeuwarden: Steenbergen van Goor, 1831 (trans. into Dutch as *Menschen en steden* by O. Grattan [*sic*]). SOURCE Alphabetische naamlijst 1790–1832 (Suppl.), p. 48.

Boston: Wells & Lilly, 1829, 2 vols. in 1. LOCATION NUC.

+ New York: J. & J. Harper, 1829, 2 vols. LOCATION NUC, InND Loeber coll.

COMMENTARY No copy of the London 1834 edn located. Includes some Irish content. 'A bone to pick: Tale of Irish revenge', 'The maison de santé', 'A soeur de charité', 'The one-handed flute player, of Arques, in Normandy', 'The nightmare', 'Laura Pemegia', 'The confessions of an English glutton', 'A Sabbath in London', 'A city feast', 'The pleasures of the table', 'The anathema', 'The tea-pot gentleman', 'The veteran', 'No fire! No fire!', 'Home service: Starving manufacturers and warlike weavers', 'Captain X—', 'The monks of Roncesvalles', 'An affair of outposts', 'Sharp fighting – spoiled feasting – blundering and burying – priests and pilgrims', 'Paris sights: The carnival, Longchamps, Horse race – fete of Rosiere – Saint Louis's day', 'The frontier', 'National traits', 'Towns and churches', 'The convent cell', 'The living alchymist', 'The Trappists of Catsberg', 'Story of the begging brother' [ML; RL].

G64   *The heiress of Bruges. A tale of the year sixteen hundred* (by Thomas Colley Grattan; dedicated to the Hon. Lady Bagot).

London: Henry Colburn & Richard Bentley, 1830, 4 vols. SOURCE Sadleir, 1062; Garside 2, 1830:57. LOCATION Corvey CME 3–628–47775–1, D (1831 edn), Dt (1831 edn), DLC.

Brussels: J. Gardiner, 1830, 3 vols. LOCATION O, NUC.

+ Paris: A. & W. Galignani; Brussels: J. Gardiner, 1830, 3 vols. LOCATION Dt, InND Loeber coll.

+ Paris: Charles Gosselin, 1831, 6 vols. (trans. by M. Delepierre as *L'Héritière de Bruges*). SOURCE Devonshire, p. 464. LOCATION L.

Deventer: A. ter Gunne, 1840, 3 vols. (trans. into Dutch as *De erfdochter van Brugge: Een vehaal uit de Nederlandsche geschiedenis*). SOURCE Adamnet. LOCATION UVA.

New York: J. & J. Harper, 1831, 2 vols. LOCATION NUC.

COMMENTARY Written when TGG was living in Brussels, this is an historical novel set in the Low Countries around 1600 when Spain occupied large parts of the country. A gold beater in Bruges finds a hoard of gold and precious stones in the grounds of a ruined house that becomes the basis of his fortune and political prominence. When his daughter returns from the convent where she has been educated, she has many suitors for her hand and fortune. These range from a lowly apprentice to the Spanish governor of Bruges to officers in the various warring parties. The ups and downs of the suitors coincide with a number of military events in which they take part [ML].

G65   *High-ways and by-ways* (by Thomas Colley Grattan).

London: H. Colburn & Richard Bentley, 1831, 6 vols (The Modern Novelists, Nos. 22–7. SOURCE OCLC. LOCATION ICU.

Berlin: Duncker & Humblot, 1828, 5 vols. (trans. as *Heer- und Querstrassen, oder, Erzählungen gesammelt auf einer Wanderung durch Frankreich, von einem fussreisenden Gentleman*). SOURCE OCLC. LOCATION Duke Univ.

COMMENTARY A reissue of the second, and third series, published in 1825, and 1827, respectively. However, it is not clear whether this also applies to the Berlin edn [RL; OCLC].

G66   *Jacqueline of Holland. A historical tale* (by Thomas College Grattan; dedicated to Sir Arthur Brooke Faulkner, Knt).

+ London: Henry Colburn & Richard Bentley, 1831, 3 vols. SOURCE Wolff, 2720; Garside 2, 1831:32. LOCATION Corvey CME 3–628–47776–X, D (1843 edn), L, MH, InND Loeber coll.

+ London: Richard Bentley; Edinburgh: Bell & Bradfute; Dublin: J. Cumming, 1843 (revsd and corrected edn; ill. J. Cawse, S. Bull; Standard Novels, No. 92). SOURCE NCBEL 3, p. 728. LOCATION D, Dt, NUC, InND Loeber coll.

New York: Harper, 1831, 2 vols. LOCATION NUC.

COMMENTARY Historical fiction set in fifteenth-century Holland dealing with the war and political intrigue between the Hoeken and the Kabbeljauwen and their relationship to the struggle between Jacqueline of Holland and Philip the Good of Burgundy. The main character is Jacqueline of Holland, who married four times. For a while, the earl of Gloucester, regent of England, supports Jacqueline but she loses her battle and is imprisoned for some time. She is released only by giving up her rights [ML; Hartman, 533].

G67   *Legends of the Rhine and of the Low Countries* [anon.].

+ London: Henry Colburn & Richard Bentley, 1832, 3 vols. SOURCE Block, p. 90;

Topp 6, 190; Garside 2, 1832:36. LOCATION Corvey CME 3–628–51087–2, D, L, NUC, InND Loeber coll.

+ London: Thomas Hodgson, 1847 (as *The curse of the black lady, and other tales. Legends of the Rhine*; Parlour Library, No. 165). SOURCE Sadleir, 1060; Jarndyce cat. 141/218. LOCATION L.

+ London: Thomas Hodgson, [1857] (as *The forfeit hand, and other tales. Legends of the Rhine*; Parlour Library, No.163). SOURCE Sadleir, 1061, 3755a. LOCATION L.

Frankfurt o.M.: C. Jugel, 1836. SOURCE NCBEL 3, p. 728. LOCATION NUC.

+ Philadelphia: E.L. Carey & A. Hart; Boston: Allen & Ticknor, 1833, 2 vols. LOCATION NUC, InND Loeber coll.

COMMENTARY Contents: 'The forfeit hand. A legend of the fifteenth century', 'The orphan of Cambray. A legend of the fourteenth century', 'The curse of the black lady. A legend of the twelfth century', 'The three foretellings. A legend of the fourteenth century', 'A year of joy. A legend of the twelfth century', 'The lady of the cold kisses. A legend of the year 1200', 'The double doubt', 'The tragedy of the Truenfels. A legend without a date', 'The prisoner of the Pfalz', 'Countess Kunigund', 'Heidelberg Castle, and its legends', 'The legend of the Wolf's Brun', 'The legend of Ruprecht's building'. The contents of the [1857] edn varies in terms of stories listed [RL].

G68   *Agnes de Mansfeldt. A historical tale* (by Thomas Colley Grattan).
London: Saunders & Otley, 1836, 3 vols. SOURCE Block, p. 90; Garside 2, 1835:50; COPAC. LOCATION D (1847 edn), L, NUC.

+ London: Richard Bentley; Edinburgh: Bell & Bratfute, 1847 (with new introd.; ill. Clara Cawse, G. Cooke; Standard Novels, No. 109). LOCATION D, InND Loeber coll. (London, Simms & M'Intyre, 1851 edn).

+ Paris: A. & W. Galignani & Co., 1836. LOCATION D, Dt, NUC.

Brussels: Wahlen, 1836 (Whalen's Modern British Authors). SOURCE NCBEL 3, p. 728. LOCATION L.

Stuttgart: Imle & Krauss, [1836] (trans. as *Agnes von Mansfeld: Ein geschichtlicher Roman*). SOURCE Garside 2, 1835:50; GLOL. LOCATION Württembergische Landesbibliothek.

+ Deventer: A. ter Gunne, 1842, 2 vols. (trans. into Dutch as *Agnes van Mansfeldt: Historisch verhaal*; ill). SOURCE Adamnet. LOCATION UVA.

+ Philadelphia: Carey, Lea & Blanchard, 1836, 2 vols. SOURCE Kaser, 558. LOCATION D (vol. 1 only), NN.

COMMENTARY Historical fiction. Introductory note locates the narrative when 'All Europe was harassed and convulsed by the "Dutch and Belgic question" of the sixteenth century' and points to the possible parallels with present events. The last volume contains notes [Garside].

G69   *Julie Corryeur, a romance of the Alps* (by Thomas Colley Grattan).
Philadelphia: A.J. Rockafellar, 1843. SOURCE OCLC. LOCATION NUC.

COMMENTARY Not known from an English edn. Possibly written when TCG was in the US. However, it may be a spurious attribution [RL].

G70   *The master passion; and other tales & sketches* (by Thomas Colley Grattan).
London: H. Colburn, 1845, 2 vols. SOURCE Block, p. 90; COPAC. LOCATION NUC.

G71   *A chance medley of light matter* (by Thomas Colley Grattan).
+ New York: Harper & Bros, 1845 (Library of Select Novels, No. 59). SOURCE OCLC. LOCATION NUC, InND Loeber coll.

COMMENTARY Contains some Irish stories. Contents: 'Mountain musings', 'Julie Corryeur; or, the master passion; a tale of Chamouny' (appeared as a volume in 1843), 'My first visit to Brussels', 'Teresa; a tale of revolutionized Rome', 'The mother's revenge', 'My travelling acquaintance', 'Sketches of Irish fools', 'The love draught; a tale of the Barrow side', 'Fragments of a diary; a memorial of the wet summer', 'The caves of Groenendael; an episode of Waterloo', 'The curate-confessor of Viroflay; a real ghost story' [RL].

G72   *High-ways and by-ways: or, tales of the roadside; picked up in the French provinces* ('by a walking gentleman'; dedicated to Washington Irving).
  + London, Belfast: Simms & M'Intyre, 1847 (Parlour Library, No. 7). SOURCE Sadleir, ii, p. 153. LOCATION InND Loeber coll.
  COMMENTARY A reissue of the first and second series, published in 1823 and 1825, respectively [RL].

G73   *Beaten paths and those who trod them* (by Thomas Colley Grattan).
  London: Chapman & Hall, 1862, 2 vols. SOURCE OCLC. LOCATION D, L.
  COMMENTARY Autobiography told in the form of stories. The first six chapters deal with life in Ireland [ML].

GRAVES, A.F. See **GRAVES, Arnold**.

GRAVES, Arnold (also known as **A.F. Graves**), fl. 1898. This writer may be identified with the AG who wrote *The complete signaller* (London, 1914). However, the NUC and RIA/DIB identify him as Arnold Felix Graves (b. Dublin 1847, d. 1930) the third son of Charles Graves, who was descended from a line of Church of Ireland ministers and was later Bishop of Limerick, and Selina Cheyne. AG graduated BA at TCD in 1868, obtained an MA, and became a barrister in 1872. He was secretary to the commissioners for endowed schools in 1879 and in 1886 was appointed secretary to the commissioners of charitable endowments and bequests in Ireland. He worked to introduce technical education into Ireland and helped found the Royal Society for the Training and Employment of Women. He married Constance Weatherley. AG wrote some poetry, and co-authored with his brothers Charles and Alfred Perceval Graves (father of poet and translator Robert Graves) two satirical verse books about politics: *The Blarney ballads* (London, 1888) and *The green above the red* (London, 1889). SOURCE BLC; Landed gentry, 1904, p. 230; Leslie, *Connor*, p. 355; NUC; O'Donoghue, p. 169; RIA/DIB.

G74   *Prince Patrick: A fairy tale* (by Arnold Graves).
  London: Downey & Co., 1898 (ill. A.D. McCormick). SOURCE Brown, 646; Hodges Figgis cat. 10 n.s./1204; OCLC. LOCATION L, NUC.
COMMENTARY A fairy tale set in old Gaelic times in Co. Kerry, around Cahirciveen and Staigue Fort. A witch substitutes a changeling for Prince Patrick. When Prince Patrick grows up he succeeds in finding a linen garment that proves his identity. He saves the Princess Nora and is acknowledged as tanist, or successor apparent to the Celtic chief [Brown].

G75   *Healthy, wealthy, and wise* (by A.F. Graves).
  London: Methuen & Co., 1925. LOCATION L.

GRAVES, Clotilde (Clotilda) Inez Mary (also known as **Clotilde Graves** and **Clo Graves**), pseud. '**Richard Dehan**' (not 'Dahen' as in OCIL), b. Buttevant Barracks (Co. Cork) 1863 (1864 according to OCIL and O'Donoghue), d. 1932. Novelist, playwright and journalist, CG was the daughter of Maj. W.H. Graves (and not of an Irish clergyman as mentioned by O'Toole) and Antoinette Deane. She studied at the Royal Female School of Art in Bloomsbury. Determined to become a playwright, she spent some time acting in travelling companies to gain experience of the stage. Sixteen of her plays were produced in London and New York between 1887 and 1913. She also wrote *The lover's battle: a heroical comedy in rhyme* (London, 1902) based on Alexander Pope's *The rape of the lock*. She supported herself by journalism and writing stories for periodicals such as the *Gentlewoman*, the *Sporting Times* (both London), and the *World* (London?). She was a regular contributor to *Judy* (London, 1889), a comic periodical. She published 27 works of fiction, including novels (some about war) and short stories. CG became a Catholic in 1896 and after her health failed retired to a convent in 1928. SOURCE Allibone Suppl., i, p. 704; Blain, p. 453; Colman, pp 102–3; NCBEL 4, p. 2045; OCIL, p. 224; O'Donoghue, p. 170; O'Toole, pp 85–6; RIA/DIB.

G76   *The belle of Rock Harbour* (by Clotilda Inez Mary Graves).
       London: 'Judy' Office, [1887] (ill. L. Willson). SOURCE Alston, p. 169; COPAC.
       LOCATION L.
       COMMENTARY 79pp [COPAC].

G77   *The pirate's hand. A romance of heredity* (ed. by Clotilde Graves).
       London: 'Judy' Office, [1889.]. LOCATION L.
       COMMENTARY Parody of the style of R.L. Stevenson [NCBEL].

G78   *A field of tares; a novel* (by 'Richard Dehan').
       New York: Harper & Bros, 1891. LOCATION NUC.

G79   *Dragon's teeth. A novel* (by 'Richard Dehan').
       London: Dalziel Bros, 1891. SOURCE Alston, p. 169; COPAC. LOCATION L.

G80   *Maids in a market garden* (by Clo Graves).
       London: W.H. Allen & Co., 1894 (ill. Maurice Greiffenhagen). SOURCE Alston, p. 169;
       COPAC. LOCATION L, Dt, NUC.
       New York: Wycil & Co., 1912. LOCATION NUC.

G81   *A well-meaning woman* (by Clo Graves).
       London: Hutchinson & Co., 1896. SOURCE Alston, p. 169; COPAC. LOCATION L.
       London: William Hutchinson, 1916 (by 'Richard Dehan'; as *The gilded vanity*). SOURCE
       Blain, p. 453. LOCATION L.

G82   *The dop doctor* (by 'Richard Dehan').
       London: W. Heinemann, 1910. SOURCE COPAC. LOCATION L (1911 edn), E, NUC.
       New York: George H. Doran, [1910]. LOCATION NUC.
       New York: Duffield & Co., 1910 (as *One braver thing*). LOCATION NUC.
       COMMENTARY Of all her novels, this was the most successful, and went through 30
       edns [RL].

G83   *Between two thieves* (by 'Richard Dehan').
       London: William Heinemann, 1912. SOURCE Blain, p. 454. LOCATION L, NUC.
       New York: Frederick A. Stokes, [1912]. LOCATION NUC.
       COMMENTARY Set in the Crimean War [Blain].

G84   *The headquarter recruit, and other stories* (by 'Richard Dehan').
       London: William Heinemann, 1913. LOCATION NUC, L.
       New York: Frederick A. Stokes, [1913]. LOCATION NUC.
COMMENTARY Contents: 'The headquarter recruit', 'Gougou', 'The man in the woods and forests', 'How Farlingby flew', 'The quality of mercy', 'A chintz-covered chair', '"Rouge gagne [*sic*]!"', 'The fourth volume', 'A stuffed lion', 'The resurrection of Freddy', 'Liege lady mine', 'Toto the tempter', 'Clairvoyance', 'In the lagoon', 'Mrs. Crichton's convert', 'Transference', 'A subaltern's healing', 'Todminster's thirst', 'White fox', 'Realization', 'Fool-sized James', 'A new leaf', 'The tribute of Offa' [NUC].

G85   *The cost of wings, and other stories* (by 'Richard Dehan').
       London: William Heinemann, 1914. LOCATION L, NUC.
       New York: Frederick A. Stokes, [1914]. LOCATION NUC.
COMMENTARY Contents: 'The cost of wings', 'A faded romance', 'An Indian baby', 'Yvonne', 'The delusion of Mrs. Donohoe', 'Ponsonby and the pantheress', 'A fat girl's love story', 'In

the fourth dimension', 'The gewgaw', 'The knight of power', 'The man who could not manage women', 'Obsessed', 'A vanished hand', 'An ordeal by fire', 'How the mistress came home', 'A motor-burglar', 'The lost room', 'Father to the man', 'The fly and the spider', 'For valor!', 'Mellicent', 'The collapse of the ideal', 'The hand that failed', 'His silhouette', 'A nocturne', 'The last expedition' [NUC].

G86   *The man of iron* (by 'Richard Dehan').
      London: William Heinemann, 1915. LOCATION NUC, L.
      New York: Frederick A. Stokes, [1915]. LOCATION NUC.
      Toronto: S.B. Gundy, 1915. LOCATION NUC.
      Paris: Thomas Nelson & Sons, 1916 (Nelson's Continental Library, vol. 15). LOCATION L.
      COMMENTARY Concerns the Franco-Prussian war [NUC].

G87   *Off Sandy Hook. Short stories* (by 'Richard Dehan').
      London: William Heinemann, 1915. LOCATION L, NUC.
      New York: Frederick A. Stokes, [1915] (as *Off Sandy Hook, and other stories*). LOCATION NUC.

COMMENTARY Contents: 'Off Sandy Hook', 'Gemini', 'A dish of macaroni', '"Freddy & C."', 'Under the electrics', '"Valcourt's grin"', 'The evolution of the fairest', 'The revolt of Rustleton', 'A dispeptic's tragedy', 'Renovation', 'The breaking place', 'Lancashire daisy', 'A pitched battle', 'The tug of war', 'Gas!', 'Air', 'Side!', 'A spirit elopement', 'The widow's might', 'Susanna and her elders', 'Lady Clanbevan's baby', 'The duchess' dilemma', 'The child', 'A hindered honeymoon', '"Clothes – and the man!"', 'The devil and the deep sea' [NUC].

G88   *Earth to earth* (by 'Richard Dehan').
      London: William Heinemann, 1916. LOCATION L.
      New York: Frederick A. Stokes, [1916]. LOCATION NUC.

COMMENTARY Contents: 'Earth to earth', 'Life and the MacWauch', 'Society and the MacWauch', 'A nursery tea', 'The self-denial of the MacWauch', 'The rising generation', 'The young man from "the shop"', 'The rout of the Royal MacTurks', 'Taken in war', 'The sin of the intention', '"Lilium peccatorum"', 'The Menards' dance', 'The infamy of the MacWaugh', 'Thinner than water', 'The half loaf', 'A royal betrothal', 'The curse of the MacWaugh', 'On the honeymoon', 'The idiocy of the MacWaugh', 'The crucial test', 'The power and glory', 'The mission Selina', 'The MacWaugh and fame', 'The hair' [NUC].

G89   *Gilded vanity* (by 'Richard Dehan').
      London: William Heinemann, 1916. LOCATION L.
      New York: George H. Doran, [1916] (as *A gilded vanity*). LOCATION NUC.

G90   *Under the Hermés, and other stories* (by 'Richard Dehan').
      London: William Heinemann, 1917. LOCATION L.
      New York: Dodd, Mead & Co., 1917. LOCATION NUC.

COMMENTARY Contents: 'Under the Hermés', 'Brother Nightingdale', 'Peter', 'The compleat housewife', 'The queen of Ruatava', 'The mortality of the divine Emilie', 'The jest', 'A speaking likeness', 'A game of faro', 'The vengeance of the cherry-stone', '"Apamé', 'White man's magic', 'Utukuluk', 'How Yamko married fourteen wives', 'The tooth of Tuloo', 'The great beast of Kafue', 'The judgement of Big man', 'The vengeance of Ounaka' [NUC].

G91   *"That which hath wings". A novel of the day* (by 'Richard Dehan').
      London: William Heinemann, 1918. LOCATION L, NUC.
      New York, London: G. P. Putnam's Sons, 1918. LOCATION NUC.
      COMMENTARY Concerns World War I [NUC].

G92   *A sailor's home, and other stories* (by 'Richard Dehan').
      London: William Heinemann, 1919. LOCATION L, NUC.

New York: George H. Doran, [1919]. LOCATION NUC.

G93 *The eve of Pascua, and other stories* (by 'Richard Dehan').
London: William Heinemann, 1920. LOCATION L.
New York: George H. Doran, [1920]. LOCATION NUC.
COMMENTARY Contents: 'The eve of Pascua', 'The mother of turquoise', 'The tribute of the kiss', 'A sight cure', 'Wanted – a king', 'How Carey came back to the mines', 'The pretender', 'The king's catharrh', 'A game of écarte', 'Johnny's case', 'An impression', 'The end of the Cotillion', 'His deceased wife's sister', 'A perfect cure', 'An Ascot hat', 'A maker of comedies' [NUC].

G94 *The villa of the peacock, and other stories* (by 'Richard Dehan').
London: William Heinemann, 1921. LOCATION L, NUC.
New York: George H. Doran, [1921]. LOCATION NUC.
COMMENTARY Contents: 'Villa of the peacock', 'The formula of Brantin', 'Dorotéa', 'At sea', 'The slug's courtship', 'The extraordinary adventures of an automobile', 'The silver birch', 'Countess and couturière' [NUC].

G95 *The just steward* (by 'Richard Dehan').
London: William Heinemann, 1922. LOCATION L.
New York: George H. Doran, [1922]. LOCATION NUC.

G96 *The pipers of the market place* (by 'Richard Dehan').
London: Thornton Butterworth, 1924. SOURCE COPAC. LOCATION L, NUC.
New York: H. Doran, [1924]. LOCATION NUC.
Toronto: McClelland & Stewart, [1924]. LOCATION NUC.

G97 *The sower of the wind* (by 'Richard Dehan').
London: Thornton Butterworth, 1927. LOCATION L, NUC.
Boston: Little, Brown & Co., 1927. LOCATION NUC.

G98 *The lovers of the market-place* (by 'Richard Dehan').
London: Thornton Butterworth, 1928. LOCATION L, NUC.
Boston: Little, Brown & Co., 1928. LOCATION NUC.

G99 *Shallow seas* (by 'Richard Dehan').
London: Thornton Butterworth, 1930. LOCATION L.

G100 *The man with the mask, and other stories* (by 'Richard Dehan').
London: Thornton Butterworth, 1931. LOCATION L.

G101 *Dead pearls. A novel of the great wide West* (by 'Richard Dehan').
London: J. Long, [1932]. SOURCE COPAC. LOCATION L, Dt, NUC.

G102 *The third graft, and other stories* (by 'Richard Dehan').
London: John Long, [1933]. SOURCE COPAC. LOCATION L, E.

GRAVES, Margaret. See **DERENZY, Mrs Margaret Graves.**

'GRAY, Russell', pseud. See **LE FANU, Eleanor Frances.**

GREELEY, Robert F., fl. 1854. American fiction writer, RFG was the author also of *The partisan's oath; or, the trooper's revenge. A tale of the revolution* (New York, [185?]. SOURCE NUC; Wright, ii, pp 136–7.

G103 *Violet, the child of the city. A story of New York life* (by Robert F. Greeley).
New York: Bunce & Brother, 1854. SOURCE Allibone Suppl., i, p. 707; Fanning, p. 381; Wright, ii, 1020. LOCATION NUC, Wright web.
COMMENTARY Concerns the Irish in New York [Fanning, p. 78].

GREEN, Mrs —. See GREEN, Sarah.

'GREEN, Ananias', fl. 1895. Pseudonym of a writer on contemporary affairs.
G104   *Interviews with the immortals or Dickens up to date* (by 'Ananias Green').
+ Salisbury: Brown & Co.; London: Simpkin, Marshall, Hamilton, Kent & Co., 1895.
LOCATION L.
COMMENTARY 112 pp. Concerns William Gladstone and Home Rule. Contents: 'The inter-
viewer's credentials', 'The real and true: A discourse by A.G.', 'Mr. Micawber on the grand
old man', 'Mrs. Micawber on Plantagenet', 'Sam Weller's valentine on Erin', 'Mark Tapley
on Jolly John', 'The Micawber congress' [RL].

GREEN, S. See GREEN, Mrs Sarah.

GREEN, Mrs Sarah, pseuds 'A cockney', 'S.G.**', and 'A Lady' (also known as **Mrs Green**
and **S. Green**), fl. 1790. Novelist and translator, SG was a native of Ireland and wrote mostly
anonymously. She translated from German and was the author of a courtesy book, *Mental
improvements for a young lady* (London, 1793). She edited and enlarged *Fatherless Fanny*
(London, 1822), a publication that has been ascribed to Mrs Edgeworth§. She wrote at least
17 mostly-Gothic novels, many with historical backgrounds, that mixed satire and humour.
In London, she lived at Dartmouth Street, Westminster. SOURCE Allibone, i, p. 732; BD, p.
136; Blain, p. 457; NCBEL 4, p. 924; NSTC, ser. 1, ii, p. 308; OCIL, pp 223–4; ODNB; RL.
G105   *Charles Henley; or, the fugitive restored* [anon.].
London: William Lane, 1790, 2 vols. SOURCE Blakey, p. 149; Raven 2, 1790:47; Forster
2, 1712.
COMMENTARY No copy located. The *Monthly Review* (London) mentions its 'jumble
of improbabilities'. Attributed to Mary O'Brien§ by Blain [Raven 2; Blain, p. 807].
G106   *Court intrigue, or the victim of constancy. An historical romance* [anon.].
London: William Lane, 1799, 2 vols. SOURCE Blakey, p. 188; Raven 2, 1799:44; ESTC
n068073. LOCATION CaACU.
G107   *Tankerville family* (by a 'Lady').
London: R. Dutton, 1808, 3 vols. SOURCE British Fiction; Garside, 1808:50. LOCATION
Corvey CME 3–628–48491–5.
G108   *The private history of the court of England* [anon.].
+ London: Printed for the author by B. Crosby, 1808, 2 vols. SOURCE British Fiction;
Garside, 1808:49. LOCATION L.
G109   *Tales of the manor* [anon.].
London: B. Crosby & Co., 1809, 2 vols. SOURCE British Fiction; Garside 1809:28.
LOCATION Corvey CME 3–628–48873–7, O, NUC.
G110   *Romance readers and romance writers. A satirical novel* (by 'S.G**')
London: T. Hookam Jnr & E.T. Hookam, 1810, 3 vols. SOURCE British Fiction;
Garside, 1810:46. LOCATION L, NUC.
G111   *The festival of St. Jago. A Spanish romance* [anon.].
London: A.K. Newman & Co., 1810, 2 vols. SOURCE Blakey, p. 232; NCBEL 4, p.
924; British Fiction; Garside, 1810:44. LOCATION Corvey CME–3–628–47497–3, L,
NUC.
COMMENTARY Gothic fiction set in Spain. In the opening scene a lecherous cavalier, Don Lopez,
attends mass in order to flirt with the women of the congregation. He is attracted by a mysteri-
ous veiled lady, attended by two Moorish guards bearing staves with thumbscrews and racks, the
emblems of the Inquisition. Lopez pursues her, and in the process kills his brother merely because

his good character annoys him. Don Lopez enlists the aid of the devil-lady, Donna Lauretta, who pursues the heroine through the catacombs and graveyards of Valladolid. In the end, the Inquisition seizes Don Lopez, but he is allowed to repent and to marry the pure Aurora [Frank, 142].

GI12   *The reformist!!! A serio-comic-political novel* [anon.] (preface signed 'S.G.**').
London: A.K. Newman & Co., 1810, 2 vols. SOURCE Blakey, p. 233; British Fiction; Garside, 1810:45. LOCATION L.
+ London: A.K. Newman & Co., 1816, 2 vols. (as *Percival Ellingford: or the reformist*). SOURCE British Fiction; Garside, 1810:45. LOCATION Corvey CME 3–628–47854–5.

GI13   *The royal exile; or, victims of human passions. An historical romance of the sixteenth century* (by Mrs Green).
London: John Joseph Stockdale, 1810, 4 vols. SOURCE British Fiction; Garside, 1810:47. LOCATION L (1811 edn), NUC (1811 edn).

COMMENTARY Gothic fiction set in the sixteenth-century. A muffled stranger assails the Count D'Amaile with the injunction to follow him to the Convent of Hilaire, a resting place for royal fugitives and regal illegitimates. Inside the convent, the count picks up the trail of Elwina, a secret daughter of Henry VIII and Anne Boleyn (executed in 1536). Volume 3 consists of an almost separate tale of Elwina's imprisonment in Castle Villebois. The novel ends with an historical verdict on Henry VIII's character [Frank, 143].

GI14   *Good men of modern date. A satirical tale* [anon.] (dedicated to 'To the Reviewers, in particular to the British and Critical Reviewers'; preface signed S. Green).
London: Thomas Tegg, 1811, 3 vols. SOURCE British Fiction; Garside, 1811:35. LOCATION George Washington Univ. (vol. 2 missing).
+ Philadelphia: Moses Thomas, 1813, 2 vols. in 1. LOCATION NUC, InND Loeber coll.

COMMENTARY A tale of family fortunes set in London. However Eliza Fitzwarren, the principal character, her uncle, and his servant Paddy, are Irish. Eliza, after the death of her father, is left with very little money and has to find employment. Her experiences teach her that many 'good' men are in fact egocentric and not helpful. Several rich relatives do want to give her a recommendation when she tries to find a position as a governess. Eventually she obtains a post in the household of a Mrs Jeffery, whose mode of bringing up her children is based on Jean-Jacques Rousseau's model, and the children are allowed to grow up like little savages. Eliza leaves because two men in the household make improper advances. Her next job is as secretary to a woman author who has no talent but is flattered by several men into thinking that she is a celebrated writer. In the end Eliza, finds out that she is actually very rich but that her relatives had hidden this fact from her. She marries the man who helped her uncover her true state in life [ML].

GI15   *Deception. A fashionable novel ... founded on facts* (by Mrs Green).
London: Sheerwood [*sic*], Neely & Jones, 1813, 3 vols. SOURCE British Fiction; Garside, 1813:20. LOCATION NUC.

COMMENTARY A story of domestic intrigue using several Gothic episodes and perilous situations encountered by the East Indian heroine, Maisuna Cleveland, who travels in England. She is both object and perpetrator of various deceptions, which bring excitement to her otherwise ordinary life through her contacts with an impoverished gambler, Mr Jefferson, and a dissipated female gamester. She rejects the wealthy Mr Berresford's proposal of marriage, whereupon he seizes her and prepares to violate her, with the encouragement of the villainous priest, Fr Jocelyn. She frightens them off by appearing as a sheeted phantom brandishing a dagger and crying for death. She then declares herself to be Mr Jefferson's benefactress, which leads him to abjure gaming and request her hand [Frank, 144].

GI16   *The fugitive; or, family incidents* [anon.].
+ London: Black, Parry & Co., 1814, 3 vols. SOURCE British Fiction; Garside, 1814:25. LOCATION Corvey (1815 edn), CME 3–628–7843–X, L.

G117 *The Carthusian friar; or, the mysteries of Montanville; a posthumous romance …
corrected and revised by an author of celebrity* [anon.].
London: Sherwood, Neely & Jones; C. Chapple, 1814, 4 vols. SOURCE British Fiction;
Garside, 1814:24. LOCATION Corvey CME 3–628–47217–2, NUC.
COMMENTARY Gothic fiction inspired by Ann Radcliffe's *The Italian* (London, 1797), and
William Henry Ireland's§ *The abbess* (London, 1799), the story features Fr Scorani, a Carthusian
friar. He conspires against the innocent Mathilda, with his partner in evil, a despicable abbess
who becomes Mathilda's keeper and tormentor at Montanville Priory. Mathilda narrowly averts
the rape attempts of both the friar and the abbess [Frank, 145].

G118 *Who is the bridegroom? or, nuptial discoveries. A novel* (by Mrs Sarah Green).
London: A.K. Newman & Co., 1822, 3 vols. SOURCE British Fiction; Garside, 1822:36;
COPAC. LOCATION Corvey CME 3–628–47852–9, L, NUC.

G119 *Gretna Green marriages; or, the nieces. A novel* (by Mrs Green).
London: A.K. Newman & Co., 1823, 3 vols. SOURCE British Fiction; Garside, 1823:40.
LOCATION Corvey CME 3–628–47907–X, L.

G120 *Scotch novel reading; or, modern quackery. A novel really founded on facts* (by 'A
cockney').
London: A.K. Newman & Co., 1824, 3 vols. SOURCE British Fiction; Garside, 1824:42.
LOCATION Corvey CME 3–628–47300–4, L.

G121 *Parents and wives; or, inconsistency and mistakes. A novel* (by Mrs Green).
London: A.K. Newman & Co., 1825, 3 vols. SOURCE British Fiction; Garside, 1825:36.
LOCATION Corvey CME 3–628–47927–4, L.

G122 *Fatherless Fanny; or, a lady's first entrance into life* (by the late Miss Taylor, ed.
and enlarged by Mrs Sarah Green).
Liverpool: H. Fisher & Caxton, 1821. SOURCE OCLC. LOCATION CtY.
London: Fisher, Son & Co., 1833. SOURCE British Fiction; Garside, 1811:31.
COMMENTARY No copy of the London, 1833 edn located. See under Mrs Edgeworth§
for more on this novel. The ending differs from earlier versions [RL; Garside].

GREENE, Mrs —. See **GREENE, the Hon. Louisa Lelias.**

GREENE, the Hon. Louisa Lelias (née Plunket, also Plunkett; also known as (**the Hon.**) **Mrs
Greene** and **Mrs R.J. Greene**), b. 1833, d. 1891. Children's writer and translator, LLG was
the daughter of the 3rd Baron Plunket of Newtown (1793–1871), crown prosecutor on the
Munster circuit, and Charlotte, daughter of Charles Kendal Bushe, chief justice of the queen's
bench. Her father lived at Old Connaught House (later called Old Conna), Bray (Co. Dublin),
and had a town residence at St Stephen's Green, Dublin. Her sister was the author the Hon.
Isabella-Catharine Plunket§. In 1852 in Dublin LLG married Richard Thomas Greene (Richard
J. according to Allibone), an Irish barrister and son of Richard Wilson Greene, a baron of the
court of exchequer in Ireland. She published mostly children's stories, and one novel. NCBEL
mentions *Harry Galbraith: or the pierced eggs*, but this has not been located. SOURCE Allibone
Suppl., i, p. 712; Burke's, p. 497; CP, x, p. 557; NCBEL 4, p. 1800; RIA/DIB.

G123 *A winter and summer at Burton Hall: A children's tale* (by Mrs R.J. Greene).
+ London: James Hogg & Sons, [1861] (ill. Kenny Meadows). SOURCE OCLC.
LOCATION L.
New York: E.P. Dutton, 1875 (ill.). SOURCE OCLC. LOCATION Boston Public Library.
COMMENTARY Fiction for juveniles [RL].

G124 *Cushions and corners or holidays at old orchard* (by Mrs Greene).
London: Smith, Elder & Co., 1864. SOURCE OCLC. LOCATION D, L (destroyed).

+ London: Frederick Warne & Co.; New York: Scribner, Welford & Co., n.d. (as *Cushions and corners: or, pleasant and awkward ways*; ill.). LOCATION InND Loeber coll. New York: E.P. Dutton, 1886. SOURCE OCLC. LOCATION Univ. of Virginia. Boston: E.P. Dutton & Co., 1867 (ill.). LOCATION L.

G125 *Filling up the chinks* (by the Hon. Mrs R. Greene).
London: Frederick Warne & Co.; New York: Scribner, Welford & Co., 1869. LOCATION L.

G126 *The little castle maiden: simple stories for young children* (by the Hon. Mrs Greene).
London: Frederick Warne & Co.; New York: Scribner, Welford & Co., 1870. LOCATION L.
+ London, Edinburgh: Frederick Warne, 1871 (ill.). SOURCE NCBEL 4, p. 1800. LOCATION L.
COMMENTARY Contents: 'The little castle maiden and the thorny zukum', 'The jewelled bridge', 'The oyster realm', 'The lost sunbeam' [RL].

G127 *The broken promise and other tales* (by the Hon. Mrs Greene).
+ London, New York: Cassell, Petter & Galpin, 1870 (ill.). LOCATION L.
COMMENTARY Contents: 'The broken promise', 'The useful holiday', 'The best joke of the season', 'The doctor's apple', 'Tom Chator's advice', 'Monday come never', 'Joseph's pit', 'The fairy's gap' [ML].

G128 *The schoolboy baronet* (by the Hon. Mrs Greene).
London: Frederick Warne & Co.; New York: Scribner, Welford & Co., 1870. LOCATION L.

G129 *The grey house on the hill or Trust in God* (by the Hon. Mrs Greene).
New York: Dutton, 1871 (ill.). SOURCE OCLC. LOCATION ICU.
London, New York, Edinburgh, T. Nelson and Sons, 1872. SOURCE OCLC. LOCATION D, Dt (1874 edn).

G130 *Gilbert's shadow or the magic beads* (by the Hon. Mrs Greene).
+ London: Frederick Warne & Co.; New York: Scribner, Welford & Armstrong, 1875 (ill.). LOCATION L.

G131 *The star in the dust-heap* (by the Hon. Mrs Greene).
London: Warne, 1876. SOURCE OCLC. LOCATION D, L (destroyed).

G132 *God's silver or youthful days* (by the Hon. Mrs Greene).
London: Warne, 1877 (ill.). SOURCE OCLC. LOCATION D, L (n.d. edn).
[London]: Warne, [1877 or later] (as *The haunted sacks*). SOURCE OCLC. LOCATION D.
COMMENTARY Contents: (n.d. edn): 'God's silver', 'The pierced eggs, and what came of them', '"What can it matter?"', 'The haunted sacks', 'Heinrich's white castles', 'The new mistletoe bough', 'Katie's jacket', 'The cherry tent', 'Harry's rash wish, and how the fairies granted it', 'Willy's trunk; or, Mrs. Lambton's legacy' [ML].

G133 *Dora's dolls' house. A story for the young* (by the Hon. Mrs Greene).
London: Nelson & Sons, [1880]. LOCATION L.

G134 *Jubilee Hall; or, "there is no place like home". A story* (by the Hon. Mrs Greene).
London: Nelson & Sons, 1881. SOURCE NCBEL 4, p. 1800. LOCATION L.

G135 *Alda's leap and other stories* (by the Hon. Mrs Lelias Greene).
London: Nelson & Sons, 1883. LOCATION L.

G136 *The babe i' the mill and Zanina, the flower girl of Florence* (by the Hon. Mrs Greene).
London: Nelson & Sons, 1883. LOCATION L.

G137 *On angel's wings; or the story of the little Violet of Edelsheim* (by the Hon. Mrs Greene).

London: Nelson & Sons, 1884. LOCATION L.

G138   *Bound by a spell; or, the haunted witch of the forest* (by the Hon. Mrs Greene).
London, Paris, New York, Melbourne: Cassell & Co., 1885. LOCATION L.

G139   *Across the garden wall, a novel* (by the Hon. Mrs Greene).
London: F.V. White & Co., 1886, 2 vols. LOCATION L.

G140   *The phantom picture, a tale* (by the Hon. Mrs Greene).
London: T. Nelson, 1896. SOURCE RLIN. LOCATION NIC.
COMMENTARY Published posthumously [RL].

G141   *The golden wrens* (by the Hon. Mrs Greene).
London: T. Nelson & Sons, 1898. LOCATION L.

G142   *The lost opal ring; or, the end crowns all* (by the Hon. Mrs Greene).
London: T. Nelson & Sons, 1898. LOCATION L.

G143   *The lost telegram: or, trust betrayed* (by the Hon. Mrs Greene).
London: T. Nelson & Sons, 1898. LOCATION L.

GREENE, Mrs R.J. See **GREENE, the Hon. Louisa Lelias**.

'GREENWOOD, Grace', pseud. See **LIPPINCOTT, Sara Jane**.

GREER, Mrs J.R. (née Sarah D. Strangman; also known as Mrs S.D. Greer), b. Waterford 1806, d. 1891. Fiction writer and poet, Mrs JRG was the daughter of John Hancock Strangman, a wealthy merchant and Quaker with commercial connections in Russia. She attended the Suir Island Quaker school. In 1829 she married John R. Greer of the Ulster Greer family and lived for some time in Bristol (Avon) and later in Devon. Around 1836 she and her husband returned to Ireland, settling at Monkstown (Co. Dublin). Eventually, she was expelled from the Quaker community and joined the Episcopal (Anglican?) church. She wrote an anonymous autobiography, *Quakerism; or, the story of my life* (Dublin, 1851), which chronicles her long struggle with her Quaker faith, different communities of Quakers, and particularly women preachers. She subsequently published a purported 'exposure' of Quakerism in a thinly disguised fiction (see below), which included unkind personal accusations and insinuations. She is the author of a volume of poetry, *The chained Bible, and other poems* (Dublin, 1857). SOURCE Allibone, i, p. 736; Colman, p. 104; ER; Harrison, pp 53, 95–6; O'Donoghue, p. 171; O'Toole, p. 87; RIA/DIB.

G144   *The Society of Friends: A domestic narrative, illustrating the peculiar doctrines held by the disciples of George Fox* (by Mrs J.R. Greer).
+ London: Saunders & Otley, 1852, 2 vols. LOCATION L, O.
+ New York: M.W. Dodd, 1853. LOCATION NYPL, NN.
COMMENTARY Irish religious fiction set in Ireland, particularly Dublin, dealing with Quakers. In the preface the author states that this narrative is 'partly fictitious. Each character introduced, has indeed had it's [*sic*] prototype in the sect, each event narrated has occurred'. However, she used fictitious names [NYPL; ER].

GREER, James, fl. 1883, d. Derry (Co. Derry) 1919 (1913 according to RIA/DIB). Ulster writer who also edited *Guide to Londonderry and the highlands of Donegal* (Londonderry, 1885). He may be related to the John Greer (1851–95) who wrote for the *Derry Journal* and the *Derry Standard*. SOURCE Brown, p. 118; Irish pseudonyms; RIA/DIB.

G145   *Three wee Ulster lasses; or, news from our Irish cousins* (by James Greer).
+ London, Paris, New York, Melbourne: Cassell & Co., 1883 (ill.). SOURCE Allibone Suppl., i, p. 715; Brown, 648; Topp 7, 382. LOCATION D (n.d. edn), BFl, L.

COMMENTARY Contrasts three girls of different backgrounds: Ulster-Saxon, Ulster-Scot, and Ulster-Gaelic. The author depicts the first two as vastly superior. In the end, Nelly, the Ulster-Gaelic girl, is converted to Protestantism and emigrates to America [Brown].

GREER, Mrs S.D. See **GREER, Mrs J.R.**

GREER, Thomas (known as **Tom Greer**), b. Anahilt (Co. Down), d. *c.*1895. Physician and writer, TG was educated at Queen's College, Belfast, and practiced medicine in Cambridge. He unsuccessfully contested North Derry as a Liberal Home Rule candidate in 1892. SOURCE Brown, p. 119; Newmann, p. 92; RIA/DIB.

G146 *A modern Daedalus* (by Tom Greer).
+ London: Griffith, Farran, Okeden & Welsh, 1885. SOURCE Allibone Suppl, i, p. 715; Brown, 649; Wolff, 2754; COPAC. LOCATION D, L, NUC, InND Loeber coll.
London: Griffith, Farran, Okeden & Welsh; New York: E.P. Dutton & Co., [1887]. LOCATION NUC.

COMMENTARY A nationalist science fiction fantasy based on the old Derry folktale of Hudy McGuiggen (see Hugh Harkin§), who learns the secret of aerial flight by watching sea birds and studying hard. His father and brothers are all involved in revolutionary activities against the English. The young inventor refuses to be drawn into the conflict and to have his flying machine used against the English. He flies over to London to make his invention known. He goes to the house of commons where he sees Parnell in action. He is imprisoned because the English want to make use of his invention, but he escapes. On his return to Ireland, he is willing to aid in the struggle against England. There is a successful rising, aided by an air fleet that bombs Dublin Castle and several warships in Dublin Bay. Features Charles Stewart Parnell [ML; Brown; Hartman, 760; Newmann]

GREGG, Revd John, b. Cappa, near Ennis (Co. Clare) 1798, d. Cork 1878. An evangelical preacher and writer, JG was the son of Richard Gregg who had a small property at Cappa. His mother, Barbara Fitzgerald, was a Catholic but was converted to protestantism by JG before her death. From 1819 he attended TCD, where he obtained his BA in 1824 and was ordained in 1826. He eventually received his DD in 1860. He was renowned for his ardent temperament and impetuous eloquence, attracting large congregations wherever he served and was considered the greatest preacher of his age. He often preached in the Irish language and was a member of the Irish Society, which advocated the distribution of bibles in Gaelic. One of the parishes of which he had the living early in his career was Kilsallaghan (Co. Dublin). Later, Trinity Church in Lower Gardiner Street, Dublin, was built for him. He became bishop of Cork, Cloyne and Ross in 1862 and built the cathedral church of St Fin Barre. JG published many sermons, lectures and tracts including *Plain teaching for little children in questions and answers* (Dublin, 1852), and *A missionary visit to Achill and Erris* (Dublin, [1850]). He married in 1830 Elizabeth Law of Dublin. Their son Robert Samuel Gregg became archbishop of Armagh. JG's portrait and a brief biographical sketch were published in W. FitzPatrick et al., *What Ireland needs: The gospel in the native tongue* (London, n.d.). For other portraits and papers, see ODNB. SOURCE Allibone Suppl., i, p. 717; B & S, p. 346; D. Bowen, *The Protestant crusade in Ireland, 1800–70* (Dublin, 1978); Brooke, p. 23; Elmes, p. 89; RIA/DIB; ODNB; RL.

G147 *Recollections of Mick Healy, an Irish peasant* (by Revd John Gregg).
+ Dublin: William Curry & Co., 1849, 5th edn. LOCATION D.
+ London: Religious Tract Society, n.d (as *Mick Healy, an Irish peasant*; Narrative Series, No. 925). LOCATION InND Loeber coll.

+ New York: Lane & Scott [for the Sunday-school Union of the Methodist Episcopal Church], [1851] (as *The history of Mick Healy, an Irish peasant, illustrating the power of scripture truth* (revsd by Daniel P. Kidder; ill.; Youth Library, No. 494). SOURCE OCLC. LOCATION Drew Univ., Madison (NJ), InND Loeber coll.

+ Nashville (TN): Southern Methodist Publishing House, 1859 (as *Mick Healy, the Irish peasant*; revsd by Thomas O. Summers, DD). LOCATION InND Loeber coll.

Toulouse: Société des Livres Religieux, 1864 (trans. as *Michel Healy, le paysan irlandais, histoire véritable*). SOURCE Bn-Opale plus. LOCATION L (destroyed; slightly different title), BNF.

+ Dublin: G. Herbert, 1886 (as *The story of Mick Healy, an Irish peasant*; with a preface by J.F. Gregg [i.e., John Gregg's son]). LOCATION L.

COMMENTARY A much reprinted work, which stayed in print until the 1880s. No copy of the 1st Dublin edn located. The title page of the 1849 Dublin edn carries a Bible quote in Gaelic. It is most likely based on the author's actual experience while minister at Kilsallaghan. He meets Mick Healy, a converted peasant, and recounts Mick's life story. In his fifties, Mick, who is a Gaelic speaker and a native of Co. Meath, discovers fragments of an English Bible in his father's trunk and reads it with great interest. The parish priest forbids him to continue, but he does and eventually acquires a complete new Bible from a local minister. People start to avoid him and his landlord discharges him, but Mick is steadfast in not giving up his new insights. He is forced to move into a mud cabin, where one of his sons dies. He finds other employment and in 1835 joins the Protestant congregation at Kilsallaghan where, among children, he attends religious instruction. Although not able to read Gaelic, he enjoys having the minister read to him from a Gaelic Bible. Mick continues to be plagued by abuse from Catholics and from a priest. He dies a strong believer in the Protestant faith [RL].

'GREGG, W.S.', also 'GREGG, William Stevenson', pseuds. See **ROBINSON, Frances Mabel**.

GREGORY, Lady (Isabella) Augusta. Co-author. See **YEATS, William Butler**.

GREGORY, Sir William. Husband of Lady Augusta Gregory. Attributed author. See **WALROND, Robert Francis**.

GRESLEY, Revd William (1801–1876). Editor. See **ALEXANDER, Cecil Frances**.

GREVILLE, Lady Beatrice Violet (née Graham; known as **Lady Violet Greville**; not Violet Beatrice as in Brown 2), b. 1842, d. 1932. Novelist, editor and feature writer, BVG was the daughter of James Graham, 5th duke of Montrose (not the 4th duke as mistakenly stated by Allibone and CP, vi, p. 117) and Caroline Agnes, daughter of John Horsley-Beresford, 2nd Baron Decies in Ireland. She married Algernon William Fulke Greville-Nugent, 2nd Baron Greville of Clonyn (also known as Cloneen, Co. Westmeath) in 1863. Her husband died in London in 1909, leaving £16,000. She is known for her eight novels written for juveniles, some of which were set in Ireland. She edited *Ladies in the field; sketches of sport* (London, 1894), to which she contributed 'Riding in Ireland and India'. She also wrote the life of the marquess of Montrose (London, 1886). *Source* Allibone Suppl., i, p. 719; Alston, p. 175; Brown 2, p. 106; Casey & Rowan, p. 215; CP, vi, p. 117; ix, p. 158; Daims, p. 295.

G148 *Faiths and fashions: short essays republished* (by Lady Violet Greville).
London: Longmans & Co., 1880. SOURCE Allibone Suppl., i, p. 719. LOCATION L, NUC

G149 *Zoe; a girl of genius. A novel* (by Lady Violet Greville).
London: Richard Bentley & Son, 1881, 3 vols. SOURCE Allibone Suppl., i, p. 719.
LOCATION L.

G150 *Keith's wife. A novel* (by Lady Violet Greville).
London: Richard Bentley & Son, 1883, 3 vols. SOURCE Allibone Suppl., i, p. 719.
LOCATION L, NUC.

G151 *Creatures of clay. A novel* (by Lady Violet Greville).
London: Chapman & Hall, 1885, 3 vols. SOURCE Allibone Suppl., i, p. 719. LOCATION
L, NUC.

G152 *The secret of Barravoe. A tale* (by Lady Violet Greville).
+ London, New York: George Routledge & Sons, [1885] (The Ludgate Novels).
SOURCE Allibone Suppl., ii, p. 719 (1886 edn). LOCATION L.
COMMENTARY Detective story set in Ireland. A lawyer searches in an obscure part of Ireland
for Myles Donovan, whose relative in America has left him a fortune [CM; Burmester list].

G153 *That hated Saxon* (by Lady Violet Greville).
London: Ward & Downey, 1892. SOURCE Alston, p. 175 (1893 edn). LOCATION L (1893
edn), NUC.
+ London: Ward & Downey, 1894 (new edn; ill. Edwin J. Ellis). SOURCE Brown 2,
571. LOCATION D.
COMMENTARY Fiction for juveniles. A story of romance and country life in Ireland, where
three charming girls live with their father, an impecunious landlord, in a rambling country
house. Two eligible Englishmen arrive: the Hon. Harry Colville and Capt. Yelverton. The
former falls in love with Kathleen and the latter eventually marries Eileen. Descriptions of
hunting scenes, a horse show, and a horse fair [Brown 2].

G154 *The home for failures* (by Lady Violet Greville).
London: Hutchinson & Co., 1896. LOCATION L.

G155 *The fighters. A novel* (by Lady Violet Greville).
London: Chapman & Hall, 1907. LOCATION L.

GREVILLE, Lady Violet. See **GREVILLE, Lady Beatrice Violet.**

GREY, Eliza, fl. 1831. Irish writer of fiction for children and friend of Mary Grey§, referred
to as Mrs Eliza Grey in an advertisement in Mary Grey's *Memoirs of Dickey* (London, 1831).
In the preface to *The history of a geranium* (London, 1831), EG mentions that the book was
'merely intended for the amusement of dear little Mary, and her cousin, the young Lord', and
may suggest that EG was a governess. SOURCE RL.

G156 *The adventures of a marmotte. Sold for the distressed Irish* (preface signed Eliza
Grey).
+ London: Simpkin & Marshall; Leeds: Spink, 1831 (ill. Brown). SOURCE OCLC.
LOCATION L, D, CLU.
COMMENTARY 50pp. Fiction for juveniles [ML].

G157 *The history of a geranium. Sold for the distressed Irish* [anon.].
+ London: Simpkin & Marshall; Leeds: Spink, 1831. LOCATION L.
COMMENTARY 48pp. Advertised in *The adventures of a marmotte*, as 'sold for the same charitable purpose', but author is not identified. In the preface, the author addresses English children on behalf of the distressed Irish children, and states that she had kept a journal of 'my
native country' [RL; BLC].

GREY, Josephine Elizabeth. See **BUTLER, Josephine Elizabeth.**

GREY, Mrs Mary, fl. 1831. Writer of fiction for juveniles and friend of Eliza Grey§, who participated in the publication of booklets for the benefit of the distressed Irish. SOURCE NCBEL 4, p. 1801; Preface to [Eliza Grey's§] *The history of a geranium* (London, 1831); RL.
G158 *Memoirs of Dickey, a yellow canary; written by himself in behalf of, and sold for, the famishing Irish* (by Mrs Mary Grey).
+ London: Simpkin & Marshall; Leeds: Spink, 1831 (ed. by his friend, Mrs. Mary Grey; ill.). SOURCE OCLC. LOCATION D (ill. lacking), L, CLU.
COMMENTARY 62pp. Title on cover: *Memoirs of Dickey, a yellow canary. Sold for the distressed Irish.* Written for English children, the 'good friends of the Irish' [RL].

GRIFFIN, Daniel. Editor. See **GRIFFIN, Gerald**.

GRIFFIN, Gerald, pseud. 'Thaddeus Flint', b. Limerick 1803, d. Cork 1840. Novelist, playwright and poet, GG was the ninth child of Patrick Griffin and his wife Ellen Geary. The family name originally was O'Griobhth. His father's business failure forced them to move to Glin (Co. Limerick) where they resided at Fairy Lawn on the river Shannon in 1810. He received part of his education at the Limerick Grammar School. His parents emigrated with some of their children to Pennsylvania (1820) and the remaining children moved to Adare and then to Pallas Kenry (both Co. Limerick), which remained the Griffin home in Ireland. GG never saw his parents again. He went to London in 1823 to make a career in literature. John Banim§ helped him to contact periodicals, and GG wrote an opera, *The Noyades*, which he produced in London. His life there proved to be too hard and he returned to Limerick in poor health in 1827 after handing in the manuscript of *Holland-tide* (London, 1827) to the publishers Simpkin and Marshall. He continued to publish in the *Literary Souvenir* (London, 1828–29); the *News of Literature and Fashion* (London, 1825–26); the *Irish Monthly Magazine of Politics and Literature* (Dublin, 1834), and other magazines. However, even in his lifetime it was difficult to identify many of his contributions to periodicals (for details, see Cronin, pp 153–5). He was back in England in 1832 to petition the author Thomas Moore§ to stand for parliamentary election in Limerick. In 1836 he spent some time in Taunton and Paris. Always withdrawn and religious, he continued writing but burnt his manuscripts when an unhappy love affair with a married woman, Lydia Fisher (daughter of Mary Leadbeater§), made GG decide to enter the Christian Brothers in 1838 and dedicate his life to teaching poor children. As Brother John, he moved to the North Monastery in Cork City and died there from typhus in 1840 at age 37. His works remained popular, and the Dublin publisher Duffy reprinted his fiction numerous times. After GG's death, his play *Gisippus* was produced successfully in Drury Lane in 1842. It is possible that GG was an artist as well and provided a sketch for the title page of the Dublin edn of *The collegians* (1842). His brother Daniel published *The life of Gerald Griffin* (London 1843). Karl von Killinger§ published a biography of GG in German in Stuttgart in 1847. Cronin mentions an unpublished work: 'Common-place book A', in which Griffin recorded his research for *The invasion* (London, 1832) and extensive notes on other topics. Some of GG's letters are among the Matthew Russell papers in the Jesuit Archives, Leeson Street, Dublin (MS J27/67), while other papers are listed in the ODNB. For his portraits, see ODNB. SOURCE Allibone, i, p. 741; M. Banim, *Here and there through Ireland* (Dublin, 1891), p. 219; Brady, p. 94; Boylan, p. 136; Clyde, p. 92; J. Cronin, *Gerald Griffin, 1803–1840: a critical biography* (Cambridge, 1978); [Aubrey de Vere] *Recollections of Aubrey de Vere* (New York, 1897), pp 27–33; Elmes, p. 90; Field Day, i, pp 1172, 1296, ii, pp 1009–10; S.C. Hall, pp 229–30; Hogan, pp 276–7; Hogan 2, pp 501–3; Irish pseudonyms; K. von Killinger (trans.), *Gerald Griffin en schriftstellerleben* (Stuttgart, 1847); W. Laffan & B. Rooney, '"One of our brilliant ornaments": the death and life of Thomas Foster' in *Irish*

Architectural and Decorative Studies, 7 (2004), pp 197–8; McKenna, pp 187–91; E. Mannin, *Two studies in integrity: Gerald Griffin and the Rev. Francis Mahony (Father Prout)* (London, 1954); J.O'K. Murray, *The prose and poetry of Ireland* (New York), 1877), pp 383–411; NCBEL 4, pp 1303–4; OCIL, pp 228–9; ODNB; O'Donoghue, pp 173–4; RIA/DIB; Rogal, p. 230; Lord J. Russell (ed.), *Memoirs, journal, and correspondence of Thomas Moore* (London, 1854), iv, p. 301.

G159 *'Holland-tide;' or, Munster popular tales* [anon.].

+ London: W. Simpkin & R. Marshall, 1827. SOURCE Rafroidi, ii, p. 175; Brown, 659; British Fiction; Garside, 1827:34; Sadleir, 1069. LOCATION Grail, Corvey CME 3–628–51038–4, Ireland related fiction, D, L, NUC, InND Loeber coll.

+ London: Saunders & Otley, 1827, 2nd edn (as *Holland-tide; or Irish popular tales*). LOCATION D, NUC.

New York: Garland, 1979 (introd. by R.L. Wolff). SOURCE COPAC. LOCATION Dt.

COMMENTARY In the introd., Griffin conducts an imaginary discussion between an old man and the novelist about the proper aims for an Irish writer in representing his people and his nation. Contents: '"Holland-tide"', 'The Aylmers of Bally-Aylmer', 'The hand and word', 'Saint Martin's day', 'The brown man', 'The persecutions of Jack-Edy', 'The unburied legs', 'Owney and Owney-na-Peak', 'Conclusion'. Additional stories in some later edns: 'The village ruin' (originally published in *Tales of my neighbourhood*), 'The knight of the sheep', 'The rock of the candle'. Simpkin and Marshall paid Griffin £70 for the copyright of *Holland-tide* [ML; J. Cronin, *Gerald Griffin*; Harris, p. 181].

G160 *Tales of the Munster festivals: containing card drawing; The half Sir; and Suil Dhuv, the coiner* [anon.].

+ London: Saunders & Otley, 1827, 3 vols. SOURCE Rafroidi, ii, p. 175 (mentions dates 1826 and 1827); McKenna, p. 190; Brown, 664a; British Fiction; Garside, 1827:35; Sadleir, 1072; Wolff, 2786. LOCATION Grail, Corvey CME 3–628–48867–2, Ireland related fiction, D, Dt (1829 edn), BFl (1829 edn), L, NUC, InND Loeber coll.

+ London, Belfast: Simms & M'Intyre, 1848 (Parlour Library, No. 15). SOURCE Sadleir, ii, p. 153. LOCATION D, InND Loeber coll.

+ London, New York: George Routledge & Co., 1857 (as *Tales of the Munster festivals*, Railway Library, No. 148). SOURCE Todd, p. 86. LOCATION D, DPL (n.d. edn).

London: Newnes, [*c.*1896–99] (as *Suil Dhuv, the coiner*; Newnes' Penny Library of Famous Books, No. 3). SOURCE Sadleir, 3643. COMMENTARY *London, Newnes edn* No copy located [RL].

London: Newnes, [*c.*1896–1899] (as *Half-sir*; Newnes' Penny Library of Famous Books, No. 44). SOURCE Sadleir, 3643. COMMENTARY *London, Newnes edn* No copy located [RL].

Glasgow: Cameron & Ferguson, [1880] (as *Castle Hamond; or, the half sir* [anon.]). SOURCE P.S. O'Hegarty, 'Notes and comment ...' in *The Bibliographical Society of Ireland*, 6(4) (1954), p. 63. LOCATION E.

COMMENTARY *Glasgow edn* Published in coloured pictorial wrappers priced at 3*d.* [RL; P.S. O'Hegarty, 'Notes and comment ...' *The Bibliographical Society of Ireland*, 6 (4) (1954), p. 63].

Leipzig: Hartman, 1829 (trans. by A. Kaiser as *Suil Dhuv der Falschminger und die Kartenschlägerin: Romantische Erzählung*). SOURCE Garside, 1827:35; GLOL. LOCATION SBB-PK, Berlin.

New York: Garland, 1979, 3 vols. (introd. by R.L. Wolff). SOURCE COPAC. LOCATION Dt.

COMMENTARY Contents: 'Card-drawing' (set in Co. Clare, and concerns superstition and the prevention of an unjust execution through a last-minute repentance by the real murderer),

'The half Sir' (set in Co. Limerick after the famine of 1822. Deals with the snobbery of the older gentry towards a new arrival in their economic class), 'Suil Dhuv, the coiner' (set in the penal days of the early-eighteenth century in Co. Limerick, and concerns outlaw violence). 'Suil Dhuv, the coiner' was reissued as a serial in *The Illustrated Dublin Journal* (Dublin, 1862) and was turned into a play (London, [18—]) [Wolff introd., pp 19–20; RL; RLIN].

G161   *The collegians* [anon.].

+ London: Saunders & Otley, 1829, 3 vols. SOURCE Rafroidi, ii, p. 175; Brown, 660 (mistakenly mentions a 1828 edn); British Fiction; Garside, 1829:41; Sadleir, 1066; Wolff, 2782. LOCATION Grail, Corvey CME 3–628–47304–7, Ireland related fiction, D, Dt, DPL (1829, 2nd edn), L, NUC, InND Loeber coll.

London: Saunders & Otley, 1829, 2nd edn., 3 vols. (with half titles: *Second series of Tales of the Munster festivals*), SOURCE Topp 4, p. 222 (who mentions this as new edn); COPAC. LOCATION E.

+ London, Belfast: Simms & M'Intyre, 1847 (as *The collegians. A tale of Garryowen*; by Gerald Griffin, Parlour Library, No. 6). SOURCE Topp 4, p. 223. LOCATION InND Loeber coll.

+ London, New York: George Routledge & Co., 1857 (as *The collegians. A tale of Garryowen*). LOCATION D, NUC.

London, New York: Routledge, Warne & Routledge, 1861 (as *The collegians; or, the Colleen Bawn. A tale of Garryowen*; new edn; Railway Library). LOCATION NUC.

London: C. Vickers, 1861 (as *The Colleen Bawn; or, the collegian's wife. A tale of Garryowen originally entitled: 'The collegians'*). LOCATION L, NUC.

+ Preston: James Askew, 1888 (as *The collegians or, the Colleen Bawn. A tale of Garryowen*; The Artisan's Cottage Library; on cover: 'Knowledge is power', on spine: 'Colleen Bawn'). LOCATION InND Loeber coll.

+ London, New York: Frederick Warne & Co., 1892 (as *The collegians, or the Colleen Bawn*; Warne's Library of Fiction; see Plate 34). LOCATION InND Loeber coll.

+ Dublin: James Duffy, [1842] (as *The collegians, a tale of Garryowen*; ill. Samuel Watson, Johnson, Mulrahy, S. Griffin). SOURCE Topp 4, pp 222–3.

+ Stuttgart, Tübingen: J.G. Gotta, 1848, 2 vols. (trans. as 'Die Schulfreunde'; in *Erin. Auswahl vorzüglicher irischer Erzählungen* by K. v. K[illinger]). SOURCE OCLC. LOCATION D.

Paris: Didier, 1872 (trans. by Thérèse Alphonse Karr as *La fille du cordier, scènes de la vie irlandaise*). SOURCE Rafroidi, ii, p. 364; Bn-Opale plus. LOCATION BNF.

New York: J. & J. Harper, 1829, 2 vols. SOURCE Topp 1, p. 84. LOCATION NUC.

New York, Boston: D. & J. Sadlier & Co., [1829?]. LOCATION NUC.

Philadelphia: J. & J.L. Gihon, [1854?] (as *The collegians. A novel*). LOCATION NUC.

Cincinnati: U.P. James, [1876] (as *The collegians. A novel*). LOCATION NUC.

+ Dublin: Talbot Press, 1953 (as *The collegians*, Everyman's Irish library; introd., Padraic Colum; ill.). LOCATION D, InND Loeber coll.

+ Belfast: Appletree Press, 1992 (introd. by John Cronin). LOCATION D.

COMMENTARY Based on a notorious murder case in the Limerick region, this was Griffin's most successful and enduring work, giving insights into the many layers of Irish society at the time. He sent the £800 he earned for it to his parents in America. His literary contemporaries admired it, among them Maria Edgeworth. The story contrasts two young Catholic men of the gentry, both educated at TCD. One is a steady, sober person; the other, the villain, is dashing and self-indulgent. He causes the girl who loves him to be murdered when she becomes an encumbrance. In the actual murder trial, Daniel O'Connell defended the prisoner, and although Griffin is said to have reported the trial for the press, this is unlikely, and is not mentioned in his brother's biography. The story was made into an opera by Jules Benedict with the words by Dion Boucicault§ and John Oxenford (*The lily of Killarney*, London, 1862), and was turned into a play, *The Colleen Bawn; or, the brides of Garryowen* (New York, [1865]) by Dion Boucicault§. An early account of the murder case can be found in [Revd Richard Fitzgerald] *Ellen Hanly or the true history of the Colleen Bawn* (Dublin, 1868) [Brady, p. 94; Brown; J. Cronin, *Gerald Griffin*; Field Day, i, pp 1081, 1150–69, iv, p. 825; ODNB; Rafroidi, ii, p. 70; Wolff introd., p. 20].

G162   *The rivals*, [and] *Tracy's ambition.* [on half page:] *Third series of Tales of the Munster festivals* [anon.].

  + London: Saunders & Otley, 1829, 3 vols. SOURCE McKenna, p. 190; British Fiction; Garside, 1829:42; Sadleir, 1071; Wolff, 2785. LOCATION Corvey CME 3–628–48613–0, Ireland related fiction, D, DPL (1830, 2nd edn), L (1830 edn), O, NUC.

  + London, Belfast: Simms & M'Intyre, 1851 (as *The rivals, and Tracy's ambition*; Parlour Library, No. 62). SOURCE Sadleir, ii, p. 154. LOCATION D.

  + New York: J. & J. Harper, 1830, 2 vols. LOCATION NUC, InND Loeber coll.

  Lille: Pui Cercuil, Irish and Anglo-Irish Texts, 1978. SOURCE COPAC. LOCATION O.

  New York: Garland, 1979, 3 vols. (introd. by R.L. Wolff). SOURCE COPAC. LOCATION Dt.

COMMENTARY Contents: 'The rivals' (a love story set in the 1820s. The main character is Esther Wilderming, a Methodist. The rivals are of different religions, and the novel contains a strong attack on Evangelicals), 'Tracy's ambition' (lured by his ambitions for an appointment as a magistrate and by the false promises of a Protestant neighbour, Tracy loses the affection and support of his tenantry, which came to him largely because of his Catholic wife. The novel describes fierce feuds among the Irish peasantry in a society already in unrest) [Wolff introd., p. 20].

G163   *The Christian physiologist. Tales illustrative of the five senses: their mechanisms, uses, and government; with moral and explanatory introductions. Addressed to a young friend* [anon.].

  London: E. Bull, 1830. SOURCE Rafroidi, ii, p. 176; Brown, 652; Sadleir, 1065; Garside 2, A:3. LOCATION Grail, Corvey CME 3–628–52902–6, L, NUC.

  + Dublin: James Duffy, 1854 (as *The offering of friendship; or, tales of the five senses*). LOCATION D, L, NUC.

  + Dublin: James Duffy, 1854 (as *The Christian physiologist and other tales*). SOURCE NCBEL 3, p. 932; Wolff, 2781 (1860 edn). LOCATION DPL (n.d. edn).

  Dublin: James Duffy, 1854 (as *A story of Psyche*; Duffy's Popular Library). SOURCE NCBEL 3, p. 932. LOCATION L.

  + Dublin, London: James Duffy & Sons, 1876 (as *Tales for youth*). LOCATION D.

  Dublin: James Duffy, 1854 (as *The kelp-gatherer. An Irish tale*; Duffy's Popular Library). SOURCE NCBEL 3, p. 932. LOCATION L (destroyed).

  Dublin: James Duffy, 1854 (as *The day of trial. An Irish tale*; Duffy's Popular Library). SOURCE NCBEL 3, p. 932. LOCATION L (destroyed).

  Dublin: J. Duffy, 1854 (as *The offering of friendship; or, Tales of the senses*). SOURCE OCLC; Garside 2, A:3). OCLC. LOCATION D, MH.

  Dublin: James Duffy, 1854 (as *The voluptuary cured: An Irish tale*; Duffy's Popular Library). LOCATION L (destroyed).

  New York, Boston, Montreal: D. & J. Sadlier, 1854 (as *Tales of the five senses*; ill.; Fireside Library, No. 7). SOURCE Rev. in the Boston *Pilot* (24 June 1854, p. 4). LOCATION NUC, InND Loeber coll. (n.d. edn).

COMMENTARY Written for the 'instruction of young persons' (preface). Arranged according to the different senses (poetry not included). Sight: 'The mechanism of sight', 'Uses and government of sight', 'The kelp gatherer: A tale'. Hearing: 'The mechanism of hearing', 'Uses of hearing', 'The day of trial: A tale' (first published in the *Juvenile Keepsake*). Feeling: 'Mechanism and uses of feeling', 'The voluptuary cured: A tale'. Smell: 'Mechanism and uses of smell', 'The self consumed: A tale'. Taste: 'Mechanism and uses of taste', 'The selfish crotarie: A tale'. The intellect: 'Of the intellect', 'A story of Psyche' [RL; Garside 2].

G164   *The invasion* [anon.].

+ London: Saunders & Otley, 1832, 4 vols. SOURCE Rafroidi, ii, p. 149; Brown, 663; Sadleir, 1070; Wolff, 2784; Garside 2, 1832:38. LOCATION Corvey CME 3–628–47457–4; Grail, D, L, NUC.

Dublin, London: James Duffy [1861] (ill.). SOURCE Advertised in the *Illustrated Dublin Journal* (Sept. 28, 1861); COPAC. LOCATION Dt.

COMMENTARY Preface warns the reader against expecting an historical novel, but the text consists of a romanticized story of life and civilization in Ireland just before the Danish invasions and featuring the fortunes of the O'Haedhas, who lived on Bantry Bay. GG did extensive research for this book in both Dublin and London, all contained in the manuscript, 'Commonplace book A', which references over sixty works on history and mythology and researches the history of ancient Ireland and the development of Irish Christianity, all of which fed into *The invasion*. Later edns contain notes supplied by antiquarian Prof. Eugene O'Curry in response to criticisms of G.G.'s amateur status as an antiquarian. Republished as a serial in the *Illustrated Dublin Journal* (1861). The Dublin edn was advertised as being ready for publication on 1 Oct. 1861 in a one volume edn in 'fancy boards' at 2s. (formerly 2 guineas). Reviewed in the *Illustrated Dublin Journal* (16 Nov. 1861) [Advertised in the *Illustrated Dublin Journal*, Sept. 28, 1861; Brown; RL; Garside].

G165   *Tales of my neighbourhood* [anon.] (introductory letter in volume 2 signed 'Thaddeus Flint').

+ London: Saunders & Otley, 1835, 3 vols. SOURCE Rafroidi, ii, p. 177; Brown, 665; Sadleir, 1073; Wolff, 2787; Garside 2, 1835:51. LOCATION Grail, L, NUC.

Philadelphia: Carey, Lea & Blanchard, 1836, 2 vols. SOURCE Kaser, 890. LOCATION NUC, ViU.

New York: Garland, 1979, 3 vols. (introd. by R.L. Wolff). SOURCE COPAC. LOCATION Dt.

COMMENTARY Contents (except poetry): 'The barber of Bantry', 'The great house', 'A night at sea', 'Touch my honour, touch my life', 'Sir Dowling O'Hartigan', 'The village ruin', 'The cavern', 'The force of conscience', 'The sun-stroke', 'Send the fool farther', 'Mount Orient', 'The philanthropist', 'The blackbirds and yellow hammers' [Harris, pp 181–2; Garside].

G166   *The Duke of Monmouth* [anon.].

London: Richard Bentley, 1836, 3 vols. SOURCE Rafroidi, ii, p. 177; Brown, 666; Sadleir, 1067; Garside 2, 1836:32. LOCATION Grail, L, NUC.

Dublin: J. Duffy, 1836. SOURCE NSTC; Garside 2, 1836:32; OCLC. LOCATION Grail, Boston College.

Philadelphia: Carey & Hart, 1837. LOCATION NUC.

COMMENTARY An historical novel set at the end of the seventeenth century dealing with the Duke of Monmouth and the battle of Sedgmoor in England during the war between King James II and King William III. Two Irish soldiers, Morty and Shemus Delany, supply the comic relief. Contains two ballads [ML; Brown].

G167   *Talis qualis; or, tales of the jury room* (by Gerald Griffin).

+ London: Maxwell & Co., 1842, 3 vols. SOURCE Rafroidi, ii, p. 177; Brown, 667; Sadleir, 1074. LOCATION Grail, D (only vols. 2, 3), Dt, L, NUC.

+ Dublin: James Duffy, 1846, 3 vols. in 1 (ill.). LOCATION D (incomplete), NUC, InND Loeber coll. (1872 edn).

+ Dublin: James Duffy, 1891 (as *Tales of the jury room*; ill. S. Watson, W. Greatbatch). LOCATION DPL.

New York: Garland, 1979, 3 vols. (introd. by R.L. Wolff). SOURCE COPAC. LOCATION Dt.

COMMENTARY Published posthumously. Contents: 'Sigismund', 'The story-teller at fault', 'The knight without reproach', 'The mistake', 'Drink, my brother', 'The swans of Lir', 'McEneiry, the covetous', 'Mr. Tibbot O'Leary, the curious', 'The lame tailor of Macel', 'Antrim Jack and his general', 'The prophesy', 'Sir Dowling O'Hartigan' (first published in *Tales from my neighbourhood*), 'The stranger's tale: The raven's nest'. The story 'McEneiry, the covetous' was republished in the *Harp* (Montreal, Aug.–Sept., 1880) [ML; RL].

+ Dublin: James Duffy & Co., [1864 or later] (as *The knight without reproach*). LOCATION D. COMMENTARY *Dublin [1864 or later] edn.* One penny edn of a single story [RL].

G168 *The young Milesian and the selfish crotarie. A tale* (by Gerald Griffin).
Dublin: James Duffy, 1854 (Duffy's Popular Library). SOURCE Falkner Greirson cat. 9/137. LOCATION L, D (n.d. edn, uncatalogued), NUC (where it listed as part of *Tales for youth*), CLU.
Dublin: Catholic Truth Society of Ireland, 1903 (as *Eagna, the bard; or, the selfish crotarie*). LOCATION NUC.

G169 *The beautiful Queen of Leix; or, the self-consumed; an Irish tale* (by Gerald Griffin).
Dublin: James Duffy, 1854 (Duffy's Popular Library). SOURCE NCBEL 3, p. 932. LOCATION L (destroyed).

G170 *Adventures of an Irish giant* (by Gerald Griffin).
+ Boston: Patrick Donahoe, 1854. SOURCE McKenna, p. 191; Brown 2, 573 (n.d. edn). LOCATION Grail, D.

COMMENTARY Serialized in *Duffy's Fireside Magazine* (Dublin, c.1850). Set partly in Ballymahon, an out-of-the-way village in the south of Ireland, and partly in Dublin. The good-natured, simple-minded giant, Patcheen Goggin, plays but a subordinate part of the tale, the central figure of which is the beautiful Erina Conway about whose birth there is a mystery which is cleared up only in the end. The story is largely concerned with the machinations of the villain, Murdo Cox, to raise himself in the world and marry Erina. It relates political events and the clearances on the Villiers estate [Brown 2; Clyde, p. 116; J. Cronin, *Gerald Griffin*, pp 142–6].

G171 *Castle Hamond; or, the half sir* [anon.].
Glasgow: Cameron & Ferguson, [1880]. SOURCE P.S. O'Hegarty, 'Notes and comment ...' in *The Bibliographical Society of Ireland*, 6(4) (1954), p. 63. LOCATION E.

COMMENTARY One of four parts of *Romances of mystery* (Glasgow: Cameron & Ferguson, [1880]). Originally published as the 'The half sir' in *Card drawing, the half sir, and Suil Dhuv the coiner* (Dublin, 1857) as part of Griffith's Collected works (see below). This edn published in coloured pictorial wrappers priced at 3*d*. [RL; P.S. O'Hegarty, 'Notes and comment ...' *The Bibliographical Society of Ireland*, 6 (4) (1954), p. 63].

— COLLECTED WORKS
The following is an approximation of the collected works, which has proven difficult to document fully because of the many undated edns and the long period over which GG's works remained in print [RL].

G172 *The life and works of Gerald Griffin.*
London: Simpkin & Marshall; Dublin: J.L. Cumming; Edinburgh: Bell & Bradfute, 1842–43, 8 vols. (ill. J. Watson, W. Greatbatch). SOURCE Rafroidi, ii, p. 178; McKenna, p. 190; Sadleir, 1075. LOCATION L, InND Loeber coll. (some vols.).

COMMENTARY [10 vols. planned, but only 8 vols. published]. The publication was supervised by GG's brother Daniel, who made alterations to several stories, omitted others, and added several published in periodicals [Cronin, p. xix; RL].

G173 *Works of G. Griffin, Esq.* [title on spine].
London: Maxwell & Co.; Dublin: John Cumming; Edinburgh: Bell & Bradfute, 1842, 6 vols. (ill. S. Watson, W. Greatbatch). LOCATION NUC, InND Loeber coll.

G174 [*Gerald Griffin's works*].
Dublin: James Duffy, 1857, 8 vols. (ill. S. Watson, W. Greatbatch). LOCATION InND Loeber coll. COMMENTARY *1857 edn* Advertised in *Card drawing* shows the order of publication. Two binding types: (a) common edn made of light green cloth, blind stamped, except spine in gold; (b) deluxe edn; red cloth, stamped in gold (see Plate 35 for *Holland-tide, The Aylmers of Bally-Aylmer, The hand and word, The barber of Bantry*). The series consists of the same selection of volumes as the London, 1842–43 edn. [RL; Sadleir, ii, pp 158–9].
Dublin, London: James Duffy, [1864–73], 9 vols. (ill.). LOCATION InND Loeber coll. COMMENTARY [*1864–73*] *edn* Unnumbered and untitled series. Common edn consisting of red cloth blind stamped, except spine in gold [RL].
Dublin: James Duffy, 1874 and n.d., 9 vols. (ill.). LOCATION D (some vols.), InND Loeber coll. (some vols.). COMMENTARY *Dublin 1874 edn* Binding types (a) Common edn; binding of medium dark green cloth blind stamped, except spine in gold; (b) Common edn; very dark green cloth blind stamped in black, except spine in gold [RL].
Dublin, London: James Duffy, [1875], 9 vols. (ill.). LOCATION InND Loeber coll. (one vol.). COMMENTARY *Dublin [1875] edn* Binding type: Common edn, consisting of beige cloth blind stamped, except spine in gold; design simpler than in earlier edns [RL].
Dublin: James Duffy & Sons, [1889], [9 vols?](ill.). LOCATION InND Loeber coll. (several vols.). COMMENTARY *Dublin [1889] edn* Three binding types: (a) red cloth binding, with bouquet of flowers on cover and spine, stamped in black and gold; (b) the same, but in green cloth; (c) different floral design, in green cloth (see Plate 36, *The invasion*) [RL].

G175 *The works of Gerald Griffin.*
Dublin: James Duffy & Sons, [9 vols?][1875 or later, incl. 1891]. LOCATION DPL (some vols.), InND Loeber coll. (some vols.).
COMMENTARY Title on cover. Paperback edn printed in green and black with Griffin's portrait, harp and shamrock; no illustrations [Adv. in *Card drawing*; RL].

G176 [*Gerald Griffin's works*].
Dublin: James Duffy, 1904, 10 vols. (ill.). LOCATION InND Loeber coll. (one vol.).
COMMENTARY Unnumbered and untitled series. Remainder issue; yellow cloth binding, with bouquet of flower printed in black on cover, title and name of author gold stamped [RL].
Dublin: James Duffy & Co., [after 1908], [10 vols?]. LOCATION InND Loeber coll. (one vol.).

G177 *Gerald Griffin's works.*
New York, Boston, Montreal: D. & J. Sadlier & Co., [1857], 10 vols. SOURCE Hogan, p. 277; Hyland cat. 210/304; Emerald Isle cat. 88/616; Adv. in T.N. Burke, *Ireland's case stated* (New York, 1873). LOCATION NUC, InND Loeber coll. (one vol.).
COMMENTARY [*1857*] *edn* Title on binding; bound in blind stamped brown cloth, except spine, black stamped. Note that this New York edn includes *The invasion*, which did not appear in the Dublin collected works until after 1857 [RL].
New York, Montreal: D. & J. Sadlier & Co., [c.1885], 10 vols. (ill. Mercier, Mulcahy, J.B. Hall). SOURCE Emerald Isle cat. 88/616. LOCATION NUC, InND Loeber coll. COM-

MENTARY [*c.1885*] *edn* Title on binding; bound in blind stamped brown cloth, except spine, gold stamped [RL].
New York, Boston, Montreal: D. & J. Sadlier, n.d., 10 vols. (ill. Mulcahy, H.B. Hall, Mercier). LOCATION InND Loeber coll. (several vols.). COMMENTARY *n.d. edn* Two binding types of the Deluxe edn: (a) dark green cloth, embossed in gold with central design of ruin and round tower surrounded by wreath of clover, with a harp below; (b) Remainder of the deluxe edn in light green cloth, blind with central design of ruin and round tower surrounded by wreath of clover, with a flower below; numbered [RL].

G178 [*Gerald Griffin's works*].
New York: P.J. Kenedy, [1895], 10 vols (ill.). SOURCE Broadsheet adv. by P.J. Kenedy, [1895]; RL.
COMMENTARY No copy located. Advertised as being published in two binding types: (a) crushed leather half morocco, gilt tops at $7; (b) half calf, gilt edges at $20. The series probably is a reissue of the collected works first published by D. & J. Sadlier. The Kenedy series of Griffin's works was advertised as part of 'Kenedy's Gilt-top Series of Irish Novelists', and included the works of John and Michael Banim§, William Carleton§, and Samuel Lover§, in total 35 uniformly bound volumes, which were priced at $22 [Broadsheet advertised by P.J. Kenedy, [1895]; RL].

GRIFFITH, Mrs —. See **GRIFFITH, Elizabeth.**

GRIFFITH, Elizabeth (née Griffith; also known as **Mrs Griffith**), pseud. 'Frances' (see under Richard Griffith), b. Glamorgan, Wales (not Dublin as in some sources) 1727?, d. Millicent, near Naas (Co. Kildare) 1793. Actress, playwright, novelist, translator and writer in many genres, EG was the daughter of Thomas Griffith, an actor of Welsh descent and manager of the Theatre Royal in Smock Alley, Dublin, and Jane, daughter of Richard Foxcroft, rector of Portarlington (Co. Laois). Early in life EG must have benefited from the excellent schools at Portarlington, where French was taught, as she later used this skill for translating. She met in 1746 a penniless Kilkenny farmer, Richard Griffith§, with whom she conducted a sentimental correspondence. Five years later they were married in secret and she bore him two children, but they rarely lived together. Her education also seems to have been designed to make her an actress. In 1749 she made her acting debut at the Smock Alley Theatre in Dublin, then managed by Thomas Sheridan, and lived in Abbey Street in Dublin and later in Chapelizod (Co. Dublin). She moved to London where she played in the theatre in minor roles. Always under financial pressure, she wrote to make money. EG jointly published some novels with her husband (see Richard Griffith§), but she also published under her own name. Under both names she and her husband published their actual courtship letters in *A series of genuine letters, between Henry and Frances* (see under Richard Griffith§). Her work included *Amana. A dramatic poem (in five acts)* (London, 1764), which had a long list of Irish subscribers but was never produced. However, her comedy *The platonic wife* premiered at Drury Lane in 1765 and *The double mistake. A comedy* (London, 1766) was a great success and had a royal command performance. David Garrick produced her translation of Beaumarchais's *Eugénie* as *The school for rakes*. EG translated the works of Voltaire, C.J. Dorat's *The fatal effects of inconstancy* (London, 1774, 2 vols.), and did a free translation of *The memoirs of Ninon de l'Enclos* (London, 1771; repr., Dublin, 1778), to which she added a 'Conclusion', addressing the reader on natural and artificial morals. She and others translated *Delicate crimes* (London, 1777, Dublin, 1782). She also undertook literary criticism in *The morality of Shakespeare's drama illustrated*

(London, 1775). She published *Essays, addressed to young married women* (London, 1782), which deal with religion, conjugal love, temper, neatness etc. Her son went to India, where be became rich. On his return to Ireland he purchased the Millicent estate, near Naas (Co. Kildare), where EG joined him and spent the rest of her life. For her portraits and papers, see ODNB. SOURCE Allibone, i, p. 742; Blain, pp 463–4; DLB, xxxix, pp 247–51; Elmes, p. 90; D.H. Eshleman, *Elizabeth Griffith, a biographical and critical study* (Philadelphia, 1949); Field Day, i, p. 686, v, p. 831; Gecker, p. 42; *Ireland's Mirror: or, a Chronicle of the Times* (Dublin, 1805), pp 362–4; H. Farrar (ed.), *Irish marriages* (London, 1897), ii, p. 517; HIP, iv, pp 316–18; Mayo, 1274; OCIL, p. 229; ODNB; Pollard 2, p. 311; J.S. Powell, *Huguenots, planters, Portarlington* ([Portarlington], 1994]), pp 92, 148–9; RIA/DIB; Summers, p. 68; Todd, pp 296–300.

G179   *The history of Lady Barton, a novel, in letters* (by Mrs Griffith).

London: T. Davies & T. Cadell, 1771, 3 vols. SOURCE Black, 499; Raven 2, 1771:41; ESTC t071307. LOCATION L, NUC.

Leipzig: Weidman, 1772 (trans. as *Geschichte der Lady Barton*). SOURCE Raven 2, 1771:41; GLOL; Rochedieu, p. 132. LOCATION Universitätsbibliothek, Bielefeld.

Londres [Paris?]: Poingot, 1788, 2 vols. (trans. as *Histoire de Lady Barton*). SOURCE Raven 2, 1771:41; ESTC t200399. LOCATION Univ. of Leeds.

Londres [Paris]: Letellier, 1788 (trans. as *Delia, ou histoire d'une jeune héritiere*). SOURCE Raven 2, 1771:41; ESTC n016962. LOCATION CtY.

Lausanne: J. Mourer, 1788, 2 vols. in 1 (trans. as *Histoire de Lady Barton*). SOURCE Streeter, 159.

Amsterdam: Johannes Allart, 1789 (trans. into Dutch as *Delia, of the jonge erfgename*). SOURCE Wintermans, 1771:41.

COMMENTARY Lord and Lady Barton are travelling to Ireland. A storm at sea precipitates Lord Lucan to express his devotion to Lady Barton, which plants the seeds of all the unhappiness that follows. The storm forces the vessel to land on the northern coast of Ireland, adding to Lady Barton's anxieties, including her fear of her husband's jealousy, and the foreign society in which she is introduced [Field Day, v, pp 775, 797–8; Kilfeather, pp 287–8].

G180   *The story of Lady Juliana Harley. A novel. In letters* (by Mrs Griffith).

London: T. Cadell, 1776, 2 vols. SOURCE Raven 2: 1776:11; Forster 2, 1741; McBurney & Taylor, 380; ESTC t066937. LOCATION L, NUC, IU.

+ Dublin: S. Price, B. Corcoran, W. Sleater, W. Whitestone, R. Cross, W. Watson, J. Hoey, J. Potts, F. Smith, J. Williams, W. Colles, W. Wilson, T. Walker, C. Jenkin, E. Cross, P. Moncrieffe, G. Burnett, M. Mills, W. Spotswood, G. Bonham, J. Mehain, S. Colbert, J. Beatty, C. Talbot & J. Exshaw, 1776, 2 vols. SOURCE Raven 2, 1776:11; ESTC t107620. LOCATION L.

Amsterdam: M. Schalekamp, 1778, 2 vols. in 1 (trans. into Dutch as *Geschiedenis van Lady Juliana Harley*). SOURCE F.A. van S., p. 37.

Paris: Veuve Duchesne; Amsterdam: D.J. Changuion, 1778, 2 vols. in 1 (trans. as *Histoire de lady Julie Harley*). SOURCE Streeter, 160; Rochedieu, p. 133; Bn-Opale plus. LOCATION BNF.

Leipzig: Junius, 1777, 2 vols. (trans. as *Geschichte der Lady Juliana Harley*). SOURCE Raven 2, 1776:11; GLOL. LOCATION Bibliotheksverbund Bayern.

Amsterdam: M. Schalekamp, 1778 (trans. into Dutch as *Geschiedenis van Lady Juliana Harley*). SOURCE Wintermans, 1776:11.

COMMENTARY Epistolary novel about a forced, loveless marriage. The heroine, who behaves impeccably with her unworthy husband, confides at the end of the book the secret of her lost love and enters a convent [Blain; Todd, p. 299)

G181 *A collection of novels* (selected and revsd by Mrs. Griffith).
London: G. Kearsley, 1777, 3 vols. (ill.). SOURCE Gecker, 387; Fraser 2, 1740. LOCATION L.
COMMENTARY Contents: 'Zayde' (by M. de Segrais), 'Oroonoko' (by Aphra Behn), 'The princess of Cleves' (by Elizabeth Griffith), 'The fruitless inquiry' (by Elizabeth Haywood) [Gecker, 387].

G182 *Novellettes, selected for the use of young ladies and gentlemen; written by Dr. Goldsmith, and Mrs. Griffith, &c. and illustrated by elegant engravings.*
+ London: Fielding & Walker, 1780 (ill.). SOURCE Raven 2, 1780:17; ESTC n005867. LOCATION L, IU.
Dublin: John Cash, 1784, 2 vols. SOURCE Raven 2, 1780:17; ESTC t131769. LOCATION D.
COMMENTARY First published in the *Westminster Magazine* (London). The preface states that the intention of the editors was to 'provide an useful instructor, in the habit of a pleasing companion, to the young of both sexes. No poisoning levity is concealed beneath the colouring of character ...' Unless indicated, the stories were written by Elizabeth Griffith. Contents: 'The unforced repentance', 'The dupe of love and friendship: or, the unfortunate Irishman', 'The triumph of constancy', 'The history of Louisa', 'The dangerous effects of a wrong education: or, the fatal contest', 'Story of Valmore and Julia', 'Story of Rosalie', 'Conjugal fidelity: or, female fortitude', 'Story of Lady Fanny Beaumont and Lord Layton', 'The story of Miss Williams', 'The story of Miss Warner', 'The story of Sir William Sidney', 'The story of the Comte De Bernis', 'Julia: or, the adventures of a curate's daughter' (Mr M'Millan), 'A register of Scotch marriages' (Dr [Oliver] Goldsmith§), 'The history of Cyrillo Padovano, the noted sleep-walker' (Dr [Oliver] Goldsmith§) [CM].

GRIFFITH, Richard, pseuds 'Henry', 'Automathes' and 'Biographer Triglyph', b. Dublin? *c.*1704, d. Naas (Co. Kildare) 1788. Novelist, playwright and letter writer, RG was the son of Edward Griffith and Abigail Handcock. Since he later lamented his lack of a liberal education, he is probably not the RG who was a scholar at TCD and graduated BA in 1721 and MA in 1724. RG farmed at Maiden Hall (Co. Kilkenny) and married Elizabeth Griffith§ in 1751 but had to keep the marriage a secret from his father for some time, so the couple lived in different locations: he at Maiden Hall, she in Abbey Street in Dublin and later in Chapelizod (Co. Dublin). With his wife he collaborated on several popular novels and, using their own correspondence, two popular epistolary novels written in the form of letters exchanged between lovers. RG also wrote poetry and a comedy, *Variety*, which was performed at Drury Lane, London, in 1782. He had met Laurence Sterne§ in 1767 and left a reminiscence of him in the final edn of *A series of letters*. This author should not be confused with a Richard Griffith who was a member of the Irish parliament and the author of political pamphlets. SOURCE Allibone, i, p. 742; Brady, p. 95; H. Butler, 'Henry and Frances' in *Jrnl of the Butler Society* 2, No. 1 (1980–81), pp 45–50; Field Day, i, pp 684, 686; Hogan 2, p. 504; *Ireland's Mirror: or, a Chronicle of the Times* (Dublin, 1805), p. 365; OCIL, pp 229–30; ODNB; O'Donoghue, p. 174; RIA/DIB [included in Elizabeth Griffith]; RL.

G183 *A series of genuine letters between Henry and Frances* [anon.; written with his wife Elizabeth Griffith§].
London: W. Johnston, 1757, vols. 1 and 2 (subscribers' list). SOURCE Raven 2, 1770:31; Forster, 1149; Gecker, 391 (3rd edn); ESTC t117316. LOCATION Dt (3rd edn, prob. printed in Dublin), L, MH.
London: W. Johnston, 1766, vols. 3 and 4. SOURCE Raven, 1013; Forster, 1150; ESTC t111107. LOCATION L, MH.

London: Richardson & Urquart, 1770, vols. 5 and 6. SOURCE Raven 2, 1770:31; Forster, 1151; ESTC t154222. LOCATION C.

London: W. Johnston, 1767, vol. 1 and 2 (revsd, corrected, and improved by the authors). SOURCE Raven, 1102; ESTC t111105. LOCATION L, MH.

Dublin: Printed for the authors by S. Powell, 1760, 2vols., 2nd edn (revsd, corrected and improved by the authors; subscribers' list). SOURCE Cole, p. 228; Raven 573; ESTC t111109. LOCATION L, MH.

Belfast: [publisher?], [*c*.1774]. SOURCE Anderson 2, p. 7. COMMENTARY *Belfast edn* No copy located [RL].

Leipzig, Berlin: [publisher?], 1770 (trans. as *Briefe zwischen Heinrich und Franziska*). SOURCE Raven 2, 1770:31

COMMENTARY No copy of the Leipzig edn located. Autobiographical, epistolary novel based on an exchange of letters between HG and Frances Griffith§ in which HG's doubts about commitment and fidelity are answered by Frances's ideas on female independence and the proper roles for women, particularly as wage-earners and intellectuals. In the first edn the Irish place names were changed to English place names, so it would have a more general appeal. The book created a literary sensation but not a fortune for the authors [Butler, p. 46; Field Day, v, pp 796–7; ODNB].

G184   *The triumvirate; or, the authentic memoirs of A[ndrew] B[eville] and C[arewe]* [anon.] (dedicated to the duke of Bedford, lord lieutenant of Ireland).

London: W. Johnston, 1764, 2 vols. (subscribers' list). SOURCE Raven, 841; Forster, 1155; Hardy, 444; Pickering & Chatto cat. 737/208; ESTC t077690. LOCATION D, L, NUC, MH.

Dublin: H. Saunders, [1764?]. SOURCE Raven, 842. COMMENTARY *Dublin Saunders edn* This edn known from advertisement only [Raven].

Dublin: J. Hoey, Snr, P. Wilson, J. Exshaw, S. Cotter, E. Watts, H. Saunders, W. Sleater, J. Potts, J. Hoey Jnr, J. Williams & J. Sheppard, 1765, 2 vols. (as *The triumvirate; or, the authentic memoirs of Andrews, Beville and Carewe*). SOURCE ESTC t212506; Dt, NUC.

COMMENTARY According to an inscription in a presentation copy at Cambridge University, the novel recounts the author's own life, and identifies the author of the poems and soliloquy as Elizabeth Griffith§. The preface is signed 'Biographer Triglyph'. An appendix refers to the works by Laurence Sterne§ [Quaritch cat. Spring 1997/35; Hardy].

G185   *Something new* [anon.] (preface signed 'Automathes').

London: Printed for the author, 1772 [*sic*, 1762], 2 vols. SOURCE Forster, 1154; Hardy, 443; McBurney & Taylor, 382; ESTC t100998; Quaritch cat. 1193/29. LOCATION IU.

London: E. & C. Dilly, 1762, 2nd edn, 2 vols. (revsd and corrected by the author). SOURCE Raven, 719; ESTC t069140. LOCATION L, YU.

COMMENTARY Written by RG only [RL].

G186   *Two novels: in letters ... In four volumes. The first and second, entitled, The delicate distress: a novel in letters, by Frances, the third and fourth, entitled, The Gordian knot, or dignus vindice nodus* (by 'Henry'; dedicated to the duke of Bedford).

+ London: T. Becket & P.A. de Hondt, 1769, 4 vols. SOURCE Raven, 1314; Forster, 1152; Hardy, 442; Gecker, 392; McBurney & Taylor, 381; ESTC n014241. LOCATION NUC, PU, MH, IU.

Dublin: P. Wilson, J. Exshaw, H. Saunders, W. Sleater, B. Grierson, D. Chamberlaine, J. Potts, J. Hoey, J. Williams, 1769, 4 vols. SOURCE ESTC n014239. LOCATION MH.

Dublin: T. Walker, 1775 (as *The delicate distress*). SOURCE Gecker, 388; ESTC n006231. LOCATION NUC, PU.

+ Dublin: United Company of Booksellers, 1787, 2 vols. (as *The delicate distress, a novel: in letters*). SOURCE Black, 498; ESTC n032594. LOCATION DPL, Dix coll.

London: T. Becket, 1769, 4 vols. SOURCE ESTC n14241. LOCATION D, L, CLU.

Londres [Paris]: n.p., 1770, 4 vols. (trans. by Anne François Joachim Fréville as *Le noeud Gordien*). SOURCE Streeter, 161, 170; ESTC n67929; Rochedieu, p. 132. LOCATION L, Univ. California, Los Angeles.

COMMENTARY Epistolary novels published at the instigation of Margaret, countess of Cork. 'Delicate distress' is by Elizabeth Griffith§. (The heroine, jilted by her unworthy lover, secretly bestows an annuity on him when he becomes impoverished. Eventually he learns the identity of his benefactor.) 'The Gordian knot' is by Richard Griffith. The latter, in contrast to the former novel, was not reprinted. C. Turner cites an eighteenth-century source stating that 'Delicate distress' was also published as two separate volumes, entitled *Delicate embarrassments* in London in 1769, but ESTC does not identify this title as by EG [Summers, p. 68; *Ireland's Mirror: or, a Chronicle of the Times* (Dublin,1805), p. 364; C. Turner, *Living by the pen* (London, 1992), pp 233–4; Marlborough cat. 176/145; Raven, 1262; RL; Todd, p. 299].

G187 *The posthumous works of a late celebrated genius, deceased* [contains] *The Koran; or, character, and sentiments of Tria Juncta in Uno, M.N.A. or Master of No Arts* [anon.] (dedicated to the earl of Charlemont).

London: Printed [for the author?] by W. & J. Robinson, 1770, 2 vols. SOURCE Forster, 1153; Raven 2: 1770:32; ESTC t044094. LOCATION L, MH.

+ Dublin: J. Exshaw, H. Saunders, W. Sleater, D. Chamberlaine, J. Potts, J. Williams & C. Ingham, 1770, 2 vols. in 1. SOURCE Raven 2, 1770:32; ESTC t120274. LOCATION Dt, InND Loeber coll.

Leipzig: Engelhart Benjamin Swickert, 1771, 3 parts in 1 (trans. as *Yoricks nachgelassne Werke*). SOURCE Burmester cat. 32/263; COPAC. Location C.

Hamburg: Heroldischen Buchhandlung, 1778 (trans. as *Der Koran oder leben under meynungen des tria juncta in uno*). SOURCE COPAC. LOCATION L.

+ Vienna: R. Sammer, 1798 (as *The Koran; or, essays, sentiments, characters, and callimachies of Tria Juncta in Uno, M.N.A. or Master of No Arts.*). LOCATION InND Loeber coll.

COMMENTARY This book was first ascribed to Laurence Sterne§. The first part is an autobiography, rambling, digressive, in the Sterne manner, and the second and third parts contain 359 maxims, called 'The Koran', usually citing famous thinkers or historical figures. Several of the aphorisms of the 'The Koran' were used by Goethe in the collection called *Aus Makariens Archiv* [Cole; L.M. Price, *The reception of English literature in Germany* (New York, 1968), p. 245].

GRIMSHAW, Beatrice Ethel (also known as **Beatrice Grimshaw**), b. Cloona House, Dunmurry (Co. Antrim), 1870, d. Bathurst (Australia) 1953. Short story and travel writer, novelist and adventurer, BEG was the daughter of William Grimshaw, a Belfast merchant, and Eleanor Newsam of Cork. She was educated in Ireland, France and at Bedford College, London, and early in her life was a convert to catholicism. Athletic, adventurous and intelligent, she became a sporting journalist for the *Irish Cyclist* (Dublin) and set a world record for women for a 24-hour bicycle road trip. She moved to London seeking independence and adventure. In 1893 she joined the *Social Review* (London) and wrote on books, the arts, employment for women, current topics, as well as publishing her own creative work: poems, dialogues and short stories. After publishing her first book, she devised an ingenious scheme of offering free newspaper publicity and good 'copy' to the shipping companies in exchange for free passage. Thus began the six-monthly voyages that took her 'between the magic lines of Cancer and Capricorn' to Fiji, the New Hebrides, the Solomon Islands, Papua New Guinea, Borneo, Java, and many other exotic and dangerous parts of the world. She was the first white woman to visit the great Sepik and Fly rivers in New Guinea. She published some 40 volumes of novels, short stories and travel books based on her experiences while living among the head-hunters and cannibals, whom she befriended. Some of her books became best-sellers in Australia, the US and England. While written for a popular market, her novels provide competent and useful information on the lives and attitudes of settlers in those parts of the world. Several of her novels were set in Ireland: *Broken away* (London, 1897), and 'A fool of forty', which was serialized in 1898 and 1899. She managed a plantation, and finally settled in Australia with her brothers Ramsay and Osborne, where she spent the last fourteen years of her life. She wrote an autobiography, *Isles of adventure: From Java to New Caledonia, but principally Papua* (London, 1930). SOURCE ADB, vol. 9; EF, pp 163–4; Hogan 2, pp 504–6; Krishnamurti, p. 54; OCIL, p. 230; RIA/DIB.

G188   *Broken away* (by Beatrice Grimshaw).
London: John Lane, 1897. SOURCE Krishnamurti, p. 54. LOCATION L, NUC.
COMMENTARY Serialized in 1895–96. Set in Ireland. Portrays Grimshaw's own circle, while casting a cynical eye on marriage [RIA/DIB].

G189   *Vaiti of the islands* (by Beatrice Grimshaw).
London: A.P. Watt & Son, [1906]. LOCATION L.
New York: A. Wessels, 1908. LOCATION NUC.

G190   *When the red gods call* (by Beatrice Grimshaw).
+ London: George Newnes, 1911. LOCATION L.
New York: Moffat, Yard & Co., 1911. LOCATION NUC.
COMMENTARY Set in British New Guinea [CM].

G191   *Guinea gold* (by Beatrice Grimshaw).
+ London: Mills & Boon, 1912. LOCATION L, NUC].
New York: Moffat, Yard & Co., 1912. LOCATION NUC.
COMMENTARY Set in New Guinea [CM].

G192   *The sorcerer's stone* (by Beatrice Grimshaw).
+ London, New York, Toronto: Hodder & Stoughton, 1914. LOCATION L.
Philadelphia: John C. Winston Co., [1914] (ill. Charles Sarka). LOCATION NUC.
COMMENTARY Set in New Guinea. The plot centres on an immense diamond belonging to a wizard. The story features an Australian narrator and his companion, a portly French anthropologist [EF, p. 163–63; CM].

G193   *Red Bob of the Bismarcks* (by Beatrice Grimshaw).
+ London: Hurst & Blackett, 1915. LOCATION NUC.
COMMENTARY The novel starts in Liverpool, after which the main characters relocate to Australia [CM].

G194   *My lady of the island; a tale of the South Seas* (by Beatrice Grimshaw).
Chicago: A.C. McClurg & Co., 1916 (ill. Harvey T. Dunn). LOCATION NUC.

G195   *Nobody's island* (by Beatrice Grimshaw).
+ London: Hurst & Blackett, 1917. LOCATION L, NUC.
Garden City NY: Doubleday, Page & Co., 1923. LOCATION NUC.
COMMENTARY Set in Ireland [CM].

G196   *Kris-girl* (by Beatrice Grimshaw).
+ London: Mills & Boon, [1917]. LOCATION L (1923 edn), NUC.

G197   *The coral queen* (by Beatrice Grimshaw).
New York: Federal Printing Co., 1917. SOURCE OCLC. LOCATION DCL, NUC.
Sydney: NSW Bookstall, 1923. SOURCE OCLC. LOCATION CLU.

+ London: George Newness, 1928. LOCATION L.
COMMENTARY Set in New Guinea [CM].

G198 *The terrible island* (by Beatrice Grimshaw).
New York: Ridgeway Co., [1919]. LOCATION NUC.
London: Hurst & Blackett, 1920. LOCATION L, NUC (1920, 2nd edn).

G199 *The coral palace: 'Twixt Capricorn and Cancer* (by Beatrice Grimshaw).
+ London: Mills & Boone, 1920. LOCATION L.
COMMENTARY Set in the South Sea islands [CM].

G200 *Queen Vaiti* (by Beatrice Grimshaw).
+ London: George Newness, [1921] (Newness Sevenpenny Novels). LOCATION L.
COMMENTARY Fictional adventures of an irresistible heroine, a half-caste, who takes what she wants in a man's world. No Irish content [RIA/DIB; CM].

G201 *My South Sea sweetheart. A novel* (by Beatrice Grimshaw).
+ London: Hurst & Blackett, 1921. LOCATION L.
New York: Macmillan, 1921. LOCATION NUC.
COMMENTARY Set in the South Sea islands [CM].

G202 *The little red speck, and other South Seas stories* (by Beatrice Grimshaw).
London: Hurst & Blackett, 1921. LOCATION NUC.
COMMENTARY Contents: 'The little red speck', 'Maddox and the Emma-pea', 'When the o.o. called', 'The bright Alaras', 'The day of the paw-paw tree', 'The brides of Tarabora', 'Through the back door', 'The shadow of the palm', 'Devil's gold', 'The beach of Vanalona', 'The man with the tail', 'Down to the sea' [NUC].

G203 *Conn of the coral seas* (by Beatrice Grimshaw).
New York: Macmillan Co., 1922. LOCATION NUC.
+ London: Hurst & Blackett, 1922. LOCATION L, NUC (n.d. edn).
COMMENTARY Set among the South Sea islands (New Cumberland Islands). Steve Conn, an Irishman, who has a TCD degree, is involved in scouting for treasures. He is a rough character but is on the right side of the law. Describes life in the islands and the trouble between France and England about possession of the various islands. The book has several other Irish characters [ML].

G204 *The valley of Never-Come-Back, and other stories* (by Beatrice Grimshaw).
+ London: Hurst & Blackett, 1923. LOCATION L, NUC.
COMMENTARY Set in Australia. Contents: 'The valley of Never-Come-Back', 'Lost wings', 'The island grave', 'Isles of peace', 'Under the Shwe-Dragon', 'The woman in the cage', 'Peak of the moon', 'Something lost', 'The long, long day' [NUC].

G205 *The sands of Oro* (by Beatrice Grimshaw).
+ London: Hurst & Blackett, 1924 LOCATION L.
Garden City (NY): Doubleday, Page & Co., 1924. LOCATION NUC.
COMMENTARY No Irish content [CM].

G206 *Helen of man o' war island* (by Beatrice Grimshaw).
London: Hurst & Blackett, 1924. SOURCE Hogan 2, p. 506.
COMMENTARY No copy located [RL].

G207 *The paradise poachers* (by Beatrice Grimshaw).
+ London: Hurst & Blackett, 1924. LOCATION L, NUC (n.d. edn).
COMMENTARY Set in New Guinea and based on the author's experiences as the first white woman to venture up the dangerous Sepik and Fly rivers in Papua-New Guinea [CM; RIA/DIB].

G208 *The candles of Katara* (by Beatrice Grimshaw).
London: Hurst & Blackett, 1925. LOCATION L, NUC.

COMMENTARY Short stories set in San Francisco (CA) and Queensland (Australia) [NUC].

G209　*The wreck of the 'Redwing'* (by Beatrice Grimshaw).
New York: Henry Holt & Co., 1926. LOCATION L (1927 edn). LOCATION NUC.
London: R. Hale, 1937. LOCATION L, NUC.

G210　*Eyes in the corner, and other stories* (by Beatrice Grimshaw).
+ London: Hurst & Blackett, 1927. LOCATION L, NUC.
COMMENTARY No Irish content [CM].

G211　*Black sheep's gold* (by Beatrice Grimshaw).
+ London: Hurst & Blackett, 1927. LOCATION L.
New York: H. Holt & Co., [1927]. LOCATION NUC.
COMMENTARY Set in Australia [CM].

G212　*My lady far-away* (by Beatrice Grimshaw).
+ London: Cassell & Co., [1929]. LOCATION L.

G213　*White savage Simon* (by Beatrice Grimshaw).
+ London: George Newness, 1929 (Newness Sixpenny Novels). LOCATION L.

G214　*The star in the dust* (by Beatrice Grimshaw).
London: Cassell & Co., 1930. LOCATION L, NUC.

G215　*The beach of terror, and other stories* (by Beatrice Grimshaw).
+ London: Cassell & Co., 1931. LOCATION L.
COMMENTARY Stories set in London, Toronto, Melbourne, Sydney, and Ireland. The Irish story is called 'Carry me out to sea' [CM].

G216　*The mystery of Tumbling Reef* (by Beatrice Grimshaw).
Boston, New York: Haughton Mifflin Co., 1932. LOCATION L, NUC.

G217　*The long beaches and other South Sea stories* (by Beatrice Grimshaw).
+ London: Cassell & Co., 1933. LOCATION L.
COMMENTARY. Set in the islands of the South Sea. Contents: 'The return of the pilot', 'Castle in the wood', 'Angel in the palms', 'Full fathom five', 'Ema, ema, e', 'Black Venus of Rubiana', 'Shane of the Sorrowful Islands', 'The long beaches', 'The Captain had a daughter' [CM].

G218　**void**

G219　*Victorian family Robinson. A novel* (by Beatrice Grimshaw).
+ London, Toronto, Melbourne, Sydney: Cassell & Co., 1934. LOCATION Dcc, NUC.
New York: Longmans, 1935. SOURCE OCLC. LOCATION NUC, CtY.

G220　*Pieces of gold and other South Sea stories* (by Beatrice Grimshaw).
+ London, Toronto, Melbourne, Sydney: Cassell & Co., 1935. LOCATION Dcc.

G221　*Rita Regina* (by Beatrice Grimshaw).
+ London: Herbert Jenkins, 1939. LOCATION L.
New York: Arcadia House, 1940. LOCATION NUC.

G222　*South Sea Sarah. Murder in paradise. Two complete novels* (by Beatrice Grimshaw).
Sydney: New Century Press, 1940. LOCATION NUC.

G223　*The lost child* (by Beatrice Grimshaw).
+ London: Herbert Jenkins, 1940. LOCATION L.
COMMENTARY Set on Thursday Island, Queensland (Australia) [CM].

G224　*The island Queen* (by Beatrice Grimshaw).
+ London: Vallency Press, 1945. LOCATION L.
COMMENTARY Set in London and on a cruise [CM].

GRIMSTONE, Mrs Leman. See **GRIMSTONE, Mrs Mary Leman.**

GRIMSTONE, Mrs Mary Leman (also known as **Mrs Leman Grimstone**), pseud. 'Oscar', b. probably Hamburg (Germany) *c.*1800, d. *c.*1851. Novelist, social reformer and women's rights activist, MLG was the daughter of an Englishman, Leman Thomas Rede, a playwright living in Germany to escape his debts. She began publishing in 1815 and in 1820 poetry under her pseudynom 'Oscar' appeared. Nothing is known about her husband but it is likely she was widowed young as she left for Van Diemen's Land (Tasmania, Australia) with her sister and brother-in-law in 1825 and remained there until 1829. There she wrote most of *A woman's love* (London, 1832, 2 vols.). Later in life she married a Scotsman, William Gillies, and continued her work for better education for women and children, reform of marriage, religious toleration and improvements in the lives of the working class. Her portrait was published in her novel *Louisa Egerton* (London, 1830). Only her works relating to Ireland are listed here. SOURCE BLC; ODNB O'Donoghue, p. 372.

G225 *The vision of Tara* (by 'Oscar').
+ London: Printed for the author, 1831. LOCATION D, Dt.
COMMENTARY 72pp. The narrator mourns the decline of Ireland and climbs a mountain to meet Liberty, Britannia and Hibernia, who discuss the fate of Ireland. Features Lennoc'o [Daniel O'Connell], and has several other names spelled backwards [ML].

G226 *Woman's love. A novel* (by Mrs Leman Grimstone).
+ London: Saunders & Otley, 1832, 3 vols. SOURCE Garside 2, 1832:39. LOCATION Corvey CME 3–628–47774–3, L.
COMMENTARY Set in England. Features characters with Irish names, such as Mrs Fitzarran, Lord Conway, and Lord Dromore, but is not set in Ireland. The novel makes a plea for the intellectual development of women [ML].

G227 *Character; or, Jew and gentile: A tale* (by Mrs Leman Grimstone).
London: Charles Fox, 1833. SOURCE Garside 2, 1833:30. LOCATION Corvey CME 3–628–44769–7, L.

G228 *Cleone. A tale of married life* (by Mrs Leman Grimstone).
+ London: Effingham Wilson, 1834, 2 vols. SOURCE ODNB; Garside 2, 1834:31; COPAC. LOCATION Corvey CME 3–628–47773–5, L, MH.
COMMENTARY Main character is an Irish-Italian from Munster named Felix Festus Connor, but most of the novel is set in Lancashire. The story deals with the impact of nationality on character [CM].

GRINDON, Maurice, fl. 1896. Fantasy fiction writer, MG was also the author of *Till the sun grows cold* (London, 1904). SOURCE RL.

G229 *Kathleen O'Leovan. A fantasy* (by Maurice Grindon; dedicated to 'my very old friend, W.H.D.').
+ London: Simpkin, Marshall, Hamilton, Kent & Co., 1896 (ill. John Fullwood). LOCATION D, L, NUC, InND Loeber coll.
COMMENTARY A story about an Englishman, Levan, who has corresponded with the Irish branch of his family, O'Leovan. Mr O'Leovan invites Mr Levan for a visit to his home, Castle Columba in Kilronan, near Carrick-on-Shannon (Co. Leitrim). Mr Levan has some mysterious experiences that are explained as the work of Kathleen, a relative of Mr O'Leovan, who is living in Castle Columba but has been kept away from the visitor because she is somewhat unusual. Once Levan and Kathleen do meet, they fall in love and become engaged. Kathleen is finishing a book, begun by her father, about the history of Ireland. When the book is finished, it seems her task in this world is done, and she dies. After her death, the book of

O'Leovan is never seen, but 'its truth and counsel [is impressed] on the hearts of the people'. The book ends with several prophetic statements about Ireland in 1950 [ML].

GROVES, Revd Edward. See **GROVES, Revd Edward Kelly**.

GROVES, Revd Edward Kelly (known as **Edward Groves**), b. Dublin *c*.1777. Minister, playwright and story writer for children, EKG was the son of James Groves, Esq. Admitted to TCD in 1790, he obtained his BA in 1794. His tragedy in verse 'The warden of Galway' was first produced on the stage in Dublin in 1831 and published in the next year. He was an ardent advocate of repeal of the Union. He was interested in linguistics, and was the author of *Summary of the history and statistics of Ireland* (n.l., 1836) prepared for the 7th edn of the *Encyclopædia Britannica*, and *The geography of Ireland* (Edinburgh, 1833), which was part of the English edn of Mate-Burn's *Universal geography*. He should not be confused with the novelist Edward Groves MA, DSc. SOURCE B & S, p. 350; COPAC; O'Donoghue, p. 174.

G230　*Stories from the history of Greece, from the earliest period to the final conquest by the Romans, adapted to the capacities of children* (by Edward Groves).
　　　Dublin: W.F. Wakeman, 1829–30, 2 vols (ill.). SOURCE O'Donoghue, p. 174; COPAC. LOCATION L.

GRUNDY, Bertha Jane. See **ADAMS, Bertha Jane**.

GUENOT, Charles, fl. 1863. French writer of fiction. SOURCE BLC.
G231　*Le Comte de Tyrone, ou l'Irlande et le protestantisme au xvie siècle* (by Charles Guenot).
　　　+ Tours: A. Mame & Co., 1863 (ill. Pontenier). SOURCE IBL, 16 (1928), p. 59. LOCATION L, NUC (1867 edn), InND Loeber coll.
　　　COMMENTARY Historical fiction. Concerns the rebellion of Hugh O'Neill, 2nd earl of Tyrone (1593–1603) [NUC].

GUERNSEY, Lucy Ellen, pseud. '**L.E.G.**', b. Rochester (NY) 1826, d. 1899. American novelist and writer on religion, according to the preface to *Irish Amy* (Philadelphia, 1854), LEG had taught in Ireland in the Spring of 1853 a sewing class for fourteen girls, ages 8 to 15 'taken indiscriminately from the streets'. In the US LEG published several books for Sunday schools and other pieces of fiction. SOURCE Allibone, i, p. 748; Allibone Suppl., i, p. 729; Burke, p. 305; NUC; RL; Wright, ii, pp 139–40 (list of novels).
G232　*Irish Amy* (by 'L.E.G.').
　　　+ Philadelphia: American Sunday-School Union, 1854 (ill.). SOURCE Burke, p. 305. LOCATION D.
　　　COMMENTARY According to the preface, the incidents in this tale 'are literally true' and were based on direct observation [RL].
G233　*Ready work for willing hands; or, the story of Comfort Allison* [anon.].
　　　+ Philadelphia, New York, Boston, Cincinnati, Louisville: American Sunday School Union, 1856 (ill.). LOCATION NUC (n.d edn), InND Loeber coll.
　　　London: T. Nelson & Sons, 1859 (as *Ready work for willing hands; or, the story of Edith Allison*). LOCATION L.
COMMENTARY Religious fiction, probably autobiographical, set in an undisclosed American city. The heroine is a Protestant young lady, who over the course of the story devotes herself more and more to Christian good works, including teaching a Sunday school, visiting the homes of her students, visiting the sick, giving sewing lessons, and teaching servants. The

recipients of these good works are mainly the Irish poor, among whom there was much drunkenness and ignorance [ML].

GUINEE, William B., fl. 1882, b. Buttevant (Co. Cork), d. Buttevant 1901. A journalist, novelist and translator, WG for many years was connected with the *Morning Advertiser* in London. He contributed short stories to various periodicals including the *Dublin Illustrated Annual*, the *Irish People* (New York) and *Tinsley's Magazine* (London). His translations of poems from Gaelic are included in contemporary anthologies. Some of his letters are among the Downey Papers (NLI, MS 10,021). SOURCE Irish pseudonyms; O'Donoghue, p. 175; RIA/DIB; RL.

G234 *Talbot's folly. A novel* (by William B. Guinee).
       London: Tinsley Bros, 1882, 3 vols. LOCATION L.
COMMENTARY Set in London. The main character is an English lawyer, Tablot Welbore, and the novel features Delaney Morgan Doherty, MP, member for Kilruddery in Ireland, whose daughter is wooed by Welbore [RL].

GUNN, Archibald, fl. 1871. Writer and teacher, AG lived in Wolverhampton (West Midlands) and is identified in Halkett and Laing. According to the title page of the following book, he also wrote 'More blunder nor one' and 'Paddy's letters', but these have not been located. SOURCE Halkett & Laing, i, p. 177; RL; COPAC.

G235 *Barney O'Toole's comic letters to his mother in Ireland on his journey to, and adventures in, London. Including his notions on passing events of the day, and some witty criticisms on the exhibition of the Royal Academy of Arts* [anon.].
       + London: Simpkin, Marshall & Co., 1871. SOURCE Topp 8, 337; COPAC. LOCATION Dt, L.

GUNN, Revd John, fl. 1890.
G236 *A casket of Irish pearls, being subjects in prose and verse, chiefly relating to Ireland* (by the Revd John Gunn).
       Dublin: M.H. Gill & Son, 1890. SOURCE O'Donoghue, p. 175; COPAC. LOCATION L.
COMMENTARY Listed as fiction in the BL cat., but also contains poetry [RL].

GUNNING, Miss —. See **PLUNKETT, Mrs Elizabeth.**

GUNNING, Elizabeth. See **PLUNKETT, Mrs Elizabeth.**

GWYNN, Stephen. See **GWYNN, Stephen Lucius.**

GWYNN, Stephen Lucius (known as **Stephen Gwynn**), b. Rathfarnham (Co. Dublin; not in Co. Donegal as in Brady and Brown) 1864, d. Dublin 1950. Scholar, soldier, politician and man of letters, SLG was the son of Revd John Gwynn and Lucy, daughter of the nationalist politician William Smith O'Brien. His early years were spent in Co. Donegal, where his father was parson in Ramelton. He was educated at St Columba's College, Rathfarnham (where his father was warden) and later at Brasenose College, Oxford, where he graduated with a first in classics in 1886. He taught classics, after which he went to London in 1896 to work as a journalist and writer. In 1904 he was secretary of the Irish Literary Society in London. He joined the Gaelic League and was a friend of William Butler Yeats§ and H.G. Wells. In 1904 he returned to Ireland and entered politics. As a supporter of John Redmond and constitutional nationalism, he published articles in favour of Home Rule. He was elected a member of the

Irish Party and nationalist MP for Galway City from 1906 to 1918. In World War I, although over 50 years old, he served in France with the Connaught Rangers, fought at the Somme and Messines, and was later awarded the *Légion d'Honneur*. After losing his seat in the election of 1918, he devoted the rest of his life to writing poetry, novels, sketches, stories, essays, books on fishing, guidebooks to Ireland, works on politics, and biographies of Oliver Goldsmith§, Thomas Moore§, Sir Walter Scott, Jonathan Swift§, Robert Louis Stevenson, his aunt, Charlotte Grace O'Brien§, and others. He was a prolific editor and an authority on the eighteenth century. He wrote *The decay of sensibility, and other essays and sketches* (London, 1900), *Irish books and Irish people* (Dublin, [1919]), a *History of Ireland* (London, Dublin 1923), and an autobiography *Experiences of a literary man* (London, 1926). His *Irish literature and drama in the English language* (London, 1936) is considered a pioneering work. SLG was awarded a DLitt from the NUI in 1941 and one from Dublin University in 1945. His wife, Mary Louisa Gwynn, was his first cousin and in 1904 she published *Stories from Irish history told for children*. For his portraits and papers, see ODNB. SOURCE Boylan, p. 141; Brady, pp 96–7; Brown, p. 124; Burke's, pp 533, 535; Donegal, p. 104; J. Foster (ed.), *Alumni Oxonienses, 1715–1886* (Oxford, 1888), ii, p. 580; Hogan 2, pp 509–10; Irish pseudonyms; OCIL, pp 231–2; ODNB; O'Donoghue, p. 176; E. Reilly, p. 245; RIA/DIB; Zimmermann, p. 321.

G237   *The repentance of a private secretary* (by Stephen Gwynn).
+ London: John Lane, 1899. SOURCE Hogan, p. 280 (1898 edn). LOCATION Dt, D, L, NUC.
COMMENTARY Partially set in Ireland. A love story with misunderstandings. The erstwhile lover is asked to become the godfather of the child of his former lover [ML].

G238   *The old knowledge* (by Stephen Gwynn; dedicated to Mabel Dearmer).
London: Macmillan & Co., 1901. SOURCE NYPL; COPAC. LOCATION NN, L, NUC.
+ New York, London: Macmillan & Co., 1901. LOCATION D.

G239   *John Maxwell's marriage* (by Stephen Gwynn).
+ London, New York: Macmillan & Co., 1903. SOURCE Hogan, p. 280; COPAC. LOCATION D, L.

G240   *The glade in the forest and other stories* (by Stephen Gwynn).
+ Dublin: Maunsel & Co., 1907. SOURCE OCLC. LOCATION D, L, NUC.
COMMENTARY Contents: 'The glade in the forest', 'Splendide Mendax', 'Cross purposes', 'The grip of the land', 'A reconciliation', 'St. Brigid's flood', 'A Sunday at Annaghmore' [ML].

G241   *Robert Emmet. A historical romance* (by Stephen Gwynn).
+ London: Macmillan & Co., 1909. SOURCE Hogan, p. 280. LOCATION D, L, NUC.
COMMENTARY Historical fiction featuring Robert Emmet [RL].

G242   *Garden wisdom; or, from one generation to another* (by Stephen Gwynn).
+ Dublin: Talbot Press; London: T. Fisher Unwin, 1921 (ill. Grace Henry). SOURCE COPAC. LOCATION L, NUC.

H

'H., A.D.', fl. 1854. Pseudonym of a writer of religious fiction for juveniles who, given the content of some of his or her stories, was probably Irish [RL].

H1　*True stories for Sunday-school children* (by 'A.D.H.').
Dublin: Samuel B. Oldham, 1854. LOCATION L (destroyed).
London: L. Seeleys, 1854. LOCATION O.
COMMENTARY No copy of the Dublin edn located. Religious fiction for children, including some poetry. Some of the stories are connected to Ireland. Contents: 'Do you go to Sunday school?', 'A short account of Elizabeth P—', 'Poor little Billy' (set in a village in post-Famine Ireland), 'The ragged school child and the dust man', 'The happy old man. A Canadian story' (anti-Catholic story), 'Saint Patrick' (sets out to prove that St Patrick was not a Catholic), 'Conclusion' [CM].

'H., A.M.', pseud. See HALL, Mrs S.C.

'H., C.F.', pseud. See ALEXANDER, Cecil Frances.

'H., C.G.', pseud. See HAMILTON, C.G.

'H., E.', pseud. See HARDY, Elizabeth.

'H., E.E.', pseud. See HORNIBROOK, Emma E.

'H., G.C.', pseud. See CURRAN, Henry Grattan.

'H., K.', pseud. See HEAD, Katherine.

'H., M.J.', pseud. See HANNAN, Miss Josephine.

'H., P.D.' probable pseud. See HARDY, Philip Dixon.

'H., R., A.B., T.C.D.', fl. 1740s. Pseudonym, perhaps of a clergyman educated at TCD, who may have been a member of the Hayman family since Alderman Samuel Hayman was among the subscribers to the following novel, buying three copies. Most of the subscribers were from Co. Cork, which probably was the author's place of origin. In the preface he states that he wrote the novel when unemployed 'for some Time past', which indicates that he most likely belonged to the middle class. SOURCE RL.

H2　*"Camillo". A novel. Calculated chiefly to expose vice and debauchery, and to espouse the lost interest of virtue and good sense* (by 'R.H.', A.B., T.C.D.').
+ Cork: Printed [for the author?] by Thomas Cumming, [1745?] (subscribers' list).
SOURCE ESTC t071887; *Jrnl of the Cork Historical & Archaeological Society*, 9 (1903), p. 99. LOCATION L.

'H., W.', pseud. Preface writer. See STERNE, Laurence.

'H., W.E.', fl. 1865. Pseudonym, possibly of an Irish author given that the only edn of this book was published in Dublin. SOURCE RL.

H3   *Scenes in the life of a planter's daughter. Fact = 25 percent; Fiction 75 percent.*
Names imaginary (by 'W.E.H.').
+ Dublin: George Herbert, 1865. LOCATION L, O.
COMMENTARY Set in Florida and New Orleans. No Irish content. There is a possibility that this is a reprint of an American original, but an earlier edn has not been located [CM; RL].

'H., W.H.' pseud. See HAMILTON, W.H.

HACKETT, Mary, fl. 1850s. Novelist, MH also translated *Josephine, a tale for young ladies. From the French* (Dublin, 1852), and Count Montalembert's *Life of St. Elizabeth, Queen of Hungary* (New York, 1854). SOURCE TCD cat.
H4   *Helena; or, hopes deceived* (by Mary Hackett).
Dublin: James Duffy, [1857 or earlier] (Duffy's Cottage Library). SOURCE Adv. in [anon.], *The young crusader* (Dublin, James Duffy, [1857]).
COMMENTARY No copy located [RL].

HALIBURTON, Thomas Chandler, b. Windsor (NS, Canada) 1796, d. Isleworth (Middx.) 1865. Canadian jurist, journalist, satirist and history writer, TCH was the son of William Otis Haliburton, a judge in the court of common pleas in Nova Scotia, and Lucy Grant, He was educated in Nova Scotia and called to the Bar there, eventually becoming a judge in the supreme court of Nova Scotia in 1842. He was popularly known as Sam Slick, and in 1835 he began to contribute sketches to a weekly newspaper that later were collected in *The clock-maker, or, the sayings and doings of Sam Slick of Slickville* (Philadelphia, 1838). In 1842 he visited England as an attaché of the American Legation and his observations were collected in *The attaché, or Sam Slick in England* (London, 1843). In 1856 he resigned his office and moved to England, becoming MP for Launceston (1859–65). He wrote also on Canada and Nova Scotia and on English rule in America. In 1889 'The Haliburton', a society to promote a distinctive Canadian literature, was established at King's College, Windsor. Its first publication was a memoir of TCH by F. Blake Crofton (1889). SOURCE Allibone, i, p. 760; Allibone Suppl., ii, p. 742; DCB; DLB, ic; ODNB; Sutherland, p. 270.
H5   *The season-ticket* [anon.] (dedicated to Cheyne Brady of Dublin).
+ London: Richard Bentley, 1860. LOCATION D, L.
London, New York: F. Warne, [18–] (new edn; Companion Library). LOCATION NUC.
COMMENTARY According to an advertisement and to the ODNB, these sketches first appeared in the *Dublin University Magazine*. They are supposedly from the journal of the narrator, Squire Shehog, who travels by train from London to Southampton on a season ticket. One of the central characters is Cary, an Irishman with whom the narrator discusses many contemporary topics. Contents: 'An evening at Cork', 'Walks, talks, and chalks', 'Homeward bound', '"A train of thought, and thoughts in a train"', 'John Bull and diggins', 'Black jobs and white favours', 'A gallimaufry', 'Our neighbours and distant relations', 'The living and the dead', 'The old and the new year; or, Quakers afloat and ashore', 'Colonial and matrimonial alliance', 'Big wigs' [RL; ODNB].

HALL, A.D. See HALL, Arthur Dudley.

HALL, Arthur Dudley (known as A.D. Hall), fl. 1885. American author, ADH adapted several plays into novels and translated several French romances. SOURCE Adv. in *Lady Clancarty*, Chicago, 1890; Allibone Suppl. ii, p. 742; Wright, iii, 2397–8.
H6   *Lady Clancarty; or, wedded and wooed* (by A.D. Hall).

+ Chicago, New York: Rand, McNally & Co., 1890 (Globe Library, vol. 1, No. 115).
LOCATION NUC, InND Loeber coll.
COMMENTARY Historical fiction based on Tom Taylor's play of the same name (London, 1877) and set in London at the end of the seventeenth century. Muriel, Lady Clancarty, had been married to her husband when only twelve as her father thought that the earl of Clancarty would be a good match because of his extensive estate in Munster. The bride and groom were separated at the church door. Soon after, the earl of Clancarty threw in his lot with James II and consequently lost his estate and had to flee to France. In disguise, he returns to England to further the Jacobite cause and to make contact again with his wife. The Jacobites want him to be involved in a plot to murder King William III. Clancarty finds the plot too ungentlemanlike and warns the king of the impending danger. Clancarty is caught and may face the death penalty, but his wife pleads for his life before the king, who gives him his freedom and a pension to live in Germany [ML].

HALL, E., fl. 1875. Regional fiction writer.
H7 *Munster firesides; or, the Barrys of Beigh* (by E. Hall).
+ Dublin: McGlashan & Gill, 1875. SOURCE Allibone Suppl. ii, p. 743; Brown, 685.
LOCATION D, InND Loeber coll.
COMMENTARY Set in the second half of the eighteenth century on the banks of the Shannon in Co. Clare, twenty miles south of Limerick, this story is about a number of young people who are left to grow up with little parental guidance. They live eccentric lives on estates in varying degrees of decay. Some of the characters have connections with the insurgent groups of the time. One is tried for murder but at the last moment word comes that the supposed victim is alive [ML].

HALL, Mrs S.C. See HALL, Mrs Samuel Carter.

HALL, Mr Samuel Carter. Co-author. See HALL, Mrs Samuel Carter.

HALL, Mrs Samuel Carter (née Anna Maria Fielding; known as Mrs S.C. Hall), pseud. 'A.M.H.', b. Anne Street, Dublin 1800, d. Devon Lodge, East Molesey (Surrey) 1881. A prolific and popular writer, editor and philanthropist, Mrs SCH was of Huguenot extraction on her mother's side of the family. Her father died soon after her birth and she and her mother lived for most of her first fifteen years at Graige House, Bannow (Co. Wexford), the estate of her mother's stepfather, George Carr. The surrounding provided much autobiographical material for her later stories. In 1815 she and her mother went to live in London, where in 1824 she married Samuel Carter Hall, Wexford-born parliamentary reporter for the house of lords and a prolific writer, editor and publisher. In later life she recalled her first publication as the short story 'Master Ben', based on a Co. Wexford schoolteacher, which appeared in *Spirit and manners of the age* (London, 1829). M. Keane points out, however, that two small stories had appeared previously in the *Amulet* (London), the magazine founded and edited by her husband. 'Master Ben' and subsequent stories were gathered into *Sketches of Irish character* (London, 1829), which was followed by a second series in 1831. The *Ladies Pocket Magazine* dedicated the second part of its London, 1833 edn to Mrs SCH, specifically mentioning her 'inimitable Sketches of Irish character'. Mrs SCH took pains to point out that her stories were mainly of peasants who were descended from 'Anglo-Norman settlers' who retained much of their English character, in contrast to Irish peasants who needed moral and practical guidance to improve their lives. At this time her husband was also editing the London *New Monthly Magazine* and she contributed to it. Rare for an Irish writer living in England, she published in Dublin periodicals in the 1830s and early 1840s, including the *Dublin Literary Gazette* (Dublin, 1830), the *Irish Penny Magazine* (Dublin, 1833), the *Dublin University Magazine* (1838), and the *Dublin Penny Journal* (Dublin, 1840). Over a period of ten years she was the editor of the Christmas annual *Juvenile Forget-Me-Not* (London, 1829–37); editor of *Sharpe's London Magazine* (1852–3), and editor of *St. James's Magazine* (London, 1861–68). She also contributed to several annuals, including *Friendship's Offering* (London, 1830–31, 1844), the *Pearl* (Liverpool, [1840?]), the *Keepsake* (London, 1845), and the *Magnet Stories* (London, 1850s onward). In addition, she contributed to *Characteristic sketches of Ireland and the Irish by Carleton§, Lover§, and Mrs. Hall* (ed. by Philip Hardy§, Dublin, 1840) and with her husband published the *Hand-books for Ireland* (Dublin, 1853, 4 vols.) and *Ireland, its scenery, character, etc.* (London, 1841–3, 3 vols.) which gave much useful advice for the traveller. The Halls' joint travel books also include *A week at Killarney* (London, 1843) and *A companion to Killarney* ([London], 1878). Mrs SCH and her husband had a literary salon in London where they entertained writers such as William Wordsworth, Charles Lamb, Samuel Taylor Coleridge and Thomas Moore§ and handled the delicate matter of visiting the countess of Blessington§ by having Mrs SCH confine herself to daytime calls, while Mr Hall attended the countess's evening events. Mrs SCH probably knew Selina Bunbury§ since she contributed a story, *The last in the lease* (published earlier), to a benefit volume for Bunbury (*Seven tales by seven authors*, edited by Frank Smedley, London, 1849). She acknowledged that the story had been told to her by 'Martin Doyle', the pseudonym of Revd William Hickey§, who was a Co. Wexford author and a personal friend. Genuinely and practically philanthropic, she donated much of her literary profits to charitable causes related to women and was instrumental in setting up the Hospital for Consumption at Brompton and the London Home for Decayed Gentlewomen. She also participated in temperance campaigns, supported woman's rights while upholding traditional views of marriage, and while remaining a devout Christian, had a deep belief in spiritualism. She revisited Ireland five times between 1825 and 1841 and again before 1865. At one point she stopped at Edgeworthstown to visit Maria Edgeworth§, to whom Mrs SCH acknowledged a great debt for her pioneering work in writing about Ireland and the Irish. Aside from novels, she wrote for children, contributed to the tract literature (but the sponsoring society is not known), and wrote plays and burlettas. She adapted her story 'The groves of Blarney' for the stage and it had a successful year-long run at the Adelphi Theatre in London with William Tyrone Power§ in the cast. She extensively edited or provided introductions for books, such as *The adventures and experiences of Biddy Dorking* (London, 1859). After her death, her husband estimated that she had written 150 books, but this may be an overestimate. M. Keane mentions the number of joint publications as 400, and Colman 500 volumes, which needs verification. What is certain is that Mrs SCH was a full-time professional writer. Among her surviving manuscripts is 'The curse of property. A tale/sketch of Irish mismanagement', now in the NLI, a story included in *Tales of woman's trials*, and her 'Waking dreams' is in the Henry E. Huntington Library, San Marino (CA). Some of her letters are in the PRONI (MS D/2922) and at Iowa State University. Her portrait was published in *The forlorn hope* (London, [1846]), while an oil painting of her is in the NGI. There are several other known portraits (e.g., by William Brocas in the NLI, No. 2127[TX]9; see also engraved portraits listed by Elmes, and ODNB). SOURCE Allibone i, p. 767; Allibone Suppl., ii, p. 742; Blain, pp 475–6; Boylan, p. 142; Browne, pp 63–4; Colman, pp 82–5 [under Fielding]; Clyde, p. 88; *Jrnl of the Cork Historical & Archaeological Society*, 85 (1980), p. 70; de Búrca cat. 37/552 and cat. 73/14 (three letters by Mrs SCH); Elmes, p. 91; Field Day, v, pp 516–17, 528–9, 836, 846–8; S.C. Hall, *Rhymes in council* (London, 1881, [introd., n.p.]); W.E. Hall, p. 65; Hogan, p. 284; Hogan 2, pp 516–17; *Illustrated Celtic Monthly* (New York, 1879), pp 83–4; Jarndyce cat. 162/492, 510, 556, 572, 598; M. Keane, *Mrs. S.C. Hall. A lit-*

erary biography (Gerrards Cross, 1997); Law, p. 155; McKenna, pp 192–3; R. Ormond, *Daniel Maclise, 1806–1870*, ([London], 1972), p. 30; NCBEL 4, pp 1304–6; preface to *Nelly Nowlan* (London, 1865), p. iv; NUC; OCIL pp 234–5; ODNB; O'Donoghue, p. 178; RIA/DIB; Rowe & Scallan, 505; Schulz, p. 273; J. Shattock, *The Oxford guide to British women writers* (Oxford, 1993); Sutherland, pp 270–1; *Transactions of the Kilkenny Archaeological Society*, i (1849–51), pp 201–2; Todd, pp 307–9; R.L. Wolff , introd. to Mrs Samuel Carter Hall, *Sketches of Irish character* (New York, 1979).

H8   *"Do you think I'd inform?": an Irish tale* (by Mrs S.C. Hall).
+ Edinburgh: [Chambers Miscellany of Useful and Entertaining Tracts], n.d. (Tract, No. 129). LOCATION PC, NUC.
COMMENTARY 32pp.

H9   *Sketches of Irish character* [first series] (by Mrs S.C. Hall; dedicated to Miss [Mary Russell] Mitford§).
+ London: Frederick Westley & A.H. Davis, 1829, 2 vols. SOURCE Rafroidi, ii, p. 181; Brown, 686; British Fiction; Garside, 1829:43; Wolff, 2923; Bradshaw, 7923. LOCATION Grail, Corvey CME 3-628-51029, Ireland related fiction, Dt, DPL (1831, 2nd edn), L, C, NUC.
London: Frederick Westley & A.H. Davis, 1831, 2nd edn (contains additional 21pp article on Bannow parish by Dr Robert Walsh). SOURCE Rowan cat. 59A/380; COPAC. LOCATION L.
+ London: John Camden Hotten, n.d. (dedicated to Francis Bennoch; author's preface to the 3rd edn, and to the 5th edn; ill. Daniel Maclise, John Gilbert, W. Harvey, G. Cruikshank, J.R. Herbert, W. Evans, R.B. McIan, W.H. Brooke, J.C. Trimbell, C.H. Weigall, J. Franklin, A. Nicholl, H.J. Townsend, H. McManus, Fanny McIan, J. Crowley, H. O'Neil, G.F. Sargent, Robinson, Walmsley, Linton, Cook, Delamotte, Landells, Cook, Smith, Gilks, Jackson, Bastin, Mason, Green, Armstrong, Sly, Slader, Wakefield, Whimper, Thompson). LOCATION InND Loeber coll.
+ New York: Printed by J. & J. Harper, 1829. LOCATION NUC, InND Loeber coll.
Philadelphia: J.W. Moore, 1853 (ill.). SOURCE Bologna cat. 4/268. LOCATION PC.
New York: Garland, 1979, 2 vols. (introd. by R.L. Wolff). SOURCE COPAC. LOCATION Dt.
COMMENTARY No copy of the Philadelphia edn located. Maria Edgeworth§ thought the book was 'touching – simple – beautiful & true Irish'. Stories about the inhabitants of the village of Bannow (Co. Wexford) originally published in magazines, and modelled on Mary Russell Mitford's§ series, *Our village* (London, 1824–32, 5 vols.). Contents: 'Lilly O'Brien', 'Kelly the piper', 'Captain Andy', 'Independence', 'Black Dennis', 'Old Frank', 'The Bannow postman', 'Father Mike' (based on the experience of Mrs Hall's grandmother, who had been saved by a priest during the rebellion of 1798), 'Master Ben' (based on a Wexford school teacher who had taught Mrs Hall when young), 'Hospitality', 'Peter the prophet' [RL; Butler, p. 456; M. Keane, pp 4–5, 19; Personal communication, Jacqueline Belanger, Mar. 2005].

H10   *Chronicles of a school room* (by Mrs S.C. Hall; dedicated to Mrs Hofland).
+ London: Frederick Westley & A.H. Davis, 1830. SOURCE Rafroidi, ii, p. 181. LOCATION L, NUC.
Boston: Cottons & Barnard, 1830. LOCATION NUC.
COMMENTARY Fiction for juveniles, reviewed in the *Dublin Literary Gazette* (1830, p. 274). Seven stories set in a village where Mrs Ashburton is the former schoolmistress and chronicles the lives of her pupils. Contents: 'Marie de Jariot', 'Millicent O'Brian', 'Sweet May Douglas', 'The two Indians', 'The painter's sister', 'Zillah Penrose', 'The deaf and blind' [RL].

H11   *Sketches of Irish character* (second series; by Mrs S.C. Hall; dedicated to Miss [Maria] Edgeworth§).

+ London: Frederick Westley & A.H. Davis, 1831. SOURCE NCBEL 4, p. 1305; Rafroidi, ii, p. 181; Garside 2, 1831:35. LOCATION Grail, DPL, L, InND Loeber coll.

New York, Philadelphia: E. Ferrett & Co., 1846. SOURCE NYPL. LOCATION NN.

COMMENTARY Stories about the inhabitants of the village of Bannow (Co. Wexford). Contents: 'Mabel O'Neil's curse', 'Annie Leslie' (first published in *The Amulet*, London, 1830), 'The rapparee', 'Norah Clary's wise thought', 'Kate Connor', 'We'll see about it', 'Jack the shrimp', 'Irish settlers in an English village', 'Mark Connor's wooing and wedding', 'Luke O'Brian', 'Larry Moore' (first published in *Friendship's Offering*, London, 1830), 'Mary MacGoharty's petition', 'The last of the line' [ML; Field Day, v, p. 886*n* ('We'll see about it'); RL].

H12   *The buccaneer. A tale* [anon.].

London: Richard Bentley, 1832, 3 vols. SOURCE NCBEL 4, p. 1305; Rafroidi, ii, p. 181; Sadleir, 1096; Wolff, 2912; Garside 2, 1832:40. LOCATION Corvey, CME 3-628-47330-6, L, NUC.

+ London: Richard Bentley; Edinburgh: Bell & Bratfute; Dublin: J. Cumming, 1840 (revised edn; ill. J. Cowse, W. Greatbatch; Bentley's Standard Novels, No. 79). LOCATION D.

Haarlem: A.C. Kruseman, 1848, 2 vols. (trans. into Dutch as *Hugh Dalton, de vrijbuiter onder Cromwell's regering*). SOURCE Alphabetische naamlijst 1833–49, p. 258. LOCATION UVA.

Philadelphia: Carey, Lea & Blanchard, 1833, 2 volumes in 1. SOURCE Kaser, 362. LOCATION MH.

COMMENTARY First edn had a print run of 1,000 copies. Historical fiction, set in England in Cromwellian times, the action takes place mainly on an island off the coast of Kent and deals with the conflicts between the Royalists and the Cromwellians. The story has many Gothic features such as a buccaneer, dark caves, people with false names, and a property owner masquerading under false pretences. Oliver Cromwell appears in the story [ML; Garside].

H13   *The outlaw* [anon.].

London: Richard Bentley, 1835, 3 vols. SOURCE Brown 2, 580; NCBEL 4, p. 1305; Rafroidi, ii, p. 181; Garside 2, 1835:52. LOCATION Dt, C, L, NUC.

+ London: Richard Bentley; Edinburgh: Bell & Bradfute; Dublin: Cumming & Ferguson, 1847 (Standard Novels Library, No. 105, ill. J. Cawse). LOCATION D, L, InND Loeber coll.

New York: Harper & Bros, 1835, 2 vols. SOURCE NYPL. LOCATION NUC, NN.

COMMENTARY First edn issued in a print run of 1,000. An historical romance set in England in the time of James II and William and Mary. Most of the characters are English. The plot revolves around the mistaken identity of a girl known by the name of Rosalind Sydney who is brought up in the household of her uncle, Sir Everard Sydney. Her Irish nurse, Alice Murrough, plays a noteworthy part in the story. Rosalind is supposed to be the illegitimate daughter of her uncle's brother. She falls in love with his nephew. However, there is saying in the family that if a Sydney were to marry a person of illegitimate birth, their fortunes would fall. In the end, nurse Murrough admits that she had switched babies and Rosalind is not illegitimate after all but comes from good Irish stock and so can marry the man of her choice [ML; Garside].

H14   *Tales of woman's trials* (by Mrs S.C. Hall; dedicated to the marchioness of Lansdowne).

+ London: Houlston & Son, 1835. SOURCE Rafroidi, ii, p. 182; COPAC; Garside 2, 1835:53. LOCATION Dt, D (London, Warne 1890 edn), L, InND Loeber coll. (London, Chapman, 1847 edn).

New York: Wallis & Newell, 1835 (Franklin Library Edition). SOURCE NYPL. LOCATION NUC, NN, InND Loeber coll. (New York, Harper 1847 edn).

+ Hartford (CT): Silas Andrus & Son, 1846 (Franklin Library Edition). LOCATION InND Loeber coll.

COMMENTARY Contents: 'The wife of two husbands: The trials of Marian Raymond' (set in Ireland), 'The old maid: The trials of Millicent Morrison', 'The struggle: The trials of Grace Huntley' (first published in the *Amulet*, London), 'The mother: The trials of Lady Elizabeth Montague', 'The mosspits: The trials of Agnes Hoskins' (first published in the *Amulet*, London), 'The merchant's daughter: The trials of Margaret Sunderland' (first published in the *New Monthly Magazine*, London; this version enlarged), 'Lost beauty: The trials of Lady Leslie' (set in Ireland; first published in the *Amulet*), 'The curse of property: The trials of Alice Lee', 'The visionary: The trials of Delphine Barrington.' The play, *The trials of Grace Huntley; or, the struggles of poverty and crime*, performed in London in 1843, was based on 'The struggle'. The New York edn has slightly different contents [RL; Bolton, p. 213; Field Day, v, pp 836, 848, 884–93 ('The curse of property ...'); M. Keane, pp 8–9].

H15   *Harry O'Reardon; or, illustrations of Irish pride* (by Mrs S.C. Hall).

+ Philadelphia: E.L. Carey & A. Hart, 1836. LOCATION Grail, D, NUC.

COMMENTARY A story set in Dublin, London and Liverpool that examines the consequences of foolish pride. It features a young Irishman, Harry O'Reardon, who is poor, but too proud of his family ancestry to take up menial work. He is unable to take advantage of the help given to him, drifts into crime, and dies in prison [M. Keane, p. 84, 106].

H16   *The juvenile budget: or, stories for little readers. Chiefly collected from the "Juvenile Forget-me-not"* (by Mrs S.C. Hall).

+ London: Chapman & Hall, 1837 (dedicated to Miss Grogan Morgan of Johnstown Castle, Co. Wexford; ill. H.K. Browne [Phiz]). SOURCE Block, p. 94. LOCATION L (1840 edn), InND Loeber coll.

COMMENTARY Moral stories for children, mostly first published in the *Juvenile Forget-Me-Not* (London), of which Mrs SCH was the editor from 1829 to 1837. In the dedication she states, 'I love little children dearly, and I never wrote a tale for their amusement, without thinking of their improvement, and endeavouring to promote it, by all means in my power'. Contents: 'Dummy', '"I was born so, mother"', 'Seven and seventeen', 'The star', 'The Savoyards', 'Little ears', 'Gaspard and his dog', 'Passages in the lives of Jenny Careless and Jane Careful', 'The young rebel', 'The Irish cabin', 'Holiday time', 'The "not" family (A letter to Miss Mary Cunningham when she was a very little girl)', 'An English farm-yard', 'The young card-play-ers', 'Madelon', 'Irish Jerry' (first published in the *Pearl*, Liverpool, [*c*.1840]), 'Papa's letter', 'The Savoyards' [*sic*, although the title of this story is repeated (see above), its contents are different], 'The gipsy girl', '"Cast thy bread upon the waters"', 'The "good" family' [RL; M. Keane, p. 23].

H17   *Uncle Horace. A novel* [anon.].

London: H. Colburn, 1837, 3 vols. SOURCE NCBEL 4, p. 1305; Rafroidi, ii, p. 182; Wolff, 2924. LOCATION L, NUC.

Philadelphia: E.L. Carey & A. Hart, 1838, 2 vols. SOURCE NYPL. LOCATION NN, NUC.

COMMENTARY Set in contemporary England. A story with a high moral tone about middle-class life [M. Keane, p. 76].

H18   *Lights and shadows of Irish life* (by Mrs S.C. Hall; dedicated to Mrs Grogan Morgan).

+ London: Henry Colburn, 1838, 3 vols. SOURCE Brown, 687; Rafroidi, ii, p. 182; Wolff, 2913. LOCATION Grail, D, L, NUC, InND Loeber coll.

Philadelphia: Carey, Lea & Blanchard, 1838, 2 vols. SOURCE Kaser, 933. LOCATION NUC, CtY.

New York: Garland, 1979, 3 vols. (introd. by R.L. Wolff). LOCATION Dt.

COMMENTARY In the introd. Mrs SCH says that most of the stories 'have already courted favour in Periodical Works conducted by my husband' (i.e. the London periodicals, the *Amulet*, the *Spirit and Manners of the Age*, and the *New Monthly Magazine*). The first volume consists entirely of 'The groves of Blarney', later adapted into a play of the same name which was performed in London in 1838. This melodramatic story of kidnapping and revenge was based on a real incident in Blarney (Co. Cork) in about 1812, and Mrs SCH acknowledges her debt to Thomas Crofton Croker§ for 'the history and character of the place'. The tales in the second volume are collectively entitled 'Sketches on Irish highways during the autumn of 1834', consisting of 'The jaunting car', 'Beggars', 'Servants', 'Naturals', 'Ruins – part I', 'Ruins – part II. The story of Clooney Blaney', 'Ruins – part III. The old eagle', Ruins – part IV. Florence O'Donnell', 'Luck – part I. Moyna Brady', 'Luck part II. Dermot O'Dwyer', 'Dummy', 'Procrastination'. The tales in the third volume: 'Illustrations of Irish pride' (consisting of 'Harry O'Reardon', 'The bocher of Red-Gap Lane'), 'The dispensation', 'Old granny' [Brown; Bolton, p. 212; M. Keane, p. 31, 75–91; Rowan cat. 62/168].

H19   *The Hartopp jubilee; or, profit from play. A volume for the young* (by Mrs S.C. Hall; dedicated to Miss Lucy Ann Johnson; dedication dated 1839).

+ London: Darton & Clark, [1839] (ill.). SOURCE Alston, p. 179; NCBEL 4, p. 1305. LOCATION D, L, InND Loeber coll.

COMMENTARY Fiction for juveniles set in England about a week-long family gathering to celebrate the fiftieth wedding anniversary of the grandparents. Several adults tell the children stories for their moral edification [ML].

H20   *Stories of the Irish peasantry* (by Mrs S.C. Hall; dedicated to the landlords and tenants of Ireland).

+ Edinburgh: William & Robert Chambers, 1840 (People's Edition). SOURCE NUC; Rafroidi, ii, p. 182; Sadleir, 1097 (1850 edn); Wolff introd., p. 27 (mistakenly states that 1851 is misprint for 1840); McKenna, p. 193 (mistakenly states 1851 edn is the first edn). LOCATION Grail, L (1848 edn), NUC, InND Loeber coll. (also 1850 edn, 1851 edn).

+ Philadelphia: Lippincott, Grambo & Co., 1854. LOCATION, InND Loeber coll.

COMMENTARY Sixteen stories, each with a distinct moral purpose, first published in *Chambers's Edinburgh Journal*. Each story deals with what Mrs SCH saw as a distinctly Irish failing: recklessness, improvidence, violence, drunkenness, etc. According to the publishers (1840 edn) they were aimed to reconcile landlords and peasantry and had the additional goal of 'leading general readers of all parts of the United Kingdom to take a kindly interest in the Irish people ...' Contents: 'Too early wed!', '"Time enough"', '"It's only a drop!"', '"Do you think I'd inform?"', 'The landlord abroad', 'The landlord at home', '"It's only a bit of a stretch!"', '"Sure, it was always so!"', '"It's only the bit and the sup"', 'The follower of the family', 'Ready Ryland', 'The crock of gold', 'The wrecker, a sea-side story', '"It's only my time"', 'Going to law!', '"Union is strength"', 'Family union', 'Going to service', 'Debt and danger'. In the 1850 edn, 'The tenant-right' was added [ML; Brown; M. Keane, pp 97–112].

H21   *Marian; or, a young maid's fortunes* (by Mrs S.C. Hall; dedicated to the author's mother, Mrs Fielding).

+ London: Henry Colburn, 1840, 3 vols. SOURCE Brown 2, 581 (mentions perhaps incorrectly Routledge, 1840 edn, 3 vols.); NCBEL 4, p. 1305; Rafroidi, ii, p. 182; Wolff, 2914. LOCATION D, L, NUC.

London: Ward & Lock, 1864 (as *Marian*; Library of Popular Authors). SOURCE Topp 2, 241. COMMENTARY *London, Ward edn* No copy located [RL].

+ London, Belfast: Simms & M'Intyre, 1847 (Parlour Library, No. 9). SOURCE Sadleir, ii, p. 153; Wolff, 2914a (1848 edn). LOCATION D, BFl, InND Loeber coll.
Dublin: Cumming, 1840. SOURCE Rev. in *The Citizen* (Dublin, 1 (1840), pp 443–7); RL. COMMENTARY *Dublin edn* No copy located [RL].
Deventer: M. Ballot, 1841, 3 vols. (trans. into Dutch by E.J. Potgieter as *Marianne*). SOURCE Alphabetische naamlijst 1833–49, p. 258; Adamnet. LOCATION UVA.
Leipzig: Bernard Tauchnitz, 1877, 2 vols. SOURCE T & B, 1657. LOCATION NUC.
New York: Harper & Bros, 1840, 2 vols. SOURCE Topp 2, p. 61. LOCATION NUC.
COMMENTARY Story of a young maid who is a foundling. Kathy Malone adopts her and watches over her with untiring affection. Includes a detailed picture of an English boarding school for girls [Brown 2, 581; M. Keane, p. 110].

H22 *Ireland, its scenery, character, etc.* (by Mr and Mrs Samuel Carter Hall).
London: Jeremiah How & Parsons, 1841, 3 vols. (ill.). SOURCE COPAC. LOCATION L.
London: Jeremiah How, 1846, 3 vols. (new edn). SOURCE COPAC. LOCATION Wellcome Library.
Berlin: W. Hertz, 1850 (trans. by Victor Aimé Huber [author according to Bn-Opale plus] as *Skizzen aus Irland*). SOURCE M. Keane, p. 143; Bn-Opale plus. LOCATION BNF.
COMMENTARY Based on five tours of Ireland undertaken between 1825 and 1841, a mixture of 'statistics and stories, fact and fiction, history and legend'. The short stories are by Mrs S.C. Hall. Every county in Ireland is included, with statistical surveys of each. Much practical advice for the tourist is given, along with suggested antiquarian sites to visit and recommended places to stay. Original drawings for these volumes are in the NLI, MS 1,979TX [RL; M. Keane pp 113–44].

H23 *Sketches of Irish character* (by Mrs S.C. Hall; dedicated to Thomas Boyse of the Grange, Bannow [Co. Wexford]).[1]
+ London: How & Parsons, 1842 (new introd.; ill. D. Mc Clise (known as Maclise) H. Robinson, J. Franklin, Jackson, W.H. Brooke, J. Nugent, J.R. Herbert, Walmsley, Linton, Cook, W. Evans (of Eton), R.R. McIan, Delamotte, J.C. Timbrell, E. Landells, C.H. Weigall, J. Gilbert, Smith, Gilks, W. Harvey, Thompson, Bastin, Green, Armstrong, A. Nicholl, H.J. Townsend, H. McManus, Sly, Fanny McIan, Slader, S. West, J. Crowley, Mason, H. O'Neil, Wakefield, G.F. Sargent, Whimper, Geo. Cruikshank). LOCATION, InND Loeber coll. COMMENTARY *London 1842 edn* The fact that this edn carries a 'new' introd. suggests that there was an earlier edn, but this has not been located [RL].
+ London: M.A. Nattali, 1844, [third revsd edn] (ill. H. McManus, D. Mc Clise, H. Robertson; new preface). LOCATION L, InND Loeber coll. COMMENTARY *London 1844 edn* The London 1844 edn is a reissue of the 1842 edn and was published in three different bindings: (a) blue cloth, impressed in gold on spine with harp; (b) marbled boards with leather spine; frontispiece a portrait of Mrs S.C. Hall at a young age; (c) title at top of spine and below that a long design of a high cross, and below that a harp design. Her preface states that she revised the stories and added several new ones [RL; Rowan cat. 62/169].
+ London: Nattali & Bond, 1855, 5th edn (ill.; with new introd.; dedicated to Francis Bennoch). LOCATION L, InND Loeber coll. (also London, Camden Hotten, [1855 or later edn]; see Plate 37).
+ New York, Philadelphia: Ferrett & Co., 1845 (ill. Spittall, W.A. Wilmer, D. Maclise, A.W. Graham). LOCATION, InND Loeber coll.

1 This was the improving landlord, Thomas Boyce of Bannow House, Grange, Bannow (Co. Wexford), also mentioned under William Hickey§.

+ Philadelphia: David McKay, n.d. ('Virtue in all its lustre may be found in an Irish cabin' on cover; ill. Spittall, D. Maclise, Mason Jackson, Hinckley, J. Gilbert). LOCATION, InND Loeber coll.

+ Philadelphia: William Flint, 1868 (as *The wearing of the green; or, sketches of Irish character*; ill.). LOCATION NUC, InND Loeber coll. COMMENTARY *Philadelphia 1868 edn* The Philadelphia 1868 edn is a reissue of Philadelphia n.d. David McKay edn, but under different title and different binding in green cloth showing a harp embossed in gold on the front and spine [RL].

+ Nashville (TN): John Locken, 1858 (ill. Sharp, Spitall, D. Maclise, A.W. Graham, W.A. Wilmer, Linton, Weigall; Welch, Walter, T. Unwin). LOCATION, InND Loeber coll. COMMENTARY *Nashville edn* The copy in InND has extra title page, Philadelphia: John Locken, n.d. [RL].

New York: Garland, 1979, 2 vols. (introd. by R.L. Wolff). SOURCE COPAC. LOCATION Dt. COMMENTARY Includes most of the stories of the first and second series with some dropped, and some new additions ('Take it easy', 'The fairy of Forth', 'Geraldine', 'Good spirits and bad' are added). Contents first London edn: 'Lilly O'Brien', 'Mary Ryan's daughter', 'The Bannow postman', '"We'll see about it"', 'The last of the line', 'Wooing and wedding', 'Jack the shrimp', 'Hospitality', 'Take it easy', 'Peter the prophet', 'Kate Conner', 'Father Mike', 'Larry Moore', 'Kelly the piper', 'The rapparee', 'Annie Leslie' (first published in *The Amulet*, London, 1830), 'Master Ben', 'The wise thought', 'Mabel O'Neil's curse', 'The fairy of Forth', 'MacGoharty's petition', 'Old Frank', 'Luke O'Brian', 'Independence', 'Black Dennis', 'Geraldine', 'Captain Andy', 'Good spirits and bad' [RL].

H24 *Little Chatterbox. A tale* (by Mrs S.C. Hall).
London: Wm. S. Orr, 1844 (ill. John Absolon). SOURCE NCBEL 4, p. 1305. LOCATION L.

H25 *Turns of fortune; and other tales* (by Mrs S.C. Hall).
New York: C.S. Francis; Boston: J.H. Francis, 1844. SOURCE COPAC. LOCATION NUC, InND Loeber coll. (New York, Miller 1864 edn). COMMENTARY *New York 1864 edn* Contents: 'Turns of fortune', '"All is not gold that glitters"', '"There is no hurry"' [RL].

+ London and Edinburgh: W. & R. Chambers, 1858 (as *Turns of fortune*; Miniature Library of Fiction, vol. 5). LOCATION L.

H26 *The Whiteboy; A story of Ireland in 1822* (by Mrs S.C. Hall).
London: Chapman & Hall, 1845, 2 vols. (Chapman & Hall's Monthly Series, Nos. 1–2). SOURCE Block, p. 85; Brown, 689; Rafroidi, ii, p. 182; Sadleir, ii, p. 133; Sadleir, 3574 (1855 edn); Topp 2, p. 262. LOCATION D ([1880] edn), Dt, L, NUC, InND Loeber coll. (1855 edn).

+ Amsterdam: P.N. van Kampen, 1846, 2 vols. (trans. into Dutch as *De withemden, of Ierland in 1822*; ill.). SOURCE Adamnet. LOCATION UVA.

+ New York: Harper & Bros, 1845. SOURCE Topp 2, p. 262. LOCATION NUC, InND Loeber coll. (also, 1871 edn).

New York: Garland, 1979, 2 vols. (introd. by R.L. Wolff). SOURCE COPAC. LOCATION Dt.

COMMENTARY First issued in four parts. This is Mrs SCH's first Irish or national novel, the central theme of which is the relationship between landlords and tenants in Ireland. In 1822, during the height of the Whiteboy agrarian protests, a young Englishman, Mr Spencer, comes to Ireland to take possession of his estate. He is intent on not choosing sides and wants to improve the condition of the peasants who work for him. Both the tenants and the landlords claim him as favouring their cause, and it requires great strength of character on Spencer's part not to be usurped by either party. He succeeds, and together with his Irish wife bestows many improvements on his tenants. In the end of the book Spencer expresses the opinion that Catholic emancipation is the first step toward righting Ireland's wrongs. A play, *The white boy; or, MacArty's fate*, based on this novel, was performed in New York in 1848 [ML; Brown; Bolton, pp 213–14; Field Day, v, p. 846; M. Keane, pp 145–76; Topp 3, p. 295].

H27 *The forlorn hope. A story of old Chelsea* (by Mrs S.C. Hall).
+ London: Printed [for the author?] and sold in aid of the fund for building the hospital for consumption and diseases of the chest in Old Brompton [1845] (ill.). SOURCE Block, p. 94; NCBEL 4, p. 1305. LOCATION D, L ([1846], destroyed).
COMMENTARY 28pp [M. Keane, p. 203].

H28 *The old governess. A story* (by Mrs S.C. Hall; dedicated to the patrons and friends of the Governesses' Benevolent Institution, and to Mrs David Laing; printed for the benefit of the Governesses' Benevolent Institution).
London: Brewster & West (printed & sold for the Asylum for Aged and Decayed Governesses), [1845]. SOURCE Wolff, 2917; NUC.
+ London: J. Nisbet & Co. [1852] (as *Stories of the governess*; ill. F.W. Fairholt, Hulme, W.T. Green, Weir, E.B., G. Dalziel, Geo. Measom, G.R. Clayton etc.). LOCATION D, InND Loeber coll., L, NUC.
COMMENTARY Stories that bemoan the plight of governesses and stress that governesses are not given the respect they deserve. Contents: 'The old governess', 'The governess', 'The daily governess', 'Working memoranda on Governesses' [ML].

H29 *The private purse; and other tales* (by Mrs S.C. Hall).
New York: C.S. Francis & Co.; Boston: J.H. Francis, 1845. LOCATION NUC, InND Loeber coll. (1850 edn).
COMMENTARY Contents: 'The private purse', 'Cleverness', 'The governess' (first published in *The old governess*, London, [1845]) 'Dummy' (first published in *The juvenile budget*, London, 1837) [RL].

H30 *Stories and studies from the chronicles and history of England* (by Mrs S.C. Hall and Mrs J. Foster).
+ London: Darton & Co., 1847 (ill.), vol. 1 [all issued]. LOCATION L.
London: Darton & Hodge, [1859] (as *Stories and studies from English history*; new edn, with additions; ill.). LOCATION BGL; InND Loeber coll. ([1866?], 9th edn).
COMMENTARY Very popular, with an 11th edn appearing about 1880. The [1859] edn states that it was brought up-to-date to 1859 [RL].

H31 *Midsummer eve. A fairy tale of love* (by Mrs S.C. Hall).
+ London: Longman, Brown, Green & Longmans, 1848 (ill. W.T. Green, G. & E. Dalziel, J. Bastin, J. Williams, H. Linton, G. Measom, W. Measom, A.J. Mason, T.R. Macquoid, Maclise, Landseer etc.; cover J. Marchant). SOURCE Rafroidi, ii, p. 182; Brown 2, 582. LOCATION D, Dt, L, NUC, InND Loeber coll.
London: John Camden Hotten, 1870 (as *Midsummer eve. A fairy tale of loving and being loved*; preface by the author, dated 1869). SOURCE Osborne, p. 892; Wolff, 2915. LOCATION CaOTP.
+ New York: Harper & Bros, 1848 (Library of Select Novels, No. 108). LOCATION, InND Loeber coll., NUC.
New York: C.S. Francis & Co., 1848 (Francis & Co.'s Cabinet Library of Choice Prose and Poetry). SOURCE NYPL. LOCATION NN, NUC.
COMMENTARY Originally serialized in the London *Art Union Journal*. The story of an Irish girl who was born, after her father's death, on Midsummer Eve and was thus the 'rightful property' of the fairies [M. Keane, p. 11; Osborne, p. 892].

H32   *Uncle Sam's money box* (by Mrs S.C. Hall).
+ Edinburgh: William & Robert Chambers, 1848 (Chambers's Library for Young People; ill. G. Millar). SOURCE NCBEL 3, p. 932. LOCATION D, L, NUC, InND Loeber coll.
COMMENTARY Fiction for juveniles. Two children are very curious to know what is in their uncle Sam's moneybox. They expect that it holds wonderful presents. However, during the course of the story it becomes clear that the moneybox is his mind, which contains good memories and useful stories [ML].

H33   *The drawing-room table-book* (ed. by Mrs S.C. Hall).
London: Virtue, Hall & Virtue, [1848?]. LOCATION BGL (1849 edn), Univ. of Leeds, InND Loeber coll. ([184?] edn).
+ London, Edinburgh, New York: T. Nelson & Sons, 1866 (as *The playfellow, and other stories*; ill. Landseer, Stone, Purser, and Wilkie). SOURCE Wolff, 2920 (1870 edn). LOCATION D (1870 edn), L, O, NUC.
COMMENTARY The London [1848?] edn includes poetry by various authors but mostly consists of short stories by Mrs SCH. Contents (excluding poetry): 'The dark lady', '"The way of the world"', '"The latest news"', 'A village sketch', 'The wishing-well. An Irish sketch', 'Mother and daughter', 'The old man's wife', 'The playfellow', 'The first sorrow', 'Titian in his studio'. The London 1866 edn has a slightly different composition [RL; CM].

H34   *Grandmamma's pockets* (by Mrs S.C. Hall).
+ Edinburgh: William & Robert Chambers, 1849 (Chambers's Library for Young People; ill. G. Millar, also contains *The whisperer*). LOCATION D, L, NUC, InND Loeber coll.
COMMENTARY M. Keane mentions a 1848 edn, but this has not been identified [RL].

H35   *The swan's egg* (by Mrs S.C. Hall).
+ Edinburgh: William & Robert Chambers, 1850 (Chambers's Library for Young People; ill. Swanston). SOURCE Block, p. 95; NCBEL 3, p. 932; Osborne, p. 893 (1851 edn). LOCATION D (1890 edn), L (1851 edn), CaOTP (1851 edn), InND Loeber coll. (1851 edn), NUC (1851 edn).
COMMENTARY A morally instructive tale contrasting the characters of two orphan girls who are being cared for by their uncle, Mr Kemp, and his sister, who have a reasonably extensive farm in England. The main servant is Simon, a good-hearted Irishman. Jane is proud and egocentric, whereas Kate is warm-hearted and considerate. Jane sets her heart on having a swan because she feels it would give their pond distinction. Because times are bad and crops fail, they lose their land and have to move to a smaller cottage. Faithful Simon goes with them. When Jane succeeds in getting a swan for the little pond near their humble cottage, it becomes the butt of neighbourhood jokes. Because of the swan and Jane's ill-will, the Kemps lose the assistance of the shopkeepers. Kate does her best to lighten the burden for her aunt and uncle. When he falls ill, she begs the doctor to come, and she negotiates with the baker to exchange her work for some bread. While in the village, she is knocked off her feet by a carriage. The person responsible turns out to be a relative who in former years had also been brought up by the Kemps. He is just in time to relieve them from extreme poverty. Jane, however, has contracted consumption and dies. They move to a new cottage, and slowly take up a little bit of farming again [ML].

H36   *The whisperer* (by Mrs S.C. Hall; dedicated to the author's nephew Bonny, also Edward).
+ London, Edinburgh: William & Robert Chambers, 1850 (ill. G. Millar; Chambers's Library for Young People). SOURCE M. Keane, p. 217 (1848 edn, which has not been identified); Osborne, p. 893. LOCATION CaOTP, InND Loeber coll., NUC.

+ Edinburgh: William & Robert Chambers, 1869 (dedicated to the author's nephew Edward; ill. G. Millar). LOCATION, InND Loeber coll.

New York: C.S. Francis, 1851 (Francis & Co.'s Little Library). LOCATION NUC, InND Loeber coll. (New York, Dodd n.d. edn).

COMMENTARY Fiction for juveniles set in north Wales. Three orphans are being brought up by their aunt, who seems incapable of refining their bad characteristics. The boy's vice is to speak the low language of the stable hands, and the vice of both girls is to whisper to each other in company. A blunt-spoken, elderly cousin comes to stay. He straightens out the children's behaviour by teaching them to listen to the whisperer, which turns out to be one's conscience. The volume also contains 'Grandmamma's pockets' (first separately published, Edinburgh, 1849) [ML; RL].

H37 *Tales of domestic life* (by Mrs S.C. Hall).

+ New York: C.S. Francis & Co.; Boston: J.H. Francis, 1850 (ill. Richardson). SOURCE OCLC. LOCATION InND Loeber coll., NjP.

COMMENTARY Contents: 'The merchant's daughter' (first published in *New Monthly Magazine*, London), 'The curse of property', 'Bear and forbear', 'Lost beauty' (first published in *Tales of women's trials*, London, 1835), 'Madelon' (first published in *The juvenile budget*, London, 1837), 'The private purse' (earlier published in *The private purse; and other tales*, New York, 1845), 'Cleverness' (first published in *The private purse*, New York, 1845), 'The governess' (first published in *The old governess*, London, [1845]), 'Turns of fortune', 'All is not gold that glitters', 'There is no hurry'. The last three stories were earlier published in *Turns of fortune; and other tales* (New York, 1844) [AMB; RL].

H38 *Time enough, an Irish tale* (by Mrs S.C. Hall).

+ [n.l.], [n.p.], [c.1850] (No. 64). SOURCE Hyland cat. 235/322. LOCATION, InND Loeber coll.

COMMENTARY 28pp, first published in *Stories of the Irish peasantry* (Edinburgh, 1840). Also published in an 16pp edn [RL; COPAC].

H39 *The merchant's daughter and other tales* (by Mrs S.C. Hall).

New York: C.S. Francis, 1850. SOURCE OCLC. LOCATION Simmons College.

COMMENTARY *New York Francis edn* Partly reprinted from *Tales of woman's trials* (London, 1835), *Tales of domestic life* (London, 1857), and *The juvenile budget* (London, 1837). Contents: 'The merchant's daughter', 'The curses [*sic*] of property', 'Bear and forbear', 'Lost beauty', 'Madelon' [OCLC].

+ New York: Allen Bros, 1869 (ill.). LOCATION InND Loeber coll. COMMENTARY *New York Allen edn* Partly reprinted from *Tales of woman's trials* (London, 1835) and *Tales of domestic life* (London, 1857). Contents: 'The merchant's daughter', 'The mosspits', 'The old maid', 'The uses of adversity', 'The private purse' [RL].

+ London: Frederick Warne & Co., 1874 (as *The merchant's daughter*; Golden Links Series). SOURCE Topp 4, p. 76. LOCATION D ([1876] edn), InND Loeber coll.

H40 *Popular tales of Irish life and character* (by Mrs S.C. Hall).

+ Glasgow: Thomas D. Morison; London: Simpkin, Marshall, Hamilton, Kent & Co., [1856] (ill. Maclise, Franklin, Brooke, Herbert Harvey, Nicholl, Weigall and others). LOCATION DPL, InND Loeber coll., NUC.

COMMENTARY Mostly reprinted from *Sketches of Irish character* (London, 1829, 2 vols., and London, 1831, first and second series). According to author's introd., these stories are among her earliest work and are mostly set on the seacoast of Co. Wexford. Contents: 'Sweet Lilly O'Brien', 'Mary Ryan's daughter', 'The Bannow postman; or, Mrs. Clavery's story', 'Philip Garraty; or, "We'll see about it"', 'The story of Sir John Clavis; or, the last of the line', 'The wooing and the wedding', 'Jack Shrimp', 'The hospitality of Barrytown', 'Aunt Alice and her niece; or, "Take it easy"', 'Peter the prophet', 'Kate Connor; or, impulse and principle', 'Father Mike', 'Larry Moore; or, think of tomorrow', 'Kelly the piper', 'The rapparee', 'Annie Leslie's troubles; or, he laughs best who laughs last', 'Master Ben; or, the dominie of Bannow', 'Norah Clarey and her lover; or, the wise thought', 'Mabel O'Neil's curse', 'John Merry's story; or, the fairy of Forth', 'The story of old Frank; or, the stout and strong of heart', 'Luke O'Brian; or, the road side adventure', 'Black Dennis; or, the story of an informer', 'Captain Andy', 'Good spirits and bad' [ML].

H41 *Popular tales and sketches* (by Mrs S.C. Hall).

+ London: Lambert & Co.; Edinburgh: Menzies, 1856 (ill., The Amusing Library for Young and Old). SOURCE Brown 2, 583; Sadleir, 3398c. LOCATION D, L, InND Loeber coll.

COMMENTARY Mostly Irish stories from Co. Wexford: 'A story of old Chelsea' (first published in *The forlorn hope*, London, [1845]), 'The old émigré', 'The Irish washerwoman', 'The forgotten friend', 'The home-deserter', 'The newspaper boy', 'The blind artist', 'The poor scholars', 'The gold-thirst', 'The young hop-picker', 'The last in the lease', 'Old Madelaine', 'Paddy the tinker', 'The lost ship', 'The wild rose of Rosstrevor', 'Never heed it', 'The master of winter's court', 'The village dressmaker' [RL].

H42 *The lucky penny, and other tales* (by Mrs S.C. Hall).

+ London, New York: George Routledge & Co., 1857 (Cheap Series, No. 166). SOURCE Sadleir, 3572; Topp 1, p. 88. LOCATION L, NUC.

COMMENTARY Contents: 'The lucky penny', 'Ronald Herbert', 'The selfish man', 'The picture', 'The woman of the world', 'Words and deeds', 'Ellen Doyle', 'The sergeant', 'The new sympathies', 'The drowned fisherman', 'Madame Raymotte', 'The inn at Tremadoc', 'Blanche of Broomonde', 'Our cousin Katharine', 'Hidden treasure' [CM].

H43 *A woman's story, written by a self-proclaimed 'Nobody'* (by Mrs S.C. Hall).

+ London: Hurst & Blackett, 1857, 3 vols. SOURCE Sadleir, 1098; Wolff, 2926. LOCATION L, NUC, InND Loeber coll.

COMMENTARY Set in England, a story of two cousins, Helen and Florence, who are kept apart by their parents but both of whom are known to the narrator, who describes herself as 'NOBODY'. Helen becomes a well-known playwright, but she seems to be under the control of a Mr Marley, who is engaged to be married to Florence. Marley has extorted money from Helen under false pretences. Eventually, he is arrested and kills himself in his cell. Florence is devastated and Helen devotes the rest of her life to her care [ML].

H44 *The governess. A tale* (by Mrs S.C. Hall).

+ London, Edinburgh: W. & R. Chambers, 1858 (Miniature Library of Fiction, No. 1). SOURCE Alston, p. 179. LOCATION L, NUC.

COMMENTARY 99pp. Fiction for juveniles originally published in *Chambers's Edinburgh Journal* and *The private purse and other tales* (New York, 1845) [RL; Topp 4, p. 76].

H45 *All is not gold that glitters. A tale* (by Mrs S.C. Hall).

London, Edinburgh: W. & R. Chambers, 1858 (Miniature Library of Fiction, vol. 2). SOURCE Alston, p. 179; M. Keane, p. 215. LOCATION L, NUC.

COMMENTARY Fiction for juveniles originally published in *Turns of fortune; and other tales* (New York, 1844) [RL].

H46 *The private purse, and Tattle; Tales from Chambers's Edinburgh Journal* (by Mrs S.C. Hall).

+ London, Edinburgh: W. & R. Chambers, 1858 (Miniature Library of Fiction, vol. 3). LOCATION L, NUC.

COMMENTARY 86pp. Fiction for juveniles originally published in *Chambers's Edinburgh Journal*. Contents: 'The private purse, a tale' (earlier published in *The private purse; and other tales*, New York, 1845), 'Tattle, a tale' [RL].

Hall

H47 *There is no hurry, and, Deeds not words. Tales* (by Mrs S.C. Hall).
+ London, Edinburgh: W. & R. Chambers, 1858 (Miniature Library of Fiction, No. 4). SOURCE Alston, p. 180. LOCATION L.
COMMENTARY Fiction for juveniles originally published in *Chambers's Edinburgh Journal.* Contents: 'There is no hurry! A tale', was published earlier in *Turns of fortune; and other tales* (New York, 1844), 'Deeds – not words, a tale' [ML; RL].

H48 *Wives and husbands. A tale* (by Mrs S.C. Hall).
+ London, Edinburgh: W. & R. Chambers, 1858 (Miniature Library of Fiction, vol. 9). SOURCE Alston, p. 180; M. Keane, p. 204; NCBEL 4, p. 1305. LOCATION L.
COMMENTARY Fiction for juveniles originally published in *Chambers's Edinburgh Journal.* This story exemplifies Mrs SCH's belief in the sanctity of the marriage bond. One character, Mrs Mansfield, expresses the understanding that no matter how a husband behaves, 'the wife was bound to fulfil her part of the contract' [M. Keane, p. 204].

H49 *Daddy Dacre's school. A story for the young* (by Mrs S.C. Hall).
+ London, New York: G. Routledge & Co., 1859. SOURCE NCBEL 3, p. 932. LOCATION L.
+ London: Routledge, Warne & Routledge, 1861 (new edn, ill.). LOCATION DPL.
+ London: George Routledge & Sons; New York: E.P. Dutton & Co., n.d. (ill.). LOCATION InND Loeber coll.
COMMENTARY Fiction for juveniles consisting of a story about a school for boys in England [ML].

H50 *Mamma Milly. A story* (by Mrs S.C. Hall).
+ London: Groombridge & Sons, 1860 (ill.; Magnet Stories for Summer Days and Winter Nights, No. 3). SOURCE Alston, p. 179; NCBEL 4, p. 1305. LOCATION L.

H51 *Fanny's fancies* (by Mrs S.C. Hall).
+ London: Groombridge & Sons, [1860] (ill.; Magnet Stories for Summer Days and Winter Nights). SOURCE Alston, p. 179; NCBEL 4, p. 1305. LOCATION L, BGL.
COMMENTARY 48pp [BGL].

H52 *Can wrong be right? A tale* (by Mrs S.C. Hall; dedicated to the author's husband [Samuel Carter Hall]).
London: Hurst & Blackett, 1862, 2 vols. SOURCE NCBEL 3, p. 932. LOCATION Dt, L.
+ Leipzig: Bernard Tauchnitz, 1868. SOURCE T & B, 978. LOCATION InND Loeber coll., NUC.
Boston: T.O.H.P. Burnham, 1862. LOCATION NUC.
COMMENTARY Story of a rural schoolmaster's daughter who has to protect her virtue against the assaults of the local lord. They marry, and the narrative follows several years of their wretched life together [Sutherland, p. 271].

H53 *There is no hurry! A tale of life-assurance* (by Mrs S.C. Hall).
New York: Baker & Godwin, 1862. LOCATION NUC.
COMMENTARY Includes a description of the Manhattan Life Insurance Company of New York; earlier published in *Turns of fortune; and other tales* (New York, 1844) [RL].

H54 *Union Jack, and other stories* (by Mrs S.C. Hall).
London: Groombridge & Sons, 1863 (ill.; Shilling Gift Books). SOURCE Topp 4, pp 237–8. LOCATION BGL.
COMMENTARY Contents: 'Union Jack', 'Mamma Milly' (published separately London, 1860), 'Fanny's fancies' (published separately London, [1860]) [BGL; RL].

H55 *The village garland. Tales and sketches* (by Mrs S.C. Hall).
+ London, Edinburgh, New York: T. Nelson & Sons, 1863 (ill. L. Corbaux, J.H. Kernot). SOURCE Alston, p. 180. LOCATION L, InND Loeber coll.
+ London, Edinburgh, New York: T. Nelson & Sons, 1868 (as *Alice Stanley, and other stories*). SOURCE M. Keane, p. 215; NCBEL 4, p. 1306. LOCATION L, O.
COMMENTARY *London 1863 edn* Contents 'The mountain daisy', The fisherman', 'The rose of Fennock Dale', 'The soldier's wife', 'The story of Edwin', 'The exile of Deira', 'Annie Leslie' (first published in *The Amulet*, London, 1830), '"We'll see about it"' (first published in *Sketches of Irish character*, London, 1831), 'The anxious wife', 'Alice Stanley', 'Seven and seventeen' (earlier published in *The juvenile budget*, London, 1837), 'The moral of a picture', 'The golden age', 'The naughty boy'. The London, 1868 edn is a subset of the above stories [RL].

H56 *The mountain daisy and other stories* (by Mrs S.C. Hall).
London: T. Nelson, 1864. SOURCE Wolff, 2916; OCLC; RLIN. LOCATION Univ. of Florida, Gainesville (FL).
COMMENTARY 'The mountain daisy' was first published in *The village garland*, London, 1863 [RL].

H57 *Nelly Nowlan and other stories* (by Mrs S.C. Hall; dedicated to Mrs John Edward Walshe).
+ London, Edinburgh, New York: T. Nelson & Sons, 1865 (ill. W. Small). SOURCE Brown, 691; NCBEL 4, p. 1305. LOCATION D (1870 edn), L, O, BGL.
COMMENTARY In the preface the author discusses the positive trend in the attitudes of the English toward the Irish. Contents: 'Nelly Nowlan' (partly set in England), 'The last in the lease' (first published in *Lights and shadows*, London, 1838, 2 vols.), 'Nobody's boat' [Brown; CM; M. Keane, p. 216].

H58 *Ronald's reason; or, the little cripple* (by Mrs S.C. Hall; dedicated to Richard Wm. Tamplin, senior surgeon of the Royal Orthopædic Hospital).
+ London: Seeley, Jackson & Halliday; S.W. Partridge, [1865] (ill.; The Children's Friend Series). SOURCE M. Keane, p. 217; NCBEL 3, p. 933. LOCATION PC, L.
London: S.W. Partridge & Co., n.d. LOCATION L.
COMMENTARY 56pp. Fiction for juveniles [RL].

H59 *The cabman's cat* (by Mrs S.C. Hall).
+ London: S.W. Partridge, [1865] (Kindness to Animals Series, No. 1). SOURCE Alston, p. 179; NCBEL 4, p. 1305. LOCATION L (destroyed), O.
COMMENTARY Religious fiction concerning the protection of animals, extracted from the *British Workman* [BLC].

H60 *"God save the green!" A few words to the Irish people* (by Mrs S.C. Hall).
London: S.W. Partridge, [1866]. SOURCE NCBEL 4, p. 1305; NYPL. LOCATION O, NN, NUC.
COMMENTARY 31pp, priced at 2*d*. An anti-Fenian pamphlet arguing that armed risings always hinder progress and that the situation in Ireland is improving. A number of people are having a chat after mass in the chapel of Ballymount. They discuss a proclamation sent down by the lord lieutenant that ends with the usual sentence 'God save the Queen'. One of the talkers would like to change this sentence to 'God save the green'. A long debate ensues about whether the Irish are really badly off or whether life has improved over the previous decades in such areas as education, unrest, Catholic representation and famine. Eventually, they all agree that life as it is now is not bad at all and the best sentence to end such proclamations would be: 'God save the Queen and the green' [ML; M. Keane, p. 210; CM].

H61 *The way of the world, and other stories* (by Mrs S.C. Hall).
+ London, Edinburgh, New York: T. Nelson & Sons, 1866. SOURCE Alston, p. 180; NCBEL 4, p. 1305. LOCATION D (1867 edn), L, O, NUC.

+ London, Edinburgh, New York: T. Nelson & Sons, 1873, on cover: *Favourite tales by Mrs. S.C. Hall* (on spine: *A Book For the Young*). LOCATION InND Loeber coll.
COMMENTARY A few of the following stories were first published in *The drawing-room table-book* (London, [1848?]). The London 1873 edn consists of reprints or remainders put in a uniform cloth binding (two versions, one brown, the other green cloth), impressed in black, with a paper medallion printed in colours. Contents: 'The way of the world', 'The moral of a picture', 'Titian in his studio', 'The naughty boy', 'The first sorrow', 'The wishing well', 'Little ears', 'Nobody's boat', 'The golden age' [ML].

H62   *The prince of the Fair family. A fairy tale* (by Mrs S.C. Hall; dedicated to the author's god-daughters Ellen Hall Radford, Alicia Maria Judd, Eva Mariamne Ward, Eva Maria Broderip, Clara Eugenie Holmes, Blanche Anna Louisa Garvock).
+ London: Chapman & Hall, [1867] (ill. J.D. Cooper, E.M. Ward, Mrs E.M. Ward, Sir Noël Paton, Walter J. Allen, W.S. Coleman, Jules Chèret, Kenny Meadows, E.M. Wimperis; cover: John Leighton; see Plate 38). SOURCE NCBEL 4, p. 1305; Osborne, p. 892; Wolff, 2921. LOCATION D, L, CaOTP, NUC, InND Loeber coll.
COMMENTARY Fiction for juveniles. Most of the story is set in South Wales and tells about a fairy prince who did not wish to follow his mother's command to marry a certain princess. As a punishment, she sends him to live with people instead of with fairies. There he falls in love with a sweet girl, who eventually proves to be the princess he had scorned [ML].

H63   *Animal sagacity* (ed. by Mrs S.C. Hall; dedicated to Alexander Home-Lyon).
+ London: S.W. Partridge, [1868] (ill. Harrison Weir, Piloty, J. Bateman). SOURCE Alston, p. 179. LOCATION D, L, NUC, InND Loeber coll.
COMMENTARY Fiction for juveniles concerning animals, interspersed with poems. Most of the stories are by other authors than Mrs SCH. 'The three bears' (by A.M.H. [Anna Maria Hall]), '"Charlie", the white sergeant', 'The lion, the king of the forest' (by R.P.S.), 'Gipsy and the chickens' (by A.M.H. [Anna Maria Hall]), 'The elephant' (by R.P.S.), 'Old Zeb' (by D.J.E.), 'The chaffinches and the nest' (by Nelsi Brook), 'The whip of straw' (by D.J.E.), 'Faithful chum' (by C.L.B.), 'Sagacity of cats' (by R.P.S.), 'Affection of the sheep' (by Abel Sunnyside), 'Rovers' one fault' (by C.L.B.), 'Sagacity of the rat' (by D.J.E.), 'Robin redbreast' (by R.P.S.), 'The dog and the nightingale' (by A.M.H. [Anna Maria Hall]), 'Dogs preserving property and life' (by R.P.S.), 'Our noble "friend"' (by Uncle John), 'Docility and affection of the horse' (by R.P.S.), 'Fidelity of the dog' (by A.M.H. [Anna Maria Hall]), 'The dog that was kind to his fellow' (by E.S.O.), 'Dandie; or, the dog that reasoned' (by E.S.O), 'The cat and the blackbird' (by R.P.S.), 'Don and Sambo' (by E.B.), 'Jack, the shepherd dog' (by E.S.O.), 'Poor Meggy's grave' (by R.P.S.), 'Saved from death' (by R.P.S.) [ML].

H64   *The flight of faith. A story of Ireland* (by Mrs S.C. Hall; dedicated to Charles Ratcliff).
+ London: Chapman & Hall, 1869, 2 vols. SOURCE Brown, 690; NCBEL 4, p. 1306; Rafroidi, ii, p. 182. LOCATION L, NUC.
COMMENTARY The dedication of this strongly anti-Catholic novel states that the story is an attack on the disestablishment of the Church of Ireland, which the author held to be a betrayal of Irish protestantism. Historical fiction set at the time of the Williamite War. It opens at Le Havre where a Huguenot family is fleeing from persecution. Their ship is wrecked off the Isle of Wight, and the girl, Pauline, is rescued by an old sea captain. The scene then changes to Carrickfergus (Co. Antrim), which at that time was held by General Schomberg, commander of part of William III's army. Revd George Walker, joint governor of the city of Londonderry during its long siege (1689), is introduced, and the story ends with the battle of the Boyne (1690), the 'fight of faith.' Both Schomberg and Walker lost their lives there [Brown; M. Keane, p. 208].

H65   *The rift in the rock. A tale* (by Mrs S.C. Hall).
London: Groombridge & Sons, [1871] (The Rainbow Stories for Summer Days and Winter Nights, No. 2). SOURCE M. Keane, p. 217; NCBEL 3, p. 933; Sadleir, 3573. LOCATION L, BGL.

H66   *Digging a grave with a wine glass* (by Mrs S.C. Hall).
London: S.W. Partridge, [1871] (ill.). SOURCE Alston, p. 179; M. Keane, p. 21. LOCATION L, NUC.
Boston: Bradley & Woodruff, [1871]. LOCATION NUC.
COMMENTARY A temperance tale that appeared later in *Boons and blessings* (1875).

H67   *Grace Huntley, and other stories* (by Mrs S.C. Hall).
+ London: Frederick Warne & Co., 1874 (Golden Links Series). SOURCE Topp 4, p. 76; seen at Jarndyce, Sept. 2001.
COMMENTARY Contents: 'Grace Huntley' (first published in *Tales of woman's trials* (London, 1835), 'The governess' (first published in *The old governess*, London, [1845]), 'The great mistake', 'The forced blooms' [RL].

H68   *The daily governess, and other stories* (by Mrs S.C. Hall).
+ London: Frederick Warne & Co., 1874 (Golden Links Series). SOURCE Topp 4, p. 76; seen at Jarndyce, Sept. 2001.
COMMENTARY Contents: 'The daily governess' (first published in *The old governess* (London, [1845]), 'The curse of property' (from *Tales of women's trial*, London, 1835), 'Lost beauty', 'The wisdom of forethought' (from *Tales of women's trial*, London, 1835), 'The mother' (from *Tales of women's trial*, London, 1835), 'The young person', '"Bear and forbear"' (first published in *Tales of domestic life*, New York, 1850) [RL].

H69   *It's only a drop* (by Mrs S.C. Hall).
Philadelphia: Thomas Wm. Stuckey, 1875. SOURCE OCLC. LOCATION NUC.
COMMENTARY 32pp. A temperance tale first published in *Chambers's Miscellany* (Edinburgh), No. 56 [ML; RL].

H70   *Chronicles of cosy nook. A book for the young* (by Mrs S.C. Hall).
London: Marcus Ward & Co.; Belfast: Royal Ulster Works, 1875 (ill.). SOURCE NCBEL 3, p. 933. LOCATION L, NUC.

H71   *Boons and blessings. Stories and sketches to illustrate the advantages of temperance* (by Mrs S.C. Hall; dedicated to the earl of Shaftesbury).
+ London: Virtue, Spalding & Co., 1875 (ill. E.M. Ward, Frederick Goodall, A.J. Woolmer, Butterworth, Heath, W.J. Allen, Dalziel brothers, J.D. Cooper, P.R. Morris, Henrietta Ward, H.R. Robertson, W.J. Palmer, F.D. Hardy, George Cruikshank, E. Sherard Kennedy, J. and J.P. Nicholls, Alfred Elmore, Erskine Nicol, G.H. Boughton, R. Thorburn, C.M. Jenkin, N. Chevalier, J.C. Griffiths). SOURCE Alston, p. 179; M. Keane, p. 215; NCBEL 4, p. 1306. LOCATION L, NUC, InND Loeber coll.
COMMENTARY Temperance stories: 'The drunkard's Bible', 'The rolling stone', 'What he lost', 'It is never too late', 'Mary Riley's simple story', 'The worn thimble', 'Rest and be thankful', 'Building a house with a tea-cup', 'Pepper and her foes', 'The two friends', 'It is only a drop' (first published Philadelphia, 1875), 'Briget Larkins', 'The true temperance cordial', 'Mrs. Grant's perplexities', 'Digging a grave with a wine glass' (first published, London, [1871]) [ML].

H72   *John Harding's locket* (by Mrs S.C. Hall).
+ London: S.W. Partridge & Co., [1875] (British Workman Series, No. 8). SOURCE NCBEL 4, p. 1306; COPAC. LOCATION C.
Philadelphia: American Sunday-School Union, n.d. SOURCE RLIN. LOCATION Free Library of Philadelphia.

COMMENTARY 31pp for the London edn (priced at 2*d*.), and 14pp for the Philadelphia edn. Temperance tale. John Harding has an Irish wife. Because of drinking he reduces his family to great poverty. However, he is given a temperance tract and decides to mend his ways, and the family's financial circumstances improve as a result. The London edn (with continuous pagination) includes *A guide to Glendalough* by Mr S.C. Hall, which also comments on temperance [OCLC; ML].

H73   *Annie Leslie and other stories* (by Mrs S.C. Hall).
+ London, Edinburgh, New York: Nelson & Sons, [1877]. SOURCE Alston, p. 179; M. Keane, p. 215 (mentions an Edinburgh edn printed in 1869, but this has not been located). LOCATION L.
COMMENTARY Stories mostly reprinted from the *Amulet* (London, 1830), *The juvenile budget* (London, 1837), and *The drawing-room table-book* (London, [1848?]). Contents: 'Annie Leslie', 'The playfellow', 'The latest news', 'The old man's wife', 'Irish Jerry', 'Papa's letter', ' The Savoyards', 'The gipsy girl' [CM; RL].

H74   *Mother and daughter, and other stories* (by Mrs S.C. Hall).
London, Edinburgh, New York: T. Nelson & Sons, [1878 or earlier]. LOCATION PC, BGL.

H75   *Tales of Irish life and character* (by Mrs S.C. Hall).
+ Edinburgh, London: T.N. Foulis, 1909 (ill. Erskine Nicol). SOURCE Brown, 692. LOCATION InND Loeber coll., NUC.
Chicago: A.C. McClurg & Co., 1910. LOCATION NUC.
COMMENTARY Published posthumously. Selections from *Sketches of Irish character* (London, 1829, 2 vols.) and *Lights and shadows of Irish life* (London, 1838, 3 vols.). Contents: 'The jaunting car', 'The Bannow postman', 'We'll see about it', 'Beggars', 'Naturals', 'Kelly the piper', 'Illustrations of Irish pride', 'Lilly O'Brien', '"Take it easy"', 'Master Ben', 'Moyna Brady' [RL; Brown].

HALPINE, Charles G. See **HALPINE, Gen. Charles Graham.**

HALPINE, Gen. Charles Graham (known as **Charles G. Halpine**), pseud. **'Private Miles O'Reilly'**, b. Oldcastle (Co. Meath) 1829, d. New York 1868. Journalist, novelist, soldier and comic poet, CGH was the son of Revd Nicholas John Halpin [*sic*], a Church of Ireland minister and poet who was for many years editor of the *Dublin Evening Mail*, and his wife Anne Grehan. The journalist William Henry Halpin, who became sub-editor of Galignani's in Paris, must have been related to CGH. CGH graduated at TCD in 1846, read for the law in London, worked as a journalist in Dublin and London, and then went to America in 1851 to make his fortune. To distinguish himself from his pro-English and anti-Catholic parents, he added an 'e' to his name and changed his middle name from Graham to Grehan. For a while he was a journalist in Boston and was later secretary to the circus owner P.T. Barnum. After moving to Washington and then New York, he worked as a journalist on several newspapers, including the *New York Herald* and the *New York Times*. He first published a poem in Horace Greeley's *Tribune* (New York) protesting the use of US troops to return a fugitive slave. He also wrote *Lyrics by the letter h* (New York, 1854), and in 1857 contributed 'Us here; or, a glimpse behind Know-nothingism in one of the rural districts' to the *Irish American* (New York), which also published at least six serial novels of his that dealt with Ireland. At the outbreak of the Civil War he joined New York's Irish 69th Regiment and was transferred to Gen. David Hunter's staff, where he helped raise the first African-American regiment. Charged with igniting support for the war among Irish-Americans, he created the character of Miles O'Reilly, whose broad burlesques – printed in the *Herald* – were often taken to be straight

news, and whose poems and stories became popular throughout the North. He was brevetted to the rank of brigadier-general of volunteers after the battle of Piedmont, when failing eyesight forced his resignation. CGH, as a dedicated Union soldier and an Irishman, helped change the image of the Irish in the North and inspired the immigrant Irish to view their new country as somewhere they could succeed and was worth fighting for. After the war he again worked as a journalist and he supported the Fenian movement in the US. He was editor of the *New York Citizen*, a journal devoted to civic reform, a prominent member of the Democratic party of his day, and an outspoken critic of municipal corruption. He was elected to the lucrative position of New York City registrar of deeds in 1867, but he died soon after of an accidental overdose of chloroform, taken to relieve the symptoms of withdrawal from alcohol. His collected verses were published in New York in 1869. The ANB states that his *Prison life of Jefferson Davis* (London, 1866), ascribed to J. Craven, MD, is a largely fictional work that aroused sympathy in the North for the ex-Confederate president and helped enable President Andrew Jackson to release him from prison in 1867. A collection of CGH's papers is at the Henry E. Huntington Library, San Marino (CA), and the DCL has scrapbooks kept by his wife, Margaret Milligan, whom he married in Ireland in 1849. For his portrait, see ODNB.
SOURCE Allibone Suppl., ii, p. 749; ANB; B & S, p. 358; Brady, pp 97–8; Burke, p. 313; Crowley, pp 183–202; Curran index [under *Fraser's Magazine*]; DAB; Irish pseudonyms; O'Donoghue, pp 179–80; Fanning, pp 75, 84–6; Hogan, p. 285; Hogan 2, pp 517–18; OCIL, p. 235; ODNB; O'Donoghue, p. 179; RIA/DIB.

H76   *The life and adventures, songs, services and speeches of private Miles O'Reilly (47th Regiment, New York Volunteers) ... From the authentic records of the New York Herald* [anon.] (dedicated to 'Our navy and our army; to all good citizens of Manhattan Island and the great state of New York; and to patriots of every class and nationality throughout the United States').
+ New York: Carleton, 1864 (ill. Mullen). SOURCE Fanning, p. 382; Wright, ii, 1073.
LOCATION L, NUC, InND Loeber coll., Wright web.
COMMENTARY Reprinted from the *New York Herald*, where the stories appeared in 1864. Set during the Civil War, Miles O'Reilly is arrested for song writing (in an Irish brogue) and interned at Morris Island (SC). President Lincoln pardons him, he is lionized at an author's reception in New York, and he ends up invited to the White House, where he meets the president and scandalizes the diplomatic corps with an irreverent song about Lord Palmerston's affair with the much younger 'Mrs. O'Kane' [Fanning, p. 86; NUC].

H77   *Baked meats of the funeral. A collection of essays, poems, speeches, histories and banquets* (by Charles G. Halpine).
New York: Carleton, 1866. SOURCE Fanning, p. 382; Wright, ii, 1072; OCLC.
LOCATION NUC, Wright web.
COMMENTARY A mixed set of newspaper stories which, although a sequel to *The life and adventures* (New York, 1864) have little to do with Private Miles [Fanning, p. 86].

H78   *The patriot brothers; or, the willows of the Golden Vale. A page from Ireland's martyrology* (by the late General C.G. Halpine).
Dublin: A.M. Sullivan, [1869]. SOURCE Hogan, p. 285; Brown, 694 (1884, 6th edn).
LOCATION Dt (1884, 6th edn), L, NUC.
COMMENTARY Published posthumously. Advertised in 1877 in *The poems of Richard D. Williams* (Dublin, 1877) at 6*d*. Historical fiction dealing with the fate of the brothers Henry and John Sheares, who were executed after the rebellion of 1798. The story very much adheres to historical facts. Describes the scenery of Co. Wicklow [Brown].

H79   *Mountcashel's brigade; or, the rescue of Cremona. An historical romance* (by Charles G. Halpine).

+ Dublin: T.D. Sullivan, 1882. SOURCE Brown, 693; COPAC. LOCATION D (1882, 5th edn), L.
COMMENTARY Episodes in the story of the Irish brigade in the service of France [Brown: RL].

HALSEY, Harlan Page, pseud '**Old sleuth**', fl. 1876. Prolific American detective writer, HPH's stories appeared in the dime serial, the *Old Sleuth Library* (New York), which was first published in the *Fireside Companion* (New York), and in a serial, *Old Sleuth's Own* (New York, 1894–98). Only works with known Irish content are listed below. SOURCE Wright, ii, 1074–6; iii, 2410; Jarndyce cat. 151/666; E. Pearson, *Dime novels; or, following an old trail in popular literature* (Boston, 1929), pp 191–2.

H80   *Faithful Mike, the Irish hero* (by 'Old sleuth').
New York: G. Munro, 1876 (Old Sleuth Library, No. 49). SOURCE Brown, 29; OCLC. LOCATION NRU.
COMMENTARY 33pp [OCLC].

H81   *The Irish detective* (by 'Old sleuth').
New York: G. Munro, 1880 (ill.; Seaside Library, No. 720). SOURCE Brown, 43. LOCATION DCL.
COMMENTARY 42pp [OCLC].

H82   *Old Ironsides abroad; or, the giant detective in Ireland* (by 'Old sleuth').
New York: G. Munro's Sons, 1888 (Old Sleuth Library, No. 38). SOURCE OCLC. LOCATION NUC.
COMMENTARY 27pp [OCLC].

H83   *The Irish detective; or, on his track* (by 'Old sleuth').
New York: George Munro's Sons, 1892 (The Calumet Series, No. 8). SOURCE OCLC. LOCATION Univ. of Delaware.

H84   *Ranelagh, the lightning Irish detective* (by 'Old sleuth').
New York: G. Munro's Sons, 1894 (Old Sleuth Library, No. 71). SOURCE Brown, 87; OCLC. LOCATION NRU.
COMMENTARY 28pp [OCLC].

H85   *The Irish detective's greatest case; or, the strategy of O'Neil McDarragh* (by 'Old sleuth').
Cleveland (OH): A. Westbrook, 1908. SOURCE OCLC. LOCATION NRU.
COMMENTARY 28pp [OCLC].

HAM, Elizabeth, b. North Perrott (Som.) 1783, d. Brislington, near Bristol (Avon) 1859. English poet, memoirist and writer, EH was the daughter of Thomas and Elizabeth Ham and was reared largely in Dorset and Wessex. Her father and she moved to Ireland in 1804, living first in Carlow and travelling through Kilkenny, Tipperary, Limerick and Clare to Ballina (Co. Mayo), where he set up a malting business. She recorded her impressions of the state of Ireland in the five years they lived there, during which time she fell in love with an officer of the local garrison. The preface to the following volume was written at Brislington where, after various employments as governess, school-keeper and companion, she died unmarried. EH wrote the *Infant's grammar* (Dorchester, 1820–2), reprinted many times; *Elgiva; or, the monks* (London, 1824); an historical poem, and an account of her life from 1783 to 1820, an abridged edn of which, *Elizabeth Ham by herself*, was published in 1945. In this she recounts stories she heard in Mayo about the French landing in 1798 and meeting Capt. William Napier§. She also describes talking with country people around Ballina who told her many legends, and one who recited for her English versions of the Ossian poems he had learned in Irish. For her portraits and papers, see ODNB. SOURCE Blain, p. 478; BLC; Field Day, iv, pp 833, 892, E. Gillett, *Elizabeth Ham by herself, 1783–1820* (London, 1945); ODNB; Rowan cat. 57A/350; RL.

H86 *The Ford family in Ireland. A novel* [anon.].

+ London: T.C. Newby, 1845, 3 vols. SOURCE Brown, 33. LOCATION L, InND Loeber coll.

COMMENTARY A largely autobiographical novel, consisting of a romance set in Connacht in the early 1800s when it was a proclaimed district suffering from agrarian unrest. The English army is stationed in the fictional town of Ballyburn. Lt. Macalbert sees that the army is repressing his country. He defects but is caught and forgiven. In the meantime, his brother has died and he succeeds him, but he is also given a commission, which he cannot immediately give up. Later he takes up the rebels' cause again. He marries one of the daughters of the Ford family, and dies on the scaffold. The novel looks forward to the future glad tidings 'that, at *last*, "JUSTICE HAS BEEN DONE TO IRELAND"' [ML; Blain; Gillett, *Elizabeth Ham*, p. 8; ODNB].

HAMILTON, Mrs. See HAMILTON, Mrs Ann (Mary).

HAMILTON, Ann. See HAMILTON, Mrs Ann (Mary).

HAMILTON, Mrs Ann (Mary; also known as **Ann Hamilton** and **Mrs Hamilton**), fl. 1806. Novelist, whose name is given is Ann Mary Hamilton in NSTC. However, it is possible that Ann Hamilton and Mary Hamilton were two different individuals. O'Donoghue lists an Ann Hamilton, an Irish author of verse, who may be identified with the author of these novels. Only works known to be related to Ireland are listed below. SOURCE Allibone, i, p. 772; Allibone, i, p. 776 [under M. Hamilton]; cat., University of Virginia, Charlottesville (VA); NSTC, ser. 1, ii, p. 342; O'Donoghue, p. 180.

H87 *The Irishwoman in London. A modern novel* (by Ann Hamilton).

London: J.F. Hughes, 1810, 3 vols. SOURCE Brown, 695; British Fiction; Garside, 1810:49. LOCATION Corvey CME 3–628–47–589–9, Ireland related fiction, L, NUC.

COMMENTARY Originally this was an epistolary novel which the publisher, without the knowledge of the author, changed from letters to chapters. Ellen O'Hara lived with her parents in Dublin. After her parents die, she lives with an aunt near Monaghan, where she marries a drunken squireen. She deserts him and goes under an assumed name to London as a companion. Her husband finds her and carries her off to Somerset. He dies and she marries the man who had been her suitor in London [Brown; Garside].

H88 *The adventures of a seven-shilling piece* (by Ann Hamilton).

+ London: M.L. Panier, 1811, 2 vols. SOURCE Block, p. 95; British Fiction; Garside, 1811:37. LOCATION L, O, NUC.

COMMENTARY Includes some Irish characters, such as Lord Fitzallan and Mr O'Hara, but the tale is not set in Ireland [ML].

H89 *The monk's daughter; or, hypocrisy punished. A novel* (by Mrs Hamilton).

+ London: Allen & Co., 1812, 3 vols. SOURCE British Fiction; Garside, 1812:32. LOCATION Corvey CME 3–628–47586.

COMMENTARY Gothic fiction which features an English heroine, Ellen Marchmont, who is imprisoned in Cromartie Castle in Connacht [*sic*] who during her incarceration is looked after by an Irish-speaking servant, Kathleen O'Connell [CM].

HAMILTON, Antoine, Comte . See HAMILTON, Anthony.

HAMILTON, Anthony (later known as **Comte Antoine Hamilton**), b. Roscrea, or more likely, Nenagh Castle (Co. Tipperary) 1645 or 1646, d. St Germain-en-Laye (Paris) 1720. AH was a poet, writer and translator whose parentage has been a matter of dispute. Traditionally he was known as the third son of Sir George Hamilton, earl of Abercorn, and Mary, daughter of Thomas Butler, Viscount Thurles, who was related on his mother's side to the earl of Ormond. However, recent research indicates that he was the son of another Sir George Hamilton, resident at Nenagh Castle, who also married a Mary Butler. Because of the aftermath of the 1641 rebellion, the family went into exile to France in 1651. AH, along with his brothers, was a soldier and courtier who served and fought for both kings Charles II and James II. A devout Roman Catholic, he was appointed governor of Limerick in 1685, fought against the Williamite forces at Enniskillen and Newtownbutler (Co. Fermanagh); the battle of the Boyne (1690); and the siege of Limerick (1691). After the war he settled in France at the court of St Germain-en-Laye where he wrote verse, carried on a lively correspondence with the duke of Berwick while the latter served in the Peninsular War, and published his famous *Memoires de la vie du Comte de Grammont* (Cologne, 1713). AH, who was known as Count Hamilton, wrote a free paraphrase in French alexandrines of Alexander Pope's *Essay on Criticism* (London, 1711). To entertain his friends, he produced a series of four *contes*. These were published posthumously in Paris in 1730 and first translated and published in English in 1760. AH also published *Le bélier* (*c.*1703), a *conte* inspired by his sister's (the countess of Grammont) new house, renamed 'Pontlie'. It aimed to furnish a romantic etymology for the new name; the principal incident being a contest between a prince and a giant for the daughter of a druid. ODNB says he also wrote two unfinished *contes*: 'Les quatre Facardins', and 'Zénéyde'. 'Les quatre Facardins' and *Histoire de fleur d'épine* (see below) were published in Paris in 1730, while 'Zénéyde' was included in *Oeuvres mêlées en prose et en vers* in 1731. For his portraits, see ODNB. SOURCE R. Clark, *Anthony Hamilton* (London, 1921); Elmes, pp 91–2; C. Manning, 'The two Sir George Hamiltons and their connections with the castles of Roscrea and Nenagh' in *Tipperary Historical Jrnl*, 150 (2001), 149–54; OCIL, p. 235; ODNB; O'Donoghue, p. 181; Raven 2, 1793:20.

H90 *Mémoires de la vie du comte de Grammont; contenant particulièrement* [*sic*] *l'histoire amoureuse de la cour d'Angleterre sous le règne de Charles II* [anon.].
+ Cologne [Rouen ?]: Pierre Marteau, 1713. LOCATION L.
+ Rotterdam: Veuve de Nicolas Bos, 1716. LOCATION L.
London: J. Round, W. Taylor, J. Brown, W. Lewis & J. Graves, 1714 (trans. by Mr [Abel] Boyer as *Memoirs of the life of Count de Grammont: Containing, in particular, the amorous intrigues of the Court of England in the reign of King Charles II*). SOURCE ESTC t113751. LOCATION D, L.
London: Barrie & Rockliff, 1965 (ed. and trans. by Nicholas Deakin). LOCATION L.
COMMENTARY A fictionalized account of the amorous intrigues at the court of Charles II, including those of the duke of York, the future king James II, with, among others, Hamilton's sister-in-law, the future duchess of Tyrconnell. Admired by Voltaire, it became a minor classic that has had over eighty editions to date. According to the ODNB, Hamilton and Philibert, count de Grammont (AH's brother-in-law) planned the work two years before the count's death in 1707. Only two of the three planned volumes were published. In 1712 the duchesse d'Orléans sent a copy to the dowager electress of Hanover, which then appeared anonymously and without authorization, supposedly in Cologne but more likely in Rouen. An English translation was published in 1714 [ODNB].

H91 *Histoire de fleur d'épine* (by the Comte Antoine Hamilton).
Paris: Jean Fr. Josse, 1730. SOURCE COPAC. LOCATION O.
London: G. & T. Wilkie, 1793 (as *History of May-Flower. A fairy tale*). SOURCE Raven 2, 1793; ESTC t219333. LOCATION O.

Salisbury: E. Newbury, 1796 (as *History of May-Flower. A Circassian tale*; ill.). SOURCE Ximenes, M11/91; ESTC t098978. LOCATION L (1796, 2nd edn).
COMMENTARY A satire of the popular imitations of the *Arabian Nights* written, according to Hamilton, in a style 'plus Arabe qu'en Arabie' [ODNB; Ximenes, M11/91].

HAMILTON, C.G. (also known as Mrs Charles Gillingham Hamilton), pseud. 'C.G.H.', fl. 1845. Religious fiction writer, only CGH's works with Irish content are listed below. SOURCE Allibone Suppl., ii, p. 752; NCBEL 4, p. 1802.

H92   *Margaret Waldegrave; or, the power of truth* (by 'C.G.H.').
+ Edinburgh: W.P. Kenny; Glasgow: D. Bryce; London: Hamilton, Adams & Co; Dublin: J.M. M'Glashan, 1846. LOCATION L.
COMMENTARY Religious fiction with Irish content [FD].

H93   *The unclaimed daughter; a mystery of our own day* (by 'C.G.H.').
+ Bath: Binns & Goodwin; London: Whittaker & Co., Hamilton & Co; Edinburgh: Oliver & Boyd; Dublin: J. M'Glashan, [1853] (ill.; cover: J.L.). SOURCE Hart cat. 36/62; NCBEL 4, 1802. LOCATION L (1853, 2nd edn), InND Loeber coll.
COMMENTARY Fiction for juveniles. Unusual account of a girl discovered in a Dublin orphanage. She gradually recovers her memory and her story involves cruel abductors, murders, sojourns in a filthy hovel in the Irish countryside, etc. From the girl's behaviour it is deduced that she is of noble birth. An investigation is mounted to find out her true origins. The whole account is given as though it was factual and is published in aid of discovering the girls' relatives [ML; Hart cat. 36/62].

HAMILTON, C.J. See HAMILTON, Catherine Jane.

HAMILTON, Catherine Jane (also known as C.J. Hamilton), pseud. 'Retlaw Spring', b. Somerset *c*.1840, d. probably in Ireland 1935. English-born novelist, biographer, religious fiction and miscellaneous writer, CJH's father was from Strabane (Co. Tyrone) and her mother from Queen's Co. (Co. Laois). Her father was a vicar of the Church of England and after his death in 1859 she moved to Ireland, where she lived for more than thirty years. She contributed to periodicals in Ireland and in addition to her novels wrote a play and children's books. She also wrote *Notable Irish women* (London, [1892]), and *Women writers: their works and ways* (London, 1892–93). She later returned to London. Because the year of her return to England is not clear, all her known works are listed below, irrespective of whether they deal with Ireland or not. SOURCE Alston, p. 182; Brown, p. 127; Colman, p. 107; EF, p. 170; NCBEL 4, p. 1802.

H94   *Marriage bonds; or, Christian Hazell's married life* [anon.].
London: Ward, Lock & Co., [1879] (Library of Favourite Authors, No. 36). SOURCE Brown, 696 (mistakenly mentions [1878] edn); Colman, p. 107 (ditto); Topp 2, 1306. LOCATION L.
COMMENTARY A girl from an English manor house, Christian, is married to a man who neglects her. She is forced to live in his ill-managed country house among disagreeable neighbours somewhere on the south-east coast of Ireland. She has no friend until the arrival of her husband's cousin Eustace. Eustace and Christian fall in love, but they are both honourable people and Christian stays faithful to her husband until the very end [Brown].

H95   *The Flynns of Flynnville* (by Catherine Jane Hamilton; dedicated to George MacDonald, LLD).
+ London: Ward, Lock & Co., [1880] (Library of Favourite Authors, No. 47; ill.). SOURCE Allibone Suppl., ii, p. 752; Alston, p. 182; Brown, 697 (mistakenly dates 1879); Colman, p 107 (ditto); Topp 2, 1382; COPAC. LOCATION L, RB.

COMMENTARY A story set in the south of Ireland based on the murder of a bank manager by a constabulary officer and the subsequent trial [Brown].

H96 *Mr. Bartram's daughter. An every-day story* (by Catherine Jane Hamilton).
London: Bemrose & Sons, [1882]. SOURCE Allibone Suppl., ii, p. 752; Alston, p. 182; COPAC. LOCATION L.

H97 *True to the core. A romance of '98* (by C.J. Hamilton).
London: F.V. White & Co., 1883, 2 vols. SOURCE Allibone Suppl., ii, p. 752; Alston, p. 182; Brown, 698 (1884 edn); COPAC. LOCATION L.
COMMENTARY Historical fiction set during the 1798 rebellion, it concerns the love of a Kerry girl for John Sheares, a rebel and son of Henry Sheares§, who with his brother Henry, was later executed [Brown].

H98 *Rivals at school; or, a lesson for life* (by C.J. Hamilton).
London: Sunday School Union, [1888]. SOURCE Alston, p. 182; NCBEL 4, p. 1802; COPAC. LOCATION L (destroyed), E.
COMMENTARY Fiction for juveniles.

H99 *The battle of the waves; or, the herring boat* (by Catherine Jane Hamilton).
London: Religious Tract Society, [1890]. SOURCE Alston, p. 182. LOCATION L.
COMMENTARY Religious fiction [BLC].

H100 *Dr. Belton's daughters* (by Catherine Jane Hamilton).
London, New York, Melbourne: Ward, Lock & Co., [1890]. SOURCE Brown, 699; Alston, p. 182; COPAC. LOCATION L.
COMMENTARY Alice, the second of Dr Belton's daughters, marries a curate in the west of Ireland and struggles to keep up a good appearance on small means [Brown].

H101 *Hedged with thorns; or, working waiting and winning* (by 'Retlaw Spring').
+ London: Ward, Lock & Tyler, [1875] (Violet Spring Series, No. 1). SOURCE Alston, p. 182; COPAC. LOCATION O.
London, New York, Melbourne: Ward, Lock & Co., 1891 (new edn; as *Hedged with thorns* by C.J. Hamilton). LOCATION L.

H102 *The merry-go-round* (by Catherine Jane Hamilton).
London: Religious Tract Society, [1894]. SOURCE Alston, p. 182; COPAC. LOCATION L (destroyed), NUC.
COMMENTARY Religious fiction [BLC].

H103 *From hand to hand; or, the adventures of a jubilee six-pence* (by C.J. Hamilton).
London: S.W. Partridge & Co., [1895]. SOURCE Alston, p. 182; COPAC. LOCATION L.

H104 *The strange adventures of Willie Norman, etc* (by Catherine Jane Hamilton).
London: Religious Tract Society, [1898]. SOURCE Alston, p. 182; COPAC. LOCATION L (destroyed).
COMMENTARY Religious fiction. No copy located [RL; BLC].

H105 *A flash of youth* (by Catherine Jane Hamilton).
London: Sands & Co., 1900. SOURCE Alston, p. 182; COPAC. LOCATION L.
COMMENTARY Concerns a marriage between a lady and a cultivated farmer's son. The relationship ends in tragedy when he flirts with a younger girl of his own class [EF].

H106 *Frank and Flo on their travels* (by Catherine Jane Hamilton).
London: Religious Tract Society, [1901]. SOURCE COPAC. LOCATION L (destroyed).
COMMENTARY Religious fiction. No copy located [BLC; RL].

H107 *Two little run-aways* (by Catherine Jane Hamilton).
London: Christian Knowledge Society, 1903. LOCATION L (destroyed).
COMMENTARY Religious fiction. No copy located. Apparently different from James Buckland's *Two little run-aways* (London, 1898) [BLC].

H108 *Crossing the dark river: Words of cheer and hope* (by C.J. Hamilton).
London: Elliot Stock, 1907. SOURCE COPAC. LOCATION L (destroyed), E.
COMMENTARY 32pp. Religious fiction [BLC].

H109 *The luck of the Kavanaghs* (by C.J. Hamilton).
Dublin: Sealy, Bryers, 1911. SOURCE Brown, 700 (1900 edn, not located); COPAC.
LOCATION E.

COMMENTARY Adventures of an emigrant Irish boy who makes a fortune in America and returns
to Ireland to marry the poverty-stricken gentlewoman he has always loved [Brown; EF].

H110 *A regular little pickle* (by Catherine Jane Hamilton).
London: Religious Tract Society, 1919 (May Blossom Series). SOURCE COPAC.
LOCATION L.
COMMENTARY Religious fiction [BLC].

H111 *Rupert's wife* (by C.J. Hamilton).
London: A.H. Stockwell, [1922]. SOURCE COPAC. LOCATION L.

H112 *The story of Steady and Sure* (by Catherine Jane Hamilton).
London: G.G. Harrap & Co., 1927. SOURCE COPAC. LOCATION L.
New York: Thomas Y. Crowell, 1928 (ill. M.D. Hardy). SOURCE OCLC; ABE Books
(website accessed, 28 Dec. 2003).
COMMENTARY Fiction for juveniles. Story about twin brother ponies [ABE Books].

H113 *The story of a little white cat* (by Catherine Jane Hamilton).
London: G.G. Harrap & Co., 1933 (ill. E.M. Starling). SOURCE OCLC. LOCATION L.

HAMILTON, Edwin, pseud. **'W. Ridley Thacker'**, b. Balbriggan? (Co. Dublin) 1849, d. 1919.
Poet, librettist, editor, barrister and humour writer, EH was the only son of Revd Hugh
Hamilton, rector of Balbriggan and master of the St Patrick Cathedral Grammar School, and
Charlotte Mary Ormsby. He was educated at the Durham Grammar School and at TCD, from
which he graduated MA in 1874. Called to the Irish Bar in 1887, he initially made writing his
profession. He published several volumes of poetry (e.g. *The moderate man*, London, 1888, ill.
Harry Furniss§) and produced libretti for *opera buffe* and pantomimes which, according to the
critic Charles Reed, he raised 'to the level of a fine art'. He edited comic journals and annuals
and various short-lived humorous magazines in Dublin, including *Zozimus*, and in 1884 launched
Ireland's Eye, followed by *Zoz*, and *Pat*. He contributed to Percy French's§ comic publication
the *Jarvey* (Dublin). He became a member of the RIA in 1879; chairman of the Conservative
Club, Dublin, 1892–94, and chairman of the Dublin District of the Institute of Journalists, 1900.
In 1891 he married Helen Delacherois of Donaghadee (Co. Down; possibly related to Maria
Henrietta de la Cherois Crommelin§, also of Donaghadee). Moving to his wife's town, he lived
at The Crossways, and became a JP and practised as a barrister. Some of his letters are among
the Downey Papers (NLI, MS 10,022). SOURCE Allibone Suppl., ii, p. 752; Brown, p. 128;
Ferguson, pp 198–9; Leslie & Wallace, p. 697; LVP, p. 208; McKenna, pp 194–5; MVP, pp
203–4; OCIL. p. 235; O'Donoghue, p. 181; RIA/DIB.

H114 *Ballymuckbeg. A tale of eighty years hence* (by 'W. Ridley Thacker').
London: Griffith, Farran & Co.; Dublin: William McGee, 1885, 2nd edn [Brown, 701
(1892 edn); McKenna, p. 195 (lists 1892 edn, as *Ballymuckbeg. A political satire*).
LOCATION Grail, Dt.
COMMENTARY Political satire. First published in London in 1884 in the form of a chap-
book of 23pp [Brown; COPAC].

H115 *Waggish tales* (by Edwin Hamilton).
+ Dublin: Sealy, Bryers & Walker, 1897. SOURCE Brown, 702. LOCATION Grail, D.
COMMENTARY Short, humorous stories of which three have an Irish subject [Brown].

Hamilton

HAMILTON, Elizabeth (also known as **Eliza Hamilton**), pseud. 'Geoffrey Jarvis', b. Belfast 1758, d. Harrogate (Yorks.) 1816. Novelist and educationalist, EH was the youngest child of Charles Hamilton and Katherine Mackay, who were well-born but poor. Her brother was the noted orientalist Charles Hamilton (1753–92). Her father died early in her life and her mother sent her to be brought up by a Scottish aunt and uncle in Stirlingshire, from whom she received a very good education. She started to write early 'by stealth', including an unpublished novel on Arabella Stuart, and other works. In 1789 she moved to London to be with her brother, who was translating a guide to Islamic law and whose work influenced her novel, *Hindoo Rajah* (London, 1796). Charles Hamilton died in 1792 and EH went to live with her sister. She was governess to Lady Elizabeth Lucan (wife of Richard Bingham, 2nd earl of Lucan) for six months, but finding the work too much of a constraint, she settled in Edinburgh in 1804, sustained by a government pension. EH wrote several other novels, as well as works on education including *Letters on education* (London, 1801, repr. Dublin, 1801), and *Letters addressed to the daughter of a nobleman* (London, 1806), explaining ethical principles to children in a comprehensible way. She also devoted herself to philanthropy. Maria Edgeworth§ visited her in 1803 and they became friends. Living much of her life in Scotland, she only occasionally returned to Belfast (in 1815 she spent three months in Ireland). She suffered from rheumatism and she moved to Harrogate (Yorks.) in 1812. Between 1809 and her death in 1816 she does not appear to have published any fiction. Plans for a series of historical lives, begun with *Memoirs of the life of Agrippina, the wife of Germanicus* (Bath, 1804, 3 vols.) were dropped because of illness. Maria Edgeworth wrote a eulogy on her death, praising her role in promoting education for women. EH's other admirers included Sir Walter Scott and Jane Austen. Some of her correspondence is in the BL and in the NLS. For her portraits, see ODNB. SOURCE Allibone, i, pp 774–5; *Belfast literary society* (Belfast, 1902), p. 31; E.O. Benger, *Memoir of the late Mrs. Elizabeth Hamilton* (London, 1818), pp 160, 218; Blain, p. 479; W. Blake (ed.), *An Irish beauty of the regency* (London, 1911), p. 26; Brady, p. 98; Butler, pp 198–9, 220n.3; Mrs [Frances] Edgeworth, *A memoir of Maria Edgeworth* (London, 1867), i, p. 293; M. Edgeworth, 'Character and writings of Mrs. Elizabeth Hamilton', *Gentleman's Magazine*, 1st ser., 86/2 (1816), pp 188, 623–4; Elmes, p. 92; Mrs Elwood's *Literary ladies of London*. [n.d.]; Field Day, v, pp 824, 832, 1090; A.J.C. Hare (ed.), *The life and letters of Maria Edgeworth* (London, 1894), i, p. 160; preface to EH's *The cottagers of Glenburnie* (Edinburgh, 1837); Hogan 2, p. 518; NCBEL 4, pp 926–7; ODNB; O'Donoghue, p. 181; RIA/DIB; Scott (correspondence with Sir Walter Scott).

H116 *Translation of the letters of a Hindoo Rajah; written previous to, and during the period of his residence in England. To which is prefixed a preliminary dissertation on the history, religion, and manners, of the Hindoos* (by Eliza Hamilton; dedicated to Warren Hastings).

London: G.G. & J. Robinson, 1796, 2 vols. SOURCE Black, 509; Blain, p. 479 (who mentions a different title); Forster 2, 1790; Gecker, 418 (1801, 2nd edn); Johnson cat. 38/28; Raven 2, 1796:49; ESTC t056854. LOCATION Dt (1801, 2nd edn), L, PU (1801, 2nd edn), NUC.

+ Dublin: H. Colbert, 1797, 2 vols. SOURCE Raven 2, 1796:49; ESTC t055907. LOCATION D, Dt (1801 edn), L, NUC.

Boston: Wells & Lilly, 1819, 2 vols. LOCATION NUC.

COMMENTARY A satire of contemporary British society, this epistolary novel commemorates EH's recently deceased brother Charles, an orientalist, who had served in India and from whom she learned much about India and its Hindu culture. It concerns a rajah who comes to England after he has heard much about it from an Englishman in India. Half of the novel is set in India and deals with Indian affairs, while the rest is a critique of English life from the rajah's viewpoint. The 55pp introd. offers a treatise of Hindu mythology, society, government and on the contrasting treatment of Hindu culture by the Mughal and British rulers. It contains a glossary of Indian terms [RL; Blain; Field Day, v, pp 824–5; ODNB; Trebizond cat. 40/146].

H117 *Memoirs of modern philosophers* (preface by 'Geoffrey Jarvis', dedicated to Mr Robinson, bookseller).

London: G.G. & J. Robinson, 1800, 3 vols. SOURCE ESTC t064746; Gecker, 417 (1800, 2nd edn); British Fiction; Garside, 1800:39; Forster 2, 1789. LOCATION Corvey CME 3-628-48063-9, Dt, L, UP (1800, 2nd edn), InND Loeber coll. (1800, 2nd edn).

Dublin: Wogan, Burnett, Gilbert & Hodges, Brown, Rice, Porter, Dornin, Folingsby & Fitzpatrick, 1800, 2 vols. SOURCE ESTC n022030. LOCATION NUC.

Paris: Le Normant, 1802, 4 vols. (trans. by M. B*** as *Bridgetina, ou les philosophes modernes*). SOURCE Streeter, 164. LOCATION L.

+ London: Routledge/Thoemmes, 1992, 3 vols. (introd. by Peter Garside). LOCATION Dt, O, InND Loeber coll.

COMMENTARY A satire attacking William Godwin's§ philosophy with some of the characters quoting from Godwin's *Political Justice* (London, 1793) and *The inquirer* (London, 1797). The characters embracing Godwin's philosophy believe in the concept of perfectibility, free love and common property, and that the Hottentot civilization is an example of these principles. These new philosophers are contrasted with characters who embody the virtues of piety, benevolence, prudence and good sense. The new philosophers are trying to live by their principles, but find in the end that the principles do not necessarily bring happiness and may even lead to misery and death. Women who try to adhere to the principle of free love find out the dangers of abandonment [ML; Field Day, v, p. 824].

H118 *Memoirs of the life of Agrippina, the wife of Germanicus* (by Elizabeth Hamilton).

+ Bath, London: G.G.& J. Robinson, 1804, 3 vols. (introd. by 'Johnson'; genealogical table of the family of the Caesars). SOURCE British Fiction; Garside, Appendix D: 2; Hardy, 461. LOCATION L, NUC, InND Loeber coll.

London: John Walker; Wilkie & Robinson, John Richardson, J.M. Richardson, A.K. Newman & Co., Jos. Johnson & Co, Geo. Robinson, 1811, 2 vols., 2nd edn. SOURCE Blakey, p. 235. LOCATION CtY.

COMMENTARY The author maintains that this work was not a novel, but an 'imaginative' biography. A review in the *British Critic* (1805) states that the work illustrates the principles accounted for in EH's *Letters on education* (London, 1801), so as to show 'the pernicious consequences of improper associations early formed, and the necessity of curbing the exorbitance of every passion' [RL; ODNB].

H119 *The cottagers of Glenburnie; a tale for the farmer's ingle-nook* (by Elizabeth Hamilton).

+ Edinburgh: Manners & Miller, S. Cheyne; London: T. Caddell, W. Davies, W. Miller, 1808. SOURCE British Fiction; Garside, 1808:52; Block, p. 96; Wolff, 2942. LOCATION L, E, NUC, InND Loeber coll. (1808, 2nd edn.).

+ Edinburgh: William & Robert Chambers; London: W.S. Orr & Co.; Glasgow: John MacLeod, 1837 (as *The cottagers of Glenburnie, a tale*; People's Edition). LOCATION InND Loeber coll.

London: Charles Tilt, 1837. LOCATION L.

+ Belfast: Printed by J. Smyth, [*c*.1835]. SOURCE Adams, p. 138; *Catalogue of the Library at Lough Fea* (London, 1872), p. 41 (where listed as a chapbook); Falkner Grierson cat. 22/249 (where this imprint is on cover only; Dublin imprint of the text). LOCATION UCD Folklore Dept.

Belfast: Simms & McIntyre, [1840]. SOURCE COPAC. LOCATION L.
COMMENTARY *Belfast Simms edn* An abridged edn 'intended to instil into the minds of youth the advantages of a tractable disposition' [COPAC].
Dublin: Printed by C.M. Warren, [*c.*1835]. SOURCE Adams, p. 138; Falkner Grierson cat. 22/249; COPAC. LOCATION O.
New York: E. Sargeant, 1808 (as *The cottagers of Glenburnie, a tale for the farmer's fireside*). LOCATION NUC.
COMMENTARY A moralistic story set in Scotland that extols the virtues of hard work, prudence and common sense. At the same time it shows how pride leads to unhappiness. It contrasts the two daughters of Mr Stewart, one who is haughty, and one who resembles her deceased mother and is generous and kind. Mrs Mason, a servant who had done their mother a great service when she was young, comes to visit and takes over the reformation of the lazy highland villagers. Her story provides opportunities to show how people can live virtuous lives. Maria Edgeworth§ spoke highly of this book [ML; ODNB; A.J.C. Hare (ed.), *The life and letters of Maria Edgeworth* (London, 1894), i, p. 160].

HAMILTON, Col. Gawin (also Gawen) William Rowan (also known as Col. Rowan Hamilton and Hamilton Rowan), b. 1844, d. 1930. Novelist and military man, GWRH was the eldest son of Archibald Rowan Rowan-Hamilton of Killyleagh Castle (Co. Down), and Catherine Anne Caldwell. He descended from the Irish nationalist Hamilton Rowan. Educated at Cheltenham and University College, Oxford, where he graduated BA in 1886, he entered the Inner Temple, London, in 1882. GWRH became a DL, a JP, and in 1875 HS of Co. Down. He reached the rank of colonel in the 3rd Royal Irish Rifles, and captain of the 7th Dragoon Guards. In 1876 he married Lina Mary Howley. He resided at Killyleagh Castle and Shanganagh Castle (Co. Dublin). SOURCE Brown 2, p. 110; Burke's p. 554; J. Foster (ed.), *Alumni Oxonienses 1715–1886* (Oxford, 1888), ii, p. 593; RIA/DIB.
H120   *The last of the cornets. A novel* (by Rowan Hamilton).
+ London: F.V. White & Co., 1890, 2 vols. SOURCE Wolff, 2945. LOCATION L, NUC, InND Loeber coll.
COMMENTARY A military novel set in England and Ireland. The story purports to be about Allan MacDonagh, the last man to hold the rank of cornet, which was abolished in 1871. The narrator is Capt. Merrilis, who has taken the Irish cornet under his wing. They both serve in a regiment of dragoons. The story describes regimental life when not on campaign. Much of military life revolves around horses, hunts, races, and balls. The life of the cornet takes a wrong turn when a servant, O'Halloran, passes a false check in his name. Even though it becomes clear who the real culprit is, the cornet is still under suspicion and many merchants present their bills for payment. The bank is not eager to prosecute the offender, leaving the cornet no choice but to go after him himself. His search leads him to the Continent and then to the US, where he tracks O'Halloran down in a gambling den in Boston. The cornet is wounded in the attempt to arrest O'Halloran. However, in an effort to atone for his misdeed, O'Halloran intercepts a second shot at the cornet. MacDonagh dies of his wound [ML].
H121   *Betwixt two lovers. A novel* (by Col. Rowan Hamilton).
+ London: F.V. White & Co., 1891, 2 vols. SOURCE Brown 2, 589; Wolff, 2944. LOCATION D, L, NUC.
COMMENTARY A romance that is set between Carrickmanor Castle (apparently near Newcastle, Co. Down), London and Zululand. Harry Kingscote and Ned Borthwick both love Effie MacDonald. She accepts Ned who shortly afterwards sails for South Africa. Harry enters on a course of dissipation. Soon he leaves for the Zulu war. Meantime Effie meets with an acci-

dent that deprives her of speech. Ned on hearing this cools considerably. Unaware that she has been cured, he breaks off the match and she and Harry become lovers [Brown 2].

H122　*The story of Sylvia* (by Hamilton Rowan [*sic*]).
　　London, New York, Melbourne: Ward, Lock, Bowden & Co., 1893. LOCATION NUC.

H123　*The second answer* (by Rowan Hamilton).
　　London: F.V. White & Co., 1908. SOURCE COPAC. LOCATION L.

HAMILTON, Revd John, pseuds 'An Irishman' and 'N.N.', b. 1800, d. St Andrews (Scotland) 1884. A reforming landlord and writer, JH was the son of James Hamilton, who owned a vast estate at St Ernan's (Co. Donegal), and his wife Helen Pakenham. By age 7, JH and his siblings were orphaned. They were mainly raised by their grandmother, Lady Longford, of Pakenham Hall (Co. Westmeath), spending some time with their uncle, Sir Arthur Wellesley (later the duke of Wellington) in Dublin where he was then chief secretary for Ireland. JH attended Armagh Royal School and Cambridge University and received an MA in 1821, without examinations. After his marriage to Mary Rose of Novar, Scotland, he returned to the family estates in Donegal and devoted himself to their improvement, at great personal expense. He was devoutly religious, hostile to Roman Catholic doctrine, but opposed to the Orange Order. Considering it unfair that Catholics and Presbyterians should have to support the established church, he relieved his tenants of this obligation. During the Famine he employed his tenants in land improvement, deploring the workhouse system, and he sharply criticized the government over its handling of landlord levies. His relief efforts left the estate diminished and in debt, and while he was remembered by the tenants with affection and respect, his grandson blamed him for reducing the family fortune. He wrote an autobiography, published posthumously: *Sixty years' experience as an Irish landlord* (London, [1894]), and two works on Ireland: *Ireland's recovery and Ireland's health* (Dublin, 1848), and *Thoughts on Ireland by an Irish landlord* (London, 1886). In addition, JH wrote several religious books. SOURCE Allibone Suppl., ii, p. 754; BLC; Brown, p. 128; Cox cat. 49/96; O'Donoghue, p. 182; RIA/DIB.

H124　*Three Fenian brothers; or, some scenes in Irish life* (by 'an Irishman'; dedication signed 'N.N.').
　　London, Cambridge: Macmillan & Co., 1866. SOURCE Brown, 704; NSTC; COPAC. LOCATION Dt.
　　COMMENTARY Set in Ireland around 1865. Three sons of a well-to-do farmer are enticed into joining the Fenian brotherhood. One of them had served in the Federal army in the US [Brown; COPAC].

H125　*Philo: A romance of life in the first century* (by John Hamilton).
　　London: Saunders, Otley & Co., 1867, 3 vols. SOURCE COPAC; OCLC. LOCATION L, Kent State Univ.
　　COMMENTARY Historical fiction of the Christians under the Roman empire in the first century [RL; Cox cat. 49/96].

'HAMILTON, M.', pseud. See **LUCK, Mrs Mary Churchill.**

HAMILTON, Margaret. See **HUNGERFORD, Mrs Margaret Wolfe.**

HAMILTON, Rowan. See **HAMILTON, Gawin William Rowan.**

HAMILTON, W.H., pseud. 'W.H.H.', fl. 1876. Humour writer and possible playwright, WHH's identity is revealed in the NLI copy of the following book, which states that this person was from Holywood (Co. Down). He or she may be identified with the author of a play,

'The portrait of Cervantes', acted in the early part of the nineteenth century at Crow Street Theatre, Dublin. However, the long interval between the play and the following book remains unexplained. SOURCE O'Donoghue, p. 182; RL.

H126   *Waifs of conversation* (by 'W.H.H.').
+ Belfast: James Magill, 1876. SOURCE Linen Hall cat. p. 106. LOCATION D, BFl, InND Loeber coll.
COMMENTARY Humorous anecdotes of Irish life, set mainly in Ulster, which were first published in the *Belfast News-Letter*. Preface dated June 1876 [Rowan cat. 62/174].

HANAN, Revd Denis. Co-author. See MORRIS, Alfred.

HANNAN, Miss Josephine, pseud. 'M.J.H.', fl. 1860s. Catholic religious fiction writer, JH also wrote a book of prayers, *Angels' whispers* (Dublin, 1883). Given her surname and that she published mostly in Dublin, she is likely to have been of Irish origin. SOURCE Allibone Suppl., ii, p. 760; BLC.

H127   *Gertrude Waynflete. A story for Christmas* (by 'M.J.H.')
+ London: Ward & Lock, [1864]. SOURCE Alston, p. 184. LOCATION L.
COMMENTARY Set in Riverford, a fictional place [CM].

H128   *Sister Agatha; or, lights and shadows in a life-work* (by 'M.J.H.').
+ Dublin: M.H. Gill & Son, 1883. LOCATION D.
COMMENTARY Religious fiction [ML].

H129   *Leo. A tale* (by 'M.J.H.').
Dublin: M.H. Gill & Son, 1883. SOURCE Alston, p. 184. LOCATION L (destroyed), E.
COMMENTARY Religious fiction [BLC].

H130   *Told in the gloaming; or, our Novena and how we made it* (by Josephine Hannan).
+ Dublin: M.H. Gill, 1884. SOURCE Allibone Suppl., ii, p. 760; Alston, p. 184; COPAC. LOCATION D (1905 edn), L (destroyed), O.
COMMENTARY Religious fiction featuring an Irish person living in a French convent [CM].

H131   *Waifs of a Christmas morning, and other tales* (by Josephine Hannan).
Dublin: M.H. Gill & Son, 1886 (ill. I.M. Whitgreave). SOURCE Allibone Suppl., ii, p. 760; Alston, p. 184; COPAC. LOCATION L (destroyed).
COMMENTARY Religious fiction [BLC].

HANNIGAN, Denis Francis, b. Dungarvan (Co. Waterford) 1855. Journalist, novelist, and barrister, DFH was the only son of Declan Hannigan, merchant, Dungarvan (Co. Waterford), and Honora Curran. DFH was educated at Queen's College, Cork, where he graduated BA and LLB. He was admitted to the King's Inns, Dublin, in 1876, to the Middle Temple, London, in 1877, and was called to the Irish Bar in 1878. He worked as a journalist in Dublin and later moved to America. His serialized novel 'The Moores of Moore's Court' appeared in the *Monitor: An Illustrated Dublin Magazine* (1879). He contributed to a variety of periodicals and translated several books from French. SOURCE Brown, p. 129; BLC; Ferguson, p. 200; Irish pseudonyms; RIA/DIB; RL.

H132   *Luttrell's doom: A narrative from the autobiography of an Irish gentlewoman (1661–1729)* (by Denis Francis Hannigan).
Aberdeen: Moran, 1896. SOURCE Brown, 708. LOCATION NUC.
COMMENTARY Historical fiction. Purports to be extracts from an Irish gentlewoman's diary kept between 1661 and 1729 [Brown; RL].

HANRAHAN, P.R., b. probably Co. Wexford *c*.1815, d. Wexford 1893 (1892 according to Browne). Teacher, poet and writer of historical fiction, PRH lived in Farnogue Cottage, Wexford, to which his family, formerly of Macmine (Co. Wexford) had moved. He was a pupil of the Lancastrian school, and became a teacher in 1831. He was in charge of the local school until it was disestablished in 1871, when he was entrusted with the National School. The story about the schoolteacher in the following book may well be autobiographical. He also published *Echoes of the past, odes on ancient Ireland, national melodies and other miscellaneous pieces* (Dublin, 1882). He died at Farnogue Cottage and was buried in Carrig churchyard, near Gorey, Wexford. SOURCE Brown, p. 130; Browne, p. 63; NUC; O'Donoghue, p. 183; RL; Rowe & Scallan, 471.

H133   *Eva; or, the buried city of Bannow. A historical tale of the early English invaders* (by P.R. Hanrahan).
+ London: For the author, 1866 (subscribers' list). SOURCE Brown, 711. LOCATION D, InND Loeber coll.
+ Wexford: John English, 1960, 3rd edn (as *Eva; or, the buried city of Bannow. An historical tale of the early English invaders* [without the second story]). LOCATION L, InND Loeber coll.
COMMENTARY Historical fiction about the Norman invasion in Co. Wexford, opening in 1169, relating the marriage of Eva MacMurrough to Strongbow (the source for the story is Giraldus Cambrensis). The remainder of the volume contains another story 'Frank Farrell, the Irish national teacher', which addresses abuses in the National schools, Frank's fondness of reading but his lack of books, and reading practices. This story is not reprinted in the 1960 edn [RL; Brown].

HARDING, Mrs Anne Raikes, b. Bath 1781, d. Boulogne (France) 1858. English novelist, ARH married a Bristol merchant, Thomas Harding, who died young and intestate. She ran a school for thirty-five years and from 1818 on published seven anonymous novels. She retired when her children (except a mentally-handicapped daughter) were settled. Shortly afterwards her banker defrauded her of her capital of £1,000. She opened a high-class boarding-house and applied to the Royal Literary Fund for assistance. Later she went to live in France, from which she addressed further pleas to the Fund for help. The following is her only known Irish novel. SOURCE Blain, p. 486; Boase, i, p. 1326; NCBEL 4, pp 927–8; NUC; ODNB.
H134   *The refugees. An Irish tale* [anon.].
London: Longman, Hurst, Rees, Orme & Brown, 1822, 3 vols. SOURCE Brown, 712; Block, p. 97; British Fiction; Garside, 1822:37. LOCATION Corvey CME 3–628–47459–0, Ireland related fiction, L, NUC.
Paris: C. Gosselin, 1830, 5 vols. (trans. by Mrs Sinclair as *Les réfugiés, histoire irlandaise*). SOURCE Garside, 1822:27; CCF. LOCATION BNF.
COMMENTARY Historical fiction. Sir Phelim O'Brien, an absentee Irish landlord, is driven from France by the revolution of 1789. He returns to Ireland with his foolish, fashionable wife, his daughter Calista, his surviving son, St Louis, and an Italian follower. Everything in Ireland seems rude and barbarous in comparison to France. Their estate in the Galtees, with its dilapidated mansion, is contrasted unfavourably with that of the neighbouring Lord Dungarron. There is a love story between Calista and Lord Dungarron's heir. St Louis joins the United Irishmen and is killed in the 1798 rising [Brown].

HARDY, Elizabeth, pseud. '**E.H.**', b. Dublin 1786 (1794 according to RIA/DIB), d. London, 1854. Novelist, EH was a zealous Protestant who was ruined by bank failure and dishonest lawyers and in 1830 turned to her pen to make a living. In 1848, while working on *Owen Glendower* (London, 1849, 2 vols.), which she intended to be her masterpiece, she ran into debt and was imprisoned in the Queen's bench prison, London, 1852, dying there two years later. The RIA/DIB states that she also wrote another work, 'Thomas Dillon' (1845), but this has not been located. SOURCE Allibone, i, p. 784; Boase, i, p. 1332; Brady, p. 101; ODNB; RIA/DIB; Sutherland, p. 276.

H135 *Michael Cassidy; or, the cottage gardener. A tale for small beginners* [anon.].
London: Seeley & Co., 1845. SOURCE Brown, 713; COPAC. LOCATION L.
COMMENTARY Improving fiction that attempts to urge people to cultivate small allotments, green crops, rotation, economy, and hard work [Brown].

H136 *Owen Glendower; or, the prince in Wales. An historical romance* [anon.].
+ London: Richard Bentley, 1849, 2 vols. SOURCE Brown, p. 130. LOCATION L, NUC.
COMMENTARY Historical novel set in Wales in the time of King Henry IV and features the Welsh hero, Owen Glendower (1359–1415). The idea of taking Glendower for a hero was suggested by Sir James Mackintosh [ML; Burmester list].

H137 *The confessor: A Jesuit tale of the times, founded on fact* (by 'E.H.').
London: Richard Bentley, 1851, 3 vols. SOURCE Brown, 713; COPAC (1854 edn). LOCATION NUC.
London: Clarke, Beeton & Co., 1853 (The Run and Read Library, No. 3). SOURCE Sadleir, 3673; Alston, p. 185. LOCATION L (1854 edn).
COMMENTARY Anti-Catholic fiction [Sadleir].

HARDY, P.D. See **HARDY, Philip Dixon.**

HARDY, P. Dixon. See **HARDY, Philip Dixon.**

HARDY, Philip Dixon (known as **P.D. Hardy** and **P. Dixon Hardy**), possible pseud. 'P.D.H.', b. *c*.1794, d. Rathmines (Dublin) 1875. Poet, bookseller, printer, editor and miscellaneous writer, PDH concentrated on publishing Irish fiction and Irish topography, and was also known for his anti-Catholic publications. He edited several Dublin periodicals, including the *Dublin Penny Journal* (published first by Folds, then by Hardy, 1833–6) with Samuel Lover§; the *Dublin Literary Gazette* (Dublin, 1830, in collaboration with W.F. Wakeman), and the literary annual *A wreath from the Emerald Isle. A new year's gift for 1826* (Dublin, 1826), which sold poorly. Together with J.J. McGregor, and G.N. Wright he published *The new picture of Dublin or a stranger's guide to the Irish metropolis* (Dublin, 1835), and wrote *Essays, and sketches of Irish life and character* (Dublin, 1827). In the realm of Irish literature, he edited several anthologies of Irish short stories (see below), and wrote a poem, *Bertha: A tale of Erin* (Dublin, 1817). It is probable that under the pseudonym 'P.D.H.' he contributed a short story to *Popular tales and legends of the Irish peasantry* (ed. by Samuel Lover§, Dublin, 1834). PDH's main occupation, however, was as a printer (in the 1830s his place of business was at Cecilia Street in Dublin). He supplied at least seven volumes for the Kildare Place Society. Judging from his *The holy wells of Ireland* (Dublin, 1840), he also had antiquarian interests. He married Marianne Hall, but the date of the marriage is not known. SOURCE Allibone, i, p. 784; Allibone Suppl., ii, p. 764; Bradshaw, i, pp 560–1; Brown, p. 130; Clyde, pp 88–9; de Búrca cat. 47/416; Garside 2, 1833:46; Hodges Figgis cat. 10 n.s./1295; Keane, p. 213; NUC; O'Donoghue, p. 184; Personal communication, Mary Pollard, Jan. 1998; RIA/DIB; RL.

H138 *A wreath from the Emerald Isle. A new year's gift for 1826* (ed. by P.D. Hardy).
+ Dublin: Wm. Curry Jnr & Co; London: James Duncan; Edinburgh: D. Lizars, [1826] (ill. Kirkwood & Son, T. Kells). LOCATION D, L.
COMMENTARY Some of the stories appeared in a periodical publication conducted by PDH 'some years ago' (possibly the *Dublin Penny Journal*). Consists of essays, poetry and stories.

The stories are: 'A party of pleasure, or a trip to the Dargle', 'Amelia and Amandis, or a cure for love', 'A water party, or a voyage to Howth', 'Memoranda of Timothy Timmins, Esq. Incorporated with his log-book', 'Jane Fitz-Charles, or the effects of indiscretion', 'The wedding of Benjamin Brimmige, gentleman. Containing some particulars of a matrimonial excursion to the County of Wicklow', 'Scenes from Ireland. Journal of an excursion equatic and pedestrian' (contains a letter from Castle Rack-Rent, inspired by Maria Edgeworth's§ novel of that name). PDH used the unsold sheets of this book in his *Essays, and sketches of Irish life and character* (Dublin, 1827) [RL].

H139   *Tales and stories of Ireland. Carleton, Lover and Mrs. Hall* [ed. by P. Dixon Hardy]. Dublin: William Curry Jnr & Co., 1834. SOURCE Hayley 2, p. 423.

+ Dublin: Hardy & Walker; London: Ball, Arnold & Co., 1840 (as *Characteristic sketches of Ireland and the Irish by Carleton, Lover, and Mrs. Hall*; ed. by P. Dixon Hardy; ill. J. Kirkwood). SOURCE Hayley, 13a; Rafroidi, ii, p. 182 (1845 edn); Sadleir, 496 (1845 edn); Topp 8, p. 39. LOCATION NUC (1844 edn), Grail, D, InND Loeber coll. (lacks pp 103–201, the 'Abduction').

+ London: Milner & Co., n.d. (as *Tales and stories of Ireland. By Carleton, Lover, and Mrs. Hall* (ill. J. Kirkwood). SOURCE Hayley, 13i. LOCATION Utrecht Univ., Utrecht, Netherlands.

+ Halifax: Milner & Sowerby, 1852 (as *Characteristic sketches of Ireland and the Irish. By Carleton, Lover, and Mrs. Hall*; ill. J. Kirkwood). LOCATION D, InND Loeber coll.

COMMENTARY PDH in the preface to the Dublin, 1840 edn relates that the stories first appeared in the *National Magazine* (Dublin, 1825–6). No copy of the Dublin, Curry, 1834 edn has been located. The Dublin, Hardy & Walker edn is bound from the parts, but without title pages. Another edn in parts was published by John Cumming in Dublin and R. Groombridge in London, starting Apr. 1841, which appears to have had the same contents and was priced at 6*d*. per part, with the same preface by PDH but dated 1841. Contents: 'The horse stealers' (William Carleton§), 'Owen M'Carthy' (William Carleton§), 'Squire Warnock' (William Carleton§), 'The abduction' (William Carleton§), 'Sir Turlough' (William Carleton§), 'Paddy Mullowney's travels in France' (Samuel Lover§), 'A legend of Clonmacnoise' (Samuel Lover§), 'Ballads and ballad singers' (Samuel Lover§), 'The Irish agent' (Mrs S.C. Hall§), 'Philip Garraty; or, "we'll see about it"' (Mrs S.C. Hall§) [RL].

H140   *Pic nics: from the Dublin Penny Journal, being a selection from the legends, tales and stories of Ireland, which have appeared in the published volumes of the Dublin Penny Journal* [ed. by Philip Dixon Hardy] (dedicated to Sir William Betham).

+ Dublin: Philip Dixon Hardy, W.F. Wakeman; London: Richard Groombridge, 1836 (ill. B. Clayton Jun; spine has title and 'Carleton' [*sic*]). SOURCE Brown, 80; Harris, p. 167. LOCATION D, L, NUC, InND Loeber coll.

+ Dublin: John Cumming, 1837 (as *Legends, tales, and stories of Ireland*, ed. by Philip Dixon Hardy; ill.). SOURCE Brown, 714; Wolff, 2969. LOCATION Dt, L, NUC, InND Loeber coll.

Philadelphia: E.L. Carey & A. Hart, 1837, 2 vols. (as *Pic nics; or, legends, tales and stories of Ireland*). SOURCE Cummins cat. 61/68; OCLC. LOCATION Virginia Tech.

COMMENTARY The Dublin (1837) edn was published in two sizes, octavo and duodecimo, with the latter in slightly smaller type. The stories deal chiefly with the south of Ireland. Contents of the Dublin, 1836 edn (excluding poetry): 'Darby Doyle's voyage to Quebec' (T.E. [Thomas Ettingsall]), 'Reminiscences of a Rockite' (M'C), 'The pooka' (E.W. [Edward Walsh]), 'The dreamers. Founded on facts' (J.L.L.), 'The smugglers' (Tim. Simkins), 'Hie over to England, or Shaun Long and the fairies' (W.B. [William Betham?]), 'Ellen Duncan' (Denis O'Donoho), 'Murtough Oge, the outlaw', 'The leprachaun' (J.L.L.). [in 1836 edn 'The leprawhaun (*sic*)'],

'The unforgiven', 'The red spirit' ([John Francis Waller§?]), 'Paddy Doyle's first trip to Cork' (E.W. [Edward Walsh]), 'Pether Brierly's inn adventure' (Denis O'Donoho), 'The pattern of the lough' (J.L.L.), 'The banshee' (J.L.L.) [ML; Brown; identification of the authors in Cummins cat. 61/68; Harris; Rowan cat. 54/361].

H141 *The Northern cottage; or, the effects of Bible-reading* (by 'P.D.H.').
+ Dublin: Philip Dixon Hardy & Sons; London: R. Groombridge (For the Religious Tract and Book Depository for Ireland), 1842. LOCATION D.
COMMENTARY 71pp. Ascribed to PDH. This appears to be an extended version of a chapbook of 24pp of the same title which was published by Bentham & Hardy in Dublin in 1827. The 1842 edn priced at 6*d*. [RL].

H142 *Hardy's tourist guide through Ireland: in four tours* [ed. by Philip Dixon Hardy].
+ Dublin: Hardy & Sons, 1858. SOURCE COPAC. LOCATION L.
COMMENTARY Travel guide interspersed with 'Legend of O'Donoghue and his white horse', 'The hermit of Muckross Abbey' and other untitled stories [RL].

HARE, Barbara. See HEMPHILL, Barbara.

HARE, M., fl. 1797. Novelist, MH probably resided in Cork or its vicinity. Perhaps he can be identified with Mark Hare, eldest son of the Rev. Patrick Hare, of Cashel (Co. Tipperary) and Mary Crozier. MH was educated at TCD; admitted to the King's Inns in 1794; to the Middle Temple (London) in 1796, and called to the Irish Bar in 1798. SOURCE Keane, p. 213; RL.

H143 *The Bastile* [*sic*]; *or, manly sensibility. A novel* (by M. Hare; dedication to countess de Civrac).
Cork: James Haly, 1797, 2 vols. SOURCE Raven 2, 1797:43; ESTC n043555. LOCATION MH.
COMMENTARY Preface mentions that subscribers had been collected but that there were so few that a list was unwarranted [Raven 2].

HARE, Mark. See HARE, M.

HARKIN, H. See HARKIN, Hugh.

HARKIN, Hugh (known as H. Harkin), b. Magillian (Co. Derry) 1791, d. Belfast (Co. Antrim) 1854. Teacher, journalist and editor of the *Lamp* (York), a Catholic periodical, and the *Bulletin: A Catholic Journal* (York, 1852). HH wrote verse and sketches of Irish life for the Catholic *Belfast Vindicator, edited* by Charles Gavan Duffy, and for the *Nation* (Dublin) and the *Dublin Penny Journal*. An ardent Catholic with the gift of oratory, he supported Daniel O'Connell and worked hard for Catholic emancipation. Several anonymous publications and one under the name 'Henry Picken' that were Presbyterian in tone were written by HH for a poor blind man of that name who sold them as his own with HH's consent. HH resided at Edinburgh and Leeds about 1842 to 1848. SOURCE BLC; Boase, v, pp 576–7; Brown, p. 131; Irish pseudonyms; O'Donoghue, p. 184.

H144 *The quarterclift; or, the adventures of Hudy McGuigan* (by H. Harkin).
Dublin: William Curry Jnr & Co.; London: Hodgson; Belfast: Hodgson, 1840. SOURCE OCLC. LOCATION KU-S.
Belfast: Vindicator, [1841] (ill.). SOURCE Brown, 715; Linen Hall cat. p. 107 ([1840] edn); OCLC. LOCATION BFl, D (parts).
Draperstown: Ballinascreen Historical Society, 1993 (as *The life and adventures of Hudy McGuigan*). SOURCE OCLC. LOCATION DCL.

COMMENTARY Originally issued by William Curry in Dublin and Hodgson in London and Belfast in parts, at 1*s*. per part (starting in Jan. 1841). The story is founded on an old Co. Derry folk tale of a 'gommeral' named Hudy McGuiggen, who did not understand why he could not fly. He made himself a pair of wings out of goose feathers with which he jumped off a high mountain, and came to grief. However, he recovered and lived to be an old man [Brown].

HARPUR, Revd W., b. *c*.1855, d. *c*.1936. Fiction writer for juveniles, WH can probably be identified with Thomas William Harpur, son of the Revd Thomas Bernard Harpur, incumbent of Ardmore (Co. Wexford). TWH was educated at TCD, where he graduated BA in 1877 and MA in 1880. He was ordained deacon in 1877 and was curate of St Chrysostom, Everton (England, 1877–80); Kilglass (Co. Sligo, 1880–1); incumbent of Clonaslee (Co. Laois, 1881–5); curate of Leighlin (Co. Carlow, 1885–6); incumbent of Muckamore (Co. Antrim, 1886–98); rector of Castlecomer (Co. Kilkenny, 1907–17); incumbent of Knocktopher (Co. Kilkenny, 1917); prebendary of Tascoffin (Co. Kilkenny, 1911–26), and treasurer of Ossory (1926). He married at Killeshin Church (Carlow) in 1887, Geraldine, eldest daughter of Major Harman Fitzmaurice, Queen's County Rifles. SOURCE: Swanzy, p. 214; Leslie, *Connor*, p. 376.
H145   *The Glen farm; or, Jim Maguire's dream, and what came of it* (by W. Harpur). London: J. Henderson, 1880 (Young Folks Illustrated Story Books). SOURCE OCLC. LOCATION D.

HARRIS, Frank. See **HARRIS, James Thomas.**

HARRIS, James Thomas (also known as **Frank Harris**), b. Galway 1856, d. Nice (France) 1931. Editor, journalist, biographer and novelist, FH was born of Welsh parents and baptized John Thomas Harris. His father was a lieutenant in the Royal Navy and a harsh disciplinarian; his mother was the daughter of a Baptist minister and died when FH was age 4. He attended the Royal Grammar School, Armagh and Ruabon Grammar School, Denbigh (Wales). At age 15 he used a school prize of £10 to run away to America. He drifted between many jobs, including cattle driving, but managed to educate himself at Kansas State University where he showed his talent for journalism. He was admitted to the Bar in Lawrence, Kansas, around 1876. He returned to London, travelled in France and Germany and attended the universities of Heidelberg and Göttingen. He studied Greek and Latin, and by his own admission his twin pleasures were Shakespeare and seduction. He returned to London, became editor of the ailing *Evening News* and with a mix of sensational politics, sport and sex, increased the circulation tenfold. By 1886 he was editor of the *Fortnightly Review* (London); married to a wealthy widow; entertaining royalty, and being considered as a candidate for parliament. This period of respectability soon passed and he reverted to his old ways. His support of Charles Stuart Parnell, coupled with his flagrant marital infidelities, ruined his political and financial circumstances. His wife separated from him in 1894. His succeeded in updating the *Fortnightly Review* (George Bernard Shaw§ was employed as a drama critic) but he was dismissed in 1894, his lifestyle too unpalatable for the proprietors. With help from wealthy friends he bought the London *Saturday Review* and made it the most brilliant – and profitable – literary and political periodical in the country. Yet only a few years later he had fallen into financial ruin and personal disgrace and served time in prison for contempt of court. He went to the US after the outbreak of the First World War where he continued editing and writing, often clashing with the censors. He settled in France in 1923. Besides his novels, Harris wrote multiple works on Shakespeare and biographies of George Bernard Shaw§ and Oscar Wilde§, to whom he remained a good friend during Wilde's trial and imprisonment. A play, *Mr. & Mrs. Daventry* was based on a scenario by Wilde, who

Harris

is quoted as having said: 'Frank Harris has been to all the great houses of England – once!' His biography *My life*, which was as scandalous as it was popular, was published privately in Paris between 1922 and 1927. For his portraits and papers, see ODNB. SOURCE EF, p. 175; Hogan 2, pp 524–7; OCIL, p. 238; ODNB; Sutherland, p. 281.

H146 *Elder Conklin and other stories* (by Frank Harris).
London: William Heinemann, 1895. SOURCE Hogan 2, p. 526; Sutherland, p. 281; COPAC. LOCATION L.
COMMENTARY Vivid recollection of rough life in Kansas. The title story is a portrait of an iron-willed Christian patriarch who stands up against General Custer's attempt to give his farmland to Indians as part of a treaty. It ends unhappily with the Elder's daughter running away from his domestic tyranny. Also includes 'The best man in Garotte, a tale of gun sling-ing in the wild west' [Sutherland].

H147 *A daughter of Eve* (by Frank Harris).
Paris: privately printed, 1898. SOURCE Hogan 2, p. 526; OCLC. LOCATION California State Univ., Northridge.

H148 *Montes de matador, and other stories* (by Frank Harris).
+ London: Grant Richards, 1900. SOURCE Hogan 2, p. 526; Sutherland, p. 281. LOCATION L.
New York: M. Kennerly, 1910. SOURCE NYPL. LOCATION NN.
COMMENTARY Contents: 'Montes de matador', 'First love: A confession', 'Profit and love', 'The interpreter: A mere episode', 'Sonia' (the story of a young MP's infatuation for a Russian nihilist) [ML] .

H149 *How to beat the Boer: A conversation in Hades* (by Frank Harris).
+ London: William Heinemann, 1900. SOURCE COPAC. LOCATION L.
COMMENTARY 29pp. Story, written in the form of a formal dialogue, concerning the Boer War in South Africa and features among the discussants, Lord Randolph Churchill, Thomas Carlyle, Charles Stewart Parnell, one Aylward, Dr. Samuel Johnson, and a Fenian [Hartman, 760; RL].

H150 *The bomb* (by Frank Harris).
London: John Long, 1908. LOCATION L.
New York: M. Kennerly, 1909. SOURCE Hogan 2, p. 526. LOCATION L.

H151 *Unpath'd waters* (by Frank Harris).
+ London: John Lane, 1913. LOCATION L.
Leipzig: Bernard Tauchnitz, 1924. SOURCE T & B, 4899. LOCATION L.
COMMENTARY Contents: 'The miracle of the stigmata', 'The holy man', 'The king of the Jews', 'The irony of chance', 'An English saint', 'Mr. Jacob's philosophy', 'The ring', 'The spider and the fly', 'The magic glasses' [RL].

H152 *Great days* (by Frank Harris).
London: John Lane; Toronto: Bell & Cockburn, 1914. LOCATION L.
New York: M. Kennerly, 1914. SOURCE Hogan 2, p. 526.
COMMENTARY No copy of the New York edn located [RL].

H153 *The yellow ticket and other stories* (by Frank Harris).
London: Grant Richards, 1914. SOURCE Hogan 2, p. 526. LOCATION L.

H154 *Undream'd of shores* (by Frank Harris).
+ London: Grant Richards, 1924. SOURCE Hogan 2, p. 526. LOCATION L.
New York: Brentano's, 1924. SOURCE Hogan 2, p. 526; RLIN. LOCATION NNC.
COMMENTARY Contents: 'A mad love', 'Akbar: "the mightiest"', 'A fit of madness', 'A Chinese story', 'Sir Peter's difficulty', 'Love is my sin', 'As others see us', 'A lunatic?', 'In central Africa', 'The extra eight days', 'The great game', 'The temple to the forgotten dead', 'My last word' [ML].

568

HARRIS, Miss S.M., pseud. 'Athène', b. probably Co. Down, fl. 1898. Historical and romance novelist, SMH was the daughter of a farmer at Ballynafern, Banbridge (Co. Down), and later lived in Belfast. SOURCE Brown, p. 131; RIA/DIB.

H155   *In the valleys of South Down* (by 'Athène'; dedicated to John Ruskin and Miss Constance F. Gordon Cumming).
+ Belfast: M'Caw, Stevenson & Orr, 1898. SOURCE Brown, 717. LOCATION D, L, NUC, InND Loeber coll.
COMMENTARY A story of thwarted love between Rupert Stanwell and Mabel Mervyn, set in south Co. Down with many descriptions of rural outings. Rupert's parents want him to marry a rich American heiress. In the end, however, Rupert and Mabel marry [ML].

H156   *Grace Wardwood; or, from the gloom of winter to the glories of summer* (by 'Athène'; dedicated to the author's mother).
+ Dublin: James Duffy & Co., 1900. SOURCE Brown, 718; OCLC. LOCATION D, L, InND Loeber coll.
COMMENTARY A domestic tale of middle-class people in Co. Down, with several love stories intertwined. Some legends, such as 'Legend of the Irish harp', are introduced [RL; Brown].

H157   *Dust of the world. Historical novel of Belfast in the seventeenth century* (by 'Athène'; dedicated to the author's mother).
+ London: George Allen & Co., 1913. SOURCE Brown, 719. LOCATION D, InND Loeber coll.
COMMENTARY An historical romance of Belfast in the seventeenth century revolving around the persecution of Presbyterians. Among various historical characters, it introduces the earl of Donegall and Lady Donegall, both of whom have hankerings after presbyterianism [ML; Brown].

HARRISON, James, pseud. 'Himself', fl. 1800? Attributed author and publisher, JH was publisher of the *British Magazine* (London), possibly the bookseller employed by Lady William Hamilton in compiling the *Genuine memoirs of Lord Viscount Nelson* (1806), and attributed author of the following text, which first appeared in periodicals. SOURCE Allibone, i, p. 793; ER; NYPL; Mayo, 565.

H158   *The exile of Ireland; or, the life, voyages, travels, and wonderful adventures of Captain Winterfield, who, after many successes and surprising escapes in Europe and America with English forces, became, at last, a distinguished rebel chief in Ireland* (by 'Himself').
London: J. Bailey, [1800?]. SOURCE NYPL. LOCATION NN.
London: Ann Lemoine, 1802 (as *The voyages, distresses, and adventures of Capt. Winterfield. Written by himself containing an account of his transactions in America, during the war; his disastrous voyage to England in which he had the misfortune to be taken by an Algerine man of war near the coast of Portugal, and carried to Barbary, where he remained in slavery upwards of six years: his miraculous escape from thence with five more, in a canvass boat of their own construction, and safe arrival at Majorca: with several remarkable circumstances after his captivity; and his safe arrival at last in Scotland*). LOCATION ViU.
London: E. Thomas, 1805 (as *The exile of Ireland; or, the wonderful adventures and extraordinary escapes of an Irish rebel officer, exhibiting the bravery of a young soldier, the passion of an ardent lover, and the skills of an intrepid commander, in travels in America, Spain and Ireland. Written by himself*). LOCATION L.
COMMENTARY 36 pp in London, J. Bailey [1800?] edn. Probably fictitious. First published in instalments under the title *The history of Captain Winterfield*, in the *British Magazine and*

Review (where signed 'H—'), and in the *Gentleman's and London Magazine* (both London, 1783) and subsequently reprinted in many other periodicals. An associated text is the possibly equally fictitious novelette *The voyages, distresses and adventures of Capt. Winterfield. Written by himself. Containing an account of his transactions in America, during the war* (London, 1799), in which Capt. Winterfield describes himself as a native of Scotland. Capt. Winterfield relates his voyage to the West Indies and how, upon returning to England after two years, his regiment is ordered to Ireland. He is moved by what he sees in Ireland and how cold the English are compared to the warmth of the common Irish people. Further voyages take him to Canada and America but he returns to Ireland, having inherited a small estate in Co. Wicklow upon the death of his father. He falls in love with an Irish rebel's daughter and is thus embroiled in the 1798 rebellion. On the point of being condemned to death in the aftermath of the rebellion, he is rescued by a former fellow British officer, escapes to the Continent to live in Hamburgh (*sic*), Germany [ER; Mayo, 565; NYPL].

HART, Elizabeth Anna (née Smedley), b. London 1822, d. Dublin 1886. Children's writer and poet, EAH was the daughter of Revd Edward Smedley and Mary Hume. Her sister, Manella Bute Smedley§, was also an author. EAH married Thomas Barnard Hart of Glen Alla (Co. Donegal), a retired officer in the British army in India, in 1848. The couple lived at Glen Alla where she partly-financed the building of the church and rectory from the proceeds of her writing. She published a novel in verse, *Mrs. Jerningham's journal* (London, 1869), and other poetry, especially for children. Under the joint pseudonym, 'Mrs. Fanny Hart', she and her sister contributed to *Aunt Judy's Magazine* (London). Some of EAH's fiction is set in Ireland. She died childless. SOURCE A. Harvey, afterword to 2002 edn of *The runaway* (London, 1872); H.T. Hart, *The family history of Hart of Donegal* (London, 1907), pp 62–4; MVP, p. 209.

H159 *The runaway. A story for the young* [anon.].
    London: Macmillan & Co., 1872. LOCATION L.
    + London: Persephone Books, 2002 (ill. Gwen Raverat; with new afterword by Anne Harvey & Frances Spalding). LOCATION InND Loeber coll.
    COMMENTARY An adventure story for juveniles set in England. Olga has run away from her boarding school and asks Clarissa, who she meets in a park, to hide her. Clarissa hides her in a closet in her bedroom, but Olga roams around the house at times and creates all kinds of upheaval. Olga has brought with her money and jewellery. An advertisement in the paper inquiring about her whereabouts implies that she has stolen these goods. The police are after her, and Clarissa gets in hot water over her. Just when things look really bleak, Olga's father appears and sets things right. Unlike many other books of juvenile fiction of the time, this volume does not have a religious message or a strong moral overtone [ML].

H160 *A very young couple* [anon.].
    + London, Belfast: Marcus Ward & Co., [1873]. LOCATION L.
    COMMENTARY No Irish content [RL].

H161 *Miss Hitchcock's wedding dress* [anon.].
    + London, Belfast: Marcus Ward & Co., 1876. SOURCE COPAC. LOCATION L.
    COMMENTARY Set in London [RL].

H162 *Freda* [anon.].
    + London: Richard Bentley & Sons, 1878, 3 vols. LOCATION L.
    COMMENTARY No Irish content [RL].

H163 *Very genteel* [anon.].
    + London: Griffith & Farran; New York: E.P. Dutton, 1880. LOCATION L.
    COMMENTARY Fiction for juveniles set in Ireland [RL].

H164 *Poor Nelly; and Polly and Joe* [anon.].
+ London, Paris, New York: Cassell, Petter, Galpin & Co., [1880] (ill.). SOURCE Topp 7, 275. LOCATION L.
COMMENTARY Fiction for juveniles; no Irish content [RL].

H165 *Two fourpenny bits* [anon.].
+ London, Paris, New York: Cassell, Petter, Galpin & Co., [1880] (ill.). SOURCE Topp 7, 266. LOCATION L.
COMMENTARY Fiction for juveniles; no Irish content [RL].

H166 *May Cunningham's trial* [anon.].
+ London, Paris, New York: Cassell & Co., [1883] (ill.). LOCATION L.
COMMENTARY Fiction for juveniles; no Irish content [RL].

H167 *Wilfred's widow* [anon.].
+ London: Richard Bentley & Son, 1883, 2 vols. LOCATION L.
COMMENTARY No Irish content [RL].

H168 *Mr. Burke's nieces* [anon.].
+ London, Paris, New York: Cassell & Co., [1883] (ill.). SOURCE Topp 7, 371. LOCATION L.
COMMENTARY Fiction for juveniles; no Irish content [RL].

HART, William, pseud. 'W.H. Floredice', b. 1816, d. near West Drayton (London) 1904. Folklore writer, memoirist and colonial administrator, WH was the son of Gen. George Vaughan Hart (not to be confused with Revd George Vaughan Hart, who died *c*.1831) and Charlotte Ellerker of Co. Donegal. WH probably grew up at Doe Castle (Co. Donegal), which his father had purchased as a residence. Educated in England at Shrewsbury and the East India College at Hailesbury, he entered the service of the East India Company in 1834. In a career that spanned over thirty years he held many appointments in India, including secretary to the government, judge of the court at Sudder Adawlut, and commissioner of revenue and police. He was also a fellow of the university and a member of the legislative council of Bombay. He returned to Ireland and lived at Fahan (Co. Donegal), where he started to cultivate oyster beds in Lough Swilly which, however, failed,. Subsequently, he lived at Westwood, Lansdowne Hill, Bath. He had married Frances Anne Frere in 1840, with whom he had eight children. He is buried at Eastbourne (E. Sussex). SOURCE H.T. Hart, *The family history of Hart of Donegal* (London, 1907), p. 56; Leslie, *Derry*, pp 267–8; Personal communications, John Hart, Sept. 2001, and Aug. 2005.

H169 *Memories of a month among the 'mere Irish'* (by 'W.H. Floredice').
London: Kegan Paul & Co., 1881. SOURCE Brown, 607. LOCATION L.
London: Kegan Paul, Trench & Co., 1886 (as *Memories of a month among the 'mere Irish'; containing legends, stories, and anecdotes*). LOCATION NUC.
COMMENTARY A record of conversations, events and stories heard from the peasantry during a stay by the author when a youth at the family home, Doe Castle near the head of Sheephaven (Co. Donegal) [Brown; Personal communication, J. Hart, Sept. 2001].

H170 *Floredice stories: Derryreel* (by 'W.H. Floredice').
+ London: Hamilton, Adams & Co.; Bath: Charles Hallett, 1886. SOURCE OCLC (1888 edn). LOCATION L.
+ London: Hamilton, Adams & Co.; Bath: Charles Hallett, 1889 (as *Derryreel: A collection of stories from North-West Donegal*). SOURCE Brown, 607a. LOCATION D, L, NUC.
COMMENTARY Interrelated stories set in north-west Donegal. Contents: 'Mrs. Herraty's wee friend', 'Nancy MacIlhenny's stories of the bad man that was good to his dog', 'The splay-footed princess of Magheroarty', 'Nancy MacIlhenny's story of how Father Bryan Hoolahan

got the better of the witch and her counsellor'. The 1889 edn contains four additional stories 'The great assault and malicious trespass trial', 'Jamie Lavery's narrative of the mystery in Mulroy', 'Nancy MacIlhenny's stories of the sore foot', 'The girl with the eye in the back of her neck' [ML].

HARTIGAN, Henry, fl. 1877. Military man and miscellaneous writer, HH was a sergeant in the Ninth Royal Lancers who served under Capt. Lord William de la Poer Beresford (probably a member of the family of the marquess of Waterford) and fought in India at the siege of Delhi and the battle of Agra. SOURCE Brown, p. 111; RL.

H171 *Stray leaves from a military man's notebook* (by Henry Hartigan; dedicated to Capt. Lord William de la Poer Beresford, a.-d.-c. to the viceroy).

+ Calcutta: Thomas S. Smith, City Press, 1877 (ed. by N.T. Walker, late 6th Dragoon Guards (Carabineers)). SOURCE Brown 2, 595. LOCATION D, L.

COMMENTARY Stories of military life in India, England, and Ireland (mostly Dublin), and describes pranks and escapades of Irish soldiers in the English army [Brown 2].

HARTLEY, Mrs Mary (May) (née Laffan), b. Dublin 1850, d. Dublin 1916. Novelist, short story writer, translator and social critic, MH was the elder daughter of Michael Laffan, a customs officer of Blackrock (Co. Dublin), and Elizabeth Fitzgibbon. Reared a Catholic like her father, and educated at a convent school, she became estranged from catholicism. In an article in *Fraser's Magazine* (London, 1874), she expressed her negative views on the influences of a Catholic education. She married in 1882 Walter Noel Hartley, a fellow of the Royal Society and professor of chemistry at King's College, London, and who later moved to Dublin to teach at the Royal College of Science. He was knighted in 1911. His wife wrote nine novels, several of which are noted for their social realism concerning issues such as education and poverty. Other themes are Irish politics, social climbing, and inter-marriage between Catholics and Protestants. In 1880 she translated as *No relations* (London, 1880) a novel by the French writer Hector Malat. Her interest in children's welfare led her to serve on the executive committee of the National Society for the Prevention of Cruelty to Children from its inception in 1889 until 1893. Her last novel appeared in 1887, perhaps because of negative reaction by the Catholic hierarchy to her criticisms of the Catholic education system and her support for mixed marriages (her husband was a Protestant). In later life she had a nervous breakdown and died in an asylum (ODNB says at her home), three years after the death of her husband, from whom she had been long-separated, and shortly after their son was killed at Gallipoli. For a document by her, see ODNB. In Dublin, she first lived at 2 Tobernia Terrace, Monkstown, and subsequently at 36 Waterloo Road, and 10 Elgin Road, Ballsbridge. SOURCE Allibone Suppl. ii, p. 780; Blain, p. 623; Field Day, v, pp 926–7, 939, 974–5 [under Laffan]; Hogan 2, pp 528–9; C. Mollan, W. Davis, & B. Finucane, *Irish innovators* (Dublin, 2002), p. 91; OCIL, p. 238; ODNB; RIA/DIB; Sutherland, p. 283; Wolff, ii, pp 195–7.

H172 *Hogan, M.P. A novel* [anon.].

London: Henry S. King & Co., 1876, 3 vols. SOURCE Wolff, 3044. LOCATION L.

+ London: Macmillan & Co., 1881 (new edn). SOURCE Brown, 721; Macmillan, p. 398; Topp 5, p. 75. LOCATION D (1882 edn), Dcc, DPL (1883 edn), NUC.

New York: Garland, 1979, 3 vols. (introd. by R.L. Wolff). SOURCE COPAC. LOCATION Dt.

COMMENTARY Set in Dublin in the early 1870s, it depicts the life of rich Dublin Catholic business families and purports to expose the wrongs of the Catholic system of education that leads to lack of learning and lack of good breeding. The hero is a nephew of a Catholic bishop – possibly based on Bishop William Whelan of Bombay – and a Home Rule MP who is manipulated by unscrupulous individuals. He tries to marry a Protestant Ascendancy heiress [Brown; Field Day, v, p. 926; Murphy, pp 29, 60*n*.1; ODNB; Wolff introd., p. 35].

H173 *King, or knave?* [anon.].

London: Chapman & Hall, 1877, 2 vols. SOURCE Burmester list; RLIN. LOCATION L, NIC.

H174 *The honourable Miss Ferrard* [anon.].

+ London: Richard Bentley & Son, 1877, 3 vols. SOURCE Brown, 722; Wolff, 3045. LOCATION DPL, L.

+ London: Macmillan & Co., 1881 (new edn). SOURCE Macmillan, p. 386; Topp 5, p. 73. LOCATION D.

New York: H. Holt & Co., 1878 (Leisure Hour Series, No. 93). SOURCE NYPL. LOCATION NUC, NN.

COMMENTARY The New York edn has some changes to the text. The story addresses, through dialogue, criticisms of Home Rule and of Irish attitudes to work and culture. The Hon. Miss Ferrard is the only daughter of the ancient house of the Darraghmores. Her father squanders his income and the family has to keep moving from place to place, living mainly on credit. She and her brothers grow up in a wild way. For a while she lives with her maiden aunts in Bath, but this is not a success. She has the choice between an Irish farmer lover and an admirable Englishman [Brown; Blain; Topp 5, p. 73].

H175 *Flitters, Tatters, and the counsellor: three waifs from the Dublin streets* [anon.].

+ London: Simpkin, Marshall & Co.; Dublin: Hodges, Foster & Figgis; Edinburgh, Glasgow: John Menzies & Co.; Aberdeen: L. Smith, [1879]. SOURCE OCLC; Topp 8, 586. LOCATION D, L.

+ London: Macmillan & Co., 1883 (new edn). SOURCE Topp 5, p. 74; Wolff, 3043a. LOCATION InND Loeber coll.

Philadelphia: Lippincott & Co., 1879. SOURCE NYPL. LOCATION NN, NUC.

New York: George Munro, 1879 (Seaside Library, No. 27). LOCATION NUC.

COMMENTARY 60pp. A 6th edn was published in 1880. Deals with street urchins of the Dublin slums and shows the brutalizing effects of poverty [COPAC; Topp].

H176 *Flitters, Tatters, and the counsellor and other sketches* [anon.].

+ London: Simpkin Marshall & Co.; Dublin: Hodges, Foster & Figgis; Edinburgh, Glasgow: John Menzies & Co.; Aberdeen: L. Smith, [1879]. SOURCE Topp 8, 586; Wolff, 3043. LOCATION Dt.

Leipzig: Bernard Tauchnitz, 1881. SOURCE Blain, p. 623; T & B, 1962; GLOL. LOCATION Staatsbibliothek zu Berlin.

New York: Garland, 1979 (introd. by R.L. Wolff). SOURCE COPAC. LOCATION Dt.

COMMENTARY Contents: 'Flitters, tatters, and the counsellor' (first published separately in [1879]), 'The game hen' (first published separately in 1880), 'Baubie Clark' (first published separately in 1880), 'Weeds' (set in Co. Tipperary) [Field Day, v, pp 927, 956–9; OCIL; ODNB; Sutherland; Topp 5, p. 74; Wolff; Wolff introd., pp 35–6; RL].

H177 *Christy Carew. A novel* [anon.].

+ London: Richard Bentley & Son, 1880, 3 vols. SOURCE Alston, p. 243; Wolff, 3042. LOCATION D (3 vols. in 1), L.

+ London: Macmillan & Co., 1882 (new edn). SOURCE Brown, 725; Macmillan, p. 410. LOCATION D, Dt (1883 edn), DPL (1893 edn), InND Loeber coll.

New York: Henry Holt, 1880 (Leisure Hour Series, No. 112). SOURCE Topp 5, p. 73. LOCATION NUC.

COMMENTARY Set in Dublin it describes social barriers and distinctions within the middle class. It also touches on Home Rule and the differences between the Irish and the English. It denounces Catholic hostility to mixed marriages, showing the social disabilities which it imposes upon Catholics. Several portraits of priests are presented. A love story is embedded [ML; Brown].

H178　*The game hen* [anon.].
　　　Dublin: M.H. Gill & Son; London: Simpkin, Marshall & Co., 1880. SOURCE Brown, 724; Topp 8, 619. LOCATION L.
　　　COMMENTARY 56pp. Shows women's vindictive and supportive treatment of one another. Also deals with street urchins of the Dublin slums [Blain; RL].

H179　*Baubie Clark* [anon.].
　　　+ Edinburgh, London: William Blackwood & Sons, 1880 (ill.). SOURCE Alston, p. 243. LOCATION D, L.
　　　COMMENTARY Set in Edinburgh [RL].

H180　*No relations* [anon.].
　　　London: Richard Bentley & Son, 1880, 3 vols. SOURCE COPAC. LOCATION L.
　　　New York: G. Munro, 1880. LOCATION NUC.

H181　*A singer's story* [anon.].
　　　London: Chapman & Hall, 1885. SOURCE Alston, p. 243; Topp 3, p. 444. LOCATION L.
　　　New York: George Munro, 1886 (Seaside Library Pocket Edition, No. 681). SOURCE Topp 3, p. 444. LOCATION NUC.

H182　*Ismay's children* [anon.].
　　　+ London, New York: Macmillan & Co., 1887, 3 vols. SOURCE Brown, 726 (mentions 1887, New York, London edn); Macmillan, p. 516; Wolff, 3046. LOCATION D (1887, 2 vol. edn), L, NUC, InND Loeber coll.

COMMENTARY A story of the problems of illegitimacy set in Co. Cork in the second half of the nineteenth century. Ismay Darcy elopes with Capt. Godfrey Mauleverer. They marry in Scotland and have three children. Ismay dies and her aunt Juliet looks after the children. She urges Mauleverer to obtain proper proof of the marriage to ensure the legitimacy of the children. He never does so and dies suddenly, just after he has inherited his uncle's estate. Juliet takes the children to Ireland, but since she has forgotten the name of the place where the marriage took place, she cannot prove that the children are heirs to the estate. It goes to Tighe O'Malley, and Juliet and the three children live in a house on the other side of the river under the protection of the parish priest. The story describes village life, concerns about advantageous marriages, the relations between peasants and landlords, and the Fenian unrest. In the end, the proof to the children's title is found, but not before Juliet dies and the boy, Godfrey, who was involved with the Fenians, is also found dead, either murdered or accidentally drowned [ML].

HARTSTONGE, Matthew Weld (name at birth, Matthew Weld), b. Dublin 1772, d. 1825. Poet and historical novelist, MWH was the son of Edmund Weld, a gentleman, and Anne Vesey, the daughter of John Hartstonge. He entered TCD in 1789 and graduated BA in 1792. He was admitted to the Middle Temple (London) in 1792, and to the King's Inns in 1795, but there is no record that he was called to the Irish Bar. He authored an anti-Act of Union pamphlet, and published several volumes of poetry, including *Marion of Drymnagh. A tale of Erin* (London, 1814), and *Minstrelsy of Erin, poems lyrical, pastoral and descriptive* (Edinburgh, 1812). At some point he changed his name to Mathew Weld Hartstonge, and lived with relatives at The Lodge (Co. Carlow). He corresponded extensively with Sir Walter Scott, to whom he dedicated the following volume. He was among the subscribers to T.M. Rafter's *Mental flowerets* (Dublin, 1829) and to Revd J.L. Villanueva's *Poesias escognidas* (Dublin, 1833).

He died unmarried. SOURCE Allibone, i, p. 796 [under Hartstonge]; B & S, p. 867; Brown, p. 133 (who appears to confuse him with Matthew Weld, son of Revd Joseph Weld, b. *c*.1779); Garside, 1825:40; JAPMDI, 4(11) (1899), p. 236; Keane, p. 505; King Bulletin 29 (1997); Landed gentry, 1912, p. 752; NCBEL 4, p. 349 [under Hartstonge]; O'Donoghue, pp 186, 394, 466; Scott (correspondence with Sir Walter Scott).

H183   *The eve of All-Hallows; or, Adelaide of Tyrconnell; A romance* (by Matthew Weld Hartstonge; dedicated to Sir Walter Scott).
   London: J.B. Whittaker, 1825, 3 vols. SOURCE Brown, 727; Block, p. 98; British Fiction; Garside, 1825:40. LOCATION Corvey CME 3–628–47630–5, E, ViU.
   COMMENTARY Reviewed in the *Dublin and London Magazine* (London, 1825, pp 287–8). Historical fiction set in Ireland during the second half of the seventeenth century, it features the duke of Tyrconnell and his chaplain, Revd Dr M'Kenzie [ML].

HARVEY, F. Editor. See **KNOWLES, James Sheridan.**

'**HASTLER, Doctor —, M.R.S.P.Q.L.M.N.A.S.T. and L.L.Z.**', pseud. See **BOSWELL, John Whittley.**

HATTON, Ann Julia (née Kemble, later Curtis), pseud. '**Anne of Swansea**', b. Wales 1764, d. Swansea (Wales) 1838. Welsh novelist, poet, lecturer and actress, AJH was the daughter of theatrical manager Roger Kemble and actress Sarah Ward, and the younger sister of Sarah Siddons and John Philip Kemble, leading actors of their day. In 1783 she married an actor named Curtis, who turned out to be a bigamist, but under the name Ann Curtis she published *Poems on miscellaneous subjects* (London, 1783). In 1792, she married William Hatton, with whom she went to New York, where he made musical instruments and she wrote libretti. The Hattons returned to Britain around 1800 and settled in Swansea. She was widowed in 1806. She gave lectures on women in society. Her *Poetic trifles* appeared in Waterford in 1811 (printed for the author by John Bull), but it is not clear why she published in that city. She attempted suicide in Westminster Abbey (London), and later received an accidental gunshot wound in the face in a bathhouse. Only one of her novels is set in Ireland. The Folger Library in Washington (DC) has many of her manuscripts. SOURCE Alston, pp 189–90; Blain, pp 498–9; Burmester cat. 31/304; NCBEL 4, pp 898–9; ODNB.

H184   *Guilty or not guilty; or, a lesson for husbands. A tale* (by 'Anne of Swansea').
   + London: A.K. Newman & Co., 1822, 5 vols. SOURCE British Fiction; Garside, 1822:39; Wolff, 3059. LOCATION Corvey CME 3–628–48803–6, L, MH.
   COMMENTARY Set in London. One of the main characters is Arthur O'Neil, an Irish lawyer [CM].

H185   *Gerald FitzGerald. An Irish tale* (by 'Anne of Swansea').
   London: A.K. Newman & Co., 1831, 5 vols. SOURCE Brown, 842; Garside 2, 1831:37. LOCATION Corvey CME 3–628–8801–X, Ireland related fiction, L.
   COMMENTARY A story of romantic intrigues set in the north of Ireland. Gerald, whose Catholic wife has deserted him, lives in an old half-ruined family castle near Armagh. The book details scandals, flirtations, gossip and match-making among titled individuals living in 'Doneraile Castle' and 'Lisburn Abbey' [Brown].

HATTON, Joseph, b. Andover (Hants.) 1841, d. London 1907. English journalist, editor and prolific author of fiction, travel books and plays, JH was the son of a writer and bookseller. He started out in the law but quickly turned to writing for a living. He edited the *Gentleman's Magazine* (London, 1868–74) and was foreign correspondent for several international papers, including the *New York Times*. He successfully dramatized several of his novels, including the volume below. Only one novel with Irish content is known. SOURCE Allibone Suppl., ii, p. 786; Brown, p. 133; NCBEL 4, pp 1575–6; ODNB; Sutherland, p. 284.

H186   *John Needham's double. A story founded on fact* (by Joseph Hatton).
    London: John & Robert Maxwell, [1885]. SOURCE Brown, 730; NCBEL 4, p. 1575; Wolff, 3066; COPAC. LOCATION L.
    New York: Harper & Bros, 1885. LOCATION NUC.
COMMENTARY Based on the true story of John Sadleir's career, including his fraud of the Tipperary Bank. Needham poisons his 'double', John Norbury, and deposits his body on Hampstead Heath (London). He then escapes to America, but is tracked and arrested. When under arrest he takes poison [Brown].

HAVERGAL, M.V.H. Editor. See ASHBY, Caroline W.

HAWTHORNE, Julian, b. 1846 Boston (MA), d. San Francisco (CA) 1934. American novelist, children's and detective fiction writer, JH was the son of noted writer Nathaniel Hawthorne and Sophia Peabody and as a child lived with his parents in Liverpool and in Italy. He entered Harvard College in 1863, but did not graduate. Later he studied civil engineering at the Lawrence Scientific School in Cambridge (MA) and in Dresden. From 1870 to 1872 he was employed as a hydrographic engineer in the department of docks in New York. In 1872 he travelled to Germany and London, where he was on the staff of the *Spectator* for two years and contributed to reviews and magazines. He returned to New York in 1882 and subsequently began his writing career. He published over 25 novels, five of which featured Inspector Thomas Byrnes of the New York City police, as well as numerous short stories. He wrote for a variety of periodicals and he and several colleagues were imprisoned for mail fraud in soliciting money by circulating fraudulent prospectuses. Only fiction with Irish content is listed here (other books also feature Chief Inspector Byrnes). SOURCE Allibone Suppl., ii, p. 792; ANB.

H187   *A tragic mystery. From the diary of Inspector Byrnes* (by Julian Hawthorne).
    New York: Cassell & Co., 1887. SOURCE Topp 7, 712; OCLC. LOCATION GEU.
    London, Paris, New York, Melbourne: Cassell & Co., 1888 (as *A tragic mystery*; Cassell's Railway Library). SOURCE Topp 7, 712. LOCATION O.
COMMENTARY Crime fiction. Chief Inspector Thomas Byrnes of the New York City police and Robert Johnson investigate Fenians for the British secret service [Personal communication Stephen Ennis, Nov. 2001].

'HAWTHORNE, Rainey', pseud. See RIDDELL, Mrs J.H.

HAY, Mary Cecil, b. Shrewsbury (Shrops.) 1840?, d. 1886. Writer of fiction for juveniles, MCH was the daughter of T.W. Hay, a watchmaker in Shrewsbury. She wrote many volumes but only her works with Irish connections are listed here. She spent her latter years at East Preston (Sussex). SOURCE Allibone Suppl., ii, p. 793; COPAC; RL.

H188   *Brenda Yorke, and other tales* (by Mary Cecil Hay).
    + London: Hurst & Blackett, 1875, 3 vols. SOURCE OCLC. LOCATION L.
COMMENTARY 'Brenda Yorke' (set at Glen Farm, and features an Irish domestic, Brenda Yorke. Part of the story takes place at Blarney, Co. Cork), 'One summer month (set in Omagh, Co. Tyrone), 'A midnight meeting', 'Two hallow eves', 'A few days', 'Well–done!', 'By the night express', 'Richardo's benefit', 'What our advertisement bought', 'One winter night', 'We four', 'He stoops to conquer', 'Stop thief!', 'Larry's hut' [RL].

H189   *Nora's love test* (by Mary Cecil Hay).

London: Hurst & Blackett, 1876, 3 vols. SOURCE COPAC. LOCATION L.
New York: Harper & Bros, 1877. SOURCE OCLC. LOCATION MH.
COMMENTARY Set in Ireland [RL].

HAYDEN, John Joseph, b. Dublin 1859, d. 1936. Poet and novelist, JJH was the son of a well-known Dublin physician, Dr Thomas Hayden. He studied medicine at the Catholic University, Dublin,. He emigrated to Vancouver (Canada), and became a lawyer in the US, in England and in Ireland. He published two collections of poetry: *Foam-bells* (Dublin, 1889), and *Chequy sonnets* (Halifax, 1898). SOURCE O'Donoghue, p. 188; RIA/DIB.

H190 *The Baron of Eppenfield; or, the Poor Clare, A medieval romance* (by John Joseph Hayden).
+ London: Samuel Tinsley & Co., 1878. SOURCE Allibone Suppl., ii, p. 794. LOCATION L.

COMMENTARY Historical fiction set in Italy during the Middle Ages. The Gothic story is interspersed with poetry from M.G. Lewis's *The monk* (London, 1796) and unsigned poetry, probably by JJH [RL].

HAYWARD, William Stephens, d. 1870. Prolific English novelist, WSH also wrote children's stories. SOURCE Allibone Suppl., ii, p. 797; Brown 2, p. 112; NCBEL 4, p. 1804.

H191 *Lord Scatterbrain; or, the rough diamond polished. A sequel to Handy Andy* (by William Stephens Hayward).
London: C.H. Clarke, [1869]. SOURCE Brown 2, 601; COPAC. LOCATION L.

COMMENTARY Likely to be a sequel to Samuel Lover's§ *Handy Andy* (London, 1842). Tells of the adventures of the hero, now Lord Scatterbrain. For the first part of the book he is an ornament of English society, but in the course of the story he relapses to his earlier ways [Brown 2].

HAYWOOD, Eliza (née Fowler), pseudo. 'A Lady', b. Shrops? (London according to Todd) 1693?, d. London 1756. English actress, prolific novelist, playwright and translator, EH was the first woman to write sustained drama criticism. Little is certain about her origins (Todd asserts she was the daughter of a London shopkeeper) but from 1714 to 1717 she was acting in Dublin, appearing at the Theatre Royal in Smock Alley. Some sources mention that she married Revd Valentine Haywood, but the ODNB says this information has been completely discredited. By 1719 she was a single woman with two children. Her first brief Irish sketch, *Irish artifice*, appeared in her *The female dunciad* (London, 1728). She was lampooned by Jonathan Swift§ and by the English poet Alexander Pope, but her books sold rapidly and her *Some memoirs of the amours and intrigues of a certain Irish dean* (London, [1728]) constituted her counter-attack on Swift. Her work became popular in Ireland: *The British recluse* (London, 1722) was reprinted in Dublin in 1724; *The fortunate foundlings* (London, 1744) was reprinted in Dublin in the next year; *The female spectator*, (London, 1744–46) was reprinted by subscription in Dublin in 1746, attracting 624 subscribers, and her *The history of Miss Betsy Thoughtless* (London, 1751) and *Jemmy and Jenny Jessamy* (London, 1753) were also reprinted in Dublin in their respective years of publication. The following volumes are her only known works with Irish content. SOURCE Allibone, i, p. 839; Blain, p. 505; Field Day, v, p. 1091; ODNB; Todd, pp 322–6.

H192 *Some memoirs of the amours and intrigues of a certain Irish Dean, who liv'd and flourish'd in the Kingdom of Ireland, not many hundred years since. Interspers'd with the gallantries of two Berkshire ladies. In which will be inserted several original letters of the said Dean, that will be well known by those that may be now living, who have ever seen the Dean's handwriting* (by 'A Lady, who was in those days well acquainted with him').

London: J. Roberts, [1728]. SOURCE NCBEL 2, p. 992; McBurney, 225; ESTC t126245; Linen Hall cat. p. 234. LOCATION BFI (1730 edn), Di, C, CtY.

H193   [Pt. II] *Being a continuation of the amours of the said Dean, and the gallanteries of two Berkshire ladies* (by 'A Lady, who was in those days well acquainted with him').

London: J. Roberts, 1728. SOURCE McBurney, 225a; ESTC t126245. LOCATION L, O.

London: Printed and Dublin reprinted by R. Dickson, 1730, 3rd edn. SOURCE McBurney, 225b; ESTC t155557. LOCATION MH, ICN.

COMMENTARY Attack on Jonathan Swift and the Blount sisters combined with a tale of extravagant passion [NCBEL 2].

HEAD, Katherine, pseud. 'K.H.', fl. 1837. Sketch writer and poet, KH's dedication of the following book was signed from Kirkdale, Liverpool. Given the many Irish subscribers, it is likely that she was Irish. Members of the Head family were among the gentry in Cos. Offaly and Tipperary at this time, but whether or not she belonged to this family is unclear. SOURCE FD; AMB.

H194   *Sketches in prose and poetry* (by 'K.H.'; dedicated to Mrs Muspratt).

London: Smith, Elder & Co., 1837 (subscribers' list with many Irish names). SOURCE Emerald Isle cat. 83/455. LOCATION L.

COMMENTARY Includes fictional reminiscences, including 'Farewell to Erin', 'Irish hospitality', 'Song of the blind harper', 'Irish cabins', 'Irish beggars', etc. [Emerald Isle cat. 83/455; FD].

HEAD, Richard, b. Carrickfergus (Co. Antrim) 1637, d. in The Solent (Hants.) 1686. Poet, novelist, miscellaneous writer and bookseller, RH was the son of a clergyman, most likely Richard Head (Hedde), who matriculated at Cambridge from Peterhouse 1616, and starting in 1633 was vicar at several parishes in Co. Antrim. He was killed in the rebellion of 1641. Richard Jnr and his mother escaped to Belfast and then to England, where he was sent to school in Bridport (Dorset) and then to Oxford. He became a successful bookseller in London but ruined himself by gambling. He moved to Dublin and wrote a well-received comedy, *Hic et ubique, or the humours of Dublin* (London, 1663), concerning the exploits of English adventurers in Ireland. Among RH's many writings is a character book, *Proteus redivivius, or the art of wheedling, or insinuation* (London, 1675), and a chapbook, *Western wonder: or O-Brazile, an inchanted island discovered* (London, 1694). For his portraits, see ODNB. SOURCE Brady, p. 103; Chronology, p. 35; DNB; Hogan 2, p. 532; NCBEL 2, pp 976–7; OCIL p. 239; ODNB; Leslie, *Connor*, p. 383; O'Donoghue, p. 189; RIA/DIB.

H195   *The English rogue described, in the life of Meriton Latroon, a witty extravagant! being a compleat history of the most eminent cheats of both sexes* [Part 1] (by Richard Head).

London: H. Marsh, 1665. SOURCE DNB; Esdaile, p. 241; ESTC r8745; NCBEL 2, p. 976; Sweeney, 2264. LOCATION L, NUC.

London: Charles Passinger, 1679 (abridgment of Part 1 as *The life and death of the English rogue; or his last legacy to the world. Containing most of his notorious robberies, cheats, and debauncht practices. With a full discovery of a high-way rogue; also directions to all travellers, how to know rogues and how to avoid them. And an infallible rule to take themm [sic] when rob'd by them*). SOURCE ESTC r9724; Sweeney, 2265. LOCATION L.

London: Henry Marsh, 1986, 4 vols. SOURCE OCLC. LOCATION CtY.

COMMENTARY First novel to feature an Irish protagonist, it is the racy story of a professional thief. Told as an 'autobiography', it became very popular. Parts 2, 3, and 4 were published in London in 1668, 1671, and 1671, respectively. Modern scholars credit RH with the first part only and attribute subsequent parts to the publisher Francis Kirkman. According to the ODNB, it is likely RH collaborated on them with the publisher [Brady; Chronology, p. 35; ODNB; Sweeney, 2264].

H196 *The canting academy, or the devil's cabinet opened: Wherein is shown the mysterious and villainous practices of that wicked crew commonly known by the name of hectors, trapanners, gilts, etc., to which is added a compleat canting dictionary, both of old words, and such as are now most in use. With several new catches, songs, compos'd by the choicest wits of the age. A book very useful and necessary to be read by all sorts of people* (preface signed by R. Head).
+ London: Mal. Drew, 1673. SOURCE DND; COPAC; ESTC r9723. LOCATION Dt, C.

COMMENTARY Consists of songs and stories of gypsies and beggars in England, and includes a canting dictionary from *The English rogue* (London, 1665) [ML; ODNB].

H197 *The complaisant companion, or new jests; witty reparties, rhodomontados, and pleasant novels* [anon.].
London: Printed [for the author?] by H.B., 1674. SOURCE ESTC r20756. LOCATION CSmH.
London: Printed by W[illiam] D[owning], 1675, 2nd edn (as *Nugæ Venalis, or a complaisant companion, being new jests, domestick and foreign, bulls, rhodomontados, pleasant novels, and miscellanies*). SOURCE ESTC. LOCATION MH.

COMMENTARY Amusing but coarse, for the most part old stories [ODNB].

H198 *The miss display'd, with all her wheedling arts and circumventions: in which historical narration are detected, her selfish contrivances, modest pretences, and subtil stratagems* [anon.].
London: [n.p]. 1675. SOURCE COPAC; DNB. LOCATION C, MH.

COMMENTARY 'Anatomizes' the story of an Irish prostitute's body in order to warn young male readers against the dangers of her 'text'. The author stresses that what matters is the description of her body rather than her body's sexual attraction [L. Vallone, *Disciplines of virtue* (New Haven, 1995), p. 8].

HECTOR, Annie (née French), pseud. **'Mrs Alexander'**, b. Dublin 1825, d. London 1902. Novelist and short story writer, AH was the only daughter of a Dublin solicitor, Robert French of Frenchpark (Co. Roscommon), and Anne Malone. In 1844 her father lost his money and the family moved to Liverpool, then settled in London where, with the encouragement of Mrs S.C. Hall§, AH became a magazine writer, publishing a short story 'Billeted in Boulogne' in *Household Words* (London, 1856). In 1858 she married Alexander Hector, a wealthy merchant and explorer who had made a fortune in opening up trade between Britain and the Persian Gulf. He disapproved of her writing but she did so in secret to help support her father. The marriage was not a happy one and the Hectors separated in 1870. After her husband's death in 1873, she adopted his Christian name as a pseudonym and, not having been left much money, supported her four children by her writing. She went on to be a prolific writer of short stories and over 40 novels, only two of which – as far as is known – have to do with Ireland. Many of her novels centre on marriage issues, money and deceit. They were popular in England and the US and were translated into many languages, from French to Polish; eleven went into second edns. For six years she lived with her family in Germany, France and Scotland but settled back in London. She returned to Ireland only once. For her portraits, see ODNB. SOURCE Allibone Suppl., ii, p. 803; Blain, p. 15 [under Alexander]; Brady, p. 104; Brown, p. 16; Field Day, v, pp 927–30; Hogan 2, pp 541–2; NCBEL 4, p. 1094–6 [under Alexander]; OCIL, p. 242; ODNB; Sutherland, p. 16 [under Alexander]; RIA/DIB; Wolff, ii, p. 208.

H199　*Kate Vernon. A tale* [anon.].
　　London: Thomas Cautley Newby, 1854, 3 vols. SOURCE Wolff, 3122. LOCATION L, NUC.

H200　*The happy cottage* [anon.].
　　London: T. Cautley Newby, 1856. SOURCE ODNB. LOCATION L.

H201　*Agnes Waring. An autobiography* [anon.].
　　London: Thomas Cautley Newby, 1856, 3 vols. SOURCE Alston, p. 194. LOCATION L.

H202　*'Look before you leap.' A novel* [anon.].
　　London: Richard Bentley, 1865, 2 vols. SOURCE Wolff, 3124; NSTC. LOCATION L.
　　London: Richard Bentley & Son, 1882 (revsd edn; Bentley's Favourite Novels, No. 87). SOURCE Topp 5, p. 155. LOCATION D, L, E, NUC.
　　New York: Henry Holt, 1882 (Leisure Hour Series, No. 139). LOCATION NUC.
　　New York: George Munro, 1882 (Seaside Library, No. 1391). LOCATION NUC.

H203　*Which shall it be? A novel* [anon.].
　　London: Richard Bentley, 1866, 3 vols. SOURCE Alston, p. 195; Wolff, 3127 (1891, 8th edn). LOCATION D (1900 edn), L.
　　London: Richard Bentley, 1867 (new edn; ill.). SOURCE Topp 5, p. 156. LOCATION L.
　　New York: Henry Holt, 1874 (Leisure Hour Series, No. 27). SOURCE Topp 5, p. 156. LOCATION MH.
　　Boston: Loring, 1874. SOURCE Topp 5, p. 156; OCLC. LOCATION CtY.

H204　*The wooing o't. A novel* (by 'Mrs Alexander').
　　+ London: Richard Bentley, 1873, 3 vols. SOURCE Sadleir, 41; Wolff, 3129. LOCATION D (1875, 3rd edn), Dt (1893, 9th edn), L, InND Loeber coll.
　　London: Richard Bentley, 1874 (new edn). SOURCE Topp 5, p. 144. LOCATION L.
　　New York: Henry Holt & Williams, 1873. SOURCE Topp 5, p. 144; OCLC. LOCATION NN.

COMMENTARY A romance first serialized in the *Temple Bar* (London, June 1872–Nov. 1873). Maggie, cruelly treated by her aunt and exploited in the shop where she works, becomes a lady's companion. Her employer takes her to France where she meets an English earl, who falls in love with her. The earl's mother is upset about this and sends over a cousin, Mr Trafford, to prevent the marriage. However, Maggie has already refused the earl's advances and becomes friendly with Mr. Trafford. She returns to England where she is engaged as a secretary to a rich heiress. In the end, despite their differences in social standing, she marries Mr Trafford, who prefers her to the rich heiress for whom Maggie works [ML; Blain, p.15; Topp].

H205　*Ralph Wilton's weird* (by 'Mrs Alexander').
　　London: Richard Bentley & Son, 1875, 2 vols. SOURCE NCBEL 4, p. 1094; Sadleir, 39; Wolff, 3125. LOCATION L.
　　+ New York: Henry Holt & Co., 1875 (The Leisure Hour Series). LOCATION InND Loeber coll.

COMMENTARY A romance set in London and Scotland and first serialized in *Temple Bar* (London, June 1875–Aug. 1876). Col. Wilton's eccentric relative, Lord St George, tells him he will inherit his title and possessions but only if he marries a gentlewoman of unblemished reputation. (Lord St George had a daughter he disinherited because she ran off with a foreign revolutionary.) Col. Wilton goes to Scotland for some shooting and shares the train compartment with a Miss Rivers, an accomplished artist. They have the same destination and sub-sequently meet by accident several times. Wilton becomes more and more enamoured of Miss Rivers and even though he knows she would not be an acceptable bride in Lord St George's eyes, he marries her anyway, thereby forfeiting his relative's estates. A search is undertaken for Lord St George's possible heirs. It turns out that Miss Rivers is his grandchild, and she inherits the estate [ML].

H206 *Her dearest foe. A novel* (by 'Mrs Alexander').
London: Richard Bentley & Son, 1876, 3 vols. SOURCE Sadleir, 36. LOCATION Dt (1899 edn), L.
London: Richard Bentley & Son, 1877 (new edn). SOURCE Topp 5, p. 144. LOCATION D, NUC.
New York: Henry Holt & Co., 1876 (Leisure Hour Series, No. 56). SOURCE Topp 5, p. 144. LOCATION NUC.
+ New York: A.L. Burt Co., n.d (as *Her dearest foe*). SOURCE NCBEL 4, p. 1094. LOCATION D.
COMMENTARY First serialized in the *Temple Bar* (London, June 1875–Aug. 1876) [Topp 5, p. 144].

H207 *The heritage of Langdale. A novel* (by 'Mrs Alexander').
London: Richard Bentley & Son, 1877, 3 vols. SOURCE Sadleir, 37. LOCATION D (1877, new edn), L, NUC.
+ London: Hutchinson & Co., 1894 (cheap edn; as *The heritage of Langdale*). LOCATION InND Loeber coll.
New York: H. Holt & Co., 1877 (Leisure Hour Series). SOURCE Nield, p. 80. LOCATION NUC.
New York: H. Munro, 1877 (Seaside Library). SOURCE OCLC. LOCATION TxU.
COMMENTARY Historical novel about Jacobites set in the time of George I in London and the south of England. The guardian of a girl, whose father had lost his lands by attainder, tries to force her into a marriage with his dissolute son because he knows that a pardon has been granted, making the girl a rich heiress. Another relative prevents this nefarious plot from suc-ceeding [ML; Nield].

H208 *Maid, wife, or widow? An episode of the '66 war* (by 'Mrs Alexander').
London: Chatto & Windus, 1879. SOURCE Alston, p. 194; Nield, p. 112. LOCATION L, NUC.
New York: Henry Holt, 1879 (as *Maid, wife, or widow?*; Leisure Hour Series, No. 105). LOCATION NUC.
New York: G. Munro, [1879] (Seaside Library, No. 532). LOCATION NUC.
Chicago: Homewood, [1880–1889?]. SOURCE OCLC. LOCATION ICU.
COMMENTARY Historical novel concerning the war between Prussia and Austria in 1866 [Nield].

H209 *The Freres. A novel* (by 'Mrs Alexander').
London: Richard Bentley & Son, 1882, 3 vols. SOURCE Sadleir, 35; Wolff, 3120. LOCATION L, NUC.
+ New York: H. Holt & Co., 1882 (Leisure Hour Series, No. 134). LOCATION NUC, InND Loeber coll.
New York: George Munro, [1882] (Seaside Library, No. 1231). SOURCE Topp 5, p. 154. LOCATION NUC.
COMMENTARY A story of family life and romance first serialized in the *Temple Bar* (London, Jan. 1881–May 1882). An impoverished Irish branch of the Freres family moves to London where the women hope to live cheaply and earn a living. The mainstay of the family is Grace, who had been

looking forward to meeting again her London cousin Max, who had stayed with them several times in Ireland. Max waxes hot and cold in his behaviour toward her. Grace is employed as a companion by Lady Elton, but when Grace refuses the hand of an eligible man, Lady Elton drops her. Grace moves with a relative to Austria. Eventually, she marries Randal Balfour, her old playfellow and neighbour from Ireland, and they move to New Zealand to start a new life [ML].

H210 *Valerie's fate* (by 'Mrs Alexander').

New York: George Munro, 1882 (Seaside Library, No. 1259). SOURCE Topp 3, p. 127. SOURCE OCLC. LOCATION DCL.

New York: J.S. Ogilvie & Co., [1882]. SOURCE Topp 3, p. 127.

London: Chatto & Windus, 1883 (in the *Gentleman's Annual*). SOURCE Topp 3, p. 127. LOCATION L.

London: Frederick Warne & Co., [1885] (as *At bay*; London Library, No. 7). SOURCE Topp 4, p. 177. LOCATION NUC.

COMMENTARY No copy of the New York Ogilvie edn located [Topp; RL].

H211 *The admiral's ward* (by 'Mrs Alexander').

+ London: Richard Bentley & Son, 1883, 3 vols. SOURCE Sadleir, 33. LOCATION D, L, NUC, InND Loeber coll. (1883, popular edn).

New York: Henry Holt, 1883 (Leisure Moment Series, No. 3). SOURCE Topp 5, p. 153. LOCATION NUC.

New York: G. Munro, 1883 (Seaside Library, No. 1595). SOURCE Topp 5, p. 153. LOCATION NUC.

New York: John Lovell, [1883] (Lovell's Library, No. 99). SOURCE Topp 5, p. 153.

COMMENTARY First serialized in *Belgravia* (London, Jan. 1882–May 1883), and in the US in *Demorest's Monthly* (New York, certainly in Sept–Oct. 1882) [Topp 5, p. 153].

H212 *The executor: A novel* (by 'Mrs Alexander').

London: Richard Bentley & Son, 1883, 3 vols. SOURCE Sadleir, 34; Wolff, 3117 (1885 edn). LOCATION D (1900 edn), L, NUC.

+ New York: Henry Holt & Co., 1883 (Leisure Hour Series, No. 155). SOURCE Topp 5, p. 154. LOCATION NUC, InND Loeber coll.

New York: John W. Lovell Co., [1883] (Lovell's Library, No. 209). SOURCE Topp 5, p. 154. LOCATION NUC.

New York: George Munro, [1883]. SOURCE Topp 5, p. 154. LOCATION NUC.

COMMENTARY A romance of inheritance and intrigue about a young girl who inherits money from her Syrian stepfather. She is underage, and one of her executors, her stepfather's relative, wants to marry her for her money. When he does not succeed, he tries to poison her slowly. A doctor falls in love with her and marries her, without the approval of her guardians, so that he can protect her [ML].

H213 *Mrs. Vereker's courier maid* (by 'Mrs Alexander').

+ London: Chatto & Windus, 1884 (in the *Gentleman's Annual*, together with Percy Greg's 'By death beleaguered'). LOCATION InND Loeber coll.

COMMENTARY Mrs Vereker, an extremely selfish widow, takes Ella Marston, a poor relative, with her to the Continent as her maid. They travel extensively in Germany where they meet Mrs Vereker's rich brother and an old acquaintance, Col. Cecil. Mrs Vereker fancies that Col. Cecil is in love with her. However, he is in love with Ella. Mrs Vereker's brother is about to change his will in favour of Ella but dies before this can be effected. Col. Cecil marries Ella regardless [ML].

H214 *A second life. A novel* (by 'Mrs Alexander'; dedicated to Mrs W.H. Wills).

London: Richard Bentley & Son, 1885, 3 vols. SOURCE Sadleir, 40. LOCATION L.

+ Leipzig: Bernard Tauchnitz, 1885, 3 vols. in 1. SOURCE T & B, 2362. LOCATION InND Loeber coll.

+ New York: Henry Holt & Co., 1885 (Leisure Hour Series, No. 163). LOCATION InND Loeber coll.

COMMENTARY Set in England and on the Continent. Mildred Carr and her mother find that upon the death of Mr Carr, they are almost penniless. One of their creditors, Mr Welby, suggests that Mildred marry him so that he can look after her and her mother. After an initial refusal, she gives in. Life with Mr Welby, however, is insufferable, but since he will not consent to a divorce, she stages her own death by supposedly falling into a ravine in the Swiss Alps. She later encounters Mr Welby, who has to leave her alone because his respectability would suffer if the story came out. In the end, Mr Welby dies, which frees Mildred to marry a man who has befriended her [ML].

H215 *By woman's wit. A novel* (by 'Mrs Alexander').

London: F.V. White & Co., 1886, 2 vols. SOURCE Alston, p. 194; Jarndyce cat. 94/7; Topp 7, 94. LOCATION D (n.d. edn), L, InND Loeber coll. ([1887?], 3rd edn).

London: Chatto & Windus, 1898 (new edn). SOURCE Topp 3, pp 254–5.

COMMENTARY *London, Chatto edn* No copy located [RL].

Leipzig: Bernard Tauchnitz, 1886. SOURCE T & B, 2432. LOCATION NUC.

New York: J.S. Ogilvie, 1886 (Fireside Series, No. 14). SOURCE Topp 3, pp 254–5; OCLC. LOCATION Univ. of Arizona.

New York: George Munro, 1886 (Seaside Library Pocket Edition, No. 900). SOURCE Topp 3, pp 254–5. LOCATION NUC.

New York: George Munro, 1886 (Munro's Library, No. 685). SOURCE Topp 7, 94; OCLC. LOCATION Univ. of Arizona.

COMMENTARY A story of theft and deception set in England. A squire, who has led a fairly dissipated life, devises a scheme to pay his debts by stealing the diamonds of one of his guests at a ball at his house. The victim expected to marry the squire, but he falls in love with an orphan who lives in a house adjoining his estate. By devious means he thwarts the girl's lover and finally makes her promise to marry him. When she finds out that the squire has misled her, she wishes to be released from her promise. In the meantime, the woman whose diamonds were stolen finds out that the squire was the culprit and threatens to tell all unless he marries her. The girl is released from her engagement and marries her true love, while the squire is forced to spend the remainder of his life with a woman who has a complete hold over him [ML].

H216 *Beaton's bargain. A novel* (by 'Mrs Alexander').

London, New York: Frederick Warne & Co., [1886] (London Library, No. 9). SOURCE Alston, p. 194; Topp 4, p. 182. LOCATION L.

+ New York: Henry Holt & Co., 1886 (Leisure Hour Series, No. 187). LOCATION InND Loeber coll.

New York: George Munro, [1886] (Seaside Library Pocket Edition, No. 794). SOURCE Topp 4, p. 182. SOURCE OCLC. LOCATION Univ. of Minnesota, St Paul (MN).

New York: J.S. Ogilvie, [1886]. SOURCE Topp 4, p. 182; OCLC. LOCATION Univ. of Illinois.

New York: Norman Munro, [1886] (Munro's Library, No. 567). SOURCE Topp 4, p. 182; OCLC. LOCATION Univ. of Minnesota, Minneapolis.

Toronto: Rose, 1886. SOURCE OCLC. LOCATION Univ. of Montreal.

COMMENTARY A story of love and money set in London. Mr Beaton, an impoverished young man of good family, is advised by his relatives to marry an heiress. He finds an advertisement in the *Times*, where the guardians of an heiress wish to meet possible suitors. Mr Beaton presents himself as a suitor to the heiress, Miss Vivian. She is a sweet but very unsophisticated girl whose personal attractions make no impression on him. However, his friend Mr Maitland, the son of the agent of the Beaton family estate, is very taken by her. When Mr Beaton and Miss Vivian are about to be married, a new claimant to her riches appears on the scene. He has a better right to the inheritance than she, so she is left in a financially poor state. Mr Beaton speedily disappears from the scene, and eventually Mr Maitland marries Miss Vivian [ML].

H217   *Forging the feathers. A novel* (by 'Mrs Alexander').
New York: F.M. Lupton, 1886. SOURCE OCLC. LOCATION Northern Illinois Univ.
Chicago: W.B. Conkey, [1880–1889?] (as *Forging the feathers*). SOURCE OCLC. LOCATION Michigan State Univ.
Toronto: W. Bryce, 1890 (as *Forging the feathers*). SOURCE OCLC. LOCATION Univ. of Montreal.
+ London: Spencer Blackett, 1890 (as *Forging the feathers*; Blackett's Select Novels). SOURCE Alston, p. 194; Topp 4, p. 244. LOCATION L.
COMMENTARY No Irish content [ML; CM; Topp].

H218   *Forging the fetters, and other stories* (by 'Mrs Alexander').
New York: Henry Holt, 1887 (Leisure Moment Series, No. 83). SOURCE Topp 4, p. 244. SOURCE OCLC. LOCATION CtY. COMMENTARY *New York Holt, 1887 edn* Contains three stories [Topp].
New York: John W. Lovell Co., [1887] (Lovell's Library, No. 1044). LOCATION NUC.
New York: George Munro, [1887] (Seaside Library Pocket Edition, No. 997). SOURCE Topp 4, p. 244. COMMENTARY *New York, Munro [1887] edn* Contains two stories [Topp].
New York: John W. Lovell, [1887]. SOURCE Topp 4, p. 244. COMMENTARY *New York Lovell [1887] edn* Contains four stories. NCBEL 4, p. 1095 mentions a New York edn of 1897 containing three stories: 'Forging the fetters', 'Mrs. Vereker's courier maid', 'The Australian maid' [Topp; NCBEL 4, p. 1095].

H219   *Mona's choice. A novel* (by 'Mrs Alexander').
London: F.V. White & Co., 1887, 3 vols. SOURCE Alston, p. 194; Topp 7, 108. LOCATION D (1888 edn), L.
Leipzig: Bernard Tauchnitz, 1887. SOURCE T & B, 2493; OCLC. LOCATION Ohio Univ.
New York: George Munro, [1887] (Seaside Library Pocket Edition, No. 1054). SOURCE Topp 3, p. 260; OCLC. LOCATION DCL.
New York: John W. Lovell Co., [1887] (Lovell's Library, No. 1105). SOURCE Topp 3, p. 260.
Chicago, New York: Rand, McNally & Co., [1890 or earlier] (Globe Library, No. 46). SOURCE advertised in A.D. Hall, *Lady Clancarty* (Chicago, 1890); Topp 7, 108.
COMMENTARY No copies of the New York and Chicago edns located. No Irish content. The orphan Mona faces a choice between two men and marries the man she first rejected [Blain; CM].

H220   *A life interest* (by 'Mrs Alexander').
London: Richard Bentley & Son, 1888, 3 vols. SOURCE Sadleir, 38; Wolff, 3123; Topp 7, 122. LOCATION D (1889 edn), L.
London: Chatto & Windus, 1898 (new edn). SOURCE Topp 3, p. 259. COMMENTARY *London, Chatto edn* No copy located [RL].
+ Leipzig: Bernard Tauchnitz, 1888, 2 vols. in 1. SOURCE T & B, 2519. LOCATION NUC, InND Loeber coll.
New York: Henry Holt & Co., 1888 (Leisure Hour Series, No. 212). LOCATION NUC.
New York: John W. Lovell, [1888] (Lovell's Library, No. 1142). LOCATION NUC.

New York: G. Munro, 1888 (Seaside Library, No. 1057). LOCATION NUC.

New York: J.S. Ogilvie & Co., 1888 (Fireside Series, No. 40). LOCATION NUC.

Chicago, New York: Rand, McNally & Co., 1888 (Globe Library, No. 51). SOURCE Topp 3, p. 259.

COMMENTARY No copy of the Chicago edn located. A story of deception and intrigue set in England and first serialized in White's *London Society* (beginning Apr. 1887). A scheming adventuress with a shady past marries Mr Acland, a fairly stiff and priggish London businessman. For both of them it is a second marriage, and the three children of the previous marriage are badly treated by Mrs Acland. The two boys have to make their own way and the girl, unguided and unprovided for, has a hard time extricating herself from the clutches of an unprincipled man. Mrs Acland's first husband, who she claimed had been drowned in America, is still alive and shows up in time to befriend his son and secure for him a large inheritance from rich relatives. Mrs Acland, who had never told Mr Acland her first husband was alive, has her scheming unmasked which leads to her separation from him, but Mr Acland's daughter marries her son [ML].

H221   *A crooked path* (by 'Mrs Alexander'; dedicated to Mrs John King).

London: Hurst & Blackett, 1889, 3 vols. SOURCE Wolff, 3116. LOCATION L, InND Loeber coll. (1889, 3 vols., 2nd edn).

Leipzig: Bernard Tauchnitz, 1889, 2 vols. SOURCE T & B, 2606. LOCATION NUC.

New York: H. Holt, 1889. LOCATION NUC.

New York: G. Munro, 1889. LOCATION NUC.

COMMENTARY Set in England, and tells a story of deception in a good cause. Catherine, the daughter of an impoverished family, tries to lighten her mother's financial burden by working for a rich but unpleasant uncle. Toward the end of his life he softens towards her but dies before he can change his will. In despair, Catherine takes away the will to make it appear that he died intestate. She inherits, and is able to make her mother's last years less stressful. She gives money to her egocentric sister-in-law, so that her two nephews will not suffer. She meets the man who ought to have inherited her uncle's money and confesses what she has done. He forgives her and destroys the original will. However, the uncle's son, presumed to be dead, returns to England and claims his father's estate. Catherine has to hand over what is left and has barely enough money to continue to look after her nephews. She and the man she had defrauded fall in love and marry [ML].

H222   *A false scent. A novel* (by 'Mrs Alexander').

+ London: F.V. White & Co., 1889. SOURCE Alston, p. 194; Topp 7, 100. LOCATION L, InND Loeber coll.

New York: J.W. Lovell, [1889] (Lovell's Library, No. 1361). LOCATION NUC.

New York: G. Munro, [1889] (Seaside Library Pocket Edition, No. 1119). LOCATION NUC.

COMMENTARY A detective story, set in England. A Russian gentleman is sought by the police for a murder that had taken place in Russia. While eluding his pursuers, he makes the acquaintance of a girl in a train by climbing into her compartment. He assures her that he is a gentleman and she believes him, although appearances are against him. Not only is he sought for the murder, but he is also accused of having robbed a gentleman in the train. When he is finally cleared of both crimes, he is free to pursue the girl [ML].

H223   *Blind fate. A novel* (by 'Mrs Alexander').

London: F.V. White, 1890, 3 vols. SOURCE Wolff, 3114. LOCATION D (1891 edn), L, NUC.

London: Chatto & Windus, 1897 (new edn). SOURCE Topp 3, p. 252; OCLC. LOCATION CLU.

+ Leipzig: Bernard Tauchnitz, 1891, 2 vols. SOURCE T & B, 2696. LOCATION NUC, InND Loeber coll.

New York: H. Holt, 1890 (Leisure Moment Series). LOCATION NUC.

New York: George Munro, 1890 (Seaside Library Pocket Edition, No. 1571). SOURCE Topp 3, 252. COMMENTARY *New York Munro edn* No copy located.

New York: M.J. Ivers & Co., 1890. LOCATION NUC.

COMMENTARY A story of romance and murder set in an English seaside resort. Col. Callander has returned from India to join his wife, Mabel, and her sister Dorothy, at the resort. Also in town is Mr Standish, Mabel's and Dorothy's guardian, as well as Mr Egerton, the colonel's friend. The dowager Mrs Callander and her niece, Miss Oakeley, are staying nearby. The dowager has never liked Mabel and had wished her son to marry the rich Miss Oakeley. She insinuates to him that Mabel and her guardian are too close. Egerton, who is a frequent visitor, proposes to Dorothy, but she declines. Egerton is not really interested in Dorothy but in Mabel, and he tries to convince Mabel to elope with him. The colonel, feeling that he is losing his wife's affection to Standish, kills her. Dorothy thinks that Egerton has done this but cannot talk about it for fear of damaging her sister's reputation, and the colonel's crime remains undetected. Standish and Dorothy care for each other, but it takes them a long time to accept that their relationship is more than one of guardian and ward. The colonel eventually finds out that his wife had always loved him and that it was not Standish but Egerton who had tried to impose himself on her. He drowns himself. Dorothy and Standish marry and take care of Mabel's children [ML].

H224   *Three notable stories* (by 'Mrs Alexander').

+ London: Spencer Blackett, 1890. SOURCE Alston, p. 194. LOCATION L, InND Loeber coll.

COMMENTARY A long story 'To be, or not to be' is by 'Mrs. Alexander'; the other stories are by the marquis of Lorne and Thomas Hardy [RL].

H225   *A woman's heart. A novel* (by 'Mrs Alexander').

+ London: F.V. White & Co., 1891, 3 vols. SOURCE Alston, p. 195; Wolff, 3128 (1894 edn); Topp 7, 228. LOCATION L.

Leipzig: Bernard Tauchnitz, 1891. SOURCE T & B, 2764; OCLC. LOCATION Univ. Lille III.

New York: John W. Lovell, 1890 (International Series, No. 82). SOURCE Topp 7, 228; OCLC. LOCATION MH.

COMMENTARY No Irish content [CM].

H226   *Well won* (by 'Mrs Alexander').

London: F.V. White & Co., 1891. SOURCE Alston, p. 194. LOCATION L.

COMMENTARY No Irish content [CM].

H227   *The snare of the fowler* (by 'Mrs Alexander').

London, Paris, Melbourne: Cassell & Co., 1892, 3 vols. SOURCE Wolff, 3126. LOCATION L.

Leipzig: Bernard Tauchnitz, 1893. 2 vols in 1. SOURCE T & B, 2881, 2882; RLIN. LOCATION MH.

H228   *Mammon. A novel* (by 'Mrs Alexander').

London: William Heinemann, 1892, 3 vols. SOURCE Alston, p. 194; COPAC. LOCATION L, NUC (1897 edn).

+ Leipzig: Heinemann & Balestier, 1892 (The English Library, No. 105). LOCATION D, NUC, InND Loeber coll.

New York: J.W. Lovell, [1891]. LOCATION NUC.

COMMENTARY A man wishes to marry a girl because of her wealth. She sees through him and declines. Over time he learns to appreciate the girl 'for what she is' and eventually they love each other mutually [ML].

H229 *For his sake. A novel* (by 'Mrs Alexander').
London: F.V. White, 1892, 3 vols. SOURCE Daims, 1366; Wolff, 3118 (n.d. edn); Topp 7, 221. LOCATION D (1893 edn), L.
Leipzig: Bernard Tauchnitz, 1892, 2 vols. SOURCE T & B, 2853, 2854. LOCATION NUC.
Philadelphia: J.B. Lippincott & Co., 1892 (Series of Select Novels, No. 136). SOURCE Daims, 1366; Topp 221. LOCATION NUC.

H230 *Found wanting. A novel* (by 'Mrs Alexander').
London: F.V. White & Co., 1893, 3 vols. SOURCE Daims, 1367; Wolff, 3119; Topp 7, 240. LOCATION D (1895 edn), L, NUC.
+ Leipzig: Bernard Tauchnitz, 1893, 2 vols. in 1. SOURCE T & B, 2940. LOCATION NUC, InND Loeber coll.
Philadelphia: J.B. Lippincott & Co., 1893 (Series of Select Novels, No. 158). SOURCE Daims, 1367; Topp 7, 240. LOCATION NUC.
COMMENTARY A romance set in Paris and London. May and her father live in Paris where she has several friends among the English. One is Mme Falk, who has been deserted by her husband, taking her son with him. After her father's death, May is left destitute. Mr Ogilvie, a rising, ambitious diplomat and her father's friend, arranges for her to work as a companion in his aunt's house in London. Ogilvie, although in love with May, plans to marry May's best friend, and proposes that May moves in with them. She refuses and takes refuge with Mme Falk, who miraculously has been reunited with her son, Bernard Carr. Bernard and May fall in love and marry [ML].

H231 *A choice of evils. A novel* (by 'Mrs Alexander').
London: F.V. White & Co., 1894, 3 vols. SOURCE Daims, 1363; Brick Row cat. 116/78; Topp 7, 269. LOCATION D (1895, 2nd edn), L, NUC.
Leipzig: Bernard Tauchnitz, 1894, 2 vols. SOURCE T & B, 3013, 3014. LOCATION NUC.
New York: Cassell, [c.1894] (as *Broken links: a love story*). SOURCE Daims, 1363. LOCATION NUC.
New York: Marathon, 1894 (as *Broken links*). LOCATION NUC.

H232 *A ward in Chancery. A novel* (by 'Mrs Alexander').
+ London: Osgood, McIlvaine, 1894, 2 vols. SOURCE Alston, p. 194. LOCATION D (1895 edn), L.
+ Leipzig: Bernard Tauchnitz, 1894. SOURCE T & B, 2977. LOCATION D.
COMMENTARY No Irish content [CM].

H233 *What gold cannot buy* (by 'Mrs Alexander').
+ London: F.V. White, 1895. SOURCE Alston, p. 194; Topp 7, 261. LOCATION L.
New York: F.M. Lupton, n.d. SOURCE Topp 7, 261; OCLC. LOCATION Univ. of Wisconsin, Madison.
New York: M.J. Ivers, n.d. SOURCE Topp 7, 261; OCLC. LOCATION OU.
Cleveland (OH): Arthur Westbrook, n.d. SOURCE OCLC. LOCATION GEU.
COMMENTARY No Irish content [CM].

H234 *A winning hazard* (by 'Mrs Alexander').
+ London: T. Fisher Unwin, 1896. SOURCE Alston, p. 195; Topp 8, 1589. LOCATION L.
Leipzig: Bernard Tauchnitz, 1896. SOURCE T & B, 3149; RLIN. LOCATION NIC.
New York: D. Appleton, 1896 (Appleton's Town and Country Library, No. 192). SOURCE RLIN. LOCATION NN.
COMMENTARY No Irish content [CM].

H235 *A fight with fate* (by 'Mrs Alexander').
London: F.V. White & Co., 1896. SOURCE Alston, p. 194. LOCATION L, NUC.
Leipzig: Bernard Tauchnitz, 1896, 2 vols. SOURCE T & B, 3135, 3136. LOCATION NUC.

Philadelphia: J.B. Lippincott & Co., 1896. LOCATION NUC.

H236 *A golden autumn. A novel* (by 'Mrs Alexander').

London: F.V. White & Co., 1896. SOURCE Alston, p. 194; Wolff, 3121 (1897, new edn); Topp 7, 348. LOCATION L, NUC (1898 edn).

Leipzig: Bernard Tauchnitz, 1897. SOURCE T & B, 3190.

Philadelphia: J.B. Lippincott & Co., 1896. SOURCE Topp 7, 348. LOCATION NUC.

H237 *Mrs. Crichton's creditor. A novel* (by 'Mrs Alexander').

London: F.V. White & Co., 1897. SOURCE Topp 7, 375. LOCATION Dt, L.

+ London. F.V. White & Co., 1898 (new edn). SOURCE Topp 7, 375. LOCATION InND Loeber coll.

Leipzig: Bernard Tauchnitz, 1897. SOURCE T & B, 3224; RLIN. LOCATION NIC.

Philadelphia: J.B. Lippincott & Co., 1897. SOURCE Topp 7, 375; OCLC. LOCATION CtY.

COMMENTARY A romance about a young navy lieutenant, Norman Adair, who, when on leave, happens to see his former love, Mrs Crichton, in a pawnshop. She is married to a rich but stingy man and the marriage is very unhappy. Norman tries to be of support to her and loans her money. Norman's mother wants to marry her son to a woman in whom he is not interested. Eventually, Mr Crichton dies and Norman and his love can marry [ML].

H238 *Barbara. Lady's maid and peeress* (by 'Mrs Alexander').

London: F.V. White & Co., 1897. SOURCE Daims, 1361; Topp 7, 367. LOCATION L.

Leipzig: Bernard Tauchnitz, 1897. SOURCE T & B, 3243. LOCATION NUC.

Philadelphia: J.B. Lippincott & Co., 1898. SOURCE Daims, 1361; Topp 7, 367. LOCATION NUC.

H239 *The cost of her pride* (by 'Mrs Alexander').

London: F.V. White & Co., 1898. SOURCE Daims, 1364. LOCATION L.

+ Leipzig: Bernard Tauchnitz, 1899, 2 vols. SOURCE T & B, 3366, 3367. LOCATION D, NUC.

Philadelphia: J.B. Lippincott & Co., 1899. SOURCE Daims, 1364. LOCATION NUC.

H240 *The step-mother* (by 'Mrs Alexander').

London: F.V. White, 1899. SOURCE Daims, 1368. LOCATION L.

Philadelphia: J.B. Lippincott & Co., 1900. SOURCE Daims, 1368. LOCATION NUC.

H241 *Brown, V.C.* (by 'Mrs Alexander').

London: T. Fisher Unwin, 1899. SOURCE Daims, 1362; Wolff, 3115. LOCATION L, NUC.

Leipzig: Bernard Tauchnitz, 1899. SOURCE T & B, 3381. LOCATION NUC.

New York: R.F. Fenno & Co., 1899. SOURCE Daims, 1362. LOCATION NUC.

H242 *Through fire to fortune* (by 'Mrs Alexander').

London: T. Fisher Unwin, 1900. SOURCE Daims, 1369. LOCATION D (n.d. edn), L.

+ Leipzig: Bernard Tauchnitz, 1900. SOURCE T & B, 3414. LOCATION InND Loeber coll.

New York: R.F. Fenno, 1900 (as *Thro' fire to fortune*). SOURCE Daims, 1369. LOCATION NUC.

H243 *A missing hero* (by 'Mrs Alexander').

+ London: Chatto & Windus, 1901. LOCATION L.

+ Leipzig: Bernard Tauchnitz, 1901. SOURCE T & B, 3480. LOCATION D, NUC.

New York: R.F. Fenno & Co.; London: Chatto & Windus, [1900].

COMMENTARY No Irish content [CM].

H244 *Stronger than love* (by 'Mrs Alexander'; dedicated to Ewing and Edith Paterson).

+ London: T. Fisher Unwin, 1902. LOCATION D.

Leipzig: Bernard Tauchnitz, 1902. SOURCE T & B, 3607; RLIN. LOCATION NIC.
H245　*The yellow fiend* (by 'Mrs Alexander').
London: T. Fisher Unwin, 1902. LOCATION O.
Leipzig: Bernard Tauchnitz, 1902. SOURCE T & B, 3562; OCLC. LOCATION Univ. of North Carolina, Chapel Hill.
H246　*Kitty Costello* (by 'Mrs Alexander').
London: T. Fisher Unwin, 1904 (biographical sketch of the author by Iza D. Hardy).
SOURCE Brown, 113 (n.d. edn); Blain, p. 15 (mentions 1902 edn, but this has not been found); Sutherland, p. 17. LOCATION L.
Leipzig: Bernard Tauchnitz, 1904. SOURCE T & B, 3719. LOCATION NUC.
COMMENTARY Published posthumously. Partly autobiographical, set around the 1840s, and describes the experiences of a beautiful and well-born Irish girl, who is suddenly plunged into commercial circles in a busy English port. The book contrasts the Irish and English temperaments [Brady; Brown].
H247　*The crumpled leaf; a Vatican mystery* (by 'Mrs Alexander').
London: H.J. Drane, [1911]. SOURCE Daims, 1365. LOCATION L (destroyed).
COMMENTARY Religious fiction concerning divorce [BLC].

'HEFFERNAN, Michael', pseud. See **FERGUSON, Sir Samuel**.

HELFFERICH, Adolf, b. 1813, d. 1894. Prolific German author, AH published on European countries, history, religion, mythology and languages. SOURCE RLIN; GLOL.
H248　*Skizzen und Erzählungen aus Irland* (by Adolf Helfferich).
Berlin: Springer, 1858. SOURCE RLIN. LOCATION CtY.

HELLEN, Robert (1725–93). Attributed author (for whom see HIP, iv, pp 390–1). See **PERY, Edmund Sexton**.

HEMPHILL, Barbara (née Hare), d. Dublin 1858. Novelist and short story writer, BH was the youngest daughter of Revd Patrick Hare, rector of Golden (Co. Tipperary) and vicar-general of the diocese of Cashel. In 1807 she married John Hemphill (of Cashel and Rathkenny, Co. Tipperary) who died in 1833. Their son, Charles Hare Hemphill, QC, became solicitor-general of Ireland and the lst Baron Hemphill. She was related by marriage to Thomas Crofton Croker§ who advised her to publish and her first story, an historical tale called 'The royal confession, a monastic legend', appeared in the *Dublin University Magazine* (1838). Most of her work appeared anonymously. For family papers, see ODNB. SOURCE Allibone Suppl., ii, p. 806; Boase, i, p. 1420; Brown, p; 134; W.E. Hall, p. 65; Landed gentry, 1904, p. 256; ODNB; RIA/DIB.
H249　*Lionel Deerhurst; or, fashionable life under the Regency* [anon.].
London: Richard Bentley, 1846, 3 vols. (ed. by Lady Blessington§). SOURCE Brown, p. 134; Alston, p. 196; Rafroidi, ii, p. 66; NCBEL 3, p. 711. LOCATION L, NUC, InND Loeber coll.
COMMENTARY Appeared under the name of Lady Blessington§, who is noted as its editor, but is by BH [COPAC].
H250　*The priest's niece; or, the heirship of Barmulph* [anon.].
London: Hurst & Blackett, 1855, 3 vols. SOURCE Brown, 734. LOCATION L, NUC.
COMMENTARY The story takes place initially in Spain and Scotland and shifts to Ireland in the third volume. The plot hinges on the dilemma in the hero's mind between his love for Ellen, a penniless peasant girl, to whom he owes several rescues from the 'Shanavests', and a

rich heiress who if he marries her, could save his father from ruin. The novel was very favourably reviewed in the *Irish Quarterly Review* (Dublin), where it was presumed the author was a man. A second edn appeared within five months of the first [Brown; ODNB].

H251 *Freida, the jongleur* (by Barbara Hemphill)
London: Chapman & Hall, 1857, 3 vols. SOURCE Brown, p. 134; COPAC. LOCATION L, NUC.
COMMENTARY An historical novel [DNB].

HENDERSON, Revd Henry, pseud. 'Ulster Scot', b. Belfast 1820, d. 1879 (Brown 2 mistakenly states 1897). Novelist and Presbyterian minister in Holywood (Co. Down), HH wrote for the *Belfast Weekly News* and also published his sermons. His fiction is anti-Catholic in tone. SOURCE Brown, p. 134; McKenna, p. 196; Newmann, p. 104; RIA/DIB.

H252 *The true heir of Ballymore: Passages from the history of a Belfast Ribbon lodge* [anon.].
+ Belfast: News-letter Office, 1859 (ill.). SOURCE Brown, 737; Linen Hall cat. p. 15; McKenna, p. 196. LOCATION D, BFL, InND Loeber coll.
COMMENTARY Originally issued in 4 parts. An anti-Catholic novel describing terrible machinations of a Ribbon lodge bent on the destruction of protestantism. The story revolves around a Catholic widow who inveigles Col. Aubrey into marriage. She drives out his relatives and their house is invaded by a low-class set of Catholics, who make the colonel's life so miserable that he dies. It transpires that the woman's first husband was alive all the time. Thus, the colonel's nephew inherits the property and the Ribbon plot fails [ML; Brown; Rowan cat. 48 pt. I/346].

H253 *The dark monk of Feola. Adventures of a ribbon pedlar* [anon.].
+ Belfast: News-letter Office, 1859. SOURCE McKenna, p. 196; Brown, 738. LOCATION D, Dt, BFl.
COMMENTARY Originally issued in 4 parts. Describes the evils which are certain to follow the union of Protestant women with Roman Catholic men [Brown; Rowan cat. 48 pt. I/346].

H254 *Flora Verner; or, the Sandy Row convert. A tale of the Belfast revival* (by Henry Henderson; preface by J. Sheridan Knowles§).
+ Belfast: George Phillips & Sons, [1859 or earlier]. LOCATION BFl, L ([1861] edn), InND Loeber coll.
Belfast: Phillips, 1861 (as *The Sandy Row convert. A tale of the Belfast revival*). SOURCE McKenna, p. 196; Brown, 739, OCLC. LOCATION Queen's University, Belfast.
COMMENTARY An anti-Catholic novel set in Belfast in 1859 when there was a strong movement of Protestant revival. Roman Catholics, particularly priests, are described in a negative manner. Stories are related of how priests stole Protestant children to take to the south of Ireland where they would be brought up as Catholics. Old people are preyed upon by priests to write their wills in favour of the Catholic church. When a mixed marriage is threatened, they entice the undesirable partner with false promises of emigration to America. Several instances are related of people who find Jesus as their saviour. The two 'saved' people love each other, come into an inheritance, and marry [ML; Brown].

H255 *Woodleigh Hall. A tale of the Fenians* (by 'Ulster Scot').
Belfast: Weekly News, 1867. SOURCE Brown 2, 605.
COMMENTARY No copy located [RL].

H256 *Sir Harry Aubrey. A tale of Indian warfare and Irish life* (by 'Ulster Scot')
Belfast: Weekly News, 1873. SOURCE Brown 2, 606.
COMMENTARY No copy located [RL].

H257 *The Mountrays of Clonkeen* (by 'Ulster Scot').
Belfast: Weekly News, 1877. SOURCE Brown 2, 606.

COMMENTARY No copy located [RL].

H258   *The squire of Ballynascree. A tale of the turn and the tent* (by 'Ulster Scot').
Belfast: Weekly News, 1877. SOURCE Brown 2, 607.
COMMENTARY No copy located [RL].

'HENRY', pseud. See GRIFFITH, Richard.

HENRY, Alexander, b. Loughbrickland (Co. Down) 1783, d. Harrogate (London) 1821.
Novelist and poet, AH is associated by O'Donoghue with the Alexander Henry who was an
eminent woollen and cotton merchant and MP for South Lancashire. Aside from the following novel, he also published *The wood-elves, a poem* (Dublin, 1820), and poems in the *Dublin
Magazine* (1820). SOURCE O'Donoghue, p. 192.

H259   *Rolando: a romance* (by Alexander Henry, Esq.).
London: A.K. Newman & Co., 1821, 2 vols. SOURCE COPAC; O'Donoghue, p. 192;
Garside, 1821:46; Corvey; CME 3-628-47778-6; NSTC 2H17522. LOCATION L.

HENRY, James, b. Dublin 1798, d. Dalkey Lodge, Dalkey (Co. Dublin) 1876. Physician,
classical scholar, poet and traveller, JH was the son of Robert Henry, a woollen draper, and
Katherine Elder. He graduated with the gold medal in classics at TCD in 1819, where he
received an MA and MB in 1822 and his MD in 1832. He became an eminent if eccentric
physician and was elected vice-president of the King and Queen's College of Physicians in
Dublin. But he alienated his colleagues by his sarcasm and his habit of charging his patients
no more than five shillings a visit, on the grounds that no doctor's opinion was worth a guinea.
After receiving a large inheritance he gave up his practice in 1845 and devoted his time to
scholarly pursuits, especially the collecting of materials for a commentary on Virgil's *Aeneid*,
which he had loved since he was a schoolboy. For twenty-five years he travelled widely
throughout Europe, mostly on foot, accompanied by his daughter Katharine and, until her
death in 1849 his wife, the former Anne Patton, visiting libraries and centres of learning, exam-
ining rare edns and manuscripts concerning Virgil and the *Aeneid*. Eventually he and his daughter returned to Dublin in 1869, where he spent most of his remaining years in the library at
TCD and was noted for his learning and kindness. JH also wrote pamphlets on religion and
politics; commentaries on the classics; on medical matters (e.g. *A dialogue between a bilious
patient and a physician*, Dublin, 1838), and *An account of the drunken sea* (Dublin, 1840), which
deal with constipation and alcoholism. His travel writing includes *Thalia petasata, or, a foot
journey from Carlsruhe to Bassano, described on the way in verse* (Dresden, 1859), and *Thalia
petasata iterum, or, a foot journey from Dresden to Venice, described on the way in verse* (Leipzig,
1877). Many of these writings were published privately and given as gifts to friends. His life-
long study of the *Aeneid* resulted in the publication of *Aeneida; or, critical, exegetical, and aes-
thetical remarks on the Aeneis* (London & Dublin 1873–79), published posthumously, which
was highly praised by the scholar J.P. Mahaffy. In his travels JH crossed the Alps seventeen
times. For his portrait and papers, see ODNB. SOURCE Allibone Suppl., ii, p. 809; Boase, i,
p. 1432; Hogan 2, p. 542; J.B. Lyons, *Scholar and sceptic: the career of James Henry M.D.
1798–1876* (Dublin, c.1985); MVP, p. 218; ODNB; O'Donoghue, p. 192.

H260   *An account of the proceedings of the government metropolitan police in the city of
Canton* (by Henry James).
+ Dublin: Hardy & Walker, 1840 (ill. J. Kirkwood). LOCATION D, InND Loeber coll.
COMMENTARY 81pp. A satire based on the founding of the Dublin Metropolitan Police (1836),
but set in Canton, China, and relating the government's introduction of a metropolitan police
force. Although the people of Canton are initially very pleased with the change, slowly the

police start to control and regulate all aspects of life. The Cantonese have to pay extremely high taxes to pay for the police. Eventually they send a petition to Peking to stop police interference. The petition is not heard and no changes are made [ML].

HENTY, G.A. See **HENTY, George Alfred**.

HENTY, George Alfred (known as **G.A. Henty**), b. Trumpington (Cambs.) 1833, d. Weymouth Harbour (Dorset) 1902. English soldier, journalist and prolific writer of adventure stories for juveniles, GAH was the son of Mary Bovill and James Henty, a stockbroker and coal mine owner. He was educated at Canterbury and Westminster schools and attended Cambridge University. Judged a born leader, he had a successful military career on the Continent and was in charge of the commissariat in Belfast and later in Portsmouth. He married Elizabeth Finucane in Dublin in 1857. For some years he engaged in mining operations in Italy before returning to England. After his wife's death in 1865, he resigned his commission and became war correspondent for the *London Standard*, reporting from the Crimea, the Franco-Prussian war, the Turco-Serbian war, and from West Africa, where he accompanied Sir Garnet Wolseley§. He used these experiences and many other foreign travels as background for his enormously popular stories for boys, which blended historical accuracy with high adventure. They remained popular well into the twentieth century. SOURCE Allibone Suppl., ii, p. 810; Brown, p. 135; EF, p. 180; NCBEL 4, pp 1576–9; ODNB; Sutherland, pp 291–2; Venn, part ii, iii, p. 334.

H261 *Friends though divided* (by G.A. Henty).
London: Griffith & Farran, 1883. SOURCE Brown, 742 (mistakes different edn, 1910). LOCATION NUC.
New York: E.P. Dutton, [1885?]. LOCATION NUC.
COMMENTARY Historical fiction for juveniles. A boy's adventure story of the English Civil War. Covers Montrose and the Covenanters. At the end of the story, the action shifts to Ireland for the siege of Drogheda [Brown; Nield].

H262 *Orange and green: A tale of the Boyne and Limerick* (by G.A. Henty).
London, Glasgow, Edinburgh, Dublin: Blackie & Son, 1887. SOURCE Brown, 743; Dixson, p. 221. LOCATION D (n.d. edn).
+ London: Blackie & Son; Toronto: Copp Clark; William Briggs, n.d (ill. Gordon Browne). LOCATION InND Loeber coll.
+ [n.l.]: The Educational Company of Ireland, n.d. (as *A young patriot*; Story Reader for Senior Standards). LOCATION DPL.
New York: Scribner, n.d. SOURCE Nield, p. 332. LOCATION NUC.
+ Akron [OH], New York: Superior Printing Co., n.d. (The Henty Series, No. 47). LOCATION InND Loeber coll.
COMMENTARY Historical fiction for juveniles. Adventures of a Protestant and a Catholic boy during the Williamite War. The battles of the Boyne and Aughrim, and the sieges of Athlone, Cork, and Limerick are described. Features Patrick Sarsfield [Brown].

H263 *With Moore at Corunna* (by G.A. Henty).
New York: C. Scribner's Sons, 1897 (ill. Wal Paget). LOCATION NUC.
+ New York: Charles Scribner's Sons, 1902 (ill. Wal Paget). LOCATION InND Loeber coll.
London, Glasgow, Edinburgh, Dublin: Blackie, 1898 (ill. Wal Paget). LOCATION NUC.
COMMENTARY Historical fiction for juveniles. Describes the adventures of Terence O'Connor during the Peninsular War. Terence's father is a captain in the Mayo Fusiliers, stationed in Athlone before their removal to the Iberian Peninsula. Terence committed many pranks in

Athlone but his quick-wittedness stands him in good stead during the campaign, where he has many adventures and rises very rapidly through the ranks [ML].

H264 *In the Irish Brigade. A tale of war in Flanders and Spain* (by G.A. Henty).
+ London, Glasgow, Edinburgh, Dublin: Blackie & Son, 1901 (ill. Charles M. Sheldon). SOURCE Brown, 744. LOCATION D, NUC, InND Loeber coll.
New York: Charles Scribner's Sons, 1900 (ill. Charles M. Sheldon). LOCATION NUC.
COMMENTARY Historical fiction for juveniles set chiefly in Flanders and Spain. Tells of the adventures of Desmond Kennedy, an officer of the Irish Brigade in the service of France during the war of the Spanish succession. The author mentions his historical sources [Brown].

HERBERT, Dorothea, b. Carrick-on-Suir? (Co. Tipperary) c.1770, d. 1829, Diarist, poet, playwright and novelist, DH was the daughter of Revd Nicholas Herbert and Martha Cuffe, daughter of the first Lord Dysart of Dysart (Co. Kilkenny). Her father descended from the Herberts of Muckross (Co. Kerry) and was minister at Carrick-on-Suir and Knockgrafton (Co. Tipperary). As a child DH was taught writing by the local parish clerk and later attended a boarding school in Carrick-on-Suir. In 1776 she accompanied her family to England. She was wooed by a curate, but her parents turned him down and she remained single all her life. Her father died in 1803, leaving the family finances in a precarious state. Around this time DH started to write her diary (later published in part), entitled 'Retrospections of an outcast or the life of Dorothea Herbert authress [*sic*] of the orphan plays and various poems and novels in four volumes written in retirement Volume the Fourth adorned with cuts' (MS in TCD). None of her plays and novels appears to have survived. In her diary she complained about family members beating her and locking her up, which may have to do with her mental instability at that time. The writer Hercules Young§ was her friend. Source O'Toole, pp 94–5; *Retrospections of Dorothea Herbert 1770–1806* (Dublin, 1988), pp 437–56.

HERBERT, Henry William, b. London 1807, d. New York 1858. English novelist, periodical writer, translator and writer on field sports, HWH was the son of the dean of Manchester, William Herbert, and the Hon. Letitia Allen. He graduated at Cambridge University and left suddenly for France and then the US in 1831, after which his family refused to acknowledge him. He worked as a classical tutor, founded the *American Monthly Magazine* in New York and wrote voluminously on outdoor sports, for which he is remembered more than for his novels. His novel on Oliver Cromwell does not deal with Ireland. He committed suicide in New York in 1858. SOURCE Allibone Suppl., ii, p. 830; Boase, i, p. 1440; Brown 2, p. 113; ODNB; RL.

H265 *Dermot O'Brien: or, the taking of Tredagh. A tale of 1649* (by Henry William Herbert).
New York: Stringer & Townsend, 1849. SOURCE Brown 2, 611; COPAC. LOCATION L, NUC.
COMMENTARY Historical fiction about the siege of Drogheda (1649) during the war in Ireland led by Oliver Cromwell [RL].

HERBERT, James Dowling, b. Dublin 1762/3, d. Jersey (Channel Islands) 1837. Artist, revolutionary, art dealer and writer, JDH was born James Herbert Dowling, son of James Dowling, an ironmonger in South Great George's Street, according to RIA/DIB. O'Donoghue says JH was an actor and a painter who studied with Robert Home (1752–1834, the leading portrait painter in Dublin at the time who was from London but settled in Dublin in 1779). He was an assistant to the American painter Gilbert Stuart and finished some of the paintings started by Stuart when he worked in Ireland before leaving hurriedly for the US in 1793 to escape his creditors. JDH was implicated in the 1798 rebellion, after which he changed his name from Dowling to Herbert (according to RIA/DIB he used the latter as a stage name). There is a satirical reference to him under his former name in John Wilson Croker's§ *Familiar epistles to Frederick Jones* (Dublin, 1804). JDH painted portraits of several of the leaders of the rebellion as well as a picture of the capture of the Irish revolutionary Lord Edward Fitzgerald, and in 1801 a portrait of Thomas Moore§, who knew him well. He opened a picture dealership in Dublin in 1811 and his premises in Exchequer Street became one of the earliest places to display art in the city. He also worked in Bath and in Cork before settling in Jersey. SOURCE A. Crookshank & the Knight of Glin, *The painters of Ireland* (Billericay, Essex, 1978), p. 156; ODNB; O'Donoghue, p. 193; RIA/DIB.

H266   *Irish varieties, for the last fifty years: written from recollections. Consisting of sketches of character, customs, manners, occurrences, events, professions, establishments, the stage, the Bar, the pulpit; and a plan for relieving the Irish peasantry* (first series; [all published]; by James Dowling Herbert; dedicated to James Sheridan Knowles§).
     + London: William Joy, 1836. SOURCE Hodges Figgis cat. 10 n.s./1355. LOCATION D, NUC.
COMMENTARY Partly essays, partly fiction. Contents: 'The actress', 'The actor, author, and liberal senator', 'The dramatic reader and general censor', 'Dinner at Mansergh St. George's', 'The poet', 'The Dublin Society's drawing academy, the masters and the pupils', 'The franchises', 'The pinling dindies', 'The Liberty and Ormond boys', 'The cutting beavers', 'Bullbaiting, etc.', 'The night of the Boyne', 'Sad affairs', 'The king of Dalkey', 'Ranelagh public walks and promenades', 'The pulpit', 'Hone, the painter', 'Patronage', 'Portrait-painting and private drama', 'Private theatricals and high life', 'Patronage slighted', 'Hypochondria cured by fright', 'The humorist', 'A critique on a private play, performed by some persons of note in Cork. Supposed to be written by Hudson', 'Leaves from my scrap-book', 'Memoir of Stuart, portrait-painter', 'The forced marriage', 'The private theatre, Fishamble Street', 'Ancient and modern times', 'Patch-work', 'Plan for relieving the Irish peasantry' [ML].

'THE HERMIT HIMSELF', pseud., fl. 1866. Pseudonym of a fantasy writer, probably American.
H267   *The monk of the mountains; or, a description of the joys of paradise: Being the life and wonderful experiences of an aged hermit, who was taken by his diseased friend to the first heaven, and there shown the beauties and the happiness of the spirited land; with the destiny and condition of earth for one hundred years to come* (by 'The hermit himself').
     + Indianapolis [IN]: Downey & Brouse, 1866. LOCATION Wright web.
COMMENTARY A hermit disappointed in life lives in the mountains of Virginia. A friend conducts him to paradise, which makes it possible for him to see in the past and in the future. He sees that America attacks England and demands the independence of Ireland and of other colonies. England also has to pay a large sum of money to Ireland. Seventy-five years later Ireland is prosperous and England, stripped of the influx of intelligent Irish people and of income from their colonies, is poor [ML].

HERON, Isaac, b. Cumberland 1735. Fictionalizing autobiographer, IH was the son of Edmund Heron and Mary Wilson. His father had a dry goods shop, probably in Coleraine (Co. Derry), where the author grew up. Later he became a sea captain. SOURCE ML; vol. below; RIA/DIB.
H268   *My own memoirs; or, the life of Isaac Heron, a loyalist on pure genuine principles* [anon.] (dedicated 'to her Majesty, Queen of Ierne, alias Eringobraugh').

+ Waterford: John Bull, 1810, vol. 1 [all published]. SOURCE OCLC. LOCATION D (incomplete).

COMMENTARY 72pp (but incomplete). A partly fictionalized autobiography containing some dialogue between the author and a London bookseller. A review in the *Hibernia Magazine* (Dublin, Jan. 1810) states that 'it is well written, and contains a variety of the most curious adventures that can be supposed to occur in human life'. Allegedly the account of a living person, a resident of the City of Waterford and holding a position in the revenue there. In the dedication the author expresses 'but very little, or rather no gratitude, I among many of your worthy sons owe *you*, who ever, ever since your cordial kind reception of STRONGBOW, have been in the unnatural monstrous habit of taking your best and most delightful children's bread, and casting it to the dogs!' [RL].

'HERRING, Geilles', pseud. See SOMERVILLE, Edith Œnone.

HERVEY, Elizabeth. Attributed author. See ELLIOTT, Rev. Robert.

HEYGATE, Revd William Edward, b. Hackney (Middx.), 1802, d. Brighstone (Isle of Wight), 1902. Church of England clergyman and author of historical novels, religious and devotional works, poetry and stories for children, WEH was the son of James Heygate and Anna Mackmurdo. He graduated at St John's College, Oxford, in 1839 and was ordained in 1840. After a series of curacies, he was made rector of Brighstone in 1869 and in 1887 became honorary canon of Winchester. He was a devoted follower of the Tractarian movement at Oxford. Several of his sons followed him into holy orders. SOURCE Allibone Suppl., ii, p. 816; Brown, p. 136; ODNB.

H269 *Wild scenes amongst the Celts. The penitent and the fugitive* [anon.].
London: James Henry & James Parker, [1859]. SOURCE Brown, 745; COPAC. LOCATION L.
New York: General Protestant Episcopal Sunday School Union and Church Book Society, n.d. SOURCE NSTC. LOCATION CtY.
COMMENTARY Historical fiction: 'The penitent' (set in the fifth century in Ireland and England), and 'The fugitive' (set in Scotland and north Connacht in the sixth century) [Brown].

HEYWOOD, Eliza. See HAYWOOD, Eliza.

'AN HIBERNIAN', attributed pseud. See DOUGLASS, Adam.

HICKEY, Revd William, pseud. 'Martin Doyle', b. Murragh (Co. Cork) 1787, d. Dublin 1875. Clergyman, pamphleteer and writer on agriculture, WH was the son of the Revd Ambrose Hickey and Jane Herrick of Shippool (Co. Cork). He was admitted at TCD in 1804, at St John's, Cambridge, in 1806 and obtained a BA from both institutions in 1809. He was ordained in 1811 and received his MA in Dublin in 1832. He served at various parishes in Carlow and Wexford and as early as 1817 his concern for the poor was evidenced in a pamphlet *The state of the poor of Ireland* (Dublin, 1820). He was vicar of Bannow (Co. Wexford, 1820–26. During this period, WH, together with Thomas Boyse of Bannow House (at Grange, Bannow), a friend of Mrs S.C. Hall§), founded an agricultural school at Bannow and the South Wexford Agricultural Society, the first of its kind in Ireland. Subsequently WH published many pamphlets and books on practical farming and improvements for the lives of the poor, some of which were cloaked as fiction. After 1826 he was transferred to Monart, near Enniscorthy (Co. Wexford), where he established another model farm at Ballyorley. He was a prolific author, writing also about gardening, emigration and about Co. Wexford. He was active in originating improvements in roads and bridges. His *Hints to the small farmers of Ireland* was published by the Kildare Place Society (Dublin, 1830). He also wrote *Hints to small holders on planting and on cattle* (Dublin, 1830); *Practical gardening* (Dublin, 1833), and the very comprehensive *A cyclopædia of practical husbandry* (Dublin, 1839). He was co-founder of the *Irish Farmer's and Gardener's Magazine* (Dublin, 1834–42) and editor of *The illustrated book of domestic poultry* (London, 1854). Many of his articles appeared in such Dublin periodicals as the *Dublin Penny Journal*, the *Irish Penny Journal* and in the Edinburgh *Blackwood's Agricultural Magazine*. Deeply concerned about relationships between landlords and tenants, he wrote *Address to the landlords of Ireland* (Dublin, 1831), and *The labouring classes in Ireland* (Dublin, 1846). WH was a member of the Royal Dublin Society, which awarded him its gold medal in recognition of his services to Ireland, and he received a pension from the Royal Literary Fund. He continued to publish until late in life, with his *Cottage farming* appearing in London in 1870. In all of his writing he studiously avoided religious and political controversy. It is not clear whether WH can be identified with the 'M. M'Donald Doyle', resident of Tintern (Co. Wexford), who published a volume of poetry, *Moorland minstrelsy ... To which is added "Bannow," a descriptive poem* (Wexford, 1833), or the Martin Doyle, author of the poem *The O'Muliganiad; or, the views, objects, and motives of O'Sullivan McGhee, and Todd detected and exposed* (Wexford, 1836), which O'Donoghue mentions as associated with New Ross (Co. Wexford). WH married in 1813 Henrietta Maria, only daughter of John Steuart (not Stewart as in some sources), of Steuart's Lodge (Leighlin Bridge, Co. Carlow), with whom he had six children and who died at Camolin Rectory in 1878, age 85. Among his friends was the author Mrs S.C. Hall§ , who attributed the source of her story 'The last in the lease' to WH. For WH's portraits, see Elmes, Strickland, and ODNB. SOURCE Allibone Suppl., ii, p. 817; Boylan, p. 156; Brady, pp 105–6; B & S, p. 395; Browne, pp 35–6; Collinson Black, 3184, 4025; P.L. Curran (ed.), *Towards a history of agricultural science in Ireland* (Dublin, 1992), p. 15; Elmes, p. 98; Hislop, p. 1039; Irish pseudonyms; JAPMDI, 5(3) (1903), p. 312; Leslie, *Ferns*, p. 217; Leslie & Wallace, p. 728; ODNB; O'Donoghue, p. 195; Reese cat. 166/178; RIA/DIB; Strickland, i, p. 595; Venn, part ii, iii, pp 357–8.

H270 **Irish cottagers** (by 'Martin Doyle').

+ Dublin: William Curry Jnr; London: Hurst, Chance & Co.; Edinburgh: Oliver & Boyd, 1830. SOURCE Jarndyce cat. 98/323; Garside 2, 1830:60. LOCATION Dt, L, NUC, InND Loeber coll.

+ Dublin: William Curry Jnr & Co.; London: Simpkin & Marshall; Edinburgh: Oliver & Boyd, 1833, 3rd edn (enlarged). LOCATION NUC, InND Loeber coll.

COMMENTARY The preface is written from Ballyorley [Co. Wexford], and states that 'some striking coincidences' between the present work and the recently published William Carleton's§ *Traits and stories of the Irish peasantry* (Dublin, 1830) 'are purely accidental, the author having not seen the prior work until after completing his own'. The *Irish cottagers* consists of a fictional, didactic tale, intended to 'convey sound practical advice'. The central theme is about an improving landlord who rewards good management in his tenants. The story presents many examples of good and bad habits for tenants. In a later edn the ending was altered [ML; Jarndyce; Garside 2].

H271 *Hints addressed to the small holders and peasantry of Ireland, on subjects connected with health, temperance, morals, &c. &c. &c.* (by 'Martin Doyle').

Dublin: William Curry Jnr & Co., 1830. LOCATION NUC.

+ Dublin: William Curry Jnr & Co.; London: Simpkin & Marshall; Edinburgh: Oliver & Boyd, 1832 (8th edn, as *Hints originally intended for the small farmers of the county of Wexford; but suited to the circumstances of most parts of Ireland*). LOCATION NUC, InND Loeber coll.

COMMENTARY A mixture of instructional text and fictional prose, including 'Story of Molly Butler and Peg. Carthy' (concerns proper dress), and stories on temperance and education, the latter set in a classroom visited by local gentry, in which a boy reads aloud an allegorical story [RL].

H272 *Common sense for common people, or illustrations of popular proverbs, designed for the use of the peasantry of Ireland* (by 'Martin Doyle').
Dublin: William Curry Jnr & Co., 1835. LOCATION NUC, InND Loeber coll. (1835 end, 13th thousand).
Dublin: William Curry & Co., 1847, 14th edn (*as Tom Brady and Dick Smith. Two popular stories of the peasantry of Ireland*). SOURCE Rowan cat. 60/207; COPAC. LOCATION C.
COMMENTARY Contents: 'Tom Brady', 'Dick Smith' [RL].

H273 *Agricultural class book; or, how to best cultivate a small farm and garden: together with hints on domestic economy* [anon.].
Dublin: Commissioners of National Education in Ireland, 1848. LOCATION D, L (1850 edn), NUC.
+ Dublin: Alex. Thom & Sons; London: Longman, Brown & Co.; Edinburgh: Fraser & Co. [for the Commissioners of National Education in Ireland], 1858 (ill.). LOCATION InND Loeber coll.
COMMENTARY The story is directed at the older children of cottagers. The person who guides the cottagers to a better lifestyle is called Mr Doyle, and the text mentions the baronies of Forth and Bargy in Co. Wexford. The text was partly or fully written prior to the famine of 1846–47 (p. 109), and contains dialogues on how to improve farming and gardening methods for cottagers. John Doran and his family want to emigrate to America because of their economic plight, but are shown how to improve their farming methods and their budget. A varied diet is advocated to counteract one based solely on potatoes. History is interwoven with information and instruction [ML; RL; D. Akenson, *The Irish education experiment* (London, 1970), p. 232)].
— COLLECTED WORKS

H274 *The works of Martin Doyle.*
+ Dublin: William Curry Jun. & Co., 1831 (4 parts). SOURCE Drury cat. 109/41. LOCATION L, InND Loeber coll.
Dublin: William Curry Jnr & Co., 1834, 2 vols. SOURCE NSTC. LOCATION Dt, Newcastle Univ. Library.
+ Dublin: William Curry & Co.; London: Simpkin, Marshall & Co.; Edinburgh: Fraser & Co., 1836, 2 vols. LOCATION InND Loeber coll.
COMMENTARY The works of Martin Doyle are known from several edns, which increasingly included more of his tracts. Starting with the 1831 edn of four parts, the 1834 edn contains 5 parts and 8 parts in different edns, compared with the 1836 edn of 9 parts. The ten 'volume' works were advertised in Mar. 1842, while the twelve-volume works were advertised in 1839 [No. 3 of Lever's *Jack Hinton*, issued in parts; advertised in M. Doyle, *A cyclopædia of practical husbandry* (Dublin, 1839); RL].

HIGGINSON, Agnes Nesta Shakespear [*sic*]. See SKRINE, Mrs Agnes Nesta Shakespear [*sic*].

HIGGINSON, Francis S., fl. 1825. History writer, poet and former commander of the cutter 'Lynx', FSH is probably a different person than the author Francis Higginson (1799–1879), who entered the navy at age 13, was appointed lieutenant in 1839, became a commander in 1860 and published his first book of fiction in 1851. SOURCE Allibone Suppl., ii, p. 819; Belanger, 86; Boase, v, pp 653–4.

H275 *Manderville; or, the Hibernian Chiliarch: A tale* (by Francis S. Higginson).
    + London: Thomas Dolby, 1825, 2 vols. SOURCE Block, p. 103; British Fiction; Garside, 1825:41; COPAC. LOCATION Corvey CME 3–628–47685–2, Ireland related fiction, L, NUC.
    COMMENTARY An historical novel set in the north of Ireland in the first half of the eighteenth century. Sir Henry Mortimer assembles a small army in order to gain independence for Ireland and to establish catholicism as the official religion in Ireland. He is aided by other Catholic Continental sovereigns, but is eventually defeated by the 'royalists' and the rather implausibly named Maj. Digby Dauntless. Mortimer's daughter Sophia is a combination of Flora MacIvor and Lady Morgan's§ Glorvina – she first appears playing the harp. Mortimer's son, who has maintained his loyalty to England and the Protestant faith throughout his father's rebellion, turns out to be of English parentage, and after this discovery marries Sophia, the woman he thought was his sister [JB].

HIGGINSON, Nesta. See SKRINE, Mrs Agnes Nesta Shakespear [*sic*].

HILDITCH, Hiram, fl. 1841. Editor, HH in the preface to the following work, describes himself as its editor and 'General Bagman, Commission Agent, and Traveller from the North of England and South of Scotland'. He visited or lived in Ireland. SOURCE CM; RL.

H276 *The humours of 99* [*sic*]: *A tale of the times after the turn-out; transcribed from the recitations of John Bell (blind from his infancy) … and printed for the blind man's benefit* (by Hiram Hilditch).
    + Newtown, Larne: M'Calmont's General Printing-Office, 1841. SOURCE Linen Hall cat. p. 126. LOCATION BFl.
    COMMENTARY The editor recorded the blind John Bell's tales over a period of seven days and nights [RL].

HILL, Benson Earle, b. Bristol (Avon), 1795, d. London, 1845. Editor, novelist and writer on theatre, BEH served in the army from 1809 to 1822. Passionate about the theatre, he tried to make a second career there but was not very successful. He was the brother of the dramatist Isabel Hill. He edited the *Monthly Magazine* in London and one of his short stories 'The Irishman in Egypt' appeared in the *Catholic Keepsake* (Philadelphia, 1845). He signed the preface to his *Recollections* from Brompton (London, 1836). He was the author of a book on cooking and entertainment, *The epicure's almanac* (London, 1841–43), based on his experiences and travels, which offered a recipe for every day of the year; hints on using exotic ingredients as well as leftovers; ways to economize on cooking, and standard British favourites. BEH never married and died in poverty. SOURCE BLC; ODNB; RL.

H277 *Recollections of an artillery officer: Including scenes and adventures in Ireland, America, Flanders, and France* (by Benson Earle Hill; dedicated to Lord Segrave, 'The drama's patron and actor's friend').
    + London: Richard Bentley, 1836, 2 vols. SOURCE Garside 2, 1836:35; COPAC. LOCATION L.
    COMMENTARY The work is a combination of autobiography and fiction and recounts the life of an artillery officer. The narrator is an officer ordered to Cork in 1810. He spends two years in Ireland in various garrisons in Dublin, Athlone and Limerick. It contains descriptions of barracks life, visits to country houses, and theatricals in which the narrator participates [ML; CM; ODNB].

H278   *Home service: or, scenes and characters from life, at out and head quarters* (by Benson Earle Hill; dedicated to George Raymond).
+ London: Henry Colburn, 1839, 2 vols. LOCATION L.
COMMENTARY Partly autobiographical and partly fiction, it refers to the 1798 rebellion in Ireland [RL].

HILL, John, d. 1904. Novelist, song writer and poet, JH was from an Ulster family of Hills. He contributed to the London *Tinsley's Magazine* and published *Songs* (London, 1881). According to O'Donoghue, he lived for some time in the Isle of Wight and later in Brussels. Some of his letters are among the Downey Papers in the NLI (MSS 10,005, 10,024–27, 10,030, 10,043). SOURCE Allibone Suppl., ii, p 822; Brown, p. 103 [under Faly]; LVP, p. 225; E. Reilly, p. 218; O'Donoghue, p. 197; RIA/DIB.

H279   *Wild rose, a romance* (by John Hill; dedicated to E.S.C.).
+ London: Tinsley Bros, 1882, 3 vols. SOURCE Brown, p. 103 (1886 edn). LOCATION L, NUC.
COMMENTARY No Irish content [CM].

H280   *The waters of Marah* (by John Hill).
+ London: Tinsley Bros, 1883, 3 vols. LOCATION L, NUC.
New York: G. Munro, [1883] (Seaside Library, No. 112). LOCATION NUC.
COMMENTARY No Irish content [CM].

H281   *Sally. A novel* (by John Hill).
London: Tinsley Bros, 1885, 3 vols. LOCATION L, NUC.
COMMENTARY No Irish content. Set in Scotland [CM].

H282   *The corsairs; or, love and lucre* (by John Hill).
+ London: Vizetelly & Co., 1885. LOCATION L, NUC.
COMMENTARY No Irish content. Author states that he is indebted to his friend Henry George Murray for his assistance in chapters 1 and 2 [CM].

H283   *A garden of tares* (by John Hill and Clement Hopkins).
+ London: Vizetelly & Co., 1888 (Vizetelly's One-Volume Edition). SOURCE Allibone Suppl., ii, p. 822. LOCATION L.
COMMENTARY Set in London [RL].

H284   *An unfortunate arrangement* (by John Hill).
+ London: Ward & Downey, 1890, 2 vols. LOCATION L, NUC.
COMMENTARY No Irish content [CM].

H285   *Treason-felony. A novel* (by John Hill).
+ London: Chatto & Windus, 1892, 2 vols. LOCATION L, NUC.
COMMENTARY No Irish content [CM].

H286   *The common ancestor* (by John Hill).
+ London: Chatto & Windus, 1894, 3 vols. LOCATION L.
COMMENTARY The main character, Sergeant Dick Scanlan, is of Irish ancestry and it tells the story of how his family had turned from protestantism to the Catholic faith [CM].

H287   *Dinah Fleet* (by John Hill).
+ London: Downey & Co., 1897. LOCATION L.
COMMENTARY No Irish content [CM].

H288   *Ninety-eight: being the recollections of Cormac Cahir O'Connor Faly (late Col. in the French service) of that awful period* (by John Hill).
London: Downey & Co., 1897 (collected and ed. by author's grandson, Patrick C. Faly, attorney-at-law; ill. A.D. M'C [A.D. McCormick]). LOCATION L.
Buffalo, N.Y.; (ill. A.D. McCormick). SOURCE Brown, 573.

+ London: Downey & Co., 1898 (new edn, as *"Ninety-eight"*, *a story of the Irish rebellion*; see Plate 39). LOCATION D, InND Loeber coll.

COMMENTARY Historical novel of the 1798 rebellion in Dublin, which details the cruelty of the English and the traitorous intrigue in the organization of the United Irishmen. The main character, Cormac Cahir O'Connor, participates in the uprising in Wexford, where he loses his fiancée and his best friend. Later he joins Humbert's forces, becomes a prisoner and is forced to leave the country. Contains an account of General Thomas Cloney and the battle of New Ross (Co. Wexford) [ML; Brown].

HILLARY, Joseph, b. Cork, fl. 1818. Journalist, poet and miscellaneous writer, JH was the son of a silversmith and was left well-off by his father. JH soon ran through his fortune, and then supported himself by journalism. He wrote for a short-lived Cork magazine, the *Munster Olive Branch*, and published *Poems* (Cork 1794), which included lyric pieces, tales, and elegies. SOURCE Brown, p. 137; O'Donoghue, p. 197; RIA/DIB.

H289 *The parish priest in Ireland* [anon.].

+ London: T. Hughes; Cork: W. Mathews, 1818, 2 vols. SOURCE Brown 2, 615 (where mistakenly, the name is spelled Hilary); British Fiction; Garside, 1818:36; Belanger, 53. LOCATION Corvey CME 3-628-48360-3, Ireland related fiction, D.

COMMENTARY Set somewhere in the south of Ireland. The story is meant to be humorous and portrays, among others, a parish priest [Brown 2].

'HIMSELF', pseud. See **CROFTS, Charley**.

'HIMSELF', pseud. See **FRENEY, James**.

'HIMSELF', pseud. See **HARRISON, James**.

'HIMSELF', pseud. See **MAC FARLAND, John**.

'HIMSELF', pseud. See **NUGENT, Robert**.

'HIMSELF', pseud. See **ST LEGER, Francis Barry Boyle**.

'HIMSELF', fl. 1847. Pseudonym of an historical fiction writer.

H290 *Henry Domville; or, a younger son* (by 'Himself').

London: Chapman & Hall, 1847, 2 vols. SOURCE Burmester list; COPAC; OCLC; RLIN. LOCATION L, Univ. of North Carolina, Chapel Hill, MH.

COMMENTARY Adventures of a young radical in Ireland and France in the last years of the eighteenth century. In part of the narrative, the hero fights with the French against the Prussians. Members of the Domvile (also Domville) family resided in Ireland from the seventeenth century on at Louglinstown House (Co. Dublin; later the residence later of Charles Lever§), but there is no clear link between this family and this novel [Burmester list; RL, Burke's, p. 375].

HINKSON, H.A. See **HINKSON, Henry Albert**.

HINKSON, Henry Albert (known as **H.A. Hinkson**), b. Dublin 1865, d. Brook Hill, Claremorris (Co. Mayo) 1919. Novelist, miscellaneous writer and barrister, HAH studied classics at TCD and in Germany and in 1890 received an MA in classics from the Royal University of Ireland. For a while he taught classics at Clongowes Wood College (Co. Kildare). He married the novelist and poet Katharine Tynan§ and converted to catholicism before their marriage in 1893. They settled initially in England where he studied law and was called to the English Bar in 1902. The family remained some years in England before returning to Ireland. HAH was appointed RM in south Mayo, living at Claremorris. Besides his historical novels and works of fiction for juveniles, he wrote stories and poems and contributed to journals, including the *Bookman* (London) and he authored *Student life at Trinity College* (Dublin, 1892). He was father of the writer Pamela Hinkson. Some of his letters are among the Downey Papers in the NLI (MSS 10,005, 10,024–27, 10,030, 10,043). SOURCE Brady, pp 106–7; Brown, p. 137; EF, p. 184; E. Reilly, pp 218, 245; Hogan 2, pp 553–4; IBL, 10 (1919), p. 72; O'Donoghue, p. 462 [under Katharine Tynan]; RIA/DIB; Sutherland, pp 296–7.

H291 *Golden lads and girls* (by H.A. Hinkson; dedicated to 'the dearest of women').
  + London: Downey & Co., 1895. SOURCE Brown, 749; Wolff, 3216. LOCATION D, Dt, DPL, L.
  COMMENTARY A love story, set in Co. Galway and depicting life in the upper-middle classes as well as student life in TCD [Brown].

H292 *O'Grady of Trinity. A story of Irish university life* (by H.A. Hinkson; dedicated to Louise Imogen Guiney).
  + London: Lawrence & Bullen, 1896 (on spine: Clery & Co.). SOURCE Brown, 761 (1909 edn). LOCATION Dt, DPL, L, NUC, InND Loeber coll.
  COMMENTARY A novel of the frolics and fun depicting the academic and athletic activities of students living in TCD. A love story is interwoven [ML; Brown].

H293 *Father Alphonsus* (by H.A. Hinkson).
  + London: T. Fisher Unwin, 1898. SOURCE Brown, 750; OCLC. LOCATION L.
COMMENTARY Describes the life of two young seminarians, one leaves before ordination, the other ignoring uneasy feelings, becomes a priest. Afterwards the priest meets a lady, a recent convert from protestantism. Eventually, they are married. The erring priest ends his life in a Carthusian monastery [Brown].

H294 *Up for the green. A romance of the Irish rebellion of 1798* (by H.A. Hinkson; dedicated to Frank Mathew§).
  + London: Lawrence & Bullen, 1898. SOURCE Brown, 751; Wolff, 3217. LOCATION D, Dt, DPL, L, NUC, InND Loeber coll.
COMMENTARY Historical fiction of the Irish rebellion of 1798. The hero, Samuel Riley, a Quaker yeoman, starts from Cork for Dublin, but only reaches the capital after falling into the hands of the rebels and undergoing many experiences. Glimpse of Lord Castlereagh, and allusions to Henry Grattan and others [Nield, 1657].

H295 *When love is kind* (by H.A. Hinkson; dedicated to H.W. Lawrence).
  + London: John Long, 1898. SOURCE Brown, 752. LOCATION D, Dt, L, NUC, InND Loeber coll.
  COMMENTARY A love story with a hero who is soldier and a soldier's son. The story brings out the comradeship that may exist between father and son [Brown].

H296 *The King's deputy. A romance of the last century* (by H.A. Hinkson).
  + London: Lawrence & Bullen, 1899. SOURCE Brown, 753. LOCATION D, Dt, DPL, L, NUC, InND Loeber coll.
  Chicago: A.C. McClurg & Co., 1900. SOURCE NYPL. LOCATION NN, NUC.
COMMENTARY Historical fiction set in Ireland during the time of Henry Grattan's parliament. The interest in the plot is divided between a love story and the efforts of the Protestant aristocracy to establish an independent Irish republic on the Venetian model. Many historical figures are introduced, including the Irish revolutionary James Napper Tandy [Brown].

H297 *Sir Phelim's treasure* (by H.A. Hinkson; dedicated to Toby and Bunny).
+ London: Society for Promoting Christian Knowledge, [1901] (ill. W.S. Stacey).
SOURCE Brown, 754. LOCATION D (n.d. edn), L (destroyed), NUC, InND Loeber coll.
COMMENTARY Story for juveniles revolving around the search for a treasure. It gives
a Crusoe-like description of living on a little island off the Irish coast [Brown].

H298 *The point of honour. Being some adventures of certain gentlemen of the pistol,*
including those of the notorious Sir Phelim Burke (by H.A. Hinkson; dedicated to
William Ernest Henley).
+ London: Lawrence & Bullen, 1901. SOURCE Brown, 755. LOCATION L, NUC.
Chicago: A.C. McClurg & Co., 1902. SOURCE NYPL. LOCATION NN, NUC.
COMMENTARY Novel consisting of stories set in Ireland about the quarrelsome, hard-
drinking, duelling gentry of the eighteenth century [Brown; RL].

H299 *Silk and steel* (by H.A. Hinkson).
London: Chatto & Windus, 1902. SOURCE Brown, 756; COPAC. LOCATION L, NUC.
COMMENTARY Historical fiction describing the adventures of an Irish soldier of fortune at the
court of Charles I, in the Netherlands and in Ireland in the seventeenth century. The main
character is Daniel O'Neill, a nephew of Owen Roe. Many historical incidents and personages, such as the earl of Essex, are featured [Brown].

H300 *Fan Fitzgerald* (by H.A. Hinkson; dedicated to William C. Sullivan).
+ London: Chatto & Windus, 1902. SOURCE Brown, 757; Wolff, 3215. LOCATION L,
D.
COMMENTARY Published in a print run of 1,500 copies. Dick Burke, brought up in England,
returns to his inherited estates in Ireland with the intent of being a model landlord. The story
details his successes and failures [Brown; E. Reilly, p. 230].

H301 *The wine of love* (by H.A. Hinkson).
London: Eveleigh Nash, 1904. SOURCE Brown, 758; COPAC. LOCATION L.
COMMENTARY Set among the upper classes in the west of Ireland, and describes horse-deal-
ing, fox-hunting and other activities. Gives pictures of good and bad landlords [Brown].

H302 *The splendid knight* (by H.A. Hinkson).
+ Dublin: Sealy, Bryers & Walker; London: F.V. White & Co., 1905 (ill. Lawson
Wood). SOURCE Brown, 759; COPAC. LOCATION L, NUC.
COMMENTARY Historical fiction for juveniles. Details the adventures of an Irish boy
in Walter Raleigh's expedition up the Orinoco River (Venezuela) in 1595 [Brown].

H303 *The castaways of Hope Island. A book for boys* (by H.A. Hinkson).
+ London, Edinburgh: T.C. & E.C. Jack, 1907. SOURCE IBL, 10 (1919), p. 72.
LOCATION L, D (1922 edn).
COMMENTARY Fiction for juveniles; no Irish content [ML; CM].

H304 *Golden morn* (by H.A. Hinkson).
London: Cassell & Co., 1907. SOURCE Brown, 760; COPAC. LOCATION Dt, L, NUC.
COMMENTARY Adventures of Capt. O'Grady in Ireland, London, and France, includ-
ing a scene at the Leopardstown races [Brown].

H305 *The King's liege. A story of the days of Charles I* (by H.A. Hinkson).
+ London, Glasgow, Dublin, Bombay: Blackie & Son, 1910 (ill. A.A. Dickson).
LOCATION L, InND Loeber coll., NUC ([1910] edn).
COMMENTARY The IBL mentions a 1909 edn, but this has not been identified. Historical fic-
tion for juveniles. The story of a young boy, Maurice Hyde, set in England in the time of
Charles I. The boy's father has come from the Continent where he had fought for Gustavus
Adolphus, but his wounds have made him unsuitable for active service. There is growing dis-
content in the country about King Charles, and a plot is hatched to take him prisoner. Maurice

is the means by which the plot is foiled. The king knights him, and gives his father a commission as colonel of horse [IBL, 10 (1919), p. 72; ML].

H306   *The house of the oak* (by H.A. Hinkson).
London: Society for Promoting Christian Knowledge, [1912] (ill. Harold Piffard).
SOURCE IBL, 10 (1919), p. 72. LOCATION L (destroyed), NUC.
COMMENTARY Historical fiction set in 1651. A tale of the escape of Charles II after Worcester, his concealment at Boscobel and his flight into Wales [NUC].

H307   *The Considine luck* (by H.A. Hinkson).
+ London: Stephen Swift & Co., 1912. SOURCE Brown, 762. LOCATION L, D.
COMMENTARY The story revolves around the popular belief that the Considine estate could not pass from Considine hands. However, when Sir Hugh Considine dies, the estate is found to have been mortgaged to Mr Smith of London. He comes to Ireland and tries to carry out his English notions of running an estate. He refuses to be bought out, but the Considine luck comes to the rescue and the estate reverts to Considine hands [Brown].

H308   *The glory of war: A story of the days of Marlborough* (by H.A. Hinkson; dedicated to Charles Lowry, head master of Tonbridge School).
+ London: Society for Promoting Christian Knowledge, [1912] (ill. W.S. Stacey).
SOURCE IBL, 10 (1919), p. 72; OCLC. LOCATION D (n.d. edn), L (destroyed), NUC.
COMMENTARY Historical fiction set in the eighteenth century and featuring the duke of Marlborough [RL].

H309   *Gentleman Jack* (by H.A. Hinkson).
+ London: Society for Promoting Christian Knowledge; New York: E.S. Gorham, 1913 (ill. Harold Piffard). LOCATION L.
COMMENTARY No Irish content [CM].

HINKSON, Mrs H.A. See TYNAN, Katharine.

HINKSON, Katharine Tynan. See TYNAN, Katharine.

HINKSON, Pamela. Novelist; completed one of her mother's novel. See TYNAN, Katharine.

HOARE, Revd Edward Newenham (Snr), b. Limerick, 1802, d. Upper Norwood, London, 1877. Clergyman, religious fiction and miscellaneous writer, ENH was the son of Revd John Hoare of Limerick and Rachel, daughter of Sir Edward Newenham, MP. He was educated at TCD, where he graduated BA in 1824 and MA in 1839. He was curate of St John's (Limerick 1830–31); rector of Raddanstown (Co. Meath, 1838); archdeacon of Ardfert (Co. Kerry, 1836–39); dean of Achonry (Co. Sligo, 1839), and dean of Waterford (1850–77). He wrote various works on the English language and on Irish matters, including *The English settler's guide through Irish difficulties* (London, 1850) and *Practical suggestions with a view to the removal of objections to the national system of education in Ireland* (Dublin, 1854). In addition, he wrote poetry and books for children. He was editor of the *Christian Herald* (Dublin?, 1831). He married first Maria (Louisa Maria according to Leslie), daughter of Lt.-Col. Daniel O'Donoghue, and second Harriet, daughter of Col. George Browne and widow of J.W. Sheppard. ENH is not be confused with his son, Revd Edward Newenham Hoare§ (by his first marriage). There is some uncertainty about which books are by each of these authors and where attributions conflict between Allibone and NCBEL, we chose the latter, despite the posthumous publication dates of all but one of these works. SOURCE Addenda, *Waterford*, p. H14; Allibone Suppl., ii, p. 829; B & S, p. 402; Boase, i, p. 1486; D. Bowen, *The Protestant crusade in Ireland 1800–70*,

p. 65 [who mentions EWH as rector of St Lawrence, Limerick]; Leslie, *Connor*, p. 391; NCBEL 4, p. 1805; RL; Rennison, p. 38.

H310   *Two voyages, and what came of them* [anon.].
London: Society for Promoting Christian Knowledge, [1877]. SOURCE NCBEL. LOCATION L.
COMMENTARY Religious fiction [BLC].

H311   *Percy Trevor's training* [anon.].
London: Society for Promoting Christian Knowledge; New York: Young & Co., 1878. SOURCE NCBEL 4, p. 1805; COPAC. LOCATION L (n.d. edn), O.

H312   *Between the locks; or, the adventures of a water-party* [anon.].
+ London: Society for Promoting Christian Knowledge; New York: Putt & Young, 1879. SOURCE NCBEL 4, 1805; COPAC; Allibone Suppl., ii, p. 829. LOCATION L (destroyed), E.

H313   *Mike. A tale of the great Irish famine* [anon.].
+ London: Society for Promoting Christian Knowledge; New York: Pott, Young & Co., [1880] (ill.). SOURCE Brown 2, 623; NCBEL 4, p. 1805. LOCATION D, Dt.
COMMENTARY An agent in Connacht, Mr Chaplin, is shot at by a tenant but is unhurt. A little boy runs out into the road in front of a cabin and is hurt by a carriage he wanted to stop because his mother is dying of hunger inside. The boy, Mike, comes to live with Mr Chaplin, whose house is besieged in 1848. Subsequently Mr. Chaplin comes into a property in England and together with Mike settles in Brighton. Mike becomes his faithful servant through life [ML].

H314   *Brave fight; being a narrative of the many trials of Master W. Lee, inventor* (by Edward Newenham Hoare).
London: Christian Knowledge Society, [1882]. SOURCE NCBEL 4, p. 1805; COPAC; Allibone Suppl., ii, p. 829. LOCATION L.
COMMENTARY Religious fiction [BLC].

H315   *Paths in the great waters; a tale wherein is comprised a record of Virginia's early troubles, together with the true history of the Bermudas or Somers Islands* (by Edward Newenham Hoare).
London: Society for Promoting Christian Knowledge; New York: E. & J.B. Young, [1883] (ill. Gordon Browne). SOURCE Allibone Suppl., ii, p. 829; NCBEL 4, p. 1805; COPAC. LOCATION L (destroyed), NUC.
COMMENTARY Religious fiction [BLC].

HOARE, Revd Edward Newenham (Jnr), b. Dublin 1842, d. Liverpool? 1909. Clergyman and religious fiction writer, ENH (Jnr) was the son of Revd Edward Newenham Hoare (Snr) §, dean of Waterford, and his first wife, Maria (Louisa Maria according to Leslie), daughter of Lt.-Col. Daniel O'Donoghue. He was educated by Dr Price, and entered TCD in 1858 at age 16, graduated BA in 1862, did his divinity test in 1865 and obtained his MA in 1877. He became curate of Dundonald (Co. Down, 1865); was at Belfast (1866–8) and Jordanstown (Co. Antrim, 1868–72). He moved to England, where he ministered in Liverpool (1872–75); Brighton (1875–7); Folkestone (1877–9); Acrise (Kent, 1879–88), and Stoneycroft (Liverpool, 1888–1909). He married in Dublin in 1870 Frances Kidd, daughter of Revd Thomas Fitzwilliam Miller, with whom he had two children. There is uncertainty about which books are by ENH (Jnr) or his father. 'Vera of Stoneycroft', attributed to him, has not been located. Our estimate is that he published 21 religious books children for children, set in various countries, many of them for the Society for Promoting Christian Knowledge. SOURCE Allibone Suppl., ii, p. 829; B & S, Appendix B, p. 56; BLC; Brown 2, p. 115; Leslie, *Connor*, p. 391; RL.

H316 *A child of the glens; or, Elsie's fortunes* [anon.].
+ London: Society for Promoting Christian Knowledge; New York: Pott, Young & Co., [1875] (ill.). SOURCE Allibone Suppl., ii, p. 829; Brown 2, 622. LOCATION D, L.
COMMENTARY Authorship is evident from a handwritten note in the NLI copy of this book. Religious fiction for children. A tale of the life of people of the Glens of Antrim. The scene is Tor Bay, near Fair Head, where the heroine Elsie, adopted daughter of an old couple, discovers the body of a drowned woman who long afterwards turns out to be her mother [Brown 2].

H317 *Motherless Maggie: A Liverpool tale* [anon.].
London: Christian Knowledge Society; New York: E. & J.B. Young & Co., [1876]. SOURCE NSTC; Allibone Suppl., ii, p. 829; Brown 2, p. 115; COPAC. LOCATION L, C.

H318 *Harvey Compton's holiday* [anon.].
London: Society for Promoting Christian Knowledge, [1878]. LOCATION L.
COMMENTARY Religious fiction [BLC].

H319 *Roe Carson's enemy; or, the struggle for self-conquest* (by Edward Newenham Hoare).
Edinburgh: Nelson & Sons, [1880]. SOURCE Allibone Suppl., ii, p. 829. LOCATION L.

H320 *The brave men of Eyam; or, a tale of the great plague year* (by Edward Newenham Hoare).
London: Society for Promoting Christian Knowledge, [1881] (ill.). SOURCE Allibone Suppl., ii, p. 829. LOCATION L (destroyed), NUC.
COMMENTARY Religious fiction [BLC].

H321 *Tempered steel; or, tried in the fire* (by Edward Newenham Hoare).
+ London, New York: T. Nelson & Sons, 1882. SOURCE Allibone Suppl., ii, p. 829. LOCATION L, NUC.
COMMENTARY Set in England. A story about two business families, who live next to each other. The Cremers are doing very well, while Mr Ridley's business runs into trouble. Mr Cremer, when asked, does not lend Mr Ridley any help, except to allow Mr Ridley's son, Edward, to come and work for him. However, Edward feels it is beneath him to work for Mr Cremer. Edward is picked up by a sailing ship after a boating accident. He stays on board and goes to South Africa, where after some hardship he finds works with a Dutch farmer. When he has saved some money, he sends it to his father with an apology for his rude behaviour. His father has received some help from an accountant, who is now about to marry Mr Ridley's daughter. Edward returns home and his father confides in him that he holds documents showing that Mr Cremer had committed fraud in the past. Father and son decide to burn the papers [ML].

H322 *Heroism in humble life; or, the story of Ben Pritchard and Charlie Champion. A temperance tale* (by Edward Newenham Hoare).
London: Nelson & Sons, 1883. SOURCE Allibone Suppl., ii, p. 829. LOCATION L (destroyed), NUC.
+ London, Edinburgh, New York: Nelson & Sons, 1890 (ill. F.A.F.). LOCATION InND Loeber coll.
COMMENTARY Religious fiction set in Liverpool. Charlie, a careless young man, marries prematurely, loses his job and leaves his mother's house. He leads a dissipated life. His mother does not want to see him anymore and he lives with his wife and children in a small room belonging to a woman who becomes involved in the temperance movement. After a terrible accident, Charlie sees the light and turns to God. He does not drink anymore and reconciles himself with his mother [ML].

H323 *A turbulent town; or, the story of the Arteveldts* (by Edward Newenham Hoare).
London: Christian Knowledge Society, [1884]. SOURCE Allibone Suppl., ii, p. 829; COPAC. LOCATION L (destroyed), E.

COMMENTARY Historical, religious fiction set in the fourteenth century and featuring Philip van Artevelde, who led the revolt of Ghent against the count of Flanders [BLC; Hartman, 52].

H324 *Perils of the deep, being an account of some of the remarkable shipwrecks and disasters at sea during the last hundred years* (by Edward Newenham Hoare).
London: Society for Promoting Christian Knowledge; New York: E. & J.B. Young, [1885]. SOURCE Allibone Suppl., ii, p. 829. LOCATION L (destroyed), NUC.
COMMENTARY Religious fiction [BLC].

H325 *Fred Turner's friends. A temperance tale* (by Edward Newenham Hoare).
London: Nelson & Sons, 1885. SOURCE Allibone Suppl., ii, p. 829; Brown 2, 624. LOCATION L (destroyed).
COMMENTARY Set in Belfast, with descriptions of the Giant's Causeway and the Carrick-a-Rede rope bridge. The story relates the ruin, through drink and reckless living, of an old business family [Brown 2].

H326 *Seeking a country; or, the home of the pilgrims* (by Edward Newenham Hoare).
London, New York: T. Nelson & Sons, 1886 (ill.). SOURCE Allibone Suppl., ii, p. 829 (who assigned a 1885 date of publication). LOCATION L (destroyed), NUC.
COMMENTARY Historical, religious fiction featuring Miles Standish, military leader at the Plymouth Colony, America's first Puritan settlement founded in Provincetown (MA) in 1620 [BLC; Hartman, 939].

H327 *Josiah Hunslet's reward* (by Edward Newenham Hoare).
London: Christian Knowledge Society, [1886]. SOURCE Allibone Suppl., ii, p. 829; COPAC. LOCATION L (destroyed), E.
COMMENTARY Religious fiction [BLC].

H328 *Foxholt, and the light that burnt there* (by Edward Newenham Hoare).
London: Society for Promoting Christian Knowledge; New York: E. & J.B. Young, [1887] (ill. Frank Dedd). SOURCE Allibone Suppl., ii, p. 829. LOCATION L (destroyed), NUC.
COMMENTARY Religious fiction [BLC].

H329 *Between two oceans; or, George Earley at Panama* (by Edward Newenham Hoare).
London: Christian Knowledge Society, [1889] (ill.). SOURCE COPAC. LOCATION L (destroyed), E.
COMMENTARY Religious fiction [BLC].

H330 *Lennard's leader; or, on the track of the Emin relief expedition* (by Edward Newenham Hoare).
+ London, Brighton: Society for Promoting Christian Knowledge; New York: E. & J.B. Young & Co., 1890 (ill. J. Nash). LOCATION L (destroyed), NUC, InND Loeber coll.
COMMENTARY Religious fiction. Story of a timid Liverpool clerk, Lennard Abberline, who in his spare time assists in a mission house in a rough part of town. He is sent by his firm to Africa to settle some matters and is accompanied by Ham, a boy from the mission house. After various adventures at sea they arrive only to find that the head of his firm has absconded with the firm's money and there is no business. They fall in with a Capt. Felton and sail with him up the Congo River, looking for work. Eventually they cross the Continent to end up at Zanzibar, more or less at the same time as Stanley who, with his expedition, follows largely the same route to rescue the Amin Pasha. The trip is beset with difficulties and adventures. Ham dies; Lennard finds his deceased brother's daughter, and Capt. Felton reveals that he is the son of the preacher in Liverpool who ran the mission house. They return to Liverpool where Lennard marries the preacher's daughter, Capt. Felton marries Lennard's niece, and Lennard and his wife return to Africa to devote their lives to mission work [ML].

H331　*The Conroy cousins* (by Edward Newenham Hoare).
London: Society for Promoting Christian Knowledge, [1892]. LOCATION L (destroyed), NUC.
COMMENTARY Religious fiction [BLC].

H332　*The Fairhope venture. An emigration story* (by Edward Newenham Hoare).
London: Society for Promoting Christian Knowledge Society, [1893]. SOURCE COPAC.
LOCATION L (destroyed), E.
COMMENTARY Religious fiction [BLC].

H333　*Rick Ralton's reconciliation* (by Edward Newenham Hoare).
+ London: Society for Promoting Christian Knowledge; New York: E. & J.B. Young,
[1894] (ill. W.H. Overend). SOURCE BLC. LOCATION L, NUC.
London: Christian Knowledge Society, [1894] (ill.). LOCATION L (destroyed); COPAC.
LOCATION E.
COMMENTARY Religious fiction [BLC].

H334　*From that lone ark* (by Edward Newenham Hoare).
London: Christian Knowledge Society; New York: E. & J.B. Young, [1895]. SOURCE
COPAC. LOCATION L (destroyed), C.
COMMENTARY Religious fiction [BLC].

H335　*By Sartal sands; or, the Thutalls of Ballskyr* (by Edward Newenham Hoare).
London: Christian Knowledge Society, [1897]. SOURCE COPAC. LOCATION L
(destroyed), E.
COMMENTARY Religious fiction [BLC].

HOARE, Mrs. —. See **HOARE, Mrs Mary Anne.**

HOARE, Mrs Mary Anne (née Pratt; also known as M.A. Hoare and **Mrs Hoare**), b. *c.*1818,
d. Monkstown (Co. Cork) 1872. Story writer, MAH was the only child of John Pratt of
Woburn Place, Cork, and Miss Hawkes of Bandon. In 1837 she married William Barry Hoare
of Monkstown (Co. Cork), solicitor and attorney and brother of the antiquary Edward Hoare,
at Glanmire (Co. Cork). The couple had six children, of whom three survived into adulthood.
She may be identified with the M.A. Hoare, who published a poem 'After visiting Exeter
Cathedral' in the *Dublin University Magazine* (April 1850, p. 434), and is known to have contributed to several London periodicals, including *Sharpe's London Magazine* (verse and prose),
Temple Bar, Howitt's Journal, and many pieces to *Household Words* (1850–54). Several of her
contributions to *Household Words* were reprinted in *Harper's* (New York). She was an ardent
admirer of the English author Mary Russell Mitford, with whom she corresponded. SOURCE
Griffith Survey of Monkstown, Co. Cork (Dublin, 1850); E. Hoare, *Some account … of the families of Hore and Hoare* (London, 1883), pp 28–9; Lohrli, pp 302–3; O'Toole, p. 97; C. Póirtéir
(ed.), *The great Irish famine* (Dublin, 1995), p. 235; Personal communication, Charles Ginnane,
May 1997.

H336　*Shamrock leaves; or, tales and sketches of Ireland* (by Mrs Hoare).
+ Dublin: J. M'Glashan; London: Partridge & Oakey, 1851 (ill. T. Minkhouse).
SOURCE Brown, 763. LOCATION NUC (where she is mistakenly identified as Mrs Louisa
Gurney Hoare). LOCATION InND Loeber coll.
COMMENTARY Earliest known fiction on the Famine of 1845, written during 1846–47. Most
of these moral stories are set in the south of Ireland. Contents: 'The beautiful city', 'The
ogham stone', 'The black potatoes', 'Irish beggars', 'The knitted collar', 'Father and son' (first
published in *Household Words*, London, 1850), 'Little Mary' (first published in *Household
Words*, London, 1850), 'The living and the dead', 'The faction fight', 'An affair of honour',

'James Cronin', 'The old Irish mansion', 'The sailor prelate', 'The bog-oak shamrocks', 'The quack-doctor', 'The brethren of the pubs', 'A sketch of the famine', 'The young painter', 'Daniel Leary' [ML; Fegan, p. 213].

HOBHOUSE, Mary Violet (née McNeill; known as **Violet Hobhouse**), b. Co. Antrim (London according to RIA/DIB) 1864, d. 1901 (1902 according to Brown, Hogan, and OCIL). Novelist, poet, linguist and political activist, MVH was the daughter of the DL of Co. Antrim, Edmund McNeill of Craigdunn. She studied Irish culture and traditions and was fluent in the Irish language. In 1887, she married Revd Walter Hobhouse, a fellow and lecturer at Christ Church, Oxford. While living in England, she maintained close contact with her family in Ulster through summer visits. She was a firm Unionist and spoke against Home Rule from English platforms. She also wrote poetry, some of which was translated from Irish. SOURCE Blain, p. 527; Brady, p. 107; Brown, p. 139; Colman, pp 151–2 [under McNeill]; Hogan 2, pp 554–5; OCIL, p. 248; RIA/DIB; Sutherland, p. 300.

H337 *An unknown quantity. A sad story of modern life* (by Violet Hobhouse).
      London: Downey & Co., 1898. SOURCE Brown, 764; Sutherland, p. 300; COPAC.
      LOCATION L.
      COMMENTARY A love story set chiefly in London and abroad. Two of the characters,
      Miss Kilmeny, the heroine, and the faithful nurse Maria are Irish [Brown].

H338 *Warp and weft. A story of the North of Ireland* (by Violet Hobhouse).
      + London: Skeffington & Son, 1899. SOURCE Brown, 765; COPAC. LOCATION L,
      InND Loeber coll.

COMMENTARY A story of coercion set in the linen weaving community and its Presbyterian culture on the Co. Derry and Co. Antrim border. Esther MacVeagh is lured, by the threat of eviction, into marriage with Samuel Martin, a selfish man. He tries to prohibit his sister from marrying a local man, and throws her out of the house when he finds she has done so. After Esther discovers his true character, she is on the point of leaving him when she realizes that he is ruined. She stays with him and eventually reforms his character [ML; Brown; Leclaire, p. 229].

HOBHOUSE, Violet. See **HOBHOUSE, Mary Violet.**

HOEY, Mrs Cashel. See **HOEY, Mrs Frances Sarah Cashel.**

HOEY, Mrs Frances Sarah Cashel (née Frances Sarah Johnston; known as **Mrs Cashel Hoey**), b. Bushy Park (Co. Dublin) 1830, d. Beccles (Suffolk) 1908. Novelist, periodical writer and translator, Mrs CH was one of eight children of Charles Bolton Johnston, registrar of Mount Jerome cemetery in Dublin, and Charlotte Jane Shaw, a relative of George Bernard Shaw§. Largely self-educated, she married at age 16 Adam M. Stewart, with whom she had two children. She met Daniel O'Connell and became a fervent nationalist, although none of her later popular novels, written in England, reflects this. Around 1853 she began to write for the Young Ireland publications the *Freeman's Journal* and the *Nation* (both Dublin). Her husband died in 1855. The young widow came to London with an introd. from William Carleton§ to William Thackeray§. She began writing reviews and was soon well-known in literary circles. In 1858 she married the journalist and Young Irelander John Cashel Hoey (1828–93), who had been the editor of the *Nation*. She converted to his catholicism and her new faith influenced many of her subsequent novels. In 1865 she began a long association with *Chambers's Journal* (Edinburgh), then edited by James Payn, and she also had a long and prolific association with the *Spectator* (London). She wrote 13 works of fiction under her own name and collaborated on the following four novels attributed to Edmund Yates: *Land at last* (London, 1866, 3 vols.); *Black sheep* (London, 1867, 3 vols.); *Forlorn hope* (London, 1867, 3 vols.), and *The rock ahead* (London, 1868, 3 vols.). It has been argued that she was the author of *A righted wrong* (1870) published under Yates's name, but the ODNB states that the story of Hoey's authorship of this 'remains barely credible' (hence this novel is not listed below). She helped Yates (who was editor of *Tinsley's Magazine*) found the *World* (London?) in 1874 and contributed often to it. In addition, she translated many volumes from Italian and French (e.g. D'Hericault's *1794. A tale of the terror*, Dublin, 1884). Mrs CH also worked as a publisher's reader and for twenty years produced a regular column, 'Lady's Letter', for the *Australasian* (Melbourne). She experienced financial difficulties throughout her career, due in part to her generosity to many Catholic charities and her support of such organizations as the Society for Sick Children and the Anti-Vivisection League, and in 1892 she was awarded a Civil List pension. For her papers, see ODNB. SOURCE Allibone Suppl., ii, p. 834; Blain, p. 529; Boase, v, p. 680 [under John Baptist Cashel Hoey]; Brady, p. 107; Brown, p. 139; Field Day, v, pp 927–9; Hogan, pp 297–8; Hogan 2, pp 555–6; NCBEL 4, pp 1579–81; OCIL, p. 248; ODNB; E. Reilly, pp 218, 225*n*.17; RIA/DIB; G.B. Shaw, *Immaturity* (London, 1931), p. xxxvi; Sutherland, p. 302; Wolff, ii, p. 222.

H339 *A house of cards. A novel* (by Mrs Cashel Hoey; dedicated to the author's father [Charles Bolton Johnston], 'by whom it was suggested').
+ London: Tinsley Bros, 1868, 3 vols. SOURCE Hogan, p. 297. LOCATION Dt, L, NUC, InND Loeber coll.
London: Chapman & Hall, 1871 (new edn; Select Library of Fiction, No. 180). SOURCE Topp 3, p. 367.
Boston: Littell & Gay, [1869]. SOURCE NYPL. LOCATION NN, NUC.
COMMENTARY No copy of the London 1871 edn located. Serialized in *Tinsley's Magazine* (London, Mar. 1868–Feb. 1869) and in *Littell's Living Age* (Boston). Set in England. Julia, who had been married to a convicted felon and has a son, is placed in a rich family as a companion to the blind mother. The family is not familiar with her antecedents. The son of the family falls in love with her, and she marries him, effectively hiding her past by having her little boy raised by a widow and her daughter. Her son grows up with some of his father's characteristics. He eventually is apprehended by the police for the murder of his young wife. His mother learns of his fate, and he learns who his mother is. Both die, he by the hand of the law, and she from misery [ML; NCBEL; Topp].

H340 *Falsely true. A novel* (by Mrs Cashel Hoey).
London: Tinsley Bros, 1870, 3 vols. SOURCE NCBEL 4, p. 1580; Wolff, 3227. LOCATION L, NUC.
London: Ward & Downey, 1890 (revised edn). SOURCE Hogan, p. 297; COPAC. LOCATION L.

H341 *A golden sorrow* (by Mrs Cashel Hoey; dedicated to Jean Ingelow§).
London: Hurst & Blackett, 1872, 3 vols. SOURCE Hogan, p. 297; NCBEL 4, p. 1580. LOCATION L, NUC.
Leipzig: Bernard Tauchnitz, 1872, 2 vols. SOURCE T & B, 1259–60. LOCATION NUC.
New York: Harper & Bros, 1872. SOURCE Hogan, p. 297. LOCATION NUC.
COMMENTARY A story of romance and family intrigue featuring Miriam Clint, who is called home from school by her father when she is age 18. She is loath to go because he is a very cold man. Her bother Walter, in disguise, asks her to engage Florence, the next door girl, who is his wife, as he has to go to America to earn money and he does not want to leave her behind without protection. In order to get out of her father's house Miriam marries the first eligible man that comes along. Her new husband proves to be very jealous. When Miriam is abroad,

her father falls ill and her husband does not allow her to go home. Florence takes her place and looks after her father-in-law, who does not know that she is married to his disgraced son. In the meantime, Walter is living in the gold fields with his friend Lawrence Daly, but he becomes severely ill and suffers memory loss. The father dies and makes Florence his heir. Miriam's husband dies and Miriam falsifies a will in her favour. This will cuts out Florence. However, Miriam and Lawrence fall in love and Miriam admits what she has done. Walter regains his memory [ML].

H342 *Buried in the deep, and other tales* [anon.].
    London: Chapman & Hall, 1872 (new edn; Select Library of Fiction, No. 209). SOURCE NCBEL 4, p. 1580; Topp 3, p. 383 ([1873] edn); COPAC. LOCATION Univ. of Newcastle.
    COMMENTARY No copy of the first edn located. NCBEL states that title story was first published in *Chambers's Journal* (Edinburgh, Feb. 1865) [NCBEL; Topp; RL].

H343 *Out of court* (by Mrs Cashel Hoey; dedicated to the author's mother [Charlotte Jane Johnston]).
    London: Hurst & Blackett, 1874, 3 vols. SOURCE NCBEL 4, p. 1580; Wolff, 3228. LOCATION L, NUC.
    Leipzig: Bernard Tauchnitz, 1874, 2 vols. SOURCE T & B, 1429–30. LOCATION NUC.
    COMMENTARY First published in the *Australasian* (Oct. 1873–Nov. 1874) [NCBEL].

H344 *The blossoming of an aloe, and the Queen's token* (by Mrs Cashel Hoey; dedicated to the author's mother [Charlotte Jane Johnston]).
    London: Hurst & Blackett, 1875, 3 vols. SOURCE Hogan, p. 297; Wolff, 3226. LOCATION D (n.d. edn), L.
    London: Spencer Blackett, 1889 (as *The Queen's token;* Blackett's Select Novels). SOURCE Hogan, p. 298 (mentions 1888 edn); OCLC; Topp 6, 382. LOCATION Univ. of Delaware.
    New York: Harper & Bros, 1875. SOURCE Topp 2, p. 157. LOCATION NUC.
    + Chicago, New York: Rand, McNally & Co., 1889 (as *The Queen's token*; Globe Library, No. 91). LOCATION InND Loeber coll.
    Toronto: W. Bryce, 1889. SOURCE OCLC. LOCATION CaACU.
    COMMENTARY Historical fiction, partly set at the Dominican abbey of Kilferran in the south-west of Ireland at the beginning of Queen Elizabeth I's reign. One of the Dominicans is a Frenchman who has withdrawn from the world after having served Queen Mary. His brother comes to visit him and tells him he has sold all his possessions and converted his money to precious stones to be ready for Queen Mary, if she is freed from prison. He tells his brother the secret of where the stones are and asks him to take up the task of helping Queen Mary if he should fail. The signal for taking action would be sent to him in the form of a special diamond 'the Queen's token'. Several centuries later the story is pieced together and the treasure is found and restored to a descendant of the family of the two brothers [ML].

H345 *Griffith's double* (by Mrs Cashel Hoey; dedicated to the author's daughter and husband [John Cashel Hoey]).
    London: Hurst & Blackett, 1876, 3 vols. SOURCE Hogan, p. 297; NCBEL 4, p. 1580. LOCATION L.
    COMMENTARY First published in *All the Year Round* (London, Dec. 1875–Aug. 1876) [NCBEL].

H346 *No sign, and other tales* (by Mrs Cashel Hoey).
    London: Ward, Lock & Tyler, [1876] (The Country House Library, No. 5). SOURCE Brown, 767; Alston, p. 201; NCBEL 4, p. 1580; Topp 2, 1097; Sadleir, ii, p. 32. LOCATION L.

COMMENTARY First published in the *New Quarterly Magazine* (London, Apr.–Oct. 1875); the title story is founded on the case of Richard Burke, hanged in Clonmel (Co. Tipperary) for murdering his wife [Brown].

H347 **Kate Cronin's dowry** (by Mrs Cashel Hoey).
New York: Harper & Bros, 1877. SOURCE Hogan, p. 297; NCBEL 4, p. 1580; NYPL. LOCATION NN, NUC.
COMMENTARY First published in the *New Quarterly Magazine* (London, Jan. 1887) [NCBEL].

H348 **All or nothing** (by Mrs Cashel Hoey; dedicated to the author's husband's mother, 'who for twenty years, was my most constant reader and most gentle critic').
London: Hurst & Blackett, 1879, 3 vols. SOURCE Hogan, p. 297; NCBEL 4, p. 1580. LOCATION D (n.d. edn), L, NUC (1888 edn).
New York: Harper & Bros, [?date] (Franklin Square Library, No. 45). SOURCE Adv. in J.T. Bent, *The life of Giuseppe Garibaldi* (New York, [after 1881], Franklin Square Library, No. 217).
COMMENTARY First published in *All the Year Round* (London, July 1878–Mar. 1879). No copy of the New York edn located [RL; NCBEL].

H349 **The question of Cain** (by Mrs Cashel Hoey).
New York: Harper, 1881. SOURCE Hogan, p. 297. LOCATION NUC.
London: Hurst & Blackett, 1882, 3 vols. SOURCE Hogan, p. 298. LOCATION L, NUC.
London: Ward & Downey, 1890 (new and revised edn). SOURCE Hogan, p. 298; COPAC. LOCATION L.
COMMENTARY First published in *All the Year Round* (London, Mar. 1881–Dec. 1882). The story of a burglary syndicate whose action goes as far afield as India and features a death-bed conversion [ODNB; NCBEL; Sutherland].

H350 **The lover's creed** (by Mrs Cashel Hoey).
London: Chatto & Windus, 1884, 3 vols. SOURCE Hogan, p. 298; Topp 3, p. 150. LOCATION L, NUC.
New York: Harper Bros, [1884] (Harper's Franklin Square Library, No. 418). SOURCE NYPL. LOCATION NN.
New York: George Munro, [1884] (Seaside Library, No. 1905). SOURCE Topp 3, p. 150. LOCATION NUC.
COMMENTARY First published in *Belgravia* (London, Jan.–Dec. 1884). The plot, which involves a love affair and a royal French diamond necklace, leads to Australia where most of the volume is set and, like *The question of Cain* (London, 1882), features a death-bed conversion [ODNB; Quaritch; Topp].

H351 **A stern chase. A novel** (by Mrs Cashel Hoey; dedicated to Robert Murray Smith, C.M.G, agent-general for Victoria).
London: Sampson Low, Marston, Searle & Rivington, 1886, 3 vols. SOURCE Hogan, p. 298. LOCATION D (n.d. edn), L, NUC, InND Loeber coll. (n.d. edn).
New York: Harper & Bros, 1886 (as *A stern chase; a story in three parts*; Harper's Franklin Square Library, No. 525). SOURCE NCBEL 4, p. 1580; NYPL. LOCATION NN, NUC.
COMMENTARY First published in *All the Year Round* (London, Aug. 1885–May 1886). Set in England and Cuba. Hugh Rosslyn, an English artist, goes to Cuba where he falls in love with a beautiful Cuban woman, Inés, who is betrothed to her cousin, whom she hates. Hugh and Inés elope and are married. Before they reach England, Hugh dies and his wife is left without resources in England. She gives birth to a child and marries another man, who leaves her.

Several years later, Inés lives with the child in a small cottage. Just after she dies her second husband shows up and claims the guardianship of the child. People think that the child is Hugh's daughter, and they make a great effort to claim her Cuban inheritance. Eventually, it transpires that Hugh's child had died and that the little girl is the daughter of the second husband [ML; NCBEL].

HOGAN, James Francis, b. Nenagh (Co. Tipperary) 1855, d. London 1924. Teacher, journalist, editor and miscellaneous writer, JFH emigrated with his parents, Roedy and Mary Hogan, to Melbourne (Australia) in 1856. He was educated at St Patrick's College, Melbourne, and became a teacher, serving as headmaster at Geelong. After contributing successfully to periodicals, he gave up teaching for a job with the *Melbourne Argus*. A prominent supporter of Irish and Roman Catholic causes in Victoria, he was an advocate of state aid to Catholic schools. He became a recognized authority on Australian affairs, moved to London and worked there as a journalist before being elected to parliament as a member from Tipperary (1892–1900). In parliament he worked on colonial affairs and took his stand as an Irish nationalist. He wrote *The Irish in Australia* (London, 1887), and a biography of the convict Jorgan Jorgenson (London, 1891). SOURCE ADB, iv; Allibone Suppl., ii, p. 835; Miller, ii, p. 630; O'Donoghue, p. 199.

H352   *An Australian Christmas collection: stories, sketches, essays* (by James Francis Hogan).
    Melbourne: Alex McKinley, 1886. SOURCE Miller, ii, p. 630; OCLC. LOCATION NUC, Univ. Of Queensland.
    COMMENTARY Reprints from Australian periodicals and newspapers, including a few short stories [Miller].

H353   *The lost explorer. An Australian story* (by James Francis Hogan).
    London: Ward & Downey, 1890. SOURCE Miller, ii, p. 630; COPAC. LOCATION L, C.
    Sydney: Edwards, Dunlop, [1890?]. SOURCE Miller, ii, p. 630; OCLC. LOCATION Univ. of Queensland.

COMMENTARY Under the name of Leonard Louvain, it presumes to tell of the supposed finding of Ludwig Leighhardt in the centre of Australia. The description is based upon Charles Sturt's *Expedition into central Australia* (London, 1849); but the story itself is largely made up of adventures with the natives [Miller].

'**HOGG, Cervantes, F.S.M.**', pseud. See **BARRETT, Eaton Stannard**.

HOLLAND, Denis, b. Cork *c*.1826, d. Brooklyn (New York) 1872. Journalist, editor and fiction writer, DH began his career with the *Cork Southern Reporter*. Around 1858 he started the *Ulsterman* in Belfast, which was transformed into the *Irishman*, based in Dublin. He wrote prose, verse and articles under a variety of pseuds. He went in 1867 to the US where he became editor of the *Emerald* (New York, 1867 onwards), to which he contributed much fiction, including a long serial entitled 'Pardoned yet guiltless. A story of real life', and 'Bartle O'Cleary's vengeance'. He also contributed in the early 1870s to the *Sunburst*, a New York Irish weekly. SOURCE Allibone Suppl., ii, p. 838; Brown, p. 140; Hogan 2, p. 559; IBL, 23 (1935), p. 148; Irish pseudonyms; McKenna, p. 201; O'Donoghue, p. 210; RL.

H354   *The landlord in Donegal, pictures from the wilds* (by Denis Holland).
    Belfast: Ulsterman Office, [*c*.1859]. SOURCE Hogan 2, p. 559; McKenna, p. 201. LOCATION Grail, NUC.
    COMMENTARY Attacks on landlordism, reprinted from the *Ulsterman* [McKenna].

H355   *Ulic O'Donnell: an Irish peasant's progress* (by Denis Holland).

+ London: Catholic Publishing & Bookselling Co.; Dublin: J. Mullany, 1860. SOURCE Hogan 2, p. 559; McKenna, p. 201; Brown, 770. LOCATION Grail, D, L. Baltimore: Murphy, 1860. SOURCE Rev. in *Brownson's Quarterly Review* (Boston, Oct., 1860, p. 535).
COMMENTARY No copy of the Baltimore edn located. A peasant lad from Newry (Co. Down) goes to England where he has many adventures. He wins his way by his good qualities and returns a prosperous man. The author contrasts the characteristics of the Irish with those of the English [Brown; RL].

H356 *Donal Dun O'Byrne: A tale of the rising in Wexford in 1798* (by Denis Holland).
+ Glasgow, London: Cameron & Ferguson, [1869]. SOURCE Hogan 2, 559; McKenna, p. 201. LOCATION Grail, D, InND Loeber coll.
+ Dublin: M.H. Gill & Son, n.d. SOURCE Brown, 769. LOCATION D, InND Loeber coll.
New York: P.M. Haverty [1871 or earlier] (as *Donal Dun O'Byrne. A tale of '98*). SOURCE Adv. in *Haverty's Irish-American Illustrated Almanac* (New York, 1871), p. 104.
COMMENTARY No copy of the New York edn located. Donal Dun O'Byrne, a tall and powerful Wicklow man, is reluctant to become involved in any uprising against the English, until an English soldier wantonly kills his last remaining child. He kills the soldier with his flail, and vows to kill as many of that soldier's regiment as possible. He joins up with the rebels and is involved in all the skirmishes in Wexford. Because of bad leadership, the Irish do not prevail. Donal turns away from the rebels and leaves Ireland with the daughter of a fellow-rebel, at whose deathbed he had promised to look after the girl [ML].

HOLLINS, Charles, d. Birmingham (W. Midlands) 1885. A memoirist, CH was a manu-facturing jeweller in Birmingham, probably of Irish descent. He left his estate to charity. SOURCE *Gifts to the Birmingham Charities. An old folk's trust for Aston* ([Birmingham], 1887 (a broadside, enclosed in the NLI copy of the following vol.).
H357 *Reminiscences and vicissitudes of human life* (by Charles Hollins).
+ Birmingham: A.E. Partridge, 1886. SOURCE COPAC. LOCATION L, D.
COMMENTARY Only fifty copies printed for private circulation. Begins at the village of Conmore in Ireland, and may be partially autobiographical. In the preface the author notes that he set 'down his thoughts upon many social, political, and religious changes, which during his life he had observed'. He recalls the 1817 famine that caused families to emigrate to Liverpool [RL; CM].

HOLLOWAY, John, fl. 1865. Soldier and periodical writer, JH served in the British army from 1865 to 1886, including during the Indian mutiny. He contributed stories to periodicals and ran a weekly called the *Boys World* (London?) from 1870 to 1886. SOURCE Allibone Suppl., ii, p. 840; Brown 2, p. 117.
H358 *Kathleen; or, the four-leaved shamrock* (by John Holloway).
+ London: C.H. Clarke, 1872 (Clarke's Standard Novel Library). SOURCE Brown 2, 633 (1871 edn, but not located). LOCATION L.
COMMENTARY Patsy Nowland, washed ashore after a shipwreck on the Antrim coast, is reared by a fisherman. After many ups and downs, his identity is revealed and he is restored to his rightful position in the world. Patsy and Kathleen are lured to the cave of Dunferry near the Giant's Causeway, where they are shown a vision of Ireland's future greatness [Brown 2].

HOLMES, Ann. See **DOHERTY, Mrs Ann.**

HOLMES, W.H.M., fl. 1842. Fiction writer, possibly American, or someone who had visited America. SOURCE Brown 2, p. 117.

H359 *Life in the West: Black-wood leaves and prairie flowers: Rough sketches of the picturesque, the sublime, and ridiculous. Extracts from the notebook of Morleigh in search of an estate* [anon.] (dedicated to the outward bound).

+ London: Saunders & Otley, 1842. LOCATION L.

COMMENTARY A novel written as a journal and narrated in the first person. On board ship the narrator listens to a gentleman who relates his adventures about trying to purchase an Irish estate. In his first foray to find one, he travels from Dublin to Athlone (Co. Westmeath). His second foray concentrates on the 'wild west' of Co. Tipperary. His final travels bring him to estates in Baltinglass (Co. Wicklow) and Ballycragmorris (not identified) [CM; RL].

H360 *Oakleigh; or, the minor of great expectations* (by W.H.M. Holmes).

+ London: T.C. Newby, 1843, 3 vols. (ill. J. Onwhyn). SOURCE Brown 2, 634; Wolff, 3246; COPAC. LOCATION D, NUC.

COMMENTARY Concerns adventures told in the first person by Eustace Oakleigh, and set chiefly in Ireland during the period 1796 to 1800. After his schooldays and wandering in Europe, Oakleigh meets for the first time his crusty old guardian, Sir Carnaby Rohan, who lives in the 'antiquated pile', Rohan Abbey, and who takes him on as a steward of the estate. Oakleigh becomes friendly with Trevordale, a nobleman of liberal views friendly to the national cause, and with Blanche Trevordale. Oakleigh wants to enlist in the regular army. He is shocked by the brutal behaviour of the yeomanry. A certain Mr Edwards (Lord Edward Fitzgerald) comes on the scene and a series of exciting adventures follow. The novel gives a satirical picture of the Ascendancy of the time. Oakleigh narrowly escapes execution and eventually gets away to France where he meets Gen. Lazare Hoche, Napoleon Bonaparte and Theobald Wolfe Tone§. He finally joins Gen. Jean Joseph Humbert's invasion force, landing at Killala in Co. Mayo in 1798. The invasion is described in detail, as well as the conditions that rendered Humbert's success impossible, especially discord between Catholics and Protestants [Brown 2; Wolff, 3246].

HOLT, Emily Sarah, b. Stubbylee (Lancs.) 1836, d. *c.*1904. English historical novelist, biographer and religious tract writer, ESH wrote *The web Isme move* for the Irish Society (no copy located; priced at 1*d.* in 1880). Much of her fiction, which provided strong, moral, female role models was written for teenage girls and was very successful. She was adamantly anti-Catholic. SOURCE Allibone Suppl., ii, p. 842; Alston, p. 203; Brown, p. 140; advertised in W. FitzPatrick et al., *What Ireland needs: The gospel in the native tongue* (London: n.d.); NCBEL 4, pp 1806–7 (list of novels); ODNB.

H361 *Under one sceptre; or, Mortimer's mission* (by Emily Sarah Holt).

London: John F. Shaw, 1884. SOURCE Brown, 771.

London: John F. Shaw & Co., n.d. (new edn; as *Under one sceptre, or Mortimer's mission; the story of the Lord of the Marches*). SOURCE RLIN. LOCATION UBP.

COMMENTARY No copy of the 1st edn located. Historical fiction for juveniles. Set in the fourteenth century, it describes the career of Roger Mortimer, earl of March and Ulster. The adventures are set in Monmouthshire (Wales), Ireland, and London. Mortimer was lieutenant of Ulster, Connacht and Meath. For a while he was the favourite of Richard II, who declared him heir to the throne but grew jealous of his popularity. Mortimer was killed at Kells in battle with Art McMurrough Kavanagh [Brown].

HOMAN-MULOCK, Anne. See KENNARD, Nina.

'THE HON. MRS. W.', pseud. See **WARD, the Hon. Mrs Mary.**

'HONORIA', pseud. See **POWER, Marguerite A.**

HOOD, Thomas. Co-editor. See **KENNEDY, Patrick.**

HOOPER, I., fl. 1897. Historical novelist.
H362 *The singer of Marly* (by I. Hooper).
    + London: Methuen & Co., 1897 (ill. W. Cubitt Cooke). SOURCE Brown 2, 636; Nield,
    p. 77. LOCATION D, L, NUC.
COMMENTARY Historical novel covering the period 1697 to 1699. The scene is set in Ireland,
Brittany, Paris and the slave market in Martinique [Brown 2; CM; Nield].

HOPE, Alexander James Beresford Beresford, b. 1820, d. Bedgebury Park, Cranbrook
(Kent) 1887. A miscellaneous writer and patron of architecture, AJBBH was the son of the
English author and art collector Thomas Hope, and Louisa, daughter of William Beresford,
1st Baron Decies and archbishop of Tuam. He was educated at Harrow and Cambridge, where
he graduated in 1841. He was a Tory MP for various English seats and represented Cambridge
University for many years. He was an unswerving supporter of the Established Church and
wrote extensively on church matters. In 1845 he published *The new government scheme for aca-*
demic education in Ireland (London, 1845), and *The Irish church and its formularies* (London,
1870). He was strongly opposed to disestablishment of the Church of Ireland. A prolific journalist, he was a co-proprietor of and contributor to the London *Saturday Review* and following his inheritance of the English estates of Marshal Lord Beresford (whose name he added
to his own), he became a committed patron of Gothic architecture in England. He restored
and built churches, wrote hymns, and published on a wide variety of topics including art,
English cathedrals, and the American Civil War. SOURCE Allibone Suppl., ii, p. 847; Boase, i,
pp 1529–30; Brown 2, p. 118; ODNB; Venn, part ii, iii, p. 434.
H363 *Strictly tied up* [anon.] (dedicated to 'the dear light and guide to the author's life').
    + London: Hurst & Blackett, 1881. SOURCE Brown 2, 637; COPAC. LOCATION D
    (1881, 3rd edn), NUC.
    New York: G. Munro, 1883. LOCATION NUC.
COMMENTARY A story of social aspirations and inheritance intrigues set in the second part of
the nineteenth century. Delicia, countess of Foulisville is, like her husband, a social climber.
Leaving Dublin they settle in a mansion in Eaton Place, London. But Lady Delicia is not a
success socially and becomes thoroughly disgruntled and blasé. Merial, a young relative and
heiress, is entrusted to the chaperonage of Lady Foulisville. An accident and other events led
to Merial's marriage to a wicked old schemer and to the danger of her property falling into
his hands. Her mother saves the situation by marrying the schemer's son. Eventually Merial
becomes free to marry a respectable gentleman [Brown 2].

HOPKINS, Clement. Co-author. See **HILL, John.**

HOPKINS, Tighe. See **HOPKINS, William Tighe.**

HOPKINS, William Tighe (also known as **Tighe Hopkins**), b. Cheshire (Nottingham
according to EF) 1856, d. 1919. English novelist and editor of Irish background, WTH was
the son of an Anglican clergyman, the Revd W.R. Hopkins, vicar of Moulton (Ches.). He was
educated at Oundle Grammar School. In 1881 he married Ellen Crump, stepdaughter of the

novelist Mortimer Collins. TH edited a number of William Carleton's§ works (e.g. *Stories by William Carleton*, London, [1905]) and wrote *Kilmainham memoirs* (London, 1896), an investigation of the Phoenix Park murders (1882). In the last years of his life he applied repeatedly for financial support from the Royal Literary Fund. In 1918, the year before his death, he moved to Ireland to live with his relatives. Some of his letters are among the Downey Papers in the NLI (MSS 10,005, 10,024–27, 10,030, 10,043). SOURCE Allibone Suppl., ii, p. 849; Brown, p. 140; EF, p. 192; E. Reilly, p. 218; Sutherland, p. 305; T & B, p. 988.

H364 *The Nugents of Carriconna. A story more or less Irish* (by Tighe Hopkins).
+ London: Ward & Downey, 1890, 3 vols. SOURCE Brown, 772; Topp 8, 127. LOCATION D, DPL (1891, 5th edn), NUC.
+ London: Chatto & Windus, 1899 (new edn; ill. F. Dadd). LOCATION InND Loeber coll.
+ New York: D. Appleton & Co., 1891 (Town & Country Library, No. 65). SOURCE Topp 8, 127. LOCATION InND Loeber coll.

COMMENTARY Published in an initial print run of 500. A story of discord over inheritance issues set in Ireland during a period of agrarian unrest and boycotting. Features an impoverished landlord, Anthony Nugent, who has come into a large fortune from his deceased brother in Australia. He purchases a telescope to be mounted atop a medieval tower in his demesne and advertises for an astronomer to help him. His brother's disinherited daughter responds, incognito. Her intent is to recover her father's fortune, but she falls in love with a neighbouring landowner, whom she saves from opium addiction, and loses interest in the money. The telescope is a bone of contention for the neighbouring peasants, because it is instrumental in catching some of them stealing turf from their landlord's bog. The niece leaves to marry the former opium addict, and Anthony dies without telling anyone where his money is when the tower collapses in a great storm. The niece returns to direct the family to the money in the hidden vault under the tower. In gratitude, Anthony Nugent's son settles some of the money on her [ML; E. Reilly, p. 230].

HOPPER, Nora (Eleanor Jane, later Mrs W.H. Chesson), b. Exeter, 1871, d. 1906. Poet and story writer, NH was the daughter of Capt. Harman Baillie Hopper, an Irish officer in the British army, and Caroline Augusta Francis. Her father died when she was very young and she was reared in London, where she enjoyed studying folklore at the British Museum. She published several volumes of verse, including *Under quicken boughs* (London, 1896), and wrote stories for periodicals. 'A northern Juliet' was serialized in *Atalanta* (London). NH was described as a 'Celtic revivalist poet', but William Butler Yeats§ and Katharine Tynan§ both believed that she had plagiarized their work. Nevertheless Yeats praised her *Ballads in prose* (London, 1894) and said that it had in turn inspired him. Although NH claimed that *Ballads* was 'spun out of the moonshine of my own brain', and that 'Irish tradition has given me nothing', Irish poet Thomas McDonough considered her to be truly Irish. NH continued to write poetry, fiction and reviews and published prolifically. She wrote the libretto for O'Brien Butler's three-act opera 'Muirgheis' ('The sea-swan'), produced in Dublin in 1903 and later translated into Irish by Tórna (Tadhg Ó Donnchadha), as well as a Celtic play, 'The dark prince' (rejected for the Abbey in 1910). After her husband suffered a breakdown, she received assistance from the Royal Literary Fund. NH went to Dublin for the first time in 1905 and from there to Portrush (Co. Antrim). Her death followed shortly after the birth of a second daughter. SOURCE Alston, p. 207; Blain, p. 537; Brown, p. 140; Colman, pp 113–14; Field Day, ii, pp 958–9, 990; Irish pseudonyms; NCBEL 4, p. 753; ODNB; O'Donoghue, p. 203.

H365 *Ballads in prose* (by Nora Hopper; dedicated to the author's mother, Caroline Augusta Hopper).

+ London: John Lane; Boston: Roberts Bros, 1894 (ill. Walter West]). SOURCE Brown, p. 140. LOCATION L, NUC, InND Loeber coll.

COMMENTARY Tales of far-off pagan days soaked with Gaelic legendary and fairy lore. The short prose pieces are interspersed with little poems. Contents of the stories: 'The sorrow of Manannan', 'The three Brigits', 'Cuchullin's belt', 'The lamp of Brighid', 'Crióch agus amen', 'Boholaun and I', 'Daluan', 'The soul of Maurice Dwyer', 'The gifts of Aodh and Una', 'The four kings', 'Aonan-na-Righ' [RL; Brown; ODNB].

HOPPUS, Mary Anne Martha (afterwards Mrs Alfred Marks; also known as Mary A.M. Marks), b. 1843, d. 1916. English novelist, poet, and popular historian, MAMH was the daughter of John J. Hoppus, professor of mental and moral philosophy, University College, London, and Martha Devenish, who was of an old west country family (the Devenish name could also be found in Dublin and Athlone). MAMH grew up in Camden Town (London), where her father taught her Latin, French and mathematics. She wrote 12 novels and stories and two works on history and economics: *England and America, 1763 to 1783* (London, 1907), and *Landholding in England considered in relation to poverty* (London, 1908). SOURCE Blain, pp 537–8; COPAC.

H366 *Thorough. A novel* (by Mary A.M. Marks).
  London: Richard Bentley & Son, 1894, 3 vols. SOURCE Burmester list; Wolff, 3279; RLIN; COPAC, OCLC. LOCATION Dt, L, NYU.
  COMMENTARY Historical novel set in Ireland in Cromwellian times [Burmester list].

HORNE, Richard Henry (also known as Richard Hengist Horne), b. Edmonton, near London 1802 (not 1803 as in Allibone and NCBEL), d. Margate (Kent) 1884. Novelist, biographer, playwright, poet and prolific writer, RHH was educated at Sandhurst and served as a mid-shipman in the Mexican navy and in Mexico's war against Spain in 1829. He became editor of the *Monthly Repository* (London, 1836–37); and as a correspondent of the *Daily News* spent a year in Ireland in 1846 reporting on the Famine. He emigrated to Australia in 1852 and held several minor government positions. He returned to England in 1869. In *A new spirit of the age* (London, 1844, 2 vols.), a cultural survey which he partly wrote and edited, commentaries on 'celebrities' included 'Banim§ and the Irish novelists' (Allibone). In the introd. to the following novel he refers to his 'Ireland, its lakes, rivers and scenery', but this volume has not been located. SOURCE Allibone, i, pp. 888–9; Allibone Suppl., ii, p. 851; *Australian Dictionary of biography* (Melbourne, 1872), iv, p. 424; Boase, i, p. 1539; NCBEL pp 618–20, 1808; ODNB; RL; L. Stuart, 'Early convict novels' in *Proceedings of the sixteenth annual conference of the Association for the Study of Australian Literature* (n.l., [1994]), pp 100–4; Sutherland, pp. 305–6.

H367 *Rebel convicts. An Australian novel* [anon.].
  Melbourne: George Slater, 1858. SOURCE Miller, ii, p. 600. LOCATION State Library of Victoria.
  [St Lucia, Queensland]: Univ. of Queensland Press, 1966 (ed. by C. Hadgraft). LOCATION Univ. of Queensland.

COMMENTARY Attribution is mentioned by Stuart. The title piece is headed: 'The fiction-fields of Australia'. Also published in the *Illustrated Journal of Australasia* (Jun. – Dec. 1856). Concerns a mixture of incidents arising out of the Irish rebellion of 1798. The two principal characters are Francis Newton and the villain, Connel O'Meara. They are transported to New South Wales and Van Diemen's Land (Tasmania), and the story describes their parallel lives. The novel condemns transportation. It is somewhat unreliable as to dates of historical events [Miller; Personal communication, Jennifer Harrison, Feb. 2005; L. Stuart, 'Early convict novels', pp 100–1].

HORNIBROOK, Mrs Emma E., pseud. 'E.E.H.', fl. 1870s. Children's and religious fiction writer, possibly of Irish origin, EEH is identified in COPAC. She was author of 15 works of fiction, at least two of which have clear Irish connections. She also was the author of 'Clouds', and 'Mad Phil', which have not been located. The Hornibrook name occurs in Cork City and West Cork and some members of this family were seated at Corrin, Ballinhassig, in that county in 1876. In Paris, EEH edited a Protestant, missionary periodical, *Send and see* (Paris, 1890). She may be related to the author Isabel Hornibrook and to John Lawrence Hornibrook, who was her co-author in *Queen of the ranch; or, life in the far west* (New York, [fl. 1880]). The topic and New York publication suggest that she emigrated to North America. SOURCE Allibone Suppl., ii, p. 852; COPAC; E. MacLysaght, *The surnames of Ireland* (Dublin, 1973), p. 162; NCBEL 4, p. 1808; OCLC; *Return of owners of land* (Dublin, 1876), p. 12; RL; RLIN.

H368   *Allie, the little Irish girl* (by 'E.E.H.').
    + London, Edinburgh: Gall & Inglis, n.d. (ill. B.B. M'L). LOCATION D.
    COMMENTARY Fiction for juveniles. According to the author's preface, the story is based on fact [RL].

H369   *Two Irish scenes* (by 'E.E.H.').
    + London: S.W. Partridge & Co., [1873]. LOCATION L (destroyed), O.
    COMMENTARY Religious fiction published in association with the Church Education Society [BLC; CM].

HOUSTON, Mrs —. See HOUSTON, Maggie J.

HOUSTOUN, Mrs —. See HOUSTOUN, Mathilda Charlotte Fraser.

HOUSTON, Maggie J. (née Sinclair; also known as **Mrs Houston**), b. Moneymore (Co. Derry), fl. 1888, d. 1895. Novelist, MJH was the daughter of a (presumably Presbyterian) minister, Revd Robert Sinclair. She married a minister, the Revd John Houston, of Portglenone (Co. Antrim). SOURCE Brown, p. 141; TK.

H370   *A bunch of shamrocks* (by Maggie J. Houston).
    + London: Hamilton, Adams & Co.; Belfast: Charles W. Olley, 1888 (ill. Marcus Ward). SOURCE Brown, 775; Brown 2, 650; COPAC. LOCATION D, L, InND Loeber coll.
COMMENTARY A story of religious and land conflict set first on the shores of Lough Swilly (Co. Donegal) and later in Belfast, Nice, London and the US. Mr Dunbar, an upright and prosperous Presbyterian tenant on Lord Lofty's estate, having favoured the tenant rights movement is refused a renewal of his lease and must quit his home. He dies of heart failure, and his son Robert emigrates to America. Returning after some time, Robert travels to Nice and to London, where he loses his Christian faith. The chance sight of a bunch of shamrocks is the beginning of his return to faith, which is completed by a prolonged inward struggle at the Giant's Causeway (Co. Antrim). Moonlighters create havoc. Peter Donovan, son of a Catholic retainer of the Dunbars, assaults and kills Lord Lofty. He is arrested but he escapes and goes to America [Brown 2].

H371   *Kathleen Carmichael's recollections* (by Mrs Houston).
    Dublin, Belfast: Eason; London: Bagster, 1894. SOURCE Brown, 776; Brown 2, 651; COPAC. LOCATION L.
COMMENTARY A moral story of love and intrigue centred around Mr Carmichael, a Presbyterian minister in a northern county, beloved by his children, Mary, Jack and Kathleen. Henrietta (also called Etta) is an American cousin who comes to live with them and is affianced to Jack. Early in the story a Mr Allingham and an agnostic Englishman come to stay. Mr Allingham

falls in love with Etta. On the day of his departure, Jack accompanies him. A telegram comes telling that Jack has been drowned while bathing. The family travels in the Middle East and on their way back they are met in London by a Mr McGregor and Jack himself. Allingham cynically confesses that he had attempted to murder Jack. Mr McGregor, on board a ship leaving Larne (Co. Antrim) saw Jack's body floating in the sea and rescued him. McGregor proposes to Kathleen, who refuses him because she could never marry the son of a crofter, but the death of her father and her own severe illness change her mind. Mary, who had volunteered for foreign missions, dies in a hotel fire [Brown 2].

HOUSTOUN, Mathilda Charlotte Fraser (née Jesse; known as **Mrs Houstoun**), b. London 1820, d. London 1892. A novelist and travel writer, MCH was a daughter of the author Edward Jesse and was educated by a Welsh governess who forbade her to read novels. Widowed from her first marriage, she married William Houstoun, a captain of the Hussars in 1842. The couple moved to Delphi, near Westport (Co. Mayo) to take over the estates of Lord Sligo, from which many of the tenants had been evicted when they could not pay rent during the Famine. Her experiences and impressions of life in Ireland are captured in *Twenty years in the wild west; or life in Connaught* (London, 1879) and in *A woman's memories of world-known men* (London, 1883). The Houstouns spent a year living on a yacht and travelling to the West Indies, the Gulf of Mexico and the US, and MCH wrote about these adventures. She wrote her most well-known novel, *Recommended for mercy* (London, 1862), while she was living in Ireland. Only novels with known Irish content are listed here; others that may have Irish content remain to be identified. SOURCE Allibone, i, pp 897–8 [under Mrs Houston, *sic*]; Allibone Suppl., ii, p. 857; Blain, pp 542–3; Burmester cat. Spring 1998/226; NUC; ODNB.

H372   *Records of a stormy life* [anon.].
  + London: Hurst & Blackett, 1879, 3 vols. SOURCE Topp 6, 349. LOCATION L.
  COMMENTARY Not set in Ireland, but one of the characters is Irish [ML].

H373   *The poor of the period; or, leaves from a loiterer's diary* (by Mrs Houstoun; dedicated to 'other folks', and to George Eliot).
  London: F.V. White & Co., 1884, 2 vols. SOURCE Burmester cat. Spring 1998/227; COPAC; OCLC. LOCATION L, NUC.
COMMENTARY Religious fiction. A collection of stories set in London concerning the poor and persons of lowly origin and deals with landlords, the law, crime, philanthropy. Has Irish content [Burmester cat.; CM].

HOWARD, Jane. Co-author. See **DENISON, Mary Andrews.**

HOWARD, Lady Harriet, b. 1820, d. 1846. A writer of religious fiction for juveniles, HH was the second daughter of William Howard, 4th earl of Wicklow, and Lady Cecil-Frances Hamilton, daughter of the marquess of Abercorn, with whom he had seven daughters. Her father had their Co. Wicklow seat, Shelton Abbey, remodelled by the architect William Morrison, and housed his daughters in a new wing called the nunnery. HH remained unmarried and died young. A visitor to the estate in 1844 related that 'One of the earl's seven daughters writes religious tales for the cottagers' children, and gives them as rewards for industry and cleanliness' (copies not located). There was some controversy whether her book *The birthday* (London, 1844) was intended as a Protestant or Catholic publication, giving rise to ([anon.], *Is 'The birthday', ... intended as a Protestant or Popish publication?* (London, 1857, copy in the BL). HH's sister, the Hon. Catherine Howard (Lady Petre), became a convert to catholicism, and published religious poetry (e.g., under the pseudonym of a 'Lady—, a convert from Anglicanism to Christianity', Dublin, 1854, and London, 1884). HH collaborated with Cecil

(Fanny) Alexander§, a childhood friend, on a number of religious tracts, she providing the prose and CA the poetry. It is quite likely that HH was involved in one or more of the three schools in the parish of Kilbride (in which Shelton Abbey is situated), under the patronage of the earl and countess of Wicklow. HH also, wrote two religious works: *Gideon "the mighty man of valour"* (London, 1838), and *Josiah* (London, 1842), the former being for the benefit of the Brighton Asylum for Female Orphans and was written when she was age 17. SOURCE Colman, p. 115; E. Lodge, *The peerage and baronetage of the British Empire* (London, 1897, 66th edn), pp 692–3; S. Lewis, *A topographical dictionary of Ireland* (London, 1837), ii, p. 55; LVP, p. 376; MPV, p. 365; A. Nicholson, *Ireland's welcome to the stranger, or an excursion through Ireland in 1844 and 1845* (New York, 1847), p. 56; NCBEL 4, p. 1808; O'Donoghue, p. 205; V. Wallace, *A life of the hymn writer Mrs. Alexander* (Dublin, 1995), pp 28–9, 32–4, 41, 43, 45–6, 63–5; Williams, p. 386.

H374   *The birthday: a tale for the young* [anon.] (dedicated to the author's younger sisters). London: James Burns, 1844 (ill.). SOURCE Osborne, p. 897; NCBEL 4, p. 1808. LOCATION L, NUC, CaOTP; InND Loeber coll. (London, Masters, 1849, 3rd edn).
COMMENTARY A moral story about the five lively children of the marquis and marchioness de Courcy who discuss Christian conduct and morality with the parish rector and his ten-year-old daughter during the summer holidays at the family's castle [Osborne, p. 897].

HOWE, W. Henry, fl 1898. There is a remote possibility that this author can be identified with William Henry Howe (1846–1929), a landscape and cattle painter, b. Ravenna (OH), d. Bronxville (NY), who studied in Europe and whose paintings hang in the National Gallery in Washington (DC) and in art museums in St Louis (MO) and Cleveland (OH), among others. But there are no author credits and no mention of Ireland in any way in his biographical sketch. SOURCE DAB; AMB.

H375   *Irish wit and humor; classified under appropriate subject headings, with, in many cases, a reference to a table of authors* (compiled by W. Henry Howe).
+ Philadelphia: George W. Jacobs & Co., 1898 (ill.). SOURCE Halkett & Laing, ix, p. 156. LOCATION InND Loeber coll.
COMMENTARY Brief anonymous sketches on Irish definitions; love; travels; Irish bulls; meeting difficulties; politics; tenants; money; literary wit and humour; the army, navy, judiciary and police; commerce; domesticity, and religion [RL].

'HUBERTO', pseud. See LAMBART, W. Huberto.

HUDDLESTON, Robert, b. Moneyrea, near Comber (Co. Down) b. 1814, d. 1887. Poet and unpublished novelist, RH was known as the bard of Moneyrea. He was the son of James and Agnes Huddleston, a farmer and gunsmith. RH also became a farmer and a fiddler and played for wedding dances. He remained a bachelor until he was age 48, when he married Margaret Ellison. He published by subscription *A collection of poems and songs on rural subjects* (Belfast, 1844), and *A collection of poems and songs on different subjects* (Belfast, 1846). He contributed poems to *Ulster Magazine* (Belfast?), between 1860 and 1863. RH's poetry was noted for its rich Ulster-Scots language and its linguistic creativity but his power of satire was feared locally. A non-subscribing Presbyterian, he held nationalistic views on politics and was interested in Gaelic traditions as well as Ulster-Scots folklore. SOURCE Newmann, p. 113; O'Donoghue, p. 206; RIA/DIB.

H376   *The adventures of Hughey Funny or the many tales of love* (by Robert Huddleston).
COMMENTARY Unpublished manuscript novel, begun in 1850 (location not known) [Newmann, p. 113].

HUDSON, Frank (Francis S. Brereton), b. Co. Offaly, fl. 1888. Writer of comedies and burlesques as well as poems and sporting pieces, FH was the son of S.B. Hudson of Skreggan House (Co. Offaly). At age 14 he wrote a three-act comedy and he published his first poem in the *Shamrock* (Dublin) at age 16. He became half-proprietor and editor of the *Turf Telegraph* (presumably, the *Irish Turf Telegraph*, Dublin) as well as editor of a comic series *Pat* (Dublin). In 1882 went to London to work as a journalist and contributed prose and verse to many of the most popular periodicals of the day. In 1881 one of his burlesques was produced at the Queen's Theatre, Dublin. Some of his letters are among the Downey Papers (NLI, MS 10,026). SOURCE Brown, p. 141; O'Donoghue, p. 206.

H377 *The last hurdle. A story of sporting and courting* (by Frank Hudson).
London: Ward & Downey, 1888. SOURCE Brown, 778. LOCATION L, NUC.
COMMENTARY A romance set among an Irish county family who have sympathy for the poor around them. The heroine is won by the hero in spite of plots by the rival. Contrasts good and bad landlords and contains an eviction scene [Brown].

H378 *The origin of plum pudding, with other fairy tales and a little burletta* (by Frank Hudson).
+ London: Ward & Downey, [1889] (ill. Gordon Browne, etc.). SOURCE Brown, 777. LOCATION L, NUC.
COMMENTARY Contents: 'The origin of plum pudding', 'The fairy of fashion', 'The fairy from France' (features a stage-Irishman), 'Shawn Murray's challenge' (set in Dalkey). Also added is a burletta in two acts [CM].

H379 *A very mad world; or, myself and my neighbour fair* (by Frank Hudson).
London: Ward & Downey, 1889, 2 vols. SOURCE Wolff, 3327. LOCATION L, NUC.

H380 *Running double: A story of the stable and the stage* (by Frank Hudson; dedicated to Edwin Hamilton§).
+ London: Ward & Downey, 1890, 2 vols. SOURCE Brown, 779. LOCATION L, NUC, InND Loeber coll.
COMMENTARY Originally printed as 'A loose rein', but since that title was already taken, it was renamed. Set in England, Dublin, and 'Ennisbeg'. The chief interests are sporting, horse racing and betting. A girl who is the bookkeeper in the hotel in Ennisbeg marries a labourer. She had been separated from her brother in youth. He has made a fortune abroad and comes looking for his only relative. When he finds out she had made such a poor marriage, he is initially disappointed but in the end comes to value his brother-in-law and to love Ennisbeg [ML; Brown].

H381 *She shall be mine! A novel* (by Frank Hudson).
London: Ward & Downey, 1894, 2 vols. LOCATION L, NUC.

HUGHES, Mrs Kate Duval. See **HUGHES, Mrs Kate Elizabeth Duval**.

HUGHES, Mrs Kate Elizabeth Duval (née Duval; known as **Kate Duval Hughes**), b. 1839, d. 1925. Probably American, a fiction writer who wrote under the name Kate Duval Hughes. SOURCE DCU, Catholic Americana files.

H382 *The fair maid of Connaught and other tales for Catholic youth* (by Mrs Kate Duval Hughes; dedicated to Cardinal Gibbons).
New York: P.J. Kenedy; Philadelphia: Kilner, 1889. SOURCE Brown, 780; DCU, Catholic Americana files; OCLC. LOCATION NUC.
+ Philadelphia: H.L. Kilner & Co., 1889 (Premium Library). LOCATION InND Loeber coll.
COMMENTARY Fiction for juveniles. Contents: 'The fair maid of Connaught' (the only Irish story), 'The lame foot', 'Eulalie, or the little miser', 'The good old priest & the snuff box',

'Lies in action and omission', 'Vanity', 'Gratitude and integrity', 'The faithful servant', 'Pamela, or the happy adoption', 'Punctuality' [RL].

HUGHES, Margaret. See **CALLAN, Mrs Margaret.**

'HUMBUG, Humphrey', pseud. See **FRICKER, Thomas.**

HUMPHREYS, Cecil Frances. See **ALEXANDER, Cecil Frances.**

HUMPHREYS, Mrs W. Desmond (née Eliza M. Gollan; formerly Mrs Otto Van Booth), pseud. **'Rita'**, b. Gollanfield, near Inverness (Scotland) 1860 (1856 according to EF), d. 1938. Novelist and writer, Mrs WDH was both prolific and successful. She spent her childhood in Sydney (Australia), returning to London when she was aged 14. Her first marriage to Otto Van Booth was unhappy and this provided background for several of her novels. She later married W.D. Humphreys of Ballintemple (Co. Cork). They stayed briefly in Youghal (Co. Cork), afterwards living at Bournemouth (Dorset) and at Bath (Avon). She continued to visit the south of Ireland and became very interested in the country, resolving to 'study its people, manners, and conditions, with a view of future use in my books'. Aside from more than 70 novels, she wrote plays and an autobiography, *Recollections of a literary life* (London, 1936). Many of her novels deal with male-female relationships, with women as the main characters. A number of them were reprinted in the US and her novel *Peg the rake* (London, 1894, 3 vols.) reached a record sale of 160,000 copies. Mrs WDH's husband became an invalid and she supported him with her writing. She applied twice to the Royal Literary Fund for financial assistance. She was a founder of the Writer's Club for Women, but she eschewed feminism. After a visit to the US she wrote a series of essays, *Personal opinions publicly expressed* (London, 1907), which contained virulently anti-American opinions. Her portrait was included in her *The man in possession* (London, [*c.*1910]). Only novels with known Irish connections are listed below. SOURCE Blain, p. 907; Brown 2, p. 121; EF, p. 343; 'Rita' (Mrs Desmond Humphreys), *Recollections of a literary life* (London, 1936), pp 66, 71–7, 79, 280; ODNB; Wolff, 5864.
H383   *The man in possession* (by 'Rita').
    + New York: Hovendon, [1891] (Metropolitan Series, No. 3). SOURCE Daims, 1477; Topp 7, 243. LOCATION NUC.
    New York: G.W. Lovell, [1891]. LOCATION NUC.
    + London: F.V. White, 1893. SOURCE Daims, 1477; Wolff, 5859 (1895 edn); Topp 7, 243. LOCATION D, L, InND Loeber coll. (London, The Goodship House, n.d. edn).
    COMMENTARY Features an actress, Kate O'Brien [RL].
H384   *Peg, the rake* (by 'Rita').
    London: Hutchinson & Co., 1894, 3 vols. SOURCE Brown, 1433; Daims, 1478; Sadleir, 2072; Wolff, 5863. LOCATION D (9th edn), L.
    [New York]: [P.F. Collier], 1895 (Once A Week Library). SOURCE Daims, 1478. LOCATION NUC.
    COMMENTARY Immensely successful novel with an Irish setting first serialized in *Household Words* (London). Emilia, a worldly woman age 40, is in conflict with her father and stepmother. She marries to escape from them, but the marriage is not happy. However, it appears that a secret marriage had taken place twenty years previously that even Emilia was not aware of. This fact sets her free from her own marriage [Recollections, p. 67].
H385   *The ending of my day. The story of a stormy life* (by 'Rita').
    + London: F.V. White, 1894, 3 vols. SOURCE Brown 2, 655; Daims, 1473; Sadleir, 2071; Wolff, 5843; Topp 7, 254. LOCATION D, L, NUC, InND Loeber coll. (1895 edn).

COMMENTARY A story in diary form concerning the English governess Belle Ffolliott in the period from 1873, when she is aged 14, to her second marriage. She comes to live with the Mac Fadyean family at Kilfane, a stereotypically Irish, tumbledown mansion. She describes the Irish Catholics of the neighbourhood as kindly, warm-hearted people, but the story is concerned with the Protestant gentry. Belle is attractive, but proud. Charley Kilmurran's affections are transferred to her from Nora Mac Fadyean who, in consequence, commits suicide. Belle refuses three suitors and then accepts Jack Trefusis, a childhood friend, who is going on the stage. Gradually estrangement comes, ending in divorce. She then marries one of her former suitors, but her life is ruined. Comic relief is introduced by Mrs Leery, a busybody, and wife of the rector of Kilfane [Brown 2].

H386   *A woman in it. A sketch of feminine misadventure* (by 'Rita').
  + London: Hutchinson & Co., 1895. SOURCE Daims, 1483; Wolff, 5878. LOCATION L, InND Loeber coll.
  Philadelphia: J.B. Lippincott & Co., 1895. SOURCE Daims, 1483. LOCATION NUC.
COMMENTARY Nina Garbett, an Irish woman, is left penniless and without reputation because her husband divorces her. She finds work as a companion to an invalid, but leaves when the woman's husband murders the invalid to have an affair with Nina. The book relates her struggles to find another job and survive and tells about her dealings with different men [ML].

H387   *Kitty the rag* (by 'Rita').
  + London: Hutchinson & Co., 1896. SOURCE Brown, p. 264; Daims, 1476; Wolff, 5854. LOCATION D (n.d. edn), L, NUC.
  New York: R.F. Fenno, [*c*.1897]. SOURCE Daims, 1476. LOCATION NUC.
COMMENTARY Story about an Irish orphan [RL].

H388   *Joan & Mrs. Carr* (by 'Rita').
  + London: F.V. White & Co., 1896. SOURCE Wolff, 5853 (1897 edn); Topp 7, 323. LOCATION L, InND Loeber coll.
COMMENTARY Some Irish content [ML].

H389   *The sinner* (by 'Rita').
  + London: Hutchinson & Co., 1897. SOURCE Daims, 1481. LOCATION L.
  Chicago, New York: Rand, McNally, 1897. SOURCE Daims, 1481; OCLC. LOCATION NUC.
COMMENTARY Detective story set in an Irish hospital [RL].

H390   *Vignette. Stories* (by 'Rita').
  London: F.V. White & Co., 1897. SOURCE Topp 7, 342. LOCATION L.
COMMENTARY Several ghost stories. Contents: 'Snow-white', 'In the vaults', 'The spectre', '"Consequences"', 'Haunted', 'The irony of fate', '"Good-bye"', 'Child Lilian', 'A knot in a handkerchief' [Topp; RL].

H391   *Petticoat loose. A novel* (by 'Rita').
  + London: Hutchinson & Co., 1898. SOURCE Brown, p. 264; Daims, 1479; Wolff, 5865. LOCATION D, L, InND Loeber coll.
COMMENTARY Story of Brianna, an Irish girl, becoming an actress [RL].

H392   *An old rogue's tragedy* (by 'Rita').
  + London: Hutchinson & Co., 1899. SOURCE Brown, p. 264 (1900 edn). LOCATION L, InND Loeber coll.
COMMENTARY Story of an old Irish woman whose profession is to bring girls out in society and to marry them off well. She is a miser, and the reason is that she has, hidden from the world, a daughter who is deformed and retarded. The daughter dies and the old woman lives only a little bit longer, but receives love from her latest protégée. In her will she bequeaths her money to a penniless young Irish writer who has been kind to her so that the writer and the protégée will have a chance to marry each other [ML].

H393 *Prince charming. Fantastic episode in court dress* (by 'Rita').
+ London: Sands & Co., 1901. SOURCE Wolff, 5867. LOCATION D.
Leipzig: Bernard Tauchnitz, 1906. SOURCE T & B, 3872; OCLC. LOCATION CLU.
COMMENTARY Irish content [ML].

H394 *The sin of Jasper Standish* (by 'Rita').
London: Constable, 1901. SOURCE Brown, 1434. SOURCE COPAC. LOCATION E.
New York: R.F. Fenno & Co.; London: Constable & Co., 1902. LOCATION NUC.
COMMENTARY Set in one of the Irish midland counties. The story is founded on a
Newtownstewart (Co. Tyrone) tragedy where an inspector of police murders the local bank
manager and then also conducts the investigation into the murder. He is unmasked and brought
to justice by the English heroine and her housekeeper [Brown].

H395 *Souls. A comedy of intentions* (by 'Rita').
London: Hutchinson, 1903. SOURCE Wolff, 5873. SOURCE COPAC. LOCATION E.
+ Leipzig: Bernard Tauchnitz, 1903. SOURCE T & B, 3363. LOCATION InND Loeber
coll.

COMMENTARY A novel written against the emptiness of society life. Mrs Brady tries to penetrate a secret group of society people because she thinks it will give her better chances in life.
Eventually, she finds out that the group mainly consists of mean, vain and empty-headed people, whose company is far from desirable [ML].

H396 *The masqueraders* (by 'Rita'; dedicated to 'two dear Irishmen').
+ London: Hutchinson & Co., 1904. SOURCE Brown, p. 264. LOCATION D, InND
Loeber coll. (1904, 2nd edn).
Leipzig: Bernard Tauchnitz, 1905. SOURCE T & B, 3799; COPAC. LOCATION L.

COMMENTARY A story of two Irish singers who perform in England under pseuds. For many
years they struggle to make ends meet. When they are about to reap success the tent in which
they perform goes up in flames and one of them is seriously hurt and cannot perform
any more. However, he comes into an inheritance which allows him to live on the Continent
[ML].

H397 *Half a truth* (by 'Rita').
London: Hutchinson & Co., 1911. SOURCE Brown, p. 264. LOCATION D (n.d. edn), L.
Leipzig: Bernard Tauchnitz, 1911. SOURCE T & B, 4270; OCLC. LOCATION NIC.
COMMENTARY Irish content [Brown].

H398 *A grey life. A romance of modern Bath* (by 'Rita').
London: Stanley Paul & Co., 1913. SOURCE Brown, 1435; Wolff, 5850. LOCATION E,
D (n.d. edn).
COMMENTARY Set in the 1870s in a boarding-house in Bath, England, which is kept by three
ladies of reduced circumstances. One of the boarders is Rosaleen O'Hara. The central figure
is the Chevalier Theophrastus O'Shaughnessy, who is a charming scholarly man with a sad
history [Brown].

H399 *The rubbish heap* (by 'Rita'; dedicated to Carrie, 'Mrs Pat').
+ New York, London: G.P. Putnam's Sons, 1917. SOURCE Brown, p. 264 (1918 edn).
LOCATION D (1918 edn), NUC.
+ New York, London: G.P. Putnam's Sons, 1918. LOCATION InND Loeber coll.

COMMENTARY Set in England and Ireland. A captain residing at a seaside town in England
brings home a little Irish girl he found wandering in the Irish countryside. The girl inspires
a young man who becomes an artist, and touches the heart of several other people. Eventually,
she flees back to Ireland and is followed by her friends who want to bring her back. It
transpires that she is related to them. She does not return to England, but enters a convent
[ML].

H400   *The ladies of Moyallo* (by 'Rita').
London: Hutchinson & Co., [1933]. SOURCE Brown 2, 656; Wolff, 5855 (n.d. edn).
LOCATION L.
COMMENTARY Told by Aunt Albreda, living in Bath, who, with her sisters, 'The Ladies of
Moyallo', belonged to the old Ascendancy class and were driven out of Ireland by 'the trou-
bles'. She watches with kindly interest the careers of several young people: Sheila, her niece;
Judy Ginsberg, the clever young American 'college dame'; and Phyllida Graeme, whom she
helps in her ambition to go on the stage [Brown 2].

HUNGERFORD, Mrs —. See HUNGERFORD, Margaret Wolfe.

HUNGERFORD, Margaret Wolfe (née Hamilton; Mrs Thomas Hungerford, formerly Mrs
Edward Argles; later published as **Mrs Hungerford**), pseud. '**The Duchess**', b. Milteen,
Rosscarbery (Co. Cork) 1852, d. Bandon (Co. Cork) 1897. Romance novelist and short story writer,
MWH was the daughter of the Revd Fitzjohn Stannus Hamilton, a clergyman at St Faughnan's
cathedral in Rosscarbery (Co. Cork), and Sarah Paye of Kilworth (Co. Cork). Her home was St
Brenda's in Bandon. MWH was educated at Portarlington College (Co. Laois). She married twice:
first in 1872 Edward Argles (d. 1878), a Dublin solicitor; and secondly in 1882 the landowner
Thomas Henry Hungerford, of Cahirmore (Co. Cork). The Irish revolutionary Jeremiah O'Donovan
Rossa grew up on the Hungerford estate but had left when MWH arrived there. MWH began
writing at an early age and wrote some 56 books of popular romantic fiction, always set among
the landed gentry, as well as publishing collections of short stories, children's fiction, and contributions to the British and American press (including the *Argosy*, London, 1884). Most of her work
consists of romances and the complications of love between women and men; some are set in
Ireland. Her novels were widely circulated in India, Australia and the US, and many of them were
reprinted by Tauchnitz in Germany. Each of her two marriages produced three children. She died
prematurely of typhoid and was buried in the church of Rosscarbery (Co. Cork), where a grave
slab and panelling around the communion table were erected in her memory. She was survived
by her husband, who died in 1906. For her portraits, see ODNB. SOURCE Allibone Suppl., ii, p.
872; Blain, p. 551; Boase, v, pp 728–9; Brady, p. 109; Brown, p. 142; Burke's, p. 609; Field Day,
iv, p. 1142, v, p. 927; Hogan 2, p. 567; JAPMDI, 5(1) (1901), p. 23, 4(1) 1904, p. 35; OCIL, p.
253; ODNB; RIA/DIB; RL; *Rossa's recollections, 1838 to 1898, memoirs of an Irish revolutionary*
(Guilford, CT, 2004), p. 15; Sutherland, p. 313; Wolff, ii, p. 248.
H401   *Phyllis. A novel* [anon.].
London: Smith, Elder & Co., 1877. SOURCE Alston, p. 8. LOCATION D (1917 edn), L.
London: Smith, Elder & Co., 1894 (new edn). SOURCE Topp 5, p. 247. LOCATION
InND Loeber coll. (1895, new edn).
Leipzig: Bernard Tauchnitz, 1883, 2 vols. SOURCE T & B, 2195. LOCATION NUC.
Philadelphia: J.B. Lippincott & Co., 1877. LOCATION NUC.
+ New York: A.L. Burt, n.d. (as *Phyllis*, by 'The Duchess'). LOCATION InND Loeber
coll.
COMMENTARY A romance set in England. A young girl marries a rich, good looking neigh-
bour. She likes him but she is not in love with him. Their first years are very stormy and
filled with jealousy until they learn to trust each other [ML].
H402   *Molly Bawn* [anon.].
+ London: Smith, Elder & Co., 1878, 3 vols. SOURCE Brown, 785; Alston, p. 8; Wolff,
3436 (1888 edn). LOCATION D (1896 edn), L, NUC, InND Loeber coll.
London: Smith, Elder & Co., 1888 (new edn). SOURCE Topp 5, p. 247. LOCATION
InND Loeber coll. (1890, new edn).

Leipzig: Bernard Tauchnitz, 1878, 2 vols. SOURCE T & B, 1788. LOCATION NUC.

+ Philadelphia: J.B. Lippincott & Co., 1878. LOCATION NUC, InND Loeber coll.

New York: George Munro, 1878 (Seaside Library, No. 393). LOCATION NUC.

COMMENTARY A romance featuring a light-hearted but irresistible Irish girl, who flirts and arouses her lover's jealousy [Brown; Sutherland].

H403 *The baby* [anon.].

New York: G. Munro, 1878. LOCATION NUC.

COMMENTARY Published together with *Michael Gargrave's harvest*, by Mrs J.H. Riddell§.

H404 *"Airy fairy Lilian"* [anon.].

London: Smith, Elder & Co., 1879, 3 vols. SOURCE Alston, p. 8. LOCATION L, NUC.

+ London: Smith, Elder & Co., 1886 (new edn). SOURCE Topp 5, p. 249. LOCATION D, InND Loeber coll.

Philadelphia: J.B. Lippincott & Co., 1879. SOURCE Topp 5, p. 250; OCLC. LOCATION Colorado State Univ., Boulder (CO).

New York: George Munro, [1879] (Seaside Library, No. 499). SOURCE Topp 5, p. 250. LOCATION NUC.

COMMENTARY A romance set in England. A girl living on an estate loses her father and a distant relative inherits the estate. The girl moves to the house of her guardian, Guy Chetwoode. While living there, she flirts with various young men and argues relentlessly with her guardian. However, in the end they declare their love for each other [ML].

H405 *Beauty's daughters. A novel* [anon.].

London: Smith, Elder & Co., 1880, 3 vols. SOURCE Wolff, 3420. LOCATION D (1886 edn), Dt (1889 edn), L, NUC.

New York: G. Munro, [c.1880] (Seaside Library). LOCATION NUC.

Philadelphia: J.B. Lippincott & Co., 1880. LOCATION NUC.

Chicago, New York: Belford, Clarke & Co., 1880. SOURCE OCLC. LOCATION Univ. of Detroit, InND Loeber coll. (Chicago, Henneberry, n.d. edn).

COMMENTARY Set in England and describes the lives of the Tremaine family, who have a son and three daughters: Kitty, Gretchen, and Flora. Kitty marries a man who is fairly flighty and when Kitty and her husband move to London, their relationship worsens because of intrigues by both of them. Gretchen marries an invalid who goes to Germany for treatment and comes back cured. Kitty and her husband reconcile after a baby has been born and some misunderstandings are cleared up [ML].

H406 *Mrs. Geoffrey* [anon.].

+ London: Smith, Elder & Co., 1881, 3 vols. SOURCE Alston, p. 8. LOCATION D, Dt (1886 new edn), L.

London: Smith, Elder & Co., 1887 (new edn). SOURCE COPAC. LOCATION Univ. of Liverpool.

+ Leipzig: Bernhard Tauchnitz, 1881, 2 vols. SOURCE T & B, 2019. LOCATION D, NUC.

New York: G. Munro, 1881 (Seaside Library). LOCATION NUC.

+ Philadelphia: J.B. Lippincott & Co., 1881. LOCATION NUC, InND Loeber coll.

COMMENTARY A story of romance between different classes set in Ireland and England. An Englishman, Geoffrey Rodney, goes to Ireland to visit a shooting lodge he has inherited. While there he falls in love with Mona, a niece of a common farmer. He marries her and brings her to his family's ancestral estate in England. His mother is extremely shocked that he has married this girl and is very rude to Mona. However, Mona is instrumental in solving a potential threat to the eldest brother's succession to the estate. Her mother-in-law is thankful for this and takes Mona to her heart [ML].

H407 *Faith and unfaith* [anon.].
London: Smith, Elder & Co., 1881, 3 vols. SOURCE Wolff, 3423. LOCATION D (1890 edn), L, NUC.
+ London: Smith, Elder & Co., 1887 (new edn). SOURCE Topp 5, p. 249. LOCATION InND Loeber coll.
Leipzig: Bernard Tauchnitz, 1882, 2 vols. SOURCE T & B, 2046–47. LOCATION NUC.
New York: George Munro, [1881] (Seaside Library, No. 010). SOURCE Topp 5, p. 249. LOCATION NUC.
New York: J.S. Ogilvie, 1881 (People's Library, No. 45). SOURCE Topp 5, p. 249.
Philadelphia: J.B. Lippincott & Co., 1881. SOURCE Topp 5, p. 249. LOCATION NUC (1882 edn).
COMMENTARY No copy of the New York Ogilvie edn located. A romance set in England. Two brothers, Dorian and Horace, are both in love. Dorian marries Georgie, a governess, who marries mainly to escape poverty. Horace is engaged to Clarissa, but before he can marry he first has to make a living in London. The disappearance of the miller's daughter from the neighbourhood causes suspicion to fall on Dorian. However, it appears that the miller's daughter is living with Horace in London. Dorian and his wife reconcile, and Clarissa marries a man who has long loved her [ML].

H408 *Portia; or, "by passions rocked". A novel* [anon.].
London: Smith, Elder & Co., 1883. 3 vols. SOURCE Topp 5, p. 253. LOCATION D (1901 edn), L.
London: Smith, Elder & Co., 1886 (new edn). SOURCE Topp 5, p. 253.
Leipzig: Bernard Tauchnitz, 1883, 2 vols. SOURCE T & B, 2130–31. LOCATION NUC.
New York: George Munro, 1883 (Seaside Library, No. 1518). SOURCE Topp 5, p. 253. LOCATION NUC.
Philadelphia: J.B. Lippincott & Co., 1883. LOCATION NUC.
COMMENTARY No copy of the London 1886 edn located. O'Toole mentions a 1878, 3 vols. edn, but this probably is in error and has not been located [RL].

H409 *Loÿs, Lord Beresford and other tales* [anon.].
London: Smith, Elder & Co., 1883, 3 vols. SOURCE Topp 5, p. 267; Wolff, 3431. LOCATION L.
London: Smith, Elder & Co., 1888 (new edn). SOURCE Topp 5, p. 267; RLIN. LOCATION Univ. of Michigan.
Leipzig: Bernard Tauchnitz, 1883, 2 vols. SOURCE T & B, 2157. LOCATION NUC.
Leipzig: Bernard Tauchnitz, 1883 (as *Her first appearance, and other tales*). SOURCE T & B, 2174. LOCATION NUC. COMMENTARY *Leipzig, 1883, one vol. edn*. Contains a subset of the stories [RL].
+ Philadelphia: J.B. Lippincott & Co., 1883 (as *Loÿs, Lord Berresford* [*sic*], *and other tales*). LOCATION NUC, InND Loeber coll.
New York: John W. Lovell, 1883 (Lovell's Library, No.126). SOURCE Topp 5, p. 267. LOCATION NUC.
New York: G. Munro, [1884] (as *The witching hour, and other stories*; Seaside Library). LOCATION NUC.
New York: G. Munro, [1884] (as *Sweet is true love and other tales*; Seaside Library). LOCATION NUC.
COMMENTARY Contents: 'Loÿs, Lord Beresford', 'Eric Dering', 'Sweet is true love', 'Lydia', 'Jocelyne', 'The witching hour'; Philadelphia edn has additional stories: 'The pity of it', 'How snooks got out of it', 'Cross-purposes', 'Her first appearance', '"Krin"', 'Beatrix', 'Clarissa's choice', '"What a mad world it is, my masters!"', 'The baby' (published earlier as a separate

volume in New York, 1878), 'The dilemma', '"That last rehearsal"'. Other edns have a slightly different selection of stories. The Munro (New York, [1884]) titles of *The witching hour, and other stories,* and *Sweet is true love and other tales* each contain a subset of the stories. Note that O'Toole mentions a London edn of *The witching hour* (1884), but this has not been located [NUC; RL; O'Toole, p. 73].

H410 *Monica* (by 'The Duchess').

New York: J.W. Lovell, [1883] (Lovell's Library). LOCATION NUC.

COMMENTARY Contents: 'Monica', 'How snooks got out of it' (first published in *Loÿs, Lord Beresford and other tales,* London, 1883), 'The baby' (published earlier as a separate volume in New York, 1878) [NUC].

H411 *Monica, and A rose distill'd* (by 'The Duchess').

New York: G. Munro, 1883 (Seaside Library). LOCATION NUC.

COMMENTARY Contents: 'Monica' (also separately published in New York by Lovell [1883] as a volume entitled *Monica*), 'A rose distill'd', 'The pity of it', 'Cross-purposes', 'Her first appearance', '"Krin"' The last four stories were published earlier in *Loÿs, Lord Beresford and other tales,* London, 1883 [NUC; RL].

H412 *Moonshine and marguerites* (by 'The Duchess').

London: Smith, Elder & Co., 1883. Source O'Toole, p. 73.

New York: J.W. Lovell & Co., 1883. SOURCE OCLC. LOCATION Cleveland Public Library (OH).

COMMENTARY No copy of the London edn located. Contents: 'Moonshine and marguerite' [*sic*], 'The witching hour', 'Cross-purposes' [OCLC; RL].

H413 *Rossmoyne* [anon.].

London: Smith, Elder & Co., 1883, 3 vols. SOURCE Alston, p. 9; Wolff, 3442 (1892, new edn); COPAC. LOCATION L, D (1885 edn).

+ London: Smith, Elder & Co., 1885 (new edn). LOCATION NUC, InND Loeber coll.

+ Leipzig: Bernard Tauchnitz, 1884, 2 vols. SOURCE T & B, 2218. LOCATION D, NUC.

New York: G. Munro, 1883 (Seaside Library, No. 1743). LOCATION NUC.

New York: John W. Lovell, [1883] (Lovell's Library, No. 284). SOURCE Topp 5, p. 251. LOCATION NUC.

Philadelphia: J.B. Lippincott & Co., 1884. LOCATION NUC.

COMMENTARY A romance set in Ireland among the landed gentry about the thwarted love between two young people. The girl's aunts believe that the boy's uncle had jilted the girl's mother in her youth. In the end the truth comes out that the mother had been the culprit rather than the boy's uncle, and the couple is united [ML].

H414 *Twitching horn and other stories* (by 'The Duchess').

New York: G. Munro, [1884]. SOURCE Hogan 2, p. 567.

COMMENTARY No copy located [RL].

H415 *A week in Killarney* (by 'The Duchess').

New York: G. Munro, 1885 (Seaside Library, No. 1910; Seaside Library Pocket Edition, No. 312). SOURCE Topp 8, 32. LOCATION NUC (1884 edn), InND Loeber coll. (n.d. edn). COMMENTARY *New York, Munro, 1885 edn* No copy located [RL].

New York: J.W. Lovell, [1885] (Lovell's Library, No. 477). SOURCE Topp 8, 32; OCLC. LOCATION PpiU.

New York: J.W. Lovell, 1886 (as *Her week's amusement*; Lovell's Library, No. 792). SOURCE Topp 8, 32; OCLC. LOCATION Arlington Library, VA.

London: Ward & Downey, 1886 (as *Her week's amusement*). SOURCE Brown, 786 (probably mistakenly mentions 1885 edn); Topp 8, 32. LOCATION D (n.d. edn), Dt (1887, 2nd edn), L.

London: Ward & Downey, 1890 (as *A week in Killarney*). SOURCE Topp 8, 32; OCLC. LOCATION LCA.

Leipzig: Bernard Tauchnitz, 1886 (as *Her week's amusement; Ugly Barrington*). SOURCE T & B, 2418. LOCATION NUC.

COMMENTARY First serialized in *Lippincott's Magazine* (Philadelphia, 1884) and the *New-York Monthly Fashion Bazar* (Nov. 1884–Jan. 1885). A holiday romance set in Killarney. Pretty Muriel Kingsley has been left by her aunt in the care of a young married couple who feel at times not equal to the task of supervising her. Muriel carries on a week's flirtation with two young men. Muriel and the couple made many excursions in the Killarney area with the two young men in tow, until her chosen lover appears [ML; Brown].

H416 *Doris* [anon.].

London: Smith, Elder & Co., 1884, 3 vols. SOURCE Wolff, 3422. LOCATION L, NUC.

London: Smith, Elder & Co., 1887 (new edn). SOURCE Topp 5, p. 252 (1888 end). LOCATION Univ. of Manchester.

Leipzig: Bernard Tauchnitz, 1884, 2 vols. SOURCE T & B, 2301. LOCATION NUC.

New York: George Munro, [1884] (Seaside Library Pocket Library, No. 284). SOURCE Topp 5, p. 252. LOCATION NUC.

New York: J.W. Lovell, [1884] (Lovell's Library, No. 451). SOURCE Topp 5, p. 252. LOCATION NUC.

Philadelphia: J.B. Lippincott & Co., 1885. LOCATION NUC.

+ Chicago, New York: Belford, Clarke & Co., n.d. (spine: *Doris. A novel*, by 'The Duchess'). LOCATION InND Loeber coll.

H417 *A maiden all forlorn, and other stories* [anon.].

London: Ward & Downey, 1885, 3 vols. SOURCE Alston, p. 8; Wolff, 3432 (5th edn). LOCATION L.

London: Ward & Downey, 1885 (new edn). LOCATION NUC.

London: F.T. Neely, [1889] (as *Nurse Eva*, by 'The Duchess'; Neely's Booklet Series). LOCATION NUC.

COMMENTARY London [*1889*] edn Only contains the story 'Nurse Eva' [NUC].

Leipzig: Bernard Tauchnitz, 1885. SOURCE T & B, 2333. LOCATION NUC.

+ Leipzig: Bernard Tauchnitz, 1885 (as *A passive crime and other stories* [anon.]. SOURCE T & B, 2354. LOCATION D, NUC, InND Loeber coll.

New York: G. Munro, 1885 (as *A passive crime and other stories*; Seaside Library). LOCATION NUC. COMMENTARY *Leipzig 1885 and New York* edns under title of *A passive crime and other stories* A selection from *A maiden all forlorn, and other stories* (London, 1885, 3 vols.) [RL].

Philadelphia: J.B. Lippincott & Co., 1885. LOCATION NUC.

COMMENTARY London new edn Contents: 'A maiden all forlorn', 'Moonshine and marguerites', 'A passive crime', 'Zara', 'Vivienne', 'A fit of the blues', 'Monica' (earlier published in New York [1883]), 'Dr. Ball', 'Barbara', 'One New Year's eve', 'Nurse Eva', 'A rose distill'd' (earlier published in *Monica, and A rose distill'd*, New York, 1883). The Philadelphia edn contains eight stories, while the New York edn contains four stories [NUC; Topp].

H418 *Mildred Trevanion* (by 'The Duchess').

New York: G. Munro, [1885] (Seaside Library). LOCATION NUC.

H419 *Dick's sweetheart* (by 'The Duchess').

New York: G. Munro, 1885 (Seaside Library). LOCATION NUC.

New York: G.W. Lovell, [1885] (Lovell's Library). LOCATION NUC.

+ London: Smith, Elder & Co., 1886, 3 vols. (*Green pleasure and grey grief* [anon.]). SOURCE Wolff, 3424. LOCATION D (1886 edn, 1 vol.), L.

London: Smith, Elder & Co., 1886 (new edn; (*Green pleasure and grey grief*). LOCATION NUC.

+ Leipzig: Bernard Tauchnitz, 1886, 2v in 1 (*Green pleasure and grey grief*). SOURCE T & B, 2384. LOCATION NUC, InND Loeber coll.

Philadelphia: J.B. Lippincott & Co., 1891 (as *O tender Dolores*). LOCATION NUC.

COMMENTARY A story of love and legitimacy set in England. Dolores has been brought up by her aunt to believe that she is an orphan, although the aunt understood that she had been born out-of-wedlock. Dick Bouverie, who lives on a neighbouring estate, falls in love with Dolores. She reciprocates his feelings. However, Dick's mother learns from a relative that the girl was born out-of-wedlock. When Dolores hears the story, she flees her home and while travelling falls sick. She is taken in by a kindly gentleman who, it transpires, is her real father and who had been married to her mother. Not only can she now prove proper parentage, her father happens also to be rich. Dick and Dolores are reunited [ML].

H420 *In durance vile, and other stories* (by 'The Duchess').

New York. G. Munro, 1885 (Seaside Library, No. 1986). LOCATION NUC.

New York: J.W. Lovell, [1885] (Lovell's Library, No. 530). LOCATION NUC.

New York: G. Munro, [1887] (as *In an evil hour, and other stories*; Seaside Library). LOCATION NUC.

COMMENTARY *New York [1887] edn* Contains a subset of the stories [RL].

Philadelphia: J.B. Lippincott & Co., 1885. LOCATION NUC.

Philadelphia: J.B. Lippincott & Co., 1889 (as *"Jerry", and other stories* [anon.]). LOCATION NUC.

COMMENTARY *Philadelphia 1889 edn* Consists of a subset of the stories [RL; NUC].

London: Ward & Downey, 1889, 3 vols. SOURCE Alston, p. 8. LOCATION L, NUC.

London: Ward & Downey, 1890 (new edn). SOURCE Wolff, 3426; OCLC. LOCATION KU-S.

Leipzig: Bernard Tauchnitz, 1889. SOURCE T & B, 2597. LOCATION Dt, NUC.

COMMENTARY The London, 1889, 3 volume edn has eleven stories. Contents: 'In durance vile', 'The haunted chamber', 'The haunted chamber, continued', '"Jerry"', 'In an evil hour', 'The last resource', '"On trial"', '"On trial", continued', '"None so blind"', '"That night in June"', 'Fortune's wheel', '"As it fell upon a day"', 'Ugly Barrington'. Contents of New York, Lovell edn: 'In durance vile', 'Dr. Ball', 'A fit of the blues'. The Philadelphia edn contains five stories only. The New York (Lovell) edn has three stories only [NUC; Topp 3, p. 208].

H421 *Lady Valworth's diamonds* [anon.].

London: Ward & Downey, 1886. SOURCE Topp 8, 15. LOCATION D (n.d. edn), Dt ([*c*.1900] edn), L.

Leipzig: Bernard Tauchnitz, 1887. SOURCE T & B, 2480. LOCATION NUC.

New York. G. Munro, 1886 (Seaside Library Pocket Edition, No. 875). LOCATION NUC.

New York: J.W. Lovell, [1886] (by 'The Duchess'; Lovell's Library). LOCATION NUC.

Philadelphia: J.B. Lippincott & Co., 1886 (by 'The Duchess'). SOURCE Topp 8, 15; LOCATION NUC (1887 edn).

COMMENTARY Philadelphia edn also contains 'The haunted chamber' [Topp 8, 15].

+ Chicago: M.A. Donohue, n.d. (by 'The Duchess'; 'Lady Walworth's [*sic*] Diamonds' on spine). LOCATION InND Loeber coll.

COMMENTARY A story of deceit, gambling and thievery set in England. Granit Boyle is engaged to be married to his cousin Millicent Gray. He leads a double life, however, and his gambling leads him to steal his mother's and Millicent's jewels. Millicent has a friend, Nadine, who teaches her German. Unbeknownst to Millicent, Granit is trying to get Nadine to agree to be his wife. The plot unravels when Nadine innocently wears a jewel from the set that Granit had stolen. When Granit realizes that all is lost, he shoots himself [ML].

H422 *Ugly Barrington* (by 'The Duchess').
New York: G. Munro, 1886. SOURCE OCLC. LOCATION DCL.
COMMENTARY First published in *In durance vile, and other stories* (New York, 1885) [RL].

H423 *The haunted chamber. A novel* (by 'The Duchess').
New York: J.W. Lovell, [1886] (Lovell's Library). LOCATION NUC.
New York: G. Munro, [1886] (Seaside Library). LOCATION NUC.

H424 *Lady Branksmere* (by 'The Duchess').
London: Smith, Elder & Co., 1886, 3 vols. SOURCE Wolff, 3427. LOCATION L, NUC.
London: Smith, Elder & Co., 1887 (new edn). SOURCE Topp 5, p. 261; COPAC. LOCATION Univ. of Manchester.
Leipzig: Bernard Tauchnitz, 1887, 2 vols. SOURCE T & B, 2457. LOCATION NUC.
New York: J.W. Lovell, [1886] (Lovell's Library, No. 721). SOURCE Topp 5, p. 261. LOCATION NUC.
New York: George Munro, [1886] (Seaside Library Pocket Edition, No. 733). SOURCE Topp 5, p. 262; OCLC. LOCATION NN.
Philadelphia: J.B. Lippincott & Co., 1886. LOCATION NUC.
COMMENTARY First serialized in Munro's *New York Monthly Fashion Bazar* (Dec. 1885–Apr. 1886) [Topp 5, p. 262].

H425 *A mental struggle. A novel* [anon.].
London: Ward & Downey, 1886, 3 vols. SOURCE Topp 3, pp 210–11; Topp 8, 53. LOCATION L.
+ London: Chatto & Windus, 1892 (new edn). SOURCE Topp 3, pp 210–11; Wolff, 3434. LOCATION D, Dt.
Leipzig: Bernard Tauchnitz, 1886, 2 vols. SOURCE T & B, 2408. LOCATION NUC.
New York. G. Munro Sons, 1886 (by 'The Duchess'; Seaside Library Pocket Edition, No. 771). SOURCE Topp 3, pp 210–11. LOCATION NUC.
New York: John W. Lovell, [1886] (by 'The Duchess'; Lovell's Library, No. 735). SOURCE Topp 3, pp 210–11. LOCATION NUC.
Philadelphia: J.B. Lippincott & Co., 1886 (by 'The Duchess'). LOCATION NUC.

H426 *A life's remorse. A novel* [anon.].
Philadelphia: Crawford & Co., 1887 (by 'The Duchess'; The Sea Shore Library). LOCATION NUC.
London: F.V. White, 1890, 3 vols. SOURCE Wolff, 3429; Topp 7, 165. LOCATION L, NUC.
Leipzig: Bernard Tauchnitz, 1890, 2 vols. in 1. SOURCE T & B, 2632. LOCATION NUC.
New York: G. Munro, [1889] (by 'The Duchess'; Seaside Library). LOCATION NUC.

H427 *The Duchess* [anon.].
New York. G. Munro, [1887] (Seaside Library). LOCATION NUC.
New York: J.W. Lovell, [1887] (Lovell's Library). LOCATION NUC.
+ Chicago: M.A. Donohue & Co., n.d. (by 'The Duchess'; Modern Authors' Library, No. 515). LOCATION InND Loeber coll.
Philadelphia: J.B. Lippincott & Co., 1887. LOCATION NUC.
London: Hurst & Blackett, [1888]. SOURCE Alston, p. 8 (1889 edn); OCLC. LOCATION L, NUC.
Leipzig: Bernard Tauchnitz, [1891]. SOURCE T & B, 2721. LOCATION NUC.

H428 *A modern Circe* [anon.] (dedicated to Alys).
+ London: Ward & Downey, 1887, 3 vols. SOURCE Brown 2, 657; Topp 8, 81.
LOCATION D (1887, 2nd edn), L, NUC (1888 edn).
London: Chatto & Windus, 1892 (new edn). SOURCE Wolff, 3435. LOCATION Dt.
Leipzig: Bernard Tauchnitz, 1888, 2 vols. SOURCE T & B, 2497. LOCATION NUC.
New York: George Munro, 1887 (Seaside Library Pocket Edition, No. 1016). SOURCE
Topp 8, 81.
COMMENTARY *New York, Munro edn* No copy located [RL].
New York: J.W. Lovell, [1887] (by 'The Duchess'; Lovell's Library). LOCATION NUC.
Philadelphia: J.B. Lippincott & Co., 1887 (Series of Select Novels, No. 76). SOURCE
Topp 8, 81. LOCATION NUC.
COMMENTARY Mrs Dundas, beautiful, heartless and fatally attractive, is 'a modern Circe'. She
deliberately seduces Lord Varley, a former admirer, but now married. Her husband discovers
the double adultery and shoots Varley and then himself, while Donna Dundas, who is pres-
ent, loses her mind. Combined with this sordid tragedy are the commonplace chronicles of
Constantia and her various admirers [Brown 2].

H429 *Under-currents* [anon.].
+ London: Smith, Elder & Co., 1888, 3 vols. SOURCE Wolff, 3443. LOCATION D, L,
NUC, InND Loeber coll.
London: Smith, Elder & Co., 1889 (new edn). SOURCE Topp 5, p. 268. LOCATION L.
Leipzig: Bernard Tauchnitz, 1889, 2 vols. SOURCE T & B, 2574. LOCATION NUC.
New York. George Munro, [1888] (by 'The Duchess'; Seaside Library Pocket Edition,
No. 1123). SOURCE Topp 5, p. 268. LOCATION NUC.
New York: John Lovell, [1888] (Lovell's Library, No. 1224). SOURCE Topp 5, p. 268;
OCLC. LOCATION Univ. of Wisconsin, Milwaukee (1892 edn).
Philadelphia: J.B. Lippincott & Co., 1888 (Lippincott's Series of Select Novels).
LOCATION NUC.
COMMENTARY A story of deception and romance first serialized in *Belgravia* (London, begin-
ning Jan. 1888). Set in England, the story opens with two girls, who have recently become
orphans, being conveyed to their uncle's house. The uncle is a miser and the girls lead a very
restricted life in his home. One of them manages to escape now and then into the woods,
where she strikes up a friendship with a young man. The uncle's plan is to marry the eldest
girl to his son, who is very willing, but the girl is not. The reason for this plan is that the
uncle had cheated his brother out of the inheritance, so that estate should have been the girl's
property. The son finds out the truth about the inheritance and makes it known to the girls,
thereby reducing himself to relative poverty. Eventually, the heiress admits that she loves the
son, and both girls marry the one they love [ML; Topp].

H430 *Marvel* [anon.].
London: Ward & Downey, 1888, 3 vols. SOURCE Topp 8, 89. LOCATION Dt, L,
NUC.
London: Chatto & Windus, 1892 (new edn). SOURCE Wolff, 3433. LOCATION Univ. of
Manchester.
Leipzig: Bernard Tauchnitz, 1888, 2 vols. SOURCE T & B, 2517. LOCATION NUC.
New York: J.W. Lovell, [1888] (by 'The Duchess'; Lovell's Library, No. 1136).
LOCATION NUC.
New York: M.J. Ivers, 1888. SOURCE Topp 3, p. 210.
Chicago, New York: Rand, McNally & Co., 1888. SOURCE Topp 3, p. 210.
Philadelphia: J.B. Lippincott & Co., 1888 (by 'The Duchess'; Series of Select Novels,
No. 83). SOURCE Topp 3, p. 210. LOCATION NUC.

COMMENTARY No copies of the New York Ivers edn and the Chicago Rand edn located. First serialized in the *New York Fashion Bazaar* (beginning Dec. 1887) [Topp; RL].

H431 *The Honble. Mrs. Vereker. A novel* [anon.].

+ London: F.V. White & Co., 1888, 2 vols. SOURCE Alston, p. 8; Jarndyce cat. 94/574; Wolff, 3425 (1889 edn); Topp 7, 188. LOCATION D (1889 edn), L, InND Loeber coll. (1889 edn).

Leipzig: Bernard Tauchnitz, 1888. SOURCE T & B, 2551. LOCATION NUC.

New York: George Munro, 1888 (Seaside Library Pocket Edition, No. 1103). SOURCE Top 7, 118.

New York: J.W. Lovell, [1880?] (by 'The Duchess'). LOCATION NUC.

Philadelphia: J.B. Lippincott & Co., 1888 (by 'The Duchess'; Series of Select Novels, No. 87). SOURCE Topp 7, 118. LOCATION NUC.

+ New York: International Book Co., n.d. (by 'The Duchess', as *The Honorable Mrs. Vereker*, Columbus Series, with quote from Thomas Carlyle on cover). LOCATION InND Loeber coll.

Chicago: T.S. Denison, 1888. SOURCE Topp 7, 118.

COMMENTARY No copies of the New York Munro edn and the Chicago edn located. St John, aged 29, returns to his estate in England after an absence of ten years. One of the people he meets is Mrs Vereker, who he remembers as Sissy, a school-fellow's sister. She is now married to an odious person, who more or less bought off her father. St John falls in love with Mrs Vereker. She is physically abused by her husband who in the end is murdered by a disgruntled tenant. For a while the suspicion rests on St John, but his name is cleared. Mrs Vereker goes abroad to forget about her husband, but also to forget about St John. When she returns, she realizes that her feelings for St John have not changed and they marry [ML].

H432 *A troublesome girl. A novel* [anon.].

+ London: F.V. White & Co., 1889. SOURCE Alston, p. 9. LOCATION L.

+ Leipzig: Bernard Tauchnitz, 1889. SOURCE T & B, 2605. LOCATION D, NUC.

New York. G. Munro, 1889 (Seaside Library). LOCATION NUC.

New York: F.F. Lovell & Co., [1889] (by 'The Duchess'; as *A troublesome girl and other stories*; Lovell's Library). LOCATION NUC.

COMMENTARY The New York, Lovell edn, consists of works by several authors [NUC].

H433 *A born coquette* (by Mrs Hungerford).

+ London: Spencer Blackett, 1890, 3 vols. SOURCE Wolff, 3421. LOCATION D (n.d. edn), L, NUC, InND Loeber coll.

Leipzig: Bernard Tauchnitz, 1891, 2 vols. SOURCE T & B, 2699. LOCATION NUC.

New York: J.W. Lovell, [1890] (by 'The Duchess'; Lovell's International Series). LOCATION NUC.

COMMENTARY A romance set in Co. Cork. Nan Delaney, the eldest daughter of a impecunious and withdrawn gentleman, is a flirt and has several lovers in tow. The neighbouring estate is inherited by Mr Hume, who also falls in love with Nan, and is intent on marrying her. Mr Hume and Nan go for a sail but a terrible storm cripples the boat and they have to make for the English coast. Mr Hume tells Nan that the way to prevent shame and being gossiped about is to marry him instantly. When she is made to see the truth of his words, she assents but tells him that she will never love him. She sticks to this for quite a while and takes up flirting with her old lovers until in the end she comes to recognize the worth of her husband [ML].

H434 *April's lady. A novel* (by 'The Duchess').

New York: J.W. Lovell, [1890]; Lovell's International Series, No. 90). LOCATION NUC.

New York: George Munro, [1890] (Seaside Library Pocket Edition, No. 1363). SOURCE Topp 3, p. 263; OCLC. LOCATION Bowling Green State Univ., OH.

+ London: F.V. White & Co., 1891, 3 vols. (by Mrs Hungerford). SOURCE Wolff, 3419; Topp 7, 160. LOCATION D (1891 edn, 1 vol.), L.

London: Chatto & Windus, 1899 (new edn). SOURCE Topp 3, p. 263; COPAC. LOCATION Univ. of Liverpool.

Leipzig: Heinemann & Balestier, 1891, 2 vols. LOCATION NUC.

H435   *A little rebel* (by 'The Duchess').

New York: J.W. Lovell, 1890 (Lovell's Westminster Series, No. 32). SOURCE Topp 7, 149.

+ London: F.V. White & Co., 1891. SOURCE Alston, p. 8; Topp 7, 149. LOCATION L. LOCATION NUC.

H436   *Her last throw. A novel* (by 'The Duchess').

+ London: F.V. White & Co., 1890. SOURCE Alston, p. 8; Topp 7, 128. LOCATION L.

Leipzig: Heinemann & Balestier, 1891 (as *Her last throw, and A little rebel*). LOCATION NUC.

New York: J.W. Lovell, [1890] (Lovell's Westminster Series). LOCATION NUC.

+ New York: J.S. Ogilvy, n.d. (The Dora Thorne Series, No. 34; see Plate 40). LOCATION InND Loeber coll.

New York: George Munro, 1890 (Seaside Library Pocket Edition, No. 1453). SOURCE Topp 7, 128.

+ Cleveland (OH): Arthur Westbrook, n.d. (published with *The moment after* by Robert Buchanan§; ill. cover). LOCATION InND Loeber coll.

COMMENTARY No copy of the New York Munro edn located. Consists of a love story set among the gentry in England [ML].

H437   *A little Irish girl, and other stories* (by 'The Duchess').

+ London: Henry & Co., 1891 (with portrait of the author; The Whitefriars Library of Wit and Humour). SOURCE Brown, 787; Wolff, 3430. LOCATION L, NUC, InND Loeber coll.

+ Leipzig: Heinemann & Balestier, 1891 (The English Library). LOCATION D, NUC.

+ New York: M.J. Ivers & Co., n.d. (American Series). LOCATION D.

+ New York: F.M. Lupton, n.d. LOCATION InND Loeber coll.

Philadelphia: J.B. Lippincott & Co., 1891 (Lippincott Select Novels). LOCATION NUC.

COMMENTARY Contents: 'A little Irish girl', 'When we two parted', 'Sans-culotte', 'Two to a quarrel', 'A wrong turning', 'Dan Cupid'. All are love stories; only the first story has Irish content [ML].

H438   *Nor wife nor maid. A novel* (by Mrs Hungerford).

New York: Hovendon, 1891. LOCATION NUC.

London: William Heinemann, 1892, 3 vols. SOURCE Alston, p. 8; Sutherland, p. 313; Wolff, 3437 (1893 edn). LOCATION D (1894 edn), L.

H439   *Lady Patty. A sketch* (by Mrs Hungerford).

London: F.V. White & Co., 1892. SOURCE Alston, p. 8; Wolff, 3428 (1894, 3rd edn); Topp 7, 210. LOCATION D (2nd edn), L, InND Loeber coll. (London, Collins' Clear-Type Press, n.d. edn).

Leipzig: Heinemann & Balestier, 1892 (The English Library). LOCATION NUC.

Philadelphia: J.B. Lippincott & Co., 1892 (by 'The Duchess'; Series of Select Novels). SOURCE Topp 3, p. 247. LOCATION NUC.

COMMENTARY First serialized in *Lippincott's Monthly Magazine* (Philadelphia, 1891). A story of a socially ambitious mother, who plots to have her daughter married to Sir Rufus Greyly, an unlovable character. The daughter refuses and is afraid that her mother will be terribly disappointed that she has chosen to marry Lord Vysely. However, the mother is more than pleased that her daughter has been able to improve on the social position that she would have had, had she married Sir Rufus [ML].

H440 *A conquering heroine* (by Mrs Hungerford).
+ London: F.V. White & Co., 1892. SOURCE Alston, p. 8; Topp 7, 180. LOCATION L, InND Loeber coll.
Leipzig: Bernard Tauchnitz, 1893 (as *A conquering heroine, and "When in doubt"*). SOURCE T & B, 2903. LOCATION NUC.
New York: Tait Sons & Co., [1892] (by 'The Duchess'). LOCATION NUC.
COMMENTARY 102pp [RL].

H441 *The O'Connors of Ballinahinch* (by Mrs Hungerford; dedicated to her cousin Mary Hamilton).
New York: Hovendon, 1892. LOCATION NUC.
New York: J.W. Lovell, [1892]. LOCATION NUC.
+ London: William Heinemann, 1893. SOURCE Brown, 788 (1896 edn). LOCATION D, Dt, L.
Leipzig: Heinemann & Balestier, 1893. LOCATION NUC.
COMMENTARY A story of love and marriage among the landed classes set in Co. Cork [Brown].

H442 *Nora Creina. A novel* (by Mrs Hungerford; dedicated to Mary Hamilton).
New York: Hovendon, 1892 (by 'The Duchess'; Metropolitan Series, No. 11). SOURCE Topp 3, p. 259. LOCATION NUC.
+ London: F.V. White & Co., 1893, 3 vols. SOURCE Alston, p. 8; Brown, 789 (1903 edn); Wolff, 3438 (1894 edn); Topp 7, 217. LOCATION D, L, InND Loeber coll (1894 edn).
London: Chatto & Windus, 1898 (new edn). SOURCE Topp 3, p. 259. LOCATION L.
Leipzig: Bernard Tauchnitz, 1893, 2 vols. SOURCE T & B, 2916-17. LOCATION NUC.
COMMENTARY A love story set in the south of Ireland, where two sisters live with their miserly and mean stepfather who thwarts the progress of their love affairs. One of the girls, Nora, has made a bad choice. Her lover cheats on her and in the end makes her extremely unhappy. Another man who has watched over her and is in love with her, proposes to marry her. She accepts for the wrong reasons. In the end she learns to love him and thoroughly rejects her former scoundrel-lover [ML].

H443 *A mad prank. A novel* (by Mrs Hungerford; dedicated to Jessie Rouse).
London: F.V. White & Co., 1893. SOURCE Alston, p. 8; Topp 7, 202; COPAC. LOCATION L.
Leipzig: Bernard Tauchnitz, 1893 (as *A mad prank and other stories*). SOURCE T & B, 2936. LOCATION NUC.
New York: J.A. Taylor & Co., 1893 (by 'The Duchess'; as *A mad prank*; Mayflower Series, No. 12). SOURCE Topp 7, 202. LOCATION NUC.

H444 *The red-house mystery. A novel* (by Mrs Hungerford).
London: Chatto & Windus, 1893, 2 vols. SOURCE Alston, p. 9; Sutherland, p. 313. LOCATION L.
Leipzig: Bernard Tauchnitz, 1894. SOURCE T & B, 2979. LOCATION NUC.
Chicago, New York: Rand McNally, 1894 (by 'The Duchess'; Rialto Series, No. 62). LOCATION NUC.

H445 *Lady Verner's flight. A novel* (by 'The Duchess').
London: Chatto & Windus, 1893, 2 vols. SOURCE Daims, 1487; COPAC. LOCATION L.
London: Chatto, Windus & Co., 1893 (new edn). SOURCE COPAC. LOCATION NUC, InND Loeber coll. (1895 edn).

Leipzig: Bernard Tauchnitz, 1893. SOURCE T & B, 2879. LOCATION NUC.

New York: J.A. Taylor, 1893 (Broadway Series). SOURCE Daims, 1487. LOCATION NUC.

H446 *The hoyden. A novel* (by Mrs Hungerford).

Philadelphia: J.B. Lippincott & Co., 1893 (by 'The Duchess'). SOURCE Daims, 1486. LOCATION NUC.

London: W. Heinemann, 1894, 3 vols. SOURCE NUC; COPAC. LOCATION D (1901 edn), L (1894 edn), NUC (1894 edn).

Leipzig: Bernard Tauchnitz, 1894, 2 vols. SOURCE T & B, 2956. LOCATION NUC.

H447 *An unsatisfactory lover. A novel* (by Mrs Hungerford).

+ London: F.V. White & Co., 1894. SOURCE Wolff, 3444 (1895, 2nd edn); Topp 7, 238. LOCATION D, Dt, L, NUC.

+ Leipzig: Bernard Tauchnitz, 1894 (as *An unsatisfactory lover*). SOURCE T & B, 3010. LOCATION NUC, InND Loeber coll.

COMMENTARY First serialized in *Lippincott's Monthly Magazine* (Philadelphia, 1893). A love story set in Ireland. The eldest daughter of an impoverished family battles after her parents' death to keep the country house in her hands. Poverty and pride separate her and her lover. However, she becomes an heiress, and eventually the lovers are united [ML; Topp 3, p. 251].

H448 *Peter's wife. A novel* (by Mrs Hungerford).

London: F.V. White & Co., 1894, 3 vols. SOURCE Topp 7, 277. LOCATION NUC, InND Loeber coll. (1895 edn).

London: Chatto & Windus, 1899 (new edn). SOURCE Topp 3, p. 264.

Leipzig: Heinemann & Balestier, 1891, 2 vols. LOCATION NUC.

Leipzig: Bernard Tauchnitz, 1895, 2 vols. SOURCE T & B, 3029–30. LOCATION NUC.

Philadelphia: J.B. Lippincott & Co., 1894 (by 'The Duchess'; Series of Select Novels, No. 161). LOCATION NUC.

COMMENTARY No copy of the London, Chatto edn located. A society romance set in England about a girl, Nell, who is left in the charge of a young guardian, Peter Wortley. Nell is not happy about having a guardian and often disagrees with him. However, in time they fall in love and eventually marry [ML].

H449 *A tug of war. A novel* (by Mrs Hungerford).

+ London: F.V. White & Co., 1895. SOURCE Topp 7, 301. LOCATION D, Dt, L, InND Loeber coll.

+ Leipzig: Bernard Tauchnitz, 1895. SOURCE T & B, 3079. LOCATION NUC, InND Loeber coll.

+ New York: The Federal Book Co., n.d. (as *A tug of war*). LOCATION InND Loeber coll.

COMMENTARY A novel of family conflict set in Ireland where a landowner, O'Neill, has three grandchildren. O'Neill hates his grandson Denis, who is his heir, and plans to leave him as little as possible. He also hates his granddaughter Ellen. He favours his grandson Strangford and he wishes Ellen to marry her cousin Strangford. Strangford encourages some peasants about to be evicted by O'Neill to kill O'Neill, but they do so before he has made a new will in Strangford's favour. Strangford sets the peasants to pursue the fleeing Denis and Ellen. Denis and Ellen spend a night in a cave but because they are unescorted, tongues in the neighbourhood wag. Denis wants to marry Ellen but she feels her name is besmirched and cannot allow Denis to marry her. Eventually, a duchess comes to the rescue and declares Ellen a hero, which stops the gossip. Strangford tries to get the peasants to kill Denis and Ellen. However, one of the peasants sees through him, kills Strangford and then commits suicide [ML].

H450 *Only an Irish girl* (by 'The Duchess').
New York: Hurst, 1895. SOURCE OCLC. LOCATION Bowling Green State Univ., OH.
+ New York: Hurst & Co., n.d. (Arlington Edition; in anthology, *Barbara's fortune by Burdette and other stories*, which includes 'Only an Irish girl'). LOCATION InND Loeber coll.

COMMENTARY The title story may allude to Horatio Alger's§ *Only an Irish boy* (Chicago, [*c*.1894]). The volume also contains some poetry and 'The mystery of a mining town', which are by other authors [RL].

H451 *Molly darling and other stories* (by Mrs Hungerford).
+ London: T. Fisher Unwin, 1895 (The Autonym Library). SOURCE Jarndyce cat. 94/577; COPAC. LOCATION D, L, NUC, InND Loeber coll.
Philadelphia: J.B. Lippincott & Co., 1895 (by 'The Duchess'). LOCATION NUC.

COMMENTARY Contents: '"Molly darling"', 'Good dog, then!', 'Romeo and Juliet', '"Was it a spirit?"', 'A false conclusion', 'A hasty judgment', 'Lady Blackmore's deliverance', 'Nellie's dilemma' [ML].

H452 *The professor's experiment. A novel* (by Mrs Hungerford).
London: Chatto & Windus, 1895, 3 vols. SOURCE Wolff, 3441; COPAC. LOCATION L, NUC.
London: Chatto & Windus, 1896 (new edn). SOURCE Topp 3, pp 255–6 (1898 edn); COPAC. LOCATION Dt.
+ Leipzig: Bernard Tauchnitz, 1896, 2 vols. in 1. SOURCE T & B, 3102. LOCATION NUC, InND Loeber coll.
New York: R.F. Fenno & Co., [1895]. LOCATION NUC.

COMMENTARY Serialized through the Tillotson's syndicate. A romance set in Ireland. A professor has developed a potion that will put people in suspended animation and needs to find a subject on whom to experiment. While he is discussing this with a former pupil, Paul Wyndham, his butler brings in a girl, Ella, he found in the street. She is very depressed and wishes to die. She agrees to be the subject for the experiment in the hope that it will fail and she will die. But while the experiment is in progress, the professor dies and leaves Ella in Wyndham's care. He tells his servant to take Ella away to a safe place, which the servant understands to be Wyndham's cottage. Wyndham is upset because it is hard to explain what a single female is doing in his cottage. Ella does not stir from the cottage because she is afraid of the man in whose house she lived before who wanted to marry her. Complications arise because people start to talk. Eventually, Wyndham falls in love with Ella and they marry [ML; Law, p. 89].

H453 *The three graces. A novel* (by Mrs Hungerford).
London: Chatto & Windus, 1895, 2 vols. SOURCE Alston, p. 9; COPAC. LOCATION D (1896 edn), L, NUC.
London: Chatto & Windus, 1897 (new edn). SOURCE Topp 3, p. 250. LOCATION Univ. of Manchester.
+ Leipzig: Bernard Tauchnitz, 1895. SOURCE T & B, 3065. LOCATION NUC, InND Loeber coll.
Philadelphia: J.B. Lippincott & Co., 1895 (by 'The Duchess'; ill. Maria L. Kirk). LOCATION NUC.

COMMENTARY The romantic adventures of three daughters of a widower and their quests for husbands, set in England. A cousin, O'Grady of Ballyclash in Ireland, plays a main role [ML].

H454 *A point of conscience* [anon.].
Philadelphia: J.B. Lippincott & Co., 1895. LOCATION NUC.
London: Chatto & Windus, 1896, 3 vols. SOURCE Wolff, 3439. LOCATION L, NUC.

+ Leipzig: Bernard Tauchnitz, 1896, 2 vols. in l. SOURCE T & B, 3117. LOCATION NUC, InND Loeber coll.

COMMENTARY Set in England, the story of Richie and Carrie, two poor cousins who are very good friends and encourage each other to marry uncongenial suitors to end their poverty. In the end, Richie comes into money and marries his cousin [ML].

H455 *A lonely girl* (by Mrs. Hungerford).

+ London: Downey & Co., 1896. SOURCE Alston, p. 9; Topp 8, 197. LOCATION L.

+ Leipzig: Bernard Tauchnitz, 1897. SOURCE T & B, 3188. LOCATION D, NUC, InND Loeber coll.

Philadelphia: J.B. Lippincott & Co., 1896 (as *A lonely maid* by the 'Duchess'; Lippincott's Select Novels, No. 186). SOURCE Topp 8, 197. LOCATION NUC, InND Loeber coll. (1901 edn).

COMMENTARY A romance set at Carrig Castle in the wilds of Carrigmahon in Ireland. The rather unpleasant owner, Sir Lucien Adare, has descended upon the castle with several relatives in quest of some priceless family jewels that disappeared at the death of his sister, who had married a mill owner. He has ignored the existence of his sister's daughter. However, Capt. Adare, Sir Lucien's heir, falls in love with her. Only after the mystery of the jewels is resolved can they marry [ML].

H456 *The coming of Chloe. A novel* (by Mrs Hungerford).

+ London: F.V. White & Co., 1897. LOCATION Dt (1898 edn), L, InND Loeber coll. (1898 edn).

+ Leipzig: Bernard Tauchnitz, 1897. SOURCE T & B, 3239. LOCATION D, NUC.

Philadelphia: J.B. Lippincott & Co., 1897. LOCATION NUC.

COMMENTARY A story of romance and intrigue involving Chloe, who comes to live in an Irish village with the Fitzgeralds, a mother and a daughter, who are hard up. Chloe has been recommended to them by a relative and the two hundred pounds she offers for the six months she will stay is very welcome. Chloe has actually run away from her titled husband, who has treated her abominably. The book abounds with love intrigues and in the end practically all major characters are about to marry their loved ones [ML].

H457 *An anxious moment etc.* (by Mrs Hungerford).

+ London: Chatto & Windus, 1897. SOURCE Alston, p. 8. LOCATION D (1897, 2nd edn), L, NUC (1897, 2nd edn).

COMMENTARY Contents: 'An anxious moment', 'Poor little Cinderella', 'Miss Saville of Thorby Hall', 'In great distress', 'A lucky ghost hunt', 'Storm-driven', 'A terrible mistake', 'Her first situation', 'A chance meeting', 'How I write my novels' [ML].

H458 *Lovice* (by Mrs Hungerford; dedicated to Lady Emily Barnard).

+ London: Chatto & Windus, 1897. LOCATION D (1904 edn), Dt, L, InND Loeber coll.

Leipzig: Bernard Tauchnitz, 1897. SOURCE T & B, 3210. LOCATION NUC.

Philadelphia: J.B. Lippincott & Co., 1897. LOCATION NUC.

COMMENTARY A story of misplaced love involving Lovice, who is engaged to a Capt. Lambert. He asks her to keep the engagement secret because he has expectations of inheritance from an uncle and does not want to upset him by his engagement. Lambert is a cad who throws over Lovice when it seems he will not inherit from his uncle. He then proposes to a rich, but ugly heiress. Lovice accepts the offer of marriage from a faithful friend. However, she pines away and dies with Lambert's name on her lips [ML].

HUNT, Kathleen. See CAFFYN, Kathleen Mannington.

HUNTER, Anna Maria. See **HUNTER, Mrs Maria Susanna.**

HUNTER, Mrs Maria Susanna (née Cooper; also known as Mrs Hunter and **Maria Hunter**), fl. 1792. Actress and novelist, there is some dispute over this author's first name: the publisher William Lane refers to her in an advertisement of 1792 as Anna Maria Hunter. MSH first appeared on the London stage at Covent Garden in 1774 and continued to perform until 1799, if not later. She made at least one trip to act in Ireland, in 1775, first performing at the Theatre Royal in Smock Alley, Dublin, and subsequently in Cork. The theatre historian Tate Wilkinson saw her perform in Doncaster in 1777 and described her as 'a woman of great good-breeding, sense, and conviviality, and knew how to *dissect* with a grace and point', but he also said that her memory on the stage was not to be depended on, 'and was a great bar to her stage success' (Wilkinson, i, p. 276). She started writing after her career as an actress was on the wane. MSH wrote her dedication to *Fitzroy* (London, 1792) from Great Tichfield Street, Portland Place, London, in which she stated that her goal was to give, in contrast to contemporary novels, 'a true and useful picture of human life'. She was the mistress of Gen. John Hayes St Leger (born at Grangemellon, Co. Kildare), from at least 1777 onward, and accompanied him to the West Indies where he was posted as a commandant in about 1781. MSH returned to England and published several novels under the name of Maria Hunter. Her novels indicate a knowledge of classical learning. SOURCE Allibone, i, p. 922; W.S. Clark, *The Irish stage in the county towns*, Oxford, 1965, p. 362; C.B. Hogan, *The London stage 1660–1800*, Carbondale, 1968, p. 5, 213; R.D. Hume (ed.), *The London theatre world 1660–1800*, Carbondale (IL), 1980, pp 91, 158; Raven 2, 1792:40; C. Turner, *Living by the pen* (London, 1992), p. 80; T. Wilkinson, *The wandering patentee; or, the history of the Yorkshire theatres* (York, 1795), i, p. 276.

H459 *Fitzroy; or, impulse of the moment. A novel* (by Maria Hunter; dedicated to John Doyle, MP, major of the late 105th Regiment, secretary to the prince of Wales)[2].
+ London: William Lane, 1792, 2 vols. SOURCE ESTC t129871; Raven 2, 1792:40; Blakey, p. 159; Hardy, p. 90; Forster 2, 2122. LOCATION L, C, MH, InND Loeber coll.

COMMENTARY A story of the adventures in Ireland and England of George Fitzroy. On the demise of his merchant father, George's uncle became executor of the estate. Although the uncle is prosperous, he appropriated most of the money for himself, and assigned very little yearly to the widow and her son. This forces George to seek his fortune in the world. When the story begins, George is arriving in Dublin on the Roscra [Roscrea] stagecoach. He is on his way to London to go to the Temple Bar. However, he meets with various adventures in Dublin, in one of which he is duped by a gambler, losing all his money. He is rescued from his sorry state by a former tutor from TCD, and arrives in England where he encounters other adventures, good and bad. He meets again his earliest love, who is now a widow, and competes for her hand with his current patron. After a bout of imprisonment under false accusations, he wins the love of his lady and inherits the estate of his uncle in Ireland, to which he returns. George Fitzroy is accompanied in all his adventures by Owen, his trusty Irish servant [ML].

H460 *Ella; or, he's always in the way* (by Maria Hunter).
London: William Lane, 1798, 2 vols. SOURCE Raven 2, 1798:31; Blakey, p. 184; Forster 2, 2121; ESTC n65935. LOCATION CtY.

COMMENTARY The *Critical Review* states that the plan of this novel 'has little regularity. It seems to have been intended only as a vehicle for the introduction of characters from what

2 Later promoted to general. He was the fourth son of Charles Doyle of Bramblestown, Co. Kilkenny (DNB).

the authoress calls *nature*. Some of these, as well as the incidents, are delineated with the pen of a caricaturist; and with the exception of a few just though trite reflections on education and seduction, the moral tendency of the work is not very obvious. The character of one of the managers of our theatres is, we hope, a gross misrepresentation' [*Critical Review* (Dec. 1798)].

HUNTINGTON, J.V. See HUNTINGTON, Jedediah Vincent.

HUNTINGTON, Jedediah Vincent (known as J.V. Huntington), pseud. 'John Vincent', b. New York 1815, d. Pau (France) 1862. American physician, novelist, editor and Episcopalian clergyman, JVH converted to catholicism in 1849. He was editor of the *Leader* (Boston?), a Catholic literary and political weekly, in 1856; a contributor to *Blackwood's Magazine* (Edinburgh); the *Knickerbocker* (New York), and other periodicals, and editor of the *Metropolitan Magazine* (London). He also wrote poetry. SOURCE Allibone, i, p. 924; Allibone Suppl., ii, p. 877; Burke, p. 367; DAB.

H461   *Lady Alice, or the new Una* [anon.].
New York: D. Appleton & Co., 1849. LOCATION L (1850 edn), NUC.
+ London: Henry Colburn, 1849. LOCATION L.
COMMENTARY Irish content [CM].

H462   *Alban. A tale of the New World* [anon.].
New York: G.P. Putnam, 1851. SOURCE OCLC.
New York: Printed for the author, 1853 (as *Alban. A tale*). SOURCE NSTC. LOCATION L.
London: Henry Colburn & Co., 1851. LOCATION L.
COMMENTARY Set in New England where the characters debate the role of catholicism in Ireland [CM].

H463   *The forest* (by J.V Huntington).
New York: Redfield, 1852. SOURCE OCLC. LOCATION L.
COMMENTARY A sequel to *Alban* (New York, 1851) [OCLC].

H464   *The pretty plate* (by 'John Vincent').
New York: D. & J. Sadlier, 1852 (ill. Darley). SOURCE OCLC.
+ New York: Redfield, 1852 (ill. Darley, Whitney, Annin, Richardson, Cox). LOCATION L, InND Loeber coll.
+ London: Addey & Co., 1854 (as *The pretty plate or honesty is the best policy*). LOCATION L.
+ London: Burns & Lambert, [1861] (new edn; as *Kate Kavanagh; or, the story of a china plate*). LOCATION L.
COMMENTARY A moral tale set in New York among the descendants of Irish Catholic immigrants. Aunt Kate tells a number of her young relatives a story of her childhood, which had been made more difficult by the fact that her parents were poor and that the Catholic Irish were despised. Aunt Kate and her sister had once stolen a pretty plate from a shop, spurred on by envy of a schoolmate who owned such a plate. The stolen plate was a great bother to them because they were in constant fear of being found out. Eventually, they secretly returned it. Since her parents did not live close to a Catholic church, the children had not benefited from proper religious instruction. When they did move near a church they were prepared for holy communion. This involved going to confession and admitting to the sin of the stolen plate. Great was their relief to be truly forgiven. The moral of the story is that parents should never neglect the religious instruction of their young ones [ML].

H465   *Rosemary; or, life and death. An interesting tale* [anon.] (dedicated to 'The dearest and truest of my friends').

+ New York, Boston, Montreal: D. & J. Sadlier & Co., 1856 (ill. George G. White). SOURCE Wright, ii, 1312 (1860 edn). LOCATION L (1860 edn), Wright web.
Dublin: James Duffy, [1865 or earlier]. SOURCE advertised in *Adventures of a watch* (Dublin, [1865]).
COMMENTARY No copy of the Dublin edn located. Set in New York and concerns the work of a group of medical students, one of whom is an Irishman named O'Callaghan [RL; CM].

HUTCHINSON, Eliza. See LESLIE, Eliza.

HUTTON, Mark, fl. 1864. Novelist, MH is known for the following novel only. SOURCE BLC.
H466   *The cruise of the "Humming Bird;" or, notes near home* (by Mark Hutton; dedicated to Ralph Bernal Osborne, MP [of Newtown Anner, Co. Tipperary]).
+ London: Tinsley Bros, 1864. SOURCE Allibone Suppl., ii, p. 881. LOCATION L, InND Loeber coll.
COMMENTARY Set on the west coast of Ireland. An English travelling party sails along the coast and visits several places such as the Claddagh, near Galway, and Achill Island, off Co. Mayo. They discuss the characteristics of the Irish, the weaknesses of their priests, and the rigidity of the scripture readers and mission workers [ML].

HYDE, Douglas, pseud. 'An Craoibhín Aoibhinn', b. Kilmactranny (Co. Sligo) 1860, d. Dublin, 1949. Poet, scholar, translator and first president of the Republic of Ireland, DH was the son of the Revd Arthur Hyde, rector of Tibohine, Frenchpark (Co. Roscommon) and Elizabeth Oldfield, whose father was the Protestant rector at Castlerea (Co. Roscommon). The Hyde family descended from Elizabethan planter stock. Educated principally at home, DH developed a great love of the Irish language, which led him while still a young man to collect the oral songs and folklore of the local country people. At TCD, he studied modern literature, divinity and law brilliantly but perfunctorily, and received his LLD in 1888. His enthusiasm was for his ongoing efforts to learn as much as possible about Irish language and culture. Fluent in French and German in addition to Irish, he studied Latin, Greek and Hebrew and spent a year in 1891 as interim professor of modern languages at the University of New Brunswick, Canada. Returning to Ireland he was disappointed in his efforts to secure a university appointment and began in earnest to write and publish poetry both in Irish and English. His early Fenianism, absorbed in Co. Roscommon, was transformed into cultural nationalism and vigorous efforts to revive Irish as a spoken language. With William Butler Yeats§, John O'Leary, George Sigerson and Thomas Rolleston, he was part of the Irish Literary Revival. He published essays and poetry in the *Dublin University Review* and other periodicals; contributed – along with Yeats and Katharine Tynan§ – to *Poems and ballads of Young Ireland* (Dublin, 1888), and to Yeats's *Fairy and Folk Tales of the Irish peasantry* (London, 1888). DH's talent in translating Irish folklore and poetry into a true Anglo-Irish poetic idiom was evident in his *Leabhair sgeulaigheachta* [*Book of story-telling*] (Dublin, 1889) and in his *Love songs of Connacht* (London,1893) and was of immense significance to the nascent movement towards a Gaelic national literature. In 1892 he was elected president of the new National Literary Society and his inaugural address was on 'The necessity for de-Anglicizing Ireland'. He was a founder and president of the Gaelic League, a non-political organization the aim of which was to restore Irish as a national language, but when in 1915 the League's constitution was amended to include the idea of a free Ireland, he resigned from the presidency in protest. DH was appointed to the chair of modern Irish at University College, Dublin, in 1905. He continued his work as a folklorist, poet, translator and professor. He was also a playwright and an amateur actor and his play *Casadh an tSugáin* (trans. by Lady Gregory as *The twisting of the rope*), the first play in Irish produced in a professional theatre, was immensely popular. Among his many works is his magisterial *A literary history of Ireland from the earliest times to the present day* (London 1889). He resigned his position as professor of modern Irish at University College in 1932 and retired to Roscommon, but when the Irish Constitution was adopted in 1938 he was elected, unopposed, as the first president of the Republic of Ireland. He served until 1944. DH's papers and correspondence are in the NUI, the NLI, TCD, NYPL, Irish Folklore dept., UCD, among other places. For his portraits and papers, see ODNB. SOURCE Brooke, p. 146; Brown, p. 143; J.E. Dunleavy & C.W. Dunleavy, *Douglas Hyde: a maker of modern Ireland* (Berkeley, CA, 1991); Field Day, vs. ii & iii (which has an extensive bibliography); Hogan 2, pp 570–4; Irish pseudonyms; LVP, p. 238; NCBEL 4, pp 757–8; OCIL, pp 254–6; ODNB; O'Donoghue, p. 209; RIA/DIB; Zimmermann, pp 312–15.

H467   *Beside the fire. A collection of Irish Gaelic folk stories* (ed., trans. and annotated by Douglas Hyde; An Chraoibhín Aoibhinn; with additional notes by Alfred Nutt; dedicated 'to the memory of ... the poet-scribes and hedge-schoolmasters').
+ London: David Nutt, 1890. LOCATION BFl, NUC, InND Loeber coll. (also 1910 edn).
Dublin: Irish Academic Press, 1978 (Irish Folklore Series). SOURCE COPAC. LOCATION Dt, L.

COMMENTARY Contents: 'The tailor and the three beasts', 'Bran', 'The king of Ireland's son', 'The Alp-Luachra', 'Paudyeen O'Kelly and the weasel', 'Leeam O'Rooney's burial', 'Guleesh na Guss Dhu', 'The well of D'Yerree-in-Dowan', ' The court of Crinnawn', 'Neil O'Caree', 'Trunk-without-head', 'The hags of the long teeth', 'William of the tree', 'The old crow and the young crow', 'Riddles' [RL].

H468   *The three sorrows of story-telling and ballads of St. Columkille* (by Douglas Hyde).
London: T. Fisher Unwin, 1895. SOURCE COPAC. LOCATION Dt, L.

H469   *Five Irish stories translated from the Irish of the "Sgeuluidhe Gaodhalach"* (by Douglas Hyde).
Dublin: M.H. Gill, [1896]. SOURCE Brown 2, 664. LOCATION L, NUC.
Paris, Rennes: J. Plihon, 1901, 2 vols. in 1 (trans. by George Dottin as *Contes irlandais*). SOURCE Healy cat. 5/753; OCLC. LOCATION D, CLU.

COMMENTARY 55pp. Literal translations of five out of the ten stories: 'The priest and the bishop', 'The going of Conn among the goats', 'The knights of the tricks', 'The boy who was long on his mother', 'Hard-Gum, Strong-Ham, Swift-Foot and Eyeless-Lad'. The first story tells how a priest, on his way home after ordination, is tempted by a woman. He resists and out of spite she gets him sentenced to be hanged for theft. He vindicates his innocence and she is hanged instead. But she returns to earth and tempts him and he falls. The bishop then gives him a wholly impossible task to perform or he will lose his soul, but he manages to perform it [Brown 2].

H470   *Four Irish stories. Tales XI., XIII., XIV., XIX., translated from the "Sgeuluidhe Gaedhealach"* (by Douglas Hyde).
+ Dublin: M.H. Gill, [1902] (Gaelic League Publications). SOURCE Brown 2, 663. LOCATION UCD, InND Loeber coll., Boston College.

COMMENTARY Sequel to *Five Irish stories* (Dublin, [1896]). Literal translation of stories 'The king of the black desert', 'Coirnín of the furze', 'The bracket bull', 'John of the two sheep'. All transcribed from stories related by Connacht storytellers. In the first story, the king's son plays cards and then ball with a grey old man and has his wish for each win. When he loses he learns that the grey old man is the king of the Black Desert and that he must find out where he lives or forfeit his own head. The second story is humorous, with a spirited description of poor Coirnín's ride on a goat [Brown 2].

H471   *Legends of saints and sinners* (collected and trans. from the Irish by Douglas Hyde).
Dublin: Talbot Press, 1914 (Every Irishman's Library). LOCATION D, L.
+ London, Dublin, Belfast: The Gresham Publishing Co., [1915?] (ill. Noel L. Nisbet).
LOCATION Dt, NUC, InND Loeber coll.
London: T. Fisher Unwin, [1916]. LOCATION L, NUC.
New York: Frederick A. Stokes, [1915]. LOCATION NUC.

COMMENTARY Contents: 'St. Patrick and Crom Dubh', 'Mary's well', 'How covetousness came into the church', 'Knock Mulruana', 'The stone of truth', 'The adventures of Léithin', 'The comparison as to ages', 'The death of Bearachan', 'Story of Solomon', 'Christmas alms', 'The burial of Jesus', 'Saint Peter', 'Legends of St. Deglan', 'St. Paul's vision', 'Oscar of the flail', 'Oisin in Elphin', 'The priest who went to do penance', 'The friars of Urlaur', 'Dialogue between two old women', 'The minister and the gossoon', 'The keening of the three Marys', 'The farmer's son and the bishop', 'Shaun the tinker', 'Mary and St. Joseph and the cherry tree', 'The student who left college', 'The help of God in the road', 'The minister's son', 'The old woman of Beare', 'The old hag of Dingle', 'The poem of the Tor', 'Columcille and his brother Dobhran', 'Bruadar and Smith and Glinn', 'Friar Brian', 'How the first cat was created', 'God spare you your health', 'Teig O'Kane and the corpse', 'Tomaus O'Cahan and the ghost', 'Prayer after tobacco', 'The Buideach, the tinker, and the black donkey', 'The great worm of the Shannon', 'The poor widow and Grania Oï', 'The gambler and the branch', 'The beetle, the dhardheel, and the prumpolaun', 'The lady of the alms', 'St. Patrick and his garron', 'How Saint Moling got his name' [ML].

H472   *Sgéalta Thomáis Uí Chathasaigh: Mayo stories, told by Thomas Casey* (collected, ed., and trans. with notes by Douglas Hyde).
Dublin: Irish Text Society, 1939, 36. SOURCE NCBEL 4, p. 758. LOCATION Dt, L.

'HYLA', pseud. See **CHAPLIN, Jane Dunbar**.

I

'IGNOTUS', pseud. See FULLER, James Franklin.

'IMO', fl. 1891. Pseudonym of a social issues novelist, apparently Scottish, who wrote a supernatural novel, *Lotus: A psychological romance* (London, 1888), *A new Marguerite* (London, 1886), and the following novel. SOURCE Brick Row cat. 137/58; COPAC.
I1   *Priests and people. A no-rent romance* [anon.].
+ London: Eden, Remington & Co., 1891, 3 vols. SOURCE Brown, 84; Wolff, 7548. LOCATION D.
+ New York: Garland, 1979, 3 vols. (introd. by R.L. Wolff). LOCATION D, Dt, L.
COMMENTARY Set in Co. Kerry and in Dublin, the novel describes the 'no rent' agitation of the Land League in the 1880s. The author is fiercely hostile to the Land League and tells of a young Catholic woman who becomes a landlord and seeks to solve discontent with kindly rule [Murphy, pp 46–7; Wolff introd., p. 39].

INGELOW, Jean, b. 1820, Boston (Lincs.) d. Kensington (London) 1897. English novelist, poet and short story writer for children, JI was the daughter of William Ingelow, a banker, and Jean Kilgour, who was Scottish. Her only novel with an Irish title, considered to be her best, has little to do with Ireland. She is not known to have visited Ireland. SOURCE Allibone Suppl., ii, p. 885; Blain, p. 559; Brown, p. 144; NCBEL 4, pp 621–3; ODNB; M. Peters, *Jean Ingelow* (Ipswich, 1972); Sutherland, p. 319.
I2   *Off the Skelligs* (by Jean Ingelow).
London: Henry S. King & Co., 1872, 4 vols. SOURCE Brown, 1872 (probably mistakenly mentions a Kegan Paul, 1872, 3 vol. edn); Wolff, 3472. LOCATION L, NUC.
+ Leipzig: Bernard Tauchnitz, 1873, 3 vols. SOURCE T & B, 1293–95. LOCATION NUC, InND Loeber coll.
+ Boston: Roberts Bros, 1879. LOCATION NUC, InND Loeber coll.
COMMENTARY Concerns the fortunes of the Mortimer family, and is largely autobiographical, drawing on the author's childhood. The family's bankruptcy is followed by the father's departure for Australia to regain his fortune. There is a minor connection with Ireland in an episode near the Skellig Islands, off Waterville (Co. Kerry), when a crew that had escaped from a burning skip is rescued. JI's *Fated to be free* (London, 1875) was the sequel to *Off the Skelligs* [RL; Brown].

INGRAHAM, Joseph Holt, b. Portland (ME) 1809, d. Holly Springs (MS) 1860. American writer of adventure, religious and historical romance novels, JHI was born into a successful merchant and shipping family. He travelled aboard his grandfather's ships before he entered Yale University, where he was dismissed after a year. He settled in Natchez (MS) and taught at Jefferson College. His writing was spurred by financial pressures and from the late 1830s onward he wrote prolifically and achieved wide popularity. Unable to support his family, despite his success, he moved to Tennessee and became an Episcopalian minister. Many of his works are set in the American south, some in other countries, and several are about seafaring. Under the pseudonym 'A Yankee' he also wrote a regional study, *The South-west* (New York, 1835). SOURCE Allibone, i, p. 932; ANB; DAB; RL; Wright, i, 1255a–1366; ii, 1315–1321.

I3   *Captain Kyd; or, the wizard of the sea. A romance* [anon.].
New York: Harper & Bros, 1839, 2 vols. SOURCE Wright, i, 1273; COPAC. LOCATION
NUC.
London: T.L. Holt, 1839 (on cover: Novel Newspaper). LOCATION NUC.
COMMENTARY A sea story which starts at old Castle Cor, the home of the earl of
Bellamont in the south of Ireland [RL].

'INVISIBLE GREEN, ESQ.', fl 1856. Pseudonym of an American story writer.
I4   *Green peas picked from the path of Invisible Green Esq.*
Cincinnati: Moore, Wilstach, Keys & Overend; New York: Livermore & Rudd, 1856
(ill. John McLenan). LOCATION Wright web.
COMMENTARY Pieces from the pen of a reporter. Six of the stories set in the US have some
Irish connection in that they contain people with Irish names and who speak with a brogue
[ML].

'IOTA', pseud. See **CAFFYN, Mrs Kathleen Mannington**.

'IOTA', pseud. See **WALLER, John Francis**.

IRELAND, W.H. See **IRELAND, William Henry**.

IRELAND, William Henry (known as **W.H. Ireland**), b. London 1777, d. London 1835.
English forger, playwright, and novelist, WHI was the son of an engraver, Samuel Henry
Ireland, and Anna Maria de Burgh Coppinger. Infamous for having created forgeries pur-
porting to be works of Shakespeare (done to please his father, a collector of Shakespeariana),
WHI's own plays and novels appeared between 1800 and 1805, all published in London. Some
were Gothic and anti-Catholic in tone. He also wrote ballads and translated from French writ-
ers such as Voltaire. Only the following novel has Irish content.. SOURCE Garside, passim;
NCBEL 4, pp 373–4; ODNB.
I5   *The Catholic, an historical romance* (by W.H. Ireland).
+ London: W. Earle, 1807, 3 vols. SOURCE Belanger, 7; British Fiction; Garside,
1807:31; NCBEL 4, p. 373. LOCATION Corvey CME 3–628–7944–4, Ireland related
fiction.
COMMENTARY An historical romance that begins in London in 1606. Moor O'Mara, an Irish
Catholic, first takes part in the Gunpowder Plot and then escapes to Ireland to aid the earl of
Tyrone. After she hears that Moor has perished in fighting in Ireland, Mabel Donovan, an
Irish Catholic woman who is the mother of Moor's child Reginald, goes to Ireland herself (disguised for the first part of her journey as an English soldier). She meets Tyrone, who proposes marriage to her, but she refuses. Tyrone takes charge of educating Reginald O'Mara,
who distinguishes himself in battle against the English. Moor O'Mara is discovered alive but
unrepentant for his 'bigoted' adherence to catholicism, and the novel ends with Mabel con-
senting to the marriage between her Catholic son and the Protestant daughter of Tyrone [JB].

IREMONGER, Henrietta. See **CHATTERTON, Lady Henrietta G.M.**

'AN IRISH ARTIST', fl. 1813. Pseudonym of a satirical writer.
I6   *A gallery of portraits, painted by an old and celebrated master; and re-touched by
an Irish artist.*
+ Dublin: John Cumming, 1813 (ill.). LOCATION UCD Folklore Dept., O.

COMMENTARY 118pp. Satire on different personalities. Contents: 'Portrait of a child', 'A raw young preacher', 'A genuine divine', 'A mere dull physician', 'The secretary', 'A raiser of the wind', 'A high-spirited man', 'A prison', 'A man of fashion', 'A lady of fashion', 'An Irish hovel', 'A smatterer', 'A young miss', 'A minute philosopher', 'The singing-men in Cathedral churches', 'An Irish fair', 'A suspicious thin-skinned man', 'A rash man', 'A flatterer', 'A hypocrite', 'A delightful evening', 'A lecturer', 'A fixture in a reading-room', 'Acquaintances', 'Finished education', 'A stayed man', 'Lady Bountiful', 'A weak man', 'A man of the world', 'A tourist', 'A detractor', 'Coterie of blue stockings' [ML].

'IRISH BACHELOR', pseud. See ABBOT, —.

'IRISH BOHEMIAN', pseud. See O'SHEA, John Augustus.

'AN IRISH BRAMWELLIAN', fl. 1885. Pseudonym of a fiction writer.
I7   *The last drop of '68. A picture of real life with imaginary characters* (by 'An Irish Bramwellian').
         + Dublin: Hodges, Figgis & Co.; London: Simpkin, Marshall & Co., 1885 (ill. cover).
         SOURCE Brown, 61. LOCATION D, L, InND Loeber coll.
COMMENTARY The narrator is a lawyer in Dublin, where the story begins, but almost all the incidents take place in London. Most of the characters are more or less disreputable drunks and swindlers. The lawyer gets involved in an extremely shady divorce case. The story mentions '"Corless" Elegant Restaurant' in Dublin, which is also advertised on the back of the volume [ML; Brown].

'AN IRISH CLERGYMAN', pseud. See KNOX, Revd James Spencer.

'AN IRISH LADY', pseud. See RUXTON, Maria.

'AN IRISHMAN', pseud. See CLAYTON, F.H.

'AN IRISHMAN', pseud. See HAMILTON, Revd John.

'AN IRISHMAN', fl. 1821. Pseudonym of a writer of political and historical fiction.
I8   *National feeling; or, the history of Fitzsimon. A novel, with historical and political remarks* (by 'An Irishman'; dedicated to 'to you, my countrymen').
         + Dublin: Printed for the author by A. O'Neil at the Minerva Printing Office, 1821, 2 vols. SOURCE Brown 70; British Fiction; Garside, 1821:9. LOCATION D, Dt, MH.
COMMENTARY Set partly in Co. Mayo and Dublin, and partly abroad. Tells the story of Edward Fitzsimon's wooing of Matilda, which is thwarted by the machinations of a wicked lord. A number of national personages appear in the book, such as the duke of Leinster and Lady Rossmore. The hero visits North and South America. The story mentions the Union, the effect of absentee landlords, and the advantages of landlords who live on their estates, and how few Irish members are attending parliament in London. Contains a brief piece on the life of a Jesuit [ML; Brown].

'AN IRISHMAN', fl. 1853. Pseudonym of a proselytizing Protestant fiction writer.
I9   *Poor Paddy's cabin; or, slavery in Ireland. A true representation of facts and characters* (by 'An Irishman').
         + London: Wertheim & MacIntosh; Dublin: M'Glashan, 1853 (ill.). SOURCE Brown, 81 (1854, 2nd edn); Sadleir, 92; NSTC. LOCATION L.

+ London: Wertheim & MacIntosh; Dublin: M'Glashan; Curry & Co., 1854, 3rd edn (with additional facts and anecdotes, ill.). SOURCE NSTC. LOCATION L, InND Loeber coll.

+ London: Wertheim & MacIntosh; Dublin: M'Glashan & W. Curry & Co., 1854, 2nd edn (with additional facts and anecdotes; ill.). LOCATION L.

+ Amsterdam: H. de Hoogh for the Evangelische Verbond, 1856 (trans. as *De hut van den armen Paddy of slavernij in Ierland*; ill.). LOCATION InND Loeber coll.

COMMENTARY Proselytizing fiction inspired by Harriet Beecher Stowe's *Uncle Tom's cabin* (Boston, 1852, 2 vols.), and like its American model a work of propaganda, in this case to show the superiority of protestantism over catholicism. The preface states that the story is interwoven with 'a representation of *facts* and *characters*' in the form of a parable. In the preface to the second edn, the author cites a review in the *London Standard* (30 Dec. 1853), which recommends the book because it documents an 'abominable system' in Ireland, 'worse than Negro Slavery ... Yes, we have a slavery in the United Kingdom, a slavery in which men and women of our own colour, race, and language are the victims ...' Against the backdrop of the Famine, the main plot is the struggle between the two theologies. A few folk songs (keens) in Irish are given. The family of Poor Paddy, a Catholic, is about to go into the poor-house for want of food, when the daughter comes home and tells them that if she and her siblings go to the Protestant school, they will get a meal a day. She is enchanted by the Bible, and finds out that her father has also been reading it. The mother tries various ploys to keep her family within the Catholic church, one of which is to encourage a Catholic young man's suit for her daughter's hand. The daughter refuses on religious grounds. In sorrow the young man goes to America. The family is eventually reduced to the poor-house, but when they are reunited the mother has also converted to protestantism. The daughter's suitor has become a Protestant in America and returns to claim her. They marry and return to Ohio, not far from the city of Pittsburgh [ML; Rowan cat. 37].

I10   *The Irish widow; or, a picture from life of Erin and her children* [anon.].

+ London: Wertheim & MacIntosh, 1855 (ill.). SOURCE Brown, 56; NSTC. LOCATION D, BFl, L.

COMMENTARY Sequel to *Poor Paddy's cabin; or, slavery in Ireland* (London, 1853). Religious fiction. Deals with the religious question in Ireland from a Protestant, evangelical point of view. The characters are drawn from the middle class. Catholics make the lives of converts very miserable [Brown; Fegan, p. 225].

I11   *Eveline; or, incidents of Irish convent life* (by the author of 'Poor Paddy's cabin').

+ London: Wertheim, MacIntosh & Hunt; Dublin: Wm. Curry & Co.; Edinburgh: Kennedy & Co.; Belfast: A.S. Mayne, 1861. LOCATION L, O.

COMMENTARY Story set in Ireland, and criticizes catholicism and convent life. In the end the girl who had been sent to the convent leaves the convent, converts to protestantism and marries [ML].

'AN IRISHWOMAN', pseud. See PECK, Mrs Frances.

IRWIN, Thomas Caulfield (not Caulfeild as in Newmann), b. Warrenpoint (Co. Down) 1823, d. Rathmines (Dublin) 1892. Journalist, poet, biographer, travel writer and editor, TCI was a son of a physician, Thomas Irwin, of Warrenpoint (Co. Down), and was privately educated. TCI travelled widely on the Continent before he lost his inheritance in 1848 and took to journalism as a livelihood. Returning to Ireland in 1853, he contributed to several Dublin periodicals, including the *Nation*, the *Dublin University Magazine* (1863), the *Shamrock*, the *Dublin Saturday Magazine* (1867), and other Irish journals, including a short-lived publication he edited himself, the *Irish Monthly Illustrated Journal*. Although TCI published over 130 prose tales, he is better known for his poetry, for example his *Versicles* (Dublin, 1856); *Songs and romances* (Dublin, 1878); *Pictures and songs* (Dublin, 1878); *Irish poems and legends* (Glasgow, [1869]), and *Poems, sketches, and songs* (Dublin, 1889). A prolific writer, he also wrote a biography of Jonathan Swift§. In old age he was increasingly eccentric and died insane and poor. In Dublin, he lived at various addresses, dying at 36 Upper Mountpleasant Ave, Rathmines. TCI's obituary appeared in *United Ireland* (Dublin, 27 Feb. 1892). He was buried in Mount Jerome cemetery, Dublin. SOURCE Allibone Suppl., ii, p. 890; Boase, v, pp 752–3; Brady, p. 112; Brown, p. 145; Clyde, pp 132, 135; Curran index; Field Day, ii, pp 113, 930; Hogan, pp 313–14; Hogan 2, pp 586–7; Igoe, pp 110–11; Irish pseudonyms; LVP, p. 242; McKenna, pp 205–6; MVP, pp 242–3; Newmann, p. 118; OCIL, p. 271; O'Donoghue, p. 211; RIA/DIB; RL.

I112 *Winter and summer stories, and slides of fancy's lantern* (by Thomas Caulfield Irwin; dedicated to Esther).
 + Dublin: M.H. Gill & Son, 1879. SOURCE Hogan, p. 313; Brown, 800; COPAC. LOCATION Grail, D, NUC.
COMMENTARY Mostly stories from foreign countries: 'Old Christmas hall', 'The first ring', 'An Irish fairy sketch', ' The miser's cottage', 'By moonlight', 'By gaslight', 'Falstaff's wake', 'A scene in Macbeth's castle', 'Julio: A little story in the manner of Boccaccio', 'A death', 'Visions of an old voyage from Rome to Asia', 'The shores of Greece', 'Theocritus', 'A glimpse of Arcadia: Greeks in the rough', 'Billy in the bowl: a ballad of old Dublin', 'Corney M'Clusky and the insurance office', 'Ethel Maccara', 'Pausias and Glycera: A tale of Cyprus', 'Manon and her spirit lover', 'An ancient Arian legend', 'A Florentine fortune', 'Insielle's dimple and fan' [ML].

ISDELL, Sarah, b. Ireland *c*.1780, d. 1811. Novelist, SI was the daughter of a government official in Dublin, but a family of this name owned a small country estate at Conlanstown and nearby Rockbrooke (both Co. Westmeath) not far from Edgeworthstown. She was governess to the children of the Denny family (probably Sir Barry Denny, 1st Bt and his wife Jane Denny) of Tralee (Co. Kerry) and she also resided in Dublin where she wrote plays. One of these, a comedy, *The poor gentleman* (1811), was produced 'with considerable success' in Dublin. In 1806 she subscribed to the publication of Revd M. Sleater's *Introductory essay to … topography of Ireland* (Dublin, 1806). After her father's death she was destitute. She is said to have been a near relation of Oliver Goldsmith§. SOURCE Allibone, i, p. 945; Blain, p. 562; Brady, p. 112; BD, p. 174; NUC; O'Donoghue, p. 212; RIA/DIB; RL; Taylor & Skinner's *Maps of the roads of Ireland* (Dublin, 1783), p. 67.

I113 *The vale of Louisiana. An American tale* [anon.] (dedicated to Mrs O.H.).
 Dublin: Printed [for the author?] by B. Smith, 1805, 2 vols. SOURCE British Fiction; Garside, 1805:40; OCLC. LOCATION MH.
COMMENTARY Reviewed in *Ireland's Mirror* (1805), where it is stated that it was published for the author by Watson, in 2 vols. at the cost of '7*d*. 7*s*.' [*sic*], but this edn has not been located. According to Blain, SI claimed that the story was based on fact. It describes the trials and adventures of an English emigrant family who suffer war, Indian captivity, shipwreck and the like before returning to a rational England that offers refuge from 'savage' exciting America [RL; Blain; *Ireland's Mirror: or, A chronicle of the Times* (Dublin, July–Aug. 1805), pp 391–2, 442–3].

I114 *The Irish recluse; or, a breakfast at the Rotunda* (by Sarah Isdell; dedicated to Sir Edward Denny, Bt, of Tralee Castle [Co. Kerry]).
 + London: J. Booth, 1809, 3 vols. (ill.). SOURCE Belanger, 16; British Fiction; Garside, 1809:34. LOCATION D, Dt (incomplete), NUC.

COMMENTARY Reviewed twice in the *British Critic*, which makes no mention of the Irish content. Starts out on the south-west coast of Ireland in 1780 where a nobleman, De Burgh, returns with his new wife to settle on his estate and build a castle at Glanmore in the place of an old castle that 'hung ... over the Atlantic coast'. He is very jealous of his wife. According to the *Critical Review*, 'Some of the scenes ... carry us back to the horror, anarchy, and confusion which prevailed during the French Revolution'. One of the characters, Emma Summers marries a young man who is 'mad after *French liberty*, and, from taking an active part in the confusion of the times, is brought to the guillotine'. An advertisement mentioned that a few copies of this novel were printed on 'fine paper with tinted Frontispieces' at the price of 18s. [RL; JB; *British Critic* 35 (Jan. 1810), p. 72 and 35 (Mar. 1810), p. 300; *Critical Review* (London, Nov. 1809); British Fiction].

I15   *FitzHerbert. A novel* [anon.].
       London: J.F. Hughes, [1810?]. SOURCE British Fiction; Garside F:1.
       COMMENTARY No copy located, but known from an advertisement. Ascribed to SI or
       to Mary Pilkington [Garside].

'IVANIONA', pseud. See **PEACOCK, Ida**.

J

'J., A.', pseud. See **JAMESON, Anna Brownell.**

'J., C.M.', pseud. See **JOHNSTON, C.M.**

'J., F.', pseud. See **MAC NALLY, Mrs Louisa.**

'J., J.', fl 1821. Pseudonym of a writer who, according to the title page of the volume below, was also a clergyman. Given that he published in Belfast only, he probably was from the north of Ireland. SOURCE RL.
J1   *Margaret Shaw* (by 'J.J.').
       Belfast: Printed [for the author?] by T. Mairs & Co., 1821. SOURCE Anderson 2, p. 13.
       COMMENTARY No copy located [RL].

'JAARVEY, Addison, Esq.', fl. 1843. Probable pseudonym of a fiction writer.
J2   *Sir Patrick Fitz-Patrick, knt., vulgarly called "Paddy from Cork" ...; translated by Addison Jaarvey, Esq.*
       + Cork: Albion & Columbian Press, 1843. LOCATION Dt (incomplete).
COMMENTARY 48pp. No evidence that this is a translated work. Starts out on the St Lawrence River in North America, at the 'Ex Disputed Territory'. Tells the story of Paddy from Cork and contains many allusions to people and events of the day. The same character features in a chapbook *The comical sayings of Paddy from Cork* (Norwich, CT, 1794) [ML].

JACOBS, Joseph, b. Sydney (Australia) 1854, d. New Rochelle (NY) 1916. Historian of Jewish life and culture, folktale writer, editor and polymath, JJ went to England as a young man and graduated from Cambridge University. He joined a group of London Jewish intellectuals and together they produced the *Bibliotheca Anglo-Judaica* (London, 1888). JJ went on to study and publish on Jewish history and ethnicity and was one of the first Jews to conduct research in Spain since the expulsion of the Jews in 1492. He was made a corresponding member of the Royal Spanish Academy and was active in drawing attention through the press to the plight of Jews in Russia and in counteracting rising anti-Semitism in England in response to increasing Jewish immigration from Europe. After the birth of his children, he turned his attention to folklore and began to write fairy and folk tales, including an edn of Aesop's fables; *English Fairy Tales* (London, 1888); *Celtic Fairy Tales* (London, 1892); *Indian Fairy Tales* (London, 1892), and *More English Fairy Tales* (London, 1893). He was honorary secretary of the International Folklore Council and editor of *Folklore* (London). In 1900 he and his family emigrated to New York where he became reviewing editor of the *Jewish encyclopedia* (New York, 1906) and continued to publish on Jewish history and civilization. SOURCE ANB; DAB; DLB, cxli; ODNB.
J3   *Celtic fairy tales* (selected and ed. by Joseph Jacobs).
       + London: David Nutt, 1892 (dedicated to Alfred Nutt; ill. John D. Batten). SOURCE Hayley, p. 184; Osborne, p. 33. LOCATION E, CaOTP, NUC, InND Loeber coll.
       New York: J.P. Putnam's Sons, 1892. LOCATION NUC.
       New York: World, 1971. LOCATION InND, MH.

London: Frederick Muller, 1972. SOURCE Hayley, p. 184. SOURCE COPAC. LOCATION L.

COMMENTARY Irish, Welsh, and Scottish Celtic stories. Contents of Irish stories: 'Connla and the fairy maiden' (from the *Book of Dun Cow*), 'Guleesh' (Douglas Hyde§), 'Field of Boliauns' (Thomas Crofton Croker§ [*sic*]), 'The horned women' (Lady Wilde§), 'Munachar and Manachar' (Douglas Hyde§), 'King O'Toole and his goose' ([Samuel] Lover§), 'Jack and his comrades' (Patrick Kennedy§), 'Shee an Gannon and Gruagach Gaire' (Jeremiah Curtin§), 'The story-teller at fault' (Gerald Griffin§), 'A legend of Knockmany' (William Carleton§), 'Fair, brown, and trembling' (Jermiah Curtin§), 'Jack and his master' (Patrick Kennedy§), 'The lad with the goat skin' (Patrick Kennedy§) [RL].

J4   *More Celtic fairy tales* (selected and ed. by Joseph Jacobs; dedicated to 'the many unknown little friends').

+ London: David Nutt, 1894 (ill. John D. Batten). SOURCE Osborne, p. 33. LOCATION CaOTP, InND Loeber coll.

New York: Dover, [1968]. LOCATION InND.

New York: World, 1971 (as *Celtic fairy tales: being the two collections Celtic fairy tales & more Celtic fairy tales*). LOCATION InND.

COMMENTARY Contents: 'The fate of the children of Lir', 'Jack the cunning thief', 'Powel, prince of Dyfed', 'Paddy O'Kelly and the weasel', 'The black horse', 'The vision of MacConglinney', 'Dream of Owen O'Mulready', 'Morraha', 'The story of the MacAndrew family', 'The farmer of Liddesdale', 'The Greek princess and the young gardener', 'The russet dog', 'Smallhead and the king's sons', 'The legend of Knockgrafton' [William Maginn§], 'Elidore', 'The leeching of Kayn's leg', 'How Fin went to the kingdom of the big men', 'How Cormac Mac Art went to the faery', 'The Ridere of riddles', 'The tail' [RL].

'JAMES, Brother', pseud. See REYNOLDS, James.

JAMES, G.P.R. See JAMES, George Payne Rainsford.

JAMES, George Payne Rainsford (also known as G.P.R. James), b. London 1799, d. Venice (Italy) 1860. Historical novelist, biographer, diplomat and writer on history, GPRJ was the son of Pinkstan James, MD, a former naval officer, and Jean Churnside. He began to write at an early age and after a period in the army settled on writing as a career. He benefited from the friendship of Washington Irving and Sir Walter Scott, who praised *Richelieu*, GPRJ's historical romance published in 1829, which was an immediate success. Starting in 1841 he published in the *Dublin University Magazine*. His *Mary of Burgundy* was published in Belfast by Simms and M'Intyre as part of the Parlour Library in 1850. They also reprinted his *The gentleman of the old school* in 1852. It is unclear whether he spent time in Ireland. Eventually, he became a highly successful novelist, producing over 100 novels, many of which became very popular, as well as books of popular history. Around 1850 GPRJ suffered a financial setback and he and his family moved to the US. They first lived in Stockbridge (MA) where he wrote, lectured and got to know American writers such as Nathaniel Hawthorne. He sought a government post and was appointed British Consul in Norfolk (VA), later moving to Venice (Italy) where he held a similar position and where he died. His *The commissioner; or, de lunatico inquirendo* was published anonymously in Dublin in 1843, after having been issued there in parts (starting in Dec. 1841) did not have Irish content, and did not sell well. GPRJ was befriended by Charles Lever§. SOURCE Allibone, i, pp 950–1; FitzPatrick, pp 136–7, 199; W.E. Hall, pp 101, 119; Kunitz & Haycraft, pp 324–5; Loeber coll. InND (copy of *The commissioner* (Dublin, 1843); NCBEL 4, pp 936–9, 1812; ODNB; RL; Sutherland, pp 325–6.

J5　*Arrah Neil; or, times of old* (by G.P.R. James).
Leipzig: Bernard Tauchnitz, 1844. SOURCE T & B, 66. LOCATION NUC.
+ London: Smith, Elder & Co., 1845, 3 vols. SOURCE Dixson, p. 220; Wolff, 3496;
NCBEL 4, p. 938; Sadleir, 1248. LOCATION L, NUC.
New York: Harper & Bros, 1844. LOCATION NUC.
COMMENTARY First published in the *Dublin University Magazine* (1843–44). Historical novel
set in the early 1640s in Ireland. Arrah Neil is a homeless 16-year-old girl, who has a myste-
rious background [CM; Dixson; W.E. Hall, pp 119–20].

JAMES, Humphrey, fl. 1896. Story writer, this HJ can perhaps be identified with the HJ
who was a schoolmaster and the brother of Revd William James, vicar of Mount Sorrell
(Leicester?) and who married in 1861 Minnie, daughter of William F. Reynett of the South
Parade in Waterford. One of their sons became Revd Albert Boyce James. SOURCE Leslie,
Connor, p. 407; RL.
J6　*Paddy's woman and other stories* (by Humphrey James).
+ London: T. Fisher Unwin, 1896. SOURCE Brown, 806. LOCATION L, NUC, InND
Loeber coll.
COMMENTARY Stories which are loosely connected and deal with Catholic peasant life in Ulster.
Contents: 'Jane's hand in it', 'A glass of whisky', 'Paddy's woman', 'A whole night of it',
'Jemmy, the Scotchman', 'Magrory's daughters', 'Got out of wing' [ML].

JAMESON, Mrs —. See JAMESON, Anna Brownell.

JAMESON, Anna Brownell (née Murphy; also known as Mrs Jameson), pseud. 'A.J.', b.
Dublin 1794, d. Ealing (London) 1860. Novelist, essayist, travel writer, art critic and feminist, ABJ was the eldest daughter of Denis Brownell Murphy, an Irish miniature painter and
painter-in-ordinary to Princess Charlotte, and his English wife. The family moved to England
in 1798, living first in Cumberland and Newcastle-on-Tyne and settling near London in 1806.
When young, ABJ wrote 'Faizy', an oriental story for children, which remained unpublished.
She became a governess at age 16 in the household of the marquess of Winchester, serving
with a number of other families until she married Robert Jameson, a lawyer, in 1825. She did
not accompany her husband to Dominica when he was appointed to a government position in
1829, but briefly joined him in Canada in 1833, where he was attorney-general, although their
marriage had broken down and he agreed to a yearly stipend for her. Her sojourn in Canada
resulted in *Winter studies and summer rambles in Canada* (London, 1838). She was deeply concerned with the legal and educational lot of women, on which topics she lectured. She wrote
widely on art and art history, on women and women's issues (e.g. *Characteristics of women,
moral poetical and historical* (Philadelphia, 1833, 2 vols.), and a well-received series of critical
sketches of heroines in the works of William Shakespeare, later reprinted as *Shakespeare's heroines* (New York, 1832). She visited Maria Edgeworth§ in 1848, travelled through much of
Ireland, and attended the opening of the Irish Exhibition in 1853. From Mullingar (Co.
Westmeath) she wrote that her impressions of Ireland were 'of pain and discord', and apparently she chose not to talk or write about the country. She was close friends with Elizabeth
and Robert Browning, who stayed with her and with whom she travelled, and with the Thomas
and Jane Carlyle, and she was befriended by the American author Catherine Sedgwick§. As
the principal breadwinner in her family, she supported her parents in their later years, as well
as her sisters, and in 1851, with the support of William Thackeray§, she was awarded a Civil
List pension. In 1855 her friends purchased an annuity for her after her husband failed to
mention her in his will. At the time of her death, she was working on *The history of our Lord*

as exemplified in works of art (London, 1892), which was completed by Lady Eastlake. For her portraits and papers, see ODNB. Her library was sold on July 19, 1861. SOURCE Allibone, i, p. 953; Blain, pp 569–70; Brady, p. 112; DCB viii, pp 649–51; DLB, ic, clxvi; Field Day, iv, pp 1187, 1155–6, v, 1103; S.C. Hall, pp 374–5; List of catalogues, p. 295; G. MacPherson, *Memoirs of the life of Anna Jameson* (Boston, 1878), passim; NCBEL 4, p. 2165–9; OCIL, p. 273; ODNB; RIA/DIB.

J7   *A lady's diary* [anon.]
      London, R. Thomas, 1826. LOCATION L.
      London: Henry Colburn, 1826 (as *Diary of an ennuyée*). LOCATION L.
      Paris: Baudry, 1836 (new edn; as *Diary of an ennuyée*). SOURCE GLOL. LOCATION
      Bayerische Staatsbibliothek, München.
COMMENTARY Contains a narrative of travels through Paris, Milan, Florence, Rome, Naples and Lucca, which became very popular. The melodramatic plot of a heroine dying for love is completely submerged by the same heroine's vibrant, humorous descriptions of travel and art in Italy. The book created a minor sensation when it was discovered not to be a true story, as this account by Fanny Kemble in 1828 indicates: 'The Ennuyée, one is given to understand, dies, and it was a little vexatious to behold her sitting on a sofa in a very becoming state of blooming *plumptitude*' [ODNB].

J8   *Visits and sketches at home and abroad with tales and miscellanies now first collected, and a new edition of the "Diary of an ennuyée"* [anon.].
      + London: Saunders & Otley, 1834, 4 vols. SOURCE Garside 2, B:15. LOCATION L.
      + Boston: Ticknor & Fields, 1859 (as *Studies, stories, and memoirs*; ill. Corregio).
      LOCATION NUC, InND Loeber coll.
COMMENTARY Preface to the reader is signed 'A.J.' The *Edinburgh Review* and Garside 2 attribute this to Mrs Jameson (her *Diary of an ennuyée* was first published in London in 1826). Contents of the stories: 'The false one' (first published in 1827; set in India), 'Halloran the peddler' (a footnote states that this story was written in 1826, and was in the hands of the publisher 'long before the appearance' of John and Michael Banim's§ story entitled 'The Nowlans'. This must have been a bit of an overstatement because *Tales by the O'Hara family. Second series. Comprising The Nowlans, and Peter of the castle* appeared in London in 1826. Both stories were based on the same incidents), 'The Indian mother', 'A dramatic proverb for little actors' [RL; Garside 2].

'JANE, Ann', pseud. See **MORGAN, Ann Jane**.

JARNAC, Philippe Ferdinand Auguste de Rohan Chabot, comte de. See **DE JARNAC, Philippe Ferdinand Auguste de Rohan Chabot, comte.**

JARROLD, Ernest, fl. 1899. American writer.
J9   *Micky Finn idylls* (by Ernest Jarrold; introd. by C.A. Dana).
      + New York: Doubleday & McClure, 1899. SOURCE Brown, 807 (1899, Harper edn);
      NUC; Wright, iii, 2955. LOCATION InND Loeber coll.
COMMENTARY Set at Coney Island near New York City and tells the story of Micky who is about nine or ten, and who is born of Irish parents. A goat figures largely in the sketches [Brown].
J10 *Micky Finn's new Irish yarns* (by Ernest Jarrold).
      New York: J.S. Ogilvie, [1902]. SOURCE Brown, 807a. LOCATION NUC.
      COMMENTARY Sequel to *Micky Finn idylls* (New York, 1899) [RL].

'JARVIS, Geoffrey', pseud. See HAMILTON, Elizabeth.

JAY, Edith Katherine Spicer, pseud. 'E. Livingston Prescott', b. London, 1847, d. Sandgate (Kent) 1901. English novelist and writer of religious fiction and fiction for juveniles, EKSJ in her writings addressed social conditions in England. She was the daughter of Samuel Jay, a barrister, and Elizabeth Spicer. Both sides of her family had strong connections with the military and many of her novels had military backgrounds. Given her pseudonym, it was often assumed they had been written by a man. In her novels and pamphlets she wrote against the practice of flogging in the army, but she was an enthusiastic and generous supporter of the military and military charities, to the extent that when she died she was buried in the military cemetery of Shorncliffe army camp (Kent). SOURCE Blain, p. 871 [under Prescott]; BLC; EF, p. 319; ODNB; Sutherland, p. 509 [under Prescott].
J11   *A small, small child. A tale* (by 'E. Livingston Prescott').
       London: J. Bowden, 1898 (ill. A.D. M'Cormick). LOCATION L.
       + Boston: L.C. Page & Co., 1901 (ill. A.D. M'Cormick; Cosy Corner Series of Charming Juveniles). LOCATION NUC, InND Loeber coll.
COMMENTARY Fiction for juveniles. A story of how the sickly daughter of a prison guard before her early death humanizes both the worst prisoner, an Irishman called Murphy, as well as her father [ML].

JAY, Harriet, b. London 1857, d. Ilford (London) 1932. Novelist and playwright, HJ was a sister-in-law, and later adopted daughter of the writer Robert Williams Buchanan§. She was educated in Scotland and lived for some years with the Buchanans in Co. Mayo when they went there to reduce their living expenses, on the strength of which she wrote a number of novels with an Irish flavour. *The Queen of Connaught* (London, 1875, 3 vols.) has been ascribed to HJ by Wolff, Brown, Blain and Sutherland, but it has also been ascribed to Buchanan. Blain explains this by stating that it was her first novel and that Buchanan rewrote it as a play, and Brown concurs with this. HJ became an actress in 1881, appearing in the title role of Buchanan's 'A nine day queen'. In a prefatory note to *My Connaught cousins*, Buchanan – at HJ's request – counters the charge that HJ was 'an enemy of Irish nationality', explaining that she wrote out of sympathy for the people. HJ collaborated with Buchanan on a number of plays, using the pseudonym 'Charles Marlowe' and travelled with him to Philadelphia in 1884 to oversee a production. She remained with Buchanan until his death in 1901 and wrote her adoptive father's biography. Several of her letters to the publisher Richard Bentley are mentioned in the Burmester list. Only her novels with known Irish content are listed below. SOURCE Allibone Suppl., ii, p. 901; Alston, p. 220; Blain, pp 571–2; Burmester list; H. Jay, *Robert Buchanan* (London, 1903); ODNB [under Robert W. Buchanan]; Sutherland, p. 328.
J12   *The Queen of Connaught* [anon.].
       London: Richard Bentley & Son, 1875, 3 vols. SOURCE Blain; Brown, 808; Sutherland; Wolff; COPAC. LOCATION L.
COMMENTARY An Englishman, John Birmingham, becomes involved with a west of Ireland community when he marries Kathleen O'Mara. He tries but fails to reform the Connacht peasantry with English ideas [Brown; Sutherland].
J13   *The dark Colleen* [anon.].
       London: Richard Bentley & Son, 1876, 3 vols. SOURCE Brown, 809. LOCATION D, L.
       New York: Lovell, Adam, Wesson & Co., 1877. LOCATION NUC.
COMMENTARY Originally titled 'Morna Dunroon'. The story of a French sailor, wrecked on Eagle Island on the west coast of Ireland, who is nursed back to health by an Irish maiden, whom he marries and deserts [Sutherland; Burmester list].

J14   *The priest's blessing; or, poor Patrick's progress from this world to a better* (by
Harriet Jay).
London: F.V. White, 1881. SOURCE Brown, 810. LOCATION L.
New York: G. Munro, 1883 (Seaside Library). LOCATION NUC.
COMMENTARY An anti-Catholic book, which describes two priests who are objection-
able characters [Brown; Sutherland].

J15   *My Connaught cousins* (by Harriet Jay).
London: F.V. White & Co., 1883, 3 vols. (preface by R. [Williams] Buchanan§). SOURCE
Brown, 811; COPAC. LOCATION L, NUC.
New York: Harper & Bros, [1883]. LOCATION NUC.
COMMENTARY Describes the life in a country house in Connacht, where Jack Kenmare visits
his uncle. He becomes engaged to one of his cousins, who writes stories, several of which are
incorporated in the book [Brown].

JEBB, Richard, b. Drogheda (Co. Louth) 1766, d. Rostrevor (Co. Down) 1834. Pamphleteer,
barrister and judge, RJ was the son of John Jebb, alderman of Drogheda, and Alice (Alicia)
Forster. He graduated at TCD in 1786 and in 1787 he inherited the estate of his uncle, Sir
Richard Jebb, who was court physician to George III, and entered Lincoln's Inns (London).
He was a friend of Wolfe Tone§ and John Radcliff§ and helped to conceive and produce with
them the novel *Belmont castle, or suffering sensibility* (Dublin, 1790), a parody of the romantic
novels of the period, which featured various Anglo-Irish personalities resident in Dublin and
London. Returning to Ireland, he was admitted to the Irish Bar in 1789. He was active in the
rebellion of 1798 with a corps of militia of Trinity College lawyers he had recruited. He supported the Union and published *A reply to a pamphlet entitled arguments for and against an
Union* (Dublin, 1798) but declined a seat in parliament and became increasingly supportive of
the Orange Order, although he never became a member. His judicial career flourished and he
became 4th justice of the Irish court of king's bench, known for his partiality to Protestant
interests and for rigorously censoring writings critical of the government. His brother John
became bishop of Limerick. SOURCE Allibone, i, p. 958; B & S, p. 436; IBL, 23 (1935), pp
47–8; Keane, p. 247; Leslie, *Ardfert*, pp 8–10; ODNB [under John Jebb, 1775–1833]; RIA/DIB.

JEFFEREYS, E.C., fl. 1890s. Novelist, ECJ also contributed 'Noblesse oblige' to the *Dublin
University Magazine* (1873). SOURCE NUC.
J16   *An Irish landlord and an English M.P. A tale* (by E.C. Jeffereys).
+ London: Digby & Long, [1890]. LOCATION D, L.
COMMENTARY Set in the west of Ireland in the village of Bally Malone [RL].

JEFFERY, Revd William, fl. 1859. English writer of evangelical religious fiction. According
to a letter to the reader in the following book, WJ resided in Torrington, Devon, in 1859. He
was invited to Ireland by Revd Robert Carson. SOURCE CM.
J17   *The Irish revival. Confessions of converts* (by Revd William Jeffery).
+ London: Houlston & Wright, 1859. LOCATION L.
COMMENTARY Religious fiction. In a letter to the reader, the author states that 'After spending many weeks journeying through Ireland, carrying out everywhere a diligent process of
examination into the reported Regeneration of the people ... the Reformation of the People
has been effected on a stupendous and unparalleled scale ... The simple object of this little
book is to furnish the best evidence of the genuine character of what is called 'The Irish
Revival.' For that purpose I have endeavoured to bring you to within the heart-breathings of
the newly-awakened. You will be able to accompany me from cottage to cottage, and hear from

the Converts what they have to say about themselves and their Saviour ...' He visits Tubbercully and Coleraine (Co. Derry) [CM].

JELF, Sir Ernest Arthur, b. 1868, d. 1941. Senior master of the supreme court of England, and king's remembrancer, EAJ married in 1895 Rose Frances Reeves, daughter of Robert William Cary Reeves and Grace Dorothea Vandeleur. He was interested in the verification of psychic phenomena and in 1938 became a member of the London Ghost Club (William Butler Yeats§ had been one of its earlier members), whose chairman was the ghost hunter Harry Price. EAJ lived in London during most of his professional life. His portrait in the National Portrait Gallery, London. SOURCE On line: Internet <http://www/pinnerlhs.freeserve.co.uk/abpeople.htm> (accessed Oct. 2005); RL.

J18   *Eileen's journey. History in fairyland* (by Sir Ernest Arthur Jelf).
London: John Murray, 1896 (ill.). SOURCE Healy cat. 5/768 (1899 edn); COPAC.
LOCATION L.

COMMENTARY Fiction for juveniles. A magical journey through history and time, featuring St Patrick at Tara, the king of Meath and his revenge against the Danes, the battle of Clontarf, Henry VIII and his dealings with Ireland, and Columbus in the New World, etc. [Healy cat.].

JELLY, Symes M., pseud. 'Le Jemlys', fl. 1885. Detective story writer, probably American, SMJ also published other detective stories. SOURCE OCLC.

J19   *Shadowed to Europe: A Chicago detective on two continents* (by 'Le Jemlys').
Chicago, New York: Belford, Clarke & Co., 1885 (Mooney & Boland Detective Series).
SOURCE BLC; OCLC (1900 edn); Wright, iii, 2957. LOCATION L, NIC (1900 edn).
COMMENTARY Features Detective James Mooney of Mooney & Boland, Consulting Detectives, and an Irish detective in Europe [RL].

'JEMLY, LE', pseud. See **JELLY, Symes M.**

JENNINGS, Revd John Andrew, b. Dublin 1855, d. Rathgar (Dublin) 1923. Clergyman, editor, hymn writer and anthologist, JAJ was the son of John Jennings, a prominent member of the Church of Ireland's YMCA, Dublin. He graduated BA at TCD in 1880 and MA in 1883. He edited the *Church of Ireland Parish Magazine* (Dublin) from 1888 to 1898, greatly increasing its circulation. He was incumbent of Portnashangan (Co. Westmeath, 1881–2); Donaghpatrick (Co. Meath, 1882–96); St Matthew's (Dublin, 1896–1901), and chaplain at Mount Jerome cemetery (Dublin, 1904). His *Hymns for private circulation* appeared in 1876 and his *Wayside restings* in Dublin in 1880. From 1902 to 1923 he was Wallace divinity lecturer at TCD, and from 1912 to 1917 professor of pastoral theology. He gave many readings to raise money for charity and his anthologies of Charles Dickens and of American writers were as popular as his Irish one. He married Jane Charlotte, widow of the Revd Samuel McCutcheon, with whom he had four children. He was buried in Mount Jerome. SOURCE Leslie & Wallace, p. 768; LVP, p. 248; O'Donoghue, p. 214; RIA/DIB; Topp 8, 810.

J20   *Readings from Irish authors, humorous and pathetic* (ed. by John Andrew Jennings, MA).
+ Dublin: Carson Bros; London: Simpkin, Marshall; Hamilton, Adams & Co., [1883] (portrait of Samuel Lover§ on cover). SOURCE OCLC; Topp 8, 657. LOCATION D, L, NjP, InND Loeber coll.
COMMENTARY Contents: excluding poetry (many of the stories are condensed): 'The gridiron: Paddy Mullowney's story' (Samuel Lover§), 'Darby's Doyle's voyage to Quebec' [Thomas Ettingsall], 'Steward Moore' (Charles Lever§), 'The country dancing-master' (William

Carleton§), 'King O'Toole and St. Kevin' (Samuel Lover§), 'The present to the priest' (Samuel Lover§), 'Paddy M'Quillan's courtships (a County Down sketch)', 'Robin' [Wesley Lyttle§], 'The Irish schoolmaster' (anon.), 'Daniel O'Rourke' (Thomas Crofton Croker§ [but actually by William Maginn§]), 'The hedge schoolmaster' (William Carleton§), 'Paddy the piper' (Samuel Lover§), 'The legend of Bottle Hill' (Thomas Crofton Croker§ [but actually by William Maginn§]), 'Frank Webber's wager' (Charles Lever§), 'The little weaver of Duleek Gate' (Samuel Lover§), 'The hedge schoolmaster and his English visitor' (William Carleton§), 'Dreaming Tim Jarvis' (Thomas Crofton Croker§[*sic*]), 'O'Dempsey and the duke' (Samuel Lover§), 'The square gander' (J.S. Le Fanu§), 'A pleasant journey' (Charles Lever§), 'Barny O'Reirdon, the navigator' (Samuel Lover§), 'Phil Purcel, the pig-driver' (William Carleton§), 'My father as sentry. Mickey Free's story' (Charles Lever§), 'Paddy Flynn. A story founded on fact' (anon.), 'The furlough' (Thomas Hood), 'The stolen sheep' (John Banim§), 'The cockney in Ireland' (Charles Lever§), 'The letter-writer' (William Carleton§), 'The three advices' (Thomas Crofton Croker§ [*sic*]) [RL].

JENNINGS, Louis John, b. London 1837, d. London 1893. English journalist, editor and miscellaneous writer, LJJ was special correspondent for the *London Times* in India and the US and became editor of the *New York Times*, in which he attacked the political corruption of Tammany Hall. He returned to England and became a Tory MP for Stockport. He was a regular contributor to the *Quarterly Review* (London) and besides some novels wrote on political history and on walking in England, as well as editing the speeches of Lord Randolph Churchill and *The Croker papers: the correspondence and diaries of the late Rt Hon John Wilson Croker*§ (London, 1884, 3 vols.; revsd edn, 1885). SOURCE Allibone Suppl., ii, p. 908; Boase, v, pp 770–1; Jarndyce cat. 123/168; ODNB; Sutherland, p. 331.

J21   *The Philadelphian* (by Louis John Jennings).
    + London: Hurst & Blackett, 1891, 3 vols. SOURCE Jarndyce cat. 123/168; Sadleir 1325; Wolff, ii, 3651. LOCATION L, NUC, InND Loeber coll.
    New York: Harper & Bros, 1891 (Harper's Franklin Square Library, No. 697). LOCATION NUC.
COMMENTARY A murder and detective story about an American, Col. Pendleton, his daughter, Edith, and his friend Mr Snapper from Philadelphia who come to England where they stay with an old friend, Roland Clavering. Clavering marries an American adventuress, whose good-for-nothing son, Sam, expects that his mother will be rich once her husband dies. He is in debt to various unsavoury characters, one of whom is an Irish-American Fenian, Patrick Daly. Daly does not want to wait for his money and murders Clavering. Clavering, however, had left his wife very little, so Sam is unable to pay off his debts. Col. Pendleton solves the mystery of the murder and brings Daly to justice, but lets Sam escape [ML].

JEPHSON, Robert, pseud. 'Jeoffry Wagstaffe', and possibly 'Jacques Bourreau', b. Mallow (Co. Cork) 1736, d. Blackrock (Co. Dublin) 1803. Satirist, librettist, playwright and poet, RJ was the son of John Jephson, archdeacon of Cloyne and uncle of Sir Richard Mounteney Jephson of Mallow, and Jane, daughter of Anthony Dopping, bishop of Ossory. RJ was admitted to TCD in 1751 at age 14 but left without taking a degree. He entered the army and served for a period in the West Indies before returning to Ireland to live on half-pay. He moved to London, where he knew Samuel Johnson and Edmund Burke, and was described by James Boswell as 'a lively little fellow and the best mimic in the world'. In 1766 he married Jane Barry, daughter of a Dublin physician, but soon he was living in France to escape creditors. Through Lord Townshend, lord lieutenant in Ireland, he was made master of horse and in 1767 returned to Ireland. There he consorted with other literati and regularly visited Dublin

Castle. He published several satirical political tracts arranged in the form of periodicals, such as *The bachelor; or, speculations by Jeoffry Wagstaffe* (Dublin, 1769, 2 vols.; further edn, Dublin, 1772). On 11 Feb. 1774 he delivered a speech opposing a bill designed to encourage Catholics to convert to protestantism, which was printed later as a pamphlet: *The better encouragement of persons possessing the Popish religion to become Protestants* (Dublin, 1774). His drama *Braganza*, about Portugal's resistance to Spain, was produced to great success in Drury Lane in 1775 and was extravagantly praised by Horace Walpole. In 1781 he dramatized Walpole's Gothic novel *The castle of Otranto* (London, 1765) as *The Count of Narbonne* (London, 1781; Dublin, 1781). He caused a stir by writing poems about Alderman Howard and the publisher George Faulkner, forging their signatures, which fuelled conflict between the two but elicited many re-printings. His three-act opera, *The Campaign*, appeared in Dublin in 1784 and at Covent Garden in 1785 and was later shortened by Irish playwright John O'Keeffe and produced to great acclaim in 1787 as the farce *Love and war*. Other operas were performed to varying degrees of success. RJ abhorred the consequences of the French Revolution, which is reflected in his poem *Roman portraits* (London, 1794; his annotated copy is in a private collection) and which compares the achievements of Rome with the excess and violence of the new French republic. For his portraits, see M.D. Jephson, Elmes, and ODNB. For his papers, see ODNB. SOURCE Allibone, i, p. 965; B & S, p. 439; Bickersteth cat. 140/24; DLB, lxxxix; Elmes, p. 103; Hogan 2, pp 590–1; S.C. Hughes, *The pre-Victorian drama in Dublin* (New York, 1970 (reprint)), p. 59; HIP, iv, pp 483–4; *Ireland's mirror: or, a chronicle of the times* (Dublin, 1805), pp 530, 583–7; M.D. Jephson, *An Anglo-Irish miscellany. Some records of the Jephsons of Mallow* (Dublin, 1964), pp 300–11; OCIL, p. 274; ODNB; O'Donoghue, pp 214–15; Rafroidi, i, p. 62, ii, pp 189–90; RIA/DIB; R.E. Ward, *Prince of Dublin printers. The letters of George Faulkner* (Lexington, KY, 1972, p. 33); T.J. Walsh, *Opera in Dublin 1705–1797* (Dublin, 1973), p. 251.

J22   *A letter from Jacques Bourreau late of Trou-la-Putain, in Dauphiné … and now of the City of Dublin, to the Whigs of the capital* [anon.].

Dublin: P. Byrne, 1791. SOURCE ESTC t37894. LOCATION L, NUC.

+ London: J. Debrett, 1791 (as *A letter from an eminent legal character, late of Trou-la-Putain, in Dauphine, and now of the City of Dublin, to the Whigs of the capital*). SOURCE Bradshaw, 7524; ESTC t148215. LOCATION C, NUC, InND Loeber coll.

COMMENTARY 37pp for the Dublin edn, and 60pp for the London edn. Possibly by Robert Jephson according to O'Donoghue, cited in Bradshaw, 7524. Prose narrative by a Frenchman, living in Dublin, addressed to the Whigs in England. It facetiously celebrates the French Revolution and agrees to live by the tenets of Thomas Paine's *The rights of man* but then shows, without admitting it, its terrible consequences, including robbery, homicide, the rejection of laws made by preceding generations of lawmakers, and the rejection of inheritance. After leaving France, the narrator moves to England, but disliking English admiration for liberty of person and property in the framework of a hereditary monarchy, he goes and lives in Ireland, 'a country where there are many men of strong hands, and of little property'. He concludes by disparaging the English constitution and wishing to overturn it [RL].

J23   *The confessions of James Baptiste Couteau, citizen of France, written by himself and translated from the original French, by Robert Jephson* [anon.].

London: J. Debrett, 1794, 2 vols. SOURCE Hardy, 514; Rafroidi, ii, p. 190; Raven 2, 1794:33; Forster 2, 2255; ESTC t129718. LOCATION Dt, L, CtY.

+ Dublin: Printed by Zachariah Jackson, 1794, 2 vols. (ill.). SOURCE Raven 2, 1794:33; ESTC n026911. LOCATION D, O, MH.

London: Printed by S. Bailey, 1808 (abbreviated as *The French rogue, or extraordinary and surprising adventures of that notorious thief, spy and murderer, J. Baptiste Couteau, alias M. Ragout, alias Dick Hell-Finch: Containing all the sconces of horror he was engaged in, during the whole of the French Revolution; ... with anecdotes of the notorious Tom Paine, Esq. and his associates the Revolutionary Societies.* SOURCE Jarndyce cat. 114/251. COMMENTARY No copy of the London 1808 edn located other than that noted by Jarndyce. Satire on the worst excesses of the French Revolution in the form of an autobiographical account. Deals with, among others, the United Irishmen. The hero is elected to the Convention with Marat and Robespierre but ends up as a Muslim convert in Turkey. Contains excursions to Dublin and Boston in North America [Rafroidi; RL; Jarndyce cat. 114/250; Jarndyce cat. 150/193].

JESSE, Mathilda Charlotte. See HOUSTOUN, Mathilda Charlotte.

JESSOP, George H. See JESSOP, George Henry.

JESSOP, George Henry (also known as George H. Jessop), b. Doory Hall (also known as Dury Hall; now ruined), near Ballymahon (Co. Longford) 1852, d. Hampstead (London) 1915. Novelist, playwright and short story writer, GHJ was the third son of Frederick Thomas Jessop of Doory Hall and Elizabeth Low, and brother of the author Mary Kathleen Jessop§. The family estate was lost before 1891 through the gambling of its last owner. GHJ studied law and letters at TCD, and subsequently wrote for London magazines. He went to California in 1873 (not 1872 as mentioned in *Exiles*), where he worked as a journalist and editor until 1878. He sometimes collaborated with Brander Matthews in his novels and plays. GHJ wrote the libretto for Charles Villers Stanford's comic opera *Shamus O'Brien* (London, c.1896). At some point he returned to Europe, possibly because his cousin Catherine Jessop, who died unmarried in 1891, left him her estate of Marlfield (Co. Dublin). Subsequently he lived in London, where he continued to write. It was reported that he was received into the Catholic church on his deathbed. As far as is known, he remained a bachelor all his life. His play 'The picture of a year' (1914) is known from a manuscript. SOURCE Brown, p. 147; Carraig cat. 1166/250; *Exiles*, p. 191–206; J.P. Farrell, *History of the County of Longford* (Dublin, 1891), p. 316; *Landed gentry*, 1904, p. 289; IBL, 6 (1915), p. 154; Preface to G.H. Jessop's *Gerald ffrench friends* (London, 1889); *Landed gentry*, 1904, p. 289; O'Donoghue, p. 215; RIA/DIB; Sutherland, p. 334; *Vanishing country houses*, p. 107.

J24   *Check and countercheck. A tale of twenty-five hours* (by Brander Matthews and George H. Jessop).
+ Bristol: J.W. Arrowsmith; London: Simpkin, Marshall & Co., 1888 (Arrowsmith's Bristol Library, vol. 32). LOCATION L, NUC.
New York: D. Appleton & Co., 1892 (as *A tale of twenty-five hours*). LOCATION NUC.
COMMENTARY First appeared in *Lippincott's Monthly Magazine* (Philadelphia, 1888); no Irish content [CM].

J25   *Gerald ffrench's friends* (by George H. Jessop; dedicated to Brander Matthews).
London: Longmans, 1889. LOCATION L.
+ London: Murray & Evenden, [1911], 2nd edn (as *Gerald ffrench's friends: the fortunes and misfortunes of an Irish family*). SOURCE Brown, 814. LOCATION D, L.
+ New York: Longman, Green & Co., 1889. SOURCE Brown, 813; Fanning, p. 383; Wright, iii, 2969. LOCATION NUC, InND Loeber coll.
+ New York: Baker & Taylor Co., [1911]. SOURCE Fanning, p. 383. LOCATION D, NUC.
COMMENTARY A collection of linked stories, the hero being a young Irishman who emigrates to San Francisco in the early 1870s, and concerns the Irish in California. Contents: 'The rise and fall of the "Irish Aigle"', 'A dissolving view of Carrick Meagher', 'At the town of the

queen of the angels', 'An old man from the old country', 'The last of the Costellos', Under the redwood tree' [Brady, p. 113; RL; Sutherland, p. 334; 'The rise and fall …' was reprinted in *Exiles*, pp 191–206].

J26 *Judge Lynch. A romance of the Californian vineyards* (by George H. Jessop).
London: Longman, Green & Co., 1889. LOCATION L, NUC.
Chicago, New York, San Francisco: Belford, Clarke & Co.; London: Henry J. Drane, [1889]. SOURCE Fanning, p. 383; Wright, iii, 2970. LOCATION NUC.

J27 void

J28 *His American wife* (dedicated to Brander Matthews).
+ London: John Long, 1913. SOURCE EF, p. 214. LOCATION L.
COMMENTARY A wife misunderstands her husband, partly because of his absorption in politics and partly because a jealous rival has spread the notion that her husband married her for her money [EF, p. 214].

J29 *Desmond O'Connor. The romance of an Irish soldier* (by George H. Jessop; dedicated to 'the countless, gallant Irishmen who have fallen in the world's battles, fighting most often in quarrels not their own').
+ London: John Long, 1914. SOURCE Brown, 815. LOCATION L, InND Loeber coll.
New York: Longman, Green & Co., 1914 (as *Desmond O'Connor*). SOURCE Fanning, p. 383.
COMMENTARY No copy of the New York edn located. Historical fiction about the Wild Geese in Flanders, where Desmond O'Connor is the 'lion' of the Irish Brigade. A love story is interwoven with various adventures [Brown].

JESSOP, M.K. See **JESSOP, Mary Kathleen.**

JESSOP, Mary Kathleen (also known as **M.K. Jessop**), fl. 1882. Poet, and author of what appears to be a single collection of short stories, MKJ was the daughter of Frederick Thomas Jessop of Doory Hall (also known as Dury Hall), now ruined, near Ballymahon (Co. Longford) and Elizabeth Low, and the sister of the author George Henry Jessop§. The family estate was lost before 1891 through its last owner's gambling. Her poems were published privately in 1882 under the title *Patchwork, a collection of poems, etc.* (n.l.). MKJ appears to have remained single. SOURCE Allibone Suppl., ii, p. 911; BLC; J.P. Farrell, *History of the County of Longford* (Dublin, 1891), p. 316; LVP, p. 248; *Landed gentry*, 1904, p. 289; O'Donoghue, p. 215; RL.

J30 *Odds and ends for platform reading* (by M.K. Jessop).
+ London: Simpkin, Marshall & Co.; Dublin: Sealy, Bryers & Walker, 1887. SOURCE Topp 8, 839; LOCATION L.
COMMENTARY Stories apparently written for railroad travel. Contents: 'Tales of my grandmother', 'Story of a gate', 'What was it?', 'Juliana's husband', 'Cross questions and crooked answers', 'The tale of Simpkins', 'My Mary', 'A girl's soliloquy', Keeping your hands out of your pockets', 'A foreshadowing', 'Mrs. Pandora Penserosa – her last poem', 'Mrs. Battery O'Bell', 'Confessions of John Thomas Jones, inside man', 'Mrs. Scribner "at home"', 'The little shoeblack', 'The lament of the Irish emigrant', 'Constantia's inside man', 'Our domestic pets', 'How I lost my watch', '"Frankie"', 'Millie's story', 'My neighbours', 'An Irish blacksmith's tale', 'Paddy's bank', 'Nugget's heir', 'Suing for damages', 'Ten thousand leagues below the sea', 'They blew away', 'Brian MacThwate', 'Three fishes', 'Two generations – A Christmas reverie', 'A dialogue', 'Biddy's Dhrame', 'A history of myself', 'A tale of Irish life' [RL].

JEWETT, Sarah Orne, b. South Berwick (ME) 1849, d. 1909. American novelist, short story writer and naturalist, SOJ was educated at home and at the Berwick Academy. She travelled extensively in Europe, Canada and the US and was a contributor to the Boston *Atlantic Monthly* and other periodicals. Taught by her doctor father to observe the details of life around her and 'write about things just as they are', her writings gave rich accounts of women's lives and documented the changing life of New England in transition from the West Indian trade to an industrial region. She frequented the Boston literary scene and was a friend of Henry Wadsworth Longfellow, Charles Eliot Norton, and Julia Ward Howe. SOURCE Allibone Suppl., ii, p. 12; ANB; Blain, pp 576–7; Brown 2, p. 127; DAB; DLB, xii, lxxiv, ccxxi; Wright, iii, 2972–85.

J31   *A native of Winby, and other tales* (by Sarah Orne Jewett).
London: Constable & Co; Boston, New York: Houghton, Mifflin & Co., 1893. SOURCE Brown 2, 682; Wright, iii, 2980; OCLC. LOCATION NUC.
COMMENTARY Includes two sketches of Irish New Englanders, with humorous broad speech [Brown 2].

JOHNSON, —. Introduction writer. See HAMILTON, Elizabeth.

JOHNSON, Mrs D. See JOHNSON, Mrs David.

JOHNSON, Mrs David (known as Mrs D. Johnson), fl. 1813. Novelist. An advertisement in the *Star* (London, 25 June 1813) lists the following novel as by Mrs David Johnson. Brown lists her as Mrs D. Johnston and mistakenly mentions a 1837 edn. SOURCE Allibone i, p. 970; RL.

J32   *The brothers in high life; or, the north of Ireland* (by Mrs D. Johnson).
London: G. Kearsley, 1813, 3 vols. SOURCE Brown, 821; Belanger, 35 (1820 edn); British Fiction; Garside, 1813:37. LOCATION CtY (1820 edn).
COMMENTARY According to Garside, no copy of the first edn has been located. Advertisement in the *Star* (London, 1813) states that the novel describes 'through the medium of fictitious Characters, the Manners of the Sister Kingdom'. A review in the *British Critic* (London, 1813) mentions that 'The laws of consistency and probability are indeed stretched to the very utmost limits and the obstinate recovery and restoration to her husband of Elvina, the Heroine of the Tale, is indeed wonderful ... ' However, the *Critical Review* (London, 1813) states that 'Mrs. D. Johnson did very right to inform the world, that the above work is a novel, or it might have puzzled the wisest of the wise to know what it is, or was intended to be. But, it is a novel; – and contains the greatest farrago of nonsense that ever was published. What the lady could be thinking of when she committed such trash to the press, is not for us to determine; but, if she had put her composition on the back of the fire, it would have been no loss to the world, and more credit to herself'. Despite this review, the novel was reprinted in 1820 [Belanger; British Fiction].

JOHNSTON, Miss —, fl. 1837. Novelist. According to the preface to the volume below, written from Stratford, Miss J states that she wrote it in 1837. She probably was a Protestant. She also published *Transition* (London, 1839, 2 vols.). SOURCE NSTC; RL.

J33   *Ellen, a tale of Ireland* (by Miss Johnston).
+ London: Painter, 1843. SOURCE Brown, 816; Block, p. 124. LOCATION D, L.
COMMENTARY Cover title: *Ellen O'Rorick. A tale of Ireland*. Ellen O'Rorick, daughter of a drunken tavern keeper in Leixlip (Co. Kildare) goes to England where she mixes in high society. She marries in succession two elderly rich men, and becomes a Protestant. She settles in Ireland to a life of philanthropy [Brown].

JOHNSTON, C.M., pseud. 'C.M.J.', fl. 1839. Novelist, short story writer and illustrator from the south of Ireland. SOURCE Linen Hall cat. p. 96, O'Donoghue, p. 262.

J34   *Waking dreams* (by 'C.M.J.').
+ London: Saunders & Otley, 1839 (ill. by the author). LOCATION L.
+ London: Saunders & Otley, 1840 (as *The four Greys, or, travelling sketches in Ireland; and other tales*; ill. C.M.J. [the author]). SOURCE Linen Hall cat. p. 96. LOCATION D, BFl.
COMMENTARY Stories set in Ireland. Contents: 'The four greys', 'Help and hold; or, the history of the Bruce', 'Love', 'Mabel Annesley, or the fairy well', 'The comet', 'Old Nick in 1700' [CM].

J35   *Cromwell in Ireland. A historical romance* [anon.].
+ London: Thomas Cautley Newby, 1847, 3 vols. SOURCE Hodgson, p. 138. LOCATION Dt, L.
COMMENTARY 'C.M.J.' is identified as the author in Falkner Greirson cat. 39/75. Historical fiction set in mid-seventeenth-century Ireland, which gives an account of a love story between Glandine O'Dempsey of Ballybrittas (Co. Laois) and Capt. Richard Power [ML].

JOHNSTON, Charles. See JOHNSTONE, Charles.

JOHNSTON, Frances Sarah. See HOEY, Mrs Cashel.

JOHNSTON, H. See JOHNSTON, Henry.

JOHNSTON, Henry (known as H. Johnston), pseud. 'Zachary Fleming, writer', b. Ireland 1844, d. 1919. Novelist and short story writer, HJ was born of Scottish parents and went to Glasgow in his youth, where he worked as an accountant, writing for magazines in his spare time. In later life he published some moderately successful and quietly humorous stories of small-town life in Scotland. SOURCE Allibone Suppl., ii, p. 917; Sutherland, p. 338.

J36   *The Dawsons of Glenara. A story of Scottish life* [anon.].
London: Sampson Low, Marston, Searle & Rivington, 1877, 3 vols. SOURCE Wolff, 3702. LOCATION L, NUC.
COMMENTARY Story of the west of Scotland [Leclaire, p. 142].

J37   *Martha Spreull: being a chapter in the life of a single wumman* [*sic*] (ed. by 'Zachary Fleming, writer', with preface by the authoress [*sic*]).
Glasgow: D. Bryce & Son, 1884 (new edn). SOURCE Leclaire, p. 142 (ill. Thym); COPAC. LOCATION L. [
COMMENTARY First edn not located. Although edited by 'Zachary Fleming', this novel is by HJ. Features a room-letting spinster in Glasgow [Leclaire, p. 142; RL].

J38   *The chronicles of Glenbuckie* (by H. Johnston).
Edinburgh: D. Douglas, 1889. SOURCE Sutherland, p. 338; COPAC. LOCATION L, NUC.
COMMENTARY A tale of Scottish village life set in an Ayrshire parish in the 1830s [Leclaire, p. 143; Sutherland].

J39   *Kilmallie* (by Henry Johnston).
London: Ward & Downey, 1891, 2 vols. SOURCE Wolff, 3703; OCLC. LOCATION L, NUC (1891, new edn).
COMMENTARY A tale of Scottish village life in the 1830s [Sutherland].

J40   *Dr. Congalton's legacy; a chronicle of North country by-ways* (by Henry Johnston).
London: Methuen & Co., 1896. LOCATION L.

New York: C. Scribner's Sons, 1896. SOURCE Sutherland, p. 338. LOCATION NUC.
COMMENTARY A story of complications that ensue when in his will a Scottish doctor
leaves his property equally among three incompatible heirs [Sutherland].

JOHNSTON, William, b. Downpatrick (Co. Down) 1829, d. 1902. Novelist, sectarian pamphleteer and Orange Order apologist, WJ was the son of John Brett Johnston, of Ballykilbeg
(Co. Down) and Thomasine Anne Brunette Scott. He graduated BA from TCD in 1852 and
inherited his father's encumbered estate in 1853. He was admitted to the King's Inns, Dublin,
in 1868, and to the Middle Temple, London, in 1869, and was called to the Irish Bar 1871,
but does not seem to have practiced. A radical Unionist and Orangeman, Johnston joined the
Orange Order in 1848 and by 1855 was deputy grandmaster of the Orange lodge of Ireland.
He resided at Ballykilbeg House and promoted the order through a newspaper called *The
Downshire Protestant* (Downpatrick, Co. Down), which ran from 1855 to 1862. He was master of his local Orange lodge from 1857 until his death, forty-five years later. WJ's fame rests
on his opposition to the Party Processions Act of 1850, legislation designed to control sectarian conflict by banning inflammatory marches and displays, when he led a protest march of
9,000 Orangemen in Co. Down. His subsequent conviction and imprisonment made him a
folk-hero among the supporters of the Orange Order and he was elected MP for Belfast from
1868 to 1878, and succeeded in winning repeal of the Party Processions Act in 1872. He left
the parliament in 1878 and was given the minor government position of inspector of Irish
Fisheries, a post he lost in 1885 due to his outspoken politics, but he was returned to parliament that year (representing Belfast South) and remained there until his death in 1902. One
of the most strenuous northern Irish opponents of Home Rule, he nevertheless supported
Gladstone's land bill of 1890 and with regard to land issues was an advocate of fair rent, free
sale, and fixity of tenure. He travelled several times to the US to promote the cause of Irish
Protestants and he was instrumental in politically allying Irish Unionists with English
Conservatives. WJ wrote numerous pamphlets expressing his sectarian fears, and edited *The
Boyne Book of poetry and song* (Downpatrick, 1859). His novels reflect his fierce anti-Catholic
politics, but he was known as an upright and honest gentleman who was beloved by his ten-
ants, Catholics included. He married three times, first Harriet Allen in 1853, Arminella Frances
Drew in 1861, and Georgiana Barbara Hay in 1863. When one of his daughters converted to
catholicism, he drove her to Mass on his way to his own church. For his portraits and papers,
see ODNB. SOURCE Allibone Suppl., ii, p. 918; Brown, p. 148; Ferguson, p. 213; A.
McClelland, *William Johston of Ballykilbeg* (Lurgan, 1990); OCIL, p. 276; ODNB;
O'Donoghue, p. 217; RIA/DIB; Sutherland, pp 338–9; N. Vance, *Irish literature* (Oxford,
1990), p. 135.
J41   *Nightshade. A novel* (by William Johnston; dedicated to the author's wife [Harriet
        Johnston]).
        + London: Richard Bentley, 1857. SOURCE Sutherland, p. 338 (1856 edn, probably in
        error); Dt cat. (mentions 1857 as first edn). LOCATION InND Loeber coll.
        + London: Simpkin, Marshall & Co., 1858 (new edn, corrected; ill.; preface by Revd
        G. Gilfillan). LOCATION L.
        + Belfast: R. Aickin & Co., [*c*.1870] (new edn; ill.). SOURCE Brown, 818. LOCATION D
        ([1869?] edn), Dt ([*c*.1900] edn).
COMMENTARY Anti-Catholic fiction, describing nunneries, Jesuits, and romanizing Oxford high
churchmen. The story is about Charles Annandale, a young Ulster landlord, who returns from
Oxford to Ireland in the midst of agrarian agitation, which is condoned by the priests. His
agent is shot by Ribbonmen. Charles is an unsuccessful candidate for parliament. The election scenes are described in detail. The sister of Charles's betrothed is entrapped by a Jesuit

and incarcerated in a Paris convent, but is eventually released [Brown; N. Vance, *Irish litera-ture* (Oxford, 1990), pp 135–6].

J42   *Freshfield. A tale* (by William Johnston).
London: James Blackwood, [1860]. SOURCE Sutherland, p. 338 (1861 edn); NSTC; BL cat. LOCATION L.
COMMENTARY Contains melodramatic scenes of political skulduggery, assassination and Catholic unscrupulousness [Sutherland].

J43   *Under which king?* (by William Johnston).
+ London: Tinsley Bros, 1873. SOURCE Brown, 819; COPAC. LOCATION NUC, InND Loeber coll.
COMMENTARY An historical tale of the events of 1688 to 1691, and the struggle between King James II and King William III, written from a Williamite point of view. Details the siege of Londonderry (1689) and the battle of the Boyne (1690). Describes the fear Protestants have of the Catholics and their hatred of Lord Tyrconnell. An Owen O'Neil is the embodiment of all the bad characteristics ascribed to the Catholics [ML; Brown].

JOHNSTONE, Charles (variant spelling Johnston), pseuds 'An adept' and 'A Briton', b. Carrigogunnel (Co. Limerick) 1719, d. Calcutta (India) *c.*1802. Novelist, satirist and journal-ist CJ, according to the 1821 edn of his *Chrysal*, was descended from the Scottish family of the Johnstones of Annandale. He was educated at TCD (admitted in 1737?), but did not take a degree. He went to London and enrolled at Middle Temple, where he was called to the Bar, but he was unable to practice because of his deafness. He took to writing and became an owner-editor of several newspapers. CJ wrote the first two volumes of his highly popular *Chrysal* (London, 1760) while on a visit to Mount Edgecumbe in Cornwall, but the third and fourth volumes did not appear until later. In 1782, when he already was a man of advanced middle-age, he went to India, possibly to escape the enmity of men he had libelled. He was saved from a shipwreck off Johanna, an island between Madagascar and the African conti-nent. In India, he employed his talents in writing essays for the Bengali newspapers under the signature 'Oneiropolos'; became a joint owner of a paper, and died a wealthy man. CJ was also the attributed author of a tragedy, *Buthred* (London, 1779). SOURCE Allibone, i, p. 985; B & S, p. 443; Brady, pp 113–14; Field Day, i, pp 684–5, 759; introd. to 1821 edn of *Chrysal* ..., pp v–viii; Hogan 2, pp 599–600; NCBEL 2, p. 1007; OCIL, p. 276; ODNB; RIA/DIB.

J44   *Chrysal; or, the adventures of a guinea. Wherein are exhibited views of several striking scenes, with curious and interesting anecdotes of the most noted persons in every rank of life, whose hands it passed through in America, England, Holland, Germany and Portugal* (by 'An adept'; dedication to William Pitt, signed 'A Briton').
+ London: T. Becket, 1760, vols. 1 and 2. SOURCE Raven, 577; Forster, 1440; McBurney & Taylor, 493; Hardy, 517; ESTC t089195. LOCATION Dt, L, YU, IU, InND Loeber coll.
+ London: T. Becket & P.A. de Hondt, 1765, vols. 3 and 4 in l. SOURCE Raven, 922; Forster, 1442; Hardy, 577; ESTC t128716. LOCATION L, InND Loeber coll.
+ London: T. Becket, 1762, 3rd edn, vol. 1 & 2 in 1 (greatly enlarged and corrected). SOURCE Raven, 846 (1764, 4th edn); ESTC t119016 (1764, 4th edn). LOCATION L (1764, 4th edn), InND Loeber coll.
+ London: T. Becket & P.A. de Hondt, 1762, 3rd edn, vol. 2 (greatly enlarged and corrected). SOURCE Raven, 846 (1764, 4th edn); ESTC t119016 (1764, 4th edn). LOCATION L (1764, 4th edn), InND Loeber coll.
London: John Hill, 1767, 4 vols. SOURCE Pollard, p. 82; Raven, 1108; ESTC t061908.

LOCATION Dt, L, NN. COMMENTARY *London 1767 edn* This is the first complete edn. Probably published in Ireland [Raven, 1108; RL].

London: J.F. & D.C. Rivington, G. Robinson, T. Cadell, T. Evans & R. Baldwin, 1783, 4 vols. (new edn). SOURCE Seen at Ximenes, Dec. 1993. LOCATION Dt.

London: J. Watson, M. Pearce, S. Lewis, G. Longman & W. Crowder, 1785, 4 vols. SOURCE Jarndyce cat. 129/884; ESTC t073508. LOCATION L. COMMENTARY *London 1785 edn* A piracy; publishers' names are fictitious, perhaps printed in Dublin [Jarndyce cat. 129/884].

+ London: Hector M'Lean, 1821, 3 vols. (a new edn, with a sketch of the author's life). SOURCE Seen at MacManus, Philadelphia, April, 1993; RL. LOCATION Univ. of Liverpool.

Dublin: Dillon Chamberlaine, 1760, 2 vols. SOURCE Raven, 578; McBurney & Taylor, 495. LOCATION O, H, IU.

+ Dublin: Henry Saunders & Hulton Bradley, 1761, 2 vols., 2nd edn ('greatly enlarged and corrected'). SOURCE Raven, 658; ESTC n000969. LOCATION O, InND Loeber coll. (vol. 2 only).

+ Dublin: Printed by Dillon Chamberlaine, 1765, 2 vols., vols. 3 and 4. SOURCE Raven, 923; ESTC n000980. LOCATION D, L (not found), InND Loeber coll.

+ Dublin: Henry Saunders & Hulton Bradley, 1766, 2 vols., 3rd edn, vols. 1 and 2 ('greatly enlarged and corrected'). SOURCE ESTC n000979. LOCATION L, InND Loeber coll. (vol. 1 only).

Londres [Paris?]: Grangé, 1767 (trans. as *Chrisal ou les aventures d'une guinée, histoire angloise*). SOURCE ESTC t185739. LOCATION O.

Leipzig: Weygand, 1775 (trans. as *Chrysal oder Begebenheiten einer Guinee*). SOURCE OCLC. LOCATION Univ. of California, Berkeley.

+ Baltimore: F. Lucas Jnr & Joseph Cushing, 1816, 4 vols. in 2. LOCATION InND Loeber coll.

+ New York: D. Huntington, 1816, 2 vols. LOCATION InND Loeber coll. (vol. 1 only), CtY.

New York: Garland, 1979, 4 vols. (introd. by Malcolm Bosse). SOURCE COPAC. LOCATION Univ. of Liverpool.

COMMENTARY A satire disguised as a chronicle of contemporary events loosely strung together in the autobiography of a guinea as it passes from hand to hand. Set in America, England, Holland, Germany and Portugal during the Seven Years War, the book pretends to reveal political secrets and to expose the private lives of various public men. Although the native Irish are generally portrayed favourably, with some criticisms of English misgovernment, there are notable anti-Catholic and anti-Semitic passages. It calls for the fair education of women and the principle of one man, one vote. The novel was admired widely, but it made Johnstone many enemies. The book was reprinted in London over a period of fifty years [Brady, p. 114; Baker; Field Day, i, pp 718–26; ODNB; RIA/DIB].

J45   *The reverie; or, a flight to the paradise of fools* [anon.].

+ Dublin: Printed [for the author?] by Dillon Chamberlaine, 1762, 2 vols. in 1. SOURCE Raven, 723 (unauthorized first edn); ESTC t066926. LOCATION Dt, L, InND Loeber coll. (vol. 1 only).

+ London: T. Becket & P.A. da [*sic*] Hondt, 1763, 2 vols. SOURCE Raven, 724 (2 vols. in 1); Forster, 1444; Hardy, 521; ESTC t126192; Gecker, 549; McBurney & Taylor, 501; Quaritch cat. 1193/35. LOCATION L, O, UP, IU, InND Loeber coll.

's Gravenhage: Pieter van Os, 1765, 2 vols. (trans. into Dutch as *De mijmering of een vlucht naar het paradijs der dwazen*; ill. S. Fokke). SOURCE F.A. v. S.

New York: Garland Press, 1975. SOURCE COPAC. LOCATION Dt.

COMMENTARY Reviewed in the *Monthly Review* (Dec. 1762). A political satire attacking Lord Bute and others. Copy in the New York Public Library has a written list of the actual names of the characters. The storyteller is in a reverie and recounts various events and philosophical thoughts that occur to him [RL; NCBEL 2].

J46   *The history of Arsaces, prince of Betlis* [anon.].

London: T. Becket, 1774, 2 vols. SOURCE Block, p. 124; Forster, 1443; Raven 2, 1774:30; Gecker, 546; Hardy, 518; McBurney & Taylor, 498; Forster 2, 2310; ESTC t117967. LOCATION L, UP, IU.

+ Dublin: W. Sleater, M. Hay, J. Williams, W. Wilson, J. Husband & L. Flynn, 1774–1775, 2 vols. SOURCE Bradshaw, 1855; Raven 2, 1774:30; Pollard 2, p. 114; ESTC t064759. LOCATION Dm, D, C, InND Loeber coll.

Dublin: Printed for the United Company of Booksellers, 1774, 2 vols. SOURCE Raven 2, 1774:30; ESTC n007597. LOCATION D, Dt, CtY.

Leipzig: [publisher?], 1775 (trans. as *Die Geschichte Arsaces, des Prinzden von Betlis*). SOURCE Raven 2, 1774:30. LOCATION Bayerlische Staatsbibliothek.

New York: Garland, 1975. LOCATION O.

COMMENTARY Comment on America using oriental allegory; criticizes policy of founding colonies. The tale is told by a person who had been taken captive during a war and who tells the story of his very eventful life [ML; OCIL; NCBEL 2].

J47   *The pilgrim; or, a picture of life. In a series of letters written mostly from London by a Chinese philosopher, to his friend at Quang-Tong. Containing remarks upon the laws, customs, and manners of the English and other nations. Illustrated by a number of curious and interesting, anecdotes, and characters drawn from real life* [anon.] ('by the editor of Chrysal; dedicated to Philip Affleck, Esq., Captain [afterwards Admiral] of his Majesty's navy').

London: T. Cadell & W. Flexney, 1775, 2 vols. SOURCE Black, 551; Block, p. 124; McBurney & Taylor, 500; Hardy, 520; Raven 2, 1775:25; Forster 2, 2312; ESTC t118158. LOCATION L, IU.

Dublin: J. Potts, J. Williams, W. Colles, R. Moncrieffe, C. Jenkins, W. Wilson, T. Walker, G. Burnett, J. Colles & M. Mills, 1775, 2 vols. SOURCE Black, 551; Raven 2, 1775:25; ESTC t116306. LOCATION L, O, Univ. of Minnesota.

Leipzig: J.F. Junius, 1775 (trans. as *Der Pilgrim, oder, ein Gemählde des Lebens*). SOURCE Raven 2, 1775:25; OCLC. LOCATION Univ. of California, Berkley.

New York: Garland, 1974. LOCATION Dt.

COMMENTARY An epistolary novel in which a Chinese spy comments to friends on English life [NCBEL 2].

J48   *The history of John Juniper, Esq. alias Juniper Jack. Containing the birth, parentage, and education, life, adventures and character of that most wonderful and surprizing gentleman* [anon.].

London: R. Baldwin, 1781, 3 vols. SOURCE Block, p. 124; Gecker, 548; McBurney & Taylor, 499; Hardy, 519; Raven 2, 1781:20; Forster 2, 2311; ESTC t073521. LOCATION L, UP, IU.

+ Dublin: S. Price, J. Sheppard, R. Cross, T. Wilkinson, W. Gilbert, E. Cross, P. Higly, W. Wilson, R. Moncrieffe, C. Jenkin, T. Walker, J. Exshaw, L. White, J. Beatty & P. Byrne, 1781, 2 vols. SOURCE Pickering & Chatto cat. 710/69; Raven 2, 1781:20; ESTC n008001. LOCATION D, O, InND Loeber coll.

COMMENTARY Episodic *Bildungsroman* with scenes set in Portarlington (Co. Laois) and Dublin about a young Irishman who leaves to seek his fortune in England and gets into trouble [Chronology, p. 54; OCIL, p. 277].

J49   *The adventures of Anthony Varnish; or, a peep at the manners of society* (by 'An adept'; dedicated to George Colman).
London: William Lane, 1786, 3 vols. SOURCE Blakey, p. 137; Block, p. 124; Raven 2, 1786:29.
Forster 2, 2307; ESTC t066944. LOCATION L.
Londres [Paris]: Regnault, 1788, 4 vols. (trans. as *Les aventures comiques et plaisantes d'Antoine Varnish*). SOURCE Raven 2, 1786:29; ESTC t149929; Streeter, 212. LOCATION L.
+ Brussels: B. LeFrancq, 1788, 4 vols. (trans. as *Les aventures comiques et plaisantes d'Antoine Varnish*). LOCATION L.
Leipzig: [publisher?],1786 (trans. as *Peregrine Pickel der Zweyte oder Tragisch-komische Abenteuer von Anton Varnish*). SOURCE Raven 2, 1786:29.
COMMENTARY No copy of the Leipzig edn located. A picaresque social satire inspired by the work of Tobias Smollett with great a variety of lively scenes in Ireland and England. The *Monthly Review* commented that this novel was 'Made up entirely of scenes of low life. And it must be acknowledged that the Author in describing them, appears to be perfectly *at home*' [NCBEL 2, p. 1007; Raven 2].

JOHNSTONE, Charles, fl. 1770. English scandal writer to whom the following work has been attributed by John Taylor. SOURCE J. Taylor, *Records of my life* [London, 1832], i, pp 58–9; Personal communication, Mary Pollard, 2001.
J50   *The genuine memoirs of Miss Faulkner otherwise D***l***n* [i.e. Donellan]; or, *Countess of H*****x* [i.e., Halifax], *in expectancy. Containing, the amours and intrigues of several persons of high distinction, and remarkable characters: with some curious political anecdotes, never before published* [anon.].
+ London: William Bingley, 1770. SOURCE Raven 2, 1770:6; Forster, 1055; McBurney & Taylor, 338; ESTC t073915. LOCATION L, IU.
COMMENTARY This novel, partly based on facts, concerns the career of Miss Anna Maria Faulkner (also Falkner, later Mrs Donaldson), the adopted niece of the Irish publisher George Faulkner, who plays a major role as 'Mr Paragraph'. The heroine, Miss Faulkner, is courted by Lord K—ngs—b—gh [Kingsborough],[1] who schemes to carry her off to the country. Contains a description of Kingsborough's seat at Rockingham (Co. Roscommon). Miss Faulkner gives birth to a boy, who dies; both return to Dublin. His lordship elopes with a Miss J—n to Paris, whereupon Miss Faulkner leaves for London. Kingsborough with his new love also comes to London, where Miss J—n engages the affection of an Irishman, Mr Fleming, who she marries. Kingsborough in vain tries to find Miss Faulkner, returns to Ireland, where he dies of apoplexy. She meets another former mistress of Kingsborough, Lady Valeria, who describes her adventures including her life at Rockingham. Miss Faulkner becomes a successful singer, marries a Mr D—ll—n [Donellan], who treats her cruelly. She receives pecuniary assistance from Lord H—x [Halifax], who eventually meets her, and assists Donellan to flee his creditors and go to America. Halifax takes Miss Faulkner in his keeping and has two children by her. She joins him in Ireland, where he is appointed to a government position, and advances the interests of her relatives there. Donellan returns to blackmail Halifax. A supplement contains several letters to the publisher Bingley about the history of Miss Faulkner, including one

1 This must be Sir Robert King, 4th Bt, of Rockingham (Co. Roscommon), who was created Baron Kingsborough in 1748, and died unmarried in 1755. He must have been a notorious rake and seducer, as is also evident from Bishop Edward Synge's letters (R.D. King-Harman, *The Kings, Earls of Kingston* (Cambridge, 1959), p. 25, and chart following p. 4; M.-L. Legg (ed.), *The Synge letters* (Dublin, 1996), pp 142-43).

referring to Kingsborough's architect Henry K—ne, [Keene] 'now [1770] of Golden Square' [London] [RL; Seen at Ximenes, New York, Dec. 1993].

JOLLY, James, fl. 1833. Fictionalizing autobiographer. Members of the Jolly (also Joly) family have lived in Ireland for a long time. The 'Biographical introduction' to the following semifictional work is followed by a 'Biographical postscript', quoting a letter sent by James Jolly dated 'Londonderry, March 18th, 1833'. SOURCE RL; Garside 2, A:24.

J51   *The young enthusiast in humble life. A simple story. Biographical introduction* [anon.].
        + London: James Fraser, 1833. SOURCE Garside 2, A:24. LOCATION L.
COMMENTARY Fictionalized autobiography set in England. Henry Martlet accompanies a friend who runs away, but they are brought back to their parents' homes. His father then places him in an apprenticeship to a respectable trade, and Henry regularly attends a dissenting chapel. After Henry and his mother die, his father falls in love with Mary, a neighbour girl, but their love is fraught with trouble. Eventually the father leaves England. He is shipwrecked and dies and his body is washed ashore on the western coast of Ireland [ML].

'JONES, James Thomas', pseud. See **LESLIE, Mary**.

JONES, T. Mason, fl. 1867. Dublin journalist, editor of the *Dublin Tribune* and later a well-known lecturer in England for the Reform League. During the American Civil War TML lectured in the US in favour of the North. Later he ran unsuccessfully for parliament. His knowledge of TCD in the volume below would suggest he had been a student there, and the defence attorney in the trial is modelled on Isaac Butt§. SOURCE Allibone Suppl., ii, p. 924; Brown, p. 149; Hogan 2, p. 602; Wolff introd., p. 34.

J52   *Old Trinity. A story of real life* (by T. Mason Jones).
        + London: Richard Bentley, 1867, 3 vols. in 1. SOURCE Brown, 822; Hogan 2, p. 602; Wolff, 3711; COPAC. LOCATION L, InND Loeber coll.
        New York: Garland, 1979, 3 vols. (introd. by R.L. Wolff). SOURCE COPAC. LOCATION Dt.
COMMENTARY Set around 1850 in TCD, Ossory, and Co. Limerick, it describes college life in detail and tells of the career and love affair of Tom Butler, a student. An evil baronet wishes to marry the heiress to whom Tom is secretly betrothed. Tom accidentally kills the baronet, but when his brother is accused of the deed, he steps forward. He is acquitted of murder, and marries his heiress. It includes some account of the land troubles of the day [ML, Brown].

JORDAN, Kate, b. Dublin 1862, d. Mountain Lakes (NJ) 1926. Novelist and playwright, KJ emigrated to New York with her parents Michael James and Katherine Jordan when she was an infant. She published her first story by age 12, and her first popular work 'The kiss of gold' appeared in *Lippincott's Monthly Magazine* (Philadelphia, Oct. 1892). After she married Fredrick Vermilye, a broker, she continued to write under her maiden name. She travelled widely and lived for some time in England and France. In London she was involved with the Pen and Brush Club, the Lyceum, and the Writer's Club. In the US she was a member of the Society of American Dramatists. Her most popular plays were: *A luncheon at Nick's* (1903); *The pompadour's protégé* (1903); *Mrs Dakon* (1909), and *The right road* (1911). She suffered from insomnia for years and eventually committed suicide by ingesting poison. SOURCE Blain, p. 591; DAB; RIA/DIB.

J53   *The kiss of gold* (by Kate Jordan).
        Philadelphia: J.B. Lippincott & Co., 1892. SOURCE Blain, p. 591; OCLC. LOCATION NN.
J54   *The other house: A story of human nature* (by Kate Jordan).
        New York: Lovell, Coryell & Co., [c.1892]. SOURCE Wright, iii, 3042. LOCATION L.

J55 *A circle in the sand* (by Kate Jordan).
Boston: Lamson, Wolffe & Co., 1898. SOURCE Wright iii, 3041. LOCATION L.

J56 *Time the comedian* (by Kate Jordan).
New York: D. Appleton & Co., 1905. LOCATION L.
COMMENTARY Portrays the effects of age and unhappiness on one whose beauty has been destroyed [Blain].

J57 *The creeping tides: A romance of an old neighborhood* (by Kate Jordan).
Boston: Little, Brown & Co., 1913. SOURCE OCLC. LOCATION NN.
London: S. Paul & Co., [1915]. SOURCE COPAC. LOCATION L.
COMMENTARY Depicts New York City's unglamorous side, especially for women striving for independence [Blain].

J58 *Against the winds* (by Kate Jordan; dedicated to Mrs Frederic J. Faulks [Theodosia Garrison]).
+ Boston: Little, Brown & Co., 1919 (ill.). LOCATION L.
London: Hutchinson & Co., [1919]. LOCATION L.
COMMENTARY Similar content to *The creeping tides* (Boston, 1913) [Blain].

J59 *The next corner* (by Kate Jordan).
London: Eveleigh Nash, 1921. LOCATION L.
COMMENTARY Set in France [Blain].

J60 *Trouble-the-house* (by Kate Jordan).
+ Boston: Little, Brown & Co., 1921. LOCATION L.
London: Methuen & Co., 1922. LOCATION L.
COMMENTARY Concentrates on childhood experiences and is partly autobiographical [Blain].

JOY, J.M., fl. 1875. Irish novelist and poet, JMJ authored a collection of poetry, *Labda, and other poems* (London, 1876). According to the title page of the following work, he or she was also the author of *A dream and the song of Caedmon* (London, 1875). SOURCE MVP, p. 251; COPAC; RL.

J61 *The two mothers* (by J.M. Joy).
+ London: George Bell & Sons, 1879. SOURCE COPAC. LOCATION L.
COMMENTARY The story begins and ends in France, but is set mainly in Italy. Features, royalists, republicans and patriots [RL].

JOYCE, Robert D. See JOYCE, Robert Dwyer.

JOYCE, Robert Dwyer (also known as Robert D. Joyce), b. Glenosheen (Co. Limerick) 1830 (1836 according to Burke), d. Dublin 1883. Poet, novelist, short story writer and translator, RDJ was the brother of Patrick Weston Joyce, a linguist and historian. Educated in local hedge-schools and trained as a teacher, he became principal of Clonmel Model School. He resigned to study medicine at Queen's College, Cork, where he graduated in 1865. Shortly after completing his medical studies, he became professor of English literature at the Catholic University, Dublin. He contributed stories to the *Harp* (Cork, 1859); the *Nation* (Dublin, under the pseudonym 'Feardana'); *Duffy's Hibernian Magazine* (Dublin, 1860–61), and the *Irish People* (Dublin, using the pseudonym 'Merulan'). According to RIA/DIB, his first collection of poetry, *Ballads of Irish chivalry* was published in 1861 when he was still a student. Frustrated by the lack of success of the Fenian movement in Ireland, he emigrated to the US in 1866 where he settled in Boston and lectured at the Harvard Medical School. He joined the Fenian movement in the US and was friends with leading Irish nationalists John Devoy and Michael Davitt. His two volumes of poetry: *Deirdre* (Boston, 1876) and *Blanid* (Boston, 1879) were immensely success-ful. The former, a narrative poem dealing with ancient Ireland, RDJ presented to Oscar Wilde§ in Boston in 1882. While primarily a poet, his serialized novel 'The squire of Castleton' appeared in the Dublin *Irishman*, and another serial, 'The whitethorn tree', appeared in the *Irish Literary Gazette* (Dublin, between 1857 and 1861). His *Old Celtic romances* (London, 1879) consists of translations from the Irish. RDJ returned to Ireland in 1883 and died just one month later. SOURCE Allibone Suppl., ii, p. 927; Boase, ii, p. 154; Brady, p. 116; Boylan, p. 177; Brown, p. 339; Burke, p. 390; Crowley, pp 253–4; Cummins cat. 57/109; Fanning, p. 383; Field Day, iii, p. 625; Hogan, pp 338–9; Hogan 2, p. 628; Irish pseudonyms; MVP, p. 251; NCBEL 4, p. 626; OCIL, pp 281–2; O'Donoghue, p. 220; RIA/DIB.

J62   *Legends of the wars in Ireland* (by Robert Dwyer Joyce; dedicated to John Savage).
+ Boston: James Campbell, 1868. SOURCE Brown, 825; Fanning, p. 383; Wright, ii, 1408. LOCATION Grail, L, NUC, Wright web.
COMMENTARY *Boston edn* Contents: 'A batch of legends', 'The master of Lisfinry', 'The fair maid of Killarney', 'An eye for an eye', 'The rose of Drimnagh', 'The house of Lisbloom', 'The White Knight's present', 'The first and the last Lords of Fermoy', 'The chase from the hostel', 'The whitethorn tree', 'Rosaleen; or, the white lady of Barna', 'The bridal ring', 'The little battle of Bottle Hill' [Wright].
+ Glasgow, London: Cameron & Ferguson, n.d. LOCATION UCD Folklore Dept.

J63   *The green and the red; or, historical tales and legends of Ireland* [anon.].
Glasgow: Cameron & Ferguson, 1870. SOURCE Brown 2, 695.
Glasgow: Cameron & Ferguson, n.d. (as *Galloping O'Hogan; or, the rapparee captains: A romance of the days of Sarsfield: to which is appended the interesting tales of The whitethorn tree; The Rose of Drimnagh; and The fair maid of Killarney*). LOCATION OCLC. SOURCE KU-S.
+ Dublin: M.H. Gill & Son, n.d. (as *Galloping O'Hogan; or, the rapparee captain: A romance of the days of Sarsfield: to which is added The whitethorn tree, The Rose of Drimnagh & The fair maid of Killarney*). SOURCE Brown 2, 695; Healy cat.5/1070. LOCATION D, DPL.
COMMENTARY No copy of the Glasgow 1870 edn located. Contents: 'Galloping O'Hogan' (Galloping O'Hogan was a rapparee in Co. Tipperary, who served as a guide to Patrick Sarsfield, Jacobite military commander in the Williamite War. Presents an accounts of fight-ing, with Black Gideon Grimes of the House of Lisbloom and the Williamites on one side, and Sarsfield, O'Hogan and Eamon an Cnuic on the other), 'The whitethorn three', The rose of Drimnagh' and 'The fair maid of Killarney'. The last three stories were first published in *Legends of the wars in Ireland* (Boston, 1868) [Brown 2; RL].

J64   *Irish fireside tales* (by Robert D. Joyce).
+ Boston: Patrick Donahoe, 1871. SOURCE Brown, 826; Fanning, p. 383; White, ii, 1407. LOCATION Grail, L, NUC.
COMMENTARY Contents: 'The Geraldine and his bride, fair Eileen', 'The pearl necklace; or, the beauty of the blossom-gate' (a love story of Kilmallock), 'Creevan, the brown-haired; or, the seventh son', 'The fisherman's daughter. A tale of Rindown castle', 'The building of Mourne', 'Madeline's vow', 'A little bit of sport' (four comic stories): 'No. 1. Ducks and divers', 'No. 2. Hunting down the walrus', 'No. 3. Otter-hunting on the Blackwater', 'No. 4. The enchanted fox of Darra', 'The buccaneers' castle', 'Mrs Carberry and the phooka; or, the return on new-year's eve', 'The old bachelor', 'The golden butterfly' (set in Co. Clare), 'The Adventures of Hugh and Brian', 'Winnifred's fortune. A story of Dublin life in the days of Queen Anne', 'Legend of Tiernan; or, the blue knight', 'The rescued bride. A legend of the Cummeraghs', 'The bible oath' [ML].

K

'K., J.M.M.', pseud. See **KEANE, J.M.**

'K., K. v.', pseud. See **KILLINGER, Karl, freiherr von**.

'K., O.C.', pseud. See **NEWELL, R.H.**

KANE, Annie (later known as **Annie Vernon**), b. 1839, d. United States? Author of a single novel. Like the novel's heroine AK probably was born in Co. Galway, emigrated to the US, and became blind. Later, as Annie Vernon, she edited *Golden gems of thought by great authors* (Baltimore, *c.*1887). SOURCE NUC; RL.

K1   *The golden sunset, or the homeless blind girl* (by Annie Kane; dedicated to Thomas C. Yearly).
+ Baltimore: J.W. Bond, 1862. SOURCE OCLC. LOCATION Syracuse Univ., *InND Loeber coll.* (1882 edn)
+ Baltimore: James Young, 1887 (by Annie Vernon). LOCATION InND Loeber coll., ViU.

COMMENTARY Autobiographical story about a girl from Co. Galway, who emigrated to the US. She becomes blind, but her faith sustains her through various trials. Contains a description of the Maryland Institution for the Instruction of the Blind [ML].

KANE, Revd J. Blackburne, b. Co. Roscommon 1832, d. 1894. Church of Ireland clergyman and writer, JBK was the son of John Kane, gentleman. Educated at Sligo School and entered TCD in 1849, obtained his BA in 1853 and MA in 1877. Became curate of Templemore (Co. Tipperary), 1853–5; curate of Annaghmore (Co. Armagh), 1855–72; and deputy secretary of the London Society in Aid of the Moravians, 1872–81. Moved to England where he became vicar of Bicester (Oxford), 1881–94. Married at Templemore in 1856, Fanny, youngest daughter of Capt. Paul K. Carden, RN., of Manna Cottage. By her he had nine children. She died in 1888, aged 49 years; and he died in 1894. He also published sermons. SOURCE B & S, Appendix B, p. 64; Brown 2, p. 131; Fleming, *Armagh*, pp 121–2.

K2   *Love's labour not lost: A new temperance tale* (by J. Blackburne Kane; dedicated to Revd Francis Close, Dean of Carlisle).
+ Belfast: Irish Temperance League, 1863. SOURCE Allibone Suppl., ii, p. 929; Brown 2, 701. LOCATION D.

COMMENTARY A temperance tale set in a northern Irish village, but there is no description of scenery nor any attempt at dialect. By the 'love's labour' of Mrs Ernestone, the principal characters, lay and clerical, are converted to total abstinence. The plot turns on a pseudo-murder and an attempted murder, for both for of which an innocent youth is blamed [Brown 2].

KARR, Miss Thérèse Alphonse. French author.
K3   *Croquis irlandais* (by Thérèse Alphonse Karr).
Poitiers: Oudin Frères, 1880. SOURCE Emerald Isle cat. 69/588; Bn-Opale plus. LOCATION BNF.

COMMENTARY Contents, among others stories, 'La veuve de Cairnlough' [Emerald Isle].

'Kate'

'KATE, COUSIN', pseud. See BELL, Miss Catherine Douglas.

KAVANAGH, Bridget, fl. 1876. BK was the mother and co-author of Julia Kavanagh§. See KAVANAGH, Julia.

KAVANAGH, Julia, b. Thurles (Co. Tipperary) 1824, d. Nice (France) 1877. Novelist and biographer, JK was the only child of Morgan Peter Kavanagh§, a writer, and his wife Bridget Fitzpatrick. Her family lived for some time in Thurles (Co. Tipperary), but mainly in Paris and Normandy, which later gave her the settings for some of her novels. The Kavanaghs returned to London in 1844, with mother and daughter separating from – or being abandoned by – the father. Thereafter JK supported herself and her invalid mother by her writing. She made contributions to *Eliza Cooke's Journal* (London), contributed to the *People's Journal* (London, 1847), to *Household Words* with W.H. Wills (London, 1850), as well as contributing essays on 'Conquered languages' to *Duffy's Hibernian Magazine* (Dublin, 1860–61). In an extraordinary literary quarrel in 1857, JK disowned any connection with a novel (*The hobbies*, London, 1857, 3 vols.), which her father had written and which he, or his unscrupulous publisher Newby, had tried to pass off as partly hers. The contretemps and subsequent lawsuit damaged her literary reputation for a period. Some of her books focus on the perils of working women (e.g., *Rachel Gray*, London, 1856) and they record much of the social history of the period. She wrote many biographical sketches of women, including *Women in France during the eighteenth century* (London, 1850); *Women of Christianity exemplary for acts of piety and charity* (London, 1852); *French women of letters* (London, 1862, 2 vols.), and *English women of letters* (London, 1863), which included the Irish authors Maria Edgeworth§ and Lady Morgan§. All of these portraits of women were meant to counter their neglect in typically male-oriented histories. She also wrote *A summer and winter in the two Sicilies* (London, 1858, 2 vols.) and with her mother a volume of fairy stories published in 1876. Many of her novels were first serialized in periodicals. *Nathalie*, which was a critical and commercial success, may have been influenced by Charlotte Brontë's *Jane Eyre*. Brontë wrote JK expressing her admiration for *Nathalie*, and it may in turn have influenced Brontë's own later novel *Villette*. JK and Brontë met in 1850. JK moved to Nice where she was a semi-invalid for several years before her death. A devout Catholic, she died unmarried. Her portrait is in the NGI. For her papers, see ODNB. SOURCE Allibone, i, p. 1007; Allibone Suppl., ii, p. 930; Blain, p. 598; Brady, p. 117; Field Day, v, pp 927–8, H. Fraser et al., *Gender and the Victorian periodical* (Cambridge, 2003), p. 97; N. Higgins, 'Julia Kavanagh (1824–1877) a novelist from Thurles', *Tipperary Historical Journal* (1992), pp 81–3; Hogan, ii, pp 630–1; J. Kestner, *Protest and reform. The British social narrative by women 1827–1867* (Madison, WI, 1985), pp 188–92; Kunitz & Haycraft, p. 338; K.S. Macquoid, 'Julia Kavanagh' in *Women novelists of Queen Victoria's reign* (London, 1897); NCBEL 4, p. 1310; OCIL, p. 283; ODNB; O'Toole, pp 103–4; RIA/DIB; Sutherland, pp 343–4; Tiger Books cat. 04/02/159; Todd, p. 376–77.

K4   *The three paths. A story for young people* (by Julia Kavanagh).
+ London: Chapman & Hall, 1848 (ill. Andrew Maclure). SOURCE NCBEL 3, p. 935; Block, p. 126; Todd, p. 377; Sutherland, p. 343 (notes 1847 edn, perhaps mistakenly). LOCATION D, L, NUC.
Concord (NH): E.C. Eastman, 1862. LOCATION NUC.
Boston: Whittemore, Niles & Hall, 1856 (as *Saint-Gildas; or, the three paths*). LOCATION NUC.

K5   *Madeleine. A tale of Auvergne. Founded on fact* (by Julia Kavanagh).
+ London: Richard Bentley, 1848. SOURCE Hodgson, p. 306; Wolff, 3720; Topp 8, 75. LOCATION L, NUC, InND Loeber coll.

+ London: Chapman & Hall, 1873 (new edn; Select Library of Fiction, No. 173). SOURCE Topp 3, p. 387. LOCATION D.

London, New York: Ward & Lock & Co. [1884] (Select Library of Fiction, No. 773, as *Madeleine*). SOURCE Topp 2, 1740; Sadleir, 3604.

New York: D. Appleton & Co., 1852. SOURCE Topp 2, p. 262. LOCATION NUC.

Philadelphia: Kilner, [1850s]. SOURCE Topp 2, p. 262. LOCATION NUC.

COMMENTARY Life of a peasant girl of the Auvergne who founded the Hospital of Mont-Saint-Jean [Todd, p. 736].

K6   *Nathalie. A tale* (by Julia Kavanagh).

+ London: Henry Colburn, 1850, 3 vols. SOURCE Hodgson, p. 306; Wolff, 3721. LOCATION D, L, NUC.

+ Leipzig: Bernard Tauchnitz, 1851, 2 vols. in 1. SOURCE T & B, 195. LOCATION Dt, NUC, InND Loeber coll.

New York: D. Appleton; Philadelphia: G.S. Appleton, 1851. SOURCE OCLC. LOCATION MH.

COMMENTARY One of the earliest school stories for young women, it is set in a girl's school in northern France. The heroine is a passionate, independent young schoolmistress who falls in love with and marries an older man [Field Day, iv, p. 1142; ODNB; Todd, p. 376].

K7   *Daisy Burns. A tale* (by Julia Kavanagh).

London: Richard Bentley, 1853, 3 vols. SOURCE NCBEL 3, p. 935. LOCATION L, NUC.

+ Leipzig: Bernard Tauchnitz, 1853, 2 vols. SOURCE T & B, 263–64. LOCATION InND Loeber coll.

New York: D. Appleton & Co., 1864. LOCATION NUC.

+ Paris: L. Hachette & Co., 1860 (trans. by Mme H. Loreau as *Tuteur et pupille*). SOURCE DNB. LOCATION L.

COMMENTARY Reviewed in the *Westminster Review* (London, 1853). Set in England. Daisy, an orphan, whose grandfather showed only an intermittent interest in her, is brought up by Cornelius O'Reilly, her father's Irish friend. The story traces the development of a father-daughter relationship between Cornelius and Daisy that leads to marital love [ML].

K8   *Grace Lee. A tale* (by Julia Kavanagh).

+ London: Smith, Elder & Co., 1855, 3 vols. SOURCE NCBEL 3, p. 935. LOCATION L.

+ Leipzig: Bernard Tauchnitz, 1855, 2 vols. SOURCE T & B, 320–21. LOCATION InND Loeber coll., NUC.

K9   *Rachel Gray. A tale founded on fact* (by Julia Kavanagh).

+ London: Hurst & Blackett, 1856. SOURCE Alston, p. 227. LOCATION D, DPL, L, InND Loeber coll.

Toulouse: Société des Livres Religieux, 1900 (as *Rachel Gray* by Mrs L. [sic] Kavanagh). SOURCE Devonshire, p. 394 (cites 1856 edn, which has not been located); B-Opale plus. LOCATION BNF.

Leipzig: Bernard Tauchnitz, 1856. SOURCE T & B, 344. LOCATION NUC.

New York: D. Appleton & Co., 1856. LOCATION NUC.

COMMENTARY Shows through the eyes of a working girl, how relentless class struggle for success affected both the working and managerial classes of northern England [Todd, p. 376].

K10   *Adèle. A tale* (by Julia Kavanagh).

London: Hurst & Blackett, 1858, 3 vols. SOURCE Wolff, 3715. LOCATION L, NUC ([1865] edn).

+ Leipzig: Bernard Tauchnitz, 1858, 3 vols. SOURCE T & B, 420. LOCATION InND Loeber coll., NUC.

+ New York: D. Appleton & Co., 1858. LOCATION InND Loeber coll., NUC.

COMMENTARY A story of bad relations between step-family members set in England and France. After his father's death, William Osborne inherits an ailing business as well as responsibility for his stepmother and her children. They make his life miserable, and when he marries in France they use many sly ways to try to wreck his and his wife's happiness. Eventually he offers his step-relatives a settlement just so he can be rid of them and be happy with his wife [ML].

K11   *Seven years, and other tales* (by Julia Kavanagh).
+ London: Hurst & Blackett, 1860, 3 vols. SOURCE Wolff, 3722. LOCATION D, L, NUC.
+ Leipzig: Bernard Tauchnitz, 1859, 2 vols. SOURCE T & B, 496–97. LOCATION NUC.
Boston: Ticknor & Fields, 1859 (as *Seven years*). LOCATION NUC.
COMMENTARY Set in France. Contents Leipzig edn: 'Seven years', 'The cheap excursion', 'The conscript', 'Gaiety and gloom', 'The little dancing-master', 'A soirée in a porter's lodge', 'A comedy in a court-yard', 'The troubles of a quiet man', 'Young France', 'Adrien', 'The mysterious lodger', 'An excellent opportunity', 'The experiences of Silvie Delmare' [NUC].

K12   *Queen Mab. A novel* (by Julia Kavanagh).
London: Hurst & Blackett, 1863–64, 3 vols. SOURCE Alston, p. 227; Sadleir, 3604 (n.d. edn). LOCATION L, NUC.
Leipzig: Bernard Tauchnitz, 1863. SOURCE T & B, 673; OCLC. LOCATION CSt.
+ New York: D. Appleton & Co., 1864. LOCATION InND Loeber coll., NUC.
COMMENTARY A story of abandonment and inheritance set partly in London and partly in Ireland. A young girl is swindled out of her inheritance by some relatives, who pretend that she has died. They had, however, dropped her at the doorstep of a Mr Ford. Even though he is somewhat suspicious of the little girl's sudden appearance, the £500 that comes with her soothes his conscience. Over time, Mr Ford finds out the real state of affairs and makes a number of efforts to rectify the girl's situation [ML].

K13   *Beatrice. A novel* (by Julia Kavanagh).
Leipzig: Bernard Tauchnitz, 1864, 2 vols. SOURCE T & B, 740. LOCATION NUC.
+ London: Hurst & Blackett, 1865, 3 vols. SOURCE Alston, p. 226. LOCATION L.
New York: D. Appleton & Co., 1865. LOCATION NUC.
COMMENTARY No Irish content. Leipzig edn may have been predated by its publisher [CM; RL].

K14   *Sybil's second love. A novel* (by Julia Kavanagh).
+ London: Hurst & Blackett, 1867, 3 vols. SOURCE Alston, p. 227. LOCATION L.
Leipzig: Bernard Tauchnitz, 1867, 2 vols. in 1. SOURCE T & B, 858. LOCATION NUC.
New York: D. Appleton & Co., 1867. LOCATION NUC.
COMMENTARY A story of intrigue and romance set on the French coast where Mr Kennedy, an Irishman and a widower, has an estate and a mill. His daughter Sybil lives with him. A mysterious Mr Smith comes to visit. He seems to have a hold over Mr Kennedy. Later, another man, presumably Mr Kennedy's brother, comes to stay, and Sybil invites a poor woman, Blanche Cains. Sybil falls in love with her uncle and Blanche secretly marries Mr Kennedy. Eventually, it transpires that the uncle is really a Mr Dermot and the actual owner of the estate. Mr Dermot and Sybil marry and Mrs Kennedy is defeated in her plans to become rich [ML].

K15   *Dora. A novel* (by Julia Kavanagh).
+ London: Hurst & Blackett, 1868, 3 vols. SOURCE NCBEL 3, p. 935. LOCATION L, NUC.
Leipzig: Bernard Tauchnitz, 1868, 2 vols. SOURCE T & B, 941–42. LOCATION NUC.

+ New York: D. Appleton & Co., 1868. 3 vols. in 1 (ill. Gaston Fay). SOURCE Wolff, 3717. LOCATION InND Loeber coll., NUC.

COMMENTARY Set in Dublin, France, and London. The New York edn was published in two similar bindings, one in dark green, the other in lighter green cloth [ML; RL].

K16   *Silvia* (by Julia Kavanagh).
+ London: Hurst & Blackett, 1870, 3 vols. SOURCE Alston, p. 227. LOCATION L, NUC.
Leipzig: Bernard Tauchnitz, 1870, 2 vols. SOURCE T & B, 1098. LOCATION NUC.
New York: D. Appleton & Co., 1870. LOCATION NUC.
COMMENTARY No Irish content [CM].

K17   *Bessie. A novel* (by Julia Kavanagh).
+ London: Hurst & Blackett, 1872, 3 vols. SOURCE Alston, p. 227. LOCATION L.
+ Leipzig: Bernard Tauchnitz, 1872, 2 vols. (as *Bessie*). SOURCE T & B, 1268–69.
LOCATION D.
New York: D. Appleton & Co., 1872 (Library of Choice Novels). SOURCE Wolff, 3716.
LOCATION NUC.
COMMENTARY No Irish content [CM].

K18   *John Dorrien. A novel* (by Julia Kavanagh).
London: Hurst & Blackett, 1875, 3 vols. SOURCE NCBEL 3, p. 935; Sadleir, 3604 (1893 edn); Topp 1, p. 443. LOCATION L, NUC.
Leipzig: Bernard Tauchnitz, 1875, 3 vols. SOURCE T & B, 1482–84. LOCATION NUC.
COMMENTARY A story of career conflict, business and misplaced trust. Mrs Dorrien, who has come down in the world, goes through much hardship to give her son, John, a good education. He wants to become a poet but his uncle summons him to join the family business. Much of the story is about business dealings and about the betrayal of a friend whom John had trusted [ML].

K19   *The pearl fountain and other fairy tales* (by Julia Kavanagh and Bridget Kavanagh).
+ London: Chatto & Windus, 1876 (ill. Moyre Smith). SOURCE NCBEL 3, p. 935.
LOCATION L.
Leipzig: Bernard Tauchnitz, 1877. SOURCE T. & B., B26. LOCATION NUC.
Detroit: Craig & Taylor, 1878 (ill. J. Moyre Smith). LOCATION NUC.
COMMENTARY Children's stories; contents: 'The pearl fountain', 'The silver fish', 'The golden hen', 'Sunbeam and her white rabbit', 'Redcap's adventures in fairyland', 'Fire and water', 'Tipsy's silver bell', 'Prince Doran', 'Fairie and Brownie', 'Batty', 'Feather head' [CM].

K20   *Two lilies. A novel* (by Julia Kavanagh).
+ London: Hurst & Blackett, 1877, 3 vols. SOURCE NCBEL 3, p. 935; Topp 6, 357.
LOCATION L, NUC.
Leipzig: Bernard Tauchnitz, 1877, 2 vols. in 1. SOURCE T & B, 1643. LOCATION NUC.
COMMENTARY No Irish content [CM].

K21   *Forget-me-nots* (by Julia Kavanagh).
London: Richard Bentley & Son, 1878, 3 vols. SOURCE Wolff, 3818. LOCATION L,
NUC.
+ Leipzig: Bernard Tauchnitz, 1878, 2 vols. SOURCE T & B, 1754–55. LOCATION D,
NUC.
COMMENTARY A series of connected short stories, all ostensibly by a French maiden living in a Norman village called Manneville. Contents: 'By the well', 'Sister Anne', 'The story of Monique', 'Annette's love-story', 'Phyllis and Corydon', 'The miller of Manneville', 'Réné', 'Charlotte Morel', 'Mimi's sin', 'My brother Leonard', 'Nina, the witch', 'Sylvie's vow', 'Cousin Jane', 'The countess's story', 'A young girl's secret', 'The broken charm', 'Clement's love [ML; Wolff].

— COLLECTED WORKS

K22 [*Julia Kavanagh's Works*].

New York: D. Appleton & Co., [1873–1881?], [16 vols?]. SOURCE Adv. in *Nathalie* (New York, 1873) and *Queen Mab* (New York, 1881). LOCATION InND Loeber coll. (3 vols. only).

COMMENTARY Unnumbered and untitled series. Advertised in *Nathalie* (New York, 1873) and *Queen Mab* (New York, 1881). No title of the works is known, but the set is uniformly bound in red cloth and impressed in gold and black. The series was issued gradually, as the 1881 list is longer than the 1873 list. Earlier edns of the 1850s and 1860s appear in different bindings and formats [RL].

KAVANAGH, M. See KAVANAGH, Fr Maurice Denis.

KAVANAGH, Fr Maurice Denis (also known as M. Kavanagh), b. Galway 1812, d. Co. Galway? 1864. Catholic priest and novelist, MDK was educated at the Christian Brothers School in Lombard Street, Galway. After ordination he ministered in Galway, at Moycullen and later at Oughterard (all in Co. Galway), where he is buried. SOURCE Galway, p. 56; RIA/DIB.

K23 *Shemus Dhu, the black pedlar of Galway. A tale of the penal times* (by M. Kavanagh).

+ Dublin, London: James Duffy, 1867. SOURCE Brown, 827; OCLC. LOCATION D (1881 edn), DPL (1881 edn), L, NUC, InND Loeber coll. (also 1881 edn).

COMMENTARY The 1881 edn was published in two different bindings: (a) cloth; (b) printed wrappers. A story of dispossession and struggle in and around Galway during the penal era. The Catholic family of O'Halloran are dispossessed of their lands and leave for France but still have a number of friends who are willing to fight for their rights. The disturbed times require great secrecy and almost nobody in the story seems to go by their real name. O'Halloran's son returns to Ireland and is eventually able to clear his father's name: in the process, however, he shoots his arch-enemy D'Arcy, which disqualifies him for restoration of his possessions and he returns to France [ML; Brown].

KAVANAGH, Morgan. See KAVANAGH, Morgan Peter.

KAVANAGH, Morgan Peter (also known as Morgan Kavanagh), b. Thurles (Co. Tipperary) 1800, d. 1874. Poet, novelist and self-proclaimed philologist, MPK was the father of Julia Kavanagh§. He and his family initially lived in Thurles (Co. Tipperary) and later in Paris and Normandy. He began his literary career as a poet: he published *Wanderings of Lucan and Dinah* (London, 1824), a poetical romance in ten cantos, and *The reign of Lockrin* (anon., London, 1838), a poem in Spenserian stanza. He wrote a work on linguistics that was challenged by critics and is described by the ODNB as ridiculous. However it was translated into French and further developed in *Myths traced to their primary source through language* (London, 1856), and in *Origin of language and myths* (London, 1871). MPK's domestic life was evidently unsettled and unhappy, his wife Bridget and daughter separating themselves from – or being abandoned by – him. His novel *The hobbies* (London, 1857, 3 vols.) involved him in public controversy with his better-known daughter when he, or his unscrupulous publisher Newby, indicated on the title page that she had edited the narrative. This was subsequently withdrawn (see below). SOURCE Allibone i, p. 1007; Allibone Suppl., ii, p. 930; Boase, ii, pp 161–2; ODNB [under Julia Kavanagh]; O'Donoghue, p. 221; Sutherland, p. 344; RIA/DIB.

K24   *Aristobulus, the last of the Maccabees. A tale of Jerusalem* (by Morgan Kavanagh).
      + London: Thomas Cautley Newby, 1855, 3 vols. SOURCE Allibone, i, p. 1007;
      Sutherland, p. 344. LOCATION L.

K25   *The hobbies; A novel* (by Morgan Kavanagh).
      + London: Thomas Cautley Newby, 1857, 3 vols. SOURCE Allibone, i, p. 1007;
      Sutherland, p. 344. LOCATION L.

COMMENTARY Allibone states it was edited by Julia Kavanagh§, who denied she had authorized the use of her name as editor of this book. The BL copy has on the page facing the title
page the following text: 'Mr. Newby has been induced to withdraw Miss Kavanagh's name
from the title page for reasons that will be publicly stated immediately' [ML].

KAYE, Revd John, pseud. 'Philalethes Cantabrigiensis', b. Hammersmith (London) 1783,
d. Riselholme (Lincoln) 1853. Anglican clergyman, church scholar and miscellaneous writer,
JK was the son of Abraham Kaye, a linen draper, and Susan Bracken. He was an outstanding student and scholar at Cambridge University where he subsequently became master and
vice-chancellor of Christ College. He was appointed bishop of Bristol and later moved to the
Lincoln see, which benefited greatly from his energetic efforts to increase the number of clergy
and to build parsonages. In 1848 he was elected a visiting fellow at Balliol College, Oxford,
and a member of the Royal Society. He was opposed to Catholic emancipation and considered the Tractarian movement a betrayal of the Reformation. Under his pseudonym he contributed papers to the *British Magazine* (London), and his writings on the church fathers, sermons, letters and addresses were collected and published in 1888. SOURCE ODNB.

K26   *Reply to the "Travels of an Irish gentleman in search of a religion"* (by 'Philalethes
      Cantabrigiensis').
      + London: J.G. & F. Rivington, 1834. LOCATION InND Loeber coll.

COMMENTARY Written in response to Thomas Moore's§ *Travels of an Irish gentleman in search
of a religion* (London, 1833, 2 vols.), Moore's defence of the Catholic nationalist position in
Ireland [RL].

KEANE, Joanna Maria, pseud. 'A Lady', and 'J.M.M.K.', fl. 1857. This historical novelist's first name is evident from an inscription in the NLI copy of *William and James*. Since
the primary place of publication of the following novel is Dublin, it is likely that she was Irish,
and judging from the subscribers' list, she might have been a resident of the north of Ireland.
SOURCE RL.

K27   *William and James; or, the revolution of 1688. An historical tale, in which the
      leading and principal events of that truly interesting and stirring period of our his-
      tory, viz., 1688–89, etc., are faithfully and truly narrated* (by 'A Lady', and
      'J.M.M.K.' according to dedication; dedicated to the author's friends, patrons, and
      subscribers).
      + Dublin: William Curry & Co., London: Wertheim & Macintosh; Edinburgh: Oliver
      & Boyd, 1857 (subscribers' list). SOURCE Cathair cat. 24/289; Brown, 109. LOCATION
      D, Di, L.

COMMENTARY Historical fiction describing the Williamite War in Ireland, including the battles of the Boyne and of Aughrim. The scene is set chiefly in Co. Fermanagh, and introduces
as characters King William III, King James II, the earl of Tyrconnell, Patrick Sarsfield, Richard
Hamilton and others. Subscribers' list is almost completely Irish, mainly from the north (almost
300 subscribers). The list does not contain Keanes, but there are 19 Irvines, and 9 Bettys
[Brown; ML].

KEARY, Anna Maria (Annie), b. Bilton, near Wetherby (Yorks.) 1825, d. Eastbourne (Sussex) 1879. A novelist and children's writer, AMK was the sixth child of an Anglican clergyman, the Revd William Keary, a former soldier from an impoverished Irish landowning family in Co. Galway, and Lucy Plumer of Bilton. AMK was educated largely at home, where her father told her stories of his early life in Ireland. She became a precocious storyteller herself. As a young woman, she took charge of her brother's motherless children for six years, for whom she wrote many children's stories. On his remarriage and their removal, coupled with the death of two of her other brothers and the breaking of her own engagement, she evidently suffered a severe breakdown. In 1858 she travelled to Egypt, where she experienced a religious crisis. Much of her later fiction was written in the south of France in a condition of semi-invalidism. She remained unmarried. Of her many novels, only two deal with Ireland. AMK paid her only visit to Ireland, two weeks in Connemara, while she was writing *Castle Daly*. She described Ireland as 'a country of contradictions—some things in it so delightful and beautiful, and others so utterly depressing and sad ...' She contributed to the *Young Ireland* magazine (Dublin). For her portrait, see ODNB. Her sister, the poet Eliza Keary, wrote *Memoir of Annie Keary* (London, 1882). SOURCE Allibone Suppl., ii, p. 931; Blain, p. 600; Brown, p. 151; Colman, pp 125–6; Field Day, v, pp 925–6, 974; Hogan 2, p. 647; Kunitz & Haycraft, p. 339; Irish pseudonyms; Leclaire, p. 139; NCBEL 4, pp 1310–11; ODNB; O'Donoghue, p. 223; Sutherland, p. 345.

K28   *Castle Daly. The story of an Irish home 30 years ago* (by Annie Keary).
     London: Macmillan & Co., 1875, 3 vols. SOURCE Brown, 828; Macmillan, p. 283; Wolff, 3728. LOCATION L.
     London: Macmillan & Co., 1875, 2 vols. (new edn). SOURCE Topp 5, p. 165. LOCATION InND Loeber coll. (1875, 2nd edn).
     Leipzig: Bernard Tauchnitz, 1875, 2 vols. in 1. SOURCE T & B, 1547–48. LOCATION D, NUC.
     Philadelphia: Porter & Coates, 1875. SOURCE Topp 5, p. 165. LOCATION D (1876 edn).
     New York: G. Munro [1880]. LOCATION NUC.
     New York: Garland, 1979, 3 vols. (introd. by R.L. Wolff). SOURCE COPAC. LOCATION Dt.

COMMENTARY First serialized in *Macmillan's Magazine*, a story that explores the differences between Celt and Saxon in Ireland. It is set in Castle Daly, an actual estate in Co. Galway, and in Connemara, in the 1840s during the Famine and the Young Ireland rebellion of 1848 led by William Smith O'Brien. The tale is sympathetic to Home Rule, to which one of the chief characters is converted. Throughout the book English and Irish standpoints are contrasted through the medium of a mixed marriage [ML; Field Day, v, pp 924, 925, 951–5; ODNB; Wolff introd., p. 34].

K29   *Father Phim* [anon.] (dedicated to Paisy).
     + London: Frederick Warne & Co.; New York: Scribner, Welford & Armstrong, [1879] (ill.). SOURCE Blain, p. 600; Brown 2, 708; Osborne, p. 1000; NCBEL 4, p. 1814. LOCATION D, NUC, InND Loeber coll., CaOTP.
     London: The Faith Press, 1962. SOURCE Blain, p. 600. LOCATION L.

COMMENTARY The story of a child's visit to Ireland during times of agrarian unrest. Helen Neale lives with her sisters and brothers in a northern English city where her father is a clergyman. She contracts smallpox and spends a year of recuperation at Castle Connell (Co. Galway), the home of her maternal grandfather. She finds herself in a strange world, quite different from England. She comes to love the people and makes friends with the real Fr Phim, of whom a very engaging portrait is painted. There are serious agrarian troubles. An attempt is made on the life of a very unpopular agent who Helen saves from death [RL; Brown 2].

KEATINGE, Mrs R.H. See **KEATINGE, Mrs Richard Harte.**

KEATINGE, Mrs Richard Harte (Harriet, née Pottinger; known as **Mrs R.H. Keatinge**), d. 1874. She was the daughter of Thomas Pottinger, of Mount Pottinger (Co. Down). She married Richard Harte Keatinge of Lynnwood, Horsham, Sussex, who served in the colonial military service. SOURCE Burke's, p. 655; RIA/DIB.

K30 *Honor Blake: The story of a plain woman* (by Mrs R.H. Keatinge).
+ London, Edinburgh: Henry S. King, 1872, 2 vols. SOURCE Allibone Suppl., ii, p. 932; COPAC. LOCATION Univ. of Manchester.
COMMENTARY An Irish family falls into poverty and moves to France, where most of the action takes place. Eventually, the main characters emigrate to Australia to make their fortune [ML].

KEDDIE, Henrietta, b. Fife (Scotland) *c.*1827, d. London, 1914. Scottish novelist and historical fiction writer for juveniles, HK was the daughter of Philip Keddie, a lawyer and mine owner, and Mary Gibb. With her sisters she ran a school before turning to writing from necessity due to straitened family resources. She published voluminously – anonymously, under her pseudonym, and under her own name and she contributed to *Fraser's Magazine* (London), *Cornhill Magazine* (London), and other periodicals. In 1869 she moved to England where she developed a wide circle of women writer friends, including Jean Ingelow§ and Anna Maria Hall§. She lived abroad for a while before settling in Oxford. HK wrote many historical tales for adolescent girls, novels in which women's roles and relationships are explored, as well as a life of Queen Victoria and a book about her own family. SOURCE Allibone iii, p. 2496 [under Tytler]; Allibone Suppl., ii, p. 932; Blain, p. 1104 [under Tytler]; NCBEL 4, p. 1815; ODNB; Sutherland, p. 346; Wolff, iv, pp 219–23 (list of novels).

K31 *Wearing the willow; or, Bride Fielding. A tale of Ireland and of Scotland sixty years ago* [anon.].
+ London: John W. Parker & Son, 1860. SOURCE Emerald Isle cat. 69/592. LOCATION D, L.
COMMENTARY Set in Dublin and Scotland before the Union between Ireland and England. The story starts in Blake's boarding-house in 'Merrion-street' in Dublin, run by Mr Blake, who was of 'ancient descent', but had been a jockey, actor and dancing master, and Mrs Blake 'of a meaner line' [RL].

KEEGAN, John, b. Shanahoe (Co. Laois) 1809, d. Dublin, 1849. Poet, story writer and journalist, JK was the son of a Mary O'Mahony. He was educated by his uncle, Thomas O'Mahony, a hedge-school master. JK began to write verse early and had a great interest in music. During his brief life he published many short stories and poems in Dublin periodicals such as the *Nation*, the *Irish Penny Journal*, the *Dublin Penny Journal* (1840) and the *Dublin University Magazine*. Included in the latter (Sept.–Nov. 1839) was a serial 'Legends and tales of the Queen's County peasantry'. He contracted an unhappy marriage in 1840. He worked as a clerk in a relief committee assisting the poor during the Famine. Separating from his wife, he moved to Dublin in 1847. There he associated with James Clarence Mangan§ and worked as a journalist. He died of cholera and was buried in a pauper's grave in Glasnevin cemetery. Some of his papers are the NLI. William Butler Yeats§ included some of JK's stories in *Fairy and folk tales of the Irish peasantry* (London, [1888]). SOURCE W.E. Hall, p. 105; Hogan 2, pp 647–8; 'John Keegan of Killeaney', *Carloviana* (Dec. 1966), pp 31–3; Irish pseudonyms; OCIL, p. 286; ODNB; O'Donoghue, p. 224; Rafroidi, ii, pp 190–1; RIA/DIB; Thuente 1, pp 52–3.

K32 *Legends and poems* (by John Keegan; ed. by J. Canon O'Hanlon§, with memoir by D.J. O'Donoghue§).

Dublin: Sealy, Bryers & Walker, 1907. SOURCE Rafroidi, ii, p. 191. LOCATION L, NUC. COMMENTARY Published almost sixty years after JK's death. Stories are set in Co. Laois. Contents: 'Tales of the Rockites – Stories I to IV', Tales of my childhood: 'St. Kenny's bush', 'A dead man's revenge', 'The trooper's ghost', Legends and tales of the Queen's County peasantry: 'The banshee', 'The bewitched butter', 'The sheoge', 'The boccough ruagh', 'A tradition of poor man's bridge', 'Puss in brogues, A legend', 'Darkyduff the madman, A tale of South Munster', 'The hornpipe, a sketch of Skariff mountains', 'Gleanings in the green isle', 'The fairy's revenge, A tale of Grantstown Lough', 'The Orangeman's tale, a reminiscence of 1798', 'The direough's legacy', 'Croibheen Dearg's story', 'The fatal flower-basket', 'The grave robber, A story of Upper Ossory' [ML].

KEELING, Elsa. See **D'ESTERRE-KEELING, Elsa.**

KEENAN, H.F. See **KEENAN, Henry Francis.**

KEENAN, Henry Francis (known as **Henry F. Keenan**), b. Rochester (NY) 1849, d. Washington (DC) 1928. American journalist and novelist, HFK was born of poor Irish immigrants. He fought in the Civil War as a private, and returned to become a journalist on the *Rochester Chronicle*. He moved to New York City around 1870, where he made a career on the *New York Tribune*. Between 1883 and 1888 he worked full-time as a novelist. Only *The aliens* (London, 1886) drew on his own family's immigrant background. Since the books failed to make money, and severely disappointed in his lack of success as a novelist, he was forced to return to journalism. SOURCE Allibone Suppl., ii, p. 933; Exiles, p. 181.

K33   *The money-makers: a social parable* [anon.].
+ New York: D. Appleton & Co., 1885. SOURCE Fanning, p. 383 (1884 edn not located). LOCATION L, NUC.
London: Ward, Lock & Co. [1885]. SOURCE COPAC. LOCATION L.
New York: Johnson Reprint Co., 1969. SOURCE Fanning, p. 383; OCLC; Wright, iii, 3060. LOCATION MH.
COMMENTARY A story of social differences in New York in 1871 describing the lives of two Irishmen, Alfred Carew and Hilliard, who both write for the *Atlas* newspaper. They help to save the life of a millionaire, Aaron Grimstone, who rewards them with money. Hilliard, who is a stubborn individual, sends the money back, but Carew keeps it [ML; CM].

K34   *The aliens. A novel* (by Henry F. Keenan).
London: Ward & Downey, 1886, 2 vols. SOURCE Brown, 830; Wright, iii, 3058; COPAC. LOCATION L.
New York: D. Appleton & Co., 1886. SOURCE Fanning, p. 383; part printed in Exiles, pp 182–190. LOCATION NUC.
COMMENTARY A story of Irish immigrants in America, it tells of the Boyne family who arrive in 'Warchester' from Belfast sometime in the 1830s. The Irish Boynes are contrasted with the German Ritter family. Hugh Boyne drinks up his stake and disappears. His wife Kate ruins her health under the strain of trying to keep the family together. Hugh's brother James, well settled in Warchester, heartlessly evicts her and her children. They end up in the almshouse, where Kate goes mad and dies at the age of thirty [Exiles, pp 181–2].

KEIGHTLEY, Sir S.R. See **KEIGHTLEY, Sir Samuel Robert.**

KEIGHTLEY, Sir Samuel Robert (known as **S.R. Keightley**), b. Belfast 1857, d. Dublin 1940 (1949 according to EF and Hogan). Historical novelist and poet, SRK was the son of

Samuel Keatly [*sic*; according to Ferguson], of Bangor (Co. Down), a JP, and Katherine Brennan. SRK graduated LLB at Queen's College, Belfast, and was admitted at the King's Inns, Dublin, in 1881, and was called to the Irish Bar in 1883. He married in 1892 and was knighted in 1912. Politically active, he contested Antrim as an Independent Unionist in 1903 and south Derry as a Liberal in 1910. He lived in Lisburn (Co. Antrim). His collection of poetry *A king's daughter* (Belfast, 1878 and 1879) was written while still a student. SOURCE Brown, p. 151; EF, p. 219; Ferguson, p. 217; Hogan 2, p. 648; MVP, p. 253; O'Donoghue, p. 224; RIA/DIB; Sutherland, pp 346–7.

K35 *The crimson sign. A narrative of the adventures of Mr. Gervase Orme, sometime Lieutenant in Mountjoy's regiment of foot* (by S.R. Keightley).
London: Hutchinson & Co., 1894. SOURCE Brown, 831; COPAC. LOCATION D (1897, 3rd edn), L.
New York: Harper & Bros, 1896. LOCATION NUC.

COMMENTARY Historical fiction. Recounts the adventures of Mr Gervase Orme, a lieutenant in Mountjoy's regiment of foot. The story is set before and during the siege of Derry in 1689 [Brown].

K36 *The cavaliers. A novel* (by S.R. Keightley).
+ London: Hutchinson & Co., 1895 (ill. Simon Harmon Vedder). LOCATION Dt (1896, 3rd edn), L.
New York: Harper & Bros, 1896. LOCATION NUC.

K37 *The last recruit of Clare's. Being passages of the memoirs of Anthony Dillon, Chevalier of St. Louis, and late Colonel of Clare's regiment in the service of France* (by S.R. Keightley; dedicated to the author's brother).
+ London: Hutchinson & Co., [1897] (ill. Paul Dare). SOURCE Brown, 832; COPAC. LOCATION D, DPL, L, NUC.
+ New York: Harper & Bros, 1897 (ill. Paul Dare). LOCATION D, NUC.

COMMENTARY Stories purportedly from the memoirs of Anthony Dillon, who had been a colonel in Clare's regiment in the service of France. Contents: 'Among the evening shadows', 'The last recruit of Clare's', 'The king's favour', 'The last sacrament', 'The case of M. de Lussac', 'The knees of fate' [ML].

K38 *The silver cross. A romance* (by S.R. Keightley).
+ London: Hutchinson & Co., 1898 (ill. Paul Dare). SOURCE Wolff, 3739; COPAC. LOCATION D, NUC.
New York: Dodd, Meade & Co., 1898. LOCATION NUC.

K39 *Heronford* (by S.R. Keightley; dedicated to Philip Russell).
+ London: C. Arthur Pearson, 1899. SOURCE Wolff, 3738. LOCATION D, InND Loeber coll.
+ New York: Dodd, Meade & Co., 1899. LOCATION InND Loeber coll., NUC.

COMMENTARY Set in England and tells the story of the Cassilis family. A young boy, John, is introduced to the family. His background is a mystery, but he is loved by the master of the house. When the master dies, two of his three children make life difficult for John. Eventually, it appears that John is the heir. He lives in Heronford Castle, and, with his family, brings happiness to the place [ML].

K40 *A man of millions* (by S.R. Keightley).
London, Paris, Melbourne: Cassell & Co., 1901. SOURCE Sutherland, p. 346; COPAC. LOCATION L.
New York: Dodd, Meade & Co., 1901. LOCATION NUC.

COMMENTARY Percival Colthurst returns from South Africa with a large amount of diamonds. He is planning to avenge himself on his cousin, who in his absence married his fiancée. The cousin conspires with Percival's Chinese servant to obtain the diamonds, but he is murdered [EF, p. 219].

K41 *The pikemen. A romance of the Ards of Down* (by S.R. Keightley).
+ London: Hutchinson & Co., 1903 (ill. Martin Stainforth). SOURCE Brown, 833. LOCATION D, DPL, NUC.

COMMENTARY The purported narrative of Revd Patrick Stirling (MA), of Drenton, Sangamon County (IL), formerly of Ardkeen in Co. Down. It relates his experiences in the Ards during the rising of 1798. The narrator describes the brutality of the British soldiers, which makes him sympathize with the United Irishmen. Descriptions of Irish scenery [Brown; EF, p. 219].

K42 *A beggar on horseback* (by S.R. Keightley).
London: John Long, 1906. SOURCE Brown, 834; COPAC. LOCATION L.

COMMENTARY The adventures in Dublin and on the Continent of a young man, set at the end of the eighteenth century [Brown].

K43 *Barnaby's bridal* (by S.R. Keightley).
+ London: John Long, 1906. SOURCE COPAC. LOCATION D, L.

KELLETT, Mrs Theodore, fl. 1880s. Given that her work appeared in Dublin only, she probably was Irish. SOURCE RL.

K44 *Lime tree hall; or, right v. might* (by Mrs Theodore Kellett).
+ Dublin: Humphrey & Armour, [not before 1886] (ill.). SOURCE Brown 2, 710; COPAC. LOCATION D, Dt.

COMMENTARY A saga concerning the Debreton family of Lime Tree Hall on the borders of Norfolk and Suffolk. Wilfred, the elder of two sons, is an officer in a cavalry regiment quartered in Ireland and marries an Irish girl, Margaret Brickson. Vernon, the younger son, is jealous and vindictive and gets his father to sign a will in his favour. Wilfred, disinherited, lives for a time in Ireland where his daughter Geraldine is born. He dies in the Crimean War. His wife is drowned on a visit to Bundoran (Co. Donegal). Meantime at Lime Hall, Mrs Hawkes, an adventuress, inveigles Vernon into marriage. Geraldine is sent to live with them and Vernon's wife plots to marry her to her son Freddy. The scheme fails. Dr Grey, Wilfred's friend, returns from a trip abroad and investigates the will. Vernon is found guilty of fraud and dies in prison. Dr Grey marries Geraldine [Brown 2].

KELLY, Mrs —, fl. 1816. A novelist who was probably resident in Ireland as her first Irish novel was co-published in Dublin. She is not to be confused with the author Mrs Isabella Kelly (1759–1857). McCormack in *Field Day* attributes the novels *The matron of Erin* (London, 1816) and *The ruins of Avondale Priory* (London, 1796) to her, but the latter is by Isabella Kelly. SOURCE Blain, p. 602 [under Isabella Kelly]; RL; Todd, pp 380–1.

K45 *The matron of Erin. A national tale* (by Mrs Kelly).
+ London: Simpkin & Marshall; Dublin: Richard Coyne, 1816, 3 vols. SOURCE Brown, 835; Block, p. 126; British Fiction; Garside, 1816:39. LOCATION Corvey CME 3–628–47463–9, Ireland related fiction, D, L, MH.

COMMENTARY A Gothic tale set in Connacht in 1798, it describes the plight of the Catholic Church in pre-emancipation days and features an exemplary heroine who survives her husband's wickedness [Blain; Brown; Field Day, ii, pp 823–33].

K46 *The fatalists; or, records of 1814 and 1815. A novel* (by Mrs Kelly).
+ London: A.K. Newman & Co., 1821, 5 vols. SOURCE Block, p. 126; British Fiction; Garside, 1821:52. LOCATION Corvey CME 3–28–48008–6, Ireland related fiction, L.

COMMENTARY A story of love and war set largely in Ireland, although some action takes place in Paris and Brussels. It revolves around Geraldine, daughter of Sir Richard Courtney, who elopes with Maj. Blandford. Blandford and Geraldine are unhappy and involve themselves in various flirtations in Paris. When war breaks out, Geraldine flees Paris for Brussels, where she learns that her husband has been killed, leaving her free to marry her first suitor, Capt. Plunkett. There is some mention of issues such as Catholic emancipation and a few descriptions of Irish 'national character' [JB].

KELLY, George C., pseud. 'Harold Payne', b. Ireland 1849, d. Brooklyn (NY), 1895. Journalist and writer of novelettes, GCK lived in New York and kept a room at 136 Concord Street in Brooklyn to work undisturbed. He is best known for writing many dime novels, including crime fiction featuring the detective Thad Burr. He wrote several dime novels of less than 24pp which are not listed below. He committed suicide in 1895. SOURCE Dime novels; RL.

K47   *The man from Mexico in New York; or, Turning down the Shylock pawnbroker: a story of Detective Burr's Wall Street stroke* (by 'Harold Payne').
New York: Street & Smith, 1890 (ill; Log Cabin Library, No. 88). SOURCE OCLC. LOCATION NRU.
COMMENTARY 32pp. Crime fiction [OCLC].

K48   *The Birchall-Benwell tragedy; or, tracing a mysterious crime* (by 'Harold Payne').
New York: Street & Smith, 1890 (Log Cabin Library, No. 92). SOURCE OCLC. LOCATION NRU.
COMMENTARY 32pp. Crime fiction [OCLC].

K49   *XX, the fatal clue, or detective Burr's master case: A romance of the silent tragedy* (by 'Harold Payne').
New York: Beadle & Adams, 1891 (ill; Beadle's New York Dime Library, No. 680). SOURCE OCLC. LOCATION NNC.
COMMENTARY 28pp. Crime fiction [OCLC].

K50   *The matchless detective; or, Thad Burr's marvellous case: A romance of the Newburg mystery* (by 'Harold Payne').
New York: Beadle & Adams, 1892 (ill.; Beadle's New York Dime Library, No. 690). SOURCE OCLC. LOCATION NNC.
COMMENTARY 29pp. Crime fiction [OCLC].

K51   *Detective Burr's seven clues; or, the studio crime* (by 'Harold Payne').
New York: Beadle & Adams, 1892 (ill.; Beadle's New York Dime Library, No. 706). SOURCE OCLC. LOCATION DCL.
COMMENTARY 30pp. Crime fiction [OCLC].

K52   *Detective Burr's spirit chase; or, the mystery of No. 13* (by 'Harold Payne').
New York: Beadle & Adams, 1892 (ill.; Beadle's New York Dime Library, No. 713). SOURCE OCLC. LOCATION DCL.
COMMENTARY 30pp. Crime fiction [OCLC].

K53   *Detective Burr, the headquarters special; or, the great shadower's baffling case. A story of false clues and a woman's art* (by 'Harold Payne').
New York: Beadle & Adams, 1892 (ill.; Beadle's New York Dime Library, No. 728). SOURCE OCLC. LOCATION DCL.
COMMENTARY 30pp. Crime fiction [OCLC].

K54   *Detective Burr's foil; or, A cunning woman's strategy* (by 'Harold Payne').
New York: Beadle & Adams, 1892 (ill.; Beadle's New York Dime Library, No. 734). SOURCE RLIN. LOCATION NRU.
COMMENTARY 30pp. Crime fiction [RLIN].

K55   *The gilded fly: A political satire* (by 'Harold Payne').

St Paul MN: Price-McGill, 1892 (Idle Moment Series, No. 18). SOURCE OCLC. LOCATION Arlington Library (VA).

K56 *Detective Burr among the New York thugs; or, the clean out of the Night Hawks* (by 'Harold Payne').
New York: Beadle & Adams, 1893 (ill.; Beadle's New York Dime Library, No. 742). SOURCE RLIN. LOCATION Florida State Univ.
COMMENTARY 31pp. Crime fiction [RLIN].

K57 *The Wall Street sharper's snap* (by 'Harold Payne').
New York: Beadle & Adams, 1893 (ill.; Beadle's New York Dime Library, No. 792). SOURCE OCLC. LOCATION Univ. of Texas, Austin.
COMMENTARY 32pp. Crime fiction [OCLC].

K58 *The Grand Street gold-dust sharpers* (by 'Harold Payne').
New York: Beadle & Adams, 1894 (ill; Beadle's New York Dime Library, No. 806). SOURCE OCLC. LOCATION NRU.
COMMENTARY 31pp. Crime fiction [OCLC].

K59 *The tramp shadower's backer* (by 'Harold Payne').
New York: Beadle & Adams, 1894 (ill; Beadle's New York Dime Library, No. 821). SOURCE OCLC. LOCATION NNC.
COMMENTARY 30pp. Crime fiction [OCLC].

K60 *The Frisco sharper's cool hand* (by 'Harold Payne').
New York: Beadle & Adams, 1894 (ill; Beadle's New York Dime Library, No. 829). SOURCE OCLC. LOCATION NNC.
COMMENTARY 31pp. Crime fiction [OCLC].

K61 *The policy brokers blind; or, detective Burr's policy puzzle* (by 'Harold Payne').
New York: Beadle & Adams, 1894 (ill.; Beadle's New York Dime Library, No. 836). SOURCE OCLC. LOCATION NNC.
COMMENTARY 31pp. Crime fiction [RLIN].

K62 *The Quaker City crook; or, Thad Burr's fight for a million. A story of Philadelphia and New York* (by 'Harold Payne').
New York: Beadle & Adams, 1895 (ill; Beadle's New York Dime Library, No. 853). SOURCE OCLC. LOCATION NNC.
COMMENTARY 32pp. Crime fiction [OCLC].

K63 *The tenderloin big four; or, Colonel Bob's trump backer* (by 'Harold Payne').
New York: Beadle & Adams, 1895 (ill; Beadle's New York Dime Library, No. 861). SOURCE OCLC. LOCATION NNC.
COMMENTARY 31pp. Crime fiction [OCLC].

K64 *The king-pin shark; or, Thad Burr's tenstrike* (by 'Harold Payne').
New York: Beadle & Adams, 1895 (ill.; Beadle's New York Dime Library, No. 872). SOURCE OCLC. LOCATION Univ. of Texas, Austin.
COMMENTARY 31pp. Crime fiction [OCLC].

K65 *Who shot Chief Hennessy; or, The New Orleans dagoes* (by 'Harold Payne').
New York: Beadle & Adams, 1895 (ill; Beadle's New York Dime Library, No. 883). SOURCE OCLC. LOCATION NRU.
COMMENTARY 32pp. Crime fiction [OCLC].

KELLY, Hugh, b. Killarney (Co. Kerry; Dublin according to Brady and O'Donoghue) 1739, d. London 1777. Playwright, theatre critic, essayist, novelist, pamphleteer and barrister, HK was brought up in Dublin where his father, following the loss of his estate, became a publican. HK had no higher education but during his apprenticeship as a stay maker he frequented the theatre and became friendly with actors. He moved to London at age 21 and worked first as a stay maker and then as a journalist, becoming successively editor of several London periodicals: the *Court Magazine*; the *Ladies Museum* and the *Public Ledger*. He was a theatre critic of some notoriety and he published several plays, the first of which, *False delicacy* (London, 1768), was enormously successful and was translated into several languages. It was translated into French by Mme Riccoboni§, friend of its producer David Garrick. Garrick had given preference to JK's play over Oliver Goldsmith's§ *The good-natured man*, sparking a bitter rivalry between the two playwrights. Years later at Goldsmith's funeral, however, HK was seen weeping. HK's *A school for wives*, produced under another writer's name, was also very successful. He published anonymously a collection of essays *The babbler* (Dublin [1770?], 2 vols.). He studied at Temple Bar to help support his large family and gave up literature for the law after being called to the Bar in 1774. He also wrote political pamphlets for the government and was rewarded with a pension. For his portraits and papers, see ODNB. *The works of Hugh Kelly* (London, 1778) includes a life of the author and was compiled to benefit his widow. ODNB says *Memoirs of a Magdalen* is his only novel, but the ESTC includes as well *The tutor; or, the history of George Wilson, and Lady Fanny Melfont* (London, 1771, 2 vols.). SOURCE Allibone, i, p. 1013; Brady, p. 121; Boylan, p. 181; Field Day, i, pp 504, 656; Hogan, pp 349–51; Hogan 2, pp 650–2; NCBEL 2, p. 1324; OCIL, p. 287; ODNB; O'Donoghue, p. 226; RIA/DIB.

K66   *Memoirs of a Magdalen; or, the history of Louisa Mildmay. Now first published from a series of original letters* [anon.] (dedicated to the duchess of Northumberland). London: W. Griffin, 1766, 2 vols. SOURCE Raven, 1017; ESTC t072182. LOCATION L, H, NUC (1767 edn), InND Loeber coll. ([1801] edn).

+ London: Harrison & Co., 1782–84 (*Harrison's Novelist's Magazine*, vol. vii). SOURCE Gecker, 558; Sadleir, 3745. LOCATION InND Loeber coll., UP.

+ Dublin: P. Wilson, J. Exshaw, J. Murphy, H. Saunders, W. Sleater, J. Potts, D. Chamberlain, J. Hoey Jnr, J. Williams & T. Ryder, 1767, 2 vols. SOURCE Raven, 1111; ESTC n035186. LOCATION Dt, Dm, L, YU, NUC.

Londres [Paris]: J.-B.G. Musier, 1773 (trans. by Mlle Matné de Morville as *Les égarements réparés, ou histoire de Miss Louise Mildmay*). SOURCE Streeter, 216. LOCATION BNF.

London: Home & Van Thal, 1947 (as *A strange adventure in the life of Miss Laura Mildmay*). SOURCE NCBEL 2, p. 1324; RLIN. LOCATION NRU.

COMMENTARY Also published as part of the *Novelist's Magazine* (London, 1780–81). Epistolary novel giving an account of a prostitute's life in England [Blain; Brady; Mayo, 864].

K67   *The tutor; or, the history of George Wilson, and Lady Fanny Melfont* [anon.]. London: T. Vernor & J. Chater, 1771, 2 vols. SOURCE Raven 2, 1771:42; ESTC n024383. LOCATION, NUC.

Dublin: S. Colbert, 1781, 2 vols. in 1 (as *The tutor; or, the history of George Wilson, and Lady Frances [sic] Melfont. In a series of letters*). SOURCE McBurney & Taylor, 505; ESTC t209247. LOCATION D (imperfect), IU, NUC.

COMMENTARY Attributed by the ESTC to Hugh Kelly. An advertisement for this epistolary novel in [anon.], *The triumph of prudence over passion* (Dublin, [1781]) states that 'These letters describe several characters and relate many interesting events in a new and agreeable manner. Throughout them are interspersed many generous sentiments and noble observations that do honour to the heart and head of the writer' [CM; ESTC n024383].

KELLY, J.J. See KELLY, Fr James J., OSF.

Kelly

KELLY, Fr James J., OSF (also known as **J.J. Kelly**), b. Co. Roscommon 1845, d. 1917. A Catholic clergyman, poet and novelist, JJK was ordained in 1866. Aside from fiction he published poetry, often under the pseudonym 'Coman', in the *Nation* (Dublin) and the *Irish Harp* (Dublin) which was collected in two volumes (Edinburgh, 1894; and Dublin, 1903). JJK may be identified with the translator of stories for juveniles from Spanish *Tales for the young* (London, 1883), listed in Allibone. The title page of *Irish varieties* mentions that he was also the author of 'The queen's confession', but this has not been located. SOURCE Allibone Suppl., ii, p. 936; BLC; Irish pseudonyms; O'Donoghue, p. 226; RL.

K68   *Irish varieties* (by James J. Kelly and J.P. O'Byrne; on cover: 'dedicated without permission to the Vinegar cruelties and the mustard pots of society').
    + Dublin: A.B. Harrison & Co.; New York: The Anglo-American Publishing Co.; London: The Hansard Publishing Union, 1891. LOCATION D, L, InND Loeber coll.
COMMENTARY Contents: 'Life and adventures of Charley Crofts – anecdotes and escapades (Cork in '98)', 'Haps and mishaps of an Irish landlord', 'Major Dismal's runaway duel', 'The friar of Dunraven's musical tribulations, with an exercise for the French horn (Mrs McGrath)', 'A lesson to lovers (poem)', 'Home rule (a farce)'. The first story is probably based on Charles Crofts§ *Memoirs of Charley Crofts* (Cork, 1829) [RL].

K69   *With lance and shield. A romance of the East* (by J.J. Kelly).
    + London: R. Washbourne; Dublin: M.H. Gill & Co., 1895. LOCATION L.
COMMENTARY Historical fiction set in Egypt and the near East at the time of the Crusades [RL].

K70   *The true story of the village priest; or, the martyr of a secret* (by J.J. Kelly; dedicated to Professor O'Byrne).
    + Dublin: Harrison & Co. [1896]. SOURCE COPAC. LOCATION L.
COMMENTARY Set in Ireland. Frank Fitzroche's horse returns riderless. Frank is engaged to Maggie. Frank has been killed by a rival to Maggie's hand. The villain confesses his deed to the priest who is the brother of Frank, who cannot tell the police about it. Eventually the criminal admits his deed to the authorities. Father Fitzroche attends him to the scaffold [ML].

K71   *The stainless sword. A romance of the crusades* (by J.J. Kelly).
    + Dublin: Talbot Press, 1919 (ill. H.A. Dixon). LOCATION D, L, NUC.
COMMENTARY Published posthumously. Historical, religious fiction [BLC].

KELLY, Mary or **May. See GORGES, Mary** or **May.**

KELLY, Peter Burrowes, pseud. **'A member of the Irish Bar'**, b. Stradbally (Co. Laois) 1811, d. Glentolka, Fairview (Dublin) 1883. Barrister, novelist, dramatist and political orator and agitator, PBK was the fourth son of John Kelly of Stradbally and Eliza Grace. PBK was admitted to TCD in 1826, to the Gray's Inn (London) in 1832, and to the King's Inn in 1835. He was called to the Irish Bar in 1837, but evidently did not practice. PBK was well-known for his political agitation, particularly in relation to the issue of tithes. However, he later became clerk of the peace for Co. Laois. He contributed to the *Dublin Review* and other periodicals. His *The Polish mother* (London, 1840), a 'tragedy in five acts and verse', was dedicated to Thomas Campbell, the poet, who was his personal friend. SOURCE B & S, p. 458; Boase, ii, p. 184; Brady, p. 121; Brown, p. 152; Keane, p. 259; O'Donoghue, p. 228; RIA/DIB.

K72   *The manor of Glenmore; or, the Irish peasant. A tale* (by 'A member of the Irish Bar'; dedicated to 'the English nation').
    + London: Edward Bull, 1839, 3 vols. SOURCE Hodgson, p. 361; Brown, 840; Block, p. 126. LOCATION D, L, InND Loeber coll.

COMMENTARY A political novel reviewed in *Dublin University Magazine* (Sept., 1839). Set at Stradbally (Co. Laois) in the Irish midlands in the time just before Catholic emancipation, when meetings were held across the country by followers of Daniel O'Connell. The story contains a cruel agent and a hypocritical Protestant minister. The Catholic clergy as well as O'Connell's party are described as vigorously trying to discourage secret societies, which might harm the political goal of emancipation. The Clare election and Bishop Doyle feature in the story. The novel describes the lives of various villagers and how they live together [ML].

KELLY, R.N. See KELLY, Richard N.

KELLY, Richard N. (known as R.N. Kelly), fl. 1821. Historical novelist who, in the introd. of the following volume, signed himself 'esquire', and was resident in Dublin. SOURCE RL.

K73　*De Renzey; or, the man of sorrow, written by himself, edited by his nephew* (introd. signed Rich. N. Kelly; dedicated to Lady Morgan§).
+ London: W. Simpkin & R. Marshall, 1821, 3 vols. SOURCE British Fiction; Garside, 1821:53. LOCATION Corvey CME 3–628–48565–7, Ireland related fiction, D.
Paris: Vernavelle & Tenon, [n.d.], 4 vols. (trans. by M*** [Dubergier] as *L'Homme de la douleur*). SOURCE Bn-Opale plus. LOCATION BNF.

COMMENTARY An historical novel set largely in Ireland, it tells the story of De Renzey, a magistrate in Ireland, whose life is destroyed by events stemming from the 1798 rebellion. He is attacked by Irish rebels for his support of the government and rescued by Capt. Shortland, who deceives De Renzey and runs away with De Renzey's wife Helena. Thinking Helena dead, De Renzey joins a regiment that first helps to quell rebellion in Ireland, then fights in Holland in the war with France. Eventually it transpires that Helena is alive and innocent of any wrongdoing. She and De Renzey meet just before her death and she tells him how she was rescued by O'Gorman, a noble leader of the rebellion and a friend whom De Renzey, in his capacity as magistrate, was earlier forced to condemn [JB].

K74　*Frederick Dornton; or, the brothers. A novel* (by R.N. Kelly).
London: A.K. Newman & Co., 1822, 4 vols. SOURCE British Fiction; Garside, 1822:50. LOCATION Corvey CME 3–628–47926–6, L.
COMMENTARY Set during the Peninsular War [ML].

KELLY, Revd Thomas, b. Kellyville, near Athy (Co. Laois) 1769, d. Dublin 1855. Anglican and non-conformist clergyman, religious fiction and hymn writer, TK was the son of Justice Thomas Kelly of the Irish court of common pleas. He was educated at schools in Portarlington and Kilkenny before entering TCD, where he obtained his BA in 1789. He initially studied for the law but rejected it in favour of the church and was ordained in the Church of Ireland in 1792. He and several of his fellow ordinates with evangelical leanings contributed to a weekly evangelical magazine, the *Inquirer* (London?). In 1795 he married the wealthy Elizabeth Tighe of Rosanna (Co. Wicklow), whose brother Henry Tighe had married the poet Mary Tighe§. TK's gradual shift towards a more evangelical stance resulted in a rebuke by the archbishop of Dublin. He began to preach and minister throughout the country and founded in 1802 the Kellyites, a religious organization based along congregational lines. The next year he seceded from the established church on the basis that a national church was incompatible with the principles of the New Testament. He was one of the early supporters of the Hibernian Bible Society and the Evangelical Alliance. His popularity as a preacher attracted many listeners, including Catholics, which brought him into conflict with the Catholic Church, although he argued that Catholics came out of their own conviction and not because of any efforts on his part to convert them. TK set up meeting houses in Athy, Cork, Dublin, Kilkenny,

Maryborough, New Ross, Portarlington, Waterford and Wexford. By the 1820s his congregations peaked, and by the time of his death had mostly dissolved. TK wrote religious tracts, including *The advantage of reading the scriptures, exemplified in the history of James Byrne of Kilberry in the county of Kildare* (1809, repr. London, 1823), and *A letter to the Roman Catholics of Athy occasioned by Mr. Hayes's seven sermons* (Dublin, 1823). He edited collections of psalms and hymns and wrote hymns himself. He may be identified with a Thomas Kelly who wrote *Thoughts on the marriages of the labouring poor* (London, 1806). SOURCE Allibone, i, p. 1014; Landed gentry, 1912, p. 692; 'Memoir of the late Rev. Thomas Kelly of Dublin', *The Evangelical Magazine*, (Feb. 1856), pp 61–70; NSTC; OCLC; ODNB; O'Donoghue, p. 228; RIA/DIB.

K75   *The history of Andrew Dunn, an Irish Catholic* [anon.].
    Chelsea: Printed for the Religious Tract Society, 1814, 5th edn SOURCE OCLC. LOCATION NUC (n.d. edn).
    + London: Religious Tract Society, [1817], 4th edn (First Series Tracts, No. 110). SOURCE Bradshaw, 7929 ([1830?] edn); OCLC (1838 edn). LOCATION L, CLU (1838 edn).
    London: William & Smith, [1820?], 4th edn (as *The converted Catholic; or, the history of Andrew Dunn. A narrative*). LOCATION L.
    Philadelphia: n.p., 1857. SOURCE OCLC. LOCATION NUC.
COMMENTARY First edn not located. Religious fiction relating the conversion of Andrew Dunn. It includes conversations with Fr Dominick, the conversion of James Nowlan's family, and the death of Fr Dominick. The text is heavily footnoted [RL].

KELLY, William Patrick, b. Co. Kilkenny 1848, d. England? 1916. A writer of historical fiction and scientific and adventure stories for juveniles, WPK was the son of P.J. Kelly of Mount Brandon, Graignamanagh (Co. Kilkenny), but B. Browne states that he was a native of nearby New Ross (Co. Wexford). WPK was educated at Clongowes Wood College. After training at the Royal Military Academy, Woolwich, he was commissioned into the Royal Artillery in which he served until 1878. He lived at Harrogate (Yorks.) thereafter and was appointed a JP. SOURCE Brown, p. 153; B. Browne, p. 81; EF, p. 220; RIA/DIB; Sutherland, p. 347.

K76   *School boys' three. A story* (by William Patrick Kelly).
    London: Downey & Co., 1895. LOCATION L.
    London: George Routledge & Sons, 1904 (as *Schoolboys three: a story of school life*). SOURCE Brown, 841. LOCATION L.
    COMMENTARY Recalls life at Clongowes Wood College (Co. Kildare) in the early 1860s and contains autobiographical material [Brown; Sutherland].

K77   *The Dolomite cavern; or, light and darkness* (by William Patrick Kelly).
    + London: Greening & Co., 1899. LOCATION D, L.
    COMMENTARY Adventure story featuring x-rays [EF, p. 220].

K78   *The Cuban treasure island: A romance of adventure* (by William Patrick Kelly).
    London: George Routledge & Sons, 1903. LOCATION L.
    COMMENTARY Adventure story featuring terrestrial magnetism [EF, p. 220].

K79   *The stone-cutter of Memphis* (by William Patrick Kelly).
    London: George Routledge & Sons, 1904. LOCATION L.
    COMMENTARY Historical fiction set in ancient Egypt [EF, p. 220].

K80   *The Assyrian bride* (by William Patrick Kelly).
    London: George Routledge & Sons, 1905. LOCATION L.
    London: George Routledge & Sons; New York: E.P. Dutton & Co., 1907. LOCATION NUC.

COMMENTARY Historical romance set in Nineveh [EF, p. 220].

K81   *The senator Licinius* (by William Patrick Kelly).
London: George Routledge & Sons, 1909. LOCATION L.
London: George Routledge & Sons; New York: E.P. Dutton & Co., 1909. LOCATION NUC.

COMMENTARY EF identified an 1907 edn, but this has not been located. Historical fiction set in Rome at the time of Caligula. The senator's daughter is kidnapped. She and her lover eventually become Christians [RL; EF, p. 220].

K82   *The stranger from Iona* (by William Patrick Kelly).
London: George Routledge & Sons; New York: E.P. Dutton & Co., 1911 (ill. Edward Read). LOCATION L, NUC.

K83   *Dr. Baxter's invention. A story* (by William Patrick Kelly).
London: Greening & Co., 1912. LOCATION L.

K84   *The house at Norwood* (by William Patrick Kelly).
Bristol: J.W. Arrowsmith, 1914. LOCATION L.

K85   *The Harrington Street mystery* (by William Patrick Kelly).
London: Simpkin, Marshall & Co., 1915. LOCATION L.

KEMBLE, Ann Julia. See HATTON, Ann Julia.

KENDALL, Mrs A., fl. 1799, d. 1816. A novelist who wrote the advertisement to her *Tales of the abbey* (London, 1800, 3 vols.) from Isleworth (London), Sept. 1, 1800. Several of her books, including *The castle on the rock* (Dublin, 1799) and *Derwent Priory* (Cork, 1799) were reprinted in Ireland. SOURCE Allibone, i, p. 1017; ESTC; RL.

K86   *Tales of the abbey, founded on historical facts* (by A. Kendall).
London: H.S. Simonds, 1800, 3 vols. SOURCE British Fiction; Garside, 1800:45; ESTC n047689. LOCATION Corvey CME 3–628– 47996–7, NUC.
+ Dublin: P. Wogan, H. Colbert, W. Porter, J. Moore, J. Rice, J. Folingsby, J. Stockdale & T. Codd, 1801, 2 vols. LOCATION Dm (vol. 1 only), NUC.

COMMENTARY Historical fiction set in the sixteenth century. Vol. 1 describes the life of the daughter of Sir Francis Walsingham and widow of Sir Philip Sidney. Lady Sidney had secretly become the wife of the earl of Essex and had given birth to a son, Dudley, who was taken care of by the earl's sister. After the earl's death, Queen Elizabeth, who did not know that Lady Sidney had married Essex, sent for her. Lady Sidney was afraid of the queen's wrath and fled to Ireland with Philippa, her daughter by Sir Philip Sidney. Many adventures beset them on the way. Finally they arrive at an abbey in Co. Wexford, where they are reluctantly admitted. While living there, they are witnesses to the unsettled times [ML].

KENDALL, Edward Augustus, b. 1776?, d. Pimlico (London) 1842. English publisher, political commentator, translator and writer of children's stories and travel accounts, EAK travelled in the US and Canada and wrote about his experiences there before beginning in London the *Literary Chronicle and Literary Review* in 1819. It was intended to provide cheap and good literature, and was as such a pioneer in weekly periodical literature. EAK wrote proposals to the government to provide new and distinct colonies for the relief of the half-castes of India and the mulattos of the West Indies. He also published *Letters to a friend on the state of Ireland* (London, 1826, 3 vols.), in which he argued that Ireland enjoyed a vigorous and paternal government whose duty it was to repress catholicism there and in England. He translated several works by Jacques-Henri Bernadin de Saint Pierre, published in Dublin in 1779 and 1800. Of his own works written for children, only the following deals, indirectly, with Ireland. His

Parental education; or, domestic lessons (London, 1803) was partly modelled on the work of Maria Edgeworth§. SOURCE Allibone, i, p. 1018; G. Gargett & G. Sheridan (eds), *Ireland and the French enlightenment* (Houndmills, 1999), p. 247; NCBEL 4, p. 1815; ODNB; Osborne, p. 271; RL.

K87   *Keeper's travels in search of his master* [anon.] (dedicated to the author's infant son William Webb Kendall).

London: E. Newbery, 1798 (ill. Dudley, John Thurston). SOURCE Osborne, p. 271. LOCATION CaOTP, NUC.

Dublin: T. Jackson, 1799. SOURCE OCLC. LOCATION CLU.

Paris: Lelong, 1822 (trans. by B.-C. Brian as *Voyage d'un chien à la recherche de son maître, anecdote morale pour l'instruction et l'amusement des enfans*). SOURCE Streeter, p. 224; Bn-Opale plus. LOCATION BNF.

Philadelphia: B. & J. Johnson, 1801. SOURCE Welch, 723.1. LOCATION NUC.

Boston: Lilly, Wait, Portman Colman & Holden, 1833. SOURCE OCLC. LOCATION NUC, InND Loeber coll. (Carter 1844 edn).

COMMENTARY Original London edn set in Gloucestershire. Dublin edn set in a town in the north of Ireland where a dog, Keeper, searches for his lost master. The Dublin edn also contains a poem set in Ireland 'The harper', which features a poor dog named Tray [ML].

KENEALY, Edward. See KENEALY, Edward Vaughan Hyde.

KENEALY, Edward Vaughan Hyde (known as Edward Kenealy), pseud. 'Y', b. Cork City 1819, d. London 1880. A barrister, scholar, linguist, poet, novelist and miscellaneous writer, EVHK was the son of William Kenealy, a merchant in Cork, and Catherine Vaughan. He received his BA at TCD in 1840, an LLB in 1846 and an LLD in 1850. He was admitted to the Gray's Inn (London) in 1838, to the King's Inn in 1840, and was called to the Irish Bar in 1840 and to the English Bar in 1847, when he settled in London. He spent a month in prison in 1850 for punishing too severely his 6-year-old illegitimate son. EVHK defended the Fenian prisoners Burke and Casey but resigned the case after the Clerkenwell prison explosion (1867) that killed twelve people, believing his clients had been aware of the escape attempt. His legal career suffered after his violent and lengthy defence of a claimant to the Tichborne baronetcy when he was disbarred for his improper conduct, contempt of the bench and groundless claims against various witnesses and Catholic institutions. (Although born a Catholic, EVHK had rejected catholicism early in his life.) He began the scurrilous periodical the *Englishman* around 1873, in which he continued to plead the cause of the Tichborne claimant and published articles deemed libellous, but its circulation mounted to over 160,000 copies a week. He founded the Magna Charta association and toured the country lecturing on the Tichborne trial. As a result, he became something of a working-class hero and was elected MP for Stoke-on-Trent in 1875. O'Donoghue describes him as 'the most extraordinary demagogue of his time' (O'Donoghue, p. 229). A prolific writer and linguist, EVHK translated from the Irish *Cahir Conri, a metrical legend* (Cork, 1860), contributed to *Fraser's Magazine* (London) and the *Dublin University Magazine*, among others, and translated poems and ballads from and into many languages. He published poetry, meditations and works of scriptural exegesis. He was the first president of the Cork Temperance Institute and wrote a series of theological works in which he set out his mystical and visionary religious ideas. His autobiographical notes were published by his daughter, Arabella. For his portraits and papers, see ODNB and the Henry E. Huntington Library, San Marino (CA). SOURCE Allibone, i, p. 1018; Allibone Suppl., ii, p. 938; B & S, p. 459; COPAC; Hogan 2, p. 656; A. Kenealy, *Memoirs of Edward Vaughan Kenealy LL.D.* (London, 1908); Irish pseudonyms; J. McCarthy, *An Irishman's story* (New York, 1904), p. 41; MVP, p. 254; ODNB; O'Donoghue, p. 229; RIA/DIB; Schulz, p. 277.

K88   *Brallaghan, or the Deipnosophists* (by Edward Kenealy; dedicated to Thomas Noon Talfour, Serjeant at law).
+ London: E. Churton, 1845. SOURCE OCLC. LOCATION Dt, L, NUC, InND Loeber coll. COMMENTARY *London edn* Spine of London 1845 edn states 'first series', but no other published.
London: [publisher?], 1847 (as *Irish wit, anecdote and table talk*). SOURCE NSTC. LOCATION Dt (not found).
Cork: George Purcel & Co., printers, 1845. SOURCE Burmester cat. 53/241. COMMENTARY *Cork edn* No copy located. Title page a cancel, showing London: E. Churton, 1845 [Burmester cat. 53/241].
COMMENTARY On cover: first series, but no other published. Humorous descriptions of members of a literary club in Cork and presumed pieces of their works. Mentions William Maginn§, Alfred Millikin§, Thomas Crofton Croker§, John Anster, Dr Porther, James Sheridan Knowles§, Samuel Lover§, and Francis Sylvester Mahoney§ (Fr Prout) [ML; Burmester cat. 53/241; OCLC].

K89   *Edward Wortley Montagu. An autobiography* (preface signed 'Y').
+ London: T. Cautley Newby, 1869, 3 vols. (ill.). SOURCE Jarndyce cat. 123/170. LOCATION L.
COMMENTARY Ascribed to Kenealy in the BLC. Fictional autobiography of Edward Wortley Montague, son of Lady Mary Wortley Montague, set in the first half of the eighteenth century [Jarndyce; RL].

KENLEY, Marianne, b. *c.*1780, possibly in Ulster. Romantic novelist who, according to the preface, was not yet seventeen when she wrote the following, her first novel. Four years elapsed between the date of the preface and publication SOURCE RL.

K90   *The cottage of the Appenines, or, the castle of Novina. A romance* (by Marianne Kenley; dedicated to the marchioness of Donegall).
+ Belfast: Printed [for the author?] at the Public Printing Office, 1806, 4 vols. in 2. SOURCE British Fiction; Garside, 1806:39. LOCATION L, InND Loeber coll.
COMMENTARY This Gothic story is set in the Apennines and recounts the maltreatment of two generations of women of noble birth at the hands of their relatives. Part of the story takes place in a rustic farmhouse and the other part in the ancestral, baronial castle, which has the usual dungeons and remote towers to serve as prisons. The greed of the male relatives is such that they try to force the women into marriages with unsuitable husbands against their wills. Eventually all the good people find love and happiness and the bad characters die or reform [ML].

KENNARD, Mrs Arthur. See **KENNARD, Nina H.**

KENNARD, Mrs Nina H. (née Anne Homan-Mulock; also known as **Mrs Arthur Kennard**), b. Bellair (Co. Offaly) 1844, d. 1926. Romantic novelist and biographer, NHK was the eleventh of fifteen children of an Irish landowner, Thomas Homan-Mulock, who changed his name from Molloy in 1843, and his second wife, Jane Elizabeth Collister. NHK wrote biographies, including one on the Irish-Greek writer Lafcadio Hearn, based on her friendship with his half-sister Mrs Atkinson; contributed articles on historical subjects to periodicals, and published five novels between 1880 and 1900. She married Arthur Challis Kennard, the son of Robert William Kennard, MP, in 1866, and had four children. SOURCE Allibone Suppl., ii, p. 939; Blain, p. 606; EF, p. 221; Landed gentry, 1912, p. 502.

K91 *There's rue for you. A novel* (by Mrs Nina H. Kennard).
London: Chapman & Hall, 1880, 2 vols. LOCATION L.
COMMENTARY Romantic novel whose heroine writes poetry [Blain].

K92 *Hélène. A novel* (by Mrs Nina H. Kennard).
London: Richard Bentley & Son, 1883, 2 vols. LOCATION L.

K93 *Rachel* (by Mrs Arthur Kennard).
London: W.H. Allen & Co., 1885 (Eminent Women Series). SOURCE COPAC.
LOCATION L.

K94 *Diogenes' sandals* (by Mrs Nina H. Kennard).
London, Sydney: Remington & Co., 1893. LOCATION Dt, L.

K95 *The second Lady Delcombe* (by Mrs Nina H. Kennard).
London: Hutchinson & Co., 1900. LOCATION L.
Philadelphia: J.B. Lippincott, 1900. SOURCE EF, p. 221. LOCATION NUC.

COMMENTARY An American heiress marries an impoverished peer. For a long time they do not consummate their marriage. The Irish problem is a major theme in the book and is viewed from an Unionist and landowner's point of view [EF, p. 221].

KENNEDY, Grace, b. Penmore, Ayr (Scotland) 1782, d. 1825. GK was a Scottish religious fiction writer and novelist who was the daughter of Robert Kennedy and Robina Agnew, a devout evangelical Protestant. She probably visited Ireland, where she had relatives. According to the introd. to her *Philip Colville; or, the covenanter's story* (Edinburgh, 1825), she also wrote *The word of God, and the word of man*, 'intended for Ireland', which was published soon after 1823, but no copy of it has been located. Her *Father Clement* (Edinburgh, 1823), a story of the Jacobite rebellion of 1715 in Scotland, provoked an anonymous author to publish in Ireland *The biblicals; or, Glenmoyle Castle. A tale of modern times* (Dublin, 1830, and London, 1831). SOURCE Allibone, i, p. 1018; Alston, p. 232; Brown 2, p. 133; introd. to *Andrew Campbell* (New York, 1829); ODNB; NCBEL 4, p. 943–44.

K96 *Andrew Campbell's visit to his Irish cousins* [anon.].
Edinburgh: William Oliphant, 1824. SOURCE COPAC. LOCATION L.
Edinburgh: William Oliphant, 1829 (new edn; ill.). SOURCE Brown 2, 712. LOCATION D (1881 edn), L (destroyed).
Rotterdam: Wed. Van der Meer & Verbruggen, 1831 (trans. by R. into Dutch as *Het bezoek aan Ierland: Jessy Allan; en Twee vertoogen van godsdienstigen inhoud*; ill.). SOURCE Adamnet. LOCATION UVA.
+ New York: Jonathan Leavitt; Boston: Croker & Brewster, 1829 (as second part to *Philip Colville; a covenanter's story. Unfinished*). LOCATION InND Loeber coll., NUC.

COMMENTARY Religious fiction. Andrew is a Scottish gardener and a Bible Christian. His aunt marries an Irish 'Papist' and goes to live in Ireland. Andrew visits and is received and treated with the greatest kindness. This is his first contact with Catholics and he sees much that he dislikes, such as the observance of the Sabbath, improvident and early marriages, and 'careless, listless idleness'. He convinces his cousin Richard that the priests keep the people ignorant and withhold the Bible from them. Richard goes to Scotland and becomes a Bible Christian also [Brown 2].

'KENNEDY, Kevin', pseud. See RYAN, W.P.

KENNEDY, Patrick, pseud. 'Harry Whitney, philomath', b. Kilmyshall (also spelled Kilmyshal) near Bunclody (Co. Wexford) 1801 (1800 according to ODNB), d. Dublin 1873. Publisher, editor and story writer, PK was educated at a school supported by the Carew fam-

Kennedy

ily after his family moved to Coolbawy, west of Courtnacuddy. In 1821 he went to Dublin and became an assistant in the Kildare Place Training School, an interdenominational education project of the Kildare Place Society. In 1832 he married Maria Kelly in the Pro-Cathedral in Dublin. He gave up teaching in 1843 and opened a bookstore and 'the English and French Library' at Anglesea Street, Dublin, where he acted also as a publisher. In 1855 he contributed a legend to the meeting of the Kilkenny and south-east branch of the Ireland Archaeological Society (see *Proceedings*, iii, pp 415–17). He became well-known to many contemporary writers, including John Banim§, Rosa Mulholland§ R.R. Madden§ and Joseph Sheridan Le Fanu§. Le Fanu, as editor of the *Dublin University Magazine*, encouraged him to write and subsequently he published over 200 pieces of PK's work in the *Dublin University Magazine*. His regional stories were based on first-hand experience but his interests extended to other literatures, including Russian, French and Breton. He also contributed to the *Irish Quarterly Review* (Dublin), the *Irish Harp* (Dublin, 1863–64) and to other periodicals. His major works are collections of stories. PK's study of and writings about Irish mythology, antiquities, legends, stories and folk tales appeared at a time when interest in them was being fostered by such writers as Isaac Butt§ and Samuel Ferguson§ and was to be important later in the works of Douglas Hyde§ and William Butler Yeats§. PK was buried at Glasnevin cemetery. Some of his correspondence is in the library of the University of Cork and his portrait is in the NGI. The NUC mentions a manuscript of 137 original poems and drawings (Newberry Library, Chicago). For his portraits, see ODNB. SOURCE Allibone, iii, p. 2702 [under Whitney]; Allibone Suppl., ii, p. 941; Boylan, p. 184; Brady, p. 122; Brown, p. 153; B. Browne, pp 81–2; Curran index; W.E. Hall, p. 175; Hogan 2, pp 656–7; Irish pseudonyms; McKenna, pp 215–16; NUC; OCIL, p. 287; ODNB; O'Donoghue, pp 230–1; RIA/DIB; Thuente 1, pp 56–9; T. Wall, *The sign of Doctor Hay's head* (Dublin 1958), p. 149.

K97   *Legends of Mount Leinster: Three months in Kildare-Place; Bantry and Duffrey traditions; The library in Patrick Street* (by 'Harry Whitney, philomath').
+ Dublin: P. Kennedy, 1855. SOURCE McKenna, p. 215; Brown, 844. LOCATION D, L, NUC, LOCATION InND Loeber coll.
London: Lambert & Co.; Dublin: P. Kennedy, 1855 (as *Legends of Mount Leinster; tales and sketches*; Lambert & Co. Amusing Library for Young and Old). SOURCE OCLC; RLIN. LOCATION D, Dt, L, NUC.
Enniscorthy: Duffry, 1989. SOURCE COPAC. LOCATION Dt.
COMMENTARY The Dublin edn was issued with an additional title page of the London and Dublin edn. Stories set in Co. Wexford. Contents: 'Legend of Lough na Piast', 'The Carlow courtship', 'The fight of Shroughmore', 'A day at Duffrey-Hall', 'Clonmullin and its traditions', 'A Sunday with Father Murphy', 'The fortunes of the Earl of Stair', 'Three months in Kildare-Place', 'The library in Patrick-street' [RL; OCLC].

K98   *Fictions of our forefathers: Fion Mac Cumhail and his warriors* [anon.].
Dublin: M'Glashan & Gill, James Duffy, P. Kennedy; London: Burns & Lambert, [c.1859–60] (Transactions of the Ossianic Society). SOURCE Rowan cat. 59A/472. LOCATION E, MH.
+ London: Burns & Lambert, [1859?]. SOURCE Brady, p. 122 (mentions 1860 edn, but location not identified); McKenna, p. 215; RLIN. LOCATION L, E, NUC.
COMMENTARY 82pp. Reprinted from the *Irish Quarterly Review* (Dublin, Oct., 1859). Translations of Gaelic stories, which PK had collected [NUC; Rowan cat. 54/462].

K99   *Legendary fictions of the Irish Celts* (by Patrick Kennedy; dedicated to Joseph Sheridan Le Fanu§).
+ London: Macmillan & Co., 1866 (collected and narrated by Patrick Kennedy; ill. W. Small). SOURCE Brown, 845; Macmillan, p. 147; McKenna, p. 215; Bradshaw, 5862. LOCATION BFl (1891, 2nd edn), L, C, NUC, InND Loeber coll. (also 1891, 2nd edn).

693

Kennedy

COMMENTARY Compiled from contributions to the *Dublin University Magazine* and based on what the author had heard in his youth among the peasantry of his native Co. Wexford. Contains a glossary for 'the mere English reader', and consists of over 100 stories, divided into: Household stories: 'Jack and his comrades', 'The bad stepmother', 'Adventures of "Gilla na Chreck an Gour"', 'Jack the master and Jack the servant', '"Ill be wiser the next time"', 'The three crowns', 'The corpse watchers', 'The brown bear of Norway', 'The goban saor', 'The three advices which the king with the Red Soles gave to his son'. Legends of the 'good people': 'The fairy child', 'The changeling and his bagpipes', 'The Tobinstown sheeoge', 'The belated priest', 'The palace in the rath', 'The Breton version of the palace in the rath', 'The fairy nurse', 'The recovered bride', 'Faction-fight among the fairies', 'Jemmy Doyle in the fairy palace', 'The fairy cure', 'The sea fairies', 'The black cattle of Durzy Island', 'The silkie wife', 'The pooka of Murroe', 'The Kildare pooka', 'The Kildare lurikeen', 'The adventures of the "Son of bad counsel"'. Witchcraft, sorcery, ghosts, and fetches: 'The long spoon', 'The prophet before his time', 'The bewitched churn', 'The ghosts and the game of football', 'The cat of the carman's stage', 'Cauth Morrisy looking for service', 'Black stairs on fire', 'The witches' excursion', 'The crock found in the rath', 'The enchantment of Garrett the earl', 'Illan Eachthach and the Lianan', 'The misfortunes of Barrett the piper', 'The woman in white', 'The Queen's County ghost', 'The ghost in Graigue', 'Droochan's ghost', 'The Kilranelagh spirit', 'The doctor's fetch', 'The apparition in Old Ross'. Ossianic and other early legends: Fann [*sic*] Mac Cuil and the Scotch giant', 'How Fann [*sic*] Mac Cuil and his men were bewitched', 'Qualifications and duties of Fianna Eirionn', 'The battle of Ventry Harbour' (first published in Limerick, 1835), 'The fight of Castle Knoc', 'The youth of Fion', 'Fion's first marriage', 'How Fion selected a wife', 'Pursuit of Diarmuid and Grainne', 'The flight of the sluggard', 'Beanriogain na Sciana Breaca', 'Conan's delusions in Ceash', 'The youth of Oisin', 'The old age of Oisin', 'Legend of Loch na Piasta', 'The king with the horse's ears', 'The story of the sculloge's son from Muskerry', 'An Broan Suan Or', 'The children of Lir', 'Lough Neagh', 'Killarney', 'Legend of the Lake of Inchiquin', 'How the Shannon acquired its name', 'The origin of the Lake of Tiis', 'The building of Ardfert Cathedral', 'How Donaghadee got its name', 'The borrowed lake', 'Kilstoheen in the Shannon', 'The isle of the living', 'Fionntuin Mac Bochna', 'The Firbolgs and the Danaans', 'Inis na Muic', 'The bath of the white cows', 'The quest for the "Tain-Bo-Cuailgne"', 'The progress of the wicked bard'. Legends of the Celtic saints: 'St. Patrick', 'How St. Patrick received the staff of Jesus', 'The fortune of Dichu', 'St. Patrick's contest with the druids', 'The baptism of Aongus', 'The decision of the chariot', 'Conversion of the robber chief Macaldus', 'Baptism after death', 'The vision of St. Brigid', 'Death and burial of St. Patrick', 'The corpse-freighted barque', 'St. Brigid's cloak', 'St. Brigid and the harps', '"Arran of the Saints," and its patrons', 'St. Fanchea's visit to Arran', 'St. Brendain's voyage', 'The island of the birds', 'The sinner saved', 'A legend of St. Mogue of Ferns', 'O'Carroll's warning', 'How St. Eloi was cured of pride', 'St. Lateerin of Cullin' [RL].

K100   *The banks of the Boro. A chronicle of the county of Wexford* (by Patrick Kennedy; dedicated to Patrick Joseph Murray, Esq., barrister-at-law, director of convict prisons and inspector of reformatory schools).

+ London: Simpkin, Marshall & Co.; Burns, Oates & Co.; Dublin: M'Glashan & Gill, P. Kennedy, 1867. SOURCE Brown, 846; McKenna, p. 215; Topp 8, 232. LOCATION D, Dcc, DPL, L, NUC, InND Loeber coll.

+ Dublin: McGlashan & Gill, 1875 (new edn; The Shamrock Series; also called The Shamrock Library in advs). LOCATION D.

+ Enniscorthy: Duffry Press, 1989 (reprint of 1875 edn). LOCATION InND Loeber coll.

COMMENTARY A collection of tales describing country life in north-west Wexford between the years 1817 and 1818, but the manuscript was finished in 1856. The story opens in

Cloughbawn during the narrator's school years. He recounts his school days before becoming a teacher. He then opens a school and becomes engaged to Eliza, who is a Protestant, but she resolves to convert to catholicism against her parents' will. The story is interspersed with folk tales, songs and poems, which describe local Wexford traditions, such as funeral wakes, marriage, and hurling. Arranged in 'books' with continuous numbering of chapters: Book I, 'The place and the people'; Book II, 'The framing of the plot'; Book III, 'Estrangement'; Book IV, 'Reconciliation'; Book V, 'Trails and troubles'; Book VI, 'Relief' [RL; Brown; CM].

K101 *Evenings in the Duffrey* (by Patrick Kennedy; dedicated to the late Lord Carew).
+ Dublin: M'Glashan & Gill, Patrick Kennedy; London: Burns, Oates & Co., 1869. SOURCE Brown, 847; Lough Fea cat. p. 168; McKenna, p. 215. LOCATION Dcc, L, NUC, InND Loeber coll.
+ Dublin: McGlashan & Gill, 1875 (new edn; The Shamrock Series; also called The Shamrock Library in advs.). LOCATION PC, NUC.
COMMENTARY Sequel to *The banks of the Boro* (London, 1867), set in Co. Wexford, describes the days of a country schoolmaster and the storytelling and singing in the houses where he goes for dinner. The book reports in detail various country walks, with an abundance of topographical detail in the area of Enniscorthy and Mount Leinster. Includes stories, poems and legends, such as 'Loch-na-Peisthe' and 'The family curse'. The Dublin 1875, new edn, actually is a reissue of unsold sheets of the 1869 printing [ML; CM; Rowan cat. 65/155].

K102 *The fireside stories of Ireland* (by Patrick Kennedy; dedicated to Edward Barrington, JP, of Fassaroe, Bray).
+ Dublin: M'Glashan & Gill, Patrick Kennedy; London: Simpkin, Marshall & Co.; Burns, Oates & Co.; Edinburgh: John Menzies & Co., 1870. SOURCE McKenna, p. 216; Brown, 848; Topp 8, 304. LOCATION InND Loeber coll., NUC.
Dublin: McGlashan & Gill, 1875 (new edn; Shamrock Series).
COMMENTARY A collection of stories based on the recording of oral traditions. Most of the stories originally appeared in the *Dublin University Review*. Contents: 'Hairy Rouchy', 'A legend of clever women', 'The twelve wild geese', 'The wonderful cake', 'The false bride', 'The end of the world', 'The three gifts', 'The unlucky messenger', 'The maid in the country underground', 'Jack the cunning thief', 'The Greek princess and the young gardener', 'The giant and the royal servants', 'The lazy beauty and her aunts', 'The Gilla na Gruaga Donna', 'Shan an omadhawn and his master', 'The princess in the cat-skins', 'The well at the world's end', 'The poor girl that became a queen', 'The grateful beasts', 'The Gilla Rua', 'The fellow in the goat-skin', 'The haughty princess', 'Doctor Cure-all', 'The wise men of Gotham', 'The good boy and the boy that envied him', 'Choosing the least of three evils', 'The hermit and the robber', 'Birth and baptism of St. Mogue', 'The greedy mason', 'The music of heaven', 'How Donn Firinne got his horse shod', 'Cliona of Munster', 'A bullock changeling', 'How John Hackett won the French princess', 'The fairy-stricken servant', 'The fairy rath of Clonnagowan', 'The fairies' pass', 'The banshee of the O'Briens', 'Tom Kiernan's visit to France', 'The love Philtre', 'The pooka of Baltracy', 'The enchanted cat of Bantry', 'How the Devil's Glen got its name', 'The Rock of Cashel', 'The tree of the seven thorns', 'Legend of the Lover's Leap in the Dargle', 'The discovery of the Mitchelstown Caves', 'Lord Clancarty's ghost', 'The treasure-seekers of Maynooth', 'The origin of Loch Erne', 'The death of the Red Earl'. Contains notes and a glossary [RL].

K103 *The bardic stories of Ireland* (by Patrick Kennedy).
+ Dublin: M'Glashan & Gill, Patrick Kennedy; London: Simpkin, Marshall & Co., Burns, Oates & Co; Edinburgh: John Menzies & Co. 1871. SOURCE McKenna, p. 216; Brown, 849; Wolff, 3782; Topp 8, 338. LOCATION L, NUC, InND Loeber coll.

Kennedy

COMMENTARY Contents: 'Partholanus and his people', 'The fight of the Southern Moytura', 'The fight of the Northern Moytura', 'The children of Tuirreann', 'The four swans', 'The last of the Danaan kings', 'How Emania was built', 'The courtship of Labradh Maen', 'Baillie and Aillinn', 'The story of Fachtna', 'Episodes of the reign of King Conor', 'The enchantment of Cuchulainn', 'The youth of Moran the Just', 'The prophecy of Conn Cead Cathach', 'The monster in Loch Ruaighre', 'The fortunes of King Cormac', 'The hill of the bellowing oxen', 'The treachery of Conla', 'The disputed Claymore', 'King Cormac in fairy land', 'Cliona of Munster', 'The first lap-dog that came to Erinn' [*sic*], 'The origin of Aileach', 'The quickbeam fort', 'The churl in the grey coat', 'The fight of Cnoc an Air', 'The Fians at the house of Cuana', 'The fortunes of Diarmuidh and Grainne', 'Oisin in Tir na-n-Oge', 'The Amadhan Mor', 'The adventures of Conall Gulban', 'Death of Niall, and a household mystery', 'The fate of Breacan', 'How it fared with the chief of Castle Knoc', 'St. Patrick's first visit to Dublin', 'How Armagh Cathedral was begun', 'Death of Milcho', 'The thievish glutton', 'The princess at the well', 'St. Brigid's charity', 'The blind nun', 'The amhra of Colum Cille', 'The legend of St. Efflamm', 'Legend of the Cathach', 'The voyage of St. Brendan', 'Some of King Guairé's doings', 'The road of the dishes', 'The chastisement of the bards', 'The desertion of Tara', 'How Brandubh saved Leinster', 'The fight at Moyra', 'The death of the wicked Thorgils', 'The fortunes of Queen Gormflaith', 'The fight in Dundalk Bay', 'The Leinster cow-tribute', 'The war-path to Clontarf', 'The last Lord of Cappa', 'The legend of Mac Corish'; and a glossary [RL].

K104 *The book of modern Irish anecdotes, humour, wit, and wisdom* (by Patrick Kennedy). + London, New York: George Routledge & Sons, [*c.*1872] (by Patrick Kennedy, compiler). SOURCE Hogan 2, p. 657; Topp 8, 1067. LOCATION InND Loeber coll., n.d., 2nd edn.
COMMENTARY Brief anecdotes told with the purpose of drawing attention to the principal events in the history of Ireland since 1691. Partly based on historical works, includes those by R.R. Madden§, W.J. FitzPatrick, J.T. Gilbert, Sir Jonah Barrington, etc.; includes index and selection of Irish proverbs [RL].

K105 *The book of modern anecdotes – English, Irish, Scotch* (by Patrick Kennedy). + London, New York: George Routledge & Sons, [1873] (ed. with Thomas Hood and Allan James Mair§). SOURCE COPAC. LOCATION E.

K106 *Legends of Irish witches and fairies* (by Patrick Kennedy). Dublin: Mercier Press, [*c.*1976]. LOCATION InND.
COMMENTARY Selection of stories from the *Legendary fictions of the Irish Celts* (London, 1866), *The fireside stories of Ireland* (Dublin, 1870), and *The banks of the Boro* (London, 1867) [InND cat.].

KENNEDY, William, b. Scotland (not near Dublin as in O'Donoghue) 1799, d. Paris 1871. Poet, journalist and novelist, WK was the son of an Ayrshire man, who became a cotton manufacturer in Dublin, and Ann Davis. His parents died when he was still a minor and Revd James Bridges of Aughnacloy (Co. Tyrone) became his guardian (O'Donoghue states that his father had property there). His father's will stipulated that WK could only inherit if he became a clergyman. WK was a student at Belfast College in 1819, undertook a theological course in Selkirk (Scotland) and returned to Aughnacloy, where he preached. Dissatisfied with this type of life, he resigned after a year and became a resident of Dublin in 1824. By 1826 he became an editor of the *Paisley Magazine* and edited the *Continental Annual* (London) in 1832. His short stories appeared in several annuals, such as the *Amulet* (London, 1829–31) and he published a moralizing prose story for children, *My early days* (London, 1826). His published poetry includes *The arrow and the rose* (London, n.d.), and *Fitful fancies* (n.l., 1827). As secretary to Lord Durham he went to Canada and soon afterwards was appointed British consul in Texas. He was the author of *Texas: Rise, progress and prospects of the Republic of Texas* (London, 1841, 2 vols.). He retired in 1847 and returned to England, but died in Paris. SOURCE Allibone, i, p. 1020; ODNB; O'Donoghue, pp 231–2; COPAC.

K107   *An only son* [anon.].
    London: Frederick Westley & A.H. Davis, 1831. SOURCE COPAC; O'Donoghue, p. 231. LOCATION Dt, Univ. of Glasgow.
    COMMENTARY Listed as Irish fiction in COPAC [RL].

KENNY, M.L., fl. 1875. Dublin novelist. Perhaps this person can be identified with Molly Kenny, whose letters are among the Downey Papers (NLI, MS 10,029). SOURCE Brown, p. 156.
K108   *The fortunes of Maurice Cronin. A novel* (by M.L. Kenny).
    + London: Tinsley Bros, 1875, 3 vols. SOURCE Allibone Suppl., ii, p. 941; Brown, 859; OCLC. LOCATION Dcc, L, NUC.
COMMENTARY The plot revolves mainly around a case of mistaken identity and is set in the 1840s. Maurice Cronin returns from soldiering in India and finds that he is heir to the estates of the Grace family in Ireland. This enables him to marry Mary Grace, his cousin, whom his putative mother had said was his sister [Brown].

KEON, Miles Gerald, b. Keon's Folly (also known as Keonbrooke), Carrick on Shannon (Co. Leitrim) 1821, d. Bermuda 1875. A novelist, journalist and religious writer, MGK came from an old Irish Catholic family. Both his father, Miles Gerald Keon, a barrister, and his mother, Mary Jane Magawly, died when he was very young, leaving MGK to be brought up by his maternal grandmother, Countess Magawly, whose husband had received his title from the kingdom of Sicily. He was educated at Stonyhurst, the Jesuit college in England, and for a while served as a soldier of fortune in the French army in North Africa. Around this time he published *The Irish revolution; or, what can the Repealers do?* (Dublin, 1843). He studied law at Gray's Inn, married Anne de la Pierre Hawkes in 1846, and drifted into writing for his living. He wrote religious works, edited Catholic periodicals such as *Dolman's Magazine* (London), wrote for the *Dublin Review*, contributed to periodical literature and worked for the *Morning Post* (London, 1847–59), mainly as a correspondent sympathetic to the conservative cause. For some time he was the paper's representative in St Petersburg, Russia. He was author of *The life of the Roman patrician Alexis* (London, 1847). Sir Edward Bulwer Lytton§ procured for him the post of colonial secretary to Bermuda in 1859, a position he held until his death. For his papers, see DNB. SOURCE Allibone Suppl., ii, p. 942; Boase, ii, p. 208; Brady, p. 123; IBL, 12 (1921), pp 81–2; Irish pseudonyms; ODNB; O'Donoghue, p. 233; RIA/DIB [under Miles Keon]; Sutherland, p. 349.
K109   *Dion and the Sibyls. A romance of the first century* (by Miles Gerald Keon).
    London: Richard Bentley, 1866, 2 vols. SOURCE Sutherland, p. 349; Sadleir, 1335; Wolff, 3783. LOCATION L, NUC.
    + New York: Catholic Publishing Co., [1871] (as *Dion and the sibyls, a classic Christian novel*). LOCATION L, NUC.
    Baltimore: McCauley & Kilner, [c.1871] (as *Dion and the sibyls, a classic Christian novel*; Catholic Library). LOCATION NUC.
    COMMENTARY Historical fiction set during the time of the Roman emperor Tiberius (AD 14–37), [RL].
K110   *Harding, the money spinner* (by Miles Gerald Keon).
    London: Richard Bentley & Sons, 1879, 3 vols. SOURCE Allibone, i, p. 1025; Sadleir, 1336; Wolff, 3784. LOCATION L, NUC.
    COMMENTARY First appeared as a serial in the *London Journal* (1852) [Brady].

Kernahan

KERNAHAN, Coulson. See **KERNAHAN, John Coulson.**

KERNAHAN, John Coulson (also known as **Coulson Kernanhan**), b. Ilfracombe (Devon) 1858, d. 1943. English novelist and miscellaneous writer. He was the son of Revd James Kernahan, a scientist and biblical scholar, possibly of Irish descent. Shan Bullock§ dedicated his *Irish pastorals* (London, 1901) to him. JCK married the author Mary Jean Hickling Bettany (née Gwynne), who as a writer is also known as Mrs Coulson Kernahan. He published a volume of recollections of authors such as Algernon Swinburne and Oscar Wilde§ (London, 1917). JCK's portrait was published in *A literary gent* (London, n.d). Only JCK's fiction connected with Ireland is listed below. SOURCE BLC; EF, p. 222; O'Donoghue, p. 234; Sutherland, p. 350.

K111   *Captain Shannon* (by Coulson Kernanhan; dedicated to Lady Seton).
+ New York: Dodd, Mead & Co., 1896. LOCATION InND Loeber coll.
+ London, New York, Melbourne: Ward, Lock & Co., 1897 (ill. F.S. Wilson). LOCATION L, InND Loeber coll. (also 1897 2nd edn).
+ New York: International Association of Newspapers and Authors, 1901. LOCATION InND Loeber coll.

COMMENTARY Crime fiction featuring an Irish-American terrorist, Capt. Shannon, who has come to England to fight for the freedom of Ireland. In a message to the people of Great Britain and Ireland he tells that various anarchists and nihilists, Fenian and other movements, have joined forces and will in the end succeed in bringing down governments such as those of England and Russia. His method is to strike terror by bombing and murdering. The explosions that follow in London are of extraordinary force. Despite large rewards, the police do not seem to be making much headway in capturing the perpetrator. Mr Rissler, an author, feels he may have met Capt. Shannon once before, and sets out to track him down. A number of his assistants die in the process. He finally tracks him to a dynamite hulk moored offshore. The ship is blown to pieces, killing Capt. Shannon [ML].

KERR, Eliza, fl. 1876. EK wrote many religious novels, of which the following have Irish content. SOURCE Allibone Suppl., ii, p. 943; Alston, p. 233.

K112   *Slieve Bloom* (by Eliza Kerr).
London: Wesleyan Conference Office, [1881]. SOURCE Brown, 860; Alston, p. 233; COPAC. LOCATION L.

COMMENTARY Religious fiction for juveniles written from a Methodist viewpoint, it tells how Mary and Willie live a very poor life with their maternal grandmother. However, the coming of their paternal grandmother raises them to better circumstances. Set in the midlands, it describes Mountmellick (Co. Laois), Slieve Bloom, and the Bog of Allen [Brown].

K113   *Kilkee* (by Eliza Kerr).
+ London, Derby: Bemrose & Son, 1881. SOURCE Alston, p. 233; Brown, 861 (1885, 3rd edn); COPAC. LOCATION L.

COMMENTARY A religious tale describing the adventures of two boys near Kilkee (Co. Clare) with descriptions of its scenery. The boys are well-versed in scripture, which they quote frequently [Brown].

K114   *Keena Karmody* (by Eliza Kerr).
London: Wesleyan Methodist Sunday School Union, [1887]. SOURCE Alston, p. 233; Brown, 862. LOCATION L (destroyed), NUC.

COMMENTARY Religious fiction. Not seen, but the name suggests some Irish content [BLC; RL].

'KERR, Orpheus C.', pseud. See NEWELL, R.H.

KETTLE, Mary Rosa Stuart. See KETTLE, Rosa MacKenzie

KETTLE, Rosa MacKenzie (also known as Mary Rosa Stuart Kettle, using her mother's maiden name, and Mary Rosa Kettle), b. Overseale (Leics.), fl. 1839, d. Mansefield, Callander, Perthshire (Scotland) 1895. Daughter of John Kettle of Overseale, near Ashby-de-la-Zouche (Leics.). Prolific English novelist who from 1863 to 1883 lived near Poole (Dorset). SOURCE Allibone Suppl., ii, pp 944–5 (list of novels); Boase, v, p. 818; Sutherland, p. 350; Wolff, ii, p. 300.

K115   *The Earl's cedars* [anon.].
London: L. Booth, 1860, 2 vols. SOURCE COPAC; Wolff, 3786. LOCATION C.
COMMENTARY Partly set in Ireland [Personal communication, John Hart, July, 2000].

K116   *The old hall among the water meadows* (by Mary Rosa Stuart Kettle).
London: T. Fisher Unwin, 1890. SOURCE Burmester list; COPAC. LOCATION L.
COMMENTARY Irish content [Burmester list]

K117   *Rose, shamrock and thistle* (by Mary Rosa Stuart Kettle).
London: T. Fisher Unwin, 1893. SOURCE Brown, 863. LOCATION L.
COMMENTARY Fiction for juveniles. Rhoda Carysfort, an Irish girl, goes to live with her English cousins and eventually marries a Scottish laird [Brown].

KICKHAM, Charles J. See KICKHAM, Charles Joseph.

KICKHAM, Charles Joseph (known as Charles J. Kickham), b. near Cashel (Co. Tipperary) 1828, d. Blackrock (Co. Dublin) 1882. Novelist, prose and verse writer and Fenian nationalist, CJK was the son of John Kickham, a prosperous shopkeeper and farmer, and his wife Anne Mahony. Schooled locally, he was intended to study medicine, but at age 13 he had an accident with gunpowder that injured his sight and hearing. An early enthusiast of the Irish nationalist cause, CJK joined the Young Ireland movement and contributed verse and tales to Dublin periodicals, including the *Shamrock* and the *Nation*. He became a Fenian around 1861, moved to Dublin in 1863 and helped to edit the Fenian newspaper the *Irish People*, to which he contributed leading articles, specializing in rebuttals to clerical opposition to Fenianism. In 1865 the Fenian leader James Stephens appointed CJK to the supreme executive of his Irish Republic. CJK was arrested in the same year and sentenced to fourteen years penal servitude. He served four years of the sentence at Pentonville, Portland and Woking prisons, but was released in poor health. From around 1873 until his death he was president of the supreme council of the Irish Republican Brotherhood and opposed Fenian support of Home Rule and the Land War. He wrote his first novel, *Sally Cavanagh* (Dublin, 1869), in prison and continued to write after his release, producing both novels and prose. His shorter pieces were published in the *Irishman* (Dublin, 1869 onward), the New York *Emerald*, the Boston *Pilot*, the Dublin *Shamrock* and the Dublin *Irish Monthly Magazine*. Although CJK was a devout Catholic, he criticized the clergy for its lack of nationalism. On account of his Fenianism he was denied the sacraments until shortly before his death. Sir Charles Gavan Duffy, politician and statesman, rated him 'next after Carleton§, Griffin§, and Banim§, and before Lever§ and Lady Morgan§ as a painter of national manners' (DNB). A volume of *Poems, sketches and narratives, illustrative of Irish life* was announced as in preparation in *Sally Cavanagh* but is not known to have been published. He became a chronicler of life in Co. Tipperary. Some of his novels, particularly *Knocknagow* (Dublin, [1873]), remained popular well into the twentieth century. Later in life he lived at 2 Montpelier Place, Stradbrook Road, Blackrock

(Co. Dublin). For his portraits and papers, see ODNB. A bronze statue of CJK by J. Hughes was erected in the main street in Tipperary in 1898. SOURCE Allibone Suppl., ii, p. 946; Boylan, p. 186; Brady, p. 123; Brown, p. 157; Clyde, p. 136; R.V. Comerford, *Charles J. Kickham, A biography* (Portmarnock [Co. Dublin], 1979), pp 102, 244 and passim; Elmes, p. 110; Field Day, ii, pp 256–9 and passim; Hogan, pp 345–55; Hogan 2, p. 664; Igoe, pp 132–5; Irish pseudonyms; R.J. Kelly, *Charles Joseph Kickham. Patriot and poet* (Dublin, 1914); McKenna, p. 217–20; Murphy, p. 81; OCIL, p. 289; ODNB; O'Donoghue, p. 235; RIA/DIB; Sutherland, p. 351; K. Tynan, *Twenty-five years: Reminiscences* (New York, 1913), opp p. 246.

K118   *Sally Cavanagh; or, the untenanted graves. A tale of Tipperary* (by Charles J. Kickham; dedicated to John O'Leary, Portland convict establishment or elsewhere, dated from Woking Invalid Convict Prison, Sept. 5, 1867; however, preface is dated from Mullinahone (Co. Tipperary), Apr., 1869).

+ Dublin: W.B. Kelly; London: Simpkin, Marshall & Co., 1869. SOURCE Hogan, p. 354. LOCATION Grail, D, Dcc, InND Loeber coll.

Dublin: James Duffy; London: Simpkin & Marshall, 1869. SOURCE Brown, 864; Comerford, p. 243. LOCATION D, Dt (1905 edn).

Boston: Patrick Donahoe, 1870. LOCATION NUC.

New York: A.E. & R.E. Ford, 1887, 2 vols. (Ford's National Library), 1887. LOCATION NUC.

+ Dublin, Cork: The Mercier Press, 1979. LOCATION L, InND Loeber coll.

COMMENTARY First serialized in the *Hibernian Magazine* (Dublin, 1864), it illustrates the difficulties of Irish peasant life under the twin evils of landlordism and emigration. Set in the 1840s in Co. Tipperary, the heroine has to fend off the lecherous attentions of a landlord while her husband is in America. He returns to find their children dead and his wife Sally a madwoman, living in a graveyard. Oliver Grinden, the cause of Sally's misfortunes, is killed in an accident and Sally dies in her former home [Clyde, p. 129; OCIL, pp 507–8; Sutherland, p. 351].

K119   *Knocknagow; or, the homes of Tipperary* (by Charles J. Kickham; dedicated to the author's nieces Annie and Josie, 'with many regrets and apologies that in spite of all their entreaties I was obliged to let poor Norah Lahy die').

Dublin: A.M. Sullivan, [1873]. SOURCE Comerford, p. 243; Brown, 865 (1879, 2nd edn); de Búrca cat. 40/541; Hogan, p. 354 (1879 edn). LOCATION Grail (Duffy 1887 edn), Dt (Duffy 1887 edn).

+ Dublin: Anna Livia, 1988. LOCATION InND Loeber coll.

New York: Garland, 1979 (introd. by R.L. Wolff). SOURCE COPAC. LOCATION Dt.

COMMENTARY No copy of the Dublin [1873] edn located. First serialized in the *Emerald* (New York, 1870) and in the *Shamrock* (Dublin, 1870). Advertised in *The poems of Richard D. Williams* (Dublin, 1877) at 6*d*. Set in CJK's birthplace, it became a very popular story (it reached a 25th Dublin edn in 1930), combining sentimentality and political anger and life in a depopulated Co. Tipperary village. It includes discussions of the land question and the Fenian tenet that violence is justified if the law is an enemy of the people. An English visitor, the nephew of the landlord, stays with the Kearneys, who introduce him to other Irish families in the locality, thereby increasing his understanding of Irish life [Brown; Comerford, p. 103; Field Day, ii, 248–52, v, 590; OCIL, p. 293–94; RL; Sutherland, p. 351].

K120   *For the old land. A tale of twenty years ago* (by the late Charles J. Kickham).

+ Dublin: M.H. Gill & Son, 1886 (ill.). SOURCE Brown, 866; Comerford, p. 243; Topp 8, 1127. LOCATION Grail, D, Dt, L, InND Loeber coll.

Dublin: M.H. Gill, 1904 (new edn). LOCATION Dt (imperfect), InND Loeber coll. (1908 edn).

+ New York: A.E. & R.E. Ford, 1887, 2 vols. (Ford's National Library, vol. 1, Nos. 5–6; vol. 2 also contains *Sally Cavanagh*). LOCATION D (vol. 2), L, NUC. InND Loeber coll.

COMMENTARY Posthumous publication. Story of peasant life in the 1870s. Describes the fortunes and the sufferings of an Irish family of small farmers under the old land system and deals with the sadness of emigration [Brown; Sutherland, p. 351].

K121 *The eagle of Garryroe* (by Charles J. Kickham).
Dublin: Martin Lester, 1920. SOURCE Brown 2, 716 (where misspelled Lister; mentions 1919 edn but this has not been located); Comerford, p. 243; Hogan, p. 354; RL. LOCATION Grail, Dcc (n.d. edn), DPL (n.d. edn), L, NUC.

COMMENTARY Published posthumously. The initial title was 'Elsie Dhuv' and it is a romance of the rising of 1798 set in Co. Tipperary. Hubert Butler, a TCD student and grandson of the local parson, is sent home by the United Irishmen to prepare for the rising. He is in love with Hester Herbert, niece of Capt. Branton of Garryroe Castle. Hubert is captured and imprisoned in the Castle. Hester is abducted, but she is rescued by the Volunteers. An old, tame eagle plays a part in Hubert's escape. He and Hester are married by his grandfather [Brown 2; Comerford, *Kickham*, p. 170].

K122 *The eagle of Garryroe and, Tales of Tipperary* (by Charles J. Kickham).
Dublin: Talbot Press, 1920, 2 vols. in 1. SOURCE OCLC. LOCATION OU.
+ Dublin: Talbot Press, [1926] (as *Tales of Tipperary*). SOURCE Brown 2, 717 (Dublin: Martin Lester, but this edn not located); Comerford, p. 243; Hogan, p. 354. LOCATION D, DPL (n.d. edn), NUC.

COMMENTARY Published posthumously. Reissue of *The eagle of Garryroe* (Dublin, 1920). The *Tales of Tipperary* consists of stories that first appeared in the *Celt* (Dublin) and *Irish Harp* (Dublin). Contents: 'White Humphrey of the Grange', 'Never give up', 'Annie O'Brien', 'Poor Mary Maher', 'Joe Lonergan's trip' [RL; Comerford, pp 192–3].

K123 *The valley near Slieveamon, a Kickham anthology* (ed. by James Maher; dedicated to editor's mother Bridget Maher, and Annie White; foreword by the Hon. John Cudahy).
+ Kilkenny: Kilkenny People, [1941]. LOCATION NUC (1942 edn), InND Loeber coll.

KILLINGER, Karl (also **Carl**) freiherr von, b. Heilbronn (Germany), pseud. 'K. v. K.', d. Karlsruhe (Germany) 1868. Translator, folklorist and biographer, KvK was the son of August von Killinger. KvK became very interested in the work of Gerald Griffin§ and published his biography in Stuttgart in 1847. He also translated Gerald Griffin's *The collegians* (as *Die Schulfreunde*, Stuttgart, 1843), published on fairy tales, and edited the following work. SOURCE OCLC; *Neue Deutsche biographie* (Berlin, 1978), xi, p. 608.

K124 *Erin: Auswahl vorzüglicher irischer Erzählungen mit lebensgeschichtlichen Nachrichten von ihren Verfassern und Sammlung der besten irischen Volkssagen, Märchen under Legenden* ([compiled and trans.] by 'K v. K').
Stuttgart, Tübingen: J.G. Cotta, 1847–8, 5 vols. SOURCE Union Cat. of Bavaria. LOCATION D (vols. 4–5 only, see below).
Stuttgart, Tübingen: J.G. Cotta, 1847–9, 6 vols [*sic*]. SOURCE Union Cat. of Northern Germany. LOCATION Weimar, Herzogin Anna Amalia Bibliothek.

COMMENTARY Numbering of volumes is not uniform in library catalogues. Contents of 1847–49 edn: *Sagen and Mährchen* (2 vols.); *Gerald Griffin – ein Schriftstellerleben* (2 vols.; biography), *Die Schulfreunde* (2 vols.; trans. of Gerald Griffin's *The collegians*). The difference between the 1847–48 edns, and between the 1847–49 edns appears to be an additional volume of *Sagen and Mährchen* [RL; OCLC; Union Cat. of Northern Germany].

KIMBER, Edward, b. 1719, d. 1769. An English novelist, editor and poet, EK was the son of Isaac Kimber, a Baptist minister and journalist (b. Wantage, Berks., 1692). His father became editor of the *London Magazine* in 1732 and EK began to contribute poetry to this journal as early as 1734, later taking over the editorship himself in 1755. He travelled in the American colonies between 1742 and 1744 and published accounts of his experiences there. These later provided grist for his seven novels, which were quite successful, several going into second edns. EK compiled indices of the *London Magazine* and the *Gentleman's Magazine* (London) and contributed to various other periodicals. He wrote *The peerage of Ireland* (London, 1768, 2 vols.); *The peerage of Scotland* (London, 1767), and *The peerage of England* (London, 1766). Allibone attributes to him also a *History of England* (London, 10 vols.), written in conjunction with R. Johnson. SOURCE Allibone, i, p. 1030; F.G. Black, 'Edward Kimber: anonymous novelist of the mid-eighteenth century', *Harvard Studies and Notes in Philology and Literature*, 17 (1935), pp 27–42; K.J. Hayes, introd., E. Kimber, *Itinerant observations in America* (Newark, NJ, 1998), pp 11–24; CM; ODNB.

K125 *The juvenile adventures of David Ranger, Esq; from an original manuscript found in the collections of a noble lord* [anon.].
+ London: P. Stevens, 1757, 2 vols. SOURCE Hardy, 533; ESTC t107720. LOCATION L, NUC.
COMMENTARY Irish content, set in Cork and Dublin [CM].

K126 *The life, extraordinary adventures, voyages, and surprizing escapes of Capt. Neville Frowde, of Cork. In four parts. Written by himself and now first published from his own manuscript* [anon.].
London: J. Wren, 1708 [mistake for 1758]. SOURCE Raven, 440; Forster, 1523; Hardy, 534; ESTC t107401. LOCATION L, YU, NUC.
Berwick: W. Phorson, B. Law & Son, 1792. SOURCE Bradshaw, 7527; ESTC t110509. LOCATION C.
COMMENTARY A romance recounting a voyage from Cork and Dublin, via Smyrna, Malta, Gibraltar, and Madeira, to the South Seas and South America, where Frowde is attacked by Indians [Bradshaw; CM; Burmester list].

KING, C., fl. 1850s. Regional religious fiction writer, probably a resident of Co. Derry. SOURCE RL.

K127 *An evening's conversation in the mountains of Derry. With a friendly enquiry into the question whether the Rev. Samuel Montgomery, or, the Rev. Patrick O'Loughlin, is the lawful pastor and parish priest of Ballynascreen* [anon.].
+ Dublin: J. M'Glashan, W. Curry, J. Robertson, S.B. Oldham & G. Herbert, 1854 (second, revsd. edn). LOCATION PC, D ([1854?] edn), L.
COMMENTARY First edn not located. A copy in a private collection is inscribed by C. King, presumably the author. The volume starts with an 'Introductory letter to a convert from the Church of Rome', which concerns the difference between the Communion of Rome and the Reformed Catholic Church of Ireland. It is followed by a prose work, 'The old church of Ballynascreen', and 'Address to the Roman Catholics of Ballynascreen', 'Historical notices of Ballynascreen', 'Successors of SS. Patrick and Columkille'. Ballynascreen is a parish in Co. Derry [RL].

KING, Jane. See **MAHON, Lady Jane**.

KING, Katherine, fl. 1875. A novelist born in England of Irish descent, KK emigrated to Toowong in Australia. Her brother, H.E. King, was an officer in the British army before becoming a member of the Queensland Legislative Assembly and later a journalist with the *Brisbane Courier*. SOURCE Bickersteth cat. 132/101; Miller, ii, pp 616–17; OCLC.

K128   *Our detachment* (by Katherine King).
London: Hurst & Blackett, 1875, 3 vols. SOURCE Jarndyce cat. 137/1008. LOCATION L.
+ London: Chapman & Hall, 1877 (new edn). LOCATION InND Loeber coll.
+ New York: Harper, 1875. LOCATION InND Loeber coll., NUC.
COMMENTARY A romance of military life set in Ireland and England during Fenian times, it tells the story of the love life of three English officers stationed in a small country town in the south of Ireland. The mother of one of the officers is violently opposed to his marrying an Irish girl, and she creates a great deal of mischief and unhappiness, ending in the death of one of the officers. Eventually, the Irish girl is accepted. The novel describes hunting, country balls, picnics, and other activities the officers engage in, including the quelling of Fenian activities [ML].

KING, Lady Margaret Jane. See **MOUNT CASHELL, Margaret Jane, Countess.**

KING, Mary. See **WARD, the Hon. Mrs Mary.**

KING, Revd Richard Ashe, pseud. 'Basil', b. Ennis (Co. Clare) 1855 (1839 according to OCIL), d. London 1932. Fiction and literary writer and clergyman, RAK was educated at TCD and was ordained into the Church of England in 1862. He was posted to Yorkshire where he was a curate in Bradford. In 1881 he gave up his living and came to London where he contributed to London periodicals such as the *Cornhill Magazine* and *Pall Mall Gazette*. King returned to Ireland for long periods in his later life but died in London, where for some years he had been president of the Irish Literary Society. He wrote works on Jonathan Swift§ and Oliver Goldsmith§ and published some stories in the *Shamrock* (Dublin, 1892). In Ireland he lived at Blackrock. Some of his letters are among the Downey Papers in the NLI (MSS 10,005; 10,024–27; 10,030; 10,043). SOURCE Allibone Suppl., ii, p. 949; Brady, p. 124; Brown, p. 158; CM; Hogan 2, p. 673; OCIL, p. 290–91; E. Reilly, p. 218, 245–46; RIA/DIB; Ryan, p. 149; Sutherland, p. 353.

K129   *Love the debt* (by 'Basil').
London: Smith, Elder & Co., 1882, 3 vols. SOURCE Wolff, 3798. LOCATION L, NUC.
New York: Harper & Bros, 1882 (Harper's Franklin Square Library, No. 234). LOCATION NUC.
COMMENTARY First serialized in *Cornhill Magazine* (London) [Personal communication, Theodore Hoffman, June 2005].

K130   *'The wearing of the green'* (by 'Basil'; dedicated to Kathleen Mary Horsfall).
London: Chatto & Windus, 1884. SOURCE Brown, 868 (1886 edn); Wolff, 3801. LOCATION D (1886 edn), L.
New York: Harper & Bros, [1885] (Harper's Franklin Square Library, No. 444). LOCATION NUC.
COMMENTARY A love story in which the lovers are kept apart by various happenings. It describes the Fenian conspiracy. Although Protestant in tenor, the author sympathizes with Irish grievances [Brown].

K131   *A drawn game* (by 'Basil').
London: Chatto & Windus, 1884. SOURCE Allibone Suppl., ii, p. 949. LOCATION L, NUC.

K132   *A coquette's conquest. A novel* (by 'Basil').

London: Ward & Downey; Richard Bentley, 1885, 3v. in 1. LOCATION L.

New York: Harper & Bros, 1885 (Harper's Franklin Square Library). LOCATION NUC.

COMMENTARY The heroine is Lucy Lisle, a vicar's daughter. Her conquest is the meek Henry Rowan, whose infatuation threatens his ordination to the priesthood. Eventually, he marries Lucy's sister Mary [Personal communication, Theodore Hoffman, June 2005].

K133   *A shadowed life* (by Richard Ashe King).
London: Ward & Downey, 1886, 3 vols. SOURCE Wolff, 3800; COPAC. LOCATION L.

K134   *A leal lass* (by Richard Ashe King).
London: Ward & Downey, 1888, 2 vols. SOURCE Wolff, 3796; COPAC. LOCATION L, NUC.

K135   *Passion's slave* (by Richard Ashe King; dedicated to the author's sister-in-law Mrs Henry King).
+ London: Chatto & Windus, 1889, 3 vols. SOURCE Wolff, 3799. LOCATION D, L.
New York: D. Appleton & Co., 1889 (as *Passion's slave. A novel*). LOCATION NUC.
New York: G. Munro, 1889. SOURCE OCLC. LOCATION L.

K136   *Love's legacy. A novel* (by Richard Ashe King).
+ London: Ward & Downey, 1890, 3 vols. SOURCE Hogan 2, p. 673; Wolff, 3797. LOCATION D, L, InND Loeber coll.

COMMENTARY A mystery romance set in Dublin, mainly at Trinity College. A girl stands to loose either her lover or her father as killers of her cousin. Her father had actually tried to kill the cousin, who was his ward and whose money he had embezzled. However, the cousin, terminally ill with a brain tumour, had saved enough laudanum and killed himself. The girl's lover is falsely framed. Although he knew of the father's attempt at murder, he tried to shield the girl from shame by being a suspect himself. Eventually, all is cleared up and the lovers marry [ML].

K137   **Bell Barry** (by Richard Ashe King).
London: Chatto & Windus, 1891. SOURCE Brown, 869. LOCATION L.

COMMENTARY The father and sister of the main character are insufferably good. In contrast, Bell is a warm, good-hearted human being. The story is partly set in America and centres on the rehabilitation of Bell's fiancée by her rejected suitor. Two minor characters are 'typically Irish' [Brown].

K138   *A Geraldine* (by Richard Ashe King).
London: Ward & Downey, 1893, 2 vols. SOURCE Brown, 870; Wolff, 3795. LOCATION L, NUC.

COMMENTARY Set in the late-nineteenth century, the story is concerned with the land troubles in Ireland. The heroine is the daughter of a rack-renting squireen and is a contrast to the rest of her family [Brown].

'KING, Toler', pseud. See FOX, Mrs Emily.

KINGSLEY, Revd Charles, b. Devon 1819, d. Eversley (Hants.) 1875. Prolific English writer, social and political activist, professor, historian and clergyman, CK is probably best known for his fantasy *The water-babies* (London, 1863), and his extravagantly heroic *Hereward the wake* (London, 1866). He is said to have written an historical volume entitled *John Inglesant*, dealing with the activities of Lord Glamorgan in Kilkenny, but this has not been located. He married Frances (known as Fanny) Eliza Grenfell, daughter of Pascoe Grenfell, MP, a wealthy industrialist who had married as his second wife Georgiana St Leger, daughter of the 1st Viscount Doneraile of Doneraile (Co. Cork). Major collections of CK's papers are in the BL and in the Morris L. Parrish collection, Princeton Univ. SOURCE Allibone, i, pp 1034–5; Allibone Suppl., ii, pp 951–2; S.M. Griffin, *Anti-Catholicism and nineteenth century fiction*

(Cambridge, 2004), pp 114–15, 121, 126; NCBEL 4, p. 1311–18; ODNB; Rafroidi, i, p. 208; Sutherland, p. 355.

K139 *Westward Ho* (by Charles Kingsley).
  Cambridge: Macmillan & Co., 1855, 3 vols. SOURCE Rafroidi, i, p. 208; Sadleir, 1340; Sutherland, pp 667–8. LOCATION L.
  Leipzig: Bernard Tauchnitz, 1855. SOURCE T & B, 329. LOCATION L.
COMMENTARY Anti-Catholic novel inspired by the Crimean War but set in the age of Sir Frances Drake. The setting is partly in Ireland. It deals with the expulsion of the Spaniards from Ireland and the story argues that for nineteenth-century England to achieve its former greatness it needs to defeat Catholic Spain, which represents an archaic religion [Rafroidi; Sutherland; S.M. Griffin, *Anti-Catholicism* (Cambridge, 2004), pp 114–15, 121, 126].

KINGSTON, William H.G. See **KINGSTON, William Henry Giles.**

KINGSTON, William Henry Giles (known as **William H.G. Kingston**), b. London 1814, d. London, 1880. English editor and writer of adventure fiction for juveniles, WHGK was the son of Lucy Henry Kingston and Frances Rooke. For many years he travelled to and from and lived in Oporto (Portugal), where his father's wine business was located and which he joined in 1833. He helped bring about a successful trade treaty with Portugal in 1842, for which he was decorated by the queen of Portugal. He began writing newspaper articles in Portugal and in 1850 gave up business to devote himself to writing. He edited two periodicals, the *Colonist* (London?) and the *Colonial Magazine and East India Review* (London) and wrote pamphlets about emigration and emigrants' welfare. WHGK travelled widely, including to the US. He was one of the most popular and prolific writers of adventure stories for boys of his time, with some of his work focusing on naval stories and others on Irish boys. SOURCE Allibone Suppl., ii, pp 954–5; Brown 2, p. 137; M.R. Kingsford, *The life, work and influence of William Henry Giles Kingston* (Toronto, 1947); NCBEL 4, pp 1319–22; ODNB; Sutherland, p. 357.

K140 *Peter the whaler. His early life, and adventures in the Arctic regions* (by William H.G. Kingston).
  London: Grant & Griffith, 1851 (ill. E. Duncan). SOURCE Brown, 872; Wolff, 3873. LOCATION L, NUC.
  New York: C.S. Francis & Co., 1852. LOCATION NUC.
COMMENTARY WHGK's best-selling adventure story for boys. The hero is Peter, the scapegrace son of a vicar in the south of Ireland, who is sent to sea as a punishment for poaching. He is subjected to harsh treatment at the hands of a brutal captain, but survives and has many adventures. In the US he joins the navy and is shipwrecked on an iceberg; saved by the crew of a whaler, which he joins, and eventually shipwrecked again off the coast of Ireland, where he is welcomed home like a prodigal son. In the course of all of these adventures, Peter develops manly Christian virtues [Brown; Sutherland, p. 500].

K141 *Salt water; or, the sea life and adventures of Neil D'Arcy, the midshipman* (by William H.G. Kingston).
  London: Griffith & Farran, 1857 (ill.). SOURCE OCLC; Wolff, 3877. LOCATION L.
  New York: C.S. Francis & Co., 1858. LOCATION NUC.
  + Philadelphia: J.B. Lippincott & Co., 1877 (ill.). LOCATION InND Loeber coll.
COMMENTARY A story of naval adventures for boys. The hero, Neil D'Arcy, was brought up in Co. Cork and has been partially under the guidance of Larry Harrigan, the family butler who had been to sea with Neil's grandfather. Neil's first assignment at sea is with his uncle, who commands a revenue cutter, after which he joins the Royal Navy and has many adventures on the Atlantic and Mediterranean and off the coast of Africa [ML].

K142 *The heir of Kilfinnan. A tale of the shore and ocean* (by William H.G. Kingston).
London: Sampson Low, Marston, Searle & Rivington, Gilbert & Rivington, 1881.
SOURCE OCLC. LOCATION L, InND Loeber coll. ([1894 or earlier] edn).
COMMENTARY A story for boys set on the west coast of Ireland. A fisher boy is befriended by
the local gentry, who teach him to read and write. After many adventures it transpires he is
the new earl of Kilfinnan. He marries the girl who made much of him when he was still a
fisher boy [ML].

K143 *Paddy Finn; or, the adventures of a midshipman afloat and ashore* (by William
H.G. Kingston).
+ London: Griffith & Farran; New York: E.P. Dutton & Co., 1883 (ill.; see Plate 41).
SOURCE Brown 2, 733; Wolff, 3870. LOCATION D, L, NUC, InND Loeber coll.
(London, Frowde, 1910 edn).
COMMENTARY A story for boys featuring Terence O'Finnahan, who grew up on an estate near
the Shannon. The family was impoverished and it was only due to the support of an uncle
that they managed at all. Terence and his servant Larry go to sea and encounter many adven-
tures, particularly during a tour of the Caribbean and, after England concludes a peace with
France, in the Mediterranean. Terence is called Paddy Finn on board, and Larry keeps crews
happy by playing his fiddle, which he manages to save from every disaster. Both Terence and
Larry behave gallantly and their adventures include saving an aristocratic family from an angry
mob in France. At the end of the story Paddy is promoted to lieutenant [ML].

'KINK, Emannuel', pseud. See DOWLING, Richard.

KINLEY, Jane, fl. 1868. Religious fiction writer, JK may have been Irish since she published
in Dublin [RL].
K144 *The Ashtons. A dark beginning with a bright ending* (by Jane Kinley).
+ Dublin: Moffat & Co., 1868 (introductory preface by Revd Frederick Whitfield,
Tunbridge, Kent). SOURCE Allibone Suppl., ii, p. 954; Alston, p. 237. LOCATION L.
COMMENTARY Religious fiction. The preface contains a tirade against the dangers of modern fic-
tion, 'the malaria of modern times, and one of the marked features of the last days' [BLC; CM].

'KINNFAELA', pseud. See MCGINLEY, Thomas Colin.

KIRBY, Alfred F.P., fl. 1869. AFPK may have been a member of the Kirby family of
Woodbrook (Co. Leitrim). SOURCE Personal communication, Harman Murtagh, May 1994.
K145 *The green island. A tale for youth* (by Alfred F.P. Kirby).
+ London, Derby, Dublin: Thomas Richardson & Son, 1869. SOURCE Allibone Suppl.,
ii, p. 955; COPAC. LOCATION L.
Baltimore: Kelly, Piet & Co., 1870. SOURCE DCU, Catholic Americana files (1871 edn).
LOCATION NUC.
COMMENTARY Religious fiction for juveniles [CM].

'KIRKWOOD, Arthur', pseud. See MCGLYNN, M.J.

'KNIGHT ERRANT', pseud. See DUBOIS, Edward.

KNORTZ, Karl, b. Garbenheim, near Wetzlar (Germany) 1841, d. Tarrytown (NY) 1918.
German-American folklorist KK was born out of wedlock, but raised by his mother and an
adoptive father. He emigrated to the US in 1863, settled in New York and became a schoolteacher. In 1868 he moved to Oshkosh (WI), and subsequently to Cincinnati (OH) and

Pittsburgh (PA). In 1882, he returned to New York, but settled in Evansville (IN). After his retirement from teaching in 1905, he moved to Tarrytown (NY). He became a prolific author of poetry and detective stories and an editor of books on German and British authors, political ideas and social theories. His principal works are on folklore, including that of the native Indian-Americans, Germans, and to a lesser extent, the Irish in America. SOURCE RLIN; E. Schamschula, *Pioneer of American folklore: Karl Knortz and his collections* (Moscow (ID), 1996).

K146   *Irländische Märchen wiederverzählt* (by Karl Knortz).
   + Zurich: Verlags-Magazine (J. Schabelitz), 1886. SOURCE RLIN. LOCATION Swiss National Library, MH.
   COMMENTARY Irish fairy stories retold by the author. Contents: 'Der Wechselbalg', 'Eine probate Kur', 'Die Geschichte von zwei Buckligen', 'Die Elfen-Amme', 'Jim Doyle im Elfenpalast', 'Nora', 'Moruach oder Die Nixen', 'Ochs, Kuh und Kalb', 'Ein Kobold in Eselsgestalt', 'Das Schloss der Ungewitzheit', 'Der Teufel und der Steuerempfanger', 'Der vorzeitige Prophet', 'Die Geschichte von drei Geistern, welche Fussball Spielten', 'Cauth Morrisy', 'Der Schatzgräber', 'Gearoidh Jarla', 'Jack Barrett', 'Eine Geistergeschichte', 'Fann Mac Cuil und der Schottische Riese', 'Fion's Jugend', 'Die Konigin von Sciana Breaca', 'Conan in Cealdh', 'Oisin's Jugend', 'Oisin's Greisenalter', 'Die Legende von Loch na Piasta', 'Der Konig mit den Pferdeohren', 'Knockseogowna, oder Der Berg des Elfen-Kalbes', 'Des Priesters Abendessen', 'Die Eierschalen-Brauerei', 'Der Flaschenberg', 'Herr und Knecht', 'Der kleine Schuh', 'Das Geister-Pferd', 'Der verwunschene See', 'Die Nixe von Gollerns', 'Die Wundermelodie', 'Donaghadee', 'Der Geborgte See', 'Königliche Lehren', 'Goban Saor oder Der Kluge Baumeister', 'Hans der Herr und Hans der Knecht', '"Das nächste Mal werde ich kluger sein!"', 'Der drei Schwestern', 'Der Braune Bär von Norwegen', 'Giolla na Choricean Gobhar oder Der Mann in dem Ziegenfelle', 'Die böse Stiefmutter', 'Shannon', 'Wie die Insel "Man" entstand', 'Wie der Killarney-See enstand', 'Der Imhiquin-See', 'An Braon Suan or', 'Lir's Kinder', 'Tiis', 'Jakob und seine Kameraden', 'Die drei Kronen', 'Die Milch der weissen Kuhe', 'St. Patrick und die Druiden', 'Wie St. Cloi von seinem Stolze kurirt wurde', 'Sculloge' [ML; RL].

KNOT, Mary John [*sic*], fl. 1835. Author of religious fiction, MJK also wrote *Two months at Kilkee* (Dublin, 1836), which consists of studies on Irish life and character. According to the title page of *The life of a thief* (Dublin, 1835), she published 'The life of Anne –, a penitent female', and 'Memoir of Jane Kenny, an infant school child', but these have not been located. It is possible that she can be identified with Mary Jane Knott, who was a Quaker. SOURCE CM; Religious Society of Friends' Historical Library, Dublin, Portfolio 2C; RL.

K147   *The life of a thief, related by herself. To which is added, some observations, &c. on the non-observance of the eighth commandment* [anon.].
   + Dublin: R.M. Timms & W. Curry Jnr & Co.; London: Edmund Fry; Liverpool: Joseph Davenport, 1835. LOCATION L.
   COMMENTARY Moralistic fiction about a female thief. The story is set in Ireland [ML].

KNOWLES, James Sheridan, b. Cork 1784, d. Torquay (Devon) 1862. Playwright, actor, Baptist preacher and novelist, JSK was a son of schoolmaster and lexicographer, James Knowles, and his wife Jane Peace Daunt. He was a cousin of playwright Richard Brinsley Sheridan on his father's side, and on his mother's side he was related to the Le Fanu family. The Knowles moved to London in 1793 after his parents boycotted the senior Knowles's school because of his support for Catholic emancipation, but JSK maintained contact with individuals in Munster (see below). With encouragement from his mother he began to write verse and plays when still young and through his family made the acquaintance of eminent writers such as William Hazlitt, Charles Lamb and Samuel Taylor Coleridge. He was in the militia for a while before studying medicine at Aberdeen University, but after completing his degree soon abandoned medicine for a successful theatrical career as actor, producer and author. He played in Ireland in Dublin, Waterford (where he acted with and married the Scottish actress Maria Charteris and wrote 'Leo, or the gypsy' (1810) as a vehicle for the actor Edmund Kean) and Belfast where, according to the ODNB he wrote and acted in a drama 'Brian Boroighme, or, the maid of Erin' in 1811 to great success. To secure a steady income, he opened a school in Belfast and later taught with his father at the Belfast Academical Institution. He went to Glasgow, where he ran a school for fifteen years. In Glasgow he also started a short-lived newspaper, the *Glasgow Free Press*. He edited *The elocutionist* (Belfast 1831), a collection of prose and verse for declamation by students, and contributed to several London periodicals including the *Keepsake* (1834), *Bentley's Miscellany* ('Glorvina, the maid of Meath', 1837), and *The Gift for All Seasons* (1840). He visited the US on a theatrical tour in 1834 and presented 'Lectures on Dramatic Literature', two of which were published posthumously (London, 1873). In the early 1840s JSK underwent a religious conversion and became a Baptist preacher. He acquired a great reputation in London as an orator and published the controversial *The idol demolished by its own priest: an answer to Cardinal* [John Henry] *Newman's§ lectures on transubstantiation* (Edinburgh, 1851). JSK wrote poetry – his *A collection of poems* was published in Waterford in 1810 – and more than twenty plays. He was widely regarded as the leading dramatist of his day. In 1838 he acted in his own play *The hunchback* (London, Theatre Royal), which proved a great success. Relatively late in life he published four works of fiction. A short story 'The Irish beauty; or Phil Brannon's marriage' appeared [anon.] in *MacNeil, the pirate; or, the man of St. Martin's* (Boston, 1848). Elizabeth Rennie described JSK as of about middle height, 'rather stout … with bright, intelligent eyes, a large well-shaped forehead, a complexion of healthful freshness … His manner was full of warmth, heartiness, and kindliness' (Rennie, ii, pp 147, 156). He was related to the novelist Caroline Norton and his son Richard Brinsley Sheridan Knowles§ was also a writer. JSK featured in Edward Kenealy's§ *Brallaghan, or the Deipnosophists* (London, 1845). He received a civil list pension in 1848. Some of his letters are in the Henry E. Huntington Library, San Marino (CA). For his portraits and papers, see ODNB. *The dramatic works of James Sheridan Knowles* (Baltimore, 1835) consists of plays only. SOURCE Allibone, i, p. 1043; R.E. Blanc, *James McHenry (1745–1845)* (Philadelphia, 1937), pp 25–8; Boylan, p. 188; D. & M. Coakley, *Wit and wine* (Peterhead, 1975), opp. p. 72; S.C. Hall, p. 236; Hogan, p. 360; Hogan 2, p. 678; R. Horne (ed.), *The new spirit of the age* (London, 1844), ii, pp 86–128; Jarndyce cat. 162/515; Mott cat. 201/139; NCBEL 4, p. 1970–71; NUC; OCIL, p. 294; ODNB; O'Donoghue, pp 238–9; [E. Rennie], *Traits of character* (London, 1860), ii, pp 147, 156; RIA/DIB; RL; Schulz, p. 278; Strickland, i, p. 478; Sutherland, p. 358; Wolff, ii, p. 321.

K148   *The Magdalen, and other tales* (by James Sheridan Knowles; dedicated to John Forster of the Inner Temple).

+ London: Edward Moxon, 1832. SOURCE Rafroidi, ii, p. 200; Hodgson, p. 316; Wolff, 3920; Garside 2, 1832:54. LOCATION Corvey CME 3–628–51070–8; InND Loeber coll., NUC.

Philadelphia: Carey, Lea & Blanchard, 1833. SOURCE Kaser, 410. LOCATION NUC, CtY.

New York: Wallis & Newell, 1835. LOCATION NUC.

COMMENTARY Short stories set mostly in England or France. One story is set in Ireland. Contents: 'The Magdalen', 'Love and authorship', 'Old adventures', 'Therese', 'The letter-de-cachet', 'The portrait: a sketch' (set in Ireland) [ML].

K149   *Fortescue. A novel* (by James Sheridan Knowles; dedicated to Caroline Norton).

London: Printed for private circulation only, 1846, 3 vols. SOURCE Quaritch cat. 1193/158. LOCATION L.

+ London: Edward Moxon, 1847, 3 vols. LOCATION InND Loeber coll., NUC.

New York: Harper & Bros, 1846 (Library of Select Novels, Nos. 92, 94). LOCATION NUC.

COMMENTARY Set in England, a story of the fortunes and loves of the scion of an Irish family. The story starts in Co. Cork where Henry Fortescue's father's unpopular political opinions bring about his downfall. The family moves to England and after Henry's parents die, he becomes a tutor to a young girl, Marian. Her mother feels that Henry and Marian would be well-suited to marry. But before this marriage takes place a number of obstacles have to be overcome, particularly those posed by a girl who has designs on Henry, and a relative of Marian's who almost forces her to marry him. All ends well [ML].

K150 *George Lovell. A novel* (by James Sheridan Knowles).

London: Edward Moxon, 1847, 3 vols. SOURCE Rafroidi, ii, p. 200; Sutherland, p. 358 (probably mistakenly mentions 1846 edn); Hodgson, p. 316; Wolff, 3918; COPAC. LOCATION L, NUC.

New York: Pursons, Stringer & Co., 1847. LOCATION NUC.

COMMENTARY The story of the adventures of a jeweller's son [Sutherland].

K151 *Tales and novelettes, collected* (by James Sheridan Knowles; revsd and ed. by F. Harvey).

London: privately printed for J. McHenry, 1874. SOURCE NCBEL 4, p. 1971; Rafroidi, ii, p. 202 ; OCLC. LOCATION NUC.

COMMENTARY Only 25 copies printed [OCLC].

KNOWLES, R.B. Sheridan. See **KNOWLES, Richard Brinsley Sheridan.**

KNOWLES, Richard Brinsley Sheridan (also known as **R.B. Sheridan Knowles**), b. Glasgow (Scotland) 1820, d. London 1882. Playwright, editor, novelist and biographer, RBSK was the son of the playwright James Sheridan Knowles§. He was educated by the Rosminian Fathers at Ratcliffe (Leics.) and after studying at the Middle Temple was called to the Bar in 1843. His interest was in writing rather than law and in 1845 he produced a comedy, *The maiden aunt*, at the Haymarket Theatre in London. That year he married Eliza Mary, youngest child of Peter and Elizabeth Crowley of Dublin. He became a Catholic in 1849 and was editor of the *Catholic Standard* (Dublin?) and later of the *London Illustrated Magazine* and the *London Review*. A lead writer for the *Standard* from 1857 to 1860, he was forced out by the anti-Catholic influence of the owners, at which the editor resigned. Later he worked for the London *Morning Post*. RBSK wrote a biography of his father *The life of James Sheridan Knowles* (London, 1872) that vividly evokes the life of the theatre at that time. In 1871 he was appointed an inspector of historical manuscripts. SOURCE Allibone, i, p. 1043; Allibone Suppl., ii, p. 961; Brown, p. 159; L.E. Dobrée, *A round table of the representative Irish and English Catholic novelists* (New York, 1897), pp 127–8; ODNB; O'Donoghue, p. 239; Wolff, ii, p. 323.

K152 *Glencoonoge. A novel* (by R.B. Sheridan Knowles).

+ Edinburgh, London: William Blackwood & Sons, 1891, 3 vols. SOURCE Brown, 873; Wolff, 3922. LOCATION L, InND Loeber coll.

COMMENTARY Published posthumously. First appeared in the *Month* (location unclear), this is a love story of an English girl of gentle birth and a young Irish peasant, set in a valley somewhere on the south-west coast of Ireland. The girl's brother had lost track of her earlier in life and is trying to find her. He is very upset with the alliance she has made. However, he comes to appreciate the character of her Irish husband and eventually buys for them the inn in which they both had been working [ML; Brown].

KNOX, Capt. —. See **KNOX, Capt. Charles H.**

KNOX, Capt. Charles H. (also known as **Capt. Knox**), d. 1855. CHK was a military historian and novelist, whose parentage is unclear. He joined the army in 1826 as an ensign, made captain in 1836, retired on half pay in 1838 and served in the royal Glamorgan militia. SOURCE Allibone, i, p. 1043; Boase, v, p. 835; Maggs cat. 1322/180; Sutherland, p. 359.

K153   *Harry Mowbray* (by Captain Knox).
    + London: John Ollivier, 1843 (ill.). SOURCE Wolff, 3923. LOCATION InND Loeber coll., NUC.
COMMENTARY A mystery and romantic adventure story set in England, Ireland, and the Middle East, with reminiscences of India. The featured family has a country house in Ireland. Harry Mowbray is an officer stationed in Ireland and there are several Irish characters in the book. The story contains a number of villains, people with secrets in their pasts, mistaken identities, and thwarted lovers. The mysteries are eventually unravelled but it requires a trip to the Middle East to visit an eccentric Englishwoman who lives in the Syrian desert to get to the bottom of the plot. By the end of the book all villains are dead and all lovers happily reunited [ML].

KNOX, Revd James Spencer, pseud. '**An Irish clergyman**', b. Co. Armagh 1789, d. Clifton, Bristol (Avon), 1862. Eldest son of Revd William Knox, bishop of Derry. Church of Ireland clergyman and writer, JSK was admitted to TCD in 1805 and obtained a BA in 1810 and an MA in 1814. Rector of Fahan (Co. Donegal), 1813–17, vicar of Innismagrath (Co. Leitrim), 1815–17, rector of Maghera and Kilcronaghan (Co. Derry), 1817–62, and later vicar-general of Derry. He married in 1813, Clara Barbara, daughter of the Hon. John Beresford, and, with her had three sons and three daughters. He was a friend of Charles Lever§. He probably is a different individual than 'An Irish clergyman,' who signed as 'H.B.' and who published his 'Reminiscences', that is, Irish religious tales, in the *Christian Lady's Magazine* (London, 1837–38; ed. by Elizabeth Tonna§). SOURCE B & S, p. 475; Brown, p. 159; Leslie, *Derry*, pp 259–60; RIA/DIB; RL.

K154   *Pastoral annals* (by 'An Irish clergyman').
    + London: R.B. Seeley & W. Burnside, 1840. SOURCE Brown, 875; Hodgson, p. 316.
    LOCATION L.
COMMENTARY Deals with the 1817 famine. Sketches of peasant life, probably from Co. Donegal. Contents: 'The sick parish', 'The first death', 'The sermon', 'The warning', 'The private still', 'The pluralist', 'The inn', 'The school', 'Ribbonism', 'The night', 'The starving family', 'The birth', 'The soup shop', 'Death by starvation', 'The confessional', 'Family worship', 'Tithe setting', 'Lough Derg' [Brown; Fegan, p. 209].

KNOX, Kathleen, fl. 1873. A poet and a children's author primarily, KK was the daughter of Charles George Knox, LLD, vicar-general of Down and Connor. Her uncle was lord primate Dr Knox. In 1879 she lived at Howth (Co. Dublin), and published poetry under the pseudonym 'Edward Kane'. SOURCE Allibone Suppl., ii, p. 962; Colman, p. 134; LVP, p. 263; NCBEL 4, p. 1819; O'Donoghue, p. 239; RIA/DIB.

K155   *Father Time's story book. For the little ones* (by Kathleen Knox).
    + London: Griffith & Farran, 1873 (ill. H.W. Petherick). SOURCE NCBEL 4, p. 1819
    LOCATION L.
    COMMENTARY Fiction for juveniles [RL].

K156   *Fairy gifts; or, a wallet of wonders* (by Kathleen Knox).
    London: Griffith & Farran, 1875 (ill. K. Greenaway, John Greenaway). SOURCE NCBEL 4, p. 1819; Osborne, ii, p. 1005. LOCATION L, CaOTP.
    COMMENTARY Fiction for juveniles [RL].

K157   *Seven birthdays; or, the children of fortune. A fairy chronicle* (by Kathleen Knox).
+ London: Griffith & Farran, 1876 (ill. K. Greenaway). SOURCE NCBEL 4, p. 1819;
COPAC. LOCATION L.
New York: Pott, Young & Co., [1880?]. LOCATION L.
COMMENTARY Fiction for juveniles [RL].

K158   *Wildflower Win: The journal of a little girl* (by Kathleen Knox).
+ London, Belfast: Marcus Ward & Co., 1876 (ill.). SOURCE NCBEL 4, p. 1819.
LOCATION L.
COMMENTARY Fiction for juveniles [RL].

K159   *Lily of the valley; a story for little boys and girls* (by Kathleen Knox).
+ London, Belfast: Marcus Ward & Co., 1876 (ill.). SOURCE NCBEL 4, p. 1819;
OCLC. LOCATION L, CtY.
COMMENTARY Fiction for juveniles set in Co. Longford [OCLC; CM].

K160   *Meadowleigh. A holiday history* (by Kathleen Knox).
+ London, Belfast: Marcus Ward & Co., 1876 (ill.). SOURCE NCBEL 4, p. 1819.
LOCATION L.
COMMENTARY Fiction for juveniles [RL].

K161   *Queen Dora: The life and lessons of a little girl* (by Kathleen Knox).
+ London: Griffin & Farran, 1879. SOURCE NCBEL 4, p. 1819. LOCATION L.
COMMENTARY Fiction for juveniles [RL].

K162   *Cornertown chronicles: New legends of old lore* (by Kathleen Knox).
+ London: Griffith & Farran; New York: E.P. Dutton & Co., 1879. SOURCE NCBEL
4, p. 1819 (1879 edn). LOCATION L.
COMMENTARY Fiction for juveniles [RL].

K163   *Captain Eva. The story of a naughty girl* (by Kathleen Knox).
London, New York: Society for Promoting Christian Knowledge, 1880. SOURCE
NCBEL 4, p. 1819. LOCATION L (destroyed).
COMMENTARY Religious fiction written for juveniles [BLC].

K164   *Poor Archie's girls. A novel* (by Kathleen Knox).
London: Smith, Elder & Co., 1882, 3 vols. SOURCE Allibone Suppl., ii, p. 962.
LOCATION L.
COMMENTARY Fiction for juveniles [RL].

K165   *The organist's baby: A story* (by Kathleen Knox).
London, Glasgow, Edinburgh, Dublin: Blackie & Son, 1895. SOURCE NCBEL 4, p.
1819. LOCATION L.
London, Glasgow: Blackie & Son, [1927] (as *Bab's two cousins. Or, the organist's baby*,
ill. R.H. Brock). SOURCE NCBEL 4, p. 1819. LOCATION L.
COMMENTARY Fiction for juveniles [RL].

KNOX, Thomas W. See **KNOX, Thomas Wallace.**

KNOX, Thomas Wallace (known as **Thomas W. Knox**), b. Pembroke (NH) 1835, d. New
York City 1896. An American journalist, traveller, inventor and newspaper correspondent,
TWK began his career as a journalist as a special reporter and editor on the Denver *Daily
News* during the gold rush. He served in the Civil War, and was war correspondent for the
New York Herald. In 1866 he travelled to Siberia for the *Herald* working with an American
company laying telegraph lines for the Russian government. The following year he was granted
a patent for an invention that transmitted plans of battlefields by telegraph. In 1875 in
Dollymount, Dublin, at an international rifle match, he invented a device that telegraphed by

Morse code the spot where the bullet struck the target. His travels around the world provided the basis for numerous travel books, biographies and many adventure stories for juveniles, including a series on *The boy travellers*. SOURCE Allibone Suppl., ii, p. 962; DAB; DLB, vol.189.

K166 *The boy travellers in Great Britain and Ireland. Adventures of two youths in a journey through Ireland, Scotland, Wales, and England, with visits to the Hebrides and the Isle of Man* (by Thomas W. Knox).
+ New York: Harper & Bros, 1890 (ill., with maps; Boy Travellers Series). LOCATION InND Loeber coll., NUC.
COMMENTARY Fiction for juveniles probably based on TK's own travels, including a visit to Dublin in 1875 [ML; DAB].

KNOX, William, b. Firth (Scotland) 1789, d. Edinburgh (Scotland) 1825. Journalist, poet and miscellaneous writer, WK was an unsuccessful farmer in Dumfries, of whom Sir Walter Scott wrote in his diaries 'he became too soon his own master and plunged into dissipation and ruin' (DNB). He moved with his family to Edinburgh in 1820 where he worked as a journalist, often supported by Scott, but his convivial nature undermined his health and he died young. His several volumes of poetry were highly regarded. He may be identified with the William Knox who contributed prose and articles to the *Belfast Magazine and Literary Journal* (Belfast, 1825). SOURCE Allibone, i, p. 1045; Clyde, p. 85; DNB; ODNB; Personal communication, Peter Garside, Nov. 2001; Personal communication, Richard Jackson, Nov. 2001; Scott (correspondence with Sir Walter Scott).

K167 *A visit to Dublin, containing a description of the principal curiosities and public buildings in the Irish metropolis* [anon.].
+ Edinburgh: John Anderson; London: Simpkin & Marshall, 1824 (ill.). SOURCE McVeagh, p. 90. LOCATION D, L.
COMMENTARY Fiction for juveniles. Quasi-fictional account with dialogues of travels from England to Belfast and Dublin and visits to sites there including the Glen of the Dargle (Co. Wicklow) and the battlefield of the Boyne (Co. Meath) [RL].

KÜHNE, Ferdinand Gustav, b. 1806, d. 1888. German author. SOURCE OCLC.

K168 *Die Rebellen von Irland. Novelle aus den Papieren und Denkwurdigkeiten der "Vereinigten Irlander"* (by Ferdinand Gustav Kühne).
Leipzig: L. Denicke, 1862, 2 vols. (vol. iii of Kühne's *Gesammelte Schriften*). SOURCE Dixson, p. 222; OCLC. LOCATION Rice Univ. (TX).
COMMENTARY Concerns the United Irishmen [RL].

KYLE, Ellen. See NOEL, Mrs John Vavasour.

KYLE, Revd Robert Wood, b. Dublin 1799, d. Melbourne (Derbys.), 1858. RWK was the fourth son of Samuel Kyle, merchant, by his wife Martha (his cousin), youngest daughter of the Revd Henry Wright. Educated by the Revd George Miller, DD (later headmaster of the Royal School, Armagh), he entered TCD in 1814, where he received his BA in 1819, and his MA in 1846. He was appointed curate of Loughgall (Co. Armagh), 1823–1825, curate of Killeavy (Killevy?, Co. Armagh), 1825, and subsequently vicar of Holy Trinity, Guernsey (Channel Islands). He married at St George's Church, Dublin, 1826, Georgina Jane, youngest daughter of the Revd George Horan, MA, curate of Castle Ellis, Enniscorthy (Co. Wexford). RWK wrote the following anonymous book, which is evident from a handwritten note on the title page of the copy at the University of California, Los Angeles. SOURCE B & S, p. 476; Fleming, *Armagh*, p. 553; OCLC; RL.

K169 *The martyr of Prusa or the first and last prayer: A tale of the early Christians* [anon.].
Dublin: William Curry Jun. & Co., 1830. SOURCE NSTC, OCLC. LOCATION CLU.
COMMENTARY Historical fiction [RL].

L

'L.', pseud. of **Lady Anne Nugent-Grenville**. Co-author. See **NUGENT-GRENVILLE, George, 3rd baron**.

'L., C.E.', pseud. See **LAMBERT, Camden Elizabeth**.

'L., E.L.', pseud. See **FALLOON, Mrs Garnet**.

'L., J.E.', pseud. See **LEESON, Jane Eliza**.

'L., M.R.', pseud. See **LAHEE, Miss M.R.**

'A LADY', pseud. See **DAVYS, Mary**.

'A LADY', pseud. See **DESPOURRINS, M.**

'A LADY', pseud. See **GREEN, Sarah**.

'A LADY', pseud. See **KEANE, Joanna Maria**.

'A LADY', pseud. See **O'BRIEN, Mary**.

'A LADY', pseud. See **O'CONNOR, E.**

'A LADY', pseud. See **PHIBBS, Mary**.

'A LADY', pseud. See **RUXTON, Maria**.

'A LADY', pseud. See **SELDEN, Catharine**.

'A LADY', pseud. See **SHACKLETON, Elizabeth**.

'A LADY', pseud. See **T., Ellen**.

'A LADY', pseud. See **TAYLOR, Emily**.

'A LADY', fl. 1760. A romantic novella writer, presumed to be Irish because the following book was published in Dublin only. SOURCE RL.

L1   *Love in several shapes: being eight polite novels, in a new taste: The titles as follow: I. The fair hermit; or, the lady of the cave. II. The treacherous uncle. III. The adventures of Philander and Altezeera. IV. Magdalena; or, the unconssumated [sic] marriage: A novel founded on recent facts: being an intrigue of a surprising nature. V. Love and honour; or, the maid's dilemma. VI. The double perfidy. VII. The abused virgin; or, history of Madame St. Clercy: A strange, yet true story.*

VIII. *The amours of Clelia and Cleomenes; or, platonik love ensnarled into conjugal* (by 'A Lady').
+ Dublin: Printed [for the author?] by James Hoey Jnr, 1760. LOCATION C.
COMMENTARY Set in England and France. No Irish content [JB].

'A LADY', fl. 1770. Epistolary romance novelist.
L2   *Fatal friendship. A novel* (by 'A Lady').
Lodon: T. Lowndes, 1770, 2 vols. SOURCE Raven 2, 1770:3; ESTC t107804. LOCATION
L.
+ Dublin: H. Saunders, D. Chamberlaine, J. Potts, W. Sleater, J. Williams, J. Porter,
R. Moncrieffe & T. Walker, 1771, 2 vols. SOURCE Falkner Greirson cat. 17/158; ESTC
t212490. LOCATION Dt.
New York: Garland, 1975. LOCATION Univ. of Glasgow.
COMMENTARY Epistolary novel set in Ireland. Anne Walpole writes from Castle Carey in the
north of Ireland. The main topic is love among the gentry. The principal couple expire on
their wedding day. The hero, O'Brian, is typical of the eighteenth-century Irish adventurer
who proved such a menace to English heiresses and their guardians [ML; Falkner Greirson
cat. 17/158].

'A LADY', fl. 1775. Epistolary novelist.
L3   *The Irish guardian. A pathetic story* (by 'A Lady').
London: Joseph Johnson, 1775, 4 vols. SOURCE Raven 2, 1775:8; ESTC t167034.
LOCATION C.
+ Dublin: W. Whitestone, 1776, 2 vols. SOURCE Brown 48; Gecker, 532; Raven 2,
1775:8; ESTC t212443. LOCATION Dt, Dm (missing), UP, InND Loeber coll.
Belfast: Printed by James Magee, 1776, 2 vols. SOURCE Anderson 3, p. 11 (known from
Pinkerton MSS).
Leipzig: [publisher?], 1776 (trans. as *Der irlandische Vormund*). SOURCE Raven 2, 1775:8.
COMMENTARY No copies of Belfast edn and the Leipzig edn located. Epistolary novel, set in
the 1770s. The correspondents are Julia Nesbitt in Dublin, Sophia Nesbitt of Brandon Castle
(Co. Antrim), and Sabina Bruce of Edenvale (Co. Antrim). Some letters are addressed from
Paris and the Isle of Man. The letters mainly describe love affairs but also provide descriptions of landscape and country house demesnes in Ulster and Kerry, and a description of the
city of Galway. Mention is made of books read by the correspondents as well as of charitable
works [ML; Brown].

'A LADY', fl. 1776. Pseudonym of a fiction writer who, given the Dublin publisher, Irish
subscribers, and Irish locations in the following novel, is presumably Irish. SOURCE RL.
L4   *The vicissitudes of human life. A narrative founded on facts. To which is added,
an account of a voyage to Jamaica ... In a series of letters from a young gentleman who went to reside there to the author* (by 'A Lady').
+ Dublin: J. Sheppard & G. Nugent, 1776, 2 vols. (subscribers' list with many Irish
names). SOURCE Black, 335; ESTC t212690. LOCATION Dt, NN.
COMMENTARY An advertisement in the *Hibernian Journal* (Dublin, 24 Apr. 1776) requested
that subscriptions for the following volumes be sent to Mrs Chamberlaine, 2 Paradise-Row in
Dublin. *An account of a voyage to Jamaica* has a separate title page and pagination but the register is continuous. *The vicissitudes of human life* is set in England, in which a wealthy gentleman lives at Belmore Park with his wife and daughter, Aminta. A young man, Raymond, supposedly falls in love with Aminta. Her father dies without a will and his brother takes over

the estate, forcing Aminta and her mother to take lodgings in town. Aminta marries Raymond in secret and elopes with him to Bordeaux. She discovers that he only wanted her for her money. Aminta is then taken care of by a Mrs Mason who recounts her life story in Dublin [Black; CM; Dt cat.; ESTC].

'A LADY', fl. 1781. Epistolary society novelist, presumed to be Irish because the following book appears to have been published in Dublin only. SOURCE RL.

L5   *The new Eloisa; or the history of Mr. Sedley, and Miss Wentworth, in a series of letters* (by 'A Lady').
+ Dublin: C. Jackson, 1781, 2 vols. in 1. SOURCE Raven 2, 1781:11; ESTC t226780. LOCATION L, Dt.
COMMENTARY Epistolary novel about love among the upper classes. Apparently a sequel to Jean-Jacques Rousseau's *La nouvelle Héloïse* (1761) [RL; Dt cat.].

'A LADY', fl. 1781. Society novelist, presumed to be Irish because the following book was published in Dublin only. SOURCE RL.

L6   *Fashionable life; or, the history of Miss Louisa Fermor. A novel* (by 'A Lady').
+ Dublin: Printed [for the author?] by C. Jackson, 1781. SOURCE Raven 2, 1781:7; ESTC n031314. LOCATION ICN.
COMMENTARY Prefatory advertisement signed by an unidentified male, T.M., who states that the author is 'a Lady of Distinction', who lives 'retired from the World ...', and 'to a fine Genius, [she] has added every Advantage, that could be derived from a polite Education'. He advises her to take the book to London for publication. It could be that T.M. was the actual author, adopting a female persona to mask his true authorship. Set in England among the upper classes, no reference to Ireland [RL; Raven 2].

'A LADY', fl. 1781. The following novel was advertised in 1781 as by 'A lady of this kingdom [of Ireland]' SOURCE Pollard 2, p. 192.

L7   *The dénouement: or, history of Lady Louisa Wingrove* (by 'A Lady').
+ Dublin: Printed [for the author?] by John Exshaw, 1781. SOURCE Raven 2, 1781:4; Black, 66; Pollard 2, p. 192; ESTC t057432. LOCATION L, PU.
London: Robinson, 1784. SOURCE Summers, p. 58; Raven 2, 1781:4. SOURCE ESTC n28179. LOCATION Indiana Univ., Bloomington (IN).
COMMENTARY Epistolary novel. No Irish content [ML; Black].

'A LADY', fl. 1787. A novelist whose nationality is unknown. For that reason, her non-Irish novels remain listed here. With one exception, her works were published by the Minerva Press in London. SOURCE RL.

L8   *Edward and Sophia. A novel* (by 'A Lady').
[London]: William Lane, 1787. SOURCE Raven 2, 1787:6; Forster 2, 1215; ESTC t120637. LOCATION L, MH.
Londres [Paris]: de Senne, 1788, 2 vols. (trans. as *Edouard et Sophie*). SOURCE Raven 2, 1787:6; Bn-Opale plus. LOCATION BNF.
COMMENTARY Mentioned on the title page of *The predestined wife; or force of prejudice* (London, 1789). The *Critical Review* stated that 'this novel is undoubtedly superior to the general herd ...' [Raven 2].

L9   *Eliza Cleland. A novel* [anon.].
London: William Lane, 1788, 3 vols. SOURCE Raven 2, 1788:14; Forster 2, 1248; ESTC n6974. LOCATION PU.

COMMENTARY Mentioned on the title page of *The predestined wife; or force of prejudice* (London, 1789). Epistolary novel. The *Critical Review* commented that this novel 'has received a temporary life from the warmth of a circulating library ...' [Raven 2].

L10   *Powis Castle; or, anecdotes of an antient family* [anon.]

London: W. Lane, 1788, 2 vols. SOURCE Raven 2, 1788:30; Block, p. 189; Blakey, p. 144; McBurney & Taylor, 707; Forster 2, 3562; ESTC n020868. LOCATION IU.

COMMENTARY Mentioned on the title page of *The predestined wife; or force of prejudice* (London, 1789) [RL].

L11   *The predestined wife; or force of prejudice; A novel. In a series of letters* (by the author of *Edward and Sophia*, *Powis Castle*, *Eliza Cleland*).

London: J. Kerby, 1789, 2 vols. SOURCE Raven 2, 1789:22; Forster 2, 3592; ESTC n020400. LOCATION PU.

L12   *Benedicta. A novel* [anon.].

+ London: William Lane, 1741 [*sic*, 1791], 2 vols. SOURCE Raven 2, 1791:3; Blakey, p. 152; Block, p. 19; Burmester cat. 36/181; ESTC t064710. LOCATION L, CaACU, CSmH.

COMMENTARY Mentioned on the title pages of *Mariamne; or, Irish anecdotes* (London, 1793). Concerns the experiences and development of the heroine, Benedicta, who comes with her parents to England from their home in Antigua in the Caribbean in order to be educated. It examines the distinction between true and false delicacy, and gives guidance on the scruples and morals of young women: the general tenor of this advice can be well surmised from the maxim with which the novel ends: 'That human happiness is the result of reason, rather than the passions' [Johnson cat. 42/6].

L13   *Ashton priory. A novel* [anon.].

London: Law, 1792, 3 vols. SOURCE Raven 2, 1792:2; Blakey, p. 294; Forster 2, 155; adv. by J. Connor, Cork, [*c.*1795].

Philadelphia: W.W. Woodward, 1795. SOURCE McBurney & Taylor, 127. LOCATION IU.

COMMENTARY Mentioned on the title page of *Mariamne; or, Irish anecdotes* (London, 1793). No copy of the first London edn located (further edn, London, 1803). Originally published in the *True Briton* (London), it contains a series of seemingly suspenseful and supernatural events, which belatedly are clarified by natural explanation. The *Critical Review* (London) mentions that the heroine is a Miss Overbery, who at the age of sixteen reasons and thinks like a woman of thirty [Frank, p. 9; McBurney & Taylor, p. 22; Raven 2].

L14   *Mariamne; or, Irish anecdotes. A novel* (by the author of *Ashton Priory*, *Benedicta*, *Powis Castle* &c.).

London: William Lane, 1793, 2 vols. SOURCE Block, p. 152; Blakey, p. 163; Raven 2, 1793:8; Forster 2, 2714. LOCATION Corvey CME 3–628–45035–7, Ireland related fiction, DCL (1801 edn).

+ Dublin: Printed by P. Wogan, P. Byrne & B. Smith, 1794, 2 vols. SOURCE Raven 2, 1793:8; ESTC t212268. LOCATION D.

Dublin: Printed by B. Smith, 1794, 2 vols. SOURCE Raven 2, 1793:8; ESTC n034819. LOCATION D, MH.

COMMENTARY Set in Ireland. The main character is found as a baby in a shipwreck. The *Critical Review* (London, Dec. 1793) noted that the novel has 'a variety of sensible remarks on the uncultivated state, both of the lands and peasantry of our sister kingdom. Amidst these, however, the machinery or romance possesses its natural movements ...' [ML; RL; Personal communication, Antonia Fraser, Sept. 1997].

'A LADY', fl. 1789. Epistolary romance novelist. SOURCE RL.

L15   *Family sketches. A novel* (by 'A Lady').

+ Dublin: P. Byrne, P. Wogan, J. Jones & J. Halpen, 1789, 2 vols. in 1. SOURCE Raven 2, 1789:7; ESTC t203189. LOCATION D.

London: Lane, [1789 or 1790?]. SOURCE Raven 2, 1789:7.

COMMENTARY No copy of the London edn located. Epistolary novel concerned with various love affairs. Setting is Wales, England, Dublin and Cork; some Irish characters [ML; RL; Raven 2].

'A LADY', fl. 1791. This historical novelist dedicated the following volume from Dublin, Aug. 1791. It is almost certain that she was a member of the Irish gentry or the official class. SOURCE RL.

L16   *Edwy, son of Ethelred the Second: An historical tale* (by 'A Lady'; dedicated to the countess of Westmorland [wife of the lord lieutenant of Ireland]).

+ Dublin: Printed for the authoress by John Rice, 1791, 2 vols. SOURCE Falkner Greirson cat. 'Jane'/103; Pollard 2, p. 492; Raven 2, 1791:9; ESTC n001241. LOCATION Dt, MH.

COMMENTARY In the preface the author entreats 'her readers to make allowances for the inaccuracies of a female pen'. The story is set in England during Saxon times and mentions the battle of Hastings [1066 AD]. A hermit opens the tale with an account of his own life. The story shifts to Ethelred (king of England, who died in 1016), who falls in love and marries several women, begetting children along the way. The kingdom is threatened when a fleet from Denmark arrives. Ethelred receives them peacefully and the Danes integrate into daily life. However, at a certain point a large number of them are slain. They are avenged by other Danes, whose leader is declared king of England. Ethelred flees to Normandy and his outcast son Edwy becomes a pilgrim [ML; Falkner Greirson; CM].

'A LADY', fl. 1797. Novelist, presumed to be Irish given that the following novel was published in Dublin only and that many of the subscribers are Irish. The largest group of subscribers consists of members of the Tandy family (to which the United Irishman James Napper Tandy belonged). SOURCE RL.

L17   *Anastatia: or, the memoirs of the Chevalier Laroux. Interspersed with a variety of anecdotes from real life* (by 'A Lady').

+ Dublin: Printed [for the author?] by John Chambers, 1797, 2 vols. (subscribers' list, mostly Irish). SOURCE Raven 2, 1797:3, McBurney & Taylor, 24; Falkner Greirson cat. 9/6; ESTC n030938. LOCATION Dt, IU.

COMMENTARY Epistolary novel, mostly set in England and America. Some letters are sent from Ireland (Cork). One letter contains questions about a debate in the Irish house of commons; other letters discuss the political situation in France [ML; Falkner Greirson].

'A LADY', fl. 1799. Novelist of contemporary political events.

L18   *The rebel. A tale of the times* (by 'A Lady').

[Southampton]: B. Law, 1799. SOURCE Raven 2, 1799:15; ESTC n014245. LOCATION CLU.

Dublin: P. Wogan, W. Porter, J. Rice, J. Halpen, H. Colbert, B. Dornin, G. Folingsby & J. Stockdale, 1801. SOURCE Falkner Greirson cat. 9/285; Raven 2, 1799:15. LOCATION Dt, D.

COMMENTARY Probably one of the first novels published about the 1798 rebellion. Set in Co. Wicklow [Falkner Greirson cat. 9/285; RL].

'A LADY', fl. 1804. Epistolary novelist, presumed to be Irish because her two novels concern Ireland. She dedicated the first to Lady Cotter (probably the second wife of Sir James Lawrence Cotter, Bt, of Rockforest, Co. Cork), and because she published her second novel initially in Cork, she probably was a resident of Cork or its vicinity. SOURCE RL.

L19 *Amasina, or the American foundling* [anon.] (dedicated to Lady Cotter).
+ London: Lane, Newman & Co., 1804, 2 vols. SOURCE British Fiction; Garside, 1804:3. LOCATION Corvey CME 3–628–47052–8, O.
COMMENTARY Epistolary novel starting out in America after the war of Independence with correspondence between C. Clindillon from Philadelphia to relatives named Belmont in Dublin [ML].

L20 *The soldier of Pennaflor; or, a season in Ireland. A tale of the eighteenth century* (by 'A lady').
+ Cork: Printed [for the author?] by John Connor, sold by A.K. Newman in London, 1810, 5 vols. SOURCE Blakey, p. 305; NSTC. LOCATION L.
London: A.K. Newman & Co., 1811, 5 vols. SOURCE British Fiction; Garside, 1810. LOCATION Corvey CME 3–628–48719–6, Ireland related fiction.
COMMENTARY The story of a soldier named Sedley who returns to England, marries, and buys a farm called Pennaflor Cottage in north Wales. His wife dies but leaves him with a boy, Alfred. Father and son move to London to live with relatives, one of whom is a young girl, Zabellina. The story recounts the love between Alfred and Zabellina and the obstacles in their way to happiness. Alfred becomes an officer and fights in a campaign in Co. Wexford during the 1798 rebellion. His further adventures in Dublin, Killarney, Glanmire (Co. Cork) and Callan (Co. Kilkenny) are described [ML].

'A LADY', fl. 1844. Religious fiction writer, presumed to be Irish because the following book was published in Dublin only. SOURCE RL.

L21 *Edward Beaumount; or, the efficacy of prayer. A narrative founded on facts* (by 'A Lady').
Dublin: Samuel B. Oldham, 1844. SOURCE Alston, p. 227; L (destroyed); Adv. in S. O'Moore's, *The voice of the new year* (Dublin, 1850).
COMMENTARY Religious fiction. No copy located [RL; BLC].

'A LADY', fl. 1860s. Religious fiction writer.

L22 *What I saw at Belfast* (by 'A Lady').
+ London: John F. Shaw, [1860]. LOCATION L.
COMMENTARY Religious fiction. Concerns Protestant religious revivalism in the north of Ireland and includes a description of Belfast [BLC; CM].

'LADY M.', pseud. See MAHON, Lady Jane.

'A LADY OF BOSTON', pseud. See WESTON, Mrs M.A.

'A LADY OF NEW YORK', pseud. See 'B., F.F.'

LAFFAN, Mrs De Courcy Laffan. See ADAMS, Bertha Jane.

LAFFAN, May. See HARTLEY, Mrs May.

'LAGENIENSIS', pseud. See O'HANLON, Canon John.

LAHEE, Miss M.R., pseud. 'M.R.L.', fl. 1860. English author, possibly of Irish descent, who wrote several Lancashire tales. SOURCE Allibone Suppl., ii, p. 966; NSTC.

L23   *Tim Bobbin's adventures with the Irishman; or, rising the dead by the art of freemasonry. A Lancashire tale* (by 'M.R.L.').
+ Manchester: John Heywood; London: Simpkin, Marshall, 1860. SOURCE Wolff, 3934.
LOCATION L, NUC, InND Loeber coll. (n.d. edn).
COMMENTARY The Manchester n.d. edn consists of 32pp, but the Manchester 1860 edn consists of 55pp. According to the preface, which is signed from Rochdale (near Manchester) where the story is set in 1739, it contrasts opposing characteristics of the Lancastrians and the Irish. It contains much northern and Irish dialect, some history of Ireland and the strife between the Irish and the English [CM].

LAMB, Lady Caroline (Louisa May Caroline, née Ponsonby), b. London 1785, d. London 1828. Novelist and poet, LMCL was the only daughter of Frederick Ponsonby, Viscount Duncannon, later 3rd earl of Bessborough (of Bessborough, Co. Kilkenny), and Lady Henrietta Frances Spencer, daughter of the 1st Earl Spencer. Highly-strung and impetuous, LMCL was brought up without much discipline in the household of her aunt, the duchess of Devonshire. She married in 1805 William Lamb, later 2nd Viscount Melbourne. She is best known for her romantic obsession and affair with Lord Byron in 1812, which led to his portrayal in her novel *Glenarvon* (London, 1816; subsequently this served as the model for a play). She lived briefly in Ireland in 1812, staying at Belline House (Co. Kilkenny) near the main family seat of Bessborough House. Her unhappy marriage with Melbourne and increasing obsession with Byron resulted in a de facto separation. She moved briefly to France but spent her last years in the Melbourne houses in Derbyshire, more or less confined as insane. She died after a long illness, her husband returning from his post as chief secretary in Ireland to be with her. Rosina Doyle Wheeler (later Lady Bulwer Lytton§) and Lady Morgan§ were among her friends; she bequeathed Lord Byron's picture to Lady Morgan. Aside from *Glenarvon* she wrote two other novels. A few years before her death, her life was turned into fiction when Thomas Henry Lister published his novel *Granby* (London, 1826, 3 vols.), depicting her (as Lady Harriet Duncan) and her circle. Some of her letters and a poem are in the Henry E. Huntington Library, San Marino (CA); for other locations of manuscript materials, see Douglass. Only fiction relating to Ireland is listed below. SOURCE Allibone, i, p. 1048; Blain, p. 624; Burke, Sir B. & A.P. Burke, *A genealogical and heraldic dictionary of the peerage and baronetage* (London, 1906, 68th edn), p. 160; H. Blythe, *Caro, the fatal passion. The life of Lady Caroline Lamb* (New York, 1973), passim; P. Douglass, *Lady Caroline Lamb* (New York, 2004), passim; NCBEL 4, p. 944; ODNB; Schulz, p. 278; Todd, pp 391–2.

L24   *Glenarvon. A tale* [anon.].
+ London: Henry Colburn, 1816, 3 vols. SOURCE British Fiction; Garside, 1816:40; Wolff, 3938. LOCATION L, NUC.
London: Henry Colburn, 1816, 3 vols., 2nd edn (with a new preface). SOURCE British Fiction; Garside, 1816:40. LOCATION Corvey (1816, 3rd edn) CME 3–628–47814–6, Ireland related fiction (1816, 3rd edn), NUC.
+ London: C.H. Clarke, [1865] (as *The fatal passion*; Capt. Mayne Reade Library [*sic*]). SOURCE Blain, p. 624. LOCATION L.
Paris: Gabriel Dufour: 1819, 3 vols. SOURCE Garside, 1816:40; Burmester, list 18/129; Bn-Opale plus. LOCATION BNF.
Philadelphia: Moses-Thomas, 1816, 2 vols. LOCATION NUC.
London: Everyman; Vermont: C.E. Tuttle, 1995. SOURCE OCLC. LOCATION L, Mount Holyoke College.

COMMENTARY Gothic novel set largely at Castle Delaval in Ireland during the late 1790s. The heroine, Calantha Delaval, marries Henry Mowbray, earl of Avondale, an Anglo-Irish captain in the army. She is introduced to Lord Glenarvon, a mysterious Anglo-Irish nobleman who is initially a leader of the 1798 rebellion, and they conduct a passionate affair that ruins Calantha and her family. It includes some descriptions of the state of Ireland previous to the 1798 uprising and of the rebellion itself, although this is limited largely to the portrayal of the activities of Ellinor St Clare, a former lover of Glenarvon's, who takes over as leader of the rebellion when Glenarvon betrays their cause and fights on the side of the government. The book is arguably autobiographical, relating to the author's affair with Lord Byron. Key to the characters: Glenarvon = Lord Byron; Calantha, Lady Avondale = Lady Caroline Lamb; Princess of Madagascar = Lady Holland; Lord Avondale = William Lamb, Lord Melbourne; Sophia = Lady Granville. A contemporary guessed that the character of Mrs Seymour was partly based on Lady Blessington§. Eaton Stannard Barrett§ made references to this novel in his *Six weeks at Long's* (London, 1817), while Maria Edgeworth§ liked best the part describing the princess of Madagascar [JB; Colvin, pp 105–6; Frank, 220; Marlborough cat. 169/145 (listing the MS key); Rose cat. 15/209; Todd, p. 392; Tracy, 83; Ximenes cat. 102/110; Ziegler, p. 75; M. Elwin, *Lord Byron's family* (London, 1975), p. 33].

LAMB, Mary Montgomerie (also Montgomery). See **SINGLETON, Mary Montgomerie**.

LAMBART, Revd W. Huberto, pseud. 'Huberto'. According to a manuscript annotation in the InND copy of the following novel, the author can be identified with WHL, who served as an incumbent of Leamington Spa (War.) and in 1888 lived in Liverpool (he is not known to have served in Ireland). Earlier in life he was a member of the Masonic 'Shakespeare Lodge' at Warwick, and probably was an Irishman by birth. SOURCE RL; TK; Ximenes cat.105/16.
L25   *The ghost of Dunboy Castle* (by 'Huberto'; dedicated to the author's parents).
      + London: Simpkin, Marshall & Co., 1889, 2 vols. SOURCE Wolff, 7644. LOCATION L, NUC, InND Loeber coll.
COMMENTARY A dream fantasy set initially in the nineteenth century. Three young men visit Dunboy Castle on Bantry Bay, which is reputed to be haunted by ghosts. They take turns to stay awake at night, and the first one to do so, Mortimer O'Sullivan, picks up a book with the story of Mary O'Sullivan, a seventeenth-century relative of his. The narrative then becomes somewhat confusing since it is not clear whether the seventeenth-century story is being narrated, or whether the seventeenth-century characters have been transposed into the nineteenth century, and some ghosts appear. The seventeenth-century story is set at the end of the siege of Limerick in 1651 when the Confederates hand over the city to Cromwell's forces, and follows the fortunes and love lives of three gallant Irishmen. Interwoven is a story of a doctor who ravishes young girls; a long discussion of the relative merits of arsenic, prussic acid and morphine for the humane killing of household pets, while freemasonry is mentioned as the means of saving the life of one of the Confederate officers when he gives the secret signal of distress, which is understood by an officer in Cromwell's army. The three principal seventeenth-century characters (and several others) seem to live on the outskirts of Kanturk (Co. Cork) in villas that have both hot and cold water in their bathrooms and were built on speculation, which points more to a nineteenth- than a seventeenth-century setting. At the end of the story, Mortimer is woken by his friends. He tells them that he has been reading a book and dreaming about it and that he has seen ghosts [ML].

LAMBERT, the Hon. Camden Elizabeth (also known as the Hon. Mrs Lambert), pseud. 'C.E.L.', fl. 1836. Novelist and short story writer, CEL dedicated the following book from

Greg Clare, Co. Galway, 14 Jan. 1836 (this country house is since destroyed). Peter Lambert of Greg Clare (d. 1844), married after 1828 a second wife, who is not named in Burke, with whom he had two daughters. It is possible that CEL was this second wife. An inscription by Lady Kirkcudbright in the volume in a private collection indirectly suggests that CEL was related to that family (judging from the similarity in the Christian name of Camden Cray MacLellan, 10th Lord Kirkcudbright). CEL's short story 'A tale of the Consulate' appeared in *Friendship's Offering* (London, n.d., pp 261–82). SOURCE Sir B. Burke, *Burke's ... landed gentry of Ireland* (London, 1958), 4th edn, p. 421; RL.

L26   *The bar-sinister, or memoirs of an illegitimate. Founded on facts* (by 'C.E.L.'; dedicated to Earl Mulgrave, lord lieutenant of Ireland).
+ London: Smith, Elder & Co., 1836, 2 vols. SOURCE Garside 1836:43. LOCATION L, E, MH, InND Loeber coll.
COMMENTARY Dedication is signed 'C.E.L.', 'Greg Clare, Co. Galway, 14th January 1836'. Postscript states that the novel 'is written by a Lady, her first essay in the arena of literature'. A bar-sinister is a heraldic term denoting bastardy. This story of tangled family relationships due to a succession of extramarital affairs is set mainly in England and on the Continent. The main character finds out in adolescence that he is an illegitimate son. He renounces his father's name and calls himself Mr Harcourt. His mother had left his father several years previously because the father had a new mistress. The father promised to make a will that would leave his personal property to his son, while the rest of his estate would go to a relative, Augustus Percival. Percival and Harcourt are enemies throughout life. At the death of Harcourt's father, Percival takes possession of everything, suppresses the will, and renders Harcourt destitute. Several illegitimate attachments of other family members are recounted in the book, and Harcourt himself almost elopes with a happily married woman but at the last moment he is told by someone who turns out to be his mother, that this woman is his step-sister. He lives for a while with his mother until she dies, after which the forgery of the will is discovered. Harcourt marries the girl he loves. After Percival dies, it transpires that she is the heiress next in line for Harcourt's father's estate [ML; Garside 2, 1836:43].

LAMBERT, Nancy Power. See O'DONOGHUE, Mrs Nancy Power.

'LAMBERT, Nannie', questionable pseud. See O'DONOGHUE, Mrs Nancy Power.

LAMOTHE, Alexandre Bessot De. See DE LAMOTHE, Alexandre Bessot.

'A LANDLORD', fl. 1886. Loyalist historical novelist.
L27   *The great Irish rebellion of 1886* (retold by 'A landlord'; dedicated to 'all who hate treason and who love God, their queen, and their country!').
+ London: Harrison & Sons, 1886. LOCATION L, C.
COMMENTARY 48pp and priced at 6*d*. Loyalist story; the orange cover of this booklet commemorates the battles of Aughrim and the Boyne and the siege of Derry. Set in Ireland in 1886 during the land troubles. A fourth edn appeared in 1886 as well [RL].

LANG, Andrew, b. 1844, d. 1912. Scottish classicist, anthropologist and historian. Co-author. See MASON, Alfred Edward Woodley. SOURCE EF, pp 231–2; NCBEL 4, p. 2363–69; ODNB.

LANGBRIDGE, Revd Frederick, b. Birmingham 1849, d. 1922. An English poet and novelist, who became a Church of Ireland clergyman and scholar, FL was the sixth son of Henry Charles Langbridge of Birmingham, an armiger, a family apparently of Irish origin. FL graduated from Merton College, Oxford. He was ordained 1876 and obtained his MA in 1883. After graduation he became incumbent at Glen Alla (Co. Donegal), 1879–81; canon, St Munchin's (Limerick), 1881–82; rector, Newcastle West (Co. Limerick), 1882–83; and St John's (Limerick), from 1883. He wrote tract fiction for the Religious Tract Society. A distinguished scholar, he was awarded a DLitt. by TCD in 1907. Joint author, with Freeman Wills, of the comedy *The Only Way* (London, 1899). He wrote six books of fiction, and contributed to the *Manchester Guardian*, the *Saturday Westminster Gazette* (London), and the *Sunday at Home* (London) and other periodicals. He married in 1878 at Kendal Parish Church, Jane Wilson, by whom he had three children. His daughter Rosamund (b. 1880) became a journalist and novelist. SOURCE Allibone Suppl., ii, p. 972; Donegal, pp 140–1 [under Rosamund Langbridge]; EF, p. 232; J. Foster (ed.), *Alumni Oxonienses 1715–1886* (Oxford, 1888), iii, p. 815; IBL, 13 (1922), p. 147; Leslie, *Raphoe*, p. 69; NCBEL 4, p. 1820; LVP, p. 267; MVP, p. 266; O'Donoghue, p. 499; O'Toole, p. 115; Sutherland, p. 362.

L28   *Miss Honoria. A tale of a remote corner of Ireland* (by Frederick Langbridge).
    + London: Frederick Warne, 1894 (The Tavistock Library). SOURCE Brown, 879.
    LOCATION L ([1894] edn), NUC ([1893, *sic*] edn), InND Loeber coll.
COMMENTARY A romance initially set on the west coast of Ireland. A pious woman, Miss Honoria, is engaged to Sebert, who writes her beautiful letters from London. However, when Honoria goes to London she finds that Sebert has been making love to her niece Daisy. Sebert and Daisy marry, but he is unfaithful to her, leading to Daisy's disappearance and the death of the girl with whom he is unfaithful. After a number of tragedies both Sebert and Daisy become missionaries in London's East End [ML; Brown].

L29   *The dreams of Dania* (by Frederick Langbridge).
    + London: James Bowden, 1897 (ill. J.B. Yeats). SOURCE Sutherland, p. 362. LOCATION L, NUC, InND Loeber coll.
COMMENTARY Chronicles the romantic upsets of a young woman [Sutherland].

L30   *Love has no pity; a novel* (by Frederick Langbridge).
    London: Digby, Long & Co., 1900. SOURCE Brown, p. 160 (1901 edn); IBL, 13 (1922), p. 147. LOCATION L, NUC.

L31   *The calling of the weir* (by Frederick Langbridge).
    London: Digby, Long & Co., 1902. SOURCE Brown, 880. LOCATION L.
COMMENTARY Set near the Shannon weir and the falls of Donass (Co. Limerick), chronicles the love story of two Protestant middle-class girls who have become engaged to two men mainly through force of circumstances. Each girl marries the other's fiancée and both find happiness [Brown].

L32   *Mack the miser* (by Frederick Langbridge).
    London: Elliott Stock, 1907. SOURCE Brown, 881; COPAC. LOCATION E.
COMMENTARY A tale of middle-class Protestant life in Limerick, turning on the vindication by a young girl of the supposed miser's character. Fairly religious in content [Brown].

LARMINIE, William. See **LARMINIE, William Rea.**

LARMINIE, William Rea (also known as **William Larminie**), b. Castlebar (Co. Mayo) 1849 or 1850, d. Bray (Co. Wicklow) 1900. A folklorist, poet, writer of stories and verse and part of the Irish Literary Revival, WRL was the son of William Larminie of Castlebar, a land agent and a descendent of Huguenots who settled in Ireland in 1721, and Bridget Jackson. After the death of his father, his maternal grandfather moved him and his mother to Co. Wicklow, where he was tutored and later attended school. He was admitted to TCD in 1854, where he obtained his BA in 1860 and an MA in classics in 1871. Initially WRL spent some years in the India Office in London. At that time he became acquainted with William Butler Yeats§ and Samuel Ferguson§. By 1884 he had begun to collect folklore (having at least some knowledge of Irish). In 1887 he gave up his job, returned to Ireland, and lived at Bray (Co. Wicklow) where he started a second career as a writer. A shy, retiring man, he contributed to the *Contemporary Review* (London) and was an active member of the National Literary Society. He travelled around the west of Ireland (see below) collecting stories, which he tried to record as accurately as possible. Field Day points out that all of his informants were male. Towards the end of his life he published some carefully collected and charmingly-told folk tales as well as two volumes of verse and a well-received translation of Johannes Scotus Eriugena's *Divisione Naturae*. WRL was highly respected by other members of the Irish Literary Revival such as Yeats§ and George Russell, who regretted that Larminie's 'many and great gifts as an imaginative poet, should have been so coldly received' (ODNB). For his portrait and papers, see ODNB. SOURCE B & S, Appendix B, p. 69; Boase, vi, p. 11; Field Day, ii, pp 722, 723, 779, 845, iv, p. 1434; Hogan, pp 361–2; Hogan 2, pp 682–3; Irish pseudonyms; LVP, p. 269; P.L. Marcus, *Yeats and the beginning of the Irish renaissance* (Ithaca, 1970), pp 207–8; NCBEL 4, p. 760; OCIL, p. 299; O'Donoghue, p. 243; RIA/DIB; RL; Ryan, p. 142.

L33 *West Irish folk-tales and romances* (collected and trans. by William Larminie).
London: Elliot Stock, 1893 (Camden Library). SOURCE Hogan, p. 362; Rowan cat. 37, part A/1076. LOCATION BFl, NUC.
Shannon: Irish University Press, 1972. SOURCE COPAC. LOCATION Dt, L.
+ Towata (NJ): Rowman & Littlefield, 1976. LOCATION O, InND Loeber coll.
COMMENTARY The author collected these tales verbatim from the peasantry of Renvyle (Co. Galway), Achill Island (Co. Mayo), and Glencolumbkille and Malinmore (Co. Donegal). Included are a phonetic text, specimens of the tales in phonetic Irish, and notes. Contents: 'The gloss gavlen', 'Morraha', 'The ghost and his wives', 'The story of Bioultach', 'King Mananaun', 'The champion of the red belt', 'Jack', 'The servant of poverty', 'Simon and Margaret', 'The son of the king of Prussia', 'Beauty of the world', 'Grig', 'The little girl who got the better of the gentleman', 'Gilla of the enchantments', 'The woman who went to hell', 'The king who had twelve sons', 'The red pony', 'The nine-legged steed' [RL].

'A LATE RESIDENT', pseud. See BARRETT, Eaton Stannard.

LA TOUCHE, Mrs —. See LA TOUCHE, Mrs Maria.

LA TOUCHE, Mrs Maria (Polly, née Price; known as Mrs La Touche), b. Desart Court (Co. Kilkenny) 1824, d. Dublin 1906. Poet, novelist and miscellaneous writer, MLT was the daughter of Lt. Rose Lambart Price (of Irish descent, whose family was seated at Trengwainston, Cornwall) and Catherine, countess of Desart of Desart Court (Co. Kilkenny). Her mother was the heiress of Maurice O'Connor of Mount Pleasant (Co. Offaly), and was thus related to the authors William O'Connor Morris and Elizabeth O'Connor Morris§. Her father died two years after his marriage, leaving a will that declared his daughter should spend six months of the year in England. Summers were usually spent at Desart Court. She started writing poetry at age 12 and accompanied her mother on a tour through France to Geneva in 1839. She married in 1843, John La Touche of Harristown (Co. Kildare) where she spent most of her subsequent life, travelling occasionally to London (where her husband had a house in Norfolk Street) and to the Continent. She developed strong intellectual interests and produced two novels which, according to Young, were written 'more as an amusement than for graver reason. Perhaps because of this they were not successful, and are now [1908] quite forgotten' (Young, p. 16). In addition to poems (see *Irish Monthly*, 1877–88) and letters, she wrote essays on a variety of topics. She was a Protestant and a staunch Unionist and identified her-self with Ireland. A selection of her *Letters of a noble woman* (London, 1908), was highly acclaimed by William O'Connor Morris and by John Ruskin. After the death of her husband in 1904 she left Harristown to the benefit of her son and settled in Dublin, where she died. Her travel diary in Ireland and France for 1864 is in the Representative Church Body Library, Dublin (MS 538). SOURCE Allibone Suppl., ii, p. 976; Burke's, p. 694; M. Bence-Jones, *Twilight of the ascendancy* (London, 1987), pp 16, passim; Colman, p. 138; RIA/DIB; M.F. Young (ed.), *Letters of a noble woman* (London, 1908), passim.

L34   *The Clintons; or, deeps and shallows of life* [anon.].
        + London: Richard Bentley, 1853, 3 vols. SOURCE Wolff, 3951. LOCATION L, NUC.
COMMENTARY Mostly set in England, but refers in negative terms to Mr Desmond's ugly and uncomfortable country house in Ireland, Slievemore, situated near the sea, with neighbours described as 'savages'. Desmond inherited the neglected estate, but his improvements are upset when his wife dies, leaving him with twin daughters [RL].

L35   *Lady Willoughby; or, the double marriage* (by Mrs La Touche).
        + London: Hurst & Blackett, 1855, 3 vols. SOURCE Allibone Suppl., ii, p. 976; Alston, p. 240; OCLC. LOCATION L.
COMMENTARY Partly set in the fictive town of Killdash in one of the Wicklow valleys [RL].

LATREICHE, Symon. See DROHOJOWSKA, Mme la Comtesse.

'LAUDERDALE, E.M.', pseud. See MOORE, Mrs Emma.

LAWLESS, the Hon. Emily, b. Lyons Castle (Co. Kildare) 1845, d. Gomshall (Surrey) 1913. A novelist, poet and short story writer, EL was the eldest daughter of Edward Lawless, 3rd Baron Cloncurry, a wealthy Anglo-Irish nobleman whose family had risen to prominence in the late-eighteenth century, and Elizabeth Kirwan. Educated at home, she spent part of her youth with her mother's relatives at Castle Hacket (Co. Galway). Her father and her two sis-ters committed suicide. She never married. Although by background and inclination a Unionist, she criticized England's treatment of Ireland and after the agitation of the Land War she spent more and more time in England, but never lost her interest in Ireland and Irish history. She counted among her friends Sir Horace Plunkett and British prime minister William Gladstone, who said of her novel *Hurrish* that it was impossible to understand Ireland without it. EL wrote short stories (e.g., in the *English Illustrated Magazine*, London, 1893; *Blackwood's Magazine* (Edinburgh); *Cornhill Magazine* (London); *Homestead* (Dublin); and other periodicals; a history of Ireland (London, 1887); *A garden diary* (London, 1901); poetry (e.g., *With the Wild Geese*. London, 1902), and a biography of Maria Edgeworth§ (London, 1904). She is best remembered for her historical fiction about Ireland's conflicts. She received a DLitt from TCD in 1905. Her last years were spent in Surrey, in poor mental and physical health. At this time she was befriended by Shan Bullock§, who completed her final novel *The race of Castlebar*. A private printing of poems, *The inalienable heritage*, appeared posthumously (London, 1914). Forty-four manuscript volumes of her writings are at Marsh's Library in Dublin (Z2/1/15), while selec-tions of her letters are in TCD (MSS 1,827–36, 2,472–82), and other papers are listed in the DLB and the ODNB. SOURCE Allibone Suppl., ii, p. 978; Blain, p. 636; Boylan, p. 195; Colman, pp 138–40; DLB, ccxl; Field Day, ii, p. 1216, v, pp 921 and passim (lists many of her essays); Hogan, pp 365–6; Hogan 2, pp 687–8; LVP, p. 271; NCBEL 4, p. 761; OCIL, p., 302; O'Donoghue, p. 244; M. O'Neill, 'Emily Lawless' in *Dublin Historical Record*, 48(2) (1995), pp 125–41; E. Reilly, p. 246; RIA/DIB; RL; Sutherland, p. 364.

L36 *A Chelsea householder* [anon.].
London: Sampson Low, Marston, Searle & Rivington, 1882, 3 vols. SOURCE Wolff, 3958. LOCATION L.
New York: H. Holt & Co., 1883 (Leisure Moment Series). SOURCE NYPL. LOCATION NN, NUC.

L37 *A millionaire's cousin* (by the Hon. Emily Lawless).
+ London: Macmillan & Co., 1885. SOURCE Wolff, 3963; Macmillan, p. 476. LOCATION L, NUC.
New York: H. Holt & Co., 1885 (Leisure Moment Series). SOURCE NYPL. LOCATION NN, NUC.

L38 *Hurrish. A study* (by Emily Lawless; dedicated to Mrs Oliphant).
Edinburgh, London: William Blackwood & Sons, 1886, 2 vols. SOURCE Quaritch cat. 1129/251; Wolff, 3960. LOCATION Dt (1887 edn), D (1887 edn), L, NUC.
Edinburgh, London: William Blackwood & Sons, 1886 (new edn). SOURCE Brown, 889 (Methuen, 1886 edn). LOCATION D (1887 edn), Dt (1887 edn), DPL (Methuen, 1895, 6th edn), InND Loeber coll. (Nelson, n.d. edn).
Arnhem: Gouda Quint, 1890 (trans. into Dutch by Anna Bok as *Hurrish: Een Iersche roman*; preface by N.G. Pierson). SOURCE Adamnet. LOCATION UVA.
+ Leipzig: Bernard Tauchnitz, 1888. SOURCE T & B, 2543. LOCATION NUC, InND Loeber coll.
New York: Harper & Bros, 1886 (Harper's Handy Series, No. 61). SOURCE NYPL. LOCATION NN.
New York: Garland, 1979, 2 vols. (as *Hurrish*; introd. by R.L. Wolff). SOURCE OCLC. LOCATION Dt, L, DCL.
+ Belfast: Appletree Press, 1992 (introd. by Val Mulkerns). LOCATION D.
COMMENTARY A melodrama set in the 1870s in the 'wildest west' of Co. Clare that describes the upheavals of the Land League, with a representation of divergent characteristics. The hero is Horatio O'Brien, known as Hurrish. He is a good man who is adverse to violence. However, he kills Mat, who had taken a farm from which the tenants had been evicted. Hurrish is acquitted at his trial for manslaughter but is subsequently killed by Mat's half-brother [ML; Field Day, ii, pp 1021–2, 1027–33; Wolff introd., p. 37].

L39 *Major Lawrence, F.L.S. A novel* (by the Hon. Emily Lawless; dedicated to the author's mother [Elizabeth Lawless]).
+ London: John Murray, 1887, 3 vols. SOURCE OCLC. LOCATION Dt, L, InND Loeber coll.
London: John Murray; New York: Holt, 1887, 3 vols. SOURCE Wolff, 3961. LOCATION Dt, L, NUC (1888, 2nd edn).
+ London: John Murray, 1888 (new edn). LOCATION D.
New York: H. Holt & Co., 1887 (Leisure Hour Series, No. 209). SOURCE NYPL. LOCATION NN, NUC.
COMMENTARY The love story of an English officer, Maj. Lawrence, returned from India who has a small cottage on the Devonshire coast where he tries to occupy himself with botany. However, he gets drawn into the affairs of the people on the neighbouring estate, particularly a Lady Eleanor. He meets her first when she is still a child and follows her through her disastrous marriage to a rich, but extremely spoiled and sickly man. Over the years he realizes that he is in love with her, but her honour does not allow her to reciprocate. In the end, however, she realizes that she has always counted on Maj. Lawrence to solve her problems and that she cannot live without him [ML].

L40 *Plain Frances Mowbray and other tales* (by the Hon. Emily Lawless; dedicated to M.A.W. and D.W.).

+ London: John Murray, 1889. SOURCE Sutherland, p. 365; OCLC. LOCATION D, DPL, L, NUC, InND Loeber coll.

COMMENTARY Contents: 'Plain Frances Mowbray' (first published in *Blackwood's Magazine*, Edinburgh; set in Venice), 'Quin Loch' (Set in Co. Clare, first published in *Murray's Magazine*), 'A Ligurian episode' (first published in *Macmillan*, London), 'Borroughdale of Borroughdale' (first published in *Macmillan*), 'Namesakes' (concerns the O'Sullivans of Ploughwell Hall in Gloucestershire, who were English, first published in *Temple Bar*, London) [RL; Burmester list].

L41   *With Essex in Ireland: Being extracts from a diary kept in Ireland during the year 1599, by Mr. Henry Harvey, sometimes secretary to Robert Devereux, Earl of Essex* [anon.] (preface by 'John Oliver Maddox').

London: Smith, Elder & Co., 1890 (ill., map; preface by John Oliver Maddox [*sic*]). SOURCE Brown, 890 (mistakenly mentions Methuen as the publisher). LOCATION D, DPL, NUC.

Leipzig: Heinemann & Balestier, 1891. LOCATION NUC.

New York: J.W. Lovell, [1890]. SOURCE NCBEL 3, p. 1907. LOCATION NUC.

New York: Garland, 1979 (introd. by R.L. Wolff). SOURCE COPAC. LOCATION Dt.

COMMENTARY Historical fiction set in the sixteenth century. Originally believed by many, including William Gladstone, to be a genuine historical document, and considered by William Butler Yeats§ to be one of the thirteen best works of Irish fiction, it is a fictional journal written in Elizabethan English by a private secretary, Henry Harvey, of Robert Devereux, the earl of Essex's 1599 expedition against the earl of Tyrone from Dublin to a point past Limerick, and the return to Dublin [Brown; RIA/DIB; Hogan; Sutherland; Wolff introd., pp 37–8].

L42   *Grania. The story of an island* (by the Hon. Emily Lawless; dedicated to M.C. [M.C. Bishop?]).

+ London: Smith, Elder & Co., 1892, 2 vols. (ill., map). SOURCE Brown, 891; Daims, 1754; Wolff, 3959. LOCATION Dt, L, NUC, InND Loeber coll.

+ London: Smith, Elder & Co., 1892 (new edn; ill.). SOURCE Hogan, p. 688. LOCATION D, DPL (1897 edn).

Leipzig: Heinemann & Balestier, 1892. LOCATION NUC.

New York, London: Macmillan & Co., 1892. SOURCE Daims, 1754. LOCATION NUC.

New York: Garland, 1979, 2 vols. (introd. by R.L. Wolff). SOURCE COPAC. LOCATION Dt, L.

COMMENTARY Set on the Aran isles off the Galway coast and predating J.M. Synge in its realistic depiction of life among the peasants there, it is the story of Grania, a young girl brought up among the island's fishing community. Her dark complexion and passion witness her Spanish blood, inherited from her mother. When she is age 18 her father dies and she is left in charge of her family. Her betrothed, Murdough Blake, does not come to her aid as she tries to cross the foggy channel to fetch a priest for her dying sister Honor, and she drowns [Field Day, iv, pp 758, 826, v, pp 977, 980–5; Hogan, Sutherland, p. 258].

L43   *Maelcho. A sixteenth century narrative* (by the Hon. Emily Lawless; dedicated to M.C. Bishop).

+ London: Smith, Elder & Co., 1894, 2 vols. SOURCE Brown, 892 (1895 edn); Daims, 1755; Wolff, 3962. LOCATION D, Dt, DPL, L, NUC.

+ New York: D. Appleton & Co., 1894. SOURCE Daims, 1755. LOCATION D, NUC.

New York: Garland, 1979, 2 vols. (introd. by R.L. Wolff). SOURCE COPAC. LOCATION Dt, L.

COMMENTARY Historical novel set in Connacht and Munster during the bloody Desmond rebellion of 1579–83. It tells the story of an English youth who is saved from a massacre of his Irish relatives and who is buffeted about by the various waves of war and unrest of the times. The novel details the political and economic causes of the war and the sufferings endured by the Irish [Field Day, v, p 905; Hogan 2, p. 687; Wolff introd., p. 38].

L44　*Traits and confidences* (by the Hon. Emily Lawless; dedicated to S.S.).
　　　 + London: Methuen & Co., 1898. SOURCE Brown, 893 (mistakenly identified a 1897 edn); Hogan, p. 366; OCLC. LOCATION DPL, L, NUC, InND Loeber coll.
　　　 New York: Garland, 1979 (introd. by R.L. Wolff). SOURCE COPAC. LOCATION Dt, L.
COMMENTARY A collection of stories that are partly autobiographical. Contents: 'A song of the hobbies', 'An entomological adventure', 'On the pursuit of marine zoology as an incentive to gossip', 'A song of "veiled rebellion"', 'Mrs. O'Donnell's report', 'Old Lord Kilconnell', 'Of the influence of assassination upon a landscape', 'What the bag contained', 'Famine roads and famine memories', 'After the famine', 'Irish history considered as a pastime', 'The song of Art Kavanagh', 'How Art Kavanagh of Wexford fought Richard the king' [RL].

L45　*The book of Gilly: four months out of a life* (by the Hon. Emily Lawless; dedicated to E.F.M.).
　　　 + London: Smith, Elder & Co., 1906 (ill. L. Leslie Brooke). SOURCE Brown, 894; Wolff, 3957. LOCATION D, DPL, NUC.
COMMENTARY Gilly is an eight-year-old boy sent to a small island in Kenmare Bay (Co. Kerry) for a few months by his father, Lord Magillycuddy, who is in India but who wants his son to experience the same happy times there he remembers from his youth. The story tells of the boy's life on the island [Brown; Field Day, iv, pp 1142].

L46　*The race of Castlebar. Being a narrative addressed by Mr. John Bunbury to his brother, Mr. Theodore Bunbury, attached to His Britannic Majesty's Embassy at Florence, October 1798, and now first given to the world* (by the Hon. Emily Lawless and Shan F. Bullock§; dedicated to S.S. and E. de V., and the latest of all the Granias).
　　　 + London: John Murray, 1913. SOURCE Brown, 895; Wolff, 3965. LOCATION D, DPL, NUC, InND Loeber coll.
COMMENTARY Published posthumously. A light-hearted rendition of Gen. Humbert's invasion in 1798 as seen by the narrator, an Englishman named Bunbury. This work is largely based on the narrative of Dr Stock, Protestant bishop of Killala. Both the rebel leaders and the Orange men come in for criticism. Shan Bullock§ wrote the last chapter [Brown; Sutherland, p. 365].

LAWLOR, Denis Shyne (also known as Denys Shine), b. Castlelough (Co. Kerry) 1808, d. Woodchester, near Stroud (Glos.) 1887. A poet and miscellaneous writer, DSL was the eldest son of Denis Shyne and Ellen Lawlor. DSL assumed his mother's name. He was a Catholic and was educated at St Mary's College, Oscott, Liverpool. He was a frequent contributor to Irish and Catholic periodicals, including the *Catholic Miscellany* (London) between 1825 and 1840. His collection of poetry *The harp of Innisfail* was published in London in 1829. He published both a story and a travel account of a trip to the Pyrenees *Pilgrimages in the Pyrenees and Landes* (London 1870). He was sheriff of Kerry in 1840, was associated with the Young Ireland movement, and is mentioned in Thomas Carlyle's account of his tour in Ireland in 1849. DSL's library was sold in Dublin in 1893. SOURCE Allibone Suppl., ii, p. 978; Boase, vi, pp 15–16; COPAC; Irish pseudonyms; O'Donoghue, p. 245; RIA/DIB.

L47　*Tales of the South* (by Denis Shyne Lawlor).
　　　 [place?]: [publisher?], [1825]. SOURCE O'Donoghue, p. 245.
COMMENTARY No copy located. A collection of legendary prose sketches, some of which were translated into German by Julius Rodenberg§ in his *Die Harfe von Erin* (Leipzig, 1861) [O'Donoghue].

L48   *Centulle, a tale of Pau* (by Denis Shyne Lawlor).
       London: Longmans, Green, Reader & Dyer, 1874. SOURCE Allibone Suppl., ii, p. 978; RLIN. LOCATION CtY.

LAWRENCE, Sir Henry Montgomery, b. Matura (Ceylon, now Sri Lanka) 1806, d. 1857. Military man and miscellaneous writer, HML was the son of Col. Alexander Lawrence of Coleraine (Co. Derry) who served much of his life in India, and Letitia Catherine, daughter of the Revd George Knox of Co. Donegal. HML was sent to school at Foyle College in Derry. Later he became a cadet in the East India Company's army, studied at Addiscombe College and obtained a commission in the Bengal artillery in 1822. He served first in Burma and later, while recovering from malaria, joined the trigonometrical survey in the north of Ireland. A talented linguist in Indian languages, HML spent the remainder of his life in civil and military service in India, where he was killed at the defence of Lucknow. He was a regular contributor to various Indian periodicals, including the *Calcutta Review*. A volume of his essays on military and political matters, written in India, was published posthumously in 1859. He married his cousin Honoria, daughter of Revd George Marshall, rector of Carndonagh (Co. Donegal), where she was born in 1808. Two of his brothers also served in India: Sir George Alexander and Lord John Lawrence, who was viceroy from 1863 to 1869. SOURCE Allibone Suppl., ii, p. 979; Boase, ii, p. 329; Landed gentry, 1912, p. 373; Newmann, p. 134; ODNB; RIA/DIB; Ximenes cat. M9/149.

L49   *Some passages in the life of an adventurer in the Punjaub* [anon.].
       Delhi: Printed at the Gazette Press, by Kunniah Lall, 1842. SOURCE Ximenes cat. M3/119; COPAC. LOCATION L.
       London: Henry Colburn, 1845, 2 vols. (as *Adventures of a officer in the service of Runjeet Singh*). SOURCE Allibone Suppl., ii, p. 979. LOCATION L.
       COMMENTARY No Irish content. Originally published in the *Delhi Gazette*; the title page of the Delhi edn states that 'Any Profits that may arise from the Sale of this Work, will be appropriated to the Support of a School in the Delhi Territory ...' The book purports to be the memoirs of Col. Belassis, who in May 1830 is employed in the service of the Sikh leader, Maharajah Ranjit Singh, and is a mixture of fact and fiction. Each chapter is accompanied by notes providing details about life in India [Ximenes cat. M3/119; Quaritch cat. 1336/55].

LEADBEATER, Mrs Mary (née Shackleton), b. Ballitore (Co. Kildare) 1758, d. Ballitore (Co. Kildare) 1826. Story writer, memoirist, poet and miscellaneous writer, ML was the daughter of a Quaker schoolmaster, Richard Shackleton, and his second wife, Elizabeth Carleton. ML had a speech defect and was much teased at the family school where she was the only female student. But she received a good education and she kept a diary from the age of 10 onward. She married a local landowner, William Leadbeater, and ran the village post office and a bonnet making business. She corresponded with Edmund Burke (who had been educated by her grandfather) and with Maria Edgeworth§ and with Maria's father, Richard Lovell Edgeworth§. Her earliest work was *Extracts and original anecdotes for the improvement of youth* (Dublin, 1794). She wrote poems and published the memoirs of her parents, *Memoirs and letters of Richard and Elizabeth Shackleton, late of Ballitore* (London, 1822), and wrote an account of the events in Ballitore from the year 1766 to 1824 (*The Leadbeater papers: the annals of Ballitore*, London, 1862, 2 volumes, a review of which was J.S. Le Fanu's§ first non-fiction piece, published in the *Dublin University Magazine*). This provides an excellent social history of the period, including the harrowing events of the 1798 uprising in and around Ballitore. An early-nineteenth-century listing of her work mentions that, at least up to 1814, 'these works were written for the most part in conjunction with her sister Miss Elizabeth Shackleton§'.

Maria Edgeworth§, upon the suggestion of her father, added many notes to ML's *Cottage dialogues* (London, 1811) to make them more intelligible to English readers. The original text was revised by ML's friend, the poet Melesina Trench, who encouraged its publication. ML also wrote *Cottage biography; being a collection of lives of the Irish peasantry* (Dublin, 1822, repr. 1987), which she dedicated to Melesina Trench, 'who suggested the plan of this little work'. An account of ML written after her death states that she took a great interest in bringing about improvements in society, prison discipline, schools, saving banks and other means of improving the condition of the poor. She was befriended by the Quaker author Abigail Roberts§ and she published *Biographical notes of Friends in Ireland* (London, 1823). For her papers, see ODNB. For her portrait, see Elmes. SOURCE Allibone, i, p. 1072; Allibone Suppl., ii, p. 982; Blain, p. 639; Boylan, p. 196; BD, p. 199; Butler, p. 211; Dean of Westminster, *The remains of the late Mrs. Richard Trench* (London, 1862), passim (many letters addressed to ML); Field Day, iv, pp 501, 502–5, 515–16, 1142, v, pp 842–3 and passim; Elmes, p. 113; A.J.C. Hare (ed.), *The life and letters of Maria Edgeworth* (London, 1894), i, pp 174–5; Harrison, p. 68; Hogan 2, p. 689; OCIL, pp 303–4; K. O'Neill, 'Almost a gentlewoman' in M. O'Dowd & S. Wichert (eds), *Chattel, servant, or citizen* (Belfast, 1995), pp 91–102; ODNB; O'Donoghue, p. 246; RIA/DIB.

L50   *Extracts and original anecdotes for the improvement of youth* [anon.].
      + Dublin: Printed [for the author?] by R.M. Jackson, 1794. SOURCE Rafroidi, ii, p. 204; ESTC t133453. LOCATION D, C, NUC.
COMMENTARY Starts with a history of the Quakers and of famous Quakers, followed by short stories for children, interspersed with Quakers' accounts of their lives, and followed by some poetry. Contents of the children's stories (a few are set in Ireland): 'The mastiff', 'Early reproofs of conscience', 'The bird's nest', 'The friend and the highwayman', 'The children in the boat', 'The orphans', 'The old nurse', 'Dispute decided by a negro', 'The dumb boy's presence of mind', 'Benevolence rewarded', 'Alleviation of pain', 'The apostle John and the robber', 'Extract of a letter from R.S.', 'Goodnature', 'Fretfulness reproved', 'The right employment of time', 'Account of the death of a child about 8 years of age', 'Visit of a negro', 'Account of a negroboy', 'Samuel', 'The Shunamite', 'The punishment of covetousness', 'The fiery furnace', 'The punishment of pride', 'Paul persecuted by the Jews, and his defence', 'Anecdotes respecting an Indian chief, who came 200 miles to Philadelphia in the year 1760 on a religious account', 'Concerning slavery' [RL].

L51   *Cottage dialogues among the Irish peasantry* (by Mary Leadbeater; with notes and preface by Maria Edgeworth§).
      + London: J. Johnson, 1811 (2 parts in 1 vol.). SOURCE Rafroidi, ii, p. 204; Brown, 1706; British Fiction; Garside, 1811:50; Wolff, 1997. LOCATION Grail, D, L, NUC, InND Loeber coll.
      + Dublin: Printed by J. & J. Carrick, 1811 (subscribers' list). SOURCE NSTC. LOCATION D, O.
      + Dublin: J. Cumming, 1813, 4th edn (as *Cottage dialogues among the Irish peasantry. Part I*). SOURCE Rafroidi, ii, p. 205; Bradshaw, 2974. LOCATION C.
      COMMENTARY *Dublin 1813 edn*. Has 45 dialogues [Rafroidi].
      Philadelphia: Samuel R. Fisher Jnr, 1811. LOCATION NUC.
      Philadelphia: Johnson & Warner, 1811. LOCATION NUC.
COMMENTARY The first edn has 54 didactic stories, directed at women cottagers, to contrast the careless, idle type of peasant with the thrifty, industrious housewife. Each story is about two pages long and contains in simple language ideas for improvement of morals and of practical matters. The volume contains an extensive 'Glossary and notes for the use of English readers' by Maria Edgeworth§. In the introd. to part II (see below), ML stated that the orig-

inal idea for the composition [of the two volumes] had been suggested by William P. Le Fanu, who had recently established 'a very useful and national publication', the *Irish Farmer's Journal* (Dublin). Melesina Trench undertook the revision of the work and encouraged its publication. The English edn was noted by the Society for Bettering the Condition of the Poor, which extracted and published some dialogues for the use of English cottagers. Contents of the dialogues (all set in Ireland): 'The child in the cradle', 'Learning to sew', 'Going to the fair', 'Returning from the fair', 'Decorum', 'The wake', 'Dress', 'Servitude' [four dialogues], 'Fidelity', 'Benevolence', 'Housekeeping', 'Matrimony', 'Nursing', 'Squabbling', 'Chastisement', 'Sunday', 'Anger', 'The quarrel', 'The reconcilement', 'The garden', 'The house', 'The pig', 'Manure', 'The dairy', 'The cupboard', 'Cookery', 'False report, and slander', 'Wise recollections', 'Cookery', 'The room', 'Starch', 'Washing', 'The weather', 'Stirabout', 'Forecast', 'Concord' [two dialogues], 'Spinning-match', 'Courtship' [two dialogues], ' 'Straw-platting', 'Cow-pock', 'Small-pox', 'Politicks', 'Charring' [two dialogues], 'The fire', 'The fever', 'Whiskey', 'Degradation', 'Death' [RL; Field Day, v, pp 469, 842–3, 846, 859–65 and passim].

L52   *Cottage dialogues among the Irish peasantry. Part II* (by Mary Leadbeater).
    + London: J. Johnson, 1813 (with glossary and notes for English readers [by Maria Edgeworth§], evident from introd. to 1841 Dublin edn containing the three parts of *Cottage dialogues*; said to be illustrated but not in Univ. of Cambridge copy). SOURCE Bradshaw, 8737. LOCATION C, InND Loeber coll.
    + Dublin: John Cumming, 1818 (new edn, corrected and revised). SOURCE Bradshaw, 2974. LOCATION C.
    COMMENTARY Forty-four dialogues set in Ireland mostly between Martin Nowlan and Thady Maguire, unless noted otherwise. Contains an extensive 'Glossary and notes, for the use of the English reader', by Maria Edgeworth§, as in the first volume. The Dublin edn of the second volume, not surprisingly, has no glossary. Contents: 'Planting', 'Brotherly care', 'Sunday school', 'Robbing birds' nests', 'Contrition. Biddy and her brother Martin', 'Victuals', 'Perseverance. Winny, and her son Martin', 'Cultivation. Barney, Martin', 'Night school', 'Cruelty (wanton)', 'Theft', 'Lancastrian school', 'Use of learning', 'Basket-making', 'Benefit society', 'Filial love', 'Swearing and lying', 'Procrastination', 'Passion', 'Punctuality', 'Independence', 'Calculation', 'Potatoes. Mr. Seymour and Barney Nowlan', 'Hospital', 'Tillage. Barney, Mr. Seymour', 'Carelessness', 'Recovery. Barney Nowlan, and his wife Winny', 'Confession. Mary Doyle and her mother Nanny', 'Dieting. Barney and his son Martin', 'Cruelty (inconsiderate). Martin and his brother Johnny', 'Vanity. Hetty Flood and Mary Doyle', 'Pride', 'Reparation. Thady, and his mother Katty', 'The funeral', 'Remorse', 'Amendment', 'Reading', 'The relapse', 'Drunkenness. Mr. Seymour, Thady', 'Elopement. Barney, Martin's father, Terry, Thady's father', 'Botany Bay. Barney, and his son Martin', 'Courtship. Martin Nowlan, and Mary Doyle', 'Matrimony. Barney and his son Martin', 'Matrimony. Nanny Doyle, and her daughter, Mary Nowlan' [RL; Field Day, v, pp 469, 842–3 and passim].

L53   *Cottage dialogues among the Irish peasantry* (by Mary Leadbeater).
    + Dublin: Hibernian Press Office, 1813, 2 parts (notes and ill. W.P. Le Fanu). SOURCE NSTC. LOCATION D (4th edn), L, O.
    COMMENTARY Combines parts I and II [RL; Field Day, v, pp 469, 842–3 and passim].

L54   *Short stories for cottagers, intended to accompany Cottage dialogues* [anon.].
    Dublin: Hibernia Press, 1813. SOURCE BD, p. 199; Emerald Isle cat. 90/1212.
    COMMENTARY No copy located. Sequel to *Cottage dialogues* (Dublin, 1811, 1813) [RL].

L55   *The landlord's friend, intended as a sequel to 'Cottage Dialogues'* (by Mary Leadbeater).
    Dublin: J. Cumming, 1813. SOURCE Rafroidi, ii, p. 205; NSTC. LOCATION Grail, L, NUC.

COMMENTARY Sequel to *Cottage dialogues* (Dublin, 1811, 1813), intended to instruct the well-to-do on matters such as beggars, spinning wheels, Sunday-schools, public institutions, lying-in-charity and the Benefit Fund [Maggs cat. 1195/159].

L56   *Tales for cottagers, accommodated to the present condition of the Irish peasantry* (by Mary Leadbeater and Elizabeth Shakleton [*sic*, Shackleton]§).

+ Dublin: John Cumming, 1814. LOCATION Di, L (incomplete), NUC.

+ Dublin: J. Cumming; London: Gale, Curtis & Fenner, 1814 (ill.). SOURCE Rafroidi, ii, p. 205; British Fiction; Garside, 1814:37; Gecker, 602. LOCATION D, Dt, L, UP.

COMMENTARY Stories set in Ireland: 'Perseverance', 'Calculation', 'Economy', 'Early training', 'Temper', 'The Scotch ploughman', 'High spirit'. Includes a play 'Honesty is the best policy' [RL].

L57   *The pedlars* [anon.].

+ Dublin: Printed by Bentham & Hardy [for the Kildare Place Society], 1826 (ill.; see Plate 42). SOURCE Adams, 190; Bradshaw, 3338; Rafroidi, ii, p. 205 (as *The pedlars, a tale*); Dm exhibit. cat., 1981, p. 31. LOCATION D, L, C, InND Loeber coll.

COMMENTARY Describes the travels through the south-east of Ireland of the peddler Darby and his son Pat, with discussions on farming practice, local industries, peasant economy, schools and finally a meeting with a book peddler, which gives occasion for great praise of the Kildare Place Society's publications and provides a list of 58 titles then available [Dm exhib. cat., 1981, p. 31].

L58   *Cottage dialogues among the Irish peasantry* (by Mary Leadbeater).

+ Dublin: P. Kennedy, 1841. SOURCE Rafroidi, ii, p. 204. LOCATION NUC, InND Loeber coll.

COMMENTARY Published posthumously. This edn contains a re-publication of parts I and II, complemented by part III. Part III contains an additional 20 dialogues between Martin and Thady, unless noted otherwise: 'The rencontre. Martin and the stranger', 'Glad tidings. Martin Nowlan, Terry Maguire, and his wife Katty', 'The interview. Martin, Mary, Terry, Katty, Thady', 'Contrition', 'Taste', 'Gardening', 'The cottager's garden calendar', 'The savings bank', 'Drunkenness', 'New South Wales', 'The good wife', 'Good management. Judy Curtis and Mary Whelan', 'Nursing. Judy, Mary', 'Boxing', 'The house', 'Harvest work', 'The hen house', 'The contrast', 'Bacon', 'Charity', 'Conclusion' [RL; Field Day, v, pp 469, 842–3 and passim].

LEAMY, Edmund, b. Waterford 1848, d. Pau (France) 1904. Poet, politician, story writer and editor, EL was educated at the Jesuit College in Tullabeg (Co. Offaly) and became a solicitor before being called to the Irish Bar in 1885. He was elected as nationalist MP for Waterford and later for Kildare, spending many years in parliament where he was known as an accomplished orator. Politically he sided with Parnell and was present at some of the stormy events in Parnell's political life. He was an editor for *United Ireland* and was later associated with the *Evening Herald* (both in Dublin). He contributed to the *Waterford Chronicle* and to the *Weekly Independent* (Dublin). His portrait was published in *By the Barrow River* (Dublin, 1907). Brown attributes to Leamy, *Leandro, or the sign of the cross. A Catholic tale* (Philadelphia 1870). Some of his letters are among the Downey Papers (NLI, MS 10,031). SOURCE Brady, p. 129; Brown, p. 164; Hogan 2, p. 690; Irish pseudonyms; OCIL, p. 304; RIA/DIB; Ryan, p. 145.

L59   *Irish fairy tales* (by Edmund Leamy).

Dublin: M.H. Gill, [1890] (ill. George Fagan). SOURCE Brown, 899; Osborne, p. 604. LOCATION L, CaOTP (1906 edn), NUC, InND Loeber coll. ([1906] edn).

+ New York: D. FitzGerald, [1911] (as *Golden spears and other fairy tales*; ill. Corinne Turner). SOURCE Hogan 2, p. 690; OCLC; NYPL. LOCATION NUC, NN.

COMMENTARY Seven fairy tales with notes, inspired by Eugene O'Curry and Robert Dwyer Joyce§, written for children. Contents: 'Princess Finola and the dwarf', 'The house in the lake',

'The little white cat', 'The golden spears', 'The fairy tree of Dooros', 'The enchanted cave', 'The huntsman's son' [RL].

L60   *The fairy minstrel of Glenmalure, and other stories for children* (by Edmund Leamy).

Dublin: James Duffy & Co., [1899] (ill. C.A. Mills). SOURCE Brown, 900. LOCATION L, NUC (n.d. edn).

COMMENTARY A small book containing adventures of Irish children in an Irish fairy land [Brown].

L61   *By the Barrow River and other stories* (by Edmund Leamy; foreword by Katharine Tynan§).

+ Dublin: Sealy, Bryers & Walker, 1907. SOURCE Brown, 901. LOCATION D, NUC.

COMMENTARY Twenty stories including several ghost stories, tales of the Irish Brigade, tales of early Ireland, and of tragedy and comedy. Contents: 'By the Barrow River', '"Bendemere Cottage"', 'A night with the rapparees', '"Worse than Cremona"', 'Maurya na Gleanna, or revenge at last', 'Story of the raven', 'The spectres of Barcelona', 'The black dog', 'The ghost of Garroid Jarla', 'True to death', '"The light that lies in woman's eyes"', 'Death by misadventure', 'A message from the dead', 'The vision of the night', 'The pretty Quakeress', 'My first case', 'A vision or a dream?', 'From the jail to the battlefield', 'All for a woman's eyes', 'The ruse of Madame Martin' [ML].

LEATHLEY, Mary Elizabeth Southwell (née Dudley), b. Clonmel (Co. Tipperary) 1818, d. Hastings (E. Sussex) 1899. A prolific writer of fiction, poetry, and religious stories for children, MESL was the daughter of George Dudley of Clonmel, a Quaker, and published her first book at age 16. It is said that she went on to write over 100 volumes (not according to our list), and among the best known of her non-fiction works were: *Children of scripture* (London, 1856), and *Requiescent: a little book of anniversaries* (London, 1888). She also did translations (e.g. *Breton legends*, London, 1857), and wrote verse (London, 1896). MESL married William Henry Leathley of London, a barrister, in 1847 and converted to catholicism the same year, when it appears she also moved to England permanently. She raised her only child, Dudley Leathley, as a Catholic. Among her most popular works was *Chick-seed* (London, [1846?]), of which almost 500,000 copies were sold. NCBEL mentions that she wrote *Tales for children* (n.d.), but this has not been located. She lived in England at Midhurst (Sussex), Ascot (Berks.), and Malvern (Herefs.). SOURCE Allibone Suppl., ii, p. 984; Boase, vi, pp 25–6; LVP, p. 273; NCBEL 4, p. 1821; RIA/DIB; *Waterford Society Jrnl*, 10 (1937) p. 337).

L62   *The child's book of country things. Containing simple lessons on agriculture, domestic animals, trees, fruit, vegetables, etc.* [anon.]

London: Darton & Clark, [c.1840] (ill.). SOURCE COPAC. LOCATION L.

COMMENTARY 60pp. Descriptions of country things rather than stories [RL; COPAC].

L63   *Mama's stories about the birds* [anon.].

London: Darton & Co., [1840s]. SOURCE OCLC. LOCATION CLU.

COMMENTARY Contents: 'The eagle', 'The duck', 'The quail', 'The robin redbreast', 'The bullfinch', 'The albatross', 'The owl', 'The goose', 'The magpie', 'The pheasant', 'The flamingo', 'The swan', 'The kestrel', 'The vulture', 'The parrot', 'The lapwing' [OCLC].

L64   *Chick-seed without chick-weed; being very easy and entertaining lessons for little children* [anon.].

London: Darton & Clark, [1846?]. SOURCE COPAC; RIA/DIB (mentions 1861 edn); RLIN. LOCATION E, Univ. of Florida.

COMMENTARY Half a million copies of this work were sold [Boase, vi, p. 26].

L65   *The cheerful companion, an easy story book for young children* [anon.].
London: Darton & Co. [1850?] (ill. George C. Leighton). SOURCE COPAC. LOCATION
L.

L66   *Plain things for little folk* [anon.].
London: Darton & Co., 1851. SOURCE RLIN. LOCATION O.

L67   *My favorite story book for the young* [anon.].
New York: T.W. Strong, 1851. SOURCE RLIN; OCLC. LOCATION Univ. of Florida.

L68   *The happy family: or, scenes in every-day life* [anon.].
London: Darton & Co., 1852 (ill.). SOURCE COPAC. LOCATION Univ. of Birmingham,
UK.

L69   *The life of a dutiful son* [anon.].
London: Darton & Co., 1854 (ill.). SOURCE COPAC. LOCATION L.

L70   *Large pictures with little stories: for children* [anon.].
London: Darton & Co., 1855 (ill.). SOURCE OCLC. LOCATION Nat. Art Library,
Victoria & Albert Museum.
COMMENTARY 32pp [RLIN].

L71   *Stories and pictures* [anon.].
London: Darton & Co., [*c*.1855]. SOURCE RLIN. LOCATION O.
COMMENTARY 32pp [RLIN].

L72   *Milk for babes: Bible stories for young children* [anon.].
London: Darton & Co., [*c*.1855], 10th edn. SOURCE COPAC. LOCATION E.
COMMENTARY No copy of the 1st edn located. Much reprinted religious stories for
children [RL].

L73   *The children of scripture* [anon.].
+ London: Darton & Co., 1856 (assisted by the Revd T. Wilson; ill.). SOURCE COPAC.
LOCATION L.
COMMENTARY Retelling of bible stories [RL].

L74   *True stories for young children* [anon.].
London: Darton & Co., 1856. SOURCE OCLC. LOCATION L ([1856], 2nd edn), NN.
COMMENTARY First published in parts. Contents: 'The best way to spend a penny', 'The two
dogs', 'A visit to the zoological gardens', 'Do as you are bid', 'Peace and war', 'The ship on
fire', 'The Russian exiles', 'The races', 'The castle and its true owners', 'The grateful dog',
'The gathering for peace', 'The young princes who were killed in the tower', 'The blue-coat
boys', 'King Richard's death', 'The little patriots', 'Penn's treaty with the Indians' [COPAC].

L75   *Stories that should be told* [anon.].
London: Darton & Co., 1858 (ill.). SOURCE COPAC. LOCATION L.

L76   *Truthful stories for the young* [anon.].
London: Darton & Co., [1860] (ill.). SOURCE COPAC. LOCATION L.

L77   *Early seeds to produce flowers* [anon.].
London: Darton & Co., 1861 (ill.). SOURCE OCLC. LOCATION Toronto Public Library.
COMMENTARY Contents: 'The pen and ink, 'The boy and the ant', 'What is tea?', 'The dark',
'The plums', 'The two pigs', 'The lazy man who had been a lazy boy', 'The boy who did not
like to go to bed', 'The storm', 'The little ducks', 'The good boy', 'The rash promise', 'The
little birds', 'The naughty dog and cat', 'The little baby', 'The silly little man', 'The kind doctor', 'The end' [OCLC].

L78   *Little crumbs for little chickens, or, reading pleasures, not a task* [anon.].
London: Darton & Co., 1861. SOURCE RLIN. LOCATION NNC.

L79   *Bible stories for young children* [anon.].
New York: T.W. Strong, 1869. SOURCE OCLC. LOCATION CLU.

COMMENTARY Retelling of Bible stories [RL].

L80   *Conquerors and captives; or, from David to Daniel* [anon.].
London: Ward, Lock & Tyler, 1873 (ill.; Beeton's Good Aim Series). SOURCE Allibone Suppl., ii, p. 984; COPAC. LOCATION L.
COMMENTARY Retelling of Bible stories [RL].

L81   *Living and moving, or how we travel* [anon.].
London: Darton & Co., [1874?]. SOURCE RLIN. LOCATION Univ. of Florida.
COMMENTARY 32pp. Also attributed to Mary Elliott [COPAC].

L82   *In the beginning, or, from Eden to Canaan* [anon.].
+ London: Ward, Lock & Tyler, 1875 (Beeton's Good Aim Series). SOURCE Allibone Suppl., ii, p. 984; COPAC. LOCATION E.
COMMENTARY Retelling of Bible stories [RL].

L83   *The story of stories for little ones* [anon.].
London: Ward, Lock & Tyler, [1875] (ill.). SOURCE Allibone Suppl., ii, p. 984; COPAC; RLIN. LOCATION L.

'LECKY, Walter', pseud. See MCDERMOTT, William A.

LEE, Hannah Farnham (née Sawyer), b. Newburyport (MA) 1780, d. 1865. American writer on history, art and self-improvement and of fiction for children, HFL was the daughter of Micajah S. Sawyer and one of three sisters whose mother died when they were very young. HFL married Dr George G. Lee, a naval officer, who died in 1816, leaving her to raise their three daughters. She lived in Boston where in 1832 she began her writing career, principally for money, publishing many works anonymously. SOURCE Allibone, i, p. 1074; Blain, p. 642; DAB; Wright, i, pp 214–17).

L84   *Rosanna; or, scenes in Boston* [anon.].
Cambridge (MA): J. Owen, 1839. SOURCE Slocum, ii, 2634; Wright, i, 1633. LOCATION NUC, NN.
COMMENTARY 'Written and sold for the benefit of the infant school in Broad Street, Boston'. Portrays some aspects of the life of poor Irish immigrants in Boston during the 1830s. Rosanna McCarty, a widow with two daughters, too often accepts the liquor her neighbour, slovenly Catty Corny, presses upon her. A sympathetic lady gives employment to Rosanna as a chambermaid. Rosanna and Dora McCree, whose husband is serving a life term in prison, are able to gain improvement in their living conditions and a better future for their children [Slocum].

LEE, Sophia Priscilla, b. London 1750, d. Clifton, Bristol (Avon), 1824. English playwright, poet and novelist, SPL was the daughter of actor and theatre manager John Lee and actress Anna Sophia Lee. The family moved between London, Dublin, Edinburgh and Bath and SPL helped to raise the younger children, including her sister the future author Harriet Lee, as her mother was often away acting. She wrote her first play *Chapter of accidents* while with her father in debtor's prison in 1772. After his death, when his four daughters were left without support, she managed to get it produced. It was a great success and with the profits SPL started a school in Bath, Belvidere House, which flourished until 1803. SPL contributed two novellas to Harriet Lee's *The Canterbury tales* (5 vols. 1797–1805). SOURCE Allibone, i, p. 1076; Blain, pp 643–4; Field Day, v, p. 1092; NCBEL 4, pp 946–7; ODNB; Todd, p. 406.

L85   *The recess; or, a tale of other times* [anon.] (dedicated to Sir John Eliot, Bt).
London: T. Cadell, 1785, 3 vols. SOURCE Hardy, 567; Gecker, 610; McBurney & Taylor, 536; Raven 2, 1785:37; ESTC n048409. LOCATION L, PU.

+ London: T. Cadell, 1787, 3rd edn, 3 vols. (corrected). SOURCE Gecker, 611; McBurney & Taylor, 537. LOCATION InND Loeber coll.

London: T. Hurst, [1802], 3rd edn. SOURCE Falkner Greirson cat. 19/385. COMMENTARY *London [1802] edn* A much abbreviated version [Falkner Greirson].

+ London: J.S. Pratt, 1843 (as *The recess. A tale of the days of Queen Elizabeth*). LOCATION InND Loeber coll.

+ Dublin: G. Burnet, R. Moncrieffe. J. Exshaw, J. Beatty, L. White, P. Byrne, S. Colbert, H. Whitestone, W. Sleater, J. Cash, R. Marchbank, T. Heary & J. Moore, 1786, 2 vols. SOURCE Falkner Greirson cat. 'Jane'/188 (1786 edn); McBurney & Taylor, 538 (1791 edn); Raven 2, 1785:37. LOCATION D (vol. 1 only), Dt, Dm (1791 edn).

Paris: Lepetit, 1797, 4 vols. (trans. by P.-B. de La Mare as *Le souterrain, ou Mathilde*). SOURCE Bn-Opale plus. LOCATION BNF.

Leipzig: Weidmanns, Erben & Reich, 1786, 3 vols. (trans. by B. Naubert as *Die Ruinen, eine Geschichte aus den vorigen Zeiten*). SOURCE Raven 2, 1785:37; COPAC. LOCATION Univ. of Leeds.

Prague: Johann Joseph Diesbach, 1788, 3 vols. (trans. as *Die Ruinen, eine Geschichte aus den vorigen Zeiten*). SOURCE OCLC. LOCATION NjP.

Lexington: University Press of Kentucky, 2000. SOURCE RLIN. LOCATION DCL.

COMMENTARY Very popular historical and Gothic romance, which went into many edns and was translated into several languages. Set in the reigns of Elizabeth I and James I, who both feature in the story, together with Francis Drake, Sir Henry Sidney, and the countess of Pembroke, it concerns the persecution by Elizabeth of two daughters supposedly born to Mary, Queen of Scots, by a clandestine marriage, and the sisters' horrid, unfortunate adventures through life. Although raised secretly, one manages to marry the earl of Leicester, while the other falls in love with the earl of Essex. She follows Essex into Ulster but is captured by the Irish, who are depicted as wild, uncivilized people. She lands in the hands of 'Tiroen' [the earl of Tyrone] and is held captive by him until she escapes. She finally is able to join Essex in Ulster, but loses track of him when he returns to England to give account to Elizabeth of his Irish actions [RL; Blain, p. 644; Field Day, v, p. 812; Frank, 240; ODNB; Todd; Tracy, 92].

LEESON, Jane Eliza, pseud. 'J.E.L.', b. 1807, d. 1882. Listed as an Irish author by Colman. JEL was a hymnist, poet, and author of stories for children as well as of many non-fiction religious works, and, given the nature of her writings, she presumably was a Irish Protestant. The introd. to her *A wreath of lilies* was written on the 'Banks of the Trent' in 1845. SOURCE Boase, vi, p. 34; Colman, p. 141; CM; NCBEL 4, p. 1822; O'Donoghue, p. 248.

L86   *A wreath of lilies. A gift of the young* [anon.].
+ London: James Burns, 1848. LOCATION L.
COMMENTARY Consists of the retelling of the Bible in verse and prose. Some chapters have been reprinted from *Burns' Magazine for the Young* (location not clear) [CM].

L87   *The orphan's home* (by 'J.E.L.').
London: Joseph Masters, 1849. LOCATION L (destroyed).
COMMENTARY Religious fiction. No copy located [BLC].

L88   *Christmas tide; or, the word of a king* (by 'J.E.L.').
London: [publisher?], 1849. LOCATION L (destroyed).
COMMENTARY Religious fiction. No copy located [RL; BLC].

L89   *The child's new lesson book; or, stories for little readers* [anon.].
London: Joseph Masters, [1850]. LOCATION L.

L90   *The story of a dream; or, a mother's version of an olden tale* [anon.].
+ London: Joseph Masters, 1850. LOCATION L.

LE FANU, Miss —. See LE FANU, Alicia.

LE FANU, Alicia (also known as **Alicia LeFanu, Miss Le Fanu** and **Miss Lefanu**), b. 1791 (*c.*1795 according to NCBEL and Blain), d. Dublin *c.*1844. Novelist, poet and memoirist, ALF was the daughter of Henry Le Fanu and Anne Elizabeth Sheridan (daughter of Thomas Sheridan and sister of Richard Brinsley Sheridan). Her first book *The flowers, or the sylphid Queen*, a tale in verse, appeared in London in 1809 (O'Donoghue mistakenly attributes this to her aunt of the same name.) She never married, and according to an inscription in her copy of Elizabeth Hamilton's§ *The cottagers of Glenburnie*, she lived at Glasnevin in 1811. The second edn of her *Strathallan* is dated from Fareham (Hants.) 29 Nov. 1816, while according to the Longman archive she was living at Northampton in 1821. She wrote memoirs of her grandmother, the author Frances Sheridan§ (*Memoirs of the life and writings of Mrs. Frances Sheridan*, London, 1824). Allibone attributes another novel *The India voyage* (London, 1804, 2 vols.) to her, but this is by Elizabeth Le Fanu§. One letter by ALF is among the Beaufort MSS in the Henry E. Huntington Library, San Marino (CA), while other letters are the NLI (P2594). She is not to be confused with her aunt, Alicia Le Fanu (1753–1817), the dramatist and daughter of Thomas Sheridan and Frances Chamberlaine. ALF's date of death is unclear, but in 1844 the writer Caroline Norton, Richard Brinsley Sheridan's granddaughter, secured for her £150 from the Royal Bounty Fund. SOURCE Allibone, i, p. 1077; Blain, pp 644–5; British Fiction; W.H. Dixon (ed.), *Lady Morgan's memoirs* (London, 1863), i, pp 247–9; Field Day, v, pp 775, 802; Hogan 2, pp 693–4; NCBEL 4, p. 947; NSTC, L1041, 1042; T.P. Le Fanu, *Memoir of the Le Fanu family* (n.p, n.d.), p. 76, Table 1; OCIL, p. 305; ODNB [under Philip Le Fanu]; O'Donoghue, p. 248; Rafroidi, ii, p. 207; RIA/DIB; RL; Wolff, iii, p. 15.

L91   *Strathallan* (by Alicia LeFanu).

+ London: Sherwood, Neely & Jones, 1816, 4 vols. SOURCE Rafroidi, ii, p. 207; British Fiction; Garside, 1816:43; Hogan 2, p. 694; Wolff, 4004. LOCATION Corvey CME 3–628–47948–9, D, DPL (1816, 2nd edn), L, ViU.

Paris: H. Nicolle, 1818, 5 vols. (trans. by C.H. de J**). LOCATION ViU.

COMMENTARY Contains several plots, one romantically melodramatic, one Gothic, and one a social comedy with a good deal of effective satire. Lord Strathallan is Scottish, but the scene is set mainly in England [Hogan; RL].

L92   *Helen Monteagle* (by Alicia LeFanu).

London: Sherwood, Neely & Jones, 1818, 3 vols. SOURCE Hodgson, p. 328; Block, p. 136; British Fiction; Garside, 1818:38. LOCATION Corvey CME 3–628–47975–4, ViU.

L93   *Leolin Abbey. A novel* (by Alicia LeFanu).

London: Longman, Hurst, Rees, Orme & Brown, 1819, 3 vols. SOURCE Rafroidi, ii, p. 207; Block, p. 136; British Fiction; Garside, 1819:44. LOCATION Corvey CME 3–628–47977–0, L, NUC.

[Paris?]: [publisher?], 1824 (trans. as *L'Abbaye de Léolin*). SOURCE Garside, 1819:44.

COMMENTARY No copy of the French edn located. The novel made little profit: in April 1821, only 279 copies out of an edn of 500 had been sold [British Fiction; RL].

L94   *Don Juan de las Sierras; or, el empecinado. A romance* (by Miss Le Fanu).

London: A.K. Newman & Co., 1823, 3 vols. SOURCE Rafroidi, ii, p. 207; British Fiction; Garside, 1823:54. LOCATION Corvey CME 3–628–47974–6, Dt, L.

L95   *Tales of a tourist. Containing The outlaw, and Fashionable connexions* (by Miss Lefanu [*sic*]).

+ London: A.K. Newman & Co., 1823, 4 vols. SOURCE Rafroidi, ii, p. 207; Block, p. 136; British Fiction; Garside, 1823:55. LOCATION Corvey CME 3–628–48046–9, Ireland related fiction, L, ViU.

COMMENTARY Consists of two tales, the first of which 'The outlaw' is set in Ireland. Geraldine Southwell is Irish but her 'ideas and habits are English'. Geraldine is orphaned, but in the course of the narrative she discovers that her father, Gerald Fitz-Clare, is alive but is an 'outlaw' after his involvement in the 1798 uprising. He has settled in America, but eventually receives a pardon and returns to Ireland to regain his Irish estates. Now an heiress to a substantial fortune, Geraldine is able to marry Ferdinand, Earl O'Melvyl. Fitz-Clare strongly condemns the aims and methods of those involved in the United Irishmen rising. It includes satirical treatment of tourists who produce travelogues of Ireland with only a superficial knowledge of the country [JB].

L96　*Henry the fourth of France. A romance* (by Alicia LeFanu).
　　London: A.K. Newman & Co., 1826, 4 vols. SOURCE Rafroidi, ii, p. 207; Block, p. 136; British Fiction; Garside, 1826:49. LOCATION Corvey CME 3–628–47976–2, L, ViU.
　　COMMENTARY A novel about Henry of Navarre, king of France, 1553–1610 [RL].

LE FANU, Eleanor Frances, pseud. **'Russell Gray'**, b. Dublin, 1845, d. probably England 1903. A poet and novelist, EFLF was the eldest daughter of the novelist and journalist Joseph Thomas Sheridan Le Fanu§, a Dublin barrister, and Susanna Bennett. She married in 1871 Col. Patrick Robertson of the 92nd Gordon Highlanders. Her three novels first appeared in the *Dublin University Magazine*, which her father owned and edited beginning in 1861 and in which her cousin, English novelist Rhoda Broughton, also published her first fiction. Her pseudonym, 'Russell Gray', is not to be confused with another author whose real name was Mrs (M.C.) Russell Gray. SOURCE T.P. Le Fanu, *Memoir of the Le Fanu family* (n.l., n.d.), p. 75, Table 1; McCormack, pp 201–2, passim; Wolff, iii, p. 21.

L97　*Never – for ever* (by 'Russell Gray'; dedicated to J. Sheridan Le Fanu§).
　　London: Richard Bentley, 1867. SOURCE Allibone Suppl., i, p. 706; Wolff, 4030. LOCATION L.
　　COMMENTARY First published in the *Dublin University Magazine* [W.E. Hall, p. 196].

L98　*John Haller's niece* (by 'Russell Gray').
　　London: Tinsley Bros, 1868, 3 vols. SOURCE T.P. Le Fanu, *Memoir of the Le Fanu family* (n.l., n.d.), p. 80; Cummins 90/82.
　　COMMENTARY First published in the *Dublin University Magazine*. The novel has long been known from a reference, but a copy surfaced only in 2004 [RL; W.E. Hall, p. 196; Cummins 90/82].

L99　*Up and down the world* (by 'Russell Gray').
　　London: Tinsley Bros, 1869, 3 vols. SOURCE Allibone Suppl., i, p. 706; T.P. Le Fanu, *Memoir of the Le Fanu family* (n.l., n.d.), p. 80. LOCATION L.
　　COMMENTARY First published in the *Dublin University Magazine* [W.E. Hall, p. 196].

LE FANU, Elizabeth ('Betsy'; née Sheridan; also known as **Mrs H. Le Fanu**), b. London 1758, d. Bath 1837. Diarist and novelist, she was the daughter of Thomas Sheridan and Frances Chamberlaine and sister of Richard Brinsley Sheridan and Alicia Sheridan Le Fanu. After her mother's death she spent three unhappy years in Dublin with her brother Charles, later living with her other brother Richard in London. Her letters to her sister Alicia, in which she gave lively accounts of Regency society, formed the basis of her posthumously published *Betsy Sheridan's Journal* (ed. by William Le Fanu, New Brunswick, NJ, 1960). She married Henry Le Fanu, younger brother of her sister Alicia's husband Joseph Le Fanu, and they lived in often straitened circumstances in Bath and Dublin. Her daughter Alicia LeFanu§ was also a writer. ELF's portrait was published by T.P. Le Fanu. SOURCE Allibone, i, p. 1077 [under Mrs Le Fanu]; Hogan 2, pp 694–5; T.P. Le Fanu, *Memoir of the Le Fanu family* (n.l., n.d.), opp. p. 37, p. 75, Table 1; McCormack, p. 206.

L100   *The India voyage* (by Mrs H. LeFanu).
+ London: G. & J. Robinson, 1804, 2 vols. SOURCE Gecker, 613 (who, along with
Allibone, mistakenly ascribes this to Alicia Le Fanu); British Fiction; Garside, 1804:39.
LOCATION Corvey CME 3-628-48047-7, L, UP, NUC.
COMMENTARY Formerly wrongly attributed to Alicia Le Fanu§. Epistolary novel. No
Irish content [British Fiction; RL].

L101   *The sister; a tale* (by Mrs H. Le Fanu).
+ London: Richards & Co., 1810, 2 vols. SOURCE British Fiction (Update 1). LOCATION
L.
COMMENTARY No Irish content. A party of travellers arrive at Sir Edward Cecil's house in
Wales. He had fled the country because of debts. However, his wife, children and Sir Edward's
sister live in the house. The sister becomes the protector of her brother's family. Only after
everyone finds their spot in life, does she die [ML].

LE FANU, Mrs H. See LE FANU, Elizabeth.

LEFANU, J. S. See LE FANU, Joseph Thomas Sheridan.

LEFANU, J. Sheridan. See LE FANU, Joseph Thomas Sheridan.

LE FANU, Joseph Thomas Sheridan (known as Joseph Sheridan Le Fanu, J. Sheridan
Le Fanu, and J.S. Le Fanu), b. Phoenix Park (but 45 Lower Dominick Street, according to
Igoe, also Dublin) 1814, d. Dublin 1873. Novelist, short story writer and journalist, JTSLF
was the eldest son of a Church of Ireland clergyman, Revd Thomas Philip Le Fanu and Emma
Lucretia, daughter of Revd William Dobbin. The Le Fanus were an old Huguenot family who
came to Ireland when JTSLF's grandfather was appointed clerk of the coast of Ireland. He
was related on his grandmother's side to the playwright Richard Brinsley Sheridan. Educated
initially at the Royal Hibernian military school, where his father was chaplain, he moved when
he was age 12 with his family to Abington (Co. Limerick), where his father was appointed
dean of Emly. There he was educated at home until he entered TCD, where he graduated
with honours. At university, Le Fanu made a name for himself as a public debater. He was
admitted to the King's Inn in 1836, to the Lincoln's Inn (London) in 1838, and was called to
the Irish Bar in the next year, but never practiced. Instead, he went into journalism. In 1838
he began contributing to the *Dublin University Magazine*, for which he wrote his first ghost
story 'The ghost and the bone setter' and was friends with founder and editor Isaac Butt§. In
the 1840s JTSLF owned and ran various Irish newspapers, including the *Warder* (Dublin) and
the *Statesman and Dublin Christian Record*, which occupied most of his creative energies for a
decade. He developed an interest in Celtic Ireland, judging from the fact that he was elected
a council member of the newly-founded Celtic Society in 1845. In 1843 (not 1844 as in OCIL)
he married Susanna§, the daughter of a barrister, George Bennett, QC, of Dublin, a member
of the Bennett family of The Grange, Clareen (Co. Offaly). They had two sons and two daughters. After the death of his wife in 1858 and his mother a few years later, he withdrew from
society and spent his time writing novels. Many of these were elaborations of earlier short stories and are remarkable for their psychological power and complex narrative schemes. From
1861 to 1870 he was editor and proprietor of the *Dublin University Magazine* in which he serialized much of his fiction and introduced writers such as Patrick Kennedy§, his wife Susanna§,
his daughter Eleanor§ and his English novelist niece Rhoda Broughton. He contributed to
many other journals (e.g., *Temple Bar*, London, 1870). JTSLF died at 18 Merrion Square,
Dublin, the Bennett family home where he and Susanna had lived for many years. His son

Philip dispersed his library. For his portrait and papers, see McCormack (p. 290) and ODNB. SOURCE Allibone Suppl., ii, p. 990; B & S, p. 492; Boylan, p. 197; Burke's, p. 707; Ellis, pp 140–191; J.C. Erck, *The ecclesiastical register* (Dublin, 1820), p. 49; Field Day, i, pp 1078, 1298–9 and passim, ii, pp 832, 840–2, 849–50 and passim, iv 1091; W.E. Hall, pp 169–72; W.V. Harris, *British short fiction in the nineteenth century* (Detroit, 1979), p. 56; Hogan, pp 369–71; IBL, 8 (1916), pp 30–3; Igoe, pp 143–8; Irish pseudonyms; Keane, p. 284; Leslie & Wallace, p. 813; McCormack, passim (pp 274–6 include a list of his writings); McKenna, pp 223–8; NUC; NCBEL 4, pp 1323–5; OCIL, p. 306; ODNB; O'Donoghue, p. 249; J. O'Donovan (ed.), *The book of rights* (Dublin, 1847), n.p., (list of officers of the Celtic Society); RIA/DIB; Sutherland, p. 368; Wilson, pp 318–24; R.L. Wolff, introd., *The Cock and Anchor* (New York, 1979).

L102 *The Cock and Anchor, being a chronicle of old Dublin city* [anon.].
+ Dublin: William Curry Jnr & Co.; London: Longman, Brown, Green & Longmans; Edinburgh: Fraser & Co., 1845, 3 vols. SOURCE Brown, 904 (Duffy edn [*sic*]); Rafroidi, ii, p. 211; Ellis, p. 184; Sadleir, 1373; Wolff, 4010. LOCATION Grail, D, Dt, L, NUC.
Dublin: William Curry Jnr & Co., 1845, 3 vols. (new edn). SOURCE Sadleir, 1373a.
COMMENTARY *Dublin Curry 1845 edn without London and Edinburgh co-publishers*. No copy located other than that reported by Sadleir, 1373a [RL].
London: Longman & Co.; Parry & Co., 1847, 3 vols. SOURCE Topp 3, p. 388. LOCATION NUC.
London: Parry & Co., 1851, 3 vols., 3rd edn (as *Sir Henry Ashwoode. The forger. A chronicle of old Dublin City*). SOURCE Falkner Greirson cat. 9/195; Sadleir, 1373b; Wolff, 4010a. LOCATION Dt.
+ London: Chapman & Hall, 1873 (new edn, as *Morley Court: being a chronicle of old Dublin City*). SOURCE Ellis, p. 184; Topp 3, p. 388; Sadleir, 1373d. LOCATION Grail, NUC, InND Loeber coll.
+ Dublin: James Duffy, [1909–10]. SOURCE Rowan cat. 62/267. LOCATION D, InND Loeber coll.
New York: W.H. Colyer, 1848. SOURCE NYPL. LOCATION NN, NUC.
+ New York: Garland, 1979, 3 vols. (introd. by R.L. Wolff). SOURCE COPAC. LOCATION Dt, InND Loeber coll.
COMMENTARY Historical fiction set in Dublin during the viceroyalty of the earl of Wharton during the beginning of the eighteenth century. The story tells of the conspiracy of a number of wicked villains to ruin a young spendthrift baronet and to compel his sister to marry one of them. She escapes to her uncle in Limerick. The conspirators plan a rising in favour of the Stuarts after Queen Anne's death [Brown; Wolff introd., pp 31–2].

L103 *The fortunes of Colonel Torlogh O'Brien. A tale of the wars of King James* [anon.].
+ Dublin: J. McGlashan; London: William S. Orr & Co., 1847 (ill. Hablot K. Browne [Phiz]). SOURCE Rafroidi, ii, p. 211; Ellis, p. 184; Sadleir, 1375a,b; Wolff, 4012; Topp 8, 178. LOCATION Grail, DPL Gilbert coll., Dt, L, NUC, InND Loeber coll.
COMMENTARY *Dublin 1947 edn* Two variant bindings with gold impressed decorative spine in blue and red cloth [RL].
+ London, New York: George Routledge, [1847] (ill. H.K. Browne [Phiz]). SOURCE Brown, 905. LOCATION D.
+ London, New York: George Routledge & Sons, n.d. [anon.] (new edn, ill. H.K. Browne [Phiz]). LOCATION D.
+ New York: W.H. Colyer, 1847. LOCATION NUC, InND Loeber coll.
Philadelphia: Carey & Hart, 1848. SOURCE Todd 8, 178.
COMMENTARY *Philadelphia edn* No copy located [RL].

+ New York: New Amsterdam Book Co.; London: Downey, 1899 (ill. Phiz). LOCATION InND Loeber coll.

COMMENTARY First issued in parts by McGlashan, Dublin (April 1846 – Jan. 1847). Historical fiction set at the turn of the seventeenth century, Torlogh O'Brien, an officer in the Jacobite army, tries to regain possession of his estates in Tipperary, which are held by the Williamite Sir Hugh Willoughby, with whose daughter O'Brien is in love. In the course of the story, an account is given of the causes of the Jacobite downfall, of James's court in Dublin and of the battle of Aughrim. The story closes shortly after the treaty of Limerick. Le Fanu incorporates into this novel the story *An adventure of Hardress Fitzgerald, a royalist captain*, published in 1840, which drew on several anonymous letters to James II in the possession of his family telling of conditions in Ireland before 1688 [Brown; McCormack, pp 89–90; Topp].

L104   *Ghost stories and tales of mystery* [anon.].

Dublin: J. McGlashan; London, Liverpool: Orr & Co., 1851 (ill. Phiz). SOURCE Rafroidi, ii, p. 211; Ellis, p. 184; Sadleir, 1376; Wolff, 4013. LOCATION Grail, NUC.

COMMENTARY Issued in three binding types: (a) red faintly-ribbed or smooth morocco cloth; (b) red rough morocco cloth; (c) violet bead-grained cloth. Published as a Christmas collection, but its publication was delayed until the New Year. Contents: 'The watcher', 'The murdered cousin', 'Schalken the painter' (first published in May 1839; a painter has a vision of his lost love beckoning from a crypt), 'The evil guest' (originally entitled 'Some account of the latter days of Richard Marston of Dunoran', and its setting changed from Ireland to England) [Carter, pp 127–8, 165; Ellis; Field Day, i, pp 1231–42 ('Strange event in the life of Schalken the painter); McCormack, pp 75, 104–7, 117].

L105   *The house by the church-yard* (by J. Sheridan Le Fanu).

Dublin: [J. McGlashan?], 1863. SOURCE Carter, pp 128–9; Brown, 906 (states 1863, James Duffy edn, but this probably is in error). COMMENTARY *Dublin 1863 edn.* No copy located. Carter, pp 128–9; R.L. Wolff, introd. *The cock and anchor* (New York, 1979), p. xvi].

London: Tinsley Bros, 1863, 3 vols. SOURCE Rafroidi, ii, p. 211; Ellis, p. 185; Sadleir, 1379; Wolff, 4016. LOCATION Grail, Dt, L, NUC.

London: Tinsley Bros, 1863, 3 vols. (second 'issue' of 1st edn, and first with English prelims.). SOURCE Topp 5, p. 145; Sadleir, 1379a; COPAC. LOCATION Dt.

London: Richard Bentley & Son, 1866 (revsd. and enlarged; ill.). SOURCE Sadleir, 1379e. LOCATION Dt.

New York: G.W. Carleton, 1866. SOURCE Topp 5, p. 145. LOCATION NUC.

+ New York: Stein & Day, 1968 (introd. by Elizabeth Bowen). LOCATION InND Loeber coll.

New York: Garland, 1979, 3 vols. (introd. by R.L. Wolff). SOURCE COPAC. LOCATION Dt.

+ Belfast: Appletree Press, 1992 (introd. by Thomas Kilroy). LOCATION D.

COMMENTARY First serialized in the *Dublin University Magazine* (Oct. 1861–Feb. 1863). This is the first novel JTSLF wrote after a hiatus from fiction writing of sixteen years. The title derives from Jonathan Swift's§ poem, 'The little house by the churchyard at Castleknock', a town close to Chapelizod (Co. Dublin) where the novel is set in 1767. Both locations are near the Phoenix Park where JTSLF lived as a child. Originally the author had the book printed and part of the edn bound in Dublin, but it was then published by Tinsley in London who stripped and rebound the volumes. However, O'Hegarty records a combined binding type. The first London edn was issued in two binding types. A Gothic story of subversion and criminality that takes place in the eighteenth century, it contains an account of murder, ghastly visions and detection and depicts in great detail social life among a group of officers and their families [Brown; Carter, pp 128–9; Field Day, ii, pp 883–9; McCormack, p. 140; P.S. O'Hegarty, 'Notes and comment ...' *The Bibliographical Society of Ireland*, 6(4) (1954), p. 61; Sutherland; R.L. Wolff, introd., *The cock and anchor* (New York, 1979), p. xvi].

L106 *Uncle Silas. A tale of Bartram-Haugh* (by Joseph Sheridan Le Fanu; dedicated to the countess of Gifford).

London: Richard Bentley, 1864, 3 vols. SOURCE Rafroidi, ii, p. 211; Ellis, p. 186; Sadleir, 1386; Wolff, 4025; OCLC. LOCATION Dt (imperfect copy), NUC.

+ London: Richard Bentley, 1865 (new edn; new preface; ill.; Favourite Novels, No. 11). SOURCE Topp 5, p. 146; Sadleir, 1386b. LOCATION Grail, D.

London: Chapman & Hall, 1879 (new edn; Select Library of Fiction). SOURCE Sadleir, 3610.

Paris: C. Lévy, 1877 (in Bibliothèque Contemporaine, trans. as *Mon oncle Silas*). SOURCE Rafroidi, ii, p. 365; RLIN. LOCATION BNF.

Leipzig: Bernard Tauchnitz, 1865, 2 vols. SOURCE T & B, 781–82. LOCATION Dt, NUC.

New York: Harper & Bros, 1865 (Library of Select Novels, No. 251). LOCATION NUC.

+ London: The Cresset Press, 1947 (introd. by Elizabeth Bowen). LOCATION D, InND Loeber coll.

+ Oxford: Oxford University Press, 1981. LOCATION Dt, L, InND Loeber coll.

COMMENTARY First serialized in the *Dublin University Magazine* (ending Dec. 1864). On the sudden death of her father, Austin Ruthyn, from a heart attack, Maud is left to the care of her uncle Silas in Derbyshire, until she comes of age. Silas is suspected of having earlier murdered in his house a man to whom he owed gambling debts, but he has never been brought to justice. Sinister in appearance and a consummate villain, Silas plots to marry Maud to his oafish son Dudley (who is, it emerges, already married). When this falls through, father and son conspire to murder the ward and so inherit her fortune. A French governess, Mme de la Rougierre, is brought in to help with the plan, by which the victim is to be killed with a spiked hammer. The plot fails, the French governess is murdered in Maud's place, and the heroine escapes in the nick of time from Silas's house in horror. Silas kills himself with an overdose of laudanum. Maud goes to live happily as Lady Ilbury, the 'wife of a noble-hearted husband' [Sutherland, pp 645–6; Topp 5, p. 146].

L107 *Wylder's hand. A novel* (by Joseph Sheridan Le Fanu; dedicated to the Hon. Mrs [Caroline] Norton).

London: Richard Bentley, 1864, 3 vols. SOURCE Rafroidi, ii, p. 211; Ellis, p. 185; Sadleir, 1389; Wolff, 4028. LOCATION Grail, L, NUC.

+ London: Hutchinson & Co., 1871 (new edn). SOURCE OCLC. LOCATION DPL (n.d. edn), CtY.

New York: G.W. Carleton, 1865. LOCATION NUC.

+ New York: Dover Publications, 1978. LOCATION InND Loeber coll.

COMMENTARY First serialized in the *Dublin University Magazine* (June 1863–Feb. 1864). A murder mystery set in England with an aristocratic cast of actors. Mark Wylder, engaged to Dorcas Brandon, disappears mysteriously. A series of letters arrive from the Continent in which he renounces his claim. Dorcas marries Stanley Lake. Eventually, Lake dies and the decomposed body of Wylder is discovered. Lake had killed his rival and had caused the forged letters to be sent [OCIL, p. 606; Topp 3, p. 367].

L108 *Guy Deverell* (by J.S. Le Fanu; dedicated to Charles Lever§).

London; Richard Bentley, 1865, 3 vols. SOURCE Rafroidi, ii, p. 211; Ellis, p. 186; Sadleir, 1377; Wolff, 4014; OCLC. LOCATION Grail, Dt, NUC.

+ London: Richard Bentley, 1866 (new edn; ill. Pearson, H. Briscoe). SOURCE Topp 3, p. 359; Sadleir, 3610 (n.d. edn). LOCATION InND Loeber coll.

+ Leipzig: Bernard Tauchnitz, 1865, 2 vols. SOURCE T & B, 803,804. LOCATION Dt, NUC, InND Loeber coll.

New York: Harper & Bros, 1866 (Library of Select Novels, No. 261). LOCATION NUC.

+ New York: Dover Publications, 1984 (ill. Pearson, H. Briscoe). LOCATION InND Loeber coll.

COMMENTARY First published in the *Dublin University Magazine* (Jan.–July 1865). A Gothic melodrama set in a country house, Marlowe Hall. The owner of the house is Sir Jekyl Marlowe, MP, who earlier in life killed Guy Deverell in a duel. The victim now has a grown-up son, also called Guy Deverell. Sir Jekyl's comfortable middle age is disturbed by a sinister, indeterminately foreign intruder, M. Varbarriere, who is actually Herbert Strangways, whose sister was married to the original Guy. Sir Jekyl is finally driven to death-bed contrition. The estate goes to his brother, Revd Dives Marlow, frustrating Varbarriere's schemes. But Guy marries Sir Jekyl's daughter [Sutherland, p. 267; Topp 3, p. 359].

L109   *All in the dark* (by J. Sheridan Le Fanu).

London: Richard Bentley, 1866, 2 vols. SOURCE Rafroidi, ii, p. 211; Ellis, p. 186; Sadleir, 1369; Wolff, 4006; OCLC. LOCATION Grail (n.d. edn), Dt, NUC.

London: Chapman & Hall, [1870] (new edn; Select Library of Fiction, No. 162). SOURCE Topp 3, p. 362; Sadleir, 3610 (n.d. edn). LOCATION D (n.d. edn).

+ New York: Harper & Bros, 1866 (Library of Select Novels, No. 276). LOCATION NUC, InND Loeber coll.

COMMENTARY First serialized in the *Dublin University Magazine* (Feb.–June 1866). Three binding variants of the first London edn: (a) cream colour; (b) claret colour; (c) dull scarlet. The central character is an old aunt, Miss Dinah Perfect of Gilroyd Hall, given to table rapping. Under the influence of a spiritual advisor, 'Henbane', she interferes in the lives of her niece Violet Darkwell (choosing marriage partners for her) and her orphaned nephew William (choosing a career). After various comic complications the young people marry happily [Sutherland, p. 18; Topp 3, p. 362; Carter, p. 129].

L110   *The tenants of Malory. A novel* (by Joseph Sheridan Le Fanu).

+ London: Tinsley Bros, 1867, 3 vols. SOURCE Rafroidi, ii, p. 211; Ellis, p. 186; Sadleir, 1385; Wolff, 4024; OCLC. LOCATION Grail (n.d.), D (vol. 2 only), NUC.

London: Chapman & Hall, 1870 (new edn; Select Library of Fiction, No. 177). SOURCE Topp 3, p. 367 (1871 edn); Sadleir, 3610 (n.d. edn); OCLC. LOCATION D (n.d. edn), CLU.

New York: Harper & Bros, 1867. LOCATION NUC.

Boston: Little & Gay, 1867. SOURCE Topp 3, p. 367.

COMMENTARY No copy of the Boston edn located. First serialized in the *Dublin University Magazine* (Feb.–Oct. 1867), and in the US in *Littell's Living Age* (Boston) [Topp 3, p. 367; RL].

L111   *Haunted lives. A novel* (by J.S. Le Fanu; dedicated to Mrs FitzGerald, of Fane Valley [Co. Louth, home of Percy Hetherington Fitzgerald§]).

London: Tinsley Bros, 1868, 3 vols. SOURCE Rafroidi, ii, p. 211; Ellis, p. 187; Sadleir, 1378; Wolff, 4015 ; OCLC. LOCATION L, NUC.

COMMENTARY First serialized in the *Dublin University Magazine* (May–Dec. 1868). Mystery novel [W.E. Hall, p. 194; Wilson, p. 321].

L112   *A lost name* (by J. Sheridan Le Fanu).

+ London: Richard Bentley, 1868, 3 vols. SOURCE Rafroidi, ii, p. 211; Ellis, p. 187; Sadleir, 1381; Wolff, 4018; OCLC. LOCATION Grail, D, NUC.

New York: Harper & Bros, [1868?]. SOURCE NYPL. LOCATION L, NN.

COMMENTARY Suspense novel, first serialized in *Temple Bar* (London), a rewritten and expanded version of the story, 'The evil guest'. Concerns the struggle of Mark Shadwell, the owner of Raby Hall, against despair after murdering his first cousin. He has an affair with his daughter's French governess and becomes estranged from his wife. At the end of the tale he commits suicide [CM; Wilson, p. 321].

L113   *The Wyvern mystery* (by J.S. Le Fanu; dedicated to Judge [William Nicholas] Keogh).
+ London: Tinsley Bros, 1869, 3 vols. SOURCE Rafroidi, ii, p. 211; Ellis, p. 187; Sadleir, 1390; Wolff, 4029; OCLC. LOCATION Grail, D, L, NUC.
London: Ward & Downey, [1891] (new edn). SOURCE Topp 8, 119; OCLC. LOCATION D, Dt, MH.
COMMENTARY First serialized in the *Dublin University Magazine* (Feb.–Nov. 1869) Mystery novel [W.E. Hall, p. 194; Wilson, p. 321].

L114   *Checkmate* (by Joseph Sheridan Le Fanu; dedicated to the Rt Hon. John Ball, MP).
+ London: Hurst & Blackett, 1871, 3 vols. SOURCE Rafroidi, ii, p. 211; Ellis, p. 187; Sadleir, 1371; Wolff, 4008; Sadleir, 3160 (Chapman & Hall, n.d. edn); Topp 8, 215. LOCATION Grail, D, L, NUC.
Philadelphia: Evans, Stoddart & Co., 1871 (ill.). LOCATION NUC.
New York: R.M. DeWitt, [1873?]. LOCATION NUC.
+ Chichester: Sutton, 1997 (introd. by Jessica de Mellow). LOCATION InND Loeber coll.
COMMENTARY Serialized in the *Cornhill Magazine* (London, Sept. 1870 – Mar. 1871) and the *Sunday Mercury* (New York, beginning Jan. 1871). A mystery to which the key is the changed facial features of a murderer. He tries to ingratiate himself into the family of the murdered person, but when this does not work he sets out to destroy them. He is unmasked with the help of the surgeon who had operated on his face [ML; Topp 4, p. 144; Topp 8, 215].

L115   *Chronicles of Golden Friars* (by J.S. Le Fanu; dedicated to Lady Fanny Cole).
+ London: Richard Bentley & Son, 1871, 3 vols. SOURCE Rafroidi, ii, p. 211; Ellis, p. 188; Sadleir, 1372; Wolff, 4009 ; OCLC. LOCATION Grail, L, NUC.
+ New York: Arno Press, 1976, 3 vols. (introd. by Devendra P. Varma). LOCATION InND Loeber coll.
COMMENTARY Three ghost stories which, according to the introduction, were recounted twenty years previously in the 'George and Dragon' inn in Golden Friars – hence the title of the collection. Contents: 'A strange adventure in the life of Miss Laura Mildmay', 'The haunted baronet', 'The bird of passage' [RL].

L116   *The rose and the key* (by Joseph Sheridan Le Fanu; dedicated to Thomas E. Beatty, MD).
London: Chapman & Hall, 1871, 3 vols. SOURCE Rafroidi, ii, p. 211; Ellis, p. 187; Sadleir, 1384; Wolff, 4023; OCLC. LOCATION Grail (n.d. edn), Dt ([1898] Downey edn), L, NUC.
+ New York: Dover Publications, 1982. LOCATION InND Loeber coll.
COMMENTARY First published in *All the Year Round* (London, 1871). Set at a country house, Roydon Hall, it tells the story of Maud Vernon, a young girl with a domineering mother, and how she keeps her sanity while vainly craving her mother's love [RL].

L117   *In a glass darkly* (by J. Sheridan Le Fanu; dedicated to Brinsley Homan).
+ London: Richard Bentley & Son, 1872, 3 vols. SOURCE Rafroidi, ii, p. 211; Ellis, p. 188; Sadleir, 1380; Wolff, 4017 ; OCLC. LOCATION Grail, D, L, NUC.
+ London: Richard Bentley & Son, 1886 (new edn). LOCATION DPL.
COMMENTARY Three ghost stories and one vampire story: 'Green tea', 'The familiar' (formerly published in *Ghost stories*, London, 1851, as 'The watcher'), 'Mr. Justice Harbottle', 'The room in the dragon volant', 'Carmilla' (a vampire story, first serialized in *Dark Blue*, London, Dec. 1871–Mar. 1872) [ML; Field Day, iv, pp 1100–1; Sutherland, p. 107].

L118   *The black lady of Duna; or, the renegade's doom* (by J.S. Le Fanu).
New York: Ornum & Co., [1872?] (Ornum's 15 Cent Romances, No. 9). SOURCE
RLIN; Dime novels; OCLC. LOCATION NYU.

COMMENTARY 99pp. Not documented in any bibliography of JTSLF's writings, therefore this
work may be spurious. The story is set on the island of Duna and in Vienna and tells of the
English duke of Wharton's intrigue against Spain. Note that JTSLF's *The Cock and Anchor*
(Dublin, 1845) is set in Ireland during the viceroyship of the earl of Wharton [Dime novels;
RL].

L119   *Willing to die* (by J. Sheridan Le Fanu).
London: Hurst & Blackett, 1873, 3 vols. SOURCE Rafroidi, ii, p. 211; Ellis, p. 189;
Sadleir, 1388; Wolff, 4027; OCLC. LOCATION Grail, L, NUC.

COMMENTARY First published in *All the Year Round* (London, 1872–73), and published posthumously in the next year. It is a sequel to *The tenants of Malory* (London, 1867). Set first in a
country house in Wales, then in London, it tells about a girl's illusions and her gradual disillusionment [RL; IBL].

L120   *The Purcell papers* (by the late Joseph Sheridan Le Fanu, with a memoir by Alfred
Perceval Graves).
+ London: Richard Bentley & Son, 1880, 3 vols. SOURCE Brown, 907; Ellis, p. 189;
Sadleir, 1383; Wolff, 4022. LOCATION Grail, D (2 of 3 vols.), DPL (2 of 3 vols.), L,
NUC.
+ Sauk City (WI): Arkham House, 1975 (introd., August Derleth, no memoir). SOURCE
Rafroidi, ii, p. 211. LOCATION InND Loeber coll., NUC.
New York: Garland, 1979, 3 vols. (introd. by R.L. Wolff). SOURCE COPAC. LOCATION
Dt.

COMMENTARY Published posthumously. Carter records four binding types of the London edn:
(a) smooth blue-black cloth; (b) smooth very dark green cloth; (c) smooth scarlet cloth; (d)
maroon coarse morocco cloth. In addition, O'Hegarty records one additional binding type.
Published seven years after the author's death, but contains some of his earliest fiction. Contents:
'The ghost and the bone-setter' (an exercise in pseudo-Gothic comedy), 'The fortunes of Sir
Robert Ardagh' (features the doomed master of the Great House, and allusions to supernatural
intrusions), ' Castle Connor' (a young heir, returning form the Continent is challenged to a duel
by a stranger named Fitzgerald, perhaps modelled on the notorious murderer-duellist, George
Robert 'Fighting' Fitzgerald). He is wounded, and though believing that he will live, he dies.
A poem entitled *Castle Connor* was published anonymously in London in 1865), 'The drunkard's dream', 'Passage in the secret history of an Irish countess', 'The bridal of Carrigvarah'
(based on a murder case of 1819 in Limerick, in which Lt. Scanlan had ordered the death of
Ellen Hanley), 'Strange event in the life of Schalken the painter', 'Scraps of Hibernian ballads',
'Jim Sullivan's adventures in the great snow', 'A chapter in the history of a Tyrone family', 'An
adventure of Hardress Fitzgerald, a royalist captain', 'The quare gander', 'Billy Malowney's taste
of love and glory' [Ellis; McCormack, p. 73–75; Carter, p. 130; P.S. O'Hegarty, 'Notes and comment ...' *The Bibliographical Society of Ireland*, 6(4) (1954), p. 61; Wolff introd., p. 31].

L121   *The watcher and other weird stories* (by J. Sheridan Le Fanu).
+ London: Downey & Co., [1894] (ill. Brinsley Le Fanu). SOURCE Ellis, p. 189; Sadleir,
1387; Wolff, 4026. LOCATION Grail, DPF, D, L, NUC.
New York: Arno Press, 1977. SOURCE OCLC. LOCATION CtY.

COMMENTARY Most of the following stories were first published in *Ghost stories* (London, 1851)
and *The Purcell papers* (London, 1880, 3 vols.). Contents: 'The watcher', 'Passage in the secret
history of an Irish countess', 'Strange event in the life of Schalken the painter', 'The fortunes
of Sir Robert Ardagh', 'The dream', 'A chapter in the history of a Tyrone family' [RL].

L122   *A chronicle of golden friars, and other stories* (by J. Sheridan Le Fanu).
+ London: Downey & Co., 1896 (ill. Brinsley Le Fanu, John F. O'Hea). SOURCE
Brown, 908; Ellis, p. 190; Sadleir, 1372; Wolff, 4009a. LOCATION Grail, D, NUC.
COMMENTARY Most of the following stories were first published in *A chronicle of golden friars*
(London, 1871, 3 vols.) and *The Purcell papers* (London, 1880, 3 vols.). Contents: 'A chroni-
cle of golden friars', 'Jim Sullivan's adventures in the great snow', 'The last heir of Castle
Connor', 'Billy Malowney's taste of love and glory', 'The ghost and the bone-cutter', 'The
quare gander' [Ellis].

L123   *A stable for nightmares* (by J. Sheridan Le Fanu [and others]).
+ New York: New Amsterdam Book Co., 1896 (ill. A. Burnham Shute). SOURCE
COPAC. LOCATION NUC, InND Loeber coll.
COMMENTARY Series of unsigned stories, some of which are by Sir Charles Young and other
writers. Contents: 'Dickson the devil', 'The debt of honour. A ghost story', 'Devereux's dream',
'Catherine's quest', 'Haunted', 'Pichon & Sons, of the croix rousse', 'The phantom fourth',
'The spirit's whisper', 'Dr. Feversham's story', 'The secret of the two plaster casts', 'What
was it?' [RL].

L124   *Madam Crowl's ghost, and other tales of mystery* (by Joseph Sheridan Le Fanu).
+ London: G. Bell & Sons, 1923 (collected and ed. by M.R. James). SOURCE Rafroidi,
ii, p. 211; Ellis, p. 191; Hogan, p. 371; Wolff, 4019; OCLC. LOCATION Grail, D, Dt,
DPL, L, NUC, InND Loeber coll.
COMMENTARY Contents: 'Madam Crowl's ghost' (first published in *All the Year Round*,
London, 1870–71, and later incorporated in *Chronicles of golden friars* (London, 1871)), 'Squire
Toby's will. A ghost story' (first published in *Temple Bar*, 1868), 'Dickon the devil' (first published in the *London Society*, Christmas, 1872), 'The child that went with the fairies' (first
published in *All the Year Round*, London, 1869–70), 'The white cat of Drumgunniol' (first
published in *All the Year Round*, London, 1869–70), 'An account of some strange disturbances
in a house in Aungier Street' [Dublin] (first published in the *Dublin University Magazine*,
1853), 'Ghost stories of Chapelizod' (first published in the *Dublin University Magazine*, 1851),
'Wicked Captain Walshawe, of Wauling' (first published in the *Dublin University Magazine*,
1869), 'Sir Dominick's bargain: a legend of Dunoran' (set in the (fictitious) village of Murroe
in Le Fanu's father's parish and the park of Cappercullen; first published in *All the Year
Round*, London, 1872), 'Ultor De Lacy' (first published in the *Dublin University Magazine*,
1861), 'The vision of Tom Chuff' (first published in *All the Year Round*, London, 1870),
'Stories of Lough Guir' (first published in *All the Year Round*, London, 1869–70) [Ellis; T.P.
Le Fanu, *Memoir of the Le Fanu family* (n.p., n.d.), pp 55–6].

L125   *No escape* (by Joseph Sheridan Le Fanu).
[Waterford]: Carthage Press, 1942. SOURCE COPAC. LOCATION O, NUC.
COMMENTARY Originally published as 'The watcher' in *Ghost stories and tales of mys-
tery* (Dublin, 1851) [COPAC].

L126   *Green tea and other ghost stories* (by J. Sheridan Le Fanu).
Sauk City (WI): Arkham House, 1945. SOURCE OCLC. LOCATION NN.
New York: Dover; London: Constable, 1993. LOCATION L.

L127   *Best ghost stories of J.S. Le Fanu* (ed. by E.F. Bleiler).
+ New York: Dover; London: Constable & Co., 1964. SOURCE Wilson, p. 320.
LOCATION L.
COMMENTARY Contents: 'Squire Toby's will' (first published in *Temple Bar*, 1868), 'Schalken
the painter', 'Madam Crowl's ghost' (first published in *All the Year Round*, London, 1870–71,
and later incorporated in *Chronicles of golden friars* (London, 1871)), 'The haunted baronet',
'Green tea', 'The familiar' (formerly published in *Ghost stories*, London, 1851, as 'The

watcher'), 'Mr. Justice Harbottle', 'Carmilla' (first serialized in *Dark Blue*, London, Dec. 1871–Mar. 1872), 'The fortunes of Sir Robert Ardagh', 'An account of some strange disturbances in Aungier street' (first published in the *Dublin University Magazine*, 1853), 'The dead sexton', 'Ghost stories of the tiled house', 'The white cat of Drumgunniol' (first published in *All the Year Round*, London, 1869–70), 'Sir Dominick's bargain' (first published in *All the Year Round*, London, 1872), 'Ultor de Lacy' [ML].

L128　*Ghost stories and mysteries* (by J.S. Le Fanu; selected and ed. by E.F. Bleiler). New York: Dover; London: Constable & Co., 1964. SOURCE Wilson, p. 320; OCLC. LOCATION L.

+ New York, Dover Publications, 1975. LOCATION InND Loeber coll.

COMMENTARY Contents: 'The room in the dragon volant', 'Laura silver bell', ' Wicked Captain Walshawe, of Wauling' (first published in the *Dublin University Magazine*, 1869), 'Ghost stories of Chapelizod' (first published in the *Dublin University Magazine*, 1851), 'The child that went with the fairies' (first published in *All the Year Round*, London, 1869–70), 'Stories of Lough Guir' (first published in *All the Year Round*, London, 1869–70), 'The vision of Tom Chuff' (first published in *All the Year Round*, London, 1870), 'The drunkard's dream', 'The ghost and the bone-setter', 'A chapter in the history of a Tyrone family', 'The murdered cousin', 'The evil guest', 'The mysterious lodger' [RL].

L129　*The hours after midnight ... Tales of terror and the supernatural* (by J. Sheridan Le Fanu; ed. by Des Hicky).

+ London: Leslie Frewin, 1975 (ill. Geoffrey Bourne-Taylor). SOURCE COPAC. LOCATION D, L.

COMMENTARY Republication of stories published earlier. Contents: 'The fortunes of Sir Robert Ardagh', 'Schalken the painter', 'A ghost story', 'A haunted house', 'My uncle Watson', 'Madam Crowl's ghost' (first published in *All the Year Round*, London, 1870–71, and later incorporated in *Chronicles of golden friars* (London, 1871)), 'The legend of Dunblane', 'Green tea', 'Dickon the devil' [ML].

L130　*Borrhomeo the astrologer: A monkish tale* (by J. Sheridan Le Fanu; introd. by W.J. McCormack). Edinburgh: Tragara Press, 1985 (limited edn of 150 copies). SOURCE Wilson, p. 320; OCLC. LOCATION L.

COMMENTARY 35pp. First published anonymously in the *Dublin University Magazine* (Jan. 1862) [BLC; Rowan cat. 62/266].

L131　*The illustrated J.S. Le Fanu. Ghost stories and mysteries by a master Victorian storyteller* (selected and introd. by Michael Cox).

+ Wellingborough, Northants: Equation, 1988. LOCATION NjP.

COMMENTARY Republication of stories published earlier. Contents: 'Schalken the painter', 'The familiar' (formerly published in *Ghost stories*, London, 1851, as 'The watcher'), 'The murdered cousin', 'An account of some strange disturbances in Aungier Street' (first published in the *Dublin University Magazine*, 1853), 'Ghost stories of the tiled house', 'Wicked Captain Walshawe, of Wauling' (first published in the *Dublin University Magazine*, 1869), 'Squire Toby's will' (first published in *Temple Bar*, 1868), 'Green tea', 'Madam Crowl's ghost' (first published in *All the Year Round*, London, 1870–71, and later incorporated in *Chronicles of golden friars* (London, 1871)), 'Mr. Justice Harbottle', 'The room in the dragon volant' [ML].

— COLLECTED WORKS

L132　[*Collected works of Joseph Sheridan Le Fanu*]. London: Downey & Co., [*c*.1894–95] (prefatory note and ill. Brinsley Le Fanu) 13 vols. SOURCE Ellis, p. 184; Sadlier, 1373c (one vol.); Wolff, 4010b (one vol.). LOCATION D (one vol.), L, InND Loeber coll. (three vols.).

COMMENTARY Unnumbered and untitled series, published posthumously. Volumes are listed in advertisements in *Wilder's hand* (London, [*c*.1894–95]), which lists 12 volumes only. Includes *The evil guest* as a separate volume [RL].

L133　*The collected works of Joseph Sheridan Le Fanu* (ed. by Sir Devendra P. Varma). New York: Arno Press, 1977, 21 vols. SOURCE Rafroidi, ii, p. 211; OCLC; NCBEL. LOCATION CtY.

LE FANU, Susanna (née Bennett), probable pseud. 'Marion Leigh', b. *c*.1823, d. Dublin 1858, A probable novelist, SLF was the third youngest child of a barrister on the Munster circuit, George Bennett, QC, of Dublin, a member of the Bennett family of The Grange, Clareen (Co. Offaly). Her sister married Delves Broughton, and was the mother of the English author Rhoda Broughton. Susanna married the author Joseph Thomas Sheridan Le Fanu§ in 1843, by whom she had two sons and two daughters. The couple lived initially in Warrington Place and then moved to 18 Merrion Square, Dublin, the family home of the Bennetts, where they continued to live under straitened financial circumstances. She fell ill in 1851 and her health remained precarious until her death in 1858. She was buried at Mount Jerome cemetery, Dublin. SLF's portrait was published by McCormack. SOURCE Field Day, i, p. 842, ii, p. 841; McCormack, pp. 288, Plate 4, and passim.

L134　*My own story* (by 'Marion Leigh').
　　+ New York: G.P. Putnam; Hurd & Houghton, 1865. SOURCE McCormack, p. 288. LOCATION L.
COMMENTARY Cautiously attributed by McCormack on the basis of a comparison between the text that first was serialized in the *Dublin University Magazine* (Sept. 1868–May 1869) under the titles 'Loved and lost' and 'My own story; or loved and lost'. Set in England near the town of 'Highbury' with characters from the middle classes. SOURCE McCormack, pp 280–9.

LEFURT, Annie B., fl. 1874. Romantic novelist.
L135　*Sweet, not lasting. A novel* (by Annie B. Lefurt).
　　London: Sampson Low, Marston, Low, & Searle, 1874. SOURCE Allibone Suppl., ii, p. 991; Brown 2, 790; COPAC. LOCATION L.
COMMENTARY An Irish story of a fatal flirtation. Nellie, whose heart is broken by the conduct of a young doctor, returns to a convent and dies a Sister of Mercy [Brown 2].

LEICESTER, Caroline, fl. 1840s. A writer of poetry and religious works for children whose earliest works were first published in Dublin, indicating a possible Irish connection. SOURCE BLC; NCBEL 4, p. 1822; RL.
L136　*History of Betsy, or the orphan. A tale* (by Caroline Leicester).
　　Dublin: P. Dixon Hardy & Sons [for the Religious Book and Tract Depository for Ireland], [1846 or earlier]. SOURCE Adv. in [anon.], *The history of Susan Blake. A true story* (Dublin, 1846).
COMMENTARY No copy of Dublin edn located [RL].
L137　*Susan and her doll. A tale founded on fact* (by Caroline Leicester).
　　Dublin: P. Dixon Hardy & Sons [for the Religious Book and Tract Depository for Ireland], [1846 or earlier]. SOURCE Adv. in [anon.], *The history of Susan Blake. A true story* (Dublin, 1846).
　　London: James Hogg & Son, 1859. SOURCE OCLC. LOCATION L ([1861] edn), CLU.
L138　*Little Arthur Lee. A short but true story for little boys and girls, in words of one and two syllables* (by Caroline Leicester).

Dublin: P. Dixon Hardy & Sons [for the Religious Book and Tract Depository for Ireland], [1846 or earlier]. SOURCE Adv. in [anon.], *The history of Susan Blake. A true story* (Dublin, 1846).
COMMENTARY No copy located [RL].

L139   *Fanny and her mamma, containing a series of interesting and useful conversations on various subjects* (by Caroline Leicester).
Dublin: P. Dixon Hardy & Sons, 1848. SOURCE Alston, p. 252. LOCATION L.
COMMENTARY *Dublin edn* The publisher Hardy used an emblem on the title page consisting of a map of Ireland with his initials superimposed [RL].
London: Grant & Griffith, 1848 (as *Fanny and her mamma; or, easy reading lessons: in which it is attempted to bring scriptural principles into daily practice: with hints for nursery discipline*). LOCATION L.
Philadelphia: American Sunday School Union, 1849 (as *Fanny and her mamma*). SOURCE OCLC. LOCATION ICU.
Philadelphia: G.S. Appleton, 1861 (as *Fanny and her mamma: or, easy reading lessons, in which it is attempted to bring scriptural principles into daily practice. With hints for nursery discipline*). SOURCE OCLC. LOCATION Univ. of Chicago.

'LEIGH, Marion', probable pseud. See LE FANU, Susanna.

'LE JEMLYS', pseud. See JELLY, Symes M.

LELAND, Thomas, b. Dublin 1722, d. Dublin 1785. Church of Ireland clergyman, historian and novelist, TL was the son of John Leland and was educated at Thomas Sheridan's school in Dublin. He graduated with a BA at TCD in 1742, MA in 1745, was elected a fellow in 1846, and received a BD in 1752 and a DD in 1757. He was appointed professor of oratory and history (1761–62) and oratory alone (1762–81). In 1868 he was appointed chaplain to the lord lieutenant, Viscount Townshend. Through Townshend he became vicar of Bray from 1768 to 1773 and prebendary of Rathmichael (Co. Dublin) in St Patrick's Cathedral, Dublin. In 1768 he started writing his *History of Ireland* (London, 1773, 3 vols.), the same year as he became vicar of St Anne's, Dublin. The history was not well received when it was finally published. In 1781 he resigned his academic fellowship and went to live at Ardstraw (Co. Tyrone) where he was rector until his death in 1785. His translation of the *Orations of Demosthenes against Philip* (Dublin, 1754–70, 3 vols.) provided a model for the Anglo-Irish tradition of parliamentary speaking, practiced by Edmund Burke, Henry Grattan and John Philpot Curran. TL's main publications were on classical scholarship, and from these it appears he was well connected. Among his friends was Edmund Burke, he often visited Lord Charlemont at the Casino in Marino, and his *The history of the life and reign of Philip, King of Macedon* (London, 1758) was underwritten by a large number of prominent Irish subscribers. His only attributed novel, *Longsword* (London, 1762, 2 vols.), was dramatized by Hall Hartson, a student at TCD, and was first performed as *The Countess of Salisbury* in Dublin and London in 1765 and 1767, respectively. TL is said to have married, but his wife's name and a record of the marriage are not known. He was buried at St Anne's Church, Dublin. For his portraits and papers, see ODNB. SOURCE Allibone, i, p. 1083; B & S, p. 494; Elmes, p. 115; Field Day, i, pp 944, 1291; R.D. Hume's introd to the 1974 edn of *Longsword*, pp xxvi–xxvii; H. Farrar, *Irish marriages* (London, 1897), ii, p. 522; Leslie & Wallace, p. 821; OCIL, pp 306–7; ODNB; W. O'Sullivan, 'Irish manuscripts', *Celtica*, 11 (1976), pp 233–4; RIA/DIB; Summers, p. 162.

L140   *Longsword, Earl of Salisbury. An historical romance* [anon.].

+ Dublin: G. Faulkner, 1762, 2 vols. SOURCE Raven, 729; ESTC t11902. LOCATION Dt (2 vols. in 1), L, NUC.

London: W. Johnston, 1762, 2 vols. SOURCE Raven, 728; Forster, 1586; Gecker, 614; McBurney & Taylor, 541; ESTC n2902. LOCATION DCL, UP, IU, NUC.

London: T. Evans, 1775, 2 vols. (new edn). SOURCE ESTC t129467. LOCATION Di, L, Johns Hopkins Univ.

New York: Arno Press, 1974, 2 vols. (foreword by P. Varma; introd. by Robert D. Hume). SOURCE COPAC. LOCATION E.

COMMENTARY A landmark novel as the first 'English' – but also Irish – historical novel with Gothic overtones, which appeared three years prior to Walpole's *Castle of Otranto* (London, 1765). The story is based on the life of William de Longspée, 3rd earl of Salisbury, and illegitimate son of Henry II. The tale is set in 1225 and 1226, and describes the struggles of Longsword to return home safely at the end of a war in France. The second part of the book describes how his wife resisted all pressures to remarry after her husband was reported dead. In the end husband, wife, and son are reunited. The story features the villainy of the odious monk, Reginhald [ML; Frank, 243; Summers, pp 158, 162; Tracy, 95].

LESLIE, —, fl. 1768. Attributed to a member of the Irish branch of the Leslie family. SOURCE Falkner Grierson cat. 23/579.

L141 *The unexpected wedding, in a series of letters* [anon.].

+ London: T. Becket & P.A. De Hondt, 1768. SOURCE Raven, 1197; ESTC t057459. LOCATION L. Dublin: H. Saunderson, W. Sleater, D. Chamberlaine, J. Potts, J. Williams & W. Colles, 1768. SOURCE Falkner Grierson cat. 23/579; Raven 1198; ESTC n035408. LOCATION Indiana Univ., Bloomington (IN).

COMMENTARY Epistolary novel with an unusually complicated plot. Set in England, no Irish content [Falkner Grierson cat. 23/579; ML].

LESLIE, Eliza (née Hutchinson), fl. 1830s. A hymn and tract writer who probably can be identified with Elizabeth Leslie, the daughter of a Church of Ireland clergyman, Revd Francis Hutchinson and Mary Angelica De la Cherois Crommelin, of Lisburn. EL married at the Abbey Church, Bath in 1816, George Leslie, son of the Revd Edmund Leslie, archdeacon of Down. EL was the author of *Sacred and moral songs* (Dublin, 1839). Not be confused with the American author on domestic science with the same name (1787–1858). SOURCE COPAC; Leslie, *Down*, p. 105; O'Donoghue, p. 250; RL.

L142 *Susan Smith, the ferry-man's daughter. A true narrative* (by Eliza Leslie).

+ London: B. Wertheim, J.L. Porter, [1830s?] (ill.; see Plate 43). LOCATION InND Loeber coll.

COMMENTARY 32 pp. Religious fiction set in Dublin where Susan Smith's father is a ferryman on the river Liffey until his livelihood is taken away by the building of a bridge. Susan attends a school set up by a Protestant lady. (The author states her opinion that much harm can be done by children of the lower classes receiving too much education.) At home, she meets her brother's friend, who is a sailor. She marries him against her parents' wishes and has three children in rapid succession. She tries to provide for her children but falls ill. She is often visited by a lady with whom she talks about religious topics. After she dies, her children are provided for by the Protestant Orphan Society [ML].

LESLIE, Mary, pseud. 'James Thomas Jones', b. Wellington County, Ontario (Canada) 1842 (Toronto according to CEWW), d. 1920. Canadian novelist and poet, ML was the daughter John Leslie, an engraver and architect, and Elizabeth Griffin. ML was educated by private tutors and by her father. She travelled to Paris and Antwerp to study art and, upon her return, taught drawing. She lived in Guelph (Ontario). ML mysteriously ends the preface of her *The Cromaboo mail carrier* by encouraging the reader to 'renew his acquaintance in a new occupation – as "The Gibbeline Flower Seller"' She continued to write serials, as for example in the *Clifford Arrow* (1891). She adhered to the Anglican religion and remained single. The Mary Leslie Papers are in the Archives of Ontario. SOURCE CEWW; index CaOONL; RL; Watters, p. 328.

L143   *The Cromaboo mail carrier. A Canadian love story* (by 'James Thomas Jones').

Guelph [Ontario, Canada]: Jos. H. Hacking, 1878. LOCATION CaOONL, NUC, InND.

COMMENTARY Very rare novel, because the book, creating an outcry, was withdrawn after a few days. A murder story, written about the village of Erin (Drumbo?), near Guelph, but in this volume it is given the name of Cromaboo, 'the most blackguarded village in Canada, and ... settled by the lowest class of Irish, Highland Scotch and Dutch', in which there are many illegitimate children. The central event is the detailed account of the impregnation of 15-year-old Mary Smith by a philandering visitor. Mary is neither martyred nor punished; she makes the best of her lot by marrying a widower and enduring the normal hardships of rural family life. The son's delinquent father returns and is reconciled with the child, but the father does not marry the mother [C. Gerson, *A purer taste. The writing and reading of fiction in English in nineteenth-century Canada* (Toronto, 1989), pp 145–6, 195; Rhodenizer, p. 717; Personal communication, Debra Deerlove, June 2004].

LESTER, Edward, fl. 1886. A political satirist who is also credited with writing two religious books. Perhaps can be identified with Edward Augustus Lester, born in Armagh, the son of George Lester. EAL was admitted to TCD in 1860, where he obtained his BA in 1864 and MA in 1868. SOURCE B & S, Appendix B, p. 71; Brown, p. 167.

L144   *The siege of Bodike: a prophesy of Ireland's future* (by Edward Lester).

+ Manchester: Heywood & Co., 1886. SOURCE Allibone Suppl., ii, p. 997 (mentions as title *The siege of Bodike: a tale of Home Rule and the great Irish rebellion of 1890: a prophecy of Ireland's future*, but this has not been located); Brown, 915. LOCATION L, NUC.

COMMENTARY A political satire in which the author tells how he would deal with the Irish question. Set in the 1880s, a Fenian rebellion is described in which Kilkenny falls into the hands of the Fenians and a bomb is dropped from a balloon on Bodike, a village in Co. Kilkenny [Brown].

LEVER, Charles James (best known as **Charles Lever**), pseuds '**Cornelius O'Dowd**', '**Harry Lorrequer**', and '**Tilbury Tramp**', b. Dublin 1806, d. Trieste (Italy) 1872. A popular and prolific novelist, song writer and editor, CJL was the son of James Lever, a building contractor from Lancashire living in Dublin, and Jane Chandler, who was of an Anglo-Irish family from Kilkenny (a brother, John, later became rector at Tullamore, Co. Offaly). Admitted to TCD in 1822, he obtained a BA in 1827. As a schoolboy and undergraduate he was renowned for his jests and irrepressible wit. In 1828 he made a tour through Germany and studied medicine at Göttingen (his diary of that period is in the RIA, MS SR.3.B.52). He returned to Dublin where he continued his medical studies desultorily and received his MB at TCD in 1831. He failed the examination of the Royal College of Surgeons and never took the MD. However, in 1832 as a dispensary doctor in Kilrush (Co. Clare) he helped out heroically during a cholera epidemic, the experience of which he used as background for his novel *St. Patrick's eve* (London, 1845). In 1829 he went to Canada and the US where he travelled to the frontier and passed some time among the settlers and native Americans, from whom he had to escape with the help of an Indian named Tahata. CJL married at Navan in 1832 Catherine Baker, his childhood sweetheart, who later contributed short fiction to the *Dublin University Magazine*. His father's death in 1833 set him up with a small legacy. At his next medical post at Portstewart (Co. Derry), he fell out with his superiors but met William Hamilton Maxwell§, who encouraged him to write and whose *Wild sports of the West* (London, 1832, 2 vols.) inspired the jaunty, comic tone of Lever's early military novels. However, losses at cards and an absence of economy soon pushed him into writing to support his family. He had contributed to the *Dublin Literary Gazette* (Dublin, 1830), and he published a short story in the *Irish Monthly Magazine of Politics and Literature* (Dublin, 1834). In 1837 he had his first big success with the first instalment in the *Dublin University Magazine* of *The confessions of Harry Lorrequer*, the rollicking adventures of an English officer in Ireland and abroad. He moved to Brussels in 1840 for a few years when invited to be the physician to the British Embassy there, while continuing to practice medicine and to publish his stories. These were so successful that he was invited to return to Dublin to edit the *Dublin University Magazine*, which he did from 1842 to 1845, while contributing much fiction to it in the form of serialized novels and short stories. His income from writing increased, allowing him to set up an elaborate household at Templeogue House (Co. Dublin). But the politics of editorship embroiled him in controversies with contributors (e.g. Samuel Carter Hall, the husband of Mrs. S.C. Hall§, and Edward Kenealy§) and kept him from the first-hand observation of events that fuelled his writing. In addition, in the pages of the rival nationalist periodical, the *Nation* (Dublin), a long article in 1843 excoriated CJL's portrayals of the Irish in fiction as stage-Irish buffoons. While acknowledging his popularity and the many comparisons of him to Charles Dickens, the magazine also pointed out what was considered evidence of plagiarism from William Hamilton Maxwell§ and other contemporary novelists. CJL eventually resigned from the *Dublin University Magazine* in 1845, and after discussions with William Thackeray§, he decided to leave Ireland. Among his best friends were Samuel Lover§, the English illustrator Hablot Brown (known as Phiz), who illustrated many of CJL's stories and who visited him in Ireland on several occasions, and Revd Samuel O'Sullivan§. After some time back in Brussels, and travelling for several years around the Continent, he and his family eventually settled at La Spezia, Italy, where he was appointed vice-consul in 1858, an arrangement that allowed him ample time for writing. He was promoted to consul at Trieste in 1867 and in conferring on Lever what was in effect a sinecure, Lord Derby declared, 'Here is £600 a year to do nothing, and you are just the man to do it' (ODNB). CJL was unhappy there but continued to write almost up to his death from heart failure. He was characterized politically in 1843 as a conservative who energetically defended the superiority of the English in Ireland. But in his novels of the 1840s he sympathetically depicted the plight of the poor peasantry and urged social responsibility and land reform on the part of landlords to quell agrarian unrest. He remained faithful to Irish publishers, despite more lucrative offers, and refused the editorship of the London *Bentley's Miscellany* because it would have meant leaving Dublin at the time. He visited Ireland after the death of his wife in 1870, and in the following year TCD awarded him an LLD by diploma. William Curry, Jnr, in Dublin in 1841 and Carey and Hart in Philadelphia in 1842 advertised that *Continental gossipings* by 'Harry Lorrequer' (2 vols.) was being prepared for publication. No such book by Lever is known but instalments of this work had appeared in the *Dublin University Magazine* (1839). Planned but aborted projects include a fictitious 'The wild songs of the west, edited by Father Malachy Duggan P.P.', 'Campaigns of Hannibal, by his aide-de-camp, Terence McHale', and an anthology, 'The Irish by themselves'. A spurious serial with the title 'Major O'Connor', by 'the author of *Charles O'Malley*', published by the *Sunday Times* in New York, is noted by CJL in 1841. Lever's work was often reprinted in England and Germany. A notice by the publisher William Curry, 1 Dec. 1841, reports that Lever's work had been pirated by 'various booksellers and newspaper proprietors in the British Colonies', but these edns have not yet been identified. In his 1875 catalogue, W.B. Kelly of Grafton Street (Dublin) announced for publication 'Leveriana – reminiscences and anecdotes of some of the characters introduced in the works of Charles Lever – ready Dec., 1875', but it never appeared. The collected edn of Lever's work published by Downey (1897–99, 37 vols.) was prepared by CJL's daughter, Julia Kate Neville, and includes memoranda and bibliographical notes. Another daughter, Sydney Lever§, became a poet and is said to have written *A rent in a cloud* (London, [1865]), which was published under Charles Lever's name. Two of Lever's plays were turned into novels after his death (*The happy man*, New York, 1883, and London, 1993; and, *For wife and child*, London, 1883). For his papers, see ODNB. His collection of books was auctioned on Aug 26, 1861. For his portraits, see ODNB. Strickland notes John Edward Jones's bust of CJL. The following list of CJL's works is complicated and tentative because of the complex publishing history of his works. SOURCE Allibone i, p. 1088; Allibone Suppl., ii, p. 998; B & S, p. 499; T. Bareham (ed.), *Charles Lever: New evaluations* (Gerrards Cross, 1981); Boylan, p. 199; Brooke, p. 164; Clyde, pp 88, 92, 94; Elmes, p. 116; Field Day, i, pp 1175, 1255–65, 1299, ii, p.1011, iii, p. 562, 665; FitzPatrick, passim; S. Haddelsey, *Charles Lever: The lost Victorian* (Gerrards Cross, 2000), p. 23; W.E. Hall, pp 72–84, 98, 110; Hogan, pp 375–7; Hogan 2, pp 708–9; Igoe, pp 53; 148. Irish pseudonyms; 'Harry Lorrequer', *Charles O'Malley, the Irish dragoon* (Dublin, 1841), ii, p. 335; LVP, p. 280; B.B. Lester, *Phiz. The man who drew Dickens* (London, 2004), pp 108–27; McKenna, pp 230–5; List of catalogues, p. 296; NCBEL 4, pp 1325–6; NUC; J.J. Prévost, *Un tour en Irlande* (Paris, 1846), p. 47; McCormack, p. 277, n. 2; OCIL, p. 309; ODNB; O'Donoghue, p. 251; Rafroidi, ii, pp 212–17; RIA/DIB; RL; Schulz, p. 280; Strickland, i, p. 559; Sutherland, pp 372–4; Wolff, iii, pp 28–31 (letters).

L145   *The confessions of Harry Lorrequer, late Captain in the –th regiment of foot* [anon.] (dedicated to Sir George Hamilton).

+ Dublin: Wm. Curry Jnr & Co.; London: Wm. S. Orr & Co., 1839 (ill. Phiz). LOCATION InND Loeber coll. COMMENTARY *Dublin, London 1839 edn* Bound from the 11 parts [RL].

+ Dublin: William Curry Jnr & Co.; London: William S. Orr; Edinburgh: Fraser & Crawford, 1839 (ill. Phiz). SOURCE Rafroidi, ii, p. 213; Brown 918; Sadleir, 1398; Wolff, 4081. LOCATION Grail, D, L, NUC, InND Loeber coll. COMMENTARY *Dublin, London, Edinburgh edn* Issued in three binding types: (a) green diaper or ribbed cloth; (b) green morocco or ribbed cloth; (c) maroon bold-ribbed cloth [Carter, p. 131].

London: Chapman & Hall, 1850. SOURCE Topp 3, p. 306; Sadleir, 3611 (1862 edn). LOCATION D (1857 edn).

+ London, New York: George Routledge & Sons, n.d. (as *The confessions of Harry Lorrequer*, ill. paper cover). LOCATION InND Loeber coll.

+ London, New York: Frederick Warne & Co., n.d. (as *Harry Lorrequer*; Crown Library). LOCATION InND Loeber coll.

+ Leipzig: B. Tauchnitz Jnr, 1847, 2 vols. in 1 (new edn, corrected by the author for continental circulation; as *The confessions of Harry Lorrequer*). SOURCE T & B, 138. LOCATION L, NUC, InND Loeber coll.

Paris: Hachette, 1859, 2 vols. (trans. by Aristide Baudéan as *Aventures d'Harry Lorrequer*; Bibliothèque des Meilleurs Romans Étrangers). SOURCE Rafroidi, ii, p. 36 (1858 edn not found); Bn-Opale plus. LOCATION BNF.

Paris: Hachette, 1861 (trans. by Aristide Baudéan as *L'Homme du jour*). SOURCE Rafroidi, ii, p. 365; Bn-Opale plus. LOCATION BNF.

+ Philadelphia: Carey & Hart, 1840 (as *The confessions of Harry Lorrequer*; ill. Phiz).

SOURCE NYPL (1840, 2nd edn). LOCATION NUC, NN (1840, 2nd edn), InND Loeber coll. (also 1842 edn).
+ Chicago: M.A. Donohue & Co., n.d. (The Modern Authors' Library, No. 289; ill. paper cover W.B.B.; see Plate 44). LOCATION InND Loeber coll.
COMMENTARY Highly popular novel, originally published as a serial in the *Dublin University Magazine* (1837–42), extending past the publication date of the book. Subsequently it was rewritten and serialized in monthly parts. The book was first issued in 11 parts in Dublin by William Curry Jnr. It features the adventures of an English officer posted with his regiment in Ireland and is set in Napoleonic times. An opening episode, in which Lorrequer (after a gregarious drunken night) goes on parade unconscious of his blackened face, sets the tone of the narrative. He is subsequently posted all round Ireland where he loves, duels, steeplechases, gambles, drives tandems and feasts. Lorrequer later travels to France, where he has various adventures with Arthur O'Leary (eponymous hero of another Lever novel), ending up with the latter's arrest and trial. The action winds up in Munich where, with the aid of a rich uncle, the hero finally wins the hand of an Irish love, Lady Jane Callonby. Her Irish country seat was modelled on the estate of Col. Macnamara outside of Kilrush (Co. Clare). CJL's introd. to the Leipzig edn states that a second series of this volume was planned, to be entitled 'Lorrequer married', but no such production is known. The edn was also to be issued in Philadelphia by Carey & Hart in parts in 1840, but similarly is not known to have been published. John Brougham§ is thought to be the model for Harry Lorrequer, while Lt.-Col. John Elliott Cairnes stood as model for Col. Kamworth. The character of Fr Malachy Brennan is based on Fr Malachy Duggan. FitzPatrick mentions several versions of the preface in different edns and that CJL wrote an alternative ending to this novel, but its whereabouts is not known [A. Blake, 'Writing from the outside in: Charles Lever' in N. McCaw (ed.), *Writing Irishness* (Aldershot, 2004), p. 117; FitzPatrick, pp 121, 125; W.E. Hall, p. 73; OBND; B. Rogers, 'Dr. Lever at Portstewart' in T. Bareham (ed.), *Charles Lever: New evaluations* (Gerrards Cross, 1981), p. 65; Sutherland, p. 145; RL; Rafroidi; Topp 4, p. 151; FitzPatrick, pp 78–9, 121].

L146 *Charles O'Malley, the Irish dragoon* (ed. by 'Harry Lorrequer'; dedicated to the marquess of Douro).
+ Dublin: William Curry Jnr & Co.; Edinburgh: Fraser & Crawford; London: W.S. Orr & Co., 1841, 2 vols. (ill. Phiz). SOURCE Brown, 919; Rafroidi, ii, p. 213; Sadleir, 1396; Wolff, 4079. LOCATION Grail, DPL Gilbert coll., DL, NUC, InND Loeber coll.
London: Chapman & Hall, 1850, 2 vols. SOURCE Topp 3, p. 305; Sadleir, 3611 (1862 edn). LOCATION D.
Amsterdam: L. Frijlink, 1845, 3 vols. (trans. into Dutch as *Zonderlinge lotgevallen en ontmoetingen van Charles O'Malley, den Ierschen dragonder*). SOURCE Adamnet. LOCATION UVA.
Stuttgart: Franckh'schen Buchhandlung, 1846, 4 vols. (trans. by Gottlob Fink as *Charles O'Malley, der irishe Dragoner*). SOURCE COPAC. LOCATION Dt.
Leipzig: Bernard Tauchnitz, 1848, 3 vols. SOURCE T & B, 142–4. LOCATION Dt, L, NUC.
Brussels: [publisher?], 1840, 2 vols. in 1. LOCATION NUC.
+ New York: W.L. Allison, [1841?]. LOCATION NUC, InND Loeber coll. (A.L. Burt ed., n.d.).
+ Philadelphia: Carey & Hart, 1841–2, 2 vols. (ill. Phiz). SOURCE Topp 3, p. 306. LOCATION NUC, InND Loeber coll. COMMENTARY *Philadelphia 1841–42 edn* This edn also issued in parts. SOURCE Topp 3, p. 306.
Philadelphia: J. Harding, 1848, 2 vols. in 1 (ill. Phiz). SOURCE NYPL. LOCATION NN.

COMMENTARY Initially entitled 'Charles O'Hara', it was originally published in the *Dublin University Magazine* (Mar. 1840–Dec. 1841), afterwards issued in 21 parts by William Curry Jnr & Co.; London: William S. Orr & Co.; Edinburgh: Fraser & Crawford (see Plate 45), and alleged to be partly copied from William Hamilton Maxwell's§ *My life* (London, 1835, 3 vols.), but CJL and Maxwell were friends, and CJL was clearly inspired by Maxwell's works. Two book versions existed, of which the first contained several extra sections in each volume, occasioned by a fire which engulfed the printing premises in Dublin (2 Jan. 1841), destroying the manuscript of, presumably, volume 2 of the text (vol. 1: 'L'Envoy', a poem by 'Harry Lorrequer', directed to the author G.P.R. James asking for help, and James's answer, with his outline of the second and third volumes, see volume 2: 'L'Envoie' by 'Harry Lorrequer', dated Brussels, Nov. 1841). There are at least two binding types: (a) dark green cloth with dragoon on horse blind impressed on cover, and standing dragoon on spine, impressed in gold, holding banner with the book's title; (b) leather binding impressed with dragoon on horse, identical to the dragoon on horse in (a), with additional garlands above and below. Both bindings lack the publisher's name and may not have been publisher's bindings. This novel, interspersed with songs, consists of a picaresque autobiography of a lovable Irish rogue, Charles O'Malley, who is first discovered as a 17-year-old bravo in Galway. On an electioneering mission for his uncle, Godfrey O'Malley, he becomes enamoured of the English beauty, Lucy Dashwood. Following a duel, Charles goes to Dublin to study law but eventually enlists in the dragoons. He sees action in the Peninsular War and rises to the rank of captain. Meanwhile, the O'Malley estates have fallen into bankruptcy and it seems they will be bought up by Gen. Dashwood, Lucy's father. The principals meet in Brussels, before Waterloo. A special courier, Charles is captured by the enemy and witnesses the battle by Napoleon's side. He contrives to save the life of Gen. Dashwood and the marriage with Lucy is allowed to go forward. The character 'Uncle Godfrey' O'Malley is based on the landowner Dick Martin of Ballynahinch, Connemara. Baby Blake in the story refers to the equestrian Miss French of Moneyvoe, near Castle Blakeney (Co. Galway). According to Oman, many of the characters are drawn from Irish officers depicted in William Grattan's *Adventures with the Connaught rangers* (London, 1847), but this does not agree with the publication of *Charles O'Malley, the Irish dragoon* about six years earlier. A dime song book, entitled *The Charles O'Malley Irish songster* was advertised by Dick & Fitzgerald in New York in the 1850s. A song by one of the characters in the book, the servant Micky, inspired by 'Boots' who worked at a Dublin hotel, was quoted by Major O'Gorman in the British parliament and the house roared with laughter [Field Day, i, pp 1255–65; cat. of Dick & Fitzgerald in O. Bradbury, *Ellen Grant* (New York, [185?]); Oman's preface to W. Grattan, *Adventures with the Connaught rangers* (London, 1902), p. vii; FitzPatrick, pp 129, 136, 140–2; W.E. Hall, p. 97; Howes cat. 294/215; and additional information from Miles Bartley); Mealy's cat. Nov. 2000/837; Rafroidi; RL; Sutherland, p. 117; Wolff, introd., *The Boyne Water*, pp xlii–xliii].

L147 *Our mess, Jack Hinton, the guardsman* (by Charles Lever; dedicated to Lord Eliot, Chief Secretary of State for Ireland).

+ Dublin: William Curry Jnr & Co; London: William S. Orr & Co; Edinburgh: Fraser & Co., 1843–44 (ill. Phiz). SOURCE Brown 920; Rafroidi, ii, p. 214; Sadleir, 1415; Wolff, 4098. LOCATION Grail, D, L, NUC, InND Loeber coll.

London: Chapman & Hall, 1850. SOURCE Topp 3, p. 305; Sadleir, 3611 (1857 edn). LOCATION D (1857 edn).

+ London, New York: Ward, Lock & Co., [1884] (as *Jack Hinton, the guardsman*; ill.). SOURCE Topp 2, 1763. LOCATION InND Loeber coll.

Amsterdam: C.F. Stemler, 1845, 2 vols. (trans. into Dutch as *De lotgevallen van Jack Hinton in Ierland*). SOURCE Alphabetische naamlijst 1833–49, p. 398.

Leipzig: Bernard Tauchnitz, 1849, 2 vols. SOURCE T & B, 165–66. LOCATION L.

Philadelphia: Carey & Hart, 1843 (ill. Phiz). SOURCE Topp 3, p. 305. LOCATION NYPL, NN. COMMENTARY *Philadelphia 1843 edn* This edn issued in parts [Topp 3, p. 305].

+ Philadelphia: Carey & Hart, 1844 (as *Jack Hinton, the guardsman*, ill. Phiz, J. Yeager). LOCATION InND Loeber coll.

COMMENTARY *Our mess*, and *Tom Burke of "ours"* (see below) were originally published in the *Dublin University Magazine* (Mar.–Dec. 1842), after which each was issued in 35 parts in 32 issues by William Curry Jnr & Co., Dublin (starting Jan. 1842). It was also issued in parts by Carey & Hart (Philadelphia, 1843). Jack Hinton is an ingenuous English officer in Ireland in the turbulent second decade of the century. He steeplechases, makes love and duels and meets many different Irish characters along the way. Hinton is accompanied by Corny Delaney, an Irish servant. In the course of his adventures Hinton learns something of the real Ireland. The last part of the novel takes place in Spain, France and Italy. The character of Fr Tom Loftus is based on the famous parish priest of Kilkee (Co. Clare), Father Comyns; Sir Harry Boyle is the MP Sir Boyle Roche; Beauchamp Bagenal was the prototype of Bagenal Daly [Brown; Field Day, i, pp 1243–8; FitzPatrick, pp 161–2, 171; W.E. Hall, p. 98; Rafroidi; Sutherland, p. 323; Topp 3, p. 305].

L148 (Our Mess, II & III) *Tom Burke of "ours"* (by Charles Lever (Harry Lorrequer); dedicated to Miss [Maria] Edgeworth§).

+ Dublin: William Curry Jnr & Co; London: William S. Orr & Co.; Edinburgh: Fraser & Co., 1844, 2 vols. (ill. H.K. Browne [Phiz], J. Jeager). SOURCE Brown, 921; Rafroidi, ii, p. 214; Sadleir, 1415; Wolff, 4098. LOCATION Grail, D, L, NUC, InND Loeber coll. COMMENTARY *Dublin 1844 edn* Bound from the 20 parts [RL].

+ London: Chapman & Hall, 1850, 2 vols. SOURCE Topp 3, p. 309; Sadleir, 3611 ([1869] edn). LOCATION InND Loeber coll. (1865 edn). COMMENTARY *London 1850 edn* No copy located [RL].

+ Leipzig: Bernard Tauchnitz, 1848, 3 vols. SOURCE T & B, 154–56. LOCATION D, L, NUC.

+ Philadelphia: Carey & Hart, 1844. LOCATION NUC, InND Loeber coll. COMMENTARY *Philadelphia 1844 edn* Second title page states as publisher: Dublin: William Curry, Jnr & Co.; London: William S. Orr. & Co.; Edinburgh: Fraser & Co., 1844; 2 vols. in 1, text was reset, however [RL].

New York: G. Munro's Sons, [18—] (as *The last campaign. Being the conclusion of Tom Burke of "Ours"*). SOURCE NYPL. LOCATION NN.

COMMENTARY First published in the *Dublin University Magazine* (starting Jan. 1843). Also issued in 22 parts in 20 issues (see *Jack Hinton*, above). The story is set initially in Ireland, where Tom Burke has enlisted, but because of a fatal quarrel he has to flee. He goes to France, then under the First Consul, and joins the army. Military adventures are described, such as the battle of Austerlitz and the campaign of Jena. Napoleon is featured and a love story is interwoven. In this novel Lever fictionalized Lt.-Col. Henry Robert Addison§ as Captain Bubbleton [Brown; Topp 4, p. 190; Sutherland, p. 632].

L149 *Arthur O'Leary: his wanderings and ponderings in many lands* (ed. 'by his friend, Harry Lorrequer').

+ London: Henry Colburn, 1844, 3 vols. (ill. George Cruikshank). SOURCE Brown, 922; Sadleir, 1393; Wolff, 4076. LOCATION Grail, D, L, NUC.

+ London: Henry Colburn, 1845 (new edn). LOCATION D.

London, New York: George Routledge & Co., 1856 (as *The adventures of Arthur O'Leary*; Railway Library, No. 118; ill. Phiz). SOURCE Sadleir, 3611; NCBEL 3, p. 943; Topp 1, p. 73. LOCATION NUC.

Meppel: P.A. Reynders , 1849, 2 vols. (trans. into Dutch as *Arthur O'Leary's omzw-ervingen en opmerkingen in verscheiden landen*). SOURCE Alphabetische naamlijst 1833–49, p. 399.

Leipzig: Bernard Tauchnitz, 1847, 2 vols. SOURCE T & B, 136–37. LOCATION NUC.

New York: G. Winchester, 1844 (as *The loiterings of Arthur O'Leary*).

COMMENTARY No copy of the New York edn located. Originally published in the *Dublin University Magazine* (Jan.–Dec. 1843) as 'The loiterings of Arthur O'Leary'. Lever's hero Harry Lorrequer writes about O'Leary's adventures. O'Leary discovers and burns this version, furnishing in its place a collection of fragments that Lorrequer then uses to construct the story of O'Leary. The novel is really a string of adventures of the hero in various parts of the world including Canada, Belgium, France and Germany. Included are descriptions of student life in Germany (based on CJL's personal experiences) and stories of the Napoleonic wars. Partly based on CJL's own experiences in North America [Brown; W.E. Hall, p. 111; Rafroidi; Sutherland, pp 29–30; Topp 4, p. 214; FitzPatrick, pp 38, 46].

L150 *St. Patrick's eve; or, three eras in the life of an Irish peasant* (by Charles Lever; dedicated to the author's children).

+ London: Chapman & Hall, 1845 (ill. Phiz). SOURCE Brown, 923; Topp 3, p. 336; Sadleir, 1420; Wolff, 4103. LOCATION Grail, D, Dt, L, NUC, InND Loeber coll. (1845, 2nd edn).

Leipzig: Bernard Tauchnitz, 1870 (as *St. Patrick's eve; Paul Gosslett's confessions*). SOURCE T & B, 1113. LOCATION NUC.

Stuttgart: Franckh, 1846 (trans. as *Der St. Patricks' Abend*). LOCATION NUC.

+ New York: Harper & Bros, 1845. SOURCE Topp 2, p. 239. LOCATION InND Loeber coll., NUC.

COMMENTARY A story of the evils of absentee landlordism set during the cholera epidemic in Co. Clare in 1832 when Lever served as a dispensary doctor there. Owen Connor, a peasant, saves the life of the landlord's son in a faction fight. The landlord rewards him by giving him his little plot rent free. However, after the landlord dies, his son's agent tries to exact back rent. Owen sets out to London to find the son but learns that he is in Paris. When he returns, rural unrest has broken out and someone has accused him of murder. He hides until the new landlord comes and hears about his rescue years earlier. He reinstates Owen rent free on his property. The landlord realizes that a lot of the evils resulted from his absence [ML; FitzPatrick, p. 235].

L151 *Nuts and nutcrackers* [anon.].

+ London: William S. Orr & Co; Dublin: William Curry Jnr & Co., 1845 (ill. Phiz). SOURCE Sadleir, 1412; Topp 2, p. 225. LOCATION InND Loeber coll., Grail, L (1857 edn), NUC.

COMMENTARY Originally published in the *Dublin University Magazine* (1842–44) in 12 issues, not monthly. Contents: 'An opening nut', 'A nut for men of genius', 'A nut for coroners', 'A nut for tourists', 'A nut for legal functionaries', 'A nut for "endearing affection"', 'A nut for the police and Sir Peter', 'A nut for the budget', 'A nut for repeal', 'A nut for national pride', 'A nut for diplomatists', 'A nut for foreign travel', 'A nut for domestic happiness', 'A nut for ladies bountiful', 'A nut for the priests', 'A nut for learned societies', 'A nut for the lawyers', 'A nut for the Irish', 'A nut for viceregal privileges', 'Rich and poor – pour et cointre', 'A nut for St. Patrick's night', 'A nut for gentlemen jocks', 'A nut for younger sons', 'A nut for the penal code', 'A nut for the old', 'A nut for the art unions', 'A nut for the Kingstown railway', 'A nut for the doctors', 'A nut for the architects', 'A nut for a new colony', 'A sweet nut for the Yankees', 'A nut for the season – Jullien's quadrilles', 'A nut for "All Ireland"', 'A nut for a new company', 'A nut for "the polished economists"', 'A nut for "grand dukes"', 'A nut for the East Indian directors', 'A filbert for Sir Robert Peel', '"The income tax"', 'A nut for the Belges', 'A nut for workhouse chaplains', 'A nut for the "house"', 'A nut for "law reform"', 'A nut for "climbing boys"', 'A nut for "the subdivision of labour"', 'A nut for a "new verdict"', 'A nut for the real "liberator"', 'A nut for "her majesty's servants"', 'A nut for the landlord and tenant commission', 'A nut for the humane society' [CM; W.E. Hall, p. 98; Topp 3, p. 299].

L152 *Tales of the trains, being some chapters of railroad romance* (by 'Tilbury Tramp, queen's messenger').

+ London: William S. Orr & Co; Dublin: William Curry Jnr & Co., 1845 (ill. Phiz). SOURCE Rafroidi, ii, p. 214; Sadleir, 1421; Topp 2, p. 234; Wolff, 4104. LOCATION InND Loeber coll., Grail, L, NUC.

+ London: Chapman & Hall, 1857 (new edn). SOURCE Topp 3, p. 299. LOCATION D.

Amsterdam: M.H. Binger & Sons, 1848 (trans. into Dutch as *Spoorwegvertellingen, of hoofdstukken uit de romantiek der spoorwegen*). SOURCE Alphabetische naamlijst 1833–49, p. 399.

COMMENTARY Originally published in the *Dublin University Magazine* (Jan.–May 1845), and then published in 5 parts at 6*d.* each. Contents: 'The coupé of the North Mid', 'The road versus the rail', 'The tunnel of Trubau', 'Mr. Blake in Belgium' [NYPL].

L153 *The O'Donoghue. A tale of Ireland fifty years ago* (by Charles Lever; dedicated to John Wilson).

+ Dublin: William Curry Jnr & Co; London: William S. Orr & Co; Edinburgh: Fraser & Co., 1845 (ill. H.K. Browne [Phiz]). SOURCE Sadleir, 1413; Wolff, 4096; Topp 8, 167. LOCATION InND Loeber coll., Grail, D, DPL, L. COMMENTARY *Dublin 1845 edn* Bound from the 11 parts, Dec. 1844 – Nov. 1845 [Topp 3, p. 307].

Niewediep: C. Bakker Bz, 1846, 2 vols. (trans. into Dutch as *O'Donohu* [sic]. *Een Iersch volksverhaal uit den tijd der Fransche landing in 1797* [sic]). SOURCE Alphabetische naamlijst 1833–49, p. 399.

Paris: Hetzel & Lacroix, 1864, 2 vols. (trans. by Charles-Bernard Derosne as *O'Donoghue, histoire d'une famille irlandaise*). SOURCE Rafroidi, ii, p. 365; OCLC. LOCATION D. COMMENTARY *Paris edn* Was also translated in *Le siècle* (Paris) [FitzPatrick, p. 215].

Leipzig: Bernard Tauchnitz, 1845. SOURCE T & B, 89. LOCATION L, NUC.

+ Philadelphia: Carey & Hart, 1846. SOURCE NYPL. LOCATION InND Loeber coll., NUC, NN.

+ New York: William H. Colyer, 1845. LOCATION InND Loeber coll., NUC.

COMMENTARY Originally issued in 11 parts by William Curry Jnr & Co. in Dublin (Dec. 1844 – Nov. 1845). Set in Glenflesk (Co. Kerry) and between Mallow and Bantry Bay (Co. Cork) in the last decade of the eighteenth century (one chapter is set in Clontarf, Co. Dublin). The hero, Martin O'Donoghue, a member of the decaying Catholic gentry, joins the United Irishmen and witnesses the French expedition of Admiral Hoche in 1796, which ended disastrously under terrible storm conditions. One of the characters is a well-intentioned English landlord who makes ludicrous attempts to better the conditions for his tenants [Brown; Nield, 651; Rafroidi; Topp 3, p. 307; FitzPatrick, p. 40].

L154 *The Knight of Gwynne. A tale of the time of the Union* (by Charles Lever; dedicated to Alexander Spencer).

+ London: Chapman & Hall, 1847 (ill. Phiz; 'Chales' [sic] Lever on half-title page). SOURCE Brown, 926; Rafroidi, ii, p. 214; Sadleir, 1407; Wolff, 4090. LOCATION Grail, D, Dt (1862–64 edn), DPL, L, InND Loeber coll. COMMENTARY *London 1847 edn* Bound from the 19 parts [RL].

+ London: Chapman & Hall, 1872 (new edn, ill. H.K. Browne 'Phiz'; 'Chales' [*sic*] Lever on half-title page). LOCATION D, InND Loeber coll.

Breslau: Grass, 1847, 3 vols. in 1 (trans. by G.N. Bärmann as *Der Ritter von Gwynne*). SOURCE OCLC. LOCATION NjP.

Leipzig: Bernard Tauchnitz Jnr, 1847, 3 vols. SOURCE T & B, 125–27. LOCATION Dt, NUC.

Philadelphia: Carey & Hart, 1847, 2 vols. SOURCE Hayley, 28a; Topp 1, p. 401. LOCATION NUC. COMMENTARY *Philadelphia 1847 edn* Also contains William Carleton's§ 'Parra Sastha' and 'O'Sullivan's love' [Hayley])

New York: W.H. Colyer, 1847 (ill. Phiz). SOURCE Topp 1, p. 401. LOCATION NUC. COMMENTARY Originally published in the *Dublin University Magazine* (1846–47), and afterwards issued in 19 parts (London, Chapman & Hall, 1847). The story starts at the time just before the Union and shows the means adopted by the English government to destroy the Irish parliament. Lord Castlereagh is featured, and the knight is a portrait of a nobly pathetic but chivalrous and courteous old Irishman. Allegedly the story features the historical highwayman, Capt. James Freney§. Part of the story is based on CJL's life in Ulster, and his experiences in Castlebar and Westport (Co. Mayo) and at the Delphi Lodge (near Louisburg, Co. Mayo), occupied by Lord John Browne, brother of the marquis of Sligo [Brown; FitzPatrick, pp 86, 204; [J.G.A. Prim], *Nooks and corners of the County Kilkenny* (Kilkenny, 2003), p. 93; Rafroidi; Topp 3, p. 307)].

L155 *Diary and notes of Horace Templeton, Esq. late secretary of legation at ...* [anon.]. London: Chapman & Hall, 1848, 2 vols. SOURCE Sadleir, 1403; Wolff, 4086. LOCATION L, NUC.

+ London, New York: George Routledge & Sons, n.d. (as *Horace Templeton*). LOCATION D.

Leipzig: Bernard Tauchnitz Jnr, 1848. SOURCE T & B, 149. LOCATION Dt, NUC.

L156 *The confessions of Con Cregan: the Irish Gil Blas* [anon.]. Dublin: James M'Glashan; London: Wm. Orr & Co., 1848. SOURCE Adv. noted by Topp 1, p. 84. COMMENTARY *Dublin 1848 edn* No copy located [RL].

+ London: W.S. Orr & Co., [1849], 2 vols. (ill. Hablot K. Browne [Phiz]). SOURCE Brown, 930 (mentions later edn); Rafroidi, ii, p. 215 (mentions 1849 or 1850?); Block, p. 138 ([1850] edn); Sadleir, 1397 (assigns 1849); Wolff, 4080. LOCATION Grail, D (2 vols. in 1), Dt (mentions [1849]), DPL, L, NUC, InND Loeber coll.

+ Amsterdam: Johs. Van Der Hey en Zoon, [1851], 2 vols. (trans. as *De Iersche Gil-Blas. Lotgevallen en avonturen van Con Cregan, op zijne zwerftogten uit Ierland naar Canada, de Vereenigde Staten, Texas, onder de goudzoekers, door Algiers, Spanje, Frankrijk, enz.; ill.* C.C.A. Last). LOCATION InND Loeber coll.

Paris: A. & W. Galignani & Co., 1850. SOURCE Carraig cat. 1164/269; Bn-Opale plus. LOCATION BNF.

Leipzig: Bernard Tauchnitz, 1860, 2 vols. SOURCE T & B, 513–14. LOCATION NYPL, L, NUC, NN.

New York: Stringer & Townsend, 1850, 2 parts. SOURCE Topp 1, p. 84. LOCATION NUC.

Philadelphia: Carey & Hart, 1849. SOURCE Topp 1, p. 84. COMMENTARY *Philadelphia 1849 edn* No copy located [RL].

Philadelphia: T.B. Peterson & Bros, [1877] (as *Con Cregan. The Irish Gil Blas. His confessions and experiences*). SOURCE NYPL. LOCATION NN, NUC.

+ Boston: Little, Brown & Co., [18–] (ill.). LOCATION InND Loeber coll., NUC.

COMMENTARY First issued in 14 (in 13) parts (London, S. Orr & Co., 1849). The wild adventures of Con Cregan, who was born on the borders of Co. Meath. He goes to Dublin, from whence he is carried off in the yacht of an eccentric baronet. He is wrecked on an island off the coast of North America, where he meets a runaway Negro slave. Other adventures follow in Quebec, Texas and Mexico. In the end he returns to Ireland and marries a Spanish lady whom he had met in Mexico [Brown; Maggs cat. 621/287].

L157   *Roland Cashel* (by Charles Lever; dedicated to G.P.R. James§).
+ London: Chapman & Hall, 1850 (ill. Phiz). SOURCE Brown, 927 (mentions 1849 edn, which may refer to the parts); Rafroidi, ii, p. 215; Hogan, p. 376; NCBEL 3, p. 943; Sadleir, 1417; Wolff, 4100. LOCATION Grail, D, Dt, DPL, L, NUC, InND Loeber coll.
London: Chapman & Hall, 1872 (new edn; Select Fiction Library). SOURCE Topp 3, p. 379; COPAC. LOCATION Univ. of Sheffield.
London: Chapman & Hall, 1877, 2 vols. (new autobiographical introd.). SOURCE Topp 3, p. 379. LOCATION E.
Leipzig: Bernard Tauchnitz, 1858, 3 vols. in 2. SOURCE T & B, 454–5. SOURCE NYPL. LOCATION L, NUC, NN.
+ New York: Harper & Bros, 1850 (Library of Select Novels, No. 99). LOCATION InND Loeber coll., NUC ([1849] edn).
+ New York: Harper & Bros, 1850 (ill. Phiz). LOCATION InND Loeber coll. (also 1856 edn). COMMENTARY *New York 1850 edn* Publishers binding, embossed with Harper's name; also issued in three parts [Topp 3, p. 308].
COMMENTARY Originally published in the *Dublin University Magazine* (1848–49), and then in 19 parts (London, Chapman & Hall, 1848–49). Starts out in Colombia, South America, where Roland Cashel, a young Irish soldier of fortune, almost promises marriage to a daughter of a Colombian adventurer. However, he learns that he is the heir to a large property in Ireland and immediately sets off for Ireland, where many adventures follow. He falls in love with a girl of no fortune and is introduced by an enemy to fast society, which gets him almost in trouble, but in the end all turns out well. One of the characters is based on the archbishop of Dublin, Richard Whately§, while the author William Thackeray§ stood for the character of Elias Howle [Brown; Rafroidi; Topp 3, p. 308; S. Haddelsey, *Charles Lever* (Gerrards Cross, 2000), p. 28].

L158   *The Daltons; or, three roads in life* (by Charles Lever; dedicated to Lord Metheun).
+ London: Chapman & Hall; Edinburgh, J. Menzies; Dublin: J. M'Glashan, June 1850, vol. 1; Oct. 1851, vol. 2 (ill. Phiz). LOCATION formerly InND Loeber coll. (1850–51 edn mislaid; also 1852 edn). COMMENTARY *London 1850–51 edn* Published from the parts (probably 24), the first one announced May 1850 [Topp 3, p. 306].
Leipzig: Bernard Tauchnitz, 1852, 4 vols. SOURCE T & B, 232–35; COPAC. LOCATION L.
New York: Harper & Bros, 1852 (Library of Select Novels, No. 170). SOURCE Topp 3, p. 306. LOCATION NUC.
New York: G.P. Putnam, 1852, 2 vols. SOURCE Topp 3, p. 306.
COMMENTARY No copy of the New York edn located. First issued in 24 (in 23) monthly parts (London, Chapman & Hall, May 1850 onward). The New York edn was also published in parts in 1850. The Irish scenes were inspired by Lever's stay at Inistioge (Co. Kilkenny). Set mainly on the Continent in Germany, Austria and Italy, it describes the life of an Irish absentee landlord and his family. Some of the characters are involved in the Austro-Italian campaign of 1848 and in the Tuscan rebellion. Pictures are given of Anglo-Italian life in Florence and of Austrian military life [Brown; Quaritch List No. 2001/12/28; Topp 3, p. 306; FitzPatrick, p. 7].

L159   *Maurice Tiernay, the soldier of fortune* [anon.].
New York: Harper & Bros, 1852 (Library of Select Novels). SOURCE Topp 3, p. 315. LOCATION NUC.

London: Thomas Hodgson, [1854] (Parlour Library, vol. 119). SOURCE Rafroidi, ii, p. 215; Sadleir, 1411; 3755a; Topp 2, p. 63; Topp 6, 250; Wolff, 4094. LOCATION Grail, Dt, L, NUC.

Leipzig: Bernard Tauchnitz, 1861, 2 vols. SOURCE T & B, 554–55. LOCATION L, NUC.

COMMENTARY Originally published in the *Dublin University Magazine* (Apr. 1850–Dec. 1851), and in Harper's *New Monthly Magazine* (June 1850–Feb. 1852), while A. Hart issued it in parts in Philadelphia in 1850. See Topp for other London edns. Historical fiction consisting of the adventures of a young Jacobite exile in many lands at the end of the eighteenth and the beginning of the nineteenth century. Opens in Paris during 'The Terror' where young Maurice Tierney's father is scheduled to be guillotined and he escapes only with the intervention of Robespierre. Later he joins the army of the Rhine and then Humbert's expedition to Ireland in 1798. The book describes the capture and death of Theobald Wolfe Tone§. Further adventures are set in America, and Italy during the Austrian siege. Eventually he joins Napoleon's army, fights in the Austrian campaign, catches the emperor's eye, marries an aristocratic bride, and ends up rich and happy [Brown; Rafroidi; Sutherland, pp 422–3; Topp].

L160 *The Dodd family abroad* (by Charles Lever; dedicated to Sir Edward Lytton Bulwer Lytton§, Bt, MP).

+ London: Chapman & Hall, 1854, 2 vols. (ill. Phiz). SOURCE Rafroidi, ii, p. 215; Brown, 937; Sadleir, 1404; Wolff, 4087. LOCATION Grail, D (2 vols. in 1), Dt (1859 edn) DPL (2 vols. in 1), L, NUC, InND Loeber coll. (1854 and 1866, 6th edns). COMMENTARY *London 1854 edn* Bound from the parts [Topp 3, p. 307].

Paris: [publisher?], 1854. SOURCE Devonshire, p. 413. COMMENTARY *Paris edn* No copy located [RL].

+ Leipzig: Bernard Tauchnitz, 1854, 3 vols. SOURCE T & B, 298–300. LOCATION InND Loeber coll.

New York: Harper & Bros, 1854 (Library of Select Novels, No. 187). SOURCE Topp 3, p. 307. LOCATION NUC (1854 edn).

COMMENTARY First issued in 19 parts (London, Chapman & Hall, 1852–54), and also in parts in New York in 1852. Epistolary novel concerning the adventures on the Continent of an Anglo-Irish family who seem to have no idea of the manners and customs of the countries they visit. Based on the Lever family's own 'Grand Tour' of Europe, 1845–47 [Brown; RIA/DIB; Sutherland, Topp 3, p. 307].

L161 *Sir Jasper Carew, Knt.: His life and experiences. With some account of his overreachings and shortcomings, now first given to the world by himself* (by Charles Lever).

+ New York: Harper & Bros, 1854 (Library of Select Novels, No. 188). SOURCE NYPL; OCLC. LOCATION InND Loeber coll., NUC, NN.

London: Thomas Hodgson, [1855] (as *Sir Jasper Carew, Knt. his life and experiences* [anon.]; Parlour Library, No. 123). SOURCE Rafroidi, ii, p. 215; Brown, 931; Sadleir, 1419, 3755a; Wolff, 4102; OCLC. LOCATION Grail, Dt, L, NUC.

Leipzig: Bernard Tauchnitz, 1861, 2 vols. SOURCE T & B, 572–73. LOCATION L, NUC.

COMMENTARY First appeared in the *Dublin University Magazine* (June 1852–June 1854). The London edn came in three binding variants: (a) boards printed in red; (b) olive-green fine-ribbed cloth; (c) boards printed in green-brown. A story about two generations of Carews, a family of Cromwellian stock. The elder Carew has an estate and copper and lead mines in Co. Wicklow. He goes to Paris, where he allies himself by a secret marriage with the party of the duke of Orleans. Upon his return to Ireland, he has a duel with a Dublin Castle official. Both parties are killed. His widow is deprived of the property and retires to Co. Mayo with her son Jasper. The early days of the Irish parliament are described and also the extravagant social life of the period. Jasper goes to France and England where, as a secret agent, he interviews William Pitt and Charles Fox and meets with many adventures. Eventually he returns to Ireland to reclaim his birthright [Brown; Topp 3, p. 313; Carter, p. 133, frontispiece].

L162 *The Martins of Cro' Martin* (by Charles Lever; dedicated to Revd Mortimer Sullivan§).

+ London: Chapman & Hall, 1856 (ill. Phiz). SOURCE Brown, 925 (mistakenly states a 1847 edn); Rafroidi, ii, p. 215; Sadleir, 1410; Wolff, 4093. LOCATION InND Loeber coll., Grail, D, L. NUC.

London: Chapman & Hall, 1859, 2 vols. (new edn; ill. Phiz). SOURCE Topp 3, p. 313. LOCATION InND Loeber coll. (1873 edn), D (1873 edn). COMMENTARY *London 1859 edn* No copy of this new edn located [RL].

Leipzig: Bernard Tauchnitz, 1856, 2 vols. SOURCE T & B, 361–2. LOCATION L (1861 edn).

+ New York: Harper & Bros, 1856 (Library of Select Novels, No. 100). LOCATION InND Loeber coll., NUC.

COMMENTARY Despite CJL's denial, it is likely that the story was inspired by the life of the Martin family and their large estate at Ballynahinch (Co. Galway, see Harriet Letitia Martin§). The novel was first published in 19 parts (London, Chapman & Hall, starting in Dec. 1854 to 1856). Set mainly in Connemara, where the Martins lead an easygoing life as Irish landlords, and also in Paris during the revolution of 1830. When Martin is rejected by his tenantry in an election, he quits the country in disgust, leaving them to the mercies of his Scottish agent. The tenants suffer from the agent's regime, as well as from cholera. Here Lever again used his own experiences as a doctor in Kilrush, Co. Clare, during the cholera epidemic of 1832 [Brown; RIA/DIB; Topp 3, p. 313; S. Haddelsey, *Charles Lever* (Gerrards Cross, 2000), p. 28; FitzPatrick, p. 85].

L163 *The fortunes of Glencore* (by Charles Lever; dedicated to Sir James Hudson, HBM's minister at Turin).

London: Chapman & Hall, 1857, 3 vols. SOURCE Rafroidi, ii, p. 215; Brown, 932; Sadleir, 1405; Wolff, 4088. LOCATION Grail, L, NUC.

+ London: Chapman & Hall, 1862 (new edn; ill. Ed. Evans). SOURCE Topp 3, p. 310; Sadleir, 3611 (n.d., 4th edn). LOCATION InND Loeber coll.

Leipzig: Bernard Tauchnitz, 1857, 2 vols. SOURCE T & B, 393–94. LOCATION L, NUC, NN.

+ New York: Harper & Bros, 1857 (Library of Select Novels, No. 203). SOURCE NYPL (1864 edn). LOCATION InND Loeber coll., NUC, NN (1864 edn).

COMMENTARY First published in the *Dublin University Magazine* (Aug. 1855–Apr. 1857). Lord Glencore, living in a castle on the shore of the Killaries between Galway and Mayo, is a proud man soured by a scandal connected with his wife. He disowns his son, who runs away from home. The book then describes the adventures in Italy and elsewhere of Sir Horace Upton, a distinguished diplomat, together with those of his Irish follower Billy Traynor, a former scholar and hedge-school master, whose character is based on a real person. In the end Lady Glencore's innocence is established [Brown; W.E. Hall, p. 180].

L164 *Davenport Dunn. A man of our day* (by Charles Lever; dedicated to the marquess of Normanby).

+ London: Chapman & Hall, 1859 (ill. Phiz). SOURCE Rafroidi, ii, p. 216; Brown, 933; Sadleir, 1401; Wolff, 4084. LOCATION InND Loeber coll., Grail, D, NUC (2 vol. edn).

Leipzig: Bernard Tauchnitz, 1859, 3 vols. SOURCE T & B, 472–74; NUPL. LOCATION L, NUC, NN.

+ Philadelphia: T.B. Peterson & Bros, [187—?]. SOURCE NYPL. LOCATION InND Loeber coll., NUC, NN.

COMMENTARY Originally published in 22 parts in 21 numbers (London, Chapman & Hall, July 1857–Apr. 1859). The history of two adventurers. Dunn is an ambitious man who lifts himself into a high position as a financier by shady deals and by swindling his fellow Irishmen after the calamities of the 1840s. The character is based on the notorious Irish politician John Sadlier Jnr, lord of the treasury, and an embezzler. Dunn tries to set up an Anglo-French alliance in the Crimean War, conquers English society, is courted by ministers, and looks to an aristocratic marriage. He is accidentally killed on a train by the other character, Grog Davis, a swindler, who engages in sporting cheats as his enterprises collapse [Brown; Sutherland, p. 172; Ximenes cat. 97–5/89].

L165   *Gerald Fitzgerald, the chevalier. A novel* (by Charles Lever).
+ New York: Harper & Bros, 1859, parts 1 and 2 (Library of Select Novels, Nos. 210, 211). SOURCE NYPL. LOCATION InND Loeber coll., NUC, NN.
COMMENTARY First published in the *Dublin University Magazine* (1858–59), followed by an American pirated edn. The first London edn was part of the collected works (*The novels of Charles Lever*, London, 1897–9). An historical romance, the hero of which is a legitimate son of the Young Pretender (grandson of James II), offspring of a secret marriage with an Irish lady. It describes his adventures in France and Italy [Brown].

L166   *One of them* (by Charles Lever; dedicated to the Rt Hon. James Whiteside, MP).
+ London: Chapman & Hall, 1861 (ill. Phiz). SOURCE Brown, 934; Rafroidi, ii, p. 216; Topp 2, p. 236–37; Sadleir, 1414; Sadleir, 3611 (1863 edn). LOCATION Grail, Dt, DPL, L, NUC, InND Loeber coll. (also 1872 edn).
Leipzig: Bernard Tauchnitz, 1860, 2 vols. SOURCE T & B, 533–34. LOCATION L, NN, NUC.
New York: Harper & Bros, 1861 (Library of Select Novels, No. 216; ill. Phiz). SOURCE Topp 2, p. 236; NYPL. LOCATION NUC, NN.
+ New York: Harper & Bros, 1862. LOCATION InND Loeber coll.
COMMENTARY First issued in 14 parts (London, Chapman & Hall, starting Dec. 1859), and in New York in parts in the same year. Set in the north of Ireland (at Port-na-Happle) and Florence (both places well known to Lever), and deals largely with the adventures of an Irish MP, but its outstanding character is Quackinbuss, a droll Yankee [Brown; B. Rogers, 'Dr. Lever at Portstewart' in T. Bareham (ed.), *Charles Lever: New evaluations* (Gerrards Cross, 1981), p. 70; Sutherland; Topp 3, p. 310].

L167   *A day's ride. A life's romance* (by Charles Lever).
+ New York: Harper & Bros, 1861 (Library of Select Novels, No. 217; ill.). SOURCE NYPL. LOCATION InND Loeber coll., NUC, NN.
London: Chapman & Hall, 1863, 2nd edn [*sic*], 2 vols. SOURCE Rafroidi, ii, p. 216 (mentions 1862); Brown, 936 (mentions 1862); Wolff, 4085; Sadleir, 1402 (mistakenly states that this is the first book edn); Grail.
+ Leipzig: Bernard Tauchnitz, 1864, 2 vols. in 1. SOURCE T & B, 694. LOCATION L, NUC, InND Loeber coll.
COMMENTARY For the history of its printing, see Topp 3, p. 314, showing that the first book edn was brought out as 'second edition'. First serialized in *All the Year Round* (London, probably in 1862). Set in Ireland and the Continent, it describes the adventures of Algernon Sydney Potts, only son of a Dublin apothecary. Sutherland says that it caused the sales of *All the Year Round* to plummet and Charles Dickens had to start publishing *Great expectations* (London, 1860–1) to restore circulation [Brown; Sutherland, p. 374; Topp 3, p. 314].

L168   *Barrington* (by Charles Lever; dedicated to Charles Dickens).
+ London: Chapman & Hall, 1863 (ill. Phiz). SOURCE Brown, 935 (1862 edn, which may refer to parts); Rafroidi, ii, p. 216; Hogan, p. 376; NCBEL 3, p. 943; Sadleir, 1394; Wolff, 4077. LOCATION Grail, D, NUC, InND Loeber coll.

+ London: Chapman & Hall, 1872 (new edn). LOCATION D.

Leipzig: Bernard Tauchnitz, 1863, 2 vols. SOURCE T & B, 652–53. LOCATION L, NUC.

New York: Harper & Bros, 1863 (Library of Select Novels, No. 226). SOURCE Topp 3, p. 327; OCLC. LOCATION Univ. of Toledo.

COMMENTARY First published in 13 (in 12) parts (London, Chapman & Hall, Feb. 1862–Jan. 1863). A novel of social and domestic life of the middle classes. The scene is set at the little inn 'The Fisherman's Home' on the River Nore (Co. Kilkenny), where the Barringtons live. The story turns on the disgrace and subsequent vindication of Barrington's son George. Apparently, the author was portraying his own son Charles (who died aged 26) and his career [Brown; RIA/DIB; Topp 3, p. 327].

L169 *Cornelius O'Dowd upon men and women and other things in general* (by 'Cornelius O'Dowd'; vol. 1, dedicated to John Anster, LLD; vol. 2, dedicated to Judge Longfield, LLD).

+ Edinburgh, London: William Blackwood & Sons, 1864 (1st series). SOURCE Sadleir, 1399; Wolff, 4082. LOCATION Grail, L, NUC, InND Loeber coll.

+ Edinburgh, London: William Blackwood & Sons, 1865 (2nd and 3rd series). SOURCE Sadleir, 1399; Wolff, 4082. LOCATION Grail, L, NUC, InND Loeber coll. (lacks vol. iii).

London: Chapman & Hall, 1873 (contains 30pp article on Lever's works). SOURCE Topp 3, p. 386; OCLC. LOCATION MH.

COMMENTARY Essays and short stories first published in *Blackwood's Magazine* (Edinburgh, Feb. 1863–Mar. 1873) [ML; Topp 3, p. 386].

L170 *Luttrell of Arran* (by Charles Lever; dedicated to Joseph Sheridan Le Fanu§).

+ London: Chapman & Hall, 1865 (ill. Phiz). SOURCE Rafroidi, ii, p. 216; Brown, 938; Sadleir, 1409; Wolff, 4092. LOCATION Grail, D, L, NUC, InND Loeber coll.

Leipzig: Bernard Tauchnitz, 1865, 2 vols. SOURCE T & B, 761–2. LOCATION L.

New York: Harper & Bros, 1865. SOURCE Topp 3, p. 335. LOCATION NUC.

COMMENTARY First published in 16 (in 15) parts (London, Chapman & Hall, Dec. 1863–Feb. 1865). The book appeared in two binding types as noted by Sadleir: (a) purple cloth with gilt decoration on the spine; (b) green cloth. Luttrell, a proud man of broken fortune, lives on Inishmore, one of the Aran Islands (Co. Galway), with his son Harry. A wealthy Englishman, Sir Gervase Vyner, visits the island and renews his acquaintance with Luttrell. Moving on to Donegal, Vyner adopts a beautiful peasant girl, who he turns into a fine lady. Eventually, Harry and the adopted daughter of Vyner marry [Brown; Topp 3, p. 335].

L171 *Tony Butler* [anon.].

+ Edinburgh, London: William Blackwood & Sons, 1865, 3 vols. SOURCE Rafroidi, ii, p. 216; Brown, 939; Sadleir, 1423; Wolff, 4106. LOCATION Grail, Dt, L, NUC InND Loeber coll.

London: Chapman & Hall, 1872, 3 vols. (new edn). SOURCE Topp 3, p. 386; Sadleir, 1423; OCLC. LOCATION CLU. COMMENTARY *London 1872 edn* Reissue of first edn with cancelled title page [Rowan cat 57A/517].

Leipzig: Bernard Tauchnitz, 1865, 2 vols. in 1. SOURCE T & B, 866. LOCATION L (1866 edn), NUC.

+ New York: Harper & Bros, 1865 (Library of Select Novels). SOURCE NYPL. LOCATION InND Loeber coll., NUC, NN.

COMMENTARY First serialized in *Blackwood's Magazine* (Edinburgh, Oct. 1863–Jan. 1865). The London 1872 edn appears to be a reissue of unsold sheets of the Edinburgh 1865 printing. Set partly in the north of Ireland and partly on the Continent. The 'big house' in the Irish part of the story probably refers to the earl bishop of Derry's country house Downhill (Co.

Antrim). Tony Butler is in the diplomatic service and he has many adventures, some of which take place during the Garibaldian war in Italy [Brown; B. Rogers, 'Dr. Lever at Portstewart' in T. Bareham (ed.), *Charles Lever: New evaluations* (Gerrards Cross, 1981), p. 71; Rowan cat. 53B/708; Topp 3, p. 386].

L172 *Sir Brook Fossbrooke* (by Charles Lever; dedicated to Philip Rose).

+ Edinburgh, London: William Blackwood & Sons, 1866, 3 vols. SOURCE Rafroidi, ii, p. 216; Brown, 940; Sadleir, 1418; Wolff, 4101; Topp 7, 53. LOCATION Grail, L, NUC InND Loeber coll.

Edinburgh, London: William Blackwood & Sons, 1867 (new edn). SOURCE Topp 3, p. 383. LOCATION L.

Leipzig: Bernard Tauchnitz, 1867, 2 vols. SOURCE T & B, 886–67. LOCATION L, NUC.

+ New York: Harper & Bros, 1866 (Library of Select Novels, No. 281). SOURCE NYPL. LOCATION InND Loeber coll., NUC, NN.

Boston: Littell & Gay, [1866] (Tales of the Living Age). SOURCE Topp 3, p. 383. LOCATION NYPL, NUC, NN.

COMMENTARY First serialized in *Blackwood's Magazine* (Edinburgh, May 1865–Nov. 1866). Set mainly in Ireland, the story revolves around members of the family of Baron Lendrick of the court of exchequer in Dublin, who is very old, extremely vain, but also very smart. He is estranged from his son, who lives a retired life with his two children in the country. Sir Brook Fossbrooke, an honourable man, befriends the baron's grandchildren. Sewell, an army officer married to the baron's stepdaughter, is a scoundrel who lives off cheating and gambling. He is about to ruin a number of people, including the baron's granddaughter and her lover, but he is unmasked by Fossbrooke and has to flee the country. The baron is reunited with his son and grandchildren and the granddaughter marries her lover. One of the characters is based on the Irish chief justice Thomas Lefroy [ML; Topp 3, p. 383; FitzPatrick, p. 146].

L173 *The Bramleighs of Bishop's Folly* (by Charles Lever; dedicated to Alexander William Kinglake, MP).

+ London: Smith, Elder & Co., 1868, 3 vols. SOURCE Rafroidi, ii, p. 216; Brown, 941; Sadleir, 1395; Wolff, 4078. LOCATION Grail, D, L, NUC.

+ London: Chapman & Hall, 1872 (new edn; ill. M.E.E., Swain). SOURCE Topp 3, p. 384. LOCATION DPL, InND Loeber coll.

Leipzig: Bernard Tauchnitz, 1868, 2 vols. SOURCE T & B, 987–88. LOCATION NUC.

New York: Harper & Bros, 1868 (Harper's Library of Select Novels). SOURCE NYPL. LOCATION NUC, NN.

COMMENTARY First serialized in the *Cornhill Magazine* (London, June 1867–Oct. 1868). Set in the north of Ireland near Coleraine (Co. Derry) and later in Italy. Deals with the experiences of a rich English banker and his family who come to Ireland and a neighbouring landowner, Viscount Culduff. Coal is found on the Culduff estate and part of the novel deals with the exploitation of the Culduff mine. The book contains a mystery that is kept unsolved to the very end. It has been suggested that the earl bishop of Derry's country house Downhill (Co. Derry) was the setting which inspired Bishop's Folly [Brown; S. Haddelsey, *Charles Lever* (Gerrards Cross, 2000), pp 28–9].

L174 *Paul Gosslett's confessions in love, law, and the civil service* [anon.].

London: Virtue & Co; New York: Virtue & Yorston, 1868 (ill. Marcus Stone). SOURCE Rafroidi, ii, p. 216; Sadleir, 1416; Wolff, 4099. LOCATION Grail, Dt, L, NUC.

New York: G. Munro, 1881. LOCATION NUC.

COMMENTARY First serialized in *Saint Paul's Magazine* (London, Feb.–July 1868). SOURCE Topp 3, p. 401.

L175 *That boy of Norcott's* (by Charles Lever).

London: Smith, Elder & Co., 1869 (ill. Joseph Swain). SOURCE Rafroidi, ii, p. 216; Sadleir, 1422; Wolff, 4105. LOCATION Grail, Dt, L, NUC.

Leipzig: Bernard Tauchnitz, 1869. SOURCE T & B, 1024. LOCATION NUC.

New York: Harper & Bros, 1869 (Library of Select Novels). SOURCE NYPL. LOCATION NUC, NN.

COMMENTARY First serialized in the *Cornhill Magazine* (London, Nov. 1868–Mar. 1869) [Topp 3, p. 384].

L176 *Lord Kilgobbin. A tale of Ireland in our own time* (by Charles Lever; dedicated to 'the memory of one whose companionship made the happiness of a long life, and whose loss has left me helpless').

London: Smith, Elder & Co., 1872, 3 vols (ill. Luke Fildes). SOURCE Brown, 942; Rafroidi, ii, p. 216; Sadleir, 1408, 1408a (1872 edn); Wolff, 4091. LOCATION Grail, L, NUC, InND Loeber coll. (1873 edn).

Leipzig: Bernard Tauchnitz, 1872, 2 vols. SOURCE T & B, 1210–11. LOCATION NUC.

+ New York: Harper & Bros, 1872 (ill. S.L.F.). LOCATION InND Loeber coll. (hardback and paperback edns), NUC.

+ Belfast: Appletree Press, 1992 (introd. by A.N. Jeffares). LOCATION D.

COMMENTARY First published in the *Cornhill Magazine* (London, Oct. 1870–Mar. 1871). Regarded by many as Lever's best work, it describes the social and political conditions in Ireland in the Fenian times of about 1865 and on the surface appears to be a Big House novel of Ascendancy decline. It is partly set in Co. Offaly and partly in Dublin (but it also describes the River Nore valley in Co. Kilkenny). A series of visitors to an isolated estate provide a mix of volatile opinions and emotions reflecting Anglo-Irish perspectives, Fenian nationalist agitation, and European diplomatic intrigue. One of the characters, Daniel Donogon, is said to be inspired by the revolutionary Jeremiah O'Donovan Rossa [Brown; RIA/DIB; OCIL, p. 316; S. Haddelsey, *Charles Lever* (Gerrards Cross, 2000), p. 149; FitzPatrick, p. 7].

L177 *A rent in the cloud and St. Patrick's eve* (by Charles Lever).

London: Chapman & Hall, [1871] (Select Library of Fiction, No. 193). SOURCE Topp 3, p. 370.

COMMENTARY The first story, *A rent in the cloud* was first published in London (1871) and is by Sidney Lever§, while *St. Patrick's eve* was first published in London (1845) [RL].

L178 *Con O'Kelly. "The smuggler's story"* (by Charles Lever).

London: Downey & Co., 1898. SOURCE Topp 8, 213; OCLC. LOCATION KU-S.

Dublin: J. Duffy & Co., 1904. LOCATION L.

COMMENTARY Posthumous publication, part of the collected works (see below). The story was originally published in the *Dublin University Magazine* (Jan.–Dec. 1843) as 'The loiterings of Arthur O'Leary'. For possible US edns, see Topp [RL; Topp].

— COLLECTED WORKS

L179 *[The Novels of Mr. Charles Lever].*

Dublin: William Curry Jnr & Co., [1850s–60s], [no. of vols. unclear]. SOURCE RL. LOCATION InND Loeber coll. (some vols.).

London: Chapman & Hall, [1850s–60s]. SOURCE RL. LOCATION InND Loeber coll. (some vols.).

COMMENTARY Unnumbered and untitled series, issued in an uniform rose-madder cloth stamped binding with the bust of an Irishman with shillelagh, hat and pipe on the spine. The volumes are remainders of earlier edns, some issued by William Curry Jnr & Co. of Dublin, and others issued by Chapman & Hall of London. The number of volumes is unclear, but is at least eleven. An advertisement in the *Irish Metropolitan Magazine* of 1857 indicates that the series is called *The Novels of Mr. Charles Lever*, and was issued in a cheap cloth edn at a cost of 4*s*., and a library edn at a cost of 7 to 21*s*., with a usual cost of 7*s*. per vol. [RL].

L180 [*Charles Lever's works*].
> London: Chapman & Hall, 1865 onwards (Select Library of Fiction), 20 vols. LOCATION NUC, InND Loeber coll. (some vols.).
> London: Chapman & Hall, 1873 (new edn, Select Library of Fiction). LOCATION InND Loeber coll. (some vols.).

COMMENTARY Unnumbered and untitled series as part of The Select Library of Fiction, which also includes novels by Anthony Trollope§ and others. All are in 'picture board' (i.e., yellowback), but the Lever volumes are distinctive in that they have a harp and shamrocks on spine (however, we have seen at least one of the yellow-backs where the harp is replaced by the 'Select Library'). Early volumes appear in a bluish cover, while later volumes (called new edn, 1873 onwards) are printed in green and yellow. The new edn is advertised in the London, 1873 edn of *A day's ride*, which is a yellow-back, but is not listed in this series. Another advertisement in *One of them* (London, 1872), lists the series as the 'Railway Edition', with picture covers by H.K. Browne [Phiz], 20 volumes (with prices varying from one to three shillings), the series could also be purchased in cloth at £3 18*s*. [RL].

L181 **Charles Lever's Works.**
> London: Chapman & Hall, 1867 (ill. Phiz.), [no. of vols. unclear]. LOCATION InND Loeber coll. (one vol.).

COMMENTARY Green cloth binding, heavily blind embossed with shamrocks in the corners, and gold embossed on the spine [RL].

L182 [*Charles Lever's works*].
> London: Chapman & Hall, 1872–73, 19 vols. (new edn; ill. H.K. Browne [Phiz]). LOCATION InND Loeber coll. (seven vols.), NUC (17 vols.).

COMMENTARY Unnumbered and untitled series. Several binding types: (a) green cloth, stamped in black and gold with military trophies on cover and spine, harp on top of spine; (b) green cloth, embossed in black and gold, showing oval with lady reading, with Chas. Lever in capitals on spine, and a harp above; (c) red cloth, embossed in black and gold, showing oval with lady reading, with Chas. Lever in capitals on spine, and a harp above; (d) crimson morocco with gilded spines [RL].

L183 **Charles Lever's novels.**
> + London, Manchester, New York: George Routledge & Sons, [1876], 24 vols. (ill. Phiz). SOURCE Topp 1, p. 362. LOCATION DPL, NUC, InND Loeber coll. (2 vols. only).

COMMENTARY Uniformly bound in cloth. Date from InND cat. Advertisement states 'Charles Lever's works, The "Harry Lorrequer" edition'. Some catalogues refer to 33 or 34 vols., but this is the total number issued over 24 titles [RL; NUC].

L184 [*Charles Lever's works*].
> Westminster [London]: Archibald Constable & Co., 1898, [no. of vols. not clear] (ed. by D.J. O'Donoghue). LOCATION DPL (2 vols.).

COMMENTARY Unnumbered and untitled series, uniformly bound in red cloth spine, gold embossed lettering, and green paper covers with dark green printing [RL].

L185 **The military novels of Charles Lever.**
> London, New York, Glasgow, Manchester: George Routledge & Sons, 1892, 9 vols. SOURCE OCLC. LOCATION D.
> + Boston: Little, Brown & Co., 1892 (ill.). LOCATION InND Loeber coll. (1 vol. only).

L186 **The novels of Charles Lever.**
> + London; Downey & Co., 1897–99, 37 vols. (ed. by his daughter [Julia Kate Neville]); ill. Phiz). LOCATION D, DPL, L, NUC, InND Loeber coll.

COMMENTARY Limited edn of 1,000 [RL].

L187   *Novels and tales.*
Leipzig: [publisher?], 1856–60, 21 vols. SOURCE NYPL. LOCATION NN, NUC.

L188   *The works of Charles Lever.*
+ New York: P.F. Collier, [1872?], 6 vols. SOURCE NYPL ([188?] edn). LOCATION NUC, NN, InND Loeber coll. (1880 edn, 2 vols. only).
+ New York: P.F. Collier, 1880 (ill. M.L. Flanery), [no. of vols. unclear]. LOCATION D (1882 edn), InND Loeber coll.
New York: P.F. Collier, 1900, 35 vols. SOURCE RLIN. LOCATION UBP.

L189   *The selected writings of Charles Lever.*
+ New York: P.F. Collier, 1905 (Irish Literature, Section Two), 10 vols. LOCATION InND Loeber coll. (vol. 9, n.d.), Boston College.

L190   *The works of Charles Lever (Harry Lorrequer). Embracing the following volumes of his works: Harry Lorrequer; Charles O'Malley, the Irish dragoon; Paul Gosslett's confessions; Jack Hinton, the guardsman; The O'Donoghue, and Roland Cashel.*
+ New York: Will. C. Sadlier, 1880, [vol. 1] 2 vols. in 1 (ill. H.K. Browne [Phiz]; The Templeogue Lever). LOCATION D (1881 edn), NUC (1881 edn), InND Loeber coll.
New York: Pollard & Moss, 1880, [vol. 2] 2 vols. in 1. Stem of title as above, with: *embracing the following volumes: Tom Burke of 'Ours'; Maurice Tiernay, the soldier of fortune; The Nevilles of Garrettsville [sic]; Martins of Cro' Martin; Con Cregan, the Irish Gil Blas; and Gerald Fitzgerald, the chevalier.* SOURCE Advertised as 'second series' in the New York: Will C. Sadleir, 1880. COMMENTARY *New York 1880 edn of this volume.* Binding consists of a deluxe edn in quarter leather. It and all following edns by Pollard & Moss contain the original plates, but coloured. The *Nevilles of Garrettsville* [sic] is not by Lever but by Mortimer O'Sullivan§ (originally published as *The Nevilles of Garretstown,* London, 1860) [RL].
+ New York: Pollard & Moss, 1880 (ill. H.K. Browne [Phiz]; stem of title as above, with: *embracing the following volumes of his works: Jack Hinton, the guardsman; The O'Donoghue, and Roland Cashel.* 'The Templeogue Lever'). LOCATION InND Loeber coll. COMMENTARY *New York 1880 edn of this volume.* Binding of brown cloth, embossed in black and gold, depicting military accoutrements; probably issued in 4 volumes [RL].
+ New York: Pollard & Moss, 1882 (ill. H.K. Browne [Phiz]; Stem of title as above, with: *embracing the following volumes of his works: Harry Lorrequer; Charles O'Malley, the Irish dragoon; and Paul Gosslett's confessions.* 'The Templeogue Lever'). LOCATION InND Loeber coll. COMMENTARY *New York 1882 edn.* Binding of reddish brown cloth, embossed in black and gold in the same manner as above; probably issued in 4 volumes [RL].

L191   *The works of Charles Lever.*
Philadelphia: T.B. Peterson, [1848 or later], 4 vols. SOURCE OCLC. LOCATION Univ. of Delaware.
COMMENTARY Dedication dates 1839 [misprint for 1849?], but the volumes must have been published after 1848 or later because of the original publication dates of the volumes in the series. Still advertised in 1855 [Adv. in E. Bennett, *Ellen Norbury* (New York, 1855); OCLC].

L192   *The novels of Charles Lever.*
Boston: Little, Brown & Co., 1894–95, 40 vols. LOCATION NUC.

LEVER, Sydney, fl. 1865–84. Novelist and poet, SL was the youngest daughter of Charles Lever§ and Catherine Baker. It is not clear when and where she was born, but she lived with her parents in Ireland for some years before the family moved abroad in 1840. A kinsman wrote that 'one of Lever's daughters [probably SL] inherited much of his literary talent; but although some things she wrote sufficiently indicated this gift, he strongly urged her against publishing them, and uniformly expressed a hope that she might never embark in a literary career' (FitzPatrick, p. 336). Aside from a volume of poetry, *Fireflies, ballads, and verses* (London, 1883; not 1833 as in O'Donoghue), she published two novels, one under her father's name. Bareham describes her as 'flighty and unstable' (p. 13). She married Crafton Edgar Smith, a wealthy merchant she met when her family was living in Trieste. She later lived in Tirnau (Slovakia). SOURCE T. Bareham, *Charles Lever: New evaluations* (Gerrards Cross, 1991), p. 13; FitzPatrick, pp 336, 344, 359*n*, 363; O'Donoghue, p. 251.

L193 *A rent in a cloud* (by Charles Lever [*sic*]).
Edinburgh, London: William Blackwood & Sons, [1865]. SOURCE Topp 2, p. 238; NCBEL 3, p. 944.
London: Chapman & Hall, 1870 (new edn). SOURCE Topp 2, p. 239.
Leipzig: Bernard Tauchnitz, 1869. SOURCE T & B, 1006. LOCATION NUC.
Philadelphia: T.B. Peterson & Bros, 1870 (ill.). SOURCE NYPL. LOCATION NUC (n.d. edn), NN.
COMMENTARY No copies of the Edinburgh and London edns located. Attributed by the *Encyclopaedia Britannica* to SL [RL].

L194 *Years ago. A story* (by Sydney Lever).
London: Remington & Co., 1884. SOURCE COPAC. LOCATION L.

LEVINGE, Elizabeth Jane. See **BRABAZON, Elizabeth Jane.**

LEVINGE, Sir Richard George Augustus, 7th Bt, b. Knockdrin Castle, near Mullingar (Co. Westmeath, but ODNB has Hertford Street, London) 1811, d. Brussels (Belgium) 1884. Army officer and miscellaneous writer, RGAL was the eldest son of Sir Richard Levinge, 6th Bt, and Elizabeth Anne, eldest daughter of Thomas Boothby, first Baron Radcliffe. He entered the 43rd Regiment as an ensign in 1828 and with it was posted to Ireland in 1832. Later the regiment went to Canada to help suppress the French-Canadian rebellion of 1837–38. He retired from the army in 1843 and became a lieutenant colonel in the Westmeath militia, HS for Westmeath, and MP for the county from 1856 to 1865. He married first in 1849, Caroline Jane, daughter of Col. Lancelot Rolleston, of Whatnall (Notts.), and secondly in 1870, Margaret Charlotte, daughter of Sir George Campbell, Knt. He was a keen sportsman and lived most of his life in Co. Westmeath. He wrote a book based on his American experiences *Echoes from the backwoods; or, sketches of transatlantic life* (London, 1846, 2 vols.), and *Traveller in the east* (London, 1849), in addition to *Historical records of the forty-third regiment* (London, 1868). SOURCE Allibone, i, p. 1089; Allibone Suppl., ii, p. 998; Boase, ii, pp 406–7; Block, p. 139; Casey & Rowan, pp 370–2; G.E.C. (ed.), *Complete baronetage* (Exeter, 1904), iv, p. 235; E. Lodge, *The peerage and baronetage* (London, 1897), p. 916; ODNB; RIA/DIB; Westmeath, p. 90.

L195 *Cromwell Doolan; or, life in the army* [anon.] (dedicated to Lord Radcliffe).
+ London: Colburn, 1849, 2 vols. SOURCE Westmeath, p. 90; Wolff 4108. LOCATION L.

COMMENTARY Set in nineteenth-century Ireland, and starts at Lough Dereverragh (Co. Westmeath), renowned for its fishing, the story chronicles the fateful history of the O'Neils, former earls of Tyfarnham, who gradually descend into poverty. The attorney Terence Doolan aims to get possession of the last remains of the Tyfarnham property. Much of the novel follows his son, Cromwell Doolin, and his career in the English army's campaigns in Spain. Some of the story is set in Switzerland [ML; RL].

L196 *A day with the Brookside Harries at Brighton* (by Sir Richard George Augustus Levinge).
London, New York: George Routledge & Co., 1858. SOURCE Topp 1, p. 101; COPAC. LOCATION L.

LEVY, —. See **RODENBERG, Julius.**

LEVY, John, pseud. 'Captain Prout', b. Glanagh? (Co. Longford) 1806, d. Dublin 1870. Journalist and novelist, JL was the son of Patrick Levy of Glanagh (Co. Longford) and Mary Tynan. Educated at Stonyhurst, according to the IBL he is said to be the author of *Bob Norberry* (Dublin, 1844). JL was admitted to Gray's Inn (London) in 1842, was called to the Irish Bar in 1845, and reported for the *Irish Jurist*, *Irish Law Reports*, and *Irish Law Times*. He was the author of *The law and practice of bankruptcy and insolvency* (Dublin, 1862, 4th edn). He dropped dead in Dame Street, Dublin, in 1870. SOURCE Boase, ii, p. 407; IBL, 14 (1924), pp 106–7; Keane, p. 287.

L197 *Bob Norberry; or, sketches from the notebook of an Irish reporter* (ed. by 'Captain Prout'; dedicated to C. Bianconi).
+ Dublin: James Duffy, 1844 (ill. W.H. Holbrooke, H. McManus, W. McDowall, I. O'Malley; cover: Fetherston). SOURCE Allibone, ii, p. 1697 [under Prout]; Brown, 9; Sadleir, 77; Wolff, 5665. LOCATION D, Dt, DPL, L InND Loeber coll. (also 1846 edn).
COMMENTARY Originally issued in parts. The number of plates of the 1844 edn varies by copy, with Sadleir's copy containing 7 plates, but the InND Loeber coll. copy contains 9 plates. However, a copy in the Marlborough cat. 186/25 contains 16 plates. The 1846 edn is a reissue of the 1844 edn, but with an additional, engraved title page, and 17 illustrated pages. The author's stated aim is to vindicate the character of his countrymen and to show to Englishmen the state of affairs in Ireland. The book is written in the form of an autobiography and begins with the marriage of the hero's grandparents in Dublin at the end of the eighteenth century. Much attention is paid to how the law works in Ireland. Young Bob Norberry was first intended for the priesthood but becomes a reporter for a Dublin newspaper, which offers an opportunity to describe a variety of events [Brown; RL].

LEWIS, Harriet Newell (née O'Brien), b. 1841, d. 1878. American writer who published several other works of fiction and was a popular writer of serials. SOURCE Allibone Suppl., ii, p. 1000; Brown, p. 174; DAB; NUC; Wright, iii (for other novels).

L198 *Lady Kildare. A novel* (by Harriet Newell Lewis).
New York: Robert Bonner's Sons, [1889]. SOURCE Wright, iii, 3298. LOCATION NUC.
New York: R. Bonner's Sons, 1889 (*As Lady Kildare; or, the rival claimants*). LOCATION NUC.

LEWIS, Mary Elizabeth. See **PENROSE, Mrs H.H.**

LEWIS, Richard, b. England, fl. 1759. Press corrector, bookseller, author and translator. RL arrived in Ireland about 1754 and published his first book, *Some thoughts on education*, in Newry (Co. Down) in 1759. He moved to Dublin, where in about 1780 he resided at 22 Bride Street. His published poetry includes *General election: A poem* (Dublin, 1768), and *A defence of Ireland* (Dublin, 1776), written in reply to Richard Twiss's *A tour in Ireland in 1775* (London, 1776). He contributed to the *Hibernian Magazine* (Dublin, 1772) and to the *Sentimental and Masonic Magazine* (Dublin, 1792–95), where he was called 'corrector of the press'. He wrote sketches such as *The candid philosopher; or, free thoughts on men, morals, and manners* (Dublin, 1778, 2 vols.) and privately published *The Dublin guide; or, a description of the city of Dublin* (Dublin, [1787]). In that year W. Wilson, the author of *The post-chaise companion*, accused RL of plagiarizing information in RL's prospective 'Irish gazetteer'. SOURCE O'Donoghue, pp 251–2; Pollard 2, pp 365–6.

L199 *Tristram Shandy's description of general elections* (by Richard Lewis).
  Dublin: [publisher?], 1762. SOURCE Pollard 2, p. 366.
  COMMENTARY Not in ESTC, and no copy located. Probably inspired by Laurence Sterne's§ *The life and opinions of Tristram Shandy, gentleman* (York, 1760) [RL].

L200 *Pleasing moralist; or, polite philosopher. Consisting of essays, poems, histories, and dialogues serious and comic* (by Richard Lewis).
  + Dublin: For the author, [1780], 2 vols. SOURCE Pollard 2, p. 365; ESTC t206933. LOCATION D.
  COMMENTARY Contains some fiction: 'The loves of Lisander and Narcissa', 'Vertue rewarded: or, the history of Fidelia' [ML].

L201 *Adventures of an actor* (by Henry Lewis).
  Dublin: [publisher?], 1780. SOURCE Pollard 2, p. 366.
COMMENTARY Not ESTC, and no copy located. Probably not the same as *The adventures of an actor, in the characters of a Merry-Andrew, a Methodist-preacher, and a fortune-teller* (London, [various attributed dates: 1770?, 1778, and1782?]) [Raven 1782:1; RL].

LEYNE, Maurice Richard. See 'ZOZIMUS'.

LIDDELL, Clara Lucas. See **BALFOUR, Clara Lucas.**

LINDSAY, Fanny E. See **FISHER, Fanny E.**

LINTON, Revd Henry P., b. Co. Tipperary, *c.*1822, d. England? Church of Ireland clergyman, novelist, and writer on religion, HPL was the son of Robert Linton, vicar choral of Cashel. He obtained his BA at TCD in 1845, and was awarded an MA in 1857. He was curate at Bray (Co. Wicklow) from 1845 to 1846, and curate of Killygordon in the diocese of Derry from 1846 to 1847. He then moved to England and served as vicar of the Holy Trinity Church, Birkenhead, Liverpool, from 1847 to 1859, and returned there in 1882. In between, he was curate and later rector of St Paul's, at Nottingham. He was divinity lecturer at St Aidan's College from 1848 to 1859. His writings from 1858–1887 are mainly on religion and biblical topics. SOURCE B & S, p. 503; CM; Leslie & Wallace, p. 828.

L202 *The curate of Elmdale. A tale of the Irish tithe agitation, during the years 1830 to 1836* (by Henry P. Linton; dedicated to the Revd J. M'Ghee, rector of Holywell-cum-Kneedingwoth).
  + London: Seeley, Burnside & Seeley; Birkenhead: R. Pinkney; Dublin: S.B. Oldham, 1848. SOURCE Allibone, i, p. 1105; Block, p. 141; Hodgson, p. 338; OCLC. LOCATION L.
COMMENTARY Probably partly autobiographical. According to the preface, the actual events related in this novel concerning the tithe agitation took place in a southern diocese in Ireland during the years 1830 to1836 [RL].

LIPPINCOTT, Sara Jane (née Clarke), pseud. '**Grace Greenwood**', b. Pompey (NY) 1823, d. New Rochelle (NY) 1904. An American newspaper correspondent, editor, poet and miscellaneous writer, SJL first became noted for her letters to the editors of the *New York Mirror*. In 1853 she married Leander K. Lippincott of Philadelphia. She edited *The Little Pilgrim*, a

Philadelphia periodical for children, and she was one of the first women in the US to become a regular newspaper correspondent. She visited Ireland before 1857, where she listened to the legends told by peasants and guides, some of which she found 'quite poetic and beautiful'. SOURCE Allibone, i, pp 1105–6; Allibone Suppl., ii, p. 1006; ANB; Blain, pp 458–9 [under Greenwood]; Burke, p. 438; DAB; DLB, vol. 43; Hart, p. 434; *Stories and legends* (Boston, [1857]), p. 215.

L203 *Greenwood leaves: a collection of sketches and letters* (by 'Grace Greenwood'; second series).
Boston: Ticknor, Reed and Fields, 1852. SOURCE Wright, ii, 1559; COPAC. LOCATION Univ. of Birmingham, Wright web.
COMMENTARY Collection of stories that includes 'The Irish patriots of '48' [Wright, ii, 1559].

L204 *Stories and legends of travel and history, for children* (by Sara Jane Lippincott).
+ Boston: Ticknor & Fields, [1857] (ill. John Andrew). LOCATION InND Loeber coll., NUC.
COMMENTARY Second half of the volume consists of brief travel descriptions, each followed by a story for children: 'The fisherman's return', 'Grace O'Malley', 'The little fiddler', 'Little Nora and the Blarney stone', 'Kathleen of Killarney', 'Little Andy and his grandfather', 'Tim O'Daly and the clericaune', 'The poor schoolmaster' [ML].

LIPSETT, Caldwell. See **LIPSETT, H. Caldwell.**

LIPSETT, H. Caldwell (also known as **Caldwell Lipsett**), fl. 1896. A probable Irish fiction and short story writer, who is likely to have served in the army in India. HCL also wrote *Lord Curzon in India* (London, 1903). Members of the Lipsett family resided at Ballyshannon (Co. Donegal) at the end of the nineteenth century. SOURCE Ferguson, p. 229; NUC, RL.

L205 *Where the Atlantic meets the land* (by H. Caldwell Lipsett; dedicated to the author's mother).
London: John Lane, 1896 (Keynote Series, No. 25; cover ill.: Patten Wilson). SOURCE Hart cat. 41/90. LOCATION L.
+ Boston: Roberts Bros London: John Lane, 1896 (ill.). SOURCE Brown, 947. LOCATION O, InND Loeber coll., NUC.
COMMENTARY Concerns Donegal peasantry. Contents: 'The unforgiven sin', 'The legend of Barnesmore gap', 'More cruel than the grave', 'The air-gun', 'The giant's castle', 'The night of the Home Rule bill', 'A border war', 'A nightmare climb', 'A peasant tragedy', 'Orange and green', 'Andy Kerrigan's honeymoon', 'A pauper's burial', 'The gauger's lep [*sic*]', 'The gillie', '"The final flicker"', 'A divided faith' [RL; Leclaire, p. 210].

L206 *A frontier officer. A tale of the Punjab* (by Caldwell Lipsett; dedicated to the author's wife).
+ London: R.A. Everett & Co., 1903. SOURCE Brown, p. 174; NSTC. LOCATION L.
COMMENTARY Features Nora, an Irish girl who comes to India [RL].

'LISTADO, J.T.' Judging from the location of the plots in these two novels, the author probably was resident in Co. Wexford. SOURCE RL.

L207 *Maurice Rhynhart; or, a few passages in the life of an Irish rebel* (by 'J.T. Listado').
+ London: Chapman & Hall, 1871, 2 vols. SOURCE Allibone Suppl., ii, p. 1007; Brown, 950. LOCATION D, L.
COMMENTARY A romantic adventure involving Maurice, a descendant of a Williamite soldier who is a Protestant and a respectable clerk in Selskar (Co. Wexford). He is in love with Miss

Rowan, who is socially much above him. He has to escape from Ireland because of his activities in the Young Ireland movement. In London he marries Miss Rowan and after many hardships they arrive in Australia, where he becomes premier and is knighted. Eventually he returns to Ireland and becomes the MP for Selskar [Brown].

L208   *Civil service* (by 'J.T. Listado').

London: H.S. King & Co., 1874, 2 vols. SOURCE Brown, 951. LOCATION NUC.

COMMENTARY Set in Selskar (Co. Wexford) and in London and tells of the fortunes of the Haughton family, who are county magnates. Events include an election and a trial involving the Haughton estate. The civil service before the days of competitive examination is described [Brown].

LITTLE, Grace. See RHYS, Grace.

LITTLE, William S. See LITTLE, William Swayne.

LITTLE, William Swayne (also known as William S. Little), b. Galway *c*.1812. Prose and verse writer, WSL was the son of Thomas Little, MD. He was admitted to TCD in 1827 where he obtained a BA in 1832 and a MB in 1838. Among the subscribers to this volume is George Little of Lilliput (Co. Wexford). SOURCE B & S, p. 504; O'Donoghue, p. 254; RIA/DIB; RL.

L209   *Leisure moments, in prose and verse* (by William S. Little; dedicated to the author's father, Thomas Little, MD).

+ Dublin: William Curry Jnr & Co.; London: L.B. Seeley & Son; Edinburgh: W. Oliphant, 1833 (subscribers' list). LOCATION D.

COMMENTARY Contents (excluding poems): 'Party of pleasure', 'The emigrant', 'Valley of La Roche', 'Emily Merville', 'Helen Lindsay', 'The student' [ML].

'LITTLEMORE, F.', pseud. See MOORE, Frank Frankfort.

LLOYD, Joseph Henry. Editor. See O'NEILL, William.

'LOCKE, Sophia Mary', pseud. See TOTTENHAM, Blanche Mary Loftus.

'LORD AND LADY THERE', pseud. See NUGENT-GRENVILLE, George, 3rd baron, and his wife, Lady Anne Lucy Poulett Nugent-Grenville.

'LORD B******', pseud. See CHICHESTER, Frederick Richard.

'LORREQUER, Harry', pseud. See LEVER, Charles James.

LOUDAN, Jack. Editor. See ROSS, Mrs Anna Margaret.

LOUDON, Margracia (née Margareta Ryves), b. Ryves Castle (also known as Castlejane, Co. Limerick) *c*.1795, d. England? 1857. Novelist and political writer, ML was the daughter of William Ryves, landowner, and his wife Frances Catherine. Her mother was the author of a volume of verse, *Cumbrian Tales* (London, 1812). The Ryves Castle estate was situated next to Ballywire House (Co. Limerick), where Rosina Wheeler (later Lady Bulwer Lytton§) spent her early years. ML married Charles Loudon, MD, in 1830 in Leamington Priors (War.), the year her first novel was published. The couple settled at Leamington Spa. Her husband published medical works and a book on the medicinal effects of the spa at Leamington. He sat on a committee to investigate child employment in factories and developed a theory about the well-being of populations that differed from that proposed by Malthus. ML also developed social interests and, aside from novels, published *Philantropic economy* (London, 1835) and *The light of mental science* (London, 1845). SOURCE Allibone, i, p. 1134; ODNB [under Charles Loudon]; O'Toole, p. 122.

L210   *First love. A novel* [anon.].
+ London: Saunders & Otley, 1830, 3 vols. SOURCE Garside 2, 1830:71; Wolff, 4190.
LOCATION L, MH.

COMMENTARY One of the characters (Fitz-Ullin) is Irish; in the final chapter Fitz-Ullin and his wife Julia visit Ireland. There are some brief comments about the state of Ireland in this chapter (e.g. 'Here [in Ireland] nature indeed had been bountiful; but her benign intentions had, hitherto, been defeated by an ill judged organization of the social system' (vol. iii, p. 427) [JB].

L211   *Fortune-hunting: A novel* [anon.] (dedicated to Charles Loudon, Esq., M.D.; dedicated written from Leamington Spa).
London: Henry Colburn & Richard Bentley, 1832, 3 vols. SOURCE Garside 2, 1832:58.
LOCATION L, MH.

L212   *Dilemmas of pride* [anon.]
London: Bull & Churton, 1833, 3 vols. SOURCE Garside 2, 1833:45. LOCATION L, MH.

L213   *The fortunes of woman* (by Mrs Loudon, the author of 'First love').
New York: Stringer & Townsend, 1849. SOURCE OCLC. LOCATION Univ. of South Carolina.

COMMENTARY Cover states that the volume is 'entire and unabridged from the London edn', but no English edn has been located. Probably different from Miss Lamont's novel of the same title (London, 1849, 3 vols.) [OCLC; RLIN; RL].

L214   *Maternal love* (by Mrs. Margracia Loudon).
+ London: Thomas Cautley Newby, 1849, 3 vols. SOURCE COPAC. LOCATION L.

LOUGHNAN, Edmond Brenan, fl. 1871. Possibly the same individual as the Irish-Australian poet represented in D. Sladen's *Australian poets* (London, 1888). SOURCE O'Donoghue, p. 255 [under Loughran].

L215   *The foster sisters. A novel* (by Edmond Brenan Loughnan).
London: Tinsley Bros, 1871, 3 vols. SOURCE Allibone Suppl., ii, p. 1019 [as Loughman, *sic*]; Brown, 957; Wolff, 4191; OCLC. LOCATION O, Dt.

COMMENTARY Set in Sligo and Paris and deals with an intricate family history which contains mysteries of identity. One of the characters is murdered and the story concerns the tracking down of the murderer [Brown].

LOVER, Samuel, b. Dublin 1797, d. St Hellier, Jersey (Channel Islands) 1868. Novelist, painter, song writer, composer and performer, the multi-talented SL was the eldest son of Samuel Lover, a stockbroker, and Abigail Maher, an accomplished singer who encouraged her son's artistic and musical interests. Against his will he went to London in 1814 to work in business, which he disliked, while enjoying the artistic life of the city. Returning to Dublin he left business and trained as a painter, working as a miniaturist and as a marine and landscape painter. He began exhibiting at the Dublin Society in 1817. His literary debut was in the *Dublin Literary Gazette*, and with a popular story 'The gridiron', he established himself as a humorist. Many of SL's drawings were engraved in the *Dublin Penny Journal* and the *Irish Penny Magazine* (Dublin, 1833), to which he also contributed 'National proverbs'. He edited the *Dublin Literary*

Gazette (1830), to which he contributed stories and ballads, the *National Magazine* (Dublin, 1830–31), and with John D'Alton the short-lived *Irish Penny Journal* (Dublin, 1833). He was one of the founders of the *Dublin University Magazine* in 1833, to which he contributed also. He published two series of short stories: *Legends and stories of Ireland* (Dublin, 1831; London, 1834), which contain oral tales collected by him in the west of Ireland. Although Lover's name is associated with *Popular tales and legends of the Irish peasantry* (Dublin, 1834), he disclaimed editorship of this anthology. Aside from his novels, he published popular ballads, sketches, plays and some poetry (e.g. *The Comic Offering*, London, 1832; *Songs and ballads*, London, 1839; (with Charles MacKay and Thomas Miller) *Original songs for the volunteers*, London, 1861). He is also known for contributions to satirical works, including *The parson's horn-book* (Dublin, 1831), and *The Valentine post-bag* (Dublin, 1831 [annotated copy in PC]). He illustrated several of his own books and also T.W. Magrath's *Authentic letters from Upper Canada* (Dublin, 1833), which contains some of his etchings. Initially in his artistic and literary career SL divided his time between Dublin and London but in 1837 he moved his household permanently to London. With Charles Dickens and others he founded *Bentley's Miscellany* (London, 1837) to which he contributed. As his accomplishments grew, he became an habitué of Lady Blessington's§ literary salon. His dramas included a stage version of his novel *Rory O'More* and, with the Irish comedian Tyrone Power playing the lead, it had a successful run at the Adelphi Theatre in London. He wrote a burlesque opera *Il Paddy Whack in Italia* (London, 1841) that was produced at the English Opera House by the Irish composer Michael Balfe, for whom he wrote libretti. When his eyesight began to fail, he toured England, and then the US from 1846 to 1848, with a popular stage entertainment of poetry, song and sketches called 'Irish evenings'. In 1856 he received a Civil List pension. SL featured in Edward Kenealy's§ *Brallaghan, or the Deipnosophists* (London, 1845). W.A. Shee recalled him as a 'liberal Irish Protestant ... what a *rara avis* is a Protestant in Ireland, who has any sympathy with her wrongs, or who is free from the most violent political predilections and sectarian politics' (Shee, pp 46–7). Bernard's biography *The life* includes unpublished poems and prose sketches, both American and Irish. Some of his letters and poems are in the Henry E. Huntington Library, San Marino (CA), while many of his drawings are the NLI. His portrait bust is in the National Portrait Gallery, London, and a memorial plaque is in St Patrick's Cathedral, Dublin. For his portraits and papers, see ODNB. SOURCE Allibone, i, p. 1135; Allibone Suppl., ii, p. 1020; B. Bernard, *The life of Samuel Lover, R.H.A.* (New York, 1874); Boylan, p. 201; B. Browne, p. 89; P. Caffrey, 'Samuel Lover's achievement as a painter' in *Irish Arts Review*, 3(1), 1986, pp 51–4; Chronology, p. 81; Clyde, pp 88–9; DLB, clix, cxc; Elmes, p. 120; Field Day, ii, p. 990, 1011; iii, p. 562; S.C. Hall, pp 231–2; W.E. Hall, pp 43–4; Hogan, pp 381–2; Hogan 2, pp 724–5; Igoe, pp 155–9; Irish pseudonyms; W. Laffan & B. Rooney, '"One of our brilliant ornaments": the death and life of Thomas Foster' in *Irish Architectural and Decorative Studies*, 7 (2004), p. 189; McKenna, pp 236–9; NCBEL 4, pp 951–2; OCIL, pp 318–9; ODNB; O'Donoghue, pp 255–6; RIA/DIB; RL; A.J. Symington, *Samuel Lover: A biographical sketch, with selections from his writings and correspondence* (London, 1880); Schulz, p. 281; W.A. Shee, *My contemporaries, 1830–1870* (London, 1893), pp 46–7; Sutherland, pp 384–5.

L216   *Legends and stories of Ireland* (compiled by Samuel Lover; dedicated to Sir Martin Archer Shee§, 'a painter, a poet and an Irishman'; spine: 'first series').

    + Dublin: W.F. Wakeman, 1831 (ill. the author). SOURCE Block, p. 144; Rafroidi, ii, p. 218 (1832 edn); Brown, 961 (1832 edn). LOCATION Corvey, CME 3–628–51096–1, D (1832, 2nd edn), Ireland related fiction, Dt, O, InND Loeber coll. (1832, 2nd edn).

    + Dublin: W.F. Wakeman; London: Baldwin & Cradock, Simpkin & Marshall, R. Groombridge, 1834, 3rd edn (ill. the author). SOURCE Garside 2, 1831:44; LOCATION InND Loeber coll.

+ London: Ward, Lock & Co., [1865] (new edn). SOURCE Topp 2, 427. LOCATION D.
London: Chapman & Hall, [1878?] (cover: *Irish stories and legends*; see Plate 46). Source
OCLC. Location InND Loeber coll.
Birmingham: Lewis, n.d. SOURCE de Búrca cat. 57/375 (only copy located); RL.
Paris: [publisher?], n.d. (adapted and trans. by Francis Nettement as *Histoires et legends irlandaises*). SOURCE OCLC. LOCATION D.
COMMENTARY Became very popular and reached at least a tenth edn. Contains an introd. and
glossary that explains the Irish words. According to the author's preface, the only story which
he himself originated was 'The gridiron'; the remaining stories are essentially of oral origin
from the west of Ireland. Two of the stories were first published in the *Dublin Literary Gazette*.
Preface to the 1831 edn mentions that 'Though the sources whence these stories are derived
are open to every one, yet chance or choice may prevent thousands from making such sources
available; and though the village crone and mountain guide have many hearers, still their circle is so circumscribed, that most of what I have ventured to lay before my readers, is, for the
first time, made tangible to the greater portion of those who do me the favour to become such'.
SL explains that the stories 'are given in the manner of the Irish peasantry; and this has led
to some peculiarities that might be objected to, were not the cause explained – namely, frequent digressions in the course of the narrative, occasional adjurations, and certain words
unusually spelt. As to the first, I beg to answer, that the stories would be deficient in national
character without it; – the Irish are so imaginative, that they never tell a story straight forward, but constantly indulge in episode: for the second, it is only fair to say, that in most
cases, the Irish peasant's adjurations are not meant to be in the remotest degree irreverent;
but arise merely from the impassioned manner of speaking, which an excitable people are prone
to'. Consists of a mixture of 'authentic' old legends, accounts of surviving superstitions, and
modern anecdotes. Contents: 'King O'Toole and St. Kevin. A legend of Glendalough', 'Lough
Corrib', 'Manuscript from the cabinet of Mrs—. A legend of Lough Mask', 'The white trout
– A legend of Cong', 'The battle of the Berrins, or the double funeral', 'Father Roach', 'The
priest's story', 'The king and the bishop. A legend of Clonmacnoise', 'An essay on fools', 'The
catastrophe', 'The devil's mill', 'The gridiron; or, Paddy Mullowney's travels in France'
[Samuel Lover], 'Paddy the piper', 'The priest's ghost', 'New potatoes – An Irish melody' [in
one version, called '"My new pittayatees!"'], 'Paddy the Sport'. Later edn has additional stories: 'National minstrelsy. Ballads and ballad singers', 'National proverbs' [RL; Harris, pp 44,
189; CM; RLIN; Topp 3, p. 333].

L217 *Legends and stories of Ireland* (second series; compiled by Samuel Lover; dedicated
to Thomas Moore§).
+ London: Baldwin & Cradock, 1834 (ill. W. Harvey, Samuel Lover). SOURCE Block,
p. 144; Rafroidi, ii, p. 218; Brown, 961; Garside 2, 1834:46. LOCATION Grail, Corvey,
CME 3–628–51095–3, Ireland related fiction, D, L, InND Loeber coll. (also 1837, 2nd
edn).
COMMENTARY Contents: 'Barny O'Reirdon, the navigator' (first published in the *Dublin
University Magazine*, 1833), 'The burial of the tithe', 'The white horse of the Peppers. A legend of the Boyne', 'The legend of the little weaver of Duleek gate', 'Conclusion of the white
horse of the Peppers',' 'The curse of Kishoge', 'The fairy finder', 'The leprechaun and the
genius', 'The Spanish boar and the Irish bull. A zoological puzzle', 'Little fairly' (first published in the *Dublin University Magazine*, 1833), 'Judy of Roundwood' [RL].

L218 *Legends and stories of Ireland* (first and second series; compiled by Samuel Lover).
Philadelphia: Carey & Hart, 1835, 2 vols. SOURCE Topp 3, p. 334. SOURCE OCLC.
LOCATION Georgetown Univ., Washington, DC.
+ New York: Dick & Fitzgerald, n.d., 2 vols. LOCATION InND Loeber coll.

+ London: H.G. Bohn, 1848, 2 vols. (new edn; ill. J. Thompson). LOCATION D, InND.
London: C.H. Clarke & Co., 1861 (new edn; Parlour Library, No. 243). SOURCE Topp 3, p. 334; OCLC. LOCATION DCL.
+ London: Newnes, [*c*.1896–1899] (as *Barney O'Reirdon and other Irish legends and stories*; Newnes' Penny Library of Famous Books, No. 22). SOURCE Sadleir, 3643. LOCATION InND Loeber coll.
[Paris?]: [publisher?], 1856 (trans. as *Légendes irlandaises*). SOURCE Garside 2, 1834:47.
COMMENTARY No copy of the Paris edn located. A combination of the first and second series of these stories (for contents of each, see above). The London, New York edn (n.d.) has an additional story, 'Ballads and ballad singers', but lacks two other stories [RL].

L219 *Rory O'More. A national romance* (by Samuel Lover).
+ London: Richard Bentley, 1837, 3 vols. (ill. the author). SOURCE Rafroidi, ii, p. 219; Brown, 958; Sadleir, 1452; Topp 8, 190. LOCATION InND Loeber coll. (also London, 1839 edn), Grail, Dt, L.
London: Richard Bentley; Edinburgh: Bell & Bradfute; Dublin: J. Cumming, 1839 (revsd and corrected; ill.; Bentley's Standard Novels, No. 76). SOURCE COPAC. LOCATION Dt.
+ Liverpool: Bon Marché, n.d. LOCATION PC.
Philadelphia: Carey, Lea & Blanchard, 1837, 2 vols. SOURCE Kaser, 658. LOCATION MH.
+ Philadelphia: Lea & Blanchard, 1844. LOCATION D (1846 edn), InND Loeber coll.
New York: Burgess & Garrett, 1851 (ill.). SOURCE NYPL. LOCATION NN.
+ Calcutta: William Rushton, 1837. LOCATION D.
COMMENTARY An often reprinted historical novel of dubious accuracy, in which the hero Rory, a comical character, tries to prove that the atrocities in 1798 were due to a few desperadoes. The songs in this volume were set to music by the author and he adapted the story as a play (London, 1837). The play was subsequently transformed into a chapbook of 24pp, entitled *Rory O'More, an Irish tale* (Durham, 1839), and a song (London, [*c*.1835]). The story became one of the first movies filmed in Ireland (1911) [RL; Brown; Figgis cat. n.s. 10/301; R. Hogan, *Dion Boucicault* (New York, 1969), p. 27; Leclaire, p. 63].

L220 *Handy Andy: A tale of Irish life* (by Samuel Lover).
+ London: Frederick Lover, Aldine Chambers & Richard Groombridge, 1842 (ill. Samuel Lover). SOURCE Brown, 959; Rafroidi, ii, p. 219; Sadleir, 1451; Wolff, 4192; Topp 8, 199. LOCATION Grail, D, DPL, L, NUC, InND Loeber coll. (n.d. edn, large binding in red cloth; also small binding in green cloth, black stamped).
Paris: M. Gautier, n.d. (trans. by A. Nettement as *L'Enterrement de la dîme, le combat des funérailles*). SOURCE Rafroidi, ii, p. 366; Bn-Opale plus. LOCATION BNF.
+ New York: D. Appleton & Co., Philadelphia: George S. Appleton, 1843 (ill. but only two, not 22 illustrations as stated on the title page). SOURCE NYPL (1851 edn). LOCATION InND Loeber coll., NUC, NN (1851 edn).
+ Chicago: Donohue Bros, n.d. (ill. the author). LOCATION InND Loeber coll.
+ Philadelphia: Henry B. Ashmead, n.d. (ill. Geo. G. White). LOCATION InND Loeber coll.
COMMENTARY An often reprinted novel. First serialized in *Bentley's Miscellany* (London, Jan. 1837–May 1839), and published in 12 monthly parts (London, Frederick Lover & Richard Groombridge, Jan.–Dec. 1842), and in parts by D. Appleton & Co. (New York, 1842). Misadventures of a comic, blundering Irish manservant, Andy Rooney, as well as episodes featuring the gentry, duellists, hedge-school masters, poteen distillers and other characters [Brown; Leclaire, p. 64; Sutherland, pp 274–5; Topp 4, p. 172].

L221 *Treasure trove: the first of a series of accounts of Irish heirs: being a romantic Irish tale of the last century* (by Samuel Lover; dedicated to the earl of Charlemont).
+ London: Frederick Lover, Aldine Chambers, 1844 (ill. the author). SOURCE Bradshaw, 5910; Brown, 960; Rafroidi, ii, p. 219; Sadleir, 1453; Wolff, 4195. LOCATION Grail, D, L, C, InND Loeber coll. COMMENTARY *London 1844 edn* Published from the parts [RL].
London: Bryce, [1854] (new edn; as *He would be a gentleman; or, treasure trove. A romance*). SOURCE Topp 3, p. 332; Sadleir, 3614. LOCATION NUC (1866 edn).
+ London, New York: Frederick Warne & Co., n.d. (as *Treasure trove; or, he would be a gentleman*). LOCATION InND Loeber coll.
New York: D. Appleton & Co., 1844 (ill.). SOURCE NYPL. LOCATION NN.
New York: J. Winchester, 1844. SOURCE Topp 2, p. 62. COMMENTARY *New York, Winchester, 1844 edn* No copy located [RL].
+ New York: D. Appleton & Co.; Philadelphia: George S. Appleton, 1847 (as *Treasure trove: A tale*; ill. the author). SOURCE Topp 3, p. 332. LOCATION InND Loeber coll., D (1849 edn).
New York: Dick & Fitzgerald, 1862 (as *Irish heirs*). SOURCE NCBEL 3, p. 745; OCLC. LOCATION Univ. of Delaware.
COMMENTARY According to OCLC and Allibone it was published first in eight parts in 1844 under the title *£ s. d.: treasure trove; a romantic Irish tale*. However, Topp states that it was first published in parts in London, starting in January 1843. A pseudo-historical tale featuring the adventures of Ned Corkery who was in the service of the Irish Brigade in France and of the Young Pretender [Allibone, i, p. 1135; Brown; Topp 3, p. 332].

L222 *Tom Crosbie and his friends* (by Samuel Lover).
Buffalo: A. Burke, [1855]. LOCATION NUC.
New York: G. Munro, 1878. SOURCE NCBEL 3, p. 745. LOCATION NUC.
COMMENTARY No European edn located [RL].

L223 *The life of Samuel Lover, R.H.A., artistic, literary, and musical, with selections from his unpublished papers and correspondence* (ed. by Bayle Bernard).
+ London: Henry S. King & Co., 1874, 2 vols. LOCATION InND Loeber coll.
COMMENTARY Posthumous publication. Author's life, Irish and American essays and fictional Irish sketches. Examples of the latter are: 'St. Patrick and the serpent', 'The Dublin fishwoman', 'Paddy and the bear' [Samuel Lover], 'The Irish post-boy', 'Paddy at sea' [RL].

L224 *Miscellaneous stories, sketches, etc., now chiefly collected for the first time* (by Samuel Lover; ed. by D.J. O'Donoghue).
Westminster [London]: A. Constable & Co., 1899. SOURCE NYPL. LOCATION NN, NUC.
+ Westminster [London]: Archibald Constable & Co., 1899 (as *Further stories of Ireland*, ed. and introd. by D.J. O'Donoghue). LOCATION InND Loeber coll., DPL, NUC.
COMMENTARY Contents: 'St. Patrick and the serpent', 'It's mighty improvin'', 'The Irish post-boy', 'Dublin porters, carmen and waiters', 'The Irish Brigade', 'Paddy at sea', 'Illustrations of national proverbs', 'The happy man, an extravaganca in one act' (a play). With notes. Some of the stories had been published earlier in *The life of Samuel Lover* (London, 1874) [NYPL].
— COLLECTED WORKS

L225 *The selected writings of Samuel Lover.*
New York: P.F. Collier & Son, [1854], 10 vols. LOCATION NUC.

L226 *The novels and tales of Samuel Lover.*
New York, Montreal: D. & J. Sadlier & Co., 1872–73, 5 vols. LOCATION DCU, InND Loeber coll. COMMENTARY *New York 1872–73 edn* Green cloth binding impressed with harp in gold [RL].

New York, Montreal: D. & J. Sadlier & Co., 1874–75, 5 vols. LOCATION InND Loeber coll. COMMENTARY *New York 1874–75 edn* Bound in half leather binding on marbled boards; spine: Lover's Works, but no publisher's name [RL].

L227　*The novels and tales of Samuel Lover.*
New York: P.J. Kenedy & Sons, [1895], 5 vols. (ill.; copyright D. & J. Sadlier & Co., 1885). SOURCE OCLC. LOCATION InND Loeber coll. (one vol.).
COMMENTARY Remainder issue of the Sadleir edn. Two binding types: (a) crushed leather half morocco, gilt tops at $3.50; (b) half calf, gilt edges at $10. Emblem on title page the same. The series probably is a reissue of the collected works first published by D. & J. Sadlier. The Kenedy series of Lover's works was advertised as part of 'Kenedy's Gilt-top Series of Irish Novelists', and included the works of the Banim brothers§, William Carleton§, and Gerald Griffin§, in total 35 uniformly bound volumes, which were priced at $22 [Sheet adv. P.J. Kenedy, [1895]; RL].

L228　[*Works of Samuel Lover*].
New York: Brentano's, 1900, 6 vols. LOCATION NUC.
COMMENTARY Unnumbered and untitled series [RL].

L229　*The collected writings of Samuel Lover.*
+ Boston: Little, Brown & Co., 1901–3, 10 vols. (Treasure Trove edn.; ill. by the author, H.L. Richardson). LOCATION InND Loeber coll.
COMMENTARY Limited edn of 900 [RL].

L230　*The novels and tales of Samuel Lover.*
London, New York: George Routledge & Sons, n.d., [no. of vols. unclear]. LOCATION D (one vol.). L231　*The works of Samuel Lover.*
New York: Athenaeum, 1901, 6 vols. SOURCE RLIN. LOCATION CSt.
Boston: Little, Brown, 1902, 6 vols. SOURCE RLIN. LOCATION NNC.

LOWELL, Robert. See **LOWELL, Robert Trail Spence.**

LOWELL, Robert Trail Spence (known as **Robert Lowell**), b. Boston (MA) 1816, d. Schenectady (NY) 1891. RTSL was the son of a Unitarian minister and of Harriet Brackett Spence. He graduated from Harvard University and trained for the ministry of the Episcopal Church. He served in Bermuda and was sent as a missionary to Bay Roberts, Newfoundland, a fishing town on Conception Bay. During 1846–7 Newfoundland experienced a severe famine, brought on by the failure of the inshore fishery and a potato blight. RTSL wrote the following novel eleven years after leaving Bay Roberts. SOURCE BLC, DCB (on line, accessed 12–12–04).

L232　*The new priest in Conception Bay* (by Robert Lowell).
+ Boston: Phillips, Sampson & Co., 1858, 2 vols. SOURCE OCLC. Location L.
Boston: E.P. Dutton, 1864 (new edn; as *The story of the new priest in Conception Bay*). LOCATION L.
COMMENTARY Set in a fishing village in Newfoundland and features an Irish priest, Fr O'Toole [Personal communication, George Casey, Nov. 2004; RL].

LOWRY, Frank M., pseud. '**Zabo**', fl. 1900. Humorous writer.
L233　*Dublin statues "at home." A new year's tale* (by 'Zabo').
+ Dublin: Sealy, Bryers & Walker, 1900 (ill. Taman; on cover: *Dublin statues alive*). LOCATION InND Loeber coll., DPL.
COMMENTARY 32pp. Comic story about Dublin statues coming alive on New Year's eve, 1900. They discuss politics and go to a party. On their way back, they are arrested and are freed only if they promise to stay on their pedestals [ML].

LOWTHER, G. See **LOWTHER, Gorges.**

LOWTHER, Gorges (known as **G. Lowther**), b. Dublin? 1769, d. Hampton Hall (Som.) 1854. Novelist and religious writer, GL was the son of Gorges Lowther of Lowther Lodge, Dublin (probably MP for Rathoath, 1739–60, and Co. Meath, 1761–92). He served in the Dragoon Guards in 1787, and later became a MP for Ratoath (Co. Meath) from 1790 to 1800, after which he sold his seat, Kilrue (Co. Meath). He was the author of *Brief observations on the state of the Waldenses, in the year 1820* (London, 1821), and a pamphlet, *Abjurations from popery* (London, 1847). SOURCE Allibone, i, p. 1141; B & S, p. 514; Boase, ii, p. 517; RL; NUC.

L234   *Gerald; a tale of conscience* (by G. Lowther).
        + London: John W. Parker, 1840, 2 vols. in 1. LOCATION InND Loeber coll., L.
COMMENTARY Probably written in response to Miss Eleanor C. Agnew's§ *Geraldine, a tale of conscience* (London, 1837–39), which describes a conversion from protestantism to catholicism. *Gerald* describes a reverse conversion from catholicism to protestantism. The main character is a Catholic Irish priest, who by reading the Bible has started to feel some doubts about his religion. In long theological conversations with his nephew Gerald he becomes convinced to convert to protestantism. The book is set partly in Ireland and partly in England and is written as a long letter of justification to a priest in Ireland, a friend from his days in the seminary at Maynooth [ML].

LUCAS, Revd Charles, b. 1769, d. Devizes (Wilts.) 1854. English clergyman, novelist and poet, CL was the son of William Lucas of Daventry (Northants.). He matriculated at Oriel College, Oxford, in 1786. He used 'A.M.' on the title pages of his books, but the university does not record him as a graduate. He became curate of Avebury (Wilts) in 1791 and devoted himself to writing religious poems and novels, using several countries as backdrops to his fiction. Only his novels with Irish links are listed below. SOURCE Allibone, i, p. 1142; Blakey, pp 183, 269; Block, p. 145; BLC; British Fiction (Update 1, under 1800 and 1802); ODNB; NCBEL 4, p. 402.

L235   *The infernal Quixote. A tale of the day* (by Charles Lucas).
        London: William Lane, 1801, 4 vols. (ill. J. Simpkins). SOURCE Blakey, p. 198; British Fiction; Garside, 1801:45; Forster 2, 2622. LOCATION Corvey CME 3–28–48119–8, Ireland related fiction, L.
        Dublin: D. Grasberry, 1801, 4 vols. in 2. SOURCE OCLC. LOCATION Dm.
        Paris: Riche, Le Normant, Maradan, 1801 (trans. as *L'infernal Don Quichotte: histoire à l'ordre du jour*). SOURCE COPAC. LOCATION Univ. of Leeds.
        Peterborough (ON): Broadview, 2004 (ed. by M.O. Grenby). SOURCE OCLC. LOCATION Boston College.
COMMENTARY An anti-Jacobin novel in the form of a Gothic fantasy, attacking the revolutionary ideas of William Godwin§ and other Jacobin authors. The novel is intended as an abrasive response and conservative answer to the radical presumptions of Godwin and the Rousseauistic theories of Robert Bage§ and Thomas Holcroft, his fellow Jacobin novelists of the 1790s. The anti-hero of the story, Lord Marauder, adopting the pseudonym of Patrick McGinnis, becomes involved with the Irish rebellion, which then allows him to reveal the real intentions of the United Irishmen. Marauder is a diabolical freethinker and predatory anarchist on the loose. His egotism helps to forment the Irish rebellion of 1798, to which Lucas appends a fictive collapse of the British government itself, followed by the dissolution of social order. When he is not undermining legal governments, the hero is defiling innocent women with his Godwinian notions of open marriage [Frank, 252; Johnson cat. 38/52; Tracy, 104; M.O. Grenby, *The anti-Jacobin novel* (Cambridge, 2001), p. 58].

L236 *The double trial; or, the consequences of an Irish clearing. A tale of the present day* [anon.].

+ London: Smith, Elder & Co., 1832, 3 vols. SOURCE Brown, 22 (1834 edn); Garside 2, 1832:59. LOCATION Corvey, CME 3–628–47648–8, Ireland related fiction, L.

COMMENTARY Attribution to Revd C. Lucas is detailed in Garside 2. The novel describes Irish economic conditions, the evils of absenteeism and the abuses of the landlords. The scene is laid in Ireland for only the first few chapters. The book is written from a Protestant point of view. James Elrington is called to the Bar in 1812 and eventually moves to a mansion in Coombhleigh in Ireland. Depressed by the poverty, starvation, fever and clearances of the local Irish population, Elrington, his wife and daughter flee Ireland. On their way to Dublin they pick up a starving child and appeal to an Irishman to bury her dead mother. The man, taking the money, declines and says: 'Let the dead bury their dead!' They take the little girl with them to Dublin where she is rejected by the Foundling Hospital. A discussion ensues about the history of the Foundling Hospitals in Ireland and the philosophy of Malthus. The main story is about two children exchanged in infancy. In adulthood several lawsuits take place, resulting in the determination of their identities and their titles to estates. Includes some poetry [Brown; CM; Garside 2, 1832:59].

LUCK, Mrs Mary Churchill (née Spottiswood-Ashe) pseud. '**M. Hamilton**', b. Kilrea (Co. Derry) 1869, d. England? 1949. She may be a descendant of Revd George Hamilton Ashe (whose father was of Ashbrook, Co. Derry) and who married in 1828, Mary daughter of the Rev. Thomas Spottiswood, by whom had two sons, William Hamilton Ashe and Thomas Spottiswood Ashe, and an unnamed daughter. Mary married Churchill Arthur Luck in Lahore, India, in 1898, where she spent the first twenty years of her marriage. She returned to England and was living in London in 1919. She wrote 18 works of fiction, of which several were set in Ireland, and most deal with man-woman relationships. Her Ulster-based novels are notable for their focus on relationships not just between individuals but between social classes. MCL is wrongly listed by Brown and Hogan as Mrs Churchill-Luck. Several of her letters are in the NLI (MS 13,825). SOURCE Brady, p. 98; Brown, p. 129; EF, p. 171–72; Hogan 2, p. 519 [under Hamilton]; Leslie, *Derry*, p. 174; NUC.

L237 *A self-denying ordinance* (by 'M. Hamilton').

New York: D. Appleton & Co., 1895 (Appleton's Town and Country Library, No. 183). SOURCE Alston, p. 262; Brown, p. 129. LOCATION L, NUC.

L238 *Across an Ulster bog* (by 'M. Hamilton').

+ London: William Heinemann, 1896 (The Pioneer Series; ill. showing a picture of Japanese ladies, after Kitagawa Utamara, 1752–1806). SOURCE Alston, p. 262; Brown, 705 (mistakenly gives title and date as 'Under an Irish bog', 1894); Hogan 2, p. 519; Personal communication, Lucille Stark, June 2000. LOCATION InND Loeber coll., Dt, D, L.

New York: E. Arnold, 1896. LOCATION NUC.

COMMENTARY Set in Co. Derry. A story about a southern Irish Protestant clergyman who seduces a northern Irish Protestant peasant girl. The complications of his position vis-à-vis the peasantry and the gentry are described and Protestant interdenominational issues explored [Brown; Hogan; Leclaire, p. 211].

L239 *McLeod of the Camerons* (by 'M. Hamilton').

London: W. Heinemann, 1897. SOURCE Alston, p. 262; Brown, p. 129. LOCATION L.

New York: D. Appleton & Co., 1897 (Appleton's Town and Country Library, No. 207). LOCATION NUC.

L240 *The freedom of Harry Meredyth* (by 'M. Hamilton').

New York: D. Appleton & Co., 1897 (Appleton's Town and Country Library, No. 230). LOCATION NUC.

London: W. Heinemann, 1898. SOURCE Alston, p. 262; Brown, p. 129. LOCATION L.

L241   *The dishonour of Frank Scott* (by 'M. Hamilton').
London: Hurst & Blackett, 1900. SOURCE Alston, p. 262. LOCATION L.
New York, London: Harper & Bros, 1900. LOCATION NUC.

L242   *Poor Elizabeth* (by 'M. Hamilton').
London: Hurst & Blackett, 1901. LOCATION L, NUC.

L243   *Beyond the boundary* (by 'M. Hamilton').
London: Hurst & Blackett, 1902. SOURCE Brown, 706; Hogan 2, p. 510. LOCATION L.
COMMENTARY Set in London and Ulster. Brian Lindsay, soldier son of Presbyterian Ulster peasants, in a moment of panic had deserted his men in action. By mistake he is decorated, instead of the man who had died to save him. In London he meets this man's sister, a working girl but a lady. They are married and he takes her home. The wife is disillusioned with the marriage and Brian is threatened with the discovery of his secret cowardice [Brown; Hogan].

L244   *On an Ulster farm* (by 'M. Hamilton').
London: R.A. Everett & Co., 1904. SOURCE Brown, 707; Hogan 2, p. 519. LOCATION L ([1905] edn), NUC ([1904] edn).
COMMENTARY The story of a workhouse child sent out to service to an unlovable set of Ulster Scots in Co. Derry [Brown; Hogan; Leclaire, p. 211].

L245   *Cut laurels* (by 'M. Hamilton').
London: William Heinemann, 1905. LOCATION L, NUC.
COMMENTARY The heroine's husband has been a prisoner in Egypt for eighteen years. In the meantime she has brought up their daughter while making a living as a dressmaker in Belfast. When he is released, she has to cope with the renewal of intimacy and the knowledge that he has an Egyptian wife and two sons. She makes the best of the situation and is rewarded with happiness [EF, p. 172].

L246   *The first claim* (by 'M. Hamilton').
London: Methuen & Co., 1906. LOCATION L.
+ New York: Doubleday, Page & Co., 1907. LOCATION InND Loeber coll., NUC.
COMMENTARY A story of the desperate choices a woman must make when locked in a stifling marriage. Valerie Palmer marries an older man with considerable wealth, but finds herself alone and unappreciated, watching her mother-in-law and the family nanny raise with an iron hand her young child; after agonizing about leaving her child, she runs off with another man, but then plots to steal her child from the other household [Sumner & Stillman cat. 99/193].

L247   *Mrs Brett* (by 'M. Hamilton').
London: Stanley Paul & Co., 1913. LOCATION L.
COMMENTARY In India, Judy Brett's sick fiancée is nursed by her mother, who long ago ran away from her odious husband. Mrs Brett goes back with the fiancée to England and embarks on a career as a successful painter [EF, p. 172].

L248   *The woman who looked back* (by 'M. Hamilton').
London: Stanley Paul & Co., 1914. LOCATION L, NUC.

L249   *The general's wife* (by 'M. Hamilton').
London: Stanley Paul & Co., 1916, 2nd edn. LOCATION L.

L250   *The locust's years* (by 'M. Hamilton').
London: Skeffington & Sons, [1919]. LOCATION L.

L251   *Anne against the world* (by 'M. Hamilton').
London: Hurst & Blackett, [1922]. LOCATION L.

L252   *The detached marriage* (by 'M. Hamilton').
London: Hurst & Blackett, [1923]. LOCATION L.

L253   *The alien child* (by 'M. Hamilton').
London: Hurst & Blackett, [1924]. LOCATION L.

L254   *The breakaway* (by 'M. Hamilton').
London: Hurst & Blackett, [1928]. LOCATION L.

LUGARD, Flora Louise, Baroness. See **SHAW, Flora Louise.**

LUNN, Mrs John Calbraith, fl. 1873. A novelist and hymn writer, Mrs JCL was the wife of a clergyman and hymn writer, Revd John Calbraith Lunn, who published a book of hymns in Leicester in 1880. Mrs JCL wrote several novels, but only one novel has Irish contents. SOURCE BLC; COPAC.

L255   *Shamrock and rose* (by Mrs John Calbraith Lunn).
+ London: T. Fisher Unwin, 1888, 3 vols. SOURCE Allibone Suppl., ii, p. 1027; OCLC. LOCATION InND Loeber coll., L.

COMMENTARY A story of love and religious differences contrasting Irish and English characters. Ethne O'Meath, a Catholic Irishwoman, marries a Protestant Englishman and finds that she can not live with the difference of their religion between them. Interwoven is another love story between her cousin Fergus who falls in love with an English lady. Their courtship is complicated by a cloud hanging over him because of his possible involvement in the murder of a landlord's son [ML].

LUPTON, William, fl. 1849. Religious writer and a Wesleyan minister. SOURCE BLC.

L256   *The Irish convert; or, Popish intolerance illustrated* (by William Lupton).
+ London: J. Mason, 1849. SOURCE OCLC. LOCATION InND Loeber coll., L, Drew Univ., Madison (NJ) (1860 edn).

COMMENTARY A proselytizing novel of religious conversion set in the north of Ireland. The story of Magorian's conversion is used as a vehicle to explain various theological controversies. The Catholic Magorian learns that the way he prays is a rigid formula in which he does not bring his concerns directly to God. He attends an evangelical meeting at a marketplace, which starts him thinking about religious matters. He begins reading the Bible and, eventually, turns away from catholicism to embrace the Protestant faith. The Catholic clergy cajole and threaten him and his family makes it difficult for him to attend Protestant religious services by hiding his socks and boots. When his life is nearing its end, he is afraid that a Catholic priest will attend to him, but a Protestant minister sits with him and he dies peacefully [ML].

LUTTRELL, Henry, b. Dublin (according to O'Donoghue) 1768, d. London 1851, probable pseud. '**A flat enlightened "experienta docet"**'. Fiction writer, poet and wit, HL is said to have been the natural son of Henry Lawes Luttrell, 2nd earl of Carhampton, who was of Irish stock, and a gardener's daughter named Harman from Woodstock. Raised under the surname of King, he studied at TCD, where he graduated BA in 1790 and LLB in 1791, in which year he was called to the Irish Bar. He took the name Luttrell, and through his father's influence obtained a seat for Clonmines (Co. Wexford) in the 1798 Irish parliament, and a post in the Irish government, which he later commuted for a pension. In about 1802 he was sent for a brief period to the West Indies to manage his father's estates there. He settled in London, where he was well-received in high society because of his great wit and easy manners, and was a frequent guest at Holland House and Lady Blessington's§ Gore House. He was a good friend of Thomas Moore§, and the pair was 'seldom apart, and always hating, abusing, and ridiculing each other' (ODNB, p. 812). HL travelled much in Europe. Moore acted as the sponsor for the volume of poetry, *Advice to Julia* (London, 1820). In 1850 HL married Ann Springer, but it is possible that he had married before. For his correspondence to Lord and Lady Holland, see ODNB. SOURCE Allibone, i, p. 1144; British Fiction; COPAC; ODNB; O'Donoghue, pp 257–8.

L257 *Life in the West; or, the curtain drawn. A novel ... Containing sketches, scenes, conversations, and anecdotes of the last importance to families, and men of rank, fashion, and fortune. Founded on facts* (by 'A flat enlightened "experienta docet"'; dedicated to the Rt Hon. Robert Peel, MP).

+ London: C. Chapple, 1828, 2 vols. in 1. SOURCE British Fiction; Garside, 1828:38; Wolff, 7637. LOCATION Corvey CME 3–628–48103–1, L, MH.

+ London: Saunders & Otley, 1828, 2nd edn, 2 vols. (as *Crockford's; or, life in the West*). SOURCE Garside, 1828:37; British Fiction; NSTC; Wolff, 7637a (1828, 3rd edn). LOCATION L.

New York: J. & J. Harper, 1828, 2 vols. (as *Crockford's; or, life in the West*). SOURCE British Fiction; OCLC. LOCATION CtY.

COMMENTARY For the attribution to Henry Luttrell (rather than – Deale) see British Fiction and Wolff. Satire on gambling. Only chapter 1 has Irish content: at a dinner party the state of catholicism in Ireland is extensively discussed. There is a new preface to a later edn, in which the author claims that the novel has already forced the closing down or curtailment of activities in gambling houses [CM; British Fiction; Wolff, 7637, 7637a; ODNB].

L258 *Craven Derby, or the lordship by tenure, includes The ladye of the rose: an historical legend, relating to the great founder of the noble house of Darbye* (by the author of *Crockford's; or, life in the West*).

+ London: Merric Smith, 1832–33, 2 vols. SOURCE Garside 2, 1837:26; British Fiction; COPAC. LOCATION Corvey CME 3–628–47351–9, Dt, L.

COMMENTARY Attributed by Halkett and Laing to Henry Luttrell. Contents: 'Craven Derby', 'The ladye of the rose'. Craven Derby visits the remains of the family castle. The family have lost all their possessions but he finds an old manuscript. He transcribes it and this is 'The ladye of the rose'. That story is set at the time of the Crusades, and contains various adventures in the Middle East. No Irish content [Halkett & Laing, i, p. 451; ML; Wolff, 7637].

'LYALL, Edna', pseud. See BAYLY, Ada Ellen.

LYNAM, Capt. William. See LYNAM, William Francis.

LYNAM, William Francis (known as Capt. William Lynam), b. Shandilla, Connemara (Co. Galway) 1845, d. Clontarf (Dublin) 1894. Humorist, dramatist and editor, WFL was an officer in the 5th Royal Lancashire militia. He wrote a large number of serials for magazines (e.g., 'The Lynaghs of Croghan; or, the three systems of courtship' in the *Dublin Saturday Magazine*, 1867), of which the most famous was *The adventures of Mick M'Quaid*. The stories of Mick M'Quaid were also published as an extended serial in the *Shamrock* (Dublin), of which he was editor from 1867 until his death, and they were reproduced in penny numbers. WFL grew tired of M'Quaid and tried to replace him with other characters, but any cessation in episodes caused an immediate drop in the circulation of the *Shamrock*. Another humorous series, 'Darby Durkan P.L.G.', was published in the *Irish Emerald* (Dublin). WFL also wrote a comic drama 'Darby the dodger' (Dublin, 1877). He lived at Churchtown House, Dundrum, and later at Clontarf and was a pious, retiring Catholic. His famous character, M'Quaid, is remembered in a popular brand of tobacco of the same name still used in Ireland. For WFL's portrait, see Elmes. SOURCE Boase, vi, p. 94; Brady, p. 137; Brown, p. 178; Elmes, p. 121; Galway, pp 65–6; Hogan 2, p. 726; McKenna, pp 240–41; ODNB; D.J. O'Donoghue, 'The author of Mick M'Quaid', IBL, 3 (1911–12), pp 4–7; RIA/DIB; RL; Sutherland, p. 387.

L259   *The adventures of Mick M'Quaid* (by Capt. William Lynam).
+ Dublin: Office of the 'Shamrock', 1875, vol. 1. SOURCE McKenna, p. 240 (mistakenly states that only one vol. was published); OCLC. LOCATION Grail, D, L.
+ Dublin: Office of the 'Shamrock', 1877, vol. 2. LOCATION D, DPL.
COMMENTARY The copy in the DPL, presumably taken from the *Shamrock* (Dublin), carries the title 'Mick M'Quaid, the evangeliser' (a satirical account of a scripture reader) [RL; Brown, 969 (lists other episodes of M'Quaid from the *Shamrock*); Sutherland].

L260   *Christ Church vaults; or, a night amongst the dead* (by William Francis Lynam).
Dublin: John Mullany, [1888 or earlier]. SOURCE Adv. in the *Irish Catholic directory* (Dublin, 1888).
COMMENTARY No copy located. First published in the *Dublin Saturday Magazine* (1867) and subsequently priced at 3*d*. [RL].

LYNCH, E.M. See **LYNCH, Edward Melville**

LYNCH, Edward Melville (known as **E.M. Lynch**), fl. 1893. Novelist EML is called a 'Miss' by Brown, but this must be in error. SOURCE Brown, p. 178; Ryan, p. 118; Wolff, iii, p. 54.

L261   *The boy-god, troublesome and vengeful* (by E.M. Lynch).
London: T. Fisher Unwin, 1893 (ill.). SOURCE OCLC. LOCATION L.
COMMENTARY Amusing novel intended as a satire on students of a girls' college who scorn love and are passionately interested in economic science. But the boy-god finds his way in and shoots his deadly arrows at their theories [Krishnamurti, p. 81].

L262   *A parish providence. A country tale* (by E.M. Lynch).
+ London: T. Fisher Unwin; Dublin: Sealy, Bryers & Walker; New York: P.J. Kenedy, 1894 (The
New Irish Library; introd. by Sir Charles Gavan Duffy, KCMG). SOURCE Wolff, 4223; COPAC. LOCATION D, DPL, Dcc, L, InND Loeber coll.
COMMENTARY Issued in two binding types: (a) cloth; and (b) wrapper. The introd. by Charles Gavan Duffy deplores the lack in Ireland of local and national initiatives for developing manufacturing and rational agriculture. He gives many examples of goods being then imported that could easily be manufactured in Ireland. The text consists of a didactic story, adapted from a French book *Medicin de campagne* (not identified), set in the mountains near Grenoble, showing how the mayor of a district has been able to turn a miserable village into a prosperous and healthy town by example and by the encouragement of good morals, initiative and hard work. The book ends with a section called 'Last words', in which adoption of the system exemplified in the main story is strongly urged for Ireland. It recommends cooperative banking and includes a table of the Irish congested districts [ML; Rowan cat. 62/278; Wolff, iii, p. 54].

L263   *Killboylan Bank; or, every man his own banker. Being the account of how Killboylan characters concerned themselves about co-operative credit* (by Miss E.M. Lynch; dedicated to Msgr. Charles Rayneri, manager of the Banque Populair, Mentone).
+ London: Kegan Paul, Trench, Trübner & Co., 1896 (The Village Library). SOURCE Brown, 970; COPAC. LOCATION InND Loeber coll., Dt, Dcc, DPL, L.
COMMENTARY Fr O'Callaghan, who has spent many years in Italy, returns to Ireland and settles in Killboylan. While living on the Continent he was greatly impressed by agricultural cooperative banks and wants to introduce the system in Killboylan. He gets together a number of prominent townspeople and reads to them extensive extracts from various books on the

subject. As can be expected, the Irish parishioners are not immediately enthusiastic, but Fr O'Callaghan explains that modern agriculture cannot succeed without capital. Eventually, a cooperative bank is established in the town and seems to fulfil its promise [ML].

LYNCH, Hannah, b. Dublin 1859, d. Paris 1904. Novelist, travel writer, and journalist, HL was the daughter a committed, non-violent Fenian father who died before she was born, and a mother with nationalist sympathies. She was raised in a cultivated, literary household and was familiar with political agitators and writers of the day. After a French convent education she supported herself as a governess, working with aristocratic families in France, Spain and Greece. Back in Ireland, she associated with Anna Parnell and she and her sisters were remembered by Katharine Tynan§ as 'confident, dynamic and bohemian young women'. She joined the Ladies' Land League and when its periodical *United Ireland* (Dublin) was suppressed, HL smuggled the type over to France and had it printed in Paris. Besides her novels she wrote for periodicals such as *Macmillan's Magazine* (London), where she used the pseudonym 'E. Enticknappe', and for newspapers such as the *Dublin Evening Telegraph*. She was imprisoned for her work with the Land League, and her health suffered. She went to the Isle of Wight to recover, later settling in Paris. She was the Paris correspondent for the *Academy* (London?) and contributed regularly to periodicals in England and France. She published 11 works of fiction, wrote on history, and produced a critical study on the writer George Meredith to whom she dedicated *Through troubled waters* (London, [1885]). Her translations from French include B.P. Gaston's *Medieval French literature* (Paris, 1903). Many of her novels contain a distinctly feminist element. Despite her literary success, HL was not financially successful and several times received grants from the Royal Literary Fund. For her papers, see ODNB. SOURCE Allibone Suppl., ii, p. 1029; Blain, pp 677–8; Brady, p. 137; Brown, p. 179; Field Day, iii, pp 418–9; Hogan 2, pp 726–7; OCIL, p. 320; ODNB; RIA/DIB; Sutherland, p. 387; K. Tynan, *Twenty-five years: reminiscences* (London, 1913), pp 76–8.

L264 *Defeated* (by Hannah Lynch).
+ London: Beeton's Christmas Annual, [1885]. SOURCE Alston, p. 264. LOCATION L.
L265 *Through troubled waters* (by Hannah Lynch; dedicated to George Meredith).
London, New York: Ward, Lock & Co. [1885]. SOURCE Brown, 971. LOCATION L.
COMMENTARY Wrongly identified in the ODNB as HL's first novel. It consists of an account of the Fenian rebellion of 1867, and it is set chiefly in a country house near Tuam (Co. Galway), and concerns the dispute about the inheritance of the house. It includes a love story that is thwarted at one point but turns out well in the end [Brown; RL].
L266 *The prince of the Glades* (by Hannah Lynch; dedicated to Anna Parnell).
London: Methuen & Co., 1891, 2 vols. SOURCE Daims, 1916. LOCATION L.
COMMENTARY A love story among Fenians, the heroine (modelled on the Land League activist Anna Parnell) is completely involved in the Fenian movement. She is beautiful but cold, although she does love another Fenian, who goes to prison. Later he shoots his own brother, who is attracted to the heroine [Daims; J. McL. Côté, *Fanny & Anna Parnell* (London, 1991) p. 156].
L267 *Daughters of men* (by Hannah Lynch).
London: William Heinemann, 1892. SOURCE Alston, p. 264. LOCATION L.
New York: J.W. Lovell, [c.1892]. SOURCE Daims, 1913. LOCATION NUC.
L268 *Rosni Harvey. A novel* (by Hannah Lynch).
+ London: Chapman & Hall, 1892, 3 vols. SOURCE Daims, 1917. LOCATION L.
COMMENTARY Chronicles the life of an Irish woman becoming a medical student [RL].
L269 *Dr. Vermont's fantasy and other stories* (by Hannah Lynch).
London: J.M. Dent & Co.; Boston: Lamson Wolffe & Co., 1896. LOCATION L, NUC.

L270 *Denys d'Auvrillac. A story of French life* (by Hannah Lynch).
London: J. Macqueen, 1896. SOURCE Daims, 1914. LOCATION L.

L271 *Jinny Blake* (by Hannah Lynch).
London: J.M. Dent & Co., 1897. SOURCE Alston, p. 264. LOCATION L.
COMMENTARY A portrait of an idealistic new woman's girlhood [Sutherland, p. 387].

L272 *An odd experiment* (by Hannah Lynch).
+ London: Methuen & Co., 1897. SOURCE Daims, 1915. LOCATION L.
COMMENTARY No Irish content. A middle-aged woman meets the mistress of her husband, and insists on a marriage *à trois* [CM; Sutherland].

L273 *The autobiography of a child* [anon.].
New York: Dodd, Mead & Co., 1899. SOURCE Daims, 1911. LOCATION NUC.
+ Edinburgh, London: William Blackwood & Co., 1899. SOURCE Brown, 972; Daims, 1911. LOCATION InND Loeber coll., D, L.
COMMENTARY Originally published in *Blackwood's Magazine* (Edinburgh). Probably an autobiographical account up to the age of twelve. Set partially in a village in Co. Kildare and in Dublin. Told by an adult, it is the story of a battered child who can forgive her mother. Angela is maltreated by her mother and her sisters, but receives love from her stepfather. At age 8, she leaves the family home to stay at a convent near Birmingham, where the treatment is not better. Contains much about the child's inner life, rebellion and pleasures [Brown; RL; Sutherland, p. 387].

L274 *Claire Monro. The story of a mother and daughter* (by Hannah Lynch).
+ London: J. Milne, 1900 (Milne's Express Series). SOURCE Daims, 1912. LOCATION L.

LYON, E.D. See **LYON, Capt. Edmund David**.

LYON, Capt. Edmund David (known as **E.D. Lyon**), fl. 1883. A soldier and novelist, EDL served in the 68th Durham Light Infantry. His only Irish novel is listed here. SOURCE Brown, p. 179.

L275 *Ireland's dream. A romance of the future* (by E.D. Lyon; dedicated without permission to Mr [William] Gladstone).
+ London: W. Swan Sonnenschein, Lowrey & Co., 1888, 2 vols. SOURCE Brown, 973; Wolff, 4225; OCLC. LOCATION D, DPL (2 vols. in 1), L, NUC.
COMMENTARY A pessimistic forecast of Ireland under Home Rule. Describes how the author sees relations between Orangemen and Catholics, and a prediction that under Home Rule there will be no security or prosperity [Brown].

LYSAGHT, Elizabeth J. See **LYSAGHT, Elizabeth Jane**.

LYSAGHT, Elizabeth Jane (née Conner; known as Mrs William Lysaght, and **Elizabeth J. Lysaght**), fl. 1872. Prolific novelist and writer of stories for children and adolescent girls, EJL was the third daughter of Daniel Conner of Manch House, Ballineen (Co. Cork), and married William Lysaght, of Beechmount, Mallow in 1857. She lived in Limerick. She wrote 24 works of fiction, which included many romantic novels for girls. On the title page of *A long madness* (London, 1877), she is listed as the author of *Barbara Vaughan*, but this has not been traced. In addition, Wolff mentioned two other works, *George Lisle* and *Norah*, which also have not been located. SOURCE Allibone Suppl., ii, p. 1030; Burke's, pp 266, 742; Field Day, iv, p. 1142; RIA/DIB; Wolff, iii, p. 55.

L276 *Building upon sand* (by Elizabeth J. Lysaght).
+ London: Samuel Tinsley, 1872. SOURCE Alston, p. 265; COPAC. LOCATION L.

L277   *Nearer and dearer. A novel* (by Elizabeth J. Lysaght).
+ London: Samuel Tinsley, 1873, 3 vols. SOURCE Alston, p. 265. LOCATION D, L, NUC.

L278   *Gaunt abbey. A novel* (by Elizabeth J. Lysaght).
+ London: Samuel Tinsley, 1874, 3 vols. SOURCE Alston, p. 265. LOCATION D, L.

L279   *Mark Brandon's wife* (by Elizabeth J. Lysaght).
+ London: Ward, Lock & Tyler, [1874], 3 vols. SOURCE Alston, p. 265; COPAC. LOCATION L.

L280   *A long madness. A novel* (by Elizabeth J. Lysaght).
London: Charing Cross Publishing Co., 1877, 3 vols. SOURCE Wolff, 4229. LOCATION L.

L281   *Over the border* (by Elizabeth J. Lysaght).
+ London, Belfast: Marcus Ward & Co., 1878 (The Blue Bell Series; ill. Catherine A. Sparkes). SOURCE Alston, p. 265. LOCATION L.

L282   *A wild white rose* (by Elizabeth J. Lysaght).
London: [publisher?], 1880. SOURCE Allibone Suppl., ii, p. 1030.
COMMENTARY No copy located [RL].

L283   *Breakers a-head! A modern romance of thrilling interest* (by Elizabeth J. Lysaght).
+ London: Milner & Co., 1880 (ill.). SOURCE Allibone Suppl., ii, p. 1030. LOCATION D (n.d. edn).
COMMENTARY No copy of the 1880 edn located [RL].

L284   *Brother and sister; or, the trials of the Moore family* (by Elizabeth J. Lysaght).
London, Glasgow, Edinburgh, Dublin: Blackie & Son, 1883. SOURCE Alston, p. 265; COPAC. LOCATION L.
+ London, Glasgow, Dublin, Bombay: Blackie & Son, 1908 (new edn; ill. Gordon Browne; see Plate 47). LOCATION InND Loeber coll.
COMMENTARY Advertised as 'A story showing, by the narrative of the vicissitudes and struggles of a family which has "come down in the world", and of the brave endeavours of its two younger members, how the pressure of adversity is mitigated by domestic affection, mutual confidence, and hopeful honest efforts' [Adv. in Rosa Mulholland§'s *Four little mischiefs* (London, 1883)].

L285   *Sealed orders* (by Elizabeth J. Lysaght).
+ London: Richard Bentley & Son, 1886, 3 vols. SOURCE Wolff, ii, p. 55. LOCATION InND Loeber coll., L, NUC.
COMMENTARY A two-generation saga of two friends Sydney Le Marchant and George Vandeleur who both love the same woman, Janet. Because of this, Sydney allows George to unknowingly enter a leper colony during their visit to the Holy Land. George subsequently dies, and Sydney now comes into a fortune. He marries Janet despite the fact that he is a Catholic and Janet is not. His spiritual mentor, a Dominican monk, denounces him. Janet dies in childbirth, and her child is brought up by a dependent who had given at birth the same time. Le Marchant believes his wife's death is his punishment for George's death and sets out to serve lepers in a colony in the South Seas, where he dies. The young Sydney inherits his father's estate and becomes engaged to Clarice Gray, whose mother George had secretly married and deserted. Sydney receives from the Dominican priest papers his father had left him and learns that he was instrumental in George's death. He tells Mrs Gray, who forbids him to see Clarice. The lovers are heartbroken. Sydney's foster mother then reveals he is not Le Marchant's and Janet's child but hers. Clarice and Sydney, now called Harold, marry and set off to Canada to start a new life, poor but happy [ML].

L286   *Aunt Hesba's charge* (by Elizabeth J. Lysaght).
+ London, Glasgow, Edinburgh, Dublin: Blackie & Son, 1888 (ill.). SOURCE Alston, p. 265. LOCATION D, L,NUC.
COMMENTARY Fiction for juveniles [RL].

L287   *Our general. A story for girls* (by Elizabeth J. Lysaght).
   + London, Glasgow, Edinburgh, Dublin: Blackie & Son, 1888 (ill.). SOURCE Alston, p. 265. LOCATION D, L, NUC, InND Loeber coll. (n.d. edn).
COMMENTARY Fiction for juveniles. A young girl named Basil looks after her family, consisting of a sickly mother and a younger brother and sister. Her siblings call her 'the general'. Their father is in Australia, trying to rescue some of his fortune. The mother dies and times are hard for the children. Their father is presumed to have died at sea in a shipwreck. However, he had been saved and with his fortune intact he returns to his children [ML].

L288   *Jasper's conquest* (by Elizabeth J. Lysaght).
   + London, Glasgow, Edinburgh, Dublin: Blackie & Son, 1889 (ill. H. Wilson). LOCATION D (n.d. edn), L, NUC.

L289   *Jack-a-Dandy; or, the heir of Castle-Fergus. A story for boys and girls* (by Elizabeth J. Lysaght).
   + London, Glasgow, Edinburgh, Dublin: Blackie & Son, [1889] (ill.). SOURCE Alston, p. 265. LOCATION InND Loeber coll., D, L.
COMMENTARY Fiction for juveniles. A deformed boy, Jack, inherits a title at the death of his father. His cousin envies him very much and ponders the possibility that if Jack were dead, his father and eventually he would inherit the title. Jack rescues his cousin when he falls through the ice and, while recovering, the cousin believes Jack is dead. He feels terribly guilty about his previous bad thoughts. However, Jack is alive and they become best friends [ML].

L290   *The veiled picture; or, the wizard's legacy* (by Elizabeth J. Lysaght).
   + London: Simpkin, Marshall, Hamilton Kent & Co., [1889] (O.U.R. Books, No. 2). SOURCE Alston, p. 266; Topp 8, 914. LOCATION L ([1890] edn).
COMMENTARY Historical novel. No Irish content [CM].

L291   *The gold of Ophir* (by Elizabeth J. Lysaght).
   + London: Ward & Downey, 1890, 3 vols. SOURCE Alston, p. 265. LOCATION D, L.

L292   *Thorns and roses. A story of home life* (by Elizabeth J. Lysaght).
   + London: George Cauldwell, [1890]. SOURCE Alston, p. 266. LOCATION L.
COMMENTARY No Irish content [CM].

L293   *Grannie* (by Elizabeth J. Lysaght).
   London, Glasgow, Edinburgh, Dublin: Blackie & Son, 1891. SOURCE Alston, p. 265. LOCATION L.
COMMENTARY Fiction for juveniles [RL].

L294   *Sharp Tommy* (by Elizabeth J. Lysaght).
   + London, Glasgow, Edinburgh, Dublin: Blackie & Son, [1891] (ill. Ph.T.). SOURCE Alston, p. 266. LOCATION InND Loeber coll., L.
COMMENTARY Fiction for juveniles set in England. The story is about a little boy who is fascinated by the romanticism of the circus that has come to town. When the circus leaves, he goes with them. Instead of leading an exciting life, he finds out that working for a circus is very hard. He returns home a wiser boy [ML].

L295   *An unexpected hero* (by Elizabeth J. Lysaght).
   London, Glasgow, Edinburgh, Dublin: Blackie & Son, 1893. SOURCE Alston, p. 265. LOCATION L.
COMMENTARY Fiction for juveniles [RL].

L296   *The squire's household* (by Elizabeth J. Lysaght).
   + London: Biggs & Co., 1894 (ill. 'W.M.B.'). SOURCE Alston, p. 266. LOCATION L.
COMMENTARY No Irish content [CM].

L297   *Rex singleton; or, the pathway of life* (by Elizabeth J. Lysaght).
   London: Wells Gardner & Co., [1894]. SOURCE Brown, 974 (1894, 3rd edn). LOCATION L.

COMMENTARY Fiction for juveniles from a Protestant point of view. The model boy Rex comes to stay with his wild Irish cousins and sets them many a good example, giving the author opportunities to develop moral lessons [Brown].

L298 *Parkington's pantry* (by Elizabeth J. Lysaght).
Westminster [London]: Church of England Temperance Society, 1893. SOURCE Alston, p. 265. LOCATION L.
COMMENTARY No Irish content [CM].

L299 *Hetty Martin's trial; or, life's thorns and roses* (by Elizabeth J. Lysaght).
+ London: Sunday School Union, [1897]. SOURCE Alston, p. 265. LOCATION L.
COMMENTARY No Irish content [CM].

LYSAGHT, Sidney Royse, b. near Mallow (Co. Cork) 1856 (1860 according to E. Reilly), d. Hazelwood House, Mallow 1941. Novelist, poet and successful businessman, SRL was the eldest son of Thomas Royse Lysaght, an architect, of Mintinna (Co. Cork) and Emily Moss. He was educated at TCD and as a young man travelled extensively through Australia, New Zealand and Polynesia and visited Robert Louis Stevenson in Samoa. SRL became a wealthy ironmaster at the family's iron works in Bristol but returned to Ireland around 1920. He was a staunch nationalist and although a Protestant, was a generous benefactor of the local Catholic church. In 1886, he married Katharine Clarke, a nationalist who was active in the independence movement and was sentenced to imprisonment in 1920. Their son was the poet Edward E. Lysaght. SRL wrote three volumes of verses and a play. He also published a philosophical work entitled *A reading of life* (London, 1936) within which both his religious faith and reactionary ideas mingle. He resided at Hazelwood House and at Raheen manor (Co. Clare), where he established a nursery industry (house now ruined). Several of his letters are in the NLI (MS 5,854). SOURCE Allibone Suppl., ii, p. 1030; Brady, p. 139; Brown, p. 179; Burke's, p. 744; EF, p. 252; Hogan, p. 386; Hogan 2, p. 734; O'Donoghue, p. 261; E. Reilly, p. 246; RIA/DIB; Sutherland, pp 387–8; H.W.L. Weir, *Houses of Clare* (Whitegate, 1986), p. 223.

L300 *The marplot* (by Sidney Royse Lysaght).
+ London, New York: Macmillan & Co., 1893, 3 vols. SOURCE Brown 2, 853. LOCATION D (1893, 1 vol. edn), Dt, L, InND Loeber coll. (1893, one vol. edn).
New York, London: Macmillan & Co., 1893. LOCATION NUC.
COMMENTARY A melodramatic romance involving a young Irishman in England, Dick Wrixon, who falls in love with an Irish girl, Elsinora, whom he cannot marry because he is already married to a circus girl, called Connie, who does not live with him. Elsinora is engaged to a Mr O'Connor. Dick and O'Connor are about to have a duel but, instead, they have a bet. Dick loses the bet and is bound by honour to take his life within a year. At the end of the year, O'Connor shoots himself and Dick sails into a storm after having spent a few days with Elsinora. Dick, however, is not killed but is cast ashore. When he makes his way back to Elsinora, he hears that she too has died [ML; AMB].

L301 *One of the Grenvilles* (by Sidney Royse Lysaght; dedicated to the author's mother [Emily Lysaght]).
+ London, New York: Macmillan & Co., 1899 (Macmillan's Colonial Library). LOCATION InND Loeber coll., D, Dt, L, NUC.
COMMENTARY A story of family honour and romance that turns around the Grenville family motto, 'Win love, lack gold'. The Grenville estate is situated near Bristol and the hero, Martin Grenville, unbeknownst to most people, was born before his parents married. A large part of the plot concerns efforts to keep this secret to preserve his mother's honour. Martin falls in love with an Irish girl from Co. Kerry who is engaged to the son of a rich merchant. Her hon-

our prevents her from breaking the engagement until she realizes that her fiancée is an unworthy person. She then marries Martin [ML].

L302   *Her Majesty's rebels* (by Sidney Royse Lysaght).

+ London, New York: Macmillan & Co., 1907. SOURCE Brown, 975. LOCATION InND Loeber coll., D, L, NUC.

COMMENTARY A political novel written mainly about the course of national life in Ireland between 1875 and 1891, and resembling in some ways the career of Charles Stewart Parnell [ML; Brown].

L303   *My tower in Desmond* (by Sidney Royse Lysaght; dedicated to the author's wife [Katherine Lysaght]).

+ London: Macmillan & Co., 1925 (ill.). LOCATION InND Loeber coll., D, DPL.

New York: Macmillan, 1925. SOURCE Brown 2, 852; Hogan, p. 386; NYPL. LOCATION L, NUC, NN.

COMMENTARY An autobiographical novel partly set in Co. Cork in the beginning of the twentieth century. Describes the lives of family members living in a country house called Ballyquin, and shows the conflicts between personal and political loyalties during the time that Ireland was gaining independence. The story focuses mainly on the narrator and his cousin Brian. Brian is a nationalist who sided with the Boers against the British in South Africa and fought with the French rather than with the British army during the First World War. He was also active in the Easter Rising. On the other hand, the narrator is much more traditional and wishes for peace with England. His role is to save the family from ruin. Initially he joins a firm run by relatives in England, but finds the life uncongenial. He goes to New Zealand, makes his fortune on a sheep ranch, and returns to Ireland. Despite the different characters and political leanings of the two young men, they are very attached to each other. An English cousin buys Ballyquin. She is in love with Brian, but there are many obstacles, mainly political, in their way to a union. Eventually they marry when Brian is in prison and it is thought he might die from his wounds. In the end, the narrator also marries an English woman [ML].

LYTTLE, W.G. See **LYTTLE, Wesley Guard.**

LYTTLE, Wesley Guard (also known as **W.G. Lyttle**), pseud. 'Robin', b. Newtownards (Co. Down) 1844, d. 1896. A journalist, school teacher, editor and writer, WGL's varied career included being a shorthand teacher, an accountant and a lecturer on Dr Corry's Irish Diorama. He began in 1880 the *North Down and Bangor Gazette*, a strongly Liberal and Home Rule newspaper. He was known all over Ulster as 'Robin', giving public entertainments of poems and sketches under that name in the dialect of a Co. Down farmer. In 1892 he advertised that he was 'prepared to make arrangements with Secretaries of Associations, Clubs, Societies, or other social organisations for giving public Recitals from His Own Writings'. The bibliographic order and origins of the following works is difficult to disentangle, and for that reason is only tentative. SOURCE Boase, vi, p. 98; Brown, p. 180; RL; O'Donoghue, p. 261; RIA/DIB.

L304   *The Bangor season. What's to be seen and how to see it* (compiled and published by W.G. Lyttle).

Bangor: W.G. Lyttle, 1885. SOURCE COPAC (based on reprint).

+ Belfast: Appletree Press, [1976]. LOCATION D.

COMMENTARY No copy of the 1895 edn located. Contents: 'The parables of the rulers: A skit upon the doings of the Bangor town commissioners'. It also contains topographical sketches [RL].

L305   *Sons of the sod. A tale of County Down* (by W.G. Lyttle).

+ Bangor: By the author at his works 'North Down Herald' office, 1886. SOURCE Brown, 977; NLI cat. LOCATION D.

Bangor: Printed by D.E. Alexander, [1911] (repr. by the author's son). SOURCE Rowan
cat. 39/528. LOCATION KU-S, InND Loeber coll. (n.d., 6th edn).
+ Belfast: R. Carswell & Son, n.d. (author's name mistakenly spelled 'W.C. Lyttle'
on the ill. cover; Robin's Readings Series). LOCATION InND Loeber coll., D.
COMMENTARY Set in north Co. Down among the peasantry. A landlord, Squire Brown, has a
bad agent who creates a lot of hardship among the peasantry. The agent wishes to marry a decent
widow, who spurns him. As a result, the agent threatens to evict tenants, particularly a very
aged retainer of Squire Brown. The neighbouring peasants prevent the eviction, but the old
retainer dies on the spot. In the end the agent is slain and an honest person put in his place.
The squire's daughter marries the old retainer's son, who has returned from abroad [ML].

L306 *Betsy Gray; or, hearts of Down. A tale of ninety-eight* (by W.G. Lyttle).
Bangor: The author, 1894. SOURCE Brown, 978 (who perhaps mistakenly mentions
1888 edn); COPAC. LOCATION Dt ([1915?], 7th edn), L, NUC [(189?] edn).
+ Newcastle, Co. Down: Mourne Observer, [1968]. LOCATION InND Loeber coll.
COMMENTARY *Newcastle edn* Also includes *Other stories and pictures of '98 as collected
and published in the 'Mourne Observer'*. SOURCE Rowan cat. 39/529. LOCATION D.
COMMENTARY First published in the *North Down Herald* (Bangor). The heroine Betsy Gray
takes part in the 1798 rebellion and fights at Ballynahinch. The story dwells on the atrocities
of the yeomanry and describes the chief incidents of the rebellion. It introduces a number of
historical characters [Brown; E. Reilly, 'Rebel, muse, and spouse: The female in '98 fiction'
in *Éire-Ireland*, 34(2), 1999, p. 144].

L307 *Daft Eddie* (by W.G. Lyttle).
Belfast: Carswell, 1914. SOURCE Brown, 980; OCLC. LOCATION D.
+ Newcastle, Co. Down: Mourne Observer Press, 1979 (as *Daft Eddie or the smugglers
of Strangford Lough*). LOCATION InND Loeber coll., D, L.
COMMENTARY According to Brown, this was first published as *The smugglers of Strangford
Lough*, c.1890, but no copy has been located. Set in the eighteenth century at Killinchy (Co.
Down), the story is an account of murder, robbery, abduction, smuggling and secret societies
[Brown, 979].

— COLLECTED WORKS
L308 *Humorous readings* (by 'Robin').
[n.l.], [date?], vol. 1.
COMMENTARY Contents: Vol. 1 'The adventures of Paddy M'Quillan' [listed in vol. iii])
[n.l.], [date?], vol. 2.
COMMENTARY Contents: Vol. 2 'The adventures of Robin Gordon' [listed in vol. iii])
+ [n.l.], [no publisher], 1892, vol. iii (Author's edn). LOCATION D, InND Loeber coll.
COMMENTARY *1892 edn* Contents: 'My brither Wully', 'Kirk music', 'The Ballycuddy
precentor', 'The general assembly of 1879', 'The Newtownbreda harmoneyum', 'The
electric light', 'The Ballycuddy meinister' [*sic*] , 'The royal visit to Ireland', 'Izek
Neelson in Ballycuddy' [RL].
+ Belfast: Allen, Son & Allen, John Robb & Co., Ollie & Co., W.E. Maine, Miss
Henderson; Londonderry: W. Graham; Glasgow: Porteous Bros; Edinburgh: John
Menzies & Co., 1886, 2nd edn, 2 vols. SOURCE Hyland cat. 218/498; OCLC. LOCATION
InND Loeber coll. (vol. 2 only), D (1892 edn), KU-S.
COMMENTARY No copies of vols. 1 and 2 located. *Belfast 1886 edn* Includes 'Life in
Ballycuddy', 'County Down', but probably included several other stories [RL].

L309 *Robin's readings.*
Belfast: Joseph Blair, 1893, 3 vols. SOURCE OCLC. LOCATION D (vol. 1), Univ. of
Kansas.

+ Belfast: R. Carswell & Son, n.d., Parts 1, 2, & 3 (of 8 parts.) in 1 vol. SOURCE Brown, 976; Emerald Isle cat. 23/627, 50/564. LOCATION InND Loeber coll., D.

COMMENTARY Republication of separately published stories, priced at 6*d*. per vol. Consists of humorous poems and sketches in the dialect of a county Down farmer. Pt. 1: 'The adventures of Paddy McQuillan'; Pt. 2: 'The adventures of Robert Gordon'; Pt. 3: 'Life in Ballycuddy, Co. Down' [Brown; Emerald Isle].

LYTTON, Edward G. Bulwer. See BULWER LYTTON, Sir Edward G.

LYTTON, Lady. See BULWER LYTTON, Lady Rosina Doyle.

LYTTON, Rosina Doyle Bulwer. See BULWER LYTTON, Lady Rosina Doyle.

LYTTON BULWER, Lady. See BULWER LYTTON, Lady Rosina Doyle.

M

'M., E.', pseud. See **EDGEWORTH, Maria**.

'M., E.', pseud. See **MANGIN, Edward**.

'M., E.', pseud. of co-author. See **WHATELY, Mary Louisa**.

'M—, G—', fl. 1833. Pseudonym of a writer who, given the Dublin publisher, was likely to be Irish. The preface suggests male authorship. SOURCE Garside 2, 1833:46; RL.

M1   *Tales of the tombs: A series of anecdotes illustrative of the affections* (by 'G—M—').
      Dublin: W.F. Wakeman; London: Simpkin & Marshall, & R. Groombridge, 1833.
      SOURCE Garside 2, 1833:46. LOCATION Corvey CME 3-628-51160-7, L.
COMMENTARY Stories about death, set in Lisbon, Paris, Scotland and England. Contents (except poetry): 'The duel', 'The protégée', 'Woman's love', 'Percival' [Garside 2, 1833:46].

'M., G.', fl. 1877. Pseudonym of an historical romance writer who, given the Dublin publisher, was probably Irish. SOURCE RL.

M2   *A winner recorded* (by 'G.M.').
      + Dublin: M.H. Gill & Son, 1877. LOCATION D, InND Loeber coll.
COMMENTARY The adventures of Edward Fitzgerald, son of humble farmers in the Vale of Ovoca [*sic*] (Co. Wicklow) who has benefited from education given by a learned priest. Edward's landlord is Col. Palley, and on several occasions Edward saves the life of his daughter Helen. This arouses the jealousy of Mr Hassard, a distant relative of the Palleys whose suit Helen has rejected. Edward goes to France to join the Irish Brigade. While there he engages in a duel with Mr Hassard and in self-defence kills him. Edward distinguishes himself in battle and returns knighted. He finds Helen ill and assumed to be dying. However, his return brings a change for the better in her condition and eventually they marry [ML].

M3   void

'M., J.M.', pseud. See **MOORE, John McDermott**.

'M., L.M.', pseud. See **MEANEY, Mary L.**

'M., M.E.', pseud. of co-author. See **WHATELY, Mary Louisa**.

'M., M.M.C.', pseud. See **METHUEN, Mary M.C.**

'M., S.', fl. 1881. Pseudonym of a novelist and poet who, given the Dublin publisher, was probably Irish. SOURCE RL.

M

M4   *A mass in the mountains and poems* (by 'S.M.').
+ Dublin: M.H. Gill & Son, 1881. SOURCE O'Donoghue, p. 262. LOCATION D, L.
COMMENTARY Fiction and poetry. An Irish couple has long lived in Spain, but toward the end of their lives they move back to Ireland to a place where a relative is a priest. A soldier who interrupts their religious activities turns out to be a long-lost relative [ML].

'M., S.G.' Pseudonym of a religious fiction writer who, given the Dublin publisher, was probably Irish. SOURCE RL.
M5   *The hillside flower* (by 'S.G.M.').
Dublin: Catholic Truth Society, [1894 or earlier]. SOURCE Adv. in R. Mulholland's§, *Marigold* (Dublin, 1894).
COMMENTARY No copy located [RL].

'M., T.' Pseudonym of a preface writer. See 'A Lady', who wrote *Fashionable life* (Dublin, 1791).

'M., T.', pseud. See CONVILLE, Thomas M.

'M., T.C.' pseud. See MACK, Thomas C.

'McD., M.', pseud. See MC DERMOTT, Mrs Mary.

'M—x—ll, K.', pseud. See MAXWELL, Katherine.

MABERLY, Mrs —. See MABERLY, the Hon. Mrs Catherine (Kate) Charlotte.

MABERLY, the Hon. Mrs Catherine (Kate) Charlotte (née Prittie; also known as **Mrs Maberly**), b. Corville (Co. Tipperary) 1805, d. 1875. Historical romance novelist, CCM was the daughter of the Hon. Francis Aldborough Prittie of Corville. In 1830 she married William Leader Maberly, an army officer and later MP and secretary of the General Post Office, who figures in Anthony Trollope's§ autobiography. She wrote *The present state of Ireland and its remedies* (London, 1847, 2nd edn), a pamphlet about the Famine. ODNB says she authored nine novels, but we have located only eight. SOURCE Allibone, ii, p. 1155; Allibone Suppl., ii, p. 1032; BLC; Boase, ii, p. 556; DNB [under William Leader Maberly]; Sutherland, p. 391.
M6   *Emily; or, the Countess of Rosendale. A novel* (by Mrs Maberly).
London: H. Colburn: 1840, 3 vols. SOURCE Sadleir, 1471; Wolff, 4250; COPAC. LOCATION L, NUC.
M7   *The love-match. A novel* (by Mrs Maberly).
London: H. Colburn, 1841, 3 vols. SOURCE Block, p. 147; OCLC. LOCATION L, NUC.
M8   *Melanthe; or, the days of the Medici. A tale of the fifteenth century* (by Mrs Maberly).
London: John Mitchell, 1843, 3 vols. SOURCE Block, p. 147; COPAC. LOCATION L, NUC.
M9   *Leontine; or, the court of Louis the fifteenth* (by Mrs Maberly).
London: H. Colburn, 1846, 3 vols. SOURCE Sadleir, 1473; OCLC. LOCATION L, NUC.
New York: Harper Bros, [1865?]. LOCATION NUC.

M10 *Fashion and its votaries* (by Mrs Maberly).
 London: Saunders & Otley, 1848, 3 vols. SOURCE Block, p. 147. LOCATION L, NUC.
M11 *The lady and the priest: An historical romance* (by Mrs Maberly).
 + London: Colburn & Co., 1851, 3 vols. SOURCE Sadleir, 1472; COPAC. LOCATION
 L, NUC.
 COMMENTARY Set in England during the twelfth century [ML].
M12 *Display. A novel* (by Mrs Maberly).
 + London: Hurst & Blackett, 1855, 3 vols. SOURCE Alston, p. 267; Wolff, 4251;
 COPAC. LOCATION L, NUC.
 COMMENTARY No Irish content [CM].
M13 *Leonora* (by the Hon. Mrs Maberly).
 + London: Smith, Elder & Co., 1856, 3 vols. SOURCE Alston, p. 267; Wolff, 4252;
 OCLC. LOCATION L, NUC.
COMMENTARY According the preface, the story is taken from real life and relates the history
of a 'bold, bad, beautiful woman who having lost her character plunges into crime to preserve
her reputation'. No Irish content [CM; Sutherland, p. 391].

'MAC', pseud. See **MAC MANUS, Séumas**.

MC ANALLY, David Rice, Jnr, fl. 1888. Irish-American anthologist, DRM travelled through
Ireland collecting stories. Allibone also lists a Revd David R. McNally (b. Tennessee, 1810),
a Methodist minister in St Louis, who may be the same author or a relation. SOURCE Allibone
Suppl., ii, p. 1033; Zimmermann, p. 290.
M14 *Irish wonders. The ghosts, giants, pookas, demons, leprechawns, banshees, fairies,*
 witches, widows, old maids, and other marvels of the Emerald Isle. Popular tales
 as told by the people (compiled by David Rice McAnally Jnr; dedicated to Joseph B.
 McCullagh).
 Boston: Houghton, Mifflin, 1888 (ill. H.R. Heaton). SOURCE Allibone Suppl., ii, p.
 1033; Fanning, p. 384. LOCATION NUC.
 + New York: Weathervane Books, n.d. (ill. H.R. Heaton). LOCATION InND Loeber
 coll.
 + London, New York: Ward, Lock & Co., 1888 (ill. H.R. Heaton). SOURCE Brown,
 982. LOCATION BFl, L, NUC, InND Loeber coll.
COMMENTARY Reviewed by William Butler Yeats§ in 1889, who found it impossible to use any
of the stories for his own anthology. Contents: 'The seven kings of Athenry', 'Taming the pooka',
'The sexton of Cashel', 'Satan's cloven hoof', 'The enchanted island', 'How the lakes were made',
'About the fairies', 'The banshee', 'The round towers', 'The police', 'The leprechawn', 'The
henpecked giant', 'Satan as a sculptor', 'The defeat of the widows' [ML; Thuente 1, p. 92].

'MAC ARTHUR, Alexander', pseud. See **NICCHIA, Mrs —**.

MAC AULIFFE, Miss E.F., fl. 1891. Historical novelist, EFM was from Cork and died at
an advanced age before 1917. SOURCE Alston, p. 268; Brown, p. 181.
M15 *Grace O'Donnell. A tale of the 18th century* (by Miss E.F. Macauliffe).
 + Cork: Guy & Co., 1891. SOURCE Brown, 984; COPAC. LOCATION D, Dt, L.
COMMENTARY Historical fiction set during the penal times in Ireland in the eighteenth cen-
tury describing the sufferings of the Catholics. It is set in Galway and Dublin, as well as
London, Madrid and Paris. Tells about the inequities of the penal laws [Brown; Fenning cat.
225/149].

MAC CABE, William Bernard, pseud. 'J.M. Piercy', b. Dublin 1801, d. Donnybrook (Dublin) 1891. Catholic journalist, scholar, translator and writer, WBM began work in 1823 as a contributor to newspapers in Dublin, then London, and later again in Dublin. He was a scholar and linguist and while working as a parliamentary reporter in London and during parliamentary recesses spent a good deal of time abroad as a foreign correspondent. From 1847 to 1851 he was consul of the Oriental Republic of Uruguay in London. In addition to seven works of fiction, he translated from the German and published *The last days of O'Connell* (Dublin, 1847), *A Catholic history of Ireland* (between 1848 and 1855), and *A Catholic history of England* (London, 1847–54, 3 vols.), based on original research in monastic records in England and abroad. In 1851, he became editor of the *Weekly Telegraph* (Dublin), a Catholic paper. He contributed to Duffy's *Hibernian Magazine* and to the *Irish Monthly Magazine of Politics and Literature* (both Dublin). WBM wrote the preface to the American edn of *Florine* (Baltimore, MD, 1855) from Vernon Avenue, Clontarf, Dublin, on 20 Jan. 1855. He later went to live in Brittany to pursue antiquarian interests and in 1858 he contributed 'The six giants of Lehon' to *Household Words* (London), which consists of a Celtic saint's legend told to him by an Irishman resident in Brittany. He returned to Dublin and died there at age 90. SOURCE Allibone, ii, p. 1161; Brady, p. 141; Brown, p. 181; Brown, 2, p. 155; Lohrli, p. 349; [J. O'Brien], *Irish Celts* (Detroit, 1884), n.p.; Irish pseudonyms; ODNB; O'Donoghue, p. 265; Sutherland, p. 391.

M16   *Bertha. A romance of the dark ages* (by William Bernard MacCabe; dedicated to Dr McCabe, JP, Hawkhurst, Kent).
+ London: T.C. Newby, 1851, 3 vols. SOURCE Sutherland, p. 391; OCLC. LOCATION D.
+ Dublin: James Duffy, 1856, 3rd edn (as *Bertha; or, the pope and the emperor. An historical tale*). LOCATION PC.
Boston: Donahoe, 1856 (as *The pope and the emperor, an historical tale*). LOCATION NUC.
COMMENTARY Deals with the struggle between Emperor Henry of Germany and Hildebrand (*c.*1020–85, became Pope St Gregory VII) [DNB].

M17   *A grandfather's story book; being the legends and tales of a poor scholar* (by William Bernard MacCabe; dedicated to Richard Robert Madden§).
+ Dublin: James Duffy, 1852 (Duffy's Cottage Library). SOURCE Brown 2, 860; OCLC. LOCATION D.
COMMENTARY Only one of these stories, 'The possessed', has an Irish subject. It tells how St Patrick's charioteer sacrificed his life to save the saint from Foilge, a pagan chief, and how at the prayer of St Patrick the devil entered into the murderer [Brown 2].

M18   *Florine, Princess of Burgundy. A tale of the first crusaders* (by William Bernard MacCabe; dedicated to Paula Josephine).
+ Baltimore: John Murphy; Pittsburgh (PA): George Quigley, 1855. SOURCE OCLC. LOCATION D, DCU, NUC, InND Loeber coll.
+ Dublin: James Duffy, 1855. LOCATION Di, L.
Paris: Putois-Cretté, 1859 (trans. as *Florine, princesse de Bourgogne, ou une page de la première croisade*). SOURCE Devonshire, p. 468; CCF. LOCATION BNF.

M19   *Adelaide, Queen of Italy; or, the iron crown. An historical tale* (by William Bernard MacCabe; dedicated to Adelaide, mother of Emperor Francis Joseph, and to the Archduchess Sophia of Austria).
+ London: Charles Dolman; Baltimore: J. Murphy, 1856. SOURCE Wolff, 4254; OCLC. LOCATION D, L, NUC.
Dublin: James Duffy, 1860, 2nd edn. LOCATION L.
Paris: Putois-Cretté, 1859 (trans. by M. de La Gracerie as *Adélaïde, reine d'Italie, ou la couronne de fer*). SOURCE Devonshire, p. 468; CCF. LOCATION BNF.

COMMENTARY Reviewed in the *Metropolitan* (4 Oct. 1856), p. 574 [RL].

M20 *Popular tales; or, deeds of genius illustrative of the moral and social virtues in the lives of eminent individuals* (by 'J.M. Piercy').

+ Dublin: James Duffy, 1860 (ill.). LOCATION L.

+ Dublin, London: James Duffy & Sons, 1880 (as *The Queen of Italy, Canova's cake, and the prudent choice*, [anon.]; ill.). LOCATION PC. COMMENTARY *Dublin 1880 edn* Consists of a selection of the stories [RL].

Dublin: James Duffy & Co., [1886 or earlier] (as *The golden pheasant*, [anon.]). SOURCE Adv. in W. Carleton, *Redmond, Count O'Hanlon* (Dublin, 1886). COMMENTARY *Dublin [1886 or earlier] edn* Priced at 6*d*. No copy located [Adv. in W. Carleton, *Redmond, Count O'Hanlon* (Dublin, 1886); RL].

Baltimore: Piet & Co., 1868 (as *The golden pheasant, Young Franklin, and Vanity corrected*, [anon.]). SOURCE OCLC. LOCATION Michigan State Univ. COMMENTARY *Baltimore edn* contains the first four stories only [RL].

COMMENTARY Part retelling of existing tales about famous individuals. Contents: 'The golden pheasant', 'Young Franklin', 'Giotto; or, the lost lamb', 'Grandfather Kerouan; or, vanity corrected', 'The founder of the Sorbonne', 'Henrietta of England', 'The goldsmith artist', 'Aline de Coulanges; or, the danger of ignorance', 'Matthew Schinner', 'William and his monkey; or, the misery of covetousness and intoxication', 'Good King Rene', 'The optimist; or, the way to be happy', 'A tale of the Napolitan revolution', 'Canova's cake', 'Adelaide, queen of Italy', 'The prudent choice', 'The zombi of the studio' [CM].

M21 *A Christmas story book being tales, traditions, chances, and mischances, of the captain, crew, and passengers of the old canal boat* (by William Bernard MacCabe).

+ Dublin: James Duffy, 1860. SOURCE Brown 2, 859; OCLC. LOCATION D, L.

COMMENTARY The book opens with a description of travel on the Royal Canal and a series of stories told by the passengers going from Mullingar to Dublin: 'The Royal Irish Rat' (a tale of a Danish fairy named Kobold who lived on the top of Tory Hill, Co. Kilkenny), 'The irresistible captain' (a facetious burlesque), 'Little Jack and his two brothers' (a story on a folktale model), 'The three jockeys' (a comedy with a preternatural elements), 'The young goose, the three ganders, and the fox' (a humorous fable describing the fox's manoeuvres in the hopes of eating the gosling protected by O'Gander, MacGander and Fitzgander), 'The wonderful doctor' (Pat Cooney becomes infatuated with a girl whom he has rescued from an accident; the story tells how he was cured) [Brown 2].

M22 *Agnes Arnold. A novel* (by William Bernard MacCabe).

+ London: Thomas Cautley Newby, 1860, 3 vols. SOURCE Brown, 985 (1861 edn); Sutherland, p. 391; OCLC. LOCATION D, NUC.

COMMENTARY Reviewed in *Duffy's Hibernian Magazine* (Dublin, 1861), pp 93–4. Historical fiction set in Wexford in 1798, and shows how the people were driven to rebellion. The author based his story on conversations he had with William Putnam MacCabe, one of the insurgent leaders [Brown].

MC CALL, Patrick Joseph, b. Dublin 1861, d. Dublin 1919. Poet, song and story writer, PJM was the son of John McCall (born at Clonmore, Co. Carlow) and Elizabeth Mary Newport (of Woodtown, Mayglass, Co. Wexford). His father ran a public house and a grocery. PJM was educated at the Catholic University School in Dublin. He owned a pub in Patrick Street and married Margaret Furlong in 1900. He became a Poor Law Guardian and nationalist representative of the Wood Quay ward, Dublin. He contributed sketches, often humorous retellings of old stories, and verses to a wide variety of magazines, including the *Shamrock* (Dublin). He is best known for his songs. 'Boulavogue', a ballad of the 1798 rebellion, and 'Follow me up to Carlow', which are still sung today. With William Butler Yeats§, Douglas Hyde§ and others, PJM was a founder-member of the Irish National Literary Society. He was also a member of the non-sectarian Pan-Celtic Society, and was active in the Gaelic League. Ryan described him as 'possessing an intimate knowledge of Old Dublin … with a knowledge nearly as thorough of the traits and traditions of Wexford and Wicklow. His command over metres and versification was almost as peculiar as that of [James Clarence] Mangan§. His mind was stored with the drollest old songs of the people, with their idioms, superstitions and fancies' (Ryan, pp 41–3). PJM's portrait was published by Ryan. SOURCE Boylan, p. 210; Brown, p. 182; Browne, p. 96; Field Day, ii, p. 105; iii, p. 494; Hogan, p. 389; Hogan 2, p. 742; Irish pseudonyms; O'Donoghue, p. 266; O'Donoghue 2, p. 429; RIA/DIB; Ryan, pp 41–3; K. Whelan, *Fellowship of freedom: the United Irishmen and 1798* (Cork, 1998), p. 127.

M23   *The Fenian nights' entertainments, being a series of Ossianic legends told at a Wexford fireside* (compiled by P.J. McCall; dedicated to author's father [John McCall]).

+ Dublin: T.G. O'Donoghue, 1897 (first series [all published]; The Shamrock Library).

SOURCE Brown, 986 (n.d. edn); Rowan cat. 37, part B/12; Hogan, p. 389. LOCATION D, L, NUC, InND Loeber coll.

COMMENTARY Ossianic legends and fairytales told in contemporary dialect at a Wexford fireside in twelve evenings by a storyteller who is purported to be a farmer. Contents: 'Cath Luan, prince of Phoenicia', 'Tuan MacCoireall', 'The origins of the harp', 'The druid's wife that couldn't be pleased', 'Cuchellin and Emir', 'Fionn MacCumhail and the giant', 'Fionn MacCumhail and the princess', 'Yellow face', 'Prince Baille and the Princess Aileen', 'How King Cormac MacArt won his wife', 'King Crimthan and Nair, the queen of beauty', 'The Amadan Mor' [RL; Brown].

MC CARROLL, James, pseud. 'Scian Dubh', b. Lanesborough (Co. Longford) c.1813–15, d. Buffalo (NY), 1896 (1892 according to RIA/DIB). Novelist, editor, critic and miscellaneous writer, JM emigrated to Canada in 1831. He was editor and proprietor of the Peterborough *Chronicle* and of the Newcastle *Courier*, both in Ontario, Canada. He later moved to New York where he was a music and drama critic and contributed to various periodicals, including *Belford's Magazine* (Chicago) and *Humanity and Health* (New York). His 'The new gauger or Jack's trainer's story' was serialized in the *Anglo American Magazine* (Toronto, 1855). Aside from four works of fiction, he wrote dramas, poems and scientific articles, and he patented several inventions. SOURCE Allibone Suppl, ii, p. 1035 [under MacCarroll]; DAB; MacDonald, pp 314–15; O'Donoghue, p. 267; RIA/DIB; Watters, p. 331.

M24   *Letters to Terry Finnegan, author of several imaginary works* [anon.] (dedicated to 'every Irishman under the sun no matter what his creed or county').

+ Toronto: [n.p.], 1863, vol. 1 ('Complete in itself' [No more vols. published]).

LOCATION NUC, Univ. of Toronto.

COMMENTARY Thirty-seven comic letters addressed by Thomas D'Arcy McGee§, MP, to his 'cousin' Terry Finnegan, written in an Irish brogue, commenting on political events in Canada [RL].

M25   *The adventures of a night* (by James McCarroll).

[place?]: [publisher?], 1865. SOURCE Allibone Suppl., ii, p. 1035; O'Donoghue, p. 267. COMMENTARY No copy located [RL].

M26   *The new life* (by James McCarroll).

Boston: [publisher?], 1866. SOURCE Allibone Suppl., ii, p. 1035.

COMMENTARY No copy located. O'Donoghue has a *The life boat* of this date, which also has not been located [RL].

M27　*Ridgeway. An historical romance of the Fenian invasion of Canada* (by 'Scian Dubh').

+ Buffalo: McCarroll & Co., 1868. SOURCE Brown 88; Fanning, p. 390; Wright, ii, 2164; Watters, p. 331. LOCATION NUC, InND Loeber coll., Wright web.

COMMENTARY A highly-charged account of the Fenian raid from Buffalo (New York) into Canada in 1866. The introd. consists of a nationalistic account of Ireland's wrongs over many centuries. The story is frequently interrupted by diatribes against the English and justifications of Fenianism. A love story is interwoven. The appendix is a report of the invasion itself by General O'Neill [ML].

MC CARTHY, Charlotte, pseud. 'A gentlewoman', fl. 1745, d. 1768. Irish poet and religious writer, CM moved to London sometime before 1745 where she published a collection of poems (many in praise of friendship between women), *News from Parnassus* (London, 1757). In addition, she published a playlet in prose, *The author and the bookseller* (London, 1765); *Justice and reason, faithful guides to truth* (London, 1767) in which she was expressed some paranoia about Catholics and Jews, and *A letter from a Lady to the Bishop of London* (London, 1768), dealing with poverty, morality and the church. SOURCE Allibone, ii, p. 1162 [under MacCarthy]; Blain, p. 683; Field Day, iv, pp 1091–2, 1137, v, pp 776, 794–6; Gecker, p. 71; O'Donoghue, p. 267; Personal communication, Andrew Carpenter, July 1996; RIA/DIB.

M28　*The fair moralist; or, love and virtue. To which is added, several occasional poems, by the same* (by 'A gentlewoman').

London: Printed for the author, and sold by B. Stichall & Messrs. Baldwin & Jefferies, 1745. SOURCE ESTC t066938; Beasley, 172; Blain, p. 683. LOCATION L.

London: B. Stichall, Baldwin & Jefferies, 1746, 2nd edn (corrected edn as *The fair moralist; or, love and virtue. A novel … To which is added, the author's observations, or, a looking-glass for the fair sex. Also several additional poems*). SOURCE Blain, p. 683; Gecker, 665; ESTC t066932. LOCATION PU, CSmH (1747 edn).

+ Dublin: William Ranson, 1747 (as *The fair moralist: or, love and duty. A novel. A narrative, which has its foundation in truth and nature, and at the same time that it agreeably entertains by a variety of curious and affecting incidents is entirely divested of all those images, which in too many pieces tend to inflame the minds they should instruct*). SOURCE ESTC n47388. LOCATION L.

New York: Garland, 1974. SOURCE Blain, p. 683. LOCATION Univ. of Glasgow, DCL.

COMMENTARY Stayed in print until at least 1783. The exemplary Emelia, a poor girl, has been orphaned. She encounters the libertine Philander, a notorious aristocratic seducer who once had debauched Melissa, her best friend and confidante. She escapes him, and wanders over the countryside. She assumes the name Vileria, dons the clothes of a page boy, and goes into service as footman to a young country squire. This man is carrying on an affair with the parson's pretty young bride. The squire's wife makes advances to Vileria/Emilia, who meets Philander again. He admits that he has wounded Melissa's brother Theodore in a duel, and she, helped by her disguise, extracts from him a promise of reformation and a declaration of love for herself. When she hears that Theodore is recovered, she forgives Philander, and the heroine tells him who she is. During the wedding preparations, she decides that Philander should redeem Melissa's honour by marrying her instead. Theodore declares his love for Emelia, and the two couples live happily ever after [J.C. Beasley, *Novels of the 1740s* (Athens, GA, 1982), pp 172–3].

MC CARTHY, Justin, b. Dunmanway (Co. Cork) 1830, d. Folkestone (Kent) 1912. Novelist, nationalist politician and literary historian, JMC was the son of Michael McCarthy, clerk to the Cork City magistrates, and Ellen Fitzgerald. His father contributed a romance to the *Cork Magazine* (which he had founded), which also at a later stage published JM's first efforts at story writing. The family was too poor to grant him his wish to read for the Bar, so at age 17 he turned to journalism with the *Cork Examiner*. For a while he allied himself with the radical Young Ireland movement. He went to London in 1852 and then to Liverpool where he worked on the *Northern Daily Times* and contributed to the *Porcupine*. He then settled in London where he was parliamentary reporter and editor of the *Morning Star*. Some of his fiction was published by the Tillotson's syndicate. In 1855 he married Charlotte Allman of Bandon (Co. Cork). JM visited the US in 1868, where he worked for the *Independent* (New York), toured extensively and was so well-received that he contemplated settling there. However, he returned to London in 1871 and became a leader writer for the liberal *Daily News*, for which he worked for twenty-three years. He contributed fiction to *Young Ireland* (Dublin, 1876) and his *History of our own times* (London, 1879, 4 vols.) made him well-known as an author. The financial success of *History* enabled him to run for parliament and he was elected for Longford in 1879, later for Derry, and then Longford again until 1900. He had joined the Westminster Home Rule Association in 1877 and when Charles Stewart Parnell became chairman of the Home Rule Party, McCarthy became vice-chairman. After Parnell was named as correspondent in the O'Shea divorce case, JM believed Home Rule would be impossible to achieve under his leadership and led the anti-Parnell faction of the Irish parliamentary party but remained on friendly terms with Parnell himself. Throughout his career in parliament, JM continued his literary§ work, and he and Thomas Power O'Connor§ were the only Irish members of parliament in London with an important literary career at that time. JM was a shareholder in the *United Ireland* (Dublin) newspaper from its inception in 1881 and with his keen interest in Irish literature published under the pseud. 'Historicus' a proposal for a national canon of Irish literature, 'The Best Hundred Irish Books', in the *Freeman's Journal* (Dublin, 23 Mar. 1886) which caused considerable reaction. In 1887 he spoke before the Southwark Irish Literary Club in London on 'The literature of '48'. Later he was active in the London Irish Literary Society. He published *Reminiscences* (London, 1899) and after he left political life in 1900, when he was almost blind, he continued his work by dictation. He co-authored the 10-volume anthology *Irish literature* (New York, 1904; Chicago, 1904), and wrote the memoir *The story of an Irishman* (London, 1904), and *Irish recollections* (London, 1911). In all JMC authored or co-authored over 50 volumes, including the 23 novels listed below, three of which – combining romance and politics – were written in collaboration with Mrs R.M. Campbell Praed§. After his death she wrote *Our book of memories* (London, 1912), which dealt with their partnership. JM had never recovered financial stability after losing a great deal of his money on the failed Irish Exhibition of 1888 and through Arthur Balfour's intercession he was awarded a Civil List pension of £300 in 1903. For JM's portraits and manuscripts, see ODNB. His son, Justin Huntly McCarthy§, became a writer and MP also. SOURCE Allibone Suppl., ii, pp 1035–6 [under MacCarthy]; Boylan, p. 211; Brady, pp 142–3; Brown, p. 182; EF, p. 254; Elmes, p. 123; Un diplomate étranger, *La société de Londres* (Paris, 1885, 2nd edn), p. 282; Field Day, v, p. 924; Hogan, pp 392–3; Hogan 2, p. 747; Irish pseudonyms; Law, pp 73, 89; J. McCarthy, *An Irishman's story* (New York, 1904); NCBEL 4, pp 2440–1; OCIL, pp 328–9; ODNB; O'Donoghue, p. 269; C.A. Read, *The cabinet of Irish literature* (London, 1880), iv, opp. p. 306; RIA/DIB; Rowan cat. 53B/1310; Ryan, pp 26, 74; Sutherland, p. 392; Wolff, iii, p. 59.

M29   *Paul Massie* [anon.].

London: Tinsley Bros, 1866, 3 vols. SOURCE Wolff, 4263. LOCATION L.

+ New York: Sheldon & Co., [1875] (as *Paul Massie. A romance*). SOURCE DCU, Catholic Americana files; NYPL ([186?] ed). LOCATION NN ([186?] edn), NUC, InND Loeber coll.

COMMENTARY Set in England and Mexico. Paul Massie who lives in Mexico comes to visit his English relatives who are distant cousins. He is not well received and the mother of the cousins is clearly upset. Eventually, she and Paul discuss a secret related to Paul's family background, but it remains a secret for the rest of the family. Unhappy, Paul returns to Mexico, taking with him the cousin's fiancée. This novel may be referred to in JMC's autobiography as the 'sensational' book which he later withdrew from circulation so that his name would not be associated with it [ML; McCarthy, *An Irishman's story*, pp 136–7].

M30   *The Waterdale neighbours* (by Justin McCarthy).
London: Tinsley Bros, 1867, 3 vols. SOURCE Wolff, 4265; Topp 6, 15. LOCATION L, NUC.
+ London: Tinsley Bros, 1868 (new edn). SOURCE Topp 6, 15. LOCATION D, InND Loeber coll. (London, Chatto n.d. edn).
Leipzig: Bernard Tauchnitz, 1868, 2 vols. SOURCE T & B, 937–38. LOCATION NUC.
New York: Harper & Bros, 1867 (Harper's Library of Select Novels, No. 302). SOURCE NYPL; Topp 6, 15. LOCATION NN, NUC.
COMMENTARY The contrasted life stories of two men: one a manly and upright worker, the other a political turncoat Chartist who joins the Tories for the sake of personal success, and, when ruin stares him in the face, commits an act of treachery that is quickly followed by retribution [Baker].

M31   *My enemy's daughter. A novel* (by Justin McCarthy).
London: Tinsley Bros, 1869, 3 vols. SOURCE Topp 6, 34. LOCATION L, NUC.
London: Chatto & Windus, 1878 (new edn; as *My enemy's daughter*). SOURCE Topp 3, p. 53. LOCATION Univ. of North Carolina, Chapel Hill.
New York: Harper & Bros, 1869 (Harper's Library of Select Novels). SOURCE McCarthy, vi, p. 2133; Topp 6, 34; NYPL. LOCATION NN, NUC.
COMMENTARY Serialized in *Harper's New Monthly Magazine* (New York, Jan.–Dec. 1869), and stayed in print until at least 1890 [Topp 3, p. 53; RL].

M32   *Lady Judith. A tale of two Continents* (by Justin McCarthy).
+ New York: Sheldon & Co., 1871. SOURCE DCU, Catholic Americana files; OCLC; NYPL. LOCATION D, NN, NUC.
COMMENTARY A melodrama set in London in the year of the Great Exhibition, 1851 [Sutherland].

M33   *A fair Saxon. A novel* (by Justin McCarthy).
London: Tinsley Bros, 1873, 3 vols. SOURCE Brown, 987; Ximenes cat. 58/528. LOCATION D (1891 edn), L, NUC.
London: Chatto & Windus, 1878 (new edn; as *A fair Saxon*). SOURCE Topp 3, pp 54, 218. LOCATION DPL (1901 edn).
+ New York: Sheldon & Co., 1873. SOURCE DCU, Catholic Americana files; NYPL. LOCATION D, NN (n.d. edn), NUC.
New York, Montreal: D. & J. Sadlier & Co., [1887?] (as *Maurice Tyrone; or, a fair Saxon. A novel*). SOURCE Brown, 988 (New York: Benziger edn); DCU, Catholic Americana files.
COMMENTARY A romance about an English girl's love for an Irish MP, Maurice FitzHugh Tyrone. She has another suitor also, who tries to supplant Tyrone and to get him to violate the conditions of a legacy: that Tyrone would not marry before age 40, that he would not join the Fenians, and that he would not fight a duel. Pro and anti-Fenian positions are expressed [Brown; Murphy, p. 20; Sutherland].

M34   *Linley Rochford. A novel* (by Justin McCarthy).
London: Tinsley Bros, 1874, 3 vols. SOURCE Topp 3, p. 54. LOCATION L.

+ New York: Sheldon & Co., 1874. SOURCE DCU, Catholic Americana files; NYPL. LOCATION NN, NUC, InND Loeber coll.

COMMENTARY Serialized in *Sheldon's Galaxy* (New York, Nov. 1873–Oct. 1874) [Topp 3, p. 54].

M35 *Dear Lady Disdain* (by Justin McCarthy).

London: Grant & Co., 1875, 3 vols. SOURCE Topp 3, p. 54. LOCATION L, NUC (1876 edn).

London: Chatto & Windus, 1887 (new edn). SOURCE Topp 3, p. 54. LOCATION D (1893 edn).

Leipzig: Bernard Tauchnitz, 1876, 2 vols. in 1. SOURCE T & B, 1580–81. LOCATION NUC.

New York: Sheldon & Co., 1876. SOURCE NYPL. LOCATION NN, NUC.

COMMENTARY Serialized in Sheldon's *Galaxy* (New York, Feb. 1875–Jan. 1876). The story of Lady Marie Challoner, an uncompromisingly scornful heroine [Sutherland; Topp 3, p. 54].

M36 *Miss Misanthrope. A novel* (by Justin McCarthy).

+ New York: Sheldon & Co., 1877. SOURCE NYPL. LOCATION NN, NUC, InND Loeber coll.

London: Chatto & Windus, 1878, 2 vols. SOURCE Sutherland, p. 392; McCarthy, vi, p. 2133 (probably mistakenly notes a London, 1877 edn); Brick Row cat. 127/173. LOCATION L.

London: Chatto & Windus, 1879 (new edn; as *Miss Misanthrope*; ill. Arthur Hopkins). SOURCE Topp 3, 68.

Leipzig: Bernard Tauchnitz, 1875, 2 vols. SOURCE T & B, 1733–34. LOCATION NUC.

COMMENTARY Serialized in *Sheldon's Galaxy* (New York, Feb.–Oct. 1877). No Irish content [Topp 3, p. 68; RL].

M37 *Donna Quixote* (by Justin McCarthy).

+ London: Chatto & Windus, 1879, 3 vols. (ill. Arthur Hopkins). SOURCE Wolff, 4259. LOCATION D, L, NUC.

London: Chatto & Windus, 1881 (new edn). SOURCE Topp 3, p. 78. LOCATION Dt.

Leipzig: Bernard Tauchnitz, 1881, 2 vols. SOURCE T & B, 2004–05. LOCATION NN, NUC.

New York: Harper & Bros, 1879 (Franklin Square Library, No. 95). LOCATION NUC.

New York: G. Munro, 1879 (Seaside Library, No. 663). LOCATION NUC.

COMMENTARY Serialized in *Belgravia* (London, beginning Jan. 1879) [Topp 3, p. 78].

M38 *The comet of a season* (by Justin McCarthy; dedicated to the Hon. Mrs F.H. Jeune).

+ London: Chatto & Windus, 1881, 3 vols. SOURCE Brady, p. 142. LOCATION D, L, NUC (1885 edn).

+ London: Chatto & Windus, 1893 (new edn). LOCATION D.

Hamburg: K. Grädener & J.F. Richter, 1881–2, 2 vols. in 1. SOURCE NYPL. LOCATION NN, NUC.

New York: Harper & Bros, [1881] (Franklin Square Library, No. 214). SOURCE OCLC. LOCATION Univ. of Chicago.

COMMENTARY First serialized in the *Gentleman's Magazine* (London, Jan.–Dec. 1881) [Topp 3, p. 117].

M39 *The maid of Athens* (by Justin McCarthy).

London: Chatto & Windus, 1883, 3 vols. SOURCE Wolff, 4260. LOCATION L, NUC.

London: Chatto & Windus, 1885 (new edn; ill. F. Barnard). SOURCE Topp 3, p. 139; COPAC. LOCATION L.

+ Chicago, New York: Belford, Clarke & Co., [1889?] (Caxton Edition). LOCATION DCU, NUC.

New York: Harper & Bros, [1883]. LOCATION NUC.

New York: John W. Lovell Co., 1883 (Lovell's Library, No. 278). SOURCE Topp 3, p. 139. LOCATION NUC.

COMMENTARY First published in *Belgravia* (London, Jan.–Dec. 1883) [Topp 3, p. 139].

M40 *'The Right Honourable.' A romance of society and politics* (by Justin McCarthy and Mrs Campbell Praed).

+ London: Chatto & Windus, 1886, 3 vols. SOURCE Wolff, 4264; OCLC. LOCATION D, L, InND Loeber coll.

London: Chatto & Windus, 1887 (new edn). LOCATION NUC.

New York: D. Appleton & Co., 1887. SOURCE DCU, Catholic Americana files; NYPL. LOCATION NN, NUC.

COMMENTARY In the preface the authors state that the work constitutes 'an experiment' which 'in the strictest sense [is] the work of a man and a woman'. Sandham Morse, ex-premier of South Britain in Australia, meets Kooràli, the daughter of the new premier on a boat. They talk through the night after which she is taken off the boat to join her father and Mr Morse continues to England. He becomes a famous politician, and she marries Crichton Kenway, a political upstart. The Kenways move to England, where Crichton uses his wife's charms to improve his chances for a government appointment. They meet Mr Morse, who in the mean-time has married a charming wife. Crichton encourages intimacy between his wife and Mr Morse, who eventually fall in love with each other. They are too high-minded to give in to this passion, but Crichton drives her out of his house. Morse offers to elope with her, which would mean the end of his political career. To spare him this sacrifice, she returns to her father in Australia. The novel suggests that elements in it are autobiographical [ML; Sutherland, p. 537].

M41 *The ladies' gallery. A novel* (by Justin McCarthy and Mrs Campbell Praed).

London: Richard Bentley & Son, 1888, 3 vols. SOURCE Sutherland, p. 392. LOCATION D (1892, 2nd edn), L, NUC (1892 edn), InND Loeber coll. (London, White 1890 edn).

New York: D. Appleton & Co., 1889 (Appleton's Town and Country Library, No. 26). SOURCE NYPL. LOCATION NN, NUC.

M42 *The rebel rose. A novel* (by Justin McCarthy and Mrs Campbell Praed).

London: Richard Bentley & Son, 1888, 3 vols. LOCATION L, NUC.

+ London: F.V. White & Co., 1890 (as *The rival princess: A London romance of to-day*). SOURCE Topp 7, 148. LOCATION D, L, NUC.

New York: Harper & Bros, 1888. SOURCE DCU, Catholic Americana files. LOCATION NUC.

New York: J.W. Lovell Co., [1890] (as *The rival princess*; Lovell's International Series, No. 84). SOURCE DCU, Catholic Americana files. LOCATION NUC.

M43 *Roland Oliver. A novel* (by Justin McCarthy).

London: Spencer Blackett & Hallam, 1889 (Blackett's Select Novels). SOURCE Topp 6, 376. LOCATION L.

New York: B. Munro, [c.1889] (Seaside Library. Pocket Edition, No. 1233). SOURCE DCU, Catholic Americana files. LOCATION NUC.

New York: F.F. Lovell & Co., [c.1889]. SOURCE DCU, Catholic Americana files. LOCATION NUC.

Chicago: Rand, McNally & Co., 1889 (Globe Library). SOURCE DCU, Catholic Americana files. LOCATION NUC.

M44 *The grey river* (by Justin McCarthy and Mrs Campbell Praed and Mortimer Menpes). London: Seeley & Collins, 1889 SOURCE NCBEL 4, p. 2441; OCLC. LOCATION L.

M45 *Red diamonds* (by Justin McCarthy). London: Chatto & Windus, 1893, 3 vols. LOCATION L, NUC.
+ London: Chatto & Windus, 1895 (new edn). SOURCE Topp 3, p. 238; NYPL. LOCATION D, NN, NUC.
New York: D. Appleton & Co., 1894 (as *Red diamonds. A novel*; Town & Country Library, No. 144). SOURCE Topp 3, p. 238. LOCATION NUC.

M46 *The dictator* (by Justin McCarthy). London: Chatto & Windus, 1893, 3 vols. SOURCE Wolff, 4258. LOCATION L, NUC.
+ London: Chatto & Windus, 1895 (new edn). SOURCE Topp 3, p. 235. LOCATION DPL.
+ New York: Harper & Bros, 1893 (as *The dictator. A novel of politics and society*). SOURCE DCU, NUC, InND Loeber coll.
COMMENTARY A political romance about a South American dictator in exile in London where he falls in love with a much younger girl. His life is threatened, but he recognizes his assailants as two South American desperados. With his new wife, he returns to South America, where he is welcomed back [ML].

M47 *The riddle ring. A novel* (by Justin McCarthy; dedicated to Courtauld Thomson).
+ London: Chatto & Windus, 1896, 3 vols. LOCATION D, L, NUC.
London: Chatto & Windus, 1898 (new edn). SOURCE Topp 3, p. 256. LOCATION NIC.
New York: D. Appleton & Co., 1896 (Town & Country Library, No. 195). SOURCE Topp 3, p. 256; NYPL. LOCATION NN, NUC.

M48 *The three disgraces, and other stories* (by Justin McCarthy).
+ London: Chatto & Windus, 1897. LOCATION NUC.
COMMENTARY None of the following stories is set in Ireland. Contents: 'The three disgraces', 'A lying vision', 'A night of terror', 'The wrong letter', 'Only a photograph', 'Was she right' [CM].

M49 *Mononia. A love-story of 'forty-eight'* (by Justin McCarthy). London: Chatto & Windus, 1901. SOURCE Brown, 989; Wolff, 4261. LOCATION L, NUC, InND Loeber coll. (1901 Colonial edn).
+ Boston: Small, Maynard & Co., 1901. LOCATION D, DCU, NUC.
COMMENTARY First edn had a print run of 4,000 copies. Presumed to be partly autobiographical, the *Athenaeum* (London) described it as 'an amiable narrative of youthful patriotism' (Sutherland, p. 392). Historical fiction set in a large southern town, presumably Cork, at the time of the 1848 attempted rising. Describes the role of several young men in the rising and their love affairs. The interaction between the Irish and the English is described in positive terms, although the standpoint of the book is nationalist. The teacher in the story, Mr. Conrad, is based on JMC's teacher Mr. Goulding [ML; Brown; E. Reilly, p. 230; Sutherland, p. 392, J. McCarthy, *An Irishman's story*, p. 20–32].

M50 *Julian Revelstone. A romance* (by Justin McCarthy).
+ London: Chatto & Windus, 1909. SOURCE NYPL. LOCATION D, L, NN, NUC.
COMMENTARY Concerns the heir of an ancient English family who returns from America a wealthy man. He visits his old home disguised as a business agent. His reforming ideas shock his neighbours, especially when he starts wooing the daughter of one of them [EF, p. 255].

M51 *Kilnahoura cottage* (by Justin McCarthy). Dublin: James Duffy & Co., [1912 or earlier] (Duffy's Penny Library). SOURCE Adv. in *Catalogue of books* (Dublin, 1912).
COMMENTARY No copy located [RL].

— COLLECTED WORKS

M52 *Justin McCarthy's novels.*
London: Chatto & Windus, 1878, onwards (new edn), [no. of vols. unclear]. SOURCE Topp 3, pp 53–4, 154, 328. LOCATION NUC
COMMENTARY Title of the series is printed on the spine [Topp].

MC CARTHY, Justin Huntly (not Huntley as in ODNB), b. London 1860, d. 1936. Dramatist, novelist, poet and translator, JHM was the only son of the author Justin McCarthy§ and Charlotte Allman. He was educated at the University College School, London, and was elected to parliament as an ardent Irish nationalist MP, first representing Athlone (Co. Westmeath) and then Newry (Co. Down). He joined his father in withdrawing support from Parnell in the split in the nationalist ranks in parliament in 1890. JHM travelled widely and published some translations of oriental literature as well as writings on political subjects. He married in 1894 Marie Cecilia [last name not known], a music hall artist whose stage name was Cissie Loftus, and who composed songs and wrote tales for young people. He edited her *Our sensation* published in 1886. Only his known Irish works are listed below. SOURCE Allibone Suppl., ii, p. 1036; Brown, p. 183; EF, p. 254; Field Day, ii, p. 328; Irish pseudonyms; OCIL, p. 329; Sutherland, p. 393.

M53 *Lily lass. A romance* (by Justin Huntly McCarthy; dedicated to 'Lel akova lil, komeli rakli. Tachenes si tutis lil: Tuti dalled mandi zi to kair lesti' [*sic*]).
London: Chatto & Windus, 1889. SOURCE Brown, 990. LOCATION D, L.
New York: D. Appleton & Co., 1890. LOCATION NUC.
COMMENTARY Historical tale of the Young Ireland movement and the brief 1848 insurrection, but opens with the American Civil War. Interwoven is a love story [ML; Brown].

M54 *The illustrious O'Hagan* (by Justin Huntly McCarthy; dedicated to author's father [Justin McCarthy§]).
London: Hurst & Blackett, 1906. SOURCE Brown, 991 (mistakenly mentions 1905 edn). LOCATION D, L, NUC, InND Loeber coll. (n.d. edn).
+ New York, London: Harper & Bros, 1906. LOCATION D, NUC.
COMMENTARY The adventures of two Irish brothers, John and Philip, who had been forced by a fall in their family fortune to seek employment in the armies on the Continent. Philip had won the heart of a titled German girl, who was later forced to marry a tyrannical German prince. Philip comes to her aid when the marriage turns truly miserable. He is helped in this by the arrival of his brother [ML].

M55 *The O'Flynn* (by Justin Huntly McCarthy; dedicated to Sir Herbert Beerbohm Tree).
London: Hurst & Blackett, 1910. SOURCE Brown, 992; Wolff, 4273. LOCATION D (n.d. edn), L, NUC.
New York, London: Harper & Bros, 1910. LOCATION NUC.
COMMENTARY Story of a swashbuckling Irish soldier of fortune who had been in the Austrian army and joins King James II's army in 1689. He and a rival are both suitors for the hand of a lady, and the scene is set in Dublin and Co. Wicklow. The story was a successful play before it was published in book form [Brown].

M56 *The fair Irish maid* (by Justin Huntly McCarthy; dedicated to George Tyler).
+ London: Hurst & Blackett, 1911. SOURCE Brown, 993. LOCATION D, L.
+ New York, London: Harper & Bros, 1911. LOCATION D, NUC, InND Loeber coll.
COMMENTARY A romantic story set a few years after the Union (1801) about a beautiful girl from Co. Kerry who comes to London where she is for a while the toast of the town. However, she is true to her Kerry lover, whom she finds in London, lost and ruined. She rescues him and enables the production of his Irish play [Brown].

McCartney

M57   *The king over the water; or, the marriage of Mr. Melancholy* (by Justin Huntly McCarthy).
+ London: Hurst & Blackett, 1911. SOURCE Brown 2, 866. LOCATION D, L.
New York, London: Harper & Bros, 1911. LOCATION NUC.
COMMENTARY Historical fiction set in the eighteenth century. Tells the story of the rescue of the Princess Clementina Sobieska by the Chevalier Wogan, Irish soldier of fortune [Brown 2].

M58   *Truth and the other thing* (by Justin Huntly McCarthy; dedicated to Leslie Purcell).
+ London: Hurst & Blackett, [1924]. SOURCE Brown 2, 867. LOCATION D, L, NUC.
COMMENTARY Purports to be written about 1914 by one James Newhouse, a descendant of the famous Chevalier Casanova de Seingalt, through a marriage contract with an Irish lady when on a visit to Dublin in 1764. Mr Newhouse intersperses his own reminiscences with those of his ancestor, Casanova on certain evenings obligingly stepping down from his picture and talked to the writer. Thus we have the supposed writer's life in London, 1870–1914, and a description of Dublin life in the eighteenth century, the period of the Hell Fire Club [Brown 2].

MC CARTNEY, J.W., fl. 1860s. Irish or Irish-American historical novelist.
M59   *The Fenians; or, Neil O'Connor's triumph. A story of old Ireland and young America* (by J.W. McCartney).
Boston: Elliott, Thomes & Talbot, [1865] (Ten Cents Novelettes, No. 26). LOCATION NUC.

M'CHESNEY, Dora Greenwell, b. 1871, d. 1912. American historical novelist, DGM wrote several works but only the one connected with Ireland is listed below. SOURCE Alston, p. 268; Brown, p. 184; Wright, iii, pp 347–8.
M60   *Kathleen Clare, her book, 1637–1641* (by Dora Greenwell M'Chesney).
Edinburgh, London: William Blackwood & Sons, 1895 (ill. James A. Shearman). SOURCE Brown, 995; OCLC. LOCATION L, NUC.
COMMENTARY Historical fiction about the viceroyalty of Thomas Wentworth, earl of Strafford, in Ireland in the seventeenth century told in the form of a diary purportedly written by a kinswoman in his household. Strafford's trial and death are narrated [Brown].

M'CLINTOCK, Maj. Henry Stanley (also known as H.S. McClintock), JP, b. 1812, d. 1898. Soldier and story writer, HSM was the sixth son of George Augustus Jocelyn McClintock, of Drumcar (Co. Louth) and his second wife, Lady Elizabeth Trench, daughter of 1st earl of Clancarty. He resided at Kilwarlin House (Co. Down) and was a JP for Down, Antrim and Kildare. He served in the Royal Horse artillery and held the rank of major in the Antrim artillery. He married in 1839 Gertrude, only daughter of Robert La Touche, of Harristown (Co. Kildare). SOURCE Landed gentry, 1904, p. 365; RIA/DIB.
M61   *Random stories; chiefly Irish* (by H.S. M'Clintock).
+ Belfast: Marcus Ward; London: Simpkin Marshall; Dublin: Hodges, Figgis & Co., [1885] (ill. SMC [probably H.S. M'Clintock], C.H.). SOURCE Brown, 997; Wolff, 4275. LOCATION BFl, L, NUC ([1895] edn), InND Loeber coll.
COMMENTARY A collection of brief anecdotes mainly about life in Ireland, interspersed with poetry [ML].

MC CLINTOCK, Letitia (also known as Letitia MacClintock and Letitia M'Clintock), fl. 1869. Novelist, short story writer and folklorist, LM can probably can be identified with the eldest daughter of William McClintock and Catherine Ramage (or Margaret Macan; the sources appear contradictory). Her father was a member of the McClintock family that had settled at Dunmore (Co. Donegal). Among her books are two works of fiction and several storybooks, set mostly in Ireland, written for juveniles. In addition, she published a great deal on Irish folklore in periodicals, including the *Dublin University Magazine* (Dublin, 1876–77), *All the Year Round* (London, 1880–2, 1888), and *Cornhill Magazine* (London). William Butler Yeats§ selected some of her stories for his *Fairy and folk tales of the Irish peasantry* (London, 1888). It is not known if LM ever married. SOURCE Allibone Suppl., ii, p. 1038; BLC; Burke's, p. 750; Field Day, iv, p 1188, v, p. 926; Landed gentry, 1904, p. 366; RIA/DIB; Thuente 1, pp 64–5; Zimmermann, p. 294.

M62   *Archie Mason. An Irish story. And other tales* [anon.].
+ Edinburgh: Johnstone, Hunter & Co., 1869 (Children's Hours Series). SOURCE Dixson, p. 373; Author identified in COPAC. LOCATION E, NUC.
COMMENTARY Published in parts (London, Oct. 1868–March 1869). Contents: 'A child's prayer', 'A golden rule', 'A king honouring the Sabbath', 'A letter from Palestine', 'A little boy moves a great ship', 'A new year's hymn', 'A true incident', 'A winter's sermon', 'Animal instinct', 'The apple tree', 'The blessed bible', 'The boy martyr', 'Catching sunbeams', 'Christmas', 'The clean aprons', 'Cousin Helen', 'Death of Mirabeau's father', 'Easter day in Russia', 'Fables from the farm-yard', 'Far from home, yet going home', 'Forget-me-not', 'Francois Huber', 'God still works miracles', 'The gold mine', 'Good works', 'Honey in Palestine', 'How they ride in Cairo', 'I shall be a man', 'I will give you rest', 'Jesus wept', 'John Clarke', 'Kara Georgii', 'Kiss me good night', 'Learn to pray', 'Little child's morning prayer', 'The little chimney sweep', 'Little Ellie's cross', 'The little helpers', 'Little Mary's thought', 'Looking up', 'Lucy's winter birthday', 'The Luther Monument at Worms', 'Maltese divers', 'Missionary address', 'Mount's Bay', 'My little boy's morning prayer', 'My little boy's evening prayer', 'On a child planting a miniature tree', 'Our darling', 'Palissy the potter', 'Sabbath school answers', 'Samoides and reindeer', 'Selling milk', 'Sketches of Italian and Swiss scenery', 'The snowball', 'The stolen boy', 'The stolen sheep', 'Stories about quadrupeds – the lion – the tiger – the elephant – the bear – the wolf – the camel', 'The story of a cold bath', 'The story of a robin redbreast', 'The lord looketh on the heart', 'The true Christmas', 'True stories of brave hearts and strong wills – Francois Huber – Palissy the potter', 'Uncle Godfrey's story of a picnic at Lob's Hole', 'Will you be there' [ID; COPAC].

M63   *Old Andy's money* (by Letitia M'Clintock).
+ [Edinburgh]: [Johnstone & Hunter], 1869 (Children's Hours Series). Source COPAC; ID. Location E.
COMMENTARY Published in parts, Oct. 1868–Mar. 1869 [COPAC].

M64   *The cottagers of Glencarran* (by Letitia McClintock).
+ Edinburgh: Johnstone, Hunter & Co., [1869]. LOCATION L.
London: Hodder & Stoughton, 1885 (Sunday Library for Young People). LOCATION L.
New York: Carlton & Lanahan; San Francisco: E. Thomas; Cincinnati: Hitchcock & Walden, [1890s?] (by Letitia M'Clintock; introd. by D.W.; ill.; Sunday School Department [Series]). SOURCE OCLC (New York: Hunt [1890s]); NYPL. LOCATION NN (New York: Hunt [1890s] edn).
COMMENTARY Religious fiction, set in Glencarran on the Co. Donegal coast, and written for children from an evangelical Protestant point of view. It contrasts people who are indifferent to religion with those who try to live by God's word. Catholics do not play a role, nor does the setting in Ireland seem to be material to the story [ML].

M65   *Fred and his friends, and the wisdom he learned* (by Letitia MacClintock).
+ Edinburgh: Johnston, Hunter & Co., [1870]. SOURCE COPAC. LOCATION L.

London: T. Nelson & Sons, 1886. LOCATION L.
COMMENTARY Animal stories for children [CM].

M66 *The story of the mice; and Of the Rover and Russ* (by Letitia MacClintock).
+ Edinburgh: Johnstone, Hunter & Co., [1870] (ill.). SOURCE COPAC. LOCATION L.
COMMENTARY Stories for children. Contents: 'The story of the mice', 'The history of Rover and Puss' [ML].

M67 *Sir Spangle and the dingy hen* (by Letitia McClintock).
London: Henry S. King & Co., 1877 (ill.). SOURCE OCLC. LOCATION L, NUC.
COMMENTARY Stories for children [RL].

M68 *A boycotted household* (by Letitia McClintock).
+ London: Smith, Elder & Co., 1881 (cover: author's name is misspelled as McClintoch). SOURCE Brown, 996; TK; OCLC. LOCATION D, L, NUC, InND Loeber coll.

COMMENTARY An anti-Land League story set around 1880 in Co. Offaly and Co. Donegal and based on the social ostracism of Capt. Henry Boycott in Co. Mayo. The main character, Mr Hamilton, is a model as a man and landlord. His family lives in very reduced circumstances because of the no-rent campaign of the Land War. They cannot sell the produce from the land nor buy victuals, and their servants leave them. Various incidents, from threatening letters to murders, are described showing the ingratitude of the peasantry. Eventually, some of the peasants start to pay their rent [ML; Brown; Field Day, v, p. 926].

M69 *Alice's pupil* (by Letitia MacClintock).
London: James Nisbet & Co., 1883. SOURCE COPAC. LOCATION L.
COMMENTARY A children's story [BLC].

M70 *The march of loyalty* (by Letitia MacClintock).
+ London: Tinsley Bros, 1884, 3 vols. SOURCE COPAC. LOCATION L.
COMMENTARY A novel containing a description of an Orange march. One of the characters is Irish-American [CM].

M71 *Old Andy's money: An Irish story. And other tales* [anon.].
+ Edinburgh: Johnstone, Hunter & Co., [late-nineteenth century] (ill.; The Children's Hour Series). LOCATION D.

COMMENTARY Short Protestant stories for children. 'Old Andy's money' was first published in Edinburgh in 1869. The remaining stories are by other authors [ML; COPAC; TK].

M72 *A little candle, and other stories* (by Letitia M'Clintock).
London: T. Nelson & Sons, 1886 (ill. Edward Dalziel, George Dalziel. SOURCE COPAC. LOCATION L (destroyed), E.
COMMENTARY Religious fiction [BLC].

MC COOK, Revd Henry Christopher, b. New Lisbon (OH) 1837. Minister, entomologist, novelist and writer on religion, HCM graduated from Washington & Jefferson College, Washington (PA) in 1859, studied theology, and became a minister at a Presbyterian church in Philadelphia. He fought on the Union side in the Civil War. Later he spent time in Cuba with the National Relief Commission after the Spanish-American War organizing hospitals and the care of the sick and wounded. He was vice-president of the American Entomological Society and of the Academy of Natural Sciences in Philadelphia. His objective in writing was to produce works he hoped would be of educational value to children and the general public. SOURCE Allibone Suppl., ii, p. 1039; ANB; DAB.

M73 *The Latimers. A tale of the Western insurrection of 1794* (by Henry Christopher McCook).
+ Pittsburgh (PA): The Gibson Press, [1897]. SOURCE OCLC. LOCATION InND Loeber coll., PpiU.

+ Philadelphia: George W. Jacobs & Co., 1898 (4th thousand, ill.). SOURCE Wright, iii, 3485. LOCATION L, NUC, InND Loeber coll.

COMMENTARY Historical fiction presenting a picture the life of the Scots-Irish pioneers on the American frontier in western Pennsylvania and Ohio in the eighteenth century. Includes an account of the Whiskey Rebellion (1794) [ML].

MC CORRY, Peter, pseud. 'Con O'Leary', fl. 1869, d. United States. Novelist, editor, periodical writer and nationalist, PM was reared a Catholic and left Ulster for the US as an adult in 1868. According to O'Donoghue he first spent time in Scotland, where he was editor of the *Glasgow Free Press*. He also lived in Boston where he edited the *Catholic World*, and perhaps worked for the publisher Patrick Donahoe. Moving on to New York City, in the early 1870s he edited the *Irish People*, which was the official organ of the Fenian Brotherhood, and wrote prose and verse for the *Catholic People*. On the title page of *Mount Benedict* (Boston, 1871), he is mentioned as the author of 'The light house of the Lagan', but this work has not been located. He is not to be confused with Con O'Leary (1887–1958), not a pseudonym, who was a journalist and novelist in Ireland and England. PM also used the pseudonym 'Shandy McSherry'. SOURCE Fanning, pp 75, 79; Hogan, pp 534–5; O'Donoghue, p. 272; RIA/DIB; Wright, ii, p. 217.

M74   *The Irish widow's son; or, the pikemen of ninety-eight. A story of the Irish rebellion, embracing an historical account of the battles of Antrim and Ballinahinch* (by 'Con O'Leary'; dedicated to Patrick Donahoe [the publisher]).
     + Boston: Patrick Donahoe, 1869. SOURCE Brown, 1342; Fanning, p. 385; Wright, ii, 1608; DCU, Catholic Americana files. LOCATION InND Loeber coll., CtY, Wright web.

COMMENTARY An historical novel that focuses on British atrocities against Ulster Catholics during the 1798 rebellion, including the burning of Catholic houses, fields and churches, and the murder of innocent women and children by a drunken soldiery. Gives an historical account of the battles at Antrim and Ballinahinch. Ultimately, the hero, Cormac Rogan, escapes to America, where he marries his Irish sweetheart and raises a large family [ML; Fanning, p. 81].

M75   *The lost rosary; or, our Irish girls, their trials, temptations and triumphs* (by 'Con O'Leary'; dedicated to 'the ever faithful Irish girls in America').
     + Boston: Patrick Donahoe, 1870. SOURCE Brown, 1342; Fanning, p. 385; Wright, ii, 1609; Brown 2, 1239. LOCATION D, Wright web.

COMMENTARY A moral and educational story tracing two pairs of emigrants from Co. Donegal to the US, Barney McAuley and Tim Heggerty, and the cousins Mary and Ailey O'Donnell, the girls who love them. The men sail first in 1845. Mary's father dies, after being rackrented out of his family's ancestral land in Donegal, and Ailey comes down with famine fever and ends up in a squalid, overcrowded fever ward. Mary heroically nurses her cousin back to health, and the two girls take ship for America in 1848. They land in New York and begin to make their way as servants. The author asks 'the pure daughters of Erin' to cultivate a list of virtues. In contrast to the Clarksons, other immigrant girls, Mary and Ailey live virtuous lives. The author advises how to find decent housing and steady work, and which men to avoid. A rosary, a parting gift from Barney to Mary, lost in the shuffle of eviction and emigration, miraculously turns up again on a Celtic cross in a New York cemetery over the grave of a child of Mr O'Meara, a successful merchant immigrant. The O'Mearas provide encouragement for the girls and good jobs for Tim and Barney, and a joyous double wedding concludes the action [Fanning, pp 82–4].

M76   *Mount Benedict; or, the violated tomb. A tale of the Charlestown convent* (by 'Con O'Leary').

Boston: Patrick Donahoe, 1871. SOURCE Wright, ii, 1610. LOCATION L, Wright web.
COMMENTARY Fiction concerning the historic burning of the Ursuline convent in Boston in
1834. The story starts with the growth of a friendship between the Boston Protestant Cecilia
Morton and the Irish Catholic immigrant Kate Crolly. The Mortons, whose son is a Methodist
minister, are vociferously anti-Catholic. Because of the encouragement of the Ursuline sisters
at Mount Benedict, Cecilia ultimately converts to catholicism and Kate joins the order as a
nun. On August 11, 1834, the nuns and pupils are driven from the convent by a Boston mob,
and the buildings are burned. The author uses the novel to denounce the botched trial of the
chief instigators that follows, and the refusal of all concerned to pay an indemnity to the
Ursuline order [Fanning, p. 72–73].

MAC CULLA, Anne Jane, fl. 1848. Writer of moral fiction for juveniles. Because the fol-
lowing work was published in Dublin only, AJM was probably Irish. SOURCE RL.
M77   *The sad consequences of evil company and disobedience to parents, illustrated in
        two narratives* (by Anne Jane MacCulla).
        Dublin: [publisher?], 1848. SOURCE Alston, p. 268; COPAC. LOCATION L (destroyed).
COMMENTARY No copy located [RL].

MAC DERMOT, Brian, fl. 1871. Romance novelist who, given the Dublin publisher, was
probably Irish. SOURCE BLC; RL.
M78   *Leigh of Lara'. A romance of a Wicklow vale* (by Brian MacDermot; dedicated to
        Tiny).
        + Dublin: M.H. Gill & Son; London: Simpkin, Marshall & Co., 1899. SOURCE Brown
        1000 (n.d. edn); COPAC. LOCATION D, L, NUC, InND Loeber coll.
COMMENTARY A romance set in the village of Laragh Bridge near Glendalough (Co. Wicklow).
An English family, Mr and Mrs Leigh and a little boy, have been staying in a hotel but Mr
Leigh is so captivated by the neighbourhood that he rents Laragh Castle. The villagers feel
there is something unusual in Mr and Mrs Leigh's relationship, but don't know what. Mr
Leigh meets Nora Mortimer, with whom he falls in love. He tells her that Mrs Leigh is the
wife of his brother who under embarrassing circumstances had left England until his financial and legal problems could be resolved. He decides to look for his brother to resolve this
awkward situation and asks Nora to keep his story secret until then. Nora's family is under
the impression that she has fallen in love with a married man. Mr Leigh disappears to America
where he finds his brother and brings him back, after which he marries Nora [ML].

'**MAC DERMOT, Murtagh**', fl. 1727. Pseudonym of a fantasy adventure writer. Given the
Irish pseudonym and the Dublin publisher, he or she may have been Irish. SOURCE RL.
M79   *A trip to the moon ... Containing some observations and reflections, made by him
        during his stay in that planet, upon the manners of the inhabitants* (by 'Murtagh
        MacDermot'; dedicated to 'Captain Lemuel Gulliver').
        Dublin: Christopher Dickson, 1727. SOURCE Esdaile, p. xxix; Personal communica-
        tion, Steve Weissman, Dec. 2000.
        [London]: Printed at Dublin: and repr. at London: J. Roberts, 1728. SOURCE
        McBurney, 227; ESTC t090098. LOCATION L, O, ICN, NUC.
COMMENTARY The [London] edn is 90pp. For a long time the Dublin (1727 edn) was known
only as a lost edn, but a copy recently surfaced at Ximenes. Inspired by Jonathan Swift's§
Travels into several remote nations (London, 1726, 2 vols.), *A trip to the moon* consists of a fantastical adventure story that is a mixture of comedy and satire throughout, always with particular reference to the idiosyncrasies of Irish life. The story begins with the narrator going

to sea as a young man on a ship bound from Dublin to Tenerife, where he climbs the island's highest peak and is blown into space by a whirlwind. Arriving on the moon, he finds himself in the midst of a society of brutes, in the shape of wolves, bears, tigers, foxes, monkeys, cats, dogs etc. Within a short time he is befriended by a creature name Tckbrff, who contrives to teach him the lunar language by boiling a dictionary in a cauldron, and serving it up to him as kind of stew. With Tckbrff as a guide, the narrator is introduced to various aspects of life on the moon, including love and courtship, the theatre, coffee-houses, a cult of Pythagorean philosophers, and a good deal more. One episode involves a machine for the creation of poetry, into which slips of paper are fed and rearranged as doggerel; the narrator is permitted to try out the device, and produces a poem entitled 'Rodomontado Bembuz', which begins: 'The happy Pa-Gods of the gloomy seas,/ Shall make the world, with Taratantara blaze'. After a stay of more than two years, the narrator decides to return to earth, and effects his voyage home by the construction of a huge device made from a network of wooden tubs and a long trail of gunpowder. This apparatus has sometimes been described as the first description of rocketry as a means of inter-planetary travel. The Dublin printing concludes with 'the end of the first part', but nothing more was ever published. An 'advertisement', quoting briefly from an article in *Dickson's Newsletter* (Dublin), describes a whirlwind which lifted four 200-pound haycocks off the ground, only to put them down half a mile away. This episode is cited as proof that the preceding voyage to the moon was not to be dismissed as 'only a mere dream' [Personal communication, Steve Weissman, Dec. 2000].

MC DERMOTT (also M'Dermott), **Mrs Mary**, pseud. 'M. McD.', b. Killyleagh Glebe (Co. Down) 1832. Poet, essayist, and short story writer who lived in Belfast or its vicinity, MM also published *Lays of love* (Dublin, 1859) and was known to have set some of her own songs to music. 'Our sister land' (published in volume below) refers to Ireland. She is known also for having made a drawing of Ballymote Castle (Co Sligo) mentioned in 1856. She may be identified with the MM whose letters are among the Gill MSS in TCD (MS10,308, ff189–201). SOURCE *Jrnl of the Kilkenny and South-East of Ireland Archaeological Society*, i (1856–57), p. 286; O'Donoghue, p. 274.

M80   *My early dreams* (by 'M. McD.'; dedicated to the marchioness of Bristol, dedication
        signed Mary M'Dermott)
        + Belfast: Printed [for the author?] by F.D. Finlay, 1832 (subscribers' list). SOURCE
        COPAC. LOCATION L.

COMMENTARY Mostly poetry, some essays and short stories. Contents: 'The young musician' (about a female musician, Emma M'Donald; set in Scotland), 'The Grecian and her daughter' [RL].

MAC DERMOTT, Will. See MC DERMOTT, Fr William A.

MC DERMOTT, **Fr William A.** (also known as **Will MacDermott**), pseud. '**Walter Lecky**', b. Stranorlar (Co. Donegal) 1863, d. United States 1913. Priest, novelist and journalist, WAM came to the US as a child and grew up in Lawrence (MA). He was educated at Villanova University in Pennsylvania and afterwards became a book canvasser in Chicago and a journalist in Chicago and in New York. As a young man he travelled widely. Later he studied for the priesthood. His last years were spent as a pastor of a parish in the Adirondack mountains (NY), where he wrote most of his books. He was the author of *Down at Caxtons* (Baltimore, 1895), which deals with Catholic thought in America. Not to be confused with the historian Walter E.H. Lecky (1838–1903). SOURCE Exiles, p. 223; NUC; O'Donoghue, p. 274; RIA/DIB.

M81   *Cremore; a village idyll* (by Will MacDermott).
New York, Montreal: D. & J. Sadlier & Co., 1886. SOURCE DCU, Catholic Americana files; OCLC. LOCATION Brooklyn Historical Society.
COMMENTARY 36pp. Perhaps by William McDermott, but not mentioned by O'Donoghue or Wright [OCLC; RL].

M82   *Mr. Billy Buttons. A novel* (by 'Walter Lecky').
New York, Cincinnati: Benziger Bros, 1896. SOURCE Wright, iii, 3494. LOCATION NUC.

M83   *Père Monnier's ward. A novel* (by 'Walter Lecky').
New York, Cincinnati: Benziger Bros, 1898. SOURCE Fanning, p. 385; part printed in *Exiles*, pp 224–30; Wright, iii, 3495. LOCATION NUC.
COMMENTARY Immigrant tale featuring James Fortune, a Catholic orphan raised as a servant by Mr Brown, a Protestant Poor Law guardian in their native Stranorlar (Co. Donegal). The boy flees to America, and on ship is befriended by a fellow Donegal man, Jamie McDade, a ward boss and tavern keeper in New York. McDade's daughter marries Fortune, who founds an Irish nationalist club and climbs the New York political ladder, from alderman to congressman to a mansion on Fifth Avenue. But having arrived, he resigns his membership in the Irish club and joins the St Andrew's Society and declares himself Scotch-Irish. In a final stroke of hypocrisy, he has his fourth child baptized Chichester Hartley Portune in the Episcopal Church [*Exiles*, p. 223].

M84   *Exiles from Erin. With the Irish fairies* (by 'Walter Lecky').
New York: C. Wildermann, 1898 (Catholic Library). LOCATION NUC.

MAC DONNELL, Eneas (also Aeneas), b. Westport (Co. Mayo) 1783, d. Laragh (Co. Kildare) 1858. Barrister, novelist, editor, pamphleteer and lobbyist, EM was the son of Charles MacDonnell of Clonagh (Co. Mayo), a merchant, and Jane Miller. EM was educated at Tuam and at the lay college of Maynooth, and was admitted to the King's Inns in 1805 and called to the Irish Bar in 1810. The preface to his *The hermit of Glenconella* (London, 1820) was signed at Rosbeg near Westport, 26 Oct. 1819.He was one of the chief promoters of the cause of Catholic emancipation and a supporter of Daniel O'Connell. He became an editor for the *Cork Chronicle* and was sentenced to six months imprisonment for his writings. He moved to London where he was a parliamentary agent for the Catholic Association and wrote many political pamphlets, including *Practical views and suggestions, on the present condition and permanent improvement of Ireland* (Dublin, 1823), written under the pseudonym 'Hibernicus'. After Catholic emancipation (1829) he parted company with Daniel O'Connell and became a conservative. SOURCE Belanger, 64; Boase, ii, p. 589; Brady, p. 145; Brown, p. 185; Drury cat. 124; W.J. FitzPatrick, *The life, times, and correspondence of the Right Rev. Dr. Doyle, Bishop of Kildare and Leighlin* (Dublin, 1861), i, pp 368–9; Hogan 2, p. 753; Keane, p. 307; Leclaire, p. 40; RIA/DIB.

M85   *The hermit of Glenconella. A tale* (by Eneas MacDonnell).
+ London: G. Cowie & Co., 1820. SOURCE Brown, 1004; British Fiction; Garside, 1820:47; OCLC. LOCATION Corvey CME 3–628–48076–0, Ireland related fiction, D, Dt, Di, L, NUC.
COMMENTARY O'Mahony, who had been involved in the Desmond insurrection at the end of the sixteenth century, retires to a cottage near the Killeries in Co. Mayo and opens a school. Later he is restored to his family and his estates. Includes descriptions of Galway and Mayo coastal scenery, and the legendary pirate-queen of Connacht, Grace O'Malley, makes an appearance. Reprinted in the *Mayo News* (1913) [Brown; Leclaire, p. 40].

MAC DONNELL, R. Wogan, fl. 1870s. Short story writer. Given his name and that he published in Dublin, RWM probably was Irish. SOURCE RL.

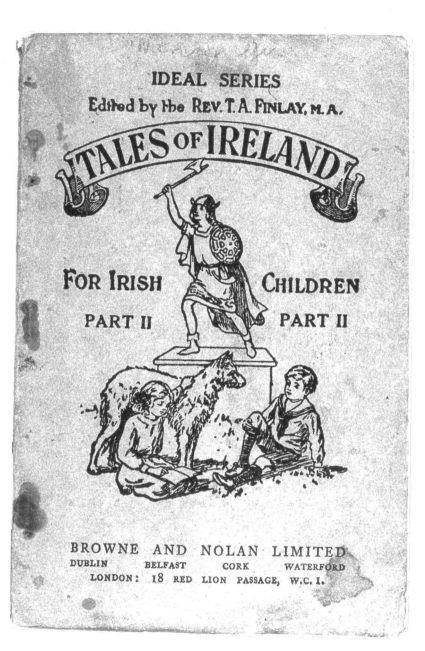

IDEAL SERIES
Edited by the REV. T. A. FINLAY, M. A.

TALES OF IRELAND

FOR IRISH   CHILDREN
PART II   PART II

BROWNE AND NOLAN LIMITED
DUBLIN   BELFAST   CORK   WATERFORD
LONDON: 18 RED LION PASSAGE, W.C. I.

33   Cover of Revd Thomas A. Finlay (ed.), *Tales of Ireland
for Irish children* (Dublin, [1917]). See **F36**.

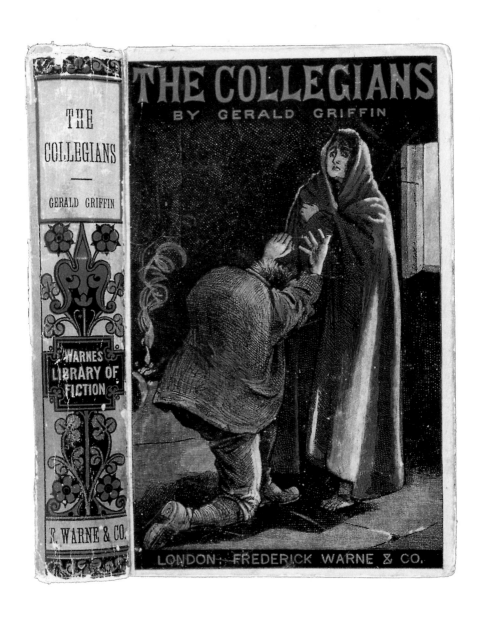

34 Cover of Gerald Griffin, *The collegians* (London, 1892). See **G161**.

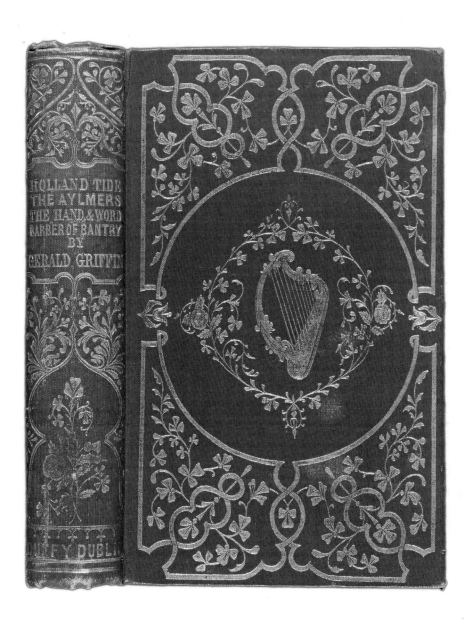

35 Cover of Gerald Griffin, *Holland-tide* (Dublin, 1857). See **G174**.

36 Cover of Gerald Griffin, *The invasion* (Dublin, [1889]). See **G174**.

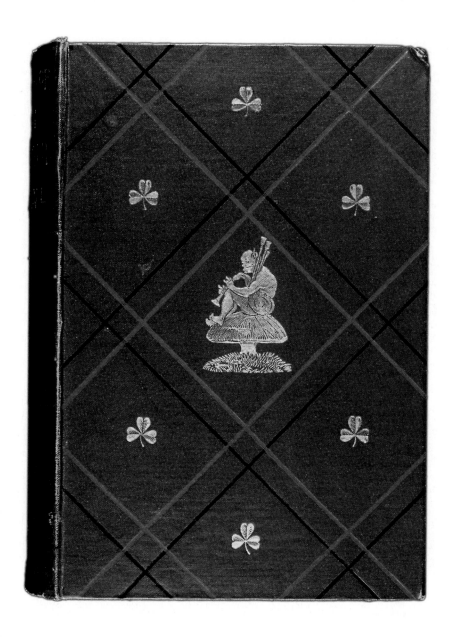

37 Cover of Mrs. S.C. Hall, *Sketches of Irish character*
(London, [1855 or later], [5th edn]). See **H23**.

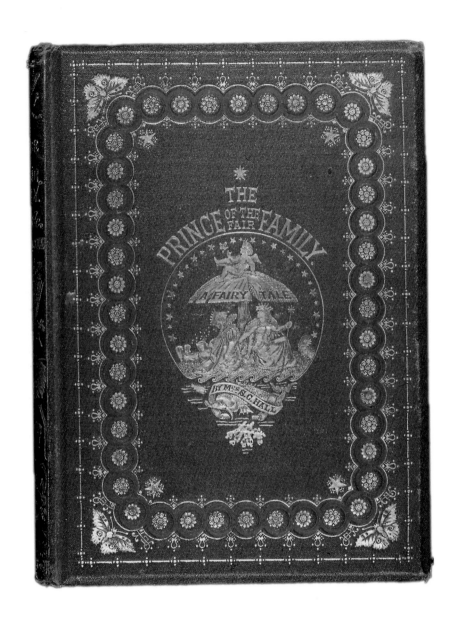

38 Cover of Mrs. S.C. Hall, *The prince of the
Fair family* (London, [1867]). See **H62**.

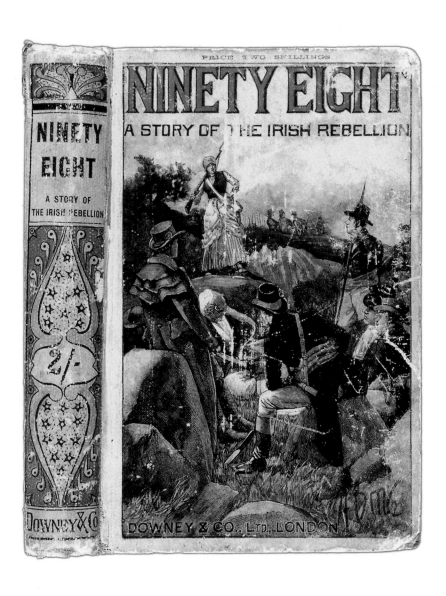

39 Cover of John Hill, *"Ninety-eight", a story of the Irish rebellion*
(London, 1898, new edn). See **H288**.

40   Cover of 'The Duchess' [Margaret Wolfe Hungerford],
Her last throw (New York, n.d.). See **H436**.

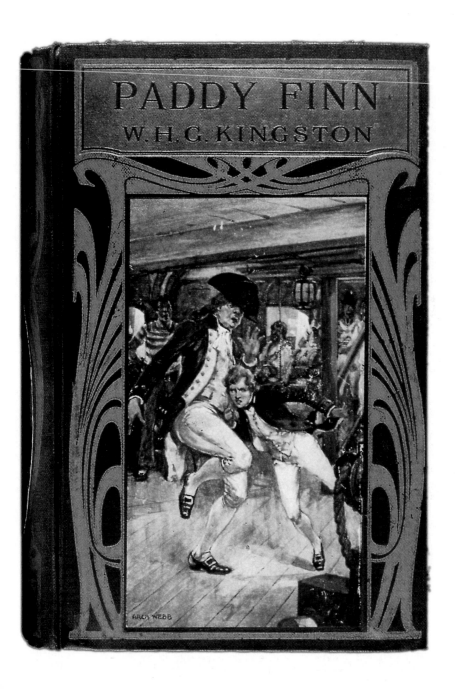

41 Cover of W.H.G. Kingston, *Paddy Finn* (London, 1883). See **K143**.

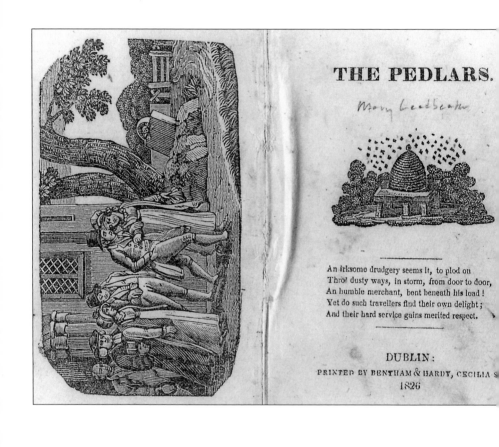

THE PEDLARS.

Mary Leadbeater

An irksome drudgery seems it, to plod on
Thro' dusty ways, in storm, from door to door,
An humble merchant, bent beneath his load !
Yet do such travellers find their own delight ;
And their hard service gains merited respect.

DUBLIN:
PRINTED BY BENTHAM & HARDY, CECILIA S
1826

42 Title of [Mary Leadbeater], *The pedlars* (Dublin, 1826). See L57.

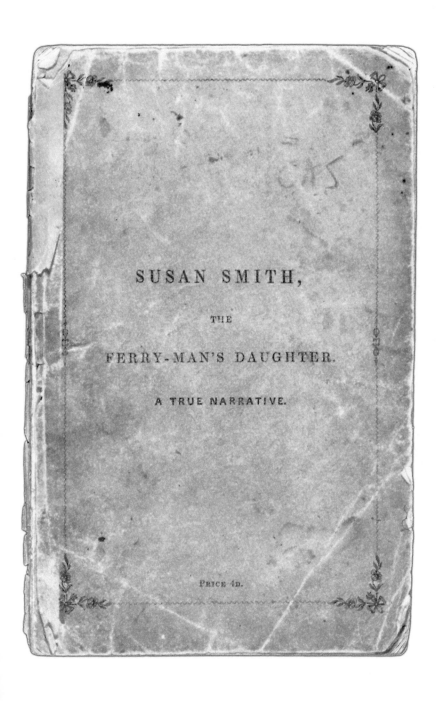

SUSAN SMITH,

THE

FERRY-MAN'S DAUGHTER.

A TRUE NARRATIVE.

PRICE 4D.

43 Cover of Eliza Leslie, *Susan Smith, the ferry-man's daughter*
(London, [1830s?]). See **L142**.

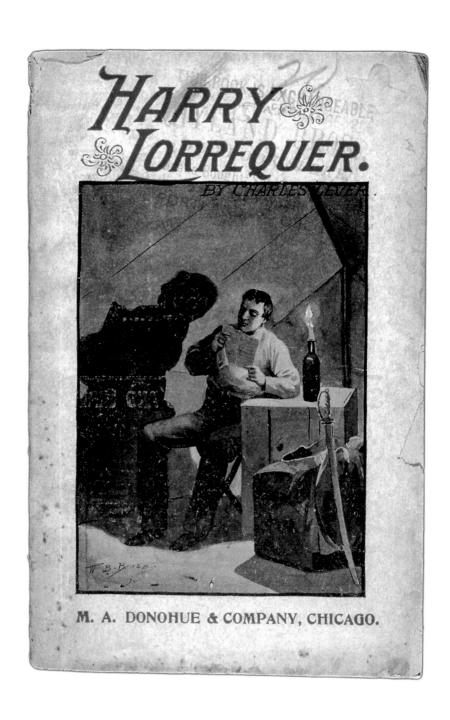

44 Cover of Charles Lever, *Harry Lorrequer* (Chicago, n.d.). See **L145**.

45 Cover of [Charles Lever], *Charles O'Malley, the Irish dragoon*
(Dublin, 1841; issued in parts). See **L146**.

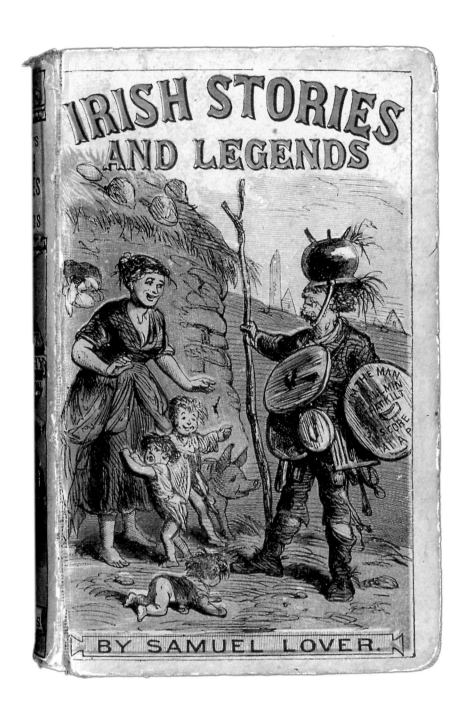

46 Cover of Samuel Lover, *Irish stories and legends* (London, [1878?];
title page: *Legends and stories of Ireland*). See **L216**.

47 Cover of Elizabeth J. Lysaght, *Brother and sister; or, the trials of the Moore family* (London, 1908, new edn). See **L284**.

48 Cover of 'Norah' [Margaret McDougall], *The days of a life*
(Almonte (ON), 1883). See **M97**.

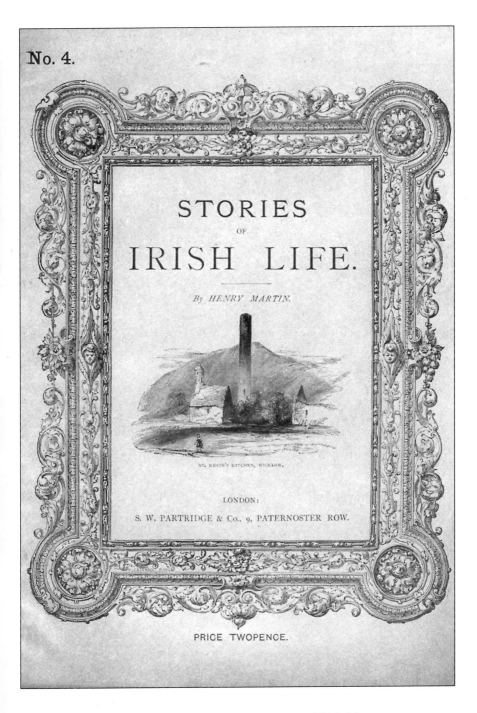

49 Cover of Henry Martin, *Stories of Irish life*
(London, [1878]; issued in parts). See **M290**.

ILLUSTRATIONS

OF

POLITICAL ECONOMY.

No. IX.

IRELAND.

A Tale.

BY

HARRIET MARTINEAU.

LONDON:
CHARLES FOX, 67, PATERNOSTER-ROW.

1832.

50   Cover of Harriet Martineau, *Ireland. A tale* (London, 1832). See **M300**.

THE

HISTORY

OF

CHARLOTTE VILLARS:

A

NARRATIVE founded on TRUTH.

Interfperfed with a

VARIETY of INCIDENTS,

INSTRUCTIVE and ENTERTAINING,

Inter Spem Curamque. HOR.

DUBLIN:

Printed by HENRY SAUNDERS, at the Corner of
Chrift-Church-Lane, in *High-Street*,

MDCCLVI.

---

51 Title page of [Isaac Mukins], *The history of Charlotte Villars*
(Dublin, 1756). See **M585**.

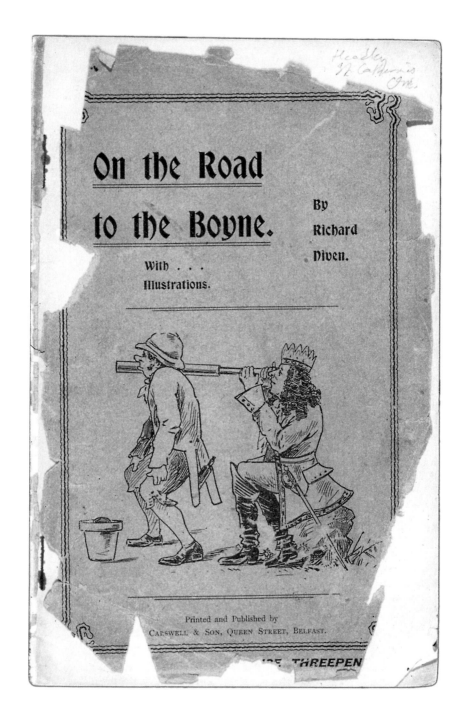

52 Cover of Richard Niven, *On the road to the Boyne*
(London, n.d.). See **N21**.

FRONTISPIECE.

See Page 9.

THE
SINGULAR AND EXTRAORDINARY
ADVENTURES
OF
POOR LITTLE BEWILDERED
HENRY,
Who was shut up in an old Abbey for three Weeks,
A STORY FOUNDED ON FACT.

By the Author of ' NOTHING AT ALL,' &c.

WELLINGTON, SALOP:
PRINTED BY AND FOR F. HOULSTON AND SON.
And sold by Harrison and Stephens, Ave-Maria
Lane, London.

1825.
[Entered at Stationers' Hall.]

53 Title page of [Mrs Margaret Graves DeRenzy], *The singular and extraordinary adventures of poor little bewildered Henry* (Wellington, 1825). See **D58**.

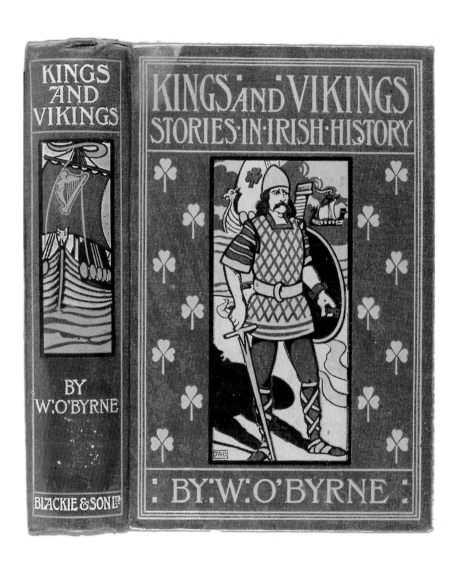

54 Cover of W. O'Byrne, *Kings and Vikings* (London, 1901). See **O58**.

55 Cover of Jane Marian Richardson, *Apples of gold: or talks with the children*
(London, 1896). See **R136**.

56 Title page of Regina Maria Roche, *The children of the abbey*
(London, [*c.* 1881?], issued in parts). See **R231**.

57   Cover of Mrs J. Sadlier, *The daughter of Tyrconnell*
(New York, 1863). See S16.

VILLA NOVA:

OR,

THE RUINED CASTLE.

A ROMANCE.

IN TWO VOLUMES.

❖

VOL. I.

BY CATHERINE SELDEN,

Author of—" Count de Santerre,"—" The Sailors,"—" English Nun,"—&c.

Cork:

PRINTED BY J. CONNOR, GRAND-PARADE.

1804.

58 Title page of Catherine Selden, *Villa Nova; or, the ruined castle* (Cork, 1804, 2 vols.). See **S82**.

59 Cover of 'L.T. Meade' [Elizabeth Thomasina Toulmin Smith], *The girls of Kings Royal* (London, 1913). See **S422**.

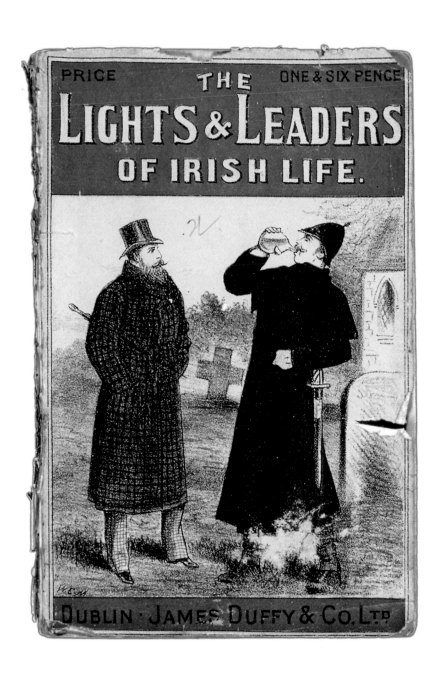

60 Cover of James Stinson, *Lights and leaders of Irish life* (Dublin, [1889]). See **S615**.

61 Cover of Bram Stoker, *Under the sunset* (London, 1882). See **S616**.

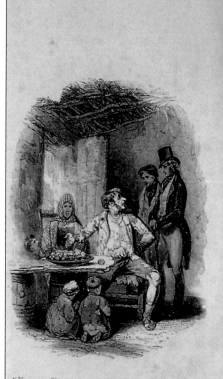

"You see, Sir," pointing to the potatoes on his board,
for he and his family were at dinner, "I am eating
dry potatoes." &c.

See page 131.

THE

IRISH TOURIST;

OR,

THE PEOPLE

AND THE

PROVINCES OF IRELAND.

Emily Taylor

LONDON:

DARTON AND HARVEY,
GRACECHURCH STREET.

———

1837.

62 Title page of [Emily Taylor], *The Irish tourist* (London, 1837). See **T12**.

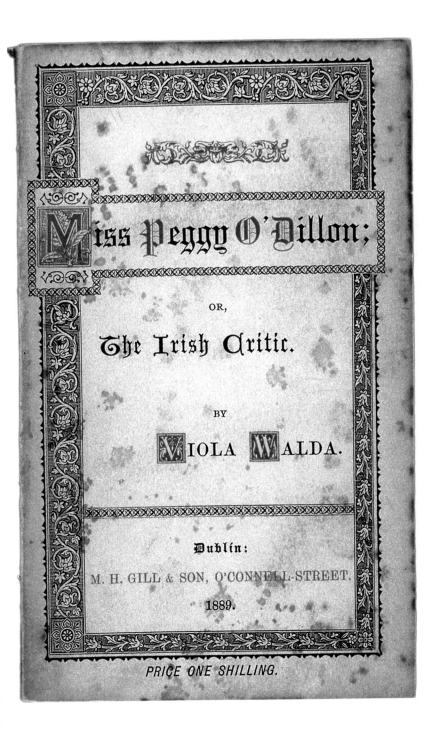

Miss Peggy O'Dillon;

OR,

The Irish Critic.

BY

VIOLA WALDA.

Dublin:

M. H. GILL & SON, O'CONNELL-STREET.

1889.

PRICE ONE SHILLING.

63 Cover of Viola Walda, *Miss Peggy O'Dillon* (Dublin, 1889). See **W**4.

64 Cover of 'Hon. Mrs W. [Mary Ward] and Lady M' [Jane, Lady Mahon],
Entomology in sport (London, [1859]). See **W26**.

M86   *The angel of snow and other stories* (by R. Wogan MacDonnell).
      + Dublin: James Duffy & Co., n.d. LOCATION D.
COMMENTARY Contents: 'Under the stone', 'Millie's trial', 'Found at last; or, the bride of Ballycrea', 'The angel of the snow', 'Gabriel Lurance, the actor', 'Only a girl's picture', 'Silver cross', 'Against hope', 'The golden crescent', 'Through fire and water', 'The old pantaloon' [RL].

M87   *Gabriel Lurance, actor; and other tales* (by R. Wogan MacDonnell).
      Dublin: James Duffy, [*c*.1870]. SOURCE Hart cat. 36/88; RLIN. LOCATION MH.
COMMENTARY A collection of short stories set in Ireland and London. The lead story appeared in *The angel of snow* (Dublin, n.d.) [Hart cat. 36/88].

MC DONNELL, Randal. See MC DONNELL, Randal William.

MC DONNELL, Randal William (known as **Randal McDonnell**), pseud. 'Kendal Roy', b. Dublin 1870, d. 1930. Historical novelist, poet and engineer, RWM was the son of Randal McDonnell, a lawyer, and Sara Carlisle of Belfast. He studied engineering at TCD, where he obtained his BA in 1855. He was an inspector for the local government board for many years and an engineer on the Great Southern and Western railroad, writing *How to become a locomotive engineer* (London, 1899). The prelude to his immensely successful *Kathleen Mavourneen* was written 15 Aug. 1897 from Natal, South Africa. For a while he was assistant librarian at Marsh's Library, Dublin, and was a reviewer for the Dublin *Freeman's Journal*. He was also a magistrate. SOURCE B & S, Appendix B, p. 76; Brady, p 145; Brown, p. 186; BLC; EF, p. 255; Hogan 2, p. 754; O'Donoghue, p. 276; E. Reilly, p. 247; RIA/DIB.

M88   *Tales of an engineer. Being facts and fancies of railway life* (by 'Kendal Roy').
      + Dublin: Sealy, Bryers & Walker, 1896. LOCATION L.
      London: T. Fisher Unwin, 1896. LOCATION L.
COMMENTARY Contents: 'The story of Kathleen Marr' (narrative told to someone on the *Kilkenny Mail* by Dr Cyril Hargrave about his life as a doctor in poorer parts of Dublin), 'With the Queen in Killarney' [CM].

M89   *Kathleen Mavourneen: A memory of the great rebellion, from the record of Hugh Tallant, rebel to King George of England in the year of grace one thousand seven hundred and ninety eight* (by Randal McDonnell).
      London: T. Fisher Unwin; Dublin: Sealy, Bryers & Walker, 1898 (photograph of Wolfe Tone's grave). SOURCE Brown, 1005. LOCATION L.
      Dublin: M.H. Gill & Son, 1901. LOCATION D (1912, 5th edn), L, NUC (1935 edn).
COMMENTARY Historical novel set in Ireland between 1792 and 1798 describing the rise of the United Irishmen movement through the eyes of Hugh Tallant, a young man who has come from Co. Wicklow to Dublin to seek his fortune. He gets involved with the United Irishmen and reports on developments taking place over the period. The novel covers the French invasion (Bantry Bay) at end of 1796, as well as the last French expedition in 1798 and the outbreak of the great rebellion. It describes the battle of New Ross (Co. Wexford). Theobald Wolfe Tone§ is prominent, and other leaders of the United Irishmen appear, including glimpses of Lord Edward Fitzgerald and of Henry Grattan speaking in the Irish parliament. In the end, Tallant flees to France with his new bride, who had helped him escape from many a difficult situation. They return to Ireland after twenty years and visit among others the graves of Lord Edward Fitzgerald, John and Henry Sheares and Wolfe Tone [ML; Nield; B. Browne].

M90   *With the Queen to Killarney and other stories* (by Randal McDonnell).
      + London: T. Fisher Unwin; Dublin: Sealy, Bryers & Walker, 1900 (new edn).
      LOCATION D, DPL.

McDonnell

COMMENTARY No copy of earlier edn located. Some of the stories are railway stories, and others are set in Dublin and Killarney. Contents: 'With the Queen to Killarney' (first published in *Tales of an engineer*, Dublin, 1896), 'Men call it chance (a tale of Southern Express)', 'A "maid of honour" or, the law of inertia', 'Told by a sad spectator', 'Half a second slow', 'The short story of Kathleen Marr' (first published in *Tales of an engineer*, Dublin, 1896), 'The tower of St. Michan's', 'Round the Inchicore works' [ML].

M91   *When Cromwell came to Drogheda; a memory of 1649, edited from the record of Clarence Stranger, a captain in the army of Owen Roe O'Neill* (by Randal McDonnell).
        Dublin: M.H. Gill, 1906. SOURCE Brown, 1006. LOCATION DPL (n.d. edn), L (destroyed), NUC (n.d. edn).
COMMENTARY Historical novel set in the seventeenth century. Tells the main events from Cromwell's landing to the subsequent confiscation and plantations. It is written from the point of view of an officer in the army of Owen Roe O'Neill [Brown].

M92   *My sword for Sarsfield. A story of the Jacobite war in Ireland, edited from the memoirs of Phelim O'Hara (1668–1750) a Colonel in Sarsfield's horse* (by Randal McDonnell).
        Dublin: M.H. Gill, 1907. SOURCE Brown, 1007; OCLC. LOCATION L.
        + Dundalk: W. Tempest, 1920. SOURCE Emerald Isle cat. 89/1117. LOCATION DPL, InND Loeber coll.
COMMENTARY Historical novel describing the main events of the Williamite War from the point of view of a colonel in Sarsfield's troop of horse [Brown].

M93   *Ardnaree. The story of an English girl in Connaught, told by herself and edited from the original mss* (by Randal McDonnell).
        + Dublin, Waterford: M.H. Gill & Son, 1911. SOURCE Brown, 1008; OCLC. LOCATION D, DPL, L, InND Loeber coll.
COMMENTARY The story of an English girl who has moved to Connacht with her family, where her father hopes to make his fortune. She gives a fairly naive picture of social life, consisting of tea parties and military balls. A love affair comes to nothing. The landing of the French at Killala in 1798 is noted but seems to have little effect on the story. Eventually, the family moves back to England, since the Irish venture failed financially [ML].

MC DONNELL, William, b. 1814, d. 1900. American novelist, WM was also the author of *The heathens of the heath. A romance* (New York, 1874), which is not a novel but a criticism of England's role in the history of Ireland that puts blame on both the English and the Irish. SOURCE Wright web.

M94   *Exeter Hall. A theological romance* [anon.].
        + New York: American News Co., 1869. LOCATION Wright web.
COMMENTARY Religious fiction. The novel starts with a description of Exeter Hall in London, a centre for evangelizing activities. The story features several Irish priests, who discuss an upheaval that had occurred at a Baptist chapel. They defend catholicism and Ireland, discuss the unfairness of tithes imposed by the Church of Ireland, and show their dislike of Bible societies [ML].

MC DOUGALL, Margaret Dixon (née Carey), pseud. 'Norah', b. Belfast (Co. Antrim) 1826, d. Seattle (WA) 1899. Novelist, journalist and poet, MDM was reared in a prosperous family in a conservative Hiberno-Scotsh environment in the north of Ireland. Her mother was Eleanor West. It is not clear when MDM and her parents emigrated to Canada, but she first lived at White River (ON), and later at Bay City (MI) in the US, where she became an active member of the Baptist Home Missionary Society. She married Alexander McDougall, a lumberman, with whom she had six children and who died in Oscoda (MI) in 1887. She later lived in Pembroke (ON) where she had her own school. Subsequently she lived in Montreal and returned to Ireland sometime before 1882 as a correspondent of the Montreal *Witness* and the New York *Witness*. She was a keen advocate of reforms in Ireland and in her letters to the newspapers reported on the conditions of the peasantry, poorhouses, landlordism, evictions, famine, tenant rights, and the activities of the Land League. The letters were published by subscription in Montreal as *The letters of 'Norah' on her tour through Ireland, being a series of letters to the Montreal 'Witness' as special correspondent to Ireland* (Montreal, 1882). Under her pseudonym she published a volume of poems, *Verses and rhyme by the way* (Pembroke, ON, 1880). The title pages of several of her publications refer to the following works: 'My young master'; 'Revenge in theory and practice'; 'Casting the lot', and 'In search of the super-natural', but none of these has been located. Revd John Boyce§ (under the pseudonym 'Paul Peppergrass') edited *The lady of the beacon of Araheera* (Quebec, 1859), which has been attributed to MDM She died on a visit to Seattle (WA). SOURCE CEWW; Personal communication, Michel Brisebois, National Library, Ottawa; Rhodenizer, p. 855; RL; Watters, p. 334; M.D. McDougall, *The letters of 'Norah' on her tour through Ireland* (Montreal, 1882), pp 167, 228, 297.

M95   *The lady of the beacon of Araheera. (A chronicle of Innishowen)* (ed. by 'Paul Peppergrass' [Fr John Boyce§]).

    + Quebec: Daniel Carey & Co., 1857. SOURCE Brown 2, 129 (1859 edn); Watters, p. 334. LOCATION CaOTP, CaOONL.

COMMENTARY Although edited by 'Paul Peppergrass', the pseudonym of Fr. John Boyce§, Watters attributed the book to MDM. In the afterword the editor relates that the male [*sic*] author of this work, whom he did not identify, on account of rheumatism did not finish the volume in Canada prior to leaving for Ireland. The story is set in Co. Donegal and concerns events surrounding the lighthouse of Araheera [RL].

M96   *Life in Glenshie, being the recollections of Elizabeth Ray, school teacher. A tale* [anon.].

    + Montreal: John Dougall & Son, 1878. LOCATION NUC, CaOONL (microfiche), CaBVAU, InND Loeber coll.

COMMENTARY Fiction, probably autobiographical in part, set in Co. Antrim [RL].

M97   *The days of a life* (by 'Norah'; dedicated to 'The exiled sons and daughters of Ireland, in the US and Dominion of Canada').

    + Almonte (ON): W. Templeman, 1883. SOURCE Watters, p. 334 (Plate 48). LOCATION NUC, InND Loeber coll.

COMMENTARY Based on Margaret Dixon McDougall's *The letters from "Norah"* (Montreal, 1882). A Canadian girl comes to visit her relatives in Ramelton (Co. Donegal). During her stay she has many occasions to comment on the landlords' abuse of power and to contrast the state of the labourers with that of the free farmers in Canada. She also comments on the Presbyterians in the North who seem to be more concerned about Scotland than about Ireland. Various evictions take place, and the law that was designed to protect the interest of the tenant in improvements made on the land, is shown in practice to be useless [CEWW; ML].

'MAC DOWELL, Lalla', fl. 1877. Probably a pseudonym, with the 'Lalla' deriving from Thomas Moore's poem *Lalla Rookh* (London, 1817). Social commentary novelist LM also published *How we learned to help ourselves* (London, 1877). The SOURCE Allibone Suppl., ii, p. 1044.

M98   *The earl of Effingham* (by 'Lalla MacDowell').

    + London: Samuel Tinsley, 1877. SOURCE Allibone Suppl., ii, p. 1044; Brown, 1011. LOCATION L.

COMMENTARY Set in Ballyquin (Co. Galway) in the 1840s and appeals to the Irish landlords to stay at home and right Ireland's wrongs [Brown].

'MAC EIRE, Fergus', fl. 1872. Pseudonym of a novelist who was Irish or of Irish descent. SOURCE RL.
M99   *The sons of Eire. A novel* (by 'Fergus Mac Eire, the last of the sons of Eire').
London: T. Cautley Newby, 1872, 3 vols. SOURCE Brown, 1013; Wolff, 4326. LOCATION Dt, L, NUC.
COMMENTARY A presumably autobiographical account of 'the last of the sons of Eire', and an old decayed Irish family living in Hampshire, England. They return to Ireland, where their sympathies lie. In the end, the storyteller marries the betrothed of his brother, who has been killed in a skating accident [Brown].

MC ELGUN, John, fl. 1873. Irish or Irish-American novelist.
M100   *Annie Reilly; or, the fortunes of an Irish girl in New York. A tale founded on fact* (by John McElgun; dedicated to Bernard Reilly).
New York: J.A. McGee, 1873 (ill. M'Donald). SOURCE Fanning, p. 385; Wright, ii, 1614. LOCATION DCU (1877 edn), NUC, InND Loeber coll. (1877 edn), Wright web.
COMMENTARY A saga of emigration that provides the fullest description available of the Queenstown (Cobh, near Cork) to Liverpool to New York journey of the Famine generation. In the 1850s Annie Reilly's family is evicted from their small Munster holding through the machinations of a despicable middleman, Ryan. At the same time, Annie's beau, James O'Rourke, is accused of conspiring to steal arms from a police barracks. Both young people flee to America, where they hope to be reunited, but they travel on different ships and lose track of each other. At his landing, James is swindled by an 'intelligence agent', who sets him up with a fictitious job. After finding another job, he heads to the Pennsylvania oil fields. Annie arrives in New York and finds her relatives, the Sweeneys, who have achieved middle-class respectability. At the end of the novel, James and Annie find each other, and get married. Catholic characters make it clear that they are carefully instructed as to the teachings of their religion and that they are not merely receptacles for information but active thinkers [Fanning, p. 84; C.M. Eagon, '"White," if "not quite"': Irish whiteness in the nineteenth century' in *Éire/Ireland*, 36 (2001), p. 71].

MC FALL, Mrs Frances Elizabeth Bellenden (née Clarke; known as **Frances Elizabeth McFall**), pseud. '**Sarah Grand**', b. Donaghadee (Co. Down) 1854, d. Calne (Wilts.) 1943. Novelist, feminist and suffragist, FEBM was the fourth daughter of Edward John Bellenden Clarke, a Royal Navy lieutenant and coastguard, and Margaret Bell Sherwood, who were of English, middle-class background. On the death of her father in 1861, the family returned to England to live in Yorkshire. She attended two boarding schools, unhappily, and at age 16 married an army surgeon, Lt.-Col. David McFall, of Magherafelt (Co. Derry) who was twenty-three years older than she and a widower with children. The marriage was not a happy one. The McFalls travelled to Hong Kong and the Far East with the army. Back in England, she began to publish in magazines and with the small profit from her novel *Ideala* (Warrington, Lancs., 1888) which she published privately, she was able to leave her husband and take her son to London, where she supported herself by writing. The enormous success of *The heavenly twins* (London, 1893) and her growing reputation for her 'new woman' novels that explored issues of social concern (e.g. *The Beth book*, London, 1897), created a career for her as a frequent lecturer on women's topics, including a tour of the US, where she stayed with Mark Twain in Connecticut. She later lived at Tunbridge Wells and in 1920 she moved to Bath and was subsequently mayoress of the city on six occasions. She was a member of the Women Writers Suffrage League and president of the Tunbridge Wells branch of the National Union of Suffrage Societies. She published 14 novels and volumes of short stories, mostly on women and social issues. *The breath of life* (Bath, [*c*.1920]) is a short anthology of quotations from her work for the days and the months of the year. An article about her was published in *Woman's life* (London, 1896). Some of her letters are in the PRONI (MS D/790). The major collection of her papers is in the Bath Reference Library; the Sadleir Collection at UCLA has seventy of her letters, and another collection is at the University of Reading (for other MS sources, see DNB). FEBM's portrait was published in her *Our manifold nature* (London, 1894). SOURCE Allibone Suppl., ii, p. 1045; H.C. Black, *Pen, pencil, baton and mask. Biographical sketches* (London, 1896), pp 70–6; Blain, p. 451 [under Grand]; T. Eakin, 'Sensational Sarah; the story of the Ulster-born woman who shocked the world' in *Ulster Local Studies*, 27(1) (Summer 1995); EF, p. 159; Field Day, iv, pp 827, 894–5, v, p. 977 [under Grand]; H. Fraser et al., *Gender and the Victorian periodical* (Cambridge, 2003), p. 43; G. Kersley, *Darling madam, Sarah Grand and devoted friend* (London, 1983); NCBEL 4, pp 1555–6 [under Grand]; OCIL, p. 223–4 [under Grand]; RIA/DIB [under Clarke]; RLIN; Sutherland, pp 257–8 [under Grand]; Todd, pp 286–7 [under Grand].

M101   *Two dear little feet* (by Frances Elizabeth McFall).
+ London: Jarrold & Sons, 1880. SOURCE Alston, p. 269; OCLC. LOCATION L.
COMMENTARY Story about a girl's maltreatment of her feet in order to keep them small as a concession to fashion by wearing pointed boots that are too narrow and short for her feet. She needs to have operations to correct her deformed feet which are only partially successful. Not a children's story [ML].

M102   *Ideala. A study from life* [anon.].
Warrington, Lancs.: Privately printed; 1888. SOURCE NCBEL 3, p. 1555. LOCATION C.
London: E.W. Allen, 1888. SOURCE Alston, p. 269; Sadleir, 1049 (London, Bentley 1889 edn). LOCATION L.
+ New York: M.J. Ivers & Co., 1893 (as *Ideala*; American Series, No. 320). LOCATION InND Loeber coll.
New York: D. Appleton & Co., 1893. SOURCE Jarndyce cat. 94/511.
COMMENTARY *New York, Appleton, 1893 edn* No other copy located than that listed by Jarndyce [RL].
+ Chicago: Donohue, Henneberry & Co., n.d. (as *Ideala*, by 'Sarah Grand'). LOCATION InND Loeber coll.
COMMENTARY Ideala is an unconventional English woman who expresses at length her ideas on marriage, social immorality, women's education, and the equality of men and women. She is tempted to leave a brutal and unfaithful husband for the protection of a man she loves. Instead, she leaves her husband's roof to spend a year in China. After her return to England she devotes the remainder of her life to the weak and erring of her own sex [ML].

M103   *A domestic experiment* [anon.].
+ Edinburgh, London: William Blackwood & Sons, 1891. SOURCE Daims, 1952. LOCATION L, NUC, InND Loeber coll.
COMMENTARY The refined Agatha Oldham is married to the brutish Paul. He is conducting an affair with a woman called Dolly, and has low-class associates. Paul invites Dolly to his house in the hopes his wife will introduce her to society. Agatha is embarrassed by her husband's move. Instead of introducing Dolly to high society, she sinks to Dolly's level and befriends her. Several men try to rescue Agatha, among whom is one Vaincrecourt. Agatha and Vaincrecourt are about to fall in love when Vaincrecourt meets with an accident and dies. She then decides to make the best of her life with her husband [ML].

M104   *The heavenly twins* (by 'Sarah Grand').
   + London: William Heinemann, 1893, 3 vols. SOURCE Daims, 1953; Sadleir, 1048; Wolff, 2669. LOCATION D (1894 edn), L.
   + New York: Cassell, [*c.*1893]. SOURCE Daims, 1953; SOURCE Krishnamurti, p. 51. LOCATION NUC, InND Loeber coll.
COMMENTARY FM had the volume typeset at her own expense, after which Heinemann published it. It became a huge success, selling about 100,000 copies in the year of publication. The story follows several young women, including twins, from girlhood to womanhood as they try to achieve independence in a male-dominated society. The double standard in sexual behaviour is seen through Edith's disastrous marriage, through which she and her baby have contracted syphilis. The story advanced the idea of sexual equality and responsibility. George Bernard Shaw§ found the novel threatening to a male, patriarchal society but acknowledged that it had made him think about issues from a woman's point of view. [Field Day, iv, pp 880–1; Krishnamurti, p. 51].

M105   *Singularly deluded. A romance* (by 'Sarah Grand').
   Edinburgh, London: William Blackwood & Sons, 1893. SOURCE Daims, 1954; Wolff, 2671. LOCATION L.
   New York: J. Munroe, [*c.*1895]. SOURCE Daims, 1954. LOCATION NUC, InND Loeber coll. (New York, Lupton n.d. edn).

M106   *Our manifold nature* (by 'Sarah Grand').
   + London: William Heinemann, 1894 (ill. with photo of author). SOURCE Wolff, 2670. LOCATION L, InND Loeber coll.
   Leipzig: Bernard Tauchnitz, 1894. SOURCE T & B, 2983; GLOL. LOCATION Die Deutsche Bibliothek.
COMMENTARY Contents: 'The yellow leaf', 'Eugenia', 'Ah man', 'Kane, a soldier's servant', 'Janey, a humble administrator', 'Boomellen'. The first two stories deal with feminist topics [ML].

M107   *The Beth book, being a study from the life of Elizabeth Caldwell Maclure, a woman of genius* (by 'Sarah Grand').
   London: W. Heinemann, 1897. SOURCE Daims, 1951. LOCATION L.
   + New York: D. Appleton & Co., 1897. SOURCE Daims, 1951. LOCATION NUC, InND Loeber coll.
   Bristol: Thoemmes, 1994 (introd. by Sally Mitchell). SOURCE RLIN. LOCATION CtY.
COMMENTARY A portrait of the new woman in fiction in the form of an autobiographical novel of the author's childhood. The main character, Elizabeth, is brought up in shabby gentility in northern Ireland where her father is a coastguard official. She is neglected, while attention is lavished on her brother. Her father is unfaithful to her mother and dies prematurely from a brain tumour. Elizabeth and her mother then move to Yorkshire to live with an unpleasant relative. Amidst this domestic upheaval, Elizabeth grows up poorly educated and at sixteen marries a doctor, Dan Maclure. He is unfaithful to her with a female patient and is secretly employed at a hospital for the forcible treatment of women prostitutes. He is also, as she discovers, a sadistic vivisectionist. She cannot surrender to him sexually and leaves to become a novelist. In the boarding-house where she takes up residence she meets an American artist and nurses him through illness, but turns down his proposal to become his mistress. In the course of her tribulations she is politicized and begins to speaks out on women's rights. At the end of the novel the heroine and the American are mystically united at harvest time in the countryside [Sutherland, pp 61–2].

M108   *The modern man and maid* (by 'Sarah Grand').
   + London: Horace Marshall & Son, 1898. SOURCE NCBEL 4, p. 1555. LOCATION L.

M109 *Babs the impossible* (by 'Sarah Grand').
  + London: Hutchinson & Co., 1901. SOURCE Wolff, 2667. LOCATION D, InND Loeber coll.
  Leipzig: Bernard Tauchnitz, 1901, 2 vols. SOURCE T & B, 3505–6; OCLC. LOCATION NIC.

COMMENTARY Set in England among the gentry of four country houses, an impetuous girl grows up without any proper guidance or intellectual training. She falls in love easily, but needs to develop her soul before she can be a worthy wife. Her mother marries a Mr Jellybond, who has moved into the area and who has charmed everyone, although he used to own a bar and is proud of that fact. The county returns him as a member of parliament. The girl finally ends up leaving the area, when she thinks that the person she truly loves, the main local landowner, is to marry her aunt [ML].

M110 *Emotional moments* (by 'Sarah Grand').
  London: Hurst & Blackett, 1908. SOURCE Wolff, 2668; OCLC. LOCATION MH.
  + Leipzig: Bernard Tauchnitz, 1908. SOURCE T & B, 4037. LOCATION InND Loeber coll.

COMMENTARY Contents: 'An emotional moment', 'From dusk till daybreak', 'A new sensation', 'The condemned cell', 'The baby's tragedy', 'She was silent', 'When the door opened –?', 'The rector's bane', 'The wrong road', 'The butcher's wife', 'The man in the scented coat', 'The undefinable' [ML].

M111 *Adnam's orchard: a prologue* (by 'Sarah Grand'; dedicated to 'the Lady').
  + London: William Heinemann, 1912. SOURCE Daims, 1950. LOCATION D, L, NUC, InND Loeber coll.
  New York: D. Appleton, 1913. SOURCE Daims, 1950. LOCATION NUC.

COMMENTARY Set in rural England, the story deals with the relationship between classes, and particularly that of employer and labourers. Modern ideas such as intensive cultivation of the land, but also socialism, radicalism, and feminism are discussed, with the conviction that 'all social remedies should be moral, not material'. The story deals with the lives of families of different classes who live in close proximity [ML].

M112 *The winged victory* (by 'Sarah Grand').
  London: W. Heinemann, [1916]. SOURCE Daims, 1955. LOCATION L, NUC.
  New York: D. Appleton, 1916. SOURCE Daims, 1955. LOCATION NUC.

M113 *Variety* (by 'Sarah Grand').
  + London: William Heinemann, 1922. SOURCE NCBEL 4, p. 1555. LOCATION L.

COMMENTARY Contents: 'The turning of the worm', 'Vanity and vexation', 'The saving grace', '"I can't explain it"', 'A thorough change', 'One of the olden time', 'Joseph recounts a remarkable experience', 'The commandant' [CM].

MAC FARLAND, John, pseud. 'Himself', fl. 1820. Novelist. The following work has been attributed to JM, who was probably Irish or Irish-American. SOURCE Exiles, p. 25.

M114 *The life and travels of Father Quipes, otherwise Dominick O'Blarney* ('by Himself').
  Carlisle (PA): Printed for the purchaser, 1820. SOURCE Fanning, p. 384; almost fully printed in Exiles, pp 25–33; RLIN. LOCATION Univ. of California, Berkeley.

COMMENTARY 32pp. The story takes its hero from Co. Kerry to Carlisle (PA), with stops along the way in Galway, Sligo and – thanks to a British press gang – Ceylon [Sri Lanka]. The satirical targets include the habits of the Pennsylvania Dutch, American political electioneering, and the fad for impossibly romantic novels [Exiles, p. 25].

'MC'GALLAGHER, Blarney', fl. 1830s. Pseudonym of a short story anthologist.

McGee

M1115 *Tales of Ireland* (by 'Blarney Mc'Gallagher').
+ London: For the Booksellers, [1834 or later]. LOCATION D.
COMMENTARY Contents: 'Rival dreamers' [John Banim§ and Michael Banim§], 'Paddy the piper' [Samuel Lover§], 'The station, an Irish sketch', 'Kate Connor' [Mrs S.C. Hall§], 'Paul Doherty', 'The gridiron' [Samuel Lover§], 'The three advices' [from *Royal Hibernian tales*, Dublin?, 1825 or earlier], 'The tough yarn', 'Flora Cantillon's funeral', 'Dreaming Tim Jarvis' [from Thomas Crofton Croker's§ *Fairy legends*], 'Rent-day', 'The little shoe', 'The black thief and the Knight of the Glen' [from *Royal Hibernian tales*, Dublin?, 1825 or earlier], 'Manus O'Mallaghan and the fairies' [from *Royal Hibernian tales*, Dublin?, 1825 or earlier], 'The hermit turned pilgrim', 'The spaeman' [from *Royal Hibernian tales*, Dublin?, 1825 or earlier], 'The priest and the robber' [from *Royal Hibernian tales*, Dublin?, 1825 or earlier], 'Teague Sloan' [from *Royal Hibernian tales*, Dublin?, 1825 or earlier], 'Story of Oldemar' [from *Royal Hibernian tales* Dublin?, 1825 or earlier], 'The wife of two husbands' [J.L.L.], 'The generous Irishman', 'Laying a ghost' [William Carleton§], 'The three devils' [B.A.P.], 'Darby Doyle's voyage to Quebec' [Thomas Ettingsall], 'Paddy Foorhane's fricassée', 'The curse of Kishoge' [Samuel Lover§], 'The mayor of Galway' [ML].

MC GEE, T.D. See MCGEE, Thomas D'Arcy.

MC GEE (also M'Gee), **Thomas D'Arcy** (also known as **T.D. McGee**), b. Carlingford (Co. Louth) 1825, d. Ottawa (Canada) 1868 (not Montreal as in Brady). Revolutionary, journalist, poet and politician, TDM was the second son of James McGee, a coastguard, and Dorcas Catherine Morgan, whose father, a Dublin bookseller, had been ruined because of his connection to the United Irishmen. TDM emigrated to Boston at age 17 and became known as such a dynamic and forceful speaker that he was made editor of the Boston *Pilot* when age 19. His political activities brought him to the notice of the Young Irelanders and he returned to Dublin in 1845, en route to London as parliamentary correspondent of the Dublin *Freeman's Journal*. In Dublin he met Charles Gavan Duffy and agreed to contribute 'Letters from London' to the nationalist paper the *Nation* (Dublin), which led to his dismissal from the *Freeman's Journal*. As secretary of the Irish Confederation, he made a secret mission to Scotland to procure arms for a rebellion, was arrested briefly for sedition, and after the unsuccessful rising of 1848 he escaped to Philadelphia, disguised as a priest. In New York he founded his own paper, the *Nation*, in which he clashed with the Irish-born bishop of New York over the Catholic church's opposition to the rebellion and to republicanism in Ireland. Moving to Boston, he founded the *American Celt and Adopted Citizen* (Boston), to which he contributed a series of articles on 'The poets and poetry of the Irish' (July 1850–Mar. 1851). Throughout his career he advanced the Irish cause in North America but gradually changed his views in favour of constitutional methods of change in Ireland, for which he was bitterly attacked by former revolutionary associates, so much so that in 1857 he moved to Canada to settle in Montreal, where he founded another paper, the *New Era*. He became an MP in 1858 and took a leading part in promoting the federation of the Canadian provinces. In 1864 he served as minister of agriculture, emigration and statistics. He denounced a threatened Fenian invasion of Canada and was assassinated outside his house in Ottawa by Patrick James Whelan, a member of the Fenian secret society. TDM wrote poetry (e.g., in the *Harp*, Montreal, Mar.–May 1880), using many pseuds, fiction, and over 20 books on Ireland including two volumes for the 'Library of Ireland': *Gallery of Irish writers* (Dublin, 1846) and *A memoir of the life and conquests of Art MacMurrogh* (Dublin, 1847). In addition he wrote *A history of the Irish settlers in North America* (Boston, 1852); *The Catholic history of North America* (Boston, 1855), which contains sections on Irish-American relations, and *A popular history of Ireland* (New York, 1865, 2 vols.). He also wrote a play *Sebastian; or the Roman martyr*

McGinley

(New York, 1861). He is one of the few Irishmen who was in a position to encourage the development of national literatures in two countries: Ireland and Canada. The Irish-American author Mary Anne Sadlier§ was his close friend and after his death she published his poems. For TDM's portraits and MS sources, see ODNB. TDM's papers can be found in Concordia University, Montreal, in a number of collections in the NLI, and in the National Archives of Canada. SOURCE Allibone, ii, p. 1169 [under MacGee]; Allibone Suppl., ii, p. 1046 [under MacGee]; Boylan, p. 219; Brady, p. 147; Browne, pp 99–100; Crowley, pp 339–74; DCB, ix, pp 489–94; DLB, ic; R. David, *The Young Ireland movement* (Dublin, 1987); Field Day, i, pp 113–14, 999; Hogan, p. 401; Hogan 2, p. 761; R.P. Holzapfel, *James Clarence Mangan*§. *A checklist of printed and other sources* (Dublin, 1969), p. 31; Irish pseudonyms; C. Murphy (ed.), *1825 – D'Arcy McGee – 1925. A collection of speeches and addresses* (Toronto, 1937); OCIL, p. 336; OCCL, p. 484; ODNB; O'Donoghue, p. 278; J. Phelan, *The ardent exile: The life and times of Thomas D'Arcy McGee* (Toronto, 1951); RIA/DIB; RL.

M1116   *Eva MacDonald. A tale of the United Irishmen and their times* (by T.D. McGee; dedicated to Thomas Colley Grattan§).
+ Boston: Charles H. Brainard & Co., 1844. SOURCE McKenna, p. 249; Rafroidi, ii, p. 227; Hodgson, p. 352. LOCATION L, NUC.
COMMENTARY Historical fiction set during the late-eighteenth century. The story starts on the Co. Antrim coast at the house of the McDonalds. There is a terrific storm outside and a boat sinks off the coast. Only the captain of the ship, an Englishman, is rescued. O'Doherty, a neighbour who is in love with Eva McDonald, leaves the area when he believes that the English captain is also enamoured of her. The story abounds with adventures of United Irishmen, and mentions Theobald Wolfe Tone§ and Napper Tandy. Eventually, O'Doherty returns to the glen and marries Eva [ML].

MAC GINLEY, P.T. See MAC GINLEY, Peter Toner.

MAC GINLEY, Peter Toner (also known as P.T. MacGinley), b. Breenagh, Glenswilly (Co. Donegal), d. Dublin, 1942. Poet, dramatist and anthologist, PTM was a customs and excise officer in the civil service who, although not a native Irish speaker, had a deep interest in the language and wrote handbooks on teaching Irish as well as poems and stories in Irish. He contributed poetry to the *Nation* (Dublin), the *Derry Journal*, the Dublin *Weekly News* and other periodicals and was instrumental in setting up the first branch of the Gaelic League in Belfast. Bridget MacGinley, who contributed to the following work, was most likely related to him. SOURCE Donegal, pp 159–61; Irish pseudonyms; O'Donoghue, p. 279; RL.

M1117   *Donegal Christmas Annual, 1883, containing stories & songs by Donegal writers* (ed. by P.T. MacGinley).
+ Londonderry: Printed at the Derry Journal Steam Printing Works, 1883. SOURCE J. Bourke, *Husbandry to housewifery* (Oxford, 1993), p. 108n.1; Donegal, p. 159; OCLC; O'Donoghue, p. 279. LOCATION D.
COMMENTARY Contents (except poetry): 'Taken at the flood' (Rebecca Scott), 'Mary McKay's Christmas' (P.T. MacGinley), 'The fairies of Kilpheak' (Bridget MacGinley), 'The three sisters' (P.T. McGinley; deals with Donegal women earning a living through skilled embroidery, which is taken over by a fairy), 'Johnny Sharky's subscription' (John M'Call), 'Na cardaibh' (P.T. McGinley), 'Paddy Timony's love story (Bridget McGinley), 'The Molly Maguire's men' (P.T. McGinley) [ML].

MC GINLEY, Thomas Colin, pseud. 'Kinnfaela', b. Meenacross, Glencolumbcille (Co. Donegal) 1830, d. Killybegs (Co. Donegal) 1887. Teacher, folklorist and textbook writer, TCM

821

was the son of Catherine Campbell Mcginley. His father died when he was six months old. He was educated at the Murray Stewart school on the estate of White House in Killybegs. Trained as a teacher in the Marlborough Street Training College in Dublin, he taught in Belfast for several years and spent over twenty years as principal teacher at the Croagh National School, Dunkineely (Co. Donegal) before becoming principal of the Commons School, Killybegs. He married Margaret Sinnott, who came from a Co. Wexford family, and they had ten children, several of whom became eminent priests. He travelled a great deal in south-west Donegal, making notes on the history, flora and fauna, the local traditions in songs, stories, and folklore, and published his notes in the *Derry Journal*. These form the basis for the following book. He encountered persistent problems with the department of education about his salary and conduct at school, which may be why he published anonymously. TCM spoke the Irish language fluently, and he published a treatise on biology, *General biology* (London, 1874) with 124 sketches, partly after his own design, as well as textbooks on mathematics. He was known for encouraging students to study beyond primary level and offered evening classes in his Classical School. He probably was related to P.T. MacGinley§ who edited the *Donegal Christmas Annual, 1883, containing stories & songs by Donegal writers* (Londonderry, 1883). Later in life many of his children died, and he suffered from ill-health. SOURCE Donegal, pp 161–2; E. Mac Cuinneagáin's preface to the (Dublin, 2000) reprint of *The cliff scenery* (Londonderry, 1867); RIA/DIB.

M118   *The cliff scenery of south-western Donegal; embracing detailed notices of St. John's Point, Killybegs, Sliabh Liag, and Glen-Head; and interspersed with a rare variety of local legends and historical annotations* (by 'Kinnfaela').
Londonderry: Printed at the Journal Office, 1867. LOCATION Magee College (Derry), L.

\+ Dublin: Four Masters Press, 2000 (preface by E. MacCuinneagáin, and comments by Michael Herity). LOCATION Dt, InND Loeber coll.
COMMENTARY Topographical and antiquarian account of south-west Donegal, interspersed with local legends: 'O'Boyle of Strabrinna', 'The child and the eagle', 'The dying Spaniard', 'A legend of Sliabh Liag', [untitled story featuring Fr Brian O'Cahan], 'Legend of Rathlin O'Byrne' [RL].

MC GLYNN, M.J., pseud. 'Arthur Kirkwood', fl. 1876. American short story writer. SOURCE Brown 2, 735.
M119   *The fortune teller of Killarney; or, the spirit of revenge, and Ever in danger* (by 'Arthur Kirkwood').
Chicago: Ottaway & Colbert, 1876. SOURCE Allibone Suppl., ii, p. 957 (under Kirkwood); Brown 2, 735. LOCATION NUC.
COMMENTARY Two stories in one volume, which were severely reviewed in *McGee's Illustrated Weekly* (New York). The author, it would seem, is ignorant of Irish names, customs etc. The first story is about ancient Ireland and the second about 1798 [Brown 2].

M'GOVERN, Revd J.B., pseud. 'J.B.S.', fl. 1883. Anglican clergyman, romance novelist and archaeologist, JBM was minister of St Stephen's rectory, Chorlton-on-Medlock, Manchester. He was interested in Irish archaeology and contributed papers on this topic to journals including the *Jrnl of the Cork Archaeological and Historical Society* and the *Antiquary* (London). SOURCE Brown, p. 188.
M120   *Imelda; or, retribution. A romance of Kilkee* (by 'J.B.S.').
London: Tinsley Bros, 1883. SOURCE Brown, 1018. LOCATION L.
COMMENTARY The story opens in 1829 and is set around Kilkee (Co. Clare) and in Italy. It describes the unfaithfulness of the Irish Imelda Lestrange to her Florentine lover Gaspar

Biccheiri, whom she met in Kilkee. Monckton, her new lover – and husband – deserts her. Forty years later Gaspar returns to Kilkee to brood on the catastrophe of his life [Brown].

'MC GRATH, Terence', pseud. See BLAKE, Sir Henry Arthur.

MAC GREGOR, Angusine. Co-author. See PRAEGER, Sophia Rosamond.

'MAC GUIRE, Cathal', pseud. See MAC MANUS, Lily.

MACHAR, Agnes Maule, b. Kingston (ON, Canada) 1837, d. Canada 1927. Novelist, poet and religious fiction writer, AMM was likely of Scottish descent and was the daughter of the Revd John Machar, a Presbyterian minister and second principal of Queen's College, Kingston, where AMM lived as a single woman for her whole life. She twice won first prize in a competition sponsored by a Toronto publisher 'for the book best suited to the needs of the Sunday School Library'. Her 'Lost and won: A Canadian romance' was serialized in the *Canadian Monthly* (Toronto) in 1875 but was never issued as a book. Known for her social criticism and her concern for issues such as poverty, temperance, and women's 'inequality in the industrial system', she also wrote (under the pseudonym 'Fidelis') *Kingston and its vicinity; a historical sketch* ([Kingston, ON], 1884), as well as poetry. She wrote eight novels, of which only one is known to deal directly with Ireland. She was the first woman to become a life member of the International Council of Women. SOURCE Allibone Suppl., ii, p. 1047; Blain, p. 691; BLC; CEWW; COPAC; DCB, ix [under John Machar]; Gerson, pp 140, 195; NUC; H.J. Morgan, *The Canadian men and women of the time* (Toronto, 1912); Watters, p. 336.

M121   *The heir of Fairmount Grange* (by Agnes Maule Machar).
+ London: Digby, Long & Co., [1895]. SOURCE Gerson, p. 195; OCLC. LOCATION NUC, D, L.
COMMENTARY Irish content. Closes with an heroic orphan displaced in the new world who is eventually restored to its rightful position in the old world [Gerson, p. 44; FD].

MC HENRY (also M'Henry), James, pseud. 'Solomon Secondsight', b. Larne (Co. Antrim) 1785, d. Larne 1845. Physician, novelist, poet, editor and dramatist, JM was the son of George McHenry, merchant, and Mary Smiley. He seems to have been a member of the Seceding Presbyterian church. He studied at TCD and medicine at Glasgow and practiced in Larne starting in 1811. His first published poem was *Patrick* (location unclear, 1810), which is a narrative of the 1798 rebellion. He married Jane Robinson of Foxhall (RIA/DIB has Cairncastle, Co. Antrim) in 1816. They emigrated to the US that year and settled first in Baltimore (MD), but soon afterwards moved to Harmony in Butler County (PA). In 1823 he opened a medical office in Philadelphia (PA), where he stayed for eighteen years. He was prominent as a physician and political leader and founder and editor of the *American Monthly Magazine* (Philadelphia). He contributed to the *Album* (Philadelphia, 1828); to the *American Quarterly Review* (Philadelphia), for which he served as the leading reviewer of poetry in the 1830s; the *Ladies Weekly Gazette* (Philadelphia?), the *Casket* (Philadelphia?), the *Atlantic Souvenir* (Philadelphia, 1831) and the *Working Man's Gazette* (Woodstock, VT). In 1825 he visited Europe, including Ireland, but returned to the US. He published four works of fiction, while another two works have been ascribed to him. His volumes of poems include *The bard of Erin* (Belfast, 1808); *Patrick, a poetic tale, founded on incidents which took place in Ireland during the unhappy period of 1798* (Glasgow, 1810); *The pleasures of friendship, a poem, in two parts; to which are added a few original Irish melodies* (Pittsburgh, PA, 1822), and *The antediluvians; or, the world destroyed* (London, 1839). An Irish blank-verse tragedy, *The usurper* (Philadelphia,

McHenry

1829), first performed in Philadelphia in 1827, led to his expulsion from the Presbyterian church. In 1837 he received a honorary degree of Doctor in Medicine from the Washington Medical College in Baltimore. Five years later, he returned to Ireland and became US consul in Derry. James Sheridan Knowles§ and the Irish-American publisher Matthew Carey were among his friends. His portrait was published by Clarke-Robinson. He was buried in the churchyard of Inver (Co. Antrim). A collection of his papers is in the Henry E. Huntington Library, San Marino (CA), MSS MH1–116. SOURCE ADB; Allibone, ii, pp 1170–1 [under MacHenry]; Allibone Suppl., ii, p. 1048 [under MacHenry]; ANB; R.E. Blanc, *James McHenry (1745–1845)* (Philadelphia, 1937); Brady, p. 148; Brown, p. 188; Burke, p. 482; W. Clarke-Robinson, 'James MacHenry' in *Ulster Jrnl of Archaeology*, 14 (1908), pp 127–32 (which contains some conflicting information); DAB; Exiles, p. 78; Hart, p. 459; Hogan 2, pp 770–1; McKenna, p. 250–1; OCIL, p. 339; ODNB; O'Donoghue, p. 281.

M122 *The wilderness; or, Braddock's times. A tale of the west* (by 'Solomon Secondsight'). New York: E. Bliss & E. White, 1823, 2 vols. SOURCE Rafroidi, ii, p. 230; Fanning, p. 386; Wright, i, 1757. LOCATION NUC.

Pittsburgh (PA): M.P. Morse; Allegheny: J.B. Kennedy, 1848, 2 vols. in 1. LOCATION NUC.

London: A.K. Newman, 1823, 3 vols. (as *The wilderness; or, the youthful days of Washington*). SOURCE Blessing, p. 150; British Fiction; Garside, 1823:61. LOCATION Corvey, CME 3-628-47501-5, L, NUC.

Vienna: C.F. Schade, 1829 (trans. by L.M. von Wedell as *Die Wildniss; oder, Washingtons Jünglingsjahre; eine west-amerikanische Geschichte*). SOURCE R.E. Blanc, *James McHenry*, pp 23, 122. LOCATION CSmH.

COMMENTARY Historical novel set during Gen. Edward Braddock's campaign in Pennsylvania in the French and Indian War (1753–64). The story revolves around the family of Gilbert Frazier, an immigrant from northern Ireland. Frazier is brought by the Indians to the western part of Pennsylvania, near what is now the town of Kittanning. Frontier life is interwoven with a love story [Blanc, *James McHenry*, pp 46–50; Hart, p. 459].

M123 *The spectre of the forest; or, annals of the Housatonic. A New England romance* (by 'Solomon Secondsight').

New York: E. Bliss & E. White, 1823, 2 vols. SOURCE Wright, i, 1756; Slocum, ii, 2965. LOCATION NUC.

London: A.K. Newman, 1824, 3 vols. SOURCE British Fiction; Garside, 1824:64. LOCATION Corvey CME 3-628-48631-9, L.

COMMENTARY Historical fiction set during the eighteenth century, presented as a manuscript written by someone else. Goffe, one of the regicides of Charles I, having been outlawed on the restoration of Charles II, finds shelter in New England. The action takes place in the region of the Housatonic River in Connecticut and in England. Goffe becomes the spectral mentor of the hero of the tale, George Parnell, who is the son of a woman who escaped the persecutions of her husband's murderer in England by emigrating to the US. The story includes the trial of a reputed witch, the mother of Amos Settle, who is saved from execution in the nick of time. Some of the characters are based on historical figures such as Joe Aiger, sometimes identified as Captain Jack, the wild hunter of the Juniata (a river in PA), and Samuel Brady, the famous 'Captain of the Spies' of the Revolutionary epoch [Blanc, *James McHenry*, pp 50–3; *The Pennsylvania Magazine*, 24 (1900), p. 40; Slocum; British Fiction].

M124 *O'Halloran; or, the insurgent chief. An Irish historical tale of 1798* (by 'Solomon Secondsight').

Philadelphia: H.C. Carey & I. Lea, 1824, 2 vols. SOURCE Fanning, p. 386; Wright, i, 1755; Garside, 1824:63. LOCATION NUC.

Philadelphia: H.C. Carey & I. Lea, repr. by A.K. Newman & Co., 1824, 3 vols. (as *The insurgent chief; or, O'Halloran, an Irish historical tale of 1798*). SOURCE Brown, 1019; Belanger, 79; Garside, 1824:63; British Fiction. LOCATION Grail, Corvey CME 3–628–48630–0, Ireland related fiction, Dt (1842 edn). COMMENTARY *Philadelphia & London edn* The author in the preface to *The hearts of steel* (Philadelphia, 1825) complained about this unauthorized edn by the Minerva Press in London [Bennett cat. 41/116].

+ London: Joseph Smith, [1838] (as *O'Halloran; or, the insurgent chief*). LOCATION NUC (1841 edn), InND Loeber coll.

Chiswick: C.S. Arnold, Simpkin & Marshall, 1824. SOURCE OCLC; British Fiction. LOCATION CtY.

+ Dublin: Tegg & Co.; London: Thomas Tegg & Son, 1838. LOCATION D, BF1.

+ Dublin: M.H. Gill, n.d. (as *The insurgent chief; or, the pikemen of '98. A romance of the Irish rebellion*, anon.). LOCATION DPL, InND Loeber coll.

Belfast: J. Henderson, 1847 (as *O'Halloran*; includes notes by the author). SOURCE Rafroidi, ii, p. 231; McKenna, p. 250; British Fiction; Garside, 1824:63; R.E. Blanc, *James McHenry*, p. 123 (notes a 1844 edn, but this has not been located). LOCATION L.

Glasgow: R. Griffin & Co., 1848 (new and revsd edn; as *The insurgent chief; a tale of the United Irishmen*). LOCATION Providence College.

+ Glasgow: Cameron, Ferguson & Co., n.d. (as *The insurgent chief; or, the pikemen of 1798. A romance of the Irish rebellion*). LOCATION D.

New York: P.M. Haverty, [1871 or earlier] (as *The insurgent chief*). SOURCE Adv. in Haverty's *Irish-American Illustrated Almanac* (New York, 1871), p. 104; OCLC (New York, Munro, 1887 edn).

COMMENTARY No copy of the New York, Haverty edn located. The first novel about northern Ireland to be published in America, it proved to be very popular and was much reprinted. It is wrongly ascribed to Thomas Berkeley Greaves in Brown 2, 563, but correctly identified in the NLI copy, and in the London edn published by Joseph Smith [1838]. The *National Gazette* of 2 May 1825 reports that a Paris edn appeared, but no copy has been located. The manuscript for this novel was sold by the dealer D.N. Mott (Sheffield, MA) about 1992 (current location unknown). The first chapters appeared in the *American Monthly Magazine* (New York), which JM edited. The book, based on the author's direct observations, describes the adventures of a young loyalist, Edward Barrymore, in Co. Antrim in 1798. Barrymore is rescued from the sea and recuperates in the insurgent O'Halloran's castle. He falls in love with O'Halloran's granddaughter, but finds himself in opposite political camps from O'Halloran, who is a member of the United Irishmen. Through the events of the rebellion, they learn to appreciate each other and eventually the granddaughter and Barrymore marry. This work gives an account of scenes in Belfast and Larne prior to the battle of Antrim. The author knew many of the leading rebels and the heroic death of Willy Nelson is described. The famous rebel ballad of Blaris-Moore is also rendered. James Allen adapted the novel into a play, which was published in Dublin in 1867. Earlier a dramatized version was planned to be performed in Belfast, but because some of the characters mentioned in the novel were still living, the magistrate requested it to be withdrawn [ML; Brown 2, 563; RL; B. Browne; Bradshaw, 4986; Blanc, *James McHenry*, pp 15–16, 31; Personal communication, D.N. Mott, 1994; RIA/DIB].

M125 *The Hearts of Steel, an Irish historical tale of the last century* [anon.].

+ London: Wightman & Cramp, 1825, 3 vols. SOURCE Brown, 1020; British Fiction; Garside, 1825:58. LOCATION Grail, Corvey CME 3–628–47718–2, Ireland related fiction, D, L.

Dublin: Thomas Tegg, 1838. SOURCE Linen Hall cat. p. 109. LOCATION BFl.

Belfast: John Henderson, 1845 (as *The Hearts of Steel. An Irish historical tale of the eighteenth century*). LOCATION BFl.

+ Glasgow: Cameron, Ferguson & Co., [1877 or earlier] (on cover: *The Hearts of Steel or the Celt and the Saxon*). LOCATION UCD Folklore Dept., L.

Paris: C. Gosselin, 1830, 4 vols. (trans. as *Les coeurs d'acier, roman l'histoire d'Irlande au dernier siècle*). SOURCE CCF. LOCATION BNF.

+ Philadelphia; A.R. Poole, 1825, 2 vols. SOURCE Fanning, p. 386; Wright, i, 1752. LOCATION NUC.

New York: P.M. Haverty, [1871 or earlier]. SOURCE Adv. in Haverty's *Irish-American Illustrated Almanac* (New York, 1871), p. 104.

COMMENTARY No copy of the New York edn located. Set in the eighteenth century in northern Ireland, it describes the adventures of various Ulster Protestant secret societies that indulge in agrarian outrages, of which the Hearts of Steel was one. It is also concerned with the evils of absentee landlordism. The Catholic McManus family loses its estate as a result of the Williamite War and one of the sons swears revenge on the family that now owns the land. After many fights, imprisonments and an abduction, the daughter of McManus falls in love with the new owner's son, which solves all animosity [R.E. Blanc, *James McHenry*, pp 64–6; Brown; RL].

M126 *The betrothed of Wyoming. A historical tale* [anon.].

+ Philadelphia: Sold by the principal booksellers, 1830. SOURCE Hogan 2, p. 770; Wright, i, 1749. LOCATION InND Loeber coll., NUC (Philadelphia, Porter 1830, 2nd edn).

COMMENTARY Ascribed to JM, but this is not certain. It tells of the strife between the colonists and the Tories. No Irish content [ADB; ML; R.E. Blanc, *James McHenry*, p. 80].

M127 *Meredith; or, the mystery of the Meschianza. A tale of the American Revolution* [anon.].

Philadelphia: Sold by the principal booksellers, 1831. SOURCE Hogan 2, p. 770; Wright, i, 1753. LOCATION NUC.

COMMENTARY Ascribed to JM, but this is not certain. Features Quakers as leading characters. No Irish content [ADB; R.E. Blanc, *James McHenry*, p. 80, 84].

M128 *McHenry's Irish tales: O'Halloran, or the insurgent chief; and The hearts of steel, or the Celt and the Saxon.*

+ Glasgow: Cameron, Ferguson & Co., [1877 or later]. SOURCE Blessing, p. 150 (mentions 1901 edn, but this has not been located); RLIN. LOCATION NN, InND Loeber coll.

COMMENTARY Reprint of JH's Irish prose works. Contents: 'O'Halloran or, the insurgent chief' and 'The hearts of steel: an Irish historical tale of last century', published in 1824 and 1825, respectively [RL].

MACHRAY, Robert, b. Fyvie, Aberdeenshire (Scotland) 1857, d. 1946. Novelist, professor and editor, RM was educated at Cambridge and became professor of ecclesiastical history at St John's University College, Manitoba (Canada). He was editor of the *Daily Mail* (London) and aside from the following title, published eleven other novels. Not to be confused with Robert Machray (1831–1904), Anglican archbishop of Rupert's Land in Canada. SOURCE Brown, p. 199; EF, p. 256; MDCB, p. 515.

M129 *Grace O'Malley, princess and pirate, told by Ruari MacDonald, redshank and rebel; the same set forth in the tongue of the English* (by Robert Machray).

New York: F.A. Stokes, [1898]. LOCATION NUC.

London, Paris, New York, Melbourne: Cassell & Co., 1898 (as *Grace O'Malley, princess and pirate*). SOURCE Brown, 1081. LOCATION L.

COMMENTARY Historical fiction set in the sixteenth century on the west coast of Ireland and deals with the life of Grace O'Malley, pirate-queen of Connacht, and her lover Richard Burke, chief of the Burkes of Mayo. Sir Nicholas Malby, president of Connacht, the earl of Desmond, and Stephen Lynch of Galway are introduced [Brown].

M'ILROY, Archibald (also McIlroy), b. Ballyclare (Co. Antrim) 1860, d. at sea on the Lusitania, 1915. Novelist and short story writer, AM worked in insurance and banking and took part in public life in Cos. Antrim and Down. In 1902 he lived at Drumcairn, Deramore Park, Belfast. He visited the Holy Land, Greece, Italy, and Egypt and privately published *Letters from the Holy Land*, n.l., [*c*.1904]. For the last three years of his life he lived in Canada. His stories are mostly set in Co. Antrim and Ulster. His portrait was published in *The humour of druid's island* (Dublin, 1902). SOURCE Brady, p. 148; Brown, p. 189; Davidson cat. 32/856; IBL, 6 (1915), p. 192; OCIL, p. 339; Hogan 2, p. 772; RIA/DIB; RL; Sutherland, p. 396.

M130 *When lint was in the bell* (by Archibald M'Ilroy; dedicated to author's wife).
+ Belfast: M'Caw, Stevenson & Orr, 1897. SOURCE Brown, 1022 (London, Unwin, 1898 edn, not located); OCLC. LOCATION D, L, NUC, InND Loeber coll.
COMMENTARY Stories of Scots-Irish life in Co. Antrim. Contents: 'The village itself', 'Fractions,' 'The quaint pastor of a quaint congregation', 'The precentor', 'A converted Calvinist', 'A Mormon invasion', 'The auld fair day', 'The selling of Danny M'Cartney's farm', 'Davy Bewhunnan's difficulties', 'The turning of a long lane', 'The sound of a voice that is still', 'The passing years' [NUC; Leclaire, p. 218].

M131 *The auld meetin'-hoose green* (by Archibald M'Ilroy; dedicated to author's parents).
Belfast: McCaw, Stevenson & Orr, 1898. SOURCE Brown, 1021. LOCATION D, Dt, L, NUC.
Toronto: F.H. Revell, 1899. LOCATION NUC.
COMMENTARY Stories, arranged in chapters, on the Co. Antrim peasantry around the middle of the nineteenth century. Contents: 'By the river banks', 'The tragedy at the Stick Brig', 'The innovation of the tuning-fork', 'The divinity student', 'Liza Lowry's retirement', 'In death they were not divided', 'The old precentor "crosses the bar"', 'Aboot the brig', 'A railway king', 'Isaac Cupples's second wife', 'The widow's son', 'The sextoness', 'Theology at the lint dam', 'A village celebrity', 'Scobes's love story', 'Twixt the cup and the lip', 'Odds and ends', 'A minister and a *man*', 'The black oaks', 'Two little green graves', 'At Jesus' feet' [ML].

M132 *By lone Craig-Linnie burn* (by Archibald M'Ilroy; dedicated author's son).
+ London: T. Fisher Unwin, 1900. SOURCE Brown, 1023. LOCATION D, L, NUC, InND Loeber coll.
COMMENTARY Stories giving pictures of various grades of Scots-Irish life in a country town in northern Ireland. Craig-Linnie is Ballyclare (Co. Antrim). Contents arranged according to chapters: '"Captain" Branningan, J.P.', 'Bell and Ailie and Rose', 'How Johnny Glenn opposed the railway', 'The Mill Lane tragedy', 'A collapse of mesmerism', 'Sacrament Sabbath', 'The burying-ground', 'Doctor Coulson', 'The ordination', 'The minister's entrangl'ment', 'Doctor Coulson's Christmas party', 'Light at eventide', 'A happy Christmas' [RL; Brown].

M133 *A banker's love story* (by Archibald M'Ilroy).
+ London: T. Fisher Unwin, 1901. SOURCE Brown, 1024. LOCATION D, L.
COMMENTARY Set in Belfast, Craig-Linnie and Ballinasloe and concerns a love story interwoven with the workings of a bank [Brown; Leclaire, p. 218].

M134 *The humour of druids' island* (Archibald M'Ilroy).
+ Dublin: Hodges Figgis; Belfast: W. Mullan, 1902 (ill.). SOURCE Brown, 1025. LOCATION D, L, NUC, InND Loeber coll.
COMMENTARY Druid's island is Islandmagee (Co. Antrim). The book contains a number of anecdotes told by Presbyterian country people in a Scots-Irish dialect [Brown; NUC].

M135 *Burnside* (by Archibald M'Ilroy).
Belfast: McCaw, Stevenson & Orr, 1908. SOURCE Brown, 1026; OCLC. LOCATION
Queen's Univ., Belfast.
COMMENTARY Stories told by an old clergyman of country life in Ulster in the 1850s
[Brown].

M136 *By the ingle nook* [anon.].
+ Belfast: M'Caw, Stevenson & Orr, 1910. SOURCE Fenning cat. 175/172. LOCATION
InND Loeber coll.

MAC INLAY-JAMIESON, Annie. Fiction writer, AM-J was a resident of Jamaica and pos-
sibly was of Irish background. SOURCE RL.
M137 *The three Kerry pearls* [anon.].
Kingston, Jamaica: [publisher?], n.d. SOURCE Halkett & Laing, vi, p. 446.
COMMENTARY No copy located [RL].

MAC INNES, Revd D., fl. 1890. Clergyman, short story anthologist and translator.
M138 *Folk and hero tales* (ed., collected, and trans. by Revd D. MacInnes).
+ London: David Nutt, 1890 (with notes by the editor and by Alfred Nutt; ill. E.
Griset; Waifs and Strays of Celtic Tradition; Argyllshire Series, No. 11). SOURCE
Brown, 1027. LOCATION L.
COMMENTARY Contents: 'The son of the of the king of Erin', 'Feunn MacCüail and the bent
grey lad', 'The herding of Cruachan', 'The kingdom of the green mountains', 'The ship that
went to America', 'Koisa Kayn, or Kian's leg', 'Lod, the farmer's son', 'The two young gentlemen', 'The tale of young Manus, son of the king of Lochlann', 'Leoän Creeäch, son of the
king of Eirin, and Laytav, son of the king of the Cola', 'A battle fought by the Lochlanners
in Dun-nac-Sneeächain'. The volume includes a chapter on the development of Fenian or
Ossianic sagas [RL].

MACK, Thomas C., pseud. 'T.C.M.', fl. 1841. American historical novelist. SOURCE Wright,
i, 1777.
M139 *The priest's turf-cutting day. A historical romance* (by 'T.C.M.').
New York: Printed for the author, 1841. SOURCE Fanning, p. 386; Wright, i, 1777.
LOCATION NUC.

MAC KAY, William, b. Belfast 1846. Novelist, poet, and journalist, WM was the son of
Revd J.W. McKay [*sic*], who was president of the Methodist College, Belfast. His brothers
Wallis and Joseph William both wrote plays and poetry. WM became a well-known London
journalist, and published poetry and short stories. Some of his letters are among the Downey
Papers (NLI, MS 10,035). SOURCE Boase, vi, p. 122 [under Joseph William MacKay]; Brady,
p. 148; Brown, p. 190; Hogan 2, p. 774; O'Donoghue, p. 283; E. Reilly, p. 247; RIA/DIB.
M140 *The popular idol. A novel* (by William MacKay; dedicated to author's sister Nell
[MacKay]).
+ London: Richard Bentley & Son, 1876, 2 vols. SOURCE Allibone Suppl., ii, p. 1049
[as *A popular idol*]; Brown, 1030. LOCATION D, L, NUC.
COMMENTARY Frank Edgehill, a young English artist, travels to Ballymareen (Co. Cork) to
visit his uncle Archibald McTavish, 'a Scotch settler', and witnesses strife between McTavish
and the proprietor of the local newspaper, 'the popular idol', firsthand. His uncle is shot, the
'idol' is suspected, eventually arrested and defended by Jacob Butler, who is modelled on Isaac
Butt§. A love story is interwoven [Brown].

M141 *Pro patria: The autobiography of a conspirator. Carefully transcribed and edited from authentic documents* (by William MacKay; dedicated to 'my compatriots … and to hereditary bondsmen in general').

+ London: Remington & Co., 1883, 2 vols. SOURCE Allibone Suppl., ii, p. 1049; Brown, 1031. LOCATION D, L, NUC, InND Loeber coll.

COMMENTARY Set in Dublin and Wicklow. Ptolemy Daly of Castle Beg is a weak, conceited youth who, full of visions of the revolutionary Robert Emmet, joins the staff of the *Sunburst*, the organ of an insurrectionary movement. This movement is led by Phil. Gallagher, who is evidently modelled on the Young Irelander, Thomas Clarke Luby (1821–1901). At the critical moment, Daly plays the traitor and leaves for England. Isaac Butt§ and John Ray, members of the Young Ireland movement, are introduced under thinly disguised names. Some of the text is addressed to the English reader [Brown; RL].

M142 *Besides still waters. A novel* (by William McKay).
London: Remington & Co., 1885, 3 vols. SOURCE Allibone Suppl., ii, p. 1049; Brady, p. 148. LOCATION L.
COMMENTARY Some copies of this edn bear the title 'Sins of the fathers' at top of page [BLC].

M143 *Unvarnished tales* (by William McKay).
London: W. Swan Sonnenschein & Co., 1886. SOURCE Brown, p. 190; COPAC. LOCATION L.

M144 *A mender of nets* (by William McKay).
London: Chatto & Windus, 1906. SOURCE Brown, p. 190; COPAC. LOCATION L.

MAC KENNA, Stephen J. See MACKENNA, Stephen Joseph.

MAC KENNA, Stephen Joseph (also known as Stephen J. MacKenna), b. Dublin, 1837, d. Chelsea (London) 1883. Journalist and writer of fiction for boys, SJM was educated at Downside, served as an ensign in the 28th Foot, and was probably stationed in Ireland. He became a sub-editor of the *Evening News* (London), which position he held until his death in 1883. He co-authored a book of military stories with John Augustus O'Shea§. He should not be confused with the translator Stephen MacKenna (1872–1934). SOURCE Allibone Suppl., ii, p. 1050; Boase, ii, p. 622; Brown 2, p. 162; NCBEL 4, p. 1827; RL.

M145 *Roddy the Rapp; or, the whiskey still of Glanvoe* (by Stephen J. MacKenna).
London: Henderson, n.d. SOURCE Brown 2, 908.
COMMENTARY No copy located. A tale of the period of insurrection between 1795 and 1798, set in Tuam (Co. Galway). A popular 3*d.* story book with spies and informers, mystery, fiction and fact. In the end Roddy and his bride escape to France and he obtains a commission in the French army [Brown 2; RL].

M146 *Off parade* (by Stephen J. MacKenna).
+ London: Hurst & Blackett, 1872, 3 vols. SOURCE Wolff, 4342. LOCATION L, InND Loeber coll.
COMMENTARY The story of two brothers, set partially in England and partially in Connacht. Randal, the younger brother, has been left in Ireland to take care of the estate but has been so miserable and lonely that he leaves Ireland and joins the army. His father is not very fond of him and thinks him a thoughtless spendthrift. Randal's brother, William, is very jealous of him and ruins the family fortune just to thwart Randal. Both brothers are in love with the same woman. In the end, William goes mad and Randal is vindicated [ML].

M147 *King's beeches. Stories of old chums* (by Stephen J. MacKenna).
London: Virtue & Sons, 1873. SOURCE COPAC. LOCATION L.

M148 *Plucky fellows, being reminiscences from the note-book of Captain Fred. A book for boys* (by Stephen J. MacKenna).
London: Henry S. King & Co., 1873. SOURCE COPAC; OCLC. LOCATION L, CtY.
COMMENTARY Fiction for juveniles [RL].

M149 *At school with an old dragoon* (by Stephen J. MacKenna).
London: Henry S. King & Co., 1874. SOURCE COPAC. LOCATION L, C.

M150 *A child of fortune* (by Stephen J. MacKenna).
+ London: Hurst & Blackett, 1875, 3 vols. LOCATION L.
COMMENTARY Set in Dumour in the south of Ireland [CM].

M151 *Handfast to strangers* (by Stephen J. MacKenna).
London: Chapman & Hall, 1876, 3 vols. SOURCE COPAC. LOCATION L.

M152 *Brave men in action; some thrilling stories of the British flag* (by Stephen J. MacKenna and John Augustus O'Shea§).
London: S. Low, Marston, Searle & Rivington, 1878. SOURCE COPAC. LOCATION NUC.
+ London: Chatto & Windus, 1899 (as *Brave men in action. Thrilling stories of the British flag*; by Stephen J. MacKenna and John Augustus O'Shea§). LOCATION L.
COMMENTARY *1899 edn* Fiction for juveniles. Contents: 'How "Charley" took Sidon', 'Sarsfield, and King William's convoy', 'A gunpowder plot of the 19th century', '"Gold, or the sword?"', 'Sixty minutes' fire and frost', 'Killing no murder', 'Vincible "invincibles"', 'Saving an emperor', 'The three John Benbows', 'Mars on crutches', 'Storm in calm', 'British schoolboys and French invincibles', 'Deed of dering-do', 'A plunge in the dark', 'Merchantmen v. men-o'-war', 'A midnight contest' [ML].

MC KENNEY, Anna Hanson. See DORSEY, Anna Hanson.

MAC KENZIE, Mrs —. See MACKENZIE, Mrs Anna Maria.

MAC KENZIE, Mrs Anna Maria (née Wright; also known as Mrs MacKenzie), d. after 1816. English novelist, AMM was left a widow with four young children and began to write from need as well as from a love of writing. Her *The gamesters. A novel* (London, 1786) was reprinted in Dublin in the same year, and her *Dusseldorf; or, the fratricide* (London, 1798), was reprinted in Dublin in the same year and in Cork before 1799. She claimed to have written 16 novels, some published anonymously and some under the name of Mrs Johnson. SOURCE Allibone ii, p. 1175; Blain, pp 694–5; BD, p. 214; Pickering & Chatto cat. 737/289; RL.

M153 *The Irish guardian; or, errors of eccentricity* (by Mrs MacKenzie).
London: Longman, Hurst, Reese & Orme, 1809, 3 vols. SOURCE BD, p. 214; Block, p. 148; Wolff, 4343 (1811 edn); British Fiction; Garside, 1809:45. LOCATION L, NUC.
London: A.K. Newman & Co., 1811 (as *Almeria D'Aveiro; or, the Irish guardian*).
SOURCE British Fiction; Garside, 1809:45; OCLC, Wolff, 4343. LOCATION Corvey CME 3-628-48094-9, Ireland related fiction, TxU.
COMMENTARY Gothic fiction largely set in Portugal and England. The preface reads: 'The Author perceives she cannot conclude without paying a feeble tribute of praise to those male writers, who have thought it no degradation of their dignity ... to ... improve and amuse in the form of a novel.' There is only one major Irish character, Capt. Derrick, Almeria's protector, whose 'eccentricity' and blundering lead to most of the adventures which Almeria and her lover undergo. Capt. Derrick speaks the last words of the novel, which are inexplicable in that the novel nowhere discusses the relationship between Ireland and England: 'the time is not far distant, when Albion and Hibernia shall know no difference of opinion, but strongly—

firmly—and invariably united in the great—the just—the glorious cause—of KING AND COUN-
TRY!' [JB; Frank, 259].

MAC KENZIE, John, fl. 1881. Fiction writer, probably Scottish. SOURCE RL.
M154 *The Blakes of Listellick, or, scenes from Irish life* (by John MacKenzie).
Castle-Douglas [Dumfries and Galloway, Scotland]: Printed at the Advertiser Steam
Press Works, 1881. SOURCE COPAC. LOCATION E.
COMMENTARY 45pp. Listellick is a townland near Tralee (Co. Kerry) [COPAC; AMB]

MC KENZIE, Robert Shelton, (also known as **R. Shelton Mackenzie**) b. Drew's Court
(Co. Limerick) 1809, d. Philadelphia (PA) 1880. Journalist, novelist, editor and miscellaneous
writer, RSM was the son of Capt. Kenneth McKenzie, who published a volume of Gaelic
poetry in Glasgow in 1796. He studied in Fermoy and in Cork, where he was apprenticed to
an apothecary, but does not seem to have practiced medicine. According to Allibone, he graduated in Dublin and was made DCL of Oxford in 1844. In 1834, he received an honorary
LLD from Glasgow University. Moving to London in 1830, RSM contributed to London
periodicals such as the *Ladies Magazine* and the *London Magazine* and the *Monthly Belle
Assemblée* (1848), and as a journalist wrote a weekly newsletter for the *New York Evening Star*,
making him the first regular salaried European correspondent of the American press. After
bankruptcy and the loss of his job as editor of the *Liverpool Journal* in 1852 he moved to New
York, and in 1857 to Philadelphia where he was foreign and literary editor of the *Press*. With
an eye to the growing market in the US for Irish writers, he wrote or edited many Irish-related
works, including *Miscellaneous writings of the late Dr. Maginn* (Baltimore, 1855–57, 5 vols.),
the New York edn of Lady Morgan's§ *The O'Briens and the O'Flahertys* (1856, 2 vols.), and
compiled an edn of *Noctes Ambrosianæ* (New York, 1863–65, 5 vols.) from *Blackwood's
Magazine* (Edinburgh, Mar. 1822–Feb. 1835), which included many sketches by William
Maginn§. His published poetry includes his first book, *The lays of Palestine* (London 1828),
and he contributed poetry to the *Friendship's Offering* (London, n.d.). He wrote biographies
of Charles Dickens (London, 1870) and Sir Walter Scott (Boston, 1871) and contributed to
the *Harp* (Montreal, Oct., 1880). At his death he had three manuscripts unfinished: 'The poets
and poetry of Ireland', 'Men of '98', and 'Actors and actresses'. RSM used the pseudonym
'Sholto' for some of his periodical work. For RSM's MSS, see ODNB. SOURCE Allibone, ii,
p. 1178 [under Mackenzie]; Boase, ii, p. 632; Brown, p. 191 [under Mackenzie]; *Catholic Mirror*
(3 Jan. 1857, p. 6); Irish pseudonyms; ODNB [under Mackenzie]; O'Donoghue, p. 284 [under
Mackenzie]; Pickering & Chatto List 208/113; RL; Rose cat. 24/135.
M155 *Titian. A romance of Venice* (by R. Shelton MacKenzie).
+ London: Richard Bentley, 1843, 3 vols. LOCATION L, NUC.
COMMENTARY Historical novel set in Italy during the fifteenth and sixteenth centuries
[RL].
M156 *Mornings at Matlock* (by R. Shelton MacKenzie).
London: H. Colburn, 1850, 3 vols. LOCATION L, NUC.
M157 *Bits of Blarney* (by R. Shelton MacKenzie; dedication to J.S. Redfield, Esq., dated
Aug. 20 1855).
+ New York: Redfield, 1854. SOURCE Brown, 1034; Fanning, p. 386; Wright, ii, 1636
(1855 edn); OCLC. LOCATION NUC, InND Loeber coll., Wright web.
COMMENTARY Contents: Legends: 'Blarney Castle', 'Con O'Keefe and the golden cup',
'Legends of Finn Mac Coul'. Irish stories: 'The petrified piper', 'The Geraldine', 'Captain
Rock' (first published in the *Monthly Belle Assemblée*, London, 1848), 'A night with the
Whiteboys' (first published in the *Dublin Monthly Magazine*, 1830), 'Buck English'. Eccentric

831

characters: 'The bard O'Kelly', 'Father Prout', 'Father Prout's sermon', 'Irish dancing masters', 'Charley Crofts'. Irish publicists: 'Henry Grattan', 'Daniel O'Connell' [RL; Clyde, p. 90].

M158 *Tressilian and his friends* (by Dr R. Shelton MacKenzie).
+ Philadelphia: J.B. Lippincott & Co., 1859. SOURCE Wright, ii, 1637; OCLC. LOCATION NUC, Wright web.
COMMENTARY Some of the stories are set in Europe and are based on historical figures. Contents: 'The gathering', 'Ensign Simmons', 'The bush guinea', 'Le millionaire malgré lui', 'Tressilian's story', 'Velasquez and his mestizo', 'A night with Burns', 'Love and phrenology', 'The composer of poetry', 'The divan', 'The heiress', 'Josephine's repeater', 'The second sight', 'The German student's story', 'Bleeding-heart yard', 'Beatrice d'Este', 'A legend of Charlemagne', 'Love and moonlight', 'An excursion', 'Legend of the maiden tower', 'The last throw of the dice', 'The great Will Cause', 'L'Envoi' [RL].

MC KIM, Joseph, b. Coolloney (Co. Sligo), fl. 1881. Novelist and poet, JM was the author also of *William the Silent* (Manchester, 1881), an historical sketch in verse. SOURCE O'Donoghue, p. 285.
M159 *Darcy and friends. An Irish tale* (by Joseph McKim).
+ London: F.V. White, 1881. SOURCE Allibone Suppl., ii, p. 1052 [under MacKim]; Brown, 1036. LOCATION L, InND Loeber coll.
COMMENTARY The downfall of John Darcy, a young landowner in the west of Ireland. He is inducted into a secret society, after which he is obliged to take refuge in the West Indies. He leaves his young wife behind, who dies in his absence. Darcy returns to Ireland to seek his daughter, but he falls ill and dies, cursing the secret society [Brown].
M160 *Fairy tales for children; Tommy Greedygrag and Wiggletum* (by Joseph McKim).
London: [publisher?], 1882. SOURCE Allibone Suppl., ii, p. 1052 (under MacKim).
COMMENTARY No copy located [RL].

MC KITTRICK, Anna Margaret. See ROSS, Anna Margaret.

MAC LAUGHLIN, Patrick O'Conor, b. Derry (Co. Derry) 1851. Poet and satirical writer, PO'CM was educated in Derry and lived for some time in London and Paris. Between 1870 and 1893 he was a frequent contributor of poetry to various Dublin periodicals, including the *Nation*, the *Shamrock*, and *Young Ireland*, among others. SOURCE O'Donoghue, p. 287.
M161 *The threatening letter-writer, and Irish loyalist's companion* (by Patrick O'Conor MacLaughlin).
+ Dublin: M.H. Gill & Son, 1889. LOCATION L.
COMMENTARY Fictional account laced with satirical humour concerning forged letters, aimed at how to calculate a fair rent, pack a jury, etc. [CM].

MAC LENNAN, William, fl. 1898. Historical fiction writer and possible song writer or translator, WM also wrote (with Jean N. MacIlwraith) another historical novel *The span o' life: A tale of Louisbourg and Quebec* (New York, 1899). He probably can be identified with the author (Allibone mentions translator) of *Songs of old Canada* (Montreal, 1886). SOURCE Allibone Suppl., ii, p. 1055; BLC.
M162 *Spanish John; being a memoir, now first published in complete form, of the early life and adventures of Colonel John McDonell, known as "Spanish John," when a Lieutenant in the Company of St. James of the Regiment Irlandia in the service of the King of Spain operating in Italy* (by William MacLennan).

London, New York: Harper & Bros, 1898 (ill. F. de Myrbach). SOURCE Brown, 1037. LOCATION L, NUC.

COMMENTARY Historical fiction describing the adventures of Col. John McDonell from the Scottish Highlands when a lieutenant in an Irish regiment in the service of the king of Spain operating in Italy (1744–46). At the Scots College in Rome, where he had been sent to become a priest, he had met a young student, a Mr O'Rourke. O'Rourke, now a chaplain in the Irish Brigade, saves McDonell's life on the battlefield. Subsequently the two are sent by the duke of York to Scotland on a mission to Prince Charlie [Brown].

MAC LEOD, Miss E.H. (later known as 'E.H.P.', which may refer to her married name), fl. 1821, d. *c.*1826. English author of moralistic, socially well-observed tales, EHM based some of her characters on actual society figures. She was a resident of East Anglia. The preface to her *Geraldine Murray* (London, 1826) is dated from Fingringhoe Hall, Essex, to which she had moved after her marriage. That volume also mentioned that she had died. The dedication of *Principle!* (London, 1824, 4 vols.) is dated from Norwich in that year. Her single work with known Irish content is listed below. SOURCE Blain, p. 696; RL.

M163 *Geraldine Hamilton; or, self-guidance* [anon.].
    + London: Richard Bentley, 1832, 2 vols. SOURCE Brown, 1038; OCLC. LOCATION L.
COMMENTARY Published posthumously. Geraldine, living at Newtown Hamilton (Co. Donegal), falls in love with Major Stuart, an officer sent with a detachment to quell disturbances. Even though he is married, she accompanies him to the Iberian Peninsula. After various adventures there and in England, she finally marries him [Brown; ML].

MAC MAHON, Ella, b. Dublin 1867?, d. England? 1956. Romance novelist and writer on religion and local history, EM was the daughter of the chaplain to the lord lieutenant of Ireland. She converted to catholicism and her first publications were translations of the writings of saints. She produced 14 works of fiction, several of which deal with adultery and marital intrigue. She moved to England, worked as a civil servant in the intelligence services, and contributed to the BBC. She was given a civil list pension for services to literature. SOURCE Allibone Suppl., ii, p. 1057; EF, p. 259; Krishnamurti, p. 84; Sutherland, p. 399.

M164 *Heathcote. A novel* (by Ella MacMahon; dedicated to M.F.S.).
    + London: Ward & Downey, 1889, 2 vols. SOURCE Wolff, 4352. LOCATION L, InND Loeber coll.
COMMENTARY A romance set in England. Heathcote works for a living as a journalist on a provincial paper. His sole joy in life is observing Violet, the daughter of the archdeacon. Someone who is in love with her tells Heathcote that Violet is going to marry his best friend, Frank. Heathcote goes off to Russia on newspaper work, thinking that Violet is lost to him forever. On his return it appears that Frank has married someone else. Heathcote and Violet come to an understanding and get married [ML].

M165 *A new note* [anon.].
    London: Hutchinson & Co., 1894, 2 vols. SOURCE Daims, 1989. LOCATION Dt, L.
    New York: R.F. Fenno, [*c.*1895]. SOURCE Daims, 1989. LOCATION NUC.
M166 *A modern man* (by Ella MacMahon).
    New York, London: Macmillan & Co., 1895 (ill. Ida Lovering). SOURCE Daims, 1988; OCLC. LOCATION L, NUC.
    London: J.M. Dent & Co., 1895. SOURCE Daims, 1988. LOCATION L.
M167 *A pitiless passion* (by Ella MacMahon).
    New York, London: Macmillan & Co., 1895. SOURCE Daims, 1990; OCLC. LOCATION NUC.

London: Hutchinson & Co., [1896] (as *A pitiful passion*). SOURCE Daims, 1990. LOCATION Dt, L.

M168 *The touchstone of life* (by Ella MacMahon).

London: Hutchinson & Co., 1897. SOURCE Daims, 1991. LOCATION Dt, L.

New York: F.A. Stokes, [*c.*1897]. SOURCE Daims, 1991; OCLC. LOCATION NUC.

M169 *An honourable estate* (by Ella MacMahon).

+ London: Hutchinson & Co., 1898. LOCATION D, Dt, L.

London: Mills & Boon, [1918] (new and revsd edn). LOCATION Dt.

COMMENTARY A romance that begins in Florence where Revd James Vincent, a Protestant clergyman from Ireland, is on holiday. He is acquainted with Lady Edward Sanquhar and falls in love with her daughter, Brenda. Brenda is in love with Rufus Holland, but she overhears Vincent declare his true feelings for her and when Vincent asks her to marry him; she consents, despite not being in love with him. They are married at the British consulate and return to Ireland to settle into parish life. When Holland comes to visit, she realizes that she has made a mistake in her hasty marriage. She contracts diphtheria and is on the verge of death. In a desperate bid to save her, Vincent risks his own life. When she recovers and learns of his heroic deed, she discovers the true love she has for her husband [CD].

M170 *The fortune's yellow* (by Ella MacMahon).

London: Hutchinson, 1900. SOURCE Alston, p. 271. LOCATION L.

COMMENTARY The sight of a rose recalls to the heroine her lover of twenty years earlier whom she gave up to marry for money [Sutherland, p. 399].

M171 *Such as have erred* (by Ella MacMahon).

+ London: Hutchinson & Co., 1902. SOURCE EF, p. 259. LOCATION L.

COMMENTARY Scrope Cuthford marries a beautiful tobacco seller while still a student at TCD. After she leaves him, he becomes secretary to the British ambassador in Rome and after ten years he meets Honor Beresford, a woman who is handsome, pure and genteel [EF, p. 259].

M172 *The court of conscience* (by Ella MacMahon).

+ London: Chapman & Hall, 1908. SOURCE EF, p. 259. LOCATION L.

COMMENTARY The daughter of disreputable parents marries a rising politician without taking the trouble to check his marital history [EF, p. 259].

M173 *Fancy O'Brien* (by Ella MacMahon).

+ London: Chapman & Hall, 1909. SOURCE Daims, 1987. LOCATION L.

COMMENTARY The sad story of an Irish couple [RL].

M174 *The divine folly* (by Ella MacMahon).

London: Chapman & Hall, 1913. SOURCE Daims, 1986. LOCATION L.

M175 *The job* (by Ella MacMahon).

London: James Nisbet, 1914. SOURCE EF, p. 259; Brown, 1049. LOCATION D.

COMMENTARY Describes a baronet's struggles to improve his Irish estate despite his amateur attempts, the fecklessness of the inhabitants and the distractions of a love affair [Brown; EF, p. 259].

M176 *Wind of dawn* (by Ella MacMahon; dedicated to 'many dear memories ...').

+ London: John Lane, 1927. SOURCE Brown 2, 927. LOCATION Dt, L.

COMMENTARY The scene is laid in rural Ireland in the truce period during the Anglo-Irish war truce of 1921 [Brown 2, 927].

M177 *Irish vignettes* (by Ella MacMahon).

London: John Lane, 1928. LOCATION D.

COMMENTARY The sketches in this volume first appeared in *Blackwood's Magazine* (Edinburgh), with the exception of 'Jinny', which was first published in the *English Review* (London), and 'Brady's auctioneer', a previously unpublished story. Contents: 'The station-master of Aghole',

'Miss Oriel', 'Flynn', 'Kate Higgin', 'The rebel', 'Jinny', 'Our gardener', 'Mary Ann', 'Her own poor boy', 'Ellen', 'Jobber Brannigan', 'The postmistress of Ballyboreen', 'Musha Andy', 'Poverina', 'Brady's auctioneer', 'Mrs. Delia Murphy', 'Owney', 'Lady Clontarf', 'The crusaders' [CD].

MC MAHON, Patrick Justin, fl. 1891. American novelist, probably of Irish Catholic birth or background.
M178   *Philip; or, the Mollie's secret. A tale of the coal regions* (by Patrick Justin Mcmahon).
  + Philadelphia: H.L. Kilner & Co., 1891 (Catholic Library). SOURCE Fanning, p. 386; Wright, iii, 3539. LOCATION L, NUC, Wright web.
COMMENTARY Starts in Schuylkill county in Pennsylvania, and tells the story of the Molly Maguires, a secret society begun in Ireland in the 1830s and later moved to the US where they were involved in labour disputes in the coal mining regions of eastern Pennsylvania. The book abounds with Irish names, and ends with a short sermon by a priest [ML].

'MAC MAHON, Thornton', pseud. See CALLAN, Margaret.

MAC MANUS, Charlotte Elizabeth (known as Lilly MacManus and L. MacManus and L. M'Manus), pseud. 'Cathal MacGuire', b. Killeaden, Castlebar (Co. Mayo) *c.*1850, d. 1941. Historical novelist, diarist and memoirist, LM was the daughter of James MacManus, a former sugar planter, and Charlotte Strong, and was born at Killeaden, her mother's family estate. Educated at home by a governess and later at Torquay (Devon), she became very interested in military history. Later she immersed herself in Irish history, travelling between Ireland and England and completing much of her historical research in the BL in London. She learned Irish, joined the Gaelic League, and established branches in Mayo. LMM wrote two popular serials for *Sinn Féin* (Dublin), 'One generation passeth' and 'The professor in Erin', later published as a book (see below). By 1902 she was writing a weekly page in the *Irish Emerald* (London). She knew the writers involved in the Irish Literary Revival and was involved in the Anglo-Irish War. She kept a diary, which includes a description of the 1916 Easter Rising, and wrote a memoir entitled *White light and flame: Memories of the Irish Literary Revival and the Anglo-Irish war* (Dublin, 1929). Many of the stories she collected appeared in the *Folklore Journal* (London) and the Educational Company of Ireland published many of these as penny pamphlets. A few of her letters are in the Allen Library, Dublin (Click Repository, Box 105, folder 3). SOURCE Blain, p. 696; Brady, p. 151; Brown 2, p. 167; EF, p. 259; E. Reilly, pp 220–2, 247; Hogan 2, p. 787; RIA/DIB.
M179   *Amabel. A military romance* (by 'Cathal MacGuire').
  + London: T. Fisher Unwin, 1893, 3 vols. LOCATION L.
M180   *The red star* (by L. MacManus; dedicated to Arthur Corrigan McManus of the Victorian Rangers).
  London: T. Fisher Unwin, 1894 (Autonym Library. SOURCE Daims, 1992; COPAC. LOCATION D (1896 edn), L, InND Loeber coll. (1896 edn).
  New York: G.P. Putnam's, 1895. SOURCE Daims, 1992. LOCATION NUC.
M181   *The silk of the kine* (by L. MacManus).
  + London: T. Fisher Unwin, 1896. SOURCE Brown, 1050; COPAC. LOCATION D, Dt, DPL, L, InND Loeber coll.
  + New York: Harper & Bros, 1896. LOCATION InND Loeber coll.
COMMENTARY Historical fiction set in Ireland during the Cromwellian period. An earl's daughter, along with many others, is transplanted to Connacht. On the way she faints and is left for

dead. When she recovers she falls into the hands of two scoundrels who plan to sell her as a slave to be sent to St Kitts in the West Indies. They are intercepted by an officer of Cromwell's army who takes charge of her to bring her before the Loughrea commissioners. The commissioners give her into the custody of a Protestant woman, who is in cahoots with the scoundrels, into whose hands she falls again. Once more she is rescued by the English officer, who claims that she is his wife. Although she still sees him as her enemy, she marries him because by his acts he has endangered his own life. They flee to the Continent until he receives a pardon, after which they happily reside on his English estates [ML].

M182 *Lally of the brigade* (by L. M'Manus).

> London: T. Fisher Unwin, 1899. SOURCE COPAC. LOCATION L.
>
> Dublin: James Duffy, 1899. SOURCE Brown, 1051. LOCATION L, InND Loeber coll. (n.d. edn).
>
> + Boston: L.C. Page & Co., 1899 (ill. H.C. Edwards). SOURCE Nield, p. 77 (1911 edn). LOCATION D.

COMMENTARY Historical fiction set in France around the time of King James II's death. The Irish Brigade is stationed in northern Italy during the war of the Spanish succession where it is fighting the Austrian advances under Prince Eugene. Lally-Tollendal is a captain in the famous Irish Dillon regiment in the French army. He has been sent to Paris to deliver and receive dispatches, from which he returns to Cremona. The book describes various political intrigues that would involve the Irish joining the Austrian army. However, none of the Irishmen agree. The battle for Cremona (1702) is vividly described. A love intrigue is intertwined with the story. Lally-Tollendal, derived from Tullinadaly, Co. Galway, was an Irishman who was colonel proprietor of a regiment in the French army; he was defeated at the battle of Wandiwash in India, and returned to France in disgrace, where he was executed [ML; Personal communication, Harman Murtagh, July 2002].

M183 *Nessa* (by L. MacManus).

> Dublin: Sealy, Bryers & Walker, 1902. SOURCE Brown, 1052 (1904 edn); COPAC. LOCATION D (n.d. edn), L.
>
> COMMENTARY Historical tale of the Cromwellian plantation set at an old castle near Lough Conn (Co. Mayo) [Brown].

M184 *In Sarsfield's days. A tale of the siege of Limerick* (by L. MacManus).

> + Dublin: M.H. Gill & Son, 1906. SOURCE Brown, 1053 (1907 edn); COPAC. LOCATION D, DPL, L.
>
> + Dublin: M.H. Gill & Son, n.d. LOCATION InND Loeber coll.
>
> New York: Buckles, [date?] (as *The wager*). SOURCE Brown, 1053.

COMMENTARY No copy of the New York edn located. Historical fiction about the 1690 siege of Limerick from the point of view of Brig. Niall McGuinness of Iveagh, an officer in Patrick Sarsfield's Horse. The plot hinges on the disappearance of Balldearg O'Donnell's cross, which this officer is suspected of having stolen. It includes an account of Sarsfield's legendry ride behind enemy lines to destroy siege equipment and the repulse of William's assault. MacMahon's play, 'O'Donnell's cross', based on this novel, was later produced in New York [Brown; RL].

M185 *Nuala. The story of a perilous quest* (by L. MacManus).

> + Dublin: Browne & Nolan, 1908 (ill. Donald H. Cuningham). SOURCE Brown, 1054. LOCATION D, L.

COMMENTARY Historical fiction for juveniles. The story of the daughter of the head of the O'Donnells, then in the service of the Austrian government. She is entrusted by her father just before his death with the mission of obtaining the Cathach, or battle book of the O'Donnells, from the monks at Louvain. This leads to many adventures, one of which involves her being captured by Napoleon's soldiers [Brown].

M186   *The professor of Erin* (by L. MacManus).
+ Dublin, M.H. Gill & Son, 1918. SOURCE Brown 2, 941; COPAC. LOCATION D, DPL, L.
COMMENTARY First serialized in *Sinn Féin* (Dublin). A German professor exploring an Irish ruin is knocked on the head. He comes to himself in an Ireland that bewilders him. He is told that the Irish won the battle of Kinsale (1601) and have developed on their own lines ever since. He has to re-read history. He is told of Sarsfield's campaign in England against King William and of a siege of Exeter instead of a siege of Limerick. He is fortunately a good Gaelic scholar, for this is an Irish-speaking Ireland. We have a picture of a medieval social system with modern transport and material progress. Tara is another Paris. After many adventures the professor comes back to the 'real' Ireland [Brown 2].

M187   *Within the four seas of Fola* (by L. MacManus).
+ Dublin: M.H. Gill & Son, 1922. SOURCE Brown 2, 942; COPAC. LOCATION D, DPL, L.
COMMENTARY Twelve sketches, all but two dealing with strange 'psychic' experiences and manifestations of the preternatural among western Irish country people. In 'The bell' (an old bell which legends says tolls six times of itself whenever someone dies for Ireland. Those who have been listening to the story suddenly hear it toll: it is Easter Monday, 1916, the date of the Easter Rising), 'The conspiracy' (tells how the phantom 'death coach' of the Burkes brings death to old Ulick Burke in spite of his attempt to substitute his nephew), 'The baptism' (tells how Our Lady appeared to a gypsy woman and helped her to have her child baptized), 'The man who must walk' (the wandering Jew appears in Mayo in 1913) [Brown 2].

MAC MANUS, James. See MACMANUS, Séumas.

MAC MANUS, L. See MACMANUS, Charlotte Elizabeth.

MAC MANUS, S. See MACMANUS, Séumas.

MAC MANUS, Séumas (also Seumas; known as S. MacManus and James MacManus), pseud. 'Mac', b. James MacManus, Mountcharles (Co. Donegal) *c.*1869 (1878 according to McCarthy), d. New York 1960. Story and verse writer, playwright and editor, SM was the son of Patrick MacManus, a peasant farmer, and Mary Molloy. Educated at Glencoagh National School (Co. Donegal), he became a teacher at age 17 and was appointed principal of his old school. He contributed articles to local papers and to the *Shan van Vocht*, the Belfast nationalist magazine. In 1899 he went to the US where he found a ready market for his stories of Donegal traditions. He returned to Donegal each year. He published 27 volumes of stories, mostly set in Co. Donegal, but some of the volumes may be US reprints. In addition, he wrote several plays, many of them published in Mountcharles, and a brief history of Ireland, *Ireland's case* (New York, *c.*1917) written for Irish-Americans. He lectured on Irish matters in many places in the US, and his virulent criticism of John Millington Synge's *Playboy of the Western World* when the Abbey Theatre toured it in the US in 1911 led Lady Augusta Gregory to describe him as 'Shame-us MacManus'. He received a LLD from Notre Dame University (IN) in 1917 and wrote a popular autobiography *The rocky road to Dublin* (New York, 1938). He edited the short-lived periodical *Chimney corners. A Journal of Recreation for the Irish Home* (1938), to which he contributed fiction. He had a loyal following in the US – many of his books were either published there for the first time or reprinted there. In 1901, he married the poet and editor Anna Johnston, who wrote under the name Ethna Carbery. She died shortly afterwards and ten years later he married Catalina Violante Paez. SOURCE Boylan, p. 228; Brady,

p. 152; Burke, p. 460; Cathach cat. Summer 2001/374; Donegal, pp 170–7 (lists also plays and short stories published in periodicals); EF, p. 259; Irish pseudonyms; McCarthy, vi, p. 2254; Hogan, pp 415–17; Hogan 2, pp 789–91; LVP, p. 309; OCIL, p. 344; O'Donoghue, p. 288; RIA/DIB; RL; Sutherland, p. 400; Zimmermann, pp 319–21.

M188 *Shuilers from heathy hills* (by 'Mac'; dedicated to Louis Ely O'Carroll).
+ Mount Charles: G. Kirke, 1893. SOURCE Brown, 1055; Hogan, p. 416 (who wrongly calls it *Shuilers of healthy hills*). LOCATION D.
COMMENTARY Poems and three prose pieces set in Co. Donegal: 'Micky Maguire, the last of the hedge schoolmasters', 'How you bathe at Bundoran', 'A trip with Phil M'Goldrick' [Brown; Leclaire, p. 189].

M189 *The leadin' road to Donegal and other stories* (by 'Mac'; dedicated to Frank MacElroy).
London: Digby, Long & Co., [1895] (ill.). SOURCE Brown, 1056 (1896 edn); Hogan, p. 416 (1896 edn); NYPL. LOCATION D (3rd edn), DPL, NN, NUC.
COMMENTARY Stories of the Donegal peasantry. Some of the stories are reprinted from *Shuilers from heathy hills* (Mount Charles, 1893). Contents: 'The leadin' road to Donegal', 'The first and last review of the prince of Wales' own Donegal militia', 'Manis, the besom man', 'Mickey Cusack's goat', 'The dhorko', 'Mickey Maguire, the last of the hedge school-masters', 'The giant of the band beggars' hall', 'Barney Roddy's penance', 'The apprentice thief', 'Dinny Monaghan's last keg', 'Buried alive; or, the fate of poor Mickey M'Gragh', 'How Con Doherty got Lord Wellington a Christmas dinner' [ML; Brown].

M190 *'Twas in dhroll Donegal* (by 'Mac'; dedicated to Fred J. Reilly, MA).
London: Downey & Co., 1897. SOURCE Brown, 1057 (mentions a 1896 edn); Topp 8, 171. LOCATION D, Dcc (1897, 3rd edn), DPL, L, NUC (1897, 2nd edn), InND Loeber coll. (1897, 3rd edn).
COMMENTARY Stories about the Donegal peasantry. Contents: 'Billy Baxter', 'Jack who was the ashypet', 'Barney Brian's bounce', 'Teddy Tiveniagh's Christmas box', 'Sergeant M'Grannigan's saizure', 'Corney Higgerty's "jewel" with Boneyparty', 'The quad-dhroop-eds', 'Jack and the Lord High Mayor of Dublin' [RL].

M191 *The bend of the road* (by James MacManus ('Mac')).
Dublin: M.H. Gill; James Duffy, 1898. SOURCE Brown, 1058 (1897 edn, but not located); Leclaire, p. 189; NYPL (1906 edn); OCLC. LOCATION D (1906, 2nd edn), NN (1906 edn), NUC (1906 edn).
London: Downey & Co., 1898. LOCATION L, NUC.
COMMENTARY No copy of the Dublin 1898 edn located. Sketches of life in an out-of-the-way part of Donegal. According to the blurb of the 1906, 2nd edn, this is a companion volume to *A lad of the O'Friel's*, with the same characters moving through its pages. Some of the stories were first published in *'Twas in dhroll Donegal* (London, 1897), and *Barney Brian and other boys* (Dublin, 1890). Contents: 'In Toal a-Gallagher's', 'Father Dan and the fiddlers four', 'In the Bummadier's', 'The counsellor', 'The master and the bocca beag', 'Jack and the king who was a gentleman', 'When the "Nation" came', 'The masther's love story', 'Padh Mullen's Nancy', 'The widow's Mary', 'The vagabone' [Brown; NYPL; Personal communication, Peter Rowan, May 2001; RL].

M192 *The humours of Donegal* (by Seamus MacManus§).
+ London: T. Fisher Unwin, 1898. SOURCE Brown, 1059; Wolff, 4353. LOCATION D, DPL, BFl, L, NUC, InND Loeber coll.
COMMENTARY Dedicated from Donegal, Apr. 1898. Contents: 'When Barney's trunk comes home', 'How Paddy M'Garrity did not get to be gauger', 'Terry M'Gowan and Father Luke', 'Shan Martin's ghost', 'One St. Pathrick's day', 'Corney Higarty's interview with the devil', 'Why Tómas Dubh walked' [Wolff].

M193 *Through the turf smoke. The love, lore, and laughter, of old Ireland* (by Seamus MacManus; dedicated to Ethna Carbery).

+ New York: Doubleday & McClure, 1899. SOURCE Hogan, p. 416; NYPL. LOCATION NN, NUC, InND Loeber coll.

Toronto: G.N. Morang & Co., 1899. LOCATION L.

London: T. Fisher Unwin, 1901. SOURCE Brown, 1060 (1899 edn, but not located); RLIN. LOCATION DPL, L, NUC.

COMMENTARY Tales of Donegal peasantry, some of which were published earlier in *The leadin' road to Donegal* (London, [1895]), *'Twas in dhroll Donegal* (London, 1897), and *The bend of the road* (Dublin, 1898). Contents: 'The leadin' road to Donegal', 'The Boyne water', 'The quad-dhroopeds', 'The prince of Wales' own Donegal militia', 'Barny Roddy's penance', 'Dinny Monaghan's last keg', 'Billy Baxter', 'The counsellor', 'The masther and the Bocca Fadh', 'Father Dan and fiddlers four', 'Jack who was the ashypet', 'Jack and the Lord High Mayor' [RL; Leclaire, p. 190].

M194 *In chimney corners. Merry tales of Irish folklore* (by Seamus MacManus dedicated to Irish emigrants).

London, New York: Harper & Bros, 1899. SOURCE Brown, 1061; Fanning, p. 386. LOCATION L.

New York: Doubleday & McClure, 1899 (ill. Pamela Coleman Smith). SOURCE Hogan, p. 416. LOCATION NUC, InND Loeber coll. (1904 edn).

COMMENTARY Some of the stories were published earlier in *The leadin' road to Donegal* (London, [1895]), *'Twas in dhroll Donegal* (London, 1897), and *The bend of the road* (Dublin, 1898). Contents of the 1904 edn: 'Billy Beg and the bull', 'Murroghoo-More and Murroghoo-Beg', 'The queen of the golden mines', 'The widow's daughter', 'Shan Ban and Ned Flynn', 'When Neil A-Mughan was tuk', 'The black bull of the Castle of Blood', 'The old hag of the forest', 'Rory the robber', 'Myles McGarry and Donal McGarry', 'Nanny and Conn', 'The apprentice thief', 'Manis the besom man', 'Jack and the king who was a gentleman', 'The giant of the band beggar's hall' [RL].

M195 *The bewitched fiddle and other Irish tales* (by Seamus MacManus; dedicated to An Roisín Dubh).

London, New York: Doubleday & McClure, 1900. LOCATION L.

+ New York: Doubleday & McClure, 1900. SOURCE Brown, 1062; NYPL. LOCATION NN, NUC, InND Loeber coll.

COMMENTARY Mainly humorous stories, presented in a Donegal dialect, heard by the author at Donegal firesides. Contents: 'The bewitched fiddle', 'The wisdom of dark Pathrick', 'When Myles Maguire melted', 'Pathrick's proxy', 'Corney Clery's balance', 'The staff of the "Universe"', 'The cadger-boy's last journey', 'The three master tradesmen', 'Condy Sheeran's courtin'', 'Billy Lappin's search for a fortune' [Brown; Leclaire, p. 190; NYPL].

M196 *Donegal fairy stories* (collected and told by S. MacManus; dedicated to the Gaelic shanachies).

London: McClure, Phillips & Co., 1900. SOURCE Brown, 1063 (1902 edn); Osborne, p. 605 (1902 edn). LOCATION CaOTP (1902 edn), L.

+ New York: McClure, Phillips & Co., 1900 (ill.). LOCATION D, NUC.

COMMENTARY Stories from Co. Donegal. Contents: 'Our tales', 'The plaisham', 'The amadan and the dough', 'Conal and Donal and Taig', 'Manis the miller', 'Hookedy-crookedy', 'Donal that was rich and Jack that was poor', 'The snow, the crow and the blood', 'The adventure of Ciad, son of the king of Norway', 'The bee, the harp, the mouse and the bum-clock', 'The old hag's long leather bag' [RL].

M197 *The red poocher* (by Seamus MacManus).

+ New York: Funk & Wagnalls, 1903 (ill.). SOURCE Brown, 1064; NYPL. LOCATION D, DPL, NN, NUC, InND Loeber coll.

COMMENTARY Four stories in which R.P., a mysterious person with great audacity, plays the central role. The stories are set in Co. Donegal and told in dialect by a gamekeeper. Contents: 'Why Tómas Dubh walked', 'Misther Kilgar of Athlone', 'Misther McCran of Belfast', 'Misther O'Mara from the County of Maith'. The first story was first published in *The humours of Donegal* (London, 1898) [RL; Brown].

M198 **Barney Brian and other boys** (by Seumas MacManus).

Dublin: 'Irish Nights' Office, 1903 (ill.). SOURCE Hogan, p. 417; NYPL; OCLC. LOCATION NN, NUC.

COMMENTARY Contents: 'Barney Brian's monument', 'Father Dan and fiddlers four', 'Billy Baxter's holiday', 'The sorrow of Phelim Ruadh', 'Dinny O'Neill', 'The parvarted bachelor', 'Two brothers', 'The jarvey', 'Larry Devenny's goose-leg' [NYPL].

M199 **A lad of the O'Friel's** (by Seamus MacManus; dedicated to Ethna).

London: Isbister & Co., 1903. LOCATION L.

Dublin: M.H. Gill; James Duffy & Co., 1903. SOURCE Brown, 1065; NYPL (1906 edn). LOCATION D (1906, 4th edn), DPL, NN (1906 edn), NUC (1906, 5th edn).

+ Dublin, Belfast, Cork, Waterford: Browne & Nolan, n.d. (as *A lad of the O'Friel's. A story of the older times in Ireland for boys; being a school-edition of the famous novel of that name*). LOCATION D.

+ New York: McClure, Phillips & Co., 1903 (as *A lad of the O'Friels [sic]*). SOURCE OCLC. LOCATION Boston College.

COMMENTARY Stories about people living in Knocknagar, south Donegal. Contains the same characters as those in *The bend of the road* (Dublin, 1898). A love story of Dinny O'Friel and Nuala Gildea is interwoven. Contents: 'Around Toal-a-Gallagher's candle', 'A donkey-load and a mission', 'The mixed delights of a schemer', 'The coming of Nuala', 'A Sunday at Knockagar', 'Uncle Donal', 'Herding in Glenboran', 'A Glenboran feast', 'A learned man and the little people', 'The little people', 'My first flogging', 'On the road to the fair', 'At the big harvest fair of Glenties', 'When Billy's temper was bruck', 'The outcast wren', 'By the yalla firelight', 'When Corney drew his pension', 'When Greek met Greek', 'After the battle', 'Intellectual feats by the fireside and elsewhere', 'The pilgrimage to Loch Dearg', 'The fall of Dunboy', 'Bonfire night', 'At uncle Donal's fireside again', 'The kindly neighbors', 'Father Dan's present', 'Five years after' [RL; Brown].

M200 **Irish nights** (by Seamus MacManus).

+ Dublin: 'Irish Nights' Office, 1903. LOCATION L, NUC (1905 edn).

COMMENTARY Some of the stories had been published earlier in *Barney Brian and other boys* (London, [1890s]) and *A bunch of shamrocks* (London, 1879). Issued monthly: volume I: 'Barney Brian's monument', 'Father Dan and fiddlers four'; volume II: 'Billy Baxter's holiday', 'The sorrow of Phelim Ruadh'; volume III: 'Dinny O'Neill: a story of 1798', 'The parvarted bachelor'; volume IV: 'Thwo brothers', 'The jarvey. A sketch'; volume V: 'Toal A. Gallagher, theologian', 'The resurrection of Dinny O'Dowd'; volume VI: 'The capture of Molly Maguire', 'The priest's boy' [CM].

M201 **Doctor Kilgannon** (by Seamus MacManus).

+ Dublin: M.H. Gill & Son, 1907 (ill.). SOURCE Brown, 1066; NYPL. LOCATION D, L, NN, NUC.

COMMENTARY A stream of loosely connected after-dinner stories, chiefly about comic duelling and electioneering in Co. Donegal. Contents: 'A County Clare angel', 'The feat of attorney Phil', 'How Conn Rafferty missed five thousand a year', 'A wife of Jack Dempsey', 'The tenantry of Lock Muck', 'How the doctor made an MP out of Brian Mulvenny', 'The doctor's first and last duel' [ML; Brown].

M202 **Yourself and the neighbours** (by Seamus MacManus; dedicated to Catalina).

+ New York: Devin-Adair, [1914] (ill. Thomas Fogarty). SOURCE Brown, 1067; Hogan, p. 416; NYPL. LOCATION D, L, NN, NUC, InND Loeber coll. (1945 edn).

+ Dublin: James Duffy & Co., 1926 (as *O, do you remember*; dedicated to Catalina). SOURCE Hogan, p. 416; Brown 2, 945; Personal communication, Peter Rowan, May 2001. LOCATION D, DPL, L, NUC, InND Loeber coll.

COMMENTARY Some of the stories had been published earlier in *A bunch of shamrocks* (London, 1879), *The bend of the road* (Dublin, 1898), *Irish nights* (Dublin, 1903), and *A lad of the O'Friel's* (London, 1903). Stories set in Co. Donegal. Contents: 'Yourself and herself', 'The lore you loved', 'The priest's boy', 'When Greek meets Greek', 'But when Greek meets Tartar', 'Your post mistress', 'The bachelor of Braggy', 'The masther', 'A day in the bog', 'The bacach', 'The conquest of Killymard', 'Denis a-Cuinn and the grey man', 'The come-home Yankee', 'The gentle people', 'Gentle-and something besides', 'When the tinkers came', 'The tales you told', 'When God sent Sunday' [ML].

M203 *Lo, and behold ye!* (by Seamus MacManus; dedicated to Bartlett Arkell).
+ New York: Frederick A. Stokes, 1919 (ill. Mabel Hatt). SOURCE Hogan, p. 416; NYPL. LOCATION D, NN, NUC.

M204 *Tales that were told* (by Seamus MacManus).
Dublin: Talbot Press; London: T. Fisher Unwin, 1920 (ill. Mabel Hatt). SOURCE Brown 2, 946 (probably published in 1919); Donegal, p. 42; Hogan, p. 416; NYPL. LOCATION NN, NUC.

COMMENTARY A few of the stories had been published earlier in *Barney Brian and other boys* (Dublin, [1890s]), and *'Twas in dhroll Donegal* (London, 1897). The stories are set in Co. Donegal. Contents: 'The mad man, the dead man and the devil', 'The queen's conquest', 'Dark Patrick's blood-horse', 'The bodach and the boy', 'The far adventures of Billy Burns', 'The tinker of Tamlacht', 'The man who would dream', 'The day of the scholars', 'Donal O'Donnell's standing army', 'The parvarted bachelor', 'The king's curing', 'Lord Thorny's son', 'Long Cromachy of the Crows', 'Jack and the Lord High Mayor', 'The quare birds', 'The son of strength', 'The resurrection of Dinny Muldoon' [NUC].

M205 *Top o' the morning* (by Seamus MacManus; dedicated to Edward Bok).
+ New York: Frederick A. Stokes, [1920]. SOURCE Hogan, p. 416; Brown 2, 947 (1921 edn); NYPL. LOCATION D (1920 edn), DPL, NN, NUC.

COMMENTARY Some of the stories were first published in *The humours of Donegal* (London, 1898), and *The bewitched fiddle* (London, 1900). Contents: 'The Lord Mayor o' Buffalo', 'The widow Meehan's cassimeer shawl', 'The cadger-boy's last journey', 'The minister's race-horse', 'The case of Kitty Kildea', 'Billy Baxter's holiday', 'Wee Paidin', 'When Barney's trunk comes home', 'Five minutes a millionaire', 'Mrs. Carney's sealskin', 'The capture of Nelly Carribin', 'The bellman of Carrick', 'Barney Brian's monument', 'All on the Brown Knowe', 'The heartbreak of Norah O'Hara' [NYPL].

M206 *The Donegal wonder book* (by Seamus MacManus).
New York: Frederick A. Stokes, 1926. SOURCE Hogan, p. 416; Brown 2, 943. LOCATION NUC.

COMMENTARY Contents: 'Tales of magic, mystery, witchery, and fairie', e.g., 'The wonders of the three Donals', 'The sword of light', 'The hound of the Hill of Spears', 'The queen of the Lonely Isle', 'The wee red man' [Brown 2].

M207 *Bold blades of Donegal* (by Seamus MacManus; dedicated to J.S., and P.D.).
New York: Frederick A. Stokes & Co., 1935. SOURCE Hogan, p. 417; Brown 2, 948. LOCATION NUC.
+ London: Sampson Low, Marston & Co., [1937]. SOURCE Hogan, p. 417; Brady, p. 152 (probably mistakenly identified a 1930 edn). LOCATION D, DPL, L, NUC, InND Loeber coll.
Dublin: Brown & Nolan, 1939 (as *The knights of Knockagar*). SOURCE OCLC. LOCATION D.

MacManus

COMMENTARY These stories are for the most part reminiscences of the author's boyhood. The main character is once more Dinny O'Friel, who was first featured in *A lad of the O'Friels* (London, 1903). Dinny and his friends often try to enact scenes from Ireland's past as well as current events [ML; Brown 2].

M208   *Dark Patrick* (by Seamus MacManus; dedicated to Molly Emerson).
+ New York: Macmillan, 1939. SOURCE Hogan, p. 417. LOCATION D, NUC.
+ Utrecht: De Lanteern, n.d. (ill. C.A.B. Bantzinger). LOCATION InND Loeber coll.

M209   *The well o' the world's end* (by Seamus MacManus).
+ New York: Macmillan, 1939 (ill. Richard Bennett). SOURCE Hogan, p. 417; Brown 2, 949; Hodges Figgis cat. 10 n.s./1884. LOCATION D, NUC.
+ New York: Devin-Adair Co., 1949 (as *The well o' the world's end and other folk tales*; ill. Richard Bennett). SOURCE Hogan, p. 417. LOCATION InND Loeber coll.

COMMENTARY Ancient folk-tales of Donegal communicated by the local seanchaite. Contents: 'The well o' the world's end', 'Conaleen and Donaleen', 'The three golden eggs', 'Jack the ashypet' (first published in *Trough the turf smoke*, New York, 1899), 'The blue scarf of strength', 'Queen o' the tinkers', 'Feather o' my wing', 'The king of Greece's daughter', 'The haggary nag', 'Jack the fool', 'The princess of the garden of Eden' [ML].

M210   *Tales from Ireland* (by Seamus MacManus).
London: Evans Bros, [1949] (ill. W.H. Conn). SOURCE Donegal, p. 173; Hogan, p. 417 ([1947] edn). LOCATION L, NUC ([1949] edn).

COMMENTARY Some of the stories published earlier in *The Donegal wonder book* (New York, 1926). Contents: 'The wonders of the three Donals', 'The mistress of magic', 'The wee red man', 'The sword of light', 'The three princesses of Connaught' [ML].

M211   *Heavy hangs the golden grain* (by Seamus MacManus).
New York: Macmillan, 1950. SOURCE Hogan, p. 417. LOCATION NUC.
Dublin: Talbot Press, [1951]. SOURCE Brown 2, 951 (mistakenly mentions 1931 edn); Hogan, p. 417. LOCATION L, NUC.

M212   *The bold heroes of Hungry Hill, and other Irish folk tales* (retold by Seamus MacManus; dedicated to Hudy and Butch).
New York: Ariel Books, [1951] (ill. Joy Chollick). SOURCE Hogan, p. 417. LOCATION NUC.
New York: Pellegrini & Cudahay, [1951] (ill. J. Chollick). SOURCE Hogan, p. 417. LOCATION NUC.
+ London: J.M. Dent & Sons, [1952] (introd. by H.E. the Irish Ambassador Frederick H. Boland, ill. Joy Chollick. SOURCE Brown 2, 950 (Cape edn); Hogan, p. 417. LOCATION L, NUC.

COMMENTARY Contents: 'The bold heroes of Hungry Hill', 'Prince Finn the fair', 'The crochera', 'Donal from Donegal', 'The king of Araby's daughter', 'The wonder ship and ship's crew', 'Donal O'Ciaran from Connaught', 'The giant of the brown beech wood', 'Manny MacGilligan's story', 'The white hen', 'The golden apples of Loch Erne', 'The wishing chair of the lord of Errigal' [ML].

M213   *The little mistress of the Eskar Mór* (by Seamus MacManus).
+ Dublin: M.H. Gill & Son, 1960. SOURCE Hogan, p. 417; Burke, p. 460 (mistakenly mentions a 1959 edn). LOCATION D, DPL.

M214   *Hibernian nights* (by Seamus MacManus; introd. by Padraic Colum).
+ New York: Macmillan, 1963 (ill. Paul Kennedy). SOURCE Hogan, p. 417. LOCATION InND Loeber coll., Boston College.

COMMENTARY Published posthumously. Some of the stories were published earlier *In chimney corners* (London, 1899), *Donegal fairy stories* (London, 1900), *Tales that were told* (Dublin,

1920), *The well o' the world's end* (New York, 1939), and *The bold heroes of Hungry Hill* (New York, [1951]). Contents: 'The son of strength', 'The tinker of Tamlacht', 'The three golden eggs', 'The king who was a gentleman', 'Nanny and Con', 'The adventures of Ciad', 'The knight of the glen's steed o' bells', 'The wee red man', 'Queen o' the tinkers', 'Prince Finn the fair', 'Jack and the Lord High Mayor', 'Nidden and Didden and Donal Beg O'Neary', 'The sword of light', 'The will of the wise man', 'The mad man, the dead man, and the devil', 'The wonders of the three Donals', 'The three tasks', 'The bold heroes of Hungry Hill', 'The day of the scholars', 'The widow's daughter', 'Donal O'Donnell's standing army', 'The well o' the world's end' [RL].

MC NAIR, Julia. See **WRIGHT, Mrs Julia McNair**.

MAC NALLY (also McNally), **Leonard**, b. Dublin 1752, d. Ireland 1820. Barrister, playwright, poet and government spy, LM was the only son of William MacNally, a Dublin merchant who died when LM was six years old. His mother, Mary Murphy of Co. Wexford, remarried Thomas Fetherston of Co. Westmeath (RIA/DIB has of St Mary's Lane, presumably Dublin), at whose house LM grew up. According to OCIL, he was educated at TCD (but not mentioned in other sources). LM spent some time in Bordeaux, but he returned to Dublin to open a fashionable grocery in St Mary's Lane in 1771, which went into bankruptcy in 1772. However, he began a legal career and was admitted to the Middle Temple (London) in 1771, to the King's Inns in 1776, and was called to the English Bar in 1783 (RIA/DIB has 1784). Combining the law with writing, he had a comic opera, *The ruling passion*, produced in Dublin in 1777, and a number of comedies performed in Covent Garden, in one of which, *The apotheosis of Punch* (London, 1779), he satirized the Irish playwright Richard Brinsley Sheridan. Returning to Dublin around 1790, he became a sworn member of the United Irishmen and was counsel to his fellow member Napper Tandy and defence counsel in several treason trials, including those of the brothers John and Henry Sheares. But while socializing with and defending his fellow United Irishmen members, he was by 1794 also in the pay of the government. His connivance is said to have aided in the capture of the revolutionary Lord Edward Fitzgerald. The ODNB points out, however, that while informing the authorities in Dublin Castle on Theobald Wolfe Tone's§ movements, he may have also provided them with disinformation about him. LM was defence counsel for the trial for treason of Robert Emmet, but for £200 he had already confided the case to the government before the trial began, kissing Emmet farewell after his conviction and sentence of death. Later he received a £300 pension from the government's secret service fund. It was his son's efforts to continue this after his father's death that uncovered LM's dual life of patriot/informer. LM made a deathbed conversion to catholicism, received absolution from a priest, and was buried in Donnybrook (Dublin). Aside from his one work of fiction, he published *The claims of Ireland, and the resolutions of the Volunteers vindicated* (London, 1782), *The justice of the peace for Ireland* (Dublin, 1808, 2 vols.), as well as various publications on the law. Sir Jonah Barrington, with whom he fought a duel, described him thus: 'His figure was ludicrous: he was very short, and nearly as broad as long: his legs were of unequal length, and he had a face which no washing could clean ...' (Barrington, ii, p. 47). He married three times: his first wife died in 1786, after which he married Frances Janson, who died in 1795 and for whom he wrote his ballad 'The lass of Richmond Hill'. He then married in 1799 Louisa Edgeworth the daughter of Revd Dr Robert Edgeworth, and relative of Maria Edgeworth§, who wrote fiction as Mrs Louisa MacNally§, and with whom he had a son. For LM's portraits, see Elmes and ODNB. SOURCE Allibone, ii, p. 1193; *Appendix to 26th Report of the Deputy Keeper of the Public Records of Ireland* (Dublin, 1895), p. 565; J. Barrington, *Personal sketches* (London, 1830, 2nd edn, ii, p.

47; Elmes, p. 126; Field Day, i, p. 1170, iii, pp 1316, 1373*n*.; Hogan 2, pp 791–2; Keane, p. 316; OCIL, pp 344–5; ODNB; O'Donoghue, p. 290; RIA/DIB; RL; T.J. Walsh, *Opera in Dublin 1705–1797* (Dublin, 1973), pp 254, 305.

M215 *Sentimental excursions to Windsor and other places, with notes critical, illustrative, and explanatory, by several eminent persons, male and female, living and dead* [anon.].

> London: J. Walker, 1781. SOURCE Johnson cat. 38/53; Raven 2, 1781:B:7; ESTC t128528. LOCATION L, CtY.

COMMENTARY An imitation and parody of Laurence Sterne§, it appeared originally in the *Public Ledger* (London) and later in the *Morning Herald* (London) and consists of thoughts that the author had while riding in a coach. It refers to Laurence Sterne and Richard Brinsley Sheridan. It mentions a sieur O'Riely and a Count O'Dunn [ML; RIA/DIB; Johnson cat. 38/53].

MAC NALLY, Mrs —. See MACNALLY, Mrs Louisa.

MAC NALLY, Mrs Louisa (née Edgeworth; known as **Mrs MacNally**), possible pseud. 'F.J.', b. after 1767. Novelist, LM was the daughter of Revd Dr Robert Edgeworth of Lissard (Co. Longford), and Charlotte Roberts. She was thus distantly related to Maria Edgeworth§ as they both had the same great-grandfather, Sir John Edgeworth. Her father was probably the brother of Abbé Henry Edgeworth of Firmount (Co. Longford). In 1799 she became the third wife of Leonard MacNally.§ LM's name as an author is evident from an extra page inserted in her novel *Eccentricity* (Dublin, 1820). Her link to the Edgeworth family is confirmed by an advertisement in the *Star* (London, 1820), which announced the novel *Eccentricity* as by 'One of the Edgeworth family'. The signed advertisement showed that the book was her first publication. She revealed her identity rather than publishing anonymously because, she stated, 'I understand that an anonymous Publication, not of very recent date, has been ascribed to my pen …' She had a son, Robert. SOURCE *Appendix to 26th Report of the Deputy Keeper of the Public Records of Ireland* (Dublin, 1895), p. 271; British fiction; Blakey, pp 49–50; Brown, p. 197; Keane, p. 316; ODNB [under Leonard MacNally]; RIA/DIB [under Leonard MacNally].

M216 *Eccentricity. A novel* (by Mrs MacNally).

> + Dublin: J. Cumming, 1820, 3 vols. SOURCE Brown, 1068; Block, p. 149 (who mentions Louisa MacNally as its author); RLIN; British Fiction. LOCATION D, L, MH.

> Dublin: J. Cumming; London: Longman, Hurst, Rees, Orme & Brown, 1820, 3 vols. SOURCE British Fiction; Garside, 1820:50. LOCATION Corvey CME 3–628–48138–4, Ireland related fiction, Dt, L.

> + London: Longman, Hurst, Rees, Orme & Brown; Dublin: John Cumming, 1820, 3 vols. SOURCE Seen at Quaritch, Oct. 1996; RL. LOCATION NUC.

COMMENTARY Country house novel, set largely in Ireland. Describes a series of love affairs among the upper class. The eccentricity refers to a hermit who resolves to return to normal life and renew acquaintance with his daughter, who he had left with friends. He descends upon the friend's family and carries off another girl by mistake. According to the preface, the 'prime object' of the novel 'is to exemplify … the undeviating and pious devotion of some children to their parents, notwithstanding the palpable dereliction … of parents … towards their offspring' [Brown; Johnson cat. 42/31].

M217 *Such is the world* [anon.].

> London: G. & W.B. Whittaker, 1822, 3 vols. SOURCE Garside, 1822:13. LOCATION Corvey CME 3–628–48790–3, L, MH.

COMMENTARY If the attribution of *The village coquette* (see below) is correct, this would also affect the attribution of this title. Preface states that the manuscript was completed on 15 Aug. 1820 and is referred to 'as my first novel', which either contradicts *Eccentricity* (London, 1820, 3 vols.), or may mean that *Such is the world* was written at an earlier date. Still, the attribution is tentative [Garside; British Fiction (Update 1); RL].

M218 *The village coquette; a novel* [anon.].
> London: G. & W.B. Whittaker, 1822, 3 vols. SOURCE Garside, 1822:13. LOCATION Corvey CME 3–628–48918–0, L.

COMMENTARY Attributed to Mrs Macnally [*sic*] in *Bettison's Library Catalogue* (London, 1829). However, the preface is signed 'F.J.', Kensington, Dec. 1821 [British Fiction (Update 1)].

MAC NALLY, Louisa, fl. 1854. Historical romance novelist. Brown is of the opinion that this author is distinct from Mrs Louisa MacNally§ (wife of Leonard MacNally§), whose *Eccentricity* appeared thirty-four years previous to the following novel. ODNB does not mention that there was a daughter by this marriage. Leonard MacNally's only known daughter was born to his second wife, Frances Janson, in 1788. SOURCE RL; Brown, p. 197; BLC; ODNB.

M219 *The pirate's fort. A tale of the sixteenth century* (by Louisa MacNally).
> Dublin: Hodges & Smith, 1854. SOURCE Allibone Suppl., ii, p. 1058; Brown, 1069; Dixson, p. 220; OCLC. LOCATION L.

COMMENTARY Attributed by Brown to Louisa M'Nally. Historical fiction set towards the close of the sixteenth century at the fort of Dunalong, on Inisherkin in Baltimore Bay (Co. Cork), a stronghold of the O'Driscolls. An English ship is captured and O'Driscoll's natural son, a ferocious pirate, falls in love with the captain's daughter. She is true to her English officer lover. O'Driscoll's beautiful daughter saves her from her brother's fury. The English destroy the fort and there is a double wedding of the two fair maids to two English officers. A prominent role is assigned to a money-grabbing, idle, besotted Franciscan friar [Brown].

MAC NAMARA, Revd Lewis, b. Cork 1869. Church of Ireland clergyman and story writer, LM was the son of Revd Arthur David MacNamara, incumbent of the Free Church in Cork, and a Miss Crawford of Roscommon. He became a curate of Killoughy (Co. Offaly). Source Leslie & Wallace, p. 861 (which mistakenly attributes the following book to LM's father); RIA/DIB.

M220 *Blind Larry: Irish idylls* (by Lewis MacNamara).
> + London: Jarrold & Sons, 1897 (ill.; The Impressionist Series). SOURCE Brown, 1071. LOCATION D, L, NUC, InND Loeber coll.

COMMENTARY A series of interrelated stories about life among the very poor in the west of Ireland: 'Blind Larry', 'Katty's wedding', 'Molly Ahearne', 'Katty's husband', 'Murty Mulligan's revenge', 'Shawn O'Brien's courtin'', 'Mauriceen Kate', 'Neil Morrogh', 'The blighting of Honor's Denis', '"The fam'ly"', 'Conolly's fool' [ML; Brown].

MAC NAUGHTON, Euphans H. See STRAIN, Euphans Helen.

MC NEILL, Mary Violet. See HOBHOUSE, Mary Violet.

MC NULTY, Edward. See MCNULTY, Matthew Edward.

MC NULTY, Matthew Edward (also known as Edward McNulty), b. Randalstown (Co. Antrim) 1856, d. Ireland? 1943. Novelist, playwright and bank manager, MEM was educated at the English Scientific and Commercial Day School, a Protestant business academy in Aungier and Whitefriars streets in Dublin, where he was a classmate and friend of George Bernard Shaw§. Together the two enjoyed afternoon classes at the Royal Dublin Society's School of Art and visits to the NGI. MEM became a schoolmaster at the same school and wrote for *Irish Society* (Dublin) and the *Occult* (London?). He had two plays produced at the Abbey Theatre: 'The Lord Mayor' (1914) and 'The courting of Mary Doyle' (1921). He lived at Ranelagh, Dublin. At his death he left an unpublished memoir of Shaw. SOURCE Brady, p. 154; Brown, p. 198; Hogan, p. 427; Hogan 2, p. 804; Newmann, p. 170; OCIL, pp 347–8; ODNB [included under G.B. Shaw]; E. Reilly, p. 247; RIA/DIB.

M221 *Misther O'Ryan. An incident in the history of a nation* (by Edward McNulty).
    + London: Edward Arnold, 1894. SOURCE Brown, 1073. LOCATION D, L, NUC.
COMMENTARY An anti-clerical novel in which a vulgar priest and a ruffian who is a relative of his organize a branch of the Land League. They boycott a farmer who will not join and as a consequence, the farmer's daughter dies [Brown].

M222 *The son of a peasant* (by Edward McNulty).
    + London, New York: Edward Arnold, 1897. SOURCE Brown, 1074; Hogan, p. 427.
    LOCATION Dt, L, InND Loeber coll. (also n.d. edn).
COMMENTARY A story of class differences and the power of money set in a small provincial Irish town in the nineteenth century. Clarence Maguire, a young schoolmaster with a physical handicap, is suspected by many people to be a changeling. He lives in the house of Mr Flanagan, a shopkeeper, who always defends him. Clarence's grandfather lives in a pitiful hovel in the bog. Clarence is in love with the daughter of Sir Herbert O'Hara, an impoverished gentleman. They are too proud to consider Clarence as a possible suitor. However, after Clarence comes into great wealth, Sir Herbert changes his tune and more or less forces his daughter to accept Clarence. On the eve of his wedding, Clarence sleeps in his grandfather's hut. His grandfather kills him in the belief that Clarence is a changeling and that by killing him he will get his true grandson back. A subplot is provided by the love affairs of Constable Kerrigan and his efforts to obtain promotion [ML].

M223 *Maureen* (by Edward McNulty).
    London: Edward Arnold, 1904. SOURCE Brown, 1075. LOCATION L.
COMMENTARY An anti-clerical story in which priests are ridiculed [Brown].

M224 *Mrs. Mulligan's millions* (by Edward McNulty).
    London: Hurst & Blackett, 1908. SOURCE Brown, 1076. LOCATION L.
COMMENTARY A stage-Irish farce in which Mrs Mulligan, a tramp-like woman, is supposed to have come in for a fortune. Her relations fall over each other to gain her favour, until the bubble bursts. The book was adapted as a comedy under the same title (Dublin, 1918) [ML; Brown].

'MAC O BONNICLABBERO', pseud. See FAREWELL, James.

MC SPARRAN, Archibald. See M'SPARRAN, Archibald.

M'SPARRAN, Archibald (also known as Archibald McSparran), b. Drumsurn (Co. Derry) 1786, d. Philadelphia (PA) 1848. Schoolmaster and story writer in prose and verse, AM was brought up by relatives at Flanders, near Dungiven (Co. Derry). He was a schoolmaster at Glenkeen (Co. Derry) and entered TCD as a pensioner in 1816. He emigrated to America in 1830 (1835 according to O'Donoghue). Brady mentions also 'Tales of the Alleghenies' ('Tales and stories of the Alleghanies' [*sic*] according to O'Donoghue) and both mention a volume of verse, 'The hermit of the Rockie Mountains', but these have not been located. SOURCE Brady, p. 154; Brown, p. 198; IBL, 23 (1935), p. 94; O'Donoghue, p. 292; RIA/DIB.

M225 *The Irish legend; or, M'Donnell and the Norman de Burgos. A biographical tale* (by Archibald M'Sparran).

+ Philadelphia: Printed [for the author?] by A. Gross, 1846 (preface by the author, dated 1 July 1846; cover: harp and label 'Erin go bragh'). SOURCE OCLC. LOCATION PVU.

+ Coleraine: at the Chronicle Office by J. M'Combie, 1854 (printed from the author's improved American edn as *The Irish legend of M'Donnell and the Norman the Burgos. A biographical tale ... with an original appendix, containing historical and traditional records of the ancient families of the North of Ulster*). SOURCE NYPL. LOCATION Dt, BFl, NN, NUC, InND Loeber coll.

+ Dublin: M.H. Gill, n.d. SOURCE Emerald Isle cat. 89/1153. LOCATION InND Loeber coll.

+ Glasgow, London: Cameron, Ferguson & Co., [1869]. SOURCE Allibone Suppl., ii, p. 1061. LOCATION D, InND Loeber coll.

Limavady: North-West Books, 1986. LOCATION Dt.

COMMENTARY Brown (1078) mentions a Belfast edn of 1829, but this has not been located. The book purports to tell the history of a number of Ulster septs. The story starts at the Anglo-Norman invasion, but most of the action seems to take place in the early part of the sixteenth century. Since no dates are given for the historical events, it is not easy to place the story in time. The tale concerns mainly the struggles between the M'Quillans, O'Donnells, O'Neills, O'Cahans, and M'Donnells. Dunluce Castle (Co. Antrim) features in the story [ML].

MC SWINEY, Paul J., b. Cork 1856, d. New York, 1890. Musical composer, poet and novelist, PJM went to London soon after 1880 and contributed verse to periodicals there. In 1883 he left for New York where he produced an Irish opera, 'An Bárd 'gus an Fo' (The bard and the knight), under the auspices of the Gaelic Society there. He wrote several dramas. Some of his songs became popular in the US. SOURCE COPAC; O'Donoghue, p. 293.

M226 *Nirvana* (by Paul McSwiney).

[Location?], [Publisher?], [date?]. Source: O'Donoghue, p. 293.

COMMENTARY No copy located [RL].

MAC VICAR, Mrs Anne. See **GRANT, Mrs Anne.**

MAC WALTER, J.G., fl. 1852. Journalist and religious history and fiction writer, JGM was, according to the preface to his *The Irish Reformation movement* (Dublin, 1852) 'of' the *Warder* and *Dublin Evening Herald* newspapers. Aside from the following book of fiction, he published between 1852 and 1854 three books on religious history, one dealing with the Irish reformation and Protestant missionary movements (Dublin, 1852). In his *Tales of Ireland* (London, 1854) he announced the planned publication of a second series, but this does not appear to have been realized. Its intended contents were: 'Biddy Bourke's bridal; or, luckless love', 'The Ballingarry hero; or, a ride with the rebels', and 'Life and times of Dr Darby; being a peep at Protestant progress'. SOURCE Allibone, ii, p. 1198; BLC; RL.

M227 *Scarlet mystery* (by J.G. MacWalter).

+ London: James Nisbet & Co, 1854. SOURCE Allibone, ii, p. 1198. LOCATION L.

COMMENTARY Narrative is cast in 'an imaginative form'. Religious fiction set in Kilkee (Co. Clare). Probably mistakenly called *Modern mystery* by Allibone [AMB; ML; Allibone, ii, p. 1198].

M228 *Tales of Ireland and the Irish* (by J.G. MacWalter; dedicated to Benjamin Disraeli).

+ London: John Farquhar Shaw, 1854 (ill.). SOURCE Allibone, ii, p. 1198; Brown, 1080; OCLC. LOCATION L, NUC, InND Loeber coll.

COMMENTARY Three stories of anti-Catholic religious fiction: 'Betty Bryan's fortune; or, the magic of May' (story about superstitions), 'The Terry Alt; or, an excursion on the hills' (about insurrection), 'A memoir of Mortimer Mack-Carthy, Esq., being, real romance in a student's life' (ups and downs of wooing) [ML].

'MADAME PANACHE', pseud. See MOORE, Frances.

MADDEN Daniel Owen (also known as Daniel Owen Maddyn), pseud. 'Danby North', b. Mallow (Co. Cork) 1815, d. Dublin 1859. Journalist, attorney, novelist and anti-Catholic writer on politics and history, DOM was the son of Owen Madden, a Cork merchant, and Margaret Quain. He was educated in Cork and worked there before being admitted to the King's Inns in 1838 (he is not known to have been called to the Irish Bar). He was opposed to repeal of the Union, a pacifist, and an admirer of British imperialism. Nevertheless he was a friend of the poet-patriot Thomas Davis. He contributed articles to the *Citizen* (Dublin?). In 1842 he moved to London and around this time converted from catholicism to anglicanism. Although he enrolled in the Inner Temple, he did little legal work and devoted himself to writing. He was a staff member of the conservative paper the *Press* (London) from 1842 to 1857. His *Ireland and its rulers, since 1829* (London, 1843–44, 3 vols.) praised Davis but bitterly attacked Daniel O'Connell, which prompted O'Connell's description of Madden as 'odious and disgusting'. In 1846 he published the first volume of his *Age of Pitt and Fox* (London, 8 vols. projected). It was scathingly reviewed by John Mitchel in the *Nation* (Dublin). DOM did not complete the work nor did he write for the *Nation* again. He wrote *Revelations of Ireland in the past generation* (London 1848) and a memoir of the patriot and parliamentary reformer Henry Grattan, published with Thomas Davis's *The life of the Right Hon. J.P. Curran* (Dublin, 1846), and edited Grattan's speeches (Dublin, 1854).. DOM returned to Dublin in 1857 as Irish correspondent for the *Daily News* with instructions from his editor to continue writing history and biography. His final volume was *The chiefs of parties, past and present* (London, 1859, 2 vols.). He died in Dublin and was buried in Upper Shandon, Cork. SOURCE Allibone, ii, p. 1198; Allibone Suppl., ii, p. 1061; Boase, ii, p. 683; Brown 2, p. 173; Field Day, ii, p. 995*n*; Keane, p. 319; RIA/DIB.

M229 *Tales of the Munster circuit* (by Daniel Owen Madden).
       [location?]: [publisher?], [1844].
COMMENTARY No copy located. Advertised in *Ireland and its rulers* (London, 1843–44). Contents as advertised: 'The elopement from Ennis', 'Nights on the Shannon', 'The white rose of east Muskerry', 'The fate of genius', 'The bride of Duhallow', 'The Kerry hero', 'The drowned judge and his ghost', 'The breach of promise', 'Fair Fanny', 'Curran's last circuit' [RL].

M230 *Wynville; or, clubs and coteries. A novel* [anon.] (dedicated to Viscount Palmerston).
       + London: Charles J. Skeet, 1852, 3 vols. SOURCE COPAC. LOCATION L, E, C, NUC.

M231 *The game of brag; or, the battery boys. A comic novel* (by Daniel Owen Madden).
       London: C.J. Skeet, 1853, 2 vols. SOURCE Brown 2, 985; COPAC. LOCATION L.
COMMENTARY An anti-Catholic and anti-clerical political satire intended to be a picture of Irish political life setting out 'the peculiar process by which Battery Boys are converted into legislators and sent to play the game of Brag before a British Parliament'. Battery Boys are the Irish Nationalist party at a time when Irish politics had sunk to its lowest. Satire is unsparing and Irish politicians are pictured as vulgar and unscrupulous place hunters. A large part of the book is taken up with an election in Rathdowney (Co. Wexford or Co. Laois) and with lurid pictures of clerical domination [Brown 2].

M232 *The Mildmayes, or, the clergyman's secret: A story of twenty years ago* (by 'Danby North'; dedicated to Q.R.).

+ London: Chapman & Hall, 1856, 3 vols. SOURCE Allibone, ii, p. 1434 [under North]; COPAC [under North]. LOCATION L, E, C.

MADDEN, Mary Anne. See **SADLIER, Mrs J.**

MADDEN, R.R. See **MADDEN, Richard Robert.**

MADDEN, Richard Robert (known as **R.R. Madden**), b. Dublin 1798, d. Dublin 1886. Physician, anti-slavery advocate, colonial administrator, historian and man of letters, RRM was the son of Edward Madden, a manufacturer of Dublin, and Elizabeth Forde of Corry (Co. Leitrim), who came from an old Irish family. He studied at Chaigneau's academy in Dublin and later studied medicine in Paris, Naples and London. His subsequent travels in the Near East are recorded in *Travels in Turkey, Nubia, Egypt, Palestine &c. in 1824–27* (London, 1833, 2 vols.). In 1828, he married Harriet Elmslie of Jamaica, and practiced as a surgeon in London until 1833. In that year he was appointed a special magistrate to administer the Abolition of Slavery statute in Jamaica. After bitter quarrels with the planters he resigned in 1834, but returned to similar work in Havana (1836–40) where he was commissioner of arbitration in the mixed court of justice. In 1841 he published a searing indictment of Ottoman rule in Egypt and its tacit encouragement of the slave trade in Egypt and Sudan in *Egypt and Mohamed Ali: illustrative of his slaves and subjects, &c, &c*, based on a series of letters he wrote for the *Morning* Chronicle (London), for which he was a special correspondent. He was a commissioner of inquiry for the government in West Africa, worked in Lisbon as a special correspondent of the London *Morning Chronicle*, and served as colonial secretary and acting governor of Western Australia in 1847. He returned to Ireland in the next year and took up the cause of the Irish peasantry with the same passion he had shown for the freed slaves and the exploited Australian settlers. He wrote several books on the West Indies including *A twelve month's residence in the West Indies* (London, 1835, 2 vols.). He wrote on the penal laws, as well as a biography of Robert Emmet (Dublin 1847). His best known works are *The United Irishmen* (London, 1842–60, 11 vols.) and *Literary remains of the United Irishmen of 1798* (Dublin, 1887). In addition, he published *The history of Irish periodical literature* (1867, 2 vols.). He was a friend of Lady Blessington§ from his time in Italy and wrote *The literary life and correspondence of the countess of Blessington* (London, 1855), and also of Mrs J. Sadlier§, for whom he wrote historical notes to her *The fate of Father Sheehy* (Dublin, *c.*1847). Aside from the following novel, he was urged by Lady Blessington in 1834 to write a 'lively novel' descriptive of 'life in the West Indies', but such a work by him has not been identified. RRM is known also for his poetry, some of which was published in his memoirs, edited by his son T.M. Madden. His library was auctioned on Nov. 20, 1865. RRM was buried in the Donnybrook churchyard, Dublin. For RRM's portraits, see ODNB. Some of his correspondence and papers are in the Catholic University of America, Washington (DC), TCD, the RIA and the BL (for additional details, see ODNB). SOURCE Allibone, ii, p. 1199; Allibone Suppl., ii, 1061; Brady, pp 154–5; *The collection of autograph letters ... historical documents formed by Alfred Morrison (second series, 1882–1893)*. *The Blessington papers* (n.l., 1895), p. 30; Elmes, p. 127; Field Day, iv, pp 855–6, 892–3; Irish pseudonyms; Landed gentry, 1904, p. 376; List of catalogues, p. 313; T.M. Madden, *Memoirs of Dr. R.R. Madden* (New York, 1892); L. Ó Broin, 'R.R. Madden, historian of the United Irishmen', *Irish University Review* (1972); OCIL, p. 349; ODNB; O'Donoghue, p. 293; RIA/DIB; RL.

M233 *The mussulman, or life in Turkey* (by R.R. Madden; dedicated to author's departed mother [Elizabeth Madden]).

+ London: Henry Colburn & Richard Bentley, 1830, 3 vols. SOURCE Wolff, 4368; NYPL; Garside 2, 1830:76. LOCATION Corvey CME 3–628–48141–4, D, L, NN, InND Loeber coll.

Philadelphia: Carey & Lea, 1830, 2 vols. SOURCE Kaser, 233. LOCATION PPL-R, NUC. COMMENTARY RRM received 300 guineas from his publishers for this novel. Set at the beginning of the nineteenth century, the story begins at the eastern part of the Mediterranean where a Turkish aga has many Greeks living under him. The hero, Mourad, has been taken into the aga's household after the aga has sent Mourad's father away to do sea duty and has driven Mourad's mother insane by his advances. Mourad grows up without knowing that his parents are Christian Greeks. When Mourad's father returns, the aga has him killed. Mourad learns of his background from an old Greek, and the rest of his life is filled with revenge and wild adventures that take him to many places around the eastern Mediterranean and Egypt. He tries his hand at various professions, including astrology and medicine, but he is best suited for the life of a soldier [ML].

MADDEN, Revd Samuel Molyneux, b. Dublin 1686, d. Drummully (Co. Fermanagh) 1765. Church of Ireland clergyman, writer and philanthropist, SMM was the second son of John Madden of Manor Waterhouse (Co. Fermanagh), and Mary Molyneux. He received his BA from TCD in 1705 and his DD degree in 1723. He became rector of Drummully, near Newtownbutler (Co. Fermanagh). Besides a heavy involvement in the civic life of the area, he was an active author, and through the Royal Dublin Society (his brother John was a founding member) he promoted his ideas on agricultural improvement, architecture, philanthropy and education. One of his most important books was *Reflections and resolutions proper for the gentlemen of Ireland* (Dublin, 1738; repr. Dublin, 1814), in which he decried landlord absenteeism and the extravagance and idleness of the people. He was known as 'Premium Madden' because of a scheme of educational grants he established at TCD, to which he contributed generously. Besides his successful *Themistocles* (Dublin, 1729), a verse tragedy, he wrote several panegyric poems, an introduction in verse to Thomas Leland's§ *The history of the life and reign of Philip, king of Macedon* (London, 1758, 2 vols.), and *A proposal for the general encouragement of learning in Dublin College* (Dublin, 1731). He was a friend of Jonathan Swift§ and of Dr Samuel Johnson. Arthur Young said SMM was 'one of the most patriotic individuals which any country has ever produced' (RIA/DIB). SMM married in 1709 Jane Magill and they had five sons and five daughters and made their home at Manor Waterhouse. For SMM's portraits, see Elmes and ODNB. SOURCE B & S, pp 543–4; Elmes, pp 127–8. Field Day, iv, pp 774–5, 823; Gilbert, p. 522; Landed gentry, 1904, p. 375; OCIL, p. 350; ODNB; O'Donoghue, p. 294; RIA/DIB.

M234 *Memoirs of the twentieth century. Being original letters of state under George the Sixth: relating to the most important events in Great-Britain and Europe, as to church and state, arts and sciences, trade, taxes, and treaties, peace and war: and characters of the greatest persons of those times; from the middle of the eighteenth, to the end of the twentieth century, and the world. Received and revealed in the year 1728; and now published for the instruction of all eminent statesmen, churchmen, patriots, politicians, projectors, Papists and Protestants. In six volumes* [anon.].
+ London: Osborn, Longmans, Davis & Batley, Strahan & Clarke, Rivington, Robinson, Astley & Austen, Gosling, Nourse, Prevost & Millar, Parker, Joliffe, Brindley, Shropshire & Smith & Gouge & Stagg, 1733, vol. 1 [all published]. SOURCE McBurney, 284; Maggs cat. 477/1093; Hodges Figgis cat. 10 n.s./1918; Gilbert, p. 522; ESTC t124606. LOCATION DPL Gilbert coll., L.

London: W. Nicholl, 1763 (as *The reign of George VI*). SOURCE ESTC t070919; Raven, 783; OCLC. Location Dt, L, MH.

COMMENTARY Satire against George II and court, written as an imaginary history of England at the beginning of the twentieth century; six volumes projected; a thousand copies printed of volume 1, but the book was suppressed within two weeks of publication, and no more volumes appeared. The author is said to have destroyed all but three volumes, but this appears unlikely [Gilbert; preface to [Samuel Madden], *Reflections and resolutions proper for the use of gentlemen of Ireland* (Dublin, 1816), p. iv; RL; Maggs].

MAGENNIS, Peter, b. near Derrygonnelly (Co. Fermanagh) 1817, d. at his birthplace 1910. Teacher, poet and fiction writer, PM was the son of a farmer and taught in the National School. He wrote the preface to *Tully Castle* (Dublin, 1877) from Knockmore (Co. Fermanagh). His poems were published in Enniskillen in 1844 and 1888. He contributed stories to periodicals and an early one, 'Mary Stuart O'Donnell', won a £10 prize in the Dublin *Freeman's Journal.* SOURCE Brady, p. 155; Brown, p. 200; Hogan 2, p. 810; O'Donoghue, p. 295; RIA/DIB.

M235   *The Ribbon informer. A tale of Lough Erne* (by Peter Magennis).
London: F. Bell & Co., 1874. SOURCE Brown, 1083; Hogan 2, p. 810. LOCATION L.
COMMENTARY The story contains local traditions and legendary lore. It also describes highway robbery, illicit distilling, rural manners, and party feelings [Brown]

M236   *Tully Castle. A tale of the Irish rebellion* (by Peter Magennis; dedicated to Lady Wilde§).
+ Dublin: M.H. Gill & Son; Enniskillen: William Trimble, 1877. LOCATION D, DPL, InND Loeber coll.
COMMENTARY Concerns the outbreak of the rebellion of 1641 in Ulster and is written from the point of view of the displaced Irish. Contains a love affair, abductions, etc. Set chiefly on the shores of Lough Erne, and describes its beauties. Tells of the unsuccessful attack on Dublin and the trial of Lord Maguire, one of the hereditary chieftains of Fermanagh. The volume abounds with poems and songs [ML; Brown].

MAGINN, Dr. —. See **MAGINN, William.**

MAGINN, Daniel Wentworth, probable pseud. '**An officer of the line**', fl. 1827. Military surgeon, possibly Irish, DWM is identified in British Fiction (Update 4). He is not be confused with the Revd Henry Woodward§, who used the same pseudonym. SOURCE RL; British Fiction (Updates 1 and 4).

M237   *The military sketch-book. Reminiscences of seventeen years in the service abroad and at home* (by 'An officer of the line').
+ London: Henry Colburn, 1827, 2 vols. SOURCE British Fiction; Garside, 1827:51. LOCATION L, InND Loeber coll.
COMMENTARY Sketches about military life mainly set during the Peninsular War, implausibly attributed to William Maginn§. Some of the stories are told in a guardhouse in the Wicklow mountains. Several stories have Irish officers and soldiers as main characters. Contents: 'First week in the service', 'The soldier's orphan', 'Nights in the guard-house', 'No. I: story of Maria de Carmo', 'Old Charley', 'Mess-table chat, No. I', 'A daughter of Ossian', 'The muleteer', 'Rations or else', 'Infernal duty', 'Nights in the guard-house, No. II', 'The fate of young Gore', 'Recollections of the Walcheren expedition', 'Journal of a campaign at the horse-guards', 'Mess-table chat, No. II', 'Geraghty's kick', 'Duelling in the service', 'Nights in the guard-house, No. III', 'The biscuit', 'The battle of the grinders', 'A rough passage to Portugal', 'Nights in the guard-house, No. IV', 'Absent without leave', 'The punishment', 'Eccentricities of the late Morris Quill', 'Mess-table chat, No. III', 'Recollections of the last campaign in the Peninsula', 'Nights in the guard-house, No. V', 'Holy orders', 'A little consequence', 'The hussar and the

commissary', 'Allemar and Ellen', 'The coup de grace', 'A volunteer of forty', 'The half-pay captain', 'Mess-table chat, No. IV (a sketch for the 'medicos')', 'Nights in the guard-house, No. VI (the bush-rangers)' [ML; NCBEL 3, p. 1294].

M238 *Tales of military life* (by the author of the *Military sketch book*; dedicated to Sir George Murray, by the author, who was an officer in his regiment).
+ London: Henry Colburn, 1829, 3 vols. SOURCE British Fiction; Garside, 1829:58; Rafroidi, ii, p. 235. LOCATION Corvey CME 3-628-48864-8, Ireland related fiction, Dt, L, MH, InND Loeber coll.
COMMENTARY Implausibly attributed to William Maginn§ (e.g., NCBEL 3, p. 1294; Garside, 1829:58; Harris, p. 190). Contents: 'Vandeleur' (initially set in Ireland, and describes Robert Emmet's rising in 1803. Most of the military action, however, takes place in the Iberian Peninsula, where the British army is fighting the French. A love story is interwoven, and a young officer who did not know his parentage turns out to be of noble origin and the owner of considerable wealth, which had been kept from him by deceit); 'Gentleman Gray' (takes place a little later when the British army is fighting Bonaparte in Belgium and northern France. Gray is a young man of good birth, but at his father's death it turns out that he is penniless and cannot fulfil his dream of becoming an officer. He decides to enroll in the ranks and hopes that by bravery he may reach his goal. He marries his childhood sweetheart, who also finds herself to be poor. The commanding officer of his regiment, unbeknownst to Gray, persecutes Gray's wife with unwanted advances. When Gray finds out, he kills him in a duel and is sentenced to death. Just before the execution the sentence is reversed and he is freed in time to see his wife die). Note that Countess Mariana Pisani (formerly Mrs Col. Garner) wrote *Vandeleur; or, animal magnetism* (London, 1836, 3 vols.), which is not related to the story in this volume [ML; Garside 2, 1836:56].

MAGINN, J.D., fl. 1889, novelis.
M239 *Fitzgerald the Fenian. A novel* (by J.D. Maginn).
+ London: Chapman & Hall, 1889, 2 vols. SOURCE Brown, 1085; Wolff, 4371; OCLC.
LOCATION D (incomplete), Dt, L, NUC.
COMMENTARY Set mainly in Co. Sligo and deals with the Fenian and Land League movements. The land agitation is represented as forced upon an unwilling peasantry by a kind of murder club in America. Home rule politicians Charles Stuart Parnell and Joseph Biggar are brought in under assumed names. Isaac Butt§ is also portrayed [Brown].

MAGINN, William (known as Dr Maginn), pseud. 'Morgan', b. Marlborogh's Fort (Co. Cork) 1793, d. Walton-on-Thames (Surrey) 1842. Writer, editor, poet and parodist, WM was the son of John Maginn, a classical scholar and schoolmaster, and Anne Eccles. A precocious and brilliant child, WM entered TCD at age 11 and graduated BA in classics in 1811. He returned to Cork to assist his father in running an academy, which he did for several years after his father's death, a task for which he was well-equipped given his knowledge of classical and English literature and his extraordinary facility with languages, including Irish. He returned to TCD and obtained his LLB and LLD in 1819. He began to contribute poems and parodies (including one of Thomas Moore§ as Maginn despised him for being what he considered pseudo-Irish) first to the *Freeholder*, a Cork newspaper, and then to *Blackwood's Magazine* (Edinburgh). In 1823 he went to London and, using innumerable pseuds, wrote stories and verse for London periodicals, including the *London Literary Gazette*, *Bentley's Miscellany*, *John Bull*, *Age* and *Argus*. He married Ellen Ryder Bullen of Cork in 1824. He contributed some stories to [Thomas Crofton Croker's§] *Fairy legends and traditions of the South of Ireland* (London, 1825), and to (anon.) *The ancient Irish tales* (Drogheda, 1829).

Despite an interest in Gaelic Ireland, he was one of the writers, along with others such as Charles Lever§ and Samuel Lover§ considered to have promoted the image of the stage-Irishman in the English press. When he was appointed joint editor of the Tory newspaper the *Standard* (London), WM used it as a vehicle in which he opposed Catholic emancipation, bitterly attacked England's treatment of Ireland, and argued against the anti-slavery campaign, saying the government should first take care of its own working poor. In 1830 he jointly founded *Fraser's Magazine* (London), for many years one of the most brilliant monthly magazines in England. WM was one of the most important contributors to *Blackwood*'s *Noctes Ambrosianæ* (Edinburgh), which ran from 1822 to 1835, and he became one of the highest-paid contributors to that magazine. But his intemperate habits and generosity brought bankruptcy, illness, and time in debtors' prison, an incident captured by Maginn's protégé W.M. Thackeray§ in his novel *History of Pendennis* (London, 1878). S.C. Hall wrote that 'through … his habits of intoxication … his position was low when it ought to have been high' (S.C. Hall, p. 159). He was a facile writer, a brilliant conversationalist (he and Francis Mahony§ played literary games in several languages), and was much admired by, among others, Edward Kenealy§, in whose *Brallaghan, or the Deipnosophists* (London, 1845) WM features, and by Robert Shelton McKenzie§ who edited a compilation of *Noctes ambrosianae* (New York, 1863–65). Both these writers wrote biographical sketches of their friend. WM collaborated with Samuel Ferguson§ and John Fisher Murray§ on *Father Tom and the Pope* (first serialized in *Blackwood's Magazine*, Edinburgh, 1838, and subsequently published as a volume in many edns; see under Samuel Ferguson§). WM also wrote 'How Father Tom taught the pope to mix punch', published in *Irish pleasantry and fun. A selection of the best humorous tales by Carleton, Lover, Lever, and other popular writers* (Dublin, 1882), which would seem to confirm a Maginn hand in the *Father Tom* stories. WM's *Shakespeare papers; pictures grave and gay* (London, 1859) was compiled from pieces that had appeared originally in the London *Bentley's Miscellany* under the title 'Shakspeare [*sic*] papers'. Some books have been ascribed to WM but have since been rejected, including *Tales of military life* (London, 1829, 3 vols.). WM died in poverty in 1842. Several of his letters and a poem are in the Henry E. Huntington Library, San Marino (CA). His letters to Thomas Crofton Croker§ are in Cork City Library and the NLI. Other papers are in the NLS and Yale University (for additional collections, see ODNB). For WM's portraits, see ODNB, Elmes, Strickland, and Laffan & Rooney (Fig. 9). SOURCE Allibone , ii, pp 1201–2; B & S, p. 546; Boylan, p. 236; D. & M. Coakley, *Wit and wine* (Peterhead, 1975), pp 6–22, 55–71; Elmes, p. 128; Field Day, ii, pp 4, 112, 1011; S.C. Hall, p. 159; Harris, p. 190; Hogan, pp 429–30; Hogan 2, pp 810–11; W. Laffan & B. Rooney, '"One of our brilliant ornaments": the death and life of Thomas Foster' in *Irish Architectural and Decorative Studies*, 7 (2004), pp 201, 203; McKenna, p. 254–6; NCBEL 4, p. 2191; OCIL, pp 350–1; ODNB; O'Donoghue, pp 295–7; M. Sadleir, *Bulwer: A panorama* (London 1931), pp 221–9; Schulz, p. 282; Strickland, i, p. 596; Sutherland, p. 402; RIA/DIB.

M240 *Whitehall; or, the days of George IV* [anon.] (dedicated to Sir Edmund Nagle). + London: William Marsh, [1827]. SOURCE Rafroidi, ii, p. 235; British Fiction; Garside, 1827:52; Sadleir, 1520; NYPL; NCBEL 3, p. 1291. LOCATION Corvey CME 3-628-48905-9, Dt, L, NN, NUC, InND Loeber coll.

COMMENTARY Rafroidi notes uncertain authorship but it is included in WM's work by ODNB and other sources. Humorous satire on the historical novels so popular at that time, particularly *Brambletye House, or, Cavaliers and Roundheads* (London, 1826, 3 vols.) by the writer and humorist Horatio Smith (1779–1849) and Benjamin Disraeli's *Popanilla* (London, n.d.). Contains footnotes referring to fake authorities [Coakley, p. 58; ODNB; Rafroidi, ii, p. 235; British Fiction; M. Sadleir, *Bulwer: A panorama* (London 1931), p. 225].

Maginn

M241 *The red barn. A tale, founded on fact* [anon.].
+ London: Knight & Lacey, 1828 (ill. R. Seymour, Phiz). SOURCE J & S, 391; Sadleir, 1521 (ascribes this book to WM); Wolff, 4376; Brown 2, 988; British Fiction; Garside, 1828:53. LOCATION L, NUC.
COMMENTARY The BL in one copy ascribes this to Robert Huish, but in another copy to WM. ODNB includes it in WM's work. Set in Suffolk and concerns the story of a murder. Folding facsimile letter in this novel contains 'Trial of William Corder, for the murder of Maria Marten'. No Irish content [ML; Garside; ODNB; British Fiction].

M242 *The suicide. A tale founded on facts* (by the author of *Red barn*).
+ London: John Knight, [1828 or later], No. 1 (all published; ill. R. Seymour). SOURCE Block, p. 150 (mentions [1825?] but this probably is incorrect); NSTC; RL. LOCATION L.
COMMENTARY 48pp. Advertisement states that the story was to be continued to 30 numbers, but only one appeared. Set in England in Cumberland and Windermere [CM].

M243 *Magazine miscellanies* (by Dr Maginn).
+ [n.l.]: [n.p.], 1841. SOURCE Rafroidi, ii, p. 235; Sadleir, 1516 (*c.*1840); Harris, p. 190 (1840 or 1841); NCBEL 4, p. 2191; COPAC. LOCATION L.
COMMENTARY Rafroidi notes uncertain authorship. Tales, verses, maxims etc. Contents of stories: 'A story without a tail', 'Bob Burke's duel with Ensign Brady of the 48th', 'First love', 'The man in the bell', 'The mask; or, part of a story', 'Pococurante', 'A love story in three chapters', 'The spear-head', 'The two Butlers' (first published in *Bentley's Miscellany*, 1837), 'My last love', 'A night of terror', 'Irish stories' [Harris; NCBEL 4, p. 2191; Rafroidi, ii, p. 235].

M244 *John Manesty, the Liverpool merchant* (by the late William Maginn, LLD; completed by the publisher Charles Ollier; dedicated by author's widow to J.G. Lockhart).
+ London: John Mortimer, 1844, 2 vols. (ill. George Cruikshank). SOURCE Hodgson, p. 357; Rafroidi, ii, p. 235 (uncertain authorship); Sutherland, p. 402; NCBEL 4, p. 2192; Sadleir, 1515; Wolff, 4374; NYPL. LOCATION L, NN ([1843] edn), NUC (1843–44 edn), InND Loeber coll.
COMMENTARY This and the following works were published posthumously. Set around 1760 in Liverpool and features John Manesty, an important and wealthy merchant who seems to lead an upright life and converses much with dissenting ministers. One topic of discussion among the merchants and the religious leaders is the slave trade and plantations that use slaves. When Manesty inherits a plantation in the West Indies, he asks the divines whether he is justified in keeping it or not. They give him their blessing with the justification that the slaves would be worse off without the plantation. Manesty then disappears regularly for months on end to attend to his plantation. At a certain point a sailor in Liverpool accuses him of being a notorious pirate and slave-trader. This seemingly preposterous accusation is slowly substantiated and in the end it appears that Manesty had led a double life [ML].

M245 *Maxims of Sir Morgan O'Doherty, Bart.* [anon.].
+ Edinburgh, London: William Blackwood & Sons, 1849. SOURCE Rafroidi, ii, p. 235 (notes uncertain authorship); Sadleir, 1517; Wolff, 4375; Brown 2, 898. LOCATION L, NUC, InND Loeber coll.
COMMENTARY A parody of La Rochefoucauld. First appeared in *Blackwood's Magazine* (Edinburgh, 1824) [NCBEL 4, p. 2191].

M246 *Miscellaneous writings of the late Dr. Maginn.*
New York: Redfield, 1855–7, 5 vols. (ed. by Dr Shelton MacKenzie§). SOURCE Rafroidi, ii, p. 236; Brown, 1086; Sadleir, 1518; NCBEL 3, p. 1293. LOCATION Grail, L, NUC.

COMMENTARY Consists mostly of nonfiction under the headings: The O'Doherty papers, Shakespeare papers, Homeric ballads and comedies of Lucian, and The Fraserian papers, with a life of the author. Fiction in the O'Doherty papers: 'Memoirs of Ensign and Adjutant O'Doherty', 'The man in the bell', 'Pococurante', 'A story without a tail', 'Bob Burke's duel with Ensign Brady'; 'Pandemus Polyglott', 'A traveller's week', 'The night walker', 'First love', 'The last words of Charles Edwards, Esq.' [Harris, p. 190; RL].

M247 *Miscellanies: prose and verse* (ed. by R.W. Montagu, with memoir of author).
+ London: Sampson Low & Co., 1885, 2 vols. SOURCE NCBEL 2, p. 1293. LOCATION Grail, L, NUC, InND Loeber coll.
COMMENTARY Contents (except poetry): 'The man in the bell', 'Pococurante', 'The last words of Charles Edwards, Esq.', 'A story without a tail', 'Bob Burke's duel with Ensign Brady of the 48th', 'A vision of purgatory' [Harris, p. 190].

M248 *A story without a tail* (by William Maginn; preface by George Saintsbury).
+ London: Elkin Mathews, 1928. SOURCE Brown 2, 987. LOCATION DPL, L, NUC.
COMMENTARY Originally published in *Magazine Miscellanies* and *Tales from Blackwood*, (Edinburgh, 1858, vol. 2) [RL; Brown 2; BLC].

M249 *Ten tales* (by William Maginn; preface signed W.B.).
+ London: Eric Partridge, 1933. SOURCE Brown 2, 986; NCBEL 4, p. 2191; McKenna, p. 255; NYPL. LOCATION D, L, NN, NUC.
COMMENTARY Ten stories along with a biographical sketch of the author. Several of the following stories originally appeared in Thomas Crofton Croker's§ *Fairy legends and traditions of the South of Ireland* (London, 1825–28), and had been wrongly attributed to TCC instead of to WM. Contents: 'The man in the bell', 'Bob Burke's duel with Ensign Brady of the 48th', 'The two Butlers of Kilkenny', 'A vision of purgatory', 'The legend of Bottle Hill', 'The legend of Knockshegowna', 'The legend of Knockgrafton', 'Daniel O'Rourke', 'Jochonan in the city of demons', 'A night of terror' [RL; NYPL].

MAGUIRE, John Francis, b. Cork 1815, d. Dublin 1872. Barrister, politician, editor, historian and biographer, JFM was the eldest son of John Maguire, a Cork merchant, and Ellen Jackson. He was educated in Cork, admitted to the Middle Temple (London) in 1838 and to the King's Inns in 1840 and called to the Irish Bar in 1843. JFM founded the pro-O'Connell newspaper the *Cork Examiner* in 1841 and was for many years its editor. He was elected an Irish Independent Party MP for Dungarvan (Co. Waterford) from 1852 to 1865, and then returned by his native city of Cork. He sat as a liberal after the demise of the Irish Independent Party. He was several times mayor of Cork. In parliament he represented the voice of a nationalist, Catholic, constitutional alternative to Fenianism. He fought hard for tenants' rights, disestablishment of the Church of Ireland, public education, and reform of oppressive poor laws, while refusing the offer of high office. He toured the US and Canada in the 1860s and his subsequent book *Ireland in America* (London, 1848–50) describing the industry of the Irish population there influenced British prime minister W.E. Gladstone to trust JFM to convey his proposed reforms through his newspaper. JFM's other works include *The industrial movement in Ireland* (Cork, 1853); *The life of Father Mathew* (London, 1863), and *Rome and its rulers* (London, 1857), which went into a second edn in 1879. In 1843 he married Margaret Bailey of Cork who, as Mrs. John Francis Maguire§, was later an author of children's books. He died in Dublin in 1872 and was buried at the St Joseph cemetery, Cork. For JFM's portrait and papers, see ODNB. SOURCE Allibone, ii, p. 1202; Allibone Suppl., ii, p. 1062; Boase, ii, p. 692; Keane, p. 322; ODNB; RIA/DIB; Wolff, iii, p. 83.

M250 *The next generation* (by John Francis Maguire; dedicated to 'one of the best of women').

+ London: Hurst & Blackett, 1871, 3 vols. SOURCE Wolff, 4388; OCLC. LOCATION D, RB, L, NUC, InND Loeber coll.

COMMENTARY Pro-feminist fiction, set twenty years into the future and describes the British parliament of 1891. A large portion of the members are female and hold important positions. India and China are part of the Commonwealth. Like men, the women have their own clubs in London. Home Rule has been restored to Ireland, and Ireland is at peace with its neighbour. Some of the main characters in the book are Irish. Although the female members of parliament are generally very intelligent and competent, their eventual lot is marriage with, as a consequence, withdrawal from public office [ML].

— COLLECTED WORKS

M251 [*John Francis Maguire's works*].
New York, Montreal: D. & J. Sadlier & Co., [1875 or earlier]. SOURCE Adv. in M.J. Hoffman, *The orphan sisters* (New York, 1875).
COMMENTARY Unnumbered and untitled series. No copy located [RL].

MAGUIRE, Mrs John Francis (née Margaret Bailey), fl. 1873, b. Cork, d. Ireland? *c*.1905. Writer of children's stories and poet, she married the author John Francis Maguire§ in 1843. SOURCE Allibone Suppl., ii, p. 1062; ODNB [under John Francis Maguire]; O'Donoghue, p. 297; RL.

M252 *Young prince Marigold, and other fairy stories* (by Mrs John Francis Maguire).
London: Macmillan & Co., 1873 (ill. S.E. Waller). LOCATION L, NUC.
COMMENTARY Listed in O'Donoghue OCLC, and ODNB under author's husband's name, but correctly attributed in COPAC. Fiction for juveniles. Contents: 'Young prince Marigold and his little ponies, Daisy and Lilly', 'Autobiography of a cat', 'Jack Tubbes; or, the happy isle' [COPAC; NUC; OCLC; O'Donoghue, p. 297].

M253 *Beauty and the beast: A play, with a new version of old fables, an episode and an allegory, also two proverbs illustrated* (by Mrs John Francis Maguire).
+ Dublin: M.H. Gill & Son, 1878. SOURCE COPAC. LOCATION UCC, L.
COMMENTARY Included with the play are: 'The mouse and the lion', 'Marry in haste, repent at leisure. A true story', 'Short accounts, make long friends', 'The man with the pail of milk on his head', 'The countryman and the adder', 'Honesty the best policy. A fable', 'The fox and the crow', 'The lion and other beasts hunting', 'The dog in the manger', 'An allegory' [RL].

MAGUIRE, Justin, fl. 1880s. Novelist.

M254 *Alastor. An Irish story of to-day* (by Justin Maguire).
+ London: Simpkin, Marshall & Co.; Dublin, Belfast: Eason & Son, [1888]. SOURCE Allibone Suppl., ii, p. 1062; Topp 8, 893. LOCATION D, Dt, L, NUC.
COMMENTARY Set in the second half of the nineteenth century in rural Ireland, it describes a tenant family losing their land, and interweaves a love story [ML].

MAHER, Mary, fl. 1898. Catholic religious writer, MM was probably Irish as she also published *Footsteps of Irish saints in the dioceses of Ireland* (London, 1927). SOURCE BLC.

M255 *Not up to date. A Catholic story* (by Mary Maher).
+ Dublin: James Duffy & Co., n.d. SOURCE OCLC. LOCATION D.

M256 *Fidelity. A Catholic story with glints from real life* (by Mary Maher).
London: Burns & Oates; New York, Cincinnati: Benziger Bros, 1898. SOURCE Brown 2, 992; Alston, p. 275; OCLC. LOCATION L.
COMMENTARY Religious fiction. The story traces the careers of two Irish convent school girls. One of them goes to America and the other to England. In spite of various temptations and

difficulties, they remain faithful to their faith and the lessons taught them in their school [Brown 2].

M257 *Her father's trust. A Catholic story* (by Mary Maher).
London: Burns & Oates, 1900. SOURCE Alston, p. 275; COPAC. LOCATION L (destroyed), E.
COMMENTARY Religious fiction [BLC].

MAHON, Lady Jane (née King), pseud. 'Lady M.', b. Co. Offaly?, d. 1895. Writer and unpublished novelist, JM was the daughter of Church of Ireland clergyman Henry King of Ballylin (Co. Offaly), and Harriet Lloyd (sister of the countess of Rosse). She married in 1853 Revd Sir William R. Mahon, 4th Bt, of Castlegar (Co. Galway). With her sister, the Hon. Mary Ward§, she wrote *Entomology in sport, and entomology in earnest* (London, [1859], using the pseudonym 'Lady M.'), which are partly in the form of dialogues with children. JM's writing desk is held by a descendant. SOURCE BLC; Personal communication, George Gossip, April 1993; Landed gentry, 1912, p. 369; ODNB [under Mary Ward]; H. Shiel, *Falling into wretchedness. Ferbane in the late 1830s* (Maynooth, 1998); Wolff, 4389.
M258 *The golden chain* (by Lady Jane Mahon).
COMMENTARY Unpublished manuscript novel, dated 1878, consisting of two note books, written on lined paper, 1st volume, 243 written pages, rest blank, with photo, presumably of author; 2nd note book consisting of 260 written pages, with label of Charles Chambers, Stationer, Dublin on front end-paper. Present location not known [Wolff, 4389].

MAHONY, Fr Francis Sylvester, pseuds 'Oliver Yorke', 'Father Prout', and 'Don Jeremy Savonarola', b. Cork 1804, d. Paris 1866. Catholic priest, poet, journalist and miscellaneous writer, FSM was the third son of Martin Mahony, a well-to-do woollen manufacturer of Blarney (Co. Cork), and Maria Reynolds. He was educated at Clongowes Wood College (Co. Kildare), which he entered in 1815. Aspiring to be a Jesuit, he studied in Amiens, Paris and Rome. He was appointed to the staff of Clongowes in 1830 but a late night frolic led to his resignation and to the termination of his membership in the society. He then entered the Irish College in Rome and was ordained priest in Lucca in 1832. He was briefly assigned to a parish outside Cork and worked valiantly during the cholera epidemic there in 1832, but after a disagreement with the bishop he went to London in about 1835 and soon after discontinued his active life as a priest. He began to write for various periodicals, especially for the London *Fraser's Magazine* (under William Maginn§, also from Cork) and later for the London *Bentley's Miscellany*, under Charles Dickens. He developed the fictional character of Fr. Prout based on a real priest from Watergrasshill in Cork (described by Mahony as the child of Jonathan Swift§ and Esther (Stella) Johnson) as a vehicle for FSM's comments on literature and the literati. His active social life included visits to Lady Blessington§ and William Makepeace Thackeray§. He left London in 1837, travelled widely, and settled first in Italy, where he was a correspondent for the London *Daily News*, and then in Paris in the early 1850s where he was a correspondent for the *Globe and Traveller* (London) and continued to contribute to *Fraser's Magazine*. Sir J. Crowe found that 'His neglect of the graces of the toilet made him difficult to approach; but he had a big voice, and he kept his hearers in fits of laughter by an inexhaustible series of anecdotes and epigrams' (Crowe, p. 72). Frank Thorpe Porter visited him in London and found his conversation remarkable for a journalist, never touching on political or religious differences. In 1835, however, William Charles Macready had found him 'churlish in his manners', and in 1847 a 'drunk, and a wild dissolute character, though certainly a clever man'. FSM was well-known for his verse, much of it humorous or satirical. He was multilingual and translated verse, including poems of Thomas Moore§, into Latin,

French and Greek and then proceeded to make mock accusations of plagiarism against Moore. He wrote almost until the end of his life and before his death he was reconciled to the church and was anointed by a priest friend. He was buried in Shandon Church in Cork, the bells of which he had immortalized in his most famous ballad. FSM featured in Edward Kenealy's§ book *Brallaghan, or the Deipnosophists* (London, 1845) and Kenealy speaks of FSM's charity towards those in need. William Allingham§ visited him in Paris in 1858, where he lived in a hotel on the rue des Moulins. For FSM's portraits and papers, see ODNB. The sculptor John Hogan made a bust of 'Father Prout'. SOURCE Allibone, ii, p. 1205; H. Allingham & D. Radford (eds), *William Allingham. A diary* (London, 1985), pp 77–8; Boase, ii, p. 695; Boylan, p. 328; D. & M. Coakley, *Wit and wine* (Peterhead, 1975), pp 42, 84; Sir J. Crowe, *Reminiscences of thirty-five years of my life* (London, 1895), pp 72, 76, 100; Crowley, pp 397–424; Field Day, ii, pp 4, 9, 38, 112, 1011; Hogan, 2. pp 1040–1 [under Prout]; A. Kenealy, *Memoirs of Edward Vaughan Kenealy LL.D.* (London, 1908), pp 101–2; J.E. McGee, *The glories of Ireland* (New York, 1877), pp 168, 175; S.C. Hall, pp 237–9; B. Jerrold, *The final reliques of Father Prout* (London, 1876); McKenna, pp 257–9; E. Mannin, *Two studies in integrity: Gerald Griffin and the Rev. Francis Mahony (Father Prout)* (London, 1954); MVP, pp 298–9; NCBEL 4, p. 2239; OCIL, p. 352; ODNB; O'Donoghue, p. 298; O'Donoghue 2, p. 428; F.T. Porter, *Gleanings and reminiscences* (Dublin, 1875), pp 468–72; RIA/DIB; Schulz, p. 282; Strickland, i, p. 495; W. Toynbee (ed.), *The diaries of William Charles Macready 1833–1851* (London, 1912), i, p. 248; ii, p. 370.

M259 *The reliques of Father Prout late P.P. of Watergrasshill in the County of Cork, Ireland* (collected and arranged by 'Oliver Yorke, Esq.').

+ London: James Fraser, 1836, 2 vols. (ill. Alfred Croquis [i.e., Daniel Maclise]). SOURCE Rafroidi, ii, p. 238; Sadleir, 1523; Wolff, 4390. LOCATION D, Dt, L, NUC, InND Loeber coll.

+ London: Henry G. Bohn, 1860 (new edn, revsd and largely augmented; ill. Alfred Croquis [Daniel Maclise]; Bohn's Illustrated Library). SOURCE Sadleir, 1523b. LOCATION BFl, InND Loeber coll.

COMMENTARY Contents: 'Father Prout's apology for lent', 'A plea for pilgrimages', 'Sir W. Scott's visit to the Blarney stone', 'The groves of Blarney', 'The Watergrasshill carousel', 'Dean Swift's madness', 'The rogueries of Tom Moore', 'Literature and the Jesuits', 'Vert-vert, a poem by Gresset', 'The songs of France', 'Wine and war', 'Women and wooden shoes', 'Philosophy', 'The songs of Italy', 'Jerome Vida's silkworm' [Rafroidi].

M260 *Facts and figures from Italy. By Don Jeremy Savonarola, Benedictine monk. Addressed during the last two winters to Charles Dickens, Esq.: being an appendix to his "Pictures".*

London: Richard Bentley, 1847. SOURCE McKenna, p. 259; Block, p. 150; Sadleir, 1522. LOCATION Grail, L, NUC.

COMMENTARY It is not clear to which of Dickens' works "Pictures" refers [RL].

— COLLECTED WORKS

M261 *The works of Father Prout (The Revd Francis Mahony).*

+ London, New York: George Routledge & Sons, [1881] (ed. and biographical introd. by Charles Kent). LOCATION Grail, L, InND Loeber coll.

COMMENTARY Includes *The reliques* (London, 1832) and 'Miscellaneous pieces', but not *Facts and figures* (London, 1847) nor certain unpublished pieces that figure in B. Jerrold's edn of *The final reliques* (London, 1876) [Rafroidi, ii, p. 239].

MAHONY, M.F. See **MAHONY, Martin Francis.**

MAHONY, Martin Francis (known as M.F. Mahony), pseud. 'Matthew Stradling', b. Cork 1831, d. 1885 (1882 according to Burke). Novelist, MFM was the eldest son of Martin Augustus Mahony, of Levenagh, Blackrock (Co. Cork) and Elizabeth Ronayne and nephew of Francis Sylvester Mahony§. MFM's novels are generally in the form of political and legal satires. His *The Irish bar sinister* (Dublin, 1871) is a non-fictional attack on the Irish legal establishment. He married Mary Copinger in 1864, and had his residence at Lotamore (Co. Cork). SOURCE Allibone Suppl., ii, p. 1064; Brady, p. 157; Burke's, p. 777; Ferguson, p. 249; Hogan 2, p. 817; RIA/DIB.

M262 *Checkmate. A tale* [anon.].
+ London: Richard Bentley, 1858. SOURCE Hogan 2, p. 817. LOCATION L.
COMMENTARY No Irish content [ML].

M263 *Cheap John's auction: A narrative in three parts* (by 'Matthew Stradling').
+ London: Simpkin, Marshall & Co.; Dublin: Hodges, Forster & Co., 1871. SOURCE Brown, p. 201 (1872 edn); Brady, p. 157; Topp 8, 341. LOCATION D, L (1871, 4th edn), NUC.
+ London: Simpkin, Marshall & Co., 1872 (7th edn, enlarged). LOCATION InND Loeber coll.
COMMENTARY Reached a 8th edn in 1872. A political satire in which England is portrayed as a firm of very corrupt peddlers, who sell only worthless goods. Ireland is portrayed as a famished female with a child at her breast. She comes to demand her rights and does not want to be put off with promises or small gifts. Various other characters portray the Irish establishment. For instance, Silken Thomas represents the Irish Bar [ML; Topp].

M264 *A chronicle of the Fermors: Horace Walpole in love* (by M.F. Mahony).
+ London: Sampson Low, Marston, Low & Searle, 1873, 2 vols. (ill. H. Adlard). SOURCE Allibone Suppl., ii, p. 1064. LOCATION D, L, NUC.

M265 *The misadventures of Mr. Catlyne, Q.C. An autobiography* (by 'Matthew Stradling').
+ London: Tinsley Bros, 1873, 2 vols. SOURCE Brown, 1089; Brady, p. 157 (mistakenly mentions Dublin 1873 edn), NUC, InND Loeber coll.
COMMENTARY First published in a shorter, serialized format in *Frazer's Magazine* (London). Describes the career of an Irish Roman Catholic barrister, Mr Catlyne, who commences his career as a repealer and a supporter of the rebellion of 1848. In later life he is elected to parliament under the protection of the clergy. The effort to maintain a balance between being a government supporter and an MP useful to the Irish Roman Catholic clergy is too much. In the end, the clergy drops him because he is not willing to speak out in parliament regarding Irish education, and the government does not come through with promised preferments [ML; Brown].

M266 *Jerpoint. An ungarnished story of the time* (by M.F. Mahony).
+ London: Chapman & Hall, 1875, 3 vols. SOURCE Brown, 1090; Brady, p. 157 (possibly mistakenly mentions Dublin 1877 edn); Wolff, 4391. LOCATION L, NUC, InND Loeber coll.
COMMENTARY A saga of family life set mostly in Ireland with some scenes in London. It revolves around the Courtneys, who had risen from a public house to a country family, and live outside of Jerpoint town (perhaps modelled on Cork city). The conflict between father and son also embroils an opportunistic English visitor, Mr Sharman, the estate agent Mr Pratt, and Courtney's daughter Lucy. The young Courtney, aided by his sister and against his father's wishes, marries the impoverished Miss Hogan. The story describes hunting scenes, electioneering, country house and club life, and some political machinations in London. Eventually, the story centres on Sharman, who loses out politically and financially, and flees from Jerpoint to meet his death. Pratt gains by his investments, is rebuffed in his social and love life, but

finds his place in society. Lucy, however, remains a spinster, stuck in her love for Sharman, who she did not realize was a charlatan [RL].

M267 *A Westminster's night's dream* (by M.F. Mahony).
London: Simpkin, Marshall & Co.; Dublin: M.H. Gill & Son, 1877. SOURCE Hogan 2, p. 817; Topp 8, 532; COPAC. LOCATION L.
COMMENTARY Irish story about the MP for Ballycostigan in Westminster [ML].

MAHONY, Richard John, b. Dromore Castle, Kenmare (Co. Kerry) 1828 (not 1827 as in Boase), d. London 1892. Miscellaneous writer, landlord, evangelic preacher, and civic leader, RJM was the eldest son of the Revd Denis Mahony, a Church of Ireland clergyman of Dromore Castle, and Lucinda Catherine Segerson. RJM matriculated for Worcester College, Oxford, in 1845, and graduated BA in 1849. Following the death of his father in 1851, he inherited the family estate in Co. Kerry, where he founded a model farm. He married Mary Henriette, eldest daughter of John Waller, of Shannon Grove (Co. Limerick). He was DL, JP, and HS of Co. Kerry. However, he lost his estate as a result of one of the acts reforming land ownership in Ireland, which is why he is probably the same person who published in 1880 and 1884 under the pseudonym of 'A working landowner' on land issues (e.g., *"Credo experto." A short statement concerning the confiscation of improvements in Ireland*, Dublin, 1880). He was involved in various Protestant, evangelical movements. He also wrote poems for private circulation and contributed to the *Kerry Magazine* (1854–56) and to *Fraser's Magazine* (London). According to O'Donoghue, he was the original of the chief in J.A. Froude's§ novel, *The two chiefs of Dunboy* (London, 1889). Froude visited him at Dromore. RJM died in London, but was buried in the family vault near Dromore Castle. SOURCE Bary, pp 102–3; BLC; Boase, ii, p. 696; Burke's, p. 776; O'Donoghue, pp 298–9; F. O'Dwyer, *The architecture of Deane & Woodward* (Cork, 1997), pp 21–2 (Dromore Castle); *Return of owners of land* (Dublin, 1876), p. 143; RIA/DIB.
M268 *Father Martin. An Irish story* [anon.].
+ London: S.W. Partridge & Co., 1876. LOCATION D ([1895?] edn), L (destroyed), O.
COMMENTARY 60pp. Religious fiction. Recounts the last days of Fr Martin, who is attended by his housemaid, Bridget. He asked her to bring him 'Thomas à Kempis' (*The imitation of Christ*) from his bookshelf, but she gives him the New Testament. The book contains a full page display of 'The New Testament', printed in Dublin by Richard Coyne. The story centres around religious beliefs and personal struggles [CM; RL].

MAIR, James Allan (not Allen as in Allibone), b. Aberdeen (Scotland) 1843, d. Aberdeen 1875. Writer and anthologist, JAM worked in Dublin in 1866 where he was assistant to the Dublin branch of the publishers W.H. Smith and Son, and is likely to have become acquainted with the Irish publisher Patrick Kennedy§ during this period. He was author of several anthologies of Scottish anecdotes, and also published with Tom Hood and Patrick Kennedy§ *The book of modern anecdotes – English, Irish, Scotch* (London, [1873]). SOURCE Allibone Suppl., ii, p. 1065; Boase, ii, p. 700; RL.
M269 *The book of Irish readings in prose and verse from the works of popular Irish authors* (ed. by James Allan Mair).
+ Glasgow, London: Cameron & Ferguson, 1873 (ill.). SOURCE OCLC. LOCATION D, InND Loeber coll. (also 1886 edn).
COMMENTARY The preface is dated from Dublin, 1 Jan. 1873. Contains prose, plays, poetry, and essays. Contents of the prose: 'The wager and the ball' (Lever§), 'King O'Toole and St. Kevin' (Samuel Lover§), 'Moll Roe's marriage' (William Carleton§), 'Paddy and the bear' [Samuel Lover], 'Captain Andy' (Mrs S.C. Hall§), 'Father Giles of Ballymoy' (Anthony Trollope§), 'The story of Colonel James Roch, the swimmer' (Sir Bernard Burke) [RL].

MALLEY, Arthur W., fl. 1870. Sketch and verse writer, AWM probably was a native of Sligo or its vicinity as he was editor of the *Sligo Independent.* SOURCE O'Donoghue, p. 299; RL.

M270 *The Garravogue papers. Tales and sketches in prose and verse* (by Arthur W. Malley). Sligo: Printed at the Sligo Independence Office, 1870. SOURCE IBL, 6 (1915), p. 90; O'Donoghue, p. 299; COPAC. LOCATION Univ. of Manchester.

'A MAN OF FASHION', pseud. See MILLS, John.

MANGAN, James Clarence, b. Dublin 1803, d. Dublin 1849. Poet, translator and prolific contributor to periodicals, JCM was born James Mangan, the son of James Mangan of Limerick, and Catherine Smith, whose family came from Co. Meath and who were poor grocers in Fishamble Street, Dublin. He later adopted the middle-name Clarence. Educated by the Jesuits in a school in Saul's Court, he studied Latin, French, Spanish and Italian and found refuge from a hard life in books. He went to work in an office at age 15 to help support his family. He began submitting miscellaneous pieces to several Dublin almanacs. Under many and varied pseuds he continued to contribute poetry and humorous verse to Dublin magazines such as the *Comet,* the *Nation,* the *Dublin Penny Journal, Dublin Monthly Magazine,* the *Dublin Satirist,* the *Irish Monthly Magazine,* and particularly the *Dublin University Magazine,* which published hundreds of his prose pieces and poems, including translations from German. He was employed for some time in the office of the Ordnance Survey where he was involved in the copying of Irish manuscripts. This encouraged him to make poetic transformations of literal translations from Irish done by himself and by others. From 1842 to 1846 he worked in the library of TCD. JCM is known for his poetry and essays more than for his fiction, which was Gothic, humorous and fantastical. For most of his life he suffered poverty and physical illnesses, and he was addicted to either alcohol or opium, or both. He was buried at Glasnevin cemetery; his bust is in St Stephen's Green, Dublin. For JCM's portrait and papers, see ODNB. SOURCE Allibone, ii, p. 1213; Boylan, p. 240; de Búrca, cat. of Mangan archive, n.d.; B. Clifford, *The Dubliner: the lives, times and writings of James Clarence Mangan* (Belfast, 1988); D. Crowley, pp 281–316; H.J. Donaghy, *James Clarence Mangan* (New York, 1974); Field Day, i, p. 1298, ii, iii, iv, and v, passim; Hogan, pp 433–4; Hogan 2, pp 818–20; Igoe, pp 166–9; Irish pseudonyms; OCIL, pp 354–5; ODNB; O'Donoghue, pp 300–1; O'Donoghue 2, p. 429; E. Shannon-Mangan, *James Clarence Mangan, a biography* (Dublin, 1996); Rafroidi, ii, pp 241–69; RIA/DIB.

— COLLECTED WORKS

M271 *Essays in prose and verse* (by James Clarence Mangan; ed. by C.D. Meehan).
+ Dublin: James Duffy, 1884. SOURCE COPAC. LOCATION L.
COMMENTARY Prose contents: 'A treatise on a pair of tongs', 'The two flats; or, our quack institution', 'My bugle, and how I blow it', 'An extraordinary adventure in the shades', 'The three rings', 'The story of the old wolf' [CM].

M272 *The prose writings of James Clarence Mangan* (ed. by D.J. O'Donoghue§; with an essay by Lionel Johnson; dedicated to William Boyle).
+ Dublin: O'Donoghue & Co.; M.H. Gill; London: A.H. Bullen, 1904 (ill.; Centenary edn). SOURCE Rafroidi, ii, p. 267. LOCATION Grail, L, NUC, InND Loeber coll.
COMMENTARY Some of the following stories had been published first in *Essays in prose and verse* (Dublin, 1884). Contents: 'The thirty flasks', 'The man in the cloak', 'The churl in the grey coat', 'Chapters on ghostcraft', 'A sixty-drop dose of laudanum', 'The three half-crowns', 'A German poet', 'A treatise on a pair of tongs', 'My bugle, and how I blow it', 'An extraordinary adventure in the shades', 'The three rings', 'The story of the old wolf' [RL].

MANGIN, Revd Edward, pseud. 'E.M.', b. Dublin 1772 (1762 according to Leslie & Wallace), d. Bath (Avon) 1852. Church of Ireland clergyman, novelist and man of letters, EM descended from two Huguenot families. He was the eldest son of Samuel Henry Mangin, an army officer whose family had come to Ireland in the middle of the seventeenth century, and Susanna Corneille. EM matriculated at Balliol College, Oxford, where he graduated BA in 1793 and MA in 1795. Subsequently he was prebendary of Dysart (Co. Clare, 1798–1800), Rathmichael, attached to St Patrick's (Dublin, 1800–03), and vicar of Bray (Co. Wicklow, 1800–03). His ultimate appointment was as prebendary of Rath (Co. Clare), which he held until his death. Like other clergymen of the Church of Ireland at that time, this left him free to live elsewhere, first in Toulouse and Paris before settling in Bath for the remainder of his life. Known for his wide reading and fascinating conversation, he was a prolific original author and translator, contributing to a variety of local and national publications. He published four works of fiction, which included short stories. His poem 'Deserted city', on Bath in the summer, was a parody of Oliver Goldsmith's§ 'A deserted village'. Among his non-fiction works were *Utopia found; being an apology for Irish absentees* (Bath, 1813), and two books on reading: *An essay on light reading* (London, 1808), and *A view of the pleasures arising from a love of books* (London, 1814). He also edited the works of Samuel Richardson (London, 1811, 19 vols.). EM married first Emily Holmes, who died in Dublin in 1801, and second, Mary Nangreave. SOURCE Allibone, ii, p. 1213; Cork, i, p. 218; J. Foster (ed.), *Alumni Oxonienses 1715–1886* (Oxford, 1888), iii, p. 907; Leslie & Wallace, p. 871; ODNB; O'Donoghue, p. 301; RIA/DIB.

M273 *Oddities and outlines* (by 'E.M.').

+ London: J. Carpenter, 1806, 2 vols. in 1. SOURCE NSTC. LOCATION Dt, L, NUC, InND Loeber coll.

COMMENTARY Epistolary novel consisting of a mixture of fact and fiction, in which a romance of the 1798 rebellion is interwoven with the facts of a tour through France, Italy, Switzerland, and Germany [ML].

M274 *George the Third. A novel* [anon.].

+ London: James Carpenter, 1807, 3 vols. SOURCE Block, p. 151; British Fiction; Garside, 1807:40. LOCATION Corvey CME 3–628–47728–X, Dt, L, NUC.

COMMENTARY According to the DNB (but not mentioned in ODNB) some copies carry EM's name on the title page. Has some Irish characters but the main character is English, born in Oakley, son of a medical doctor. The Irish character is called Dyer and he sometimes speaks with the accent of Sir Lucius O'Trigger. Several references to Laurence Sterne§ and to Oliver Goldsmith§ [ML].

M275 *Stories for short students; or, light lore for little people* (by Edward Mangin).

+ London: John Harris, 1829 (ill.). SOURCE Osborne, p. 908; OCLC. LOCATION L, CaOTP, NUC.

COMMENTARY Described in the preface as 'a new species of book for the juvenile library'. Stories written for children, but omitting the then usual religious allusions. Contents: 'Sense in a brute', 'Honour', 'Swimming', 'Story of William Tell', 'Firmness of character', 'George Washington', ' General Lally', 'Real feelings', 'Economy', 'Ferocity of the tiger', 'Long life', 'Benjamin Franklin', 'Sagacity of a dog', 'An Irish chieftain', 'A lesson for a prince', 'Sir Thomas More and Sir Walter Raleigh', 'William Shakespeare', 'Admiral Byng', 'Presence of mind', 'Bertholde', 'The generous dog', 'The ape the best doctor', 'The siege of Londonderry', 'The good son', 'Sir Joshua Reynolds', 'Delicacy of feelings in the people', 'Buonaparte', 'Greatness of mind', 'The diving-bell', 'Howard', 'Courage', 'The air-balloon', 'Louis XVIII', 'Sealing wax', 'The river under ground', 'Mistakes of history', 'Wonderful memories' [ML; Quaritch cat. Summer 2005/69].

M276 *More short stories* (by Edward Mangin).
London: Whittaker, Treacher; Bath: John Upton, 1830 (ill.). SOURCE Block, p. 151; Wolff, 4425. LOCATION L.
COMMENTARY Contents: 'The spring lock', 'The absent man', 'The mother', 'Danger', 'The life of the Pope, the poet', ' The sea', 'The black hole of Calcutta', 'Remorse', 'Remorse concluded', 'The friars', 'A noble countenance', 'Prince Charles Edward', 'General B.', 'Adversity', 'The hat', 'King William III', 'The life and character of Jonathan Swift', 'Monkies', 'Major Andre', 'Adrien', 'Malesherbes', 'Mr. Smith', 'Poor Jack', 'Peter Pullen', 'Young Fitzhugh' [Wolff].

MANNIX, Mrs Mary Ellen (née Walsh), b. New York 1846, d. 1938. American religious fiction and children's writer, MEM was educated in the convent of Notre Dame, Reading (OH). She wrote a great deal for Catholic and Irish periodicals in the US. SOURCE Brown, p. 201; O'Donoghue, p. 302.
M277 *Michael O'Donnell; or, the fortunes of a little emigrant* (by Mrs Mary Ellen Mannix).
Notre Dame (IN): Ave Maria, 1900 (as *The fortunes of a little emigrant*; on cover: *Michael O'Donnell; or, the fortunes of a little emigrant*). SOURCE OCLC. LOCATION DCL.
Boston: Flynn, [1900]. SOURCE Brown, 1093.
COMMENTARY No copy of the Boston, Flynn [1900] edn located. Michael, an industrious Irish boy, comes to the US. After walking across the Continent for three months, he finds an excellent position. However, by a series of misunderstandings and hostile malice, he is made to appear guilty of theft. In the end the truth comes out [Brown].

MANT, Miss —. See MANT, Alicia Catherine.

MANT, Alicia Catherine (also known as Miss Mant), b. *c*.1788, d. 1869. Prolific English writer of fiction for juveniles, ACM also wrote *The study of heavens at midnight … arranged as a game of astronomy* (London, 1814). In 1835 she married Revd James Russell Philpott, the rector of Bath, after which date she appears to have stopped writing. She may have been related to Richard Mant, bishop of Down, Connor and Dromore (d. 1847). SOURCE Allibone, ii, p. 1216; Bradshaw, ii, p. 982; Burmester cat. 50, Part I/66; NCBEL 4, p. 1829; Osborne, pp 153, 909; RL.
M278 *Poor old Peggy, or the discovery. An amusing tale* [anon.].
+ London: D. Carvalho, [1825?] (ill.). SOURCE Bennett cat. 33/132. LOCATION L, InND Loeber coll.
COMMENTARY 55pp. Fiction for juveniles, set in England, but some of the characters are Irish. An old woman is instrumental in saving the little son of a man who, it turns out, she nursed when he was a baby. A servant of the man turns out to be her grandson [ML].

MAPOTHER, Mary J., fl. 1878. Novelist, MJM came from an old Catholic family residing at Kilteevan (Co. Roscommon). She is known to have contributed to the *Young Ireland* magazine (Dublin). SOURCE Brown, p. 202; Irish pseudonyms; Landed gentry, 1912, pp 458–9.
M279 *The Donalds* (by Mary J. Mapother).
+ Dublin: M.H. Gill & Son, 1878. SOURCE Brown, 1093 (1883 edn); Topp 8, p. 94 (1883 edn); OCLC. LOCATION D, Dt, InND Loeber coll.
COMMENTARY Set in Ireland in a country house. Alfred Donald, a young man of self-indulgent character, degenerates morally until he commits the terrible crime of killing his younger sister. This brings him to his senses and he tries to gain the affection of his fellow creatures.

However, one by one his friends fall away from him. Eventually, he is homeless and jobless and dies in a roofless cottage [ML; Brown].

'MARCELLINA', fl. 1881. Pseudonym of a romance novelist.
M280 *Ireland's true daughter. A novel* (by 'Marcellina'; dedicated to the Rt Hon. W.E. Gladstone, 'England's greatest statesman, with his kind permission').
+ London: Remington & Co., 1881, 3 vols. SOURCE Brown 2, 12; Wolff, 7654. LOCATION D, L, NUC.
COMMENTARY A love story set in Co. Galway concerning a Marion Burke [ML].

'MARCHMONT, A.C.U.', pseud. See CORDNER, Catherine Adelaide.

'MARCLIFFE, Theophilus', pseud. See GODWIN, William.

MARKS, Mary A.M. See HOPPUS, Mary Anne Martha.

MARLAY (or Marley), Daniel, fl. 1770. Irish novelist, DM is identified as the author of the following volume in ESTC. The Marlay family was seated at Belvedere (Co. Westmeath) and Crevagh (Co. Longford) but no Daniel Marlay has been identified. He may be related to Chief Justice Thomas Marlay, who had seven sons. SOURCE Block, p. 152; Commoners, iv, p. 13; Landed gentry, 1912, p. 459; Personal communication, Jeremiah Falvey, Jan. 1998.
M281 *The history of Mr. Charles Fitzgerald and Miss Sarah Stapleton. In five books.* [followed by] *Fugitive pieces by the author of the preceding memoirs* [anon.].
+ Dublin: Printed [for the author?] by James Hoey Jnr, 1770. SOURCE Block, p. 152; Gecker, 498; Raven 2, 1770:8; ESTC n007818. LOCATION C, PU.
COMMENTARY Second part has separate title page: Dublin: Printed in the year 1770, but continuing pagination. Probably the first regional Irish novel, published thirty years before Maria Edgeworth's§ *Castle Rackrent.* Set in Co. Westmeath, the story starts in Randalstown, the country house residence of Mr Stapleton and his daughter Sarah. Features a Mrs Wheeler from Castlepollard in the same county. Sarah has rejected many suitors because she is in love with her kinsman, Charles Fitzgerald of Summer-hill. She admits this to her father when a report comes in that Charles has been killed in Phoenix Park. However, the report is false, and the two lovers are pledged to be married. They are separated, however, by the machinations of a rejected suitor with the result that Sarah drowns herself. Presents satirical portraits of a minister and a country doctor. Mr Stapleton gives extensive advice on how to be a good housewife. The 'fugitive pieces', which follow the novel, include poems taken from the *Batchelor* (Dublin), starting with 'The battle of the chaunters, fought near Castleblakeney in the County of Galway, July 27th, 1767' [ML; RL].

MARLEY, Daniel. See MARLAY, Daniel.

MARRYAT, Capt. Frederick, b. Westminster (London) 1792, d. Langham (Norfolk) 1848. Prolific English author of adventure stories, FM was the son of Joseph Marryat, MP, a merchant, and Charlotte Geyer, an American. He was educated in private schools but ran away several times, wishing to go to sea. In 1806 his father secured him service on a frigate that saw much action in naval warfare with the French. On this and subsequent ships he observed the heroic actions that were later to be part of his novels. He rose quickly in the ranks and gained a high reputation for bravery. His novels were noted for their adventure, scientific content, and their skilful depiction of naval customs, characters and scenes. After leaving the navy, he supported himself and a large family through writing. His *Diary in America* (London, 1839, 3 vols.) was deplored by Daniel Webster for adding to the misinformation about America in England. He was one of the most highly-paid, popular, and reprinted authors of the nineteenth century, despite his slapdash style, which was lambasted by critics. Only his works with Irish content are listed below. SOURCE Allibone, ii, pp 1222–3; DLB, xxi, p. 163; NCBEL 4, pp 953–6; 1830; ODNB; Sutherland, p. 412.

M282 *Japhet in search of a father* [anon.].

London: Saunders & Otley, 1836, 3 vols. SOURCE Sadleir, 1579; Wolff, 4518. LOCATION L, NUC.

Leipzig: Bernard Tauchnitz, 1843. SOURCE T & B, 49; COPAC. LOCATION L.

+ New York: Wallis & Newell, 1835 (Franklin Library). SOURCE Sadleir, 1579a (parts only). LOCATION NUC, InND Loeber coll.

Philadelphia, Baltimore: Carey & Hart, 1835, 2 vols. SOURCE Sadleir, 1579b. LOCATION NUC.

Trenton: H.C. Boswell, 1835. SOURCE Topp 2, p. 222. LOCATION NUC.

COMMENTARY First serialized in the *Metropolitan Magazine* (London, Oct. 1834–Jan. 1836). Partly set in Ireland. A foundling hero devotes himself to finding a father whom he feels must be a great man [RL; Sutherland, p. 413; Topp 4, p. 113].

M283 *Joseph Rushbrook, or the poacher* [anon.].

+ London: Longman, Orme, Brown, Green & Longmans, 1841, 3 vols. SOURCE Topp 4, p. 159. LOCATION L, NUC.

+ London, New York: George Routledge & Co., 1856 (as *The poacher*; Routledge Standard Novels; ill. J. Cawse, S. Fisher). LOCATION InND Loeber coll.

Paris: Baudry's European Library, 1841. LOCATION NUC.

Philadelphia: Carey & Hart, 1841, 2 vols. SOURCE Topp 4, p. 159. LOCATION NUC.

New York: Derby & Jackson, 1857. LOCATION NUC.

COMMENTARY Opens in Grassford (Devon) in 1812, and is only briefly set in Ireland at the home of the Capt. O'Donoghue's parents. A Capt. Mc'Shane is also mentioned. Both figures appear frequently in the story, but are not the main characters. Joseph Rushbrook and his son Joey go poaching. A peddler, Mr Byres, tries to catch Rushbrook, who shoots him dead. Joey leaves his satchel at the scene of the crime so the police will suspect him instead of his father. He runs away and meets Capt. Patrick O'Donahue, who knew his father from a regiment. Joey becomes his servant and they make a trip to St Petersburg, where O'Donoghue fights in the Russian dominions. Back in Grassford, Joey is convicted of murder and a reward is offered for his capture. He returns but is discovered and in terror runs away again. He falls in love with Emma Phillips but is captured and taken to prison. His parents have inherited an estate and have changed their name to Austin. Mr Austin comes to the aid of his son and confesses the true circumstances of the murder of Mr Byres. He dies after the confession and Joey is released [CD].

MARSHALL, Thomas Henry, fl. 1821. Gothic novelist.

M284 *The Irish necromancer; or, Deer Park. A novel* (by Thomas Henry Marshall).

+ London: A.K. Newman & Co., 1821, 3 vols. SOURCE Brown, 1097; British Fiction; Garside, 1821:59. LOCATION Corvey CME 3–628–48092–2, Ireland related fiction, L.

Mannheim: Löffler, 1824, 2 vols. (trans. as *Der irländische Schwarzkünstler und die Giftmischerin*). SOURCE Garside, 1821:59; GLOL. SOURCE Bibliotheks- und Informationssystem der Universität, Oldenburg.

Paris: de Lavigne, 1824 (trans. by M*** [Dubergier] as *Le nécromancien irlandais*). SOURCE British Fiction; Bn-Opale plus. LOCATION BNF.

COMMENTARY Gothic fiction inspired by Karl Friedrich Kahlert's *The necromancer; or, the tale of the Black Forest* (London, 1794), possibly after an unidentified German original. Love story among the nobility. Some characters, such as Lucius O'Brien, are Irish. The scene in the second volume starts out in the vice-regal court in Dublin. The setting is more or less immaterial to the plot [ML; Frank, 263].

MARTIN, Miss. See **MARTIN, Mary Letitia.**

MARTIN, Ewan, fl. 1899. Historical novelist, possibly American, EM also wrote *The knight of King's Guard* (London, 1899). SOURCE BLC; RL.
M285 *Dauntless. A story of a lost and forgotten cause* (by Ewan Martin).
+ Boston: L.C. Page & Co., 1900 (ill. Harry C. Edwards). LOCATION D, NUC.
+ London: C. Arthur Pearson, [1901] (ill. H.C. Edwards). SOURCE Brown, 1098; COPAC. LOCATION L, E, InND Loeber coll.
COMMENTARY Historical fiction, this is a love story set in the middle of the seventeenth century. Harry Dauntless, of a Norman-Irish family from the vale of Shanganagh (Co. Dublin), first serves in the Royalist army of the earl of Ormond and then with the Confederates. Owen Roe O'Neill, Ormond, Ever MacMahon, Daniel O'Neill, and Sir Hardress Waller figure in the tale. The story presents a picture of the changing allegiances of the various parties [ML; Brown].

MARTIN, Harriet (née Evans; known as H. Martin), fl. 1788, d. 1846. Novelist and critic, she was the daughter of Hugh Evans, Senior Surgeon of the 5th Dragoon Guards. She first married Capt. Robert Hesketh, RN. After he died she married Richard Martin ('Humanity Dick'), the owner of a large estate at Ballynahinch (Co. Galway). Their eldest daughter was the writer Harriet Letitia Martin§. Aside from two novels, HM also wrote *Remarks on … J. Kemble's performance of Hamlet and Richard III* (London, 1802). She dedicated the following volume to George Evans, 4th Baron Carbery, who probably was a relative on her father's side of the family. SOURCE BLC; Garside, 1802:41; HIP, v, p. 196; ODNB [under Richard Martin].
M286 *Historic tales. A novel* [anon.] (dedicated to George Evans, 4th Baron Carbery).
Dublin: Printed [for the author?] by P. Byrne, 1788, 2 vols. in 1. SOURCE Raven 2, 1788:17; ESTC t212454. LOCATION Dt, ICN.
+ London: C. Dilly, 1790. SOURCE Summers, p. 355; Raven 2, 1788:17; ESTC t127176. LOCATION L, C.
COMMENTARY Author identified on title page of *Helen of Glenross* (London, 1802, 4 vols.). Historical fiction with no Irish content. Set in France and in England, and features Anna [*sic*] Boleyn [ML; CM].
M287 *Helen of Glenross. A novel* [anon.] (dedicated to **** *****).
+ London: G. & J. Robinson, 1802, 4 vols. SOURCE Block, p. 161; Gecker, 706; British Fiction; Garside, 1802:41. LOCATION Corvey CME 3–628–47724–7, PU, NUC, InND Loeber coll. (vols. 3 and 4).
Paris: F. Béchet, 1812, 3 vols. (trans. as *Hélène de Glenross*). SOURCE Garside, 1802:41; CCF. LOCATION BNF.
Boston: Joseph Nancrede, 1802. SOURCE OCLC. LOCATION NUC.
COMMENTARY Epistolary novel, mainly about connections among the upper class and the unhappiness that pride can bring. One of the families with English estates also has an Irish estate. Part of the story was serialized under the title of 'The history of Mr. Frazer' in the *Universal Magazine* (London, 1802) [ML; Mayo, 615].

MARTIN, Harriet Letitia, b. London, 1801, d. Dublin 1891. Novelist, HM was the eldest daughter of Richard Martin of Ballynahinch (Co. Galway) and his second wife Harriet Evans Martin§ (widow of Robert Hesketh) and aunt of Mary Letitia Martin§. Her father, known as 'Humanity Dick', inherited over 200,000 acres in Connemara and was renowned for his kindness and generosity to his tenants. He was MP for Co. Galway from 1801 to 1826, which would explain HLM's London birth. She travelled widely in America and on the Continent and stayed with John Banim§ and his wife in Paris, where she wrote *Canvassing* (see below), which was published with work by the Banim§ brothers. She remained unmarried. SOURCE Blain, p. 723 [see Mary Letitia Martin]; Boase, ii, p. 766; OCIL, p. 358 [see Mary Letitia Martin]; A.S.E. Martin, *Genealogy of the family of Martin* (Winnipeg, 1890); ODNB [see Richard Martin]; RIA/DIB.

M288   *The Mayor of Windgap (and Canvassing)* (by 'the O'Hara family' [*sic*, see commentary below]).

London: Saunders & Otley, 1835, 3 vols. SOURCE Sadleir, 147; Wolff, 230; Garside 2, 1835:22. LOCATION L, NUC.

Dublin, London: James Duffy, 1865. SOURCE Brown, 1099. LOCATION C.

+ Brussels: Ad Wahlen, 1835 (Wahlen's Modern British Authors). LOCATION InND Loeber coll.

+ Paris: Ambroise Dupont, 1836, 2 vols. (trans. by Mme la baronne de Los Valles as *Le candidat – moeurs irlandaises*, by 'Banim' [*sic*]). SOURCE Rafroidi, ii, p. 366; Devonshire, p. 455; Robertshaw cat. 78/86. LOCATION BNF, InND Loeber coll. COMMENTARY *Paris 1836 edn* Although it carries the name 'Banim' as its author, it is the translation of HLM's *Canvassing*. Each volume contains explanatory notes about the Irish setting of the text [RL].

Philadelphia: Carey, Lea & Blanchard, 1835 (by 'the O'Hara family' [*sic*]). SOURCE Kaser, 480. LOCATION MH, NUC.

+ New York: Harper & Bros, 1835 (*The Mayor of Wind-Gap* by 'the O'Hara Family' [*sic*]). LOCATION NUC, InND Loeber coll. COMMENTARY *New York 1835 edn* This edn does not include *Canvassing* [RL].

+ New York, Montreal: D. & J. Sadlier & Co., 1881 (as *Canvassing. A tale of Irish life* (by 'the O'Hara family' [*sic*], a new edn, with introd. and notes by Michael Banim§; Sadlier's Household Library). LOCATION D, DCU.

COMMENTARY Two stories: 'Canvassing' only is by Harriet Martin, whereas 'The Mayor of Windgap' is by 'the O'Hara family', that is the brothers John Banim§ and Michael Banim§. 'Canvassing' is a story of match-making and marriage among the upper class in Ireland. Describes an election contest in the first quarter of the nineteenth century [Brown].

M289   *The changeling* [anon.].

+ London: Saunders & Otley, 1848, 3 vols. SOURCE Boase, ii, p. 766 (has as title *The changeling, a tale of the year '47*, but this has not been located); Brown, 150; Rafroidi, ii, p. 269; Block, p. 154; Wolff, 4591. LOCATION L (3 vols. in 1), NUC.

COMMENTARY Wrongly attributed by Brown to John Banim§. Set in the city of Galway and Connemara and concerns the mystery surrounding the heir of Ballymagawley who was removed from his home by the present owner, Whaley. The heir returns in disguise to claim his rights. The novel is at the expense of the Galway bourgeoisie and the squirearchy [Brown; Wolff].

MARTIN, Revd Henry, fl. 1878, d. 1906? Religious fiction writer HM can perhaps be identified with Henry Francis John Martin, third son of the Revd John Charles Martin, Church of Ireland archdeacon of Kilmore. HM graduated BA at TCD and was ordained rector of Ballysax (Co. Kildare, 1863–65, then as rector of Kilmacrenan (Co. Donegal, 1865–73), and rector of Christ Church (Derry, 1873–78). He was curate and then rector of Killeshandra (Co. Cavan, 1878–1906). He married in 1865 Barbara, daughter of Robert Collins, MD, of Ardsallagh, Co. Meath (d. 1902). Among his publications is *Spiritual Life as illustrated by the Book of Psalms* (Dublin, 1905, Donnellan Lectures). He should not be confused with Henry Newell Martin, MD, b. Newry (Co. Down) 1848, an eminent biologist who after studying in London was associated with Johns Hopkins University in Baltimore (MD). SOURCE Allibone Suppl., ii, p. 1081; AMB; Leslie, *Derry*, p. 146.

M290   *Stories of Irish life* (by Henry Martin).

+ London: S.W. Partridge & Co., [1878] (ill. A.W. Cooper; see Plate 49). SOURCE Brown 2, 1012; OCLC. LOCATION D, L, NUC, InND Loeber coll. (Parts 1, 2–3, 4, 5, 6, 7, 8, 9, 10–11, 12).

COMMENTARY Issued in 12 parts and priced at 2*d*. each (some are double issues priced at 4*d*.) in London. Each part has an Irish antiquity on the front cover. Consists of a series of short stories, the purpose of which is to dispute some doctrine or doctrines of the Catholic church and to inculcate Protestant principles and teachings. Contents: 'Farmer O'Shaugnessy and his son; or, "saved; yet so as by fire"', 'The Mitchelstown caves; or, "De profundis"', 'Brian Gallagher, the Irish fisherman and pilot; and old Jack Sibley, the turf carrier', 'The last of the O'G's; or, the lost inheritance restored; and the reformed Irish republican', 'Phelim M'Carthy; or, the pilgrim of the holy wells', 'Ned Cassidy of the lakes; or "The blessed virgin Mary's creed"' and 'Michael Donovan; or, the "order" of Jesus Christ', 'Ned Cassidy on the lakes; or the eagle's nest', 'Larry O'Toole; or, "do you know your road?"', 'Ned Cassidy of the lakes in "the steel bracelets"', 'Barny O'Brien on "Home Rule"' [ML; Brown 2].

MARTIN, Josephine M. See **CALLWELL, Josephine M**.

MARTIN, Mary Letitia (also known as **Miss Martin** and **Mrs Martin Bell**), b. Ballynahinch Castle (Co. Galway) 1815, d. New York 1850. Novelist, MLM was the only child of Thomas Barnewall Martin, MP, of Ballynahinch Castle and Julia Kirwan. Her father's stepmother, Harriet Martin§, and stepsister, Harriet Letitia Martin§, were writers. MLM was said never to have had a governess and to have been entirely self-taught. Her scholarly interests included literature, science, Hebrew, Latin, Greek, French and engineering. Maria Edgeworth§ stayed for a few weeks at Ballynahinch Castle in 1834 and initially found MLM self-centred and opinionated, but noted that she had 'more knowledge of books, both scientific and learned, than any female creature I ever saw or heard of at her age'. When MLM visited Edgeworthstown (Co. Longford) in that year, Maria Edgeworth's esteem for her increased. In 1838, MLM composed articles for the French *Encyclopédie des gens du monde*, including one on Maria's father, Richard Lovell Edgeworth§. She married her cousin Arthur Gonne Bell of Brookhill (Co. Mayo) in 1847. One of her friends was Revd Henry Woodward§. On her father's death in that year, she inherited heavily-mortgaged estates of about 200,000 acres. During the Famine years of 1846–7 the family had spent large sums to relieve the suffering of their tenants and MLM made additional borrowings to continue the relief. The property was brought into the encumbered estates court; she lost every acre and became almost penniless. She went to Belgium and later to France, where she tried to support her family with her writing. In 1850, according to a contract for her *Julia Howard* (London, 1850) with the publisher R. Bentley, she resided at Chaudfontaine in France. That same year she and her husband sailed for New York to try to better their fortunes, but having given birth prematurely on board, she died in New York ten days after her arrival in America. Charles Lever§ based his novel *The Martins of Cro' Martin* on her family. Maria Edgeworth§ planned to write a novel about MLM, but never followed through. SOURCE Blain, p. 723; Boylan, p. 243; BL, MSS 46,615, f.250; Brown, p. 202; Burke's, p. 787; H.E. Butler (ed.), *Maria Edgeworth. Tour in Connemara and the Martins of Ballinahinch* (London, 1950), passim; Field Day, iv, p. 1142; Hogan 2, pp 826–7; OCIL, p. 358; ODNB; H. Woodward, *Essays, thoughts and reflections, and letters* (London, 1864), pp xxiv–xxvi; Mrs Edgeworth, *A memoir of Maria Edgeworth* (London, 1867), iii, p. 135; RIA/DIB.

M291   *St. Etienne. A romance of the first revolution* (by Miss Martin, dedicated at Ballynahinch Castle to Miss [Maria] Edgeworth§).

London: T.C. Newby, 1844, 3 vols. SOURCE Rafroidi, ii, p. 271; Hodgson, p. 484; Wolff, 4592; NSTC (1845 edn). LOCATION L (1845 edn), DCL, NUC (1845 edn).

COMMENTARY Reviewed in the *Dublin University Magazine* (1845). A tale set in the Vendée region of France during Napoleonic times, 1793–1800. Blain mistakenly contends MLM's authorship of this novel [Blain; Rafroidi].

M292   *Eda Morton and her cousins; or, school-room days* [anon.].

+ London: John Olivier, 1848. SOURCE NSTC. LOCATION L.

COMMENTARY Set in Scotland. A story for young people. No Irish content [ML].

M293   *Julia Howard. A romance* (by Mrs Martin Bell).

London: Richard Bentley, 1850, 3 vols. SOURCE Hodgson, p. 304; Rafroidi, ii, p. 271; Brown, 1097a; Block, p. 154; NSTC. LOCATION L.

New York: Harper, 1850. SOURCE NSTC. LOCATION NUC.

COMMENTARY Reviewed in *Bentley's Miscellany* (London, Aug., 1850). A partly autobiographical story set around 1740 in Connemara during a famine. Alister O'Connor loses his estates and becomes a soldier of fortune. Col. Herbert, a member of the Irish parliament and tolerant of Catholics, purchases the estates. His niece and heiress Julia Howard is the friend and protector of the estate's peasants. Julia is abducted by Alister's apostate brother. Alistair rescues her, but all three die. The book shows the workings of the penal laws and how they fostered dissension in families [Brown; Brady, p. 159; Curran index, BentM 1849; ODNB].

MARTIN, Robert Jasper, b. Ross House, Killanin (Co. Galway) 1846, d. Oughterard (Co. Galway) 1905. Journalist and stage-Irish humour writer and singer whose pseud., 'Ballyhooly', was the title of one his best known songs, RJM was the eldest son of James Martin and Anna Selina Fox of Ross House (Co. Galway) and brother of Violet Florence Martin§. He was educated at TCD and then went to London where he worked as a society journalist on the *Sporting Times*, using his pseudonym. After his father's death in 1872 he leased out Ross House for five years as it was encumbered by heavy debts stemming from mis-management and the family's care for their tenants during the Famine. He returned to Dublin in 1877 as a journalist. His income was further reduced through his agent's embezzlement of rent and by the increasing tensions of the Land War. Some of his anti-Land League and anti-government songs were collected in *Days of the Land League* (London, 1882) and were popular with the landlord class who felt threatened by Prime Minister William Gladstone's eagerness to settle the land question in Ireland. In 1886 RJM married Amelia Constance, daughter of Johan Jacob Schmidt and widow of Victor Baddely Roche of Killuntin (Co. Cork) and re-settled in London. Much of his work was based on the stage-Irish images of drunken peasantry and benign landlords popularized by writers such as Charles Lever§ and William Maginn§. He used his anti-Land League material to speak for Unionist candidates to parliament but he declined to run himself, being financially dependent on his stage career. He frequently returned to Connemara for charity concerts – where he would sing his famous songs – and for local civic activities, including overseeing famine relief there, but he did not settle in Ireland again until shortly before his death. RJM also wrote an opera, *Dr. Faust and Miss Marguerite* (Dublin], [1885]). SOURCE Burke's, p. 788; G. Lewis, *Somerville and Ross* (London, 1987), pp 28, 76, 250; LVP,

p. 317; NUC; O'Donoghue, p. 303–04; E.O. Somerville and 'Martin Ross' (Violet Martin), *Irish memories* (London, 1917); RIA/DIB.

M294 *Bits of Blarney* (by Robert Jasper Martin).
+ London: Sands & Co., 1899. SOURCE Brown, 1101; COPAC. LOCATION L, NUC, InND Loeber coll.

COMMENTARY Humorous stories, sketches and verse, almost all dealing with Irish life. Contents: 'Ballyhooly', 'St. Patrick's day in the morning', 'Killaloe', 'A parliamentary candidate', 'The priest's mare', 'Mulrooney's dog', 'Catching a poacher', 'Mullingar', 'A Kerry recruit', 'Enniscorthy', 'The wrong man', 'The two leaders', 'The Derby dog', 'How the masther stopped the scandal', 'The Ballymacslattery card party', 'Ballyhooly in Morocco', 'Spanish Cork, or Ballyhooly in Spain', 'Hearts around the queen', 'The adventures of a breast-pin', 'Donegal', 'Seaside excursion', 'Very extraordinary, isn't it?', 'An Irish fairy', 'A gentleman jockey', 'A man of iron constitution', 'Miles from anywhere', 'The prodigal son', 'The "Ballybunion sentinel"', 'Mrs. Burke's café Shong-Tong', 'Mulligan's English cook', 'Through darkest Ireland', 'An English tenant in Ireland', 'A voter by profession', 'An alternative', 'Family feuds', 'Miss Sarah Jenkins' sea bath', 'The Blatherumskite', 'A Connemara short cut', 'The submerged shamrock', 'The queen at Netley', 'A cheery wrong 'un', 'Under county guarantee', 'Flannigan's football team', 'A marrying man', 'The old woman of Elbow Lane' [RL].

MARTIN, Selina, fl. 1828. Religious, history, travel, and children's fiction writer, SM was the elder of two daughters of Revd Robert Martin who was curate of Ballymoyer (Co. Armagh) in 1765, and rector of Newtownhamilton in the same county from 1787 until his death in 1796. Her father married first Ann Brownrigg, of St Peter's Parish, Dublin, and second in 1762, Sarah Gaskell. SM's sister married in 1804 Sir Walter Synott, of Ballymoyer (Co. Armagh). SM is likely to have lived in Ulster judging from the fact that when she was leaving for Italy in 1819 she sailed from Warrenpoint (Co. Down). She lived and travelled in Italy until 1822, resulting in her *A narrative of three years residence in Italy* (London, 1828). In addition, she published five works of fiction, mostly written for juveniles, as well as historical and religious works, including *Sketches of Irish history. Antiquities, religion, customs, and manners* (London, 1844). SM was friendly with Charlotte Elizabeth (pseud. of Mrs Tonna§) who wrote an introd. to SM's *Sketches of Irish history* (London, 1844). The NLI copy of her *The Protestant rector* (Dublin, 1830) has an endorsement in her hand, written from 'Dunstaffnage, Dec. 17, 1831'. SM is not known to have married. SOURCE Fleming, *Armagh*, pp 702–3; RL.

M295 *Eglantine; or, the flower that never fades; An allegorical tale, altered from the French* [anon.] (dedicated to the children of St George Smith of Green-hills, near Drogheda).
+ Dublin: Richard Moore Tims; London: Hamilton & Adams, Hatchard & Son, J. Nesbitt; Edinburgh: W.M. Oliphant, 1828. LOCATION L.

COMMENTARY Advertised in George Brittaine's *Irish priests and English landlords* (Dublin, 1830) as by 'Miss Martin', author of *A narrative of three years residence in Italy* (London, 1828) [Garside 2, 1830:28].

M296 *Little Georgiana; or, conversations for children* [anon.] (dedicated to Lady Mary Stopford).
+ Dublin: Richard Moore Tims; London: Hamilton & Adams, J. Nesbitt, Hatchard & Son; Edinburgh: W.M. Oliphant, Waugh & Innes; Glasgow: Chalmers & Collins, 1829. LOCATION L.

COMMENTARY Religious narrative in a series of conversations between 'Georgiana, and her mamma and pappa' [CM].

M297 *The Protestant rector; or, a tale of other times in Ireland* [anon.].
+ Dublin: William Curry Jnr & Co., 1830. LOCATION D.
+ London: J. Nesbit, 1830. SOURCE Brown, 85; Block, p. 192; Garside 2, 1830:79.
LOCATION L.
COMMENTARY Religious fiction. At the Protestant rectory a priest is received even though he
is frequently drunk. While visiting Rome, the priest is converted to protestantism by seeing
the pope being treated as God. On his return, the priest is again welcomed at the rectory; he
converts many Protestants and dies a holy death [Brown].

M298 *Georgiana and her father, or conversations on natural phenomena* [anon.].
+ London: R.B. Seeley & W. Burnside, 1832. SOURCE Heath cat. Nov. 2000/63.
LOCATION L, InND Loeber coll.
COMMENTARY Religious fiction for children arranged in dialogues, a continuation of *Little
Georgiana; or, conversations for children* (Dublin, 1829). Georgiana is a little older now and
holds religious conversations with her father while walking together. The topic of the con-
versation is usually sparked by a natural phenomenon such as the stars or rainstorms. The
text is replete with quotations from the Bible [ML].

M299 *A sister's stories* [anon.].
+ Kirkby Lonsdale: A. Foster; London: L.B. Seeley & Sons, 1833 (ill.). SOURCE Block,
p. 154. LOCATION L, NUC.
COMMENTARY Fiction for juveniles with many stories dealing with biology [ML].

MARTIN, Violet Florence, pseud. '**Martin Ross**', b. Ross House, Killanin (Co. Galway)
1862, d. Cork 1915. Novelist, VFM was the youngest daughter of James Martin of an old
landed Norman family, one of the legendary 'tribes of Galway', and Anna Selina Fox. VFM
spent her early life at Ross House, where she learned Irish, after which she studied at Alexandra
College, Dublin, where she obtained a solid literary education. In 1886 she met her cousin,
Edith Œ. Somerville§, of Drishane (Co. Cork), with whom she established a correspondence
while Edith studied art abroad. This friendship blossomed into a literary partnership that was
to last until VFM's death – and beyond – since Somerville continued to publish under their
joint names. Before moving to Drishane in 1906, VFM helped her mother manage the estate
at Ross after her father's death. In the straitened financial circumstances common to many
Anglo-Irish families of the time, she witnessed the gradual decline of that class against a rising Irish middle-class, experiences that were central to many of the novels she co-authored
with Somerville. VFM shared a common great-grandmother with Maria Edgeworth§ and she
followed Edgeworth's example of using Irish vernacular dialogue in the novels. An enthusiastic suffragette, she became vice-president of the Munster Women's Franchise League. In 1898
she was severely hurt in a fall from her horse and was thereafter more or less an invalid, perhaps in part due to the brain tumour that eventually killed her. She was awarded a posthumous DLitt. by TCD. An ardent Unionist and anti-nationalist, she nevertheless had tremendous sympathy for Irish people of the countryside and a deep love of the Irish language. Some
of her travel writing (e.g. 'An outpost of Ireland' about a visit to the Aran Islands) was partly
anthologized in the *Oxford book of English prose* (Oxford, 1925). For her joint books with her
cousin, see Somerville. VFM was a cousin of Lady Augusta Gregory, co-founder of the Abbey
Theatre. VFM's brother Robert Jasper Martin§ was a writer noted for his humorous songs
and entertainments. For VFM's portraits and papers, see ODNB. SOURCE Blain, p. 1006 [under
Somerville and Ross]; Boylan, p. 245; Brady, p. 213; Burke's, p. 788; DLB, cxxxv [under
Ross]; Field Day, ii, p. 1217; v, p. 1072 [under Ross]; Galway, pp 79–80; Hogan 2, pp 1132–4
[under Somerville and Ross]; ODNB; Rogal, p. 141; RIA/DIB [under Somerville]; Sutherland,
pp 415–16.

MARTIN-BELL, Mrs. See **MARTIN, Mary Letitia.**

MARTINEAU, Harriet, b. Norwich 1802, d. Ambleside (Cumbria) 1876. Prolific English writer on economics, religion, travel and social conditions and a didactic novelist, HM was the daughter of Thomas Martineau, a cloth manufacturer of Huguenot descent, and Elizabeth Rankin. Her early writings dealt mostly with religious topics – she was a committed Unitarian – and in 1831 she won all three prizes in a Unitarian contest for the best essays aimed at converting Roman Catholics, Jews, and Muslims. Her *Letters from Ireland* (London, 1852, repr. Dublin, 2001) first appeared in the *Daily News* (London). These were the result of a tour through Ulster, the west, and the midlands and were in the form of a series of essays. In them she intelligently analyses the woes of and solutions to Irish national and personal dilemmas. Her *Endowed schools of Ireland* (London, 1859), derives from a series of articles also published in the *Daily News*. She also contributed articles about Ireland to *Household Words* (London, 1852). Several of HM's letters to Thomas Wyse§, MP, are in the NLI (MSS 15,025). Her brother, James Martineau, was minister of the Eustace Street Presbyterian congregation in Dublin from 1828 to 1832 and was the author of *Ireland and her famine* (London, [1847]). SOURCE Allibone, ii, p. 1232; Allibone Suppl., ii, p. 1084; Blain, p. 724; Brown, p. 203; DLB, vols. xxi, lv, clix, clxiii, clxvi, cxc; Field Day, v, pp 837–8, 843; A. Hall, *James Martineau* (London, 1906), pp 39–41; McVeagh, p. 98; NCBEL 4, pp 1344–7; ODNB; Todd, pp 452–6; *Ordination service ... Delivered by the ministers of Dublin, at the ordination of the Rev. James Martineau* ([Dublin], 1829); Sutherland, p. 417.

M300   *Ireland. A tale* (by Harriet Martineau).
+ London: Charles Fox, 1832 (in *Illustrations of Political Economy*, vol. 9; see Plate 50). SOURCE Brown, 1102; Wolff, 4610. LOCATION L, NUC, InND Loeber coll.
Hartford (CT): S. Andreus & Son, 1845 (as *Glen of the echoes; or, Van Mahoney and Dora Sullivan: A tale of Ireland*). LOCATION NUC.
New York: J.W. Lovell, 1884 (as *Glen of the echoes; or, Van Mahoney and Dora Sullivan: A tale of Ireland*). SOURCE OCLC. LOCATION NUC.
New York: Garland, 1979 (introd. by R.L. Wolff). LOCATION D, Boston College.
COMMENTARY This story illustrates aspects of the misgovernment of Ireland, focusing on the evils of the subdivision of leases, tithes, lack of rewards for improvements to the land, poor laws, and the beneficial effects of the personal interest of landlords in the welfare of their estates and those living on them [ML].

MARTYN, Edward Joseph, pseud. 'Sirius', b. Tullira, Ardrahan (Co. Galway) 1859, d. Tullira 1923. Playwright, theatrical entrepreneur and novelist, EJM came from a Catholic landed gentry background, and was the son of John Martyn, JP, of Tullira (not Tillyra as in ODNB) and Masonbrook (also Co. Galway), and Annie Mary Josephine Smith (Smyth according to ODNB). EJM succeeded to his father's estate in 1860. He was educated at Belvedere College, Dublin, and Beaumont (a Jesuit school outside London), after which he entered Christ Church College, Oxford, in 1877, but studied without distinction. He travelled on the Continent with his cousin George Moore§, furthering his interests in the music of Giovanni Palestrina and Richard Wagner and returning to his ancestral home with contemporary French and Japanese works of art. A devout Catholic, strict JP, and confirmed bachelor, he founded the Dublin Palestrina Choir in 1899 and was active in improving the standard of ecclesiastical art in Ireland. Together with Augusta Lady Gregory and William Butler Yeats§, and joined later by George Moore§, he founded in the same year the Irish Literary Theatre, forerunner of the Abbey Theatre, for which he wrote plays (the most successful was *The heather field* (London, 1899) and which he supported financially). Personality clashes with Moore and aesthetic differences with Yeats§ eventually made him break away from the partnership. Increasingly anti-English, he was a member of the ruling council of the Gaelic League and was president of the nationalist Sinn Féin party from 1904 to 1908, when he withdrew from politics in favour of writing. Subsequently he co-founded the Theatre of Ireland and then, with Joseph Mary Plunkett and Thomas McDonagh, the Irish Theatre, for the purpose of performing plays of contemporary Irish life as well as Gaelic and Continental masterpieces in translation. Its first production, in 1914, was EJM's drama *The dream physician*, in which he caricatures George Moore§, who had lampooned him with malicious wit in *Hail and farewell* (London, 1911). Plunkett and McDonagh were both executed after the Easter Rising of 1916 and the Irish Theatre eventually folded in 1920. EJM died at Tullira after surgery for a brain tumour. He left his library to the Carmelites in Clarendon Street, Dublin. For EJM's portraits and papers, see ODNB. SOURCE DLB, x; J. Foster (ed.), *Alumni Oxonienses 1715–1886* (Oxford, 1888), iii, p. 922; Field Day, ii, pp 562, 716–17, 847, iii, p. 495, 665; Hogan, pp 438–40; Hogan 2, pp 827–9; IBL, 14 (1924), p. 16; Igoe, pp 170–2; Kersnowski, pp 80–1; Landed gentry, 1904, p. 392; OCIL, pp 358–9; ODNB; RIA/DIB.

M301 *Morgante the Lesser. His notorious life and wonderful deeds* (arranged and narrated for the first time by 'Sirius').
+ London: W. Swan Sonnenschein & Co., 1890. SOURCE Kersnowski, p. 81. LOCATION L, NUC.
COMMENTARY Mixture of Rabelaisian satire and utopianism set in the nineteenth century. Morgante was born in a very old family, which included Greek and Roman philosophers. He is an atheist who formulated a philosophy called 'enterism'. Characters in the story have partly historical names, such as Dr Galen McGuesswork [ML; Hogan].

'MARY ELIZA', fl. 1785. Possible pseudonym of a writer and/or translator. The periodical version of the following volume appeared in the *New Lady's Magazine* (London, 1787) and the *Berwick Museum* (Berwick-upon-Tweed, 1787) version is accompanied by a letter of the editor, signed 'Mary Eliza. / Primrose St.', presumably in London. It is not clear whether this person is the translator of the French volume or is the author of the original volume. SOURCE Mayo, 612; RL.

M302 *Histoire de Miss Sydney Hamilton* [anon.].
Londres [Paris]: Mérigot Jeune, 1785. SOURCE H. Nicholson, *The desire to please* (New York 1943, pp 49–54); GLOL. LOCATION Universitätsbibliothek, Augsburg.
COMMENTARY Probably can be identified with *The history of Miss Sidney* [*sic*], which was serialized in the *New Lady's Magazine* (London), the *Hibernian Magazine* (Dublin), and in the *Berwick Museum* (Berwick-upon-Tweed), all in 1787. Apparently based on a true story, the history of Sydney Hamilton, daughter of Galen Hamilton and his wife Jane, and sister of Archibald Hamilton Rowan (1751–1834), all of Killeagh Castle (Co. Down). For the French court proceedings, see G. Marquis de Limon, *A question of public right* ([London?, 1782?]) (copy of this translation is in the King's Inns, Dublin). The story is set in England and on the Continent. Sydney, at age 15 and assisted by Sarah Dawson (daughter of a former Irish neighbour), elopes with Revd Benjamin Beresford, chaplain to the duke of Bedford. They marry at Gretna Green. Sydney's mother appeals to the English lord chancellor for an injunction. Beresford, realizing his dangerous position having abducted a child below the age of consent, hides her in Marylebone, and marries her again according to English law. He is fired by the duke and, as a consequence, they have to live in poverty. Beresford begs Mrs Hamilton for forgiveness, but she rejects him and her daughter. Sydney, however, visits her mother, and is forgiven, on the condition that she goes abroad. She is confined in an asylum in Lille, but Beresford finds her. Soon she gives birth to a daughter. Mrs Hamilton appeals to Louis

XVI and obtains a *lettre de cachet*. A legal battle ensues. Sydney's descent from the earls of Clanbrassil, the dukes of Hamilton, but also from Henry I of France and all the kings of Scotland is emphasized. Judgment is pronounced against Mrs Hamilton, who is ordered to pay £50,000 to Beresford for unwarranted arrest, to be held in trust for Sydney's infant. The order of court is reversed by a royal decree, stipulating that Beresford is to be released if he promises not to molest Sydney [Nicholson; Mayo, 612; RL].

MASON, Miss —, fl. 1853. Novelist.
M303 *Kate Geary; or, Irish life in London. A tale of 1849* (by Miss Mason).
+ London: Charles Dolman, 1853. SOURCE Brown, 1103. LOCATION D, L.
Paris: Putois-Cretté, 1859 (trans. by M. William O'Gorman as *Catherine Geary ou les Irlandais à Londres*). SOURCE Devonshire, p. 469; CCF. LOCATION BNF.
COMMENTARY Reviewed in *Dublin Review* (35 (1853), pp 522–3). The novel exemplifies the hard life of the Irish poor in London and describes the life of a charitable female, who has witnessed the incidents of the tale. Intermixed is a love story. According to the author's preface, most of the scenes described were written from personal experience [Brown; *Dublin Review*; Burmester list].

MASON, Mrs —. See **MOUNT CASHELL, Margaret Jane, Countess.**

MASON, A.E.W. See **MASON, Alfred Edward Woodley**.

MASON, Alfred Edward Woodley (known as **A.E.W. Mason**), b. Camberwell (London) 1865, d. London 1948. English historical, adventure and detective novelist, AEWM was educated at Dulwich College and Oxford and initially tried his hand at acting, appearing in the first production of George Bernard Shaw's§ *Arms and the man* ([London], 1910). He fought in the First World War, travelled extensively, and was for a time an MP. Encouraged by Sir Arthur Quiller Couch and Oscar Wilde§, he began to write and was quite prolific. His novels, capitalizing on British patriotism, included many bestsellers and several became films. Some of his books were translated into Gaelic. Only his works with Irish links are listed below.
SOURCE Brown, p. 203; BLC; EF, pp 270–1; ODNB; Sutherland, pp 418–19.
M304 *Parson Kelly* (by A.E.W. Mason and Andrew Lang; dedicated to Baron Tanneguy de Wogan).
New York, London: Longmans, Green & Co., 1899. SOURCE COPAC. LOCATION L (1900 edn), NUC, InND Loeber coll. (1900 edn).
COMMENTARY Historical fiction set in early-eighteenth-century England and France, the story is founded on the deeds of the Chevalier Nicholas de Wogan. Wogan and his friend, Parson Kelly, are both Irish and have known each other since childhood. They are engaged in the Jacobite cause but the safety of the cause is endangered by the parson's love affair with Lady Oxford. However, both Kelly and Wogan are able to escape to France [ML].
M305 *Clementina* (by A.E.W. Mason).
London: Methuen & Co., [1901] (ill. Bernard Partridge). SOURCE Brown, 1104; OCLC. LOCATION L.
COMMENTARY Historical romance about the escape in 1720 of the Princess Clementina Sobieski from Austria and how she is conducted to Rome to be married to the Pretender by the Chevalier Charles Wogan, member of an Anglo-Irish family of Clongowes Wood (Co. Kildare). Some glimpses of the Irish Brigade [Brown].
M306 *The four feathers* (by Alfred Edward Woodley Mason).
London: Smith, Elder & Co., 1902. SOURCE Brown, 1105. LOCATION L.

Leipzig: Bernard Tauchnitz, 1903. SOURCE T & B, 3630. LOCATION L.
COMMENTARY A moral story set in London, Devonshire, the Sudan, and Donegal (Ramelton and Glenalla). The hero, an English soldier, is all his life haunted by the fear of showing 'the white feather' at a critical moment. He resigns his commission rather than risk his reputation for courage in a campaign. This action brings on him the dreaded imputation of cowardice, but he redeems his honour [Brown].

'MASSINGBERD, Godfrey', pseud. See STARKEY, Digby Pilot.

MATHEW, Frank. See MATHEW, Frank James.

MATHEW, Frank James (known as Frank Mathew), b. Bombay (India) 1865, d. 1924. Historical novelist and story writer, FJM was the son of a civil engineer; a nephew of Cork-born judge and Home Rule supporter Sir James Mathew, and great-nephew of the Irish temperance advocate Fr Theobald Mathew, whose biography he wrote (London, 1890). FJM was educated at Beaumont, King's College, and London University, became a solicitor and lived in London. His romantic Irish stories appeared in the *Idler* (London). He also wrote the text to two books, both titled *Ireland*, with paintings by Francis S. Walker in one (London, 1905), and by Alfred Heaton Cooper in the other (London, 1916). He was one of the founders of the Irish Literary Society in London. Only FJM's known Irish fiction is listed below. SOURCE Brady, p. 160; Brown, p. 204; IBL, 14 (1924), p. 124; Hogan 2, p. 829; O'Donoghue 2, p. 429; Quinn, 6207; E. Reilly, p. 247; Ryan, p. 115; Sutherland, p. 422.

M307 *At the rising of the moon. Irish stories and studies* (by Frank Mathew; dedicated to Jerome K. Jerome).
+ London: McClure & Co.; Simpkin, Marshall, Hamilton, Kent & Co., 1893 (ill. Fred Pegram, A.S. Boyd, J. Stafford). SOURCE Brown, 1106; OCLC. LOCATION D, DPL, L, NUC, InND Loeber coll.
+ New York: Tait, Sons & Co., [1893]. LOCATION D, NUC, InND Loeber coll.
COMMENTARY Interconnected stories set in the parish of Moher (Co. Clare). Contents: 'The Reverend Peter Flannery', 'A Connemara miracle', 'Shane Desmond', '"The other country"', 'By the devil's mother', 'Colonel Hercules Desmond', 'The white witch of Moher', 'Their last race', 'The snipe's luck', 'At the rising of the moon', 'The dark man', 'Aileen Desmond', 'A prodigal', 'A prodigal's return', 'The heroism of Larry Ronan', 'In the black valley', 'The leenaun shee', 'Bishop O'Halloran', '"A letter for Ireland"', 'Constable Coyne', 'Epilogue [treasure trove]' [ML].

M308 *The wood of the brambles* (by Frank Mathew; dedicated to Lady Davern).
+ London: John Lane; Chicago: Way & Williams, 1896 (ill.). SOURCE Brown, 1107; OCLC. LOCATION D, L, NUC, InND Loeber coll.
COMMENTARY Historical fiction set during the 1798 rebellion. The rebels are portrayed as comic savages and their leaders little better than buffoons. Portrays the uncertainty of who is on what side. The main character is repeatedly taken captive and has to take part into various trials, his own and that of others [ML; Brown].

M309 *A child in the temple* (by Frank Mathew).
+ London, New York: John Lane, 1897. SOURCE Quinn, 6202; OCLC. LOCATION D (1897, 2nd edn), L, NUC, InND Loeber coll.
COMMENTARY A romance set in Ireland and London. Florence Kilmorna grows up in the house of his aunt and uncle in the country. His uncle is relatively poor and has to press his tenants for rent. When his tenants start to threaten him, policemen are stationed on the estate. Florence's best friend is Curly Adair, who promises to marry him when he grows up to be

six feet tall and has become a policeman. Eventually, Kilmorna goes to London and studies law at the Temple. Curly enters a convent in London and they happen to meet. They realize that they still love each other and Curly leaves the convent [ML].

M310 *The Spanish wine* (by Frank Mathew).

+ London, New York: John Lane, 1898. SOURCE Brown, 1108; Hogan 2, p. 829; OCLC. LOCATION D, L, NUC, InND Loeber coll.

COMMENTARY Historical fiction set in the sixteenth century in the form of the reminiscences of Lady Dunluce of Dunluce Castle (Co. Antrim) at the time that the MacDonnells from Scotland are lords of Antrim and Sir John Perrott is Queen Elizabeth's deputy in Ireland (1584–88). The author's sympathies are with the MacDonnells, who are on the side of the English at the time. Lady Dunluce, at the end of her life, remembers the men who had been important to her [ML; Brown].

M311 *Love of comrades. A romance* (by Frank Mathew).

+ London, New York: J. Lane, 1900. SOURCE Brown, 1109; OCLC. LOCATION D, NUC.

COMMENTARY Historical fiction set in early-seventeenth-century Ireland. The daughter of a Wicklow squire, bosom friend of the lord deputy Strafford, goes on a perilous journey disguised as a man with a life or death message for Strafford in Dublin [Brown].

MATTHEWS, Brander. Co-author. See JESSOP, George Henry.

MATURIN, Revd Charles Robert, pseud. 'Dennis Jasper Murphy', b. Dublin 1780 (1782 according to Allibone), d. Dublin 1824. Church of Ireland clergyman, novelist, playwright and poet, CRM was the son of Fidelia Watson and William Maturin, who was of Huguenot extraction and a clerk in the Irish post office. As a boy, he loved poetry and wrote dramas for his siblings to perform. He read widely, especially the Gothic romances popular at the time. He graduated BA at TCD in 1800 and in 1803 married Henrietta, daughter of Revd Thomas Kingsbury, archdeacon of Killala (Co. Mayo). He was ordained for the curacy at Loughrea (Co. Galway) the same year but in 1805 he was transferred to St Peter's, Dublin. CRM supplemented his small clerical income by tutoring and by writing novels. Sir Walter Scott's positive review of his first effort *The fatal revenge* (London, 1807) in 1810 began a relationship between the two authors that greatly benefited CRM, and although the two men had a life-long friendship they never met. Scott edited CRM's manuscript copy of a play *Bertram; or, the castle of St. Aldobrand*, and through his efforts – with the assistance of Lord Byron – it was staged at Drury Lane in 1816 and was an immediate success. The publisher John Murray printed an amended version of the play that sold out seven printings within a year. It was transposed into the novel *The history of Count Bertram, an Italian nobleman* (London, [1816?]), but the author of that is unknown. CRM's acclaim as a playwright was short-lived and subsequent dramas met with little success. His writings and love of entertainment allegedly precluded his advancement in the church, but his eccentricity of manner and deviations from religious orthodoxy may have been equally to blame. CRM was known to compose while walking around the house with 'a wafer on his forehead', as a sign that no one should address him lest he lose his thought. He and his family were often in financial difficulties. He published seven novels, mostly in a Gothic mode. CRM's poem *The universe* (London, 1821) has been ascribed also to James Wills who, Scholten asserts, allowed Maturin to use it when he needed to fulfil a promise made to the publisher Colburn. Another poem, *Lines on the battle of Waterloo*, published under the name of John Shee, an undergraduate at Trinity, is attributed to Maturin by his anonymous biographer. His 'Leixlip Castle, an Irish family legend' is a short story that posthumously appeared in the *Literary Souvenir* (London, 1825). CRM was very much against catholicism and presbyterianism and his *Five sermons on the errors of the Roman Catholic Church* (Dublin, 1824, repr. 1826) were drawn from his preaching at St Peter's and were very popular. His novel, *Melmoth* (Edinburgh, 1820, 4 vols.) was praised by Balzac as 'the greatest creation of one of the greatest geniuses in Europe' (ODNB). CRM was buried in the churchyard of St Peter's, Dublin. His son Edward Maturin§ emigrated to the US and became a writer also. For CRM's portraits and papers, see ODNB. SOURCE Allibone, ii, p. 1246; B & S, p. 563; Boylan, p. 247; Brooke, pp 6–7; Brown, p. 205; *Catalogue of the library at Abbotsford* (Edinburgh, 1837), pp 208, 335–6; DLB, clxxviii; Field Day, i, p. 1171, ii, pp 832–4 and passim, iii, p. 562; S.C. Hall, p. 234; Hogan, pp 441–2; Hogan 2, p. 831–2; Igoe, pp 173–7; D. Kramer, *Charles Maturin* (New York, 1973), passim; McKenna, p. 269–72; Leslie & Wallace, p. 881; NCBEL 4, pp 956–8; NSTC; G.N. Nuttall-Smith, *The chronicles of a puritan family in Ireland* [*Smith (formerly) of Glasshouse*] (Oxford, 1923), pp 92–6; OCIL, pp 359–60; ODNB; O'Donoghue, p. 305; F. Ratchford & W.H. McCarthy (eds), *The Scott-Maturin correspondence* (Austin, TX, 1937); RIA/DIB; W. Scholten, *Charles Robert Maturin the terror-novelist* (Amsterdam, 1933); Scott (correspondence with Sir Walter Scott); Summers, p. 193; H.A. Wheeler & M.J. Craig, *The Dublin city churches of the Church of Ireland. An illustrated handbook* (Dublin, 1948), p. 35; Ximenes cat. 97–5/150.

M312 *Fatal revenge; or, the family of Montorio. A romance* (by 'Dennis Jasper Murphy').
+ London: Longman, Hurst, Rees & Orme, 1807, 3 vols. SOURCE Rafroidi, ii, p. 271; British Fiction; Garside, 1807:42; Wolff, 4647. LOCATION Corvey CME 3–628–48395–6, Grail, D, Dt, L, NUC.
Paris: G.C. Hubert, 1822, 5 vols. (trans. by J. Cohen as *La famille de Montario, ou la fatale vengeance*). SOURCE Rafroidi, ii, p. 367; Bn-Opale plus. LOCATION BNF.
+ New York: I. Riley, 1808, 2 vols. LOCATION NUC, InND Loeber coll. (vol. 2 only).
New York: Arno Press, 1974, 3 vols. SOURCE Rafroidi, ii, p. 271. LOCATION L, E.
COMMENTARY In the preface to this Gothic story of mystery and terror set in Italy in the late-seventeenth century, Maturin asserts that the most powerful and universal source of emotion is the 'fear arising from objects of invisible terror'. The story begins when Orazio returns to Muralto Castle to revenge himself on his usurping brother, the count of Montorio. Earlier the count had led Orazio to believe his wife Erminia was unfaithful to him with the handsome young officer, Verdoni, which was untrue. But Orazio had gruesomely killed Verdoni, causing Erminia's death and the onset of his own madness. Having been away for many years, during which time he studied occultism, Orazio comes back disguised as the monk Schemoli and becomes the confessor to the household at Muralto Castle. Orazio persuades his brother's sons to kill their father. It turns out that the two young men are in fact his own sons, adopted by the count in atonement for his wrongdoing, and Orazio has made them murderers. Orazio confesses and dies from a burst blood-vessel. His sons are pardoned on condition they leave Italy. They take service in the French army and are killed in the siege of Barcelona in 1697. The book was reviewed by Sir Walter Scott in the *Quarterly Review* (1810) [OCIL, p. 182; Frank, 265; Scholten, pp 15–20].

M313 *The wild Irish boy* [anon.] (dedicated to the earl of Moira).
+ London: Longman, Hurst, Rees & Orme, 1808, 3 vols. SOURCE British Fiction; Garside, 1808:75; Rafroidi, ii, p. 272; Brown, 1110; Sadleir, 1669. LOCATION Corvey CME 3–628–48922–9, Grail, Ireland related fiction, D (1808, 2nd edn), Dt, L, NUC, InND Loeber coll.
Paris: Mame et Delauney-Vallée, 1828, 4 vols. (trans. by Comtesse*** [de Molé] as *Le jeune Irlandais*). SOURCE Rafroidi, ii, p. 367. LOCATION Dt.
+ New York: E. Sargeant, 1808, 2 vols. (by Dennis Jasper Murphy). LOCATION NUC, InND Loeber coll.

New York: E. Sargeant; Baltimore: Geo. Hill; Charleston: E. Morford; Boston: Hastings, Atheridge & Bliss, Munroe, Francis & Parker, 1808, 2 vols. SOURCE NCBEL 3, p. 746. LOCATION D.

Buffalo (NY): G. & M. Morse, [1850–1870?]. SOURCE RLIN. LOCATION Brown Univ.

New York: Arno Press, 1977, 3 vols. SOURCE Rafroidi, ii, p. 272. LOCATION E.

New York: Garland, 1979, 3 vols. (introd. by R.L. Wolff). LOCATION Dt.

COMMENTARY Epistolary novel, partly inspired by Lady Morgan's *The wild Irish girl* (London, 1806, 3 vols.). *The wild Irish boy* is set in Dublin, the west of Ireland, and London in the period 1806 to 1808. Intended as an exposition of the unhappy condition of Ireland and as a picture of the life and manner of the time, it features a wild young Irishman, Ormsby Bethel, who eventually finds his real father. The novel features his irascible but generous uncle in the person of an old Irish chieftain full of Gaelic patriotism; a stern father who is not actually the wild Irish boy's father after all; a domineering governess (Miss Percival), and several other women who compete for the young man's affections. The major action occurs in London where Ormsby lives a dissipated life, encouraged by his cousin, Deloraine, and his partner in intrigue, Lady Delphina. Ormsby's real father appears and is anxious to teach his son in the degenerate ways of the world and thus cure his son's wildness. In the preface Maturin noted that he had been criticized for the lack of female presence and female interest in his first novel and in this one tried to remedy that [Brown 1110; Wolff introd., p. 14; Frank, 266; Scholten, pp 20–1].

M314 *The Milesian chief. A romance* [anon.] (dedicated to the *Quarterly* reviewers).

+ London: Henry Colburn, 1812, 4 vols. SOURCE Rafroidi, ii, p. 272; Brown, 1112; British Fiction; Garside, 1812:46; Sadleir, 1668; Wolff, 4651; Bradshaw, 5997. LOCATION Grail, Corvey CME 3-628-48130-9, Ireland related fiction, D, Dt, L, C, NUC.

Paris: Mame & Delauney-Vallée, 1828, 4 vols. (trans. by comtesse de Molé as *Connal, ou les Milésiens*). SOURCE Rafroidi, ii, p. 367. LOCATION L.

Philadelphia: Bradford & Innskeep; New York: Innskeep & Bradford, 1812, 2 vols. SOURCE NCBEL 3, p. 746. LOCATION NUC.

New York: Garland, 1979, 4 vols. (introd. by R.L. Wolff). LOCATION Dt.

COMMENTARY The author explains in the preface to this tragic tale his reasons for mixing nationalism with Gothicism into a Hibernian Gothic: The ways of the Gothic are appropriate to 'the only country on earth, where, from the strange existing opposition of religion, politics, and manners, the extremes of refinement and barbarism are united, and the most wild and incredible situations of romantic story are hourly passing before modern eyes'. The imputed time is the early-nineteenth century in the west of Ireland where the old Milesian chief O'Morven has barricaded himself within his grim turret as a last act of defiance against the English. His grandson, the gallant patriot, Connal, carries on the fight against the oppressors of Irish liberty. He opposes the brutal English officer, Wandesford, vying with him for the love of Ireland and the love of Armida Fitzalan, daughter of Lord Montclare who has bought the O'Morven's land. Armida is at the mercy of Wandesford who displays all of the usual wicked drives of the Gothic villain. A haunted castle on the Connacht seacoast serves as Wandesford's emporium of terror. Connal kills Wandesford, and he is seized and condemned to death by the English. Armida, who is slowly dying of poison arrives at the place of execution too late for a final farewell. A subplot involves the growing love between Connal's brother Desmond, an officer in the English army, and Armida's brother who, unbeknownst to Desmond, is in reality her sister who has been disguised by her mother to ensure the succession of the estates [Frank, 267; Scholten, pp 22–6].

M315 *Women; or, pour et contre. A tale* [anon.] (dedicated to the countess of Essex).

+ Edinburgh: Archibald Constable & Co.; London: Longman, Hurst, Rees, Orme & Brown, 1818, 3 vols. SOURCE Rafroidi, ii, p. 272; Brown, 1114; British Fiction; Garside,

1818:41; Sadleir, 1670; Wolff, 4653. LOCATION Grail, Corvey CME 3–628–48977–6, Ireland related fiction, D, L, ViU, InND Loeber coll.

Paris: J.G. Dentu, 1818, 4 vols. (trans. by M.***** as *Eva, ou amour et religion*). SOURCE Rafroidi, ii, p. 366; Burmester list. LOCATION Dt.

Paris: Grandin, 1820, 3 vols. (trans. by Mme E. de Bon as *Les femmes, ou rien de trop*). SOURCE Rafroidi, ii, p. 366; Bn-Opale plus. LOCATION BNF.

New York: C. Viley, 1818, 2 vols. LOCATION NUC.

Philadelphia: Moses Thomas, 1818, 2 vols. SOURCE NCBEL 3, p. 746. LOCATION MH.

New York: Garland, 1979, 3 vols. (introd. by R.L. Wolff). LOCATION D, Dt, CtY.

COMMENTARY The original title *De Courcy: Pour et contre*, was rejected by the publisher Constable. The author states in the preface to this psychological study that, in contrast to his earlier novels, which wanted reality, he now presents some characters 'which experience will not disown'. Set in Dublin; the hero is De Courcy, a Trinity College undergraduate. He rescues Eva Wentworth, who has been carried off by a fanatical grandmother to be made a Catholic. He falls in love with her and this brings him into Calvinistic and Methodist circles in Dublin. The Methodist gloom drives the hero to the company of a brilliant actress (in reality Zaira, Eva's mother, who does not know where her daughter is). He is torn between the two, but finally goes to Paris with Zaira. There his passion for Zaira wanes and hearing Eva is ill, he returns to Dublin. Zaira learns that Eva is her daughter and is in despair that she had destroyed her happiness. Eva dies and De Courcy, repentant, soon follows [Brown; Field Day, i, p. 949, 1078, 1081, 1115–25, 1150; Wolff, introd., p. 15; Scholten, pp 57–75; D. Kramer, *Charles Maturin* (New York, 1973), p. 150, *n.*1].

M316 *Melmoth the wanderer. A tale* [anon.] (dedicated to the marchioness of Abercorn).

+ Edinburgh: Archibald Constable & Co.; London: Hurst, Robinson & Co., 1820, 4 vols. SOURCE Rafroidi, ii, p. 272; British Fiction; Garside, 1820:51; Sadleir, 1667; Wolff, 4650. LOCATION Grail, Corvey CME 3–628–48054–X, Ireland related fiction, D, Dt, L, NUC.

+ London: Richard Bentley & Son, 1892, 3 vols. (with a memoir and bibliography of Maturin's work). SOURCE Rafroidi, ii, p. 272. LOCATION InND Loeber coll.

Paris: Librarie Nationale et Étrangère, 1821, 3 vols. (trans. by Mme Emile Bégin as *L'Homme du mystère, ou histoire de Melmoth le voyageur*). SOURCE Rafroidi, ii, p. 367; Sadleir, 1667a; Bn-Opale plus. LOCATION BNF.

Paris: G.C. Hubert, 1821, 6 vols. (by Mathurin [*sic*]; very free trans. by J. Cohen as *Melmoth ou l'homme errant*). SOURCE Rafroidi, ii, p. 367; Bn-Opale plus. Location BNF.

Arnstadt: Hildenbrand'schen Buchhandlung, 1821 (trans. by C.v.S. as *Melmoth, der Wanderer*). SOURCE Belanger, 65; OCLC. LOCATION Brown Univ.

Boston: Wells & Lilly, 1821, 2 vols. LOCATION Dt (4 vols. in 2), NUC.

+ Lincoln: Univ. of Nebraska Press, 1961. SOURCE Rafroidi, ii, p. 272. LOCATION D.

+ London: Oxford Univ. Press, 1968 (ed. by Douglas Grant). SOURCE Rafroidi, ii, p. 272; Hogan, p. 442; COPAC. LOCATION InND Loeber coll.

+ London: Penguin, 2000 (ed. with an introd. by Victor Sage). LOCATION Dt, L, C.

COMMENTARY A novel fusing Gothic modes with tragic themes inspired, according to Maturin in the preface (omitted in later edns), by the theme of one his sermons in which he speculated whether anyone in the congregation would be prepared to sacrifice his eternal salvation for temporal power and riches. Melmoth, the hero, had bargained away his soul in return for 150 years of power and knowledge on earth. The book abounds in lurid scenes. The novel's poetic and tragic elements include Faustian betrayal of soul and loss of self, the moral problem of confronting and controlling the darkest facets of self, the riddle of suffering in an absurd and unheroic universe, the dilemma of the overreaching personality entrapped by a limited cosmos, and the metaphysical catastrophe of the never-ending life which becomes the wanderer's ironic damnation. Structurally, it consists of five novelettes: 'The tale of Stanton' (the prisoner, Stanton, confined to a madhouse where slowly he is going mad), 'The tale of the Spaniard' (Don Alonzo de Monçada, a kindly hidalgo in the clutches of the Spanish Inquisition; 'Tale of the Indians', about the lovely Immalee, a young woman living in a deserted tropical paradise), 'The tale of Guzman's family' (the starving Walberg family and the horrible temptations to end their misery), 'The lover's tale' (the thwarted love of the pathetic Elinor Mortimer). The novel was transformed by B. West into a play, which was published in 1823; Honoré de Balzac wrote a sequel *Melmoth réconcilié à l'église* (Paris, 1866), and Oscar Wilde§, related to CRM through his mother, used the name Sebastian Melmoth after his release from prison [Jarndyce cat. 106/1672; OCIL, pp 362–3; Field Day, ii, pp 832–4, 854–6; Frank, 268; Hogan 2, pp 831–2; ODNB; Scholten, pp 76–108].

M317   *The Albigenses. A romance* [anon.] (dedicated to Mrs Smith, Fitzwilliam Street, Dublin).

+ London: Hurst, Robinson & Co.; Edinburgh: A. Constable & Co., 1824, 4 vols. SOURCE Rafroidi, ii, p. 272; British Fiction; Garside, 1824:66; Sadleir, 1662. LOCATION Grail, Corvey CME 3–628–47036–6, D, L, NUC.

Paris: Gosselin, Mame & Delauney-Vallée, 1825, 4 vols. (trans. as *Les Albigeois, roman historique du xiie siècle*). SOURCE Rafroidi, ii, p. 367; Bn-Opale plus. Location BNF.

Philadelphia: S.F. Bradford & J. Laval, 1824, 3 vols. SOURCE NCBEL 3, p. 746. LOCATION NUC.

New York: Arno Press, 1974, 4 vols. (introd. By Dale Kramer). SOURCE Rafroidi, ii, p. 272. LOCATION Univ. of Southampton.

COMMENTARY Fiction integrating Gothic devices with historical drama, set in thirteenth-century France and giving an account of the campaign of Simon de Montfort to exterminate the sect of the Albigenses, a large group of Manichean heretics living in communities in the south of France. The main characters are two brothers: Sir Paladour is a vigorous proponent of the crusade against the Albigenses; the other brother, Almirald, takes the side of the threatened heretics and falls in love with Genevieve, an Albigensian maid. The novel describes their adventures in the campaigns and the ups and downs in their love life, ending with a double wedding. Along with the expected Gothic themes of castles, curses, and vocal spectres, the novel introduces lycanthropy, or werewolfism, as a terror motif for the first time in Gothic fiction [Frank, 269; OCIL, p. 10; Scholten, pp 104–92].

MATURIN, Edward, b. Dublin 1812, d. New York 1881. Professor, novelist, poet and playwright, EM was the son of Charles Robert Maturin§ and Henrietta Kingsbury. He was admitted to TCD and received his BA in 1832. After becoming a barrister he emigrated to the US where he became professor of Greek, first in Charleston (SC), and later in New York. He was involved in the translation of the *Gospel of St Mark* for the American Bible Union and was the author of *Lyrics of Spain and Erin* (Boston, 1850). EM wrote five novels, some of which were historical fiction. SOURCE Allibone, ii, p. 1247; Brady, p. 161; Burke, p. 474; ODNB [under Charles Maturin]; OCLC; O'Donoghue, p. 305; Sutherland, p. 422.

M318   *Sejanus, and other Roman tales* [anon.].

New York: F. Saunders, 1839. SOURCE Wright, i, 1842. LOCATION NUC.

New York: Printed by Jared W. Bell, 1839. SOURCE Wright, i, 1843; OCLC. LOCATION CtY.

COMMENTARY Historical fiction set during Roman times [RL].

M319   *Montezuma, the last of the Aztecs* (by Edward Maturin).

New York: Paine & Burgess, 1845, 2 vols. SOURCE Wright, i, 1841. LOCATION NUC.

COMMENTARY Historical fiction set during Aztec times [RL].

M320 *Benjamin, the Jew of Grenada. A romance* (by Edward Maturin).
New York: Richards & Co., [1847]. SOURCE Wright, i, 1839. LOCATION NUC.

M321 *The Irish chieftain; or, the isles of life and death* (by Edward Maturin).
+ Glasgow: R. Griffin & Co., 1848. SOURCE Rafroidi, ii, p. 275; Brown, 1116. LOCATION D, Dt, NUC.
New York: Stringer & Townsend, 1848, 2 vols. (as *Eva; or, the isles of life and death*). SOURCE Allibone, ii, p. 1247; Wright, i, 1840.
COMMENTARY No copy of the New York edn located. Historical fiction set in the time after the Norman invasion of Ireland. Historical names are used, but the incidents described have no foundation in history [Brown].

M322 *Bianca. A tale of Erin and Italy* (by Edward Maturin; dedicated to Jesse W. Benedict).
+ New York: Harper & Bros, 1852. SOURCE Brown, 1117; Rafroidi, ii, p. 275; Wright, ii, 1684. LOCATION L, NUC, InND Loeber coll., Wright web.
COMMENTARY A story set in Ireland and Italy full of murders, terrible secrets and illegitimate children [Brown].

MAUNSELL, Dorothea (later Dorothea Kingsman), b. probably Limerick *c*.1745–48 or 1751, d. 1820. Fictionalizing autobiographer, DM was the fourth daughter of Thomas Maunsell, LLD, county court judge and MP for Kilmallock (Co. Limerick), and Dorothea Waller, of Castle Waller (Co. Tipperary). According to Burke's, she married William Long Kingsman in 1762, but this date is in error. Her own account of her life up to 1765, fictionalized below, indicates that she married first the Italian soprano and composer Giusto Ferdinando Tenducci (*c*.1735–1790) in 1766. Tenducci had become friendly with the Mozart family in England, and had sung at the Theatre Royal in Smock Alley, Dublin, in 1765. According to later court proceedings he was a castrato. In the summer of 1766 he was introduced to the Maunsell family. DM was a minor under age 15, but Tenducci married her on 19 Aug. 1766 at the house of a 'Romish priest' Patrick Egan. After the dramatic sequence of events recounted in the volume below, the couple left Ireland and went to Edinburgh, where he renounced 'the Errors of Popery', and then to London in early 1770 or 1771 where DM made her first appearance in a musical entertainment. They then travelled to Florence, where he called her Signora Dorothea but did not reveal his marriage to her. They continued to live together there until 1772, when the Irishman William Long Kingsman convinced her to leave Italy. Before doing so, she and Kingsman, to whom she was married, were painted in Naples in 1773 by the Limerick painter Timothy Collopy, who also gave her drawing lessons. After her marriage to Kingsman, she made her stage début as an actress in the Theatre Royal in Cork city in 1775. Tenducci eventually returned to Ireland to sing in the Dublin opera in 1784. Clark ascribes three subsequent marriages, or relationships, to DM: first to William Farren, an actor, then to Thomas Orton, and last to one Bell, but it is likely that he confused the actor Mary Mounsell with Dorothea Maunsell (see ODNB under Thomas Orton). It is not clear whether DM or someone else wrote the following work. Another related work, referred to as *Mrs. Tenducci, letters*, was published in Cork in 1774, but is not in ESTC and no copy has been located. SOURCE Burke's, pp 811, 813; W.S. Clark, *The Irish stage in the county towns* (Oxford, 1965), pp 94–5, 98, 367; *Dorothea Kingsman against Ferdinando Tenducci, libel given in Oct. 1775. In Trials for adultery: or, the history of divorce. Being select trials at Doctors Commons* (London, 1780), vii, pp 1–4; HIP, v, pp 210–20; J. Ingamells, *A dictionary of British and Irish travellers in Italy* (New Haven, 1997), pp 231, 578; Personal communication, Toby Barnard, Oct. 2004 (based on Revd James Hingston, 'An alphabetical catalogue of my books', Representative Church Body Library,

Dublin, MS 521.3); S. Sadie (ed.), *The new Grove dictionary of music and musicians* (London, 1977), xviii, p. 687; T.J. Walsh, *Opera in Dublin 1705–1797* (Dublin, 1973), passim.

M323 *A true and genuine narrative of Mr. and Mrs. Tenducci. In a letter to a friend at Bath. Giving a full account, from their marriage in Ireland, to the present time* [anon.].
+ London: J. Pridden, 1768. SOURCE Raven, 1249; Pollard 2, p. 62; ESTC t117835. LOCATION L, InND Loeber coll.

COMMENTARY Pencil endorsement in the Notre Dame copy identifies the author of this somewhat fictionalized autobiography as 'Miss Maunsell'. Giusto Ferdinando Tenducci is an Italian opera singer who in his early thirties comes to London and Dublin to appear on stage and to give music lessons. In Ireland, he gives lessons to Dora Maunsell, a young lady from a good family who is staying with friends in a house outside Dublin. In a letter, she relates the subsequent story to a correspondent in England. She falls in love with her teacher, but she returns with her father and mother to Limerick, where she is pressed to marry a man whom she thought unsuitable. The family moves to Cork for the assizes (her father is a judge), and she meets Tenducci who is performing in the city. She secretly marries him, but the news leaks out before she returns without him to Limerick. She leaves for G—h—ll, her sister's house about 12 miles from Limerick, from where she elopes with Tenducci to Cork. There, she is surprised by armed men, who confine her to a house in the city. In the meantime, Tenducci is arrested by virtue of court proceedings instigated by Dorothea's father. Dora and her husband are temporarily united, but her father reinstigates court proceedings, resulting in Tenducci's imprisonment. Dorothea's father, mother and other relatives try to change her mind about Tenducci and threaten to lock her up in a private madhouse near Dublin. She is sent to her sister G., where her parents threaten to confine her on a remote mountain, and where the clergyman from Nenagh pleads with her in vain. She is subsequently transported to a ruinous castle of the O'd family in the west of Co. Clare, where she is forced to stay for a few months under deplorable circumstances, and has to defend herself against the advances of O'D's son. She manages to escape and finds her way to Mr P—'s house at Ballymacarbarry [Ballymacarbry] in Co. Waterford, where her husband had stayed. However, he has left for Dublin but because of the machinations of Dorothea's family is not able to exercise his profession. Dorothea joins him in Dublin. Eventually, her father drops all court proceedings and Dorothea and Tenducci are married again. A postscript is dated 1767 from Clogheen (prob. Co. Tipperary). Key: W.H. of G—h—ll is Dorothea's brother-in-law Henry White of Greenfield (Co. Tipperary); R.M. is Robert Maunsell, her uncle; F— is her father; M— is her mother; S— is her sister, Elizabeth; cousin W. is cousin Waller, probably of Castle Waller (Co. Tipperary); sister G. is Margaret, who had married Robert Going of Traveston Hall (near Nenagh, Co. Tipperary); O'D may be O'Dea of Dysart O'Dea Castle [RL].

MAUNSELL, W.P. See **MAUNSELL, William Pryce.**

MAUNSELL, W. Pryce. See **MAUNSELL, William Pryce.**

MAUNSELL, William Pryce (also known as **W. Pryce Maunsell** and **W.P. Maunsell**), b. probably Limerick 1828, d. 1920. Solicitor, novelist, and miscellaneous writer, WPM was the second son of Henry Maunsell of Fanstown, Kilmallock (Co. Limerick) and Elizabeth Peacocke, and perhaps was related to Dorothea Maunsell§ and Ida Peacocke§. WPM graduated BA at TCD and was admitted as a student to the King's Inns in Dublin in 1848. Subsequently he became a solicitor and married Richarda, youngest daughter of Richard Gabbett, of Strand House (Limerick) in 1861. He lived at Fairyfield, Kilmallock, and also at

Dun Laoghaire (Co. Dublin). He wrote a drama 'Alfieri' (not located), *The idler in college, or the student's guide* (Dublin, 1850), and a volume on the Church of Ireland entitled *Old England's Union Jack, our disestablished church* (London, 1880). There is an unexplained 30-year gap between these two publications. SOURCE B & S, p. 566 (possible identification); Brown 2, p. 177; Burke's, p. 813; Keane, p. 332; Landed gentry, 1904, p. 394.

M324 *Our disestablished parish: A story of the Church of Ireland* (ed. by W.P. Maunsell).
+ London: Simpkin, Marshall & Co., 1880. SOURCE COPAC. LOCATION L.
COMMENTARY 40pp. Fiction set in the south of Ireland. The preface states that the work had been written to expose to the General Synod 'some of the defects in the working of the constitution of our Church. Secondly, to try to point out the dangers which follow if all independent thought is crushed out of the Church ...' [CM].

M325 *The poisoned chalice. A novel* (by W. Pryce Maunsell).
London: Roper & Drawley, 1888. LOCATION L.
+ London: W.H. Beer & Co., 1888. SOURCE Allibone Suppl., ii, p. 1092; Brown 2, 1014. LOCATION NUC, InND Loeber coll.
COMMENTARY The background is garrison and country society in Limerick in the early years of the nineteenth century. Annabel Elton breaks her engagement on learning of a moral lapse in the past life of her fiancée. She instead marries a worthless man. The rejected lover rejoins his regiment in England and dies there. The story is apparently founded on family records [Brown 2].

MAXWELL, Mrs —. See MAXWELL, Mrs Caroline.

MAXWELL, Mrs Caroline (also known as Mrs Maxwell). fl. 1808. Novelist, poet and miscellaneous writer, CM was probably English. Her *Feudal tales* (London, [1810?]) contains a poem 'The heir of Tyrconnell', which has Irish content. Her only novel linked to Ireland is listed below. SOURCE Allibone, ii, p. 1251; Garside, 1812:47; NCBEL 4, p. 958.

M326 *The Earl of Desmond; or, O'Brien's cottage. An Irish story* (by Mrs Maxwell).
+ London: J.F. Hughes, 1810, 3 vols. SOURCE British Fiction; Garside, 1810:62; Block, p. 156. LOCATION Corvey CME 3–28–48203–8, Ireland related fiction, L.
COMMENTARY A complicated plot centring on the Desmond family. The earl of Desmond's brother Frederick Fitzhugh and his wife Ophelia take refuge in Denis O'Brien's cottage in northern Ireland. During their stay Ophelia dies in childbirth. Their daughter Georgiana is looked after for fifteen years by the O'Briens while the father returns to fight in the East Indies. The earl of Desmond's nephew turns up at the O'Brien's cottage when Georgiana is age 16. Disguised as his uncle (whose assassination he has plotted in Italy) he kidnaps the girl, telling her that her father is dead. He takes her to London and forces her into marriage. Georgiana is accidentally reunited with her father who has returned from the East Indies. The identity of her husband is soon revealed and he is forced to flee to Italy. Just as he leaves, the real earl of Desmond returns and the murder plot is uncovered. Eventually Georgiana's evil husband returns to his castle and repents before committing suicide [CM].

MAXWELL, Herbert. See MAXWELL, Sir Herbert Eustace, 7th Bt.

MAXWELL, Sir Herbert Eustace, 7th Bt (known as Herbert Maxwell), b. Edinburgh (Scotland) 1845, d. Monteith Wigtownshire (Scotland) 1937. Novelist, historian and man of letters, HEM was the son of Sir William Maxwell and Helenora Shaw-Stewart. He studied at Eton, which he described as a time of 'insensate indolence', and spent a year at Christ Church, Oxford. He returned to Scotland to assist his father in the running of the estate. He was widely-read and maintained scholarly interest in numerous subjects, including archaeology, antiquities, horticulture and natural history. He married Mary, eldest daughter of Henry Fletcher-Campbell, of Boquan, Stirling. HEM succeeded his father in 1877, and was MP for Wigtownshire from 1880 to 1906. He was a prolific writer on topics such as topography, natural history, biography, fishing and sport. A declining income spurred his literary output. He was president of the Society of Antiquaries of Scotland and chairman of the NLS. Only one of his novels is known to have a connection with Ireland. SOURCE Allibone Suppl., ii, p. 1094; BLC; Burke, 1878, pp 808–9; Personal communication, John Hart, Mar. 1994; ODNB; RL; Sutherland, p. 423.

M327 *The letter of the law* (by Herbert Maxwell).
+ London: Henry & Co., [1892] (The Whitefriars Library of Wit and Humour; ill.).
LOCATION L, InND Loeber coll.

COMMENTARY To while away the time on a rainy day in a Scottish country house, the company of residents perform a wedding mass composed by an ancestor. Nobody thinks much about it, but later when the girl who played the bride is engaged to be married, a person in love with her tells her that according to Scottish law she is already married to Arthur Knatchbull, the dashing Irish officer who had played the bridegroom. Knatchbull, when confronted, declines to undo the marriage and retires with his wife to his impoverished Irish estate. The marriage is an unhappy one. Knatchbull is threatened by his tenants and eventually is shot. The widow finds a new love and she and her husband buy her first husband's bankrupt estate to complete the plans for improvement that she had developed [ML].

MAXWELL, Katherine, pseud. 'K. M—x—ll', fl. 1750s. Novelist.
M328 *The history of Miss Kitty N—. Containing a faithful and particular relation of her amours, adventures, and various turns of fortune, in Scotland, Ireland, Jamaica, and England. Written by herself* (by 'K. M—x—ll').
+ London: F. Noble & J. Noble, [1757]. SOURCE Raven, 393; McBurney & Taylor, 456; ESTC t191251. LOCATION L, IU, NUC.

COMMENTARY Written as a supposed autobiography, with all names changed or only partially spelled out, this is the saga of a young woman who is born into a Scottish family with noble connections, but who ends up impoverished and alone. Katty is left an orphan at an early age and is boarded out in several relatives' houses where she learns to enjoy high life but gets little guidance. At age 13 she is almost raped by an earl, and her relatives think that she is a flirt and encourages undue attention from gentlemen. They decide she must leave and she moves to another house, where she is visited by Sir James who proposes marriage to her. He cannot marry her yet, he says, since he has an uncle from whom he will inherit only if he marries with his consent. He tries to seduce her and when he is not successful he gives her the love story of Eloise and Abelard to read in the hope to change her mind. Eventually she lives with him but his behaviour towards her changes quickly and he leaves. After various adventures her relatives decide to put her in a nunnery in Ireland, and later she stays in a boarding school in Dublin. She falls in love with a Mr Betterton, a journeyman, who seduces and marries her. He is arrested by the bailiff for debt. Katty is with child, but miscarries. The only one of her family interested in helping her is a brother, but he dies in a battle. She goes to Scotland to procure some money and comes back to Dublin where her husband is still in jail. Her letter of credit from Scotland is not honoured. When her husband comes out of jail he squanders what money there is. They live in England and Scotland for a while; she has another child, and her husband grows cold towards her. After many more misadventures she sets sail for Jamaica where her brother has possessions. Her stay there is also unhappy, and she returns to England. She ends in poverty and writes this book in the hope of earning some money [ML].

MAXWELL, W.H. See MAXWELL, Revd William Hamilton.

MAXWELL, Revd William Hamilton (known as W.H. Maxwell), b. Newry (Co. Down) 1792 (1794 according to OCIL), d. Musselburgh, near Edinburgh (Scotland) 1850. Church of Ireland clergyman, novelist and short story writer, WHM was the son of James Maxwell, a merchant. His mother was the daughter of William Hamilton. As a young boy, WHM witnessed the hanging of two United Irishmen in Newry in 1798, an event later recreated in his *O'Hara; or 1798* (London, 1825). He matriculated at TCD at age 15 and graduated BA in 1812, afterwards enjoying his favourite sports of hunting, shooting and fishing, while reading extensively. There is some confusion about WHM's life after university. He was inclined to a military career while his family preferred the church or the law. His obituary in the *London Illustrated News* (25 Jan. 1851) stated he had served in the 88th Regiment, participated in the Peninsular War and was present at the battle of Waterloo. Both the RIA/DIB and the ODNB state this was not so, although WHM may have fostered the idea himself. His knowledge of these events could have come from his acquaintance later with military officers stationed in Co. Mayo. After being left out of an expected inheritance from his aunt, WHM married in 1817 an heiress, Mary, second daughter of Thomas Dobbin, MP, of Armagh. He entered the church and was ordained deacon at Carlow in 1813 and became a minister at Clonallon, near Newry, in the same year. But some prankish behaviour caused him to be transferred to Ballagh (also known as Balla, Co. Mayo), six miles from Castlebar, around 1820. There were very few Protestants in this parish, leaving him free to pursue field sports, a very active social life and writing. He contributed to various periodicals, including the *Dublin University Magazine*, the *New Monthly Magazine* (London), and *Bentley's Miscellany* (London, 1837, 1850). Charles Dickens included WHM's story 'The expedition' in *The pic nic papers* (London, 1841, 3 vols.). WHM, who wrote 20 novels in as many years, is credited with inventing two genres of fiction: the dashing military novel and the novel of rollicking Irish life. He was a mentor to Charles Lever§ and the similarity of many of their stories may spring in part from their many exchanges of experiences and tales. Lever described him as 'a tall, distinguished-looking person' (FitzPatrick, p. 87). WHM also wrote travel books, a popular life of the duke of Wellington (London, 1839), and a *History of the Irish rebellion in 1798* (London, 1845), in part in reaction to R.R. Madden's§ *The lives and times of the United Irishmen* (London, 1842–46, 7 vols.). He subscribed to Matthew Archdeacon's§ *Legends of Connaught* (Dublin, 1839). WHM lost the living of Ballagh for non-residence in 1844 and went to Portrush (Co. Antrim) and then to Scotland. The last years of his life were plagued by financial difficulties and ill-health. He was a witty conversationalist and a great raconteur. William Maginn§ said of him, 'he flings off his tales as if they were so many tumblers of punch, hot and strong, pleasant and heart-cheering, hastily mixed, and hastily disposed of' (Brown, p. 206). For WHM's portraits and papers, see ODNB. SOURCE Allibone, ii, p. 1251; B & S, p. 568; J. Barrow, *A tour round Ireland* (London, 1836), p. 87; Boylan, p. 247; Brady, p. 161; Brown, p. 206; Brown 2, p. 14; Curran index, BentM 92; Elmes, p. 133; J.C. Erck, *The ecclesiastical register* (Dublin, 1820), p. 115; Field Day, i, p. 1256, ii, pp 833 and passim, iv, p. 892; FitzPatrick, pp 87–8, 99–104, 108–9, 380; W.E. Hall, pp 43, 66; Hogan, pp 444–5; Hogan 2, p. 836; S. Lewis, *A topographical dictionary of Ireland* (London, 1837), i, p. 102; ii, p. 467; McKenna, pp 273–5; NCBEL 4, pp 958–9; OCIL, p. 361; ODNB; O'Donoghue, p. 305; RIA/DIB; Swanzy, pp 105–6; Sutherland, pp 423–4.

M329 *O'Hara; or, 1798* [anon.] (dedicated to Howe Peter Browne, marquess of Sligo).
    + London: J. Andrews; Dublin: Milliken, 1825, 2 vols. (ill. J. Kirkwood, C. Grey, G.A. Hanlon, G. Du Noyer, E. Evans, H.K. Browne [Phiz]). SOURCE Rafroidi, ii, p. 276; Brown, 1118; Brown 2, 46; British Fiction; Garside, 1825: 59; Wolff, 4669. LOCATION Grail, Corvey CME 3–628–48244–5, Ireland related fiction, D, Dt, L, NUC.

+ New York: Garland, 1979, 2 vols. LOCATION Dt, E, InND Loeber coll.

COMMENTARY This novel has also been attributed to Robert Ashworth§, but according to RIA/DIB it is by WHM and said to have been written when he was given the use of a shooting lodge at Ballycroy on the marquess of Sligo's estate. Historical fiction, which begins with the Protestant hero's adventures during the American Revolution, followed by a period of retirement on his land near the Mourne Mountains (Co. Down). He subsequently joins the United Irishmen, is accused of treason by the government, and is hanged. His embittered son then throws himself into the rebellion and fights with the rebels in Antrim and Down. The story shows the friction between Catholic and Protestant commanders that often threatens to disrupt the rebel forces [Brown; ODNB; RIA/DIB; Wolff introd., p. 28].

M330 *Stories of Waterloo and other tales* [anon.] (dedicated to Arthur, duke of Wellington). London: Henry Colburn & Richard Bentley, 1829, 3 vols. SOURCE Rafroidi, ii, p. 27; British Fiction; Garside, 1829:60; Sadleir, 1682; Wolff, 4672. LOCATION Grail, Corvey CME 3–628–51133–X, Dt, L, NUC (1833 edn).

+ London, New York: George Routledge & Sons, n.d. (new edn; as *Stories of Waterloo* by W.H. Maxwell; Novels at Two Shillings). LOCATION InND Loeber coll. (also [1892] edn).

+ New York: J. & J. Harper, 1830, 2 vols. LOCATION D, NUC.

COMMENTARY Soldiers amuse each other by telling stories. Contents: 'My own adventure', 'The detachment', 'The adventure of the Captain of Grenadiers', 'The route', 'The outlaw's story' (set in Ireland), 'The march', 'Sarsfield', 'Frank Kennedy', 'The story of Colonel Nilson' (connected with the 1798 rebellion), 'Napoleon's return', 'The champ de Mai', 'Belgium', 'The park', 'The little Major's love adventure', 'The tall Major's story', 'The interview', 'The ball', 'Letters, and a lost mistress', 'Quatre-bras', 'Ligny', 'The seventeenth of June', 'The cavalry picket', 'Maurice Mac Carthy', 'Maurice Mac Carthy, continued', 'Waterloo', 'The field of battle', 'Napoleon and his army', 'Brussels', 'The dead dragoon', 'Stephen Purcell', 'The gazette', 'Captain Plinlimmon', 'Conclusion' [RL; W.E. Hall, p. 72; British Fiction].

M331 *Wild sports of the West, with legendary tales and local sketches* [anon.].

+ London: Richard Bentley, 1832, 2 vols. (ill. Bonner, T. Bagg). SOURCE Leclaire, pp 61–2; Rafroidi, ii, p. 276; Sadleir, 1683; Wolff, 4673; Garside 2, D:3. LOCATION Grail, Dt (1834 edn), L, NUC, InND Loeber coll.

London: Richard Bentley, 1833, 2 vols. (new edn, revsd and corrected; ill.). SOURCE de Búrca cat. 38/1242. LOCATION BFl.

+ Dublin: Talbot Press, n.d. (as *Wild sports of the West*; introd. by the earl of Dunraven; ill.; Every Irishman's Library). SOURCE OCLC. LOCATION NUI (Galway), InND Loeber coll.

New York: J. & J. Harper, 1833, 2 vols. in 1. SOURCE NCBEL 3, p. 747. LOCATION NUC.

+ Philadelphia: T.B. Peterson, [1870 or earlier]. SOURCE Adv. in A. Trollope's *MacDermots* (New York, 1870). LOCATION InND Loeber coll.

+ Southampton: Ashford Press, 1986 (new edn with biography by Colin Laurie McKelvie; The Field Library; ill.). LOCATION NUI (Galway), InND Loeber coll.

COMMENTARY First edn had a print run of 1,250 copies. This novel on hunting in the west of Ireland appeared in at least nine London edns. In 'Dull evening-memoir of Hennessy', WHM's account of Hennessy's elopement draws attention to the way in which a figure could become an outcast in a rural community, and describes the traditional customs that accompanied country weddings [Field Day, iv, pp 764, 849–52, 1169; Leclaire, pp 61–2; Garside 2].

M332 *The dark lady of Doona* [anon.].

London: Smith, Elder & Co., 1834 (Library of Romance, No. 9). SOURCE Sadleir, ii, p. 172; Rafroidi, ii, p. 276; Hogan, p. 445; Brown, 1102 (1836 edn); Garside 2, 1834:52. LOCATION Grail, Corvey CME 3–628–47420–5, Dt, D (1837 edn), L, NUC.

London, Belfast: Simms & M'Intyre, [1854] (Parlour Library, No. 113). SOURCE Sadleir, ii, p. 155.

Belfast: Simms & M'Intyre; London: W.S. Orr & Co., 1846 (The Parlour Novelist, No. 10). SOURCE Topp 1, pp 139–40. LOCATION D, Dt, NUC.

Paris: Allardin, 1834, 2 vols. (trans. by Paquis as *La dame noire de Doona*). SOURCE Rafroidi, ii, p. 368. LOCATION NUC.

New York: Wallis & Newell, 1835 (Franklin Library). SOURCE Topp 1, p. 140; NYPL. LOCATION NN, NUC.

COMMENTARY Historical fiction in which the heroine is the legendary pirate 'queen' of Connacht, Grace O'Malley. The story starts in 1601 but her earlier life is told in retrospect. The heir of the Geraldines (who marries Grace's granddaughter), Hugh O'Neill and Sir Richard Bingham figure in the story [Brown].

M333 *My life* [anon.].

+ London: Richard Bentley, 1835, 3 vols. SOURCE Rafroidi, ii, p. 276; Sadleir, 1680; Garside 2, 1835:69. LOCATION Grail (1838 edn), Dt (1838 edn), L, NUC, InND Loeber coll.

London: Richard Bentley, 1836 (as *The adventures of Captain Blake; or, my life*; Bentley's Standard Novels, No. 70). SOURCE Brown, 1121 (1857 edn); Sadleir, 3622 (1857 edn). LOCATION NUC, InND Loeber coll. (1856 edn).

New York: Harper & Bros, 1835, 2 vols. SOURCE NCBEL 3, p. 747; Topp 1, p. 87. LOCATION NUC.

COMMENTARY Historical fiction. Consists of two practically independent stories, that of Maj. Blake and that of his son, Capt. Blake. The first story contains the account of Gen. Jean-Joseph Humbert's invasion of Ireland in 1798 and the manner of the peasantry at the time. In the second part of the story, John Blake, the son, is often confused with his scapegrace cousin, Jack Blake. The action takes place in Paris, Portugal and London. Love affairs are interwoven in both parts of the story and the life histories of a number of other characters are recounted [ML; Brown].

M334 *The bivouac; or stories of the Peninsular War* (by W.H. Maxwell; dedicated to the earl of Musgrave).

+ London: Richard Bentley, 1837, 3 vols. SOURCE Sutherland, p. 424 (mistakenly mentions 1834 edn); Rafroidi, ii, p. 276; Hogan, p. 445; Sadleir, 1676; Wolff, 4662. LOCATION Grail (1839 edn), D (1839 edn), DPL, L, NUC (1839 edn).

Philadelphia: E.L. Carey & A. Hart, 1837, 2 vols. LOCATION NUC.

+ New York: Garrett & Co., n.d. (with *The rival suitors*). LOCATION InND Loeber coll.

COMMENTARY Contents: 'The village; the gipsy; and the route', 'The forest and the fortune-teller', 'The rejection', 'The churchyard meeting', 'The rival suitors', 'Jealousy', 'The gypsy's story', 'The mess-table', 'The captain's story', 'The gypsy's story continued', 'Departure from the country quarters – a parting interview', 'The march from Ashfield', 'The card-case', 'The rival armies', 'Opening of the campaign; affair of St. Millan; the bivouac', 'Vittoria', 'The mountain combat; French bivouac; Military reminiscences', 'Confessions of a gentleman who would have married if he could (first confession)', 'Night in the Pyrenees; The murdered sentinel; and the guerrilla chief', 'The guerrilla bivouac', 'El manco, A guerrilla breakfast', 'Confessions of a guerrilla', 'The fall of St. Sebastian', 'The storm of Badajoz', 'The dead lieutenant', 'Barbara Maxwell', 'Life in the mountains', 'Confessions of a gentleman who would have married if he could (second confession)', 'The major's story', 'Entrance into France', 'Battles of the Bidassoa and the Nivelle', 'Sick quarters; depression; an unexpected letter', 'Arrival in London – a scoundrel's villainy confirmed', 'Memoir of a ruined beauty', 'The house of death', 'The house of feasting', 'The duel', 'Conclusion' [Wolff].

M335 *Rambling recollections of a soldier of fortune* (by W.H. Maxwell).
+ Dublin: William Curry Jnr & Co.; London: Longman, Brown & Co., 1842 (ill. H.K. Browne [Phiz]). SOURCE Sadleir, 1681; Wolff, 4671. LOCATION Grail, DPL, L, NUC, InND Loeber coll. COMMENTARY *Dublin 1842 edn* The copy in the Public Library, Pearse Street, Dublin, is bound in ribbed cloth with a gold embossed harp on front [RL].
London, New York: George Routledge & Co., 1857 (as *Flood and field; or, recollections of a soldier of fortune*; ill. H.K.B. [Phiz]; Cheap Series, No. 159). SOURCE Topp 1, p. 87; Sadleir, 3622. LOCATION L, NUC.
COMMENTARY First published in the *Dublin University Magazine* (1834–35). On a dark and rainy night, several gentlemen ask for shelter at a country house in Scotland. All have a military background and to while away the hours they tell each other the following stories: 'The outcast', 'The unknown', 'My first steeple chase', 'Leaves of a journal of a deceased pluralist', 'A tour-not sentimental', 'Mr. Mac Dermott's story', 'Mr. Mac Dermott's story continued', 'The condemned soldier', 'Leaves from a game book' [ML; W.E. Hall, p. 66].

M336 *The fortunes of Hector O'Halloran and his man, Mark Antony O'Toole* (by W.H. Maxwell).
+ London: Richard Bentley; Dublin: John Cumming; Edinburgh: Bell & Bradfute, [1842–43] (ill. J. Leech, Dick Kitcat [i.e., Richard Doyle]). SOURCE Brown 1122 (mistakenly mentions Tegg, 1842, which should be 1845); Rafroidi, ii, p. 277; Wolff, 4665, 4665a. LOCATION Grail, D, Dt, DPL (1846 edn), L, NUC, InND Loeber coll. COMMENTARY *London [1842–43] edn* Bound from the parts, according to Topp 4, p. 174; but this is not the case in the Notre Dame copy.
London: William Tegg, 1845 (new edn). SOURCE Topp 4, p. 174. LOCATION InND Loeber coll. (n.d. edn).
+ New York: D. Appleton & Co.; Philadelphia: George S. Appleton, 1843 (ill. Leech). LOCATION NUC, InND Loeber coll. COMMENTARY *New York 1843 edn* Cloth binding, decoration on spine taken from cover of parts as published in London [RL].
New York: Garland, 1979 (introd. by R.L. Wolff). SOURCE COPAC. LOCATION Dt, L.
COMMENTARY First published in 13 parts by Bentley, London, 1842–43, and in parts by D. Appleton & Co., New York, 1843. The hero is the son of a landlord and ex-soldier living in the south of Ireland. Hector and his servant pass through a series of adventures, beginning with an attack on his father's castle by local malcontents. Other adventures are encountered in Dublin, London, and in the Peninsular War [Brown].

M337 *Wanderings in the highlands and islands. With sketches taken on the Scottish border, being a sequel to 'Wild Sports of the West'* (by W.H. Maxwell).
+ London: A.H. Bailly, 1844, 2 vols. (ill. with portrait of author). SOURCE Rafroidi, ii, p. 277. LOCATION Grail, L, NUC, InND Loeber coll.
London: George Routledge & Co., 1852, 2 vols. (as *Highlands and islands, being a sequel to 'Wild Sports of the West'*). SOURCE Wolff, 4666. LOCATION NUC.
London: George Routledge & Co., 1853 (as *Sports and adventures in the highlands and islands of Scotland*). SOURCE NCBEL 3, p. 747; Topp 1, p. 33. LOCATION L, NUC.
COMMENTARY Set in Scotland [ML].

M338 *Captain O'Sullivan; or, adventures, civil, military, and matrimonial of a gentleman on half pay* (by W.H. Maxwell).
+ London, Henry Colburn, 1846, 3 vols. SOURCE Rafroidi, ii, p. 278; Brown, 1123; Sadleir, 1677. LOCATION Grail, D, L.
+ London: David Bryce, [1858] (new edn; as *Adventures of Captain O'Sullivan*). SOURCE Sadleir, 3622. LOCATION D, Dt, L, InND Loeber coll.

New York: Harper & Bros, 1846. SOURCE NCBEL 3, p. 747; Topp 1, p. 100. LOCATION NUC.

COMMENTARY Capt. O'Sullivan is stationed in Connacht where his duties consist mainly of keeping down the Ribbonmen and hunting for illicit stills. Includes some recounting of the duties of the tithe-proctor, who grinds money 'out of the wretched serfs' [Brown].

M339 *Hill-side and border sketches. With legends of the Cheviots and the Lammermuir* (by W.H. Maxwell; dedicated to Archibald Douglas of Glenfinnart).

+ London: Richard Bentley, 1847, 2 vols. (ill. Leech, G. Measom). SOURCE Rafroidi, ii, p. 278; Wolff, 4667. LOCATION Grail, D, L, NUC, InND Loeber coll.

London: Richard Bentley, 1849, 2 vols. in 1 (as *Legends of the Cheviots and the Lammermuir: a companion to Wild sports of the West*). SOURCE NCBEL 3, p. 747. LOCATION NUC.

London: Richard Bentley, 1852 (as *Border tales and legends of the Cheviots and the Lammermuir*; cover ill. Phiz; Bentley's Railroad Library). SOURCE Sadleir, 3622; Topp 8, 9. LOCATION L, NUC. COMMENTARY *London 1852 edn* first six chapters of the original edn are omitted [Topp 8, 9].

+ New York: D. Appleton & Co.; Philadelphia: Geo. S. Appleton, 1847. SOURCE NCBEL 3, p. 747. LOCATION NUC, InND Loeber coll.

COMMENTARY A collection of stories and sketches about Scotland, describing a trip through Scotland to visit angling spots. The account is interspersed with stories about people met on the road and about Scottish historical events [ML].

M340 *Brian O'Linn; or, luck is everything* (by W.H. Maxwell).

London: Richard Bentley, 1848, 3 vols. (ill. John Leech). SOURCE Rafroidi, ii, p. 278. LOCATION Grail (1856 edn), L.

+ London, New York: George Routledge & Co., 1856 (new edn; as *Luck is everything; or, the adventures of Brian O'Linn*; Railway Library, No. 121). SOURCE Topp 1, p. 74; Brown, 1125 (1860 edn); NCBEL 3, p. 474. LOCATION D (1857 edn), Dt (1858 edn), L, InND Loeber coll.

New York: Burgess, Stringer & Co., 1848 (ill.). SOURCE Topp 1, p. 74; NYPL. LOCATION NN, NUC.

Philadelphia: T.B. Peterson & Bros, [18—]. LOCATION NUC.

COMMENTARY First serialized in *Bentley's Miscellany* (London, 1846). Set in Ireland, on the Scottish border, and in London. An abducted infant, child of a dying mother, is landed on Innisturk in the west of Ireland. He is adopted and does not know his real name. When he grows up he goes to England and after many adventures he finds his origins with the help of a Scottish friend's mysterious relative. Brian succeeds to ancestral estates that had been kept from him by a distant relative who had caused the deaths of both his mother and father. Note that *Fraser's Magazine* (London, 1841) published by an anonymous author, 'Lin the commissioner: An autobiogram ... transmitted from the island of Tchousang' by 'Brian O'Lynn'. A play of the title, *Brian O'Linn: A farce in two acts* by Samuel D. Johnson came out in 1853, while 'Brian O'Linn' (also O'Lynn) was a popular ballad around this time [ML; Brown; Curran index, FM 1533].

M341 *The soldier on service; or, adventures in the camp and field* (by W.H. Maxwell).

+ London: T.C. Newby, 1849, 2 vols. LOCATION NUC, InND Loeber coll.

COMMENTARY Epistolary novel consisting of letters by an Irish father to his son embarking on a military career. The letters contain advice to the son on such matters as duelling and gambling, and reminiscences of the father's own military career in the Peninsular war [ML].

M342 *Erin-go-bragh; or, Irish life pictures* (by W.H. Maxwell).

London: Richard Bentley, 1859, 2 vols. (with a memoir of W.H. Maxwell by W. Maginn§; ill.). SOURCE Rafroidi, ii, p. 278; Brown, 1124; Sadleir, 1678; Wolff, 4664;

NYPL. LOCATION Grail, D, L, NN, NUC, InND Loeber coll. (1859, 2 vols. in 1).
London: Richard Bentley, 1860 (new edn). SOURCE Topp 8, 69. LOCATION L.
COMMENTARY *London 1860 edn* Omits seven of the 'papers' [Topp 8, 69].
New York: Garland, 1979, 2 vols. (introd. by R.L. Wolff). LOCATION Dt, CtY.
COMMENTARY Published posthumously. First appeared in an unidentified 'popular' periodical. Miscellany of fiction and essays. Contents: 'Biographical sketch of the author by Dr.
Maginn§', 'Frank Hamilton; or, the confessions of an only son', 'An incursion into Connemara, with an account of a traveller who survived it', 'Albert Murdock', 'Dionysius Dogherty, Esq.', 'A short biography of a gentleman from Ireland', 'Last scenes of the condemned', 'Terence
O'Shaughnessy's first attempt to get married' (first published in *Tales from Bentley*, i, 1859), 'Robert Emmet and Arthur Aylmer; or, Dublin in 1803', 'Richard Rafferty; or, the Irish fortune-hunter', 'Adventures of a freshman fifty years ago', 'The forest ride of a West India planter', 'Queen's bench sketches', 'Inconvenience of a "Suspicion of debt"', 'The two funerals', 'John Campbell, the homicide', 'The sporting outlaw', 'Song from the Gaelic', 'Anecdotes of duelling', 'The devil and Johnny Dixon', 'The regatta', 'Legends', 'Boulogne, en route to Paris', 'Memoir of the Rev. Robert Hogg', 'Familiar epistles from an elderly gentleman on half-pay' [Wolff].

— COLLECTED WORKS

M343 *W.H. Maxwell's novels*
London, New York: George Routledge & Sons, n.d. [no. of vols. not clear]. SOURCE
OCLC. LOCATION College of St Catherine (1 vol.)

M344 *Maxwell's novels.*
New York: Dick & Fitzgerald, [1850s], 5 vols. SOURCE Adv. in O. Bradbury, *Ellen Grant* (New York, [185?]).
COMMENTARY Advertised at 50¢ per vol. (but *Hector O'Halloran* was sold in a 2 vol. edn). Also advertised in Haverty's *Irish-American Illustrated Almanac* (New York, 1872) as *Maxwell's works*, but does not mention a publisher. No copy located [RL; Adv. in O. Bradbury, *Ellen Grant* (New York, [185?])].

— POSSIBLY SPURIOUS WORK

M345 *Grace Willoughby. A tale of the wars of King James* (by the author of *Brian O'Linn*).
Cincinnati: Edwards & Goshorn, [1848 or later]. SOURCE OCLC. LOCATION NUC.
COMMENTARY Not known in book form in an English or Irish edn and, therefore, possibly spurious [RL].

'MAY, Sophia', pseud. See **CLARKE, Rebecca Sophia.**

MAY, Thomas P., fl. 1879. American novelist, TPM also wrote *Illan Yenrutt* (New Orleans, 1880), and *The Earl of Mayfield* (Philadelphia, 1879), a novel about the US Civil War. SOURCE
Allibone Suppl., ii, p. 1096; BLC; NUC; Wright iii, 3667–9.

M346 *A Prince of Breffny* (by Thomas P. May; dedicated to author's wife).
+ Philadelphia: T.B. Peterson & Bros, [1881]. SOURCE Allibone Suppl., ii, p. 1096;
Wright, iii, 3369. LOCATION L, NUC, InND Loeber coll.
Philadelphia: T.B. Peterson & Bros, [1882] (as *Lady Edith, or Alton towers*). LOCATION
NUC.
COMMENTARY An historical novel set in the early-seventeenth century and begins at Lough
Erne. Alexander O'Reilly, descendant of the prince of Breffny, is poor and decides to leave
Ireland for the Continent to make his fortune as a soldier. On his way through England he
stops at the castle of Gilbert Talbot, marquess of Shrewsbury, and falls in love with Talbot's
niece, Edith, who lives with her uncle. He sets out for the Continent and joins the army in

Italy. Finally he goes to Spain when king Charles raises an Irish Brigade under the command of General Preston. Alexander distinguishes himself but cannot leave Spain to claim his bride. Eventually, Edith sets out for Spain but perishes in a shipwreck. Several years after Edith's death he marries Doña Rosa, a proud Spanish lady who has been in love with him for years, and they provide a home for the ageing General Thomas Preston [ML].

MAYHEW, Augustus Septimus, b. London 1826, d. Richmond (London) 1875. English novelist, journalist and dramatist, ASM was one of the sixteen children of Joshua Mayhew and Mary Ann Fenn. His brothers Henry and Horace were collaborators with him on several popular works. Henry was one of the founders of the humorous magazine *Punch* (London) and another brother, Thomas, was renowned for his efforts to promote inexpensive education and for starting *The Penny National Library*. ASM assisted Henry on his *London labour and the London poor* (London, 1851), a pioneering study of the lives of the labouring classes in Victorian London based on a series of articles for the London *Morning Chronicle*. SOURCE Allibone, ii, p. 1254; Allibone Suppl., ii, p. 1097; NCBEL 4, p. 1347; ODNB; Sutherland, p. 424.

M347 *The greatest plague of life: or, the adventures of a lady in search of a good servant. By one who has been "almost worried to death"* (ed. by the brothers Mayhew [with Henry Mayhew]).
London: George Routledge & Sons, [1847] (ill. George Cruikshank). LOCATION Corvey CME 3–628–47486–8, L, InND Loeber coll. (n.d. edn).
COMMENTARY A lady's tale provides a device for the Mayhew brothers to attack the morals and manners of domestic servants in a way reminiscent of Jonathan Swift's§ *Directions to servants* (London, 1745). The satirical narrative is told by a lady of a household in London who feels harassed by the servants she employs. It soon becomes clear that she is as much to blame for her misadventures as those she abhors. Chapter six considers her Irish servant Norah O'Connor. The narrator follows this servant about the house, exploiting O'Connor by continually increasing her work load. The servant looses respect for her mistress when the latter declares Ireland to be '"a filthy dirty place, and only fit for a set of pigs to wallow in". No sooner were the words out of my mouth , than she turned round sharp upon me, and shrieking out, '"Hoo! Hubbaboo!" (or some such gibberish), seized the kitchen carving knife, which was unfortunately lying on the table, and kept brandishing it over her head, crying out, "Hurrah for ould Ireland! The first jim of the sa! – and a yard of cowld steel for them as spakes agin' her!" Then she set to work, chasing me round and round the kitchen table, jumping up in the air all the while, and screaming like one of the celebrated wild cats of Kilkenny.' The servant continually reverses the meaning of her mistress' frustrated anger by, for example, accepting a seeming apology from Lady Caroline rather than giving one. Charles Chamberlain§ published an American version of this volume, under the title *The servant-girl of the period, the greatest plague of life. What Mr. and Mrs. Honeydew learned of housekeeping* (New York, 1873) [D. Attar (ed.), *A bibliography of household books published in Britain 1800–1914* (London, 1987), p. 241; RL; CM].

MAYHEW, Henry. Co-author. See **MAYHEW, Augustus Septimus.**

MAYNE, Thomas E. See **MAYNE, Thomas Ekenhead.**

MAYNE, Thomas Ekenhead (known as **Thomas E. Mayne**), b. Belfast (Co. Antrim), 1867 (1866 according to LVP), d. Belfast? 1899. Short story writer and poet, TEM was the son of a Belfast bookseller, probably W. Erskine Mayne (who advertised in the following volume, and was its co-publisher). TEM contributed to several Irish newspapers including the *Limerick Leader*. He was a member of the Henry Joy McCracken Society and wrote for its journal, the Belfast *Northern Patriot*, between Oct. and Dec. 1895. After Alice Milligan§ and Anna Johnston left the Society in 1896 to establish the *Shan Van Vocht* (Belfast), TPM gave them his full support by contributing several articles, poems and stories to this new magazine. The *Shan Van Vocht* became his most important forum until his death in 1899, publishing his poems (including 'Kitty of the North', 'Nora Oge' and 'Hic Sepultus') and his short stories (including 'The O'Farrell's fortune' and the series 'In the byways of Ballindreen'). While relations between TEM and his editors were generally harmonious, Milligan did take issue with his bloodthirsty article concerning the French Revolution, 'The Development of Ireland' (Oct. 1896). In 1897 he published his poems in the collection *Blackthorn blossoms* (Belfast). After his early death Milligan and Johnston raised funds for the republication of TEM's short stories in *The heart o' the peat* (London, [1900]). SOURCE Brady, p. 162; Brown, p. 208; CM; Hogan 2, p. 838; Irish pseudonyms; LVP, p. 321; O'Donoghue, p. 306.

M348   *The heart o' the peat. Irish fireside and wayside sketches* (by Thomas E. Mayne).
+ London: Simpkin, Marshall, Hamilton, Kent & Co.; Belfast: W. Erskine Mayne, 1899. SOURCE Brown, 1127; OCLC. LOCATION BFl, L.
COMMENTARY Published posthumously and contains an obituary of TEM by Ethna Carbery (pseud. of Anna Johnston, co-founder of the magazine the *Shan Van Vocht* (Belfast) and wife of Seumas MacManus§). Contents: 'Dead man's gold', 'Tim Hogan, moonlighter', 'The rearing of Roddy Ranagan', 'A marriage portion', 'The poteen drinkers', 'Seeking for Tir na n-Og', 'The mysteries of Roslyn', 'Epilogue' [RL].

MAYO, the earl of. See **MAYO, Dermot Robert Wyndham Bourke, 7th earl of.**

MAYO, Dermot Robert Wyndham Bourke, 7th earl of (known as **the earl of Mayo**), b. 1851, d. Ireland? 1927. Novelist, politician and travel writer, DRWBM was the son of Richard Southwell, 6th earl of Mayo and governor-general of India, and the Hon. Blanche Julia Wyndham, daughter of George, Lord Leconfield. Styled Lord Naas from 1867 to 1872, he succeeded his father in 1872, the year he married Geraldine, daughter of the Hon. Gerald Henry Brabazon Ponsonby. Educated at Eton, he served as a cornet in the 10th Hussars and later in the Grenadier Guards. His works include a single novel; works on Africa; *The Irish land bill* (London, 1909), and *A history of the Kildare hunt* (London, 1913). His main residence was Palmerstown House, Straffan (Co. Kildare). He was childless and was buried in Johnstown cemetery (Co. Kildare). SOURCE E. Lodge, *The peerage and baronetage* (London, 1897), pp 463–4; CP, viii, pp 610–11; COPAC.

M349   *The war cruise of the 'Aries'* (by the earl of Mayo).
+ Dublin: Edward Ponsonby; London: Simpkin, Marshall, Hamilton, Kent & Co., 1894 (ill. William B. Boulton). SOURCE COPAC; Topp 8, 1309. LOCATION L.
COMMENTARY At the beginning of the story, England is on the verge of war with France; France is 'intriguing with the ruler of Egypt against England'. When war begins, Lord Mainland, 'an Irish nobleman very fond of yachting' proposes the building of a ship 'for attack by ramming' in the war. In-depth descriptions and a diagram of the ship (the *Aries*) are given. The *Aries* is built in Belfast and is captained by the Irishman, Capt. Duke. Letters between Lord Mainland and Capt. Duke are included. Descriptions are given of 'The History of the War', dealing with various incidents and engagements between the French and the English. Much of the book is written in the first person, with some dialogue, but mostly in a straightforward narrative description. About midway through is 'Captain Duke's narrative,' which is apparently taken from his journals, and which includes various letters between Duke and oth-

ers. The last chapter is 'Last Cruise of the Aries', in which Capt. Duke and the Aries sail to Killala Bay in Ireland to intercept a French squadron. The book ends quite abruptly with the destruction of the *Aries* by the French [JB].

MEADE, Elizabeth Thomasina. See **SMITH, Elizabeth Thomasina Toulmin.**

'MEADE, L.T.', pseud. See **SMITH, Elizabeth Thomasina Toulmin.**

MEANEY, Miss Mary L., pseud. **'M.L.M.'**, fl. 1865. American Catholic novelist, MLM lived in Philadelphia. Only her single novel with known Irish content is listed here. SOURCE Adv. of books published by F. Cunningham in [anon.], *Leandro* (Philadelphia, 1879). Allibone Suppl., ii, pp 1099–100; RL.

M350   *The confessors of Connaught; or, the tenants of a Lord Bishop. A tale of our times* (by 'M.L.M.').
+ Philadelphia: Peter F. Cunningham, 1865. SOURCE Allibone Suppl., ii, pp 1099–100; Brown, 1135; Fanning, p. 386; Wright, ii, 1691. LOCATION D, Dcc, NUC, InND Loeber coll. (1867 edn), Wright web.
COMMENTARY Fictional account of the real eviction by the Protestant bishop of Tuam (i.e., Power Le Poer Trench) in 1860 of Catholic tenants who had refused to send their children to his school. Contains dramatic scenes of families driven into the November cold, with clusters of small children huddled around piles of furniture in the rain [Fanning, p. 81].

MEANY, J.L., fl. 1891. American novelist.
M351   *The lovers; or, cupid in Ireland* (by J.L. Meany).
Havana (IL): Democrat Power Printing House, 1891. SOURCE Fanning, p. 386; Wright, iii, 3677; OCLC. LOCATION L, CtY.

MEANY, Stephen Joseph, b. New Hall, near Ennis (Co. Clare) 1822 or 1825, d. Waterbury (CT) (New York according to Boase) 1888. Journalist, poet, novelist and radical nationalist, SJM was the son of Mary Sheehan Meany and attended a classical school in Ennis in the mid-1830s. He published a volume of his poetry, *Shreds of fancy*, with local subscribers, in Ennis in 1841. He moved to Dublin where he worked briefly as a constable but was dismissed. He contributed to the *Clare Journal* (Ennis), the *Limerick Chronicle*, and became a reporter for the Dublin *Freeman's Journal* and rose in the ranks, reporting steadily from Westminster. He was a friend of Daniel O'Connell and was involved in Young Ireland politics, founding a short-lived Dublin *Irish National Magazine* that ran from May to Aug. 1846. He left the *Freeman's Journal* in 1848 to participate more fully in the revolutionary activities of the time, later joining the staff of the Dublin *Irish Tribune*. He was imprisoned for some months for his revolutionary activities and rhetoric. He became editor of the *Drogheda Argus* (Co. Louth). Afterwards he moved to Liverpool where he founded the *Lancashire Free Press*, the first English Catholic paper outside of London. In the 1860s he went to the US where he wrote for numerous publications and owned and edited the *Commercial* in Toledo (OH). He was active in the Fenian movement in the US, founding and editing the organization's *Irish Press* (location not clear, 1866) and editing the New York *Irish Democrat* later. Returning to England in 1866, he was arrested on a charge of Fenianism and sentenced to fifteen years in prison, but was released on the condition that he not return to Ireland. SJM spent the remainder of his life in the US where he was active in Irish-American organizations. He made frequent though illegal visits to Ireland to lecture on nationalist topics. His biography, *Fenian convict 3498*, was written by John Augustus O'Shea§ and published in Dublin in 1869. SJM's remains were returned to

Ireland for burial. SOURCE BLC; Boase, ii, p. 828; Brown, p. 209; Irish pseudonyms; NUC; O'Donoghue, p. 307; RIA/DIB; Sutherland, p. 427.

M352 *The Terry Alt. A tale of 1831* (by Stephen Joseph Meany).
[location?]: [publisher?], 1841, 3 vols. SOURCE Brown, 1136; Sutherland, p. 428.
COMMENTARY No copy located. The Terry Alts was the name of a secret society of agrarian agitators in Munster, previously known as Whiteboys [Brown].

MEARS, A. Garland. See **MEARS, Amelia.**

MEARS, Amelia (née Garland; known as **A. Garland Mears**), b. Freshford (Co. Kilkenny). Poet and fiction writer, AM was the daughter of the schoolmaster and poet John Garland. The family moved to England when she was still a child. In 1864 she married an Ed. Mears, a merchant of West Hartlepool (Yorks.). Aside from four works of fiction, she wrote on public speaking. Her portrait was published on the cover of *Tales of our town* (London, [1893]). SOURCE BLC; Colman, p. 91; LVP, p. 322; O'Donoghue, p. 307.

M353 *Sketches of life: Tales of West Hartlepool* (by Amelia Mears?).
London: [publisher?], n.d. SOURCE Colman, p. 91.
COMMENTARY No copy located [RL].

M354 *The story of a trust; and other tales* (by A. Garland Mears).
London: Simpkin & Marshall, 1893. SOURCE Adv. in *Tales of our town* (London, [1893 edn]). LOCATION L.

M355 *Tales of our town* (by A. Garland Mears).
+ London: Simpkin, Marshall, Hamilton, Kent & Co., [1893] (new edn, 3rd edn).
SOURCE COPAC; Topp 8, 1256. LOCATION L.
COMMENTARY No copy of first edn located. The [1893] edn was priced at 6*d.* Contents: 'The undertaker's wife' (set in Yorkshire), 'How she plagued them', 'The open door (A Yorkshire idyll)', 'Too modest by far', 'The real Roger (a story of the Tichborne Trial)', 'Our cremation craze, or, the fake of Parson Rudd' (set in West Hartlepool) [RL].

M356 *Mercia, the astronomer royal: A romance* (by A. Garland Mears).
+ London: Simpkin, Marshall, Hamilton, Kent & Co., 1895. SOURCE COPAC.
LOCATION L.
COMMENTARY Futuristic novel set in 2002, a time when peace reigns and women have more power. Set partially in India where Mercia is crowned astronomer royal and marries Swami, leaving behind a desolate Geometricus. The book is mostly about women's roles in modern society. No Irish content [ML].

MEEHAN, Fr Charles Patrick, pseud. 'Father Charles', b. Dublin 1812, d. 1890. Catholic priest, historian, poet, translator and novelist, CPM came from a farming family from Ballymahon (Co. Longford), where he was taught in a hedge-school. Early in life he became interested in history and archaeology. He went to Rome in 1828 to join the Irish College and was ordained there in 1834. His first contact with Irish historical documents took place in Rome. He returned to Ireland where he was a curate, first at Rathdrum (Co. Wicklow) and then at SS Michael and John in Dublin until his death. A member of the nationalist Young Ireland association, he published poetry and prose in its magazine the *Nation* (Dublin) but after the failed rising of 1848 dropped out of public life. He was a prolific author of historical and literary works, many critical of the oppression of Gaelic and Catholic Ireland, including *The Confederation of Kilkenny* (Dublin, 1860), and *The fate and fortunes of Hugh O'Neill, Earl of Tyrone, and R. O'Donel, Earl of Tyrconnel* (Dublin, 1868). His series *Flowers from foreign fields* (Dublin, 1857) was published by James Duffy in six parts, and consists of translations from French stories. His *The poets and poetry of Munster; a selection of Irish songs* appeared in Dublin in 1833. CPM was a friend of James Clarence Mangan§ and collected and edited his works as well as re-editing Robert R. Madden's§ *Literary remains of the United Irishmen* (Dublin, 1887). He was a member of the RIA. For CPM's portrait and papers, see ODNB. SOURCE Allibone Suppl., ii, p. 1101; BLC; Boase, ii, p. 833; F.P. Carey, *Father Charles P. Meehan* (Dublin, [1933]); M. Russell, 'Rev. C.P. Meehan', *Irish Monthly*, 18 (Apr. 1890), pp 218–19; Field Day, ii, p. 267; Irish pseudonyms; OCIL, p. 362; ODNB; O'Donoghue, p. 307; RIA/DIB; RL.

M357 *Lucy and Isabella; or, the lady and the maid* (by 'Father Charles').
+ Dublin: James Duffy, 1860 (ill.). SOURCE Adv. in 'The adventures of a watch', [1865]. LOCATION L.
COMMENTARY Set in Paris and features a charitable Mrs Dermody [RL].

M358 *Ferdinand; or, the triumphs of filial love* (by 'Father Charles').
Dublin: James Duffy, 1860. LOCATION L (missing), InND Loeber coll. (n.d. edn).
COMMENTARY A Catholic moral story set in France. A dissolute notary marries a Christian woman and tries to make her partake in parties and the theatre. She bears him a son and tries to spend her time in the upbringing of her baby. When her health is failing, she settles her estate on her son and makes sure that her mother will bring up the boy. He grows up a good boy, steeped in the Catholic faith. His father remarries a woman as dissolute as himself. When the grandmother dies the boy joins his father and stepmother, who both try to draw him into un-Christian entertainment. He refuses and eventually is the tool for saving his father from ruin. His father reforms his life and becomes a good Catholic [ML].

M359 *Matilda; or, the orphans of the Pyrenees* (by 'Father Charles').
Dublin: [James Duffy?], 1860. LOCATION L (destroyed).
COMMENTARY No copy located [RL].

MEEHAN, M., fl. 1860s, Novelist, MM and her co-author and sister, R. Meehan, were probably Irish because they were the daughters of Capt. Francis Meehan of the Peninsular and Oriental Steam Navigation Company, an offshoot of the City of Dublin Steam Navigation Company. SOURCE Title page of *The haunted castle* (London, [1862]); Personal communication, Maurice Craig, Nov. 1998.

M360 *The haunted castle* (by M. and R. Meehan).
+ London: Ward & Lock, [1862]. SOURCE Allibone Suppl., ii, p. 1101. LOCATION L, InND Loeber coll.
COMMENTARY The haunted castle is Lewellen Castle in the neighbourhood of Canterbury, England. The previous lord of Lewellen Castle had an unacknowledged son from a marriage in Spain. At his deathbed, he charges his brother with his son's upbringing. However, his brother gives the child a different last name and claims the title and the possessions for himself. The actual heir is treated very badly. A servant who knows the truth but who has his own reasons for not revealing it, acts as the ghost of the dead lord to make sure that the heir is not treated too severely. In a parallel story, a general casts his wife out as a result of false stories told to him by his sister. After many adventures, all wrongs are righted. One chapter deals with a party of servants, butlers and housekeepers of different houses, several of whom are Irish and speak with an Irish brogue [ML].

MEEHAN, R. Co-author. See **MEEHAN, M.**

MEEKINS, Isaac. See **MUKINS, Isaac.**

MEIKLE, James, fl. 1837. Novelist, JM was an Ulster-Scots Presbyterian schoolmaster in Co. Down. He may have been related to William Meikle of Falkirk, Stirlingshire (Scotland), who published *Don Roderick: A Spanish tale* (Dublin, 1868). SOURCE Brown, p. 210; MVP, p. 309.

M361 *Our Scottish forefathers: A tale of the Ulster Presbyterians* (by James Meikle; dedicated to the Revd Henry Cooke DD).
+ Belfast: William M'Comb; London: J. Nisbet & Co.; Edinburgh: Fraser & Co.; Glasgow: W. Collins; Dublin: William Curry Jnr & Co., 1837. LOCATION D.

M362 *Killinchy; or, the days of Livingston. A tale of the Ulster Presbyterians* (by the author of *Our Scottish forefathers*).
+ Belfast: William McComb; London: J. Nisbet & Co.; Edinburgh: Fraser & Crawford; J. Johnstone; Glasgow: W. Collins; Dublin: Wm. Curry Jnr & Co., 1839. SOURCE Brown, 1137. LOCATION D, Dt, InND Loeber coll.
Pittsburgh (PA): [publisher?], [*c*.1870]. SOURCE Emerald Isle cat. 83/697.
COMMENTARY No copy of the Pittsburgh edn located. Set in the early-seventeenth century after the Scottish settlement of Ulster, it describes Presbyterian life in a rural parish in Co. Down and contains biographical details of the Revd John Livingston, who was a minister at Killinchy (Co. Down, 1630–35) and later in Scotland. The story describes the outbreak of the 1641 rebellion in Ireland. It includes an appendix of historical notes and sources [ML; Brown].

'MELUSINE', pseud. See **THOMPSON, Emily Skeffington**.

MELVILLE, Theodore, fl. 1802. Gothic novelist. It is unclear whether this is the author's real name or a pseudonym. SOURCE Allibone, ii, p. 126; BD, p. 232; Brown, p. 210; Summers, p. 92.

M363 *The White Knight; or, the monastery of Morne. A romance* (by Theodore Melville).
London: Crosby & Letterman, 1802, 3 vols. SOURCE Brown, p. 210; Summers, p. 92; British Fiction; Garside, 1802:44. LOCATION Corvey CME 3–624–48057–4, NUC.
COMMENTARY Gothic romance mingling pseudo-feudal history with elements of terror set in Avonmore, Co. Cork. In the introduction, the author stresses that romance writers are often 'content to amuse the fancy, without the smallest regard to moral or probability. I have, however, endeavoured to connect fancy, moral, and probability ...' The story concerns the extinct Fitzgerald branch of the White Knight. The disinherited hero, Allan, encounters the ghost of his revenge-demanding father and proceeds to the monastery of the Morne to learn his destiny. The monastery is already the home of Allida, a standard Gothic heroine who endures numerous torments at the hands of the White Knight. Like the hero, Allida is also engaged in a quest for her missing father who may, or may not, turn out to be her current tormentor and the master of the monastery. The White Knight meets his end by plunging from one of the towers of his crumbling monastery [CM; Frank, 280].

M364 *The benevolent monk; or, the castle of Olalla. A romance* (by Theodore Melville).
+ London: B. Crosby & Co., 1807, 3 vols. SOURCE Allibone Suppl., ii, p. 1102; Block, p. 157; Brown, p. 210; British Fiction; Garside, 1807:43. LOCATION Corvey CME 3–628–48055–8, L.
COMMENTARY Gothic story set in Spain. An O'Reilly makes an appearance, but not as a main character. The plot pits a bad brother against a good brother in a struggle for ownership of Olalla Castle. It portrays a benevolent cleric in a probable attempt to revise the standard Gothic image of the lecherous or fiendish priest [ML; Frank, 281].

M365 *The Irish chieftain, and his family. A romance* (by Theodore Melville).
London: Lane, Newman & Co., 1809, 4 vols. SOURCE Blakey, p. 228; Brown, 1138; British Fiction; Garside, 1809:49. LOCATION Corvey CME 3–628–48056–6, Ireland related fiction, L, ViU.

COMMENTARY A romantic adventure story set in the eighteenth century, chiefly around Killarney. The O'Donoghue of Killarney is dispossessed for loyalty to the Stuarts. Lord Roskerrin, a Williamite, is rewarded with an estate. Conrad O'Donoghue falls in love with the daughter of the hated Lord Roskerrin. This leads to sensational adventures, including the reinstatement of an exiled Venetian grandee [Brown].

'A MEMBER OF THE IRISH BAR', pseud. See KELLY, Peter Burrowes.

'A MEMBER OF THE HOUSE OF MERCY', pseud. See CARROLL, Mary Augustine.

'A MEMBER OF THE COMMITTEE OF THE JUVENILE DEAF AND DUMB ASSO-CIATION', fl. 1830. Pseudonym of a writer of fiction for children who was a minister and probably Irish. SOURCE RL.
M366 *The children of sorrow; a tale* (by 'A member of the Committee of the Juvenile Deaf and Dumb Association').
+ Dublin: Printed [for the author?] by P.D. Hardy, 1830. LOCATION D.
COMMENTARY Religious fiction set in England in Westmoreland and Cumberland. The story is about a deaf-and-dumb child learning about religion [ML].

MENPES, Mortimer. Co-author. See MC CARTHY, Justin.

MEREDITH, Mrs —. See MEREDITH, Mrs Charles.

MEREDITH, Mrs Charles (Louise Anne), b. Birmingham 1812, d. 1895. Didactic story writer, this author can be identified with the Mrs Meredith who ran the Adelaide school in Dublin, which presumably specialized in lace making (p. 15 of the following book). The Library of Congress cat. identifies this person as the author of the following book, and possibly is the same person who in 1839 married Charles Meredith, an Australian squatter and politician. Subsequently, she published several works on Tasmania, where prior to 1853 she resided for nine years, and about New South Wales where she lived from 1839 to 1844. The reason for her later connection with Ireland is not clear. Her portrait is in the Allport Library and Museum of Fine Arts, Tasmania. SOURCE Allibone Suppl., ii, p. 1104; On line: Internet http://images.statelibrary.tas.gov.au (access date: Nov. 2005); DCL cat.
M367 *The lacemakers: sketches of Irish character, with some account of the effort to establish lacemaking in Ireland* (by Mrs Merdith; dedicated to Miss Burdett Coutts).
+ London: Jackson, Walford & Hodder, 1865 (ill.). SOURCE Brown, 1139. LOCATION MChB, InND Loeber coll.
COMMENTARY Written to advocate industrial training for the female poor in Ireland to allow them to earn a living. In the preface, the writer gives the history of the lace industry in the 1850s when, after the Famine, industrial lace-making schools were set up in various parts of the country (listed in the appendix). The lace produced was sold in England and America. The women could earn very good salaries; however, the fashion for Irish lace died down after a number of years. To illustrate the economic and social influence of the industry, three didactic tales follow: 'Ellen Harrington' describes the heroine as a child during the Famine looking after people dying from fever. An English captain who had brought famine relief takes pity on her and places her in a lace-making school. She excels, and her work, together with that of other girls from the village, helps the local doctor to move to America where, instead of practicing medicine, he becomes an agent for selling Irish lace. After the demand for Irish lace dies down, Ellen goes to London to attend an art school and one day meets the doctor who,

after his American adventure, has become a sheep farmer in Australia. They marry and return to Australia. 'The redeemed estate' tells the story of Catherine and Margaret Fitzwalter who keep their father's estate in the family with the money earned by making lace. To avoid creditors, their father fled the country but his family intimated he had died. Many neighbours are aware of the deceit. Mr Fitzwalter returns to die for real, but by that time, his daughters have been able by their lace-making to satisfy the creditors. The story of 'Mary Desmond' concerns a worker in a lace school who is very artistic and quick. She earns a good living, but spends her money easily and does not follow rules very well. She becomes a servant and companion to a Miss Black. While there she is seduced by Miss Black's fiancée and is involved in letting others do serious harm to the Black family. Eventually, she rights the wrongs done to the Black family and atones for her sins [ML].

'MEREDITH, Francis', pseud. See **CHAPMAN, Mary Francis**.

MEREDITH, Louise Anne. See **MEREDITH, Mrs Charles**.

METHUEN, Mary M.C., pseud. 'M.M.C.M.', fl. 1850s. Anti-Catholic fiction writer. SOURCE BLC.

M368 *The morning of life: A memoir of Miss A—N, who was educated for a nun. With many interesting particulars and original letters by Dr. Doyle* (by 'her friend M.M.C.M.').
+ Bath: Binns & Goodwin; London: J. Nisbet & Co., Whittaker & Co.; Edinburgh: Oliver & Boyd; Dublin: J. M'Glashan, [1850] (ill.). Location D, L.
COMMENTARY Anti-Catholic fiction with Irish content, written as a memoir. According to inscription in BL copy, Miss A—N is a short for Bessie Anderson. Details the struggles of Miss Anderson, who was educated as a nun, to retain her catholicism [Adv. in C.G.H., *The unclaimed daughter* (Bath, [1853]); RL; FD; CM].

M369 *Pearls from the deep, comprising the remains and reminiscences of two sisters … Forming a sequel to 'The morning of life'* [anon.].
London: Hamilton, Adams & Co.; Sheffield: J. Pearce, Jun., [1852]. LOCATION L.
COMMENTARY Mentioned in J.E. Howard's anti-Catholic *"The island of saints"; or, Ireland in 1855* (London, 1855, p. 219), which alludes to the 'Popish' misrepresentations of 'the numerous conversions in the West of Ireland'. Religious fiction set in Ireland, and contains religious discussions and letters to show the alleged errors of the Catholic faith [ML; RL].

MILDMAY, Jacob, fl. 1888. Novelist, JM possibly was Irish. SOURCE RL.

M370 *Hopelessly Irish; some chapters from the domestic history of a respectable Irish family* (by Jacob Mildmay).
+ Dublin: M.H. Gill & Son, 1888 (ill.). SOURCE Allibone Suppl., ii, p. 1111. LOCATION L.
COMMENTARY Set in Ireland (at Cahircorry, not identified) and England. Master Ethelred O'Fogerty, a dandy, is sent to school at Beowolf Hall in England, where he turns out to be a bully. He is then sent to TCD where he leads a life that includes heavy drinking. It the end he falls ill and dies [ML; CM].

MILIKIN, Anna. See **MILLIKIN, Anna**.

MILLE, James de. See **DE MILLE, James**.

MILLIGAN, Alice L. See MILLIGAN, Alice Letitia.

MILLIGAN, Alice Letitia (known as Alice L. Milligan), b. Omagh (Co. Tyrone) 1866 (not in 1865 as in Boylan), d. Tyrcur (Co. Tyrone) 1953. Novelist, poet, playwright, biographer and periodical proprietor, ALM was the daughter of Seaton Forest Milligan of Belfast, a wealthy businessman and antiquary, and Charlotte Burns of Omagh. She was educated at the Methodist College in Belfast, Magee College (Derry) and King's College (London), where she studied English history and literature. Her great-uncle, Armour Alcorn, a farmer who spoke with his workers in Irish, introduced her to the Irish language and cultivated her interest in it. Her first published work, written with her father, was a travel book: *Glimpses of Erin; civilization, manners, &c.* (London, 1888). She went to Dublin to study Irish, joined the Irish Literary Society, met William Butler Yeats§ and George Russell, who encouraged her to write, and became involved in Irish nationalist politics. She was a founder and first president of the Irish Women's Association in Belfast and other northern cities and one of the founders of the Henry Joy McCracken Society in Belfast in 1896. With Anna Johnston (who wrote under the pseudonym Ethna Carbery) she joined the organization's newspaper, the Belfast *Northern Patriot*. They were dismissed when it was discovered Johnston's father was a Fenian. Instead, they launched the *Shan Van Vocht* (Belfast), which supported the Irish nationalist agenda and which ALM edited from 1896 to 1899. She wrote for a variety of periodicals and while serving on a committee to commemorate the centenary of the 1798 rebellion, she wrote a life of Theobald Wolfe Tone§ (Belfast, 1898). She contributed to the *Irish Homestead* (Dublin, 1895 onward), *Sinn Féin, United Irishmen* (both Dublin), the *Derry Journal*, and many other periodicals. She was a member of the Gaelic League and involved in its organization in Ulster. In 1904 she was appointed by the League to be a full-time travelling lecturer. Among her eleven plays is *Last feast of the Fianna* (London, 1900), the first Irish drama to be based on an Irish saga. Her 'The deliverance of Red Hugh' was produced by the Irish Literary Theatre in 1900 and by William Fay's Irish National Dramatic Society in 1902. She wrote some of her works with her brother W.H. Milligan. She supported Eamon de Valera and the anti-partition faction and found the division between the Republic of Ireland and Northern Ireland and the subsequent civil war very difficult to accept. She lived with her brothers – on whom she increasingly depended – in Bath and later back in Tyrone and was one of the founders of the Anti-Partition League in the 1930s. She was a founding member of the Irish Academy of Letters and she received an honorary degree from the NUI in 1941. Her later life was beset by poverty. For ALM's portraits, see ODNB, while a painting of her is in the Ulster Museum, Belfast. Several of her letters are in the Allen Library, Dublin (Click Repository), the NLI (MSS 10,864, 13,161), and the Belfast Central Library (Bigger collection). SOURCE Allibone Suppl., ii, p. 1116 [under S.F. Milligan]; Alston, p. 301; Boylan, p. 249; Brady, p. 163; Brown, p. 213; Clyde, pp 140, 143; Colman, pp 157–8; Field Day, ii, p. 990, v, pp 898, 900, 922–3; Hogan, p. 447; Hogan 2, pp 841–2; Irish pseudonyms; OCIL, p. 366; ODNB; O'Donoghue, p. 309; Personal communication, Catherine Morris, May 2001; E. Reilly, p. 248; RIA/DIB; Ryan, p. 118.

M371 *A royal democrat. A sensational Irish novel* (by Alice L. Milligan).
+ London: Simpkin, Marshall, Hamilton, Kent & Co.; Dublin: M.H. Gill & Son, [*c.*1892]. SOURCE Brown, 1153; Hogan, p. 447. LOCATION D, Dt, NUC.
COMMENTARY Historical fiction written after the death of Charles Stuart Parnell and affirming the case for Protestants to be involved in Home Rule for Ireland, the story is set in Donegal and Dublin, a fanciful forecast of Irish political history covering 1892 to 1948 as told in a story of Arthur Cormac Christian Frederick, prince of Wales. The rebellion of 1895 had been crushed and the national leaders had been killed in action or had been executed. Prince Cormac,

on a tour around the world, is shipwrecked on the Donegal coast. He keeps his identity secret and enters a secret society in order to turn it from agrarian murder to mere cattle driving. He is arrested and sentenced to death. He is saved by his cousin who has become queen, but his identity is never disclosed [Brown; Field Day, v, p. 926; ODNB].

M372 *Sons of the sea kings* (by Alice and W.H. Milligan; dedicated to George Coffey).
+ Dublin: M.H. Gill & Son, 1914 (ill. J. Carey). SOURCE Brown, 1154. LOCATION D, DPL, L, NUC, InND Loeber coll.
COMMENTARY A romantic tale of ancient Iceland, mainly based on the Laxdale saga written in the twelfth century. This book describes the voyages, battles, love intrigues, and deeds of prowess in the realm of the Norsemen, including Ireland [ML].

M373 *The dynamite drummer* (by Alice and W.H. Milligan; dedicated to the memory of Seaton Forrest Milligan and William Gray).
+ Dublin: Martin Lester, [*c.*1927]. SOURCE Brown 2, 1029; Rowan cat. 47/411. LOCATION D, DPL, NUC.
COMMENTARY Serialized in the *Derry Journal* (Apr.–Nov. 1920). The adventures of two wealthy Americans in Ulster during the Home Rule agitation. Telemachus Du Querne inherits a property in Donegal. He is in the dynamite business and takes leave to visit Ireland with a friend named McGilligan, but gets into trouble as a supposed Mormon. A big deal in the sale of dynamite provides misunderstandings and excitement [Brown; CM; Rowan cat.].

MILLIGAN, W.H., fl. 1887. Co-author and brother of Alice Letitia Milligan. See MILLIGAN, Alice Letitia.

MILLIKEN, Anna. See MILLIKIN, Anna.

MILLIKEN, Richard Alfred. See MILLIKIN, Richard Alfred.

MILLIKIN, Anna (also Milliken) probably born at Castlemartyr (Co. Cork), fl. 1793, d. Ireland 1824? Novelist and periodical founder, AM was the daughter of Robert Millikin, a Quaker of Scottish descent, and Elizabeth Battaley from a Wilts. (England) family, who brought some fortune into the family. AM's brother was the author and artist Richard Alfred Millikin§. Her grandfather, Robert Millikin, a Belfast linen merchant, with the encouragement of Henry Boyle (later earl of Shannon), had settled on the Boyle estate at Castlemartyr. AM started writing novels in order to restore the family finances, but 'either from locality of situation, or some other cause, her labours proved unproductive' (Millikin, pp xv–xvi). Together with her brother, she founded and contributed to the literary periodical the *Casket or Hesperian Magazine* (Cork, 1797–98), which was said to have been successful, but its publication was interrupted by the outbreak of the rebellion of 1798. She published her last novel in 1804. In that year, the publisher John Connor advertised her *An historical epitome, for the use of schools*, which had been just published; a copy of this work has not been located. Her letters to Thomas Crofton Croker§ (now in the Public Library, Cork) show that she lived in the city of Cork between 1819 and 1824. The Dublin bookseller and printer John Milliken, who published AM's *Eva* (Dublin, 1796), may have been a relative. SOURCE Crookshank, p. 307; A. Millikin (ed.), *Poetical fragments of the late Richard Alfred Millikin* (London, 1823), pp xv–xvi; Personal communication, Charles Ginnane, May 1995; Pollard 2, p. 408.

M374 *Corfe Castle; or, historic tracts. A novel* (by Anna Millikin; dedicated to Lord Boyle).
+ Cork: Printed [for the author?] by J. Haly, 1793, 2 vols. (subscribers' list). SOURCE Raven 2, 1793:29; McBurney & Taylor, 655; ESTC n032906. LOCATION D, IU, NUC, InND Loeber coll. (vol. 2 only).

COMMENTARY Reviewed in *Anthologia Hibernica* (2 (1793), pp 366–7). Historical fiction at the time of Ethelred, king of England (968?–1016); no Irish content [ML; RL].

M375 *Eva. An old Irish story* [anon.].
Cork: J. Connor, 1795. SOURCE Brown 2, 1030; Raven 2, 1795:31; ESTC t19330. LOCATION L.
Dublin: John Milliken, 1796. SOURCE Pollard 2, p. 408.
COMMENTARY No copy of the Dublin edn located. Historical fiction about the story of Eva, daughter of Dermot MacMurrough, king of Leinster, from the period of his visit to Henry in Aquitaine to solicit help for Eva's marriage to Strongbow (Richard de Clare, earl of Pembroke). A romance is provided by the love of Regan MacDonagh for Eva, but he is killed while defending her and bequeaths her to Strongbow [Brown 2].

M376 *Plantagenet: or, secrets of the house of Anjou. A tale of the twelfth century* (by Anna Millikin).
+ Cork: Printed [for the author?] by J. Connor, 1802, 2 vols. SOURCE Allibone, ii, p. 1288; NSTC; Block, p. 161 (infers a London 2 vols. edn, by referring to Allibone, but no such edn has been located); British Fiction; Garside, 1802:45. LOCATION Corvey CME 3–628–48132, D, Dt, CtY, MH, NUC, InND Loeber coll.
COMMENTARY Partly serialized in the *Casket or Hesperian Magazine* (Cork, 1797–98). Historical Gothic novel set in twelfth-century France after the battle between King Henry I of England and Robert, duke of Normandy. Henry wins and is eager to take captive William, the duke's son. William escapes and in his wanderings finds out various awful secrets about successive dukes of Anjou. William had hoped to marry the daughter of the current duke of Anjou, whom he had considered his friend but who is intent on betraying William to Henry. In the end the duke of Anjou admits his crimes and allows his daughter to marry William, who has succeeded to the dukedom of Flanders [ML].

M377 *The rival chiefs; or, battle of Mere. A tale of ancient times* (by Anna Millikin).
Cork: Printed [for the author?] by J. Connor, 1804. SOURCE Allibone, ii, p. 1288; British Fiction; Garside, 1804:50. LOCATION L.
London: Lane, Newman & Co., 1805. SOURCE Blakey, p. 217; British Fiction.
COMMENTARY No copy of the London edn located. The battling chiefs make war against foreign invaders and one another. All the events and characters are pseudo-historical and the exact century in the which the action takes place is difficult to place. Gaelic, Celtic, Elizabethan, and fantastic ancient Irish material is freely mixed with contemporary Anglo-Irish politics. The rival chiefs destroy themselves, their heirs, and the cause of Irish freedom [Frank, 285].

MILLIKIN (also Milliken), **Richard Alfred**, b. Castlemartyr (Co. Cork) 1767, d. Douglas (Cork) 1815. Poet, playwright, writer and artist, RAM was the son of Robert Millikin, a Quaker of Scottish origin, and Elizabeth Battaley of Wilts. (England), and sister of the author Anna Millikin§ (see under her name for more details about the Millikin family). RAM was educated at Midleton (Co. Cork), and started writing poetry at age 13. He became an attorney at the Irish Exchequer in 1792, but decided instead to devote himself to literary and artistic pursuits. Initially he published poetry in the *Monthly Miscellany* (Cork, 1795), and with his sister founded the *Casket or Hesperian Magazine* (Cork, 1797–98). On the outbreak of the rebellion of 1798 he joined the Royal Cork volunteers and fought with notorious 'zeal and efficiency' (DNB) against the rebels. RAM wrote short fiction, drama, verse, and comic ballads that were popular on the London stage. He is mostly known for his poem 'The groves of Blarney', a satire on Munster politics of the 1780s and a burlesque on an earlier ballad, which is remembered in Lady Morgan's§ novel *The O'Briens and the O'Flaherty's* (London, 1827). RAM also published a volume of poems, *The river-side* (Cork, 1807). He executed watercolours and became a set designer for the Apollo Society of Amateur Actors, whose theatre was in Patrick Street, Cork (later the *Cork Examiner* building). At the end of his life RAM established the first society for artists and their patrons in Cork, which became known as the Cork Society of Arts and which posthumously exhibited twenty-two of RAM's pictures in 1816. RAM featured in Edward Kenealy's§ *Brallaghan, or the Deipnosophists* (London, 1845) After his death his widow presented his papers to Thomas Crofton Croker§ but, with one exception, these have not been traced. Croker published some of RAM's poems in *Popular songs of Ireland* (London, 1839). RAM's portrait appeared in his sister Anna's *Poetical fragments of the late Richard Alfred Millikin with an authentic memoir of his life* (London, 1823). Henry Kirchhoffer wrote a poem to the memory of RAM. He was buried at Douglas, Cork, where his tomb survives. SOURCE Brady, p. 163; *Biographia Hibernica* (London, 1822), ii, pp 426–9 Carpenter, pp 523–5; T. Crofton Croker, *Popular songs of Ireland* (1839, ed. by H. Morley, 1890), pp 88–92, 260–2; Crookshank, p. 307; DNB; Field Day, i, pp 1081, 1170; C. Foley, *A history of Douglas* (Cork, 1991, 2nd edn), p. 44; Hogan, p. 449; Hogan 2, pp 843–4; Keane, p. 339; *Jrnl of the Cork Historical & Archaeological Society*, 19 (1913), pp 169–70; O'Donoghue, pp 237, 309–10; P. O'Flanagan & C.G. Buttimer (eds), *Cork history & society* (Dublin, 1993), p. 821; A. Millikin (ed.), *Poetical fragments of the late Richard Alfred Millikin* (London, 1823); McKenna, pp 276–7; NCBEL 3, p. 1899; NCBEL 4, pp 407–8; OCIL, pp 366–7; ODNB; O'Donoghue, pp 309–10; Personal communication, Charles Ginnane, May 1995; Public Library, Cork (Thomas Crofton Croker§ MSS); RIA/DIB.

M378   *The slave of Surinam; or, innocent victim of cruelty* (by Richard Millikin).
   + Cork: Printed [for the author?] by Mathews, 1810. SOURCE Rafroidi, ii, p. 280.
LOCATION D.
COMMENTARY A tale, written after the manner of Bernadin de St Pierre, but 'in haste, and without proper attention'. Mr Walton from England has a plantation in the Dutch colony of Surinam. Walton returns to England to discover his relatives. His friend, Mr Willenstein, promises to look after his affairs in his absence. Willenstein had married a native, who bore him a son, Joseph. News comes to Surinam that the ship Walton took was wrecked. Willenstein sells Walton's estate, including a female slave who had given birth to a daughter conceived by Walton, to a Mr Dunker. Willenstein leaves for Europe to contact Walton's relatives, leaving Joseph behind. Joseph falls in love with Walton's daughter Mary, but Mary's master has designs on her and imprisons her. After Dunker has been rebuked, he lets her out of prison but tries to rape her and is prevented from doing this by Joseph. Joseph and Mary flee into the woods, pursued by Dunker's people. Throughout all their adventures they are faithful to each other and, eventually, they both die and are buried close to each other [ML; *Biographia Hibernica* (London, 1822), ii, p. 429].

MILLINGEN, John Gideon, b. Westminster (London) 1782, d. London 1862 (1849 according to Curran). Physician, novelist and playwright, JGM was the son of Michael Millingen, a Dutch merchant, and was taken to Paris in childhood, where he witnessed the horrors of the French Revolution and frequently met Maximilien Robespierre, Georges-Jacques Danton and other Jacobin leaders. He studied medicine at the École de Médicine in Paris and took a medical degree in 1802. Joining the British army that same year, he served as a surgeon in the Peninsular War and was chief surgeon of the cavalry at Waterloo (1815). After service in the West Indies undermined his health, he retired on half-pay. He lived for a while in Boulogne but moved to England in the 1830s where he was medical officer to various lunatic asylums and wrote about the management and treatment of the insane. He also contributed to *Bentley's Miscellany* (London) and wrote a number of farces. His *Recollections of Republican France from 1790 to 1801* appeared in London in 1848. Only works with Irish connections are listed below.

SOURCE Allibone, ii, p. 1288; Boase, ii, p. 887; Brady, p. 164; Brown, p. 213; Curran index; ODNB; O'Donoghue, p. 310; Sutherland, p. 435.

M379 *The adventures of an Irish gentleman* [anon.].
+ London: Henry Colburn & Richard Bentley, 1830, 3 vols. SOURCE Hodgson, p. 379; Brown, 1155; Rafroidi, ii, p. 281; Garside 2, 1830:82. LOCATION Corvey CME 3–628–47019–6, Ireland related fiction, D, L, NUC, InND Loeber coll.
COMMENTARY Reviewed in the *Dublin Literary Gazette* (1830) as belonging to a class of books 'which lends its name to a certain plan and pungent species of snuff: it is a course [*sic*] nasty book'. Consists of the story of the life of a Mr O'Shannon, who, we are to believe, had given a manuscript to the author. Only the beginning and the end of the story are set in Ireland. In the interval, O'Shannon has adventures in Portugal and France at the time of the French Revolution. O'Shannon is a sceptic where religion or love are concerned. He takes a dim view of the Inquisition and of convents. His love affairs never lead to a long-lasting relationship. At the end of his life, he leads a very solitary existence in Dublin [ML; RL; *Dublin Literary Gazette* (1830), p. 107].

M380 *Jack Hornet; or, the march of intellect* [anon.].
+ London: Richard Bentley, 1845, 3 vols. SOURCE Hodgson, p. 379; Rafroidi, ii, p. 281. LOCATION L.
COMMENTARY Set in England and features a Lord Killfair who is an Irish libertine, but not a main character [ML].

MILLS, John, pseud. 'A man of fashion', fl. 1844, d. *c.*1885. Novelist, very little is known about JM other than he lived in Essex and wrote rollicking hunting books. SOURCE NCBEL 4, pp 1355–6; Sutherland, p. 436.
M381 *D'Horsay; or, the follies of the day* (by 'A man of fashion').
London: William Strange, 1844 (ill. George Sandfast). SOURCE Sadleir, 1736; Wolff, 4801. LOCATION L, NUC.
COMMENTARY Satire on Count D'Orsay, Lady Blessington's§ lover, and the *beau monde* of the 1840s. The novel depicts many of his contemporaries and friends in thin disguises: Lady Blessington§ as 'Lady Rivington', etc. The book was instantly suppressed; but as Sadleir observed, 'one is less surprised that it should have been withdrawn than that in 1844 it should ever have been published' [M. Sadleir, *Blessington-D'Orsay* (London, 1933), pp 311–14].

'A MINISTER OF THE CHURCH OF ENGLAND'. Pseudonym of a religious fiction writer. Judging from the following book, its author probably was resident in Ulster. SOURCE RL.
M382 *Mary, the factory girl; or, a brief memorial of the conversion and happy death of one of the Lord's dear children* (by 'A minister of the Church of England').
Belfast: Geo. Phillips, Wm. M'Comb & Geo. Druitt, 1838. SOURCE Scott cat. 15/15.
COMMENTARY No copy located other than that mentioned in the Scott cat. Religious fiction. Even though the locales are disguised, evidently the pious biography of a young Irish girl who was lured at an early age from her factory employment 'by one [of] those unprincipled persons, whose gain is founded on the corruption of the morals of their neighbours, and the deprivation of the young especially – I mean strolling stage players'. Happily, she is rescued and enters school, only to succumb to consumption. The volume includes an extended deathbed debate between Mary and a Catholic priest (with Mary, of course, victorious) [Scott cat. 15/15].

'A MISSIONARY PRIEST', pseud. See **QUIGLEY, Fr Hugh**.

MITCHELL, A.W., fl. 1846. American anthologist of religious fiction tracts, AWM may be identified with Agnes Woods Mitchell, author of *The smuggler's son* (Philadelphia, 1842).
M383 *Interesting narratives; or, religion the great concern* (compiled by A.W. Mitchell).
+ Philadelphia: Presbyterian Board of Publication, 1846. LOCATION InND Loeber coll.
COMMENTARY Religious fiction, compiled chiefly from the publications of the London Religious Tract Society, and containing several stories, of which the following have Irish content: 'The weaver's daughter. A narrative of facts', 'Power of religion', 'Old Andrew; or, happiness in a workhouse' [RL; Wright, i, 1880].

MITCHELL, Edward, pseud. 'Étoile', fl. 1886. Novelist. SOURCE Brown 2, 1031.
M384 *Events in an Irish country house in 1880* (by 'Étoile').
+ Manchester: J. Heywood, 1886. SOURCE Brown 2, 1031. LOCATION L.
COMMENTARY 48pp. Set in Ireland. Most of the action takes place at Ballydonard House, the residence of Sir Henry Simpson, a land agent and ex-officer. The book is interspersed with long discussions with another ex-officer and a Liberal MP on the land question and disestablishment. Intertwined is a love story and an attempted shooting [ML; Brown 2].

MITFORD, Mary Russell, b. Alresford (Hants.) 1787, d. Swallowfield (Berks.) 1855. English dramatist, poet and prose writer, MRM was the daughter of George Mitford, who squandered her mother's money, leaving the family in straitened circumstances. In 1820 they moved from Grazely, an estate in Berkshire, to a labourer's cottage at nearby Three Mile Cross. Well-educated and an extraordinary reader, she became a prolific writer in order to support the family's finances. Her *Our village: sketches of rural character and scenery* (London, 1824–32) was the inspiration for Mrs Marianne Croker's§ *My village, versus "our village"* (London, 1833).
SOURCE Allibone, ii, pp 1330–3; Blain, p. 746; NCBEL 4, pp 960–2; ODNB; Sutherland, p. 441; Todd, pp 470–1.
M385 *Belford Regis. Sketches of a country town* (by Mary Russell Mitford; dedicated to the duke of Devonshire).
London: Richard Bentley, 1835, 3 vols. SOURCE Brown 2, 1033 (1896 edn); Sadleir, 1742; Wolff, 4820; Garside 2, 1835:70. LOCATION L, NUC.
Philadelphia: Carey, Lea & Blanchard, 1835, 2 vols. LOCATION NUC.
COMMENTARY Describes life in and around the town of Reading (Berks.). One of the sketches is 'The Irish haymaker', about migratory labour in England during famine years [Brown 2].
M386 *Country stories* (by Mary Russell Mitford; dedicated to Revd William Harness).
+ London: Saunders & Otley, 1837. LOCATION NUC.
Philadelphia: Carey, Lea & Blanchard, 1838. LOCATION L, NUC.
COMMENTARY Includes 'Honor O'Callaghan', a story about an Irish girl [NUC].

'MITZEN, Mat.', pseud. See **WILLIAMS, Henry Llewellyn**.

MOLLOY, J. Fitzgerald. See **MOLLOY, Joseph Fitzgerald**.

MOLLOY, Joseph Fitzgerald (known as J. Fitzgerald Molloy), b. New Ross (Co. Wexford) 1858, d. London 1908. Catholic novelist, poet, historian and biographer, JFM was the son of Pierce Molloy and Catherine Byrne. He was educated at St Kieran's College, Kilkenny. Intended by his parents for the priesthood, he was for a time the organist at the Augustinian friary church in New Ross (Co. Wexford), but decided to become a professional writer and went to London in 1878 with introductions to the Irish-born writers Mr and Mrs S.C. Hall§. The Halls proved to be good supporters; initially he was given a position by Samuel Hall in the office of his *Art Journal*. He became secretary to Sir Charles Gavan Duffy, who had been MP for New Ross, and through him secured employment in the office of the agent-general of New Zealand. JFM published ten novels, and a volume of poetry: *Songs of passion and pain* (London, 1881). In addition, he wrote about theatrical history in the popular *The romance of the Irish stage* (London, 1897) and a history of Irish drama in Dublin in the eighteenth century. His *Court below stairs, or London under the first Georges 1714–1760* (London, 1882–83, 4 vols.) details George III's slights to Daniel O'Connell. He also wrote a history of the Russian court in the eighteenth century (London, 1905) and a biography of the countess of Blessington§ (London, 1896, 2 vols.). In London he was part of a literary circle and entertained both Oscar Wilde§ and George Bernard Shaw§. In all, he published 23 books. His novels were written for serial publication and to order for leading London and Liverpool newspapers and for the *Temple Bar* (London), *English Illustrated Magazine* (London), *Graphic* (London), *Illustrated London News* and other periodicals. He died unmarried. Some of his letters are among the Downey Papers (NLI, MS 10,038). SOURCE Allibone Suppl., ii, p. 1124; H.C. Black, *Pen, pencil, baton and mask. Biographical sketches* (London, 1896), pp 287–93; Brady, p. 165; ODNB; O'Donoghue, pp 311–12; RIA/DIB; Sutherland, p. 442.

M387 *Merely players. A novel* (by J. Fitzgerald Molloy).
London: Tinsley Bros, 1881, 2 vols. SOURCE Burmester cat. 34/229. LOCATION L.
COMMENTARY A story of crossed love in high places set against the background of a touring theatre company [Burmester].

M388 *It is no wonder. A story of bohemian life* (by J. Fitzgerald Molloy).
London: Hurst & Blackett, 1882, 3 vols. SOURCE Wolff, 4835. LOCATION L, NUC.

M389 *What hast thou done?* (by J. Fitzgerald Molloy; dedicated to Mr & Mrs John Braye).
+ London: Hurst & Blackett, 1883, 3 vols. SOURCE Sutherland, p. 442; Topp 8, 62. LOCATION L, InND Loeber coll.
New York: Harper & Bros, 1883 (Franklin Square Library, No. 326). Source Topp 8, 62. LOCATION NUC.

COMMENTARY A romance set in Ireland and London featuring Maurice Fitzmaurice, who comes from an impoverished but proud Irish family and goes to London to make his way in the world. Before he leaves, he realizes that he should give up the idea of ever marrying his childhood friend, Madge, who is in love with him. He becomes secretary to Sir Lawrence Usher, an important British government official but also a great landlord in the region where Fitzmaurice's family lived. On a visit to Ireland, Sir Lawrence falls in love with Madge. She is aghast at the idea of marrying him. Maurice writes her a cold letter indicating that marrying Sir Lawrence is the best thing she can do for herself. Madge, realizing that her love for Maurice is not reciprocated and that her parents insist that she marry Sir Lawrence, does so in the end. He dies after six months and Maurice destroys a will, which he thinks was the last, so that a previous will, more favourable to Madge, will stand. He renews his pursuit of Madge, but she has seen through him and does not want him anymore. Another man, Purcell, also loves Madge, but is troubled by the fact that she is rich. Eventually, the real last will, which gives Madge only a small portion if she marries again, is discovered,. This takes away Purcell's compunction and he asks her hand in marriage [ML].

M390 *The life and adventures of Peg Woffington; with pictures of the period in which she lived* (by J. Fitzgerald Molloy).
London: Hurst & Blackett, 1884, 2 vols. LOCATION L.
+ London: Downey & Co., 1897 (new and revsd edn; ill. with portrait). LOCATION Univ. of Manchester, InND Loeber coll.
COMMENTARY Historical fiction set in the eighteenth century, consisting of a fictionalized biography of Peg Woffington, the Irish actress [RL].

M391 *That villain Romeo* (by J. Fitzgerald Molloy).
London: Ward & Downey, 1886. SOURCE Sutherland, p. 442; Topp 8, 44. LOCATION
L, NUC.

M392 *A modern magician* (by J. Fitzgerald Molloy).
London: Ward & Downey, 1887, 3 vols. SOURCE Sutherland, p. 442; Topp 8, 332.
LOCATION L, NUC.
New York: J.W. Lovell, [1888]. LOCATION NUC.

M393 *How came he dead?* (by J. Fitzgerald Molloy).
New York: J.W. Lovell, [1890]. LOCATION NUC.
COMMENTARY No known London edn [RL].

M394 *An excellent knave* (by J. Fitzgerald Molloy).
London: Hutchinson & Co., 1893, 3 vols. SOURCE Wolff, 4833. LOCATION L.
New York: Lovell, Coryell & Co., [1892]. LOCATION NUC.
COMMENTARY Detective fiction featuring Inspector Jacob Inquies of Scotland Yard,
and Geoffrey Gillesby, private (formerly police) detective [RL].

M395 *His wife's soul* (by J. Fitzgerald Molloy).
London: Hutchinson, 1893, 3 vols. SOURCE Wolff, 4834; COPAC. LOCATION L.
+ London: Hutchinson & Co., [1895] (Cheap Edition; as *Sweet is revenge; or, his wife's soul*). LOCATION RB, L.
New York: J.A. Taylor & Co., [1891] (as *Sweet is revenge; or, his wife's soul*; Broadway Series, No. 1). SOURCE NYPL. LOCATION NN, NUC.
COMMENTARY A contemporary melodrama of crime, death, and distraught spouses [Sutherland].

M396 *A justified sinner* (by J. Fitzgerald Molloy).
London: Downey & Co., 1897. SOURCE Sutherland, p. 442. LOCATION L.
COMMENTARY A highly-coloured story of deceit in love with the kind of tremendous emotional climax that was the author's speciality [Sutherland].

MONAHAN, Henry J., Jnr, b. Dublin *c*.1833. Novelist, HJM probably can be identified with Henry James Monahan, a Catholic and the son of the Rt. Hon. James Henry Monahan (Snr), a judge (d. 1878), and Fanny Harrington. HJM Jnr was admitted at TCD in 1851 and graduated BA in 1856 and MA in 1864. He may be identified with HJM who became registrar of the consolidated nisi prius court. *Irish pseudonyms* lists a HJM who contributed to *Duffy's Fireside Magazine* (Dublin). SOURCE B & S, Appendix B, p. 83; Ferguson, p. 255; Irish pseudonyms; ODNB [James Henry Monahan Snr]; RL.

M397 *O'Ruark; or, the chronicles of the Balliquin family, detailing what they did, and what they did not; the wise maxims that they didn't put in practice, and the good resolutions which they left to be performed by their descendants: and laying the whole of their private transactions fully before the public* (by Henry J. Monahan; dedicated to the public at large).
+ Dublin: James Duffy, 1852. SOURCE Brown, 1156; OCLC. LOCATION D, Dt, L, NUC.
London: [publisher?], 1852. SOURCE Allibone Suppl., ii, p. 1125.
COMMENTARY No copy of London edn located. The story begins with the Great Famine and closes at the Special Commission of Clonmel (Co. Tipperary) in 1849. Included are humorous descriptions of life in Balliquin [Brown; RL].

'**MONGO, Baba**', pseud. See **DRISCOL, Denis**.

MONSELL, Revd John S.B. See MONSELL, Revd John Samuel Bewley.

MONSELL, Revd John Samuel Bewley (known as John S.B. Monsell), b. St Columb's (Derry) 1811, d. Guildford (Surrey) 1875. Church of Ireland clergyman, hymn writer, religious poet and prose writer, JSBM was the son of Thomas Bewley Monsell, archdeacon of Derry. After graduating at TCD, he was ordained deacon in 1834 and priest in the following year. He ministered in the north of Ireland, but then left for England to become rector of St Nicholas, Guildford, and was appointed honourable chaplain to Queen Victoria. He wrote many volumes of verse on religious themes as well as nursery carols for children. Among these are: *Hymns and miscellaneous poems* (Dublin, 1837); *Spiritual Songs* (London, 1857), and *The parish hymnal* (London, 1873). Eight of his hymns are included in the Revd William M'Ilwaine's *Lyra Hibernica sacra* (Belfast, 1878). He married in 1835 Anne Waller, daughter of Bolton Waller of Shannon Grove (Co. Limerick) and with her had three children. For JSBM's manuscripts, see ODNB. SOURCE Boase, ii, p. 927; Leslie, *Connor*, p. 505; ODNB; O'Donoghue, p. 313; RIA/DIB.

M398 *Cottage controversy; or, dialogues between Thomas and Andrew on the errors of the Church of Rome* (by John S.B. Monsell).
Limerick: Printed [for the author?] by George M. Goggin, 1839. SOURCE de Búrca cat. 68/242 (1839, 2nd edn); DNB ; OCLC. LOCATION L.
COMMENTARY 122pp. Dialogues between Thomas (Protestant) and Andrew (Catholic) on the following topics: The novelty of the church of Rome; transubstantiation; infallibility; the church of Rome is not the mother and mistress of all churches, nor the church of Christ; purgatory; the sacrifice of the mass; invocation of saints and angels; and penance. In the end, Andrew accepts the protestant view and dies happily [ML; BLC].

MONTAGUE, Louisa Julia. See CRAWFORD, Louisa Julia.

MONTAGU, R.W. Editor. See MAGINN, William.

MONTGOMERY, Alexander. See MONTGOMERY, Alexander Esme De Lorges.

MONTGOMERY, Alexander Esme De Lorges (known as Alexander Montgomery), b. Derry (Co. Derry) 1847, d. Australia 1922. Adventure travel writer and journalist, AEDLM was intended for diplomatic service but went to sea and rambled around the world. At age 23 he arrived in Melbourne (Australia) and worked as a journalist. Later he travelled through the Malay archipelago, after which he worked as a journalist in Sydney. SOURCE Miller, ii, p. 674; OCLC.

M399 *Five skull island and other tales of the Malay archipelago* (by Alexander Montgomery).
Melbourne: G. Robertson, 1897. SOURCE Miller, ii, p. 647; OCLC. LOCATION Univ. of Queensland.
COMMENTARY Sketches of traders, Dyaks, Chinese, and other natives of Java, Borneo, the Celebes, etc. [Miller].

M400 *The sword of a sin* (by Alexander Montgomery).
Melbourne: G. Robertson, 1898. SOURCE Miller, ii, p. 647; OCLC. LOCATION Univ. of Queensland.
+ London: Swan Sonnenschein & Co.; Melbourne, Sydney, Adelaide, Brisbane: George Robertson & Co., 1898 (Robertson's Library of Australian Authors). SOURCE COPAC. LOCATION Dt.

COMMENTARY An historical novel based on a double tragedy in 1889 when Crown Prince Rudolph of Austria and Marie Vetserea were found dead after having been forbidden to marry [Miller].

MONTGOMERY, John Wilson, b. Virginia (Co. Cavan) 1835, d. Bangor (Co. Down) 1911. Poet, antiquarian and law enforcement officer, JWM was master of the workhouse in Bailieborough (Co. Cavan) for some years and became known as the Bard of Bailieborough. He spent much of his life in Downpatrick, where he was clerk to the Poor Law Board of Guardians. He wrote extensively on antiquarian subjects and also published verse, including *Rhymes Ulidian* (Downpatrick, 1887) and *Fireside lyrics* (Downpatrick, 1887). According to O'Donoghue, he spent time on the police force and wrote a book about his experiences under an assumed name. SOURCE Brown, p. 213; Newmann, p. 185; O'Donoghue, p. 314; RIA/DIB.

M401 *Mervyn [or Merven] Gray [or Grey]; or, life in the Royal Irish Constabulary* (by John Wilson Montgomery).

Glasgow: Cameron & Ferguson, [c.1875]. SOURCE Brown, 1157; Adv. in *McHenry's Irish tales* (Glasgow [190—?]); H. Herlihy, *The Royal Irish Constabulary* (Dublin, 1997), p. 245.

COMMENTARY No copy located. Mention of title varies as indicated above [RL].

M402 *Round Mourne* (by John Wilson Montgomery; dedicated to Samuel Coyne Hunter). + Bangor: Printed [for the author?] by D.E. Alexander, 1904. SOURCE Newmann, p. 185. LOCATION D, BF1.

MONTGOMERY, Jemima. See **TAUTPHOEUS, Baroness Jemima von.**

MOORE, A., fl. 1861. Although this volume was published in Holland, it is unlikely that AM was Dutch. The name suggests an Irish or English origin. However, no such work in the English language has been located. Source RL.

M403 *Schetsen uit het Iersche volksleven van den tegenwoordigen tijd* (by A. Moore). Rotterdam: G.W. van Belle, 1861. SOURCE Mes, p. 165.

COMMENTARY No copy located. The title refers to sketches of contemporary Irish folk life [RL].

MOORE, Mrs Emma, pseud. 'E.M. Lauderdale', fl. 1880, d. 1916. Novelist and miscellaneous writer. She married George F. Moore of Guys' Printing Works in Cork, and became the compiler of many of the *Guy's Directories* for the city and county. In addition, she contributed to the *Munster Journal* (Limerick, 1888–90), *Southern Industry* (Cork, 1889), and *Shandon Bells* (location not clear, 1889). SOURCE O'Toole, pp 155–6.

M404 *Tivoli. A story of Cork* (by 'E.M. Lauderdale').

London, Cork: Guy, 1886. SOURCE Allibone Suppl., ii, p. 977 [under Lauderdale]; Brown, 888; IBL, 6 (1915), p. 104; Alston, p. 245. LOCATION L.

COMMENTARY A story of a family of the landlord class. Set first at Deer Park, near Cork, and afterwards in England where the family had retired to avoid the Land League agitation. The story turns largely on a mystery of identity [Brown].

MOORE, Revd (Canon) Courtenay, b. Ballymoney (Co. Antrim) 1840, d. 1922 (1916 according to Maher). Church of Ireland clergyman, religious history and liturgical writer, antiquarian and novelist, CM was the son of Alexander Moore. He was admitted at TCD in 1858, graduated BA in 1861 and MA in 1871. He was minister at Brigown, Mitchelstown (Co. Cork, 1865–71). He contributed to various archaeological journals and was editor of the *Irish*

Ecclesiastical Gazette (Dublin, 1893–97). His daughter, Mrs. Victor Rickard, was a popular novelist in the early-twentieth century. SOURCE B & S, Appendix B, p. 84; BLC; Brown 2, p. 182; J. Maher (ed.), *Chief of the Comeraghs* (Mullinahone [Co. Tipperary], 1957), p. 267; RIA/DIB; RL; Ryan, p. 161.

M405 **Con Hegarty. A story of Irish life** (by the Revd Courtenay Moore).
+ Dublin: Church of Ireland Publishing Co., 1897. SOURCE Brown 2, 1047. LOCATION D.
COMMENTARY Through the machinations of an enemy, Con, a hard-working young farmer, is arrested for the murder of an estate agent. He is tried and acquitted, the real murderers being punished. The author introduces many personal recollections and defends the antiquarian trade. Describes priests and parsons of the old school [Brown 2].

MOORE, E.M. Co-author. See **WHATELY, Mary Louisa**.

MOORE, Frances, pseud. 'Madame Panache', b. Carlingford (Co. Louth) *c.*1789/91, d. Exeter (Devon) 1881. Novelist and historian, FM was the daughter of Peter Moore, a former civil servant in India and MP for Coventry, and Sarah, daughter of Lt.-Col. Richmond Webb of Bandon (Co. Cork). One of a family of seven, it is not known if she went with her father when – after the collapse of his businesses and the loss of his parliamentary seat in 1826 – he fled to France to escape arrest. She published anonymously and also under her pseudonym. Her *Historical life of Joanna of Sicily, Queen of Naples* (London, 1824, 2 vols.) was influential but controversial. In her preface to her translation of Carlo Botta's *History of Italy during the consulate and empire of Napoleon Buonaparte* (London, 1828, 2 vols.) she discusses issues of history and biography. Both ODNB and Blain list *Manners* (London, 1817) as FM's second novel, but a first novel has not been identified. SOURCE Blain, p. 755; NCBEL 4, p. 2446; ODNB.

M406 **Manners. A novel** [anon.].
+ London: Baldwin, Cradock & Joy, 1817, 3 vols. SOURCE Blain, p. 755; British Fiction; Garside, 1817:43; Wolff, 4858. LOCATION Corvey CME 3–628–48081–7, Ireland related fiction, L, NUC.
New York: William B. Gilley, 1818, 2 vols. LOCATION NUC.
COMMENTARY A novel that sharply outlines social distinctions in an English village and in Ireland. It displays FM's learning and includes comments on other novelists, including female novelists. Block and other sources have erroneously attributed this novel to Frances Brooke (née Moore) [Blain; British Fiction].

M407 **A year and a day** (by 'Madame Panache').
London: Baldwin, Cradock, & Joy, 1818. SOURCE Blain, p. 755; British Fiction; Garside, 1818:43; ODNB. LOCATION L.
New York: C. Wiley & Co., 1819. SOURCE COPAC. LOCATION NUC.
[location?], [publisher?], 1820 (trans. as *Un an et un jour*). Source Garside, 1818:43; Bn-Opale plus. LOCATION BNF.
COMMENTARY A silver fork novel presenting two heroic young women: one shy, self-sacrificing yet strong; one a dazzling young countess whose grand marriage, unconventionality, and goodness combine to destroy her. It may have been inspired by the life of Lady Caroline Lamb§. Block has erroneously attributed this novel to Frances Brooke (née Moore) [Blain, ODNB; British Fiction].

MOORE, Frank Frankfort, pseuds 'F. Littlemore' and 'Bernard O'Hea', b. Limerick 1855 (1850 according to Brady; not 1885 as in OCIL), d. St Leonard's (Sussex) 1931.

Journalist, poet, novelist and miscellaneous writer, FFM was the son of John Moore of Belfast and brother-in-law of Bram Stoker§. He was educated at the Royal Academical Institute, Belfast, and by a private tutor. He joined the staff of the *Belfast Newsletter* and by age 20 had published two volumes of poetry and his first novel. He was an inveterate and adventurous traveller and many of the exotic locations he visited were used as backdrops for his novels. Some of his experiences are recorded in *A journalist's note-book* (London, 1894). When once asked how he managed to write a novel on Australia without having visited it, he remarked that 'any journalist can mug up a continent in a week'. His 'A whirlwind harvest' was serialized in the Melbourne *Age* (1898–9). Many of his works of fiction were published under the auspices of the Society for Promoting Christian Knowledge. He settled in London, wrote several historical dramas, a biography of Oliver Goldsmith§, and several books about English life. His *The truth about Ulster* (London, 1914) argued that Ulster should not be included in any Home Rule plan because of its urban, manufacturing nature. FFM wrote 81 works of fiction, some of which were written for juveniles, and some set in Ireland. Many of his fiction books were reprinted in Germany. SOURCE Allibone Suppl., ii, p. 1131; Brady, p. 167; Brown, p. 214; EF, p. 283; Hogan 2, p. 859–60; IBL, 3 (1911–12), p. 76; Law, p. 230; MVP, p. 322; OCIL, p. 373; O'Donoghue, p. 315; E. Reilly, p. 248; RIA/DIB; Sutherland, p. 445; Wilson, p. 371.

M408 *Kathleen Mavourneen* (by Frank Frankfort Moore).
    London: Lloyds, n.d. SOURCE Brown 2, 1050.
    COMMENTARY No copy located. Major Ainlie, an Englishman, buys an estate in Co. Mayo on which the mortgages have foreclosed. His coming is resented by the people and the former owner, Mahony, father of Kathleen, refuses all intercourse with him. Ainlie poses as his steward and gets to know the Mahonys. Kathleen falls in love with him. Complications ensue, which are solved by the homecoming of a son of the Mahonys, whom Ainlie had befriended in South Africa. This book is not to be confused with R.W. McDonnell's§ work of the same title [RL; Brown 2].

M409 *Sojourners together. A story* (by Frank Frankfort Moore).
    + London: Smith, Elder & Co., 1875. LOCATION D, L, NUC.
    + London: Hutchinson & Co., [1894], 2nd edn (as *Sojourners together. A holiday romance*; Hutchinson's Popular Novels). LOCATION NUC, InND Loeber coll.
    COMMENTARY Love story among English vacationers in an Alpine setting [ML].

M410 *Where the rail runs now: A story of the coaching days* (by Frank Frankfort Moore).
    + London, Belfast: Marcus Ward & Co., 1876 (ill.). LOCATION D, RB, L, NUC, InND Loeber coll.
    COMMENTARY Detective fiction that unravels a murder mystery. Set in England around the time the railways were introduced. The main character is a coachman who travels daily the stretch of road close to where a murder was committed. On the day in question, he had picked up a woman. A Capt. Saxeby has come home from service abroad. The coachman is suspicious of him but does not know why. Saxeby woos a rich girl and is about to announce his engagement to her when her brother recognizes him as a scoundrel he had known in Malta. The coachman realizes that the 'woman' he had picked up had been Capt. Saxeby in disguise and that he must be the murderer. Saxeby is caught while attempting to elope. He is shackled to be taken to London but jumps out of the carriage and drowns [ML].

M411 *Told by the sea: Tales of the coast* (by Frank Frankfort Moore).
    London. Belfast: Marcus Ward & Co., 1877. LOCATION NUC.

M412 *Daireen* (by Frank Frankfort Moore).
    + London: Smith, Elder & Co., 1879, 2 vols. SOURCE Brown, 1158 (1893 edn).
    LOCATION D, L, NUC.

New York: Harper & Bros, 1880 (Franklin Square Library, No. 115). LOCATION NUC.
COMMENTARY A romantic story featuring Daireen Gerald who is courted by The O'Dermot MacNamara, an example of broken-down Irish gentry, and by Standish MacNamara. All three are passengers on a ship to Cape Town. At the end of the story the issue of who Daireen will marry is left undecided [Brown].

M413 *Mate of the Jessica. A story of the South Pacific* (by Frank Frankfort Moore).
+ London, Belfast, Philadelphia: Marcus Ward & Co., 1879, 2 vols. SOURCE Wolff, 4874. LOCATION D, L.
COMMENTARY Set in the south Pacific [Sutherland, p. 445].

M414 *The mutiny on the Albatross* (by Frank Frankfort Moore).
+ London, Brighton: The Society for Promoting Christian Knowledge; New York: E. & J.B. Young, 1885 (ill. W.H. Overend). SOURCE Wolff, 4876; Sutherland, p. 445. LOCATION D, NUC.

M415 *The fate of the "Black swan." A tale of New Guinea* (by Frank Frankfort Moore).
+ London: Society for Promoting Christian Knowledge, [1885] (ill. L.H. Overend). SOURCE Wolff, 4864. LOCATION D, L.

M416 *The great Orion* (by Frank Frankfort Moore).
+ London: Society for Promoting Christian Knowledge; New York: E. & J.B. Young & Co., [1886] (ill. J. Nash). SOURCE Sutherland, p. 445; Wolff, 4867. LOCATION D, L, NUC.

M417 *Will's voyages* (by Frank Frankfort Moore).
+ London: Society for Promoting Christian Knowledge; New York: E. & J.B. Young & Co., [1886] (ill. W.H. Overend). LOCATION D, L.

M418 *Tre, pol, and pen* (by Frank Frankfort Moore).
+ London: Society for Promoting Christian Knowledge, [1887] (ill. W.H. Overend). SOURCE Wolff, 4881. LOCATION D, L.
COMMENTARY Historical fiction for juveniles set in Cornwall about 1798–1800 at the time of Admiral Nelson's victories, featuring smugglers [Nield].

M419 *Under hatches: or, Ned Woodthorpe's adventures* (by Frank Frankfort Moore).
+ London, Glasgow, Edinburgh, Dublin: Blackie & Son, 1889 (ill. A. Forestier). SOURCE Wolff, 4882; Osborne, p. 375. LOCATION D, CaOTP, L, NUC.
COMMENTARY Story for boys [ML].

M420 *Fire-flies and mosquitoes* (by Frank Frankfort Moore).
+ London: Society for Promoting Christian Knowledge; New York: E. & J.B. Young & Co., [1888]. SOURCE Wolff, 4865. LOCATION D, L, NUC.
COMMENTARY Tale of adventures in the East Indies [NUC].

M421 *The slaver of Zanzibar* (by Frank Frankfort Moore).
+ London, Brighton: Society for Promoting Christian Knowledge; New York: E. & J.B. Young & Co., [1889] (ill. J. Nash). SOURCE Wolff, 4880. LOCATION L, InND Loeber coll.
COMMENTARY Adventure story for boys about a young midshipman on the HMS Pelican in the 1880s. The ship is stationed at Zanzibar for the purpose of preventing the Arab slave trade from Africa. The midshipman is responsible for seizing an English ship involved in the trade [ML].

M422 *Coral and cocoa-nut. The cruise of the yacht "Fire-fly" to Samoa* (by Frank Frankfort Moore).
+ London: Society for Promoting Christian Knowledge, 1890 (ill. A. Forestier). SOURCE Wolff, 4862. LOCATION D, L, NUC.
+ New York: E. & J.B. Young & Co., n.d. (ill. W.H. Overend). LOCATION D.

M423 *Highways and high seas. Cyril Harley's adventures on both* (by Frank Frankfort Moore).
London, Glasgow, Edinburgh, Dublin: Blackie & Son, 1890. LOCATION L, InND Loeber coll. ([1890] edn).
New York: Scribner & Welford, [1889]. LOCATION NUC.
COMMENTARY A story for boys [ML].

M424 *The silver sickle* (by Frank Frankfort Moore).
+ London, Sidney: Griffith, Farran, Okeden & Welsh; Belfast: Charles W. Olley, 1891 (ill.). LOCATION D, L.
COMMENTARY Collection of stories [Topp 8, 1252].

M425 *The ice prison* (by Frank Frankfort Moore).
+ London, Brighton: Society for Promoting Christian Knowledge: New York: E. & J.B. Young & Co., 1891 (ill. W.H. Overend). SOURCE Wolff, 4868. LOCATION D, L.

M426 *Larry O'Lannigan, J.P. His rise and fall* [anon.].
+ Belfast: Olley & Co., 1892. SOURCE Linen Hall cat. p. 172. LOCATION D, BFl.
Belfast: Olley & Co.; London: Simpkin, Marshall, Hamilton, Kent & Co., 1893. SOURCE Topp 8, 1230.
COMMENTARY The Belfast 1892 and 1893 edns each was 38pp; no copy of 1893 edn located. A 26th edn appeared in that year [L; Topp 8, 1230; OCLC; RL].

M427 *Sailing and sealing. A tale of the North Pacific* (by Frank Frankfort Moore).
London: Society for Promoting Christian Knowledge, [1892]. LOCATION L, NUC.

M428 *From the bush to the breakers* (by Frank Frankfort Moore).
+ London: Society for Promoting Christian Knowledge, [1893] (ill. W.H. Overend). SOURCE Sutherland, p. 445. LOCATION D, L, NUC (n.d. edn).
COMMENTARY Set in Australia [Sutherland, p. 445].

M429 *"I forbid the banns". The story of a comedy which was played seriously* (by Frank Frankfort Moore).
+ London: Hutchinson & Co., 1893, 3 vols. SOURCE Wolff, 4869. LOCATION D, L, NUC.
Leipzig: Bernard Tauchnitz, 1893, 2 vols. SOURCE T & B, 2908–9. LOCATION NUC.
New York: Cassell, [1893]. LOCATION NUC.

M430 *The two clippers* (by Frank Frankfort Moore).
London: Society for Promoting Christian Knowledge, [1893] (ill. W.H. Overend). LOCATION NUC.

M431 *A gray eye or so* (by Frank Frankfort Moore).
London: Hutchinson & Co., 1893, 3 vols. SOURCE Brown 2, 1048; Wolff, 4866. LOCATION D (n.d., 7th edn), L, NUC, InND Loeber coll. (n.d., 7th edn.).
Leipzig: Bernard Tauchnitz, 1894, 2 vols. SOURCE T & B, 3000–1. LOCATION NUC.
New York: D. Appleton, 1894. LOCATION NUC.
COMMENTARY A love-tale with pictures of house-party life in Ireland. Harold Wynne is meant to be marrying the rich Helen Craven. However, he falls in love with Beatrice, a girl without a fortune. His friends and father try to discourage him, but Harold and Beatrice avow their love for each other. Eventually, Harold's father dies and leaves him a title and a small income [ML; Brown 2].

M432 *The diary of an Irish cabinet minister: being the history of the first (and only) Irish national administration, 1894. Printed from the MS of the Right Hon. Phineas O'Flannagan, late secretary of state for foreign affairs* (by 'Bernard O'Hea').
+ Belfast: Olley & Co., 1893 (ill.). LOCATION L.
Belfast: Olley & Co., 1893 (as *Ireland a nation! The diary of an Irish cabinet minister: being the history of the first (and only) Irish national administration, 1894. Printed from*

the MS of the Right Hon. Phineas O'Flannagan, late secretary of state for foreign affairs,
by 'Bernard O'Hea'). LOCATION D.
Belfast: Olley & Co., 1893 (new and up-to-date 15th edn; Ireland a Nation! series).
SOURCE OCLC. LOCATION D.
COMMENTARY 37pp. The 30th edn was advertised in *The viceroy Muldoon* in 1893. A
satire on Ireland imagined under Home Rule [RL; Murphy, p. 60].

M433   *The viceroy Muldoon: His court and courtship. Including the true record of His
Excellency's encounter with the Right Honourable Timothy Moriarty, prime min-
ister, in the Lower Castle Yard, Dublin, A.D. 1895* (by 'Bernard O'Hea').
+ Belfast: Olley & Co., 1893 (ill.; Ireland a Nation! Series). SOURCE OCLC. LOCATION
D, InND Loeber coll.
Belfast: Olley & Co., 1893 (as *Ireland a nation! The viceroy Muldoon: His court and
courtship. Including the true record of His Excellency's encounter with the Right Honourable
Timothy Moriarty, prime minister, in the lower castle yard, Dublin, A.D. 1895*, by 'Bernard
O'Hea'). LOCATION D.
Belfast: Olley & Co.; London: Simpkin, Marshall, Hamilton, Kent & Co., 1893. SOURCE
Topp 8, 1238.
COMMENTARY 33pp. No copy of the Belfast 1893 edn located. A satirical story written from
a Unionist point of view about Ireland having its own parliament and the power to select the
lord lieutenant. It describes the chaos that arises from the move of a parliament to Dublin.
Most of the constabulary resigns and moves to the north, while most of the gentry close up
their houses and leave the south. A plan is developed to make Ulster pay for most of the taxes
and to encourage alcohol consumption so as to increase the excise tax. Eventually rioting takes
place in Dublin and William Gladstone ends Home Rule [ML].

M434   *One fair daughter: Her story* (by Frank Frankfort Moore).
+ London: Hutchinson & Co., 1894, 3 vols. SOURCE Sutherland, p. 445; Jarndyce cat.
110/730. LOCATION L, NUC, InND Loeber coll.
Leipzig: Bernard Tauchnitz, 1895, 2 vols. SOURCE T & B, 3037–38. LOCATION NUC.
Chicago: E.A. Weeks & Co., [1895]. LOCATION NUC.
COMMENTARY Set in England. A daughter whose father is in debt stages his death by secretly
sending him to America and claiming a dying man as her father. She goes to London, where she
is a popular figure in the social scene and has various lovers. Her father returns, but he is not welcome. In the end, she marries the young man from her village who has always loved her [ML].

M435   *A journalist's note book* (by Frank Frankfort Moore).
+ London: Hutchinson & Co., 1894. LOCATION L, NUC.
COMMENTARY Contains anecdotes and dialogues of people the author had met [ML;
RIA/DIB].

M436   *They call it love* (by Frank Frankfort Moore).
+ London: Hutchinson & Co., [1895]. LOCATION D, L, NUC (1896, 2nd edn).
Leipzig: Bernard Tauchnitz, 1895, 2 vols. SOURCE T & B, 3074–75. LOCATION L,
NUC.
Philadelphia: J.B. Lippincott, 1895. LOCATION L, NUC.

M437   *Phyllis of Philistia* (by Frank Frankfort Moore).
London: Hutchinson & Co., 1895. LOCATION L, NUC (1895 edn).
New York: Cassell, [1895]. LOCATION NUC.

M438   *The secret of the court. A romance of life and death* (by Frank Frankfort Moore).
+ London: Hutchinson & Co., 1895 (ill. G.H. Edwards). LOCATION D, L.
Philadelphia: J.B. Lippincott, 1895 (ill. G.H. Edwards). SOURCE OCLC. LOCATION
NN.

M439   *The sale of soul* (by Frank Frankfort Moore).
London: Hutchinson, [1895] (Zeit-Geist Library). LOCATION L.
New York: F.A. Stokes, [1895] (ill. G.H. Edwards). LOCATION NUC.

M440   *Two in the bush and others elsewhere* (by Frank Frankfort Moore).
+ London: A.D. Innes & Co., 1895. LOCATION D, DPL, L, NUC.
COMMENTARY Contents: 'Two in the bush and others elsewhere', 'A colourable imitation', 'Under royal patronage', 'The cruise of the "Diana"', 'Sylvia the sorceress', 'At the king's head' [RL].

M441   *Dr. Koodmadhi of Ashantee* (by Frank Frankfort Moore).
+ London: A. Constable & Co., 1896 (The Acme Library). SOURCE Wolff, 4863.
LOCATION L, NUC, InND Loeber coll.
COMMENTARY Set in Africa where an English-trained African doctor is on somewhat friendly terms with the government's commissioner. This relationship is severely disturbed when Dr Koomadhi asks the commissioner's daughter to marry him. Mysterious happenings take place as a result of Dr Koomadhi obtaining some magic from his mother. However, he is not careful with his magic and, as a consequence, a large group of monkeys kill him [ML].

M442   *In our hours of ease* (by Frank Frankfort Moore).
+ London: Mentz & Co., 1896. SOURCE Wolff, 4871 (1897 edn). LOCATION L, NUC (1897 edn).
COMMENTARY No Irish content. Contents: 'The tender heart', 'Reggie's rival', 'The prince of the Schwabs', 'The iconoclast', 'Sally', 'The waits of Taragonda Creek', 'A lead over', 'The duke', 'Highwaymen for an hour' [ML].

M443   *The impudent comedian and others* (by Frank Frankfort Moore).
+ London: C. Arthur Pearson, 1897 (ill. Robert Sauber). SOURCE Wolff, 4870.
LOCATION DPL (1898 edn), L, InND Loeber coll.
+ Chicago: H.S. Stone & Co., 1897 (ill. Robert Sauber). LOCATION InND Loeber coll.
COMMENTARY Historical fiction about people associated with the theatre world in the eighteenth century. Contents: ' The impudent comedian', 'Kitty Clive', 'A question of art', 'The muse of tragedy', 'The way to keep him', 'The capture of the duke' [ML].

M444   *The Jessamy bride* (by Frank Frankfort Moore).
+ London: Hutchinson & Co., 1897 (ill. A. Forestier). SOURCE Brown, 1159; Wolff, 4872. LOCATION D (1897, 2nd edn), DPL (n.d., 7th edn), Dt, L, NUC (1898 edn), InND Loeber coll.
Leipzig: Bernard Tauchnitz, 1897. SOURCE T & B, 3242. LOCATION NUC.
New York: New Amsterdam Book Co., [c.1896]. LOCATION NUC, InND Loeber coll.
(New York, Duffield 1906 edn).
Chicago: H.S. Stone & Co., 1897. LOCATION D (1898 edn), NUC.
COMMENTARY Historical fiction set in the eighteenth century. The story relates Oliver Goldsmith's§ last years of life in London. The story describes the success of his play *She stoops to conquer* and his attachment to Mary Horneck. Various celebrities of the day make their appearance in the story, including Edmund Burke and Dr Johnson [ML].

M445   *The fatal gift* (by Frank Frankfort Moore).
London: Hutchinson & Co., 1898 (ill. Sauber). SOURCE Brown 2, 1049. LOCATION D, L.
New York: Dodd, Mead & Co., 1898. LOCATION NUC.
COMMENTARY Historical fiction. One of the characters is Heffernan, landlord of the Cruiskeen Beg, Dunleary (Co. Dublin), but the story is written around the lives of Miss Elizabeth Gunning (see Mrs Elizabeth Plunkett§) and Miss Maria Gunning, celebrated Irish beauties of the eighteenth century [Brown 2].

M446   *The millionaires* (by Frank Frankfort Moore).
+ London: Hutchinson & Co., 1898 (ill. M. Grieffenhagen). SOURCE Wolff, 4875.
LOCATION D (n.d., 4th edn), Dt, L, NUC, InND Loeber coll.
Leipzig: Bernard Tauchnitz, 1898. SOURCE T & B, 3291. LOCATION NUC.
New York: D. Appleton & Co., 1898 (Appleton's Town and Country Library). SOURCE
NYPL. LOCATION NN, NUC.
COMMENTARY Set in the Riviera in France among the rich and those who aspire to
catch a rich spouse. American millionaires are the targets of matrimonial plans [ML].

M447   *Well, after all —* (by Frank Frankfort Moore).
+ London: Hutchinson & Co., 1899. SOURCE Wolff, 4883. LOCATION DPL, L.

M448   *Nell Gwynn – comedian. A novel* (by Frank Frankfort Moore).
London: Hutchinson, 1899. SOURCE Wolff, 4877 (1900 edn). LOCATION L (1900 edn),
NUC.
+ London: C. Arthur Pearson, n.d. (as *The adventures of Nell Gwynn*). LOCATION D.
Leipzig: Bernard Tauchnitz, 1900. SOURCE T & B, 3449. LOCATION NUC.
New York: Dodd, Mead & Co., 1899. LOCATION NUC.
COMMENTARY Historical fiction about Nell Gwynn, who was king Charles II's mis-
tress [RL].

M449   *The conscience of Coralie* (by Frank Frankfort Moore).
+ London: C. Arthur Pearson, 1900 (ill. F.H. Townsend). LOCATION D, L, NUC.
+ Chicago, New York: Herbert S. Stone & Co., 1900 (ill. F.H. Townsend). LOCATION
NUC, InND Loeber coll.
COMMENTARY Coralie, an American girl of Irish extraction, visits some Irish friends of her
father who are living in London. She is sorely disappointed by English society, whose members she finds extremely insipid and superficial. One man, however, stands out. He is of humble background but has made himself the 'socialist' leader. Most people consider him a bounder,
but for Coralie he seems to be the only person in England who takes life seriously. Attracted
by her father's millions, the bounder asks her to marry him. Her friends are distraught and
do not know how to intervene. The tactic that eventually has the desired effect is to give
Coralie a heavy dose of her lover's presence. She finds out by herself that he is a coward and
a dishonest person [ML].

M450   *According to Plato* (by Frank Frankfort Moore).
+ London: Hutchinson & Co., 1901. SOURCE Wolff, 4860. LOCATION D, DPL, L,
NUC.
New York: Dodd, Mead & Co., 1901. LOCATION NUC.

M451   *A nest of linnets* (by Frank Frankfort Moore).
London: Hutchinson & Co., 1901 (ill. J. Jellicoe). SOURCE Wolff, 4878. LOCATION D,
L, NUC (n.d. edn).
New York: D. Appleton, 1901. LOCATION NUC.
COMMENTARY Historical fiction set in Bath in the eighteenth century featuring all the well-
known figures of that time such as Dr Oliver Goldsmith§, Horace Walpole, Dr Samuel
Johnson, David Garrick, Richard Brinsley Sheridan, etc. The main character is a beautiful
singer who is exploited by her father and who shrinks from displaying her emotions and artistic talent in public. To avoid having to sing, she accepts an offer of marriage from Mr Long,
an elderly gentleman. He is not in love with her but wants to protect her, and the marriage
does not take place. Sheridan, who is in love with her, learns from Mr Long how to behave
unselfishly. In the end he marries the singer with the full approbation of Mr Long [ML].

M452   *A damsel or two* (by Frank Frankfort Moore).
London: Hutchinson & Co., 1902. LOCATION L, NUC.

Leipzig: Bernard Tauchnitz, 1902. SOURCE T & B, 3593. LOCATION NUC.
+ New York: D. Appleton & Co., 1902. LOCATION D, NUC.

M453 *Castle Omeragh* (by Frank Frankfort Moore).
+ Westminster [London]: Archibald Constable & Co., 1903 (2nd impression). SOURCE Brown, 1160; Wolff, 4861. LOCATION D, DPL, L, NUC, InND Loeber coll.
Leipzig: Bernard Tauchnitz, 1903. SOURCE T & B, 3669. LOCATION NUC.
New York: D. Appleton & Co., 1903. LOCATION NUC.

COMMENTARY An historical novel set in Co. Clare during Cromwell's invasion. The central figures are the Fawcetts, a Protestant planter family whose sympathies are with the Irish. The oldest son, is an officer in the army of O'Neill. The second son is unwarlike and inclined to Quakerism. By having taken precautions against an attack, Castle Omeragh is not taken by Cromwellian soldiers. A Jesuit friend of the family figures prominently in the story. Describes the Drogheda massacre and Cromwell's repulse at Clonmel [Brown; ML].

M454 *Shipmates in sunshine. Their romance on the Caribbean cruise* (by Frank Frankfort Moore).
London: Hutchinson & Co., 1903. SOURCE Wolff, 4879. LOCATION L, NUC.
Leipzig: Bernard Tauchnitz, 1904, 2 vols. SOURCE T & B, 3717–18. LOCATION NUC.
New York: D. Appleton & Co., 1903. LOCATION NUC.

M455 *The original woman* (by Frank Frankfort Moore).
+ London: Hutchinson & Co., 1904. SOURCE Brown, 1161. LOCATION DPL, L, NUC.
Leipzig: Bernard Tauchnitz, 1904. SOURCE T & B, 3749. LOCATION NUC.

COMMENTARY The heroine is a modern girl. The hero, who is also the villain, has a very attractive personality. The scene is first set in a country house in Galway, but later shifts to Martinique, where an element of the supernatural enters the story. The thesis of the story is that whatever culture might have done for the modern woman, in crises she reverts to female instincts [Brown].

M456 *Sir Roger's heir* (by Frank Frankfort Moore).
+ London: Hodder & Stoughton, 1904. SOURCE Nield, p. 411. LOCATION D, DPL, L ([1904] edn), NUC (1904, 2nd edn), InND Loeber coll.
COMMENTARY Historical fiction depicting English country life in the time of Queen Anne [Nield].

M457 *The other world* (by Frank Frankfort Moore).
+ London: Eveleigh Nash, 1904. LOCATION L, NUC.

COMMENTARY Ghost stories. Contents: 'A providential escape', 'Magic in the web of it', 'The baseless fabric', 'Black as he is painted', 'The ghost of Barmouth Manor', 'The blood oranges', 'The strange story of Northavon priory' [ML].

M458 *The white causeway* (by Frank Frankfort Moore).
+ London: Hutchinson & Co., 1905 (ill.). LOCATION D, L, NUC.
Leipzig: Bernard Tauchnitz, 1905. SOURCE T & B, 3815. LOCATION NUC.
COMMENTARY A love story containing supernatural motifs [Wilson, p. 370].

M459 *He loved but one. The story of Lord Byron and Mary Chaworth* (by Frank Frankfort Moore).
+ London: Hutchinson & Co., 1905. LOCATION D, Dt.
+ London: Eveleigh Nash, 1905. LOCATION L, NUC.
New York, London: G.P. Putnam's Sons, 1905 (as *Love alone is lord*). LOCATION NUC.
COMMENTARY Love story [ML].

M460 *The artful Miss Dill* (by Frank Frankfort Moore).
+ London: Hutchinson & Co., 1906. LOCATION D, L, NUC.

Leipzig: Bernard Tauchnitz, 1906. SOURCE T & B, 3887. LOCATION NUC.

COMMENTARY Set in Venezuela and England, featuring the manipulations of the daughter of a shady diplomat who had served various South American presidents and patriots [EF, p. 283].

M461 *Captain Latymer. A romance* (by Frank Frankfort Moore).

+ London: Cassell & Co., 1907 (ill. S. Seymour Lucas). SOURCE Nield, p. 318; Brown, 1162 (1908 edn). LOCATION D, L, NUC.

COMMENTARY A sequel to *Castle Omeragh* (Westminster, 1903). Historical novel of the seventeenth century set in Barbados and in Ireland (just after the siege of Drogheda) in the Civil War time. The oldest son of the Fawcett family, who has served in the army of Owen Roe O'Neill, is condemned by Cromwell to be exiled to the West Indies, but escapes along with the daughter of Hugh O'Neill. Among the characters is Prince Rupert [Nield; Brown].

M462 *The marriage lease: The story of social experiment* (by Frank Frankfort Moore).

London: Hutchinson & Co., 1907. LOCATION L, NUC.

+ Leipzig: Bernard Tauchnitz, 1907. SOURCE T & B, 3985. LOCATION NUC, InND Loeber coll.

COMMENTARY Set in an imaginary state where things are organized along scientific principles. The latest experiment is that marriages will only be valid for three years. While many people initially applaud this sensible law, eventually the experiment fails and people clamour for the old fashioned marriage ceremony and for being allowed to have churches again [ML].

M463 *The messenger* (by Frank Frankfort Moore).

+ London: Hodder & Stoughton, 1907. LOCATION D, L, NUC.

New York: Empire Book Co., [1907] (as *The love that prevailed*; ill. H.B. Matthews).

COMMENTARY No copy of the New York edn located. Historical novel portraying John Wesley as lover and preacher [Baker; RL].

M464 *An amateur adventuress* (by Frank Frankfort Moore).

London: Hutchinson & Co., 1908. LOCATION L, NUC.

Leipzig: Bernard Tauchnitz, 1908. SOURCE T & B, 4053. LOCATION NUC.

M465 *A Georgian pageant* (by Frank Frankfort Moore).

London: Hutchinson & Co., 1908 (ill.). LOCATION L, NUC.

New York: Dutton & Co., 1909. LOCATION NUC.

COMMENTARY Many of the following stories are set in London. Contents: 'The monarch of the pageant', 'A comedy in St. Martin's Street', 'A tragedy in the Haymarket', 'The fatal gift', 'The fête champetre', 'The plot of a lady novelist', 'Tragedy with a twinkle', 'The best comedy of the century', 'The Jessamy bride', 'The amazing elopement', 'The amazing jewels', 'A melodrama at Covent Garden', 'The comedy at Downing Street' [NUC]

M466 *Love and the interloper* (by Frank Frankfort Moore).

London: Hutchinson & Co., 1908. SOURCE Wolff, 4873. LOCATION L, NUC.

M467 *Priscilla and Charybdis: A story of alternatives* (by Frank Frankfort Moore).

+ London: Archibald Constable & Co., 1909. LOCATION D, L, NUC.

Leipzig: Bernard Tauchnitz, 1909, 2 vols. SOURCE T & B, 4134–35. LOCATION NUC.

M468 *The food of love* (by Frank Frankfort Moore).

London: Eveleigh Nash, 1909. LOCATION L, NUC.

Leipzig: Bernard Tauchnitz, 1909. SOURCE T & B, 4153. LOCATION NUC.

M469 *The laird of Craig Athol* (by Frank Frankfort Moore).

London: Constable & Co., 1910. LOCATION L, NUC.

Leipzig: Bernard Tauchnitz, 1910. SOURCE T & B, 4198. LOCATION NUC.

M470 *The marriage of Barbara* (by Frank Frankfort Moore).

London: Constable & Co., 1911. LOCATION L, NUC.

Leipzig: Bernard Tauchnitz, 1911. SOURCE T & B, 4267. LOCATION NUC.

M471 *A keeper of the robes* (by Frank Frankfort Moore).
+ London, New York, Toronto: Hodder & Stoughton, [1911] (ill.). LOCATION NUC, InND Loeber coll.
COMMENTARY Historical fiction set in the eighteenth century with Fanny Burney as the main character [BLC].

M472 *The narrow escape of Lady Hardwell* (by Frank Frankfort Moore).
+ London: Constable & Co., 1912. LOCATION D, L, NUC.
Leipzig: Bernard Tauchnitz, 1912. SOURCE T & B, 4358. LOCATION NUC.
COMMENTARY A saga of the Hardwell family set in the South Downs in Sussex. Jasper Brooke, a student of the supernatural, visits Chalford Castle. He sees a sleepwalker on the roof of the castle and saves her, only to discover that she is the wife of Sir Hubert Hardwell and wanted to kill herself. Lady Hardwell was forced into an unhappy marriage by her mother. Brooke's fiancée, Hilda, becomes suspicious of his conduct towards Lady Hardwell. The castle is set on fire and the cruel Sir Hubert escapes, with his wife locked in a room. She is saved, and leaves her husband. Meanwhile, Brooke learns that while Hilda has been in France, she married Revd Lindsay Fellowes. Brooke is relieved, as he is in love with Lady Hardwell although she does not return the sentiment. Sir Hubert is found dead in a mantrap in his own demesne. It is revealed that Tom Tompsett, who started the fire, has killed him [CD].

M473 *The red man's secret. A romance of the stage prairie* (by Frank Frankfort Moore).
London: Hutchinson & Co., 1912. LOCATION L, NUC.

M474 *The rescue of Martha* (by Frank Frankfort Moore).
London: Hutchinson & Co., 1913. LOCATION L, NUC.

M475 *The lighter side of English life* (by Frank Frankfort Moore).
+ London, Edinburgh: T.N. Fowlis, 1913 (ill. George Belcher). LOCATION L, NUC.
Boston: L. Phillips, [1913]. LOCATION NUC.
COMMENTARY Contents: 'The village', 'Outside the village', 'The village villas', 'The comedies of the country house', 'The county, old and crusted', 'The old county town', 'The people of Mallingham', 'The pushing provincial town', 'Red-tiled society', 'The lesser English country towns', 'The cathedral towns', 'A close corporation', 'Among the amateurs', 'The lighter side of clerical life', 'The croquet lawns', 'Art and the artful in the provinces' [ML].

M476 *The Ulsterman. A story of to-day* (by Frank Frankfort Moore).
+ London: Hutchinson & Co., 1914. SOURCE Brown, 1163. LOCATION D, DPL, BFl, L, NUC, InND Loeber coll.
Leipzig: Bernard Tauchnitz, 1914. SOURCE T & B, 4477. LOCATION NUC.
COMMENTARY Portrayal of Ulster society and political attitudes at the beginning of the twentieth century. Describes the good and bad qualities of people in Co. Antrim. The sons of a bigoted Ulster Protestant mill owner eventually marry into Catholic families. This brings an end to the romance of one of the mill owner's daughters with an up-and-coming politician, who decides he does not want to be associated with the family any longer [ML; Brown].

M477 *The lady of the reef* (by Frank Frankfort Moore).
+ London: Hutchinson & Co., 1915. SOURCE Brown, 1164. LOCATION D, L, NUC.
COMMENTARY A young English artist in Paris unexpectedly inherits a property in Co. Down. When he arrives there he finds himself in a puzzling environment [Brown].

M478 *The romance of a Red Cross hospital* (by Frank Frankfort Moore).
London: Hutchinson & Co., 1915. LOCATION L, NUC.

M479 *A friend indeed* (by Frank Frankfort Moore).
+ London: Hutchinson & Co., 1916. SOURCE Brown, 1165. LOCATION D, L, NUC ([1916] edn).

COMMENTARY Two friends are in love with the same girl. After many events and adventures, the best of the two friends is united with his first love. Scenes are set in England, Ireland and Australia and discussion of the Land League and its efforts is included [Brown].

M480　*The rise of Raymond* (by Frank Frankfort Moore).
London: Hutchinson & Co., 1916. LOCATION L, NUC.

M481　*The fall of Raymond* (by Frank Frankfort Moore).
London: Hutchinson & Co., 1917. LOCATION L.

M482　*A garden of peace. A medley in quietude* (by 'F. Littlemore'; dedicated to Dorothy, Rosamund, Francie, Olive, Marjorie, Ursula).
+ London, Glasgow, Melbourne, Auckland: W. Collins Sons & Co., 1919 (ill.). LOCATION D, NUC.
New York: George H. Doran, [1920]. LOCATION NUC.

M483　*The courtship of Prince Charming; a modern romance* (by Frank Frankfort Moore).
London, Glasgow, Melbourne, Auckland: W. Collins, Sons & Co., 1920. LOCATION L, NUC ([1920] edn).

M484　*The 9.15. A novel* (by Frank Frankfort Moore).
+ London: Hutchinson & Co., [1921]. SOURCE Brown 2, 1051. LOCATION D, L, NUC.
COMMENTARY An adventure story with political overtones. Capt. Storrington, son of an English baronet, while on a train to Southaven is kidnapped by a member of Sinn Féin, who suspects him of being a spy. He is held prisoner on board a steamer flying the Venezuelan flag. On a voyage to South America he learns too much about a great Hispano-Sinn Féin conspiracy against England and in consequence is marooned on an island. There he finds hidden treasure and a charming young lady. The Sinn Féin adherent, evidently intended as typical, is depicted as a low, ignorant and despicable rascal [Brown 2].

M485　*The hand and dagger* (by Frank Frankfort Moore; dedicated to Olive).
+ London: Eveleigh Nash & Grayson, 1928. LOCATION D, L.

M486　*That holy kiss* (by Frank Frankfort Moore; dedicated to Rosamund).
+ London: Eveleigh Nash & Grayson, 1928. LOCATION D, L.

M487　*The awakening of Helen* (by Frank Frankfort Moore).
London: E. Nash & Grayson, 1929. LOCATION L.

MOORE, George, b. [1778?], d. 1830. Romance novelist, who, according to O'Donoghue was possibly Irish. He may be identified with a GM (b. 1778), fifth son of John Moore of Summerhill, Dublin, and Mary Anne Moore. This GM was educated at TCD, admitted to the King's Inns in 1796, and to Gray's Inn (London) in 1798, and was called to the Irish Bar in 1800. An alternative is that GM is the same person as Revd George Moore (mentioned by Mayo, but does not cite a source). This GM wrote *Observations on the Union, Orange associations and other subjects of domestic policy, with reflections on the late events on the Continent* (Dublin, 1799), and probably the tragedy *Montbard, or the buccaneer* (London, 1804) and *The minstrel's tale and other poems* (London, 1826). SOURCE Allibone, ii, p. 1352; Black, 2247; W.J. McCormack, *The pamphlet debate on the Union* (Blackrock, 1996), p. 65; Keane, p. 347; Mayo, p. 350; O'Donoghue, p. 315; RL.

M488　*Grasville Abbey. A romance* [anon.].
London: G.G. & J. Robinson, 1797, 3 vols. SOURCE Raven 2, 1797:58; Forster 2, 2931; ESTC n047440. LOCATION Corvey CME 3-628-45051-9, NUC.
+ Cork: Printed by J. Connor, 1798, 2 vols. SOURCE Raven 2, 1797:58; ESTC n030851. LOCATION CKu, CSmH, InND Loeber coll.
+ Dublin: P. Wogan, P. Byrne, G. Burnet, H. Colbert & J. Rice, 1798, 2 vols. SOURCE Summers, p. 343; Raven 2, 1797:58; ESTC n002356. LOCATION D, Dt, NUC.

Prague: Politischen Buchhandlung, 1799, 3 vols. in 1 (trans. as *Die Abten von Grasville*). SOURCE Raven 2, 1797:58. LOCATION ViU.

+ Paris: Maradan, 1798, 3 vols. (trans. by B. Ducos as *L'Abbaye de Grasville*; ill. Challiou, Bovinet). SOURCE Streeter, 269. LOCATION NUC, InND Loeber coll.

Leiden: P.A. Trap, 1803 (trans. into Dutch as *De abdij van Grasville*). SOURCE Wintermans, 1797:58.

Amsterdam: J.C. van Kesteren, 1804 (trans. into Dutch from the French as *De abdij van Grasville*). SOURCE Alphabetische naamlijst 1790–1832, p. 142.

Salem (MA): T.C. Cushing & B.B. Magannulty, 1799, 2 vols. in 1. SOURCE ESTC w020412. LOCATION NUC.

New York: Arno Press, 1974, 3 vols. (introd. by Robert D. Mayo). LOCATION E.

COMMENTARY A Gothic novel set in France, Italy and England, which first appeared in the *Sentimental and Masonic Magazine* (Dublin, 1793–95) and in 47 instalments in the *Lady's Magazine* (London, 1793–97). A French nobleman, Maserini, prevails upon his two younger daughters to enter a convent so that the marriage portion of the eldest sister will be sufficient to attract an appropriate suitor. One of the sisters is reluctant and falls in love with the brother of a fellow inmate of the convent. She escapes with this man and leaves for Italy where his father has a large estate. Before they reach the ancestral home, they marry. However, the father has died and a Spanish relative has inherited all. The castle, Grasville Abbey, seems to be shrouded in mystery and the son is intent on getting to the bottom of it. He breaks in, but the castle comes alive with spectral events, a corps de ballet of ghosts, yelling portraits, and restless cadavers. After one fact-finding excursion to the Abbey, the son never returns and leaves his young wife with a twin son and daughter, Edward and Mathilda. The children grow up in Paris and before their mother's demise, she gives Edward an unfinished memorandum about their father's death. They go to England to stay with a distant relative but this is unsatisfactory since the relatives lead a fairly dissipated life. The Spanish relative, D'Ollifont, turns up in London and tries to seduce Mathilda. Her brother defends her and wounds D'Ollifont, causing them to flee to the Continent, leaving behind a young nobleman, Milverne, with whom Mathilda is in love, and Lady Albourne, with whom Edward is in love. They go to Grasville Abbey and try to penetrate the mysterious events surrounding the death of their father and grandfather. Eventually, it turns out that D'Ollifont was the murderer of both. Edward and Mathilda are reinstated in their rights and marry their lovers [ML; Frank, 295; Mayo, 478].

M489 *Theodosius de Zulvin, the monk of Madrid: a Spanish tale, delineating various traits of the human mind* (by George Moore; dedicated to the inhabitants of the Isle of Wight).

London: G. & J. Robinson, 1802, 4 vols. SOURCE Block, p. 165; British Fiction; Garside, 1802:46. LOCATION Corvey CME 3–628–48279–8, ViU.

COMMENTARY Issued in a print run of 1,000 copies. A novel comprising two stories about the disastrous effects of a closed education, both set in Spain and both featuring the murderous monk, Fr Theodosius. The separate tales of the twin brothers, Orlando and Osmund, are connected through the sexual misfortunes and parental deprivations of the monk's mistress, Leonora. The twin brothers receive opposite upbringings: Orlando is given a virtuous and sheltered education from his patron, Don Diego; hence, when he arrives in Madrid he goes on a wild sexual spree and destructive rampage, abetted by the evil influence of Fr Theodosius. His brother Osmund is thoroughly instructed in the ways of the world and is thus much better able to control himself when turned loose in the metropolis. They both secretly observe Fr Theodosius gloating over the blood-smeared body of a young woman he has concealed [Frank, 296; Garside].

M490   *Tales of the passions; in which is attempted an illustration of their effects on the human mind: each tale comprised in one volume, and forming the subject of a single passion* (by George Moore; dedicated to 'a British public').
+ London: G. Wilkie & J. Robinson, 1808, 1811, 2 vols. SOURCE British Fiction; Garside, 1808:80; Block, p. 165. LOCATION Dt, L, NUC, InND Loeber coll. (vol. 1 only).
COMMENTARY Contents: 'The Courtezan, an English tale: in which is attempted an illustration of the Passion of Revenge' (this tale is dedicated to J.P. Kemble; in the preface, the author states that the plan was taken from 'Miss Baillie's Series of Plays, in which the delineation of one of the stronger passions of the mind forms a subject for a tragedy and a comedy'). The second story is 'The married man; an English tale: in which is attempted an illustration of the passion of jealousy, in its effects on the human mind' (dedicated to author's mother). There are no further volumes as the series did not proceed [RL; Block, p. 165].

MOORE, George. See MOORE, George Augustus.

MOORE, George Augustus (known as George Moore), b. Moore Hall, Ballyglass (Co. Mayo) 1852, d. London 1933. Novelist, playwright, short story writer, crusading journalist, art critic and poet, GAM was the son of George Henry Moore of Moore Hall, a wealthy Catholic landowner and poet, Liberal MP, and one of the founders of the Catholic Defence League, and Mary Blake. GAM was educated at Oscott College, Birmingham, where he did not distinguish himself academically. He inherited the Moore estate after his father's death in 1870, but he rarely lived there (the house was burnt in 1923). His father's death allowed him to escape a military career and in 1873 he went to Paris to become a painter. Finding his talent for painting insufficient, he went to London where he started writing in earnest. His novel *A modern lover* (1883), which showed the influence of Henry James, Honoré de Balzac and Émile Zola and was notable for its realism, was suppressed by Mudie's, the popular lending library. In retaliation, GAM wrote 'A new censorship of literature' in the *Pall Mall Gazette* (London, 10 Dec. 1884) and *Literature at nurse or circulating morals* (London, 1885), an attack on Mudie's and the powerful lending library system that enshrined literary Victorianism and was hostile to new fiction. During his time in London he wrote extensively on modern French art and literature. Collections of this writing appeared as *Impressions and opinions* (London, 1891) and *Modern painting* (London, 1903) and added to his stature as an art critic. His interest in the works of Henrik Ibsen and August Strindberg and other new European playwrights led him to co-found the Independent Theatre in London. His own drama, *The strike at Arlingford*, was presented there and later published (London, 1893). In reaction to British atrocities in the war in South Africa (recounted to him by his brother Maurice), he returned to Dublin in 1901. With William Butler Yeats§, Lady Gregory and Edward Martyn§ he helped to launch the new Irish Literary Theatre, forerunner of the Abbey Theatre. Yeats, Gregory and Martyn all later decried GAM's satirical and humorous account of the Irish Literary Revival in *Hail and farewell*, his three-part autobiography (London, 1911–14). Unhappy at his standing in the literary life of Ireland, and increasingly disenchanted with catholicism, he returned to London in 1911, becoming a Protestant before he did so. He settled in Ebury Street, continued to write, and lived the life of a man of letters. Owing to legal problems with his publications starting with his *A story-teller's holiday* published in 1918, GAM decided that his books would be issued privately in limited edns under the sign of Cumann Sean-eaolais na h-Éireann (Society for Irish Folklore). No such society existed. GAM often painstakingly revised his books several times. Revisions are noted below, but for details, see E. Gilcher's *A bibliography of George Moore* (DeKalb, 1970). GAM had a long-standing friendship with Lady Cunard, but never married. His ashes were buried on Castle Island in

Moore

Lough Carra across the lake from Moore Hall. For GAM's portraits and papers, see ODNB. SOURCE Allibone Suppl., ii, p. 1132; *Bibliographies of modern authors, no. 3*, compiled by I.A. Williams (New Haven, 1921); Boylan, p. 254; DLB, x, xviii, lvii, ciiiv; EF, pp 283–4; Field Day, ii, pp 560–1 and passim, iii, p. 2 and passim; A. Frazier, *George Moore, 1850–1933* (New Haven, 2000); Gilcher, passim; Hogan, pp 458–66; Hogan 2, pp 860–6; Igoe, pp 177–84; Landed gentry, 1904, p. 418; G. Moore, *Hail and farewell* (London, 1911, 1912, 1925), 3 vols.; S.L. Mitchell, *George Moore* (Dublin, 1916); MVP, p. 322; NCBEL 4, pp 1647–55; OCIL, pp 373–5; ODNB: O'Donoghue, p. 316; RIA/DIB; Schulz, p. 284; Sutherland, p. 445.

M491 *A modern lover* (by George Moore).
London: Tinsley Bros, 1883, 3 vols. SOURCE Gilcher, A5/1a; Sadleir, 1767; Wolff, 4892. LOCATION L, NUC.
+ London: William Heinemann, 1917 (as *Lewis Seymour and some women*). SOURCE Gilcher, A36/2a. LOCATION D, L, NUC ([1916] edn).
Paris: L. Conrad, 1917 (as *Lewis Seymour and some women*; Standard Collection). SOURCE Gilcher, A36/3a (1918 edn); OCLC. LOCATION D.
+ Chicago: Laird & Lee, 1890 (as *A modern lover. A realistic novel*; ill.). SOURCE Gilcher, A5/2b. LOCATION D (n.d. edn), NUC, InND Loeber coll.
New York: L. Lipkind, [190?]. SOURCE Gilcher, 5A/2b4. LOCATION NUC.
+ New York: Brentano's, 1917 (as *Lewis Seymour and some women*). SOURCE Gilcher, A36/a; NYPL. LOCATION D, NN, NUC.
COMMENTARY Two binding variants of the first London edn: (a) putty-coloured cloth; (b) blue cloth. Tells the story of a young London artist, Lewis Seymour, who callously betrays the three women who sacrifice their virtue to him [Burmester cat. 33/261; Carter, p. 142].

M492 *A mummer's wife* (by George Moore; dedicated to James Davis).
+ London: Vizetelly & Co., 1885 (Vizetelly's One-Volume Novels, No. 3). SOURCE Gilcher, A6/a; Wolff, 4893. LOCATION D (1886, 7th edn), L (1885, 2nd edn), NUC, InND Loeber coll.
London: Vizetelly & Co., 1886 (revsd edn; Vizetelly's One-Volume Novels). SOURCE Gilcher, A6/b; COPAC. Location Dt (1886, 7th edn).
London: William Heinemann, [1918] (revsd edn). SOURCE Gilcher, A6/2c. LOCATION Dt, O.
Paris: G. Charpentier, 1888 (trans. as *La femme du cabotin*). SOURCE Gilcher, D:Fr-8; NCBEL 3, p. 1015; CCF. LOCATION L.
Chicago: Laird & Lee, 1889 (as *An actor's wife; a realistic novel*). SOURCE Gilcher, A6/2b; NYPL. LOCATION NN. COMMENTARY *Chicago 1889 edn* First US, unauthorized edn [Gilcher, A6/2b.].
+ New York: Brentano's, 1903 (revsd edn; dedicated to Robert Ross). SOURCE Gilcher, A6/3b; NYPL. LOCATION D (1908 edn), NN, NUC. COMMENTARY *New York 1903 edn* First US authorized edn [Gilcher, A6/3b.].
New York: Liveright, 1966 (Black and Gold Library). SOURCE Gilcher, A6/3c; OCLC. LOCATION D, NN.
COMMENTARY Regarded as the first English novel with a naturalistic setting, it deals with alcoholism and the seedy side of theatrical life. A travelling actor seduces a draper's wife, and she leaves with him. When she becomes pregnant the actor marries her, but life is very hard because there is no work. The child dies, and the marriage disintegrates because of the actor's association with other women. Depressed, she drinks herself to death [OCIL, p. 381; ODNB].

M493 *A drama in muslin. A realistic novel* (by George Moore).
London: Vizetelly & Co., 1886 (Vizetelly's One-Volume Novels, No. 15; ill. J.E. Blanche). SOURCE Gilcher, A9/a; Brown, 1166. LOCATION L, NUC.

+ London; William Heinemann, 1915 (as *Muslin*). SOURCE Gilcher, A34/a. LOCATION D, L, NUC ([1915] edn) , InND Loeber coll.

+ Leipzig: Bernard Tauchnitz, 1920. 2 vols. (as *Muslin*). SOURCE Gilcher, A34/2a; T & B, 4541–42. LOCATION InND Loeber coll.

+ New York: Brentano's, 1915 (as *Muslin*). SOURCE Gilcher, A34/a2. LOCATION D, NUC.

+ Belfast: Appletree Press, 1992 (introd. by James Plunkett). LOCATION D.

COMMENTARY First published as a serial in *Court and Society Review* (1886). Set around the time of the Land War and the murder of two British officials in the Phoenix Park (Dublin) in 1882, and highlighting intense feminine friendships, it describes a group of girls educated at a convent school and their subsequent adventures in Irish society looking for husbands. Except for two of the girls, all of them go to the bad. The exceptions are a mad Protestant missionary who becomes a Catholic nun, and an authoress who is a free-thinker, which GAM considered a natural combination [Brown; Field Day, iv, pp 1101–2; ODNB].

M494 *A mere accident* (by George Moore).

+ London: Vizetelly & Co.; New York, Washington, Chicago: Brentano's, 1887 (Vizetelly's One-Volume Novels, No. 26). Gilcher, A10/a; SOURCE Wolff, 4890. LOCATION Dt, L, NUC, InND Loeber coll.

COMMENTARY The story was reprinted as *John Norton* in *Celibates* in 1895. John Norton, a well-to-do young man, decides to live a celibate life and dedicate himself to the Roman Catholic church. His mother would like him to marry, but initially he does not like his mother's choice. Over time, however, he falls in love and decides to give his up his celibacy [ML; Gilcher A10/a].

M495 *Parnell and his island* (by George Moore).

+ London: W. Swan Sonnenschein, Lowrey & Co., 1887 SOURCE Gilcher, A11/a. LOCATION L, NUC, InND Loeber coll.

COMMENTARY Semi-autobiographical sketches at the time of the Land League. Contents: 'Dublin', 'An Irish country house', 'The house of an Irish poet', 'The landlord', 'The tenant farmer', 'The priest', 'The patriot', 'A castle of yesterday', 'A castle of to-day', 'An eviction', 'A hunting breakfast'. The volume concludes with an overview of the ills of Ireland [RL].

M496 *Confessions of a young man* (by George Moore).

+ London: W. Swan Sonnenschein, Lowrey & Co., 1888 (ill., William Strang). SOURCE Gilcher, A12/a; Wolff, 4886. LOCATION D, Dt, L, NUC.

London: W. Swan Sonnenschein & Co., 1889 (revsd edn). SOURCE Gilcher, A12/b. LOCATION NUC.

London: T. Werner Laurie, 1904 (revsd edn). SOURCE Gilcher, A12/c. LOCATION L, NUC.

London: William Heinemann, 1917 (revsd edn). SOURCE Gilcher, A12/2d. LOCATION L.

London: William Heinemann, 1926 (expanded edn). SOURCE Gilcher, A12/2d2. LOCATION L, NUC.

Leipzig: Bernard Tauchnitz, 1905. SOURCE Gilcher, A12/2c; T & B, 3812. LOCATION NUC.

+ Leipzig: Bernard Tauchnitz,1920 (dedicated to Jacques Blanche). SOURCE T & B, 3812. LOCATION InND Loeber coll.

Paris: A. Savine, 1889 (trans. as *Confessions d'un jeune anglais*). SOURCE Gilcher, D:Fr-9. LOCATION NUC.

Chicago, New York, Paris: Brentano's, 1888. SOURCE Gilcher, A12/a2. COMMENTARY *Chicago edn* No copy located [RL].

New York: Brentano's, 1917 (revsd edn). SOURCE Gilcher, A12/d. LOCATION NUC.
+ New York: Boni & Liveright, 1917 (introd. by Floyd Dell; The Modern Library; ill.). LOCATION InND Loeber coll.
+ Montreal, London: McGill-Queen's Univ. Press, 1972 (annotated edn by Susan Dick with all the changes over time). LOCATION InND Loeber coll.
COMMENTARY A pseudo-autobiographical account of the author's formative years in Paris, when he tried to become an artist, and in London when he decides to become a writer. Gives vivid descriptions of Parisian artistic life and established GAM as an expert in impressionism and symbolism [OCIL, p. 111; ODNB].

M497 *Spring days. A realistic novel, a prelude to "Don Juan"* (by George Moore; dedicated to Frank Harris§).
+ London: Vizetelly & Co., 1888 (Vizetelly's One-Volume Novels, No. 29). SOURCE Gilcher, A13/a. LOCATION Dt, L, NUC, InND Loeber coll.
London: T. Werner Laurie, 1912 (revsd edn; as *Spring days*). SOURCE Gilcher, A13/2a2. LOCATION L, NUC ([1912] edn).
Leipzig: Bernard Tauchnitz, 1912. SOURCE Gilcher, A13/2b; T & B, 4364. LOCATION NUC.
Chicago: G.E. Wilson, 1891 (as *Shifting love, a realistic novel*; Wilson's Library of Fiction). SOURCE Gilcher, A13/2a. LOCATION NUC.
New York: Brentano's, [1912]. LOCATION NUC.
COMMENTARY First published in the *Evening News* (London, 1888) [Gilcher, A13/a].

M498 *Mike Fletcher. A novel* (by George Moore; dedicated to author's brother Augustus [Moore]).
+ London: Ward & Downey, 1889. SOURCE Gilcher, A14/a; Wolff, 4891. LOCATION L, Dt, NUC, InND Loeber coll.
New York: Minerva, 1889 (Minerva Series, No. 17). SOURCE Gilcher, A14/2a; NYPL (1890 edn). LOCATION NN (1890 edn), NUC.
COMMENTARY Describes a poet's dissolute life and suicide in bohemian London [Sutherland, p. 446].

M499 *Vain fortune* (by George Moore).
+ London: Henry & Co., [1891] (ill. Maurice Greiffenhagen). SOURCE Gilcher, A16/a. LOCATION D, L, NUC.
London: Henry & Co., [1891] (ill. Maurice Greiffenhagen; limited edn of 150 copies). SOURCE Gilcher, A16/a2. LOCATION L, NUC.
London: Walter Scott, 1895 (new edn, completely revsd; ill. Maurice Greiffenhagen). SOURCE Gilcher, A16/c. LOCATION Dt, L, NUC.
New York: P.F. Collier, 1892. SOURCE Gilcher, A16/2a; OCLC. LOCATION Duke Univ.
+ New York: Charles Scribner's Sons, 1892 (revsd edn). SOURCE Gilcher, A16/b; NYPL. LOCATION D, NN, NUC.
COMMENTARY Serialized as by 'Lady Rhone' in *Lady's Pictorial* (London, July–Oct.1891), the story of an author who comes into an inheritance. He decides to live with his disinherited niece and her companion. He falls in love with the companion and when they marry, the niece kills herself. Richard Ellmann, biographer of James Joyce, said it was admired by Joyce and the inspiration for his short story 'The dead' [ODNB; Welch, p. 585].

M500 *Esther Waters. A novel* (by George Moore; dedicated to author's brother Major Maurice Moore).
+ London: Walter Scott, 1894. SOURCE Gilcher, A19/a; Wolff, 4887. LOCATION D, Dt, L, NUC, InND Loeber coll.
London: Walter Scott, 1899 (revsd edn). SOURCE Gilcher, A19/b. LOCATION NUC.

London: William Heinemann, 1920 (revsd edn; as *Esther Waters. An English story*; dedicated to 'My dear Rolleston'). SOURCE Gilcher, A19/c. LOCATION D (1922 edn), L, NUC.
London: Cumann Sean-eaolais na h-Éireann, 1920 (limited edn of 750 copies). SOURCE Gilcher, A19/c2. LOCATION L, NUC.
Leipzig: Heinemann & Balestier, 1894, 2 vols. SOURCE Gilcher, A19/2a. LOCATION NUC.
Paris: Hachette, 1907. SOURCE Gilcher, D:Fr-12; OCLC. LOCATION D, Arizona State Univ. Library.
Chicago: C.H. Sergel, 1894. SOURCE Gilcher, A19/a2. LOCATION NUC.
Chicago, New York: H.S. Stone & Co., [1894] (revsd and enlarged edn). SOURCE Gilcher, A19/2b. LOCATION NUC.
+ Oxford, New York: Oxford Univ. Press, 1983 (introd. by David Skilton; The World Classics). LOCATION D.
COMMENTARY Considered a breakthrough in subject matter in its non-judgmental depiction of a 'fallen woman' and a turning point in English fiction, it tells the story of a Plymouth Sister driven from her home by her stepfather. She becomes pregnant and struggles to survive with her young son. Her religious convictions and support from a few friends carry her through her difficulties. The novel was dramatized by Henry D. Davray. It has never been out of print since publication. In 1994 at the Cheltenham festival it was awarded a spoof centennial '1894 Booker prize' [Holmes cat. 81/168; OCIL, p. 176; ODNB].
M501 *Celibates* (by George Moore).
+ London: Walter Scott, 1895. SOURCE Gilcher A21/a. LOCATION D, Dt, L, NN, NUC, InND Loeber coll.
+ Leipzig: Bernard Tauchnitz, 1895. SOURCE Gilcher, A21/3a; T & B, 3068; NYPL. LOCATION D, NN.
+ New York, London: Macmillan & Co., 1895. SOURCE Gilcher, A21/2a. LOCATION Dt, NUC, InND Loeber coll.
COMMENTARY Three stories dealing with celibacy, repression and art. Contents: 'Mildred Lawson', 'John Norton', 'Agnes Lahens'. The stories became part of a larger collection under the title *In single strictness* (London, 1920) [ML].
M502 *Evelyn Innes* (by George Moore; dedicated to Arthur Symons and W.B. Yeats§).
+ London: T. Fisher Unwin, 1898. SOURCE Gilcher, A22/a; Wolff, 4888; NYPL. LOCATION D, Dt, L, NN, NUC, InND Loeber coll.
London: T. Fisher Unwin, 1898 (2nd, revsd edn). SOURCE Gilcher, A22/b. LOCATION L, NUC.
Leipzig: Bernard Tauchnitz, 1898, 2 vols. SOURCE Gilcher, A22/2a; T & B, 3294–95. LOCATION NUC.
Berlin: Fleischel & Co., 1904 (trans. by A. Neuman-Hofe as *Arbeite und Bete*). SOURCE Gilcher, D:Ge-5; OCLC. LOCATION Univ. of Calgary.
+ New York: D. Appleton & Co., 1898. SOURCE Gilcher, A22/2a; NYPL. LOCATION D, NN, NUC, InND Loeber coll.
COMMENTARY Initially published in an edn of 10,000 copies. The story of an opera singer who is torn between her world of art and religion. Eventually, she enters a convent [OCIL, p. 177; Gilcher A22/a].
M503 *Sister Teresa* (by George Moore).
London: T. Fisher Unwin, 1901. SOURCE Gilcher, A25/a; Wolff, 4894; NYPL. LOCATION NN, NUC.
London: T. Fisher Unwin, [1909] (rewritten edn; Adelphia Library). SOURCE Gilcher, A25/c; RLIN. LOCATION L, NUC.

Leipzig: Bernard Tauchnitz, 1901, 2 vols. (rewritten edn). SOURCE Gilcher, A25/2b; T & B, 3535–36. LOCATION NUC.

Berlin: Egon Fleischel & Co., 1905, 2 vols. SOURCE Gilcher, D:Ge-6.

+ Philadelphia: J.B. Lippincott, 1901. SOURCE Gilcher, A25/2a. LOCATION NUC, InND Loeber coll.

COMMENTARY No copy of the Berlin edn located. Sequel to *Evelyn Innes* (London, 1898) in which Evelyn wavers between her life in the convent and the world outside [OCIL, p. 177].

M504 *The untilled field* (by George Moore).

+ London: T. Fisher Unwin, 1903. SOURCE Gilcher, A26/a; Brown, 1167; Wolff, 4894A. LOCATION D, L, NUC, InND Loeber coll.

+ London: William Heinemann, 1914 (revsd edn). SOURCE Gilcher, A26/c. LOCATION L, NUC, InND Loeber coll.

London: William Heinemann, 1931, 2nd edn [revsd]. SOURCE COPAC. LOCATION Dt, C.

+ Leipzig: Bernard Tauchnitz, 1903 (revsd edn). SOURCE Gilcher, A26/b; T & B, 3656. LOCATION D, NUC.

Philadelphia: J.B. Lippincott, 1903. SOURCE Gilcher, A26/2a; NYPL. LOCATION NN, NUC.

COMMENTARY Written after GAM's return to Ireland from Paris and London and first published in the *Irish Monthly* (Dublin, 1902), with Irish translations. Inspired by *The sportsman's sketch-book* by Ivan Turgenev, whom GAM knew in Paris, the stories are written with colloquial language and are concerned with the social realities of rural Ireland rather than myth or legend. Frank O'Connor, a later novelist and short story writer, said that with them 'the Irish short story became a fact'. Contents: a series of sketches about country life in the west of Ireland: 'In the clay', 'Some parishioners', 'The exile', 'Home sickness', 'A letter to Rome', 'Julia Cahill's curse', 'A play-house in the waste', 'The wedding gown', 'The clerk's quest', 'Alms giving', 'So on he fares', 'The wild goose', 'The way back'. The London, 1931 edn contains a new story: 'Fugitives'. The 1914 Heinemann edn does not contain 'In the clay' or 'The way back', but includes 'The wedding feast' and 'The window' [ML; AMB; Field Day, ii, pp 520, 549–53 ('The wedding gown'), 1022, 1034–40 ('A letter to Rome'); Gilcher; OCIL, p. 267; Leclaire, p. 242].

M505 *The lake* (by George Moore; dedicated to Edouard Dujardin).

+ London: William Heinemann, 1905. SOURCE Gilcher, A27/a; Brown, 1168; Wolff, 4889. LOCATION D, L, NUC, InND Loeber coll.

London: William Heinemann, 1921 (revsd edn). SOURCE Gilcher, A27/d. LOCATION L, NUC.

Paris: Stock, 1923 (trans. by Mme W. Laparre as *Le Lac*). SOURCE Gilcher, D:Fr-21. LOCATION NUC.

Leipzig: Bernard Tauchnitz, 1906 (revsd edn). SOURCE Gilcher, A27/b; T & B, 3863. LOCATION NUC.

+ New York: D. Appleton & Co., 1906. SOURCE Gilcher, A27/2a; NYPL. LOCATION D, NN, NUC.

+ Gerrards Cross: Colin Smythe, 1980 (with preface to 1921 edn; Appendix A chapter 9 of the 1905 edn; Appendix B consists of 'Gogarty's dinner party' from second 1905 edn; Appendix C contains 'King and hermit' and 'The monk and his pet', translated by Kuno Meyer). SOURCE OCLC. LOCATION InND Loeber coll., Boston College.

COMMENTARY Set in Connacht and Kilronan Abbey and detailing a young priest's rebellion against celibacy stimulated by the attractions of a woman he had driven from the parish because she had gone wrong [Brown].

M506 *Memoirs of my dead life* (by George Moore).
    + London: William Heinemann, 1906. SOURCE Gilcher, A29/a; NYPL. LOCATION L,
    NN, NUC, InND Loeber coll.
    + London: William Heinemann, 1915 (expanded edn). SOURCE Gilcher, A29/c.
    LOCATION NUC, InND Loeber coll.
    London: William Heinemann, 1921 (limited edn of 1,030 copies; dedicated to
    [?Edmund] Gosse). SOURCE Gilcher, A29/2d. LOCATION L.
    London: William Heinemann, 1928 (revsd edn). SOURCE Gilcher, A29/e. LOCATION NUC.
    Leipzig: Bernard Tauchnitz, 1906 (revsd edn). SOURCE Gilcher, A29/b; T & B, 3921.
    LOCATION NUC.
    Berlin: Egon Fleischel & Co., 1907 (trans. as *Aus toten Tagen*). SOURCE Gilcher, D:Ge-
    11; OCLC. LOCATION CtY.
    Paris: B. Grasset, 1922 (trans. by G. Jean-Oubry as *Mémoires de ma vie morte; galanter-
    ies, méditations, souvenirs, soliloques et conseils aux amants avec des réflexions variées sur
    la vertu et les mérites*). SOURCE Gilcher, D:Fr-20. LOCATION L, NUC.
    New York: D. Appleton & Co., 1906. SOURCE Gilcher, A29/2a. LOCATION D (1915
    edn), L (1907 edn), NN (1907 edn), NUC.
    + New York: Boni & Liveright, 1920 (revsd and expanded edn, limited edn of 1,500
    copies; dedicated to T.R. Smith). SOURCE Gilcher, A29/d; NYPL. LOCATION NN,
    InND Loeber coll.
    COMMENTARY A semi-autobiographical book of reveries. Contents: 'Spring in London',
    'Flowering Normandy', 'A waitress', 'The end of Marie Pellegrin', 'La Butte', 'Spent love',
    'Ninon's table d'hôte', 'The lovers of Orelay', 'In the Luxembourg gardens', 'A remembrance',
    'Bring in the lamp', 'Sunday evening in London', 'Resurgam'. 'Euphorion in Texas' was added
    to the Heinemann, 1915 edn, and 'Lui et elles' to the Boni & Liveright, 1920 edn [AMB;
    NYPL; ODNB].

M507 *The Brook Kerith. A Syrian story* (by George Moore; dedicated to Mary Hunter).
    London: T. Werner Laurie, 1916. SOURCE Gilcher, A35/a. LOCATION L, NUC.
    London: T. Werner Laurie, 1916 (limited edn of 250 copies). SOURCE Gilcher, A35/a2.
    LOCATION L.
    London: William Heinemann, 1927 (revsd edn; limited edn of 250 copies). SOURCE
    Gilcher, A35/b. LOCATION NUC.
    Paris: Cres, 1927, 2 vols. (trans. by Philippe Neel as *Solitude de Kerith*). SOURCE
    Gilcher, D:Fr-24. LOCATION L.
    + Leipzig: Bernard Tauchnitz, 1920, 2 vols. SOURCE T & B, 4536–37; Gilcher, A35/3a;
    T & B, 4536. LOCATION D, InND Loeber coll.
    New York: Macmillan, 1916. SOURCE Gilcher, A35/2a. LOCATION NUC.
    + New York: Macmillan, 1916 (new edn with a preface). SOURCE Gilcher, A35/2a2;
    NYPL. LOCATION NN, NUC, InND Loeber coll.
    COMMENTARY Written after a trip to the Holy Land in 1914 and partly as a riposte to Catholic
    dogmatism, it retells the life of Jesus. But instead of dying on the cross, Jesus goes into a coma
    and is revived through human healing and meets Paul twenty years after the crucifixion. Jesus
    is depicted as a person who moves from simplicity to contempt for man's venality and to the
    craving for discipleship. Rather than ascending to heaven, Jesus finds peace in a community
    of Essenes. GAM wrote several stage versions of the theme: 'The apostle' (1911), revised as
    The passing of the Essenes (London, 1930) [OCIL, pp 65–6; ODNB; COPAC].

M508 *A story-teller's holiday* (by George Moore; dedicated to Lady Cunard).
    London: Cumann Sean-eaolais na h-Éireann, 1918 (limited edn of 1,000 copies).
    SOURCE Gilcher, A37/a; Brown, 1169. LOCATION L, NUC.

London: William Heinemann, 1928, 2 vols. (revsd with additional tales). SOURCE Gilcher, A37/2b. LOCATION NUC.

+ New York: Cumann Sean-eaolais na h-Éireann, 1918 (limited edn of 1,250 copies). SOURCE Gilcher, A37/2a; Brown, 1169. LOCATION NUC, InND Loeber coll.

New York: Horace Liveright, 1928, 2 vols. (revsd and expanded edn; limited edn of 1,250 copies). SOURCE Gilcher, A37/b. LOCATION NUC, InND Loeber coll. (1929 edn).

COMMENTARY Stories supposedly told by the character Alec Trusselby of Westport (Co. Mayo). He is a fern gatherer who has had a sunstroke in America and is now a shanachie. Trusselby is supposed to have heard the stories from his grandfather. The author reciprocates by telling stories to Alec [Brown].

M509 *Héloïse and Abélard* (by George Moore).

London: Cumann Sean-eaolais na h-Éireann, 1921, 2 vols. (limited edn of 1,500 copies). SOURCE Gilcher, A40/a. LOCATION L, NUC.

New York: Boni & Liveright, 1921, 2 vols. (limited edn of 1,250 copies). SOURCE Gilcher, A40/b. LOCATION NUC.

COMMENTARY A re-telling of the story of the twelfth-century lovers Héloise and Abélard. GAM separately published corrections and insertions as *Fragments of Héloïse & Abélard* (London, 1921, 23pp) [OCIL, p. 243].

M510 *In single strictness* (by George Moore).

+ London: William Heinemann, 1922 (limited edn of 1,030 copies). SOURCE Gilcher, A44/a. LOCATION L, NUC, InND Loeber coll.

+ London: William Heinemann, 1927 (as *Celibate lives*). SOURCE Gilcher, A52/a; Brown 2, 1052. LOCATION D, NUC.

+ Leipzig: Bernard Tauchnitz, 1927 (as *Celibate lives*). SOURCE Gilcher, A52/3a; NYPL; T & B, 4793. LOCATION D, NN, NUC.

New York: Boni & Liveright, 1922 (limited edn of 1,050 copies). SOURCE Gilcher, A44/2a. LOCATION NUC.

New York: Boni & Liveright, 1923 (revsd edn). SOURCE Gilcher, A44/b. LOCATION NUC.

New York: Boni & Liveright, 1927 (as *Celibate lives*). SOURCE Gilcher, A52/2a. LOCATION NUC.

COMMENTARY Contents: 'Wilfred Holmes', 'Priscilla and Emily Lofft', 'Albert Nobbs', 'Henrietta Marr'. Short stories of so-called celibates. 'Albert Nobbs' is the story of a girl assuming the role of a man and marrying one of her own sex. There are criticisms of the Catholic religion, especially in 'Henrietta Marr'. The scenes are laid in Dublin, England and France [Brown 2].

M511 *Conversations in Ebury Street* (by George Moore).

+ London: William Heinemann, 1924 (limited edn of 1,030 copies). SOURCE Gilcher, A46/a. LOCATION L, NUC, InND Loeber coll.

+ London: William Heinemann, 1930 (revsd edn). SOURCE Gilcher, A46/b. LOCATION D, NUC.

+ New York: Boni & Liveright, 1924 (limited edn of 1,000 copies). SOURCE Gilcher, A46/2a. LOCATION D, NUC, InND Loeber coll.

COMMENTARY Some of GAM's critical writings for periodicals formed the basis of sections of this volume [ODNB].

M512 *Daphnis and Chloë. Perronik the fool* (by George Moore).

New York: Boni & Liveright, 1924 (limited edn of 1,000 copies). SOURCE Gilcher, A50/a. LOCATION NUC.

Mount Vernon (NY): William Edwin Rudge, 1926 (as *Peronnik the fool*; limited edn of 785 copies). SOURCE Gilcher, A50/2a. LOCATION NUC.

Chapelle-Réanville, Eure: The Hours Press, 1928 (revsd, limited edn of 200 copies). SOURCE Gilcher, A50/b. LOCATION NUC.

London: William Heinemann, 1933 (as *The pastoral loves of Daphnis and Chloe ... together with Peronnik the fool*). SOURCE Gilcher, A50/2b. LOCATION O.

+ London: George G. Harrap & Co., 1933 (as *Peronnik the fool*; limited edn of 525 copies, ill. Stephen Gooden). SOURCE Gilcher, A50/3b. LOCATION L, NUC, InND Loeber coll.

COMMENTARY *Peronnik the fool* was first published in the *London Mercury* [NUC].

M513 *Ulick and Soracha* (by George Moore; dedicated to Lady Cunard).

+ London: Nonsuch Press, 1926 (limited edn of 1,250 copies; ill. Stephen Gooden). SOURCE Gilcher, A51/a; Brown 2, 1053. LOCATION L, NUC, InND Loeber coll.

+ New York: Boni & Liveright, 1926 (limited edn of 1,250 copies; ill.). SOURCE Gilcher, A51/2a. LOCATION NUC, InND Loeber coll.

COMMENTARY An historical adventure story of the period of Bruce's invasion of Ireland in 1315 set in Danish Dublin, on the Waterford coast, in England and in France. Ulick is the bastard son of Richard de Burgo by Louise Chastel, a French singer. After her death, Richard sends his son to France in company with Tadhg O'Dorachy, a harper. Ulick sees in France a portrait of the beautiful Soracha, daughter of O'Melaghlin of Meath. He returns to take her from the convent of Durrow. The faithful Tadhg throughout plays Sancho to Ulick's Quixote. He has various comic adventures and then comes back to Ireland in search of his master [Brown 2].

M514 *Aphrodite in Aulis* (by George Moore; dedicated to Sir John Thomson Walker).

+ London: William Heinemann; New York: The Fountain Press, [1930] (same limited edn of 1,825 copies). SOURCE Gilcher, A56/a; NYPL. LOCATION L, NN, NUC, InND Loeber coll.

London: William Heinemann, 1931 (revsd edn). SOURCE Gilcher, A56/2b. LOCATION D, NUC.

+ New York: Brentano's, 1931 (revsd edn). SOURCE Gilcher, A56/b. LOCATION D, NUC, InND Loeber coll.

COMMENTARY A family saga of ancient Greece, set in Aulis in the fifth century BC [OCIL, p. 18].

M515 *A flood* (by George Moore).

New York: G.G. at the Harbor Press, 1930. SOURCE Gilcher, A57/a; NYPL. LOCATION NN.

COMMENTARY Originally published in the *Irish Review* (Dublin, 1911) [Gilcher].

M516 *In minor keys. The uncollected stories of George Moore.*

+ Syracuse (NY): Syracuse Univ. Press, 1985 (ed. by David B. Eakin and Helmut E. Gilcher). LOCATION, InND Loeber coll.

+ London: Fourth Estate, 1985. LOCATION D.

COMMENTARY Published posthumously. Contents: 'Under the fan', 'A Russian husband', 'Dried fruit', 'Two men, a railway story', 'A strange death', 'A faithful heart', 'Parted', 'An episode in bachelor life, 1', 'An episode in bachelor life, 2', '"Emma Bovary"', 'The voice of the mountains', 'A flood', 'At the turn of the road', 'The strange story of the three golden fishes' [AMB].

— COLLECTED WORKS

M517 *The works of George Moore.*

+ New York: Brentano's, 1920, [no. of vols. unclear]. SOURCE RLIN. LOCATION InND Loeber coll. (some vols.), NYU.

Moore

+ New York: Brentano's, 1925, [no. of vols. unclear] (new and revsd edn). LOCATION InND Loeber coll. (some vols.).

M518 *The Carra edition. The collected works of George Moore.*
New York: Boni & Liveright, 1922–4, 21 vols. (limited edn of 1,000 sets). SOURCE Gilcher, p. 99, n. 2; RLIN. LOCATION NUC, InND Loeber coll. (some vols.), CSt.

M519 *The works of George Moore.*
London: William Heinemann, 1924–33, 20 vols. (Uniform edn). LOCATION L, NUC.
London: William Heinemann, 1937, 20 vols. (Ebury edn). LOCATION L, NUC.

MOORE, John, b. Stirling (Scotland) 1729, d. Richmond (London) 1802. Scottish physician and man of letters, JM was the son of a Presbyterian minister, Charles Moore, and Marion Anderson. He was educated at the University of Glasgow and studied medicine in London and Paris. He was surgeon to the North Belfast Fusiliers and attended the wounded after the battle of Maastricht (1748). Returning to Glasgow, he had a busy public and private practice and introduced the idea of vaccination to the city. He later served in the British ambassador's household in Paris and spent five years travelling on the Continent as surgeon to the duke of Hamilton. These experiences were recorded in his *Zeluco* (London, 1789, 2 vols.) and his *Edward* (London, 1796, 2 vols.), which were republished in Dublin in 1789 and 1797 respectively. JM was the father of five sons who distinguished themselves in the military services, medicine and the law, including Gen. Sir John Moore who commanded English forces against the rebels led by Fr Roche in the battle of New Ross (Co. Wexford) in 1798, and subject of the Revd Charles Wolfe's famous poem, 'The burial of Sir John Moore at Corunna' (1817). SOURCE Allibone, ii, p. 1353; Block, p. 165; ODNB; RL; UCD Folklore Dept.

M520 *Mordaunt. Sketches of life, characters, and manners in various countries; including the Memoirs of a French lady of quality* [anon.].
London: G.G. & J. Robinson, 1800, 3 vols. SOURCE Block, p. 165; British Fiction; Garside, 1800:56; ESTC t057357. LOCATION L, NUC.
Dublin: W. Watson & Son, G. Burnet, P. Wogan, P. Byrne, H. Colbert, W. Porter, W. M'Kenzie, B. Dugdale, W. Jones, J. Rice, H. FitzPatrick, N. Kelly, G. Folingsby, J. Stockdale, R. Mercier & Co., P. Moore & J. Parry, 1800, 3 vols. SOURCE ESTC t077681. LOCATION L, NUC.
New York: E. Duyckinck, 1801, 2 vols. LOCATION NUC.
COMMENTARY The first volume consists of a travel journal by Mr Mordaunt, which features as minor characters an Irish priest and an Irish officer in Spanish service, both living in Spain. An additional character with Irish connections is an English peer with land holdings in Ireland [ML].

MOORE, John M. See **MOORE, John McDermott**.

MOORE, John McDermott (known as **John M. Moore**), pseud. '**J.M.M.**', fl. 1834. Journalist, editor, novelist and poet, JMM emigrated from Ireland to New York City sometime before 1830. He wrote for literary periodicals such as *Brother Jonathan* (New York), edited at least two New York newspapers in the 1830s: the *Irishman and Foreigners' Advocate* and the *European*, and produced burlesque dramas. SOURCE Exiles, p. 61.

M521 *Lord Nial. A romance* (by J.M.M').
New York: John Doyle, 1834. SOURCE Exiles, p. 61; Wright, i, 1914; OCLC. LOCATION NUC.
COMMENTARY Contains one story and poems [Exiles].

M522 *The adventures of Tom Stapleton; or, 202 Broadway* (by John M. Moore).
New York: W.F. Burgess, 1850 (ill.). SOURCE Wright, i, 1913; partly repr. in Exiles,
pp 62–77. LOCATION NUC.
London: J. Lofts, [18—] (as *Life in America; or, the adventures of Tom Stapleton*).
SOURCE Exiles, p. 61. LOCATION NUC.
COMMENTARY A novel interspersed with poetry, featuring Philip O'Hara from Donnaraile [*sic*],
in a satirical presentation of various aspects of life in New York in the 1830s. The bulk of the
story is about the campaign for a New York alderman [Exiles, pp 61–2].

MOORE, Lady. See **MOORE, Lady Margaret Mathilda**.

MOORE, Margaret Jane. See **MOUNT CASHELL, Margaret Jane, Countess**.

MOORE, Lady Margaret Mathilda (née O'Connor; known as **Lady Moore**), fl. 1860.
Novelist, MMM was the daughter of Roger O'Connor (it is uncertain whether this is the
author Roger O'Connor§), and she became the second wife of Sir Richard Emanuel Moore,
9th Bt, in 1851. Note that Sir B. Burke's *A genealogical and heraldic dictionary of the peerage
and baronetage* (London, 1878, p. 847), states that Sir Richard Emanuel Moore was the 10th
Bt, and married in 1839, Mary-Anne, daughter of A.-R. O'Connor, Esq. SOURCE Sir B. Burke
& A.P. Burke, *A genealogical and heraldic dictionary of the peerage and baronetage* (London,
1906, 68th edn), p. 1162; NUC.
M523 *De La More; or scenes in many lands* (by Lady Moore).
+ Cork: Printed [for the author?] by Guy Bros, 1860 (ill.). SOURCE Brown 2, 1043.
LOCATION D, L, NUC.
COMMENTARY A romance set around 1820 or 1830. The hero, De La More, sails for Liverpool
across the Irish Sea. He and his friend Dillon fall in with Count O'Donnell and his two daughters. O'Donnell relates to them his life story: the troubles of his Catholic ancestors, and his
own unhappy love for Ella Herbert. The two friends and the O'Donnells have various adventures, first in England, then, after De La More and Dillon have been elected MPs for English
boroughs, on the Continent. In the end there is a double wedding [Brown 2].

MOORE, Oliver. b. Ireland 1777. Military man and autobiographer, OM states in the text
of the following work that his father was from the south of Ireland, a town which 'derives its
name from being the burial place of the clan …' He attended the academy of Samuel White
in Dublin and spent his summers with relatives in Lucan (Co. Dublin). In 1790 he went with
his father to England for the first time and at age 17 enlisted as an ensign in the army. After
serving in Ireland, he was posted to the West Indies. SOURCE de Búrca cat. 46/320.
M524 *The staff officer; or, the soldier of fortune. A tale of real life* (by Oliver Moore).
+ London: Cochrane & Pickersgill, 1831, 3 vols. SOURCE Wolff, 4897. LOCATION
Corvey CME 3–628–48285–2, D, L.
Philadelphia: E.L. Carey & A. Hart, 1833. SOURCE Allibone, ii, p. 1354; OCLC.
LOCATION DCL.
COMMENTARY A largely autobiographical account in a semi-fictional format, which starts with
the author's early life and education in Ireland. It tells of the suppression of the United
Irishmen, gives brief biographical details of various illustrious characters in Ireland, and includes
military adventures in Ireland and the West Indies [de Búrca cat. 46/320].

MOORE, Sidney O. (also known as **Sidney O'Moore**), fl. 1840s. Protestant novelist, religious fiction and children's writer, SOM is probably the same individual as Sydney O'Moore,

known from advertisements. He or she wrote at least one anti-Catholic work as well as *Sacred symbols* (London, 1852). SOURCE Allibone, ii, p. 1354; RL.

M525 *Kate Connor; or, a text for all things* (by Sidney O'Moore).
Dublin: J. Robertson, [1849 or earlier]. SOURCE Adv. in Mrs Margaret Percival, *The Irish dove* (Dublin, 1849).
COMMENTARY No copy located [RL].

M526 *The fatal lie* (by Sidney O'Moore).
Dublin: J. Robertson, [1849 or earlier]. SOURCE Adv. in Mrs Margaret Percival, *The Irish dove* (Dublin, 1849).
COMMENTARY No copy located [RL].

M527 *Annie Gray; or, the experience of a week* (by Sidney O'Moore).
London: [publisher?], 1850. SOURCE Allibone, ii, p. 1354; Block, p. 165; Adv. in S.O Moore's *The family of Glencarra* (Bath, [1851 or earlier]).
COMMENTARY No copy located. Fiction for children [RL].

M528 *The voice of the new year* (by Sidney O'Moore).
+ Dublin: Samuel B. Oldham; London: Seeleys, 1850. LOCATION L (1850, 2nd edn), InND Loeber coll.
COMMENTARY A moral tale written to secure subscriptions to support twenty girls and boys who had been orphaned by the Famine. The volume consists of little essays about the fleeting nature of time and the importance of dedicating one's time to good works and preparations for the hereafter [ML].

M529 *The family of Glencarra. A tale of the Irish rebellion* (by Sidney O. Moore).
+ Bath: Binns & Goodwin; London: Whittaker & Co., Hall, Virtue & Co., Nisbet & Co., Hamilton, Adams & Co., Simpkin & Co., R.B. Blackader; Edinburgh: Oliver & Boyd; Dublin: John Robertson & Co., [1851 or earlier] (ill. George Measom, S.W.).
SOURCE Allibone, ii, p. 1354; Brown, 1170; Hodgson, p. 387. LOCATION D, L (1858 edn), NUC, InND Loeber coll.
COMMENTARY Religious fiction set in a fishing village on the Donegal coast around the time of the 1798 rebellion. Written in support of evangelical efforts such as those of the Irish Reformation Society, the book is at pains to point out superstitions in the Catholic religion. Several characters in the novel are converted to protestantism [ML].

MOORE, Thomas, b. Dublin 1779, d. Sloperton Cottage (Wilts.) 1852. Poet, lyricist, biographer and historian, TM was a son of John Moore, a Catholic grocer and wine merchant who was a native of Co. Kerry, and Anastasia Codd of Cornmarket (Co. Wexford). TM was admitted at TCD in 1794, one of the first Catholics to attend after the ban on Catholics had been lifted. He graduated in 1798 or 1799. He became friendly with the revolutionary Robert Emmet, but did not become involved in the activities of the United Irishmen, although he remained an apologist for the United Irishmen all his life. In 1799 he entered the Middle Temple in London where he was an immediate social success because of his ability to sing and act. In 1803 he was appointed registrar of the admiralty prize court in Bermuda, but he did not like the isolation of living there. He soon appointed a deputy and returned to London via the US and Canada. In London he resumed his career as poet and socialite. In 1811 he married Elizabeth (Bessy) Dyke. His *Irish melodies* (London, 1808, 2 vols.) was followed by an additional 8 vols. up to 1834 that include such famous songs as 'The last rose of Summer' and 'Believe me if all those endearing young charms'. The success of the early *Irish melodies* and verse epistles such as *Intercepted letters, or, the two-penny postbag* (London, 1813) led to a bidding war between the publishers Murray and Longman for his oriental verse romance *Lalla rookh* (London, 1817), which Longman purchased for £3,000. It proved hugely successful and went into many edns, proving to be the 'cream of the copyrights'. In 1818 it was found that TM's deputy in Bermuda had absconded, leaving him responsible for debts of £6,000. Unable to pay, and in order to avoid prison, he went abroad for three years. In Italy he resumed his friendship with Lord Byron, who gave him his memoirs. Moore used them as collateral for a loan from the publisher Murray, but after Byron's death Lady Byron, fearing the memoirs would be incriminating, sued TM. He bought them back from Murray and burnt them, writing a critically-acclaimed life of Byron himself instead as well as editing his poetry. He also wrote biographies of the revolutionary Lord Edward Fitzgerald and playwright Richard Brinsley Sheridan and a *History of Ireland* (London, 1835–46, 4 vols.). TM's prose works are limited to three works of fiction, which became highly popular. He received a Civil List pension in 1835. Elizabeth Rennie characterized him as 'a very well-dressed, bright, sparkling-looking little man ...' and although, he liked to sing, 'his voice was weak power he had none' (Rennie, i, p. 170). His last years were saddened by the loss of his two sons and by mental illness. He is best remembered for his satiric verse and for his enduring and beautiful melodies, which are still popular worldwide. TM was buried at Bromham, near Sloperton. S.C. Hall published *A memory of Thomas Moore* (London, [*c.*1852]) to raise money for a memorial window at the church there. His collection of books is in the RIA, Dublin (but part of his collection of papers was sold in June 1863). For TM's portraits and papers, see Elmes and ODNB. SOURCE Allibone, ii, pp 1354–9; B & S, p. 595; Boylan, p. 255; Browne, p. 93; DLB, xcvi, cxliv; Elmes, pp 137–8; Field Day, i, pp 1053–69 and passim, ii, pp 3–6 and passim, iii p. 673 and passim; S.C. Hall, pp 1–20; Hodgson, p. 207; Hogan 2, pp 867–70; Igoe, pp 184–7; List of catalogues, p. 261; S. MacCall, *Thomas Moore* (London, 1935), pp 128, 188; McKenna, pp 280–7; NCBEL 4, pp 411–13; OCIL, pp 375–7; ODNB; O'Donoghue, pp 317–18; [E. Rennie], *Traits of character* (London, 1860), i, p. 170; RIA/DIB; Schulz, p. 284; W.A. Shee, *My companions, 1830–1870* (London, 1893), pp 204–5; T. de Vere White, *Tom Moore: the Irish poet* (London, 1977).

M530 *Memoirs of Captain Rock, the celebrated Irish chieftain, with some account of his ancestors, written by himself* [anon.] (preface signed by the editor, S.E.).
London: Longman, Hurst, Rees, Orme, Brown & Green, 1824. SOURCE Rafroidi, ii, p. 289; Wolff, 4900; Bradshaw, 6025 (1824, 4th edn); British Fiction; Garside, 1824:69. LOCATION Grail, Dt, L, NUC.
+ Paris: A. & W. Galignani & Co., 1824. LOCATION NUC, InND Loeber coll.
Paris: E. Dentu, 1829 (trans. by L. Nachet as *Insurrections irlandaises depuis Henri II jusqu'à l'union, ou mémoires du Capitaine Rock*). SOURCE Rafroidi, ii, p. 373. LOCATION D, Univ. of Missouri, Columbia.
+ Paris: Baudry's European Library, 1835. LOCATION InND Loeber coll.
Breslau: J. Max & Co., 1825 (trans. as *Memoiren des Hauptmann's Rock*). SOURCE Belanger 80; OCLC. LOCATION Syracuse Univ.
+ New York: J. M'Loughlin, 1824. LOCATION NUC, InND Loeber coll.
New York: William Durel & Co., 1824. LOCATION Dt, NUC.

COMMENTARY Inspired by TM's visit with his patron Lord Lansdowne to Ireland, it is an indictment of English misrule in Ireland and a history of Ireland from the standpoint of a Whiteboy agrarian agitator. It argues that English misrule begets Irish violence. Capt. Rock was the name given to a fictitious leader of an agrarian protest movement among the poor in the southern counties of Ireland in the early-nineteenth century. The Dublin publisher Millikin reported that 'the people through the country are subscribing their sixpences and shillings to buy a copy' of this book (Drury cat.129/111). Roger O'Connor§ was the prototype of the captain, and O'Connor wrote a non-fictional rejoinder, *Captain Rock in Rome. Written by himself in the capital of the Christian world* (London, [*c.*1833], 2 vols.). Another response was written by Mortimer O'Sullivan§ and anonymously published under the title *Captain Rock detected* (London, 1824). The Irish artist Daniel Maclise painted 'The installation of Captain Rock', which was exhibited in London in 1834, the subject of which was said to have been taken from 'Tipperary tales', but clearly refers to TM's character Capt. Rock [Drury cat.129/111; RL; W.G. Neely, *Kilcooly, land and people in Tipperary* (n.l., 1983), p. 95; OCIL; p. 376; ODNB; W.J. O'Driscoll, *Memoirs of Daniel Maclise* (London, 1871), pp 49–51].

M531 *The epicurean. A tale* (by Thomas Moore; dedicated to Lord John Russell).
+ London: Longman, Rees, Orme, Brown & Green, 1827. SOURCE Rafroidi, ii, p. 290; British Fiction; Garside, 1827:53; Bradshaw, 6026 (1827, 2nd edn); Wolff, 4898. LOCATION Grail, D, Dt, L, UC, NUC, InND Loeber coll. (also 1827, 3rd edn).
Paris: J. Renouard, 1827 (trans. by A. Renouard as *L'Epicurien*). SOURCE Rafroidi, ii, p. 372. LOCATION Dt, NUC.
Paris: Béchet, 1827 (trans. by Mme A. Aragon as *L'Épicurien, ou la vierge de Memphis*). SOURCE Rafroidi, ii, p. 372. COMMENTARY *Paris, Béchet edn* No copy located [RL].
Paris: A. & W. Galignani & Co., 1828 (as *The epicurean. A tale*). SOURCE Hodges Figgis cat. 10 n.s./2113. LOCATION L.
+ Innsbruck: Wagner'schen Buchhandlung, 1828 (trans. by Johannes J. as *Der Epikuräer*). SOURCE COPAC. LOCATION L. COMMENTARY *Innsbruck edn* The BL has TM's copy, with a manuscript translation in English of the preface to this German edn [RL].
Deventer: A.J. van den Sigtenhorst, 1829 (trans. into Dutch as *De epicurist*). SOURCE Wintermans: 1827:53. LOCATION UVA.
Philadelphia: Carey, Lea, Carey & R.H. Small, 1827. SOURCE Kaser, 75. LOCATION PPL-R, NUC.
Boston: Wells & Lillie, 1827. LOCATION NUC, InND Loeber coll. (Boston, Whitaker 1831 edn).
+ New York: Charles S. Francis; Boston: Joseph H. Francis, 1841 (a new edn, revsd and corrected by the author). SOURCE NYPL. LOCATION DCU (1846 edn), NN, NUC.
COMMENTARY The 1st and 2nd edns were published in a combined total of 2,000 copies. Allegedly based on a manuscript found in the monastery of St Macarius, in the valley of the Lakes of Natron, which the author claims to have translated. Set in third century AD in the reign of the Roman emperor Valerian. A young man sets out from Egypt in the hope of learning the secret of immortality. He is converted by the hermit monks of the Thebaïd, but then dies as a martyr under Valerian. ODNB says this is a prose version of verse letters first published as *Alchipron* (not located, 1839) [RL; ODNB; British Fiction].

M532 *Travels of an Irish gentleman in search of a religion. With notes and illustrations* [anon.] (dedicated to 'the people of Ireland this defence of their ancient, national faith').
+ London: Longman, Rees, Orme, Brown, Green & Longman, 1833, 2 vols. SOURCE Rafroidi, ii, p. 290; Wolff, 4902; NSTC. LOCATION Grail, Dt, L, DLC, NUC, InND Loeber coll.
+ London: Longman, Rees, Orme, Brown, Green & Longman, 1833, 2nd edn, 2 vols. (preface by E.C.R.). LOCATION InND Loeber coll.
's Gravenhage: A.P. van Langenhuisen, 1835 (trans. into Dutch as *Reizen eens Ierschen edelmans om eene godsdients te zoeken*). SOURCE Alphabetische naamlijst 1833–49, p. 458.
Paris: Gaume, 1833 (trans. by Abbé Didon as *Voyages d'un jeune Irlandais à la recherche d'une religion*). SOURCE Rafroidi, ii, p. 373. LOCATION D (1835 edn), BNF (1836 edn).
+ Paris: A. & W. Galignani & Co., 1833. LOCATION L, InND Loeber coll.

+ Lyons: Perisse Frères; Paris: Au dépôt central de librarie, 1834, 2 vols. (trans. by M.D.**, 'professeur de philosophie' as *Voyages d'un irlandais a [sic] la recherche d'une religion*; introd. by the translator. LOCATION PC.

Cologne: M. DuMont-Schauberg, 1834 (trans. as *Wanderungen eines irländischen Edelmannes sur Entdeckung einer Religion. Mit Noten und Erläuterungen*). SOURCE Burmester cat. 64/55.

+ Köln am Rhine: J.P. Bachem, 1835 (trans. by D. Johann Christian Wilhelm Augusti as *Die Religiones-Wanderungen des Herrn Thomas Moore, eines irlandischen Romantikers, beleuchtet von einigen seiner Landsleute*). SOURCE OCLC. LOCATION NNC, InND Loeber coll.

Aschaffenburg: Theodor Pergay, 1847 (trans. as *Reisen eines Irländers um die wahre Religione zu suchen*). SOURCE OCLC. LOCATION St John's Univ.

The Hague: A.P. Van Langenhuysen, 1835 (trans. and introd. by F.J. Hoppenbrouwers as *Reizen eens Ierschen edelmans om eene godsdienst te zoeken*; ill. Last, Langenhuysen).

+ New York: M. Carey, 1833, 2 vols. in 1. LOCATION NUC.

+ Philadelphia: Carey, Lea & Blanchard, 1833. SOURCE Kaser, 367. LOCATION DCU, NN, NUC, InND Loeber coll.

Baltimore: J. Murphy, [1833]. LOCATION NUC, DCU (1844 edn).

+ Baltimore: J. Murphy & Co.; Philadelphia: James Fullerton; Pittsburgh (PA): George Quigley, n.d. (ill., with notes). LOCATION D, InND Loeber coll.

+ Baltimore: J. Murphy & Co.; Pittsburgh (PA): George Quigley, [186?]. SOURCE NSTC. LOCATION DCL, InND Loeber coll.

COMMENTARY A defence of the Catholic nationalist position in Ireland, which engendered at least four responses: Revd Mortimer O'Sullivan§, *A guide to an Irish gentleman in his search for a religion* (Dublin, 1833), 'Philalethes Cantabrigiensis' [pseud. of Bishop John Kaye§], *Reply to the "Travels of an Irish gentleman in search of a religion"* (London, 1834), Joseph Blanco White§, *Second travels of an Irish gentleman in search of a religion. With notes and illustrations NOT by the author of "Captain Rock's memoirs"* (Dublin, 1833, 2 vols.), and perhaps, [J.F. Waller's§] *The adventures of a Protestant in search of religion* (London, 1873) [RL; OCIL, p. 377].

— COLLECTED WORKS (except collected poetic works).

M533 *The works of Thomas Moore, Esq. With critical notes and sketch of his life* [by J.W. Lake].

+ Leipzig: Ernst Fleischer, 1826. SOURCE Ximenes cat. 105/278. LOCATION NUC, InND Loeber coll.

+ Leipzig: Ernst Fleischer, 1833 (new edn, 2 vols. in 1, vol. 2 dated 1840). LOCATION InND Loeber coll.

COMMENTARY Poetry and prose: 'The Fudge family in Paris' [not by TM], 'Epicurean', 'Fudges in England' [not by TM] [RL].

M534 *[The works of Thomas Moore].*

New York: D. Longworth, 1805–7, 4 vols. LOCATION NUC.

M535 *The works of Thomas Moore.*

New York: W.B. Gillie, 1821, 5 vols. LOCATION NUC.

M536 *The works of Thomas Moore.*

New York: G. Smith, 1825, 6 vols. LOCATION L, NUC.

M537 *The works of Thomas Moore.*

Philadelphia: Washington Press, 1827–28, 2 vols. SOURCE OCLC. LOCATION L (1829 edn), NUC.

MORAN, Edward, b. Waterford 1845, d. US 1915. Lawyer and novelist, EM was the brother of D.P. Moran, editor of the *Leader* (Dublin). EM practiced as a solicitor in Waterford, where he belonged to the literary circle of Richard Dowling§ and Edmund Downey§, and emigrated to the US where he was a lawyer in Brooklyn (NY) and served on the staff of the *Irish World* (New York). SOURCE Brown, p. 216; Dixson, p. 222; E. Reilly, p. 248.

M538   *Edward O'Donnell. A story of Ireland of our day* (by Jeremiah O'Donovan Rossa [*sic*; by Edward Moran]).
+ New York: S.W. Green's Son, 1884. SOURCE Brown, 1172; NYPL; OCLC. LOCATION D, NN.
COMMENTARY The author is not Jeremiah O'Donovan Rossa, the Fenian. Set somewhere near Fethard (Co. Tipperary) during the Land League agitation, the story is bitterly anti-landlord and abounds with eviction scenes, boycotting, and midnight conspiracies. The book contains many discussions of the agrarian question [Brown].

MORAN, James J., fl. 1893. Novelist, writer of humorous stories and publisher of Irish books at Aberdeen (Scotland). Given that JJM's prose includes five works of fiction with Irish content, it is likely that he was Irish. He inaugurated the Dundee Catholic Literary Society in 1893. His first literary effort was a dramatic serial, 'Pat O'Neill's vow', which was published in *Young Ireland* (Dublin), and which he prepared for the stage. He eschewed the prototype of the stage-Irishman. Later he moved to Durban, Natal Province, South Africa. A work, entitled *Runs in the blood* is mentioned on the title page of *The Dunferry risin'* (London, 1894), but has not been located. SOURCE Brown, p. 217; RL; Ryan, pp 171–2.

M539   *A deformed idol* (by James J. Moran).
+ London: Digby & Long, 1893. SOURCE Brown, p. 217; COPAC. LOCATION L.
COMMENTARY Love story set in England and on the Continent. No Irish content [ML].

M540   *The Dunferry risin'. A tale of the I.R.B.* (by James J. Moran).
+ London: Digby, Long & Co.; Dublin: J.J. Lalor, 1894. SOURCE Brown, 1173. LOCATION D, L.
COMMENTARY First appeared in the *Irish Emerald* (London). A vivid picture of the Irish Republican Brotherhood and the Fenian movement [Brown; Ryan, p. 171].

M541   *Irish stew* (by James J. Moran).
London: Digby, Long & Co., 1894. SOURCE Brown, 1174. LOCATION L.
+ Aberdeen: Moran & Co., 1900 (on cover: Dublin: Clery & Co.). LOCATION D.
COMMENTARY Contents: 'Jack Arnold's tour', 'Malrooney's banshee', 'Paddy Cassidy's return from spirit-land', 'Mick Mourican's mare', 'Nancy Mulligan's blankets. A story of 47', 'Tim Davey's strange bed-fellow. A tale of a double resurrection', 'The Land League donkey' [ML].

M542   *Stories of the Irish rebellion* (by James J. Moran).
+ Aberdeen: Moran & Co., [1898] (ill.). SOURCE Brown, 1175. LOCATION L.
COMMENTARY Contents: 'O'Ryan's brigade', 'Eily's friend in need', 'A fair insurgent', 'A bullet's billet', 'A ghostly executioner', 'Maureen's find', 'The bell of Doonmorey' [CM].

M543   *Two little girls in green. A story of the Irish Land League* (by James J. Moran).
+ Aberdeen: Moran & Co., [1898]. SOURCE Brown, 1176. LOCATION D, L.
COMMENTARY A story about the Land League. It contains an amiable Englishman who sees justice done for his tenants [Brown].

M544   *Irish drolleries* (by James J. Moran).
+ London: Henry J. Drane, [1909]. SOURCE Brown, 1177. LOCATION D, L.
COMMENTARY Humorous stories: 'Judy Hogan's patchwork quilt', 'Pat Mulligan's love-making', 'M'Cann's day at the waxworks', 'Miss Mullen's mistake', 'Pat Torsney's ghost',

'O'Hagan's golden weddin'', 'Mrs. Muldoon and the specialist', 'Tim Mannion the hero', 'The wake at Mrs. Doyle's', 'Mullarkey's American tour' [Brown].

M545 *Irish smiles* (by James J. Moran).

+ Aberdeen: W. Jolly & Sons, [1932]. SOURCE Brown 2, 1055. LOCATION L, NUC, InND Loeber coll.

COMMENTARY Published posthumously. Humorous stories: 'The duel at Ballyslash', 'Mulloney's lost notes', 'The beatin' of boxer Jim O'Connor', 'The Carryshanny poets', 'Dan Casey's imprisonment' [RL].

MORAN, Michael, pseud. 'Zozimus', b. The Liberties (Dublin) 1794, d. Patrick Street, Dublin 1846. MM, whose pseudonym is the name of a fifth-century pagan historian and chronicler of the decline of the Roman Empire, was a near-blind composer and ballad singer who was sometimes called 'the Last Gleeman'. He became blind when two weeks old. According to Boylan, he became known as Zozimus because he used to recite a poem by Dr Coyle, bishop of Raphoe, about St Mary of Egypt who, after fifty years of penance in the desert, is found by the Blessed Zozimus. William Butler Yeats§ in *The Celtic twilight* (London, 1893) mentions MM's poem 'The finding of Moses' (*Songs of Dublin*, ed. F. Harte, 1898). Some of Zozimus's lines are still current in Dublin speech. A Dublin version of the London *Punch*, under the title *Zozimus*, appeared as a 1d. weekly from May 1870 to Aug. 1872. MM married twice and his second wife's name was Curran. She and their son and daughter emigrated to the US shortly after his death. For MM's portraits, see Elmes and ODNB. SOURCE [anon.] *Memoir of the great original Zozimus* (Blackrock, 1976, which is a reprint of his life, with a selection of his ballads); J.P. Curtis, *Apes and angels. The Irishman in Victorian caricature* (Washington, DC, 1971), p. 88; Elmes, p. 243; Hogan 2, p. 1294; OCIL, p. 614; ODNB; O'Donoghue, p. 319.

M546 *Memoir of the great original Zozimus (Michael Moran) the celebrated Dublin street rhymer and reciter with the songs, sayings and recitations by Gulielmus Dubliniensis Humoriensis* [anon.].

Dublin: M'Glashan & Gill, Joseph Tully, 1871. SOURCE Fenning cat. 131/456. LOCATION Univ. of Manchester. COMMENTARY Dublin edn 34pp [COPAC].

New York: J.A. McGee, 1878 (as *The Zozimus papers. A series of comic and sentimental stories and legends, being the edited, unedited and pilfered works of Michael Moran, the blind story-teller of Dublin* [anon.] (Running title: *Half Hours with Irish Authors*; ill.). SOURCE Brown, 503; Hogan, p. 211 (1909 edn by 'Marcus Fels' [i.e., Richard Dowling], but this seems to be mistaken); OCLC (1882 edn); RLIN. LOCATION NN.

+ New York: J.A. McGee, 1879 (as *"Zozimus" or Michael Moran, the blind story teller of Dublin*). LOCATION D (New York, Kenedy 1886 edn), NN, PVU.

+ Dublin: Carraig Chapbooks 6, 1976 (facsimile edn; with an introd. by Dr Thomas Wall). SOURCE COPAC. LOCATION Dt.

COMMENTARY Humorous tales attributed to MM, published posthumously. However, many of the stories cannot be traced directly to him and one, 'A Fenian tale', postdates his era. Contents of New York, 1879 edn: 'The "Zozimus" papers', 'The prophecy man', 'The deserter', 'The matchmaker', 'The ghost', 'An Irish pic-nic', 'The Irish parliament and the Turk', 'Bothering an editor', 'A Fenian tale', 'Handy Andy's little mistakes', 'Puss in brogues', 'The wise simpleton', 'Peggy the pishogue', 'An Irish dancing-master', 'A dance at Pat Malone's', 'Mike Driscoll and the fairies', 'Tom Kearney', 'Paddy Corbett's first smuggling trip', 'Hannaberry the piper', 'The Irish fiddler', 'Barney O'Grady', 'Orohoo, the fairy man', ' A tale of other days', 'What Mr Maguire saw in the kitchen', 'The will', 'Serving a writ', 'The gauger outwitted', 'The will o' the wisp', 'The flower of the well' [RL; AMB].

MORGAN, Ann Jane, pseud. 'Ann Jane', fl. 1848. English novelist and religious fiction writer. SOURCE Alston, p. 309 (for her other novels); Block, p. 166; NSTC.

M547 *Irish Dick* (by 'Ann Jane').
London: Benjamin L. Green, 1848. SOURCE Block, p. 166; NSTC. LOCATION L (destroyed).
COMMENTARY Religious fiction [BLC].

MORGAN, Revd Henry, b. Newtown (CT) 1824, d. 1884. Clergyman, lecturer and religious fiction writer, HM moved to Boston in 1859 where he was pastor of Indiana Place Chapel. SOURCE Allibone Suppl., ii, p. 1135.

M548 *Ned Nevins, the news-boy; or, street life in Boston* (by Henry Morgan).
Boston: Lee & Shepard, 1866. SOURCE Allibone Suppl., ii, p. 1135. LOCATION NUC.
COMMENTARY According to the advertisement in *The fallen priest* [1883], this story won the author 'the friendship of the Irish'. The book became very popular and reached a 35th edn in about 1881 [NUC].

M549 *The fallen priest: Story founded on fact. Key and sequel to "Boston inside out."* (by Henry Morgan).
Boston: Shawmut, 1883. SOURCE Slocum, ii, 3099; Wright, iii, 3837; OCLC. LOCATION NUC, InND Loeber coll. ([1883], 3rd edn).
COMMENTARY The 3rd edn has 11 extra chapters. Consists of three books with some Irish characters: 'The story. Forty chapters', 'Catholic church in politics: For sale or to let', 'Key and appendix'. Fr Jerome Keenan has fallen into disgrace because of an affair with Maria McShea. He sinks into further degradation, but through the power of personality and his own efforts to change his ways remains a force to be contended with even up to his death. Fr Leonard, on the other hand, is an old formalist who disapproves of Fr Jerome and any ceremony outside the guidelines of the Church. Includes the seamier aspects of Boston [RL; Slocum].

MORGAN, Lady (née Sydney Owenson; also known as **Miss Owenson**), pseud. 'S.O.', b. Dublin 1775 or 1776 (she kept it a secret), baptized 1783, d. London 1859. Novelist, poet and socialite, LM was the daughter of Robert Owenson (born MacOwen), a theatre manager and former steward to Sir John Browne of Co. Mayo, and Jane Mill (Hill according to Todd and ODNB), an English Methodist and daughter of a Shrewsbury tradesman. Her paternal grandmother was Sydney Crofton, the disowned daughter of the Croftons of Longford House, landed gentry from west of Sligo town. Her sister Olivia was an accomplished songwriter and a dramatist. She was educated at the Huguenot school in Clontarf (Dublin) and a finishing school in Dublin before joining her widowed father in Sligo. Her father's theatrical undertakings were not very successful and she became a governess in the family of Fetherstonhaugh at Bracklyn Castle (Co. Westmeath)[1]. She published her first volume of verse in 1801, and in 1802 in the *Hibernian Magazine* (Dublin) a long elegy on the death of the poet Tom Dermody, who had tutored her and her sister. Her first novel, *St. Clair*, was published in Dublin in 1803. Its heroine – like all future heroines in her novels – was based on herself. The popularity of her writing, especially *The wild Irish girl* (London, 1806, 3 vols.), led to an invitation to become part of the household of the marchioness of Abercorn. She continued to publish fiction and poetry and in 1807 a single comic opera, *The first attempt, or, the whim of a moment*. She liked to collect Irish songs, to which she furnished English translations, and some of these were

1 Probably, James Fetherstonhaugh, who settled at Bracklin (also known as Bracklyn) Castle, and married Margaret, daughter of Sir Richard Steele, Bt. (A.J. Fethersonhaugh, *The history of the Fethersonhaugh family* (Dublin, 1879), p. 24).

published as *Twelve original Hibernian melodies* (London, [1805]) and *Lay of an Irish harp* (London, 1807). She also wrote on Irish customs and antiquities in her *Patriotic sketches of Ireland, written in Connaught* (London, 1807, 2 vols.), a work that also included pointed social criticism. In 1812 she married the Abercorn family surgeon, Thomas Charles Morgan, for whom the marquess had arranged a knighthood. The Morgans moved to Dublin and her salon in 35 (now 39) Kildare Street (where they lived from 1812 to 1837) was celebrated. She travelled extensively in France and Italy and wrote about her experiences, notably in *France* (London, 1817, 2 vols.), and *Italy* (London, 1821, 2 vols.), and in *The life and times of Salvator Rosa* (London, 1824, 2 vols.). She published nine novels, of which *The wild Irish girl* (London, 1806, 3 vols.) became the most well-known. She also produced a book of essays, *Absenteeism* (London, 1825), and autobiographical sketches in a collection called *The book of the boudoir* (London, 1829). Through her Irish, or national, novels she worked tirelessly for the cause of Catholic emancipation and freedom for Ireland from English domination. Both she and her husband were interested in Irish history and they subscribed to J.L. Villanueva's *Ibernia Phoenicea* (Dublin, 1831). Elizabeth Ham§, who met her in Dublin at the height of her popularity, recalled in her autobiography that Lady Morgan's 'figure was small and slightly awry … she had a decided cast in one eye … her hair was cropped and worn in short curls on her head' and 'she was excessively fond of dancing' (Ham, p. 139). In 1837 the Morgans moved to London where, turning her attention from Irish politics to feminism, she wrote *Woman and her master: a history of the female sex from the earliest period* (London, 1841). Living at 11 William Street in Knightsbridge, she was well-known in society and with her husband published a collection of essays *The book without a name* (London, 1841, 2 vols., which contains a single short story). Her works elicited both fierce criticism and ardent admiration. They were severely criticized in the *Quarterly Review* by John Wilson Croker§, without impairing their success, but Lord Byron, Percy Bysshe Shelley, Sir Walter Scott and Maria Edgeworth§ all had praise for various novels (although Edgeworth decried LM's *Florence McCarthy* (London, 1818), see below). She was granted a civil list annual pension of £300 in 1837, the first woman to receive one. Her later work includes contributions to the London *Athenaeum* and some autobiographical sketches in *An odd volume extracted from an autobiography* (London, 1859). Among her friends was Charlotte Brooke§, to whom she claimed to be related. The Morgans had no children. She outlived her husband and was interred in Brompton (London) cemetery where a monument by Sherrard Westmacott was erected by her niece. It shows a carved Irish harp propped by two books: *France* and *The Wild Irish girl*. For her portraits and papers, see ODNB. Her books were sold by Sotheby's in 1863. SOURCE Allibone, ii, pp 1366–7; Allibone Suppl., ii, pp 1136–7; Blain, pp 762–3; Boylan, p. 256; Brady, p. 169; BL, S.-C.S. 529(3); C. Connolly, '"I accuse Miss Owenson": The Wild Irish Girl as a media event' in *Colby Quarterly*, 36(2) (2000), pp. 98–115; W.H. Dixon (ed.), *Lady Morgan's memoirs* (London, 1862), 2 vols., passim; Elmes, pp 140–1; *The Emerald* (New York, 19 Sept. 1868), p. 105; Field Day, i, pp 1080 and passim, ii, pp 836–7, 840–1, 948, v, pp 11, 836–7 and passim; W.J. Fitzpatrick, *Lady Morgan; her career, literary and personal, with a glimpse of her friends and a word to her calumniators* (London, 1860); T. Flanagan, *The Irish novelists 1800–1850* (New York, 1958), pp 109–64; F.A. Gerard, *Some fair Hibernians* (London, 1897), pp 180–1; E. Gillett (ed.), *Elizabeth Ham by herself* (London, 1945), p. 139; S.C. Hall, pp 214–27; Hogan, pp 469–71; Hogan 2, pp 871–2; Igoe, pp 187–90; List of catalogues, p. 302; McKenna, p. 288–91; G.N. Nuttell-Smith, *The chronicles of a puritan family in Ireland* (Oxford, 1923), pp 89–92; NCBEL 4, pp 967–9 [under Sydney Owenson]; OCIL, pp 378–9; ODNB [under Sydney Morgan]; O'Donoghue, p. 319–20; RIA/DIB; Schulz, p. 284; M.A. Shee, *My contemporaries, 1830–1870* (London, 1893) pp 97–9, 307; B. Sloan, *The pioneers of Anglo-Irish fiction* (Gerrards Cross, 1986), p. 8; Todd, pp 523–4; Wolff introd., p.12.

M550   *St. Clair; or, the heiress of Desmond* (by 'S.O.'; dedicated to author's sister Lady Clarke).
Dublin: Wogan, Brown, Halpin, Colbert, John Dornin, Jackson & Medcalf, 1803. SOURCE Wolff, 4917; British Fiction; Garside, 1803:55; Pollard 2, p. 316. LOCATION Ireland related fiction, Dt, NUC.
London: E. Harding & S. Highley; Dublin: J. Archer, 1803 (ill. Dighton). SOURCE Brown, 1178; Rafroidi, ii, p. 293; Sadleir, 1782; British Fiction; Garside, 1803:55. LOCATION Corvey CME 3–628–7460–4, Dt, L, NUC.
+ London: J.J. Stockdale, 1812, 3rd edn, 2 vols. (corrected and much enlarged; by Miss Owenson). SOURCE Sadleir, 1782a. LOCATION NUC, InND Loeber coll.
Leipzig: [publisher?], 1827 (trans. by Otto Christoph freiherr von Budberg as *Saint Clair*). SOURCE Garside, 1803:55. LOCATION Niedersächsische Staats-und-Universitätsbibliothek.
Paris: J.G. Dentu, 1813, 2 vols. (trans. by H. Vilmain as *Saint-Clair, ou l'héritière de Desmond*). SOURCE Rafroidi, ii, p. 374. LOCATION NUC.
+ Amsterdam: Johannes van der Heij, 1816 (trans. into Dutch by F. van Teutem as *St. Clair en Olivia*). SOURCE Brown, 1179; Wintermans, 1803:55. LOCATION L.
+ Philadelphia: S.F. Bradford, 1807. SOURCE NSTC; Gecker, 758. LOCATION D, L, PU, NUC.
London: Routledge/Thoemmes, 1995. LOCATION Dt, C.
COMMENTARY Originally listed in *Lady Morgan's memoirs* (London, 1863, 2nd edn, i, p. 223) as *St. Clair, or first love* and dedicated to Lady Clonbrock, but both title and dedication were changed later. An imitation of Goethe's *Die Leiden des jungen Werther* (Leipzig, 1774), this epistolary novel is set in Connacht. A sensitive young man, St Clair, living in the household of Lord L., his rich relative, finds the environment uncongenial and seeks the company of Olivia, who lives on the next estate. Olivia is engaged to be married to one of St Clair's relatives, who is on the Continent with his regiment. The relationship between St Clair and Olivia grows from sympathy to friendship to love. Just before Olivia's marriage, her fiancée finds Olivia and St Clair together in what he construes to be a compromising situation. He challenges St Clair to fight him, and in the ensuing duel St Clair is mortally wounded. The fiancée flees to the Continent. St Clair dies and Olivia dies also after a long illness and decline [ML; Ximenes cat. 58/745].

M551   *The novice of Saint Dominick* (by Miss Owenson).
London: Richard Phillips, 1806, 4 vols. SOURCE Rafroidi, ii, p. 293; Gecker, 755; British Fiction; Garside, 1806:52. LOCATION Grail, Corvey CME 3–628–48373–5, D, Dt, L, PU, NUC, InND Loeber coll. (1806, 2nd edn, 4 vols.).
Paris: H. Nicolle, 1816, 4 vols. (trans. by Victomtesse de Ruolz as *La novice de Saint Dominique*). SOURCE Rafroidi, ii, p. 374; Sadleir, 1788 (1817 edn); Bn-Opale plus. LOCATION BNF.
+ Philadelphia: T.S. Manning, 1807, 4 vols. SOURCE Gecker, 756. LOCATION PU (lacking vols. 2 and 4), NUC, InND Loeber coll.
+ Philadelphia: Hugh Maxwell & Thomas S. Manning, 1807, 4 vols. in 2. LOCATION InND Loeber coll.
COMMENTARY This volume was originally called *The minstrel* and it begins with an idealized portrait of Thomas Moore§, who had performed for the Fetherstonhaughs when LM was governess there. An historical novel set in fourteenth-century France, whose heroine crosses the country as a troubadour. The story attacks religious and political oppression [Blain; ODNB].

M552 *The wild Irish girl. A national tale* (by Miss Owenson).
+ London: Richard Phillips, 1806, 3 vols. SOURCE Brown, 1180; Rafroidi, ii, p. 293; British Fiction; Garside, 1806:54; Sadleir, 1783; Wolff, 4918; NSTC. LOCATION Corvey CME 3-628-48373-5, Ireland related fiction, Grail, D, DPL (1807, 3rd edn), L, NUC, InND Loeber coll.
London: H. Colburn, 1846 (revsd edn). SOURCE Wolff, 4918a. LOCATION NUC.
+ Paris: Gide Fils, 1813, 4 vols. (trans. by P.L. Dubuc as *Glorvina, ou la jeune irlandaise. Histoire nationale*). SOURCE Rafroidi, ii, p. 374; Sadleir, 1787. LOCATION D, NUC.
Leipzig: W. Rein, 1809–10, 3 vols. (trans. as *Glorvina, das wilden Mädchen in Irland*). LOCATION NUC.
Philadelphia: S.F. Bradford, 1807. SOURCE Topp 1, p. 309. LOCATION E, NUC, InND Loeber coll. (1807, 3rd American edn).
Baltimore: John Vance & Co., 1807. SOURCE OCLC. LOCATION College of William & Mary.
New York: Alsop, Brannan & Alsop, 1807. SOURCE Topp 1, p. 309. LOCATION NUC.
+ New York: Richard Scott, 1807, 4th American edn. LOCATION NUC, InND Loeber coll.
+ Hartford: Silas Andrus & Son, 1853. SOURCE NYPL (1855 edn). LOCATION NN (1855 edn), InND Loeber coll.
New York: Garland, 1979, 3 vols. (introd. by R.L. Wolff). LOCATION Dt.
+ London, Brookfield (VT): Pickering & Chatto, 2000 (ed. with introd. and notes by C. Connolly and Stephen Copley; foreword by K. Whelan). SOURCE OCLC. LOCATION Dt, L, InND Loeber coll.
COMMENTARY A heavily-researched and footnoted epistolary novel set in a remote and desolate part of Connacht, its planned title was *Princess of Inismore*. The novel is a plea for the oppressed Irish people expressed through the love affair between Horatio, a profligate Ascendancy hero, and the mysterious Glorvina, the beautiful harpist and daughter of the dispossessed local Catholic ancestral chieftain, the prince of Inismore, a survivor of the Cromwellian occupation. Horatio is banished by his stern father to his Connacht estates. There he falls in love with Glorvina. Towards the close of the novel she is forced into the castle chapel and confronted with a bridegroom who insists that the ceremony of marriage proceed. Horatio intervenes; the bridegroom turns out to be Horatio's son, who has been hiding in the castle to observe Glorvina. Although the father's methods are sinister, they are intended to bridge the historical breach between the English and the Irish. The story ends with the match between the Catholic Gaelic princess and Horatio. As in many of LM's novels, the heroine was assumed to be a portrait of the author. After its publication LM was known as Glorvina [W.H. Dixon (ed.), *Lady Morgan's memoirs* (London, 1862), i, p. 276; Field Day, v, pp 837–41, 849–57; Frank, 313; ODNB; Wolff, introd. pp 12–13].

M553 *Woman; or, Ida of Athens* (by Miss Owenson).
+ London: Longman, Hurst, Rees & Orme, 1809, 4 vols. SOURCE Rafroidi, ii, p. 293; Gecker, 759; Sadleir, 1785; British Fiction; Garside, 1809:55. LOCATION Grail, Corvey CME 3-628-48374-3, D, L, PU, NUC.
Paris: H. Nicolle, 1812, 4 vols. (trans. by P.L. Dubuc as *La femme, ou Ida l'Athénienne*). SOURCE Rafroidi, ii, p. 374; Streeter, p. 223. LOCATION D (1817 edn).
Amsterdam: J. Radink, 1813, 2 vols. (trans. into Dutch as *Ida, of het meisje van Athene*). SOURCE Alphabetische naamlijst 1790–1832, p. 411.
Magdeburg: Rubach, 1820, 4 vols. (trans. by Leopold Marsch von Wedell as *Ida von Athen*). SOURCE Garside, 1809:55. LOCATION Staatsbibliothek, Berlin.

+ Philadelphia: Bradford & Inskeep; New York: Inskeep & Bradford; Baltimore: Coale & Thomas, 1809, 2 vols. SOURCE Gecker, 760. LOCATION PU, NUC, InND Loeber coll.

COMMENTARY LM described this as an attempt to delineate perfect feminine character in its natural state, with the perfect place to do this being Greece. It tells of the romantic adventures of the learned heroine Ida, whose lover had to flee Greece after a revolt against the Turks. She travels to London and experiences a time of poverty and misfortune. However, eventually she inherits a fortune and is reunited with her lover and concludes 'it is for men to perform great actions, for women to inspire them' [Blain, p. 762; ODNB; Welch, p. 605].

M554 *The missionary. An Indian tale* (by Miss Owenson; dedicated to Ann Jane, marchioness of Abercorn).

London: J.J. Stockdale, 1811, 3 vols. (ill. James Gosby). SOURCE Rafroidi, ii, p. 293; British Fiction; Garside, 1811:61; Sadleir, 1775. LOCATION Corvey CME 3–628–48324–7 (1811, 3rd edn), Dt, L, NUC.

London: Westerton, 1859 (as *Luxima, the prophetess. A tale of India*). SOURCE NCBEL 3, p. 754; Rafroidi, ii, p. 293. LOCATION NUC.

+ Utrecht: J. Herfkens Fz, 1861 (trans. into Dutch as *Luxima, the profetes: Een geschiedenis in Indië*; ill.). SOURCE Adamnet. LOCATION UVA.

+ Paris: H. Nicolle, 1812, 3 vols. in 1 (trans. by [P.L. Dubuc] as *Le missionaire, histoire indienne*). SOURCE Rafroidi, ii, p. 374; Streeter, p. 223. LOCATION NUC, InND Loeber coll.

Vienna: C.F. Schade, 1827 (trans. As *Die Prophetin von Caschimir, oder Glaubenskraft und Liebesglück*). SOURCE Garside, 1811:61; OCLC. LOCATION Univ. of Virginia.

+ New York: Franklin Co., Butler & White, 1811, 3 vols. in 1. SOURCE NYPL. LOCATION NN, NUC, InND Loeber coll.

COMMENTARY Written at Barons Court (Co. Tyrone), a story that deals with religious differences between Christians and Hindus and between the Franciscan and Dominican orders. A Portuguese monk of high birth is sent to India to convert the natives. His austere and unwordly manner does not endear him to the church hierarchy in Goa. He travels to Kashmir but realizes that it will not be easy to convert anyone. He plans and succeeds in converting the Brahmin priestess, Luxima, who lives not far from the cave where he lives. In so doing he commits the sin of falling in love with Luxima, who becomes an outcast because of her conversion. They travel back to Goa, with the priest struggling continuously with having given in to his love. He is arrested by an officer of the Inquisition, accused of having a concubine, and is to be burnt at the stake. Luxima jumps on to the pyre and in the ensuring confusion they flee. Luxima dies and in her last moments reverts to the religion of the Brahmins. The missionary returns to Kashmir, there to end his days as a hermit [ML; *Lady Morgan's memoirs* (London, 1863, 2nd edn), i, p. 407; ODNB].

M555 *O'Donnel. A national tale* (by Lady Morgan, late Miss Owenson; dedicated to the duke of Devonshire).

+ London: Henry Colburn, 1814, 3 vols. SOURCE Brown, 1181; Rafroidi, ii, p. 293; Gecker, 757; Sadleir, 1779; British Fiction; Garside, 1814:41; Wolff, 4914. LOCATION Grail, Corvey CME 3–628–48329–8, Ireland related fiction, D, L, PU, NUC, InND Loeber coll.

+ London: Henry Colburn, 1815, 3 vols. (new edn). SOURCE Bradshaw, 6031; NSTC. LOCATION L, C, InND Loeber coll.

+ London: H. Colburn, 1835 (revsd edn; Colburn's Modern Novelists, vol. 3). SOURCE NCBEL 3, p. 754; Rafroidi, ii, p. 293 (1836 edn). LOCATION D (1836 edn), NUC, InND Loeber coll.

Paris: Le Normant, 1815, 3 vols. (trans. by P.A. Lebrun de Charmettes as *O'Donnel, ou l'Irlande, histoire nationale*). SOURCE Rafroidi, ii, p. 374. LOCATION D.

Amsterdam: H. Molenyzer, 1815, 2 vols. (trans. into Dutch as *O'Donnel; een Iersch volksverhaal*). SOURCE Alphabetische naamlijst 1790–1832, p. 411.

Haarlem: François Boon, 1815 (trans. into Dutch as *O'Donnel. Een Iersch volksverhaal*). SOURCE Wintermans, 1814:41.

Berlin: Voss, 1825, 2 vols. (trans. by Leopold Marsh von Wedell as *O'Donnel, oder die Reise nach dem Riessendam: Irishes National-Gemählde*). SOURCE Garside, 1814:41 (1823 edn); GLOL. LOCATION Bibliotheks – und Informationssystem der Universität, Oldenburg.

New York: Van Winkle & Wiley, 1814. SOURCE NYPL. LOCATION NN, NUC.

New York: Garland, 1979, 3 vols. (introd. by R.L. Wolff). LOCATION Dt.

COMMENTARY Set in Ulster and England in the 1810s and with barely-disguised portraits of Lady Abercorn and others, the novel begins in an epistolary form. The hero is the Catholic Red Hugh O'Donnel, earl of Tyrconnell, who is dispossessed and impoverished but proud and honourable and the veteran of heroic service in the Austrian and French armies. The novel describes rural Ulster with much local colour, and then life in fashionable society in England. The heroine is a brilliant young Irish woman, whom the reader first meets as a governess. She becomes a portrait painter and captures an aged duke, who promptly dies. The novel condemns British laws that penalize Roman Catholics [ODNB; Wolff introd., p. 13].

M556 *Florence Macarthy: An Irish tale* (by Lady Morgan; preface by T.C.M. [Thomas Charles Morgan, author's husband]).

+ London: Henry Colburn, 1818, 4 vols. SOURCE Brown, 1182; Rafroidi, ii, p. 293; Sadleir, 1769; Wolff, 4909; Gecker, 754 (1819 edn); British Fiction; Garside, 1818:44. LOCATION Grail, Corvey, CME 3–628–8327–1 (1819, 4th edn), Ireland related fiction, D, Dt (1819, 4th edn), DPL, L, PU, NUC, InND Loeber coll. (1819, 4th edn).

+ Paris: H. Nicolle, 1819, 4 vols. (trans. by A.J.B. Defauconpret as *Florence Macarthy*). SOURCE Rafroidi, ii, p. 374; Sadleir, 1786. LOCATION D.

+ Paris, Strasbourg, London: Treuttel & Würtz, 1819, 4 vols. (trans. by J.T. Parisot as *Florence Macarthy, nouvelle irlandaise*; ill. Croizier; preface by Lady Morgan for this edn). SOURCE Rafroidi, ii, p. 374. LOCATION InND Loeber coll.

Leipzig: Hinrichssche Buchhandlung, 1821 (trans. by Johann Friedrich von Bernard as *Florentina Macarthy: eine irländische Novelle*). SOURCE Belanger, 55; GLOL. LOCATION Union Cat. Northern Germany.

Arnhem: C.M. Thieme, 1823, 2 vols. (trans. into Dutch as *Florence Macarthy, een Iersch verhaal*). SOURCE Wintermans, 1818:44. LOCATION Koninklijke Bibliotheek, The Hague.

Baltimore: N.G. Maxwell, 1819, 2 vols. LOCATION NUC.

Philadelphia: M. Carey & Son, 1819. LOCATION NUC.

New York: W.B. Gilley, 1819. SOURCE NYPL. LOCATION NN, NUC.

New York: Garland, 1979, 4 vols. (introd. by R.L. Wolff). LOCATION Dt.

COMMENTARY Set on the picturesque south coast of Munster, it examines contemporary Ireland in a story in which ancient Irish tribal loyalties triumph over both Anglo-Norman aristocrats and the vicious self-seeking new men, who are profiting by their roles as agents to acquire land and power. The Anglo-Norman Protestant hero's exploits in South American revolutions afford opportunities for comparisons between the persecuted Indians in South America and the Irish peasantry. The Catholic heroine is a successful novelist, victim of brutally unfair reviewers, castigated here in the satirical portrait of John Wilson Croker§, LM's own worst enemy, who appears as an upstart agent, Crawley Jnr. Maria Edgeworth§ commented 'What a shameful mixture in this book of the highest talent and the lowest malevolence ... My general feelings in closing the book are shame and disgust and the wish never more to be classed with *novel* writers when the highest talents in that line have been so disgraced. Oh that I could prevent people from ever naming me along with her [LM] either for praise or blame' (Colvin, pp 166–7). The castle Dunore in the novel has been identified as Lismore (Co. Waterford) and the character of Lord Rosbrin said to be based on the earl of Blessington§. Maria Edgeworth§ thought that the Lord Adelm in the novel was based on Lord Byron. The novel was adapted into a play by Michael Bryant with the title 'Florence MacCarthy, or life in Ireland' (London, 1823) [M. Bence-Jones, *Life in an Irish country house* (London, 1996), pp 160–1; Colvin, pp 166–7; Bolton, p. 217; [F. Edgeworth], *A memoir of Maria Edgeworth* (London, 1867), ii, p.28; S.C. Hall, p. 16; ODNB; M. Sadleir, *The strange life of Lady Blessington* (Boston, 1933), p. 31; Wolff introd., p. 13].

M557 *The O'Briens and the O'Flahertys. A national tale* (by Lady Morgan).
+ London: Henry Colburn, 1827, 4 vols. SOURCE Brown, 1183; Rafroidi, ii, p. 293; Bradshaw, 6032; British Fiction; Garside, 1827:54; Sadleir, 1777; Wolff, 4913. LOCATION Grail, Corvey CME 3–628–48328–X, D, Dt (1838 edn), Ireland related fiction, DPL, L, C, NUC, InND Loeber coll. (1828, 2nd edn, 4 vols.).
London: Henry Colburn & Richard Bentley; Edinburgh: Bell & Bradfute; Dublin: John Cumming, 1834, 3 vols. (Colburn's Irish National Tales Nos. 13–16). SOURCE Sadleir 3736c(ii); Rowan cat. 45/330. COMMENTARY *London, Colburn edn* No copy located [RL].
+ Paris: Charles Gosselin, 1828, 3 vols. (trans. by J. Cohen as *Les O'Brien et les O'Flaherty*). SOURCE Rafroidi, ii, p. 375; NYPL. LOCATION D, NN.
Heidelberg: Engelmann, 1828, 4 vols. (as *The O'Briens and the O'Flanértys [sic]: A national tale*). SOURCE Garside, 1827:53; GLOL. LOCATION Union Cat. Bavaria.
Philadelphia: Carey, Lea & Carey, 1828, 4 vols. in 2. SOURCE NYPL. LOCATION NN, NUC.
New York: Redfield, 1856, 2 vols. (annotated by R. Shelton MacKenzie§). SOURCE Rose cat. 24/135; NYPL. LOCATION NN, NUC.
New York: Garland, 1979, 4 vols. (introd. by R.L. Wolff). LOCATION Dt.
+ London, Sydney, Wellington: Pandora, 1988 (introd. by Mary Campbell). LOCATION Dt, O, InND Loeber coll.
COMMENTARY A partly-epistolary novel, it is said to have been based in part on an Elizabethan document concerning the O'Bryens of the Aran Islands. It deals with the survivors of each successive wave of settlement and conquest in Ireland and is emblematic of the frustrations and final defeat of the author's own form of patriotism. After a prologue set in the 1770s, the main story unfolds in the 1790s and closes after the Act of Union in 1800. The scene is set in Dublin and the wild regions of Connacht, not far from Galway. The hero, Murrough O'Brien, nominally a Protestant, joins the United Irishmen but has to flee after the rebellion of 1798. The heroine, nominally a Catholic abbess, comes and goes freely in the secular world and within the church works against 'vulgar bigotry'. Eventually she abandons her order to marry O'Brien. O'Brien's father, a declassed descendant of an ancient family, compromises with the Ascendancy, converts to protestantism, makes his fortune and becomes a successful politician, only to revert to his ancestral faith and turn into a secret, half-mad revolutionary [J. Burke, *A ... history of the commoners* (London, 1835), i, p. 671n.; Field Day, i, p. 1080, ii, pp 867–83; Wolff introd., p. 13].

M558 *The princess; or, the beguine* (by Lady Morgan).
+ London: Richard Bentley, 1835, 3 vols. SOURCE Rafroidi, ii, p. 294; Sadleir, 1781; Wolff, 4916; Garside 2, 1835:71. LOCATION Grail, D, Dt, L, DLC.

+ Paris: Baudry, 1835 (Baudry's European Library). SOURCE NYPL. LOCATION NN, NUC, InND Loeber coll.

Paris: A. & W. Galignani & Co., 1835. LOCATION Dt.

Paris: A. Betrand, 1835, 3 vols. (trans. by Mlle A. Sobry as *La princesse*). SOURCE Rafroidi, ii, p. 375. LOCATION UBP.

+ Brussels: Ad. Wahlen, 1835. LOCATION D.

Berlin: Duncker & Humblot, 1835, 3 vols. (trans. by Georg Nicolaus Bärman as *Die Princessin*). LOCATION NUC.

Philadelphia: Carey, Lea & Blanchard, 1835, 2 vols. SOURCE Kaser, 468. LOCATION ViU, NUC.

COMMENTARY Depicts the life of English high society and is set in England and Belgium, just after Belgium has become independent from Holland. It has extensive descriptions of Bruges, Ghent, and Brussels. LM bore a grudge against Hermann von Puckler-Muskau and she lampooned him in this novel [ML; Scott cat. 15/118].

MORAN, Thomas Charles. Preface writer. See MORGAN, Lady.

'THE MORIARTY FAMILY', pseud. See DAUNT, W.J. O'Neill.

'MORIARTY, Denis Ignatius', pseud. See DAUNT, W.J. O'Neill.

MORLEY, Mabel, fl. 1889. Novelist, possibly English, MM, according to the title page of the following book, also wrote 'When we two parted', 'Snowdrop', and other tales, but these have not been located. SOURCE Brown, p. 219; RL.

M559 *Boycotted. A story* (by Mable Morley).

+ London: Remington & Co., 1889. SOURCE Brown, 1186. LOCATION D, L, InND Loeber coll.

COMMENTARY A romance set during the nineteenth century at the time of agrarian agitation in the west of Ireland. The owner of a small estate near Athenry (Co. Galway), Capt. Boyd, is boycotted. A company of dragoons under Capt. St Heliar is sent down to protect the labourers brought in from Dublin to harvest Capt. Boyd's crops. St Heliar falls in love with Capt. Boyd's sister-in-law. He is shot in the arm by one of the disgruntled peasants. After he has recuperated, he is allowed to go on leave and crosses over to England in the same boat as the Boyd family, who are leaving Ireland for the time being. He confesses his love, which is reciprocated [ML; Brown].

MORRIS, Alfred, fl. 1900. Historical novelist, AM probably had died by 1900 when his portrait was prefixed to this volume. SOURCE RL.

M560 *Eochaid the heremhon; or, the romance of the Lia Phail* (by Alfred Morris).

+ London: Robert Banks & Son, 1900 (ed. and compiled by Revd Denis Hanan). LOCATION D, L, NUC.

COMMENTARY An unfinished biblical story in the guise of an historical romance that portrays some of the rituals of pagan settlements in Ireland before the arrival of Christianity. The editor explains that he has not altered the story, but has filled in some blanks. It includes extracts from the Bible. Set around 580 BC, it features Eochaid son of the king of the Tuatha de Danaan who has succeeded to the crown of Ulster. Meanwhile in Egypt, Jeremiah the prophet is going to establish his own kingdom. He retrieves the Pillar of Wisdom stone from the ruins of the temple at Jerusalem and learns about the tribe of fierce colonists who are settled in Ulster [CD].

MORRIS, Elizabeth Georgiana Catherine O'Connor (also known as E. O'Connor Morris), b. probably Blackrock (Co. Dublin) 1861, d. Gortnamona (not 'Gartnamona' as in ODNB; also known as Mount Pleasant, Co. Offaly) 1917. Novelist and short story writer, EGCO'CM was the youngest of five daughters of Judge William O'Connor Morris, who was involved in land rights issues and was a writer of works on history and politics, and Georgiana Kathleen Lindsay. She was a keen student of Irish affairs and a staunch Unionist. In 1880 her father moved the family from Dublin back to Gortnamona. Her short stories appeared in the *Church of Ireland Parish Magazine* (Dublin), the *Fireside*, and the *Church Monthly* (both London). SOURCE Brown, p. 219; Landed gentry, 1904, p. 422; ODNB [under W.O'C. Morris]; W.O'C. Morris, *Memories and thoughts of a life* (London, 1895); Personal communication, Kevin Whelan, April 1993.

M561 *Killeen. A study of girlhood* (by E. O'Connor Morris).
London: Elliot Stock, 1895. SOURCE Brown, 1187; COPAC. LOCATION Dt.
COMMENTARY A romance among upper-class Anglo-Irish and English characters set in 'Killeen Castle', in Queen's County (Co. Laois). The story revolves around misunderstandings that keep lovers apart [Brown].

M562 *Clare Nugent* (by E. O'Connor Morris).
London: Digby, Long & Co., 1902. SOURCE Brown, 1188; COPAC. LOCATION L.
COMMENTARY An Irish girl goes to work in England to restore the fallen fortunes of her family. She succeeds by marrying well [Brown].

M563 *Finola* (by E. O'Connor Morris).
London: Digby, Long & Co., 1910. SOURCE Brown, 1189; COPAC. LOCATION L.
COMMENTARY Set mainly in Dublin in the early-twentieth century. Murrough O'Brien is to get a large inheritance on condition that he marries Finola de Burgh. He consents, but is then ordered to South Africa. On his return he falls in love with a certain Kathleen Burke and resolves to lose his inheritance for her sake. The situation has been planned by the romantic Lady Mary Eustace and revolves around the real identity of Kathleen Burke [Brown].

MOSSE, Mrs —. See MOSSE, Henrietta.

MOSSE, Henrietta (née Rouvière; known as **Henrietta Rouvière, Henrietta Rouvière Mosse** and **Mrs Mosse**), b. Ireland, d. England? 1834. Little is known about romance novelist HM's childhood, but she may have been related to Joseph Rouviere [*sic*], an oculist who lived in 24 Great Ship Street, Dublin. She moved to London, where she wrote eleven novels for the Minerva Press and developed a reputation for work that was both marketable and moral. Her first novel, *A peep at our ancestors* (London, 1807, 4 vols.), initially was to have been published in Dublin, but its sponsors were said to have failed. Before 1812 she married Isaac Mosse, a businessman and author of a work on grammar. Her husband became an invalid by 1822 and her writing provided their financial support. The preface to her *Woman's wit and man's wisdom* (London, 1827, 4 vols.) was signed from Queen Street, Camden-Town, London. Although she received support from the Royal Literary Fund, she died in miserable circumstances and the fund declined to contribute to her burial. Her portrait was published in *A peep at our ancestors* (London, 1807, 4 vols.). For her manuscript letters, see ODNB. SOURCE Allibone, ii, p. 1378; Blain, p. 766; Blakey, p. 224; Garside (2003); M. Lyons (ed.), *The memoirs of Mrs. Leeson* (Dublin, 1995), pp 217, 265; NCBEL 4, pp 964–5; ODNB.

M564 *Lussington Abbey. A novel* (by Henrietta Rouviere [*sic*]).
+ London: William Lane, 1804, 2 vols. SOURCE Blakey, p. 212; Summers, p. 85; British Fiction; Garside, 1804:51. LOCATION Corvey CME 3–628–48348.

COMMENTARY No Irish content. Gothic fiction featuring gloomy castles and sinister abbeys, several perpetually pursued maidens, abductions, escapes, passageways, mild-mannered phantoms and colossal coincidences [ML].

M565 *The heirs of Villeroy. A romance* (by Henrietta Rouvière).
London: Lane, Newman & Co., 1806, 3 vols. (ill.). SOURCE Blakey, p. 215; Summers, p. 86; British Fiction; Garside, 1806:49. LOCATION Corvey CME 3–628–48347–6, O.
COMMENTARY This novel was well-received [ODNB].

M566 *A peep at our ancestors. An historical romance* (by Henrietta Rouvière; dedicated to the late duke of Leinster).
London: Lane, Newman & Co., 1807, 4 vols. (subscribers' list; ill. H.R. Cook, Ramsey). SOURCE Blain, p. 766; British Fiction; Garside, 1807:47; Blakey, p. 224; Garside (2003). LOCATION Corvey CME 3–628–48350–6, L.
COMMENTARY Subscribers' list is predominantly Irish names from Dublin and Irish towns, and includes five members of the La Touche family, the earl of Ormond and the duke of Leinster. Historical fiction. According to the author, the writing of this novel, set in the twelfth century, was aided by 'records and documents', but this is debatable (however, Blain mentions she did research in the British Museum). A thinly-disguised romance novel, it contains many footnotes explaining historical details and relates the adventures of the peerless Adelaide and her suitor, Walter of Gloucester [Blain; ODNB; Summers, p. 177; Garside (2003)].

M567 *The old Irish baronet; or, manners of my country* (by Henrietta Rouvière).
+ London: Lane, Newman & Co., 1808, 3 vols. SOURCE Blakey, p. 226; British Fiction; Garside, 1808:83. LOCATION Corvey CME 628–48349, Ireland related fiction.
COMMENTARY Modelled on Clara Reeve's successful Gothic novel *The old English Baron* (London, 1788) and set in Ireland and on the Continent, particularly Spain, it concerns the lives of Baronet O'Callaghan and his daughter Ellen, whose courtship adventures are described [ML; ODNB].

M568 *Arrivals from India; or, time's a great master. A novel* (by Henrietta Rouvière Mosse, dedicated to the Princess Mary).
London: A.K. Newman & Co., 1812, 4 vols. SOURCE Blakey, p. 237; British Fiction; Garside, 1812:50; ODNB. LOCATION Corvey CME 3–28–48339–5, ViU.

M569 *Craigh-Melrose Priory; or, memoirs of the Mount Linton family. A novel* [anon.]
London: C. Chapple, 1816, 3 vols. SOURCE British Fiction; Garside, 1816:45; NCBEL 4, p. 964. LOCATION Corvey CMH 3–628–47347–0, L.
Paris: Ledoux & Tenré, 1817, 4 vols. (trans. by Jean Cohen as *L'Abbaye de Craigh-Melrose, ou mémoires de la famille de Mont-Linton*). SOURCE Bn-Opale plus. LOCATION BNF.
COMMENTARY ODNB, Block and Summers 2 suggest authorship, but it is debatable that this novel is by HM. The story is a family saga of the Mount Lintons and contains lengthy landscape descriptions and fondness for the picturesque [Frank, 378; Garside; ODNB].

M570 *A bride and no wife. A novel* (by Mrs Mosse, late Henrietta Rouvière).
London: A.K. Newman & Co., 1817, 4 vols. SOURCE British Fiction; Garside, 1817:44; Blakey, p. 257. LOCATION Corvey CME 3–28–48340–9, L.

M571 *A father's love and a woman's friendship; or, the widow and her daughters. A novel* (by Henrietta Rouvière Mosse).
London: A.K. Newman & Co., 1825, 5 vols. SOURCE Blain, p. 766; British Fiction; Garside, 1825:60. LOCATION Corvey CME 3–628–48343–3, L.
COMMENTARY Describes the courtship of four lively sisters and, in letters, their mother's marriage against her rich father's will [Blain].

M572 *Gratitude and other tales* (by Henrietta Rouvière Mosse).
London: A.K. Newman & Co., 1826, 3 vols. SOURCE Blain; British Fiction; Garside, 1826:59. LOCATION Corvey CME 3–628–48346–8, L.

Mount Cashell

M573 *Woman's wit and man's wisdom; or, intrigue. A novel* (by Henrietta Rouvière Mosse). London: A.K. Newman & Co., 1827, 4 vols. SOURCE Blain, p. 766; British Fiction; Garside, 1827:55. LOCATION Corvey CME 3–628–48351–4, L.

M574 *The Blandfords; or, fate and fortune* (by Henrietta Rouviere [*sic*] Mosse). London: A.K. Newman & Co., 1829, 4 vols. SOURCE Blain, p. 766; British Fiction; Garside 1829:61. LOCATION Corvey CME 3–628–48342, L.

MOUNT CASHELL, Margaret Jane, Countess (née King, later known as Mrs Mason), b. Dublin 1771 or 1772, d. Leghorn (Italy) 1835. Novelist, short story and miscellaneous writer, MJMC was the eldest daughter of Robert, 2nd Viscount Kingsborough (later 2nd earl of Kingston), of Mitchelstown Castle (Co. Cork) and Caroline Fitzgerald. Mary Wollstonecraft was her governess in 1786 and 1787 and spoke highly of her. Wollstonecraft may have influenced her pupil with her enlightened views on education and women's rights. MJMC learned French and Italian and was fluent in German, Latin and Greek, and later in life translated from German. Lady Moira, a patron of Irish literature, encouraged her to read widely in Irish history. She married in 1791 Stephen Moore, 2nd earl of Mount Cashell, and lived with her husband at Moore Park (Co. Cork) and at Mount Cashell House on St Stephen's Green in Dublin. During this period of her life she met some liberals and radicals and became a supporter of the United Irishmen. Unusual for a woman of her time, she wrote several pamphlets against the Union, including *A hint to the inhabitants of Ireland* (Dublin, 1800), which expressed a strong sense of Irish nationality. In 1801 she and her husband travelled through France and Italy. In Rome, she met George William Tighe (of the Rossana, Co. Wicklow branch of that family) and, her marriage not being a success, she parted from her husband on their journey home to Ireland in 1805, being forced to leave her seven children with him. She assumed the name of Mrs Mason and moved with Tighe to London and then to Pisa (Italy) where initially they were short of money, which may have prompted her to publish her first book in 1808. In Pisa she befriended the poet Percy Bysshe Shelley (who wrote of her in his poem 'The sensitive plant') and his wife, Mary, daughter of Mary Wollstonecraft and William Godwin§. In turn, MJMC wrote a poem about Shelley. The adoption of the name Mrs Mason was probably inspired by the main character of that name in Wollstonecraft's children's book, *Original stories from real life* (London, 1788), which was published a year after Wollstonecraft had left Mitchelstown Castle. MJMC studied medicine and ran a dispensary for the poor of Pisa, which led to her writing the pioneering *A grandmother's advice to young mothers on the physical education of children* (London, 1823), reprinted (and probably enlarged) as *Advice to young mothers on the physical education of children* (Florence, 1835), which has been compared as a practical companion volume for children to Wollstonecraft's *The rights of woman* (London, 1792). MJMC organised a literary society, Accademia dei Lunatici, in 1827. She wrote short stories for M.J. and William Godwin's§ juvenile publications. Her husband died in 1822, after which she married Tighe in 1826. They had two daughters. In a family picture done when she was a child, she is shown with a book in her hands. Her portrait in adulthood was published by McAleer. Her manuscripts, formerly the Mount Cashell-Cine papers, are now in the NYPL (Pforzheimer collection). SOURCE Bennett cat. 33/146; Burke's, p. 819; Sir B. Burke & A.P. Burke, *A genealogical and heraldic dictionary of the peerage and baronetage* (London, 1906, 68th edn), p. 1175; Commoners, iii, p. 514; W. Godwin, *Memoirs of the author of A vindication of the rights of woman* (1798, Oxford, 1990), p. 56; E.C. Denlinger, *Before Victoria. Extraordinary women of the British romantic era* (New York, 2005), pp 44–9, 169; R.D. King-Harman, *The Kings, Earls of Kingston* (Cambridge, 1959), pp 125–6; E.C. McAleer, *The sensitive plant. A life of Lady Mount Cashell* (Chapel Hill, NC, 1958); NCBEL 4, p. 1838; O'Toole, pp 156–7; V. Pakenham, *The big house in Ireland* (London, [2000]), p. 111; RIA/DIB [under Margaret

Jane Moore]; T.U. Sadleir (ed.), *An Irish peer on the Continent, 1801–1803* (London, 1920), passim; J. Todd, *Rebel daughters. Ireland in conflict 1798* (London, 2003); J. Todd, 'Ascendancy: Lady Mount Cashell, Lady Moira, Mary Wollstonecraft and the Union pamphlets' in *Eighteenth-Century Ireland*, 18 (2003), pp 98–117; C. Tomlin, introd. to *Maurice, or the fisher's cot*, by Mary Shelley (New York, 1998), which contains MJMC's poem about Shelley.

M575 *Chieftain of Erin. Romance of the time of Queen Elizabeth* (by Lady Margaret Jane Mount Cashell).

COMMENTARY Unpublished historical manuscript novel of three volumes. It is shown on an Italian engraving of 'Mrs. Mason'. Written around 1800, it is set in Elizabethan Ireland and features Irish chieftains who, facing English tyranny, plot the expulsion of the English. The historical details are inspired by the works of Joseph Cooper Walker and Charlotte Brooke§. MJMC abandoned the volume, and looking back on it later, expressed the view that 'the spirit of party ... ran too high and the prejudices of those days were too bitter, to allow such a composition to be viewed with impartial eyes'. Todd suggests that the main Irish lord was modelled on Lord Edward Fitzgerald, the revolutionary who was her personal friend. The story also features an Irishman who is disloyal and treacherous to his clan [McAleer, opp. p. 147; Todd, *Rebel daughters*, passim].

M576 *Selene* (by Lady Margaret Jane Mount Cashell).

COMMENTARY Unpublished manuscript of an utopian novel about an ideal society on the moon. It features a rich boy who is taught by an austere and benevolent tutor. It is set in a classical republican government with a prince chosen by the nobility over age 25 and the plebeians over age 50. The story features a moon man who is appalled by the English legislature [Todd, *Rebel daughters*, pp 115, 156, 167; Todd, Ascendancy, p. 103].

M577 *Stories of old Daniel; or, tales of wonder and delight* [anon.].

+ London: Printed for the proprietors of the Juvenile Library 1808 (ill. S. Springsguth, H. Corbould). SOURCE Osborne, p. 915. LOCATION L, CaOTP, InND Loeber coll.

London: M.J. Godwin, 1810, 2nd edn (as *Stories of old Daniel; or, tales of wonder and delight. Containing narratives of foreign countries and manners, and designed as an introduction to the study of voyages, travels, and history in general*). SOURCE Osborne, p. 916. LOCATION D (1813, 3rd edn), L, CaOTP, InND Loeber coll. (1820, 7th edn).

[Toronto]: S.R. Publishers & Johnson Reprint Corp., 1969. SOURCE Osborne, p. 916. LOCATION CaOTP.

COMMENTARY A fourteenth edn appeared in 1868. Moral stories for juveniles wrongly advertised by Godwin as by Charles Lamb. Old Daniel, the principal storyteller, was probably patterned on a retired soldier who apparently lived at the green of Kingston College in Mitchelstown, home to decayed gentlemen and gentlewomen. Contents: 'The church-yard', 'The robbers' cave', 'The same continued', 'The bog-trotter', 'The fortunate reproof', 'Father Giacomo', 'The same concluded', 'The little pedlar', 'The man-hater', 'The passing of the Pyrenean mountains', 'Dog Trusty's ancestor' (probably a reference to 'The little dog Trusty', a story by Maria Edgeworth's *The parent's assistant*, London, 1796, 3 vols.), 'The boy who was forgot at school', 'The man-hater resumed', 'The same concluded' [RL; Jarndyce cat 106/922].

M578 *Continuation of the stories of old Daniel; or, tales of wonder and delight. Containing narratives of foreign countries and manners, designed as an introduction to the study of voyages, travels, and history in general* [anon.].

London: M.J. Godwin, 1820 (ill. S. Springsguth). SOURCE Osborne, p. 915; Ximenes cat. 58/732; OCLC. LOCATION L, CaOTP.

Boston: Munroe & Francis, [1816–24] (as *Stories of Old Daniel*; ill.). SOURCE Advertised in Mrs S.C. Hall, *The private purse* (New York, 1850); RLIN. LOCATION Free Library of Philadelphia.

COMMENTARY Children's stories. In the introd., William Godwin§ stated that he doubted whether two stories, 'The murderer', and 'The blind man', 'might not be thought too horrible for a publication of this nature ...' [Osborne, p. 915].

M579 *The sisters of Nansfield. A tale for young women* [anon.].
+ London: Longman, Hurst, Rees, Orme, Brown & Green, 1824, 2 vols. SOURCE McAleer, p. 188. LOCATION Corvey CME 3–628–48749–8.

M580 *Stories for little boys and girls, in words of one syllable* [anon.].
London: M.J. Godwin, [1810–26]. Source McAleer, p. 172. LOCATION Smith College (Northampton, MA).
London: J. Harris & Son, 1824 (new edn; ill.). SOURCE COPAC. LOCATION L, C.
COMMENTARY 34pp for 1824 edn [COPAC].

MOUNTPLEASANT, J.J.R., fl. 1831. Historical novelist. Probably a pseud., named after Mountpleasant Avenue, Rathmines (Dublin), or a country seat of that name. SOURCE RL.

M581 *William Clarke. A story of ninety eight* (by J.J.R. Mountpleasant).
London: [publisher?], 1831. SOURCE B. Browne.
COMMENTARY No copy located. Concerns Billy Byrne of Ballymanus and guerrilla leader Michael Dwyer during the 1798 rebellion [B. Browne; RL].

MOUNT SANDFORD, George Sandford, 3rd baron, b. Ireland? 1756, d. Stowey Mead (Som.) 1846. Attributed author, GSMS was the third son of Henry Sandford and Sarah, daughter of 1st Viscount Mount Cashell. He was sometime captain of the 18th Dragoons and was MP for Roscommon (1783–97 and 1798–99). His elder brother, who had been created Baron Mount Sandford of Castlerea in 1800, died in 1814. GSMS succeeded to the title and the estate of Castlereagh (Co. Roscommon; the house since demolished) after the death of his nephew, the 2nd Baron Mount Sandford in 1828. He also had an English residence at Stowey Mead. Mrs Charlotte Elizabeth Tonna§ became acquainted with him when she was in Ireland and in 1829 dedicated to him her *The Rockite. An Irish story* (London, 1829). He probably was the same person who offered to employ her to rewrite a novel he had written previously, but to republish the new version under his name, which she declined (the title of the novel is not known). He died unmarried. SOURCE Charlotte Elizabeth, *Personal recollections* (London, 1843), p. 150, 239–40; CP, ix, p. 363; HIP, vi, p. 233; S. Lewis, *A topographical dictionary of Ireland*. London, 1837, i, pp 306–7; C.G. Luard (ed.), *The journal of Clarissa Trant 1800–1832* (London, 1925), p. 66, 129ff; chapter on 'Charlotte Elizabeth' in [Erskine Neale], *The closing scene* (London, 1848), pp 130–1.

MOWATT, James Alexander, b. Manorhamilton (Co. Leitrim) 1834. Temperance writer and editor, JAM was a reporter for the Cork *Daily Reporter*, the *Belfast News* and the Dublin *Irish Times*. In Dublin he was active in the temperance movement and helped to establish the *Irish Temperance Star* in 1866. He published *The temperance glee book* (New York, 1874), a collection of songs, and travelled in Ireland, England and the US lecturing on temperance. The preface to the following book is signed from Dublin, 4 Feb. 1869. In the US he edited the New Haven (CT) *Commonwealth* and wrote for the Boston *Pilot*. SOURCE BLC; Brown 2, p. 185; O'Donoghue, p. 321; RIA/DIB.

M582 *The autobiography of a brewer's son* (by James Alexander Mowatt; dedicated to the Rt. Hon. Thomas O'Hagan).
+ London: Heywood & Co., 1869. SOURCE Allibone Suppl., ii, p. 1149; Brown 2, 1064.
LOCATION D, L, NUC, InND Loeber coll.
COMMENTARY A temperance tale featuring Timotheus Makedrink, a brewer's son, who is rusticated from TCD on account of a drunken spree. He goes to America, enduring the horrors

of an emigrant ship, which is nearly lost through the drunkenness of the captain and crew. He attends a total abstinence meeting and signs the pledge. While teaching in a school in Maine and taking an active part in the electoral campaign that brings about the liquor laws, he is called home by the death of his father. He returns, converts the family brewery into a linen factory and changes a poverty-stricken and drink-sodden district in the west into a prosperous and temperate community [Brown 2].

MUDDOCK, Joyce Emerson Preston (known as **Joyce Emerson Muddock**), b. Southampton (Hants.) 1843, d. 1934. English novelist and journalist, JEPM was educated partly in India and began work there in a gun foundry. Several of his novels have as background the Indian mutiny of 1857, which he witnessed. He travelled widely in the east, was Swiss correspondent for the London *Daily News*, and was proprietor of a newspaper. Under his pseudonym he wrote about two dozen volumes of crime detection, which were immensely successful, and many other novels with international themes. His autobiography, *Pages from an adventurous life*, appeared in London in 1907. SOURCE Alston, p. 311 (list of novels); Allibone Suppl., ii, p.1150; Brown 2, p. 185; NCBEL 4, p. 1839; Sutherland, pp 448–9; Wolff, iii, pp 171–4.

M583 *Grace O'Malley. An Irish historical romance* (by Joyce Emerson Muddock).
+ London: James Henderson, 1873. SOURCE Brown 2, 1065 (1874 edn); Alston, p. 311.
LOCATION L.
COMMENTARY Historical fiction set in the sixteenth century. Based on the career of the historical heroine, the pirate queen of Connacht. Principal personages: Grania (i.e. Grace) herself, Hubert Dillon (her husband), Sir Conyers Clifford and Thomas Radcliffe (earl of Sussex and chief governor of Ireland) [Brown 2].

M584 *The two Queens. A sequel to Grace O'Malley* (by Joyce Emerson Muddock).
London: Henderson, 1874. SOURCE Brown 2, 1066. LOCATION L.
COMMENTARY A slender thread of historical incident holding together plotting, fighting, romance and revenge. The central incident is Grania's visit to London and her meeting with Queen Elizabeth I. It ends with a highly emotional description of Grania's death and funeral [Brown 2].

MUKINS, Isaac, b. Dublin *c.*1727. Historical novelist, IM was the son of John Mukins, a gentleman, and can be identified with the IM, also known as Meekins, who was admitted at TCD in 1743 at age 16 but does not appear to have obtained a degree. Members of the Mukins family resided in Kilkenny in the eighteenth century. Alderman Isaac Mukins, who died in Kilkenny in 1706, had purchased in 1703 for £45 the large brick mansion in Kilkenny forfeited by Jacobite supporter Michael Rothe who had fled Ireland to join the French service after the Treaty of Limerick (1691). In the dedication to the following work, IM states that this is 'the first Essay of my Pen', with no other works known. SOURCE B & S, p. 573; ODNB [under Michael Rothe]; A. Vicars (ed.), *Index to the prerogative wills of Ireland, 1526–1810* (Dublin, 1897), p. 340.

M585 *The history of Charlotte Villars: A narrative founded on truth. Interspersed with a variety of incidents, instructive and entertaining* [anon.] (dedicated to Viscount Mayo).
London: S. Crowder & H. Woodgate, 1756. SOURCE Raven, 351; Forster, 1937; ESTC t070077. LOCATION L, C.
+ Dublin: Printed [for the author?] by Henry Saunders, 1756 (see Plate 51). SOURCE Raven, 352 (who mentions an incomplete title); Burmester cat. 36/220; ESTC n033063. LOCATION PU, InND Loeber coll.

COMMENTARY The author is identified from the dedication in the London edn. A picaresque, historical novel set in Ireland, London and France during the time of William III. Mr. Villars leaves his Irish estate for England but his ship founders and he is presumed dead. His brother attempts to deprive Mrs Villars of the estate by producing a false will and bringing a lawsuit against her. Together with her daughter Charlotte, she flees the Irish family home for England to fight the lawsuit. Mrs Villars marries a man who hopes that she will regain her estate. He wishes his son to marry Charlotte, but she refuses. She and her mother lose the lawsuit. The new husband dies and Mr Villars, who had not died but had been captured as a slave, reappears on the scene and confronts his brother with his villainy [ML; Burmester cat. 36/220].

MULHOLLAND, Clara, b. Belfast (Co. Antrim), fl. 1878. Catholic novelist and translator, CM was the daughter of Dr Joseph Stevenson Mulholland, and younger sister of the author Rosa Mulholland§. CM left Belfast at an early age and was educated at convents in England and Belgium. She wrote 15 works of fiction, much of it with Catholic overtones, aimed primarily at adolescent girls. Her translations include *The little hunchback* (Dublin, [1884]), from the French of Comtesse de Ségur. She contributed to the *Irish Fireside* (Dublin, 1883–84); a novel 'A perplexing promise' to the *Irish Monthly* (Dublin, 1887), and a short story 'Ma[e]ve's repentance' to *A round table of the representative Irish and English Catholic novelists* (New York, Cincinnati, Chicago, 1897). SOURCE Allibone Suppl., ii, p. 1154; Brown, p. 220; Field Day, iv, p. 1142; Murphy, pp 26, 158; NCBEL 4, p. 1839; RIA/DIB; RL; Rowan cat. 53A/594; Sutherland, p. 450 [under Rosa Mulholland].

M586 *The little bog-trotters; or, a few weeks at Conmore* (by Clara Mulholland).
    + London: Marcus Ward & Co.; Belfast: Royal Ulster Works, 1878. SOURCE Alston, p. 311; Brown, 1192. LOCATION L.
    + Baltimore: John Murphy & Co., 1892 (as *The little bog-trotters or, a few days at Conmore*; ill.). SOURCE Brown, 1192; OCLC. LOCATION D, NUC.
COMMENTARY Fiction for juveniles. Elsie's father is to remarry and Elsie is looking forward to having a stepmother. During her parents' honeymoon, Elsie visits her cousins in Ireland, where she has many adventures [Brown].

M587 *Naughty Miss Bunny* (by Clara Mulholland).
    + London, Glasgow, Edinburgh, Dublin: Blackie & Son, 1883 (ill.). LOCATION DPL.
    + London, Glasgow, Edinburgh, Dublin: Blackie & Son, [1904] (as *Naughty Miss Bunny: A story for little children*; ill.). LOCATION NUC, InND Loeber coll.
    New York: The Catholic Publication Society, [1887?]. SOURCE DCU, Catholic Americana files.
COMMENTARY Fiction for juveniles. A story about a young girl, Bunny, who is very spoiled. While holidaying at the seaside, a cousin comes to join her and slowly helps to change Bunny's behaviour [ML].

M588 *Linda's misfortunes, and Little Brian's trip to Dublin* (by Clara Mulholland).
    + Dublin: M.H. Gill & Son, 1885. SOURCE Brown, 1195 (1892 edn); Alston, p. 311. LOCATION D (1924 edn), DPL (1904 edn), L, InND Loeber coll. (also n.d. edn).
    New York: The Catholic Publication Society, [1887?]. SOURCE DCU, Catholic Americana files.
COMMENTARY No copy of the New York edn located. Consists of two stories for children: 'Linda's misfortunes' (set in England and tells how two little girls come to terms with a new stepmother), and 'Little Brian's trip to Dublin' (set in Ireland and tells the story of a little boy from Co. Wicklow who goes to Dublin to beg so that he can help his mother pay the rent. While in Dublin, he is taken up by a deranged rich girl who thinks that Brian is her lost brother. She dies, but her father settles some money on Brian) [ML].

M589 *The miser of King's Court* (by Clara Mulholland).
London: Burns & Oates, [1887]. SOURCE Alston, p. 311. LOCATION L.
New York: The Catholic Publication Society, [1887?]. SOURCE DCU, Catholic Americana files.
COMMENTARY No copy of the New York edn located [RL].

M590 *Percy's revenge. A story for boys* (by Clara Mulholland).
Dublin: M.H. Gill & Son, 1887. SOURCE Alston, p. 311. LOCATION L (destroyed).
Boston: Thomas B. Noonan & Co., 1887. SOURCE DCU, Catholic Americana files; OCLC. LOCATION CLU.
COMMENTARY Fiction for juveniles. No copy of Dublin edn located [RL].

M591 *The strange adventures of little snowdrop, and other tales* (by Clara Mulholland).
London: R. Washbourne, 1889. SOURCE Brown, 1191 (who mentions a slightly different title); Alston, p. 311. LOCATION L.
Boston: Noonan & Co., 1885 (*as Adventures of a little snowdrop, and other stories. A book for girls*). LOCATION NUC.
COMMENTARY Stories for children. Contents: 'The strange adventures of little snowdrop' (set in Killiney, near Dublin, tells of a child kidnapped by the gypsies), 'The tale of a green coat', 'A bunch of violets', 'Lazy Nancy' [ML; Brown].

M592 *Kathleen Mavourneen* (by Clara Mulholland).
Baltimore: John Murphy & Co., 1890. SOURCE Brown, 1194; DCU, Catholic Americana files; Sutherland, p. 450. LOCATION NUC.
COMMENTARY Fiction for juveniles. A cruel Donegal landlord, fearing that his son is getting attached to Kathleen Burke, daughter of a poor tenant, evicts her mother. The blow kills her mother and Kathleen goes as a governess to London. There she meets again the landlord's son who has seen the errors of his father's ways and who enters parliament. In the end both father and son become Catholics and all ends well [Brown].

M593 *Little merry face and his crown of content, and other tales* (by Clara Mulholland).
London: Burns & Oates, [1895]. SOURCE Alston, p. 311; NCBEL 4, p. 1839. LOCATION L.
COMMENTARY Fiction for juveniles [RL].

M594 *A striking contrast* (by Clara Mulholland).
+ Dublin: M.H. Gill & Son, 1895. SOURCE Alston, p. 312 ([1895] edn). LOCATION D (n.d. edn), DPL (n.d. edn), L, InND Loeber coll.
COMMENTARY Fiction for juveniles first published in the *Irish Monthly* (Dublin, 1890). Sylvia and Nora, while travelling from Australia to England, are involved in a shipwreck near the English coast. Sylvia's governess and Nora are rescued, but Sylvia is nowhere to be found. The governess does not dare let her employer know that Sylvia has disappeared and she presents Nora as Sylvia to Sylvia's grandfather. Sylvia, however, has survived and the story deals with the eventual revelation of the deception and Nora's usurpation of Sylvia's place [ML; Murphy, p. 158].

M595 *Dimplings' success* (by Clara Mulholland).
New York, Cincinnati: Benziger Bros, 1901. SOURCE Brown, 1193 (n.d. edn). LOCATION NUC.
COMMENTARY Fiction for juveniles. Dimpling O'Connor not only wins her stern old grandfather's heart, but wins him to the Catholic church [Brown].

M596 *Bunt and Bill* (by Clara Mulholland).
New York, Cincinnati: Benziger Bros, [1902]. LOCATION NUC.

M597 *The lost chord. A story for girls* (by Clara Mulholland).
+ London, Glasgow: Collins, [1905] (ill. Miss Clarke). LOCATION D, NUC.

+ London, Glasgow: Collins, n.d. (as *The lost chord*; ill.). LOCATION D.
COMMENTARY Fiction for juveniles [RL].

M598 *In a roundabout way. A story* (by Clara Mulholland).
+ London, Glasgow: R. & T. Washbourne; New York, Cincinnati, Chicago: Benziger
Bros, 1908. SOURCE Brown, 1196. LOCATION D, NUC.
COMMENTARY A failed plot to defraud an orphan girl of her inheritance. Scenes are
set in London and Co. Donegal [Brown].

M599 *Terence O'Neill's heiress* (by Clara Mulholland).
+ Dublin: Browne & Nolan, 1909 (ill. C.A. Mills). SOURCE Brown, 1197. LOCATION
D, NUC ([1910] edn).
COMMENTARY Fiction for juveniles. A young girl is left an orphan with no provision for her
upkeep. She is cared for by generous relatives, whom she strives to repay in their hour of
need. She is suspected of a theft and is vindicated only after much sorrow [Brown].

M600 *Sweet Doreen* (by Clara Mulholland).
London: Washbourne, 1915. SOURCE Brown, 1198.
COMMENTARY No copy located. Fiction for juveniles. A landlord's agent urges the local priest
in Ballygorst to go to Dublin to try to get the landlord to do something for his tenants, who
are extremely poor and miserable. Although the landlord is respectful, he is not willing to
help. Just as Fr Ryan is leaving, the landlord's daughter and her American friend come in.
The girls persuade him to go with them to Ballygorst where they all meet the peasants and
try to do good [RL; Brown].

MULHOLLAND, Rosa (Lady Gilbert), pseud. '**Ruth Murray**', b. Belfast 1841, d. Dublin
1921. Novelist, poet and children's writer, RM was the second daughter of Dr Joseph Stevenson
Mulholland and sister of Clara Mulholland§. After her father's death, the family spent some
years in Letterfrack (Co. Galway), which provided background for some of her later work.
Educated at home, RM later studied at the South Kensington School of Art in London. Fr
Matthew Russell, founder of the Dublin *Irish Monthly*, noted that RM's first prose story printed
in London was 'My first picture', which appeared in *London Society*. Many of her early stories
appeared in Charles Dickens's London-based *Household Words* and *All the Year Round* and as
early as 1864 she had a comic story 'Mrs Archie' published in *Cornhill Magazine* (London). She
contributed a story to *Now-a-Days* (Dublin, 1874) and published 'Letters from the South of
Ireland' in the *Irish Monthly* (Aug.–Sept. 1881). Her stories celebrate female independence and
are heavily religious, without being anti-Protestant. Her later work was directed at the young
girl reader. William Butler Yeats§ included several of her stories in *Representative Irish Tales*
(New York, 1891) and described her as 'the novelist of contemporary Catholic Ireland' (Field
Day, iv, p. 1138). She published over 40 works of fiction. In addition to contributing to a vari-
ety of periodicals, she wrote poetry, at least one play, and many small books for the *Catholic
Truth Society*. In 1891 she married John Thomas Gilbert (later knighted), the Irish historian
and secretary of the Public Record Office of Ireland. They lived at Villa Nova in Blackrock (Co.
Dublin). He died in 1898 and she wrote his biography, *Life of Sir John T. Gilbert* (London,
1907). RM was a supporter of the suffragette movement and her writing influenced younger
Catholic writers, including Katharine Tynan§. Many of her letters are in the NLI (MS 8,615).
SOURCE Allibone Suppl., ii, p. 1154; Blain, p. 774; Boylan, p. 258; Brown, p. 221; V. Blain, P.
Clements, & I. Grundy, *The feminist companion to literature in English* (New Haven, CT, 1990);
Colman, pp 162–3; Clyde, pp 137–8; EF, p. 151; Field Day, iv, pp 1137–8, 1142, v, p. 929;
Hogan, pp 261–2; Hogan 2, pp 479–80 [under Gilbert]; IBL, 8 (1921), pp 21–2; Irish pseudo-
nyms; Jesuit archives, Leeson St., Dublin, Matthew Russell papers, J27/106; McVeagh, p. 104;
Murphy, p. 16; NCBEL 4, p. 1839; K. & C. Ó Céirín, *Women of Ireland* (Kinvara, 1996); OCIL,

p. 380; O'Donoghue, p. 161 [under Gilbert]; E. Reilly, p. 248; RIA/DIB; Sutherland, p. 245 [under Gilbert], p. 450 [under Mulholland]; Wilson, p. 371.

M601   *Dunmara* (by 'Ruth Murray').
> London: Smith, Elder & Co., 1864, 3 vols. SOURCE Brown, 1199. LOCATION L, C.
> London: Burns & Oates, 1907 (as *The story of Ellen*). SOURCE Brown, 1214; Hogan, p. 262. LOCATION L.
> + New York, Cincinnati, Chicago: Benziger Bros, n.d. (as *The story of Ellen*, ill. T.B.). LOCATION DCU.
> COMMENTARY Ellen is wrecked on the Irish coast and taken into the family of Mr Aungier of Dunmara Castle. The household has some strange inmates. A will is discovered making Ellen heiress of Dunmara. The will also reveals that Ellen is the daughter of a man who was slain by Mr Aungier. Mr Aungier asks Ellen to marry him, but the revelations of the will keeps them apart for a while. In the end they are married [Brown].

M602   *Hester's history* [anon.].
> London: Chapman & Hall, 1869, 2 vols. SOURCE Brown, 1200; Hogan, p. 262. LOCATION L.
> COMMENTARY A love story set in the glens of Antrim and in London at the time of the Act of Union in 1800. It describes incidents of the rebellion of 1798. The story was written at the request of Charles Dickens for *All the Year Round* (London) [Brown].

M603   *The wicked woods of Tobereevil* (by Rosa Mulholland).
> London: Chapman & Hall, 1872, 2 vols. SOURCE Hogan, p. 262. LOCATION L.
> + London: Burns & Oates, [1897] (as *The wicked woods*; ill.). SOURCE Brown, 1219; IBL, 13 (1921), p. 22. LOCATION D, Dt, NUC.
> Boston: J.R. Osgood & Co., 1873. SOURCE DCU, Catholic Americana files. LOCATION NUC.
> COMMENTARY First published in Dickens's *All the Year Round* (London), the novel has supernatural touches. A curse, which had been uttered against a family by poor peasants who had been dispossessed, wreaked ruin for many generations. The last representative of the family, although wholly unlike his ancestors, falls under its influence and the story tells how he escapes from terrible trials [RL; Brown; Wilson, p. 371].

M604   *The little flower seekers: being adventures of Trot and Daisy in a wonderful garden by moonlight* (by Rosa Mulholland; dedicated to Tarl and Eily).
> + London, Belfast: Marcus Ward & Co., [1873] (ill. W.H. Fitch, W. French, F.E. Hulme; Juvenile Gift Books). SOURCE Alston, p. 312; *Irish Monthly* (1874), p. 61. LOCATION DPL, D, L, NUC.
> COMMENTARY Christmas stories for juveniles, consisting of two parts: 'Midsummer's eve' and 'Midsummer's night', with stories in each [RL].

M605   *Puck and blossom, a fairy tale* (by Rosa Mulholland; dedicated to Cyril and Sweeto).
> + London, Belfast: Marcus Ward, [1874] (ill. [attributed to Kate Greenaway]). SOURCE Emerald Isle cat. 87/937; Mott cat. 197/234. LOCATION D, NUC.
> COMMENTARY Fiction for juveniles [RL].

M606   *Eldergowan; or, twelve months of my life, and other tales* (by Rosa Mulholland).
> + London: Marcus Ward & Co.; Belfast: Royal Ulster Works, 1874 (ill.). SOURCE Brown, 1201. LOCATION D, L, NUC, InND Loeber coll. (1875 edn).
> COMMENTARY Contents: 'Eldergowan', 'Mrs. Archie' (first appeared in *Cornhill Magazine*, London, 1864), 'Little Peg O'Shaughnessy' [ML; Blain].

M607   *Five little farmers* (by Rosa Mulholland).
> London, Belfast: Marcus Ward & Co., 1875. SOURCE Hogan, p. 262 (1876 edn); OCLC. LOCATION L.

M608 *Four little mischiefs* (by Rosa Mulholland).
+ London, Glasgow, Edinburgh, Dublin: Blackie & Son, 1883 (ill.). SOURCE Brown, 1202. LOCATION D, L, InND Loeber coll. ([1902 or later] edn).
Chicago: Donahue & Co., [189?]. LOCATION NUC.
COMMENTARY Fiction for juveniles. Adventures of four London children who have been sent to a farm to recover strength after the mumps. The story focuses on building character [ML; Brown].

M609 *The wild birds of Killeevy* (by Rosa Mulholland).
+ London: Burns & Oates & Washbourne, [1883]. SOURCE Brown, 1203; Hogan, p. 262. LOCATION D, DPL, L, NUC, InND Loeber coll. (n.d., 4th edn).
New York: The Catholic Publication Society, [1890?]. SOURCE DCU, Catholic Americana files.
COMMENTARY RM states in the preface that, 'At the present moment when the Irish peasant is under a terrible cloud, it may not be uninteresting to some readers to get a glimpse of him from a favourable point of view'. Set in Killeevy, which is an Irish-speaking district where people treasure their Irish manuscripts. Kevin and Fanchea are peasant playmates. Kevin is dull at his books, but full of the love of nature. Fanchea is fairy-like. One day she is stolen by the gypsies and ends up in the upper stratum of society. Kevin goes out into the world to look for her. He becomes educated and writes poetry. After a number of years they meet again [Brown; Hogan 2, pp 479–80; Murphy, p. 33].

M610 *Hetty Gray; or, nobody's bairn* (by Rosa Mulholland).
London, Glasgow, Edinburgh, Dublin: Blackie & Son, 1884. SOURCE Hogan, p. 262. LOCATION D (n.d. edn), DPL (n.d. edn), L, InND Loeber coll. (n.d. edn).
New York: Scribner & Welford, [1889?]. SOURCE DCU, Catholic Americana files. LOCATION NUC.
New York: Vatican Library Co., [1890?]. SOURCE DCU, Catholic Americana files. LOCATION InND.
COMMENTARY Fiction for juveniles. Set in England, where a little baby is washed ashore and found by peasants, Mr Kane and his wife. Hetty grows up happily until she comes to the attention of a rich woman, who takes her to live with her. She spoils her, but when she dies she leaves her nothing. Relatives of the rich woman take her in, not to treat her as one of the family, but to train her to become a governess. She gets re-acquainted with Mr and Mrs Kane, and slowly learns humility. A rich visitor determines that Hetty is her lost sister. Hetty goes to live with her sister in London and does not need to become a governess [ML].

M611 *The walking trees, and other tales* (by Rosa Mulholland).
+ Dublin: M.H. Gill & Son, 1885 (ill. W.O.M.). SOURCE Brown, 1204. LOCATION D, L, NUC (1897 edn).
COMMENTARY Contents: 'The walking trees', 'Little Queen Pet and her kingdom', 'The girl from under the lake', 'Floreen's golden hair' [ML].

M612 *Marcella Grace. An Irish novel* (by Rosa Mulholland).
+ London: Kegan Paul, Trench & Co., 1886. SOURCE Brown, 1205. LOCATION D, Dt (1898 edn), L.
+ London: Kegan Paul, Trench, Trübner & Co., n.d. (new edn; ill.). LOCATION D.
+ Braunschweig: Grüneberg, 1891 (trans. as *Marcella Grace*). LOCATION D.
New York: Harper & Bros, 1886. SOURCE DCU, Catholic Americana files. LOCATION NUC.
Philadelphia: H.L. Kilner, [18??] (as *Marcella Grace*). LOCATION NUC.
COMMENTARY An historical tale with an elaborate plot in which the evils of landlordism and Fenianism are dwelt upon, it was first published in the *Irish Monthly* (Dublin, 1885). A pop-

ular story, it highlights the changes in a nationalist's attitudes on becoming a landowner. The Phoenix Park murders (1882) are mentioned. The main character is Bryan Kilmartin who, as a youth, becomes interested in the sufferings of the people and joins the Fenian movement. Later he goes to Cambridge where education makes him realize that nothing can be obtained by rebellion. He withdraws from the Fenian organization, but the Fenians mark him for destruction for his action, and Kilmartin is convicted of murder [Brown; Field Day, v, pp 926, 929; Kelley, p. 193].

M613 *The late Miss Hollingford* (by Rosa Mulholland).

+ London, Glasgow, Edinburgh, Dublin: Blackie & Son, [1886] (ill. E.L. Willson). SOURCE Wolff, 4980. LOCATION D, DPL (n.d. edn), L, NUC (n.d. edn), InND Loeber coll.

New York: G. Munro, [1887] (Seaside Library Pocket Edition, No. 921). SOURCE DCU, Catholic Americana files. LOCATION L, NUC.

COMMENTARY Fiction for juveniles [RL].

M614 *A fair emigrant. A novel* (by Rosa Mulholland).

+ London: Kegan Paul, Trench & Co., 1888 (ill.). SOURCE Brady, p. 90; Brown, 1206 (1889 edn); Hogan, p. 262. LOCATION D, L, NUC.

Dublin: M.H. Gill, [1920s]. SOURCE Rowan cat. 34/1082.

COMMENTARY *Dublin edn* No copy located other than the one listed by Rowan [RL].

New York: D. Appleton & Co., [1889]. SOURCE DCU, Catholic Americana files. LOCATION NUC.

Philadelphia: H.L. Kilner, n.d. LOCATION D.

COMMENTARY A love story set in the 1870s initially in rural America and then on the north coast of Co. Antrim. The heroine is an only daughter whose mission in life is to clear her dead father's reputation. It describes the landlord class and discusses the vexed social and economic questions of the day [Brown].

M615 *Giannetta. A girl's story of herself* (by Rosa Mulholland).

+ London, Glasgow, Edinburgh, Dublin: Blackie & Son, 1889 (ill. Lockhart Bogle). SOURCE Brown, 1208. LOCATION D, L, NUC.

New York: Scribner & Welford, 1889. SOURCE DCU, Catholic Americana files. LOCATION NUC.

COMMENTARY A story for girls. Giannetta, an Italian girl, is claimed by an Irish gentleman as his long lost daughter. She comes to Ireland where she does much good. Eventually it turns out that she is not the true heiress and she becomes an artist. An eviction scene, based on the well-known Glenbeigh (Co. Kerry) evictions, is incorporated in the story. During the evictions, some of the landed gentry side with the tenants [Brown; Murphy, p. 41].

M616 *Kathleen's motto* (by Rosa Mulholland).

New York: Vatican Library Co., [1890?]. SOURCE DCU, Catholic Americana files.

COMMENTARY No copy located, and the attribution solely rests with the DCU, Catholic Americana files. Note that a novel *Kathleen's motto; or, the sea king* by one 'S.D.B.'§ was published in Barnet [London] in 1898 [RL].

M617 *Hetty Gray; or, nobody's bairn, and The late Miss Hollingford* (by Rosa Mulholland).

Baltimore: McCauley & Kilner, [189—?]. LOCATION NUC.

COMMENTARY Republication of *Hetty Gray; or, nobody's bairn* (London, 1884) and *The late Miss Hollingford* (London, [1886]) [RL].

M618 *The victor's laurel* (by Rosa Mulholland).

New York: Vatican Library Co., 1889. SOURCE DCU, Catholic Americana files; OCLC. LOCATION Fordham Univ.

Mulholland

M619 *The haunted organist of Hurly Burly, and other stories* (by Rosa Mulholland).
+ London: Hutchinson & Co., 1891 (Idle Hours Series). SOURCE Alston, p. 312; Wolff, 4979; COPAC. LOCATION L, NUC (1901 edn).
COMMENTARY Supernatural tales: 'The haunted organist of Hurly Burly', 'The ghost of the rath', 'The country cousin', 'The hungry death' (first published in W.B. Yeats§ (ed.) *Representative Irish tales* (New York & London, 1891, republished with changes in the *Irish Monthly* (Dublin, June–July, 1914)), 'Krescenz', 'A strange love story', 'The signor John', 'The fit of Ailsie's shoe', 'A will o' the wisp', 'The ghost of wildwood chase'. Wolff say this volume was edited by Alfred Miles, but is not evident from the copy in the BL [Field Day, v, pp 925, 959–66 ('The hungry death'); ML; Wolff; Wilson, p. 371].
M620 *The mystery of Hall-in-the-Wood* (by Rosa Mulholland).
London: Sunday School Union, [1893]. SOURCE Hogan, p. 262. LOCATION D (n.d. edn), L.
M621 *Marigold and other stories* (by Rosa Mulholland).
+ Dublin: Eason & Son; London: Simpkin, Marshall, Hamilton, Kent & Co., 1894. SOURCE Hogan, p. 262; Topp 8, 1303. LOCATION D, L.
London: Catholic Truth Society, 1901. LOCATION NUC.
COMMENTARY Contents: 'Marigold', 'The mystery of Ora', 'Mr. Hansard's ward', 'The story of a poor relation', 'Molly the tramp', 'Maureen Lacey', 'The five cobblers of Brescia'. The stories were published separately for the *Catholic Truth Society* in about 1901 [ML].
M622 *Banshee Castle* (by Rosa Mulholland).
+ London, Glasgow, Edinburgh, Dublin: Blackie & Son, 1895 (ill. John H. Bacon). SOURCE Hogan, p. 262. LOCATION D, L, NUC ([1894] edn).
+ London, Glasgow, Bombay: Blackie & Son, [1925] (as *The girls of Banshee Castle*: ill. John H. Bacon). SOURCE Brown, 1207 (mistakenly mentions 1894 edn under this title). LOCATION D, Dt, DPL, L, NUC, InND Loeber coll.
COMMENTARY Three girls have been brought up in London by a governess, who is more like a grandmother to them. They inherit a very small sum of money and come to Galway to occupy a castle, pending the discovery of their half-brother, the missing heir. The latter arrives and although he turns out to be only a very distant relation he has indeed inherited the title. Their actual half-brother had been a wastrel and had died of consumption. Seeing a chance of easing the girls' lives, he lets them believe that he is the long-lost brother. The truth comes out, and he disappears in disgrace for a while. In the end he is forgiven and he marries one of the girls. Interwoven with the story are various fairy and folk tales, collected by one of the sisters. There is also a description of the establishing of a model fishing community on a small island [ML].
M623 *Our own story and other tales* (by Rosa Mulholland).
+ London: Catholic Truth Society, [1896]. SOURCE Hogan, p. 262; Brown, 1222. LOCATION L, NUC.
COMMENTARY Contents: 'Our own story', 'The rescue of Madge O'Driscoll', 'A home across the ocean', 'Bet's match-making', 'That snowy Christmas', 'Sketched from life', 'An angel's visit', 'In a forest country', 'Jim Riley's luck' [NUC].
M624 *Nanno, a daughter of the State* (by Rosa Mulholland).
+ London: Grant Richards, 1899. SOURCE Brown, 1209; Daims, 1171. LOCATION Dt, L, NUC, InND Loeber coll.
COMMENTARY A rural love story centring on a young girl, Nanno, who was born in a Dublin workhouse, is saved from the degradation of the workhouse by kind country people, from whom she learns morality and self-sacrifice [Burmester list].
M625 *Onora* (by Rosa Mulholland).
London: Grant Richards, 1900. SOURCE Brown, 1210. LOCATION L, NUC.

London, Edinburgh: Sands & Co., 1915 (as *Norah of Waterford*). SOURCE Brown, 1226. LOCATION L, InND Loeber coll. (1927, 2nd impr.).

+ New York: P.J. Kenedy, 1915 (as *Norah of Waterford*). LOCATION D, NUC.

COMMENTARY A story of country life in Co. Waterford in the days of the Land League. It contains eviction scenes and shows life in the huts of Land Leaguers on the Ponsonby estate. The daughter of the evicted family goes into service with the Aherne family. Joe Aherne falls in love with Norah, but his mother wants him to marry for money Sabina Doolan, who is much older than he is, but who has returned rich from the US. Norah's father wants her to marry the gombeen man, the local moneylender, to avert further ruin. Eventually Norah's noble character makes Sabina give up her designs on Joe, and she furthers Joe and Norah's happiness [Brown].

M626 *Dympna Tyrconnell* (by Rosa Mulholland).
+ Dublin: Educational Co. of Ireland, 1900 (ill.). LOCATION D (n.d. edn), SUNY at Buffalo.

M627 *Cynthia's bonnet shop* (by Rosa Mulholland).
London, Glasgow, Edinburgh, Dublin: Blackie & Son, 1900. SOURCE Brown, 1211; OCLC. LOCATION D, L (1901 edn), Boston Public Library, InND Loeber coll. (n.d. edn).

COMMENTARY Widow Mrs M'Shane O'Naughten lives with her three daughters, Cynthia, Befind, and Morrie, in reduced circumstances in the west of Ireland. Their father's sister is quite rich but looks down on her poor relatives and does not support them. When the three girls prepare to visit her, Cynthia has no hat and makes one out of heather and feathers. The aunt admires it and tells Cynthia that she could make a fortune as a milliner in London. A guest of the aunt, Professor Anstruther, overhears the conversation and copies part of it in a letter to his friend Mr Bartram. Befind, an amateur astronomer, is very interested in Professor Anstruther. Cynthia frets how she can ease her mother's life as she has no opportunities to earn any money. One day an anonymous letter arrives with a large sum of money for Cynthia to start a bonnet shop in London. Cynthia and Befind set off for London, and the shop is a huge success. The aunt is indignant that her niece has gone into trade, but when the girls are patronized by high society, she softens somewhat. Cynthia speculates about who the anonymous benefactor could be and comes to the reluctant conclusion that it is her aunt. She makes the acquaintance of Mr Bartram, who is extremely rich and who and falls in love with her. Befind marries the astronomy professor and Mr Bartram, the actual anonymous benefactor, marries Cynthia [ML].

M628 *Terry; or, she ought to have been a boy* (by Rosa Mulholland).
London, Glasgow, Edinburgh, Dublin: Blackie & Son, [1900]. SOURCE Brown, 1212 (1902 edn); Hogan, p. 262. LOCATION L, NUC.

COMMENTARY A children's story set in the west of Ireland. A girl and a boy have various adventures while they are living with their grandmother and their nurse, their parents being away in Africa [Brown].

M629 *The tragedy of Chris. The story of a Dublin flower girl* (by Rosa Mulholland).
London, Edinburgh: Sands & Co., 1903. SOURCE Brown, 1213; Weekes, p. 239. LOCATION L.

+ London, Edinburgh: Sands & Co., n.d. (as *The tragedy of Chris*). LOCATION D.

St Louis: B. Herder, 1904. SOURCE Daims, 1172. LOCATION D (2nd edn).

COMMENTARY The story begins in rural Ireland and describes the friendship between two women who sell flowers. One of them gets into bad company and disappears, to be made a white slave, the other searches all over London for her. She finds her, but in the saddest circumstances [Brown; EF, p. 151; Field Day, iv, pp 827, 1104–5].

Mulholland

M630   *The squire's grand-daughters* (by Rosa Mulholland).
    + London: Burns & Oates; New York, Cincinnati, Chicago: Benziger Bros, 1903.
    SOURCE Hogan, p. 262; Brown, p. 221 (mistakenly mentions 'The squire's grand-
    daughter'). LOCATION L.
    Baltimore: McCauley & Kilner, [1903?] (as *The squire's grand-daughter*). LOCATION
    NUC.

M631   *A mother of emigrants* (by Rosa Mulholland).
    + Dublin: Catholic Truth Society, 1905. LOCATION D.

M632   *A girl's ideal* (by Rosa Mulholland).
    London, Glasgow, Dublin, Bombay: Blackie & Son, 1905 (ill. R. Hope). SOURCE
    Hogan, p. 262; Brown, 1217 (1908 edn). LOCATION D (n.d. edn), L, NUC (n.d. edn).
    New York: Benziger, [1905]. LOCATION NUC.

COMMENTARY A romance featuring Tabby Chaigneau, an American girl of Irish extraction
who inherits an oil fortune, but only permanently if she marries a Dermod MacMurrough,
who lives in Ireland. Both Tabby and Dermod reject this condition, with the result Tabby
will have the use of the fortune for twelve years only. She travels with her aunt to Ireland,
where the first person she meets is Dermod, who is a doctor. They are antagonistic towards
each other. She uses her fortune to do a lot of good and to resurrect her ancestors' poplin factory in the Dublin Liberties. After a number of years, the oil wells stop producing and Tabby
is left with practically no money. At that point, Dermod proposes to her. She is at first reluctant to accept because she feels that a poor wife is a hindrance to his medical career. They
marry, the oil starts to flow again, and she can give Dermod a laboratory to pursue his medical research. The book includes a description of the Dublin Horse Show [ML].

M633   *Our sister Maisie* (by Rosa Mulholland).
    + London, Glasgow, Dublin, Bombay: Blackie & Son, 1907 (ill. G. Demain Hammond)
    SOURCE Brown, 1215. LOCATION D, L, NUC, InND Loeber coll.

COMMENTARY Maisie, an Irish girl, is the protégée of a rich English woman in Rome. At age
18 she decides to leave and take charge of a large family of stepbrothers and sisters in Ireland,
incurring the displeasure of her protectress. Maisie and her family go to an island off the west
coast, which she owns. They live as frugally as possible. After many adventures the children
develop special aptitudes and put these to use to help the poor islanders. Maisie's admirers
follow her from Rome, and eventually she marries one of them, showing that her self-imposed
exile did not lead to social disadvantage [ML; Brown].

M634   *The return of Mary O'Murrough* (by Rosa Mulholland).
    London, Edinburgh: Sands & Co., 1908. SOURCE Brown, 1218; Hogan, p. 262.
    LOCATION D (1910 edn), L, NUC, InND Loeber coll. (1910 edn).
    + Dublin: Phoenix, n.d. (ill.; The Library of Modern Irish Fiction). LOCATION D,
    InND Loeber coll.

COMMENTARY Set in the mountains above Killarney (Co. Kerry), the story deals with the pain
of depopulation and emigration. Mary O'Murrough had temporarily emigrated to America to
earn money until her fiancée, Shan, and his family would be able to buy the small farm they
are living on. When she comes back she finds Shan in prison on a false charge. Because of
the tough life in America, she has changed so much that none of the villagers recognize her.
Shan's love seems to have disappeared altogether after the shock of seeing her so altered.
However, her good character wins it back [ML].

M635   *Cousin Sara. A story of arts and crafts* (by Rosa Mulholland).
    + London, Glasgow, Edinburgh, Bombay: Blackie & Son, 1909 (ill. Frances Ewan).
    SOURCE Brown, 1216 (mistakenly mentions 1908 edn); Hogan, p. 262; IBL, 8 (1921),
    p. 22. LOCATION D, L, NUC.

COMMENTARY A love story set in the north of Ireland, Italy and London. Sara's father is a retired soldier who has a talent for inventing machinery. One of his inventions is stolen and patented by one whom he had trusted. Sara then shows her true worth [Brown].

M636 *Father Tim* (by Rosa Mulholland).
+ London, Edinburgh: Sands & Co., 1910 (ill.). SOURCE Brown, 1221; Hogan, p. 262. LOCATION DPL (1927 edn), L, NUC, InND Loeber coll. (1927, 2nd impr.).
COMMENTARY The story of a curate who initially works in a parish in the Co. Dublin mountains among poor people, whom he helps with spiritual and temporal problems. He saves a gentleman, at least for a while, from destroying himself with drink. Later he works unceasingly in the Dublin slums [ML].

M637 *The O'Shaughnessy girls* (by Rosa Mulholland).
+ London, Glasgow, Bombay: Blackie & Son, 1911 (ill. G. Demain Hammond). SOURCE Brown, 1220 (mentions perhaps mistakenly 1910 edn); Hogan, p. 262; IBL, 13 (1921), p. 22. LOCATION D, L.
+ New York: Benziger, 1910. LOCATION NUC, InND Loeber coll.
COMMENTARY Set partly by the Blackwater River in Munster and partly in London, the story is about Lady O'Shaughnessy and her two unmarried daughters. Lavender lives at home and takes an interest in Gaelic matters. The other runs away and goes on stage. The search for the runaway and the discovery of the identity of a mysterious young man on the estate constitute the main incidents. The book contrasts the simple virtues of Irish country life with the temptations life in London [Brown; ML].

M638 *Agatha's hard saying* (by Rosa Mulholland).
New York: Benziger Bros, 1912. SOURCE Daims, 1170. LOCATION NUC.

M639 *Fair Noreen. The story of a girl of character* (by Rosa Mulholland).
+ London, Glasgow, Bombay: Blackie & Son, 1912 (ill. G. Demain Hammond). SOURCE Brown, 1223. LOCATION D, L.
+ London, Glasgow, Bombay: Blackie & Son, n.d. (ill. G. Demain Hammond). LOCATION InND Loeber coll.
COMMENTARY Set on the west coast of Ireland where Noreen, a ten-year-old girl, claims to be the daughter of Lord Finbarr, who had gone on a polar expedition and who has since not been heard of. She is brought up by relatives and after many adventures her father returns [Brown].

M640 *Twin sisters. An Irish tale* (by Rosa Mulholland).
London, Glasgow, Bombay: Blackie & Son, 1913 (ill. Frank E. Wiles). SOURCE Brown, 1224 (mentions mistakenly a 1912 edn); Hogan, p. 262; IBL, 13 (1921), p. 22. LOCATION L, NUC.
COMMENTARY Pippa and Sue Hurley, left poorly off, return from Spain to relatives in Ireland. The story tells of the different reactions of the two girls to the life provided for them in Ireland [Brown].

M641 *The Cranberry claimants* (by Rosa Mulholland).
New York: P.J. Kenedy & Sons, [1914]. SOURCE NYPL. LOCATION NN.
+ Dublin, Belfast: Talbot Press, n.d. SOURCE OCLC. LOCATION D, InND Loeber coll.
+ London, Glasgow: Sands & Co., [1932] (ill.). SOURCE Hogan, p. 262. LOCATION DPL, L.
COMMENTARY Set in England, where an uncle claims that his nephew is the heir to an estate while an American woman claims that her niece is the real heiress. The children are taught to hate each other and the villagers also take sides. This situation continues for several years until the boy rescues the girl from drowning. The young people fall in love and when the real claimant appears, everybody seems to be relieved and happy. The boy becomes an engineer, marries his sweetheart, and distinguishes himself in his profession [ML].

'*A Munster Farmer*'

M642   *Old school friends. A tale of modern life* (by Rosa Mulholland).
+ London, Glasgow, Bombay: Blackie & Son, 1914 (ill. G. Demain Hammond).
SOURCE Brown, 1225 (mistakenly mentions 1913 edn); Hogan, p. 262; IBL, 13 (1921), p. 22. LOCATION D, L, NUC.
COMMENTARY Fiction for juveniles. A character study of two girls and the story of their careers. Bridget is Irish, and when her friend Jessica falls on hard times owing to sudden deafness, Bridget invites her to Ireland. Jessica is continuously in difficulties, from which Bridget extricates her [Brown].

M643   *The daughter in possession. The story of a great temptation* (by Rosa Mulholland).
+ London, Glasgow, Bombay: Blackie & Son, 1915 (ill. G. Demain Hammond).
SOURCE Hogan, p. 262. LOCATION D, L, InND Loeber coll.
COMMENTARY The story starts in London where a famous opera singer adopts a girl, Stine, the only survivor of a shipwreck, who lives in the slums with the family of the sailor who rescued her. Stine has a friend, Keefe, a young man whose antecedents are also vague. Stine and Keefe lose track of each other but, after a long series of adventures, they marry [ML].

M644   *Narcissa's ring. The story of a strange quest* (by Rosa Mulholland).
+ London, Glasgow, Bombay: Blackie & Son, 1916 (ill. G. Demain Hammond).
SOURCE Brown, 1227. LOCATION DPL, L.
+ London: Blackie & Son, n.d. (as *Narcissa's ring*; ill. G. Demain Hammond).
LOCATION D.
COMMENTARY The story is set in Ireland, Egypt and Russia. The main characters are in quest of a mysterious perfume [Brown].

M645   *O'Loughlin of Clare* (by Rosa Mulholland).
+ London, Edinburgh: Sands & Co., 1916. SOURCE Brown, 1228; Hogan, p. 262.
LOCATION D, L.
+ New York: P.J. Kenedy & Sons, 1916. LOCATION NUC, InND Loeber coll.
COMMENTARY An historical novel set in Co. Clare around 1746 during the time of the penal laws. Morrogh O'Loghlin is a Catholic gentleman living almost surreptitiously in his Clare home with his daughter Brona, his Frenchified sister and his chaplain. Brona is brought to Dublin by Mrs Delaney, wife of the dean of St Werburgh's, where she meets Hugh Ingoldesby, a Co. Clare landowner of English origin. Differences of religion bar the way to their union. Morrogh's worthless son turns Protestant to gain the family estates, but Ingoldesby intervenes and later, becoming a Catholic, marries Brona [Brown].

'A MUNSTER FARMER', pseud. See O'SULLIVAN, Revd Mortimer.

MURDOCH, John A., fl. 1896. Canadian novelist from Pilot Mount, MB. SOURCE *Literary history of Canada* (Toronto, 1976), i, pp 394–5; RL; Watters, p. 351.
M646   *In the woods and on the waters* (by John A. Murdoch).
+ Winnipeg: Stovel Co., 1896 (ill.). SOURCE Watters, p. 351; OCLC. LOCATION InND Loeber coll., Univ. of British Columbia.
COMMENTARY One of the first Canadian books dealing extensively with natural history, it tells the story of a number of United Empire Loyalists settling in the wilds of eastern Ontario in the second half of the eighteenth century. Among their number is a servant, lately come from Ireland. His ignorance of how to settle in the wilderness provides an opportunity for many explanations and instructions. The settlers are rescued from dangerous situations several times by a hunter who lives alone in the wilderness. For a while, the Irishman attaches himself to the hunter, who falls in love with and marries the daughter of the principal settler [ML].

MURPHY, Anna Brownell. See JAMESON, Anna Brownell.

MURPHY, Arthur, b. Clooniquin (Co. Roscommon) 1727, d. London 1805. Playwright, actor, novelist, theatrical critic and biographer, AM was related through his mother to the French family of Co. Roscommon. His father Richard – who died when he was age 2 – was a Dublin merchant. AM was educated under the name of Arthur French at the English College of St Omer in France. Destined by his maternal uncle, Jeffrey French, MP, for a career in the family business, he was apprenticed in Cork. He moved to London to work in a bank there in 1749. He disliked business, and by refusing to transfer to Jamaica offended his uncle, who later disinherited him. AM's brother, known as James Murphy French, was also a lawyer and although an unsuccessful dramatist, he introduced AM to the world of the London theatre. He became a journalist, actor, theatrical critic, biographer and prolific playwright, contributing to many periodicals, including the *Covent-Garden Journal*, the *Craftsman*, the *Chronicle*, the *Gray's Inn Journal*, and the *Literary Gazette* (all London). He also edited the *Test*, a political journal supporting Henry Fox. His first farce, *The apprentice*, was performed at Drury Lane in Jan. 1756 and his first tragedy, *The orphan of China* in 1759. Many of his dramas were translations and adaptations of French works. After he gave up acting he was admitted at Lincoln's Inn and was called to the Bar in 1762. He combined a successful career in the law with his work as an equally-successful dramatist, best remembered for comedies and dramas, including *The Grecian daughter*, *Know your own mind* and *Zenobia*. He was a friend of Dr Samuel Johnson and of the actor David Garrick, both of whose biographies he wrote, and he edited the works of Henry Fielding and translated from the classics. From 1765 to 1778 and again from 1797 to 1805 he served as a commissioner of bankruptcy. His collected works were published in 1786. For AM's portraits and papers, see ODNB. SOURCE Allibone, ii, pp 1389–90; Brady, p. 171; J.P. Emery, *Arthur Murphy, an eminent dramatist of the eighteenth century* (Philadelphia, 1946); Field Day, i, pp 506, 546–54, 656; Hogan, pp 474–5; Hogan 2, p. 881; OCIL, pp 382–3; ODNB; O'Donoghue, p. 325; RIA/DIB.

M647 *Isabella; or, the memoirs of a coquette* (by Arthur Murphy).
    Dublin: James Hoey, 1761. SOURCE Brown, 1229.
    COMMENTARY No copy located, and not in ESTC. The reminiscences of an elderly lady, who had been an inveterate, though harmless, flirt and had turned over a new leaf in her old age [Brown].

M648 *The triumph of benevolence; or, the history of Francis Wills* [anon.].
    + London: T. Vernor & M. Chater, 1772, 2 vols. SOURCE Block, p. 189; Raven 2, 1772:24; ESTC t138879. LOCATION L.
    Dublin: J. Potts, W. Sleater, D. Chamberlaine, J. Williams, T. Walker & C. Jenkins, 1772, 2 vols. SOURCE Block, p. 197; Raven 2, 1772:24; ESTC n021546. LOCATION Dt (2 vols. in 1).
    Amsterdam: D.K. Changuion, 1773, 2 vols. in 1 (trans. as *Histoire de François Wills, ou le triomphe de la bienfaisance*, by the author of '*Ministre de Wakefield*' [*sic*]). SOURCE Streeter, 388; Raven 2, 1772:24; OCLC. LOCATION C, MH.
    Berlin: Sold by August Mylius, 1786, 2 vols. (as *The triumph of benevolence; or, the history of Francis Wills*, by the author of *The vicar of Wakefield* [*sic*]). SOURCE Maggs cat. 1162/419; GLOL. LOCATION Universitätsbibliothek Hohenheim.
    Breslau, Leipzig: I.F. Korn der älte, 1776 (trans. as *Geschichte des Herrn Franz Wills, Esquire, oder der Triumph der Mildhäertigkeit*, by the author of *Wakefield* [*sic*]). SOURCE Raven 2, 1772:24; GLOL. LOCATION Universitätsbibliothek Hohenheim.
    COMMENTARY Attributed to Arthur Murphy, but according to the BLC has in the past been attributed to Oliver Goldsmith§. No Irish content. The story is set in England and the main character is a son of a well-to-do farmer. It includes a love story [ML].

MURPHY, Con T., b. Ireland 1841, d. United States 1907. Playwright and novelist, CTM emigrated to the US. According to the title page of the following volume, his plays included 'Fairies' well', and 'Killarney' (performed in New York in 1892). SOURCE RL; OCLC.

M649   *The miller of Glanmire. An Irish story* (by Con T. Murphy).
    + Chicago: George W. Baker, 1895 (ill.; The Ivy Leaf Series, No. 1). SOURCE Brown, 1230. LOCATION NUC, InND Loeber coll.

COMMENTARY A story of romance and inheritance set in Glanmire (Co. Cork) at the end of the nineteenth century, centred around a flour mill and an inn. One of the lessees of the flour mill conspires with the innkeeper to break up the relationship between the owner of the mill and her lover. They also try to prove that she should not have inherited the mill. Their various plots are all thwarted [ML].

'**MURPHY, Dennis Jasper**', pseud. See **MATURIN, Charles Robert**.

MURPHY, James, b. Glynn (Co. Carlow) 1839, d. Dublin 1921. Historical novelist, teacher and professor, JM was educated locally and at St Patrick's College, Dublin. He was principal of public schools in Bray (Co. Wicklow), where he was also town clerk. He later was appointed professor of mathematics at the Catholic University, Dublin. He lived at Kingstown (now Dún Laoghaire). He wrote many poems, some of which were collected in *Lays and legends of Ireland* in the 1880s and a few copies published privately. A second volume under the same title was published in 1911. Only a portion of his novels were published; many of them have nationalist themes and some were translated into Irish. He contributed to the *Nation*, the *Shamrock* and *Young Ireland* (all Dublin) and was editor of the *Irish Fireside* (Dublin), and *Irish Bits: A Journal of Irish Story, Romance, and Scenery* (Dublin, 1897–8?), to which he contributed fiction. The title page of *Hugh Roach* (Dublin, *c*.1887) mentions that he also wrote 'Ulic FitzMaurice' and 'Nollie, or the lost treasure', but these have not been located. Similarly, 'The cross of Glencarrig' and 'Maureen's sorrow' are mentioned on the title page of *The forge of Clohogue* (Dublin, 1885), but remain to be located also. SOURCE Allibone Suppl., ii, p.1157 [under J. Murphy]; Brady, p. 172; Brown, p. 226; Hogan 2, p. 883; OCIL, p. 383; O'Donoghue, p. 327; E. Reilly, p. 248; RIA/DIB; Sutherland, p. 451.

M650   *The fortunes of Maurice O'Donnell: An Irish-American story* (by James Murphy; dedicated to Edward Murphy, JP, of Montreal, Canada).
    + Dublin: John Falconer; London: Simpkin, Marshall & Co.; New York: A.E. & R.E. Ford, [1877]. SOURCE Brown, 1237; Topp 8, 824. LOCATION D, DPL, Dcc, L, NUC, InND Loeber coll.

COMMENTARY Published in two binding types: (a) green boards, M.H. Gill on spine, gold-embossed, with gold harp on cover; (b) a yellow-backboards, ill. cover, contents the same, but advertised of James Duffy on inside of cover, which implies that it might have been a reissue. The hero, although innocent, is implicated in an affray between smugglers and revenue officers off the west coast of Ireland and is forced to flee the country. He has many adventures in the American Civil War. Meanwhile his betrothed in Ireland has been abducted and shut up in a lonely tower near the Killaries in Connemara. She escapes, the hero returns, a hidden treasure is discovered, and all ends well. [RL; Brown].

M651   *The forge of Clohogue. A story of the rebellion of '98* (by James Murphy).
    + Dublin: Sealy, Bryers & Walker, 1885. SOURCE Brown, 1234 (1912, 5th edn). LOCATION D, NUC, InND Loeber coll.

COMMENTARY A story of the rebellion of 1798, it opens at Christmas Eve 1797, covers the rebellion of '98, and ends with the battle of New Ross (Co. Wexford). The main character is Col. Walter Malone, who returns to Clohogue after four years' service in the French armies under Napoleon. A dramatized version of the book was first performed in Dublin in 1918. Topp mentions that the volume was a joint publication with the London firm of Simpkin, Marshall & Co., but this has not been located [Brown; Browne; Kelley; Topp 8, p. 99].

M652   *The Shan van Vocht. A tale of '98* (by James Murphy).
        Dublin: M.H. Gill, 1886. SOURCE Brown, 1232 (mentions [1883] edn, but this may be wrong). LOCATION NUC, Wake Forest Univ.
        + Dublin: M.H. Gill & Son, 1889 (new edn, as *The Shan van Vocht. A story of the United Irishmen*; on cover: *The Shan van Vocht*). SOURCE OCLC; Topp 8, 863 (Dublin, London, 1888 edn, but not located). LOCATION D, Dt, L, InND Loeber coll.
COMMENTARY Published in a print run of 2,700 copies. Historical novel of the rebellion of 1798, it tells of Theobald Wolfe Tone's§ negotiations in Paris leading to the various attempted French invasions of Ireland, including the defeat of Admiral Bompart in Lough Swilly. It also relates the capture of Wolfe Tone and his trial and sentence of death [Brown; E. Reilly, p. 230].

M653   *The house in the rath* (by James Murphy).
        + Dublin: Sealy, Bryers & Walker, [1886]. SOURCE Brown, 1235; OCLC. LOCATION DPL, Univ. of Kansas.
COMMENTARY Historical novel of the rebellion of 1798, it deals with Wolfe Tone's§ efforts to obtain aid from France for the United Irishmen and includes appearances by Lord Edward Fitzgerald and Oliver Bond. The atrocities of the yeomanry are described and a love story is interwoven [Brown].

M654   *'Convict No. 25'; or, the clearances of Westmeath. A story of the Whitefeet* (by James Murphy; dedicated to Michael Davitt).
        Dublin: Sealy, Bryers & Walker, 1886. SOURCE Brown, 1236 (probably mistakenly mentions Dublin, Duffy [1886] edn). LOCATION Dt.
COMMENTARY Dealing with the worst aspects of landlordism in Ireland and set in the middle of the nineteenth century, it features Kevin Moore, a Catholic, who is sentenced to transportation for involvement in the nationalist movement of the Ribbonmen. Subsequently he is charged with murder on the false evidence of Keliff McNab, a former land steward [Brown; Murphy, p. 19].

M655   void

M656   *Hugh Roach, the Ribbonman. A story of thirty years ago* (by James Murphy).
        Dublin: James Duffy & Sons, [*c.*1887]. SOURCE Brown, 1238. LOCATION Dt, NUC.
        + Dublin: James Duffy & Co., 1909 (new edn). LOCATION DPL, InND Loeber coll.
COMMENTARY A fast-paced adventure story of a member of the secret society of Ribbonmen set in Templemore (Co. Tipperary), England and the Crimea. An absentee landlord's insatiable appetite for money drives his tenants into the secret society. Hugh Roach, the son of a tenant, has an altercation with the agent which leaves the agent lying stunned. Hugh flees to London to explain to the landlord what had happened and to relate the sufferings of the tenants. On leaving the landlord's house he meets with a small accident that leaves his mind befuddled. In this state he enlists and is shipped off to Sebastopol, where he acquits himself well. He returns to London with a stash of Russian roubles and diamonds. Meantime in Tipperary the agent has truly been killed. The Ribbonmen had drawn lots for who would kill the agent. A Mr Dwyer, who is innocent, is accused of the crime because he had had a disagreement with the agent over Mr Dwyer's daughter. At his trial all comes out and he has to be released. Hugh returns to Tipperary and is united with Mr Dwyer's daughter, Nelly [ML].

M657   *The haunted church. A novel* (by James Murphy).

+ London: Spencer Blackett, 1889. SOURCE Sutherland, p. 451; Brown (1889, 4th edn). LOCATION L, InND Loeber coll.

COMMENTARY A mystery involving a number of seafaring men who, after a life of plunder, end up in Dublin where in an old church they hide a treasure, stolen from a palace in Lima (Peru). An intricate set of coincidences reveals all the treachery and reunites the Spaniard from Lima with his lost treasures and his abducted daughter in Dublin. The persons instrumental in the unravelling of the plot marry the Spaniard's two daughters, and the main villain dies a horrible death [ML].

M658 *Luke Talbot; or, the cliffs of Mullawn-Mor* (by James Murphy).

+ Dublin: Sealy, Bryers & Walker, 1890. SOURCE Brown, 1239. LOCATION DPL, Dt.

COMMENTARY A murder mystery about a crime committed by a wicked land agent in Ireland, but of which the hero Luke Talbot is suspected. All through the various adventures in the book, until just the end, the land agent is on top, but eventually the truth comes out [Brown].

M659 *The flight from the cliffs. A story of troubled times. A tale of the Catholic Confederation of Kilkenny* (by James Murphy).

+ Dublin: James Duffy & Co., 1911. SOURCE Brown, 1240. LOCATION DPL, D.

COMMENTARY An historical adventure tale set in Ireland, Spain and Rome in the middle of the seventeenth century. The story presents the Irish and Catholic view of the wars of Confederation. A romance between the Confederate Walter Butler and the daughter of Lord Inchiquin is included and there are descriptions of many parts of Ireland [Brown].

M660 *Lays and legends of Ireland* (by James Murphy).

+ Dublin: James Duffy, 1911. SOURCE Brown, 1241 ([1912] edn). LOCATION D, DPL ([1912] edn), NUC ([1911] edn).

Dublin: Mercier, [c.1980] (as *Tales from an Irish fireside*). LOCATION D.

COMMENTARY Contents (excluding poems): 'In sands of gold', 'The stranger warner', 'The midnight train', 'On the Dublin mountains', 'Maureen's sorrow', 'The tower of doom', 'Neil O'Neill', 'Una of the streams', 'At noon by the ravine', 'Handwriting on the wall', 'The captain's story', 'Grace Elmwood's peril' [ML].

M661 *The inside passenger; a story of the old castles and caves of Dalkey* (by James Murphy).

+ Dublin: James Duffy & Co., [1913] (on cover: *The inside passenger; a story of the castles and caves of Dalkey*). SOURCE Brown, 1242. LOCATION D, Dcc, DPL, InND Loeber coll.

COMMENTARY A mystery story about the mail coach from Limerick which gets stuck in a snow-drift at the old castle of Bullock, near Dalkey (Co. Dublin). The passengers take shelter in the castle and entertain each other by telling stories, which all refer somehow to the inside passenger of the coach. In the morning the inside passenger, the coachman and six boxes have disappeared. The story tells how the mystery is solved [Brown].

M662 *In the days of Owen Roe. A story of the great Catholic rebellion of 1641* (by James Murphy).

+ Dublin: M.H. Gill & Son, 1920. SOURCE Brown 2, 1083. LOCATION DPL, L, NUC, InND Loeber coll.

COMMENTARY An historical tale of the rebellion of 1641 and of Maurice O'Donnell who had fought on the Continent and is now a captain in Charles I's army. He visits Ireland on the eve of the rebellion and gets drawn into the action. Sir William Parsons and Sir Charles Coote feature, and Charles is depicted as a man who betrays his friends and is willing to sacrifice them. Owen Roe O'Neill has not set foot in Ireland by the end of the novel [ML].

M663 *The priest hunters. A story of the penal days* (by James Murphy).

+ Dublin: Talbot Press, [1924]. SOURCE Brown 2, 1084. LOCATION D, Dt, DPL, L, InND Loeber coll.

COMMENTARY Published posthumously. The scene of this historical romance is the Clare-Galway district of Connacht, the period is around 1668. To speak, as the writer does, of the penal laws as being in force at that time is not correct as they were introduced beginning 1695. The plot centres on the romance between the rightful heir of the Monivea estate (now in the possession of the Puritan planter, Col. Everard) and the planter's daughter. With this are interwoven the fortunes of the fugitive priest, Cahir O'Flaherty. The father of the true heir comes back to avenge himself on Everard. Fr Cahir intervenes to unite the families by a marriage alliance. The fierce old Cromwellian is softened and the hero and heroine are married. Note the similarity of this title with M. Archdeacon's§ *Shawn na soggarth, the priest-hunter. An Irish tale of the penal times* (Dublin, 1844) [RL; Brown 2].

M664 *In Emmet's days. The story of Eamon Revelle* (by James Murphy).
   Dublin: Talbot Press, [1925]. SOURCE Brown 2, 1085; COPAC. LOCATION D ([1926] edn), NUC (n.d. edn), InND Loeber coll. (Dublin, Lester, n.d. edn).
COMMENTARY An historical story centring on the adventures of Eamon Revelle who had fought as a boy in the rebellion of 1798 but when the story opens in 1801, is on his way to Dublin as apprentice to a wool merchant and means to settle down quietly in business. Events, however, are too much for him. He meets the revolutionary Robert Emmet. He rescues his employer's daughter from a fire, but falls under suspicion of theft. A series of mishaps brings him on board a British warship. In an attack on a fort in Brittany he is taken prisoner and sent to Toulon. Thence he escapes and in Paris again meets Emmet and is one of a deputation from Ireland that is received by Tallyrand and the emperor. He is left in Paris to bring Emmet word of the date at which he is to expect a French expedition. But Napoleon suddenly changes his plans and Eamon reaches Dublin too late to stop the rising [Brown 2].

'MURPHY, Paddy', pseud. See BRACKEN, Thomas.

'MURPHY, Patrick', fl. 1866. Pseudonym of an anti-Catholic novelist and song writer who also published a volume of songs entitled *Murphy is coming (the blighted potatos)* ([Dublin], [1866?]). The author is described in the BLC as a Protestant lecturer. SOURCE OCLC; COPAC.
M665 *Patrick Murphy on popery in Ireland; or, confessionals, abductions, nunneries, Fenians, and Orangemen. A narrative of facts.*
   + London: Jarrold & Sons, 1866 (ill. W. Cheshire). SOURCE OCLC. LOCATION D, L, InND Loeber coll. (n.d. edn).
COMMENTARY An anti-Catholic novel describing the persecution of a young woman and a man, Patrick Murphy, who start to doubt the tenets of the Catholic religion. Eventually, she is whisked away from her home and put in a nunnery, from whence she is rescued by Murphy and his friend. They flee to Belfast where they continue to live. Contains an appendix satirizing a confession [ML].

MURRAY, Anna Maria. See BUNN, Anna Maria.

MURRAY, Henry George. Possible co-author. See HILL, John.

MURRAY, John Fisher, b. Belfast 1811, d. Dublin 1865. Poet, pamphleteer, periodical writer and novelist, JFM was the eldest son of Sir James Murray, an eminent doctor, and Mary Sherlock. He was educated at Belfast and TCD, where he graduated BA in 1830 and MA in 1832, and was admitted to the King's Inns in 1832, but does not appear to have been called to the Irish Bar. He began contributing light sketches to *Blackwood's Magazine* (Edinburgh), where he worked with William Maginn§ and Samuel Ferguson§, and over the years contributed to many other journals, such as the *Belfast Vindicator* and Dublin periodicals including the *Dublin University Magazine*, the *Nation* and the *United Irishman*. He was a member of the Young Ireland movement. In 1838 *Father Tom and the Pope* (listed under Samuel Ferguson§) was serialized in *Blackwood's Magazine* (Edinburgh) and although published under JFM's name in Philadelphia (1868), the ODNB states that it is now understood to be a collaboration between Samuel Ferguson§, William Maginn§, and JFM. JFM also wrote several books about London and its environs. His work for the *Nation* was represented by his best-known piece 'War with everybody' (1844) in *The voice of the Nation* (Dublin, 1844), a collection of articles from the paper. Some of his poems were included in Edward Hayes's *Ballads of Ireland* that appeared in 1855 (and many subsequent edns). He was buried in Glasnevin cemetery, Dublin. For some of his manuscripts, see ODNB. SOURCE Boase, ii, p. 1049–50; Brady, p. 173; Brown, p. 228; W.E. Hall, p. 114; Hogan 2, p. 891; Irish pseudonyms; Keane, p. 358; ODNB; O'Donoghue, p. 330; Sutherland, p. 452.

M666   *The viceroy* (by John Fisher Murray).

+ London: John Murray, 1841, 3 vols. SOURCE Brown, 1244; OCLC. LOCATION L.
COMMENTARY A satirical novel about Dublin society and the Protestant Ascendancy written from a Protestant point of view, while even-handedly lampooning the Catholics [Brown, Sutherland].

'MURRAY, Ruth', pseud. See **MULHOLLAND, Rosa**.

'MYSELF', pseud. See **PURCELL, Mrs** —.

N

N1   void

'N.N.', pseud. See **HAMILTON, Revd John**.

NAPIER, Maj.-Gen. See **NAPIER, Sir William Francis Patrick**.

NAPIER, Sir Charles. See **NAPIER, Gen. Sir Charles James**.

NAPIER, Gen. Sir Charles James (known as **Sir Charles Napier**), b. Whitehall (London) 1782, d. Oaklands, near Portsmouth (Hants.) 1853. Military man and miscellaneous writer, CJN was the son of Col. George Napier and his second wife, Lady Sarah Bunbury, daughter of the duke of Richmond and sister of the duchess of Leinster. One of his brothers was Sir William Napier§. When he was age 3, the family moved to Celbridge (Co. Kildare). He joined a regiment at age 12 but when it went abroad he was sent to study with William at a grammar school in Celbridge. During the rebellion of 1798 his father fortified the house, armed Charles and his four brothers, and offered his home as a haven from the rebels. In 1803 CJN served with his cousin, Gen. Edward Fox, in subduing rebel forces in Ireland. According to his brother's biography, CJN was acutely conscious of the sufferings of the poor Irish that had led them to revolt, and English misgovernment in Ireland became for him the example of what he endeavoured to avoid in his later military and colonial career in the Ionian Islands and in India. He became a distinguished, if controversial, military commander and civil administrator, known as the 'conqueror of Scinde' (also known as Sind), and wrote about military life and law and issues in Britain's colonies. He married in 1827 Elizabeth Oakeley, a writer on childrearing, whose work he edited after her death in 1833. CJN resigned from the army in 1850 and settled near Portsmouth. Aside from the following novel, CJN was the author of a pamphlet, *An essay on the present state of Ireland* (London, 1839). He died after catching a cold as a pallbearer at the duke of Wellington's funeral. His statue in Trafalgar Square in London was erected by public subscription, with ordinary soldiers comprising the majority of the subscribers. For CJN's portraits and papers, see ODNB. SOURCE Allibone, ii, p. 1397; P. Napier, *Raven Castle: Charles Napier in India, 1844–1851* (Salisbury, 1991); W.F.P. Napier, *The life and opinions of General Sir Charles James Napier* (London, 1857, 4 vols.); ODNB; Quaritch cat. Spring 1997/66; W.A. Shee, *My contemporaries, 1830–1870* (London, 1893), pp 209–10.

N2   *William the Conqueror: a historical romance* (by Sir Charles Napier; ed. by Sir W. Napier§).
    + London, New York: George Routledge & Co., 1858. SOURCE Topp 1, p. 132 (1859 edn). LOCATION L (1859 edn), NUC, InND Loeber coll.
COMMENTARY Published posthumously. Originally entitled 'Harould'. Set in France and England during the eleventh century before and during the battle of Hastings (1066), it describes the lives of William the Conqueror and Harold, who was briefly king in England. Strife and battles on both sides of the English Channel are described. The main characters have all been converted to the Christian faith but still entertain pagan beliefs. The volume ends with the battle of Hastings, in which Harold is killed and William is victorious [ML; Allibone, ii, p. 1397].

NAPIER, Sir William Francis Patrick (known as Maj.-Gen. Napier, b. Celbridge House (later known as Oakley Park, Co. Kildare), but Allibone states Castletown House) 1785, d. Clapham Park (Surrey) 1860. Military officer and historian, WFPN was the son of Col. George Napier and his second wife, Lady Sarah Bunbury, daughter of the duke of Richmond and sister of the duchess of Leinster. One of his brothers was Sir Charles Napier§. WFPN was educated at a local grammar school in Celbridge and joined the army at age 14. He participated in the Peninsular War, commanded a regiment under Wellington, and was wounded severely several times. In 1812 he married Caroline Amelia, daughter of British statesman Henry Fox, who later assisted him in the research and writing of his historical works. By 1813 he had reached the rank of colonel but because of ill-health retired on half-pay in 1819. In retirement he wrote, painted and sculpted (he was an honorary member of the Royal Academy) and was an incessant letter-writer to newspapers and periodicals on topics such as national security, injustice, foreign affairs and history. He probably can be identified with the William Napier who wrote in 1833 a short manuscript, *Remarks on the invasion and defence of Ireland*, which deals with the 1798 rebellion, since as a young boy his father had armed him and his brothers in defence of their home. He contributed to the *Dublin University Magazine*. From 1842 to 1848 WFPN was lieutenant-governor of Guernsey, and was then knighted and made a general. He is best known for his *History of the war in the Peninsula and the South of France* (London, 1828–40, 6 vols.), and for the several books on the life of his brother Charles, whose military and civilian career he actively defended. He edited Charles Napier's§ novel *William the Conqueror: a historical romance* (London, 1858) after the latter's death. He also wrote on the poor laws and the corn laws. He knew Thomas Moore§, to whom he offered financial assistance on at least one occasion. A statue of WFPN inscribed 'Historian of the Peninsular War' was installed in St Paul's cathedral (London). For WFPN's portraits and papers, see ODNB. SOURCE Allibone, ii, pp 1400–1; Boylan, p. 262; Burke, 1878, p. 871; *Catalogue of … books … by … Dr. J. Orr Kyle* (New York, 1924), i, p. 17; S.C. Hall, p. 26; W.E. Hall, p. 60; ODNB; P. Napier, *Revolution and the Napier brothers, 1820–1840* (London, 1973); OCIL, p. 389; NCBEL 4, pp 2446–7; RIA/DIB; W.A. Shee, *My Contemporaries, 1830–1870* (London, 1893), pp 209–10.

N3   *Tales* (by Maj.-Gen. Napier).
      Guernsey: Printed [for the author?] by Stephen Barbet, 1846. SOURCE Wolff, 5063; OCLC. LOCATION TxU.
      COMMENTARY Contents: 'Griffone' (a story about Portugal; first published in London *Bentley's Miscellany*, 1838), 'How the fairy of Rocquaine was tamed' (a story of Guernsey) [Wolff].

'NASEBY', pseud. See FITZGERALD, Geraldine Penrose.

NAUTA, Abraham, b. Alkmaar (Netherlands) 1820, fl. 1853. Dutch historical fiction writer. AN published several novels between 1853 and 1858. SOURCE Adamnet.

N4   *Elizabeth Edmunds of de redding der Iersche Protestanten, Eene episode uit de regering van Mary Tudor* (by A. Nauta).
      Amsterdam: Allart & Van der Made, 1855, 2 vols. (ill.). SOURCE Adamnet. LOCATION UVA.
      COMMENTARY Historical fiction about the saving of Irish Protestants during the reign of Queen Mary in the sixteenth century [RL].

'A NATIVE OFFICER', pseud. See ARNOLD, Lt. —.

'A NAVAL OFFICER', pseud. See ARNOLD, Lt. —.

'NAVERY, Raoule de', pseud. See DAVID, Mme Marie.

NEALE, Capt. William Johnson Nelson, b. Devon 1812, d. Cheltenham (Glos.) 1893. English novelist and miscellaneous writer, WJNN was the son of Adam Neale, a military physician and writer, and Margaret Johnston Young. After serving as a naval officer he entered Lincoln's Inn and subsequently the Middle Temple (both London) and was called to the Bar in 1836. WJNN wrote popular nautical novels, naval histories, an anonymous satire, and a book about the law of parliamentary elections. He modelled his work on that of Frederick Marryat§ with whom he quarrelled over WJNN's novel *The port admiral* (London, 1833), and according to Sutherland and ODNB, he challenged Marryat to a duel, which Marryat declined on the grounds of WJNN's social inferiority. The two writers subsequently scuffled publicly in Trafalgar Square. WJNN's brother Erskine was also a novelist. SOURCE Allibone, ii, p. 1405; Boase, ii, p. 1090; NCBEL 4, pp 1360–1; ODNB; Sutherland, p. 457.
N5   *Paul Periwinkle; or, the press-gang* [anon.].
    London: Thomas Tegg, 1841 (ill. Phiz). SOURCE Brown 2, 1095; NCBEL 4, p. 1361. LOCATION L, NUC.
COMMENTARY WJNN's most popular novel, it was initially published in parts from 1839 to 1841. The story opens in England but about midway the scene shifts to Ireland. The novel is hostile to the insurgents of 1798 and the atrocities are attributed to them [Brown 2; ODNB].

'NECESSITY', pseud. See 'AN UNWILLING AUTHOR' (pseud.).

NEEDHAM, Ellen Creathorne. See CLAYTON, Ellen Creathorne.

NEEDHAM, George Carter (known as Geo. C. Needham), b. 1840, d. 1902. American novelist, GCN may be identified with the author of several works on religious themes. SOURCE Allibone Suppl., ii, p. 1167; RLIN.
N6   *Father Flynn, an Irish tale of conflict and victory* (by Geo. C. Needham).
    New York: James A. O'Connor, 1890. SOURCE Wright, iii, 3939; OCLC. LOCATION L, CtY.
    Boston: Bradley & Woodruff, [c.1890]. SOURCE RLIN; NYPL. LOCATION NN.
    Philadelphia: American Baptist Publication Society, 1896 (as *Conflict and conquest: the experiences of Father Flynn*). SOURCE RLIN; OCLC. LOCATION DCL.

NELSON, Mrs Lucy, fl. 1864. Writer on religious and domestic themes, LN also wrote *The voice of the prayer-book and the holy communion* (London, 1877), and a reply to M.F. Sadler's *The one offering* (London, 1875). Given the story line of the following book, she may have been the wife of an officer stationed in Ireland for some time. SOURCE Allibone Suppl., ii, p. 1168; BLC.
N7   *Wandering homes, and their influences* [anon.] (dedicated to the young wives and daughters of military officers subject to colonial service).
    London: James Nisbet & Co., 1864. SOURCE OCLC. LOCATION L, InND Loeber coll. (1868 edn).
    London: James Nisbett & Co., 1902 (as *Wandering homes: A tale of military life*). SOURCE OCLC. LOCATION CaOK.

COMMENTARY The story starts at Kilnock in Ireland, but moves to Canada. The book describes the duties of officers' wives and life in a garrison. A number of useful hints are provided for the smooth running of a household, either while travelling or while settled abroad. The story contrasts virtuous, intellectual and religiously-minded people with those who dance, gamble, and suffer from jealousies. Interwoven is a tale of thwarted love with a happy ending [ML].

NETHERCOTT, Margaret, fl. 1878. Novelist, MN is mentioned as the author of 'The witch-thorn' on the title page of *Verney Court* (London, 1878, 3 vols.), while the title page of *The tenants* (Aberdeen, 1895) mentions that she also wrote 'Who can he be?', but neither of these titles has been located. SOURCE RL.

N8   *Verney Court. An Irish novel* (by Margaret Nethercott).
      + London: Remington & Co., 1878, 2 vols. SOURCE Allibone Suppl., ii, p. 1168; Brown 2, 1096. LOCATION D.

COMMENTARY A mystery romance in which Grace Melville at age 15 is sent to stay with her guardian, Mr. Verney, in a ruined mansion on the Irish Atlantic coast. Mr Verney is harsh, unscrupulous and, as it later transpires, a criminal. His only daughter, Catherine, lives with him in a kind of captivity. She is engaged to Cecil Nugent, a neighbouring landowner and a noble character. But Percival, a handsome stranger, appears and Catherine is captivated. Mr Verney is furious and Cecil breaks off the engagement. Catherine and Percival disappear, the latter apparently killed in a train accident. Verney schemes to marry Grace and acquire a fortune. But gradually all his villainies are revealed. A climax is reached when Verney Court goes up in flames. Catherine, who had been hidden in a remote tower, is burnt to death. Verney commits suicide, and Grace is rescued and marries Cecil [Brown 2].

N9   *The tenants of the grey house and other stories* (by Margaret Nethercott).
      + Aberdeen: Moran & Co., 1895. SOURCE OCLC. LOCATION D, L.

COMMENTARY Superstitious tales concerning love, loss and death. Contents: 'The twelfth rig' (mentioned on the title page of *Verney Court*, London, 1878, and, therefore, may have been published separately prior to that date), 'The black glen', 'The tenants of the grey house' (Capt. Bowring visits his family home in Ireland. The new tenants, an old woman and her daughter, Caroline M'Carthy, are not very sociable people and are viewed with suspicion by the local villagers. Bowring falls in love with Caroline and they plan to marry. However, Caroline is very temperamental and subject to bouts of insanity. Bowring tries to resolve the mystery of her strange behaviour. One night, he finds her trying to throw herself off a cliff. It transpires that this is not Caroline, but her twin sister, whose lover was killed. Since then, she has tried to kill herself many times. She eventually manages to commit suicide. Caroline and Bowring marry) [CD].

'NETTERVILLE, Luke', pseud. See **O'GRADY, Standish.**

NEVILLE, Ralph, fl. 1864. Historical novelist.

N10   *Lloyd Pennant. A tale of the West* (by Ralph Neville).
      London: Chapman & Hall, 1864, 2 vols. SOURCE Allibone Suppl., ii, p. 1169; Brown, 1247. LOCATION L.
      New York: P.J. Kenedy, 1886 (Library of Catholic Stories). LOCATION NUC.

COMMENTARY First serialized in Duffy's *Hibernian Magazine* (Dublin, 1863), the novel is set at the end of the eighteenth century. The hero, who bears an assumed name and is really the heir of an old Anglo-Irish family, joins the British navy. He is unjustly accused of disloyalty and intimacy with the revolutionary leader Lord Edward Fitzgerald. All ends well, including his love affair. The French invasion under Gen. Jean-Joseph Humbert in 1798 is mentioned [Brown].

N11   *The squire's heir* (by Ralph Neville).
+ London: W.H. Allen, 1881, 2 vols. SOURCE Allibone Suppl., ii, p. 1169; Brown, p. 228. LOCATION L.
COMMENTARY The story starts out in the west of Ireland in the Killery mountains at the time of the Act of Union (1800). It features the illicit distilling of whiskey, Whiteboys and the burning of homes. The main character moves to France to fight in Napoleon's Russian campaign [ML].

NEWCOMEN, George. See **NEWCOMEN, George Arnold.**

NEWCOMEN, George Arnold (also known as **George Newcomen**), b. 1855, d. Vichy (France) 1932. Miscellaneous writer, poet, and barrister, GAN was the son of Capt. George Newcomen of Camla, Co. Roscommon, and Harriet O'Donnell. GAN graduated LLB at TCD, and was admitted to the King's Inns, Dublin, in 1883, and to the Middle Temple, London, in 1884, and was called to the Irish Bar in 1886. He reviewed for the *Academy* (London), and contributed to *Kottabos* (Dublin). He published a volume of poetry, *The passing of years: A miscellany of verse* (London, [1926]). SOURCE Ferguson, p. 264; Foreword to *The passing of years* (London, [1926]), p. v.
N12   *The maze of life* (by George Newcomen).
London: Bellairs & Co., 1898. LOCATION L.
COMMENTARY Set in Ireland. Contents: 'The career of Charlie Browning', 'The vanities of Jasper West' [ML; CM].
N13   *A left-handed swordsman. A romance of the eighteenth century* (by George Newcomen).
London: L. Smithers & Co., 1900. SOURCE Brown, 1248. LOCATION L, NUC.
COMMENTARY Set in Dublin society during the eighteenth century, it features the lives of Cicely Grattan and her adopted son, Victor La Roche. Victor is a noble youth and his successful love affairs are described. In contrast, Cicely has not much luck in love [Brown].

NEWELL, R.H., pseuds '**Orpheus C. Kerr**' and '**O.C.K.**', b. New York City 1836, d. 1901. American editor, novelist and poet, RHN was literary editor of the New York *Mercury* (1858–62); associated with the New York *World* (1869–74), and edited *Hearth and Home* (New York, 1874–76). His published poetry includes *The palace beautiful, and other poems* (New York, 1864), and *The martyr president* (New York, 1865). SOURCE Allibone Suppl., ii, pp 1170–1; Wright, iii, p. 397; Wright web.
N14   *Avery Gilburn; or, between two fires. A romance* (by 'Orpheus C. Kerr'; preface signed 'O.C.K.').
+ New York: G.W. Carleton & Co.; London: S. Low, Son & Co., 1867. SOURCE Allibone Suppl., ii, p. 1170. LOCATION Wright web.
COMMENTARY Set in the US and deals with politics. O'Murphy is a political candidate who is against abolitionism. The story depicts many Irish Catholics who criticize England and complain that the US does not demand Ireland's freedom [ML].

NEWLAND, Henry. See **NEWLAND, Revd Henry Garrett.**

NEWLAND, Revd Henry Garrett (also known as **Henry Newland**), b. London 1804, d. Torquay (Devon) 1860. Anglican clergyman, writer on religion and on travel, HGN was the son of Richard Bingham Newland, lord of the manor of Havant. HGN lived abroad with his father before entering Cambridge, where he graduated BA in 1827 and MA in 1830. He was rector and vicar of Westbourne (Sussex), where because of his high anglicanism he was known as 'the Pope of Westbourne'. Later he was transferred to St Mary-Church, Torquay, where he died. It is likely that there were two individuals under the name of Revd Henry Newland writing at this time: one in England, the other in Ireland. The latter was the author of *Apology for the church in Ireland* (London, n.d.) and *An examination ... on tithes in Ireland* (Dublin, 1832) and was dean of Ferns in 1832. SOURCE Allibone, ii, p. 1412; Allibone Suppl., ii, p. 1171; BLC; Boase, ii, pp 1120–1; V. Fletcher, *Three before the altar* (London, 1859); ODNB; RL; R.N. Shutte, *A memoir of the late Henry Newland* (London, 1861).

N15 **The Erne. Its legends and fly-fishing** (by Henry Newland; dedicated to Sir Charles Taylor of Hollycombe).

+ London: Chapman & Hall, 1851 (ill.). SOURCE COPAC; Allibone, ii, p. 1463; Emerald Isle cat. 91/1213; ODNB. LOCATION D, BFl, L, NUC.

COMMENTARY Explains the geographical features of the river Erne. Dialogues, stories and legends are woven into the narrative. Examples of some of the stories: 'An evening at Belleek', 'Ennis and Shia', 'A day up the river', 'The upper rapids', 'The entomology of the Erne', 'Lough Derg', 'A well-spent Sunday', 'The falls of Ballyshannon', 'The river', 'Tubber Turner', 'A morning at Ballyshannon', 'The breaking up of the party' [CD].

NEWMAN, Cardinal John Henry, b. London, 1801, d. Birmingham (War.) 1890. Theologian, prolific writer on religion and education, influential churchman and novelist, JHN was the son of John Newman, a banker, and Jemima Fourdrinier, descendant of a Huguenot family long-established in London. He won a scholarship to Trinity College, Oxford, and in 1822 was elected a fellow of Oriel College where Richard Whately§, later archbishop of Dublin, was a colleague and mentor. JHN was ordained a priest in the Church of England in 1825. He became vicar of St Mary's (Oxford) in 1828 and a select university preacher soon after. Although his first published piece was an anti-Catholic verse romance 'St Bartholomew's Eve' (1818), JHN's religious views evolved to where he embraced the idea of a church independent of the state and one that emphasized spirituality, the mysteries of Christian revelation, the Holy Spirit and the sacraments. These ideas he promulgated in a series of tracts that gave the Oxford Tractarian movement its name. JHN was accused of undermining the Protestant nature of the established church but argued that the Anglo-catholicism of the Tracts was not the same as Roman catholicism. However, his evolving theory of doctrinal development led him more and more towards the idea of infallibility and in 1845 he was received into the Roman Catholic church. He left for Rome in 1846 to study for the priesthood and was ordained in 1847. He introduced to England a branch of the Congregation of the Oratory, founded by St Philip Neri. He was appointed vicar of the new Catholic University of Ireland in Dublin in 1851, after the Catholic bishops had refused to support the new Queen's universities. He delivered the next year the first five lectures of what became *The idea of a university; nine lectures addressed to the Catholics of Dublin* (1859; New Haven, 1996) but did not take up his position in Dublin until 1854. He began the *Catholic University Gazette* (Dublin) right away and later an academic journal, the *Atlantis* (London). JHN held the position of vicar until 1858, when he resigned over disagreements with the Catholic archbishop of Dublin over the character and staffing of the university. In 1863 Charles Kingsley§ in a pamphlet accused JHN and the Roman Catholic church of preferring cunning to truth. In response, JHN wrote an explanation of his conversion in tracts that were published as *Apologia pro vita sua* (London, 1864), which became a best-seller. JHN was appointed a cardinal by Pope Leo XIII in 1879, a position he acquiesced to because he felt it signified a more liberal stance by the church on the acceptance of converts. SOURCE Allibone, ii, p. 1413; Allibone Suppl., ii, pp 1171–2; DLB, xviii, xxxii, lv; Field Day, ii, p. 479; Igoe, pp 191–4; NCBEL 4, p. 2246; OCIL, p. 391; ODNB; RIA/DIB; Sutherland, p. 463.

N16   *Loss and gain* [anon.].
       London: James Burns, 1848. SOURCE DNB; Sutherland, p. 463; NCBEL 4, p. 2252;
       Sadleir, 1825; Wolff 5096, 5096a. LOCATION L.
       Zwolle: Thomas a Kempis Vereeniging, 188[?] (trans. into Dutch as *Verlies and winst*).
       SOURCE Mes, p. 169.
COMMENTARY A novel of moral growth through ordeal, which can be compared to William
Makepeace Thackeray's§ *History of Pendennis* (London, 1849–50, 2 vols), which it may have
influenced [Sutherland].

N17   *Callista: A sketch of the third century* [anon.].
       London: Burns & Lambert; Cologne: J.P. Bachem, 1856. SOURCE NCBEL 4, p. 2253;
       Sutherland, p. 463; Wolff, 5095; Sadleir, 1824. LOCATION L.
       Leipzig: Bernard Tauchnitz, 1869. SOURCE T & B, 1021. LOCATION NUC.
       's Hertogenbosch: P. Verhoeven, 1856 (trans. into Dutch as *Callista, eene schets uit de
       IIIe eeuw*). SOURCE Mes, p. 168; Adamnet. LOCATION UVA.
       Amsterdam: C.L. van Langenhuysen, 1868 (trans. into Dutch as *Callista, eene schets
       uit de IIIe eeuw*). SOURCE Mes, p. 168.
       New York, Boston, Montreal: D. & J. Sadlier & Co., 1861. LOCATION NUC, DPL
       (Burns & Oates, n.d. edn), InND Loeber coll. (n.d. edn).
       Paris, Tournai: Casterman, 1860 (trans. as *Callista, scènces de l'Afrique Chrétienne aux
       iiime siècle*). SOURCE Fotheringham cat. 36/93.
       Limoges: Barbou frères, 1868 (trans. by Marie Guerrier de Haupt as *Callista, esquisse
       du IIIe siècle*). SOURCE Bn-Opale plus. LOCATION BNF.
       Brussels: [publisher?], 1857 (trans. by Abbé A. Goemaere as *Callista, ou tableau his-
       torique du IIIe siècle*). SOURCE Bn-Opale plus. LOCATION BNF.
COMMENTARY Historical fiction consisting of an imaginative melodrama of conversion, faith,
persecution and martyrdom in Roman pro-consular Africa. It recreates the world of the early
church, with Christians facing persecution in the Roman empire – implying an analogy with
the position of Catholics in nineteenth-century Britain. It contains an existential theology of
hell. Adapted into a French play (Paris, 1874) [ODNB; Sutherland; Bn-Opale plus].

NEWMAN, M.W., pseud. 'An exile of Erin', fl. 1874. American Catholic novelist, pre-
sumably Irish-born given pseudonym. Perhaps this author can be identified with the Mary
(May) Wentworth Newman (fl. 1867–1915) who published in both San Francisco and London.
However, neither COPAC or Allibone lists under her name the novels below. SOURCE Allibone
Suppl., ii, p. 1172; COPAC.
N18   *Alice Harmon; and the mother and her dying boy* (by 'An exile of Erin').
       New York, Montreal: D. & J. Sadlier & Co., 1874. SOURCE; DCU, Catholic Americana
       files; RLIN. LOCATION UBP.
COMMENTARY Advertised in 1875 as *Alice Harmon: and other tales*. Regular edn sold for $1.25,
and in cloth gilt for $1.75 [Adv. in M.J. Hoffman, *The orphan sisters* (New York, 1875)].
N19   *The adventures of Sidney Flint* (by 'An exile of Erin').
       New York, Montreal: D. & J. Sadlier & Co., 1875. SOURCE DCU, Catholic Americana
       files.
COMMENTARY No copy located [RL].

NICCHIA, Mrs — (née Lily MacArthur), pseud. 'Alexander MacArthur', fl. 1893. Novelist,
Mrs N lived at one point in New York, but she may be identified with the author of several
religious works published in London. Only her known Irish work is listed below. SOURCE
Allibone Suppl., ii, p. 1033 [under A. Macarthur]; Brown, p. 181.

N20   *Irish rebels. A novel* (by 'Alexander MacArthur').
London: Digby, Long & Co., 1893. SOURCE Brown, 983. LOCATION L, NUC.
COMMENTARY O'Donoghue, a Catholic student at TCD, is deputed by a secret society to shoot a landlord. He escapes, has a successful career at the Bar and in parliament, and marries the daughter of Judge Kavanagh, a bitter Orangeman. Later his crime becomes known and the discovery kills his wife [Brown].

NICHOLSON, Marianne. See **CROKER, Mrs Marianne.**

NIVEN, Richard, fl. 1892. Comic novelist, miscellaneous writer and angler, RN wrote *The British angler's lexicon* (London, 1892); *Orangeism as it was and is* (London, 1899), and *The life of St. Patrick ... for the use of schools* (n.l., 1901). SOURCE BLC; OCLC.
N21   *On the road to the Boyne* (by Richard Niven).
+ London, Dublin, Belfast: R. Carswell & Son, n.d. (ill.; see Plate 52). LOCATION InND Loeber coll.
COMMENTARY 48pp. A comic story of the landing of King William in Ireland, his trip to the River Boyne and the battle there (1690). The story is told by a fisherman who served as the king's guide [ML].

NOBLE, Annette Lucille, b. Albion (NY) 1844, d. Albion 1932. American writer on religion, ALR was also a contributor to periodicals. She was the daughter of Dr William Noble and his wife Amelia Stiles. She made numerous trips to Europe, the last entailing a hasty evacuation to Switzerland at the outbreak of the First World War. SOURCE Allibone Suppl., ii, p. 1178; Wright, iii, pp 398–9.
N22   *Out of the way* (by Annette Lucille Noble).
+ New York: American Tract Society, 1879 (ill. E.J.V.). SOURCE OCLC. LOCATION DCL, InND Loeber coll.
COMMENTARY Christian ladies in New York who are engaged in good works in the course of their ministrations come across some poor people of Irish descent [ML].

NOBLE, E., fl. 1873. Short story and religious fiction writer, EN was probably female and Catholic. According to the title page of *An Irish decade* (London, [1890]), EN was also the author of 'Dora's diamonds' which has not been located. SOURCE Alston, p. 318; RL.
N23   *The story of Marie, and other tales* (by E. Noble).
+ London: [n.p.], 1873. LOCATION L.
COMMENTARY Catholic religious fiction consisting of a volume of separately published tracts, each with its own title page and pagination. With one exception, the stories are set in England or in unspecified locales. Contents: 'The story of Marie', 'Nelly Blane', 'A conversion and a deathbed', 'Herbert Montague', 'Jane Murphy', 'The dying gypsy', 'The beggars', 'The nameless grave', 'A contrast', 'Pat and his friend' (The Irishman Patrick O'Connor is seeking work in England. He meets the young Protestant boy Tom Allen. Tom and Pat debate the merits of catholicism versus protestantism, before Pat leaves 'to return to his lowly Irish cabin' (p. 22). After a few years, Tom visits Pat in Ireland, having converted to catholicism as a result of his discussions with the Irishman. Tom eventually marries Pat's daughter Kathleen and they settle in Ireland), 'True and false riches' [JB].
N24   *Irish pride: an unsocial tale of social life* (by the author of *Dora's diamonds*).
London: Bevington & Co., 1885. SOURCE Allibone Suppl., ii, p. 1178; COPAC.
LOCATION L.]
N25   *An Irish decade* (by E. Noble).

London: Digby, Long & Co., [1890]. SOURCE Brown, 1252; COPAC. LOCATION Dt, L.

London: Digby, Long & Co., [1893] (new edn). LOCATION L.

COMMENTARY Consists of three stories about land agitation: 'The O'Donol [*sic*] rent', 'Rosie', 'By Kerry moonlight' [Brown].

NOBLE, Vere D'Oyly, fl. 1895. Military man, editor and miscellaneous writer, VD'ON served in the Inniskillings 27th Regiment and is likely to have been Irish. SOURCE AMB.

N26 *Military yarns* (selected and arranged by Vere D'Oyly Noble).
+ London: Harrison & Sons, 1895 (ill. F.D. Notermann, A.E. Francis, F.J. Duncan; first series [all published]). SOURCE Scott cat. 3/103. LOCATION L, InND Loeber coll.
COMMENTARY A collection of anecdotes, caricatures and stories on military topics, some with Irish content. According to the preface, the text and illustrations were originally published in the regimental periodical of the 27th Inniskillings, *The sprig of shillelagh* (Portsmouth, 1891 onwards), of which VD'ON was editor (1891–95). By 1895 he had retired from the Inniskillings, where he must have been a commanding officer [RL; Scott cat. 3/103].

NOEL, Ellen. See NOEL, Mrs. John Vavasour.

NOEL, Mrs J.V. See NOEL, Mrs John Vavasour.

NOEL, Mrs John Vavasour (née Ellen Kyle; known as **Mrs J.V. Noel**), b. Ireland 1815, d. Kingston (ON, Canada) 1873 (not 1875 or 1878 as in some sources). Short story writer and novelist, Mrs JVN emigrated to Kingston in 1832. Her husband, whom she married the next year, was a clerk and insurance agent, and they had a daughter, also Ellen, who later published poetry. The family moved to Savannah (GA), where Mrs JVN conducted a seminary for ladies. They returned to Canada in 1847 (or possibly 1857). Several of her stories and serial novels were published in American and Canadian periodicals, such as 'The secret of Stanley Hall' in the *Saturday Reader* (Montreal, 3 Feb.–10 Mar. 1866), and 'The cross of pride' in the *Canadian Illustrated News* (Hamilton, 1863). According to Watters, she also wrote 'Hilda; or, the merchant's secret' and 'Passion and principle', but these have not been located. SOURCE Blain, p. 796; CEWW; C. Gerson, *A purer taste* (Toronto, 1989), p. 170; NUC; O'Donoghue, p. 335; Rhodenizer, p. 708; RL; Watters, p. 354.

N27 *The abbey of Rathmore, and other tales* (by Mrs J.V. Noel).
+ Kingston, C[anada] W[est], Printed [for the author?] by J.M. Creighton, 1859. SOURCE Wolff, 5126. LOCATION NUC, Univ. of Toronto.
COMMENTARY Contents: 'The abbey of Rathmore' (situated on Ireland's west coast, the abbey serves as setting for the French invasion in 1798), 'Madeline Beresford; or, the infidel's betrothed' (set in high society in London), 'Grace Raymond; or, the slave's revenge' (an 1840 Irish emigration story), 'Moonlight thoughts' (written by the author's daughter, Ellen, and relates what can be seen of the sadness and happiness of different individuals by peering into their windows at night [ML; Blain, p. 796].

NOLAN, Alice, fl. 1869. American novelist, AN was possibly of Irish birth, given her name and subject matter. SOURCE RL.

N28 *The Byrnes of Glengoulah. A true tale* (by Alice Nolan; dedicated 'to the faithful people of Ireland and their descendants, scattered over ... the habitable globe, victims of British rule and landlord rapacity, exiles from our beautiful and poetic land ...').
+ New York: P. O'Shea, 1869. SOURCE Allibone Suppl., ii, p. 1179; Brown, 1253 (who mentions a Baltimore *c*.1876 edn published by O'Shea, but this probably is an error);

Fanning, p. 387; Wright, ii, 1797. LOCATION Dcc (1870 edn), NUC (1870 edn), Wright web.

COMMENTARY Details evictions and a rigged murder trial in Wicklow, based on a real case in Co. Westmeath in 1846, the upshot of which was the unjust execution of an innocent man at Mullingar for the murder of Sir Francis Hopkins [Brown; Fanning, p. 81].

NOLAN, Mary, fl. 1884. American novelist.

N29 *Biddy Finnegan's botheration; or, that romp of a girl* (by Mary Nolan).
+ St Louis: Ev.E. Carreras, 1884 (ill.). SOURCE Fanning, p. 387; Wright, iii, 3984; COPAC. LOCATION C, NUC.
COMMENTARY Comical story about an Irishwoman's life in America. A large portion of the text is in Irish brogue [ML].

'NORAH', pseud. See MC DOUGALL, Margaret.

NORAKIDZE, Vladimir Georgievich, fl. 1855. Probably the pseudonym of a religious fiction writer. While the first names are Russian, the surname has a typically Georgian ending. However, given the subject of some of the books, it is tempting to think of this as a joking take on 'Norah kids ye'. SOURCE COPAC; AMB.

N30 *Norah and her Kerry cow; or, the Bible the best guide* [anon.].
London: Religious Tract Society, 1855. Loca*tion* D, L (destroyed).
+ London: Religious Tract Society, [1884] (as *Norah and her Kerry cow*, by the author of *Johnny McKay*; ill. Whymper). LOCATION L (destroyed), O, InND Loeber coll.
COMMENTARY Religious fiction. The author states that 'This happened before the potato blight, when no cabin door was ever closed against the wayfaring man, nor seat at the hospitable hearth and board denied him'. Set near Glena Mountain, Killarney (described in a verse by Richard Chester), Norah and her father, together with their only possession, a young Kerry cow, are on the road after they have lost their farm due to their inability to pay the rent. They are taken in by a kind family, where the father earns enough to emigrate to North America and tries to set up a home for his daughter. The girl places her faith in God, and when confused or worried she reads her Bible as her best guide. Through various adventures she is never separated from her little cow. After a number of years her father and the young man who was fond of her return to Ireland. She ends up setting up a school. In the 1878 edn, the second story in this book is also religious fiction involving Bertha Connor retaining her Irish methodism when adopted by cousins in England [RL; CM].

N31 *Johnny McKay; or, the sovereign* [anon.].
London: Religious Tract Society, 1855. SOURCE COPAC ([1877] edn). LOCATION L (destroyed), E ([1877] edn).
COMMENTARY No copy of first edn located [RL].

N32 *The little guide of Adrighoole; or, how to be happy* (by the author of *Norah and her Kerry cow*; *Johnny McKay*).
+ London: Religious Tract Society, [1858] (ill. W.C.B.). SOURCE NSTC. LOCATION D, L (destroyed), InND Loeber coll.
+ Boston: Henry Hoyt; New York: Sheldon & Co.; Cincinnati: George Crosby; Chicago: Wm. Tomlinson, 1859 (as *The little mountain guide; or, how to be happy*). LOCATION InND Loeber coll.
COMMENTARY Religious fiction. The story is about finding happiness in Christianity. An uneducated peasant girl shows some visitors in Adrighoole (also known as Adrighole, Castlehaven, Co. Cork) the way to inner contentment and happiness [ML].

N33   *Norah, the flower-girl* [anon.].
+ London: Religious Tract Society, [1872]. SOURCE COPAC. LOCATION L.
+ Boston: D. Lothrop, n.d. (ill.). LOCATION InND Loeber coll.
COMMENTARY Religious fiction featuring Norah Brady, a flower girl in London,
ascribed to Vladimir Georgievich Norakidze in the BLC [RL].

N34   *Norah and her Kerry cow, and Cousin Bertha* [anon.].
London: Religious Tract Society, [1878] (Monthly Shilling Volumes). SOURCE COPAC.
LOCATION L (destroyed), O, Univ. of Southern Mississippi.
COMMENTARY The first story was published in London in 1855 [RL].

NORMAN, Sir Henry, Bt (also known as **Henry Norman**), fl. 1887. Journalist and politi-
cian, HN probably can be identified with the HN, who was b. Leicester (Leics.) 1858, d.
Chiddingfold (Surrey) 1939, but the linkage through writing for the London *Pall Mall
Magazine* remains tentative. HN was the son of a merchant (also Henry) and his wife Sarah
Riddington Norman. He was educated privately in France, received a degree in theology from
Harvard University (Boston) and studied further in Leipzig, but gave up his faith and a career
in the church when he returned to England in 1883. He joined the staff of the *Pall Mall
Gazette* and later worked on the editorial staff of the *News Chronicle* (both London). He was
a prolific journalist, writing on literary, political and theatrical topics and working as London
correspondent for the *New York Times*. A four-year tour around the world beginning in 1877
resulted in several books on Japan and the Far East. He joined the staff of the *Daily Chronicle*
(London) as assistant and literary editor. He was elected a Liberal MP in 1900, served until
1923 and was created baronet in 1915. A collection of glass negatives of photographs of his
travels in French Indo-China, China, Malaya, Siam, Korea and Japan with hand-written cap-
tions is in the Royal Commonwealth Society Library at Cambridge Univ. SOURCE AMB;
ODNB; RL.

N35   *Bodyke. A chapter in the history of Irish landlordism* (by Henry Norman).
+ London: T. Fisher Unwin, 1887. SOURCE Allibone Suppl., ii, p. 1180. LOCATION L.
New York: Putnam's Sons, 1887 (Questions of the Day, No. 42; ill.). LOCATION NUC.
COMMENTARY Printed with several additional chapters from the *Pall Mall Magazine*. Based
on historical incidents but set in the fictional village of Bodyke (Co. Clare), outside Limerick,
it features Col. O'Callaghan and his tenants and describes a number of evictions [RL; BLC].

NORRIS, Mrs —, fl. 1805. Novelist, Mrs N. was probably Irish and from Munster given that
most of the subscribers to her *The strangers; A novel* (London, 1806, 3 vols.) have Irish addresses
and include many officers of the Kerry militia, and some individuals from Tralee (Co. Kerry).
Two clusters of subscribers, members of the Brooke family and members of the Kirchhoffer
family stand out, and may have been related to Mrs Norris. The preface 'To the reader' in *The
strangers* is dated from London, Apr. 1806, and mentions that the author is separated 'from her
native country, and consequently from friends and connections'. SOURCE RL; Garside (2003).

N36   *Second love; or, the way to be happy. A novel* (by Mrs Norris).
+ London: B. Crosby & Co., 1805, 2 vols. SOURCE Block, p. 174; Garside, 1805:56.
LOCATION Corvey CME 3–628–48237–2.
COMMENTARY No Irish content [CM].

N37   *The strangers; A novel* (by Mrs Norris; dedicated to the duchess of Devonshire).
+ London: For the author, [printed] by Vernor, Hood & Sharpe, 1806, 3 vols. (sub-
scribers' list). SOURCE British Fiction; Garside, 1806:51. LOCATION Dt, NUC.
London: B. Crosby & Co., 1807 (as *Olivia and Marcella; or, the strangers*). SOURCE
Garside, 1805:51. LOCATION Corvey CME 3–628–48236–4.

COMMENTARY Set in England and, to a lesser extent, India. No Irish content [RL; Garside (2003)].

N38   *Julia of England. A novel* (by Mrs Norris).
    + London: Samuel Tipper, 1808, 4 vols. SOURCE British Fiction; Garside, 1808:86. LOCATION Corvey CME 3–628–48235–6.

COMMENTARY One of the main characters, Julia, encounters a kind Irish couple, Nell and Paddy, after the boat on which she is travelling down the Reuss River to Waldshut capsizes. Despite troubles of their own, they nurse and comfort her and the child she carries. Eventually they decide to leave her on the coast of Yarmouth so she can find refuge in England [CM].

N39   *Euphronia, or the captive; a romance* (by Mrs Norris).
    + London: Henry Colburn, 1810, 3 vols. SOURCE Block, p. 174; Garside, 1810:64. LOCATION Corvey CME 3–628–48234–8, NUC.
    COMMENTARY No Irish content [CM].

NORRIS, W.E. See **NORRIS, William Edward**.

NORRIS, William Edward (known as **W.E. Norris**), b. London 1847 (not 1817 as in Brown 2), d. Torquay (Devon) 1925. Prolific English author, WEN was educated at Eton and was called to the Bar at the Middle Temple (London), but never practiced. He wrote a number of novels, most of which were serialized first in London periodicals such as the *Cornhill Magazine, Temple Bar,* and others. SOURCE Allibone Suppl., ii, p. 1181; Brown 2, p. 192; EF, pp 297–8; Sutherland, p. 468; T & B, pp 1002–3 (list of novels).

N40   *The fight for the crown* (by W.E. Norris).
    London: Seeley, 1898. SOURCE Brown 2, 1107; Wolff, 5148. LOCATION D (1900, 3rd edn), L.
    New York: Harper & Bros, 1897. LOCATION NUC.
    Leipzig: Bernard Tauchnitz, 1898. SOURCE T & B, 3284. LOCATION NUC.

COMMENTARY Chronicles the humours of political differences between a liberal husband and a conservative wife when the Home Rule question is much to the fore. Wilfred Ellis is divided between his love for the daughter of a ruined Irish landlord and his allegiance to a Lady Virginia [Brown 2; Sutherland].

'**NORTH, Danby**', pseud. See **MADDEN, Daniel Owen**.

'**A NORTHERN MAN**', pseud. See **BROWN, David**.

NORWAY, Arthur Hamilton. Co-author. See **RIDDELL, Mrs J.H.**

NUGENT-GRENVILLE, Lady Anne Lucy Poulett, pseud. 'L.'. Co-author. See **NUGENT-GRENVILLE, George, 3rd baron**.

NUGENT-GRENVILLE, George, 3rd Baron, pseuds '**G.**', '**Lord and Lady there**' (with his wife Anne Lucy Poulett), and '**William Spurstowe**', b. Kilmainham (Dublin) 1788, d. Lilies (Bucks.) 1850. Short story and miscellaneous writer and politician, GN-G, 3rd Baron Nugent of Carlanstown (Co. Westmeath), was the second son of George and Mary Elizabeth, marquess and marchioness of Buckingham. His mother was the daughter and co-heir of Robert Nugent, 1st Earl Nugent, and in 1800 she was created Baroness Nugent of Carlanstown with special remainder of the dignity to GN-G. GN-G matriculated at Oxford (Brasenose College) in 1804 and probably served with the army in the Peninsular War. He succeeded as Baron Nugent of Carlanstown in 1812, became MP for Buckingham (1810–12), and lord high commissioner for the Ionian Islands

(1832–35). In 1813 he married Anne Lucy, second daughter of Maj.-Gen. the Hon. Vere Poulett, who became his co-author. GN-G wrote short stories and poetry for periodicals, including the *Keepsake* (London, 1831) and *Bentley's Miscellany* (London, 1843). He published his *Some memorials of John Hampden* (London, 1832), and *Lands, classical and sacred* (London, 1845) based on his travels. A Whig radical in politics, GN-G espoused parliamentary reform, religious liberty, anti-slavery, free trade, Roman Catholic relief and education reform, frequently writing pamphlets on various topics. Maria Edgeworth§ in 1831 described Lord Nugent as 'a humorous Irishman and doats on Ireland after a short visit there but is not Irish and has not a foot of land there or anywhere else I believe – poor and married for love and seems still very glad of it' (Colvin, p. 491). She found his wife to be 'a great beauty'. Elizabeth Rennie mentions that GN-G was 'a literary man', who frequently contributed stories and political articles to the annuals. In appearance he was 'extremely stout … it is not often you see a man so badly made as he was' (Rennie, pp 212–13). A poet and classicist also, GN-G welcomed to his home at Lilies literary and political figures of the day. When he died, his peerage became extinct. For GN-G's portraits and papers, see ODNB. SOURCE Allibone, i, p. 738 [under Grenville]; Allibone, ii, p. 1444; Colvin, pp 491–2; CP, ix, pp 795–6; Curran index, BentM 861a, 891a, 899a; NCBEL 4, p. 345 [under Grenville]; [E. Rennie], *Traits of character* (London, 1860), ii, pp 212–13; O'Donoghue, p. 337; ODNB [under Grenville]; RIA/DIB.

N41   *Legends of the library at Lilies* (by the 'Lord and Lady there').
        London: Longman, Rees, Orme, Brown, Green & Longman, 1832, 2 vols. SOURCE Block, p. 174; Garside 2, 1832:67. LOCATION Corvey CME 3–628–51074–0, Dt, L, DCL, InND Loeber coll. (1837 edn).
        Philadelphia: Carey, Lea & Blanchard, 1833, 2 vols. SOURCE Kaser, 350. LOCATION PPL-R, NUC.
        COMMENTARY Collection of 17 stories and 2 poems, a few with Irish content, the joint production of Baron Nugent ('G.') and his wife, Anne Lucy Poulett ('L.'). Contents (excluding poetry): 'Isabel; or, the old angler's story' (by 'L.'), 'The confessions of a suspicious gentleman' (by 'L.' and 'G.'), 'The shooting star' (by 'G.'; first published in the *Keepsake*, London, 1830), 'The first fit of the gout, the end of man's happiness. A journal' (by 'G.'), 'The convent in the forest' (by 'L.'), 'The witch. A tale' (an Irish story by 'L.' and 'G.'), 'The old soldier' (by 'L.'), 'The odious Catholick question' (by 'L.'), 'The costlye dague – the ladyes counselloure' (by 'L.'), 'Misadventures of a short-sighted man. Written by himself' (by 'L.' and 'G.'), 'On superstition; with O'Sullivan's story of O'Donnell's breann' (an Irish story by 'G.'), 'Mrs. Allington's pic nic' (by 'G.'), 'A notion of convenience; with other solecisms in language' (by 'G.'), 'The promise kept' (by 'L.'), 'The man and the lioness' (by 'G.'), 'A propos of bread' (by 'G.'), 'La belle Chanoinesse' (by 'G.') [RL; Ximenes cat. 105/345].

N42   *Tract entitled true and faithful relations of a worthy discourse between Colonel John Hampden and Colonel Oliver Cromwell* (by 'William Spurstowe').
        London: Chapman & Hall, 1847. SOURCE COPAC. LOCATION L.
        COMMENTARY 61pp. Historical fiction. ODNB lists this as 'an agreeable fictional persiflage' [ODNB].

NUGENT, John F., fl. 1850s. Catholic publisher in Dublin who printed and sold the following work and probably compiled it. JFN published several Irish song and comical books. SOURCE COPAC; RL.

N43   *Nugent's Irish national winter evening tales, specially intended for the perusal of the Irish peasantry, young and old, – eminently calculated to subvert those stories previously printed, which jibed the Irish character and insulted the Celtic name!* [anon.].

+ Dublin: Printed [for the author?] by John F. Nugent, [185?], vol. 1 [all published] (ill.). SOURCE COPAC. LOCATION D, O.
COMMENTARY 36pp. Contents: 'Truly-interesting tale of Cauthleen and Darby, or, truth rewarded', 'Poor Paddy Connor and the broken fiddle [on title page, but in text: 'The broken fiddle!!']. A sketch from life', 'The Dutchman and the ruined forge' [on title page, but in text: 'The affecting tragic story of the ruined forge'], 'The beggarman and the blacksmith', 'Dhirro Dheerlha, or the sleeping warriors' [text has additional subtitle, 'A legend of Kildare'] (first published in the *Irish Penny Magazine* (Dublin, 1833), pp 309–10), 'Paul Doherty's visit to squire Beamton's', 'Ireland as it now is, and as it was 60 years ago!', 'Paul Murphy and the piano thirty!' [*sic*] [ML].

NUGENT, Robert (also known as **Robert Plunkett**), pseud. 'Himself', b. 1730. Fiction-alizing autobiographer, RN was from Co. Westmeath. According to the imprint of *The supplement* (London, 1755), the author was a prisoner in Fleet Street prison in London, where he remained at least as late as 1757, and from where he sold his books about his conflict with his father. According to the *Memoir of Robert, Earl Nugent* (Chicago, 1898), RN was the illegitimate son of Robert Craggs Nugent and his cousin Clare Nugent of Donore (Co. Westmeath). However, RN was also known as Robert Plunkett, named after one his father's wives, and the name he was asked to assume by his father when he joined the East India Company. The different names led to the author's paternity being called into question. The poet William Dunkin wrote in the early 1740s 'An epistle to Robert Nugent Esq. with a picture of Dr Jonathan Swift§' (published in *Select poetical works by the late William Dunkin D.D.*, Dublin, 1770, 2 vols., and repr. by Fagan). RN's father is not to be confused with another Robert Craggs Nugent of Carlanstown (Co. Westmeath), who was created Earl Nugent in 1767. SOURCE Allibone, ii, p. 1444; P. Fagan, *A Georgian celebration. Irish poets of the eighteenth century* (Dublin, 1989), pp 109–11, 115*n*.4; Field Day, iv, p. 823; C. Nugent, *Memoir of Robert, Earl Nugent* (Chicago, 1898), pp 316–44; R. Nugent, preface to *The unnatural father* (London, 1755); ODNB [under Earl Nugent]; RL.

N44   *The unnatural father; or, the persecuted son. Being a candid narrative of the most unparallleled [sic] sufferings of Caius Silius Nugenius, now under confinement in the Fleet Street Prison, at the suit of an implacable and relentless parent* (by 'Himself').
London: Printed for the author, 1755. SOURCE Allibone, ii, p. 1444; ESTC t050504. LOCATION Di.
COMMENTARY An annotated copy of this volume was for sale in 2004, giving part identification of the characters. For content, see next entry [Price cat., Sept. 2004/130].

N45   *The unnatural father, or the persecuted son, being a candid narrative of the most unparrellelled [sic] sufferings of Robert Nugent, junr. by the means and procurement of his own father. Written by himself, and earnestly recommended to the perusal of all those whose goodness gives them the inclination to alleviate the distress of the fellow-creatures, and are blest with the means* (by 'Himself').
+ London: Printed for the author and sufferer, now a Prisoner in the Fleet; and sold by him, and all the Booksellers in Town and County, 1755. LOCATION L.
COMMENTARY 64 pp. In this version of the above book, the names are not 'latinized', simply given with the first and last letter only in each name (e.g. name of father is given as R—t N—t, Esq.). Text deals with how paternity is established (his mother gives RN a statement before her death, signed by a witness, stating that RN is the 'real son' of R—t N—t, (p. 8)) This was done to ensure that his father treated him properly. The story details RN's disputes with his father. The close of the text is signed Robert Nugent, Jun., Fleet Prison, Feb 30, 1755 [JB].

N46   *A supplement to* The unnatural father, *or, the persecuted son: Being a candid nar-*
rative of the most unparalleled sufferings of Robert Nugent, Jun., by means and
procurement of his own father ... To which is prefixed an address to Stephen
Theodore Janssen Esq. (by 'Himself').
London: Printed for the author, 1755. SOURCE ESTC n024804; Field Day, iv, pp
785–6. LOCATION L.
COMMENTARY 36pp. The text raises the problem of how the author's paternity is established [ESTC; Field Day].

N47   *The oppressed captive. Being an historical novel, deduced from the distresses of real*
life, in an impartial and candid account of the unparalleled sufferings of Caius Silius
Nugenius, now under confinement in the Fleet Street Prison, at the suit of an implaca-
ble and relentless parent [anon.] (dedicated to the 'generous and humane reader').
+ London: Sold by the author and 'sufferer' in the Fleet Prison, 1757. SOURCE Forster,
2031; ESTC t92960. LOCATION L.
COMMENTARY The BL catalogue notes that 'Name of Plunkett occurs in Preface, that of Nugent
at p. 175. Autobiographical account with latinized names for historical figures. The main character is Caius Silius Nugenius who describes his background in Ireland. His father is Tiberium
Nugenius from Carlingstown [Carlanstown] in Co. Westmeath. His mother's father was Caius
Attilius Nugenius of Donore (Co. Westmeath). Caius Silius is the natural son of the two
cousins. He lived in Castle Pollard (Co. Westmeath) as an infant and later with Fr Lynch in
Galway (as related in the *Memoir*). He moves to England where he is denied help by his father
who puts him in prison, where he writes his life story [ML; C. Nugent, *Memoir of Robert,*
Earl Nugent (Chicago, 1898), pp 316–44; RL].

'THE NUN OF KENMARE', pseud. See **CUSACK, Margaret Anna**.

NUNN, John J., fl. 1869. Miscellaneous writer and poet, JJN can be identified with John Joshua
Nunn, second son of Joshua Nunn of St Margaret's and Hill Castle (Co. Wexford) and Mary
Westby. JJN first married Gertrude White, and secondly, Elizabeth Frances Peers, and had issue
from each marriage. In England, he must have lived at Cheltenham (Glos.) where his son Arthur
Westby Nunn also lived. According to the cover of *Portraits* (Cheltenham, [1893]), JJN also
wrote *Poetic waifs and strays* (not located); *A handy-book on agriculture* (Dublin, [1869]), and
"Spero Meloria": or, Ireland in 1869–70 (Dublin, 1869). SOURCE Burke's, p. 886; RIA/DIB; RL;
Rowe & Scallan, 538, 909.

N48   *Mrs. Montague Jones' dinner party; or, reminiscences of Cheltenham life and man-*
ner (by John J. Nunn).
+ London: John Camden Hotten, 1872 (ill. Harry Furniss§). LOCATION L.

N49   *Portraits of the people. English, Irish and Scotch* (by John J. Nunn).
+ Cheltenham: Horace Edwards, [1893]. LOCATION D, L.
COMMENTARY 190pp. Character sketches originally published in the *Clifton Chronicle* and the
Wexford Independent. Contents: 'The English farm labourer', 'The widow', 'The money lender
and his clients', 'Mrs. Nippers, a boarding house proprietor', 'The auctioneer', 'The fashion-
able physician', 'The Muldoon, M.P.', 'Sir Charles Kingsley, Bart.', 'The young squire',
'Madame de Barri', 'The curate', 'Sawney Muddyman, Esq.', 'Lacy Lound Fitzshirker, Esq.',
'The undergraduate' [RL].

NUNN, Mrs Lorenzo N., fl. 1852. Novelist, Mrs LNN can in all likelihood be identified
with Harriet Baker, who married in 1842 Lorenzo Nickson Nunn, barrister-at-law, third son
of John Nickson Nunn of Rosehill (Enniscorthy Castle, according to Keane, both Co. Wexford).

Nutt

Or he may be identified with the Lorenzo Nunn who resided at Medhop Hall, near Camolin (Co. Wexford) in 1853, and who was the son of John Miles Nunn, and had been admitted at TCD in 1825. Mrs LNN also wrote 'That developed age' and 'Hubert Dane', but these have not been located. SOURCE B & S, p. 625; Brown 2, p. 193; Burke's, p. 886; Keane, p. 368; RL; Rowe & Scallan, 693.

N50   *The militia major. A novel* (title on first page of each of the three vols: *The militia major or the social system of Tipperary*) [anon.].

+ London: Thomas Cautley Newby, 1852, 3 vols. SOURCE Allibone Suppl., ii, p. 1184; Brown 2, p. 193; Wolff, 5196. LOCATION L, NUC.

COMMENTARY A political novel. In the preface the author states that she attempted to express in a tale of fiction 'some leading facts connected with the 'Social System' that has plunged this unhappy land in all the barbarism of moral evil, beat back from her shores English capital, and Scottish enterprise, whilst her own industrial energies lie paralyzed and collapsed'. She protests that 'in our day [Ireland is] a vast pauper house seeking alimony from the land whose people she has fed with her grain'. Although admitting that agrarian outrages have occurred, she contends that most people trace their effects rather than their causes [RL].

N51   *Heirs of the soil* (by Mrs Lorenzo N. Nunn).

+ Dublin, London: Moffat & Co., [1870]. SOURCE Allibone Suppl., ii, p. 1184 (London, 1869 edn); Brown 2, 1109; Wolff, 5195 ([1869] edn). LOCATION D, Dt, L, NUC, InND Loeber coll.

COMMENTARY An anti-Catholic novel of post-Famine land agitation and romance set in Co. Cork. At the end of the Famine, a farmer is behind in his rent and is evicted by solicitors acting for Ormsby, the absentee landlord. The McCarthy family splits up; the parents to go into the workhouse, and the son, Owen, and daughter go to America. The local priest is also evicted and he curses the landlord and his family in church. The landlord is succeeded by his son, Arthur Ormsby, who lives with family and his cousin May and her fiancée in Glensallagh, the big house. Dudley Ormsby, a cousin from the north of Ireland, comes to visit. Owen McCarthy returns from America where he has been an officer in the Federal army. He wants to get back his father's farm and marry Alley Doran. Through his stay in America, Owen is more like a Protestant. The priest denounces him for his independent stand. In reaction, Owen agrees to train the Fenians at night. They are surprised by the police, and Owen flees with a bullet wound. In retaliation, Alley Doran's family is evicted. In the meantime, May falls in love with Dudley Ormsby. He loves her but fights against his love because of his friendship with May's fiancée. Arthur Ormsby finds a document that proves Dudley is the real owner of the estate. He clears the way for Dudley and May to declare their love. Arthur is killed by the Fenians in an ambush. Dudley and May reign with benevolence on the Glensallagh estate, granting tenants security of leases. Owen and his wife become important tenants [ML].

N52   *Sybarite and Spartan* (by Mrs Lorenzo N. Nunn).

London: Remington & Co., 1880, 3 vols. SOURCE Allibone Suppl., ii, p. 1184; Brown 2, p. 193; COPAC. LOCATION L, C.

NUTT, Alfred. Editor. See MACINNES, Revd D.

O

'O., S.', pseud. See **MORGAN, Lady.**

OAKMAN, John, b. Hendon (Middx.) *c.*1748, d. London 1793. English engraver, novelist, songwriter and print shop owner, JO wrote popular songs; burlesques for the theatre, and made wood engravings for children's books. In one of his volumes he attacked the institution of slavery. SOURCE ODNB.

O1   *The life and surprising adventures of Benjamin Brass, an Irish fortune-hunter* [anon.].
+ London: W. Nicoll, 1765, 2 vols. SOURCE Hardy, 105; Raven, 933; ESTC to57358. LOCATION D, L.
COMMENTARY The main character, a shoemaker and the son of Denis Brass, sets out from Munster to England to make a fortune. His fortune-hunting lands him in prison [ML].

'O'BARRY, Bartle', fl 1866. Story writer, B'OB is perhaps a pseudonym.

O2   *Queer customers: What they did and what they didn't. Promiscuously set down by their contemporary* (by 'Bartle O'Barry').
London, New York: George Routledge & Sons, 1866. LOCATION L, NUC.
+ London: Tindall Cox, 1871 (as *Queer customers (What they did and what they didn't); and the revelations of the Red Lamp Club*). SOURCE Brown 2, 1110. LOCATION D (1871, 2nd edn), L (1871, 2nd edn).
COMMENTARY Stories dealing with leprechauns, farcical characters and impossible situations, set mainly in Galway and Limerick [Brown 2].

'O BONNICLABBERO, Mac', possible pseud. See **FAREWELL, James.**

O'BRIEN, Charlotte. See **O'BRIEN, Charlotte Grace.**

O'BRIEN, Charlotte Grace (known as Charlotte O'Brien), pseud. 'Katherine Roche', b. Cahermoyle (also known as Cahirmoyle) House (Co. Limerick) 1845, d. Foynes (Co. Limerick) 1909. Novelist, children's writer, poet and social activist, CGO'B was the daughter of William Smith O'Brien, the nationalist politician, and Lucy Caroline Gabbett of High Park (Co. Limerick). She suffered from deafness and spent part of her childhood abroad with her father after his return in 1854 from Van Diemen's Land (Tasmania), where he had been transported for his part in the 1848 rebellion. She lived with him in Brussels from 1854 to 1856, when he was allowed to return to Ireland. After her father died in 1864, she moved back to the family house at Cahermoyle to live with her brother. Like her father, she became active in nationalist politics and was a supporter of Charles Stewart Parnell, the Land League and the Gaelic League. She was also active in social causes and wrote for *United Ireland*, the *Irish Monthly* and the *Nation* (all Dublin) and contributed articles and letters to the *Limerick Field Club Journal*; the *Irish Naturalist* (Dublin); *Nineteenth Century* (London) and the *Pall Mall Gazette* (London), often attacking government policies in Ireland. After the famine of 1879 increased the number of young women emigrating to the US, she worked strenuously to improve conditions on board emigrant ships and to establish boarding-houses for women at ports on both sides of the Atlantic, making the trip several times herself to observe conditions first hand. An article by her in the *Pall Mall Gazette* (London, 1881) led to an investigation of the White Star Line by the Board of Trade. CGO'B became a Catholic in 1887. Aside from novels and religious fiction, she wrote a play and poetry (including nationalist ballads and poems on emigrant life), which appeared in *Lyrics* (London, 1886). After the remarriage of her brother in 1870, she moved to Foynes, where she had built a house called 'Ardnanoir'. The Limerick author and carpenter William C. Upton§ was among her friends. CGO'B published at least 30 works of fiction, mostly aimed at juvenile readers (it is likely that more titles listed in an advertisement in her *Mary's visits to the gold fields* (London, [1858?]), eventually will be attributed to her). Many of her early works were issued in the Buds and Blossom Series in the form of chapbooks of 32pp each and priced at 2d. Before her conversion to catholicism, some of her work was sponsored by the Religious Tract Society. She contributed a story, 'The nine sisters, a legend of the O'Clerys', to E.W. Jacob's anthology, *Something new; or, tales for the times* (London, 1863). Her nephew Stephen Gwynn§ published selections of her poetry and essays and her portrait posthumously in 1909. 'Eleanor's story', mentioned by Murphy, probably appeared as a serial in 1878. For correspondence regarding her death, see ODNB; a large collection of pamphlets from the library of Cahirmoyle House is now in the NLI. SOURCE Allibone Suppl., ii, p. 1185; Blain, pp 804–5; Brady, p. 176; Brown, p. 230; Burmester list; Colman, pp 169–72; Field Day, v, p. 926; S. Gwynn, *Charlotte Grace O'Brien* (Dublin, 1909); Hogan 2, pp 905–6; Irish pseudonyms; LVP, p. 357; C. Miller, 'Tumbling into the flight': Charlotte Grace O'Brien (1845–1909), the emigrant's advocate' in *History Ireland*, 4 (1996), pp 44–8; Murphy, p. 28; NCBEL 4, p. 1842; OCIL, p. 399; O'Donoghue, p. 340; ODNB (which notes that some works by English author Charlotte O'Brien have been attributed to Charlotte Grace O'Brien); O'Toole, pp 228–30; RIA/DIB; Sutherland, p. 470.

O3 *Paddy Kiely* (by Charlotte O'Brien).
COMMENTARY Unpublished manuscript, a semi-autobiographical sketch. Contains the account of a farm labourer, just returned to Ireland from America, and tells harrowing family tales [J.McL. Côté, *Fanny & Anna Parnell* (London, 1991), p. 45].

O4 *The coral necklace* (by Charlotte O'Brien).
+ London: Office of the Family Economist, 1855 (Buds and Blossom Series). SOURCE Alston, p. 320. LOCATION L.
COMMENTARY A girl wavers between purchasing Maria Edgeworth's§ tales or a coral necklace. She buys the necklace but then regrets it. Also issued in London by Groombridge & Co., n.d., in the series Buds and Blossoms, and Stories for Summer Days and Winter Nights [RLIN; Adv. in C. O'Brien, *Mary's visits to the gold fields* (London, [1858?])].

O5 *Lady Eva: or rich and poor. A Christmas story* (by Charlotte O'Brien).
London: Office of the Family Economist, 1855 (ill. E. Whimper). SOURCE NCBEL 4, p. 1842; COPAC. LOCATION E, Univ. of Florida, Gainesville (FL).
COMMENTARY 31pp [RLIN].

O6 *Midsummer holidays at Beechwood farm* (by Charlotte O'Brien).
London: William Wesley, 1856 (ill. E. Whimper). SOURCE NCBEL 4, p. 1842; COPAC. LOCATION E, Univ. of Florida, Gainesville (FL).
COMMENTARY 32pp. Fiction for juveniles. Later reissued in London by Groombridge & Sons (1858) in the Buds and Blossom Series, and Stories for Summer Days and Winter Nights, priced at 2d. [RLIN; COPAC; Adv. in C. O'Brien, *Mary's visits to the gold fields* (London, [1858?])].

O7 *Primrose gathering* (by Charlotte O'Brien).
London: William Wesley, 1856 (ill. E. Whimper; Stories for Summer Days & Winter Nights). SOURCE NCBEL 4, p. 1842; RLIN. LOCATION Univ. of Florida.
COMMENTARY 32pp. Fiction for juveniles. Also issued in London by Groombridge & Co., n.d., in the series Buds and Blossoms, and Stories for Summer Days and Winter Nights, priced at 2d. [RLIN; Adv. in C. O'Brien, *Mary's visits to the gold fields* (London, [1858?])].

O8   *The cottagers' Christmas: The sequel to Lady Eva* (by Charlotte O'Brien).
      London: Office of the Family Economist, 1856 (ill. E. Whimper). SOURCE RLIN.
      LOCATION Univ. of Florida, Gainesville (FL).
      COMMENTARY 32pp. Fiction for juveniles [RLIN].

O9   *The children's visit to the water-fowl in St. James Park* [anon.].
      London: William Wesley, 1856 (ill.; Buds and Blossoms Two Pence Stories). SOURCE
      RLIN. LOCATION CSt.
COMMENTARY 32pp, priced at 2*d.* Fiction for juveniles. Author identified from *The coral neck-
lace, and other tales* (London, [1858?]) [RL; Adv. in C. O'Brien's *Mary's visit to the gold fields*
(London, [1858?])].

O10   *Ernest's dream. A Christmas story* (by Charlotte O'Brien).
      London: Groombridge & Sons, 1858 (Buds and Blossoms Series). SOURCE NCBEL 4,
      p. 1842; RLIN; Adv. in C. O'Brien, *Mary's visits to the gold fields* (London, [1858?]).
      LOCATION CSt.
      COMMENTARY 31pp, priced at 2*d.* Fiction for juveniles [RLIN].

O11   *The Irish emigrants* (by Charlotte O'Brien).
      London: Groombridge & Sons, [1858 or earlier?] (Buds and Blossoms, and Stories for
      Summer Days and Winter Nights). SOURCE Adv. in C. O'Brien's *Mary's visit to the
      gold fields* (London, [1858?]).
      COMMENTARY No copy located. Fiction for juveniles. Priced at 3*d.* [Adv. in C.
      O'Brien's *Mary's visit to the gold fields* (London, [1858?]); RL].

O12   *The lost letter* [anon.].
      London: Groombridge & Sons, [1858?] (ill. E. Whimper; Buds and Blossoms, and
      Stories for Summer Days and Winter Nights). SOURCE RLIN. LOCATION CSt.
COMMENTARY 32pp, priced at 2*d.* Fiction for juveniles. Author identified from *The coral neck-
lace, and other tales* (London, [1858?]) [RL; Adv. in C. O'Brien's *Mary's visit to the gold fields*
(London, [1858?])].

O13   *The coral necklace, and other tales* [anon.]
      London: Tallant & Allen, [1858?] (ill. E. Whimper). SOURCE RLIN. LOCATION Univ.
      of Florida, Gainesville (FL).
COMMENTARY Fiction for juveniles. Author identified according to sources mentioned in RLIN.
Contents: 'The coral necklace' (first published separately in London in 1855), 'The children's
visit to the water-fowl' (first published separately in London in 1856), 'The lost letter' (first
published separately in London in 1858?), 'Garden worthies', 'Round the world' (first published separately in London in 1858?), 'The Irish emigrants' (first published separately in
London before 1858?) [OCLC; RL].

O14   *The queen of the May* (by Charlotte O'Brien).
      London: Groombridge & Sons, 1858 (Buds and Blossoms, and Stories for Summer
      Days and Winter Nights; ill. E. Whimper). SOURCE NCBEL 4, p. 1842; RLIN.
      LOCATION L, Univ. of Florida.
      COMMENTARY 32pp, and priced at 2*d.* Fiction for juveniles [Adv. in C. O'Brien, *Mary's
      visits to the gold fields* (London, [1858?])].

O15   *Mary's visit to the gold fields* (by Charlotte O'Brien).
      + London: Groombridge & Sons, [1858?] (Buds and Blossoms, and Stories for Summer
      Days and Winter Nights). LOCATION Univ. of London; PC.
      COMMENTARY 32pp, priced at 2*d.* Fiction for juveniles. Contents: 'Mary's visit to the
      gold fields', 'The gold fish' [RL].

O16   *Margaret and her friends* [anon.].
      Philadelphia: James S. Claxton, 1859. SOURCE OCLC. LOCATION L (destroyed), NN.

London: John Morgan, [1864] (by Charlotte O'Brien; ill. W. Dickens). SOURCE Allibone Suppl., ii, p. 1185 (attributes this to Mrs Charlotte O'Brien [*sic*]); Alston, p. 320 LOCATION L (destroyed), O.

COMMENTARY Fiction for juveniles. Set among the poor in London [RL].

O17   *Gipsy Jem, or Willie's revenge* [anon.].
+ London: Society for Promotion of Christian Knowledge, [1861]. LOCATION L. Dublin: Catholic Truth Society, n.d. SOURCE Adv. in R. Mulholland's§ *Marigold* (Dublin, 1894) where listed as by 'Katherine Roche'.
Philadelphia: Alfred Martien, 1870 (ill.). SOURCE NCBEL, 4, p. 1842 (1872 edn); OCLC. LOCATION Gettysburg College, PA.
COMMENTARY No copy of the Dublin edn located [RL].

O18   *The young folks of Hazelbrook* [anon.].
London: Religious Tract Society, 1864. SOURCE NCBEL 4, p. 1842. LOCATION L.

O19   *Bessie Field: A cottage story* (by Charlotte O'Brien).
London: Christian Knowledge Society, [1864]. SOURCE Allibone Suppl., ii, p. 1185 (attributes this to Mrs Charlotte O'Brien [*sic*]); Alston, p. 320. LOCATION L (destroyed), NUC.
COMMENTARY Religious fiction [BLC].

O20   *Oliver Dale's decision* (by Charlotte O'Brien).
London: John Morgan, [1864]. SOURCE Allibone Suppl., ii, p. 1185 (attributes this to Mrs Charlotte O'Brien [*sic*]); Alston, p. 320; OCLC; COPAC. LOCATION L (destroyed), E.
+ London: Wells Gardner, Darton & Co., 1889 (as *Oliver Dale*; ill.). SOURCE D (1898 edn). LOCATION InND Loeber coll.
Philadelphia: James S. Claxton, [1867]. SOURCE NYPL. LOCATION L (destroyed), NN
COMMENTARY Religious fiction about a young boy who learns responsible behaviour and work skills through practicing religion [ML].

O21   *Basil: or, honesty and industry* (by Charlotte O'Brien).
+ London: Religious Truth Society, [1865] (ill.). LOCATION L.

O22   *Mother's warm shawl. A tale* (by Charlotte O'Brien).
+ London: John Morgan, [1865]. SOURCE Allibone Suppl., ii, p. 1185 (attributes this to Mrs Charlotte O'Brien [*sic*]); Alston, p. 320. LOCATION D (1893 edn), L, InND Loeber coll. (London: Wells, 1890 edn).
Philadelphia: James S. Claxton, [1870?]. LOCATION L.

COMMENTARY Set in England where Mary, the daughter of respectable cottagers, is going out to service in a big house. Her mother presents her with a warm cloak she has made from her own cloak. Mary promises to buy her mother a shawl from the money that she will earn. In the big house she falls under the influence of other servant girls who are interested in dresses and parties. Instead of buying her mother a shawl, she spends money on finery for herself. She is dismissed from her employment because she went to a party at an inn. She returns home without a shawl, but in a repentant mood, not planning to leave her neighbourhood again. A kindly woman in the village gives Mary a warm shawl to present to her mother [ML].

O23   *Owen Netherby's choice* (by Charlotte O'Brien).
London: Christian Knowledge Society, [1866]. SOURCE Alston, p. 320. LOCATION L (destroyed).
COMMENTARY Religious fiction [BLC].

O24   *Cottage stories* (by Charlotte O'Brien).
[London]: [publisher?], 1866. SOURCE Allibone Suppl., ii, p. 1185.
COMMENTARY Priced at 2*d*. No copy located. Allibone attributes this to Mrs Charlotte O'Brien [*sic*] [RL; Allibone Suppl., ii, p. 1185].

O25   *George Wayland: the little medicine carrier* (by Charlotte O'Brien).

London: Religious Tract Society, 1866. SOURCE NCBEL 4, p. 1842. LOCATION L.

O26   *Ben Holt's good name* [anon.].
London: Religious Tract Society, [1867]. LOCATION L (destroyed).
COMMENTARY Religious fiction [BLC].

O27   *Little gipsy Marion: A tale* (by Charlotte O'Brien).
Edinburgh: [publisher?], [1870]. SOURCE Alston, p. 320; COPAC. LOCATION L
(destroyed), E.
London: Gall & Inglis, [1895] (as *Gipsy Marion. A story of the New Forest*). SOURCE
Alston, p. 320; COPAC. LOCATION L.
COMMENTARY Fiction for juveniles. Classified in the BL cat. as religious fiction [RL;
BLC].

O28   *Walter and Frank; or, the two paths* (by Charlotte O'Brien).
+ Edinburgh: Gall & Inglis, [1870]. SOURCE Alston, p. 320; COPAC. LOCATION L
(destroyed), E.
COMMENTARY Allibone attributes this to Mrs Charlotte O'Brien [*sic*] [Allibone Suppl.,
ii, p. 1185].

O29   *Dominick's trials. An Irish story* (by Charlotte O'Brien).
Edinburgh: Gall & Inglis, [1870]. SOURCE Brown, 1255. LOCATION L.
COMMENTARY Religious fiction relating how Dominick is converted to protestantism through
reading his Bible. As a result of his conversion, he loses his job as a farmer's scarecrow. He
converts his sister Judy and is sent with her to a Protestant orphanage in England, after which
they never lose an opportunity to try to convert Roman Catholics to protestantism [Brown].

O30   *Light and shade* (by Charlotte O'Brien).
+ London: Kegan Paul & Co., 1878, 2 vols. SOURCE Allibone Suppl., ii, p. 1185 (attributes this to Mrs Charlotte O'Brien [*sic*]); Brown, 1256. LOCATION L, NUC.
New York: Harper & Bros, 1878 (Franklin Square Library, No. 29). LOCATION NUC.
COMMENTARY Serialized in the *Illustrated Celtic Monthly* (New York, 1879), the novel concerns the Fenian uprising and shows the sufferings of the Irish peasants and their consequent
resentment. Some gestures of goodwill are by the landlords as well by the Fenians. It includes
a strong protest against conditions for interned Irishmen held in Mountjoy Prison under the
suspended Habeas Corpus act, and ends with the hero and heroine emigrating to America.
Stephen Gwynn stated that CGO'B gathered much of the information for this novel from 'the
lips of men who had been active in the Fenian rising' [RL; Brown; Blain; Field Day, v, p.
926; S. Gwynn, *Charlotte Grace O'Brien* (Dublin, 1909); Murphy, p. 41; OCIL, p. 399;
Sutherland, p. 471].

O31   *Northcliffe boys* (by Charlotte O'Brien).
+ London: Religious Tract Society, [1880] (ill.). SOURCE Alston, p. 320. LOCATION L
(destroyed), InND Loeber coll.
COMMENTARY Religious fiction [BLC].

O32   *Frank Hardy's choice, and what came of it* (by Charlotte O'Brien).
London: Gall & Inglis, [1897]. SOURCE Alston, p. 320; COPAC. LOCATION L
(destroyed), E.
COMMENTARY Religious fiction [BLC].

O'BRIEN, Fr Cornelius, b. New Glasgow, PEI (Canada) 1843, d. 1906. Catholic priest,
writer on religion, biographer, poet and novelist, CO'B was the son of Irish-born parents
Terence O'Brien, from Munster, and Catherine O'Driscoll. He was educated at St Dunstan's
College, Charlottetown, and later at the College of Propaganda in Rome. He was ordained in
1871 and became Roman Catholic archbishop of Halifax in 1882, in which position he served

until his death. Aside from religious works, a biography of Edmund Burke (first bishop of Halifax, Ottawa, 1894), and the following novel, he also published a narrative poem, *Aminta. A modern life drama* (New York 1890), and contributed verse to the Boston *Pilot.* SOURCE Allibone Suppl., ii, p. 1185; DCB; MDCB, pp 622–3; ODNB; O'Donoghue, p. 340.

O33   *After weary years* (by Cornelius O'Brien).
+ Baltimore, New York: John Murphy & Co., 1885. SOURCE Allibone Suppl., ii, p. 1185; Watters, p. 355 (who added *A novel* to the title, but this is not on the title page of the book). LOCATION DCU, NUC.
COMMENTARY A partly-autobiographical novel featuring Morgan Leahy, of Irish extraction born in Canada, his journey to Italy, the Catholic church in Rome, and his return to Canada [RL; DCB].

'O'BRIEN, Desmond', pseud. See **KING, Richard Ashe**.

O'BRIEN, Dillon, b. Kilmore, Co. Roscommon (Tullabeg, according to OCIL) 1817 (1818 according to Fanning), d. St Paul (MN) 1882. Novelist son of a prosperous Catholic landowner with estates in Roscommon and Galway, DO'B was educated at St Stanislaus College, Tullabeg, and later by the Jesuits at Clongowes Wood College (Co. Kildare). He married Elizabeth Kelly, daughter of a respected Galway magistrate and huntsman, and began married life as a country squire on one of the family's holdings. However, the Famine ruined the O'Brien family and their generosity to Catholic tenants during those years rendered them landless by 1850. Shortly after, DO'B with his wife and children sailed for America. After a few years in Detroit, he took a job running the Indian school at LaPointe, Madeline Island (WI), an isolated fishing and trading post on Lake Superior, where he wrote his first novel. In 1863 the family moved to St Paul where DO'B became editor of the Catholic weekly newspaper, the *Northwestern Chronicle.* After 1869 he lived on his own farm until his death. He spent years working towards the founding of the Irish Catholic Colonization Association in 1879. SOURCE Brown, p. 230; Fanning, pp 88, 93; OCIL, p. 400; O'Donoghue, p. 340; RIA/DIB; Roscommon, p. 105.

O34   *The Dalys of Dalystown* (by Dillon O'Brien).
+ St Paul: Pioneer Printing Co., 1866. SOURCE Brown, 1257; Fanning, p. 387; Wright, ii, 1808. LOCATION D, NUC, Wright web.
COMMENTARY Most likely this novel about Godfrey Daly, a Catholic landlord in a 'big house' in the northeast corner of Co. Galway near the border with Mayo and Roscommon, is partly-autobiographical. A compassionate landlord, Daly has come under the power of the evil middleman, O'Roarke, who holds mortgages on the Dalystown estate. Vowing vengeance on O'Roarke for having driven scores of tenants from their homes, the Ribbonmen plot his death. The murder exposes the group, which has been infiltrated by an English spy. When the mortgage becomes due, Godfrey Daly falls ill and dies. His son Henry sets off for America in 1825 in search of fortune and Rose O'Donnell, his lost love. He finds Rose in a backwoods Canadian cabin and earns a substantial living as a farmer in Michigan. In 1848 the now wealthy Henry hears about the Famine in Ireland, and that Dalystown is up for sale. He sails back and purchases the ancestral and neglected estate [Fanning, pp 89–91].

O35   *Dead broke. A Western tale* (by Dillon O'Brien; dedicated to the author's wife [Elizabeth O'Brien]).
St Paul: Pioneer Printing Co., 1873. SOURCE Fanning, p. 388; Wright, ii, 1809. LOCATION NUC, Wright web.
COMMENTARY Serialized in the *Irish Monthly* (Dublin, 1882), as 'Dead broke'. The story of a Scottish immigrant to the Michigan Territory whose son wanders out west and ultimately returns to his home [Brown, p. 230; Fanning, p. 92].

O36   *Frank Blake* (by Dillon O'Brien).
St Paul: Pioneer Printing Co., 1876. SOURCE Allibone Suppl., ii, p. 1185; Brown, 1258; Fanning, p. 388; Wright, iii, 4017. LOCATION NUC.
COMMENTARY A romance set in the village of 'Renville' [perhaps Renvyle], a seaside resort town in Connemara in the early-nineteenth century. The courtship between the Catholic royal navy lieutenant Frank Blake, who is in charge of the coast guard detachment at Renville, and Susan Howard, daughter of the village's Church of Ireland rector, culminates in Susan's conversion to catholicism. Frank is arrested for the murder of Robert Eyre, the dissolute, fox-hunting son of the district's big landlord, Lord Eyrecourt. A surprise witness, the returned immigrant Willie Joyce who found the real murderer in New York and extracted a signed confession before his death, saves Frank. Frank and Susan marry and Willie Joyce remains in Ireland as head gamekeeper for Lord Eyrecourt [Fanning, p. 92].

O37   *Widow Melville's boarding house* (by Dillon O'Brien).
St Paul: Pioneer Printing Co., 1881. SOURCE Fanning, p. 388; Wright, iii, 4018. LOCATION NUC.
COMMENTARY Set in Fairoaks, a town in one of the western states of America, where the widow Melville supports herself and her son Harry by feeding and housing a pleasant group of boarders. The boy grows up and wanders off to make his fortune, returning to settle in his hometown after having struck it rich in the California gold fields [Fanning, p. 93].

O'BRIEN, Fitz-James. See **O'BRIEN, Michael Fitz-James.**

O'BRIEN, Frances Marcella (also known as Attie O'Brien), b. near Ennis (Co. Clare) 1840, d. Dublin 1883. Poet and serial fiction writer, AO'B came from a Catholic family from Peafield, near Ennis. Her mother, Margaret Burke-Browne, died when she was very young and her father, William O'Brien, an unsuccessful farmer, emigrated with his new wife, and 'all his sons'. AO'B was brought up by her grandmother at the town of Tulla (Co. Clare), later moving to Kildysart (also known as Killadysart) to live her aunt and grandmother. She did not enjoy good health and did not receive much formal education, but she read widely. She received intellectual direction from the parish priest and from Fr Matthew Russell, who published her poetry in a local newspaper in Ennis (Co. Clare) and fiction in the Dublin *Irish Monthly* (1878–98), including the serials, 'Won by worth' in 1892, and 'Through the dark night' in 1898. The RIA/DIB mentions that each serial was published as a book, but we were unable to locate such volumes. She contributed also to the *Nation, Weekly Freeman, Young Ireland* (all Dublin) and *Tinsley's Magazine* (London). She had difficulty in breaking into the English market, which she attributed to reluctance by publishers to feature writings with a Catholic focus, but in Ireland she met with conservative criticism for featuring contemporary social issues. Some of her work appeared posthumously. She suffered from asthma all her life but was actively engaged in charitable works. Her journal, which records what she used to read, was excerpted by Mrs Morgan John O'Connell (Dublin, 1887), who also may have acted as an editor of *The Carradassan family* (New York, 1897), which appeared posthumously. Toward the end of her life she moved to Dublin. She was buried at Killadysert graveyard (Co. Clare). SOURCE Brown, p. 230; Colman, pp 172–3; Field Day, v, p. 929; Irish pseudonyms; McKenna, p. 294–5; Murphy, pp 31, 36, 41; M.J. O'Connell, *Glimpses of a hidden life: Memories of Attie O'Brien* (Dublin, 1887); OCIL, p. 399; O'Donoghue, pp 340–1; O'Toole, pp 225–7, 239; RIA/DIB.

O38   *The monk's prophecy and other tales* (by Frances Marcella O'Brien?).
New York: Hickey & Co., n.d. SOURCE DCU, Catholic Americana files.

COMMENTARY No copy located. First published in the *Irish Monthly* (1882–3). The story delights in the embarrassment of Mrs Hassett, who had opposed the association of her brother, Eugene, and Ida Lestrange, as she had planned for him to marry an heiress. Ida's impoverished brother Frank is engaged to Sydney Ormsby, an orphaned girl, who had once looked in vain to Mrs Hassett, a family friend, for help. Mrs Hassett is humiliated when Frank inherits a lucrative earldom, Sydney becomes socially significant and Ida becomes a desirable heiress [RL; Murphy, pp 26–8; O'Toole, p. 227].

O39   *The Carradassan family: An Irish tale* (by Mrs Morgan John O'Connell [*sic*]).
       New York: Vatican Library, 1891. SOURCE OCLC; Brown, 1254 (New York, Sadleir, 1897 edn). LOCATION D.
COMMENTARY Published posthumously. Author attribution to AO'B was established by Brown. However, OCLC lists the New York edn under Mrs Morgan John O'Connell, who later published a memoir about AO'B (see above), and may have acted as editor of this novel, which was first serialized in the *Irish Monthly* (Dublin, 1888). Carradassan is an estate on the Shannon, home to a Col. Fitzgerald and his family. They have taken in an orphan, Charlie McCarthy. Charlie is in love with Letty, the eldest daughter, but the English Capt. Calvert and family misfortunes come between them. After many adventures Charlie comes back from America to save the family estate and to marry Letty [RL; Brown; Murphy, p. 37].

O'BRIEN, Harriet Newell. See **LEWIS, Harriet Newell**.

O'BRIEN, Mary, pseud. '**A Lady**', fl. 1790. Poet, playwright and prose writer, MO'B was married to Patrick O'Brien. She stayed at least for a while in London in the 1780s. She wrote the comedy *The fallen patriot* (Dublin, 1790) that satirizes the search for titles in exchange for Irish rights. According to Blain and O'Donoghue, she published the novel *Charles Henley* (London, 1790; no copy located), but Raven 2 attributes this to Sarah Green§. The BL has the manuscript of her opera 'The temple of virtue'. SOURCE Blain, pp 807–8; O'Donoghue, p. 341; Raven 2, 1790:47.

O'BRIEN, Mary, fl. 1838. Instructional and fiction writer who, judging from the following volume, may have been born and reared in the barony of Forth (Co. Wexford). However, names mentioned in the volume appear fictitious. SOURCE Personal communication, Kevin Whelan, Nov. 1997; RL.
O40   *The guide to service. The dairy-maid* (by Mary O'Brien).
       + London: Charles Knight & Co., 1838 (ill.). LOCATION L, InND Loeber coll. (1843 edn).
COMMENTARY 71pp. Part of the series *The guide to service* (London, 1838–44, 17 parts). This separately-numbered part of the series, set in the barony of Forth (Co. Wexford), is an instructional and autobiographical story about the life of a dairymaid who has injured her back and will not be able to work anymore. The daughter of a labourer, she became a dairymaid to the wife of the agent of the absentee landowner. In the story, she needs some convincing to become an author, and she tells all she knows about being a proper dairymaid for the benefit of other girls who have to go into service. It includes specific instructions on how to prepare dairy products [ML; RL].

O'BRIEN, Michael Fitz-James (also known as **Fitz-James O'Brien**), b. most likely Co. Cork (RIA/DIB says lived on the South Mall in Cork, but Co. Limerick is mentioned in some sources) 1828, d. Cumberland (MD) 1862. Short story writer, poet, playwright and soldier, MF-JO'B was the son of a lawyer, James O'Brien, and his wife Eliza O'Driscoll of Baltimore, west Cork, and was raised on the family estates there. After his father's death and his mother's remarriage, he moved with her and her new husband to Castleconnell (Co. Limerick) where he was educated privately and had an active, outdoor life. He was educated at TCD (RIA/DIB says this is a fallacious claim but that he probably spent time in France since he spoke the language fluently). He observed the effects of the Famine first-hand, especially since Skibbereen, one of the hardest hit areas, was close to his mother's family home. This prompted him to write a poem calling for the relief of the suffering peasantry and advocating emigration to America. It was published in the *Nation* (Dublin) and was followed by more poems, some published in the *Cork Magazine* and in the *Irishman* (Dublin). In 1849 he came into a considerable inheritance, which he took to London and squandered in a little over two years while publishing in the *Metropolitan* (London) and the *Parlour* (location unclear) magazines. His first story, 'The phantom light', appeared in the *Home Companion* (London, n.d.). When the money ran out, he emigrated to New York in 1852 and quickly established himself as a leader of the bohemian literary group that included Walt Whitman. His first literary contribution in New York was to the *Lantern*, a comic magazine founded by the Irish actor and theatre manager John Brougham§. MF-JO'B became drama editor of the *Saturday Press* (New York) and took a position on the staff of the *New York Daily Times*, contributing stories, poems, literary reviews and essays. He also contributed essays, stories, and poems to New York magazines including *Harper's* and *Scribner's*, as well as to the Boston *Atlantic Monthly*. A story, 'Bob O'Link', appeared in *Tales of the time* (New York, Boston, 1861), and 'From hand to mouth' and 'Three of a trade; or, red little Kris Kringle' in *Good stories* (Boston, 1867–8). For about nine months in 1857 he contributed a 'Man about town' column to *Harper's Weekly* (New York) which, while it brought him fame, he could not sustain. He also wrote six plays (ten according to OCIL), including 'A gentleman of Ireland', about an Irishman in London, which opened to great success in 1854 with the lead role played by John Brougham. At the outbreak of the Civil War, he joined the Union army's Seventh Regiment and was killed in action at Cumberland (MD) in 1862. All of his books were published posthumously. Some of MF-JO'B's stories are still anthologized and he was described in the US as the Celtic [Edgar Allan] Poe. His work has been translated into French, Spanish, Italian and Japanese (RIA/DIB). His manuscripts are in the NYPL (Berg collection). His portrait was published by Wolle. SOURCE Allibone Suppl., ii, p. 1185; Brown, p. 231; Burke, p. 538; DAB; DLB, vol. 74; Fanning, p. 87; Irish pseudonyms; McKenna, p. 296; OCIL, p. 401; O'Donoghue, p. 340; RIA/DIB; J.A. Salmonson (ed.), *The supernatural tales of Fitz-James O'Brien* (New York, 1988); Wilson, pp 386–7; F. Wolle, *Fitz-James O'Brien, a literary Bohemian of the eighteen-fifties* (Boulder, CO, 1944).

O41   *The poems and stories of Fitz-James O'Brien.*

+ Boston: James R. Osgood & Co., 1881 (collected and ed., with a sketch of the author, by William Winter and recollections of the author, dedicated to the army of the Potomac; ill.). SOURCE Brown, 1259; Rafroidi, ii, p. 300; Wright, iii, 4020. LOCATION D, NUC, InND Loeber coll.

+ New York: Charles Scribner's Sons, 1885 (as *The diamond lens with other stories*; ed. by William Winter). SOURCE Blessing, p. 152. LOCATION D, L, NUC, InND Loeber coll. (1893 edn).

Philadelphia: H. Altemus, 1909 (as *The diamond lens*). SOURCE Blessing, p. 152. SOURCE OCLC. LOCATION NUC (n.d. edn), Univ. of Iowa.

+ London: Ward & Downey, 1887. SOURCE Brown, 1260. LOCATION DPL, L, NUC.

COMMENTARY Contents (Boston edn; excluding poetry): 'The diamond lens' (about a man who commits murder to obtain the perfect lens, which enables him to see a sylph in a drop of water but when the water evaporates he goes mad), 'The wondersmith' (about diabolic toys that eventually attack their creators), 'Tommatoo', 'Mother of pearl', 'The Bohemian', 'The lost room', 'The pot of tulips', 'The golden ingot', 'The wife's temper', 'What was it?', 'Duke Humphrey's dinner', 'Milly Dove', 'The dragon fang' [RL; RIA/DIB].

O42   *Collected stories* (by Fitz-James O'Brien; ed. and introd. by Edward J. O'Brien).
+ New York: Albert & Charles Boni, 1925. SOURCE Blessing, p. 152. LOCATION NUC, MH.

COMMENTARY Contents: 'The diamond lens', 'The wondersmith', 'The lost room', 'The pot of tulips', 'The golden ingot', 'My wife's temper', 'What was it?', 'The dragon fang possessed by the conjurer Piou-Lu' [MLa].

O43   *What was it? and other stories* (by Fitz-James O'Brien).
London: Ward & Downey, 1889. SOURCE Blessing, p. 152; Topp 8, 87. LOCATION L, NUC.

COMMENTARY 'What was it' concerns an encounter with an invisible monster [RIA/DIB].

O44   *The fantastic tales of Fitz-James O'Brien.*
+ London: John Calder, 1977 (ed. by Michael Hayes). SOURCE Rafroidi, ii, p. 300. LOCATION DPL, L, InND Loeber coll.

COMMENTARY Contents: 'The diamond lens', 'The lost room', 'What was it?', 'The wonder-smith', 'Seeing the world', 'The pot of tulips', 'The dragon fang possessed by the conjurer Piou-Lu' [RL].

O'BRIEN, Fr (Msgr) Richard Baptist, pseud. **'Father Baptist'**, b. Carrick-on-Suir (Co. Tipperary) 1809, d. Newcastle West (Co. Limerick) 1885. Novelist RBO'B was a member of the staff of All Hallows College, Dublin, and resided for a number of years in North America. Returning to Ireland, he became parish priest at Newcastle West before being made dean of Limerick. He was well-known for his religious and philanthropic works and was the founder of the Catholic Young Men's Society. He wrote poems for the Dublin *Nation* under his pseu-donym and contributed to two Dublin periodicals, the *Irish Catholic Magazine* and the *Irish Monthly*. In 1853 he lectured on Irish history and poverty before the Young Men's Society of Cork. He resigned from the society to get more involved in politics, and was a supporter of Home Rule. SOURCE Boase, vi, p. 315; Brady, p. 179; Brown, p. 231; Hogan 2, p. 916; Irish pseudonyms; McKenna, p. 297; Murphy, p. 55; R.B. O'Brien, *Ireland and the invasion: and why Ireland is poor* (Cork, 1854); OCIL, pp 402–3; O'Donoghue, p. 342; E. Reilly, p. 249; RIA/DIB; Sutherland, p. 471.

O45   *Ailey Moore. A tale of the times; showing how evictions, murder, and such-like pas-times are managed and justice administered in Ireland. Together with many stir-ring incidents in other lands* (by 'Father Baptist', dedicated to the Rt Revd Dr Moriarty, co-adjutor bishop of Kerry).
+ London: C. Dolman; Baltimore: J. Murphy & Co., 1856. SOURCE NSTC. LOCATION D, L.
+ Paris: P. Lethielleux; Tournai: H. Casterman, 1859 (trans. by Joseph Chantrel as *Ailey Moore, scènes irlandaises contemporaines* par le 'R.P. Baptiste' [*sic*]). SOURCE NSTC. LOCATION L.
+ New York: Edward Dunigan & Brother, 1856. LOCATION DCU.
Dublin: James Duffy, 1867. SOURCE Brown, 1264 (mentions [1856] edn, 3 vols., but this must be mistaken); McKenna, p. 297 (1856 edn [*sic*]); OCLC. LOCATION D, Dt (1867, 3rd edn), DPL (1867, 4th edn), InND Loeber coll. (1867, 4th edn).

COMMENTARY A somewhat anti-Protestant historical story set in Ireland around 1848. Gerald Moore, a Catholic, is accused of the murder of the landlord, Skerin. The murder had been committed by a Protestant land agent attorney named Snapper, who has had false evidence brought against Gerald in revenge for Gerald's sister's rejection of his marriage proposal. Eventually Gerald is vindicated and he receives the congratulations and admiration of the trial judge. The story condemns converts [Murphy, p. 19; Fegan, p. 223; Hartman, 345].

O46 *Jack Hazlitt, A.M. A Hiberno-American story in which the indisputable advantages of unsectarian education and free thought are illustrated, and some startling scenes, at home and abroad, are set forth* (by Richard Baptist O'Brien).

+ Dublin, London: James Duffy & Sons, 1875. SOURCE McKenna, p. 297. LOCATION D (n.d. edn), DPL, L, InND Loeber coll.

New York: Benziger, [1875]. SOURCE Brown, 1265.

COMMENTARY No copy of the New York edn located. First serialized in the *Irish Monthly Magazine* (Dublin, 1874) as 'Jack Hazlitt, M.A.' The story, purportedly founded on facts, sets out to show the dangers of a lax religious education. Jack Hazlitt, born near the Shannon, had a Roman Catholic mother, but his father was indifferent to religion. He was educated in one of the Queen's Colleges, and grows up to be no good. He is heavily in debt, abducts a girl, and goes to the US where he lives under an assumed name and is involved in dreadful scams, in which some people lose their lives. Eventually he is caught by the police, and dies. His mode of living is contrasted with the Catholics in the story, who seem to be the only ones to lead virtuous lives. A critique of the book was published as a separate pamphlet (C.F. Desmond, *The Very Reverend Dean O'Brien and "Jack Hazlitt": A review and criticism,* Dublin, 1878) [ML; Clyde, p. 136; RL].

O47 *The D'Altons of Crag. A story of '48 and '49* (by Richard Baptist O'Brien).

+ Dublin: James Duffy & Sons, 1882. SOURCE Brown, 1266; McKenna, p. 297. LOCATION D, Dt ([1920] edn), L, NUC, InND Loeber coll. (n.d. edn).

New York: Benziger, [1882]. SOURCE Brown, 1266.

COMMENTARY No copy of New York edn located. First serialized in the *Harp* (Montreal, 1879) and starting in 1883 in *Donahoe's Magazine* (Boston). Set mainly in Carrick-on-Suir (Co. Waterford) at the time of the Young Ireland movement in the late 1840s where Mr D'Alton is threatened with murder by a secret society. However, a bigger threat comes from his nephew, who stands to inherit after his death. Eventually Mr D'Alton's disinherited son returns and is reunited with his father. The benevolent power of the Catholic clergy is in evidence throughout the book. It describes the consequences of the Famine and the spread of fever and presents an unfavourable account of the soupers and converts [ML; RL; Fegan, p. 223].

O'BRIEN, William, b. Mallow (Co. Cork) 1852, d. London 1928. Patriot, politician, journalist and writer, WO'B was the son of a solicitor's clerk, and Kate Nagle. Although of Catholic parentage, he was educated at the Protestant Cloyne Diocesan College and at Queen's College, Cork, where he studied law but did not graduate as he was needed to support the family's finances. He began work as a journalist on the *Cork Daily Herald*, where the plight of tenant farmers first drew his attention. Later he joined the Dublin *Freeman's Journal* in 1875 and published a pamphlet *Christmas in the Galtees* (Dublin, 1878) that described the condition of poor tenants on the Buckley estate threatened with eviction. It set out his aspirations for government reform and the redress of Irish issues through constitutional means. He became editor of the Land League journal *United Ireland* (Dublin) in 1881, conducting it with such militancy that it was suppressed, leading to his arrest. In Kilmainham Jail, at Parnell's urging, he wrote 'The no rent manifesto' (published in *United Ireland*, 22 Oct. 1881) urging farmers to withhold rent until the land question was resolved. He was released in 1883 and elected MP for Mallow and, despite his repugnance for serving in the English parliament, was a member almost continuously from then until 1918, representing a number of different constituencies and being imprisoned again and again for his activities. He continued his no rent campaign in *United Ireland* and was active in land politics for several decades, having a crucial hand in the passage of Wyndham's Land Act of 1903, which effectively ended agitation over land issues. WO'B remained personally loyal to Parnell after the split in the Irish Parliamentary Party following the O'Shea divorce case, but joined the anti-Parnell group for reasons of political effectiveness and ceded leadership to Justin McCarthy§. He founded the United Irish League in 1898 to promote tenant rights and the ideal of 'conference, conciliation, consent'. Gradually he became the dominant figure in the Irish nationalist movement. In 1909 he formed the All-for-Ireland League, an attempt to win over Protestant enthusiasm for Irish nationalism. Such ideas were gradually overtaken by the rise of Sinn Féin militancy and he effectively retired from political life after the Easter Rising (1916). He believed in the ideal of a united, non-sectarian, autonomous Ireland and feared that conflict would destroy the chance to achieve it. He did not contest his seat in the 1918 election. Besides *United Ireland*, WO'B was actively involved with the *Irish People* (Dublin 1899–1909), the *Cork Accent* (1910), and the *Cork Free Press* (1910–16). His 'Kilsheelan; or, the old place and the new people' appeared as a serial in a Montreal magazine and in the *Shamrock* (Dublin, 1872), but it was not published in book form. He had plans to write a sequel to his *When we were boys* (London, 1890) to redeem the clergy, whom he had seriously criticized in the volume, but the plans were not realized. He advocated the revival of Gaelic literature in his lecture, 'The influence of the Irish language on Irish national literature and character', before the Cork National Society in 1892. His *Recollections*, which contains his photograph, appeared in 1905, and his *Irish fireside hours* (Dublin, 1927) is a selection of autobiographical sketches and essays. He married Sophie Raffalovich, daughter of a Russian Jewish banker, who as Mrs WO'B published *Silhouettes Irlandaises* (Paris, 1904), an account of their visits to the Mayo/Sligo area, and a work of fiction, *Rosette, a tale of Dublin and Paris* (London, 1907). She greatly supported her husband's political efforts. WO'B died in London and was buried in Mallow. For WO'B's portraits and papers, see ODNB. SOURCE Boylan, p. 269–70; Brown 2, 1133; EF, p. 332; Field Day, ii, p. 370 and passim, iii, p. 425 and passim; Hogan 2, pp 916–18; Irish pseudonyms; Murphy, p. 66; OCIL, p. 403; J.V. O'Brien, *William O'Brien* (Berkeley, CA, 1976); W. O'Brien, *Recollections* (London, 1905); ODNB; O'Donoghue, p. 343; E. Reilly, p. 249; Ryan, pp 84, 86–8; Sutherland, p. 471.

O48   *'Neath silver mask; or, the cloudland of life* (by William O'Brien).
       + Boston: Patrick Donahoe, 1871. SOURCE Brown 2, 1132; DCU, Catholic Americana files (1872 edn); OCLC. LOCATION DPL, NN.
       New York: N.L. Munro, [1887] (as *O'Hara's mission; or, hope on, hope ever*). SOURCE DCU, Catholic Americana files. LOCATION DCL.
       COMMENTARY Set in Ireland [ML].

O49   *When we were boys. A novel* (by William O'Brien; dedicated to John Dillon).
       + London, New York: Longmans, Green & Co., 1890. SOURCE Brown, 1268. LOCATION D, Dt, DPL, L, InND Loeber coll.
       + Dublin, London: Maunsel & Co., 1920. LOCATION DPL, L.
       New York: Garland, 1979 (introd. by R.L. Wolff). SOURCE COPAC. LOCATION Dt.

COMMENTARY Written during two separate terms of imprisonment in a Galway jail and set in Glengariff (Co. Cork) in Fenian times, it describes the excitement and enthusiasm of young men willing to take their turn in contributing to yet another rising. It ends with the hero, Ken Rohan, sentenced to life imprisonment for murder. The real murderer goes free and kills the son of a Protestant landowner. WO'B's brother, the Fenian James Nagle O'Brien, is said to have been the original of Ken Rohan. The novel chronicles the progress of American republican ideas in Ireland. It also exposes the effects of the clergy's aloofness from nationalist politics. The Irish revolutionary Jeremiah O'Donovan Rossa read it when young and remarked that 'It is a libel on the character of the Fenian movement in Ireland' [ML; Leclaire, p. 173; Murphy, pp 67–8; J.V. O'Brien, *William O'Brien* (Berkeley, CA, 1976), pp 70–1; *Rossa's recollections, 1838 to 1898, memoirs of an Irish revolutionary* (Guilford, CT, 2004), p. 129; Ryan, p. 87; Sutherland, p. 471].

O50   *A queen of men* (by William O'Brien; dedicated to the author's wife [Sophie O'Brien]).
    + London: T. Fisher Unwin, 1898. SOURCE Brown, 1269; Wolff, 5197. LOCATION D, DPL, L, InND Loeber coll. (1899 edn, 3rd impr.).
    + Dublin: Clonmore & Reynolds; London: Burns Oates & Washbourne, 1958. LOCATION DPL, L.
COMMENTARY Written when WO'B spent time in Galway prison. Historical fiction set in Galway, on the coast and on Clare Island toward the end of the sixteenth century, it tells the story of the pirate queen, Grace [Grania] O'Malley. The Composition of Connacht (a tripartite tax agreement between the crown, lords and commons), the disgrace of the lord deputy, Perrott, the wrecking of the Armada on the Connacht coast, and Grania's visit to Queen Elizabeth are all related. Sir Richard Bingham, governor of Connacht, and his successor, Sir William Fitzwilliam, figure among the actors. Some events in the book are fictitious. The writing is full of Spanish, native Irish, and slang [Baker; Brown; O'Brien, p. 96].

O'BYRNE, J.P. Co-author. See KELLY, Fr James J., OSF.

O'BYRNE, M. L. See O'BYRNE, M. Louise.

O'BYRNE, M. Louise (known as M.L. O'Byrne), pseud. 'Emilobie de Celtis', fl. 1876. Historical novelist, MLO'B was a Catholic and a resident of Dublin and died some years before 1919. She published six historical novels. SOURCE Allibone Suppl., ii, p. 1186; Brown, p. 234.

O51   *The Pale and the septs; or, the Baron of Belgard and the chiefs of Glenmalure. A romance of the sixteenth century* (by 'Emilobie de Celtis').
    + Dublin: M.H. Gill & Son, 1876, 2 vols. SOURCE Brown, 1274. LOCATION D, DPL.
    + Dublin: M.H. Gill & Son; London: Simpkin, Marshall & Co., 1885 (new edn, as *The Baron of Belgard; or, the Pale and the septs. An Irish romance*). SOURCE Topp 8, 716. LOCATION D, L, InND Loeber coll.
COMMENTARY The Dublin 1876 edn was published double-decker format, which was rare for Irish publishing at this time. Historical fiction, which aims to illustrate the advance of the English settlement in sixteenth-century Ireland, and gives an account of intrigues within the government. It describes such individuals as Archbishop Loftus of Armagh and Gerald Fitzgerald, 11th earl of Kildare. Events such as the battle of Glenmalure, Hungerford's massacre at Baltinglass, and the capture and recapture of Glenchree (now known as Glencree) (all Co. Wicklow) are recounted [RL; Brown].

O52   *Leixlip Castle. A romance of the penal days of 1690* (by 'Emilobie de Celtis').
    + Dublin: M.H. Gill & Son, 1883. SOURCE Brown, 1275. LOCATION D, DPL (incomplete), L, InND Loeber coll.
COMMENTARY Historical fiction describing the time from just before James II came to Ireland (Mar. 1689) until after the treaty of Limerick (Oct. 1691). The characters are delineated by their descent and their religion, with the Cromwellians as the villains of the story. The book is written from a strongly nationalist and Roman Catholic point of view and details the change in the fortunes of the Catholics and their eventual persecution after the treaty of Limerick. The book ends by pointing out that at the time of its writing, the English were still oppressing the Irish and attempting to convert them [ML].

O53   *Ill-won peerages; or, an unhallowed union* (by M.L. O'Byrne).
+ Dublin: M.H. Gill & Son, 1884. SOURCE Brown, 1276. LOCATION D, Dcc, DPL, L, InND Loeber coll.
COMMENTARY Ultra-nationalist adventure and romantic novel of the 1798 rebellion. Many historical figures appear [Brown].

O54   *Art M'Morrough O'Kavanagh, Prince of Leinster. An historical romance of the fourteenth century* (by M.L. O'Byrne).
+ Dublin: M.H. Gill & Son, 1885 (ill. W.C.M.). SOURCE Brown, 1277; Baker, p. 28. LOCATION D, Dcc, L, InND Loeber coll.
COMMENTARY Set in the thirteenth and fourteenth centuries, it tells of the career of Art M'Morrough (also known as Art Kavanagh), chieftain of Leinster, whom Richard II tried to appease by entertaining and knighting, but who defeated the English forces, killed Richard's heir, and ruled his country until he died [Baker].

O55   *The court of Rath Croghan; or, dead but not forgotten* (by M.L. O'Byrne).
+ Dublin: M.H. Gill & Son, 1887. SOURCE Brown, 1278; Wolff, 5198. LOCATION D, Dcc, DPL, L, InND Loeber coll.
Dublin: M.H. Gill & Son; London: Simpkin, Marshall, Hamilton, Kent & Co., 1891 (new edn). SOURCE Topp 8, 1891.
COMMENTARY No copy of the Dublin/London edn located. Historical fiction of the story of the Norman invasion of Ireland, and how it was abetted by the treachery and disunion of her own princes. The last *ard righ* (high king), Roderick, is shown weak and unfit to rule in perilous times. Richard Strongbow is a leading character, while Dermod MacMurrough is represented as the villain. Historical notes are appended [Brown].

O56   *Lord Roche's daughters of Fermoy. An historical romance of the seventeenth century founded upon authentic incidents of the Cromwellian era in Ireland* (by M.L. O'Byrne).
+ Dublin: Sealy, Bryers & Walker, 1892. SOURCE Brown, 1279; Alston, p. 321. LOCATION D, DPL, L.
New York: Pratt, 1892. SOURCE Brown, 1279.
COMMENTARY No copy of New York edn located. Historical romance set at the time of the wars of the Confederation of Kilkenny in the 1640s and the Cromwellian invasion. It features Owen Roe O'Neill [Brown; Hartman, 748].

O'BYRNE, W. Lorcan, b. Dublin 1845, d. 1913. Historical story writer, especially for children, WLO'B was the son of Christopher O'Byrne, of Ballinacor (Co. Wicklow). From an early age he was much interested in Irish lore and his stories for juveniles are notable for their depth of historical accuracy. He held a position in the department of Education during the greater part of his life. SOURCE Brown, p. 235.

O57   *A land of heroes. Stories from early Irish history* (by W. Lorcan O'Byrne).
London: Blackie & Son; New York: C. Scribner's Sons, [1899] (ill.). SOURCE Brown, 1281; RLIN. LOCATION Univ. of Pennsylvania.
+ London, Glasgow, Edinburgh, Dublin: Blackie & Son, 1900 (ill. John H. Bacon). SOURCE Brown, 1281. LOCATION D (n.d. edn), DPL (n.d. edn), InND Loeber coll.
COMMENTARY Fiction for juveniles. Contents: 'Nuada of the silver arm (or the sons of Turenn)', 'Lir's children', 'The Milesians', 'Tara of the kings', 'Queen Macha', 'Lavra Main', 'Little Setanta', 'Fosterage', 'The champion's hand-stone', 'The poet's journey', 'Deirdré', 'Queen Maeve', 'Boher na Breena', 'Dun Angus', 'Carbry Cat-head', 'Tuathal the legitimate', 'Conn of the hundred fights', 'Cormac Mac Art', 'Finn and the Feena', 'The three Collas', 'The Picts and Scots', 'Niall of the nine hostages', 'The druid's prophecy' (contains a list of Gaelic proper-names) [RL].

O58   *Kings and Vikings* (by W. Lorcan O'Byrne).
       Dublin: Talbot Press, 1900 (ill. Paul Hardy). SOURCE OCLC. LOCATION D.
       London: Blackie & Son; New York: C. Scribner's Sons, 1900. SOURCE Brown, 1282;
       OCLC. LOCATION Dt (1901 edn), Cleveland Public Library (OH).
       + London, Glasgow, Edinburgh, Dublin: Blackie & Son, 1901 (ill. Paul Hardy; cover:
       JAD; see Plate 54). LOCATION D, DPL, L, InND Loeber coll.
COMMENTARY Drawn from the published translations of Gaelic manuscripts and tells stories
of early Christian times, particularly about the Irish saints. Contents: 'Erin's days of faith',
'An Irish Laura', 'St. Columbkille', 'The trial of the bards', 'The battle of Dunbolg', 'The
banquet of Dun-na-gay', 'Till doomsday', 'Glendalough', 'Queen Gormilla', 'Malachi and
Brian' [ML; Brown].
O59   *Children of kings* (by W. Lorcan O'Byrne).
       + London, Glasgow, Edinburgh, Dublin: Blackie & Son, 1904 (ill. Paul Hardy).
       SOURCE Brown, 1283. LOCATION D, L.
COMMENTARY Tales from the Cuchulain, the Ossianic, and the Arthurian literature. The chief
characters of these appear in various stories. Contents: 'The tribute of Cornwall', 'How the
tribute was lost', 'Beneath the sands of time', 'Chapelizod', 'The coming of Cuchulain', 'The
knighting of Cuchulain', 'The tochmarc of Eimer', 'In the Isle of Skye', 'How Eimer was
won', 'The discovery of the sword', 'The battle of Knocka', 'The betrothal of Isoud', 'The
two dreams', 'The charmed cup', 'Little Britain', 'Tristam's marriage', 'The tournament',
'The story of Balin', 'Tristam made knight of the round table', 'The second tribute of
Cornwall', 'The betrothal of Grania', 'Flight of Dermot and Grania', 'Over stream and moor-
land', 'The hurling match of Loch Lein', 'The handful of berries', 'The glen of the cattle',
'The hunt on Benbulben', 'Two victims', 'The quest for Sir Tristam', 'Over the Iccian sea'
[ML; Brown].
O60   *The knight of the cave; or, the quest of the Pallium* (by W. Lorcan O'Byrne).
       + London, Glasgow, Dublin, Bombay: Blackie & Son, 1906 (ill. Paul Hardy). SOURCE
       Brown, 1284. LOCATION D (n.d. edn), DPL, L, InND Loeber coll.
COMMENTARY Fiction for juveniles set in medieval Christian times. The hero arrives in Ireland
from England, laid waste by the wars of Stephen's reign. Civil and ecclesiastical life of the
day is detailed. The hero accompanies St Malachi on a visit to St Bernard at Clairvaux, thence
to Italy and Rome, after which he returns to Ireland [Brown].
O61   *The falcon King; or, the romance of the Anglo-Norman invasion of Ireland* (by W.
       Lorcan O'Byrne).
       + London, Glasgow, Dublin, Bombay: Blackie & Son, 1907 (ill. Paul Hardy). SOURCE
       Brown, 1285; Baker, p. 17. LOCATION DPL, L, InND Loeber coll.
       + Dublin: Talbot Press, n.d. (as *The falcon king. Stories of the Anglo-Norman invasion
       of Ireland*; ill. Paul Hardy). LOCATION DPL.
       + Dublin, Belfast: Talbot Press, n.d. (as *The falcon king; or, the story of the Anglo-
       Norman invasion of Ireland*; ill. Paul Hardy). LOCATION D, DPL.
COMMENTARY Fiction for juveniles. A series of historical episodes starting in the twelfth century illustrating events, manners and religion of the time, including stories from Celtic and
Icelandic sagas and French *chansons de geste*. The conquest of Ireland by Henry II and his
barons is described and Dermot MacMurrough and life in Dublin feature [Baker; Brown].

'O'C., G.', pseud. See **WRIGHT, E.H.**

O'CALLAGHAN, J.P. Co-author. See **FENNELL, Charlotte.**

O'CONNELL, Mrs Morgan John (née Mary Anne Bianconi); d. 1908. Possible editor. See **O'BRIEN, Frances Marcella**.

O'CONNOR, Barry, fl. 1890. Irish-American poet and short story writer, BO'C published his poems in the New York *Daily News* and other papers. SOURCE O'Donoghue, p. 346.

O62 *Turf-fire stories and fairy tales of Ireland* (compiled by Barry O'Connor).
+ New York: P.J. Kenedy, 1890 (ill.). SOURCE Brown, 1288; Wright, iii, 4022 (1891 edn); DCU, Catholic Americana files. LOCATION D, L, NUC, InND Loeber coll.
COMMENTARY In the introduction, the compiler states that the stories had first appeared in various journals. He added that 'the greater number of the ... sketches are original; the others have been transcribed and in most cases materially altered, from the musty pages of some "quaint and curious volumes of forgotten lore"'. Contents: 'His Lordship's coat', 'Corney's fiddle', 'Suil-levwan', 'The O'Sheas', 'Blarney Castle', 'Clouds and sunlight', 'Knockfierna', 'Grassy hollow', 'The sumachaun', 'Her gra bawn', 'The hag's bed', 'The gold seeker', 'Outwitted', 'The highest penny', 'The fairy's curse', 'The angelus', 'The magic clover', 'Owney's kish', 'The turf cutters', 'How I got my passage money', 'Innisfallen', 'The leprachaun', 'The pike heads', 'The luckpenny', 'Dan Doolin's ghost', 'O'Carrol's dream', 'The wishing stone', 'The fairy boy', 'The emigrants', 'An Irish whistle', 'The prediction', 'The miller's trap', 'The cluricaun', 'The Fenian scare', 'Christmas eve', 'The diving cap', 'The golden turf', 'The Irish carman', 'The hunchbacks', 'The phooka', 'Squire Darcy's fetch', 'The poetical prisoner', 'The horse tamer', 'Serving a writ', 'Gra-geal-machree', 'The red knight', 'The silver snuff box', 'Rosaleen', 'Purcel the piper', 'An Irish chameleon', 'The haunted cliff', 'The rival giants', 'Murder will out', 'Smuggle poteen', 'The four leaved shamrock', 'The priest's leap' [ML].

O'CONNOR, E., fl. 1789, pseud. 'A Lady'. Attributed to E. O'Connor in ESTC. Novelist. Given that EO'C's *Emily Benson* was published in Dublin only, it is likely that she was Irish. SOURCE ESTC t212437; RL.

O63 *Almeria Belmore. A novel, in a series of letters* (by 'A Lady').
London: C.G.J. & J. Robinson, 1789. SOURCE Raven 2, 1789:59; Raven 2, 1791:54 (mentioned on title page of author's *Emily Benson*); Forster 2, 3098.
Utrecht: J. Altheer, 1792 (trans. into Dutch as *Almeria Belmore, in brieven*). SOURCE Alphabetische naamlijst 1790–1832, p. 11. LOCATION UVA.
Rotterdam: B. Wild, J. Altheer & J. Meijer, 1792 (trans. into Dutch as *Almeria Belmore, in een reeks van brieven*). SOURCE Wintermans, 1789:59.
COMMENTARY No copy of the London edn located. Judged by Mary Wollstonecraft as having 'no discrimination of character, no acquaintance with life, nor, do not start, fair lady! any passion' [S.M. Conger, ed., *Sensibility in transformation* (Cranbury, NJ, 1990), p. 128; Raven 2].

O64 *Emily Benson. A novel* (by the author of *Almeria Belmore*).
+ Dublin: Printed [for the author?] by P. Byrne, 1791. SOURCE Raven 2, 1791:54; McBurney & Taylor, 680; ESTC t212437. LOCATION Dt, IU, NUC.
COMMENTARY Epistolary novel. The author's prefatory address concerns the 'bad tendency of Novels in general' and the need to 'raise those works of fancy, from the abject state into which they are sunk'. The story is a sequel to *Almeria Belmore* (London, 1789) and concerns Lord Montalta, the brother of Lady Almeria and his love, Miss Emily Benson. She was taken away from him, but she escapes from her captors, wanders through a dark wood, and finally escapes to a nunnery. Eventually, she is reunited with Lord Montalta. Baron Luneville, who also had wanted to marry Emily, finds happiness with another woman, Eliza [ML; Raven 2].

O'CONNOR, Margaret Mathilda. See **MOORE, Lady Margaret Mathilda.**

O'CONNOR, Roger, pseud 'Captain Rock', b. Connorville, Bantry (Co. Cork) 1762 or 1763, d. Ballincollig, Kilcrea (Co. Cork) 1834. Miscellaneous writer, RO'C was the fourth son of Roger Connor (previously Conner) and Anne Longfield, sister of Richard, Viscount Longueville. He was the brother of the poet Daniel Roderick O'Connor (known as O'Conor) and, under the name of Roger Connor, was admitted at TCD in 1777. He was subsequently called to the Bar, but did not practice seriously. Another brother, Arthur, owned the Cork property but because he was exiled in France, entrusted its running to RO'C, who swindled him out of most of it. Living in Munster, RO'C, joined the Muskerry yeomanry as a loyalist and aided in suppressing the Whiteboy agrarian protest outbreaks. However, influenced by the French Revolution, he – along with Arthur – became a leader of the United Irishmen in Co. Cork before the rebellion of 1798 and founded a radical newspaper, the *Harp of Erin* (Cork). He was betrayed to the government by his brother Robert, imprisoned in Cork, but later released. He fled to England, where he was again arrested and sent to Newgate prison in Dublin, from where he probably published a flattering catalogue of his virtues which, with his portrait, appeared in *Walker's Hibernian Magazine* (Dublin, Mar. 1798). After several years of incarceration he was released in 1801, but as he was not allowed to live in Ireland, he settled in London. He did get permission to return to Ireland and disposed of the family estate, which had been ransacked by government forces. He rented the former estate of the Wellesley family in Dangan (Co. Meath). Living beyond his means, he became linked to an insurance fraud in the burning of Dangan castle, and in a mail-coach robbery in which he tried to retrieve incriminating letters for a friend. He married Louisa Anna Strachan, and later Wilhelmina Bowen of Bowenscourt (Co. Cork). After 1817 he seems to have wandered a good deal, ending up in a cottage at Ballincollig with a peasant girl whom he called his 'Princess of Kerry'. ODNB states that RO'C's claims to Irish heritage were spurious as the family 'Conner' was descended from a rich London merchant. In his *Chronicles of Eri; being the history of the Gaal Sciot Iber; or, the Irish people; translated from the original manuscripts in the Phoenician dialect of the Scythian language* (London, 1822) he attempted to prove that the pagan civilization of Ireland had been ruined by the advent of Christianity. RO'C was the prototype of Captain Rock in Thomas Moore's§ *Memoirs of Captain Rock* (London, 1824), to which RO'C wrote a non-fictional rejoinder *Captain Rock in Rome. Written by himself in the capital of the Christian world* (London, [*c.*1833], 2 vols.), and a more fictional *Letters to his Majesty, King George IV* (London, 1828). It is possible that the author Lady Moore§ was his daughter. His son Fergus became a Chartist. The agrarian and anti-tithe protest organization, the Rockites, took its name from his initials. For RO'C's portrait and papers, see ODNB. SOURCE B & S, p. 170; B. Burke, *A second series of vicissitudes of families* (London, 1860), pp 30–56; Landed gentry, 1912, pp 128–9; J. Leerssen, *Remembrance and imagination* (Notre Dame, IN, 1996), pp 82–7; OCIL, p. 414; ODNB; D. Reid & E. Glasgow, *Feargus O'Connor* (London, 1961), pp 12–14.

O65 *Letters to his Majesty, King George IV* (by 'Captain Rock').

+ London: B. Steill, 1828. LOCATION L, InND Loeber coll.

COMMENTARY Published in response to Thomas Moore's§ *Memoirs of Captain Rock* (London, 1824), and continues its conceit by opening the book with an introductory letter from New York by Captain Rock in sham-Irish addressed to King George IV [J. Leerssen, *Remembrance and imagination* (Notre Dame, IN, 1996), p. 87].

O'CONNOR, T.P. See **O'CONNOR, Thomas Power.**

O'CONNOR, Thomas Power (also known as T.P. O'Connor), b. Athlone (Co. Westmeath) 1848, d. London 1929. Journalist, politician, historian and writer, TPO'C was the son of Thomas and Theresa Power O'Connor (Teresa in RIA/DIB), he was educated at Queen's College, Galway, where he graduated BA in 1866 and MA in 1873. He worked as a journalist, first in Dublin, where he was employed by the government to report on political demonstrations, and then in London on the staff of the *Daily Telegraph* and as a correspondent to the *New York Herald*. His biography of Benjamin Disraeli, in which he was extremely critical of the prime minister, was published initially anonymously in serial form in 1877 and in London in 1879 under his name. It drew attention to him and spurred him to enter politics, which he did as a Home Rule candidate for Galway in 1880. He founded a number of periodicals, including *T.P.'s Magazine* (London, 1910–12). He completed the last volume and edited the *Cabinet of Irish literature* (London, 1876–78). In 1885 he won a seat for Liverpool, which he held until his death. He and Justin McCarthy§ were the only Irish MPs in the London parliament to maintain literary careers. He was elected president of the Irish National League of Great Britain in 1883 after returning from the US where he lectured on the Irish cause and raised money for the Irish Parliamentary Party. In 1917 he became the first film censor, and was made a privy councillor in 1924. Aside from fiction, he wrote biographies and histories of the English parliament, including *The Parnell movement* (London, 1886), and *Memoirs of an old parliamentarian* (London, 1929). For TPO'C's portraits and papers, see ODNB. SOURCE Allibone Suppl., ii, pp 1186–7; Boylan, p. 279–80; Brady, p. 193; L.W. Brady, *T.P. O'Connor and the Liverpool Irish* (London, 1983); Field Day, ii, p. 370 and passim, iii, p. 72; OCIL, p. 414; ODNB; RIA/DIB; Westmeath, p. 141.

O66   *Pat O'Rourke; or, the deed in the dark avenue* (by T.P. O'Connor).

London: Henderson, 1875. SOURCE Brown 2, 1167.

COMMENTARY No copy located. Reprinted from the *Weekly Budget* (London?) where it appeared as a serial, the story opens in the town of Kilbay in the 1850s. It tells how Pat was wrongfully convicted of complicity in a murder and transported to Norfolk Island (South Pacific), and how the real murderer was afterwards discovered. The scene shifts continuously between Ireland and the Antipodes [RL; Brown 2].

O67   *Some old love stories* (by T.P. O'Connor).

+ London: Chapman & Hall, 1895 (ill.). SOURCE Westmeath, p. 142. LOCATION L, NUC, InND Loeber coll.

COMMENTARY Fictionalized historical sketches. Contents: 'Abraham Lincoln and his wife', 'Mirabeau and Sophie de Monnier', 'William Hazlitt and Sarah Walker', 'Fersen and Marie Antoinette', 'Carlyle and his wife' [RL].

O'CONOR, Charles, b. Kilmactranny (Co. Sligo) 1710, d. Belanagare (Co. Roscommon) 1791. Scholar, antiquary, Catholic advocate, writer and a descendant of the last high king of Ireland, CO'C was the eldest son of Denis O'Conor, a farmer reduced to poverty by the confiscation of the O'Conor lands after the Williamite War, and Mary O'Rourke. He learned Irish and Latin from Franciscan fathers in nearby Crieveliagh and studied further with Dominic O Duigenan, a local historian, and with his uncle, Bishop O'Rourke of Killala. After restoration of part of their estates, the family moved to a restored seat at Belanagare, where the harper Turlough O'Carolan was a frequent visitor and taught CO'C music. He had begun to translate and copy old Irish manuscripts under O Duigenan's guidance. He later started a collection of manuscripts and through dissemination of his translations and copies provided a direct link between medieval scribes and contemporary scholars. He planned, in collaboration with Revd Thomas Contrarine and Henry Brooke§, a 'fictionalised history of Ireland to be called the *Ogygian tales*', which was never published. However, it formed the basis for CO'C's later

Dissertation on the antient history of Ireland (Dublin, 1753). *Ogygian tales* alludes to Roderick O'Flaherty's *Ogygia* (London, 1685), an 'alternative to the Anglo-Irish chronicles and the first work of Gaelic historiography to be printed in London', and itself a blend of fact and fiction (OCIL, pp 431, 435–6). CO'C later published *The Ogygia vindicated ... (a posthumous work) by Roderic O'Flaherty* (Dublin, 1775). CO'C was a major influence on translator and anthologist Charlotte Brooke§ and one of the driving forces behind a renewed interest in Irish history and antiquities, particularly among the Protestant elite, at the end of the eighteenth century. His grandson (also Charles) wrote *Memoirs of the life and writings of Charles O'Conor of Belanagare* in 1796 but it was quickly dismissed because of inaccuracies. For CO'C's portraits and papers, see ODNB. SOURCE Allibone, ii, p. 1448; Field Day, i, pp 857, 858, 937, iii, pp 619–20; OCIL, pp 414–15, 435 [re Ogygian tales]; ODNB; RIA/DIB; R. Ward (ed.), *Letters of Charles O'Conor of Belanagare* (Washington, DC, 1988), p. xxiii.

O'DOHERTY, Margaret T. See PENDER, Mrs Margaret T.

'O'DOHERTY, Morgan', pseud. See MAGINN, William.

O'DONNELL, Hugh Joseph, fl. 1850s. Religious fiction writer, HO'D calls himself on the title page of the following work an 'esquire' and 'a Mayo layman'. SOURCE AMB.

O68   *David and Goliah; or, the complete victory of a Mayo hedge-school pupil, over Sir Thomas Dross, a souper knight, and three bible and tract-distributing ladies, in which is shewn, beyond the possibility of refutation, that Protestants, as such, have not the divine law, the divine word, nor divine faith, and that the Protestant heresy is less just, less philanthropic, and, less humane than Mohammedism, less scriptural than Judaism, more absurd and inconsistent than Sabianism; and, that the pious monk of Partree, in Mayo, was perfectly justified before, in burning the spurious Protestant version of the scriptures* (by Hugh Joseph O'Donnell).
+ Dublin: Printed [for the author?] by John F. Nugent, [1853]. SOURCE OCLC. LOCATION L, KU-S.
COMMENTARY Anti-Catholic religious fiction. The author states in the preface that the controversy related in this volume took place recently on the top of 'a green hill, which overlooks Clew Bay, and the entrance to the towns of Westport, and Newport Pratt'. The story features the discussions with Sir Thomas Dross, 'a chivalrous Knight in the service of Proselytism; the three ladies were Miss Ling, Miss Bored, and Mrs. Cocoon – three very amiable tract-distributors'. The authors date the preface from Grace O'Malley's Castle, 12 July 1853. It was reviewed in the *Nation* (Dublin, 12 Aug. 1854) [RL].

O'DONNELL, John Francis, pseud. 'Caviare', b. Limerick 1837, d. London 1874. Journalist, poet and periodical writer, JFO'D began to write for the press at age 14. He started work in Limerick, where he joined the *Munster News*, moving after two years to Clonmel where he was an editor on the *Tipperary Examiner*. He spent some time in London, working on the Catholic and Irish nationalist newspaper the *Universal News*. Returning to Dublin in 1862 he worked for and contributed to the *Nation* and contributed to and edited *Duffy's Hibernian Magazine* (Dublin). He became editor of the *Lamp* (Dublin, London) and wrote for many Irish magazines, such as the *Dublin Review*, as well as for various English journals, including those of Charles Dickens, who befriended him. JFO'D became editor of the *Universal News* and from 1865 to 1868 editor of the *Tablet* (London?), another Irish Catholic paper. Moving back and forth between London and Dublin, he was a supporter of the Fenian movement and one of its ablest advocates. He is best known for his poetry, much of which expressed his ardent nationalism, a selection of which was published after his death by the Southwark Irish Literary Club Society to raise money for a monument over his grave. Brown mentions two serialized novels: 'Evictions and evicted', and 'Sadleir the banker; or the Laceys of Rathcore', which appeared in the *Lamp* (Dublin, London) and the *Nation* (Dublin), respectively. In 1870, JFO'D contributed to *Zozimus*, a comic paper edited by Richard Dowling§, who later edited an edn of JFO'D's poems. For JFO'D's portrait, see ODNB. SOURCE Boase, ii, p. 1213; Brown, p. 237; Field Day, ii, pp 3, 8, 114; Hogan 2, pp 941–2; Irish pseudonyms; McKenna, pp 298–9; MVF, p. 345; OCIL, p. 422; O'Donoghue, pp 349–50; ODNB; O'Donoghue 2, p. 430; RIA/DIB.

O69   *The emerald wreath. A fireside treasury of legends, stories, &c.* (by 'Caviare').
+ Dublin: James Duffy, 1864 (ill. Brothers Dalziel). SOURCE McKenna, p. 299; Brown, 1292 (1865 edn). LOCATION Grail, D, L ([1864] edn).
COMMENTARY Consists of stories and ballads: 'Sybil Gray's secret', 'Tom Hickey and the good people', 'The old house by the mere', 'Benevolent freak of an odd gentleman', 'Mike Driscoll and the fairies', 'The double shadow' [CD].

O'DONNELL, Lucy, fl. 1855. Historical novelist, L'OD possibly was Irish, given her name and the fact she published in Dublin. SOURCE RL.
O70   *St. Patrick's cathedral. A tale of the sixteenth century* (by Lucy O'Donnell).
+ Dublin: William Curry & Co., 1855. SOURCE Brown, 1293; COPAC. LOCATION L.
COMMENTARY Historical fiction describing the fortunes of the house of Desmond in the sixteenth century, particularly those of Lord James Fitzgerald, son of the great earl. He becomes a Protestant; is rejected by his people, and retires to England [Brown].

O'DONOGHUE, D.J. See **O'DONOGHUE, David J.**

O'DONOGHUE, David J. (known as **D.J. O'Donoghue**), b. Chelsea (London) 1866, d. Dublin, 1917. Literary historian, biographer, scholar and bibliographer, DJO'D was the son of Cork-born parents. He was self-educated, primarily through time spent at the British Museum library. He was a member of the Southwark Irish Literary Society and contributed literary pieces to the *Dublin Evening Telegraph* (collected later as *Ireland in London*, [London], 1889) and wrote sketches of Irish authors for the DNB and for Justin McCarthy's§ anthology *Irish literature* (Chicago, 1904). He moved to Dublin in 1896 where he became a bookseller and in 1909 librarian at UCD. He contributed to several literary journals. His *The poets of Ireland* (1892–93) contained over 2,000 biographical and bibliographical entries (enlarged for later edns.) and became a standard reference work. He championed the work of William Carleton§ and edited new edns of several of his works, arranged for financial support for Carleton's daughters—for which in gratitude they gave him several of Carleton's manuscripts and an unfinished autobiography, which became the basis of his *Life of William Carleton* (London, 1896; introduction by Mrs Cashel Hoey§), considered a major work of literary scholarship. He also wrote *Life and writings of James Clarence Mangan* (Edinburgh, 1897), as well as *Life of Robert Emmet* (Dublin, 1902). His *Sir Walter Scott's tour of Ireland in 1825* (Glasgow, 1905) deals with Scott's relationship with Maria Edgeworth§ and with Revd Charles Maturin§. He published two volumes of stories by Samuel Lover§: *Miscellaneous stories, sketches, etc.* (Westminster, 1899), and *Further stories of Ireland* (Westminster, 1899). He wrote *The geographic distribution of Irish ability* (Dublin, 1906). To the *Shamrock* (Dublin) he contributed a series on 'Some minor Irish poets' and on 'The literature of '67'". He was a member of the libraries committee of Dublin Corporation and with Douglas Hyde§ appraised the library of Sir John T. Gilbert, which later became part of the Dublin City Library. Many of DJO'D's papers are in UCD (MSS IE UCDAD LA15), and some of his correspondence is among the

Downey Papers (NLI, MS 10,041). SOURCE Field Day, iii, pp 391–9; Hogan 2, pp 945–6; Irish pseudonyms; OCIL, pp 424–5; RIA/DIB; RL.

O71 *The humour of Ireland* (ed. by D.J. O'Donoghue).

+ London: Walter Scott, 1898 (ill. Oliver Paque; Humour Series). LOCATION Dt, InND Loeber coll.

+ London, Felling-on-Tyne, New York: Walter Scott, n.d. (ill. Oliver Paque). LOCATION InND Loeber coll.

COMMENTARY Contains poetry, drama, belle-lettres, and fiction, along with biographical sketches of the authors. Contents of fiction only: 'Exorcising the demon of voracity' (trans. by Douglas Hyde§), 'The fellow in the goat-skin' (Patrick Kennedy§), 'Often-who-came' (trans. by Douglas Hyde§), 'The old crow and the young crow' (trans. by Douglas Hyde§), 'Will o' the wisp' ([Royal] Hibernian tales), 'Donald and his neighbours' ([Royal] Hibernian tales), 'In praise of digressions' (Jonathan Swift§), 'Letter from a liar' (Sir Richard Steele), 'Widow Wadman's eye' (Laurence Sterne§), 'Beau tibbs' (Oliver Goldsmith§), 'Bulls' (Sir Boyle Roche), 'Ana', 'A warehouse for wit' (George Canning§), 'Montmorency and Cherubina' (Eaton Stannard Barrett§), 'Modern medievalism' (Eaton Stannard Barrett§), 'Darby Doyle's voyage to Quebec' (Thomas Ettingsall), 'Thoughts and maxims' (William Maginn§), 'Daniel O'Rourke' (William Maginn§), 'Giving credit' (William Carleton§), 'The turkey and the goose' (Joseph A. Wade), 'Handy Andy and the postmaster' (Samuel Lover§), 'The little weaver of Duleek Gate' (Samuel Lover§), 'The loquacious barber' (Gerald Griffin§), 'Bob Mahon's story' (Charles Lever§), 'How Con Cregan's father left himself a bit of land' (Charles Lever§), 'Father Tom's wager with the pope' (Sir Samuel Ferguson§), 'The quare gander' (Joseph Sheridan Le Fanu§), 'Table talk' (Edward V.H. Kenealy§), 'Rackrenters on the stump. A remarkable demonstration' (T.D. Sullivan§), 'The thrush and the blackbird' (Charles Kickham§), 'Paddy Fret, the priest's boy' (John Francis O'Donnell§), 'An Irish story-teller' (Patrick O'Leary), 'The first Lord Liftinant (as related by Andrew Geraghty, philomath)' (William Percy French§), 'How to become a poet' (Francis A. Fahy), 'Musical experiences and impressions' (George Bernard Shaw§), 'From Portlaw to paradise' (Edmund Downey§), 'Fionn MacCumhail and the princess' (Patrick J. McCall§), 'Their last race' (Frank Mathew§) [RL].

O'DONOGHUE, Revd F. Talbot. See **O'DONOGHUE, Revd Francis Talbot.**

O'DONOGHUE, Revd Francis Talbot (known as **F. Talbot O'Donoghue**), b. Tipperary 1817. Anglican clergyman and novelist, FTO'D can probably be identified with Francis O'Donoghue, who was admitted at TCD in 1833. He was the son of Daniel O'Donoghue, JP. FTO'D was ordained in the Church of England and was vicar of Twickenham (London), Walsden (Yorks.), and Davenport (Ches.). He was also chaplain to the marquess of Westmeath. In Feb. 1867 he was living at Walsden vicarage. SOURCE Allibone Suppl., ii, pp 1187–8; B & S, p. 632; Hart cat. 56/36; RIA/DIB.

O72 *St. Knighton's keive: A Cornish tale. With a postscript and glossary* (by the Revd F. Talbot O'Donoghue).

London: Smith, Elder & Co., 1864. SOURCE OCLC. LOCATION L.

O73 *Donnington Hall. A novel* (by Francis Talbot O'Donoghue; dedicated to the author's wife).

+ London: Saunders, Otley & Co., 1865. SOURCE BL cat. LOCATION L.

COMMENTARY No Irish content [ML].

O'DONOGHUE, Mrs Nancy (Nannie) Power (née Lambert; also known as **Nannie Power O'Donoghue** and **Mrs Power O'Donoghue**), b. Dublin (Athenry, Co. Galway, according to

MVP), 1858. Novelist, poet, and journalist, NPO'D was the daughter of Charles Lambert of Castle Ellen, Athenry (Co. Galway). She became a notable journalist who contributed to women's and other papers, and wrote manuals of instruction for women riders. Blain ascribes to her *The knave of clubs* (London, 1868, by Nannie Lambert), but considering the date of publication it is likely to be by a different author as NPO'D was then ten years old. Some of her novels were enormously popular, selling upwards of 100,000 copies. Her poems were published in *Spring leaves* (London, 1877) and *Rhymes for readers and reciters* (Dublin, 1895). Her 'You should' is mentioned on the title page of *Ladies on horseback* (London, 1891), but has not been located. She married William Power O'Donoghue, a professor of music, in Dublin. SOURCE Allibone Suppl., ii, p. 1188; Alston, p. 321; Blain, p. 808; Burke's, p. 685 (does not clearly identify her); Colman, pp 135–6; MVP, p. 346; O'Donoghue, p. 350; RIA/DIB; Wolff, iii, p. 214.

O74   *Unfairly won. A novel* (by Nannie Power O'Donoghue).

+ London: Chapman & Hall, 1882, 3 vols. SOURCE Alston, p. 321. LOCATION L.

COMMENTARY Set in England. Concerns horseracing and the Derby and describes a spirited heroine. The author states in the preface that the (French) priest in the story 'is a veritable life study' [RL; Blain].

O75   *A beggar on horseback* (by Mrs Power O'Donoghue).

London: Hurst & Blackett, 1884, 3 vols. SOURCE Alston, p. 321. LOCATION L.

COMMENTARY Provides a picture of provincial society [Blain].

O'DRISCOLL, John, fl. 1825, d. 1828. Barrister, novelist and miscellaneous writer, JO'D was possibly a Protestant and certainly a Unionist. He may be identified with the John O'Driscol, only son of John O'Driscol, a merchant of Cork City, who was a student at the King's Inns in 1812 and was called to the Irish Bar in 1816. He became a judge in the island of Dominica, where he died in 1828. In Oct. of the next year, Owen Rees of the publishing firm Longman & Co. in London contacted N. Vincent, a lawyer in Cork, about the funds due to JO'D's widow, who presumably was living in Cork. The letter mentions that JO'D was the author of the following novel and of two nonfiction works: *Views of Ireland, moral, political and religious* (London, 1823), commended by Thomas Moore§ in his *Memoirs of Captain Rock* (London, 1824), and *The history of Ireland* (London, 1827, 2 vols.). JO'D wanted the latter to be a history without 'heavy detail of Irish grievances and disasters', and based much of it on Thomas Leland's§ *History of Ireland* (London, 1773, 3 vols). JO'D also wrote *Thoughts and suggestions on the education of the peasantry of Ireland* (London, 1820), and *Review of the evidence taken before the Irish committees of both houses of parliament* (Dublin, 1825). SOURCE Allibone, ii, pp 1449–50; Longman Archives, Letter Books, Longman I, 102, no. 106D; Personal communication, Jacqueline Belanger, Jan. 2003; Keane, p. 377; RIA/DIB; RL.

O76   *The adventurers; or scenes in Ireland, in the reign of Elizabeth* [anon.].

+ London: Longman, Hurst, Rees, Orme, Brown & Green, 1825, 3 vols. in 2. SOURCE Brown, 1; British Fiction (also Update 3 under 1825); Garside, 1825:2. LOCATION Corvey CME 3-628-47021-8, Ireland related fiction, Dt (imperfect), L, InND Loeber coll.

COMMENTARY Attribution to JO'D is evident from the Longman Letter Books. Initially issued in 750 copies, of which almost 600 remained unsold in Dec. 1828, which were then sold at a much reduced price. Briefly mentioned in the *Dublin and London Magazine* (London, 1825), p. 287 as 'very sad stuff indeed'. Historical fiction set in late-sixteenth-century Ireland, the story mainly centres on Hugh O'Neill and begins with O'Neill accompanying the troops of lord deputy Perrott to subdue the Ulster lords. It relates O'Neill's hostile relations with Sir Henry Bagenal, particularly after O'Neill's marriage to Bagenal's sister. Military encounters are included, particularly at the Blackwater and the battle at the Yellow Ford where Sir Henry Bagenal is killed, and it gives an account of Lord Deputy Essex's tenure in Ireland. The book takes some artistic license with historical facts [ML; British Fiction (also Update 3 under 1825)].

'AN OFFICER', fl. 1886. Pseudonym of an allegorical novelist.

O77 *Albion and Ierne. A political romance* (by 'An officer'; dedicated to the people of Great Britain and Ireland and of the British dominions).
+ London, Belfast, New York: Marcus Ward & Co., 1886. SOURCE Brown, 3. LOCATION D, Dt, L, InND Loeber coll.
COMMENTARY An allegory in which the characters stand for England and Ireland. Albion, who is visiting Ireland, is well meaning and willing to protect the Irish. However, he is misunderstood, and subversive forces in Ireland foment unrest. The relations between the two countries deteriorate and the possible results of separation are shown. It ends with the happy marriage of Albion with Ierne's sister, Kathleen, and the burial of the hereditary feud. Ierne dies in the strife, but not until after he has seen that Albion's intentions are the best [ML; Brown].

'AN OFFICER'S DAUGHTER', pseud. See SCOTT, H.

'AN OFFICER OF THE LINE', probable pseud. See WOODWARD, Revd Henry.

'AN OFFICER OF THE LINE', pseud. See MAGINN, Daniel Wentworth.

'AN OFFICER OF RANK', pseud. See GLASCOCK, Capt. William Nugent.

'AN OFFICER'S WIDOW', pseud. See PATRICK, Mrs F.C.

O'FLANAGAN, J.R. See O'FLANAGAN, James Roderick.

O'FLANAGAN, J. Roderick. See O'FLANAGAN, James Roderick.

O'FLANAGAN, James Roderick (known as J.R. O'Flanagan and J. Roderick O'Flanagan), b. Fermoy (Co. Cork) 1814, d. Grange House, Fermoy 1900. Novelist, barrister and man of letters, JRO'F was the son of John Fitch O'Flanagan, barracks-master at Fermoy, and Eliza Glissan. He was educated at Fermoy College and at TCD and was admitted to the King's Inns in 1834, Gray's Inn (London) in 1836 and to the Inner Temple (London). He was later called to the Irish Bar in 1838. In 1836 he travelled on the Continent and his diary of that trip was published as *Impressions at home and abroad; or, a year of real life* (London, 1837, 2 vols.). Beginning in 1838, he practiced on the Munster circuit but relied on journalism for his livelihood, contributing to the London *Law Times* and the *Cork Southern Reporter*. He also contributed to the *Dublin University Magazine*, the *Harp* (Cork, 1859), and the *Dublin Journal* (Dublin, 1858). In addition, he became editor of the *Irish National Magazine* (Dublin, 1846), the *Irish Teachers' Magazine* (Dublin, from 1860), and was chief writer for the *Dublin Saturday Magazine* (1865–67). By 1846 he had risen to the position of crown prosecutor in Cork. In 1847 he secured a post in the insolvency court in Dublin but, his sight failing, he retired on a pension. He moved to London around 1870, but returned to Ireland in 1872 and built a mansion on the family property on the Blackwater River near Fermoy. He was editor of the *Fermoy Monthly Illustrated Journal: A Magazine of Literature and Local Intelligence* (Fermoy, 1885–86). He had a very productive literary career. His works of fiction consist of Irish stories, set in Munster, and hunting novels. Aside from fiction, he wrote much history: *The Blackwater River in Munster* (London, 1844), a pioneering regional study; with John Dalton *The history of Dundalk* (Dublin, 1864); *The lives of the Lord chancellors of Ireland* (London, 1870), as well as other books of Irish legal history and memoirs of himself and his contemporaries in *The Munster circuit* (London, 1880). He wrote a travel book, *Through North Wales with my wife: An Arcadian tour* (London, [1884]), and his *The O'Connell anecdotes* (Dublin, 2 vols.) and *The Bar anecdotes of O'Connell* were advertised in the *Irish Catholic Directory* (Dublin, 1888) as having been published by John Mullany. According to the RIA/DIB, his serialized novel 'Galtymore, a tale of '98' (1874), published in an unidentified periodical, is based on the Kingston elopement case of 1798. He also wrote *Annals, anecdotes, traits and traditions of Irish parliaments 1172–1800* (Dublin, [1893]) and *An octogenarian literary life* (Cork, 1896). Although a supporter of Parnell and Home Rule, JRO'F was intensely loyal to the British empire and to Queen Victoria. SOURCE Allibone, ii, p. 1450 [under J.R. O'Flanagan and Rod. O'Flanagan]; Allibone Suppl., ii, p. 1188; Boase, vi, pp 319–20; Boylan, p. 292; Brady, p. 189; Brown, p. 239; Clyde, p. 126; R. Day's, Cork Printed Books at Myrtle Hill (MS, 1904); W.E. Hall, p. 164; Hogan 2, p. 969; Keane, p. 378; OCIL, p. 431; J.R. O'Flanagan, *Impressions at home and abroad* (London, 1837), i, p. 113; RIA/DIB; Sutherland, p. 472.

O78   *The Blackwater in Munster* (by J.R. O'Flanagan; dedicated to Sir Richard Musgrave of Tourin, Co. Waterford).

+ London: Jeremiah How, 1844 (subscribers' list; ill.). SOURCE OCLC. LOCATION D, NN.

COMMENTARY A regional study that contains stories: 'The enchanted horse of Cloghleagh castle', 'The haunted huntsman. A tale of the Blackwater side', 'The haunted huntsman. A legend of Blackwater side' [*sic*], 'Legendary tales: No. 1. Fion Macoul', 'No. 2. The leprechaun's bottle', 'An old follower. Part I.', 'The dying huntsman's last request, Part II.' 'The chase from Glenabo wood, Part III', 'The huntsman's end' [RL].

O79   *Gentle blood; or, the secret marriage. A tale of high life* (by J.R. O'Flanagan).

Dublin: McGlashan & Gill, 1861. SOURCE Brown, 1302; Bradshaw, 3984. LOCATION C (only parts 2 and 4).

COMMENTARY First issued in parts. Based on the Yelverton (Lord Avondale) bigamy case of the 1850s. Descriptions of sporting events, such as coursing in the Galtees [Brown; Sutherland, p. 472].

O80   *The life and adventures of Bryan O'Regan. An Irish sporting tale* (by J. Roderick O'Flanagan; dedicated to Edmund Burke Roche, Baron Fermoy).

Dublin: P.C.D. Warren, [1866]. SOURCE Brown, 1303. LOCATION Dt (1869 edn), NUC.

COMMENTARY First serialized in the *Dublin Journal* (1858) and later in the *Dublin Saturday Magazine* (1865), a biographical account of a young squireen at the beginning of the nineteenth century. He hunts with the Duhallows (north Cork) and is generally engaged in sports. He is the defendant in a breach of promise case, but marries happily and has many adventures [Brown; Clyde, p. 126].

O81   *Captain O'Shaughnessy's sporting career. An autobiography* [anon.].

+ London: Chapman & Hall, 1873, 2 vols. SOURCE Brown, 1304; Brady, p. 189 (mistakenly mentions 1872 edn). LOCATION D, L, NUC.

COMMENTARY The hero, after a childhood spent at his ancestral home near the Blackwater River in Munster, joins the army. He is first stationed in Ireland and afterwards in India and returns to be aide-de-camp to the lord lieutenant in Ireland. It gives descriptions of field sports and of the manners of the time and is filled with topographical and antiquarian digressions [Brown; RIA/DIB].

O'FLANAGAN, Thomas, pseud. 'Samoth' [the reverse spelling of Thomas], fl. 1871. Novelist, TO'F was a native of Castlefin (Co. Donegal). According to the title page of *Ned McCool*, below, he was also author of 'Strabane and Lifford', and 'The consequences of a refusal', both of which have not been identified. SOURCE RL; Brown, p. 239. Donegal, p. 214.

O82　*Ned McCool and his foster brother. An Irish tale, founded on facts* (by 'Samoth'; dedicated to Vere Foster).

　　+ Londonderry: Printed at the offices of the *Derry Journal*, 1871. SOURCE Brown, 1305; COPAC. LOCATION D, Dt.

　　COMMENTARY In the preface the author states that his purpose is to 'redeem from oblivion some of our local incidents' [ML].

'O'FLANNIGAN, Tague', fl. 1872. Pseudonym of a writer of anti-Catholic humorous fiction.

O83　*Tenant right in Tipperary. A series of humorous epistles bearing on the superstitions of Catholicism, from T. O'Flannigan ...to Mike Collins.*

　　Paisley: J. & J. Cook, 1872, 2nd edn. SOURCE COPAC. LOCATION L (1876, 3rd edn), Univ. of Glasgow, NUC (1876, 3rd edn).

　　+ Glasgow: Bogie & Morrison; Edinburgh: John Menzies; Dublin: Hodges Figgis & Co.; London: Houlston & Sons; Melbourne, Sydney: George Robertson, 1881 (new and enlarged edn). LOCATION D, L.

　　+ Glasgow: William Love; Edinburgh, Glasgow: John Menzies & Co.; Dublin: Hodges, Figgis & Co.; London: Houlston & Sons; Melbourne, Sydney: George Robertson, 1883 (new and enlarged edn [1st and 2nd series]; as *Tenant right in Tipperary: being a series of humorous epistles from Tague O'Flannigan, Ballinamuck, to Mike Collins, Renfrewshire* (dedicated to Sir Archibald C. Campbell, Bt, of Blythswood; ill.). LOCATION InND Loeber coll.

　　Dublin: Stationers' Hall, 1903. LOCATION NUC.

　　COMMENTARY No copy of the 1st Paisley edn located. Comic epistolary fiction that first appeared in the *Paisley and Renfrewshire Gazette* and stayed in print until at least 1903. The letters are dated from 1 Jan. 1870 to 18 Mar. 1874 (1st series), and from the 1880s (2nd series), and are directed from the fictitious Ballinamuck ['town of the pigs'] (Co. Tipperary) by Tague O'Flannigan to his friend Mike Collins in Glasgow. The letters are ostensibly written from the nationalist, Catholic point of view and strike out at Protestants, landlords, and the English government. However, the stories are tongue-in-cheek, and gently ridicule the power of the priest, the Catholic religion, the Land League and Irish political figures. At the same time, the letters report the events in the village, pilgrimages and faction fights [ML; RL].

'O'FLANNIGAN, Teddy', fl. 1820s. Pseudonym of a writer of satirical fiction.

O84　*Irish bulls, selected by that tight lad, Teddy O'Flannigan, the great little man of Killarney, Professor of "St. Giles's Greek, and other slack chatter." Whack, Erin go brah.*

　　+ London: Printed for R. Rusted, [1820?] (ill.). LOCATION L, ViU.

　　COMMENTARY No pagination, 34 pp; priced at 6*d*. [RL].

'O'FLESH, Phelim F.', fl. 1841. Pseudonym of a religious education writer.

O85　*The only genuine and authenticated report of Mogue More O'Molahan's dream on the school question, as dreamed by him on the night of the 3rd, or morning of the 4th November 1841; with a biographical sketch of Mr. O'Molahan himself, and some account of the Pharao-like manner in which "the thing had gone from him"*

while in the act of changing "his weary side." Together with its miraculous restora-
tion to his memory by the use of "the Apollo pil, or mental regenerator." The whole
published under the editorial supervision of Phelim F. O'Flesh.
New York: Casserly, 1841. LOCATION NUC.
COMMENTARY 43pp. Binder's title states *Religious education* [NUC].

OGLE, T. Acres. See **OGLE, Thomas Acres.**

OGLE, Thomas Acres (known as **T. Acres Ogle**), fl. 1873. Military man, memoirist and
poet, TAO was born into a distinguished Irish naval family. He became a captain in the militia and resided at Logan Shade, Carn (Carna?, Co. Wexford). According to the title page of
his *The Irish militia officer* (Dublin, 1873), he was 'late 1st Royal Cheshire Light Infantry'. He
wrote two volumes of poetry, both published in 1865. While a resident at Verona House,
Enniscorthy (Co. Wexford), he was recorded as subscribing to two of P.R. Hanrahan's§ books:
Eva; or, the buried city of Bannow (London, 1870), and *Echoes of the past* (Dublin, 1882). SOURCE
Brown, p. 240; MVP, p. 347; O'Donoghue, p. 354; RIA/DIB; RL; Rowe & Scallan, 1009.
O86   *The Irish militia officer* (T. Acres Ogle; dedicated to 'the Irish people').
    + Dublin: [Privately published], 1873. SOURCE Brown, 1307. LOCATION L, NUC, InND
    Loeber coll.
COMMENTARY Presumably partly-autobiographical, it traces the history of the Old Wexford
Regiment from 1810 to its disbandment in 1816. The volume consists mainly of anecdotes
about its members and the events taking place during their service. Part of the volume describes
the involvement of the main character, O'Brien, in the suppression of the 1798 rebellion.
Mention is made of a corps of yeomanry called Ogle's Blues, raised by the Rt Hon. George
Ogle, who lived at Belview on the banks of the Slaney (Co. Wexford) and who was married
to a Miss Moore. Another part describes the life of a highwayman, Jeremiah Grant, a nineteenth-century incarnation of James Freney§, a highwayman of earlier times (for Grant, see
also *A biographical sketch of the adventures of Jeremiah Grant*, Dublin, [1816]) [ML; Brown].

O'GRADY, Standish. See **O'GRADY, Standish James.**

O'GRADY, Standish James (known as **Standish O'Grady**), pseud. **'Luke Netterville'**, b.
Castletown Berehaven (also known as Castletown Bearhaven, Castletownbere, and Bearhaven,
Co. Cork) 1846, d. Isle of Wight 1928. Novelist, historian, and editor whose writings became
a foundation for the Irish Literary Revival, SJO'G was the son of Revd Thomas O'Grady, of
Castletown Berehaven, and Susanna Dowe. He was educated at Tipperary Grammar School,
studied at TCD, and was called to the Irish Bar in 1872. However, he soon turned to writing for a living. A chance reading of Sylvester O'Halloran's *History of Ireland* (London, 1778,
2 vols.) began for him a life-long fascination with Irish history and legend and led him to the
RIA, where he continued his reading and research. This resulted in his *History of Ireland*
(London, 1878–80, 3 vols.), which is an elaborate re-telling of the ancient Irish hero-myths
and romances, and he followed it in 1881 with a less romantic *History of Ireland: critical and
philosophical* (London). These works greatly contributed to the Irish Literary Revival by shaping a picture of the Irish past that was to inspire writers such as William Butler Yeats§ and
George Russell (AE). Yeats included six of SJO'G's books in his list of the thirty best Irish
books in 1895. SJO'G published archaeological articles in the *Dublin University Magazine* and
contributed to the *Irish Homestead* (Dublin, 1895 onward). He was editor and publisher of the
All Ireland Review (Kilkenny, 1900–06) and edited several periodicals, including the *Kilkenny
Moderator*, which was the first Irish newspaper of consequence to print a weekly Irish lesson.

However, as a result of a conflict with the 3rd marquess of Ormond, he was forced to resign as editor. A staunch Unionist, SJO'G wrote extensively on efforts to reform landlordism and on the necessity of the Anglo-Irish Ascendancy playing its part in shaping a future for Ireland based on its heroic past. After the demise of the *All-Ireland Review*, he withdrew from political affairs and left Ireland in 1918, eventually moving to the Isle of Wight. He is not to be confused with a poet of the same name, who emigrated in 1836 from Ireland to Canada, or with the Gaelic scholar Standish Hayes O'Grady, the son of Viscount Guillamore (OCIL adds to the confusion by stating that SJO'G was the son of Viscount Guillamore, rector of Castletown Berehaven). For SJO'G's portrait and papers, see ODNB. SOURCE Allibone Suppl., ii, p. 1189; M. Bence-Jones, *Twilight of the ascendancy* (London, 1987), pp 82–9; Boylan, p. 294; Brown, p. 240; Clyde, pp 140, 146; Field Day, i, p. 1053, ii, pp 521–5, 559 and passim, iii, pp 411 and passim; W.E. Hall, p. 225; Hogan, pp 529–30; Hogan 2, pp 973–5; Irish pseudonyms; MacDonald, p. 317; P.L. Marcus, *Standish O'Grady* (Lewisburg, PA, 1970); P. Maume, 'Standish O'Grady' in *Éire/Ireland* 39 (Summer 2004), pp 11–35; OCIL, pp 434–5; NCBEL 4, p. 1842; ODNB; O'Donoghue, p. 354; Quinn, 7355; E. Reilly, p. 218; RIA/DIB; Sutherland, p. 473.

O87   *Cuculain. An epic* (by Standish O'Grady).
        London: Sampson, Low, Searle, Marston & Rivington; Dublin: E. Ponsonby, 1882. SOURCE Hogan, p. 531; OCLC. LOCATION Univ. of California, Berkeley.
        COMMENTARY SJO'G, who did not read or speak Irish, misspelled the name of Cú Chulainn in this book. The story is based on the life of Cú Chulainn, who was the hero of the Ulaid, a powerful prehistoric people of the north of Ireland. Chulainn was the chief figure in the epic tale of the conflict between the Ulaid and Connachta (Connacht), the 'Táin bó Cuailgne' (cattle raid of Cooley), one of the oldest stories in European vernacular history [OCIL, pp 125–6, 551–2; ODNB].

O88   *Red Hugh's captivity. A picture of Ireland, social and political, in the reign of Queen Elizabeth* (by Standish O'Grady).
        London: Ward & Downey, 1889. SOURCE Brown, 1309; Hogan 2, p. 974; Kersnowski, p. 104. LOCATION L, Dt, NUC.
        + London: Lawrence & Bullen, 1897 (as *The flight of the eagle*). SOURCE Brown, 1318; Hogan 2, p. 975; Kersnowski, p. 103. LOCATION D, Dt, DPL, InND Loeber coll.
        Dublin: Sealy, Bryers & Walker, 1908 (as *The flight of the eagle*). SOURCE Brown, 1318. LOCATION NUC.
        New York: Benziger, [date?] (as *The flight of the eagle*). SOURCE Brown, 1318.
        COMMENTARY No copy of the New York edn located. Set in the late-sixteenth century at the end of the lord deputyship of Perrott and the beginning of that of Fitzwilliam, it describes the kidnapping of Hugh Roe O'Donnell and his escape, twice, from Dublin Castle. The author in the preface states that he based the story on several historical sources. An appendix contains historical notes. O'Grady probably adapted it into a play, *Hugh Roe O'Donnell, a 'sixteenth century Irish historical play'*, which was performed in Kilkenny in 1902 (published, Belfast, 1902) [ML; Brown; N.G. Bowe, 'Arts and crafts in early 20th century Kilkenny', *Irish Architectural and Decorative Studies*, 1999, ii, p. 70; RL].

O89   *Finn and his companions* (by Standish O'Grady).
        + London: T. Fisher Unwin, 1892 (Unwin, Children's Library; ill. J.B. Yeats). SOURCE Brown, 1310; Hogan 2, p. 974; Osborne, p. 12. LOCATION D, BFl, L, CaOTP, NUC, InND Loeber coll.
        + Dublin: Talbot Press; London: T. Fisher Unwin, 1921 (new edn; ill.). LOCATION DPL, L, NUC.
        New York: Cassell, 1892 (ill. J.B. Yeats). LOCATION NUC.

O'Grady

COMMENTARY Children's stories about the third-century Irish hero Finn [Brown; Osborne].

O90 *The bog of stars and other stories and sketches of Elizabethan Ireland* (by Standish O'Grady).

+ London: T. Fisher Unwin; Dublin: Sealy, Bryers & Walker; New York: P.J. Kenedy, 1893 (The New Irish Library; ill.). SOURCE Brown, 1311; Hogan 2, p. 974; Kersnowski, p. 103. LOCATION D, DPL, BF1, L, NUC (1893, 2nd edn), InND Loeber coll.

Dublin: Educational Company of Ireland, [1901?]. LOCATION NUC.

COMMENTARY Stories of Ireland in the days of Queen Elizabeth I, 'not so much founded on fact as in fact true'. Contents: 'Mona-reulta; or, the bog of stars', 'Philip O'Sullivan, historian, soldier, and poet', 'Kiegangair', 'The vengeance of the O'Hagans', 'Sir Richard Bingham', 'The outlawed chieftain', 'Brian-of-the-Ramparts O'Rourke', 'Don Juan del Aquila, hero of Kinsale', 'The battle of the Curlew mountains' [RL].

O91 *The coming of Cuculain. A romance of the heroic age of Ireland* (by Standish O'Grady).

+ London: Methuen & Co., 1894 (ill. D. Murray Smith). SOURCE Brown, 1312; Hogan 2, p. 975; Kersnowski, p. 103. LOCATION D, Dt, DPL, BFl, NUC, InND Loeber coll.

+ Dublin: Talbot Press; London: T. Fisher Unwin, n.d. (as *The coming of Cuculain*; ill. P. Tuohy). LOCATION DPL, NUC.

COMMENTARY The story of Cuculain's boyhood where 'the great shadows of ancient De Danann gods are never far from the mortal heroes who figure in the sagas' [Brown].

O92 *Lost on Du-Corrig; or, twixt earth and ocean* (by Standish O'Grady).

London, Paris, Melbourne: Cassell & Co., 1894 (ill. Tuohy). SOURCE Brown, 1314; Hogan 2, p. 975; Kersnowski, p. 103. LOCATION Dt, NUC.

+ Dublin: Talbot Press; London: T. Fisher Unwin, n.d. (ill. Tuohy). LOCATION D, DPL, NUC.

COMMENTARY Fiction for boys first published in *Chums* (London, 1893), this is a tale of adventures among the caves and cliffs of the west coast of Ireland. Two brothers disappear, seemingly without a trace. They are in a cave, where they are kept alive by befriending the seals that enter with fish. To free themselves they have to build stairs against a very steep slope [ML; Brown].

O93 *The chain of gold; or, in crannied rocks. A boy's tale of adventure on the wild West coast of Ireland* (by Standish O'Grady).

London: T. Fisher Unwin, 1895 (ill. E. Capper). SOURCE Brown, 1315; Hogan 2, p. 975; Osborne, p. 376. LOCATION D, Dt, L, CaOTP, NUC.

+ Dublin, London: Talbot Press; London: T. Fisher Unwin, [1921] (as *The chain of gold. A tale of adventure on the west coast of Ireland*; ill. Tuohy). SOURCE NYPL. LOCATION DPL, NN, NUC, InND Loeber coll.

New York: Dodd, Mead & Co., 1895. LOCATION NUC.

COMMENTARY Fiction for boys of adventures on the west coast of Ireland with an element of the supernatural [Brown].

O94 *Ulrick the ready; or, the chieftain's last rally* (by Standish O'Grady).

+ London: Downey & Co., 1896 (ill. John F. O'Hea). SOURCE Brown, 1316 (n.d. edn); Hogan, p. 531. LOCATION D, L, NUC, InND Loeber coll.

+ Dublin: Talbot Press; London: T. Fisher Unwin, n.d. (ill. Tuohy). LOCATION D, DPL, NUC.

New York: Dodd, Mead & Co., 1896. SOURCE NYPL. LOCATION NN, NUC.

New York: Dodd, Mead; London: Downey & Co., 1896. SOURCE Kersnowski, p. 104. LOCATION Dt.

COMMENTARY An historical novel set in the last years of the reign of Elizabeth I in O'Sullivan Beare country on the Beara Peninsula in Co. Cork. It describes the power struggles within the territory of the O'Sullivans, and the guarded game that O'Sullivan Beare plays with Sir George Carew at the time of the Spanish invasion. The battle of Kinsale and the siege of Dunboy are woven into the story of the young Ulrick O'Sullivan. Ulrick, on his trips to Cork for his master O'Sullivan Beare, falls in love with a Puritan girl, whose father, Capt. Egerton, is constable of Carrickfergus (Co. Antrim). When O'Sullivan Beare leaves the country, he bestows £1,000 on Ulrick, who then rides to Carrickfergus to ask permission of Capt. Egerton to marry his daughter. They marry and live in Ulster [ML; Brown].

O95   *In the wake of King James; or, Dun-Randal on the sea* (by Standish O'Grady).
       + London: J.M. Dent & Co., 1896. SOURCE Hogan 2, p. 975; Kersnowski, p. 104.
       LOCATION D, Dt, L, DPL, NUC.
       London: J.B. Dent; Philadelphia: J.B. Lippincott, 1896. LOCATION NUC.
       + London, Toronto: J.M. Dent & Sons, [1896] (new edn; as *In the wake of King James*;
       Wayfarers' Library). SOURCE Brown, 1317. LOCATION D (1897, 2nd edn), DPL.
COMMENTARY An historical novel set in the seventeenth century. The scene is set on the west coast of Ireland where a gang of Jacobite desperadoes inhabits a lonely castle. It mentions king James II and William III [Brown; Hartman, 1036].

O96   *The queen of the world or under the tyranny* (by 'Luke Netterville').
       + London: Lawrence & Bullen, 1900. SOURCE Hogan 2, p. 975; Kersnowski, p. 104.
       LOCATION D, DPL, NUC, InND Loeber coll.
COMMENTARY Science fiction. The main character, Gerald Pierce De Lacy, was born at Forres (Co. Westmeath). He travels all over the world before he becomes interested in spiritualism, through which powers he is transferred to the year 2179. He finds that the whole world is under the tyranny of Chinese overlords. They patrol the earth with gigantic aerial machines, which are a cross between a boat and a bird. England, which had been a very strong colonial power before the Chinese took over, has been destroyed. However, in the last battle with the Chinese, one English aerial machine has escaped to a secret haven. The story describes the flight of a rebel lord, accompanied by Gerald Pierce De Lacy, to the English stronghold. A giant battle ensues and the tyrants are destroyed [ML].

O97   *In the gates of the North* (by Standish O'Grady).
       + Kilkenny: Standish O'Grady, 1901 (Library of the Nore). SOURCE Hogan 2, p. 975;
       Kersnowski, p. 104. LOCATION D, L, NUC, InND Loeber coll.
       London: J. Watkins, 1901. LOCATION NUC.
       + Dublin: Sealy, Bryers & Walker, 1908. SOURCE Brown, 1313. LOCATION D, NUC.
       New York: Frederick A. Stokes, [19??]. LOCATION NUC.
       COMMENTARY Sequel to *The coming of Cuculain* (London, 1894) and tells how the hero held the forts of Ulster alone against the hosts of Queen Maeve of Connacht [Brown].

O98   *The masque of Finn* (by Standish O'Grady).
       Kilkenny: O'Grady, 1907. SOURCE Hogan 2, p. 975; Kersnowski, p. 104; COPAC.
       LOCATION Dt.
       Dublin: Sealy, Bryers & Walker, 1907. SOURCE J. MacKillop, *Fionn mac Cumhaill*
       ([Syracuse], 1986), p. 202. LOCATION NUC (n.d. edn).

O99   *The departure of Dermot* (by Standish O'Grady).
       + Dublin: Talbot Press, 1917. SOURCE Brown, p. 240; Brown 2, 1231; Kersnowski, p.
       103. LOCATION D, L, NUC.
COMMENTARY Historical fiction. An evocation of the circumstances and the actual scene of Dermot MacMurrough's departure for Bristol from the cove of Cork in the year 1166 and his mission to Henry II [Brown 2].

O100   *The triumph and passing of Cuculain* (by Standish O'Grady).
        Dublin: Talbot Press; London: T. Fisher Unwin, [1919]. SOURCE Hogan 2, p. 975;
        Brown 2, 1232 (n.d edn); Kersnowski, p. 104 (n.d. edn). LOCATION DPL (n.d. edn),
        NUC, InND Loeber coll. (n.d. edn.).
        New York: Frederick A. Stokes, [1919?]. LOCATION NUC.
COMMENTARY The third member of O'Grady's trilogy of Cuculain. Tells how Maeve and the
men of Erin invade Ulster, outnumbering and defeating the Red Branch. How Cuculain,
thought to be dead, returns and after a long sleep throws himself into the fight and routs
Maeve's army. Maeve gathers a fresh host and overwhelms the Ultonians. Cuculain and Laeg
fight their last fight and perish [Brown 2].

O101   *The Cuculain cycle* (by Standish O'Grady).
        Dublin, Talbot Press, [1938], 3 vols. SOURCE Kersnowski, p. 103; OCLC. LOCATION
        UCD, Boston College.
COMMENTARY Volume 1: 'The coming of Cuculain' (introd. by AE [George Russell]); volume
2: 'In the gates of the North'; volume 3: 'The triumph and passing of Cuculain'. The three
stories were separately published in London (1894), Kilkenny (1901), and Dublin (1920),
respectively [Kersnowski; RL].

O'HANLON, Alice, fl. *c.*1878. Novelist and religious fiction writer, AO'H probably lived in
Lancashire. Only one of her works is known to have Irish content, but given her name it is
likely she may have had Irish connections. SOURCE Allibone Suppl., ii, p. 1189.

O102   *Chance? or fate? A novel* (by Alice O'Hanlon).
        + London: Chatto & Windus, 1889, 3 vols. SOURCE Allibone Suppl., ii, p. 1189 ([1888]
        edn). LOCATION L.
        New York: F.F. Lovell & Co., 1889. (as *Chance or fate*. Lovell's Household Library).
        SOURCE OCLC. LOCATION C, Cleveland Public Library (OH).
COMMENTARY Contains some Irish characters and scenes [ML].

O'HANLON, Canon John, pseud. 'Lageniensis', b. Stradbally (Co. Laois) 1821, d.
Sandymount (Dublin) 1905. Cleric, folklorist, poet and editor, JO'H was the son of Edward
O'Hanlon, a tanner or farmer, and his wife Honor. He studied at Carlow Ecclesiastical College
but was there only a year when the family decided to emigrate to Quebec (Canada) in 1842
and then to St Louis (MO), where he was ordained in 1847. He ministered initially to the
immigrant Irish community in St Louis, but ill-health forced him to return to Ireland in 1853
where, after he had recuperated, he volunteered for the Dublin archdiocese. He had begun
writing while a seminary student, contributing to the *Catholic Cabinet* (St Louis) and *Donohue's
Magazine* (Chicago?) and while still in St Louis wrote *Abridgement of Irish history* (1849); *An
emigrant's guide to the USA* (Boston, 1851); *Catechism of Irish history* (Dublin, 1864), and *Life
and scenery in Missouri* (Dublin, 1890). He wrote extensively on Irish folklore, including *Irish
folk-lore* (Glasgow, [1870]), and *Irish local legends* (Dublin, 1896). In preparation for the work
for which he is best-known: the *Lives of Irish saints* (Dublin, 1875–1903, 9 vols.), he visited
many of the premier libraries in England and Europe. The tenth volume remained unfinished
at his death. He also wrote on the history of the Irish in America and contributed to a wide
number of newspapers and periodicals. In Dublin, he was Roman Catholic curate first at SS
Michael and John and then at St Mary's in Sandymount. As such he features as the Canon
O'Hanlon who celebrates benediction in James Joyce's *Ulysses* (Paris, 1922). Several of his stories concern north Co. Tipperary, Queen's County [Co. Laois], and southwest Co. Offaly. He
published in verse *The buried lady: a legend of Kilronan* (Dublin, 1877), and his poetical works
were advertised by Duffy in 1886. He was an elected member of the RIA. His portrait appeared

in his *Irish local legends* (Dublin, 1896). Some of his papers are in St Patrick's College, Maynooth. SOURCE Allibone Suppl., ii, p. 1189; Adv. in W. Carleton's *Redmond Count O'Hanlon* (Dublin, 1886); Brady, p. 191; Irish pseudonyms; Lough Fea cat. p. 148; MVP, p. 347; OCIL, p. 436; ODNB; O'Donoghue, pp 355–6; RIA/DIB; RL; Thuente 1, pp 59–60; Zimmermann, pp 292–3.

O103 *Irish folk-lore: traditions and superstitions of the country; with humorous tales* (by 'Lageniensis'; dedicated to Denis Florence MacCarthy, M.R.I.A.).

+ Glasgow, London: Cameron & Ferguson, [1870]. SOURCE Brown, 1323; Lough Fea cat. p. 150 (where wrongly dated 1869). LOCATION L, Univ. of Utrecht, Utrecht, Netherlands, NUC.

COMMENTARY Contents: 'The living ghost; or, fallacies from over-hasty conclusions', 'Lackeen Castle, O'Kennedy, and the phooka', 'Fairy mythology of the Irish', 'Apparitions and fetches', 'Changelings, fairy-men, and fairy-women', 'Buried treasures', 'The merrow-maiden and mer-row-man', 'The lianhaun shee', 'O'Carroll's banshee and Terryglass castle', 'The three wishes; or, all is not gold that glitters', 'Fairy haunts and fairy celebrities', 'Lake habitations and spir-its', 'Monument bushes and road-side cairns', 'Mr. Patrick O'Byrne in the Devil's Glen; or, folly has a fall', 'Hy-Breasail; or, the blessed island', 'The féar gortha; or, hungry grass: A tale of the Irish famine', 'Various popular fancies', 'Traces of druidism in Ireland', 'The wizard earl of Kildare', 'The realms of fairydom', 'The water-sheerrie; or, bog-sprite', 'The fomorian warrior, Balor of the Evil Eye', 'Ancient planetary, elementary, and idolatrous worship of the pagan Irish', 'Ancient festival celebrations in Ireland', 'All-Hallows' eve, with its various div-inations and festive customs', 'Memorials of Redwood Castle', 'Irish marriage customs', 'The solitary fairies', 'Divinations, enchantments, astrology, and nostrums', 'Dungal the recluse, a learned Irishman of the ninth century', 'Popular notions concerning good and ill luck', 'Tir-na-n-og', 'Saint legends', 'Sprite frolics and peculiarities', 'Irish fortune-tellers, and predic-tions' [RL].

O104 *Irish local legends* (by 'Lageniensis').

+ Dublin: James Duffy, 1896 (ill.). SOURCE Brown, 1325. LOCATION L, NUC, InND Loeber coll.

COMMENTARY Stories accumulated by the author during holidays in various parts of Ireland. Contents: 'The rival professors. Legend of Howth, County of Dublin', 'The gobban saor and his critics. Legend of Ardmore, County of Waterford', 'The baboon's rescue. Legend of Woodstock Castle, County of Kildare', 'Romantic birth of St. Fursey. Legend of Inchiquin or Insiquin, County of Galway', 'The garran bawn. Legend of Moghia, near Lismore, Queen's County', 'Conla the artist and the dead bones. Legend of Dub-Cruithne, Innishowen, County of Donegal', 'The tyrant chieftainess and her punishment. Legend of Lios Na Eiblin Oge O Coille Mor, County Cork', 'The water monster. Legend of the river Lagan, County Down', 'Naomh Greoihir, or St. Gregory of the golden mouth. Legend of Inishmaan, Aran Islands, County of Galway', 'The black man's apparition. Legend of Mundrehid, Queen's County', 'The sea-syren's revenge. Legend of the river Delvin, County of Meath', 'Contests of the clans. Legend of Mullaghmast, County of Kildare', 'The captive piper. Legend of Knockaney, County of Limerick', 'The peistha discomfited. Legend of Drumsna, County of Monaghan', 'The Leinster tribute. Legend of Tara, County of Meath', 'Fin-Mac-Cool's stone-throw. Legend of the Clough-Mor, County of Down', 'The death-coach. Legend of Timogue, Queen's County', 'The blessed trouts. Legend of the three wells, County of Wicklow', 'Mistaken iden-tity. Legend of Sandymount, County of Dublin', 'The druid's betrayal. Legend of the river Bann, County of Londonderry', 'The gobban saor's ingenuity. Legend of St. Mullins, County of Carlow', 'The peistha of Saint's Island. Legend of Lough Derg, County of Donegal', 'The witch transformed. Legend of Cullenagh, Queen's County', 'The fool's fantasies. Legend of

Cloonfush, County of Galway', 'Tipperary tactics. Legends of Upper and Lower Ormond, County of Tipperary', 'The battle of the cats. Legend of Irishtown, County of Dublin', 'Humours and humorists. Legends of Ballyroan, Queen's County', 'The witch's fate. Legend of Antrim, County of Antrim', 'The Confederate peddlers. Legend of Dingle, County of Kerry', 'The storm spectre. Legend of the Mullet, County of Mayo' [RL].

O'HARA, Cassie M., fl. 1880. Poet and writer of Catholic religious fiction for children, CMO'H lived near Ballymena (Co. Antrim). She won the tercentenary of St Teresa prize for *Saint Teresa of Jesus; a poem in four cantos* (London, 1883). She was a regular contributor to the *Catholic Fireside* (Dublin, Liverpool) and she published poetry in the Dublin *Irish Monthly*. SOURCE Colman, p. 177; Irish pseudonyms; O'Donoghue, p. 356; RIA/DIB.

O105   *Clare's sacrifice: A tale for first communicants* (by Cassie M. O'Hara).
        London: R. Washbourne, 1880. SOURCE Allibone Suppl., ii, p. 1189; Colman, p. 177;
        COPAC. LOCATION L (destroyed), E.
        COMMENTARY 64pp. Catholic religious fiction [RL].

'THE O'HARA FAMILY', pseud. See **BANIM, John**, and **BANIM, Michael**.

'O'HARA, Hardress', fl. 1874. Pseudonym of a family saga novelist.
O106   *Conquered at last: from "Records of Dhu Hall and its inmates."* A novel (by
        'Hardress O'Hara'; dedicated to the Hon. Mrs J.A. Caulfeild).
        London: Sampson Low, Marston & Searle, 1874, 3 vols. SOURCE Brown, 1328.
        LOCATION L.
COMMENTARY Set in Ireland. The narrator's father, Capt. Hardress O'Hara had married a daughter of Capt. Henry Ireton of Castle-Ireton. Another Ireton lives at Dhu Hall, a 'fine old mansion in a neighbouring county'. The narrator spends part of his youth with his aunt at Castle-Ireton and during that time lives at a fishing village near the Giant's Causeway in Co. Antrim. The remaining story is set in Dublin, France and Italy. It features The O'Shaugnessy of Castle Ruinous [ML; RL].

'O'HEA, Bernard', pseud. See **MOORE, Frank Frankfort**.

O'HEGERTY, Caroline, fl. 1812. Story writer for children, CO'H may have been Irish, given her Irish name and the place of publication of the following volume. SOURCE RL.
O107   *Contes moraux* (by Caroline O'Hegerty; dedicated to Mme la duchesse de Richmond; dedication signed Caroline O'Hegerty).
        + Dublin: James Jones, 1812 (subscribers' list). SOURCE Pollard 2, p. 323; COPAC.
        LOCATION E.
COMMENTARY French reader for children. Unusual as a French children's book being published in Dublin. Contents: 'Les deux cousines', 'L'irlandaise', 'La jalouse', 'Le Comte d'Elvarsi' [ID].

O'KEEFFE, Miss —. See **O'KEEFFE, Adelaide D.**

O'KEEFFE (also **O'KEEFE**), **Adelaide D.** (also known as **Miss O'Keeffe**), b. Dublin, 1776, d. *c*.1855. Novelist and poet, ADO'K was the daughter of the very popular Irish dramatist John O'Keeffe, a Catholic, and an Irish Protestant mother, Mary Heaphy, an actress, whose father was the proprietor of the Theatre Royal in Dublin. After her parents' marriage broke down, AO'K went with her father to London, where she was sent to school. When her father heard that his wife was secretly visiting her, she was sent to a French convent until 1799. After her education, Adelaide became helper to her father, who at that time was nearly blind. She is known for five novels and several educational works for children. She contributed 34 poems to *Original poems for infant minds* (London, 1804), which established her reputation and which she followed with her own *Original poems calculated to improve the mind of youth* (London, 1808) and a variety of other volumes of verse for children, including *Poems for young children* (London, 1849). She also wrote for children *A trip to the coast* (London, 1819). The preface to her *Patriarchal times* (London, 1811, 2 vols.) is from Greenford (Middx) Apr. 1811, while that to her *Dudley* (London, 1819, 3 vols.) is signed from Chichester (Sussex). In 1830 she resided at Carlton Place, Southampton (Hants.). To supplement her income she sometimes worked as a governess and in 1840 wrote to the Royal Literary Fund concerning the 'wretched pittance' of her annual pension of £50. She wrote a tribute to her father in the *New Monthly Magazine* (London, 1833) and contributed a memoir of him that was published in his *O'Keefe's legacy to his daughter* (London, 1834). April, 1811. The DNB, but not the ODNB, refers to one of her letters bound in a BL copy of her father's *Recollections*. Other papers are in the BL. SOURCE Alston, p. 321; Blain, p. 811; BD, p. 257; Boase, ii, pp 1226–7; British Fiction; DNB [included in John O'Keeffe]; Field Day, iv, pp 1144–5, 1187; NCBEL 4, p. 416; 1842; ODNB; O'Donoghue, p. 358; RIA/DIB.

O108 *Llewellin: A tale* [anon.] (dedicated to Princess Charlotte Augusta of Wales).
   London: G. Cawthorn, 1799, 3 vols. SOURCE Block, p. 175; Raven 2, 1798:51; Forster 2, 3179; ESTC t070092. LOCATION L, McMaster Univ.
   COMMENTARY This has also been attributed to Grace Buchanan Stevens. Historical fiction set in England, Scotland, Wales and Ireland in about 1282 during the English conquest of Wales, and continues into the fourteenth century. It includes a history of Norman O'Connor, an Irish prince [AD; Raven 2].

O109 *Patriarchal times; or, the land of Canaan: A figurative history. In seven books. Comprising interesting events, incidents, and characters, founded on the holy scriptures* (by Miss O'Keeffe; dedicated to Revd Joseph Holden Pott).
   London: Gale & Curtis, J. Hatchard & T. Williams, 1811, 2 vols. SOURCE Allibone, ii, p. 1451; BD, p. 257; Block, p. 175; DNB; British Fiction; Garside, 1811:60. LOCATION D (1826, 4th edn), L, NUC.
   Franeker: G. Ypma, 1825, 2 vols. (trans. into Dutch as *Tafereelen uit de tijden der aartsvaderen, naar de heilige schrift*). SOURCE Alphabetische naamlijst 1790–1832, p. 437. Philadelphia: Jewish Publication Society, 5608 [1848] (The Jewish Miscellany, No. 8–10). SOURCE NYPL. LOCATION NN.
   COMMENTARY Prefatory statement mentions that 'the subject of this Work begins at the Eighth Verse of the Twenty-first Chapter of Genesis, and ends at the Twenty-ninth verse of the Forty-sixth Chapter'. In this re-interpretation of biblical stories the author examines assumptions about women's guilt in Hebrew texts and critiques partriarchism [Field Day, iv, pp 1145–8; Garside].

O110 *Zenobia, Queen of Palmyra. A narrative, founded on history* [anon.].
   London: F.C. & J. Rivington, 1814, 2 vols. SOURCE Allibone, ii, p. 1451; Block, p. 175; DNB; British Fiction; Garside, 1814:43. LOCATION Corvey CME 3–28–48247–X, Dt, L, NUC.
   COMMENTARY Historical fiction set in the third century at the time of Zenobia, queen of Palmyra, who led a war against Rome [Blain; RL].

O111 *Dudley* (by Miss O'Keeffe).
   London: Longman, Hurst, Rees, Orme & Brown, 1819, 3 vols. SOURCE Allibone, ii, p. 1451; Block, p. 175; DNB; British Fiction; Garside: 1819:52; Wolff, 5206. LOCATION Corvey CME 3–628–48245–3, L, NUC.

Paris: A. Betrand, 1824, 5 vols. (trans. by Mme de Montolieu as *Dudley et Claudy ou l'isle de Ténériffe*). LOCATION NUC.

COMMENTARY Epistolary novel written after the sudden death of the author's only brother in 1803 but not published until 1819, it deals with the topic of bereavement. Set in Tenerife and relates the history of Don Zulvago. The *Monthly Review* (London, Sept. 1819) criticized the novel for its 'few Hibernicisms and grammatical errors'. Issued in an edn of 500 copies, with the remaining 108 copies sold to Newman in 1825 [Blain; RIA/DIB; British Fiction].

O112   *The broken sword, or, a soldier's honour; a tale of the allied armies of 1757* (by Adelaide D. O'Keeffe),

    + London: Groombridge & Sons, 1854 (ill.). SOURCE Allibone, ii, p. 1451; Alston, p. 321; DNB. LOCATION L, InND Loeber coll.

COMMENTARY Given that the publication date of this book was more than twenty years following the preceding title, it is plausible that its author was another Miss O'Keeffe, but ODNB points out that it mirrors the O'Keeffe children's own experiences with their parents' separation and time in France. Set in mid-eighteenth-century England and France, featuring two children suffering from their parents' estrangement, which has come about through the presumed dishonour of their French father who was in the French army fighting against the Prussians. The mother returns to her native England and takes her son with her. He grows up thinking his father is dead. The father rears the daughter in France. When the children are older they are, by prearrangement, switched to the other parent. Neither child is happy with the new situation, and each makes an effort to return. In the meantime, it transpires that the father had not acted dishonourably. The parents reunite, and the children marry their chosen loves. In the end everyone is rich and happy [ML; ODNB].

O'KEEFFE, Christopher. See **O'KEEFFE, Christopher Manus**.

O'KEEFFE, Christopher Manus (also known as **Christopher O'Keeffe**), d. Brooklyn (NY) *c*.1889. Historical novelist and political agitator, CMO'K was sentenced about 1866, presumably in Ireland, to penal servitude for Fenianism. He had been contributing to various nationalist periodicals during the 1860s under the pseudonym 'Ollamh Fodhla', and he published the *Life of Daniel O'Connell* (Dublin, 1864, 2 vols.). According to the title page, the following novel was written when CMO'K was a political convict (No. 2873). He went to the US after his release, where he published *The liberation of Ireland* (New York, 1875). He wrote a short story, 'Killoch Hill, a fireside story', set in Co. Tipperary and published in New York periodicals, including poems in the *Illustrated Celtic Monthly* (New York, 1879) and articles in the *Catholic World* (New York). SOURCE BLC; Brown, p. 245; Irish pseudonyms; O'Donoghue, p. 358; RIA/DIB; RL.

O113   *The knights of the Pale; or, Ireland 400 years ago. A historical romance* (by Christopher O'Keeffe, political convict 2873; dedicated to Dixon C. O'Keeffe, Esq., Templemore, Ireland).

    + Glasgow: Cameron & Ferguson, 1870. SOURCE Allibone Suppl., ii, p. 1189; Brown, 1337. LOCATION D, Dcc (n.d. edn), L, InND Loeber coll.

    New York: P.M. Haverty, [1871 or earlier]. SOURCE Adv. in Haverty's *Irish-American illustrated almanac* (New York, 1871), p. 104.

COMMENTARY No copy of the New York edn located. First appeared in the *Celt* (Dublin) in 1857. Historical fiction. The author's stated aim was to bring to nineteenth-century readers aspects of war-like Ireland of the fifteenth century. The scene is set in the Pale and the story starts with a postulant knight, Christopher St Lawrence, son the baron of Howth, who as part of his initiation has to spend a night in the Cathedral of Holy Trinity (Christ Church) in

Dublin. There he meets a half-mythical person called the Dollaher. The tale is loosely connected by the love story of Maude Barnewall and The O'Ferrall of Annaly. There are long descriptions of events such as a tournament, the burning of a bard at the stake, and the life and manners of the O'Byrnes of Glenmalure (Co. Wicklow). The text contains many Irish words, which are explained in footnotes [ML; Brown].

'AN OLD BOY', pseud. See FULLER, James Franklin.

'AN OLD COMMERCIAL TRAVELLER', pseud. See CAHILL, Charles.

'AN OLD HAND', pseud. See BELL, Charles Dent.

'AN OLD SAILOR', pseud. See BARKER, Matthew Henry.

'THE OLD SAILOR', pseud. See BARKER, Matthew Henry.

'OLD SLEUTH', pseud. See HALSEY, Harlan Page.

'AN OLD SOLDIER', pseud. See BUTLER, Gen. Sir William Francis.

'O'LEARY, Con', pseud. See MC CORRY, Peter.

O'LEARY, Joseph, b. Cork *c*.1795, d. London? *c*.1845. Poet, balladeer and journalist, JO'L was a strolling player before he became a contributor to papers in Cork such as the scurrilous *Freeholder*, the *Bagatelle* and the *Cork Mercantile Chronicle*, of which he was an editor. He wrote the infamous ballad 'Whiskey, drink divine' (1818), and contributed poems and sketches to the *Dublin and London Magazine* (London, 1825–27). In 1834 he went to London and acted as a parliamentary reporter for the *Morning Herald*. His published poetry includes the anonymous *The Tribute* (Cork, 1833) for which see below, and *Odes to Anacreon* (location?, *c*.1840), while some of his poems are included in *Poems of Ireland* (London, 1858), edited by Samuel Lover§. Between 1840 and 1850 JO'L disappeared, and is said to have committed suicide in the Regent's Canal (London), but this has not been confirmed, although O'Donoghue said he spent considerable effort in investigating the matter. JO'L should not be confused with the author of the same name who was admitted to Gray's Inn (London) in 1820 and who wrote several works on tithe and rent law in Ireland. SOURCE Irish pseudonyms; ODNB; O'Donoghue, p. 362; RIA/DIB.

O114 *The tribute; a miscellaneous volume in prose and verse* [anon.] (dedicated to William Crawford Jnr).
 + Cork: Printed for the author by F. Jackson, 1833 (ill. 'a Cork artist' [Mr James M'Daniel and his thirteen-year-old son]). SOURCE Ximenes cat. 98/223 (mentions the attribution). LOCATION D (also mentions attribution), DCU, InND Loeber coll.
COMMENTARY One of the author's aims was to prove that 'a Cork press may produce a work, which those of London, Edinburgh or Dublin, need not blush to acknowledge'. Aside from poetry, it contains the following sketches: 'Passages in the life of an actor' (an autobiographical account in rural Ireland), 'When I was a boy!', 'The phrenologist', 'Mr. O'Connell', '"As Shakespeare says"', 'First love. A fragment', 'Repeal: Whigs and Tories', 'The late John Boyle', 'On the character of Hamlet' [ML].

OLIVER, Laetitia S. See OLIVER, Laetitia Selwyn.

Oliver

OLIVER, Laetitia Selwyn (known as **Laetitia S. Oliver**), fl. 1887. Religious fiction writer and translator, LSO was possibly an Irish Catholic. SOURCE Allibone Suppl., ii, p. 1193; RL.

O115 *Annunziata; or, the gipsy child* (by Laetitia S. Oliver).
+ Dublin: M.H. Gill & Son, 1887. SOURCE Allibone Suppl., ii, p. 1193; OCLC (1914 edn). LOCATION D (1914 edn), L.
COMMENTARY Set in England, but the story contains an Irish nurse and an Irish priest. The main characters convert to the Catholic faith [ML].

OLLIER, Charles. Publisher and co-author. See **MAGINN, William**.

O'MEARA, Kathleen, pseud. 'Grace Ramsay', b. Dublin 1839, d. Paris 1888. Novelist and religious biographer, KO'M was the daughter of Dennis O'Meara of Tipperary and grand-daughter of Barry Edward O'Meara, who was Napoleon's surgeon on St Helena. She was taken to Paris as a child (her mother may have received a pension because of her father's service to Napoleon) and KO'M remained in France until her death, although she travelled widely. She published stories in the *Irish Monthly* (Dublin, 1877), including a pro-Catholic novel 'Robin Redbreast's victory'. She also contributed to the *Monitor: An Illustrated Dublin Magazine* (1879), to the *Atlantic Monthly* (Boston), and to *Harper's* (New York). It is unlikely that she returned to Ireland but it features prominently in some of her fiction. She wrote a biography of St Gaston de Louise de Marillac Ségur (1591–1662) as *The blind apostle: and a heroine of charity. Being the third series of "Bells of the sanctuary"* (London, 1890). For many years she was the Paris correspondent of the *Catholic Journal* (London?) and the *Tablet* (London). She published 12 works of mostly Catholic fiction, including fictionalized biographies of notable Catholics. KO'M never married and her last work, a biography of Jean Baptiste Vianney, curé d'Ars, was published posthumously in 1891. Some of her papers are in the NLS. SOURCE Allibone Suppl., ii, p. 1194; Blain, p. 814; Boase, ii, p. 1244; Brady, p. 195; Brown, p. 247; Colman, pp 179–80; Murphy, p. 62; OCIL, p. 446; ODNB; RIA/DIB; Sutherland, p. 479.

O116 *A woman's trials* (by 'Grace Ramsay').
London: Hurst & Blackett, 1867, 3 vols. SOURCE ODNB; Sutherland, p. 479. LOCATION L, NUC.
COMMENTARY Concerns a young English girl who is educated in Paris and who becomes a Catholic, thus provoking her father into disowning her [Blain; Sutherland].

O117 *Iza's story* (by 'Grace Ramsay'; dedicated to Charles, Comte de Montalembert).
+ London: Hurst & Blackett, 1869. SOURCE DNB; Sutherland, p. 479. LOCATION L.
London: Burns, 1877 (by Kathleen O'Meara; as *Iza: A story of life in Russian-Poland*). SOURCE Alston, p. 321. LOCATION L, NUC.
COMMENTARY Set in Russia and Poland [ML].

O118 *The bells of the sanctuary: Mary Bendedicta, Agnes, Aline, One of God's heroines, Monseigneur Darboy* (by Kathleen O'Meara (Grace Ramsay)).
+ London: Burns & Oates, 1871. SOURCE OCLC (1879 edn); COPAC. LOCATION InND (1879 edn), E.
COMMENTARY Contents: 'Mary Bendedicta' (extended Irish Catholic tale), 'Agnes', 'Aline', 'One of God's heroines', 'Monseigneur Darboy' (concerns Georges Darboy, 1813–1871) [OCLC; RL].

O119 *The bells of the sanctuary. A daughter of St. Dominick* (by 'Grace Ramsay').
London, [publisher?], 1871. LOCATION L (destroyed).
COMMENTARY No copy located. Reprinted from the *Catholic World* (London or New York) [RL; COPAC].

O120 *Mary Benedicta, and other stories* [anon.].

+ New York: The Catholic Publication Society, 1873 (ill.). LOCATION InND Loeber coll.

COMMENTARY Contents: 'Mary Benedicta' (first published in *The bells of the sanctuary*, London, 1871), 'The two portraits', 'The pierced rock', 'The glass of brandy'. Aside from the first story, it is not clear whether the remaining stories are by Kathleen O'Meara [RL].

O121   *A salon in the last days of the empire, and other stories* (by 'Grace Ramsay').
+ London: Richard Bentley & Son, 1873. SOURCE Allibone Suppl., ii, p. 1194; Sutherland, p. 479. LOCATION L, NUC.
London: Richard Bentley & Son, 1885 (as *Madame Mohl, her salon and her friends; a study of social life in Paris*). SOURCE COPAC. LOCATION L.
Paris: Plon, Nourrit, 1886 (as *Un salon à Paris; Madame Mohl et ses intimes: Chateaubriand, Madame Récamier, Fauriel, Ampère, Mérimée, Tocqueville, Manzoni, Madame Ristori, La reine de Hollande, Le duc Broglie, Maupas, Thiers, Guizot, Loménie, Jules Simon, M. Renan*). SOURCE Bn-Opale plus. LOCATION BNF.
COMMENTARY According to Allibone it was first serialized in the *Atlantic Monthly* (Boston). Contents: 'The Parisienne en deshabille', 'The business of life', 'Extremes meet', '"Wanted three million"', 'A Berlin', '"Awakening"', 'Excelsior!', 'Mademoiselle Adrienne: a sketch after the Blocus', 'Number thirteen: an episode of two sieges' [RL; Allibone].

O122   *Alba's dream and other stories* [anon.].
New York: Catholic Publication Society, 1878. SOURCE DCU, Catholic Americana files; RLIN. LOCATION UBP.

O123   *Are you my wife? A novel* (by 'Grace Ramsay').
+ London: Samuel Tinsley, 1878, 3 vols. SOURCE ODNB; Sutherland, p. 479; Wolff, 5297. LOCATION L.
New York: The Catholic Publication Society, 1876. SOURCE DCU, Catholic Americana files. LOCATION NUC.
COMMENTARY The story begins in Wales and then moves to Russia [ML].

O124   *The battle of Connemara* (by Kathleen O'Meara).
+ London: R. Washbourne, 1878. SOURCE Brown, 1347; ODNB; Sutherland, p. 479. LOCATION D, Dcc, L (destroyed).
COMMENTARY A story of priests and people in Connacht in the days of the 'soupers', with part of the story taking place in Paris. The plot turns mainly on the conversion of an English woman, Lady Peggy Blake, who has married an Irish Protestant landlord and has settled in Connacht where the faith of the peasants inspires her to become a Catholic [Brown; ODNB].

O125   *Pearl* (by Kathleen O'Meara).
+ New York: The Catholic Publication Society Co., 1879. LOCATION DCU.
New York: Christian Press Association, [1879]. LOCATION NUC.
London: Burns & Oates, 1879. LOCATION L.

O126   *Diane Coryval* [anon.].
+ Boston: Roberts Bros, 1884 (No Name Series). SOURCE Allibone Suppl., ii, p. 1194. LOCATION L, NUC, InND Loeber coll.
London: Richard Bentley & Son, 1887 (as *The old house in Picardy*). SOURCE Allibone Suppl., ii, p. 1194; Alston, p. 321. LOCATION L, NUC.
COMMENTARY Set in France. Diane Coryval is a student at an art academy and is in love with Réné, a fellow artist. However Réné's father wants him to marry a rich girl. Diane's mother dies and Diane moves to the country to be with her relatives who are good-natured but fairly uncouth farmers. It appears as if Réné has deserted her and she marries one of her cousins. Réné reappears and eventually they are united [ML].

O'Moore

O127 *Queen by right divine, and other tales. Being the second series of "Bells of the sanctuary"* (by Kathleen O'Meara).
London: Burns & Oates; New York: The Catholic Publication Society Co., 1885. SOURCE Alston, p. 321; COPAC. LOCATION L (destroyed; also n.d. edn), E. COMMENTARY Religious fiction. Consists of fictionalized sketches of Jeanne Rendu, Sr Rosalie, Mme Swetchine, and the Abbé Lacordaire [NUC; RL].

O128 *Mabel Stanhope. A story* (by 'Grace Ramsay').
Boston: Roberts Bros, 1886. SOURCE Allibone Suppl., ii, p. 1194; DCU, Catholic Americana files. LOCATION NUC.

O129 *Narka, the nihilist* (by 'Grace Ramsay').
New York: Harper & Bros, 1887. SOURCE Allibone Suppl., ii, p. 1194; ODNB; DCU, Catholic Americana files. LOCATION NUC.
London: Richard Bentley & Son, 1888, 2 vols. (by Kathleen O'Meara; as *Narka. A novel*). SOURCE Wolff, 5298. LOCATION L, NUC.
COMMENTARY Partly serialized in *Harper's Magazine* (New York). A suspense story of a young Russian singer caught up in political intrigue, a murder, court scenes – including her own trial – and ending in her triumph at La Scala in Milan. ODNB lists the 1888 edn. as *Narka, a story of Russian life*, but such a title has not been located [Bennett cat. 33/160; ODNB; RL].

O'MOORE, Sidney. See **MOORE, Sidney O.**

O'NEILL, Henrietta Bruce. See **BOATE, Mrs Edward Wellington.**

O'NEILL, John, b. Waterford 1787, d. London 1858. Poet, playwright and novelist, JO'N was the son of Thomas O'Neill, a poor shoemaker at Carrick-on-Suir, and Jane English. He was mainly self-educated and followed in his father's trade. He married Mary Dollard in Carrick-on-Suir around 1800 and they moved to London in 1808. He combined his work as a shoemaker with his literary activity, writing some plays and poetry on temperance. He wrote the poem *The drunkard* (London, 1842, ill. by JO'N's friend, George Cruikshank), which he dedicated to Fr Theobald Mathew, pioneer of the temperance movement in Ireland, and which earned JO'N the sobriquet of laureate of the temperance movement. It vividly depicts the destructive power of drink in a labouring-class family. JO'N wrote 'Fifty years experience as an Irish shoemaker in London', published posthumously in serial form in *St Crispin* (1869–70), a boot and shoe trade magazine, which described his struggles to support his large family, their life in the slums – including their diet and entertainment – the decline of his trade, and his efforts through writing songs, plays and articles to earn money. He remained poor all his life but he did receive support from the Royal Literary Fund. For JO'N's portraits, see ODNB. SOURCE Allibone, ii, p. 1458; Boase, ii, p. 1246; Brady, p. 196; Brown, p. 248; Hogan 2, p. 985; NUC; OCIL, pp 449–50; ODNB; O'Donoghue, p. 366; RIA/DIB.

O130 *Handerahan the Irish fairy man; and legends of Carrick* (by John O'Neill; introd. by Mrs S.C. Hall§).
+ London: For the author by W. Tweedie, 1854 (subscribers' list). SOURCE Brown, 1349; Bradshaw, 6129. LOCATION C, NUC.
COMMENTARY Contents: 'Handerahan, the Irish fairy man' (a story of an herb doctor skilled in potions and charms against the fairies), 'Paddy Galagher and his horse', 'Memoir of Will Handerahan', 'The phantom bride', 'Paddy Mulcahy and the enchanted potatoes', 'The changeling', 'The evil eye'; 'Legends of Carrick' [Carrick-on-Suir], containing: 'The race and the duke and the devil', 'Biddy and the enchanted spancels', 'Jemmy-on-occasion, and the weaver', 'The first brogue maker', 'The doodheen, a sheogue', 'Going for the midwife',

'Pinning-fe-clough', 'The boleen skeigh', 'The four-leaf shamrock' (contains a list of Irish phrases) [RL; Brown].

O131 *Mary of Avonmore; or, the foundling of the beach* (by John O'Neill). [location?], [publisher?], [1855?], 3 vols. SOURCE Brown, 1350; OCIL, p. 450. COMMENTARY No copy located [RL].

'O'NEILL, Moira', pseud. See SKRINE, Agnes Nesta Shakespear [*sic*].

O'NEILL, William, b. Mooretown Great, Tomhaggard (Co. Wexford), 1823, d. 1890. Schoolteacher and miscellaneous writer, WO'N taught at Rathgarogue and Tomhaggard and later at the Tenacre School in the barony of Forth. He married Ann, daughter of the architect and builder Richard Piece of Tenacre (*c.*1810–54). WO'N was active in the Land League. He wrote much on the castles and the Norman families of Co. Wexford. His son collected his father's writing with an eye to publication, including the 200pp manuscript listed below. He was buried at Tomhaggard church grounds. SOURCE Browne, pp 115–16; Personal communication, Ann Martha Rowan, Sept. 2005.

O132 *Tales of Forth and Bargy. A description of the two south eastern baronies of County Wexford* (by William O'Neill).
COMMENTARY Unpublished manuscript, *c.*1875, edited by Joseph Henry Lloyd, consisting of loose handwritten sheets enclosed in two folders (NLI, MS 10,674). According to the first page of the manuscript, O'Neill was the principal at Tenacre School. Written in both English and Yola, a dialect unique to the barony of Forth and Bargy that survived until the middle of the nineteenth century, it contains accounts of several parishes in the area. Interspersed are some stories and legends and songs in Yola with literal translations. It also contains the following anecdotes: 'The two fits of ill-humour of the two Corishes, the father and the son, in the alehouse', 'Dickeen Corish's the son's fit of ill-humour in the alehouse', 'Synnott the tanner's fright', 'Translation of the second version', 'Michael Cahill's trick', 'Jean Corish's mix-up of grains', 'Michael Cawl's bunk', as well as short stories: 'The lucky crust of bread: a true tale of "98"', 'The ghost of Leache's cross', 'The rise and fall of Ballyhealy', 'Wexford tenants and Carlow landlords one hundred years ago', 'Treasure-findings in the barony of Forth', 'Redmond O'Hanlon and the priest hunter', 'The sad fate of Browne of Mulrankin', 'The military raid on Denistown in '98' [CD].

'ONE OF AMERICA'S MOST FAMOUS DETECTIVES', fl. 1889. Pseudonym of a mystery writer. SOURCE RL.

O133 *The great Cronin mystery or the Irish patriot's fate. A complete and accurate history of the assassination of Dr. Patrick Henry Cronin, the search for the murderers, the inquest, the trial, and the verdict* (by 'One of America's most famous detectives').
+ Chicago: Laird & Lee, 1889 (ill.). LOCATION InND Loeber coll.
+ [Chicago]: Laird & Lee, 1889 (salesman's dummy). LOCATION InND Loeber coll.
COMMENTARY Set among the Chicago Irish, the story is presumed to relate the actual course of events leading to the murder of Dr Patrick Henry Cronin, in which Irish organizations were involved because Dr Cronin had become aware of some irregularities of their members. The book is written by a private detective and gives details as the case unfolds. A related publication is H.M. Henry's *The crime of the century, or the assassination of Dr. Patrick Henry Cronin* ([Chicago], 1889) [ML; RL].

'ONE OF THE BOYS', pseud. See FITZGERALD, Percy Hetherington.

'ONE OF THEMSELVES', fl. 1888. Pseudonym of a writer of police stories and history, who probably was Irish. SOURCE RL.

O134   *Tales of the Irish police* (by 'One of themselves').
+ Dublin: Printed at the Office [*sic*], 1888 (ill.). SOURCE de Búrca cat. May, 1998. LOCATION InND Loeber coll.
COMMENTARY Contents: 'No. I. Royal Irish Constabulary', 'No. II. The Dublin Metropolitan Police', 'No. III. The Revenue Police'. Each section starts with a brief history and is then followed by anecdotes [ML].

'ONE JONES', fl. 1890s. Pseudonym of a humour writer, most probably American. SOURCE RL.

O135   *A peculiar Irishman; or, Johnny Dooley loved the girl and said to the world: "Git out of the rut and see what's to be seen on the other soide of the fince"* (by 'One Jones').
+ New York: The Truth Seeker Co., [1896]. LOCATION PC, L.

'ONE WHO WAS THERE', fl. 1890s. Pseudonym of a military veteran.

O136   *Sword and lance. A story of Indian mutiny* (by 'One who was there').
+ London: Charles Fox, [1891]. LOCATION L.
COMMENTARY 68pp. Story populated with Irish soldiers and other Irishmen [RL].

OPIE, Mrs —. See OPIE, Amelia.

OPIE, Amelia Alderson (née Alderson; known as Mrs Opie), b. Norwich (Norfolk) 1769, d. Norwich 1853. Popular English novelist, poet and prose writer, AO was the daughter of John Alderson, a doctor, and Amelia Briggs, after whose death she assumed the role of housekeeper for her father. As a young woman she spoke French; wrote; acted in a drama ('Adelaide'), and began to publish poetry. In London she was part of the literary circle around William Godwin§ and Mary Wollstonecraft. There she met the painter and portraitist John Opie, whom she married in 1798 and who encouraged her in her literary work. AO later became a Quaker and devoted herself to philanthropy. Only one of her novels is known to have Irish content. SOURCE Allibone, ii, pp 1458–60; Blain, pp 815–16; NCBEL 4, pp 965–7, 1843; ODNB; RL.

O137   *Adeline Mowbray; or, the mother and the daughter: A tale* (by Mrs Opie).
London: Longman, Hurst, Reese & Orme; Edinburgh: A. Constable, 1805, 3 vols. SOURCE British Fiction; Garside, 1805:57; NCBEL 4, 966; COPAC. LOCATION Corvey CME 3–628–48260–7, L.
COMMENTARY Suggested in part by Mary Wollstonecraft and William Godwin's§ attempt to counter the subordination of women within conventional marriage, the novel features Adeline Mowbray, whose mother betrays her daughter by letting her second husband, the Irish Sir Patrick O'Carroll, come between them. After O'Carroll attempts to rape Adeline, she flees with her lover, Glenmurray, and lives openly with him outside of marriage until a series of disasters forces her to repent of such a free-thinking relationship [ODNB; D. Spender (ed.), *Living by the pen* (New York, 1992), pp 208–9].

'OPTIC, Oliver', pseud. See ADAMS, William Taylor.

O'REILLY, Eleanor Grace (also known as Mrs Robert O'Reilly), fl. 1868. Writer of stories and religious fiction for juveniles and a novelist, EGO'R was Irish, according to the publisher Edmund Downey§. Some of her stories are set in Sussex, where she probably lived for some of her life. She published 22 works of fiction, mostly for children, none of which has Irish content. SOURCE Allibone Suppl., ii, pp 1195–6; BLC; IBL, 9 (1918), p. 71 (by Edmund Downey); NCBEL 4, p. 1843; RIA/DIB; RL.

O138   *Grandmamma's nest: a child's story-book* (by Eleanor Grace O'Reilly).
London: Saunders, Otley & Co., 1868. SOURCE Allibone Suppl., ii, p. 1195; OCLC. LOCATION Univ. of Florida.
COMMENTARY Fiction for juveniles [RL].

O139   *Daisy's companions; or, scenes from child life. A story for little girls* [anon.].
London: Bell & Daldy, [1869]. LOCATION L.
Boston: Roberts Bros, 1872. SOURCE NCBEL 4, p. 1843; OCLC. LOCATION CLU.
Philadelphia: J.B. Lippincott, 1881. SOURCE OCLC. LOCATION Boston Public Library.
COMMENTARY Fiction for juveniles [RL].

O140   *Deborah's drawer* (by Eleanor Grace O'Reilly).
+ London: Bell & Daldy, 1871 (ill.). SOURCE Allibone Suppl., ii, pp 1195–6. LOCATION L.
Boston: Roberts, 1871. SOURCE OCLC. LOCATION Brown Univ.
New York: [publisher?], 1875 (ill.). SOURCE NCBEL 4, p. 1843.
Philadelphia: J.B. Lippincott, 1881. SOURCE NCBEL 4, p. 1843. LOCATION Univ. of Alabama, Birmingham.
COMMENTARY No copy of the New York edn located. Fiction for juveniles set in America [ML].

O141   *Doll world; or, play and earnest* (by Eleanor Grace O'Reilly).
+ London: Bell & Daldy, 1872 (ill. C.A. Saltmarsh). SOURCE Allibone Suppl., ii, p. 1195. LOCATION L.
Philadelphia: J.B. Lippincott, 1881 (by Mrs Robert O'Reilly). SOURCE OCLC. LOCATION Free Library of Philadelphia.
COMMENTARY Fiction for juveniles, no Irish content [ML].

O142   *Little Grig: and the tinker's letter* (by Eleanor Grace O'Reilly).
London: [publisher?], [1872], 2 parts. SOURCE Allibone Suppl., ii, pp 1195; NCBEL 4, p. 1843. LOCATION L (destroyed).
Nashville (TN): Publishing House of the Methodist Episcopal Church South, n.d. (ill.). SOURCE OCLC. LOCATION GEU.
New York: Phillips & Hunt; Cincinnati: Hitchcock & Walden, n.d. SOURCE OCLC. LOCATION Univ. of Southern Mississippi.
COMMENTARY No copy of the London edn located. Religious fiction for juveniles [BLC; RL].

O143   *The stories they tell me, or Sue and I* (by Eleanor Grace O'Reilly).
+ London: William Wells Gardner, [1873] (ill.). SOURCE Allibone Suppl., ii, p. 1195; NCBEL 4, p. 1843 (1877 edn). LOCATION L.
COMMENTARY Stories for children. Contents: 'The ferns' story', 'The cowslips' story', 'Naughty Tiny's trip to America', 'Spotted cottons', 'The wind's story', The plumcake's story', 'Limited incomes', 'Thin bread-and-butter', 'Old boats', 'Our half-holiday', 'The white violets' story', 'The kettle's story', 'At court' [JB].[ML].

O144   *Giles's minority; or, scenes at the red house* (by Eleanor Grace O'Reilly).
+ London: George Bell & Sons, 1874 (ill.). SOURCE Allibone Suppl., ii, p. 1195; NCBEL 4, p. 1843. LOCATION L.
COMMENTARY Fiction for juveniles. No Irish content [ML].

O145   *Little prescription, and other tales* (by Eleanor Grace O'Reilly).

+ London: George Bell & Sons, 1875 (ill.). SOURCE Allibone Suppl., ii, p. 1195 (mentions 1872 edn, which has not been located); NCBEL 4, p. 1843. LOCATION L.
COMMENTARY Fiction for juveniles. Contents: 'Little prescription', 'My sister Bliss', 'An unbidden guest', 'May's mail-cart', 'London daisies', 'The balcony boys', 'Grandmamma's nest', 'Princess Lina' [JB].

O146   *Cicely's choice* (by Eleanor Grace O'Reilly).
+ London: George Bell & Sons, 1875 (ill. A.J. Pasquier). SOURCE NCBEL 4, p. 1843; Allibone Suppl., ii, p. 1195 (mentions a 1874 edn, which has not been located). LOCATION L.
COMMENTARY Fiction for juveniles. No Irish content [ML].

O147   *The girls of the square, and other tales* (by Eleanor Grace O'Reilly; dedicated to Kathleen, Kit, and Katie, 'in memory of their schoolroom days').
+ London: Strahan & Co., [1878]. SOURCE Allibone Suppl., ii, p. 1195; NCBEL 4, p. 1843. LOCATION L.
COMMENTARY Fiction for juveniles. No Irish content. Contents: 'The girls of the square', 'My mistakes', 'A speaking likeness', 'Linda's girls', 'The red villa children' [RL].

O148   *The story of ten thousand homes* (by Eleanor Grace O'Reilly).
+ London: Strahan & Co., [1878]. SOURCE Allibone Suppl., ii, p. 1195. LOCATION L.
COMMENTARY No Irish content [ML].

O149   *Phoebe's fortunes* (by Eleanor Grace O'Reilly).
+ London, Aylesbury: Strahan & Co., 1879, 3 vols. SOURCE Allibone Suppl., ii, p. 1195; NCBEL 4, p. 1843. LOCATION L.
COMMENTARY Fiction for juveniles. No Irish content [ML].

O150   *Sussex stories* (by Eleanor Grace O'Reilly).
+ London: Strahan & Co., [1880], 3 vols. SOURCE Allibone Suppl., ii, p. 1195. LOCATION L.
+ London: Hodder & Stoughton, 1884 (as *Meg's mistake, and other Sussex stories*; ill. Fred Barnard). SOURCE Allibone Suppl., ii, p. 1195. LOCATION L (destroyed), E.
COMMENTARY Stories set in Sussex. Contents: 'The burden and the blessing', 'Meg's mistake', 'The little blue band-box', 'Waiting', 'Our Rosie', 'A golden wedding', 'Miss Olive's boys', 'Fairy gold', 'Master Judd's daughter', 'Little Grig', 'Two girls', 'A twelvemonth's good character', 'The tinker's letter', 'Darby and Joan' [JB].

O151   *Reed farm* (by Eleanor Grace O'Reilly).
London: Strahan & Co., [1880]. SOURCE Allibone Suppl., ii, p. 1195. LOCATION L.
London: Hodder & Stoughton, 1887 (as *Kitty Deane of Reed farm*; ill. Townley Green). SOURCE NCBEL 4, p. 1843 (1894 edn); OCLC (1897 edn); COPAC. LOCATION E.

O152   *The red house in the suburbs: a story* (by Eleanor Grace O'Reilly).
London: Strahan & Co., [1881] (ill.). SOURCE COPAC; Allibone Suppl., ii, p. 1195 (mentions wrong title). LOCATION E, L (London, Hodder 1884 edn).

O153   *David Broome, artist* (by Mrs Robert O'Reilly).
London: Sampson Low & Co., 1881, 3 vols. SOURCE Allibone Suppl., ii, p. 1195; COPAC. LOCATION L.
London: Ward & Downey, 1886 (new edn). SOURCE IBL, 9 (1918), p. 71. LOCATION L.

O154   *Dinglefield* (by Eleanor Grace O'Reilly).
London, New York: George Routledge & Sons, 1883 (ill. A.C. Corbould). SOURCE Allibone Suppl., ii, p. 1195. LOCATION L.

O155   *Kirke's mill and other stories* (by Eleanor Grace O'Reilly).
London: Hatchards, 1885. SOURCE Allibone Suppl., ii, p. 1195. LOCATION L (destroyed), E.

COMMENTARY Religious fiction. Contents: 'Kirke's mill', 'A sister of charity', 'Set to music', 'A rare case', 'Ray', 'Joshua Long's superstition', '"Only right"' [ID; BLC].

O156   *Our hero* (by Eleanor Grace O'Reilly).
+ London, New York: George Routledge & Sons, 1885 (ill. E.T. Garland). SOURCE COPAC. LOCATION L.
COMMENTARY Fiction for juveniles, no Irish content [ML].

O157   *Holiday tasks* (by Eleanor Grace O'Reilly).
London, New York, Glasgow, Manchester: George Routledge & Sons, 1890 (ill. M.E. Edwards). SOURCE COPAC. LOCATION L.

O158   *Hurstleigh Dene* (by Eleanor Grace O'Reilly).
London: Longmans & Co., 1890 (ill. M.E. Edwards). SOURCE COPAC. LOCATION L.

O159   *Joan and Jerry* (by Eleanor Grace O'Reilly).
London: W. & R. Chambers, 1891 (ill.). SOURCE COPAC. LOCATION L.

O160   *The sound of the streets* (by Eleanor Grace O'Reilly).
London: Wells Gardner & Co., [1892]. LOCATION L (destroyed), E.
COMMENTARY Religious fiction [BLC].

O161   *When we were young* (by Eleanor Grace O'Reilly).
London: W. & R. Chambers, 1892. LOCATION L.

O'REILLY, John Boyle, b. Castle Dowth (Co. Meath) 1844, d. Boston (MA) 1890. Poet, patriot, newspaperman and novelist, JBO'R was the son of David O'Reilly and Eliza Boyle. His father was master of a school attached to the Netterville institution for widows and orphans at Castle Dowth. He apprenticed as a compositor to the *Argus* newspaper in Drogheda at age 11 but left Ireland in 1859 and became a compositor and reporter on the *Guardian* in Preston, England. He returned to Ireland in 1863 and enlisted with the British army's 10th Hussars, then stationed in Dublin, so that he could recruit Irishmen for the Fenian movement. His activities were uncovered in 1866 and he was sentenced to death. The sentence was commuted to life imprisonment and he was transported to Fremantle, Australia. He escaped in 1869 and went to the US where he settled in Boston and worked for the *Pilot*, with which he was associated for the rest of his life. As a reporter for the *Pilot*, he accompanied the 'Fenian invasion' of Canada under Gen. John O'Neill in 1870, and in 1876 he was one of the organizers – along with John Devoy –of the rescue of his comrades still in convict prisons in Australia and their transport to America on a whaler. He made a name as a lecturer, a writer and poet; he was a contributor to a wide variety of periodicals, and he became joint-owner of the *Pilot*, which was then the country's foremost Catholic newspaper. In his writing he supported Irish nationalism and land reform and was an advocate for the poor and downtrodden and for workers' rights, opposing racial discrimination and religious prejudice. He was a leader in civic life in Boston, supporting the Democratic party; founding a literary society in 1873 called the Paphyus Club; serving as president of the Boston Press Club, and founding the Cribb Club, dedicated to boxing, his favourite sport. He was a leading figure in Irish-American political efforts, helping to organize support for Parnell's Home Rule initiative; one of the founders of the Irish National Land League, and involved with the Irish National League of America. In 1881 he received an honorary doctor of laws from Notre Dame University (IN) and an honorary Phi Beta Kappa from Dartmouth College (NH), and in 1889 an honorary doctorate from Georgetown University (Washington, DC). JBO'R was one of the first novelists to write about western Australia. His books of poetry include *Songs of the southern seas* (Boston, 1873); *Songs, legends and ballads* (Boston, 1878), and *Poetry and song of Ireland with biographical sketches of her poets* (New York, 1887). A workaholic, he suffered from chronic insomnia and died of an overdose of chloral. In the ruined Dowth parish church JBO'R is commemorated by a monument of his bust flanked by allegorical figures of Ireland and America. Other memorials are in Australia and Charlestown (MA). Some of his papers are at Boston College (MA) and in the John Devoy collection in the NLI. For JBO'R's portrait, see ODNB. SOURCE Allibone Suppl., ii, p. 1196; ANB; S. Ashton, 'John Boyle O'Reilly & Moondyne (1878)' in *History Ireland* (2002), pp 38–42; Boylan, pp 310–11; Casey & Rowan, p. 230; DAB; A.G. Evans, *Fanatic heart: a life of John Boyle O'Reilly* (Boston, 1997); Fenning, pp 161–6; Field Day, ii, p. 999; Hogan, p. 542; Hogan 2, pp 991–2; Irish pseudonyms; LVP, p. 361; McKenna, pp 304–6; Macartney, p. 367; F.G. McManamin, *The American years of John Boyle O'Reilly* (New York, 1959, revsd 1976); OCIL, pp 453–4; ODNB; O'Donoghue, pp 367–8; RIA/DIB; RL; J.J. Roche, *Life of John Boyle O'Reilly together with his complete poems and speeches* (ed. by Mrs. John Boyle O'Reilly; New York, 1891); W.G. Schofield, *Seek for a hero* (New York, 1956); Wolff, iii, p. 229.

O162   *Moondyne. A story from the under-world* (by John Boyle O'Reilly; dedicated to 'the prisoner, whoever and wherever he may be').

Boston: Pilot Publishing Co., 1879. SOURCE McKenna, p. 306; Fanning, p. 388; Wright, iii, 4040; Wolff, 5302. LOCATION Grail, NUC.

Boston: Roberts Bros, 1879. SOURCE Blessing, p. 154 (1883 edn); Miller, ii, p. 623. LOCATION InND Loeber coll. (1879, 3rd edn).

+ New York: P.J. Kenedy & Sons, 1879 (as *Moondyne Joe, a story from the underworld*). LOCATION D, NUC, InND Loeber coll.

Philadelphia: H.L. Kilner & Co., [188?] (ill.). SOURCE Macartney, p. 367; NYPL. LOCATION NN, NUC.

+ Melbourne, Sydney, Brisbane, Adelaide: George Robertson, 1880 (as *Moondyne. A story of life in West Australia*). SOURCE Macartney, p. 367; Miller, ii, p. 623. LOCATION DPL.

Melbourne: E.W. Cole, 1887 [anon.] (as *The golden secret; or, bond and free. A tale of bush and convict life in Western Australia*). SOURCE Miller, ii, p. 623; RLIN. LOCATION NUC, Univ. of Iowa.

+ London, New York, Glasgow, Manchester: George Routledge & Sons, 1889 (as *Moondyne. A story of the under-world*; dedicated to 'all who are in prison'). SOURCE Topp 1, p. 397; Macartney, p. 367. LOCATION D, Dcc, DPL, L. NUC (n.d. edn).

COMMENTARY Autobiographically inspired. Description of life in the Australian bush by a convict who befriends aborigines, through whom he learns of a rich vein of gold. This enables him to return to England and, under the name of Wyville, effect prison reforms there. He takes up the cause of a young woman who was falsely accused of murdering her own child. Eventually, he dies in an attempt to save a villain from death in a brush fire [ML; Fanning, p. 163; Macartney].

O163   *The King's men. A tale of tomorrow* (by John Boyle O'Reilly; written by Robert Grant, John Boyle O'Reilly, J.S. of Dale, and John T. Wheelwright).

+ New York: Charles Scribner's Sons, 1884. SOURCE Blessing, p. 154; Fanning, p. 388; McKenna, p. 306; Wright, iii, 2236. LOCATION C, CtY, InND Loeber coll.

COMMENTARY A futuristic novel about England in the twentieth century: England is described as a republic, the old guard has lost power, and the king is in exile in America. An uprising is planned to bring the king back but a woman who feels scorned in love betrays the insurgents. The insurgent leader is executed and others are given long prison sentences. Some of the prisoners escape to America, where one of them tells the king he will no longer be loyal to such a weak person as the king has proved to be. The treacherous role of the woman comes out and she disappears. One of the prisoners marries the American girl he has loved for a long time [ML].

O164   *Stories and sketches* (by John Boyle O'Reilly).
       Boston: [publisher?], 1888. SOURCE Allibone Suppl., ii, p. 1196.
       COMMENTARY No copy located [RL].
O165   *Watchwords* (by John Boyle O'Reilly; ed. by Katherine Eleanor Conway).
       Boston: T.J. Flynn, 1907. SOURCE OCLC. LOCATION Boston College.

'O'REILLY, Private Miles', pseud. See HALPINE, Gen. Charles Graham.

O'REILLY, Mrs Robert. See O'REILLY, Eleanor Grace.

O'RIORDAN, Conal. See O'RIORDAN, Conal Holmes O'Connell.

O'RIORDAN, Conal Holmes O'Connell (known as **Conal O'Riordan**), pseud. '**F. Norreys Connell**', b. Dublin 1874, d. Ealing (London) 1948. Novelist, playwright, actor and theatre manager, CHO'R was the younger son of Katherine O'Neill O'Riordan and her cousin Daniel O'Connell O'Riordan, QC, JP, of Dublin and Cork. CHO'CO'R was educated at home and at Belvedere and Clongowes Wood colleges and abroad. At Sandhurst military college a riding accident prevented him from obtaining a commission in the British army. However, his interest in the military influenced much of his later writing, particularly his critically-acclaimed series of novels featuring soldiers. His play *The piper* was performed at the Abbey Theatre (Dublin) in 1907. For a short while he was managing director of the Abbey, chosen by William Butler Yeats§ and Lady Gregory to replace J.M. Synge, and while in this position several other of his plays appeared on its stage. He then lived in London, visiting Ireland frequently, where he was friendly with such contemporary writers as Joseph Conrad, John Galsworthy, William Butler Yeats§, and Wilfred Owen. Rejected by the army for service in the First World War because of his injury, he served on the front at a YMCA rest hut. After the war he gave up his pseudonym and published under his own name. He was active in a number of literary societies, including the Irish Literary Society, of which he was president (1937–39). He published 21 works of fiction, many with strong autobiographical elements. He contributed to as variety of periodicals and magazines, including drama criticism to the *Westminster Review* (London) and the *Stage* (London?). His autobiography, *A plain tale from the bogs*, was published in London in 1937. SOURCE Boylan, p. 312; Brady, p. 197; Hogan 2, pp 992–5; OCIL, p. 455; O'Donoghue, pp 368–9; RIA/DIB; Ryan, pp 118–19; RL.
O166   *In the green park or half-pay deities* (by 'F. Norreys Connell'; dedicated to the
       author's brother).
       + London: Henry & Co., 1894 (ill. F.H. Townsend). SOURCE Brady, p. 197; Hogan
       2, p. 994. LOCATION D, L, NUC.
       COMMENTARY A story about an Irishman in London [RL].
O167   *The house of the strange woman* (by 'F. Norreys Connell').
       London: Henry & Co., 1895. SOURCE Hogan 2, p. 994; OCIL, p. 455; Wolff, 1406.
       LOCATION L, NUC.
COMMENTARY A story about upper-class bohemian life that includes a Foreign Legion plot
and ends in the mock-heroic suicide of the heroine [Hogan; OCIL; Wolff].
O168   *The fool and his heart. Being the plainly told story of Basil Thimm* (by 'F. Norreys
       Connell').
       London: Leonard Smithers, 1896. SOURCE Brady, p. 197; Hogan 2, p. 994. LOCATION
       L.
       New York: G.H. Richmond & Co., 1897. SOURCE NYPL. LOCATION NN, NUC.
       COMMENTARY An often autobiographical story satirizing Bohemian life in *fin de siècle*
       London [Hogan].

O169   *The nigger knights* (by 'F. Norreys Connell').
London: Methuen & Co., 1900. SOURCE Hogan 2, p. 994. LOCATION L.

O170   *The follies of Captain Daly* (by 'F. Norreys Connell').
London: Grant Richards, 1901. LOCATION L.
+ New York: Grant Richards, 1901. LOCATION D.

O171   *The pity of war* (by 'F. Norreys Connell').
London: Henry J. Glaiser, 1906. SOURCE Hogan 2, p. 993. LOCATION L.
COMMENTARY Stories of military life [Hogan].

O172   *The young days of Admiral Quilliam* (by 'F. Norreys Connell').
Edinburgh, London: William Blackwood & Sons, 1906. SOURCE Hogan 2, p. 994.
LOCATION L.

O173   *Adam of Dublin. A romance of to-day* (by Conal O'Riordan; dedicated to Jane).
+ London, Glasgow, Melbourne, Auckland: W. Collins Sons & Co., 1920. SOURCE
Brown 2, 1259; Hogan 2, p. 994. LOCATION DPL, L, NUC (n.d. edn).
Dublin: W. Collins Sons & Co., 1923. LOCATION NUC.
+ New York: Harcourt, Brace & Howe, 1920. LOCATION NUC, InND Loeber coll.
COMMENTARY A roman-à-clef of the literary revival period. The story of a poor boy in Dublin
whose parents send him out into the street at an early age to peddle newspapers so that his
father can buy alcohol. An illness takes the boy to a hospital, and after that a convalescent
home. Through charity he enters Belvedere College, which is an unhappy experience for him.
This book is the first in a series of four depicting Adam's life, and stops rather abruptly. It
describes the squalor of the poor in Dublin as well as giving portraits of Belvedere College
and the Abbey Theatre [ML; Hogan; OCIL, p. 455].

O174   *Adam and Caroline. Being the sequel to Adam of Dublin* (by Conal O'Riordan; ded-
icated to Francis R. Pryor).
+ London, Glasgow, Melbourne, Auckland: W. Collins Sons & Co., 1921. SOURCE
Brown 2, 1260 (1926, 3rd edn). LOCATION DPL, L, NUC, InND Loeber coll. (London:
Collins 1927 edn).
+ New York: Harcourt, Brace & Co., 1922. LOCATION NUC, InND Loeber coll.
COMMENTARY A sequel to *Adam of Dublin* (London, 1920), largely dealing with the sexual dif-
ficulties or adventures of adolescence, including a brief love affair with Caroline Brady [Brown
2].

O175   *In London. The story of Adam and marriage* (by Conal O'Riordan; dedicated to J.D.
Beresford).
+ London, Glasgow, Melbourne, Auckland: W. Collins Sons & Co., 1922. SOURCE
Brown 2, 1261; NYPL. LOCATION NN, NUC (n.d. edn).
+ London, Glasgow, Melbourne, Auckland: W. Collins Sons & Co., 1927. LOCATION
InND Loeber coll.
+ New York: Harcourt, Brace & Co., 1922. LOCATION NUC, InND Loeber coll.
COMMENTARY A continuation of *Adam and Caroline* (London, 1921). Adam goes to London
and drifts into a stage career. The novel covers the war period 1914–18 [Brown 2].

O176   *Rowena Barnes* (by Conal O'Riordan).
London: W. Collins Sons & Co., 1923. SOURCE Hogan 2, p. 994; NYPL. LOCATION
L, NN, NUC (n.d. edn).

O177   *Married life* (by Conal O'Riordan; dedicated to Katie and Bill Gouldsmith).
+ London, Glasgow, Melbourne, Auckland: W. Collins Sons & Co., 1924. SOURCE
Brown 2, 1262. LOCATION DPL, NUC (n.d. edn).
COMMENTARY A continuation of *In London* (London, 1922). This novel opens with Adam's
marriage to Barbara Burns, a conceited, heartless beauty, who makes life unbearable for him.

It recounts his experiences as an actor on tour. His Irish friends reappear and there are glimpses of Black and Tan atrocities in Ireland. Finally he returns home, accompanied by his little crippled son David and his staunch friend and guardian, Stephen MacCarthy [Brown 2].

O178 *The age of miracles. A novel of our time* (by Conal O'Riordan; dedicated to Constance Sylvester).
+ London, Glasgow, Sydney, Auckland: W. Collins Sons & Co., 1925. LOCATION DPL, L, NUC (n.d. edn).

O179 *Young Lady Dazincourt, a discovery* (by Conal O'Riordan).
London: W. Collins Sons & Co., 1926. SOURCE Kennys cat. 45/669; COPAC. LOCATION D, CtY, NUC (n.d. edn).

O180 *Soldier born. A story of youth* (by Conal O'Riordan).
London: W. Collins Sons & Co., 1927. SOURCE Brown 2, 1263. LOCATION D, O, CtY, NUC (n.d. edn).

COMMENTARY First of the tetralogy featuring David Quinn, son of a Quaker banker's daughter and a dissolute and irreligious Irish captain who has been made a baronet because he voted for the Union. Born about 1797, David passes his first ten or twelve years in a house in Gardiner's Row, Dublin. The Dublin of that day is carefully sketched. His father takes him first to Mallow and then to the ancestral home Derryvoe, in Muskerry, where owing to the penal laws his grandparents live a retired and almost secretive life. As his Quaker relatives are paying for his education at Westminster School, his father sends him there and the rest of the book describes his schooldays [Brown 2].

O181 *Soldier of Waterloo. A story of manhood* (by Conal O'Riordan; dedicated to Wijnand and Jeanne Mees-Hudig).
London, Glasgow, Sydney, Auckland: W. Collins Sons & Co., 1928. SOURCE Brown 2, 1264; Hogan 2, p. 994; OCLC. LOCATION DPL (1929 edn), NUC (n.d. edn).

COMMENTARY A sequel to *Soldier born* (London, 1927). The hero fights at Waterloo, which is vividly depicted, and where he is so horribly mutilated that for the rest of his life he is obliged to wear a mask. David's mental and moral reactions to this fate are analyzed [Brown 2; Hogan].

O182 *Yet do not grieve* (by Conal O'Riordan; dedicated to Wijnand and Jeanne Mees-Hudig).
+ New York: Charles Scribner's Sons, 1928. LOCATION NUC, InND Loeber coll.
COMMENTARY Joint edn of *Soldier born* (London, 1927) and *Soldier of Waterloo* (London, 1928) [RL].

O183 *Soldier's wife* (by Conal O'Riordan; dedicated to Wijnand and Jeanne Mees-Hudig).
+ London: Arrowsmith, 1935. SOURCE Brown 2, 1265; Hogan 2, p. 994. LOCATION DPL, L, NUC (n.d. edn).

COMMENTARY A further account of the Quinn family and the ramshackle, racy, shabby genteel Dublin of the nineteenth century. Daniel O'Connell is introduced [Brown 2].

O184 *Soldier's end* (by Conal O'Riordan; dedicated to Wijnand and Jeanne Mees-Hudig).
+ London: Arrowsmith, 1938. SOURCE Brown 2, 1266; Hogan 2, p. 994. LOCATION DPL, L, NUC (n.d. edn), InND Loeber coll.

COMMENTARY This completes the series about David Quinn. He returns in middle-age to the Dublin of the Famine years. He is full of good intentions and philanthropic ideals but his attempts to carry them into practice are thwarted by his rascally brother, Bonaventure, and also by family troubles and sorrows, which drive him to London. There he meets, at a public execution, Mazzin, and also the quixotic Lord Ashley (afterwards earl of Shaftesbury) [Brown 2].

O185 *Judith Quinn. A novel for women* (by Conal O'Riordan; dedicated to Brigid Brophy).
+ London: Arrowsmith, 1939. SOURCE Brown 2, 1267. LOCATION DPL, L, NUC (n.d. edn).

O'Rourke

COMMENTARY Historical fiction set in Dublin in Victorian days. Judith is a Dublin girl whose father has been shot dead by the military commanded by his brother during a political disturbance. The story tells of her series of unsuccessful approaches to matrimony: her first prospect refuses her and enters a seminary; the second is proposed to by old Lady Dazincourt, but, owing to muddling, this does not come off. In the end she marries beneath her; one Dinny Muldoon, whom she does not love [Brown 2].

O186 *Judith's love* (by Conal O'Riordan; dedicated to Dorothy and June Damant).

+ London: Arrowsmith, 1940. SOURCE Brown 2, 1268. LOCATION DPL, L, NUC (n.d. edn).

COMMENTARY A sequel to *Judith Quinn* (London, 1939). Judith is now Mrs Muldoon. All her love is concentrated – not on her lout of a husband – but on her son. The story follows her further fortunes and gives a picture of Dublin in the late-nineteenth century. The religion of the Catholic characters is presented as a compound of hypocrisy and superstition [Brown 2].

O'ROURKE, Fr John, pseud. 'Anthony Evergreen', b. 1809, d. Maynooth (Co. Kildare) 1887. Catholic cleric and writer, JO'R was trained at Maynooth, where he began his studies in 1845 at age 36. He was ordained four years later and served as a curate at Castledermot and Athy (both Co. Kildare), and Kingstown (Co. Dublin) for twenty years. In 1869 he became parish priest at St Mary's (Maynooth), and served there for the remainder of his life. Aside from the work of fiction below, he wrote a devotional manual, *The lamp of the soul* (Dublin, 1862); an influential *History of the Irish famine* (Dublin, 1875), compiled in great part from the archives of the *Freeman's Journal* (Dublin) and not from oral accounts; a life of Daniel O'Connell (Dublin, 1875), and *The battle of the faith in Ireland* (Dublin, 1887), all of which are strongly Catholic in tone. He may be identified with the contributor to the Dublin *Nation* and the *Irishman* (Dublin?) in the 1850s, who wrote under the pseudonym 'Miro'. He was buried in Laraghbryan cemetery (Co. Kildare) and there is a memorial to him in the Maynooth College chapel. SOURCE Allibone Suppl., ii, p. 1197 [under J. O'Rourke and John O'Rourke]; R.V. Comerford, 'Canon John O'Rourke' in T. Kabdebo (ed.), *Beyond the library walls* (Maynooth, 1995), pp 58–68; Irish pseudonyms; O'Donoghue, p. 370; RIB/DIB.

O187 *Holly & ivy for the Christmas holidays* (by 'Anthony Evergreen').

+ Dublin: Bellew, [1852] (ill. W.C. Forster). SOURCE Brown 2, 1269. LOCATION D, L, InND Loeber coll. (Dublin, Duffy [1868] edn).

COMMENTARY The story is set in Co. Wicklow where the main character is a dishonest land agent who defrauds both the tenants and the landlord. He is unmasked by a brave young man who has returned from America where he had made some money in the gold fields. The young man becomes the landlord's new agent and peace and happiness return to the village. The holly and ivy in the story are sold at Christmastime in Dublin by poor Wicklow people. In the preface, O'Rourke alludes to the Synod of Thurles (1850) when the Irish hierarchy, led by archbishop Paul Cullen, warned the faithful of the dangers of modern literature and suggests that his story could both amuse and edify the reader [ML; RIA/DIB].

ORPEN, Mrs —. See **ORPEN, Mrs Adela Elizabeth**.

ORPEN, Mrs Adela E. See **ORPEN, Mrs Adela Elizabeth**.

ORPEN, Mrs Adela Elizabeth (née Richards; also known as **Mrs Orpen, Mrs Goddard Orpen**, and **Adela E. Orpen**), pseud. 'An Ulster clergyman', b. 1856, d. 1928 (1927 according to Browne). Novelist and storywriter, AEO was the eldest daughter and heiress of Edward Moore Richards of Monksgrange (Co. Wexford), and Sarah Elizabeth Tisdale (of Virginia,

US). She married the historian Goddard Henry Orpen (1852–1932) in 1880, thereby bringing the Monksgrange property into the Orpen family. She was buried at Killanne graveyard (Co. Wexford). SOURCE Brown 2, p. 216; Browne, pp 117–18; Burke's, p. 938; Landed gentry, 1904, p. 508; D. Walsh, *100 Wexford country houses* (Enniscorthy, 1996), pp 71–2; Rowe & Scallan, 738.

O188   *Stories about famous precious stones* (by Mrs. Goddard Orpen).
>   Boston: D. Lothrop, 1890. SOURCE OCLC; COPAC. LOCATION L, Cleveland Public Library (OH).

O189   *The chronicles of the Sid; or, the life and travels of Adelia Gates* (by Adela E. Orpen).
>   London: Religious Tract Society, 1893. SOURCE Alston, p. 326. LOCATION L, NUC.
>   New York, Chicago: Fleming H. Revell, 1897. LOCATION NUC.

O190   *Perfection city* (by Mrs Orpen).
>   London: Hutchinson & Co., 1897. SOURCE Daims, 2291. LOCATION Dt, L.
>   New York: D. Appleton & Co., 1897. SOURCE Daims, 2291. LOCATION NUC.

O191   *Corrageen in '98. A story of the Irish rebellion* (by Mrs Orpen).
>   + London: Methuen & Co., 1898. SOURCE Brown, 1353; Brown 2, 1270. LOCATION D, Dt, L, NUC, InND Loeber coll.

COMMENTARY Historical fiction set in Co. Wexford in the days before and during the rising of 1798. The author's residence, Monksgrange, becomes the Corrageen of the novel, the seat of the Rossiters. The story opens with Lady Laura Rossiter and a Mr Brandon discussing, in poetic terms, the national cause. Her husband is pro-English and does not expect any trouble from the tenants on his estate. But all the tenants of Corrageen are swept up in the rebellion. The country around is convulsed with atrocities committed on both sides. Lady Rossiter is captured and temporarily loses her infant child; her husband is wounded and Mr Brandon dies [ML; Brown 2; Browne, p. 117].

O192   *The jay-hawkers; a story of free soil and ruffian days* (by Adela E. Orpen).
>   New York: D. Appleton & Co., 1900. LOCATION NUC

O193   *The downfall of Grabbum. An Ulster fable* (by 'An Ulster clergyman').
>   Belfast: Carswell & Son, 1912. SOURCE Brown 2, 1271. LOCATION L.

COMMENTARY Authorship is established by Brown 2, but its proof is not clear. This is not so much a fable as an allegory, the personages standing for countries, systems or groups. Thus Pat, John, Uncle Sam, and Dugald stand respectively for Ireland or the Irish, England, the US, and Scotland. Drudge represents the peasant; Grabbum the land grabber or landlord from England. The allegory represents the English treatment of Ireland as seen from a nationalist point of view [Brown 2].

ORPEN, Mrs Goddard. See **ORPEN, Mrs Adele Elizabeth.**

ORRERY, first earl of. See **BOYLE, Roger.**

ORSAY, Harriet Anne D'. See **D'ORSAY, Harriet Anne.**

ORSONNENS, Eraste D'. See **D'ORSONNENS, Eraste.**

O'RYAN, Edmund. Co-author. See **O'RYAN, Julia.**

O'RYAN, Julia M., b. Cork City 1823, d. 1887. Novelist, verse and storywriter, JO'R and her brother Edmund O'Ryan (sometimes appeared as Ryan), contributed to the *Irish Monthly*

(Dublin, 1874), *Dublin Journal of Temperance*, the *Catholic World* (New York), and *Chamber's Journal* (Edinburgh). She also submitted to periodicals under the initials 'JMOR' and 'JMR'. SOURCE Brown, p. 249; Irish pseudonyms; O'Donoghue, p. 371; RIA/DIB.

O194 *In re garland, a tale of a transition time* [anon.; with Edmund Ryan] (dedicated to the authors' father, 'A true patriot, an honest man and a good father').

+ London, Dublin, Derby: Thomas Richardson & Son; New York: Henry H. Richardson & Co., 1870. SOURCE Brown, 1354 (1873 edn); Fegan, p. 230. LOCATION L.

COMMENTARY Set in Munster during the time after the Famine of 1846 when the encumbered estates court is in operation. An aristocrat, being entirely impoverished by the Famine, has to rely on the support of his illegitimate daughter who had grown up as a peasant [RL; Brown; Fegan, p. 230].

O'RYAN, W.P. See RYAN, W.P.

OSBORNE, Catherine Isabella, b. Newtown Anner (Co. Tipperary) 1817 or 1818, d. Newtown Anner 1880. Novelist, memoirist, artist and travel writer, CIO was the daughter of Sir Thomas Osborne, Bt, MP, a prominent landowner of Newtown Anner, and Catherine Smith, who was English. After the death of her brother at age 8, CIO became the heiress to the Osborne estate. The anonymous author, 'An officer of the line', who inscribed a copy of his *Sketches, scenes and narratives* (Dublin, 1828; private collection) to her, was Revd Henry Woodward§, a good friend of her mother's. In 1844 at the home of Lady Morgan§, she met and later married Ralph Bernal, a politician, who added Osborne to his name by royal license and in his political career was known as Bernal Osborne. She continued to live at Newtown Anner while her husband spent a great deal of time in London. CIO was a patron of artists and was a talented artist herself. She financed the library at nearby Knockmahon (Co. Waterford). CIO wrote about her mother in *Memorials of the life and character of Lady Osborne and some of her friends* (Dublin, 1870, 2 vols.). Her daughter, Edith, became the second wife of the author Sir Henry Arthur Blake§. The Osborne family papers are in the National Archives, Dublin. SOURCE Allibone Suppl., ii, p. 1198 [under Mrs Osborne and Mrs C.I. Osborne]; BLC; A. Crookshank & the knight of Glin, *The watercolours of Ireland* (London, 1994); M. Girouard, *Town and country* (New Haven, CT, 1992), pp 121–34; L.W. McBride, *Reading Irish histories* (Dublin, 2003), p. 25n.26; ODNB [under Ralph Bernal Osborne]; Mrs [Catherine Isabella] Osborne, *Memorials of the life and character of Lady Osborne and some of her friends* (Dublin, 1870, 2 vols.); Personal communication, Mary Pollard, Aug. 2001; RIA/DIB; RL.

O195 *False positions; or, sketches of character* [anon.].

+ London: Chapman & Hall, 1863, 2 vols. LOCATION PC, L.

COMMENTARY The annotations in the author's corrected copy indicate that this novel, which is set in England with a short excursion to Ireland, was based on the murder in 1862 of Gustave Thiebault by one Halloran. Despite the evidence, Halloran was acquitted in the trial, which was reported in the *Clonmel Chronicle* (9 Dec. 1865), but part of the proceedings must have happened earlier [P.C. Power, *History of South Tipperary* (Cork, 1989), p. 172; Personal communication, Mary Pollard, Aug. 2001].

O196 *A few pages from real life; or, a guide book from notes of impressions received from well-known places* (by Catherine Isabella Osborne).

+ London: Chapman & Hall, 1874, 2 vols. SOURCE Allibone Suppl., ii, p. 1198; COPAC. LOCATION L.

COMMENTARY Stories of travel through Europe to Turkey, Greece, and Italy, containing discussions [ML].

'OSCAR', pseud. See **GRIMSTONE, Mrs Mary Leman.**

O'SHAUGHNESSY, P., fl. 1848. Novelist.
O197 *The miser's fate: embracing the life and adventures of Bob Norberry an Irish reporter* (by P. O'Shaunghnessy).
+ London: G. Purkess, Lloyd, [1848]. SOURCE Block, p. 177. LOCATION L.
COMMENTARY The story of an Irish reporter, Bob Norberry, but it mainly concerns Norberry's grandfather, a rich miser living in Ireland. His grandson leads a hard life until it is revealed that he is the heir to his grandfather's fortunes. He marries, returns to Ireland and recovers the estate [ML].

O'SHAUGHNESSY, Tom, fl. 1887. Anti-Catholic religious fiction writer.
O198 *Terence O'Dowd; or, Romanism to-day. An Irish story, founded on facts* (by Tom O'Shaughnessy).
+ Philadelphia: Presbyterian Board of Education and Sabbath-School Work, 1887.
SOURCE Allibone Suppl., ii, p. 1198. LOCATION L, NUC.
COMMENTARY A highly anti-Catholic novel set in Ireland in which Terence differs from his parents in that he does not believe what the priest teaches him and also has a regard for the British government. The book makes fun of the priests and the village schoolmasters. Terence's father had intended him for the church, but he has become acquainted with a girl called Nelly who has opened his eyes to the real truth. Nelly had been abducted and placed in a convent. She converts a nun and leaves the convent. Nelly and Terence and some other converts leave Ireland [ML].

O'SHEA, Geraldine, fl. 1870s. Novelist, GO'S probably came from the Co. Waterford area. According to the dedication of her only novel, her brother was exiled, but the reason is not made known. SOURCE RL.
O199 *Armidale's fortunes; or, the hunted heir* (by Geraldine O'Shea; dedicated to the author's brother).
+ Dublin: Gerald P. Warren; Cork: D. Mulcahy & Co., [c.1877]. LOCATION D, Dt, InND Loeber coll. (n.d. edn).
COMMENTARY A romance and family saga set at Armidale Castle on the coast of Co. Waterford, home of the widowed Lady Armidale. She plans to marry her son Walter to Lady Moreton, but he falls in love with Eva Clare, who lives with her mother in a cottage. Walter introduces himself to the Clares as Mr Fitzgerald, a tutor staying at Armidale Castle, and marries Eva in secret. When his mother finds out, she lures Eva away from her home by saying that her husband has met with an accident. After Eva has been brought to Dublin with her children, she is told that her husband was previously married and that she will never see him again. Eva is left to fend for herself. When Walter cannot find his family, he goes to Germany as a tutor. Walter and Eva's son, Henry, grows up to be a journalist in Dublin. He saves a rich man whose horse had bolted, and becomes the suitor of his daughter. A jealous competitor trumps up a charge of rebellion against Henry, who is sentenced to death but is smuggled out of prison and flees to France. Nearing the end of her life, Lady Armidale confesses to her daughter what she had done to separate her son from his wife. They go to Dublin to find Eva, who forgives her mother-in-law. Walter, who has just returned from Germany, finds his wife and mother reconciled. Henry comes back from France and marries his love at Castle Armidale, where everybody lives happily together [ML].

O'SHEA, John, fl. 1838. Journalist, translator, and writer of poems, songs and stories, JO'S was connected with the Munster press for many years. He worked for and contributed poems

to the *Clonmel Advertiser* (afterwards the *Nenagh Guardian*) and other southern journals, pub-lishing his *Nenagh minstrelsy: a volume of original poems, songs and translations* at Nenagh in 1839. He was the father of the writers John Augustus O'Shea§ and Mrs J.J. O'Shea Dillon§.
SOURCE ODNB [under John Augustus O'Shea]; O'Donoghue, p. 372.

O200   *The legends of Dromineer Castle and Poulshesereigh* [anon.] (dedicated to J. Egerton Carroll of the 46th Regiment).
Nenagh: [n.p.], Dec. 1838. LOCATION L.
COMMENTARY 56pp. Includes 'The legend of Dromineer Castle' (on the river Shannon), 'Poulshesereigh; a legend' (separate pagination, but no title page). The sheets were re-used in *Nenagh minstrelsy: a volume of original poems, songs and translations, compiled, revised and published by John O'Shea* (Nenagh, 1839) [RL].

O'SHEA, John Augustus (also known as John A. O'Shea), b. Nenagh (Co. Tipperary) 1839, d. London 1905 (1906 according to Gleeson). Journalist, writer, dramatist and composer, JAO'S was the son of John O'Shea§, a journalist and poet. The young JAO'S entered the newly-estab-lished Catholic University of Ireland in Dublin in 1856 and went to London in 1859. He reported on the Austro-Prussian war for an American journal; settled in Paris, where he was correspon-dent for the *Irishman* (Dublin), and contributed to the *Shamrock* (Dublin). He joined the staff of the London *Standard* in 1869 and wrote a personal account of Paris under siege in the Franco-German war in 1870: *An iron-bound city* (London, 1886, 2 vols.). Later he worked in Spain and wrote *Romantic Spain: a record of personal experience* (London, 1870). The *Shamrock* published some of his best stories, including 'Memoirs of a white cravat' (1868). A versatile journalist (he reported on the Carlist war and famine in Bengal, among other topics and wrote on Irish and Continental politics), he contributed to various periodicals and newspapers, including to the *Freeman's Journal* (Dublin) and the *Dublin Evening Telegraph* and, after leaving the *Standard,* was on the staff of the *Universe*, a London Catholic newspaper. In addition he was a lecturer, dramatist and a composer, particularly of music for the organ. He joined the Southwark Irish Literary Club in London in 1885 and, according to W.P. Ryan§, he was 'one of its most faith-ful friends ever after' (Ryan, pp 23–4, 90–1). Later he was active in the London Irish Literary Society. Ryan favourably commented on his 'many diverse traits', including his advocacy of Irish nationalism and his skills as an historian. JAO'S was paralyzed by a traffic accident towards the end of his life and he died in poverty. He collaborated with Stephen J. MacKenna§ in the writ-ing of *Brave men in action* (London, 1899). His fiction includes five books, some on war (set on the Continent) and some on the life of journalists. He wrote two autobiographies: the partly-fictionalized *Leaves of the life of a special correspondent* (London, 1885, 2 vols.), and *Roundabout recollections* (London, 1892, 2 vols.) in which he describes his time as a student in Dublin (Brown 2 mis-attributes this book to JAO'S's sister J.J. O'Shea Dillon§, who was also an author). He died in London and was buried in Kensal Green cemetery. Some of JAO'S's letters are among the Downey Papers (NLI, MS 10,045). JAO'S's portrait was published by Ryan (see ODNB for an additional portrait). SOURCE Allibone Suppl., ii, pp 1198–9; Brady, p. 198; Brown, p. 250; Brown 2, p. 72; Field Day, iii, p. 419; J. Gleeson, *History of the Ely O'Carroll territory* (Kilkenny, 1982), i, p. 217; Irish pseudonyms; NUC; OCIL, p. 457; ODNB; J.A. O'Shea, *Roundabout rec-ollections* (London, 1892, 2 vols.); RIA/DIB; Ryan, pp 23–4, 90–1; Sutherland, p. 482; Wolff, iii, p. 230.

O201   *Leaves from the life of a special correspondent* (by John Augustus O'Shea).
+ London: Ward & Downey, 1885, 2 vols. SOURCE OCLC. LOCATION D, NUC.
COMMENTARY Autobiography with dialogues [ML].

O202   *An iron-bound city; or, five months of peril and privation* (by John Augustus O'Shea; dedicated to Col. Frederick Gustavus Burnaby§).

+ London: Ward & Downey, 1886, 2 vols. SOURCE Wolff, 5310. LOCATION L, NUC, InND Loeber coll.

COMMENTARY Graphic account of author's adventures during the Franco-German war. Set mainly in Paris. A journalist, O'Donovan, features in the story [ODNB; RL].

O203 *Military mosaics. A set of tales, and sketches on soldiery themes* (by John Augustus O'Shea; dedicated to Tommy Atkins).

+ London: W.H. Allen & Co., 1888. SOURCE Brown, 1358. LOCATION D, L, C, NUC.

COMMENTARY Contents: 'Fred Burnaby: In memoriam', 'Gunner Molampy's conversion', 'The war crisis in Monaco', 'The regimental pet', 'A reminiscence of General Buonaparte', 'Drummer Brien of the Rovers', 'With the Carlists', '"Much-a-wanted"', 'A little dinner at Kiko', 'A Breton group in besieged Paris', '"The devil's own"; a tale of the Crimea', 'Major Moriarty', 'The true story of the "Gineral"', 'Cipriano', 'Trooper Tom Sturps' [RL].

O204 *Mated from the morgue. A tale of the second empire* (by John Augustus O'Shea).

London: Spencer Blackett, 1889 (Blackett's Select Novels). SOURCE OCLC; Wolff, 5311; Topp 6, 373. LOCATION D, L, NUC.

COMMENTARY Historical fiction. A tale of France during the second empire [Sutherland, p. 482].

O'SULLIVAN, Dennis, pseud. '"Corporal" Morgan Rattler', b. possibly Co. Cork 1838. writer of fiction for juveniles, popular serials and poetry, and a printer, DO'S emigrated to the US prior to 1856, when he is first known to have lived in New York, and where he resided until at least 1901. He contributed serials such as 'The angel of the scourge. A romance of our day' (*Illustrated Celtic Monthly*, New York, 1879) to various American periodicals, some of which were republished in the *Shamrock* (Dublin) in the 1880s and later in book form. O'Donoghue states that he was the founder and editor of the *Irish People* and the *Emerald* (both New York). He published many dime novels for boys concerning Irish matters (24pp or less, and thus not listed below), such as *Brian the brave; or, the hero minstrel boy* (New York, 1877); *Brian the bear, or, the pranks of a wild Irish boy* (New York, 1888); *Detective Dan; or, the Irish ferret* (New York, 1877); *Gallant Sarsfield; or, the young hero of Limerick* (New York, 1882), and *Danny the clown: a story of circus life in Ireland* (New York, 1887). He contributed '"Ireland will be free;" or, a message from the dead' to the *New York Family Story Paper* (1887, vol. 13, No. 642), and 'The young Captain Rock; or, the first of the Whiteboys' to the *Boys of New York* (1896, vol. 12, Nos. 606–7). In 1853 *Irlande, poesies de bardes, legendes, ballades, chant populaires. Precédés d'une essaie sur ses antiquités et sa litterature* appeared in Paris, but it is unclear whether it was by this DO'S or a namesake. O'Donoghue lists a DO'S who edited a volume of poetry, *Popular songs and poetry of the Emerald Isle* (New York, 1880), that includes his poem 'Will my soul pass through Erin', based on Charles Kickham's§ *Knocknagow* (Dublin, [1873]). A Mrs Denis O'Sullivan, possibly his wife, published *Mr. Dimock* (New York, 1920). DO'S is not to be confused with 'Dennis Barrington O'Sullivan', pseudonym of William Beresford. SOURCE Brown 2, p. 216; D & P; Dime novels (biographical sketch); NUC; O'Donoghue, p. 373; RIA/DIB; RLIN.

O205 *A fool's advice; or blundering Barney O'Hare* (by '"Corporal" Morgan Rattler').

London: Henderson, 1880 (Weekly Budget People's Pocket Story Books). SOURCE Brown 2, 1272.

COMMENTARY No copy located. The story of a murder and of a young surgeon who is falsely accused of it. Set in Ireland, it includes some local colour. Brown 2 mentions an American edn, but this has not been identified [Brown 2, 1272; RL].

O206 *The Irish detective evil genius* (by '"Corporal" Morgan Rattler').

New York: N.L. Munro, 1883 (Old Capt. Collier Library). LOCATION NUC.

COMMENTARY 44pp [NUC].

O207 *The lion of Limerick* (by '"Corporal" Morgan Rattler').
New York: N.L. Munro, 1885 (Munro's Library of Popular Novels). LOCATION NUC.
COMMENTARY Historical fiction concerning Patrick Sarsfield. Perhaps based on D'OS's dime novel, *Gallant Sarsfield; or, the young hero of Limerick* (New York, 1882) [AMB; NUC].

O208 *The beauty of Benburb. A romance of the days of Owen Roe O'Neill* (by '"Corporal"' Morgan Rattler').
New York: N.L. Munro, 1885 (Munro's Library of Popular Novels). LOCATION NUC.
COMMENTARY Historical fiction, first published in serial form as 'The hero of Benburb'. Set in the seventeenth century and features Owen Roe O'Neill [RL; Brown 2; Hartman, 748].

O209 *Mary Mavourneen; or, the bride child of sorrow* (by '"Corporal" Morgan Rattler').
New York: N.L. Munro, 1885 (Munro's Library of Popular Novels). LOCATION NUC.

O210 *O'Driscoll of Darra* (by '"Corporal" Morgan Rattler').
New York: N.L. Munro, 1885 (Munro's Library of Popular Novels). LOCATION NUC.

O211 *Famed Fontenoy; or, the brothers of bivouac* (by '"Corporal" Morgan Rattler').
New York: N.L. Munro, 1886 (Munro's Library of Popular Novels). LOCATION NUC.
COMMENTARY First published in serial form but unclear where [Brown 2].

O212 *Eileen Alanna* (by '"Corporal" Morgan Rattler').
New York: N.L. Munro, 1886 (Munro's Library of Popular Novels). LOCATION NUC.
COMMENTARY First published in serial form as 'Eileen Alanna; or, the dawning of the day' in the Waverly Library (Aug. 16, 1881) and previously in the *Family Story Paper* (New York, beginning Aug. 23, 1880) [Brown 2; Dime novels].

O213 *Robert Emmet; or, true Irish hearts* (by '"Corporal" Morgan Rattler').
New York: N.L. Munro, 1886 (Munro's Library of Popular Novels). LOCATION NUC.
COMMENTARY First published in serial form but unclear where [Brown 2].

O214 *Corney of the cliff; or, the bold Irish smuggler* (by '"Corporal" Morgan Rattler').
New York: F.A. Tousey, 1887 (The Boys' Star Library, No. 15). SOURCE RLIN.
LOCATION NUC; Univ. of Minnesota.
COMMENTARY 30pp [NUC].

O215 *The brave Captain Kelly, or the brave Irish privateers* (by '"Corporal" Morgan Rattler').
New York: F. Tousey, 1888 (The Boys' Star Library, No. 52). SOURCE RLIN.
LOCATION Univ. of Minnesota.
COMMENTARY 27pp. A shorter edn appeared in New York in [1881] [RLIN; NUC].

O216 *Tracked for years* (by '"Corporal" Morgan Rattler').
New York: F. Tousey, 1890 (The Boys' Star Library, No. 143). SOURCE RLIN.
LOCATION Univ. of Minnesota.
COMMENTARY 29pp [RLIN].

O217 *Galloping O'Hogan, or the bold free rider: A thrilling story of Ireland* (by '"Corporal" Morgan Rattler').
New York: F. Tousey, 1891 (The Boys' Star Library, No. 195). SOURCE RLIN.
LOCATION Univ. of Minnesota.
COMMENTARY 30pp [RLIN].

O218 *Tracked by a friend* (by '"Corporal" Morgan Rattler').
New York: F. Tousey, 1891 (The Boys' Star Library, No. 213). SOURCE RLIN.
LOCATION Univ. of Minnesota.
COMMENTARY 28pp [RLIN].

O'SULLIVAN, Revd Mortimer (earlier named Murtagh O'Sullivan), pseud. **'A Munster farmer'**, b. Clonmel (Co. Tipperary) 1793 (1791/2 according to RIA/DIB) d. Dublin 1859. Church of Ireland clergyman, polemicist and writer, MO'S was the son of John O'Sullivan, a Catholic schoolmaster. He joined the Church of Ireland under the influence of his own schoolmaster, a Revd Carey, a Protestant clergyman at the Clonmel (Co. Tipperary) endowed school. MO'S was admitted at TCD in 1811. He graduated BA in 1816; was ordained the same year, and graduated MA in 1832 and BD and DD in 1837. He taught at the Tipperary Grammar School and at the Royal School in Dungannon (Co. Tyrone), and in 1827 was made prebendary of St Audoen's (Dublin, 1827–30), after which he became rector at Killyman (Co. Armagh) and later prebendary at Ballymore (Co. Armagh, 1830 until his death). In 1824 he published in London *Captain Rock detected* in response to Thomas Moore's§ *Captain Rock* (London, 1824), in which he attacked landlordism and advocated more education and better living-conditions for Catholics while defending the established Church of Ireland. His testimony before a select committee in 1825 was published as *The evidence of the Rev. Mortimer O'Sullivan, before the Select Committees of the Houses of Lords and Commons on the state of Ireland* (Dublin, 1825). He argued before another select committee in 1835 that the Orange lodges preserved the peace in Ulster. The Catholic archbishop of Dublin, Dr. Daniel Murray, accused him in 1835 of misquoting his testimony before a committee investigating the circulation of the Bible among the laity, and MO'S wrote about the controversy in his *Case of the Protestants in Ireland stated* (London, 1836). He lectured extensively on the state of the Protestant clergy in Ireland, England and Scotland and published (with Revd Robert M'Ghee) an attack on the Roman Catholic church in *Romanism as it rules in Ireland* (London, 1840, 2 vols.). Together with his brother, Revd Samuel O'Sullivan§, he was heavily involved in the early years of the *Dublin University Magazine*, and was a friend of the later editor, Charles Lever§. MO'S published three works of anti-Catholic fiction. He married Elizabeth Bloomfield Baker (Elizabeth Bloomfield according to Fleming) in 1824 and with her had three children. According to William Connor Magee, later archbishop of York, MO'S was his 'favourite orator' (MacDonnell, i, p. 77), who could hold 'an audience of two thousand people spellbound for nearly two hours'. Allegedly, he features in John Banim's§ 'The Nowlans', a story from *Tales by the O'Hara family* (London, 1826). In his later life he lived in Dublin where he was chaplain to the lord lieutenant and to the duke of Manchester. He was buried in Chapelizod churchyard. For his portrait, see Elmes and ODNB. Some of his papers are in the NLS. SOURCE Allibone, ii, p. 1466; B & S, p. 646; Brady, p. 199; Brooke, pp 172–3; Davidson cat. 33/138; Elmes, p. 163; Field Day, i, p. 1136; FitzPatrick, passim; Fleming, *Armagh*, p. 204; W.E. Hall, pp 38–9; *The Irish pulpit: A collection of original sermons by clergymen of the established Church of Ireland* (Dublin, London, 1827), pp 145–64, 185–234; Leslie & Wallace, p. 945; McCormack, p. 13; J.C. MacDonnell (ed.), *The life and correspondence of William Connor Magee, archbishop of York, bishop of Peterborough* (London, 1896), i, p. 77; ODNB; RIA/DIB; Sutherland, p. 482.

O219   *Captain Rock detected; or, the origin and character of the recent disturbances, and the causes, both moral and political of the present alarming condition of the South and West of Ireland, fully and fairly considered and exposed* (by 'A Munster farmer').

+ London: T. Cadell; Dublin: E. Milliken; Edinburgh: William Blackwood, 1824. SOURCE Bradshaw, 6144; Wolff, 4903 (see also Wolff, iii, p. 231). LOCATION L, C, NUC, InND Loeber coll.

COMMENTARY Written in response to Thomas Moore's§ *Memoirs of Captain Rock* (London, 1824) [Bradshaw].

O220   *A guide to an Irish gentleman in his search for a religion* (by Mortimer O'Sullivan; dedicated to 'To those of the people of Ireland who are willing to believe that their

country had a national faith and a national church before the Papacy of Adrian IV
...').
+ Dublin: William Curry Jnr & Co.; London: Simpkin & Marshall, 1833. LOCATION
L, NUC, InND Loeber coll.
Philadelphia: Carey, Lea & Blanchard, 1833. SOURCE Kaser, 409. LOCATION DLC,
NUC.
COMMENTARY Written in response to Thomas Moore's§ *Travels of an Irish gentleman
in search of a religion* (London, 1833) [RL].

O221   *The Nevilles of Garretstown. A tale of 1760* [anon.].
New York: Harper & Bros, 1844. SOURCE NYPL. LOCATION NN.
Philadelphia: J. & J.L. Gihon, [1844?]. SOURCE NYPL. LOCATION NUC, NN.
+ London: Saunders, Otley & Co., 1860, 3 vols. (as *The Nevilles of Garretstown: A
tale of 1760*, preface by the author of *Emilia Wyndham* [Anne Marsh]). SOURCE Brown,
1096; Sadleir, 1956. LOCATION D, Dt, L, NUC, InND Loeber coll.
Stuttgart: Franckh, 1846, 5 vols. in 1 (trans. by Gottlob Fink as *Die Nevilles von
Garretstown. Eine Erzählung aus dem Jahr 1760, aus den Dublin University Magazine*).
SOURCE OCLC. LOCATION Center for Research Library (IL).
COMMENTARY First published in the *Dublin University Magazine* (1844–45), the earliest book
edn appeared in a pirated form in the US. The London edn appeared sixteen years later.
Falsely advertised and titled in the American edns as by Charles Lever§ (e.g., in the American
edn of Charles Lever's *The Martins of Cro' Martin*), and sometimes mis-attributed to Mrs.
A.M. Marsh, who wrote the preface to the London 1860 edn. Historical fiction set in the middle of the eighteenth century, partly in Clonmel (Co. Tipperary), but Dublin, Bantry and
places on the Continent feature as well. It deals with the suspicion with which Catholics are
regarded in Ireland. Throughout the story there is the threat of a Jacobite rising. A lost heir
returns to claim his inheritance, which had been usurped by his uncle. Numerous side incidents and transgressions are included, one of which is a description of a hedge-school. It introduces historical personages, such as archbishop George Stone, primate of Armagh, Archbishop
Arthur Richard Dillon of Narbonne (France), Charles Stuart, known as Bonnie Prince Charlie,
and the French privateer François Thurot. A love story is interwoven [ML; Brooke, pp 172–3;
Brown; W.E. Hall, p. 128; Hartman, 310, 952, 970].

O'SULLIVAN, Murtagh. See **O'SULLIVAN, Revd Mortimer.**

O'SULLIVAN, Richard, fl. 1882. Fiction writer, RO'S was probably from the south of
Ireland, perhaps Co. Wexford. He is possibly the same individual who contributed a short
story 'A "ninety-eight" scene' to [anon.], *Penny readings for the Irish people* (Dublin, 1871 and
1876). SOURCE AMB.

O222   *"Three stories for the fireside." The privateer's revenge; Full retribution; and, The
smuggler* (by Richard O'Sullivan).
Dublin: Sullivan, 1882, 3rd edn. SOURCE OCLC. LOCATION D (1884, 4th edn), L
(1884, 4th edn.).
COMMENTARY First edn not located. The Dublin, 1884 edn consisted of 63pp. Contents of
Irish stories in the 4th edn: 'The privateer's revenge' (set in Ireland; starts out in the Hook,
Co. Wexford), 'Full retribution' (set on the coast of Bantry Bay), 'The smuggler' (set in Ireland,
but no clear location) [ML; RL].

O'SULLIVAN, Revd Samuel, b. Clonmel (Co. Tipperary) 1790, d. Dublin 1851. Church
of Ireland clergyman and writer on religion and history, SO'S – like his brother Revd Mortimer

O'Sullivan§ – came from a Roman Catholic background, the eldest son of John O'Sullivan, a Catholic schoolmaster. He matriculated at TCD in 1812 where he was a member of the historical society and distinguished himself as a debater. He graduated BA in 1818; MA in 1825; and, like his brother, received his BD and DD in 1837. He was ordained in 1818 and served as curate at St Catherine's and as chaplain at Marshalsea prison (both Dublin). For many years he was chaplain to the Royal Hibernian military school in the Phoenix Park (Dublin). He married in 1827 Henrietta Armstrong and had two children. With his brother and Isaac Butt§, among others, he was involved in the early years of the *Dublin University Magazine*. He contributed to *Blackwood's Magazine* (Edinburgh) and to *Fraser's* (London) and wrote on the rebellion of 1798 and on a wide range of religious topics. After his death, a collection of his unpublished articles was edited by his brother and published in three volumes as *Remains of the Rev. Samuel O'Sullivan* (Dublin, 1853). He is buried in Chapelizod (Dublin). SOURCE Allibone, ii, p. 1466; B & S, p. 646; Boase, ii, p. 1272; Brooke, p. 172; Leslie & Wallace, p. 945; ODNB [under Mortimer O'Sullivan]; RIA/DIB; Ximenes cat. 105/362.

O223 *College recollections* [anon.].
+ London: Longman, Hurst, Reese, Orme, Brown & Green, 1825. SOURCE Block, p. 43. LOCATION D, L, NUC, InND Loeber coll.
COMMENTARY Inter-related sketches about life at TCD. Contents: 'Lorton', 'Waller' (the main character represents the Revd Charles Wolfe), 'An idler', 'Travers', 'Sidney', 'The funeral', 'The last night of the Historical Society'. Wrongly attributed to Revd Mortimer O'Sullivan§ in the IBL [ML; IBL, 16 (1924), pp 76–7].

'O'TARA, MacErin', fl. 1825. Pseudonym of a writer of historical fiction.
O224 *Thomas Fitz-gerald, the Lord of Offaley. A romance of the sixteenth century ... Being the first of a projected series illustrative of the history of Ireland* (by 'MacErin O'Tara, the last of the Senachies').
London: A.K. Newman & Co., 1825, 3 vols. SOURCE Brown, 100 (1836 edn); Block, p. 177; British Fiction; Garside, 1825:64; Wolff, 7665. LOCATION Corvey CME 3–628–48071–X, Ireland related fiction, D (1836 edn), L, ViU.
COMMENTARY Advertised in several London newspapers as a history book, but mentioned as a novel in the *Dublin and London Magazine* (London, Aug. 1825, p. 287) and as 'not a bad one for the Minerva Press'. Historical fiction about the rebellion of Lord Thomas Fitzgerald ('Silken Thomas') in 1534. The conversations are in Elizabethan English, redolent of Shakespeare. The story opens with a description of Christmas in Dublin in 1533 [British Fiction; Brown; Wolff].

OTWAY, Revd Caesar, b. Co. Tipperary 1780, d. Dublin 1842. Church of Ireland evangelical clergyman, periodical founder and writer, CO was the son of Loftus Otway a merchant of Nenagh (Co. Tipperary), and Sarah Woodward. He was admitted at TCD in 1796, graduated BA in 1801 and subsequently was ordained. He was curate of Drung (Co. Cavan, 1808–11), Leixlip (Co. Kildare, 1811–22), followed by Lucan (Co. Dublin, 1822–26), and then at St George's church and the Leeson Street Magdalen church (Dublin), until the end of his life. He wrote about his extensive travels through Ireland, and while not a fiction writer in the traditional sense, in some of his travelogues he reports extensively on tales and stories he heard from local inhabitants. He was a founder and editor of the anti-Catholic *Christian Examiner* (Dublin) in 1825, the first magazine in Ireland to promote the established church, in which he launched his protégé William Carleton§. He gave up the editorship in 1831 and with landscape painter and antiquary George Petrie edited the *Dublin Penny Journal* (Dublin, 1832–33) and was among the founders and a contributor (often under the pseudonym 'Terence

O'Toole') to the *Dublin University Magazine*. He was an advocate of the humane treatment of animals (see his lecture 'The intellectuality of domestic animals' before the Royal Zoological Society of Ireland, Dublin, 1847). CO married firstly in 1803 Frances, daughter of the Revd James Hastings, dean of Achonry (Co. Sligo), and secondly in 1837 Elizabeth, daughter of William Digges La Touche, with whom he had four children. He is buried in St Anne's churchyard (Dublin). For CO's portrait, see Elmes, Strickland and ODNB. SOURCE Allibone, ii, p. 1468; B & S, p. 646; Brooke, pp 169–70; Burke's, pp 616–17; Clyde, pp 92–13; Elmes, p. 163; Hogan 2, p. 1002; B. Hayley & E. McKay (eds), *Three hundred years of Irish periodicals* (Mullingar, 1987), p. 32; Leslie & Wallace, p. 965; OCIL, p. 463; ODNB; Rafroidi, ii, p. 319; RIA/DIB; Strickland, i, p. 595; Zimmermann, p. 162.

O225   *Sketches in Ireland, descriptive of interesting and hitherto unnoticed districts in the North and South* [anon.].
+ Dublin: William Curry Jnr & Co; London: Charles Tait; Edinburgh: William Blackwood, 1827. SOURCE Emerald Isle cat. 93/1560. LOCATION L, NUC.
+ Dublin: William Curry Jnr & Co., 1839, 2nd edn (corrected; as *Sketches in Ireland, descriptive of interesting portions of the Counties of Donegal, Cork and Kerry*). SOURCE Leclaire, p. 48; Lough Fea cat. p. 229. LOCATION L.
COMMENTARY First published in the *Christian Examiner* (Dublin), this book consists of letters detailing the author's travels in the north and south of Ireland. His impressions, meetings and discussions with people and descriptions of the scenery are intermixed with contemporary and historical stories [ML].

O226   *A tour in Connaught: Comprising sketches of Clonmacnoise, Joyce Country, and Achill* [anon.].
+ Dublin: William Curry Jnr & Co., 1839 (ill. A. Nicholl, L.A. Wheeler). SOURCE Bradshaw, 3515; de Búrca cat. 30/597. LOCATION C, L, NUC.
COMMENTARY Antiquarian sketches in the west of Ireland along with a few stories as told by country people [RL].

O227   *Sketches in Erris and Tyrawley* [anon.].
+ Dublin: William Curry Jnr & Co.; London: Longman, Orme & Co., 1841. SOURCE Lough Fea cat. p. 229. LOCATION L, NUC.
COMMENTARY Descriptions of author's travels and stays on the coast and in inland parts of Co. Mayo. Contains many stories collected from the native Irish and others living in the area [RL].

OUSELEY, John Mulvey (not Ousley as in mentioned by Galway), b. Dunmore (Co. Galway) in the second half of the nineteenth century. Novelist JMO was a member of the family of the publishing firm Ouseley, whose seat for many years was at Dunmore. Aside from fiction, he published one play. He may be the same person as the John M. Ouseley who wrote guides for businesses. Several of the following novels were published by John Ouseley, probably the author. SOURCE BLC; Galway, p. 99; RIA/DIB; RL.

O228   *The spirit of the day. A novel* (by John Mulvey Ouseley).
London: Beeton & Co., 1897. SOURCE Galway, p. 99. LOCATION L.

O229   *Kitty and the viscount* (by John Mulvey Ouseley).
London: Gay & Bird, 1905. SOURCE Galway, p. 99. LOCATION L.

O230   *The sorrows of Michael* (by John Mulvey Ouseley).
London: Gay & Bird, 1906. SOURCE Galway, p. 99. LOCATION L.

O231   *A guilty silence: A novel* (by John Mulvey Ouseley and Sidney Warwick).
London: Gay & Bird, 1907. SOURCE COPAC. LOCATION L.

O232   *A blind goddess. A novel* (by John Mulvey Ouseley).
London: John M. Ouseley, 1909. SOURCE Galway, p. 99. LOCATION L.

O233   *The Jewess. A novel* (by John Mulvey Ouseley).
        London: John M. Ouseley, [1911]. SOURCE Galway, p. 99. LOCATION L, NUC.

O234   *What should a woman do. A novel based on Herbert Darnley's successful play* (by John Mulvey Ouseley and Walter Burton Baldrey).
        London: John M. Ouseley, 1912. SOURCE Galway, p. 99. LOCATION L.
        COMMENTARY Herbert Darnley was a well-known playwright, but the play on which this volume was based has not been identified [RL].

O235   *Dunmóhr of the Guards: A military history society novel* (by John Mulvey Ouseley).
        London: John M. Ouseley & Son, [1916]. SOURCE Galway, p. 99. LOCATION L.

O236   *In the land of lost illusions* (by John Mulvey Ouseley).
        London: Grafton & Co., 1918. SOURCE Galway, p. 99. LOCATION L.

O237   *A lady of a thousand hearts* (by John Mulvey Ouseley).
        + London: Aldine Publishing Co., [1922] (Mascot Novels, No. 177). LOCATION L.

O238   *A snake in Eden. A novel* (by John Mulvey Ouseley).
        London: John M. Ouseley & Son, [1922]. SOURCE Galway, p. 99. LOCATION L.

O239   *The banker's secret: A modern romantic novel* (by John Mulvey Ouseley).
        + London: Henry Walker, [1928]. LOCATION L.
        COMMENTARY The prologue starts in the newsroom of a London daily [RL].

'OUTIS', pseud. See **WHITE, Richard Grant**.

OWENSON, Miss —. See **MORGAN, Lady**.

OWENSON, Sydney. See **MORGAN, Lady**.

P

'PANACHE, Madame', pseud. See MOORE, Frances.

'PARADOX, Peter, M.D., deceased', fl. 1860. Pseudonym of an historical fiction writer.

P1　*The land of the Kelt. A tale of Ierne in the days of '98 from an unpublished manuscript* (by 'Peter Paradox, M.D., deceased').
+ London: Saunders & Otley, 1860, 3 vols. SOURCE Brown, 60. LOCATION RB, L.
COMMENTARY Historical fiction set at the time of the rebellion of 1798, the story concerns a lawsuit in which Stephen Bingham is declared to be Stephen FitzStephen, heir to the earldom of Glanmore. Another character, Sir Roderick O'Conor, is arrested for high treason, escapes, but is killed at Castlebar (Co. Mayo) [RL; Brown].

PARKER, Helen F. (née Helen Eliza Fitch), b. 1827, d. 1874. American novelist and miscellaneous writer who under the pseudonym 'H.F.P.' wrote *Constance Aylmar: a story of the seventeenth century* (New York, 1869), set in New Amsterdam (New York), as well as other works of fiction. Her *Morning stars of the New World* (New York, 1854) and *Discoverers and pioneers of America* (New York, 1856) are portraits of the explorers of the Americas. SOURCE Allibone, ii, p. 1501; Allibone Suppl., ii, p. 1210; Wright, ii, p. 149; Wright web.

P2　*Sunrise and sunset. A true tale* (by Helen F. Parker).
Auburn: Derby & Miller; Buffalo: Derby, Orton & Mulligan; Cincinnati: Henry W. Derby, 1853. SOURCE OCLC (1854 edn). LOCATION Wright, ii, 1842; Wright web.
COMMENTARY A story about domestic life in Ireland and in America. It starts in Ireland with descriptions of various parts of the country. The main character, Kathleen, grew up in a family belonging to a church of seceders [ML].

PARKES, William Theodore, pseud. 'Barney Bradey', fl. 1868, d. London *c.*1908. Artist, poet and prose writer, WTC probably was from Dublin, which he celebrated in his *Tails an' ballads iv Dublin's grate methropolis* (Dublin, 1866). He was a frequent contributor to many periodicals, listed by O'Donoghue, both under his name, his pseudonym, and one or two other signatures. In addition he published several books of poetry, such as his *Napoleon's christening cake, an extravaganza of the war* (Dublin, n.d.). In Dublin, he appears to have published his own works. He moved to London where he died in or about 1908. SOURCE O'Donoghue, p. 376; RL.

P3　*Tails an' ballads iv Dublin's grate methropolis* (by 'Barney Bradey').
Dublin: William Theodore [Parkes], 1866. SOURCE COPAC. LOCATION L.
COMMENTARY 32pp [COPAC].

P4　*Queer papers* (by 'Barney Bradey').
Dublin: Moffat & Co., 1868. SOURCE OCLC. LOCATION UCD.
COMMENTARY Contains poetry and prose [OCLC].

'PARLEY, Peter', pseud. See GOODRICH, Samuel Griswold.

PARNELL, William (later Parnell-Hayes), b. *c.*1780 Avondale (Co. Wicklow), d. Castle Howard (Co. Wicklow) 1821. Politician, political pamphleteer and novelist, WP was the son of Sir John Parnell and Letitia Charlotte Brooke of Colebrook (Co. Fermanagh) and brother of Lord Congleton. WP was educated at Eton and TCD and as a young man moved in literary circles and was a friend of the authors Thomas Moore§ and Mary Tighe§, who dedicated one her poems to him. A large landowner, he was knight of the shire for Co. Wicklow and was elected Liberal MP in 1817, holding the seat until his death. He was opposed to the Act of Union and, although a Protestant, was protective of Catholics and favoured Catholic emancipation. Besides two novels, he wrote several political treatises, including *An enquiry into the causes of popular discontent in Ireland* (London, 1805) and *An historical apology for the Irish Catholics* (Dublin, 1807), which linked the disaffection of Catholics with their persecution. Most likely he is the Mr Parnell, MP for Co. Wicklow, who was responsible for introducing into schools *A selection from the New Testament* (Dublin, 1818), which created a negative response among Catholics. He married Frances Howard in 1810 and was the grandfather of the statesman Charles Stewart Parnell. For WP's manuscript papers, see ODNB. SOURCE Allibone, ii, p. 1511; Brady, p. 201; Brown, p. 251; IBL, 8 (1921), p. 79; H. Kingsmill Moore, *An unwritten chapter in the history of education* (London, 1904), pp 258–9; ODNB; O'Donoghue, p. 377; RIA/DIB; M. Tighe, *Psyche* (London, 1811), p. 236.

P5   *Julietta; or, the triumph of mental acquirements over personal defects* [anon.].
+ London: J. Johnson, 1802. SOURCE Hardy, 660; British Fiction; Garside, 1802:52; ODNB. LOCATION Corvey CME 3–628–8014–0, Dt, L, InND Loeber coll.
Dublin: Rowland Hunter & C.P. Archer, 1817.
COMMENTARY No copy of the Dublin edn located. Attribution to WP by Block (p. 179), ODNB and Garside, but not by Allibone or Summers. Julietta, born a hunchback, is ignored by her parents and relegated to the regions of the housekeeper. She is intelligent and of a sweet disposition. While walking, she saves from drowning Lord Marsham, who is known to be a miser and who lives in a haunted house. The two strike up a friendship and he asks her parents to allow her to live in his house. He teaches Julietta that to overcome her physical defect she must acquire many accomplishments so that her personality and skills will outshine her deformity. When Lord Marsham dies, Julietta finds herself the heiress to his estate. She is very generous in her gifts, and she marries a man she loves but whom she suspects of marrying her for her possessions. By not forcing her presence upon her husband, and by not demanding physical affection from him, she gives him time to recognize the beauty of her mind. In the end, both husband and wife are truly happy [ML; Allibone, ii, p. 1511; Block, p. 179; Colvin, p. 401 (incorrectly identified this novel as WP's later *Maurice and Berghetta*, London, 1819); Garside, 1802:52; Jarndyce cat. 98/384; ODNB; Summers, p. 379].

P6   *Maurice and Berghetta; or, the priest of Rahery. A tale* [anon.] (dedicated to the Catholic priesthood of Ireland).
+ London: Rowland Hunter; Dublin: C.P. Archer, 1819. SOURCE Block, p. 179; British Fiction; Garside, 1819:53; Jarndyce cat. 98/385. LOCATION Corvey, CME 3–628–8198–8, Ireland related fiction, D, InND Loeber coll.
London: Rowland Hunter; Dublin: C.P. Archer, 1825 (as *The priest of Rahery. A tale*). SOURCE IBL, 8 (1921), p. 79, ODNB. LOCATION L.
Dublin: Printed by Richard Coyne, 1820, 2nd edn. LOCATION Dt.
+ Boston: Wells & Lilly, 1820. LOCATION NUC, InND Loeber coll.
COMMENTARY The drop-head title reads: 'The priest of Rahery's tale'. Written in support of Catholic grievances regarding extreme poverty. The narrator is a Fr O'Brien, who tells the story of several generations of O'Neals. They are poor and, although conscious of their noble lineage, they are down-to-earth and work hard. This is in contrast to the O'Sullivans of Berehaven, who cannot free themselves of the memory of their once-exalted position. The hardworking Maurice marries Berghetta Tual. He prospers, particularly because he acquires new agricultural tools and skills on a trip to England, where he has secured a place for his sis-

ter with a Catholic gentlewoman. The children of Maurice and Berghetta end up in Spain, as do their aunt and the last of the O'Sullivans, where all of them are treated as grandees because of their lineage. The novel was severely critiqued in the *Quarterly Review*, which provoked WP to write *A letter to the editor of the Quarterly Review* (Dublin, 1820) stating that he planned to make changes in later edns [ML; Fenning cat. 188/211; ODNB; British fiction].

PARTRIDGE, Blanche. See **ANDERDON, Blanche.**

'PATRICIA', fl. 1877. Pseudonym of an American writer.

P7   *Blanche Carey; or, scenes in many lands* (by 'Patricia').
+ New York: P. O'Shea, 1877. LOCATION DCU.
COMMENTARY Travels by an Irish girl in several countries in Europe and in North America [RL].

PATRICK, Mrs F.C., pseuds 'The wife of an officer' and 'An officer's widow', fl. 1797. Irish novelist and poet, it is not clear to which branch of the Patrick family Mrs FCP and her husband belonged but members of the Patrick family had settled at Dunminning (Co. Antrim). By 1798 her first husband must have died because she signed the preface to her novel *More ghosts!* (London, 1798) with 'An officer's widow'. Her *Poems founded on the events of the war in the Peninsula* (by 'the wife of an officer') was printed at Hythe (in either Kent or Hants.) in 1819, where she may have resided, and was probably published privately. Her (probably second) husband most likely served in the Peninsular War. SOURCE Allibone, ii, p. 1524; Blain, p. 837; Field Day, ii, p. 832; L.G. Pine (ed.), *Burke's landed gentry of Ireland* (London, 1958, 4th edn), p. 564; C.R. Johnson, *Provincial poetry 1789–1839* (Otley, 1992), No. 691; RIA/DIB.

P8   *The Irish heiress. A novel* [anon.].
London: William Lane, 1797, 3 vols. (ill.). SOURCE Brown, 1367; Brown 2, 1282; Blakey, p. 182; Block, p. 180; Forster 2, 3254; Raven 2, 1797:63; ESTC t130394. LOCATION Corvey CME 3–628–45094–2, Ireland related fiction, L, PU.
COMMENTARY The *Critical Review* (Jan. 1799) includes this note: 'While *The Irish Heiress* remained in her own country, the narrative bore many marks of reality'. The story is set in Ireland and France. The heroine (the 'heiress' of the title) is a Catholic girl, the rejected daughter of an Irish squire and an English mother. She travels to revolutionary France, and the story blends fiction with real events and character connected with the revolution. The duke of Orleans is represented as being enamoured of the heiress, and Maximilien Robespierre is the agent employed to solicit her favours [Blain; Brown 2; JB].

P9   *More ghosts!* (by 'The wife of an officer').
+ London: William Lane, 1798, 3 vols. SOURCE Blakey, p. 185; Block, p. 180; Forster 2, 3256; Raven 2, 1798:53; ESTC n010225. LOCATION Corvey CME 3–628–45132–9, Ireland related fiction, MH.
Philadelphia: Caritat, [date?]. SOURCE Frank, 324.
COMMENTARY No copy of the Philadelphia edn located. The preface, signed 'An officer's widow', states that the novel is 'a burlesque upon the multitude of ghosts and mysteries which have excited public curiosity …' Set in and around an ancient abbey in Yorkshire, residence of the ghost of a wronged relative, it makes fun of claims of unearthed old manuscripts and gives a picture of the hardships of military families. The *Critical Review* (Oct. 1798) stated that 'The ghosts in this piece are rather cunning than terrible; and they add considerably to our entertainment … [and the book contains] reflections on the errors of education and the irregularity of the passions.' The story reverses the standard conditions of Gothic misery and matrimony by featuring two women of opposite natures, the selfless Mary Morney and the

selfish Betsey Bolton, both seeking after Thomas Grey. Betsey plants the idea in Thomas's mind that Mary is his sister and throws him into despair. He leaves for London. Betsey, who is carrying his child, follows him, but Mary's brother, Charles, intervenes, admitting that he too had slept with Betsey and that the child is his. In a denouement, Thomas's mother's ghostly apparition in the abbey transmits an unexpected message: she is an escaped nun, who has come back to shield her son from a match with the wrong woman. Spectral appearances and ghostly sounds are presented and explained away [Blain; CM; Personal communication, Antonia Fraser, Sept. 1997; Frank, 324].

P10   *The Jesuit: or, the history of Anthony Babington, Esq. An historical novel* [anon.]. Bath: Printed for the authoress by R. Cruttwell, 1799, 3 vols. SOURCE Block, p. 180; McBurney & Taylor, 693; Forster 2, 3255; Raven 2, 1799:71; ESTC n048921. LOCATION Corvey CME 3–628–45088–8, Ireland related fiction, IU.
Berlin, Stettin: Nicholai, 1800 (trans. as *Der Jesuit, eine wahre Geschichte*) SOURCE Union Cat. Bavaria.
COMMENTARY Historical fiction describing the story of a sixteenth-century Catholic martyr, Anthony Babington, who had planned to murder Queen Elizabeth I and place Mary Queen of Scots on the throne. He was hanged, drawn and quartered [Blain; AMB].

PAUL, Maj. Norris, fl. 1888. Military officer and novelist.
P11   *Moonlight by the Shannon shore. A tale of modern Irish life* (by Norris Paul). London: Jarrold & Sons, 1888. SOURCE Allibone Suppl., ii, p. 1218; Brown, 1368; OCLC. LOCATION NUI, Galway, InND.
+ London: Jarrold & Sons 1892 (as *Eveline Wellwood*). SOURCE Brown, 1369. LOCATION L, InND Loeber coll.
COMMENTARY An anti-Land League novel set on the shores of the Shannon (Cos. Clare and Limerick). The story starts in India, where six Irish soldiers of a mule battery are about to be discharged. They want to thank their English sergeant, John Seebright, and present him with a document stating that he can always count on their help in Ireland. At the time it seems unlikely that he would ever avail himself of this offer. However, not long afterwards he inherits his uncle's estate, part of which is a large farm in Ireland. Incognito, he goes to Ireland to have a look at the farm and accidentally meets his former soldiers. Eveline Wellwood, a charming Irish girl, and her mother occupy the farm. They are being boycotted at the instigation of a lover whom Eveline rejected. The sergeant organizes his band of soldiers to provide help and protection for the girl and her mother without anyone's knowledge. The neighbours attribute the help to the 'good people' from the fairy rath on the farm. One night the rejected lover goes to see what he thinks will be the destruction of the farm. When he rides over the rath it caves in, and he falls to his death in the ancient burial chamber beneath, which contains a mass of treasures. The girl and the sergeant marry. The book contains vivid descriptions of boycotting techniques [ML].

PAYN, James, b. Cheltenham (Glos.), 1830, d. London 1898. English novelist and editor, JP was the son of William Payn of Kidwells, Maidenhead (Berks.). He graduated from Trinity College, Cambridge, in 1853. He contributed to *Household Words* (London), becoming a friend of Charles Dickens, and to *Chambers's Journal* (Edinburgh) where many of his novels appeared in serial form and increased the circulation greatly. He spent a few years in Edinburgh as editor of *Chambers's Journal* but disliked living there and returned to London in 1861 where he continued to edit the magazine until 1871. He was a reader for the publisher Smith, Elder & Co. and in 1883 he became editor of the London *Cornhill Magazine*. He was a prolific and popular writer of novels, but the *Saturday Review* (London) regretted that his 'genuine sense of humour [was] marred by a reprehensible love of bad puns'. SOURCE Allibone, ii, p. 1531; Allibone Suppl., ii, p. 1219; Boase, vi, p. 368; NCBEL 4, pp 1380–5 (list of novels); NUC; ODNB; RL; Sutherland, pp 493–4.

P12   *Murphy's master and other stories* [anon.].
+ London: Tinsley Bros, 1873. 2 vols. SOURCE Wolff, 5458. LOCATION L, NUC.
Leipzig: Bernard Tauchnitz, 1873. SOURCE T & B, 1312. SOURCE RLIN. LOCATION MH.
New York: Harper & Bros, 1873. LOCATION NUC.
COMMENTARY An adventure story set in England and Australia. Murphy is the servant of a Mr Kavanagh who, as the story begins, has just killed his brother. While Murphy and Kavanagh are making their escape they are helped by a boy, Robert Chesney, who decides to join them. Kavanagh and Murphy are Irish and have been involved in insurrections in Co. Tipperary. They decide to go to Australia in the company of a number of Irish followers. They are shipwrecked on an island near Australia, and while there, Kavanagh's behaviour becomes rather strange. Chesney escapes from the island and sees it disappear into the ocean [ML].

'PAYNE, Harold', pseud. See KELLY, George C.

PEACOCKE, Ida (née Tufnell), pseud. 'Ivaniona', b. Co. Dublin, fl. 1870. Novelist and poet, IP was the daughter of Dr. Jolliffe Tufnell, sometime president of the Royal College of Surgeons of Ireland. She married Capt. P.L. Peacocke. In her dedication in *Cásga*, she mentioned that her father was indebted to the duke of Cambridge. SOURCE O'Donoghue, p. 379 (where her name is misspelled 'Peacock'); RL.

P13   *Brought to light* [anon.].
+ London: Ward, Lock & Tyler, [1870] (Library of Popular Authors). SOURCE Topp 2, 686. LOCATION L.
+ Dublin: Hodges Figgis & Co., [1885] (by 'Ivaniona'; ill. Walter C. Mills). SOURCE Alston, p. 217. LOCATION L.
COMMENTARY Contents: 'Muriel's vision', 'A living death', 'How it will end'. Said to have been copublished with the London firm of Simpkin, Marshall & Co., but that edn has not been located [CM; Topp 8, p. 99].

P14   *Cásga* (by 'Ivaniona'; dedicated to HRH the duke of Cambridge, 'from permission given to me during his recent visit to Ireland … in grateful remembrance of the unvaried kindness shown by him towards my beloved father for many years – From the time his Royal Highness held command of the Dublin district in 1846 until my father's death in 1885').
+ London: Simpkin, Marshall & Co., 1889. SOURCE Alston, p. 217; Topp 8, 911. LOCATION L.
COMMENTARY Published posthumously. A novel set in Ireland, mainly at the Castlemore estate on Achill Island (Co. Mayo). One of the characters is Cásga O'Donnell [CM; RL].

PECK, Mrs — . See PECK, Mrs Frances.

PECK, Mrs Frances (also known as Mrs Peck), pseuds 'An Irishwoman' and 'Candida', fl. 1808. Novelist, FP's mother's maiden name was Andrews and she was a niece of Dr Francis Andrews, provost of TCD. Sometime before 1809 she married a Capt. Peck, who inherited some property in Dublin, where she lived. She herself inherited income from the Deragmaglochney estate (location unknown) from her mother. Capt. Peck was a lieutenant in the 13th Light Dragoons and was severely wounded in Egypt. He retired on half-pay and afterwards was appointed captain and adjutant in the Royal South Down militia. She 'lived happily' with her husband for twenty years, but his infatuation with a young girl led to their separation, and the subsequent slander also implicated their son, a lieutenant in the 11th Foot. At this time FP was living at Carlow. She mentions that she had visited Paris and that she was for some time in bad health, 'her nervous system, being much impaired'. She suffered from eye problems in 1812, which made it impossible for her to write. A poem dedicated to her appeared in the *Hibernian Magazine* (Dublin, 1810, p. 61). In 1812 she remonstrated with Primate George Robinson for going back on his promise to publish her novel. She became a convert to her father's catholicism and was an enthusiastic advocate of repeal of the Act of Union. She published seven novels (many for the London Minerva Press), of which her *The bard of the West* (London, 1818, 3 vols.) became the most popular. She had a hand in a weekly periodical entitled *Emun ac Knuck*, the location of which has not been identified. Her portrait was published in *Vaga* (London, 1813) and in *The last conquest of Ireland* (Dublin, 1836). She was still alive in 1835. SOURCE Author's circular letter, in her *The life and acts of ... Edmund of Erin* (Dublin, 1842); Blain, p. 840; BD, p. 267; Letter to George Robinson, Dublin, from Dublin, 6 Oct. 1812 (Univ. of Iowa Libraries (IA), Special Coll., MsL\P3665r).

P15   *The maid of Avon. A novel, for the haut ton* (by 'An Irishwoman').
+ London: Lane, Newman & Co., 1808, 3 vols. SOURCE Blakey, p. 223 (who mistakenly lists it under 1807); British Fiction; Garside, 1808:87. LOCATION Corvey CME 3–28–48147, Ireland related fiction.
COMMENTARY Set in Ireland in the late 1790s. Ainsford, an English clergyman, raises Josephina, the orphan daughter of his friend Maj. Darnley. The life of quiet contemplation and retirement led by Ainsford and Josephina (the 'maid' of the title) is compared favourably to the dissipations of the fashionable life led by Josephina's aunt, Lady Avon. After being attacked by a Catholic mob and receiving warning letters about his and his ward's safety, Ainsford and Josephina are forced to leave Ireland as the state of the country becomes increasingly dangerous prior to the 1798 rebellion. Once the rebellion is over, they return to Ireland and Josephina marries an Anglo-Irish nobleman, Lord Mount Errin [JB].

P16   *The Welch peasant boy. A novel* [anon.].
London: Lane, Newman & Co., 1808, 3 vols. SOURCE Blakey, p. 226; Block, p. 181; British Fiction; Garside, 1808:88. LOCATION Corvey CME 3–628–48882–6, L.
COMMENTARY The Welsh hero is actually not a peasant. The story opens with a mysterious baby deposited with humble foster-parents. The hero's mother had once 'supported herself by writing for the press' [Blain].

P17   *The young Rosinière; or, sketches of the world. A novel* (by Mrs Peck; dedicated to the countess of Londonderry; dedication signed Frances Peck).
London: Henry Colburn, 1809, 3 vols. SOURCE British Fiction; Garside, 1809:57. LOCATION Dt.
COMMENTARY Reviewed in the *Hibernia Magazine* (Jan. 1810). Part of the story concerns a young female miniature painter [RL].

P18   *Vaga; or, a view of nature. A novel* (by Mrs Peck).
London: Robinson, 1813, 3 vols. SOURCE Blakey, p. 306; Block, p. 181 (1815 edn); British Fiction; Garside, 1813:46. LOCATION Corvey CME 3–628–48410–3 (1815 edn), Ireland related fiction, NUC (1815 edn).
COMMENTARY No copy of the first edn located [Garside].

P19   *The bard of the West; commonly called Eman ac Knuck, or Ned of the Hills. An Irish historical romance, founded on facts of the seventh century* (by Mrs Peck; dedicated to Prince Edward; dedication signed Frances Peck).

+ London: Baldwin, Cradock & Joy; Dublin: John Cumming, 1818, 3 vols. SOURCE Block, p. 181; British Fiction; Garside, 1818:49; Hardy, 669. LOCATION Corvey CME 3–628–48408–1, Ireland related fiction, D, L, NUC.

Dublin: S.J. Machen, 1836 (as *The last conquest of Ireland, the life and adventures of Ned of the Hills, historical legends of Ireland*; ill. B. Clayton). SOURCE Brown, 1373 (Tegg edn, 2 vols., not identified).

+ Dublin: Published for the authoress by Samuel J. Machen, 1842, 4th edn, 2 vols. in 1 (as *The life and acts of the renowned and chivalrous Edmund of Erin, commonly called Emun ac Knuck; or, Ned of the Hills. An Irish historical romance of the seventh century. Founded on facts. Blended with a brief and pithy epitome of the origin, antiquity, and history of Ireland. With copious notes, critical and historical*; dedicated to the Irish people; includes a letter to Daniel O'Connell; ill. B. Clayton). SOURCE Hodges Figgis cat. 10 n.s./2596; Rowan cat. 43/171 (where called the 4th issue). LOCATION Dt, NUC (3rd edn), InND Loeber coll.

COMMENTARY No copy of Dublin 1836 edn located. Ned of the Hills was an old story, which the actor and playwright John O'Keeffe transformed into an opera, *The Wicklow Mountains, or the lad of the hills* (first performed and published in Dublin in 1797). The story, set in seventh-century Ireland, is told in Peck's book, but it is mainly a vehicle for the exultation of Ireland and the vilification of England. Emun, in a dream, foresees the events of the nineteenth century. The book contains many prefaces and addenda, among which is a letter relating FP's matrimonial differences with her husband. Some parts of the book have extensive footnotes with digressions, quotes and elaborations. The number of plates in the Dublin 1842 edn usually ranges from 10 to 11, but a copy with 12 plates is known [ML; Brown; Personal communication, Peter Rowan, n.d.; T.J. Walsh, *Opera in Dublin 1705–1797* (Dublin, 1973), p. 307].

P20 *Napoleon; or, the mysteries of the hundred days. An historical novel* (by Mrs Peck). London: Simpkin & Marshall; Dublin: Westley & Tyrrell, 1826, 2 vols. SOURCE Block, p. 181; British Fiction; Garside, 1826:61. LOCATION Corvey CME 3–628–48409–X, C.

COMMENTARY Historical fiction illustrating, according to the author's preface, 'the human character [of Napoleon], by decorating simple facts; with the drapery of fancy'. The introd. is dated Dublin, 1 June 1826 [Johnson cat. 38/69; British Fiction].

P21 *Tales for the British people* (by 'Candida'; dedicated to 'the man of all people!!! Daniel O'Connell').

+ London: James Ridgeway & Sons, 1834. SOURCE Garside 2, 1834:16. LOCATION L.

COMMENTARY Stories exposing the moral evils of the time. Contents (excluding a play): 'The sojourner in Dublin', 'Life in the Irish militia', 'A visit to Killarney', 'An allegorical tale', 'A new earth, a new heaven' [ML].

PECK, George W. See **PECK, George Wilbur**.

PECK, George Wilbur (known as **George W. Peck**), Jnr, b. Henderson (NY) 1840, d. Milwaukee (WI) 1916. American novelist, GWP was a journalist, editor of the *Milwaukee Sun*, and Democratic governor of Wisconsin (1891–95). He came to national attention in 1869 in the New York *Democrat* with his letter, using the pseudonym Terence McGrant, in Irish dialect satirizing the nepotism of the administration of President Ulysses S. Grant. He was offered a staff job on a new newspaper if he would continue the McGrant letters, which proved very popular and were later published. He was also the author of a series of books about a character named Peck. SOURCE Allibone Suppl., ii, p. 1222; ANB; DAB; DLB, xxiii, xlii; Wright, iii, pp 415–16 (list of novels).

P22   *Adventures of one Terence McGrant, a brevet Irish cousin of President Ulysses S. Grant* (by George W. Peck).

New York: James H. Lambert, 1871 (ill. H.L. Stephens). SOURCE Wright, ii, 1865. LOCATION L, NUC, Wright web.

COMMENTARY A fictional distant cousin of President Ulysses S. Grant and an office-seeker, McGrant, an Irish character, reports weekly in an Irish dialect about administration scandals, including the gold conspiracy and the disbursement 'of office and stalings' to a large circle of relatives. In the course of these violently racist letters, McGrant also beats up a black door-man at the White House and a black senator from Mississippi and complains of Reconstruction that Grant 'thinks more of nagers and dogs than he does of his relatives' [DLB].

P23   *Peck's Irish friend, Phelan Geoheagan* (by George W. Peck).

+ Chicago, New York: Belford, Clarke & Co., 1888. SOURCE Wright, iii, 4145. LOCATION NUC, InND Loeber coll. (Chicago: Conkey, [1900] edn).

COMMENTARY Set in Milwaukee among the Irish, written in an exaggerated Irish brogue [ML].

PENDER, Mrs M.T. See PENDER, Mrs Margaret T.

PENDER, Mrs Margaret T. (née O'Doherty; known as Mrs **M.T. Pender**), b. Ballytweedy (Co. Antrim) 1865, d. Belfast (Co. Antrim) 1920. A novelist and poet, MTP was the daughter of Daniel O'Doherty, a Catholic farmer, and Margaret White, a Presbyterian, whose family disowned her when she married. She was educated at the Ballyrobin National School and the Convent of Mercy, Belfast. Both her mother and maternal grandfather wrote poetry and MTP began to write poetry herself at an early age. She contributed to Irish periodicals, including the *Belfast Morning News*, the *Nation*, the *Shamrock* (both Dublin), and the *Shan Van Vocht* (Belfast) and won a £50 prize for a short story on the 1798 rebellion in the *Weekly Freeman* (Dublin), which spurred her to continue writing fiction. She went on to publish stories and novels, mostly historical and dealing with Ulster's resistance to English rule, many of which were serialized in the Irish, Irish-American and Irish-Australian press. Active in support of the nationalist cause, MTP succeeded Alice Milligan§ as president of the Belfast branch of the Nationalist Association of Irishwomen and lectured frequently on Irish history to nationalist groups. Her story 'O'Neill of the Glens' was used as the Irish Film Company's first production and employed some members of the Abbey Theatre company. Some of MTP's letters are at UCD (MS LA15). SOURCE Brady, p. 202; Brown, p. 253; Brown 2, p. 219; Hogan 2, p. 1014; Irish pseudonyms; A. Millar, 'Discovering Mrs Pender', *Causeway*, 11 (1998), pp 49–52; NLI, MS 8,411; O'Donoghue, p. 380; E. Reilly, p. 250.

P24   *The green cockade. A tale of Ulster in 'ninety-eight* (by Mrs M.T. Pender).

+ Dublin: Sealy, Bryers & Walker; London: Downey & Co., 1898. SOURCE Brown, 1375. LOCATION D, L, NUC.

+ Dublin, Belfast: The Phoenix Publishing Co., n.d. (as *The green cockade*; Library of Modern Irish Fiction). LOCATION InND Loeber coll.

COMMENTARY An historical novel of love and hate, imprisonment and escape set in the north of Ireland (the Belfast region) in 1797–98 at the time of the rebellion. The book is written entirely from the rebel standpoint. William Putnam M'Cabe, the 'Unitedman' is much to the fore, while Lord Edward Fitzgerald, Lord Castlereagh, and other historical figures are introduced. The battle of Antrim is described [Brown; RL].

P25   *The last of the Irish chiefs* (by Mrs M.T. Pender).

+ Dublin: Martin Lester, [1920]. SOURCE Brown 1376; Brown 2, 1289. LOCATION D, DPL.

COMMENTARY An historical novel set in and around Derry during the period following the Flight of the Earls, including the rebellion of the ill-fated Sir Cahir O'Doherty. It contains many incidents, battles, burnings, torturings and hairbreadth escapes [Brown 2].

P26 *Married in May* (by Mrs M.T. Pender).

Dublin: Martin Lester, [1920]. LOCATION D (Dublin: Talbot n.d. edn), L, NUC.

COMMENTARY A bankrupt landlord tries to marry his daughter to a rascally attorney. The girl escapes with her lover and marries him in Scotland. The lover is tried and imprisoned for marrying a girl under sixteen while, with the rector's help, the girl escapes to Australia. On his release, the hero follows her but is flung overboard by the villain, but he swims ashore. After having made a fortune in the gold fields, he becomes (under another name) a famous poet and woos again successfully his wife, who had believed him dead and who has not recognized him [Brown 2].

P27 *The outlaw* (by Mrs M.T. Pender).

+ Dublin: Martin Lester; London: Leonard Parsons, [1925]. SOURCE Brown 2, 1290. LOCATION D, DPL, InND Loeber coll.

COMMENTARY This and the following novels were published posthumously. A romantic tale of Ireland in the days of highwaymen. Squire Adair of Castle Adair, near Carrickfergus (Co. Antrim), wants his daughter Eileen to marry Sir Samuel Shaw, who is old but rich and who holds a mortgage on the castle. But Eileen is in love with Dick Desmond. With the help of the mysterious Aeneas O'Haughan, a highwayman, the lovers defeat the designs of Sir Samuel [Brown 2; ML].

P28 *The bog of lilies* (by Mrs M.T. Pender).

+ Dublin, Cork: Talbot Press, 1927. SOURCE Brown 2, 1291. LOCATION D, DPL, InND Loeber coll.

COMMENTARY A romance set mainly in Ireland where Ever Magennis and Nora O'Heyne fall in love with each other. However, Ever marries Jem Calderwood, who felt rejected by Ever and had made it her business to ensnare him into marriage. The marriage is absolutely miserable and Jem leaves him. Eventually, the true lovers get together [ML].

P29 *The spearmen of the North* (by Mrs M.T. Pender).

+ Dublin, Cork: Talbot Press, 1931. SOURCE Brown 2, 1292. LOCATION D, L, NUC, InND Loeber coll.

COMMENTARY First serialized as 'Red Hugh O'Donnell; or, the Northern chiefs' in the *Shamrock* (Dublin, 1900). An historical novel about the O'Donnells and the O'Neills, late-sixteenth-century earls of Ulster, with Hugh O'Donnell as the main character. He is incarcerated in Dublin Castle for many years. After his release he helps to organize the uprisings against the incursions of the English soldiers in the North. It describes the battle of Kinsale and O'Donnell's journey to Spain to request more help. The book ends with the deaths of O'Donnell and his wife [ML].

PENROSE, Ethel (née Coghill), b. 1857, d. 1938. Children's writer, EP was the daughter of Sir Jocelyn Coghill of Glen Barrahane, Castletownshend (Co. Cork), and cousin of Edith Somerville§, who illustrated EP's second children's book. She married James Penrose in 1880 and with him had a large family. They probably lived at Lismore (Co. Waterford). She contributed to *Argosy* (London). SOURCE O'Toole, p. 253.

P30 *The fairy gobbler's gold* (by Ethel Penrose).

London: T. Nelson & Sons, 1890. SOURCE COPAC; OCLC. LOCATION L, ICU.

COMMENTARY Story for children [RL].

P31 *Clear as a noon day* (by Ethel Penrose).

London: Jarrold & Sons, [1893] (ill. E.Œ. Somerville§). SOURCE O'Toole, p. 253; COPAC; OCLC. LOCATION L, ICU.

New York: E.P. Dutton, n.d. SOURCE OCLC. LOCATION Univ. of Southern Mississippi.
COMMENTARY Story for children [O'Toole, p. 253].

P32 *Darby and Joan. Being the adventures of two children* (by Ethel Penrose).
London, Glasgow, Edinburgh, Dublin: Blackie & Son, [1894]. SOURCE COPAC.
LOCATION L.
COMMENTARY Story for children [RL].

PENROSE, Mrs H.H. (née Mary Elizabeth Lewis), b. Kinsale (Co. Cork) 1860. Novelist and fiction writer, Mrs HHP was born to a Protestant family and was educated at Rochelle School, Cork. She contributed fiction to magazines such as the *Temple Bar* and *Windsor Magazine* (both London), and wrote 16 novels. Her husband may be identified with Henry Herbert Penrose, second son of Robert William Henry Penrose of Riverview, Ferrybank, and Seaville, Tramore (Co. Waterford). However, this is not certain because he was born in 1874, which would make him fourteen years younger than his wife. SOURCE EF, pp 312–13; Landed gentry, 1912, p. 556.

P33 *The love that never dies: A study* (by Mrs H.H. Penrose).
London: Jarrold & Sons, 1898 (The Greenback Series, No. 48). LOCATION L.

P34 *The modern gospel* (by Mrs H.H. Penrose).
London: A. Constable & Co., 1898. LOCATION L.

P35 *Chubby: A nuisance. A study of child life* (by Mrs H.H. Penrose).
+ London: Longmans & Co., 1902 (ill.). LOCATION L.
COMMENTARY Fiction for children. The story of Chubby who lives on a country estate and has an Irish nurse, Bridget [RL].

P36 *As dust in the balance* (by Mrs H.H. Penrose).
London: Alston Rivers, 1905. LOCATION L.

P37 *The unequal yoke: A study in temperament* (by Mrs H.H. Penrose).
London: Alston Rivers, 1905. LOCATION L.

P38 *Rachel the outsider* (by Mrs H.H. Penrose).
London: Chapman & Hall, 1906. LOCATION L.

P39 *The given proof* (by Mrs H.H. Penrose).
+ London: T. Werner Laurie, [1907]. LOCATION D, L.
COMMENTARY A love story featuring Kenneth Stanford, who takes an interest in Mrs Theodosia Wynne, and wonders why she ever married George Wynne. Stanford becomes Theodosia's good friend as they share similar interests in art, literature and theatre. George Wynne invites Stanford to spend the winter with them in Florida. They arrive at Fort Ballantyne, where Stanford declares his love for Theodosia. He asks her to get a divorce, but she refuses. Wynne becomes violent when intoxicated and Theodosia escapes from him. Meanwhile, enemies pursue Stanford. Theodosia urges him to disguise himself as her, and he escapes. She confronts the enemies in Stanford's clothes and sacrifices her life for him [CD].

P40 *The grey above the green* (by Mrs H.H. Penrose).
London: Hodder & Stoughton, [1908]. LOCATION L.

P41 *Denis Trench. A plotless history of how he followed the gleam and worked out his salvation* (by Mrs H.H. Penrose).
+ London: Alston Rivers, 1911. LOCATION D, L, NUC.
COMMENTARY Set in Guernsey in the Channel Islands where Denis and Kathleen have been deserted by their father, a rector. Their mother dies of a broken heart and they are reared by an aunt. Denis wins a scholarship. He is a born writer and later writes for magazines such as *Punch* (London). Lady Laurence adopts Kathleen. A priest named Fr Desmond, who comes to attend to Lady Laurence, turns out to be Kathleen's and Denis's father. He had changed

his religion to catholicism. Fr Desmond makes peace with his children before his death. Denis travels to Cork. He falls in love with Stella Delaney. In a hasty decision, he asks her to marry him. A friend tells Denis about Stella's scheming ways and he returns to London alone. His sister introduces him to Grace Diston, who writes literary reviews. She gives Denis's book *The temple of Janus* a glowing review. He realizes that they have much in common and they become closer [CD].

P42   *A sheltered woman* (by Mrs H.H. Penrose).
        London: Alston Rivers, 1911. LOCATION L, NUC.

P43   *A faery land forlorn* (by Mrs H.H. Penrose).
        London: Alston Rivers, 1912. LOCATION L.

COMMENTARY A romance set in a seaside town in the south of Ireland among upper-class Protestants. The story revolves around the sad love tale of Evelyn Eyre, separated from her lover forever [Brown, 1378].

P44   *Charles the Great. A very light comedy* (by Mrs H.H. Penrose).
        + London: Methuen & Co., 1912. LOCATION L, NUC.

COMMENTARY A story of deceit about a vain man who poses as a genius by having someone else write a brilliant novel, for which he takes the credit. In the end his duplicity is exposed [EF, p. 312].

P45   *The brat. A trifle* (by Mrs H.H. Penrose).
        London: Mills & Boon, 1913. SOURCE EF, p. 312; COPAC. LOCATION L.

COMMENTARY Fiction for juveniles. Three children who torment their ageing governess are checked, not by their mother, but by the governess's young niece. A fierce old admiral who stays in the village turns out to be the governess's lost love [EF, p. 312–13].

P46   *The house of Rennel* (by Mrs H.H. Penrose).
        London: Alston Rivers, 1913. LOCATION L, NUC.

P47   *Burnt flax* (by Mrs H.H. Penrose).
        London: Mills & Boon, 1914. LOCATION L.

COMMENTARY An historical novel concerned with Land League agitation [EF, p. 312].

P48   *Something impossible. An extravaganza* (by Mrs H.H. Penrose).
        London: Mills & Boon, 1914. LOCATION L.

COMMENTARY Doctor Marks is convinced that his wife cannot love a man as ugly as he is. A friend gives him an Indian charm, which allows the possessor one wish. He uses the wish to become like the handsome Capt. Darlington. This leads to great confusion for his wife and for the captain [EF, p. 313].

'PENSEVAL, Guy', pseud. See **DARLEY, George**.

'PEPPERGRASS, Paul', pseud. See **BOYCE, Fr John**.

PERCIVAL, Mrs Margaret, pseud. 'A young Lady', d. prior to 1852. A Protestant religious fiction writer, MP lived in the countryside in Ireland and visited London at least once, according to the introd. to her *The Irish dove* (Dublin, 1849). She held strong nationalist feelings for Ireland and advocated – through the Irish Society – the religious instruction of the Irish through Gaelic translations of the Bible. She saw the necessity of the survival of Gaelic alongside the English language. SOURCE RL.

P49   *Rosa, the work-girl. A tale* (by 'A young Lady').
        Dublin: J. Robertson, 1847. SOURCE Block, p. 182; Rafroidi, ii, p. 324. LOCATION L.

COMMENTARY According to an advertisement in *The Irish dove*, profits arising from *Rosa* were for the benefit of the Association for the Relief of Distressed Seamstresses [RL].

P50   *The Irish dove; or, faults on both sides. A tale* [anon.].
+ Dublin: John Robertson; London: Simpkin, Marshall & Co., 1849. SOURCE Brown, 1380; Rafroidi, ii, p. 324; NSTC. LOCATION D, Dt, DPL, L, NUC, InND Loeber coll.

COMMENTARY Evangelical fiction published for the benefit of the 'Irish Society for promoting the Education of the Native Irish, through the medium of their own language; to which any profits arising from its sale are to be devoted'. In the introd., the author states that she received the anonymous manuscript from a friend in London, who had acquired it in an auction. She changed the document very little and left the Irish pronunciation intact. The story is set during a famine prior to 1845 and recounts that Helen Wilson inherits, through her mother, an estate in Co. Kerry. After years of residence in India and then England, she comes to live in Ireland. She is able to speak Gaelic, which she has learned from Corny, an Irish servant employed by her family. Helen is passionately interested in converting the Catholics to protestantism, and finds that providing Gaelic bibles is the key to this process. The more successful she is, the more bitterly priests oppose her, and ugly scenes follow. The book is written as an attempt to describe the work of the Irish Society, but it is also aimed at defending Ireland and the Irish against English ignorance and hostility [ML; Fegan, p. 220].

P51   *The fisherman's daughter, a tale* (by the author of *Rosa, the work girl*).
+ Dublin: John Robertson, 1852. LOCATION L (not found).
London: Simpkin, Marshall & Co., 1853. SOURCE Topp 8, 15.
Boston: [publisher?], 1852. SOURCE Topp 8, 15.

COMMENTARY No copies of the London and Boston edns located. Sunday school book, published posthumously, consisting of religious fiction set in Ireland. In the preface the author states that profits from the sale will be devoted to charitable purposes. Reviewed in the *Christian Penny Journal* (location unclear, 1853, p. 54) [ML; RL; Topp].

'PEREGRINUS', pseud. See **TRACY, Henry**.

'A PERSON OF HONOUR', pseud. See **BOYLE, Roger**.

'A PERSON OF HONOUR', pseud. See **BOYLE, Robert**.

PERY, Edmund Sexton, first Viscount Pery, b. Limerick 1719, d. London 1806. Parliamentarian, barrister, patriot and novelist, ESP was the eldest son of Revd Stackpole Pery, a Church of Ireland clergyman of Stackpole Court (Co. Clare), and Jane Twigg, daughter of the archdeacon of Limerick. He was educated at TCD (entered 1736), admitted as a student to the Middle Temple (London) in 1739 and admitted to the King's Inns in 1745 and called to the Irish Bar in 1745. He was MP for Wicklow (1751–60), and for Limerick (1761–85). As a councillor of the city of Dublin he worked for the city's interests and as MP for Limerick he steered funds to the city for construction, particularly the building of new roads and quays. He became speaker of the house of commons in Ireland in three successive parliaments: 1771, 1776, and 1783. Independent in his views, he worked consistently to promote Irish interests, pressing parliamentary reform; supporting Henry Grattan's efforts on legislative independence; promoting free trade, an Irish Habeas Corpus act and the passage of the Relief Bill. Due to ill-health, he resigned as speaker in 1785 and was created in that year Viscount Pery of Newtown-Pery, near Limerick. As a peer he opposed the Act of Union between Ireland and England and the anti-union members of parliament met at his Dublin house before the vote to discuss strategy. He married first Patty Martin of Dublin, who died in 1757, and second, Elizabeth (née Vesey), widow of Robert Handcock, and daughter of the 1st Baron Knapton.

'Petrel'

Respected and admired by Edmund Burke, he was described by Henry Grattan as 'one of the most honest men in existence' and is recognized as one of the leading political figures in eighteenth-century Ireland. Some of his papers and manuscripts are in the Henry E. Huntington Library, San Marino (CA), the PRONI, the NLI, and the BL (Add. MSS 38,213–26, 38, 306–10). For ESP's portraits and papers, see ODNB. SOURCE B & S, p. 665; W. Blake (ed.), *An Irish beauty of the regency* (London, 1911), pp 62–3, opp. p. 61; HIP, vi, pp 55–9; Keane, p. 400; ODNB; RIA/DIB.

P52   *Letters from an Armenian in Ireland to his friend in Trebisond &c. Translated in the year 1756* [anon.].

London: Printed in the year [i.e., published privately] 1757. SOURCE ESTC t05733. LOCATION D, Dt, BFl, L, C.

London: W. Owen, 1757. SOURCE Black, 648; Raven, 423; Collinson Black, 317; Hardy, 673; Bradshaw, 7418; ESTC n018913. LOCATION DPL Gilbert Coll., D, L, C, NN, NUC.

COMMENTARY This 250pp novel has been ascribed to ESP by Barnard and in the *Modern Language Review*, but Raven, BLC, and Collinson Black give as its author Robert Hellen, one of the justices of the court of common pleas in Ireland. It is probably the first pseudo-oriental, epistolary novel written by an Irishman. The running title is 'Aza to Abdallah from Dublin', imitating Montesquieu's *Lettres Persanes* (Amsterdam, 1721). The volume consists of thirty-one letters written by Aza to his daughter. His guide is an Irish friend, whose comments and explanations help Aza understand many things happening in Ireland. These include the passion for card playing; the daring behaviour of a gallant and of the women who accept his attentions; the activities in the assembly of the house of commons; the defects of the system of education; the way justice is administered; the manner of conducting funerals and the use of professional mourners; the eating habits of the Irish; the behaviour of Irish orators and the abuse of eloquence. Much of Oliver Goldsmith's§ *The citizens of the World* (London, 1762) is based on *Letters from an Armenian* [T. Barnard, *A new anatomy of Ireland* (New Haven, 2003), p. 341n.22; DNB; *Modern Language Review*, 14(2) 1953, pp 209–16; ODNB; Raven, 423; Collinson Black, 317].

'PETREL, Fulmar', fl. 1895. Pseudonym of an adventure novelist.

P53   *Grania Waile: A West Connaught sketch of the sixteenth century* (by 'Fulmar Petrel').

+ London: T. Fisher Unwin, 1895 (ill. F.R.). SOURCE Brown, 1381. *Location* DPL, L, NUC.

COMMENTARY Historical fiction set in sixteenth-century Ireland and tells the story of the life of Grace (Grania) O'Malley, the legendary pirate 'queen of Connacht'. Few of the incidents are historical facts [Brown].

'PETRILL, Mrs Frank', pseud. See **CAREW, Miss**.

PHELPS, Elizabeth Stuart (also known as Elizabeth Stuart Ward), b. Andover (MA) 1844, d. 1911. American novelist and temperance and feminist writer, ESP was the daughter of the novelist Elizabeth Wooster Stuart. She wrote many books for juveniles, some religious in nature. She was an advocate of temperance and women's equality in voting, marital relationships, employment and education. Well-known for her popular book on the afterlife, *The gates ajar* (1868; repr. Cambridge (MA), 1964), she contributed to periodicals such as New York's *Harper's*, Boston's *Atlantic Monthly* and the New York *Century*. After the death of her fiancée in the Civil War she vowed not to marry, but in 1888 she married Herbert Dickinson Ward, editor of the *New York Independent*. She is credited with being the first person to write a full-length novel about urban industrial problems and about a failed marriage. SOURCE Allibone, ii, p. 1576; Allibone Suppl., ii, pp 1485–6 [under Ward]; ANB; Blain, p. 849; BLC; DAB [under Ward]; DLB, ccii; L.D. Kelly *The life and works of Elizabeth Stuart Phelps, Victorian feminist writer* (New York, 1983).

P54 **Donald Marcy** (by Elizabeth Stuart Phelps).
+ Boston: Houghton, Mifflin & Co.; Cambridge: Riverside Press, 1893. SOURCE Doolin Dinghy cat. 15/129; OCLC; Wright, iii, 5759. LOCATION InND Loeber coll.
COMMENTARY Fiction for juveniles featuring life in a New England college where two of the characters, a policeman and one of the students, are Irish. This student is depicted as very strong and good-hearted, but not very intelligent. A love story is interwoven [ML].

PHIBBS, Mary, pseud. 'A Lady', fl. 1813. Irish novelist, as identified in the University of Virginia (Charlottesville, VA) copy of the following volume, but this is doubted by Sadleir and Garside. However, that copy also carries an inscription by William H. Phibbs, who in all likelihood was William Harloe Phibbs of Bloomfield, sheriff of Co. Sligo in 1814. William married in 1778 Susan, daughter of John Lloyd of Croghan, and died in 1827. He had four sons and three daughters, of whom MP may have been one. Several members of the Phibbs family are among the subscribers, including Mr and Mrs Wm H. Phibbs, and members of the Phibbs family of Lisheen (formerly known as Seafield, Co. Sligo). Other Irish subscribers, some from the west and the midlands of Ireland, include Lady Gore-Booth, members of the Crofton and Wynne families, Miss [Maria] Edgeworth§ (who ordered two copies), William Le Fanu, and Charles Phillips§. The preface to the following novel is written from Laura House, Bath (Avon), Dec. 1812. MP dedicated the book to the marchioness of Ely, who belonged to the Irish nobility. MP may be identified with the person of this name who published a drama *Alice Western; or, the dangers of coquetry* (London, 1855). SOURCE British Fiction; CM; COPAC; Garside, 1813:47; Landed gentry, 1912, pp 562–3; W.G. Wood-Martin, *Sligo and the Enniskilleners from 1688 to 1691* (Dublin, 1880), p. 177.

P55 **The lady of Martendyke; an historical tale of the fifteenth century** (by 'A Lady'; dedicated to the marchioness of Ely).
+ London: For the author by Henry Colburn, 1813, 3 vols. (subscribers' list). SOURCE British Fiction; Garside, 1813:47. LOCATION Corvey CME 3–628–47892–8, L.
COMMENTARY In the preface the author argues that the historical novel has a greater authenticity and usefulness than mere fictional romance. The novel is set against the civil wars in Holland, Zealand and Hainault (Belgium). It relates the reluctant visit of the countess of Hainault to the Magronnel family of Killarney. The countess is on her way to visit King Henry in England but is inconvenienced by the hospitality of Irish acquaintances, who insist on her staying a week in their country. The Magronnels are of Scottish descent and the leader Magronnel 'is now vassal to the king of England, dependent on his favour, and must attend his court'. Her entertainment includes watching a wolf chase through the woods of Killarney, a banquet at Ross Castle, a trip along the river Shannon, a visit to a grotto near Kilkenny and to the monastery at Boyle Abbey. The king of Connacht gives a banquet in her honour at the Castle of Sligo where she witnesses sports such as 'throwing the sledge'. From there she travels to the Kilmantine Abbey. On her way to England she stays at the Friary of St Saviour, on Usher's Island, Dublin. At first she is amazed by the beauty of Ireland and continually draws comparisons between its landscape and architecture with that of Europe: 'Instead of savage wilds, and savage mountains, she had found a country rich in natural beauty, richer in natural merit; and she became hourly interested for people doomed to be slandered and misrepresented by those who do not know it, loved and neglected by those who do'. A discussion

about whether Ireland will be dominated by England and the pros and cons of such a conquest is included [CM].

'PHILALETHES CANTABRIGIENSIS', pseud. See KAYE, Bishop John.

'PHILANTROPOS', pseud. See DELAP, James.

PHILLIPS, Charles, b. Sligo *c.*1787, d. London 1859. Barrister, novelist, pamphleteer and miscellaneous writer, CP was the son of William Phillips of Consity (not identified), Co. Sligo, who was a member of Sligo corporation, a tax-collector and a publican. CP was admitted at TCD in 1802 and graduated BA in 1806. He entered King's Inns the same year and was admitted to the Middle Temple (London), where he wrote his only novel. He was called to the Irish Bar in 1812 and joined the Connacht circuit, where he gained a reputation for his florid oratory. CP, a Protestant, was a supporter of Catholic emancipation and a friend and advisor to Daniel O'Connell. He married a Miss Whalley of Camden Town (London) in 1819. In 1821 he was called to the English Bar and became a leader at the Old Bailey. In 1842 he was made commissioner of the bankruptcy court in Liverpool and in 1847 appointed a commissioner of the court of insolvent debtors. He wrote several works relating to Ireland: a poetic eulogy, *The consolations of Erin* (London, 1811); a poem, *The Emerald Isle* (London, 1812); *A garland for the grave of R.B. Sheridan* (London, 1816), and *Recollections of Curran and his contemporaries* (London, 1818). In addition, he wrote *The queen's case stated in an address to the king* (London, 1820), a defence of Queen Caroline, the repudiated wife of George IV, *Historical sketch of Arthur, Duke of Wellington* (Brighton, 1852), and in 1857 *Vacation thoughts on capital punishment* (London, 1856), a pamphlet urging abolition of the death penalty. Judging from the following novel, he may have visited France. He is buried in Highgate cemetery, London. For CP's portraits, see Elmes and ODNB. His extensive correspondence with Henry Brougham, lord chancellor, is in the library of University College, London (for additional papers, see ODNB). SOURCE Allibone, i, pp 1581–2; B & S, p. 667; Brady, p. 205; Elmes, p. 167; Garside 1811:67; Keane, p. 401; NCBEL 4, p. 419; OCIL, p. 472; ODNB; O'Donoghue, pp 381–2; RIA/DIB.

P56   *The loves of Celestine and St. Aubert; a romantic tale* (by Charles Phillips; dedicated to the comtesse de St Marguerite).

London: J.J. Stockdale, 1811, 2nd edn, 2 vols. SOURCE British Fiction; Garside 1811:67.
LOCATION O (1811, 2nd edn; which contains the dedication).
COMMENTARY No copy of the first edn located. A second edn (London, 1811) carries the dedication to Mme la comtesse de St Marguerite. The story starts with the burial of Celestine and the discovery shortly after of the drowned body of a stranger, a monk with the message 'Let me rest beside my Celestine' attached. The novel then moves backward in time to the first-person memoir of Celestine, who had been brought up in France where she meets and falls in love with the Swiss St Aubert, son of her father's old friend. Before he is sent off to fight in the American War of Independence, they plight their troth. The last that is heard of him is his capture by the native Americans and his supposed death. The second part of the narrative shows Celestine caught up in the French Revolution in Paris, where she and her father face a tribunal headed by Maximilien Robespierre. Their accuser is the perfidious L'Enfer, a tyrannical and duplicitous monk who appeared in the first part of the novel. Celestine eventually finds security of a sort through marriage to La Motte, who proves a jealous and intractable husband. The text has praise for Thomas Paine and the Marquis de Condorcet. The denouement comes with the unexpected return of St Aubert. Overwhelmed with passion, Celestine agrees to meet him, and the premature birth of a dead child results [Personal communication, Peter Garside, Oct. 2002; Garside 1811:67].

'A PHYSICIAN', pseud. See ADAMS, Alexander Maxwell.

'PIERCY, J.M.', pseud. See MAC CABE, William Bernard.

PIGOTT, Miss H. Bouverie. Novelist, HBP may be of Irish origin because her first book was published in Dublin. An annotation in the NLI copy of *Walter Chetwynd* (Dublin, 1862) states that the Pigott family formerly owned Chetwynd Park (Shrops.). The author Harriet Pigott (1775–1846) belonged to this family but clearly is a different person from HBP. SOURCE Blain, p. 854; ML; RL.

P57   *Walter Chetwynd. A novel* (by Miss H. Bouverie Pigott).
        + Dublin: M'Glashan & Gill; London: Kent & Co.; Edinburgh: John Menzies, 1862. SOURCE Allibone, ii, p. 1594 (mentions a London, 1862 edn); COPAC. LOCATION Dt, L, InND Loeber coll.
COMMENTARY A romance set in England where Mrs Chetwynd raises three children: her daughter Alice, Walter, an orphan nephew, and a ward, Etta. Walter and Etta are very fond of each other, but before they become formally attached, Mrs Chetwynd sends Walter to his guardian to be trained in business. Walter's and Alice's money is invested in this business. When Mrs Chetwynd is dying, she extracts from Walter the promise that he will marry Alice, which he does. In the meantime, the business goes bankrupt and Walter tries to make a living by writing. His wife dies. He inherits Chetwynd Park from an uncle and eventually marries Etta [ML].

P58   *Grace Clifford. A novel* (by Miss H. Bouverie Pigott).
        + London: John Maxwell & Co., 1865, 3 vols. SOURCE Allibone, ii, p. 1594; COPAC. LOCATION L. COMMENTARY No Irish content [ML].

P59   *The Cravens of Cravenscroft* (by Miss H. Bouverie Pigott).
        + London: Tinsley Bros, 1873, 3 vols. SOURCE Wolff, 5563; COPAC. LOCATION L. COMMENTARY No Irish content [ML].

PILKINGTON, Miss, fl. 1790. Novelist, Miss P was possibly Irish as she wrote two Irish novels. Two other novels are set in revolutionary France, and all were printed by the Minerva Press in London. In 1806, a Miss Pilkington married Charles Carrothers in Ireland. A branch of the Pilkington family had an estate at Tore (near Tyrrelspass, Co. Westmeath; probably also known as Torr, now ruined). Miss P should not be confused with the author Mary Pilkington or the poet and memoirist Laetitia Pilkington (1701–50). SOURCE Blain, p. 855; H. Farrar (ed.), *Irish marriages* (London, 1897), ii, p. 358; *Landed gentry*, 1904, p. 486; *Vanishing country houses*, p. 144; G. Taylor & A. Skinner, *Maps of the roads of Ireland* (Dublin, 1783), 2nd edn, p. 74.

P60   *Delia, a pathetic and interesting tale* [anon.].
        + London: William Lane, 1790, 4 vols. SOURCE Blakey, p. 150; Blain, p. 855; Block, p. 184 (who mistakenly identifies Mary Pilkington as its author); Forster 2, 3341; Raven, 1790:59; ESTC t107742. LOCATION L, NUC.
        Dublin: P. Byrne, P. Wogan, Grueber & M'Allister. J. Moore, J. Jones & W. Jones, 1790, 2 vols. SOURCE Raven 2, 1790:59; ESTC n00635. LOCATION Dt, PU.
COMMENTARY Epistolary novel set largely in Ireland in which women's abilities and education are discussed. Delia, one of the novel's heroines, survives the malicious breaking of her first love affair; but her lover's return and violent reproaches on her marriage kill her [Blain].

P61   *Rosina. A novel* [anon.].
        + London: William Lane, 1793, 5 vols. SOURCE Blakey, p. 163; Blain, p. 855; McBurney & Taylor, 776; Forster 2, 3342; Raven 2, 1793:35; ESTC t066923. LOCATION L, IU.

Dublin: P. Wogan, P. Byrne, J, Moore, W. Jones & J. Rice, 1793, 3 vols. SOURCE Raven 2, 1793:35; ESTC no12943. LOCATION CtY.
COMMENTARY Concerns the FitzOsborne family residing in Ireland [ML].

P62 *The subterranean cavern; or, memoirs of Antoinette de Montflorance* [anon.].
London: William Lane, 1798, 4 vols. SOURCE Blakey, p. 187; Blain, p. 855; Gecker, 812; Forster 2, 3343; Raven 2, 1798:55; ESTC no24522. LOCATION PU.
COMMENTARY Set in revolutionary France [Blain].

P63 *The accusing spirit; or, De Courcy and Eglantine. A romance* [anon.].
+ London: Lane & Newman, 1802, 4 vols. (ill. Rothwell, Richter). SOURCE Blakey, p. 201; British Fiction; Garside, 1802:54. LOCATION Corvey CME 3–628–47004–8, O.
COMMENTARY Attribution to Miss Pilkington mentioned in the Minerva Library Catalogue of 1814. Set in revolutionary France and contains a plea to philosophers to keep their dangerous notions to themselves and enjoy toleration without disturbing society. Despite the Marquis De Courcy's name, there are no clear Irish connections [Blain; RL; Blakey].

PINKERTON, Allan, b. Glasgow (Scotland), 1819, d. Chicago 1884. Novelist and detective, AP was the son of William Pinkerton, a sergeant in the police force, and the founder of the detective agency that bears his name. As a young man he was a Chartist. He emigrated to the US in 1842 and settled in Chicago where he worked as a cooper and as an abolitionist, worked for the underground railroad. He became deputy sheriff of Cook Co. and in 1850 was appointed the first detective in the city, while establishing his private detective agency. In 1861 he organized the US secret service and he was an agent during the Civil War and organized counter-espionage activities from Washington (DC). After the war which he moved to New York and then Philadelphia. His agency tracked railroad and bank robbers, including a botched ambush on the outlaw Jesse James. Between 1874 and 1884 he published 16 detective stories, some imaginative and some based on true cases, where he was helped by agents who shared their memories. SOURCE Allibone Suppl., ii, p. 1237; ANB; DAB; Wright, ii, p. 258, iii, pp 426–7.

P64 *The Molly Maguires and the detectives* (by Allan Pinkerton).
New York: G.W. Carleton, 1877. SOURCE Wright, iii, 4167; OCLC. LOCATION MH.
New York: G.W. Dillingham, 1887 (new and enlarged edn). SOURCE OCLC. LOCATION CtY.
COMMENTARY Based on the episode of a Pinkerton agent, James McParlan, infiltrating the Molly Maguires, a secret agrarian agitation society begun in Ireland in the early-nineteenth century that spread to the US around 1835 and became active in the coal fields of eastern Pennsylvania. The arrest and execution of several members of the group led to accusations of Pinkertons as *agents provocateur*, while others considered the incident as a blow against terrorism in the US [ANB; DAB].

PIPER, A.G., pseud. 'F. Clinton Barrington', fl. 1850. American novelist, AGP was possibly of Scottish or perhaps Irish descent since his only known publication outside of America, *Fitz-Hern; or, the Irish patriot chief* (Boston, 1865) deals with Ireland and was also published in Glasgow. He specialized in maritime fiction. In America he published, among other works, *The Lady Imogen; or, the wreck and the chase* (Boston, 1850), *Conrado de Beltran; or, the buccaneer of the gulf* (Boston, 1851), and *The young fisherman; or, the cruiser of the English Channel* (Boston, 1853). SOURCE Allibone Suppl., i, p. 100 [under Barrington]; NSTC; Wright, i & ii (list of novels).

P65 *Fitz-Hern; or, the rover of the Irish seas. A story of Galway bay* (by 'F. Clinton Barrington').

Boston: Elliott, Thomes & Talbot, 1865 (Ten Cent Novelettes, No. 15). LOCATION NUC.

Glasgow, London: Cameron & Ferguson, [1870?] (as *The free flag; or, the Irish patriot chief: A story of Galway Bay*). SOURCE OCLC; Brown, 181. LOCATION KU-S.

COMMENTARY Brown mentions a Glasgow edn by the same publishers under the title *Fitz-Hern; or, the Irish patriot chief*. This edn has not been identified, and must be the same as F. Clinton Harrington's [*sic*] *FitzHern; or, the rover of the Irish seas. A story of Galway bay* by the same publisher and advertised in McHenry *Irish tales* (Glasgow, [190?]). Gothic fiction set around Galway Bay telling the story of wicked married bishops, scheming foreign monks, and friars in the role of villains. The hero is a smuggler of noble birth who always escapes from their clutches, and finally marries the heroine [Brown].

'A PLAIN ENGLISHMAN', pseud. See SHEAHAN, Thomas.

PLUNKET, the Hon. Frederica. See PLUNKET, the Hon. Frederica Louisa Edith.

PLUNKET, the Hon. Frederica Louisa Edith (known as the Hon. Frederica Plunket), fl. 1880s. Novelist, FLEP was the daughter of Thomas Span Plunket, 2nd Baron Plunket (1792–1866), who became bishop of Tuam, Killala, and Achonry, and Louisa Jane Foster of Fane Valley (Co. Louth). The authors the Hon. Isabella-Catharine Plunket§ and the Hon. Louisa Greene§ were her nieces. SOURCE CP, x, p. 557.

P66   *Taken to heart. A novel* (by the Hon. Frederica Plunket).
       + London: John & Robert Maxwell, [1885]. SOURCE Allibone Suppl., ii, p. 1240.
LOCATION L.

COMMENTARY Beechwood, an Elizabethan house, is owned by Mr. Vaughan, who is single. After the death of a friend, he takes it upon himself to look after the friend's daughter, Tommy. He does not realise that this girl is 17 years old and very good-looking. Eventually Mr. Vaughan marries her off and he marries her governess. No Irish content [ML].

PLUNKET, the Hon. Isabel. See PLUNKET, the Hon. Isabella-Catharine.

PLUNKET (sometimes spelled Plunkett), the Hon. Isabella-Catherine (also Katherine; known as the Hon. Isabella Plunket), b. 1847. Writer of religious and moral stories for children, I-CP was the youngest daughter and one of fourteen children of John Span Plunket, 3rd Baron Plunket of Newton (1793–1871), crown prosecutor on the Munster circuit, and Charlotte, daughter of Charles Kendal Bushe, chief justice of the queen's bench. Her father was seated at Old Connaught House (later called Old Conna), Bray (Co. Wicklow), and had a town residence at St Stephen's Green, Dublin. The family included the great Catholic MP and orator the Rt Hon. William Conygham, Lord Plunket, whose eloquence and advocacy on behalf of Catholics' rights was crucial to the passage of the emancipation act of 1829. Aside from children's books, I-CP wrote two works for mothers: *Words of help for working women* [Edinburgh, 1877], and *Thoughts of peace. Six short addresses for mothers meetings*, London, 1889). Her *More than conqueror* (London, 1871) consists of a series of moral and religious tracts. Her sister, the Hon. Emmeline-Mary, published a children's book of singing games with music *Merrie games in rhyme from ye olden time* (London, [1886]). Another sister, the Hon. Louisa Greene§, was also a children's writer. SOURCE Allibone Suppl., ii, p. 1240; BLC; CP, x, p. 557; E. Lodge, *The peerage and baronetage* (London, 1897), 66th edn, p. 536; NCBEL 4, p. 1850; Osborne, p. 852; RIA/DIB.

P67   *Hester's fortune; or, pride and humility* (by the Hon. Isabella Plunket).
       + London: Frederick Warne & Co.; New York: Scribner, Welford & Co., [1870] (ill.).
       SOURCE Allibone Suppl., ii, p. 1240; NCBEL 4, p. 1850 ([1871] edn); OCLC.
       LOCATION L.
       New York: E.P. Dutton & Co., J. & W. Rider, 1871. SOURCE OCLC. LOCATION NN.

P68   *The children's band; or, the trial of Paul's faith* (by the Hon. Isabella Plunket).
       London: Frederick Warne & Co., [1874] (ill.). SOURCE Allibone Suppl., ii, p. 1240;
       NCBEL 4, p. 1850; OCLC. LOCATION L.

P69   *"The cricket green" or "Malcolm's luck"* (by the Hon. Isabella Catherine Plunket).
       + Edinburgh, London: Gall & Inglis, [1876]. SOURCE COPAC. LOCATION L.
       + London: Gall & Inglis, [1897] (as *Malcolm's luck; or, the cricket green*). LOCATION
       L.

P70   *Harold Hardy's revenge: the cruise of the 'Merry Mermaid'* (by the Hon. Isabella
       Catherine Plunket).
       London: Gall & Inglis, [1886] (ill.). SOURCE Allibone Suppl., ii, p. 1240; COPAC.
       LOCATION L.

P71   *Kathleen's desire* (by the Hon. Isabella Catherine Plunket).
       London: Gall & Inglis, [1889]. SOURCE COPAC. LOCATION L.
       COMMENTARY 60pp [BLC].

PLUNKET, the Hon. Louisa Lelias. See GREENE, the Hon. Louisa Lelias.

PLUNKETT, Mrs. See PLUNKETT, Mrs Elizabeth.

PLUNKETT, Mrs Elizabeth (née Gunning; also known as **Miss Gunning** and **Mrs
Plunkett**), b. 1769, d. Melford House (Suffolk) 1823. Novelist, translator, story writer and
children's writer, EP was a daughter of Gen. John Gunning of Castle Coote (Co. Roscommon),
who 'was then deputy adjutant-general in north Britain', and Susannah Minifie of Fairwaters
(Som.). She grew up in Edinburgh (and not in Ireland as far as is known). Her mother and
aunt were both novelists and their reputation for breathless prose gave rise to a writing style
called 'minific'. EP, at age 21, caused a major scandal when she – or her mother – was accused
of forging letters implying that the marquess of Blandford, heir to the duke of Marlborough,
was her suitor. She was disowned by her father who dismissed her and her mother from his
household, but she won the patronage of the duchess of Bedford, Blanford's grandmother.
She married in 1803 the Irish major James Plunkett of Kinnaird (Co. Roscommon), an officer of slender means, with whom she had several children. She translated novels, drama, science and other works from French and German. Her portrait was published in *The farmer's
boy* (London, 1802, 4 vols.). Since EP is not known to have lived in Ireland for an extended
period of time, only those novels with Irish content are listed below. For her portrait, see
Elmes, and the frontispiece of her *The farmer's boy* (London, 1802), vol. 1. SOURCE Allibone,
ii, p. 1612 [under Mrs Plunkett]; Alston, p. 178; BD, p. 278 (list of novels); Blain, pp 468–9
[under Gunning]; Elmes, p. 169; I. Gantz, *The pastel portrait* (London 1963); NCBEL 4, pp
983–4; ODNB [under Gunning]; RIA/DIB.

P72   *The farmer's boy; a novel* (by Miss Gunning).
       London: B. Crosby & Co., 1802, 4 vols. (ill.). SOURCE British Fiction; Garside, 1802:26.
       LOCATION Corvey CME 3–628–47582; L, NUC.
       Dublin: William Porter, 1803. SOURCE British Fiction; OCLC. LOCATION D.
       COMMENTARY The story is set entirely in Ireland. The main character is Lord Mount
       Talbot who in the end is reunited with his children [ML].

P73　　*The exile of Erin. A novel* (by Mrs Plunkett, late Miss Gunning).
London: B. Crosby & Co., 1808, 3 vols. SOURCE Blain, p. 468; Brown 2, 1308; British Fiction; Garside, 1808:90; Gecker, 822. LOCATION Dt, L, MH, PU, NUC.
+ Alexandria (VA): Printed by Cotton & Stewart, 1809. LOCATION DCU, NUC.
COMMENTARY Epistolary family and romantic saga set in Ireland, England and America. In the dedication to the public the author asserts the story is based on fact and states that as a woman she has avoided anything like a political discussion, well aware how ill-qualified one of her sex is to enter on such a topic. Francis Portland is left responsible for the welfare of his mother and sister, Rosanna, after his father's banishment to America. Rosanna is sent to Lady Avenmore, a relative in England, who receives her with great kindness. The separation of the family creates extreme distress. Mr Portland lives in a cottage near Philadelphia, which he bought from another exiled Irish family, Mr and Mrs and Erin Fitzgerald. Mr Fitzgerald, descended from a noble family, had participated in the rebellion of 1798, which he realized too late led his country into ruin. Rosanna writes to her mother that Avenmore Castle has become gay since the return of the son, the earl of Avenmore. Also present is the marquis of Desmond who is the fiancée of one of Lady Avenmore's daughters. Lord Desmond has taken an interest in the fate of Mr Portland and is willing to exert himself on his behalf. Mrs Portland writes an account of the troubles that her husband encountered and mentions that on their estate there was a family named Jenkins who had a daughter, Emma, who was an exceptional child. Francis Portland was very attached to Emma, but an alliance was out of the question. A letter arrives explaining that Emma is in reality the daughter of Lord and Lady Stanley, to whom she must return. The earl of Avenmore falls in love with Rosanna but does not want to marry her because of the blot on her father's name. However, her father returns from exile, Rosanna marries the earl, and her brother marries his Emma. The book contains a play written by Revd Osmond, the minister of Avenmore [ML].

PLUNKETT, Mary Sophia Elizabeth. See PONSONBY, the Hon. Mary Sophia Elizabeth.

PLUNKETT, Robert. See NUGENT, Robert.

POLLARD, Eliza Fanny. See POLLARD, Eliza Frances.

POLLARD, Eliza Frances (known as Eliza Fanny Pollard), d. before 1917. Novelist and children's writer, probably English, EFP wrote a large number of historical works for juveniles. SOURCE Allibone Suppl., ii, p. 1241; Alston, p. 350; Brown, p. 255; Daims, pp 564–5.
P74　　*The king's signet; or, the story of a Huguenot family* (by Eliza Fanny Pollard).
London, Glasgow, Edinburgh, Dublin: Blackie & Son, 1900 (ill. G. Demain Hammond). SOURCE Alston, p. 350; Brown, 1384; COPAC. LOCATION L (1909 edn), NUC.
+ London, Glasgow, Bombay: Black & Son, n.d. (new edn; ill. G. Demain Hammond). LOCATION InND Loeber coll.
COMMENTARY An historical novel for juveniles set in France during the revocation of the Edict of Nantes, which tells of the scattering of some Huguenot families from Normandy. Via different routes they end up in England and a number of them enlist under William III. One of the characters, the marquis de Ruvigny, fights in Ireland and is made earl of Galway and given the confiscated estate of Portarlington (Co. Laois), where he settles with a large number of Huguenots [ML].

POLSON, Thomas R.J., b. Enniskillen (Co. Fermanagh) 1823, d. Ireland? 1908. Novelist, poet and newspaperman, TRJP was, according to Brown, an Englishman, but this appears to be an error. Originally a private soldier who owned and managed the *Fermanagh Mail* (Enniskillen) for about forty years, according to O'Donoghue he was a town councillor, a poet, and a member of the RIA. SOURCE Brady, p. 206; Brown, p. 255; O'Donoghue, p. 386; RIA/DIB.

P75   *The fortune teller's intrigue; or, life in Ireland before the Union. A tale of agrarian outrage* (by Thomas R.J. Polson; dedicated to Henry T.L. Corry).
Dublin: James McGlashan; London: Wm. S. Orr, 1848, 3 vols. SOURCE Brown, 1385 (mistakenly states as date 1847); Block, p. 187. LOCATION Dt, L.
COMMENTARY Set in Co. Clare in the late-eighteenth century, and is anti-Catholic in tone [Brown].

PONSONBY, Mrs. See **PONSONBY, Mrs Catherine**.

PONSONBY, Mrs Catherine (also known as **Mrs Ponsonby**), fl. 1841. Novelist, poet and biographer, CP is included in O'Donoghue's *Irish poets* and so she probably was Irish. According to Colman, she 'evidently emigrated to Scotland, or lived there for an extensive period of time'. She was the editor of the annual *Forget-Me-Not* (London, 1847; to which she had contributed in 1845), and contributed to the *Christian Family Advocate* (London, 1852), and the *Keepsake* (London, 1853). She also wrote *Lays of the lakes, and other poems of description and reflection* (Edinburgh, 1850) and a religious work. SOURCE Allibone, ii, p. 1620 [under Mrs Ponsonby]; BLC; Colman, p. 190; Jarndyce cat. 162/491, 563; O'Donoghue, p. 386; Sutherland, p. 508 [under Lady Emily Ponsonby§].

P76   *The Countess D'Auvergne; or, sufferings of Protestants in France in the sixteenth century* (by Mrs Catherine Ponsonby).
Edinburgh: William Whyte & Co., 1841. SOURCE Allibone, ii, p. 1620; COPAC.
LOCATION E.

P77   *Border wardens. A historical romance* (by Mrs Catherine Ponsonby).
+ London: John Mortimer, 1844, 3 vols. SOURCE Allibone, ii, p. 1620. LOCATION L.
COMMENTARY Historical novel set in England in the time of Queen Elizabeth I [RL].

P78   *The Desborough family; A novel* (by Mrs Ponsonby).
+ London: John Mortimer, 1845, 3 vols. SOURCE Allibone, ii, p. 1620. LOCATION L (3 vols. in 1).
COMMENTARY The title could be an allusion to the author's family's title, the earl of Bessborough. The novel is set in Kent among the upper classes [RL].

P79   *The protégé; A novel* (by Mrs Ponsonby).
+ London: H. Hurst, 1847, 3 vols. SOURCE Allibone, ii, p. 1620. LOCATION L.
COMMENTARY Set in England, and features Walter Euston, who becomes the protégé of the duke of Basenthwaite [RL].

PONSONBY, Lady Emily. See **Mary PONSONBY, Lady Emily Charlotte Mary**.

PONSONBY, Lady Emily Charlotte Mary (known as **Lady Emily Ponsonby**), b. London 1817, d. London 1877. English novelist, ECMP was the third daughter of John William Ponsonby, 4th earl of Bessborough (lord lieutenant of Ireland, d. 1847) and Lady Maria Fane, daughter of the 10th earl of Westmoreland. She was the sister of the author Lady Georgiana Ponsonby§, and a niece of the author Lady Caroline Lamb§. Her father's family estate was at Bessborough (Co. Kilkenny), and from 1826 to 1832 he represented the Kilkenny constituency in parliament. He was lord lieutenant of Co. Carlow from 1831 to 1838 and of Co. Kilkenny from 1838 until his death. After ECMP's mother's death in 1834, she took over the management of the household at Bessborough and acted as her father's secretary, a duty that became more onerous after the earl had a bad fall. ECMP never married. She began to publish only after her father's death, and published 15 novels anonymously. Most of her books were romances about the upper classes. She died 'at her home' in London in 1877. Some of her letters are listed in Sutton. SOURCE Allibone, ii, p. 1620; Allibone Suppl., ii, p. 1243; Blain, p. 863; Sir B. Burke & A.P. Burke, *A genealogical and heraldic dictionary of the peerage* (London, 68th edn), p. 160; Colman, p. 191; ODNB; O'Donoghue, p. 386; Sutherland, pp 507–8; Sutton, ii, p. 766.

P80   *The discipline of life* [anon.].
     London: Henry Colburn, 1848, 3 vols. SOURCE Alston, p. 352; Block, p. 187; DNB.
     LOCATION L.
     COMMENTARY Deals with two sisters and the trials and temptations of common life, and advocates self-sacrifice for women [Blain].

P81   *Pride and irresolution. A new series of the discipline of life* [anon.].
     London: Henry Colburn, 1850, 3 vols. SOURCE Wolff, 5590. LOCATION L.
     COMMENTARY Contents: 'Susan Greville; or, irresolution. A domestic story', 'Ada Mowbray; or, pride' [Wolff].

P82   *Clare abbey; or, the trials of youth* [anon.].
     + London: Colburn & Co., 1851, 2 vols. SOURCE Alston, p. 352; DNB. LOCATION D, L.
     COMMENTARY No Irish content [ML].

P83   *Mary Gray, and other tales and verses* [anon.].
     London: G. Hoby, 1852. SOURCE Wolff, 5587. LOCATION L.
     COMMENTARY Contents: 'Mary Gray', 'Passage of my life' [by another hand], 'A tale of second love', and verse [Wolff].

P84   *Edward Willoughby. A tale* [anon.].
     + London: Hurst & Blackett, 1854, 2 vols. SOURCE Alston, p. 352. LOCATION L.

P85   *The young Lord* [anon.].
     + London: Hurst & Blackett, 1856, 2 vols. SOURCE Alston, p. 352. LOCATION L.

P86   *The two brothers* [anon.].
     London: Richard Bentley, 1858, 3 vols. SOURCE Wolff, 5592. LOCATION L.
     COMMENTARY Not to be confused with Mathilde Raven's *The two brothers* (London, 1850, 2 vols.) which is a translation from the German [Wolff, iii, p. 281].

P87   *A mother's trial* [anon.].
     London: Hurst & Blackett, 1859. SOURCE Wolff, 5588. LOCATION L.

P88   *Katherine and her sisters* [anon.].
     London: Hurst & Blackett, 1861, 3 vols. SOURCE Wolff, 5586. LOCATION L.
     COMMENTARY A Cinderella tale of three sisters [Blain].

P89   *Mary Lyndsay* (by Lady Emily Ponsonby).
     + London: Hurst & Blackett, 1863, 3 vols. SOURCE Alston, p. 352; OCLC; DNB.
     LOCATION L.
     New York: Harper & Bros, 1863 (Library of Select Novels, No. 235). SOURCE OCLC.
     LOCATION MH.

P90   *Violet Osborne* (by Lady Emily Ponsonby).
     London: Hurst & Blackett, 1865, 3 vols. SOURCE Wolff, 5593; OCLC. LOCATION L.

P91   *Sir Owen Fairfax* (by Lady Emily Ponsonby).
     London: Hurst & Blackett, 1866, 3 vols. SOURCE Wolff, 5591; COPAC. LOCATION L.

P92   *A story of two cousins* (by Lady Emily Ponsonby).
+ London: Smith, Elder & Co., 1868. SOURCE Alston, p. 352; OCLC. LOCATION L.

P93   *Nora* (by Lady Emily Ponsonby).
+ London: Hurst & Blackett, 1870, 3 vols. SOURCE Alston, p. 352; OCLC. LOCATION L.

P94   *Oliva Beaumont and Lord Latimer* (by Lady Emily Ponsonby).
London: Hurst & Blackett, 1873, 3 vols. SOURCE Wolff, 5589; COPAC. LOCATION L.

PONSONBY, Lady Georgiana, b. 1807, d. 1861. Novelist, GP was the eldest daughter of John William Ponsonby, 4th earl of Bessborough (who died in 1847 as lord lieutenant of Ireland) and Lady Maria Fane, daughter of the 10th earl of Westmoreland. She was the sister of the author Lady Emily Ponsonby§ and niece of the author Lady Caroline Lamb§. GP married Revd Sackville-Gardiner Bourke (a close relative of the earl of Mayo) in 1839, with whom she had five children. The authorship of the following book is evident from a copy in the University of Texas, Austin, where she is referred to as Lady Georgiana Bourke. However, she was single when she wrote this work. SOURCE E. Lodge, *The peerage and baronetage of the British Empire* (London, 1897), pp 75, 464; Personal communication, Steve Weissman, Feb. 2002; RL.

P95   *The Etheringtons* [anon.].
+ London: George Wightman, 1833. SOURCE OCLC; Garside 2, 1833:61. LOCATION TxU, InND Loeber coll.

COMMENTARY William Etherington is the son of a farmer descended from Puritans at the time of Cromwell. Despite a proper upbringing, his reckless nature leads him to drink and gambling and the companionship of unsuitable friends. The loss at dice of his mother's legacy prompts William to go to sea, but in the end he returns a reformed man, and marries his childhood sweetheart Kathleen O'Neil. The story includes descriptions of an Irish wake ('barbarous') and a county fair; some attempt is made to reproduce Irish dialect [Personal communication, S. Weissman, Feb. 2002].

PONSONBY, Lady Louisa May Caroline. See LAMB, Lady Caroline.

PONSONBY, the Hon. Mary Sophia Elizabeth (née Plunkett), d. London 1921. Unpublished novelist, MSEP was the daughter of Edward Plunkett, 16th Lord Dunsany, and Anne Constance Dutton, daughter of Lord Shelburne. Her brother was Horace Plunkett, who pioneered the agricultural cooperative movement in Ireland. She married Capt. Chambré Ponsonby in 1873. He inherited Kilcooly Abbey estate (Co. Tipperary) and other lands in 1880. She had a reputation as a bluestocking, and started writing either before or just after her marriage. Her husband, seeing the worsening situation over land issues and agitation in Ireland, travelled to America to investigate settling there, but died on the return voyage in 1884. For a while, with the help of her brother, she continued to live at Kilcooly Abbey. She spent the last years of her life in London. SOURCE W.G. Neely, *Kilcooly, land and people in Tipperary* (n.l., 1983), pp 115–16, 119, 121, 128, 164; Burke, Sir B. & A.P. Burke, *A genealogical and heraldic dictionary of the peerage and baronetage* (London, 1906, 68th edn), p. 549.

P96   *[Untitled novel]* (by the Hon. Mary Sophia Elizabeth Ponsonby).

COMMENTARY Unpublished novel, set probably in Co. Tipperary against the background of the Fenian rising, and which was critical of the lower class of Irish Protestants. The manuscript is now lost, but a few extracts were published by Neely [W.G. Neely, *Kilcooly, land and people in Tipperary* (n.l., 1983), pp 115–16, 119, 121, 128, 164; Personal communication, Mrs M. Turnton, Kildale, Whitby (north Yorks.), Feb. 1997].

PORTER, Miss A.M. See **PORTER, Anna Maria.**

PORTER, Anna Maria (also known as **Miss A.M. Porter**), b. Salisbury (Wilts.) 1778 (according to ODNB and not 1780 as in many other sources), d. Bristol (Avon) 1832. English historical novelist and poet of Irish background, AMP was the daughter of Jane Blenkinsop and William Porter, surgeon to the 6th Inniskilling Dragoons, who was of Ulster extraction and who died in 1779 when she was one year old. Her sister was the well-known novelist Jane Porter, with whom she co-authored several works (see below), while her brothers William Ogilvie Porter and Robert Ker Porter were also writers of fiction. Her preface to *The lake of Killarney* (London, 1804) is dated from Thames Ditton (Surrey) in that year. She was described by Mrs S.C. Hall as 'blonde, and by nature gay'. Only AMP's known Irish works are listed below. For her portrait, see Elmes. SOURCE Allibone, ii, p. 1644; Belanger, 5; Blain, pp 865–6; British Fiction (Update 4, under 1809); Brown, p. 255; BD, p. 280; Elmes, p. 170; Frank, pp 335–8; S.C. Hall, pp 128–31; NCBEL 4, pp 985–6; ODNB; O'Donoghue, p. 386; PRONI, MS D/2922; Todd, pp 540–2.

P97   *The lake of Killarney. A novel* (by Anna Maria Porter; dedicated to Revd Percival Stockdale, rector of Lesbury, Northumb.).
+ London: T.N. Longman & O. Rees, 1804, 3 vols. SOURCE British Fiction; Garside, 1804:57; Wolff, 5601. LOCATION Corvey CME 3–628–8345–X, Ireland related fiction, L (1838 edn), O, NUC.
London: Tegg, 1839 (new edn). SOURCE Brown, 1387. LOCATION NUC.
+ London: Charles H. Clarke, 1856 (as *Rose de Blaquière; or, the lake of Killarney*). SOURCE NCBEL 3, p. 757. LOCATION L.
+ New York: Inskeep & Bradford; Boston: William M'Ilhenny, 1810. LOCATION D.
Philadelphia: Thomas De Silver, 1810, 2 vols. LOCATION NUC.
COMMENTARY Set in the late-eighteenth century in Killarney (Co. Kerry) and Dublin, the plot concerns the events and misunderstandings that keep apart the hero and the heroine [Brown].

P98   *Honor O'Hara. A novel* (by Miss A.M. Porter).
+ London: Longman, Rees, Orme, Brown & Green, 1826, 3 vols. SOURCE Block, p. 188; Brown, 1386; British Fiction; Garside, 1826:63; Wolff, 5598. LOCATION Corvey CME 3–628–48299–2, Ireland related fiction, L, ViU, InND Loeber coll.
Paris: Pigoreau, 1827, 4 vols. (trans. by Jean Cohen as *Honorine O'Hara*). LOCATION Dt.
New York: J. & J. Harper, 1827, 2 vols. LOCATION NUC.
COMMENTARY A romantic tale set in Northumbria where the heroine Honor O'Hara, a young Irish woman who has lost both her parents in Ireland, has come with her Irish nurse to stay with her uncle, a minister. Her uncle's coarse wife makes it difficult for Honor to become acquainted with society people. Over time, however, her pleasant character endears her to the people she meets. Honor becomes fond of Delaval FitzArthur, but pride forbids her to accept his proposal. She regrets this decision, but she believes that he is going to marry an heiress who will be able to restore the fallen fortunes of the FitzArthurs. Eventually, fate brings Honor and Delaval together again and they marry [ML].

P99   *Tales round a winter hearth* (by Jane Porter and Anna Maria Porter).
+ London: Longman, Rees, Orme, Brown & Green, 1826, 2 vols. SOURCE British Fiction; Garside, 1826:64; NCBEL 4, p. 985; Wolff, 5610. LOCATION Corvey CME 3–628–54704–0, Dt, L, ViU, InND Loeber coll.
COMMENTARY Some of the following stories are a retelling of existing tales. AMP contributed, 'Glenowan, a Scottish tradition', 'Lord Howth, an Irish legend' (a little rat attaches itself to an Irish nobleman, Lord Howth. He ties a gold thread to one of the animal's legs so that he

may recognize it but in a fit of irritation, he kills the rat. Later on, he rescues a girl from the waves and marries her. She wears a gold bracelet that he is told she can never take off. One day, while she is sleeping, he removes the bracelet and finds inside it the rat's gold thread and she dies on the spot), 'Jeannie Halliday, a tale of our own times', 'My chamber in the old house of Huntercombe', 'The pilgrimage of Berenice, a record of Burnham Abbey' [ML; Garside; NCBEL].

P100　*Coming out; and the field of the forty footsteps* (by Jane Porter and Anna Maria Porter).

　　London: Longman, Rees, Orme, Brown & Green, 1828, 3 vols. SOURCE British Fiction; Garside, 1828:64; NCBEL 4, p. 985; Wolff, 5609. LOCATION Corvey CME 3–628–8357–3, Ireland related fiction, Dt, L.

　　Paris: Mame & Delauney-Vallée, 1828 (trans. by Comtesse Molé as *Entrée dans le monde*). SOURCE Garside, 1828:64; CCF. LOCATION BNF.

　　New York: J. & J. Harper, 1828. SOURCE Garside, 1828:64; OCLC. LOCATION MH.

COMMENTARY 'Coming out; a tale of the nineteenth century' (by AMP: Alicia, the daughter of Col. and Mrs Barry is educated at home in Ireland. The parents hope that Alicia may come out in London under the patronage of Lady Donnington. However, the family is threatened with financial ruin, and to escape arrest the colonel leaves Ireland to visit his Jamaican property. The only family with which Alicia has been intimate is that of Mr M'Manus, who had taken care of an orphan boy, Jocelyn Hastings. She is wooed by earl St Lawrence, who turns out to have seduced a young Italian woman. Eventually, Hastings marries Alicia), 'The field of the forty footsteps, a romance of the seventeenth century' (by Jane Porter) [RL; *La Belle Assemblée*, 3rd ser. 7 (Mar. 1828, pp 128–30)].

PORTER, Classon, b. (Co. Antrim?) 1858, d. 1944. Barrister and short story writer. Can be identified with CP, the son of Revd Classon Porter of Larne (Co. Antrim) and E. Wallace. CP graduated BA at TCD, and was admitted to the King's Inns, Dublin, in 1879, Gray's Inns, London, in 1882, and was called to the Irish Bar in 1882. SOURCE Ferguson, p. 283.

P101　*Witches, warlocks, and ghosts* (by Classon Porter).

　　+ Belfast: Reprinted from the *Northern Whig*, 1885. LOCATION InND Loeber coll.

COMMENTARY 31pp. Ghost stories. Contents: 'Ulster sketches: The witches of Islandmagee', 'Witches and warlocks', 'Some ghost stories: Lord Tyrone's ghost', 'Haddock's ghost', 'Mrs. Loslin's ghost' [RL].

PORTER, Francis (Frank) Thorpe, b. Dublin 1801, d. Ireland? 1882. Miscellaneous writer and translator, barrister and magistrate, FTP was the son of William Porter of Willmount, Rathfarnham (Co. Dublin), a bookseller and printer who was implicated in the 1798 rebellion, and Susanna Bacon. He entered TCD in 1817 and graduated BA in 1823 and MA in 1832. He was admitted to the King's Inns in 1823, to Gray's Inn (London) in 1825, and called to the Irish Bar in 1827. He was on the Leinster circuit from 1827 to 1840. Between 1840 and 1870 he was a police magistrate in Dublin. He contributed a serial, 'The romance of life – old prisons' to *Duffy's Hibernian Sixpenny Magazine* (Dublin, 1860–61). He published *Gleanings and reminiscences* (Dublin, 1875), a collection of historical accounts and memories. He also translated Elie-Bertrand Berthet's§ *The drapier's daughter. A tale of Paris in the olden time* (Dublin, 1852), and occasionally he wrote songs. He was a member of a social circle that included Revd Mortimer O'Sullivan§, Charles Lever§, and other notables, who often met for dinner at P. Brophy's residence in Dawson Street, Dublin. FTP may be identified with the F.T. Porter who wrote on legal issues in Ireland. An American eulogy in the *Illustrated Celtic Monthly* (New York, 1879) praises him as 'a true Irishman in temperament and intellect, a walking repository of anecdote and information ...' SOURCE Allibone, ii, p. 1645; Allibone Suppl., ii, p. 1245; B & S, p. 675; Boase, ii, p. 1590; Emerald Isle cat. 23/926; FitzPatrick, pp 142, 145; *The Illustrated Celtic Monthly*, 1 (1879), pp 13–15; Irish pseudonyms; Keane, p. 406; O'Donoghue, p. 387; RIA/DIB; Wolff, 410.

P102   *Twenty years' recollections of a Irish police magistrate* (by Frank Thorpe Porter). Dublin: Hodges, Foster & Figgis; London: Simpkin, 1880, 6th edn. SOURCE Sadleir, 3519 (1880, 8th edn); Topp 8, 618. LOCATION NUC (1880, 8th edn), InND Loeber coll. (1880, 9th edn.).

COMMENTARY No copy of the 1st edn located; a 10th edn appeared in 1880. This appears to be based on FP's *Gleanings and reminiscences* (Dublin, 1875). Anecdotes about Irish judicial matters in the eighteenth and nineteenth centuries, mainly from the author's own experiences as a magistrate in Dublin. Written in semi-fictional style with the use of dialogues [ML; Topp].

PORTER, Revd James, b. Tamna Wood, near Ballindrait (Co. Donegal) (Strabane, Co. Tyrone, according to Brady) *c*.1753, d. Co. Down? 1798. Presbyterian clergyman, songwriter, satirist and nationalist, JP was the son of Alexander Porter, a farmer and scutch miller. He was a schoolmaster at Dromore (Co. Down) and after his marriage to Anna Knox in 1780, he moved to Drogheda (Co. Louth). He studied divinity at Glasgow College *c*.1784 and became a Presbyterian minister at Greyabbey (Co. Down) in 1787, supplementing his income by farming and introducing many mechanical and scientific advances to his work. He was a supporter of Catholic emancipation and joined the Volunteers, a part-time military force raised for defence in 1778 and 1779 that later became a political force until it was suppressed in 1793. He was a contributor to a collection of patriotic songs, *Paddy's resource*, which was published in the *Northern Star* (Belfast, 1795), the literary organ of the nationalist movement. A critic of the government, he travelled in 1796 throughout the province of Ulster, supposedly for the purpose of delivering lectures on his study of natural philosophy. In reality he was spreading the principles of the League of United Irishmen. That same year he wrote a series of letters to the marquess of Downshire attacking prime minister William Pitt's policies, which caused the paper to be suspended. On the outbreak of the rebellion in 1798, a large reward was offered for JP's capture, although he had never been a rebel and had advocated peaceful reform. However, his satire *Billy Bluff and squire Firebrand*, published in 1796 (a later edn of *Billy Bluff and the 'squire; or, a sketch of the times'*), which was immensely popular, was considered to be treasonable. His hiding-place was found and after false testimony he was found guilty of treason and hanged before his meetinghouse. According to the ODNB, his wife's efforts to have her husband's sentence suspended resulted only in having the order for quartering commuted. Lord Londonderry, to whom she appealed, could not forgive JP for depicting him as Lord Mountmumble in *Billy Bluff*. He was buried in the Cistercian abbey at Greyabbey. Two of his sons emigrated to Louisiana, where one became a senator and the other state attorney-general. For JP's portrait, see ODNB. SOURCE Adam, pp 86, 180; Boylan, pp 330–1; Brady, p. 206; Donegal, pp 225–7; Field Day, iii, p. 329; Hogan 2, pp 1029–30; IBL, 8 (1922), pp 126–31; ODNB; O'Donoghue, p. 387; RIA/DIB.

P103   *Billy Bluff and the 'squire; or, a sketch of the times* [anon.].
        Belfast: [n.p.], 1796. SOURCE IBL, 8 (1922), p. 126. SOURCE ESTC t228610. LOCATION BFl.
        + Belfast: Printed at the Star Press, 1796. SOURCE IBL, 8 (1922), p. 126; ESTC t219762. LOCATION Dm.
        Belfast: Printed at the Northern Star, 1796 (by 'a Presbyterian'; as *Billy Bluff and Squire Firebrand; or, a sample of the times*). SOURCE Adams, pp 78, 86, 180; Bradshaw, 5001; Donegal, p. 226; Linen Hall cat. p. 33; ESTC t228610. LOCATION BFl, D (1797 edn), C (1797 edn).

Belfast: Reprinted for the purchasers, 1812 (as *Billy Bluff and Squire Firebrand; or, a sample of the times ... With a selection of songs from 'Paddy's resource'*). SOURCE Donegal, p. 227; Emerald Isle cat. 68/910. LOCATION D, UCD Folklore Dept., L.

+ Belfast: Printed for the purchasers, 1840, 13th edn (as *Billy Bluff and Squire Firebrand: or, a sample of the times. As it appeared periodically, in five letters*). SOURCE Adams, p. 149; IBL, 8 (1922), p. 127. LOCATION Belfast Free Library, InND Loeber coll.

Dublin: Printed privately, 1798. SOURCE IBL, 8 (1922), p. 126. COMMENTARY *Dublin 1798 edn* No copy located [RL].

Glasgow, London: Cameron & Ferguson, 1886 (as *Billy Bluff and the squire. A picture of Ulster in 1796*). SOURCE Brown, p. 320; OCLC. LOCATION D.

New York: American News Co., 1868 (as *Billy Bluff, the spy, and Firebrand, the magistrate. A relic of the United Irishmen. Reprinted from the text of 1796 by the son of a United Irishman*). LOCATION NUC.

+ [Belfast]: Athol Books, 1991 (ed. and introd. by Brendan Clifford as *Billy Bluff and the squire (a satire on Irish aristocracy) and other writings by Rev. James Porter who was hanged in the course of the united Irish rebellion of 1798*). LOCATION D.

COMMENTARY *Belfast, 1991 edn* Contents: 'Billy Bluff & Squire Firebrand', 'Paddy's resource', 'Letters to Downshire', 'Wind and weather', 'Courtmartial'. 'Billy Bluff ...' is a Presbyterian satire on the gentry and aristocracy in Co. Down in the 1790s. First published in the *Northern Star* as serialized letters in 1796, it is characterized as a United Irishmen prose satire attacking the conservative British elements in Ulster and a tale of two regions located near Strangford Lough. Key: Rosemount is the domain of the Montgomery family, the older gentry of the region, who had settled there from Scotland around 1600, before the plantation of Ulster. The Stewarts are the proprietors of Mountstewart. There are three characters in the Billy Bluff dialogue. Lord Mountmumble is a caricature of Robert Stewart, 1st marquess of Londonderry. Squire Firebrand represents the Revd Hugh Montgomery of Greyabbey, while Billy Bluff represents Billy Lowry, a bailiff who spies on Montgomery's estate. Porter gives a graphic portrayal of the system of espionage and feudal tyranny of the times [Adams, p. 86; CD; IBL 8 (1922), p. 127; Thuente 2, p. 235; Whelan, K., 'The United Irishmen, the enlightenment and popular culture' in D. Dickson, D. Keogh, & K. Whelan (eds), *The United Irishmen* (Dublin, 1993), p. 280; ODNB].

P104 *Wind and weather. A sermon on the late providential storm which dispersed the French fleet off Bantry Bay* (by James Porter).

Belfast: [n.p.], 1797. SOURCE Donegal, p. 227; Hogan 2, pp 1029–30; ESTC t95336. LOCATION Belfast Central Library, L.

COMMENTARY A satire in the form of a sermon on the British government's order for a fast day in thanksgiving for the storm that battered the French fleet under General Lazare Hoche en route to Bantry Bay in 1796 carrying troops to aid the Irish rebels [Hogan (where mistakenly called 'Wind and water'; ODNB]

PORTER, Jane. Co-author. See **PORTER, Anna Maria**.

POSNETT, Mrs George, fl. 1880s. Novelist, Mrs GP in the dedication of *The touch of fate* (London, [1884], 3 vols.) acknowledges her gratitude to the surgeon Sir George Hornidge Porter for treating her 'during a long and painful illness'. The Posnett name is known to occur in Belfast. A George Posnett was the owner of 48 acres in Co. Antrim in 1870. SOURCE RL; COPAC; http://genforum.genealogy.com/macaulay/messages/453.html (access date: 15 Feb. 2005).

P105 *The touch of fate* (by Mrs George Posnett; dedicated to Sir George Hornidge Porter, Surgeon in Ordinary to the Queen in Ireland).

London: J. & R. Maxwell, [1884], 3 vols. SOURCE COPAC. LOCATION L.

COMMENTARY The story starts with Mrs Fortham, who lives at the dower house of the Forthams in the outskirts of Dublin, and then introduces James Patrick O'Grady, a widower whose wife had been Mrs Fortham's cousin. He lives at Ballydoo Farm in the north of Ireland and goes on a visit to London [RL].

P106   *On the square* [anon.].

+ Dublin: Hodges, Figgis & Co.; London: Simpkin, Marshall & Co.; Edinburgh: Andrew Elliot, 1885. LOCATION Dt, L.

COMMENTARY Set in the diamond fields of South Africa and in Scotland. The characters are Scottish [ML].

P107   *Who am I?* [anon.].

+ London: Simpkin, Marshall & Co.; Dublin: Sealy, Bryers & Walker, 1885. SOURCE COPAC. LOCATION L.

COMMENTARY No Irish content [ML].

P108   *Her golden forget-me-not* (by Mrs George Posnett).

Dublin: Sealy & Co., 1886. SOURCE COPAC. LOCATION L.

COMMENTARY No Irish content. Concerns a love story set in England [ML].

'POSTERITAS', fl. 1884. Pseudonym of a political fantasy novelist.

P109   *The siege of London* (by 'Posteritas').

London: Wyman & Sons, 1884. SOURCE COPAC. LOCATION L.

Paris: [n.p.], [1885?] (trans. as *La siége de Londres*). SOURCE COPAC. LOCATION C.

+ Paris: [n.p.], n.d. (trans. by A. Garçon as *Les battailes imaginaires. Le battaile de Londres en 188 ...*). SOURCE COPAC. LOCATION L.

COMMENTARY 68pp for the London edn. A fantasy war novel sold at 1*s*.: mismanagement of the nation at the hands of a contemporary Gladstone government, coupled with the perfidy of the Fenians, leads to the French army on English soil. Contains elaborate scenarios on the perils of a light hand in governing the Empire, noting unrest in Egypt and (presciently) among the Boers in southern Africa [COPAC; Scott cat. 15/147].

POTTER, Matilda, fl. 1813. Novelist, presumably Irish, to whom both Block and Allibone attribute another volume, *Matilda. An Irish tale* (1813), which has not been located and is possibly is a mix-up between the author's first name and part of the title of the following novel of the same date, or a misattribution of *Matilda; a tale of the day* by Constantine Henry Phipps (London, 1825). SOURCE Allibone ii, p. 1652; Block, p. 188.

P110   *Mount Erin. An Irish tale* (by Matilda Potter).

London: J. Souter, 1813, 2 vols. SOURCE Allibone, ii, p. 1652; Belanger, 36; Block, p. 188; Brown 2, 1320; British Fiction; Garside, 1813:50. LOCATION Corvey CME 3-628-48366-2, Ireland related fiction, NUC.

COMMENTARY Mount Erin is the estate around which the action of the story revolves. Nearby is the castle of Sir Hubert Fitzmaurice who has been 'importuned by our misguided countrymen when making what they termed a struggle for liberty, to join their party'. He refuses, saying that his arm would never be raised against a monarch in whose defence he would die. The story chiefly concerns the love of his daughter, Ella, for the man of her choice instead of her father's. In a weak moment she elopes with the former. The result is a violent breach with her father, but in the end Fitzmaurice is reconciled to his grandson [Brown 2].

POTTER, Thomas J. See **POTTER, Fr Thomas Joseph**.

POTTER, Fr Thomas Joseph (known as **Thomas J. Potter**), b. Scarborough (Yorks.) 1828, d. All Hallows College, (Dublin) 1873. English-born Catholic priest, poet and religious fiction writer, TJP was the son of George Potter. After training for the priesthood, he became professor and director of All Hallows College, Dublin. He published seven works of fiction, a volume of poetry, *Legends, lyrics and hymns* (Dublin, 1862), as well as *The panegyric of St. Patrick* (London, 1864). His fiction remained in print after his death and was reprinted by M.H. Gill in Dublin in 1891. SOURCE Allibone, ii, p. 1653; Allibone Suppl., ii, p. 1247; Boase, ii, p. 1603; Fenning cat. 147/300; O'Donoghue, p. 387; RL.

P1111   *The two victories. A Catholic tale* (by Thomas J. Potter; dedicated to the Reverend the Director and students of the Foreign Missionary College of All Hallows).
Dublin, London: James Duffy, 1860. SOURCE Adv. in *The adventures of a watch* (Dublin, [1865]). LOCATION D (1862, 2nd edn), L, NUC ([1865?], 5th edn).
New York, Montreal: D. & J. Sadlier & Co., [1875 or earlier]. SOURCE Adv. in M.J. Hoffman, *The orphan sisters* (New York, 1875); OCLC (1880 edn). LOCATION Central Connecticut State Univ. (1880 edn).

P1112   *The rector's daughter; or, love and duty. A Catholic tale* (by Thomas J. Potter).
Dublin, London: James Duffy, 1861. SOURCE OCLC. LOCATION D (1862, 2nd edn), L.
+ Dublin: James Duffy & Co., [1864 or later], 5th edn (as *The rector's daughter. A Catholic tale*). LOCATION InND Loeber coll.
Brussels: H. Goemaerts, 1863 (trans. by Guillaume Lebrocquy as *Edith, la fille du recteur*). SOURCE Devonshire, p. 471; Adv. in T.J. Potter's *Legends, lyrics and hymns* (Dublin, 1862).
COMMENTARY Rev. in *Duffy's Hibernian Magazine* (1861, No. 13, p. 48). Catholic religious fiction set in England. The story involves Mr Mason, a Church of England clergyman, who was educated at Oxford where the Oxford movement had deeply affected him. He often feels that in conscience he should become a Catholic but to do so would be financially disastrous as he has a wife and children to support. His neighbour Mrs Clifford, a lapsed Catholic, has set her mind on her son Alfred marrying Mr Mason's daughter Edith, although Edith is against this. Mr Mason suffers a stroke and on recovery converts to catholicism, along with Edith, to the great horror of his wife. Two other children, Katy and Walter, follow suit. The family lives in poverty and depends on Edith's work as a teacher to support them. Walter goes to college to become a priest, supported financially by the bishop. Katy dies young. The day after Katy's death, when there is neither money or food in the house, Mrs Mason's brother appears, just returned from India. He is extremely rich, and they move to the countryside. Edith marries Lord Oakenshaw, who has also converted to catholicism. Walter, after becoming a priest, ministers to the sick in a foreign land. On her deathbed, Mrs Clifford calls for Edith and returns to her Catholic faith. All the surviving characters live happily and count their blessings [ML].

P1113   *Light and shade; or, the manor house of Hardirge* (by the Revd Thomas J. Potter; dedicated to Msgr Bartholomew Woodlock, DD, rector of the Catholic Univ. of Ireland).
+ Dublin: James Duffy, 1864. SOURCE OCLC. LOCATION D (1875 edn), DPL (n.d. edn), L, RB (1875 edn), NUC (n.d. edn).
COMMENTARY An advertisement in *The adventures of a watch* (Dublin [1865]) states that this book had been 'particularly adapted for school premiums' [RL].

P1114   *Percy Grange; or, the ocean of life. A tale in three books* (by Thomas J. Potter; dedicated to the Rt Revd the Bishop, the Chapter and the Very Revd and Revd the Clergy of the Diocese of Beverley).
Dublin: James Duffy, 1864. SOURCE COPAC. LOCATION D (1865, 2nd edn), L, NUC (1887 edn).

P115   *The Farleyes of Farleye; or, faithful and true. A tale in three books* (by Thomas
        Joseph Potter; dedicated to the Rt Revd Robert Cornthwaite, Bishop of Beverley).
        + Dublin, London: James Duffy, 1867. SOURCE OCLC. LOCATION D (Dublin, M.H.
        Gill, 1891 edn), NUC, InND Loeber coll.
        Boston: Patrick Donahue, 1868. SOURCE OCLC. LOCATION Kent State Univ.

P116   *Sir Humphrey's trial: or, the lesson of life. A book of tales, legends and sketches,
        in prose and verse* (by Thomas J. Potter; dedicated to the Rt Revd David Moriarty,
        DD, Bishop of Kerry).
        Dublin: James Duffy, 1869 (ill.). SOURCE OCLC. LOCATION L, InND Loeber coll.
        (1883, 3rd edn.).
        COMMENTARY Contents (other than poetry) 1883 edn: 'Our uncle Humphrey's budget',
        'Atherby House; or, our school and our scholars', 'Tom Bowman; or, coming right', 'The con-
        spiracy; a tale of a horrible murder, and what came of it', 'Walter Mason; or, the story of a
        noble life', 'Ethel: a sketch' (first published in *The Farleyes of Farleye*, Dublin, 1867), 'Faithful
        evermore; or, a mother's love. A contrast' [RL].

P117   *Rupert Aubrey of Aubrey Chase. An historical tale of 1681* (by Thomas J. Potter;
        dedicated to Revd Daniel M'Gettigan, DD, Archbishop of Armagh).
        Boston: Patrick Donahoe, 1873. SOURCE DCU, Catholic Americana files; OCLC.
        LOCATION NUC, InND Loeber coll. (Dublin, M.H. Gill, 1891 edn).
        COMMENTARY Historical fiction set in the late-seventeenth century in England, the tale is about
        the persecution of the English Catholics, particularly by Dr Oates who 'uncovered' the
        Yorkshire Plot in which a number of Catholics had been accused of plotting to overthrow the
        king and the government. Rupert Aubrey, a young Catholic nobleman, is unjustly accused of
        having had connections with this group. When he is imprisoned in Newgate, his cell is next
        to the one occupied by Oliver Plunkett, archbishop of Armagh. Part of the story deals with
        Oliver Plunkett's trial, imprisonment and execution. The story ends with Rupert being set
        free by intercession of the king [ML].

POTTINGER, Harriet. See **KEATINGE, Mrs Richard Harte.**

POULETT, Anne Lucy. See **NUGENT-GRENVILLE, George, 3rd Baron Nugent.**

POWELL, Harcourt. See **POWELL, Revd Harcourt Morley Isaac.**

POWELL, Revd Harcourt Morley Isaac (known as **Harcourt Powell**), fl. 1880s. Anglican
clergyman and novelist, HMIP graduated at TCD in 1872 and was ordained a year later. From
1881 on he was vicar at Wollaston (Northhamptonshire) He wrote the preface to *Ewart Conroy*
from Crawleydown (Sussex) in July 1881. SOURCE Allibone Suppl., ii, p. 1248; ML.

P118   *Ewart Conroy* (by Harcourt Powell; dedicated to Sir Herbert Miller, Bt, of the
        Coldstream Guards).
        + Dublin: M.H. Gill, [c.1881]. SOURCE Allibone Suppl., ii, p. 1248; OCLC. LOCATION
        L.
        COMMENTARY Irish content. In the preface the author states: 'If there be any real danger to
        the stability of the British empire, it will partly consist in prejudice and in a tendency to con-
        clude hastily whereby the countries and communities forming this empire are taught to dis-
        trust and dislike each other ...' [ML].

POWER, Marguerite. See **BLESSINGTON, Marguerite, countess of.**

Power

POWER, Marguerite A. See **POWER, Marguerite Agnes**.

POWER, Marguerite Agnes (known as **Marguerite A. Power**), pseud. 'Honoria', b. Ireland 1815?, d. Bushy Heath (Herts.) 1867. Novelist, journalist and poet, MAP was the daughter of an army colonel and a niece of the countess of Blessington§, with whom she and her sister Ellen went to live in London around 1839. Her mother was a daughter of Thomas Brooke of St Helena. After her father's army career he became agent for the Blessington estates in Co. Tyrone. MAP lived with her aunt, Lady Blessington, from at least 1840 onward, and in that year was noted by William Archer Shee who found her 'pretty and attractive' at one of Lady Blessington's soirées. When Lady Blessington became bankrupt and broke up her residence at Gore House in 1849, MAP accompanied her to Paris and took care of her during her last illness. Aside from novels, MAP wrote poetry, including *Virginia's hand* (London, 1860) and a book on her travels in Egypt, *Arabian days and nights, or rays from the East* (London 1863). After her aunt's death, she worked as Paris correspondent for the *Illustrated London News* and edited the *Keepsake* (London, 1851–57). She also contributed to the *Irish Metropolitan Magazine* (Dublin); *Forget-me-not*; *Household Words*; *Once a Week* (all London), and *Friendship's Offering* (London, 1842–43). In addition, she wrote a biographical sketch of her aunt, included in Lady Blessington's *Country Quarters* (London, 1850, 3 vols.). Some of her poems were included in A.B. Stopford and T.W. Rolleston's anthology, *A treasury of Irish poetry in the English tongue* (London, 1900). She seems to have remained single all her life. For MAP's portraits, see ODNB. SOURCE Allibone, ii, p. 1657; Jarndyce cat. 162/508; Lohrli, p. 402; MPV, p. 373; ODNB; O'Donoghue, p. 388; RIA/DIB; RL; M. Sadleir, *The strange life of Lady Blessington* (Boston, 1933); W.A. Shee, *My contemporaries, 1830–1870* (London, 1893), p. 97; Sutherland, p. 508.

P119   *Evelyn Forester: A woman's story* (by Marguerite A. Power).
London, New York: George Routledge & Co., 1856 (Routledge's New Series of Original Novels, No. 9). SOURCE Alston, p. 354; OCLC; Sadleir, 3672. LOCATION L, NUC.
Paris: G. Havard, 1856, 2 vols. (trans. by M.A. Rolet as *Evelyn Forester, histoire d'une femme*; Bibliothèque Choisie des Romans Anglais). SOURCE Devonshire, p. 394; Bn-Opale plus. LOCATION BNF.

P120   *The Foresters. A novel* (by Marguerite A. Power).
+ London: T. Cautley Newby, 1857, 2 vols. SOURCE Alston, p. 354 (1857 edn); COPAC; OCLC (where misspelled 'The Forsters'). LOCATION L (1858 edn), C.

P121   *Too late* (by Marguerite A. Power).
[location?]: [publisher?], 1858. SOURCE Sutherland, p. 508.
COMMENTARY No copy located [RL].

P122   *The letters of a betrothed* (signed by 'Honoria').
+ London: Longman, Brown, Green, Longmans & Roberts, 1858. SOURCE COPAC; RIA/DIB; Sutherland, p. 508. LOCATION L, NUC.

P123   *Nelly Carew. A novel* (by Marguerite A. Power; dedicated to the marquess of Lansdowne).
+ London: Saunders, Otley & Co., 1859, 2 vols. (ill. De Veria, Chas. Rolls). SOURCE Brown, 1388; RIA/DIB; Sadleir, 1973. LOCATION D, L, NUC.
COMMENTARY The daughter of an Irish landlord is driven into marriage to an Irish roué by the scheming of her crafty French stepmother, who once was her governess. Her life is miserable, but her honour is stainless. The story ends happily [Brown].

P124   *Sweethearts and wives* (by Marguerite A. Power).
London: Saunders, Otley & Co., 1861, 3 vols. SOURCE RIA/DIB; Sadleir, 1974; Sutherland, p. 508; Wolff, 5614. LOCATION L (1861, 2nd edn), NUC.

POWER, Revd P.B. See **POWER, Revd Philip Bennett**.

POWER, Revd Philip Bennett (known as the **Revd P.B. Power**), b. Co. Waterford 1822, d. The Cliff, Eastbourne (Sussex) 1899. Anglican clergyman, religious tract writer and poet, PBP was the son of John Power. He studied at TCD and graduated BA in 1843, was ordained in 1845 and received his MA in 1846. He left for England shortly after, worked as a curate, and became incumbent of Christ Church, Worthing (Sussex), and subsequently several other parishes in England. He was well known as a prolific evangelical tract writer (41 works), published both in England and the US. His *The lost sunbeam; shady tree; the woven sunbeams* (London, 1861) consists of little sermons and moral lessons for children. His daughter, Eileen Power, became an economic and social historian. SOURCE Allibone, ii, p. 1657; Allibone Suppl., ii, p. 1248; Boase, vi, pp 421–2; ML; MVP, p. 373; NCBEL 4, pp 1850–1; O'Donoghue, p. 388; O'Dowd, M., & S. Wichert (eds.), *Chattel, servant, or citizen* (Belfast, 1995), pp 12–13; RIA/DIB.

P125 *The man without a master* (by P.B. Power).
London: Hamilton, Adams & Co., n.d. LOCATION L.
COMMENTARY Religious fiction [BLC].

P126 *The last shilling; or, the selfish child. A story founded on fact* (by P.B. Power).
London: Charles Haseldon, 1853. SOURCE Allibone, ii, p. 1657. LOCATION L.
New York: Robert Carter & Bros, 1863. SOURCE NCBEL 4, p. 1850; OCLC. LOCATION Univ. of Florida.
Philadelphia: American Sunday School Union, [1867]. SOURCE NCBEL 4, p. 1850. LOCATION NN.

P127 *Three cripples* (by P.B. Power).
London: Society for Promoting Christian Knowledge, [1853?]. SOURCE Allibone, ii, p. 1657 ([1853] edn; not located); RLIN ([18??] edn). LOCATION State Univ. of New York, Albany ([18??] edn]).
New York: R. Carter & Bros, 1864. SOURCE OCLC. LOCATION CtY.

P128 *The two brothers, and the two paths* (by P.B. Power).
London: Wertheim & MacIntosh, [1854]. LOCATION L (destroyed), E.
COMMENTARY Religious fiction [BLC].

P129 *John Clipstick's clock* (by P.B. Power).
[London?]: [publisher?], 1858. SOURCE Allibone, ii, p. 1657.
COMMENTARY No copy located. Later published in P.B. Power's *The oiled feather tracts* (London, 1866–68) as 'Mr. Clipstick's clock' [RL].

P130 *The one moss-rose* (by P.B. Power).
London: T. Nelson & Sons, 1860. SOURCE NCBEL 4, p. 1650 (1867, 1872 edns). SOURCE COPAC. LOCATION L (destroyed), E.
COMMENTARY 67pp. Religious fiction [BLC].

P131 *Little Kitty's knitting needles* (by P.B. Power).
London: T. Nelson & Sons, 1860. SOURCE NCBEL 4, p. 1650 (1861, 1868 edns). SOURCE COPAC. LOCATION L (destroyed), E.
Boston: Henry Hoyt, 1863. SOURCE Allibone, ii, p. 1657 (1862 edn, not located). SOURCE RLIN. LOCATION American Antiquarian Society.
COMMENTARY Religious fiction [BLC].

P132 *The talking fire-irons* (by P.B. Power).
London: W. MacIntosh, [1860s]. SOURCE Allibone, ii, p. 1657; NYPL; OCLC. LOCATION NN.
Philadelphia: American Sunday-School Union, n.d. SOURCE OCLC. LOCATION Kent State Univ. (OH).
COMMENTARY 35pp. Temperance fiction. The 40th edn appeared in 1868 [Allibone; OCLC].

P133 *Croaking Kate and chirping Jane* (by P.B. Power).

+ London: William MacIntosh, [1866?]. SOURCE Allibone, ii, p. 1657. LOCATION L.
COMMENTARY 30pp. Priced at 2*d*. According to Allibone, the 15th edn appeared in 1868 [Allibone; RL; BLC].

P134 *The eye doctor* (by P.B. Power).
+ London: William MacIntosh, [1866?]. SOURCE Allibone, ii, p. 1657. LOCATION L.
COMMENTARY 31pp. Over 23,000 copies sold [RL; BLC].

P135 *The oiled feather* (by P.B. Power).
[n.l., n.p.], 1868. SOURCE Allibone, ii, p. 1657; Boase, vi, p. 422.
+ London: Hamilton, Adams & Co., 1871 (ill.). LOCATION L.
COMMENTARY 30pp. Religious fiction of which nearly 200,000 copies were sold. It was also published as part of *The oiled feather tracts* (London, 1866–68). '*The oiled feather*' was first published in the *Worthing Messenger* [RL; BLC; Boase, vi, p. 422].

P136 *The oiled feather tracts* (by P.B. Power).
London: William MacIntosh, 1866–68, 2 vols. SOURCE Allibone, ii, p. 1657; COPAC. LOCATION L.
+ New York: Robert Carter & Bros, 1872 (as *Stamp-on-it John, and other narratives*; ill.; Fireside Library). LOCATION InND Loeber coll.
COMMENTARY *New York edn* Contains a subset of the stories.
Philadelphia: American Sunday-School Union, n.d., 12 vols. SOURCE Allibone, ii, p. 1657.
COMMENTARY No copy of the Philadelphia edn located. Religious fiction for juveniles. Contents: 'The oiled feather', 'Mr. Clipstick's clock' (first separately published, London?, 1858), 'The talking fire-irons' (first separately published in London, 1860s), 'Reports and the mischief they do', 'Croaking Kate and chirping Jane' (first separately published in London, 1866), 'The eye doctor' (first separately published in London, 1866), 'Stamp-on-it John' [OCLC].

P137 *A faggot of stories for little folk* (by P.B. Power).
London: W. MacIntosh, [1866]. SOURCE Allibone, ii, p. 1657. LOCATION L.
New York: [publisher?], 1868. SOURCE NCBEL 4, p. 1850.
COMMENTARY No copy of the New York edn located [RL].

P138 *The ill-used postman: being an account of who beat him, and why they beat him, and what came of their beating him* (by P.B. Power).
+ London: William MacIntosh, [1866?]. SOURCE Allibone, ii, p. 1657. LOCATION L.
COMMENTARY 31pp [BLC].

P139 *Experiences of a church plate* (by P.B. Power).
+ London: William MacIntosh, [1867?]. SOURCE Allibone, ii, p. 1657. SOURCE BLC. LOCATION L.
COMMENTARY 31pp. Priced at 2*d*. The 8th edn appeared in 1868 [Allibone; RL].

P140 *The man who kept himself in repair* (by P.B. Power).
+ London: William MacIntosh, 1867. SOURCE Allibone, ii, p. 1657; COPAC. LOCATION L.
COMMENTARY 30pp [BLC].

P141 '*After all!*' (by P.B. Power).
London: [publisher?], 1868. SOURCE Allibone, ii, p. 1657; COPAC. LOCATION E ([1870?] edn).
COMMENTARY No copy of the London 1868 edn located [RL].

P142 *Appointed times* (by P.B. Power).
London: [publisher?], 1868. SOURCE Allibone, ii, p. 1657.
COMMENTARY No copy located [RL].

P143 *The man who ran away from himself* (by P.B. Power).
London: Society for Promoting Christian Knowledge, 1868. SOURCE Allibone, ii, p. 1657; OCLC. LOCATION GEU.

+ London: Society for Promoting Christian Knowledge, [1893] (*as The man who ran away with the leg of mutton and the leg mutton ran away with him*). SOURCE COPAC. LOCATION E.
Philadelphia: American Sunday-School Union, [1868?]. SOURCE RLIN. LOCATION Free Library of Philadelphia.

P144   *Paddle your own canoe* (by P.B. Power).
London: [publisher?], 1868. SOURCE Allibone, ii, p. 1657.
Philadelphia: American Sunday-School Union, [1868?] (*as Paddle your own canoe, or, Harry Bray's disappointment*; ill.; Oiled Feather Series). SOURCE RLIN. LOCATION Free Library of Philadelphia.
COMMENTARY No copy of the London edn located. The Dublin ballad publisher Brereton published a ballad *Parody your own canoe* in 1868, but it is not clear whether this relates to the above title [OCLC; RL].

P145   *"This day month!"* (by P.B. Power).
Philadelphia: American Sunday-School Union, [1868] (ill.; Oiled Feather Series). SOURCE Allibone, ii, p. 1657; RLIN. LOCATION Free Library of Philadelphia.

P146   *It only wants turning round* (by P.B. Power).
London: W. MacIntosh, [1869]. SOURCE COPAC. LOCATION L (destroyed), E.
COMMENTARY Religious fiction [BLC].

P147   *Sambo's legacy* (by P.B. Power).
London: W. MacIntosh, [1869]. SOURCE COPAC. LOCATION L (destroyed), E.
COMMENTARY Religious fiction [BLC].

P148   *The bag of blessings; or, the singing tailor* (by P.B. Power).
London: Hamilton, Adams & Co., [1870]. SOURCE NCBEL 4, p. 1851 (1872 edn).
LOCATION L (destroyed).
COMMENTARY Religious fiction. No copy located [BLC; RL].

P149   *Truffle nephews; or on repairing and keeping in repair London city missionaries* (by P.B. Power).
[London]: Printed [for the author?] by Alexander & Shepheard, 1870. SOURCE OCLC.
LOCATION Guild Hall Library.
COMMENTARY Reprinted from *Sunday at Home* (London, Mar. 1869) [OCLC].

P150   *Born with a silver spoon in his mouth* (by P.B. Power).
London: W. MacIntosh, [1870]. SOURCE COPAC. LOCATION L (destroyed), E.
COMMENTARY Religious fiction [BLC].

P151   *He's overhead* (by P.B. Power).
London: Hamilton, Adams & Co., [1871]. LOCATION L.
COMMENTARY Religious fiction [BLC].

P152   *Truffle nephews and how they commenced* (by P.B. Power).
London: S.W. Partridge & Co., [after 1874?] (ill. Barnard Frank). SOURCE NCBEL 4, p. 1851 (1874 edn); RLIN. LOCATION UBP.
COMMENTARY Story about the London city mission [RL].

P153   *Little Kitty's knitting-needles; and The one moss-rose* (by P.B. Power).
London: [publisher?], 1882. SOURCE Allibone Suppl., ii, p. 1248. LOCATION InND Loeber coll. (1886 edn).
COMMENTARY The two stories were first published separately in London (1860). 'Little Kitty's knitting-needles' is set in Yorkshire. No Irish content [ML; RL].

P154   *The further proceedings of Mr. Truffle* (by P.B. Power).
+ London: Hamilton, Adams & Co., S.W. Partridge & Co., [1885] (ill.). SOURCE Allibone Suppl., ii, p. 1248. LOCATION L.
COMMENTARY A story of the London city mission [BLC].

P155 *The cup and the kiss and other sketches* (by P.B. Power).
London: Religious Tract Society, 1888. SOURCE Allibone Suppl., ii, p. 1248; NCBEL
4, p. 1851 (1894 edn). LOCATION L (destroyed).
COMMENTARY Religious fiction. No copy located [BLC; RL].

P156 *Cured by an incurable. A tale* (by P.B. Power).
London: Elliot Stock, 1888, 2nd edn (ill. E. Fitzpatrick). LOCATION L (destroyed).
COMMENTARY No copy of first edn located [RL].

P157 *The one-talented people* (by P.B. Power).
London: Religious Tract Society, [1889]. SOURCE COPAC. LOCATION L (destroyed), E.
COMMENTARY Religious fiction [BLC].

P158 *Mr. Stepaway's two feet and other sketches* (by P.B. Power).
London: Religious Tract Society, [1889]. SOURCE COPAC. LOCATION L (destroyed), E.
COMMENTARY Religious fiction [BLC].

P159 *The heart of Tommy Titt; or, the big man and the bigger* (by P.B. Power).
London: Christian Knowledge Society, [1890]. SOURCE COPAC. LOCATION L
(destroyed), E.
COMMENTARY Religious fiction [BLC].

P160 *The split navvy, and other sketches* (by P.B. Power).
London: Religious Tract Society, [1890]. LOCATION L (destroyed).
COMMENTARY Religious fiction. No copy located [BLC; RL].

P161 *Linked to a thought* (by P.B. Power).
London: Church of England Temperance Society, [1891]. LOCATION L.
COMMENTARY Religious fiction [BLC].

P162 *The flag & the tunnel; and The talking fire-irons* (by P.B. Power).
London: Society for Promoting Christian Knowledge, [1896]. SOURCE COPAC.
LOCATION E.
COMMENTARY *The talking fire-irons* was first published in London in the 1860s [AMB].

P163 *"This day month"; and The fifth "P."* (by P.B. Power).
London: Society for Promoting Christian Knowledge, [1896]. SOURCE COPAC.
LOCATION E.
COMMENTARY *This day month* was first published in Philadelphia in [1868], or proba-
bly earlier in London [RL].

P164 *Going on wheels; and Mr. Clipstick's clock* (by P.B. Power).
London: Society for Promoting Christian Knowledge, [1896]. SOURCE COPAC.
LOCATION E.
COMMENTARY The second story, *Mr. Clipstick's clock*, was first published separately
in 1858 [RL].

POWER, Tyrone. See **POWER, William Grattan Tyrone**.

POWER, Victor O'Donovan, b. Chilcombe House, Rosbercon, New Ross (Co. Wexford)
c.1860, d. New Ross 1933. Novelist, periodical writer and playwright, VO'DP was the son of
Michael Power, an ardent nationalist. His mother was a poet. He was educated at St Patrick's
College, Carlow, and he contributed a considerable amount of literary work to Irish and
American periodicals such as the *Lamp* (New York), the *Irish Fireside*, the *Shamrock*, *Weekly
Freeman* (all Dublin), and *Ireland's Own* (Wexford, later Dublin), including many serialized
novels, such as 'The footsteps of fate' (1930). He also wrote plays that were performed by his
own company. He is buried in the graveyard at Shanbogh (Co. Kilkenny). SOURCE Brown, p.
255–56; Browne, p. 121; Hogan 2, pp 1036–7; IBL, 23 (1935), p. 93; RIA/DIB.

P165 *Bonnie Dunraven. A story of Kilcarrick* (by Victor O'Donovan Power).
London: Remington, 1881, 2 vols. SOURCE Allibone Suppl., ii, p. 1248; Brown, 1389.
LOCATION L.
COMMENTARY A contemporary love story set in Co. Cork [Brown].

P166 *The heir of Liscarragh* (by Victor O'Donovan Power; dedicated to T. Richard Hammond).
+ London, Lemington: Art & Book Co.; New York: Benziger & Co., 1891 (ill.).
SOURCE Brown, 1390 (1892 edn). LOCATION L, InND Loeber coll.
COMMENTARY First serialized in the *Catholic Times* (London?). A story of love and mystery set in Co. Cork. Mona O'Brien is engaged to Richard Lushmore, who has gone to the Continent to recover from consumption under the care of his cousin, Leonard Markham. Lushmore is reported to have died and Markham inherits his estate. Markham tells Mona that the last wish of her fiancée was that she should marry Markham. Mona does marry Markham, but the truth comes out that Lushmore is not really dead. Markham dies, and Lushmore and Mona are reunited [ML; Brown].

P167 *A secret of the past. A novel* [anon.].
London: Ward & Downey, 1893, 3 vols. SOURCE Wolff, 5615. LOCATION L.

P168 *At the eleventh hour* (by Victor O'Donovan Power).
Dublin: James Duffy, [1912 or earlier] (Duffy's Penny Library). SOURCE Adv. in *Catalogue of books* (Dublin, 1912).
COMMENTARY No copy located [RL].

P169 *Tracked* (by Victor O'Donovan Power).
Dublin: Ireland's Own Library, 1914. SOURCE Brown, 1391.
COMMENTARY No copy located. A tale of unrequited love and jealousy set in Innishowen (Co. Donegal) [Brown].

P170 *Some strange experiences of Kitty the Hare, the famous travelling woman of Ireland* (by Victor O'Donovan Power).
Dublin, Cork: Mercier, 1981. SOURCE Brown, p. 256; Hogan 2, p. 1037; COPAC.
LOCATION L.
COMMENTARY Published posthumously. According to Brown, writing before 1919, this novel was serialized over a long period in *Ireland's Own* (Wexford) and was 'about to be published'. It consists of comic, romantic and melodramatic tales related by Kitty the Hare, a wandering woman of the roads [Brown; Hogan].

POWER, William Grattan Tyrone (also known as Tyrone Power), b. near Kilmacthomas (Co. Waterford) 1797, d. while crossing the Atlantic, 1841. Actor, comic dramatist and fiction writer, WGTP was the son of an itinerant actor who came from a prosperous Waterford family, and Maria Maxwell. When he was one year old, his father died in America, and his mother then settled at Cardiff (Wales), where a relative was a printer and produced handbills for the local theatre. At age 14 WGTP joined a company of strolling players and succeeded in getting small roles before marrying Anne Gilbert of the Isle of Wight. His wife's money allowed him to leave the stage and he spent a year in South Africa before trying an acting career again in London. He made a breakthrough specializing in comic Irish parts such as Sir Lucius O'Trigger in Richard Brinsley Sheridan's *The rivals* (1775) and thereafter confined himself to these roles. He returned to the Theatre Royal in Dublin frequently, where he was very popular, and he made several successful American tours. Aside from fiction and his comic dramas – many featuring genial Irishmen – he contributed to the *Dublin University Magazine* and wrote *Impressions of America during the years 1833, 1834, and 1835* (London, 1836). He was lost at sea on his return from a trip to check on investments he had made in the US. His grandson and great-grandson achieved fame in American film and theatre. For WGP's portraits, see ODNB. SOURCE Allibone, ii, p. 1657; Boylan, p. 332; J.W.C., 'Tyrone Power: a biography [pts 1–3], *Dublin University Magazine*, 40, (1852), pp 257–73, 577–81, 715–34; Hogan 2, pp 1034–5; Irish pseudonyms; McKenna, pp 315–16; OCIL, pp 480–1; ODNB; O'Donoghue, p. 389; RIA/DIB.

P171   *The lost heir, and the prediction* [anon.].

London: Edward Bull, 1830, 3 vols. SOURCE Rafroidi, ii, p. 327; Sadleir, 1975; Garside 2, 1830:91. LOCATION Corvey CME 3–628–48115–5, L, NUC.

London, Belfast: Simms & M'Intyre, 1853 (as *Cauth Malowney*; Parlour Library, No. 183). SOURCE Sadleir, ii, p. 157.

COMMENTARY *London, Belfast edn* No copy located [RL].

+ London: Thomas Hodgson, n.d. (as *Cauth Malowney; or, the lost heir*). LOCATION D, NUC.

New York: J. & J. Harper, 1830, 2 vols. LOCATION NUC.

COMMENTARY Rev. in the *Dublin Literary Gazette* (16 Jan. 1830), where the reviewer complains that the Irish language is 'miserably bad, so is the radicalism'. Contents: 'The lost heir', 'The prediction' [RL; British Fiction].

P172   *The King's secret* [anon.].

London: Edward Bull, 1831, 3 vols. SOURCE Garside 2, 1831:58; Rafroidi, ii, p. 327. LOCATION Corvey CME 3–628–47917–7, Dt, L (2nd edn), NUC.

Paris: E. Renduel, 1832, 2 vols. (by Philip Bennet Power [*sic*], trans. by A.J.B. Defauconpret as *Le secret du roi*). SOURCE Rafroidi, ii, p. 376; Bn-Opale plus. LOCATION BNF.

New York: J. & J. Harper, 1831, 2 vols. LOCATION NUC.

PRAED, Mrs R.M. Campbell (Rosa Caroline, née Murray-Prior), b. near Brisbane (Australia), d. Torquay (Devon) 1935. Co-author, Mrs RMCP wrote over 50 books, including four novels in collaboration with Justin McCarthy§. See **MC CARTHY, Justin.**

PRAEGER, S. Rosamond. See **PRAEGER, Sophia Rosamond.**

PRAEGER, Sophia Rosamond (known as **S. Rosamond Praeger**), b. 1867 Holywood (Co. Down), d. Ulster? 1954. Children's writer and an artist, SRP was the daughter of William Emilius Praeger, a Dutch linen merchant, and Maria Patterson, and the sister of the author and naturalist Robert Lloyd Praeger. SRP studied art at the Slade School in London and later in Paris. She established her own studio, first at Belfast and then at Holywood where she worked as an illustrator and sculptor. SRP mainly wrote for children, occasionally in verse, for example, *The old Irish rimes of Brian O'Linn* (London, 1901), and a language education book, *The child's picture grammar* (London, 1900). She illustrated books, including her own. Her plaster sculpture 'Fionnula, the daughter of Lir' can be seen in the Ulster Museum in Belfast, where her portrait by Wilhelmina Geddes is also located. Drawings for her *The dragon and the three bold babies* are in the NLI. Other drawings by her can be found in the National Botanic Gardens, Glasnevin, Dublin. In 1939 she was awarded the OBE and in 1941 she was elected president of the Ulster Academy. SOURCE BLC; Brady, p. 207; Personal information, Pat Donlan, May 1997; P. Donlan, 'Drawing a fine line. Irish women artists as illustrators' in *Irish Arts Review*, 18 (2002), pp 80–92; Emerald Isle cat. 72/back leaf; C. Mollan, W. Davis, & B. Finucane, *Irish innovators* (Dublin, 2002), p. 113; K. & C. Ó Céirín, *Women of Ireland: a biographical dictionary* (Kinvara [Co. Galway], 1996); RIA/DIB; RL.

P173   *The adventures of three bold babes* (by S. Rosamond Praeger).

London: Longmans & Co., 1897 (ill. S. Rosamond Praeger). SOURCE *Irish Arts Review*, 18 (2002), p. 82 (notes a 1896 edn which has not been located); OCLC. LOCATION L (missing).

COMMENTARY 38pp. Fiction for children. The names of the three babies are Hector, Honoria, and Alisander. Set in a fairytale world of dragons and evil kings [RL; Lullaby cat. 1/192].

P174 *Further doings of the three bold babes* (by S. Rosamond Praeger).
+ London: Longmans & Co., 1898 (ill. S. Rosamond Praeger). SOURCE OCLC. P. Donlan, *Irish Arts Review*, 18 (2002), p. 82 (notes a 1897 edn which has not been located). LOCATION L.
COMMENTARY Fiction for children. Sequel to *The adventures of the three bold babes* (London, 1897). The three bold babes, Hector, Honoria and Alisander meet a sea serpent who transports them into the Kingdom of the Head Hoppers. There they promise to help the king to reunite with his banished daughter, which leads them into various adventures [Lullaby cat. 1/195; ML].

P175 *The tale of the little twin dragons* (by S. Rosamond Praeger).
London: Macmillan & Co., 1900 (ill. S. Rosamond Praeger). LOCATION L.

P176 *How they went to school* (by S. Rosamond Praeger).
London, Glasgow, Edinburgh, Dublin: Blackie & Son, [1903] (ill. S. Rosamond Praeger). SOURCE OCLC. LOCATION L.

P177 *How they went to the seaside* (by S. Rosamond Praeger).
London, Glasgow, Edinburgh, Bombay: Blackie & Son, [1909] (ill. S. Rosamond Praeger). LOCATION L.

P178 *How they came back from school* (by S. Rosamond Praeger).
London, Glasgow, Bombay: Blackie & Son, [1911] (ill. S. Rosamond Praeger; title on cover: *How they came from school*; Tiny Tots Series). LOCATION L.

P179 *Wee Tony. A day in his life* (by S. Rosamond Praeger).
London, Glasgow, Bombay: Blackie & Son, [1913] (ill. S. Rosamond Praeger). LOCATION L.

P180 *Me (baby writes a book)* (by S. Rosamond Praeger).
London, Glasgow, Bombay: Blackie & Son, [1915] (ill. S. Rosamond Praeger). SOURCE P. Donlan, *Irish Arts Review*, 18 (2002), p. 81. LOCATION L.
COMMENTARY 52pp [BLC].

P181 *Billy's garden plot* (by S. Rosamond Praeger).
London, Glasgow, Bombay: Blackie & Son, [1918] (ill. S. Rosamond Praeger). LOCATION L.

P182 *How they came from school* (by S. Rosamond Praeger).
London, Glasgow, Bombay: Blackie & Son, [1919] (ill. S. Rosamond Praeger). LOCATION L.

P183 *To school and back, and another story* (by S. Rosamond Praeger and Angusine Macgregor).
London, Glasgow: Blackie & Son, [1928] (ill. S. Rosamond Praeger). SOURCE OCLC. LOCATION L.
COMMENTARY Originally published separately in the Tiny Tots series. Contents: 'How they went to school' (by S. Rosamund [*sic*] Praeger), 'How they came back from school' (by S. Rosamund [*sic*] Praeger), 'The story of Snips' (by Angusine Macgregor) [OCLC].

P184 *The young stamp-collectors* (by S. Rosamond Praeger).
+ Limavady: Portmoon Press, 1985 (ed. by Godfrey Vinycomb; ill. S. Rosamond Praeger). SOURCE Reeve cat. 42/561. LOCATION L.

PRATT, Mary Anne. See **HOARE, Mrs Mary Anne.**

PRATT, Mathilda. See **DESPARD, Mathilda.**

'*Prescott*'

'PRESCOTT, E. Livingston', pseud. See JAY, Edith Katherine Spicer.

PRÉVOST, Antoine-François, b. France, 1697, d. 1765. French novelist, translator and author of over 200 volumes, A-FP was a French abbé who was educated by the Jesuits and left the novitiate twice, first to join the army and second in consequence of a love affair. A third attempt to follow a life in religion led to his unauthorized departure from the Benedictine house near Rouen, and a warrant for his arrest. He fled to England in 1728, where he stayed until 1730 as companion and tutor to Francis, only son of Sir John Eyles. From London he went to Holland, but was back in London in 1733. Having obtained a dispensation from Pope Clement XII, he was able to return to France in the next year, where he reconciled with the church. He is most famous as the author of *Manon Lescaut* (1731). He wrote two historical novels about Ireland but is not known to have visited the country. He translated several English novels into French, including Frances Chamberlaine Sheridan's§ *Memoirs of Miss Sidney Bidulph* (London, 1761–67) and several of his novels were translated into English, including *The life and entertaining adventures of Mr. Cleveland* (Dublin, 1736, 2 vols.). SOURCE Allibone, ii, p. 1677; Brown, p. 256; Falkner Greirson cat. 25/334; G. Gargett & G. Sheridan (eds), *Ireland and French enlightenment, 1700–1800* (Houndmills, 1999), p. 267; J. Henning, 'The historical and geographical background of Prévost's Irish novels', in *Ulster Jrnl of Archaeology*, 12 (1912), pp 89–97; B.G. MacCarthy, *The later women novelists* (Oxford, 1947), p. 21; Summers, pp 109–10.

P185   *Le doyen de Killerine, histoire morale, composée sur les mémoires d'une illustre famille d'Irlande, & ornée de tout ce qui peut rendre une lecture utile et agréable* [anon.].
Paris: Didot, 1735, vol. 1. SOURCE Henning, 'Prévost's Irish novels', p. 90; Brown, 1393; CCF. LOCATION BNF.
+ The Hague: Pierre Poppy, 1739, vol. 2. SOURCE Henning, 'Prévost's Irish novels', p. 90. SOURCE COPAC. LOCATION Dt.
[n.l]: [publisher?], 1739, vol. 3. SOURCE Henning, 'Prévost's Irish novels', p. 90. LOCATION InND Loeber coll.
+ Paris: Didot, 1739, parts 1 & 2. SOURCE Henning, 'Prévost's Irish novels', p. 90. LOCATION D, NUC, InND Loeber coll.
+ [n.l.]: [publisher?], 1739–40, parts 3 & 4. SOURCE Henning, 'Prévost's Irish novels', p. 90. LOCATION D, InND Loeber coll.
+ [n.l.] [publisher?], 1740, parts 5 & 6. LOCATION InND Loeber coll.
Amsterdam: François Changuion, 1742, 6 vols. in 3. SOURCE Henning, 'Prévost's Irish novels', p. 90; de Búrca cat. 35/807. LOCATION L.
The Hague: Pierre Poppy, 1741, 6 vols. in 3. SOURCE Falkner Greirson cat. 24/410, NUC (1744 edn).
+ Dublin: R. Gunne, S. Hyde, G. Risk, J. Leathley, W. Smith, P. Crampton, G. Faulkner, A. Bradley, T. Moore, E. Exshaw, C. Wynne, C. Connor, O. Nelson, J. Kelly & J. Keating, & booksellers, 1742, 3 vols. (ill.). SOURCE ESTC n470. LOCATION D (vols. 2, 3), L (vols. 2, 3), O (vol. 1).
Dublin: E. Exshaw, 1742, 3 vols. (ill.). SOURCE Munter, pp 19, 62; ESTC t225315. LOCATION Dt (vols. 2, 3), L (vol. 1 only).
Dublin: John Smith, George Ewing & Thomas Bacon, 1742, 2 vols. (trans. by Mr Erskine as *The Dean of Coleraine, a moral history. Composed from the memoirs of an illustrious Irish family; by the author of the Memoirs of a man of quality* [*sic*]; ill.). SOURCE Bradshaw, 1270; Brown, 1393 (incorrectly mentions London: 1742, vol. 1; Dublin, vol. 2 and 3); ESTC t190823; Linen Hall cat. p. 211. LOCATION D, Dt, BFl (mentions 1742, 3 vols.), C.

Dublin: R. Gunne, S. Hyde, G. Risk, J. Leathley [and 11 others], 1742, 3 vols. (trans. as *The Dean of Coleraine. A moral history. Founded upon the memoirs of an illustrious family in Ireland*; (ill.). SOURCE ESTC n000470. LOCATION D, NUC.

London: T. Cooper, 1742, vol. 1 (trans. as *The Dean of Coleraine. A moral history, founded on the memoirs of an illustrious family in Ireland*). SOURCE Beasley, 108; McBurney & Taylor, 714; ESTC t118773. LOCATION Dt (vol. 1), BFl, L, IU, NUC.

London: M. Cooper, 1742–43, vols. 2 and 3. SOURCE ESTC t118773. LOCATION O.

London: T. Jullion, 1780, 3 vols. (new edn, corrected and improved). SOURCE Gecker, 848; ESTC t117601. LOCATION PU.

COMMENTARY Note that the London, 1780 edn appeared posthumously and it is therefore unclear how and by whom it was corrected and improved. A very popular novel, with different Dublin publishers commissioning translations and competing for its publication in 1742. The story starts in Ireland after the Cromwellian settlements of the 1650s. The dean of Coleraine watches with a father's anxious care over the fortunes of his two half-brothers and sister. He tries to keep his wayward charges on the straight path amid the allurements of Paris. Towards the close of the story, the dean acts as a Jacobite agent in Ireland [Brown; G. Gargett & G. Sheridan, *Ireland and the French enlightenment 1700–1800* (Houndmills, 1999), pp 191–2].

P186 *Campagnes philosophiques ou mémoires de M. de Montcal, aide-de-champ de M. le Maréchal de Schomberg, contenant l'histoire de la guerre d'Irlande* [anon.]. Amsterdam: Desbordes, 1741, 4 vols. in 2. SOURCE Henning, 'Prévost's Irish novels', p. 95. LOCATION NUC.

COMMENTARY A story of the Williamite campaign in Ireland and the Huguenot troops at the Battle of the Boyne (1690) [G. Gargett & G. Sheridan (eds), *Ireland and French enlightenment, 1700–1800* (Houndmills, 1999), p. 138].

'PREVOST, H.F.', pseud. See **BATTERSBY, Henry Francis Prevost**.

'PREVOST, Francis', pseud. See **BATTERSBY, Henry Francis Prevost**.

PRÉVOST, J. Joseph, fl. 1836. French travel writer and reputed novelist, JJP was one of the collaborators in the fourth series of the *Revue Brittanique* (Paris, 1836–40). An advertisement in *Un tour en Irlande* (below) mentions that he was the author of 'Le Comte de Dromore; ou, la terreur irlandaise', but no such volume has been located. SOURCE BLC; Brown, 1394; Brown, p. 257; RL.

P187 *L'Irlande au dix-neuvième siècle* (by J. Joseph Prévost; preface by M. le Bon Taylor). Paris: L. Curmer, 1845–52. SOURCE Bn-Opale plus. LOCATION BNF.

COMMENTARY Title on cover: *Un tour en Irelande*. Brown, p. 257 mistakenly lists this under *Un tour en Irelande*. Contains standard travel descriptions but also accounts of legends, which is why this volume is included here [RL].

PRICE, Fr Edward, fl. 1850. Catholic priest, editor and fiction writer, EP was the editor of *Dolman's Magazine* (London). In 1846 he violently attacked in that magazine the writings of Fr William Faber, a colleague of John Henry Newman§, on the asceticism of St Rose of Lima in a projected series of *Lives of the Saints* (London, 42 vols., 1847–56). The series was suspended, defended by Newman (against his later better judgment), and restarted by the Oratory of St Philip Neri. SOURCE COPAC; ODNB [see William Faber].

P188 *Sick calls from the diary of a missionary priest* (by Edward Price; dedicated to the Catholic clergy of England). London: Charles Dolman, 1850. SOURCE COPAC. LOCATION L.

COMMENTARY Stories mostly reprinted from *Dolman's Magazine*. Contents: 'The infidel' (mentions Daniel O'Connell and the suffering Irish), 'The dying banker', 'The drunkard's death' (about an Irishman), 'The miser's death', 'The wanderer's death', 'The dying shirt-maker', 'The broken heart', 'The destitute poor', 'The cholera patient', 'The merchant's clerk', 'Death beds of the poor', 'A missioner's Sunday work', 'The dying burglar', 'The Magdalen', 'The famished needlewoman' [ML].

P189 *The strike and the drunkard's death* [anon.].
+ London: Burns & Oates, 1880. SOURCE COPAC. LOCATION L, O.
COMMENTARY 31pp. A note stating that 'The names of persons and localities are, of course altered', suggests that the story was based on fact. Concerns an Irish alcoholic in London [RL].

PRICE, Maria. See LA TOUCHE, Mrs Maria.

PRITTIE, Catherine Charlotte. See MABERLY, Catherine Charlotte.

'PROUT, Captain', attributed pseud. See LEVY, John.

'PROUT, Father', pseud. See MAHONY, Fr Francis Sylvester.

PURCELL, Mrs —, pseud. 'Myself', fl. 1820. Novelist.
P190 *The orientalist, or electioneering in Ireland; a tale* (by 'Myself'; dedicated to 'Myself').
+ London: Baldwin, Cradock & Joy; Edinburgh: J. Thomson & Co.; Dublin: William Gribbin; Belfast: Samuel Archer, 1820, 2 vols. SOURCE Block, p. 193; Brown, 1395; British Fiction; Garside, 1820:59. LOCATION Corvey CME 3–628–48312–3, Ireland related fiction, D, L, NUC, InND Loeber coll. (vol. 1 only).
COMMENTARY Advertisements in 1820 in the London *Morning Chronicle* and the *Star* announce this volume as an Irish novel. The story is set in Co. Antrim where an absentee landlord and his family come to secure a parliamentary seat for their son. His opponent is a mysterious gentleman of Indian extraction, who later turns out to be the long-lost Lord Dalkeith [Brown; British Fiction].

'PUZZLEBRAIN, Peregrine', fl. 1818. Pseudonym of a novelist who calls himself the 'assistant to the schoolmaster of Gandercleugh' (alluding to Sir Walter Scott's pseud.). SOURCE Garside, 1818:53; RL.
P191 *Tales of my landlady* (ed. by 'Peregrine Puzzlebrain').
+ London: M. Iley, 1818, 3 vols. SOURCE Belanger, 57; British Fiction; Garside, 1818:53. LOCATION Corvey CME 3–628–48869–9, Ireland related fiction, L.
COMMENTARY Contents: 'The uses of adversity' (a rich English heiress, Caroline Mordaunt, loses her fortune when her father dies. As a result of her sudden loss she is forced to take up a position as a governess to a family in Ireland. Later she becomes a companion to an Irish gentleman's English wife, who considers the Irish as savage and barbaric. Caroline refuses to accept such views of the Irish. She returns to London and marries well, having undergone while in Ireland a series of learning experiences that make her less vain and proud), 'The prejudiced pair' (contains descriptions of Irish society), 'Affluence, poverty, and mediocrity' (an Irish servant saves his French master from prison during the French Revolution), 'Hear before you judge'. Not to be confused with William Thomas Haley's *Tales of my landlady* (London, 1843–4) [ML; JB; British Fiction].

Q

'QUANTOCK, Andrew', pseud. See FISHER, Walter Mulrea.

QUIGLEY, Dr—. See QUIGLEY, Fr Hugh.

QUIGLEY, Fr Hugh (known as Dr Quigley), pseud. 'A missionary priest', b. near Tulla (Co. Clare) 1819 (1818 according to Boase), d. Troy (NY) 1883. Priest, anti-Baptist fiction writer and historian, HQ was designated by his father for the church at an early age. Harsh treatment at school made him run away to Killaloe (Co. Offaly) where he received tuition at Madden's classical school. He worked as a topographer at the office of the ordnance survey in Dublin and declined a government scholarship to Maynooth because he did not want to take the required oath of loyalty. Subsequently he was educated at the University of Sapienza in Rome and, returning to Ireland, worked in Tulla and Killaloe during the Famine. He then served in Sheffield (England); was involved in the rebellion of 1848 in Ireland, and asked to be posted to the American mission in New York. He was assigned to Troy (NY) and spent ten years there before being appointed rector of the University of St Mary in Chicago. After a few years he resigned to become a missionary to the Chippewa Indians and in 1875 to gold miners in Eureka (CA). Later in life, he returned to Troy. Besides his novels, he wrote *The Irish race in California and on the Pacific coast* (San Francisco, 1878). SOURCE Boase, vi, p. 445; Brady, p. 208; Brown, p. 257; Fanning, pp 75, 141; biography in the introd. to HG's *The Irish race*, pp iii–xvi; RIA/DIB; Sutherland, p. 516; H.J. Walsh, *Hallowed were the gold dust trails: the story of the pioneer priests of northern California* ([Santa Clara], 1947).

Q1   *The cross and the shamrock; or, how to defend the faith. An Irish-American Catholic tale of real life, descriptive of the temptations, sufferings, trials and triumphs of the children of St. Patrick in the great republic of Washington. A book for the entertainment and special instruction of the Catholic male and female servants of the United States* (written by 'A missionary priest'; dedicated to the faithful Irish-American Catholic citizens of the Union).
+ Boston: Patrick Donahoe, [1853]. SOURCE Brown, 1399; Fanning, p. 389; Wright, ii, 1986; partly printed in Exiles, pp 121–7. LOCATION InND Loeber coll., Wright web.
+ Boston: Thomas Noonan & Co., 1853. LOCATION D, DCU.
Dublin: James Duffy & Co., [1886 or earlier]. SOURCE Adv. in W. Carleton, *Redmond Count O'Hanlon* (Dublin, 1886). LOCATION L ([c.1900], new edn).
COMMENTARY Religious and moral instruction in the form of a story of the trials of a family of orphan children at the hands of various types of proselytizers. The book speaks harshly of American protestantism. It describes various aspects of American life, such as railroad construction [Brown].

Q2   *The prophet of the ruined abbey; or, a glance of the future of Ireland. A narrative founded on the ancient prophesies of Culmkill and on other predictions and popular traditions among the Irish* [anon.] (dedicated to Emperor Napoleon III, 'the expected conqueror of England, and the true liberator of Ireland'; dedication dated New York, 20 Nov. 1854).
+ New York: Edward Dunigan & Brother, 1854. SOURCE Fanning, p. 389 (1855 edn); Wright, ii, 1988 (1855 edn). LOCATION NUC, Wright web.
+ Boston: Patrick Donahoe, 1860. LOCATION DCU, InND Loeber coll.

+ Dublin, London: James Duffy & Sons, [1863]. SOURCE Brown, 1400. LOCATION Dt, C.

's Hertogenbosch: Maatschappij Katholieke Illustratie, 1880 (trans. into Dutch as *De profeet van de verwoeste abdij. Een blik in het verleden van Ierland*). SOURCE Mes p. 198. COMMENTARY Historical fiction set in Ireland in the second half of the eighteenth century. The main character is a priest who is under sentence of death at the hands of the British government but who is rescued by his brother, a captain in the French army who has secretly come to Ireland. Many wild adventures befall him. He lives for years in a cave in the Cliffs of Moher (Co. Clare), where at one time he rescues a little boy from the eagles. The book is anti-English in sentiment [ML; Brown].

Q3 *Profit and loss. A story of the life of a genteel Irish-American, illustrative of godless education* (by Dr Quigley).
    + New York: T. O'Kane, 1873. SOURCE Brown, 1401; Fanning, p. 389; Wright, ii, 1987. LOCATION L, InND Loeber coll., Wright web.
COMMENTARY Religious and moral instruction to guard youth from danger, particularly from the Baptist church. The story is mainly concerned with how the main character, Michael Mulrooney, who was driven out of Ireland by his landlord, maintains his faith in America [Brown].

QUIN, Michael. QUIN, Michael Joseph.

QUIN, Michael Joseph (known as Michael Quin), b. Thurles (Co. Tipperary) 1796, d. Boulonge-sur-Mer (France) 1843. Catholic journalist, translator, novelist, travel writer and editor, MJQ was the son of Morty Quin, a distiller. He entered TCD in 1811 and was called to the Bar at Lincoln's Inn in London in 1823, but instead of the law he devoted his life to writing. He made a name as a journalist contributing articles on foreign affairs to the *Morning Chronicle* and the *Morning Herald* (both London). *A visit to Spain 1822–23* (London, 1823), a collection of some of his reactions to anti-clerical extremists in Spain, was favourably reviewed by Joseph Blanco White§. In 1823 he wrote on French plans for military intervention in Spain in *A secret history of the Council of Verona* (London, 1823), and he translated from Spanish the memoirs of Ferdinand VII written by José Joaquín de Mora. He also translated an apologia by the former Mexican emperor Agustín de Iturbide, then in London and looking to return to power; lobbied the British government on his behalf, and took care of Iturbide's daughters when he returned to Mexico, where he was executed. MJQ was editor of the *Monthly Review* (London) from 1825 to 1832; the *Catholic Journal* (London, 1833), and he was the first editor of the *Dublin Review*, a joint effort with Daniel O'Connell and Nicholas, later cardinal, Wiseman§ in 1836. MJQ resigned to accept a posting to Cuba in the Spanish colonial service but when this did not work out he returned to London where he later edited the *Tablet*. Many of his books deal with travels in Europe, including *A steam voyage down the Danube* (London, 1835), and *Steam voyages on the Seine, the Moselle and the Rhine* (London, 1843). He also wrote on banking and property issues and in 1839 he translated the account of French explorer Léon de Laborde's journey through the Sinai to the lost city of Petra in Jordan. MJQ died in poverty after a long illness, survived by his widow and three daughters. For MJQ's papers, see ODNB. SOURCE Allibone, ii, pp 1717–18; B & S, p. 689; ODNB; D.J. O'Donoghue, *Geographic distribution of Irish ability* (Dublin, 1906), p. 306; RIA/DIB.

Q4 *Nourmahal; an oriental romance* (by Michael Quin).
    + London: Henry Colburn, 1838, 3 vols. SOURCE OCLC. LOCATION L.
COMMENTARY A romance supposedly related by a storyteller in Kashmir [ML].

R

'R.-A., A.', fl. 1877. Pseudonym of a travel writer and illustrator.

R1   *A rollicking tour in Ireland. By Rag, Tag, and Bobtail* (by 'A. R.-A.').
+ Paisley: Alex. Gardner, 1877 (ill. A. R.-A.). LOCATION D.
COMMENTARY A humorous travelogue which, according to the preface dated 1877 from Moors, Tobersnorey, N.B. (New Brunswick, Canada?) first appeared in an unidentified periodical [RL].

'R., E.C.' Pseudonym of author of preface. See MOORE, Thomas.

RADCLIFF, John. See RADCLIFFE, John.

RADCLIFFE (also spelled Radcliff), John, b. Co. Fermanagh *c.*1765, d. 1843. Jurist and co-author, JR was the son of the Revd Richard Radcliffe and Catherine Mason. He studied at TCD where he graduated BA in 1787 and LLD in 1795. He was admitted to the Middle Temple (London) in 1784, and to the King's Inns in 1789. He became judge of the prerogative court in 1816 and privy councillor in 1818. JR was co-author with Theobald Wolfe Tone§ and Richard Jebb§ of the mock Gothic novel *Belmont Castle* (Dublin, 1790), for which he wrote the background. SOURCE B & S, p. 690; M. Deane, introd. to *Belmont Castle or suffering sensibility* (Dublin, 1998), p. 2; IBL, 23 (1935), pp 47–8; Keane, p. 414; Leslie & Wallace, pp 997–8.

RAM, Revd Stopford James, b. Co. Cork? 1826, d. England? 1881. Clergyman and religious and temperance writer, SJR was the son of Revd Digby Joseph Stopford Ram, a Church of Ireland clergyman of Brookeville (Co. Cork), and Penelope Wallis of Renny (Co. Cork). He was descended from the Ramsford and Clonattin (Co. Wexford) branches of the Ram family and was a cousin of the Revd Richard Sinclair Brooke§. He received his education at St John's College, Cambridge, graduating BA in 1849 and MA in 1852. He was ordained in 1849 in Armagh and became minister at Tynan (Co. Armagh, 1849–51), after which he moved to England. He ministered at Elkstone (Staffs., 1841–54); Christ Church, Stratford (Essex, 1854–58); Pavenham (Beds., 1859), and was then vicar of Christ Church, Battersea (London). He was appointed associate secretary for the Irish Church Missions in 1858. His writings reflect the aims of this organization. He was author of *The temperance movement, its importance and Christian character* (London, 1856), and other tracts. He married in 1849 Eleanor Mary Hawkshaw (d. 1881), with whom he had nine children. SOURCE Allibone, ii, 1731; BLC; Brooke, p. 121; Burke's, p. 978; Fleming, *Armagh*, pp 815–16; RIA/DIB; RL.

R2   *The unseen hand; or, episodes in an eventful life* (by Stopford James Ram).
+ Bath: Binns & Goodwin, [1852] (ill. H. Anerla). SOURCE Adv. in C.G.H [C.G. Hamilton], *The unclaimed daughter* (Bath edn); COPAC. LOCATION L.
COMMENTARY Protestant religious fiction. Henry, the son of Emma Carlton and Robert de Courcy, leaves Ireland to travel to Italy and eventually to study at Cambridge. He becomes a minister and goes to Ireland, but decides to attend to the poor in Liverpool. Later he returns to Ireland, but ends up at Tunbridge (Kent), after which he marries Florence, his childhood love [RL; chapter headings advertised in C.G.H., *The unclaimed daughter* (Bath, [1853]); BLC].

R3   *Dale end; or, six weeks at the vicarage* [anon.].
+ Dublin: George Herbert; London: Hamilton, Adams & Co., 1854. SOURCE COPAC; NSTC. LOCATION L (destroyed), O.

COMMENTARY Protestant religious fiction set in Ireland. The preface states that the representation of the minister in the story is based on ministers of the Church of England, who are 'commonly called "Evangelical"'. The preface also states that the village dialogues and parochial visitations 'are authentic' [RL].

RAMBAUT, A. Beatrice, pseud. '**A.B. Romney**', fl. 1900. Fiction writer for juveniles, ABR was the author of several books for young children and probably was Irish. It is likely that she was a member of the Rambaut family that descended from William Rambaut, a wine merchant, whose father, Jean, was from France and had settled in Dublin in 1754. SOURCE BLC; Fleming, *Armagh*, pp 334–5.

R4 *Little village folk* (by 'A.B. Romney').
London, Glasgow, Edinburgh, Dublin: Blackie & Son, 1900 (ill. Robert Hope). SOURCE OCLC. LOCATION L.
London, Glasgow, Bombay: Blackie & Son, 1909 (new edn). LOCATION L.
COMMENTARY Fiction for juveniles advertised as 'A series of delightful stories of Irish village children' [Adv. in K. Tynan§, *Three fair maids* (London, 1901)].

'**THE RAMBLER FROM CLARE**', fl. 1880s. Pseudonym of a miscellaneous anthologist, who judging from his pseudonym was a resident of Co. Clare.
R5 *Recreative reading for the million. Being a collection of original poems, palindromes, puns, quips, cranks and oddities* (by 'The rambler from Clare').
+ Dublin: James Duffy & Co. [1886 or earlier]. SOURCE Adv. in W. Carleton, *Redmond Count O'Hanlon* (Dublin, 1886); OCLC. LOCATION D.
COMMENTARY Contents other than poems and songs: 'Thought reading; or, how Professor Von-Muxen found the pin', 'Wife's mother – a parody', 'Lines showing the feelings and sentiments of an N (INN) Totaller, who afterwards became a T-Totaller', 'To a young lady with a huge "dress-improper"', 'The pleasures of love; or, the course of true love for once running smooth', 'Demonstrating a fact', 'An alarming fate', 'The wife's farewell to her husband', 'The grand old man', 'Waiting for the May', 'The married man's complaint', 'The seasons in and around Norbeech', 'The ups and downs of a (K)night of the fog; or, how Robert Leach reached the "Downs"', 'A "jubilee" moment of Norbeech "mop"', 'Sound and sense', 'A satire on the dynamite scare', 'Be true to truth and honour', 'An abstraction on social vanity', 'An early serenade of the long ago – as a novel contrast to the modern late ones', 'Carrol Cody and Betsy Betsy's love affair', 'The traveller and home', 'Autumn – a reverie', 'True fame and universal duty', 'Thought on walking through a country church-yard', 'The kite and wind – an illustration of man and the world', 'Address to morning's dawn', 'The season's changes', 'Thoughts and aspirations at the close of the year', 'A toast', 'The husband's lament', 'Lines on the death of my young wife', 'A wail – in memoriam', 'Beauty and the flower', 'Norbeech bells', 'Lesson from a tempest', '"The grand old man"', 'The devils and the "times"', 'The "ball o' blue" – a starchy lucubration', 'A Tory dinner', 'Chamberlain', 'Down Unionists, lie down', 'Joseph's coat of many turns', 'Returning thanks for a sprig of shamrock', 'Ireland – a retrospection', 'The exile's return', 'The Irish nation's appeal to their liberal brethren in Great Britain', 'God save Ireland – new version', 'How coercion was defeated', 'A government lying at full length', 'The charge of the Enniskilling dragoons', 'The crime of being an Irishman' [CD].

'**RAMSAY, Grace**', pseud. See **O'MEARA, Kathleen**.

RANDALL, Alfred, fl. 1880. American novelist, AR lived for some time on the western shore of Lake Michigan. SOURCE Ximenes cat. 61/139.

R6   *Harrington's fortunes. A novel* (by Alfred Randall).
      London: Samuel Tinsley, 1880, 3 vols. SOURCE Allibone Suppl., ii, p. 1262; Wolff,
      5689. LOCATION L.
      COMMENTARY Humorous Irish-American novel about the adventures of a sea captain
      in the troubled Ireland of 1848 [Ximenes cat. 61/139].

RANKIN, Emily. RANKIN, Emily Elizabeth.

RANKIN, Emily Elizabeth (known as **Emily Rankin**), fl. 1829. Fiction writer for juveniles
and, judging from the dedication, probably a teacher. EEK perhaps can be identified with the
Miss Rankin who contributed to *Household Words* (London, 1854). SOURCE Lohrli, p. 410; RL.
R7   *Ellen Cameron. A tale for youth* (by Emily Rankin; dedicated to 'The young people
      of Mrs. Kirnan's school').
      + London: Baldwin & Cradock, 1829 (ill. W. Harvey, I.W. Cook). SOURCE Allibone,
      ii, p. 1740. LOCATION L, InND Loeber coll.
COMMENTARY Fiction for juveniles. Ellen Cameron, born in India, is more or less neglected
after her mother's death. Eventually her father sends her to England. Her aunt does not want
her in her house and she is sent to a school. Later on she meets some Irish cousins and stays
with them in Ireland. When her father has remarried, she returns to India. It requires some
adjustment for her to feel part of the family. After a fire in the house, they all return to
England [ML].

'RATTLER, Capt. Morgan', pseud. See **O'SULLIVAN, Dennis.**

RAYMOND, Rossiter Worthington, b. Cincinnati (OH) 1840. American mining engineer,
novelist, travel and children's writer and translator, RWR graduated from the Brooklyn
Polytechnic Institute in 1858, studied mining in Heidelberg and Munich and became a min-
ing engineer in New York City. He was later secretary of the American Institute of Mining
Engineers; US commissioner of Mining Statistics; editor of the *Engineering and Mining Journal*
(New York?), and author of *Mineral resources ... of the states and territories west of the Rocky
Mountains* (Washington, DC, [1868]–77, 8 vols.). With Mrs S.J. Lippincott§ he authored
Treasures from fairy-land (New York, 1870), and under the pseudonym 'Robertson Gray' wrote
the novel *Brave Hearts* (London, 1873). His one work with an Irish connection is listed below.
SOURCE Allibone, ii, p. 1750; Allibone Suppl., ii, p. 1266; DAB; RL.
R8   *Camp and cabin: Sketches of life and travel in the west* (by Rossiter Worthington
      Raymond).
      + New York: Fords, Howard & Hulbert, 1880 (ill. Karst). SOURCE Allibone Suppl.,
      ii, p. 1266; Wright, iii, 4448; COPAC. LOCATION C, DCL, InND Loeber coll.
COMMENTARY Set in a mining village in the western US. 'Agamemnon', one of the six stories
in this volume, has as one of the main characters a Mr O'Ballyhan, a graduate of TCD, but
now a good-for-nothing spendthrift. His 16-year-old son has taken him in hand and has forbidden drinking and gambling. The son is also the main economic force in the village in that
he had discovered deposits of ore. The father peppers his speech with Latin phrases and unsuccessfully tries to outsmart his son in obtaining money for gambling and drinking [ML].

REA, K.G., fl. 1885. Temperance writer, KGR probably was Irish given the setting of this
novel and the fact that he or she published in Dublin. SOURCE RL.
R9   *Neta Carleton and her Irish cousins* (by K.G. Rea).
      + Dublin: Robert Chapman, 1885. SOURCE Brown 2, 1345. LOCATION D.

Read

COMMENTARY Neta is a West Indian girl who comes to Ireland to stay with relatives, including Revd Norwood, rector of 'Marshborough'. This rectory is near the village of Castlegeoghegan (Castletown Geoghegan?, Co. Westmeath). The rector and his family are ardent teetotallers and temperance is the main interest of the story. Many examples are given of the evil effects of drink. There is a happy love story [Brown 2].

READ, Mrs C.A. (also known as **Mrs R.H. Read** and **Mrs R.H. Reade**), fl. 1882. Mrs CAR was the novelist wife of the author Charles Anderson Read§. Her 'When Malachi wore the collar of gold', a series of Irish folktales, probably appeared in a periodical in 1886, and she contributed to Henderson's *Our Young Folks Weekly Budget* (London), edited by her husband. She published eight works of fiction, some written for children. SOURCE Allibone Suppl., ii, p. 1266 [under Mrs C.A. Read and Mrs R.H. Read]; Boase, iii, p. 61; Brown 1408; Brown 2, p. 227; M. Kelleher, 'The cabinet of Irish literature' in *Éire-Ireland*, 38 (2003), p. 76; RL.

R10   *Phyllis and Corydon; or from the mountain shadow to the footlights* (by Mrs C.A. Read).
London: James Henderson, 1882 (ill.; Sixpenny Pocket Library). SOURCE Brown 2, 1346.

COMMENTARY No copy located. Phyllis Ross, defrauded of her birthright, goes to London and there becomes a great actress. After a successful career the mystery of her birth is cleared up. She returns to her old home in Co. Down and marries Gerald Corydon, the hero of the tale. Written for the readers of *Our Young Folks* (London). 'Phyllis and Corydon' is the name of a musical piece based on the story of Phyllis and Corydon in Virgil's *Ecologue* VII [Brown 2; RL].

R11   *Fairy fancy; what she saw and what she heard* (Mrs R.H. Read).
London: Blackie & Son, 1883 (ill.). SOURCE Allibone Suppl. ii, p. 1266. LOCATION L.
COMMENTARY Identified as by Mrs C.A. Read in Allibone in a London 1882 edn, but not located [Allibone; RL].

R12   *Our Dolly: her words and ways* (by Mrs R.H. Read).
London, Glasgow, Edinburgh, Dublin: Blackie & Son, 1883 (ill.). SOURCE Allibone Suppl. ii, p. 1266. LOCATION L.
COMMENTARY Identified as by Mrs C.A. Read in Allibone in a London 1882 edn, but not located [Allibone; RL].

R13   *Dora: a girl without a home* (by Mrs R.H. Read).
London, Glasgow, Edinburgh, Dublin: Blackie & Son, 1883. SOURCE Allibone Suppl., ii, p. 1266; Brown, p. 259. LOCATION L.

R14   *Silver mill: A tale of the Don Valley* (by Mrs R.H. Read).
London, Glasgow, Edinburgh, Dublin: Blackie & Son, 1886. SOURCE Allibone Suppl. ii, p. 1266 (1885 edn); Brown, p. 259. LOCATION L.
London, Glasgow, Edinburgh, Bombay: Blackie & Son, 1908 (new edn; as *Silver mill*). SOURCE COPAC. LOCATION E.

R15   *The goldsmith's ward; a tale of London city in the 15th century* (by Mrs R.H. Reade).
London: Chapman & Hall, 1891. LOCATION L, NUC.

R16   *Milly Davidson* (by Mrs R.H. Read).
[location?], [publisher?, [prior to 1889]. SOURCE Adv. on title page in *Puck's Hall* (London, 1889); Brown, p. 259]
COMMENTARY No copy located [RL].

R17   *Puck's Hall. A romance* (by Mrs R.H. Reade).
Belfast: Charles W. Olley, 1889. SOURCE Brown, 1408.

+ London: Hamilton, Adams & Co.; Belfast: Charles W. Olley, 1889. LOCATION D, Dt.
COMMENTARY Set in Newcastle (Co. Down) [Brown].

READ, Charles Anderson (also known as Charles Anderson Reade and **Charles A. Read**), pseud. '**Harry Scrimshaw**', b. Kilsella House, near Sligo (Co. Sligo) 1841, d. Thornton Heath (Surrey) 1878. Novelist, poet, periodical writer and editor, CAR was the son of the schoolmaster at Hilltown, close to Newry (Co. Down), who came there after he lost his inheritance and estate. CAR tried his luck in business for some years as a merchant at Rathfriland (Co. Down), but after he failed in this he obtained a post in James Henderson's publishing house in London in 1863, and was one of the editors of Henderson's *Our Young Folks Weekly Budget* (London), to which he contributed stories. Some of his sketches, poems and short tales were published in the *Dublin University Magazine*. He is best known for his editing of the first three of four volumes of the *Cabinet of Irish literature* (London, 1876–8), which contain selections from noted authors, the last volume of which was completed by T.P. O'Connor§ and includes samples of CAR's prose and poetry. It provided much background for Justin McCarthy's§ anthology, *Irish literature* (New York, 1904; Chicago, 1904, 10 vols.). CAR published several stories in newspapers, including 'Dark deeds! A tale of underground London'. Another, 'The mystery of Hazel Lodge', set in Ireland, was published in May Agnes Fleming's§ *The star of De Vere; or, the mysteries of Bantry Hall* (London, 1871–2, vol. 2). It is possible that some of his stories were published in the US. According to an advertisement in [anon.] *The queen of the night* (New York, 1871), its author also wrote several works with presumed Irish content, including 'The red MacMahon', 'Peep o' Day Boys', and 'Savourneen delish'. The latter story was published by CAR in London in 1867, but since the US copy has not been located yet, it is not possible to compare the two. CAR's wife was the author Mrs C.A. Read§ who also published under the name Mrs R.H. Read. CAR is not to be confused with English novelist and playwright Charles Reade (1818–84). SOURCE Boase, iii, p. 61; Boylan, p. 336; Brown, p. 258; Hogan 2, pp 1047–8; OCIL, p. 491; ODNB; O'Donoghue, p. 395; RIA/DIB; RL; Sutherland, p. 521.

R18   *Confessions of a jockey: A betting man's career* (by 'Harry Scrimshaw').
        [location?]: [publisher?], [date?]. LOCATION D (title page missing).
        COMMENTARY No other copy located [RL].

R19   *Savourneen dheelish; or, one true heart* (by Charles A. Read).
        London: James Henderson, 1867 (The People's Pocket Story Books). SOURCE Brown,
        1405 (1869 edn); Sutherland, p. 521. LOCATION L (1870, 3rd edn).
COMMENTARY The story is set around Dundalk (Co. Louth) and based on the same incident told by William Carleton§ in his 'Wildgoose lodge' (first published in his *Traits and stories of the Irish peasantry* (London, 1833, 3 vols.). One of the main characters is Kate Costelloe, who gives evidence that will bring her brother and her lover to the gallows [Brown].

R20   *Aileen Aroon; or, the pride of Clonmore* [anon.].
        London: James Henderson, 1867 (The People's Pocket Story Books). SOURCE Brown, 1406
        (1870 edn); NSTC (1870 edn); Sutherland, p. 521. LOCATION D (n.d., 6th edn), L.
COMMENTARY Set in Ireland in Fenian times where Garret O'Neill is falsely accused of murder. His sweetheart, Aileen, is abducted by his enemy while on her way to stand by him. She is suspected of infidelity and driven from her home, but is befriended by Fr Nugent and his Fenian band. In the end the lovers are united [Brown].

R21   *Eileen Oge; or, dark's hour before dawn. A romance of Irish life and character* [anon.].
        New York: Richmond & Co., 1871 (Richmond's Novels, n.s., No. 19). SOURCE Adv.
        and partly published in [anon.] *The queen of the night* (New York, 1871).

Read

COMMENTARY Tentatively attributed to CAR (see biographical sketch). No full copy located. A penny dreadful issued monthly at 10¢. Either preceded or followed by Edmund Falconer's play *Eileen Oge, or, dark's hour before the dawn* (London, New York, 1871). The first few chapters of Eileen Oge had been first published in [anon.], *The queen of the night. A story of love, crime and intrigue in wicked New York* (New York: Richmond & Co., 1871). Crime fiction set in Ireland. Contents as advertised in this booklet: 'The fairy man. Eileen's fortunes. Mark Logen's suit. Eileen's vow. The lover trapped. A vile scheme. An ace for clubs. Jimmy the innocent. Fair and foul. A new device. Eileen's resolve. The lead mine. A dark web of treachery. The ruined abbey. The vaults. The death-fetch. A good deed. The devil's pool. Conclusion and Frank's prosperity' [ML].

READ, Mrs R.H. See **READ, Mrs C.A.**

'READE, Amos', pseud. See **ROWAN, Anne Margaret.**

READE, Charles. Co-author. See **BOUCICAULT, Dionysius Lardner.**

READE, Charles Anderson. See **READ, Charles Anderson.**

READE, Mrs R.H. See **READ, Mrs C.A.**

'A REAL PADDY', pseud. See **EGAN, Pierce.**

REED, Talbot Baines, b. Hackney (London) 1852, d. Highgate (London) 1893. Popular English author of adventure stories for boys, TBR was the son of Sir Charles Reed and Margaret Baines. His father was an MP, deputy governor of the Irish Society, and a nephew of John Anderson, the Belfast bibliographer. His family were devout Congregationalists and he is described by the ODNB as a sportsman and the 'best kind of Victorian, a man of high principle, enormous industry, strong social conscience, and a robust sense of humour'. His stories for boys celebrated the public school cult of manliness and remained popular well into the twentieth century. He married in 1876 Elizabeth Greer, daughter of Samuel Macurdy Greer, a Presbyterian and MP for Derry and county court judge for Cavan and Leitrim. TBR had a great fondness for Ireland, and loved to visit. He was an expert on typography and was a founding member of the Bibliographical Society. SOURCE Allibone Suppl., ii, p. 1269; Boase, iii, p. 82; Brown, p. 259; NCBEL 4, p. 1853; ODNB; Sutherland, p. 527.

R22   *The adventures of a three guinea watch* (by Talbot Baines Reed).
       London: Religious Tract Society, [1881?] (The Boy's Own Bookshelf). LOCATION L (1883 edn), NUC.
       COMMENTARY Some Irish figures feature at the end of the story [ML].

R23   *Sir Ludar: A story of the days of the great Queen Bess* (by Talbot Baines Reed).
       London: Sampson Low & Co., 1889. SOURCE Brown, 1409; Baker, p. 55. LOCATION L, NUC (n.d. edn).
COMMENTARY Historical fiction for juveniles. It tells the adventures of an English apprentice boy in the company of Sir Ludar, who is a son of Sorley Boy MacDonnell of Dunluce Castle (Co. Antrim). Some of the adventures recounted are the re-taking of Dunluce from the English and the naval battle between the Armada and the English fleet in 1588 [Brown].

R24   *Kilgorman. A story of Ireland in 1798* (by Talbot Baines Reed).
       + London, Edinburgh, New York: T. Nelson & Sons, 1895 (ill. J.W.; includes memorial to TBR by John Sime). SOURCE Brown, 1410; Wolff, 5722. LOCATION L, NUC, InND Loeber coll.

COMMENTARY A tale of land and sea adventures set in Derry, Dublin, Paris and other foreign localities, mainly in the period 1793 to 1797 although the last few pages carry the reader through 1798 and 1799. It covers the Terror and Maximilien Robespierre's fall in France; the United Irishmen movement in the years before the 1798 rebellion; and other events, such as the mutiny at the Nore (1797) and the battle of Camperdown (Kamperduin, off the Netherlands, 1797) when the British defeated a Dutch fleet launched to aid in the French expedition to Ireland. The work is hostile to the aims of the United Irishmen. It features the Irish revolutionary Lord Edward Fitzgerald [Nield, 1649; B. Brown].

REEVE, Clara, b. Ipswich (Suffolk) 1729 (1725 in Allibone), d. Ipswich 1807 (1803 in Allibone). English moral and didactic novelist and poet, CR was the daughter of Revd William Reeve and Hannah Smithies. After her father's death she wrote to support herself and published over 20 volumes and numerous pamphlets. According to the ODNB, troubles with her London publisher spurred her to write to the Dublin publisher Archer, requesting that he republish some of her work, if not contrary to copyright law. In a letter to J.A. Walker in 1791 she said 'I would rather finish one of my beginnings, of which I have many by me, and send it to Dublin to seek its fortune ...' Only one of her works deals with Ireland. SOURCE Allibone, ii, p. 1762; Blain, p. 890; C. Reeve, letters to Joseph Cooper Walker, TCD, MS 1461; *Jrnl of English Literary History*, 9 (1942), p. 225; ODNB; Summers, p. 188.
R25   *Castle Connor. An Irish story* (by Clara Reeve).
COMMENTARY Manuscript, written 1787 or earlier. According to a preface in CR's *Exiles* (London, 1788, 3 vols.), the manuscript for this novel was lost when it was sent by means of the Ipswich coach to London in May 1787. However the theme (or parts of the novel) may have been printed later as *Fatherless Fanny* (see Mrs Edgeworth§). The original was characterized as a ghost story [*Jrnl of English Literary History*, 9 (1942), pp 224–6; NCBEL 2, p. 1005; Summers, p. 188].

REEVES, Jeanie Selina. See DAMMAST, Jeanie Selina.

REID, Mayne. See REID, Capt. Thomas Mayne.

REID, Capt. Thomas Mayne (also known as Capt. Mayne Reid), pseuds 'Charles Beach' and 'Charles A. Beach', b. Ballyroney (Co. Down) 1818, d. Ross (Herts.) 1883. ODNB says he died in Maida Hill, London, and this would seem right since he was buried at Kensal Green cemetery three days after his death. An adventure novelist, journalist and playwright, TMR was the son of a clergyman (also known as Thomas Reid) who was senior clerk of the Irish general assembly. His mother was the daughter of the Rev. Samuel Rutherford. TMR was educated at the Royal Academical Institution in Belfast but refused his father's plans for him to enter the Presbyterian ministry. After running a school for a while he emigrated to America. He travelled widely for five years in the south, west and north before settling down in 1843 as a journalist in Philadelphia, where he met Edgar Allan Poe, who described him as 'a colossal but most picturesque liar' (RIA/DIB). He moved to New York, where he worked for the *New York Herald* but he enlisted and was commissioned a second lieutenant in a regiment of New York volunteers for the Mexican war of 1846, where he served with bravery and was wounded, later recounting his experiences in *War life* (New York, 1849). His first play, *Love's martyr*, was produced in New York in 1848. In 1849 he sailed for continental Europe, visiting Ireland en route, to take part in the revolution in Hungary, but he arrived too late. He settled in London where he worked as a writer and journalist and with his novel *The rifle rangers* (London, 1860), based partly on his experiences in Mexico, established himself as an internationally-popular novelist, writing mainly adventure stories for boys, many of them featuring the American West and young heroes who overcome tremendous odds. His work influenced such later writers as Arthur Conan Doyle and Robert Louis Stevenson, who described TMR as 'that cheerful, ingenious, romantic soul' (Hogan 2, p. 1055). He went bankrupt in about 1866 and returned to New York and embarked on a successful lecture tour to replenish his finances. He went back to England in 1870. Over a period of almost forty years he published 'seventy-five novels of adventure and many short stories and sketches' (Dime novels). His books were translated into several languages, but it has not yet proved possible to assign all French and Dutch translations (listed in BNF and Adamnet) to their English-language originals. TMR founded a short-lived magazine *Onward* (probably NY), and edited the *Boys' Illustrated News* (London). His later years were clouded by depression and financial difficulties. Thus far we have found only one Irish work of fiction by TMR, the serial 'The Irish night mail' (*Young Ireland*, Dublin, 1876). His portrait was published in the biography written by his wife, the former Elizabeth Hyde (London, 1900), with whom he had fallen in love when she was only age 13, and had married when she was age 15. For his portraits and papers, see ODNB. SOURCE Allibone, ii, pp 1766–7; Allibone Suppl., i, p. 113 [under Charles Beach]; Allibone Suppl., ii, p. 1271; Boase, iii, pp 103–4; Boylan, p. 338; Brown, p. 343; Burke, p. 609; DLB, xxi, clxiii; Dime novels; Hogan 2, pp 1054–5; Holmes cat. 64/116; Law, p. 140; NCBEL 4, p. 1389; OCIL, p. 495; ODNB; O'Donoghue, p. 396; E. Reid, *Mayne Reid, a memoir of his life* (London, 1890); E. Reid & C.H. Coe, *Captain Mayne Reid. His life and adventures* (London, 1900); RIA/DIB; Sutherland, pp 527–8.

R26　　*The land pirates; or, the league of Devil's Island. A tale of the Mississippi* (by Capt. Mayne Reid).
New York: n.p., n.d., Half-dime Library No. 87. SOURCE Dime novels.

R27　　*War life; or, the adventures of a light infantry officer* (by Capt. Mayne Reid).
New York: A.J. Townsend, 1849. LOCATION NUC.
COMMENTARY 70pp. Story based on author's experiences in the Mexican war [NUC; RL].

R28　　*The rifle rangers, or, adventures of an officer in Southern Mexico* (by Capt. Mayne Reid).
London: William Shoberl, 1850, 2 vols. SOURCE Osborne, p. 1024 ([*c*.1860] edn); Sadleir, 2029; Wolff, 5756; Topp 6, 232. LOCATION L, CaOTP ([*c*.1860] edn), NUC.
London, Belfast: Simms & M'Intyre, 1853 (Parlour Library, No. 98) ([enlarged edn]; as *The rifle rangers; or, adventures in Southern Mexico*). SOURCE Topp 1, p. 285; Sadleir, ii, p. 155. LOCATION NUC.
London: Darton & Hodge, [1862–5?] (ill.). SOURCE Topp 3, p. 389; Wolff, 5756a; OCLC. LOCATION CtY.
COMMENTARY London n.d. edn Greatly enlarged edn [Topp 3, p. 389].
+ London: Blackie & Son, n.d., as *The rifle rangers or adventures in South Mexico* (ill. Stanley L. Wood; Blackie's Library of Famous Books). LOCATION InND Loeber coll. (also 1905 edn).
Paris: Georges Barba, 1864 (trans. by Raoul Bourdier as *Les tirailleurs ou Mexique*). SOURCE Bn-Opale plus. LOCATION BNF.
New York: DeWitt & Davenport, 1851. SOURCE Topp 3, p. 389; OCLC. LOCATION CtY.
New York: C. Lasalle, 1855 (trans. as *Les tirailleurs ou Mexique*). LOCATION NUC.
New York: Grosset & Dunlap, [1889] (as *The rifle rangers, a thrilling story of daring adventure and hairbreadth escapes during the Mexican war*). LOCATION NUC.
COMMENTARY An adventure story about soldiers in the American army in the Mexican war of 1846, based on the author's own experiences. One of the soldiers is an Irishman [ML].

R29　*The scalp hunters; or, romantic adventures in Northern Mexico* (by Capt. Mayne Reid).
London: Charles J. Skeet, 1851, 3 vols. SOURCE Sadleir, 2030; Wolff, 5757; Topp 6, 233. LOCATION L, NUC.
London, Belfast: Simms & M'Intyre, 1852 (Parlour Library, No. 77). SOURCE Sadleir, ii, p. 154; Topp 6, 233. LOCATION Dt, L.
Stuttgart: K. Thienemann, [1893] (trans. by Otto Hoffmann as *Der Kriegspfad; oder, die Skalpjäger auf dem Kriegszuge gegen die Navajos*). LOCATION NUC.
Philadelphia: J.B. Lippincott & Grambo, 1851. SOURCE Topp 1, p. 285. LOCATION L, NUC.
New York: Robert M. DeWitt, 1856 (ill. N. Orr). LOCATION NUC.
New York: C. Lasalle, 1854 (trans. as *Les chasseurs de chevelures*). LOCATION NUC.
COMMENTARY Issued in 31 parts by Henry Lea, London, n.d. Set around the border between the US and Mexico. The story relates the life of traders who traverse this wild area. The main exploit is the recovery of white women and children from the camps of Indians [ML; Topp 3, p. 390].

R30　*The English family Robinson. The desert home* (by Capt. Mayne Reid).
Boston: Ticknor & Fields, 1851. SOURCE OCLC. LOCATION InND.
Boston: Ticknor, Read & Fields, 1852 (as *The desert home*). SOURCE Topp 1, p. 342; Wolff, 5734a (1856 edn). LOCATION NUC.
New York: Worthington, 1890. LOCATION NUC.
London: David Bogue, 1852 (ill. William Harvey). SOURCE NCBEL 4, p. 1389; OCLC. LOCATION GEU.
London: David Bogue, 1852 (as *The desert home; or, the adventures of a lost family in the wilderness*; ill. William Harvey). SOURCE NCBEL 3, p. 958; Topp 1, p. 342; Wolff, 5734 (1854, 4th edn). LOCATION D (1857, 6th edn), L, NUC.
+ Paris: L. Hachette & Co., 1856 (trans. by Armand Le François as *L'habitation du désert ou aventures d'une famille perdue dans les solitudes de l'Amerique*; ill. Gustave Doré). LOCATION NUC (1859 edn), InND Loeber coll.
Stuttgart: Deutsche Verlaggesellshaft, 1893 (trans. by Richard Roth as *Die Heimat in der Wueste. Erzählung aus den Wildnissen des Südwestens von Nordamerika*). LOCATION NUC.

R31　*The boy hunters, or, adventures in search of a white buffalo* (by Capt. Mayne Reid; dedicated to the boy readers of England and America).
London: David Bogue, 1853 (ill. William Harvey). SOURCE NCBEL 3, p. 958; Topp 1, p. 343; Wolff, 5725. LOCATION NUC.
Stuttgart: Schmidt & Spring, 1858 (trans. by Franz Hoffmann as *The Büffeljäger am Lagerfeuer; Reisebilder und Naturschilderungen aus dem Westen*). LOCATION NUC.
Boston: Ticknor, Read & Fields, 1853 (ill. William Harvey). SOURCE Topp 1, p. 343. LOCATION L, NUC.
+ New York, London: G.P. Putnam's Sons, 1896 (ill.; Nimrod edn). LOCATION InND Loeber coll.
+ Dublin: Oifig Díolta Foillseacháin Rialtais, 1934 (as *Na Sealgairí Óga, i.e. The boy hunters of the Mississippi*). LOCATION InND Loeber coll.
Paris: H. Plon, 1856 (trans. by Raoul Boundier as *Les forêts vierges*). SOURCE Bn-Opale plus. LOCATION BNF.
COMMENTARY Catalogue at the end states that 'This book has been written for boys. In the endeavour to interest the juvenile intellect, it is necessary to deal with physical rather than moral facts ...' Three boys living with their father in Louisiana set out to obtain the skin of

a white buffalo. They traverse a large part of America, have many adventures, and return with the skin. The story is interspersed with many observations on natural history [ML; COPAC].

R32 *The hunters' feast; or, conversations around the camp-fire* (by Capt. Mayne Reid). London: Thomas Hodgson, [1854] (The Parlour Library, No. 120; cover ill. Alfred Crowquill). SOURCE Sadleir, 3662 (mentions [1855] as first edn), 3755a; Topp 1, p. 287; Topp 6, 340; Wolff, iv, p. 16. LOCATION L (1907 edn), NUC ([1855] edn). Paris: L. Hachette, 1861 (trans. by Bénédict H. Revoil as *Les veillées de chasse*). LOCATION NUC.

New York: DeWitt & Davenport, [1856] (ill. N. Orr). SOURCE Topp 1, p. 287; Topp 6, 340; Wolff, 5744 (n.d. edn). LOCATION NUC ([1855?] edn), InND Loeber coll. (n.d. edn).

COMMENTARY A hunting party sets out from St Louis to go west to hunt for buffalo. They cross different landscapes and come across a variety of wildlife, each species of which gives rise to biological discussions and hunting stories. When they finally reach a place where they can hunt the buffalo, they meet with several misfortunes. Their horses are stolen by the Indians and their camp burns down. Later they lose a raft with all their rifles, dried meat, and part of their clothing. After many hardships they return [ML].

R33 *The young voyageurs; or, the boy hunters in the North* (by Capt. Mayne Reid; dedicated to author's mother and father [Thomas Reid]). London: David Bogue, 1854. SOURCE Osborne, p. 1024; Wolff, 5764. LOCATION CaOTP, L, NUC.

+ Boston: Ticknor & Fields, 1854 (ill. W. Harvey). SOURCE Topp 1, p. 343. LOCATION NUC, InND Loeber coll.

+ New York: James Miller, 1879 (ill. W. Harvey). LOCATION InND Loeber coll.

COMMENTARY A story of the Canadian north [Osborne].

R34 *The forest exiles; or, the perils of a Peruvian family amid the wilds of the Amazon* (by Capt. Mayne Reid).
+ London: David Bogue, 1855 (ill.). SOURCE Topp 1, p. 343; NCBEL 3, p. 958; Osborne, p. 1024 (1856, 3rd edn). LOCATION CaOTP (1856, 3rd edn), L, NUC (1856 edn), InND Loeber coll.

Paris: L. Hachette & Co., 1855 (trans. by H. Loreau as *Les exiles dans la forêt*). SOURCE Topp 1, p. 343. LOCATION CCF, NUC (1863 ed.).

Leipzig: C.E. Kollmann, 1855 (trans. by W.E. Drugulin as *Die Verbannten. Naturbilder aus den Wildnissen Amazonenstrome*). LOCATION NUC.

Boston: Ticknor & Fields, 1855 (ill.). SOURCE Topp 1, p. 343; Wolff, 5737. LOCATION NUC.

COMMENTARY A family of Spanish heritage flees the regime in Peru. They cross the mountains and descend into the forest. There they gather products that they transport by raft to the mouth of the Amazon. The story abounds with descriptions of nature and encounters with various wild animals [ML].

R35 *The white chief: a legend of Northern Mexico* (by Capt. Mayne Reid). London: David Bogue, 1855, 3 vols. SOURCE Sadleir, 2031; Wolff, 5761; Topp 6, 234. LOCATION L, NUC.

+ London: Published for the author, n.d. LOCATION InND Loeber coll.

+ Gouda: G.B. Van Goor Zonen, 1878 (ill.; trans. into Dutch as *Het blanke opperhoofd. Eene legende uit Noord-Mexico*). LOCATION InND Loeber coll.

New York: DeWitt & Davenport, [1856] (ill.). SOURCE Topp 3, p. 387; Wolff, 5761c ([1858?] edn). LOCATION NUC.

COMMENTARY Set in contemporary Mexico. A white hunter who comes to the aid of an Indian tribe is selected as their chief. He uses the tribe to destroy a town whose inhabitants had committed atrocious acts. There are many pages of factual and explanatory notes [ML].

R36   *Wild life; or, adventures of the frontier. A tale of the early days of the Texan republic* (by Capt. Mayne Reid).

New York: R.N. DeWitt, [1856] (ill. N. Orr). LOCATION NUC.

R37   *The bush-boys; or, the history and adventures of a Cape farmer and his family in the wild karoos of Southern Africa* (by Capt. Mayne Reid; dedicated to Franz, Louis, and Vilma, the children of Louis Kossuth).

+ London: David Bogue, 1856 (ill. Gus. Janet). SOURCE Osborne, p. 1023; Wolff, 5729. LOCATION D, L, CaOTP, NUC.

Paris: Theodore Lefèvre, [1899] (trans. as *Les enfants des bois*; cover: Engel). SOURCE Mott cat.241/142; OCLC. LOCATION Johns Hopkins Univ.

COMMENTARY Fiction for juveniles. A father of Dutch extraction in South Africa has lost his property in the war against the English. He and his four children and two servants try to keep their stock by a nomadic existence, moving from place to place. Locusts devastate the crops on his temporary farmstead and the farmer moves away to find new pasture and water. Many adventures beset the little group. They lose all their livestock except one milk cow. In a very remote part of the country they build a house in a tree to be safe from predators. They keep domesticated zebras and wild dogs to help them in their hunt for elephants. When they have a huge pile of ivory they return to the settled world, sell the ivory, repurchase their old property, and prosper. The book is interspersed with little lessons on the biology of animals and plants the group encounters [ML].

R38   *The quadroon; or, a lover's adventures in Louisiana* (by Capt. Mayne Reid; dedicated to Thomas James Marshall).

+ London: George W. Hyde, 1856, 3 vols. SOURCE Wolff, 5753. LOCATION L, NUC, InND Loeber coll.

London: J. & C. Brown, [1856] (as *The quadroon; or, adventures in the far West*). SOURCE Sadleir, 3664. LOCATION NUC.

Leipzig: C.E. Kollmann, 1857 (trans. as *Die Quadrone; oder, Abenteuer in Louisiana*). SOURCE OCLC. LOCATION Niedersachsischen Staats und Univ.

New York: Robert M. DeWitt, [1856] (ill. Richardson, Cox). SOURCE Wolff, 5753a. LOCATION Dt, NUC.

New York: J.W. Carleton & Co.; London: S. Low, Son & Co., 1880 (as *Love's vengeance. A novel*). LOCATION NUC.

COMMENTARY A story of miscegenation set in Louisiana, where a young Englishman arrives in New Orleans in the heat of summer. He moves upstream to escape the unhealthy climate. The boat has an accident and he is instrumental in saving the life of Mlle Eugénie Besaçon. In the process, the hero receives a wound from which he recovers at Eugénie's plantation. Here he meets a beautiful quadroon slave with whom he falls in love. Eugénie's guardian is a ruffian who tries to disinherit her and possess the quadroon. After many adventures the guardian is unmasked and the hero and the quadroon marry. The novel was made into the play *The Octroon* by Dion Boucicault§ (RIA/DIB says Boucicault plagiarized TMR's work) and was first performed in New York in 1859 [ML; R. Hogan, *Dion Boucicault* (New York, 1969), p. 73; RIA/DIB].

R39   *The war-trail; or, the hunt of the wild horse. A romance of the prairie* (by Capt. Mayne Reid).

London: J. & C. Brown, 1857 (ill.). SOURCE NCBEL 3, p. 959; Topp 1, p. 121. LOCATION D (n.d. edn), L, NUC ([1857] edn).

London: [publisher?], [1857] (as *Adventures among the Indians; or, the war trail and the hunt of the wild horse*). LOCATION NUC.

New York: Robert M. DeWitt, [1857]. SOURCE Wolff, 5760. LOCATION NUC.

+ 's Gravenhage: Uitgevers-Maatschappij, Nederland, n.d., 6th edn (trans. by Frans Hoffman into Dutch as, *Op het oorlogspad. Een verhaal uit Mexico*). LOCATION InND Loeber coll.

+ New York: Carleton; London: S. Low, Son & Co., 1874 (ill.). LOCATION InND Loeber coll.

COMMENTARY Set in Mexico at the time of the Mexican wars. The American soldiers have to fight the Comanche Indians as well as the Mexicans. A captain of the rangers falls in love with an American girl, Isolina, whose beautiful horse he had killed when he thought that she was a Mexican insurgent. Her request to him is to capture a wild, white mustang, which is roaming the prairie. After many adventures he succeeds. Isolina's cousin, Igurra, has a deadly hatred of the captain. Through traitorous acts Igurra tries to take over Isolina father's land. He ties her on top of her white steed and ties firecrackers to the horse and sends it into the desert. The captain and his men try to rescue her, but only after the Indians capture Isolina do they succeed. Eventually, Isolina and the captain move to Texas where they marry [ML].

R40   *The young yägers; or, a narrative of hunting adventures in Southern Africa* (by Capt. Mayne Reid).

London: David Bogue, 1857. SOURCE Wolff, 5765. LOCATION L, NUC.

+ London, Glasgow, Manchester, New York: George Routledge & Sons, n.d. (ill.). LOCATION InND Loeber coll.

Paris: L. Hachette & Co., 1859 (trans. by Henriette Loreau as *Les vacances des jeunes boërs*). LOCATION NUC.

COMMENTARY Set in South Africa, it tells the story of a hunting expedition of two sets of three brothers. They are accompanied by two servants, a bushman and a Kaffir. They encounter all kinds of adventures in their search for game [ML].

R41   *The plant hunters; or, adventures among the Himalayan mountains* (by Capt. Mayne Reid).

London: J. & C. Brown & Co., 1858. SOURCE NCBEL 3, p. 959 (probably mistakenly states 1857 edn); Topp 1, p. 343; Wolff, 5752. LOCATION L, NUC.

Paris: Hachette, 1859 (trans. by Henriette Loreau as *Les chasseur de plantes*). SOURCE NCBEL 3, p. 959; Topp 1, p. 343. LOCATION NUC (1861, 2nd edn).

New York: James Miller, 1880. LOCATION NUC.

R42   *Ran away to sea: an autobiography for boys* [anon.].

London: J. & C. Brown, 1858. SOURCE NCBEL 3, p. 959; Topp 1, p. 343; Wolff, 5755 ([1858] edn). LOCATION L, NUC (1859 edn).

+ Rotterdam: D. Bolle, n.d. (trans. into Dutch by H.T. Chappuis as *De scheepsjongen*; ill. Riou). LOCATION InND Loeber coll.

Paris: L. Hachette, 1859 (trans. by Henriette Loreau as *À la mer*). SOURCE CCF. LOCATION L, BNF.

New York: J.W. Lovell, [1869]. LOCATION NUC.

R43   *Osceola the Seminole; or, the red fawn of the flower-land* (by Capt. Mayne Reid).

New York: R.M. DeWitt, 1858. SOURCE Topp 1, p. 286; Wolff, 5749a (n.d. edn). LOCATION NUC.

+ London: Hurst & Blackett, 1859, 3 vols. (as *Oçeola*; ill. Pearson, H. Weir). SOURCE Topp 1, p. 286; Sadleir, 2027; Wolff, 5749. LOCATION L, InND Loeber coll.

London: Chapman & Hall, 1861 (as *The half-blood; or, Oceola the Seminole*). SOURCE Topp 3, p. 389; Sadleir, 3755a (n.d. edn). LOCATION L, NUC.

London, New York: George Routledge & Sons, [1875?] (as *The half-blood, a tale of the flowery land*). SOURCE Topp 3, p. 389; Allibone Suppl., ii, p. 1271 ([1875?] edn); OCLC. LOCATION NUC, CtY.

COMMENTARY First serialized in *Chambers's Journal* (Edinburgh, Jan.–June 1858). Set in Florida around the time of the Seminole wars. The sympathies of the main character are with the Indians, who are badly treated by the whites who covet their lands [ML; Topp].

R44   *The wood-rangers* (by Capt. Mayne Reid).
London: Hurst & Blackett, 1860, 3 vols. SOURCE Topp 3, 215; Wolff, 5763. SOURCE COPAC. LOCATION C.
London: Charles H. Clarke, 1861 (new edn). SOURCE Topp 3, 215. SOURCE COPAC. LOCATION L.
New York: Robert M. de Witt, 1860 (as *The wood-rangers. The trappers of Sonora*). SOURCE Topp 3, 215; OCLC; Wolff, 5763b. LOCATION NjP.
COMMENTARY Based on Gabriel Ferry's (Luis de Bellemare) *Le coureur des bois*, published in Paris in 1850 and translated by TMR [RL].

R45   *The boy tar; or, a voyage in the dark* (by Capt. Mayne Reid).
+ London: W. Kent & Co. (late D. Bogue), 1860 (ill. Charles S. Keene). SOURCE NCBEL 3, p. 959; Osborne, p. 1023; Wolff, 5727. LOCATION L, CaOTP, NUC, InND Loeber coll.
Paris: L. Hachette, 1861 (trans. by Henriette Loreau as *A fond de cale*; ill.). SOURCE CCF; NCBEL 3, p. 959. LOCATION L.
+ Paris: Hachette & Co., 1882 (by Captaine Mayne-Raid [*sic*]; trans. by Henriette Loreau, as *A fond de cale. Voyage d'un jeune marin a travers les ténèbres*; ill. Loudan; Bibliothèque Rose Illustrée). LOCATION InND Loeber coll.
COMMENTARY An old seaman tells an audience of boys the story of his early experiences on the water. The main adventure consists of the seaman as a young boy first trying to join a ship. He is refused, but he gets into the hold, where he falls asleep. When he wakes up he finds himself imprisoned in a very small space. Nobody hears him, and his survival depends on his own ingenuity [ML].

R46   *Bruin; or, the grand bearhunt* (by Capt. Mayne Reid).
London, New York: Routledge, Warne & Routledge, 1861. SOURCE NCBEL 3, p. 959 (mentions 1860 first edn); Topp 1, p. 342; Wolff, 5728. LOCATION L, NUC.
COMMENTARY Author's note acknowledges the assistance of an American author (unidentified), whose contribution was incorporated in this volume. [RL].

R47   *Despard, the sportsman* (by Capt. Mayne Reid).
+ London: H. Lea, 1861. SOURCE OCLC. LOCATION O.
COMMENTARY 30pp [AMB].

R48   *Despard, the sportsman and other tales* (by Capt. Mayne Reid).
+ London: Miles & Miles, [1861 or later] (ill.). LOCATION InND Loeber coll., Univ. of Calgary.
COMMENTARY Contents: 'Despard, the sportsman', 'The will' [AMB; RL].

R49   *A hero in spite of himself* (by Capt. Mayne Reid).
London: Hurst & Blackett, 1861, 3 vols. SOURCE Topp 6, 254; COPAC. LOCATION E
London: C.H. Clarke [1862] (as *The tiger hunter, or a hero in spite of himself*). SOURCE Topp 6, 254; OCLC. LOCATION MH.
New York: R.M. De Witt, [*c*.1865] (as *The tiger hunter; or, a hero in spite of himself*). LOCATION NUC.
COMMENTARY Adapted by TMR from the French of Gabriel Ferry's (Louis de Bellemare) *Costal l'indien* (Paris, 1852), which appeared in an English translation in London in 1857. Set

in Mexico during the war of independence from the Spaniards. The tiger hunter falls in love with a woman above his station. He saves her family by urging them to leave Mexico. After peace has been concluded, the family returns to their estate [Allibone, ii, p. 1766; ML; NCBEL 4, p. 1389; Topp].

R50   *The wild huntress* (by Capt. Mayne Reid).
London: Richard Bentley, 1861, 3 vols. SOURCE NCBEL 3, p. 959; Sadleir, 2033; Wolff, 5762. LOCATION L, NUC.
Paris: J. Hetzel, [1875] (adapted by Stella Blandy as *Les deux filles du squatter*; ill. J. Davis). SOURCE NCBEL 3, p. 959. LOCATION L.
+ Gouda: G.B. Van Goor, 1877 (trans. into Dutch as *De dochter van den squatter*; ill.). LOCATION InND Loeber coll.
New York: Robert M. DeWitt, [1861] (as *The wild huntress; or, love in the wilderness*). SOURCE Wolff, 5762a. LOCATION NUC.
COMMENTARY First serialized in *Chambers's Journal* (Edinburgh, beginning July, 1860) [Topp 3, p. 389].

R51   *The maroon. A novel* (by Capt. Mayne Reid).
London: Hurst & Blackett, 1862, 3 vols. SOURCE Sadleir, 2025, 3663 (n.d. edn); Wolff, 5746. LOCATION L, NUC.
Paris: J. Hetzel & Co., [1874] (trans. as *Les planteurs de la Jamaïque*). SOURCE NCBEL 3, p. 959. LOCATION NUC ([1875], 4th edn).
+ Groningen: Noordhof & Smit, 1879 (trans. into Dutch by S.J. Andriessen as *De planters van Jamaica*; ill.). SOURCE Topp 1, p. 285; Adamnet. LOCATION UVA.
New York: Robert M. DeWitt, 1864 (as *The maroon: or, planter life in Jamaica*). SOURCE Topp 1, p. 285; RLIN. LOCATION Library Co. of Philadelphia.
COMMENTARY No copy of the New York edn located. Describes life on a plantation on Jamaica. The owner, Mr Vaughan, has a daughter who is of a mixed race (a maroon). She is looked after by an African slave who in her own land had been a princess and whose brother has come after her to free her. Mr Vaughan is expecting a guest, Mr Smith, who will be the owner of a neighbouring plantation. Mr Vaughan hopes that Mr Smith will marry his daughter. A penniless nephew arrives with the same boat, but he is not welcomed. A Jewish slave dealer has designs on Mr Vaughan's plantation because he has married a relative and Mr Vaughan's daughter cannot inherit because of her mixed-race status. Various people are killed, but the nephew rescues his cousin, whom he then marries. The African princess and prince return to Africa. TMR later adapted this novel for the stage [ML; ODNB].

R52   *Andrew Deverel: The history of an adventurer in New Guinea* (by 'Charles Beach').
London: Richard Bentley, 1863, 2 vols. SOURCE Allibone Suppl., i, p. 113. LOCATION NUC.

R53   *Lost Lenore; or the adventures of a rolling stone* (by 'Charles Beach', ed. and largely rewritten by Mayne Reid).
London: Charles J. Skeet, 1864, 3 vols. SOURCE Allibone Suppl., i, p. 113; Topp 1, p. 287; Topp 6, 282; NCBEL 3, p. 959. LOCATION L, NUC.
Wurzen: Verlags-Comptoir, 1866, 5 vols. (trans. by A. Kretzschmar as *Die verlorene Lenore*). LOCATION NUC.
New York: Robert M. DeWitt, [1866]. SOURCE Topp 1, p. 287. LOCATION NUC.

R54   *The cliff-climbers; or, the lone home in the Himalayas* (by Capt. Mayne Reid).
London: Ward & Lock, [1864]. SOURCE Topp 2, p. 138; Topp 6, 278; Wolff, 5731. LOCATION L.
+ London: Charles H. Clarke, [1864] (Clarke's Standard Novel Library; ill. E. Evans). SOURCE Osborne, p. 1024. LOCATION CaOTP, NUC, InND Loeber coll.

Boston: Ticknor & Fields, 1864. SOURCE Wolff, 5731a; Topp 6, 278. LOCATION NUC.

Paris: Hachette, 1865 (trans. by Henriette Loreau as *Les grimpuers de roches*). SOURCE NCBEL 3, p. 959. LOCATION NUC.

New York: James Miller, 1880 (ill.). SOURCE OCLC. LOCATION NIC.

COMMENTARY A sequel to *The plant hunters* (London, 1858). Set in a valley in the Himalayas where two brothers and their guide are trapped. They have various adventures but most of their time is taken up trying to devise ways to escape from the valley. Finally, when some cranes land near their hut, they notice that they are ringed. They tie a message in leather bags to the legs of two cranes. The cranes fly south, the messages are found, and the boys are subsequently rescued [ML].

R55   *The ocean waifs. A story of adventure on land and sea* (by Capt. Mayne Reid).
London: David Bryce, 1864. SOURCE Osborne, p. 1024 ([1871] edn); Topp 1, p. 288; OCLC. LOCATION L (1871 edn), CaOTP ([1871] edn), NUC (1871 edn), CLU.
Boston: Ticknor & Fields, 1865. SOURCE Wolff, 5748; OCLC. LOCATION NUC (1867 edn), NN.

R56   *The boy slaves; or, life in the desert* (by Capt. Mayne Reid).
Boston: Ticknor & Fields, 1865. SOURCE Topp p. 1, p. 287; Topp 6, 293; Wolff, 5726. LOCATION NUC.
New York: J. Miller, 1876. LOCATION NUC.
+ New York: Worthington, 1889 (new edn; with memoir by R.H. Stoddard; as *The boy slaves*; ill.). LOCATION InND Loeber coll.
+ New York: Hurst & Co., n.d. (as *The boy slaves*; ill.). LOCATION InND Loeber coll.
London: C.H. Clarke, [1865]. SOURCE NCBEL 3, p. 959; Topp 1, p. 287; Topp 6, 293. LOCATION L.
Paris: J. Hetzel, [1866] (trans. by Emma Allonard as *Les jeunes esclaves*). SOURCE CCF; NCBEL 3, p. 959. LOCATION L.
COMMENTARY First serialized in the *Boy's Journal* (Brooklyn?, 1864). The 1889 New York edn shows that Ticknor and Fields registered this story in 1852; the verso of the title page has an author's note acknowledging significant help of an unidentified American author. The story relates the adventures of some sailors wrecked on the Barbary coast in North Africa. They are taken as slaves through the desert and change owners frequently. Eventually, they come to a town where the English consul redeems them [ML; RL; Topp].

R57   *The guerilla chief and other tales* (by Capt. Mayne Reid).
London: C.H. Clarke, [1865]. SOURCE Topp 1, p. 288; Topp 6, 287; Wolff, 5740 (1867 edn). LOCATION NUC.
+ London, Manchester, New York: George Routledge & Sons, [1895 or earlier]. LOCATION InND Loeber coll.
COMMENTARY Contents: 'The guerilla chief', 'Despard, the sportsman' (first published separately in 1861), 'A case of retaliation', 'The broken bit', 'A turkey hunt in Texas', 'Trapped in a tree', 'The black jaguar: an adventure of the Amazon' [ML; RL].

R58   *The headless horseman. A strange tale of Texas* (by Capt. Mayne Reid).
London: Chapman & Hall, 1865, vol. 1. SOURCE Sadleir, 2023a; Topp 1, p. 296; Wolff, 5742a; OCLC. LOCATION MH.
London: Richard Bentley, 1866, vol. 2. SOURCE Sadleir, 2023a; Topp 1, p. 296; Wolff, 5742a. LOCATION L, MH, NUC.
New York: R.M. DeWitt, 1867. SOURCE Topp 1, p. 287.
New York: G.W. Carleton & Co., 1881 (as *Sounding the signal; or, the headless horseman*). SOURCE Topp 3, p. 324.
COMMENTARY No copies of both New York edns located. First issued in parts in London in 1865 by Chapman & Hall (parts 1–17), and Bentley (parts 18–20). SOURCE Topp 3, p. 324.

R59   *The white gauntlet. A romance* (by Capt. Mayne Reid).
London: Charles J. Skeet, 1865, 3 vols. SOURCE NCBEL 3, p. 959; Sadleir, 2023; Topp
1, p. 286; Topp 6, 292. LOCATION L, NUC.
Paris: G. Barba, 1865 (trans. by M.A. Kervigan as *Le gantelet blanc*). SOURCE CCF;
NCBEL 3, p. 959; Topp 1, p. 286. LOCATION L.
COMMENTARY First serialized in the *National Magazine* (Dublin, beginning May, 1863)
[Topp 3, p. 390].

R60   *Left to the world* (by 'Charles Beach').
London: John Maxwell, 1865, 3 vols. SOURCE Allibone Suppl., i, p. 113; OCLC.
LOCATION Univ. of N. Carolina, Chapel Hill.

R61   *The bandolero; or, a marriage among the mountains* (by Capt. Mayne Reid).
+ London: Richard Bentley, 1866 (ill.). SOURCE Sadleir, 2108; Wolff, 5724. LOCATION
L, NUC, InND Loeber coll.
+ London: Ward, Lock & Co., [1867] (as *The mountain marriage; or, the bandelero*).
SOURCE NCBEL 3, p. 959. LOCATION D, L, NUC.
COMMENTARY Set in Mexico where an officer of the conquering American army falls in love
with a woman, of whom he catches only a glimpse. Great confusion arises from the fact that
the woman has a sister who is very like her. The officer considers the sister's lover a rival.
This leads to various plots, counterplots and perilous adventures until eventually the mystery
is cleared up [ML].

R62   *Afloat in the forest* (by Capt. Mayne Reid).
London: C.H. Clarke, 1866. SOURCE Topp 1, p. 288; Topp 6, 297; Osborne, p. 1023
([1868] edn). LOCATION L (1868 edn), CaOTP ([1868] edn).
Boston: Ticknor & Fields, 1867. SOURCE Topp 1, p. 288. LOCATION NUC.
+ Chicago: M.A. Donahue & Co., n.d. (Fireside Henty [*sic*] Series). LOCATION InND
Loeber coll.
New York: R.R. Knox, [*c.*1860]. LOCATION NUC.
COMMENTARY First serialized in the US in the *Boy's Journal* (Brooklyn?, 1865), and in *Our
Young Folk's Magazine* (London?, 1866). Describes an adventurous and dangerous trip cross-
ing the South American continent by boat and getting lost in the Gapo, a large tract of land
submerged by floodwaters from a river. Problems of food and transportation need to be resolved
and an assortment of dangerous animals cross the travellers' path [ML; Topp].

R63   *The giraffe hunters* (by Capt. Mayne Reid).
+ Boston: Ticknor & Fields, 1867 (ill.). SOURCE Topp 1, p. 288; Wolff, 5739a.
LOCATION NUC, InND Loeber coll.
London: Hurst & Blackett, 1867, 3 vols. SOURCE Wolff, 5739; Topp 6, 314. LOCATION
L, NUC.
COMMENTARY Set in South Africa where several young friends set out on a hunting expedi-
tion to obtain hippopotamus teeth and a young male and female giraffe. They are
accompanied by a bushman and a Kaffir. They encounter many wild animals and have life-
threatening adventures. However, they are successful and return with the two young giraffes
[ML].

R64   *The Creole forger; a tale of the cresent* [*sic*] *city* (by Capt. Mayne Reid).
New York: George Munro, 1868 (Munro's Ten Cent Novels, No. 125). LOCATION
NUC.

R65   *The child wife. A tale of the two worlds* (by Capt. Mayne Reid).
London: Ward, Lock & Tyler, 1868, 3 vols. SOURCE Sadleir, 2019; Wolff, 5730.
LOCATION L, NUC.
+ New York: Sheldon & Co. LOCATION NUC, InND Loeber coll.

COMMENTARY Some elements of this story are probably semi-autobiographical as TMR wooed his wife as a 13-year-old girl and married her when she was age 15. It tells of the romantic adventures of the hero, Capt. Maynard, a true republican who has fought in Mexico and is travelling to Europe to assist in various ill-fated republican uprisings in the late 1840s. While still in the US, he rescues a rich girl from drowning. She and her mother ignore him but are captivated by an Englishman, Swinton, who tells them that he has a title. Swinton is already married, but wishes to snare a rich heiress. Maynard knows that he is a swindler. On his way to Europe, Maynard falls in love with a young girl, Blanche Vernon. Her father, an English diplomat, holds very different views than Maynard does. There are several encounters between Maynard and Swinton, with the latter always in the role of villain. When Blanche is a little older she falls in love with Maynard, but her father forbids her to see or correspond with him. At the end of Mr Vernon's life, however, he realizes that Capt. Maynard is the best person to take care of his daughter after his death [ML].

R66　　*The way to win: a story of adventure afloat and ashore* (by 'Charles Beach').
London: Lockwood & Son, 1869. SOURCE Allibone Suppl., i, p. 113; COPAC.
LOCATION L.

R67　　*The fatal cord. A tale of backwood retribution* (by Capt. Mayne Reid).
London: Ward, Lock & Tyler, [1870]. SOURCE NCBEL 3, p. 959 [1869 edn]; Topp
1, p. 288. LOCATION L ([1870] edn).
New York: Beadle & Adams, 1868 (as *The helpless hand. A tale of backwoods and ret-ribution*; Beadle's New Dime Novels. Old Series, No. 624). LOCATION NUC.

R68　　*The castaways. A story of adventure in the wilds of Borneo* (by Capt. Mayne Reid).
London, Edinburgh, New York: T. Nelson & Sons, 1870 (ill.). SOURCE NCBEL 3, p.
959. LOCATION D, L, NUC.
+ London, Edinburgh, Dublin, New York: Thomas Nelson & Sons, n.d. (as *The cast-aways*; ill.). LOCATION InND Loeber coll.
+ New York: Sheldon & Co., 1870 (ill.). LOCATION NUC, InND Loeber coll.

COMMENTARY Five people are castaways on the lonely shore of the island of Borneo. They are a ship's captain, a ship's carpenter, a servant of Malay background, and the captain's two chil-dren. They have a number of adventures finding food and meeting dangerous animals. They realize that they cannot stay on the coast but have to cross the perilous interior of the island. They successfully reach a settler outpost [ML].

R69　　*The white squaw* (by Capt. Mayne Reid).
+ London: Ward, Lock & Tyler, [1870]. SOURCE COPAC. LOCATION C.
COMMENTARY A white woman becomes the happy wife of an Indian chief [ML].

R70　　*The yellow chief. A romance of the Rocky Mountains* (by Capt. Mayne Reid).
London: Ward, Lock & Tyler, [1870]. SOURCE Allibone Suppl., ii, p. 1271 (mentions
The yellow chief: a romance published in London in 1869, but this edn has not been
located); NCBEL 3, p. 959; OCLC. LOCATION L, Univ. of Southern Carolina.
COMMENTARY A black slave who has been mistreated by his owner flees and becomes
the leader of an Indian tribe and exacts vengeance on his former owners [ML; RL].

R71　　*The white squaw and The yellow chief, a romance of the Rocky Mountains* (by
Capt. Mayne Reid).
London: C.H. Clarke, [1871], 2 parts (Standard Novel Library; ill.). SOURCE NCBEL
3, p. 959; Osborne, p. 1024; Topp 6, 337. LOCATION L, CaOTP, NUC.
New York: Beadle, 1868 (Dime Novel, No. 155). SOURCE Topp 6, 337; OCLC.
LOCATION Jacksonville Public Library, FL.
COMMENTARY Contents: 'The white squaw' (first published in London, [1870]), 'The
yellow chief' (first published in London, [1870]) [RL].

R72   *The lone ranche. A tale of the 'staked plain'* (by Capt. Mayne Reid).
  London: Chapman & Hall, 1871, 2 vols. SOURCE Allibone Suppl., ii, p. 1271; Sadleir,
  2024. LOCATION L, InND Loeber coll. (London, Routledge, n.d. edn).
COMMENTARY J.W. Hammersley, an intimate friend of TMR, was the model for the hero of
this novel [James Cummins Bookseller, New York, annotated slip in inscribed copy of TMR's
The white gauntlet (London, 1865)].

R73   *The fatal cord: and The falcon rover* (by Capt. Mayne Reid).
  London: C.H. Clarke, 1872. SOURCE Topp 1, p. 288; Topp 6, 354. LOCATION L, NUC.
  COMMENTARY *The fatal cord* was first published in London, 1869 [Topp].

R74   *The finger of fate. A romance* (by Capt. Mayne Reid).
  London: Chapman & Hall, 1872, 2 vols. SOURCE Allibone Suppl., ii, p. 1271; NCBEL
  3, p. 959. LOCATION L, NUC.
  + London: James Bowden, 1899 (new edn; as *The finger of fate*; ill. Stanley L. Wood;
  preface by Elizabeth Reid). LOCATION InND Loeber coll.
  New York: G. Munro, [1885]. LOCATION NUC.
COMMENTARY Set in Rome where Luigi Torreani, an Italian artist, is captured by soldiers
because he is a member of a subversive organization. He escapes and makes his way to England
where he meets Henry Harding, who has just been disowned by his father because of false
stories told about his behaviour by his half-brother. Henry goes to Italy to bring a message to
Luigi's family. He is caught by bandits who wish to ransom him. The bandits also abduct
Luigi's beautiful sister. Both are freed by Garibaldi's army and are united with Luigi [ML].

R75   *The death shot. A romance of forest and prairie* (by Capt. Mayne Reid).
  London: Chapman & Hall, 1873, 3 vols. SOURCE Allibone Suppl., ii, p. 1271; Wolff,
  5733. LOCATION L, NUC.
  New York: Hurst, [1874] (as *The death-shot: A story retold*). LOCATION NUC.
  + New York, London: White & Allen, [1874] (as *The death-shot: A story retold*; ill.).
  LOCATION NUC, InND Loeber coll.
COMMENTARY Set in Mississippi and Texas at the time Texas is being settled. Two men who
love the same girl are deadly enemies. Their hatred for each other involves them in various
adventures, such as being buried up to the head in the desert and the abduction of the girl in
question by a party of ruffians [ML].

R76   *The island pirate. A tale of the Mississippi* (by Capt. Mayne Reid).
  New York: Beadle & Adams, [1874] (Beadle's Pocket Novels, No. 10). LOCATION
  NUC.

R77   *Pitzmaroon; or, the magic hammer* (by 'Charles Beach').
  Springfield (MA): Whitney & Adams, 1874. SOURCE Allibone Suppl., i, p. 113.
  LOCATION NUC.

R78   *Too good for anything; or, a waif in the world.* (by 'Charles Beach').
  London: F. Warne, [1874?]. SOURCE Allibone Suppl., i, p. 113 (1874 edn). SOURCE
  OCLC. LOCATION OU.

R79   *The flag of distress: A tale of the South Sea* (by Capt. Mayne Reid; dedicated to
  Charles Ollivant).
  + London: Tinsley Bros, 1876, 3 vols. SOURCE Sadleir, 2021; Wolff, 5736. LOCATION
  L, NUC, InND Loeber coll.
  + London, Belfast: William Mullan & Son, 1879. LOCATION D.
  + New York: Worthington, 1890 (ill.; with a memoir by R.H. Stoddard). SOURCE
  Wolff, 5736a. LOCATION D.
COMMENTARY Two British naval officers fall in love with two ladies of Spanish descent who live
in San Francisco. The two women are also pursued by two ruffians, who plan to marry them.

The women leave San Francisco with their male relative in a ship specifically hired to convey the family's great wealth of gold back to Cadiz. The ruffians and their accomplices, in disguise, are hired as seamen on the ship. They steal the gold, take the girls, and leave the ship to its fate. Eventually, the British officers rescue the ship and find the ruffians, the gold, and the girls on an uninhabited island. They return safely to Cadiz, where the four young people marry [ML].

R80   *Gwen Wynn. A romance of the Wye* (by Capt. Mayne Reid).
London: Tinsley Bros, 1877, 3 vols. SOURCE Allibone Suppl., ii, p. 1271; Wolff, 5741. LOCATION L, NUC.
New York: White & Allen, [1877?]. LOCATION NUC.

R81   *The queen of the lakes. A romance of the Mexican valley* (by Capt. Mayne Reid).
+ London, Belfast: William Mullan & Son, 1879. SOURCE NCBEL 3, p. 959; Sadleir, 2028 (1880 ed.). LOCATION L.

R82   *The specter barque: A tale of the Pacific* (by Capt. Mayne Reid).
New York: Beadle & Adams, 1879 (Beadle's Dime Library, No. 66). LOCATION NUC.
COMMENTARY 38pp [NUC].

R83   *Chris Rock, or a lover in chains. A novel* (by Capt. Mayne Reid).
+ New York: Robert Bonner's Sons, 1879 (ill.). LOCATION NUC, InND Loeber coll.
+ New York: Hurst & Co., [189–] (as *The free lances. A romance of the Mexican valley*). LOCATION NUC, InND Loeber coll.
London: Remington, 1881, 3 vols. (as *The free lances. A romance of the Mexican valley*). SOURCE Allibone Suppl., ii, p. 1271; Sadleir, 2022; Wolff, 5738. LOCATION L, NUC.
COMMENTARY The main character is an Irishman, Florence Kearney, who volunteers as an irregular in Texas. He is selected to be a captain and before he sets off he takes lessons in Spanish from a man who had been dispossessed of his lands in Mexico. This man has a beautiful daughter, with whom Kearney falls in love. However, he has a formidable rival who is able to promise the Mexican the return of his lands in exchange for his daughter. Exciting adventures take place in the interior of Mexico, with the Mexican girl as a pawn. Eventually she is saved by Kearney, who then marries her [ML].

R84   *Gaspar the gaucho. A tale of the Gran Chaco* (by Capt. Mayne Reid).
London, New York: George Routledge & Sons, 1880. SOURCE Allibone Suppl., ii, 1271 (1879 edn); NCBEL 3, p. 959; Topp 1, p. 344. LOCATION L, NUC.
New York: Beadle & Adams, 1883 (as *Gaspar the gaucho; or, lost on the pampas. A tale of the Gran Chaco*). LOCATION NUC.
COMMENTARY The New York 1883 edn consists of 31pp [NUC].

R85   *La chasse au Leviathan* (by Capt. Mayne Reid).
Paris: Hachette & Co., 1882 (freely trans. by Jules Girandin). SOURCE NCBEL 3, p. 959. LOCATION NUC.
London, New York: George Routledge & Sons, [1884] (as *The chase of the Leviathan; or, adventures on the ocean*). SOURCE NCBEL 3, p. 959 (1885 edn); COPAC. LOCATION L, NUC.
COMMENTARY Original English text of the French edn is unclear [RL].

R86   *The lost mountain: A tale of Sonora* (by Capt. Mayne Reid).
London, New York: George Routledge & Sons, [1884]. SOURCE Allibone Suppl., ii, 1271; NCBEL 3, p. 959. LOCATION L (1885 edn), NUC.
New York: Robert M. DeWitt, [*c.*1860] (as *The woodrangers, or, the trappers of Sonora*). LOCATION NUC.
COMMENTARY Fabian, a young boy of noble birth, and his mother are abducted from their castle in Spain by his uncle, who wants to inherit the title and the wealth of the estate. The

mother is killed and the boy is left to float at sea in a little boat. He is rescued by a sailor who takes fatherly care of him for a number of years, but they are separated in a sea battle. The boy is given to a gold-seeker in northern Mexico, with whom he grows up. All of the main characters of the story converge in northern Mexico in search of gold. Various adventures, such as battles with the Indians, ensue. Fabian is reunited with the sailor who is now a woods ranger and pieces together his background. He metes out justice to his uncle, his mother's murderer, and to the murderer of the gold-seeker with whom he grew up. He marries the girl he loves but had previously felt too humble to claim [ML].

R87   *The land of fire. A tale of adventure* (by Capt. Mayne Reid).
    London: Frederick Warne & Co., [1884]. SOURCE Allibone Suppl., ii, 1271; Wolff, 5745. LOCATION L, NUC ([1883] edn).

R88   *Les émigrants du Transvaal* (by Capt. Mayne Reid).
    + Paris: Bibliothèque d'Education et de Recréation, [1884] (trans. by J. Lermount). SOURCE NCBEL 3, p. 959; Topp 1, p. 383. LOCATION L.
    London, New York: George Routledge & Sons, [1885] (as *The Vee-Boers. A tale of adventure in Southern Africa*). SOURCE Allibone Suppl., ii, 1271; NCBEL 3, p. 959; Topp 1, p. 383. LOCATION L, NUC.
    New York: Routledge, 1885. SOURCE Topp 1, p. 383; OCLC. LOCATION CLU.
    COMMENTARY Original English text of the French edn is unclear [RL].

R89   *The pierced heart and other stories* (by Capt. Mayne Reid).
    London: John & Robert Maxwell, [1885]. SOURCE Allibone Suppl., ii, 1271 ([1884] edn); Wolff, 5751 ([1884] edn); Topp 6, 192. LOCATION L, NUC.

R90   *The star of empire. A romance* (by Capt. Mayne Reid).
    London: John & Robert Maxwell, [1885]. SOURCE Allibone Suppl., ii, 1271; Wolff, 5758. LOCATION L ([1888] edn), NUC (n.d. edn).

R91   *No quarter! A romance* (by Capt. Mayne Reid).
    London: W. Swan Sonnenschein, Lowrey & Co., 1888, 3 vols. SOURCE Allibone Suppl., ii, p. 1271 (mentions a London, 1887 edn, but this has not been located); Sadleir, 2026; Wolff, 5747; Baker, p. 64. LOCATION D (n.d. edn), L, NUC.
    New York: White & Allen, n.d. LOCATION NUC.
COMMENTARY Historical fiction set in the middle of seventeenth-century England and features the siege of Bristol (1642), the battle of Roundway Down (1643), the Royalist reverse at Chepstow, etc. [Baker].

— COLLECTED WORKS

R92   *The Mayne Reid Library*.
    London: C.H. Clarke, [1864–65?], 9 vols. SOURCE Topp 6, 277–78, 346. LOCATION L (1864 edn, 1 vol. at least).
    COMMENTARY Issued in yellow-back, which has 'The Mayne Reid Library' on its spine. Advertisement mentions nine vols [Topp].

R93   [*Capt. Mayne Reid's works*].
    London, New York, Glasgow, Manchester: George Routledge & Sons, n.d., 17 vols. (Routledge's Florin Library; ill. E. Evans). SOURCE RL. LOCATION InND Loeber coll. (several vols.). COMMENTARY *London n.d. edn* Unnumbered and untitled series. Adv. in the series [RL].
    London, New York: George Routledge & Sons, 1884, 12 vols. (Railway Library). SOURCE Topp 1, pp 342–3. COMMENTARY *London 1884 edn* Untitled series. Perhaps the same as the 'Mayne Reid Library', mentioned in RLIN [RL].
    + London: George Routledge & Sons; New York: E.P. Dutton, n.d. and 1905, 30 vols. SOURCE Rowan cat. 37, part B/764. LOCATION D, L.

COMMENTARY Unnumbered and untitled series [RL].

R94   [*Captain Mayne Reid's books of adventure for boys*].
New York: Ticknor & Fields, 1856–58, 11 vols. (ill., Harvey). SOURCE RL; Topp 1,
p. 343. LOCATION InND Loeber coll. (1 vol.).
COMMENTARY *New York 1856–58 edn* Unnumbered and untitled series. Series title advertised
in *Bruin; or, the grand bear hunt* (New York, 1861). Bound in dark brown cloth, blind
embossed on cover and back; wild animal design of different types embossed in gold on spine
[RL].
Boston: Ticknor & Fields, [1860–61], 11 vols. (ill.). SOURCE RL, Topp 1, p. 342.
LOCATION InND Loeber coll. (2 vols.).
COMMENTARY *Boston edn* Unnumbered and untitled series. Probably a reprint of the New York
edn. Series title advertised in *Bruin; or, the grand bear hunt* (Boston, 1861). Binding: brown
cloth, embossed [RL].
New York: Ticknor & Fields, 1865–66, 11 vols. (ill. William Harvey). SOURCE RL;
Topp 1, p. 343; Wolff, 5727a, 5755a, 5764a, 5752b; title from advertisement in *Bruin*.
LOCATION InND Loeber coll. (2 vols.).
COMMENTARY *New York, 1865–66 edn* Unnumbered and untitled series. Bound in (a)
dark reddish or (b) green cloth, embossed [RL].

R95   [*Mayne Reid's popular works*].
New York: R.M. de Witt, 1863, 11 vols. (ill. N. Orr). SOURCE RL, Topp 1, p. 285.
LOCATION NUC (some vols.), InND (1 vol.).
COMMENTARY Unnumbered and untitled series. Adv. in *The scalp hunters* in this series
(New York, 1863) [RL].

R96   *Popular Novels by Captain Mayne Reid.*
New York: Carleton; London: S. Low & Co., 1868, 16 vols. SOURCE RL; Topp 1, p.
286. LOCATION NUC, InND Loeber coll. (2 vols.).
COMMENTARY Unnumbered and untitled series. Adv. in the InND Loeber coll. copies of *The
war-trail*, and *The white gauntlet*. Two binding types, one in green cloth (1868), the other in
reddish brown (1874), both with the name Mayne Reid on the spine, but the former in 16-
pointed emblem, and the latter set in a diamond pattern [RL].

R97   [*Captain Mayne Reid's works*].
Chicago: M.A. Donohue & Co., [1900?], [no. of vols. not known]. SOURCE RL; OCLC.
LOCATION InND Loeber coll. (2 vols.).
COMMENTARY Unnumbered and untitled series. Series evident from InND copy of
Woodrangers; or, the trappers of Sonora (Chicago, n.d.). Bound in grey cloth, impressed with
black, blue and yellow, showing huntsman with rifle; spine showing several rifles and hand-
guns [RL].

RENNIE, James, pseud. 'An antiquary', fl. 1819. Historical fiction writer. According to the
preface to *Saint Patrick* (Edinburgh, 1819) the author lived on St Stephen's Green, Dublin,
in 1818, but his identity is unclear. Maria Edgeworth mentions a Mr Rennie, an engineer, in
1810. He could also be identified with James Rennie (1787–1867), a naturalist and later first
professor of natural history and zoology at King's College, London. This JR was most likely
the natural son of Thomas Rennie (or Rainey) of Aldenholme, Sorn, Ayrshire (Scotland), and
Margaret Edwards. He matriculated at Glasgow University, graduated MA in 1815, and took
holy orders. He moved to London in 1821. In 1840 he emigrated to Adelaide (Australia). It
is unclear whether Elizabeth Rennie, the anonymous author of *Traits of character* (London,
1860, 2 vols.), which contains biographical sketches of English and Irish authors, is related to

him. SOURCE Mrs [Frances] Edgeworth, *A memoir of Maria Edgeworth* (London, 1867), i, p. 201; Fenning cat. 169/319; COPAC; ODNB; RL.

R98   *Saint Patrick: A national tale of the fifth century* (by 'An antiquary').

+ Edinburgh: Archibald Constable & Co.; London: Longman, Hurst, Rees, Orme & Brown; Hurst, Robinson & Co., 1819, 3 vols. SOURCE Allibone, ii, p. 1773 (mentions Rennie as the author); Brown, 91; Block, p. 196; British Fiction; Garside, 1819:57. LOCATION Corvey CME 3–628–48576–2, Ireland related fiction, Dt, D, L.

+ Glasgow, London: Cameron & Ferguson, [1877 or earlier] (as *The mistletoe and the shamrock; or, the chief of the North. A national tale of the fifth century*, by 'An antiquary'). SOURCE Brown, 68; RL. LOCATION D.

COMMENTARY Historical fiction set in fifth-century Ireland. Describes the conflict between druidism and Christianity during the lifetime of St Patrick, who enters the story. The scenes are set at Tara (Co. Meath), Dunluce, the Giant's Causeway and the river Bann (Co. Antrim),. King Laogaire's son is in love with the druidess Ethne. The London edn, 100 copies of which had been sent to the Dublin bookseller John Cummings, was remaindered in 1822. The Glasgow yellow-back edn has an illustrated cover of 'The druids altar – rescue of Aoine' [ML; RL; Brown; British Fiction].

RENTOUL, Erminda. See ESLER, Mrs Erminda Rentoul.

RENZY, Capt. S. Sparow de. See DE RENZY, Capt. S. Sparow.

'A RESIDENT', pseud. See WHATELY, Miss Elizabeth Jane.

RESTIF DE LA BRETONNE, N.E. See RESTIF DE LA BRETONNE, Nicholas-Edmé.

RESTIF DE LA BRETONNE, Nicholas-Edmé (known as N.E. Restif de la Bretonne, b. Sacy, near Auxerre (France), 1743, d. Paris 1806. French writer who came from a farming family but because of his delicate health, received education. He settled in Paris, where he became a prolific author, publishing more than 200 books. His *La découverte australe* (Leipzig, 1781), was an imitation of Jonathan's Swift's§ *Travels into several remote nations of the world* (London, 1726, 2 vols.). SOURCE *Biographie universelle* (Paris, 1843–65), xxxv, pp 462–6.

R99   *Les veilées du Marais, ou histoire du Grand Prince Oribeau, Roi de Mommonie, au pays d'Envinland, et de la verteuse Princesse Oribelle de Lagenie: tirée des anciénnes-annales–irlandaises [sic], & recenment-tranlatée en-français [sic], par Nichols-Donneraill, du comté de Korke, descandant de l'auteur* (by N.E. Restif de la Bretonne).

+ Waterford [Paris?], capital de Mommonie: [n.p.], 1785, 2 vols. in 1. SOURCE ESTC t213953; Gilbert, p. 695. LOCATION DPL Gilbert coll., Dt.

COMMENTARY Probably the imprint is not genuine. No other French edn published in England, Ireland, or France. The reference to Donneraill may refer to the village of Doneraile in Co. Cork [Gilbert; ESTC; AMB].

'A RETIRED PRIEST', pseud. See CROLLY, Fr William.

'RETLAW SPRING', pseud. See HAMILTON, Catherine.

REYNOLDS, James, pseuds 'Brother James', 'E.L.A. Berwick', d. Booterstown (Co. Dublin) 1866. A surgeon and apothecary, novelist and fiction writer for juveniles, JR had a medical practice in Booterstown. He contributed anonymously the serials 'The consequences' (a tale of the Bodkins of Ballycastle) and 'The heiress of Glenloe' to the *Irish Literary Gazette* (Dublin, 1857–61) and under the signatures 'E.L.A. Berwick' and 'A well-known novelist' as to *Duffy's Fireside Magazine* (Dublin). Under 'E.L.A. Berwick' he regularly wrote stories for the *Cork Herald* newspaper, including 'Glen Abbey Castle', and contribute also to *Duffy's Hibernian Magazine* (Dublin, 1861). He was known by his chapbooks, written for juveniles, published at 4*d*. each by James Duffy in Dublin, and for a series on Irish medical celebrities in the *Irish Literary Gazette*. Father of the later famous chemist James Emerson Reynolds. SOURCE Allibone Suppl., ii, p. 1274; Boase, iii, p. 123; Brown, pp 261, 338; C. Mollan, W. Davis, & B. Finucane, *Irish innovators* (Dublin, 2002), p. 89; NUC; Personal communication, Charles Ginnane, Feb. 1999; RIA/DIB.

R100   *The dwarf; or, mind and matter. A novel* (by 'E.L.A. Berwick').
　　　London: T.C. Newby, 1855, 3 vols. SOURCE NSTC. LOCATION L.
　　　London: C.H. Clarke, [1861] (as *The Queen's dwarf*; Parlour Library, vol. 248). SOURCE Allibone Suppl., ii, p. 1274; Sadleir, ii, p. 159; NSTC (another edn, allegedly [1855]); Topp 6, 221. LOCATION O, NUC.

R101   *Eveleen* (by 'E.L.A. Berwick'; dedicated to Charles Dickens).
　　　London: Smith, Elder & Co., 1856, 3 vols. SOURCE Allibone Suppl., ii, p. 1274; NSTC; Wolff, 5779. LOCATION L.

R102   *Miles O'Donnell; or, a story of a life* (by 'Brother James').
　　　+ Dublin: James Duffy, 1856. LOCATION D (n.d. edn), L.
　　　COMMENTARY Fiction for juveniles priced at 4*d*. [ML].

R103   *The cousins; or, a test of friendship* (by 'Brother James').
　　　+ Dublin: James Duffy, 1856. LOCATION L.
　　　COMMENTARY Fiction for juveniles priced at 4*d*. [ML].

R104   *Gerald O'Reilly; or, the triumph of principle* (by 'Brother James')
　　　Dublin: James Duffy, 1856, 9th edn. SOURCE OCLC. LOCATION Wright web.
　　　COMMENTARY 32pp. Fiction for juveniles priced at 4*d*. [Wright web; RL].

R105   *Eva O'Beirne; or, the little lace maker* (by 'Brother James').
　　　+ Dublin: James Duffy, 1856. LOCATION L.
　　　COMMENTARY Fiction for juveniles priced at 4*d*. [ML].

R106   *Gerald O'Reilly; or, the triumph of principle. And Eva O'Beirne. Two tales* (by 'Brother James').
　　　+ Dublin: James Duffy, 1856. SOURCE OCLC. LOCATION L, Stetson Univ. (Deland, FL).
　　　Baltimore: J. Murphy & Co., 1857 (as *Gerald O'Reilly; or, the triumph of principle, and Eva O'Beirne; or, the little lace maker*). SOURCE Wright, ii, 993 (who mistakenly has O'Brien). COMMENTARY 32pp. Dublin edn contains separately bound stories: 'Gerald O'Reilly; or, the triumph of principle', and 'Eva O'Beirne', first issued as chapbooks (Dublin, 1856). Reviewed in the *Metropolitan* (London, July, 1857, p. 375) [RL; OCLC].

R107   *Little Mary; or, the child of providence* (by 'Brother James').
　　　+ Dublin: James Duffy, 1856. LOCATION L.
　　　COMMENTARY Fiction for juveniles priced at 4*d*. [ML].

R108   *O'Hara Blake; or, the lost heir* (by 'Brother James').
　　　+ Dublin: James Duffy, 1856. LOCATION L.
　　　COMMENTARY Fiction for juveniles priced at 4*d*. [ML].

R109   *Rody O'Leary; or, the young outlaw* (by 'Brother James').
　　　+ Dublin: James Duffy, 1856. LOCATION L.
　　　COMMENTARY Fiction for juveniles priced at 4*d*. [ML].

R110 *The bequest; or, all is not gold that glitters* (by 'Brother James').
+ Dublin: James Duffy, 1856. LOCATION L.
COMMENTARY Fiction for juveniles priced at 4*d*. [ML].

R111 *The rose and the lily; or, the twin sisters* (by 'Brother James').
+ Dublin: James Duffy, 1856. LOCATION L.
COMMENTARY Fiction for juveniles priced at 4*d*. [ML].

R112 *The two friends: or, the reward of industry* (by 'Brother James').
+ Dublin: James Duffy, 1856. LOCATION L.
COMMENTARY Fiction for juveniles priced at 4*d*. [ML].

R113 *Catherine Hall; or, the deserted child* (by 'Brother James').
+ Dublin: James Duffy, 1856. LOCATION L.
COMMENTARY Fiction for juveniles priced at 4*d*. [ML].

R114 *Clare Costello; a true story* (by 'Brother James').
+ Dublin: James Duffy, 1856. LOCATION L.
COMMENTARY Fiction for juveniles priced at 4*d*. [ML].

R115 *After dark* (by 'Brother James').
[London?, n.p.], [1856 or earlier]. SOURCE Advertised in Wolff's copy of 'E.L.A. Berwick', *Eveleen* (London, 1856); Wolff, 5779.
COMMENTARY No copy located [RL].

R116 *The partners; or, fair and easy goes far in the day* (by 'Brother James').
+ Dublin: James Duffy, 1857. SOURCE Allibone Suppl., ii, p. 896 [under B. James]; Wolff, 7620 (1882 edn). LOCATION D (1874 edn), L.
COMMENTARY Fiction for juveniles [ML].

R117 *Tales and stories for the amusement and instruction of youth* (by 'Brother James').
+ Dublin: James Duffy, 1856 (ill. George Measom). SOURCE Brown, 1418 (1858 edn). LOCATION L.

R118 *The false friend. A tale of the times* (by 'Brother James').
Dublin: James Duffy, 1857. LOCATION D (1880 edn), L.
COMMENTARY Fiction for juveniles [ML].

COMMENTARY *Duffy 1856 edn* Originally published in parts for 4*d*. each. Contents of 1856 edn is a recompilation of separately paged parts, with one story per part. All stories have a moral and sometimes a Catholic slant and were written for juveniles. Contents: 'O'Hara Blake; or, the lost heir', 'Clare Costelloe. A true story', 'Gerald O'Reilly; or, the triumph of principle', 'Catherine Hall; or, the deserted child' [short title: 'The foundling'], 'Eva O'Beirne; or, the little lace maker', 'The two friends; or, the reward of industry', 'Miles O'Donnell; or, the story of a life', 'The cousins; or the test of friendship', 'Little Mary; or, the child of providence', 'The rose and the lily; or, the twin sisters', 'Rody O'Leary; or, the young outlaw', 'The bequest; or, all is not gold that glitters' (the latter included in 1864 or later edn). The binding of the BL copy of the 1856 edn is gold impressed on cover with decoration of shamrock, roses, and thistle, and child and adult. Priced at 4*s*. [RL].

+ Dublin: James Duffy & Co., [1864 or later] (as *Tales and stories*; ill. Geo. Measom). LOCATION InND Loeber coll.

Dublin: James Duffy, [1886 or earlier] (as *Brother James's Tales*). SOURCE Adv. in W. Carleton, *Redmond Count O'Hanlon* (Dublin, 1886).

COMMENTARY *Duffy [1886 or earlier edn]* No copy located, but contents known from advertisement in W. Carleton, *Redmond Count O'Hanlon* (Dublin, 1886): 'The city man, and the cousin in the third degree', 'Little St. Agnes, and frost land', 'The rosary of pearl; or, the ordeal by touch', 'True to the last, and other tales'. It is not clear whether this publication consisted of a combination of separate publications [RL].

R119   *Nettlethorpe; or, the London miser* (by 'Brother James').
    + Dublin: James Duffy, 1857 (ill. Geo. Jameson). LOCATION L.
    + New York: The Catholic Publication Society, 1868. SOURCE OCLC. LOCATION
    Cleveland Public Library (OH).
    COMMENTARY About a young Irishman in London [RL; DCU].

R120   *Brother James's holiday* (by 'Brother James').
    + Dublin: James Duffy, [1860]. LOCATION L.
    London: Burn & Lambert, n.d. LOCATION L.

R121   *The gift of friendship for 1860. Containing Nettlethorpe, the London miser, The
    partners. A true tale and The false friend* (by 'Brother James').
    Dublin: James Duffy, [1860]. LOCATION L.
    + Dublin, London: James Duffy & Sons, 1874 (ill. Geo. Measom). LOCATION D.
    COMMENTARY An unusual Dublin annual, which appears to have been published for one year
    only. Consists of a collective reissue of stories (first published in Dublin in 1857) each under
    its own title page and page numbering. 'A true tale' is not in the NLI copy, nor is it a sub-
    title to 'The partners' [RL].

R122   *The adventures of Mr. Moses Finegan, an Irish pervert. A true story* (by 'Brother
    James', the late Dr James Reynolds of Booterstown, Co. Dublin).
    London: [n.p.], [1870]. SOURCE Allibone Suppl., ii, p. 1274. SOURCE COPAC.
    LOCATION L.
    + Dublin: James Duffy, [1871]. SOURCE Brown 1416. LOCATION Dt ([*c.*1885] edn), C,
    InND Loeber coll.
    COMMENTARY No copy of the London edn located. Religious fiction of an anti-Protestant
    thrust, set in Ireland. Finnegan, a carpenter by trade but an idler and drunkard, seeing that
    converts could have money for drink without labour, becomes a Bible reader. He practices his
    trade with a similar convert named Gilhooly. They do not always find a friendly reception.
    Finnegan, though a married man, seduces a daughter of a magistrate. He promises that he will
    marry her when they go off to America. However, he only takes her to Liverpool, where he
    proceeds to spend the money the girl has brought with her. When she insists on being mar-
    ried, he kills her. His son, having just returned from America, surprises his father in the das-
    tardly act. Finnegan is sentenced to death, but before his sentence is executed he returns to
    the Catholic religion [ML; Brown].

R123   *The juvenile library* (by 'Brother James').
    Dublin: James Duffy, [1886 or earlier]. SOURCE Brown, 1417; Adv. in W. Carleton,
    Redmond Count O'Hanlon (Dublin, 1886).
    COMMENTARY No copy located. Contents: 'Busy Peter', 'White lies', 'The two boys', 'The lit-
    tle drummer', 'Fidelity rewarded', 'The little adventurer', 'Cathleen', etc. [Brown; RL].

RHYS, Grace (née Little), b. Knockadoo, Boyle (Co. Roscommon) 1865, d. England? 1929.
Novelist, poet and editor, GR was the youngest daughter of Joseph Bennett Little and was
educated by governesses. Her father had a country estate at Kilrush (Co. Roscommon) and a
house in Dublin. Because of his improvidence the family lost their estate. She and her sisters
went to London where she earned her living by teaching. In 1891 she married Ernest Rhys,
the Anglo-Welsh poet, friend of William Butler Yeats§ and founder of *Dent's Everyman Library*
(London), who described her then as a blue-eyed girl 'with a merry dance in her eyes' (Rhys,
165, 169–70). She began to write after her marriage, and she edited the Banbury Cross series
for children, which was published by Dent in 12 volumes. She wrote ten novels; published
several songbooks and volumes of poems; made translations, and wrote many introductions to
other books. Some of her works were illustrated by Megan Rhys, a probable relative. Some

of her letters are in the RIA (MS 12/0/24). SOURCE Brown, p. 261; Brown 2, p. 231; Colman, pp 145–6; Daims, p. 593; EF, pp 340–1; OCIL, p. 496; E. Rhys, *Everyman remembers* (London, 1931), pp 165, 169–70; Roscommon, p. 131; Sutherland, p. 533.

R124 *Mary Dominic* (by Grace Rhys).
+ London: J.M. Dent & Co., 1898. SOURCE Brown, 1419; Daims, 2537; Roscommon, p. 131. LOCATION Roscommon County Library, L.
Leipzig: Bernard Tauchnitz, 1899. SOURCE Daims, 2537; T & B, 3364. LOCATION NUC.

R125 *The wooing of Sheila* (by Grace Rhys).
London: Methuen & Co., 1901. SOURCE Brown, 1420. LOCATION L.
+ Leipzig: Bernard Tauchnitz, 1901. SOURCE T & B, 3531. LOCATION D, InND Loeber coll.
New York: H. Holt & Co., 1901. LOCATION D (1908 edn), NUC.
COMMENTARY Set in Ireland. A gentleman deliberately brings up his son as a common labourer. The son falls in love with and marries a peasant girl he had saved from a young squire. On her marriage morning she learns that her husband has killed the young squire. She leaves him, but the priest induces her to return, and the crime is hushed up [Brown].

R126 *The diverted village. A holiday book* (by Grace Rhys).
+ London: Methuen & Co., 1903 (ill. Gwen Jeffreys). LOCATION L, InND Loeber coll.
COMMENTARY Describes a London family's summer stay in a cottage in Norfolk and their interactions with the local villagers [ML].

R127 *Five beads on a string* (by Grace Rhys).
+ Hampstead: Sidney C. Mayle, 1903 (The Priory Press Booklets). LOCATION L, NUC (1907 edn).
COMMENTARY Contents: 'Eidola', 'The squirrel on the nut tree', 'The cool of the day', 'The church roof', 'The daughters of the green bay tree' [ML].

R128 *The Prince of Lisnover* (by Grace Rhys).
+ London: Methuen & Co., 1904. SOURCE Brown, 1421; McCarthy, viii, p. 2940 (mistakenly lists this as 'The prince of Lismore'). LOCATION D, L, NUC.
COMMENTARY Set in Ireland in the early 1860s and shows the devotion of the Irish people to the old, dispossessed families [Brown].

R129 *The bride* (by Grace Rhys).
London: Methuen & Co., 1909. SOURCE Roscommon, p. 131. LOCATION L.
COMMENTARY Concerns the marriage of a girl to a sculptor [EF, p. 341].

R130 *The charming of Estercel* (by Grace Rhys).
+ London: J.M. Dent, 1913. SOURCE Brown, 1422. LOCATION D, L.
New York: E.P. Dutton & Co., 1913. LOCATION NUC.
COMMENTARY Historical fiction of the adventures of Estercel in the service of Hugh O'Neill set in sixteenth-century Ireland in the days of O'Neill and Essex. A love story is interwoven [Brown].

R131 *In wheelabout and cockalone* (by Grace Rhys).
London: G.G. Harrap & Co., 1918 (ill. Margaret W. Tarrant, Megan Rhys). SOURCE Roscommon, p. 131. LOCATION L.
London: G.G. Harrap & Co., 1931 (as *The magic wood beyond the world*). LOCATION L.
New York: Frederick A. Stokes, [1918] (ill. Margaret W. Tarrant, Megan Rhys). LOCATION NUC.

R132 *About many things* (by Grace Rhys).
+ London: Methuen & Co., 1920. LOCATION L.

Leipzig: Bernard Tauchnitz, 1921. SOURCE T & B, 4557; COPAC. LOCATION L.
COMMENTARY Stories, largely reprinted from magazines: 'The quest', 'The vineyard', 'The venturer', 'The voice of India', 'The shanachie', 'The nation' [CM].

R133 *Eleanor in the loft* (by Grace Rhys).
London: J. Cape, 1923. SOURCE Brown 2, 1372a; Roscommon, p. 131. LOCATION L.
COMMENTARY A story about the unpleasant household of the Ropers, an impoverished family of Protestant landowners living in the Irish midlands. The parents, with a background of drink, treat their children harshly. Mr Roper economizes by stinting the children of all but the bare necessities of life. Even Eleanor, who is age 17, is relegated to the nursery. During a questionable house party the children are banished to a loft. But this leads to a romance between Eleanor and one of the guests, Felix Armore, a rich American. The party is broken up by a Sinn Féin raid on Doon House, setting all Mr Roper's plans awry. Armore comes back for Eleanor [Brown 2].

RICCOBONI, Marie-Jeanne (née Labouras de Mezière), b. France 1714, d. 1792. French epistolary novelist and actress who was convent-educated, this author married an Italian actor, whom she later left. She supported herself on the stage and by writing, including eight novels. Many of her works were reprinted in Dublin between 1760 and 1784, including *The history of Miss Jenny Salisbury* (Dublin, 1764, 2 vols.), dedicated to the countess of Roscommon. Her work was admired by Elizabeth Griffith§. SOURCE Blain, p. 897; G. Gargett & G. Sheridan (eds), *Ireland and the French enlightenment, 1700–1800* (Houndmills, 1999), pp 270–1; RL.

R134 *Lettres de Milady Juliette Catesby, à Milady Henriette Campley, son amie* [anon.].
Amsterdam: [n.p.], 1759. SOURCE *Catalogue of the library of Dr. R.R. Madden§* (Dublin, 1865), p. 44; CCF. LOCATION BNF, InND Loeber coll. (1759, 2nd edn).
London: R. & J. Dodsley, 1759 (trans. by Frances Brooke as *Letters from Lady Juliet Catesby, to her friend Lady Henrietta Campley*). SOURCE Raven, 502. LOCATION E.
London: R. & J. Dodsley; Dublin: repr. by J. Potts, 1760 (trans. as *Letters from Juliet Lady Catesby, to her friend Lady Henrietta Campley*). SOURCE ESTC n18905. LOCATION Dt, NYU.
Dublin: Printed by J. Potts, 1763, 2nd edn (trans. by Frances Brooke as *Letters from Lady Juliet Catesby, to her friend Henrietta Campley*). SOURCE Raven, 789. LOCATION L, O.
Dublin: Printed by J. Potts, 1773, 3rd edn (trans. by Frances Brooke as *Letters from Juliet Lady Catesby, to her friend Henrietta Campley*).
COMMENTARY Epistolary novel relating information about the earl of Ormond, Lord Ossory, and other Irish celebrities of the time [RL; *Catalogue of the library of Dr. R.R. Madden§*].

RICE, (Samuel) James (1844–1882). English co-author. See BESANT, Walter.

RICHARDS, Adela Elizabeth. See ORPEN, Mrs Adela Elizabeth.

RICHARDSON, Mrs Abby Sage (known as Abby Sage), b. 1837, d. 1900. American poet and writer of songs and miscellaneous works, ASR was previously married to a D. McFarland. SOURCE Allibone Suppl., ii, p. 1276; NUC.

R135 *Pebbles and pearls for the young folks* (by Mrs Abby Sage).
Hartford (CT): American Publishing Co.; New York: Bliss & Co.; Philadelphia, Chicago, St Louis, Cincinnati: Zeigler, Mc'Curdy [*sic*] & Co., 1868 (ill.). SOURCE RLIN; OCLC. LOCATION NUC.
COMMENTARY Classified as Irish fiction for juveniles [RLIN].

RICHARDSON, Jane Marian (née Wakefield; known as **Jane M. Richardson**), fl. 1893. Religious and miscellaneous writer, JMR came from a Quaker family and married another Quaker, John Grubb Richardson of Moyallon House (Co. Down), probably in 1850. Her husband, a linen bleacher and warehouseman, had purchased a linen mill and other property at Bessborough (Co. Armagh) in 1845 where he began a model village without public house, pawnshop, or police. Under the pseudonym 'J.M.R.', his wife authored *Six generations of Friends in Ireland* (London, 1893). According to the introduction to the following volume, she was living at Moyallon House in 1896. Her correspondence is in the Religious Society of Friends' Historical Library, Dublin (portfolio 19). SOURCE BLC; Harrison, pp 87–8, 94, 99; T.W. Moody, F.X. Martin & F.J. Byrne (eds), *A new history of Ireland, vol. VIII* (Oxford, 1982), p. 321; RL.

R136   *Apples of gold: or talks with the children* (by Jane M. Richardson).
+ London: Headley Bros, 1896 (ill. William Miller; see Plate 55). LOCATION InND Loeber coll.
COMMENTARY Religious stories for children. Contains semi-fictional accounts of Quakers in England, Scotland and Ireland [RL].

RICHARDSON, Maj. John, b. near Niagara Falls (Upper Canada) 1797, d. 1852. Military officer and novelist, JR was the son Robert Richardson, a Scottish army surgeon, and a Miss Askin from Detroit (MI). He served in the Canadian militia (41st Regiment) during the Anglo-American War of 1812 to 1814 and was taken prisoner at the battle of the Thames. When liberated, he joined the British army and left for England in 1815, where he married a woman from Essex. He lived in Paris, which provided the setting of a few of his novels. In 1835 he joined the British Auxiliary Legion raised to fight in the Carlist war. However, he quarrelled with his commander, the Irishman George DeLacy Evans. In 1838, he became the Canadian correspondent for the London *Times* and the publisher of several newspapers. He moved to New York about 1849. Only his work with Irish links is listed here. Given his blatant ignorance of Irish topography, it is unlikely that JR was an Irishman by origin. SOURCE COPAC (List of the principal publications issued from New Burlington Street during the year 1830); Garside 2, 1830:92; ODNB; RL.

R137   *Frascati's; or, scenes in Paris* [anon.].
+ London: H. Colburn & Rich. Bentley, 1830, 3 vols. SOURCE COPAC (which mentions the attribution); Garside 2, 1830:92. LOCATION L.
Philadelphia: A.L. Carey & A. Hart, 1836, 2 vols. in 1. SOURCE COPAC. LOCATION L.
COMMENTARY Features The O'Flaherty of Flaherty Hall, Co. Connaught [*sic*], but the story is also set in France. Frascati's refers to a gambling club [RL].

RICHARDSON, Robert, b. Sydney, NSW (Australia) 1850. Australian novelist and periodical writer, RR graduated BA at Sydney University in 1870. He followed a career in journalism and literature in Sydney, London and Edinburgh, writing for periodicals and as a correspondent for several newspapers. He published travel stories and at least one contribution to the *Dublin University Magazine*. Most of his works (see Allibone) were published in Edinburgh. SOURCE Allibone Suppl., ii, p. 1277; NUC.

R138   *The young cragsman, and other stories* (by Robert Richardson).
Edinburgh: William Oliphant & Co., 1878. SOURCE Allibone Suppl., ii, p. 1277. LOCATION NUC.
COMMENTARY Contents: 'The young cragsman', 'How the fight was stopped; or, Ralph and Kenneth's quarrel', 'Adam Ransome's nephew', 'An Irish girl' [NUC].

R139   *Phil's champion. An Irish story* (by Robert Richardson).
       Edinburgh: W. Oliphant, 1880. SOURCE Allibone Suppl., ii, p. 1277. LOCATION L
       (destroyed), NUC.
COMMENTARY Based on 'Frankie', a ballad poem by Lord Southesk, which in turn is based
on a short narrative by a Miss Davis in *The helping hand* (location unclear, 1875) [BLC].

RICHARDSON, Samuel. See **RICHARDSON, Samuel Thomas Stanislaus.**

RICHARDSON, Samuel Thomas Stanislaus (also known as **Samuel Richardson**), b.
Clonmel (Co. Tipperary) 1844. Moralizing Catholic novelist and barrister, SR was the only
son of Thomas Samuel Richardson of Clonmel and Marianne Mulcahy. He was educated at
Clongowes Wood College (Co. Kildare, 1858–63) and at TCD where he graduated BA.
Subsequently he was admitted to the King's Inns in 1868, the Middle Temple, London, in
1866, and was called to the Irish Bar in 1868. SOURCE Brown, p. 262; Ferguson, p. 289; Keane,
p. 422; RL.
R140   *Noel d'Auvergne: A novel* (by Samuel Richardson).
       + London: R. Washbourne; Dublin: W.B. Kelly, 1869. SOURCE Brown, 1424. LOCATION
       D, L.
COMMENTARY A religious novel from the Catholic point of view set in Dublin and Killarney in
the 1860s. Noel, a Dublin law student of French origin, becomes engaged to Madeleine, his
friend's sister. A villain, the Hon. O'Malley Oranmore, comes between them. Madeline accepts
him, but when she is reduced to poverty, he throws her over and enters on a career of crime.
She dies. Years later, Noel meets Madeleine's younger sister Mary and they are united [Brown].
R141   *Killed at Sedan. A novel* (by Samuel Richardson).
       + London: R. Washbourne; Dublin: M.H. Gill, 1882. SOURCE Allibone Suppl., ii, p.
       1277. LOCATION L.
COMMENTARY A military novel, which starts with soldiers arriving in Cork and then moves to
Co. Tipperary, before ending in France during the Franco-Prussian war [RL].

RIDDELL, Mrs J.H. (née Charlotte Eliza Lawson Cowan), pseuds '**R.V.M. Sparling**',
'**Rainey Hawthorne**', and '**F.G. Trafford**', b. The Barn, Carrickfergus (Co. Antrim) 1832,
d. Isleworth (Middx.) 1906. Novelist, periodical writer and editor, Mrs JHR was the daughter of James Cowan, a flax and cotton spinner of Carrickfergus and sheriff for Co. Antrim,
and Ellen Kilshaw, who was English. Her father died when she was young, greatly reducing
the family's standard of living. She and her mother moved to Dundonald (Co. Down) and
then to London in 1855. She began writing early in life to support herself and her mother,
who died in 1856, the year her first novel was published. In 1857 she married Joseph Hadley
Riddell, a boiler and stove merchant. Although very despondent about her initial lack of success as an author and ready to give up writing, she persevered and gained recognition for her
work. She published 56 novels (some in collaboration with Arthur Hamilton Norway) and
books of short stories, which fall into three principal categories: tales of commerce and City
life (she was one of the first novelists writing in English to feature business life), tales of the
supernatural, and tales of everyday life. In 1867 she became editor and part-proprietor of the
St. James's Magazine (London), founded in 1861 by Mrs S.C. Hall§, in which her novel *A
life's assize* was serialized between 1866 and 1870. She revised Sir Cusack P. Roney's *How to
spend a month in Ireland* (London, 1872), and she contributed to annuals such as the *Broadway
Annual* (London, 1868), the Christmas number of the *London Society* (1867), and *Routledge's
Christmas Annual* (London, 1875, 1877) and to the periodical *Once A Week* (London). Because
of reduced finances due to her husband's failed business enterprises, she moved to Addlestone,

near Weybridge (Surrey) in 1875. Five years later her husband died, forcing further financial retrenchments and a move back to London. She visited Ulster with her friend Arthur Hamilton Norway in 1885, with whom she collaborated on *The government official* (London, 1887, 3 vols.) and to whom she dedicated *A mad tour* (London, 1891). Upon her return, she moved with him to Upper Halliford, near Shepperton (Middx). Four years later, she paid her last visit to Ireland. She became seriously ill with cancer in 1892, and even more impoverished before her death in 1906. At the end of her life she received the first pension of the Society of Authors. Despite her efforts, she did not succeed in clearing all her husband's debts. Several of her novels and short stories are set in Ireland but the majority of her works are set in London, particularly around the financial and commerial life of the City, as well as in Surrey and in Middlesex. She kept an affinity for Ireland, however, and in a letter of 1902 she wrote longingly of her childhood home: 'where such magnificent scenery ... makes one hold one's breath ... How I should like were I young & strong to take you with me to that lovely land'. A set of her letters is in the NLI (MS 10,048). For her portrait, see ODNB. SOURCE Allibone, ii, p. 1803, iii, p. 2443 [under F.G. Trafford], Allibone Suppl., ii, p. 1279; Blain, pp 901–2; Brady, p. 210; Cox cat. 41/172; DLB, clvi; Ellis, p. 266–335; Field Day, v, pp 769, 927, 928, 929, 975; Hogan 2, pp 1056–7; Holmes cat. 59/184; NCBEL 4, pp 1679–80; M. Kelleher, 'Charlotte Riddell's struggle for fame' in *Colby Quarterly*, 36(2) (2000), pp 116–31; OCIL, p. 497; ODNB; Sutherland, pp 535–6; Todd, pp 568–70; Wilson, pp 422–5.

R142 *Zuriel's grandchild* (by 'R.V.M. Sparling').

London: Thos. Cautley Newby, 1856. SOURCE Ellis, p. 323; Todd, p. 569; Sotheby's cat. LN6731/594; Quaritch cat. Spring 1997/71.

London: Tinsley Bros, 1873 (new edn; as *Joy after sorrow*). SOURCE Topp 4, p. 93; Ellis, p. 323.

COMMENTARY No copy of the London 1873 edn located other than that mentioned in the Sotheby's cat.[RL].

R143 *The ruling passion* (by 'Rainey Hawthorne').

London: Richard Bentley, 1857, 3 vols. SOURCE NCBEL 3, p. 1073; Sadleir, 2065. LOCATION L, NUC.

London: Frederick Warne & Co., 1876 (revsd edn). SOURCE Jarndyce cat. 117/450; Topp 4, p. 98. LOCATION NUC.

R144 *The moors and the fens* (by 'F.G. Trafford').

London: Smith, Elder & Co., 1857, 3 vols. SOURCE Allibone, iii, p. 2443 (1858 edn); Sadleir, 2058; Wolff, 5816; Ellis, p. 323 (1858 edn). LOCATION L (1858 edn), C, TxU.

London: Smith, Elder & Co., 1863 (new edn, revsd; ill.). SOURCE Allibone, iii, p. 2443; Topp 5, p. 231. LOCATION NUC.

COMMENTARY Features a writer heroine who unhappily marries a baronet [Sutherland, p. 536].

R145 *Poor fellow!* [anon.].

New York: Dick & Fitzgerald, 1858. LOCATION L (destroyed), NUC.

London: F.V. White & Co., 1902. SOURCE Ellis, p. 335; NCBEL 4, p. 1680; Wolff, 5821. LOCATION L, NUC.

COMMENTARY The story of an unsuccessful man who ends his career by suicide. Categorized as religious fiction in BLC [RL; Ellis].

R146 *The rich husband. A novel of real life* [anon.].

London: Charles J. Skeet, 1858, 3 vols. SOURCE Ellis, p. 323–24; NCBEL 3, p. 1073. LOCATION L.

London: Tinsley Bros., 1867 (new edn). SOURCE Allibone, ii, p. 1803 (1866 edn); Ellis, p. 324; Topp 4, p. 88; Wolff, 5823; OCLC. LOCATION L.

COMMENTARY *London 1867 edn* Preface by the author states that in this edn there is a slight shortening and correction of errors [Topp].

+ Philadelphia: T.B. Peterson & Bros, [1867], 3 vols. in 1 (as *The rich husband. A novel*). SOURCE Allibone, ii, p. 1803. LOCATION NUC, InND Loeber coll.

COMMENTARY Set in Wales and London and recounts the unhappiness brought on several generations of a family by flirtatious women who marry for wealth [ML].

R147 *Too much alone. A novel* (by 'F.G. Trafford').
London: Charles J. Skeet, 1860, 3 vols. SOURCE Allibone, iii, p. 2443; Ellis, p. 324. LOCATION D (n.d. edn), Dt (1865 edn), L.
London: Charles J. Skeet, 1861 (new edn). SOURCE Topp 4, p. 97.
COMMENTARY *London 1861 edn* No copy located [RL].
Boston: T.O.H.P. Burnham, 1866. LOCATION NUC.
COMMENTARY Set in Eastcheap and Bow (England) [Ellis].

R148 *City and suburb. A novel* (by 'F.G. Trafford').
+ London: Charles J. Skeet, 1861, 3 vols. SOURCE Allibone, iii, p. 2443; Ellis, p. 23. LOCATION Dt (1862, new edn), L, NUC.
London: Charles J. Skeet, 1862 (new edn). SOURCE Topp 4, p. 87; RLIN. LOCATION NN.

COMMENTARY Alan Ruthven, a former member of the Irish gentry, comes to London to try and become a success in business in order to provide for himself, his brother, a sister and a ward of his father. Pride stands in his way and he is not very successful. Although he is very fond of and dependent on the ward, he cannot truly love her because he thinks she is beneath him. In the end they do marry, but are never very happy [ML].

R149 *The world in the church* (by 'F.G. Trafford').
London: Charles J. Skeet, 1863, 3 vols. SOURCE Allibone, iii, p. 2443 (1862, 1865 edns); Ellis, p. 324 (1863, 2nd edn); Todd, p. 569; Wolff, 5829. LOCATION L.
London: Warne, [1875] (Companion Library). SOURCE Sadleir, 3668. LOCATION NUC.

R150 *George Geith of Fen Court. A novel* (by 'F.G. Trafford'; dedicated to Alexander Johns, Esq., of Sunnylands, Carrickfergus).
London: Tinsley Bros, 1864, 3 vols. SOURCE Allibone, iii, p. 2443; Ellis, pp 324–5; Sadleir, 2050; Wolff, 5805; COPAC. LOCATION L, NUC (1865 edn).
London: Tinsley Bros, 1865 (new edn). SOURCE Allibone, iii, p. 2443; Topp 5, p. 154; COPAC. LOCATION L.
Leipzig: Bernard Tauchnitz, 1865, 2 vols. SOURCE T & B, 770–71; Wolff, 5805c. LOCATION L, NUC.
Boston: T.O.H.P. Burnham; New York: O.S. Felt, 1865. SOURCE Allibone, iii, p. 2443; Topp 5, p. 154. LOCATION DCL.

COMMENTARY Still in press in 1886. Set in the financial and business world of London. A clergyman who runs away from a disastrous marriage becomes a successful accountant. The story was turned into a play [Sutherland, p. 536; Todd, p. 568].

R151 *Maxwell Drewitt. A novel* (by 'F.G. Trafford').
London: Tinsley Bros, 1865, 3 vols. SOURCE Allibone, iii, p. 2443; Brown, 1426; Ellis, p. 325; Sadleir, 2056; Wolff, 5813. LOCATION L, NUC.
+ London: Tinsley Bros, 1866 (new edn). LOCATION D.
+ Leipzig: Bernard Tauchnitz, 1866, 2 vols. SOURCE T & B, 809–10. LOCATION D, L, NUC.
New York: Harper & Bros, 1866 (Library of Select Novels, No. 266). LOCATION NUC.
+ New York: Garland, 1979, 3 vols. (introd. by R.L. Wolff). LOCATION D, Dt, InND Loeber coll.

Riddell

COMMENTARY Set in Connemara around the middle of the nineteenth century, it describes an election and a trial for robbery. The background of the story is formed by a family grudge vigorously pursued over three generations [Brown; Wolff, introd. p. 33].

R152 *Phemie Keller. A novel* (by 'F.G. Trafford').

London: Tinsley Bros, 1866, 3 vols. SOURCE Allibone, ii, p. 1803; Ellis, p. 325; Wolff, 5820. LOCATION L (1867 edn), NUC.

London: Frederick Warne & Co., 1875 (new edn; Companion Library, No. 66). SOURCE Topp 4, p. 84.

COMMENTARY *London 1875 edn* No copy located [RL].

New York: Harper & Bros, 1866 (Library of Select Novels, No. 272). LOCATION NUC.

New York: American News Co., 1866. SOURCE Topp 4, p. 84.

COMMENTARY No copy of the New York, American News edn located. First serialized in the *Shilling Magazine* (London, May 1865–May 1866) [Topp; RL].

R153 *The race for wealth. A novel* (by Mrs J.H. Riddell).

+ London: Tinsley Bros, 1866, 3 vols. SOURCE Allibone, ii, p. 1803; Ellis, p. 325; Sadleir, 2064. LOCATION L, NUC.

Leipzig: Bernard Tauchnitz, 1866, 2 vols. in 1. SOURCE T & B, 864. LOCATION NUC.

New York: Harper & Bros, 1866 (Library of Select Novels, No. 278). SOURCE Allibone, ii, p. 1803. LOCATION NUC.

COMMENTARY First serialized in *Once a Week* (London). Set in London and its outskirts among the business classes, it tells the story of two young men who have to make their way and who are rivals in business and in love [ML].

R154 *Far above rubies. A novel* (by Mrs J.H. Riddell).

London: Tinsley Bros, 1867, 3 vols. SOURCE Allibone, ii, p. 1803; Ellis, p. 326; NCBEL 3, p. 1073; Sadleir, 2049. LOCATION L, NUC.

+ London: Tinsley Bros, 1868 (new edn). SOURCE Ellis, p. 326. LOCATION InND Loeber coll.

Leipzig: Bernard Tauchnitz, 1867, 2 vols. in 1. SOURCE T & B, 912–13. LOCATION NUC.

Philadelphia: J.B. Lippincott & Co., 1867. LOCATION NUC.

COMMENTARY Set in Hertfordshire and London. Mr Arthur Dudley lives with his wife and children in a small country place. He is a dissatisfied man who feels he should be rich but does not undertake anything practical to improve his situation. A relative persuades him to invest in a company that in reality is set up to fleece people. Dudley sells his cattle and crops in order to put as much money as possible into the company. He loses all and is about to set fire to the company premises to hide the swindle and then to commit suicide when he is rescued. He decides to be better satisfied with his lot and to pay more attention to his family [ML].

R155 *My first love* (by Mrs J.H. Riddell).

London: F. Enos Arnold, 1869. SOURCE Topp 4, p. 97. LOCATION L ([1891] edn).

COMMENTARY First published in *St. James' Magazine's Christmas Box* [Topp 4, pp 97–8].

R156 *My last love* [anon.].

London: F. Enos Arnold, 1870. SOURCE Topp 4, p. 98. SOURCE COPAC. LOCATION E.

COMMENTARY 70pp [COPAC]

R157 *Austin Friars. A novel* (by Mrs J.H. Riddell).

+ London: Tinsley Bros, 1870, 3 vols. SOURCE Allibone Suppl., ii, p. 1279; Ellis, p. 326; Wolff, 5795. LOCATION L, NUC.

London: Frederick Warne; New York: Scribner, Welford & Armstrong, [1875] (new edn; as *Austin Friars*). LOCATION NUC.

COMMENTARY First serialized in *Tinsley's Magazine* (London, beginning Apr. 1869). A story about merchant life and convoluted romantic relationships in London in which the main characters are Austin Friars, Yorke Forde, and Luke Ross. Yorke is married off by her father at a very young age. On the day of her wedding she realizes that she does not wish to be married, leaves her husband, and goes to live with Austin, whose business partner she is. Austin is a heartless opportunist and drops Yorke when the chance to better himself occurs. After Austin disappears, Yorke continues in business with the help of Luke, who is in love with Yorke but who knows her history and has decided nonetheless to stand by her. Luke has great difficulty extracting from Austin money that is owed to Yorke, and Austin involves Luke in disastrous business dealings. Mr Forde appears on the scene and when he falls ill, Yorke lives with him for a number of years to look after him. She ends up a rich widow and marries Luke [ML; Topp].

R158   *Long ago: Part I* (by Mrs J.H. Riddell).
   London: F. Enos Arnold, 1870. SOURCE Sadleir, 2055.
   COMMENTARY No copy located [RL].

R159   *A life's assize. A novel* (by Mrs J.H. Riddell; dedicated to C. Skey).
   London: Tinsley Bros, 1871, 3 vols. SOURCE Allibone Suppl., ii, p. 1279 (1870 edn, 1875 new edn); Ellis, p. 326; Sadleir, 2054. LOCATION L, NUC.
   London: Tinsley Bros, 1871 (new edn). SOURCE Topp 4, p. 87.
   COMMENTARY No copy of the London new edn located [RL].
   New York: Harper & Bros, 1871 (Library of Select Novels, No. 360). SOURCE Topp 4, p. 87. LOCATION NUC.

COMMENTARY First serialized in the London *St. James's Magazine* (beginning Mar. 1868), the story of a murder in Scotland, with later scenes laid in the Essex marshes. Two friends, Andrew and Anthony, having just finished their studies, make a tour through Scotland. Anthony seduces the wife of an acquaintance. Her husband thinks that Andrew is the culprit. In an encounter, Andrew accidentally kills the husband. Eventually, he is discharged from jail for lack of evidence. However, his whole life is blighted. Anthony takes his money and disappears to the Continent, and Andrew takes Anthony's name and becomes a curate in a poor parish, and lives for the rest of his life very unhappily under this disguise [ML; Ellis; Topp].

R160   *The Earl's promise. A novel* (by 'F.G. Trafford').
   London: Tinsley Bros, 1873, 3 vols. SOURCE Allibone Suppl., ii, p. 1279; Ellis, p. 327; Sadleir, 2047; Topp 6, 66. LOCATION L, NUC.
   London: Frederick Warne & Co., [1875] (new edn). SOURCE Topp 6, 66; OCLC. LOCATION GEU, InND Loeber coll. (1890 edn).
   + Leipzig: Bernard Tauchnitz, 1873, 2 vols. in 1. SOURCE T & B, 1355–56. LOCATION NUC, InND Loeber coll.

COMMENTARY First serialized in the London *People's Magazine* (Society for the Promotion of Christian Knowledge) beginning July 1872. Set in Ulster, it deals with small town class differences and the effects of a money-grabbing landlord. Much mischief arises from the earl's promise to one of his tenants to renew a lease for which a lot of money was given to the earl but nothing was recorded. The farmer loses out, because nobody wants to honour the promise. The heroine is an heiress for whom money does not bring happiness because it makes every suitor look suspect. It is also difficult for her to decide what are worthwhile projects on which to spend her money. The villain seduces girls and sets out to financially wreck his neighbours. Many other characters appear and their adventures are interwoven with those of the preceding actors [ML].

R161 *Home, sweet home. A novel* (by Mrs J.H. Riddell; dedicated to Mrs Frederick Nolan).

London: Tinsley Bros, 1873, 3 vols. SOURCE Allibone Suppl., ii, p. 1279; Ellis, p. 327; Wolff, 5810; Topp 6, 62. LOCATION L, NUC.

London: Frederick Warne & Co., 1875 (new edn). SOURCE Topp 4, p. 93; OCLC. LOCATION D (n.d. edn).

Berlin: A. Asher, 1873, 2 vols. LOCATION NUC.

COMMENTARY Set in England, the story deals extensively with class differences and features an orphan, Annie, who is brought up by her grandmother in a tiny cottage overlooking a large country house. The girl has a gift for singing and is eventually taught by a German professor in London, who takes her on as a speculation. She is successful as a singer, but the professional singing life has its problems and dangers. Eventually, she marries a cousin of the old ladies who live in the big house, opposite to where she grew up [ML].

R162 *Fairy water. A Christmas story* (by Mrs J.H. Riddell).

+ London, New York: George Routledge, 1873 (Routledge's Christmas Annual; ill. R. Caldecott, Edmund Evans). LOCATION L.

London: Chatto & Windus, 1885 (new edn; as *Fairy water. A novel*). SOURCE Topp 3, p. 137; Sadleir, 3668. LOCATION NUC.

COMMENTARY Ghost story set in Essex. The London, Routledge edn is 96pp, while the London new edn of 1885 consists of 252pp [Ellis; NUC; Topp 1, p. 236; Sadleir, 2048; Wolff, 5802].

R163 *Frank Sinclair's wife, and other stories* (by Mrs J.H. Riddell).

London: Tinsley Bros, 1874, 3 vols. SOURCE Allibone Suppl., ii, p. 1279 (1873 edn); Ellis, p. 327; Wolff, 5804; Topp 6, 68. LOCATION L, NUC.

London: Hutchinson, [19—] (new edn; as *Frank Sinclair's wife, and Forewarned, forearmed*). LOCATION NUC.

COMMENTARY Contents: 'Frank Sinclair's wife' (first published in *Cassell's Magazine*, London, Jan.–June 1871), 'My first love' (first published London, 1869), 'My last love, a sequel to my first love' (first published as a separate vol., 1870), 'Forewarned, forearmed' (ghost story), 'Hertford O'Donnell's warning' (ghost story; first published in *London Society*, 1867) [Ellis; Wilson, p. 423; Topp 6, 68; RL].

R164 *Mortomley's estate. A novel* (by Mrs J.H. Riddell; dedicated to Emma Martin, of Wadesmill, Herts.).

London: Tinsley Bros, 1874, 3 vols. SOURCE Allibone Suppl., ii, p. 1279; Ellis, p. 32; Sadleir, 2059; Wolff, 1817; Topp 6, 71. LOCATION L, NUC.

+ Leipzig: Bernard Tauchnitz, 1874, 2 vols. in 1. SOURCE T & B, 1464–65. LOCATION NUC, InND Loeber coll.

COMMENTARY At the time this book was being written, the author's husband's business was in serious financial trouble. Set in England, the novel describes the working of the Bankruptcy Act of 1866. Mr Mortomley's colour works are in deep financial trouble and his former associates and acquaintances only expedite his total financial ruin. His wife's little legacy is also claimed by the creditors. His wife, described initially as a cheerful, mindless thing, stands by him and she eventually opens up a small colour works again [ML].

R165 *The uninhabited house* (by Mrs J.H. Riddell).

London, New York: George Routledge & Sons, 1875 (ill. A. Chantrey Corbould; Routledge's Christmas Annual). SOURCE COPAC. LOCATION C.

COMMENTARY 96pp. Ghost story [RL].

R166 *My first love and My last love ('a sequel')* (by Mrs J.H. Riddell).

London: Frederick Warne & Co., 1876 (Companion Library, No. 80). SOURCE Allibone Suppl., ii, p. 1279; Topp 4, p. 97. LOCATION L ([1891] edn).

COMMENTARY *London edn* No copy of the 1876 edn located [RL].

New York: John W. Lovell, [1891]. SOURCE Topp 4, p. 98. LOCATION NUC.

COMMENTARY The first story was first published in *St. James' Magazine's Christmas Box* and separately in 1869; the second story was first published in 1870. They were then incorporated in *Sinclair's wife* (London, 1874) before being published together in this volume [ML; Topp 4, pp 97–98].

R167 *Above suspicion. A novel* (by Mrs J.H. Riddell).

+ London: Tinsley Bros, 1876, 3 vols. SOURCE Allibone Suppl., ii, p. 1279 (1875 edn); Ellis, p. 328; Wolff, 5794. LOCATION Dt, L.

Boston: Esters & Lauriat, [1876?] (as *Above suspicion*). LOCATION NUC.

New York: G. Munro, 1879 (as *Above suspicion*; Seaside Library). LOCATION NUC.

COMMENTARY First serialized in *London Society* (Aug. 1874–Jan. 1876). Set in England around 1858, it features an illegitimate son of minor gentry who has to make his own way in life. His dream is to be rich and to buy his parent's estate. He becomes a money counterfeiter and, in the process of stealing silver, kills a man. He is sent to Australia and his brother-in-law takes care of his young daughter. The story centres on the deception needed to hide the girl's background. When she is about to be married, she wishes to tell her fiancée about it, but he does not wish to hear. Nevertheless, the secret continues to press on her mind and before she dies she does tell her husband [ML; Topp 4, p. 103].

R168 *Her mother's darling. A novel* (by Mrs J.H. Riddell; dedicated to Eliza, Harriet, Lois and Constance Margaret Greene).

London: Tinsley Bros, 1877, 3 vols. SOURCE Allibone Suppl., ii, p. 1279; Ellis, p. 328. LOCATION L, NUC.

London: Chatto & Windus, 1879 (as *Her mother's darling*). SOURCE Topp 3, p. 215.

COMMENTARY *London 1879 edn* No copy located [RL].

New York: G. Munro, 1880 (Seaside Library, No. 847). SOURCE Topp 3, p. 58. LOCATION NUC.

R169 *The haunted river. A Christmas story* (by Mrs J.H. Riddell).

London, New York: George Routledge & Sons, 1877 (ill.; Routledge's Christmas Annual). SOURCE Topp 3, p. 137; OCLC. LOCATION CLU.

COMMENTARY 95pp. Ghost story [RL].

R170 *The disappearance of Mr. Jeremiah Redworth* (by Mrs J.H. Riddell).

+ London, New York: George Routledge & Sons, [1878] (Routledge's Christmas Annual; ill. D.H. Friston). SOURCE Allibone Suppl., ii, p. 1279 (1879 edn). LOCATION InND Loeber coll.

New York: George Munro, 1878 (Seaside Library, No. 429). SOURCE Topp 1, p. 298. LOCATION NUC.

COMMENTARY Mystery story or supernatural novella set in England about the death of a well-to-do man, whose spoiled, youngest son is suspected of having killed him [ML; Topp; Sadleir, 2046; Wolff, 5800; Wilson, p. 424].

R171 *The mystery in Palace Gardens. A novel* (by Mrs J.H. Riddell).

London: Richard Bentley & Son, 1880, 3 vols. SOURCE Allibone Suppl., ii, p. 1279; Ellis, p. 329; Sadleir, 2061; Wolff, 5818. LOCATION L, NUC (1881, 3rd edn).

New York: G. Munro, 1881. LOCATION NUC.

COMMENTARY First published in *London Society*. Set in Forest Gare and Epping (Essex) [Ellis].

R172 *Alaric Spenceley; or, a high ideal* (by Mrs J.H. Riddell).

London: Charles J. Skeet, 1881, 3 vols. SOURCE Allibone Suppl., ii, p. 1279; Ellis, p. 329. LOCATION L.

COMMENTARY Set in West Ham (London) and the possibly fictive Abbey Marsh [Ellis; RL].

R173 *The senior partner. A novel* (by Mrs J.H. Riddell).
London: Richard Bentley & Son, 1881, 3 vols. SOURCE Allibone Suppl., ii, p. 1279; Ellis, p. 329; Sadleir, 2066; Wolff, 5824. LOCATION L, NUC.
+ London: Sampson Low, Marston, Searle & Rivington, 1883 (new edn). LOCATION D (1888 edn), InND Loeber coll.
Hamburg: K. Grädener & J.F. Richter, 1882, 3 vols. LOCATION NUC.
New York: Harper & Bros, [1882] (Franklin Square Library, No. 223). LOCATION NUC.
New York: George Munro, 1882 (Seaside Library, No. 1160). SOURCE Topp 4, p. 358.
COMMENTARY No copy of the New York, Munro edn located. First serialized in *London Society* (beginning Jan. 1881). Mr McCullagh is a Scotsman with a thriving business selling Scottish products in London. He has three sons of whom he thinks very little and does not help. When Robert, his oldest son, needs money to become a partner in the firm of Mr Pousnett, he has to borrow it. The firm goes bankrupt and Robert goes to America to seek his fortune, leaving behind his wife and children until he can bring them over. Mr McCullagh falls ill and is on the point of death when Robert's wife comes to nurse him. He only finds out later who saved him. Robert's wife, however, brings the fever home and her little daughter succumbs. Mr McCullagh genuinely repents that he has treated his daughter-in-law so badly and invites her and her children to live with him, which she does. Eventually, he brings Robert back to England and offers him a job [ML; Ellis; Topp].

R174 *The curate of Lowood; or, every man has his golden chance* (by Mrs J.H. Riddell).
London: Office of 'London Society', [1882] (The Golden Acorn Series). SOURCE Ellis, p. 329; Wolff, 5799. LOCATION L.
COMMENTARY Also contains three stories by other authors [NCBEL 4, p. 1679].

R175 *The Prince of Wales's garden party and other stories* (by Mrs J.H. Riddell).
London: Chatto & Windus, 1882. SOURCE Allibone Suppl., ii, p. 1279; Ellis, p. 329; Sadleir, 3668 (1884 edn). LOCATION L.
New York: George Munro, 1882 (Seaside Library, No. 1427). SOURCE Topp 3, p. 113. LOCATION NUC.
COMMENTARY Contents: 'The Prince of Wales's garden party', 'Lady Dugdale's diamonds', 'Far stranger than fiction', 'Captain Mat's wager' (set in Carrickfergus), 'Margaret Donnan' (set in Carrickfergus), 'Miss Molloy's mishap', 'Mrs. Donald' [Ellis].

R176 *Weird stories* (by Mrs J.H. Riddell).
London: J. Hogg, 1882. SOURCE Allibone Suppl., ii, p. 1279; Sadleir, 2070; Wolff, 5828; OCLC. LOCATION TxU.
London: Chatto & Windus, 1885 (new edn). SOURCE Ellis, p. 331; Topp 3, p. 135; Sadleir, 3668 (1891 edn); COPAC. LOCATION Univ. of Glasgow.
London: Home & Van Thal, 1946. SOURCE Wilson, p. 423; COPAC. LOCATION Dt, O.
COMMENTARY Ghost stories, first published in *London Library*, (Christmas, No. 1880). Contents: 'Walnut-tree house', 'The open door', 'Nut-bush farm', 'The old house in Vauxhall Walk', 'Sandy the tinker', 'Old Mrs. Jones' [Ellis; Todd; Topp].

R177 *Daisies and buttercups. A novel* (by Mrs J.H. Riddell; dedicated to Col. and Mrs Kilshaw Irwin of Mobile, Alabama).
London: Richard Bentley & Son, 1882, 3 vols. SOURCE Allibone Suppl., ii, p. 1279; Ellis, p. 330; Sadleir, 2045. LOCATION D (1883 edn), L, NUC.

+ London: Sampson Low, Marston, Searle & Rivington, [1890] (new and cheaper edn; as *Daisies and buttercups. A novel of the Upper Thames*; ill.). SOURCE Topp 4, p. 364. LOCATION NUC, InND Loeber coll.

New York: George Munro, 1882 (Seaside Library, No. 1451). SOURCE Topp 4, p. 364. LOCATION NUC.

New York: Harper & Bros, [1882] (Harper's Franklin Square Library, No. 279). SOURCE LOCATION NUC.

COMMENTARY A story of Weybridge and Addlestone (both Surrey) [Ellis].

R178   *A struggle for fame. A novel* (by Mrs J.H. Riddell; dedicated to Mrs Skirrow).
London: Richard Bentley & Son, 1883, 3 vols. SOURCE Allibone Suppl., ii, p. 1279; Brown, 1427; Ellis, p. 331; Sadleir, 2067; Wolff, 5825. LOCATION L, NUC.

New York: Harper & Bros, [1883]. LOCATION NUC.

New York: G. Munro, [1883]. LOCATION NUC.

COMMENTARY A somewhat-autobiographical novel about the struggles of a female novelist who moves with her father from Belfast to London to find a publisher for her manuscript [Brown].

R179   *The uninhabited house and The haunted river* (by Mrs J.H. Riddell).
London, New York: George Routledge & Sons, 1883. SOURCE Allibone Suppl., ii, p. 1279; Topp 1, p. 335. LOCATION L.

London: Chatto & Windus, 1885 (new edn). SOURCE Allibone Suppl., ii, p. 1279; Topp 3, p. 137; OCLC. LOCATION KU-S.

COMMENTARY Contents: 'The uninhabited house' (a ghost story, first appeared in Routledge's Christmas Annual, London, 1875), 'The haunted river' (first appeared in Routledge's Christmas Annual, London, 1877) [Topp 3, p. 137; Sadleir, 2069; Wolff, 5827].

R180   *Susan Drummond. A novel* (by Mrs J.H. Riddell; dedicated to Mr and Mrs Colin Campbell Wyllie, of Walden, Chislehurst).
London: Richard Bentley & Son, 1884, 3 vols. SOURCE Allibone Suppl., ii, p. 1279; Ellis, p. 330; Sadleir, 2068; Wolff, 5826. LOCATION L, NUC.

New York: Harper & Bros, [1884] (Franklin Square Library, No. 361). SOURCE Topp 5, p. 155. LOCATION NUC.

New York: George Munro, 1884 (Seaside Library, No. 1801). SOURCE Topp 5, p. 155; OCLC. LOCATION Arlington Library, DC (N.L. Munro, n.d. edn).

COMMENTARY The original title was 'Three wizards and a witch' as published in *London Society* [Ellis].

R181   *Berna Boyle. A love story of the County Down* (by Mrs J.H. Riddell).
+ London: Richard Bentley & Sons, 1884, 3 vols. SOURCE Allibone Suppl., ii, p. 1279 (mistakenly given as 'Co. Devon'); Brown, 1428; Ellis, p. 331; Sadleir, 2043; Sutherland, p. 535 (mistakenly mentions a 1882 date). LOCATION L, NUC, InND Loeber coll. (also London, Macmillan, 1900 edn).

New York: George Munro, 1884 (Seaside Library, No. 1859). SOURCE Topp 5, p. 153. LOCATION NUC.

COMMENTARY A love story set in Co. Down around 1850. Young Berna Boyle lives with her mother, a vulgar and foolish woman. Her suitor, although brought up by a rich uncle, has a peasant farmer as a father. The love affair does not progress because of excessive pride and fear that family traits might reveal themselves later on. The dejected lover joins the army. When he comes back after a few years, Berna is happy to see him and they marry [ML].

R182   *Mitre Court. A tale of the great city* (by Mrs J.H. Riddell).
London: Richard Bentley & Son, 1885, 3 vols. SOURCE Allibone Suppl., ii, p. 1279; Ellis, p. 331; Sadleir, 2057; Wolff, 5815. LOCATION L.

COMMENTARY First published in *Temple Bar* (London). Set in an old house off Botolph Lane, Eastcheap [Ellis].

R183 *For Dick's sake* (by Mrs J.H. Riddell).

London: Society for the Promotion of Christian Knowledge, 1886 (Penny Library of Fiction). SOURCE Ellis, p. 331; Wolff, 5803 (n.d. edn). SOURCE COPAC. LOCATION C.

New York, Boston: T.Y. Crowell & Co., 186–. LOCATION NUC.

COMMENTARY 32pp for the London edn [COPAC].

R184 *The government official. A novel* [anon.].

London: Richard Bentley & Son, 1887, 3 vols. SOURCE Sadleir, 2051; Wolff, 5806. LOCATION L, NUC.

COMMENTARY Written in collaboration with Arthur Hamilton Norway [RL].

R185 *Miss Gascoigne. A novel* (by Mrs J.H. Riddell).

+ London: Ward & Downey, 1887. SOURCE Allibone Suppl., ii, p. 1279; Ellis, p. 332; Todd, p. 568 (mistakenly as *Miss Gascoyne*); Wolff, 5814; Topp 8, 36. LOCATION L, NUC, InND Loeber coll.

New York: D. Appleton & Co., 1887 (Gainsborough Series). SOURCE Topp 8, 36. LOCATION NUC.

New York: G. Munro, 1887 (Seaside Library Pocket Edition, No. 1007). SOURCE Topp 8, 36. LOCATION NUC.

COMMENTARY Ostensibly set in an English seaside resort, but the author told the publisher Edmund Downey§ that she had in mind a particular spot in her native Ulster. Miss Gascoigne, a rich spinster, is the only one of her family left. She has come into money and lives comfortably. An old family friend who had emigrated to Canada writes to ask if she could look after his son, who needs a change of climate. Thinking that this is a child, she agrees. However, when the visitor arrives he is a young man in his twenties. After a while they find that despite the large age difference, they are attracted to each other. However, Miss Gascoigne breaks off the liaison as unsuitable. The young man leaves and marries someone else. Miss Gascoigne becomes engaged to a man more suitable in age. According to Ellis the setting is actually Carrickfergus (Co. Antrim), and the heroine is possibly the author who, according to Todd, was seeing a younger man, Arthur Hamilton Norway, around this time [ML; Ellis, p. 305*n*.1; IBL, 9 (1918), p. 124; Todd].

R186 *Idle tales* (by Mrs J.H. Riddell; dedicated to Mrs Whittle, 'in remembrance of days spent at Larchmount, Co. Londonderry').

London: Redway, 1888, 3 vols. SOURCE Allibone Suppl., ii, p. 1279; Topp 3, p. 210. LOCATION L (Ward & Downey, 1888, 2nd edn).

New York: George Munro, 1891 (Seaside Library Pocket Edition, No. 1842). SOURCE Topp 3, p. 210.

COMMENTARY No copies of the London, Redway, 1888 edn and the New York edn located. There is some confusion about whether Redway or Ward & Downey issued the first edn. Contents: 'The run on Connell's bank', 'Only a lost letter', 'He loved and he rode away', 'Pretty Peggy', 'A slight misapprehension', 'The Misses Popkin', 'The last of squire Ennismore' (supernatural story, set in Co. Antrim), 'A storm in a tea cup' [Ellis; Topp; Wilson, p. 423; RL].

R187 *The nun's curse. A novel* (by Mrs J.H. Riddell; dedicated to Dr and Mrs George Harley).

London: Ward & Downey, 1888, 3 vols. SOURCE Allibone Suppl., ii, p. 1279; Brown, 1429 (both Allibone and Brown give 1887, which refers to date of issue); Sadleir, 2062; Wolff, 5820; Topp 8, 84. LOCATION L, NUC.

London: Ward & Downey, 1889 (new edn). SOURCE Sadleir, 3668; OCLC. LOCATION CLU.

New York: D. Appleton & Co., 1888. SOURCE Topp 3, p. 209; OCLC. LOCATION
NYU.

New York: G. Munro, 1888 (Seaside Library Pocket Edition, No. 1077). SOURCE Topp
3, p. 209. LOCATION NUC.

+ New York: John W. Lovell, [1888.] (Lovell's Library, No. 1134). SOURCE Topp 3,
p. 209. LOCATION NUC, InND Loeber coll.

New York: M.J. Ivers, 1888. SOURCE Topp 3, p. 208.

Toronto: William Ryce, [1897 or earlier]. SOURCE Adv. in E. Downey, A *house of tears*
(Toronto, 1897).

+ New York: Garland, 1979, 3 vols. (introd. by R.L. Wolff). LOCATION D, Dt, InND
Loeber coll.

COMMENTARY No copies of the Toronto edn and the New York, Ivers edn located. A mystery
novel with supernatural features set in Co. Donegal near Dunfanaghy around 1850. There is
an inherited curse, pronounced by an Elizabethan nun, on the family of Terence Conway. He
tries to take if off by being a model landlord. While Terence is engaged to be married, he has
an affair with a peasant girl and his fiancée forces him to marry the girl. After having given
birth to a son, the wife pines away and dies. The son is kidnapped and years later returns as
priest of the parish. Throughout his life, Terence feels the curse, the lifting of which is suddenly achieved just before the end of the story [Brown; Wilson, p. 424; Wolff, introd. p. 34].

R188 *Princess Sunshine and other stories* (by Mrs J.H. Riddell).
      London: Ward & Downey, 1889, 2 vols. SOURCE Ellis, p. 332. LOCATION L.
      New York: J.W. Lovell, 1890 (Lovell's International Series, No. 116). LOCATION NUC.
      COMMENTARY Contents: 'Princess Sunshine', 'A terrible vengeance' (supernatural story),
      'Why Dr. Cray left Southam' (supernatural story) [Ellis; Wilson, p. 423].

R189 *A mad tour; or, a journey undertaken in an insane moment through central Europe
      on foot* (by Mrs J.H. Riddell; dedicated to Arthur Hamilton Norway, Esq.).
      + London: Richard Bentley & Son, 1891. SOURCE Daims, 2561; Ellis, p. 333; NCBEL
      4, p. 1679; Wolff, 5812. LOCATION L, NUC, InND Loeber coll.
      New York, Chicago: U.S. Book Co., [c.1891] (as *A mad tour*). SOURCE Daims, 2561.
      LOCATION NUC.
      New York: J.W. Lovell, 1891 (as *A mad tour*).
      COMMENTARY No copy of the New York, Lovell edn located [RL].

R190 *The head of the firm. A novel* (by Mrs J.H. Riddell; dedicated to Mrs J. Gibson
      Bennett).
      + London: William Heinemann, 1892, 3 vols. SOURCE Daims, 2560; Ellis, p. 333;
      NCBEL 4, p. 1679; Wolff, 5809. LOCATION L, NUC, InND Loeber coll.
      Leipzig: Heinemann & Balestier, 1892, 2 vols. (The English Library). LOCATION NUC.
      New York: J.W. Lovell, [c.1891]. SOURCE Daims, 2560. LOCATION NUC.

COMMENTARY Set in London where Aileen, a girl of Irish extraction, sells fruits and vegetables on the street. She stops her business when she receives a legacy. The firm that handles
the legacy is headed by Edward Desborne, who regularly gives money to charity but who does
not work hard to increase the firm's business. When he runs into financial trouble, he takes
money from Aileen's trust. Edward is tried and convicted, but Aileen forgives him [ML; Ellis].

R191 *A silent tragedy. A novel* (by Mrs J.H. Riddell).
      London: F.V. White & Co., 1893. SOURCE Ellis, p. 333; NCBEL 4, p. 1680; Topp 7,
      192. LOCATION L.

R192 *The rusty sword; or, thereby hangs a tale* (by Mrs J.H. Riddell).
      + London: Society for Promoting Christian Knowledge, [1893]. SOURCE Alston, p.
      366; NCBEL 4, p. 1680. LOCATION L.

COMMENTARY First serialized in the *Dawn of Day* (London, 1893). Set mainly in Ireland where a rusty sword extracted from a bog in the middle of the nineteenth century recalls the tale of a duel fought between a Mr Conmore and a Mr Kernigan. Conmore was in love with Kernigan's sister. Kernigan dies in the duel and Conmore leaves the country. After many years Conmore is returning from abroad by boat. Another passenger is Kernigan's youngest brother, whose life he saves. The young Kernigan insists on Conmore coming home with him, not knowing who he really is. Conmore finds that the sister has been faithful to him throughout the years, but although her father is grateful to him for saving the life of his youngest son, he will not forgive the killing of his older son, and therefore will not permit a marriage [ML].

R193　*The banshee's warning and other tales* (by Mrs J.H. Riddell).

　　　+ London: Remington & Co., 1894. SOURCE Alston, p. 366; Brown, 1430 (1903 edn); NCBEL 4, p. 1680; Wolff, 5796 (1903 edn). LOCATION L.

COMMENTARY Contents: 'The banshee's warning', 'Mr. Marbot's fright', 'A vagrant digestion', 'Bertie Evering's experience', 'Little Jane', 'So near; or, the pity of it' [ML; Ellis, p. 333; note that Topp 6, 68 states that it also contained 'Hertford O'Donnell's warning', but this is not in the BL copy].

R194　*A rich man's daughter* (by Mrs J.H. Riddell; dedicated to Mrs Helen C. Black).

　　　New York: The International News Co., [1895]. SOURCE Topp 7, 361. LOCATION NUC.

　　　London: F.V. White, 1897. SOURCE Ellis, p. 334; NCBEL 4, p. 1680; Topp 7, 361. LOCATION D (1898, 2nd edn), L.

COMMENTARY A story set in North Kensington, London. A sixth edn appeared in 1899 [Ellis; Topp 7, 361].

R195　*Did he deserve it?* (by Mrs J.H. Riddell; dedicated to Annette Haddock).

　　　London: Downey & Co., 1897. SOURCE Ellis, p. 334; NCBEL 4, p. 1680; Topp 8, 210. LOCATION L, NUC.

R196　*Handsome Phil and other stories* (by Mrs J.H. Riddell).

　　　London: F.V. White & Co., 1899. SOURCE Ellis, p. 334; NCBEL 4, p. 1680; Sadleir, 2052; Wolff, 5807. LOCATION L, NUC.

COMMENTARY Contents: 'Handsome Phil', 'Diarmid Chittock's story' (supernatural story, set in Ireland), 'Out in the cold' (a story about the difficulties facing women writers), 'Mr. Polzoy's little Katey', 'In deadly peril', 'Conn Kilrea' (supernatural story set in Ireland), 'Dr. Varvill's prescription', 'A personal experience' [Ellis; Field Day, v. pp 966–73 ('Out in the cold')].

R197　*The footfall of fate* (by Mrs J.H. Riddell).

　　　London: F.V. White & Co., 1900. SOURCE Ellis, p. 335; NCBEL 4, p. 1680. LOCATION L.

　　　+ London, Bombay: George Bell & Sons, n.d. (Bell's Indian and Colonial Library). LOCATION InND Loeber coll.

COMMENTARY When Mrs Lyle, a widow, comes to settle in Abbotsmead near the Thames, there is talk and conjecture about her past. She does not provide any information about herself but leads a quiet life and unobtrusively does a lot of good. Eventually, however, it appears that she is not Mrs Lyle, but someone who was instrumental in her scoundrel husband's death. She goes to prison, where she dies [ML].

R198　*The collected ghost stories of Mrs. J.H. Riddell* (introd. by E.F. Bleiler).

　　　+ New York: Dover; London: Constable & Co., 1977. SOURCE Wilson, p. 423. LOCATION L.

COMMENTARY Contents: 'Nut bush farm', 'The open door', 'The last of squire Ennismore', 'A strange Christmas game', 'The old house in Vauxhall walk', 'Sandy the tinker', 'Forewarned, forearmed', 'Hertford O'Donnell's warning', 'Walnut-tree house', 'Old Mrs. Jones', 'Why Dr. Cray left Southam', 'Conn Kilrea', 'Diarmid Chittock's story', 'A terrible vengeance' [ML].

— COLLECTED WORKS

R199   *Mrs. Riddell's novels.*
        London: Frederick Warne & Co., [1873], [no. of vols. not clear]. LOCATION NUC.
R200   [*Mrs. Riddell's novels*].
        London: Hutchinson & Co., [*c*.1890] (new edn), [at least 6 vols]. LOCATION D, InND
        Loeber coll.
COMMENTARY Unnumbered and untitled series in two types of uniform bindings: (a) red cloth,
blind stamped binding with Japanese-styled chrysanthemums; (b) red cloth with green mot-
tled printing [RL].
— SPURIOUS WORK

R201   *Which: the right, or the left?* [anon.] (dedicated to Anson G. Phelps).
        + New York: Garrett & Co., 1855. LOCATION InND Loeber coll., CtY.
COMMENTARY This anonymous novel, concerned with commercial life in America, has been
ascribed to Mrs JHR in the NUC (repeated by Hogan). However, it is practically certain
that she was not its author, because she never published first edns outside of England and
is not known to have written about commercial life in America [RL; ML; Hogan 2, pp
1056–7].

'RITA', pseud. See HUMPHREYS, Mrs Desmond.

ROBERTS, Abigail, b. *c*.1748, d. Mountrath (Co. Laois) 1823. Poet and writer of didactic
fiction for children, AR was the daughter of George Roberts of Kyle (Co. Laois) and Dorothy
Craven of Woodhouse (Co. Tipperary), who were Quakers. A speech impediment hindered
her conversation as a child, but she had 'uncommon brightness and natural genius'. She taught
herself to read the Bible by age 5. She was employed as a teacher at the house of her cousin,
William Walpole of Cloncourse (Co. Laois). By the time AR was age 25, her father's finances
were in a bad state. With her sister Dolly, she borrowed funds from the local landlord, Sir
Charles Coote, and set up a shop in Borris-in-Ossory (Co. Laois). This they ran until the
early-nineteenth century when at age 60 she and Dolly moved to Mountrath and set up a new
shop selling drapery, worsted, crockery and plants. AR wrote poetry, much of which remains
unpublished. Her fiction, mostly tales for juveniles, was written for the Kildare Place Society.
A few of her books were published posthumously. A collection of her letters to Mary
Leadbeater§ is in the Religious Society of Friends' Historical Library in Dublin (MS Box 30).
SOURCE Blain, p. 908; Harrison, p. 88; E.J.A. Impey, *A Roberts family quondam* (Birmingham,
1939*)*, passim*; Jrnl of the Association for the Preservation of the Memorials of the Dead*, v (1903),
pp 477–8; NCBEL 4, p. 1855; O'Donoghue, p. 400; Osborne, p. 928; *The Leadbeater papers*
(London, 1861), i, p. 425; RIA/DIB.

R202   *The entertaining medley, being a collection of true histories and anecdotes, calcu-*
        lated for the cottager's fireside [anon.].
        Dublin: John Jones [for the Kildare Place Society], 1818. SOURCE Gilbert, p. 269.
        LOCATION D (1826 edn), DPL Gilbert coll., L (1822 edn), InND Loeber coll. (Dublin,
        Thomas Courtney, 1826 edn).
COMMENTARY Authorship indicated by Mary Pollard. Contents of 1826 edn: 'Remarkable story
of a sleep walker', 'Account of the Edison light-house', 'Description of a curious cavern near
Kilkenny', 'Account of a moving bog in the County of Galway', 'Account of enormous ser-
pents', 'Account of the Arabs of the desert', 'Awful account of a woman burnt to death',
'Narrative of the shipwreck of the Doddington East Indiaman', 'History of the benevolent Mr.
Howard', 'Account of the snakes of North America and of the humming bird', 'The case of
Richard Parsons', 'Account of the tarantula', 'Account of the pearl-fishery', 'Singular history

of a miser', 'Narrative of the sufferings of several Englishmen, imprisoned by the Indians in the black-hole of Calcutta', 'Account of the carrier pigeons', 'Account of the eruption of Mount Vesuvius', 'Account of the Polish dwarf and the Irish giant', 'Affecting account of a sale of slaves', 'Account of a caravan which perished in the deserts of Africa', 'Account of the camel of Africa' [RL; Forster, 768; Personal communication, Mary Pollard, Aug. 1997].

R203   *The cottage fire-side* [anon.].
         Dublin: Printed by C. Bentham [for the Kildare Place Society], 1821. SOURCE Adams, pp 104, 190; O'Donoghue, p. 400. SOURCE COPAC. LOCATION PC, D (1826 edn), L.
         + Dublin: Printed by Napper & White [for the Kildare Place Society], 1821 (ill.). SOURCE Bradshaw, 2777 (1826 edn); Gilbert, p. 171. LOCATION D (1826 edn), DPL Gilbert coll., C, MChB (1826 edn), InND Loeber coll. (Dublin, W. Folds, 1822 edn).
         Belfast: Joseph Smyth, [1826?]. SOURCE Adams, p. 195.
COMMENTARY No copy of the Belfast edn located. Not to be confused with Revd Duncan's *The cottage fireside, or, the parish schoolmaster* (Edinburgh, 1815). This volume consists of a series of didactic conversations between a grandmother and her granddaughter during which much advice is given respecting potatoes, pigs, spinning, gardening, nursing, and the advantages to be gained from a frugal and moral life. Twenty thousand copies were printed, of which 15,000 had been sold by the middle of 1821. Contents: 'Filial love', 'Scandal', 'Dress: a single life', 'The cottage winter night', 'Economy of time', 'Family love', 'Potatoes', 'The pig', 'Sickness', 'Vaccination', 'The scriptures', 'The Sabbath', 'The garden', 'Butter', 'Cleanliness', 'The annals of the poor. Part 1', 'The annals of the poor. Part 2', 'Tea-drinking', 'The Lord's prayer', 'Whiskey-drinking at fairs', 'The cottager's morning hymn', 'Advice', 'Perseverance', 'The farmers', 'Never despair', 'The history of Paddy. Part 1', 'The history of Paddy. Part 2', 'The history of Paddy. Part 3', 'Going out to service', 'Savings banks', 'Savings banks, continued', 'Fever hospital', 'The village doctor, or, every man his own physician', 'The husbandman's prayer', 'The conclusion' [Adams, p. 104; RL].

R204   *The history of Tim Higgins, the cottage visitor* [anon.].
         Dublin: Printed by C. Bentham, [for the Kildare Place Society], 1823 (ill.). SOURCE Adams, pp 198, 202 (where mistakenly called 'Tom Higgins'); Emerald Isle cat. 55/101; NCBEL 4, p. 1855. LOCATION L (destroyed), NUC.
         + Dublin: Printed by John Jones [for the Kildare Place Society], 1825 (as *The history of Tim Higgins, the cottage visiter* [sic]; ill.). SOURCE Adams, p. 107; Osborne, p. 928; NCBEL 4, p. 1855. LOCATION D, CaOTP, InND Loeber coll.
         Belfast: Simms & M'Intyre, [date?]. SOURCE Adams, p. 198 (where mentioned as 'Tom Higgins').
COMMENTARY No copy of Belfast edn located. A didactic story about an upright Irishman who becomes crippled after rescuing a child but who continues to live a useful life. He gives advice to servants and the poor, counselling his neighbours to invest their money in savings banks. The booklet contains a printed plan of Tim's cottage, and much information on how schools were conducted at the time. It refers to the advantages of Bible reading and includes references to an earlier famine [RL; Osborne].

R205   *The history of Richard Mac Ready, the farmer lad* [anon.].
         Dublin: Printed by Bentham & Gardiner [for the Kildare Place Society], 1824 (ill.). SOURCE Adams, pp 106, 190; Bradshaw, 3327; Osborne, p. 894. LOCATION D (1830 edn), L, C, CaOTP (1830 edn).
         Belfast: Joseph Smyth, [1826?]. SOURCE Adams, p. 195.
         + Linfield: Printed by C. Greene at the Schools of Industry, 1832. LOCATION L.
COMMENTARY No copy of the Belfast edn located. Attributed to AR since her *The history of Tim Higgins* (Dublin, 1823) is referred to in the text (p. 128). A didactic story, set in Munster,

of a poor farmer lad, Richard, whose father is a layabout who chooses to live in a hovel rather than work hard to better himself. Richard, however, is noticed by his landlord, who places him with his gardener. He is sent to school for several hours a day and works in the kitchen garden of the estate part of the time. He is very assiduous and writes a calendar of activities for kitchen gardens. He is frugal and puts his money in a savings bank. After a number of years his landlord places him as manager on a farm. Over time he introduces many improvements and the booklet contains dissertations on the improvement of land, management of cows, pigs, and poultry, the value of manure etc. When Richard is an adult and has saved enough money he rents from his landlord a farm that is vacant through eviction. He gets attacked by the previous owner, but recovers. He marries a girl who is equally frugal and active. They build a new cottage and learn how to brew beer and grow flax. Richard is ever-conscious of the blessings received from God [ML; RL; Adams; Fenning cat. 138/130].

R206　*The schoolmistress; or, instructive and entertaining conversations between a teacher and her scholars* [anon.].
　　+ Dublin: Printed by Bentham & Gardiner [for the Kildare Place Society], 1824 (ill.).
　　SOURCE Bradshaw, 3328; O'Donoghue, p. 400. LOCATION D (1832 edn), C, L, InND Loeber coll.
COMMENTARY Mrs Molony, a schoolteacher in a country school, injects moral, Protestant religious values as well as practical lessons into the conversations she has with her pupils. Contains a list of duties for schoolteachers [RL].

ROBERTS, Sir Randal H., Bt. See **ROBERTS, Sir Randal Howland, 4th Bt**.

ROBERTS, Sir Randal Howland, 4th Bt (known as **Sir Randal H. Roberts, Bt**), b. Britfieldstown (Co. Cork) 1836 (1837 in Allibone and O'Donoghue), d. London 1899. Military man, novelist, journalist, playwright and sport and travel writer, RHR was the only son of Sir Thomas Howland Roberts, 3rd Bt (sheriff of Co. Cork, 1837) and Eliza Caroline Maitland of Eccles, Drumfries (Scotland). He succeeded his father in 1864. He served with the British army in the Crimea and during the Indian mutiny. He was a special correspondent for the *Daily Telegraph* (London) during the Franco-German war and wrote *Modern war; or, the campaign of the First Prussian Army during the war 1870–71* (London, 1871), which won him the Iron Cross of Prussia and decorations from France and Italy. RHR married in 1858 Mary, daughter of Col. Sydney Turnbull. He was a painter, actor and tennis player. He translated *The fellah: an Egyptian novel* by Edmond About (London, 1870), and wrote on fishing and on travel. In later years he concentrated on writing sports novels, for which he achieved limited success. He died in poverty in a London nursing home. SOURCE Allibone Suppl., ii, p. 1285; Boase, vi, p. 479; J. Foster (ed.), *The baronetage and knightage of the British Empire* (Westminster, [1883]), p. 543; O'Donoghue, p. 400; RIA/DIB; RL.

R207　*In the shires. A sporting novel* (by Sir Randal H. Roberts, Bt).
　　London: F.V. White, [1887]. SOURCE Allibone Suppl., ii, p. 1285; Topp 7, 91; OCLC. LOCATION L.

R208　*Curb and snaffle* (by Sir Randal H. Roberts).
　　+ London: F.V. White & Co., 1888. SOURCE Allibone Suppl., ii, p. 1285; OCLC. LOCATION D, L, InND Loeber coll.
COMMENTARY Set in England, a novel about different approaches to child-rearing. It contrasts the upbringing of the son of a bishop, a stiff and heartless person, with the upbringing of the bishop's nephew. The bishop's brother is a good-natured person who had married an Irish woman. He gets along well with his son and allows the son to develop as he wishes. In contrast, the bishop tries to impose his iron will on his son. Eventually, some youthful sins of the

bishop are uncovered when his nephew falls in love with a girl who had been born out of wedlock and whose father turns out to be the bishop [ML].

R209   *The silver trout and other stories* (by Sir Randal H. Roberts, Bt).
London: W.H. Allen & Co., 1888. SOURCE Allibone Suppl., ii, p. 1285. LOCATION L.

R210   *Hard held. A sporting novel, being the sequel to "Curb and snaffle"* (by Sir Randal H. Roberts).
London: Spencer Blackett & Hallam, 1889. LOCATION L.

R211   *Ridge and furrow. A novel* (by Sir Randal H. Roberts, Bt).
London: Ward & Downey, 1892. LOCATION L.

R212   *Not in the betting. A novel* (by Sir Randal H. Roberts, Bt).
London: F.V. White, 1893. LOCATION L.

R213   *High-flyer Hall. Joshua Blewitt's sporting experiences* (by Sir Randal H. Roberts, Bt).
+ London: Spencer Blackett, [1893] (ill. G. Bowers). LOCATION L.
COMMENTARY No Irish content [CM].

R214   *Handicapped. A novel* (by Sir Randal H. Roberts, Bt).
London: F.V. White, 1895. LOCATION L.
+ London: F.V. White, 1896, 2nd edn (ill. boards). LOCATION InND Loeber coll.
COMMENTARY A romantic adventure story that starts with the shipwreck of the Bristol to Cork ferry. The passengers are saved by the bravery of a woman, who pays with her life. Her son, Ralph Rowlands, needs to make his living and joins the army. He falls in love with Estelle Vigoreaux, who lives in Mauritius. They become engaged, but her cousin, Paul Vigoreaux, who also wants to marry her, pursues Ralph when he is sent to India. Paul also causes his uncle to go bankrupt. Ralph inherits several properties and he hires a detective in London to find Paul's whereabouts. When Paul is cornered, he commits suicide. The majority of the money he had swindled from his uncle is found on his person [ML].

R215   *A hasty marriage. A story of two lives. A novel* (by Sir Randal H. Roberts).
London, New York, Manchester: George Routledge & Sons, 1895. LOCATION L.

ROBERTSON, Alexander, fl. 1889. Physician and novelist, possibly American.

R216   *The Irish Monte Christo abroad; or, the secrets of the catacombs* (by Alexander Robertson).
New York: Street & Smith, 1889. LOCATION NUC.

R217   *The Irish Monte Christo trail; or, hunted from the pyramids to Berlin* (by Alexander Robertson).
New York: Street & Smith, 1890. LOCATION NUC.

ROBERTSON, Miss Anne J., fl. 1863. Novelist, AJR's Wexford ancestors include the Harveys of Kyle and Bargy Castle. She is considered one of the founders of the women's rights movement, receiving the support of Lord Salisbury and Sir John Talbot, MP for Co. Wexford. She published some of her writing in the *Dublin University Magazine*. Only her works connected with Ireland are listed below. SOURCE Allibone Suppl., ii, p. 1285; Browne, p. 128; W.E. Hall, p. 196.

R218   *Yaxley and its neighbourhood. A novel* [anon.] (dedicated to Lady Wilde§).
+ London: T. Cautley Newby, 1865, 3 vols. LOCATION L.
COMMENTARY First published as a serial in the *Dublin University Magazine*. The preface states that it is a story of 'bigamy, lately so much the fashion among novelist writers' [Browne; CM].

R219   *The story of Nelly Dillon* [anon.].
London: T. Cautley Newby, 1866, 2 vols. SOURCE Brown, 98. LOCATION L.

COMMENTARY Nelly Dillon, daughter of Tipperary farmers, is abducted by a former lover who is now a Ribbonman and an illicit distiller. Her parents disown her, but Bet Fagan shelters her and when the abductor has been sentenced to death, Bet prevails on him to clear Nelly's character in the presence of the parish priest. The priest then tells the facts from the altar. The parents wish to reconcile with Nelly but she rejects their advances and dies [Brown].

R220   *Society in a garrison town* [anon.].
    + London: T. Cautley Newby, 1869, 3 vols. LOCATION L.
COMMENTARY Set in England and concerns the amorous adventures of the officers in the garrison and the ladies in the town. One of the officers, St George, is Irish. At the end of the book the hope is expressed that Lord Killeevan, as St George has become, will persuade his love to retire with him to his estate in Co. Donegal [ML].

'ROBIN', pseud. See LYTTLE, Wesley Guard.

ROBINSON, Charles. Co-author. See TYNAN, Katharine.

ROBINSON, Frances M. See ROBINSON, Frances Mabel.

ROBINSON, Frances Mabel (also known as F. Mabel Robinson), b. Leamington Spa (War.) 1858, d. Paris 1956. Novelist, educator, translator and periodical writer, FMR was the daughter of the architect George Thomas Robinson and Frances Sparrow. She attended a finishing school in Brussels between 1872 and 1873, received further education in Italy, and enrolled as one of the first women students of the University of London. She later became secretary of Bedford College, London University's principal college for women. She developed an interest in Irish politics following discussions in parliament about the introduction of Home Rule in Ireland and became so engaged politically that she carried secret messages back and forth between England and Ireland. As 'W.S. Gregg' she wrote *An Irish history for English readers* (London, 1886; repr. New York, 1886). She translated from the French and contributed many reviews to the *Athenaeum* (London) in the late 1880s and 1890s, concentrating on Irish historical, political and literary publications. She also contributed to *Atalanta* (London), the magazine for young women founded by Mrs Elizabeth Toulmin Smith§ (better known as 'L.T. Meade'). FMR's sister, Agnes Mary Robinson Darmesteter, was also a novelist and a poet. After the death of their father in 1897, the two daughters and their mother lived in France. Only those works by FMR with known Irish content are listed below. SOURCE Allibone Suppl., ii, p. 1287; Blain, p. 914 [under A.M.F. Robinson]; BLC; Brown, p. 264; Personal communication, Marysa Demoor, Dec. 2000; NCBEL 4, p. 1682; ODNB; E. Reilly, p. 250; Sutherland, p. 541.
R221   *Mr. Butler's ward* (by F. Mabel Robinson).
    London: Vizetelly, 1885. SOURCE Brown, 1436. LOCATION L, NUC (4th edn).
    New York: Harper & Bros, 1885. LOCATION NUC.
COMMENTARY Set mainly in the west of Ireland where a bailiff is murdered as the result of a cruel eviction. The bailiff's daughter, Deirdre, is adopted by Mr Butler, her father's employer. She is sent to a French convent and afterwards works as governess to Mr Butler's daughters. She marries twice. Her second husband is the son of her father's murderer. Upon discovering this, she goes mad [Brown].
R222   *The plan of campaign. A story of the fortune of war* (by F. Mabel Robinson).
    London: Vizetelly & Co., 1888, 2 vols. SOURCE Brown, 1437. LOCATION L, NUC.
COMMENTARY A novel of the Land War, set mainly in Dublin, that deals with the agrarian 'plan of campaign' in the 1880s and the politics of the time. Written from a nationalist point of view [Brown].

ROBINSON, Admiral Hercules, b. Granard (Co. Longford) 1789, d. Southsea (Hants.) 1864. Naval officer and novelist, HR was the son of Revd Christopher Robinson, Church of Ireland rector of Granard, and Elizabeth, daughter of landowner and politician Sir Hercules Langrishe of Knocktopher (Co. Kilkenny). HR entered the navy in 1800 and was present at the battle of Trafalgar (1805). His naval career took him to the Baltic, the West Indies and North and South America. He retired from service in 1846 but later made a trip to look for the spoils of a Spanish galleon on the Salvages, a group of barren rocks between Madeira and the Canaries. This gave him the opportunity to write *Sea drift* (Portsea, 1858) and provided the background for *Harry Evelyn* (London, [1859]). In 1842 he was sheriff of Co. Westmeath. He married Frances Wood of Rosmead (Co. Westmeath) in 1822 and their son, Hercules, became 1st Baron Rosmead and a colonial administrator in Ceylon, Australia and South Africa. For HR's portrait, see ODNB. SOURCE Allibone, ii, p. 1837; Longford, pp 130–1; ODNB.

R223   *Sea drift* (by Hercules Robinson; dedicated to Leopold, King of Belgium). Portsea: Hinton, 1858. SOURCE Allibone, ii, p. 1837 (mentions a London, 1858 edn and an 1866 edn); Longford, p. 131. LOCATION L, NUC.
        COMMENTARY A small volume of reminiscences in a fictional format of the voyage to the Salvages to search for the spoils of a Spanish galleon [Allibone; BLC; ODNB].

R224   *Harry Evelyn; or, a romance of the Atlantic. A naval novel, founded on facts* (by Hercules Robinson; dedicated to Admiral William Bowles, in part because of WB's 'acquaintance with Ireland').
        + London: James Blackwood, [1859] (ill.; map of the battle of Trafalgar). SOURCE Allibone, ii, p. 1837; Longford, p. 131; Quaritch cat. 1193/206. LOCATION L, NUC, InND Loeber coll.

COMMENTARY Two friends set out by yacht to find a hidden treasure near Madeira. The treasure allows one of them to buy back his Irish estate and to marry the girl he loves. The other is already rich, but he falls in love with a woman in Madeira whom he marries against his father's wishes. Interwoven are many naval anecdotes [ML].

ROBSON, Margaret Ann. Co-author. See **STACPOOLE, Henry de Vere**.

ROCHE, Hamilton. See **ROCHE, John Hamilton**.

ROCHE, James Jeffrey, b. Mountmellick (Co. Laois) 1847, d. Berne (Switzerland) 1908. Journalist, novelist and poet, JJR was the son of Edward Roche and Margaret Doyle. The family moved to Prince Edward Island (Canada) when he was a child and he was educated at St Dunstan's College there. He went to Boston in 1866 where he worked at the Boston *Pilot* under John Boyle O'Reilly§, becoming assistant editor and later editor (1883–90). He wrote for numerous periodicals, including the *Atlantic* (Boston), *Harpers* (New York) and the *Irish Packet* (Dublin). He wrote the *Life of John Boyle O'Reilly* (Chicago, [1891]), and *The story of the filibusters …to which is added the life of Colonel David Crockett* (London, 1891). He contributed a biographical and critical introd. to *The collected writings of Samuel Lover*§ (Boston, 1901–03, 10 vols.), and edited William Makepeace Thackeray's § *The mahogany tree* (Boston, 1887). He was an assistant editor of Justin McCarthy's § *Irish literature* (Chicago, 1904, 10 vols.). A strong nationalist, he was active in Irish circles in Boston. He was appointed American consul first in Genoa (Italy) and then in Switzerland, where he died. He was buried in Brookline (MA). SOURCE Burke, p. 624; DAB; Irish pseudonyms; NUC; O'Donoghue, p. 402; RIA/DIB.

R225   *Her Majesty the King. A romance of the harem: done into American from the Arabic* (by James Jeffrey Roche).

Boston: Richard G. Badger & Co., 1899. SOURCE Wright, iii, 4601; OCLC. LOCATION L, CtY.

R226 *The v-a-s-e & other bric-a-brac* (by James Jeffrey Roche).
Boston: R.G. Badger & Co., 1900. LOCATION NUC.

R227 *The sorrows of Sap'ed: a problem story of the East* (by James Jeffrey Roche).
New York, London: Harper & Bros, 1904. LOCATION L.

ROCHE, John Hamilton (also known as **Hamilton Roche**), fl. 1810. Gothic novelist, poet and army officer, according to O'Donoghue, JHR was Irish. He was an army captain and his poetic subjects included among others, Salamanca, Russia, Waterloo and France. The dedication of the following book was dated Sudbury (Suffolk), 1809. For his portrait, see Elmes. SOURCE Allibone, ii, p. 1843; Elmes, p. 175; Frank, 362; British Fiction; NCBEL 4, p. 428; O'Donoghue, p. 402.

R228 *A Suffolk tale: or, the perfidious guardian* (by Hamilton Roche; dedicated to Lady Hippisley).
London: Printed for the author by T. Hookham Jnr & E.T. Hookham, 1810, 2 vols.
SOURCE Allibone, ii, p. 1843; Frank, 362; British Fiction; Garside, 1810:69; British Fiction. LOCATION L.
COMMENTARY Gothic fiction, a story of deception and betrayal featuring two soldiers, one naïve and young, the other intelligent and evil. Marshal Duroc leaves France for political reasons to settle in Ireland under the name De Claridge. His son Alfred goes to an English military academy, where he falls under the control of a sinister and ambitious cadet, the Irish renegade William O'Connor who, as a perfidious guardian, dedicates himself to the destruction of Alfred's life and the overthrow of the Duroc family. O'Connor sends fraudulent letters to the Marshal, gains his confidence, undermines Alfred's desire to marry Louisa, and obstructs Alfred's military career by gaining control of all money allotted to Alfred by his father. Posted to duty in New Brunswick in Canada, Alfred manages to take Louisa abroad with him as his wife, but she dies soon afterwards. Meanwhile, O'Connor cheats Alfred out of his inheritance and plots to have him jailed for debt when he comes home from his Canadian duty. The broken Alfred kills himself while languishing in prison. O'Connor then assumes all the wealth and prestige of the Duroc family [Frank, 362, Tracy, 146].

'**ROCHE, Katherine**', pseud. See **O'BRIEN, Charlotte Grace**.

ROCHE, Mrs Regina Maria (née Dalton; also known as **Regina Maria Dalton**), b. Waterford 1764 (1765 in Allibone), d. Waterford 1845. Gothic and romantic novelist, RMR was the daughter of Blundell Dalton (also mentioned as Capt. Blundell), who owned an estate at Edenderry (Co. Offaly). Her father is likely to have descended from Sir George Blundell, 2nd Bt, who married about 1642, Sarah, daughter of Sir William Colley, of Edenderry. One of their descendants was Viscount Blundell, baron of Edenderry, whose only son died in 1756, making the family extinct in the male line. Most of the Edenderry estate descended to the marquess of Downshire through a female heiress. RMR was brought up in Dublin. She started writing fiction at a very young age. She may have been well-connected, since in 1789 she dedicated her first novel to the marquess of Buckingham, the Irish lord lieutenant, when she was still single and living in Dublin. She is said to have moved to England in the same year, but she married Ambrose Roche of Waterford at Rathkyran parish (Co. Kilkenny), close to Waterford, in 1792 (her father was no longer alive at this date). The remains of the ancient Rochestown Castle is in this parish. RMR's husband descended from the Rochs of Glyn Castle, near Carrick-on-Suir (Co. Waterford) and of Lehard (not located), and he was brother to Sampson Toogood Roche, a deaf-mute water colourist and miniaturist. Ambrose Roche was a captain of the 40th Regiment. RMR lived with her husband some time in London (while there in 1796, she wrote the dedication of her *The children of the abbey*). Between 1802 and 1804, she and her husband were swindled out of their Irish estates by a crooked lawyer and the ensuing legal fees absorbed the settlement when it did come after ten years of legal effort. In 1825 her husband had a stroke and they lived under even more dire financial circumstances. In 1827 she received the first support from the Royal Literary Fund. Her husband died in Nov. 1829. About two years later she returned to Ireland, first to Cloncunny, near Piltown (Co. Kilkenny), and then to the city of Waterford, where she lived on the fashionable Mall (her name does not appear in city directories of the period, which means that she may have rented accommodation). She was the author of 16 novels; there is an unexplained gap in her publications between 1828 and 1836. Her early work is Gothic and sentimental and follows in the tradition of the overwrought, suspenseful novels of English Gothic novelist Ann Radcliffe. Her later work is set mostly in Ireland. Her *The children of the abbey* became very popular, going through at least 80 editions, many of them published in the US. Several of the English reprints were issued in penny parts. An undated poem by her, 'Oh calm be each night, and sunny each day', is at the University of Newcastle-upon-Tyne. Her will was registered in 1845 but does not appear to have survived. Several of her letters to the Royal Literary Fund are at the BL. Her novels prompted several spurious works, which are separately listed below. SOURCE Allibone, ii, p. 1844; Blain, p. 917; BL, M 1077, reel 17, No. 590; J.H. Blundell & H. Blundell, *The Blundells* (privately published, 1912), pp 165–7; Brady, p. 211; Brown, pp 265–6; N. Schroeder, 'Regina Maria Roche and the early nineteenth-century Irish novel', *Éire-Ireland*, 19 (1984), pp 116–30; H. Farrar (ed.), *Irish marriages* (London, 1897), ii, p. 380; Field Day, i, p. 687, ii, p. 832, v, pp 831–2; Hogan 2, p. 1063; Landed gentry, 1912, p. 599; McKenna, p. 318; National Archives, Dublin, WW23; NCBEL 4, p. 989; OCIL, p. 499; ODNB; Personal communication, Jack Burtchaell, Jan. 2002; Personal communication, Charles Ginnane, Feb. 1996; RIA/DIB; RLIN; Robertshaw cat. 79/226; Summers 2, p. 163; Todd, pp 578–9; *Waterford Herald*, (5 May 1792).

R229   *The vicar of Lansdowne; or, country quarters. A tale* (by Maria Regina Dalton; dedicated to the marquis of Buckingham [lord lieutenant of Ireland]).
London: Printed for the author, and sold by J. Johnson, 1789, 2 vols. SOURCE Allibone, ii, p. 1844 (mistakenly mentions 1793 date); Block, p. 200; DNB (mistakenly mentions 1793 date; corrected in ODNB); Forster 2, 3853; ESTC t071894; Raven 2, 1789:64; Todd, p. 579. LOCATION L, NUC.
London: William Lane, 1800, 2nd edn (revsd and corrected edn; dedicated to the public). SOURCE Blakey, p. 197; McBurney & Taylor, 771 (1800, 4th edn); Raven 2, 1789:64; ESTC t108468. LOCATION L, IU (1800, 4th edn), NUC.
+ Paris: Rue des Poitevins, Hôtel Bouthilier, 1789, 2 vols. ('Imité de l'anglois de Miss Dalton' as *Le curé de Lansdowne, ou les garnisons*). SOURCE Rafroidi, ii, p. 376; Rochedieu, p. 284 (probably mistakenly gives 1787 edn). LOCATION D, L, NUC, InND Loeber coll.
Mayence: Kupferberg, 1789 (trans. as *Le curé de Lansdowne, ou les garnisons*). SOURCE Rochedieu, p. 284. COMMENTARY Mayence edn No copy located [RL].
Leipzig: Weygand, 1790, 2 vols. (trans. as *Der Landsprediger von Landsdowne und seine Familie*). LOCATION NUC.
+ Baltimore: Printed by W. Pechin & S. Sower, 1802, 2 vols. in 1 (dedicated to author's public). LOCATION NUC, InND Loeber coll.
New York: T.B. Janson & Co., 1802, 2 vols. SOURCE Raven 2, 1789:64; OCLC. LOCATION E, CtY.

New York: J. Harison, 1802, 2 vols. in 1. SOURCE OCLC. LOCATION Smith College, Northampton (MA).

COMMENTARY This book reached a third edn in 1825. A cautionary story of flirtation and its consequences set in the village of Lansdowne in England where an army detachment is quartered. Two daughters of the vicar strike up acquaintance with two officers. Rosina, the eldest, is a flirt whose behaviour encourages the less positive qualities in her suitor, Melford. Lydia is more careful, and her friend Manning has more exalted ideas of honour. Melford suggests elopement to Rosina, whereas Manning tells Lydia that although he loves her, he is bound to honour a previous engagement. Melford fights a duel with Francis, the sisters' brother. Francis is brought home near death, but recovers slowly. He is visited by a Miss Douglas, who has left her home to avoid marriage to someone not of her choosing. This person happens to be Manning, who is immensely relieved because now he can marry Lydia. Francis marries Miss Douglas. Manning brings back Melford, now a reformed character. Both Rosina and Melford have learned from their former errors and marry each other [ML].

R230 *The maid of the hamlet. A tale* (by Regina Maria Roche).

London: H. Long, 1793, 3 vols. SOURCE Allibone, ii, p. 1844; Block, p. 200; Forster 2, 3852; Raven 2, 1793:38; Todd, p. 579. LOCATION L (1800, 2nd edn), NUC (1800, 2nd edn).

Dublin: G. Burnett, H. Colbert, E. Dornin & T. Todd, 1802. SOURCE Raven 2, 1793:38; Rafroidi, ii, p. 332; NSTC; Gecker, 911. LOCATION L, PU.

Paris: J.G. Dentu, 1801 (trans. by Dubergier as *La fille du hameau*). SOURCE Rafroidi, ii, p. 376. LOCATION NUC, DCL.

Boston: Lincoln, 1801. LOCATION NUC.

COMMENTARY No copy of the first London edn located. A fourth edn was published in 1834. A romantic novel with some Gothic themes whose heroine, Matilda, experiences great terror when she visits a ruined abbey. After the death of her parents, she is taken in by the kind but stern Mr Belmore and is raised in rural seclusion. She meets with two morally opposite men. Her naivety and inexperience hamper her ability to judge each man for what he truly is. She is pursued by the young profligate, Mr Bromley, and is befriended by the misogynistic Charles Howard. Impulsively, Matilda marries a Mr Hartland, even though her deepest feelings are for Charles, himself the victim of a bad marital choice. Hartland dies and Charles's wife is lost in a shipwreck, removing the barriers to their union [Raven 2; Tracy, 153].

R231 *The children of the abbey. A tale* (by Regina Maria Roche; dedicated to Major-General Sir Adam Williamson, K.B.).

London: William Lane, 1796, 4 vols. SOURCE Allibone, ii, p. 1844 (1898 edn, 4 vols.); Blakey, pp 57, 92, 174; Block, p. 199; Brown, 1441 (1798, 3rd edn); Forster 2, 3850; Grail (1798, 3rd edn); Todd, p. 579; Wolff, 5948 (1800, 4th edn). LOCATION Ireland related fiction (1801 edn), L, NUC, InND Loeber coll. (1797, 2nd edn, vol. 2, imperfect).

+ London, Bristol: George Virtue, 1825 (ill. Fussell [John Henry Fuseli?], Rogers). SOURCE Jarndyce cat. 151/363. LOCATION InND Loeber coll. COMMENTARY *London Virtue 1825 edn* Published in 32 parts; first title page Manchester; second title page 1825, 6th edn [RL].

+ London: Printed by Maddick & Pottage, [*c.*1865] (ill.). LOCATION InND Loeber coll. COMMENTARY *London Maddick edn* Printed in a penny dreadful format; issued in 25 parts [RL].

+ London: [Charles Fox?], [*c.* 1881?] (ill.; see Plate 56). SOURCE Jarndyce cat. 151/366. LOCATION InND Loeber coll. COMMENTARY *London Fox edn* Published in 25 penny parts [Jarndyce cat.].

London: W. Mason, [n.d.], 2nd edn (ill.) (as *Children of the abbey, an interesting novel, founded on facts, descriptive of the adventures & misfortunes of Oscar and Amanda Fitzalan, grandchildren of Earl Dunreath*). LOCATION PpiU. COMMENTARY London Mason edn Chapbook of 32pp [PpiU].

Manchester: J. Gleave, 1823 (ill. Pigot, Hopwood Jnr). SOURCE COPAC. LOCATION Dt, InND Loeber coll. (1824 edn). COMMENTARY *Manchester Gleave edn* Issued in 32 parts [RL].

+ Glasgow: Richard Griffin & Co., 1826 (adapted for youth, by 'A Lady'; Griffin's Juvenile Library, No. 1). LOCATION InND Loeber coll.

+ Exeter: J. & B. Williams, 1834, 3 vols. (ill.). LOCATION InND Loeber coll.

+ Wakefield: William Nicholson & Sons; London: S.D. Ewins Jnr & Co., [*c.*1875] (as *The children of the abbey; a sweet and interesting tale, rendered immortal by its simple and beautiful narrations*; ill.). LOCATION InND Loeber coll.

+ Portsea: Printed for G.A. Stephens, n.d., 2 vols. (as *The children of the abbey. An authentic, moral, and interesting narrative*). LOCATION PC. COMMENTARY *Portsea edn* A much abbreviated edn [RL].

+ Cork: Printed by J. Haly, M. Harris & J. Connor, 1798, 3rd edn, 2 vols. SOURCE J. Cork Hist. & Archaeol. Soc., viii (1902), p. 251; ESTC t165215. LOCATION D, ICN, NUC, InND Loeber coll.

Dublin: C.M. Warren, [1830?] (new edn), 5 vols. in 1. SOURCE OCLC. LOCATION D.

Belfast: John McClune, 1824. SOURCE Anderson 1, p. 71. LOCATION BFl, InND edn (Joseph Smyth, 1835, 5 vols. edn. only vol. 4 in that coll.).

Paris: Denné Jeune, 1797, 6 vols. (trans. by André Morellet as *Les enfants de l'abbaye*; ill.). SOURCE Rafroidi, ii, p. 376. LOCATION Dt.

Paris: Theophilus Barrois, 1807, 5 vols. (ill. L'Epine; English edn). LOCATION NUC.

Amsterdam: G. Roos, 1802–10 (trans. into Dutch as *De abdij kinderen*). SOURCE Wintermans, 1796:78. LOCATION Koninklijke Bibliotheek, The Hague.

Braunschweig: Friedrich Vieweg, 1803, 2 vols. (trans. by Ludwig Ferdinand Huber as *Die Erben von Dunreath-Abbey*). LOCATION Staatsbibliothek, Berlin.

Hartford (CT): Goodsell & Wells, 1822, 2 vols. SOURCE NCBEL 3, p. 760. LOCATION NUC.

New York: H. Caritat, 1798, 4 vols. in 2. SOURCE Topp 1, p. 326. LOCATION NUC.

Philadelphia: W.A. Leary, 1845, 3 vols. in 1. SOURCE OCLC. LOCATION Temple Univ., Philadelphia (PA).

Philadelphia: John B. Perry, 1850 (as *Mortimer and Amanda, or the children of the abbey*; ill.). SOURCE Adv. in L.S. Stanhope, *The bandit's bride*, 1851; OCLC. LOCATION Univ. of Florida.

COMMENTARY Illustrations were only introduced in the second London edn (1797). This is one of the most frequently reprinted Irish novels of the nineteenth century – Milner's edition alone sold over 75,000 copies. It went through at least 80 editions, became very popular in the US, is referred to in Jane Austen's *Emma* (1815), and was most likely an influence on her *Pride and prejudice* (1813). Very little of the plot is set in Ireland, most of the action taking place in England. The settings include a convent, a Welsh mansion, an Irish castle, and the 'haunted' Abbey of Dunreath. The Irish part of the story is set at Enniskillen (Co. Fermanagh). The story combines, with some Gothic touches, a sentimental love and marriage plot and intrigue over a lost inheritance. The 'children of the abbey' are the brother and sister, Oscar and Amanda. Their father, the Irish soldier Fitzalan, married Malvina, daughter of the earl of Dunreath, which infuriated the earl. He disinherited her, which brought on her death and the children's loss of name. Amanda is stalked by Col. Belgrave, a seducer who, because of his military rank, holds power over the father and son. Belgrave's villainy is abetted by Amanda's aunt Augusta and her disgusting cousin Euphrasia. Amanda falls in love with Lord Mortimer of Cherbury, but their plans to marry are defied by Lord Mortimer's father. Oscar falls in love with Adela, daughter of Gen. Honeywood, but the general presents her to Col. Belgrave. Amanda returns to Dunreath Abbey in an effort to establish her heritage and name. In her mother's bedchamber she has a spectral confrontation with her dead mother. The abbey is full of supernatural surprises, all of which turn out to be hoaxes. Confirmation of Amanda's and Oscar's claim is found, and the fraud by the wicked aunt and cousin exposed. Col. Belgrave perishes of delirium tremens. Sophia Woodfall's *Rose: or, the child of the abbey* (London, 1804, 4 vols.) appears to be an expanded version of RMR's *The children of the abbey*. The book inspired two songs published in Philadelphia around 1800, 'Adieu sweet girl' and 'Song from the children of the abbey'. E.N.F. Desanteul wrote a play *Amanda* (Paris, 1803) based on this novel [ML; Blain; Field Day, v, pp 814–16; Frank, 364, 493; V.E. Neuburg, *Popular literature. A history and guide* (Harmondsworth, 1977), p. 184; OCLC; RLIN, Tracy, 149].

R232   *Clermont. A tale* (by Regina Maria Roche).

London: William Lane, 1798, 4 vols. (ill. G. Murray, Richter). SOURCE Allibone, ii, p. 1844; Blakey, opp. p. 59, p. 183; Block, p. 200; ESTC t144530; Forster 2, 3851; Raven 2, 1798:61; Todd, p. 579. LOCATION L (incomplete), NUC.

Dublin: P. Wogan, H. Colbert, W. Porter & N. Kelly, 1799. SOURCE Raven 2, 1798:61; ESTC n003015. LOCATION NUC.

Paris: Denné Jeune, 1799, 3 vols. (trans. by A. Morellet as *Clermont*). SOURCE Rafroidi, ii, p. 376 (mistakenly gives 1798 edn); Rochedieu, p. 283; OCLC. LOCATION New York Historical Society (incomplete).

Philadelphia: J. Conrad & Co., 1802. LOCATION NUC.

London: Folio Society, 1968 (ed. by D.P. Varma). SOURCE NCBEL 3, p. 760; Rafroidi, ii, p. 332; COPAC. LOCATION Dt, L.

COMMENTARY One of the seven 'horrid' titles for Isabella Thorpe's Gothic education mentioned by Jane Austen in her *Northanger Abbey* (London, 1818). Adjacent to the cottage where the heroine, Madeline Clermont, lives with her reclusive mother is a spectacular ruin that tempts her with 'horrid noises and still more horrid sights' (Frank, 365). When she explores the ruin at night, she meets a melancholy stranger, De Sevignie. However, before the attachment has time to develop, it is cut short by the countess de Merville. Madeline is sent to a remote castle. The countess's son-in-law, D'Alembert, and his ruffian partners pursue Madeline in the dark castle, but she finds an unexpected friend in Viola, D'Alembert's mistreated wife. Many events take place at a frenzied pace. After the countess's removal and murder by D'Alembert's ruffians, Madeline and Viola escape from the castle and, aided by De Sevignie, find their way to Paris [Frank, 365; Tracy, 150].

R233   *Nocturnal visit. A tale* (by Regina Maria Roche).

London: William Lane, 1800, 4 vols. SOURCE Allibone, ii, p. 1844; Blakey, p. 196; Block, p. 200; McBurney & Taylor, 772; British Fiction; Garside, 1800:63; Todd, p. 579; ESTC t127131l. LOCATION Corvey CME 3–628–48463–4, IU, ViU.

Dublin: Printed by J. Stockdale, [1801?], 4 vols. SOURCE Adv. in L. Goldsmith, *The crimes of cabinets* (Dublin, 1801); RL.

Paris: Michel et le Normant, 1801, 5 vols. (trans. by P.L. Lebas as *La visite nocturne*; ill. Challiou). SOURCE Rafroidi, ii, p. 376. LOCATION L.

Paris: Gueffier, 1801, 6 vols. in 3 (trans. by J.B.J. Breton as *La visite nocturne*). LOCATION NUC.

Philadelphia: John Conrad & Co.; Baltimore: M. & I. Conrad; Washington City: Rapin, Conrad & Co., 1801. LOCATION NUC.

Philadelphia: Maxwell, 1801, 2 vols. SOURCE RLIN. LOCATION PU.

+ New York: Arno, 1977, 4 vols. (introd. by F.G. Atkinson). LOCATION InND Loeber coll.

COMMENTARY No copy of the Dublin edn located. A synthesis of domestic and Gothic fiction, the novel features Jacintha, whose parentage is unknown and who is hated by her stepsister Gertrude, brutalized by her adoptive mother Mrs Greville, and subjected to the sexual caprices of the seducer Lord Gwytherin. Jacintha encounters adventures and abductions, imprisonment in a castle in the Pyrenees, an escape to a convent where she is again imprisoned, and attempts on her virtue in England, France, and Ireland. Eventually her noble parents claim her and Jacintha gains a surname and acquires a mother and a father. Her fiancée, Egbert Oswald, who experiences his own set of adventures and reversals of fortune, inherits a title. In the end, the pair is united. A description of Killarney is included [ML; RL; Frank, 366; Tracy, 154].

R234　*The discarded son; or, haunt of the banditti. A tale* (by Regina Maria Roche).

London: Lane, Newman & Co., 1807, 5 vols. SOURCE Allibone, ii, p. 1844 (1806 edn); British Fiction; Garside, 1807:55; Blakey, p. 222; Block, p. 200; Todd, p. 579. LOCATION Corvey CME 3–628–48458–8, L, C, NUC, InND Loeber coll. (1825, 2nd edn).

Paris: Chaumerot, 1808, 4 vols. (trans. by M. et Mme de Sennevas as *Le fils banni, ou, la retraite des brigands*). SOURCE Rafroidi, ii, p. 376; Streeter, p. 223. COMMENTARY *Paris edn* No copy located [RL].

Zaltbommel: Johannes Noman, 1818, 2 vols. (trans. into Dutch as *De verbannen zoon of de verblijfplaats der struikrovers*). SOURCE Wintermans, 1807:55.

New York: P. Burtsell, 1807, 2 vols. LOCATION NUC.

New York: Alsop, Brannan & Alsop, M. Ward & E. Sargeant, 1807–08, 2 vols. LOCATION NUC.

COMMENTARY A romantic adventure story featuring a Capt. Munro, who falls in love with a Spanish girl and marries her. His father disapproves and, aided by a wicked new stepmother, disinherits him. His Spanish father-in-law disavows his daughter also. The newlyweds establish themselves on a farm where by hard work they make a living. They are very happy and have two children, Osmond and Elizabeth. Osmond's father wants him to have a good education and does all he can to send him to university. A wicked absentee neighbour, Lord O'Sinister, re-establishes himself on his estate and although married, wants to possess Elizabeth. To achieve this, he offers Capt. Munro a position in Ireland and gives him a loan. After the captain has left, he introduces himself to Elizabeth under an assumed name and makes an offer of marriage, which is accepted. Capt. Munro writes from Ireland that the marriage should be postponed until he looks into the suitor's antecedents. O'Sinister hires someone to kill Munro in Ireland, but this fails. He tries various nefarious schemes to get Elizabeth into his clutches but in the meantime she meets the truly noble Delacour, to whom she becomes engaged. O'Sinister next tries to get Osmond out of the way by offering him a living in Jamaica. However, Delacour suggests that Osmond be a chaplain on his ship. Together they sail off, but they are shipwrecked in the Gulf of Biscay. Many adventures with pirates and robbers befall Osmond. O'Sinister calls in Munro's debt to him and since Munro cannot pay he is taken into custody. In the end, all turns out well. O'Sinister dies truly repentant and betroths his beautiful daughter to Osmond. Capt. Munro's father accepts him again, and Mrs Munro's father comes to England to make peace with his daughter. Delacour returns home and marries Elizabeth, and all are happy [ML; Frank, 367; Tracy, 152].

R235　*The houses of Osma and Almeria; or, the convent of St. Ildefonso. A tale* (by Regina Maria Roche).

London: A.K. Newman & Co., 1810, 3 vols. SOURCE Allibone, ii, p. 1844; Blakey, p. 232; Block, p. 200; British Fiction; Garside, 1810:70; Todd, p. 579. LOCATION Corvey CME 3–628–48462–6; L, NUC.

Philadelphia: Bradford & Inskeep; New York: Inskeep & Bradford; Boston: William M'Ilhenny, 1810. LOCATION NUC.

COMMENTARY A Gothic novel with scenes set in forests, castles, and monasteries. The two Spanish families of Osma and Almeria have long been at odds, and the feud manifests itself in the victimization of the novice, Elvira of Osma, by Rodolph of Almeria. Elvira is held prisoner in an obscure cloister of the convent of Ildefonso, where the abbot, Fr Anselm, who is in the pay of Rodolph, persecutes her. In an underground passage Elvira meets the Castillian warrior Eustace St Valery of the house of Almeria, the brother of Don Ferdinand St Valery, with whom Elvira had fallen in love. After many complicated adventures, Eustace destroys his evil brother, Rodolph, and reunites Don Ferdinand with Elvira [Frank, 368].

R236　*The monastery of St. Columb; or, the atonement. A novel* (by Regina Maria Roche).
London: A.K. Newman & Co., 1813, 5 vols. SOURCE Allibone, ii, p. 1844; Blakey, p. 242; Block, p. 200; Gecker, 912; British Fiction; Garside, 1813:51. LOCATION Corvey CME 3–628–48460–X, L, PU.
Paris: J.G. Dentu, 1819, 3 vols. (trans. as *Le monastère de St. Columba, ou le chevalier des armes rouges*). SOURCE Rafroidi, ii, p. 376. LOCATION NUC.
[German]: [publisher?], 1816 (trans. as *Die Geheimnisse der Abtei von Santa Columba, oder der Ritter mit den rothen Waffen*). SOURCE Garside, 1813:51.
New York: Inskeep & Bradford; Philadelphia: Bradford & Inskeep, 1813. LOCATION NUC.

COMMENTARY The story starts at St Cuthbert's Abbey in Yorkshire, is partly set in Spain, and culminates beneath 'the mouldering arches' of the monastery of St Columb in Ireland. The plot relates the interaction between two families, the Pontefracts and Lord Hexham, his sister, Rosamund, and his daughter, Angeline. Delays, separations, and entrapments interfere with the union of the children of the two families [Frank, 369].

R237　*Trecothick bower; or, the lady of the West Country. A tale* (by Regina Maria Roche).
+ London: A.K. Newman & Co., 1814, 3 vols. SOURCE Allibone, ii, p. 1844; Blakey, p. 247; Block, p. 200; British Fiction; Garside, 1814:50. LOCATION Corvey CME 3–628–8465–5, L, O, ViU.
Philadelphia: Mathew Carey; Boston: Wells & Lilly, 1816. LOCATION NUC.

COMMENTARY A Gothic historical tale. The *Critical Review* stated that the story tells of 'improbable events arising from impossible causes, a wild and disjointed plot ... [in] the most bombastic and inflated language' [ODNB; *Critical Review*, 4th ser. 5 (Jan. 1814), pp 99–101].

R238　*The Munster cottage boy. A tale* (by Regina Maria Roche).
+ London: A.K. Newman & Co., 1820, 4 vols. SOURCE Allibone, ii, p. 1844 (1819 edn); Blakey, p. 270; Brown, 1442; Block, p. 200; British Fiction; Garside, 1820:60; Todd, p. 579. LOCATION Corvey CME 3–628–48461–8, Grail, Ireland related fiction, D, L, ViU.
Paris: Locard & Davy, 1820, 5 vols. (trans. by Mme L. Girard de Caudenberg as *L'enfant de la chaumiere de Munster*). SOURCE Rafroidi, ii, p. 377. LOCATION ViU (1821 edn).
+ New York: A.T. Goodrich & Co., W.B. Gilley, C. Wiley & Co., Kirk & Mercein, 1820, 2 vols. in 1. LOCATION NUC, InND Loeber coll.

COMMENTARY Set in Ireland, the story is populated with a deserving peasantry and a predatory middle-class. The heroine is an orphaned child of an ancient Irish family, who lives in England, visits the home of her ancestors, but in the end willingly returns to England with her English lover [N. Schroeder, *Éire-Ireland*, 19 (1984), pp 122–3].

R239 *The bridal of Dunamore; and Lost and won. Two tales* (by Regina Maria Roche). London: A.K. Newman & Co., 1823, 3 vols. SOURCE Allibone, ii, p. 1844; Brown, 1443; Rafroidi, ii, p. 333; British Fiction; Garside, 1823:72; Todd, p. 579. LOCATION L, C, Corvey CME 3-628-48428-6, Ireland related fiction, ViU.

Paris: Haut-Coeur & Gayet Jeune, 1824, 4 vols. (trans. by M*** [Dubergier] as *Le marriage de Dunamore*). SOURCE Rafroidi, ii, p. 377; Bn-Opale plus. LOCATION BNF.

COMMENTARY 'The bridal of Dunamore' is a Gothic fiction set in Ireland. It is a character study of Rosalind Glenmorlie, beautiful but haughty and ambitious, and of the misery she causes to others and finally to herself. It traces the Glenmorlie family through six generations. The Dunamore property is the cause of a long-lasting rift in the family, because at one stage the eldest son was passed over in the inheritance of the estate. 'Lost and won' is about a haughty girl who comes down in the world and eventually marries someone whom she always thought beneath her [Brown; N. Schroeder, *Éire-Ireland*, 19 (1984), p. 123; Tracy, 147].

R240 *The tradition of the castle; or, scenes in the Emerald Isle* (by Regina Maria Roche). + London: A.K. Newman & Co., 1824, 4 vols. SOURCE Allibone, ii, p. 1844; Brown, 1444; Block, p. 200; British Fiction; Garside, 1824:80; Todd, p. 579. LOCATION Corvey CME 3-628-48464-2, Grail, Ireland related fiction, D, L, ViU.

Paris: Tardieu, Boulland & Co., 1824, 3 vols. (trans. by M** [Dubergier] as *La tradition du château, ou scenes de l'îsle d'émeraude*). SOURCE Rafroidi, ii, p. 377; Bn-Opale plus. LOCATION BNF.

COMMENTARY A sentimental novel with some Gothic elements in the ghost stories told by the O'Brien family. Set at Altoir-na-Greine, Howth (near Dublin), and at Killarney, it is a coming-of-age story featuring Donoghue, a descendant of Brian Boru, whose indolent, easy-to-influence father, O'Brien, returns to Ireland after refusing to support a bill for Irish independence in the English parliament. He turns over his estate to an agent, who steals the property. O'Brien leaves Ireland and becomes an absentee landlord. Donoghue, corrupted by his English education, is vain, conceited, and arrogant and believes that Ireland is a country to be avoided at all cost. On a visit with his mother, however, he is impressed by its scenery, and falls in love with Eveleen Erin, a simple natural girl who rejects him, as he has not won her esteem. He returns to England where he grows more aware of the failings of his gambler father, who dies, and of Ireland's tragic fate. Donoghue accepts a commission in the army on the Continent, and is wounded at Waterloo. After many adventures, he feels compelled to return to Ireland. Although a Protestant, he is convinced that religious freedom is essential for the peace of the country. At his return to his ancestral castle, Altoir-na-Greine, his attitude undergoes further change when he discovers an ancient manuscript that contains a Gothic love story. He learns that the agent has illegally deprived his family of their estate, and the lands are restored to him. He also discovers that Eveleen is now the heiress of a large estate. Once she recognizes the changes her lover has undergone, she is able to return his love [N. Schroeder, *Éire-Ireland*, 19 (1984), pp 125-9; Brown; Frank, 455].

R241 *The castle chapel. A romantic tale* (by Regina Maria Roche). London: A.K. Newman & Co., 1825, 3 vols. SOURCE Allibone, ii, p. 1844; Brown, 1445; Rafroidi, ii, p. 333; British Fiction; Garside, 1825:71; Todd, p. 579. LOCATION Corvey CME 3-628-48429-4, Grail, Ireland related fiction, D, L, ViU.

[German trans.], 1827 (trans. as *Die Kapelle des alten Schlosses von Saint-Doulagh, oder die Banditen von Newgate*). SOURCE Garside, 1825:71.

Paris: Corbet Âiné, 1825, 4 vols. (trans. as *La chapelle du vieux château de St. Doulagh, ou les bandits de Newgate*). SOURCE Rafroidi, ii, p. 377. LOCATION L.

COMMENTARY A Gothic story set in Ulster in the early-nineteenth century in which O'Shaugnessy O'Neill, weary of modern living, purchases a collapsed castle once owned by his family. He moves in with his children Eugene and Grace, accompanied by their maniacal aunt who believes in phrenological alteration using metallic hoods. The story turns Gothic when the children reach adulthood and the villain, Mr Mordaunt, enters the story. He is the former owner of the castle, the cruel father of Grace's friend, Rose, and his wife's murderer. Grace and Rose are able to escape, but not before seeing Mordaunt's henchmen retrieve a box of human bones. Rose is carried off by Mordaunt to a dark cottage and dies there of horror. Grace regains her freedom with the help of a local lad, William Delamore, who has returned rich from the East Indies. Prior to Grace's liberation, Eugene departs to fight for Greek independence. At the end of the story, Mordaunt's fate remains uncertain [Frank, 370; Tracy, 148].

R242　*Contrast* (by Regina Maria Roche; dedicated to Princess Augusta).
  + London: A.K. Newman & Co., 1828, 3 vols. (subscribers' list). SOURCE Allibone, ii, p. 1844; Block, p. 200; British Fiction; Garside, 1828:67; Todd, p. 579. LOCATION Corvey CME 3–628–48457–X, Grail, D, L, ViU.
  New York: J. & J. Harper, 1828, 2 vols. LOCATION NUC.
COMMENTARY The subscribers' list mostly consists of London residents, including Thomas Crofton Croker§, a few of RMR's friends in Waterford, and the authors 'L.E.L.', Robert Southey, and William Wordsworth. A subscription advertisement for this novel (now among the records of the Royal Literary Fund) shows a different title: *Contrast, or Helena and Adelaide: A novel*. The story concerns the religious persecution of the Irish and the evil effects of absenteeism. The major emphasis is on the consolations of religion. The Irish countryside is compared with that of urban London. The 'contrast' is drawn between the successful and happy marriage of Horatio de Montville and Adelaide and the unsuccessful and unhappy marriage of Montflorence and Helena. The domestic plot is mixed with Gothic features, which include the imprisonment of Adelaide in a dismal country house where she passes the time reading Samuel Richardson's *Clarissa* until she is released by Horatio. Helena, who had formerly been married to a profligate, leaves Monflorence out of shame when her first husband reappears to claim her. Because of further complications, the two are never reunited and Helena dies in miserable self-exile [Frank, 371; *Éire-Ireland*, 19 (1984), pp 129–30; L, Royal Literary Fund, Loan 96 590(17); Tracy, 151].

R243　*The nun's picture. A tale* (by Regina Maria Roche).
  + London; A.K. Newman, 1836, 3 vols. SOURCE Allibone, ii, p. 1844; Rafroidi, ii, p. 333; Todd, p. 579; Garside 2, 1836:62. LOCATION Dt (1843 edn), L.
COMMENTARY Starts out in Cumberland in England [ML].
— SPURIOUS WORKS

R244　*Eliza; or, the pattern of women. A moral romance* ('translated from the German of Maria Regina Roche').
  Lancaster, [PA]: Chr. Jac. Hutter , 1802. SOURCE RLIN. LOCATION CSt.
COMMENTARY The German original of this work has not been located [RL].

R245　*Melinda, or the victim of seduction. A moral tale* (by Mrs Roche).
  Danbury (CT): Printed for the booksellers, 1804. SOURCE Welch, 1126; OCLC. LOCATION MH.

R246　*Alvondown vicarage. A novel* [anon.].
  London: Lane, Newman & Co., 1807, 2 vols. SOURCE Blakey, p. 222; Block, p. 199; British Fiction; Garside, 1807:54; Rafroidi, ii, p. 332; Todd, p. 579. LOCATION Corvey CME 3–628–47051–X, O.
COMMENTARY Although authorship has been widely ascribed to RMR, Garside states that this is uncertain [Garside].

R247　*London tales; or, reflective portraits* [anon.].
  London: J. Booth, 1814, 2 vols. SOURCE Allibone, ii, p. 1844; Block, p. 200; British Fiction; Garside, 1814:48. LOCATION Corvey CME 3–28–51094–5, L, NUC.

COMMENTARY Attributed to RMR, but her authorship is doubtful [Garside; NCBEL 4, p. 989].

R248   *Plain tales* (by Mrs Roche).
London: G. Walker, [1814], 2 vols. SOURCE British Fiction; Garside, 1814:49; RLIN. LOCATION ViU.

COMMENTARY Attributed to RMR, but her authorship is doubtful. Contents: 'Edward; or, the unfortunate', 'Henry or the poor tutor', 'The misanthrope', 'The philanthropist', 'Lydia', 'Selena' [Garside; NCBEL 4, p. 989; cat. ViU].

R249   *Anna; or, Edinburgh. A novel* (by Mrs Roche).
London: R. Hill, 1815, 3 vols. SOURCE British Fiction; Garside, 1815:42. LOCATION Corvey CME 3–628–48427–8]

COMMENTARY Attributed to RMR, but her authorship is doubtful [Garside; NCBEL 4, p. 989].

R250   *Le père coupable, ou, les malheurs de la famille Lewison* (by Regina Maria Roche [*sic*]).
Paris: Corbet, 1821, 3 vols. SOURCE RLIN; Bn-Opale plus. LOCATION NjP.

COMMENTARY In all likelihood a spurious edn. The title page states that it was translated from the English by RMR, but an English original is not known [RLIN; RL].

ROCHFORT, Edith, fl. 1890. Novelist.
R251   *The Lloyds of Ballymore* (by Edith Rochfort).
+ London: Chapman & Hall, 1890, 2 vols. SOURCE Brown, 1446. LOCATION D, L, NUC.

COMMENTARY Set in the 1880s in the midlands and Dublin with characters mostly from the Protestant landlord class. A love story is interwoven with agrarian murder and suspicion of a bank robbery [Brown].

'ROCK, Captain', pseud. See **O'CONNOR, Roger**.

'ROCKINGHAM, Sir Charles', pseud. See **DE JARNAC, Philippe Ferdinand Auguste de Rohan Chabot, comte**.

ROCKWELL, Mrs M.E. American writer of religious fiction, MER is known from a single novel. SOURCE RL; OCLC.
R252   *Tom Miller; or, after many days* (by Mrs M.E. Rockwell; dedicated to 'poor, uneducated, Christian mothers ... and to faithful teachers ...').
+ Philadelphia: J.C. Garrigues, 1867 (ill.). LOCATION Wright, ii, 2103; Wright web.

COMMENTARY An emigration tale featuring Tom Miller, an Irish boy from Co. Tyrone who at age 9 arrives with his parents, two brothers and two sisters in Philadelphia in 1833. He is scared of the first black man he encounters. Two older children are already settled in Philadelphia. They are a Protestant family and Mrs Miller has trouble finding a church where she feels at home. Finally, a Sunday school is found for Tommy. The father and the older boys are not interested in religion. The mother tries to maintain interest in religion in her family and in the end she succeeds [ML].

RODDAN, Fr John T., b. Boston (MA) 1819, d. 1858. American priest and writer, JTR was born of Irish immigrant parents. He was age 8 or 9 when his father died. He entered the priesthood and because of his brilliance was sent by Bishop John Fitzpatrick to Rome to study at the College of Propaganda. Returning home after his ordination in 1848, he became a missionary priest ministering to a wide area south of Boston. He was appointed editor of the Boston *Pilot*, the official organ of the Roman Catholic diocese of Boston, a post he held until his death at age 39. SOURCE Fanning, p. 93.

R253 *John O'Brien; or, the orphan of Boston. A tale of real life* (by the Revd John T. Roddan; dedicated to 'The Roman Catholic orphan boys of America').

+ Boston: Patrick Donahoe, 1850. SOURCE Fanning, pp 118, 389; partly reprinted in Exiles, pp 98–108; Slocum, ii, 3824; Wright, i, 2143 (1851 edn). LOCATION NUC, DCU (1851 edn).

COMMENTARY Possibly written in response to a suggestion by Orestes Browne and published in his *Quarterly Review* (London), that someone ought to 'write a tale entitled the Orphan of New York or the Orphan of Boston, the Irish Orphan or the Catholic Orphan, which would be adapted to the condition of the poor orphan *boys* among ourselves'. The winner of the subsequent competition, however, was Mary Anne Sadlier's§ *Willy Burke; or, the Irish orphan in America*. The present work is probably partly autobiographical. In the introd. the author states that the book had been written especially for literary Catholics, and especially for those 'who move in ... the middle and the lower ranks of society ... If Protestants choose to read it, I have nothing to say ...' He endeavoured to 'give a faithful account of some of the difficulties which an unprotected boy in our cities faces', based on the accounts of twenty persons he could name. The main character is John O'Brien, who is orphaned at age 8, and who encounters numerous Protestants at his various jobs, in lodging houses, and in the streets. The novel deals with the problematic relations between Catholics and Protestants in New England before 1850 and how John O'Brien survives through many trials. As an adult, he sets straight Gallagher, an Irish errand boy, who is about to repeat all of John's youthful errors [RL; Fanning, pp 94–6, 118; DCU].

RODENBERG, Julius (also known as Levy), fl. 1860. Austrian folklore editor and travel writer, JR's *The island of the saints. A pilgrimage through Ireland* was published in translation in London in 1860. SOURCE RL; Zimmermann, p. 137.

R254 *Die Harfe von Erin: Märchen und Dichtung in Irland* (ed. by Julius Rodenberg; dedicated to Frau Lili Schenk zu Schweinsberg).

+ Leipzig: Fr. Wilh. Grunow, 1861. SOURCE OCLC. LOCATION Dt, L, MH.

COMMENTARY Along with Irish poetry and music and a long introd. on Irish fairytales, this contains some stories by Michael James Whitty§ from his *Tales of Irish life* (London, 1824, 2 vols.) and by Denis Shine Lawlor§. Contents of the stories: 'Die Stadt in Meere', 'Der Hexenmeister von Crunaan', 'Der Banschi-Brunnen', 'Von Luprechaun, dem Seenschuster', 'Die Schwarzbraune Kuh', 'Das Land der weigen Jugend', 'Der Unkel aus der Seenwelt', 'Das Seen-Handtuch', 'O'Donoghue's Dudelsack', 'Der Phuka', 'Seen-Ummen', 'Schöne Nora' [RL; IBL, 8 (1916–17), p. 53].

ROGERS, R.D., fl. 1897. Writer of humorous sketches.

R255 *The adventures of St. Kevin, and other Irish tales* (by R.D. Rogers).

+ London: W. Swan Sonnenschein & Co., 1897. SOURCE Brown, 1448. LOCATION NUC.

COMMENTARY Humorous sketches rendering old legends in a modern, comic form. Contents: 'Saint Kevin and the Welsh miner', 'Saint Kevin and the bishop of Kerry', 'Saint Kevin and the temperance reformer', 'Saint Kevin's visit to purgatory', 'Saint Kevin and the goose', 'Saint Kevin and the importunate damsel', 'The conversion of Saint Kevin', 'The widow O'Slane', 'The tale of paradise valley', 'The marvellous shillalah', 'The waters of Schlossboschen', 'Mr. Browne and Mr. Brown' [ML; Brown].

'ROMNEY, A.B.', pseud. See RAMBAUT, A. Beatrice.

ROONEY, Miss Teresa J. (also known as T.J. Rooney), pseud. 'Eblana', b. 1840, d. 1911. Catholic novelist and history writer and possibly also a contributor to periodicals, TJR lived in Dublin. Her *Erin Quintiana; or, Dublin Castle and the Irish Parliament, 1767–1772* (Dublin, 1898), appeared under her pseudonym and is a collection of historical notes. An 'Eblana' was Irish correspondent for the *Gentlewoman's Magazine* (London) in the late-nineteenth and early-twentieth centuries. The pseudonym was also used by periodical contributors Revd Thomas A. Butler and W.J. Fitzpatrick. In 1879 TJR wrote to the Catholic archbishop of Dublin that, since she had been refused absolution for upholding the rights of women, she would refrain from approaching the sacraments again until she heard from the archbishop. SOURCE Brown, p. 268; CM; Dublin [RC] Diocesan Archives (MS AB 5/File II, 337/615); Irish pseudonyms; RIA/DIB; RL; Ryan, p. 148.

R256 *Ard Righ Deighionach na Teamhrach ... The last monarch of Tara. A tale of Ireland in the sixth century* (by 'Eblana'; revsd and corrected by the Very Revd U.J. Canon Bourke, MRIA).
+ Dublin: M.H. Gill & Son, 1880 (title page in Irish and English). SOURCE Brown, 1452. LOCATION D, DPL, L, NUC, InND Loeber coll.
+ Dublin: M.H. Gill & Son, 1887 (as *The last monarch of Tara. A tale of Ireland in the sixth century*). SOURCE Falkner Greirson cat. 'Jane'/276. LOCATION Dt, NUC, InND Loeber coll.
New York: Benziger 1889 (as *The last monarch of Tara*). SOURCE Brown, 1452.
COMMENTARY No copy of New York edn located. Adv. in 1887 by Simpkin, Marshall & Co., but no copy by this firm located. Historical fiction, set during the reigns of Tuathal and Diarmaid O Cearbhail, mainly in the district around Tara (Co. Meath). It is meant to give a picture of daily life in Ireland in the sixth century. The chief events are the murder of Tuathal, the judgment of Diarmaid against Columbkille, the battle of Cooldrevne, and the cursing and abandonment of Tara [Brown; Topp 8, 840].

R257 *Eily O'Hartigan. An Irish-American tale of the days of the Volunteers* (by 'Eblana').
Dublin: Sealy, Bryers & Walker; London: Simpkin, Marshall & Co., 1889. SOURCE Alston, p. 373; Brown, 1453; Topp 8, 950. LOCATION L, E.
COMMENTARY Nationalist historical fiction, set in the time of the Volunteer movement in Ireland (1778–79). The chief incidents are the battle of Bunker Hill (Charlestown, MA, 1775) and the Irish Declaration of Independence in 1782 [Brown].

R258 *The strike: A tale of the Old Dublin Liberties* (by T.J. Rooney).
Dublin: Sealy, Bryers & Co., [1910]. SOURCE Brown, 1454 (1909 edn, but not located).
SOURCE COPAC. LOCATION L.
COMMENTARY Historical fiction. A tale of industrial activity in eighteenth-century Dublin centred on the Liberties, an area of the city outside royal governance [Brown].

R259 *Elemental drifts* (by 'Eblana').
London: A.H. Stockwell, 1920. SOURCE OCLC. LOCATION L (missing).
COMMENTARY 30pp [OCLC].

ROOPER, George, fl. 1869. Sport and sketch writer, probably English of Irish background, GR wrote books on fishing and hunting, including *Flood, field, and forest* (London, 1869) and *Thames and Tweed* (London, 1870). SOURCE Allibone Suppl., ii, p. 1295).

R260 *Tales and sketches* (by George Rooper).
+ London: Land and Water Office, 1872. SOURCE Allibone Suppl., ii, p. 1295.
LOCATION L, NUC.

COMMENTARY Contains one Irish story: 'Three days at Ballinahinch' (Co. Galway) [ML].

R261 *A month in Mayo: comprising characteristic sketches (sporting and social) of Irish life; with miscellaneous papers* (by George Rooper).
+ London: Robert Hardwicke, 1876. SOURCE Allibone Suppl., ii, p. 1295. LOCATION PC, L, NUC.

'ROS, Amanda McKittrick', pseud. See ROSS, Anna Margaret.

'ROSE', fl. 1869. Pseudonym of a children's story writer, presumably Irish, who published in Dublin moral fiction for juveniles. SOURCE RL.

R262 *Spring stories, and others* (by 'Rose'; dedicated to Evory Kennedy, MD).
+ Dublin: Thomas Webb, 1869. LOCATION D, L.
COMMENTARY Stories for juveniles. Contents: 'Spring stories' (in 12 chapters), 'A tree story', 'A rose story', 'A meadow story', 'A bog story', 'A pic-nic story', 'A sleep story', A sunbeam story', 'A little flower story', 'A story of three roses' [RL].

R263 *Leaves, blossoms, and thorns, being stories, fancies, and thoughts* (by 'Rose'; dedicated to M.B. and L.F.).
+ Dublin: Thomas Webb, 1870. LOCATION D, L.
COMMENTARY Contents: 'A story of sorrow' (in 5 chapters), 'A midsummer's night dream', 'Story of a little angel', 'Story of a garden', 'That unanswerable why?', 'An old woman's sermon', 'Allegory of a rose who envied a sensitive plant', 'An afternoon in March' (2 parts), 'A story of three children' (3 parts), '"So he bringeth them unto their desired haven"', 'Thoughts on temper' [ML].

ROSE, Edward H. See ROSE, Edward Hampden.

ROSE, Edward Hampden, b. Dublin, fl. 1811, d. Naval Hospital, Stonehouse (Scotland), 1810 (but see below). Seaman, poet and fiction writer, HER wrote for various papers over the signature 'A foremast man'. O'Donoghue mentions that HER died in 1810, but it is unclear why the following two works would have appeared posthumously. SOURCE Allibone, ii, p. 1869; O'Donoghue, p. 405.

R264 *The sea-devil, or son of a bellows-mender, a tragic-comic romance of the present day* (by Edward H. Rose).
Plymouth-Dock: J. Roach, 1811. SOURCE Allibone, ii, p. 1869; OCLC; COPAC. LOCATION L.

R265 *Trifles, in verse and prose* (by Edward H. Rose).
Plymouth-Dock: [publisher?], 1811. SOURCE Allibone, ii, p. 1869; O'Donoghue, p. 405. LOCATION L.

ROSS, Anna Margaret (Mrs Andrew Ross, also Mrs Thomas Rodgers, née McKittrick, also M'Kittrick), pseud. 'Amanda McKittrick Ros', b. near Drumaness (Co. Down) 1860, d. Larne (Co. Antrim) 1939. Novelist and poet, AMR was the daughter of Edward McKittrick, headmaster of Drumaness high school, and Eliza Black. She claimed that her mother named her Amanda after the protagonist in Regina Maria Roche's§ *The children of the abbey* (London, 1796). She was trained as a teacher in Marlborough College, Dublin, and married the stationmaster at Larne Harbour in 1887. Her novels, which were self-published, had conventional plots and often included personal attacks on those she believed had wronged her. In England they had somewhat of a cult following, which varied from kindly laughter to derision. Aldous Huxley wrote of her work as 'the discovery of art by an unsophisticated mind'

(ODNB). She also wrote several VOLUMES of verse. An *Amanda McKittrick Ros Reader* was issued by Frank Ormsby in 1988. For her portrait and papers, see ODNB. SOURCE Blain, p. 921; Boylan, p. 343; Colman, pp 150–1 [under M'Kittrick]; Hogan 2, pp 1068–9; J. Loudan, *O rare Amanda! The life of Amanda McKittrick Ros* (London, 1954); OCIL, pp 500–1; ODNB; Sutherland, p. 545.

R266   *Irene Iddesleigh* (by 'Amanda McKittrick Ros').
    + Belfast, London, Dublin: Printed [for the author?] by W. & G. Baird, 1897. SOURCE Sutherland, p. 545; Wolff, 5958. LOCATION D, Dt, L, NUC, InND Loeber coll.
    + London: The Nonsuch Press, 1926 (ill.). LOCATION L, NUC, InND Loeber coll.
    New York: Boni & Liveright, 1927. SOURCE NYPL. LOCATION NN, NUC.

R267   *Delina Delaney* (by 'Amanda McKittrick Ros'; dedicated to author's husband).
    + Belfast: R. Aickin & Co., [1898]. SOURCE Brown 2, 1394 (1902 edn); Sutherland, p. 545; Wolff, 5956. LOCATION Dt, L, NUC, InND Loeber coll.
    + London: Chatto & Windus, 1935 (this edn dedicated to John Coghlan of Vincent Street, Dublin). LOCATION D, DPL, NUC (1936 edn).
COMMENTARY The first few pages are a criticism of Barry Pain's review of *Irene Iddesleigh* (Belfast, 1897). Delina Delaney is left penniless by the death of her father, a Connemara fisherman. Lady Gifford of nearby Columba Castle offers her work. Lady Gifford's son takes a fancy to Delina, but Delina's mother warns her not to associate with him. Lord Gifford's mother wants him to marry his cousin, Lady Mattie Maynard, but he suggests to Delina that she come with him to his London house and he will marry her. Delina consents, and both mothers die from the shock of the elopement. Since Delina is a raw country girl, her husband-to-be hires Madam-de-Maine to teach her the ways of the world. She is such a tyrant that Delina leaves. She earns her own living and becomes an apprentice nurse. Lord Gifford is distracted by the loss of Delina but does not get rid of Madam-de-Maine, who takes on the role of housekeeper. One evening he is brought home after a serious accident. Madam-de-Maine does not immediately get a doctor, hoping he might die. When a doctor finally comes, he orders a nurse, and Delina happens to be the one sent. Under her care, Lord Gifford slowly improves. Madam-de-Maine adds arsenic to the flour from which Delina makes Lord Gifford's food. He does not die but Delina is convicted of attempted murder. Madam-de-Maine, on her deathbed, admits that she is Lady Mattie Maynard, and that she had added arsenic to the food. Delina is released from Mountjoy prison and marries Lord Gifford [ML].

R268   *Donald Dudley, the bastard critic* (by 'Amanda McKittrick Ros').
    [London]: Thames Ditton, 1954. SOURCE Sutherland, p. 545 ([*c.*1900] edn). LOCATION L.
COMMENTARY Published posthumously [RL].

R269   *Helen Huddleson* (by 'Amanda McKittrick Ros'; ed. by Jack Loudan).
    London: Chatto & Windus, 1969. SOURCE OCIL, p. 501. LOCATION L.
COMMENTARY Published posthumously. Jack Loudan wrote the last chapter [RL].

ROSS, Charles H. See **ROSS, Charles Henry.**

ROSS, Charles Henry (known as **Charles H. Ross**), b. London *c.*1842, d. London 1897. Novelist, cartoonist, children's writer, theatre manager and inventor of Ally Sloper, the first continuing comic-strip character in England, CHR was the son of Charles Ross, chief parliamentary reporter for the London *Times*. He entered the civil service and wrote for magazines and newspapers in his spare time. He edited *Judy*, subtitled the *London Serio-Comic Journal*, which was a rival to *Punch* magazine. CHR was a prolific and popular author. SOURCE Allibone Suppl., ii, p. 1297; Boase, vi, pp 497–8; ODNB [under Ally Sloper group]; Sutherland, p. 545.

R270   *The strange adventures of two single gentlemen, a big black box, and a green cot-*
ton umbrella, with some particulars respecting a young lady in curl-papers (by
Charles H. Ross).
+ London: Arthur Hall, Smart & Allen, [1870] (ill. H.K. Browne [Phiz], Victor Ravel,
Eugene Seys, and the author). SOURCE COPAC. LOCATION D, L.
COMMENTARY Some Irish content [ML].

'ROSS, Martin', pseud. See **MARTIN, Violet Florence.**

ROSSA, Jeremiah O'Donovan (1831–1915), attributed author, Fenian revolutionary, periodical writer and founder of the literary and political Phoenix Society. See **MORAN, Edward.**

ROUVIÈRE, Henrietta. See **MOSSE, Henrietta.**

ROVIGO, countess of. See **STAMER, Harriet Elizabeth.**

ROWAN, Anne M. See **ROWAN, Anne Margaret.**

ROWAN, Anne Margaret (known as **Annie M. Rowan**), pseud. 'Amos Reade', b.
Blennerville (Co. Kerry), probably prior to 1844, d. 1913. Historian, antiquarian and novelist, AMR probably grew up in Co. Kerry. She was the daughter of the antiquarian and Church
of Ireland clergyman, the Revd Arthur Blennerhassett Rowan, and Alicia, daughter of Peter
Thompson of Tralee. Her father became curate of Blennerville (c.1825–1844), rector of
Kilgobbin (Co. Kerry, 1846–61), and archdeacon of Ardfert (Co. Kerry, 1856–61). AMR was
a political activist in the Unionist cause, and was for twenty-five years honorary secretary of
the Kerry branch of the Irish Unionist Alliance. She was the author of *History of Ireland as
disclosed by Irish statutes passed by Irish parliaments between 1310 and 1800* (London, [1893]).
SOURCE Allibone Suppl., ii, p. 1266 [under A. Reade and Amos Reade], p. 1301 [under Annie
M. Rowan]; Leslie, *Ardfert and Aghadoe*, pp 38–9; Personal communication, Marc Caball, Sept.
2001; RIA/DIB [under Arthur Blennerhassett Rowan]; RL.
R271   *Percy Smythe: A tale of duty* (by Annie M. Rowan).
+ London: Charing Cross Publishing Co., 1878. SOURCE RIA/DIB. LOCATION L (n.d.
edn).
COMMENTARY No Irish content [ML].
R272   *Rendelsholme. A novel* (by Annie M. Rowan).
+ London: Remington & Co., 1880, 2 vols. SOURCE Allibone Suppl., ii, p. 1301.
LOCATION L.
COMMENTARY Set in England, where an Englishman has married a French Catholic girl. The
reverberations of this step are traced through several generations of the family. No Irish con-
tent [ML]
R273   *Norah Moriarty, or, revelations of modern Irish life* (by 'Amos Reade').
+ Edinburgh, London: William Blackwood & Sons, 1886, 2 vols. SOURCE Allibone
Suppl., ii, p. 1266 [under A. Reade]; Brown, 1407; Wolff, 5702. LOCATION D, L, NUC.
COMMENTARY A romance intertwined with the story of the Land League set around 1880 and
written against the Land League agitations. People flee the country to preserve their lives. It
describes the nocturnal raids of the agitators [ML; Brown].
R274   *Life in the cut* (by 'Amos Reade').
London: W. Swan Sonnenschein & Co., 1888. SOURCE Allibone Suppl., ii, p. 1266.
LOCATION L.

COMMENTARY No Irish content. Concerns canal people in England who are drunk and degraded [ML].

ROWAN, Hamilton. See **HAMILTON, Gawin William Rowan.**

'ROY, Gordon', pseud. See **WALLACE, Helen.**

'ROY, Kendal', pseud. See **MC DONNELL, Randal William.**

'A ROYALIST', fl. 1867. Pseudonym of an historical novelist who, judging from the inscription in the InND Loeber coll. copy, was an accomplished calligrapher. SOURCE RL.
R275   *The loyalist's daughter. A novel or tale of the revolution* (by 'A royalist').
+ London: Adams & Francis, 1867, 4 vols. SOURCE COPAC; Johnson cat. 44/24.
LOCATION L, InND Loeber coll.
COMMENTARY Probably privately printed, because the imprint of Adams & Francis is not known. Historical fiction set in the late-seventeenth century, featuring King James II and his family, with a decidedly pro-Jacobite perspective. It begins at the time the queen and her small son leave Whitehall and flee to France. It portrays James's indecisiveness and the uncertainty of allegiances at that time. The story follows James's career through various battles against the Williamite forces, his campaigns in Ireland, and his eventual residence in France. One of the loyalists in his retinue is an O'Brien. A presumably Irish horse, Faugh-a-ballagh (meaning in translation, 'yield the way') performs greats feats of skill during the whole story, which ends shortly after the deposed king's death. The author concludes that the book provided 'the most pleasing task of the author's life' [ML; Johnson cat.44/24; AMB; Johnson cat. 48/28].

RUFFIN, Mrs R.M., fl. 1858. American story and sketch writer, Mrs RMR was from Uniontown (AL), according to the title page of the following volume. SOURCE OCLC.
R276   *Tales and sketches for the fireside* (by Mrs R.M. Ruffin; dedicated to 'every Southern home circle').
+ Marion (AL): Printed at the Book and Job Office of Denis Dykous, 1858. LOCATION Wright, ii, 2133; Wright web.
COMMENTARY Contains several stories, the last of which is called 'The Irish immigrant', inspired by the song, 'I am sitting on the stile Mary'. The main character is Dennis O'Connel, an orphan who becomes a groom on the old squire's estate. He falls in love with Mary. The squire's son comes for a visit from London and wants to take Dennis back with him as his valet. Dennis refuses. When the old squire dies the young squire requests all outstanding fees to be paid. Dennis and Mary run into difficult times. Mary dies after childbirth and Dennis is left with the baby and his ailing mother-in-law. After both die, he emigrates to Charleston (SC) [ML].

RUNDLE, Elizabeth. See **CHARLES, Mrs Elizabeth.**

RUSSELL, Maud Mary, fl. 1900. Story and sketch writer, MMR was presumably Irish, given her subject matter and the fact that she published in Dublin. SOURCE RL.
R277   *Sprigs of the shamrock; or, Irish sketches and legends* (by Mary Maud Russell).
+ Dublin: Browne & Nolan, 1900. SOURCE McVeagh, p. 124. LOCATION D.
COMMENTARY A story of travel up the Shannon River to Athlone, then to the Giant's Causeway and Lough Neagh (Co. Antrim). Contains dialogues [ML; McVeagh].

RUSSELL, Lady Rachel Evelyn. See BUTLER, Lady Rachel Evelyn.

RUSSELL, Thomas O'Neill, pseud. 'Reginald Tierney' (not 'Reginald Massey' as in OCIL), b. Lissanode (burnt in the Anglo-Irish War, now rebuilt), near Moate (Co. Westmeath) 1828, d. Dublin 1908. Novelist, poet, translator and Irish language revivalist, TO'NR was the son of Joseph Russell, a Quaker gentleman farmer, and Sarah Broadman. In 1855 he stated the case for the revival of the Irish language in the *Irishman* (London). He spent some time as a commercial traveller in Ireland for a fellow Quaker, W.R. Jacob, then went to America in 1867 (RIA/DIB says he was implicated in the Fenian rising), where he lived for nearly thirty years, with lengthy return visits to Dublin. During this period he devoted himself to the promotion of the Irish language and music. In Dublin in 1877 he formed, with George Sigerson, the Society for the Preservation of the Irish Language, which Douglas Hyde§ joined the following year. On TO'NR's return to Dublin in the early 1890s he continued this work, becoming one of the most notable figures in the Irish language revival movement and one of the founding members of the Gaelic League. His love of and adherence to classical Irish was at odds with the efforts of the League to promote Irish as a vernacular language, and James Joyce refers to him in *Ulysses* (Paris, 1922): 'O'Neill Russell? O, yes, he must speak the grand old tongue.' TO'NR wrote voluminously for the Irish and American press, both in prose and in verse, chiefly for propagandistic purposes. He translated some of Thomas Moore's§ melodies into Irish, wrote a series of articles on historic Irish places in the Dublin *Freeman's Journal* in 1895, and published *The beauties and antiquities of Ireland* ([London], 1897) as well as several verse dramas. His final work was *Is Ireland a dying nation?* (Dublin, 1906). SOURCE Boylan, p. 345; Brown, p. 269; L. Cox, *Moate county, Westmeath: a history* (n.l., 1981); Hogan 2, p. 1073; Irish pseudonyms; McKenna, pp 319–20; OCIL, p. 504; O'Donoghue, p. 408; Sutherland, p. 547; Westmeath, p. 168.

R278   *The struggles of Dick; or, the battles of a boy* (by 'Reginald Tierney').
+ Dublin: James Duffy, 1860. LOCATION Grail, D, L.
+ Dublin, London: James Duffy, 1861, 2nd edn (as *The adventures of Dick Massey. A tale of Irish life*; ill. Fitzpatrick). SOURCE McKenna, p. 319. LOCATION D.
+ Dublin: M.H. Gill, n.d. (as *Dick Massey. A tale of the Irish evictions*; with preface). SOURCE Brown, 1461. LOCATION DPL, InND Loeber coll.
+ Glasgow, London: Cameron & Ferguson, [1871 or earlier] (as *Dick Massey: A tale of the Irish evictions*). SOURCE Allibone, ii, p. 1900 [under T.O. Russell] (London, 1869 edn); mentioned in cat. of *McHenry's Irish tales* (Glasgow, [19—]); ODNB. LOCATION D (n.d., 5th edn).
New York: P.J. Kenedy, [1856 or earlier] (as *Dick Massey. An Irish story*). SOURCE Adv. in A.D Dorsey, *Conscience* (New York, 1856). COMMENTARY *New York, Kenedy 1856 or earlier edn* No copy located [RL].
+ New York: P.J. Kenedy & Sons, [1881 or earlier] (as *Dick Massey. A tale. The Irish evictions*; The Irish Fireside Library). LOCATION InND Loeber coll.
New York: P.M. Haverty, [1871 or earlier] (as *Dick Massey. A tale of the Irish evictions*). SOURCE Adv. in Haverty's *Irish-American Illustrated Almanac* (New York, 1871), p. 104. LOCATION NUC (1887 edn).
COMMENTARY Set during the Famine of 1845–47 (and not the 1814 famine as stated in Brown), it paints a faithful picture of social life in rural Ireland at the time. Dick Massey, younger son of a country gentleman, feels more at home with the honest tenants than with the gentry. He urges his neighbours not to evict tenants. Nevertheless, one named Parsons evicts a widow and her daughter, Norah. The two women, accompanied by Norah's nephew, leave for the US. It describes the horrors of the journey aboard an emigrant ship. The widow soon dies in

America, after which Norah and the nephew return home. Dick has more success with other gentry, influencing them to treat their tenants more humanely [ML; Brown; Fegan, p. 210; ODNB].

R279   *True heart's trials: A tale of Ireland and America* (by Thomas O'Neill Russell). Dublin: M.H. Gill, 1872. SOURCE Brown, 1460; McKenna, p. 319. LOCATION Grail, Dt ([*c.*1900] edn), DPL (n.d. edn), L, InND Loeber coll. (n.d. edn).
+ Glasgow, London: Cameron & Ferguson, n.d. LOCATION D.
COMMENTARY A story of lovers' trials set first in the lake district of Cos. Cavan and Meath, and afterwards in the backwoods north of Albany (NY). Hubert Daly and his brother inherit a farm but it does not yield enough income to allow him to marry Emily Hudson. Her mother strongly discourages Emily's attachment. Hubert sells his share of the farm to his brother and emigrates to America. He lives with a friend and a servant in the backwoods where they try to create a farm from scratch. Eventually Emily and Hubert are reunited when Emily escapes from her home and travels to America [ML; Brown].

RUSSELL, William, pseud. 'Thomas Waters', fl. 1870s. Historical fiction writer.
R280   *The Ribbonman; or, the secret tribunal: An Irish romance* (by 'Thomas Waters'). Glasgow: Cameron & Ferguson, [1871]. SOURCE Brown, 1655; COPAC. LOCATION L.
New York: P.M. Haverty, [1871 or earlier]. SOURCE Adv. in Haverty's *Irish-American Illustrated Almanac* (New York, 1871), p. 104.
COMMENTARY No copy of the New York edn located. The story consists of a series of terrible plots by Ribbonmen against the life of a landlord, Mr Bolivor. These are frustrated by a faithful groom and his sweetheart, one of the maids, and by a policeman who is in love with another servant in the house. Mr Bolivor is shot, but recovers, and a priest saves the mother and sister of the groom from the Ribbonmen [Brown].

RUSSELL, Sir William Howard, b. Jobstown (Co. Dublin) 1820, d. England? 1907. Journalist, barrister, war correspondent, writer and novelist, WHR was the son of John Russell, an editor, of Co. Limerick and Mary Kelly of Jobstown. He was reared by both his grandfathers as a member of the Church of Ireland. He entered TCD in 1838 but left in 1841 without taking a degree. That year his cousin, who worked for the *Times* in London, asked him to cover the elections in Ireland for the newspaper. Later he moved to London where he read for the Bar and did occasional reporting for the *Times*, which sent him back to Ireland to report on the agitation for repeal of the Union and the monster meetings led by Daniel O'Connell. He also reported on O'Connell's trial in 1844. He worked as a parliamentary reporter in London and joined the staff of the *Morning Chronicle*. He married Mary Burrowes of Howth (Co. Dublin) in 1846, rejoined the *Times* in 1848 and was called to the Bar in 1850 but did not pursue a legal career with much enthusiasm. He covered various foreign wars and his big break came when he went to the Crimea, where he covered the battle of Balaklava (1854) and the siege of Sevastopol (1855). His reports on the sufferings of the troops through army inefficiency spurred improvements in supplies of food, clothing and medicine to the soldiers. He was praised in England for his reportage from the front and encouraged by Charles Dickens to lecture on the war in England, Ireland and Scotland. He was awarded an honorary doctorate by TCD. Later he reported on the atrocities after the mutiny in India, on the Civil War in the US, on the Franco-Prussian and the Anglo-Zulu wars, where his reports on alleged misconduct of British troops created tension between him and Gen. Garnet Wolseley§. In 1860 he helped to found the *Army and Navy Gazette* (London), which he also owned in whole or in part, and he edited it until 1901. WHR was known for his pioneering and even-handed reporting. His fellow Irish correspondent, E.L. Godkin, said that in Russell's hands, 'correspondence from the field really became a power before which generals began to quail', demonstrating the emerging power of the press to curb military excesses (Sutherland, p. 548). Friendly with royalty and with writers such as William Makepeace Thackeray§ and Charles Dickens, WHR published many books based on his dispatches from the front, as well as on his tours with Edward VII to the Near East and to India. After the death of his first wife, he married in 1884 an Italian Catholic, Countess Antoinette Mathilde Malvezzi, and in 1895 he was knighted. He is commemorated in a memorial bust in St Paul's cathedral (London) with the inscription 'the first and greatest of War Correspondents'. The manuscript, 'Retrospective', an account of his early life in Dublin, disappeared but had been consulted by John B. Atkins in preparing WHR's biography, *The life of Sir William Howard Russell, C.V.O., LL.D.: the first special correspondent* (London, 1911, 2 vols.). For WHR's portraits and papers, see ODNB. SOURCE Allibone, ii, pp 1901–2; Allibone Suppl., ii, p. 1307; B & S, p. 722; Brown 2, p. 236; A. Hankinson, *Man of wars: William Howard Russell of the Times* (London, 1982); ODNB; RIA/DIB; Sutherland, p. 548.

R281 *The adventures of Doctor Brady* (by Sir William Howard Russell; dedicated to Gen. Sir de Lacy Evans).
 London: Tinsley Bros, 1868, 3 vols. SOURCE Brown 2, 1400; Wolff, 6081. LOCATION L, NUC.
 + London: Tinsley Bros, 1869 (new edn). SOURCE COPAC. LOCATION L.
COMMENTARY An semi-autobiographical novel, originally published in *Tinsley's Magazine* (London), at the beginning of which is a largely historical account of the Brady family. While the narrator is in his infancy, his father dies in India and his mother is supposed to have been drowned at sea when on her way home. The child lives at his grandfather's residence, Bradystown House. He falls in love with his mother's picture, but as his life goes on doubts as to her character and the circumstances of her death enter his mind. He is sent to Dr Ball's Academy near Dublin. In this rowdy school he becomes famous at hurling. While fishing on the river Dodder he meets a sea captain who takes him for a great cruise in pursuit of smugglers. Later he studies at Sweatenham College in England and at TCD. There is a description of a meeting in Conciliation Hall, with a speech by Daniel O'Connell. The third volume is largely taken up with the Crimean War and the Indian mutiny. Gradually the full truth emerges about his mother, who is alive [Brown 2].

RUXTON, Maria, pseuds **'An Irish Lady'** and **'A Lady'**, fl. 1780s, d. 1830. Minerva novelist and children's writer, MR is identified in the TCD copy of *The reconciliation* (London, 1783). Mary (query later Maria?) Ruxton was the daughter of John Ruxton of Ardee House (Co. Louth) and Letitia Fitzherbert. Her brother John (of Black Castle, Co. Meath) in 1770 married Margaret Edgeworth, sister of Richard Lovell Edgeworth§. This Margaret became a friend and confidant to Maria Edgeworth§. Mary Ruxton married John Corry, Esq. of Shantonagh (also known as Chantinee, Co. Monaghan), who as King Corny featured in Maria Edgeworth's§ 'Ormond' (published in *Harrington, a tale; and Ormond, a tale*, London, 1817, 3 vols.). Maria Edgeworth stayed in this country house in 1808, and in a letter relates events that were incorporated in 'Ormond', namely that Corry after building the house, blasted the rock to enlarge the basement and subsequently lifted the roof structure to heighten it. This Corry should not be confused with the author John Corry§. SOURCE F.V. Barry (ed.), *Maria Edgeworth: Chosen letters* (Boston, [1931]), pp 153–5; J. Burke, *A history of the Commoners* (London, 1838), iv, p. 566; Butler, pp 126, 250n.2; Colvin, xxxvi, passim; J.C. Curwen, *Observations on the state of Ireland* (London, 1818), i, pp 279–83, 309; HIP, vi, p. 205; Personal communication, Chris R. Johnson, Nov. 2003; RL.

R282 *Emeline: A moral tale* (by 'An Irish Lady'; dedicated to Lady Arabella Denny).

Dublin: S. Colbert?, [1781 or earlier]. SOURCE Adv. in *The triumph of prudence over passion* (Dublin, 1781).

+ London: W. Lane, 1783 (by 'A Lady'; as *The fairy ring, or Emeline, a moral tale*). SOURCE Raven 2, 1783:2; ESTC n047307. LOCATION ICN.

COMMENTARY No copy of the Dublin edn located. An early Irish book for children. An advertisement for it in the Dublin edn of *The triumph of prudence over passion* (1781) states that 'This tale is written in a pleasing manner, and displays much merit and literary talents, distinguished by many just and pertinent remarks'. The *Critical Review* (London) mentioned that 'The Fairy, in this little tale, performs her office with wonderful dexterity. She is always ready to support the heroine, and cheerfully engages the cause of virtue and religion. Besides, we find excellent lessons for princes and ministers; but unfortunately in a place where they will do little service, as they probably will be never read'. The story shows the eventual rewards of fortitude in the face of adventures, dangers, and distresses. Emeline, an orphan princess, lives in obscurity. She is visited by a beautiful fairy who gives her a magic key. She escapes and is restored to the throne. However, the restoration is dependent on her acceptance by the senate, representing the people. There are laws against animal cruelty and a requirement for all boys to be trained in the defence of their country so that the inhabitants can enjoy liberty and happiness [RL; Raven 2; CM; Personal communication, S. Kilfeather, 2000].

R283 *The triumph of prudence over passion: or, the history of Miss Mortimer and Miss Fitzgerald* (by the authoress of 'Emeline').

+ Dublin: For the author by S. Colbert, 1731 [*sic*, error for 1781], 2 vols. SOURCE Field Day, i, pp 751–8; Hardy, 180; Raven 2, 1781:14; ESTC t135343. LOCATION Dt, L.

London: W. Lane, 1783, 2 vols. (as *The reconciliation; or, the history of Miss Mortimer and Miss FitzGerald. In a series of letters. An Hibernian novel* (by 'An Irish Lady'). SOURCE Black, 798; Falkner Greirson supplemental list No. 1/111; Forster 2, 3704; Raven 2, 1781:14; Blakey, p. 135. LOCATION Univ. of Bristol.

COMMENTARY Rev. in the *Critical Review*, which criticized it on the grounds that it did not have a reason to be called a Hibernian novel. It was advertised by James Magee in Belfast around 1782, but no Belfast imprint has been located. The London edn consists of a reissue of the Dublin edn with new title pages. An epistolary novel set in Ireland and France, with the latter of subsidiary interest. In Ireland there are two settings: Dublin and Castle Skeffington, a landed estate possibly near the Shannon. The narrative is told through letters between Louisa Mortimer (in Dublin) and Eliza Fitzgerald (in the country). Eliza hesitates before marrying Charles Skeffington, but Louisa refuses to marry her admirer, Harry Maunsell. Eliza does marry, but Louisa retains her independence. The theme of women's subjugation to men is echoed in the story's account of Ireland's subjugation to England. Women's intellectual equality with men and their ability to be patriots is emphasized. The novel adopts a pro-Irish stance, at one point describing Irish-nationalist Volunteers as 'staunch patriots' [Adams, p. 28; *Critical Review* (55 [1783], p. 74); Kilfeather, pp 322–77; Ross, *Irish University Review*, 10(2), (1980), pp 233–4; Chronology, p. 54; Rauchbauer, pp 19–20; Raven 2].

RYAN, Edmund. Co-author. See **O'RYAN, Julia.**

RYAN, William Patrick (also known as **W.P. Ryan, William Patrick O'Ryan**, O'Ryan and Liam P. Ó Riain), pseud. **'Kevin Kennedy'**, b. Templemore (Co. Tipperary) 1867, d. London 1942. Journalist, novelist, poet and social and literary critic, WPR worked in London but returned to Ireland in 1905 or 1906 to edit the *Irish Peasant* and its successor, the *Peasant*, which later became the *Irish Nation* (all Dublin). He was editor of *An tÉireannach* (Dublin) for the Gaelic League. He returned to London in 1910 or 1911 where he was involved in journalism for the rest of his life. Aside from fiction, he published drama, essays, poetry and philosophy in English and Irish and wrote for such publications as the *Irish Emerald*, the *Nation*, the *Irish People* and the *Weekly News* (all Dublin). In London he was involved in the Southwark Irish Literary Club and the Irish Literary Society. He was the first to chronicle the history of various Irish literary societies founded from the 1880s onwards in England and Ireland, which he published in *The Irish literary revival* (London, 1894). He also published a series of essays, *Literary London* (London, 1898). Critical of the influence of the clergy in Ireland, he wrote *The Pope's green island* (London, 1912). He also wrote *The Irish labour movement* (London, 1919), and many other works. Some of his letters are among the Downey Papers (NLI, MS 10,051). SOURCE Boylan, p. 348; Brown, p. 249; Hogan 2, pp 1077–8; Irish pseudonyms; OCIL, pp 504–5; O'Donoghue, p. 411; E. Reilly, p. 250; RIA/DIB; RL.

R284   *The heart of Tipperary. A romance of the Land League* (by W.P. Ryan; introd. by William O'Brien§, MP).
    + London: Ward & Downey, 1893. SOURCE Brown, 1463; Hogan 2, p. 1078. LOCATION D, DPL, L, NUC.
COMMENTARY A story about the Land League in Co. Tipperary, written from a nationalist point of view. Cultural renewal is advocated as the key to a new Ireland [Brown; Murphy, p. 74].

R285   *Starlight through the roof* (by 'Kevin Kennedy').
    London: Downey & Co., 1895. SOURCE Brown, 1464; Hogan 2, p. 1078 (London, 1895 edn as *Starlight through the thatch*, but no such title located). LOCATION L, NUC.
COMMENTARY Set in an inland village of Munster where Utopian reforms are introduced by a returned emigrant and are opposed by land agents and a landlord's priest. The reformer is arrested on a false charge of murder. He is rescued from prison. Written from a nationalist point of view [Brown].

R286   *The plough and the cross; a story of new Ireland* (by William Patrick O'Ryan).
    Point Loma (CA): Aryan Theosophical Press, 1910. SOURCE Hogan 2, p. 1078. LOCATION L.
COMMENTARY Largely autobiographical, this is a novel with a hero named Fergus O'Hagan who experiences the full contrast between his own hopes for socialism and liberal democracy and the petty, bourgeois nationalism he sees around him [OCIL, p. 504].

R287   *Daisy Darley; or, the fairy gold of Fleet Street* (by W.P. Ryan).
    London, Toronto: J.M. Dent & Sons, 1913. SOURCE Hogan 2, p. 1078. LOCATION L.

RYVES, Elizabeth (also Eliza), b. Ireland *c*.1750, d. London 1797. Poet, journalist, translator and writer of historical fiction, ER was the daughter of an Irish officer and descended from an old Irish family, perhaps that of Sir William Ryves (d. 1648), justice of the king's bench in Ireland. She was cheated out of her inheritance by a lawsuit and was forced to generate an income for herself, which she did by writing. Possibly she belonged to the Ryves family seated at Ryves Castle (also known as Castlejane, Co. Limerick, since demolished), but according to Blain she was not related to Mrs Frances Catherine Ryves of Ryves Castle, who published in verse, *Cumbrian legends* (London, 1812). ER moved to London, where she earned her living as a journalist and by translating works from French. Aside from a single novel, she wrote political articles for newspapers, plays, and her *Poems on several occasions* (London, 1771) included a comic opera, 'The prude'. A Miss Ryves, perhaps the same person, was a subscriber to Samuel White's *Poems on several subjects* (Dublin, 1790). ER died in poverty in London. SOURCE Allibone ii, p. 1908; Blain, p. 936; Brady, p. 216; Carpenter, p. 377; DNB; H. Farrar (ed.), *Irish marriages* (London, 1897), ii, p. 485; Hogan 2, p. 1078; Kilfeather, p.

331; *Monthly Magazine*, 4 (1797), p. 213; OCIL, p. 505; ODNB; O'Donoghue, p. 412; O'Toole, p. 269 [Francis [*sic*] Ryves]; Vanishing country houses, p. 104.

R288   *The hermit of Snowden: or memoirs of Albert and Lavinia. Taken from a faithful copy of the original manuscript, which was found in the hermitage by the late Rev. Dr. L— and Mr.— in the year 17§* [anon.].

+ London: Printed [for the author?] at the Logographic Press under the directions of The Literary Society, 1789. SOURCE Raven 2, 1789:67; Gecker, 925 (1793 edn); Forster 2, 3910; ESTC t120591. LOCATION L, CSmH.

Dublin: Printed by H. Colbert, 1790. SOURCE Gecker, 924; Raven 2, 1789:67; ESTC t108168. LOCATION L, PU, NUC.

COMMENTARY Historical fiction, partly autobiographical and political, this novel purports to be copied from an old manuscript. It tells the story of Lavinia, an author as unsuccessful as ER herself. Set in Wales, Devonshire and London, it opens in a cave inhabited for thirty years by a hermit where a traveller discovers 'a highly finished portrait of a very beautiful woman, indisputably not a Madonna'. The long introd. contains a poem. Albert accepts a post as secretary to the Irish lord lieutenant, but resigns in disgust when he realizes that his allotted task is to bribe members of the Irish parliament to vote in favour of a proposed union between Ireland and England [RL; Kilfeather, p. 331; ODNB; Rafroidi, i, p. 63].

RYVES, Margareta. See **LOUDON, Margracia**.

S

'S., E.A.', fl. 1854. Pseudonym of a religious fiction writer.

S1 *The talk of the road: showing how Irish people talk about Irish doings, when they get a quiet place at the back of a ditch or under a hedge* (preface in later edns signed 'E.A.S.').

+ Dublin: William Curry & Co., 1854, 2 parts. SOURCE Bradshaw, 3548. LOCATION L, C, InND Loeber coll. (part 1 only; also Dublin, 1910 edn).

+ London: S.W. Partridge & Co.; Dublin: Hodges, Foster & Co.; Edinburgh: George McGibbon, 1876, 3rd edn (ill. J. Bolton). LOCATION Dt, InND Loeber coll.

COMMENTARY An 8th edn appeared in Dublin in 1910. Reprinted from the *Catholic Layman* (Dublin). A story of religious conversion from catholicism to protestantism written in didactic form; two peasants converse with each other about religious matters and find answers in the Bible. A priest is portrayed as an ignorant bully who does not wish to answer his parishioners' questions, whereas the Protestant ministers are described as helpful but not exerting pressure to convert [ML; RL].

'S., J.', fl. 1690s. Pseudonym of a fictionalizing autobiographer.

S2 *The Irish rogue; or, the comical history of Teague O'Divelley, from his birth to the present year, 1690* (preface by 'J.S.').

+ London: G. Conyers, [1690]. SOURCE Esdaile, p. 250; ESTC r33613. LOCATION L.

COMMENTARY The purported autobiography of an Irishman whose father was hanged and whose mother became a fortune-teller, and thief. The son also becomes a robber and adventurer [ML; RL].

'S., J. OF DALE', fl. 1884. Co-author. See O'REILLY, John Boyle.

'S., J.B.', pseud. See M'GOVERN, Revd J.B.

'S., L.J.', pseud. See 'TRAVERS, F.'

'S., M.', pseud. See SMEDLEY, Menella Bute.

'S., R.'. Possible editor. See FINNY, Revd Thomas Henry Cotter.

SADLIER, Anna Theresa (1854–1932). Co-author and daughter of Mrs J. Sadlier. See SADLIER, Mrs J.

SADLIER, Mrs J. (née Mary Anne Madden; not Sadleir as in OCIL and O'Donoghue; known as Mrs M.A. Sadlier), b. Cootehill (Co. Cavan) 1820, d. Montreal (Canada) 1903. Catholic novelist, dramatist, editor, publisher and translator, Mrs JS was the daughter of Francis Madden, a merchant, and was related to Thomas D'Arcy McGee§. At a young age she had already contributed to literary journals such as *La Belle Assemblée* (London). In 1844, after the death of her father, she emigrated to Canada. There her contributions to periodicals (e.g., the *Literary Garland*, Montreal) helped to support the family. She married James Sadlier in the parish of St Marthe in Montreal in 1846. He was an Irish Catholic who had arrived in New York from Tipperary and entered the publishing and bookselling trade with his brother Denis in 1836. Their firm grew to be the principal publisher of Bibles and school texts for the North American Catholic population. The Sadliers first lived in Montreal, but moved to New York in 1860. Mrs JS was visited by the Irish Revd M.B. Buckley in 1870, who described her as 'a nice, good lady, kind and gentle' (Buckley, pp 23, 247). She wrote primarily for immigrant Roman Catholic readers. She published 26 works of fiction, mostly historical novels and stories about the struggles of Catholics in Ireland, but also novels and stories about the immigration experience of the Irish in the US. In addition to her fiction, she wrote plays, many for girls, including *Julia; or, the golden thimble* (New York, 1861), *The Talisman* (New York, 1863) and *Secret* (New York, 1865). In 1869 she published the poems of Thomas D'Arcy McGee§, for which she wrote an introd. and biographical sketch. She also published translations from French novels. She edited a New York Catholic journal, the *Tablet*, the successor to McGee's magazine the *American Celt*, and religious works such as *A new catechism of sacred history* (New York, 1866) and *Purgatory* (New York, 1886). She contributed to the Boston *Pilot*, the New York *Freeman's Journal*, the Montreal *True Witness*, and other papers. She must have greatly benefited from the fact that her husband widely advertised her work through his publishing house. She returned to Montreal in 1885 after her husband and his brother had died, and with the help of her daughter Anna Theresa Sadlier, also a novelist and editor, she continued to run the publishing company for another ten years. She lost control of it and her copyrights to her nephew, William Sadlier, in 1895. Mrs JS had seven children, including one foster child. Unlike most American-Irish authors, her work was much reprinted in Dublin and she had a wide readership on both sides of the Atlantic. She was actively philanthropic until her financial circumstances were reduced after the loss of the publishing company, when friends created a testimonial fund in her aid. Her literary contribution and service to the Catholic church were recognized when she received the Lætare Medal from the University of Notre Dame (IN) in 1895. Letters by Thomas D'Arcy McGee§ to her are among the Sadlier Papers, National Archives of Canada. SOURCE Allibone, ii, p. 1199 [under Madden], p. 1911 [under Sadlier]; Allibone Suppl., ii, p. 1309; Blain, p. 939; Boylan, p. 349; Brown, p. 270; M.B. Buckley, *Diary of a tour in America* (Dublin, 1889), pp 23, 247; CEWW; Colman, pp 152–3 [under Madden]; DAB; DCB; DLB, ic; e-mail from Rosemary O'Flaherty to Patricia Smyth, 9 Oct. 2001 (details of Mrs JS's marriage); Field Day, v, pp 924, 928; Hogan 2, p. 1079; Irish pseudonyms; M. Lacombe, 'Frying pans and deadlier weapons: the immigrant novels of Mary Anne Sadlier' in *Essays on Canadian Writing*, 29, Summer 1984; pp 96–116; MacDonald, pp 279, 314; [J. O'Brien], *Irish Celts* (Detroit, 1884), n.p.; J.O'K. Murray, *The prose and poetry of Ireland* (New York), 1877), pp 690–708; OCIL, p. 506; O'Donoghue, p. 413; RL; Sutherland, p. 549; Watters, pp 383–4.

S3   *Tales of the olden times, a collection of European traditions* [anon.].
     Montreal: Lovell & Gibson, 1845. SOURCE MacDonald, p. 331; DLB, ic.
COMMENTARY No copy located. Ascribed by MacDonald to M.A. Madden, the DLB states that this volume was sold by subscription when the author was experiencing financial difficulties and is a farewell to Ireland and youth. This was reprinted in a series of pamphlets in Montreal in 1847 [MacDonald, pp 314, 331; RL].

S4   *Willy Burke; or, the Irish orphan in America* (by Mrs J. Sadlier; dedicated to the young sons of 'my native land').
     Boston: Patrick Donahoe, 1850. SOURCE Allibone, ii, p. 1199 [under Madden]; Fanning, pp 118, 390. LOCATION D (n.d. edn), NUC, InND Loeber coll. (1851 edn).
     Dublin: James Duffy, [c.1850] (Duffy's Cottage Library). SOURCE Brown, 1467 (mistakenly states 2 vols.). LOCATION DPL, InND Loeber coll. ([c.1889–90] edn).
COMMENTARY A story of courage and survival with religious underpinnings, written in response to a contest initiated by Orestes Browne, published in his *Quarterly Review*, challenging some-

one to 'write a tale entitled the Orphan of New York or the Orphan of Boston, the Irish Orphan or the Catholic Orphan, which would be adapted to the condition of the poor orphan *boys* among ourselves', (see also under Revd John T. Rodden§). Mrs JS's book won the subsequent contest. In the dedication from Montreal, Nov. 1850, the author notes that the book had been expressly written for the young sons of 'my native land', showing that they did not have to become Protestant to obtain wealth and honour. An Irish farmer named Andy Burke sets out for America with his family. He dies on the voyage. His wife and son, Billy, arrive in New York. Billy's mother dies. Billy does many charitable acts as he struggles for independence in New York even as he is attacked because of his Catholic religion. He receives $5,000 on the death of a Mr Weiniar, who he discovers lying in an alleyway after being beaten up [RL; Fanning, p. 118; CM].

S5   *The red hand of Ulster; or, the fortunes of Hugh O'Neill* (by Mrs J. Sadlier).
+ Boston: Patrick Donahoe, 1850. SOURCE Brown 2, 1405; Hogan 2, p. 1079; Fanning, p. 390. LOCATION DCU, InND Loeber coll. COMMENTARY *Boston edn* Two different binding types: (a) one slightly larger than the other with blind embossed central decoration; (b) the smaller with corner decorations only [RL].
Boston: P. Donahoe, 1859 (new edn). SOURCE Rev. in Boston *Pilot* (5 Feb. 1859, p. 7).

COMMENTARY London edn not located. Historical fiction telling the story of Hugh O'Neill, earl of Tyrone, from the time he settled in Ireland until his death in Rome. A large part of the story concerns how he formed alliances with all the northern chiefs while trying to allay the suspicions of Sir Henry Bagnal, the lord deputy, and Queen Elizabeth. His marriage with Arabella Bagnal is recounted and reports are given of the various battles he waged against the English [ML].

S6   *The hermit of the rock of Cashel. A tale of landlordism in Tipperary* (by Mrs J. Sadlier).
Glasgow, London: Cameron & Ferguson, 1850. SOURCE Blessing, p. 156; OCLC (n.d. edn). LOCATION D (n.d. edn). COMMENTARY *Glasgow, 1850 edn*. No copy other than the n.d. edn located [RL].
+ Dublin: M.H. Gill, 1863 (as *The hermit of the rock. A tale of Cashel*). SOURCE Brown, 1473. LOCATION DPL (n.d. edn). LOCATION InND Loeber coll.
New York, Boston, Montreal: D. & J. Sadlier & Co., 1863 (as *The hermit of the rock. A tale of Cashel*). SOURCE Alston, p. 378; Fanning, 390; Hogan 2, p. 1079. LOCATION L.
London: M.H. Gill, [1893]. LOCATION L.

COMMENTARY The story gives a picture of Irish society in the 1860s. The 'hermit' tends the graves and the monuments on the Rock of Cashel (Co. Tipperary). He is a storehouse of legends and traditions [Brown].

S7   *Alice Riordan. The blind man's daughter. A tale for the young* (by Mrs J. Sadlier).
Boston: P. Donahoe, 1851. SOURCE OCLC. LOCATION Univ. of Florida (location unclear).
Dublin: M.H. Gill & Son, 1884. SOURCE Brown 2, 1406 (mistakenly mentions 1854 edn); Hogan 2, p. 1079. LOCATION L.

COMMENTARY Religious fiction for juveniles, reviewed in the Boston *Pilot* (6 Dec. 1856, and again 4 June 1859). Set in the 1840s, it is a story of Irish immigrants in Canada. Cormac Riordan, a blind man in the west of Ireland, has a brother-in-law in Montreal who pays the passage for him and his daughter to emigrate to Canada. They find that the brother-in-law has married a Protestant and given up the faith. Cormac refuses to live in his public house. Instead he enters an almshouse till his daughter is able to support him. The rest of the story deals with her fortunes, her good work at the dressmakers, her success and happy marriage [Brown 2].

S8   *New lights; or, life in Galway. A tale* (by Mrs J. Sadlier; dedicated to the people of
Ireland).
+ New York, Boston, Montreal: D. & J. Sadlier & Co., 1853 (ill. T. Horton). SOURCE
Brown, 1468 ([1853] edn); Fanning, p. 390. LOCATION D, Dt ([c.1885] edn), InND
Loeber coll. (also combined 1853/1859 edn).
COMMENTARY The InND copy of the New York 1859 edn is bound in brown cloth, has two
title pages, one dated 1853, the other 1859. An advertisement in this edn lists this title under
Sadlier's Fireside Library, No. 5. The book stayed in print until at least 1903. Advertised in
the 1850s with the subtitle 'A tale of the new Reformation' (in *New lights*, New York, 1853).
Religious fiction set in Co. Galway around 1850 in the aftermath of the Famine, the story attacks
the evils of Protestant proselytism or 'souperism', from which spring all the bad events in the
book. The two Protestants in the story, who are sympathetic figures, convert to catholicism.
The 'souperism' does not succeed in permanently converting Catholics to protestantism. The
book has an addendum, which serves as a testimonial to the many virtues of the Irish [ML; RL].
S9   *The Blakes and Flanagans. A tale, illustrative of Irish life in the United States*
(by Mrs J. Sadlier; dedicated to the author's mother and father [Francis Madden]).
New York, Boston: D. & J. Sadlier & Co., 1855. SOURCE OCLC. LOCATION DCL.
New York, Montreal: P.J. Kenedy, 1855. SOURCE Fanning, p. 390; OCLC. LOCATION
Dt (1896 edn), Pepperdine Univ. (CA).
+ Dublin: James Duffy & Sons, [1855]. SOURCE Brown, 1469; DLB, ic. LOCATION D,
DPL.
COMMENTARY The 16th printing (1,000 per printing) appeared in New York in 1879, and it
was still in print in New York in 1896. Religious fiction in which the lives of the Blakes and
the Flanagans, Irish immigrants who have settled in New York City, are contrasted. Both families are comfortably off. The Flanagans send their children to parochial schools to protect
them from being influenced by Protestants, while the Blakes send their children to city schools
run by Protestants. The beneficial effects of Roman Catholic education are shown in that the
Flanagan children honour their parents and their church, and have a great love for Ireland,
marry Roman Catholics, and lead virtuous lives. In contrast, the Blake children become hyp-
ocrites, look down upon their parents and their Irish heritage, disregard their church and their
religion, and lead unhappy lives [ML].
S10   *A collection of Irish tales* (by Mrs J. Sadlier).
New York, Boston, Montreal: D. & J. Sadlier & Co., [1859 or later], 3 vols. (Sadlier's
Fireside Library, Nos. 9–11). SOURCE Adv. in Mrs J. Sadlier, *New lights* (New York,
1859).
COMMENTARY Announced as in press in 1859, but no copy located. Some of the tales appeared
first in the Boston *Pilot* and others were published in collected form in *Tales of the olden time*
(Montreal, 1845). The stories in *A collection of Irish tales* were revsd and corrected by the
author. Contents, among others: 'Father Sheehy', 'The daughter of Tyrconnell', 'Fate of the
Sheares', 'Norman Steel, or the priest hunter', 'The later days of the O'Reillys', 'O'Grady,
or, the expatriated', 'Granu Wail, a tale of the Desmonds', etc. [Adv. in Mrs J. Sadlier, *New
lights* (New York, 1859); RL].
S11   *The Confederate chieftains. A tale of the Irish rebellion of 1641* (by Mrs J. Sadlier).
+ New York, Boston, Montreal: D. & J. Sadlier & Co., 1860, 2 vols. in 1 (ill.). SOURCE
Fanning, p. 390. LOCATION D (1864 edn), DPL (n.d. edn), Dt, InND Loeber coll.
+ London, Glasgow: Cameron & Ferguson, [c.1860]. SOURCE Allibone, ii, p. 1911
(1860 edn); COPAC. LOCATION D (n.d. edn), Dt (n.d. edn), DPL (n.d. edn), E
([c.1860] edn), InND Loeber coll. ([c.1862]).
COMMENTARY The London edn has two binding types: (a) decorative, and (b) plain. Includes

appendix of narrative of the war by 'an officer of the Parliamentary army of England'. Brown mentions a Dublin, M.H. Gill, 1859 edn, but this probably is in error, and no such publication has been located. Historical fiction about O'Neill during the Confederacy, written from a Catholic point of view. The London *c.*1862 edn. is dated by the author mentioning Thomas Moore's§ *History of Ireland*, which did not appear until that year. The volume was reissued in 24 serial parts by Cameron and Ferguson in London and Glasgow (*c.*1880), priced at 1*p.* per part [RL; Brown, 1470; Rowan cat. 50/A135].

S12   *Elinor Preston; or, scenes at home or abroad* (by Mrs J. Sadlier; dedicated to 'My friends in Canada').
    New York, Boston, Montreal: D. & J. Sadlier & Co., [*c.*1861]. SOURCE Blessing, p. 156; Hogan 2, p. 1079. LOCATION SUNY at Buffalo (NY), InND Loeber coll. (1889 edn).
COMMENTARY A somewhat-autobiographical novel whose heroine, Elinor Preston, is the daughter of a member of the Irish Bar. They live in reasonably comfortable circumstances. However, her parents and some of her siblings die and she emigrates to Canada with one of her brothers, who joins the military. For a while she lives in the house of a Protestant lady, but eventually she becomes a teacher in a Catholic school in a small village. When she – the last of her siblings – dies, she is sorely missed by the villagers [ML].

S13   *Bessy Conway; or, the Irish girl in America* (by Mrs J. Sadlier).
    New York, Boston, Montreal: D. & J. Sadlier & Co., 1861. SOURCE Fanning, p. 390; RLIN. LOCATION D (1879 edn), NN (1877 edn), InND Loeber coll. (1879 edn), Boston College.
    New York: P.J. Kenedy, [1861]. SOURCE Brown, 1471; OCIL, p. 506; OCLC. LOCATION Vassar College (1863 edn, Ploughkeepsie, NY).
COMMENTARY No copy of New York, Kenedy, 1861 edn located. An idealistic story about the lives of Irish servant girls in the New World. Bessy, daughter of a Catholic farmer in Co. Tipperary, emigrates to America. On board ship she finds that the son of her father's Protestant landlord has followed her, out of love. In the New World, the wild young man changes, becomes a Catholic and marries Bessy. They make their fortune in New York. The story ends with Bessy coming home to Ireland just in time to stop the eviction of her father during a famine [Brown; ML.; OCIL].

S14   *Old and new; or, taste versus fashion* (by Mrs J. Sadlier).
    New York, Boston, Montreal: D. & J. Sadlier & Co., 1862. SOURCE Fanning, p. 390; Hogan 2, p. 1079. LOCATION DCU (1863 edn, and [1862] edn).
COMMENTARY No copy of the first New York, 1862 edn located. The story concerns the dangers of making it into the upper classes [Exiles, p. 109; RL].

S15   *The fate of father Sheehy. A tale of Tipperary eighty years ago* (by Mrs J. Sadlier).
    + New York, Boston, Montreal: D. & J. Sadlier & Co., 1863 (Catholic Youth's Library, first series; ill. A. Williams). SOURCE Adv. in T.N. Burke, *Ireland's case stated* (New York), 1873; Fanning, p. 390. LOCATION D, DCU.
    + Dublin, London: James Duffy & Sons, 1864 (new edn with historical appendix by R.R. Madden§, as *The fate of Father Sheehy. A tale of Tipperary in the olden time*). LOCATION Dt (1864 edn), InND Loeber coll.
COMMENTARY Brown and Sutherland mention a Dublin [1845] edn, but this has not been located. Historical fiction set in the neighbourhood of Clonmel in Co. Tipperary in the second half of the eighteenth century, at the time of Whiteboy unrest. It is based on the story of a priest, Fr Nicholas Sheehy (d. 1766), who was falsely accused of having been an accessory to the murder of a man who was a witness against him. The evidence against the priest was fabricated; the witness had emigrated. Fr Sheehy was condemned to be hanged, drawn

and quartered, together with some other innocent people. The Dublin 1864 edn has an appendix by Dr R.R. Madden§, giving the details of the trial [ML; Hartman, 903; Brown, 1466; Sutherland, p. 548].

S16 *The daughter of Tyrconnell. A tale of the reign of James the First* (by Mrs J. Sadlier).
+ New York, Boston, Montreal: D. & J. Sadlier & Co., 1863 (Catholic Youth's Library, first series; see Plate 57). SOURCE Alston, p. 378; Fanning, p. 390; Hogan 2, p. 1079; OCLC. LOCATION L (destroyed), Mount St Mary's College; PC.
+ Dublin, London: James Duffy & Sons, [1864 or later]. SOURCE Brown, 1474 (Dublin, Duffy, 1863 edn, which has not been located). LOCATION InND Loeber coll.
COMMENTARY Historical fiction founded on a tradition recorded in MacGeoghegan's *History of Ireland* (Paris, 1758–62, 3 vols.) that describes the life of Mary O'Donnell, daughter of the exile earl of Tyrconnell. James I adopts her and wishes her to marry a Protestant and give up the Catholic faith. Although she loves this person, her faith cannot allow her to marry him. She dresses as a man and escapes to the Continent where she meets with her brother, who is at the court of Isabella, queen of Spain. Finally, she enters a convent [ML; Brown].

S17 *Confessions of an apostate* (by Mrs J. Sadlier).
+ New York, Boston, Montreal: D. & J. Sadlier & Co., 1864 (ill. Pease). SOURCE Fanning, p. 390 (with title *Confessions of an apostate; or, leaves from a troubled life*); 1864; Hogan 2, p. 1079; OCIL, p. 506 (mistakenly mentions the title as *Agnostic*). LOCATION D (1887 edn), L (destroyed), DCL, InND Loeber coll.
Dublin: James Duffy & Co. [1886 or earlier] (as *Simon Kerrigan; or, confessions of an apostate*). SOURCE Adv. in W. Carleton, *Redmond Count O'Hanlon* (Dublin, 1886); Brown, 1475.
+ New York: Arno Press, 1978 (The American Catholic Tradition [series]). LOCATION DCL.
COMMENTARY No copy of Dublin edn located. Religious fiction set partly near Glendalough (Co. Wicklow) and partly in Boston and New Haven (CT). A poor Catholic boy leaves his family to emigrate to the New World and better his life. In Boston he finds that the Irish are ridiculed, and slowly he distances himself from his background and his religion. He changes his name from Kerrigan to Kerr, marries a Protestant girl, and joins a Protestant congregation. Although he prospers financially, his life is unhappy because of his denial of his past and his religion. His wife and all but one of his children die. He does not get along with his surviving son who has found out about his father's background and who calls him a hypocrite and an apostate. He returns to the fold of the Catholic church, gives his son his business, and leaves town. At the end of his life he returns to Co. Wicklow, where nobody knows him anymore, to pray at the grave of his parents [ML].

S18 *Con O'Regan; or, emigrant life in the New World* (by Mrs J. Sadlier).
New York, Boston, Montreal: D. & J. Sadlier & Co., 1864. SOURCE Fanning, p. 390; Hogan 2, p. 1079; Slocum, ii, 3899. LOCATION L.
New York: P.J. Kenedy, 1864. SOURCE Brown, 1476; OCLC. LOCATION Boston College.
COMMENTARY Set in New England in the 1840s, it depicts the hardships of Irish emigrants who suffer hostility but go on to settle happily on an Iowa farm where there is no prejudice [Brown; Slocum].

S19 *The old house by the Boyne; or, recollections of an Irish borough* (by Mrs J. Sadlier).
New York, Boston, Montreal: D. & J. Sadlier & Co., [c.1865]. SOURCE Fanning, p. 390; Hogan 2, p. 1079; RLIN. LOCATION NN.
Dublin: M.H. Gill & Son, [1865] (as *The old house by the Boyne*). SOURCE Brown, 1477; Colman, p. 153. LOCATION D (n.d. edn), Dt ([c.1910] edn), DPL (n.d. edn), L (1888 edn), InND Loeber coll. (1904 edn).

COMMENTARY Set in and near Drogheda (Co. Louth). A love story is interwoven with legendary lore and descriptions of many old, historic spots [Brown; RL].

S20   *Aunt Honor's keepsake. A chapter from life* (by Mrs J. Sadlier; dedicated to Revd Wm. Quinn, Pastor of St Peter's Church, New York, and Dr L. Silliman Ives, President of the Society for the Protection of Destitute Catholic Children in the City of New York).
+ New York, Boston, Montreal: D. & J. Sadlier & Co., 1866. SOURCE Fanning, p. 389; Hogan 2, p. 1079. LOCATION D.
COMMENTARY Concerns the plight of Irish children in public orphanages [Exiles, p. 109].

S21   *The heiress of Kilorgan; or, evenings with the old Geraldines* (by Mrs J. Sadlier).
+ New York, Boston, Montreal: D. & J. Sadlier & Co., 1867. SOURCE Brown, 1478 (New York, Kenedy, 1867 edn, which has not been located); Fanning, p. 390; Hogan 2, p. 1079. LOCATION D, L (n.d. edn), InND Loeber coll. ([1867] edn).
COMMENTARY Partly historical fiction. Mr Howard, an Englishman, arrives at the country house of the FitzGeralds near the Maigue River (Co. Limerick). He asks for shelter for the night, and is welcomed by the three inhabitants of the house: Margaret, a young woman who is the owner, and her blind aunt and invalid uncle. The estate is in the hands of the encumbered estates court. While Mr Howard is staying with them, they find out that the estate has been sold to an Englishman of the same name, who Mr Howard claims is his cousin. Mr Howard falls in love with Margaret. In the end he marries her and reveals that he is the purchaser of the estate. The story forms the backdrop of tales told each evening by the uncle about the Geraldines from the Norman invasion, through the sixteenth and seventeenth centuries, and ending with Lord Edward Fitzgerald at the close of the eighteenth century. It has an appendix with several historical documents [ML].

S22   *MacCarthy More; or, the fortunes of an Irish chief in the reign of Queen Elizabeth* (by Mrs J. Sadlier).
+ New York, Boston, Montreal: D. & J. Sadlier & Co., 1868. SOURCE Fanning, p. 390; Hogan 2, p. 1079. LOCATION L, DCU, InND Loeber coll.
+ New York: P.J. Kenedy, 1868. SOURCE Brown, 1479. LOCATION InND Loeber coll.
COMMENTARY Historical fiction set in the late-sixteenth century describing the life and character of Florence MacCarthy More, based on D. MacCarthy's *Life and letters of Florence MacCarthy Reagh* (London, 1867). The novel relates the struggles of the great Irish families to preserve faith and property in the reign of Queen Elizabeth. The chief events are the battles of the Pass of Plumes, Curlew Mountains, and Bealanathabuidhe. The scene varies between west Cork and the council chamber of Queen Elizabeth in the Tower of London [Brown].

S23   *The whisperer* (by Mrs J. Sadlier; dedicated to Bonny, alias Edward).
+ London, Edinburgh: William & Robert Chambers, 1869 (ill. G. Millar). LOCATION L.
COMMENTARY Fiction for children [ML].

S24   *Maureen Dhu, the admiral's daughter. A tale of the Claddagh of Galway* (by Mrs J. Sadlier).
New York, Boston, Montreal: D. & J. Sadlier & Co., 1870. SOURCE Brown, 1480 (New York, 1869 edn, which has not been located); Fanning, p. 390; Sutherland, p. 549. LOCATION D (n.d. edn), L, InND Loeber coll. (1873 edn).
COMMENTARY A tale of the Claddagh (Co. Galway) in which the manners and ways of its inhabitants are described. The beautiful daughter of the chief fisherman is wooed by a wealthy young merchant from Galway. According to an inscription by Mrs Sadlier in the InND Loeber coll. copy, the book 'was written from vivid descriptions of the place and the people given her

by a Dominican father, since dead, who had spent several years at St Mary's on the Hill, the Dominican monastery [in the city of Galway] introduced in the story' [ML; Brown].

S25   *Stories of the promises and other tales* (by Mrs M.A. Sadlier and her daughters [*sic*, Anna Theresa Sadlier]).

+ Montreal, Toronto: D. & J. Sadlier, [1895?]. SOURCE Watters, p. 384. LOCATION L. COMMENTARY First published in the *Canadian Messenger* (Montreal). Stories are by Mrs JS unless indicated otherwise. Contents: 'Little Harry's legacy', 'A band of soldiers', 'Sam Allen's little joke', 'That picture of the Sacred Heart' (Anna T. Sadlier), 'A grandfather's story', 'What came of it', 'A separate school-boy' (Anna T. Sadlier), 'How peace came to the Doyles', 'Two new years' (Anna T. Sadlier), 'Through darkness light', 'The criminal' (Anna T. Sadlier), 'Our Lady's May-day gift', 'A bunch of June roses' (Anna T. Sadlier), 'A tryst in the Sacred Heart', 'The widow's only son' (Anna T. Sadlier), 'The intention-box' [author not indicated], 'Father Sheehan's parish', 'St. Joseph's client' (Anna T. Sadlier), 'The children's prayer' (Anna T. Sadlier), 'How it came to pass', '"The worthless lad"' (Anna T. Sadlier), 'The story of Mary Marson' (Anna T. Sadlier), 'The message of the Christmas bells' (Anna T. Sadlier), 'Aunt Isabel's new year's gift', 'A month of Mary idyl', 'The story of two brothers', 'St. Joseph's basket' (Anna T. Sadlier) [ML].

S26   *The minister's wife and other stories* (by Mrs J. Sadlier).

+ New York: C. Wildermann, 1898 (The Catholic Library). SOURCE Hogan 2, p. 1079. LOCATION DCL.

S27   *O'Bryne; or, the expatriated* (by Mrs J. Sadlier).

+ New York: C. Wildermann, 1898. SOURCE Watters, p. 384; OCLC. LOCATION L, DCL.

COMMENTARY 64pp [Watters].

S28   *Short stories. Series II* (by Mrs J. Sadlier).

New York: C. Wildermann, 1900, 3 vols. in 1 (The Catholic Library, vols. 32, 42, 52). SOURCE Watters, p. 384. LOCATION DCL.

COMMENTARY Series I not located [RL].

— COLLECTED WORKS

S29   [*Mrs James Sadlier's works*].

New York, Montreal: D. & J. Sadlier, [1875 or earlier]. SOURCE Adv. in M.J. Hoffman, *The orphan sisters* (New York, 1875). COMMENTARY *New York, Sadlier edn* Possible collected works. Adv. mentions 'Sadleir, Mrs. J., Original works of', and lists 26 works, each sold at different prices. The advertisement also mentions 'Sadleir's [*sic*], Mrs. J., Translations from the French', and lists 34 works, each sold at different prices [Adv. in M.J. Hoffman, *The orphan sisters* (New York, 1875)].

New York: P.J. Kenedy, [1895], 14 vols. SOURCE Adv. in a broadsheet by the publisher P.J. Kenedy. COMMENTARY *Kenedy edn* Unnumbered and untitled series, bound in cloth, with shamrocks impressed in gold and ink. The boxed was priced at $7.50. The advertisement mentions that Mrs JS had been awarded the Lætare Medal from the University of Notre Dame, which took place in 1895, which is the date assigned to the collected works. The collected works do not include *Maureen Dhu*, which was first published in New York in 1870 [Broadsheet adv. by the publisher P.J. Kenedy, [1895]; RL].

— POSSIBLE SPURIOUS WORK

S30   *Alt-Irland und Amerika; Sittengemälde aus den Vereinigten Staaten* (by Mrs J. Sadlier).

Cologne: J.P. Bachem, 1866 (Sammlung Unterhaltender Schriften der Neuern Englischen Literatur), SOURCE OCLC. LOCATION InND, NN.

COMMENTARY Although published under Mrs JS's name, no English original with this type of title is known and, therefore, it may be a spurious work. However, there is a possibility that this is a German translation of one of Mrs JS's immigrant novels [RL].

SADLIER, Mrs M.A. See SADLIER, Mrs J.

SAGE, Abbey. See RICHARDSON, Mrs Abby Sage.

'SAILOR, The Old', pseud. See BARKER, Matthew Henry.

ST CLAIR, Rosalia, fl. 1810s. Novelist and poet, RStC has thirteen volumes to her credit, but very little is known about her. Blain and Garside suggest that this is a pseudonym. However, members of the St Clair family were resident in Ireland at least as late as the 1780s. RStC also translated F.G. Ducray-Dumenil's *The blind beggar* (London, 1817, 4 vols.). Her novels often contain poems. Only Ireland-related works are listed below. SOURCE Blain, p. 940; H. Farrar (ed.), *Irish marriages* (London, 1897), ii, p. 389; NCBEL 4, p. 1080; Summers 2.

S31   *The son of O'Donnel. A novel* (by Rosalia St Clair).
       + London: A.K. Newman & Co., 1819, 3 vols. SOURCE Blakey, p. 268; British Fiction; Garside, 1819:59. LOCATION Corvey 3–628–8501–0, Ireland related fiction, L.
COMMENTARY Historical fiction in which Lionel O'Donnel, the 'youngest son of an ancient family' in Queen's County (Co. Laois), enlists in the British army and fights in the American War of Independence. O'Donnel's father is a benevolent landlord, and the Protestant clergyman and Catholic priest in his village work together to educate the poor of the village. Lionel marries the daughter of an American 'rebel', and they return to Ireland, where Lionel's wife dedicates herself to encouraging industry and thrift among the peasantry [JB].

S32   *The banker's daughters of Bristol; or compliance and decision. A novel* (by Rosalia St Clair).
       + London: A.K. Newman & Co., 1824, 3 vols. SOURCE British Fiction; Garside, 1824:81. LOCATION Corvey CME 3–624–48595–9, L, ViU.
COMMENTARY No Irish content, but some Irish characters [ML].

S33   *The first and the last years of wedded life. A novel* (by Rosalia St Clair).
       + London: A.K. Newman & Co., 1827, 4 vols. SOURCE British Fiction; Garside, 1827:59; Blain, p. 940 (where mistakenly called *The first and last years of married life* and mistakenly dated 1821). LOCATION Corvey CME 3–628–48496–0, Ireland related fiction, L, ViU.
COMMENTARY Set in 1821 and reconciles Irish Protestants and Catholics and praises the US system of government [Blain].

S34   *The sailor boy; or, the admiral and his protégée. A novel* (by Rosalia St Clair).
       + London: A.K. Newman & Co., 1830, 4 vols. SOURCE Alston, p. 379; Garside 2, 1830:94. LOCATION Corvey CME 3–628–48500–2, L.
COMMENTARY One of the main characters is Frank O'Neil, whose parentage is in doubt. Eventually it is established that he is the heir to an estate in Ireland [ML].

S35   *The pauper boy; or, the ups and downs of life. A novel* (by Rosalia St Clair).
       + London: A.K. Newman, 1834, 3 vols. SOURCE Alston, p. 379; Blain, p. 940; Garside 2, 1834:66. LOCATION Corvey CME 3–628–48498–7, L.
COMMENTARY Told in the first person by a young girl and consists of the story of a boy, Tony O'Neal, who with the girl has become a resident of a workhouse at Bethnal Green in London. Tony dies of consumption and after his death, his mother drowns herself. Philip O'Gorman, the paternal uncle of Mrs. O'Neal, 'a distinguished member of the Irish bar',

wants to marry his son to Mrs O'Neal's orphan daughter, but she loses her heart to Tyrone O'Neal, 'an aspirant for legal honours'. The rest of the story continues in a series of unabated misfortunes [RL].

ST JOHN, Vane Ireton Shaftsbury, b. London? 1839, d. Peckham Rye, London 1911. Novelist, editor and periodical entrepreneur, VISStJ was the son of James Augustus St John and Eliza Caroline Hansard. He was a pioneer of boys' journals, starting and editing *Boys of England* (London) and similar periodicals. SOURCE Allibone, ii, p. 1914; NCBEL 4, p. 1859; ODNB [under Sir Spenser Buckingham St John].

S36   *Larry O'Calloran's school days: or the boys of Bally Botherum* (by Vane Ireton Shaftsbury St John).
       [location?]: [publisher?], n.d. SOURCE NCBEL 4, p. 1859.
       COMMENTARY No copy located [RL].

ST LEGER, Barry. See **ST LEGER, Francis Barry Boyle**.

ST LEGER, Francis Barry Boyle, pseud. 'Himself', b. 1799, d. 1829. Novelist and editor, FBBStL was the son of Richard St Leger, second son of the 1st Viscount Doneraile, and Anne Blakenly of Holywell (Co. Roscommon). He was educated at Rugby and obtained an appointment to the East India Company, where he worked until 1821 when he resigned and became editor of a fashionable publication called the *Album* (London, 1822–5). Later he also edited the *Brazen Head* (London). He published for private circulation *Remorse and other poems* (London, 1821). His letters to the publisher Blackwoods are in the NLS. SOURCE Allibone, ii, p. 1915 [under Barry St Leger]; A. Sullivan (ed.), *British literary magazines* (Westport, CT, 1983), pp 3–4; ODNB; O'Donoghue, p. 414; Sadleir, p. 316; Wolff, iv, p. 80.

S37   *Some account of the life of the late Gilbert Earle, Esq.* ('by Himself').
       + London: Charles Knight, 1824. SOURCE Allibone, ii, p. 1915; British Fiction; Garside, 1824:82; Sadleir, 3022; Wolff, 6088. LOCATION Corvey CME 3–628–48670–X, Dt, L, InND Loeber coll.
COMMENTARY First published the *Album* (London) in 1822. Presented as an autobiography, it recounts the romantic life of a man made wretched by falling in love with a married woman in India. Even though he marries her after the death of her husband, the illicit beginning casts a pall over the relationship. After her death, he returns to England but finds everything stale and depressing rather than comforting, which he had expected it to be [ML; Sullivan, *British literary magazines*, pp 3–4; JB].

S38   *Mr. Blount's Mss. being selections from the papers of a man of the world* [anon.].
       + London: Charles Knight, 1826, 2 vols. SOURCE Allibone, ii, p. 1914; British Fiction; Garside, 1826:67; Sadleir, 3021; Wolff, 6087. LOCATION Corvey CME 3–628–47231–8, D, L, InND Loeber coll. (1826 1 vol. edn).
COMMENTARY According to the introd., this work is the result of the author arranging selections of a diary given to him. The diary describes the romances of Mr Blount, who tours the Continent and falls in love with an Italian woman. She is forced to enter a convent but eventually Mr Blount convinces her to come to England and marry him. The boat in which she travels is wrecked in a storm and she perishes. For a number of years Blount leads a dissipated life and, when reduced to poverty, he marries a rich lady and spends time on the Continent with her. However, his constitution has been undermined by his dissipation and he dies in the south of France. The story contains a description of the storming of the Bastille at the beginning of the French Revolution [ML].

S39   *Tales of passion: Lord Lovel's daughter. The bohemian.– Second love* [anon.].

+ London: Henry Colburn, 1829, 3 vols. SOURCE Allibone ii, p. 1319; British Fiction; Garside, 1829:70; Sadleir, 3024. LOCATION Corvey CME 3-628-48872-9, Dt, L, MH, InND Loeber coll.

COMMENTARY Contents: 'Lord Lovel's daughter; a tale of the Reformation' (set in England at the time of the dissolution of the monasteries; a daughter of one of King Henry VIII's courtiers is in love with a priest who is burnt at the stake), 'The bohemian' (set in Germany in the last quarter of the seventeenth century; a German nobleman falls in love with a gipsy girl, who he takes to live with him in his castle. Eventually, he feels the need to marry and parts with the girl. She vows revenge and after a few years steals his daughter, and brings her up to be a high-class prostitute. The father finds out who his daughter is after he has been instrumental in introducing her to the king for his pleasure), 'Second love' (set in Portugal during the Peninsular War; an English soldier falls in love with a nun and helps her escape from the convent. She maintains that she has never taken religious vows and he marries her. When he joins the campaign again, she is stolen back by her father, who insists that she rejoin a convent. After much suffering she is liberated from her father's house by her husband and, though severely wounded, taken on board a ship heading for England. She recovers and they live happily on her husband's English estate), 'Second love' (set at the close of the Peninsular War, the story is based on the belief that only the first attachment can be strong, deep, and permanent. Tells of a high-born woman who elopes from a convent with an English officer) [ML; *La Belle Assemblée*, 3rd ser. 9 (Mar. 1829), pp 123-5].

S40   *Froissart, and his times* (by Barry St Leger; ed. by S.B. [Samuel Bentley]).
London: Henry Colburn & Richard Bentley, 1832, 3 vols. SOURCE Garside 2, 1832:74. LOCATION L.

COMMENTARY Published posthumously. Contents: 'Historical notice of the English power in Aquitaine', 'The battle of Poitiers', 'Historical notices of Peter the Cruel', 'The Black Prince in Spain', 'Biographical notice of Froissart', 'The court of Gaston de Foix', 'Historical notice of the companions', 'Aymergot Marcel', 'Historical notice of the border-feuds between England and Scotland', 'The battle of Otterbourne', 'Historical notice of the reign of Bajazet I', 'The siege of Nicopolis', 'Historical notice of the (second) House of Burgundy', 'The last days of Charles the Bold' [Garside].

SAFFRON, Marie de. See **DAVID, Mme Marie.**

'SAIX, Tyler de', pseud. See **STACPOOLE, Henry De Vere.**

'SAMOTH', pseud. See **O'FLANAGAN, Thomas.**

SAMPSON, William, pseud. **'A barrister',** b. Derry (Co. Derry) 1764, d. New York 1836. A barrister, nationalist, pamphleteer and memoirist, WS was the third son of Revd Arthur William Sampson, a Church of Ireland clergyman of Lisburn (Co. Antrim), and Mrs Mary Mercer, daughter of George Spaight, alderman of Carrickfergus (Co. Antrim). As a young man WS joined the Irish Volunteers, attended TCD, was admitted to Lincoln's Inn (London) in 1790, and was called to the Irish Bar. He practiced on the north-east circuit and started writing. Some of his early contributions to the radical newspaper the *Northern Star* (Belfast) were reprinted as pamphlets. In 1794, under his pseudonym, he wrote *A faithful report of the second trial of the proprietors of the Northern Star* (Belfast, 1795), a trial in which he had acted as junior counsel to John Philpot Curran, and with Thomas Russell composed *Review of the Lion of Old England* (Belfast, 1794), a satirical epic on contemporary British politics. He stated that he was a reformer and not a revolutionary, and openly took the oath of the United Irishmen because 'I hated dissimulation', claiming that the government was fomenting rebellion in order to bring about the Act of Union. As a result of his efforts to document military excesses in Ireland and the general turmoil of 1798 he was arrested on a charge of treason, imprisoned and banished to Portugal, then France, and eventually sent at government expense to New York in 1806 where he returned to the profession of law. In the next year he published his *Memoirs of William Sampson* (New York, 1807) and through it joined in the debate over the meaning of the 1798 rising, the consequences of the revolution, and the character of Irish republicanism. He also expressed strong criticism of France and the French and denounced British policy in Ireland. The memoirs also contained an essay on the history of Ireland, which he probably later used for his emendations to the American edn of William Cooke Taylor's *History of Ireland* (New York, 1836, 2 vols.). In New York he became involved in Irish causes, working tirelessly for the defence and benefit of less-fortunate Irish immigrants. He was an advocate of personal rights and of the reform of common law in the US, believing it to be incompatible with American democracy. He contributed essays to the *Beauties of the Shamrock* (Philadelphia, 1812). He married Grace Clarke in 1790. Their daughter married Theobald Wolfe Tone's§ son. For WS's portraits and papers, see ODNB. SOURCE Allibone, ii, pp 1920–1; ANB; R.J. Bayor & T.J. Meagher (eds), *The New York Irish* (Baltimore, 1996), pp 64–6; Bigger, p. 198; M. Burke, 'Piecing together a shattered past' in D. Dickson, D. Keogh & K. Whelan (eds), *The United Irishmen* (Dublin, 1983), pp 304–5; DAB; Elmes, p. 179; Keane, p. 436; Leslie, *Connor*, p. 579; ODNB; O'Donoghue, p. 414; RIA/DIB; K. Whelan, *Fellowship of freedom. The United Irishmen and 1798* (Cork, 1998), p. 111.

S41   *A faithful report of the trial of Hurdy Gurdy at the bar of the court of king's bench, Westminster ... on an information, filed ex-officio, by the attorney general* (by 'A barrister').

+ Belfast: Printed [for the author?] by John Rabb, 1794. SOURCE M. Deane (ed.), *Belmont Castle* (Dublin, 1998), p. 26*n*.7; ESTC t186475. LOCATION D, Di, UCD.

Dublin: [n.p.], 1794 (as *Report of the trial of the king versus Hurdy Gurdy, alias barrel organ, alias grinder, alias seditious organ*). SOURCE Falkner Greirson cat. 7/568; ESTC t064183. LOCATION L.

COMMENTARY One of the three books confiscated from Wolfe Tone§ when taken prisoner off a French warship at Buncrana (Co. Donegal). Political satire on the increasing number of prosecutions for seditious libel in the form of a court case against a street player, Hurdy Gurdy, who played seditious melodies such as 'The volunteer's march', 'Rouse Hibernia', 'A wack of the shillelagh', and 'Protestant boys'. He is found guilty of a very grievous misdemeanour. One of the individuals who is called in to give evidence is called French Horn, and replies to questions by citing the apt titles of popular tunes [ML; Deane; ODNB].

SANBORN, Alvan F. See **SANBORN, Alvan Francis.**

SANBORN, Alvan Francis (known as **Alva F. Sanborn**), fl. 1895. American story writer.

S42   *Moody's lodging house, and other tenement stories* (by Alvan Francis Sanborn; dedicated to author's father and mother).

+ Boston: Copeland & Day, 1895. SOURCE Wright, iii, 4757. LOCATION InND Loeber coll.

COMMENTARY The main character makes it his business to become acquainted with the cheapest lodging houses to be found in Boston. He gives descriptions of the kind of bed to be had for different sums of money. In his wanderings he comes across many bums and beggars, several of whom are of Irish extraction. Contents: 'Becoming a cheap lodger', 'Moody's', 'A free breakfast', 'Riley's', 'The bed I earned', 'Joe Gunn's', 'Brewster's', 'Whiting's', 'The Fairmont House', 'Appreciation', 'A tenement street', 'A tough alley', 'Among the sandwich men' [ML; Wright].

S43   *Meg McIntyre's raffle, and other stories* (by Alvan F. Sanborn).
Boston: Copeland & Day, 1896. SOURCE Brown, 1481 (Boston, Small & Maynard, 1896 edn, which has not been located); Fanning, p. 390; Wright, iii, 4756; OCLC. LOCATION C, NN.
COMMENTARY Some Irish stories. Contents: 'Mrs. Molly's revenge', 'The clinging leaf', 'A celebrated case', 'Baucis and Philemon in Bigelow Street', 'Molly and Giuseppe', 'Trousers', 'Heroism up to date', 'Episodes in the career of a lodging-house bum', 'De Mortuis nil nisi bonum', 'Suffer little children' [Wright; RL].

SANDARS, Virginia. See SANDARS, Lady Virginia Frances Zerlina.

SANDARS, Lady Virginia Frances Zerlina (known as Virginia Sandars), b. 1828, d. after 1915. Novelist, VFZS was the daughter of Thomas Taylour, the 2nd marquess of Headfort of Headfort (Co. Meath) and his first wife, Olivia Stevenson of Dublin. She married in 1850 Joseph Sandars, MP for Yarmouth (Isle of Wight). He died in 1893, and she was still living in 1915. She contributed to the *Argosy* (London) in 1884. SOURCE Allibone Suppl., ii, p. 1313; Boase, vi, p. 527 [under Joseph Sandars]; Burke 1878, p. 608; CP, vi, p. 427; RIA/DIB; RL.

S44   *The heiress of Haredale* (by Virginia Sandars).
+ London: F.V. White & Co., 1886, 3 vols. SOURCE Allibone Suppl., ii, p. 1313; OCLC. LOCATION L.
COMMENTARY Set in the north of England and London among the upper classes [RL].

S45   *A bitter repentance* (by Lady Virginia Sandars).
+ London: Hurst & Blackett, 1888, 3 vols. SOURCE Allibone Suppl., ii, p. 1313; OCLC. LOCATION L.
COMMENTARY Set in London among the upper classes [RL].

S46   *A life's devotion* (by Virginia Sandars).
+ London: Hurst & Blackett, 1891, 3 vols. SOURCE OCLC. LOCATION L.
COMMENTARY A romance set in Co. Leitrim where the English Capt. Carmichael is visiting his friend Lord Ballina, whose wife has died. Before he reaches the house, he rescues the daughter, Shelah, who had fallen into a bog hole. Capt. Carmichael continues to be a close friend to the little girl, particularly when her father's fortunes fail. Lord Ballina decides to marry a rich woman, whom he does not love, to save his estate. At the end of the story Capt. Carmichael and Shelah marry [ML].

SANDFORD, George. See MOUNT SANDFORD, George Sandford, 3rd baron.

'SARA, DELLE', pseud. See AIKEN, Albert W.

SARGENT, George E. Co-author. See WALSHE, Miss Elizabeth Hely.

SARGENT, Lucius Manlius, b. Boston (MA) 1786, d. Roxbury (MA) 1867. American periodical and temperance writer, translator and poet, LMS was educated at Phillips Exeter Academy and entered Harvard College in 1804. He did not graduate but later studied law and was admitted to the Bar. He preferred writing to the law and contributed widely to newspapers and periodicals. He became an increasingly vociferous supporter of the temperance movement, and his stories – lambasting saloon-keepers – were widely distributed by religious and temperance societies. SOURCE Allibone, ii, pp 1932–3; DAB; ML.

S47   *An Irish heart. Founded on fact* [anon.].
　　　　Boston: William S. Damrell; Gould, Kendall, & Lincoln, 1836. SOURCE Fanning, p.
　　　　390; Wright, i, 2290; OCLC. LOCATION Univ. of North Carolina, Chapel Hill.
　　　　Boston: Whipple & Damrell, 1837 (as *The temperance tales. Vol. 3, An Irish heart, well
　　　　enough for the vulgar*). SOURCE MacLeod, p. 183. LOCATION CtY.
COMMENTARY A temperance tale that traces the downfall of an Irish immigrant who ruins his
own and his family's lives and highlights the twin morals of total abstinence and immigrant
restrictions. Fashionable people, who scorned temperance as fit only for servants and other
poor folk, meet their just fate when their son, whom they had taught to drink, becomes a
hopeless drunkard. The 1837 edn of this work should not be confused with Harriet Beecher
Stowe's *The temperance tales* (London, 1853, 2 vols.) [Fanning, p. 78; MacLeod, p. 110].

'SAUNTER, DICK', pseud. See WILSON, Charles Henry.

SAVAGE, M.W. See SAVAGE, Marmion Wilme.

SAVAGE, Marmion Wilme (not Wilmo as in several sources; known as M.W. Savage), b.
Dublin 1804, d. Torquay (Devon) 1872. Barrister, journalist and satirical novelist, MWS was
the son of a Church of Ireland clergyman, the Revd Henry Savage of Dublin, and Sarah
Bewley, and grew up in his father's parish in Ardkeen (Co. Down). He entered TCD in 1817
and graduated BA in 1824. He was admitted to the King's Inns in 1829, studied law at the
Inner Temple (London), and was called to the Irish Bar in 1832. MWS began to contribute
to periodicals the same year and wrote for the *Amulet*, the *Westminster Review* and the *Examiner*
(all London) while holding a job as a minor official at Dublin Castle. Later he wrote for the
Edinburgh Review and the *Dublin University Magazine*. He married Lady Morgan's§ niece,
Olivia Clarke. His wife died in 1843 and between then and his remarriage in 1855 he wrote
four novels, all published anonymously because of his government job. His only child, a son
from his first marriage, died as a young man. In 1856 he moved to London where he worked
as a journalist and until 1859 was editor of the *Examiner*. He died after a prolonged illness.
MWS was known for his classical learning, his knowledge of Irish folklore, and his kindliness.
Some of his papers are at the University of Iowa. SOURCE Allibone, ii, p. 1938; Allibone Suppl.,
ii, p. 1317; B & S, p. 736; Boase, iii, p. 424; Brady, p. 217; Brown, p. 272; DLB, xxi; W.E.
Hall, p. 175; Hogan 2, p. 1082; Irish pseudonyms; Keane, p. 439; NCBEL 4, pp 1398–9;
OCIL, p. 509; ODNB; O'Donoghue, pp 415, 500; N. Paralee, 'A neglected Irish novelist:
Marmion W. Savage' in *Books at Iowa*, 35 (1981); RIA/DIB; Sutherland, p. 554.

S48   *The Falcon family; or, Young Ireland* [anon.].
　　　　+ London: Chapman & Hall, 1845 (Chapman & Hall's Monthly Series, No. 6). SOURCE
　　　　Brown, 1482; Rafroidi, ii, p. 335; Sadleir, 3033, 3742. LOCATION D, DPL (1846, 2nd
　　　　edn), BFl, L, InND Loeber coll. (also 1846, 2nd edn).
　　　　Boston: T.W. Wiley Jnr, 1846. SOURCE Topp 3, p. 293 (1848 edn); OCLC. LOCATION
　　　　Massachusetts Historical Soc.
COMMENTARY Highly-politicized satire on the leaders of the Young Ireland party and the early
Tractarian movement at Oxford, with the Falcons serving as a metaphor for the Anglo-Irish
[Brown, Hogan; *Éire-Ireland*, 23/1 (1988), pp 129–43; ODNB].

S49   *The bachelor of the Albany* [anon.] (dedicated to Lady Morgan§).
　　　　+ London: Chapman & Hall, 1848 (Chapman & Hall's Monthly Series, No. 15, but
　　　　with the 'Monthly' deleted). SOURCE Hogan 2, pp 1082–3 (1847 edn); Rafroidi, ii, p.
　　　　335 (issued 1847); Sadleir, 3032, 3742; Topp 3, p. 292; Wolff, 6181; NSTC; Ximenes
　　　　cat. 99/414. LOCATION D, Dt, L, InND Loeber coll.

+ New York: Harper & Bros, 1848. SOURCE Allibone, ii, p. 1938. LOCATION InND Loeber coll.

COMMENTARY *New York edn* Two binding types, one in dark green cloth, the other in mauve cloth [RL].

+ London: Elkin Mathews & Marrot, 1927 (introd. by B. Dobrée; The Rescue Series). SOURCE NCBEL 3, p. 964. LOCATION D, InND Loeber coll.

COMMENTARY Issued in 1847, but imprint is 1848. The story loosely chronicles the commercial doings of 'Spread, Narrowsmith and Co.' as they affect Mr Barker, 'the bachelor of the Albany', while he develops into a responsible husband. The Albany was a set of fashionable West End apartments in London. Contains some satire of the Oxford Movement and the English and Irish clergy [Hogan; ODNB; Sutherland, p. 555].

S50   *My uncle the curate. A novel* [anon.].
        + London: Chapman & Hall, 1849, 3 vols. SOURCE Brown, 1712; Hogan 2, p. 1083; Rafroidi, ii, p. 335; Sadleir, 3034; Wolff, 6183. LOCATION D, Dt, L, InND Loeber coll. ([*c*.1865], 4th edn).
        New York: Harper & Bros, 1849 (Library of Select Novels, No. 128). SOURCE Topp 3, p. 295; OCLC. LOCATION CtY.

COMMENTARY A satire of out-dated Irish customs and self-indulgence set chiefly on the coast of Co. Donegal in the 1830s. A curate plays a heroic part in various calamities such as shipwrecks, highway robbery, and abduction. The intolerance of both Orangeism and the repeal movement are condemned, and toleration is preached. The villain of the story, Dawson of Castle Dawson, tries to curry favour with the rector because he is in love with his daughter, who despises him. He gains power over the rector's son by lending him money. When his plans do not succeed, he makes it appear as though the rector's son robbed the tithe proctor. The truth comes out and Dawson disappears from the scene. His skeleton is found in a cave under his castle [ML; Brown; Hogan].

S51   *Reuben Medlicott; or, the coming man* (by M.W. Savage).
        London: Chapman & Hall, 1852, 3 vols. SOURCE Allibone, 2, p. 1938; Hogan 2, p. 1083; Rafroidi, ii, p. 336; Sadleir, 3035; Wolff, 6184. LOCATION Dt, L.
        + New York: D. Appleton & Co., 1852. SOURCE Topp 3, p. 323. LOCATION InND Loeber coll.
        + New York: A.A. Kelley, 1860 (as *The lights and shadows of real life*, containing 'The universal genius; or, the coming man'). LOCATION InND Loeber coll.
        + Cincinnati: A.A. Kelley, 1861 (as *The lights and shadows of real life*). LOCATION InND Loeber coll.

COMMENTARY A satire of complacency and sensibility set mainly in England and telling the story of the life of Reuben Medlicott, who becomes a parliamentarian and gets involved with the Quakers. In his travels as a politician he visits Ireland [ML].

S52   *Clover cottage; or, I can't get in. A novelette* [anon.].
        + London: Chapman & Hall, 1856. SOURCE Rafroidi, ii, p. 336; Sutherland, p. 555; Wolff, 6182, LOCATION L.
        London: Chapman & Hall, 1867 (new edn). SOURCE Topp 3, p. 343.

COMMENTARY No copy of the London 1867 new edn located. A story about a bachelor who finally takes a bride, it was dramatized by Tom Taylor as *Nine points of the law* (London, 1859) and performed a the Olympia Theatre in London in that year [Hogan; Sutherland].

S53   *The woman of business; or, the lady and the lawyer. A novel* [anon.].
        + London: Chapman & Hall, 1870, 3 vols. SOURCE Allibone Suppl., ii, p. 1317; Rafroidi, ii, p. 336; Wolff, 6185. LOCATION L.
        New York: D. Appleton & Co., 1870 (ill. Alfred R. Woud). SOURCE Mott cat. 201/220; OCLC. LOCATION NN.

COMMENTARY First published in serial form, it concerns a feud over an estate between two sisters-in-law; one worthy, one vulgar. Although lightly satirical in parts, it is an affirmation of human nature in the face of the seemingly de-humanizing aspects of Darwin's theories [ML; Hogan 2, p. 1083].

SAVILE, H. See **SAVILE, Mrs Helen V.**

SAVILE, Mrs Helen V. (also known as **H. Savile** and **Helen Savile**), fl. 1899. Novelist, HVS has at least seven titles to her credit. She is known to have had two children, Lilith and Jack. Only her works with Irish connections are listed here. SOURCE COPAC; Dedication to her *The wings of the morning* (London, 1901).
S54   *Love, the player* (by Helen V. Savile).
       London: W. Swan Sonnenschein & Co., 1899. SOURCE Brown, 1484; Daims, 2674; OCLC. LOCATION L, NUC.
COMMENTARY Tragic plot containing sketches of Irish life, which includes an Irish woman's betrayal by her lover, and the birth of her child. Features the rector and the rector's wife in the Protestant community of Tuleen [Burmester list].
S55   *A poor buffer* (by Helen Savile).
       London: W. Swan Sonnenschein & Co., 1900 (ill. Nancy Ruxton). SOURCE Brown 2, 1413; OCLC. LOCATION L.
COMMENTARY A soldier of the 21st Lancers, the 'poor buffer' of the tale, returns from the Egyptian campaign to his native Donegal and loses his life in saving Molly Camolin from drowning. She is 'the little lady of the Castle', a child who had become attached to him, in accordance with an old legend [Brown 2].
S56   *Micky Mooney, M.P.* (by H. Savile).
       + Bristol: J.W. Arrowsmith; London: Simpkin, Marshall, Hamilton, Kent & Co., 1902 (ill. Nancy Ruxton). Location L.
COMMENTARY Partly set in Ireland. Chronicles Micky Mooney's rise from poverty to being an M.P. [RL].

'SAVONAROLA, Don Jeremy', pseud. See **MAHONY, Fr Francis Sylvester.**

SAWYER, Hannah Farnham. See **LEE, Hannah Farnham.**

SCANLAN, Anna C., fl. 1895. American novelist. The following book was completed and illustrated by Charles M. Scanlan, perhaps the author's husband. SOURCE RL.
S57   *Dervorgilla; or, the downfall of Ireland* (by Anna C. Scanlan).
       Milwaukee (WI): J.H. Yewdale & Sons Co., 1895 (completed and revsd with preface, map, ill., and notes by Charles M. Scanlan). SOURCE Fanning, p. 390; Wright, iii, 4807; OCLC. LOCATION C, CtY.

SCANLAN, Charles M. Co-author. See **SCANLAN, Anna C.**

SCANNELL, Florence, fl. 1880s. Children's writer, possibly Irish. A person of this name published a collection of verse in Cork in 1848. FS and her sister Edith authored a number of stories on Christmas in different countries, including *The highwaymen. Christmas in England* (London, 1888). SOURCE Allibone Suppl., ii, p. 1319; Alston, p. 384.
S58   *Sylvia's daughters* (by Florence Scannell).
       + London, New York: Frederick Warne, [1888] (ill. Edith Scannell). SOURCE Alston, p. 384. LOCATION L.

COMMENTARY Fiction for juveniles. No Irish content. Set in France and concerns Gabrielle, whose mother was English. At the beginning of the French Revolution, the children are being sent to England, where they have to do their own housekeeping. Master Ralph, son of the neighbouring squire, falls in love with Gabrielle. In the end they marry [ML].

SCARGILL, William Pitt. Attributed author. See CHETWODE, Anna Marie.

'SCIAN DUBH', pseud. See MC CARROLL, James.

SCHLICHTKRULL, Aline von, fl. 1859. German writer of historical fiction.
S59   *Der Agitator von Irland* (by Aline von Schlichtkrull).
       Berlin: Otto Janke, 1859, 4 vols. SOURCE Brown, 1486; COPAC. LOCATION L.
COMMENTARY A story about Daniel O'Connell from the Catholic point of view. The scene is set partly in Ireland and partly in England and speeches in the house of lords are incorporated in the story [Brown].

'SCOTT, George Gordon', pseud. See BULWER LYTTON, Rosina Doyle.

SCOTT, H., pseud. 'An officer's daughter', fl. 1790. Novelist, HS was probably a resident in the Cork area, where her novel *Helena* was published. Several of the subscribers were women of the Irish nobility, including the marchioness of Antrim; Lady Harriet Bernard; Lady Harriet Daly; the countess of Ely and Viscountess Kingsborough. HS was possibly related to Col. Hedges, who was the biggest subscriber with nine copies. SOURCE RL.
S60   *Helena: or, the vicissitudes of a military life* (by 'An officer's daughter'; dedicated
       to Lady Elizabeth Irving [second daughter of the earl of Howth]; dedication signed
       H. Scott).
       + Cork: James Haly, 1790, 2 vols. (subscribers' list). SOURCE Black, 718; Raven 2,
       1790:66; ESTC t084550. LOCATION Dt, L, MH.
COMMENTARY Epistolary novel set in America and Ireland at the time of the American War of Independence. Vol. 2 particularly concerns a stay in Dublin [ML; CM].

SCOTT, J.F., fl. 1860s. Religious fiction writer, JFS perhaps can be identified with John Fitzwilliam Scott, son of a William Scott, who was born in Co. Clare *c*.1820, entered TCD in 1835 and became a soldier. SOURCE B & S, p. 739.
S61   *The hunchback of Carrigmore. An Irish tale* (by J.F. Scott).
       + London: S.W. Partridge & Co., [*c*.1869] (ill. H.P.). LOCATION L, InND Loeber coll.
COMMENTARY Two binding types: one in a red cloth, and another in a green cloth decorative binding. An anti-Catholic story set on the coast of Co. Mayo in which Bible readers are persecuted. Willy, a crippled Catholic boy, had sheltered a dying Bible reader and for this he and his grandmother are exiled to an uninhabited island. He takes with him the Bible given to him by his late friend. After several years, survivors of a shipwreck come to the island and take the boy back to the mainland, where eventually he becomes a Protestant minister in his native village [ML].

'SCRIMSHAW, Harry', pseud. See READ, Charles Anderson.

SCULLY, W.C. See SCULLY, William Charles.

SCULLY, William Charles (known as W.C. Scully), b. Dublin 1855, d. Umbogintwini (South Africa) 1943. Botanist, poet, fiction writer and memoirist, WCS was the son of John

Scully

Joseph Scully, who came from a landed gentry family in Tipperary, and Elizabeth Mary Creagh of Co. Clare. Raised in Co. Wicklow, he emigrated with his family to South Africa in 1867. He farmed with his father and had little schooling, later prospecting for diamonds in Kimberly with the Rhodes brothers. He moved to Cape Town, where he studied botany and collected specimens for museums in South Africa, Europe and the US. He published *Poems* (London 1892) and contributed to *Pall Mall* (London), *Atlantic Monthly* (Boston), and *Scribner's* (New York) magazines. WCS wrote mostly about Africa, often in fiction but also in poetry and in travel books. He was chairman of the committee that investigated war losses after the Anglo-Boer War, which prompted him to write *The harrow* (Cape Town, 1921). His *Reminiscences of a South African pioneer* (London 1913) and other memoirs are valuable resources for historians and sociologists. His portrait was published in *Voices of Africa* (Durban, 1943). According to Field Marshal J.C. Smuts, in his preface to this volume, WCS spent a lifetime in African administration, and studied the native people. O'Donoghue lists WCS's pseudonym as 'A South African Colonist', presumably for his published poetry. SOURCE DSAB; O'Donoghue, p. 417; RIA/DIB.

S62   *Kafir stories* (by W.C. Scully; dedicated to Kate Freiligrath Kroekker and J.H. Meiring Beck).

+ London: T. Fisher Unwin, 1895 (Autonym Library). SOURCE OCLC. LOCATION D (1898, 2nd edn), L, NUC, InND Loeber coll.

New York: H. Holt & Co., 1895. LOCATION NUC.

COMMENTARY Set in South Africa and contains a glossary of Afrikaans. The stories depict the Kafir and other natives of South Africa as inherently inferior. Contents: 'The Eumenides in Kafir land', 'The fundamental axiom', 'Kellson's nemesis', 'The quest of the copper', 'Ghamba', 'Ukushwama', 'Umtagati' [ML].

S63   *The white hecatomb and other stories* (by W.C. Scully).

+ London: Methuen & Co., 1897. LOCATION D, L.

COMMENTARY Contents: 'The white hecatomb', 'The vengeance of Dogolwana', 'Gquma; or, the white waif', 'The tramp's tragedy', 'The seed of the church', 'Little Tobè', 'The imishologu', 'The madness of Gweva', 'The love charm', 'Derelicts', 'The return of Sobèdè', 'The quick and the dead', 'Aiāla' [RL].

S64   *The vendetta of the desert* (by W.C. Scully).

London: Methuen & Co., 1898. SOURCE OCLC. LOCATION L.

S65   *Between the sun and sand: A tale of an African desert* (by W.C. Scully).

London: Methuen & Co., 1898. SOURCE OCLC. LOCATION L.

S66   *By veldt and kopje* (by W.S. Scully; dedicated to Lt.-Gen. Sir William Francis Butler§).

+ London: T. Fisher Unwin, 1907. SOURCE OCLC. LOCATION L, NUC.

COMMENTARY Stories set in South Africa. Contents (excluding poetry): 'The lepers', 'The writing on the rock', 'Tommy's evil genius', 'The wisdom of the serpent', 'Rainmaking', 'The gratitude of a savage', 'Mr Bloxam's choice', 'A case for physical research', 'Chicken wings', 'Afar in the desert', 'By the waters of Marah', 'The hunter of the Didma', 'A forgotten expedition', 'Kafir music' [RL].

S67   *The harrow (South Africa, 1900–1902): a novel* (by W.C. Scully).

Cape Town: Nationale Pers, 1921. SOURCE COPAC. LOCATION L, NUC.

COMMENTARY Written in response to the government's refusal to honour its pledge to hold an inquiry after the Anglo-Boer war, it shows 'what happened to our Dutch fellow-subjects when the orgy of imported financial and spurious imperialism swept over the land' [DSAB].

S68   *Daniel Vananda, the life story of a human being* (by W.S. Scully).

+ Cape Town: Juta & Co., 1923. SOURCE OCLC. LOCATION L.

COMMENTARY The book is a fictional account of 'those unscrupulous whites who exploited the Bantu races' [DSAB].

S69 *Voices of Africa* (by W.C. Scully; introd. by Field Marshal J.C. Smuts).

+ Durban: Knox, 1943 (ill.). LOCATION L.

COMMENTARY Stories interspersed with poems. Several of the stories were published earlier in *Kafir stories* (London, 1895), *The white hecatomb and other stories* (London, 1897), and *By veldt and kopje* (London, 1907). Contents: 'The writing on the rock', 'Laughter is no laughing matter', 'The battle of Ezinyoseni', 'By the waters of Marah', 'Kellson's nemesis', 'The leepers', 'Tommy's evil genius', 'The flood', 'On picket', 'The return of Sobèdè' [ML].

SEALLY, Mr —. See SEALLY, Revd John.

SEALLY, Jean. See SEALLY, Revd John.

SEALLY, Revd John (also known as Mr Seally and Jean Seally), b. Som. 1741 or 1742, d. Westminster, (London) 1795. Novelist, educationalist, opera and miscellaneous writer, JS may have come from an Irish background because he published two novels with distinct Irish characters in the main roles. Also, his first known novel was dedicated to the Irish lord lieutenant, George, Viscount Townshend. Members of the Sealy [*sic*] family resided mostly in Munster during the eighteenth century. He possibly was the same person as John Sealy of Bridgewater (Som.), who matriculated from Hertford College, Oxford, in 1760. JS wrote both in French and in English (as in his *Les délices du sentiment; or the passionate lovers*, London, 1781). He was involved with several magazines in London; wrote an opera; *A complete geographical dictionary* (London, 1787, 2 vols.); *Belles letters for the ladies* (London, [1772?]) and *The Lady's encyclopaedia* (London, 1788, 3 vols.). His career also involved producing educational books and handbooks. He took holy orders and in 1790 was presented to the vicarage of East Meon and two other locations in Hants. In the next year he was elected fellow of the Royal Society. Only his works with Irish connections are listed below. SOURCE T. Barnard, *A new anatomy of Ireland* (New Haven, 2003), p. 246; Pickering & Chatto cat. 275/256; Raven 2, 1782:11; RL.

S70 *The Irishman; or, the favourite of fortune: A satirical novel founded upon facts* [anon.] (dedicated to George, Viscount Townshend).

London: W. Goldsmith, 1772, 2 vols. SOURCE Forster, 1379; Brown, 51; ESTC n016832; Raven 2, 1772:14. LOCATION L (apparently lost).

Amsterdam, Paris: Veuve Duchesne, 1779 (trans. by Jean-Baptiste René Robinet as *Le favori de la fortune*; 'd'apres Barbier' [*sic*, but this author has not been identified]. SOURCE Raven 2, 1772:14; Rochedieu, p. 291. LOCATION BNF.

Amsterdam [Paris]: Veuve Duchesne, 1784, 2 vols. (trans. as *Le beau garçon, ou le faveur de la fortune*). SOURCE Raven 2, 1772:14; ESTC t209211. LOCATION L (vol. 1 only).

Breslau: W.G. Kern, 1780 (trans. by Karl Conrad Streit as *Der Günstling des Glücks*). SOURCE Raven 2, 1772:14; GLOL. LOCATION Staatsbibliothek zu Berlin.

COMMENTARY Author, John Seally is identified on the title page of the Amsterdam 1780 edn. In addition, the *European Magazine* (London) mentions as its author a Mr Seally, who also wrote *The young philosopher* (London, 1782, 2 vols.). According to a contemporary review, 'This novel will neither instruct or entertain the reader. The facts are destitute of probability, and the narration is without humour. A young Irishman, by a series of unnatural and dull adventures, rises from an obscure station to splendour and rank'. The dedication to Lord Townshend, who was the Irish lord lieutenant, is 'teeming with nonsense and absurdity' [*Critical Review*, xxxiv (1772), p. 472].

S71   *Colonel Ormsby; or, the genuine history of an Irish nobleman, in the French service* [anon.].

London: J. Macgowan, 1781, 2 vols. SOURCE Forster 2, 797; Raven 2, 1781:2; ESTC n014767. LOCATION PU.

+ Dublin: Price, Whitestone, Sleater, W. Watson, Sheppard, Burnet, Moncrieffe, Walker, E. Cross, Jenkin, Beatty, Burton & Byrne, 1781, 2 vols. in 1. SOURCE Brown, 18; Black, 54; Raven 2, 1781:2; ESTC t055922. LOCATION D, L.

Leipzig: [publisher?], 1781 (trans. as *Der Oberste Ormsby, oder eine wahre Geschichte eines Irlaendischen von Adel in französischen Diensten*). SOURCE Raven 2, 1781:2.

COMMENTARY No copy of the Leipzig edn located. Since *Colonel Ormsby* carries the endorsement 'by the author of *Les délices du sentiment; or the passionate lovers* and *The young philosopher or the natural son*', published in London in 1781 and 1782 respectively, it is plausible Mr [John] Seally was the author of all three works. Epistolary novel of letters between Col. Ormsby and Lady Beaumont. There is no reference to Ireland and very little about the history of the colonel. The letters are filled with the love affairs of the writers. However, the novel also concerns the Irish Brigades in France [Brown; IBL, 6 (1915), p. 179].

'SECONDSIGHT, Solomon', pseud. See **MC HENRY, James**.

SEDDALL, Revd Henry. Editor. See **BRITTAINE, Revd George**.

SEDGWICK, Catharine Maria, b. Stockbridge (MA) 1789, d. Roxbury (MA) 1867. American novelist, self-help and travel writer, CMS was the daughter of Theodore Sedgwick, speaker of the house of representatives during George Washington's administration, and Pamela Dwight. CMS was befriended by Anna Brownell Jameson§ and visited England in the summer of 1839. Her diary of that trip, *Letters from abroad*, also covered Italy, Belgium, Germany and Switzerland and was published in New York in 1841. She dedicated her *A New-England tale* (New York, 1822) to Maria Edgeworth§. Her novels lauded personal goodness and wholesome living and contain realistic presentations of domestic scenes. She also wrote self-help books. She was among the first internationally-known American authors and was admired by Nathaniel Hawthorne, Ralph Waldo Emerson and Herman Melville. Only works with Irish content are listed below. SOURCE Allibone, ii, pp 1987–8; ANB; Blain, p. 926; DAB; G. MacPherson, *Memoirs of the life of Anna Jameson* (Boston, 1878), pp 136–8, 151–2, 160–1; NUC.

S72   *Clarence: or, a tale of our own times* (by Catharine Maria Sedgwick; dedicated to author's brothers).

+ London: H. Colburn & Richard Bentley, 1830, 3 vols. SOURCE Garside 2, 1830:97. LOCATION L.

London: A.K. Newman, 1830, 3 vols. SOURCE Garside 2, 1830:97.

COMMENTARY *London, Newman edn* No copy located [Garside 2].

+ Belfast: Simms & McIntyre, 1846 (as *Clarence; or, a tale of our times*; Parlour Novelist Series, No. 6). LOCATION NUC, InND Loeber coll.

New York: George P. Putnam; London: David Bogue, 1849. SOURCE OCLC. LOCATION MH.

+ New York: G.P. Putnam & Co., 1856 (author's revsd edn). LOCATION InND Loeber coll., NUC.

COMMENTARY Set in New York, both city and state, and featuring one Irish character, a male nurse who is willing to perjure himself in a court case but who, at the last moment, decides to speak the truth. According to Holzapfel, another character is not unlike the Irish poet James

Clarence Mangan§ [ML; R.P. Holzapfel, *James Clarence Mangan. A checklist of printed and other sources* (Dublin, 1969), p. 23].

S73   *Live and let live; or, domestic service illustrated* [anon.] (dedicated to 'my young countrywomen the future ministers of the charities of home').
New York: Harper & Bros, 1837. LOCATION OCLC. LOCATION NUC, InND Loeber coll. (1871 edn).

COMMENTARY Set in New York City, it tells the story of Lucy, a young girl who is forced into service by the poverty of her parents. She works in a number of families and experiences both strict and lax mistresses. The story makes the point that a good mistress needs to be aware of the tasks that her servants have to accomplish and to train them properly and treat them well. Some of the fellow servants Lucy meets are Irish [ML].

S74   *A love token for children* [anon.].
New York: Harper & Bros, 1838. SOURCE MacLeod, p. 100; COPAC. LOCATION NUC.
London: Richard Bentley, 1838. LOCATION L.

COMMENTARY 'Designed for the Sunday-School libraries'. Fiction for juveniles set in America and concerning an Irish labourer who is advised by a Miss Leslie not to drink so he can send his children to school. It describes Americans' prejudiced views of the Irish when a new railroad that brings in the Irish is laid out [MacLeod, pp 100, 103].

S75   *Tales and sketches* (second series) (by Catharine Maria Sedgwick).
New York: Harper & Bros, 1844. SOURCE RLIN. LOCATION UBP, NUC.
+ London: H.G. Clarke & Co., 1845 (as *The Irish girl, and other tales*). SOURCE Seen at Jarndyce, Sept. 2001; RL. LOCATION InND Loeber coll. (Slater, 1850 edn).
London: Kent & Richards; Edinburgh: J. Menzies, 1850 SOURCE OCLC. LOCATION Univ. of Oregon.

COMMENTARY Content of the New York edn: 'Wilton Harvey', 'Cousin Frank', 'A day in a railroad car', 'The Irish girl' (set America in an Irish encampment along a railroad during its construction), 'Daniel Prime', 'A Huguenot family', 'The post office' (Irish content), 'A vision', 'Second thoughts best', 'Our burial place'. London, 1850 edn contains an extra story, 'Home' [RLIN; RL].

'SEDLEY, Charles', pseud. See ELRINGTON, John Battersby.

SELDEN, Catharine (not Catherine as in Allibone and Blain), pseud. 'A Lady', fl. 1797. Novelist, CA probably was Irish and was a resident in Munster for part of her life. She may have been related to Richard Selden, who married Barbara Browne in 1747 in the diocese of Cork and Ross. CS wrote at least seven novels and in her work praised the authors Mary Robinson and Frances Sheridan§. SOURCE Allibone, ii, p. 1991; Blain, p. 963; Frank, pp 395–6; H.W. Gillman, *Index to the marriage licence bonds of the diocese of Cork and Ross, Ireland* (Cork, 1896–97), p. 115.

S76   *The Count de Santerre: A romance* (by 'A Lady').
Bath: Printed [for the author?] by R. Crutwell, 1797, 2 vols. SOURCE Forster 2, 4002; Raven 2, 1797:72; ESTC n004710. LOCATION MH.

COMMENTARY Gothic fiction. The heroine, Elinor, is in quest of her abducted mother, Olivia de Santerre, a mission which causes her to be imprisoned in the ruinous abbey of St Austin [Frank, 395].

S77   *The English nun. A novel* [anon.].
London: William Lane, 1797. SOURCE Blain, p. 963; Blakey, p. 181; Forster 2, 4003; Raven 2, 1797:73; ESTC n002258. LOCATION MH.
Paris: Maradan, [1799], 4 vols. (trans. by Comtesse L.-A. de Guibert as *Agatha, ou la religieuse anglaise*). SOURCE CCF. LOCATION BNF.

Rotterdam: Van den Dries, 1802 (trans. into Dutch as *Agatha of the Engelse non: ene hedendaagsche Fransche kloostergeschiedenis*). SOURCE Wintermans, 1797:63.
COMMENTARY A sympathetic account of convent life, probably written in response to Diderot's *La religieuse* (Paris, 1796; trans. published London, 1797; Frank hypothesizes that CS was the translator). In *The English nun*, the heroine, Louisa, is confronted with threats to her virginity and life. In the end, she is freed from the convent by a chivalrous young man, Edmund Lumley [Blain; Frank, p. 22; Frank, 396].

S78   *Lindor; or, early engagements. A novel* [anon.].
      Reading: Printed [for the author?] by Snare & Co., 1798, 2 vols. SOURCE Raven 2, 1798:63; Forster 2, 4004; ESTC n063612. LOCATION CaACU.
      COMMENTARY Privately published [RL].

S79   *The sailors. A novel* [anon.].
      Reading: Printed [for the author?] by R. Snare & Co., 1800, 2 vols. LOCATION ViU.
      London: Crosby & Letterman, 1800, 2 vols. (as *The sailors*). SOURCE British Fiction; Garside, 1800:65; ESTC t178629. LOCATION O, Univ. of North Carolina, Chapel Hill.
      COMMENTARY Privately published [RL].

S80   *Serena. A novel* (by Catharine Selden).
      + London: William Lane, 1800, 3 vols. SOURCE Blain, p. 963; Blakey, p. 181; British Fiction; Garside, 1800:66. LOCATION Corvey CME 3–628–48637, Ireland related fiction, L (incomplete).
COMMENTARY This novel defends Ireland against literary attack, and features a benevolent nobleman who supports liberty in America and France, but opposes women's education lest it makes them less docile and agreeable [Blain].

S81   *German letters, translated into English* (trans. [*sic*] by Catharine Selden).
      + Cork: J. Connor, 1804. SOURCE Blain, p. 963; Garside, 1804:59. LOCATION Corvey CME 3–28–48636–X, D, L, C.
      London: Lane, Newman & Co., 1805. SOURCE Blakey, p. 215.
      COMMENTARY No copy of the London edn located. This original novel poses as a work of translation, with modifications by the 'translator' [RL; Blain].

S82   *Villa Nova; or, the ruined castle. A romance* (by Catherine [*sic*] Selden).
      + Cork: Printed [for the author?] by J. Connor, 1804, 2 vols (see Plate 58). SOURCE Gilbert, p. 734. LOCATION DPL, Gilbert coll., InND Loeber coll.
      + London: Lane, Newman & Co. (printed by J. Connor, Cork), 1805, 2 vols. SOURCE Blakey, 218; British Fiction; Garside, 1805:63. LOCATION Corvey CME 3–628–8638–6, L.
COMMENTARY A Gothic novel set in southern Europe. The plot revolves around establishing the identity of a girl called Paulina, who had been brought up by the Sisters of Mercy until a cavalier took her away with him. At his death, she is put in the charge of a priest and he deposits her in a cloister. Paulina possesses some mysterious letters that might give an indication of her parentage. After many adventures, the girl's true identity is established. She is rich and marries happily. The story is sometimes difficult to follow because many of the characters are related to each other [ML; Frank, 397].

S83   *Villasantelle; or, the curious impertinent. A romance* (by Catharine Selden).
      + London: A.K. Newman & Co., 1817. SOURCE Blakey, p. 261; Blain, p. 963 (where mistakenly called 'Villa Santelle'); British Fiction; Garside, 1817:52. LOCATION Corvey CME 3–628–48639–4, L.
COMMENTARY A comic Gothic novel set in Spain. The hero falls over while hiding in a suit of armour and has to be rescued by his lady. He feels 'veneration' for a girl seen with her ille-

gitimate baby, the eventual result of a course of action begun by 'perpetually outraging custom and propriety by thinking for [her]self' [Blain].

SERGEANT, John, b. Barrow-upon-Humber (Lincs.) 1622, d. 1707. English religious writer and novelist, JS was a convert to catholicism who joined the English mission in 1652 and wrote widely on religious controversies. He is the attributed author of the following work, according to NCBEL 2 and Dix. Given that he published in Dublin (unless the 'Doublin' is a false imprint) and dealt with the Williamite War in Ireland, it is likely that JS had a link with the country. However, the ODNB does not mention such a connection or the following satire. SOURCE E.R. McC. Dix, *Catalogue of early Dublin-printed books* (repr. New York, 1971), ii, p. 263; NCBEL 2, p. 983; ODNB; Sweeney, 4661.

S84   *An historical romance of the wars, between the mighty giant Gallieno and the great knight Nasonius, and his associates* [anon].
        + Doublin [*sic*]: [n.p.], [1694]. SOURCE Esdaile, p. 228; Gilbert, p. 375; Sweeney, 4661; ESTC cr19614. LOCATION DPL Gilbert coll., D, L.
COMMENTARY 88pp. A satire on the wars between kings Louis XIV and William III (Gallieno and Nasonius respectively), contributing to the cult of the Irish Brigades and applauding their strength, even though they were defeated in Ireland [Esdaile; Gilbert; É. Ó Ciadrha, *Ireland and the Jacobite cause, 1685–1766* (Dublin, 2002), p. 106].

SEVEY, Louis, fl. 1862. Novelist, LS was a university-educated estate agent and son of a clergyman, according to the preface to the following work. SOURCE RL.
S85   *The dark cloud. A tale of priestly influence in Ireland in the present. A tale* (by Louis Sevey).
        + London: Saunders & Otley, 1862. SOURCE Allibone, ii, p. 1998; Brown 2, 1423; OCLC. LOCATION DPL, L.
COMMENTARY A story about an estate agent in Ireland who tries to do his duty. A considerable part of the tale is taken up with an account of his happy family life. The other element is his relations with the tenants and with the local clergy. The agent founds a new school, stipulating that the Bible should be read daily in it. Years later, after the Famine, misunderstandings arise. The Catholic teacher, Mrs Brady, is dismissed. Matters develop into a bitter quarrel with the Catholic clergy, ending in the school being attended by Protestant children only [Brown 2].

SEWELL, Revd William, b. Newport (Isle of Wight) 1804, d. Litchford Hall, near Manchester (Lancs.) 1874. Cleric, scholar, novelist, education reformer and translator, WS was a prolific writer on religion, philosophy and the classics. He graduated BA at Merton College, Oxford, in 1827, and MA in 1829. Later he received a BD in 1841 and a DD in 1859. He was a fellow of and lecturer at Exeter College, a colleague of John Henry Newman§ and J.A. Froude§ and an early member of the Tractarian movement, from which he later withdrew as it drew closer to Rome. At the invitation of Lord Adare, WS founded in 1843 St Columba's College, first in Stackallan (Co. Meath) and then in 1849 at Rathfarnham (Co. Dublin). St Columba's was designed to promote WS's high-church ideas and to convert Irish Catholics by using the Irish language in its proselytising work, as well as to provide the gentry of Ireland with an educational institution equivalent to Eton or Winchester. The venture rapidly incurred large debts, which were paid off by Lord J.G. Beresford, archbishop of Armagh, on condition WS dissociate himself from the school. He published *Journal of a residence at the college of St. Columba in Ireland* (Oxford, 1847). WS returned to England and began a similar school, St Peter's in Radley near Oxford, which also incurred debt problems.

He published four novels, one of which has Irish content, and edited several written by his sister, Elizabeth Missing Sewell. Among his many other publications are 'Romanism in Ireland' (*Quarterly Review*, 67 (Dec. 1840), pp 118–71), and *Christian politics* (Oxford, 1848). For his portraits and papers, see ODNB. SOURCE Allibone, ii, p. 2002; Boase, iii, p. 499–500; Griffin, passim; NCBEL 4, pp 1400, 2668; ODNB.

S86   *Hawkstone: A tale of and for England in 184–* (by William Sewell).
London: Murray, 1845, 2 vols. SOURCE COPAC. LOCATION C.
New York: Garland, 1976. SOURCE COPAC. LOCATION O.
COMMENTARY The novel describes the newly-industrialized English town of Hawkstone as a religious, political and cultural Babel. Irish immigrants are everywhere and revolution is imminent. Lord Ernest Villiers, owner of the town and son of a Catholic mother and a nominally Protestant, libertine father, returns and rescues a poor youth (actually his own child) from a fiery death. His public goal is the reestablishment of religious authority in the form of the Anglican Catholic church. Villiers is summoned to Italy by his dying father, whom he leaves in the care of his brother Pearce, a secret Jesuit. Villiers finds happiness in a secret marriage to Pauline, an Italian Catholic who previously had rejected Pearce's attentions. Pearce manages to displace Villiers as his father's heir. Villiers' son, also called Ernest, is kidnapped by Pearce, raised in an atmosphere of depravity, and eventually placed in the household of Connell, an Irishman who murdered a Protestant minister in Ireland and fled to England. The young Villiers is encouraged in lawlessness until his father rescues him [Griffin, pp 69–71].

SHACKLETON (sometimes spelled **Shakleton**), **Elizabeth (Betsy)**. pseud. **'A Lady'**, fl. 1821. Temperance writer, probable poet, and memoirist, ES was the daughter of Richard Shackleton, a Quaker schoolmaster, and his second wife Elizabeth Carleton, and sister of Mary Leadbeater§. An early-nineteenth-century listing of Mary Leadbeater's work mentions that, at least up to 1814, 'these works were written for the most part in conjunction with her sister Miss Elizabeth Shackleton'. She may be identified with the 'E.S.' who contributed some pieces to the *Ballitore Magazine* (Co. Kildare) in 1821. She is probably the same person as Betsy Shackleton, who wrote *Ballitore and its inhabitants seventy years ago* (Dublin, 1872). ES must have shared her sister's charitable interests. She probably also wrote a few chapbooks (smaller than 25 pp), including *James and George: or, dialogues between two servant-men* (Dublin, 1831), and *Dialogues on whiskey* (Dublin, 1832). Her reminiscences of her childhood can be found in the Religious Society of Friends' Historical Library, Dublin (MS Box 34). She is not to be confused with a 'Miss E.S.', author of verse for *Walker's Magazine* in 1773 who, O'Donoghue believes, was the sister of Richard Shackleton. SOURCE BD, p. 199; Harrison, p. 68; E. Malcolm, *Ireland sober, Ireland free* (Syracuse, 1986), p. 75; O'Donoghue, p. 419; RL (MS annotations in the *Ballitore Magazine*).

S87   *Philip and his friends: or, cottage dialogues on temperance societies and intemperance* (by 'A Lady').
+ Dublin: Printed by R.D. Webb [for the Hibernian Temperance Society], 1830.
LOCATION D.
COMMENTARY 47pp. Temperance tale in the form of 13 dialogues directed at servants and labourers and set in several Irish cabins [RL].

SHACKLETON, Mary. See LEADBEATER, Mrs Mary.

SHAND, **Alexander Innes**, b. Fetterkin (Kinardshire, Scotland) 1832, d. Edenbridge (Kent) 1907. Journalist, novelist, biographer and miscellaneous writer, AIS was the son of William Shand and his wife Christina Innes. He was educated at the University of Aberdeen and travelled widely afterwards, becoming a contributing journalist to the London *Times, Blackwood's Magazine* (Edinburgh), the *Saturday Review* and *Cornhill Magazine* (both London) as well as a biographer of Alfred Tennyson and Napoleon III, among others. He was interested in the Irish land question and wrote *Letters from the West of Ireland* (Edinburgh, 1885; repr. from the *Times*, 1884). This interest is reflected in his one novel known to have Irish content. SOURCE Allibone Suppl., ii, p. 1334; Brown, p. 274; ODNB; E. Reilly, p. 250.

S88   *Kilcarra* (by Alexander Innes Shand).
       London: Blackwood & Sons, 1891, 3 vols. SOURCE Brown, 1492; OCLC. LOCATION L.
COMMENTARY Set in Co. Galway at the time of the Land League agitation, the plot revolves around the efforts of the hero to trace the murderer of a landlord. The story deals extensively with the relations between tenants and landlords [Brown].

SHAPLEY, Rufus Edmonds, fl. 1860s. American satirist, RES was a resident of Pennsylvania and with C.W. Brook published *Pennsylvania criminal cases* (Philadelphia, 1869). SOURCE Allibone, ii, p. 2055; Fanning, p. 309.

S89   *"I', fur 'im." Solid for Mulhooly: A sketch of municipal politics under the leaders, the ring, and the boss* [anon.].
       New York: G.W. Carleton & Co., 1881. SOURCE Fanning, p. 309 (who mistakenly mentions as author 'Rufus Shavley'); Wright, iii, 4879; BLC. LOCATION L.
       + Philadelphia: Gebbie & Son, 1889 (new edn by Rufus E. Shapley; as *Solid for Mulhooly. A political satire*; ill. Thomas Nast). LOCATION L, InND Loeber coll.
COMMENTARY A satire on the Irish political machine in Philadelphia, it tells the tale of Michael Mulhooly who was born in a lowly cabin in Co. Tyrone and grew up without education. When he is aged 18, an American cousin who visits Ireland takes him back to work in his saloon in a city, probably Philadelphia. Here he is educated in the machine of municipal party politics. The story tells of his rise through municipal government until he eventually becomes a member of Congress. The political scene is depicted as being completely in the hands of the Irish and riddled by fraud, kickbacks, nepotism and crime [ML].

SHARP, Katharine Dooris, fl. 1888 to 1904. Poet and novel writer, KDS was born in Ulster of French descent. She was taken to the US when very young and settled in Ohio, where she later married a Dr Sharp of London. She published her first volume of poetry, *Eleanor's courtship and The songs that sang themselves* in Cincinnati (OH) in 1888. She was also the author of *Summer in a bog* (Cincinnati, 1913). SOURCE Allibone Suppl., ii, p. 1334 [under Kate Dooris Sharp]; O'Donoghue, p. 420; OCLC.

S90   *The south ward* (by Katharine Dooris Sharp).
       Cinninnati [OH]: Cranston & Stowe; New York: Hunt & Eaton,1891. SOURCE OCLC. LOCATION DCL.

S91   *The doctor's speaking tube* (by Katharine Dooris Sharp).
       Boston: R.G. Badger, 1904. SOURCE OCLC. LOCATION Ohio Univ.

SHARP, William (best known under the pseud. 'Fiona MacLeod'), b. Paisley (Scotland) 1855 (1856 according to Brown), d. 1905. Novelist, dramatist and biographer, WS spent his boyhood in the western highlands and islands of Scotland. He was educated at Glasgow University, became an editor of the *Canterbury Poets* (London, published from 1884 onward), and a contributor to periodicals. He spent time in Australia and lived also in Italy and Germany. For his pseudonym, he created a separate identity, even listing Fiona MacLeod in *Who's Who* (1900), and describing 'her' as a native of the Hebrides, resident in Iona, a hill-walker, sailor, and unmarried. Mrs Hinkson (Katharine Tynan§) in her *Twenty-five years rem-*

iniscences (London, 1913) said that she was not convinced that WS and Fiona MacLeod were the same person. WS edited an anthology, *Lyra Celtica* (Edinburgh, 1896), wrote plays, and biographies of Dante Gabriel Rossetti, Heinrich Heine, Percy Bysshe Shelley and Robert Browning. After his death, his widow edited the collected works published under MacLeod's name (London, New York, 1910). SOURCE Allibone Suppl., ii, pp 1334–5; Brown, pp 192–3; EF, pp 258–9; NCBEL 4, 1627–9; OCIL, p. 514; ODNB; Sutherland, p. 398 [under Macleod] and 568–9 [under Sharp]).

S92   *Songs and tales of Saint Columba and his age* [anon.].
    Edinburgh: Patrick Geddes, 1897. SOURCE COPAC. LOCATION Dt, L.
COMMENTARY Historical fiction set in the sixth century and concerns the life of the Irish missionary St Columba. Contents (excluding songs): 'The festival of the birds', 'The Sabbath of the fisher and flies', 'The moon-child', 'The flight of the culdees' [ML; Hartman, 255].

SHAW, Emily Elizabeth. See BEAVAN, Emily Elizabeth.

SHAW, Flora Louise (later Baroness Lugard), b. Woolwich, London (not Dublin as in some sources) 1851, d. Abinger Common (Surrey) 1929. Foreign correspondent, crusading journalist, novelist and children's writer, FLS was the daughter of Capt. George Shaw of the Royal Artillery and his wife, Marie Adrienne Desfontaines of Mauritius. Her grandfather was Sir Frederick Shaw, 3rd Bt, MP, of Bushy Park (Dublin), parliamentary leader of the Irish Conservatives. As a child she spent time with relatives in both France and Ireland. FLS had no formal education but read widely at the library of the Royal Military Academy in Woolwich. At age 20 she left home, spent time in France and Ireland and, encouraged by John Ruskin, began to write novels. In 1883 she secured a position on the *Pall Mall Gazette* (London) where she began a career of crusading journalism, which she considered a political activity. She was the first woman on the permanent staff of the *Times* (London) and rose to the senior position of editor of the paper's colonial department (1893–1900). In 1902 she married Sir Frederick Lugard, a colonial administrator. She travelled extensively with him and continued to work as correspondent for the *Times*. Throughout her career she followed Irish politics closely, initially approving of Gladstone's efforts towards Home Rule, but siding with Unionist opposition to it in 1914. Several of her works were reprinted in London (1930–31). Only one of her novels has Irish content. SOURCE Allibone Suppl., ii, pp 1335–6; Brown 2, p. 240; Hogan 2, p. 1104; Kunitz & Haycraft, p. 554; NCBEL 4, p. 1866; ODNB [under Lugard]; Sutherland, pp 569–70.

S93   *Castle Blair. A story of youthful days* (Flora Louise, Baroness Lugard).
    London: Kegan Paul, Trench & Co., 1878, 2 vols. SOURCE RLIN; Brown 2, 1424 (1883, 5th edn); Wolff, 6275 (1878, 2nd edn); OCLC. LOCATION D (1883, 5th edn), L (1878 edn), PU.
    + Boston: Roberts Bros, 1881. LOCATION InND Loeber coll.
    London: Rupert Hart-Davis, 1966. LOCATION L.
COMMENTARY The setting recalls the author's time as a child with her relatives in Ireland. Adrienne, an orphan whose mother was French, arrives at ramshackle Castle Blair in Ireland where she finds five unruly children living in the charge of their Uncle Blair, a retiring man who lives with his books. The children are a bone of contention between kindly Mrs Donegan, who spoils them, and Mr Plunkett the agent, who treats them harshly. The latter is an upright, well-meaning man who understands neither children nor the peasantry and is hated by both. When an attempt is made on his life, the children start to understand him better [Brown 2; Sutherland].

SHAW, George Bernard, b. Dublin 1856, d. Ayot St Lawrence (Herts.) 1950. Noted playwright, critic, novelist and man of letters, GBS was the son of an unsuccessful wholesale merchant, George Carr Shaw, and Lucinda Elizabeth Gurly, an accomplished musician. His father's alcoholism contributed to the break-up of his parents' marriage in 1873, when his mother moved to London with his two sisters, following her music colleague and teacher George Lee, with whom the Shaws had shared a house in Hatch Street, Dublin. GBS was educated intermittently at Wesley College and other educational institutions and spent two years at the Protestant Dublin English Scientific and Commercial Day School. At age 15 he was employed in an estate office as a junior clerk, which work he disliked intensely, but collecting rents around Dublin exposed him to elements of poverty and inequality that would feature in his later work. In 1876, he left for London. He worked initially ghost-writing reviews for George Lee for the *Hornet* (location unclear), educated himself by reading in the BL – where he met many of the radical intellectuals who were to influence his future socialism – and began to experiment writing fiction, drama and verse. He worked unsuccessfully on five novels, some of which were published only after his later success as a playwright. A segment of one of these, 'The Legg papers', was published as a short story in William Butler Yeats's§ miscellany *The shanachie* (Dublin, 1906). Another short story, 'The serenade', was published after several rejections in the *Magazine of Music* (London, Nov. 1885). His first gleam of success was with *Cashel Byron's profession* (London, 1886). But the succeeding, and final, novel, *The unsocial socialist*, after serialization in *To-day* (London), was published only in 1887 and after many rejections. He joined and became very active in the Fabian Society in 1884 and began to lecture, to review books and to work for several journals as an art and music critic. GBS's subsequent fame rests on his numerous and successful plays, which were remarkable for their treatment of serious themes and for their sparkling dialogue. Many, such as *St. Joan*, *Arms and the Man*, *Heartbreak House* and *Major Barbara* remain in the popular theatrical repertoire. William Butler Yeats§ commissioned *John Bull's other island* (London, 1904) for the new Abbey Theatre but delayed production as he was afraid Irish audiences would reject GBS's view of Ireland. Besides his dramas, he wrote widely on Irish issues; pacifism; religion; socialism; politics and other issues. In 1925 he was awarded the Nobel Prize for literature. He was made an honorary freeman of the City of Dublin when he was age 90, and his will benefited the NGI. In 1898 GBS married Charlotte Frances Payne-Townshend, who was wealthy and had been born in Derry. For a critical evaluation of GBS as playwright, see Hogan 2, Field Day, ODNB, RIA/DIB and sources below, and for a list of archival sources, see ODNB. For his portraits and papers, see also ODNB. SOURCE Allibone Suppl., ii, p. 1336; Boylan, pp 353–5; Field Day, i, pp xxiii, 505, 507, ii, p. 296 and passim, iii, p. 2 and passim; Hogan 2, pp 1087–105; R. Hogan, 'The novels of Bernard Shaw', *English Literature in Transition*, 8, (1965), pp 63–114; M. Holroyd, *Bernard Shaw* (London 1988–93, 4 vols.); Igoe, pp 219–22; OCIL, pp 514–17; ODNB; RIA/DIB; B.C. Rosset, *Shaw of Dublin: the formative years* (University Park, PA, 1964); Sutherland, p. 570; S. Weintraub, *Journey to heartbreak: the crucible years of Bernard Shaw, 1914–18* (New York, 1971); S. Weintraub (ed), *Shaw: an autobiography*, (New York, 1969–70, 2 vols.); S.A. Yorks, *The evolution of Bernard Shaw*, (Washington, DC, 1981).

S94   *Cashel Byron's profession. A novel* (by George Bernard Shaw).
[London]: The Modern Press, 1886. SOURCE Allibone Suppl., ii, p. 1337. LOCATION Dt.
London: Walter Scott, [1889] (revsd edn). SOURCE NCBEL 3, p. 1170. LOCATION L.
London: G. Richards, 1901 (newly revsd edn, as *Novels of his nonage*). SOURCE NCBEL 3, p. 1170. LOCATION MH.
Leipzig: Bernard Tauchnitz, 1914. SOURCE T & B, 4468. LOCATION Univ. of Manchester.

New York: George Munro, 1887. SOURCE OCLC. LOCATION NN. COMMENTARY *New York edns* This and another New York edns were unauthorized [Kersnowski, p. 126]. + Carbondale, Edwardsville (IL): Southern Illinois Univ. Press; London, Amsterdam: Feffer & Simons, 1968. LOCATION D.

COMMENTARY Written in 1882 and first appeared in *To-day* (London, April 1885 – Mar. 1886). Various explanations have been given for the variations in page size (normally 22 x 14 cm.). According to GBS, 'The size of the bigger copies is due to the fact that they reproduced not only the type but the format of *To-day*. But the booksellers objected that in this form it occupied too much room ... It was probably cut down as far as the margins would allow to meet this objection'. Set in England, it deals with the relationship between a rich young woman and a prize-fighter, each defying the rules of their class [ML; COPAC; ODNB].

S95 *The unsocial socialist* (by George Bernard Shaw).
London: W. Swan Sonnenschein, Lowrey & Co., 1887. SOURCE Allibone Suppl., ii, p. 1337; Kersnowski, p. 126. LOCATION Dt, L.
New York: Brentano's, 1888. SOURCE Kersnowski, p. 126. LOCATION D (1900 edn), C (1900 edn), InND Loeber coll. (New York, Modern Library, n.d.).
COMMENTARY No copy of the New York 1888 edn located. First serialized in *To-Day* (London, 1884), GBS's original title was 'The heartless man' and he intended this volume as 'a gigantic grapple with the whole social problem'. It paraphrased some of Karl Marx's *Das Capital* (Moscow, 1887), featured a runaway husband, a finishing school for girls, and a socialist agitator and handsome hero who was a prototype of John Tanner in GBS's *Man and superman* [ODNB; Sutherland, p. 570].

S96 *Love among the artists* (by George Bernard Shaw).
Chicago: Herbert S. Stone, 1900. SOURCE Kersnowski, p. 126. LOCATION D (1905 edn), L.
+ New York: Brentano's, 1910. LOCATION D.
London: Constable, 1914. SOURCE Kersnowski, p. 126. LOCATION Dt, Univ. of Leeds.
COMMENTARY Written in 1881, and first published in *Our Corner* (London, 1887–88). It consists of a study of a musical genius [Sutherland, p. 570].

S97 *The irrational knot, being the second novel of his nonage* (preface by George Bernard Shaw).
+ London: Constable & Co., 1905. LOCATION D, L, Pierpont Morgan Library, New York.
+ New York: Brentano's, 1905. SOURCE NCBEL 3, p. 1171; Kersnowski, p. 126. LOCATION D, CtY, InND Loeber coll.
COMMENTARY According to the preface, the novel was written in 1880 and first appeared in *Our Corner* (London, 1885–7). Marion Lind marries an engineer, Mr Conolly. He is considered by her circle to be beneath her. He has a sister who is an actress and who becomes an alcoholic. The pair drift apart, partly by Mr Conolly's lack of emotion and extreme rational behaviour. Marion escapes to America with an old flame, but finds no happiness. Eventually her husband turns up and reclaims her [ML].

S98 *Immaturity* (by George Bernard Shaw).
London: Constable & Co., 1930. LOCATION D (1931 edn), L (1931 edn), Univ. of Bristol.
COMMENTARY Written in 1879 but published fifty years later. Set in London, the story describes the lives and interactions of a number of young persons of different social classes living in a boarding-house: a clerk, minister, seamstress, painter, poet, a society girl, etc. [ML; Sutherland, p. 570].

S99 *Adventures of a black girl in her search for God* (by George Bernard Shaw).
+ London: Constable & Co., 1932. LOCATION D, L.

+ New York: Dodd, Mead & Co., 1933 (ill. John Farleigh). SOURCE Kersnowski, p. 126. LOCATION L, InND Loeber coll.

S100   *Short stories, scraps and shavings* (by George Bernard Shaw).
London: Constable & Co., 1932 (ill. John Farleigh). SOURCE NCBEL 3, p. 1173. LOCATION D (1934 edn), L, InND Loeber coll. (1934 edn).
Leipzig: Bernard Tauchnitz, 1935. SOURCE T & B, 5199. LOCATION L.
New York: Dodd, Mead, 1934. SOURCE Hogan 2, p. 1104; RLIN. LOCATION NNC.
COMMENTARY Contents: 'Aerial football: the new game', 'The emperor and the little girl', 'The miraculous revenge', 'The theatre of the future', 'A dressing room secret', 'Don Giovanni explains', 'Beauty's duty', 'Still after the doll's house', 'The domesticity of Franklyn Barnabas', 'Death of an old revolutionary hero', 'The serenade', 'A Sunday on the Surrey hills', 'Cannonfodder', 'The adventures of the black girl in her search for god' (first published in London, 1932) [ML].

S101   *An unfinished novel* (by George Bernard Shaw).
+ London: Constable; New York: Dodd, Mead, 1958 (ed. with introd. by Stanley Weintraub; preface by Bernard Shaw; limited edn). SOURCE Hogan 2, p. 1104; NCBEL 3, p. 1173; SOURCE Kersnowski, p. 126. LOCATION D, L, InND Loeber coll.
COMMENTARY Published posthumously [RL].

SHAW, John, fl. 1880. Novelist and story writer, JS was from the north of Ireland, most likely Belfast. According to the title page of *The golden Halcombes* (Belfast, 1880) he also wrote 'Wanted, a tenor' and 'The Christmas eve', but these have not been located as separate publications, although 'Wanted a tenor' is included in the collected stories in *The diamond merchant* (Belfast, 1898). SOURCE RL.

S102   *The golden Halcombes* (by John Shaw).
+ Belfast: Charles W. Olley, 1880. SOURCE Allibone Suppl., ii, p. 1336; OCLC (1888 edn). LOCATION PC.

S103   *An actor's daughter* (by John Shaw).
London: Griffith Farran, Okeden & Welsh, 1890. SOURCE COPAC. LOCATION L.

S104   *The diamond merchant* (by John Shaw).
+ Belfast: R. Aicken & Co., 1898. SOURCE Brown, 1493; Brown 2, 1425 (n.d. edn). LOCATION D.
COMMENTARY Six stories set in Belfast, written from a Protestant point of view: 'The diamond merchant' (deals with Belfast in the 1820s), 'Wanted a tenor', 'Ramore Hill', 'Jack Temple's detective experience', 'Only a poor actor', 'The widow's might' [RL].

SHEAHAN, Thomas, pseud. **'A plain Englishman',** fl. 1825. Journalist and miscellaneous writer TS was from Cork and started his career as tutor to the children of Richard Deasy of Clonakilty (Co. Cork), in which town he acted as secretary of the first Clonakilty Parochial Catholic meeting in 1824. A year later he went to London. He returned to Ireland and as a journalist reported for Cork papers on such topics as the need for Irish manufactures; tithes; the Cork Brunswick Club; Orangemen; poor laws; the Doneraile conspiracy, and the movement to repeal the Act of Union. Aside from his *'Articles'* (Cork, 1833), he planned to publish another book on Irish manufactures, the Cork tithe campaign, and the repeal movement, but this did not appear. SOURCE *'Articles'* (Cork, 1833); BLC; RL.

S105   *Excursions from Bandon, in the South of Ireland* (by 'A plain Englishman').
+ London: Longman, Hurst, Rees, Orme, Brown & Green, 1825. LOCATION L.
COMMENTARY An account of travel in the south of Ireland that recounts conversations with local people. The trip was made to 'see if the Irish are more sinned against than sinning'. It

contains notes, a chart of ships and tonnage in 1824, and a chart of comparisons between Britain and Ireland [ML; CM].

S106   *"Articles" or Irish manufacture; or, portions of Cork history* (by Thomas Sheahan; dedicated to the members of the Cork Trades' Association for the Encouragement of Irish Manufacture).

+ Cork: Printed [for the author?] by James Higgins, 1833. LOCATION L, InND Loeber coll.

COMMENTARY Largely based on newspaper articles and letters written in the 1820s and early 1830s dealing with legal proceedings in Cork City, landlords, absenteeism, and religion. Some of the writings consist of fiction in the form of dialogues with a satirical, political intent: 'The mirror of justice' (in three parts), 'Election sketch', 'Dialogues for the day', 'Mr. G—d C—n and a true Protestant', 'Scene, Humbug Hall', 'Table talk', 'Absenteeism, the unknown tongue', 'The question stated', 'A hard case', 'Measuring a face' [RL].

SHEARES, Henry (also Sheers), b. 1728, d. 1776. Miscellaneous writer, HS was the son of Henry Sheares and Mary, daughter of John Bayley of Castlemore (Co. Cork). HS Jnr was trained for the law, entered TCD in 1744, where he graduated BA in 1748. He became a banker, and was MP for Dundalk 1692–3. He married Jane Anne Bettesworth (d. *c.*1803) of Glasheen (Co. Cork). One of their sons died in a swimming accident, two more died in the 1770s while serving with the military in the West Indies, and their sons John and Henry Sheares were executed as a result of the rebellion of the United Irishmen in 1798 (John had written poetry). HS must have been wealthy: he left the bulk of his estate to his son Henry, and to John £3,000. SOURCE HIP, vi, pp 265–6; R.R. Madden, *Literary remains of the United Irishmen* (Dublin, 1887); ODNB [under John Sheares]; O'Donoghue, p. 421 [under John Sheares]; RL.

S107   *The modern monitor; or, Flynn's speculations* [anon.] (dedicated to Mrs Elizabeth Gray).

+ Cork: Printed [for the author?] by William Flynn, 1771 (subscribers' list with mostly Irish names). LOCATION UCD Folklore Dept., L.

COMMENTARY Not in ESTC. Indicated on flyleaf of the UCD copy as by the father of the Sheers brothers (Henry and John Sheares). A miscellany, issued periodically and addressed to female readers. Handwritten annotations in the copy at UCD show that O = Henry Sheers; and that T = Longfield; 3 = Mrs Gray; 1 = Miss Waterhouse; 39 = P.D.K., who remains to be identified [ML].

SHEE, Sir Martin Archer, b. Dublin 1769 (1770 in Allibone), d. Brighton (East Sussex) 1850. Painter, novelist and poet, MAS was, according to Allibone, a 'descendant of the Princess O'Shee of Kerry and Tipperary'. Son of Martin Shee, Esq. of Dublin and Mary Archer, who died when he was an infant, MAS studied painting in the school of the Royal Dublin Society under Francis Robert West. At age 15 he set himself up successfully as a portrait painter. In 1788 he went to London at the suggestion of Gilbert Stuart and for several years painted portraits, two of which were accepted by the Royal Academy in 1789. His cousin, Sir George Shee, introduced his work to Edmund Burke, who in turn introduced him to Sir Joshua Reynolds, on whose advice he entered the school of the Royal Academy. He was elected a full member in 1800, and eventually became its president in 1830, when he was knighted. In 1796 he married Mary Power, whose father James came from Youghal (Co. Cork). MAS became known chiefly for his portraits for an increasingly aristocratic clientele, but he also executed history paintings which he exhibited at the British Institution, in which he was very involved. He was instrumental in getting a royal charter for the RHA and was made an honorary member in 1826. Byron said of Shee's twinned talents of painting and writing that his 'pen and pencil yield an equal grace'. Aside from his novels, he published poems, including *Rhymes on art* (London, 1805); *Alasco*, a tragedy on the partition of Poland published in 1824, and a verse memoir of Sir Joshua Reynolds (1814). He served as president of the Royal Academy until 1845 and was rewarded with a pension when he retired. His son published in 1860 a biography, *Life of Sir Martin Arthur Shee, president of the Royal Academy, F.R.S., D.C.L.* A self-portrait is in the National Portrait Gallery, London, and further portraits are listed by Elmes and ODNB. For MAS's manuscript papers, see ODNB. SOURCE Allibone, ii, pp 2065–6; Boylan, pp 355–6; J. Burke, *A history of the commoners* (London, 1835), i, pp 405–6; Elmes, p. 181; ODNB; NCBEL 4, p. 1983; OCIL, p. 518; O'Donoghue, p. 421; RIA/DIB; W.G. Strickland, *A dictionary of Irish artists* (Shannon, 1969), ii, pp 329–47.

S108   *Oldcourt; A novel* [anon.].
London: Henry Colburn, 1829, 3 vols. SOURCE British Fiction; Garside, 1829:76; NCBEL 4, p. 1984; Strickland, p. 334; Wolff, 6277. LOCATION Corvey CME 3–628–48248–8, L, MH.
COMMENTARY Set in Ireland. A Catholic girl, Grace Oldcourt, is educated by a priest. Her beauty attracts many suitors, among whom are Sir Walter D'Arcy, the owner of an adjoining estate, and his foster brother, Doran Conolly. She accepts D'Arcy's hand, and Conolly becomes despondent and is committed to an asylum for the insane. He escapes in time to interrupt the wedding by announcing that D'Arcy had seduced his sister, and then dies from a self-administered poison. Grace breaks off her relationship with D'Arcy, who dies in a duel with Grace's brother. She goes to live in a convent [*La Belle Assemblée*, 3rd ser. 10 (Sept. 1829), pp 127–8; British Fiction).

S109   *Cecil Hyde. A novel* [anon.].
London: Saunders & Otley, 1834, 2 vols. SOURCE Hodgson p. 99; NCBEL 4, p. 1984; Strickland, p. 334; Wolff, 6276; Garside 2, 1834:69. LOCATION Corvey CME 3–628–47242–3, Dt (1834, 2nd edn), L, C, E.
Philadelphia: Carey, Lea & Blanchard, 1834, 2 vols. SOURCE Kaser, 452. LOCATION NjP.

S110   *Harry Calverley. A novel* [anon.].
London: Saunders & Otley, 1835, 3 vols. SOURCE NCBEL 4, p. 1984; Hodgson p. 502; Block, p. 213; Garside 2, 1835:88. SOURCE COPAC. LOCATION L, O.
Philadelphia: Carey, Lea & Blanchard, 1836, 2 vols. SOURCE Kaser, 569; OCLC. LOCATION CLU.

SHEEHAN, Canon P.A. See **SHEEHAN, Canon Patrick Augustine**.

SHEEHAN, Canon Patrick Augustine (known as **Canon P.A. Sheehan**), b. Mallow (Co. Cork) 1852, d. Doneraile (Co. Cork) 1913. Priest, novelist, poet, social reformer and miscellaneous writer, Canon Sheehan – as he was popularly known – was the son of Patrick Sheehan, a small businessman, and Joanna Regan. He was educated at St Coleman's College, Fermoy (Co. Cork), and at St Patrick's College, Maynooth (Co. Kildare), and was ordained in Cork in 1875. He served for a while in Plymouth, England, where he ministered to the prisoners of Dartmoor. He was appointed parish priest of Doneraile (Co. Cork) in 1895, the year in which he started writing novels. He completed 14 works of fiction, several of which deal with the life and dilemmas of the Catholic clergy and of individuals living in small communities in Co. Cork. In 1903 he was made the canon of Cloyne. From 1903 to 1907 he led negotiations between landlords and tenants leading to a land transfer settlement, and he was instrumental in bringing improvements to the village of Doneraile. He supported the United Irish League,

Sheehan

founded by his friend William O'Brien§, and his vision for an independent Ireland was one of inclusivity and cooperation among classes and religions achieved through constitutional means. He was a brilliant linguist, a man of wide culture and learning, and the author of a collection of poems and essays published as *Literary life, essays* [and] *poems* (Dublin, [1930]). But he is known most for his novels, which remained popular with Catholic readers well into the twentieth century. Some of his letters are at the St Joseph's Presentation Convent, Doneraile, and his statue is in the parish churchyard. For his portraits, see ODNB. SOURCE Boylan, p. 356; C. Candy, *Priestly fictions: popular Irish novelists of the early 20th century* (Dublin, 1995); EF, p. 359; Field Day, i, p. 1070, ii, pp 1022, 1216–17; R. Fleischman, *Catholic nationalism in the Irish revival. A study of Canon Sheehan, 1852–1913* (Basingstoke, 1997); J.A. Gaughan, *Doneraile* (1968); H. Heuser, *Canon Sheehan of Doneraile* (London, 1917); Hogan 2, pp 1105–7; Irish pseudonyms; L. McBride, 'A literary life of a socially and politically engaged priest: Canon Patrick Augustine Sheehan (1852–1913)', in G. Moran, (ed), *Radical Irish priests, 1660–1970*, (Dublin, 1998); OCIL, p. 518; ODNB; O'Donoghue, pp 422–3; RIA/DIB; Sutherland, p. 571.

S111   *Geoffrey Austin: student* [anon.] (dedicated to the Catholic youth of Ireland).
+ Dublin: M.H. Gill, 1895. SOURCE Brown, 1495; COPAC. LOCATION D, L , InND Loeber coll. (1897 edn).
COMMENTARY Set in a college near Dublin that prepares students for the entrance exams of the English civil service and military. The school is nominally controlled by the clergy, but in reality left to the care of a grinder of more than doubtful character. The standards of student conduct and religion are very low. Both the hero, Geoffrey Austin, and his friend fail their exams and have to face the world and somehow make a living. They feel the lack of a good education, but even more so the lack of spiritual guidance during their years at school [ML; Brown].

S112   *The triumph of failure. A sequel to "Geoffrey Austin, student"* (by Canon P.A. Sheehan).
+ London: Burns & Oates; New York, Cincinnati, Chicago: Benziger Bros, 1899. SOURCE Brown, 1496; Hogan 2, p. 1107. LOCATION L, InND Loeber coll.
+ Dublin: Phoenix Publishing Co., n.d. (as *The triumph of failure*). LOCATION D.
+ Steyl: Missionsdruckerei, 1902 (trans. by Oskar Jacob as *Der Erfolg des Miszerfolgs*). LOCATION D.
+ New York, Cincinnati, Chicago: Benziger Bros, 1924 (as *The triumph of failure*). LOCATION D.
COMMENTARY A sequel to *Geoffrey Austin, student* (Dublin, 1897), a study of a priest losing and regaining his faith [Brown].

S113   *My new curate. A story gathered from the stray leaves of an old diary* (by Canon P.A. Sheehan).
+ Boston: Marlier, Callahan & Co., 1899 (ill. Louis Meynell). LOCATION D, L (1900 edn), InND Loeber coll. (1900 edn and 1925 edn).
+ Dublin, Cork: Talbot Press, n.d. LOCATION D.
+ Cork, Dublin: Mercier Press, 1989. LOCATION D.
+ Cologne: J.P. Bachem, n.d. (trans. by J. Nemo as *Mein neuer Kaplan*). LOCATION D.
COMMENTARY First serialized in the *American Ecclesiastical Review*, it describes the effect of the arrival of a young, energetic curate in a sleepy, out-of-the-way parish in the author's district in Co. Cork. The curate's projects to raise the people's standards of living fail. The village comes to his support to save him from bankruptcy. It gives a vivid account of daily life and the central role of the clergy in a rural Irish parish in the late-nineteenth century [Brown; Field Day, ii, pp 1040–5; Hogan; OCIL, pp 385; EF, p. 359; Leclaire, p. 233].

1186

S114   *Luke Delmege* (by Canon P.A. Sheehan).
   + London, New York, Bombay: Longmans, Green & Co., 1901. SOURCE Brown, 1498; Hogan 2, p. 1107. LOCATION D, L.
   + Paris: P. Lethielleux, n.d. (trans. as *Luke Delmege*). LOCATION D.
   + Munich: Allgemeine Verlags-Gesellschaft, n.d. (trans. by Anton Lohr as *Lukas Delmege. Ein moderner Seelsorger-Roman*). LOCATION D.
   + New York, London, Bombay: Longmans, Green & Co., 1907. LOCATION InND Loeber coll.

COMMENTARY First serialized in the *American Ecclesiastical Review* (New York), the life story of an Irish priest who comes out of the seminary laden with prizes and finds that in general the world does not appreciate these triumphs. A theme throughout the book is the struggle between humility and intellectual pride. For a number of years Luke Delmege works in the missions in England, where he feels most at ease among the rich, more intellectually-minded Catholics. His return to Cork gives rise to many comparisons between England and Ireland [ML; EF, p. 359; Hogan; Leclaire, p. 233].

S115   *Lost angel of a ruined paradise* (by Canon P.A. Sheehan).
   London: Longmans, Green & Co., 1904. SOURCE Brown, 1500; Hogan 2, p. 1107; COPAC. LOCATION L.

COMMENTARY Three girls on leaving college take part in a *tableau vivant* as the Fates. They announce the imagined fates of their companions, and a mysterious voice from the audience announces their own. The story tells how their fates worked out. Set in Dublin and London [Brown].

S116   *Glenanaar. A story of Irish life* (by Canon P.A. Sheehan).
   + London, New York, Bombay: Longmans, Green & Co., 1905. SOURCE Brown, 1499; Hogan 2, p. 1107; RLIN. LOCATION D, L.
   Paris: Lethielleux, [1907] (trans. as *Ange égaré d'un paradis ruiné*). SOURCE Brown; RLIN. LOCATION BNF.
   + Steyl: Missionsdruckerei, 1906 (trans. by Oskar Jacob as *Das Christtagskind. Eine Erzählung aus Irland*). LOCATION D.
   + Dublin: The O'Brien Press, 1989 (introd. by Con Houlihan, ill. cover Mildred Anne Butler). LOCATION D, L, InND Loeber coll.

COMMENTARY First published in the US in the *Dolphin* (New York, 1904–05), the story is set in Doneraile (Co. Cork) and based on conspiracy trials that took place there in 1829 when, after an attempt to kill a landlord, a number of peasants were rounded up on the evidence of an informer and Daniel O'Connell came to defend them. Several of the peasants are then temporarily released. In the story, one of the defendants, Edmund Connors, meets a woman who, he realizes, is about to throw a baby in the river. Later the baby is found in his stable. He suspects that she is the child of the informer, but he does not tell this to his family. The baby, called Nodlag, grows up in their household until the neighbours find out who she is and start threatening the Connors. Nodlag's son grows up not knowing his mother's history until one day he is told that he is the grandson of an informer. He leaves Ireland, refusing to let the woman he loves accompany him. After many years in America, where he makes his fortune, he returns to Ireland to see her. She is now a widow, old and poor, and she refuses to marry him because she knows he is looking for her young self that he left behind. Eventually, he marries her daughter, who looks very much like her mother when young. By this time, the hatred against the informer's offspring has finally died down [ML].

S117   *A spoiled priest and other stories* (by Canon P.A. Sheehan).
   + London: Burns & Oates; Dublin: M.H. Gill & Son, 1905 (ill. M. Healy). SOURCE Brown, 1501; Hogan 2, p. 1107. LOCATION D.
   London: T. Fisher Unwin, 1905. LOCATION L.

Sheehan

London: Burns & Oates; New York: Benziger, 1908 (as *Canon Sheehan's short stories*; ill. M. Healy). SOURCE Hogan 2, p. 1107; OCLC. LOCATION D (1911 edn), L (1911 edn), Boston College.

COMMENTARY Stories set in Co. Cork. Contents of the London 1905 edn: 'A spoiled priest' (a glimpse of the workings of an ecclesiastical seminary and the attitude of Irish peasants towards a student who has been refused ordination), 'A thorough gentleman' (does not deal with Ireland), 'The monks of Trabolgan' (a curious, fanciful story of Ireland in the future), 'Rita, the street singer' (does not deal with Ireland), 'Remanded' (based on fact, the story of a hero-priest of Cork) , 'How the angel became happy', 'Frank Forest's mince-pie' (does not deal with Ireland), 'Topsy'. The story of 'Rita, the street singer' was published as a separate booklet by the Catholic Truth Society of Ireland [ML; Brown; Leclaire, p. 234; RL].

S118   *Lisheen; or, the test of the spirits* (by Canon P.A. Sheehan).

+ London, New York, Bombay, Calcutta: Longmans, Green & Co., 1907. SOURCE Brown, 1502; Hogan 2, p. 1107. LOCATION D, L, InND Loeber coll.

COMMENTARY The concept of the story is based on Tolstoy's *Resurrection*. Set in Co. Kerry where a young Irish landlord determines to put to the test his ideals of altruism and commences the life of a labourer. He finds out how full of disappointments the way of the reformer is, but he persists. He loses his erstwhile fiancée to an unscrupulous man, who does not tell her that he has leprosy. The hero finds love and peace in his mode of life. Two main themes are the greed and callousness of Irish landlords and the inability of the Englishman to understand the Irish character [ML; Brown].

S119   *The blindness of Dr. Gray; or, the final law* (by Canon P.A. Sheehan).

+ London, New York, Bombay, Calcutta: Longmans, Green & Co., 1909. SOURCE Brown, 1503; Hogan 2, p. 1107. LOCATION D, L.

+ Dublin: Talbot Press, 1953. LOCATION D.

COMMENTARY Set in Ireland and South Africa, it pictures clerical life and has a love story interwoven. Dr Gray is a strict disciplinarian who adheres to the law with narrowness and hardness. However, by the end he finds out that it is love, not law, that rules the world. It contains some criticism of various features of Irish life, such as popular politics, religious divisions and the Gaelic League [Brown].

S120   *The intellectuals. An experiment in Irish club-life* (by Canon P.A. Sheehan).

+ London, New York, Bombay, Calcutta: Longmans, Green & Co., 1911. SOURCE Hogan 2, p. 1107. LOCATION D, L.

New York, London: Longmans, Green & Co., 1911. LOCATION NUC.

COMMENTARY In the preface, the author states his purpose in writing the book is to show that 'there are really no invincible antagonisms amongst the peoples who make up the commonwealth of Ireland, no mutual repugnances that may not be removed by a freer and kindlier intercourse with each other'. A group of men and women, both Catholic and Protestant, from Ireland, England and Scotland form a club to discuss current issues of the day, which allows the author to express his vision of the society possible in an independent Ireland [ODNB].

S121   *The Queen's fillet* (by Canon P.A. Sheehan).

London: Longmans, Green & Co., 1911. SOURCE Hogan 2, pp 1106–7. LOCATION D (1914 edn), L, NUC.

New York: Longmans, Green & Co., 1911. LOCATION NUC.

Dublin: Phoenix, 1969 (new edn). SOURCE OCLC. LOCATION St Patrick College, Dublin, Univ. of Glasgow.

COMMENTARY Historical fiction set during the French Revolution. It warns the Irish of the dangers of demagoguery and excess in political uprisings [Hogan 2, pp 1106–7; ODNB].

S122 *Miriam Lucas* (by Canon P.A. Sheehan).

+ London: Longmans, 1912. SOURCE Brown, 1504; Hogan 2, p. 1107. LOCATION Dt, L.

COMMENTARY Set in Co. Cork. Miriam is the daughter of wealthy Protestant parents. Her mother, on becoming a Catholic, is driven by domestic persecution into evil ways, and subsequently disappears. Miriam is ostracized by society; she goes to Dublin where she flings herself into the socialist movement. Her efforts end in a disastrous strike, and crime and tragedy follow. She goes to New York in search of her mother, whom she finds sunk to the lowest moral depths. The book is meant to deal with Irish social and religious problems and draws a severe and satirical picture of the Protestant upper classes [ML; Brown; Leclaire, p. 234].

S123 *The graves at Kilmorna. A story of '67* (by Canon P.A. Sheehan).

+ New York, London, Bombay, Calcutta, Madras: Longmans, Green & Co., 1915. SOURCE Brown, 1505; Hogan 2, p. 1107. LOCATION D, L, InND Loeber coll.

COMMENTARY Historical fiction about the Fenian movement of 1867. The author describes the Fenians of that period as unselfish patriots who knew that they could not win but were willing to sacrifice themselves in order to keep the idea of nationalism alive. The author feels that patriotism has more or less died since then. The hero, Miles Cogan, was imprisoned for ten years in England. When he returns to Ireland he stays away from politics because he is disillusioned by what he sees. Eventually, he is willing to stand on the platform with a young candidate for a parliamentary seat. He makes a brief speech in support of the candidate and is hit by a rock and dies [ML; Brown].

S124 *Tristram Lloyd. A novel* (by Canon P.A. Sheehan; ed. and completed by Revd H. Gaffney, OP).

+ New York, London, Toronto: Longmans, Green & Co., 1928. SOURCE Brown 2, 1429. LOCATION D.

+ Dublin, Cork: Talbot Press, [1929] (as *Tristram Lloyd. The romance of a journalist*). SOURCE Hogan 2, p. 1107. LOCATION D, L.

COMMENTARY The story depicts the struggle of a young man to reconcile his high ideals of life with material and moral wretchedness revealed to him by his work as a journalist. An erring sister adds to his troubles. He is sent to Poland and is a witness there to Russian oppression. He returns to Ireland full of the idea of doing something for the poor and oppressed at home. But the tragedy of his sister's murder turns all to bitterness. Gradually faith, human love and happiness come back into his life [Brown 2].

— COLLECTED WORKS

S125 *The works of Canon Sheehan of Doneraile.*

Dublin: Phoenix, [1930], 12 vols. SOURCE COPAC. LOCATION Dt.

SHEEHY, David, b. Broadford (Co. Limerick) 1844, d. Dublin 1932. Nationalist politician and radical agrarian agitator, DS was the son of Richard Sheehy, a mill owner, and Johanna O'Shea. He was educated at St Munchin's Jesuit college in Limerick and at the Irish College in Paris, but did not – as his father intended – follow his brother Eugene into the Catholic priesthood. As a young man he joined the IRB and fled to the US for a time after raiding an RIC barracks. Back in Ireland, he married Elizabeth McCoy of Curraghmore (Co. Limerick), ran mills in Cork and Tipperary, and as a result of his friendship with the politician William O'Brien§ ran for parliament as the Parnell candidate for Galway in 1885. Always sympathetic to the plight of the rural poor, his career as a politician was punctuated by six periods of imprisonment for promoting land agitation. He backed the anti-Parnell faction after the split in the Irish Parliamentary Party in 1890 and campaigned against Parnellite candidates. He continued to support land issues, O'Brien's United Irish League, and Irish involvement in the

'Sheelah'

First World War. DS's daughter, Hannah, married the pacifist and socialist Francis Skeffington, who added her name to his; daughter Mary, later a Dublin city councillor, married Tom Kettle, one of the founders of the Land League, who was executed after the Easter Rising of 1916; and daughter Kathleen was the mother of the politician and writer Conor Cruise O'Brien. SOURCE Boylan, pp 208 [under Thomas Kettle], 397 [under Francis Sheehy-Skeffington]; RIA/DIB.

S126   *Prison papers* (by David Sheehy).
+ Dublin: Weldrick Bros, 1888. SOURCE COPAC. LOCATION D (uncatalogued), Dt.
COMMENTARY First serialized in the newspaper *United Ireland* (Dublin). According to the introd., the author's purpose was to 'portray the salient features of gaol life', recorded 'whilst cheating prison of its monotony'. Appended is a brief narrative of his own experiences [ML; COPAC].

'SHEELAH', pseud. See **FLETCHER, Miss A.**

SHELLEY, Mary Wollstonecraft (née Godwin), b. London 1797, d. London 1851. English novelist, editor and biographer, MWS was the daughter of the philosopher and novelist William Godwin§ and Mary Wollstonecraft, pioneering feminist and author of *Vindication of the rights of woman* (London, 1792) who had spent time in Ireland as governess to Margaret King, later Lady Mount Cashell§. MWS left England in 1814 with the poet Percy Bysshe Shelley, whom she married in 1816. After his drowning in 1822, she returned to England and supported herself and her only surviving child by writing. She is famous for her novel *Frankenstein* (London, 1818). For a detailed biography, see ODNB. SOURCE Allibone, ii, p. 2068; Blain, p. 974; NCBEL 4, pp 1063–72; ODNB; Todd, pp 605–10.
S127   *The fortunes of Perkin Warbeck. A romance* [anon.].
+ London: Henry Colburn & Richard Bentley, 1830, 3 vols. SOURCE Garside 2, 1830:99. LOCATION Corvey CME 3–628–47771–9, L, C.
London: [publisher?], 1830 (revsd, corrected, ill., new introd.). SOURCE NSTC; RLIN. LOCATION C.
Philadelphia: Carey, Lea & Blanchard, 1834, 2 vols. SOURCE NSTC. LOCATION L.
[New York?]: Norwood, 1976, 3 vols. SOURCE RLIN. LOCATION DCL.
London: William Pickering, 1996. LOCATION L.
COMMENTARY Historical fiction reviewed in the *Dublin Literary Gazette* (1830, pp 354–5). Set in the fifteenth century, Perkin Warbeck is actually the lost young duke of York. It describes Warbeck's two visits to Ireland and the attack on Waterford in 1497 by the duke of York and the earl of Desmond and his allies [*Dublin Literary Gazette*; Todd, p. 609].

SHELTON, James S., fl. 1893. American writer of moral fiction.
S128   *The strike at Shane's. A prize story of Indiana* [anon.].
+ Boston: American Humane Education Society, 1893 (Goldmine Series, No. 2). SOURCE OCLC. LOCATION MH, InND Loeber coll.
COMMENTARY The story relates how the animals at Shane's farm are abused. The only person on the farm who is friendly to them is an Irish farmhand. The animals get together and decide to go on strike. After a while, the effect on the farm is apparent. While the farm owner's son is sick, the Irish farmhand looks after the animals and under kind treatment they decide to work again. The owners realize that kindness pays [ML].

SHEPPARD, Bithia Mary. See **CROKER, Mrs Bithia Mary.**

SHERIDAN, Caroline Henrietta (née Callendar), b. 1779, d. London 1851. Novelist, CHS was the daughter of Col. James Callandar, later Sir James Campbell, and Lady Elizabeth Macdonnel, youngest daughter of the 5th earl of Antrim. The ODNB does not give a birthplace for CHS, but her father served in Ireland before returning to Scotland in 1789. She married Thomas Sheridan, son of Irish playwright Richard Brinsley Sheridan, in 1805 and accompanied him to the Cape of Good Hope, where he was colonial treasurer and where he died of consumption in 1817. A great beauty, she was the mother of three beautiful daughters known as 'The Graces': novelist Caroline Norton; Lady Dufferin§, and the duchess of Somerset. Only one of CHS's works has Irish associations. SOURCE Boase, iii, p. 548; ODNB; Sadleir, i, p. 321.

S129 *Aims and ends: and Oonagh Lynch* [anon.].

+ London: Edward Bull, 1833, 3 vols. SOURCE Brown 2, 1431; Sadleir, 3053; Garside 2, 1833:67. LOCATION Corvey CME 3–628–47028–5, D, L, InND Loeber coll.

COMMENTARY 'Aims and ends' is set in England and chronicles the ill results to a girl who prefers flirtation and riches over true affection. 'Oonagh Lynch' is an historical romance set at the end of the seventeenth century about the ill-fated love of Oonagh Lynch and Sir Maurice Bellew. Oonagh's father and Sir Maurice are Jacobites, and Sir Maurice is involved in the Jacobite campaign in Ireland. The scene is set partly at Kiltarle Castle, a tower house in Co. Kerry, and in Paris where Jacobite court life is described. Oonagh wants to be a nun, but her father insists on taking her from the convent and her vocation soon fades. Her relationship with Sir Maurice is a series of misunderstandings and sudden separations. In the end, she finds him in Spain, just as he is dying [ML; Brown 2].

SHERIDAN, Elizabeth. See **LE FANU, Elizabeth.**

SHERIDAN, Frances (née Chamberlaine), b. Dublin 1724, d. Blois (France) 1766. Novelist and dramatist, FS was the daughter of a Church of Ireland clergyman, the Revd Philip Chamberlaine, prebendary of Rathmichael (Co. Dublin), vicar of Bray (Co. Wicklow), and rector of St Nicholas Without (Dublin), and Anastasia Whyte, who came from a Co. Wexford family. Her mother died young and FS was brought up by her father in Dublin. He disapproved of his daughters being taught to read or write, but her older brother taught her privately. By the time she was age 15, she had written a two-volume novel, *Eugenia and Adelaide* (published posthumously, London, 1791), which was adapted later for the Dublin stage by her daughter, Alicia Sheridan Le Fanu. FS had a great interest in theatre and after a dispute in which Thomas Sheridan, manager of the Theatre Royal in Dublin's Smock Alley, was embroiled, she wrote a pamphlet in his defence, as well as a set of verses that appeared in Faulkner's *Dublin Journal* (Dublin) as 'The owls: a fable addressed to Mr Sheridan on his late affair in the theatre' (1746). In 1747 she married Sheridan, and together they had six children, including the playwright and politician Richard Brinsley Sheridan. She is not known to have written during her married life in Dublin when she was occupied with child-rearing and entertaining friends. After her husband's misfortunes in theatre management, the family moved to London in 1754. There, with the encouragement of Samuel Richardson, she wrote her highly-acclaimed novel, *Memoirs of Miss Sidney Bidulph* (London, 1761, 3 vols.), and two plays, including the successful drama *The discovery* (London, 1762). The celebrated actor David Garrick, who played the lead, considered it one of the best pieces he had ever read. Later, she and her husband moved to France to escape their creditors and there she wrote the play 'A journey to Bath', which, although not successful itself and not published until 1890, provided her son RBS with inspiration for his famous play *The Rivals* (first performed 1775, published London, n.d.). At her death, Faulkner's *Dublin Journal* announced that she was 'a Lady well known to the World by [her book] the *History of Miss Sydney Bidulph*, and other excellent productions of her Pen, with a moral and benevolent Tendency'. Her granddaughter Alicia Le Fanu§ wrote *Memoirs of the life and writings of Mrs Frances Sheridan* (London 1824). For FS's portraits, see ODNB. SOURCE Allibone, ii, p. 2077; Blain, pp 975–6; Boylan, p. 398; Brady, p. 220; Faulkner's *Dublin Journal* (25–8 Oct. 1766); Elmes, p. 182; Field Day, i, p. 759; Hogan 2, pp 1111–12; E. Kuti, 'Rewriting Frances Sheridan', *Eighteenth-century Ireland*, 2 (1996), pp 120–8; Leslie & Wallace, p. 475; T.P. Le Fanu, *Memoir of the Le Fanu family* (n.l., 1924); OCIL, p. 519; ODNB; O'Donoghue, p. 424; RIA/DIB; E.K. Sheldon, *Thomas Sheridan of Smock-Alley* (Princeton, 1967), pp 44–5, citing Letitia Le Fanu, pp 4–11; preface to Dublin, 1802 edn of *The history of Nourjahad;* preface to the London 1927 edn of *The history of Nourjahad*; Todd, pp 610–12.

S130 *Memoirs of Miss Sidney Bidulph, extracted from her own journal & now first published* [anon.] (dedicated to Samuel Richardson).

> London: R. & J. Dodsley, 1761, 3 vols. SOURCE Black, 729; Forster, 2537; McBurney & Taylor, 819; Raven, 670; Todd; p. 612. LOCATION L, MH, IU, InND Loeber coll. (London, Harrison 1787 edn).
>
> Dublin: G. Faulkner, 1761, 2 vols. SOURCE McBurney & Taylor, 820; Raven, 672; ESTC t064723. LOCATION L, MH, IU.
>
> Dublin: Printed by H. Saunders, 1761, 3 vols. SOURCE ESTC n035377. LOCATION Univ. of Chicago.
>
> Paris: Saillant & Desaint, 1762, 2 vols. (trans. as *Mémoires de Miss Sidney Bidulph*). SOURCE Streeter, 326. LOCATION L.
>
> + Amsterdam: Aux depens de la Companie, 1762[–1768], 5 vols. (trans. as *Mémoires de Miss Sidney Bidulph, extraits de son journal*). SOURCE Rochedieu, p. 299. LOCATION Dt, L (3 vols. edn).
>
> Utrecht: G.T. van Paddenburg & Zoon, 1803, 5 vols. (trans. into Dutch as *Historie van Juffrouw Sidney Bidulph* by [Samuel] Richardson [*sic*]). SOURCE F.A. van S.
>
> Cologne: [n.p.], 1762, 4 vols. (trans. by A.F. Prévost d'Exiles§ as *Mémoires pour servir à l'histoire de la vertu: extraits du journal* [*sic*] *d'une jeune dame*). SOURCE Streeter, 326; COPAC. LOCATION Leeds Univ. COMMENTARY *Cologne edn* For a long time thought to be a translation of *Memoirs of Miss Sidney Bidulph*, but it is at the least a very free translation and may be simply a continuation, owing very little to the original [Hall cat. 8/110].
>
> Leipzig: Bey M.G. Weidmanns Erben & Reich, 1762, 3 vols. (trans. as *Geschichte der Miss Sidney Bidulph: aus ihrem eignen Tagebuche gezogen und izt zum erstenmahle bekannt gemacht*). SOURCE OCLC. LOCATION MH.
>
> London: Pandora, 1987 (introd. by Sue Townsend). SOURCE Weekes, p. 322. LOCATION Dt, O.

COMMENTARY Reprinted in the *Novelist's Magazine* (1767). One of the first novels centring around the relationship between a heroine and her mother rather than between a heroine and her lover, it features at the beginning negotiations by Lady Bidulph and Sidney's brother George over Sidney's proposed marriage to Orlando Faulkland. Orlando had left Ireland in late June 1708 leaving his wife and lover for dead. The story continues through the ups and downs of Sidney's romantic and married life, leading to Alicia Le Fanu's advice that this book should be read 'in solitude and with the door locked to prevent interruption, for the mind hangs suspended in breathless anxiety upon the catastrophe' [Field Day, i, pp 726–38; D. Spender (ed.), *Living by the pen* (New York, 1992) p. 201; Todd; A.M. Fitzer, 'Mrs Sheridan's active demon …' in *Eighteenth-Century Ireland*, 18 (2003), pp 39, 43*n*.17].

S131 *The history of Nourjahad* [anon.].

+ London: J. Dodsley, 1767. SOURCE Forster, 2536; McBurney & Taylor, 817; Raven, 1134; Todd, p. 612; ESTC t147336. LOCATION L, MH, IU, InND Loeber coll.

+ London: John Walker & Co., 1814 (ill. T. Unwins, C. Heath). LOCATION InND Loeber coll. COMMENTARY *London, Walker edn* Abbreviated edn in 82pp [RL].

+ London: John Limbird, 1827. SOURCE OCLC. LOCATION CtY. COMMENTARY *London, Limbird edn* Condensed version of 26pp [RL].

Dublin: P. Wilson, J. Murphy, W. Sleater, D. Chamberlaine, J. Potts, J. Mitchell, J. Williams & W. Colles, 1767. SOURCE Raven, 1135; McBurney & Taylor, 818; ESTC t18782. LOCATION Dt, L, CtY, IU.

+ Dublin: John Parry, 1802 (as *The history of Nourjahad ... To which for the first time is prefixed a genuine account of the author* [by Thomas Sheridan]). SOURCE Falkner Greirson cat. 'Jane'/290. LOCATION Dt, InND Loeber coll.

+ Cork: Edward Henry Morgan at the Classic Novels Office, 1803 (new edn, as *The history of Nourjahad, the Persian*). SOURCE Fenning cat. 138/343, LOCATION L, InND Loeber coll.

Londres, Paris: Ganguery, 1769 (trans. Mme de Sérionne as *Nourjahad, histoire orientale*). SOURCE Rochedieu, p. 299; OCLC. LOCATION Linkoping Stadsbibliotek.

Londres [i.e. Frankfort], n.p., 1771 (trans. as *Les désires accomplis, et les plaisirs trompeurs*). SOURCE Hall cat. 8/137; Bn-Opale plus. LOCATION BNF.

London: E. Mathews & Marrot, 1927 (ill. Mabel Peacock; preface by H.V.M., by 'the ed. of Sidney Bidulph'. LOCATION L.

COMMENTARY The first in a planned series of moral tales, it was published posthumously and republished many times, including in periodicals, as in a condensed form in the *Universal Magazine* (London, 1767); in the *Novelist's Magazine* (London, 1788), and as a chapbook (London, 1827). Intended by the author to show that happiness depends more on the 'due regulation of the passions' than on good fortune, it is one of the first pseudo-oriental tales by an Irish author. A courtier is asked by his sultan what he values most in life, and his answer is that he would like to have inexhaustible riches and endless life. He finds that these do not give him true happiness after all. The novel was adapted to several plays, initially by Sophia Lee§ in 1788, and subsequently as *Illusion; or, the trances of Nourjahad; an Oriental romance* (London, 1813) [ML; RL; Bolton, pp 307–8; Field Day, i, p. 687; Mayo, pp 620–1; Todd, p. 612].

S132   *Conclusion of the memoirs of Miss Sidney Bidulph, as prepared for the press by the late editor of the former part* [anon.].

London: J. Dodsley, 1767, 2 vols. SOURCE Forster, 2538; Raven, 1137; ESTC n26662. LOCATION L (1770 edn), MH.

Dublin: G. Faulkner, 1767, 3 vols. in 2. SOURCE Block, p. 214; Raven, 1137; ESTC t221973. LOCATION Dt.

Paris: Saillant, 1767, 2 vols. (trans. by Jean-Baptiste-René Robinet as *Mémoires pour servir à l'histoire de la vertu: extraits du journal d'une jeune dame*). SOURCE Bn-Opale plus. LOCATION BNF.

COMMENTARY Sequel to *Memoirs of Miss Sidney Bidulph* (London, 1761, 3 vols.). Narrates the misfortunes of the heroine's daughter [ODNB].

S133   *Eugenia and Adelaide* [anon.].

London: C. Dilly, 1791, 2 vols. SOURCE Field Day, p. 759; Raven 2, 1791:11; Todd, p. 610; ESTC t074438. LOCATION L, CtY.

COMMENTARY A romance written in 1739 in Ireland when FS was age 15 and published posthumously in 1791. Set in Spain and Italy, the novel was dramatized by FS's daughter Alicia [Todd, p. 610; Kuti, 'Rewriting Frances Sheridan'].

Sheridan

SHERIDAN, Helen Selina. See DUFFERIN, Lady Helen Selina Blackwood.

SHORTER, Dora Sigerson. See SIGERSON, Dora Mary.

SIDDONS, Henry, b. Wolverhampton (Staffs.) 1774, d. Edinburgh (Scotland) 1815. Actor, theatrical entrepreneur and novelist, HS was the son of the noted actress Sarah Siddons and husband of actress Harriet Murray, known on the stage as Mrs Henry Siddons. He was the author of several dramas and an instructional work on acting. He wrote four novels between 1803 and 1809. Through the offices of Sir Walter Scott he obtained the patent for the Theatre Royal in Edinburgh and opened a New Theatre Royal in 1809, where both he and his wife acted and to which he invited his mother to perform also. He appeared on the stage in Edinburgh for the last time in 1815. His portrait is in the National Portrait Gallery, London. SOURCE Allibone, ii, p. 2094; British Fiction; OCLC; ODNB.

S134 *The son of a storm. A tale* (by Henry Siddons; dedicated to B.C. Griffinhoofe, Esq., a former school-fellow of the author).
+ London: Longman, Rees, Hurst & Orme, 1809, 4 vols. SOURCE British Fiction; Garside, 1809:64; OCLC; COPAC. LOCATION Corvey CME 3–628–48696–3, L.
COMMENTARY Lord John Oceanus O'Carroll was born aboard a ship, crossing from Ireland to England. His mother was heiress to an O'Carroll, an uncle in Ireland. As an adult, he finds twin orphans, Henry and Laura, whom he adopts. Henry becomes a clergyman and Laura, having refused an offer from Dalton, becomes his housekeeper. O'Carroll appears to have fits of lunacy, and once a year sees his father's ghost, who represents his guilty conscience. He discovers that the twins are his own children by a marriage he had kept secret from his father. Laura eventually marries Dalton. O'Carroll is instrumental in solving the problems of several other people in the novel [Tracy, 169; ML].

SIGERSON, Dora Mary (also known as **Dora Sigerson Shorter** and **Dora Sigerson**), b. Dublin 1866, d. St John's Wood (London) 1918 (not 1925 as in OCIL). Poet, novelist, journalist and sculptor, DMS was the eldest daughter of the surgeon and Gaelic scholar Dr George Sigerson, and the poet and novelist Hester Varian (known as Hester Sigerson§). With her sister Hester, who also became a writer, she was educated at home. She and her mother became members of the Pan-Celtic Society in Dublin and she joined the National Literary Society in 1892. Known mainly for her poetry, she contributed verse to several Dublin periodicals: the *Irish Monthly*, the *Nation*, and *Young Ireland*, and published over twenty volumes of verse, much of which was admired by Douglas Hyde§, who called her 'the greatest mistress of the ballad and the greatest story-teller in verse that Ireland has produced' (RIA/DIB). In 1896 she married Clement K. Shorter, an English author and editor of the *Illustrated London News* (1891–1900) and the *Sphere* (London, 1900–26) and subsequently lived in England where, according to Ernest Rhys, her husband 'was able to give [her] all the openings she desired for her poetry' (Rhys, pp 207–9). She was active in the Irish Literary Society and the Irish National Club in London and wrote a pamphlet dissuading Irish men from enlisting in the British army in the Boer War. An ardent nationalist, she worked on behalf of the prisoners taken after the Easter Rising of 1916, her reactions to which were published posthumously in *The Tricolour* in 1922, which contains elegies for the executed leaders of the rebellion. She and her husband led an unsuccessful campaign to prevent the execution of Irish revolutionary Roger Casement for treason.. She was a close friend of the writer Katharine Tynan§ who wrote the preface to her volume of poetry, *The sad years* (London, 1918). Some of her correspondence is in the NLI (MSS 18,517, 13,688); the Allen Library, Dublin (box 117); Irish Jesuit Archives, Dublin (MS J27/128–29), while her sketchbook is in UCD (Curran coll.) and her notebooks are in

TCD. Her portrait was painted both by J.B. Yeats and by Sir John Lavery, the latter is in the NGI. Her most famous sculpture is a memorial to the Easter Rising of 1916 in Glasnevin cemetery, where she is buried. SOURCE Blain, p. 982; Brady, p. 222; Brown, p. 277 [under Shorter]; Brown 2, p. 243 [under Shorter]; Colman, pp 203–5; EF, p. 361; Field Day, iv, p. 895, v, p. 900 [under Shorter]; Hogan 2, p. 1122 [under Shorter]; IBL, 9 (1918), p. 86; Irish pseudonyms; LVP, pp 432–3; NCBEL 4, p. 813; OCIL, pp 522–3 [under Shorter]; ODNB [under Shorter]; O'Donoghue, p. 426 [under Shorter]; E. Rhys, *Everyman remembers* (London, 1931), pp 207–9; RIA/DIB [under Shorter]; Ryan, pp 146–8; Sutherland, p. 574–5 [under Shorter]; Weekes, p. 323.

S135   *The father confessor. Stories of death and danger* (by Dora Sigerson Shorter).
+ London, New York, Melbourne: Ward, Lock & Co., 1900. SOURCE Alston, p. 396; Brown, 1507; Hogan 2, p. 1122; Weekes, p. 323; OCLC. LOCATION D (n.d., 2nd edn), L.
COMMENTARY Supernatural tales. Contents: 'The father confessor', 'The three travellers', 'Priscilla', 'A dreamer', 'Transmigration', 'The broken heart', 'The other woman's child', 'A question of courage', 'The strange voice' (Irish peasant setting), 'The twin brothers', 'The fourth generation', 'Walter Barrington', 'All Souls' eve', 'The lion-tamer' (Irish hero and hero-ine, final scene in Ireland), 'The women's progress club', 'The mother', 'The jealousy of Beatrix' [ML; Brown; EF, p. 361].

S136   *The country house party* (by Dora Sigerson Shorter).
London: Hodder & Stoughton, 1905. SOURCE Brown 2, 1437; Hogan 2, p. 1122. LOCATION L.
COMMENTARY A series of stories told in the evening by various members of a country house party. For the most part they illustrate various aspects of married life and of women's char-acters. Two of the stories deal with Ireland [Brown 2].

S137   *The story and song of Black Roderick* (by Dora Sigerson).
+ London: Alexander Moring, 1906. SOURCE Hogan 2, p. 1122; OCLC. LOCATION D, L.
+ New York, London: Harper & Bros, 1906. LOCATION VU.
COMMENTARY Historical fiction consisting of a tale of ancient Ireland written in archaic language and partly in verse [ML].

S138   *Through wintry terrors* (by Dora Sigerson Shorter).
London: Cassell & Co., 1907. SOURCE Hogan 2, p. 1122; Weekes, p. 323. LOCATION L.
COMMENTARY A poor artist takes in a girl thrown out by her drunken father. He is made to marry her; they struggle with poverty, part, and are reconciled [EF, p. 361].

S139   *Do-well and do-little. A fairy tale* (by Dora Sigerson).
London: Cassell & Co., [1913] (ill. Alice B. Woodward). SOURCE Hogan 2, p. 1122; Weekes, p. 323; OCLC. LOCATION L.
COMMENTARY A fairy tale written for juveniles [Weekes].

S140   *A dull day in London, and other sketches* (by Dora Sigerson; prefatory note by Thomas Hardy).
+ London: Eveleigh Nash, 1920. SOURCE Weekes, p. 324; OCLC. LOCATION D, L, InND Loeber coll.
COMMENTARY Contents: 'A dull day in London', 'The last of summer', '"Not without hon-our"', 'The child', 'The fear of the sheep', 'The skylark', 'The gift of the white rose', 'The footfall', '"The eyes"', 'Contentment', 'Christmas-tide', 'The little hero of High Wycombe', 'The city', 'The return of winter', 'Waste', 'The passing of the fairies', 'The one left behind', 'The earthquake', 'The return', 'Sunshine in rain' [RL].

SIGERSON, Hester (née Varian), b. Cork 1828, d. Dublin 1898. Periodical writer and author of one novel, HS was the daughter of Amos Varian. She married the author and Gaelic scholar Dr George Sigerson in 1865. Their home in Dublin was a meeting-place for politicians and artists and influenced their daughters Dora Sigerson§ (Shorter) and Hester (Piatt), both of whom became writers. HS and Dora were members of the Pan-Celtic Society in Dublin, and HS wrote for periodicals such as the *Harp* (New York); *Cork Examiner*; Boston *Pilot*; the *Gael* (New York); and *Young Ireland, Irish Fireside* and *Irish Monthly* (all Dublin). SOURCE Brown, p. 278; Colman, p. 229 [under Varian]; Field Day, v, p. 926; Irish pseudonyms; O'Donoghue, p. 427; O'Toole, p. 277; E. Reilly, p. 250; RIA/DIB; Sutherland, p. 575 [under Dora Sigerson Shorter]; Weekes, p. 323.

S141   *A ruined race; or, the last MacManus of Drumroosk* (by Hester Sigerson; dedicated to Mrs Gladstone).

+ London: Ward & Downey, 1889. SOURCE Brown, 1511 (1890 edn); Weekes, p. 323 (mistakenly mentions as title *A ruined place*). LOCATION D, Dt, L.

COMMENTARY Set in Ireland in the middle of the nineteenth century and describes the misfortunes of a once happy and prosperous couple of the well-to-do peasant class. The misfortunes are partly blamed on the old land system [Brown].

SIME, William, b. Wick, Caithness (Scotland) 1851, d. Calcutta (India) 1895. Scottish author of several works of fiction, one of which is set in Ireland. SOURCE Allibone Suppl., ii, p. 1346; Boase, iii, p. 575; Brown, p. 278.

S142   *The red route; or, saving a nation* (by William Sime).

London: W. Swan Sonnenschein & Co., 1884, 3 vols. SOURCE Allibone Suppl., ii, p. 1346; Brown, 1512. LOCATION L.

+ New York: Henry Holt & Co., 1885 (as *The red route*; author's edn; Leisure Moment Series). SOURCE OCLC. LOCATION InND Loeber coll., NN.

COMMENTARY Two love stories set in the west and south of Ireland. The hero, Finn O'Brien, goes to college in Galway where he suffers much from collegians and from the peasantry. He becomes a Fenian and falls in love with an English widow, who had become a Catholic to escape the pursuits of bishops and parsons of her own church. The heroine is a girl from the Claddagh, whose love for an English captain is crossed by the fact that she is a Fenian [Brown].

'SINCERITAS', pseud. See **'A CITIZENS OF THE UNITED STATES'**.

SINCLAIR, Catherine, b. Edinburgh (Scotland) 1800, d. London, 1864. Scottish moralistic and evangelical novelist, travel and children's writer, CS was the daughter of Sir John Sinclair, a well-known politician and agriculturist. From age 14 until her father died when she was age 35, CS was his secretary, taking dictation for hours a day. Her first books were written for her sister's children; she also contributed stories to *Blackwood's Magazine* (Edinburgh), but after her father's death she began her writing career in earnest. She was very active in civic and philanthropic work in Edinburgh, including the installation of public benches, drinking fountains and soup kitchens for the poor. She was a member of the Church of Scotland and several of her writings have a distinct anti-Catholic thrust. She died in London in 1864, but was buried in Edinburgh. SOURCE Allibone, ii, p. 2111; Blain, p. 986; Boase, iii, pp 536–7; Griffin, pp 141–2; NCBEL 4, pp 1401, 1867; ODNB; Todd, pp 616–17.

S143   *Beatrice; or, the unknown relatives* (by Catherine Sinclair).

London: Richard Bentley, 1852. SOURCE Griffin, p. 269; COPAC. LOCATION L.

New York: Garland, 1975. SOURCE Griffin, p. 269; COPAC. LOCATION Univ. of Glasgow, DCL.

COMMENTARY Anti-Catholic fiction. The preface to this book was separately reprinted as a tract under the title *Modern superstition* (London, 1857). Set in the Scottish Highlands in the village of Clanmarina. Two rival aristocrats live in the area: the Protestant Sir Evan McAlpine and the Catholic earl of Eaglescairn, who is ruled by his confessor, Father Eustace. Visiting the Catholic sections of the village is depicted as travelling to primitive Ireland. The author compares the Catholics to the Hindu Thuggee, a fraternity of trained assassins. The priest imports both a candidate from Ireland and a gang of reapers to sway the local election [Griffin, pp 132–47].

SINCLAIR, Maggie J. See HOUSTON, Mrs Maggie J.

SINGLETON, Mary Montgomerie (also Montgomery, née Lamb, afterwards Lady Currie), pseud. **'Violet Fane'**, b. Littlehampton (W. Sussex) 1843, d. 1905. English-born novelist and poet, MMS was the eldest daughter of Charles J.M.S. Lamb and Anna Charlotte Grey, and sister of Sir Archibald Lamb, 7th Bt, of Beauport. Raised in an unorthodox fashion and educated privately, she began to write at an early age, first using her pseudonym to avoid parental disapproval. She married in 1864 Henry Sydenham Singleton of Mell (Co. Louth, just outside of Drogheda) and Hazeley (Hants.), HS of Co. Louth (1862) and Co. Cavan (1867). They lived at Piers Court (Co. Louth) and at Grosvenor Square (London), where Oscar Wilde§ was a frequent visitor. Wilde published several of MMS's poems in *Women's World* (London). Her social circle in London included Algernon Swinburne, Robert Browning, James McNeil Whistler and Lily Langtry. She and her husband had four children. In Co. Louth, they founded Piers Court Industries (home industries for tenants). Writing under her pseudonym, she produced fiction, essays, several volumes of poetry and some drama. She was involved in several affairs, which were the subject of much gossip, including one with Philip Henry Wodehouse Currie, Lord Currie, whom she married after her husband's death in 1893. She lived with her second husband in Constantinople and Rome, where he was ambassador. Her novels, although mostly written during her life in Ireland and London, do not deal with Ireland, but some of her poetry does (see her *Collected verses*, London, 1880). Only works of fiction written during the Irish period of her life are listed below. SOURCE Allibone Suppl., ii, p. 1349; Blain, p. 355 [under Fane]; BLC; Landed gentry, 1912, p. 640; MVP, p. 199 [under Currie]; NCBEL 4, p. 733; ODNB [under Currie]; K. Tynan, *Twenty-five years* (New York, 1913), pp 263–4.

S144   *Sophy; or, the adventures of a savage* (by 'Violet Fane').
+ London: Hurst & Blackett, 1881, 3 vols. LOCATION L, NUC.
COMMENTARY No Irish content [ML].

S145   *Thro' love and war* (by 'Violet Fane').
+ London: Hurst & Blackett, [1885], 3 vols. SOURCE Topp 6, 335. LOCATION L, NUC (1886 edn).
COMMENTARY No Irish content [ML].

S146   *The story of Helen Davenant* (by 'Violet Fane').
+ London: Chapman & Hall, 1889, 3 vols. LOCATION L.
COMMENTARY No Irish content [ML].

'SIRIUS', pseud. See MARTYN, Edward.

'SISTER MARY', fl. 1845. Religious and children's fiction writer, who is unidentified. Since she published in Dublin, and since her books deal with Irish topics, she probably was Irish. Note that *Sister Mary's recreations. Tales for girls* (London, 1845) may be by the same hand.

Note that the American author Andrew Jackson published under the pseudonym of 'Sister Mary'. SOURCE Brick Row cat. 145/52; ML; OCLC.

S147   *Maria; or, the good little girl* (by 'Sister Mary').
+ Dublin: James Duffy, 1857 (Sister Mary's Tales; a Series of Tales, Written Expressly for the Amusement and Instruction of Youth). LOCATION L.
COMMENTARY Fiction written for juveniles set in the south of Ireland [ML].

S148   *Louisa; or, the learned girl* (by 'Sister Mary').
+ Dublin: James Duffy, 1857 (Sister Mary's Tales; a Series of Tales, Written Expressly for the Amusement and Instruction of Youth). LOCATION L.
COMMENTARY Fiction with Irish content, written for juveniles [ML].

S149   *New year's day* (by 'Sister Mary').
+ Dublin: James Duffy, 1857 (Sister Mary's Tales; a Series of Tales, Written Expressly for the Amusement and Instruction of Youth). LOCATION L.
COMMENTARY Fiction with Irish content, written for juveniles [ML].

S150   *The poor old soldier* (by 'Sister Mary').
+ Dublin: James Duffy, 1857 (Sister Mary's Tales; a Series of Tales, Written Expressly for the Amusement and Instruction of Youth). LOCATION L.
COMMENTARY Fiction for juveniles set in Cork [ML].

S151   *Reminiscences of my parish priest* (by 'Sister Mary').
+ Dublin: James Duffy, 1857 (Sister Mary's Tales; a Series of Tales, Written Expressly for the
Amusement and Instruction of Youth). LOCATION L.
COMMENTARY Fiction for juveniles with Irish content. Includes 'The reward', 'The punishment', 'Michael the pedlar' [ML].

S152   *Little black people* (by 'Sister Mary').
London: Groombridge & Sons, [1858?] (ill. E. Whimper; Buds and Blossom, and Stories for Summer Days and Winter Nights). SOURCE RLIN. LOCATION Univ. of Florida.
COMMENTARY 32pp. Priced at 2*d.* Fiction for juveniles [RLIN; Adv. in C. O'Brien's *Mary's visit to the gold fields* (London, [1858?])]

S153   *Sister Mary's annual. A series of delightful tales and stories, expressly written for the amusement & instruction of youth* (by 'Sister Mary').
+ Dublin: James Duffy, 1859. LOCATION L.
COMMENTARY Fiction for juveniles. The book consists of smaller booklets, each with its own pagination, all published earlier (but not all individual booklets have been located). Contents: 'The reward', 'The punishment' (set in Dublin), 'Michael the pedlar', 'The poor old soldier' (set in Cork), 'New Year's day' (mentions Father Charles's [Fr Charles Patrick Meehan's§] *Tales* and the *Young Christian's Library*), 'Maria, or the good little girl', 'Louisa; or, the learned little girl', 'Peter the hermit and the crusades', 'Recollections of the Holy Land', 'The Holy House of Loretto', 'Scenes and adventures in the land of the East' [CM; ML].

SKRINE, Mrs (Agnes) Nesta Shakespeare (née Higginson), pseud. **'Moira O'Neill'**, b. Rockport Lodge, Cushendun (Co. Antrim) 1865, d. Co. Wexford 1955. Poet and fiction writer, ANSS was the daughter of Charles Henry and Mary Higginson and was distantly related to William Makepeace Thackeray§ through the Shakespeare side of her family. She married Walter Clarmont Skrine (d. 1930), governor of Mauritius, and was the mother of the writer Molly Keane, who wrote under the pseudonym 'M.J. Farrell'. The Skrines lived for some time on the Bar-S ranch in Pekisko, Alberta (Canada), and after returning to Ireland, settled first in Co. Kildare and then in Bunclody (Co. Wexford). ANSS mostly wrote poetry, including her celebrated *Songs of the glens of Antrim* (Edinburgh, 1900), but also contributed prose to *Blackwood's Magazine* (Edinburgh). A large number of her manuscripts were destroyed when Ballyrankin House (Co. Wexford) was set on fire by the IRA during the Anglo-Irish War in 1921 (presently ruined). ANSS died at age 90 and was buried in the Kiliane cemetery near Enniscorthy (Co. Wexford). SOURCE Brady, p. 196; Brown, p. 248 [under O'Neill]; Browne, p. 115; Colman, p. 111; Hogan 2, p. 988 [under O'Neill]; Lord Killanin & M.V. Duignan, *Shell guide to Ireland* (London, 1976), 2nd edn, p. 194; NCBEL 4, p. 804 [under O'Neill]; OCIL, p. 450 [under O'Neill]; ODNB [under Molly Keane]; O'Donoghue, p. 366 [under O'Neill]; RIA/DIB; Rowe & Scallan, 179; Ryan, p. 148; Weekes, pp 294–5.

S154　*An Easter vacation* (by 'Moira O'Neill').

　　+ London: Lawrence & Bullen, 1893. SOURCE Brown, p. 248; Hogan 2, p. 988; Weekes, p. 295 (mistakenly states that this is a volume of poetry). LOCATION D, L, InND Loeber coll.

　　New York: E.P. Dutton, 1894. SOURCE Colman, p. 111; Hogan 2, p. 988; NYPL. LOCATION NN.

COMMENTARY Set in England where Mac, a young boy whose parents are abroad, goes with his tutor for the Easter vacation to a hotel in a seacoast town, chosen because he has weak lungs. Some of his relatives live nearby and he becomes very fond of one of his cousins, as does his tutor. Mac dies, but before he does he asks his tutor to marry his cousin, which in the end he does [ML].

S155　*The elf-errant* (by 'Moira O'Neill').

　　+ London: Lawrence & Bullen, 1895 (ill. W.E F. Britten). SOURCE Brown, 1351; Hogan 2, p. 988. LOCATION Dt, D (1902, new edn), L, InND Loeber coll.

　　New York: E.P. Dutton, 1894. SOURCE Colman, p. 111; Hogan 2, p. 988; OCLC. LOCATION Univ. of Illinois (1895 edn).

COMMENTARY A fanciful tale with elves and fairies. Throughout, there is a subtle comparison between English and Irish character [Brown].

S156　*From two points of view* (by 'Moira O'Neill').

　　+ Edinburgh, London: William Blackwood & Sons, 1924. SOURCE Hogan 2, p. 988. LOCATION L, D.

'SLINGSBY, Jonathan Freke', pseud. See **WALLER, John Francis**.

SMART, Hawley. See **SMART, Henry Hawley**.

SMART, Henry Hawley (known as **Hawley Smart**), b. Dover (Kent) 1833, d. Budleigh Salterton (Devon) 1893. Army officer and novelist, HHS was the son of Maj. George Smart and Katherine Hawley. He served in the Crimean War, in India during the mutiny, and in Canada, before becoming a prolific writer, well-known for his stories of hunting and horse racing, which he modelled on the works of Charles Lever§ and George Whyte-Melville§. SOURCE Allibone Suppl., ii, p. 1354; Boase, iii, p. 609; Brown, p. 279; NCBEL 4, p. 1688; ODNB; Wolff, iv, p. 126.

S157　*The master of Rathkelly. A novel* (by Hawley Smart).

　　London: F.V. White, 1888, 2 vols. SOURCE Brown, 1516; Wolff, 6391. LOCATION L, InND Loeber coll. (1889, 4th edn).

COMMENTARY Set in 'County Blarney' in the 1880s and describes the clash between the Land Leaguers and Mr Eyre, a landlord of the old stock. Disaffected tenants stop the hunt and loyal tenants are attacked. Eventually, Mr Eyre and his family move to England [ML].

SMEDLEY, Elizabeth Anna. See HART, Elizabeth Anna.

SMEDLEY, Menella Bute, pseud. 'S.M.', b. Westminster (London), 1820, d. Regent's Park (London) 1877. English novelist and poet, MBS was a daughter of an Anglican clergyman, Revd Edward Smedley, and his wife Mary Hume; sister of Elizabeth Anna Hart§, and a cousin of the author Francis Edward Smedley, to whom MBS later acted as companion and literary assistant. She became her father's scribe when he fell ill and after his death in 1836 she lived in the house of her cousins, the Dogdsons. Later she showed some work of Charles Dodgson (better-known as Lewis Carroll) to Francis Smedley who got it published in the *Comic Times* (location unclear). In spite of MBS's delicate health, she travelled to Ireland to visit her sister Elizabeth, who had married Thomas Barnard Hart of Glen Alla (Co. Donegal). MBS published poetry and many works of fiction from 1849 onwards. She was active in education for working-class women and for paupers. Her only work with an Irish connection is listed below. SOURCE Allibone, i, p. 2123; Alston, p. 401; Boase, iii, p. 611; Blain, p. 994; H.T. Hart, *The family history of Hart of Donegal* (London, 1907), p. 64; MVP, p. 423; NCBEL 4, p. 670; ODNB.

S158   *The use of sunshine. A Christmas narrative* (by 'S.M.').
+ London: George Hoby, 1852 (Rice's Library). SOURCE NCBEL 4, p. 670. LOCATION L.
+ New York: D. Appleton & Co., 1852. SOURCE OCLC. LOCATION MH, InND Loeber coll.
+ New York: Worthington Co., 1886 (by Marella [*sic*] Bute Smedley; as *The use of sunshine: A tale of northern Irish life*; ill.). SOURCE Kunitz & Haycraft, p. 564; OCLC. LOCATION D, InND Loeber coll.
COMMENTARY A tale of life in northern Ireland, probably based on MBS's visits to her sister's home in Glen Alla (Co. Donegal) [RL].

SMITH, Agnes (Mrs Samuel Lewis) , b. Ayrshire (Scotland), 1843, d. Cambridge (Cambs.) 1926. Scottish novelist and travel writer and Arabic and Syriac scholar, AS and her identical twin sister Margaret were the daughters of John Smith, of Irvine (Scotland), and his wife Margaret Dunlop, who died shortly after their birth. Educated by tutors, the twins received a large inheritance on their father's death, which enabled them to travel widely through Greece, Turkey, Egypt and Palestine, resulting in their joint book *Eastern Pilgrims* (London, 1870). On her return, AS began to study eastern languages and this enabled her to translate Syriac manuscripts, on which she published extensively. After the deaths of both their husbands, the twins lived together in Cambridge and travelled in the Middle East. AS's scholarly achievements were acknowledged with several honorary doctorates, including one from TCD in 1911. She wrote three novels, only one of which is associated with Ireland. SOURCE Allibone Suppl., ii, p. 1355; ODNB.

S159   *The brides of Ardmore. A story of Irish life* (by Agnes Smith).
+ London: Elliott Stock, 1880 (ill. W.G. Smith). SOURCE Allibone Suppl., ii, p. 1355; Brown, 1517; Wolff, 6408. LOCATION D, L, InND Loeber coll.
COMMENTARY Historical fiction, purportedly based on a manuscript found in the nunnery at Kilcheechan, near Waterford. Set in Ardmore (Co. Waterford) in the twelfth century, it describes the primitive Irish church, unconnected with Rome and resembling the modern Church of Ireland in some of its features. The priests are all married. The decrees from Rome, interrupting their matrimonial affairs, provide the greater part of the incidents. Living conditions in the monastic settlement are described [ML; Brown].

SMITH, Charlotte (née Turner), b. London 1749, d. Tilford (Surrey) 1806. Novelist, poet and translator, CS was the daughter of Nicholas Turner, a prosperous landowner, and Anna Towers. She was educated in boarding-schools and in 1765 was married off by her father to Benjamin Smith, a young merchant whose father had estates in England, Ireland, Scotland and Barbados, and who was a director of the East India Company. CS's family was constantly in financial difficulties. When her husband was jailed for debts, she joined him in debtors' prison and began to write for a living to support herself and her twelve children. Her *Eligiac sonnets and other poems* (London, 1784) was supported by subscriptions from some Irish individuals and acknowledged the assistance of the Irish antiquarian Joseph Cooper Walker, who also thought very highly of CS's novel *Emmeline* (London, 1788). He also probably facilitated the publication of the second volume of her poems (London, 1797), which again was largely supported by Irish subscribers. The Irish poet the Hon. Henrietta O'Neill published a poem in CM's novel *Desmond* (London, 1792, 3 vols.). SOURCE Allibone, ii, p. 2132; Blain, p. 996; Blakey, p. 255; Adv. in C.T. Bowden, *A tour through Ireland* (Dublin, 1791); F.M.A. Hilbish, *Charlotte Smith, poet and novelist (1749–1806)* (Philadelphia, 1941); ODNB; O'Donoghue, p. 365; Quaritch cat. on women authors (1994)/252; Raven 2, 1782:11; RL; Todd, pp 623–6.

S160 *Emmeline: the orphan of the castle. A novel* (by Charlotte Smith).
London: T. Cadell, 1788, 4 vols. SOURCE Block, p. 230; Gecker, 983; Forster 2, 4138; McBurney & Taylor, 829; Raven 2, 1788:72; Todd, p. 625; ESTC t073502. LOCATION L, PU, IU.
Dublin: White, Wogan, Byrne, Moore, Jones & Halpen, 1788, 2 vols. SOURCE Raven 2, 1788:72; ESTC t212504. LOCATION Dt.
Belfast: Doherty & Simms, 1799, 3 vols., 2nd edn. SOURCE Raven 2, 1788:72; ESTC t138544. LOCATION L.
Maastricht: J.P. Roux & Co., 1788, 4 vols. (trans. as *L'orpheline du château, ou Emmeline*). LOCATION L.
Londres [Paris]: Letellier, Desenne, 1788, 4 vols. (trans. as *Emmeline, ou l'orpheline du château*). SOURCE Raven 2, 1788:72. LOCATION L.
Vienna: J. Stahel, 1790, 4 vols. (trans. as *Emmeline, oder die Wayse des Schlosses*). SOURCE Raven 2, 1788:72. LOCATION Österreichischen Landesbibliotheken.
Philadelphia: J. Conrad & Co.; Baltimore: M. & J. Conrad & Co.; Washington: Rapin, Conrad & Co., 1802. SOURCE Hilbish, p. 583; OCLC. LOCATION MH.
Baltimore: M. & J. Conrad & Co., 1802, 3 vols. SOURCE Hilbish, p. 583.
COMMENTARY No copy of the Baltimore edn located. The novel, which was very popular, was severely critiqued in Theobald Wolfe Tone's§ *Belmont Castle* (Dublin, 1790; republ. Dublin, 1998, p. 40). Set in Switzerland, Wales, and very slightly in Ireland. Emmeline is confined to the castle of Mowbray by her miscreant guardian, Montreville. She searches to establish her heritage in the face of relatives bent upon her ruin. She is consoled in her trials by her handsome cousin, Delamere, who declares his love for her and arouses the wrath of his father, Montreville. Her uncle removes her from the castle and attempts to coerce her to marry several unattractive suitors, but she succeeds in escaping with Delamere. They cannot marry, however, because they are cousins. Her persistence is rewarded when she becomes the owner of Mowbray Castle. Once wealthy, she is the fitting wife for a fine gentleman, Godolphin [ML; Frank, 421].

S161 *The letters of a solitary wanderer: containing narratives of various description* (by Charlotte Smith).
London: Sampson Low, 1800–1, 3 vols. SOURCE ESTC n3685; British Fiction. LOCATION O. COMMENTARY *London 1800–01 edn* Hilbish and Todd note a London, 1799 edn, but this is not in ESTC [Hilbish, *Charlotte Smith*, p. 585; Todd, p. 625; RL].

London: T.N. Longman & O. Rees, 1802, 2 vols., vols. 4 and 5. SOURCE Hilbish, *Charlotte Smith*, p. 585; British Fiction. LOCATION O.

Dublin: Burnet, Wogan, Brown, Porter, Dornin, Colbert, Folingsby, Rice, Jones, Stockdale, Jackson, Mercier & Co., Kelly & Parry, 1801, 2 vols. SOURCE Quaritch cat. [Nov.] 1994/252. LOCATION Dm.

COMMENTARY The story, 'Leonora' in volume 5, is set in Ireland, and contains descriptions of the Irish landscape and coast. The story deals with the persecution of the Irish Protestants by Catholics, but was written against British prejudice concerning the Irish. It contains a scene in which a Catholic mob burns the house of a benevolent Englishwoman [Hilbish, *Charlotte Smith*, pp 209, 296, 308; Personal communication, Jacqueline Belanger, May 2002; *Critical Review*, 37 (Jan. 1803), pp 54–8].

SMITH, Elizabeth (Lillie) Thomasina Toulmin (née Meade), pseuds 'Elizabeth Thomas', 'L.T. Meade', 'Mrs L.T. Meade', 'Evelyn Beacon', and possibly, 'Aunt Penn', b. Bandon (Co. Cork) 1844 (not 1854 as stated in some sources), d. Oxford 1914 (not 1915 as in Sutherland). Acknowledged as the most prolific novelist of her time, ETTS was the daughter of the Revd Richard Thomas Meade, a Church of Ireland clergyman, and Sarah Lane. It is likely that she descended from the Meade family of Ballintobber, outside Kinsale (Co. Cork), one branch of which became earls of Clanwilliam (later resident at Gill Hall, Co. Down), but her precise ancestry is not clear. She grew up at Nohaval, a hamlet and parish about four miles east of Kinsale where her father was rector. Educated by governesses, she may later have gone to a girls' school, given that she wrote many books on life in such schools. Remarkably, there is no monograph on her life and work and manuscripts and letters are practically unknown. It is likely, however, that some of her correspondence is still lodged in the archives of the many publishers who produced her works. She is known from several interviews, one published in the *Strand Magazine* (16 Dec 1898, p. 674), another in the *Young Woman* (London, 1893–3), and a third in *Pen, pencil, baton and mask* (London, 1896, pp 222–9). She always wrote under her maiden name but used different versions – initially 'Elizabeth Thomas,' and later 'L.T. Meade', under which name most of her books appeared. ETTS published her first novel, *Ashton-Morton*, anonymously in 1866, after which she did not appear in print for nine years. In 1874, after the death of her mother and the remarriage of her father, she went to London where she studied in the reading room at the British Museum and lived with a doctor and his wife, who encouraged her to write. Formerly, her output had been estimated at 280 titles. However, the authors of *Edwardian Fiction* conclude that 'Meade's bibliography exhausts the most enthusiastic investigators'. We counted about 300 titles (the exact number is elusive because some volumes may have been reprinted in the US under different titles). ETTS had no rival during her lifetime (the contemporary English author Annie J. Swan came a distant second with over 200 titles). Between 1887 and 1898 she averaged about four novels a year, with some intense activity in 1890, 1896 and 1898, when she produced nine to ten novels in each of these years. Between 1900 and 1909, she averaged over eleven titles yearly. Leaving aside the known co-authored books and stories, the sheer volume of her work raises the question of whether she had help in writing. As far as we can judge, there are no inconsistencies of style that would point to a ghost-writer. Almost all of ETTS's works first appeared in London, and many of her books were subsequently reprinted on a very large scale in the US. Some of her reputation rests on books written about and for adolescent girls, particularly the genre of school stories, and her fame tends to be based on this narrow segment of her work without crediting her for her other writings. In fact, ETTS's prodigious output evolved in at least seven categories: social protest fiction, crime stories, science fiction, medical fiction, books for young children, school and adventure stories for adolescent girls,

and books about young women and careers. She contributed with 'Robert Eustace' (Robert Eustace Barton, a medical doctor) to the *Harmondsworth Magazine* (London, 1899–1900), the *Strand Magazine* (London, 1898) and the *Windsor Magazine* (London, 1899). With Clifford Halifax, MD (under the pseud. of 'Edgar Beaumont') she contributed crime stories featuring Miss Cusack, a female detective, to the *Strand Magazine* (London, 1896–7). Over a dozen of her books for girls are set in Ireland. She contributed innumerable short stories to periodicals, which in addition to those above include the following London-based periodicals: *Sunday Magazine*; *Cassell's*; *Woman at Home*; *Young Woman*; *Temple Magazine*; *Lady's World*; *Quiver*; *Girl's Realm*, and the Tillotson's syndicate. She also contributed to short story collections, and wrote articles on art, literature and travel. From 1887 to 1898 (NCBEL has from 1887 to 1893) she edited the *Atalanta*, a magazine for girls, the main aim of which was to show that girls and young women could have intellectual interests and sophisticated tastes in literature. The magazine contained much quality fiction by established authors and digested versions of classic works by writers such as Sir Walter Scott, Charles Dickens and Jane Austen. It encouraged girls to engage in employment, but rarely in pioneering occupations. A feature of *Atalanta* was 'The Atalanta Scholarship, Reading Union, and School of Fiction', which encouraged girls to write. Her advice to individuals writing articles can be found in *On the art of writing fiction* (London, 1894). In 1879 she had married a solicitor, Alfred Toulmin Smith, with whom she had three children. They lived in Dulwich but she retired to Oxford some time before her death. At one point in her life she belonged to a feminist club, The Pioneers, where members socialized and discussed contemporary issues. She considered herself a professional who balanced home, children and a professional and social life. ETTS is not be confused with the author Lucy Toulmin. The titles *Miss Toosey's mission, Laddie, Tip cat*, and *Our little Ann: A tale*, have been attributed to ETTS but, although included by Allibone, they are more likely by Evelyn Whitaker§ (Personal communication, Mary Pollard, Sept. 1999, citing BLC and Halkett & Laing). The publisher Hurst printed a photograph of ETTS as the frontispiece in many of her books (for other portraits, see ODNB). She was buried at Wolvercote cemetery, Oxford, where there is a tombstone commemorating her.
SOURCE Allibone Suppl., ii, pp 1356–7; [anon.], *Return of owners of land* (Dublin, 1876), p. 129; H.C. Black, *Pen, pencil, baton and mask* (London, 1896), pp 222–9 (interview); Blain, p. 729 [under Meade]; Brady, p. 162; Brown, p. 208 [under Meade]; Cork, i, p. 349; EF, pp 276–7; R. ffolliott, *The Pooles of Mayfield* (Dublin, 1958), pp 142–8 (the connection with ETTS is not clear from the Meade pedigrees presented here); Field Day, iv, pp 1142, 1188; Hogan 2, p. 838 [under Meade]; Law, p. 91; *Location register of twentieth-century English manuscripts and letters* (Boston, MA, 1988), ii, p. 633; NCBEL 4, pp 1635–42 [under Meade]; ODNB; O'Toole, pp 143–9; K. Reynolds, *Girls only? Gender and popular children's fiction in Britain, 1880–1910* (Philadelphia, 1990), p. 113; RIA/DIB; J. Rowbotham, *Good girls make good wives* (Oxford, 1989), passim; S. Sims & H. Clare, *The encyclopaedia of girls' school stories* (Aldershot, 2000), pp 227–30; Sutherland, p. 427 [under Meade]; Wolff, iii, p. 133 [under Meade]; W.B. Yeats, *Collected Letters* (Oxford, 1986), i, p. 59.

S162 *Ashton-Morton, or memories of my life* [anon.].
London: T.C. Newby, 1866. SOURCE DLB, cxli, p. 186. LOCATION L.
COMMENTARY Written when the author was aged 17. The story of a woman's life from the age of 17 to old age. The heroine's daughter was based on friend who died of fever at age 15, and other characters were drawn from people the author knew [DLB, cxli, p. 193; H.C. Black, *Pen, pencil, baton and mask* (London, 1896), pp 224–5].

S163 *Lettie's last home* (by 'L.T. Meade').
London: John F. Shaw, [1875]. SOURCE Allibone Suppl., ii, p. 1356; DLB, cxli, p. 186. LOCATION L.

COMMENTARY Fiction for juveniles. Portrays a little girl in London's East End whose drunken mother sells unwanted babies to rich clients. Influenced by a sermon, the girl returns a little boy to his real mother. For this deed she is beaten to death by her drunken mother [DLB, cxli, p. 194].

S164 *Great St. Benedict's. A tale* (by 'Elizabeth Thomas')
London: John F. Shaw & Co., 1876. SOURCE Allibone Suppl., ii, p. 1356 (1877 edn); Alston, p. 296. LOCATION L, NUC.
London: John F. Shaw & Co., [1879?] (as *Dorothy's story; or, great St. Benedict's*). SOURCE Alston, p. 296. LOCATION L, D (n.d. edn), InND Loeber coll. (n.d. edn).
COMMENTARY The theme was suggested by a doctor. It concerns the abuses at the outpatient unit of a London teaching hospital which favoured the rich and was hard on the poor. The novel describes the work of a doctor and his half-sister in the slums of London's East End [ML; J.C. Black, *Pen, pencil, baton and mask* (London, 1896), p. 225].

S165 *Little trouble-the-house* (by 'Aunt Penn').
London: John F. Shaw & Co. [1877]. SOURCE Baldwin, p. 145; COPAC. LOCATION L.
London: John F. Shaw & Co. [c.1898] (new edn; by 'L.T. Meade'). SOURCE OCLC. LOCATION NIC.
COMMENTARY Fiction for juveniles [RL; Baldwin, ii, p. 145].

S166 *A knight of to-day* (by 'L.T. Meade').
London: John F. Shaw & Co., 1877. SOURCE Allibone Suppl., ii, p. 1356; Alston, p. 296. LOCATION D (n.d. edn), L, NUC.
New York: Robert Carter, n.d. SOURCE FFF, p. 636.
COMMENTARY No copy of the New York edn located [RL].

S167 *Scamp and I: A story of city-byways* (by 'L.T. Meade').
London: John F. Shaw, [1877]. SOURCE DLB, cxli, p. 186. LOCATION D (n.d. edn), L.
New York: Robert Carter & Bros [1878?]. SOURCE FFF, p. 636. LOCATION NUC.
COMMENTARY Fiction for juveniles that ran to many edns and was eventually published in a sixpenny form. It concerns Little Flo, an orphan from London's East End who earns a living by mending old boots. Her comfort is the companionship of the mongrel Scamp [DLB, cxli, p. 195; J.C. Black, *Pen, pencil, baton and mask* (London, 1896), p. 226].

S168 *David's little lad* (by 'L.T. Meade').
London: John F. Shaw & Co., [1877]. SOURCE Allibone Suppl., ii, p. 1356; Alston, p. 296. LOCATION L, NUC, InND Loeber coll. (n.d. edn).
New York: Robert Carter & Bros, [c.1877] (ill.). SOURCE Baldwin, p. 145; OCLC. LOCATION Univ. of Florida.
New York: Harper & Bros, 1878. LOCATION NUC.
New York: G. Munro, 1878. LOCATION NUC.
COMMENTARY Fiction for juveniles set in Wales and concerns a family that owns some land and mines. The eldest son, David, is a very steady and honourable man who has a little son who is blind. David's brother, Owen, is much more brilliant and is adored by his mother and younger sister. While at university Owen dishonours the family name. He has asked to come back to Wales to manage an unprofitable mine. David tells his sister as much as he feels she should know about Owen's problems. The sister is very shocked that her hero is not perfect any more. Owen is meant to make the mine profitable as well as more safe. However, he focuses on profit with the result that his little nephew dies in a disused mineshaft and a large group of people, including his brother David, are trapped in a flooded mine. Owen redeems himself by his extraordinary efforts to save the trapped miners, and his sister realizes that Owen has some good qualities after all [ML].

S169 *White lilies and other tales* (by 'L.T. Meade').
+ London: John F. Shaw, [1878] (ill.). SOURCE Allibone Suppl., ii, p. 1356; DLB, cxli, p. 186. LOCATION L.
COMMENTARY Fiction for juveniles. Contents: 'White lilies', 'A peep into paradise, Part I. Paradise in this country', 'Part II. Paradise in a better country', 'A big surprise' [ML].

S170 *Your brother and mine. A cry from the great city* (by 'L.T. Meade').
London: John F. Shaw & Co., 1878. SOURCE Allibone Suppl., ii, p. 1356; Alston, p. 297. LOCATION L.
+ London: John F. Shaw & Co., [1878] (as *Outcast Robin; or, your brother and mine. A cry from the great city*; ill. M. Irwin, H. Petherick). LOCATION D, NUC, InND Loeber coll.
New York: Robert Carter, n.d. SOURCE FFF, p. 637.
COMMENTARY No copy of the New York edn located. Fiction for juveniles [RL].

S171 *Bel-Marjory. A story of conquest* (by 'L.T. Meade').
London: John F. Shaw & Co., 1878. SOURCE Allibone Suppl., ii, p. 1356; DLB, cxli, p. 186. LOCATION D (n.d. edn), L, NUC ([1894?] edn), InND Loeber coll. (n.d. edn).
New York: Robert Carter, n.d. SOURCE FFF, p. 635.
COMMENTARY No copy of the New York edn located. Fiction for juveniles [RL].

S172 *The children's kingdom. The story of a great endeavour* (by 'L.T. Meade'; dedicated to 'all the children of every kingdom, everywhere').
London: John F. Shaw & Co., [1878]. SOURCE Allibone Suppl., ii, p. 1357 (1879 edn); Alston, p. 296. LOCATION D (n.d. edn), L, NUC ([1879] edn).
New York: Robert Carter, n.d. SOURCE FFF, p. 635.
Boston: [publisher?], 1893. SOURCE DLB, cxli, p. 186.
COMMENTARY No copies of the New York and Boston edns located. Fiction for juveniles. The Fitzgerald family, living in Geraldstown in Ireland, lead a happy life on their dilapidated, encumbered estate. They lose the estate to their creditors and move to London where the proud father has to take a job to support his family. The eldest son seems to go astray, and the coldness of his father makes it impossible for him to confide in his parents. However, in the end parents and son are reconciled and all is well [ML].

S173 *Water gipsies; or, the adventures of Tag, Rag, and Bobtail* (by 'L.T. Meade').
+ London: John F. Shaw & Co., 1879 (ill. H. Petherick). SOURCE Allibone Suppl., ii, p. 1357; DLB, cxli, p. 186. LOCATION D, NUC.
+ London: John F. Shaw & Co., [1895 or earlier] (new edn; ill. H. Peterick). LOCATION InND Loeber coll.
New York: R. Carter & Bros, 1879 (as *Water gipsies: A story of canal life in England*; ill.). SOURCE Baldwin, p. 146; DLB, cxli, p. 186. LOCATION L, NUC.
New York: G. Munro, 1879 (as *Water gipsies: A story of canal life in England*). SOURCE DLB, cxli, p. 186. LOCATION NUC.
COMMENTARY A religious and moral story set in England, it describes the generally awful circumstances under which children on barges grew up. Rag, Tag, Bobtail, and Curly are children who live with their aunt and father on a barge that travels between London and Staffordshire. The father treats the children very badly and after the aunt dies, life becomes worse for them. Curly is the first to run away. She wants to find the Sunday-school in London where she once heard about Jesus. Soon after, the other three also set out for London and end up in a thieves' den. The little boy, Bobtail, earns money by singing about Jesus, while his associates pick pockets. One of the older boys is picked up by the police and Bobtail runs away once more. The head of the thieves decides to save Bobtail's brother by confessing his role. Eventually, everybody ends up back on the barge together with a minister who tells them

more about Jesus. The father, who was near death before his children's return, recovers and turns over a new leaf [ML].

S174   *Dot and her treasures* (by 'L.T. Meade').
London: John F. Shaw & Co., 1879. SOURCE Alston, p. 296. LOCATION D (n.d. edn), L, NUC (n.d. edn), InND Loeber coll. (n.d. edn).
New York: Robert Carter, n.d. SOURCE FFF, p. 635.
COMMENTARY No copy of the New York edn located. Fiction for juveniles [RL].

S175   *Golden apple and other stories* (by 'L.T. Meade').
New York: E.P. Dutton, [1880–1899?] (ill.). SOURCE OCLC. LOCATION NIC.
COMMENTARY 48pp [OCLC].

S176   *A dweller in tents* (by 'L.T. Meade').
+ London: Wm. Isbister & Co., 1880 (ill.). SOURCE Allibone Suppl., ii, p. 1357; Alston, p. 2. LOCATION D, L.
+ London, New York, Melbourne: Ward, Lock & Co., n.d. (The Lily Series, No. 47; ill.). LOCATION InND Loeber coll.

S177   *The floating light of Ringfinnan and guardian angels* (by 'L.T. Meade').
Edinburgh: MacNiven & Wallace; London: Simpkin, Marshall & Co., 1879. SOURCE Topp 8, 591; COPAC (1880 edn). LOCATION E (1880 edn), NUC (1880 edn).
London: Thomas Nelson & Sons, 1904 (ill.). LOCATION L.
New York: Thomas Whittaker, 1888 (ill.; Whittaker Select Books). SOURCE FFF, p. 635.
COMMENTARY No copies of the Edinburgh 1879 edn and the New York edn located. Set in Ireland. Ringfinnan is near Kinsale (Co. Cork), where the author grew up [AMB].

S178   *Andrew Harvey's wife* (by 'L.T. Meade').
London: Wm. Isbister & Co., 1880. SOURCE Allibone Suppl., ii, p. 1357; Alston, p. 295. LOCATION D (n.d. edn), L.
New York: Robert Carter, n.d. SOURCE FFF, p. 635.
COMMENTARY No copy of the New York edn located [RL].

S179   *Mou-Setsé, a negro hero* (by 'L.T. Meade').
London: Wm. Isbister & Co., 1880 (ill.). SOURCE Allibone Suppl., ii, p. 1357; Alston, p. 297; Baldwin, p. 146. LOCATION L, NIC.

S180   *Mother Herring's chicken* (by 'L.T. Meade').
London: Wm. Isbister & Co., 1881 (ill.). SOURCE Allibone Suppl., ii, p. 1357; Alston, p. 297. LOCATION L, NIC ([c.1890] edn).
New York: Robert Carter, 1881. LOCATION NUC.
COMMENTARY Fiction for juveniles [RL].

S181   *A London baby: the story of King Roy* (by 'L.T. Meade').
London: James Nisbet & Co., 1882. SOURCE Allibone Suppl., ii, p. 1357 (1883 edn); Alston, p. 297. LOCATION L, NUC.
New York: Thomas Nelson & Co., [1883 or earlier] (ill.). SOURCE Thomas Nelson & Co. cat. of books, 1883–4; RL.
COMMENTARY Fiction for juveniles [RL].

S182   *Nobody's neighbours* (by 'L.T. Meade').
London: Wm. Isbister & Co., 1882 (The Sunday Magazine Christmas Story). SOURCE Allibone Suppl., ii, p. 1357 (1888 edn); Alston, p. 297; Baldwin, p. 146. LOCATION L ([1888] edn), NIC (1902 edn).
New York: G. Munro, [1833, *sic*, 1888] (Seaside Library). SOURCE DLB, cxli, p. 187. LOCATION NUC.

S183   *A band of three* (by 'L.T. Meade').
    New York: G. Munro, [1882] (Seaside Library). SOURCE DLB, cxli, p. 186. LOCATION NUC.
    New York: Thomas Whittaker, 1886 (ill. R. Barnes). SOURCE Baldwin, p. 144.
    London: Wm. Isbister & Co., 1884. SOURCE Allibone Suppl., ii, p. 1357; Alston, p. 295. LOCATION L.
COMMENTARY No copy of the New York edn located. Fiction for juveniles [RL].

S184   *The children's pilgrimage* (by 'L.T. Meade').
    London: James Nisbet & Co., 1883. SOURCE Alston, p. 296. LOCATION D (n.d. edn), L.
    Boston: [publisher?], 1893. LOCATION NUC.
    + New York: Grosset & Dunlap, n.d. (ill.). LOCATION InND Loeber coll.
COMMENTARY Set in England, the story opens with a deathbed scene in which a stepmother asks her stepchild, Cecile, to promise that she will look after her own daughter, who had left her when she married Cecile's father. The stepmother had put away money to give to her daughter once she had found her. She entrusts this money to Cecile and warns her that after she is dead Cecile and her brother will be entrusted to her sister who is an avaricious woman who is only willing to take them because of a regular remittance from their father's French farm. Their life with Aunt Lydia is unhappy and Cecile is in continuous danger of losing the money to her. Finally she decides to look for her stepsister, who might possibly be in France. Since Cecile and Maurice are also of French origin, they set out. After many dreadful adventures, they locate the girl, who is now married in the south of France. Cecile feels that Jesus protected her through all her adventures and pointed her in the right direction [ML].

S185   *Hermie's rose-buds: and other stories* (by 'L.T. Meade').
    + London: Hodder & Stoughton, 1883 (ill.). SOURCE Allibone Suppl., ii, p. 1357; Alston, p. 296. LOCATION L.
    New York: Thomas Whittaker, 1888 (ill.). SOURCE FFF, p. 636.
COMMENTARY No copy of the New York edn located. Contents: 'Hermie's rose-buds', '"The least of these, my brethren"', 'How Nora Crena saved her own' (set in Ireland), 'Umbrella hospital', 'A wild rose. The story of a very short visit to London', '"Jack Daring's conqueror"', 'Little black sheep' [RL].

S186   *How it all came round* (by 'L.T. Meade').
    London: Hodder & Stoughton, 1883 (ill. Robert Barnes). SOURCE Allibone Suppl., ii, p. 1357; DLB, cxli, p. 186. LOCATION D (1885 edn), L.
    New York: J.W. Lovell, [1883] (by 'T.T. Meade' [*sic*]). LOCATION NUC.
COMMENTARY Charlotte Home, wife of a poor curate in London and mother of three young children, smarts under her poverty. Her mother, on her deathbed, had told Charlotte that her two much older stepbrothers had illegally kept her from inheriting some of her father's considerable wealth. Accidentally, she comes into contact with the daughter of one of the stepbrothers, and slowly the story of the deceit comes to light. The oldest stepbrother, who is about to die from a serious disease, repents under the guidance of the curate, and repairs the wrong that he has done to Charlotte [ML].

S187   *Scarlet anemones* (by 'L.T. Meade').
    London: Hodder & Stoughton, 1884 (ill.). SOURCE Allibone Suppl., ii, p. 1357; Alston, p. 297. LOCATION L.

S188   *The autocrat of the nursery* (by 'L.T. Meade'; dedicated to author's 'little son and daughter', Alfie and Hope [Smith]).
    London: Hodder & Stoughton, 1884 (ill. T.O. Pym [pseud. of Clara Creed]). SOURCE Allibone Suppl., ii, p. 1357; Osborne, p. 1027. LOCATION L, CaOTP.

New York: A.C. Armstrong & Sons, 1886 (ill. T.O. Pym). SOURCE FFF, p. 635 (n.d. edn). LOCATION NUC.

COMMENTARY Fiction for juveniles [RL].

S189 *The two sisters* (by 'L.T. Meade').
+ London: Hodder & Stoughton, 1884 (ill.). SOURCE Alston, p. 297. LOCATION L, InND Loeber coll.

COMMENTARY Fiction for juveniles. A romantic story of two English girls. On her deathbed, Esther's mother had put her in charge of her twin sister, Ellie. While growing up, Ellie got her way in everything. When the girls are aged about 18 their cousin, Jack Graham, returns from India. Esther falls in love with him but thinks that Ellie is in love with him too. She secretly leaves and goes into hiding in Ireland, where she lives in a barn on the southern coast. Ellie writes her a letter that she is engaged to Jack. Esther, while trying to suppress the pain in her heart, strays to the entrance of a cave. When the tide comes in, she cannot return to higher ground. Fortunately, Ellie and Jack arrive and rescue her. It transpires that Ellie is engaged to a Jack Montfort. So, eventually, both sisters marry [ML].

S190 *The angel of love* (by 'L.T. Meade'; dedicated to 'A little brown-eyed boy called Tonie, and his three sisters, Annabel, Rachel, and Emily').
+ London: Hodder & Stoughton, 1885 (ill. T. Pym [pseud. of Clara Creed]). SOURCE Allibone Suppl., ii, p. 1357; Osborne, p. 1026. LOCATION D (1903, 5th edn), L, CaOTP, NUC, InND Loeber coll. (also 1892 edn).
+ Boston: James H. Earle, [1887] (ill.). LOCATION NUC, InND Loeber coll.

COMMENTARY Fiction for children. A story of three little English girls and their efforts to be good [ML].

S191 *A little silver trumpet* (by 'L.T. Meade').
London: Hodder & Stoughton, 1885 (ill. T. Pym [pseud. of Clara Creed]). SOURCE Allibone Suppl., ii, p. 1357; Osborne, p. 1027. LOCATION D (n.d. edn), L, CaOTP, NUC, InND Loeber coll. (London, Milford, 1921 edn).

COMMENTARY Fiction for juveniles [RL].

S192 *A world of girls: The story of a school* (by 'L.T. Meade').
London, Paris, New York, Melbourne: Cassell & Co., 1886. SOURCE Allibone Suppl., ii, p. 1357; Alston, p. 297; COPAC; Osborne, p. 1028 (1888 edn). LOCATION D (1894 edn, 21st thousand), L, E, CaOTP (1888 edn), NUC (1888 edn).
New York: Mershon, [189?]. LOCATION NUC.

COMMENTARY Very popular fiction for juveniles, much reprinted in the US. Twenty-one thousand copies had been printed in London by 1894. Hester Thornton is sent to school after her mother's death. Her arrival causes a disturbance of established routines and loyalties. She has to chose between allegiance to a good girl or to a dangerous one. Eventually, Hester recognizes that secrecy and scheming have endangered the life and health of other girls, and she embraces the school community [DLB, cxli, p. 196; RL].

S193 *Letters to our working-party* (by 'L.T. Meade').
London: [publisher?], 1887. SOURCE Allibone Suppl., ii, p. 1357; DLB, cxli, p. 187.

COMMENTARY No copy located [RL].

S194 *Beforehand* (by 'L.T. Meade').
London, New York, Glasgow: George Routledge & Sons, 1887 (Tillotson's Shilling Fiction). SOURCE Allibone Suppl., ii, p. 1357; Topp 1, p. 375.
New York: Frank F. Lovell, 1887. SOURCE Topp 7, 371.

COMMENTARY No copies of the London and the New York edns located [RL].

S195 *"Sweet Nancy"* (by 'L.T. Meade').

+ London: S.W. Partridge, [1887] (ill. R. Barnes). SOURCE Allibone Suppl., ii, p. 1357; Alston, p. 297. LOCATION L, D, InND Loeber coll..

New York: Thomas Whittaker, 1891. SOURCE FFF, p. 637.

COMMENTARY No copy of the New York edn located. Fiction for juveniles. At least nineteen thousand copies were printed. Contents: 'Sweet Nancy', 'Two lilies' [ML; RL].

S196   *The O'Donnells of Inchfawn* (by 'L.T. Meade').

+ London: Hatchards, 1887 (ill. A. Chasemore). SOURCE Allibone Suppl., ii, p. 1357; Brown, 1128. LOCATION D, L, NUC.

New York: Harper, 1887. LOCATION NUC.

COMMENTARY Set in Donegal. Fergus O'Donnell, a Catholic, marries a Protestant from Derry. Mrs. O'Donnell is very unhappy and is not received well by her neighbours. She has two children, Geoffrey and Ellen, but then becomes an invalid. Aunt Bridget looks after the household. Fergus sells his estate in the hope that a rich relative will die soon and he can reclaim it. After many misfortunes and illnesses, Ellen and her lover Arundel decide to go to America to found a new Inchfawn. Many of the people in the neighbourhood come with them [ML].

S197   *The palace beautiful: A story for girls* (by 'L.T. Meade').

London, Paris, New York, Melbourne: Cassell & Co., 1887. SOURCE Allibone Suppl., ii, p. 1357; Alston, p. 297. LOCATION D (1891, 4th edn), L, NIC (1892, 5th edn).

+ New York: The Platt & Peck Co., n.d. (ill. W.S. Storey, cover: R. Ford Horpery). LOCATION InND Loeber coll.

New York: A.L. Burt, [189?] (as *The beautiful palace*; The Fireside Series for Girls). SOURCE FFF, p. 635. LOCATION NUC.

New York, Boston: H.M. Caldwell, n.d. SOURCE FFF, p. 636.

Philadelphia: David McKay, n.d. (The Girls' Own Library). SOURCE FFF, p. 636.

No copies of the New York, Caldwell, the New York, Boston, and the Philadelphia edns located [RL].

COMMENTARY Fiction for juveniles, which became very popular and was much reprinted. Three middle-class orphan girls are exploited and physically abused by the other inhabitants of their derelict tenement while they try to earn their living [DLB, cxli, p. 197].

S198   *Pen* (by 'L.T. Meade').

London: [publisher?], 1888. SOURCE Allibone Suppl., ii, p. 1357; DLB, cxli, p. 187. COMMENTARY No copy located [RL].

S199   *Deb and the duchess: A story for boys and girls* (by 'L.T. Meade').

London: Hatchards, [1888]. SOURCE Allibone Suppl., ii, p. 1357; DLB, cxli, p. 187. LOCATION L.

London, New York, Bombay: Longmans, Green & Co., 1896 (new edn; ill. M.E. Edwards). SOURCE Baldwin, p. 145. LOCATION Richmond Public Library.

New York: White & Allen, 1889. LOCATION NUC.

+ Rahway (NJ), New York: Mershon, n.d. (ill. M.E. Edwards). LOCATION InND Loeber coll.

COMMENTARY Fiction for juveniles [RL].

S200   *Daddy's boy* (by 'L.T. Meade').

+ London: Hatchards, 1888 (ill. Laura Troubridge). SOURCE Allibone Suppl., ii, p. 1357 (1887 edn); Alston, p. 296. LOCATION D, L, NIC.

New York: White & Allen, 1889 (ill. Laura Troubridge). LOCATION NUC.

COMMENTARY Fiction for juveniles. A story about a boy whose parents have died. He is heir to a large estate and is being brought up by his aunt and uncle with the help of a governess. Their style of childrearing is very different from what the boy had been used to when his father lived. The story describes the clashes between the boy's former upbringing and his new regime [ML].

S201   *The lady of the forest. A story for girls* (by 'L.T. Meade').
London: S.W. Partridge & Co., [1889]. SOURCE Allibone Suppl., ii, p. 1357 (1888 edn); Alston, p. 296. LOCATION L.
+ London: S.W. Partridge & Co., n.d. (as *The lady of the forest*; ill.). SOURCE Wolff, 4708. LOCATION D, InND Loeber coll.
New York: F. Warne, 1889. LOCATION NUC.
COMMENTARY Fiction for juveniles. A poor mother makes terms with the rich relatives of her dead husband to leave her children with their aunts. The aunts are in search of the true heir to their family fortune. Many pretenders present themselves, but in the end a young boy from Australia satisfies all requirements [ML].

S202   *A farthingful* (by 'L.T. Meade').
London, Edinburgh: W. & R. Chambers, 1889. SOURCE Alston, p. 296. LOCATION D (1890 edn), L.
New York: Thomas Whittaker, 1891 (Dickory Dock Series). SOURCE FFF, p. 635.
COMMENTARY No copy of the New York edn located [RL].

S203   *The golden lady* (by 'L.T. Meade').
London, Edinburgh: W. & R. Chambers, 1889 (ill.). SOURCE Alston, p. 296. LOCATION L, NIC.
New York: Thomas Whittaker, [190?] (Dickory Dock Series). SOURCE FFF, p. 635. LOCATION NUC.
COMMENTARY 64pp for the London edn [RL].

S204   *Polly: a new-fashioned girl* (by 'L.T. Meade').
London, Edinburgh: W. & R. Chambers, 1889 (ill. M.E. Edwards). SOURCE Alston, p. 297. LOCATION D (1908 edn, 32nd thousand), L.
London, Paris, New York, Melbourne: Cassell & Co., 1889. LOCATION NUC.
Philadelphia: David McKay, [1890?] (The Girls' Own Library). SOURCE FFF, p. 636. LOCATION NUC.
COMMENTARY Fiction for juveniles. The 32nd thousandth copy of this book was published in London in 1908. Based on Charlotte Yonge's *The daisy chain* (London, 1856), in which a young girl attempts to manage the household after her mother has died [DLB, cxli, p. 197; RL].

S205   *The little princess of the Tower Hill* (by 'L.T. Meade').
+ London: S.W. Partridge, [1889] (ill. S.B.). SOURCE Allibone Suppl., ii, p. 1357 (1888 edn); Alston, p. 297. LOCATION D, L.
New York: Thomas Whittaker, 1891. SOURCE FFF, p. 636.
COMMENTARY No copy of the New York edn located. Fiction for juveniles [RL].

S206   *Poor Miss Carolina* (by 'L.T. Meade').
London, Edinburgh: W. & R. Chambers, 1889. SOURCE Alston, p. 297. LOCATION L.
New York: Thomas Whittaker, 1891 (Dickory Dock Series). SOURCE FFF, p. 636.
COMMENTARY No copy of the New York edn located. Fiction for juveniles [RL].

S207   *Marigold* (by 'L.T. Meade').
+ London: S.W. Partridge & Co., [1890] (ill. Sarah Birch). SOURCE Alston, p. 297. LOCATION L, InND Loeber coll.
COMMENTARY Fiction for juveniles [RL].

S208   *Just a love story* (by 'L.T. Meade').
London: Spencer Blackett, 1890 (ill.). SOURCE Alston, p. 296. LOCATION L, NIC.

London: Griffith & Farran, 1900 (as *The Beauforts*). SOURCE DLB, cxli, p. 187. LOCATION L.

S209   *The home of silence* (by 'L.T. Meade').
+ London: Sisley's, [*c.*1890]. SOURCE Tiger cat. 10/95/163. LOCATION L (1907 edn), InND Loeber coll.

COMMENTARY Crime fiction set in England and Ireland and written for adult readers. Nigel Dering, son of an Irish father and an English mother, is about to leave for Ireland to visit his relatives for the first time. His mother has some misgivings and hopes that he will not fall in love with an Irish girl. Her reason is that her husband had been very charming but also a drunkard whose life had gone downhill very fast. In the end, he had even killed a servant, which was kept a secret. Once in Ireland, Nigel falls in love with his cousin Molly. Despite the entreaties of his mother and the revelation of his father's life (about which Molly does not want to be informed), they are planning to marry. The story ends tragically when the brother of the dead Irish servant finds out about the secret, hurries to Molly to disclose it, but accidentally steps off the path and drowns in a bog, taking the secret with him [ML].

S210   *The Beresford prize* (by 'L.T. Meade').
+ London: Longman, Green & Co., 1890 (ill. M. Ellen Edwards). SOURCE Alston, p. 296. LOCATION D (1902 edn), L, InND Loeber coll.

COMMENTARY Fiction for juveniles. A story about girls attending a prestigious boarding school. In order to compete for the school prize, girls must not only be very clever, but also honourable and have clear consciences. One girl cannot accept the prize because she has promised a rich, charming but very manipulative and deceitful girl not to tell on her. Eventually, the deceitful girl learns that it is better to admit her sins and to try to be honest [ML].

S211   *Engaged to be married. A tale of to-day* (by 'L.T. Meade').
London: Simpkin, Marshall & Co., 1890. SOURCE DLB, cxli, p. 187. LOCATION L.
London: Henry Frowde; Hodder & Stoughton, 1917 (as *The daughters of today*). SOURCE DLB, cxli, p. 187. LOCATION D (n.d. edn), L.
New York: United States Book Co., [1891] (as *A life for a love: A story of to-day*). LOCATION NUC.

COMMENTARY A story of three young women who share a flat in London and try to make a living. One of the girls is engaged but has not heard from her fiancée in India, thanks to the machinations of the young man's father. The girl becomes known as a painter and accidentally meets her fiancée again. The father's nefarious plot is uncovered and the two marry [ML].

S212   *Dickory Dock* (by 'L.T. Meade').
London, Edinburgh: W. & R. Chambers, 1890. SOURCE Alston, p. 296. LOCATION L.
New York: Thomas Whittaker, [1890 or later] (Dickory Dock Series). SOURCE FFF, p. 635.

COMMENTARY No copy of the New York edn located [RL].

S213   *Frances Kane's fortune* (by 'L.T. Meade').
London: Frederick Warne & Co., 1890 (London Library, No. 37). SOURCE Alston, p. 296; Topp 4, p. 213. LOCATION L.
New York: John W. Lovell, [1890] (Westminster Series, No. 8). SOURCE Topp 4, p. 213. LOCATION NUC.
New York, Boston: H.M. Caldwell, 1900. SOURCE FFF, p. 635 (n.d. edn); OCLC. LOCATION Univ. of Wisconsin, Eau Claire.

S214   *A girl of the people: A novel* (by 'L.T. Meade').
London: Methuen, 1890. SOURCE DLB, cxli, p. 187. LOCATION D ([1912] edn), L ([1912] edn).
New York: F.F. Lovell, [1890]. LOCATION NUC.

New York, Boston: H.M. Caldwell, n.d. SOURCE FFF, p. 635.

Montreal: J. Lovell, [1890?]. SOURCE COPAC. LOCATION L.

COMMENTARY No copy of the 1st London edn located. Also, no copy of the New York, Boston edn located. Fiction for juveniles. After her mother's death, Bet – daughter of a drunken and violent father – is left to protect herself and her brothers from her father's attempts to sell the boys into apprenticeships and her into marriage. She succeeds with the help of two women who galvanize the community into action against the sadistic sailor to whom her father has promised her [DLB, cxli, p. 197; RL].

S215   *Heart of gold* (by 'L.T. Meade').

+ London, New York: Frederick Warne & Co., 1890 (ill. Bernard Partridge, Stanley Thorn). SOURCE Topp 4, p. 242. LOCATION D (1891 edn), L, InND Loeber coll.

New York: Frederick Warne & Co., [1890]. LOCATION NUC.

New York: United States Book Co., [1890]. LOCATION NUC.

S216   *The honourable Miss. A story of an old-fashioned town* (by 'L.T. Meade').

London: Methuen & Co., 1891, 2 vols (ill. Edward Hopkins). SOURCE Wolff, 4704. LOCATION L, NUC.

New York: United States Book Co., [1890]. LOCATION NUC.

New York, Boston: H.M. Caldwell & Co., n.d. SOURCE FFF, p. 636.

COMMENTARY No copy of the New York, Boston edn located. The story of a draper's rich daughter who saves a proud family from scandal and unhappiness [ML].

S217   *Hepsy Gipsy* (by 'L.T. Meade').

London: Methuen & Co., 1891 (ill. Everard Hopkins). SOURCE Baldwin, p. 145; Alston, p. 296. LOCATION L, NUC.

S218   *The children of Wilton Chase* (by 'L.T. Meade').

+ London, Edinburgh: W. & R. Chambers, 1891 (ill. Everard Hopkins). SOURCE Alston, p. 296. LOCATION L, InND Loeber coll.

New York: Cassell & Co., [1891] (ill. Everard Hopkins). SOURCE Baldwin, p. 145. LOCATION NUC.

COMMENTARY Fiction for juveniles [RL].

S219   *Little Mary and other stories* (by 'L.T. Meade').

London, Edinburgh: W. & R. Chambers, 1891. SOURCE Alston, p. 297. LOCATION L, InND Loeber coll. (n.d. edn), NIC.

New York: Thomas Whittaker, 1891. SOURCE FFF, p. 636.

COMMENTARY No copy of the New York edn located. Fiction for juveniles. Contents 'Little Mary', 'Cassie', 'A lonely puppy', 'The tambourine girl' [RL].

S220   *A sweet girl graduate* (by 'L.T. Meade').

+ London, Paris, Melbourne: Cassell & Co., 1891 (ill. Hal Ludlow). SOURCE Daims, 2864. LOCATION D, L, NUC, InND Loeber coll. (1892 edn).

New York: Alisson, [1890s]. SOURCE DLB, cxli, p. 187; OCLC. LOCATION Duke Univ.

New York: Cassell & Co., 1892 (ill.; Story Books for Girls). SOURCE FFF, p. 636 (n.d. edn); OCLC. LOCATION InND.

New York: Grosset & Dunlap, n.d. (The Good Value Books). SOURCE FFF, p. 637; DLB, cxli, p. 187; OCLC. LOCATION Univ. of South Florida.

New York: American News Co., n.d. (Empire Edition). SOURCE FFF, p. 637.

New York, Boston: H.M. Caldwell, n.d. (ill.; The Young Folks Library). SOURCE FFF, p. 637.

Philadelphia: David McKay, n.d. (The Girls' Own Library). SOURCE FFF, p. 637.

COMMENTARY No copies of the New York, Boston edn and the Philadelphia edn located. Fiction for juveniles. Priscilla Peel, a virtuous but awkward and poor girl, enters an English women's college. She is not popular but gains the friendship of one of the more popular girls. Another girl makes it appear as if Priscilla has stolen £5 from her friend. The actual thief is found out and leaves the college in disgrace and Priscilla becomes an example to the other girls [ML].

S221 *Four on an island. A story of adventure* (by 'L.T. Meade').

  + London, Edinburgh: W. & R. Chambers, [1892] (ill. W. Rainey). SOURCE Osborne, p. 1027. LOCATION L, CaOTP, InND Loeber coll.

  New York: Cassell, [1892] (as *Four on an island; a book for the little folks*). LOCATION NUC.

  + New York: Grosset & Dunlap, n.d. [1915 according to inscription] (as *Four on an island. a book for little folks*; ill.). LOCATION InND Loeber coll.

  New York: Chatterton & Co., 1892 (ill.; Fascinating Stories for Girls). SOURCE FFF, p. 635 (n.d. edn); OCLC. LOCATION Univ. of Connecticut.

  COMMENTARY Fiction for juveniles. Four young children drift out to sea and land on an island off the coast of Brazil. Two of the children are British and show British pluck. All of them have to be very inventive to survive the dangers they meet before they are rescued [ML].

S222 *Bashful fifteen* (by 'L.T. Meade').

  + London, Paris, Melbourne: Cassell & Co., 1892. SOURCE Alston, p. 295. LOCATION D, L, InND Loeber coll. (1898 edn).

  New York: Grosset & Dunlap, [*c*.1892]. SOURCE Baldwin, p. 144; OCLC. LOCATION NN.

  New York: Cassell, [1892]. LOCATION NUC.

  COMMENTARY Fiction for juveniles. Bridget 'Biddy' O'Hara, an independent-minded Irish girl, enters an English boarding school and turns the place upside-down with her rebellious ways [OCLC; RL].

S223 *Out of the fashion* (by 'L.T. Meade').

  + London: Methuen, 1892. SOURCE Daims, 2858. LOCATION L.

  New York: Cassell, [1892]. SOURCE Daims, 2858. LOCATION NUC.

  New York: A.L. Chatterton, 1892 (ill.; Fascinating Stories for Girls). SOURCE FFF, p. 636 (n.d. edn); OCLC. LOCATION Free Library of Philadelphia.

  COMMENTARY Fiction for juveniles [ML].

S224 *A ring of rubies* (by 'L.T. Meade').

  London: A.D. Innes, 1892 (ill. L.L.B. [Leonard Leslie Brooke]). SOURCE Osborne, p. 1028. LOCATION D (1903 edn), L, CaOTP.

  New York: Cassell, [1892]. LOCATION NUC.

  New York: A.L. Chatterton-Peck, [1892] (Fascinating Stories for Girls). SOURCE FFF, p. 636. LOCATION NUC.

  + New York: Grosset & Dunlap, [1892] (ill. L.L. Roush). LOCATION InND Loeber coll.

  New York: Mershon, [1892]. LOCATION NUC.

  COMMENTARY No copy of the New York, Chatterton-Peck edn located. Fiction for juveniles. A poor girl who has some talent for drawing visits her eccentric, very rich, uncle who has never paid any attention to his relatives, to ask him for money to go to the Slade School in London. The uncle refuses, but a few weeks later he dies and leaves her a ruby ring. His will is extremely mysterious. Even though the girl is very poor and she is tempted many times to sell the ring, she holds on to it and it eventually leads her to fulfil the conditions of the will and become the heiress, together with a distant relative, whom she must marry to come into the fortune. Fortunately, they love each other [ML].

S225 *The medicine lady* (by 'L.T. Meade').

London, Paris, Melbourne: Cassell & Co., 1892, 3 vols. SOURCE Daims, 2855; Wolff, 4711 (1893 edn); Topp 7, 1074. LOCATION L, NUC (n.d. edn), InND Loeber coll. (1893 edn).

New York: Cassell, [1892]. SOURCE Daims, 2855; Topp 7, 1074. LOCATION NUC.

COMMENTARY Set in East London where a nurse marries a doctor. After he dies, his wife finds that she has consumption and tries the drug that he had developed. The drug works and she distributes the drug to other patients. However, she finds that the drug is imperfect and that it is dangerous to try to heal people without the appropriate medical training [ML].

S226   *Jill, a flower girl* (by 'L.T. Meade').

+ London: Wm. Isbister & Co., [1892] (ill. F.H. Townsend). SOURCE Osborne, p. 1027. LOCATION L, CaOTP, NUC, InND Loeber coll.

New York, Chicago: United States Book Co., [1892]. LOCATION NUC.

S227   *This troublesome world* [anon.].

London: Edward Arnold, 1893, 3 vols. SOURCE Wolff, 4723; OCLC. LOCATION L.

London: Chatto & Windus, 1901, 2nd edn (by 'L.T. Meade' and 'Clifford Halifax, M.D.'). LOCATION NIC.

New York: Macmillan & Co., 1893. SOURCE NUC.

COMMENTARY A crime story, featuring William Green, private detective [EF, p. 276].

S228   *Beyond the blue mountains* (by 'L.T. Meade').

+ London, New York, Toronto, Melbourne: Cassell & Co., 1893 (ill. Helen Jacobs). SOURCE Osborne, p. 389. LOCATION D, L, CaOTP, InND Loeber coll. (n.d. edn).

COMMENTARY Fiction for juveniles [RL].

S229   *A young mutineer. A story for girls* (by 'L.T. Meade'; dedicated to author's daughter Hope [Smith], 'the real Judy').

+ London: Wells Gardner, Darton & Co., [1893] (ill. Gordon Browne). SOURCE Osborne, p. 389. LOCATION D, L, CaOTP.

New York: Wm. L. Allison, [189?]. LOCATION NUC.

New York: A.L. Burt, n.d. (ill.; Fireside Series for Girls). SOURCE FFF, p. 637; OCLC. LOCATION DCL.

+ New York: Grosset & Dunlap, n.d. (ill. cover: Ford Horpery). LOCATION InND Loeber coll.

+ Chicago: M.A. Donohue & Co., 1893 (ill. G.B. [probably Gordon Browne]). LOCATION InND Loeber coll.

COMMENTARY Fiction for juveniles. First serialized in *Atalanta* (London, 1892–93). Set in England, a story of two sisters whose extreme attachment to each other makes their separation by the marriage of the older sister a wrenching experience. It also has a bad effect on the relationship between the married couple until, finally, the younger sister learns to let go and love her sister from a distance [ML].

S230   *Red Rose and Tiger Lily; or, in a wider world* (by 'L.T. Meade').

+ London, Paris, Melbourne: Cassell & Co., 1894 (ill. M.E.E. [Mary Ellen Edwards]). SOURCE Osborne, p. 389. LOCATION D, L, CaOTP, NUC.

+ New York: Grosset & Dunlap, 1894 (ill. M.E.E). LOCATION NUC, InND Loeber coll.

COMMENTARY Fiction for juveniles. Continues the story of the characters first introduced in *A world of girls* (London, 1886). The girls become involved with neighbours threatened with losing their ancestral home [DLB, cxli, p. 197].

S231   *In an iron grip* (by 'L.T. Meade').

London: Chatto & Windus, 1894, 2 vols. SOURCE Daims, 2851; Wolff, 4706. LOCATION L, NUC.

S232   *A soldier of fortune* (by 'L.T. Meade').
London: Chatto & Windus, 1894, 3 vols. SOURCE Wolff, 4719. LOCATION L, InND
Loeber coll. (1895, new edn).
New York: Grosset, 1894. SOURCE DLB, cxli, p. 187.
COMMENTARY No copy of the New York edn located. John Smith, son of a gentleman farmer,
is sent for a trip to the Continent because his mother feels that he is too good to become a
farmer. In Switzerland he meets a rich and extremely egocentric girl, Phyllis Martindale, who
accepts his proposal. Miss Martindale's aunt whisks her away because she wants to profit from
the girl's riches. John returns to England and tells all his woes to his long-time friend Nancy
Browne. He becomes a writer for a magazine in London. Phyllis comes back into the picture
but eventually realizes that John and his family are too good for her. John is successful as a
writer and marries Nancy [ML].

S233   *Stories from the diary of a doctor (first series)* (by 'L.T. Meade' and 'Clifford
Halifax, M.D.').
+ London: George Newnes, 1894. SOURCE DLB, cxli, p. 187; Wolff, 4722. LOCATION
L, NUC (n.d. edn).
Philadelphia: J.B. Lippincott, 1895. LOCATION NUC.
COMMENTARY First published in the *Strand Magazine* (London, 1893–95). Short stories of
crime fiction. Contents: 'My first patient', 'My hypnotic patient', 'Very far west', 'The heir
of Chartelpool', 'A death certificate', 'The wrong prescription', 'The horror of Studley Grange',
'Ten years' oblivion', 'An oak coffin', 'Without witnesses', 'Trapped', 'The Ponsonby dia-
monds' [ML; Reilly, p. 639].

S234   *The least of these, and other stories* (by 'L.T. Meade').
New York: Hunt & Eaton, 1895. SOURCE DLB, cxli, p. 187.
Cincinnati: Granston & Curtis; New York: Hunt & Eaton, 1895. LOCATION NUC.
COMMENTARY No copy of the New York edn located. The story, 'The least of these' was first
published in *Hermie's rose-buds* (London, 1883) [RL].

S235   *Minister* (by 'L.T. Meade').
[place?]: [publisher?], 1895 (ill.). SOURCE NCBEL 4, p.1637.
COMMENTARY No copy located [RL].

S236   *Betty a school girl* (by 'L.T. Meade').
London, Edinburgh: W. & R. Chambers, 1895 (ill. Everard Hopkins). SOURCE Osborne,
p. 388; D (n.d. edn). LOCATION L, CaOTP, InND Loeber coll. (n.d. edn).
+ New York: Grosset & Dunlap, n.d. (ill.). LOCATION InND Loeber coll.
New York: Cassell, [1894] [*sic*]. LOCATION NUC.
COMMENTARY Fiction for juveniles [RL].

S237   *The voice of the charmer* (by 'L.T. Meade').
London: Chatto & Windus, 1895, 3 vols. SOURCE Alston, p. 297. LOCATION D (1910
edn), L.
+ London: Chatto & Windus, 1896 (new edn; ill. Walter Paget). LOCATION InND
Loeber coll.
COMMENTARY Crime fiction. Patty Neville lives with her aunt at Red Lodge, an estate in
England. Her aunt has been planning to leave her property to Patty, but Patty takes up with
a Mr Ward, who is considered an undesirable character by the aunt, and she disinherits Patty.
Patty leaves and marries Mr Ward in secret. Ward plans to take possession of Red Lodge. He
had planted a false will in the house and after the aunt dies, he sends Patty to visit Mrs
Fletcher and her daughter Margot, who have inherited the estate. Mrs Fletcher and Margot
take Patty in because they feel sorry for her impecunious state. Ward is secretary to Sir Wilfrid
Dering and with him visits the lodge. Ward forces Patty to go through the house and find the

false will. Although Ward attains his goal and becomes a rich man, Patty is terribly unhappy and eventually posts a letter to Margot explaining the truth. Her husband finds out and on the way back from the post-box both drown in a swollen river. Margot, who in the meantime has married Dering, takes possession of Red Lodge and vows to keep Patty's story secret from the village [ML].

S238 *A princess of the gutter* (by 'L.T. Meade').
London: Wells Gardner, Darton & Co., 1895. SOURCE Daims, 2859; Wolff, 4715. LOCATION L.
New York, London: J.P. Putnam's Sons, [1896]. SOURCE Daims, 2859. LOCATION NUC.

S239 *Playmates. A story for boys and girls* (by 'L.T. Meade').
+ London, Edinburgh: W. & R. Chambers, 1896 (ill. G. Nicolet). SOURCE Osborne, p. 1028. LOCATION D (n.d. edn), L, CaOTP, NUC, InND Loeber coll. (n.d. edn).
New York: A.L. Burt, 1905 (St Nicholas Series). SOURCE FFF, p. 636; OCLC. LOCATION InND (n.d. edn).
COMMENTARY Fiction for juveniles [RL].

S240 *Stories from the diary of a doctor (second series)* (by 'L.T. Meade' and 'Clifford Halifax, M.D.').
+ London: Bliss, Sands, 1896. SOURCE DLB, cxli, p. 188. LOCATION L.
COMMENTARY Short stories of crime fiction. Contents: 'Creating a mind', 'The seventh step', 'The silent tongue', 'The hooded death', 'The red bracelet', 'Little Sir Noel', 'A doctor's dilemma', 'On a charge of forgery', 'With the eternal fires', 'The small house on Steven's heath', '"To everyone his own fear"' [Reilly, p. 639; ML].

S241 *A little mother to the others* (by 'L.T. Meade').
London: F.V. White & Co., 1896 (ill. Fred Barnard). SOURCE Alston, p. 297. LOCATION L, NIC.
+ New York: A.L. Burt, n.d. (as *Their little mother. A story for girls*). LOCATION InND Loeber coll.
New York: Frederick Warne & Co., n.d. (ill.; The Albion Library). SOURCE FFF, p. 637; OCLC. LOCATION D, NIC.
COMMENTARY Fiction for juveniles. Iris, Apollo, Diana, and Orion are left orphans at an early age. At her mother's deathbed, Iris, aged 10, was charged to be a little mother to her siblings and to help them all to live up to their names. All kinds of adventures befall the children, but they are brave and survive well [ML].

S242 *The white tzar* (by 'L.T. Meade').
London: Marshall, Russell & Co., [1896]. SOURCE Alston, p. 297. LOCATION L.

S243 *Dr. Rumsey's patient. A very strange story* (by 'L.T. Meade' and 'Clifford Halifax, M.D.').
London: Chatto & Windus, 1896. SOURCE Alston, p. 298. LOCATION L, NUC.
COMMENTARY A crime story [EF, p. 276].

S244 *Girls, new and old* (by 'L.T. Meade').
London, Edinburgh: W. & R. Chambers, 1896 (ill. J. Williamson). SOURCE Osborne, p. 389. LOCATION L, CaOTP.
New York: Cassell, [1895]. LOCATION NUC.
COMMENTARY Fiction for juveniles [RL].

S245 *A girl in ten thousand* (by 'L.T. Meade').
Edinburgh, London: Oliphant, [1896]. SOURCE Daims, 2848. LOCATION L.
New York: Thomas Whittaker, 1897. SOURCE Daims, 284. LOCATION NUC.
COMMENTARY Fiction for juveniles [RL].

S246   *Good luck* (by 'L.T. Meade').
      London: James Nisbet & Co., 1896. SOURCE Daims, 2850. LOCATION L, NIC.
      London, New York, Melbourne: Ward, Lock & Co., 1896. SOURCE RLIN. LOCATION
      NIC.
      New York: Grosset & Dunlap, [19??]. LOCATION NUC.
      + New York: The Platt & Pack Co., n.d. (ill.). LOCATION InND Loeber coll.
      COMMENTARY Grannie Reed, living in London's East End, earns a meagre living by her won-
      derful needlework. She loses the use of her arm. Her granddaughter is accused of stealing
      money in the shop where she works and loses her job. While living under a cloud of suspi-
      cion, the girl does not want to marry her fiancée and rejects him. The family disperses and
      Granny Reed goes into a workhouse. However, in the end the girl is cleared, her fiancée
      returns, and her grandmother is retrieved from the workhouse [ML].

S247   *Merry girls of England* (by 'L.T. Meade').
      London, Paris, Melbourne: Cassell & Co., 1896 (ill. W.S. Stacey). SOURCE Daims,
      2856; Osborne, p. 389. LOCATION D (1897 edn, 6th thousand), L, CaOTP.
      Boston: A.I. Bradley & Co., [1897] (ill. W.S. Stacey). SOURCE Daims, 2856. LOCATION
      NUC.
      New York: Grosset & Dunlap, 1897. SOURCE Baldwin, p. 145; OCLC. LOCATION
      Cleveland Public Library (OH).
      COMMENTARY Fiction for juveniles [ML].

S248   *Catalina: art student* (by 'L.T. Meade').
      + London, Edinburgh: W. & R. Chambers, 1896 (ill. W. Boucher). SOURCE Daims,
      2844. LOCATION D (n.d. edn), L, InND Loeber coll.
      Philadelphia: J.B. Lippincott, 1897 (ill. Boucher). SOURCE Daims, 2844. LOCATION
      NUC.
      COMMENTARY Catalina Gifford, a promising art student, lives at home with her parents, sev-
      eral sisters and a young brother. Her father is a well-known but poor professor. Her mother
      and sisters are shallow people who care more for appearances than for intellectual or artistic
      achievements. When Catalina's father falls ill and requires an extensive period of rest, she
      saves the family from poverty by visiting her rich uncle in Manchester who had been estranged
      from her mother for twenty years. At the art school, Catalina is accused of making unflatter-
      ing caricatures of her teachers and is threatened with expulsion. It transpires that a jealous
      fellow student is the culprit, and Catalina is exonerated [ML].

S249   *A son of Ishmael. A novel* (by 'L.T. Meade').
      London: F.V. White & Co., 1896. SOURCE Alston, p. 297. LOCATION D (1918 edn),
      L, NUC.
      New York: New Amsterdam Book Co., [1896] (ill. A. Burnham Shute). LOCATION
      NUC.
      COMMENTARY Crime fiction [Reilly, p. 638].

S250   *The house of surprises* (by 'L.T. Meade').
      London, New York, Bombay: Longman, Green & Co., 1896 (ill. Edith Scannell).
      SOURCE Baldwin, p. 145; DLB, cxli, p. 188. LOCATION D (1898 edn), NUC (1898 edn).

S251   *Wild Kitty: A school story* (by 'L.T. Meade').
      London, Edinburgh: W. & R. Chambers, 1897 (ill. J. Ayton Symington). SOURCE DLB,
      cxli, p. 188. LOCATION D (n.d. edn), L, NIC.
      + London, Edinburgh: W. & R. Chambers, n.d. (as *Wild Kitty*; ill. J. Ayton
      Symington). LOCATION InND Loeber coll.
      New York: A.L. Burt, n.d. (as *Wild Kitty: A story of Middleton school*; Fireside Series
      for Girls; ill.). SOURCE FFF, p. 637; DLB, cxli, p. 188. LOCATION NUC.

New York, Boston: Caldwell, n.d. (ill.). SOURCE FFF, p. 637.
New York: E.P. Dutton & Co., n.d. (ill.). SOURCE FFF, p. 637.
Rahway (NJ): Mershon, n.d. SOURCE Baldwin, p. 146.
Philadelphia: David McKay, [1913] (The Girls' Own Library). SOURCE FFF, p. 637. LOCATION NUC.
COMMENTARY No copies of the New York, Boston edn and the New York, Dutton edn located. Fiction for juveniles, which was much reprinted. [RL].

S252 *Andrew Sargeant's wedding* (by 'L.T. Meade').
London: Jarrold, 1897 (ill.). SOURCE NCBEL 4, p. 1637 (1896 edn not located); COPAC. LOCATION Univ. of Liverpool (1897, 2nd edn).
COMMENTARY No copy of the 1897 1st edn located [RL].

S253 *Eleanor Halliday's rebellion* (by 'L.T. Meade').
London, Edinburgh: W. & R. Chambers, [1897]. SOURCE Alston, p. 296. LOCATION L.
COMMENTARY Fiction for juveniles [RL].

S254 *Bad little Hannah* (by 'L.T. Meade').
London: F.V. White & Co., 1897. SOURCE Alston, p. 295. LOCATION L.
New York: Frederick Warne & Co., n.d. (The Albion Library). SOURCE FFF, p. 635; OCLC. LOCATION Univ. of Newcastle.
New York: A.L. Burt, n.d. (ill.; The Wellesley Series for Girls). SOURCE FFF, p. 635; OCLC. LOCATION Richmond Public Library.
New York: Grosset & Dunlap, n.d. SOURCE Baldwin, p. 144.
New York: Mershon, [190?]. LOCATION NUC.
COMMENTARY No copy of the New York, Grosset edn located. Fiction for juveniles [RL].

S255 *Under the dragon throne* (by 'L.T. Meade' with Robert Kennaway Douglas).
+ London: Wells Gardner & Co. [1897]. SOURCE DLB, cxli, p. 188. LOCATION C, L, NIC.
COMMENTARY Short stories of crime fiction. Contents: 'Richard Maitland, consul', 'A victim of the Kolao-Hwuy', 'Mrs. Wyndham's season of terror', 'Trapped by a Chinaman', 'A dangerous experiment' [ML; Reilly, p. 639].

S256 *The way of a woman* (by 'L.T. Meade').
London: F.V. White & Co., 1897. SOURCE Alston, p. 297. LOCATION L.

S257 *A handful of silver* (by 'L.T. Meade').
+ Edinburgh, London: Oliphant, Anderson & Ferrier, 1897 (ill. Ida Lovering). SOURCE Wolff, 4702. LOCATION D, L, InND Loeber coll.
New York: E.P. Dutton & Co., 1898 (ill. Ida Lovering). LOCATION NUC.
COMMENTARY A mother falsely claims a small inheritance so that she can satisfy her daughter's whims. The daughter tries to steal the lover of the girl who should have inherited the money. In the end the true lovers are united [ML].

S258 *Me and my dolls; the story of the joys and troubles of Miss Beau-Peep and her doll family, to which is added The strange adventures of Mopsy and Hans* (by 'L.T. Meade').
Boston: D. Lothrop, [1898] (ill.; Little Wanderer Series). SOURCE Baldwin, p. 145; FFF, p. 636. LOCATION NUC.
Boston: D. Lothrop, 1898. SOURCE OCLC. LOCATION DCL.
Boston: D. Lothrop, n.d. (as *The strange adventures of Mopsy and Hans*; Sunny Lands Series). SOURCE FFF, p. 636.
COMMENTARY No copy of the Boston n.d. edn located. Fiction for children [RL].

S259   *A master of mysteries* (by 'L.T. Meade' and 'Robert Eustace').
        + London, New York, Melbourne: Ward, Lock & Co., [1898] (ill. J. Ambrose Walton).
        SOURCE Sotheby's cat. LN6731/430. LOCATION L, NUC (n.d. edn), InND Loeber
        coll.
COMMENTARY Stories, set in England about supposedly supernatural events that are shown by
the main character to be caused naturally. Contents: 'The mystery of the circular chamber',
'The warder of the door', 'The mystery of the Felwyn tunnel', 'The eight-mile lock', 'How
Siva spoke', 'To prove an alibi' [ML].
S260   *Cave perilous* (by 'L.T. Meade').
        + London: Religious Tract Society, [1898] (ill.). SOURCE Alston, p. 296; Wolff, 4696.
        LOCATION D, L, InND Loeber coll.
COMMENTARY Historical fiction set during the Chartists' revolt in the 1840s. Three children
of a village miller discover a secret cave in which they hide when bread riots break out in their
neighbourhood. They survive because they had planned carefully what they needed for their
stay [DLB, cxli, p. 193].
S261   *A bunch of cherries: A story of Cherry Court School* (by 'L.T. Meade'; dedicated to
        'the girls whom I love everywhere').
        London: Ernest Nister, 1898 (ill. E. Start Hardy). SOURCE DLB, cxli, p. 188; Wolff,
        4695. LOCATION L, NIC.
        Rahway (NJ), New York: Mershon, [189?]. LOCATION NUC.
        New York: E.P. Dutton, 1898. LOCATION NUC.
COMMENTARY Fiction for juveniles [RL].
S262   *Mary Gifford, M.D.* (by 'L.T. Meade'; with thanks to 'Clifford Halifax, M.D.')
        + London: Wells Gardner, Darton, 1898. SOURCE Daims, 2854. LOCATION L, NUC,
        InND Loeber coll.
COMMENTARY The story of the life of a female doctor, dealing with the difficulties of being
accepted as a professional and the persistence it takes to start a career. The main character
Mary finds her place working as a doctor for the poor in the slums of London [ML].
S263   *The cleverest woman in England* (by 'L.T. Meade').
        London: James Nisbet & Co., 1898. SOURCE Daims, 2845. LOCATION D (n.d. edn), L,
        InND Loeber coll. (n.d. edn).
        Boston: A.I. Bradley & Co., 1899. SOURCE Daims, 2845. LOCATION NUC.
COMMENTARY An emancipated woman marries a man whose views are opposite of hers. They
think they can make their marriage work by agreeing not to interfere with each other's activities. However, the husband finds it impossible to stick to this contract and he gives an ulti-
matum that one of them must give up their work, implying that she should devote her time
to being a perfect wife and mother. Before she has to make her decision, she falls ill and dies
[ML; Sutherland].
S264   *The girls of St. Wode's* (by 'L.T. Meade').
        + London, Edinburgh: W. & R. Chambers, 1898 (ill. W. Rainey). SOURCE Daims,
        2849. LOCATION D (n.d. edn), L.
        New York: Mershon, [1902?]. SOURCE Daims, 2849. LOCATION NUC.
COMMENTARY Fiction for juveniles [ML].
S265   *On the brink of a chasm. A record of plot and passion* (by 'L.T. Meade').
        + London: Chatto & Windus, 1898. SOURCE Daims, 2857. LOCATION L, InND Loeber
        coll.
        New York: F.M. Buckles & Co., 1899. SOURCE Daims, 2857. LOCATION NUC.
COMMENTARY Crime fiction. A nurse uses her knowledge of hypnotism to rescue a young,
rich boy from a brain specialist who plots to kill him and then accuse his heir of poisoning

him. The prospective heir had married the woman the doctor was in love with and he wants to punish her for not returning his feelings [ML].

S266   *The rebellion of Lil Carrington* (by 'Mrs L.T. Meade').

+ London, Paris, New York, Melbourne: Cassell & Co., 1898 (ill. Hal Ludlow). SOURCE Alston, p. 297. LOCATION D, L, InND Loeber coll. (1910 edn).

New York: A.L. Chatterton & Co., n.d. (as *Lil Carrington*; Fascinating Stories for Girls; ill.). SOURCE FFF, p. 636.

COMMENTARY No copy of the New York edn located. Fiction for juveniles. The story traces the life of a young girl after she is left at age 15 in the care of a harsh aunt [Sutherland].

S267   *The siren. A novel* (by 'L.T. Meade').

+ London: F.V. White, 1898. SOURCE Alston, p. 297; Sutherland, p. 427. LOCATION D, L.

COMMENTARY The heroine is a socialist and nihilist ordered by her Russian masters to assassinate her own father [Sutherland].

S268   *The gold star line* (by 'L.T. Meade' and 'Robert Eustace').

+ London, New York, Melbourne: Ward, Lock & Co., 1899 (ill. Adolf Thiede). LOCATION D, L, NIC.

New York: New Amsterdam Book Co., [189?]. LOCATION NUC.

COMMENTARY Short stories of science fiction. Contents: 'The jewelled cobra', 'The cypher with the human key', 'The rice-paper chart', 'In the jaw of the dog', 'The yellow flag', 'The sacred chank' [ML; EF, p. 276].

S269   *Light o' the morning. The story of an Irish girl* (by 'L.T. Meade').

+ London, Edinburgh: W. & R. Chambers, [1899] (ill. W. Rainey). SOURCE Osborne, p. 1027. LOCATION D, CaOTP.

+ Toronto: W.J. Gage & Co., 1899 (ill., W. Rainey). LOCATION L, InND Loeber coll.

New York: Dutton & Co., [1900?] (ill.). LOCATION NUC.

+New York: A.L. Burt, n.d. (ill.; The Wellesley Series for Girls). SOURCE FFF, p. 636. LOCATION InND Loeber coll. (has 1910 inscription).

New York: Robert Carter, n.d. (as *How Nora Crena saved her own*). SOURCE FFF, p. 636; OCLC. LOCATION Free Library of Philadelphia.

New York: Grosset & Dunlap, [19??]. LOCATION NUC.

COMMENTARY Fiction for juveniles. Nora Crena first featured in *Hermie's rose-buds* (London, 1893). This story contrasts Irish and English character. Nora lives in a ruined castle with her Irish father and her English mother. Her father has mortgaged everything and is about to lose his home. Nora goes to England to ask her very rich uncle for help. The uncle buys the castle and does it up in English fashion. Nora's father is thoroughly unhappy about this, but has to give in for the sake of his wife. He moves into part of the barn where he can receive his Irish friends and does not feel so oppressed by the new opulence around him [ML].

S270   *The brotherhood of the seven kings* (by 'L.T. Meade' and 'Robert Eustace').

London, New York, Melbourne: Ward, Lock & Co., 1899 (ill. Sidney Paget). SOURCE Topp 2, p. 377; Wolff, 4694. LOCATION L, NIC.

New York: New Amsterdam Book Co., n.d. SOURCE DLB, cxli, p. 188.

COMMENTARY No copy of the New York edn located. Short stories of science fiction first published in the *Strand Magazine* (London, 1898). Contents: 'At the edge of the crater', 'The winged assassin', 'The swing of the pendulum', 'The luck of Pitsey Hall', 'Twenty degrees', 'The star-shaped marks', 'The iron circlet', 'The mystery of the strong room', 'The bloodhound', 'The doom' [EF, p. 276; Wolff, 4694].

S271   *The desire of men. An impossibility* (by 'L.T. Meade').

London: Digby, Long & Co., 1899. SOURCE Alston, p. 296. LOCATION L, NIC (1899 3rd edn).

S272   *An adventuress* (by 'L.T. Meade').
London: Chatto & Windus, 1899. SOURCE Alston, p. 297. LOCATION L, NIC.
S273   *The odds and the evens* (by 'L.T. Meade').
+ London, Edinburgh: W. & R. Chambers, 1899 (ill. Percy Tarrant). SOURCE Alston,
p. 297; Wolff, 4714. LOCATION D (n.d. edn), L, NUC (n.d. edn), InND Loeber coll.
Toronto: W.J. Gage & Co., [1899]. LOCATION L.
Philadelphia: David McKay, n.d. (The Girls' Own Library). SOURCE FFF, p. 636.
New York: A.L. Burt, 1899 (ill). SOURCE FFF, p. 636 (n.d.); OCLC. LOCATION InND.
COMMENTARY No copy of the Philadelphia edn located. Fiction for juveniles [RL].
S274   *All sorts* (by 'L.T. Meade').
London: James Nisbet & Co., 1899. SOURCE Daims, 2839. LOCATION L, NUC.
S275   *The kingfisher's egg* (by 'L.T. Meade').
+ London: Ernest Nister; New York: E.P. Dutton, [1899] (ill. S. Stuart Hardy, E.
Nister). SOURCE NCBEL 4, p. 1637. LOCATION D.
Philadelphia: Henry Altemus, 1900. SOURCE FFF, p. 636 (1905 edn); OCLC. LOCATION
ViU.
New York: E.P. Dutton & Co., 1899 (ill.). SOURCE Baldwin, p. 145; FFF, p. 636 (1900
edn); OCLC. LOCATION C.
COMMENTARY New York and London edns are 48pp. Fiction for juveniles. The London edn
also contains stories by Ellis Walton, Geraldine R. Glasgow, and Olive Molesworth [RL;
Baldwin, p. 145].
S276   *The temptation of Olive Latimer* (by 'L.T. Meade').
+ New York: Chatterton-Peck, 1899 (ill.). LOCATION InND Loeber coll.
+ London: Hutchinson & Co., 1900 (ill. I. Watkin). SOURCE Alston, p. 297. LOCATION
D, L, NIC.
S277   *A brave poor thing* (by 'L.T. Meade').
London: Wm. Isbister & Co., 1900. SOURCE Alston, p. 296; Daims, 2842. LOCATION
L, NUC.
COMMENTARY A story about a secretary, Dorothea Moore, who emerges from the slums of
London, and eventually marries her boss. She was a member of the Guild of the Brave Poor
Things, run by the novelist Grace Kimmins (known as 'Sister Grace') and part of the novel
centres on the Guild. The plot revolves around a stolen ring; the wealthy boss makes amends
for suspecting his virtuous secretary by distributing his wealth among the needy [Burmester
list].
S278   *The sanctuary club* (by 'L.T. Meade' and 'Robert Eustace').
+ London, New York, Melbourne: Ward, Lock & Co., 1900. (ill. Sidney Paget).
LOCATION D (n.d. edn), L, NIC.
COMMENTARY Interlocking short stories of science fiction first published in the *Strand Magazine*
(London) as 'Stories of the Sanctuary Club' and featuring the detective Dr Cato, founder of
the Sanctuary Club, and Dr Henry Chetwynde, his partner [RL; EF, p. 276].
S279   *Where the shoe pinches* (by 'Mrs L.T. Meade' and 'Clifford Halifax, M.D.').
+ London, Edinburgh: W. & R. Chambers, [1900]. SOURCE Alston, p. 298; Wolff,
4726 (n.d. edn). LOCATION L, NUC.
COMMENTARY Short stories of crime fiction. Contents: Introduction, 'Till death us do part',
'Fraser's old mate', 'Perrott's girl', 'A white elephant', 'How Dolly saved West', 'Wholesale
Philip', 'A king's ransom', 'Sunshine Susannah', 'A charm of opals', 'Her satin slipper', 'The
mystery of number eight', 'Surgeon Lily Langley', 'How Athole-Daisy was scratched for the
Derby', 'His old wife Joan', 'Heart's delight', 'At the mercy of his wife' [JB; EF, p. 276].
S280   *Wages. A novel* (by 'L.T. Meade').

London: James Nisbet & Co., 1900. SOURCE Alston, p. 297; NCBEL 4, p. 1637. LOCATION D (n.d. edn), L, InND Loeber coll. ([1900] edn).

S281   *The time of roses* (by 'L.T. Meade').
+ London: Ernest Nister; New York: E.P. Dutton & Co., [1900] (ill., F.S. Wilson; cover title: *In the time of roses*; ill. F.S. Wilson). SOURCE Osborne, p. 389. LOCATION D, L, CaOTP.
+ New York: A.L. Burt, [189?] (as *The time of roses. A story for girls* by T.L. Meade [*sic*]). LOCATION InND Loeber coll.
New York: Grosset & Dunlap, n.d. (as *In time of roses*). SOURCE Baldwin, p. 145. LOCATION NUC.
COMMENTARY Fiction for juveniles. A sequel to *A bunch of cherries* (London, 1898) [Osborne].

S282   *Miss Nonentity* (by 'L.T. Meade').
+ London, Edinburgh: W. & R. Chambers, 1900 (ill. W. Rainey). SOURCE Alston, p. 297; Osborne, p. 1028; Wolff, 4712. LOCATION D, L, CaOTP, NUC.
New York, Boston: H.M. Caldwell & Co., n.d. SOURCE FFF, p. 636.
New York: Grosset & Dunlap, [19??] (as *Miss Nonentity; a girls' story*). LOCATION NUC.
+ New York: Platt & Peck, n.d. (*Miss Nonentity; a girls' story*; ill. RM). LOCATION InND Loeber coll.
Philadelphia: J.B. Lippincott, 1900. SOURCE FFF, p. 636.
COMMENTARY No copies of the New York, Boston edn and the Philadelphia edn located. Fiction for juveniles [RL].

S283   *Seven maids* (by 'L.T. Meade').
London, Edinburgh: W. & R. Chambers, 1900 (ill. Percy Tarrant). SOURCE Alston, p. 297; Wolff, 4718. LOCATION D (n.d. edn), L, NIC.
New York: A.L. Burt, n.d. (ill. P. Tarrant; The Wellesley Series for Girls). SOURCE FFF, p. 636; OCLC. LOCATION CtY.
Philadelphia: David McKay, n.d. (The Girls' Own Library). SOURCE FFF, p. 636.
COMMENTARY No copy of the Philadelphia edn located. Fiction for juveniles. Set in England where a minister and his wife set up a small school for girls to augment their income. Their daughter is unhappy with the influx of other girls. Her character flaws are exposed, but all ends well [ML].

S284   *A very naughty girl* (by 'L.T. Meade').
New York: A.L. Burt, 1900 (ill.; The Wellesley Series for Girls). SOURCE FFF, p. 637; OCLC. LOCATION Univ. of Southern Florida.
London, Edinburgh: W. & R. Chambers, 1901 (ill. W. Rainey). LOCATION L, NIC.
New York, Boston: H.M. Caldwell & Co., [1906] (ill.; Famous Books for Girls Series). SOURCE FFF, p. 637. LOCATION NUC.
COMMENTARY Fiction for juveniles [RL].

S285   *A sister of the Red Cross; A tale of the South African war* (by 'L.T. Meade').
London: T. Nelson & Sons, 1900. SOURCE Alston, p. 297; Daims, 2863. LOCATION L, NIC.
+ London: Thomas Nelson & Sons, n.d. (as *A sister of the Red Cross*; cover title: *A story of Ladysmith*; ill.). LOCATION D, InND Loeber coll.

S286   *Stories from the diary of a doctor (third series)* (by 'L.T. Meade' and 'Clifford Halifax, M.D.')
+ London: Sands & Co., 1901. LOCATION Seen at Brick Row, San Francisco (CA) Nov. 2000; RL.

COMMENTARY No other copy located. Crime fiction issued in paperback. Contents: 'A doctor's dilemma', 'On a charge of forgery', 'The strange case of Captain Gascoigne', 'With the eternal fires', 'The small house on Steven's Heath', '"To overcome his own fear"' [RL].

S287 *Those boys. A story for all little fellows* (by 'L.T. Meade').
London: John F. Shaw & Co., [c.1901] (new edn). SOURCE Baldwin, p. 146; OCLC.
LOCATION Univ. of Texas at Arlington.
COMMENTARY Fiction for juveniles. NCBEL has a 1876 edn, by 'Aunt Penn', but this has not been located [RL].

S288 *A race with the sun* (by 'L.T. Meade' with 'Clifford Halifax, M.D.')
+ London, New York, Melbourne: Ward, Lock & Co., 1901 (ill. J. Finnemore).
LOCATION L, NIC.
COMMENTARY Short stories of crime fiction featuring Paul Gilchrist, traveller and experimental scientist. Contents: 'The snake's eye', 'Ought he to marry her?', 'Lady Tregenna', 'The sleeping sickness', 'At the steps of the altar', 'The panelled bedroom', 'A race with the sun', 'The man who smiled' [ML; Reilly, p. 639].

S289 *Daddy's girl* (by 'L.T. Meade').
+ London: George Newnes, 1901 (as *Daddy's girl;* ill. Gordon Browne). LOCATION D (n.d. edn), L,
+ New York: Grosset & Dunlap, [19??]. LOCATION PpiU, InND Loeber coll.
+ New York: The New York Book Co., 1910 (as *Daddy's girl, and Consuelo's quest of happiness*; Famous Fiction Library, No. 16). LOCATION NUC (1911 edn), InND Loeber coll.
Philadelphia: Lippincott, 1901. LOCATION NUC.
COMMENTARY Fiction for juveniles. Moralizing story about Sybil Ogilvie, an only child who is doted on by her father. Her mother is a cold-hearted, egocentric woman. Sybil thinks that, next to Jesus, her mother and father are perfect. Her father, however, is about to go out to Australia to appraise a gold mine and to submit a false report as to its possible yield. He will be well paid for this, and he needs the money as his wife is extremely extravagant. While he is in Australia, Sybil falls off her pony and is seriously injured. Her father sees the accident as a punishment from God. He returns to England, tells the board of directors of the gold mine company the actual state of affairs, and withdraws from business. Before Sybil dies, her father confesses to her that he has been far from perfect. Sybil assures him that Jesus and she herself will love him all the more for his failings. After she dies, her father spends his life in trying to do good and looks forward to being reunited with his daughter in heaven [ML].

S290 *Cosey corner; or, how they kept a farm* (by 'L.T. Meade').
+ London, Edinburgh: W. & R. Chambers, 1901 (ill. Percy Tarrant). SOURCE Wolff, 4698. LOCATION D (n.d. edn), L, InND Loeber coll.
Philadelphia: David McKay, n.d. (The Girls' Own Library). SOURCE FFF, p. 635.
COMMENTARY No copy of the Philadelphia edn located. Fiction for juveniles. Four children propose to keep a small farm to help their parents pay off a debt they owe to a businessman. The children are helped in their efforts by a neighbouring farmer and his wife who supply foodstuffs and implements when the children need them [DLB, cxli, p. 196].

S291 *The new Mrs. Lascelles* (by 'L.T. Meade').
London: James Clarke & Co., 1901 (ill.). LOCATION L, NIC.
London, Edinburgh: W. & R. Chambers, 1916 (as *Mother Mary: A story for girls*).
SOURCE DLB, cxli, p. 189. LOCATION L.
Philadelphia: J.B. Lippincott, n.d. (as *Mother Mary*). SOURCE FFF, p. 636.

COMMENTARY No copy of the Philadelphia edn located. Fiction for juveniles [RL].

S292　*The girls of the true blue: A school story* (by 'L.T. Meade').
London, Edinburgh: W. & R. Chambers, 1901 (ill. Percy Tarrant). LOCATION D (n.d. edn), L, NIC.
New York: E.P. Dutton & Co., 1901 (ill. Percy Tarrant). LOCATION NUC.
+ New York: A.L. Burt, n.d. (as *Girls of the true blue*; ill.; The Wellesley Series for Girls). SOURCE FFF, p. 636. LOCATION InND Loeber coll. (copy has inscription '1909').
New York, Boston: H.M. Caldwell & Co., 1905. (ill.; Famous Books for Girls). SOURCE FFF, p. 636; OCLC. LOCATION Univ. of Illinois.
Philadelphia: David McKay, n.d. (The Girls' Own Library). SOURCE FFF, p. 636.
COMMENTARY No copy of the Philadelphia edn located. Fiction for juveniles [RL].

S293　*The blue diamond* (by 'L.T. Meade').
London: Chatto & Windus, 1901. LOCATION L, NUC.
COMMENTARY Crime fiction [Reilly, p. 638].

S294　*The secret of the dead* (by 'L.T. Meade').
London: F.V. White & Co., 1901. LOCATION L.
COMMENTARY Crime fiction [Reilly, p. 638].

S295　*Wheels of iron* (by 'L.T. Meade').
London: James Nisbet & Co., 1901 (ill.). LOCATION L, NIC.

S296　*Through peril for a wife* (by 'L.T. Meade').
London: Digby, Long & Co., 1901 (ill. C. Dudley Tenant). SOURCE COPAC. LOCATION L (1902, rd edn), C.

S297　*The princess who gave away all, and the naughty one of the family* (by 'L.T. Meade').
+ London: Ernest Nister; New York: E.P. Dutton & Co, [1902]. LOCATION L.
New York: E.P. Dutton & Co., n.d. SOURCE FFF, p. 636.
COMMENTARY No copy of the New York edn located. 31pp for the London edn. Fiction for juveniles. Story of a spoiled little girl who feels very lonely [Reilly, p. 641; ML].

S298　*The lost square* (by 'L.T. Meade' and 'Robert Eustace').
+ London, New York, Melbourne: Ward, Lock & Co., [1902] (ill. Adolf Thiede). LOCATION L.
COMMENTARY Crime fiction issued in paperback [ML; Reilly, p. 638].

S299　*A stumble by the way* (by 'L.T. Meade').
London: Chatto & Windus, 1902. LOCATION L.

S300　*Confessions of a court milliner* (by 'L.T. Meade').
London: John Long, [1902]. LOCATION L, NUC.
COMMENTARY Crime fiction [Reilly, p. 638].

S301　*Drift* (by 'L.T. Meade').
+ London: Methuen & Co., 1902 (ill.). LOCATION D (n.d. edn), L, NIC.

S302　*The squire's little girl* (by 'L.T. Meade').
London, Edinburgh: W. & R. Chambers, 1902 (ill.). SOURCE Wolff, 4721. LOCATION D (n.d. edn), L, NIC.
COMMENTARY Fiction for juveniles [RL].

S303　*Girls of the forest* (by 'L.T. Meade').
London, Edinburgh: W. & R. Chambers, 1902 (ill. Percy Tarrant). SOURCE Osborne, p. 1027. LOCATION D (n.d. edn), L, CaOTP, NUC.
New York: E.P. Dutton & Co., [1912?]. LOCATION NUC.
New York: A.L. Burt, n.d. (ill.; The Wellesley Series for Girls). SOURCE FFF, p. 636; OCLC. LOCATION Michigan State Univ.

Akron (OH): Superior Printing Co., [1915?]. LOCATION NUC.
COMMENTARY Fiction for juveniles [RL].

S304 *Queen Rose* (by 'L.T. Meade').
+ London, Edinburgh: W. & R. Chambers, 1902 (ill. J.T. Murray). SOURCE Osborne,
p. 1028. LOCATION D, L, CaOTP, InND Loeber coll.
New York: Dutton, 1902. SOURCE DLB, cxli, p. 189.
Philadelphia: David McKay, n.d. (The Girls' Own Library). SOURCE FFF, p. 636;
OCLC. LOCATION Free Library of Philadelphia.
COMMENTARY No copy of the New York edn located. Fiction for juveniles. A story
about a girl who has to overcome extreme jealousy [ML].

S305 *The rebel of the school* (by 'L.T. Meade').
+ London, Edinburgh: W. & R. Chambers, 1902 (ill. W. Rainey). SOURCE Osborne,
p. 389; Wolff, 4699. LOCATION D (n.d. edn), L, CaOTP, NUC, InND Loeber coll.
New York: A.L. Burt, n.d. (ill.; The Wellesley Series for Girls). SOURCE FFF, p. 636.
LOCATION NUC.
New York, Boston: H.M. Caldwell, n.d. (ill.). SOURCE FFF, p. 636.
Philadelphia: David McKay, n.d. (The Girls' Own Library). SOURCE FFF, p. 636.
Philadelphia: J.B. Lippincott, n.d. SOURCE FFF, p. 636.
COMMENTARY No copies of the New York, Boston edn and both Philadelphia edns located.
Fiction for juveniles. Kathleen O'Hara, a rich, spoiled, but basically lovable Anglo-Irish girl
from a castle in west Cork enters an English school for girls. For a while she leads many
students astray, causing the poorer girls to almost lose their scholarship status by joining a
group she has dubbed the 'Wild Irish Girls'. Her passionate nature and support for the
underdog, which she sees as Irish virtues, undermine the school's culture and are seen by
the administration as a political threat. In the end, she mends her ways [ML; Field Day, v,
pp 1160–4].

S306 *Margaret* (by 'L.T. Meade').
London: F.V. White & Co., 1902. SOURCE Topp 7, 428. LOCATION L, NIC.

S307 *A double revenge* (by 'L.T. Meade').
London: Digby, Long & Co., 1902. LOCATION L.
COMMENTARY Crime fiction [Reilly, p. 638].

S308 **void**

S309 *The witch maid* (by 'L.T. Meade').
+ London: James Nisbet & Co., 1903. LOCATION D (n.d. edn), L, InND Loeber coll.
COMMENTARY Historical fiction set in Essex in the beginning of the nineteenth century, and
concerns the Quakers, Newgate, and the persecution of a girl for witchcraft [Baker].

S310 *Stories from the old, old Bible* (by 'L.T. Meade'; dedicated to Sir George
Newnes).
+ London: George Newnes, 1903 (ill. T.H. Robinson). LOCATION D, L, NUC.
+ London, Edinburgh: W. & R. Chambers, n.d. (dedicated to Elizabeth Douglas, the
author's first grandchild). LOCATION D.

S311 *A gay charmer. A story for girls* (by 'L.T. Meade').
+ London, Edinburgh: W. & R. Chambers, 1903 (ill. W.H.C. Groome). LOCATION D,
L, InND Loeber coll.
New York: A.L. Burt, n.d. (ill.; The Wellesley Series for Girls). SOURCE FFF, p. 635;
OCLC. LOCATION OU.
New York, Boston: H.M. Caldwell, n.d. SOURCE FFF, p. 635.
Philadelphia: J.B. Lippincott, n.d. SOURCE FFF, p. 635.
Chicago: Donohue, [190?]. LOCATION NIC.

COMMENTARY No copies of the New York, Boston and the Philadelphia edns located. Fiction for juveniles [RL].

S312 *Peter the pilgrim* (by 'L.T. Meade').
+ London, Edinburgh: W. & R. Chambers, 1903 (ill. Harold Copping). LOCATION D, L, NUC, InND Loeber coll.
New York: A.L. Burt, n.d. (The Little Man Series). SOURCE FFF, p. 636; OCLC. LOCATION OU.
New York: A.L. Burt, [1900] (as *Peter the pilgrim: The story of a boy and his pet rabbit*; The Rugby Series). SOURCE FFF, p. 636 (n.d. edn); OCLC. LOCATION Univ. of Southern Florida.
COMMENTARY Fiction for juveniles [RL].

S313 *Rosebury* (by 'L.T. Meade').
London: Chatto & Windus, 1903. SOURCE Daims, 2861. LOCATION L.

S314 *The sorceress of the Strand* (by 'L.T. Meade').
+ London, New York, Melbourne: Ward, Lock & Co., 1903 (ill. Gordon Browne). LOCATION D, L, NUC (1904 edn).
COMMENTARY Short stories of crime fiction featuring Mme Koluchy, the sorceress of the Strand. Contents: 'Madame Sara', 'The blood-red cross', 'The face of the abbot', 'The talk of the town', 'The bloodstone', 'The teeth of the wolf' [ML; Reilly, p. 639; Sotheby's cat. 19 Dec. 2000/470].

S315 *By mutual consent* (by 'L.T. Meade').
London: Digby, Long & Co., 1903. LOCATION L.

S316 *The burden of her youth* (by 'L.T. Meade').
London: J. Long, 1903. SOURCE Daims, 2843. LOCATION L, NUC (n.d. edn).

S317 *Resurgam* (by 'L.T. Meade').
London: Methuen & Co., 1903. LOCATION L.

S318 *The manor school* (by 'L.T. Meade').
+ London, Edinburgh: W. & R. Chambers, 1903 (ill. Lewis Baumer). SOURCE Osborne, p. 389. LOCATION D (n.d. edn), L, CaOTP, InND Loeber coll.
+ New York: Grosset & Dunlap, 1903 (ill.). LOCATION InND Loeber coll.
Rahway (NJ), New York: Mershon, [1903]. LOCATION NUC.
COMMENTARY Fiction for juveniles [RL].

S319 *That brilliant Peggy* (by 'L.T. Meade').
London: Hodder & Stoughton, 1903 (ill.). LOCATION L, NIC.
COMMENTARY Fiction for juveniles [RL].

S320 *Love triumphant* (by 'L.T. Meade').
London: T. Fisher Unwin, 1904. LOCATION L.

S321 *Petronella; and the coming of Polly* (by 'L.T. Meade').
+ London, Edinburgh: W. & R. Chambers, 1904 (ill. W. Rainey). LOCATION D, L, NUC.
New York: A.L. Burt, [1900] (ill.; The Wellesley Series for Girls). SOURCE FFF, p. 636; OCLC. LOCATION InND.
Philadelphia: J.B. Lippincott, n.d. SOURCE FFF, p. 636.
COMMENTARY No copy of the Philadelphia edn located. Fiction for juveniles [RL].

S322 *The lady cake-maker* (by 'L.T. Meade').
+ London: Hodder & Stoughton, 1904. SOURCE DLB, cxli, p. 191. LOCATION L.
COMMENTARY Contents: 'The cake with the strange flowers', 'The little hand', 'Josephine's laugh', 'Midnight', 'The brake in the motor', 'The rival shop', 'The devil's spur', 'Death's messengers'[ML].

S323 *A maid of mystery* (by 'L.T. Meade').
London: F.V. White & Co., 1904. SOURCE EF, p. 276. LOCATION L, NIC.
COMMENTARY Crime fiction involving a young woman living in a convent in Rouen and her father, who communicates with her by way of a sinister man, who preys on both. Eventually, this man and his companion are unmasked as burglars [EF, p. 261].

S324 *Bride of to-morrow* (by 'L.T. Meade').
London: Daily Mail, [1904]. SOURCE DLB, cxli, p. 191.
COMMENTARY No copy located [RL].

S325 *Castle Poverty* (by 'L.T. Meade').
London: James Nisbet & Co., 1904. SOURCE EF, p. 276. LOCATION L, NIC.
COMMENTARY A girl finds employment as a companion in a vulgar family [EF, p. 276].

S326 *At the back of the world* (by 'L.T. Meade').
London: Hurst & Blackett, 1904. SOURCE Brown, 1134. LOCATION L.
COMMENTARY Set on the coast of Co. Cork. Sheila O'Connor is long separated from her lover by the suspicion that he is her father's murderer. In the end, Sheila and her lover are united [Brown].

S327 *The girls of Mrs. Pritchard's school* (by 'L.T. Meade').
+ London, Edinburgh: W. & R. Chambers, 1904 (as *Mrs. Pritchard's school*; ill. Lewis Baumer; cover: Lewis Baumer). LOCATION L, InND Loeber coll.
New York: Grosset & Dunlap, [1904]. LOCATION NUC.
Rahway (NJ), New York: Mershon, [1904]. LOCATION NUC.
COMMENTARY Fiction for juveniles [RL].

S328 *Nurse Charlotte* (by 'L.T. Meade').
London: John Long, 1904. LOCATION L, NIC ([1915] edn).
COMMENTARY A story of genteel poverty [EF, p. 276].

S329 *Silenced* (by 'L.T. Meade').
+ London, New York, Melbourne: Ward, Lock & Co., 1904. SOURCE EF, p. 276.
LOCATION L.
COMMENTARY Crime stories told to a doctor by his patients. Contents: 'Silenced', 'The man who disappeared', 'Spangle-winged', 'Followed', 'The mystery of Susanna Tankerville', 'The blue laboratory' [ML; EF, p. 276].

S330 *A madcap* (by 'L.T. Meade').
London: Cassell & Co., 1904 (ill. Harold Copping). SOURCE Wolff, 4710. LOCATION D (n.d. edn, 15th thousand), L, NIC.
+ New York: Stitt, 1905 (ill. Harold Copping). LOCATION InND Loeber coll.
+ Rahway (NJ), New York: Mershon, [1904] (ill. Harold Copping). LOCATION NUC, InND Loeber coll.
COMMENTARY Fiction for juveniles; this work became very popular, with at least 15,000 copies printed. Set in England, where Mrs Dering and her children are left badly off after her husband's death in South Africa. However, they own Dering Towers, where they live happily until Mr. Dering's imperious niece, Inez – who is part Spanish – comes to stay with them. She has many character faults, but under the influence of her aunt and cousins she improves greatly [ML].

S331 *The adventures of Miranda* (by 'L.T. Meade').
+ London: John Long, 1904. LOCATION D, L, NIC.
COMMENTARY Crime fiction [Reilly, p. 638].

S332 *The oracle of Maddox Street* (by 'L.T. Meade').
+ London, New York, Melbourne: Ward, Lock & Co., 1904. LOCATION L, NUC.

COMMENTARY Crime stories. Contents: 'The dead hand', 'Finger tips', 'Sir Penn Caryll's engagement', 'The "D" line', 'Eyes of terror', 'The secret of Emu Plain', 'The black ball', 'The best brother-in-law in the world', 'The ruby bracelet', 'The love adventures of Primrose Ward' [ML; Reilly, p. 639].

S333   *A modern tomboy* (by 'L.T. Meade').
+ London, Edinburgh: W. & R. Chambers, 1904 (ill. Percy Tarrant). SOURCE Wolff, 4713. LOCATION D, L, NIC.
New York: E.P. Dutton, n.d. LOCATION NUC.
New York: Grosset & Dunlap, [1890s]. SOURCE Baldwin, p. 145; OCLC. LOCATION DCL.
New York: Chatterton Peck Co., [190?]. LOCATION NUC, NN.
COMMENTARY Fiction for juveniles [RL].

S334   *Toch overwonnen* (by 'L.T. Meade').
+ Tiel: H.C.A. Campagne & Son, n.d. [1905 or earlier] (trans. into Dutch by A.C. Kuiper; ill. Tresling). LOCATION InND Loeber coll.
COMMENTARY Fiction for juveniles. It is unclear from what original work this book has been translated [RL].

S335   *The other woman* (by 'L.T. Meade').
London, Felling-on-Tyne: Walter Scott, 1905. LOCATION D (n.d. edn), L (1905, 2nd edn), NUC.
+ London: Wm. Collins, n.d. (The Novel Library). LOCATION InND Loeber coll.
COMMENTARY Set in England and on the Continent. Lucy Hamilton marries a well-known author, Mark Stanhope, only to find out that he has previously lived with a woman by whom he had a son. Lucy leaves Mark because she feels that the other woman has a moral right to be his wife. After Mark pursues Lucy, she consents to live with him but plans to give up her position once she has found the other woman. When she does, the woman turns out to be mentally unstable. Lucy secretly looks after her and when she dies, Lucy once again leaves her husband, taking the little boy with her. Later she realizes that the boy needs a father and forgives her husband [ML].

S336   *His mascot* (by 'L.T. Meade').
London: John Long, 1905. SOURCE NCBEL 4, p. 1638. LOCATION L.

S337   *Old Readymoney's daughter* (by 'L.T. Meade').
London: S.W. Partridge & Co., 1905 (ill.). SOURCE NCBEL 4, p. 1638. LOCATION L, NIC.

S338   *Dumps; A plain girl* (by 'L.T. Meade').
+ London, Edinburgh: W. & R. Chambers, 1905 (ill. R. Lillie). SOURCE NCBEL 4, p. 1638. D, L, InND Loeber coll.
New York: E.P. Dutton & Co., 1905. LOCATION NUC.
COMMENTARY Fiction for juveniles [RL].

S339   *Wilful cousin Kate. A girl's story* (by 'L.T. Meade').
+ London, Edinburgh: W. & R. Chambers, 1905 (ill. W. Rainey). SOURCE NCBEL 4, p. 1638; Wolff, 4727. LOCATION D, L, NIC.
New York: A.L. Burt, n.d. (ill.; Fireside Series for Girls). SOURCE FFF, p. 636; OCLC. LOCATION Free Library of Philadelphia.
COMMENTARY Fiction for juveniles [RL].

S340   *A bevy of girls* (by 'L.T. Meade').
+ London, Edinburgh: W. & R. Chambers, 1905 (ill. Lewis Baumer). SOURCE NCBEL 4, p. 1638. LOCATION D, L, NUC.
+ New York: Grosset & Dunlap, 1905 (ill., cover: R. Ford Horpery). LOCATION NUC, InND Loeber coll.

New York: Stitt, 1905. LOCATION NUC.

COMMENTARY Fiction for juveniles [RL].

S341 *Little wife Hester* (by 'L.T. Meade').

London: John Long, 1905. SOURCE NCBEL 4, p. 1638. LOCATION L, NIC ([1910?] new edn).

S342 *Virginia* (by 'L.T. Meade').

London: Digby, Long & Co., 1905. SOURCE NCBEL 4, p. 1638. LOCATION L.

S343 *Loveday: The story of an heiress* (by 'L.T. Meade').

London: Hodder & Stoughton, 1905. SOURCE NCBEL 4, p. 1638. LOCATION L.

S344 *Bess of Delany's* (by 'L.T. Meade').

London: Digby, Long & Co., 1905. SOURCE Daims, 2841; NCBEL 4, p. 1638. LOCATION L.

S345 *The heart of Helen* (by 'L.T. Meade').

London: John Long, 1906. SOURCE NCBEL 4, p. 1638. LOCATION L.

S346 *Victory* (by 'L.T. Meade').

London: Methuen & Co., 1906. SOURCE NCBEL 4, p. 1638. LOCATION L.

S347 *In the flower of her youth* (by 'L.T. Meade').

+ London: James Nisbet & Co., 1906 (ill. A.A. Dixon). SOURCE NCBEL 4, p. 1638. LOCATION D (n.d. edn), L, NIC.

S348 *Sue: The story of a little heroine and her friend* (by 'L.T. Meade').

+ London, Edinburgh: W. & R. Chambers, 1906 (ill. Clement Flower). SOURCE NCBEL 4, p. 1638. LOCATION D, L.

New York: A.L. Burt, n.d. (as *A young heroine. A story of Sue and her friend*). SOURCE OCLC. LOCATION InND

COMMENTARY Fiction for juveniles [RL].

S349 *The girl and her fortune* (by 'L.T. Meade').

London: Hodder & Stoughton, 1906 (ill.). SOURCE NCBEL 4, p. 1638. LOCATION L, NIC.

COMMENTARY Fiction for juveniles [RL].

S350 *The Colonel and the boy* (by 'L.T. Meade'; dedicated to 'all those brave men and true, who understand the sacred heart of a little child').

London: Hodder & Stoughton, [1906] (ill. Harold Copping). SOURCE NCBEL 4, p. 1638; Wolff, 4697. LOCATION L, InND Loeber coll. (n.d., 2nd edn).

COMMENTARY Fiction for juveniles. A lame boy whose mother is an extremely self-indulgent woman is willing to undergo an operation to straighten his leg so his mother can be more proud of him. The colonel, who is the mother's second husband and who married her to protect the boy, is against the operation because it might endanger the boy's life. The boy insists, and the operation is a success [ML].

S351 *A golden shadow* (by 'L.T. Meade').

London, Melbourne, Toronto: Ward, Lock & Co., 1906 (ill. J. MacFarlane). SOURCE NCBEL 4, p. 1638. LOCATION D (n.d. edn), L, NIC.

COMMENTARY Crime fiction [Reilly, p. 639].

S352 *From the hand of the hunter* (by 'L.T. Meade').

+ London: John Long, 1906. SOURCE Daims, 2847; Wolff, 4699. LOCATION L, InND Loeber coll.

COMMENTARY Crime fiction. A mother and her daughter are more or less fugitives because they think that a child in their care was killed. The father of the little girl comes to look for her but cannot find her. After he places an advertisement, a child is presented to him as his daughter. Slowly the mystery is unravelled and it appears that this child is indeed his daughter [ML].

S353   *The hill-top girl* (by 'L.T. Meade').
+ London, Edinburgh: W. & R. Chambers, 1906 (ill. Lewis Baumer). SOURCE Osborne,
p. 1027; Wolff, 4703. LOCATION L, CaOTP, NUC, InND Loeber coll.
Chicago: David McKay, n.d. (The Girls' Own Library). SOURCE FFF, p. 636.
Philadelphia: J.B. Lippincott, n.d. SOURCE FFF, p. 636.
COMMENTARY No copy of the Philadelphia edns located. Fiction for juveniles [RL].

S354   *Turquoise & ruby* (by 'L.T. Meade').
London, Edinburgh: W. & R. Chambers, 1906 (ill. Percy Tarrant). SOURCE NCBEL
4, p. 1638; Wolff, 4725. LOCATION L, NIC.
New York: Chatterton-Peck, [1906]. LOCATION NUC.
+ New York: Grosset & Dunlap, 1906 (ill.). LOCATION NUC, InND Loeber coll.

S355   *The face of Juliet* (by 'L.T. Meade').
London: John Long, 1906. SOURCE NCBEL 4, p. 1638 (1905 edn). LOCATION L.

S356   *The home of sweet content* (by 'L.T. Meade').
London: F.V. White & Co., 1906. SOURCE NCBEL 4, p. 1638. LOCATION L.

S357   *The maid with the goggles* (by 'L.T. Meade').
London: Digby, Long & Co., 1906. SOURCE Daims, 2853; NCBEL 4, p. 1638.
LOCATION L.

S358   *Queen of the day* (by 'L.T. Meade').
Philadelphia: Henry Altemus, 1906 (Dainty Series). SOURCE FFF, p. 636; OCLC.
LOCATION Univ. of Chicago.
COMMENTARY Fiction for juveniles. Probably a reprint of an unidentified original work
published in London [RL].

S359   *Little Josephine* (by 'L.T. Meade').
+ London: John Long, 1907 (ill. E.F. Sherie). SOURCE NCBEL 4, p. 1638 (1908 edn).
LOCATION D (n.d. edn), L, InND Loeber coll.
COMMENTARY Set in England, where a young, innocent woman falls in with the wrong set of
people. Although warned by her friend who has married just for money, she marries a rich
scoundrel, after which her father does not want to see her anymore. Later, her father shows
some interest in a reconciliation and in adopting her son. However, her son dies. She has
another child abducted to take its place but, eventually, the scheme falls through [ML].

S360   *The red Ruth* (by 'L.T. Meade').
London: T. Werner Laurie, [1907]. SOURCE NCBEL 4, p. 1638. LOCATION L.
COMMENTARY Crime fiction [Reilly, p. 639].

S361   *Kindred spirits* (by 'L.T. Meade').
London: John Long, 1907. SOURCE NCBEL 4, p. 1638. LOCATION L.

S362   *The little school-mothers* (by 'L.T. Meade').
+ London, Paris, New York, Melbourne: Cassell & Co., 1907 (ill.). SOURCE NCBEL
4, p. 1638. LOCATION D, L, NIC.
Philadelphia: D. McKay, [1907] (as *The little school mothers. A story for girls*; The Girls'
Own Library). SOURCE FFF, p. 636; OCLC. LOCATION NUC.
COMMENTARY Fiction for juveniles [RL].

S363   *The scamp family* (by 'L.T. Meade').
+ London, Edinburgh: W. & R. Chambers, 1907 (ill. A. Talbot Smith). SOURCE
NCBEL 4, p. 1638. LOCATION D, L.
COMMENTARY Fiction for juveniles. Four orphans are growing up wild under the care of their
great-uncle. They are taken in by a wonderful couple who already have three children of their
own. With great patience and perseverance the best in the orphans is brought out, reducing
their selfishness and making them able to think of the comfort of others [ML].

S364   *A girl from America* (by 'L.T. Meade').
+ London, Edinburgh: W. & R. Chambers, 1907 (ill. Lewis Baumer). SOURCE NCBEL 4, p. 1638. LOCATION D, L, InND Loeber coll.
New York: New York Book Co., n.d. SOURCE FFF, p. 635; OCLC. LOCATION Michigan State Univ.
COMMENTARY Fiction for juveniles. A very rich, selfish girl from America comes to visit England to learn about English ways. In the process of her stay, she learns that to be happy it is necessary to use her wealth for the good of people less fortunate than herself [ML].

S365   *The red cap of liberty* (by 'L.T. Meade').
+ London: James Nisbet & Co., 1907 (ill. A.A. Dixon). SOURCE NCBEL 4, p. 1638. LOCATION D, L, NIC.

S366   *Three girls from school* (by 'L.T. Meade').
London, Edinburgh: W. & R. Chambers, 1907 (ill. Percy Tarrant). SOURCE NCBEL 4, p. 1638; Wolff, 4724. LOCATION L, NIC.
New York: A.L. Burt, n.d. (ill.; The Wellesley Series for Girls). SOURCE FFF, p. 637; OCLC. LOCATION Michigan State Univ.
Philadelphia: J.B. Lippincott, n.d. SOURCE FFF, p. 637.
COMMENTARY No copy of the Philadelphia edn located. Fiction for juveniles [RL].

S367   *The curse of the Ferverals* (by 'L.T. Meade').
London: John Long, 1907. SOURCE NCBEL 4, p. 1638. LOCATION L.

S368   *The lady of delight* (by 'L.T. Meade').
London: Hodder & Stoughton, 1907. SOURCE NCBEL 4, p. 1638. LOCATION L, NIC.

S369   *The lady of Jerry Boy's dreams: A story for girls* (by 'L.T. Meade').
London, Edinburgh: W. & R. Chambers, n.d. SOURCE DLB, cxli, p. 191.
Philadelphia: Jacobs, 1907. SOURCE DLB, cxli, p. 191.
COMMENTARY No copies of the London and the Philadelphia edns located. Fiction for juveniles [RL].

S370   *The château of mystery* (by 'L.T. Meade').
London: Everett & Co., 1907. SOURCE DLB, cxli, p. 191. LOCATION L.
COMMENTARY Crime fiction [Reilly, p. 639].

S371   *The love of Susan Cardigan* (by 'L.T. Meade').
London: Digby, Long & Co., 1907. SOURCE NCBEL 4, p. 1638. LOCATION L, NIC.

S372   *The school favourite* (by 'L.T. Meade').
+ London, Edinburgh: W. & R. Chambers, 1908 (ill. Percy Tarrant). SOURCE NCBEL 4, p. 1638. LOCATION D (n.d. edn), L, InND Loeber coll.
Philadelphia: David McKay, n.d. (The Girls' Own Library). SOURCE FFF, p. 636.
Philadelphia: J.B. Lippincott, n.d. SOURCE FFF, p. 636.
COMMENTARY No copy of the Philadelphia edn located. Fiction for juveniles [RL].

S373   *The Court-Harman girls* (by 'L.T. Meade').
+ London, Edinburgh: W. & R. Chambers, 1908 (ill. W. Rainey). SOURCE NCBEL 4, p. 1638. LOCATION D, L, NIC.
COMMENTARY Fiction for juveniles [RL].

S374   *A lovely fiend, and other stories* (by 'L.T. Meade').
+ London: Digby, Long & Co., 1908. SOURCE NCBEL 4, p. 1639. LOCATION L.
COMMENTARY Contents: 'A lovely fiend', 'An up to date patient', 'A queer consultation', 'Dr. Ford's lie', 'A hard bargain', 'The woman with the hood', 'The vanishing of the tea service', 'Two letters' [ML].

S375   *Betty of the rectory* (by 'L.T. Meade').

+ London, New York, Toronto, Melbourne, [1908] (ill. C. Morse). SOURCE NCBEL 4, p. 1638. LOCATION L, InND Loeber coll.

New York: Grosset & Dunlap, [1908]. LOCATION NUC.

S376 *The courtship of Sybil* (by 'L.T. Meade').
London: John Long, 1908. SOURCE NCBEL 4, p. 1638. LOCATION L.

S377 *The aim of her life* (by 'L.T. Meade').
London: John Long, 1908. SOURCE NCBEL 4, p. 1638. LOCATION D (n.d. edn), L, NIC.

S378 *The school queens* (by 'L.T. Meade').
+ London, Edinburgh: W. & R. Chambers, 1908 (ill. W. Rainey). SOURCE NCBEL 4, p. 1639. LOCATION D, L, InND Loeber coll.
New York: New York Book Co., 1910. LOCATION NUC.
COMMENTARY Fiction for juveniles [RL].

S379 *Hetty Beresford* (by 'L.T. Meade').
London: Hodder & Stoughton, 1908. SOURCE NCBEL 4, p. 1638. LOCATION L.

S380 *Aylwyn's friends* (by 'L.T. Meade').
London, Edinburgh: W. & R. Chambers, 1908 (ill. H.C. Earnshaw). SOURCE NCBEL 4, p. 1638 (1909 edn). LOCATION L, NUC.
COMMENTARY Fiction for juveniles [RL].

S381 *Sarah's mother* (by 'L.T. Meade').
London: Hodder & Stoughton, 1908. SOURCE NCBEL 4, p. 1639. LOCATION L.
London: Aldine, 1914 (as *Colonel Tracy's wife*). SOURCE DLB, cxli, p. 191. LOCATION L.

S382 *Oceana's girlhood* (by 'L.T. Meade').
New York: Hurst & Co., [1909]. LOCATION L.
COMMENTARY Possibly based on an unidentified London edn [RL].

S383 *Blue of the sea* (by 'L.T. Meade').
London: James Nisbet & Co., 1909. SOURCE NCBEL 4, p. 1639. LOCATION L, InND Loeber coll. (n.d. edn).

S384 *Brother or husband* (by 'L.T. Meade').
London: F.V. White & Co., 1909. SOURCE EF, p. 276; NCBEL 4, p. 1639. LOCATION L.
COMMENTARY Sir Auston Grave insists on marrying his deceased wife's sister [EF].

S385 *The fountain of beauty* (by 'L.T. Meade').
London: John Long, 1909. SOURCE EF, p. 276; NCBEL 4, p. 1639. LOCATION L, NUC (n.d. edn).
COMMENTARY Crime fiction. An oriental jewel, originally stolen from the Shah of Persia, is stolen once again from the English woman who has inherited it [EF].

S386 *I will sing a new song* (by 'L.T. Meade').
London: Hodder & Stoughton, 1909. SOURCE EF, p. 276; NCBEL 4, p. 1639. LOCATION L.
COMMENTARY Crime fiction. An organist marries his pupil and gets involved in a murder mystery [EF].

S387 *Betty Vivian. A story of Haddo Court School* (by 'L.T. Meade').
+ London, Edinburgh: W. & R. Chambers, 1909 (ill. A.S. Boyd). SOURCE NCBEL 4, p. 1639. LOCATION D, L, InND Loeber coll. (1921 edn).
Philadelphia: David McKay, n.d. (The Girls' Own Library). SOURCE FFF, p. 635.
COMMENTARY No copy of the Philadelphia edn located. Fiction for juveniles [RL].

S388 *The stormy petrel* (by 'L.T. Meade').
London: Hurst & Blackett, 1909. SOURCE EF, p. 276; NCBEL 4, p. 1639. LOCATION L.

COMMENTARY Historical novel about the Irish Famine that details the sufferings of the peasantry and their hatred of the English [EF].

S389   *Wild Heather* (by 'L.T. Meade').

+ London, New York, Toronto, Melbourne: Cassell & Co., 1909 (ill. Elizabeth Earnshaw). SOURCE NCBEL 4, p. 1639. LOCATION D (n.d. edn), L, NUC.

COMMENTARY The heroine leaves her maiden aunt's care for London society. She is courted by a wealthy, middle-aged peer, but marries for love [EF, p. 276].

S390   *The princess of the revels* (by 'L.T. Meade').

+ London, Edinburgh: W. & R. Chambers, 1909 (ill. Percy Tarrant). SOURCE NCBEL 4, p. 1639; Wolff, 4716. LOCATION D, L, InND Loeber coll.

New York: New York Book Co., 1910. LOCATION NUC.

COMMENTARY Fiction for juveniles. Faith, whose mother has died, is sent to rich relatives because her father, a minister, does not have time for her. One of the girl's cousins is jealous of her. She causes her to be accused of something terrible. Faith loses the regard of an old lady who had started to love her. In the end the truth comes out [ML].

S391   *The pursuit of Penelope* (by 'L.T. Meade').

+ London: Digby, Long & Co., 1909. SOURCE Daims, 2860; DLB, cxli, p. 189 (probably mistakenly mentions 1902 edn); NCBEL 4, p. 1639. LOCATION L.

COMMENTARY Crime fiction [RL].

S392   *The necklace of Parmona* (by 'L.T. Meade').

London: Ward, Lock & Co., 1909 (ill. A. Forestier). SOURCE NCBEL 4, p. 1639. LOCATION L, NIC.

COMMENTARY Crime fiction [Reilly, p. 639].

S393   *Micah Faraday, adventurer* (by 'L.T. Meade').

+ London: Ward, Lock & Co., 1910 (ill.). SOURCE NCBEL 4, p. 1639. LOCATION L, NIC.

COMMENTARY Crime stories. Contents: 'Copper-head', 'The tabloids', 'A cup of coffee', 'The lady gardener', 'The clock went wrong', 'Marked C-1507', 'Absent—on your service', 'I descended in the dark', 'The pivot', 'The woman on the cliff', 'The ides of march', 'West of here' [ML; Reilly, p. 639].

S394   *Rosa Regina. A story for girls* (by 'L.T. Meade').

London, Edinburgh: W. & R. Chambers, 1910 (ill. A.S. Boyd). SOURCE NCBEL 4, p. 1639. LOCATION L, NIC.

Philadelphia: J.B. Lippincott, n.d. SOURCE FFF, p. 636; OCLC. LOCATION Free Library of Philadelphia.

COMMENTARY Fiction for juveniles [RL].

S395   *Nance Kennedy* (by 'L.T. Meade').

+ London: S.W. Partridge & Co., [1910] (ill.). SOURCE NCBEL 4, p. 1639. LOCATION D, L.

S396   *A wild Irish girl* (by 'L.T. Meade').

+ London, Edinburgh: W. & R. Chambers, 1910 (ill. Lewis Baumer). SOURCE Brown, 1129; NCBEL 4, p. 1639. LOCATION D, L, InND Loeber coll.

COMMENTARY Fiction for juveniles. Impulsive Patricia had been allowed to run wild while growing up in Ireland. She is brought to London where she gets into many harmless scrapes because she does not fit within the conventional constraints of society [Brown].

S397   *Pretty-girl and the others* (by 'L.T. Meade').

London, Edinburgh: W. & R. Chambers, 1910 (ill. Percy Tarrant). SOURCE NCBEL 4, p. 1639. LOCATION L, NIC.

COMMENTARY Fiction for juveniles [RL].

S398   *The A.B.C. girl* (by 'L.T. Meade').
London: F.V. White & Co., 1910. SOURCE NCBEL 4, p. 1639. LOCATION L.
COMMENTARY Fiction for juveniles [RL].

S399   *Belinda Treherne* (by 'L.T. Meade').
London: J. Long, 1910. SOURCE Daims, 2840; NCBEL 4, p. 1639. LOCATION L.

S400   *A girl of to-day* (by 'L.T. Meade').
London: John Long, 1910. SOURCE NCBEL 4, p. 1639. LOCATION L.
COMMENTARY Fiction for juveniles [RL].

S401   *Lady Anne* (by 'L.T. Meade').
+ London: James Nesbit & Co., 1910 (ill. Arthur Gwidle). SOURCE NCBEL 4, p. 1639.
LOCATION D, L, InND Loeber coll.

S402   *Miss Gwendoline* (by 'L.T. Meade').
London: John Long, 1911. SOURCE NCBEL 4, p. 1639 (1910 edn). LOCATION L.

S403   *Mother and son* (by 'L.T. Meade').
London: Ward, Lock & Co., 1911. SOURCE NCBEL 4, p. 1639. LOCATION L.

S404   *The girls of Merton College* (by 'L.T. Meade').
+ London, Edinburgh: W. & R. Chambers, 1911 (ill. W. Rainey). SOURCE NCBEL 4,
p. 1639. LOCATION L, InND Loeber coll.
COMMENTARY Fiction for juveniles [RL].

S405   *For dear dad* (by 'L.T. Meade').
+ London, Edinburgh: W. & R. Chambers, 1911 (ill. Lewis Baumer). SOURCE NCBEL
4, p. 1639. LOCATION D, L, InND Loeber coll. (n.d. edn).
COMMENTARY The daughter of a Scottish minister ensures that her father, who has developed
diabetes, goes to North Africa to try and regain his health. She stays behind and is placed in
a private school where some girls gang up against her. She leaves the school and makes her
own way to Tangiers where her appearance gives her father the strength to fight his illness
[ML].

S406   *A bunch of cousins, and The barn "boys"* (by 'L.T. Meade').
London, Edinburgh: W. & R. Chambers, 1911 (ill. Hilda Cowham). SOURCE NCBEL
4, p. 1639. LOCATION L, NIC.
COMMENTARY Fiction for juveniles [RL].

S407   *The doctor's children* (by 'L.T. Meade').
+ London, Edinburgh: W. & R. Chambers, [1911] (ill. A.S. Boyd). SOURCE NCBEL
4, p. 1639. LOCATION D, L, InND Loeber coll. (n.d. edn).
Philadelphia: Lippincott, [1911]. LOCATION NUC.
COMMENTARY Fiction for juveniles [RL].

S408   *Twenty-four hours. A novel of to-day* (by 'L.T. Meade').
+ London: F.V. White & Co., 1911. SOURCE NCBEL 4, p. 1639. LOCATION L, InND
Loeber coll.
COMMENTARY Crime fiction. Barbara Rashleigh, the daughter of a rich businessman, is in love
with Jim Havergal, whom she plans to marry. However, her father's business dealings go astray
and he is in the power of Julius Hillyard, an unscrupulous man who plans to expose Mr
Rashleigh unless he gives him his daughter in marriage. Eventually, Barbara accedes when she
finds that her brother is also in Mr Hillyard's power. She leads a miserable life with Mr
Hillyard, who is later shot dead, for which Jim Havergal goes to prison. As a widow, Barbara
tries to do good by helping other people. Eventually, it turns out that Jim had not fired the
fatal shot but had taken the blame upon himself because he thought that Barbara had killed
her husband. He is freed from prison and Barbara and Jim marry [ML].

S409   *Desborough's wife* (by 'L.T. Meade').

London: Digby, Long & Co., 1911. SOURCE Brown, 1130; NCBEL 4, p. 1639. LOCATION L.

COMMENTARY Set near Tralee, Co. Kerry, where Patrick Desborough elopes with a beautiful peasant girl. He falls heavily in debt and finds that his mother – on whom he had counted to relieve his financial embarrassment – is even more in debt. The only way out is a marriage with a rich heiress. Patrick yields to this plan and his wife consents to 'disappear'. However, in the end things right themselves [Brown].

S410   *The soul of Margaret Rand* (by 'L.T. Meade').
London: Ward, Lock & Co., 1911 (ill.). SOURCE NCBEL 4, p. 1639; Wolff, 4720. LOCATION L, NIC.

S411   *"Ruffles"* (by 'L.T. Meade').
+ London: Stanley Paul & Co., [1911]. SOURCE Daims, 2862; NCBEL 4, p. 1639. LOCATION L.
COMMENTARY Crime fiction, which was reprinted many times in the early-twentieth century [NCBEL; RL].

S412   *The girl from Spain* (by 'L.T. Meade').
London: Digby, Long & Co., 1911. SOURCE NCBEL 4, p. 1639. LOCATION L.
COMMENTARY Fiction for juveniles [RL].

S413   *Love's cross roads* (by 'L.T. Meade').
London: Stanley Paul & Co., [1912]. SOURCE NCBEL 4, p. 1639. LOCATION L, NIC.

S414   *Peggy from Kerry* (by 'L.T. Meade').
London, Edinburgh: W. & R. Chambers, 1912 (ill. Miss A. Anderson). SOURCE Brown, 1131; NCBEL 4, p. 1639. LOCATION L, InND Loeber coll. (n.d. edn).
COMMENTARY Fiction for juveniles. A story set in an English boarding school where an Irish girl is first ridiculed but in the end becomes popular [Brown].

S415   *Lord and Lady Kitty* (by 'L.T. Meade').
London: F.V. White & Co., 1912. SOURCE NCBEL 4, p. 1639. LOCATION L, NIC.

S416   *Kitty O'Donovan* (by 'L.T. Meade').
+ London, Edinburgh: W. & R. Chambers, 1912 (ill. J. Finnemore). SOURCE Brown, 1132; NCBEL 4, p. 1639. LOCATION D, L, NIC.
COMMENTARY Fiction for juveniles. Set in an English boarding school where many spiteful plots are laid for a girl from Co. Kerry. However, in the end she becomes popular and is crowned the queen of May. The theme of this story is very similar to that of *Peggy from Kerry* (London, 1912) [Brown; ML].

S417   *The house of black magic* (by 'L.T. Meade').
London: F.V. White, 1912. SOURCE NCBEL 4, p. 1639; Wolff, 4705. LOCATION L, NUC.
COMMENTARY Crime fiction [Reilly, p. 639].

S418   *Corporal Violet* (by 'L.T. Meade').
London: Hodder & Stoughton, [1912]. SOURCE NCBEL 4, p. 1639. LOCATION L.

S419   *Once of the angels* (by 'Evelyn Beacon').
London: Methuen & Co., 1913. SOURCE NCBEL 4, p. 1639; COPAC. LOCATION L.

S420   *The girls of Abinger Close* (by 'L.T. Meade').
London, Edinburgh: W. & R. Chambers, 1913 (ill. Percy Tarrant). SOURCE NCBEL 4, p. 1639. LOCATION L, NIC.
+ London, Edinburgh: W. & R. Chambers, n.d. (ill. Percy Tarrant). LOCATION InND Loeber coll.
Philadelphia: J.B. Lippincott, n.d. SOURCE FFF, p. 635.
COMMENTARY No copy of the Philadelphia edn located. Fiction for juveniles [RL].

S421 *The passion of Kathleen Duveen* (by 'L.T. Meade').
+ London: Stanley Paul & Co., 1913. SOURCE Brown, 1133; NCBEL 4, p. 1639.
LOCATION D, L, NIC ([*c*.1920] edn).
COMMENTARY A tale about a young Irishman, forced into crime and unfaithfulness to
his young wife by his family's need of money [Brown].

S422 *The girls of King's Royal* (by 'L.T. Meade').
+ London, Edinburgh: W. & R. Chambers, 1913 (ill. Gordon Browne; cover title: *The
girls of Kings* [*sic*] *Royal*; see Plate 59). SOURCE NCBEL 4, p. 1639; Wolff, 4700.
LOCATION D (n.d. edn), InND Loeber coll.
COMMENTARY Fiction for juveniles [RL].

S423 *The Chesterton girl graduates* (by 'L.T. Meade').
London, Edinburgh: W. & R. Chambers, 1913 (ill. Harold C. Earnshaw). SOURCE
NCBEL 4, p. 1639; COPAC. LOCATION Univ. of Liverpool.
COMMENTARY Fiction for juveniles [RL].

S424 *The great Lord Masareene* (by 'L.T. Meade').
London: F.V. White, 1913. SOURCE NCBEL 4, p. 1639 (1912 edn but not located);
Wolff, 4701; COPAC. LOCATION E, NIC.

S425 *The wooing of Monica* (by 'L.T. Meade').
London: John Long, 1914 (new edn). LOCATION L, NIC.
COMMENTARY First edn not located [RL].

S426 *The queen of joy* (by 'L.T. Meade').
London, Edinburgh: W. & R. Chambers, 1914 (ill. Percy Tarrant). SOURCE NCBEL
4, p. 1639. LOCATION L, NUC.

S427 *Her happy face* (by 'L.T. Meade').
London: Ward, Lock & Co., 1914. SOURCE NCBEL 4, p. 1639. LOCATION L.

S428 *A girl of high adventure* (by 'L.T. Meade').
London, Edinburgh: W. & R. Chambers, 1914 (ill. Gordon Browne). SOURCE NCBEL
4, p. 1639. LOCATION L, NIC.

S429 *Elizabeth's prisoner* (by 'L.T. Meade').
London: Stanley Paul & Co., 1914. SOURCE NCBEL 4, p. 1639. LOCATION D (1925
edn), L.

S430 *A band of mirth* (by 'L.T. Meade').
London, Edinburgh: W. & R. Chambers, 1914 (ill. Mabel Lucie Attwell). SOURCE
NCBEL 4, p. 1639. LOCATION L, NIC.

S431 *The girls of Castle Rocco. A home story for girls* (by 'L.T. Meade').
New York: A.L. Burt & Co., 1915 (ill.; The Meade Series for Girls). SOURCE Baldwin, p.
145; FFF, p. 636; OCLC (n.d. edn). LOCATION Free Library of Philadelphia (n.d. edn).
COMMENTARY This and the following volumes were published posthumously, and became part
of the collected works, listed below. No British edn of this title has been identified. Fiction
for juveniles [RL].

S432 *Greater than gold* (by 'L.T. Meade').
London: Ward, Lock & Co., 1915. SOURCE NCBEL 4, p. 1639. LOCATION L, NIC.

S433 *Jill, the irresistible* (by 'L.T. Meade').
London, Edinburgh: W. & R. Chambers, 1915. SOURCE NCBEL 4, p. 1639; Wolff,
4707. LOCATION L.

S434 *The darling of the school* (by 'L.T. Meade').
+ London, Edinburgh: W. & R. Chambers, 1915 (ill. W.A. Cuthbertson). SOURCE
NCBEL 4, p. 1639. LOCATION D (n.d. edn), L, NIC.
Philadelphia: J.B. Lippincott, n.d. SOURCE FFF, p. 635.

COMMENTARY No copy of the Philadelphia edn located. Fiction for juveniles [RL].

S435   *The daughter of a soldier, a colleen of South Ireland* (by 'L.T. Meade').
London, Edinburgh: W. & R. Chambers, 1915 (ill. Gordon Browne). SOURCE DLB, cxli, p. 193; NCBEL 4, p. 1639. LOCATION E, NIC.
New York: Hurst & Co., [1915]. SOURCE COPAC. LOCATION L.

S436   *Hollyhock. A spirit of mischief* (by 'L.T. Meade').
+ London, Edinburgh: W. & R. Chambers, 1916 (ill. W. Rainey). SOURCE NCBEL 4, p. 1639. LOCATION D (n.d. edn), L, NIC.

S437   *The maid indomitable* (by 'L.T. Meade').
London: Ward, Lock & Co., 1916 (ill.). SOURCE NCBEL 4, p. 1639. LOCATION L, NIC.

S438   *Madge Mostyn's nieces* (by 'L.T. Meade').
London, Edinburgh: W. & R. Chambers, 1916 (ill. W. Rainey). SOURCE NCBEL 4, p. 1639. LOCATION L, NIC.

S439   *Better than riches* (by 'L.T. Meade').
London, Edinburgh: W. & R. Chambers, 1917 (ill. J. Petts). SOURCE NCBEL 4, p. 1640. LOCATION L, NIC.

S440   *The fairy godmother* (by 'L.T. Meade').
+ London, Edinburgh: W. & R. Chambers, 1917 (ill. W. Rainey). SOURCE NCBEL 4, p. 1640. LOCATION L, NIC.
Philadelphia: J.B. Lippincott, n.d. SOURCE FFF, p. 365.
COMMENTARY No copy of the Philadelphia edn located. Fiction for juveniles [RL].

S441   *Miss Patricia* (by 'L.T. Meade').
London: J. Long & Co., 1925 (People's Friend Library, No. 153). LOCATION L.

S442   *Roses and thorns* (by 'L.T. Meade').
London, Dundee: J. Long & Co., 1928 (People's Friend Library, No. 214). LOCATION L.

— COLLECTED WORKS

COMMENTARY The following are series published in the US that list L.T. Meade's books for girls only. In each of the series, the total number of volumes issued is estimated from sources available to us, but cannot be called final. Since most of the volumes are undated, the assignment of dates remains to be solved. Also, although each of the following series appeared in distinct bindings, some variations exist, and their chronological order remains to be established. SOURCE RL.

S443   *Mrs L.T. Meade Series.*
Chicago: George M. Hill, n.d., [at least 20 vols] (ill.). SOURCE FFF, p. 635–37; DLB, cxli, p. 187. LOCATION InND Loeber coll. (some vols.), NUC.

S444   *Mrs L.T. Meade Series.*
Chicago: M.A. Donohue, [1890s–1913?], [at least 27 vols] (ill). SOURCE DLB, cxli, p. 191; Adv. in 'L.T. Meade', *A girl in ten thousand* (Chicago, n.d.). LOCATION D (some vols.), InND Loeber coll. (some vols.), NUC.
COMMENTARY Two binding types: (a) beige cloth impressed in black and red; (b) brown cloth with printed picture on front cover [RL].

S445   *Mrs L.T. Meade Series.*
Cleveland (OH): Arthur Westbrook, n.d., 32 vols. LOCATION InND Loeber coll. (one vol.).

S446   *The Meade Series for girls.*
New York: A.L. Burt, [1897]–1915, 47 vols. (ill.). SOURCE FFF, pp 635–7; RL. LOCATION InND Loeber coll. (many vols.), NUC.

COMMENTARY The titles are sometimes shorter than those of the English edns. The publisher Burt also published many of L.T. Meade's books in other series: The Wellesley Series for Girls, and The Fireside Series for Girls, and several other, smaller series [RL].

S447   *L.T. Meade Series.*
New York: Hurst & Co., [up to 1915?], [at least 30 vols] (ill.). SOURCE FFF, pp 635–7; DLB, cxli, p. 192–93; RL. LOCATION InND Loeber coll. (some vols.), NUC.
— SPURIOUS WORKS

S448   *A pluckie girl* (by 'Laura [*sic*] T. Meade').
Philadelphia: G.W. Jacobs, [1900] (ill. Ida Waugh). LOCATION NUC.
COMMENTARY Fiction for juveniles. Given the variant pseudonym, this volume may be spurious [RL].

S449   *The Colonel's conquest* (by 'Laura [*sic*] T. Meade').
Philadelphia: George W. Jacobs & Co., 1907 (Pastime and Adventure Series). SOURCE FFF, p. 635 (n.d. edn). LOCATION NUC.
COMMENTARY Possibly an imitation of L.T. Meade's work [RL].

SMITH, Francis Shubael, b. 1819. American poet and fiction writer, FSS was, according to the title page of the following book, the author of several works which have not been located, such as 'Kit Clayton; or, the hero of the road', and 'Silver and pewter; a tale of high and low life in New York', in addition to *The vestmaker's apprentice: or, The vampyres of society* (New York, 1863), and *Bertha the sewing-machine girl, or, death at the wheel* (New York, 1896). SOURCE RL; OCLC.

S450   *Eveleen Wilson; or, the trials of an orphan girl* [anon.].
+ Philadelphia: T.B. Peterson & Bros, [before 1853?], 7th thousand (ill.). LOCATION Wright web.
New York: H. Long & Brother, 1853. SOURCE OCLC. LOCATION DCL.
COMMENTARY Eveleen Wilson was born in Dublin 1834. Her mother died soon afterwards, leaving her with her father, who doted on her. After her father's death, she lived with an uncle. Her cousin, Bernard Wilson, does not want his father to become too fond of Eveleen and he makes up stories about her lover, William Haviland, so that the uncle forbids Eveleen to have contact with him. Bernard continues to persecute Eveleen even after she has emigrated to New York, where she attempts to drown herself. Eventually, William Haviland prevents Bernard from killing Eveleen, after which she and William are united. The story gained in popularity with the publication of the play by James Pilgrim, *Eveleen Wilson, the flower of Erin* (New York, 1853), reinforced by the appearance of *Pictorial life and adventures of Eveleen Wilson, or, The trials of an orphan girl* (Philadelphia, n.d.) [ML; OCLC].

SMITH, J.A., fl. 1875. Canadian short story writer and humorist, JAS was a resident of Burford (near Brantford, ON) according to the title page of the following book. SOURCE RL.

S451   *Humorous sketches and poems* (by J.A. Smith).
+ Toronto: Dudley & Burns, 1875 (ill.). LOCATION InND Loeber coll.
COMMENTARY Contents (excluding poetry): 'Courtship in smoky hollow', 'Bill and the widow', 'Donald and Hans', 'Old Bob and young Bob', 'Ike Sickle's quilting scrape', 'A lost Irishman. Jimmy Butler and the owl' (Irish content), 'Teddy O'Brian' (Irish content), 'Timothy Hay's address to the electors of Stumpfield' (Irish content), 'Pat and the Yankee orange', 'Ben Wagstaff's horse', 'The Mapleton girls', 'Jerry Jones. A romance of Mt. Pleasant', 'Mr. John Jackson goes to hear the Mormon missionary, and Mrs J.J. gives him a talking to', 'Tastes and propensities', 'Love, courtship and matrimony', 'The brown nose, and how I sold a small portion of it for $50,000' [RL].

SMITH, Mrs James Burnett. See SWAN, Annie Shepherd.

SMITH, John, fl. 1847. Humour writer, JS was also a lecturer on education. According to Brown, at the time this book was written he was one of the editors of the *Liverpool Mercury*. SOURCE Brown, 1518; Ximenes cat. 27/335.

S452   *Irish diamonds; or, a theory of Irish wit and blunders: combined with other kindred subjects* (by John Smith; dedicated to Henry Woollcombe, patron of the Plymouth Institution).

+ London: Chapman & Hall, 1847 (ill. Phiz). SOURCE Allibone, ii, p. 2146 (1846 edn); Brown, 1518; Hodgson, p. 515. LOCATION D, L, InND Loeber coll.

COMMENTARY Mostly nonfiction, but contains a number of brief dialogues, vignettes and anecdotes illustrative of blunders and 'Irish wit'. Contents: 'The English, the Scotch, and the Irish', 'Definitions of wit and blunder', 'The author's theory of Irish wit, etc.', 'Genuine Irish bulls', 'Genuine Irish wit', 'A few English specimens', 'Genuine Irish wit continued', 'Wit of all nations', 'Blunders of all nations', 'Irish humour', 'English humour', 'Conclusion: the theory submitted to a verdict' [JB; RL].

'SMITH, Mrs John', pseud. See ARTHUR, Timothy Shay.

SMITH, John Frederick, b. Norwich (Norfolk) 1806, d. New York City 1890. Popular English Gothic and historical novelist, JFS was the son of James Smith, a theatre manager, and Elizabeth Taylor. He spent some time in Rome and published several plays and novels before returning to England in 1849 when he began to write serialized novels for the *London Journal* that substantially raised its circulation. Later he wrote for *Cassell's Illustrated Family Journal* (London) for some years. He emigrated to the US around 1880 and, despite previously having a lucrative career, died in obscurity and poverty. He never married, and his deafness cut him off from society. SOURCE Allibone, ii, p. 2140 [under J. Frederick Smith]; Allibone Suppl., ii, p. 1360 [ditto]; Boase, iii, p. 637; Brown 2, p. 244; Sutherland, p. 588; Wolff, iv, p. 138.

S453   *Redmond O'Neill; or, the substance and the shadow* (by John Frederick Smith).

New York: Dick & FitzGerald, [*c*.1875]. SOURCE Brown 2, 1444.

COMMENTARY No copy located. Redmond O'Neill, an Irish officer in the Swiss Guard of Louis XV, deceived by the schemes of his cousin Ulick Blake, believes his wife unfaithful. Maddened by this false accusation, his wife leaves France and dies in childbirth on her way to Ireland. Grown to manhood, her son, young Redmond O'Neill, goes to France to clear up the mystery of his father. After a long search he discovers him a prisoner in the Bastille. Incidents from the French Revolution and the 1798 insurrection in Ireland are included [Brown 2].

SMITH, Fr John Talbot, b. Saratoga (NY) 1855. American priest, religious novelist and editor, JTS was the son of Bernard Smith, a railroad worker, and Brigid O'Donnell. Most likely he was of Irish origin and certainly, judging his fiction, he was very interested in Irish matters. He was ordained in 1881 and in 1889 his superiors released him from his mission duties to pursue a writing career in New York City, where he lived for twenty years and where for a while he was editor of the *Catholic Review*. Among his various works of fiction, the following have some Irish content. SOURCE Allibone Suppl., ii, p. 1185 [under O'Brien], p. 1361 [under Smith]; Fanning, p. 189; Wright, iii, pp 501–2.

S454   *Solitary island. A novel* (by John Talbot Smith).

+ New York: P.J. Kenedy, 1888 (cover: *The solitary island*; School Premium Library). SOURCE DCU, Catholic Americana files, 1889 edn; Fanning, p. 391; Wright, iii, 5028. LOCATION D, InND Loeber coll.

COMMENTARY The story is set partly on an island in the St Lawrence River near Lake Ontario and partly in New York City. Florian Wallace is an ambitious young lawyer who plans to make his mark in politics. Before he leaves for New York City, he consults a hermit on an island. The girl he wishes to marry cannot make up her mind to become a Catholic, and he leaves her behind. In politics he makes his way by eloquent speeches on behalf of Daniel O'Connell and Irish freedom in order to win the votes of the Irish, for whom he does not really care. The young man's ambition corrupts his high ideals. While in New York, he is pursued by some Russians who think he is a descendant of a Russian prince. They are in the pay of a rival prince who wishes his enemies and their descendants to be destroyed. Florian takes the Russians to his hometown to meet his parents to convince them that he is not the Russian they are looking for. In transpires that Florian is the son of the hermit, who was originally a Russian prince. The hermit is shot by the agents. Florian stays alone for a while on the island considering his past life. He returns to catholicism and marries a Catholic girl and after some persuasion decides to stay in politics but now to do good [ML; Fanning, p. 190].

S455 *His honor, the mayor, and other tales* (by John Talbot Smith).
New York: The Vatican Library, 1891. SOURCE Fanning, p. 192; Wright, iii, 5027. LOCATION CtY.
COMMENTARY Several of the following stories concern the conflict between immigrants and natives. Contents: 'The deacon of Lynn', 'The four sons of Jael', 'One of many', 'A novel experiment', 'The baron of Cherubusco', 'A voice from the wilderness', 'His honor, the mayor', 'How the McGuinness saved his pride' [Fanning, p. 192].

S456 *Saranac. A story of Lake Champlain* (by John Talbot Smith).
New York: The Catholic Publication Society Company, 1892. SOURCE Fanning, p. 192. LOCATION InND.
COMMENTARY The story is about the friction between two immigrant cultures in upstate New York: the Irish and the French Canadians. One of the main characters is Mrs Sullivan, a matriarch from Limerick. Her Francophobia is tempered only when a neighbour reminds her of the French support for Ireland in the 1798 rising [Fanning, p. 192].

S457 *A woman of culture: A Canadian romance* (by John Talbot Smith).
New York: W.H. Young, 1897. SOURCE Fanning, pp 190, 391; OCLC. LOCATION MH.
COMMENTARY A contrast of New World materialism and Irish spirituality, the story concerns a lapsed Catholic who pursues money and power through unscrupulous means. He is brought to his senses when he finds out that his daughter has become an atheist, for which he blames himself. An Orange-Green riot in Toronto reawakens his faith. His daughter refuses to return to the church [Fanning, p. 190].

S458 *The art of disappearing* (by John Talbot Smith).
New York, Cincinnati: Benziger Bros, 1902. SOURCE Fanning, p. 193; OCLC. LOCATION C, Spring Hill College, Mobile, AL.
COMMENTARY Set in New England, New York and Ireland and describes the failed Fenian rising in Ireland in 1867 and the dedication of St Patrick's Cathedral in New York in 1879. The story centres around a person from New England who, upon witnessing the adultery of his wife, leaves her and assumes the identity of an Irishman. This gives him the opportunity to observe from inside the Irish community of the east side of New York [Fanning, p. 193].

SMITH, Mary E., pseud. 'Christine Faber', b. Savannah (GA) 1849, d. 1918. American Catholic writer, MES had many titles to her credit. According to the newspaper obituary in *Carroll O'Donoghue* (New York, [1881]), she taught in public schools and was active in social work. She was formerly editor of *Redpath's Magazine* (not located) and was a frequent contributor to Catholic periodicals. The obituary lists *Carroll O'Donoghue* and *Reaping the whirl-*

wind as among her best-known novels. For her other novels, see Allibone, Brown, Wright, and DCU, Catholic Americana files. Only one novel, listed below, is known to have Irish content. SOURCE AMB; Allibone Suppl., i, p. 570 [under Faber]; Brown, p. 102 [under Faber]; Wright, iii, pp 502–3.

S459 *Carroll O'Donoghue. A tale of the Irish struggles of 1866, and of recent times* (by 'Christine Faber').
+ New York: P.J. Kenedy, [1881] (ill.). SOURCE Brown, 571; Wright, iii, 5036. LOCATION D (1900 edn), L, DCU (1889 edn), NUC, InND Loeber coll. (n.d. edn and 1904 edn).
+ Dublin: James Duffy & Co., [1903]. LOCATION D, L.

SMYTH, Amelia Gillespie (erroneously spelled Smythe by Howard), fl. 1828. Scottish story writer, AGS was also the author of 'Selwyn in search of a daughter', and 'The bachelor's beat' which had been published in *Blackwood's Magazine* (Edinburgh; the former serialized starting Feb. 1827), according to the title page of the following novel. Several of AGS's letters are in the Blackwood letter books. SOURCE RL; Howard, 67; British Fiction; Scott (correspondence with Sir Walter Scott).

S460 *Tales of the moors: or, rainy days in Ross-shire* [anon.] (dedicated to Sir Walter Scott).
Edinburgh: William Blackwood & T. Caddell, 1828. SOURCE British Fiction; Garside 2, 1828:76; Howard, 67. LOCATION Corvey CME 3–628–48865–6, Dt, L.
COMMENTARY This series of tales told by four gentlemen (two Englishmen, one Irishman, and one Scotsman) during several rainy days when they are on a sporting holiday in Scotland. The work is sometimes misattributed to Caroline Anne Bowles. First serialized in *Blackwood's Magazine* (Edinburgh). Contents: 'The return', 'My last day in Rome', 'Adventures of an attaché', 'A day in the Isle of Wight' [Howard; Garside].

SMYTH, Patrick G., b. Ballina (Co. Mayo) 1857, d. United States? Historical novelist, PGS wrote the preface to *King and Viking* (Dublin, 1889) from Ballina in 1888. The title page of *The wild rose* (Dublin, [1883]) mentions that he wrote 'The duchess of Inver', but this has not been located. According to O'Donoghue, he was originally a schoolteacher who wrote verse for Dublin periodicals such as the *Irishman*, the *Shamrock*, *Young Ireland* and *Weekly News*. PGS emigrated to the US in 1889 and for some time worked as a journalist on a Chicago newspaper and was editor of the *Western People*. SOURCE Allibone Suppl., ii, p. 1366 (erroneously combines the work of P.G. Smyth with that of P.J. Smyth, the Irish politician); Boase, iii, pp 656–67; Irish pseudonyms; O'Donoghue, p. 432; E. Reilly, p. 250; RIA/DIB; RL.

S461 *The wild rose of Lough Gill: A tale of the Irish war in the seventeenth century* (by Patrick G. Smyth; dedicated to Timothy D. Sullivan§, Esq., MP for Westmeath).
+ Dublin: M.H. Gill & Son; Simpkin, Marshall & Co., [1883]. SOURCE Brown, 1520; Topp 8, 686. LOCATION D, Dcc (1898 edn), Dt (1909 edn), DPL, L, InND Loeber coll. (1904, 5th edn).
New York: Benziger, 1904, 5th edn. SOURCE Brown, 1520.
COMMENTARY No copy of New York edn located. Two thousand copies of the first Dublin edn were printed. It reached a sixth edn in 1903. Historical fiction covering the period from 1641 to 1652 and describing the various battles and sieges across Ireland, but particularly in Co. Leitrim, where the Hamiltons of Manorhamilton terrorized the countryside. Many historical personages, such as Rory O'More and Owen Roe O'Neill, play a role. The hero, a young man attached to the O'Rourke household in Leitrim, survives many bloody battles and in the end emigrates with his bride to Spain [ML; E. Reilly, p. 228; RL].

S462   *King and Viking; or, the ravens of Lochlan. A tale of the Danish invasion of Ireland*
(by Patrick G. Smyth).
+ Dublin: Sealy, Bryers & Walker; London: Simpkin, Marshall & Co., 1889 (Irish
Standard Novel Series). SOURCE Brown, 1521 (n.d. edn). LOCATION D.
COMMENTARY Historical fiction of Irish life at the period of the Danish invasions (795–1014).
Set in Co. Sligo around 888, the date assigned in the Annals of the Four Masters to a great
battle between the men of Connacht and the Danes. Much information on clan life in Ireland
at the time is included [Brown].

SMYTHE, Alfred, b. Dublin 1856. Poet, opera writer, dramatist and novelist, AS wrote for
Chambers's Journal (Edinburgh); *Pen and Pencil* (Glasgow); *Irish Society* (Dublin); *Whitehall
Review* and *Pictorial World* (both London), and *Dramatic Review* (Edinburgh, Glasgow or
London). His opera *The warlock* was published in Dublin in 1892; his poetry included *The
Lady Elwynore* (Dublin, 1879) and a collected volume published in London in 1931. SOURCE
BLC; LVP, p. 443; MVP, p. 428; O'Donoghue, p. 433; RIA/DIB.
S463   *A new Faust* (by Alfred Smythe).
+ London: Digby & Long, [1896]. LOCATION L.
New York: American Publishing Corp., [1897] (as *Van Hoff, or the new Faust*).
LOCATION L.
COMMENTARY No Irish content. In a Dutch town, a medical doctor engages in experiments
and he sells his soul to the devil. His idea is to rejuvenate blood by electricity. In the end, the
concoction he makes kills him [ML].

SNEYD, Honora. See EDGEWORTH, Honora.

SOMERVILLE, Edith Anna Œnone, pseud. 'Geilles Herring', b. Corfu (Italy) 1858, d.
Drishane (Co. Cork) 1949. Irish novelist, poet, editor, short story writer and artist, EAŒS was
the daughter and eldest of the eight children of Thomas Somerville, Col. of the Buffs, and
Adelaide Eliza Coghill. When she still a baby, the family retired to Drishane, their country house
near Skibbereen. EAŒS was educated informally by governesses in Castletownshend and for one
term at Alexandra College (Dublin), where she developed a serious interest in art. She studied
painting in London, Düsseldorf and Paris before returning to west Cork. Riding and painting
were her absorbing interests (she was the first woman master of the West Carbery Foxhounds,
from 1903 to 1908 and again from 1912 to 1919) but she worked as an illustrator to generate
income. In 1886, she met her cousin Violet Martin§ (they were both great-granddaughters of
Chief Justice Charles Kendal Bushe). After an enjoyable collaboration on a dictionary of family
slang, EAŒS and Martin wrote – for financial reasons – a 'shilling shocker' that began a life-
long literary partnership (Violet Martin wrote under the pseud. 'Martin Ross'). Together they
chronicled the culture of the Anglo-Irish 'big house' and relationships between the big house
inhabitants and the locals. EAŒS, after the death of her mother in 1895, was responsible for the
running of Drishane which, given the family's perilous finances, was partly-supported by her
writing. The success of the series beginning with *Some experiences of an Irish R.M* (London, 1899).
finally gave her and Martin the income to help sustain their lifestyles. Much of their collaboration over twenty years took place by letter. Only after Martin's mother died in 1906 did she move
to Drishane. Both women began to learn Irish, and they allied themselves with the suffragette
movement. Martin died of a brain tumour in 1915, but EAŒS continued to publish her work
under their joint names (she is said to have maintained spiritual contact with her through a
medium). She was the organist for her local parish church in Castlehaven, managed the family
farm and was active in local civic matters, beside illustrating many of her books. In 1922, Dublin

University conferred on her an honorary D.Litt. She was a founding member of the Irish Academy of Letters, from which she received their principal literary honour in 1941. EACES published two autobiographical works: *Irish memories* (London, 1917) and *Wheel-tracks* (London, 1923). She also published *Records of the Somerville family* (Cork, 1940). Many of her papers are in TCD (MSS 3,330–1, 4,276–77, 7,673–84), and at Queen's University, Belfast. For her portraits and papers, see ODNB. SOURCE Blain, pp 1006–7; Boylan, pp 364–5; J. Cronin, *Somerville and Ross* (Lewisburg, PA 1972); EF, p. 368; Field Day, ii, pp 1009–10, 1021–2, 1026, 1217, iv, pp 1071–3, 1105–7, v, p. 126 and passim; Hogan 2, pp 1132–3; Landed gentry, 1904, p. 560; G. Lewis, (ed.), *Somerville and Ross: the world of the Irish R.M.* (London, New York 1985); G. Lewis, (ed), *The selected letters of Somerville and Ross* (London, 1989); OCIL, pp 530–1; ODNB; O'Toole, pp 279–82; V. Powell, *The Irish cousins* (London, 1970); O. Rauchbauer (ed.), *The Edith Œnone Somerville archive* (Dublin, 1995); RIA/DIB; H. Robinson, *Somerville and Ross: a critical appreciation* (Dublin, New York 1980); Sutherland, pp 594–5; Todd, pp 629–31.

S464 *An Irish cousin* (by 'Geilles Herring' and 'Martin Ross').
  + London: Richard Bentley & Son, 1889, 2 vols. SOURCE Brown, 1522; Lewis, p. 241; Sadleir, 3123. LOCATION D, Dt, L.
  + London, New York, Bombay: Longmans, Green & Co., 1903 (new and revsd edn). LOCATION L, InND Loeber coll.
COMMENTARY 'Martin Ross' supplied the text for this novel, which recreates the social setting of the Anglo-Irish ascendancy in a country house and describes the awakening of a young man, Theo Sarsfield, to the realization that there are things in life beyond horses and dogs. His love for a clever cousin, returned from Canada, has a tragic ending [Brown; Sutherland, p. 594].

S465 *Naboth's vineyard. A novel* (by E.Œ. Somerville and 'Martin Ross').
  London: Spencer Blackett, 1891. SOURCE Brown, 1523; Lewis, p. 241; Sadleir, 3126. LOCATION D (n.d. edn), Dt, L.
  Leipzig: Bernard Tauchnitz, 1891. SOURCE T & B, 2775; OCLC. LOCATION NNC.
COMMENTARY Describes the sordid aspects of Irish-Catholic village life. The village is set at the border of Co. Cork and Co. Kerry [Brown].

S466 *Through Connemara in a governess cart* [anon.].
  [London]: W.H. Allen & Co., 1893 (ill. W.W. Russell, E.Œ. Somerville). SOURCE Lewis, p. 241; Sadleir, 3132. LOCATION L.

S467 *In the vine country* (by E.Œ. Somerville & 'Martin Ross').
  + London: W.H. Allen & Co., 1893 (ill. F.H. Townsend, E.Œ. Somerville). SOURCE Lewis, p. 241; Sadleir, 3122. LOCATION D, L.
COMMENTARY Originally published in the *Lady's Pictorial* (London). There are two binding variants: (a) dark-green glazed cloth; (b) grass-green unglazed cloth [Carter, p. 152; RL].

S468 *The real Charlotte* (by E.Œ. Somerville and 'Martin Ross').
  London: Ward & Downey, 1894, 3 vols. SOURCE Brown, 1524; Daims, 2883; Lewis, p. 241; Sadleir, 3127; Wolff, 6480. LOCATION Dt, L, NUC (1901 edn).
  + London: Quartet Books, 1986. LOCATION InND Loeber coll.
  + New Brunswick (NJ): Rutgers University Press, 1986 (introd. by Virginia Beards). LOCATION InND Loeber coll.
COMMENTARY Issued in two binding variants: (a) scarlet cloth; (b) purple cloth. Also published in 1948 in the World Classics series, an honour rarely awarded to a living author. Set in a west Co. Cork village, it features Charlotte Mullen, a social climber of middle-class origins who is ruthless in her business contacts and who fails in her personal relationships. She cheats her young cousin out of her inheritance, and in vain tries to marry into the local ascendancy [Carter, pp 152–3; Field Day, ii, pp 1046–59, iii, p. 104; Hogan 2, p. 1132; OCIL, p. 491; ODNB; Todd].

S469 *Beggars on horseback. A riding tour in North Wales* (by 'Martin Ross' and E.Œ. Somerville).
+ Edinburgh, London: William Blackwood & Sons, 1895 (ill. E.Œ. Somerville). SOURCE Lewis, p. 241; Sadleir, 3115. LOCATION D, Dt, L.
COMMENTARY Told in a semi-fictional manner. Issued in two binding variants: (a) powder-blue buckram; (b) darker blue smooth cloth [RL; Carter, p. 153].

S470 *The silver fox* (by 'Martin Ross' and E.Œ. Somerville).
London: Lawrence & Bullen, 1898. SOURCE Brown, 1525 (1897 edn not documented); Lewis, p. 241; Sadleir, 3128. LOCATION D, Dt, L.
COMMENTARY First appeared in the *Minute* (London?). Set in the west of Ireland, it describes the plight of the English in an unfamiliar country where the peasants still believe in superstitions. The story describes sporting scenes [Brown; E. Hudson (ed.), *A bibliography* (New York, 1942); Sutherland, p. 595; Todd].

S471 *Some experiences of an Irish R.M.* (by E.Œ. Somerville and 'Martin Ross').
+ London: Longmans, Green & Co., 1899 (ill. E.Œ. Somerville). SOURCE Brown, 1526; Lewis, p. 241; Sadleir, 3129. LOCATION Dt, L, InND Loeber coll.
COMMENTARY Humorous stories first published in the *Badminton Magazine* (London). The stories follow the adventures of a resident magistrate in the Irish countryside as he deals with the peasantry and the aristocracy. Contents: 'Great-uncle McCarthy', 'In the Curranhilty country', 'Trinket's colt', 'The waters of strife', 'Lisheen races, second hand', 'Philippa's fox-hunt', 'A misdeal', 'The holy island', 'The policy of the closed door', 'The house of Fahy', 'Occasional licenses', '"Oh love! Oh fire!"' [ML; Todd; EF, p. 368].

S472 *A Patrick's day hunt* [anon.] (dedicated to J.E.P., Professor of Embroidery, and Collector of Irish Point).
+ Westminster [London]: Archibald Constable, [1902] (ill. E.Œ. Somerville). SOURCE Lewis, p. 241. SOURCE COPAC. LOCATION Dt, L.

S473 *All on the Irish shore. Irish sketches* (by E.Œ. Somerville and 'Martin Ross').
+ London, New York, Bombay: Longmans, Green & Co., 1903 (ill. E.Œ. Somerville). SOURCE Brown, 1528; Lewis, p. 241; Sadleir, 3114. LOCATION D, L, InND Loeber coll.
+ Leipzig: Bernard Tauchnitz, 1903. SOURCE T & B, 3672. LOCATION D.
COMMENTARY According to the RIA/DIB, these hunting stories were written by Violet Martin. Contents: 'The tinker's dog', 'Fanny Fitz's gamble', 'The Connemara mare', 'A grand filly', 'A nineteenth-century miracle', 'High tea at McKeown's', 'The bagman's pony', 'An Irish problem', 'The Dane's "breechin"', '"Matchbox"', '"As I was going to Bandon fair"' [ML].

S474 *Slipper's ABC of fox hunting* (by E.Œ. Somerville).
London: Longmans, Green, 1903. SOURCE Lewis, p. 241. LOCATION L.
COMMENTARY 85pp [COPAC].

S475 *Some Irish yesterdays* (by E.Œ. Somerville and 'Martin Ross').
+ London: Longmans, Green, 1906 (ill. E.Œ. Somerville). SOURCE Brown, 1529; Lewis, p. 241; Sadleir, 3130. LOCATION L, InND Loeber coll. (n.d. edn).
COMMENTARY According to the RIA/DIB, Violet Martin wrote the following stories, consisting of short sketches about life in the country. Contents: 'An outpost of Ireland', 'Picnics', 'Boon companions', 'The biography of a pump', 'Hunting mahatmas', 'A Patrick's day hunt', 'Alsatia', '"In sickness and in health"', 'Horticultural', 'Out of hand', 'A record of holiday', 'Lost, stolen, or strayed', 'Children of the captivity', 'Slipper's A B C of fox-hunting' [RL].

S476 *Further experiences of an Irish R.M.* (by E.Œ. Somerville and 'Martin Ross').
+ London, New York, Bombay, Calcutta: Longmans, Green & Co, 1908 (ill. E.Œ. Somerville). SOURCE Brown, 1527; Lewis, p. 241; Sadleir, 3120. LOCATION D (1911 edn), L, InND Loeber coll.

+ Oxford: Isis, 1985. LOCATION D.

COMMENTARY A sequel to *Some experiences of an Irish R.M.* (London, 1899) and continues in the same vein. Contents: 'The pug-nosed fox', 'A royal command', 'Poisson d'Avril', '"The man that came to buy apples"', 'A conspiracy of silence', 'The boat's share', 'The last day of shraft', '"A horse! A horse!"' (Part I), '"A horse! A horse!"' (Part II), 'Sharper than a ferret's tooth', 'Oweneen the sprat', 'The Whiteboys' [ML; Todd].

S477 *Dan Russell, the fox: an episode in the life of Miss Rowan* (by E.Œ. Somerville and 'Martin Ross').
+ London: Methuen & Co., 1911. SOURCE Brown, 1530; Lewis, p. 241; Sadleir, 3117. LOCATION D, L, InND Loeber coll.
Leipzig: Bernard Tauchnitz, 1911. SOURCE T & B, 4298. LOCATION L.

COMMENTARY Miss Rowan, an English heiress, comes to Ireland and rents a country house in the middle of the West Carbery hunting district in Co. Cork. She falls in love with a huntsman, but he is absorbed in hounds and horses. It contains many descriptions of hunting scenes [Brown].

S478 *In Mr. Knox's country* (by E.Œ. Somerville and 'Martin Ross').
+ New York, London, Bombay, Calcutta, Madras: Longmans, Green & Co., 1915 (ill. E.Œ. Somerville). SOURCE Brown, 1531; Lewis, p. 241; Sadleir, 3121. LOCATION D, L, InND Loeber coll.
+ Oxford: Isis, 1985. LOCATION D.

COMMENTARY A series of eleven humorous episodes of country life in west Cork, forming the third instalment after *Some experiences of an Irish R.M.* (London, 1899), and *Further experiences of an Irish R.M.* (1908) [Brown; Sutherland, p. 595].

S479 *Mount Music* (by E.Œ. Somerville and 'Martin Ross').
+ London, New York, Bombay, Calcutta, Madras: Longmans, Green & Co., 1919. SOURCE Brown 2, 1467; Lewis, p. 241; Sadleir, 3125. LOCATION D, L, InND Loeber coll. (London, Nelson, n.d. edn).

COMMENTARY The plot turns on a mixed marriage between offspring of the Protestant Talbot-Lowrys of Mount Music and the Coppingers of Coppinger Court, who had become Catholics to the general scandal of their social circle. Tragedy impends from the beginning. The sinister Dr Mangan, egged on by the equally sinister Fr Green, nearly succeeds in coming between the lovers [Brown 2].

S480 *Stray-aways* (by E.Œ. Somerville and 'Martin Ross').
+ London, New York, Bombay, Calcutta, Madras: Longmans, Green & Co., 1920 (ill. E.Œ. Somerville). SOURCE Brown 2, 1468; Lewis, p. 241; Sadleir, 3131. LOCATION D, L, InND Loeber coll.

COMMENTARY A collection of essays and short stories. Contents: 'In explanation', 'At the river's edge' (a record of a conversation with an old Irishwoman about fairies, priests, and the Irish language), 'A delegate of the National League', 'Cheops in Connemara', 'Cartier Latinities I, II, III, IV', 'The dog from Doone', 'Waters of Babylon', 'In the fighting-line', 'The old station-master', 'A subterranean cave at Cloonabinnia', 'In the state of Denmark', 'The Anglo-Irish language', 'An incorrigible Unionist', 'Ireland, then and now', 'A pool of siloam', 'A fox hunt in the southern hills', '"En costume de ville"', '"*Not* the woman's place"', 'Stage Irishmen and others', 'Two Sunday afternoons', 'Extra-mundane communications' [ML; Brown 2].

S481 *An enthusiast* (by E.Œ. Somerville and 'Martin Ross'; dedicated to 'my collaborator').
+ London, New York, Bombay, Calcutta, Madras: Longmans, Green & Co., 1921. SOURCE Brown 2, 1469; Lewis, p. 241; Sadleir, 3118. LOCATION D, L.

S482 *The big house of Inver* (by E.Œ. Somerville and 'Martin Ross'; dedicated to 'Our intention 1912–1925').

+ London: William Heinemann, 1925. SOURCE Lewis, p. 241; Sadleir, 3116. LOCATION D, L, InND Loeber coll.

Garden City (NY): Doubleday, Page & Co., 1925. SOURCE RLIN. LOCATION DCL.

+ Toronto, New York, London, Bombay, Calcutta: Longmans, Green & Co., 1925. LOCATION InND Loeber coll.

COMMENTARY Set in the west of Ireland and describes the deterioration of an Ascendancy family, the Prendevilles. Shibby Pindy, one of the family members, tries to reverse the family's decline by marrying off her half-brother to a wealthy heiress. However, he foils her plans by forming a liaison with a village girl. In the end the 'big house' burns to the ground [Field Day, iii, p. 665; Hogan 2, p. 1133; OCIL, p. 46].

S483 *French leave* (by E.Œ. Somerville and 'Martin Ross'; dedicated to 'my collaborator').

+ London: William Heinemann, 1928. SOURCE Brown 2, 1470; Lewis, p. 241; Sadleir, 3119. LOCATION D, L, InND Loeber coll.

+ London: Tom Stacey, 1973. LOCATION D.

S484 *The smile and the tear* (by E.Œ. Somerville and 'Martin Ross').

+ London: Methuen & Co., 1933 (ill. E.Œ. Somerville). SOURCE Brown 2, 1472; Hogan 2, p. 1134. LOCATION D, L.

COMMENTARY Stories about people and places in West Carbery [ML; Leclaire, p. 172].

S485 *The Irish R.M. complete. All the stories in one volume* (by E.Œ. Somerville and 'Martin Ross').

London: Faber & Faber, 1936. SOURCE Brown 2, 1476. LOCATION L.

COMMENTARY Originally published in 1928, under the title: *The Irish R.M. and his experiences*, the stories are reprinted from the author's *Some experiences of an R.M., Further experiences of an Irish R.M.*, and *In Mr. Knox's country*. Contents: 'Great-uncle McCarthy', 'When I first met Dr. Hickey', 'In the Curranhilty country', 'Trinket's colt', 'The waters of strife', 'Lisheen races, second-hand', 'Philippa's fox-hunt', 'A misdeal', 'Holy island', 'The policy of the closed door', 'The house of Fahy', 'Occasional licenses', '"Oh love! Oh fire!"', 'The pug-nosed fox', 'A royal command', 'Poisson d'Avril', '"The man that came to buy apples"', 'A conspiracy of silence', 'The boat's share', 'The last day of Shraft', '"A horse! A horse!"', 'Sharper than a ferrett's tooth', 'Oweneen the sprat', 'The Whiteboys', 'The Aussolas Martin cat', 'The finger of Mrs. Knox', 'The friend of her youth', 'Harrington's', 'The maroan pony', 'Major Apollo Riggs', 'The bosom of the McRorys', 'Put down one and carry two', 'The Comte de Pralines', 'The shooting of Shinroe' [ML].

S486 *The sweet cry of hounds* (by E.Œ. Somerville and 'Martin Ross').

+ London: Methuen & Co., 1936 (ill. E.Œ. S. [Somerville]). SOURCE Brown 2, 1473; Lewis, p. 241. LOCATION D, L.

+ Boston, New York: Houghton Mifflin Co., 1937 (ill. E.Œ. Somerville). LOCATION L, InND Loeber coll.

COMMENTARY Contents (excluding a song): 'Commencing Master', 'Hounds', 'Hunting-horses', 'The field', 'The kennel-terrier', 'Dan Russell the fox' (first published as a separate vol. in London in 1911), 'Little red riding-hood in Kerry', 'A betrayal of confidence', '"*Not* the woman's place"' (first published in *Stray-aways*, London, 1920), 'A foxhunt in the southern hills' [ML].

S487 *Sarah's youth* (by E.Œ. Somerville and 'Martin Ross').

+ London, New York, Toronto: Longmans, Green & Co., 1938. SOURCE Brown 2. 1474; Lewis, p. 242. LOCATION D, L.

S488 *Notions in garrison* (by E.Œ. Somerville and 'Martin Ross').

London: Methuen & Co., 1941. SOURCE Brown 2, 1475; Lewis, p. 242. LOCATION L.

S489 *Maria and some other dogs* (by E.Œ. Somerville and 'Martin Ross').

+ London: Methuen & Co., 1949 (ill. E.Œ. Somerville). SOURCE Lewis, p. 242. LOCATION DPL, L.

— COLLECTED WORKS

S490 *The Hitchcock edition of Somerville and Ross.*
New York: Privately printed, The Derrydale Press, 1927, 7 vols. SOURCE OCLC. LOCATION CtY.

SOUTHWELL, Walter Sims, fl. 1875. Novelist.
S491 *Rupert Redmond. A tale of England, Ireland and America* (by Walter Sims Southwell).
+ London: Samuel Tinsley, 1875, 3 vols. SOURCE Allibone Suppl., ii, p. 1369; Brown 2, 1478. LOCATION D, L.
COMMENTARY Rupert, born in England, comes to live with an uncle in Donegal and goes to a local school with the country boys, making both friends and enemies. At age 15 he falls in love with Kathleen, who is a year younger. For a time he goes back to England and renews acquaintance with relatives, some of whom later come to Ireland. Meantime, owing to false rumours, there is estrangement between the lovers, but a meeting sets things right. Rupert goes to America, joins the Union army in the Civil War and is severely wounded. He hears that Kathleen and her father have come to New York. After a long search he finds her there and all is well. They return to Ballycranaght where a series of weddings takes place [Brown 2].

'SPARLING, R.V.M.', pseud. See **RIDDELL, Mrs J.H.**

SPENCE, Elizabeth Isabella, b. Dunkeld (Scotland) 1768, d. Chelsea (London) 1832. Anglo-Scottish novelist and travel writer, EIS was the only daughter of Dr James Spence and his wife Elizabeth Fordyce. She lost her parents at an early age and went to live with relatives in London. After their deaths, she supported herself by writing. Rosina Bulwer Lytton§ (then Rosina Wheeler) claimed to have contributed to the following novel. EIS's travel writing concerns England, Scotland and Wales. SOURCE Allibone ii, p. 2197; Blain, p. 1013; NCBEL 4, p. 1079; ODNB; M. Sadleir, *Bulwer: A panorama* (London 1931), p. 84.
S492 *Dame Rebecca Berry; or, court scenes in the reign of Charles the Second* [anon.].
+ London: Longman, Rees, Orme, Brown & Green, 1827, 3 vols. SOURCE Seen at Ximenes, New York, July 1993; British Fiction; Garside, 1827:65. LOCATION Corvey CME 3–628–47417–5, L, MH.
Stuttgart: Gebr. Franckh, 1827, 3 vols. (trans. as *Rebekka Berry, oder Scenen und Charaktere am Hofe Carls des Zweiten*). SOURCE Garside, 1827:65. LOCATION Staatsbibliothek, Berlin.
COMMENTARY Historical fiction set in London in the second half of the seventeenth century, which prominently features the marquess of Ormond and the earl of Ossory, both Irish peers [RL].

SPOTTISWOODE-ASHE, Mary. See **LUCK, Mrs Mary Churchill.**

'SPRING, Retlaw', pseud. See **HAMILTON, Catherine Jane.**

'SPURSTOWE, William', pseud. See **NUGENT-GRENVILLE, George.**

STACPOOLE, H. de Vere. See **STACPOOLE, Henry de Vere.**

STACPOOLE, Henry de Vere (known as H. de Vere Stacpoole), pseud. 'Tyler de Saix', b. Kingstown (Dun Laoghaire, Co. Dublin) 1863, d. Shanklin, Isle of Wight 1951. Novelist, short story writer, poet and translator, HdeVS was the son of a Church of Ireland clergyman and schoolteacher, the Revd William Church Stacpoole, and his wife Charlotte Mountjoy of Tallaght (Co. Dublin). As a child he travelled widely with his mother, who was of Irish origin but who had been born in Canada. He attended a boarding school in Portarlington (Co. Laois), studied at Malvern College (Worcs.) and trained as a doctor in London. However, he practised only intermittently, first as a ship's doctor, travelling the world and gaining experiences that inspired and provided background for his later novels. His books did not immediately make money and in 1904 he applied for assistance from the Royal Literary Fund. He married Margaret Ann Robson of Tynemouth in 1907, with whom he later jointly wrote some novels. Never aspiring to be part of the Irish Literary Revival, or interested in Irish nationalism, he lived in rural Essex, where he was a JP, and later moved to Bonchurch on the Isle of Wight, which is rendered in his fiction. He published over 60 volumes; his fiction was translated into several languages and was reprinted over the course of fifty years. He contributed short stories to the *Anglo-Saxon Review* (London, Dec. 1899); published several volumes of poetry; translated the work of Sappho and François Villon and wrote a popular biography of Villon (London,1916). He wrote two volumes of autobiography: *Mice and men, 1863–1942* (London, 1942), and *More mice and men* (London, 1945). He is described as having had 'typical Irish geniality mixing with an occasional dash of hot temper' (DNB). For his portraits and papers, see ODNB. SOURCE Brady, p. 226; Brown, p. 283; DNB; EF, pp 371–2; Hogan 2, pp 1137–8; OCIL, p. 533; ODNB; O'Donoghue, p. 436; RIA/DIB; Sutherland, p. 600.

S493   *The intended: A novel* (by H. de Vere Stacpoole).
London: Richard Bentley & Son, 1894. SOURCE Hogan 2, p. 1138; Sutherland, p. 600. LOCATION L.

S494   *Pierrot! A story* (by H. de Vere Stacpoole).
+ London: John Lane; Philadelphia: Henry Altemus, 1896 (Pierrot's Library; ill. C.H.). SOURCE Hogan 2, p. 1138; Wolff, 6503. LOCATION D, L, InND Loeber coll.
COMMENTARY Set during the Anglo-Prussian war and concerns a French boy's sinister relationship with a patricidal double [ODNB].

S495   *Death, the knight and the lady. A ghost story* (by H. de Vere Stacpoole).
London: John Lane, 1897. SOURCE Wolff, 6502. LOCATION L.
COMMENTARY Deals with (at least in part) reincarnation, transvestism, and murder [ODNB].

S496   *The doctor. A study from life* (by H. de Vere Stacpoole).
London: T. Fisher Unwin, 1899. SOURCE Hogan 2, p. 1138 (John Lane, 1895 edn, not located). LOCATION L.
COMMENTARY A story of English village life featuring an old doctor and his French niece who comes to upset his routine [ODNB].

S497   *The Rapin* (by H. de Vere Stacpoole).
+ London: William Heinemann, 1899. LOCATION D, L.

S498   *Pierrette* (by H. de Vere Stacpoole).
+ London, New York: John Lane, 1900 (ill. Charles Robinson). SOURCE Osborne, p. 391. LOCATION CaOTP, D, L, InND Loeber coll.
COMMENTARY Children's stories as told by a relative. Contents, Part 1: 'Pierrette' consisting of: 'The story of the stork', 'The story of the mysterious garden', 'The story of the great bronze tulip', 'The marvellous story of the jar babies and three other entertaining tales' (concerns the overcrowding in China and the ways in which parents can deal with that problem), 'In which the adventures of Queen Cophetua and the story of the jade dragon are

recounted, and the reader is introduced to the novel of the little prince'; Part 2: 'The little prince' [ML].

S499   *The bourgeois* (by H. de Vere Stacpoole).
London: T. Fisher Unwin, 1901. LOCATION D (n.d. edn), L.

S500   *The lady-killer* (by H. de Vere Stacpoole).
London: T. Fisher Unwin, 1902. LOCATION L.

S501   *Fanny Lambert. A novel* (by H. de Vere Stacpoole).
+ London: T. Fisher Unwin, 1906. LOCATION D (1913 edn), L.
+ London: George Newnes, n.d. (as *Fanny Lambert*; ill. F.C. Dickinson). LOCATION D.

S502   *The golden astrolabe* (by H. de Vere Stacpoole and William A. Bryce).
London: Wells Gardner, 1906. LOCATION D (1949, L.

S503   *The crimson azaleas. A novel* (by H. de Vere Stacpoole).
+ London: T. Fisher Unwin, 1907. LOCATION D, L.
+ London: George Newnes, n.d. (as *The crimson azaleas*; ill. F.C. Dickinson). LOCATION D, L.
Philadelphia: Lippincott, 1907. SOURCE Hogan 2, p. 1138.

COMMENTARY No copy of the Philadelphia edn located. Set in Japan where two rough sailors bring up a young Japanese girl. One of the men becomes involved with an old flame, now married [EF, p. 372].

S504   *The meddler. A novel of sorts* (by H. de Vere Stacpoole and W.A. Bryce).
+ London: Alston Rivers, 1907 (ill. Tho. Downey). LOCATION D (n.d. edn), L, InND Loeber coll.

COMMENTARY Set in England, it tells the story of an old general, his son and niece. The general is an inveterate meddler who tries to influence the life of the village parson, which leads to a series of incidents that involve a large part of the village before matters are straightened out again [ML].

S505   *The cottage on the Fells* (by H. de Vere Stacpoole).
London: T. Werner Laurie, [1908]. LOCATION L.

S506   *The blue lagoon. A romance* (by H. de Vere Stacpoole; dedicated to Derek Van Ulsen).
+ London, Leipzig: T. Fisher Unwin, 1908. SOURCE Sutherland, p. 600. LOCATION D, L, InND Loeber coll. (1924, 2nd edn, 30th impr.).
New York: Duffield, 1910. SOURCE Hogan 2, p. 1138 (1908 edn); OCLC. LOCATION MH.

COMMENTARY This was Stacpoole's most successful novel. It was reprinted 23 times in the first 12 years after publication. It captured public imagination, was adapted for the stage in 1920, and was the subject of three films. A romantic adventure story that evoked the wonders of a tropical paradise, it begins when an old sailor, Paddy Button, is shipwrecked and finds himself in a dinghy with two 8-year-old cousins, Dick and Emmeline Lestrange. They land on an idyllic South Seas island where, after some adventures, Button dies of alcoholism. The two children grow up, have a child, and experience a loss of innocence [EF, p. 36; Hogan 2, p. 1137; OCIL, p. 533; ODNB; Sutherland, p. 600].

S507   *The reavers. A tale of wild adventures on the moors of Lorne* (by H. de Vere Stacpoole).
London: Society for Promoting Christian Knowledge, [1908]. LOCATION L.

S508   *Patsy, a story* (by H. de Vere Stacpoole).
+ London: T. Fisher Unwin, 1908 (ill. Thomas Downey). LOCATION D, L, InND Loeber coll.

COMMENTARY Set in Ireland where Patsy, a peasant boy, plays an important role in the life of various people living in or visiting Glen Druid House, Tullagh (Co. Meath). He serves as an (unlikely) page in the house, and is highly popular among its residents because of his cunning spirit. Patsy's uncle, who has escaped from jail and is living in the woods, is plotting with a robber to break into the house to steal the guests' jewellery. They terrorize Patsy into letting them in on a specific night, but the robbers get caught before they can do any harm. Patsy also helps in facilitating a love affair between two guests. When the happy couple marry, they take Patsy with them [ML].

S509   *The pools of silence* (by H. de Vere Stacpoole).
+ London: T. Fisher Unwin, 1909. LOCATION D (n.d. edn), L, InND Loeber coll.
COMMENTARY Prompted by the author's visit to Africa, and set in France and in the Belgian Congo. An American doctor who has just finished his studies in Paris accompanies a big-game hunter on an expedition to the Congo. During the expedition, the doctor realizes the cruelty of the Belgian regime towards the natives and the fact that his employer participates in atrocities. The expedition comes to a halt when a large group of elephants charges the camp and kill practically everyone. On his return to Paris, the doctor takes with him the skull of a little boy who had been wantonly killed by the Belgians. He tries to interest people in Europe in the plight of the natives in the Congo, but he is unsuccessful. This story appeared five years after Roger Casement wrote a report to the British government on the atrocities in the Belgian Congo and it prompted Sir Arthur Conan Doyle to call a meeting to discuss the subject [ML; ODNB].

S510   *Garryowen. The romance of a race-horse* (by H. de Vere Stacpoole; dedicated to author's dog 'Whiskey, a thorough sportsman and faithful friend').
+ London: T. Fisher Unwin, 1909 (ill. photo of author, dedicated on photo to his dog 'Whiskey'). LOCATION D, L, InND Loeber coll.
London: George Newnes, [1913] (as *Garryowen*; ill.). LOCATION D, L,
COMMENTARY A horseracing story set in Ireland and England, it describes the machinations of an Irish landlord to avoid his creditors and to restore his fortunes by training a horse to win an important race. After many adventures, the horse wins, allowing the landlord to pay off his debt and stay on his estate [ML].

S511   *The vulture's prey* (by 'Tyler de Saix').
London: T. Fisher Unwin, 1909. SOURCE RLIN. LOCATION CSt.

S512   *The cruise of the "Kingfisher." A tale of deep-sea adventure* (by H. de Vere Stacpoole; dedicated to author's nephews and niece).
+ London: Wells Gardner, Darton & Co., [1910] (ill. William Rainey). LOCATION D (n.d. edn), L.

S513   *Toto. A Parisian sketch* (by H. de Vere Stacpoole).
+ London: W. Heinemann, 1910 (Popular Edition). SOURCE OCLC. LOCATION D (n.d. edn), TxU.

S514   *The drums of war* (by H. de Vere Stacpoole).
+ London: John Murray, 1910. SOURCE Hogan 2, p. 1138. LOCATION D (n.d. edn), L.

S515   *The ship of coral: A tropical romance* (by H. de Vere Stacpoole).
London: Hutchinson & Co., 1911. SOURCE Hogan 2, p. 1138; RLIN. LOCATION L ([1914] edn).
New York: Duffield & Co., 1911 (as *The ship of coral*). SOURCE RLIN. LOCATION NN.
COMMENTARY Adventures set in the South Pacific where two French sailors are shipwrecked on a reef. They discover the remains of a galleon on the sea floor. Further adventures follow [EF, p. 372].

S516   *The order of release* (by H. de Vere Stacpoole; dedicated to the countess of Warwick).
+ London: Hutchinson & Co., [1912] (ill.). LOCATION D, L.

S517   *The street of the flute-player* (by H. de Vere Stacpoole).

+ London: John Murray, 1912. SOURCE Hogan 2, p. 1138 (Hutchinson, 1912 edn). LOCATION D, L.

COMMENTARY Historical fiction set in Athens, Greece, in the fifth century BC. Both Socrates and Aristophanes feature [EF, p. 372].

S518 *The children of the sea. A romance* (by H. de Vere Stacpoole).
+ London: Hutchinson & Co., 1913. SOURCE Hogan 2, p. 1138. LOCATION D, L.

S519 *Bird cay* (by H. de Vere Stacpoole).
+ London: Wells Gardner, Darton & Co., [1913] (ill.). LOCATION D, L, InND Loeber coll.

COMMENTARY Fiction for juveniles. The hero, a young boy, runs off to sea in a ship that his uncle has sent out to recover a treasure in the Caribbean. After many adventurers, including a mutiny and a shipwreck, the gold is recovered and brought safely home [ML].

S520 *The new optimism* (by H. de Vere Stacpoole).
London: John Lane, 1914. SOURCE Hogan 2, p. 1138. LOCATION L.

S521 *Monsieur de Rochefort. A romance of old Paris* (by H. de Vere Stacpoole).
+ London: Hutchinson & Co., 1914. LOCATION D, L, InND Loeber coll.

S522 *Father O'Flynn* (by H. de Vere Stacpoole).
+ London: Hutchinson & Co., 1914. SOURCE OCIL, p. 533. LOCATION D.

COMMENTARY A sketch of an Irish priest who acts as mediator between social classes. The book was dedicated to opposing politicians Edward Carson, leader of the Irish Unionist Council, and nationalist John Redmond, leader of the Irish Parliamentary Party and supporter of Home Rule for Ireland [OCIL].

S523 *Poppyland* (by H. de Vere Stacpoole).
London: John Lane, 1914 (ill. Laiton Pearce). LOCATION L.

S524 *The beach of dreams. A story of the true world* (by H. de Vere Stacpoole).
+ London: Hutchinson & Co., [1914]. LOCATION D (n.d. edn), L.
+ New York: John Lane, 1919 (as *The beach of dreams. A romance*). LOCATION D.

S525 *The red days. Being the diary of a Prussian officer in France and Belgium during the autumn and early winter of 1914* (as communicated by H. de Vere Stacpoole).
London: Arthur Pierson, 1915. LOCATION L.
Paris: Bloud & Gay, 1916 (trans. by Henry Frichet as *Journal d'un officier Prussian*). SOURCE Hogan 2, p. 1138. LOCATION L.

S526 *The pearl fishers* (by H. de Vere Stacpoole).
+ London: Hutchinson & Co., 1915. SOURCE Hogan 2, p. 1138. LOCATION D, L.

S527 *The blue horizon. Romance from the tropics and the sea* (by H. de Vere Stacpoole).
+ London: Hutchinson & Co., 1915. LOCATION D, L, InND Loeber coll.

COMMENTARY Stories of adventure on land and sea all over the world. The first set of stories all concern sea fishing: 'Skeleton Island', The buccaneers', 'The derelict', 'High tide', 'The great ray', 'The pilot-fish', 'The hunger of the sea'. The second set consists of stories set on land: 'The love offering', 'Under the palms', 'The return of the Viking', 'A love-story', 'The hundred and fifth dream', 'The girl at the gate' [ML].

S528 *Corporal Jacques of the foreign legion* (by H. de Vere Stacpoole).
+ London: Hutchinson & Co., [1916]. LOCATION D, L.

S529 *The reef of stars. A romance of the tropics* (by H. de Vere Stacpoole).
+ London: Hutchinson & Co., [1916]. LOCATION Hogan 2, p. 1138. SOURCE D, L, InND Loeber coll.

COMMENTARY Set in Australia and New Guinea where a number of adventurers are planning to retrieve a cargo of gold, presumed to be buried near a river in New Guinea. The various characters involved in the expedition cannot trust each other and a number of plots and counterplots evolve. Eventually, the best people survive and return to Sydney with the gold [ML].

Stacpoole

S530 *The gold trail, a romance of the South Seas* (by H. de Vere Stacpoole).
New York: John Lane, 1916. SOURCE Hogan 2, p. 1138 (where title is misspelled);
RLIN. LOCATION CSt.

S531 *Sea plunder* (by H. de Vere Stacpoole).
New York: John Lane, 1917. SOURCE Hogan 2, p. 1138; OCLC. LOCATION CtY.

S532 *The starlit garden. A romance of the south* (by H. de Vere Stacpoole; dedicated to
Mary Paterson).
+ London: Hutchinson & Co., 1917. LOCATION D, L.

S533 *In blue waters* (by H. de Vere Stacpoole).
+ London: Hutchinson & Co., 1917. LOCATION D, L.

S534 *The man who lost himself* (by H. de Vere Stacpoole).
+ London: Hutchinson & Co., 1918. SOURCE Hogan 2, p. 1138. LOCATION D, L.

S535 *Under blue skies* (by H. de Vere Stacpoole).
+ London: Hutchinson & Co., [1919]. LOCATION D, L, InND Loeber coll.
COMMENTARY Almost all of the following seafaring stories are set in the South Pacific.
Contents: 'The frigate bird', 'The bay of pearls', 'The long reach', 'Trapped', 'The king of
Maleka', 'A problem of the sea', 'Mrs. Shane', 'De profundis', 'The slayer', 'The message',
'Skies of France' [ML].

S536 *Uncle Simon* (by Margaret [Stacpoole] and H. de Vere Stacpoole).
+ London: Hutchinson & Co., [1920]. LOCATION D, L.

S537 *A man of the islands* (by H. de Vere Stacpoole).
+ London: Hutchinson & Co., [1920]. LOCATION D, L.

S538 *The man who found himself* (by Margaret [Stacpoole] and H. de Vere Stacpoole).
New York: John Lane, 1920. SOURCE Hogan 2, p. 1138; COPAC. LOCATION O.

S539 *Satan: A story of the sea king's country* (by H. de Vere Stacpoole).
+ London: Hutchinson & Co., [1922]. LOCATION D, L.

S540 *Men, women, and beasts* (by H. de Vere Stacpoole).
+ London: Hutchinson & Co., [1922]. SOURCE Hogan 2, p. 1138. LOCATION D, L.
COMMENTARY Contents: 'The monster', 'Was she?', 'Cocktail, Sar?', 'O mommer!', 'The hunter
and the hunted', 'Did Kressler kill his wife?', 'The story of Gombi', 'The story of the three
stiffs', 'The problem', 'The mystery of Captain Knott', 'Luck', 'Kadjaman', 'Mary Jane Somers'
[ML].

S541 *Vanderdecken (the story of a man)* (by H. de Vere Stacpoole; dedicated to S.B. of
San Francisco).
+ London: Hutchinson Co., [1923]. SOURCE COPAC. LOCATION D.
New York: R.M. McBride & Co., 1923 (as *Vanderdecken*). SOURCE Hogan 2, p. 1138;
OCLC. LOCATION MH.

S542 *The garden of God* (by H. de Vere Stacpoole).
+ London: Hutchinson & Co., [1923]. LOCATION D (n.d., 5th edn), L.
+ New York: Dodd, Mead & Co., 1923. SOURCE Hogan 2, p. 1138. LOCATION InND
Loeber coll.
COMMENTARY A sequel to *The blue lagoon* (London, 1908) [ODNB].

S543 *Golden ballast* (by H. de Vere Stacpoole).
London: Hutchinson & Co., [1924]. LOCATION D (n.d. edn), L.
+ New York: Dodd, Mead & Co., 1924. SOURCE Hogan 2, p. 1138 (a Jacobson edn).
LOCATION InND Loeber coll.
COMMENTARY An old boat appears to have an unusual ballast of gold. In order to claim it, the
owner has to first bury it on an island in the Caribbean and then dig it up. Various adven-
tures take place before this is accomplished [ML].

S544   *The house of crimson shadows* (by H. de Vere Stacpoole).
London: Hutchinson & Co., [1925]. SOURCE Hogan 2, p. 1138 (mentions a 1920 edn, but not found). LOCATION L.

S545   *The gates of morning* (by H. de Vere Stacpoole).
London: Hutchinson & Co., [1925]. SOURCE Hogan 2, p. 1138. LOCATION L.
COMMENTARY Another sequel, along with *The garden of God* (London, [1923]), to *The blue lagoon* (London, 1908) [ODNB].

S546   *Stories East and West. Tales of men and women* (by H. de Vere Stacpoole).
+ London: Hutchinson & Co., [1926]. LOCATION D, L.
COMMENTARY Contents: 'The story of a girl', 'The confession', 'The shoe pinches', 'The story of Dakea and the charm', 'The voice of the torrent', 'Story of Kanoa and the djin', 'In the house of the Russian', 'The case of Mrs. Keller', 'The ten-franc counter', 'The hoof of Hiram Schumways', 'Where the great stars burn', 'Chattering Jimmy', 'Johnson and the viatique', 'Kitiwik' (in 2 parts and 12 chapters) [RL].

S547   *The city in the sea* (by H. de Vere Stacpoole).
London: Hutchinson & Co., 1926. LOCATION L.

S548   *The mystery of uncle Bollard* (by H. de Vere Stacpoole).
+ London, Toronto, Melbourne, Sidney: Cassell & C., 1927. LOCATION D, L.
Garden City (NY): Doubleday, Doran, 1928. SOURCE Hogan 2, p. 1138 (where Bollard is misspelled 'Ballard'). LOCATION DCL.

S549   *Goblin market. A romance of to-day* (by H. de Vere Stacpoole).
+ London, Toronto, Melbourne, Sydney: Cassell & Co., [1927]. SOURCE Hogan 2, p. 1138. LOCATION D (n.d. edn), L.
+ New York: George H. Doran, 1927 (as *Goblin market. A romance of to-day telling how Anthony Harrop, a respectable citizen, met in with the goblin folk, how he attended their market, what he bought there, and how it served him*). LOCATION InND Loeber coll.

S550   *Roxanne* (by H. de Vere Stacpoole; dedicated to all young married people).
+ London, Toronto, Melbourne, Sydney: Cassell & Co., 1928. LOCATION D, L.

S551   *Tropic love* (by H. de Vere Stacpoole).
London: Readers Library Publishing Co., [1928]. LOCATION L.

S552   *Eileen of the trees* (by H. de Vere Stacpoole).
London: Cassell & Co., 1929. LOCATION L.
Garden City (NY): Doran, 1929. SOURCE Hogan 2, p. 1138. LOCATION O, Los Angeles Public Library.

S553   *The chank shell. A tropical romance of love and treasure* (by H. de Vere Stacpoole).
+ London: Hutchinson & Co., [1930]. LOCATION D, L.

S554   *The girl on the golden reef. A romance of the blue lagoon* (by H. de Vere Stacpoole).
+ London Hutchinson & Co., [1930]. SOURCE Hogan 2, p. 1138 (1929 edn). LOCATION D, L.
COMMENTARY Another sequel to *The blue lagoon* (London, 1908) [RL].

S555   *The tales of Mynheer Amayat* (by H. de Vere Stacpoole).
+ London: George Newnes, [1930]. LOCATION D, L, InND Loeber coll.
COMMENTARY Detective stories set mainly in the Dutch East Indies. Contents: 'The raja of Gool', 'The necklace of Mynheer Van Maurick', 'Kohn', 'The witch doctor', 'Lantern Lane', 'Kow Loon', 'The house of the clouds', 'The place of confusion', 'The glass of Constantia', 'The bag of sapphires', 'The killing of Madame Hildebron', 'The amazing story of Wang', 'The story of O Toyo', 'Dead girl finotte' [RL].

S556   *Pacific gold* (by H. de Vere Stacpoole).
London: W. Collins Sons & Co., [1931]. LOCATION D (n.d. edn), L.

New York: Sears, 1931. SOURCE Hogan 2, p. 1138. LOCATION MH.

S557   *Love on the Adriatic* (by H. de Vere Stacpoole).
+ London: Ernest Benn, 1932. LOCATION D (n.d. edn), L.

S558   *The lost caravan* (by H. de Vere Stacpoole).
+ London, Glasgow, Sydney, Auckland: W. Collins Sons & Co., 1932. LOCATION L, InND Loeber coll.

COMMENTARY Set in the Balkans and North Africa. Jean Matisse, a young French artist, travels in the Balkans where he falls in love with a gipsy girl. After a quarrel with a German baron, he believes he has killed the baron and he escapes in a boat. At a Moroccan port he joins the Foreign Legion. When he hears that the baron is not dead after all, he escapes and meets up with the girl. They join someone who travels in the desert, but they are deserted and die [ML].

S559   *The blue Lagoon omnibus* (by H. de Vere Stacpoole).
London: Hutchinson & Co., [1933]. LOCATION L.

COMMENTARY Reprint of five related volumes in one single volume: 'The blue lagoon' (first published separately in London in 1908), 'The garden of God' (first published separately in London in [1923]), 'The gates of morning' (first published separately in London in [1925]), 'The girl of the golden reef' (first published separately in London in 1930), 'The beach of dreams' (first published separately in London in [1914]) [RL].

S560   *Molly Beamish. A mid summer-day's dream* (by H. de Vere Stacpoole).
London: Ernest Benn, 1933. LOCATION L.

S561   *Mandarin gardens* (by H. de Vere Stacpoole).
+ London: Hutchinson & Co., [1933]. LOCATION D, L.

S562   *The naked soul* (by H. de Vere Stacpoole).
London: W. Collins, 1933. SOURCE Hogan 2, p. 1138. LOCATION L.

S563   *The vengeance of Mynheer Van Lok and other stories* (by H. de Vere Stacpoole).
+ London: Hutchinson & Co., [1934]. SOURCE Hogan 2, p. 1138. LOCATION D, L.

COMMENTARY Contents: 'The vengeance of Mynheer Van Lok', 'The lost Diana', 'The children of Dr. Hoffmeyer', 'The last voyage of Capt. McGovern', 'A rum story', 'The story of Nan Tok the fisherman', 'The seeds of dissension', 'The ho-ho bird', 'Deep in the forest', 'The man from Sulu', 'The story of Captain Kane', 'The head of the postmaster-general', 'The girl and the joss', 'The luck of the Templetons', 'William Brown' [ML].

S564   *Green coral* (by H. de Vere Stacpoole).
London: Hutchinson & Co., [1935]. LOCATION L.

S565   *The longshore girl. A romance* (by H. de Vere Stacpoole).
London: Hutchinson & Co., [1935]. SOURCE Hogan 2, p. 1138. LOCATION L.

S566   *The sunstone* (by H. de Vere Stacpoole).
+ London: Hutchinson & Co., [1936]. LOCATION D, L.

S567   *Ginger Adams* (by H. de Vere Stacpoole).
+ London: Hutchinson & Co., [1937]. LOCATION D (n.d. edn), L.

S568   *High-yaller* (by H. de Vere Stacpoole).
London: Hutchinson & Co., [1938]. LOCATION L.

S569   *Old sailors never lie, and other tales of land and sea. By one of them* (by H. de Vere Stacpoole).
London: Hutchinson & Co., [1938]. LOCATION L.

S570   *Due East of Friday* (by H. de Vere Stacpoole).
London: Hutchinson & Co., [1939]. LOCATION L.

S571   *The ghost girl* (by H. de Vere Stacpoole).
London: Hutchinson & Co., 1940. SOURCE Brown 2, 1481. LOCATION D (n.d. edn), L.

COMMENTARY Jimmy Tassel comes to Ireland to purchase a colt out of his uncle's stables, in the hope that his father might pay off an old grudge against the uncle if the colt turns out to be valuable. The result is tragic, however: a girl who loves the horse and tries to kill it rather than let it go, meets her own death [Brown 2].

S572 *An American in Oxford* (by H. de Vere Stacpoole).
London, Melbourne: Hutchinson & Co., 1941. LOCATION L.

S573 *Oxford goes to war. A novel* (by H. de Vere Stacpoole).
London: Hutchinson & Co., [1943]. LOCATION L.

S574 *The doctor's love story and that kid!* (by H. de Vere Stacpoole).
London: Todd, 1943. LOCATION L.

S575 *Harley Street. A novel* (by H. de Vere Stacpoole).
London, Melbourne: Hutchinson & Co., 1946. SOURCE Brown 2, 1482. LOCATION D (n.d. edn), L.

COMMENTARY Dr O'Flynn is a busy doctor in a London slum largely populated by the Irish; he is helped by Biddy, his housekeeper from Kerry. One day he finds on his doorstep a baby, apparently abandoned. He takes it to Miss Julia Corkran of an Irish country family who is single and rich, but ailing, in the hope that mothering the infant will cure her. However, he discovers that the baby was not abandoned but left for a few minutes by its elder sister. In the end, the baby dies [Brown 2].

S576 *The story of my village* (by H. de Vere Stacpoole).
+ London, Melbourne: Hutchinson & Co., [1947]. LOCATION D, L.
COMMENTARY Set in Bonchurch, Isle of Wight, where the author settled in 1922 [ODNB].

S577 *The man in armour* (by H. de Vere Stacpoole).
London, Melbourne: Hutchinson & Co., [1949]. LOCATION L.

STACPOOLE, Margaret Anne. Co-author. See **STACPOOLE, Henry de Vere.**

STAMER, Harriet Elizabeth (later countess of Rovigo), b. Ennis (Co. Clare) 1816, d. Co. Clare? 1875. Unpublished short story writer and autobiographer in novel form, HES was the daughter of Col. Stamer of Stamer Park, near Ennis (Co. Clare) and likely grew up on this estate. She travelled extensively abroad and became a fluent linguist. Her short stories, contained in ten large quarto volumes, which she illustrated in an oriental style, were never published (present whereabouts not known). In 1839 she married Marie Napoleon Rene Savary, son of Gen. Savary, who had been an aide-de-camp to Napoleon (later created duke of Rovigo). In 1840 she and her husband settled at Stamer Park and she was buried at the family vault at Killoo. SOURCE G. O'Connell, 'Harriet Elizabeth Stamer duchess of Rovigo (1816–1875)' in C. Ó Murchadha (ed.), *County Clare Studies* (Ennis, 2000), pp 207–9; RL; *Connaught Journal*, April 9, 1840.

STARKEY, Digby Pilot, b. Dublin 1806, d. 1876. Poet, miscellaneous writer and barrister, DPS graduated BA at TCD in 1827 and MA in 1833. He was called to the Irish Bar in 1831 and became accountant-general in the court of chancery. He contributed poetry and prose to the *Dublin University Magazine* (largely under the pseuds 'Advena' and 'Godfrey Massingberd'); to *The book of Irish ballads* (ed. by D.F. M'Carthy, Dublin, 1846), and to *Chambers's Journal* (Edinburgh). He wrote three volumes of poetry: *Judas: A tragic mystery* (Dublin, 1843); *Theoria* (Dublin, 1847), and *Anastasia* (London, 1858). He was the author also of *Ireland. The political tracts of Menenius* (Dublin, 1849). SOURCE Allibone, ii, p. 2227; BLC; Boase, vi, p. 609; W.E. Hall, pp 42–3, 117; Irish pseudonyms; NYPL; O'Donoghue, p. 436; RIA/DIB.

S578   *John Twiller: A romance of the heart* (by Digby Pilot Starkey LLD; dedicated to Sir Bernard Burke, Ulster king of arms).
   + London: Tinsley Bros, 1869. SOURCE Rafroidi, ii, p. 343; OCLC. LOCATION L.
COMMENTARY First serialized in the *Dublin University Magazine* (1856–57), under the pseudonym 'Godfrey Massingberd'. No Irish content; it is the story of a would-be poet who has fantasies about being discovered [ML; RL; W.E. Hall, p. 190].

'STARR, Sidney', pseud. See **GALLAHER, Miss Fannie**.

STEIN, C., fl. 1897. Short story writer, CS must have been a military officer. The following is the only book listed by this author in the BLC. SOURCE RL.
S579   *Self and comrades. "Tales by a soldier"* (by C. Stein).
   + London: Vinton & Co., 1897. LOCATION PC, L.
COMMENTARY Stories of soldiers' lives in various parts of the world, some of which take place in Ireland. The stories were first published in *Baily's Magazine* (London) [ML].

STEPHENS, Mrs Ann S. See **STEPHENS, Mrs Ann Sophia**.

STEPHENS, Mrs Ann Sophia (née Winterbotham; known as **Ann S. Stephens**), b. Derby (CT) 1810, d. Newport (RI) 1886. American novelist, ASS was the daughter of John Winterbotham. In 1831 she married Edward Stephens, a newspaper man. They moved to Portland (ME), where she became the editor of the *Portland Magazine*. After moving to New York, she edited the *Ladies' Companion*. She travelled in Europe from 1850 to 1852, after which she conducted her own magazine, *Mrs. Stephens' Illustrated New Monthly*. She wrote over 30 novels and several dime novels published by Beadle in New York, but the following is her only novel with known Irish content. SOURCE Allibone, ii, pp 2237–8; Dime novels (biographical sketch); Wright, ii, p. 315 (list of novels); Wright web.
S580   *The curse of gold* (by Ann S. Stephens).
   + Philadelphia: T.B. Peterson, 1869. SOURCE Wright, ii, 2356. LOCATION Wright web.
COMMENTARY The story begins in Bellevue hospital in New York City; an Irish woman, Margaret Dillon, saves the life of a baby and its young mother, Catharine, both of whom are threatened by a cruel nurse. Mrs Dillon takes in the baby as her own (unbeknownst to Catherine), and attempts to assist Catharine herself by taking her to a benevolent society. In the end, Catharine's missing husband returns and the child is restored to them [ML; JB].

STERNE, Laurence, pseud. 'Mr. Yorick', b. Clonmel (Co. Tipperary) 1713, d. London 1768. Novelist and clergyman, LS was the Irish-born son of an impoverished English army ensign and an Irish mother, Agnes Nuttle. According to the DNB, he spent his early years in Irish garrison towns with various Irish relatives, living at Clonmel (Co. Tipperary), Annamoe (Co. Wicklow), Dublin, Mullingar (Co. Westmeath), Tullynally (Co. Westmeath), and Carrickfergus (Co. Antrim). At age 10 he was sent to school in Halifax (Yorks.) and later went to Jesus College, Cambridge, where he graduated BA in 1736 and MA in 1740. After taking orders, he secured a living near York in 1738. He married in 1741 and lived at Stillington (Yorks.) where he was attached to the nearby church of Sutton. He preached there regularly at the weekends and during the week spent his time reading (John Locke, Cervantes and Rabelais were formative influences) and painted, played music and went hunting. He also dabbled in farming to supplement his income. He contributed to various periodicals, published several sermons, one of which – *Abuses of conscience* (York, 1750) – was influenced by Jonathan Swift's§ sermon on the same topic and later appeared in *Tristam Shandy*. The publication of the first two volumes of *Tristam Shandy* at his own expense in York in 1759 made him famous and thereafter he spent much of his time in London overseeing publication of further volumes of *Tristam*, or abroad in France and Italy in search of better health. In addition to *Tristam Shandy*, LS published in 1760 *The sermons of Mr. Yorick*, and he also used the name 'Yorick' for the narrator of *A sentimental journey* (London, 1768). His work later proved influential on such Irish writers as James Joyce and Samuel Beckett. Sterne died of pleurisy in London in 1768. For his portraits and papers, see ODNB and Elmes. SOURCE Allibone, ii, p. 2242–4; Boylan, p. 369; M. Byrd, *Tristam Shandy* (London, 1985); A.H. Cash, *Laurence Sterne: the early and middle years* (London, 1975); DLB, xxxix; P. de Voogd & J. Neubauer, *The reception of Laurence Stone in Europe* (London, 2004); Elmes, pp 190–2; Field Day, i, pp 684, 758–9, ii, p. 1006; L. Hartley, *Laurence Sterne: a biographical essay* (1943, repr. Chapel Hill, NC, 1968); Hogan 2, pp 1147–8; K. Monkman (ed.), *Sterne's memoirs. A hitherto unrecorded holograph now brought to light in facsimile* (Shandy Hall, 1985); OCIL, pp 539–40; ODNB; O'Donoghue, pp 438–9; RIA/DIB.

S581   *A political romance addressed to —, Esq. of York* [anon.].

London: Printed [for the author?] by J. Murdoch, 1759. SOURCE DNB; OCIL, p. 539; Raven, 508; ESTC t014710. LOCATION MH.

York: [n.p.], 1759. SOURCE Black, 743; DNB; Raven, 509. LOCATION L, CtY.

Menston: Scholar Press, 1971 (ed. by K. Monkman). SOURCE COPAC. LOCATION E.

COMMENTARY Not published and, therefore, exceedingly rare. Epistolary pamphlet satirizing ecclesiastical lawyers and based on a real dispute around 1749 between Dr Francis Topham, an ecclesiastical lawyer, the bishop of York, and Dean Fountayne. Reprinted many times as *The history of a warm watch-coat* (e.g., in *The complete works of Laurence Sterne*, Berwick, 1800) [M. Byrd, *Tristram Shandy* (London), p. 21–2] ...

S582   *The life and opinions of Tristram Shandy, gentleman* [anon.].

[York]: [Printed by Ann Ward], 1760, vols. 1 and 2. SOURCE Forster, 2634; Raven, 507; ESTC t014780. LOCATION L, ViU.

London: R. & J. Dodsley, 1761, vols. 3 and 4. SOURCE Forster, 2635; Raven, 673; ESTC t014705. LOCATION L, MH.

London: T. Becket & P.A. de Hondt, 1762, vols. 5 and 6. SOURCE Forster, 2636; Raven, 677; ESTC t014706. LOCATION L, MH.

London: T. Becket & P.A. de Hondt, 1765, vols. 7 and 8. SOURCE Raven, 940; Forster, 2637; ESTC t014820. LOCATION L, MH.

London: T. Becket, 1767, vol. 9. SOURCE Block, p. 225; Forster, 2638. LOCATION L.

+ Dublin: D. Chamberlaine & S. Smith, 1760 [1761], vols. 1 and 2. SOURCE Cole, p. 240; Munter, p. 42; Raven, 587 (see also 588, 589); Pollard 2, p. 97; ESTC t014717. LOCATION D, Dt, L. COMMENTARY *Dublin edn* Dillon Chamberlaine's two Dublin printings of the first two vols preceded the first printing in London by Dodsley [M. Pollard, *Dublin's trade in books 1550–1800* (Oxford, 1989), p. 98].

Dublin: H. Saunders, D. Chamberlaine & S. Smith, 1761, vols. 3 and 4. SOURCE Cole, p. 240; Raven, 676; ESTC t014691. LOCATION L.

Dublin: H. Saunders, 1765, vols. 5 to 8. SOURCE Cole, p. 240; Raven, 942; ESTC t014738. LOCATION C, CtY.

Dublin: W. & W. Smith, J. Exshaw, H. Saunders, S. Watson & W. Colles, 1767, vol. 9. SOURCE Cole, p. 241; ESTC t168420. LOCATION C, CtY.

Amsterdam: A.E. Munnikhuisen, 1776–79, 5 vols. (trans. into Dutch by Bernardus Brunius as *Het leven en de gevoelens van Tristram Shandy*). SOURCE Pickering & Chatto cat. 735/152; COPAC. LOCATION L.

Neuchâtel: La Société Typographique, 1777, 2 vols. SOURCE Rochedieu, p. 316; COPAC. LOCATION C.

Berlin, Stralsund: Gottlieb August Langen, 1762–72, 9 parts in 1 vol. (trans. as *Das Leben und die Meynungen des Herrn Tristram Shandy*). SOURCE Burmester cat. 32/261; COPAC. LOCATION Univ. College, London (1769 edn).

A Yorcke, et ce trouve à Paris: Ruault, 1776, 4 vols. in 2 (trans. by M. Frénais (vols. 1–2) and [marquis] Charles François de Bannay (vols. 3–4) as *La vie et les opinions de Tristram Shandy*). SOURCE Hall cat. 8/125; ESTC t14762; COPAC. LOCATION CtY.

Hamburg: Bode, 1774, 9 vols. in 8 (trans. by Johann Joachim Christian Bode as *Tristram Schandis. Leben unde Meynungen*). SOURCE Spelman cat. 45/247.

Vienna: R. Sammer, 1798. SOURCE Gecker, 1013. LOCATION PU.

COMMENTARY Written in a form of an autobiography, it tries to find an explanation of Tristram's character in the circumstances of his conception. The text is constructed as a series of digressions to a story that never takes off and includes multitudinous unrelated thoughts that go through the minds of the characters involved [Field Day, i, pp 705–17; OCIL, p. 311; ODNB].

S583   *A sentimental journey through France and Italy* (by 'Mr. Yorick').

London: T. Becket & P.A. de Hondt, 1768, 2 vols. SOURCE Raven, 1234; Forster, 2640; Gecker, 1014; ESTC t014747; McBurney & Taylor, 869. LOCATION L, PU, IU.

Dublin: G. Faulkner, J. Hoey Snr, J. Exshaw & H. Saunders, 1768, 2 vols. SOURCE Cole, p. 242; Raven, 1237; ESTC t014769. LOCATION D, L.

Belfast: Printed by James Magee, 1768. SOURCE Anderson 3, p. 8 (known from Pinkerton MSS). COMMENTARY *Belfast edn* No copy located [RL].

Amsterdam: M.-M. Rey; Paris: Ganguery, 1769, 2 vols. in 1 (trans. by M. Frénais as *Le voyage sentimental*). SOURCE Rochedieu, p. 317; COPAC. LOCATION L.

Amsterdam: Munnikhuisen, 1778 (trans. into Dutch by Bernarus Brunius as *Sentimenteele reis door Frankrijk en Italië. Gedaan door den Heer Yorick*). SOURCE Cat. Koninklijke Bibliotheek, The Hague. LOCATION Koninklijke Bibliotheek, The Hague.

Hamburg: J.H. Cramer, 1769 (trans. as *Yoricks empfindsame Reise durch Frankreich und Italien*). SOURCE Burmester cat. 58/194; OCLC (1771 edn). LOCATION MH (1771 edn).

Lausanne: Mourer, Cadet, 1786, 2 vols. in 1 (trans. by Mr Frenais as *Voyage sentimental*). SOURCE Burmester cat. 58/195.

Geneva: [publisher?], 1779 (trans. by Frénais as *Voyage sentimentale, suivi des Lettres d'Yorick à Éliza*). SOURCE Rochedieu, p. 317.

Philadelphia: Robert Bell, 1770. SOURCE Cole, p. 77; OCLC. LOCATION Rutgers Univ.

COMMENTARY Loosely based on the author's trips to the Continent after 1762 [OCIL, p. 512].

— COLLECTED WORKS (a selection only).

S584   *The beauties of Sterne; Including all his pathetic tales, and most distinguished observations on life. Selected for the heart of sensibility* (dedication and preface signed 'W.H.').

London: T. Davies, J. Ridley, W. Flexney, J. Sewel & G. Kearsley, 1781. SOURCE ESTC n32755. LOCATION C, CtY.

Dublin: Printed by Stephen Colbert, 1784 (with considerable additions). SOURCE Pollard 2, p. 110; ESTC t188316. LOCATION O, Univ. of Michigan.

Philadelphia: William Spotswood, 1789. SOURCE Cole, p. 242; OCLC. LOCATION Rutgers Univ.

Boston: Andrews & Cummings, 1807. SOURCE OCLC. LOCATION CtY.

S585   *The works of Laurence Sterne, A.M. prebendary of York, and vicar of Sutton on the Forest, and of Stillington, near York. With the life of the author.*

Dublin: H. Saunders, D. Chamberlaine & J. Potts, 1770, 4th edn, 6 vols. SOURCE Cole, p. 242; ESTC n25772. LOCATION D.

[Philadelphia]: London printed, Philadelphia re-printed: James Humphreys Jun., 1774, 6 vols. SOURCE ESTC w20946. LOCATION American Antiquarian Society, Worcester (MA).

S586 *The works of Laurence Sterne. To which is prefixed an account of the life and writings of the author.*
London: n.p., 1775, 7 vols. SOURCE ESTC n25747. LOCATION O, MH.

S587 *The works of Laurence Sterne in ten volumes complete. With a life of the author written by himself.*
London: W. Strahan, J. Rivington & Sons, J. Dodsley, G. Kearsley, T. Lowndes, G. Robinson, T. Cadell, J. Murray, T. Becket, R. Baldwin & T. Evans, 1780, 10 vols. SOURCE McBurney & Taylor, 870; ESTC t14823. LOCATION L (1788 edn), TxU.

S588 *The works of Laurence Sterne.*
Berwick: John Taylor, 1800, 8 vols. SOURCE OCLC. LOCATION PU.

S589 *The Shakespeare Head edition of the writings of Laurence Sterne.*
Oxford: Basil Blackwell, 1926–27 (7 vols.). SOURCE Hogan, 2, p. 1147; OCLC. LOCATION LCA.

S590 *The Florida edition of the works of Laurence Sterne.*
Gainesville (FL): University Presses of Florida, 1978–2002, 6 vols. SOURCE Hogan, 2, p. 1147; OCLC. LOCATION NYU.

STEUART, John A. See **STEUART, John Alexander**.

STEUART, John Alexander (know as **John A. Steuart**), b. Perthshire (Scotland) 1861, d. 1932. Scottish adventure and melodrama novelist, journalist and editor, JAS worked in a bank before travelling to Ireland and then to the US, where he worked as a journalist in the west. He returned to England in the late 1880s and edited and modernized *Publisher's Circle* (not identified). He also wrote about his countryman, Robert Louis Stevenson. SOURCE Allibone Suppl., ii, p. 1385; EF, pp 373–4; Sutherland, p. 603.

S591 *Kilgroom. A story of Ireland* (by John A. Steuart; dedicated to William Ewart Gladstone, MP).
+ London: Sampson Low & Co., 1891. SOURCE Brown, 1544 (probably mistakenly identified a 1890 edn); Dixson, p. 223. LOCATION L.
+ New York: Belford & Co. [1890]. LOCATION L.
COMMENTARY A story about the land war in the south of Ireland, describing the evils of landlordism. The thirst for vengeance, engendered by oppression, takes possession of a young peasant, almost stifling his love for his betrothed and ruining his life [Brown].

STEWARD (also Stewart), **Mrs T.F.** (née Isabella Travers), b. Cork, d. Suffolk 1857 (1867 according to O'Donoghue). Novelist and poet, Isabella was the daughter of Robert Travers, a Cork solicitor. She married Thomas Steward of Yarmouth in 1827. ODNB records an army officer James Travers (1820–1884) of Cork who served mainly in India and was survived by his widow Mary Isabella Travers, but it is not known if or how these persons were related to this author. O'Donoghue lists as one of her uncles Admiral Sir Eaton Stannard Travers, whose names recall author Eaton Stannard Barrett§, also of Cork. SOURCE Brown 2, p. 251; BLC; ODNB; O'Donoghue, p. 439; J. Windele, *Historical and descriptive notices of the City of Cork and its vicinity* (Cork, [c.1843]).

S592 *The prediction* [anon.].

+ London: Saunders & Otley, 1834, 3 vols. SOURCE Block, p. 226; J. Windele, *Historical and descriptive notices of the City of Cork and its vicinity* (Cork, [*c*.1843]). SOURCE Garside 2, 1834:73. LOCATION Corvey CME 3–628–48369–7, L, MH.

COMMENTARY The novel starts out in Killarney and is set mainly in Ireland. One of the main characters is called Lady Blessingham (possibly an allusion to the countess of Blessington§) [ML; RL].

S593 *The Mascarenhas; a legend of the Portuguese in India* [anon.].
London: Smith, Elder & Co., 1836, 3 vols. SOURCE Block, p. 226; J. Windele, *Historical and descriptive notices of the City of Cork and its vicinity* (Cork, [*c*.1843]). SOURCE Garside 2, 1834:73. LOCATION L, NUC.

COMMENTARY There are notes at the end of each vol. [Garside 2].

S594 *The interdict. A novel* [anon.].
+ London: T. & W. Boone, 1840, 3 vols. SOURCE Block, p. 226; J. Windele, *Historical and descriptive notices of the City of Cork and its vicinity* (Cork, [*c*.1843]). LOCATION L, NUC.

COMMENTARY Set in Ireland and features the O'Toole and Fitzgerald families, who live near the Sugar Loaf Mountain in Co. Wicklow. Contains a description of a country house library, and refers to current literary tastes. Grace McQuillan tells fairy tales and fortunes. There is an interdict preventing both Walter and his sister from marrying. Walter and other relatives travel to England and Germany. Eventually all is resolved – Walter and his sister do marry and return to visit Ireland once more [RL].

S595 *Catherine Erlof. A tale of the Thirty Years War* (by T.F. Steward).
London: T.C. Newby, 1851, 3 vols. SOURCE Brown 2, 1493. LOCATION L, NUC.

COMMENTARY Historical fiction set in Germany during the early-seventeenth century. In this story, the Irishman Tyrell of Tyrone takes a leading part, and his follower, Danny Neal, provides comic interludes [RL; Brown 2].

S596 *Marguerite's legacy. A novel* (by T.F. Steward).
+ London: Hurst & Blackett, 1857, 3 vols. LOCATION L.

COMMENTARY Set in France: the story starts in the Dordogne in 1810 and deals with contemporary political events. There are some connections with the south of Ireland. A Miss Kitty McCarthy features. There is also an Irish servant, Clara, who dreams of cluricaunes [RL; ML].

STEWART, Mrs Agnes M., fl. 1846. Novelist, biographer, writer of devotional works and fiction for juveniles, AMS was most likely an Irish Catholic but she probably lived in London, since the preface to the London edn of her *Florence O'Neill* is dated from that city in 1873, but the preface to her *Earl Nugent's daughter* (London, [1883]) is dated from Bowdon, Cheshire. She contributed to periodicals such as *Young Ireland* (Dublin, 1876). In 1862 she was the editor of the *Rose & Shamrock Magazine*, which was co-published in London and Dublin, suggesting an Irish connection. The following list gives only those works with Irish content. It is likely that a further investigation will add to this list. She was also the author of *Original poetry, for young persons* (London, 1846). In addition, she wrote a biography of John Fisher, cardinal bishop of Rochester (London, 1879). SOURCE Allibone, ii, p. 2253; Allibone Suppl., ii, p. 1389; BLC; Brown, p. 285; Personal communication, Mary Pollard, Oct. 1994; NCBEL 4, p. 1872; RL; Rowan cat. 53B/1310.

S597 *The world and the cloister, to which is added, prefatory remarks on a lecture on nunneries, lately delivered at Bath by the Rev. Herbert Seymour* (by Agnes M. Stewart; dedicated to the cardinal archbishop of Westminster).
+ London, Dublin, Derby: Richardson & Son, 1852 (subscribers' list). SOURCE Alston, p. 415; COPAC. LOCATION L (destroyed), C.

COMMENTARY Religious fiction with Irish content. Many of the subscribers are Irish and include Irish convents. A long preface by the author is directed against the Revd M. Hobart Seymour's writing on nunneries (n.l., 1852) [BLC; CM; RM].

S598 *Grace O'Halloran; or, Ireland and its peasantry. A tale of the day* (by Agnes M. Stewart).

+ London: Charles Dolman; Dublin: Powell & Bellew, 1857 (subscribers' list). SOURCE Brown, 1546 (Dublin, Gill, 1857 edn, which has not been located). LOCATION D.

Baltimore: Kelly, Hedian & Piet, 1860. LOCATION Univ. of Maryland, College Park.

+ Baltimore: John B. Piet, n.d. LOCATION DCU.

COMMENTARY Rev. in *Catholic Mirror* (17 Mar. 1860, p. 6). According to the preface, the vol. was addressed to Catholic readers. Many of the subscribers are Roman Catholic clergy [RL].

S599 *Justice & mercy; or, a tale of All-Hallows e'en* (by Agnes M. Stewart).

+ London: C. Dolman, 1858 (subscribers' list). LOCATION D.

COMMENTARY Among the subscribers are many Irish names, including members of the clergy and nuns [RL].

S600 *The O'Donnells of Innismore; or, the two Marys* [anon.] (dedicated to Laura Southwell).

+ London, Dublin, Derby: Richardson, 1864. LOCATION D, Dcc.

COMMENTARY According to the preface, the author founded the story on a tale from Mrs S.C. Hall's§ *Ireland, its character, and its scenery* (London, 1841–3, 3 vols.). General O'Donnell, of Irish descent, who lives in Coblenz (Germany) has poor relatives, the Flohrbergs. Maria, their daughter, visits the O'Donnells to ask for help to obtain a position in England and become a governess in the Montague family. The family is not sympathetic to her. Another main character, Mary O'Donnell, lives in Innismore in Ireland, and is the daughter of a servant. Maria and Mary meet in England and become friends. Maria is accused of theft and is tried and acquitted. She is also confronted with her real mother. She moves to the O'Donnell house in the south of Ireland, and Mary becomes a nun [ML; RL].

S601 *Father Cleveland; or, the Jesuit* [anon.].

+ London: Burns, Lambert, Oates, 1867 (subscribers' list). SOURCE Alston, p. 415. LOCATION L, InND Loeber coll.

Boston: Patrick Donahoe, 1867. SOURCE COPAC. LOCATION L.

New York, Boston, Montreal: D. & J. Sadlier & Co., [1869?]. SOURCE DCU, Catholic Americana files.

COMMENTARY No copy of the New York, Sadlier edn located. Religious fiction about the Catholic gentry, supposedly based on a true story. An Irish girl, Aileen Desmond, is staying with the family of squire Cleveland who has in mind that she should marry his oldest son, a good-for-nothing. Aileen does not care for him and feels more at ease with the younger son, Edward, who is planning to enter a religious order. The daughter Maude is a frivolous girl and is about to marry a spendthrift. Aileen's parents fall on hard times and in order to support them, she becomes a governess. She emigrates to Canada where she assumes a new name to dissociate her parents from the shame of having a daughter who earns a living. Initially she teaches music and later sings on the stage. She becomes well-to-do but, envious of her success, women spread the rumour that she is living under an assumed name and must be concealing a serious blot on her character. She loses all patronage. When a well-meaning young woman tells her why, Aileen becomes ill. The young woman feels extremely guilty and decides not to leave Aileen. The priest of the parish happens to be Father Cleveland, the squire's younger son. He clears her name, eases her last days, then organizes a subscription for her parents, which he delivers after her death. He finds them living with his sister Maud, who is now living a respectable life. The main perpetrator of the slander is so shocked by the effects of her words that she enters the convent of the Poor Clares [ML].

S602   *Florence O'Neill, the rose of St. Germains; or, the siege of Limerick* (by Agnes M. Stewart).

+ Baltimore: Kelly, Piet & Co., 1872 (ill. John Karst). SOURCE Brown, 1547 (1871 edn, but this may be mistaken). LOCATION D, NUC.

+ New York: P.J. Kenedy, 1884 (ill. P.J. Kenedy). LOCATION D (n.d. edn), DCU.

+ London: Burns & Oates, 1873 (subscribers' list). SOURCE COPAC. LOCATION PC, Dt.

COMMENTARY Historical fiction set in Ireland during the late-seventeenth century [RL].

S603   *The Limerick veteran; or, the foster sisters* (by Agnes M. Stewart).

+ Baltimore: Kelly, Piet & Co., 1873. SOURCE Brown, 1548; DCU, Catholic Americana files. LOCATION D, NUC, InND Loeber coll.

+ New York: P.J. Kenedy, 1895 (Library of Catholic Stories). LOCATION D.

COMMENTARY Historical fiction. A Catholic story of the Jacobite invasions of Scotland and France in 1715 and 1745. The story does not deal with Ireland, except in the person of Denis O'Sullivan, a veteran of the siege of Limerick (1691) [ML; Brown].

S604   *Sir Thomas Gascoigne, or, the Yorkshire plot* (by Agnes M. Stewart).

London: Burns & Oates, 1880. SOURCE RLIN; OCLC. LOCATION CSt, Boston College.

S605   *Earl Nugent's daughter; or, the last days of the penal laws. A true story* (by Agnes M. Stewart; dedicated to Mrs Laura De Lisle of Grace Dieu, Loughborough).

+ London: Burns & Oates, [1883] (ill.). SOURCE Alston, p. 415. LOCATION D, L, InND Loeber coll. (cover imprint: Dublin, London: Duffy & Sons).

COMMENTARY Historical fiction. According to the preface, the story is based on the life of the marchioness of Buckingham. The narrative is set in England in the late-eighteenth century when catholicism was suppressed. Robert Nugent, of Irish extraction, becomes a Protestant and profits by this conversion, being made Earl Nugent. His daughter Mary has secret leanings toward catholicism but is forced by her father to marry a rich and powerful Protestant. She suffers from having to hide her beliefs but is eventually able to make her husband accept more liberal religious views [ML].

STEWART, Miss Elizabeth M. (known as **E.M. Stewart** and probably **Mrs E.M. Berens**), f. 1840s. Novelist, textbook writer, and short story writer, EMS was possibly an Irish Catholic author. Several of her books carry Duffy (Dublin) imprints but have not been located, and may have been reprints from unidentified original English editions. Her *Original poetry for young persons* was published in London in 1844. Although some of EMS's works deal with Ireland, it is not clear whether she was of Irish birth. She probably can be identified with Mrs E.M. Berens (née Stewart, according to dedication in *A woman with a past*, London, 1886, 3 vols.), who married a Mr Berens sometime prior to 1880. As Mrs E.M. Berens, she wrote a schoolbook, *Myths and legends of ancient Greece and Rome* (London, 1880). Her *A woman with a past* (London, 1886, 3 vols.) does not have Irish content. SOURCE BLC; COPAC; RL.

S606   *All for Prince Charlie; or, the Irish cavalier* (by Miss E.M. Stewart).

+ Dublin: James Duffy & Sons, [c.1870]. SOURCE Falkner Greirson cat. 9/334. LOCATION D, DPL, PC.

S607   *The king and the cloister; or legends of the dissolution* (by Miss Elizabeth M. Stewart).

London: D. Stewart, 1872. SOURCE ABE Books (accessed 1 Feb. 2004).

Dublin: James Duffy & Co. [1886 or earlier]. SOURCE Adv. in W. Carleton, *Redmond Count O'Hanlon* (Dublin, 1886).

New York, Montreal: D. & J. Sadlier & Co., 1874. SOURCE RLIN; American Antiquarian Soc.

COMMENTARY No copies of London and Dublin edns located. Contents: 'The disinherited son', 'The acolyte at the Newgate', 'The dark lady of Sunningdale', 'The ward of the prioress', 'A monarch's lyke-wake', 'The abbot's vigil' [RL; OCLC].

S608   *The victims of the penal laws, or, legends of history* (by Miss E.M. Stewart).
London: D. Stewart, 1878. Source OCLC. LOCATION MH.
+ Dublin, London: James Duffy & Sons, [1886 or earlier]. SOURCE Adv. in W. Carleton, *Redmond Count O'Hanlon* (Dublin, 1886). LOCATION D.
COMMENTARY Set in England and Italy. Includes a few poems, including 'On the ruins of Tintern Abbey', and 'O'Neill of Innismore' [ML].

S609   *Steadfast unto death. A tale of the Irish famine of to-day* (by Mrs E.M. Berens).
London: Remington, 1880 (ill. Fairfield). SOURCE Allibone Suppl., i, p. 136; Brown, 190. LOCATION L.
COMMENTARY Deals with the 1879–80 famine, and written at that time. Set in Ballinaveen, near Cork, where the outlaw Black Hugh had loved Mrs Sullivan before she married her good-for-nothing husband Pat. Black Hugh promises her on her deathbed to take care of her family. He goes so far as to take the blame for a crime committed by Pat, and he is hanged in Dublin. The family is rescued by well-meaning English people [Brown; Fegan, pp 209, 213].

S610   *The rosary of pearl, and six other tales* (by Miss E.M. Stewart).
Dublin: James Duffy & Co. [1886 or earlier]. SOURCE Adv. in W. Carleton, *Redmond Count O'Hanlon* (Dublin, 1886).
COMMENTARY No copy located [RL].

S611   *Apparition at Edendale* (by Miss E.M. Stewart).
Dublin: James Duffy, [1912 or earlier] (Duffy's Penny Library). SOURCE Adv. in *Catalogue of books* (Dublin: James Duffy & Co., 1912). LOCATION C (not found).

S612   *At his post to the last* (by Miss E.M. Stewart).
Dublin: James Duffy, [1912 or earlier] (Duffy's Penny Library). SOURCE Adv. in *Catalogue of books* (Dublin: James Duffy & Co., 1912). LOCATION C (not found).

S613   *Lost in frost land* (by Miss E.M. Stewart).
Dublin: James Duffy, [1912 or earlier] (Duffy's Penny Library). SOURCE Adv. in *Catalogue of books* (Dublin: James Duffy & Co., 1912). LOCATION C (not found).

STEWART, Revd J., fl. 1827. Writer of moral fiction for juveniles, JS was, according to the title page of *The Killarney poor scholar* (Swaffham, Norfolk, 1830), the author of *Bible gems* (London, 1827), written when he was curate of Sporle (Norfolk). The following work is based on his personal observations at Killarney and its environs. He may be identified with Revd John Stewart, a Church of Ireland clergyman, who married Celia Gillespie in Ireland in 1801. Another Church of Ireland clergyman, Revd John Stewart, the fifth son of Henry Stewart of Co. Meath, was ordained at Cork in 1809. In 1810 he was licensed to preach within the diocese of Cork and Ross. He was rector of Killowen (Co. Cork, 1832–40), and at Templetrine (Co. Cork) from 1840 to his death in 1852. He married Anne, daughter of Samuel Austen, Esq., of Crookstown (Co. Cork) with whom he had seven children. A third candidate is Revd James Stewart, who was rector of Ballinadee in the Cork diocese in 1820, served as treasurer of the diocese, and in 1825 became archdeacon of Ross. SOURCE Cork, i , pp 17, 24, 348; ii, p. 534; J.C. Erck, *The ecclesiastical register* (Dublin, 1820), pp 94–5; H. Farrar (ed.), *Irish marriages* (London, 1897), ii, p. 421; RL.

S614   *The Killarney poor scholar. Comprising the most remarkable features of the enchanting scenery of the Irish lakes; enlivened with sketches of real character and anecdotes from life* (by J. Stewart).
+ Swaffham, Norfolk: F. Skill, 1830 (ill.). SOURCE OCLC; Garside 2, A:8. LOCATION L (1840 edn), O, PC, InND Loeber coll.

London: Whittaker, 1845. SOURCE Brown, 1550; Hodgson, p. 311; OCLC (J. Graham, 1846, 3rd edn). LOCATION D (J. Graham, 1846, 3rd edn).
COMMENTARY No copy of London, 1845 edn located. Fiction for juveniles set in Killarney (Co. Kerry). The object of the book is to 'extend the knowledge, improve the taste, and correct the judgement of youth'. Mrs Clinton, an Englishwoman, is visiting Killarney with her son and daughter and Mr Meredith, the son's tutor. The son has been to a public school and has acquired the objectionable trait of pride. Occurrences during the trip are taken as lessons for improving the young people's minds. The Killarney scholar is initially despised by the son until he learns to view his values in their true light. The story includes a stag-hunt near the lakes of Killarney [ML].

STEWART, Mrs T.F. See **STEWARD, Mrs T.F.**

STINSON, James, fl. 1880s. Short story writer, probably Irish, who according to the title page of *Lights and leaders of Irish life* (Dublin, [1889]) also published 'The wrong man; Arrant knaves', and 'The Ferguson brothers', which have not been located. SOURCE RL.
S615   *Lights and leaders of Irish life* (by James Stinson; dedicated to Thomas Sexton, MP, Lord Mayor of Dublin).
+ Dublin: James Duffy & Co., [1889] (see Plate 60). LOCATION D, InND Loeber coll.
COMMENTARY Contents: 'The policeman', 'The T.C.', 'The P.L.G.', 'Belles', 'The national teacher', 'The attorney-at-law', 'The gentleman of the press', 'Justice o' Peace', 'Drummers', 'Our own M.P.' [RL].

STOKER, Abraham (Bram), b. Dublin 1847, d. London 1912. Novelist and theatre manager, AS was a son of a government clerk, also Abraham Stoker, and of Charlotte Thornley, a social activist. He was the third of seven children. Illness kept him bedridden from age 3 to 7, during which time he learned to read and was read to by his parents. He was educated at TCD, becoming an orator and athlete and receiving degrees in science and mathematics in 1871 and 1874. On graduating, he entered the civil service in Dublin. He was later called to the Bar in London, but never practiced. AS was interested in the theatre and started reviewing drama for the *Evening Mail* (London; ODNB possibly mistakenly has *Daily Mail*) and the *Warder* (Dublin?). His first horror story, 'The chain of destiny', and his novella 'The primrose path' appeared in the *Shamrock* (Dublin, 1875). When the actor Henry Irving gave a season in Dublin in the next year, AS became acquainted with him and two years later left for London to become Irving's manager at the Lyceum Theatre, a position he held for twenty-seven years. Before leaving, he wrote *Duties of the clerks of petty sessions in Ireland* (Dublin, 1879). AS was a pioneer in theatrical management, introducing numbered theatre seats, advance reservations and promotion of the season rather than individual plays. He managed the company's eight tours of the US and published *A glimpse of America* (London, 1886). After Irving's death in 1905, AS's health and fortunes declined but he continued to write fiction. He married in 1878 Florence Anne Lemon Balcombe, who had refused the suit of Oscar Wilde§ in his favour. Later in life he applied for assistance from the Royal Literary Fund. He died of Bright's disease and, according to the ODNB, the syphilis attributed to him has never been confirmed. For his portraits and papers, see ODNB. SOURCE Allibone Suppl., ii, p. 1394; B. Belford, *Bram Stoker* (1996); Boylan, p. 370; Brown, p. 286; Dalby, passim; EF, p. 375; Field Day, ii, p. 831 and passim; Hogan 2, p. 148; Igoe, pp 243–8; P. Murray, *From the shadow of Dracula: A life of Bram Stoker* (London, 2004); NCBEL 4, pp 1702–3; OCIL, pp 540–1; RIA/DIB; Sutherland, pp 605–6; Wilson, pp 459–64.
S616   *Under the sunset* (by Bram Stoker; dedicated to author's young son).
+ London: Sampson, Low, Marston, Searle, and Rivington, 1882 (ill. W. Fitzgerald, W.V. Cockburn; see Plate 61). SOURCE Dalby, p. 9. LOCATION L, InND Loeber coll.

COMMENTARY Consists of a number of fairy and supernatural tales written for children. Contents: 'Under the sunset', 'The rose prince', 'The invisible giant', 'The shadow builder', 'How 7 went mad', 'Lies and lilies', 'The castle of the king', 'The wondrous child' [EF, p. 375; Wilson, p. 460; RL)

S617   *The snake's pass* (by Bram Stoker).

+ London: Sampson, Low, Marston, Searle & Rivington, 1891. SOURCE Brown, 1551; Dalby, p. 15. LOCATION D, L.

+ Dingle, Co. Kerry: Brandon, 1990. LOCATION D.

COMMENTARY A tale written around the strange phenomenon of a moving bog in Co. Mayo. The narrator is a young English visitor to Connemara [Brown].

S618   *The man from Shorrox's* (by Bram Stoker).

New York: Theo L. De Vinne & Co., 1894. SOURCE Dalby, p. 17. LOCATION NUC.

S619   *The crooken sands* (by Bram Stoker).

New York: Theo L. De Vinne & Co., 1894. SOURCE Dalby, p. 17; OCLC. LOCATION DCL.

S620   *The watter's mou'* (by Bram Stoker).

New York: Theo L. De Vinne & Co., 1894. SOURCE Dalby, p. 17; Hogan 2, p. 1148. LOCATION L.

+ Westminster [London]: A. Constable, 1895. SOURCE Dalby, p. 19. LOCATION D.

COMMENTARY An adventure romance [ODNB].

S621   *The shoulder of Shasta* (by Bram Stoker; dedicated to author's brother Sir Thornley Stoker, president of the Royal College of Surgeons in Ireland).

+ Westminster [London]: Archibald Constable & Co., 1895. SOURCE Dalby, p. 22; Hogan 2, p. 1148. LOCATION D, L.

COMMENTARY An adventure romance [ODNB].

S622   *Dracula* (by Bram Stoker).

Westminster [London]: Archibald Constable & Co., 1897. SOURCE Dalby, p. 26; Hogan 2, p. 1148; Wolff, 6581. LOCATION L.

New York: Doubleday & McClure Co., 1899. SOURCE Dalby, p. 27; OCLC. LOCATION DCL.

+ New York: Clarkson N. Potter, 1975 (as *The annotated Dracula* [dedicated to Bela Lugosi]; ill. Sätty, with maps and photographs; introd., notes and bibliography by Leonard Wolf). LOCATION InND Loeber coll.

+ Dingle, Co. Kerry: Brandon, 1992. LOCATION D.

COMMENTARY The novel began as a short story, 'Dracula's guest', which, according to the ODNB, harkens back to Joseph Sheridan Le Fanu's§ story 'Carmilla', published in *In a glass darkly* (London, 1872, 3 vols.), and was originally titled 'The Un-dead'. In Stoker's *Dracula*, the Eastern European background details were supplied by the author's brother George, a medical officer who had served in the war between Russia and Turkey (1874–5). Count Dracula's persona combines the fifteenth-century Walachian tyrant, Vlad Dracul, with the vampire of European folklore. Jonathan Harker travels to Transylvania on behalf of his law firm to meet the mysterious Count Dracula. Count Dracula then travels to England where his first victim is Lucy Westenra, who preys on children on Hampstead Heath until, on the instructions of the philosopher-scientist Van Helsing, her tomb is opened and a stake driven through her heart [Field Day, ii, pp 889–98; OCIL, p. 154; RL].

S623   *Miss Betty* (by Bram Stoker).

London: C. Arthur Pearson, 1898. SOURCE Dalby, p. 33; Hogan 2, p. 1148; Wolff, 6583. LOCATION L.

S624   *The mystery of the sea* (by Bram Stoker; dedicated to Daisy Gilbey Riviere).
London: William Heinemann, 1902. SOURCE Dalby, p. 36. LOCATION L, InND Loeber
coll. (London, Rider, 1913 edn).
New York: Doubleday, Page & Co., 1902. SOURCE Dalby, p. 36. LOCATION L.

COMMENTARY Historical fiction set on the coast of Scotland, it tells of the fulfilment of an old
legend concerning a treasure hidden in a cave by a Spanish nobleman during the time of the
Armada. A descendant of the nobleman and an American girl descended from Sir Francis
Drake are involved in the hunt for the treasure [ML].

S625   *The jewel of seven stars* (by Bram Stoker; dedicated to Eleanor and Constance Hoyt).
+ London: William Heinemann, 1903. SOURCE Dalby, p. 41; Hogan 2, p. 1148; Wolff,
6584. LOCATION D, L, InND Loeber coll.
London: William Rider & Son, 1912 (revsd edn). LOCATION L.
New York, London: Harper & Bros, 1904. SOURCE Dalby, p. 41; RLIN. LOCATION
DCL.

COMMENTARY No copy of the New York edn located. Inspired by the Egyptian adventures of
Sir William Wilde§ (as related in his *Narrative of a voyage to Madeira, Teneriffe, and along the
shores of the Mediterranean*, Dublin, 1840) and set in England and Egypt, where an Egyptologist
has pieced together the secrets of a long-dead Egyptian princess. Her tomb had been first discovered in the seventeenth century, and many people had died over time in trying to discover
its secrets. The Egyptian princess apparently had powers to manifest herself after death and
possibly come to life again if the circumstances were right. When the Egyptologist has arranged
everything to make the circumstances right, strange things happen, and almost everyone is
killed in the experiment [ML; ODNB].

S626   *The man* (by Bram Stoker; dedicated to Gladys Helen Burrell).
+ London: William Heinemann, 1905. SOURCE Dalby, p. 45; Hogan 2, p. 1148; Wolff,
6582. LOCATION D, L.
New York: Cupples & Leon Co., [*c*.1908] (abridged as *The gates of life*). SOURCE Dalby,
p. 47; RLIN. LOCATION UBP.
COMMENTARY No copy of the New York edn located [RL].

S627   *Lady Athlyne* (by Bram Stoker; dedicated to the Lady Athlyne).
+ London: William Heinemann, 1908. SOURCE Dalby, p. 53; Hogan 2, p. 1148.
LOCATION L, InND Loeber coll.
New York: P.R. Reynolds, 1908. SOURCE OCLC. LOCATION DCL.

COMMENTARY Set mainly in America and England. On a trip across the Atlantic, a stewardess
mentions that Joy Ogilvy is good for only one man, and that is the earl of Athlyne, and jok-
ingly calls her Lady Athlyne. When the earl of Athlyne returns from the Boer War, he hears
that somebody in New York calls herself Lady Athlyne and he sets out, under a false name,
to find out who is using his name. He is not successful in New York, but he saves Joy from
the dangers of a runaway horse. He has to introduce himself under his false name. In England,
he secretly takes her out for a ride in his motorcar, and gets arrested for speeding. To protect the girl's identity, he calls her his wife. A denouement takes place, and Joy becomes Lady
Athlyne in reality [ML].

S628   *Snowbound. The record of a theatrical touring party* (by Bram Stoker).
+ London: Collier & Co., 1908 (Collier's Shilling Library). SOURCE Dalby, p. 55;
Hogan 2, p. 1148. LOCATION D, L.

S629   *The lady of the shroud* (by Bram Stoker; dedicated to the comtesse de Guerbel
[Geneviève Ward]).
London: William Heinemann, 1909. SOURCE Dalby, p. 57; Hogan 2, p. 1148. LOCATION
L.

+ London: William Rider & Son, n.d. LOCATION InND Loeber coll.

+ London: Jarrold, 1966. LOCATION D.

COMMENTARY The story is set mainly in the Balkans, where Rupert St Leger (who has an English mother and an Irish father) has inherited an estate from his English uncle. At night he encounters a beautiful woman in a shroud. He falls in love and marries her, despite the fact that he thinks she might be dead or a vampire. In fact she is only thought to be dead by her enemies, and is on display in her coffin, from which she escapes only now and then. Rupert helps to defend his adopted country (called 'The Land of the Blue Mountains') against invaders. He is aided by the vast fortune he has inherited. In the end, he and his wife are pronounced king and queen [ML; JB].

S630   *The lair of the white worm* (by Bram Stoker; dedicated to Bertha Nicoll).

+ London: William Rider & Son, 1911 (ill.). SOURCE Dalby, p. 63; Hogan 2, p. 1148. LOCATION L, InND Loeber coll.

London: W. Foulsham & Co., [1925] (Foulsham's Mayflower Library, No. 8). SOURCE Wilson, p. 461. LOCATION L. COMMENTARY *London [1925] edn* Abridged and partially rewritten [Wilson, p. 461].

New York: Paperback Library, 1966 (as *Garden of evil*). SOURCE Wilson, p. 461. LOCATION McMaster Univ., Hamilton, (ON).

+ Dingle, Co. Kerry: Brandon, 1991. LOCATION D, Dt.

COMMENTARY Set in England. The story concerns two evil people: Lady Arabella, who lives in Diana's Grove, and a Mr Caswall, who has come to live at Castra Regis. Diana's Grove contains a very deep well in which a prehistoric monster dwells, of which Lady Arabella seems to be the human incarnation. Mr Caswell has mesmeric powers that he uses for evil ends. Adam Salton, recently arrived from Australia, and Sir Nathaniel De Salis plan to rid the neighbourhood of the monster. After many dangerous adventures they succeed. This was made into a film by Ken Russell in 1988 [ML; ODNB].

S631   *Dracula's guest and other weird stories* (by Bram Stoker; dedicated to author's son; compiled by author's wife [Florence Stoker]).

London: George Routledge & Sons, 1914. SOURCE Dalby, p. 67; Hogan 2, p. 1148. LOCATION L.

+ Dingle, Co. Kerry: Brandon, 1990. LOCATION D.

COMMENTARY This work and the following were published posthumously. Contents: 'Dracula's guest' (first appeared as 'Walpurgis night' in the *Story Teller* (London, May 1914), 'The judge's house', 'The squaw', 'The secret of growing gold', 'The gipsy prophesy', 'The coming of Abel Behenna', 'The burial of the rats', 'A dream of the red hands', 'Crooken sands' (first published separately, New York, 1894) [CM; Wilson, p. 460].

S632   *The Bram Stoker bedside companion: Stories of fantasy and horror.*

+ London: Victor Gollancz, 1973 (ed. by Charles Osborne). LOCATION D, L.

COMMENTARY Contents: 'The secret of growing gold', 'Dracula's guest' (first appeared as 'Walpurgis night' in the *Story Teller*, London, 1914), 'The invisible giant', 'The judge's house', 'The burial of the rats', 'A star trap', 'The squaw', 'Crooken sands' (first published separately, New York, 1894), 'The gombeen man' (from *The snake's pass*, London, 1891), 'The Watter's mou' (first published separately, New York, 1894) [ML].

S633   *Shades of Dracula. Bram Stoker's uncollected stories.*

+ London: William Kimber, 1982 (ed. by Peter Haining). SOURCE Hogan 2, p. 1148; Wilson, p. 460. LOCATION L.

COMMENTARY Contents: 'The crystal cup', 'The chain of destiny', 'The castle of the king', 'The fate of Fenella', 'Vampires in New England', 'Walpurgis night', 'The seer', 'Another Dracula?', 'At last', 'In the valley of the shadow' [RL].

S634   *The dualists, or, the death doom of the double born* (by Bram Stoker).
Edinburgh: Tragara Press, 1986 (introd. by Richard Dalby; limited edn). SOURCE
Wilson, p. 460. LOCATION L.
COMMENTARY 29pp. Supernatural story [Wilson, p. 460].

S635   *Midnight tales* (by Bram Stoker).
+ London: Peter Owen, 1990 (ed. and introd. by Peter Haining). LOCATION D, L.
COMMENTARY Contents: 'The dream in the dead house', 'The spectre of doom', 'The dual-
ists', 'Death in the wings', 'The gombeen man', 'The squaw', 'A deed of vengeance?', 'The
man from Shorrox's' (first published separately, New York, 1894), 'The red stockade',
'Midnight tales', 'A criminal star', 'The bridal of death' [RL].

STOKER, Florence Anne Lemon. Editor. See STOKER, Abraham.

STONEY, H. Butler. See STONEY, Henry Butler.

STONEY, Henry Butler (also known as H. Butler Stoney), b. Portland Park? (Co.
Tipperary) 1818, d. Australia? 1880. Soldier, military story and travel writer, HBS was the
third son of Richard Falkiner Stoney, of Portland Park (Co. Tipperary, burnt in 1920) and
Sarah Eliza, eldest daughter and co-heiress of Robert Fannin, of Dublin (Jane Butler, according to *Landed gentry*). He entered TCD in 1833 but appears to have left without taking a
degree. He married Fanny, daughter of Benjamin Wilson, of Sledagh (Co. Wexford) and they
had one son, who died unmarried. HBS was a captain of the 40th and the 99th regiments
(Burke's and Landed gentry attribute to him the rank of major of the 40th Regiment). He
lived in Australia, about which he wrote several descriptive, topographical books. SOURCE
Allibone, ii, p. 2270; B & S, p. 786; Burke's, p. 1060; Landed gentry, 1904, p. 569; Miller, ii,
p. 600; *Vanishing country houses*, p. 136.

S636   *Reginald Mortimer; or, truth more strange than fiction: a tale of a soldier's life
and adventures* (by Henry Butler Stoney).
Melbourne: W. Fairfax & Co., 1857. SOURCE COPAC. LOCATION L.
COMMENTARY An account of the life of a young Irish university graduate and officer who
serves in Spain during the Carlist rebellion in 1836 and spends several years with his regiment in England, Malta and the West Indies. He is killed in action in the Crimea [Miller].

S637   *Taranaki, a tale of the war: with a description of the province previous to and during the war. Also an account (chiefly taken from the despatches) of the principal
contests with the natives during that eventful period* (by H. Butler Stoney).
+ Auckland [New Zealand]: W.C. Wilson, 1861. SOURCE COPAC. LOCATION C.
COMMENTARY Describes the Maori war in a fictional form [RL].

STORY, Louise Frances. See FIELD, Louise Frances.

'STRADLING, Matthew', pseud. See MAHONY, Martin Francis.

STRAHAN, Samuel A.K., fl. 1889. Novelist and physician, SAKS lived in Belfast; however,
the dedication to the following book is from London, 3 Sept. 1889. SOURCE Brown, p. 287; RL.

S638   *The resident magistrate. An Irish novel of yesterday* [anon.] (dedicated to W.E.
Gladstone, MP 'in admiration of his powerful and fearless advocacy of the cause of
Ireland').
London: Alexander & Shepheard, 1889. SOURCE Brown, 1553; Wolff, 6588; COPAC.
LOCATION D, DPL.

COMMENTARY A tale of the 'Jubilee Coercion days'. The leading character is based on Captain Plunket of 'Don't hesitate to shoot fame'. Intermingled is the story of a persecuted heroine suffering from an uncommon form of mania (in which the author was a specialist) [Brown].

STRAIN, E.H. See STRAIN, Mrs Euphans Helen.

STRAIN, Mrs Euphans Helen (née MacNaughton; known as E.H. Strain), fl. 1895, d. 1934. Scottish novelist who lived in Ayrshire and who married John Strain. She published other works of fiction in addition to the volume below. SOURCE Brown, p. 287; Daims, p. 687; EF, p. 376; E. Reilly, p. 251.

S639   *A man's foes* (by Mrs E.H. Strain).
        London, New York: Ward, Lock & Bowden, 1895, 3 vols. SOURCE Topp 2, p. 368; Brown, 1554; Daims, 2960. LOCATION L, NUC.
        + New York: Ward, Lock & Bowden, 1895. LOCATION NUC.
COMMENTARY Historical fiction. A story about the siege of Derry in 1689, from an anti-Catholic point of view. It features Lord Massareene, Lord Mountjoy, Sir Arthur Rawdon, and a Capt. Hamilton whose wife is the narrator. The story describes the uncertainty of allegiances and the resulting mistrust among people during the time that King James II's influence is waning. Many officers switch to align themselves with King William III and make heroic efforts to save the city of Derry [ML; Baker].

STRAKER, Fiorentina, fl. 1860. Religious fiction writer, FS was a Catholic. She travelled in Italy and France, dedicating her only book ('these flow'rets of catholicism, culled on the Italian soil') to her mother from St Pons, Nice, 8 Dec. 1859. SOURCE BLC; RL.

S640   *Immacolata, the convent flower. A Catholic tale* [anon.] (dedicated to author's mother).
        + London: W. Knowles; Catholic Publishing & Bookselling Co.; Dublin: J. Mullany; Baltimore: J. Murphy & Co., 1860. LOCATION L.
COMMENTARY Author identified from the dedication. Religious fiction featuring Immacolata, born of a Catholic Italian mother and a Protestant English father, who is sent to an English convent school after her mother's death. There she meets a girl of Irish extraction, Ellen O'Sullivan, and they become lifelong friends. After Immacolata leaves school, she influences many lives. Through her, Ellen's brother reverts to catholicism and, before his death, Immacolata's father also converts to catholicism. Immacolata enters the convent but dies soon after [ML].

STRANGMAN, Sarah D. See GREER, Mrs J.R.

'A STUDENT OF GRAY'S INN', fl. 1834. Pseudonym of a short story and sketch writer who states that he was born in the Vale of Glenagh not far from the mountain of Carron. These may be fictional places, but there is a townland of Glenagh near Killala (Co. Mayo), and several townlands of Carron in Co. Tipperary. The author travelled as a correspondent for an (unidentified) English journal. SOURCE IBL, 9 (1917), p. 15.

S641   *The sketch book or spectator* (by 'A student of Gray's Inn').
        London: Printed for the author, 1834, 2nd edn. SOURCE IBL, 9 (1917), p. 15.
COMMENTARY No copy located. Contains 15 chapters dealing with subjects such as 'The Catholic Association', 'The Waterford election', 'Sheil and the Clonmel bootmaker', 'The squireens of Westmeath', 'The Orangeman of Portadown' [RL; IBL].

SULLIVAN, Alexander Martin (also known as A.M. Sullivan), b. Bantry (Co. Cork) 1830, d. Dublin 1884. Publisher, editor, journalist, barrister, anthologist and history writer, AMS was the second of six sons of Daniel Sullivan of Dublin, and brother of the publishers Timothy Daniel and Donal Sullivan, with whom he collaborated. He worked for the Bantry poorhouse during the Famine in 1846 and 1847, appalled by the effects of hunger, death and emigration on the west Cork area, and became a member of the Young Ireland movement. He turned to becoming an illustrator and journalist, working for the Dublin *Expositor*, the *Tipperary Leader* and then the Liverpool *Daily Post*. Returning to Dublin in 1855, he became proprietor of the *Nation* (Dublin, 1855–74). In 1859 he founded the penny daily, the Dublin *Evening News* and a year later the *Morning News*, which ceased publication in 1864. The comic weekly *Zozimus* was published from the office of the *Nation*. He was a member of the Dublin Corporation (1862–67). In his various publications, especially the *Nation*, AMS promoted the idea of constitutional self-government. Because he opposed the militancy of the Fenians, an order for his assassination was passed by the Fenian council in 1865, but no attempt was made to execute it, given AMS's high-standing with the Fenian rank and file. Later he defended the Fenians after their failed rising. British authorities sentenced him to imprisonment for an article he published on the execution of the Fenian 'Manchester Martyrs'. He used the funds collected on his behalf to erect a statue of Henry Grattan, now in College Green (Dublin). With Isaac Butt§, AMS in 1870 formed the Home Government Association (later the Home Rule League). He was elected MP for Louth (1874–80) and for Meath (1880–82) and was called to the Irish Bar in 1876 but practiced only in England, by special permission of the Inner Temple. He deplored the excesses of the Land War, but the government's response in the Coercion Acts made him join Charles Stewart Parnell's parliamentary obstructionist tactics. He published *Speeches from the dock* (Dublin, 1867); wrote *The story of Ireland* (Dublin, 1867), which remained popular for many years, and followed it with *New Ireland* (London, 1877) and *A nutshell history of Ireland* (London, 1883). As publishers, AMS and his brothers had extensive influence on the publication of Irish nationalist work and the promotion of cultural nationalism and the Irish language. AMS married in 1861 Frances G. Donovan, daughter of John Donovan of New Orleans. SOURCE Boase, iii, p. 822; Brady, pp 230–1; S.J. Connolly (ed.), *The Oxford companion to Irish history* (Oxford, 1998), p. 528; Irish pseudonyms; OCIL, p. 545; ODNB; O'Donoghue, p. 444 [under Timothy Daniel Sullivan]; RIA/DIB; RL; A.M. Sullivan, *The story of Ireland ... continued to the present time by James Luby, of New York* (New York, 1892), pp iii–ix.

S642   *Penny readings for the Irish people* [anon.].
Dublin: A.M. Sullivan, [between 1871 and 1876], 3 vols. (conducted by the editors of the *Nation* [A.M. Sullivan and Timothy Daniel Sullivan]). SOURCE OCLC. LOCATION ICU.
+ Dublin: T.D. Sullivan, 1879, 4 vols. (compiled by the editors of 'The Nation' [Timothy Daniel Sullivan]). SOURCE O'Donoghue, p. 444; Hayley, p. 178 ([1880] edn. LOCATION InND Loeber coll.
+ Dublin: M.H. Gill & Son, 1898, 2 vols. (as *Irish readings*, ed. by A.M. Sullivan & T.D. Sullivan). LOCATION Dcc, InND Loeber coll. (n.d. edn).
COMMENTARY Originally issued in 36 parts. A miscellany taken from the *Nation* (Dublin), consisting of historical and political pieces, poetry and some fiction, often taken from novels or collections of stories. Contents of the 1879 edn: 'The Irish dancing master' (William Carleton§), 'The marriage of Florence MacCarthy More' (Mrs J. Sadlier§), 'How Tom Dillon became a Zouave' (by 'Brigid'), 'Personal recollections of the Galway election' (T.F. Meagher), 'A Union prophesy – 1799' ([William Joseph O'Neill] Daunt§), 'The Irish fiddle' (William Carleton§), 'A 'ninety-eight scene' (Richard O'Sullivan§), 'An unexpected interview' (Charles Lever§),

'Scene from "The poor scholar"' (William Carleton§), 'The defence of Limerick' (John Banim§), 'Creatures of the castle' (Lady Morgan§), 'An Irish eviction' (William Carleton§), 'The Galway election – the last of it' (T.F. Meagher), 'Died of the fever' (William Carleton§), 'All Hallow's eve' (T.C. Irwin§), 'Mr. O'Leary in trouble' (Charles Lever§), 'The death of Owen Roe O'Neill' (Thomas A. Finlay§), 'A joyful reunion' (T.D. Sullivan), 'Evicted' (Thomas Sherlock), 'Taking the "Popery" out of a tombstone' (Samuel Lover§) [RL; OCLC].

SULLIVAN, J.W. See **SULLIVAN, James William**.

SULLIVAN, James William (known as **J.W. Sullivan**), b. Carlisle (PA) 1848, d. 1938. American writer on social issues, journalist, novelist and trade unionist, JWS moved to New York and first worked there as a printer. Characterized as a 'reforming sociologist', he was involved in the American Federation of Labor. He wrote a single novel and treatises about labour and the urban poor. SOURCE DAB; Exiles, p. 207.

S643　*Tenement tales of New York* (by J.W. Sullivan).
　　　New York: Henry Holt, 1895. SOURCE Fanning, p. 391; part printed in Exiles, pp 207–22; OCLC. LOCATION CtY.
COMMENTARY Fictionalized lives of Irish, Jewish, and Italian immigrants. One of the stories, 'Slob Murphy', features the unfortunate end of an 8-year-old street urchin [Exiles, p. 207].

SULLIVAN, Timothy Daniel (also known as T.D. Sullivan and Timothy D. Sullivan) (1827–1914). Co-author. See **SULLIVAN, Alexander Martin**.

SULLIVAN, W.F. See **SULLIVAN, William Francis**.

SULLIVAN, William Francis (known as **W.F. Sullivan**), b. Dublin 1756, d. 1830. Novelist, poet, playwright and children's writer, WFS was the son of Francis Stoughton Sullivan, a barrister and distinguished jurist who was born in Co. Galway. WFS entered TCD in 1773, but his studies were interrupted by his father's death in 1776. He became a naval officer, serving from 1776 to 1783, throughout the American War of Independence. He settled in England, where he lived from his writings and his dramatic readings, publishing mostly novelettes for juveniles. He translated from the French (e.g., *Emily and Henrietta, or, a cure for idleness: An improving tale for youth* (London, 1816). His farce 'The rights of man' was printed in the *Thespian Magazine* (London, 1792) and *The flights of fancy*, a collection of poems, epigrams and trifles, appeared in Leeds in the same year. SOURCE Allibone, ii, p. 2300; B & S, p. 793; NCBEL 4, p. 1874; ODNB [under Francis Stoughton Sullivan]; O'Donoghue, p. 444; Rafroidi, ii, pp 345–6.

S644　*Early habits; or, the effects of attention and neglect: exemplified in the history of Master Thomas Towardley, and Laurence Lacey, alias Lazy* (by W.F. Sullivan).
　　　London: Whittingham & Arlis, 1816 (ill.). LOCATION L.
COMMENTARY Fiction for juveniles [RL].

S645　*The history of Mr. Rightway and his pupils; an entertaining and instructive lesson for young gentlemen* (by W.F. Sullivan).
　　　London: W. Darton Jnr, 1816. LOCATION L, NUC.
COMMENTARY 85pp. Fiction for juveniles [NUC].

S646　*Juvenile sketches; or, the history of Mrs. Barton and her little family. Illustrated with some instructive stories for the youth of both sexes* (by W.F. Sullivan).
　　　London: A.K. Newman & Co., 1817 (ill. I. Cruikshank). LOCATION L.
COMMENTARY 56pp. Fiction for juveniles [OCLC].

S647   *The young truants. An interesting and instructive lesson for the youth of both sexes* (by W.F. Sullivan).
London: Dean & Munday, 1817 (ill.). SOURCE OCLC. LOCATION L (1818 edn, printed for A.K. Newman), O, Cleveland Public Library (OH).
COMMENTARY 58pp. Fiction for juveniles [OCLC].

S648   *Portraits from life; or, the history of Charles and Charlotte. An instructive and entertaining tale, founded on truth* (by W.F. Sullivan).
London: Printed [for the author?] by Dean & Munday, 1817 (ill.). LOCATION L.
Boston: Munroe & Francis, David Francis, [1824–41?] (Juvenile Classicks [*sic*], No. 6; ill. Alonzo Hartwell, Childs). SOURCE OCLC. LOCATION NjP.
COMMENTARY Fiction for juveniles. Includes Alexander Pope's 'An essay on man' [OCLC].

S649   *The young liar!!: A tale of truth and caution; for the benefit of the rising generation* (by W.F. Sullivan).
London: Printed by [for the author?] Dean & Munday, 1817. SOURCE NCBEL 4, p. 1874 (1818 edn); OCLC. LOCATION Indiana Univ.
London: Dean & Munday, 1821 (new edn; as *Young Wilfred, or, the punishment of falsehood: A tale of truth and caution, for the benefit of the rising generation*). SOURCE OCLC. LOCATION Indiana Univ., Bloomington, (IN).
COMMENTARY 59pp. Fiction for juveniles [RL].

S650   *The history of Ben the sailor, and Ned the soldier, containing numerous entertaining and interesting anecdotes and adventures of real life vouched as genuine and authentic* (by W.F. Sullivan).
London: A.K. Newman & Co., 1818. LOCATION NUC.
London: Dean & Munday, [1818] (as *Pleasant stories; or, the histories of Ben, the sailor, and Ned, the soldier*). SOURCE DNB. LOCATION L.
New Haven (CT): J. Babcock & Son; Charleston (SC): S. Babcock & Co., 1824 (as *Pleasant stories: or, the histories of Ben, the sailor, and Ned the soldier*). SOURCE OCLC. LOCATION NUC.
COMMENTARY The two London edns are 58pp each, while the New Haven edn is 48pp. Fiction for juveniles [NUC; COPAC].

S651   *Emulation, or, the benefit of good example. An interesting narrative, for the attentive perusal of young persons* (by W.F. Sullivan).
London: A. K. Newman, 1818. SOURCE OCLC. LOCATION CtY.
London: A.K. Newman, [1820–29?] (new and improved edn). SOURCE OCLC. LOCATION Cleveland Public Library (OH).
New Haven (CT): J. Babcock, 1824 (as *Emulation, or, the benefit of good example*). SOURCE OCLC. LOCATION CtY.
COMMENTARY 52pp. Fiction for juveniles [RL].

S652   *The recluse, or the hermit of Windermere: a narrative founded upon facts; being an important lesson for youth* (by W.F. Sullivan).
London: C. Chapple, 1818 (ill.). SOURCE British Fiction; Garside, A:4. LOCATION Corvey CME 3–628–48730, L.
COMMENTARY Fiction for juveniles [RL].

SUMMERS, Thomas O. Text reviser. See **GREGG, Revd John.**

SUMNER, Revd Charles Richard, pseud. 'A young gentleman of note', b. Kenilworth (War.) 1790, d. Winchester (Hants.) 1874. Church of England bishop and novelist, CRS was the son of the Revd Robert Sumner and his wife Hannah Bird. CRS was a student at Eton when he wrote *The white nun* (London, [1809?]), which he sold to a local bookseller named Ingalton for £5, the publisher taking pains to point out to the author that everyone would see that 'note' was Eton spelled backwards. CRS was ordained in 1817 and later became private chaplain to King George IV at Windsor Castle and bishop of Winchester. He edited and translated the Latin treatises of John Milton. He voted for Catholic emancipation in 1829, which cost him the favour of the king. His portrait was painted in 1832 by Sir Martin Archer Shee§. SOURCE Allibone, ii, pp 2302–3; Boase, iii, p. 828; DNB; NCBEL 4, p. 2635; ODNB.

S653   *The white nun; or, the black bog of Dromore: A novel* (by 'A young gentleman of note').

    Eton: [publisher?], [1809?]. SOURCE C.N. Greenough card coll.; Boase, iii, p. 828. LOCATION MH.

    COMMENTARY It is not clear from the novel the location of the bog of Dromore, but there is a Dromore in Co. Down and one in Co. Tyrone [AMB].

'A SUNDAY-SCHOOL TEACHER', fl. 1820s. Pseudonym of a religious fiction writer. In all likelihood this was a woman and possibly the daughter of a clergyman, and because of her Dublin publications, she probably was Irish. SOURCE RL.

S654   *Little Mary, a true story* (by 'A Sunday-school teacher').

    Dublin: William Curry Jnr & Co., [1829 or earlier]. SOURCE Adv. in S. Bunbury, *The abbey of Innismoyle* (Dublin: William Curry Jnr & Co., 1829).

    COMMENTARY Fiction for juveniles, priced at 6*d*. [RL].

S655   *The pastor's daughter: Intended as an incentive to early piety and usefulness* (by the author of *Little Mary*).

    Dublin: Robertson, 1835, 2nd edn. SOURCE OCLC. LOCATION D.

    COMMENTARY No copy of the first edn located [RL].

SUTHERLAND, Alexr. See SUTHERLAND, Lt. Alexander.

SUTHERLAND, Lt. Alexander (known as Alexr Sutherland), fl. 1819. Novelist and military officer, AS most probably was Scottish as he was in the Cromarty Rangers and was involved with the *Edinburgh Magazine*. SOURCE BLC.

S656   *Redmond the rebel; or, they met at Waterloo. A novel* (by Alexr Sutherland).

    + London: A.K. Newman & Co., 1819, 3 vols. SOURCE British Fiction; Garside, 1819:65; Blakey, p. 267; Block, p. 231; Brown, 1555a. LOCATION Corvey CME 3–628–48519–3, Ireland related fiction, L.

    COMMENTARY Partly set in Ireland (Kilkenny) and on the Continent where an Irish rebel and other Irish characters are fighting [ML].

S657   *St. Kathleen; or, the rock of Dunnismoyle. A novel* [anon.].

    London: A.K. Newman & Co., 1820, 4 vols. SOURCE Blakey, p. 271; Block, p. 231; Brown, 1555 (mistakenly mentions 'Dunismoyle'); British Fiction; Garside, 1820:67. LOCATION Corvey CME 3–628–48490–1, Ireland related fiction, L.

    COMMENTARY Romantic adventure set in 1798 in Ireland and Scotland. In the story, St Kathleen is a name in the family of the earl of Innishboyne [Brown].

SWAN, Annie S. See SWAN, Annie Shepherd.

SWAN, Annie Shepherd (later Mrs Burnett Smith; known as Annie S. Swan), b. Edinburgh (Scotland) 1859, d. Gullane, Fife (Scotland) 1943. Prolific Scottish writer of fiction for women and children, ASS was the daughter of Edward Swan, a farmer and merchant, and Euphemia Brown. She wrote 162 novels under her own name and at least 40 under her pseudonym 'David Lyall', many of which remained popular for many years. She was educated at Queen Street Ladies College (Edinburgh) and lived in both England and Scotland, where many of her novels are set. She married James Burnett Smith in 1883. She was a contributor to several periodicals; editor of the *Woman at Home* (London, from 1893 on); and a popular public speaker. SOURCE Allibone Suppl., ii, p. 1409; Blain, pp 1049–50; Brown, p. 287; EF, pp 380–1; ODNB; Reilly, p. 251; Sutherland, p. 615; A.S. Swan, *My life* (London, 1934).

S658 *A son of Erin* (by Annie S. Swan).
+ London: Hutchinson & Co., 1899 (ill.). SOURCE Brown, 1556. LOCATION L, InND Loeber coll.
COMMENTARY Set in Edinburgh and Co. Wicklow, just before the retirement of Isaac Butt§ and the rise of Charles Stewart Parnell, who features in the tale. The story centres on the discovery of the identity of a child abandoned in Edinburgh when an infant [Brown].

SWAN, N. Walter SWAN. See **Nathaniel Walter**.

SWAN, **Nathaniel Walter** (known as **N. Walter**), b. Monaghan (Co. Monaghan) 1835 (1843 according to RIA/DIB), d. Australia? 1884. Novelist and short story writer, NWS was educated at Glasgow University. In the early 1850s he emigrated to Australia where he went to the gold diggings in Victoria. He met Henry Kingsley, an Australian author, who influenced him in taking up writing. He contributed to many journals, and also became editor and proprietor of a newspaper. SOURCE Boase, vi, p. 651; Miller, ii, 618; RIA/DIB; Sutherland, p. 616.

S659 *Tales of Australian life* (by N. Walter Swan).
London: Chapman & Hall, 1875. SOURCE Allibone Suppl., ii, p. 1409; Miller, ii, p. 618. LOCATION L.
COMMENTARY Consists of a novella and short stories. The novella *Marie Denton* relates the social incidents of a gold-mining centre with Tasmanian convict contacts in north-west Victoria. The short stories are mainly sketches of life on the diggings in the 1860s, with some references to sheep-station work [Miller].

S660 *A couple of cups ago and other stories* (by N. Walter Swan).
Melbourne: Cameron, Laign & Co., 1888. SOURCE Miller, ii, p. 618. LOCATION National Library of Australia.

S661 *Luke Mivers' harvest* (by N. Walter Swan).
Stawell (Australia): Stawell News & Pleasant Creek Chronicle, 1889. SOURCE Miller, ii, p. 618; OCLC. LOCATION Univ. of Queensland.
Kensington, NSW (Australia): New South Wales Univ. Press, c.1991. SOURCE COPAC. LOCATION L.
COMMENTARY This story won the *Sydney Mail* prize in 1878 for the best tale by a colonial author. It concerns the domestic affairs of a squatter in the western district of Victoria; and the social life of a seaport town, including the doings of a racing fraternity [Miller].

SWEETMAN, Agnes. See **CASTLE, Mrs Egerton**.

SWEETMAN, Mary E. See **BLUNDELL, Mary E.**

SWEETMAN, **Walter**, b. Clohamon, Ferns (Co. Wexford) 1830, d. Clohamon, 1905. Novelist, short story writer and poet, WS was the fourth son of Michael Sweetman of Longtown (Co.

Kildare) and came from a Catholic family. He was educated at Stonyhurst College and London University and was called to the Bar in 1852 but preferred the life of a country gentleman. Aside from his fiction and poetry, he wrote on religious and philosophical subjects. He married the eldest sister of Gen. Sir William Francis Butler§. He was related to Mary E. Blundell§, who wrote under the pseudonym 'M.E. Francis', and to Agnes Sweetman Castle§. Some of his correspondence is in the library at Sioux Falls (IA). SOURCE Allibone Suppl., ii, p. 1410; Brown, p. 288; Browne, p. 137; Murphy, p. 59; MVP, p. 447; O'Donoghue, p. 446; E. Reilly, p. 251; Rowe & Scallan, 337; Sutherland, p. 616; Personal communication, Kevin Whelan, Dec. 2000.

S662   *Through the night. A tale of the times. To which is added Onward; or, a summer sketch* (by Walter Sweetman).
    London: Longmans, Green, Reader & Dyer, 1869, 2 vols. SOURCE Allibone, ii, p. 2310; Brown, 1557; OCLC. LOCATION L.
COMMENTARY Marcus Brown comes home from the Continent to a neglected estate in Ireland. He is full of Continental liberal and democratic notions and proceeds to apply them. The author brings out the evils of absenteeism, the need for proper housing and for old age pensions. An episode in the Fenian movement is described. The second story features the life of an English family in Switzerland. The principal character discusses at great length his hope to unite religion and liberality in Ireland [Brown; Murphy, p. 59].

S663   *Libertas; or, through dreamland to truth* (by Walter Sweetman).
    London: Eden, Remington & Co., 1891, 3 vols. SOURCE Wolff, 6642. LOCATION L.
S664   *Schoolfellows' stories* (by Walter Sweetman).
    + London, Sydney: Eden, Remington & Co., 1893. LOCATION L, InND Loeber coll.
COMMENTARY Contents: 'Father Francis's dream' (set in Africa), 'William Nugent's discipline' (set in a boy's college, likely to be England), 'A friend in need' (set in O'Byrne's country, South of Dublin) [ML; JB].

S665   *Roland Kyan. An Irish sketch* (by Walter Sweetman).
    + London: Digby, Long & Co., [1896]. SOURCE Brown, 1558. LOCATION DPL, L, InND Loeber coll.
COMMENTARY A story of the holidays of Roland Kyan, scion of an Irish clan, his French friend, Jules de Gernon, and his English friend, Henry Smith, who have been educated together in England. Other young people live in neighbouring country houses. Politics and religious doubts are extensively discussed. Roland, who had more or less left catholicism, is gradually won back [ML].

SWIFT, Jonathan, b. Dublin 1667, d. Dublin 1745. Novelist, political satirist, poet, patriot and advocate of Irish rights, JS was the son of Jonathan Swift, a steward of the King's Inns, and Abigail Erick, born in Dublin, whose family came from Leicester. His parentage has been disputed. He attended Kilkenny College, where William Congreve§ was a younger colleague, and entered TCD in 1682 where graduated BA in 1686 and BD and DD in 1702. In 1689 he received an appointment as secretary to Sir William Temple, grandson of the first provost of TCD, first at Sheen and then at Moor Park (Surrey). One of his duties was to be tutor to Esther Johnson (Stella), the daughter of Temple's housekeeper Bridget Johnson. Esther and a companion moved to Dublin in 1701 where JS supported them financially. He spent a short time in Ireland during the Williamite War as secretary to Sir Robert Southwell, secretary of state for Ireland, but returned to Moor Park at the end of 1690. His first published poem was 'Ode: to the king on his Irish expedition', published in Dublin in 1691. He graduated MA from Oxford in 1692 and in 1694 he was ordained deacon at Christ Church Cathedral, Dublin, and priest in January the following year, after which he became prebendary of Kilroot (Co. Antrim).

He did not like the isolated life and returned to Moor Park in 1696, where he remained until Temple's death in 1699. JS, as literary executor, was to edit and publish Temple's memoirs and unpublished work. In 1700 he was appointed vicar of Laracor, near Trim (Co. Meath) and became prebendary of Dunlavin (Co. Wicklow) in St Patrick's Cathedral in Dublin in 1701. JS's writings on politics and in defence of the established church began to draw increasing attention. He regularly travelled between Dublin and London, where he represented Archbishop King in negotiations on ecclesiastical benefices. In London around 1707 he met Esther Van Homrigh (Vanessa), twenty-one years his junior, who (along with Stella) was to be the other enduring female presence in his life. In 1710 he became unpaid editor of the Tory weekly, the *Examiner* (London), and contributed over 30 essays asserting the principles of the new government. JS's hopes for preferment to an English bishopric did not materialize but he was appointed to the deanery of St Patrick's Cathedral in Dublin, which he regarded as a banishment, but which he held from 1713 to 1745. He was unhappy to be in Ireland, which he described as 'the most miserable country on earth', and continued to spend much time in London before settling permanently in Dublin at the end of the Tory administration. He then turned his talent to exposing social injustice, poverty and England's domination of Irish trade. His prodigious writings, in addition to his poetry and fiction, include his famous series of letters published under the pseudonym 'M.B. Drapier' attacking the disastrous undermining of the Irish currency by the introduction of Wood's copper halfpence and asserting Irish political equality with England. In 1727 he published *A short view of the state of Ireland* (Dublin, 1727-8). Even though he despaired at times of the power of satire to bring about reform, he published in 1729 one of his most biting satires: *A modest proposal for preventing the children of poor people in Ireland from being a burden to their parents or country and for making them beneficial to the public* ([London], 1729; Dublin, 1729). JS had been followed to Ireland by Esther Van Homrigh, whose mother had a property at Celbridge (Co. Kildare). He evidently did not reciprocate her passion for him and her presence in Dublin was a great embarrassment to him. Stella, to whom he was devoted, died in 1728. JS's remaining years were clouded by infirmity and loneliness but he remained active in Dublin's literary life and continued to write and to encourage other writers until his death. His literary fame rests mainly on his powers as a satirist, exemplified by his masterpiece, *Gulliver's travels* (London, 1726, 2 vols.). The catalogue of his library is at King's College, Cambridge. Some of his books are at Marsh's Library, Dublin. For his portraits and papers, see ODNB. For details of Swift's political writings see Hogan, Field Day, ODNB and RIA/DIB and other sources below. SOURCE Allibone, ii, pp 2311-18; B & S, pp 795-6; Boylan, p. 374-75; J.A. Downie, *Jonathan Swift: political writer* (London, 1984); I. Ehrenpreis, *Swift: the man, his works and the age* (Cambridge, MA, 1962-1983); Field Day, i, pp 327-94 and passim, ii, p. 217 and passim, iii, p. 55 and passim, iv, p. 454 and passim; v, p. 10 and passim; C. Fox (ed.) *The Cambridge companion to Jonathan Swift* (Cambridge, 2003); Hogan 2, pp 1157-77 (includes extensive biography and references); Igoe, pp 254-9; D. Nokes, *Jonathan Swift: A hypocrite reversed. A critical biography* (Oxford, 1985); OCIL, pp 546-7; ODNB; O'Donoghue, 446; RIA/DIB.

S666   *The tale of a tub. Written for the universal improvement of mankind. To which is added, an account of a battel [sic] between the antient and modern books in St. James's Library* [anon.] (dedicated to the Rt Honourable, John Lord Somers).
London: John Nutt, 1704. SOURCE McBurney & Taylor, 879; McBurney, 13; Teerink/Scouten, 217; ESTC t49834. LOCATION L, MH, IU.
London: John Nutt, 1704 (2nd edn corrected). SOURCE Teerink/Scouten, 218. LOCATION PU.
Dublin: Sold only at Dick's and Lloyd's Coffee-Houses, 1705, 4th edn (as *The tale of a tub: Written for the universal improvement of mankind. To which is added, an account*

of a battle between the antient and modern books in St. James's Library. SOURCE Teerink/Scouten, 221; ESTC t1866. LOCATION PU.

Dublin: n.p., 1721 (trans. by Réné Macé as *Les trios justaucorps, conte bleu*). SOURCE Rochedieu, p. 322; COPAC. LOCATION L.

The Hague: Henri Scheurleer, 1721, 2 vols. (trans. by Justus Van Effen as *Le conte du tonneau contentant tout ce que les arts et les sciences ont de plus sublime, et de plus mystérieux. Avec plusieurs autres pièces très curieuses*). SOURCE Streeter, 355; Pickering & Chatto cat. 737/481; Teerink/Scouten, 263; OCLC. LOCATION MH.

Altona: Auf Kosten guter Freunde, 1729 (trans. as *Des ber?mten Herrn D. Schwifts Mährgen von der Tonne, sum allgemeinen Nutzen des menschlichen Geschlechts abgefasset, nebst einem vollständigen Begriffe einer allgemeinen Gelehrsamkeit*). SOURCE Teerink/Scouten, 271. LOCATION PU.

Oxford: Oxford Univ. Press, 1990 (as *A Tale of the tub and other works*; ed. and introd. by Angus Ross and David Woolley). SOURCE COPAC. LOCATION Univ. College, London.

COMMENTARY A satire on religious fanaticism influenced by Sir William Temple's treatise on ancient and modern learning that ridicules the pride, delusion and irrationality of some forms of religious dissent. It is cast in mock-heroic Augustan form, using an allegory of a bee and a spider to present the conflict. It contrasts three brothers, one of whom is a Catholic, another an Anglican, and the third a Dissenter [Field Day, i, pp 327, 329, 330–8; Hogan 2, p. 1160; OCIL, p. 552].

S667   *Travels into several remote nations of the world. In four parts. By Lemuel Gulliver, first a surgeon, and then a captain of several ships* [anon.].

London: Benjamin Motte, 1726, 2 vols. (ill.). SOURCE Bradshaw, 6337; McBurney, 199; McBurney & Taylor, 889; Teerink/Scouten 389–91 (3 impressions). LOCATION Dt, L, C, IU.

Dublin: J. Hyde, 1726, 2 vols. (ill.). SOURCE Teerink/Scouten 297; ESTC t1862. LOCATION Dt (1727, 2nd edn), Univ. of Michigan.

Dublin: G. Risk, G. Ewing & W. Smith, 1727. SOURCE Teerink/Scouten 298; ESTC t208193. LOCATION L, D.

The Hague: Alberts & Van der Kloot, 1727, 4 vols. (trans. as *Reisbeschryving na verscheyde afgelegene natien in de wereld*). SOURCE Teerink/Scouten 366. LOCATION Univ. of Michigan.

The Hague: P. Gosse & J. Neaulme, 1727–28, 3 vols. (trans. as *Voyages du Capitaine Lemuel Gulliver en divers pays éloignez*). SOURCE Edwards cat. 30/93; Teerink/Scouten 371, 373. LOCATION DPL Gilbert coll. (1730 edn).

Paris: Hypolite-Louis Guerin, 1727, 2 vols. (trans. as *Voyages des Gulliver*). SOURCE Hall cat. June 2003/174; Teerink/Scouten 383. LOCATION BNF, PU.

COMMENTARY Intended as a political and social satire, and based on the author's experiences of politics, it is a mixture of fantasy, travel, parody, scientific discourse, fiction and philosophy, in a purportedly-autobiographical account of Lemuel Gulliver's voyages to Lilliput (inhabited by diminutive people), Brobdingnag (inhabited by giants), Laputa (where the inhabitants are obsessed by abstract science), and the country of the Houyhnhnm (where rational horses rule degenerate people called Yahoos) [Field Day, i, pp 352–91, iv, p. 1147; Hogan, 2, pp 1167–70; OCIL, p. 231; ODNB].

— COLLECTED WORKS

S668   *The works of J.S., D.D., D.S.P.D.*

Dublin: G. Faulkner, 1735, 4 vols. SOURCE McBurney & Taylor, 898; Teerink/Scouten 41. LOCATION IU.

Dublin: G. Faulkner, 1738, 6 vols. SOURCE Teerink/Scouten 42. LOCATION O.

Dublin: G. Faulkner, 1741–46, 8 vols. (revsd and corrected). SOURCE ESTC t52746. LOCATION D, O.

S669 *The works of Jonathan Swift, D.D., Dean of St. Patrick's, Dublin, accurately revised in twelve volumes.*
London: C. Bathurst, C. Davis, C. Hitch, L. Hawkes, J. Hodges & J. Dodsley, 1754–79, 25 vols. in 26. SOURCE McBurney & Taylor, 900; Teerink/Scouten 88. LOCATION IU.

'SYMINGTON, Maggie', pseud. See BLATHWAYT, Mrs Sarah Margaret.

SYNGE, Revd Edward, b. Inishannon (Co. Cork) 1659, d. Ireland? 1741. Cleric and religious writer, ES was the son of Edward Synge, bishop of Cork, Cloyne and Ross, and Barbara Latham of New Place (Co. Derry). He was educated at Christ Church, Oxford, were he graduated BA in 1677. He returned to Dublin and graduated MA at TCD. ES was first rector at Laracor (Co. Meath) and spent twenty years as a priest in Cork before becoming chancellor of St Patrick's Cathedral (Dublin); vicar of St Werburgh's (Dublin), bishop of Raphoe, and later archbishop of Tuam (Co. Galway) from 1716 until his death. He was recommended in 1714 for a bishopric by archbishop William King in a letter to the archbishop of Canterbury as 'a learned, prudent, pious and active man, the only objection against him was that he was a Whig!' ES married Anne Proude of Co. Cork, and they had five children: Edward, later bishop first of Ferns and Leighlin, then of Elphin; Nicholas, later bishop of Killaloe (ancestor of playwright John Millington Synge); two sons who died young, and a daughter. ES published many religious tracts and over 60 vols of sermons and was an ardent advocate of a moderate protestantism in an effort to convince Catholics to convert. His writings on religion include *A gentleman' religion* (London, 1693, part l; 1697, parts 2 and 3); *An appendix to a gentleman's religion* (London, 1698); *A plain and easy method* (London, 1715), and *Freethinking in matters of religion stated and recommended* (London, 1727). He was intensely interested in education and published anonymously *An account of the ... charity-schools in Ireland* (Dublin, 1717). For his portrait and papers, see ODNB. SOURCE Allibone, ii, p. 2325; BLC; Field Day, i, pp 760–4, 768, 804; Leslie, *Raphoe*, pp 8–9; K. Milne, *The Irish charity schools* (Dublin, 1997), pp 13–14; ODNB; RIA/DIB.

S670 *A sincere Christian and convert from the Church of Rome, exemplified in the life of Daniel Herly, a poor Irish peasant* [anon.].
London: Thomas Trye, 1742. SOURCE ESTC t74375. LOCATION L, O.
+ London: Thomas Trye, 1746 (new edn, corrected by the most Reverend Dr Edward Synge, late Lord Archbishop of Tuam in Ireland). SOURCE ESTC t074510. LOCATION L, InND Loeber coll.
+ Dublin: Printed by John Murphy, 1766, 4th edn. SOURCE Falkner Greirson cat. 17/427; ESTC t118799. LOCATION D.
COMMENTARY The earliest Dublin edn is known only from the 1766, 4th edn imprint. The 1764 London edn, which was priced at 3*d*. or 20*s*. per hundred, consists of 37pp, and the Dublin 1766 edn of 83pp. One of the earliest Irish religious-fiction stories, it is based on the account by Daniel Herly of his conversion from catholicism to protestantism. The story tells of the books he enjoys reading, including 'The seven wise masters, The history of Fortunatus, Gesta Romanorum, Valentine and Orson, the seven champions of Christendom, with diverse others of the like sort'. He also reads several books for and against popery. All these use the holy scriptures for their authority, so Daniel decides to read the Bible himself and asks permission from the priest to do so. The priest refuses and argues with him, but Daniel persists [ML; RL].

T

'T., C.J.', fl. 1889. Pseudonym of an anthologist who also edited *Oriental folktales* (London, 1905) and several other volumes of folklore and legends from different countries. SOURCE RL.

T1   *Folk-lore and legends (Ireland)* (ed. by 'C.J.T.').
+ London: W.W. Gibbings, 1889. SOURCE Brown 32; OCLC (1891 edn). LOCATION L (1891 edn), InND Loeber coll.
COMMENTARY Contents: 'Larry Hayes and the enchanted man', 'Jack o' the lantern', 'Flory Cantillon's funeral' [from Thomas Crofton Croker's§ *Fairy legends*, London, 1828], 'Saint Brandon and Donagha', 'Hanlon's mill', 'The song of the little bird', 'The rock of the candle' [Gerald Griffin§], 'The legend of Knockgrafton' [William Maginn§], 'Fuin Mac Cumhal and the salmon of knowledge', 'Legend of Garadh Duff', 'The young piper' [from Thomas Crofton Croker's§ *Fairy legends*], 'The headless horseman of Shanacloch', 'Legend of Bottle-hill' [William Maginn§], 'The spectre of Erigle Truagh', 'The O'Donoghue in the lake', 'The lord of Ballyteagh', 'The brewery of egg-shells' [from Thomas Crofton Croker's§ *Fairy legends*], 'Daniel the outlaw', 'The nurse's adventure', 'The pilfered corn', 'The changeling' [from Thomas Crofton Croker's§ *Fairy legends*], 'Stephen Sinnott's plough', 'The haunted cellar' [from Thomas Crofton Croker's§ *Fairy legends*], 'Legend of Ossheen', 'Fior Usaga' [from Thomas Crofton Croker's§ *Fairy legends*], 'The fairies and the butler', 'The legend of Sgarrive-a-Kuilleen', 'The tailor and the changeling', 'The lady of Gollerus', 'Darby, the red cat', 'Carrig-Cleena', 'The field of boliauns' [from Thomas Crofton Croker's§ *Fairy legends*], 'The fairy's quern' [RL].

'T., Ellen', pseud. 'A Lady', fl. 1845. Novelist, 'Ellen T.' (a pseud.) probably was Irish because she published her first work in Dublin. SOURCE RL.

T2   *Ravensdale. A tale* (by 'A Lady').
Dublin: William Curry Jnr; London: Longmans, Brown & Co., 1845, 2 vols. SOURCE Block, p. 194; Wolff, 7651. LOCATION L.
+ London: G. Purkess, [1847] (ill.). SOURCE Jarndyce cat. 151/418. LOCATION InND Loeber coll.
COMMENTARY Later serialized in the *Ladies' Journal* (London, 1847) and then published in parts. The London edn is bound from the parts. Set in England among the gentry [ML; RL; Jarndyce].

T3   *Rose Sommerville; or, a husband's mystery and a wife's devotion. A romance* (by 'Ellen T.').
+ London: E. Lloyd, 1847. SOURCE Block, p. 201. LOCATION L.
COMMENTARY Preface is written from London. Set in England; no Irish content [ML].

T4   *Eardley Hall. A tale* (by 'Ellen T.', authoress of *Rose Sommerville*, *Ravensdale*).
+ London: E. Lloyd, [1850]. SOURCE Block, p. 64. LOCATION L, InND Loeber coll.
COMMENTARY No Irish content [CM].

T5   *Emily Percy; or, the heiress of Sackville* (by 'Ellen T.')
+ London: J. Purkess, W. Strange, [c.1850]. SOURCE Alston, p. 426. LOCATION L.
COMMENTARY No Irish content [CM].

'T., M.E.', pseud. See DOYLE, M.

1279

TALBOT, the Hon. Thomas, fl. 1882. Novelist, translator and poet, TT's parentage is unclear. O'Donoghue believes he is Irish, but has no particulars. Apparently he is not a member of the Talbot family of Malahide (Co. Dublin). He translated classical Greek and Latin poetry and wrote *Greece and the Greeks; or a historic sketch of Attic life and manners* (London, 1880). SOURCE Allibone Suppl., ii, p. 1416; MVP, p. 451; O'Donoghue, p. 449; RL.

T6   *The Granvilles. An Irish tale* (by the Hon. Thomas Talbot; dedicated to Lady Lovedale [granddaughter of Herbert Granville]).
+ London: Sampson Low, Marston, Searle & Rivington, 1882, 3 vols. SOURCE Brown 2, 1523 (mistakenly states author is Thorpe Talbot); Watters, p. 404; Wolff, 6656.
LOCATION D, L, InND Loeber coll.
COMMENTARY Historical fiction set in the south of Ireland in the time of Daniel O'Connell. The book tells the story of Herbert Granville, whose family has fallen on hard times, partly through the machinations of a land agent. Herbert is in love with Fanny Moore, whose brother is in love with Herbert's sister Julia. Mrs Moore is very much against the matches since the Granvilles are now poor. Fanny is pursued by the coarse but rich Joe Whitmore, who plots against Herbert and who tries to separate Herbert and Fanny. He is unsuccessful, mainly because of the interventions of Capt. Gorman and Denny Mullins, a piper. In the end, the Granvilles are restored to their fortune and all barriers to the unions between the two families are removed. Interspersed are descriptions of Capt. Gorman's travels to Canada, and his report on how seals were caught on the ice. The novel criticizes the Whitefeet, a local group of the Whiteboy agrarian protest organization founded in the 1760s in Cos. Tipperary and Waterford, who are mainly portrayed as unthinking peasants [ML].

TAUNTON, M. See **TAUNTON, Mrs Margaret Theodosia**.

TAUNTON, Mrs Margaret Theodosia (also known as Margaret T. Taylor and M. Taunton), fl. 1851. Catholic religious and historical fiction writer, MTT's nationality is unclear. She also wrote under the pseudonym 'M.T.A.C. Dolman'. Her only known Irish work is listed here. SOURCE Alston, p. 427; COPAC.

T7   *The last of the Catholic O'Malleys. A tale* (by M. Taunton).
+ London: R. Washbourne, 1870. SOURCE Allibone Suppl., ii, p. 1418; Alston, p. 427.
LOCATION D, L.
+ New York: P.J. Kenedy, 1905 (Catholic Fireside Library). SOURCE Brown, 1560.
LOCATION InND Loeber coll.
COMMENTARY Set in western Mayo in 1798. At age 15 Grace is married against her will to a disreputable young man. He grows fond of her and dies penitent three years later. Their child, stolen from their mother by his nurse, grows up to join the navy. Grace in the meantime has married a naval officer. In the end, she gets her son back [Brown].

TAUTPHOEUS, Baroness. See **TAUTPHOEUS, Baroness Jemima von**.

TAUTPHOEUS, Baroness Jemima von (née Montgomery; known as **Baroness Tautphoeus**), b. Seaview (Co. Donegal) 1807, d. Munich (Germany) 1893. Romance novelist, Jemima was the daughter of James Montgomery, a landowner at Seaview, and Jemima Glasgow of Co. Leitrim. According to the ODNB, she was a cousin to Maria Edgeworth§, who considered her to be 'one of the most interesting people it was possible to know' (Thompson, pp 114–19). Jemima was educated at home and in 1838 married Cajetan Joseph Friedrich, baron von Tautphoeus of Marquartstein (Bavaria), who was chamberlain to the king of Bavaria. The remainder of her life was spent in Germany and on the Continent, which formed the backdrop to her four novels. These were initially published in London but all were reprinted in Leipzig and three in the US. Her husband died in 1885, a few days after the death of their only son, Rudolf Edgeworth Joseph, who had been appointed Bavarian minister to the Italian court. At home in court or middle-class circles, JvT wrote novels that were popular in their day and were ranked by the *Critic* (London) as English classics. SOURCE Allibone, iii, p. 2338; Blain, p. 1055; Boase, iii, p. 883; Brady, p. 234; Donegal, p. 252; Kunitz & Haycraft, p. 603; NCBEL 4, pp 1404–5; ODNB; RIA/DIB; Sadleir, p. 337; Sutherland, pp 619–20; M.L. Thompson, 'Baroness Tautphoeus', *Atlantic Monthly* (Boston), 74, (July 1894), pp 114–19; L. Thorpe, *Baroness Tautphoeus: an early Victorian novelist* (Rome, 1962).

T8 *The initials. A novel* [anon.].

London: Richard Bentley, 1850, 3 vols. SOURCE Sadleir, 3176; Wolff, 6662. LOCATION D (1886 edn), L.

London: Richard Bentley, 1853 (new edn). SOURCE Topp 8, 52. LOCATION C.

+ Leipzig: Bernard Tauchnitz, 1854, 2 vols. SOURCE T & B, 288–89. LOCATION D, InND Loeber coll.

Philadelphia: A. Hart, 1850 (as *The initials. A story of modern life*). SOURCE Topp 5, p. 157; OCLC. LOCATION Dartmouth College, Hanover, NH.

COMMENTARY An immensely popular novel, it is the story of Alfred Hamilton, second son of an English family, who is sent abroad to be groomed for the diplomatic service. He has no financial expectations from his family, except perhaps from an uncle. He lives in Munich with a family with two daughters. He falls in love first with a flighty girl who is betrothed to a much older major. Alfred quarrels with the eldest daughter, who professes to despise him. Over time, they learn to love each other, but the lack of money on both sides is a great impediment. Eventually, they decide to live very plainly in a farmhouse in Bavaria, where they remain until they are recalled to England by the death of Alfred 's uncle. The story gives numerous descriptions of German customs and the scenery of the Bavarian Alps [ML; ODNB].

T9 *Cyrilla. A tale* [anon].

+ London: Richard Bentley, 1853, 3 vols. SOURCE Sadleir, 3175; Wolff, 6661. LOCATION L, InND Loeber coll.

London: Richard Bentley, 1872 ([revsd edn]; Bentley's Favourite Novels). SOURCE Burmester list; COPAC. LOCATION L.

Leipzig: Bernard Tauchnitz, 1853, 2 vols in 1. SOURCE T & B, 282–83; OCLC. LOCATION NIC.

COMMENTARY The ODNB states that this novel is based on the criminal trial of Assessor Zahn, which it accurately follows, thus refuting criticism of the novel as melodramatic. Set in Germany among the titled-classes where a rich countess wants Rupert, her nephew and heir, to marry Cyrilla, her poor niece. Neither nephew or niece is interested in this scenario. Cyrilla secretly marries Count Zorndorff, who was destined to marry Margaret, a rich heiress. Zorndorff is forced by his father – who does not know that he has already married – to wed Margaret. Margaret is in poor health and Zorndorff hopes that she will die soon as he does not wish to release Cyrilla. In the meantime, Cyrilla and Rupert become very fond of each other. Zorndorff is jealous and is instrumental in killing Rupert. Cyrilla dies of grief and Zorndorff goes to prison for twenty years. When objections were made to the novel's ending, the author rewrote the novel, omitting the death of Cyrilla and Rupert and the trial of Count Zorndorff and his accomplices. This revision was published in 1872 [ML; ODNB; Burmester list].

T10 *Quits. A novel* [anon.].

+ London: Richard Bentley, 1857, 3 vols. SOURCE Sadleir, 3177; Wolff, 6663; Topp 8, 74. LOCATION D (incomplete), L.

+ Leipzig: Bernard Tauchnitz, 1858, 2 vols. in 1. SOURCE T & B, 428. LOCATION D, InND Loeber coll.

Philadelphia: J.B. Lippincott, 1857, 2 vols. SOURCE Topp 5, p. 1567; OCLC. LOCATION NN.

COMMENTARY Lord Medway's younger brother prevents him from marrying Nora, a distant relative. She is an intellectual young woman and has been brought up on the Continent by her wandering parents who are, to some extent, social outcasts. Nora comes to England to live with an uncongenial relative after both her parents have died and after the sudden end of the budding love affair. She inherits a vast fortune from her relative and travels on the Continent, mostly in Bavaria, of which there are many descriptions. There she meets the brother who had thwarted her union with Lord Medway and who has come into the title after his brother's death. After initial antipathy to each other, they eventually fall in love [ML; ODNB].

T11   *At odds* (by the Baroness Tautphoeus).
    London: Richard Bentley, 1863, 2 vols. SOURCE Sadleir, 3174. LOCATION L.
    Leipzig: Bernard Tauchnitz, 1863, 2 vols. SOURCE T & B, 663–64; OCLC. LOCATION DCL.
    + Leipzig: L. Wiedemann, 1863 (trans. as *Uneins*). SOURCE Alston, p. 427; NCBEL 3, p. 968. LOCATION L.
    + Philadelphia: J.B. Lippincott & Co., 1863. LOCATION InND Loeber coll.

COMMENTARY Written when the author was ill for an extended period, it is a romance set in Bavaria and Austria at the beginning of the 1800s, during the Napoleonic campaigns. Several people of Irish extraction feature in the story, which deals with the fortunes of war interwoven with various romantic alliances [ML; ODNB].

TAYLOR, Miss —. Attributed author. See **EDGEWORTH, Mrs** —.

TAYLOR, Emily, pseud. 'A Lady', b. Banham (Norfolk) 1795, d. London 1872. English educator, novelist, biographer and children's writer, ET lived in New Buckenham (Norfolk). She was the author of *Tales of the Saxons* (London, 1832); *Tales of the English* (London, 1833), and a popular biography of Sir Thomas More. She wrote also about poetry and poets, was a contributor to the *Magnet Stories* and a hymnist of note. In London she established a school for middle-class girls. According to the preface to the following work, she had visited Ireland. Only her works with Irish content are listed below. SOURCE Allibone, iii, p. 2343; Boase, iii, p. 889; BLC; NCBEL 4, pp 1875–6 (list of publications); ODNB [under Edgar Taylor].

T12   *The Irish tourist; or, tales of the people and the provinces of Ireland* [anon.].
    + London: Harvey & Darton, 1837 (ill.; see Plate 62). LOCATION CaOTP (1843 edn), DCL (1843 edn), InND Loeber coll.

COMMENTARY A fictional account of travel, written for children. In the preface, the author expresses the intention 'to present juvenile readers with as lively and graphic a view of Ireland as a diligent study of the best tourists, some personal knowledge of the country, and a memory, early filled with details gathered from the lips of those who knew well the land they spoke of, would permit me to put before them ... a book of travels in Ireland, comprehending accounts of the local curiosities, the scenery, situation of towns, and the general state of the country'. The sections cover the four provinces, each in a different story, often dealing with the relations between Catholics and Protestants. It contains a map showing the places visited [ML].

T13   *Norah Toole, and other tales, illustrative of national and domestic manners* (by 'A Lady').
    + London: John W. Parker, 1844 (ill.). SOURCE Allibone, iii, p. 2343; Block, p. 173; Osborne, p. 919. SOURCE Dt, L, CaOTP, NUC.

COMMENTARY Written for juveniles. Contents: 'Nora Toole; a tale of Ireland' (set among poor labourers near Westport, Co. Mayo), 'Rob Maxwell; or, the Highland shepherd', 'Felix Jansen; or, life in Norway', 'Leonard Hartmann, the Swiss traveller' [ML; Osborne].

TAYLOR, Frederick, pseud. '**Ballinasloe**', fl. 1861. Writer of fiction dealing with horses and horse dealers, FT was possibly an Englishman. He belonged to the Eighth Royal Irish Hussars and was probably stationed in Ballinasloe (Co. Galway), famous for its horse and cattle fair. Under his pseudonym he contributed to the *Field* (London) [RL].

T14   *Recollections of a horse dealer* (by Frederick Taylor, 'Ballinasloe').
+ London: Ward & Lock, 1861. SOURCE Topp 2, 272. LOCATION L, RB.
COMMENTARY Set in Ireland and contains anecdotes and information about horses and horse dealing [ML].

T15   *Confessions of a horse coper, comprising many curious revelations in horse dealing* (by 'Ballinasloe').
+ London: George Vickers, [1861]. SOURCE Sadleir, 3517. LOCATION L.
COMMENTARY The page header is 'The revelations of a horse dealer'. Long autobiographical account of a horse dealer (presumably the author), followed by shorter pieces of lore about horses. The horse dealer was born in north Derbyshire but at age 16 he joined an Irish regiment of Hussars where he perfected his knowledge of horses [ML; Sadleir].

TAYLOR, Col. Meadows. See **TAYLOR, Col. Philip Meadows**.

TAYLOR, Col. Philip Meadows (also known as **Col. Meadows Taylor**), b. Liverpool (Lancs.) 1808, d. Mentone (France) 1876. Military man, administrator, Indian expert and popular novelist, PMT moved as a boy to his father's native Dublin, where the senior Philip Meadows Taylor was executive manager of a large brewery. PMT was also named after his grandfather, Revd Philip Meadows Taylor, who published a series of Irish stories and articles in *Bentley's Miscellany* (London, 1839–42) and the *Dublin University Magazine* (1850). At age 15 the youngest PMT was sent to Bombay, and when only age 18 he was appointed assistant police superintendent for the Nizam of Hyderabad. He taught himself surveying, engineering, English and Indian law, botany and geology. He remained in the Nizam's service and became an effective governor of several provinces, proving to be an able and popular administrator and maintaining peace over the province of Booldana during the time of the Indian mutiny by 'moral strength' (DNB) in the absence of troops. For a time he was the London *Times* correspondent in India. Eventually his health suffered and he returned first to England and then to Dublin in 1860, and settled at his grandfather's house, Old Court, Harold's Cross. There he wrote several novels on Indian life, featuring many of the people and situations he had known. In a review of his last novel in the *Spectator* (London), he was acclaimed for educating English people on India through his fiction more than any formal history had done. He was an authority on Indian literature and lectured on the topic in Dublin in 1864. He contributed to periodicals such as the *Keepsake*, *Fraser's Magazine* (both London), *Household Words* (London, 1850), and the *Foreign Quarterly Review* (London, 1845–46). He wrote several articles on Indian antiquities, including 'Description of cairns, cromlechs, kistvaens and other Celtic, Druidical or Scythian monuments in the Dekhan', which was first published in the journal of the Bombay branch of the Royal Asiatic Society and later by the RIA (xxiv (1865)). His *A student's manual of the history of India from the earliest period to the present* (London, 1870) was reprinted many times. His daughter Alice edited his biography, *The story of my life* (London, 1877, 1878 and 1882). PMT's papers are in the BL and the NLS and his family tree and coat of arms are in the NLI. He was featured in 'Our portrait gallery' in the *Dublin*

University Magazine (April, 1841). His portraits are listed by Elmes. SOURCE [anon.], *The afternoon lectures on literature and art* (Dublin, 1864), pp 101–50; Allibone, iii, p. 2358 [under Meadows Taylor]; Allibone Suppl., ii, pp 1421–2; Boase, iii, pp 899–900; Curran index; Elmes, p. 201; D. Finkelstein, *Philip Meadows Taylor (1808–1876): A bibliography* ([Brisbane], 1990); NCBEL 4, p. 1405; ODNB; RL; Rowan cat. 60/447; Sutherland, pp 620–1.

T16   *Confessions of a Thug* (by Meadows Taylor; dedicated to George Lord Auckland, Gov.-Gen. of India, 'who is vigorously prosecuting those admirable measures for the suppression of thuggees').

+ London: Richard Bentley, 1839, 3 vols. SOURCE DNB; Sutherland, p. 620; Topp 8, 50; COPAC. LOCATION L.

+ Oxford: Univ. Press, 1986. SOURCE NCBEL 4, p. 1405. LOCATION L.

COMMENTARY The preface to the 1873 edn is dated from Old Court, Harold's Cross (Dublin), Apr. 1873. Suggested by Bulwer Lytton§ while PMT was in England recovering from a bout of malaria, this novel was an immediate success in England and was reprinted well into the twentieth century. Queen Victoria read it eagerly in sheets as it appeared. Set in India, it tells of the life of a thug-murderer who, usually operating in a like-minded group, offered protection to travellers but murdered them, mainly by strangling them with a handkerchief. Thugs believed that their work was in the service of the goddess Bhowanee and that they were doing the world a service by removing as many people from it as possible. The story is told to an English officer (i.e., the author) by an erstwhile thug, Ameer Ali, while imprisoned. PMT had regretted that his military service at the time prevented him from investigating and suppressing the movement, later accomplished by Col. Sir H.W. Sleeman [ML; ODNB; Quaritch cat. 1336/97].

T17   *Tippoo Sultaun: A tale of the Mysore War* (by Meadows Taylor; dedicated to William Newnham).

+ London: Richard Bentley, 1840, 3 vols. SOURCE DNB; NCBEL 4, p. 1405; Sutherland, p. 62; OCLC. LOCATION GEU.

New Delhi: Asian Education Services, 1986. SOURCE NCBEL 4, p. 1405; OCLC. LOCATION MH.

COMMENTARY A novel of the Mysore War climaxing in the battle of Seringapatem. It was reprinted many times [RL].

T18   *Tara: A Mahratta tale* (by Meadows Taylor; dedicated to the earl of Carlisle, viceroy of Ireland).

+ Edinburgh, London: William Blackwood & Sons, 1863, 3 vols. SOURCE NCBEL 4, p. 1405; CCOPAC. LOCATION L, NUC (probably mistakenly mentions 1843 edn).

+ London: Kegan Paul, Trench & Co., 1884 (5th edn; ill. W.C.R.B.). LOCATION InND Loeber coll.

Leipzig: Bernard Tauchnitz, 1864, 3 vols. SOURCE T & B, 702–04. LOCATION NUC.

COMMENTARY First tale in a trilogy illustrating three epochs in the history of India. Set in India around 1657 when the Mahrattas cast off their allegiance, rose to power under Sivajee, and defeated the army of Beejapoor. The tale describes religious and territorial conflicts, while depicting the life of a girl who has dedicated herself to a goddess. Eventually, she marries a man from a different religion [ML; Sutherland, p. 620; Tiger cat. 6/98/254].

T19   *Ralph Darnell* (by Capt. Meadows Taylor).

+ Edinburgh, London: William Blackwood & Sons, 1865, 3 vols. SOURCE COPAC. LOCATION L.

COMMENTARY Second tale in a trilogy, starting with *Tara* (Edinburgh, 1863, 3 vols.), illustrating three epochs in the history of India. This volume follows the conquests of Clive at Plassey, marking the rise of English power in India, and deals with the events of 1757 and the terrible Black Hole tragedy [Sutherland, p. 620; Tiger cat.].

T20   *Seeta* (by Meadows Taylor; dedicated to the author's daughters, Alice and Amy [Taylor]).
+ London: Henry S. King & Sons, 1872, 3 vols. SOURCE OCLC. LOCATION L, InND Loeber coll. (London, Kegan [1880] edn).
COMMENTARY Third tale in the trilogy of *Tara* (Edinburgh, 1863, 3 vols.) and *Ralph Darnell* (Edinburgh, 1865, 3 vols.), illustrating three epochs in the history of India. In this volume, the literal fulfilment of a prediction that the rule of the English Company should come to an end in a hundred years is a motive for the narrative of the Indian mutiny (1857) [ML].

T21   *A noble queen: a romance of Indian history* (by Meadows Taylor).
+ London: C. Kegan Paul & Co., 1878. SOURCE Allibone Suppl., ii, p. 1422; NCBEL 4, p. 1405; Sutherland, pp 620–1; OCLC. LOCATION C.
New Delhi: Asian Educational Services, 1968. SOURCE OCLC. LOCATION DCL.
COMMENTARY First serialized in the *Overland Mail* (London, Feb.–Dec. 1875), it was published posthumously. Set in the early-seventeenth century, the novel chronicles Indian resistance to the Mogul invasion and the siege of Ahmednuggar [Sutherland, p. 620].

— COLLECTED WORKS
T22   *Colonel Meadows Taylor's Indian Tales.*
London: Henry S. King & Co., 1873–74, [3 vols?]. SOURCE RL; COPAC. LOCATION PU (1 vol.).

TAYLOUR, Lady Virginia Frances Zerlina. See SANDARS, Lady Virginia Frances Zerlina.

TEEGAN, Thomas Henry, fl. 1887. Historical novelist, THT was probably Irish, given that he published his fiction in Dublin. SOURCE RL.

T23   *The fall of Moscow. March of the grand army to the Niemen. A military novel* (by Thomas Henry Teegan; dedicated to Marshal Ney).
+ Dublin: Sullivan Bros; London: Simpkin, Marshall & Co., 1887 (ill.). SOURCE Topp 8, 858. LOCATION L.
+ London: Simpkin, Marshall, Hamilton, Kent & Co., [1900] (as *With the grand army to Moscow. An historical novel*; ill.). LOCATION D (n.d. edn), L, NUC.
COMMENTARY Historical narrative of the feats of Napoleon Bonaparte as told by Camille Dumont, who joins the Military School of Paris in 1808. By 1811 Bonaparte's relations with Russia have ceased to be friendly. In 1812 Bonaparte orders Dumont's army to march to Germany. Contained within the military narrative is a love story between Dumont and Mlle Caroline d'Aubrey. The story shifts to the frontiers of Russia and includes a history of Russia from the twelfth century. Dumont tells of the departure of the army from Moscow and Napoleon's gradual downfall. Dumont returns to the hill of Ponari where he sees Caroline's father, Gen. Baron d'Aubrey, lying ill. Dumont saves his life and proves to d'Aubrey his nobility of soul. D'Aubrey gives permission to Dumont to marry his daughter. The narrative follows the march of the European army against Napoleon and his abdication in 1814, the year in which Dumont marries Caroline. An advertisement in this volume states that 'The second volume, *The advance on Moscow*, is in preparation', but this does not appear to have been published separately. However, *With the grand army to Moscow. An historical novel* (London, [1900]) contains the full sequence of 'The march to the Niemen', 'The war', 'Moscow', and 'Retreat' [CD; RL].

TEELING, Bartholomew (Bartle) J., pseud. 'The governor', b. 1848, d. Rome 1921. Novelist, military man and papal privy chamberlain, BJT was the son of Charles George Teeling and Mary

Anna McCarthy. His grandfather had been a United Irishman and his eponymous uncle had served with Gen. Jean-Joseph Humbert, who led a French expeditionary force to Ireland, and was executed in the rebellion of 1798. BJT served in the pontifical Zouaves during Garibaldi's campaign of 1867; was governor of a prison in Ireland (described in his novel below); a captain in the Longford militia, and in the Second South African War became a captain in the Irish Royal Rifles. He devoted a great deal of his life to the Roman Catholic church and was a papal privy chamberlain to Leo XIII, Pius X and Benedict XV. In Ireland, he was secretary of the Catholic Association and a frequent public speaker on the Catholic church in Ireland. He wrote *Military maxims* (London, 1881); *My weatherwise companion* (Edinburgh, 1895), and historical and genealogical articles. His first wife, Theodora Lane Clark, was a writer who published under Mrs Bartle Teeling and the pseuds 'Norman Stuart' and 'Isola'. Two of their sons were killed in the First World War. Some of BJT's papers are in the NLI and in St Patrick's College, Maynooth. His portrait is listed in Elmes. SOURCE Allibone Suppl, ii, p. 1423; Brown 2, p. 255; IBL, 7 (1921), p. 118; RIA/DIB.

T24 *My first prisoner* (by 'The governor'; dedicated to the memory of a good Irish landlord and his only son, called 'my brother Zouave').
    Aberdeen: Moran & Co., 1897. SOURCE Brown 2, 1524. LOCATION D (n.d. edn), L (1898 edn).
COMMENTARY Autobiographical novel set in Ireland. The governor's first prisoner is Robert MacMurrough, nephew of a local landlord, who is arrested in Fenian times on a trivial charge and later liberated, but not until he and the governor become friends. They both go to Italy as Zouaves to fight for the independence of the pope. On their return, they make a tour round Ireland to study the conditions of the people. In 1870 they go again to Italy to take part in the defence of Rome, and MacMurrough is killed there [Brown 2].

'TELL-TALE, Thomas', fl. 1760s. Pseudonym of a story and novella writer. Since the only known work under this pseudonym was published first in Dublin, it is probable the author was Irish [RL].

T25 *The new story teller; or, universal entertainer. Being a certain method to cast off care, an infallible cordial for low-spirits, and a help to conversation* (by 'Thomas Tell-tale').
    Dublin: James Hoey Jnr [1764?], 2 vols. SOURCE Adv. in *The orientalist. A volume of tales after the Eastern taste* (Dublin, 1764).
    London: Printed for the author, 1767 (as *The new modern story teller, or universal entertainer; being a collection of merry, polite, grave, moral, entertertaining [sic] and improving tales*). SOURCE ESTC t010036. LOCATION L, MH.
COMMENTARY No copy of the Dublin edn located. It may be based on or inspired by *The modern story-teller: or, a general entertainer. Being a collection of … tales and novels, all entirely new* (London, 1748–49, 2 vols.). An advertisement for the Dublin edn states that this work is interspersed with 'several new Novels, and each volume concludes with a long one; the first with the *History of Julia*; the second, with that of *Arabella* … [The work] consists chiefly of new stories; many of them equal to the best and most laughable now on draught among Good Companions' [RL; ESTC n039906].

TEMPLE, Mrs —. See TEMPLE, Mrs Ferdinand.

TEMPLE, Mrs Ferdinand (Laura Sophia; also known as Mrs Temple), b. 1763, d. after 1820. Epistolary novelist and poet, Mrs FT published poems in *Flowers of literature* (London, 1806), which identified her as the author of the following novel. SOURCE British Fiction; introductory section on 'Novelists' in *Flowers of literature* (London, 1806).

T26   *Ferdinand Fitzormond; or, the fool of nature* (by Mrs Temple).
+ London: Richard Phillips, 1805, 5 vols. SOURCE Allibone iii, p. 2367; BD, p. 342;
British Fiction; Garside 1805:68. LOCATION Corvey CME 3–628– 48948, L.
COMMENTARY Adv. at the beginning of the volume signed F. Temple, dated London, May
1805. Epistolary novel set in England with some Irish characters [ML].

TEMPLE, Laura Sophia. See **TEMPLE, Mrs Ferdinand.**

TENCH, Mary F.A. See **TENCH, Mary Frances Alicia.**

TENCH, Mary Frances Alicia (known as **Mary F.A. Tench**), fl. 1870s. Writer of religious
fiction for juveniles, MFAT was a Protestant of Irish birth. She spent her childhood and youth
at the family home on the Wexford coast, probably Ballyhealy, south of Bridgetown. Later
she lived in Ceylon (and probably Australia) for sixteen years and also in London. She pub-
lished six novels, of which three are set in Ireland and Australia. SOURCE Brown, p. 289;
Browne, p. 138; RL; Rowe & Scallan, 143.
T27   *Little Ned Mason; or, the beauty of holiness* [anon.].
London, Chilworth: Society for Promoting Christian Knowledge, [1879]. LOCATION
L.
T28   *The young Draytons; or, "lost in the bush"* (by Mary F.A. Tench).
London: Christian Knowledge Society, [1881]. SOURCE Allibone Suppl., ii, p. 1425;
OCLC. LOCATION L.
T29   *Madge and her friends; or, living unto others* (by Mary F.A. Tench).
London, Paris, New York: Cassell, Petter, Galpin & Co., [1881]. SOURCE Allibone
Suppl., ii, p. 1425. LOCATION L.
T30   *Where the surf breaks* (by Mary F.A. Tench; dedicated to the author's father).
+ London: Hurst & Blackett, 1897. SOURCE Brown, 1563; COPAC. LOCATION D, L.
COMMENTARY A series sketches and tales, set in the barony of Forth in Co. Wexford
[Brown].
T31   *A prince from the great never never* (by Mary F.A. Tench).
London: Hurst & Blackett, 1899. SOURCE Brown, p. 289; COPAC. LOCATION L.
COMMENTARY Opens in Ireland and then the scene shifts to Australia [Brown].
T32   *Against the pikes* (by Mary F.A. Tench).
London: W.R. Russell & Co., [1903]. SOURCE Brown, 1564; COPAC. LOCATION L.
COMMENTARY The story of Phil O'Brien who returns to Ireland after many years of sin and
suffering in Australia. He finds his first love unchanged in heart, only to see her die. For her
sake, he forgoes revenge on the man who had wrecked his life and dies to save his enemy
[Brown].

'THACKER, W. Ridley', pseud. See **HAMILTON, Edwin.**

THACKERAY, William Makepeace, b. Calcutta (India) 1811, d. London 1863. Prominent
English novelist, WMT was the son of Richmond Thackeray, an East India Company official, and
Anne Becher. He was educated at Charterhouse and Trinity College, Cambridge, studied at the
Middle Temple but disliked the law as a career and turned to journalism and illustration. He married Isabella Creagh Shawe, daughter of Col. Shawe of Doneraile (Co. Cork), at the British Embassy
in Paris in 1836. Many characters in his novels are Irish. He spent some time in Ireland in 1840
when he took his ailing wife to visit her mother, and later in 1842 when he made an extended tour
of the country. In 1843 he illustrated and published in London *The Irish sketch book*, based on his

travels. It gives a vivid description of pre-Famine Ireland, but he remarked, 'A man ought to be forty years in Ireland, not three months, to begin to understand it'. The book gave offence to many, and Samuel Ferguson§ severed his connection with the *Dublin University Magazine* as Charles Lever§, then editor, had accepted Thackeray's dedication. WMT's *The luck of Barry Lyndon* (New York, 1853, 2 vols.), which some critics believe is his most powerful novel, draws on his time in Ireland. For further biographical and bibliographical details, see ODNB. SOURCE Allibone, iii, pp 2377–81; Brown, p. 290; Crookshank, p. 312; Field Day, ii, pp 385, 498, 1007; Hogan 2, p. 1187; OCIL, pp 556–7; NCBEL 4, 1406–13; ODNB; Sutherland, pp 623–5.

T33 *The luck of Barry Lyndon: A romance of the last century* (by William Makepeace Thackeray).
+ New York: D. Appleton & Co., 1853, 2 vols. SOURCE OCLC. LOCATION Bloomsburg Univ. (PA), InND Loeber coll.
+ London: Bradbury & Evans, 1856 (as *The memoirs of Barry Lyndon, Esq., of the kingdom of Ireland. Containing an account of his extraordinary adventures; misfortunes; his sufferings in the service of his late Prussian Majesty; his visits to many of the courts of Europe; his marriage, and splendid establishments in England and Ireland; and the many cruel persecutions, conspiracies, and slanders of which he has been a victim*). SOURCE Sutherland, p. 50; Topp 5, p. 255. LOCATION L, InND Loeber coll.
Paris: L. Hachette & Co., 1857 (trans. by Léon de Wailly§ as *Mémoires de Barry Lyndon du royaume d'Irlande*). SOURCE Devonshire, p. 477; OCLC. LOCATION L.
Leipzig: Bernard Tauchnitz, 1856, in *Miscellanies: Prose and Verse, Vol. VI.* SOURCE T & B, 369; COPAC. LOCATION L.
COMMENTARY First serialized in *Fraser's Magazine* (London, Jan.–Dec. 1844). The US edn was reprinted from this source, which contains more text than the London edn in book form. The self-justifying autobiography, written in prison, of a quick-tempered Irishman called Redmond Barry, who leads the life of a blackguard, gamester and army deserter. He marries the rich Lady Lyndon, to whom he is cruel and thoughtless and who soon dies. He assumes her name, then squanders her fortune. The tale is founded in part on the marriage of Andrew Bowes and the countess of Strathmore at the end of the eighteenth century. In 1975 the novel was made into a film, directed by Stanley Kubrick [Brown; Sutherland; ODNB; Topp].

THÉBAUD, A.J. See THÉBAUD, Fr Augustus J.

THÉBAUD, Fr Augustus J. (known as A.J. Thébaud), b. Brittany (France) 1807, d. Fordham (NY) 1890. French Jesuit, educator and religious fiction writer, AJT went to America in 1839 and was president of St John's College, Fordham University (NY), from 1846 to 1863. He later lived at St Francis Xavier's College (New York City). He also published *The Irish race in the past and in the present* (New York, 1873). SOURCE Allibone Suppl., ii, p. 1427; Brown, p. 290.

T34 *Louisa Kirkbride; a tale of New York* (by A.J. Thébaud).
+ New York: Kenedy, 1878 (ill.). SOURCE Brown, 1566. LOCATION D, InND Loeber coll. (New York, Collier 1879 edn).
COMMENTARY Catholic religious fiction set in New York City in the 1860s, just after the Civil War, featuring two families: the O'Byrnes, newly arrived from Co. Wexford, who are poor but virtuous, and the Kirkbrides, a rich merchant family of Ulster origin. The book has several themes: hatred of the Irish (who in the novel actually possess an abundance of good qualities), criminal greed for money, dangers of the stock exchange, and the Catholic church as the only church in which to find peace and true religion. Mrs Kirkbride is the only admirable character in the book who is not Irish and she converts to catholicism in the end [ML; Brown].

THOMAS, Annie. See THOMAS, Annie Hall.

THOMAS, Annie Hall (later Cudlip; known as **Annie Thomas**), b. Aldborough (Suffolk) 1838, d. 1918. English popular romance novelist and periodical writer, AHT was the daughter of Lt. George Thomas, a member of the Coastguard. In 1867 she married Revd George Pender Cudlip. She wrote more than 60 popular novels and contributed to periodicals including the *Broadway* (London) and *Appleton's Journal* (New York). SOURCE Allibone iii, p. 2385; Allibone Suppl., i, p. 427 [under Cudlip]; Alston, p. 431; Blain, pp 1073–4; Sutherland, p. 165 [under Cudlip]; T & B, p. 1016 (list of novels).

T35   *Barry O'Byrne* (by Annie Thomas).
    + London: John Maxwell & Co., 1865. 3 vols. SOURCE Alston, p. 431; OCLC.
    LOCATION L.
    COMMENTARY Set primarily in England but the main character is Irish [ML].

'THOMAS, Elizabeth', pseud. See SMITH, Elizabeth Thomasina Toulmin.

THOMES, William H. See THOMES, William Henry.

THOMES, William Henry (known as **William H. Thomes**), b. Portland (ME) 1824, d. 1895. American adventure writer, WHT was the son of Job Thomes and Mary Lewis. He became a printer, then a journalist and a contributor to periodicals. He travelled in California, Australia and India and wrote a number of stories based on his travels, including *The gold hunter's adventures or life in Australia* (Boston, 1864), and *The bushrangers* (Boston, 1866). For other novels, see Allibone and Wright. SOURCE Allibone, iii, p. 2390; Allibone Suppl., ii, p. 1430; ANB; DAB; R.L. Kilgour, *Lee and Shepard. Publishers for the people* (n.l., 1965), pp 46–9; Wright, ii, p. 329; Wright, iii, p. 543; Wright web.

T36   *The gold hunters in Europe; or, the dead alive* (by William H. Thomes).
    + Boston: Lee & Shepard, 1869 (ill. John Andrews; The Gold Hunter's Library).
    SOURCE Allibone, iii, p. 2390; Wright, ii, 2465; OCLC. LOCATION Wright web.
COMMENTARY Four American men, who have been adventurers in Australia and in America, set out by boat to go to Europe. They land at Queenstown (Cobh, Co. Cork). The adventurers want to have a look at what the Fenians are doing in Ireland, and the Irish think they have come to help the Fenians. After a series of adventures, they leave Ireland and travel to France [ML].

THOMPSON, Mrs A.M. See THOMPSON, Mrs D.P.

THOMPSON, Mrs D.P. (also known as **Mrs A.M. Thompson**), fl. 1846. Religious and historical fiction writer, Mrs DPT was possibly an Irish author. The initials D.P. are those of her husband. According to the title page of *The galley slave* (Dublin, 1858), she was the author of *A brief account of change of religious opinion in Dingle* (London, 1846), which chronicles the evangelizing work of an Anglican curate, Revd Gubbbins, at Dingle (Co. Kerry). Dingle is also the setting of one of her novels. In addition, she wrote *Notes on scriptures* (London, 1846). An inscription in the NLI copy of her *The galley slave ...* (below) shows that she lived at Uptown Park, near Slough (Berks.) in 1880. SOURCE Allibone, iii, p. 2391; COPAC; RL; Rowan cat. 59B/848.

T37   *Ellen of Dingle. A narrative of facts* (by Mrs A.M. Thompson).
    + London: James Nisbet & Co., 1850. SOURCE Block, p. 235. LOCATION L.
COMMENTARY A Protestant orphan servant girl dies and another servant, a Catholic, is upset thinking that the dead girl could not have gone to heaven because she was not a Catholic [ML].

T38   *The galley slave and his daughter. A tale, founded on French Protestant history*
(by Mrs D.P. Thompson).
+ Dublin: Madden & Oldham; London: Hamilton, Adams & Co., Seeley, Jackson,
Halliday, 1858. LOCATION L, InND Loeber coll.
COMMENTARY Historical fiction set in France at the time of Henry IV (1553–1610)
[ML].

THOMPSON, Emily Skeffington (also known as E. Skeffington Thompson), pseud.
'Melusine', fl. 1879. Novelist and miscellaneous writer, EST was the granddaughter of John
Foster, probably the JF who was the last speaker of the Irish house of commons and whose
son Thomas married Lady Harriet Skeffington. She lived in England where she published an
Irish short story for children in the *Bairns' Annual* (London, [1885–86]). EST was one of the
members of a central council of the Junior Irish Literary Clubs in the 1880s or 1890s. With
her sister, Mrs Rae, she founded the Southwark Junior Irish Literary Society in 1889. She
was the author of the *Irish birthday book* (London, 1884), a series of short quotes for each day
of the year. SOURCE JB; ODNB [see John Foster 1714–1828]; NYPL; E. Reilly, p. 251;
RIA/DIB; RL; Ryan, p. 12.
T39   *Moy O'Brien. A tale of Irish life* (by 'Melusine').
New York: Harper & Bros, 1879 (Harper's Franklin Square Library, No. 72). SOURCE
NYPL. LOCATION NN.
+ Dublin: M.H. Gill & Son, [1887]. SOURCE Brown, 1568. LOCATION Dt, L.
Dublin: M.H. Gill & Son; London: Simpkin, Marshall & Co., 1888. SOURCE Topp 8,
901.
COMMENTARY No copy of the Dublin, London edn located. First published as a serial in
Harper's Magazine (New York), and subsequently as a book in a print run of 2,000 copies.
Treats of social and political life in Ireland in the 1880s and ends with many happy marriages
[Brown].

THOMPSON, James Maurice (also known as Maurice Thompson), b. Fairfield (IN) 1844.
American romance novelist, periodical contributor and expert on archery, MT was of Scots-
Irish heritage, the son of Revd Matthew Grigg Thompson, a Baptist minister, and Diantha
Jaeger. He grew up in northern Georgia. He was a Confederate soldier; an engineer; a lawyer,
and state geologist of Indiana. He contributed prose and verse to periodicals such as the Boston
Atlantic Monthly, *New York Tribune*, *Harper's Magazine* and the *Independent* (both New York),
and wrote a collection of dialect sketches of Indiana, *Hoosier mosaics* (New York, 1875). SOURCE
Allibone Suppl., ii, p. 1431; ANB; DAB; DLB, lxxi, lxxiv; RL; Wright, iii, pp 543–4 (list of
novels).
T40   *A banker of Bankersville. A novel* (by Maurice Thompson; dedicated to the Hon.
D.W. Voorhees).
+ New York: Cassell & Co., 1886. SOURCE Allibone Suppl., ii, p. 1431; Wright, iii,
5447. LOCATION L, NUC, InND Loeber coll.
COMMENTARY Describes the lives of the residents of a New York boarding-house run by Mrs
O'Slaughtery, who was born in Co. Kerry. One of her lodgers is Jear Downs, an Irishman.
Mr Milford, another lodger who is a lawyer, enters into business with a Mr Lawson, who
turns out to be a crook. When his wicked ways are discovered, Lawson flees to Canada. Milford
marries Marion, whom he has long admired, and Mrs O'Slaughtery marries Mr Downs [ML].

THOMPSON, Maurice. See THOMPSON, James Maurice.

THOMS, William John, b. London 1803, d. London 1885. Antiquary, bibliographer, editor, novelist and miscellaneous writer, WJT was the son of Nicholas Thomas Thoms, a treasury clerk, and his wife Ruth Ann. WJT edited a series, *Lays and legends of various nations, illustrative of their traditions, popular literature, manners, customs and superstitions* (London, 1834, 5 vols.), of which the following volume is part. WHT was appointed first clerk and then deputy librarian to the house of lords in 1862. In 1864 he persuaded the *Athenaeum* (London) to include pieces on 'old-world manners, customs, and popular superstitions' and in an introductory article coined the term folk-lore to describe such contributions (DNB). SOURCE Allibone, iii, p. 2396; Allibone Suppl., ii, p. 1432; Boase, iii, pp 943–4; OCLC; ODNB; Zimmermann, pp 170, 618.

T41 *Lays and legends of Ireland* (by William John Thoms).
London: George Cowie, 1834. SOURCE Zimmermann, p. 170; OCLC. LOCATION Univ. of Chicago (not found), MH.
COMMENTARY Forms Vol. 3 of *Lays and legends of various nations, illustrative of their traditions, popular literature, manners, customs and superstitions* (London, 1834), 5 vols. [RL].

THOMSON-GREGG, W., fl. 1873. Novelist, possibly Irish, WT-G at some point had probably been resident in Australia. SOURCE RL.

T42 *A desperate character. A tale of the gold fever* (by W. Thomson-Gregg).
+ London: Samuel Tinsley, 1873, 3 vols. SOURCE Figgis cat. 47/332. LOCATION L, InND Loeber coll.
COMMENTARY Hubert de Burgh, having inherited little, leaves Ireland to find his fortune in Australia where, after trials and tribulations, he eventually obtains what he seeks. Set in Melbourne and adjacent areas, it contains lively descriptions of the Australian goldfields, bush rangers, various criminal types, and other descendants of the Irish gentry, who are not fit for the hard work in the mines [ML; Figgis cat.].

T43 *Doctor Middleton's daughter. A novel* [anon.].
+ London: Samuel Tinsley, 1874, 3 vols. SOURCE Wolff, 6713. LOCATION L.
COMMENTARY The narrator is an Australian and the story is set in Ireland [ML].

THYNNE, Lady Charles (née Harriet Frances Bagot), b. 1816, d. London 1881. English novelist with possible Irish connections, HFT was the daughter of Richard Bagot, bishop of Bath and Wells (1845–54). She married in 1837 Revd Lord Charles Thynne, son of the 2nd marquess of Bath (d. 1894), rector of Longbridge and Kingston Deverell (Wilts.). Some years before 1861 they both converted to catholicism under the influence of their friend John Henry Newman§. The fact that several of HFT's works were published first in Dublin suggests an Irish connection, but details remain unclear. Only her books in first Irish edns are listed here. SOURCE Allibone, iii, p. 2414; Blain, p. 1080; Boase, iii, p. 969; *Burke's genealogical and heraldic history of the peerage* (London, 1956), p. 162; *Duffy's Hibernian Magazine* (Dublin, 1861), No. 9, p. 140; Sutherland, p. 629.

T44 *The orange girl. A tale* (by Lady Charles Thynne).
+ Dublin: James Duffy & Co., 1860 (ill.). SOURCE OCLC. LOCATION L.
COMMENTARY Set in London; no Irish content [ML].

T45 *Eleanor Morrison; or, home duties* (by Lady Charles Thynne).
+ Dublin: James Duffy, 1860. SOURCE COPAC. LOCATION L.
COMMENTARY No Irish content [ML].

T46 *Charlcote Grange: A tale* (by Lady Charles Thynne).
Dublin, London: James Duffy, 1861. SOURCE OCLC. LOCATION L.
COMMENTARY Religious fiction reviewed in *Duffy's Hibernian Magazine*. Concerns the feelings of unease with the established church felt by individuals in fashionable society, and their move-

ment towards catholicism, eventually leading to conversion [*Duffy's Hibernian Magazine*, 1861, No. 9, p. 140].

T47   *The orange girl: A tale* [with] *Sebastian's one thousand francs, and The secret of riches* (by Lady Charles Thynne).
+ Dublin, London: James Duffy, 1876. LOCATION InND Loeber coll.
COMMENTARY Fiction with a moral message written for juveniles. Contents: 'The orange girl: a tale' (originally published in 1860; set in England), 'Sebastian's one thousand francs' (set in France), 'The secret of riches' (set in France) [ML].

THYNNE, Robert, b. Clondalkin (Co. Dublin) 1827, d. 1907. Fiction writer for juveniles and adults, RT was the son of the Revd William S. Thynne. He was admitted at TCD in 1848 but does not appear to have taken a degree. He lived in Australia for ten years. On his return to Ireland, he contributed to various periodicals, including *Fraser's Magazine* and *All the Year Round* (both London). He published 12 novels, many of which have Irish and Australian connections. In politics he was an Unionist. Some of his novels for adults deal with land agitation from the viewpoint of the Ascendancy. SOURCE B & S, Appendix B, p. 118; Brown, p. 293; E. Reilly, p. 251; RL.

T48   *Ravensdale* [anon.].
London: Samuel Tinsley, 1873, 3 vols. SOURCE Brown, 1579; OCLC. LOCATION L.
COMMENTARY Historical fiction that attempts to represent the motives of Robert Emmet's insurrection (1803). Michael Dwyer and other patriots are introduced. The point of view is Unionist. Set in England, Dublin and Co. Wicklow [Brown].

T49   *Tom Delaney. A novel* (by Robert Thynne).
London: Samuel Tinsley, 1873, 3 vols. SOURCE Allibone Suppl., ii, p. 1437; Brown, 1580; OCLC. LOCATION Dt, L.
COMMENTARY Begins with the sale in the encumbered estates court of Mrs Delaney's property in the west of Ireland. The family then emigrates to Melbourne, Australia. Most of the characters are Irish. The fortunes of various love affairs are followed. Eventually, the estate is restored and the family returns to Ireland [Brown].

T50   *For this cause* (by Robert Thynne).
London: Sampson Low, 1877, 3 vols. SOURCE Allibone Suppl., ii, p. 1437; Brown, 1581. LOCATION L.
COMMENTARY Set mostly in Dublin. Ross and John Carberry are co-trustees of the will of the eccentric Lord Killery. Ross misappropriates the property to meet his liabilities. His daughter is unhappily married and has separated and lost her marriage portion. Fortunately, John returns to Ireland from Australia and saves the situation [Brown].

T51   *Sisters ever! An idea and its consequences* [anon.].
+ London: W. Swan Sonnenschein & Co., 1892. SOURCE COPAC. LOCATION L.
COMMENTARY A satire concerning the general election of 1892. Characters include John Bull, Hibernia, Britannia, and Scotia [ML; BLC].

T52   *The story of an Australian exploration* (by Robert Thynne).
London: T. Fisher Unwin, 1894. LOCATION L.
COMMENTARY Fiction for juveniles: an adventure story for boys [BLC].

T53   *Mathew Flinders; or, how we have Australia. Being the true story of Captain Flinders' explorations and adventures* (by Robert Thynne).
London: J. Hogg, [1896]. LOCATION L.

T54   *The turn of the tide. An Irish story of the day* (by Robert Thynne).
London: Roxburgh Press, 1896. SOURCE Brown, 1582. LOCATION L.

London: J. Long, 1899 (as *The story of a campaign estate; or, the turn of the tide*). SOURCE Brown, 1583. LOCATION L.

COMMENTARY Story of the boycotting of an estate in Co. Meath, written from an Ascendancy point of view. Blame for the unrest is not laid on the local people, but more on the anonymous organizers of the boycotts who select estates that cannot bear the burden of a large rent reduction. The role of the Catholic clergy is exemplified by two clergyman: one a fanatical curate, the second a more rational older priest who does not want his people to be hurt. Several hunting scenes are described. The book has many sub-plots [ML].

T55   *Irish holidays; or, studies out of school* (by Robert Thynne).

+ London: John Long, 1898. SOURCE Brown, 1584. LOCATION D, L, InND Loeber coll.

COMMENTARY The story of an Englishman who spends his holiday with Revd John Good, curate of Coolgreany in the Bog of Allen, six miles from Birr and six from Banagher (both Co. Offaly). Apart from some sporting incidents, it is chiefly concerned with aspects of agrarian agitation [Brown].

T56   *Boffin's find: A tale of the 'fifties* (by Robert Thynne).

+ London: John Long, 1899 (ill.). SOURCE Brown, 1585. LOCATION L, InND Loeber coll.

COMMENTARY Possibly autobiographical fiction. A tale of Australian life in the 1850s. One of the characters, an Irishman, while with a party searching for gold, relates his experiences with the Ribbonmen in Australia. The Ribbonmen were Irish convicts, members of a secret Catholic sectarian organization transported to Australia in the 1800s [ML; Brown].

T57   *King Radéma's word: or, John Aiken's adventures in Madagascar* (by Robert Thynne).

London: J. Hogg, 1899 (ill. J.A. Simington). LOCATION L.

T58   *John Townley. A tale for the times* (by Robert Thynne).

+ London: Henry J. Drane, 1901. SOURCE Brown, 1586. LOCATION D, L.

COMMENTARY An Anglican clergyman becomes a Catholic and later a priest. He comes to Ireland where he finds that priests are immersed in politics and use the confessional for political purposes. He is involved in tragic circumstances, and to escape from the disagreeable situation he goes to South Africa, where he reverts to protestantism [Brown].

T59   *Facing the future; or, the parting of the ways. A novel* (by Robert Thynne).

London: T. Fisher Unwin, 1904. LOCATION L.

'TIERNEY, Reginald', pseud. See RUSSELL, Thomas O'Neill.

TIGHE, Mary (née Blachford), b. Dublin 1772, d. Woodstock (Co. Kilkenny) 1810. Poet and unpublished novelist, MT was the daughter of Revd William Blachford, a Church of Ireland clergyman, keeper of Marsh's Library and prebendary at St Patrick's Cathedral, Dublin, and Theodosia Tighe, of Rosanna (Co. Wicklow). Her father died when she was still a baby, and her mother – who knew John Wesley – brought her up on strict religious principles. In 1793 MT married her first cousin, Henry Tighe, also of Rosanna (sometimes known as Rosannagh) who represented the borough of Inistioge (Co. Kilkenny) in the Irish parliament from 1790 until the Act of Union in 1800. He was known as 'by no means a faithful husband' (HIP, vi, p. 395). John Keats admired her poetry, and she is said to have been the inspiration for Thomas Moore's§ lyric, 'I saw thy form in youthful prime'. MT was mostly known for her long, allegorical poem *Psyche; or the legend of love* (London, 1805). It was reprinted and widely circulated after her death from consumption at age 37. A volume of her book reviews (1806–09) is in the NLI (MS 4,804), where there is also a journal (1788–1802, MS 4,810), partly-reprinted in Field Day, iv, pp 509–10. The Tighe mausoleum at Inistioge contains a sculpture of MT by John Flaxman, while a large statue of her was formerly in one of the rooms at her home at Woodstock. For her portraits, see ODNB. SOURCE Allibone, iii, p. 2419; Blain, p. 1081; Burke's, p. 1102; Field Day, iv, pp 509–10, 516, 1099–100; P. Henchy, 'The works of Mary Tighe published and unpublished' in *The Bibliographical Society of Ireland*, 6(6) (1957), pp 8, 10; HIP, vi, pp 394–5; Leslie & Wallace, p. 399; H.K. Linkin (ed.), *The collected poems of Mary Tighe* (Lexington, KY, 2005); NCBEL 4, pp 483–4; ODNB; O'Donoghue, p. 454; H. Potterton, *Irish church monuments* ([Belfast], 1975), pp 45–6, 67; RIA/DIB; Vanishing country houses, pp 33, 155, 157.

T60   *Selena* (by Mary Tighe).
COMMENTARY Unpublished novel (NLI, MSS 4,742–46, 5 vols.). A partly-autobiographical novel whose heroine, Selena, is tricked by parental manoeuvring into marrying her first cousin with whom she is not in love. The novel contains seven poems interwoven with the text, some of which were published in *Psyche, with other poems* (London, 1811), pp 269, 313 [Henchy].

'A TIPPERARY BOY', pseud. See **CONYNGHAM, David Power**.

TONE, Theobald Wolfe (popularly known as Wolf Tone), b. Dublin 1763, d. Dublin 1798. A revolutionary nationalist, political writer and novelist, TWT was the son of Margaret Lamport and Peter Tone, a coach-maker, When the family's wealth declined, they moved to Bodenstown (Co. Kildare), the home of TWT's godfather, Theobald Wolfe. TWT entered TCD in 1781 (not 1784 according to OCIL), where graduated BA in 1786 and LLB in 1789. He studied at the Middle Temple in London and was admitted to the Irish Bar in 1789. Having little inclination for law, he turned to politics. He wrote a number of pamphlets attacking excessive government power and promoting the republican ideal of power residing in the people, with government as a trust. He was co-founder with Thomas Russell of the Society of United Irishmen in Belfast, the resolutions of which were initially rejected by the Presbyterians as they included the idea of Catholic emancipation. This provoked TWT, an agnostic and of Protestant background, to publish *An argument on behalf of the Catholics of Ireland* (Dublin, 1791), the most widely-read pamphlet in Ireland after Thomas Paine's *The rights of man*. It was around this time he began his journals, which along with his autobiography were to become immensely influential on future Irish nationalism. In 1792 he became assistant secretary of the Catholic Committee; organized a Catholic Convention in Dublin (the first national meeting of lay Catholics in over a century), and became effectively a propagandist for Catholic relief. To escape capture when the authorities found out he was in correspondence with the French, he sailed with his wife (the former Martha Witherington) and children for the US, where he began negotiations to buy a farm in Princeton, (NJ). However TWT disliked America and the pro-British, anti-French tone of the Federalists, and when the United Irishmen asked him to seek aid from the French he went to Paris and obtained a commitment of French help. As an officer in the French army, he sailed with Gen. Hoche's doomed expedition to Bantry Bay in 1796 and with a later French fleet in 1798, but was taken prisoner, tried by court martial, and condemned to death. His request to be shot, as well as a writ of habeas corpus, were both refused by Lord Cornwallis. TWT slit his throat the night before his scheduled execution, dying in prison a week later. He wrote most of the chapters of his only novel, *Belmont Castle* (Dublin, 1790), with the remaining chapters written by his youthful friends John Ratcliffe§ and Richard Jebb§. He acted as a literary reviewer for three years. His son, William Theobald Wolfe Tone, published his father's journals and political writings and an account of TWT's last days in *Life of Theobald Wolfe Tone* (Washington, DC, 1826). For his portraits and papers, see ODNB. SOURCE Allibone, iii, p. 2431; B & S, p. 816;

Boylan, p. 384; Field Day, i, pp 926–30, 1076, ii, p. 77 and passim, iii, p. 8 and passim; Hogan 2, pp 1194–5; IBL, 23 (1925), pp 47–8; M. Deane's preface to 1998 edn of *Belmont Castle;* Keane, p. 482; OCIL, pp 564–5; ODNB; O'Donoghue, p. 457; RIA/DIB.

T61   *Belmont Castle; or, suffering sensibility, containing the genuine and interesting correspondence of several persons of fashion* [anon.; written with Richard Jebb§, and John Ratcliffe§] (dedicated to Mrs Carden¹).
    + Dublin: P. Byrne, 1790. SOURCE Brown 2, 1532; Raven 2, 1790:71; ESTC t191367. LOCATION D, O.
    + Dublin: Lilliput Press, 1998 (ed. by M. Deane, as *Belmont Castle or suffering sensibility*).

COMMENTARY The original edn is 223pp. Epistolary novel, written as a satire of the sentimental novel. It was reviewed in *Universal Magazine and Review* (Dublin, Nov., 1790). Several letters purport to be written from Belmont Castle, somewhere in Ireland, by Lady Georgina Shirley and Lord Mortimer. Other letters are written from London or Brussels. All of them deal in a highly sentimental and emotional fashion – including frequent mention of fainting and tears – with the love affairs of the writers or others. M. Deane has pointed out that 'Belmont Castle is a veiled account of real events ...' in the authors' 'personal affairs and in the enclosed world of several famous and interconnected families of the Anglo-Irish ruling class' (Deane, pp 19–22). These include the escapades of Mr Middleton, brother of the Irish Lord Middleton, and TWT's love affair with Lady Elizabeth Vesey of Lucan (Co. Dublin), who is represented as Lady Eliza Clairville. The main character, the earl of Belmont, is modelled on William, 4th earl of Inchiquin. Sir John Fillamar is based on James Caulfeild, earl of Charlemont. Belmont Castle represents Lord Charlemont's house and estate at Marino, Dublin [ML; IBL, 23 (1935), p. 47; M. Deane, introd. to *Belmont Castle*, pp 19–22].

TONNA, Mrs Charlotte Elizabeth (née Browne, not Phelan, as in Alston), pseud. 'Charlotte Elizabeth', b. Norwich (England) 1790, d. Ramsgate (Kent) 1846. English novelist, evangelical religious fiction and social protest writer, editor and poet, CET was the daughter of Michael Browne, a minor canon of the cathedral of Norwich. At an early age she learned to read and was taught French by an uncle. But she strained her eyes so much in the process that she became blind for a few months, a period in which she developed her passion for music before becoming totally deaf at age 10. Once recovered from her temporary blindness, she became highly-religious; her strong Protestant convictions influencing her behaviour much of her life. In London she met her future husband, George Phelan, an army officer of the 60th Rifle Corps in Ireland, and married him in 1813. He was directed to join his regiment at Halifax (NS), and she followed him there. She stayed in North America for two years and then returned to England. Seized by a religious 'mania', she decided to become 'a sort of Protestant nun'. Her husband was once more ordered to North America, but she declined to accompany him. However, probably following her husband, she moved to Ireland around 1819, where her mother joined her. They initially stayed at Vicarsfield, the parsonage of one Dr Hamilton at Knocktopher (Co. Kilkenny), and later settled in the town of Kilkenny, where she lived in virtual isolation. The unhappiness of her marriage, in which she claimed her husband abused her, led to a separation before his death in 1837, and she never mentioned him by name in her memoirs. She lived on her own, possibly with her mother in residence with her, spending time in writing out documentary matters for lawyers, probably to earn a living. After receiving publications of the Religious Tract and Book Society for Ireland, she decided

---

1 Probably Elizabeth, wife of John Carden, lieutenant in the Royal Artillery (M. Deane, introd. to *Belmont Castle* (Dublin, 1998), p. 33).

to try her hand at writing. Subsequently, she wrote many small tracts for the Dublin Tract Society (some of these were published under her initials 'Ch. E.'), and for the Religious Book and Tract Society for Ireland (as 'Charlotte Elizabeth'). In addition, she wrote verse, of which two Orange songs became well known, and she composed *A friendly address to converts from the Roman Catholic church* (Dublin, 1827), and *A letter to a friend ... on ... the church* (London, 1831). She developed a strong interest in the education of deaf and mute children. She identified closely with Protestant Ireland, and combined this with a strong anti-Catholic passion. After a stay of just over five years in Ireland, she had to return to England where she and her mother settled first at Clifton, and then in London in the house of her brother, Capt. John Browne. Here, in the course of just over two years, she wrote over 30 of her works, but her husband managed to claim part of the proceeds of her writings. She did not return to Ireland until 1837, probably shortly after her husband's death that year, making a tour through much of the country, which she recorded in a series of letters published the following year (*Letters from Ireland*, London, 1838). She married secondly the author Lewis Hippolytus Joseph Tonna in 1841, and lived at Clapham Common, near London in 1844 (he held an office with the United Services Museum in Whitehall). She was friendly with Lord Mount Sandford§, to whom she dedicated *The Rockite* (London, 1829), and with Selina Martin§, for whom she wrote an introd. to her *Sketches of Irish history. Antiquities, religion, customs, and manners* (Dublin, 1844). CET also met and admired the author Hannah More, to whom she dedicated her volume of poems, written in Ireland, *Osric: A missionary tale; with The garden* (Dublin, [1826?]). She moved to social activist and protest literature: her *The system* (London, 1827) was aimed at improving the fate of slaves; while the plight of female factory workers was featured in *Helen Fleetwood* (London, 1841), and the ills of strikes and unions in which Irish immigrants became involved in Manchester were the subject of *Combination* (Dublin, 1832). She published anonymously *The perils of the nation* (London, 1843) at the behest of Lord Ashley. She remained intensely interested in advancing the Protestant cause in Ireland and wrote the preface to R. Murray's *Outlines of the history of the Catholic church in Ireland* (London, 1840). She was a principal in the task of building and endowing the Irish Episcopal church in St Giles's, London, which was opened in 1830, and helped to provide relief for the Irish poor in its neighbourhood. In 1834 CET became the editor of the *Christian Lady's Magazine* (London), a position she held until close to her death. In this magazine she continued to publish articles and fiction pertaining to Ireland, some written by Selina Bunbury§ and Maria Frances Dickson§. In addition, she edited the *Protestant Annual* (London, 1841 [not 1840 as in ODNB]), and the *Protestant Magazine* (London, 1841–46). She also published *The wrongs of woman* (London, 1843–44) in which she argued that women are 'the weaker vessel', hampered by lack of education, and vulnerable to exploitation. Only her works published in Ireland or of known Irish content are listed below. An anthology of poems compiled by her, which includes two poems in Irish (written in 1833–49) can be found in the NLI (MS 3,783), where there is also biographical material (MS 8,350). Some of her letters are in the Dreer Collection at the Historical Society of Pennsylvania in Philadelphia, and the John Rylands University Library of Manchester (see ODNB for additional manuscript material). For her portraits, see ODNB. SOURCE Allibone, iii, p. 2432; biographical details from Mrs Tonna's *Letters from Ireland MDC-CCXXXVII* (London, 1838), and *Personal recollections* (London, 1843) [see Field Day, iv, pp 542–4]; C.L. Balfour, *A sketch of Charlotte Elizabeth* (London, 1854); Blain, p. 1087; D. Bowen, *The Protestant crusade in Ireland* (Dublin, 1978), pp 330*n*.110, 335*n*.198; chapter on 'Charlotte Elizabeth' in [E. Neale], *The closing scene* (London, 1848), pp 105–31; Field Day, iv, pp 538, 542–4, 560, 757; J. Kestner, *Protest and reform. The British social narrative by women 1827–1867* (Madison, WI, 1958), passim; C. Murphy, 'The destruction of the Protestant church and dismemberment of the empire: Charlotte Elizabeth, evangelical Anglican in pre-famine Ireland' in *Women's Studies*, 30 (2001), pp 741–61; NCBEL 4, pp 1413–17; OCIL, p. 565; ODNB; O'Donoghue, p. 457; RIA/DIB; Sutherland, pp 632–3; Todd, pp 67–71.

T62   *Little Nannette. A narrative of facts* (by 'Charlotte Elizabeth').
Dublin: Religious Tract and Book Society for Ireland, 1821, 3rd edn. LOCATION D.
Salem: Whipple & Lawrence, 1825. SOURCE OCLC. LOCATION NN.
[New York]: American Tract Society, n.d. (by 'A bereaved mother'). SOURCE RLIN. LOCATION American Antiquarian Society.
COMMENTARY No copy of the first edn located. 33pp for the Dublin edn [TCD cat.].

T63   *The laundry maid. A narrative of facts* [anon.].
Dublin: M. Goodwin, 1824. LOCATION D (1825, 2nd edn), Univ. of California, Davis.
COMMENTARY 1st edn is 12 pp, but the 2nd edn is 31pp. The 2nd edn identifies the author as 'Charlotte Elizabeth' [TCD cat.; RL; OCLC].

T64   *The two friends; or, the history of Hugh MacNeil and John Grant* (by 'Charlotte Elizabeth').
Dublin: Religious Tract and Book Society for Ireland, 1825, 2nd edn. LOCATION D.
COMMENTARY 40pp [NLI cat.].

T65   *The simple flower* (by 'Charlotte Elizabeth').
+ Dublin: Printed [for the author?] by M. Goodwin, 1826 (2nd edn; ill.). LOCATION InND Loeber coll.
+ Dublin: Printed by M. Goodwin [for the Religious Tract and Book Society for Ireland], 1826, 2nd edn (enlarged; ill.). LOCATION D, InND Loeber coll.
+ New York: John S. Taylor & Co., 1845 (as *The simple flower and other tales*). LOCATION L, InND Loeber coll.
COMMENTARY The enlarged edn consists of 54pp, compared to 43pp for the earlier, 2nd edn. Religious fiction for juveniles with religious lessons on how to thrive even under adversity [ML; RL].

T66   *Interesting narratives* (by 'Charlotte Elizabeth').
+ Dublin: Religious Tract and Book Society for Ireland, 1826, 2 vols? LOCATION D (vol. 1 only).
COMMENTARY No copy of volume 2 located. Bound from chapbooks, each with its own pagination. Contents: Vol. 1: 'The simple flower' (first published separately, Dublin, 1826), 'John Pascal: or the temptation of the poor', 'Naimbanna, the black prince. A narrative of facts', 'Paul, the martyr of Palestine', 'The Waldenses; or, an account of an excursion of the mountains of Piedmont', 'The laundry maid. A narrative of facts' (first published Dublin, 1825 or earlier), 'Little Nannette. A narrative of facts' (first published, Dublin, 1821 or earlier), 'The two friends; or, the history of Hugh MacNeil & John Grant' (first published, Dublin, 1825 or earlier), 'The life of Caroline E. Smelt, who died on 21st September 1817, in the city of Augusta, in North America, in the 17th year of her age. A narrative of facts', 'The pensioner; an interesting narrative' [RL].

T67   *Philip, and his garden* (by 'Charlotte Elizabeth').
Dublin: Printed by Thomas I. White [for the Religious Tract and Book Society for Ireland], 1826. LOCATION D, InND Loeber coll. (1827 edn).
COMMENTARY *Dublin edn* 50pp for the 1827 edn. Religious fiction for juveniles. Lessons in religion, culled from the experience of tending a little garden [ML; RL].

T68   *The two servants* (by 'Charlotte Elizabeth').
Dublin: [sold at 22 Upper Sackville St., which was the address for the Religious Book and Tract Society for Ireland], [1827 or earlier]. SOURCE Adv. in C. Elizabeth, *The moth* (Dublin), 1827.

Tonna

COMMENTARY Dublin edn priced at 2*d.*; no copy located [RL].

T69   *The red berries* (by 'Charlotte Elizabeth').
Dublin: [Religious Tract and Book Society for Ireland], [1827 or earlier]. SOURCE Adv.
in C. Elizabeth, *The moth* (Dublin, 1827).
COMMENTARY No copy located [RL].

T70   *Where are you going?* (by 'Charlotte Elizabeth').
+ Dublin: Printed by R. Napper [for the Religious Tract and Book Society for Ireland],
1827. SOURCE Adv. in C. Elizabeth, *The moth* (Dublin, 1827); OCLC. LOCATION D.

T71   *Joseph, or humility before honour* (by 'Charlotte Elizabeth').
+ Dublin: Printed by Thomas I. White [for the Religious Tract and Book Society for
Ireland?], 1827. LOCATION InND Loeber coll.
COMMENTARY 40pp [RL].

T72   *The two carpenters* (by 'Charlotte Elizabeth').
Dublin: [Religious Tract and Book Society for Ireland], [1827 or earlier]. SOURCE Adv.
in C. Elizabeth, *The moth* (Dublin), 1827.
+ Philadelphia: American Sunday-School Union, 1847 (as *The two carpenters; or, the
fruits of sloth and thrift illustrated*; ill. G.T. Devereauxidel). LOCATION InND Loeber coll.
COMMENTARY Price 4*p.* for the Dublin edn. No copy of that edn located. The Philadelphia
edn may refer to another book, because title page refers to having been written 'for the
American Sunday-School Union, and revised by the Committee of Publication' [RL; adv. in
C. Elizabeth, *The moth* (Dublin), 1827].

T73   *Little Frank, the Irish boy* (by 'Charlotte Elizabeth').
London: Frederick Westley & A. H. Davis, 1828, 2nd edn. SOURCE COPAC. LOCATION
D (London, Broom, 1873 edn), C.
Boston: Massachusetts Sabbath School Society, 1838, 2nd edn (as *Frank, the Irish boy*).
SOURCE OCLC. LOCATION Earlham College, Richmond (IN).
COMMENTARY First edn not located. Religious fiction for juveniles set in south-west
Ireland, featuring Jane Ryan and little Frank [RL].

T74   *The Rockite, an Irish story* (by 'Charlotte Elizabeth'; dedicated to Lord Mount
Sandford§).
+ London: James Nisbet, 1829. SOURCE Block, p. 237; Brown, 556 (1832 edn); British
Fiction; Garside, 1829:79. LOCATION Corvey CME 3–628–48833, Ireland related fic-
tion, D (1830, 2nd edn), BFl, L, NUC, InND Loeber coll.
London: James Nisbet & Co., 1846, 4th edn (enlarged). SOURCE Jarndyce cat. 139/256.
LOCATION NUC.
+ New York: John S. Taylor & Co., 1844, 4th edn (with preface to 3rd edn). LOCATION
InND Loeber coll.
COMMENTARY Probably written in response to Thomas Moore's§ *Memoirs of Captain Rock*
(London, 1824), which ET much disliked. Her book was reviewed in the *Dublin Family
Magazine* (Dublin, 1829, No. 5) and tells the story of Maurice Delany, an Irish soldier dis-
banded from an English regiment of dragoons, who is lured into becoming a Rockite in the
anti-tithe war. He participates in several atrocities, but he draws the line when his group wants
to attack the house of his former captain in the army and abduct the daughter of the house.
He uses all his wiles to prevent harm to this family. Eventually, this costs him his life [ML;
Personal communication, Jaqueline Belanger, Dec. 2000].

T75   *Short stories for children* (by 'Charlotte Elizabeth').
Dublin: Religious Tract and Book Society for Ireland, 1831, 2 vols. (ill.). SOURCE
Burmester cat. 34/257; Dm exhib. cat. 1981, p. 34. LOCATION PC, DPL (1832 edn,
vol. 2 only), InND Loeber coll. (1838, 3rd edn).

+ Dublin: Religious Tract and Book Society for Ireland; London: J. Nisbet, Houlston & Son; Edinburgh: Waugh & Innes, W. Oliphant, J. Robinson & Co; Glasgow: W. Collins & J. Gallie, 1830, 2nd edn, 2 vols. (as *Tales and illustrations chiefly intended for young persons*; dedicated to the eldest son of the author's departed brother). LOCATION L (missing) ([1854] edn), PC.

+ Edinburgh: Gall & Inglis; London: Houlston & Wright, [1861]. SOURCE Osborne, p. 950. LOCATION L, CaOTP ([1861] edn).

+ London, Edinburgh: Gall & Inglis, [*c.*1874] (as *Little tales for little readers*; ill. Kronheim). SOURCE Emerald Isle cat. 88/1370 (vol. 2 only). LOCATION InND Loeber coll. (vol. 2 only).

+ [New York]: American Tract Society, [1858?]. SOURCE RLIN. LOCATION American Antiquarian Society, PC.

COMMENTARY Stories for juveniles which have a Christian moral and contain extensive quotations from the Bible. The stories stayed in print until the 1870s. No Irish content. Every story ends with a poem. Contents of Dublin edn, volume 2 only: 'The swan', 'The fortune teller', 'The dying sheep', 'The burying ground', 'The sinful laugh', 'The oak-grove', 'Little oaths', 'White lies', 'The wasp', 'Answering again', 'The baby', 'Try again'. These stories also are contained in the London edn. Contents of the [?New York] edn: 'Anna Bell, or the faults', 'The moth', 'The bow in the cloud', 'The rose-bud', 'The willow-tree', 'The hated task', 'Good and bad luck', 'The fortune teller', 'The dying sheep', 'The burying-ground', 'The sinful laugh', 'The oak-grove', 'White lies', 'Answering again', 'The baby', 'Try again' [ML; RL].

T76 *Combination. A tale founded on facts* (by 'Charlotte Elizabeth').

Dublin: Religious Tract and Book Society for Ireland, 1832 (ill. John Kirkwood). SOURCE COPAC; Kestner, p. 42; Garside 2, 1832:83. LOCATION Dt, L.

+ New York: M.W. Dodd, 1844. LOCATION NUC, InND Loeber coll.

COMMENTARY Early labour novel based on the middle-class fear of unions. The story opens in Ireland but after Thomas Riley is implicated in a murder, he, his brother William and their sister Judy, leave for Manchester to stay with their aunt. The brothers are employed by Mr Hall, who is a very benevolent man, while their sister is employed temporarily by a beneficent gentleman, Mr Bolton. The labour agitator Smith argues to strike, but Bolton presents counter arguments. He regards oath-taking as inconsistent with being a Christian. The Riley's cousin, Michael Burke, a soldier quartered in Manchester to prevent dissension, repents of his dissolute life and becomes 'a true soldier of the Cross'. A fever infects the workers' district, which the narrator interprets as a visitation from God. The two brothers contract the fever [Kestner, pp 42–5].

T77 *The museum* (by 'Charlotte Elizabeth').

+ Dublin: Religious Tract and Book Society for Ireland, 1832. SOURCE Wolff, 6740; Garside 2, 1832:84. LOCATION Dt, D, L, InND Loeber coll. (1837, 3rd edn).

New York: Taylor & Gould, 1835. SOURCE Garside 2, 1832:84; OCLC. LOCATION MH.

COMMENTARY Remained in print until at least 1844. Fiction for juveniles in which visits to a natural history museum are used by the author to teach two children lessons about natural history and religion. The Scriptures are frequently quoted [ML; RL].

T78 *White lies* (by 'Charlotte Elizabeth').

Dublin: [Religious Tract and Book Society for Ireland], 1833. SOURCE Alston, p. 342. LOCATION L.

COMMENTARY 32pp [ML].

T79 *Derry. A tale of the revolution* (by 'Charlotte Elizabeth'; dedicated to Robert Boyd of Ballymacool).

+ London: James Nisbet, 1833. SOURCE Brown, 557 (1886, 6th edn); Bradshaw, 8009 (1835, 4th edn); Garside 2, 1833:75. LOCATION Dt, D, DPL (1833, 2nd edn), L, C, NUC.

London: James Nisbet & Co., 1859 (new edn). LOCATION PC.

+ London: James Nisbet & Co., 1875 (new edn; with preface to 6th edn; ill. H. Gastineau, R. Woodman, G. Mottram). LOCATION InND Loeber coll.

+ London: James Nisbet & Co., n.d. (new introd. by the author for the 6th edn; as *Derry. A tale of the revolution of 1688*; ill.). LOCATION InND Loeber coll.

+ New York: John S. Taylor & Co., 1841 (as *The siege of Derry, or, sufferings of the Protestants. A tale of the revolution*). LOCATION NUC, InND Loeber coll.

COMMENTARY The NLI copy has a note by CET to a Mrs Hamilton: 'If the scenes recorded in this volume awaken bitter recollections in the mind of my dear friend and her honoured Partner, may the consolations that so richly abounded to the suffering Protestants of 1688–9 be yet more abundantly experienced by them!' First semi-fictional, anti-Catholic account of the unsuccessful Jacobite siege of Derry in 1689. It ridicules Catholic superstition, and high-lights popish cruelty [Field Day, v, pp 839–40; McBride, *The siege of Derry in Ulster Protestant mythology* (Dublin, 1997), p. 57].

T80   *Grumbling* (by 'Charlotte Elizabeth').
       Dublin: Religious Tract and Book Society for Ireland, 1834. LOCATION L.
       London: [publisher?], 1834. SOURCE Alston, p. 342. LOCATION L (not found).
       COMMENTARY No copy of the London edn located [RL].

T81   *The visit. A narrative of facts* (by 'Charlotte Elizabeth').
       + Dublin: Religious Tract and Book Society for Ireland, 1834. LOCATION D.
       COMMENTARY 28pp Religious fiction [RL].

T82   *The mole* (by 'Charlotte Elizabeth').
       Dublin: Religious Tract and Book Society for Ireland, 1835. SOURCE DNB. LOCATION L.
       London: [publisher?], 1835. SOURCE Alston, p. 342. LOCATION L (not found).
       COMMENTARY No copy of the London edn located [RL].

T83   *The industrious artist* (by 'Charlotte Elizabeth').
       Dublin: Religious Tract and Book Society for Ireland, 1836. SOURCE Alston, p. 342. LOCATION L.

T84   *The deserter* (by 'Charlotte Elizabeth').
       + Dublin: Religious Tract and Book Society for Ireland; London: J. Nisbet; Edinburgh: Waugh & Innes; Glasgow: G. Gallie, 1836. SOURCE Brown 2, 442; Block, p. 237; Garside 2, 1836:73. LOCATION D, Dt, L, NUC, InND Loeber coll. (1837 edn).
       New York: M.W. Dodd, 1845. SOURCE Garside 2, 1836:73: OCLC. LOCATION D, CtY.
       COMMENTARY Proselytizing religious fiction in which Dennis O'Brien, who enlists in the British army, falls into depraved habits, is flogged and deserts. He works as a farm labourer among other Irish-speaking harvesters in England. They are instructed by an Irish Bible-reader. Arrested as a deserter, Dennis is sent to India. Falling from bad to worse, he is tried and con-demned to death. Faced with death, he repents of his errors, rejects the Catholic priest, and goes to death attended by the Protestant chaplain. His last message to his country is 'Give them the Irish Bible'. Much of the novel is given over to discussions among officers and men about the Scriptures [Bennett cat. 7/204; Brown 2].

T85   *Glimpses of the past; being a continuation of chapters on flowers* (by 'Charlotte Elizabeth').
       London: Seeley & Burnside, 1839 (ill.). LOCATION PC, L.
       + New York: Taylor, 1841. LOCATION NUC, InND Loeber coll.

COMMENTARY Some of the following stories are set in Ireland. Contents: 'The cathedral', 'The meeting', 'Ireland', 'The oak-stump' (set in the kitchen of an Irish country house), 'William III', 'The eclipse', 'The yew-tree', 'The cadet', 'The school', 'Edward', 'Idolatry', 'The lonely wreck', 'The fallen oak', 'The white chrysanthemum', 'The daisy', 'The wall-flower', 'The white clover', 'The hawthorn', 'The yellow broom', 'The widow's tale', 'Budding', 'Derry', 'Patriotism', 'The geranium', 'The mignonette', 'The violet', 'The bishop', 'Conclusion' [RL].

T86   *Golden image* (by 'Charlotte Elizabeth').
Dublin: Religious Book and Tract Society, [1842 or earlier]. SOURCE Adv. in 'P.D.H.', *The Northern Cottager* (Dublin, 1842).
COMMENTARY Priced at 4*d.* No copy located [RL].

T87   *The star* (by 'Charlotte Elizabeth').
Dublin: Religious Book and Tract Society, [1842 or earlier]. SOURCE Adv. in 'P.D.H.', *The Northern Cottager* (Dublin, 1842).
New York: The Sunday School and Juvenile Publishers and Booksellers, John S. Taylor & Co., n.d. LOCATION NUC.
COMMENTARY Dublin edn priced at 3*d.* No copy located [RL].

T88   *The widow of Zarephath* (by 'Charlotte Elizabeth').
Dublin: Religious Book and Tract Society, [1842 or earlier]. SOURCE Adv. in 'P.D.H.', *The Northern Cottager* (Dublin, 1842).
COMMENTARY Dublin edn priced at 1*d.* No copy located [RL].

T89   *The Riley family* (by 'Charlotte Elizabeth').
Dublin: P.D. Hardy & Sons, [after 1842–3]. LOCATION PC.

T90   *Second causes; or, up and be doing* (by 'Charlotte Elizabeth').
Dublin: John Robertson, 1843. SOURCE Alston, p. 342. LOCATION L.
London: Groombridge [?date]. SOURCE Hodgson, p. 563.
New York: M.W. Dodd, 1843. SOURCE OCLC. LOCATION NN.
COMMENTARY No copy of the London edn located [RL].

T91   *The military Samaritan. A narrative* (by 'Charlotte Elizabeth').
Dublin: J. Robertson, [1844 or earlier]. SOURCE Adv. in [S. Martin], *Sketches of Irish history* (Dublin, 1844).
COMMENTARY No copy of this children's book has been located [RL; Adv. in [S. Martin], *Sketches of Irish history* (Dublin, 1844)].

T92   *Philip and his garden. With other stories* (by 'Charlotte Elizabeth').
+ London: J. Hogg & Sons, [1861] (ill. W. Coleman). SOURCE Alston, p. 342. LOCATION L.
COMMENTARY Contents: 'Philip and his garden' (first published in 1826), 'The simple flower', 'The faithful dogs', 'The premium' [JB].

— COLLECTED WORKS

T93   *The works of Charlotte Elizabeth.*
+ New York: M.W. Dodd, 1844, 2 vols. (ill. J. Dickson, T. Greswich, F. Halpin, M.W. Dodd, T. Allom; introd. by Mrs H.B. Stowe). SOURCE OCLC. LOCATION D, L, NUC.

T94   *The works of Charlotte Elizabeth.*
New York: Baker & Scribner, 1846, 13 vols. SOURCE Adv. in A. Nicholson, *Ireland's welcome to the stranger* (New York, 1847). LOCATION InND Loeber coll. (several vols.).

T95   *Charlotte Elizabeth's juvenile works.*
New York: Baker & Scribner, [1847 or earlier], 8 vols. SOURCE Adv. in A. Nicholson, *Ireland's welcome to the stranger* (New York: Baker & Scribner, 1847).

COMMENTARY No copy of this collected work located. Probably different from the 1846 edn of the collected works, and consisting of 8 volumes only and not the 13 volumes of the 1846 edn [RL].

T96   *Charlotte Elizabeth's stories.*
New York: [publisher?], 1868, 8 vols. SOURCE DNB.
COMMENTARY No copy located [RL]

TORRENS, Robert, b. Hervey Hill (Co. Derry) 1780, d. London 1864. Soldier, political economist, novelist and editor, RT was the son of Robert Torrens of Hervey Hill (Co. Derry) and Elizabeth Bristow (Robert Torrens the elder should not to be confused with Revd Robert Torrens, son of Thomas Torrens of Dungiven, Co. Derry). The young RT was probably educated at the Derry diocesan school. He was commissioned in the Royal Marines in 1796 and served on the Cork station, where he married in 1801 his first wife, Charity, daughter of Richard Chute of Roxburgh (Co. Kerry). Their four children were born in Cork and Kerry. Later he served in Denmark and at Walcheren in the Dutch campaigns and as colonel of a Spanish legion in the Peninsular War – before retiring fully from military life in 1835. RT's support for Catholic emancipation (see his *Thoughts on the Catholic question*, London, 1813) blocked his initial political ambitions but he was MP intermittently for Ipswich, Ashburton and Bolton between 1826 and 1835. He is known mainly for his writings on economics, finance, trade and social topics, producing over 90 books and pamphlets, and for his advocating the commercialisation of the colonies. He supported the New Zealand Company; chaired the National Colonization Society; was an original member of the South Australian Land Company that advocated the colonization of the area, and chaired the commission established by the South Australia Act that organized land sales and recruited emigrants. Lake Torrens and the River Torrens, on which Adelaide is located, were named for him. RT believed emigration to be the solution to Ireland's problems, envisioning Australia as a 'New Hibernia', but his opponents cast him as 'the Irish exterminator' as emigration from Ireland increased in the early 1840s. He published *Self-supporting colonization: Ireland saved* (London, 1847) in renewed support of emigration to help alleviate the effects of the Famine in 1847. RT was an original member of the Political Economy Club. He is credited with formulating the law of comparative advantage in international trade, and with Malthus and David Ricardo, the law of diminishing returns. RT supported himself through journalism. He was part owner and editor of the *Traveller* evening newspaper in London, which merged with the *Globe* in 1822. A collection of pamphlets associated with his tenure at the *Globe* was on the market in 2004. His later years were occupied with banking law and his work was influential in creating the Bank of England Charter Act in 1844. His son, Sir Robert Richard Torrens, became first premier of South Australia. For RT's portraits and papers, see ODNB. SOURCE Allibone, iii, p. 2435; *Belfast Monthly Magazine*, Apr. 1814, p. 302; M. Blaug, *Great economists before Keynes* (Cheltenham, 1986); Boase, iii, pp 991–2; Boylan, p. 384; Brady, p. 237; Brown, p. 295; BD, pp 351–2; C. Johnson cat. 47/178–318; TK; Newmann, p. 257; NCBEL 4, pp 2509–10; ODNB; RIA/DIB; L.C. Robbins, *Robert Torrens and the evolution of classical economics* (London, 1958); G. de Vivo (ed.), *Collected works of Robert Torrens* (Bristol, 2000, 8 vols.).

T97   *Coelibia choosing a husband; A modern novel* (by Robert Torrens).
London: J.F. Hughes, 1809, 2 vols. SOURCE Block, p. 238; Brady, p. 238; British Fiction; Garside, 1809:72. LOCATION L.
COMMENTARY This title is related to a spate of novels inspired by Hannah More's best-selling *Coelebs in search of a wife* (London, 1809). Other related titles include [anon.], *Celia in search of a husband* (London, 1809) and [anon.] *Coelebs married, being intended as a continuation of Coelebs in search of a wife* (London in 1814). Maria Edgeworth§ considered writing a

sequel, called *Caelia in search of a husband*, but rejected the idea. RT's novel advocated higher education for women and features a heroine who is a budding political economist. She refuses a wealthy baronet, but at a third try meets a compatible man [RL; ODNB].

T98   *The victim of intolerance; or, the hermit of Killarney. A Catholic tale* (by Robert Torrens; dedicated to the people of Ireland).

+ London: Gale, Curtis & Fenner, 1814, 4 vols. SOURCE Brown, 1588; British Fiction; Garside, 1814:56. LOCATION Corvey CME 3–628–47458–2, Ireland related fiction, D, L.

COMMENTARY This book was mentioned as being read in Irish schools in 1825. The hermit, O'Connor, who lived in the ruins of Muckross abbey, dies, and papers are found recording his history. They tell how the penal laws closed every avenue of advancement to him and crossed him in love, causing him to retire from the world. The story may have expressed the author's frustration at the failure of efforts for emancipation, which he supported. An announcement of the novel in the London *Morning Chronicle* cites a review in the *Monthly Review* stating that it 'cannot fail of being extremely acceptable to the Catholic population of Ireland, whose situation and feelings are painted to the life' [Brown; *First report of the Commission of Education Inquiry* (London, 1825), appendix No. 221, p. 556; ODNB; British Fiction; *Morning Chronicle* (London, 2 Dec. 1815].

TOTTENHAM, B., fl. 1851. Religious fiction writer, BT probably was a resident of the south of Ireland. SOURCE RL.

T99   *The emigrant: A story for Ireland* (by B. Tottenham).

+ Cork: Cork Religious and Tract Society, 1851. SOURCE COPAC. LOCATION L.

COMMENTARY Farmer Pat Dooling is pressured by the local squire, Ambrosius Tierney, to join the Young Ireland Society. Pat begins to arrive home drunk and his farm goes to rack and ruin. He is forced to participate in the murder of magistrate Fenton. 'When he found out that the Young Irelanders were soon to have a great rising, and that there would be bad doings, and slaughterings, and burning, Peggy urged him strongly; so he resolved to go to America, and have no more hand in it'. He finds forgiveness in Jesus through a priest on the ship [CM].

TOTTENHAM, B. Loftus. See TOTTENHAM, Blanche Mary Loftus.

TOTTENHAM, Blanche Mary Loftus (known as B. Loftus Tottenham), pseud. 'Sophia Mary Locke', fl. 1892. According to the BLC, the pseudonym 'Sophia Mary Locke' is shared by this author and probable co-author Amelia Sophia Coates Young. Novelist, BMLT was probably a member of the Tottenham family of Tudenham Park (near Molyskar, Co. Westmeath, now ruined) or the Tottenhams of Glenfarne Hall (Co. Leitrim), who often used 'Loftus' as a middle name. The author George Charles Loftus Tottenham§ was probably a relative. SOURCE Casey & Rowan, pp 397–8; Landed gentry, 1904, pp 596–7; A.P.W. Malcomson, 'A house divided' in D. Dickson & C. Ó Gráda (eds), *Refiguring Ireland* (Dublin, 2003), p. 198; RIA/DIB; Vanishing country houses, pp 144–5.

T100   *More kin than kind* (by B. Loftus Tottenham).

London: Hurst & Blackett, 1892, 3 vols. SOURCE Wolff, 6747; COPAC. LOCATION L.

T101   *Who wins – loses* (by 'Sophia Mary Locke').

+ London: Richard Bentley & Son, 1893, 3 vols. SOURCE Alston, p. 481; COPAC. LOCATION L.

COMMENTARY No Irish content. Set in England and on the Continent and contains a love story [ML].

T102   *A heart's revenge* (by B. Loftus Tottenham).

London: Hurst & Blackett, 1894, 3 vols. SOURCE Daims, 3050; Wolff, 6747; OCLC. LOCATION L.

T103 *The unwritten law* (by B. Loftus Tottenham).

+ London: A. & C. Black, 1895. SOURCE OCLC. LOCATION L, InND Loeber coll.

COMMENTARY Set in Connacht at the time of agrarian unrest where Brian, one of the tenants who does not pay his rent, is in love with Rose, the daughter of the one farmer who does. Rose's father does not accept Brian's suit but they decide to get married anyway. Before this can take place, Brian has to flee from the police. Forced to hide her pregnancy, Rose marries a man she has always disliked. Her husband realizes that the baby is not his child and throws his wife and baby out of the house. She dies in Brian's house. Brian kills Rose's husband, but Rose's father is arrested for the deed. However, Brian admits to the crime. The peasants try to free Brian from the police and in the ensuing tussle he is killed [ML].

T104 void

T105 *In the shadow of the three* [*sic*] (by B. Loftus Tottenham).
London: Hutchinson & Co., 1898. LOCATION L.

TOTTENHAM, G.L. See **TOTTENHAM, George Charles Loftus.**

TOTTENHAM, George L. See **TOTTENHAM, George Charles Loftus.**

TOTTENHAM, George Charles Loftus (known as **G.L. Tottenham** and **George L. Tottenham**), b. Co. Leitrim 1844, d. London 1910. Novelist and miscellaneous writer, GCLT was the second son of Nicholas Loftus Tottenham, of Glenfarne Hall (Co. Leitrim), later of Rodfort House, Mullingar (Co. Westmeath) and Anna Maria Hopkins, and brother of Arthur Loftus Tottenham, MP for Leitrim and later Winchester. GCLT received his early schooling at Harrow and entered Trinity College, Cambridge, in 1861, where he graduated BA in 1867. He was admitted at the Inner Temple, London, in 1866. Aside from fiction, he wrote *The peasant proprietors of Norway* (Edinburgh,1889), a study connected with the Irish land question. He held an estate, Glenade, near Kinlough (Co. Leitrim); served as JP and as HS in 1888. He is not known to have married. His obituary appeared in the *Times* (London), 1 June 1910. The author Blanche Mary Loftus Tottenham§ was probably a relative. SOURCE Boase, iii, p. 994; Brown, p. 295; Burke's, pp 1110–11; Landed gentry, 1904, p. 597; A.P.W. Malcomson, 'A house divided' in D. Dickson & C. Ó Gráda (eds), *Refiguring Ireland* (Dublin, 2003), p. 198; RIA/DIB; Venn, part ii, vi, p. 212.

T106 *Charlie Villars at Cambridge* (by George L. Tottenham).
London: Hurst & Blackett, 1868, 2 vols. SOURCE Allibone Suppl., ii, p. 1443; Wolff, 6749; OCLC. LOCATION L.

T107 *Harry Egerton; or, the younger son of the day* (by G.L. Tottenham).
London: Chapman & Hall, 1869, 3 vols. SOURCE Allibone Suppl., ii, p. 1443; Brown, p. 295; Wolff, 6750. LOCATION L.

T108 *Terence McGowan, the Irish tenant* (by G.L. Tottenham).
+ London: Smith, Elder & Co., 1870, 2 vols. SOURCE Allibone Suppl., ii, p. 1443; Brown, 1589; OCLC. LOCATION D, Dt, L, InND Loeber coll.

COMMENTARY Set in the 1860s. Describes from the landlord's point of view the land struggles of the 1860s. Interwoven is a love story. Priests are described as evil, and the Irish people as lawless and unreasonable [Brown].

T109 *Harcourt* (by G.L. Tottenham).
+ London: Smith, Elder & Co., 1873, 3 vols. SOURCE Allibone Suppl., ii, p. 1443; Brown, p. 295; OCLC. LOCATION D, L.

TOWNSEND, C.C., See TOWNSEND, Revd Chambre Corker.

TOWNSEND, Revd Chambre Corker (known as C.C. Townsend), b. Cork *c*.1797, d. Co. Cork? 1852. Religious fiction writer, CCT was the eldest surviving son of the Revd Horatio (Horace) Townsend (d. 1837), rector of Carrigaline (Co. Cork), who wrote prose and verse. CCT was admitted at TCD in 1813, graduating BA in 1818 and MA in 1832. In 1825, he was licensed to the curacy of Castleventry (Co. Cork). Also in Co. Cork he was minister of Island and vicar of Desert (1829–40); vicar of Kilmaccabea (1840 to his death). He married in 1824, Frances Vere-Stewart, daughter of Robert Vere-Stewart, of St James's London (d. 1824), and they had a son Horatio, whose daughter Charlotte married George Bernard Shaw§. CCT married secondly in 1831, Eliza (only child of Maj.-Gen. Nathaniel-Wilmot Oliver, RA), with whom he had three sons and several daughters. Aside from the following work, CCT also authored *Oral teachings not oral tradition* (London, 1843). A monument to his memory was erected by his parishioners in Leap Church (Co. Cork), and another erected in Ross cathedral to the united memory of CCT and his bothers Horatio (also rector of Carrigaline, Co. Cork) and Richard William (a civil engineer). SOURCE Allibone, iii, p. 2440; B & S, p. 818; Cork, ii. p 514–15; COPAC; JAPMDI, 5(3) (1903), p. 331.

T110 *Happy Mary. A narrative of facts* (by C.C. Townsend).
Dublin: P. Dixon Hardy & Sons [for the Religious Book and Tract Depository for Ireland], [1846 or earlier]. SOURCE Adv. in [anon.], *The history of Susan Blake. A true story* (Dublin, 1846).
COMMENTARY No copy located. Likely to be religious fiction [RL].

TOWNSEND, Edward W. See TOWNSEND, Edward Waterman.

TOWNSEND, Edward Waterman (known as Edward W. Townsend), fl. 1895. American novelist and short story writer. SOURCE Wright, iii, p. 553 (list of titles).

T111 *'Chimmie Fadden', Major Max and other stories* (by Edward W. Townsend).
+ New York: Dodd, Mead & Co., 1895. SOURCE Blessing, p. 158. LOCATION D.
New York: Lovell & Coryell, 1895. SOURCE Wright, iii, 5536; OCLC. LOCATION D.
[New York]: Garrett, 1969. SOURCE OCLC. LOCATION PpiU.
COMMENTARY Stories first written for newspapers in New York and San Francisco. Some of the stories are told in an Irish dialect [ML].

TOWNSHEND, Dorothea. See TOWNSHEND, Dorothea Baker.

TOWNSHEND, Dorothea Baker (née Baker; later known as Mrs R.B. Townshend and Dorothea Townshend), fl. 1892. Novelist, biographer, poet and children's writer, DBT was the daughter of Revd Ralph Bourne Baker of Hasfield Court (Glos.). She married Richard Baxter Townshend of Castle Townshend (Co. Cork and later of Rievera Lodge in the same county). She wrote several biographies, including *Life and letters of Mr. Endymion Porter* (London, 1897); *Life and letters of the great Earl of Cork* (London, 1904), and *George Digby, second Earl of Bristol* (London, 1924). The title page of the following book indicates that she co-authored with her husband *An officer of the Long Parliament and his descendants; being some account of the life and times of Colonel Richard Townesend of Castletown (Castletownshend) & a chronicle of his family* (London, 1892). She also published poetry, *Broken lights* (London, 1932). Only her work with Irish content is listed below. SOURCE Brown, p. 295; Brown 2, p. 258; COPAC, D.B. Townshend & R.B. Townshend, *An officer of the Long Parliament* (London, 1892).

T112   *The strange adventures of a young lady of quality: MDCCV. In six chapters* (by Dorothea Townshend).
+ London: Digby, Long & Co., [1893]. SOURCE Wolff, 6754; COPAC; OCLC. LOCATION L.
COMMENTARY Historical fiction set in Ireland. It features a girl who is descended from supporters of King James. The family had been divided in the past between those who had sympathies with the English and those who had not. The two branches meet and intermarry. Eventually the family repurchases the estate that they had lost in the war [ML].

T113   *The faery of Lisbawn and Dennis Roe's tower* (by Dorothea Townshend).
+ London: Thomas Nelson & Sons, 1900 (ill.). SOURCE Alston, p. 439; Brown 2, 1537. LOCATION L, D.
COMMENTARY Historical fiction. In '*The faery of Lisbawn*', the scene is laid near Bandon (Co. Cork) in the period following the efforts to pacify Munster after the Desmond wars (1569–73 and 1579–83). John Hull, an Englishman, settles with his family near Lisbawn, a ruined castle of the MacCarthys. His children meet an old man and the three become friends. He teaches them 'to love the conquered Irish they live among'. The old man turns out to be the outlawed MacCarthy himself. He saves the Hull family from a raid of the Barbary corsairs at the cost of his own life. 'Dennis Roe's tower' concerns the 1798 uprising [Brown 2].

T114   *A lost leader: A tale of Restoration days* (by Dorothea Townshend).
+ London: Society for Promoting Christian Knowledge; New York: E. & J.B. Young & Co., [1902] (ill. Harold Piffard). SOURCE COPAC. LOCATION L.
COMMENTARY Historical fiction set in 1648 in England and Ireland, featuring Maj.-Gen. Harrison [RL].

T115   *A Saint George of King Charles's day. A story* (by Dorothea Townshend).
+ London: Christian Knowledge Society, [1906] (ill. W.S. Stacey). SOURCE COPAC. LOCATION L.
London: Society for Promoting Christian Knowledge; New York: E.S. Gorham [1906] (ill. W.S. Stacey). SOURCE COPAC. LOCATION C.
COMMENTARY Historical fiction set during the time of Cromwell and the Restoration. Not set in Ireland, but mentions Roger Boyle, earl of Orrery§ [ML].

T116   *The children of Nugentstown and their dealings with the Sidhe* (by Dorothea Townshend).
London: David Nutt, 1911 (ill., Ruth Cobb). SOURCE Brown, 1590. LOCATION L.
COMMENTARY Three young Nugents go to visit their aunt in her tumbledown family place in Co. Cork. The children get in touch with the fairies and as a result family papers are recovered and fortune smiles once more on the Nugents [Brown].

TOWNSHEND, Richard Baxter. Co-author. See **TOWNSHEND, Dorothea Baker.**

TRACY, Revd Bernard. See **TRACY, Henry.**

TRACY, Henry, pseud. '**Peregrinus**', fl. 1863. Historical fiction writer, HT was the brother of the Revd Bernard Tracy. His identity is confirmed in the NLI copy of the following volume and by the story's subsequent publication as a supplement to the *Dublin Saturday Magazine*. HT was the publisher of the story in book form when he resided in Glasgow. However, its preface is dated 1 Aug. 1864 [*sic*], from Lille, France. Probably a different person than the barrister Henry Tracy (b. 1844) [RL; Ferguson, p. 310].

T117   *The adventures of Bernard O'Loughlin: A tale of the north of Ireland, illustrative of the character and condition of the people some years back. Founded on facts* (by 'Peregrinus'; dedicated to Marshal MacMahon, duke of Magenta).

+ Glasgow: Henry Tracy, 1863. LOCATION D.
Dublin: *Dublin Saturday Magazine*, [between 1865 and 1867] (Supplement to this newspaper, as *The groundless accusation; or, the sufferings of Bernard O'Loughlin, a successful candidate for the priesthood*; revsd by the author's brother, Revd Bernard Tracy, resident of Mount St Mary's, Pollockshaws, Glasgow). LOCATION PC.

'TRAFFORD, F.G.', pseud. See RIDDELL, Mrs J.H.

'TRAMP, Tilbury', pseud. See LEVER, Charles.

TRAVERS, Eva L. (later Mrs Evered Poole), fl. 1886. Religious fiction writer for children and a poet; according to Colman ELT was Irish. She also wrote *The life and letters of a soldier* (London, 1883), which concerns a soldier in South Africa. SOURCE Allibone Suppl., ii, p. 1243 [under Poole], p. 1445; BLC; Colman, pp 216–17.

T118   *Golden links in a life chain* (by Eva L. Travers).
London: James Nisbet & Co., 1886. SOURCE Allibone Suppl., ii, p. 1243 [under Poole]. LOCATION L (destroyed), E.
COMMENTARY Religious fiction [BLC].

T119   *Lamps for little feet: A series of tracts for the young* (by Eva L. Travers).
London: Morgan & Scott, [1886]. LOCATION L (destroyed).
COMMENTARY No copy located. Religious fiction [BLC; RL].

T120   *Lotta's life mistake* (by Eva L. Travers).
+ London: James Nisbet & Co., 1887. SOURCE Allibone Suppl., ii, p. 1243 [under Poole]. LOCATION L.
COMMENTARY Set in England and relates the story of a sacrifice dictated by religion and its eventual reward [ML].

T121   *Jewel series: Booklets for the young* (by Eva L. Travers).
Sterling [Scotland]: Drummond's Tract Depot, [1888–1893], 12 parts. LOCATION L (destroyed).
COMMENTARY No copy located. Religious fiction [BLC; RL].

T122   *Booklets for the young. Series B* (by Eva L. Travers).
London: Religious Tract Society, [1889], 2 parts. LOCATION L.

T123   *Flower stories for our little folks* (by Eva L. Travers).
London: Religious Tract Society, [1891]. LOCATION L (destroyed).
COMMENTARY Religious fiction [BLC]

T124   *Golden grain. Booklets for the young* (by Eva L. Travers).
London: Religious Tract Society, [1891], 10 parts. LOCATION L.

T125   *Helpful messages* (by Eva L. Travers).
Sterling [Scotland]: Drummond's Tract Depot, [1891], 4 parts. LOCATION L (destroyed).
COMMENTARY No copy located. Religious fiction [BLC; RL].

T126   *His troublesome sister* (by Eva L. Travers).
+ London: Digby & Long, [1894]. LOCATION L.
COMMENTARY Set in England. A brother and a sister have lost their parents and find that they have to earn their living. They go through many tribulations and romantic intrigues; however their trust in God leads them through [ML].

'TRAVERS, F.', fl. 1860s. Writer of moral fiction for juveniles. It is possible that this is a pseudonym for the author, who signed the preface to the following volume with 'L.J.S.' SOURCE RL.

T127   *Too late for the train: or, the autobiography of Reginald Beresford. With a few*
supplementary particulars (by F. Travers; introd. signed 'L.J.S.').
+ Bath: Binns & Goodwin; London: E. Marlborough & Co., [1860]. SOURCE Allibone,
iii, p. 2446; Fenning cat. 182/27. LOCATION L, InND Loeber coll.
COMMENTARY The introd. claims that this story is based on facts, with a veil of fiction, is and
suitable for the entertainment of young persons. Set in England, but appears to be inspired
by events in Ireland. Reginald Beresford starts out life from a well-to-do background and is
an amiable person. Beresford's family title and estate is Blessington, where they keep an Irish
butler. Beresford has several shortcomings. He is not punctual, he is lazy, and he does not
take his religious duties seriously. The shortcomings have serious consequences and lose him
the esteem of his friends. At the very end of his life, he writes a document pointing out all
his shortcoming in the hope that others may benefit from his mis-spent time on earth [ML;
RL].

TRAVERS, Isabella. See **STEWARD, Isabella**.

TRENCH, Miss —, fl. 1852. Novelist, daughter of Power Le Poer Trench, archbishop of
Tuam (d. 1839), and Anne, daughter of Walter Taylor of Castle Taylor (Co. Galway), with
whom he had two sons and four daughters. Initially, the family lived at Raford, near Ballinasloe
(Co. Galway). Miss T's authorship of the following work is revealed in an advertisement by
the publisher Oldham in 1855, which mentions that it was written by 'a daughter of the late
Archbishop of Tuam' (adv. in E. Morse, *Lucy; or, scene on Lough Neagh*, Dublin, 1855). The
author Charlotte Elizabeth (Elizabeth Tonna§) contributed personal recollections to his entry
in the DNB, indicating a probable familiarity between the noted writer and the archbishop's
daughters. SOURCE DNB; ODNB [under Power Le Poer Trench]; RL.
T128   *The rectory of Glenmurragh. A tale* [anon.].
+ Dublin: Samuel B. Oldham; London: Seeley, 1852 (ill. H. Anelay; W. Dickes).
SOURCE Brown 2, 23. LOCATION D, Dt, L.
COMMENTARY Fanny Tyrrell, an Irish orphan, goes to England as a governess where she meets
an uncle who adopts her. She marries a minister who is tutor to the family of Lady Trevelyan
of Glenmurragh Castle in Ireland. The minister is presented with the living of Glenmurragh
rectory, where the couple settles down happily. Reviewed in the *Christian Penny Journal* (1853,
p. 53), which indicates that the volume was written in aid of an orphaned daughter of a minister [RL; Brown 2].

TRENCH, Richard William Steuart (also known as **William Richard Trench**; not 'Stuart'
as in Hogan), b. Bellegrove, near Portarlington (Co. Laois) 1808, d. Carrickmacross (Co.
Monaghan) 1872. Land agent, miscellaneous writer and novelist, RWST was the son of dean
Thomas Trench and Mary Weldon of Rahinderry (Co. Laois), whose father was MP for Athy
(Co. Kildare). He was educated at the Royal School (Armagh) and entered TCD in 1826, but
does not appear to have taken a degree. He chose the profession of land agent, studying agriculture and land management. He became an agent on the Shirley estate in Co. Monaghan in
1843, which he left to work on his own lands in Co. Laois and to become agent on Lord
Lansdowne's Co. Kerry estate from 1849 on. Here he organized the controversial mass emi-
grations at the charge of the estate, much-criticized by Irish nationalists. He was agent also
for the marquess of Bath (Co. Monaghan), and Lord Digby (Co. Offaly). He wrote about his
experiences in *Realities of Irish life* (London, 1868), which gives a graphic and powerful picture of the fate of the peasantry during the Famine. The illustrations by his son depicting
peasant mobs attacking righteous land agents incensed Irish readers, but the book was an imme-

diate success and was likened to the work of Charles Dickens. RWST contributed short pieces to magazines, including 'Sketches of life and character in Ireland', published in the *Evening Hours* (London, 1871–72). In the preface to *Ierne* (London, 1871), his only novel, he mentions that he had written a sketch of the history of Ireland to trace the roots of Irish disaffection, but it was suppressed after a large portion of it had been printed. He was buried in the church of Donaghmoyne (not Donaghmore as in OCIL) in Co. Monaghan where a monument to his memory was erected. His portrait was published by Lyne. SOURCE Allibone, iii, p 2450–1; B & S, p. 823; Boase, iii, pp 1014–15; Boylan, p. 386; Field Day, ii, pp 145–58, 206; Hogan 2, p. 1199; G.L. Lyne, *The Lansdowne estate in Kerry under W.S. Trench 1849–72* (Dublin, 2001); OCIL, p. 570; ODNB; RIA/DIB; *Rossa's recollections, 1838 to 1898, memoirs of an Irish revolutionary* (Guilford, CT, 2004), pp 157–8; E.P. Shirley, *The history of the County of Monaghan* (London, 1879), p. 357; Vanishing country houses, p. 97.

T129　*Ierne. A tale* (by William Richard Trench).

　　+ London: Longmans, Green & Co., 1871, 2 vols. SOURCE Brown, 1591. LOCATION D, Dt, DPL, InND Loeber coll. (1871, 2nd edn).

　　Paris: Perrin, 1879 (trans. by J. Améro as *Les Ribboniens. Scènes de la vie réelle en Irlande*). SOURCE Brown 2, 40; IBL, 16 (1928), p. 59 (attributes it to 'Stuart'); OCLC (1897 edn). LOCATION Univ. of Missouri, Columbia (1897 edn).

COMMENTARY A study of agrarian crime in which the author endeavours to show the causes of the obstinate resistance by the Irish to measures undertaken for their benefit, and the method of cure, as well as the belief of Irish peasants in their ownership of the land [Brown; ODNB].

TRENCH, William Richard. See **TRENCH, Richard William.**

TROLLOPE, Anthony, b. London 1815 (not 1812 as in OCIL), d. London 1882. Noted English novelist, AT was the son of Thomas Anthony Trollope and his wife Francis who, after the failure of her husband's business, wrote to support the family, publishing over 40 novels dealing with social issues. AT lived in Ireland from 1841 to 1851 at Banagher (Co. Offaly), Clonmel (Co. Tipperary), and Mallow (Co. Cork), and after a three-year hiatus back in England, lived in Donnybrook (Dublin), finally leaving Ireland in 1858. He taught himself about Irish life by reading the works of Maria Edgeworth§, William Carleton§, John and Michael Banim§ and Gerald Griffin§. In his capacity of inspector of the postal service, he travelled widely through the country and observed first-hand much of the material for his Irish novels, the first two of which were written while he was in Ireland and were neither popular or financial successes. AT wrote some Irish short stories for periodicals. To the London *Examiner* he contributed 'Irish distress' in 1849 and 'The real state of Ireland' in 1850. In the same year he partly-prepared a handbook for travellers in Ireland, but after writing the sections on Dublin and Killarney and the route between the two locations, abandoned the project. He revisited Ireland twice during the year of his death. For an extensive biography see ODNB, and see Sadleir for bibliographical details. Only AT's works with Irish content are included below. For his portraits and papers, see ODNB. SOURCE Allibone, iii, pp 2454–5; Allibone Suppl., ii, pp 1448–9; Brown, p. 295; T.H.S. Escott, *Anthony Trollope* (repr. Port Washington, NY, 1967); V. Glendenning, *Trollope* (London, 1992); N.J. Hall, *Trollope: a biography* (Oxford, 1991), passim; J.P. Hennessy, *Anthony Trollope* (London, 1971); Hogan 2, pp 1203–7; Igoe, pp 271–3; NCBEL 4, pp 1418–37; OCIL, p. 571; ODNB; RL; M. Sadleir, *Trollope: A bibliography* (Folkestone, 1927, repr. 1977); M. Sadleir (ed.), *An autobiography by Anthony Trollope* (London, 1923), pp 79–80; D. Smalley (ed.) *Trollope: the critical heritage* (London, 1969); Sutherland, pp 634–7.

T130　*The MacDermots of Ballycloran* (by Anthony Trollope).

Trollope

London: T.C. Newby, 1847, 3 vols. SOURCE Brown, 1592 (who mistakenly states [1844]); Hall, p. 560. LOCATION L.
London: T.C. Newby, 1848, 3 vols. (as *The MacDermots of Ballycloran. A historical romance*). SOURCE M. Sadleir, *Trollope: A bibliography* (Folkestone, 1927), p. 6.
+ London: Chapman & Hall, 1866 (new edn). LOCATION D, L.
+ Philadelphia: T.B. Peterson & Bros, [*c*.1871]. SOURCE Sadleir, 3203. LOCATION InND Loeber coll.
+ New York: Garland, 1979, 3 vols. (introd. by R.L. Wolff). LOCATION Dt, InND Loeber coll.
+ New York: Dover, 1988. LOCATION InND Loeber coll.
COMMENTARY Written between 1843 and 1845, AT shortened the later edn by three chapters. Inspired by his visit to the abandoned ruins of a country house (called Headfort), the former seat of the Jones family, near the village of Drumsna (Co. Leitrim), the novel exploited contemporary English interest in Ireland. It is a story of decline featuring the MacDermots, a broken-down landowning Catholic family that the author saw as emblematic of the decline of the country. Larry MacDermot cannot keep up the mortgage of Ballycloran, held by the vulgar Joe Flannelly – whose daughter he had refused to marry. Larry's own daughter is seduced by Capt. Miles Usher, a sub-inspector of police who enforces the excise laws against poteenmaking. Certain difficulties stand in the way of their marriage and the sub-inspector attempts to elope with her. Her brother Thady comes on the scene, and in the affray the sub-inspector is killed. Thady MacDermot is tried and publicly hanged. His father goes mad, Miss MacDermot loses her mind and dies in childbirth, and the MacDermots vacate Ballycloran. The novel is one of the rare works of Irish fiction to be cited in court proceedings – at Tralee (Co. Kerry) in 1848 [Brown; J. Burke, *A history of the commoners* (London, 1836), iii, p. 267–69); N.J. Hall, pp 91, 107; OCIL, p. 332; M. Sadleir, *Trollope, a commentary* (Oxford, 1927, repr. 1961), pp 5, 141; M. Sadleir (ed.), *An autobiography by Anthony Trollope* (London, 1923), pp 63–4, 67; Sutherland, p. 393; Wolff introd., p. 30].
T131   *The Kellys and the O'Kellys; or, landlords and tenants. A tale of Irish life* (by Anthony Trollope).
London: Henry Colburn, 1848, 3 vols. SOURCE Brown, 1593; Hall, p. 560. LOCATION L.
+ London: Chapman & Hall, 1859 (new edn). SOURCE Topp 3, p. 334. LOCATION L, InND Loeber coll.
+ New York: Rudd & Carleton; London: Chapman & Hall, 1860. LOCATION InND Loeber coll.
New York: Garland, 1979, 3 vols. (introd. by R.L. Wolff). SOURCE COPAC. LOCATION Dt.
+ Oxford, New York: Oxford University Press, 1982 (introd. by William Trevor). LOCATION InND Loeber coll.
COMMENTARY Only 375 copies of the first edn were printed. Most of the story takes place in the village of Dunmore near Tuam (Co. Galway). While opening with the famous trial of Daniel O'Connell in 1844 for conspiracy against the crown, this is a love story among landed families of the Ascendancy set in Co. Galway, with two intertwining plot lines. The first concerns Frank O'Kelly's (Lord Ballindine's) quest for the hand of the heiress Fanny Wyndham. He is frustrated in his suit by her guardian, the earl of Cashel, who wants Fanny for his own wastrel son, Lord Kilcullen. The other plot line concerns the progeny of Simeon Lynch, who has made a dishonest fortune managing Frank's family estate. Lynch's son, Barry, drunkenly tries to murder his sister Anty so as to inherit her half of the money. Taking refuge with the innkeeper Mrs Kelly, Anty eventually finds a husband, Martin Kelly, to protect her. Frank finally overcomes all obstacles and marries Fanny. The villains Barry and Lord Kilcullen are

driven abroad. The London 1859 new edn has four additional chapters [N.J. Hall, p. 103; OCIL, p. 571; Sutherland, p. 347; Topp].

T132   *Castle Richmond. A novel* (by Anthony Trollope).
London: Chapman & Hall, 1860, 3 vols. SOURCE Brown, 1594; Hall, p. 560; Sadleir, 3202; Wolff, 6770. LOCATION L.
+ Amsterdam: J.D. Sijbrandi, 1861, 2 vols. (trans. into Dutch as *Het kasteel Richmond: Een verhaal tijdens de hongersnood in Ierland*; ill. Emmerick, Binger). SOURCE Adamnet. LOCATION UVA.
+ Leipzig: Bernhard Tauchnitz, 1860, 2 vols. SOURCE T & B, 520. LOCATION DPL, L, InND Loeber coll.
+ New York: Harper & Bros, 1860. SOURCE NCBEL 3, p. 882. LOCATION InND Loeber coll. (also 1862 edn).
+ New York: Garland, 1979, 3 vols. (introd. by R.L. Wolff). SOURCE COPAC. LOCATION Dt, InND Loeber coll.
+ New York: Dover, 1984. LOCATION InND Loeber coll.
COMMENTARY AT notes in the preface that 'Irish novels were once popular enough. But there is a fashion in novels as there is in colours and petticoats; and now I fear they are drugs in the market'. Set around Mallow (Co. Cork) during the Famine years, which are described in harrowing detail, the novel contrasts the lives of two Irish families, one of which has hung on to the old Irish traditions, while the other has become more English. The novel includes a picture of an evangelical proselytizer at work among the starving Catholics [ML; N.J. Hall, pp 109, 104; OCIL, p. 571; Sutherland, p. 110; Wolff introd., p. 30].

T133   *Tales of all countries* (by Anthony Trollope).
London: Chapman & Hall, 1861. SOURCE NCBEL 4, p. 1429; Sumner & Stillman cat 98/106; COPAC. LOCATION Univ. of Sheffield.
COMMENTARY Eight stories, one set in Ireland: 'The O'Conors of Castle Conor' (first published in *Harper's New Monthly Magazine*, New York, May 1860) is a story about hunting and the hospitality of the Conors [RL].

T134   *Lotta Schmidt and other stories* (by Anthony Trollope).
+ London: Alexander Strahan, 1867. SOURCE NCBEL 4, p. 1429; Wolff, 6785. LOCATION L.
London: Chapman & Hall, [1871] (new edn; Select Library of Fiction, No. 188). SOURCE Topp 3, p. 372; COPAC. LOCATION L.
New York: George Routledge & Sons, [1867]. SOURCE Topp 3, p. 372.
COMMENTARY No copy of the New York edn located. Repr. from *Good Words* (London) and other periodicals. Contains one Irish story, 'Father Giles of Ballymoy' (first published in *Argosy*, London, May 1866). Fr Giles befriends a traveller with whom he shares a room in an inn in Co. Galway, close to Lough Corrib [RL; RLIN].

T135   *Phineas Finn, the Irish member. A novel* (by Anthony Trollope).
London: Virtue & Co., 1869, 2 vols. (ill. J.E. Millais). SOURCE Brown, 1595 (mistakenly mentions a 1866 edn); NCBEL 4, p. 1424; Hall, p. 561; Sutherland, p. 504. LOCATION L.
London: Chapman & Hall, 1871 (new edn; Select Library of Fiction, No. 186). SOURCE Topp 3, p. 368. LOCATION L.
Leipzig: Bernhard Tauchnitz, 1869, 3 vols. SOURCE T & B, 1016–18. LOCATION L.
+ New York: Harper & Bros, 1868 (issued 1869, see Brick Row cat. 116/194, citing I.R. Brussel, *Anglo-American first editions, East to West*, p. 154; ill.). SOURCE Brick Row cat. 116/194. LOCATION InND Loeber coll.

COMMENTARY First published in *Saint Paul's Magazine* (London, Oct. 1867–May 1869), and in the US in *Littell's Living Age* (Boston, Nov. 1867–Apr. 1869). The manuscript of this novel is in Yale University's Beinecke Library. The title character is Irish, but the story mainly concerns Finn's romantic involvements in London and his political life at Westminster – which eventually he gives up because of his views on tenant rights in Ireland. He returns to Ireland, marries his Irish sweetheart Mary Flood Jones, and becomes a Poor Law commissioner [OCIL, p. 571; Sutherland, p. 504; Topp 3, pp 368–9].

T136   *Phineas redux* (by Anthony Trollope).

    + London: Chapman & Hall, 1874, 2 vols. (ill. Frank Holl). SOURCE Hall, p. 561; NCBEL 4, p. 1425; Wolff, 6790. LOCATION L, InND Loeber coll.

    Berlin: Cohn, 1874, 3 vols. LOCATION Union cat. Bavaria.

    + New York: Harper & Bros, 1874. SOURCE Seen at MacManus, Philadelphia, April 1993; RL; OCLC. LOCATION CtY.

COMMENTARY First serialized in the *Graphic* (London, July 1873–Jan. 1874). A continuation of *Phineas Finn* (London, 1869, 2 vols.) in which Finn returns to Westminster after the death of his Irish wife Mary and is involved in romantic and political webs that result at one point in a murder accusation. He is eventually acquitted but resigns from parliament [OCIL, p. 571; Sutherland, p. 504].

T137   *An eye for an eye* (by Anthony Trollope).

    London: Chapman & Hall, 1879, 2 vols. SOURCE Hall, p. 561; Sutherland, p. 219. LOCATION L.

    + London, New York, Melbourne: Ward, Lock & Bowden, n.d. (new edn). LOCATION InND Loeber coll.

    Leipzig: Bernard Tauchnitz, 1879. SOURCE T & B, 1805; GLOL. LOCATION Universitätsbibliothek, Eichstätt.

    + New York: Garland, 1979, 2 vols. (introd. by R.L. Wolff). LOCATION Dt, InND Loeber coll.

COMMENTARY Written in 1870, but held back for nine years. First serialized in the *Whitehall Review* (London, Aug. 1878–Feb. 1879), this is a story of love, betrayal and murder set in Co. Clare. An English cavalry officer seduces a young Irish girl who becomes pregnant. When he is about to desert her after inheriting an earldom, her mother murders him by pushing him off a cliff. AT blames the man's passions while exculpating the woman as his victim. A priest is kind to the woman in her trouble [Sutherland, p. 219; Wolff introd., p. 30; Quaritch cat. 1323/106].

T138   *The Landleaguers* (by Anthony Trollope).

    London: Chatto & Windus, 1883, 3 vols. SOURCE Brown, 1597; Hall, p. 562; NCBEL 4, p. 1428; Wolff, 6783. LOCATION L.

    + New York: Geo. Munro's Sons, 1883 (Seaside Library, No. 32, as *The land leaguers*). SOURCE NCBEL 3, p. 884. LOCATION InND Loeber coll.

    + New York: Garland, 1979, 3 vols. (introd. by R.L. Wolff). LOCATION Dt, InND Loeber coll.

    + Ann Arbor: Univ. of Michigan Press, 1992 (introd. by R.H. Super; ill.). SOURCE OCLC. LOCATION Dt, C, InND Loeber coll.

COMMENTARY AT's final, unfinished novel is the story of an English Protestant family that purchases a property under the Encumbered Estates Act and settles in Co. Galway. The main character, Philip Jones, is a hardworking, improving landlord who treats his tenants fairly but refuses to reduce rent for Pat Carroll, a Fenian activist. As a result, his lands are despoiled, the family is boycotted and tenants refuse to pay rent. The landlord's little son is the only witness against the peasant, and the child is murdered for what he knows by a Land Leaguer filled with American ideas of autonomy. A sub-plot concerns a young American singer, Rachel O'Mahony, and ridicules her Irish-American father and Irish-American interest in Ireland. It ends with an essay on the degeneration of life in Ireland since AT had lived there [Brown; Hogan 2, p. 1206; OCIL, p. 297].

T139   *Collected short stories* (by Anthony Trollope).
    + New York: Dover, 1987 (ed. by John Hampden; ill. Joan Hassall). LOCATION InND Loeber coll.
COMMENTARY Contents: 'The parson's daughter of Oxney Colne', 'La mère bauche', 'Father Giles of Ballymoy' (first published in *Argosy*, London, May 1866), 'The spotted dog', 'Alice Dugdale', 'The O'Conors of Castle Conor' (first published in *Harper's New Monthly Magazine*, New York, May 1860), 'The journey to Panama', 'Katchen's caprices', 'The Turkish bath', 'Mary Gresley' [RL].

TROLLOPE, Henry M. See **TROLLOPE, Henry Merivale**.

TROLLOPE, Henry Merivale (known as **Henry M. Trollope**), b. Clonmel (Co. Tipperary) 1846, d. 1926. Novelist son of the English novelist Anthony Trollope§ and Rose Heseltine. Aside from the following volume, HMT was the author of *Corneille and Racine* (London, 1881). According to the ODNB, he did not have much success as a writer. SOURCE ODNB; Sutherland, p. 637 [under Anthony Trollope].

T140   *My own love story* (by Henry M. Trollope).
    + London: Chapman & Hall, 1887, 2 vols. SOURCE Sutherland, p. 637; OCLC. LOCATION L.
COMMENTARY Set in England [RL].

TROTTER, Frederick A., fl. 1894. Novelist, FAT's only known work is listed below. SOURCE RL.

T141   *The hand on the helm. A story of Irish life* (by Frederick A. Trotter).
    + London: Charles H. Kelly, 1894 (ill. A.E. Line, W & S). LOCATION D, L. InND Loeber coll.
COMMENTARY Binding types: (a) beige cloth; (b) red cloth, impressed in gold and black. Story set somewhere on the Atlantic coast of Ireland where Denis O'Sullivan, who is about to marry Rosie O'Meara, is lured under false pretences into guiding the English lieutenant Crosbie and his men to a smugglers' cave. The smugglers recognize Denis and brand him as a traitor. Denis has to flee for his life, and Rosie promises to be faithful to him. While they are separated, both Rosie and Denis become Protestants. Rosie's conversion makes Mr Swanby, who wants to marry her, turn from her in disgust, thus leaving her free for Denis, who returns and whose innocence with regard to the discovery of the smugglers is proven [ML].

TROTTER, John Bernard, b. Co. Down 1774 (not 1775 as in several sources), d. Cork 1818 (1819 according to O'Donoghue). Barrister, miscellaneous writer, poet and unpublished novelist, JBT was the son of Revd Edward Trotter, a Church of Ireland clergyman in Co. Down, and Mary Dickson. He was initially educated at the grammar school in Downpatrick and graduated BA at TCD in 1795. He was admitted at the Middle Temple (London) in 1797, at the King's Inns in 1800 and was called to the Irish Bar in 1802. In 1799 he published a pamphlet on the Union, which he sent to the statesman Charles James Fox, a lifelong friend of his uncle, William Dickson, bishop of Down. Later JBT became private secretary to Fox while he was foreign secretary. After Fox's death he published his controversial *Memoirs of the latter years of the Rt. Hon. Charles James Fox* (London, 1811), which was described as 'an ill work by a

Tufnell

weak man'. JBT was a Protestant of liberal views, he wrote on Irish politics and he founded the *Irish Harp Society* in 1809. He lived in Co. Down near Dundrum in 1808 when he was visited by the American traveller, John Melish, but his dedication to *Stories for calumniators* is dated from Richmond (Surrey) in 1809. His fortunes declined and to earn money he wrote at Dalkey (Co. Dublin) a novel *Margaret of Waldemar* (not published). His poem, *Leipsick; or Germany restored* appeared in Dublin in 1813. He died in poverty in Cork. His *Walks through Ireland in ... 1812, 1814, and 1817* (London, 1819) was published posthumously and contained a short biography of his chequered life. Maria Edgeworth§ in one of her letters communicated a very poor picture of him. His portrait is listed by Elmes. SOURCE Allibone, iii, p. 2458; BD, p. 354; B & S, p. 824; Bradshaw, 2536, 2932–34; Collinson Black, 2176; Colvin, p. 320; Elmes, p. 205; Leslie, *Down*, p. 60; J. Melish, *Travels through the United States of America ... Britain, Ireland, and Canada* (London, 1818), p. 247; ODNB [included in Edward (formerly Trotter) Ruthven]; O'Donoghue, p. 460; RIA/DIB; biographical sketch in *Walks through Ireland in ... 1812, 1814, and 1817* (London, 1819).

T142   *Margaret of Waldemar* (by John Bernard Trotter).
COMMENTARY An unpublished manuscript novel, which bearing 'the stamp of a wild and morbid imagination', was rejected by the booksellers, as 'too extravagant even for the regions of romantic fiction'. Present location of the manuscript not known [Introd. to J.B. Trotter, *Walks through Ireland* (London, 1819), pp xvii–xviii; RL].

T143   *Stories for calumniators: Interspersed with remarks on the disadvantages, misfortunes, and habits of the Irish* (by John Bernard Trotter; dedicated to Lord Holland). + Dublin: Printed [for the author?] by H. Fitzpatrick, 1809, 2 vols. SOURCE Brown, 1598; British Fiction; Garside, 1809:73; Pollard 2, p. 212. LOCATION D, L.
COMMENTARY The running title of this work is *Stories for Irish calumniators*. Extensively reviewed in the *Hibernia Magazine* (Dublin, Jan. 1810). In the preface, the author states that the work was written 'to promote the welfare of my native country'. It consists of three stories, largely based on fact and describes the aftermath of the 1798 rebellion, illustrating the tragic consequences that can ensue if those in authority listen to the voice of slander. The stories are told to a Mr Fitzmaurice by persons related to the victims, and Fitzmaurice's own romance is interwoven with the tale. The author gives his own views on Irish politics, and is sympathetic to the Catholic cause. He writes strongly in favour of the Irish language, land reform, and higher education for women. He depicts himself as Fitzmaurice; Frank is his secretary, and the vicar and his family are based on the Revd Dr Dobbyn [Brown; biographical sketch in *Walks through Ireland in ... 1812, 1814, and 1817* (London, 1819)].

TUFNELL, Ida. See **PEACOCKE, Ida.**

TUITE, Lady Elizabeth Dorothea (née Cobbe), b. Newbridge House, Donabate (Co. Dublin) 1764, d. 1850. Poet and writer of religious and other fiction for children, EDT was the second daughter of Thomas Cobbe of Newbridge and Lady Elizabeth Beresford, daughter of the 1st earl of Tyrone and niece of the countess-dowager of Moira. She married in 1784, Sir Henry Tuite, 8th Bt, of Sonnagh (also known as Sonna, a country house in Co. Westmeath, since demolished), who was an officer in the Royal Navy. EDT should not be confused with Mrs Tuite, also from Sonnagh, who was member of the literary circle on the Co. Westmeath and Co. Longford border to which Maria Edgeworth (who stayed at Sonna in 1809) and her father, Richard Lovell Edgeworth§ belonged. EDT is known mainly as a poet. Her *Poems* was published in London in 1796. After the death of her husband in 1805, she lived for many years on the Circus at Bath. She was described by a Mrs Calvert in 1807 as 'entertaining, but very eccentric. She is more like a man than woman ..., but she rather amuses me' (Blake, p.

88). A probable portrait of her is mentioned by Strickland. She was related to the author Frances Power Cobbe§. SOURCE Allibone, iii, p. 2469 (listed twice); F.V. Barry (ed.), *Maria Edgeworth: Chosen letters* (Boston, [1931]), p. 213; Blain, p. 1099; W. Blake (ed.), *An Irish beauty of the regency* (London, 1911), p. 88; Sir B. Burke & A.P. Burke, *A genealogical and heraldic dictionary of the peerage and baronetage* (London, 1906, 68th edn), p. 1622; Butler, pp 180–1, 206; Dean of Westminster, *The remains of the late Mrs. Richard Trench* (London, 1862), pp 378, 480–1; H. Farrar (ed.), *Irish marriages* (London, 1897), ii, p. 442; *Life of Frances Power Cobbe by herself* (Boston, 1895), i, p. 14; Mrs Edgeworth, *A memoir of Maria Edgeworth* (London, 1867), ii, p. 268; Landed gentry, 1912, p. 118; RIA/DIB; Strickland, I, p. 177.

T144 *Edwin and Mary. A tale. A book for youth* (by Lady Elizabeth Dorothea Tuite).
  + London: Simpkin & Marshall, 1818. SOURCE Blain, p. 1099; BD, p. 572; COPAC.
  LOCATION L.
  COMMENTARY Fiction for juveniles [ML].

T145 *The reclaimed family. A tale for youth* [anon.] (dedicated to the Board of Education in Ireland).
  + London: Simpkin, Marshall & Co., 1838. SOURCE BD, p. 572. LOCATION L.
COMMENTARY Religious fiction for juveniles set in England about lapses in temperance as told in several life stories. In the preface, the author expresses her wish that her work be placed 'under the protection' of the Board of Education in Ireland 'for the benefit of the children of the working classes' [RL].

TURNER, Charlotte. See **SMITH, Charlotte.**

TURNERELLI, Edward Tracy, b. London 1813, d. Tracy Lodge, Leamington Spa (War.) 1896. Novelist and writer on Russia, ETT was the son of Belfast-born sculptor Peter Turnerelli, who executed portrait busts of notable Irishmen such as John Philpot Curran, Henry Grattan and Daniel O'Connell, and of his first wife, Margaret Mary Tracy. ETT was educated at Carlow College (1829–30), after which he studied modelling at the Royal Academy in London. He travelled extensively in Russia, living and sketching there for eighteen years and publishing *Kazan, the ancient capital of the Tartar khans* (London, 1854). Afterwards he devoted himself to the cause of the Conservative party in England. He is the author also of several political pamphlets and his autobiography, *Memories of a life of toil, or, the autobiography of the old conservative*, was published in 1884. For his portrait, see ODNB. SOURCE Allibone, iii, p. 2483; BLC; Boase, iii, p. 1050; ODNB [under Peter Turnerelli]; W.G. Strickland, *A dictionary of Irish artists* (Shannon, 1969), 2, pp. 466–70.

T146 *A night in a haunted house! A tale of facts … The ghost story recently related* [anon.] (published in aid of a public charity in Ryde [Isle of Wight]).
  + London: Ward & Lock, [1859] (Truth is Strange, Stranger than Fiction, No. 1).
  LOCATION L, InND Loeber coll.
  London: Thomas Bosworth, 1866, 2nd edn (*A night in the haunted house in Ireland: My guitar! Whose it was and how I got it. A ghost story*). SOURCE Sotheby's cat. LN6731/469; Tiger cat. 4/97/258. LOCATION L.
COMMENTARY 71pp. Set in a haunted house on the outskirts of Kilkenny where a man spending the night there sees the ghost of another man who had died in the same room. The next day he hears the story of the dead man and visits a priest who has letters belonging to him. It appears that he died of a broken heart, and so had his beloved. The Irish setting is of no consequence to the story [ML].

TYNAN, Katharine (later known as Mrs H.A. Hinkson), b. Dublin, 1859, d. Wimbledon (London) 1931. Prolific novelist, poet, journalist and woman of letters, KT was the daughter of Andrew Cullen Tynan, a livestock farmer and enthusiastic nationalist, and Elizabeth O'Reilly. She was educated at the Dominican Convent school in Drogheda. When still very young she joined the Ladies' Land League and, like her father, supported the statesman Charles Stewart Parnell. She was encouraged to write by Rosa Mulholland§ and by Fr Matthew Russell, founder of the *Irish Monthly* (Dublin), and began to publish verse while still a teenager. Her first volume of verse, *Louise de la Valliere*, underwritten by her father, appeared in 1885. At Whitehall, the family home, she had a literary salon and visitors included Mulholland, Dora Sigerson§, George Russell (A.E.) and William Butler Yeats§. Yeats greatly admired her work and regarded it as a significant contribution to the development of the Irish literary renaissance. She became the first literary editor of the Parnellite *Irish Daily Independent* (Dublin). In 1893 she married Henry Albert Hinkson§, an Irish barrister and writer and with him lived for many years in London, where their children were born and where she supported the family with a prodigious output of novels, poems, reviews, biographies and miscellaneous writings. In London, she was a member of the Irish Literary Society and was friends with leading Irish literary figures, renewing friendships with Yeats and Russell, who described her as 'happy in religion, friendship, children ...instantly kindling to beauty'. While in Ireland she had contributed to journals such as *United Ireland, Irish Fireside* and *Irish Monthly,* in which she published *'The old country'* (Dublin, 1893), and in London she continued her periodical submissions to such publications as the *Graphic; British National Observer; Pall Mall Gazette; Tinsley's; Merry England* (all London), and to L.T. Meade's (Elizabeth Toulmin Smith§) magazine for girls, *Atalanta* (London, 1892–93). She had met Constance and Oscar Wilde§ in London in the 1880s and had contributed a series of articles to *Woman's World* (London), then edited by Wilde. Her work also appeared in the *Catholic World* (New York) and the Boston *Pilot* and she wrote some works for the Catholic Truth Society (Dublin). Many of her articles concerned social issues such as the mistreatment of shop girls, unwed mothers, capital punishment, and the education of the poor. The Hinksons returned to Dublin in 1911 for financial reasons and through KT's friendship with the wife of the lord lieutenant, her husband was appointed RM of Ballinrobe (Co. Mayo). Despite her earlier nationalism (she contributed to the feminist and nationalist paper *Bean na hÉireann*, 1908–11), KT supported British policies in Ireland, particularly after her two sons enlisted in the British army in the First World War, and she considered the Easter Rising of 1916 a 'rebellion' and vividly recorded it in her *The years of the shadow* (London, 1919), one of the volumes of her autobiography. Her literary activities continued to support the family, especially after her husband's sudden death in 1919, after which she moved to Dublin and travelled on the Continent before settling in Wimbledon. She produced several other autobiographical works: *Twenty five years* (London, 1913); *The middle years* (London, 1916); *The wandering years* (London, 1922), and *Memories* (London, 1924), all of which chronicle developments in Irish and English literary history. In addition, she wrote *Peeps at many lands: Ireland* (London, 1909). She published 'Talk about literature' in the *Women's Signal* (location not clear) and lectured in 1909 to the Cork Literary and Scientific Society on the topic of 'Books Irish people ought to read'. She authored 132 works of fiction and many other non-fiction books. A collection of her papers is in UCD (LA 32), the RIA (MS SR/12/X/19), and the NLI (MSS 10,000–10,069, 10,657, 21,754), while other papers are listed in ODNB. A bust of KT is displayed in the Dublin Writers Museum. For her portraits, see ODNB. Her daughter Pamela Hinkson became a novelist also, writing sometimes under the pseudonym 'Peter Deane'. She finished her mother's book, *Connor's wood* (London, 1933). SOURCE Allibone Suppl., ii, p. 1457; Blain, p. 1103; Boylan, p. 388; Brady, p. 239; Brown, p. 297; CM; Colman, pp 219–28; EF, p. 394; Field Day, i, p. 416–21, 557–8, iv, p. 562 and passim, v, pp 73*n*, 661–2, and passim; R.F. Foster, *W.B. Yeats: a life* (Oxford, 1997, 2003); Irish pseudonyms; R. McHugh (ed.), *W.B.*

Yeats letters to Katharine Tynan (Dublin, 1953); Hogan 2, pp 1207–10; Igoe, pp 273–7; LVP, p. 483; NCBEL 4, pp 848–50; OCIL, pp 267 [under *Irish Monthly*], 573; ODNB; E. Reilly, p. 218; RIA/DIB; RL; M.G. Rose, *Katherine Tynan* (Lewisburg, PA, 1974); *A round table of the representative Irish and English Catholic novelists* (New York, 1897), pp 321–2; Ryan, p. 117; Sutherland, p. 644; Todd, pp 682–3; P. van de Kamp (ed.), *Katharine Tynan: Irish stories 1893–1900* (Leiden, 1993).

T147   *The land I love best* (by Katharine Tynan).
Woking, London: Unwin Bros, 1890. SOURCE Kersnowski, p. 138. LOCATION L, NUC.
COMMENTARY Stories set in the west of Ireland. Contents: 'A daughter of Erin', 'A penitent', 'Joanna', 'Two swains and a maid', 'A scapegoat', 'A returned emigrant', 'A priest from the Rockies', 'A monk's garden' [Leclaire, p. 198; NUC].

T148   *A cluster of nuts, being sketches among my own people* (by Katharine Tynan; dedicated to Mary Gill).
+ London: Lawrence & Bullen, 1894. SOURCE Brown, 1601; Kersnowski, p. 136. LOCATION D, L, NUC, InND Loeber coll.
COMMENTARY Sketches of village life in the west of Ireland. Contents: 'A village genius', 'Wayfarers', 'A country auction', 'A house of roses', 'A book-lover', 'Harvesters', 'Shameen', 'A martyr indeed', 'A farmer's tragedy', 'Farewell to Ballyshannon', 'Cissy: an exile', 'A spoilt priest', 'Waifs', 'A descendant of Irish earls', 'Mad Molly', 'Rose: from an Irish hedgerow', 'A village priest' [ML; Leclaire, p. 197].

T149   *An isle in the water* (by Katharine Tynan; dedicated to Jane Barlow§).
+ London: Adam & Charles Black, 1895. SOURCE Brown, 1602; Hogan 2, p. 1209 (mistakenly listed as 'An isle of water'); Kersnowski, p. 138 (1896 edn). LOCATION D, L, NUC.
London: A. & C. Black; New York: Macmillan & Co., 1896. LOCATION NUC.
COMMENTARY Sketches of peasant life, mostly set on an unnamed island off the west coast of Ireland. Contents: 'The first wife', 'The story of Father Anthony O'Toole', 'The unlawful mother', 'A rich woman', 'How Mary came home', 'Mauryeen', 'A wrestling', 'The sea's dead', 'Katie', 'The death spancel', 'A solitary', 'The man who was hanged', 'A prodigal son', 'Changes the nurseries', 'The fields of my childhood' [Brown; NUC].

T150   *The way of a maid* (by Katharine Tynan).
+ London: Lawrence & Bullen, 1895. SOURCE Brown, 1603; Hogan 2, p. 1209; Kersnowski, p. 141. LOCATION D, L, NUC.
New York: Dodd, Mead & Co., 1895. LOCATION NUC.
COMMENTARY Depicts domestic and social life in a typical Irish country town, called Coolavera (probably in Co. Sligo), chiefly among Catholic middle-class people [Brown; Leclaire, p. 197].

T151   *The land of mist and mountain* (by Katharine Tynan; dedicated to Hester Sigerson§).
+ London: Catholic Truth Society, [1895]. SOURCE Alston, p. 445; Brown, 1604. LOCATION D, L, NUC.
London: Unwin Bros, 1895. SOURCE Kersnowski, p. 138. LOCATION L.
COMMENTARY Short sketches of Irish life. Contents: 'The emigrant', 'A saint', 'A poor little thing', 'An exile's return', 'A prodigal', 'Two exiles', 'Jimmy of the birds', 'A long quest' [RL].

T152   *Oh, what a plague is love!* (by Katharine Tynan).
London: Adam & Charles Black, 1896. SOURCE Kersnowski, p. 140. LOCATION L, NUC.
+ Chicago: A.C. M'Clurg, 1900. SOURCE Kersnowski, p. 140. LOCATION NUC.
COMMENTARY Set in England. A widower with grown-up children has many love affairs, but his children always prevent their father from marrying again. The most likely candidate is Mrs Mellor, a neighbour in Kent. After he brings home a very young woman with whom his son falls in love, he eventually marries Mrs Mellor to the satisfaction of everyone [ML].

T153   *The dear Irish girl* (by Katharine Tynan).
London: Smith, Elder & Co., 1899. SOURCE Brown, 1605; Daims, 1401. LOCATION D, L, NUC.
+ Chicago: A.C. McClurg, 1899. SOURCE Daims, 1401. LOCATION NUC, InND Loeber coll.
COMMENTARY The Chicago edn came in two bindings, both green cloth, but embossed in either light green or black. A romance set in Dublin and Connacht where Biddy O'Connor grows up motherless with her father Dr O'Connor, a professor at TCD. She meets Maurice O'Hara, a young man from Connacht who gets along well with her father, since they have the same anti-quarian interests. Biddy and her father visit Maurice but a misunderstanding between the young couple arises when Biddy thinks he is about to marry another girl. Biddy's father dies and she moves to a relative's house in England, where she is unhappy. Despite several men falling in love with her, she continues to think about Maurice, while Maurice continues to look for her. In the end they are reunited, marry, and live happily in Connacht [ML; Leclaire, p. 198].

T154   *She walks in beauty* (by Katharine Tynan).
+ London: Smith, Elder & Co., 1899. SOURCE Brown, 1606; Kersnowski, p. 141. LOCATION D, NUC.
+ Chicago: A.C. McClurg & Co., 1900. SOURCE Kersnowski, p. 141. LOCATION D, NUC.
COMMENTARY The story of the love affairs of three girls from the impoverished gentry class [Brown].

T155   *Led by a dream, and other stories* (by Katharine Tynan).
+ London: [Catholic Truth Society], 1899. SOURCE Brown, 1607; Kersnowski, p. 138. LOCATION D, L, DCU, InND Loeber coll.
COMMENTARY Stories about Irish country people. Contents: 'Led by a dream', 'An adopted son', 'An Irish peasant woman', 'Two sisters', 'The seventh son', ' Poor Peggy', 'Where are you going to, my pretty maid?' [RL].

T156   *The handsome Brandons. A story for girls* (by Katharine Tynan).
+ London, Glasgow, Edinburgh, Dublin: Blackie & Son, 1899 (ill. Gertrude Demaine Hammond). SOURCE Brown, 1626; Kersnowski, p. 137. LOCATION D (n.d. edn), L, NUC, InND Loeber coll.
Chicago: A.C. McClurg, 1900. LOCATION NUC.
COMMENTARY Set in the west of Ireland and details the vicissitudes of a group of orphan children brought up by their sister on an impoverished estate, probably in Co. Kerry, which they stand to lose at any moment to a neighbour who is an ogre and an enemy of the family. The oldest son goes to Africa with a benefactor, but returns dying of consumption. One girl marries well, but on the death of her husband finds that she is practically penniless. Another girl falls in love with the son of the ogre. The godmother of yet another girl takes her godchild into her house and makes her an heiress. A bog slide removes the castle of the neighbour from the scene, with him in it, leaving the lovers to get married. The old rich benefactor returns and marries the eldest of the siblings, thereby saving the estate from having to be sold [ML; Leclaire, p. 198].

T157   *The queen's page* (by Katharine Tynan).
London: Lawrence & Bullen, 1899. SOURCE Colman, p. 222; Hogan 2, p. 1209.
New York, Cincinnati, Chicago: Benziger Bros, 1900 (as *The queen's page. A story of the days of Charles I of England*). SOURCE Kersnowski, p. 140; OCLC. LOCATION NUC.
COMMENTARY No copy of the London edn located. Historical fiction [RL].

T158   *A daughter of the fields* (by Katharine Tynan).
London: Smith, Elder & Co., 1900. SOURCE Brown, 1610; Daims, 1400. LOCATION D (1901 edn), L, NUC.

Chicago: A.C. McClurg, 1900. SOURCE Brown, 1610; Kersnowski, p. 136 (where indicated [190?]); Daims, 1400. LOCATION NUC (1901 edn).
COMMENTARY No copy of the New York, 1900 edn located. The heroine comes home to Ireland from a French convent where she has been brought up to a refined and easy life. However, she applies herself to helping her mother run the farm rather than desert her. The hardships are eased when she finds a husband [Brown; RL].

T159   *The adventures of Carlo* (by Katharine Tynan).
         + London, Glasgow, Edinburgh, Dublin: Blackie & Son, [1900] (ill.). SOURCE Kersnowski, p. 136. LOCATION L, InND Loeber coll. (n.d. edn).
         COMMENTARY Fiction for juveniles [RL].

T160   *Her father's daughter. A novel* (by Katharine Tynan).
         New York, Cincinnati: Benziger Bros, 1900. SOURCE Hogan 2, p. 1210; Kersnowski, p. 138. LOCATION NUC.

T161   *The golden lily* (by Katharine Tynan).
         London: Constable, [1901]. SOURCE Colman, p. 223.
         New York, Cincinnati: Benziger, 1902. SOURCE Kersnowski, p. 137. LOCATION NUC.
         COMMENTARY No copy of the London edn located [RL].

T162   *That sweet enemy* (by Katharine Tynan).
         + Westminster [London]: Archibald Constable & Co., 1901. LOCATION InND Loeber coll.
         London: Archibald Constable & Co.; Philadelphia: Lippincott, 1901. SOURCE Brown, 1612; Hogan 2, p. 1209; Kersnowski, p. 141. LOCATION L.
         + Philadelphia: J.B. Lippincott, 1901. LOCATION D, NUC.
         COMMENTARY Novel about two Irish girls living in a decayed house and the ups-and-downs of their love affairs [Brown].

T163   *A union of hearts* (by Katharine Tynan).
         + London: James Nisbet & Co., [1901]. SOURCE Brown, 1611 ([1900] edn); Kersnowski, p. 141. LOCATION D, L, NUC ([1900] edn).
COMMENTARY Set in the west of Ireland where the English hero, Rivers, tries to do good for his Irish tenants but for a time incurs their hatred. The heroine is an heiress of old stock. She consults with the priest about how to temper the anger against Rivers, and how to protect Pat O'Driscoll – who had been deputed to kill Rivers – from reprisals for not killing him. The priest diverts public attention by getting the police to arrest several people for making poteen, and uses his sermons to soften the anger against Rivers [Brown; Leclaire, p. 198; Murphy, p. 61].

T164   *Three fair maids; or, the Burkes of Derrymore* (by Katharine Tynan).
         + London, Glasgow, Edinburgh, Dublin: Blackie & Son, 1901 (ill. G. Demain Hammond). SOURCE Brown, 1609 ([1900] edn, where misspelled 'Barrymore'); Kersnowski, p. 141. LOCATION D, L, NUC, InND Loeber coll. (n.d. edn).
         + New York: Scribner, 1909. SOURCE Brown, 1609. LOCATION InND Loeber coll.
COMMENTARY The family of Sir Jasper Burke lives in reduced circumstances. They take in paying guests to alleviate the situation, which results in matrimony for the three girls [Brown].

T165   *The great captain* (by Katharine Tynan Hinkson).
         London: Constable, [1901]. SOURCE Colman, p. 222.
         + New York, Cincinnati, Chicago: Benziger Bros, 1902 (as *The great captain: A story of the days of Sir Walter Raleigh*). SOURCE Kersnowski, p. 137. LOCATION D ([c.1920] edn), NUC, InND Loeber coll.
COMMENTARY No copy of the London edn located. Historical fiction set in Ireland and England concerning the life of Sir Walter Raleigh as told by a man who was rescued as a small child during the Desmond wars. He stays with Raleigh and is treated by him almost as a son. The

child has no name and Raleigh calls him Wat. Wat looks after Raleigh in his various stays in the Tower of London and accompanies him on his sea journeys. Raleigh knew that the boy was of noble birth and planned to give him part of his Munster estate, held in trust by Lord Boyle. After Raleigh's death Wat goes to Boyle but Boyle never mentions the estate he holds for Wat, and Wat never asks. The story ends with Wat going to France where the joins a Catholic order in Douai [ML].

T166 *A girl of Galway* (by Katharine Tynan).

+ London, Glasgow, Edinburgh, Dublin: Blackie & Son, 1902 (ill. John H. Bacon). SOURCE Brown, 1608 (probably mistakenly mentions 1900 edn); Colman, p. 223; Kersnowski, p. 137. LOCATION D, L, NUC.

London, Glasgow, Bombay: Blackie & Son, 1914 (new edn; ill. John H. Bacon). SOURCE OCLC. LOCATION NUC, InND Loeber coll. (n.d. edn).

COMMENTARY A 'a story about Bertha, who on the threshold of young womanhood' goes to stay with her grandfather in Connemara, entrusted by her mother with the task of reconciling him to his son, Bertha's father. Bertha finds her grandfather to be a recluse and a miser and in the power of an underling, who is an evil genius. How she keeps faith with her mother and finds her own fate, through many strange adventures, is the subject of the story [adv. in Rosa Mulholland's§ *Four little mischiefs* (London, 1883)].

T167 *A king's woman. Being the narrative of Miss Penelope Fayle, now Mistress Frobisher, concerning the late troublous times in Ireland* (by Katharine Tynan).

+ London: Hurst & Blackett, 1902. SOURCE Brown, 1613; Kersnowski, p. 138. LOCATION D, L.

COMMENTARY Historical fiction set in a Co. Kildare country house in 1798, it is the story of a young Quaker gentlewoman named Penelope Fayle [Brown].

T168 *The handsome Quaker; and other stories* (by Katharine Tynan; dedicated to May Sinclair).

+ London: A.H. Bullen, 1902. SOURCE Brown, 1614; Kersnowski, p. 137. LOCATION D, L, NUC.

COMMENTARY Stories that nearly all deal with the lives of the poorest peasantry. Contents: 'The handsome Quaker', 'The politician', 'A castle in Spain', 'The widower', 'Gipsies both', 'A pack o' children', 'A ridiculous affair', 'The cry of the child', 'The forge', 'The enemy of God', 'The three sons', 'A benefactor', 'The wardrobe', 'A childless woman', 'Pinch and the poorhouse', 'The French wife', 'Hunting-cap', 'The castle of Dromore' [RL; Brown].

T169 *Love of sisters* (by Katharine Tynan).

+ London: Smith, Elder & Co., 1902. SOURCE Brown, 1615; Kersnowski, p. 139. LOCATION D, L, NUC.

COMMENTARY A love story set in the west of Ireland and in Dublin concerning two sisters who have contrasting characters. One believes that her lover has transferred his affections to her sister, and with unselfish devotion stands aside. All ends well [Brown].

T170 *The honourable Molly* (by Katharine Tynan).

London: Smith, Elder & Co., 1903. SOURCE Brown, 1617; Kersnowski, p. 138. LOCATION D (1914 edn), L, NUC (1919 edn).

COMMENTARY A romance set in the west of Ireland featuring Molly, who is of mixed Anglo-Irish aristocratic and Scots-Irish middle-class origins. One of her suitors comes from her mother's people, the other is heir to a title and castle. The story is about which of her lovers Molly will accept [Brown; Leclaire, p. 199].

T171 *A red, red rose* (by Katharine Tynan).

London: Eveleigh Nash, 1903. SOURCE Kersnowski, p. 140. LOCATION D ([1931] edn), L.

T172   *The French wife* (by Katharine Tynan).
+ London: F.V. White & Co., 1904. SOURCE Kersnowski, p. 137; Colman, p. 223 (has a London, Hodder & Stoughton, 1904 edn, which probably is mistaken); RLIN. LOCATION D, L.
Philadelphia: Lippincott, 1904. SOURCE Kersnowski, p. 137.

T173   *Judy's lovers* (by Katharine Tynan).
London: F.V. White & Co., 1904. SOURCE Kersnowski, p. 138. LOCATION L.

T174   *Julia* (by Katharine Tynan).
London: Smith, Elder & Co., 1904. SOURCE Brown, 1618; Hogan 2, p. 1209; Kersnowski, p. 138. LOCATION L, NUC.
Chicago: A.C. McClurg & Co., 1905. SOURCE Kersnowski, p. 138. LOCATION NUC.
COMMENTARY A romance set in Co. Kerry where Julia, the Cinderella of her family, is nearly ruined and almost loses her lover because of a baseless slander. She takes refuge in a convent [Brown; Murphy, p. 37].

T175   *For the white rose* (by Katharine Tynan).
London: Constable, [1905]. SOURCE Colman, p. 223.
New York, Cincinnati: Benziger Bros, 1905. SOURCE Kersnowski, p. 137. LOCATION NUC.
COMMENTARY No copy of the London edn located [RL].

T176   *A daughter of kings* (by Katharine Tynan).
London: Eveleigh Nash, 1905. SOURCE Brown, 1616 (1905 edn); Colman, p. 222 (mentions 1900 edn, but not located); Hogan 2, p. 1209 (mentions 1900 edn, but not located); Kersnowski, p. 136; OCLC. LOCATION L, NUC.
New York, Cincinnati: Benziger Bros, [1905]. SOURCE Brown, 1616 (mistakenly mentions 1903 edn); RLIN. LOCATION NUC, NN.
COMMENTARY A daughter of a broken-down aristocratic Irish county family is obliged to take a job as a chaperone in an English family. The pride and poverty of Witche's Castle (Co. Donegal) and the opulence of the English home are contrasted [Brown].

T177   *Fortune's favourite. A novel* (by Katharine Tynan).
London: F.V. White & Co., 1905. SOURCE Kersnowski, p. 137. LOCATION L.

T178   *Luck of the Fairfaxes. A story for girls* (by Katharine Tynan).
+ London, Glasgow, New York: Collins, [1905] (ill. Frances Ewan). SOURCE Kersnowski, p. 139. LOCATION D, L, NUC.

T179   *Dick Pentreath* (by Katharine Tynan).
London: Smith, Elder & Co., 1905. SOURCE Kersnowski, p. 137. LOCATION L, NUC.
Chicago: A.C. McClurg, 1906. SOURCE Kersnowski, p. 137. LOCATION NUC.

T180   *For Maisie. A love story* (by Katharine Tynan).
London: Hodder & Stoughton, 1906. SOURCE Kersnowski, p. 137. LOCATION L, NUC.
Chicago: A.C. McClurg, 1907. LOCATION NUC.

T181   *The adventures of Alicia* (by Katharine Tynan).
London: F.V. White & Co., 1906. SOURCE Brown, 1619; Kersnowski, p. 136. LOCATION L.
COMMENTARY A poor young Irish girl has to serve English employers but in spite of all temptations, remains true to her Irish lover [Brown].

T182   *The yellow domino and other stories* (by Katharine Tynan).
+ London: F.V. White & Co., 1906. SOURCE Kersnowski, p. 141. LOCATION D, L.
COMMENTARY Contents: 'The yellow domino', 'At the spotted lamb', 'The meeting in the library', 'Yesterday's roses', 'The heart of a grandfather', 'The master', 'Miss Mary', 'Prisoner in the tower', 'The pheasant', 'Children in the wood', 'Désirée's friend', 'The heart of the

hill', 'Rollo's playmate', 'A halleluja lady', 'Matthew', 'A long rest', 'That heavenly woman', 'Jim' [RL].

T183   *The story of Bawn* (by Katharine Tynan).
+ London: Smith, Elder & Co., 1906. SOURCE Brown, 1620; Hogan 2, p. 1209; Kersnowski, p. 141. LOCATION D, L, NUC.
Chicago: A.C. McClurg, 1907. SOURCE Brown, 1620; Kersnowski, p. 141. LOCATION NUC.
COMMENTARY Set in Co. Kerry in the early 1860s where a family of high standing falls into the net of a moneylender [Brown].

T184   *A little book for Mary Gill's friends* (by Katharine Tynan).
Petersfield, Hampshire: Pear Tree Press, 1906. SOURCE Quinn, 10402. LOCATION L.
COMMENTARY Only 75 copies were printed [BLC].

T185   *A little book of courtesies* (by Katharine Tynan and Charles Robinson).
+ London: J.M. Dent & Co., 1906 (ill. Charles Robinson). SOURCE Colman, p. 223; NCBEL 4, p. 849. LOCATION L.
COMMENTARY Children's book [RL].

T186   *Her ladyship* (by Katharine Tynan).
London: Smith, Elder & Co., 1907. SOURCE Brown, 1621; Hogan 2, p. 1209; Kersnowski, p. 138. LOCATION L, NUC.
Chicago: A.C. McClurg, 1907, 2nd impr. SOURCE Brown, 1621; Kersnowski, p. 138 (1908 edn). LOCATION D (1908 edn), NUC (1908 edn).
COMMENTARY Set in Dublin and Co. Kerry where Lady Anne Chute owns a vast estate. She sets about improving the condition of her dependants. Interwoven is a love story [Brown; Leclaire, p. 199].

T187   *The house of the crickets* (by Katharine Tynan; dedicated to the dear lady of the manor).
+ London: Smith, Elder & Co., 1908. SOURCE Brown, 1622; Daims, 1403. LOCATION D, L, NUC.
COMMENTARY A story of Irish peasant life in the west of Ireland. The heroine and her brothers and sisters live lives of abject slavery ruled by a tyrannical father. But she and one of her brothers develop noble qualities of character and mind. After they escape from her father, the heroine finds a husband [Brown; Leclaire, p. 199].

T188   *Men and maids; or, the lovers' way* (by Katharine Tynan).
+ Dublin: Sealy, Bryers & Walker, 1908 (ill. Dorothea Preston). SOURCE Brown, 1623; Kersnowski, p. 139. LOCATION L, NUC, InND Loeber coll.
COMMENTARY Stories set in Ireland. Contents: 'The last dance', 'Love and an umbrella', 'The whistling thief', 'A question of age', 'Ailsie: A vixen', 'A very wise girl', 'The match-maker', 'Jim', 'The young mistress', 'A big lie', 'The returned emigrant', 'The honourable Madge', 'An international arrangement', 'Over the telephone', 'The ragged princess', 'Judy: An ugly duckling', 'The bank loan', 'Billy and lovers', 'The banshee of the O'Moores' [RL].

T189   *Mary Gray* (by Katharine Tynan).
London, New York, Toronto, Melbourne: Cassell & Co., 1908 (ill. C.H. Taffs). SOURCE Daims, 1405; Hogan 2, p. 1209; Kersnowski, p. 139. LOCATION D (1909 edn), L, NUC (1909 edn).

T190   *The lost angel* (by Katharine Tynan).
London: John Milne; Philadelphia: Lippincott, 1908. SOURCE Hogan 2, p. 1209; Kersnowski, p. 139. LOCATION L.
Philadelphia: J.B. Lippincott, 1908. SOURCE Colman, p. 224. LOCATION NUC.
COMMENTARY Contents: 'The lost angel', 'An old couple', 'The judgement of Solomon', 'St. Mary of the Isles', 'The fox', 'The interview', 'A homeless couple', 'A letter of introduction',

'A telephone message', 'The children at Okeovers', 'The kind saint', 'Aunt Betty', 'Princess Molly', 'His lordship and the poet', 'The king Cophetua', 'Billy and the bonnets', 'The old hero', 'The knocking at the door' [NUC].

T191 *Her mother's daughter* (by Katharine Tynan).
London: Smith, Elder & Co., 1909. SOURCE Kersnowski, p. 138. LOCATION L, NUC.

T192 *Kitty Aubrey* (by Katharine Tynan).
London: James Nisbet & Co., 1909. SOURCE Daims, 1404. LOCATION L.

T193 *Peggy, the daughter* (by Katharine Tynan).
London, New York, Toronto, Melbourne: Cassell & Co., 1909. SOURCE Brown, 1624; Colman, p. 224 (mentions 1907 edn, which probably is mistaken); Hogan 2, p. 1209; Kersnowski, p. 140. LOCATION L, NUC.
COMMENTARY The plot was suggested by the attempted abduction by Sir H.B. Hayes of the Quaker woman Miss Pike, of Cork. Set in Cork during the early Victorian era, a spendthrift nobleman who is a widower, runs away with a woman who is a Quaker. The penalty is a long imprisonment, from which he emerges a sadder and wiser man. While he is in prison the Quaker woman takes care of his little daughter, Peggy [Brown; Leclaire, p. 199].

T194 *Cousins and others* (by Katharine Tynan).
+ London: T. Werner Laurie, [1909]. SOURCE Brown, 1625; Kersnowski, p. 136. LOCATION D, L.
COMMENTARY Consists of eleven inter-connected stories mainly about life in Irish county society [Brown].

T195 *Freda* (by Katharine Tynan).
London, New York, Toronto, Melbourne: Cassell & Co., 1910 (ill. Gilbert Wright). SOURCE Hogan 2, p. 1209; Kersnowski, p. 137. LOCATION L, NUC.

T196 *The house of the secret* (by Katharine Tynan).
London: James Clarke & Co., 1910 (ill. E.F. Skinner). SOURCE Brown, 1627; Kersnowski, p. 138. LOCATION L, NUC.
COMMENTARY Apparently set in the west of Ireland, it is the story of Maeve Standish's self-sacrifice in the home of her father's old friend, Miss Henrietta O'Neill, and of her ultimate good fortune and happy marriage [Brown, Leclaire, p. 200].

T197 *Betty Carew* (by Katharine Tynan).
London: Smith, Elder & Co., 1910. SOURCE Hogan 2, p. 1209; Kersnowski, p. 136. LOCATION L, NUC.

T198 *The story of Cecilia* (by Katharine Tynan).
London: Smith, Elder & Co., 1911. SOURCE Brown, 1629; Colman, p. 224 (who mistakenly lists this as 'Celia'); Hogan 2, p. 1209 (who mistakenly mentions 'The story of Celia'); Kersnowski, p. 141. LOCATION L, NUC.
New York, Cincinnati: Benziger Bros, 1911. SOURCE Brown, 1629; Kersnowski, p. 141. LOCATION NUC.
COMMENTARY Set among the Irish upper classes in Co. Kerry and Dublin. The love stories of a mother and daughter are interwoven [Brown].

T199 *The story of Clarice* (by Katharine Tynan).
London: James Clarke & Co., 1911. SOURCE Kersnowski, p. 141. LOCATION L.

T200 *Paradise farm* (by Katharine Tynan).
New York: Duffield & Co., 1911. SOURCE Kersnowski, p. 140. LOCATION NUC.
London: Smith, Elder & Co., 1913 (as *Mrs. Pratt of Paradise Farm*). SOURCE Kersnowski, p. 140 (mistakenly mentions 1911 edn); Colman, p. 225; COPAC; RLIN. LOCATION L, NUC.

COMMENTARY The principal character in the New York edn was called Mrs Cripps instead of Mrs Pratt as in the London edn [NUC].

T201 *Princess Katharine* (by Katharine Tynan).
+ New York: Duffield & Co., 1911. SOURCE Daims, 1406. LOCATION D, L, NUC.
London, Melbourne, Toronto: Ward, Lock & Co., 1912. SOURCE Brown, 1930; Daims, 1406; Hogan 2, p. 1209; Kersnowski, p. 140. LOCATION L, NUC.
COMMENTARY The story of a young, educated Irish woman returning home to find her mother an alcoholic [RL].

T202 *Happy days at Glenart* (by Katharine Tynan).
Dublin: James Duffy, [1912 or earlier] (Duffy's Penny Library). SOURCE Adv. in *Catalogue of books* (Dublin: James Duffy & Co., 1912).
COMMENTARY No copy located [RL].

T203 *Heart o' gold; or, the little princess. A story for girls* (by Katharine Tynan; dedicated to Kitty King).
+ London, Victoria: S.W. Partridge & Co., [1912]. SOURCE Brown, 1628; Kersnowski, p. 137. LOCATION D, L, NUC.
COMMENTARY Two Irish orphan girls are carried off from their tumbledown Irish home to be brought up at Tunbridge Wells in England. One of them returns at age 21, full of dreams for the improvement of Ireland. She is aided in her plans by a young man, whom she afterwards marries [Brown].

T204 *Honey, my honey* (by Katharine Tynan).
+ London: Smith, Elder & Co., 1912. SOURCE Colman, p. 224; Kersnowski, p. 138 (mistakenly mentions 1903 edn). LOCATION D, L, InND Loeber coll.
COMMENTARY A story of romance and property set in England in a village where the de Crepignys have lived for centuries. They are now impoverished, but their daughter Honey is set to inherit an estate. However, the estate's owner failed to make a will and the property goes to another relative, who sells it to a rich family from Pittsburgh by the name of Fairbrother. Honey is meant to marry a family friend, but she falls in love with Denis Fairbrother. She gets out of her engagement, because her fiancée falls in love with Denis's sister. All marry happily [ML].

T205 *Rose of the garden. The romance of Lady Sarah Lennox* (by Katharine Tynan; dedicated 'to the one of Lady Sarah's blood in whom live her wit, her immortal charm, her kindness').
London: Constable & Co., 1912. SOURCE Brown, 1631; Kersnowski, p. 140. LOCATION L, NUC.
+ Indianapolis: Bobbs-Merrill Co., [1913] (with reproductions of portraits by Sir Joshua Reynolds). SOURCE Hogan 2, p. 1209; Kersnowski, p. 140. LOCATION D, NUC, InND Loeber coll.
COMMENTARY Historical fiction set in the eighteenth century. Story of the life of Lady Sarah Lennox (1745–1826), sister to Lady Louisa Conolly of Castletown (Co. Kildare) and to Emily, countess of Kildare. She is courted by King George III, but his mother makes him marry a German princess. She has a great but unhappy attachment to her cousin, Lord William Gordon. She marries Charles Bunbury, whom she leaves, and lives a number of years in retirement. Her husband divorces her. Eventually she marries Col. George Napier with whom she leads a happy life and becomes the mother of three daughters and five sons, including Charles James Napier§ and William Francis Napier§ [ML; DNB [under George Napier]].

T206 *A misalliance* (by Katharine Tynan).
New York: Duffield & Co., 1913. SOURCE Colman, p. 225; Kersnowski, p. 139. LOCATION NUC.

T207 *A midsummer rose* (by Katharine Tynan).
+ London; Smith, Elder & Co., 1913. SOURCE Hogan 2, p. 1209; Kersnowski, p. 139. LOCATION D, L, NUC.

T208 *Pat* (by Katharine Tynan).
New York, Cincinnati, Chicago: Benziger Bros, 1913. SOURCE Kersnowski, p. 140. LOCATION NUC.

T209 *A shameful inheritance* (by Katharine Tynan).
London, New York, Toronto, Melbourne: Cassell & Co., 1914. SOURCE Brown, 1632; Kersnowski, p. 140. LOCATION L, NUC.
COMMENTARY A young boy grows up in ignorance of the disgrace of his mother and the suicide of his father. The story describes the effects of the disclosure. The boy finds his mother in time to comfort her on her deathbed [Brown].

T210 *Lovers' meetings* (by Katharine Tynan).
London: T. Werner Laurie, [1914]. SOURCE Kersnowski, p. 139. LOCATION L, NUC.
London: E. Mathews, 1932 (as *Lovers' meeting* [sic]). LOCATION L.
+ London, Melbourne: Ward, Lock & Co., 1932 (as *Lovers' meeting* [sic]). LOCATION D, NUC.
COMMENTARY Contents: 'A night journey', 'The West wind', 'The little ghost', 'Mrs. Green's outing', 'A lost sheep', 'The pavilion in the garden', 'That sweet enemy', 'The convent on the dunes', 'The link in the chain', 'The evil guest', 'The heir-at-law', 'The leopard cup', 'The house of a dream', 'The house of the cherry orchard', 'The widower', 'The gentlemen in possession' [NUC].

T211 *The daughter of the manor* (by Katharine Tynan).
London, Glasgow, Bombay: Blackie & Son, 1914 (ill. John Campbell). SOURCE Kersnowski, p. 136. LOCATION L.

T212 *Men, not angels, and other tales told to girls* (by Katharine Tynan; dedicated to Margreita Beer).
+ London: Burns & Oates, [1914] (ill.) SOURCE Brown, 1635 (1915 edn); Kersnowski, p. 139 (1915 edn). LOCATION D, L.
New York: P.J. Kenedy & Sons, [1915]. SOURCE Kersnowski, p. 139. LOCATION NUC.
COMMENTARY Contents: 'All talk about vocations', 'Voices in the night', 'An understudy to St. Anthony', 'The child to whom everybody was kind', 'Father James, match maker', '"Wine that maketh glad"', 'Heart spake unto the heart', 'But in England!', 'His word or his wife?', 'The schooling of the schoolmaster', 'The abbé's indiscretions', 'The gift of God' [RL].

T213 *John Bulteel's daughters* (by Katharine Tynan).
+ London: Smith, Elder & Co., 1914. SOURCE Kersnowski, p. 138. LOCATION D, L, NUC.

T214 *A little radiant girl* (by Katharine Tynan).
London, Glasgow, Bombay: Blackie & Son, 1914 (ill. John Campbell). SOURCE Colman, p. 225; Kersnowski, p. 139. LOCATION L, NUC.

T215 *Molly, my heart's delight* (by Katharine Tynan).
+ London: Smith, Elder & Co., 1914. SOURCE Kersnowski, p. 139. LOCATION D, L, NUC.

T216 *Countrymen all* (by Katharine Tynan).
+ London, Dublin: Maunsel & Co., 1915. SOURCE Brown, 1633; Kersnowski, p. 136. LOCATION D, L, NUC.
COMMENTARY Consists of stories and sketches some of which are set in the neighbourhood of Dublin. Contents: 'The mother of Jesus', 'The mother', 'A thing seen', 'Chiefly Ted', 'The forge', 'The lark', 'General Burton's ghost', 'The abhorred impost [sic]', 'The fox-hunter';

'May-day', 'The whistling thief', 'John-a-dreams', 'Per istam sanctam unctionem', 'Owney', 'The daisy', 'The crickets', 'An O'Malley comes home again', 'A great ould [*sic*] bigot', 'The ruling passion', 'A strayed innocent' [JB; Brown].

T217   *The house of the foxes* (by Katharine Tynan).
+ London: Smith, Elder & Co., 1915. SOURCE Brown, 1634; Kersnowski, p. 138. LOCATION D, L, NUC.

COMMENTARY Based on an old legend from the west of Ireland still current at the time of the novel. The Turloughmores are overshadowed by a curse made long ago by an old woman wounded to death by a former Lord Turloughmore's hounds. According to the curse, every head of the house must die a violent death, which is presaged by foxes visiting about the house. The current Lord Turloughmore is wrecked on a yachting cruise and considered lost, but a woman staying at the castle discovers the dying lord in mysterious circumstances. He dies in his bed and his heir is married into a lucky house and the curse is said to be lifted [Brown; Leclaire, p. 200].

T218   *The curse of Castle Eagle* (by Katharine Tynan).
New York: Duffield & Co., 1915. SOURCE Kersnowski, p. 136; OCLC. LOCATION NUC.

T219   *"Since first I saw your face"* (by Katharine Tynan; dedicated to Mrs Rowan Hamilton).
+ London: Hutchinson & Co., 1915. SOURCE Kersnowski, p. 141. LOCATION D (1915, 2nd edn), L.

T220   *The squire's sweetheart* (by Katharine Tynan).
+ London, Melbourne, Toronto: Ward, Lock & Co., 1915 (ill.). SOURCE Colman, p. 225 (mistakenly mentions a 1913 edn); Kersnowski, p. 141. LOCATION D, L.

T221   *John-a-dreams* (by Katharine Tynan).
London: Smith, Elder & Co., 1916. SOURCE Brown, 1636; Kersnowski, p. 138. LOCATION L, NUC.

COMMENTARY The youngest son of Sir Anthony McGrady is a sensitive person who shrinks from publicity. He stays at home in Co. Clare to write his poems and to be a comfort of his mother. Into his life comes Octavia from the US. She is of peasant stock, but accepted by New York society. They fall in love and after various ups-and-downs they are happily married [Brown].

T222   *Margery Dawe* (by Katharine Tynan).
+ London, Glasgow, Bombay: Blackie & Son, 1916 (ill. Frank E. Wiles). SOURCE Kersnowski, p. 139; Colman, p. 225 (1934 edn). LOCATION D, L, NUC, InND Loeber coll.

COMMENTARY Fiction for juveniles set in Kent. After their father's death the children of a gentleman farmer are left to the mercy of their vicious stepmother. She takes them out of school, makes them work, neglects the farm, and keeps them out of their inheritance. With the help of kindly neighbours and a distant aunt, the children are saved from misery. Margery, the oldest daughter, marries the son of the landlord. A will is found, showing that the stepmother had not inherited the farm and that it belonged to the children [ML].

T223   *The web of Fraulein* (by Katharine Tynan).
London, New York, Toronto: Hodder & Stoughton, 1916. SOURCE Kersnowski, p. 141. LOCATION L.

T224   *Lord Edward. A study in romance* (by Katharine Tynan; dedicated to the Wyndhams, Lord Edward's grandchildren).
+ London: Smith, Elder & Co., 1916 (ill.). LOCATION D, InND Loeber coll.
COMMENTARY Historical fiction presenting an account of the 1798 rebellion and the life of Lord Edward Fitzgerald [RL].

T225   *The West wind* (by Katharine Tynan).
+ London: Constable & Co., 1916. SOURCE Kersnowski, p. 141. LOCATION D, L, NUC.

T226   *Miss Mary* (by Katharine Tynan).
London: John Murray, 1917. SOURCE Brown, 1637; Kersnowski, p. 139. LOCATION L, NUC.

COMMENTARY A romance set in Castle Morrogh, seat of Sir Hugo de Burgh, in the west of Ireland. Maurice Roche, a stable boy but of good old stock, is devoted to Mary, de Burgh's daughter. Maurice is taken up and educated by a de Burgh family friend. Mary is engaged to a man who during the courtship tries to seduce a peasant girl. The engagement is broken off and in the end Mary marries Maurice [Brown].

T227   *Kit* (by Katharine Tynan).
London: Smith, Elder & Co., 1917. SOURCE Brown, 1638; Kersnowski, p. 138. LOCATION L, NUC.

COMMENTARY Kit, a peasant girl in the west of Ireland, is driven from her village by the cruelty of the neighbours when her mistress's daughter dies trying to save Kit's life. She is befriended and educated by upper-class people in England. However, she remains true to her early love and returns to marry Donal, who has returned rich from America [Brown].

T228   *The rattlesnake* (by Katharine Tynan).
+ London, Melbourne, Toronto: Ward, Lock & Co., 1917 (ill.). SOURCE Kersnowski, p. 140. LOCATION D, L, NUC.

T229   *Miss Gascoigne* (by Katharine Tynan).
London: John Murray, 1918. SOURCE Hogan 2, p. 1210; Kersnowski, p. 139. LOCATION L, NUC.

T230   *My love's but a lassie* (by Katharine Tynan).
+ London, Melbourne, Toronto: Ward, Lock & Co., 1918 (ill.). SOURCE Kersnowski, p. 140. LOCATION D, L, NUC (n.d. edn).

T231   *The love of brothers* (by Katharine Tynan).
+ London: Constable & Co., 1919. SOURCE Brown 2, 1547; Hogan 2, p. 1210; Kersnowski, p. 139; OCLC. LOCATION D, L, NUC.
+ New York, Cincinnati, Chicago: Benziger Bros, 1920. LOCATION NUC, InND Loeber coll.

COMMENTARY Sir Shaun O'Gara and his wife have an idolized only son Terry, just out of Sandhurst. He falls in love with Stella Comerford, the adopted daughter of old Mrs Comerford. Sir Shaun opposes the match because twenty years previously he had, in a sudden fit of rage, killed his friend Terence Comerford. The secret still haunts him and his fears of discovery are enlivened by the arrival of a strange tramp and the appearance of a Mrs Wade. He recognizes her as Bridie Sweeney, once a local beauty. The tramp dies, and Mrs Wade turns out to be the younger Mrs Comerford, the mother of Stella. In the end the way is smoothed for Terry and Stella to marry [Brown 2].

T232   *The man from Australia* (by Katharine Tynan).
+ London, Glasgow, Sydney, Auckland: W. Collins Sons & Co. [1919]. SOURCE Brown 2, 1548; Hogan 2, p. 1210; Kersnowski, p. 139. LOCATION D, L, NUC.

COMMENTARY A rich young man returns from Australia to act as father to a poor and shiftless family of cousins in the west of Ireland [Brown 2].

T233   *Denys the dreamer* (by Katharine Tynan).
+ London, Glasgow, Melbourne, Auckland: W. Collins, Sons & Co., 1920. SOURCE Brown 2, 1549; Hogan 2, p. 1210; Kersnowski, p. 137. LOCATION D, L, NUC.
+ New York, Cincinnati: Benziger Bros, 1921. SOURCE Kersnowski, p. 137. LOCATION D, NUC.

Tynan

COMMENTARY The old family of the Fitzmaurices has fallen on hard times, and their home at Murrough by the Atlantic is in ruins. Denys Fitzmaurice lives with his father on a nearby farm. Denys dreams of better days for the family. He drains the bog, including the holy well, thereby for a time incurring the anger of the country people. He helps to nurse the typhus-stricken people on Carra Island and marries the pretty daughter of the impoverished Lord Leane [Brown 2].

T234   *The house* (by Katharine Tynan).
> + London, Glasgow, Sydney, Auckland: W. Collins Sons & Co., [1920]. SOURCE Daims, 1402; Hogan 2, p. 1210. LOCATION D, L, NUC.

T235   *Bitha's wonderful year. A story for girls* (by Katharine Tynan).
> + London: Humphrey Milford, [1921] (ill. Grace Lodge). SOURCE Brown 2, 1550 (1922 edn); Kersnowski, p. 136. LOCATION D, L.

COMMENTARY Bitha Casey lives slighted and snubbed by snobbish relatives in a London suburb and longs for Castle O'Grady in Ireland. By a stroke of luck, Bitha is taken up by society, and gets her handsome man and unexpected legacy [Brown 2].

T236   *Sally Victrix* (by Katharine Tynan).
> London: W. Collins Sons & Co., [1921]. SOURCE Kersnowski, p. 140. LOCATION L.

T237   *The second wife; together with A July rose* (by Katharine Tynan).
> London: John Murray, 1921. SOURCE Hogan 2, p. 1210; Kersnowski, p. 140. LOCATION L, NUC.

T238   *A mad marriage* (by Katharine Tynan).
> London, Glasgow, Sydney, Auckland: W. Collins Sons & Co., [1922]. SOURCE Kersnowski, p. 139. LOCATION D, L, NUC.

COMMENTARY The story of a love affair between Hester Ponsonby and Lord Malvern. Their courtship is complicated by revelations surrounding Hester's birth. It transpires that she is the adopted daughter of Lady Ponsonby, and that her real parents are Rose Donoghue and Harry Lambert. Years earlier, Rose was put on trial for the murder of her first husband, Teague Donoghue. Rose was forced to marry the violent and abusive Donoghue when she was 17 and he was 65. Although she was acquitted of his murder, she and her second husband Harry Lambert were ostracised from their community and kept the existence of their daughter a secret. Theirs is the 'mad marriage' of the title [JB].

T239   *The house on the bogs* (by Katharine Tynan).
> London, Melbourne: Ward, Lock & Co., 1922. SOURCE Brown 2, 1551; Kersnowski, p. 138. LOCATION L.

COMMENTARY Doreen O'Kelly lives in a house on the Mall in Cork. On her mother's death she is adopted by Miss Hamilton and sent to a college near Vienna, the abbess of which is her guardian's friend. Miss Hamilton meets with trouble when she is deserted by her fiancée. Doreen returns from school to find her guardian at the mercy of two French servants in her tumbledown house in the bogs. Doreen eventually thwarts the servants and all turns out for the best [Brown 2].

T240   *White ladies* (by Katharine Tynan).
> London: Eveleigh Nash & Grayson, 1922. SOURCE Kersnowski, p. 141. LOCATION L, NUC.

T241   *Mary Beaudesert, V.S.* (by Katharine Tynan).
> + London, Glasgow, Sydney, Auckland: W. Collins Sons & Co., 1923. SOURCE Kersnowski, p. 139; Colman, p. 226 (where wrongly spelled 'Beaudesart'). LOCATION D, L.
> Nottingham: Boots Drug Co., [1923] (The Piccadilly Novels). LOCATION NUC.

T242   *Pat the adventurer* (by Katharine Tynan).

+ London, Melbourne: Ward, Lock & Co., 1923. SOURCE Hogan 2, p. 1210; Kersnowski, p. 140. LOCATION D, L, NUC.

T243   *They loved greatly* (by Katharine Tynan).
    London: E. Nash & Grayson, 1923. SOURCE Brown 2, 1552 (1924 edn); Hogan 2, p. 1210; Kersnowski, p. 141. LOCATION L, NUC ([1923] edn).
COMMENTARY Aimée Kilmorna leaves her wild drinking husband, Lord Kilmorna, in the west of Ireland and goes to Alured Sacheverel, scion of an old family. Aimée's love for Alured is pure. They live in Florence where there is a little Irish colony. When Lord Kilmorna loses his life in an act of heroism, Aimée and Alured marry. Desirée, her daughter, however, has a deep concern for her mother's reputation and returns to Ireland when her parents die and finally wins the regard of the crazed old Lady Sacheverel [Brown 2].

T244   *The golden rose* (by Katharine Tynan; dedicated to Frank Mathew§).
    + London: Eveleigh Nash & Grayson, 1924. SOURCE Brown 2, 1553; Hogan 2, p. 1210; Kersnowski, p. 137. LOCATION D, L, NUC.
COMMENTARY A study of Irish country life and class prejudice in the years of the First World War. It depicts the gradual change in the outlook of the people after the Easter Rising of 1916 through means of a conventional love story. Carmel O'Reilly, daughter of a dispensary doctor, is engaged to Beaufoy Molyneux, the son of the lord of the manor. They are separated owing to his imprisonment in Germany and through the scheming of his unscrupulous mother, Lady Cresslough [Brown 2; Todd, p. 638].

T245   *The house of doom* (by Katharine Tynan).
    London: Eveleigh Nash & Grayson, 1924. SOURCE Hogan 2, p. 1210; Kersnowski, p. 138l. LOCATION L, NUC.

T246   *Wives. A novel* (by Katharine Tynan).
    + London: Hurst & Blackett, [1924]. SOURCE Kersnowski, p. 141. LOCATION D, L.

T247   *Dear Lady Bountiful* (by Katharine Tynan).
    London, Melbourne: Ward, Lock & Co., 1925. SOURCE Kersnowski, p. 137. LOCATION L, NUC.

T248   *Miss Phipps* (by Katharine Tynan).
    London, Melbourne: Ward, Lock & Co., 1925. SOURCE Hogan 2, p. 1210; Kersnowski, p. 139. LOCATION L, NUC.

T249   *The moated grange* (by Katharine Tynan).
    + London, Glasgow, Sydney, Auckland: W. Collins Sons & Co., 1925. SOURCE Hogan 2, p. 1210; Kersnowski, p. 139. LOCATION D, L ([1926] edn), NUC ([ca.1925] edn).
    + London, Glasgow, Sydney, Auckland: W. Collins Sons & Co., 1932 (as *The night of terror*). LOCATION D, L.

T250   *Kitty at school and college* (by Katharine Tynan).
    Dublin, Cork: The Educational Company of Ireland, [19–]. SOURCE Brown 2, 1554 (1926 edn); RLIN. LOCATION MH.
COMMENTARY An Irish story for juveniles. Kitty O'Driscoll lives with her father near the village of Glena. Her daily life, her pets, her garden, her first day at the National School and also her friends and her one enemy, Janie, daughter of the gombeenman (a moneylender) are described. Later she is sent to Rathdangan Abbey where she is very popular, but encounters her enemy. When riding in the Phoenix Park she rescues a child, and later the child's father rescues Kitty's father from financial ruin and disgrace [Brown 2].

T251   *The briar bush maid* (by Katharine Tynan).
    + London, Melbourne: Ward, Lock, 1926. SOURCE Kersnowski, p. 136. LOCATION D, L.

T252   *The heiress of Wyke* (by Katharine Tynan).

+ London, Melbourne: Ward, Lock & Co., 1926. SOURCE Kersnowski, p. 137. LOCATION D, L.

T253 *The infatuation of Peter* (by Katharine Tynan).
+ London, Glasgow, Sydney, Auckland: W. Collins Sons & Co., 1926. SOURCE Kersnowski, p. 138. LOCATION D, L, NUC.

T254 *The face in the picture* (by Katharine Tynan).
+ London, Melbourne: Ward, Lock & Co., 1927. SOURCE Hogan 2, p. 1210; Kersnowski, p. 137. LOCATION D, L, NUC.

T255 *Haroun of London* (by Katharine Tynan).
+ London, Glasgow, Sydney, Auckland: W. Collins Sons & Co., 1927. SOURCE Kersnowski, p. 137. LOCATION D, L, NUC.

T256 *The wild adventure* (by Katharine Tynan).
+ London, Melbourne: Ward, Lock & Co., 1927. SOURCE Kersnowski, p. 141. LOCATION D, L.

T257 *The respectable lady* (by Katharine Tynan).
+ London, Glasgow, Sydney, Auckland: W. Collins Sons & Co., 1927. SOURCE Kersnowski, p. 140. LOCATION D, NUC.
New York: D. Appleton & Co., 1928. SOURCE Kersnowski, p. 140. LOCATION NUC.

T258 *Castle Perilous* (by Katharine Tynan).
+ London, Melbourne: Ward, Lock & Co., 1928. SOURCE Hogan 2, p. 1210; Kersnowski, p. 136. LOCATION D, L, NUC.

T259 *The house in the forest* (by Katharine Tynan).
+ London, Melbourne: Ward, Lock & Co., 1928. SOURCE Hogan 2, p. 1210; Kersnowski, p. 138. LOCATION D (n.d. edn), L.

T260 *Lover of women* (by Katharine Tynan).
+ London, Glasgow, Sydney, Auckland: W. Collins Sons & Co., 1928. SOURCE Hogan 2, p. 1210; Kersnowski, p. 139; Todd, p. 683. LOCATION D, L, NUC.
COMMENTARY A social issue novel exposing the miserable working conditions of Irish shop girls [Todd].

T261 *A fine gentleman* (by Katharine Tynan).
+ London, Melbourne: Ward, Lock & Co., 1929. SOURCE Hogan 2, p. 1210; Kersnowski, p. 137. LOCATION D, L, NUC.

T262 *The most charming family* (by Katharine Tynan).
+ London, Melbourne: Ward, Lock & Co., 1929. SOURCE Hogan 2, p. 1210; Kersnowski, p. 139. LOCATION D, L, NUC.

T263 *The rich man* (by Katharine Tynan).
+ London, Glasgow, Sydney, Auckland: W. Collins Sons & Co., 1929. SOURCE Hogan 2, p. 1210; Kersnowski, p. 140. LOCATION D, L, NUC.

T264 *The river* (by Katharine Tynan).
+ London, Glasgow, Sydney, Auckland: W. Collins Sons & Co., 1929. SOURCE Brown 2, 1555; Hogan 2, p. 1210; Kersnowski, p. 140. LOCATION D, L, NUC.
COMMENTARY A novel about the problem of marriages between Catholics and Protestants in Ireland. Kitty, the daughter of a mixed-marriage, comes to stay with her aunt who had remained a spinster rather than marry a Protestant, Mr. Carew, and has regretted it ever since. When Kitty becomes engaged to Carew's son, her aunt plucks up her courage and marries the father [Brown 2].

T265 *Denise the daughter* (by Katharine Tynan).
+ London, Melbourne: Ward, Lock & Co., 1930. SOURCE Kersnowski, p. 137. LOCATION D (n.d. edn), L, InND Loeber coll.

COMMENTARY Set in England, Rome, and France. Mr and 'Mrs' Talbot are very attached to each other and to their daughter Denise, who is illegitimate since Mr Talbot is actually married to a woman who has lost her mind. The illegitimacy casts a shadow over all their lives. When Mr Talbot's legal wife dies, he marries his companion in secret in a church in Rome. A young man falls in love with Denise but she is afraid that when his father hears about her illegitimacy they will not be allowed to marry. She tries to withdraw from the world, but in the end she admits that she has always loved a friend of her parents who, even though he is much older than she, loves her too, so they marry [ML].

T266   *The admirable Simmons* (by Katharine Tynan).
       London, Melbourne: Ward, Lock & Co., 1930. SOURCE Hogan 2, p. 1210; Kersnowski, p. 136. LOCATION D (n.d. edn), L, NUC.

T267   *Grayson's girl* (by Katharine Tynan).
       + London, Glasgow, Sydney, Auckland: W. Collins Sons & Co., 1930. SOURCE Hogan 2, p. 1210; Kersnowski, p. 137. LOCATION D, L, NUC (n.d. edn).
       COMMENTARY The volume presupposes knowledge of *Lover of women* (London, 1928), and discusses the conditions of Irish girls working in England [RL; Todd].

T268   *The playground* (by Katharine Tynan; dedicated to the marchioness of Aberdeen and Temair).
       + London, Melbourne: Ward, Lock & Co., 1930. SOURCE Brown 2, 1556; Hogan 2, p. 1210; Kersnowski, p. 140; Todd, p. 683. LOCATION D, L, NUC.
COMMENTARY John Tracy, born in a Dublin slum, is brought up in poverty-stricken surroundings. But early in life he and his mother move to a pleasant farm near Clondalkin in Co. Dublin. Thanks to the influence of some priests, he goes to England and gets a position in Sir Joshua Dent's great garden. He marries, serves in the First World War, and lives to fulfil his life's ambition, which is to endow the poor children of Dublin with playgrounds [Brown 2; Todd].

T269   *The forbidden way* (by Katharine Tynan).
       London, Glasgow, Sidney, Auckland: W. Collins Sons & Co., [1931]. SOURCE Brown 2, 1559; Kersnowski, p. 137. LOCATION D (1934 edn), L, NUC.
COMMENTARY Cynthia Roseveare comes to Ireland to take up the duties of a 'Lady help' to Mrs Harry Burke. She finds a real home at Inishgolden, wins the hearts of her two little charges, Maeve and Brigid, and also of the servants. Mrs Burke is a pleasure-loving woman and she and her husband are quite out of sympathy. Mr Burke is attracted to Cynthia who, however, will not enter an illicit relationship and ends the dangerous situation by marrying Sir Francis McGregor [Brown 2].

T270   *Delia's orchard* (by Katharine Tynan).
       + London, Melbourne: Ward, Lock & Co., 1931. SOURCE Brown 2, 1557; Kersnowski, p. 137 (mentions a 1930 edn but this has not been located). LOCATION D, L, InND Loeber coll.
COMMENTARY The scene of the early part of this story is laid in Brittany towards the end of the nineteenth century. Odette St Hilaire grew up thinking that she would have to enter a convent because she did not have a dowry. The tale centres on Odette's love affair and happy marriage to an Irishman in the British navy. Odette has an Irish nurse, Nellie, who is deeply attached to her native land. For her sake and Odette's health, the family visits Ireland shortly before the Great War, choosing to stay in Killarney. After the war they return to Ireland for good [ML; Brown 2].

T271   *A lonely maid* (by Katharine Tynan).
       + London, Melbourne: Ward, Lock & Co., 1931. SOURCE Brown 2, 1558; Kersnowski, p. 139. LOCATION D, L.

COMMENTARY Doreen Egerton lives in Castle Inch in the west of Ireland with her grandfather, Lord Kilmore. The old man dislikes the child because he has never forgiven her mother, his daughter, for her unhappy marriage. The coming of Hilda Devine as a governess improves matters. When Hilda marries Everard Marsh, Doreen goes to school. At age 18 she discovers that her mother is still alive and goes to her. Her mother dies a year later and Doreen returns to Ireland to marry her childhood friend, Terence Burke [Brown 2].

T272   *Philippa's lover* (by Katharine Tynan).
+ London, Melbourne: Ward, Lock & Co., 1931. SOURCE Kersnowski, p. 140. LOCATION D, L.

T273   *All for love* (by Katharine Tynan).
London: Collins, 1932. SOURCE Kersnowski, p. 136. LOCATION D (n.d. edn).
COMMENTARY No copy of the 1932 edn located [RL].

T274   *The other man* (by Katharine Tynan).
+ London, Melbourne: Ward, Lock & Co., 1932. SOURCE Kersnowski, p. 140. LOCATION D, L.
COMMENTARY This novel and the following works appeared posthumously [RL].

T275   *The pitiful lady* (by Katharine Tynan).
+ London, Melbourne: Ward, Lock & Co., 1932. SOURCE Kersnowski, p. 140. LOCATION D, L, NUC.

T276   *Connor's wood* (by Katharine Tynan; completed by Pamela Hinkson, Katherine Tynan's daughter).
+ London: Collins, 1933. SOURCE Brown 2, 1560 (mentions a 1932 edn but this has not been located); Kersnowski, p. 136. LOCATION D, L.

COMMENTARY The story is set in Ireland during the penal days. To gain possession of the property of Connor's Wood, Anthony Connor had disinherited his cousin's wife and son. The story tells of the career of John Connor, descendant of that disinherited boy, his adventures in love and war and his return to his country in the post-war years. Eventually, the old wrong is righted and John becomes owner of Connor's Wood and marries the girl of his choice [Brown 2].

T277   *An international marriage* (by Katharine Tynan).
+ London, Melbourne: Ward, Lock & Co., 1933. SOURCE Kersnowski, p. 138. LOCATION D, L.

T278   *The house of dreams* (by Katharine Tynan).
+ London, Melbourne: Ward, Lock & Co., 1934. SOURCE Brown 2, 1561; Kersnowski, p. 138. LOCATION D, L, NUC.

T279   *A lad was born* (by Katharine Tynan).
+ London: Collins, 1934. SOURCE Kersnowski, p. 138. LOCATION D, L.
London: Mellifont Press, 1945 (abridged). SOURCE Colman, p. 228; COPAC. LOCATION L.

— COLLECTED WORKS

T280   [*Katharine Tynan's works*].
Chicago: A.C. M'Clure & Co., [1899–1901] (ill). [no. of vols. not clear]. LOCATION InND Loeber coll. (some vols.).
COMMENTARY Untitled and unnumbered, uniformly bound in light brown cloth binding, embossed in black [RL; adv. in K. Tynan, *The dear Irish girl* (Chicago, 1899)].

U

'ULIDIA', fl. 1883. Pseudonym of a writer of futuristic political fiction,

U1   *The battle of Newry: or the results of thirty years' liberal legislation* (by 'Ulidia').
       + Dublin: Hodges, Figgis & Co.; London: Simpkin, Marshall & Co., 1883, 2nd edn.
       LOCATION L.
COMMENTARY 42pp. No copy of the 1st edn located. Futuristic account of the English parliament in 1910 when the house of lords is being permanently dissolved. Account of the results of the Irish land legislation [RL].

'AN ULSTER CLERGYMAN', pseud. See **ORPEN, Mrs Adela Elizabeth**.

'ULSTER SCOT', pseud. See **HENDERSON, Revd Henry**.

'UNCLE WILLIAM', fl. 1848. Pseudonym of a writer of moral fiction who probably also wrote *Kind words for his young friends* (London, [?1842]), published for the Religious Tract Society. SOURCE COPAC.

U2   *The dog days, or Denis O'Flagerty* (by 'Uncle William').
       + Philadelphia: Griffith & Simon, 1848. LOCATION InND Loeber coll.
COMMENTARY A story for children set in an American town relating the moral teachings of the Hill family, including admonitions against frightening others; teasing unfortunate people and being cruel to animals, while admonishing generosity to others. Several characters are Irish [ML].

'AN UNKNOWN', fl. 1824. Pseudonym of a novelist who wrote about romance and high society.

U3   *Caprice; or, anecdotes of the Listowel family. An Irish novel* (by 'An unknown').
       + London: Sherwood, Jones & Co.; Dublin: C.P. Archer, 1824, 3 vols. SOURCE
       Belanger, 78; Block, p. 34; Brown, 13; British Fiction; Garside, 1824:2. LOCATION
       Corvey CME 3–628–47211–3, Ireland related fiction, L.
       + London: G. Lutz & R.P. Moore, 1828 (as *Caprice. A novel*). SOURCE Brown 2, 4.
       LOCATION D.
COMMENTARY Starts in Killarney, with other scenes laid in Dublin and London. A wealthy man, Capt. Listowel, in order to preserve his infant daughter, Louisa, from the pernicious influence of her mother, places her under the care of the Revd Kelly, who resides in the mountains of Co. Kerry. Years later, Louisa attempts to discover the mystery of her birth as it is an impediment to her marrying Mr Talbot, owner of a large estate. Eventually, she is claimed by her father, who allows her to marry Mr Talbot [British Fiction; *La Belle Assemblée* (n.s. 30 Oct. 1824, p. 170); ML].

'AN UNWILLING AUTHOR', also 'Necessity', fl. 1818. Pseudonyms of a writer of fiction who, given the publication of the following novel in Dublin and the Irish subscribers in volume 2, is likely to be Irish. The subscribers' list includes the bishops of Derry and Kildare (each 10 copies) and others with Irish names and addresses. SOURCE British Fiction; Garside (2003); RL.

U4   *Tales* (by 'An unwilling author'; preface signed 'Necessity').
+ Dublin: Richard Milliken, 1822, 2 vols. (2nd vol. has subscribers' list). SOURCE Block, p. 232; British Fiction; Garside, 1822:11. LOCATION D, L.
+ London: Longman, Hurst, Rees, Orme, Brown & Green, 1825. SOURCE British Fiction; Garside, 1822:11. LOCATION Corvey CME 3–628–48866–4.
COMMENTARY The preface is dated Feb. 1818. Set in Ireland. Contents: 'The agent; or, Jacob Corr', 'The pavilion; or, Mrs Evan's tale' [RL; CM; Garside (2003)].

UPTON, William C., fl. 1882. Historical novelist and Fenian supporter, WCU was a carpenter at Ardagh (Co. Limerick). He was a friend of Charlotte Grace O'Brien§, who gave him guidance in the publication of his *Uncle Pat's cabin* (Dublin, 1882), and with whom he corresponded from Ardagh in 1878. Stephen Gwynn§, O'Brien's nephew, said that WCU was 'a head centre in the Fenian organisation'. According to one reviewer, *Uncle Pat's cabin* was recommended strongly for anyone who wanted to understand the Land League and was 'more timely than a score of Harry Lorrequers' (Charles Lever's§ fictional hero and pseudonym). WCU emigrated to America, where he lived in New York at 419 West 18th Street. He became affluent enough to privately publish a revised edn of his *Uncle Pat's cabin* in New York in 1914. SOURCE Allibone Suppl., ii, p. 1460; Brown, p. 303; S. Gwynn, *Charlotte Grace O'Brien* (Dublin, 1909), p. 44; O'Donoghue, p. 463; RIA/DIB; RL.

U5   *Uncle Pat's cabin; or, life among the agricultural labourers in Ireland* (by William C. Upton; dedicated to Michael Davitt [a Fenian and founder of the Land League]). Dublin: M.H. Gill & Son, 1882. SOURCE Allibone Suppl., ii, p. 1460; Brown, 1639. LOCATION L.
+ New York: [Printed] for the author by P.J. Kenedy & Sons, 1914 (revsd edn as *Uncle Pat's Cabin, a story of Irish life*). SOURCE NYPL. LOCATION NN, InND Loeber coll.
COMMENTARY As the title indicates, the allusion is to Harriet Beecher Stowe's *Uncle Tom's cabin* (Boston, 1852), reinforced by parallels drawn between slavery in America and the state of the Irish peasantry. The story is set mainly in Co. Limerick from the time of the Famine to about 1880; it deals with the hard life of the peasants, who are being evicted from their few acres. Some of them go to America to make a living. The landowner, a Mr Pakenham, thoughtlessly condones the evictions. Later on his daughter marries an American and tries to make up for all the hardship that her father's actions caused [ML].

V

VAHLE, Joseph, fl. 1896. American writer, perhaps a Mason. JH was the author also of *The Jerico papers: a quaint and amusing side of early New England life* (New York, [1893]). SOURCE COPAC; Wright, iii, p. 562.

V1   *The Irish prince and the Hebrew prophet; a Masonic tale of the captive Jews and the Ark of the Covenant* (by Joseph Vahle).

New York: Masonic Publishing Co., 1896 (ill.). SOURCE Wright, iii, 5632; RLIN. LOCATION GEU.

VAN DOORNE, Fr Hendrik, b. Poeke (Belgium), d. Poeke 1914. Historical novelist and Catholic priest, HVD was trained at the English seminary in Bruges (Belgium); ordained in London in 1865, and served in England until 1901. He was very interested in folklore and archaeology. He organized the building of the Catholic church at Brixton (London), and was one of the founders of the religious guild of St Gregory. SOURCE J. de Mûelenaere, 'Henrik van Doorne uit Poeke in Engeland', in On line: Internet <http://home.scarlet.be/~lvn-evele/artikelen/1976_3b.htm> (access date 6-5-05).

V2   *Jan van Noorde of onderwerping en betrouwen* (by the Revd Fr Hendrik Van Doorne).

Ghent: Huis Heiligen Joseph, 1881, 3 vols. SOURCE Burmester cat. 32/215.

COMMENTARY No copy located. A novel with historical and Roman Catholic overtones, set mainly in Belgium around 1830 but part of the action takes place in London and Ireland, where a character named Paddy is involved [Burmester].

VARIAN, Hester. See SIGERSON, Hester.

VEREKER, the Hon. Lt.-Col. C.S. See VEREKER, the Hon. Lt.-Col. Charles Smyth.

VEREKER, the Hon. Lt.-Col. Charles Smyth (known as the Hon. Lt.-Col. C.S. Vereker), b. London 1818, d. Bournemouth (Dorset) 1885. Novelist and travel writer, CSV was the younger son of Charles, 2nd Viscount Gort and his second wife, Elizabeth Palliser of Derryluskan (Co. Tipperary). He was commandant of the Limerick City artillery militia and commanding officer of the 4th Brigade S. Irish Div. RA. He moved to England, where he was captain of the South Middlesex Volunteer Rifles (1860–65). He wrote *Scenes in the sunny South* (London, 1871), an account of his travels in Spain and North Africa. He may be the anonymous author of a serial, 'Life's foreshadowings', in the *Irish Metropolitan Magazine* (Dublin, 1857), where it is cited as by the author of 'Old times', but a much earlier date than the published volume mentioned below. He married Kate, youngest daughter of a Robert Fannin, in 1842. SOURCE Allibone Suppl., ii, p. 1467; Boase, vi, pp 741–2; Brown, p. 304; Sir B. Burke & A.P. Burke, *A genealogical and heraldic dictionary of the peerage and baronetage* (London, 1906), 68th edn, p. 712; RIA/DIB; RL.

V3   *Old times in Ireland* (by the Hon. Lt.-Col. C.S. Vereker).

    + London: Chapman & Hall, 1873, 3 vols. SOURCE Brown, 1644; COPAC. LOCATION D, L.

COMMENTARY The author's stated aim is to portray 'the disruption of society, and the triumph of terror and crime as well as the more genial and sunny side of the Irish character'. A comical tale that features a lord lieutenant, a duke, and the Terry Alts – a group of agitators against prevailing land ownership [Brown; ML].

V4   *The child of the desert* (by the Hon. Charles Smith [*sic*] Vereker).
      + London: Chapman & Hall, 1878, 3 vols. SOURCE Allibone Suppl, ii, p. 1467; COPAC. LOCATION L.
      COMMENTARY Set in Algeria [RL].

VERNE, Jules. VERNE, Jules Gabriel.

VERNE, Jules Gabriel (known as **Jules Verne**), b. Nantes (France) 1828, d. Amiens (France) 1906. French science fiction writer, poet, playwright and author of fiction for juveniles, JGV was the son of Pierre Verne, a lawyer, and Sophie Allotte de la Fuye. His father intended his son to follow in his footsteps in the law. Instead, he became a highly prolific author of adventure stories for juveniles and science fiction stories (what he called *roman de la science*). He often produced three or more novels per year. Many of his stories achieved enormous success worldwide; he is ranked as the fifth most-translated author of all time, and some of his stories were adapted into famous films. JGV travelled widely, including to the US, and he visited Ireland in 1888. He wrote the preface to Robert Cromie§'s *A plunge into space* (London, 1891, 2nd edn). SOURCE Brown, p. 304; DLB, cxxiii.

V5   *P'tit bonhomme* (by Jules Verne).
      + Paris: J. Hetzel & Co., [1893], 2 parts (ill. L. Benet; Les Voyages Extraordinaires). LOCATION L.
      + London: Sampson Low & Co., 1895 (as *Foundling Mick*; ill.). SOURCE Brown, 1645. LOCATION L, InND Loeber coll. (incomplete copy).
COMMENTARY The varied and exciting adventures of a poor Irish waif rescued from a travelling showman at Westport (Co. Mayo) who is sent to a school for the poor in Galway. Further adventures bring him to many other parts of Ireland, including Dublin, Belfast and Killarney. The effects of the land laws are described as well as an eviction scene. The boy never forgets those individuals who were good to him when he was a poor child. At a fairly young age, he becomes a successful merchant and goes out of his way to find these individuals and to repay them [ML; Brown].

'VERNON, Adelaide', pseud. See **BRABAZON, Elizabeth Jane.**

VERNON, Annie. See **KANE, Annie.**

'VIDI', fl. 1853. Pseudonym of an American social issues novelist.
V6   *Mr. Frank, the underground mail-agent* (by 'Vidi').
      + Philadelphia: Lippincott, Grambo & Co., 1853 (ill. Wright). LOCATION Wright web.
      COMMENTARY An Irish character, Jimmy, compares the lot of the slaves to that of the Irish peasants and decides that the slaves are far better off [ML].

VINCENT, Henry, fl. *c*.1800. Romance novelette writer.
V7   *The Irish assassin; or, the misfortunes of the family of O'Donnell* (by Henry Vincent).
      + London: Thomas Tegg, [1800?] (ill. T. Rowlandson). SOURCE Figgis cat. 48/264; Block, p. 245; Summers, p. 83. LOCATION L (1840 edn), InND Loeber coll.
COMMENTARY 28pp. It was later reprinted as a 24pp chapbook in Falkirk [1835?], and in Glasgow [1840?]. A tragic love story. Sir Neale O'Donnell, his wife, and their son Arthur live

on an estate in Co. Donegal. Sir Neale is very proud of his ancestry and expects his son to marry well. Arthur, however, falls in love with Maria, the daughter of a soldier who has retired to a cottage on the estate. The O'Donnell's estate agent, M'Pherson, wishes to marry Maria but she secretly marries Arthur. M'Pherson lays his hands on the couple's wedding certificate and hands it over to Sir Neale. He is so angry that he locks up his wife and attacks Maria, who dies. During the funeral, Arthur kills his father in revenge. As a last act, he also kills the estate agent. He is caught and while standing in the dock, dashes his brains out, thereby bringing to an end the family line of the O'Donnells [ML; RL].

'VINCENT, John', pseud. See HUNTINGTON, Jedediah Vincent.

'VIRGILIUS PENMAN', fl. 1858. Pseudonym of a short story and sketch writer, possibly of Scottish origin. SOURCE RL.

V8   *Ballytubber; or, a Scotch settler in Ireland. With advice to his countrymen* (by 'Virgilius Penman').
    + London: Houlston & Wright, 1858. SOURCE Dixson, p. 305. LOCATION UCD Folklore Dept., L.

COMMENTARY Stories set in the north of Ireland and Dublin. Contents: 'Voyage to Belfast', 'Arrival in Belfast; strange incidents', 'Journey to, and adventures in Dublin', 'Adventures in Dublin continued', 'Farm-hunting; its vicissitudes', 'Hercules farming in Ireland', 'Ballytubber and its inmates', 'Building in Ireland; its difficulties', 'Ballytubber receives visitors; miscellaneous topics discussed', 'Ballangeigh and Stenmure at an evening party', 'Captain Bottom returns to Ballytubber', 'Stenmure's address to the ladies of Leinster', 'Agricultural labourers in Ireland; their character', 'Social and political observations', 'Social and political observations continued', 'Education in Ireland', 'Dialogue between Ballangeigh and Stenmure', 'Ballangeigh on beauty, with miscellaneous topics' [ML].

VON KILLINGER, Freiherr, Carl. See KILLINGER, Freiherr von, Carl.

VON SCHLICHTKRULL, Aline von. See SCHLICHTKRULL, Aline von.

VON TAUTPHOEUS, Baroness Jemima. See TAUTPHOEUS, Baroness Jemima von.

VOYNICH, E.L. See VOYNICH, Ethel Lillian.

VOYNICH, Ethel Lillian (née Boole; known as E.L. Voynich), b. Ballintemple (Co. Cork) 1864, d. New York City, 1960. Novelist, translator, composer and revolutionary, Ethel was the daughter of professor George Boole, a notable mathematician and logician, and Mary Everest, a feminist philosopher and niece of the explorer Sir George Everest. The family moved to England after the death of EV's father, when she was an infant, but she returned to Ireland for periods of time as a child. She studied music in Berlin; lived in Paris, and – eager to study nihilism in Russia – learned Russian from the exiled revolutionary Sergei Kravchinskii, known as Stepniak, in London. For two years she travelled in Russia, where she gave music lessons, worked with the poor, and associated with the families of political prisoners. She translated the journals of Stepniak, published in *Free Russia* (London). Stepniak later wrote introductions for her translations *Stories from Garshin* (London, 1893) and *The humour of Russia* (London, 1895). She also translated Stepniak's pamphlets that appeared with Felix Volkhofsky's 'Claims of the Russian liberals' in *Nihilism as it is* (London, 1894). In 1891 she married a Polish count, Wilfred Habdank-Woynich, who had been a prisoner in Siberia.

(He later anglicized his name to Voynich.) She and her husband assisted Stepniak in his propaganda work and ELV journeyed to Ukraine alone to organize the smuggling of contraband
propaganda. Her novel *The gadfly* (London, 1897) was inspired by a portrait of a young man
in black by the Florentine painter Franciabigio (1484–1525) she had seen in the Louvre, and
by the early life of Sigmund Rosenblum, or Sidney Reilly, the 'Ace of Spies', with whom she
had an affair in the 1890s. According to ELV, the heroine is based on Charlotte Wilson, the
mistress of Prince Peter Kropotkin, a Russian anarchist. *The Gadfly* sold over five million
copies; was translated into over thirty languages; dramatized by George Bernard Shaw§, and
made into a film with a score by Dmitri Shostakovich. It became immensely-popular in Russia,
where it was translated into the eighteen languages of the USSR, transformed into operas and
much reprinted. She received royalties from the USSR only in 1955. None of her succeeding
novels enjoyed such success. Her husband became a noted bibliographer and antiquarian bookseller in London and New York, where ELV settled also in 1920. In America, she did translations from Russian and she also translated Chopin's letters. She devoted herself principally
to music, teaching and composing and she dedicated one of her cantatas to the Irish revolutionary Roger Casement. Some of her papers are at the Boole Library at NUI Cork (Ms
BP/1/); the Gurney Archive, Gloucester Public Library, and the G.I. Taylor Archive,
Cambridge Univ. Library. P.J. Kavanagh ed. her *Letters* (Oxford, 1982). For her portraits, see
ODNB. SOURCE Blain, pp 1117–18; Brady, p. 241; EF, p. 401; Hogan 2, pp 1214–15; A. Kettle,
'E.L. Voynich: a forgotten English novelist' in *Essays in criticism*, 7 (1957), pp 163–74; NCBEL
4, p. 1709–10; OCIL, pp 588–9; ODNB; O'Toole, pp 306–7; RIA/DIB; Sutherland, p. 654;
Todd, pp 686–7.

V9   *The gadfly* (by E.L. Voynich).

    London: W. Heinemann, 1897. SOURCE Daims, 3142; Todd, p. 686. LOCATION D (1901
    edn), L.

    + New York: Henry Holt & Co., 1897. SOURCE Daims, 3142. LOCATION D, NUC,
    InND Loeber coll.

    + New York: International Book & Publishing Co., 1900. LOCATION InND Loeber
    coll.

    + Moscow: Co-operative Publishing Society of Foreign Workers in the U.S.S.R., 1936.
    LOCATION D, InND Loeber coll. (1958, 4th edn).

COMMENTARY In the preface the author thanks 'many people who helped me to collect, in
Italy, the materials for this story'. The story is set in Italy at the time of the nationalist revolt
against Austrian domination that resulted in the revolution of 1848. Gemma, active in efforts
to reduce the powers of the Catholic church in Italy, gives up her politically-involved lover
Arthur Burton. She marries his comrade. Burton discovers that the priest who has been his
friend and spiritual advisor is actually his father. Disillusioned with humanity, he feigns death,
and lives for 13 years in South America, returning to resume his political agitation under an
alias, the Gadfly. He is eventually captured. His father, now a cardinal, agrees to the execution of his beloved son. The story was dramatized by George Bernard Shaw§ and made in to
a film [ODNB; Todd; O'Toole, p. 307].

V10   *Jack Raymond* (by E.L. Voynich).

    + London: William Heinemann, 1901. SOURCE Todd, p. 686. LOCATION D, L, InND
    Loeber coll.

COMMENTARY The original manuscript is in the Grolier Club, New York. A fiercely anti-clerical story of a boy mistreated by his family who finds understanding in a friend's mother, Mrs
Mirski, widow of a Polish patriot who died in Siberia [ODNB; Todd].

V11   *Olive Latham* (by E.L. Voynich).

    + London: W. Heinemann, 1904. SOURCE Daims, 3143. LOCATION D, L.

+ Philadelphia, London: J.B. Lippincott, 1904. SOURCE Daims, 3143. LOCATION NUC, InND Loeber coll.

COMMENTARY Set in England and Russia at the turn of the century before the communist revolution. Story of an English nurse who becomes involved with Russian anarchists, nihilists and Polish revolutionaries. She goes to Russia to be with her consumptive lover. He is arrested by the police and dies in prison. After she returns to England, she is mentally unstable. A Polish friend, also a revolutionary and a doctor who had been imprisoned in Siberia, insists on her going back to work. Eventually, she nurses him too after he has been shot. He does not expect to recover, but does. They admit their love for each other [ML; Todd].

V12 *An interrupted friendship* (by E.L. Voynich).

London: Hutchinson & Co., 1910. LOCATION L.

New York: Bee De Publishing, 1910. LOCATION Cleveland (OH) Public Library.

+ New York: Macmillan, 1910. SOURCE Sutherland, p. 655. LOCATION D.

COMMENTARY Sequel to *The gadfly* (London, 1897). Historical fiction set in nineteenth-century France. A young man goes on an expedition to South America to raise money for his crippled sister. There he meets a broken man, the Gadfly of the earlier book, who saves his life and becomes his friend [EF, p. 402; Sutherland].

V13 *Put off thy shoes* (by E.L. Voynich; dedicated to Anne M. Nill).

+ London, Toronto: William Heinemann, 1946. SOURCE Brady, p. 241; Sutherland, p. 655 (1947 edn). LOCATION D.

COMMENTARY Last in the trilogy concerning *The gadfly* (London, 1897) and *An interrupted friendship* (London, 1910), this novel takes the heroine back to her Cornish roots [Sutherland].

W

'W., A.M.', fl. 1861. Pseudonym of a novelist, probably American.

W1   *Patty Williams's voyage. A story almost wholly true* (by 'A.M.W.')
+ Boston: Walker, Wise & Co., 1861. LOCATION D, NUC (1863 edn).
COMMENTARY Patty Williams is a rich girl on an emigrant ship travelling from the east coast of the US to California. During the voyage she befriends the Irish Bridget Bryan, who is travelling in steerage, to whom she gives food [ML].

'W—, G—', pseud. See WOLLASTON, George.

'W., G.', fl. 1880s. Pseudonym of a writer of Protestant religious fiction.

W2   *Letters from a stranger in Ireland* (by 'G.W.').
+ London: G. Morrish, [1885] (ill. M.E.E.). SOURCE Hyland cat. 219/879. LOCATION D, L, InND Loeber coll.
COMMENTARY Two binding types, one reddish-brown cloth, the other green cloth, both with floral design stamping in black on boards and spine. Ten stories written in the form of ten letters for juveniles, conveying Protestant Christian sentiment and morals. Although the setting is Ireland, the Irish content is slim. Contents: '"The Emerald Isle"', 'The winter of age', 'Spring days', 'The spring-time of youth', 'Seed sown in spring', 'Summer months', 'Summer scenes', 'Autumn memories', 'A Scotch refugee in Irish soil', 'Autumn's departure' [ML; CD; RL].

'W., G.R.' pseud. See WYNNE, Revd George Robert.

'W., H.', pseud. of H. Wale. Co-author. See WHATELY, Mary Louisa.

'W., M.J.', pseud. See WHITTY, Michael James.

'W., M.L.', pseud. See WHATELY, Mary Louisa.

'WAGSTAFFE, Jeoffry', pseud. See JEPHSON, Robert.

WAILLY, Armand François Léon de. See DE WAILLY, Armand François Léon.

WAKEFIELD, Jane Marian. See RICHARDSON, Jane Marian.

WAKEFIELD, Priscilla (née Bell), b. Tottenham (London), 1751, d. Ipswich (Suffolk) 1832. English author of moral tales and instructional books for children, PW was the daughter of Quakers Daniel Bell and Catherine Barclay. In 1771 she married Edward Wakefield, a London merchant with Irish connections, and became involved in charitable works. When her family fell on hard times, she started writing textbooks for children. In all she published 17 works. Edward Wakefield, her older son, published *An account of Ireland. Statistical and political* (London, 1812, 2 vols.). SOURCE Allibone, iii, p. 2536; Blain, p. 1121; BLC; Falkner Greirson cat. Maud/777; ODNB; Todd, pp 688–9.

W3 *A family tour through the British empire; containing some account of its manu-factures, natural and artificial curiosities, history and antiquities; interspersed with biographical anecdotes, particularly adapted to the amusement and instruction of youth* (by Priscilla Wakefield).
London: Printed [for the author?] by Darton & Harvey, 1804. SOURCE Osborne, p. 194. LOCATION CaOTP, L.
+ London: Printed by Darton & Harvey, 1805, 2nd edn (improved; ill. with map engraved for author's tour). LOCATION L (1808 edn), InND Loeber coll.
+ Philadelphia: Jacob Johnson & Co., 1804 (ill.). SOURCE Welch, 1396. LOCATION L, InND Loeber coll.
COMMENTARY Fiction for children, supplemented by letters. It contains a section on Ireland and an itinerary [RL].

WALDA, Viola, fl. 1889. Probable pseudonym of an Irish author of contemporary commentary fiction. SOURCE RL.
W4 *Miss Peggy O'Dillon; or, the Irish critic* (by Viola Walda).
+ Dublin: M.H. Gill & Son, 1889 (see Plate 63). SOURCE Topp 8, 971. LOCATION L, InND Loeber coll.
COMMENTARY Stream-of-consciousness monologue about life in Ireland, Ireland's relationship with England, nationalism, and the role of women. Various contemporary figures such as Charles Stewart Parnell are mentioned [RL].

WALE, H. Co-author. See WHATELY, Mary Louisa.

WALFORD, L.B. See WALFORD, Lucy Bethia.

WALFORD, Lucy Bethia (née Colquhoun; known as L.B. Walford), b. Edinburgh (Scotland) 1845, d. London 1915. Prolific and popular novelist, biographer and artist, LBW was the daughter of the Scottish writer and military man John Colquhoun, and of Frances Maitland, a hymn writer and poet. She married Alfred Sanders Walford of Ilford, Essex, in 1869 and lived in London. She contributed to various periodicals including *Blackwood's Magazine* (Edinburgh) and the *World* (London) and was the London correspondent of the New York magazine the *Critic*. She published more than 45 books between 1874 and 1914, including two memoirs. To date, only one of her novels is known to have Irish content. SOURCE Allibone Suppl., ii, p. 1476; Alston, p. 451; Blain, pp 1122–3; Daims, p. 737; EF, p. 403; NCBEL 4, pp 1710–13 (list of novels); ODNB; Sutherland, p. 655; T & B, p. 1018; Todd, pp 689–90; Wolff, iv, pp 230–1.
W5 *Iva Kildare. A matrimonial problem* (by L.B. Walford).
+ London, New York: Longmans & Co., 1897. SOURCE Daims, 3156. LOCATION L, NUC.
COMMENTARY The story of an Irish widow marrying the lover rejected by her daughter [RL].

WALKER, N.T. Editor. See HARTIGAN, Henry.

'WALKING GENTLEMAN', pseud. See GRATTAN, Thomas Colley.

WALLACE, Helen, pseud. 'Gordon Roy', fl. 1889. Novelist with over a dozen titles to her name, HW was the daughter of a Scottish clergyman. SOURCE Blain, p. 1127; BLC; EF, p. 404.

W6   *For her sake. A tale of life in Ireland* (by 'Gordon Roy').
+ London: Thomas Nelson & Son, 1889. SOURCE Brown, 1458. LOCATION Dt (1891 edn), L.
COMMENTARY Capt. Stanford brings his Scottish bride to Ireland. They live in a dilapidated mansion near a squalid village. Leslie is depressed by the place and neglected by her husband, but learns to love the poor people around her. An eviction is followed by a murder and Stanford is suspected. Leslie is able to prove her husband's innocence, and they are reconciled [Blain; Brown].

WALLER, John Francis, pseuds **'Jonathan Freke Slingsby',** and **'Iota',** b. Limerick 1809 (not 1810 as in MVP), d. Bishop's Stortford (Herts.) 1894. Barrister, novelist, poet, popular song writer and editor, JFW was the third son of Thomas Maunsell Waller, of Finoe House (Co. Tipperary) and Margaret Vereker. He graduated BA at TCD in 1831; was admitted to the King's Inns in 1829; to Gray's Inn (London) in 1831, and called to the Irish Bar in 1833. Two years later he married Anna Hopkins. He had begun writing for periodicals while studying for the law and was one of the founders of the *Dublin University Magazine*, to which he contributed for over forty years. He succeeded Charles Lever§ as editor (1845–55), and he bought the magazine from Joseph Sheridan Le Fanu§ in 1870. He wrote pantomimes (e.g. *Harlequin Fulminoso: or, the Ganders of Glen Fearna: a grand Christmas pantomime* (Dublin, 1851), and became well-known for his poems, many of which became popular songs. Collections of his verse include *Ravenscroft hall* (London, 1852), and *Poems* (Dublin, 1854). Among the books he edited are *The works of Oliver Goldsmith§*, with an introduction and life, (London, 1864); Thomas Moore's§ *Irish melodies* (London, 1867), and Jonathan Swift's§ *Gulliver's Travels* (London, 1864–65). He edited the *Imperial dictionary of universal biography* (Glasgow, 1866); contributed to *Cassell's Biographical dictionary* (London, 1869) and to a variety of periodicals, including those edited by Mrs S.C. Hall§. He became vice-president of the RIA in 1864 and was appointed registrar of the rolls court in 1867. The preface to his *The Slingsby papers* is dated Feb. 1852 from Carrigbawn (Co. Cork). He was awarded an LLB and an LLD from TCD in 1852 for his scholarly and legal work. After his retirement he moved in 1870 to London, where he did literary work for Cassell and Co. and published *Boswell and Johnson: their companions and contemporaries* (London, 1881). Some of his correspondence can be found at the BL and at the NLS. JFW is not to be confused with Kathleen Mannington Caffyn§, who also used the pseudonym 'Iota'. SOURCE Allibone, iii, p. 2551; B & S, p. 851; Boase, iii, p. 1166; Boylan, p. 394; Brady, p. 242; Burke's, p. 1178; W.E. Hall, pp 43, 116, 137–8; Hogan 2, p. 1221; Irish pseudonyms; Keane, p. 496; McKenna, pp 332–4; MVP, pp 482–3; OCIL, p. 592; O'Donoghue, p. 469; ODNB; O'Donoghue 2, p. 432; RIA/DIB.

W7   *The Slingsby papers. A selection from the writings of Jonathan Freke Slingsby* (dedicated to Charles Lever§).
+ Dublin: J. M'Glashan; London: Wm. Orr & Co., 1852 (Readings in Popular Literature). SOURCE Brown 2, 1571; Rafroidi, ii, p. 351; McKenna, p. 332; Bradshaw, 3950. LOCATION Grail, D, L, C.
+ Dublin: McGlashan & Gill, [1852?] as *St. Patrick's day in my own parlour: with tales and thoughts in prose and verse (selected from the Slingsby papers)*. SOURCE Gilbert, p. 879. LOCATION DPL Gilbert coll., D.
COMMENTARY Sentimental and humorous essays, with poems and stories, reprinted from the *Dublin University Magazine* [Brown 2].

W8   *The dead bridal. A Venetian tale of the fourteenth century* (by 'Jonathan Freke Slingsby').

+ London: Ward & Lock, 1856. SOURCE Hogan 2, p. 1221; McKenna, p. 333. LOCATION L.
COMMENTARY Historical fiction. No Irish content. ODNB mistakenly mentions this as a poem [ML; RL].

W9   *From darkness to light. A confirmation tale* (by 'Iota'; preface by T. Fenton).
+ London: J.T. Hays; New York: Pott & Amery, 1870. LOCATION L.
COMMENTARY Religious fiction with Irish content [BLC; CM].

W10   *Kooroona. A tale of South Australia* (by 'Iota').
+ Oxford: Mowbray & Co., 1871; London: Simpson, Marshall & Co., 1871. SOURCE Alston, p. 65. LOCATION L, NUC.
COMMENTARY Set in Australia [ML].

W11   *Festival tales* ([ed.] by John Francis Waller).
+ Dublin: McGlashan & Gill; London: Simpkin, Marshall & Co.; Edinburgh: John Menzies & Co., 1873. SOURCE McKenna, p. 333. LOCATION D, InND Loeber coll.
COMMENTARY Contents: 'New Year's Day. – Abraham Scrimble's will', 'St. Valentine's Day. The martyr', 'Easter Day. St. Mary's-super-mare', 'All Hallow Eve. Snap-apple night at Castle Slingsby' (set in Ireland), 'The Feast of All Souls. The Count of Castel Vecchio', 'Christmas Eve. A tale of two travellers', 'Innocents Day. Turned to the wall', 'New Year's Eve – Snowed up balancing the books' (set in Ireland) [ML; RL].

W12   *The adventures of a Protestant in search of religion* (by 'Iota').
London: R. Washbourne, 1873. SOURCE COPAC; RLIN. LOCATION L (destroyed), E, Pittsburgh Theological Seminary Library.
New York, Montreal: D. & J. Sadlier & Co., 1874. SOURCE Hogan 2, p. 1221; OCLC (1879 edn).
COMMENTARY Perhaps inspired by Thomas Moore's§ *Travels of an Irish gentleman in search of religion* (London, 1833, 2 vols.). JFW's version was very popular in the US and had three edns in New York in a decade [AMB; ODNB].

W13   *The court of divorce in golden land. A legend* (by 'Iota').
+ London: Remington & Co., 1877. LOCATION L.
COMMENTARY A fable written against divorce [ML].

WALROND, Robert Francis, pseud. '**Adam Blenkinsop**', fl. 1845. A short story and miscellaneous writer, RFW also wrote *Hot water cure, sought out in Germany in the summer of 1844* (London, 1845), and *Memoirs of Dr. Blenkinsop, written by himself. Including his campaigns, travels, and adventures; with anecdotes of graphiology, and some of the letters of his correspondents* (London, 1852, 2 vols.), neither of which has Irish content. RFW is the attributed author of *A transport voyage to the Mauritius and back: touching on the Cape of Good Hope & St. Helena* (London, 1851). SOURCE ML: COPAC.

W14   *Paddiana; or, scraps and sketches of Irish life, present and past* [anon.].
+ London: Richard Bentley, 1847, 2 vols. (ill. G. Measom). SOURCE Brown, 222; Block, p. 91; Wolff, 6995. LOCATION Dt, D.
+ London: Richard Bentley, 1851 (new edn). LOCATION L, InND Loeber coll.
London: C.H. Clarke, n.d. (as *Larry Lynch or Paddiana: Irish life, past and present* by 'Adam Blenkinsop'). SOURCE Sadleir, 3448; OCLC. LOCATION Univ. of Illinois.
COMMENTARY Block attributes this to Sir William Gregory, but this is not supported by other sources. Contents: 'Mr. Smith's Irish love', '"Mick Doolan's head"', 'Still-hunting', 'A mystery amongst the mountains', 'The adventure of Tim Daley', 'Mrs. Fogarty's tea-party', 'A quiet day at Farrellstown', 'A duel', 'Mr. H.', 'The Old Head of Kinsale', 'Barney O'Hay', 'Head-breaking', 'Cads, fools and beggars', 'The mendicity association', 'The dog-fancier',

'Dublin carmen', 'Horses', 'Priests: Catholic and others', 'An Irish stew', 'Executions', 'Ronayne's ghost', 'The last pigtail', 'The green traveller', 'Larry Lynch', 'Potatoes'. The stories are followed by four chapters on Irish history [RL; Block, p. 91].

WALSH, Miss (according to Summers 2; Mrs Walsh according to Allibone; mistakenly called Mrs Wash by Gecker), pseud. **'The daughter of a Captain in the Navy, deceased'**, fl. 1810. Novelist, possibly Irish. SOURCE RL.

W15 *The officer's daughter; or, a visit to Ireland in 1790* (by 'The daughter of a Captain in the Navy, deceased'; dedicated to the Hon. Mrs Fane[1]).
+ London: Printed [for the author?] by Joyce Gold, 1810, 4 vols. (subscribers' list). SOURCE Allibone, iii, p. 2560 (n.d. edn); BD, p. 371; Block, p. 175; Gecker, 1076; Wolff, 6997; British Fiction; Garside, 1810–85. LOCATION PU.
COMMENTARY The subscribers are mostly English, but include some Irish ones, with Sir Charles Vernon, Dublin Castle, subscribing ten copies. The review in the *British Critic* makes no mention of the 'Irish' content, but the review in the *Critical Review* mentions that the heroine, Louisa Courtney, lives in Dublin with her aunt, Mrs Conolly, and participates in the gaieties of the city. One of her many admirers is a Mr Morrice, a presumptive heir of his brother, the earl of Rossmore. However, Morrice's past catches up when the woman he had seduced appears. A duel follows in which Morrice is killed. Louisa inherits some property from her aunt and marries a Mr Tarleton, who is the next heir to Lord Rossmore. Contains descriptions of the landscape of Co. Wicklow, including the river Dargle, and the waterfall close to the Powerscourt demesne [RL; JB; *British Critic* 36, (Aug. 1810), pp 184–5; *Critical Review*, 3rd ser., 21 (Sept. 1810), p. 49].

WALSH, Elizabeth A. See FITZSIMON, Elizabeth A.

WALSH, Mary E. See MANNIX, Mrs Mary E.

WALSHE, E.H. See WALSHE, Miss Elizabeth Hely.

WALSHE, Miss E. Hely. See WALSHE, Miss Elizabeth Hely.

WALSHE, Miss Elizabeth Hely (known as E.H. Walshe and E. Hely Walshe), b. Limerick 1835, d. Isle of Wight 1868 (1869 according to Allibone and Watters). Protestant evangelical writer, EHW spent part of her life in Canada. Her father was a clergyman and a member of the RIA. Her brother was a resident of Kilkenny. It is not clear when she emigrated, but she was influenced by the evangelist Revd H. Grattan Guinness, who visited Canada in 1861. By 1865 she was back in Limerick, where she wrote the preface to *Golden hills* (London, [1865]). She was a dedicated Sunday-school teacher, an accomplished musician and artist, and she was interested in the education of the poor. She regularly contributed to the *Leisure Hour Magazine* and *Sunday At Home* (both London). She died of consumption in the Isle of Wight. Several of her publications were reprinted long after her death. SOURCE Allibone, iii, p. 2561; Brown 2, p. 263; Field Day, v, p. 924; IBL, 14 (1924), p. 125; NCBEL 4, p. 1885; O'Toole, p. 94; Osborne, p. 1035; RIA/DIB; Watters, p. 412.

W16 *Cedar Creek; from the shanty to the settlement. A tale of Canadian life* [anon.].
+ London: The Leisure Hour Office, Religious Tract Society, [1863] (ill.). SOURCE Alston, p. 453; Osborne, p. 1035; Watters, p. 411–12. LOCATION CaOTP, D, L, InND Loeber coll.

1 Probably, daughter of the 10th earl of Westmoreland.

London: Religious Tract Society, 1902 (as *Cedar creek. A tale of Canadian life*). SOURCE Osborne, p. 1035; Watters, p. 412. LOCATION CaOTP ([1905] edn), InND Loeber coll. (n.d. edn).
COMMENTARY Tells of Irish immigrants who settle near the upper Ottawa River in Canada [Osborne].

W17 *The foster-brothers of Doon, a tale of the Irish rebellion of 1798* [anon.].
+ London, Religious Tract Society, [*c*.1865] (ill.). SOURCE Brown, 1651; Nield, p. 369; Wolff, 6998; Watters, p. 412 (assigns 1866 date). LOCATION D, L, InND Loeber coll. (also n.d. edn.).
COMMENTARY The n.d. edn comes in two versions, with one having a different title page, preface and pagination. First published in 26 parts in the *Leisure Hour Magazine* (London, 1864). Set during the 1798 rebellion, it contains accounts of events at Vinegar Hill, Wexford Bridge, and features foster brothers Myles Furlong, a County Wexford blacksmith, and Capt. Butler, a loyalist. The story leans to the loyalist side and is written from a Protestant point of view [Brown; Doolin Dinghy cat. 16/159; Nield, p. 369].

W18 *Golden hills. A tale of the Irish famine* [anon.].
+ London, Religious Tract Society, [1865] (ill.). SOURCE Brown, 1652; Brown 2, 1575; Wolff, 6999. LOCATION D, Dt, DPL, L.
London: Religious Tract Society, [1917] (as *Kingston's revenge: A story of bravery*; ill. J. Finnemore). SOURCE Watters, p. 412; BLC. LOCATION L.
COMMENTARY According to the BLC, the [1917] edn is possibly another version of *Golden hills. A tale of the Famine and also of the Ribbonmen*. In her preface the author writes: 'We pray that the religion of the Bible may yet be the religion of Ireland'. She considers the Famine an opportunity for conversion of Catholics [Brown 2; Fegan, p. 220].

W19 *The manuscript man; or, the Bible in Ireland* (by Miss E.H. Walshe).
+ London: Religious Tract Society, [1869] (ill.). SOURCE Brown, 1653. LOCATION D, L.
+ Philadelphia: Presbyterian Board of Publication. Printed by Westcott and Thomson, n.d. (ill.). LOCATION InND Loeber coll.
New York: Carlton & Lanahan, [1876?] (ill.). SOURCE NYPL. LOCATION NN, InND Loeber coll. (New York, Hunt & Eaton, [1895] edn).
COMMENTARY A story of proselytizing in west Connacht and the distribution of the Bible in Irish to Catholic tenantry by Protestant landowners. The life of one family becomes less congenial after converting to protestantism and they subsequently emigrate to America [RL].

W20 *Within sea walls; or, how the Dutch kept faith* (by Miss Elizabeth H. Walshe and George E. Sargent).
+ London: Religious Tract Society, [1880] (ill.). SOURCE Watters, p. 412. LOCATION D, L.
Boston: Bradley, 1881. SOURCE Watters, p. 412; OCLC. LOCATION DCL.
COMMENTARY This and the following work were published posthumously [RL].

W21 *Under the inquisition. Story of the inquisition in Italy* (by Miss E.H. Walshe).
London: Religious Tract Society, 1904 (ill. Alfred Pearse). SOURCE Watters, p. 412; OCLC. LOCATION L.

WARBURTON, Bartholomew Eliot George (also known as **Eliot Warburton**) b. near Tullamore (Co. Offaly, not northern Ireland as in Sutherland) 1810 (and not 1818 as in Boylan), d. at sea, off Land's End (Cornwall), en route to the West Indies, 1852. Barrister, editor and historical fiction, history and travel writer, BEGW was the eldest son of Maj. George Warburton, of Aughrim (Co. Galway), formerly inspector-general of the constabulary in Ireland,

and Anna Acton of Co. Wicklow. He entered Queen's College, Cambridge, in 1828, migrated to Trinity College, Cambridge, in 1830, where he graduated BA in 1833 and MA in 1837. He was admitted at the Inner Temple (London) in 1832; to the King's Inns in 1837, and was called to the Irish Bar in the same year. However, he abandoned the law to manage his estates, travel and write. He contributed to the *Dublin University Magazine* and, at the urging of Charles Lever§, compiled from articles printed there a sociological travel book, *The crescent and the cross, or romance and realities of Eastern travel* (London, 1845) based on his extensive travels in Syria, Palestine and Egypt, which reached at least 17 edns. In 1848 he married Mathilda Jane, daughter of Edward Grove, of Shenstone Park (Staffs.). BEGW led a roving life and was described as 'generous, high-spirited and unselfish ... with the Irish love of adventure' (DNB). Frances Cobbe§ referred to him as 'very refined ... and rather effeminate' (*Life of Frances Power Cobbe*, i, p. 166). In 1849 he published *Memoirs of Prince Rupert and the Cavaliers* (London, 1849, 3 vols.) and in 1851 he edited *Memoirs of Horace Walpole and his contemporaries*, compiled by Robert Folkestone Williams. His plans for a history of Ireland came to naught for want of a publisher and he also planned a 'History of the poor', for which he visited Dublin to look at poverty there. In 1852 he set sail for Central America at the request of the Atlantic and Pacific Junction Company to establish friendly relations between the Indian tribes on the Isthmus of Darien (he had published a novel on the area in that year, see below). His ship caught fire off Land's End and he was one of the many who perished. A memorial window was placed in Iffley church, near Oxford. His younger brother, George Drought Warburton (1816–1857), wrote extensively about Canada. SOURCE Allibone, iii, pp 2568–9; Boase, iii, pp 1185–6; Boylan, p. 395; Brady, p. 244; W.E. Hall, p. 114; Herlihy, p. 312; *Life of Frances Power Cobbe* by herself (London, 1895), i, p. 166; Keane, p. 500; Landed gentry, 1904, p. 637; Venn, part ii, vi, p. 339; NCBEL 4, p. 2305; OCIL, p. 593; ODNB; RIA/DIB; Sutherland, p. 657.

W22   *Zoë: An episode of the Greek war* [anon.].
    London: M. Sharpe, 1847. SOURCE BLC. LOCATION L.
COMMENTARY This 30pp story was told to Warburton on his travels and he had it printed in 1847 to help a bazaar for the distressed Irish, presumably a post-Famine relief effort [BLC; DNB].

W23   *Reginald Hastings; or, a tale of the troubles in 164–* [anon.].
    London: H. Colburn, 1850, 3 vols. SOURCE Sutherland, p. 657 (1849 edn, but this may be in error); Wolff, 7002. LOCATION L, NUC.
    New York: Harper & Bros, 1850. SOURCE OCLC. LOCATION ViU.
COMMENTARY Historical fiction. A tale of Ireland in the seventeenth century. A shipwrecked Irish boy turns out to be the relation of the dispossessed Irish prince 'The O'Connor of Connaught', and to be a zealot for the Royal cause in the face of republican roundhead scoundrels. He is later knighted by Prince Rupert [Rowan cat. 62/556].

W24   *Darien; or, the merchant prince. A historical romance* (by Eliot Warburton; dedicated to 'my friends on Tweed and Yarrow').
    + London: H. Colburn & Co., 1852, 3 vols. SOURCE Wolff, 7000. LOCATION InND Loeber coll.
    Leipzig: Bernard Tauchnitz, 1853, 2 vols. in 1. SOURCE T & B, 252; OCLC. LOCATION NIC.
COMMENTARY An historical novel set in 1697 concerning William Patterson and the Darien Scheme on the isthmus between South and Central America to drive a British wedge in the Spanish possessions at a point where a trade route could be made to the Pacific Ocean. The settlement was not a success and within a year those of the Scottish settlers still alive returned home. The story of the actual settlement is only dealt with in the third volume. The previ-

ous two volumes are taken up with scenes in Scotland, the south of Spain, the Caribbean islands and Cartagena (Colombia). Through most of the story, the Scotsman William Patterson and a Spanish Moor, Alvarez, are close friends and business partners. They share many adventures, some concerning pirates, and marry two Scottish women. The novel describes the horrors of a fire at sea, presaging Warburton's actual fate [ML].

WARBURTON, Eliot. See **WARBURTON, Bartholomew Eliot George.**

'WARD, Artemus', pseud. See **BROWNE, Charles Farrar.**

WARD, Mrs —, fl. 1869. Writer of historical fiction, Mrs W was from Ulster.
W25   *Waves on the ocean of life. A Dalriadian tale* (by Mrs Ward; dedicated to the earl of Antrim).
       + London: Simpkin, Marshall & Co.; Dublin: Moffat & Co., 1869. SOURCE Brown, 1654; OCLC. LOCATION D, L, InND Loeber coll.
COMMENTARY Historical fiction presenting a picture of life in Ulster in the eighteenth century and describing the interior of a typical farmhouse and the daily activities of its inhabitants. The story revolves around religious friction between the old-line Covenanters and a son whose outlook is less strict. It describes the political upheavals of the end of the eighteenth century, including the rise of the United Irishmen [ML; Brown].

WARD, Elizabeth Stuart. See **PHELPS, Elizabeth Stuart.**

WARD, the Hon. Mrs Mary (née King), pseud. 'The Hon. Mrs. W.', b. Ferbane (Co. Offaly) 1827, d. 1869. Entomologist, artist and one of Ireland's early women science writers, MW was the youngest daughter of Revd Henry King of Ballylin (near Ferbane), a Church of Ireland clergyman, and Harriet Lloyd (sister of the countess of Rosse). Her early interest in science was fostered by her mother's first cousin, the noted astronomer William Parsons, 3rd earl of Rosse, from whom she received her first microscope. She illustrated her own works, including *Sketches with the microscope. In a letter to a friend* ([Parsonstown], 1857); *A world of wonders revealed by the microscope. A book for young students* (London, 1858); *Microscope teachings* (London, 1864); *The microscope* (London, 1869, 3rd edn), and *Telescope teachings* (London, 1859). She contributed to the monthly, the *Intellectual Observer* (London). Her sister Jane (later Lady Mahon§) collaborated on some of MW's writings. In 1854 she married the Hon. Henry William Crosbie Ward, 5th Viscount Bangor, of Castleward (Co. Down), with whom she had eight children. She died from a fall from a steam road carriage at Birr. Her portrait was published by Ryan. Some of her illustrations, books and her telescope are on exhibition at Castleward. SOURCE Allibone, iii, p. 2573; A. Crookshank & The Knight of Glin, *The watercolours of Ireland* (London, 1994), pp 209–10; Field Day, iv, pp 642–4, 653, 681; O.G. Harry, 'The Hon. Mrs Ward' in *The Irish Naturalists' Jrnl*, 21 (Jan. 1984), pp 193–200; C. Mollan, W. Davis, & B. Finucane, *Irish innovators* (Dublin, 2002), p. 75; RIA/DIB; RL; B. Ryan, *A land by the river of God. A history of Ferbane parish from the earliest times to c.1900* (Ferbane, 1994), pp 122–5; H. Shiel, *Falling into wretchedness. Ferbane in the late 1830s* (Maynooth, 1998).
W26   *Entomology in sport, and Entomology in earnest* (by the 'Hon. Mrs W. [Mary Ward] and Lady M.' [Jane, Lady Mahon]; dedicated to H.K. [Harriet King]).
       + London: Paul Jerrald & Son, [1859] (ill. M.W. [Mary Ward], Crane; see Plate 64).
       LOCATION L, InND Loeber coll.
COMMENTARY The preface states that the authors aimed at making the study of entomology entertaining for children 'rather than complete or systematic ... by which unwary youth may

find themselves caught in the meshes of science, while seeking only for amusement'. 'Entomology in sport' is a poem, written 'years ago' for the authors' mother. The second part, 'Entomology in earnest', is written in dialogues, and was added to make the work more instructive [RL].

WARD DE CHARRIÈRE, Mrs E., fl. 1884. Travel and fiction writer, probably Swiss, Mrs WdeC wrote *Une dette d'honneur* (Lausanne, 1888) and several other works of fiction. SOURCE BLC.

W27   *La tour de Lough-Erne. Nouvelle irlandaise* [anon.].
        + Lausanne: Henry Mignot, 1884. LOCATION DPL.

WARNER, Biddulph, fl. 1858. Novelist and poet, BW was, according to the dedication of *The coquette* (Dublin, 1858), a cousin of Richard Grattan of Drummin (Co. Kildare) and may be identified with Henry Biddulph Warner (b. Co. Meath) who entered TCD in 1825 at age 16, where he graduated BA in 1831. BW also wrote *Poems and sketches* (Dublin, 1857). SOURCE B & S, p. 860; BLC; O'Donoghue, p. 472; RIA/DIB.

W28   *The coquette. A novel of Dublin life* (by Biddulph Warner; dedicated to Richard Grattan, Esq., of Drummin, Co. Kildare).
        Dublin: William Robertson, 1858. SOURCE Allibone, iii, p. 2584; Bradshaw, 3994; Brown 2, 1598; OCLC. LOCATION L, C.
        Dublin: W. Robertson; London: David Bryce, n.d. (as *The coquette. A novel*). LOCATION D.

COMMENTARY Set in Dublin in the second quarter of the nineteenth century where Henry Leslie, an undergraduate at TCD, is in love with a coquette, Adeline Marshen, of Ely Place, who on the advice of her worldly mother rejects him. He is taken in hand by Mrs. McAdnam, who contrives to transfer his affections to the poor but virtuous Mary Denning. But in the meantime, Adeline has conceived a passion for Henry and tries to ruin her rival by involving her in a theft, but she is thwarted by the astuteness of Henry's servant, Phil [Brown 2].

W29   *Adrift; or, the fortunes of Connor Blake* (by Biddulph Warner).
        + London: James Blackwood, [1860]. SOURCE Allibone, iii, p. 2584. LOCATION L.
        COMMENTARY Contains Irish characters [ML].

'WARREN, Mr. —', fl. 1878. Pseudonym of a writer of satire.

W30   *How they mismanaged their house on £500 a year. A narrative* (by Mr. Warren).
        + London: Remington & Co., 1878. SOURCE Allibone Suppl., ii, p. 1490. LOCATION L

COMMENTARY The title refers to Mrs Liza Warren's *How I managed my house on two hundred pounds a year* (London, 1864), and the author's name is clearly a pseudonym. The narrative is intended as a satire on popular domestic manuals and centres on the spendthrift O'Lavishes, originally from Ireland, and their extravagant housekeeping [D. Attar (ed.), *A bibliography of household books published in Britain 1800–1914* (London, 1987), p. 213; CM].

WARWICK, Sidney. Co-author. See **OUSELEY, John Mulvey**.

WATERMAN, Rhoda Elizabeth. See **WHITE, Rhoda Elizabeth**.

'WATERS, Thomas', pseud. See **RUSSELL, William**.

WAUGH, Edwin, b. Rochdale (Lancs.) 1817, d. New Brighton (Lancs.) 1890. Song and sketch writer and poet, EW was the son of Edwin Waugh, a shoemaker, and Elizabeth Howarth

Hawkward. After his father's death when he was age 9, the family was reduced to poverty. He was apprenticed to a printer, which gave him the opportunity to read widely. Not finding work in his trade, he travelled around the country, finally settling in Lancashire, where he began a literary society and worked for the Lancashire Public School Association. After separating from his wife, the former Mary Ann Hill, he moved in with a wealthy Irish widow, Mrs. Moorhouse, in 1856. His *Sketches of Lancashire life and localities* (London, 1855), reprinted from the *Manchester Examiner* and using local dialect, rode on his success as a songwriter and inspired similar volumes based on travels in the Lake District, the south of England, Scotland, Ireland and the Rhineland. One of his temperance songs sold millions of copies in sheet music and EW was described as 'the Lancashire Burns'. SOURCE Allibone, iii, pp 2616–17; BLC; NCBEL 4, pp 690–2; ODNB; Sutherland, pp 662–3.

W31   *Irish sketches; and miscellany* (by Edwin Waugh; dedicated to Thomas Read Wilkinson).
+ Manchester: John Heywood; London: Simpkin, Marshall & Co., [1869]. LOCATION L, InND Loeber coll. (1882 edn).
COMMENTARY A volume of miscellaneous travel sketches in Ulster with some short stories: 'The Irish fishwife', 'The old coal man (an Irish tale)', 'The twelve apostles (an Irish anecdote)', 'Denis: or the Irish oyster man' [RL].

'WAYDE, Bernard', pseud. See CARLETON, Gerald.

WELD, Matthew. See HARTSTONGE, Matthew Weld.

WERNER, A., fl. 1892. Story writer and novelist, AW may be identified with the A. Werner who published ballads and stories in London in 1886. SOURCE Allibone Suppl., ii, p. 1503.
W32   *O'Driscoll's weird and other stories* (by A. Werner).
London, Paris, Melbourne: Cassell & Co., 1892. SOURCE Brown, 1659. LOCATION L.
COMMENTARY A volume of sketches, only the first of which, 'O'Driscoll's weird', is Irish in subject. O'Driscoll is a patriotic Irishman who joins the dynamiters in America. He is sent to England on a mission, but his better feelings get the upper-hand, and he returns to New York to face his doom [Brown].

WESLEY, Revd John. Editor. See BROOKE, Henry.

'WESTBURY, Hugh', pseud. See FARRIE, Hugh.

WESTON, Mrs M.A., pseud. 'A Lady of Boston', fl. 1820s. Story writer, MAW was a resident of Boston (MA) but probably came from Co. Roscommon or Co. Galway, which serve as settings for some of the stories published in her *Tales of the Emerald Isle* (Boston, 1828). SOURCE RL.
W33   *Tales of the fireside* (by 'A Lady of Boston').
Boston: Hilliard, Gray, Little and Wilkins, 1827. SOURCE Wright i, 2535; OCLC. LOCATION C, MH.
COMMENTARY Contents: 'The fortune teller: a tale of the eighteenth century, founded on fact', 'The house on the heath: a tale of real life', 'The miniature picture; or love at first sight', 'The battle of Monmouth; or, the fair Quaker: a tale of the American Revolution', 'Rose Bradshaw; or, the curate of St. Mark's', 'The emigrants; or, Aspasia de Nemours, founded on fact'. Does not appear to have Irish content [RL; Wright].

W34　*Stories for children* (by Mrs M.A. Weston).
[Boston?]: [publisher?], [1828 or earlier]. SOURCE Mentioned on title page of *Tales of the Emerald Isle* (Boston, 1828).
COMMENTARY No copy located [RL].

W35　*Tales of the Emerald Isle; or, legends of Ireland* (by 'A Lady of Boston', author of *Tales of the fireside* and *Stories for children*).
Boston: W. Borradaile, 1828. SOURCE Wright i, 2534; OCLC. LOCATION CtY (n.d. edn).
COMMENTARY Contents 'Tradition; or, St. Kevin's Bed', 'Carol More O'Daly; or, the constant lover', 'Humble life; or, the sycamore-tree: a true story', 'Retribution', 'The victim', 'Mystery: a modern story', 'Bran, the bloodhound; or, the heir of De Burgo' [Wright].

WHATELY, Mrs —. See WHATELY, Mrs Elizabeth Pope.

WHATELY, Miss E. Jane. WHATELY, Miss Elizabeth Jane.

WHATELY, Miss Elizabeth Jane (also known as Jane Whately and E. Jane Whately), pseud. 'A resident', b. Oxford 1822, d. St Peter's Port, Guernsey (Channel Islands) 1893. Religious writer, editor, biographer and educationalist, EJW was the eldest daughter of Richard Whately§, DD, archbishop of Dublin, and his wife Elizabeth Pope Whately§, and sister of Mary Louisa Whately§. She spent her formative years in Dublin, to where the family moved in 1831 when her father was appointed archbishop. Here she and some of her siblings were taught by the Joseph Blanco White§, who lodged in their home. The Whatelys divided their time between their Dublin residence and a country seat at Redesdale (near Stillorgan, Co. Dublin). EJW was active in relief work during the Famine and in other philanthropic works with her mother and sisters. After her mother's death in 1860, she took over the domestic responsibilities of the archbishop's household and looked after him in the last years of his life (he died in 1863). Her own writing and missionary career took off only after his death, when she no longer resided permanently in Dublin. She and Mary Louisa both taught for the Irish Church Mission Society. EJW conducted a mission at Madrid (partly through the Spanish Evangelization Society of Edinburgh) in 1872 and assisted at others held in Italy and France in 1868.. She assisted her sister Mary Louisa's teaching in Cairo (Egypt) where the latter had established a school for girls. She was an enthusiast of the Irish proselytizing societies In Dublin she aided the Luke Street girls' home and later wrote *"Call them in." The story of the Luke Street girls home* [Dublin, 1872]). She never married and for health reasons often spent the winters in Italy, Spain, Switzerland, France, and in Egypt with Mary Louisa. She wrote a biography of Martin Luther and became the family chronicler, publishing a collection of her father's sermons, *Miscellaneous remains from the commonplace book of Richard Whately* (London, 1864) and the *Life and correspondence of Richard Whately, D.D.* (London, 1866, 2 vols.) with the assistance of her father's pupil and friend, the economist Nassau Senior. In addition, she published a biography of her sister Mary Louisa (London, [1890]). EJW is best known for her six works of fiction, many of them anti-Catholic, which she wrote mostly for the Religious Tract Society. Her diaries are cited by Wale, but their whereabouts are not known. Boase assigns to her *The story of Ulrich Zwingli and the Reformation in German Switzerland* (London, 1863), but OCLC gives Elizabeth Allred (1786–1879) as the author. SOURCE D.H. Akenson, *A Protestant in purgatory: Richard Whately, archbishop of Dublin* (South Bend, IN, 1981), pp 159ff.; Allibone, iii, p. 2662; Allibone Suppl., ii, p. 1507; Boase, vi, p. 837; Leslie & Wallace, p. 1168; B. MacMahon, *Eccentric archbishop. Richard Whately of Redesdale* (Stillorgan, 2005); ODNB; RL; [H. Wale], *Elizabeth Jane Whately: Reminiscences of her life and work* (London, 1894).

W36 *Cousin Mabel's experiences of ritualism* (by Miss E. Jane Whately).
London: Religious Tract Society, 1867. SOURCE Allibone, Suppl., ii, p. 1507; COPAC.
LOCATION Dt.
COMMENTARY 52pp [COPAC].

W37 *Cousin Mabel's experiences: sketches of religious life in England* (by Miss E. Jane Whately).
London: Religious Tract Society, [1870]. SOURCE Allibone, Suppl., ii, p. 1507.
LOCATION Brotherton Library, Leeds.

W38 *Esther's journal; or a tale of Swiss pension life* (by 'A resident').
+ London: James Nisbet & Co., 1876 (ill. C.O.M.). SOURCE Allibone, Suppl., ii, p. 1507; NSTC; COPAC. LOCATION L (destroyed), O.
COMMENTARY Preface by J. [*sic*] Jane Whately is dated from Clarens [Switzerland], Dec. 1875, and may refer to Elizabeth Jane Whately. Allibone attributes this work to her [RL; Allibone].

W39 *Cousin Mabel's sketches of character* (by Miss E. Jane Whately).
+ London: Religious Tract Society, [1881]. SOURCE Allibone, Suppl., ii, p. 1507; COPAC; NSTC. LOCATION L (destroyed), O.
COMMENTARY Religious fiction set in England [RL].

W40 *Stray leaves from Cousin Mabel's sketch-book; or tolerance and intolerance* (by Miss E. Jane Whately).
London: Religious Trace Society, [1883]. SOURCE Allibone, Suppl., ii, p. 1507; COPAC; OCLC. LOCATION L (destroyed), Auburn Univ., Auburn (AL).

W41 *The banished family and The Bohemian confessor* (by Miss E. Jane Whately).
+ London: Religious Tract Society, [1886]. SOURCE Allibone, Suppl., ii, p. 1507; Alston, p. 462. LOCATION L.
COMMENTARY Both stories are set on the Continent and concern the persecution of Lutherans by Catholics (in 'The banished family'), and Mennonites by Catholics (in 'The Bohemian confessor') [ML].

WHATELY, Mrs Elizabeth Pope (also known as **Mrs Whately**), d. 1860. Religious and miscellaneous writer, EPW was the third daughter of William Pope of Hillingdon Hall, Uxbridge (Middx). She married in 1821 Revd Richard Whately§, who later became Church of Ireland archbishop of Dublin. She was the author of *Conversations on the life of Christ* (London, 1833); *English life, social and domestic in the middle of the nineteenth century* (London, 1847), and she contributed a short story to *Friendly contributions for the benefit of three infant schools in the parish of Kensington* (privately printed for Lady Mary Fox, 1834). Her book of geography and travel, *Quicksands on foreign shores* (London, 1854), was published anonymously. She came under the influence of Revd Alexander Dallas of the Irish Church Missions, but her husband was much against the Irish missions, which he thought were ineffective. During the Famine she was a member of a ladies' relief committee. She was the mother of two sons and four daughters, of whom Elizabeth Jane Whately§ and Mary Louisa Whately§ became writers, while Blanche (later Mrs B. Wale) became a poet and published *Songs of the night* (Dublin, 1858). The author Joseph Blanco White§ lived in her home for some time, where he tutored her children. There is an unexplained gap of more that twenty years in the publication of EPW's works. SOURCE D.H. Akenson, *A Protestant in purgatory: Richard Whately, archbishop of Dublin* (South Bend, IN, 1981), pp 208ff; Colman, p. 236; COPAC; DNB [under Richard Whately]; Leslie & Wallace, p. 1168–69; B. MacMahon, *Eccentric archbishop. Richard Whately of Redesdale* (Stillorgan, Co. Dublin, 2005); MVP, p. 481; ODNB; O'Donoghue, p. 477 [see B. Whately]; T. O'Neill, 'The charities and famine ...' in J. Hill & C. Lennon (eds), *Luxury and austerity* (Dublin, 1999), p. 148. E.J. Whately, *The life and work of Mary Louisa Whately* (London, [1890]).

W42   *Village conversations in hard times* (by Mrs Elizabeth Pope Whately).
London: B. Fellowes, 1831. SOURCE OCLC. LOCATION CLU.

W43   *Reverses, or memoirs of the Fairfax family* [anon.].
+ London: B. Fellowes, 1833. SOURCE Allibone, Suppl., iii, p. 2662 (1846 edn);
COPAC; Garside 2, A:26. LOCATION L.

COMMENTARY Sometimes attributed to 'J.W. Parker', but assigned by Garside 2 to EPW.
Fiction for juveniles, written for the author's children 'with the view (beyond mere amusement) to the improvement and correction of their moral tendencies'. The Fairfax family eventually emigrates to Canada [RL; Garside 2].

W44   *The roving bee: or, a peep into many hives* (ed. by Mrs Whately).
+ London: James Nisbet & Co., 1855, 2 vols. (ill. Evans, of the Customs House,
Dublin). LOCATION D, L.

COMMENTARY Given that EPW only edited this volume, it is likely that someone else, perhaps
a relative, was its author. The story tells of the trials and romances of Dora Leighton who,
due to the death of her father and the necessity of putting her brothers through college, has
to work as a governess. The Delaney family in Dublin hires her, but she is fired because she
spends too much time in secret with her brother Jemmy. On her journey home to Cork, she
meets Mr Conyngham, a barrister, and falls in love with him. She secures a position as governess for the Mulhall family at Mulhall Castle, Cork. Mr Conyngham visits, not realizing
that Dora is a governess. Dora is devastated when he proposes to Anna Maria Mulhall, and
becomes very ill. Her uncle, Dr McNeill, visits her and persuades her to leave. She then works
for the Loftus family, but after a year they are in financial straits and go to Germany. Dora
goes to stay at the Delaney's home in Dublin. She becomes religious and tries to repent for
her sins. Mr O'Brien, a clergyman, asks her to marry him [CM].

WHATELY, Miss Jane. See WHATELY, Elizabeth Jane.

WHATELY, M.L. See WHATELY, Mary Louisa.

WHATELY, Mary L. See WHATELY, Mary Louisa.

WHATELY, Mary Louisa, pseud. 'M.L.W.' (known as M.L. Whately and Mary L.
Whately), b. Hailesworth (Suffolk) 1824, d. Egypt 1889. Missionary, poet and religious writer,
MLW was the daughter of Richard Whately§, DD, archbishop of Dublin, and his wife
Elizabeth Pope Whately§ and sister of Elizabeth Jane Whately§. She spent her formative years
in Dublin, to where the family moved in 1831 when her father was appointed archbishop.
They divided their time between a residence in Dublin and a country seat at Redesdale (near
Stillorgan, Co. Dublin). Her sister described her as 'impulsive, hot-tempered, and generous',
and a good storyteller. Her parents encouraged reading, contact with poor neighbours, assistance with the school founded by her father, and the writing of 'simple tales'. MLW went to
Nice and Italy in 1849 and 1850. Around this time, some members of the family were drawn
toward supporting the work of the Irish Missions to the Catholics and numerous poor Italians
in Dublin. In 1856 MLW made her first visit to the East, spent the winter at Cairo (her diaries
of this trip were lost later), and visited the Holy Land. After the death of her mother and
younger sister, she returned to Egypt in 1861 to recover her health, where, using mostly her
own funds, she established Christian schools for the purpose of proselytizing Muslim girls –
and later boys – and to teach them reading and some crafts. For several decades she lived
mostly in Egypt, returning to England only on occasion (her last visit was in 1888). She added
a medical mission to her work in 1879. Among her autobiographical sketches are *Ragged life*

in Egypt (London, 1863), followed by *More about ragged life in Egypt* (London, 1864). From the 1860s to the 1880s she wrote fiction concerning Egypt for the Religious Tract Society. Her sister Elizabeth Jane Whately§ wrote her biography. SOURCE Allibone, iii, pp 2662–3; Allibone Suppl., ii, p. 1507; Boase, iii, p. 1295; Leslie & Wallace, p. 1168; B. MacMahon, *Eccentric archbishop. Richard Whately of Redesdale* (Stillorgan, 2005); E.J. Whately§, *The life and work of Mary Louisa Whately* (London, [1890]).

W45   *The story of a diamond: Illustrative of Egyptian manners and customs* [anon.].
      London: Religious Tract Society, [1867]. SOURCE Allibone, iii, p. 2663; COPAC.
      LOCATION L (destroyed), ICU.
      Philadelphia: American Sunday-School Union, 1868. SOURCE OCLC. LOCATION Univ.
      of Florida.

W46   *Among the huts in Egypt: scenes from real life* (by M.L. Whately).
      Philadelphia: [publisher?], 1868. SOURCE Allibone Suppl., ii, p. 1507.
      New York: Dodd & Mead, [187–] (as *Among the huts in Egypt*). SOURCE RLIN.
      LOCATION NN.
      + London: Seeley, Jackson, & Halliday, 1871. SOURCE Allibone Suppl., ii, p. 1507;
      OCLC. LOCATION L, CtY.
      COMMENTARY No copy of the Philadelphia edn located. Interrelated stories, told in the
      present tense, about life for ordinary Egyptians [ML].

W47   *The prism: Unequally yoked; a tale of Egyptian life, Life in a Swiss chalet; or, the
      good stepmother, From darkness to light; A tale of Spanish life* (by 'M.L.W.', and
      two members of her family, H.W [Wale] and E. M. [Moore]), ed., with a preface by
      E. Jane Whately§).
      + London: Religious Tract Society, [1878]. SOURCE Allibone Suppl., p. 1507; COPAC.
      LOCATION L.
COMMENTARY 'Life in a Swiss chalet' is by H.W. [i.e. Henrietta Wale]; 'From darkness to light' is by E.M. [i.e., Elizabeth Moore], and other stories are by M.L. Whately [COPAC].

W48   *Lost in Egypt, a story from life* (by Miss E.J. [or rather, M.L.] Whately).
      London: Religious Tract Society, [1881]. SOURCE Allibone Suppl., ii, p. 1507; COPAC.
      LOCATION L (destroyed).
      COMMENTARY No copy located. Allibone lists this under MLW [Allibone; RL].

W49   *Scenes from life at Cairo, behind the curtain* (by Mary L. Whately).
      London: Jackson & Halliday, 1883 SOURCE Allibone Suppl., ii, p. 1507 (1882 edn);
      OCLC. LOCATION L.
      COMMENTARY Novel set in Egypt [ML].

W50   *Stories of peasant life on the Nile* (by M.L. Whately).
      London: Religious Tract Society, 1888. SOURCE Allibone Suppl., ii, p. 1507; COPAC.
      LOCATION Univ. of Liverpool.

WHATELY, Revd Richard, b. London 1787, d. Dublin, 1863. Church of England clergy-man, social scientist and prolific man of letters, RW was the son of Joseph Whately of Surrey and Jane Plumer. He studied at Oriel College, Oxford, graduating BA in 1808 in classics and mathematics and MA in 1812. He was ordained and in 1825 took the degrees of BD and LLD. After several years working in a parish, he returned to Oxford as principal of St Alban Hall and professor of political economy at a time when John Henry Newman§ was also there. In 1831 he became archbishop of Dublin and took his seat in the house of lords in 1833. His only known work of fiction was written in Dublin. He spoke out and wrote against trans-portation and slavery, and while opposing public relief during the Famine, was personally gen-erous to voluntary relief organizations. He was one of the commissioners of National Education in Ireland, a vice president of the RIA, and a pioneering social scientist who wrote extensively on religion, on logic, and on political economy. His mannerisms were gently satirized by Charles Lever§ in his *Charles O'Malley* and *Roland Cashel*. His wife, Elizabeth Pope Whately§, and his daughters Elizabeth Jane Whately§ and Mary Louisa Whately§ were also writers, and another daughter, Blanche (later Mrs B. Wale) was a poet. The author Joseph Blanco White§ lived for some time in RW's house as tutor to his children. SOURCE D.H. Akenson, *A Protestant in purgatory: Richard Whately, archbishop of Dublin* (South Bend, IN, 1981); Allibone, iii, pp 2663–5; FitzPatrick, pp 226–7; NCBEL 4, p. 2203, 2512, 2616, 2658; Leslie & Wallace, pp 1168–9; B. MacMahon, *Eccentric archbishop. Richard Whately of Redesdale* (Dublin, 2005); ODNB; RIA/DIB; E.J. Whately, *The life and correspondence of Archbishop Whately* (London, 1866), with two portraits.

W51   *Account of an expedition to the interior of New Holland* [anon.].
       London: Richard Bentley, 1837 (ed. by Lady Mary Fox). SOURCE Ximenes M11/70. LOCATION L.
       London: J.W. Parker, 1860 (as *The Southlanders*). SOURCE Hart cat. 72/174. LOCATION L, E.

COMMENTARY A utopian novel set in central Australia where a group of travellers sets out in Aug. 1835 and discovers a lost civilization of some three or four million people of European origin who have intermixed with tribes of Aborigines. The political, social and religious systems of this nation are described in detail. The system of deporting convicts to Australia is condemned: 'A new settlement with convicted criminals – to form a new nation of the scum and refuse of mankind – appeared to them so preposterous, that for some time they could not help supposing they must have misunderstood their informants'. Note that RW's wife Mrs Elizabeth Pope Whately§ contributed to *Friendly contributions for the benefit of three infant schools* (London, 1834), which was privately printed for Lady Mary Fox [Ximenes M11/70; RL].

WHEELER, Rosina Doyle. See **BULWER LYTTON, Rosina Doyle.**

WHEELWRIGHT, John T. Co-author. See **O'REILLY, John Boyle.**

WHELAND, May. See **BYRNE, May.**

WHITAKER, Evelyn, b. 1857, d. 1903. Prolific author of children's books, mostly religious in nature, EW was probably English. Several of her works were written with an unidentified co-author. Only those with known Irish content are listed below. SOURCE NCBEL 4, p. 1888; NUC; RL.

W52   *Honor Bright; or, the four-leaved shamrock* [anon.].
       + London: W. Wells Gardner, [1879] (ill.). LOCATION L.
       COMMENTARY Children's story about the Brights, an Irish family living in London [ML].

W53   *Peas-blossom* [anon.].
       New York: Young & Co., [188–]. LOCATION NUC.
       London: Wells Gardner, Darton, 1907. SOURCE COPAC. LOCATION Univ. of Liverpool.
       COMMENTARY Fiction for juveniles. An Irish story with a pair of heroines, Nolly and Molly [CM].

'WHITE, Babington', pseud. See **BRADDON, Mary Elizabeth.**

WHITE, J. See **WHITE, James.**

WHITE, James (also known as **J. White**), b. Dublin 1759, d. Wick (Glos.) 1799. Writer of historical fiction, poet and translator, JW was elected a scholar at TCD in 1778 and graduated in 1780. He moved to London, where his interest in contemporary public affairs (the impeachment of a governor of the East India Company) was mirrored in his translation of *The orations of Marcus Tullius Cicero against Caius Cornelius Verres* (London, 1787). His fiction is full of humour and parody and reflects his on-going interest in civic life. He was well-versed in Greek and he was the author of an abolitionist tract, *Hints of a specific plan for the abolition of the slave trade* (London, 1788) which combined satire, economics, a wide knowledge of the law and indignation with powerful appeals to Britons' sense of humanity, stating 'British brutality has become proverbial'. After the French Revolution he published two translations of the work of Rabaut de Saint-Etienne: *The speeches of M. de Mirabeau* (London, 1792) and *The history of the revolution in France* (London, 1792). JW believed the French Revolution could be the inspiration for political reform in England, but he stated that England, unlike France, did not need a revolution. ODNB suggests that some of JW's later conspiratorial delusions could have had some basis in the strong anti-Jacobinism of the government. Some of his poetry was published in *Conway Castle* (London, 1789). His 'Letters to Lord Camden on the state of Ireland', which were praised in the *Gentleman's Magazine* (London, 1799), have not been traced. He wrote three historical novels. Toward the end of his life he became more and more eccentric and he died almost destitute. SOURCE Allibone, iii, pp 2686–7; Brady, p. 245; ODNB; O'Donoghue, p. 478; RIA/DIB; J.M.S. Tompkins, 'James White, esq.: a forgotten humorist', *Review of English Studies*, 3 (1927), pp 146–56.

W54   *Earl Strongbow; or, the history of Richard de Clare and the beautiful Geralda* [anon.].

London: J. Dodsley, 1789, 2 vols. (ill.). SOURCE Allibone, iii, p. 2686; Raven 2, 1789:71; Forster 2, 4774; ESTC t033003. LOCATION C, CtY.

London: Dodsley; Dublin: P. Byrne, L. White, P. Wogan, P. Parker, J. Moore & H. Halpin, 1789, 2 vols. SOURCE Brown 2, 1613; Block, p. 251; McBurney & Taylor, 957; Hardy, 814; ESTC t33003. LOCATION Di, L, IU.

+ Dublin: P. Byrne, L. White, P. Wogan, P. Parker, J. Moore & J. Halpin, 1789, 2 vols. in 1. SOURCE Allibone, iii, pp 2686–7; Raven 2, 1789:71; ESTC t133456. LOCATION Dm, L.

Londres [Paris]: Maradan, 1789, 2 vols. (trans. as *Le Comte Strongbow ou l'histoire de Richard de Clare et de la belle Geralde*). SOURCE Raven 2, 1789:71; ESTC 133456. LOCATION L.

Helmstädt: Fleckeisen, 1790 (trans. by Georg Friedrich Beneke as *Graf Strongbow oder die Geschichte Richard's de Clare und der schönen Geralda*). SOURCE Raven 2, 1789:71. LOCATION Staatsbibliothek, Berlin.

COMMENTARY A Gothic historical novel. The narrator visits Chepstow Castle on the Wye in Wales, a former castle of Strongbow. He settles in a part of the castle that is still inhabited. There he encounters Strongbow's ghost who appears to him night after night and tells the story of his life: how he was trained in chivalry under the earl and countess of Shrewsbury, how he fell in love with Lady Geralda. He describes great tournaments between the Welsh and English knights and other events. Then Diarmuid MacMurrough, king of Leinster, appears and prevails on Strongbow and the other knights to conquer Ireland. There is a description of the invasion and the capture of Wexford and it includes a burlesque and satire of contemporary manners. Some of the characters are parodies of English statesman Charles James Fox, prime minister William Pitt, and the playwright Richard Brinsley Sheridan. Tompkins suggests the character of Strongbow is a direct reference to Lord Temple, former lord lieutenant of Ireland [ML; Brown 2; Frank, 472; ODNB; Tompkins, p. 151].

W55 *The adventures of John of Gaunt, Duke of Lancaster* (by James White).
London: G.G.J. & J. Robinson, 1790, 3 vols. SOURCE Allibone, iii, p. 2686; Forster 2, 4771; Raven 2, 1790:72; ESTC n004252; NYPL. LOCATION L, NN.
+ Dublin: J. Jones, W. Jones, Grueber & M'Allister & R. White, 1790. SOURCE Raven 2, 1790:72; ESTC t107032. LOCATION PC, Dt.
Helmstädt: Fleckeisen, 1791 (trans. as *Johann von Gaunt, Herzog von Lancaster*). SOURCE Raven 2, 1790:72. LOCATION Union cat. Northern Germany.
COMMENTARY An historical novel set in England in the fourteenth century. Extracts from the novel were published in the *Lady's Magazine* (London, 1790), the *Weekly Entertainer* (Shelburne, 1790), and the *Hibernian Magazine* (Dublin, 1790) [Mayo, 659–60].

W56 *The adventures of King Richard Coeur-de-Lion. To which is added, The death of Lord Falkland: a poem* (by J. White).
London: T. & J. Evans, 1791, 3 vols. SOURCE Allibone, iii, p. 2687; Forster 2, 4772; Raven 2, 1791:72; Hardy, 813; ESTC t057805. LOCATION L, IU.
Dublin: Arthur Grueber, 1791, 2 vols. SOURCE Raven 2, 1791:72; ESTC t217606. LOCATION Dt.
Dublin: James Moore, 1791, 2 vols. SOURCE Jarndyce cat. 129/402. COMMENTARY No copy of the Dublin, Moore edn located other than the one listed by Jarndyce [RL].
Dublin: Printed by Zachariah Jackson for the Company of Booksellers, 1791, 2 vols. SOURCE Rowan cat. 55/372; ESTC t208324. Location D.
COMMENTARY This historical novel may have been inspired by Gréty's opera *Richard Coeur de Lion*, which was performed in Dublin in 1787 (first performed in Paris in 1784). Embedded in the story are two travellers' tales related to Richard Coeur-de-Lion: one of travels in central Asia, and the other of travels in arctic Asia or Siberia [Rowan cat. 55/372; T.J. Walsh, *Opera in Dublin 1705–1797* (Dublin, 1973), p. 260].

WHITE, Joseph, fl. 1774. Epistolary novelist, JW probably was Irish since he published only in Dublin. SOURCE RL.
W57 *Charles and Teresa. An original novel, in a series of letters, founded on truth* (by Joseph White; dedicated to Mrs Christmas).
Dublin: Printed [for the author?] by J. Williams, J.A. Husband, T. Walker & C. Jenkin, 1774. SOURCE Raven 2, 1774:35; ESTC t064458. LOCATION Dt, L, CSmH.
COMMENTARY Epistolary novel, said to have been based on *Anecdotes of the reigns of Henry III of France, and Henry of Navarre*, but no such book has been identified. The closest is L.L. Prault's *L'Esprit d'Henri IV, ou anecdotes les plus intéressantes* (Paris, 1770) [Raven 2].

WHITE, Joseph Blanco (Don José Maria Blanco y Crespo), b. Seville (Spain) 1774, d. Liverpool (Lancs.) 1841. Spanish priest, religious writer and poet of Irish ancestry, JBW's family was part of a small Irish colony in Seville. Although ordained, he later abandoned the church of Rome, moved to Liverpool and became a Unitarian. He had roots in Oxford, and appears in many contemporary memoirs of the early Tractarian days, including those of John Henry Newman§ and Richard Whately§, in whose home in Dublin he lived for several years while tutoring Whately's children. Along with Mrs Elizabeth Whately§ he contributed a short story to *Friendly contributions for the benefit of three infant schools in the parish of Kensington* (privately printed for Lady Mary Fox, 1834), and also contributed to *Forget-Me-Not* (London, 1825) and the *Bijou* (London, 1828). He was described by A.S. Farrar in *Critical history of free thought* (London, 1862) as having 'a mind in which faith and doubt were perpetually wag-ing war, till the grave closed over his truth-searching and care-worn spirit'. SOURCE Allibone, iii, pp 2689–90; British Fiction (Update 1, under 1822); *Dublin and London Magazine* (London), 1825, p. 286; Jarndyce cat. 162/477; NCBEL 4, p. 2649; ODNB; O'Donoghue, p. 478; T & B, 1751; Wolff, iii, p. 163, iv, p. 259.

W58   *Vargas: A tale of Spain* [anon.].
London: Baldwin, Cradock & Joy, 1822, 3 vols. SOURCE British Fiction; COPAC; Garside, 1822:80. LOCATION Corvey CME 3–628–48858–3.
COMMENTARY Attribution is defended by Martin Murphy's 'The Spanish "Waverley" …' in *Atlantis* 17 (1995), pp 168–80 [British Fiction].

W59   *Second travels of an Irish gentleman in search of a religion. With notes and illustrations, NOT by the editor of "Captain Rock's Memoirs"* [anon.] (dedicated to the people of Ireland).
+ Dublin: Richard Milliken & Son; London: B. Fellowes, 1833, 2 vols. SOURCE Block, p. 251; Wolff, 4903; Garside 2, C:8. LOCATION Dt, L, DLC.
COMMENTARY The dedication addresses the people of Ireland 'whose virtue, improvement and happiness must depend, not on the antiquity or nationality but on the truth of the religion'. Prompted by Thomas Moore's§ *Travels of an Irish gentleman in search of a religion* (London, 1833), and concerns religious controversies between Protestants and Roman Catholics [RL].

WHITE, L. Esmonde. See WHITE, Capt. Laurence Esmonde.

WHITE, Capt. Laurence Esmonde (know as L. Esmonde White), b. Newlands, Ferns (Co. Wexford) 1809. Story writer, LEW became a JP for Cos. Wexford and Carlow and served in the army. He was resident at Newlands (later called Ballyrankin, Co. Wexford) in 1868. SOURCE Browne, p. 152; RIA/DIB; Rowe & Scallan, 178.

W60   *Irish coast tales of love and adventure* (by L. Esmonde White).
+ London: Smith, Elder & Co., 1865. SOURCE Allibone, iii, p. 2690; Brown, 1665. LOCATION D, Dt, L, MH, InND Loeber coll.
London: Chapman & Hall, [1869] (as *The lovers of Ballyvookan; Irish coast tales of love and adventure*). SOURCE Topp 3, p. 357. LOCATION GEU.
COMMENTARY Contents: 'The black channel of Cloughnagawn', 'The lovers of Ballyvookan' [RL].

WHITE, Rhoda E. See WHITE, Rhoda Elizabeth.

WHITE, Rhoda Elizabeth (née Waterman; known as Rhoda E. White), b. probably New York *c.*1820, d. 1866. American instructional and moral fiction writer and biographer, REW was the daughter of Thomas and Whitney Waterman, prominent New York Episcopalians, but she converted to catholicism and married James W. White, a lawyer of Irish descent who later became a judge. Her books of instruction for young mothers were based on her experiences as a mother of eight children. She wrote a memorable biography of her daughter, *Memoirs and letters of Jenny C. White Del Bal* (Boston, 1868), that describes life in Panama during the 1860s revolution. SOURCE Allibone, iii, p. 2690; Allibone Suppl., ii, p. 1513; Blain, p. 1159.

W61   *What will the world say? An American tale of real life* (by Rhoda E. White; preface by Bernard O'Reilly, DD, DLit, dated from Dublin, 8 Mar. 1885).
+ Dublin, London: James Duffy & Sons; New York: Laurence Kehoe, [1885].
LOCATION L, NUC, InND Loeber coll.
COMMENTARY The preface states that the story is based on facts. The main character is Daniel Courtney of Louisiana, a very rich Irish-American who is a representative in Congress in

Washington (DC). He has secretly married a young girl, Angelina, who has borne him a daughter, Pura. He keeps postponing the announcement of his marriage, which leads to many complications and misery. Angelina hears malicious stories about his romantic involvements in Washington and decides to leave for France. She leaves Pura behind to be taken care of by her husband, not realizing that the stories are false. Since Pura's presence is awkward for him, he finds a couple to adopt her. Daniel's estate agents work on him to write a will in their favour. When he dies, he has not acknowledged his marriage or his daughter. Angelina leads a sad existence in France, but eventually accepts a marriage offer [ML].

WHITE, Richard Grant, pseud. **'Outis'**. Novelist, possibly of Scottish background, it is very likely that this RGW is different from a namesake (1821–85), who was an American editor, philologist and author. SOURCE Halkett & Laing, iii, p. 173; RL.

W62 *The Irish middleman; a true story of a Scotch settler* (by 'Outis').
    + London: R. Sutton & Co., [1892]. SOURCE Halkett & Laing, iii, p. 173. LOCATION L.

COMMENTARY Set in Ireland, England and America and describes political unrest in the second-half of the nineteenth century. Prime minister William Gladstone's policies are derided and those of the Unionists praised [ML].

WHITE, Revd Robert, pseud. **'Owen Blayney'**, fl. 1898. Historical novelist, RW was of possible Irish origin and perhaps can be identified with Revd Robert White (1839–1913) who was educated at St Bee's College, Cambridge, and was ordained in 1878. He became curate of Ballinderry (Co. Antrim, 1878–80); Aghaderg (1880–82); rector of Drumgath (1882–84); rector of Magherally (1884–90); and curate of Annaclone (1886–90), all in Co. Down. His election to Annaclone led to a bitter parochial dispute. A large number of parishioners wished to have a different minister and set up a rival congregation in the Orange Hall, but RW by his gentle, consistent character won them all round. He married Anna Maria, daughter of William Matthews of Grange (Co. Tyrone), who died in Belfast in 1927. SOURCE Leslie, *Down*, p. 119; RL.

W63 *The MacMahon; or, the story of the seven Johns* (by 'Owen Blayney'; dedicated to 'my country and to her children everywhere').
    + Westminster [London]: Archibald Constable & Co., 1898. SOURCE Brown, 221 [under Blayney]. LOCATION Dt, D, L, InND Loeber coll.

COMMENTARY Historical fiction set in Ulster during the Williamite War (1689–91) and its aftermath and based on a Co. Monaghan tradition. Art MacMahon of Corraglen, an officer in King James's army, leaves his expectant wife at the house of a Protestant neighbour, John McKinley. He returns to be present at the baptism of his son, after which he is killed at the siege of Athlone. His wife and son stay with the McKinleys, and the son is brought up in the Catholic faith and to regard himself as The MacMahon. McKinley's wife dies and he continues to look after the young MacMahon, who is a good-for-nothing. He and McKinley's daughter fall in love. Her father forbids this association, and sends MacMahon on his way. Eventually, MacMahon joins the rapparees, and kidnaps the daughter. McKinley and six of his Protestant neighbours, all named John, go in pursuit and McKinley hangs MacMahon on the windmill at Carrickmacross (Co. Monaghan). After his daughter dies, McKinley moves to America [ML; Brown].

'WHITELOCK, A.', pseud. See **FINLAY, Fr Thomas A.**

WHITING, Mary Bradford, fl. 1892. Novelist and writer of religious fiction. OCLC lists her as Mary Bradford-Whiting. SOURCE Alston, p. 464; OCLC.

W64   *Denis O'Niel* (by Mary Bradford Whiting).
    + London: Richard Bentley & Son, 1892. SOURCE Alston, p. 464. LOCATION L.
COMMENTARY Set in Ireland, England and Australia. Denis, a medical student, has been convicted for his involvement with an insurrectionist group and is transported to Australia. In prison he is allowed to practice as a doctor. He falls in love with a nurse, who dies. Denis is killed soon after by a bullet from a member of the insurrectionist group, who had come to consider him a traitor [ML].

'WHITNEY, Harry', pseud. See KENNEDY, Patrick.

WHITTAKER, Capt. Frederick, b. London 1838, d. Mount Vernon (New York) 1889. Historical and adventure novelist and biographer, FW grew up partly on the Continent and went with his family to the US about 1850. He studied architecture and served as a volunteer in the New York cavalry during the Civil War. He worked as a book agent; taught school; and contributed to Mayne Reid's§ magazine *Onward* (1869–70) and to other periodicals such as the Galaxy, the *Fireside Companion*, Beadle's *Young New Yorker, Saturday Journal* and the *Army and Navy Journal* (all New York), for which he worked as assistant editor before his death from an accidental gun shot wound. In addition to his many swashbuckling nickel and dime novels he wrote a sympathetic biography of Gen. George Custer. Only works with an Irish connection are listed below. SOURCE Allibone Suppl., ii, pp 1517–18; Brown 2, p. 270; Dime novels; ODNB; Wright, iii, p. 591.
W65   *The Irish Brigade. A tale of Fontenoy* (by Capt. Frederick Whittaker).
    London: Henderson, 1874. SOURCE Brown 2, 1618.
    New York: Beadle & Adams, 1879 (as *The Irish captain: A tale of Fontenoy*; Beadle's New York Dime Library). SOURCE OCLC. LOCATION NRU (1879, 4th edn).
COMMENTARY No copy of the London edn located. Historical fiction recording the dashing exploits of Gerald Desmond, an officer in Clare's Brigade; his adventures on campaign and in the French court. It introduces historical personages such as King Louis XIV, François-Marie Voltaire, Madame de Pompadour and the duc du Richelieu [Brown 2].
W66   *The brave boy hunters of Kentucky* (by Capt. Frederick Whittaker).
    New York: Beadle & Adams, 1876. SOURCE Brown 2, 1617; RLIN (New York, Ivers, 1908 edn). LOCATION DCL (New York, Ivers, 1908 edn).
    Cleveland: A. Westbrook, 1908. SOURCE RLIN. LOCATION DCL.
COMMENTARY No copy of New York, 1876 edn located. Set in Kentucky around 1786. Terence O'Flynn manages to extricate his boy hunter friends from many a tight corner [Brown 2; RL].
W67   *Seamus O'Brien. A tale of '98* (by Capt. Frederick Whittaker).
    New York: Beadle & Adams, 1880. SOURCE Brown 2, 1619.
COMMENTARY No copy located. Historical fiction: A tale of the 1798 uprising [Brown 2; RL].
W68   *The mad hussars; or, the Os and the Macs* (by Capt. Frederick Whittaker).
    New York: Beadle & Adams; London: Aldine Publishing Co., 1883–1884. SOURCE Brown 2, 1620; OCLC. LOCATION Univ. of Texas, Austin.
COMMENTARY Dime novel. Historical fiction relating the adventures of four Irish soldiers of fortune in the army of Frederick the Great [Brown 2].

WHITTY, Michael James, pseud. 'M.J.W.', b. Enniscorthy (Bog West, Mayglass, according to Browne, also Co. Wexford) 1795, d. Liverpool (Lancs.) 1873. Short story writer, journalist, editor and civic leader, MJW was the son of a maltster and was intended for the priesthood. His family lived at Nicharee, near Duncormick (Co. Wexford; the house much altered now). He moved to London in the early 1820s and his *Tales of Irish life* appeared in 1824 (a year before John§ and Michael Banim's§ *Tales by the O'Hara family*). This was among the earliest published collections of Irish short stories in the English language. Several translations appeared in France and Germany soon after. The stories were illustrated by, among others, his friend George Cruikshank. MJW contributed regularly to Irish periodicals and became the editor of and chief writer for the London-based *Dublin and London Magazine* in 1825 (published Jan.–June 1827 as *Robbin's London and Dublin Magazine*). Much of what he wrote for this periodical appeared under various pseuds (e.g. 'Captain Rock' and 'Rory O'Rourke') and included several series such as, 'Superstitions of the Irish peasantry'; 'Legendary tales of the Irish peasantry'; and in the 3rd volume (1827), 'Traditional tales of the Irish peasantry'. He also contributed short stories to the *Pocket Magazine* (*Robin's series*, London, 1828), and from 1833 onward to the *Ladies Pocket Magazine* (London). Politically, he was an advocate of Catholic emancipation. In London, he married a sister of the journalist E.B. Neill, with whom he had a daughter and a son. MJW moved to Liverpool to become editor of the *Liverpool Journal*, which began in 1830, and he held that position until he was appointed chief constable of Liverpool in 1836. He organized the first police force outside of London, as well as an efficient fire brigade. When he retired in 1848, he purchased the *Liverpool Journal* and later, when the stamp duty on newspapers was removed, he published in 1855 the Liverpool *Daily Post*, the first penny-daily newspaper in England. MJW also published *A proposal for diminishing crime, misery, and poverty* (Liverpool, 1865) and wrote a guide to Liverpool (1868). He was buried in Anfield cemetery, Liverpool. SOURCE Allibone, iii, p. 2706 [under J.M. Whitty]; Boase, iii, pp 1329–30; Boylan, p. 400; Brady, p. 246; Brown, p. 308; Browne, pp 153–4; W. Graham, *English literary periodicals* (London, 1930), p. 273; J. Hennig, 'Michael Whitty', IBL, 1, (Feb. 1947), pp 39–44; Hogan, 2, p. 1238; IBL, 8 (1916–17), pp 53–6; Irish pseudonyms; McKenna, p. 337; J. O'K. Murray, *Prose and poetry of Ireland* (New York, 1877), p. 436; ODNB; O'Donoghue, pp 479–80; RIA/DIB; RL; Rowe & Scallan, 783; Tiger cat. 4–98/260.

W69   *Tales of Irish life, illustrative of the manners, customs, and condition of the people* [anon.; compiler: Michael James Whitty].

+ London: J. Robins & Co., 1824, 2 vols. (ill. George Crookshank, Bonner, J. Thompson, W. Hughes). SOURCE Brown, 1666; British Fiction; Garside, 1824:96; Grail; McKenna, p. 337; Rafroidi, ii, p. 354; Wolff, 7204. LOCATION Corvey CME 3–628–51018–X, Ireland related fiction, Dt, L, MH, InND Loeber coll.

+ Paris: Pillet Âiné, 1826, 2 vols. (trans. as *L'Hermite en Irlande, ou observations sur les moeurs et usages des Irlandais au commencement du xixᵉ siècle; faisant suite à la collection des moeurs françaises, anglaises, italiennes, espagnoles* [anon.] (ill., including map of Ireland). SOURCE Brown, 37; Hogan 2, p. 1238. LOCATION Heavey coll., Athlone Public Library, L, InND.

COMMENTARY *Paris edn* See notes below.

+ Breslau: Josef Mar & Romp, 1826, 2 vols. (trans. as *Irländische Erzählungen. zur Kenntniss der Sitten, der Gebrauche und des Volksleben in Irland*). SOURCE NSTC, 2I4038. LOCATION L, NUC.

COMMENTARY Stories that probably originate in Co. Wexford. The preface mentions that 'Less is actually known in [England] of the real state of Ireland than of the regions beyond the Ganges and Mississippi ...', and that this volume is an attempt to correct the situation. MJW stated that he had 'witnessed most of the scenes he described, and knew several of the persons whose characters he has delineated'. John Banim§ in a letter to his brother Michael§ may have referred to the appearance of this title, and writes about the race, 'pen against pen', between the two brothers and MJW to get their book out first. MJW's volumes, judging from the imprint, were published first. They consist of sixteen tales about Irish peasant life and were reviewed in Whitty's *Dublin and London Magazine* (London, 1825), pp 36–41. Contents of the London edn: 'Limping Mogue', 'The rebel', 'The absentee', 'The robbery', 'The witch of Scollough's gap', 'The informer', 'The poor man's daughter', 'Poor Mary', 'North and South; or, prejudice removed', 'The priest's niece', 'The common', 'Turncoat Watt; or, village politics', 'The last chieftain of Erin', 'The fair maniac', 'Protestant Bill', 'Indulgent landlord'. The French edn has been wrongly ascribed in RLIN to Felix MacDonagh, while Brown (37) ascribes it to MJW. However, the French edn has twice as many stories, and probably includes some by poet and periodical writer Thomas Furlong, which under his pseud. 'The hermit in Ireland' (the title given to the French edn) were first published in the *Dublin and London Magazine*. Contents of the French edn: 'Le Cunnemarra', 'Le naufrage', 'Le bandit', 'L'indolence', 'Mogue le boiteux', 'Dissentions religieuses', 'Le rebelle', 'La sorcière de Scollough's Gap', 'La contrebande', 'Le propriétaire', 'Distillation frauduleuse', 'Le marécages', 'Les bonnes gens', 'Le cluricaunes', 'La pêche', 'Le dernier des chefs de la verte Erin', 'La veillée des morts', 'Les esprits', 'La pauvre Marie', 'Les absents', 'Le retour de l'absent', 'Les paysans', 'Bill le Protestant', 'La rivière de Lee', 'Le préjugé vaincu', 'Forêts souterraines', 'Turncoat Watt, ou l'apostat', 'Le tours rondes', 'Le lac de Killarney', 'Le double vengeance', 'La chaussée des géans', 'Dublin' [ML; RL; IBL, 8 (1916–17), p. 53; J.O'K. Murray, *The prose and poetry of Ireland* (New York, 1877), p. 436].

W70   *Robert Emmet* (preface by 'M.J.W.').

+ London: Longmans, Green & Co.; Dublin: McGlashan & Gill; Liverpool: R.H. Fraser, [1870]. LOCATION L.

COMMENTARY First serialized in the *London and Dublin Magazine* (London, 1825), where it was signed by 'Godfrey K—n'. Considerably revsd by MJW when published later. A story about the last few months of Robert Emmet's life, told by an Englishman, who came to visit his relatives in Co. Wicklow. Little action ensues. Most of the novel consists of discussions by the Englishman, his relatives, Emmet, and others about nationalism, Irish history, religion, and previous uprisings as early as the fourteenth century. The narrator considers Emmet naïve and misguided. Contains an appendix on the relationship between Thomas Moore§ and Emmet, and between Emmet and Sarah Curran [ML].

WHYTE-MELVILLE, G.J. See **WHYTE-MELVILLE, Maj. George John**.

WHYTE-MELVILLE, Maj. George John (known as **G.J. Whyte-Melville**), b. Fife (Argyll, Scotland) 1821, d. Vale of Pewsey (Wilts.) 1878. Army officer and novelist, GJW-M was the son of John Whyte-Melville and Catherine Osborne. Eton-educated and a member of the Coldstream Guards, he fought in the Crimean War and his novel *The interpreter* (London, 1858) vividly describes the siege of Sevastopol and trench slaughter. After retiring from the army he wrote popular novels, many about hunting and racing and many with historical topics. He used the proceeds for philanthropic causes and especially to create reading rooms for grooms and stable boys. He encouraged Sophia Florence Montgomery§ to publish her stories. He died in a hunting accident. SOURCE Allibone, ii, p. 1264 [under Melville]; Allibone Suppl., ii, p. 1102 [under Melville]; Brown, p. 308; NCBEL 4, p. 1439 (list of novels); ODNB; Sutherland, pp 671–2; Wolff, iv, pp 262–4.

W71   *Satanella: a story of Punchestown* (by G.J. Whyte-Melville).

London: Chapman & Hall, 1872, 2 vols (ill. Lucy E. Kemp-Welch). SOURCE Brown, 1667 (1873 edn); Topp 2, p. 386; NCBEL 3, p. 971; OCLC. LOCATION L, InND Loeber coll. (London, Ward [1902] edn).

Berlin: Asher & Co.; New York: J.B. Lippincott & Co. (Asher's Collection of English Authors, vol. 3). SOURCE OCLC. LOCATION NN.

'Wife of a Chergyman'

COMMENTARY A romance set around horses and riding. An English officer, Mr Walters (called Daisy by his friends), buys a horse in Connemara. He takes it to London, where he lends it to Miss Douglas, a mysterious young woman who is called Satanella. Miss Douglas is in love with Daisy, who thinks of her as a friend, while the older Gen. St Josephs is in love with her. Daisy takes his horse to Ireland to train it for a race at Punchestown (Co. Kildare). He needs to win this race, because he is deeply in debt. Miss Douglas and her chaperone go to Ireland to watch the race. They stay with the Macormacs, whose daughter Nora is in love with Daisy. Daisy's horse loses the race by a fraction. The loss ruins Daisy as he is £3,000 in debt. He hides from his creditors in Ireland. In the meantime, Miss Douglas accepts the general's suit and asks to borrow £3,000, which she sends anonymously to Daisy. He finds out who his benefactress is and feels that the least he can do is to offer to marry her. Since Miss Douglas is already betrothed, she refuses. Daisy is visibly relieved and marries Nora. Miss Douglas feels that she can not love the general as he should be loved, and she disappears without a trace. Daisy and his wife and the general meet at a hunt where there is a splendid horsewoman on a splendid horse: Miss Douglas and Daisy's horse. She is far ahead of the other riders. Her horse stumbles and breaks its neck, and Miss Douglas is also mortally injured. Before she dies she tells the general that she loves him [ML].

'WIFE OF A CLERGYMAN', fl. 1846. Pseudonym of a religious fiction writer.

W72   *Fanny and Lucy; or, nature and grace exemplified* (by 'The wife of a clergyman'). Dublin: P. Dixon Hardy & Sons [for the Religious Book and Tract Depository for Ireland], 1846, 3rd edn. SOURCE OCLC. LOCATION UCD.
COMMENTARY Advertised in [anon.], *The history of Susan Blake. A true story* (Dublin, 1846) [RL].

'WIFE OF AN OFFICER', pseud. See **PATRICK, Mrs F.C.**

WIL, Ernest de. See **DE WIL, Ernest**.

'A WILD IRISHMAN', fl. 1860s. Pseudonym of a writer of 'penny dreadfuls'.

W73   *The boy brigand; or, the dark king of the mountains. A tale of Italy* (by 'A wild Irishman').
London: Henry Lea, [c.1865] (ill. Robert Prowse, Edward Brewtnall or T. Shepherd, E. Brett, Falcon Coullie, Edwin Jewitt, George Measom, E. Whymper). SOURCE J & S, 41. LOCATION L.
COMMENTARY Published as a 'penny dreadful' in 33 parts [J & S, 41].

WILDE, Lady Jane Francesca Agnes (née Elgee; known as **Lady Wilde**), b. Dublin (not Wexford as in Hogan) 1821 (but she claimed 1826), d. London 1896. Poet, translator and woman of letters, JFAW was the daughter of a solicitor, Charles Elgee, (and not Archdeacon Elgee as stated by Brady) and Sarah Kingsbury and was a grand-niece of novelist Charles Maturin§. Little is known of her childhood but she was well-educated and was fluent in French, German and Italian and studied Greek and the classics. As a young woman she became an ardent nationalist and Young Irelander, contributing nationalistic verse to the *Nation* (Dublin) under her pseudonym, which became famous throughout Ireland and the US. Several leaders she wrote for this magazine were considered so seditious it was temporarily closed down. Besides poetry, she wrote stories, essays, travel accounts and biography and undertook numerous translations. She was a committed feminist; advocating women's rights and campaigning for education for women. She wrote 'A new era in Irish and English social life'

(*Gentlewoman*, [London] Jan. 1883) in support of the Married Women's Property Act of 1883 that gave married women control over their own money within marriage. In 1851 she married Dr William R.W. Wilde§, a prominent Dublin opthamological surgeon. She befriended the authors William Carleton§, Samuel Ferguson§ and Charles Lever§. After a series of family tragedies and her husband's death in 1876 she moved to London to be near her sons. Needing money, she published a number of volumes on folklore based on her husband's works, and wrote for London periodicals including *Pall Mall Gazette*, the *Queen*, *Tinsley's* and the *Burlington Magazine*. She completed and published in 1880 her husband's biography as well as his *Memoir of Gabriel Beranger*, and edited two of his books on Irish folklore (listed under Sir William R.W. Wilde§). In London she was friendly with Irish writers George Moore§, George Bernard Shaw§ and William Butler Yeats§. She was a founder-member of the Irish Literary Society in London. A collection of essays, *Notes on men, women, and books* (London, 1891), included pieces on – among others – Lady Blessington§ and Thomas Moore§. In her later years she was supported by a grant from the Royal Literary Fund, a pension from the civil list in recognition of her husband's work, and by her son Oscar Wilde§. After his conviction for homosexuality she became a recluse and died in poverty soon after his incarceration. She was buried in Kensal Green cemetery (London), where her grave remained without a headstone and from whence she was removed to an unmarked grave in the same cemetery. For her portraits and papers, see ODNB. SOURCE Allibone, iii, p. 2718; Allibone Suppl., ii, p. 1521; Blain, pp 1015–16 [under Speranza]; Boylan, p. 401; Brady, p. 247; Brown, p. 308; Colman, pp 76–80 [under Elgee]; Field Day, iv, p. 894, v, p. 12 and passim; W.E. Hall, p. 163; Hogan 2, pp 1243–4; Irish pseudonyms; McKenna, pp 338–41; J. Melville, *Mother of Oscar. The life of Jane Francesca Wilde* (London, 1994); MVP, pp 496–7; NCBEL 4, p. 693; OCIL, p. 599; ODNB; O'Donoghue, p. 481; RIA/DIB; RL; T. de Vere White, *The parents of Oscar Wilde* (London, 1967); H. Wyndham, *Speranza. A biography of Lady Wilde* (London, 1951).

W74   *Essays and stories* (by Lady Wilde).
    London: A. Keller, 1907. SOURCE NCBEL 3, p. 1905; OCLC. LOCATION NN.
    + Boston: C.T. Brainard, 1909. SOURCE NCBEL 3, p. 1905; OCLC. LOCATION MH.
    New York: Lamb, [*c*.1909]. SOURCE RLIN.
COMMENTARY Contents of the Boston edn (excluding poetry): 'American women', 'Irish leaders and martyrs', 'The pet as teacher', 'The vision of the Vatican', 'Suitability of dress', 'The destiny of humanity', 'Venus victrix', 'Spiritual affinity', 'The world's new phases', 'The bondage of woman', 'A night with the fairies', 'A Legend of shark', 'The doctor's visit', 'Fairy help', 'Western isles', 'St. Patrick and the witch' [ML].

WILDE, Oscar. See Wills WILDE, Oscar Fingal O'Flahertie Wills.

WILDE, Oscar Fingal O'Flahertie Wills (known as Oscar Wilde), b. Dublin 1854, d. Paris 1900. Playwright, poet, novelist, short story writer, wit and aesthete, OFO'FWW was the son of Sir William R. Wilde§ and Lady Jane Francesca Elgee Wilde§. He had a brilliant career as a student at TCD and at Magdalen College, Oxford, where he graduated BA in 1878 and won the Newdigate Prize for his poem 'Ravenna'. At Oxford, he expounded his aesthetic philosophy, 'art for art's sake', and was renowned for his brilliance, wit and eccentricity. He was in love with a Dublin woman, Florence Balcombe, but she transferred her affections to Bram Stoker§. He published in a number of Dublin publications such as the *Dublin University Magazine*, the *Nation* and the *Irish Monthly* before moving to London in 1879, where his mother and brother Willie also lived following the death of his father in 1876. There he published poems; worked as a book reviewer; and later as an editor (*Woman's World*, London,

1887). In 1882, to make some money, he made a successful tour of the US, lecturing on such topics as 'The house beautiful'; 'The English renaissance'; 'The decorative arts'; and 'Irish poets and poetry in the nineteenth century'. In New York he made the acquaintance of Dion Boucicault§, whose friendship enabled an early play of his, *Vera*, to be produced, with mixed success. After a stay in Paris, where he met Victor Hugo, Paul Verlaine, Stephane Mallarmé and Émile Zola, he returned to England and married Constance Mary Lloyd of Dublin in 1884. His literary life flourished as he became celebrated for his poems, stories, and art and social criticism. In his review of J.A. Froude's§ *The two chiefs of Dunboy* (London, 1889), which appeared in the *Pall Mall Gazette* (London, 1889), he severely critiqued British imperialism in Ireland. In a critical essay 'Intentions: the decay of dying' published in 1891 he used a dialogue form for juxtaposing ideas that was later imitated by William Butler Yeats§ and James Joyce. Of his stories written for his children, the most famous is 'The little prince', which remains popular. His most famous fictional prose work, *The picture of Dorian Gray* (London, 1891), appeared first in *Lippincott's Magazine* (New York, 1890). It produced a storm of criticism and Wilde re-wrote much of it before publication in 1891. He is best known for his brilliant epigrams and for his plays, many of which remain part of the backbone of the theatrical repertoire worldwide, including 'Lady Windemere's fan' (first performed, 1892); 'A woman of no importance' (first performed, 1892); 'Salomé' (initially banned by the censor); 'An ideal husband' (first performed, 1895); and 'The importance of being Earnest' (first performed, 1895). His friendship and infatuation with Lord Alfred Douglas brought him notoriety and ruin. The marquess of Queensberry, Lord Douglas's father, objected to the liaison, and Wilde took action against Queensberry for criminal libel. Wilde lost the case and was later arrested for homosexual offences. He was sentenced to two years' imprisonment with hard labour, part of which he spent in Reading Jail, which became the subject of his most famous poem 'The ballad of Reading Gaol'. The family home and possessions were sold and, to avoid the scandal, his wife and sons left for her brother's home in Switzerland, where they changed their last name to Holland. His experiences in prison spurred him to write movingly to the press on the plight of prisoners and the mistreatment of young children committed for petty crimes. While incarcerated, he wrote an apologia, *De profundis*, in the form of a long letter to Douglas, the first complete publication of which was not until 1962. On his release in 1897, ill and impoverished, he left England and spent the rest of his life in Italy and France, living off an allowance from his wife, which ceased when he took up with Douglas again, and a small annuity provided to him by friends. For a while he used the name Sebastian Melmoth, the doomed hero of *Melmoth the wanderer*, a novel by his ancestor Charles Maturin§. He died in Paris of cerebral meningitis, after receiving the last rites of the Roman Catholic church. He is buried at Père Lachaise cemetery. For a detailed biography and critical assessment of Wilde as a playwright, see Hogan 2, ODNB, RIA/DIB and sources below. His manuscripts, notebooks, letters and other papers can be found in libraries in Ireland, England and the US (see lists in NCBEL and ODNB). For his portraits, see ODNB. SOURCE Allibone Suppl., ii, p. 1521; P.B. Behrendt, *Oscar Wilde: Eros and aesthetics* (London, New York, 1991); Boylan, pp 401–2; Burke's, p. 1217; R. Ellmann, *Oscar Wilde* (New York, London, 1987); Field Day, i, pp 505, 507, ii , pp 380–3, 514 and passim, iii, p. 2 and passim, iv, p. 756 and passim, v, pp 756 and passim; Hogan 2, pp 1244–9 (includes extensive list of reference works); Igoe, pp 277–82; Irish pseudonyms; LPV, p. 512; NCBEL 4, pp 2060–76; OCIL, pp 599–601; ODNB; O'Donoghue, pp 481–2; RIA/DIB; P.E. Smith & M.S. Holland (eds.), *Oscar Wilde's Oxford notebooks: a portrait of a mind in the making*, (New York, 1989); Sutherland, pp 673–4.

W75   *The happy prince and other tales* (by Oscar Wilde; dedicated to Carlos Blacker). London: David Nutt, 1888 (ill. Walter Crane, Jacomb Hood). SOURCE Osborne, p. 1038. LOCATION L, CaOTP.

Leipzig: Bernard Tauchnitz, 1909. SOURCE T & B, 4141. LOCATION Dt.

COMMENTARY Contents: 'The happy prince', 'The nightingale and the rose', 'The selfish giant', 'The devoted friend', 'The remarkable rocket' [Field Day, ii, pp 376–80; Osborne].

W76 *A house of pomegranates* (by Oscar Wilde; dedicated to Constance [Wilde]).
London: James R. Osgood, McIlvaine & Co., 1891 (ill. C. Ricketts, C.H. Shannon). SOURCE NCBEL 3, p. 1183. LOCATION L.
Leipzig: Bernard Tauchnitz, 1909. SOURCE T & B, 4095; OCLC. LOCATION D, O, Boston Univ.

COMMENTARY Contents of the London edn: 'The young king', 'The birthday of the Infanta', 'The fisherman and his soul', 'The star-child'. Contents of Leipzig edn: 'The picture of Dorian Gray', 'Lord Arthur Savile's crime and other stories', ' A house of pomegranates', 'The happy prince and other tales' [RL].

W77 *The picture of Dorian Gray* (by Oscar Wilde).
London, New York, Melbourne: Ward, Lock & Co., 1891. SOURCE NCBEL 3, p. 1183. LOCATION L.
Leipzig: Bernard Tauchnitz, 1908. SOURCE T & B, 4049; COPAC. LOCATION C.
+ New York: The Heritage Press, 1957 (introd. by André Maurois; ill. Lucille Corcos, Hallward). LOCATION InND Loeber coll.
+ London: Laurel Press, 1987 (as *The picture of Dorian Gray and the complete short stories*). LOCATION InND Loeber coll.

COMMENTARY A parable of decadence in the story of a beautiful and captivating young man, Dorian Gray, painted by the artist Basil Hallward, who has come under his spell but who feels he cannot exhibit the painting because he has put too much of his own soul into it. At the studio Dorian meets Lord Henry Wotton, who leads him on a path of moral disintegration. As Dorian loses his youthful innocence and purity, it is the painting that shows the effects of his debauchery while Dorian himself stays beautiful and young. He hides the painting, afraid that anyone will see what is happening to it, but Hallward eventually does, and Dorian kills him. He then tries to destroy the painting with a knife. Later the servants find an ugly old man with a knife in his chest, while the painting has been restored to its original beauty [ML; Field Day, ii, pp 383–4; Sutherland, p. 507].

W78 *Lord Arthur Savile's crime and other stories* (by Oscar Wilde).
London: James R. Osgood, McIlvaine & Co., 1891 (ill. C. Ricketts). LOCATION L.
Leipzig: Bernard Tauchnitz, 1909. SOURCE T & B, 4096; OCLC. LOCATION NN.
New York: Dodd, Mead & Co., 1891. SOURCE NCBEL 4, p. 2066; OCLC. LOCATION NN.

COMMENTARY Contents: 'Lord Arthur Savile's crime' (a ghost story), 'The sphinx without a secret', 'The Canterville ghost', 'The model millionaire'. William Butler Yeats§ reviewed this volume in *United Ireland* (26 Sept. 1891) [RL; Field Day, ii, pp 915–19; NCBEL 4].

W79 *The fisherman and his soul* (by Oscar Wilde; dedicated to H.S.H. Alice, princess of Monaco).
+ Portland (ME): Thomas B. Mosher, 1905. SOURCE NCBEL 4, p. 2066. LOCATION D.
COMMENTARY First published in *A house of pomegranates* (London, 1891) [NCBEL 4].

W80 *The complete shorter fiction of Oscar Wilde* (ed. and introd. by Isobel Murray).
+ Oxford, New York, Toronto, Melbourne: Oxford University Press, 1979. LOCATION D.

COMMENTARY Five sets of tales. Contents: [1.] 'Lord Arthur Savile's crime and other stories' (first published as a book in London, 1891): 'Lord Arthur Savile's crime', 'The sphinx without a secret', 'The Canterville ghost', 'The model millionaire'. [2.] 'The happy prince and other tales' (first published as a book in London, 1888): 'The happy prince', 'The nightingale and the rose', 'The selfish giant', 'The devoted friend', 'The remarkable rocket'. [3.] 'The portrait of Mr. W.H.' (first published in *Blackwood's Magazine*, Edinburgh, 1889). [4.] 'A house of pomegranates' (first published as a book in London, 1891): 'The young king', 'The birthday of the Infanta', 'The fisherman and his soul', 'The star-child'. [5.] 'Poems in prose': 'The artist', 'The doer of good', 'The disciple', 'The master', 'The house of judgement', 'The teacher of wisdom' [ML].

COLLECTED WORKS

W81   *The collected works of Oscar Wilde.*
      London: Routledge/Thoemmes, 1993, 15 vols. (ed. by Robert Ross, with introd. by Joseph Bristow). SOURCE COPAC. LOCATION O.

WILDE, W.R. See **WILDE, Sir William Robert Wills**.

WILDE, Sir William Robert Wills (known as **W.R. Wilde**), b. Kilkeevin, Castlereagh (Co. Roscommon) 1815, d. Dublin 1876. Surgeon, antiquarian, folklorist and miscellaneous writer, WRWW was the son of Dr Thomas Wilde and of Emily (ODNB has Amelia) Fynne of Co. Mayo. He was educated at the Elphin Diocesan School, trained as a surgeon in Dublin, and spent nine months as personal physician to a wealthy businessman who was on a cruise for health reasons. From this voyage came WRWW's *Narrative of a voyage to Madeira, Teneriffe and along the shores of the Mediterranean* (Dublin, 1840). The £250 he received for the manuscript enabled him to study in London, Berlin, and Vienna, and letters of introduction from Maria Edgeworth§ made sure he had entrée to literary society in various cities he visited. He settled in Dublin in 1841, where he practiced as an oculist and ear specialist, establishing a dispensary to treat the poor of Dublin and a hospital that later became part of the Royal Victoria Eye and Ear Hospital on Adelaide Road. In 1851 he married Jane Francesca Elgee (see Lady Wilde§). At their home on Merrion Square, the Wildes welcomed leading literary and political figures of the day. WRWW was a medical and surgical innovator; a statistician; and he published widely on issues relating to his specialities. In 1853 he was appointed surgeon oculist-in-ordinary to the queen in Ireland and in 1864 he was knighted for his work on the censuses of 1851 and 1861. He founded and edited the *Dublin Journal of Medical Science*. He wrote a book on Jonathan Swift's§ mental and physical condition at the end of his life that refuted the idea of Swift's insanity (Dublin, 1849). His antiquarian interests led him to write *The beauties of the Boyne and the Blackwater* (Dublin, 1849) and *Lough Corrib and Lough Mask* (Dublin, 1867), and various shorter pieces. He was the first to compile catalogues on the ancient objects held in the RIA (published, Dublin, 1858–62, 3 vols.), of which he was a vice-president. These are described by the DNB as 'a monumental work of archaeological erudition and insight'. He had a keen interest in folklore stemming from his boyhood in Castlereagh and its surroundings, evidenced in the following volumes, which are collections of stories gathered in the area. Much of his writing on folklore was published after his death by his wife, who wrote of him: 'There was probably no man of his generation more versed in our national literature, in all that concerned the land and the people, the arts, architecture, topography, statistics, and even the legends of the country'. One of his patients, Mary Josephine Travers, accused him of improprieties and published *Florence Boyle Price; or, a warning* (Dublin, [1865?]). In a subsequent court case, WRWW was fined limited damages but he had to pay court costs amounting to thousands of pounds, greatly damaging his reputation. In 1873 he was awarded the Cunningham medal, the highest award of the RIA. His death left his widow in comparative poverty and she subsequently completed and published in 1880 WRWW's biography as well as his *Memoir of Gabriel Beranger*, a French expert on Irish antiquities who had resided in

Dublin in the late-eighteenth century. WRWW's achievements have been overshadowed to some extent by the literary renown and notoriety of his son, the author Oscar Wilde§. WRWW's portrait was published in *Portraits of Irish archaeologists from original drawings by B. Mulrenin, R.H.A.* (Dublin, n.d.); other portraits (and papers) are listed in ODNB. He was buried in Mount Jerome cemetery, Dublin. SOURCE Allibone, iii, pp 2718–19; Boylan, p. 402; Brady, pp 248–9; R. Ellmann, *Oscar Wilde* (New York, London, 1987; Field Day, ii, p. 373, iv, pp 913–14, v, p. 709; Hogan 2, pp 1250–1; Igoe, pp 282–6; J. Melville, *Mother of Oscar. The life of Jane Francesca Wilde* (London, 1994), passim; NCBEL 4, p. 2305; OCIL, pp 601–2; ODNB; RIA/DIB; T. de Vere White, *The parents of Oscar Wilde* (London, 1967); T.G. Wilson, *Victorian doctor: being the life of Sir William Wilde* (London, 1947, repr. 1974); Zimmermann, p. 285.

W82 *Irish popular superstitions* (by W.R. Wilde; dedicated to 'Speranza' [Lady Wilde§]).
+ Dublin: James McGlashan, [1852] (ill. C.M. Grey; Readings in Popular Literature). SOURCE Bradshaw, 3951. LOCATION D, L, C, InND Loeber coll.
Shannon: Irish University Press, [*c*.1972]. SOURCE COPAC. LOCATION Dt, C.
COMMENTARY Partly written in the autumn of 1849 in the aftermath of the Famine, it is a review of popular superstitions, customs, and legends interwoven with stories. WRWW had asked many people – mainly village schoolmasters – who could speak both Irish and English, to collect these for him. The stories are untitled and are set in the area of Ballintober Castle (Co. Roscommon), where WRWW grew up. One of the central characters is the river fisherman, Paddy Welsh. The volume has an index [RL; Field Day, iv, pp 905–7; Melville, p. 53].

W83 *Ancient legends, mystic charms and superstitions of Ireland with sketches of the Irish past to which is appended a chapter on "The Ancient races of Ireland" by the late Sir William Wilde* ([ed.] by Lady Wilde).
+London: Ward & Downey, 1887, 2 vols. SOURCE Hogan 2, p. 1244; McKenna, p. 340; Rafroidi, ii, p. 355. LOCATION Grail, BFl, L, InND Loeber coll. (vol. 1 only).
Galway: O'Gorman, 1971. SOURCE Rafroidi, ii, p. 355; COPAC. LOCATION L, Univ. of Aberdeen.
New York: Lemma, 1973. SOURCE OCLC. LOCATION McMaster Univ., Hamilton, Ontario, Canada.
COMMENTARY Based on material collected from the west of Ireland by WRWW. Contents: 'The horned women', 'The legend of Ballytowtas Castle', 'A wolf story', 'The evil eye', 'The stolen bride', 'Fairy music', 'The fairy dance', 'Fairy justice', 'The priest's soul', 'The fairy race', 'The trial by fire', 'The lady witch', 'Ethna the bride', 'The fairies' revenge', 'Fairy help: the phouka', 'The farmer punished', 'The farmer's wife', 'The midnight ride', 'The leprechaun', 'The legends of the Western islands', 'The bride's death-song', 'The child's dream', 'The fairy child', 'The doom', 'The clearing from guilt', 'The holy well and the murderer', 'Legends of Innis-sark: a woman's curse', 'Legends of the dead in the Western islands', 'Superstitions concerning the dead', 'The fatal love-charm', 'The Fenian knights', 'Rathlin island', 'The strange guests', 'The dead soldier', 'The three gifts', 'The fairies as fallen angels', 'The fairy changeling', 'Fairy wiles', 'Shaun-mor', 'The cave fairies', 'Evil spells', 'An Irish adept of the islands', 'The May festival', 'May-day superstitions', 'Festivals', 'November spells', 'November eve', 'A terrible revenge', 'Midsummer', 'Marriage rites', 'The dead', 'The wake orgies', 'The ancient mysteries', 'The power of the word', 'The poet and the king', 'The sidhe race', 'Music', 'Poet inspiration: Eodain the poetess', 'The banshee', 'Queen Maeve', 'Death signs', 'Superstitions', 'The fairy rath', 'Fairy nature', 'Irish nature'. The second volume contains legends of animals (dogs, cats, cows, birds etc.), the properties of herbs, medical superstitions and ancient charms, various superstitions and cures, and omens. In addition, the volume contains legends of the saints, mysteries of fairy power, the holy wells, popular notions

concerning the sidhe (fairy) race, and sketches of the Irish past. The book failed to sell well [RL; Field Day, iv, pp 877–8; Melville, p. 211].

W84   *Ancient cures, charms, and usages of Ireland. Contributions to Irish lore* ([ed.] by Lady Jane Francesca Wilde).

+ London: Ward & Downey, 1890. SOURCE Hogan 2, p. 1244; Rafroidi, ii, p. 355; McKenna, p. 340. LOCATION Grail, L, InND Loeber coll.

COMMENTARY Based on material collected by WRWW from the west of Ireland. Consists mostly of written illustrations of Irish popular beliefs, and some stories, probably taken from oral history. Contents: 'Peasant tales': 'A night with the fairies', 'A legend of shark', 'The doctor's visit', 'Fairy help', 'The Western Isles'. Peasant tales of the dead: 'The spectre bride', 'The witch-girl', 'The headless horses', 'The woman with the teeth', 'The punishment' [RL].

WILLIAMS, A. Co-author. See CROMMELIN, Maria Henrietta (May).

WILLIAMS, Charles. See WILLIAMS, Charles Frederick.

WILLIAMS, Charles Frederick (known as Charles Williams), b. Coleraine (Co. Derry) 1838, d. Brixton (London) 1904. Journalist, foreign correspondent and miscellaneous writer, CFW was descended from English and Scottish settlers in Ulster. He was educated at the Belfast Academy and at a school in Greenwich. For health reasons, he spent some time in the southern states of America. He took part in a filibuster on Nicaragua and gained the reputation of a fearless blockade-runner. After his return from America, he joined the London *Evening Herald* and in 1859 began an association with the *Standard* (London) that was to last until 1884. He was the first editor of the London *Evening News* and later wrote for the *Morning Advertiser* and the *Daily Chronicle* (both London). He served as a special correspondent reporting on – among other conflicts – the Franco-Prussian war; the Turkish-Armenian conflict; the war in Afghanistan; the war between Turkey and Greece in 1898; as well as on the British expedition up the river Nile to relieve Gen. Gordon at Khartoum in 1885. Later he reported on Gen. Kitchener's campaign in Sudan and on the re-taking of Khartoum in 1898. Outspoken in his criticisms of the government's handling of war, he championed ordinary soldiers and enlightened officers. He published several books based on his wartime experiences; wrote stories and articles for the *Temple Bar* (London); and also wrote on ecclesiastical matters in addition to 'Songs for soldiers'. He was the founder of the Press Club in London. SOURCE Allibone Suppl., ii, p. 1525; Boylan, p. 403; Brady, p. 249; Brown, p. 308; ODNB; RIA/DIB.

W85   *John Thaddeus MacKay. A study in sects* (by Charles Williams).

London: Burleigh, 1889. SOURCE Brown, 1670. LOCATION L.

COMMENTARY Set partly in Ulster and in India. Two religious men are sent to India. Both learn charity and come to recognize the narrowness of their own views through mixing with the natives [Brown].

WILLIAMS, Henry L. See WILLIAMS, Henry Llewellyn.

WILLIAMS, Henry Llewellyn (also known as Henry L. Williams), pseud. 'Mat. Mitzen', fl. 1860s. Prolific American author, HLW's eclectic writings include religious subjects; travel; translations of French classics; biographical sketches; and stories based on popular dramas, including one by Dion Boucicault§. He is especially known for his 25¢ novels. SOURCE Allibone, iii, p. 2739; Allibone Suppl., ii, pp 1525–6; Wright ii, pp 366–8 (list of novels).

W86   *Arrah-na-pogue (Arrah-of-the-kiss); or, the Wicklow wedding. Founded on the same incidents as the celebrated drama by Dion Bourcicault* [anon.].

+ New York: Robert M. DeWitt, [1865] (DeWitt's Twenty-Five Cent Novels, No. 58). SOURCE Wright, ii, 2739. LOCATION L, Wright web.

COMMENTARY 96pp. Set in Ireland and describes various conflicts between the Irish people and English soldiers. Based on a drama by Bourcicault (also known as Boucicault§). The story starts at Glendalough (Co. Wicklow) at the time that Lord Castlereagh had committed suicide. Beamish McCoul tries to organize an insurrection. He robs the man who has been collecting rent from McCoul's former property. McCoul is in love with Fanny Power, but he has to leave the county because of his outlawry. Various clashes between the Irish and the English in which the Terry Alts are involved are described [BLC; ML].

W87   *Shamus O'Brien* (by Henry L. Williams).
New York: Robert M. DeWitt, [1865 or later] (DeWitt's Twenty-Five Cent Novels, No. 49). SOURCE Adv. in *Arrah-na-pogue* (New York, [1865]).
COMMENTARY No copy located [RL].

W88   *The Fenian chief; or, the martyr of '65. Founded on recent events in Ireland's struggle for liberty* (by the author of *Arrah-na-pogue* and *Shamus O'Brien*).
+ New York: Robert M. DeWitt, [1865] (DeWitt's Twenty-Five Cent Novels, No. 51). SOURCE Wright, ii, 2754. LOCATION L, Wright web.
COMMENTARY Set in Co. Cork. The main character is Maurice O'Connell and he is associated with the Fenians. Various clashes between the Fenians and the English are described. Maurice is falsely accused of a murder and is killed. The person who had committed the murder is hounded by Maurice's friends and in the end drowns [ML].

W89   *L'Africaine; or, the maid of Madagascar* (by Henry L. Williams).
+ New York: Robert M. DeWitt, 1866. SOURCE Wright, ii, 2738. LOCATION Wright web.
COMMENTARY Contains two Irish stories, among others: 'A sporting bet' (in the garrison at Athlone an Irish soldier is bragging about his horse. A Scottish soldier suggests a race in a month's time for a 10 guinea prize. At the time of the race, the Scotsman enters a pig – it had not been stipulated that it had to be a horse. The course is very short and the pig wins), 'An incident in ninety-eight' (set close to Derry where the king's troops are escorting some prisoners. The major is stopped on the road by the mother of one of the prisoners. She tells him to take one prisoner – her son – apart unbeknownst to the remainder of the prisoners because he has important information. The young man says that the house of his friend where he and his wife are staying will be attacked, and the butler will let the attackers in. The host does not believe that his butler would be unfaithful. However, the butler lets in the attackers but soldiers have been brought into the house and the attackers and the butler are defeated. The informer is attacked on his way to his mother's house and takes a long time to recover. He is helped in his recovery by the people he had warned [ML].

W90   *Murty, the rover; or, the Irish buccaneer. Full of wild and thrilling romance* (by 'Mat. Mitzen').
New York: Robert M. DeWitt, 1868. SOURCE Wright, ii, 2750. LOCATION L, Wright web.

WILLS, Samuel R. See WILLS, Revd Samuel Richard.

WILLS, Revd Samuel Richard (known as **Samuel R. Wills**), b. Co. Leitrim *c*.1826. Church of Ireland clergyman, poet, and novelist, SRW was the son of Robert Wills, a gentleman. He graduated BA in 1854 and MA in 1858 at TCD. He was curate of Birr (Co. Offaly, 1855–67); vicar of Kilfinaghty (Co. Clare, 1867–72); rector of Rathkeale (Co. Limerick, 1872); canon of Limerick; and chaplain to the Rathkeale Workhouse. His volumes of poems included *Childhood*

(Dublin, 1851); *Wellington* (1885); and *Kilkee* (Limerick, 1889). SOURCE B & S, p. 885; LVP, p. 516; O'Donoghue, p. 484; RIA/DIB; RL.

W91   *Affection's tribute; or, the voice of the old year* (by Samuel R. Wills).
    + Dublin: Samuel B. Oldham; London: Seeleys, 1852 (ill. C.M. Grey). SOURCE Allibone, iii, p. 2762. LOCATION D, L.

COMMENTARY A morbid tale about courage and overcoming a fear of death, set in England in the 1840s. A young man named William walks pensively through a village on New Year's Eve. During the year that is ending, his mother died of consumption. He resolves to learn more about love and redemption, but in the following year he dies. The story extols the virtues of Bible-reading and preparation for death [ML; CD].

WILLS, W.G. See **WILLS, William Gorman.**

WILLS, William. See **WILLS, William Gorman.**

WILLS, William Gorman (known as **William Wills** and **W.G. Wills**), b. Blackwell Lodge, Kilmurry (Co. Kilkenny, but Co. Clare according to Boase) 1828, d. London 1891. Painter, illustrator, playwright, novelist and poet, WGW was the son of a Church of Ireland clergyman, the Revd James Wills, a prolific writer, who was related to Violet Martin§ and Edith Somerville§, and edited *Lives of illustrious and distinguished Irishmen* (Dublin, 1840–47)) and Katherine, daughter of the Revd W. Gorman. WGW was sent at age 12 to a small school at Lucan (Co. Dublin) and later to the Waterford Grammar School. He entered TCD in 1845, but does not appear to have taken a degree. He studied painting at the RHA and earned a living with some painting commissions and literary work. In 1862 he settled in London. His career as a painter took off, but he lost patrons because of his absentmindedness, eccentricity and bohemian ways. He wrote about 40 plays, many based on historical events (including *Olivia* (London, [1879]), a dramatization of Oliver Goldsmith's§ *The Vicar of* Wakefield) that were vehicles for prominent actresses and actors of the time, but only two of which were printed. He was retained as a dramatist by the Lyceum Theatre at the salary of £300 per annum, but he took little interest in his dramas after their completion, rarely attended rehearsals, and was never present at a premiere. His real love remained painting and he spent time between plays in Normandy and Paris, where he rented a studio. In between these activities, he managed to publish seven novels. His brother, Revd Freeman Crofts Wills, also succeeded as a dramatist producing, with F. Langridge, *The only way*, an adaptation of Charles Dickens' *Tale of Two Cities* (London, 1899), as well as a biography that includes WGW's portrait. Some of WGW's letters to fellow Irish writer Bram Stoker§ are at the Brotherton Library, University of Leeds. For his portrait and papers, see ODNB. SOURCE Allibone, iii, p. 2762; B & S, p. 885; Boase, iii, pp 1395–6; Brady, p. 249; Brown, p. 309; Hogan 2, pp 1252–3; Leslie, *Ossory*, p. 196; LVP, p. 516; NCBEL 4, p. 2027; OCIL, p. 603; ODNB; O'Donoghue, p. 484; RIA/DIB; W.G. Strickland, *A dictionary of Irish artists* (repr. Shannon, 1968) ii, pp 541–4; F.G. Wills, *W.G. Wills, dramatist and painter* (London, 1898).

W92   *Old times. A novel* (by William Wills; dedicated to H.T. Humphreys).
    + London: Saunders & Otley, 1857 (ill. the author). SOURCE Brown, 1671; Hogan 2, p. 1253. LOCATION D, Dt, L, InND Loeber coll.

COMMENTARY First serialized in the *Irish Metropolitan Magazine* (Dublin). ODNB says WGW had this bound as if in monthly parts, like a novel of Charles Dickens, and distributed on the tables of coffee houses in Fleet Street, London. Set in Dublin and Kingstown (now Dun Laoghaire, Co. Dublin), the story is partly-based on the author's experience as a portrait painter. The main characters are Mr David Cordell and his young French wife; Mary, a daughter from an earlier marriage; Bridget, his sister; and Charlie and Marguerite. a nephew and niece who are the children of David's brother, John. John has emigrated to America and set up farming based on an old book on agriculture by Martin Doyle§. The story follows the children growing up and their tribulations in love. After many obstacles, Charlie and Mary marry [ML; Brown; ODNB].

W93 *Life's foreshadowings. A novel* (by W.G. Wills).
  + London: Hurst & Blackett, 1859, 3 vols. SOURCE Brown, p. 340; Hogan 2, p. 1253; OCLC. LOCATION L.
  COMMENTARY First serialized in the *Irish Literary Gazette* (Dublin, [between 1857–61]). However, the ODNB says it appeared in *Irish Metropolitan Magazine*. The story is set in Ireland [ML; Brown, 340; ODNB].

W94 *Notice to quit* (by W.G. Wills).
  + London: Hurst & Blackett, 1861, 3 vols. SOURCE Brown, p. 309; Hogan 2, p. 1253; OCLC. LOCATION L.
  COMMENTARY No Irish content [ML].

W95 *The wife's evidence* (by W.G. Wills; dedicated to Loftus Bushe Fox).
  + London: Hurst & Blackett, 1864. SOURCE Brown, p. 309; Hogan 2, p. 1253. LOCATION L.
  COMMENTARY No Irish content [ML].

W96 *The three watches* (by W.G. Wills; dedicated to Arthur Bushe, master of the queen's bench in Ireland).
  + London: Hurst & Blackett, 1865. SOURCE Brown, p. 309. LOCATION L.
  COMMENTARY Written for *Tinsley's Magazine* (London). No Irish content [ML].

W97 *David Chantry* (by W.G. Wills; dedicated to the author's mother [Katherine Wills]).
  + London: John Maxwell & Co., 1865, 3 vols. SOURCE Brown, p. 309; Hogan 2, p. 1253. LOCATION; L.
  COMMENTARY Written for *Temple Bar* (London). No Irish content [ML].

W98 *The love that kills* (by W.G. Wills).
  London: Tinsley Bros, 1867, 3 vols. SOURCE Brown, 1672; Hogan 2, p. 1253. LOCATION L.
COMMENTARY Written for *Tinsley's Magazine* (London) and set in Ireland during the Famine and the rebellion of 1848. It describes relations between landlords and tenants. The Catholic land-agent is brought into the Young Ireland movement by his confessor, but after a while loses trust in the leaders. ODNB points out that some material from *Old times* is reworked in this volume [Brown; Fegan, p. 227; ODNB].

WILMOT, —. See BRADSHAW, Mrs John.

WILMOT, Mrs —. Ascribed novelist. See CHETWODE, Anna Maria. Note that a Mrs Wilmot, perhaps the same person, was the ascribed author of *A word to the landholders of Ireland* (Cork, 1822). SOURCE H. Blythe, *Caro, the fatal passion. The life of Lady Caroline Lamb* (New York, 1973), p. 186; COPAC.

WILMOT, Mr, fl. 1828. Ascribed novelist, known from a letter of 13 Sept 1831 by the publisher R. Bentley to a Mr Wilmot of Woodbrook, Portarlington (Co. Laois). It mentions Bentley's refusal of a manuscript, saying that the previous one has not done as well as hoped, and that if another manuscript is in the making Bentley would like to consider it, but hopefully not that year. The titles of the novels are not known. Two individuals are possible candidates to be this Mr. Wilmot. Edward Wilmot was the son of Robert Wilmot, barrister and deputy recorder of Cork, and Elizabeth Hester Chetwode. Through his mother he was related to Miss Anna Maria Chetwode§, author of *Bluestocking Hall* (London, 1827, 3 vols.). EW was admitted at TCD in 1819 and graduated BA in 1824. O'Donoghue mentions Edward Wilmot as author of *Ugoline and other poems* (London 1828). On becoming heir to the estates of his kinsman, Jonathan Chetwode, he assumed the additional surname Chetwode in 1839. EW married Lady Jean Janet Erskine, younger daughter of John Thomas, earl of Mar. The second possible author is a Robert Wilmot. Little is known about his family other than that he was disinherited by his father, had an older brother (a lawyer, who died about 1823), and two sisters. It is not clear whether this RW was Irish, but the possibility cannot be excluded. He was trained as a surgeon and published a history of his bachelor days: *Ardent, a tale of Windsor Forest* (London, 1832, 4 vols.), which is an educational tale with no Irish content. In addition, he published *Disinherited* (no copy located), which also was autobiographical. Some time before 1839, RW and his wife and children left for America to settle on cheap land. However, his wife and children were abducted at Fort Wayne (IN) on 26 Dec. 1839. RW returned to England and was living at Chalvey, near Slough (Bucks.), in needy circumstances. In 1848 he wrote petitions to members of the royal household, and a small, rambling tract on the advantages of England paying off its national debt without raising taxes. This Robert Wilmot should not be confused with a namesake, a relative of Lord Byron and heir to a baronetcy. Note that a possible relative of Mr. Wilmot, Alice Wilmot Chetwode (probably of Woodbrook, Co. Laois), and possibly daughter of Edward Wilmot Chetwode, translated Mme Marie David's§ *The treasure of the abbey* (Dublin, 1886; New York, [1886?]) and *John Canada or New France* (Dublin, 1887). SOURCE Bentley MS L81, 65, 31, microfilm in C; B & S, p. 885; W.M. Brady, *Clerical and parochial records of Cork, Cloyne, and Ross* (London, 1864), i, p. 53; P. Douglass, *Lady Caroline Lamb* (New York, 2004), p. 190; M. Elwin, *Lord Byron's family* (London, 1975), p. 32; Garside 2, 1832:87 ([R. Wilmot], *Ardent* (London, 1832, 4 vols.); ML; O'Donoghue, p. 485; R. Wilmot, *The plan to pay off the interest and principal of England's great national debt without taxes* (London, [1848]).

WILMOT, Edward. See **WILMOT, Mr.**

WILMOT, Robert. See **WILMOT, Mr.**

WILSON, C.H. See **WILSON, Charles Henry.**

WILSON, Charles Henry, pseud. 'Dick Saunter' (known as **C.H. Wilson**), b. Bailieborough (Co. Cavan) 1757, d. London? 1808. Translator and writer, CHW was the son of the rector of Bailieborough. He was educated at TCD and studied at the Inner Temple, London. He published a collection, *Poems, translated from the Irish into the English* (Dublin, 1782), which was the first known volume of Irish poetry ever translated into English, and *Select Irish poems translated into English* (n.l., [1792]). In the same year he documented the proceedings of the Volunteer convention at Dungannon (Co. Tyrone) in *A complete collection of the resolutions of the Volunteers* (Dublin, 1782). He published edns of the works of Jonathan Swift§ and Henry Brooke§; authored *Brookiana: anecdotes of Henry Brooke* (under his initials 'C.H.W.', London, 1804, 2 vols.); and *The beauties of Edmund Burke* (London, 1798, 2 vols.). He was a parliamentary reporter; he contributed translations of works from Latin, German and Danish to periodicals; and edited the *Gazette* (London?) for several years. James Hardiman stated that he was 'a youth of promise ... [who moved to London] where he sunk ... unnoticed and unknown', but Hardiman does acknowledge CWH's productivity during his time there. SOURCE Allibone, iii, pp 2767–8; Brown 2, p. 271; Field Day, i, pp 917–18, 957; Garside, 1811:80; J.

Hardiman, *Irish minstrelsy* (London, 1831), i, p. 171; M. Mac Craith, 'We know all these poems: The Irish response to Ossian', in H. Gaskill (ed.), *The reception of Ossian in Europe* (London, 2004), pp 91–108. NSTC, W2252–W2258; OCIL, p. 603; O'Donoghue, p. 485; Personal communication, Joep Leerssen, Mar. 2005; RIA/DIB; R. Welch, *A history of verse translation from the Irish, 1789–1897* (Gerrards Cross, 1988), pp 25–6.

W99   *The wandering islander; or, the history of Mr. Charles North* (preface signed 'Dick Saunter'; dedicated to Lord Rawdon).
> + London: J. Ridgeway, 1792, 2 vols. SOURCE Raven 2, 1792:57; O'Donoghue, p. 485; ESTC t117013. LOCATION L (vol. 1, incomplete).

COMMENTARY The preface to this epistolary novel (interspersed with poems) contains a section on 'Privileges of a novel writer'. Some of the letters deal with the construction and assembly of the main character's library [RL].

W100   *The beauties of Tom Brown: consisting of humorous pieces in prose and verse selected from the works of that satirical and lively writer. To which is prefixed A life of the author* [anon.].
> + London: T. & R. Hughes, 1808 (ill. Rowlandson). SOURCE Allibone, iii, p. 2767. LOCATION L.

COMMENTARY Attribution mentioned by Allibone. Published posthumously. Recounts the life in London of Thomas Brown, the son of a Shropshire farmer [RL; Allibone, iii, p. 2767].

W101   *The Irish valet; or, whimsical adventures of Paddy O'Haloran who, after being servant to several masters, became master of many servants* (by the late C.H. Wilson; dedicated to the earl of Moira; dedication signed 'The editor').
> + London: M. Allen, 1811 (preface with a biographical sketch of the author). SOURCE Allibone, iii, p. 2767; Brown 2, 1625; *Éire-Ireland* 19 (1984), p. 118; British Fiction; Garside, 1811:80; OCIL, p. 603. LOCATION D, O.

COMMENTARY Published posthumously. A comic tale written in the first person in which the valet tells us he was born at Kilcock in 1770. After a few episodes in Ireland involving an old miser named Muckeridge and O'Haloran's first master, Luke O'Neill, who was a rake and a disreputable person, he goes off to Bristol. On the boat he falls in love with Isabella Mahon. Then begins a series of service with one master after another. He ends by marrying Isabella at Gretna Green, wins a fortune with a lottery ticket and returns to Ireland to settle down [Brown 2; OCIL].

WILSON, John Crawford, b. Mallow (Co. Cork) 1825, d. England? 1890. Poet, novelist and dramatist, JCW contributed poetry to many English periodicals and to the *Dublin University Magazine*. He lived in London and was a member of the Savage Club. His several volumes of poetry include *The village pearl and other poems* (London, 1852), and *Elsie, flights into fairyland, and other poems* (London, 1864). Brady describes him as a 'popular mid-Victorian novelist'. Of his work of fiction, only the following novel is known to have Irish content. SOURCE Allibone, iii, p. 2780; Brady, p. 250; Irish pseudonyms; LVP, p. 517 [under Crawford Wilson]; MVP, p. 502; O'Donoghue, p. 486; RIA/DIB.

W102   *Jonathan Oldaker; or, leaves from the diary of a commercial traveller* (by John Crawford Wilson).
> + London: Ward & Lock, 1859. SOURCE Allibone, iii, p. 2780 (includes 1856 and 1865 edns); OCLC. LOCATION L, Univ. of North Carolina, Chapel Hill.

COMMENTARY The main character is an Englishman, who meets on a train an Irishman who convinces him that he is at least half-Irish. He visits Ireland and, after further travels elsewhere, returns to Ireland and marries an Irishwoman [ML].

WILSON, Joseph. Editor. See **COLTHURST, Miss E.**

WILSON, Revd Plumpton, fl. 1830. Writer on religion and of religious fiction and Anglo-Irish clergyman, PW was rector of Ilchester and later of Newmarket and Ruaptoft ([*sic*] Leics.). SOURCE Allibone, iii, pp 2781–2.

W103 *Protestant truth and Roman Catholic errors; A tale* (by Plumpton Wilson).
+ London: Longman, Rees, Orme, Brown & Green, 1830. SOURCE NSTC; OCLC. LOCATION Dt, L.
COMMENTARY Possibly written in response to Noel Thomas Ellison's *Protestant errors and Roman Catholic truths. A tale* (London, 1829). Religious stories all set in Co. Wexford. The first story starts at Bannow [RL].

WILSON, S. Co-author. See **CROMIE, Robert.**

WILSON, Revd T. Co-author. See **LEATHLEY, Mary Elizabeth Southwell.**

'WILTON', pseud. See **CARLETON, William.**

WILTON, Maurice, fl. 1879. Novelist, MW also was the author of *The sole reward for so much love* (London, 1879). Among his works only the following novel is known to have connections with Ireland. SOURCE RL.

W104 *The old love is the new. A novel* (by Maurice Wilton).
+ London: Samuel Tinsley & Co., 1880, 3 vols. SOURCE Allibone Suppl., ii, p. 1535; Dixson, p. 223; Jarndyce cat. 98/396. LOCATION L, InND Loeber coll.
COMMENTARY A romance set in the nineteenth century in west Cork against a background of agrarian agitation. Mr Cecil Clavering's son, Francis, is the inseparable companion of Kathleen O'Moore, whose father is Mr Clavering's neighbour and friend. Before Francis goes off to fight in the Peninsular War he asks Kathleen to marry him, but she is not sure she wants to. A disgruntled tenant makes an attempt on Mr Clavering's life. The tenant goes to prison, but Mr Clavering makes sure that his family is well cared for. He takes a particular liking to and brings to live with him a blind boy who plays the violin. Kathleen's father dies and she goes to live with Mr Clavering, her guardian, who is moving to England because of repeated attempts on his life. Francis returns from the war and marries Kathleen. The blind boy becomes a famous musician [ML].

WINGFIELD, the Hon. Lewis. See **WINGFIELD, the Hon. Lewis Strange.**

WINGFIELD, the Hon. Lewis Strange (known as the **Hon. Lewis Wingfield**), b. Powerscourt (Co. Wicklow,) 1842, d. London 1891. Novelist, journalist, painter and adventurer, LSW was the third son of Richard, 6th Viscount Powerscourt and Lady Elizabeth Frances Charlotte Jocelyn, eldest daughter of the 3rd earl of Roden. He was educated at Eton and Bonn and married in 1868 the Hon. Cecilia Emily Emma FitzPatrick (d. 1918), daughter of the 1st Baron Castletown. He had a varied life, travelling widely in Europe, the Far East and North Africa. His first book was *Under the palms of Algeria and Tunis* (London, 1868, 2 vols.). He acted in London; designed theatre costumes; and for a while was an attendant in a mental asylum. He was also a painter and exhibited at the RHA, where he became a member, and he decorated one of the salons at Powerscourt with paintings. In 1870 he reported on the siege of Paris by the Prussians for the London *Times* and London *Daily Telegraph*, communicating by balloon, while also tending the wounded and qualifying as a surgeon. In 1884 he went as a war correspondent with the British army to the Sudan, a trip that adversely affected his health. Aside from his novels, he wrote drama criticism for the London *Globe*; adapted works for the stage; and wrote travel books based on his experiences. He published ten novels, some of which dealt with historical topics. He died childless. Strickland notes John Edward Jones's bust of LSW, carved in 1854. For his portraits and papers, see ODNB. SOURCE Allibone, iii, p. 2791; Allibone Suppl., ii, p. 1536; Boase, iii, p. 1440; Boylan, p. 405; Burke's Peerage, 1963, ii, p. 1985; ODNB; Viscount Powerscourt, *Muniments of the ancient Saron family of Wingfield* (London, 1894), p. 44; RIA/DIB; Strickland, i, p. 560; Sutherland, p. 675; Vanishing country houses, pp 154–6.

W105 *Slippery ground* (by the Hon. Lewis Wingfield; dedicated to E. Got).
+ London: Tinsley Bros, 1876, 3 vols. SOURCE Sutherland, p. 675; Wolff, 7250.
LOCATION L, InND Loeber coll.
COMMENTARY Set in a German university town and in England, the novel deals with people who are engaged in commerce. One of the characters – who appears extremely trustworthy – is actually a crook who creates havoc in the lives of his relatives and acquaintances. The story contains a description of the German siege of Paris [ML].

W106 *Lady Grizel: an impression of a momentous epoch* (by the Hon. Lewis Wingfield).
London: Richard Bentley, 1878, 3 vols. SOURCE Sadleir, 3321; Sutherland, p. 675.
LOCATION L.
COMMENTARY An historical romance set in the eighteenth century [Sutherland].

W107 *My Lords of Strogue. A chronicle of Ireland, from the 1798 Convention to the Union* (by the Hon. Lewis Wingfield; dedicated to E.W.B.).
+ London: Richard Bentley & Son, 1879, 3 vols. SOURCE Allibone Suppl., ii, p. 1536; Brown, 1675; Sadleir, 3323. LOCATION D, L.
COMMENTARY An historical romance set in Ireland mainly in the period 1795–1800, but beginning in 1793. Robert Emmet's insurrection is purposely antedated by 2 1/2 years. It depicts the politics and manners of the time, with special emphasis on the British prime minister William Pitt's policies towards Ireland. The author's sympathies are with the Irish, and he exhibits unsparingly the errors of English rule. The novel covers the 1798 rebellion, and introduces Sarah Curran, Wolfe Tone, the Emmet brothers, Lord Cornwallis and Lord Castlereagh [Brown; Nield, p. 99].

W108 *In her Majesty's keeping. The story of a hidden life* (by the Hon. Lewis Wingfield).
London: Richard Bentley & Son, 1880. SOURCE Allibone Suppl., ii, p. 1536; Sutherland, p. 675; Wolff, 7246. LOCATION L.
COMMENTARY A story of prison life on Dartmoor heath (Devon) [Sutherland].

W109 *Gehenna; or, havens of unrest* (by the Hon. Lewis Wingfield; dedicated John Laurence Toole).
New York: George Munro, 1881. SOURCE Topp 6, 348.
London: Hurst & Blackett, 1882. SOURCE Allibone Suppl., ii, p. 1536; Topp 6, 348.
LOCATION D (n.d. edn), L.
COMMENTARY No copy of the New York edn located [RL].

W110 *Abigel Rowe. A chronicle of the Regency* (by the Hon. Lewis Wingfield; dedicated to George Lean).
+ London: Richard Bentley & Son, 1883, 3 vols. SOURCE Allibone Suppl., ii, p. 1536; Sadleir, 3318; Sutherland, p. 675. LOCATION L, InND Loeber coll.

W111 *Barbara Philpot. A study of manners and morals (1727–1737)* (by the Hon. Lewis Wingfield; dedicated to Sir Henry Thompson).
+ London: Richard Bentley & Son, 1885, 3 vols. SOURCE Allibone Suppl., ii, p. 1536; Sadleir, 3319; Sutherland, p. 675; Wolff, 7246. LOCATION Dt, L, InND Loeber coll.

COMMENTARY Historical fiction set in eighteenth-century England among actors and politicians [ML].

W112 *The lovely Wang. A bit of China* (by the Hon. Lewis Wingfield; dedicated to H.P. Tennant and A. Gibb).

+ Bristol: J.W. Arrowsmith; London: Simpkin, Marshall & Co, 1887 (Arrowsmith's Bristol Library, vol. 21). SOURCE Allibone Suppl., ii, p. 1536; Wolff, 7248. LOCATION L.

COMMENTARY A romance set in Foochow, China, where a merchant, Mr. Hung, has two children. His daughter is engaged to the son of the rich Mr. Wang, who lives in another city. The fiancée falls ill and requests that his betrothed come and nurse him. This is a terrible request because engaged couples are not supposed to see each other. However, Mr. Hung does not dare to refuse because his business is about to go under and he is counting on the fiancée's father to rescue him. Instead of his daughter he sends his son, disguised as a woman. His son falls in love with Miss Wang. The young Mr. Hung and Miss Wang participate in a wedding ceremony, each impersonating their sibling. Mr. Hung flees the city for fear of being found out and goes to Peking. After many adventures, he and Miss Wang meet again and acknowledge their true identities and their strong love for each other [ML].

W113 *The curse of koshiu. A chronicle of old Japan* (by the Hon. Lewis Wingfield).

London: Ward & Downey, 1888. SOURCE Allibone Suppl., ii, p. 1536; Sadleir, 3320. LOCATION L.

COMMENTARY Historical fiction set in Japan [RL].

W114 *The maid of honour. A tale of the dark days of France* (by the Hon. Lewis Wingfield).

London: Richard Bentley & Son, 1891, 3 vols. SOURCE Sadleir, 3322; Sutherland, p. 675; Wolff, 7249. LOCATION L.

COMMENTARY Historical fiction set during the French Revolution [Sutherland].

WINTER, M. See **WINTER, Mary**.

WINTER, Mary (known as **M. Winter**), fl. 1830. Religious fiction writer, playwright and poet, MW is listed by O'Donoghue as an Irish author. She published some of her works in Dublin. Among her poetry is a translation, *The Hermann and Dorothea of Goethe* (Dublin, 1849), and among her plays is *Where there's a will there is a way, an old-fashioned Irish comedy* (Dublin, 1886). She married a Mr John Winter, but the date of the marriage is not known. Allibone notes an M. Winter and a Mary Winter, but it is not clear if these are this author. SOURCE Allibone, iii, p. 2795; COPAC; O'Donoghue, p. 487; OCLC.

W115 *Alton Park, or conversations on religious and moral subjects, chiefly designed for the instruction and amusement of young ladies* (by M. Winter; dedicated to the countess of Shrewsbury).

London: Printed and published for the author by Keating & Brown, 1830, 2 vols. SOURCE COPAC; Garside 2, App. C:3. LOCATION L.

COMMENTARY Contains chapters on religious and moral issues, with a narrative that offers a continuous sequence involving characters and conversations in the style of a novel. Alton Park may be a reference to Albury Park, home of Henry Drummond in Surrey, in which were held meetings of the millenarians, who believed Christ would return and reign on earth for a thousand years before the end of the world [D. Bowen, *The Protestant crusade in Ireland 1800–70*, pp 64–5; Garside 2, App. C:3].

WINTERBOTHAM, Ann Sophia. See **STEPHENS, Mrs Ann Sophia**.

WISEMAN, Cardinal Nicholas Patrick, b. Seville (Spain) 1802, d. London 1865. Theologian, cleric, poet and writer on religion, NPW was the son of James Wiseman and an Irish mother, the daughter of Peter Strange of Aylwardstown Castle (Co. Kilkenny), whose family came from Waterford. Brought up in Waterford after his father's death, NPW was educated at St Cuthbert's College, Upshaw, and then in the English College in Rome and received his DD in 1824. He was ordained priest in 1825. Together with Daniel O'Connell and Michael Joseph Quinn, he helped to establish a Catholic quarterly magazine, the *Dublin Review* (first published May 1836).

When the Catholic hierarchy in England was restored by Pope Pius IX in 1850, NPW was appointed cardinal archbishop of Westminster. He became a distinguished writer on theology and a friend and colleague of John Henry Newman§. He also wrote drama, and to counteract anti-Catholic propaganda a novel, *Fabiola* (anon., London, 1854), that became one of the most popular Catholic books in England and Ireland both in its time and well into the twentieth century when it was still in circulation. It was widely translated, including into Esperanto. NPW was instrumental in persuading Newman to write *Callista* (London, 1856) for the same series. SOURCE Allibone, iii, pp 2801–3; MVP, p. 504; NCBEL 4, p. 2669; ODNB; O'Donoghue, p. 487; Sutherland, pp 675–6.

W116 *Fabiola, or the church of the catacombs* [anon].
> London: Burns & Oates,1854. SOURCE OCLC. LOCATION DCL.
> Amsterdam: J.H. Laarman, 1856 (trans. into Dutch by N.C. Scheffers as *Fabiola, of de kerk der katakomben*). SOURCE Mes, p. 264.
> Zwolle: Thomas a Kempis Vereeniging, 1879 (trans. into Dutch by P.J. van Spijk as *Fabiola of de kerk der catacomben*). SOURCE Mes, p. 264.
> New York: P.J. Kenedy & Sons, 1854. SOURCE OCLC. LOCATION PpiU.
> COMMENTARY Historical fiction. The story of a young girl in the Roman catacombs. SOURCE ODNB.

WOLLASTON (or Woollaston?) George, pseud. '**G—W—**', fl. 1753. Novelist, GW was probably an Irishman. He may be identified with George Woollaston, an attorney in the king's bench in Ireland *c*.1734. He is unlikely to be have been the well-known mathematician of that name, who would have been only age 15 at the time of publication of the following work. SOURCE Figgis cat. 47/358; Keane, p. 520; ODNB.

W117 *The life and history of a pilgrim. A narrative founded on fact* (by '**G—W—**').
> + Dublin: Printed [for the author?] by Oli Nelson, 1753. SOURCE Allibone, iii, p. 2813; Raven, 197; ESTC t070274; McBurney & Taylor, 963. LOCATION Dt, L, IU, PU, InND Loeber coll.
> Dublin printed: London, repr.: J. Whiston, B. White & M. Sheepey, 1753 (by George Wollaston, Esq.) SOURCE Raven, 198; ESTC t057813; McBurney & Taylor, 964. LOCATION Dt, L, PU, IU.

COMMENTARY This tale begins with the hero's boyhood in England and continues with his adventures as a soldier in Spain, where he is taken prisoner. After he leaves prison, he takes on the character of a pilgrim and happily escapes from the Iberian Peninsula. He returns to London and finally takes up residence in Dublin. Throughout the novel there are various references to Irish people and Irish situations in, among other locations, Italy and Spain [ML].

WOLSELEY, Garnet Joseph, 1st Viscount Wolseley. Editor. See ANONYMOUS AUTHOR, fl. 1877.

WOODS, Margaret L. See WOODS, Margaret Louisa.

WOODS, Margaret Louisa (née Bradley; known as Mrs Henry George Woods and Margaret L. Woods), b. Rugby (War.) 1855, d. Thursley (Surrey) 1945. English novelist, poet and woman of letters, MLW was the daughter of Marianne Philpot and Dr George Bradley, later a master at University College, Oxford. Her four sisters were also writers. She was educated at home and at Miss Gawthorp's school in Leamington. Her husband became president of Trinity College, Oxford. She was acquainted with Oscar Wilde§. MW wrote poetry, stories, and essays on philosophy, literary criticism, biography, and travel. SOURCE Allibone Suppl., ii, p. 1546; Blain, p. 1185; ODNB.

W118 *Esther Vanhomrigh* (by Margaret L. Woods; dedicated to the author's husband [Henry George Woods]).

+ London: John Murray, 1891, 3 vols. SOURCE Brown, 1676; Sadleir, 3365; Wolff, 7307. LOCATION DPL (1892 edn), L, InND Loeber coll.

COMMENTARY An historical novel set in England and Ireland about the love story of Jonathan Swift§ and the two Esthers: Esther Vanhomrigh and Esther Johnson (Stella). Swift had kept his friendship with each woman a secret to the other. Other members of their circle – Joseph Addison, Richard Steele, Alexander Pope and Henry St John, Viscount Bolingbroke – cross the stage. The novel ends with the last tragic interview between Cadenus (Swift) and Vanessa (Esther Vanhomrigh) and her early death [ML; Quaritch cat. 1193/255].

W119 *The King's revoke. An episode in the life of Patrick Dillon* (by Margaret L. Woods). London: Smith, Elder & Co., 1905. SOURCE Brown, 1677; Wolff, 7308; OCLC. LOCATION L.

New York: Dutton, 1906 (as *The King's revoke*). SOURCE OCLC. LOCATION NN.

COMMENTARY Historical novel. The adventures of Patrick Dillon, an Irish officer in the Spanish army, who attempts to set free Ferdinand VII of Spain (1784–1833) and is imprisoned in France by Napoleon I. It gives pictures of Catholic life in Spain [Brown].

WOODWARD, Revd Henry, probable pseud. 'An officer of the line', b. Clogher (Co. Tyrone) 1775, d. Fethard (Co. Tipperary) 1863. Church of Ireland clergyman and religious writer, HW was the son of Revd Richard Woodward, dean of Clogher and later bishop of Cloyne, and Susanna Blake. He studied at Corpus Christi College, Oxford, and became a preacher in Co. Cavan for a few years before moving to the parish of Glankeen (Co. Tipperary). He was rector of Fethard for over fifty years (1812–63). He was reticent about the proselytizing activities of some Protestants; disliked Protestants who attacked Irish Catholicism; and opposed tithe collection. However, rioting broke out in 1827 when he introduced fourteen converts in church. He spoke out against souperism during the Famine years. Under his pseudonym, he published a poem 'To an early primrose' in the *Dublin Monthly Magazine* (Apr. 1830). He was characterized by his contemporary Revd Richard Sinclair§ as an 'accomplished writer'. Internal evidence in the anonymous *Sketches, scenes and narratives* (Dublin, 1828, copy in private collection) suggests that HW was probably its author.[2] He inscribed a copy of this book to Catherine Osborne§, who with her mother Lady Osborne, of Newtown Anner (Co. Tipperary) were among his friends. HW married Melesina Henrietta, daughter of Revd Verney Lovett. His memoirs, including his portrait, were published by his son Thomas Woodward, dean of Down, in 1864. HW is not to be confused with Daniel Wentworth Maginn§, who probably used the same pseudonym. SOURCE Allibone, iii, p. 2832; BLC; D. Bowen, *Souperism: Myth or reality?* (Cork, 1970), pp 73–5; Brooke, p. 169; Cork, i, p. 527; Leslie & Wallace, p. 1198; S. Lewis, *A topographical dictionary of Ireland* (repr.,

---

1 The volume on p. 164 refers to the *Irish Pulpit* (first series) Sermon II. By Revd H. Woodward. The text refers both to military and religious matters.

Baltimore, MD, 1984), i, p. 627; Mrs FitzMaurice, *Recollections of a rifleman's wife, at home and abroad* (London: Hope & Co., 1851), pp 19–20; W. Nolan & T.G. McGrath (eds), *Tipperary: History and society* (Dublin, 1985), p. 258; Mrs Osborne, *Memorials of the life and character of Lady Osborne and some of her friends* (Dublin, 1870), ii, pp 44–5, passim (which contains several of HW's letters); RIA/DIB; RL; H. Woodward, *Essays, thoughts and reflections, and letters* (London, 1864), passim.

W120 *Sketches, scenes, and narratives, chiefly of a religious tendency* (by 'An officer of the line'; dedicated to Lt.-Gen. Neville by 'his faithful servant and obliged friend').
+ Dublin: James Marshall Leckie; Edinburgh: W. Whyte & Co., W. Oliphant, Brown & Ward-Law; Glasgow: W. Collins; London: James Duncan, James Nisbet, Houlston & Son, 1828. LOCATION Corvey 3–628–51138–0; L, InND Loeber coll.
COMMENTARY Religious stories told by a military officer, set mostly in Ireland. The stories constitute a pretext for extensive sermonizing. Contents: 'The student's funeral', 'The suicide', 'The sick pensioner', 'The post captain and his family', 'The murderess, an Irish peasant's tale', 'The wanderer, a tale of the Scottish border', 'The Christian soldier', 'The dead soldier's letter', 'The stormy sky' [ML; RL].

WOOLAM, Wilfred, fl. 1895. Novelist, WW is also the author of *With the help of angels* (New York, 1894). SOURCE Brown 2, p. 272.
W121 *The friends of Innisheen* (by Wilfred Woolam).
+ London: Ward & Downey, 1895, 2 vols. SOURCE Brown 2, 1631. LOCATION D, L, RB.
COMMENTARY Innisheen is a small island. The story of a warm friendship between an Englishman, Ernest Armstrong, and Eustace Delamere, who – when they first meet – is 16 years old and who is the nephew of a retired clergyman living at Tullanhough, apparently in the west of Ireland. Armstrong is separated from his wife Norah, who is selfish, irresponsible and reckless, but not morally corrupt. She ruins the lives of more than one man – first her former lover, Robert Farran, then Armstrong. She comes to Tullanhough and Eustace falls deeply in love, not knowing who she is. Ernest comes back to save him, but at a tragic cost [Brown 2].

WOOLLASTON, George. See **WOLLASTON, George**.

WRAY, Denis, fl. 1893. Romance novelist.
W122 *The hermit of Muckross* (by Denis Wray).
London: W. Swan Sonnenschein & Co., 1893. SOURCE Brown 2, 1632 (mistakenly mentions a New York, Sonnenschein, 1893 edn). LOCATION L.
COMMENTARY A romance with an unusual ending featuring Arthur and Herbert, who are candidates for the hand of their old playmate, Maud. During a holiday in Killarney it appears that Arthur seduces her and then abandons her. She attempts suicide with her child but is rescued. Herbert for a time loses his reason but slowly recovers and takes up his abode in the ruins of Muckross Abbey in Killarney. Here he learns that Maud is living at Bruges in Belgium, but deeming himself unworthy he does not go to her but takes to working in the slums of London [Brown 2].

WRIGHT, Anna Maria. See **MAC KENZIE, Mrs Anna Maria**.

WRIGHT, E.H., pseud. 'G. O'C.', fl. 1889. Writer of historical fiction. The title page of *André Besnard* mentions that EHW was the author also of 'Heart and trumps', which has not been located. SOURCE RL.

W123 *André Besnard. A tale of old Cork* (by 'G. O'C.').

+ Cork: J. Mahony, 1889 (ill. Grogan). SOURCE Brown, 1678. LOCATION D, DPL, L. COMMENTARY Historical fiction set in Cork during the time preceding the Volunteers (before 1782). A love story is interwoven with various adventures. One of the chief characters is John Paul Jones, the celebrated American admiral [Brown].

WRIGHT, Revd John, b. Monaghan (Co. Monaghan) *c.*1765, d. London 1847. Church of Ireland clergyman and writer of historical fiction, JW was the son of Thomas Wright, a solicitor living at Monaghan. He entered TCD in 1780 and graduated BA in 1785 and MA in 1794. JW was appointed canon of Clones (1796); rector of Clontibret (1803–08); and rector of Killeevan in 1808 (all Co. Monaghan). At Killeevan he oversaw the (re?)building of the church and the glebe house. He was married and had children but his wife's name is not known. SOURCE B & S, p. 897; Brown, p. 310; J.C. Erck, *The ecclesiastical register* (Dublin, 1820), pp 11–12; Leslie, *Clogher*, p. 213; RIA/DIB; E.P. Shirley, *The history of the County of Monaghan* (London, 1879), pp 231, 337, 342.

W124 *The last of the corbes, or, the MacMahon country: A legend connected with Irish history in 1641* (by John Wright).

+ London: John Macrone, 1835. SOURCE Allibone, iii, p. 2862; Brown, 1679; Block, p. 256; Hodgson, p. 621. LOCATION D, L, InND Loeber coll.

COMMENTARY An historical tale said to be based on a manuscript, and is mainly concerned with the MacMahons and their corbe (a Roman Catholic religious dignitary) of Clones (Co. Monaghan), and a family named Willoughby in the years prior to the 1641 rebellion. It starts with a brief history of the MacMahons in Monaghan. At the opening of the action, the Willoughbys have already settled there, but are eyed with suspicion. On a visit of Sir Edward Blaney, the governor of the county, the MacMahons finally declare allegiance to the crown, after which a period of great harmony between the Irish and the settlers follows. However, after Strafford, the lord lieutenant, is recalled to England and troubles with the Parliamentarians grow, the harmony disappears. The MacMahons become heavily involved in the 1641 uprising. Events are viewed from a Protestant point of view, mention is made of the deed of the traitor O'Connolly, and the story dwells much on the excesses of the insurgents. Heber MacMahon (afterwards bishop of Clogher), Sir Phelim O'Neill, and Roger Moore are introduced. The financial decline of the Irish is imputed to their improvident living, which causes them to mortgage their estates [ML; Brown].

WRIGHT, Mrs Julia (née McNair), b. Oswego (NY) 1840, d. 1903. Proselytizing American religious and temperance writer, JW was the daughter of John McNair, and she married William James Wright in 1859. Several of her works are very anti-Catholic, and only those with an Irish connection are listed here. JW published many volumes, 12 of which – at 64pp each – were boxed and sold as *The True Story Library* (Philadelphia, 1869). SOURCE Allibone, iii, p. 2862; Allibone Suppl., ii, p. 1553; RLIN; Wright, i, pp 375–6.

W125 *Biddy Malone, or, the bundle of silk* [anon.].

Philadelphia: Presbyterian Board of Publication, [*c.*1863] (Series for Youth). SOURCE Allibone, iii, p. 2862; RLIN. LOCATION Rutgers Univ., New Brunswick (NJ).

W126 *Priest and nun* [anon.].

Philadelphia: Crittenden & McKinney, [1869] (ill.). SOURCE Allibone, iii, p. 2862; Wright, ii, 2814. LOCATION CtY, Wright web.

+ Cincinnati: Western Tract and Book Society, 1871 (16th thousand; ill. F.B. Schell). LOCATION InND Loeber coll.

+ London: Hodder & Stoughton, 1869 (as *Priest and nun: A story of convent life*; by the author of *Almost a nun*; ill.). SOURCE NSTC. LOCATION L (destroyed), O, E.

COMMENTARY An anti-Catholic religious novel, the aim of which is to show the perfidious methods Roman Catholic priests and nuns in the US use to convert Protestants to the Catholic religion. Rich Protestant girls who are sent to convent schools are especially in danger of falling into these snares. Priests and nuns lie and even resort to abduction to secure girls for their convents and lay their hands on their wealth. A prominent role in the story is played by an Irish priest, Fr Murphy, who incites Irishmen to become Fenians, and aids the nuns in their various schemes of deception. In the end, several individuals turn away from the Roman Catholic religion and find 'true' faith in protestantism. The book ends with an appendix containing newspaper reports of various other 'atrocities' committed by the Catholic clergy [ML].

W127   *Secrets of the convent and confessional: An exhibition of the influence and workings of the papacy upon society and republican institutions* (by Julia Wright; introd. by Revd Daniel March).
        + Cincinnati, Memphis, Atlanta: National Publishing Co.; Chicago: Jones Bros & Co., 1872 (ill. H. Sebald). LOCATION Wright web.
COMMENTARY An anti-Catholic story about the dangerous influence of the Catholics and the fear that they will overrun American politics, education and other areas of life. Set in New York. Catholics complain that the Orange Order is allowed to parade. The judge explains that the Irish Catholics are allowed to celebrate St Patrick's day and that it is part of the American constitution to have this freedom. The judge is warned that it will lead to a fight, which it does. The army is called out and many of the Catholic protesters are killed. An appendix gives details of convent life, the confessional, Romanism and education, and Romanism and politics [ML].

WYNNE, Revd G.R. See WYNNE, Revd George Robert.

WYNNE, Revd George R. See WYNNE, Revd George Robert.

WYNNE, Revd George Robert (also known as G. R. Wynne and George R. Wynne), pseud. 'G.R.W.', b. Dublin 1838, d. Dublin? 1912. Church of Ireland clergyman and writer of evangelical fiction, GRW was the son of George Wynne and Clara (née Wynne). He graduated BA at TCD in 1861; MA in 1875; and BD and DD in 1889. He was ordained in 1861 and served at Whitechurch (Dublin), Holywood (Co. Down), Killarney (Co. Kerry) and was archdeacon of Aghadoe (Co. Kerry), rector of St Michael's (Limerick) and canon of St Patrick's (Dublin). He published 19 works of religious fiction, mostly written for juveniles. He married Ellen Lees in 1863, with whom he had six children. He published many works on religion. SOURCE Allibone Suppl., ii, p. 1556; B & S, Appendix B, p. 129; Brown, p. 311; Brown 2, p. 272; Burke's, p. 1228; Landed gentry, 1904, p. 668; Leslie, *Ardfert*, p. 45; Leslie & Wallace, pp 1203–4; NCBEL 4, p. 1891; RIA/DIB.

W128   *Zoë's Bible. The story of an orphan* [anon.].
        London: [publisher?], 1864. SOURCE Allibone, iii, p. 2877. LOCATION L (destroyed).
        COMMENTARY No copy located [RL].
W129   *Tales for the train. Overton's question* (address to reader signed 'G.R.W.')
        + London: S.W. Partridge, 1865. LOCATION O.
        London: [publisher?], [1868] (as *Overton's question and what became of it*). SOURCE Allibone Suppl., ii, p. 1556; COPAC. LOCATION L.
        COMMENTARY Religious fiction set in England [RL].
W130   *Henry Hilliard: or, the three college friends* [anon.].
        + London: S.W. Partridge, 1867. SOURCE NSTC. LOCATION L, C, O.
        COMMENTARY Religious fiction [NSTC].

W131 *The O'Tooles of Glen Imaal* [anon.].
　　　London: S.W. Partridge & Co., 1868. SOURCE Allibone Suppl., ii, p. 1556; Brown 2, 1633; OCLC. LOCATION Dt, L.
COMMENTARY Religious fiction. The scene is laid in Donard (Co. Down) and the Glen of Imaal (Co. Wicklow). The story relates how a Bible reader converts a farmer named O'Toole to protestantism by the simple process of selling him a Catholic version of the New Testament [Brown 2].

W132 *The curate of West Norton* [anon.].
　　　London: S.W. Partridge, 1868. SOURCE Allibone, iii, p. 2877; Wolff, 7335 (n.d.); RLIN. LOCATION L (destroyed), E.

W133 *The converts of Kilbann. An Irish story* (by George R. Wynne).
　　　+ London: S.W. Partridge, [1869] (ill.). SOURCE Allibone, iii, p. 2877 (1868 edn); Brown 2, 1634; OCLC. LOCATION D, L.
COMMENTARY In the bitter winter of 1854–55, Hugh Kavanagh is forced with his children to take refuge in Kilbann workhouse. There, under the influence of the rector's daughter, he becomes a Protestant. When he comes out he is boycotted and obliged to seek work in Liverpool. Returning to Dublin, he becomes a coal porter and his children are put into a home for Protestants. It describes incidents of the alleged Bible burning at Kingstown (Dún Laoghaire, Co. Dublin) with which Thomas, Lord O'Hagan was associated [Brown 2].

W134 *Horace Harwood. A tale* [anon.] (dedicated to the dear memory of H.M.W.).
　　　+ London: S.W. Partridge, [1873]. SOURCE Allibone Suppl., ii, p. 1556. LOCATION L.

W135 *Evening chimes. A book for the little ones to read at bedtime* (by George Robert Wynne).
　　　London: Christian Knowledge Society, [1885]. SOURCE Allibone, Suppl., ii, p. 1556. LOCATION L.

W136 *Only my sister. A story* [anon.].
　　　London, Brighton: Society for Promoting Christian Knowledge; New York: E. & J.B. Young, [1893] (ill. L. Speed). LOCATION L.
COMMENTARY Fiction for juveniles. A minister in Manchester is told by his doctor that he needs to find a very quiet country parish. He and his children, Mabel and Tom, end up in a small village on the west coast of Ireland. They live there happily and have all kind of adventures, such as finding elk antlers in the dunes, and after a storm uncovering a hermit's stone hut, the outline of houses and a graveyard of great age. They have a scary adventure in a cave, and help to catch some smugglers. Tom is hired as a secretary on a ship that is making a tour to various lighthouses in the North Atlantic. While in Canada, he hears much about the opening up of the West. He convinces his father and sister to emigrate with him. They live happily in Manitoba but a prairie fire destroys their home. However, as true pioneers they start all over again and lead good lives in Canada [ML].

W137 *Crossing the ferry; or, from old England to New Brunswick* [anon.].
　　　London: Christian Knowledge Society, [1894]. LOCATION L.
COMMENTARY Story of emigration to Canada [RL].

W138 *Ralph Clifford: A tale of country life in Virginia after the Civil War* [anon.].
　　　London: Christian Knowledge Society, [1894]. SOURCE NCBEL 4, p. 1891 (London & New York 1895 edn). LOCATION L.
COMMENTARY Historical fiction set during the American Civil War [RL].

W139 *The story of Frank and his missionary-box* [anon.].
　　　London: Christian Knowledge Society, [1897]. SOURCE L.

W140 *Not peace but a sword* [anon.].
　　　London: Religious Tract Society, [1897]. SOURCE Brown, 1686. LOCATION L.

COMMENTARY A young Englishwoman, Sybill Marchant, succeeds in converting to protestantism some members of a poor family of Joyces in Connemara. The story is chiefly concerned with the trials of the new converts at the hands of their former friends and the clergy [Brown].

W141 *Nellie and her models* (by G.R. Wynne).
London: Christian Knowledge Society, [1898]. SOURCE COPAC. LOCATION L.

W142 *Ballinvalley; or, "a hundred years ago"* [anon.].
+ London, Brighton: Society for the Promoting Christian Knowledge; New York: E. & J.B. Young & Co., 1898 (ill. J. Nash). SOURCE Brown, 1687; Nield, p. 369 (which mentions a NY, Gorham edn). LOCATION D, L.
COMMENTARY Fiction for juveniles. An historical tale of the rebellion of 1798 set in Wicklow and describing the battles of New Ross and Hacketstown. The story is from a Protestant and loyalist standpoint and the author says in the preface that he drew on historical accounts. It also presents details on gold mining in Co. Wicklow; illicit distilling; and stage-coach travelling [Brown; Nield].

W143 *Sand-larks: A tale of two* [anon.].
London: Christian Knowledge Society, [1900]. LOCATION L.

W144 *The children's world. A story without an end* (by G.R. Wynne).
London: Christian Knowledge Society, [1903]. SOURCE COPAC. LOCATION L.

W145 *The Neville twins. The story of a missionary exhibition* [anon.].
London: Christian Knowledge Society, [1905]. LOCATION L.

W146 *His father's son: A tale* [anon.].
London: Christian Knowledge Society, [1908]. LOCATION L.

WYSE, Sir Thomas, pseud. 'Dr. Abraham Eldon', b. Waterford (Co. Waterford) 1791, d. Athens (Greece) 1862. Education reformer, liberal politician, translator, linguist and man of letters, TW was the eldest son of Thomas Wyse and Frances Bagge and scion of a staunchly Catholic family whose ancestor came to Ireland with Strongbow and who played a prominent role in Waterford history. He was one of the first students to attend Stonyhurst, the newly-opened Jesuit college in Lancashire, later studying at TCD, where he graduated BA in 1812, and was later admitted to Lincoln's Inn (London). After extensive travel on the Continent (France, Italy, Greece) and various countries in the Middle East, he married in March 1821 the much-younger Laetitia Bonaparte, daughter of Napoleon's brother Lucien, prince of Canino, whom he had met in his travels. The marriage was not a happy one and ended in 1828 with a deed of separation; he never saw his wife again. However, he expended much energy and funds subsequently in legal matters relating to his former wife, their two sons, and her children of a second marriage, who to his chagrin used the surname Bonaparte Wyse. WS's travels provided the material for 30 unsigned articles in the *New Monthly Magazine* (London, 1826 30). He had returned to Waterford in 1825, involving himself actively in the movement for Catholic emancipation, which he believed would strengthen the ties between Ireland and England. Later he represented Tipperary and then Waterford in parliament where he became an energetic advocate on Irish matters, particularly on the need for a national education system, publishing *Education reform, or, the necessity of a national system of education* (London, 1836). Appointed a lord of the treasury in the government of Lord Melbourne, he served from 1839 to 1841. Lord Palmerston subsequently named him British minister at Athens, and there he spent the rest of his life. TW wrote extensively on education and on catholicism in Ireland, on art, and on his travels. He translated from German the story of *Little Red Riding Hood*, as well as from the original Anglo-Saxon *The history of King Leir and his three daughters* (Hertford, n.d.). Two sonnets from a manuscript collection by him were published posthumously in 1902. His *An excur-*

sion in the Peloponnesus in the year 1858 (London, 1865, 2 vols.) and *Impressions of Greece* (London, 1871) were edited by his niece, Winifrede M. Wyse, who lived with him in Athens and accompanied him on his travels. The NLI has some of TW's correspondence, papers, diaries and notebooks. His portraits are listed in Strickland and ODNB, while the ODNB lists his papers. SOURCE J.J. Achmuty, *Sir Thomas Wyse* (London, 1939); Allibone, iii, p. 2879; Boase, iii, pp 1548–9; O. Bonaparte-Wyse, *The spurious brood: Princess Letitia Bonaparte and her children* (London, 1969); ODNB; O'Donoghue, p. 490; RIA/DIB; Strickland, i, p. 455.

W147 *Everard Aylmer, or memoirs of a papist: by one of his descendants* (by Thomas Wyse).

COMMENTARY A manuscript written in Italy and consisting of a composite picture of several of his ancestors, mainly TW's great-grandfather 'Square' Wyse, who had been persecuted for adhering to the Catholic faith. The hero Everard fights against the British at Fontenoy, but amid the victorious French finds time to deplore their callous treatment of the British wounded. In 1939 the manuscript was in the possession Mr A.N. Bonaparte Wyse, permanent secretary to the minister of education in Northern Ireland [J.J. Achmuty, *Sir Thomas Wyse* (London, 1939), p. v, 67; O. Bonaparte-Wyse, *The spurious brood* (London), 1969, p. 40].

W148 *The continental traveller's oracle; or, maxims for foreign locomotion* (by 'Dr. Abraham Eldon, ed. by his nephew').

+ London: Henry Colburn, 1828, 2 vols. SOURCE COPAC. LOCATION L.

COMMENTARY Ascribed to TW in COPAC from the copy in the NLS. It was probably written in response to William Kitchiner's *The traveller's oracle; or, maxims for locomotion* (London, 1827, 2 vols.) and consists of a satire on the 'modern' tourist. The main character, a Cambridge graduate intended for holy orders, travels from England to the Continent and is extremely insular and ignorant of other countries. The traveller makes a comment on Ireland, 'if anyone travels there, now that they can travel anywhere else' [J.J. Achmuty, *Sir Thomas Wyse* (London, 1939), p. 66; ODNB; RL].

Y

'Y', pseud. See **KENEALY, Edward Vaughan Hyde**.

'Y., O.D.', fl. 1874. Romance novelist.

Y1   *By hook or by crook: A novel* (by 'O.D.Y.').
+ London: Town and Country Publishing Co., 1874. LOCATION InND Loeber coll.
COMMENTARY A love story set among the minor gentry in the west of Ireland, not far from Limerick, in which an artless girl is contrasted with her cousin, who considers herself most attractive. The story relates a dispute between English fishing boats and the fishermen of the west of Ireland. An excursion is made to Castleconnell and to Askeaton (both Co. Limerick). It also contains an account of travels in Persia [ML].

YATES, Edmund. Attributed author. See **HOEY, Mrs Cashel**.

YEATS, W.B. See YEATS, **William Butler**.

YEATS, **William Butler** (known as W.B. Yeats), pseud. 'Ganconagh', b. Dublin 1865, d. Roquebrune (France) 1939. Nobel prize-winning poet, dramatist, essayist, theatrical entrepreneur and senator, WBY was the son of the painter John Butler Yeats and Susan Pollexfen of Co. Sligo. He had further ties to Sligo through his great-grandfather Yeats, who had been rector of the parish of Drumcliff. Shortly after his birth, the family moved to London where they remained until 1881, when they returned to Dublin. During these years, WBY often spent holidays in Sligo among his relatives and Sligo remained an inspiration for many of his poems. He studied at the Metropolitan School of Art in Dublin where he became friendly with George Russell, who introduced him to the occultism that was to be an ongoing element in his personal and artistic life. He had been writing poems for some time and his first published poetry was in the *Dublin University Magazine* (Mar. 1885). Under the influence of the Fenian patriot John O'Leary and writer and historian Standish James O'Grady§, he became interested in Ireland's literary past and he published in the *Irish Fireside* (Dublin, 9 Oct. 1886) an essay praising Sir Samuel Ferguson§ for his efforts to rescue Irish poetry and folklore from neglect. He acknowledged the influence of James Clarence Mangan§ on his poetry and in prose he respected the story writers and novelists John and Michael Banim§ and William Carleton§. During the summer of 1887 he collected folklore around Sligo. In the same year, the family went back to London, where he was one of the founders of the Irish Literary Society. Later he also helped found the National Literary Society in Dublin, whose stated objective was to publicize the literature, folklore and legends of Ireland. In Ireland at that time his friends included the poet and novelist Katharine Tynan§ and the poet and later statesman Douglas Hyde§. In 1896, through his friend Arthur Symons, WBY met George Moore§ and his cousin Edward Martyn§, and through Martyn, Lady Augusta Gregory, who became his patron and muse. With her he gathered folk stories and poems from the Irish-speaking neighbours around the Gregory home in Coole Park (Co. Galway). Already intrigued with theatre (his first play *The land of heart's desire* had been produced in London as a curtain-raiser to George Bernard Shaw's§ *Arms and the man* in 1894), he planned with Lady Gregory, Martyn, and Moore an Irish literary theatre in which his interests in Celticism, patriotism and occultism could be fused. The first production was his 'Countess Cathleen'

1385

in May 1899, the beginning of a long series of plays by WBY, Lady Gregory and J.M. Synge (whom he had encouraged to seek inspiration in the Aran Islands), that constituted the dramatic arm of the Irish Literary Revival. WBY's poetic output began with the publication of the collection *The wanderings of Oisin* (London, 1889). He received the Nobel Prize for Literature in 1923. Aside from his poetry and a book of fiction, WBY is best known for his essays and his anthologies of Irish short stories (see below). He also published *Irish tales by Maria Edgeworth and John and Michael Banim* (New York, n.d.). In addition, he prepared an anthology, 'Irish adventurers', which was to contain six sections (one on '[John] Freney§ the robber', another on 'Rogues and rapparees'), but this work was not published. After a series of intense romantic liaisons, especially with the nationalist Maud Gonne, WBY married in 1917 Bertha George Hyde-Lees who collaborated with him in his work; edited it after his death; and was a willing partner in his experiments in automatic writing and occult research, sharing his belief in connections between the natural and supernatural worlds. They lived first in England but returned to Ireland in 1922. WBY was nominated a senator of the new Irish Free State, where he fought against censorship and the imposition of Catholic social teaching in Irish law. He died in France and the outbreak of the Second World War prevented his remains from being interred in Drumcliff Churchyard until 1948, which resting place he had designated in an epitaph written years previously. For critical, biographical, archival and reference information, see Field Day; Foster; Hogan 2, RIA/DIB and ODNB, which also has a list of numerous portraits. SOURCE Allibone Suppl., ii, p. 1557; Boylan, pp 409–11; Field Day, i, ii, iii, iv, v, passim; R.F. Foster, *W.B. Yeats: a life* (Oxford, 1997, 2003, 2 vols.); Hogan 2, pp 1267–92; Igoe, pp 286–92; Irish pseudonyms; OCIL, pp 609–11; ODNB; O'Donoghue, p. 492; RIA/DIB; Thuente 1, passim.

Y2   *Fairy and folk tales of the Irish peasantry* (ed. and selected by W.B. Yeats; dedicated to 'my mystical friend G.R.' [George William Russell]).

+ London: Walter Scott, [1888] (spine: Camelot Series). LOCATION InND Loeber coll.

+ London: Walter Scott; New York: Thomas Whittaker; Toronto: W.J. Gage & Co., 1888 (The Camelot Classics). SOURCE Roth, 3; Thuente 1, passim; OCLC; Wade, 212. LOCATION L, InND Loeber coll.

London, New York: Walter Scott, [c.1888]. SOURCE Fenning cat. 222/284. COMMENTARY *London, New York edn* Variant binding not noted by Wade, and consisting of half red cloth over green silk with an overall pattern of winged cherubs in a decorated cartouche [Fenning cat. 222/284].

+ London: Walter Scott, [1893] (as *Irish fairy and folk tales*; ill. James Torrance). SOURCE Hayley, p. 180. LOCATION L, InND Loeber coll.

New York: A.L. Burt, [1902] (as *Irish fairy and folk tales*). SOURCE Wade, 212A; OCLC. LOCATION NN.

+ New York: Dorset Press, 1986 (ill.) LOCATION InND Loeber coll., NN.

COMMENTARY Yeats considerably adapted the stories that he included in this anthology, which was compiled from other printed sources (poetry is excluded here). Tales are arranged under the following categories: [a] The trooping fairies; 'Frank Martin and the fairies' (William Carleton§), 'The priest's supper' (Thomas Crofton Croker§ [*sic*]), 'Teig O'Lane and the corpse' (trans. by Douglas Hyde§), 'Paddy Corcoran's wife' (William Carleton§), 'The white trout; a legend of Cong' (Samuel Lover§), 'The legend of Knockgrafton' (Thomas Crofton Croker [but actually by William Maginn§]), 'A Donegal fairy' (Letitia Maclintock [McClintock§]). [b] Changelings: 'The brewery of egg-shells' (Thomas Crofton Croker [sic]), 'Jamie Freel and the young lady. A Donegal tale' (Letitia Maclintock [McClintock§]). [c] The merrow: 'The soul cages' (Thomas Crofton Croker §[*sic*]), 'Flory Cantillon's funeral' (Thomas Crofton Croker§ [*sic*]). [d] The solitary fairies: 'Master and man' (Thomas Crofton Croker§ [*sic*]), 'Far Darrig in Donegal' (Letitia Maclintock [McClintock§]). [e] The Phooka: 'The piper and the puca' (trans. by Douglas Hyde§), 'Daniel O'Rourke' (Thomas Crofton Croker [but actually by William Maginn§]), 'The Kildare phooka' (Patrick Kennedy§). [f] The banshee: 'How Thomas Connolly met the banshee' (J. Todhunter), 'The banshee of the Mac Carthys' (Thomas Crofton Croker §[*sic*]). [g] Ghosts: 'Grace Connor' (Letitia Maclintock [McClintock§]), 'The black lamb' (Lady Wilde§), 'The radiant boy' (Mrs [Louisa?] Crow), 'The fate of Frank M'Kenna' (William Carleton§). [h] Witches, fairy doctors: 'Bewitched butter' (Letitia Maclintock [McClintock§]), 'A Queen's County witch' [John Keegan§], 'The witch hare' (Mr and Mrs S.C. Hall§), 'Bewitched butter (Queen's County)' [John Keegan§], 'The horned women' (Lady Wilde§), 'The witches' excursion' (Patrick Kennedy§), 'The confessions of Tom Bourke' (Thomas Crofton Croker§ [*sic*]), 'The pudding bewitched' (William Carleton§). [i] T'yeer-na-n-oge: 'The legend of O'Donoghue' (Thomas Crofton Croker§ [*sic*]), 'Rent-day', 'Loughleagh (Lake of Healing)', 'The phantom isle' (Giraldus Cambrensis). [j] Saints, priests: 'The priest's soul' (Lady Wilde§), 'The story of the little bird' (Thomas Crofton Croker§ [*sic*]), 'Conversion of King Laoghaire's daughters', 'King O'Toole and his goose'. [k] The devil: 'The demon cat' (Lady Wilde§), 'The Countess Kathleen O'Shea', 'The three wishes' (William Carleton§). [l] Giants: 'The giant's stairs', 'A legend of Knockmany' (William Carleton§). [m] Kings, queens, princesses, earls, robbers: 'The twelve wild geese' (Patrick Kennedy§), 'The lazy beauty and her aunts' (Patrick Kennedy§), 'The haughty princess' (Patrick Kennedy§), 'The enchantment of Gearoidh Iarla' (Patrick Kennedy§), Munachar and Manachar (trans. by Douglas Hyde§), 'Donald and his neighbours' (from [*Royal*] *Hibernian tales*, Dublin, 1825 or earlier), 'The jack-daw' [from *Royal Hibernian tales*, Dublin, 1825 or earlier], 'The story of Conn-eda; or, the golden apples of Lough Erne' (by Abraham McCoy, trans. by Nicholas O'Kearney) [RL; Thuente 1, p. 93].

Y3   *Representative Irish tales* (ed. and introd. by W.B. Yeats).
   + New York, London: G.P. Putnam's Sons (The Knickerbocker Press), [1891], 2 vols. (first and second series). SOURCE Hayley, p. 183; Thuente 1, passim; Linen Hall cat. p. 266; Wade, 215. LOCATION Dt, BFl, InND Loeber coll.
   Gerrards Cross: Smythe, 1979 (foreword by Mary Helen Thuente). LOCATION L.
   + Atlantic Highlands (NJ): Humanities Press, 1979 (foreword by Mary Helen Thuente). LOCATION InND.
   COMMENTARY 1st series. Contents: 'Castle Rackrent' [fragment] (Maria Edgeworth§), 'The stolen sheep', (John and Michael Banim§), 'The mayor of Windgap' (John and Michael Banim§); 'Wildgoose Lodge' (William Carleton§), 'Condy Cullen and the gauger' (William Carleton§), 'The curse' (William Carleton§), 'The battle of the factions' (William Carleton§). 2nd series: 'Barny O'Reirdon' (Samuel Lover§), 'Paddy the piper' (Samuel Lover§), 'Father Tom and the Pope' (William Maginn§), 'Confessions of Tom Burke' (Thomas Crofton Croker§ [*sic*]), 'Knight of the sheep' (Gerald Griffin§), 'Death of the huntsman' (Gerald Griffin§), 'Trinity College' (Charles Lever§), 'Pig-driving peelers' (Charles Kickham§), 'Hungry death', (Rosa Mulholland§), 'The jackdaw' (Rosa Mulholland§), 'Darby Doyle's visit to Quebec' (Rosa Mulholland§) [Linen Hall cat.].
Y4   *Sherman, and Dhoya* (by 'Ganconagh').
   London: T. Fisher Unwin, 1891 (The Pseudonym Library). SOURCE Brown, 1690; Hogan 2, p. 1272; Roth, 10. LOCATION Dt, L (1891, 2nd edn).
   New York: Cassell, 1891 (The 'Unknown' Library). SOURCE Roth, 11; OCLC. LOCATION Boston College.
   COMMENTARY Written in 1888, consists of stories that illustrate WBY's leanings towards escapism and rebellion. Contents: 'Ganconagh's apology', 'John Sherman', 'Dhoya' [Hogan; Roth; Foster, i, pp 68–9].

Y5 *Irish fairy tales* (introd. by W.B. Yeats).
London: T. Fisher Unwin, 1892 (ill. Jack B. Yeats; The Children's Library). SOURCE
Roth, 15; Brown, 1691 (1892, 3rd. edn); Brown 2, 1641; Osborne, p. 47 ([1892], 3rd
impr.), Wade, 216. LOCATION CaOTP ([1892], 3rd impr.), CtY.
New York: Cassell, 1892. SOURCE Roth, 16; Wade, 217; OCLC. LOCATION CLU.
London: Pan Books, 1979 (as *Fairy and folktales of Ireland*; foreword by Kathleen
Raine). SOURCE Thuente 1, p. 283. LOCATION Dt, L.
Melbourne, Sydney, Adelaide: Cole, n.d. (Victoria Library). SOURCE Hayley, p. 181.
COMMENTARY No copy of the Melbourne edn located. Includes stories from *Fairy and folk
tales of the Irish peasantry* (London, [1888]) and *Irish fairy tales* (London, 1892). Four sets of
stories for children. [1.] 'Land and water fairies': 'The fairies' dancing-place', 'The rival kem-
pers', 'The young piper', 'A fairy enchantment', 'Teigue of the Lee', 'The fairy greyhound',
'The Lady Gollerus'. [2.] 'Evil spirits': 'The devil's mill', 'Fergus O'Mara and the air-demons',
'The man who never knew fear'. [3.] 'Cats': 'Seanchan the bard and the king of the cats',
'Owney and Owney-na-peak'. [4.] 'Kings and warriors': 'The knighting of Cuculain', 'The little weaver of Duleek gate' (Samuel Lover§) [RL].

Y6 *The Celtic twilight. Men and women, dhouls and faeries* (by W.B. Yeats) .
London: Lawrence & Bullen, 1893 (ill. J.B. Yeats). SOURCE Hogan 2, p. 1285; Roth,
20; Brown, 1693; Wade, 8. LOCATION L.
+ London: A.H. Bullen, 1902 (revsd. with additions, as *The Celtic twilight*; with por-
trait of the author by Jack B. Yeats). SOURCE Roth, 64; Thuente 1, p. 124, 141.
LOCATION L, InND Loeber coll.
New York, London: Macmillan & Co., 1894. SOURCE Roth, 30; Wade, 9. LOCATION
GEU.
COMMENTARY Consists of legends rather than folktales. A note by WBY in Quinn's copy
(Quinn 11354) states that these are 'All real stories heard among the people or real incidents
but with a little disguise in names & places'. Contents (excluding poetry): 'This book', 'A teller
of tales', 'Belief and unbelief', 'A visionary', 'Village ghosts', 'A knight of the sheep', 'The
sorcerers', 'The last gleeman', 'Regina, Regina, Pigmeorum, Veni', 'Kidnappers', 'The untiring ones', 'The man and his boots', 'A coward', 'The three O'Byrnes and the evil fairies',
'Drumcliff and Rosses', 'The thick skull of the fortunate', 'The religion of the sailor',
'Concerning the nearness together of heaven, earth and purgatory', 'The eaters of the precious
stones', 'Our lady of the hills', 'The golden age', 'A remonstrance with Scotsmen of having
soured the disposition of their ghosts and fairies', 'The four winds of desire', 'Into the twilight' [Roth; Thuente, pp 121–9, 137–41].

Y7 *The secret rose: Irish folk-lore* (by W.B. Yeats; dedicated to AE [George Russell]).
London: Lawrence & Bullen, 1897 (ill. J.B. Yeats). SOURCE Brown, 1692 (1898 edn);
Roth, 39. LOCATION Dt, L.
+ Dublin: Maunsel & Co., 1905 (as *The secret rose*; ill. J.B. Yeats). LOCATION D, L.
New York, London: Dodd, Mead & Co., 1897; London: Lawrence & Bullen. SOURCE
Quinn, 11369; Roth, 40; OCLC. LOCATION CtY.
COMMENTARY Contents (except poetry): 'The binding of the hair', 'The wisdom of the king',
'Where there is nothing, there is God', 'The crucifixion of the outcast', 'Out of the rose', 'The
curse of the fires and of the shadows', 'The heart of the spring', 'Of Costello the Proud, of
Oona the daughter of Dermott and of the bitter tongue', 'The book of the great Dhoul and
Hanrahan the Red', 'The twisting of the rope and Hanrahan the Red', 'Kathleen the daugh-
ter of Hoolihan and Hanrahan the Red', 'The curse of Hanrahan the Red', 'The death of
Hanrahan the Red', 'The rose of the shadow', 'The old men of the twilight', 'Rosa alchemica' [Roth; Quinn 11369].

Y8   *Stories of Red Hanrahan* (by William Butler Yeats [with Lady (Isabella) Augusta Gregory]).

Dundrum (Co. Dublin): Dun Emer Press [Cuala Press], 1904. SOURCE Quinn, 11460. LOCATION L.

London, Stratford-upon-Avon: A.H. Bullen, 1913 (as *Stories of Red Hanrahan. The secret rose. Rosa alchemica*). SOURCE Brown 2, 1642; Roth, 138. LOCATION L.

New York: Macmillan Co., 1914 (as *Stories of Red Hanrahan. The secret rose. Rosa alchemica*). SOURCE Quinn, 11541. LOCATION L.

COMMENTARY The Dundrum edn is a limited edn of 500 copies. A collection of folk-tales dealing with the life, adventures and death of Red Hanrahan. Written in collaboration with Lady Gregory. WBY noted in 1904 that 'I am re-writing all the Hanrahan stories in this book in very simple words like those the country people tell their stories in.' The London 1913 edn also contains a group of formless tales issued under the title *The Secret Rose*, which is a revision. Contents of the Dundrum edn: 'Red Hanrahan', 'The twisting of the rope', 'Hanrahan and Cathleen the daughter of Hoolihan', 'Red Hanrahan's curse', 'Hanrahan's vision', 'The death of Hanrahan' [Thuente 1, pp 194–238; Brown 2; Quinn; RL].

Y9   *Mythologies* (by W.B. Yeats).

London: Macmillan, 1959. SOURCE Brown 2, 1643. LOCATION L.

COMMENTARY Contains a collection of tales published originally in *The Celtic twilight* (London, 1893), *The secret rose* (London, 1897), and *Stories of Red Hanrahan* (Dundrum, 1904). Many of these tales were told to the author by Paddy Flynn, who lived in village of Ballysodare (Co. Sligo), and may be described as folk tales [Brown 2].

YONGE, Charlotte Mary, b. Otterbourne, near Winchester (Hants.) 1823, d. 1901. Prolific English writer of moral fiction, history, biography, and religious works – principally for juveniles – with over 150 titles to her name, most of them published anonymously. CMY was the daughter of William Yonge, a magistrate, and Frances Bargus. Educated at home 'on the Edgeworth system', a reference to the educational theories of Richard Lovell Edgeworth§, she later came under the influence of the cleric John Keble, who encouraged her to use her writing talent as an instrument in God's service. She was associated with the Tractarian movement at Oxford and for almost 40 years was the editor of an educational magazine. She donated the proceeds from her work to Anglican charities. In 1857 she made a trip to Dublin. Katharine Tynan§ recalled reading one of CMY's novels when she was at boarding-school. SOURCE Allibone, iii, pp 2887–8; Allibone Suppl., ii, pp 1558–9; Blain, pp 1198–9; B. Dennis, *Charlotte Yonge (1823–1901): novelist of the Oxford Movement* (Lewiston, NY, 1992); Field Day, v, p. 661; NCBEL 4, p. 1443–48; ODNB; J. Sturrock, *'Heaven and home': Charlotte Mary Yonge's domestic fiction and the Victorian debate over women* (Victoria, BC, 1995); Sutherland, pp 685–6.

Y10   *The Danvers papers. An invention* [anon.].

+ London: Macmillan & Co., 1867. SOURCE Baker, p. 91; Wolff, 7361. LOCATION L.

Leipzig: Bernard Tauchnitz, 1867 (as *The Danvers papers; The prince and the page*). SOURCE T & B, 914; COPAC. LOCATION L.

COMMENTARY Historical fiction for juveniles. Based on letters found in a family home, it concerns a Protestant family on the north-east coast of Ireland from 1680 onwards and relates the ensuing troubles in Ireland [ML; Baker].

'YORICK, Mr.', pseud. See STERNE, Laurence.

'YORKE, Oliver', pseud. See MAHONY, Fr Francis Sylvester.

'A Young Lady'

'A YOUNG LADY', pseud. See FULLER, Anne.

'A YOUNG LADY', pseud. See PERCIVAL, Mrs Margaret.

'A YOUNG LADY', fl. 1786. Pseudonym of a writer who was well-read, given the diversity of writers quoted in the following volume Considering that she published only in Dublin, she may have been Irish. SOURCE RL.

Y11 *The history of Jessy Evelin* [and] *Hassan, an Oriental tale* (by 'A young Lady').
+ Dublin: Printed for the authoress by W. Sleater, 1786. SOURCE ESTC t059654. LOCATION D.
COMMENTARY Content: 'The history of Jessy Evelin' (Jessy Evelin, the daughter of a curate, lives in a single-storey cottage next to a Gothic 'structure'), 'Hassan, an Oriental tale' [RL].

Y12 *The history of Jessy Evelin* [and] *Armine the hermit, an Oriental tale.* (by 'the authoress of Jessy').
+ Dublin: Printed for the authoress by W. Sleater, 1786. SOURCE ESTC t59654. LOCATION D.
COMMENTARY 'The history of Jessy Evelin' was published earlier in the same year. Continuous pagination in the Dublin edn, but the book has two title pages. The first story (104pp); the second story, 'Armine ...', 40pp [RL].

'A YOUNG LADY', fl. 1787. Pseudonym of a novelist.

Y13 *Georgina; or, memoirs of the Bellmour family* (by 'A young Lady'; dedicated to Lavinia, Countess Spencer; introd. addressed to Mrs Montague).
London: Printed for the author, 1787, 4 vols. SOURCE Falkner Greirson cat. 14/224; Forster 2, 429; Raven 2, 1787:31; ESTC t732360. LOCATION L.
Geneva, Paris: Maradan, 1788 (trans. as *Georgina, histoire véritable*) SOURCE Raven 2, 1787:31.
Tübingen: [publisher?], 1790–92 (trans. as *Georgina. Eine wahre Geschichte*). SOURCE Raven 2: 1787:31.
COMMENTARY *Tübingen and Amsterdam edns* No copies located [RL].
Amsterdam: W. Holtrop, 1789 (trans. into Dutch as *Georgina. Eene waare geschiedenis* by Miss Burney [*sic*]). SOURCE Wintermans, 1787:31.
COMMENTARY Sometimes attributed to Georgina Bouverie, who is actually the protagonist of the novel. The action is set in Ireland, America (during the War of Independence), and India. It purports to have been written on the voyage home from Bengal [Falkner Greirson].

'A YOUNG LADY', fl. 1797. Pseudonym of a novelist who died young and who probably lived in Cork or its vicinity. SOURCE RL.

Y14 *The history of Julia & Cecilia de Valmont* (by 'A young lady, lately deceased').
+ Cork: Printed [for the author's relatives?] by J. Connor, 1797, 2 vols. (subscribers' list). SOURCE Raven 2, 1797:11; ESTC t167609. LOCATION D (vol. 1 only), CSmH.
COMMENTARY According to Raven, this was formerly attributed to Sophia Briscoe. A relative of the 'young lady' wrote the preface to the novel, which was written when the author was aged 17. An extract from the novel appeared in the *Casket or Hesperian Magazine* (Cork, May, 1797) [RL; Raven 2, 1797:11].

'A YOUNG LADY', fl. 1801. Pseudonym of a novelist.

Y15 *The monastery of Gondolfo. A romance* (by 'A young Lady').

+ Limerick: John & Thomas M'Auliff, 1801. SOURCE British Fiction; Garside, 1801:9; Herbert, p. 18; NSTC. LOCATION Dt.
COMMENTARY 142pp. A Gothic novel set in Italy. The publishers John and Thomas M'Auliff owned a circulating library in the city of Limerick [ML].

'A YOUNG LADY', fl. 1845. Pseudonym of an American writer of fiction for juveniles.
Y16   *The Morton family* (by 'A young Lady').
Boston: James Munroe & Co., 1845. SOURCE MacLeod, p. 182; OCLC. LOCATION CtY.
COMMENTARY Fiction for juveniles. It describes the bad condition of an Irish household of immigrants in America and contains a narrative of the deaths, one by one, of an entire family. This volume appears to be different from *The Morton family; or, "In God we trust"*, published by one 'H.L.E.' in Edinburgh in 1873 [MacLeod, pp 64, 102; CM].

'A YOUNG GENTLEMAN OF NOTE', pseud. See SUMNER, Charles Richard.

YOUNG, Amelia Sophia Coates. Co-author. See TOTTENHAM, Blanche Mary Loftus.

YOUNG (or YOUNGE), Hercules (also known as 'Heck'), b. Waterford *c*.1763, d. London? Unpublished writer of fiction for juveniles, HY was the son of the poet Revd Hercules Drelincourt Young (also Younge, d. 1798), a Church of Ireland clergyman, who held a living at or near Carrick-on-Suir (Co. Tipperary) and was the author of *Select odes of Anacreon* (London, 1802). HY entered TCD in 1779 and graduated BA in 1783. Dorothea Herbert§ characterized 'Heck' Young in 1777 as 'a most Eccentrick Being with all the ingenious Qualities of his father, and a double Portion of his Satire'. He wrote an unidentified book for Dorothea Herbert and her siblings, in which he made 'Master Otway, Master Thomas [Dorothea's brothers], Miss Dolly [Dorothea] and Miss Fanny [Dorothea's sister] the principal Personages of his Epic Labours'. He was still noticed at Carrick-on-Suir in 1785, but died at a young age 'in the Temple' (the Inns of court, London?). Published works by HY are not known. SOURCE B & S, p. 902; O'Donoghue, p. 493; *Retrospections of Dorothea Herbert 1770–1806* (Dublin, 1988), pp 34, 131.

YOUNG, M.J. See YOUNG, Maria Julia.

YOUNG, Mary Julia. See YOUNG, Maria Julia.

YOUNG, Maria Julia (also known as M.J. Young and Mary Julia Young), fl. 1791. English poet and novelist, MJY lived in London and was a relative of Edward Young, author of *The complaint; or, night thoughts* (London, 1751). She published a collection of poems; translated French and German novels; and produced many novels of her own. Given that a few of them have Irish characters, she may have had Irish connections. SOURCE Allibone, iii, p. 2900; BD, p. 405; Blain, p. 1201; Blakey, p. 186; RL; NCBEL 4, pp 1088–9.
Y17   *Rose-Mount Castle; or, false report. A novel* (by M.J. Young; dedicated to Mrs Trant).
London: William Lane, 1798, 3 vols. SOURCE Blakey, p. 186; Raven 2, 1798:75; ESTC n013327.
COMMENTARY Corvey CME 3–628–45219–8, Ireland related fiction, O.
COMMENTARY The main character is a Frenchman, Villiers De Rousillon, whose mother was the daughter of a noble Irish family. Her brother was the earl of Claranbridge. De Rousillon goes to Ireland to claim an inheritance. The novel was unfavourably reviewed in the *Critical*

Review (Dec. 1798), which stated that 'It is almost destitute of fable or of any excitement to curiosity, if we accept the introduction of a gang of Irish *defenders*, who rob and murder in a very *sentimental* style, and one of whom becomes afterwards a personage of high consequence in the group of lords and dukes, having relinquished his *youthful errors*' [ML; Personal communication, Antonia Fraser, Sept. 1997].

Y18　**Right and wrong; or, the kinsmen of Naples. A romantic story** (by Mary Julia Young).

+ London: Crosby & Co.; Hughes, 1803. 4 vols. SOURCE British Fiction; Garside, 1803:79. LOCATION Corvey CME 3–628–48995–4, L.

COMMENTARY Opening in Italy and closing in Wales, the story contains a few Irish characters, for example, a Dr O'Brien. The main character chooses the name Fitzalvin as a disguise [ML; Blain].

Y19　**Donalda; or, the witches of Glenshiel. A Caledonian legend** (by Mary Julia Young). London: J.F. Hughes, 1805, 2 vols. SOURCE BD, p. 405; British Fiction; Garside, 1805:74. LOCATION Corvey CME 3–628–48991–1, L ([1843] edn).

COMMENTARY Set in Ireland and on the Scottish Aran Islands. The heroine deals boldly with supposed ghosts and corpses [Blain; CM].

Y20　**The heir of Drumcondra; or, family pride** (by Mary Julia Young).

+ London: A.K. Newman & Co., 1810, 3 vols. SOURCE BD, p. 405; Blakey, p. 232; British Fiction; Garside, 1810:89. LOCATION Corvey CME 3–628–48992–X, Ireland related fiction, E.

COMMENTARY Set largely in England, although many of the characters are Irish. The venal and greedy Anglo-Irish earl of Drumcondra usurps his title and Irish estates from his brother, whom he believes to be dead. The real earl, however, has disguised himself as a Mr Collier. After exposing his brother's crimes, Mr Collier is restored to his place as the earl of Drumcondra. His daughter marries Valentine Kennedy and settles on an Irish estate granted to them by the earl. The novel ends in Ireland with the newly-married couple improving the estate and encouraging industry among the tenants [JB].

YOUNG, Marian A.F., fl. 1862. Novelist, MAFY is likely to be Irish since she published only in Dublin. SOURCE COPAC; RL.

Y21　**Arragon House; or, the banker's son** (by Marian A.F. Young).

Dublin: James Duffy, 1862. SOURCE Adv. in *The adventures of a watch* (Dublin, [1865]); Alston, p. 481. LOCATION Dt, L.

COMMENTARY Announced to be ready for publication, 5 Apr. 1862. Set in England, the story opens with a bank failure. The family involved is Roman Catholic. No Irish content [ML; COPAC; *The Illustrated Dublin Jrnl*, 5 Apr. 1862].

YOUNGE, Hercules. See **YOUNG, Hercules.**

Z

'ZABO', pseud. See **LOWRY, Frank M.**

'ZERO', fl. 1890s. Pseudonym of a writer of moral stories.

Z1   *A gentleman of the nineteenth century. An anachronism in six parts. Two chronicles* (by 'Zero').

+ London: Digby, Long & Co., [1896]. LOCATION L, InND Loeber coll.

COMMENTARY Contents: 'A gentleman of the nineteenth century' (set in England among the gentry and revolves around the problem of how to do good), 'An anachronism in six parts' (centres on the themes of honesty and bravery. Kenneth Vivian unexpectedly inherits an estate in Ulster, where he lives happily with his mother. One day he comes across a piece of paper indicating that there might be a prior claimant in America. He engages a lawyer to seek out the heir, who is found and who takes possession. Kenneth then joins the army and on a trip back from the Continent drowns when he refuses to leave the sinking ship and insists that his friend, who has a wife and children, take his place in the lifeboat). The volume also has a 'Prologue' of 4 lines of verse, and an 'Epilogue' of 6 lines of verse [ML; JB].

'ZOZIMUS', pseud. See **MORAN, Michael**. This pseudonym is also credited to Maurice Richard Leyne, b. Tralee (Co. Kerry) 1820, d. Thurles (Co. Tipperary) 1854, a poet and patriotic journalist who contributed to the *Nation* (1844–54). SOURCE Irish pseudonyms; O'Donoghue, p. 252.

Addenda

Anon.105   *The Irish girl; or, the true love and the false.*
Improved date:
Glasgow: Cameron & Ferguson, [1877 or later]. SOURCE Brown, 47; advertised in A.M. Sullivan, *New Ireland* (London, Glasgow, [1877 or later]).

Anon.110   *The Irish pearl. A tale of the time of Queen Anne.*
Additional edn:
+ [Boulogne-sur-Mer]: [n.p.], 1855, 2nd edn (ill. Ch. Aigre). LOCATION PC.
ADDITIONAL COMMENTARY The Boulogne-sur-Mer edn is likely because the illustration of its title page is dated from that location, and the printing is French in character [RL].

Anon.134a   *De levensgevallen en bedryven van Vlaamsche Mie, welke zich door haar gedrag en wisselvalligheden in Engeland zeer berucht gemaakt heft; Gepaard met de levensgevallen en bedryven van Yrsche Beth.*
Amsterdam: Steven van Esveldt, 1752 (trans. from English into Dutch).
COMMENTARY The first story is said to be by the English author Daniel Defoe (probably a translation of his *Fortunes and misfortunes of... Moll Flanders*, London, 1722); the second story has its own title page: *Levensgevallen van Jonkvrouwe Elizabeth*** bygenaamt Yrsche Beth*, which in English would be something like *The life of Lady Elizabeth****, also known as *Irish Beth*. The English original of this story is not apparent from McBurney, Raven, or the ESTC. SOURCE *Mateboer*, 996; RL; McBurney, 128. LOCATION Koninklijke Bibliotheek, The Hague.

Anon.160   *The maid of Erin: or, the lily of Tyrconnel.*
ADDITIONAL COMMENTARY Set in Co. Donegal [Snell, p. 150].

Anon.254   *Vertue rewarded; or, the Irish princess. A new novel.*
ADDITIONAL COMMENTARY It is possible that the date of this novel (1693) is perhaps an intentional misprint. The text has more in common with novels of the 1730s than of the 1690s, and may actually have been published after Samuel Richardson's famous *Pamela; or, virtue rewarded* (London, 1742–3, 2 vols.) [Personal communication, Andrew Carpenter, Feb. 2006; RL].

Anon.254a   *De verwonderenswaardige levens-gevallen van den Graaf van Yrland door een voornaam history-schryver in 't Nederduits beschreven.*
Amsterdam: Arnoldus Olofsen, 1737 (ill.). SOURCE Mateboer, 1573. LOCATION UVA.
COMMENTARY Dutch novel. A free translation of the title would be: 'The wonderful adventures of the Count [or Earl] of Ireland written by a famous historian writing in lower German'. Such a title, however, is not apparent from McBurney or ESTC [RL].

BANIM, John.
B20   *The Boyne water. A tale* (by 'the O'Hara family').
ADDITIONAL COMMENTARY Also set on the Co. Antrim coast [Leclaire, p. 45].
B21   *The Anglo-Irish of the nineteenth century. A novel* [anon.].
ADDITIONAL COMMENTARY Also set in the west of Ireland [Snell, p. 168].
B24   *The bit o' writin' and other tales* (by 'the O'Hara family').
ADDITIONAL COMMENTARY Some of the stories illustrate peasant life in Co. Kilkenny [Leclaire, p. 47].

BARLOW, Jane.

B70   *Kerrigan's quality* (by Jane Barlow).
ADDITIONAL COMMENTARY Set in the west of Ireland [Snell, p. 168].

B71   *Strangers at Lisconnel. A second series of Irish idylls* (by Jane Barlow).
ADDITIONAL COMMENTARY Set in the west of Ireland [Snell, p. 168].

B73   *Mrs. Martin's company and other stories* (by Jane Barlow).
ADDITIONAL COMMENTARY Set in the west of Ireland [Snell, p. 169].

B74   *A creel of Irish stories* (by Jane Barlow).
ADDITIONAL COMMENTARY Set in the west of Ireland [Snell, p. 169].

B76   *From the land of the shamrock* (by Jane Barlow).
ADDITIONAL COMMENTARY Set in the west of Ireland [Snell, p. 169].

B77   *The founding of fortunes* (by Jane Barlow).
ADDITIONAL COMMENTARY Set in the west of Ireland [Snell, p. 169].

B78   *By beach and bog-land. Some Irish stories* (by Jane Barlow).
ADDITIONAL COMMENTARY Set in the west of Ireland [Snell, p. 169].

B79   *Irish neighbours* (by Jane Barlow).
ADDITIONAL COMMENTARY Set in the west of Ireland [Snell, p. 169].

B85   *Doings and dealings* (by Jane Barlow).
ADDITIONAL COMMENTARY Set in the west of Ireland [Snell, p. 169].

BARRY, Msgr William Francis.

B99   *The wizard's knot* (by William Francis Barry).
ADDITIONAL COMMENTARY Set in Co. Cork [Snell, p. 148].

BARTER, Miss, fl. 1793.

ADDITIONAL AUTHOR Novelist, whose name is sometimes spelled Bartar, lived near Derry. Miss B initially§ contacted the English novelist Charlotte Smith§ in 1793, stating that her father was unwell, and requested Charlotte Smith to correct her novel. Later she asked whether she could publish her novel under Charlotte Smith's name and share the profits. However, once Charlotte Smith had looked at the manuscript, she realized that it was not saleable, and referred her to Lane, the Minerva publisher in London. Nothing is further known about Miss B. or her novel. However, there is a small possibility that she can be identified with Miss Mary Barker§, who published *A Welsh story* (London, 1798, 3 vols), but which was not published at the Minerva Press. SOURCE J.P. Stanton, *The collected letters of Charlotte Smith* (Bloomington, IN, 2003), pp 80, 94.

BEDDOES, Thomas.

B134   *The history of Isaac Jenkins, and of the sickness of Sarah, his wife, and their three children* [anon.].
Additional edn:
Haarlem: François Bohn, 1794 (trans. into Dutch as *De geschiedenis van Isaac Jenkins en Sara zijne vrouw èn derzelver drie kinderen: Een volksboek*). SOURCE Mateboer, 508.
LOCATION UVA.

BIRD, May, fl. 1877.

ADDITIONAL AUTHOR Catholic religious fiction writer, who was also the author of Marion *Howard; or, trials and triumphs* (London, 1880, which must have been published earlier), and *Maggie's rosary, and other tales* (London, [1871]). Snell identifies her as May Bird, but provides no further information. SOURCE BLC; RL; Snell, p. 169.

Addenda

B150a *The Lady of Neville Court. A tale of the times* (by the author of *Marion Howard*).
London: [publisher?], 1877. SOURCE COPAC; Snell, p. 169. LOCATION L.
ADDITIONAL COMMENTARY Set in the west of Ireland [Snell, p. 169].

BLUNDELL, Mary E.
B200 *Maime o' the corner* (by 'M.E. Francis').
ADDITIONAL COMMENTARY Set in Liverpool and Lancashire [Leclaire, p. 187].

BOYCE, Fr John.
ADDITIONAL BIOGRAPHICAL INFORMATION See P. Maume, 'Father Boyce, Lady Morgan and
Sir Walter Scott: A study of intertextuality and Catholic polemics' in J.H. Murphy (ed.),
Evangelicals and Catholics in nineteenth century Ireland (Dublin, 2005), pp 165–78, and C. Boyce,
Biographical sketch of Rev. John Boyce, D.D. (1810–64) (Dublin, 1941).
B298 *Shandy McGuire; or, tricks upon travellers. Being a story of the North of Ireland*
(by 'Paul Peppergrass, Esq.').
ADDITIONAL COMMENTARY Col. Templeton in the story was based on the landlord
E.M. Connolly [Maume, 'Father Boyce', p. 169].

BROOKE, Henry.
B355 *The fool of quality; or, the history of Henry, Earl of Moreland* (by Mr Brooke).
Additional edn:
Amsterdam: Erven van F. Houttuyn, 1782, 5 vols. SOURCE Mateboer, 1789–01/05.
LOCATION UVA.

CANNING, the Hon. Albert Stratford George.
C61 *Baldearg O'Donnell. A tale of 1690–91* (by Albert S.G. Canning).
ADDITIONAL COMMENTARY Set in Co. Donegal [Snell, p. 150].

CARLETON, William.
C72 *Father Butler. The Lough Dearg pilgrim. Being sketches of Irish manners* [anon.].
ADDITIONAL COMMENTARY 'Father Butler' is set in the Clogher Valley of Co. Tyrone
[Leclaire, p. 56].
C73 *Traits and stories of the Irish peasantry* [anon.; first series].
ADDITIONAL COMMENTARY Set mostly in Co. Tyrone, except 'The station', which is
set in Co. Donegal [Leclaire, p. 57].
C75 *Traits and stories of the Irish peasantry* (second series) [anon.].
ADDITIONAL COMMENTARY Set mostly in Co. Tyrone, except 'Phil Purcell', which is
set in Connacht, and 'Wildgoose Lodge', which is set in Co. Louth [Leclaire, p. 57].
C79 *Fardorougha, the miser; or, the convicts of Lisnamona* (by William Carleton).
ADDITIONAL COMMENTARY Set in south Co. Tyrone [Leclaire, p. 58].
C88 *The black prophet. A tale of Irish famine* (by William Carleton).
ADDITIONAL COMMENTARY Set in Co. Tyrone [Leclaire, p. 58].

CASEY, Elizabeth Owens Blackburne.
C132 *A bunch of shamrocks. A collection of Irish tales and sketches* (by 'E. Owens
Blackburne').
ADDITIONAL COMMENTARY Set in Co. Meath [Snell, p. 164].

CHAIGNEAU, William.
ADDITIONAL BIOGRAPHICAL INFORMATION WC was one of the subscribers to the reprint of
Charlotte MacCarthy's§ *The fair moralist* (n.l., 1752). SOURCE RL.

CONYNGHAM, Major David Power.

C347 *Rose Parnell, the flower of Avondale. A tale of the rebellion of '98* (by D.P. Conyngham).
ADDITIONAL COMMENTARY Set in Co. Wicklow [Snell, p. 171].

COTTON, Revd Samuel George.

C386 *The three whispers, and other tales* (by Samuel George Cotton).
ADDITIONAL COMMENTARY Set in Dublin [Snell, p. 154].

CROKER, Marianne.

C472 *The adventures of Barney Mahoney* (by T. Crofton Croker§ [*sic*]).
ADDITIONAL COMMENTARY Set in the south-west of Ireland [Leclaire, p. 43].

CROMIE, Robert.

C489 *Kitty's Victoria Cross* (by Robert Cromie).
ADDITIONAL COMMENTARY Set in Ulster [Snell, p. 166].

DAUNT, William Joseph O'Neill.

D20 *The wife hunter & Flora Douglas. Tales by the Moriarty family* (ed. by 'Denis Ignatius Moriarty, Esq.').
ADDITIONAL COMMENTARY Set in Co. Cork [Snell, p. 148].

DAVYS, Mary.

D33 *The reform'd coquet; A novel* (by Mary Davys).
Additional edn:
Belfast: Simms & M'Intyre, 1811 (as *The reformed coquet; or, memoirs of Amoranda. A surprising novel*). LOCATION PC.
ADDITIONAL COMMENTARY Unusual late reprint of a novel first published in 1724 [RL].

DE GENLIS, Mme Stephanie-Félicité, marquise de Sillery, comtesse de Genlis.

ADDITIONAL BIOGRAPHICAL INFORMATION See also C. Ó Gallchoir, 'Orphans, upstarts and aristocrats: Ireland and the idyll of adoption in the work of Madame de Genlis'. In O. Walsh (ed.), *Ireland abroad* (Dublin, 2003), pp 36–46.

DE RENZY, Capt. S. Sparow.

D63 *Life, love, and politics; or the adventures of a novice. A tale* (by Sparow De Renzy).
ADDITIONAL COMMENTARY Satirical novel on the politics of the day [Burmester cat. 65/108].

DOWLING, Richard.

ADDITIONAL BIOGRAPHICAL INFORMATION He published an autobiographical fragment in J. White's *My Clonmel scrap book* (Waterford, 1907), pp 126–31. SOURCE RL.

EDGEWORTH, Mrs Frances (Fanny) Anne.

ADDITIONAL BIOGRAPHICAL INFORMATION Some of her drawings are in the Irish Architectural Archive in Dublin (Edgeworth Ms 82/7).

ESLER, Mrs Erminda Rentoul.

E127 *Almost a pauper. A tale of trial and triumph* (by Mrs E. Rentoul Esler).
ADDITIONAL COMMENTARY Set in Co. Donegal [Snell, p. 150].

E128   *The way of transgressors. A novel* (by Mrs E. Rentoul Esler).
ADDITIONAL COMMENTARY Set in Co. Donegal [Snell, p. 150].

E131   *'Mid green pastures. Short stories* (by E. Rentoul Esler)
ADDITIONAL COMMENTARY Set in Co. Donegal [Snell, p. 150].

E132   *The Wardlaws* (by E. Rentoul Esler).
ADDITIONAL COMMENTARY Set in Co. Donegal [Snell, p. 150].

E133   *Youth at the prow. A tale* (by E. Rentoul Esler).
ADDITIONAL COMMENTARY Set in Co. Donegal [Snell, p. 150].

E134   *The awakening of Helena Thorpe* (by E. Rentoul Esler).
ADDITIONAL COMMENTARY Set in Co. Donegal [Snell, p. 150].

FRANCILLON, Robert Edward.
F113   *Under Slieve-Ban: a yarn in seven knots* [anon.].
ADDITIONAL COMMENTARY Set in Co. Wexford [Snell, p. 170].

GLASCOCK, Capt. William Nugent.
ADDITIONAL BIOGRAPHICAL INFORMATION It is very likely that he can be identified with the
Capt. Glascock, who in about 1838 resided at Killowen, on the river Barrow, north of Ross
(Co. Wexford). SOURCE J. Fraser, *Guide through Ireland* (Dublin, 1838), p. 49.

GRIFFITH, Elizabeth.
G180   *The story of Lady Juliana Harley. A novel. In letters* (by Mrs Griffith).
Additional edn:
Amsterdam: M. Schalekamp, 1778, 2 vols. in 1 (trans. into Dutch as *Geschiedenis van
Lady Juliana Harley*). SOURCE F.A. van S., p. 37; Mateboer, 503–01/02. LOCATION
UVA.

GRIFFITH, Richard.
G185   *Something new* [anon.] (preface signed 'Automathes'; dedicated to 'All the world').
ADDITIONAL COMMENTARY Barchas called this 'highly experimental fiction' (Barchas, p. 239*n*.33).
Each of the two volumes is closed by a musical score of a dirge [J. Barchas, *Graphic design, print
culture, and the eighteenth century novel* (Cambridge, 2003), pp 212–3, 239*n*.33, 244*n*.71].

HALL, Mrs S.C.
H26   *The Whiteboy; A story of Ireland in 1822* (by Mrs S.C. Hall).
ADDITIONAL COMMENTARY Set in Co. Cork [Snell, p. 148].

HAMILTON, Catherine Jane.
H97   *True to the core. A romance of '98* (by C.J. Hamilton).
ADDITIONAL COMMENTARY Set in Dublin [Snell, p. 155].

HARDY, Philip Dixon
ADDITIONAL BIOGRAPHICAL INFORMATION He became editor of the *Irish Times* in 1824. He
introduced the first steam-powered printing press in Ireland in the early 1830s. Proprietor of
the profitable *Dublin Penny Journal*, which was published from 1832 onward. In 1841 he took
over the business and premises of the Religious Tract and Book Society for Ireland [C. Benson,
The Dublin book trade 1801–1850. Unpublished Ph.D. dissertation, Trinity College, Dublin,
2000, pp 36, 41, passim].

'HARRINGTON, F. Clinton', probably an incorrect version of 'F. Clinton Barrington',
pseud. of **A.G. PIPER.**

JOHNSTONE, Charles.
J44   *Chrysal; or, the adventures of a guinea. Wherein are exhibited views of several striking scenes, with curious and interesting anecdotes of the most noted persons in every rank of life, whose hands it passed through in America, England, Holland, Germany and Portugal* (by 'An adept'; dedication to William Pitt, signed 'A Briton').
Additional edn:
Den Haag [The Hague]: H. Bakhuysen, 1763–67, 4 vols (trans. into Dutch by E.B**s [E.Buys] as *Chrysal of: De gevallen van een guinie*). SOURCE Mateboer 218–op1/04. LOCATION Koninklijke Bibliotheek, The Hague.

J45   *The reverie; or, a flight to the paradise of fools* [anon.].
Additional detail
's Gravenhage: Pieter van Os, 1765, 2 vols. (trans. into Dutch as *De mymering, of: een vlucht naar het paradys der dwazen*; ill. S. Fokke). SOURCE F.A. v. S.; Mateboer, 1088. LOCATION UVA.

JOYCE, Robert Dwyer.
J63   *The green and the red; or, historical tales and legends of Ireland* [anon.].
ADDITIONAL COMMENTARY Advertised in A.M. Sullivan, *New Ireland* (London, Glasgow, [1877 or later], 8th edn) priced at 1*s*.

KEARY, Anna Maria (Annie).
K28   *Castle Daly. The story of an Irish home 30 years ago* (by Annie Keary).
Recent edn:
+ London: Routledge/Thoemmes, 1998 (introd. by V. Crossman). LOCATION D.
ADDITIONAL COMMENTARY Based on AMK's memory of stories told by her father [Leclaire, p. 139].

KICKHAM, Charles Joseph.
K119   *Knocknagow; or, the homes of Tipperary* (by Charles J. Kickham).
ADDITIONAL COMMENTARY No copy of the Dublin [1873] edn located. Advertised in the Shamrock (Dublin) 17 May 1873 that the book would 'be ready for delivery on Saturday, 31st May' at a price of 3*s*. 6*d*., and in a 'superior binding, cloth gilt' at 5*s*. [RL].

K120   *For the old land. A tale of twenty years ago* (by the late Charles J. Kickham).
ADDITIONAL COMMENTARY Set in Co. Tipperary [Snell, p. 166].

LARMINIE, William Rea.
ADDITIONAL BIOGRAPHICAL INFORMATION WRL published his 'Legends as material for literature' in *Literary ideals in Ireland*, edited by W.B. Yeats, 'A.E.' [George Russell], and himself (London, 1899, pp 57–65).

LAWLESS, Emily.
L44   *Traits and confidences* (by the Hon. Emily Lawless).
ADDITIONAL COMMENTARY Set in Cos. Cork, Galway, and Donegal [Leclaire, p. 156].

L46   *The race of Castlebar. Being a narrative addressed by Mr. John Bunbury to his brother, Mr. Theodore Bunbury, attached to His Britannic Majesty's Embassy at Florence, October 1798, and now first given to the world* (by the Hon. Emily Lawless and Shan F. Bullock§).
ADDITIONAL COMMENTARY Set in Co. Mayo [Snell, p. 164].

Addenda

LEADBEATER, Mary.
ADDITIONAL BIOGRAPHICAL INFORMATION ML's story 'Domestic virtue' was published posthumously in the *Amulet* (London, 1827). SOURCE RL.

LEVER, CHARLES.
L145   *The confessions of Harry Lorrequer, late Captain in the –th regiment of foot* [anon.].
ADDITIONAL COMMENTARY Partly set in and about Cork [Leclaire, p. 66].
L148   (Our Mess, II & III) *Tom Burke of "ours"* (by Charles Lever).
ADDITIONAL COMMENTARY Set in the west of Ireland [Leclaire, p. 66].
L152   *Tales of the trains, being some chapters of railroad romance* (by 'Tilbury Tramp, queen's messenger').
ADDITIONAL COMMENTARY Issued first in parts. Part No.1, entitled 'The coupé of the North Midland: A tale of the trains' announced that the second issue would be 'The white lace bonnet', but this title was not issued [RL].

LOVER, Samuel.
L216   *Legends and stories of Ireland* (compiled by Samuel Lover; [first series]).
ADDITIONAL COMMENTARY Set in the south and west of Ireland [Leclaire, p. 65].
L217   *Legends and stories of Ireland* (second series; compiled by Samuel Lover).
ADDITIONAL COMMENTARY Set in the south and west of Ireland [Leclaire, p. 65].
L219   *Rory O'More. A national romance* (by Samuel Lover).
ADDITIONAL COMMENTARY Set in the south of Ireland [Leclaire, p. 64].

LUCK, Mrs Mary Churchill.
L254   *The breakaway* (by 'M. Hamilton').
London: Hurst & Blackett, [1928]. LOCATION L.
ADDITIONAL COMMENTARY Set in Ulster [Snell, p. 167].

LYNAM, William Francis.
ADDITIONAL BIOGRAPHICAL INFORMATION WFL mentioned holding the rank of lieutenant colonel when writing 'Mick M'Quaid, workhouse master' in the *Shamrock* (Dublin) in 1904. SOURCE RL.

MC CARTHY, Miss Charlotte.
ADDITIONAL BIOGRAPHICAL INFORMATION It is assumed that CMC grew up in Ireland. She referred to her father as a 'gentleman', who died destitute after fifty years of government service. Born a Catholic, she was orphaned and raised a Protestant. She tried to publish in Ireland, but was initially thwarted in this by printers and a relative. Moving to London, she published there her novel, *The fair moralist* in 1745, supported by subscribers who were largely trades people. Although she published several volumes of poetry in London, she must have been poor and found herself selling theatre tickets in Twickenham and Richmond in 1749. It is probable that she returned to Ireland, where she privately republished her novel in 1752, with the aid of subscribers in Cos. Kilkenny, Tipperary, and Waterford (it had been initially published and reprinted in Dublin in 1747). This suggests that she had become resident in one of these counties. The subscribers' list largely consisting of trades people, mentions a few possible relatives, including Mr John McCarthy of Spring House (possibly Spring House, near Cahir, Co Tipperary), Mrs McCarthy, possibly of the same location, and Mr Denis McCarthy of Carrick-on-Suir (Co. Tipperary). SOURCE Field Day, iv, p. 1137; J. Fraser, *Guide through Ireland* (Dublin, 1838), p. 148; RL.

M28　*The fair moralist; or, love and virtue. To which is added, several occasional poems, by the same* (by 'A gentlewoman').
Additional edn:
[Ireland], [n.p.] Printed for the author, 1752 (as *The fair moralist; or, love and virtue: A novel. To which is added, several occasional poems*; by Miss Charlotte McCarthy; dedicated to Mrs Standish Howard; subscribers' list). LOCATION PC.
ADDITIONAL COMMENTARY The text of the Dublin 1747 edn consists of 69pp, while that of the 1752 consists of 126pp. The title page does not indicate a publisher, but the absence of Dublin subscribers suggests that the novel may have been published in either Kilkenny or Waterford. The volume was reprinted in Dublin by Richard Cross in 1783 (in 144pp), and thus stayed in print for an unusual length of time.

MC CARTHY, Justin Huntly.
M53　*Lily lass. A romance* (by Justin Huntly McCarthy).
ADDITIONAL COMMENTARY Set in Co. Cork [Snell, p. 148].

MC CLINTOCK, Letitia.
M67　*Sir Spangle and the dingy hen* (by Letitia McClintock).
ADDITIONAL COMMENTARY Set in Co. Donegal [Snell, p. 151].
M72　*A little candle, and other stories* (by Letitia M'Clintock).
ADDITIONAL COMMENTARY Set in Co. Donegal [Snell, p. 151].

MAC MANUS, Charlotte Elizabeth.
M181　*The silk of the kine* (by L. MacManus).
ADDITIONAL COMMENTARY Set partly in Co. Fermanagh [Snell, p. 158].

MAC MANUS, Séumas.
M194　*In chimney corners. Merry tales of Irish folklore* (by Seamus MacManus).
ADDITIONAL COMMENTARY Set in Co. Donegal [Snell, p. 151].
M198　*Barney Brian and other boys* (by Seumas MacManus).
ADDITIONAL COMMENTARY Set in Co. Donegal [Snell, p. 151].
M200　*Irish nights* (by Seamus MacManus).
ADDITIONAL COMMENTARY Set in Co. Donegal [Snell, p. 151].
M205　*Top o' the morning* (by Seamus MacManus).
ADDITIONAL COMMENTARY Set in Co. Donegal [Snell, p. 151].
M208　*Dark Patrick* (by Seamus MacManus).
ADDITIONAL COMMENTARY Set in Co. Donegal [Snell, p. 151].
M211　*Heavy hangs the golden grain* (by Seamus MacManus).
ADDITIONAL COMMENTARY Set in Co. Donegal [Snell, p. 151].
M212　*The bold heroes of Hungry Hill, and other Irish folk tales* (retold by Seumas MacManus).
ADDITIONAL COMMENTARY Set in Co. Donegal [Snell, p. 151].
M213　*The little mistress of the Eskar Mór* (by Seumas MacManus).
ADDITIONAL COMMENTARY Set in Co. Donegal [Snell, p. 151].

MAGENNIS, Peter.
M235　*The Ribbon informer. A tale of Lough Erne* (by Peter Magennis).
ADDITIONAL COMMENTARY Set in Co. Fermanagh [Snell, p. 158].

MAXWELL, William Hamilton.

M333   *My life* [anon.].
ADDITIONAL COMMENTARY Partly set in the west of Ireland [Leclaire, p. 62].

MONAHAN, Henry J., Jnr.

M397   *O'Ruark; or, the chronicles of the Balliquin family, detailing what they did, and what they did not; the wise maxims that they didn't put in practice, and the good resolutions which they left to be performed by their descendants: and laying the whole of their private transactions fully before the public* (by Henry J. Monahan).
ADDITIONAL COMMENTARY Also set in Co. Kerry [Snell, p. 161].

MORGAN, Lady.

M552   *The wild Irish girl. A national tale* (by Miss Owenson).
ADDITIONAL COMMENTARY Set in Co. Sligo [Leclaire, p. 20].

M555   *O'Donnel. A national tale* (by Lady Morgan, late Miss Owenson).
ADDITIONAL COMMENTARY Also set in Connacht [Leclaire, p. 21].

MULHOLLAND, Rosa.

M601   *Dunmara* (by 'Ruth Murray').
ADDITIONAL COMMENTARY Set in the west of Ireland [Snell, p. 170].

M632   *A girl's ideal* (by Rosa Mulholland).
ADDITIONAL COMMENTARY Partly set in the west of Ireland [Snell, p. 170].

M633   *Our sister Maisie* (by Rosa Mulholland).
ADDITIONAL COMMENTARY Set in the west of Ireland [Snell, p. 170].

MURPHY, James.

ADDITIONAL BIOGRAPHICAL INFORMATION JM also published novels in the *Irish Emerald* (Dublin, 1899, viii), for example, 'A sheaf of wheat. A tale of the rising of 1803'. SOURCE RL.

NAUTA, Abraham.

N4   *Elizabeth Edmunds of de redding der Iersche Protestanten, eene episode uit de regering van Maria Tudor* (by A. Nauta).
ADDITIONAL COMMENTARY According to the preface, the story is based on information in the *Gentleman's Magazine* (1760, iii), a memorial on Richard Boyle, earl of Cork, and the works of James Ware. Part of the story is set in Cos. Dublin, Wicklow and the city of Dublin. One of the characters is Capt. O'Noodle [RL].

NEVILLE, Ralph.

N10   *Lloyd Pennant. A tale of the West* (by Ralph Neville).
ADDITIONAL COMMENTARY Also set in the west of Ireland [Snell, p. 170].

NUGENT-GRENVILLE, Lady Anne. Co-author. See **NUGENT-GRENVILLE, George,** 3rd baron.

O'CONNOR, Thomas Power.

ADDITIONAL BIOGRAPHICAL INFORMATION He was editor of *T.P.'s Weekly* (London, 1902–16). SOURCE RL; OCLC.

O'FLANAGAN, James Roderick.

ADDITIONAL BIOGRAPHICAL INFORMATION Since there were two residences called the Grange (both close to Fermoy), it is important to point out that JRO'F resided from at least 1844 onward at Grange Farm (and not at Grange Hill), situated between the river Blackwater and the road. He laid out the gardens and grounds of about twenty acres. SOURCE J.F. O'Flanagan, *The Blackwater in Munster* (London, 1844), p. 102.

O'GRADY, Standish James.
O97   *In the gates of the North* (by Standish O'Grady).
ADDITIONAL COMMENTARY First serialized in the *Old Ireland Review* (Kilkenny, 1900). SOURCE RL.

O'SHAUGHNESSY, Tom.
O198   *Terence O'Dowd; or, Romanism to-day. An Irish story, founded on facts* (by Tom O'Shaughnessy).
ADDITIONAL COMMENTARY Set in Co. Mayo [Snell, p. 164].

O'SHEA, John.
ADDITIONAL BIOGRAPHICAL INFORMATION Perhaps can be identified with the John J. O'Shea who wrote a serial 'Alive or dead; or, the days of the rapparees', which was published in the *Shamrock* (Dublin, 1889), although this publication date would be relatively late. SOURCE RL.

O'SULLIVAN, Dennis, pseud. '"Corporal" Morgan Rattler'.
ADDITIONAL BIOGRAPHICAL INFORMATION It is likely that this author's work was republished in the *Shamrock* (Dublin) under D. O'Sullivan. An example is cited below, while another example is DO'S's 'Julia O'Connor; or, Erin's friends and foe. A thrilling story of the dynamite scare' (1886, xxiii) [RL].
O213   *Robert Emmet; or, true Irish hearts* (by '"Corporal" Morgan Rattler').
New York: N.L. Munro, 1886 (Munro's Library of Popular Novels). LOCATION NUC.
ADDITIONAL COMMENTARY First published in serial form but unclear where. Republished in serial form in the *Shamrock* (Dublin, 1886, xxiii) under the name of D. O'Sullivan as 'Ireland will be free; or, at Robert Emmet's call' [Brown 2; RL].

POWER, William Grattan Tyrone.
P171   *The lost heir, and the prediction* [anon.].
+ London: Edward Bull, 1830, 3 vols.
ADDITIONAL COMMENTARY 'The lost heir' is set in France during the French Revolution. Features several Irishmen, including Major O'Dillon and one Milligan [RL].

PRÉVOST, Antoine-François.
P185   *Le doyen de Killerine, histoire morale, composée sur les mémoires d'une illustre famille d'Irlande, & ornée de tout ce qui peut rendre une lecture utile et agréable* [anon.].
ADDITIONAL EDN
+ Lille: J.B. Henry, 1771, 6 vols in 3 (ill.). SOURCE Jarndyce cat. 166/302.

ROCHE, Regina Maria.
R231   *The children of the abbey. A tale* (by Regina Maria Roche).
ADDITIONAL COMMENTARY The book formed the basis of an early silent film [C. Connolly, 'Irish romanticism' in M. Kelleher & P. O'Leary (eds.), *The Cambridge history of English literature* (Cambridge, 2006), i, p. 415].
R239   *The bridal of Dunamore; and Lost and won. Two tales* (by Regina Maria Roche).
ADDITIONAL COMMENTARY Set in Munster [Snell, p. 165].

Addenda

RYAN, William Patrick.
R286   *The plough and the cross; a story of new Ireland* (by William Patrick O'Ryan).
ADDITIONAL COMMENTARY Set in Co. Meath [Snell, p. 164].

SADLIER, Mrs J.
S16   *The daughter of Tyrconnell. A tale of the reign of James the First* (by Mrs J. Sadlier).
ADDITIONAL COMMENTARY Set partly in Co. Donegal [Snell, p. 152].

SHAW, Flora Louise.
S93   *Castle Blair. A story of youthful days* (Flora Louise, Baroness Lugard).
ADDITIONAL COMMENTARY Set in Co. Tipperary [Snell, p. 166].

SHAW, John.
ADDITIONAL VOLUME
S103a   *The old diamond merchant: A Belfast story of sixty years ago* (by John Shaw). [Belfast]: Weekly Northern Whig, 1887. SOURCE Snell, p. 146; OCLC. LOCATION D.
Correction
S104   *The diamond merchant, and other stories* (by John Shaw).
+ Belfast: R. Aikin & Co., 1898. SOURCE Brown, 1493; Brown 2, 1425 (n.d. edn). LOCATION D.

SHEEHAN, Canon Patrick Augustine.
S119   *The blindness of Dr. Gray; or, the final law* (by Canon P.A. Sheehan).
ADDITIONAL COMMENTARY Set in Co. Cork [Snell, p. 149].
S123   *The graves at Kilmorna. A story of '67* (by Canon P.A. Sheehan).
ADDITIONAL COMMENTARY Set in Co. Cork [Snell, p. 149].

SHERIDAN, Frances.
S130   *Memoirs of Miss Sidney Bidulph, extracted from her own journal & now first published* [anon.].
EARLIER DUTCH EDN
Amsterdam: Cornelius van Tongerlo, 1761, 3 vols (trans. into Dutch as *Historie van Juffrouw Sidney Bidulph. Uit eigenhandige gedenkschriften by een verzameld. Geschreven in de smaak van Pamela, Clarissa en Grandison*). SOURCE Mateboer 651-01/03, 651-04, 933-04/05. LOCATION UVA.

SMITH, Charlotte.
ADDITIONAL BIOGRAPHICAL INFORMATION Further research shows that this English novelist had more intense contacts with Ireland than were formerly known. Although she never went to Ireland, two Irish individuals provided her, as Stanton states, 'genuine and sustained friendships (Stanton, p. xix). In addition to the antiquarian the Revd Joseph Cooper Walker (1761–1810), she shared her literary interests with the Hon. Henrietta O'Neill (1758–93; only daughter and heiress of Charles Boyle, Viscount Dungarvan, whose husband was John O'Neill of Shane's Castle, Co. Antrim). She also maintained relationships with Lady Armida (Anne) Crofton of Mote (Co. Roscommon), and Mrs St Leger (probably the Hon. Mrs Anne St Leger, d. 1809, wife of Col. Richard St Leger, younger brother of Hayes, 2nd Viscount Doneraile); Henrietta Frances, countess of Bessborough (1761–1821); John Thomas, earl of Clanricarde and his wife, and Andrew Caldwell of Co. Fermanagh. CS included two poems by Henrietta

O'Neill in her *Rural walks* (London, 1795), which contained a drawing by the countess of Bessborough. With Walker acting as an intermediary, at least two of CS's novels, immediately after publication in London, were published by John Rice and his associates in Dublin under copyright rather than in pirated editions (*The banished man*, London, 1794, 4 vols, followed by Dublin, 1794, 2 vols; *The old manor house*, London, 1793, 4 vols, and followed by Dublin, 1793, 2 vols, and possibly other novels). Her Emmeline (London, 1788) was republished in Belfast in 1799.[1] She dedicated her *Minor morals* (London, 1816) to Lady Caroline Ponsonby, daughter of the countess of Bessborough. A Cork edition of her *The young philosopher. A novel* (London, 1798, 4 vols) was advertised in 1799. A Cork edition of her *Rural walks* was advertised in 1799, while its sequel, *Rambles further*, was republished in Dublin in 1796. SOURCE J.P. Stanton, *The collected letters of Charlotte Smith* (Bloomington, IN, 2003), pp xix, 53, 57, 149, 248*n*.3, 304*n*.4, 404*n*.2, passim; RL.

SMITH, Mary E.

S459 *Carroll O'Donoghue. A tale of the Irish struggles of 1866, and of recent times* (by 'Christine Faber').
ADDITIONAL COMMENTARY Set in Co. Kerry [Snell, p. 161].

SOMERVILLE, Edith Anna Œnone.

S464 *An Irish cousin* (by 'Geilles Herring' and 'Martin Ross').
ADDITIONAL COMMENTARY Set in Co. Cork [Snell, p. 149].

S471 *Some experiences of an Irish R.M.* (by E.Œ. Somerville and 'Martin Ross').
ADDITIONAL COMMENTARY Set in the south-west of Ireland [Leclaire, p. 171].

S473 *All on the Irish shore. Irish sketches* (by E.Œ. Somerville and 'Martin Ross').
ADDITIONAL COMMENTARY Set in Co. Cork [Snell, p. 149].

S475 *Some Irish yesterdays* (by E.Œ. Somerville and 'Martin Ross').
ADDITIONAL COMMENTARY Set in Connemara and the Aran Islands [Leclaire, p. 171].

S476 *Further experiences of an Irish R.M.* (by E.Œ. Somerville and 'Martin Ross').
ADDITIONAL COMMENTARY Set in Co. Cork [Snell, p. 149].

S479 *Mount Music* (by E.Œ. Somerville and 'Martin Ross').
ADDITIONAL COMMENTARY Set in Co. Cork [Snell, p. 149].

S487 *Sarah's youth* (by E.Œ. Somerville and 'Martin Ross').
ADDITIONAL COMMENTARY Set in Co. Cork [Snell, p. 149].

'A SUNDAY-SCHOOL TEACHER'.

S655 *The pastor's daughter: Intended as an incentive to early piety and usefulness* (by the author of *Little Mary*).
ADDITIONAL EDN
Dublin: William Curry Jnr & Co., [1832 or earlier]. Source Adv. in cat. of books by William Curry Jnr & Co., bound with [anon.], *Klosterheim: or, the mask* (London, 1832); RL.

'T., C.J.'

T1 *Folk-lore and legends (Ireland)* (ed. by 'C.J.T.').
+ London: W.W. Gibbings, 1889. SOURCE Brown 32; OCLC (1891 edn). LOCATION L (1891 edn), InND Loeber coll.

---

1 Her novels became very popular in Ireland, and were read by the marchioness of Downshire and the duchess of Leinster (R.J. Kurtz & J.L. Womer, 'The novel as political marker. Women writers and their female audiences in the Hookham and Carpenter archives, 1791-1798' in Cardiff Corvey 13 (Winter 2004). Online: Internet (accessed April 2006): <http://www.cf.ac.uk/encap/corvey/articles/cc13_no2.html>.

ADDITIONAL COMMENTARY 'The song of the little bird' first appeared in the *Amulet* (London, 1827) and was written by Thomas Crofton Croker§. SOURCE RL.

TALBOT, the Hon. Thomas.
T6   *The Granvilles. An Irish tale* (by the Hon. Thomas Talbot).
ADDITIONAL COMMENTARY Set in Co. Waterford [Snell, p. 168].

TIGHE, Mary.
ADDITIONAL BIOGRAPHICAL INFORMATION MT's father died when she was in her infancy, and she was brought up as a Methodist by her mother. After her marriage, MT and her husband resided in London, where they led a social and literary life. She spent her last years in Dublin and Rosanna (Co. Wicklow). SOURCE Field Day, iv, pp 509, 516.

TYNAN, Katharine.
ADDITIONAL BIOGRAPHICAL INFORMATION She was one of the editors of the revised edition of *Cabinet of Irish Literature* (London, 1902–3). SOURCE OCLC.
T151   *The land of mist and mountain* (by Katharine Tynan; dedicated to Hester Sigerson§).
ADDITIONAL COMMENTARY Set in Co. Wicklow, Dublin, etc. [Leclaire, p. 198].
T227   *Kit* (by Katharine Tynan).
ADDITIONAL COMMENTARY Set in the west of Ireland [Snell, p. 170].

WHITELAW, Revd James, b. Co. Leitrim, 1749, d. Dublin 1813.
ADDITIONAL AUTHOR Church of Ireland clergyman, statistician and philanthropist, JW graduated BA at TCD in 1771. After ordination, he became a tutor to the earl of Meath, who presented him with the living first of St James's and after that of St Catherine's in Dublin. JA was interested in the well-being of the poor, which led him to found several charitable institutions. His primary area of work was the Liberties area of Dublin, where he founded the Meath charitable loan organisation and a school. He became most known for the census of Dublin he undertook in 1798 (published in 1805), which was the first ever undertaken in any Irish city. A member of the RIA, JW died in Dublin of a malignant fever contracted while visiting the poor. He collaborated with John Warburton on *The history of Dublin*, which was completed by Robert Walsh and published posthumously in Dublin in 1818. SOURCE DNB.
W63a   **Parental solicitude or, moral lessons for the instruction of youth** [anon.] (dedicated to Lady Arabella Denny).
Dublin: Printed for [for the author by] J. Exshaw, [*c*.1780?], 2 vols. (ill.). SOURCE Burmester cat. 65/75; ESTC t198038. LOCATION Dt.
COMMENTARY Moral tales, dialogues, and fables, some of them extracted from other writers; interspersed with poetry by Young, Goldsmith, Cotton, and others. The long introduction is addressed to Mrs Sophia Burrowes. The DNB assigned the date 1800? to this vol. [Burmester cat. 65/75].

YEATS, William Butler.
Y4   *Sherman, and Dhoya* (by 'Ganconagh').
ADDITIONAL COMMENTARY The story 'John Sherman' is set in Co. Sligo [Snell, p. 165].

Index of Persons

Index of Persons

Index of Persons

Johns, Alexander (ded.) R150
Johnson, — 661
Johnson, Mrs David 661, J32
Johnson, Esther (Swift's 'Stella') 367, 857, 1275, D32, W118
Johnson, Lucy Ann (ded.) H19
Johnson, Dr Samuel 492, 657, 850, 963, B265, H149, M444, M451
Johnston, Miss — 661, J33
Johnston, Anna 837, 899, M347, M348
Johnston, C.M. 662
Johnston, Charles 662
Johnston, Charles Bolton (ded.) H339
Johnston, Charlotte Jane (ded.) H343–344
Johnston, Frances Sarah 662
Johnston, Harriet (ded.) J41
Johnston, Henry 662, J36–40
Johnston, William 663, J41–43
Johnstone, Charles, 1719–1802, 664, 1399, J44–49
Johnstone, Charles, fl. 1770, 667, J50
Joliffe, Lady (ded.) A58
Jolly, James 668, J51
Jones, E. Anon.13
'Jones, James Thomas' (pseud.) 668, 749, L143
Jones, Owen (ill.) C88
Jones, T. Mason 668, J52
Jordan, Kate 668, J53–60
Joseph II, (Holy Roman Emperor) 370
Joy, J.M. 669, J61
Joyce, James 1014, 1149, 1257, 1364, M499
Joyce, Robert Dwyer 669–670, 1399, J62–64, L59
'J.P.G.' (pseud.) 481, G2
'J.S.' (pseud.) 1155, Anon.14, S2
'J.S. of Dale ' (coa) O163
Judd, Alicia Maria (ded.) H62
Jun, B. Clayton (ill.) H140
'J.W.' (ill.) R24

'K. v. K.' (pseud.) 671, 701, K124
Kahlert, Karl Friedrich M284
Kane, Annie (later Vernon) 671, K1
'Kane, Edward' (pseud.) 710
Kane, Revd J. Blackburne 671, K2
Kant, Immanuel 281, C369
Karr, Thérèse Alphonse 671, K3
Karst, — (ill.) R8
Karst, John (ill.) S602
Kavanagh, Bridget (coa) 672, K19, K22
Kavanagh, Julia 672, 676, K4–22
Kavanagh, Maurice Denis 676, K23
Kavanagh, Morgan Peter 672, 676, K24–25
Kaye, Revd John 677, K26
Kean, Edmund 497, 708, E105 (ded.)
Keane, Joanna Maria 677, K27
Keane, Molly 1198
Keary, Anna Maria (Annie) 678, 1399, K28–29
Keating, — (ill.) B300
Keating, Geoffrey B501
Keatinge, Mrs Richard Harte (Harriet, née Pottinger) 679, K30
Keats, John 1293
Keddie, Henrietta 679, K31
Keegan, John 679, K32, Y2
Keeling, Elsa (see D'Esterre-Keeling, Elsa)
Keenan, Henry Francis 680, K33–34
Keene, Charles S. (ill.) R45
Keightley, Sir Samuel Robert 680–681, K35–43
Keightley, Thomas Anon.30, C474–475
Keller, Arthur I. (ill.) E98
Kellett, Mrs Theodore 682, K44
Kells, T. (ill.) H138
Kelly, Mrs — 682, K45–46

Kelly, George C. 683, K47–65
Kelly, Hugh 684–485, K66–67
Kelly, Fr James J., OSF 686, K68–71
Kelly, Mary (May) 686
Kelly, Ned B286
Kelly, Peter Burrowes 686, K72
Kelly, Richard N. 687, K73–74
Kelly, Revd Thomas 687–688, K75
Kelly, William Patrick 688, K76–85
Kemble, Ann Julia 689
Kemble, E.W. (ill.) D242
Kemble, John Philip 575, M490 (ded.)
Kemp-Welch, Lucy E. (ill.) W71
Kendall, Mrs A. 689, K86
Kendall, Edward Augustus 689–690, K87
Kendall, William Webb (ded.) K87
Kenealy, Edward Vaughan Hyde 323, 690–691, 708, 751, 774, 853, 858, 902, K88–89, O71
Kenedy, P.J. (ill.) C267, S602
Kenley, Marianne 691, K90
Kennard, Nina H. (née Homan-Mulock) 691, K91–95
Kennedy, E. Sherard (ill.) H71
Kennedy, Grace 692, K96
'Kennedy, Kevin' (pseud.) 692, 1152, R285
Kennedy, Patrick 110, 692–693, 738, 860, Anon.30, Anon.50, F143, J3, K97–106, M214, O71, Y2
Kennedy, Paul (ill.) M214
Kennedy, William 696–697, K107
Kenny, M.L. 697, K108
Keogh, Judge William Nicholas (ded.) L113
Keon, Miles Gerald 697, K109–110
Kernahan, John Coulson 698, B408 (ded.), K111
Kernot, J.H. (ill.) H55
Kerr, Lady Anabel Anon.219
Kerr, Eliza 698, K112–114
'Kerr, Orpheus C.' (pseud.) 699, 973, N14
Kettle, Rosa MacKenzie 699, K115–117
Keynes, John Maynard 454
'K.H.' (pseud.) 578, H194
Kickham, Charles Joseph 220, 296, 699–700, 1037, 1399, K118–123, O71, Y3
Kiely, Benedict 199
Killinger, Karl freiherr von 513, 701, K124
Kimber, Edward 702, K125–126
King, C. 702, K127
King, Sir Edward, Bt. Anon.201
King, Harriet (ded.) W26
King, Lady Isabella (ded.) Anon.201
King, Jane 702
King, Mrs John (ded.) H221
King, Katherine 702–703, K128
King, Kitty (ded.) T203
King, Lady Margaret Jane 703
King, Mary 703
King, Richard Ashe 703, K129–138
'King, Toler' (pseud.) 704
Kinglake, Alexander William (ded.) L173
Kingsley, Revd Charles 704–705, 974, B355, K139
Kingston, William Henry Giles 705, K140–143
'Kink, Emmanuel' (pseud.) 378, 706, D124, D141
Kinley, Jane 706, K144
'Kinnfaela' (pseud.) 706, 821, M118
Kinsale [sic, Kingsale], Lady (ded.) D74
Kipling, Rudyard 481
Kirby, Alfred F.P. 706, K145
Kirk, Maria L. (ill.) H453
Kirk, Thomas 113
Kirkwood, — (ill.) Anon.217, E19

Kirkwood & Son (ill.) Anon.275, H138
'Kirkwood, Arthur' (pseud.) 706, 822, M119
Kirkwood, John (ill.) Anon.289, H139, H260, M329, T76
Kitcat, Dick (Richard Doyle) (ill.) M336
'K. M—x—ll' (pseud.) 794, 884, M328
Knight, C. (ill.) E110
'Knight Errant' (pseud.) 391, 706, D225
Knortz, Karl 706–707, K146
Knot, Mary John 707, K147
Knowles, J. Sheridan 707–708, 709, 824, H254, H266 (ded.), K88, K148–151
Knowles, Richard Brinsley Sheridan 708, 709, Anon.219, K152
Knox, Capt Charles H. 710, K153
Knox, Revd James Spencer 710 K154
Knox, John A27
Knox, Kathleen 710, K155–165
Knox, Thomas Wallace 711, K166
Knox, William 712, K167
Kroekker, Kate Freiligrath (ded.) S62
Kronheim, J.M. & Co. (ill.) Anon.78
Kühne, Ferdinand Gustav 712, K168
Kyle, Ellen 712
Kyle, Revd Robert Wood 712, K712

'L.' (pseud.) 713, 980, N41
La Touche, Maria (née Price) 362, 723–724, L34–35
'Lady, A' (pseud.) fl. 1704 353, D31
'Lady..., A' (pseud.) fl. 1728 577–78, H192–193
'Lady, A' (pseud.) fl. 1760 713, L1
'Lady, A' (pseud.) fl. 1770 714, L2
'Lady, A' (pseud.) fl. 1775 714, L3
'Lady, A' (pseud.) fl. 1776 714, L4
'Lady, A' (pseud.) fl. 1781 715, L5
'Lady, A' (pseud.) fl. 1781 715, L6
'Lady, A' (pseud.) fl. 1781 1151, R282
'Lady, A' (pseud.) fl. 1782 715, L7
'Lady, A' (pseud.) fl. 1787 715, L7–14
'Lady, A' (pseud.) fl. 1789 717, L15
'Lady, A' (pseud.) fl. 1789 1000, O63,
'Lady, A' (pseud.) fl. 1791 717, L16
'Lady, A' (pseud.) fl. 1797 717, L17
'Lady, A' (pseud.) fl. 1797 1175, S76
'Lady, A' (pseud.) fl. 1799 717, L18
'Lady, A' (pseud.) fl. 1804 718, L19–20
'Lady, A' (pseud.) fl. 1808 505, G107
'Lady, A' (pseud.) fl. 1812 1057, P55
'Lady, A' (pseud.) fl. 1814 365, D74
'Lady, A' (pseud.) fl. 1830 1178, S87
'Lady, A' (pseud.) fl. 1844 718, L21
'Lady, A' (pseud.) fl. 1844 1282, T13
'Lady, A' (pseud.) fl. 1847 1279, T2
'Lady, A' (pseud.) fl. 1857 677, K27
'Lady, A' (pseud.) fl. 1860s 718, L22
'Lady M.' (pseud.) 718
'Lady of Boston, A' (pseud.) 718
'Lady of New York, A ' (pseud.) 718
Laffan, Mrs De Courcy 718
Laffan, May 718
'Lageniensis' (pseud.) 718, 1014, O103–104
Lahee, Miss M.R. 719, L23
Laing, Mrs David (ded.) H28
Lamb, Lady Caroline (née Ponsonby) 202, 719–720, 1064, 1066, B94, L24, M407
Lamb, Charles 348, 535, 707, Anon.268
Lamb, Mary Montgomerie 720
Lambart, Revd W. Huberto 720. L25
Lambert, the Hon Camden Elizabeth 720–721, L26
Lambert, Nancy Power 721
'Lambert, Nannie' (pseud.) 721
Lamothe, Alexandre Bessot De 721
Landells, E. (ill.) H23

1417

Index of Persons

Maunsell, William Pryce 882–883, M324–325
Maurois, André W77
Maximilian (emperor of Mexico) 372
Maxwell, Mrs Caroline 883, M326
Maxwell, Sir Herbert Eustace 883–884, M327
Maxwell, Katherine 884, M328
Maxwell, Revd William Hamilton 95, 220, 751, 885–886, 1402, Anon.11, Anon.268, L146, M330–345
'May, Sophia' (pseud.) 890
May, Thomas P. 890, M346
Mayhew, Augustus Septimus 891, C190, M347
Mayhew, Henry 891, C190 (coa), M347 (coa)
Mayne, Thomas Ekenhead 891–892, M348
Mayo, Dermot Robert Wyndham Bourke, 7th earl of 892, M349
Mayo, Viscount (ded.) M585
'M.B.' (ed.) 99, F41
M'acConnell, — (ill.) C389
Meade, Elizabeth Thomasina 893
'Meade, L.T.' (pseud.) 893, 1131, 1202, 1316, Anon.262, S163, S165–170, S172–401, S402, S403–408, S410–418, S420–449
Meade, Dr Richard 377
Meadows, Kenny (ill.) G123, H62
Meagher, Gen Thomas Francis 220, 296, S642
Meaney, Mary L. 893, M350
Meany, J.L. 893, M351
Meany, Stephen Joseph 893–894, M352
Mears, Amelia (née Garland) 894, M353–356
Measom, George (ill.) Anon.19, Anon.215, C81, C94–95, C99, H28, H31, M339, M529, R118, R121, W14, W73
Measom, W. (ill.) H31
'M.E.E.' (ill.) L173, W2
Meehan, Charles Patrick 894–895, M357–358
Meehan, M. 895, M360
Meehan, R. (coa) 895, M360
Meeke, Mary Anon.77
Meekins, Isaac 895
Mees-Hudig, Wijnand and Jeanne (ded.) O181–184
Meikle, James 896, M361–362
Melior Anon.214
'Melusine' (pseud.) 896, 1290, T39
Melville, Herman 1174
Melville, Theodore 896, M363–365
Melvin, Revd John (ded.) B399
'M.E.M.' (pseud.) 793
'Member of the Committee of the Juvenile Deaf and Dumb Association, A' (pseud.) 897, M366
'Member of the Irish Bar, A' (pseud.) 686, 897, K72
'Member of the Order of Mercy, A' (pseud.) 254, C127
Menpes, Mortimer (coa) 897, M44
Mercier, — (ill.) G177
Meredith, Mrs Charles (Louise Anne) 897, M367
'Meredith, Francis' (pseud.) 266, 898, C193
Meredith, George 785, L265 (ded.)
'Merulan' (pseud.) 669
'M.E.T.' (pseud.) 386, 1279, D181
Methuen, Lord (ded.) L158
Methuen, Mary M.C. 898, M368–369
Meyer, Henri-Horace B293
Meynell, Louis (ill.) S113
'M.F.D.' (pseud.) 367, D86, D88–92

Mildmay, Jacob 898, M370
Milikin, Anna 898
Millais, J.E. (ill.) 81, T135
Millar, G. (ill.) E43, H32, H34, H36, S23
Millard, — (ill.) F41
Mille, James de 898
Miller, Sir Herbert (ded.) P118
Miller, William (ill.) R136
Milligan, Alice Letitia 892, 899, 1051, M371–373
Milligan, Seaton Forrest (ded.) M373
Milligan, W.H. (coa) 900, M372–373
Milliken, Richard Alfred 900
Millikin, Anna 900, 901, M374–377
Millikin, Richard Alfred 324, 900 901, K88, M378
Millingen, John Gideon 902–903, M379–380
Mills, C.A. (ill.) L60, M599
Mills, John 146, 903, M381
Mills, Walter C. (ill.) P13
Milton, John 1273, F137
'Minister of the Church of England, A' (pseud.) 903, M382
Minkhouse, T. (ill.) H336
'Miriam D—' (pseud.) 274, C128
'Miro' (pseud.) 1032
'Missionary Priest, A' (pseud.) 903, 1085, Q1
Mitchell, A.W. 904, M383
Mitchell, Edward 904, M384
Mitford, Mary Russell 607, 904, 536 (ded), C473, M385–386
Mitford, Miss — Anon.268
'Mitzen, Mat.' (pseud.) 904
'M.J.H.' (pseud.) 532, 562, H127–129
'M.J.W.' (pseud.) 1340, 1359, W70
'M.L.C.' (pseud.) 222, C1
'M.L.M.' (pseud.) 793, 893, M350
'M.L.W.' (pseud.) 1340, 1352, W47
'M.M.C.M.' (pseud.) 794, 898, M368
Moira, earl of (ded.) C263, M313, W101
Molière, Jean-Baptiste Poquelin 172, Anon.5, B425
Molloy, Joseph Fitzgerald 904–905, M387–396
Monahan, Henry J., Jnr 906, 1402, M397
'Mongo, Baba' (pseud.) 906
Monsell, Revd John Samuel Bewley 907, M398
Montagu, R.W. (ed.) M247
Montague, Louisa Julia 907
Montgomery, Alexander Esme Le Lorges 907, M399–400
Montgomery, Jemima 908
Montgomery, John Wilson 908, M401–402
Montgomery, Sophia Florence 1361
Mooney, P. Anon.79
Moore, A. 908, M403
Moore, Revd Courtenay 908–909, M405
Moore, E.M. (coa) W47
Moore, Mrs Emma 908, M404
Moore, Frances 909, M406–407
Moore, Frank Frankfort 909–910, M408–487
Moore, George 919, M488–490
Moore, Revd George 919
Moore, George Augustus 468, 485, 872, 872, 873, 921–922, 1363, 1385, M491–520
Moore, John 930, M520
Moore, John McDermott 930, Anon.28, M521–522
Moore, Margaret Jane 931
Moore, Lady Margaret Mathilda (née O'Connor) 931, 1001, M523
Moore, Maj. Maurice (ded.) M500
Moore, Oliver 931, M524

Moore, Sidney O. 931–932, M525–529
Moore, Thomas 309, 323, 327, 335, 337, 369, 497, 513, 531, 535, 594, 782, 852, 857, 932–933, 970, 1001, 1006, 1039, 1045, 1149, 1293, 1342, 1363, Anon.268, B19 (ded.), B94, C550 (ded.), K26, L217 (ded.), M530–557, M551, O65, O219–220, T74, W12, W59, W70
Moran, Edward 936, M538
Moran, James J. 936, M539–545
Moran, Michael 937, M546
Moran, Thomas Charles 945
More, Hannah 75, 1296, Anon.272, B64, B333, T97
More, Sir Thomas 1282
Morgan, Lady (née Sydney Owenson) 145, 305, 321, 322, 672, 719, 831, 901, 938–939, 1034, 1168, 1402, Anon.40, Anon.133, Anon.194 (ded.), Anon.196, B175, C35, C550, E117, H275, K3, K73 (ded.), M313, M550–558, S49 (ded.), S642
Morgan, Ann Jane 938, M547
Morgan, Edward 98
Morgan, Miss/Mrs Grogan (ded.) H16, H18
Morgan, Revd Henry 938, M548–549
Morgan, Thomas Charles M556
Moriarty, Rt Revd David (ded.) O45, P116
'Moriarty, Denis Ignatius' (pseud.) 350, 945, D20–22
'Moriarty Family, The' (pseud.) 945
Morley, Mabel 945, M559
Morley, Rt Hon. John (ded.) C558
Morris, Alfred 945, M560
Morris, Elizabeth Georgiana Catherine O'Connor 723, 946, M561–563
Morris, Lewis Anon.88
Morris, P.R. (ill.) H71
Morris, William O'Connor 723–724
Morse, C. (ill.) S375
Morton, J.L. (ill.) E71
Moser, Joseph Anon.59
Mosse, Henriette (née Rouvière) 946, M564–574
Mount Cashell, Margaret Jane, countess (née King) 490, 948–949, 1190, M575–580
Mount Sandford, George Sandford, 3rd baron 950, 1296, T74 (ded.)
Mountpleasant, J.J.R. 950, M581
Mowatt, James Alexander 950, M582
'Mr. C—D' (pseud.) 222, 270, C205
'Mr Yorick' (pseud.) 1256, 1389, S583
'M.R.L.' (pseud.) 713, L23
'Mrs. John Smith' (pseud.) 92, 1239, A88
'M.S.' (pseud.) 1155
'M.T.C.' (pseud.) 216, 222
Muddock, Joyce Emerson Preston 951, M583–584
Mukins, Isaac 951, M585
Mulcahy, — (ill.) G177
Mulgrave, Earl (ded.) L26
Mulholland, Clara 952, 954, Anon.219, M586–600
Mulholland, Rosa (Lady Gilbert) 693, 952, 954–955, 1316, 1402, Anon.219, B2, M601–645, Y3
Mullen,— (ill.) H76
'Munster Farmer, A' (pseud.) 962, 1039, O219
Murdoch, John A. 962, M646
Murphy, Anna Brownell 963
Murphy, Arthur 963, M647–648
Murphy, Con T. 964, M649

Index of Persons

Index of Persons

'Old Commercial Traveller, An' (pseud.) 228, 1019, C34
'Old Hand, An' (pseud.) 135, 1019, B137
'Old Sailor, An' (pseud.) 116, 1019, B65
'Old Sailor, The' (pseud.) 116, 1019, B66–67
'Old Sleuth' (pseud.) 552, 1019, H80–85
'Old Soldier, An' (pseud.) 219, 1019
'O'Leary, Con' (pseud.) 809, 1019, M74–76
O'Leary, John 454, 641, K118 (ded.)
O'Leary, Joseph 1019, O114
O'Leary, Patrick O71
Oliver, Laetitia Selwyn 1020, O115
'Oliver Optic' (pseud.) 70, A7
'Ollamh, Fodhla' (pseud.) 1018
Ollier, Charles (coa) 1020
Ollivant, Charles (ded.) R79
O'Malley, Grace (Grania) M129, M332, M583, O50, P53
O'Malley, I. (ill.) L197
O'Meara, J.B. Anon.259
O'Meara, Kathleen 1020, O116–129
O'Moore, Sidney 931–932, 1022, M525–529
O'Neil, H. (ill.) H9, H23
O'Neill, Henrietta 1404
O'Neill, Henrietta Bruce 1022
O'Neill, Hugh 442, C259, G231, O76, S5
O'Neill, John 1022, O130–131
'O'Neill, Moira' (pseud.) 1023, 1198, S154–156
O'Neill, Owen Roe A2, M91, M285, O56, O208, S461
O'Neill, William 1023, O132
'One Jones' (pseud.) 1024, O135
'One of America's Most Famous Detectives' (pseud.) 1023, O133
'One of the boys' (pseud.) 459, 1023, F69
'One of Themselves' (pseud.) 1024, O134
'One Who Was There' (pseud.) 1024, O136
O'Nial, George, Esq. Anon.70
Onwhyn, J. (ill.) H360
Opie, Amelia (née Alderson) 1024, O137
Opper, F. (ill.) D242
'Optic, Oliver' (pseud.) 1024
O'Reilly, Eleanor Grace 1024–1025, O138–161
O'Reilly, John Boyle 1027, 1132, O162–165
O'Reilly, Robert 1029
'O'Reilly, Private Miles' (pseud.) 550, 1029
O'Riordan, Conal Holmes O'Connell 1029, O16–186
Orleans, duke of 356
Orleans, Henrietta Maria, duchess of B305
Ormond, duke of 348
Ormond, earl of B393, F137
O'Rourke, John 353, 1032, O187
Orpen, Adela Elizabeth (née Richards) 1032–33, O188–193
Orpen, Mrs. Godard 1033
Orpen, R. Caulfeild (ill.) F137
Orrery, first earl of 171, 1033
Orr, N. (ill.) R29, R32, R36, R95
Orsay, Harriet Anne D' (see D'Orsay) 1033
Orsonnens, Eraste D' (see D'Orsonnens) 1033
O'Ruarc, prince of Breffini Anon.94
O'Ryan, Edmund (coa) 1033
O'Ryan, Julia M. 1033–1034, 194
O'Ryan, W.P. (see also Ryan, William Patrick) 1034
Osborne, Catherine Isabella 142, 1034, 1378, O195–196
Osborne, Ralph Bernal MP (ded.) H466
Osborne, Walter F. (ill) Anon.88
'Oscar' (pseud.) 528, 1035, G225
O'Shaughnessy, P. 1035, O197
O'Shaughnessy, Tom 1035, O198, 1403

O'Shea, Geraldine 1035, O199
O'Shea, John 1035–36, O200, 1403
O'Shea, J.J. (see Dillon, J.J. O'Shea)
O'Shea, John Augustus 369, 829, 893, 1036, Anon.27, D96, M152 (coa), O201–204
O'Sullivan, Dennis 1037, O205–18, 1403
O'Sullivan, Mortimer 1039, 1040–1041, 1068, B19, L190, M530, M532, O219–21
O'Sullivan, Murtagh 1040
O'Sullivan, Richard 1040, O222, S642
O'Sullivan, Samuel 751, 1039–1041
'O'Tara, MacErin' (pseud.) 1041, O224
Otway, Caesar 237, 1041–42, B306, O225–27
Ouseley, John Mulvey 1042, O228–239
'Outis' (pseud.) 1043, 1358, W62
Overend, W.H. (ill.) H333, M414–415, M417–418, M422, M425, M428, M430
Owen, Robert 196
Owenson, Sydney (see also Morgan, Lady) 1043
Owen, Wilfred 1029

Paget, Sidney (ill.) S270, S277
Paget, Walter (ill.) S263, S237
Paine, Thomas 658, 1294, C203, C369
Pakenham, Admiral Thomas E32
Pakenham, Charlotte (ill.) E19
Pakenham, Hon Francis (ded.) C516
Pakenham, Mrs (ded.) C516
Palestrina, Giovanni 872
Palmerston, Viscount 1383, G34 (ded.), M230 (ded.)
Palmer, W.J. (ill.) H71
Pamphili, Princess Doria (ded.) A12
'Panache, Madame' (pseud.) 848, 1044
Paque, Oliver (ill.) O71
Parallel, Jacob (ill.) Anon.31
Parker, Emma 129
Parker, Helen F. (née Fitch) 1044, P2
Parker, Lord (ded.) C162
Parker, Theodore 281
Parkes, William Theodore 1044, P3–4
Parke, Walter Anon.88
'Parley, Peter' (pseud.) 493, 1044, G49–52
Parnell, Anna 785, L266 (ded.)
Parnell, Charles Stewart 172, 220, 567, 731, 800, 805, 986, 995–996, 1045, 1270, 1316, H149, L303, M239, M371
Parnell, William 1044–45, P5–6
Parris, E.T. 146
Parry, Edward B49
Partridge, Bernard (ill.) M305, S215
Partridge, Blanche 1046
Pasqer, A.J. (ill.) O146
Paterson, Ewing and Edith (ded.) H244
Paterson, — (ill.) E2
Paterson, Mary (ded.) S532
Patmore, Coventry 81
Paton, Sir Noël (ill.) H62
'Patricia' (pseud.) 1046, P7
Patrick, F.C. 1046, P8–10
Patrick, St 342, 375, 976, Anon.41, C267–268, J18, M17, R98
Paul, Maj Norris 1047, P11
Payn, James 1047–48, P12
'Payne, Harold' (pseud.) 683, 1048, K47–65
'P.D.H.' (pseud.) 564 (see Hall, S.C.)
Peacocke, Ida (née Tufnell) 882, 1048, P13–14
Peacock, Mabel (ill.) S130
Pearce, Laiton (ill.) S523
Pearse, Alfred (ill.) W21
Pearson, — (ill.) L108
Pease, — (ill.) S17
Peck, Frances 1048–49, P15–21

Peck, George Wilbur 1050, P22–23
Pedersen, Knut 394
Peel, Sir Robert 237, L257 (ded.)
Pegram, Fred. (ill.) C441, C449, M307
Pender, Margaret T. (née O'Doherty) 1003, 1051, P24–29
Pender, M.T. Anon.27
Pendleton, — (ill.) E71
Penrose, Ethel (née Coghill) 1052, P30–32
Penrose, H.H. (née Mary Elizabeth Lewis) 1053, P33–48
'Penseval, Guy' (pseud.) 348, 1054, D16
'Peppergrass, Paul' (pseud.) 167, 1054, B299–300, C147, M95
Pepys, Hon Everard (ded.) C147
Percival, Margaret 1054, P49–51
'Peregrinus' (pseud.) 1055, 1306, T117
'Person of Honour, A' (pseud.) 169, 171, 1055, B303, B306
Pery, Edmond Sexton, first Viscount Pery 1055, B330, G43, P52
'Peter Paradox, M.D., deceased' (pseud.) 1044, P1
Petherick, H. (ill.) B505, K155, S170, S173
'Petrel, Fulmar' (pseud.) 1056, P53
Petrie, George (ill) 1041, C72, G33
'Petrill, Frank' (pseud.) 236, 1056, C65–66
Petts, J. (ill.) S439
Phelps, Anson G. (ded.) R201
Phelps, Elizabeth Stuart 1056–57, P54
Phibbs, Mary 1057, P55
'Philalethes Cantabrigiensis' (pseud.) 677, 1058, K26, M532
'Philantropos' (pseud.) 358, 1058, D50
Philleo, Calvin Wheeler Anon.71
Phillips, Charles 1058, P56
Phillips, Sheriff (ded.) E117
Phiz (ill.) 751, C73, C77, C81, C86, C90, C104, F69, H16, L103–104, L145–154, L156–158, L160, L162, L164, L166, L168, L170, L180–183, L190, M241, M329, M335, N5, R270, S452
'Physician, A' (pseud.) 70
'Physician, A' (pseud.) 1059
'Physician, A' (pseud.) A5
'Piercy, J.M.' (pseud.) 796, 1059, M20
Piffard, Harold (ill.) H306, H309, T114
Piggot, Charles Anon.102
Piggott, Miss H. Bouverie 1059, P57–59
Pigot, — (ill.) R231
Pigot, John 324n, C474
Pilkington, Miss 1059, P60–63
Piloty, — (ill.) H63
Pinkerton, Allan 1060, P64
Pinkerton, William 1060
Piper, A.G. 1060, P65
Pirrie, Rt Hon W. and (ded.) D155
Pitt, William 1069, B255, J44 (ded.), W54, W107
Pius IX, Pope 1377
'Plain Englishman, A' (pseud.) 1061, 1183, S105
Plunkett, Hon Isabella-Catherine 507, 1061, P67–71
Plunket, Lord (see Conyngham, William)
Plunkett, Elizabeth (née Gunning) 355, 1062, M445, P72–73
Plunket, the Hon Frederica Louisa Edith 1061, P66
Plunket, the Hon Louisa Lelias 1062
Plunkett, Sir Horace 399, 724
Plunkett, Joseph Mary 873
Plunkett, Mary Sophia Elizabeth 1063
Plunkett, Oliver 327, P117
Plunkett, Robert 982, 1063

Index of Persons

Index of Book Titles

The following index alphabetically lists shortened titles mentioned in this *Guide*. The references are to book identification numbers (e.g., C41) and to page numbers if a title was included in the Addenda (e.g., 1410). With the exclusion of translations, variant titles are also provided in this index. Note that (a) stands for anthology and (MS) for manuscript.

Index of Book Titles

Index of Book Titles

Index of Book Titles

Index of Book Titles

Works by the Banim brothers B28
Works of Canon. Sheehan S125
Works of Charles Lever L188, L190, L191
Works of Charlotte Elizabeth T93, T94
Works of Father Prout M261
Works of G. Griffin, Esq. G173
Works of George Moore M517, M519
Works of Gerald Griffin G175
Works of J.S., D.D., D.S.P.D. S668
Works of Jonathan Swift S669
Works of Lady Blessington B191
Works of Laurence Sterne S585, S586, S587, S588
Works of Maria Edgeworth E70
Works of Martin Doyle H274
Works of Mrs. Davys D36
Works of Samuel Lover L228, L231
Works of the Banim brothers B30
Works of Thomas Moore M533, M534, M535, M536, M537
Works of William Carleton C122, C124
World and his wife B428
World and the cloister S597
World in the church R149
World of girls S192
World turned upside-down C241
Worldlyman F87
Wreath from the Emerald Isle H138
Wreath of friendship Anon.267
Wreath of lilies L86
Wreck of the 'Redwing' G209
Wreckers. A social study D123

Wroth C152
Wylder's hand L107
Wynville; or, clubs and coteries M230
Wyvern mystery L113

XX, the fatal clue K49

Yaxley and its neighbourhood R218
Year and a day M407
Years ago L194
Yellow aster C16
Yellow chief R70
Yellow domino T182
Yellow fiend H245
Yellow ticket H153
Yeoman Fleetwood B203
Yesterday in Ireland C547
Yet do not grieve O182
Young Beck B271
Young Coelebs F78
Young cragsman R138
Young Dave's wife B240
Young days of Admiral Quilliam O172
Young Draytons T28
Young enthusiast in humble life J51
Young folks of Hazelbrook O18
Young foresters B377
Young heroine S348
Young hussar F9
Young idea F152
Young Ishmael Conway B161
Young ladies' book of romantic tales (a)

Anon.268
Young Lady Dazincourt O179
Young liar S649
Young Lord P85
Young Milesian G168
Young musicians Anon.269
Young mutineer S229
Young Navarre D223
Young patriot H262
Young prince Marigold M252
Young Rosinière P17
Young stamp-collectors P184
Young truants S647
Young voyageurs R33
Young Wilfred S649
Young yägers R40
Youngest Miss Mowbray C448
Your brother and mine S170
Yourself and the neighbours M202
Youth at the prow E133, 1398
Yusef B388

Zanthon D111
Zelda D56
Zenobia O110
Zoë: An episode W22
Zoe; a girl of genius G149
Zoë's Bible W128
Zozimus M546
Zuriel's grandchild R142
S YL LETOMENA of the antiquities B291

1456

Index of Historic Periods, Themes and Settings

The following index alphabetically lists historic periods, themes and settings of works of fiction, where mentioned. The references are to book identification numbers (e.g., C41). Note that the classification of topics is often difficult, and is dependent on the nature of its abstract and our knowledge of the books. Therefore, the topics listed are more for illustrative purposes than an exhaustive survey of all topics in the books. The classification of the topics does not apply to books that have not been seen or books for which no abstract was available.

HISTORIC PERIODS

Index of Historic Periods, Themes and Settings

Index of Publishers

The following index lists only the publishers of a given title for the primary reference to a title (in other words publishers of later reprints or translations are not included here). Publishers' names are located under the city or town in which they are based. The references are mostly to book identification numbers (e.g., C41) and very occasionally to page numbers (e.g., 1394).

Index of Publishers

Index of Publishers

Index of Publishers

Index of Places Relating to Authors

The following index alphabetically lists place names mentioned in the biographical sketches. The references are to the page numbers (e.g., 1102). A given place name is listed both as a main entry and under its larger geographic area (e.g., Ballinderry, Co. Antrim is listed under Ballinderry, and under Co. Antrim). In addition, some entries are listed under a country's name.

Index of Places Relating to Authors

Index of Places Relating to Authors